ISSN 0952-620X

April 1995
Published Monthly

THOMAS COOK

EUROPEAN

——TIMETABLE——

CONTENTS

INHALT   *TABLE DES MATIÈRES*   *CO...*

——INFORMATION——

Auskunft   *Renseignements*   *Información*

——TIMETABLES——

Fahrpläne   *Tableaux*   *Cuadros horarios*

SUMMER SUPPLEMENT : Advance summer timings for selected international services appear on pages **508 - 556**

Publishing Manager : Jennifer Rigby

Editor : Brendan Fox
Senior Compiler : David Gunning
Compilers : Peter Hedderly, Kevin Flynn
International Section : Bernard Horton

☎(Sales) 01733 505821   (Editorial) 01733 267023   (fax) 01733 267052

Thomas Cook Publishing,
P. O. Box 227,
Peterborough, England,
PE3 8BQ.

Registered Office:
45 Berkeley Street,
London, W1A 1EB.
(Company Registration No. 198600 London)

Originated in-house using '3B2' from Advent DTP
Filmset by Riverhead Typesetters, Grimsby
Printed and bound in Great Britain by Albert Gait Ltd., Grimsby

1995

Summer services commence May 28 — Winter services commence September 24

1995

JANUARY	FEBRUARY	MARCH	APRIL	MAY	JUNE
M T W T F S S	M T W T F S S	M T W T F S S	M T W T F S S	M T W T F S S	M T W T F S S
① ② ③ ④ ⑤ ⑥ ⑦	① ② ③ ④ ⑤ ⑥ ⑦	① ② ③ ④ ⑤ ⑥ ⑦	① ② ③ ④ ⑤ ⑥ ⑦	① ② ③ ④ ⑤ ⑥ ⑦	① ② ③ ④ ⑤ ⑥ ⑦
30 31 1	.. .. 1 2 3 4 5	.. .. 1 2 3 4 5	.. .. 1 2	1 2 3 4 5 6 7	.. .. .. 1 2 3 4
2 3 4 5 6 7 8	6 7 8 9 10 11 12	6 7 8 9 10 11 12	3 4 5 6 7 8 9	8 9 10 11 12 13 14	5 6 7 8 9 10 11
9 10 11 12 13 14 15	13 14 15 16 17 18 19	13 14 15 16 17 18 19	10 11 12 13 14 15 16	15 16 17 18 19 20 21	12 13 14 15 16 17 18
16 17 18 19 20 21 22	20 21 22 23 24 25 26	20 21 22 23 24 25 26	17 18 19 20 21 22 23	22 23 24 25 26 27 28	19 20 21 22 23 24 25
23 24 25 26 27 28 29	27 28	27 28 29 30 31	24 25 26 27 28 29 30	29 30 31	26 27 28 29 30 .. ..

JULY	AUGUST	SEPTEMBER	OCTOBER	NOVEMBER	DECEMBER
M T W T F S S	M T W T F S S	M T W T F S S	M T W T F S S	M T W T F S S	M T W T F S S
① ② ③ ④ ⑤ ⑥ ⑦	① ② ③ ④ ⑤ ⑥ ⑦	① ② ③ ④ ⑤ ⑥ ⑦	① ② ③ ④ ⑤ ⑥ ⑦	① ② ③ ④ ⑤ ⑥ ⑦	① ② ③ ④ ⑤ ⑥ ⑦
31 .. .. 1 2	.. 1 2 3 4 5 6	.. .. 1 2 3	30 31 1	.. .. 1 2 3 4 5	.. .. 1 2 3
3 4 5 6 7 8 9	7 8 9 10 11 12 13	4 5 6 7 8 9 10	2 3 4 5 6 7 8	6 7 8 9 10 11 12	4 5 6 7 8 9 10
10 11 12 13 14 15 16	14 15 16 17 18 19 20	11 12 13 14 15 16 17	9 10 11 12 13 14 15	13 14 15 16 17 18 19	11 12 13 14 15 16 17
17 18 19 20 21 22 23	21 22 23 24 25 26 27	18 19 20 21 22 23 24	16 17 18 19 20 21 22	20 21 22 23 24 25 26	18 19 20 21 22 23 24
24 25 26 27 28 29 30	28 29 30 31	25 26 27 28 29 30 ..	23 24 25 26 27 28 29	27 28 29 30	25 26 27 28 29 30 31

1996

Summer services commence June 2 — Winter services commence September 29

1996

JANUARY	FEBRUARY	MARCH	APRIL	MAY	JUNE
M T W T F S S	M T W T F S S	M T W T F S S	M T W T F S S	M T W T F S S	M T W T F S S
① ② ③ ④ ⑤ ⑥ ⑦	① ② ③ ④ ⑤ ⑥ ⑦	① ② ③ ④ ⑤ ⑥ ⑦	① ② ③ ④ ⑤ ⑥ ⑦	① ② ③ ④ ⑤ ⑥ ⑦	① ② ③ ④ ⑤ ⑥ ⑦
1 2 3 4 5 6 7	.. .. .. 1 2 3 4	.. .. 1 2 3	1 2 3 4 5 6 7	.. .. 1 2 3 4 5	.. .. 1 2
8 9 10 11 12 13 14	5 6 7 8 9 10 11	4 5 6 7 8 9 10	8 9 10 11 12 13 14	6 7 8 9 10 11 12	3 4 5 6 7 8 9
15 16 17 18 19 20 21	12 13 14 15 16 17 18	11 12 13 14 15 16 17	15 16 17 18 19 20 21	13 14 15 16 17 18 19	10 11 12 13 14 15 16
22 23 24 25 26 27 28	19 20 21 22 23 24 25	18 19 20 21 22 23 24	22 23 24 25 26 27 28	20 21 22 23 24 25 26	17 18 19 20 21 22 23
29 30 31	26 27 28 29	25 26 27 28 29 30 31	29 30	27 28 29 30 31	24 25 26 27 28 29 30

PUBLIC HOLIDAYS 1995

FEIERTAGE   *JOURS FÉRIÉS*   *DÍAS FESTIVOS*

The dates given below are those of public holidays (other than those which fall on a Sunday) on which normal weekday train services are liable to be **considerably altered**. Passengers intending to travel on these dates, or on days immediately before or after public holidays, are strongly recommended to reserve seats and to confirm timings locally. Further information on conditions applying on holiday dates may be found in the introduction to each country.

Austria : Jan. 6, Apr. 17, May 1, 25, June 5, 15, Aug. 15, Oct. 26, Nov. 1, Dec. 8, 25, 26.

Belarus (‡) : Jan. 7, Mar. 8, Apr. 18, May 1, 9, July 27, Nov. 2, Dec. 25.

Belgium : Apr. 17, May 1, 25, June 5, July 21, Aug. 15, Nov. 1, 11, Dec. 25, 26.

Bulgaria (‡) : Mar. 3, Apr. 24, May 1, 24, 25, Dec. 25.

Croatia : Jan. 6, 7, Apr. 17, May 1, 30, June 22, Aug. 15, Nov. 1, Dec. 25, 26.

Czech Republic : Apr. 17, May 1, 8, July 5, 6, Oct. 28, Dec. 25, 26.

Denmark : Apr. 13, 14, 17, May 12, 25, June 5, Dec. 25, 26.

England and Wales : Jan. 2, Apr. 14, 17, May 8, 29, Aug. 28, Dec. 25, 26.

Estonia : Feb. 24, Apr. 14, May 1, June 5, 23, 24, Dec. 25, 26.

Finland : Jan. 6, Apr. 14, 17, May 1, 25, June 23, 24, Nov. 4, Dec. 6, 25, 26.

France : Apr. 17, May 1, 8, 25, June 5, July 14, Aug. 15, Nov. 1, 11, Dec. 25.

Germany : Apr. 14, 17, May 1, 25, June 5, Oct. 3, Nov. 22, Dec. 25, 26.

Great Britain : see England and Wales / Scotland.

Greece : Jan. 6, Mar. 6, 25, Apr. 21, 24, May 1, June 12, Aug. 15, Oct. 28, Dec. 25, 26.

Hungary : Mar. 15, Apr. 17, May 1, Oct. 23, Dec. 25, 26.

Ireland (Northern) : Jan. 2, Mar. 17, Apr. 14, 17, May 8, 29, July 12, Aug. 28, Dec. 25, 26.

Ireland (Republic of) : Jan. 2, Mar. 17, Apr. 14, 17, May 1, June 5, Aug. 7, Oct. 30, Dec. 25, 26.

Italy : Jan. 6, Apr. 17, 25, May 1, Aug. 15, Nov. 1, Dec. 8, 25, 26.

Latvia : Apr. 14, May 1, June 23, 24, Nov. 11, 18, Dec. 25, 26.

Lithuania : Feb. 16, Apr. 17, May 1, July 6, Nov. 1, Dec. 25, 26.

Luxembourg : Jan. 2, Feb. 27, Apr. 17, May 1, 25, June 5, 23, Aug. 15, Nov. 1, Dec. 25, 26.

Moldova (‡) : Jan. 7, Mar. 8, May 1, 9, Aug. 27.

Netherlands : Apr. 17, May 25, Dec. 25, 26.

Norway : Apr. 13, 14, 17, May 1, 17, 25, June 5, Dec. 25, 26.

Poland : Apr. 17, May 1, 3, June 15, Aug. 15, Nov. 1, 11, Dec. 25, 26.

Portugal : Feb. 28, Apr. 14, 25, May 1, June 10, 15, Aug. 15, Oct. 5, Nov. 1, Dec. 1, 8, 25.

Romania : Jan. 2, Apr. 24, May 1, Dec. 1, 25.

Russia (‡) : Jan. 2, 3, 7, Feb. 23, Mar. 8, May 1, 2, June 12, Nov. 7, 8.

Scotland : Jan. 2, 3, Apr. 14, May 1, 8, 29, Aug. 7, Dec. 25, 26.

Slovakia : Jan. 6, Apr. 14, 17, May 1, July 5, Aug. 29, Sept. 1, 15, Nov. 1, Dec. 25, 26.

Slovenia : Jan. 2, Feb. 8, Apr. 17, 27, May 1, June 25, Aug. 15, Oct. 31, Nov. 1, Dec. 25, 26.

Spain : Jan. 6, Apr. 14, May 1, Aug. 15, Oct. 12, Nov. 1, Dec. 6, 8, 25.

Sweden : Jan. 6, Apr. 14, 17, May 1, 25, June 5, 24, Nov. 4, Dec. 25, 26.

Switzerland : Jan. 2, Apr. 14, 17, May 25, June 5, Aug. 1, Dec. 25, 26.

Ukraine (‡) : Mar. 8, May 1, 9, Aug. 24.

Yugoslavia : Jan. 2, 3, 7, Mar. 28, Apr. 24, May 1, 2, July 4, 7, 13, Nov. 29, 30.

‡ : *Subject to confirmation - complete information not to hand.*

MOVABLE HOLIDAYS

Bewegliche Feste   Fêtes mobiles
Fiestas movibles

	1995	1996
Good Friday	Apr. 14	Apr. 5
Easter Monday	Apr. 17	Apr. 8
Ascension Day	May 25	May 16
Whit Monday (Pentecost)	June 5	May 27
Corpus Christi	June 15	June 6

INTERNATIONAL TIME

INTERNATIONALE ZEITEN   *HEURE INTERNATIONALE*   *HORA INTERNACIONAL*

Winter time : September 25, 1994 - March 25, 1995
Summer time : March 26, 1995 - September 23, 1995

	GMT / WEZ HEOc	GMT +1 / MEZ HEC	GMT +2 / OEZ HEOr	GMT +3 / MZ HM
WINTER :	GMT / WEZ HEOc	GMT +1 / MEZ HEC	GMT +2 / OEZ HEOr	GMT +3 / MZ HM
SUMMER :	GMT +1 / MEZ HEC	GMT +2 / OEZ HEOr	GMT +3 / MZ HM	GMT +4 / MZ+1 HM+1
	Canary Isles	Austria / Albania	Belgium / Austria	Belarus / Bulgaria	Georgia

Canary Isles	Albania	Austria	Belgium	Belarus	Bulgaria	Georgia
Faroes	Bosnia	Croatia	Czech Republic	Cyprus	Estonia	Russia
Iceland **c**	Denmark	France	Germany	Finland	Greece	(European)
Ireland **a**	Gibraltar	Hungary	Italy	Latvia	Lithuania	
U.K. **a**	Luxembourg	Macedonia	Netherlands	Moldova	Romania	
	Norway	Poland	Portugal	Turkey	Ukraine	
	Slovakia	Slovenia	Spain			
	Sweden	Switzerland	Yugoslavia			

a -   Last day of summer time is Oct. 21, 1995.   **c -**   GMT all year.

What's new this month

The rail services in this issue are valid to **May 27**, except where indicated in the heading to each country or in individual tables. An exception is **Sweden**, where the current timings are valid to **June 11**. The **Summer International Supplement** (pages 508 - 556) shows provisional timings for principal international services, valid from **May 28** to **September 23**. The Summer Supplement will be further updated for the next issue as more accurate information is received from the railways.

The 'turn up and go' service has now been introduced on *Le Shuttle*, the car-carrying service through the Channel Tunnel between Folkestone and Calais. Tickets can be obtained on arrival at the terminal, or alternatively in advance from travel agents or by phone from Eurotunnel. Trains are currently running hourly, except between 2300 and 0700 when there is a train every two hours. However, the daytime frequency will be increased to two trains per hour from early April and up to four departures per hour are planned for mid-summer. Coaches and pedal cycles are not currently carried on the service, but this is likely to start in mid-May.

The summer timetable will see the introduction of high-quality overnight services using new 'hotel train' rolling stock operated by DACH Hotelzug A.G. and consisting of sleeping berths and 'sleeperette' reclining seats. They will be marketed as 'CityNightLine' and will run initially on two routes, **Köln - Wien**, as the *Donau-Kurier*, and **Zürich - Wien**, named *Wiener Walzer*. A third service, named *Komet*, will start from September 24 and will run between **Hamburg** and **Zürich**.

From **May 28**, most railway services throughout Europe will be retimed. The Summer Supplement at the back of this edition gives provisional details for most international services and a summary of the principal changes is given below:

International services from May 28

Tables 1/2: New international car-sleeper services (Table **1**) include Avignon - Berlin, München - Rimini and Budapest - Thessaloniki. The Calais - Innsbruck service will not run. The Motorail car-carrying trains in Great Britain, most of which link London with principal cities in Scotland, will be withdrawn after May 27.

Tables 10/12: The London - Paris and London - Brussels *Eurostar* service will be increased in frequency from May 28, and again from July 2 on the Paris service. There will be a connecting train on weekdays from Manchester to London Waterloo via Birmingham, and from July 3 this will be joined by an Edinburgh - London Waterloo train via Newcastle and York. Details are shown below Table **10**. Details of the London - Paris rail/sea service had not been announced as we went to press.

Table 11: More *Eurostar* trains will be calling at Lille Europe and this new table shows the service from London to the south of France using the TGV trains from Lille Europe via Charles de Gaulle airport, avoiding a change of train in Paris.

Table 18: There will be four TGV services between Paris and Brussels, of which three will take the high-speed line between Paris and Lille. Contrary to the information shown in the table, they will not pick up or set down passengers at Lille.

Table 22: Amsterdam - Berlin trains are speeded up by 30 - 50 minutes, with further improvements to follow when electrification is completed. The early morning train from Amsterdam to Hannover will be extended to Berlin, but this and the later morning train will terminate at Berlin Charlottenburg due to capacity problems at Berlin Zoo. The Berlin - Amsterdam overnight train is accelerated by about 90 minutes in this direction only.

Table 24: The once-weekly through car between Brussels and Kyïv will run twice-weekly in high summer, and modern rolling stock will be provided.

Table 28: The two-hourly Den Haag - Rotterdam - Köln service formerly shown in this table will cease, and will be replaced by two-hourly Eindhoven - Köln trains with connections to and from Den Haag.

Table 30: EuroCity *Heinrich Heine* will be extended to give a daytime Paris - Praha service, thanks to a time saving of nearly one hour between Frankfurt and Leipzig following the completion of electrification and construction of a new curve avoiding Bebra. The overnight Paris - Praha train will be speeded up by about two hours, but will run for a shorter season.

Table 31: Paris - Innsbruck passengers will have an additional change at Feldkirch. The *Arlberg Express* which ran once weekly in July and August will not run this summer.

Table 33/4: The overnight train from Oostende to München and Wien will continue to serve Oostende until September 3, but after that will start and finish at Brussels.

Table 48: There will be a daily TGV train between Brussels and Nice via Lille Europe, taking the *Jonction* route east of Paris via Marne-la-Vallée (Disneyland).

Table 51: The additional summer train between København and Berlin will not run. The *Neptun* and *Ostsee Express* will only run to September 23 as the Gedser - Warnemünde ferry will not carry passenger coaches after this date.

Table 56: Berlin and Kraków will be linked by a daytime train, named *Wawel*. The *Moskwa Express* is retimed to leave Berlin and Moskva in the evening and to arrive on the morning of the third day. This train conveys the Berlin - Kyïv cars formerly conveyed by the *Kiew Express*, which is withdrawn between Berlin and Warszawa.

Table 57: The Köln - Praha night train starts from Dortmund and is combined with the Stuttgart - Praha train for part of the journey. The *Franz Kafka* runs München - Praha (formerly from Nürnberg) and becomes an **IR** train.

Table 60: The Berlin - Praha *Comenius* is extended through to Budapest, giving two EuroCity trains each way on this route. The overnight Hamburg - Praha train (**476/7**) is withdrawn. The Berlin - Bucureşti *Balt Orient Express* becomes summer only as a better service is available by using a EuroCity train between Berlin and Budapest and changing there.

Table 61: The *Avala* (Wien - Beograd) now starts and finishes at Wien West instead of Wien Süd in order to connect with the new CityNightLine 'hotel' trains from Basel and Köln.

CONTINUED ON PAGE 27

EXPLANATION OF SIGNS	ZEICHENERKLÄRUNG		EXPLICATION DES SIGNES	EXPLICACIÓN DE LOS SIGNOS
TRANSPORT SERVICES	**BEFÖRDERUNGSDIENSTE**		**SERVICES**	**SERVICIOS DE TRANSPORTE**
Through carriage (1st and 2nd class seats)	Kurswagen (durchlaufender Wagen 1. und 2. Klasse)	🚃	Voiture directe (avec places assises 1re et 2^e classe)	Coche directo (con asientos de 1^a y 2^a clase)
Sleeping Car	Schlafwagen		Voiture-lit	Coche-camas
Couchette Car	Liegewagen		Couchettes	Coche-literas
Restaurant Car	Speisewagen	✕	Voiture-restaurant	Coche-restaurante
Buffet car or light refreshments available	Buffet-Wagen oder Verkauf von Erfrischungen	♟	Voiture-bar ou vente ambulante	Servicio de cafetería o bar móvil
Bus or coach service	Buslinie	🚌	Service autobus ou autocar	Servicio de autobuses
Shipping service	Schiffahrtslinie	⚓	Service maritime	Servicio marítimo
Airport	Flughafen	✈	Aéroport	Aeropuerto
DAYS OF RUNNING	**VERKEHRSTAGE**		**JOURS DE CIRCULATION**	**DÍAS DE SERVICIO**
Daily except Sundays and holidays	Täglich außer Sonntag und Feiertage	✕	Tous les jours sauf les dimanches et fêtes	Diario excepto domingos y festivos
Mondays to Fridays only, except holidays	Montag bis Freitag außer Feiertage	Ⓐ	Des lundis au vendredi, sauf les fêtes	De lunes a viernes, excepto festivos
Daily except Saturdays	Täglich außer Samstag	Ⓑ	Tous les jours sauf les samedis	Diario excepto sábados
Saturdays, Sundays and holidays	An Samstagen, Sonn- und Feiertagen	Ⓒ	Les samedis, dimanches et fêtes	Sábados, domingos y festivos
Sundays and holidays	An Sonn- und Feiertagen	†	Les dimanches et fêtes	Domingos y festivos
Mondays, Tuesdays	Montag, Dienstag	①②	Les lundis, mardis	Lunes, martes
Wednesdays, Thursdays	Mittwoch, Donnerstag	③④	Les mercredis, jeudis	Miércoles, jueves
Fridays, Saturdays	Freitag, Samstag	⑤⑥	Les vendredis, samedis	Viernes, sábados
Sundays	Sonntag	⑦	Les dimanches	Domingos
Mondays to Thursdays	Montag bis Donnerstag	①-④	Des lundis aux jeudis	De lunes a jueves
OTHER SYMBOLS	**WEITERE SYMBOLE**		**AUTRES SIGNES**	**OTROS SÍMBOLOS**
Train numbers (**bold figures** above train times)	Zugnummer (über den Fahrplanzeiten in **fetter Schrift** gesetzt)	IC345	Numero du train (en **caractères gras** au-dessus de l'horaire du train)	Número del tren (figura **en negrita** encima del horario del tren)
See footnotes (listed by train number)	Siehe die nach Zugnummern geordneten Fußnoten	◆	Renvoi aux notes données en bas de page (dans l'ordre numérique des trains)	Véase al pie de la página la nota correspondiente al número del tren
Reservation obligatory	Reservierung erforderlich	Ⓡ	Réservation obligatoire	Reserva obligatoria
Frontier station	Grenzbahnhof	🏛	Gare frontalière	Estación fronteriza
Train does not stop	Zug hält nicht	¦	Pas d'arrêt du train	El tren no para aquí
Separatès two trains in the same column between which no connection is possible	Trennt zwei in derselben Spalte angegebene Züge, die kein Anschluß miteinander haben	━	Sépare deux trains de la même colonne qui ne sont pas en correspondance	Separa dos trenes de la misma columna entre los cuales no hay correspondencia
Continued in later column	Fortsetzung weiter rechts	→	Suite dans une colonne à droite	Continuación a la derecha
Continued from earlier column	Fortsetzung von links	←	Suite d'une colonne à gauche	Continuación desde la izquierda
Vice versa	Umgekehrt	v.v.	Inversement	A la inversa

Other symbols are explained in the footnotes to each table or in the introduction to each country.

For dates of public holidays, see page 2.

Sonstige Symbole sind in den Fußnoten zu den einzelnen Fahrplänen oder in der Einführung zu den einzelnen Ländern erklärt.

Die öffentlichen Feiertage sind auf Seite 2 angeführt.

Les explications des autres signes se trouvent dans les notes en bas de la page de chaque tableau ou dans l'introduction de chaque pays.

Pour les dates des jours fériés voir page 2.

Los demás símbolos se explican en las notas al pie de cada cuadro o en la introducción a cada país.

Para días festivos véase la página 2.

The timetable is published twelve times a year at the beginning of each month. The services shown are liable to change at short notice, and a full subscription is recommended to maintain accurate information.

Every care has been taken to render the timetable correct in accordance with the latest advices, but changes are constantly being made by the administrations concerned and the publishers cannot hold themselves responsible for the consequences of either changes or inaccuracies.

L'indicateur paraît douze fois par an, au début de chaque mois. Les services indiqués peuvent subir des modifications de dernière minute; pour s'assurer des renseignements les plus exacts il est donc recommandé de prendre un abonnement annuel à l'indicateur.

Toute précaution est prise pour assurer l'exactitude de l'indicateur en fonction des dernières notifications reçues de la part des administrations responsables, mais comme celles-ci font constamment des modifications, les éditeurs ne peuvent être tenus responsables des conséquences des changements ou inexactitudes.

Das Kursbuch wird zwölfmal im Jahr jeweils am Monatsanfang herausgegeben. Die angeführten Verkehrsdienste unterliegen kurzfristigen Änderungen; aus diesem Grund empfehlen wir ein volles Abonnement, damit eine umfassende und genaue Information gewährleistet ist.

Das Kursbuch entspricht den zum Zeitpunkt der Drucklegung vorhandenen Kenntnissen. Für mögliche Fahrplanänderungen oder Druckfehler sowie die daraus resultierenden Folgen übernimmt der Herausgeber keinerlei Haftung.

El horario se publica doce veces al año al comienzo de cada mes. Los servicios incluidos están sujetos a cambios previa notificación a corto plazo, por lo que se recomienda una suscripción completa para mantener una información precisa.

Se ha hecho todo lo posible para ofrecer el horario correcto de acuerdo con la última información, pero como las administraciones están haciendo cambios continuamente, la editorial no se responsabiliza de las consecuencias que puedan acarrear tanto alteraciones como inexactitudes.

HOW TO USE THE TIMETABLE

HOW TO FIND YOUR SERVICES

Where the locations of the start and finish points of the journey are known, the easiest and quickest way of finding the table or tables required is to refer to the map of the country concerned.

The lines on the maps show rail, bus and shipping services and the numbers against the lines refer to the table required. In the case of a journey from Turku to Seinäjoki there is no direct line between the towns, but there is a line joining the two via Tampere. Turku to Tampere is on table 494, Tampere to Seinäjoki is on table 492.

Where the locations of the start and finish points are not known, look up the towns in the index (pages 11-26) and find a table number common to both stations.

Where no common table number is shown, look up the smaller of the two places between which you are travelling. Use the tables shown, together with the maps, to find the best place to change trains.

COMMENT TROUVER VOTRE SERVICE

Si vous savez où se trouvent les points de départ et d'arrivée de votre voyage, la manière la plus facile et la plus rapide de trouver le ou les tableaux demandés est de se reporter à la carte du pays en question.

Les lignes tracées sur les cartes indiquent les services ferroviaires, routiers et maritimes tandis que les numéros sur les lignes renvoient au tableau demandé. Dans le cas d'un voyage de Turku à Seinäjoki, aucune ligne directe ne joint les villes, mais il y a une ligne qui joint les deux villes par Tampere. Le tableau 494 donne la liaison Turku-Tampere, et le tableau 492, celle de Tampere à Seinäjoki.

Si l'on ignore où se trouvent les points de départ et d'arrivée, il faut consulter l'index des villes (page 11-26) et trouver un numéro de tableau qui soit commun aux deux gares.

Dans le cas où il n'y aurait aucune indication d'un numéro de tableau commun, cherchez d'abord la localité plus petite des deux points de votre parcours. Utilisez les tableaux indiqués, ainsi que les cartes, pour trouver le meilleur endroit pour changer de trains.

WIE SIE IHRE VERBINDUNG FINDEN

Wenn Sie die geographische Lage Ihrer Ausgangs- und Bestimmungsorte kennen, finden Sie die erforderlichen Fahrpläne am einfachsten mit Hilfe der Karte des entsprechenden Landes.

Die Linien auf den Landkarten zeigen die Eisenbahn-, Bus- und Schiffsverbindungen, und die Nummern an den Linien sind die entsprechenden Fahrplannummern. Zwischen Turku und Seinäjoki gibt es z.B. keine Direktverbindung. Es gibt jedoch eine Verbindung über Tampere. Für die Fahrt von Turku nach Tampere kommt der Fahrplan 494 in Frage; für jener von Tampere nach Seinäjoki der Fahrplan 492.

Wenn die geographische Lage der Ausgangs- und Bestimmungsorts Ihnen unbekannt ist, suchen Sie dann im alphabetisch geordneten Ortsregister (Seite 11-26) die für beide Orte geltenden Fahrplannummern.

Wenn keine gemeinsame Fahrplannummer angegeben ist, schauen Sie unter dem Namen des kleineren der beiden Orte nach. Mit Hilfe der Fahrpläne und Landkarten finden Sie dann den optimalen Umsteigebahnhof.

COMO ENCONTRAR LA RELACIÓN QUE DESEA

Si ya sabe localizar en el mapa los puntos de comienzo y final de su viaje, lo más sencillo y rápido para determinar el cuadro o los cuadros que requiere es referirse al mapa del país pertinente.

Las líneas trazadas en los mapas indican las relaciones por tren, autobús y buque, y los números que figuran al lado de ésas le remitirán al itinerario que debe consultar. En el caso de un viaje de Turku a Seinäjoki, por ejemplo, no hay relación directa entre las dos poblaciones, pero existe una línea que, pasando por Tampere, permite completar el trayecto. Para la relación Turku - Tampere consulte el cuadro 494, y para aquélla de Tampere a Seinäjoki, refiérase al cuadro 492.

Si desconoce la localización de los puntos de comienzo y final de su viaje, consulte el índice de lugares (páginas 11-26) y busque un número de cuadro horario común a ambas estaciones.

Si no existe ningún cuadro común, fíjese en la menor de las dos poblaciones y a partir de la lista de cuadros en que figura ésa busque en el mapa el punto de correspondencia con otro itinerario que más conviene al viaje que desa efectuar.

THE TABLES

Not every station on a line is necessarily shown – the omission of any station does not imply that the station does not have a service.

Kilometres shown are from the station marked 0 by the most direct route. On some routes 'tariff kilometres' (from which the fares are calculated) may be different to those shown.

Stations on branch lines are shown indented. In the example below there is a service from Göteborg to København but not from København to Malmö.

Stations where connections with other tables are possible have the table number of the other table shown in **bold**. Where the same table number is shown more than once in a station list, alternative services between the stations concerned may be shown in that table.

Stations the full service to or from which is given in another table are shown in *italics* together with the number of the other table.

All timings are departures (dep. or d.) unless noted as arr. or a. for arrival.

Any notes which apply to the whole table appear either under the heading or at the top of the station list.

Any symbols against station names are explained in the footnotes - see below.

POUR CONSULTER LES TABLEAUX

Il se peut que toutes les gares d'un parcours ne soient pas indiquées – l'omission d'une gare ne signifie pas pourtant qu'elle soit hors de service.

Les kilomètres indiqués donnent les distances par l'itinéraire le plus direct à partir de la gare signalée par 0. Sur certains itinéraires il est appliqué pour le calcul du prix des billets un kilométrage tarifaire qui peut varier de celui indiqué sur le tableau.

Sont présentés en retrait les noms des gares situées sur les lignes d'embranchement. Dans l'exemple ci-dessous il y a un service reliant Göteborg à København, mais aucun de København à Malmö.

Les numéros en caractères **gras** à droite des noms de gare renvoient aux tableaux des lignes en correspondance. Lorsque le même numéro figure plus d'une fois dans la manchette des gares d'un tableau cela signifie que sur le parcours entre les gares concernées circulent d'autres trains qui sont repris dans le tableau qui porte ce numéro..

L'ensemble des relations avec une gare dont le nom est imprimé en caractères *italiques* est repris dans un autre tableau, le numéro de celui-ci figurant à côté du nom de la gare.

Tous les horaires et dates sont ceux des départs (dep. ou d.) à moins que ne soit mentionné arr. ou a. pour arrivée.

Toutes les notes qui s'appliquent à l'ensemble du tableau apparaissent soit sous la rubrique, soit en haut de la machette des gares.

Tout signe en face du nom de la gare est expliqué dans la note au bas de la page - voir ci-dessous.

Table 466   GÖTEBORG - KØBENHAVN/MALMÖ

km		1431 12 Ⓐ	383 2Ⓡ S	383 2Ⓡ R	621 12 Ⓐ	1405 12	[bus]	397 12Ⓡ VY	697 12Ⓡ VY	601 12Ⓡ ✕	603 12Ⓡ ✕	1413 12	607 12Ⓡ ✕	391 12Ⓡ T	691 12Ⓡ T	609 12Ⓡ ✕
	Oslo Sentral **480** ...... d.	...	2240	2240	...	...	...	...	...	...	...	...	...	0730	...	...
0	Göteborg Central ...... d.	...	0320	0320	...	...	...	0600	...	0640	0754	...	1055	1212	...	1335
28	Kungsbacka ...... d.							0620		0705	0821		1122			1402
77	Varberg ...... d.							0659		0739	0850		1157	1300		1438
108	Falkenberg ...... d.							0721		0803	0915		1216			1504
151	Halmstad ...... d.		0454	0454	0540		0700	0750		0839	0944		1248	1350		1532
175	Laholm ...... d.				0557	0725				0857	1007		1305			1549
191	Båstad ...... d.				0609	0750				0908	1019		1316			1601
216	Ängelholm ...... d.				0630	0820		0834		0928	1039		1336	1435		1621
243	Helsingborg ...... a.		0555	0555	0648	0850		0852		0946	1057		1354	1458		1639
243	Helsingborg **463** ...... a.	0545	0555	0608	0658	0800		0852	0900	0948	1100	1210	1356	1458	1503	1645
283	Helsingør **463** ▲ ...... a.							0950						1550		
283	Helsingør **463** ...... a.							1010						1610		
327	København H. **463** ...... a.		0820					1050						1650		
	Hamburg Hbf. **661** ...... a.							1631						2231		
309	Lund ...... a.	0626		0651	0734	0839			0938	1024	1138	1248	1437		1552	1727
326	Malmö ...... a.	0643		0708	0747	0851			0951	1040	1152	1300	1450		1607	1740

HINWEISE ZUM GEBRAUCH DER FAHRPLÄNE

Es werden nicht alle Bahnhöfe einer Verkehrsverbindung zwangsläufig angegeben. Die Nichtangabe eines Bahnhofs bedeutet jedoch nicht, daß Aus- oder Zusteigen an diesem Ort nicht möglich ist.

Die Entfernungsangaben (km) gelten für die kürzeste Verbindung von dem mit 0 bezeichneten Ausgangsort. Auf einigen Verbindungen können die Tarifkilometer (die die Grundlage für die Fahrgeldberechnung bilden) von den angegebenden Entfernungen abweichen.

Bahnhofsnamen auf Nebenlinien sind eingerückt. Im vorliegenden Beispiel besteht zwar eine Verbindung von Göteborg nach København, jedoch nicht von København nach Malmö.

Bei Bahnhöfe mit Anschluß an andere Fahrpläne ist die Nummer des Anschlußfahrplans **fettgedruckt**. Wenn nach einer Gruppe Bahnhofsnamen die gleiche Fahrplannummer mehrere Male abgedruckt ist bedeutet dies, daß auf dem entsprechenden Fahrplan alternative Verbindungen möglich sind.

Bahnhöfe, deren sämtliche Verbindungen auf einem anderen Fahrplan angegeben sind, werden *kursiv* zusammen mit der Nummer des anderen Fahrplans angezeigt.

Die mit „arr." oder „a." bezeichneten Zeitangaben sind Ankunftszeiten; andernfalls sind alle Zeitangaben Abfahrtszeiten.

Anmerkungen, die sich auf den gesamten Fahrplan beziehen, sind entweder unter der Überschrift oder am Anfang der Stationsliste abgedruckt.

Die in Verbindung mit Stationsnamen abgedruckten Symbole sind in den Fußnoten erklärt (siehe unten).

COMO USAR LOS HORARIOS

En los cuadros no aparecen forzosamente todas las estaciones de cada trayecto. La omisión de una estación no implica sin embargo que ésta no tenga servicio.

El kilometraje se calcula a partir de la estación de orígen (señalada con 0) por el itinerario más directo. En ciertos itinerarios rige un kilometraje de tarifa (a base del cual se calcula el precio de los billetes) que puede ser distinto del indicado.

Se imprimen sangrados los nombres de estaciones situadas en ramal. En el ejemplo arriba expuesto existe una relación entre Göteborg y København, pero ninguna de København a Malmö.

Al lado de las estaciones que ofrecen posibilidades de correspondencia viene indicado en **negrita** el número de cuadro pertinente. Cuando varias estaciones llevan el mismo número este significa que entre estas estaciones pueden circular otros trenes que se verán indicados en el cuadro que lleva este número.

Las estaciones con las cuales las relaciones completas están indicadas en otro cuadro figuran en *cursiva* junto con el número de ese otro cuadro.

Todos los horarios son horarios de salida (dep. o d.) salvo indicación de "arr." o "a." que signfican llegada.

Las notas de aplicación general a un cuadro determinado aperecen o bajo el título del cuadro o en el encabezamiento de la columna de las estaciones.

Todo símbolo que figure al lado del nombre de una estación vendrá explicado en las notas al pie de la página (véase más abajo).

TRAIN COLUMNS

The top of each column shows the train number (**in bold**), train type (where important for fare calculation), classes of accommodation, catering provided and days of running. Any symbols or letters used are explained in the footnotes - see further below.

Trains run daily unless otherwise shown. Where a train does not run daily, the days or dates of running given are those that apply at the train's station of **origin** (which will be shown in a footnote if not appearing in the table itself).

Timings are all given in local time. A time comparison chart appears on page 2. Connecting times (where a change of train is necessary) are shown in *italics*.

Where two or more trains appear in the same column, each train has a separate heading. Where no connection is possible between trains in the same column, a bold line separates them.

Timings are shown in the 24 hour system. A conversion clock to am/pm times appears on page 9.

LES COLONNES HORAIRES

Le numéro du train est indiqué (**en gras**) en haut de chaque colonne ainsi que la qualité du train (là ou celle-ci influe sur le prix du billet), les classes de voitures comportées, les prestations de services et les jours ou périodes de circulation. Pour chaque signe ou lettre utilisé, consulter les notes explicatives au bas de la page - voir ci-dessous.

Les trains circulent tous les jours sauf indication contraire. Lorsqu'un train ne circule pas tous les jours, le régime de circulation indiqué est celui applicable à la gare d'**origine** du train (mentionnée, au cas où elle n'apparaît pas sur le tableau même, dans une note en bas de la page).

Les horaires sont donnés en heures locales. La page 2 donne un tableau de comparaison des heures.

Les heures *en italique* se rapportent aux correspondances (avec changement de train).

Au cas où les horaires de deux ou plusieurs trains sont présentés dans la même colonne, chaque train a son propre en-tête. Si deux trains de la même colonne n'assurent pas de correspondance entre eux, ils sont séparés par une ligne en gras.

L'heure sur 24 h. est utilisée pour les horaires. Un tableau de conversion horaire est donné en page 9.

ZUGSPALTEN

Im Kopf jeder Zeitenspalte sind Zugnummer (**fettgedruckt**), Zuggattung (da wo diese die Fahrpreisberechnung beeinflussen kann) und Hinweise über Beförderungsklassen, Service und Verkehrszeitbeschränkungen angegeben. Übrige Zeichen bezw. Buchstaben sind in den Fußnoten erklärt (siehe weiter unten).

Sofern nicht anders angegeben, verkehren die Züge täglich. Fährt ein Zug nicht jeden Tag, gelten die angezeigneten Verkehrstage oder Zeitabschnitt für den **Ausgangsbahnhof** des Zuges (dieser wird nötigenfalls in einer Fußnote angeführt).

Die angegebenen Abfahrts- und Ankunftszeiten sind jeweils Ortszeit. Eine Vergleichstabelle der verschiedenen Ortszeiten ist auf Seite 2 abgedruckt.

Die Fahrplanzeiten von Anschlußzüge (wenn ein Umsteigen erforderlich ist) sind in *Kursivschrift* angegeben.

Wenn zwei oder mehr Züge in derselben Spalte erscheinen hat jeder Zug eine separate Überschrift. Wenn zwischen Zügen, die in derselben Spalte angeführt sind, keine Anschlußmöglichkeit vorhanden ist, sind diese Züge durch eine fettgedruckte Linie getrennt.

Die Fahrplanzeiten sind nach dem 24-Stunden-System angegeben. Eine Umrechnungs-Uhrskala auf die englische Uhrzeitangabe am/pm ist auf Seite 9 abgedruckt.

Table 745   STUTTGART - NÜRNBERG

km		IR 2606	E 3193	IR§ 2665	IR 2465	3447	E 3103	IR 2467
		12	12	12	12	12	12	12
		♦⚹	W	♦⚹	⚹		⚹	⚹
	Karlsruhe 760 .... d.	0505			0706	...		*0909*
0	**Stuttgart** .... d.	0608	0635	0745	0808	0921	0928	1008
51	Schwäbisch Gmünd .... d.	0640	0715		0840	1003		1040
76	Aalen .... d.	0658	0744		0859	1022		1059
	Backnang .... d.			0815			1002	
113	Schwäbisch Hall Hessental .. d.			0847			1038	
113	Crailsheim .... d.	0725		0909	0924		1102	1124
159	Ansbach .... d.	0749		0938	0948		1133	1148
203	**Nürnberg** .... a.	0816		1010	1016		1208	1213

LAS COLUMNAS DE TRENES

El encabezamiento de cada columna indica el número del tren (**en negrita**), su categoría (cuando importa al cálculo de billete), las clases de coche que lleva, las prestaciones ofertas y el régimen de circulación. Todo signo o letra adicional remite a una nota al pie de la página (véase abajo).

Si no hay indicación contraria la circulación de los trenes es diaria. En el caso de que no circule todos los días un tren, el período de circulación indicado vale para la estación de **origen** del tren (mencionada, si no aparece en el cuadro mismo, en una nota al pie de la página).

Los horarios se dan siempre en hora local. Un cuadro de comparación de horas locales aparece en la página 2.

La presentación de un horario *en cursiva* da a entender que la relación de que se trata se efectúa mediante un cambio de trenes.

En el caso de que aparezcan dos o más trenes en la misma columna cada uno llevará su propio encabezamiento. Una línea en negrita separa dos trenes de la misma columna entre los cuales no hay correspondencia.

Los horarios se dan según el sistema de 24 horas. Una table de conversión al sistema con *am* y *pm* aparece en la página 9.

♦ – **NOTES** (LISTED BY TRAIN NUMBERS)
D738 – 🛏 1,2 cl. and 🍴 Leipzig - Schwerin - Rostock (Table **665**).
IR2140/1 – 🍴 Leipzig - Hannover - Norddeich and v.v.
L – 🍴 Köln - Hannover - Leipzig and v.v. (Table **670**).
R – 🍴 Leipzig - Schwerin - Rostock and v.v. (Table **665**).
c – Runs 5 minutes earlier on ⑥.

FOOTNOTES

Footnotes are used to give more detail of days of running, through cars to other lines, or accommodation available. A symbol or letter is used in the table against the train heading, time or station concerned, and is repeated at the foot of the table with an explanation. Standard symbols used throughout the book are explained on page 4.

More details of catering, accommodation available and supplements payable are given in the introduction to each country.

Footnotes are very important and must always be referred to when planning a journey.

FUSSNOTEN

Die Fußnoten enthalten weitere Angaben in bezug auf Verkehrstage, Kurswagen und Beförderungsklassen. Die Fußnoten sind durch ein Symbol oder einen Buchstaben gekennzeichnet. Die in diesem Kursbuch verwendeten Standard-Symbole sind auf Seite 4 erklärt.

Weitere Angaben in bezug auf Restaurant- und Schlafwagen sowie Fahrgeldzuschäge finden sich in der Einführung zu jedem einzelnen Land.

Die Fußnoten enthalten wichtige Informationen und müssen bei der Reiseplanung berücksichtigt werden.

NOTES EN BAS DE LA PAGE

Les notes en bas de la page servent à donner des renseignements complémentaires sur les jours de circulation, les voitures directes et la prestation de services dans les trains. Les signes ou lettres figurant éventuellement à côté des noms de gares ou dans les colonnes des trains renvoient à des notes explicatives en bas de page. L'explication des signes conventionnels utilisés dans tout l'indicateur se trouve en page 4.

Dans les notes préliminaires qui figurent en tête des sections réservées à chaque pays sont présentés d'autres renseignements sur les conditions de transport, les prestations, les catégories de train, les suppléments, etc.

Les notes en bas de la page sont d'une importance capitale et il faut toujours les consulter lors de la préparation d'un voyage.

NOTAS A PIE DE PÁGINA

Las notas a pie de página sirven para dar información complementaria sobre la circulación y composición de los trenes (coches directos) y las prestaciones ofertas en ellos. Las llamadas (símbolo o letra) que figuran en el encabezamiento de una columna al lado de un horario o estación remiten al pie de la página, donde vienen repetidas con su explicación. Los signos convencionales de aplicación general se explican en la página 4.

En las notas preliminares que encabezan las secciones dedicadas a cada país se encontrará una información más amplia sobre condiciones especiales en el país, servicios, categorías y clases de tren, suplementos, etc.

Las notas a pie de página son de suma importancia y deben consultarse siempre que se prepara un viaje.

KEYWORDS	STICHWORTVERZEICHNIS	GLOSSAIRE	GLOSARIO
January (Jan.)	Januar	janvier	enero
February (Feb.)	Februar	février	febrero
March (Mar.)	März	mars	marzo
April (Apr.)	April	avril	abril
May	Mai	mai	mayo
June	Juni	juin	junio
July	Juli	juillet	julio
August (Aug.)	August	août	agosto
September (Sept.)	September	septembre	septiembre
October (Oct.)	Oktober	octobre	octubre
November (Nov.)	November	novembre	noviembre
December (Dec.)	Dezember	décembre	diciembre
weekdays	Wochentage	jours ouvrables	días laborables
returning	Rückreise	retour	vuelta
sleeping car	Schlafwagen	voiture-lits	coche-camas
couchette car	Liegewagen	voiture-couchettes	coche-literas
restaurant car	Speisewagen	voiture-restaurant	coche-restaurante
buffet car	Buffetwagen	voiture-buffet	coche-bar
train number	Zugnummer	numéro du train	número de tren
and v.v.	und umgekehrt	et inversement	y a la inversa
catering service	Restaurationsdienst	service de restauration	servicio de restaurantería
change at	umsteigen in	changer à	cambiar en
footnotes	Fußnoten	notes en bas de la page	notas a pie de página
through service	Direktverbindung	service direct	servicio directo
day service	verkehrt tagsüber	service de jour	servicio de día
connection	Anschluß	correspondance	correspondencia
information not available	Angaben liegen nicht vor	renseignements non disponibles	información no disponible
subject to confirmation	noch zu bestätigen	sous réserve de confirmation	sujeto a confirmación
also	auch	aussi	también
not	nicht	non pas	no
except	außer	sauf	excepto
arrive (arr.)	Ankunft	arrivée	llegada
depart (dep.)	Abfahrt	départ	salida
runs	verkehrt	circule	circula
to	bis	jusqu'à	hasta
conveys	befördert	achemine	lleva
journey	Reise	voyage	viaje
minutes (mins.)	Minuten	minutes	minutos
hours (hrs.)	Stunden	heures	horas
every	alle	chaque	cada
later	später	plus tard	más tarde
earlier	früher	plus tôt	más temprano
daily	täglich	tous les jours	diario
one day later	ein Tag später	un jour plus tard	un día más tarde
timings	Fahrplanzeiten	horaires	horarios
runs in two portions	verkehrt als zwei Zugteile	circule en 2 tranches sauf lors	circula en dos secciones excepto en
except when train A runs	außer wenn Zug A verkehrt	de la circulation du train A	período de circulación del tren A
calls at	hält in	s'arrête à	para en
supplement payable	zuschlagpflichtig	supplément à payer	tren sujeto a suplemento
extended to	erweitert bis	prolongé à	continúa a
relief train	Entlastungszug	train supplémentaire	tren de complemento
days of running	Verkehrstage	jours de circulation	días de circulación
see page	siehe Seite	voir page	véase la página
table	Tabelle	tableau	cuadro
one class only	nur eine Klasse	classe unique	clase única
runs via	über	passe par	circula por
on these dates	an diesen Tagen	à ces dates	en estas fechas
stops to pick up only	Halt nur zum Einsteigen	arrêt seulement pour laisser monter	parada solo para recoger pasajeros
stops to set down only	Halt nur zum Aussteigen	arrêt seulement pour laisser descendre	parada solo para dejar pasajeros

PICTOGRAMS

Information
Information
Renseignements
Información

Ticket office
Fahrkartenschalter
Guichet
Despacho de billetes

Luggage office
Gepäckaufbewahrung
Consigne
Consigna

Luggage lockers
Gepäckschließfächer
Consigne automatique
Taquillas de equipaje

Ladies
Damen
Dames
Señoras

Gentlemen
Harren
Hommes
Caballeros

Lost property
Fundbüro
Objets trouvés
Oficina de objetos perdidos

Bureau de change
Geldwechsel
Bureau de change
Cambio

Post office
Postamt
Poste
Correos

Telephone
Telefon
Téléphone
Teléfono

Restaurant
Restaurant
Restaurant
Restaurante

Buffet
Buffet
Buffet
Comedor

Meeting point
Treffpunkt
Point rencontre
Lugar de reunión

Entrance
Eingang
Entrée
Entrada

Exit
Ausgang
Sortie
Salida

Bus
Bus
Bus
Autobuses

Boat
Schiff
Bateaux
Barcos

Tram
Straßenbahn
Tramways
Tranvias

HEALTH REQUIREMENTS

It is not mandatory for visitors to Europe to be vaccinated against infectious diseases unless they are travelling from endemic areas. For travellers' peace of mind, however, protection against the following diseases should be considered:

AIDS	Cholera
Hepatitis A	Hepatitis B
Polio	Rabies
Tetanus	Typhoid

Full information is available from the manual published by the World Health Organisation, or from the Thomas Cook Vaccination Centre, Berkeley Street, London W1A 1EB.

WATER: Tap water is 'generally' safe to drink in most parts of Europe. Passengers travelling in some southern countries or who doubt the purity of the tap water are recommended to boil it, use sterilisation tablets or to drink bottled water. The water in washrooms or toilets on trains is not suitable for drinking.

WEATHER

The weather in Europe is generally mild and pleasant. However, it varies greatly between the North and the South and between the East and the West as show below. Temperature is also affected by altitude.

	London	Roma	Stockholm	Budapest
JANUARY				
Highest	6	12	2	0
Lowest	1	4	- 4	- 5
Rain days	15	8	7	8
APRIL				
Highest	13	20	17	7
Lowest	4	8	6	0
Rain days	13	6	8	6
JULY				
Highest	22	31	28	21
Lowest	12	18	16	13
Rain days	13	3	7	9
OCTOBER				
Highest	14	23	16	9
Lowest	6	11	7	4
Rain days	16	9	8	9

Highest = Average highest daily temperature in °C.
Lowest = Average lowest daily temperature in °C.
Rain days = Average number of rainy days.

PASSPORTS AND VISAS

Nationals of one country intending to travel to or pass through another country normally require a valid passport and will also require a visa unless a special visa-abolition agreement has been made between the countries concerned. The limit of stay permitted in each country is usually 3 months.

Applications for visas must be on special consular forms, and in most cases one or more passport size photographs are also required. The consuls usually make a charge for issuing a visa. Before issuing a transit visa, a consul usually requires to see the visa of the country of destination.

Applications for visas should be made well in advance of the date of travel to the local consulate of the country concerned. Most can be supplied through branches of Thomas Cook for an additional fee.

The possession of a valid passport or visa does not necessarily grant the holder automatic access to all areas of the country to be visited. Certain countries have zones which are restricted or prohibited to foreign nationals.

CURRENCY

Most countries restrict the import and or export of foreign currency. In addition the countries listed below restrict the import and or export of their own currency. Certain Eastern European countries prohibit the import and export of their own currency (see below), and normally require all foreign currency to be declared on entry. To export foreign currency you must present your entry declaration, and you are unable to export more than you originally imported.

Prohibited import and export: Bulgaria, Czech Republic, Poland, Romania, Slovakia, and former U.S.S.R.

Restricted export only: Norway, Sweden.

Restricted import only: Greece, Hungary, Italy, Malta.

Full details of the amounts allowed are available from your travel agent or the embassy of the country concerned.

CURRENCY CONVERSION RATES

The information shown below is subject to alteration without notice. Tourist rates of exchange may differ from those shown.

COUNTRY	Unit	£1 =	$1 =	DM1 =	¥100 =
Albania	Lek	159.19	100.49	72.48	112.56
Austria	Schilling	15.46	9.76	7.04	10.93
Belarus	Rubl'	18486.50	11670.00	8416.88	13072.00
Belgium	Franc	45.41	28.67	20.68	32.11
Bulgaria	Lev	105.57	66.65	48.07	74.65
Croatia	Kuna	8.00	5.05	3.64	5.66
Czech Republic	Koruna	41.12	25.96	18.72	29.08
Denmark	Krone	8.86	5.59	4.03	6.26
Estonia	Kroon	17.62	11.12	8.02	12.46
Finland	Markka	6.88	4.34	3.13	4.87
France	Franc	7.85	4.96	3.57	5.55
Germany	Mark	2.19	1.38	1.00	1.55
Greece	Drakhmí	359.98	227.25	163.90	254.55
Hungary	Forint	185.60	117.17	84.51	131.25
Iceland	Krona	101.35	63.98	46.15	71.67
Irish Republic	Punt	1.00	0.63	0.46	0.71
Italy	Lira	2745.79	1733.40	1250.20	1941.64
Latvia	Lats	0.82	0.52	0.38	0.58
Lithuania	Litas	6.34	4.00	2.89	4.48
Luxembourg	Franc	45.41	28.67	20.68	32.11
Malta	Lira	0.55	0.35	0.25	0.39
Moldova	Leu	7.00	4.42	3.19	4.95
Netherlands	Gulden	2.46	1.55	1.12	1.74
Norway	Krone	9.86	6.22	4.49	6.97
Poland	Złoty	3.70	2.34	1.69	2.62
Portugal	Escudo	232.86	147.00	106.02	164.66
Romania	Leu	2908.42	1836.00	1324.20	2056.57
Russia	Rubl'	7615.60	4807.50	3467.36	5385.05
Slovakia	Koruna	46.27	29.21	21.07	32.72
Slovenia	Tolar	179.82	113.51	81.87	127.15
Spain	Peseta	203.87	128.70	92.82	144.16
Sweden	Krona	11.46	7.23	5.22	8.10
Switzerland	Franc	1.83	1.15	0.83	1.29
Turkey	Lira	66347.90	41885.00	30209.20	46916.80
Ukraine	Kupon	205173.70	129520.00	93415.10	145079.80
United Kingdom	Pound	1.00	0.63	0.46	0.71
Yugoslavia	New Dinar	+	+	+	+

+ Refer to a bank or foreign exchange dealer.

METRIC CONVERSION TABLES

The Celsius system of temperature measurement, the metric system of distance measurement and the twenty-four hour clock are used throughout this book. The table below gives Fahrenheit, mile and twelve hour clock equivalents.

TEMPERATURE

°C	°F
-20	-4
-15	5
-10	14
-5	23
0	32
5	41
10	50
15	59
20	68
25	77
30	86
35	95
40	104

Conversion formula
°C x 9 ÷ 5 + 32 = °F

DISTANCE

km	miles	km	miles	km	miles
1	0.62	45	27.96	300	186.41
2	1.24	50	31.07	400	248.45
3	1.86	55	34.18	500	310.69
4	2.49	60	37.28	600	372.82
5	3.11	65	40.39	700	434.96
6	3.73	70	43.50	800	497.10
7	4.35	75	46.60	900	559.23
8	4.97	80	49.71	1000	621.37
9	5.59	85	52.82	1100	683.54
10	6.21	90	55.92	1200	745.68
15	9.32	95	59.03	1300	807.82
20	12.43	100	62.14	1400	869.96
25	15.53	125	77.67	1500	932.10
30	18.64	150	93.21	2000	1242.74
35	21.75	175	108.74	3000	1864.11
40	24.85	200	124.27	4000	2485.48

TIME

Midnight depart	=	0000
1 am	=	0100
5 am	=	0500
5.30 am	=	0530
11 am	=	1100
12 noon	=	1200
1 pm	=	1300
3.45 pm	=	1545
Midnight arrive	=	2400

BUYING YOUR TICKET

Train tickets must be purchased before travelling, either from travel agents or at the station ticket office (or machine) unless using an unstaffed station when the ticket must be purchased on the train.

In Eastern Europe foreign nationals may have to buy international rail tickets at the office of the state tourist board concerned and not at the railway station. The tickets can usually only be purchased in Western currency and buying tickets can take a long time. It is recommended that all tickets are purchased before visiting Eastern Europe if at all possible.

All tickets for main line services (except in France) are dated when purchased and must be used within the time limit shown, usually 2 months. In France, tickets must be date-stamped by a machine (composteur) at the entrance to the station platform.

RESERVATIONS

Many express trains in Europe are restricted to passengers holding advance seat reservations. Seat reservations for most express trains can be made up to two months in advance. A small fee is charged. Many trains are not reservable, but where reservation is possible it is usually worthwhile.

SUPPLEMENTS

Many countries have faster or more luxurious train services for which an extra charge is made. This supplement is payable when the ticket is purchased and often includes the price of seat reservations. In the case of Italian ETR 450 trains, the cost of meals is also included. The supplement can sometimes be paid on the train, but usually at extra cost.

RAILPASSES

Tickets are available which give unlimited travel on all trains in a given area. These railpasses range from Eurail and Inter-Rail passes which cover the whole of Western Europe for up to 1 month, to local passes which cover limited areas for 1 day. Passports may need to be shown when purchasing such tickets.

FINDING YOUR TRAIN

At most stations departures are listed on large paper sheets (often yellow), and/or on electronic departure indicators. These sheets or indicators list trains by departure, giving principal stops, and indicate which platform they leave from.

On each platform of principal European stations, a noticeboard can be found, giving details of the main trains calling at that platform. This includes the location of individual carriages, type of accommodation provided and their destinations.

A sign may be carried on the side of the carriage indicating the train name, principal stops and destination and a label or sign near the door will indicate the number allocated to the carriage, which is shown on reservation tickets.

A sign above the compartment door will indicate seat numbers and which seats are reserved. In non-compartment trains, reserved seats have labels on their headrests. In some countries, notably Sweden and Yugoslavia, reserved seats are not marked and occupants will be asked to move when the passenger who has reserved the seat boards the train.

The above is designed to be a concise guide to travelling in Europe by train. For more details of accommodation available, catering, supplements etc. see the introduction to each country.

TRAIN SERVICES

All countries in Europe offer two classes of rail accommodation, usually 1st and 2nd class. 1st class is more comfortable and therefore more expensive than 2nd class. 1st class accommodation is usually indicated by a yellow band above the windows and doors and/or a figure 1 near the door or on the windows.

In Southern and Eastern Europe, 1st class travel is advisable for visitors as fares are reasonable and 2nd class can be very overcrowded.

CATERING

Most long distance trains in Europe have restaurant cars serving full meals or buffet cars serving light snacks. Increasingly light refreshments are being served from a trolley wheeled through the train. Not all catering cars are open for the whole length of the train journey and restaurant cars may have set times of meal sittings. Catering cars usually have a red band above the windows and doors.

OVERNIGHT ACCOMMODATION

Sleeping cars (🛏) have bedroom style compartments with limited washing facilities and full bedding. Toilets are located at one or both ends of the coach. An attendant travels with each car or pair of cars and will serve drinks and continental breakfast at an extra charge. 1st class sleeping compartments have one or two berths (in Britain and Norway two berths is 2nd class) and 2nd class compartments have three berths. Some trains convey 'special' T2 cabins, shown as (T2) in the tables, with one berth in 1st class and two berths in 2nd class. In Spain, T2 cars are first class and Talgo trains have four berths in second class.

Compartments are allocated exclusively for the use of men or women except when married couples or families occupy all berths. Children travelling alone, or who cannot be accommodated in the same compartment as their family, are placed in women's compartments. In the former U.S.S.R however, berths are allocated in strict order and men and women often share compartments.

Some trains have communicating doors between sleeping compartments which can be opened to create a larger room if both compartments are occupied by the same family group.

Berths can be reserved up to 3 months before the date of travel and early reservation is recommended as space is limited, especially on French ski trains and in Eastern Europe. Berths must be claimed within 15 minutes of boarding the train or they may be resold.

Couchettes (🛏) are a more basic form of overnight accommodation consisting of simple bunk beds with a sheet, blanket and pillow. The couchettes are converted from ordinary seat cars for the night, and usually consist of 4 berths in 1st class and 6 in 2nd. Washing and toilet facilities are provided at the ends of each coach. Males and females are booked into the same compartment and are expected to sleep in their daytime clothes.

CAR-SLEEPERS

Car-sleeper services operate throughout Europe. Cars are conveyed in special wagons while passengers travel in sleeping cars or couchettes, often in different trains. To book these services passengers should contact the tourist office of the country concerned.

LUGGAGE

Luggage may be registered at many larger stations and sent separately by rail to your destination. However, it is no longer possible to register luggage in Britain for consignment to other European countries. In some countries, bicycles may also be registered in advance and certain local and some express trains will convey bicycles for an extra charge. The relevant railway administrations will advise exact details on request.

INDEX
(by Table Number)

🚋 Local train service from nearest rail station shown.
🚎 Tram service from nearest rail station shown.
🚠 Cable car service from nearest rail station shown.
(🚗) Service provided by car-sleeper train only.

🚌 Bus service from nearest rail station shown.
⛴ Boat service (usually summer only) from nearest rail station shown.
✈ Rail station at airport.
10/159 Use both Tables to find the best connecting services.

INDEX

For places outside Europe, see the

THOMAS COOK OVERSEAS TIMETABLE

Probably the most adventurous timetable ever published, the Thomas Cook Overseas Timetable brings together in one book surface travel timetables for virtually every country outside Europe. Published every two months, it contains much information not readily available in any other form. See the back of this book for further details.

International services from May 28

CONTINUED FROM PAGE 3

Table 62: The München - Zagreb night train will carry the name *Lisinski*.

Table 66: The *Donau Kurier* will become a 'hotel' train running between Köln and Wien only and marketed as CityNightLine (see above).

Table 69: Train **EC12/3** is renamed *Leonardo da Vinci* and is diverted at Verona to run to and from Milano instead of Venezia. The once-weekly *Vorarlberg Express* will no longer run in summer.

Table 73: The Dortmund - Roma *Italia Express* will only run during the summer.

Table 76: Services over the Brenner route will be reorganised. There will be a new EuroCity train named *Tiepolo* running between München and Venezia, replacing train **EC12/3** which is diverted to Milano. The München - Ancona day train (**488/9**) is withdrawn.

Table 77: The *Schweiz Express* will not convey through cars to Dortmund in summer.

Table 78: The name *Thunersee* is transferred to a new **ICE** train between Berlin and Interlaken taking the direct route via Kassel and Frankfurt.

Table 86: The *Wiener Walzer* becomes a 'hotel' train running between Zürich and Wien only. Train **464/5** becomes a EuroNight train named *Zürichsee* running between Zürich and Graz and conveying the Zürich - Budapest cars formerly in the *Wiener Walzer*. As a result these cars now run via Sopron. The *Robert Stolz* from Zürich to Graz and Klagenfurt is withdrawn.

Table 90: The Milano - Bordeaux train is withdrawn, but is partially replaced by extending a Basel - Milano train through to Nice. The *Ligure* is withdrawn between Nice and Marseille.

Table 97: New train **492/3** provides a second service on the Beograd - Sofija - Istanbul route, which also conveys reinstated through cars from Moskva (Table **94d**) running twice weekly.

Other news is that the overnight sleeper trains from **London** to **Fort William** and from **Plymouth** to **Glasgow** via Edinburgh are expected to cease after May 27, together with the **London - Carlisle** sleeping car. The overnight **Penzance - London** train will be diverted to London Waterloo.

Shipping News

Scandinavian Seaways (Table **1040**) are to introduce sailings between **Newcastle** and **Amsterdam** on alternate days from late May to mid September, using the m.v. *Winston Churchill*. The terminal is actually at IJmuiden, some 30 km from Amsterdam, but there is a coach connection to and from Amsterdam Centraal station.

Stena Sealink's new *HSS* (High-speed Sea Service) is due to be introduced on the **Holyhead - Dun Laoghaire** route towards the end of the year. This revolutionary new twin-hulled craft, hailed as the world's largest fast ferry, will make four or five crossings each way daily, with an advertised journey time of 99 minutes. Stena Sealink also plans to introduce a *Sea Lynx* catamaran onto the **Newhaven - Dieppe** route from June 16, with a crossing time of 2 hours 15 minutes, compared to 4 hours by ship.

News of **Helsinki - Tallinn** services is that **Tallink** (Table **1295**) will be moving their terminal to the western harbour in Helsinki from May 1. **Viking Line** are to reintroduce their catamaran service on the route from April 15, but there is an unconfirmed report that **Estonian New Line** may not be operating this summer.

Ystad will cease to be served by **Polferries** from May 1, when the service to Świnoujście will switch to **Malmö** (Table **1270**).

Two more shipping companies introducing high-speed car carrying vessels this year are **SNCM** and **Larvik Line**. The former operator expects its 'NGV' to commence service from July 17 on the routes between **Nice** and **Bastia**, **Calvi** and **Ajaccio**, almost halving the journey times. The new craft will also participate in the **Livorno - Bastia** service. Further details will be found in Table **1430**. The **Larvik Line** catamaran, to be named *Juan L.*, will commence a new route between **Larvik** (Norway) and **Skagen** in Denmark, which is linked to Frederikshavn by a privately operated local railway. Journey time will be just 2 hours and 45 minutes, and the service will run from May 5 to September 29.

A new operator on the Ancona - Patras route from this summer will be **Superfast Ferries** (Table **1530**), who will be using two brand new vessels designed to make the voyage in only 20 hours. **Strintzis Lines** and **Minoan Lines**, who also operate on the Ancona - Patras route, have co-ordinated their timetables and are marketing the route as a joint service (Table **1535**).

Two new guidebooks in the Thomas Cook *On the Rails* series are now available. On the Rails around Britain and Ireland is ideal for days out by train or extended rail tours. *On the Rails around France, Belgium, the Netherlands and Luxembourg* is another practical guide to holidays by train and covers over 40 selected rail routes and over 150 popular destinations. Further details can be found on page 341, and there is an order form for all of our publications on pages 559/60.

Finally, the next edition of the European Timetable will be dated **May 1 - 27**. The June edition will be dated **May 28 - June 30** and will show the new summer services, except for a few cases where it is not possible for us to obtain the information in time.

CITY CENTRE PLANS

The following plans are intended to help travellers in a strange city
locate and use the main public transport termini and to transfer between them.

The plans show the location of the main railway, bus and shipping stations in relation to the the city centres
and the direction and distance to the main airport(s). Underground and metro lines are only
shown where they are of use to passengers transferring between stations or to the city centres.

KEY

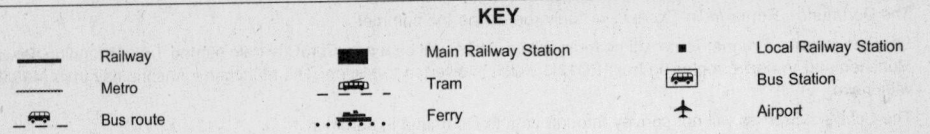

▬▬	Railway	🚈	Main Railway Station	■	Local Railway Station
═══	Metro	🚊	Tram	🚌	Bus Station
🚌	Bus route	⛴	Ferry	✈	Airport

AMSTERDAM

Sloterdijk
De Vlugtlaan
CENTRAAL
1 km
Muiderpoort
Weesp
Lelylaan
✈ 10 km
Amstel
Zuid   RAI   Duivendrecht

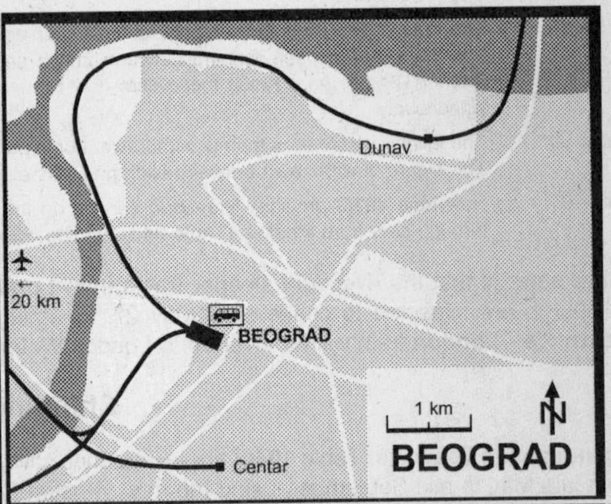

BEOGRAD

Dunav
✈ 20 km
BEOGRAD
1 km
Centar

BARCELONA

SANTS
✈ 10 km
Pas de Gracia
Plaça d'Espanya
Arc del Triomf
Plaça de Catalunya
1 km
Drassanes
FRANÇA
Barceloneta

BOULOGNE

½ km
Tintelleries
Ferryport
VILLE

BASEL

½ km
Badischer
✈ 8 km
SNCF/SBB

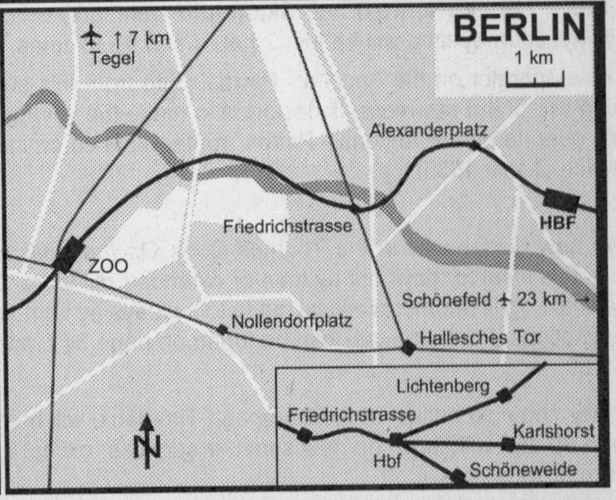

BERLIN

✈ 7 km Tegel
1 km
Alexanderplatz
Friedrichstrasse
HBF
ZOO
Schönefeld ✈ 23 km
Nollendorfplatz
Hallesches Tor
Lichtenberg
Friedrichstrasse
Karlshorst
Hbf
Schöneweide

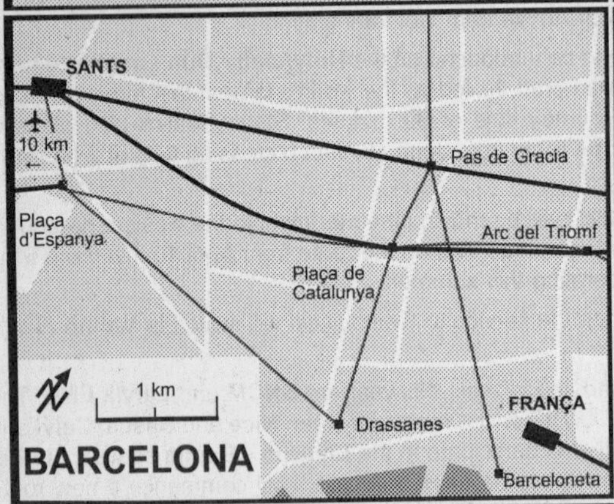

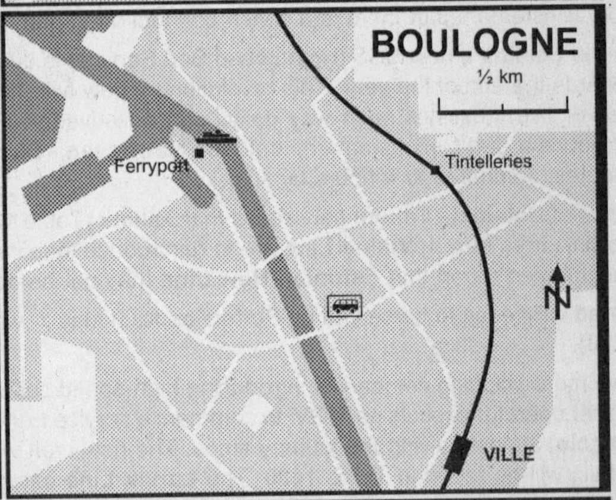

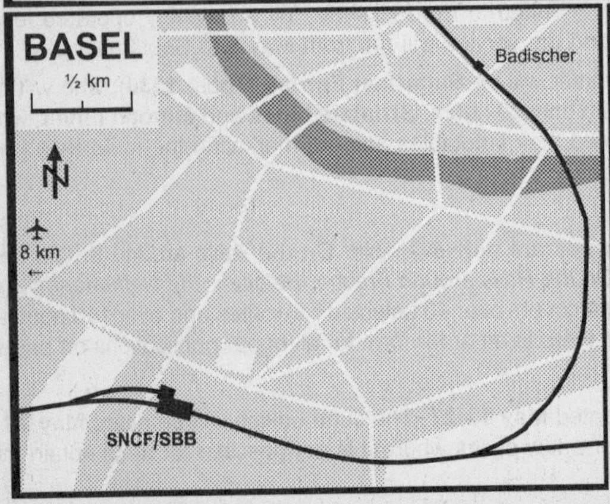

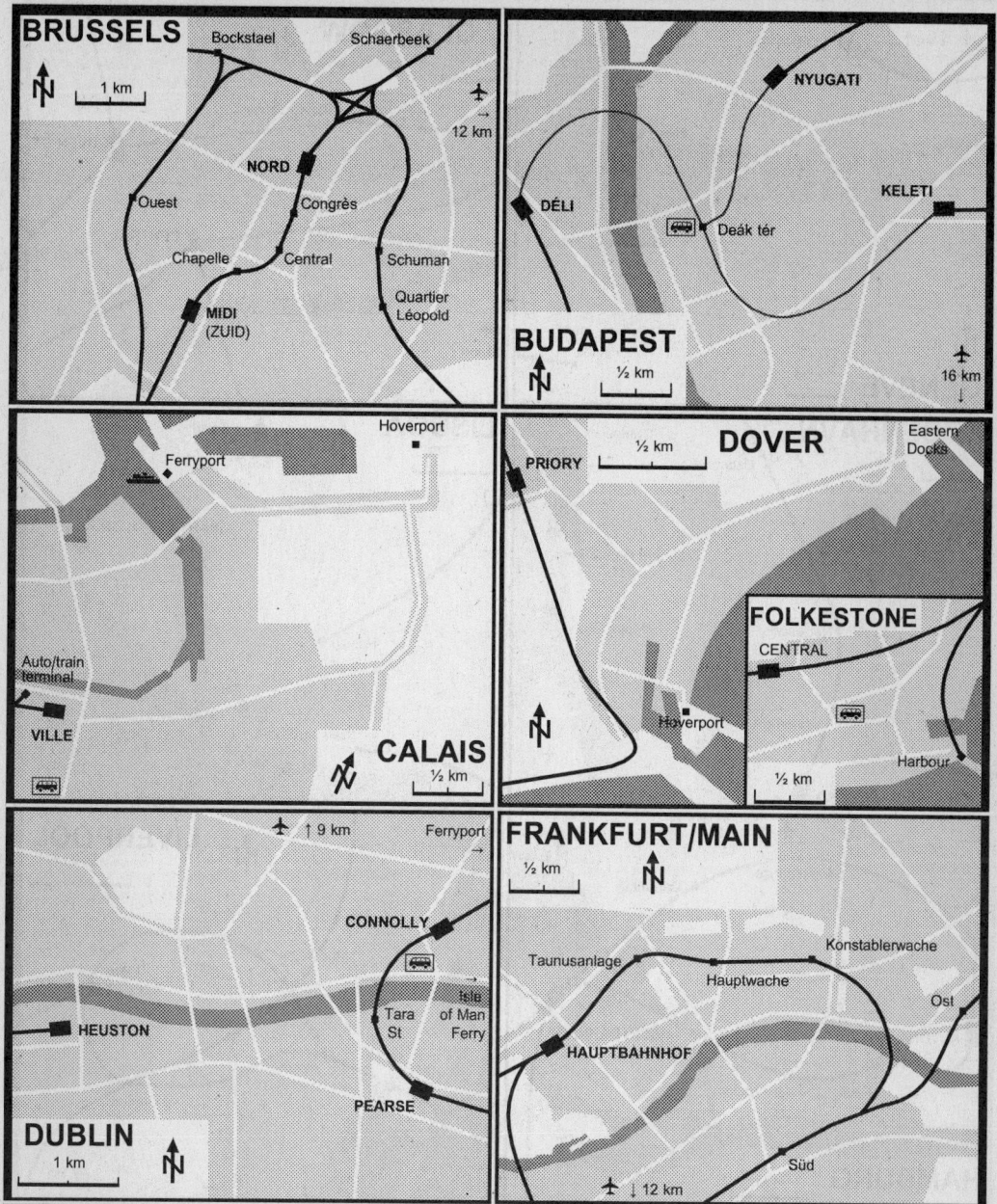

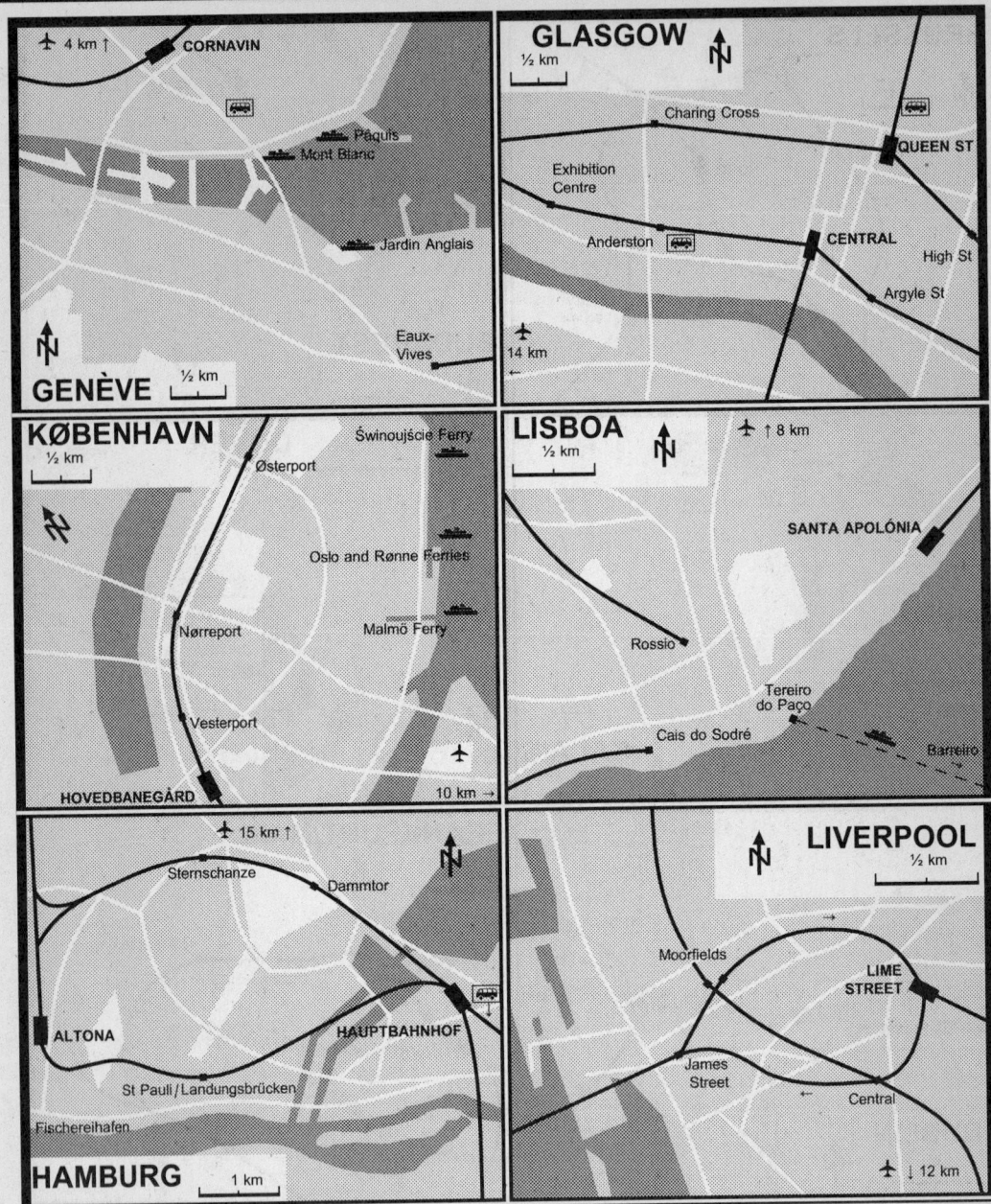

✈ 4 km ↑   CORNAVIN

Pâquis
Mont Blanc

Jardin Anglais

Eaux-Vives

GENÈVE   ½ km

GLASGOW
½ km

Charing Cross   QUEEN ST

Exhibition Centre

Anderston   **CENTRAL**

High St

Argyle St

✈ 14 km ←

KØBENHAVN
½ km

Świnoujście Ferry

Østerport

Oslo and Rønne Ferries

Nørreport   Malmö Ferry

Vesterport

HOVEDBANEGÅRD   10 km →

LISBOA
½ km   ✈ ↑ 8 km

SANTA APOLÓNIA

Rossio

Tereiro do Paço

Cais do Sodré   Barreiro

✈ 15 km ↑

Sternschanze   Dammtor

ALTONA   **HAUPTBAHNHOF**

St Pauli / Landungsbrücken

Fischereihafen

HAMBURG   1 km

LIVERPOOL
½ km

Moorfields

LIME STREET

James Street

Central ←

✈ ↓ 12 km

5254

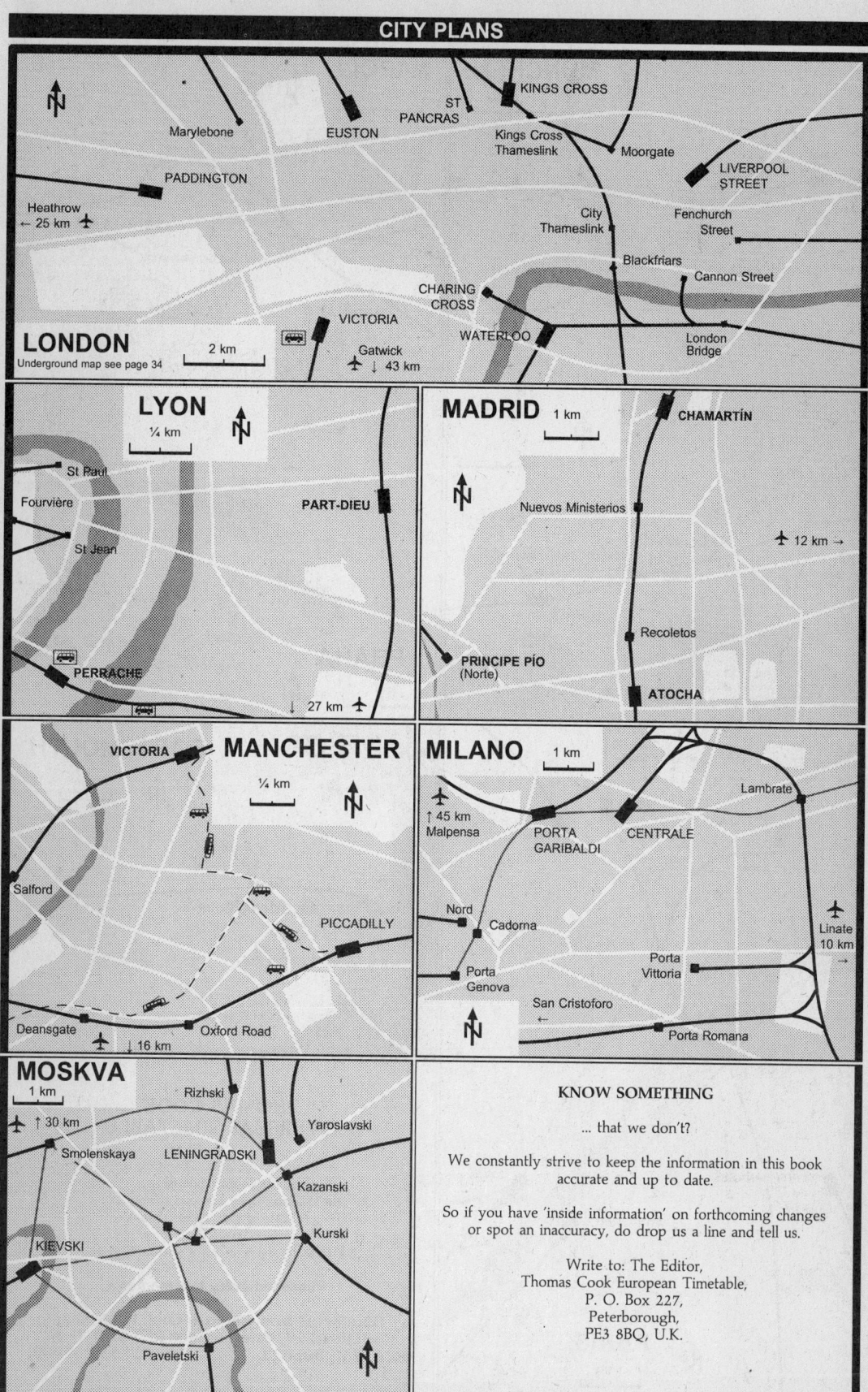

LONDON
Underground map see page 34
2 km

Marylebone
EUSTON
ST PANCRAS
KINGS CROSS
Kings Cross Thameslink
Moorgate
PADDINGTON
LIVERPOOL STREET
Heathrow ← 25 km
City Thameslink
Fenchurch Street
Blackfriars
Cannon Street
CHARING CROSS
VICTORIA
Gatwick ↓ 43 km
WATERLOO
London Bridge

LYON
¼ km
St Paul
Fourvière
PART-DIEU
St Jean
PERRACHE
↓ 27 km

MADRID 1 km
CHAMARTÍN
Nuevos Ministerios
12 km →
Recoletos
PRINCIPE PÍO (Norte)
ATOCHA

MANCHESTER
¼ km
VICTORIA
Salford
PICCADILLY
Deansgate
Oxford Road
↓ 16 km

MILANO 1 km
↑ 45 km Malpensa
Lambrate
PORTA GARIBALDI
CENTRALE
Nord
Cadorna
Linate 10 km →
Porta Genova
Porta Vittoria
San Cristoforo
Porta Romana

MOSKVA
1 km
↑ 30 km
Rizhski
Yaroslavski
Smolenskaya
LENINGRADSKI
Kazanski
KIEVSKI
Kurski
Paveletski

KNOW SOMETHING

... that we don't?

We constantly strive to keep the information in this book accurate and up to date.

So if you have 'inside information' on forthcoming changes or spot an inaccuracy, do drop us a line and tell us.

Write to: The Editor,
Thomas Cook European Timetable,
P. O. Box 227,
Peterborough,
PE3 8BQ, U.K.

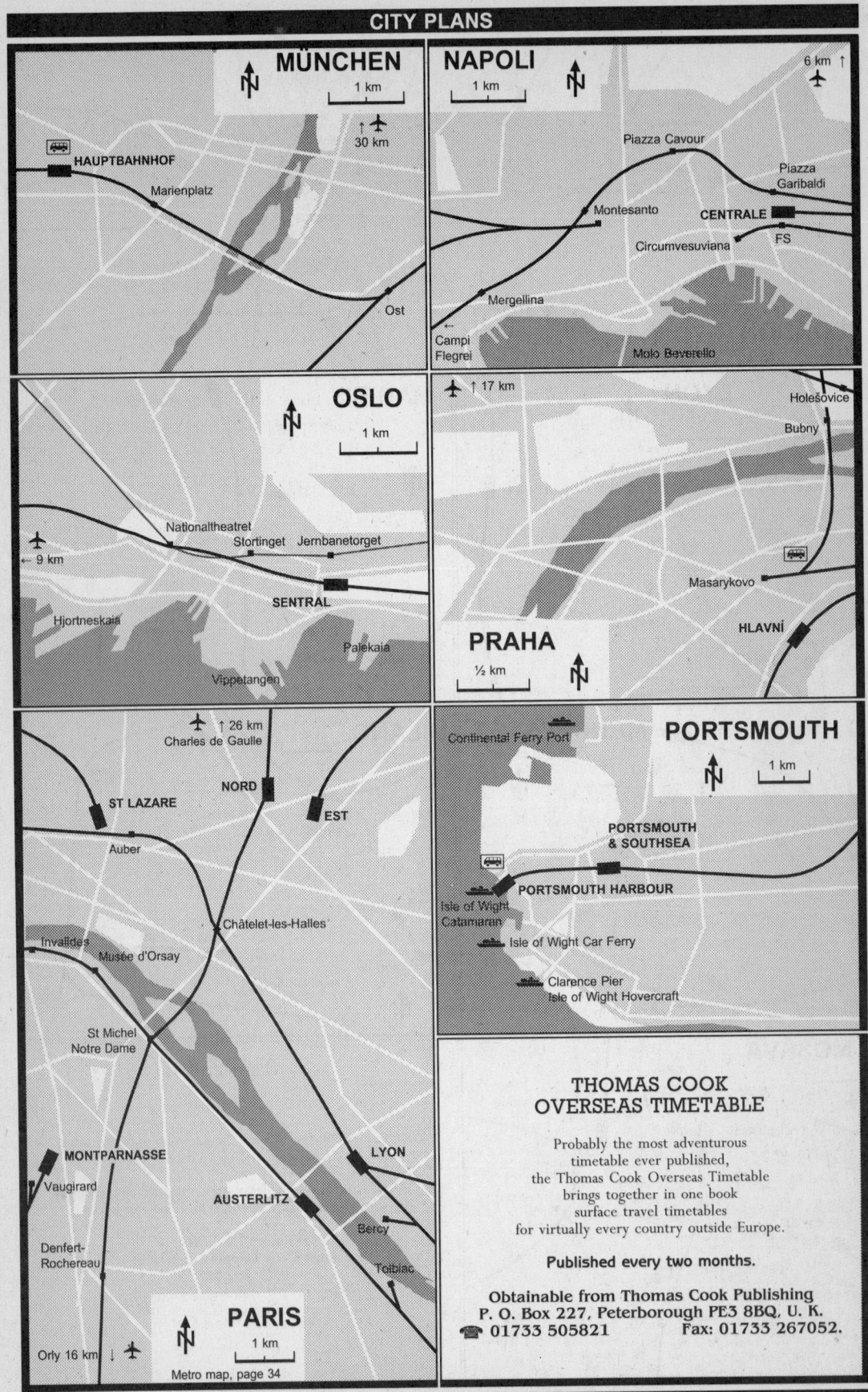

MÜNCHEN

1 km

↑ 30 km ✈

HAUPTBAHNHOF

Marienplatz

Ost

NAPOLI

1 km

6 km ↑ ✈

Piazza Cavour

Piazza Garibaldi

Montesanto

CENTRALE

Circumvesuviana

FS

Mergellina

Campi Flegrei

Molo Beverello

OSLO

1 km

Nationaltheatret

Stortinget   Jernbanetorget

← 9 km ✈

SENTRAL

Hjortneskaia

Palekaia

Vippetangen

✈ ↑ 17 km

Holešovice

Bubny

Masarykovo

HLAVNÍ

PRAHA

½ km

✈ ↑ 26 km
Charles de Gaulle

NORD

ST LAZARE

EST

Auber

Châtelet-les-Halles

Invalides

Musée d'Orsay

St Michel
Notre Dame

MONTPARNASSE

Vaugirard

LYON

AUSTERLITZ

Bercy

Denfert-
Rochereau

Tolbiac

Orly 16 km ↓ ✈

PARIS

1 km

Metro map, page 34

PORTSMOUTH

1 km

Continental Ferry Port

PORTSMOUTH
& SOUTHSEA

PORTSMOUTH HARBOUR

Isle of Wight
Catamaran

Isle of Wight Car Ferry

Clarence Pier
Isle of Wight Hovercraft

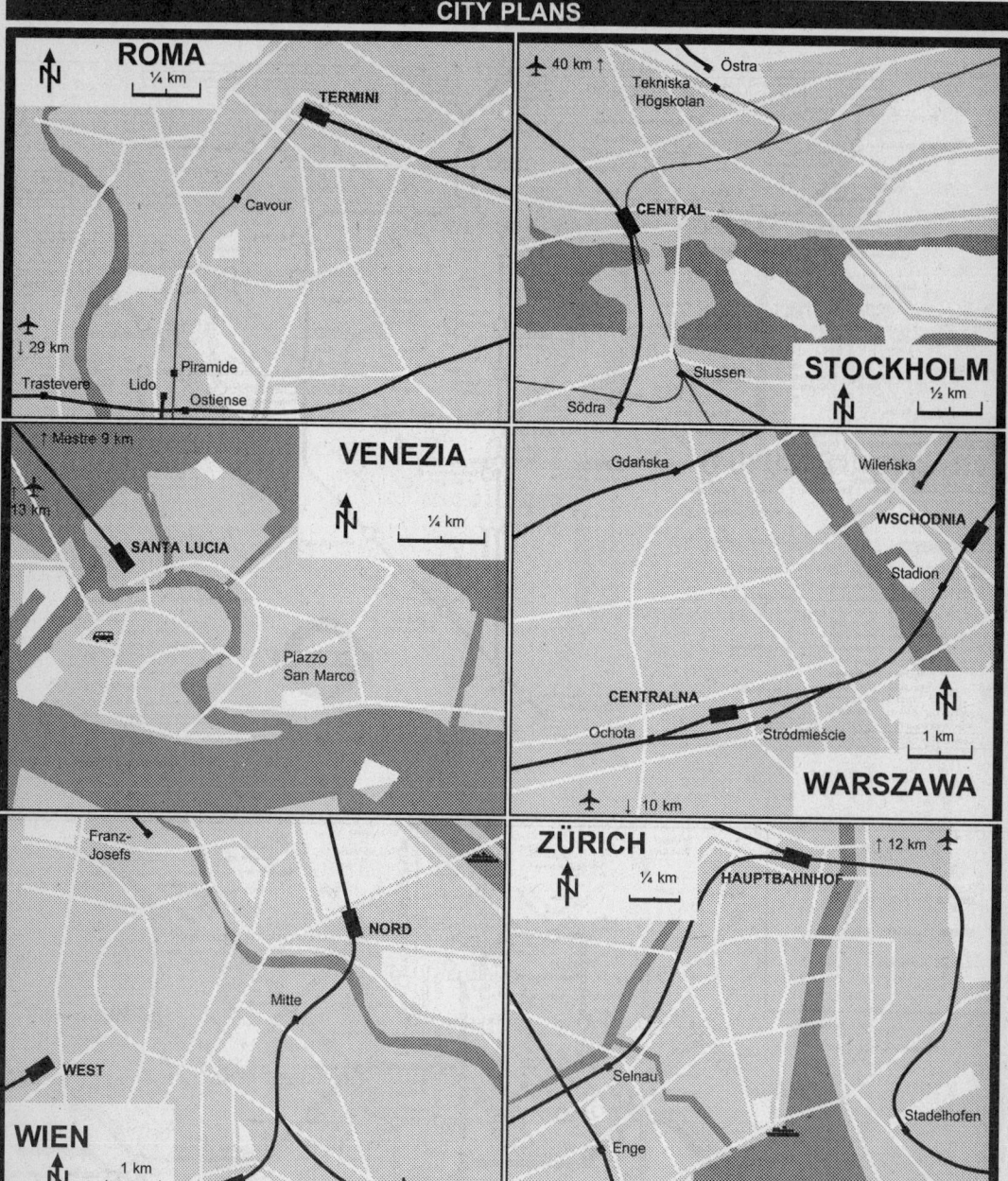

VISITOR'S RAIL MAP OF BRITAIN AND IRELAND

This map of Great Britain and Ireland is intended for tourists travelling around by rail and includes principal routes of interest and top visitor attractions accessible by rail. The main map covers most of England and Wales, the reverse side carrying separate maps of Scotland (with Northern England) and Ireland, and an enlargement of the London area. The map provides detailed visitor information on the top 200 tourist attractions of the British Isles.

Obtainable through Thomas Cook U.K. retail shops at £4.95, or by post at £5.65 (U.K.), £6.25 (Europe) or £6.85 (overseas air mail) from Thomas Cook Publishing (TPO/FE), P.O.Box 227, Thorpe Wood, PETERBOROUGH PE3 6SB, U.K.

☎ (01733) 505821/268943.

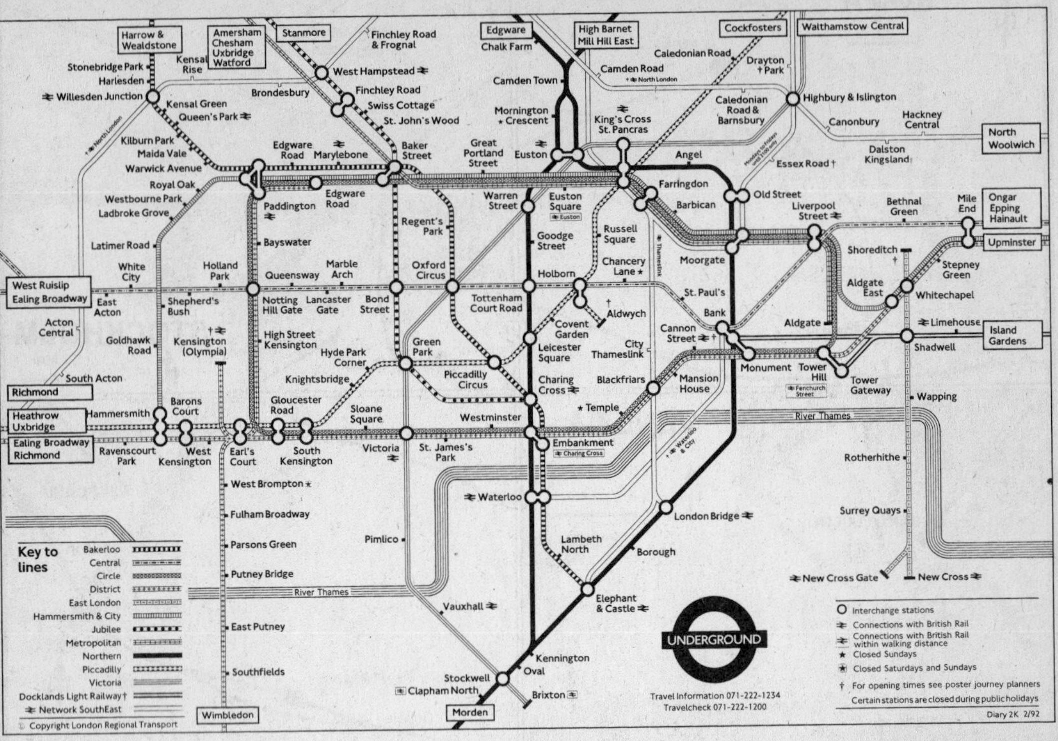

Key to lines

- Bakerloo
- Central
- Circle
- District
- East London
- Hammersmith & City
- Jubilee
- Metropolitan
- Northern
- Piccadilly
- Victoria
- Docklands Light Railway †
- Network SouthEast

© Copyright London Regional Transport

UNDERGROUND

Travel Information 071-222-1234
Travelcheck 071-222-1200

○ Interchange stations
≈ Connections with British Rail
≈ Connections with British Rail within walking distance
★ Closed Sundays
★ Closed Saturdays and Sundays
† For opening times see poster journey planners
Certain stations are closed during public holidays

Diary 2K 2/92

LRT Registered User No. 94/1969

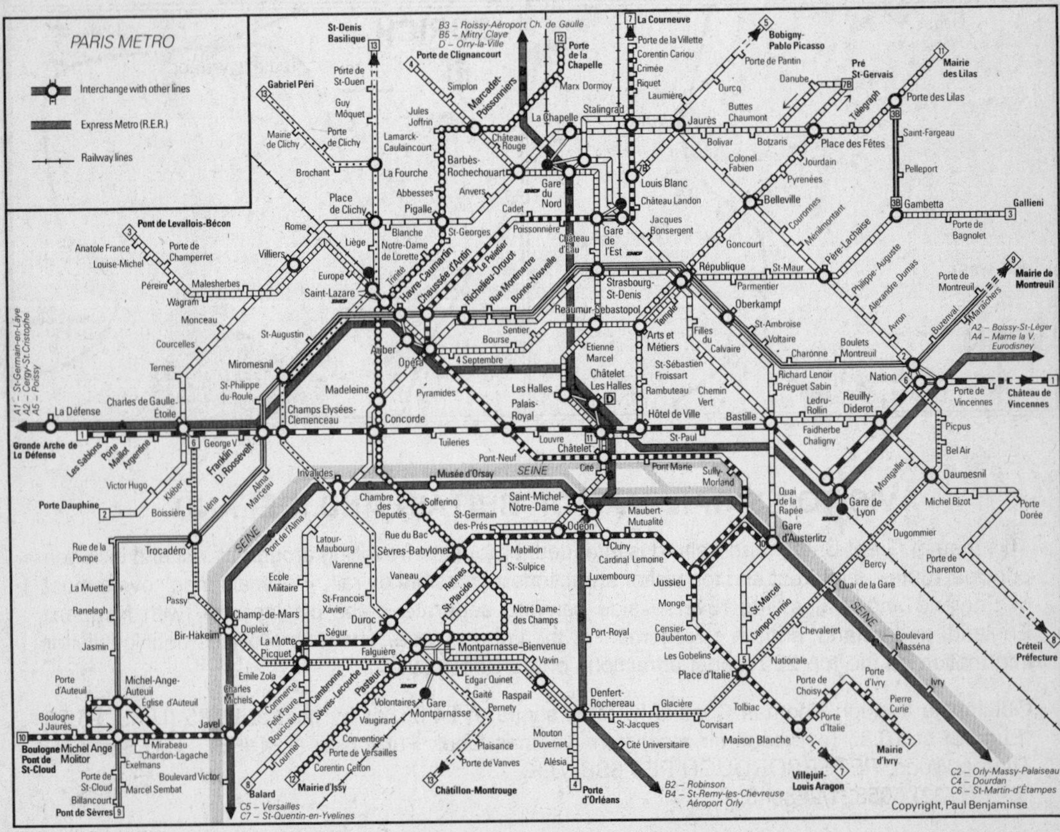

PARIS METRO

○ Interchange with other lines
Express Metro (R.E.R.)
Railway lines

A1 — St-Germain-en-Laye
A2 — Cergy-St Christophe
A3 — Poissy

A2 — Boissy-St-Léger
A4 — Marne la V. Eurodisney

B3 — Roissy-Aéroport Ch. de Gaulle
B5 — Mitry Claye
D — Orry-la-Ville

B2 — Robinson
B4 — St-Remy-les-Chevreuse Aéroport Orly

C2 — Orly-Massy-Palaiseau
C4 — Dourdan
C6 — St-Martin-d'Étampes

C5 — Versailles
C7 — St-Quentin-en-Yvelines

Copyright, Paul Benjaminse

SCENIC RAIL ROUTES OF EUROPE

The following is a list of some of the most scenic rail routes of Europe.
Routes marked * are the Editor's personal favourites.
This list does not include specialised mountain and tourist railways.

Detailed timings for most of these routes can be found within the timetable.

Types of scenery : C-Coastline, F-Forest, G-Gorge, L-Lake, M-Mountain, R-River.

AUSTRIA

Bruck an der Mur - Villach*	R
Gmunden - Stainach Irdning	ML
Innsbruck - Brennero	M
Innsbruck - Garmisch*	M
Innsbruck - Salzburg	M G
Klagenfurt - Unzmarkt	M
Landeck - Bludenz*	M
Linz - Krems	R
St Pölten - Mariazell*	M
Salzburg - Villach*	M G
Selzthal - Hieflau - Steyr	M G R
Wiener Neustadt - Semmering - Graz	M

BELGIUM AND LUXEMBOURG

Liège - Luxembourg*	R
Liège - Marloie	R
Namur - Dinant	R

BULGARIA

Septemvri - Dobriniste	M
Sofija - Burgas	M
Tulova - Gorna Orjahovitza	M

CROATIA AND SLOVENIA

Jesenice - Sežana	M R
Maribor - Zidani Most	M
Rijeka - Zagreb	M
Trieste - Ljubljana - Zagreb	G R

CZECH REPUBLIC AND SLOVAKIA

Praha - Děčín	R
Žilina - Poprad	M

DENMARK

Struer - Thisted	C

FINLAND

Kouvola - Joensuu	L F

Many other lines run through scenic areas.

FRANCE

Aurillac - Neussargues	M G
Bastia - Ajaccio	M
Chambéry - Bourg St Maurice	M
Chambéry - Modane	ML
Chamonix - Martigny*	M G
Clermont Ferrand - Béziers	M G
Clermont Ferrand - Nîmes	M G R
Gap - Briançon	ML
Genève - Aix les Bains	M R
Grenoble - Veynes - Marseille	M
Marseille - Ventimiglia	C
Nice - Digne	M
Nice/Ventimiglia - Cuneo*	M G
Perpignan - La Tour de Carol*	M G
Port Bou - Perpignan	C
Sarlat - Bergerac	G
Toulouse - La Tour de Carol	M
Valence - Veynes	M

GERMANY

Arnstadt - Meiningen	M
Bonn - Siegen	R
Dresden - Děčín	G R
Freiburg - Donaueschingen	F
Garmisch Partenkirchen - Kempten	M
Heidelberg - Neckarelz	R
Koblenz - Mainz*	G R
München - Lindau	M
Murnau - Oberammergau	ML
Naumburg - Saalfeld	R
Niebüll - Westerland	C
Nürnberg - Pegnitz	G R
Offenburg - Konstanz	M F
Pforzheim - Nagold/Wildbad	F
Plattling - Bayerisch Eisenstein	F
Rosenheim - Berchtesgaden*	ML
Rosenheim - Salzburg/Wörgl	ML
Stuttgart - Singen	F
Trier - Koblenz - Giessen	R
Ulm - Göppingen	M
Ulm - Tuttlingen	R

GREAT BRITAIN AND IRELAND

Alnmouth - Dunbar	C
Barrow-in-Furness - Maryport	C
Coleraine - Londonderry	C
Dun Laoghaire - Wicklow	C
Edinburgh - Aberdeen	C
Exeter - Newton Abbot	C
Glasgow - Oban/Mallaig	ML
Inverness - Kyle of Lochalsh*	M C
Liskeard - Looe	R
Llanelli - Craven Arms	M
Machynlleth - Pwllheli	M C
Perth - Inverness	M
Plymouth - Gunnislake	R
Rosslare - Waterford	C
St Erth - St Ives	C
Sheffield - New Mills	M
Shrewsbury - Aberystwyth	M R
Skipton - Carlisle	M R

GREECE

Korinthos - Patras	C

HUNGARY

Székesfehérvár - Balatonszentgyörgy	L
Budapest - Esztergom	R
Budapest - Szob	R

ITALY

Bologna - Pistoia	M
Bolzano - Merano	M
Brennero - Verona*	M
Brig - Arona	ML
Domodossola - Locarno*	M G
Firenze - Viareggio	M
Fortezza - San Candido	M
Genova - Pisa	C
Genova - Ventimiglia	C
Lecco - Tirano	ML
Messina - Palermo	C
Napoli - Sorrento	C
Roma - Pescara	M
Salerno - Reggio Calabria	C
Taranto - Reggio Calabria	C
Torino - Aosta	M
Udine - Villach	M

NORWAY

Bergen - Oslo*	ML
Bodø - Trondheim	ML
Dombås - Åndalsnes	M
Drammen - Larvik	C
Lillestrom - Kongsvinger	R
Myrdal - Flåm	M C
Oslo/Røros - Trondheim	ML
Stavanger - Kristiansand	M

POLAND

Jelenia Góra - Walbrzych	M
Kraków - Zakopane	M
Olsztyn - Morag	L
Olsztyn - Elk	L
Tarnów - Krynica	M

PORTUGAL

Porto - Coimbra	C R
Porto - Orense	M R
Porto - Pocinho*	R
Porto - Valença	M C
Tua - Mirandela*	M G R

ROMANIA

Braşov - Ploeşti	M
Caransebeş - Craiova	M G R
Feteşti - Constanţa	R R
Oradea - Cluj Napoca	R

SPAIN

Barcelona - La Tour de Carol	M
Bilbao - Santander	M
La Roda de Andalucia - Málaga	G
Ferrol - Gijón*	C
Granada - Almería	M
Huesca - Canfranc	M R
León - Monforte de Lemos	M
León - Oviedo	M
Málaga - Fuengirola	C
Santander - Oviedo	M C

SWEDEN

Bollnäs - Änge - Sundsvall	ML
Borlänge - Mora	ML F
Borlänge - Ludvika - Frövi	ML F
Narvik - Kiruna	M F
Östersund - Storlien	L F

Many other lines run through scenic areas.

SWITZERLAND

Andermatt - Göschenen	G
Basel - Delémont - Moutier	M R
Chur - Arosa	M G
Chur - Brig - Zermatt*	M
Chur - St Moritz*	M G
Davos - Filisur	M G
Davos - Landquart	M
Interlaken Ost - Luzern	ML
Interlaken West - Spiez	L
Lausanne - Neuchâtel - Biel	M
Lausanne - Brig	ML R
Montreux - Zweisimmen - Lenk	ML G
Rorschach - Kreuzlingen	L
Spiez - Zweisimmen	G
St Moritz - Scuol Tarasp	M
St Moritz - Tirano*	M
Thun - Brig	ML
Zürich/Luzern - Chiasso	ML
Zürich - Chur	ML

Many other lines run through scenic areas.

YUGOSLAVIA

Priboj - Bar	ML

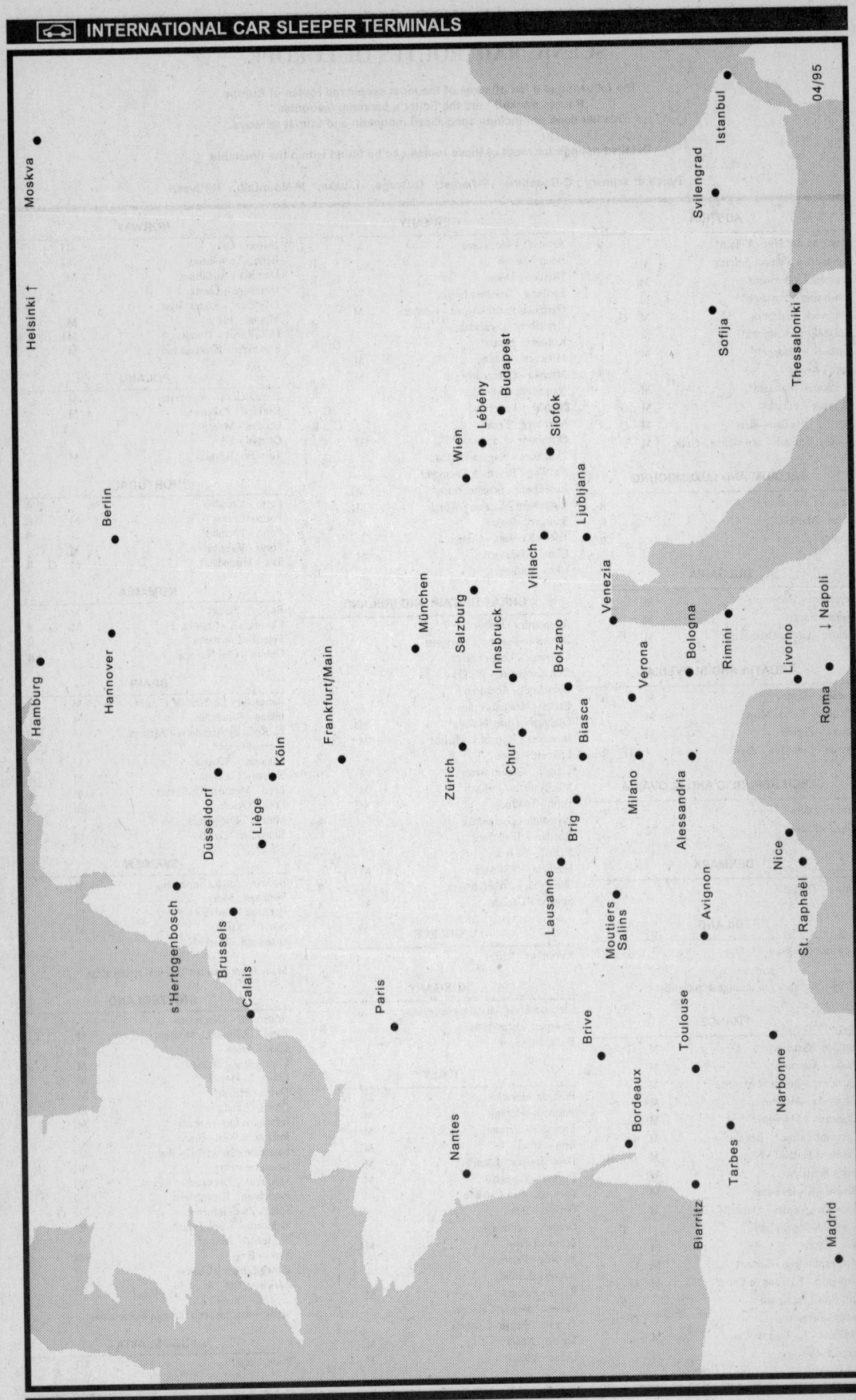

04/95

Moskva

Helsinki ↑

Istanbul

Svilengrad

Thessaloniki

Sofija

Berlin

Wien
Lébény
Budapest
Siofok

Hamburg

Hannover

Ljubljana

Villach

Venezia

München

Salzburg
Innsbruck
Bolzano

Frankfurt/Main

Verona
Bologna
Rimini

Düsseldorf

Köln
Liège

Zürich
Chur
Biasca

Milano
Alessandria

Livorno
↓ Napoli

Roma

Brig

Lausanne

Brussels

s'Hertogenbosch

Calais

Moutiers
Salins

Avignon

Nice

St. Raphaël

Paris

Brive

Toulouse

Bordeaux

Narbonne

Nantes

Tarbes

Biarritz

Madrid

CAR SLEEPER TRAINS
AUTO/TRAIN, AUTOREISEZÜGE, MOTORAIL

Car sleeper trains are composed of special wagons or vans for the conveyance of motor-cars, with sleeping cars and couchettes enabling the driver and passengers to travel overnight in comfort in the same train. Some shorter distance services run by day and convey seats coaches. The car-sleeper trains from Calais run in connection with the cross-Channel car ferries.

Cars are often loaded on the trains at separate stations from the passenger station and may be loaded some time before the passenger train leaves. International car trains are shown in Table 1, Internal car trains in Table 2. Internal services run overnight except where shown as "day train". Some services also carry passengers without cars.

Table 1   INTERNATIONAL CAR SLEEPER TRAINS

ALESSANDRIA to

HANNOVER: ④ June 2 - Oct. 6, 1994; ④ May 4-25, 1995.
Alessandria load 1900 - 2000, depart 2120,
Hannover Hbf arrive 1251.
Train **13102**: 🛏 2 cl. and 🍴.

KÖLN: ④ June 2 - Oct. 6, 1994; ④ May 4-25, 1995.
Alessandria load 1900 - 2000, depart 2120,
Köln Deutz arrive 1121.
Train **13102**: 🛏 2 cl. and 🍴.

AVIGNON to

BERLIN: ⑥ June 3 - Sept. 23, 1995.
Avignon Sud load 1800 - 1900, 🚗 connection,
Avignon Ville depart 2013, Berlin Wannsee arrive 1523.
Train **19014/5**: 🛏 1,2 cl. and 🛏 2 cl.

BRUSSELS: ① throughout the year; ④ June 15 - Aug. 31;
⑥ June 24 - Sept. 2, 1995.
①⑥: Avignon Sud load 1830 - 2030, 🚗 to Ville, Avignon
Ville depart 2219, Brussels Schaerbeek arrive 0934.
④: Avignon Sud load 1500 - 1800, depart 1900,
Brussels Schaerbeek arrive 0752.
Train **1378/7** or **1387/8**: 🛏 1,2 cl., 🛏 1,2 cl. (T2) and 🛏 2 cl.
and ✕.

CALAIS: Apr. 8,15,22, May 20,27; ①③⑥ May 29 - Sept. 23;
④⑤ July 7 - Sept. 8, 1995.
On ① May 29 - July 17, Sept. 4-18: Avignon Sud load 1830 -
2030, 🚗 connection, Avignon Ville depart 2125, Calais
auto/train arrive 0930.
On ③ Sept. 6-20: Avignon Sud load 1730 - 1900, 🚗,
Avignon Ville depart 2003, Calais auto/train arrive 0650.
On other dates: Avignon Sud load 1530 - 1830, depart
1930, Calais auto/train arrive 0736.
Train **1524**, **1430** or **1560**: 🛏 1,2 cl., 🛏 2 cl. and 🍴.

FRANKFURT: ① May 29 - Sept. 18, 1995.
Avignon Sud load 1700 - 1830, 🚗 connection, Avignon
Ville depart 2000, Frankfurt Neu Isenburg arrive 0748.
Train **19004/5**: 🛏 1,2 cl. and 🛏 2 cl.

HANNOVER: ④ May 4 - 25; ①④ May 29 - Sept. 21, 1995.
①: Avignon Sud load 1700 - 1830, 🚗 connection,
Avignon Ville depart 2000, Hannover Hbf arrive 1128.
④: Avignon Sud load 1530 - 1730, 🚗 connection,
Avignon Ville depart 1908, Hannover Hbf arrive 0952.
Train **19004/5** or **19018/9**: 🛏 1,2 cl. and 🛏 2 cl.

's-HERTOGENBOSCH: ② June 20 - Aug. 29; ④ Apr. 27 -
May 25; ⑥ Mar. 25 - Sept. 23; ⑦ June 4 - Sept. 10; also
Sept. 14,21, 1995.
Avignon Sud load 1500 - 1700, 🚗 connection, Avignon
Ville depart 1905, 's-Hertogenbosch arrive 0921.
Train **1374/1398**: 🛏 1,2 cl., 🛏 2 cl. and ✕.

's-HERTOGENBOSCH: ④ June 15 - Aug. 31, 1995.
Avignon Sud load 1630 - 1800, depart 1900,
's-Hertogenbosch arrive 0951.
Train **1387/8**: 🛏 1,2 cl., 🛏 2 cl. and ✕.

KÖLN: ④ May 4 - 25; ①④ May 29 - Sept. 21, 1995.
①: Avignon Sud load 1700 - 1830, 🚗 connection,
Avignon Ville depart 2000, Köln Deutz arrive 1029.
④: load 1600 - 1730, depart 1908, arrive 1011.
Train **19005/5** or **19012/3**: 🛏 1,2 cl. and 🛏 2 cl.

LIÈGE: ② June 20 - Aug. 29; ④ Apr. 27 - May 25 and Sept.
14,21; ⑥ Mar. 25 - Sept. 23; ⑦ June 4 - Sept. 10, 1995.
Avignon Sud load 1600 - 1730, 🚗 connection, Avignon
Ville depart 1905, Liège Bressoux arrive 0616.
Train **1374/3** or **1398/9**: 🛏 1,2 cl., 🛏 2 cl. and ✕.

MÜNCHEN: ① May 29 - Sept. 18, 1995.
Avignon Sud load 1700 - 1830, 🚗 connection,
Avignon Ville depart 2000, München Ost arrive 1049.
Train **19004/5**: 🛏 2 cl.

BERLIN to

AVIGNON: ⑤ June 2 - Sept. 22, 1995.
Berlin Wannsee load 1100 - 1200, depart 1233,
Avignon Ville arrive 0751, 🚗 to Avignon Sud.
Train **13771**: 🛏 1,2 cl. and 🛏 2 cl.

BOLZANO: ⑤ Apr. 28 - Oct. 27, 1995, also May 24.
Belin Wannsee load 2000 - 2100, depart 2138,
Bolzano arrive 1120.
Train **D1283**: 🛏 1,2 cl., 🛏 2 cl., 🚗 and 🍴.

INNSBRUCK: ⑤ Jan. 6 - Apr. 7, 1995 (also Apr. 13, 21).
Berlin Wannsee load 2000 - 2045, depart 2125,
Innsbruck Hbf arrive 0849.
Train **1183**: 🛏 1,2 cl., 🛏 2 cl., 🚗 and 🍴.

VILLACH: ⑤ Jan. 6 - Apr. 7; ⑤ June 2 - Oct. 6, 1995.
To Apr. 7: Berlin Wannsee load 1830 - 1930, depart 2022,
Villach Hbf arrive 0954.
From June 2: Berlin Wannsee load 1800 - 1845, depart
1926, Villach Hbf arrive 0855.
Train **1209**: 🛏 1,2 cl. and 🛏 2 cl. 🚗 and 🍴.

BIARRITZ to

BRUSSELS: ④ June 22 - Aug. 31, 1995.
Biarritz load 1400 - 1715, depart 1806,
Brussels Schaerbeek arrive 0741.
Train **1487/8**: 🛏 1,2 cl., 🛏 1,2 cl. (T2) and 🛏 2 cl.

CALAIS: ① June 19 - Sept. 4, 1995
Biarritz load 1430 - 1715, depart 1806,
Calais auto/train arrive 0755.
Train **1550/1**: 🛏 1,2 cl., 🛏 1,2 cl. and 🍴.

DÜSSELDORF: ① May 29 - Sept. 18, 1995.
Biarritz load 1200 - 1430, depart 1517,
Düsseldorf arrive 1107.
Train **19042/3**: 🛏 1,2 cl. and 🛏 2 cl.

FRANKFURT: ① May 29 - Sept. 18, 1995.
Biarritz load 1200 - 1430, depart 1517,
Frankfurt Neu Isenburg arrive 0726.
Train **19042/3**: 🛏 1,2 cl. and 🛏 2 cl.

's-HERTOGENBOSCH: ⑤ May 26 - Sept. 8, 1995.
Biarritz load 1400 - 1715, depart 1806, 's-Hertogenbosch
arrive 1047.
Train **1334/3**: 🛏 1,2 cl., 🛏 2 cl. and ✕.

LIÈGE: ⑤ May 26 - Sept. 8, 1995.
Biarritz load 1400 - 1715, depart 1806,
Liège Bressoux arrive 0758.
Train **1334/3**: 🛏 1,2 cl., 🛏 2 cl. and ✕.

BIASCA to

's-HERTOGENBOSCH: ⑦ May 7 - Sept. 24, 1995.
Biasca load 2000 - 2100, depart 2205,
's-Hertogenbosch arrive 1021.
Train **1304**: 🛏 1,2 cl. 🛏 2 cl. and 🍴.

BOLOGNA to

BRUSSELS: ⑥ June 3 - Sept. 23, 1995.
Bologna load 1400 - 1500, depart 1748,
Brussels Schaerbeek arrive 0911.
Train **1290**: 🛏 1,2 cl., 🛏 1,2 cl. (T2), 🛏 2 cl. and 🍴.

CALAIS: ③ July 5 - Sept. 6; ⑥ May 27 - Sept. 23, 1995.
Bologna load 1530 - 1700, depart 1808,
Calais auto/train arrive 1115.
Train **1412/3**: 🛏 1,2 cl., 🛏 1,2 cl. and 🍴.

FRANKFURT: ① May 30 - Sept. 26, 1994.
Bologna load 1700 - 1730, depart 1835,
Frankfurt Neu Isenburg arrive 0941.
Train **13386**: 🛏 1,2 cl., 🛏 2 cl. and 🍴.

HANNOVER: ① May 30 - Sept. 26, 1994; ① May 8-22,
1995.
Bologna load 1530 - 1600, depart 1835,
Hannover Hbf arrive 1051.
Train **13386**: 🛏 1,2 cl., 🛏 2 cl. and 🍴.

BOLOGNA (continued) to

KÖLN: ① May 30 - Sept. 26, 1994; ① May 8-22, 1995.
Bologna load 1615 - 1645, depart 1835,
Köln Deutz arrive 1249.
Train **13386**: 🛏 1,2 cl., 🛏 2 cl. and 🍴.

PARIS: ⑤ July 7 - Sept. 1, 1995.
Bologna load 1600 - 1800, depart 1923,
Paris Bercy arrive 0904.
Train **1324**: 🛏 1,2 cl. (T2) and 🛏 2 cl.

BOLZANO to

BERLIN: ⑥ Apr. 29 - Oct. 28, 1995, also May 25.
Bolzano load 1500 - 1600, depart 1756,
Berlin Wannsee arrive 0721 (0833 to May 27)..
Train **D1282**: 🛏 1,2 cl., 🛏 2 cl., 🚗 and 🍴.

FRANKFURT: ⑥ June 4 - Oct. 29, 1994; ⑥ Jan. 7 - May 27,
1995, also Dec. 22,25, Jan. 1.
Jan. 2 - Apr. 1: Bolzano load 1400 - 1530, depart 1650,
Frankfurt Neu Isenburg arrive 0503.
Other dates: load 1600 - 1725, depart 1830, arrive 0503.
Train **13382**: 🛏 1,2 cl., 🛏 2 cl. and 🍴.

HAMBURG: ⑥ June 4 - Oct. 29, 1994.
Bolzano load 1600 - 1725, depart 1830,
Hamburg Altona arrive 1044.
Train **13382**: 🛏 1,2 cl., 🛏 2 cl. and 🍴.

HANNOVER: ⑥ June 4 - Oct. 29, 1994; ⑥ Jan. 7 - May 27,
1995, also Dec. 22,25, Jan. 1.
Jan. 2 - Apr. 1: Bolzano load 1400 - 1530, depart 1650,
Hannover Hbf arrive 0703.
Other dates: load 1600 - 1725, depart 1830, arrive 0826.
Train **13382**: 🛏 1,2 cl., 🛏 2 cl. and 🍴.

KÖLN: ⑥ June 4 - Oct. 29, 1994; ⑥ Jan. 7 - May 27, 1995,
also Dec. 22,25, Jan. 1.
Jan. 2 - Apr. 1: Bolzano load 1400 - 1530, depart 1650,
Köln Deutz arrive 0824.
Other dates: load 1600 - 1725, depart 1830, arrive 0824.
Train **13382**: 🛏 1,2 cl., 🛏 2 cl. and 🍴.

BORDEAUX to

BRUSSELS: ④ June 22 - Aug. 31, 1995.
Bordeaux St. Jean load 1700 - 1930, depart 2046, Brussels
Schaerbeek arrive 0741.
Train **1487/8**: 🛏 1,2 cl., 🛏 1,2 cl. (T2) and 🛏 2 cl.

CALAIS: ① June 19 - Sept. 4, 1995.
Bordeaux St. Jean load 1700 - 1930, depart 2046,
Calais auto/train arrive 0755.
Train **1550/1**: 🛏 1,2 cl., 🛏 1,2 cl. and 🍴.

FRANKFURT: ①⑥ May 29 - Sept. 23, 1995.
①: Bordeaux St. Jean load 1230 - 1615, depart 1517,
Frankfurt Neu Isenburg arrive 0726.
⑥: load 1230 - 1430, depart 1603, arrive 0606.
Train **19032/3** or **19042/3**: 🛏 1,2 cl. and 🛏 2 cl.

HAMBURG: ⑥ June 3 - Sept. 23, 1995.
Bordeaux St. Jean load 1230 - 1430, depart 1603,
Hamburg Altona arrive 1211.
Train **19032/3**: 🛏 1,2 cl. and 🛏 2 cl.

HANNOVER: ⑥ June 3 - Sept. 23, 1995.
Bordeaux St. Jean load 1230 - 1430, depart 1603,
Hannover Hbf arrive 0952.
Train **19032/3**: 🛏 1,2 cl. and 🛏 2 cl.

's-HERTOGENBOSCH: ⑤ May 26 - Sept. 8, 1995.
Bordeaux St. Jean load 1700 - 1930, depart 2046,
's-Hertogenbosch arrive 1047.
Train **1334/3**: 🛏 1,2 cl., 🛏 2 cl. and ✕.

KÖLN: ①⑥ May 29 - Sept. 23, 1995.
①: Bordeaux St. Jean load 1230 - 1615, depart 1517,
Köln Deutz arrive 1020.
⑥: load 1230 - 1430, depart 1603, arrive 0858.
Train **19032/3** or **19042/3**: 🛏 1,2 cl. and 🛏 2 cl.

LIÈGE: ⑤ May 26 - Sept. 8, 1995.
Bordeaux St. Jean load 1700 - 1930, depart 2046,
Liège Bressoux arrive 0758.
Train **1334/3**: 🛏 1,2 cl., 🛏 2 cl. and ✕.

Table 1
INTERNATIONAL CAR SLEEPER TRAINS

BRIG to

HANNOVER: ⑥ Jan. 7 - Apr. 22, 1995, also Jan. 2,4.
Brig load 1815 - 1900, depart 2030,
Hannover Hbf arrive 0859.
Train **13308**: 🛏 1,2 cl. and 🛏 2 cl.

KÖLN: ⑥ Feb. 18 - Apr. 22, 1995, also Jan. 2,4,7.
Brig load 1900 - 1945, depart 2030, Köln Deutz arrive 0851.
Train **13308**: 🛏 1,2 cl. and 🛏 2 cl.

BRIVE to

BRUSSELS: ⑥ June 3 - Sept. 23, 1995.
Brive load 1530 - 2145, depart 2334, arrive Brussels
Schaerbeek 1015.
Train **1230/1**: 🛏 1,2 cl. (T2) and 🛏 2 cl.

CALAIS: Apr. 8,15,22, May 20,27; ①③⑤ May 29 - July 5;
①③⑤⑥⑦ July 7 - Sept. 4; daily Sept. 8-11,16,23, 1995.
On ⑥ July 8 - Sept. 16: Brive load 1600 - 2015, depart 2140,
Calais auto/train arrive 0654.
On other dates: Brive load 1600 - 2115, depart 2241, Calais
auto.train arrive 0845.
Train **1534/5** or **1540/1**: 🛏 1,2 cl., 🛏 1,2 cl. and ⏲.

'S-HERTOGENBOSCH: ① May 22 - Sept. 4; ③ June 28 -
Aug. 9, 1995.
Brive load 1600 - 1930, depart 2057, 's-Hertogenbosch
arrive 0951.
Train **1338/7**: 🛏 1,2 cl., 🛏 2 cl. and ✕.

LIÉGE: ① May 22 - Sept. 4, 1995.
Brive load 1600 - 1930, depart 2057,
Liège Bressoux arrive 0702.
Train **1338/7**: 🛏 1,2 cl., 🛏 2 cl. and ✕.

BRUSSELS to

AVIGNON: ⑦ throughout the year; ③ June 14 - Aug. 30;
⑤ June 23 - Sept. 1.
③: Brussels Schaerbeek load 1400 - 1715, depart 1811,
Avignon Sud arrive 0648.
⑤⑦: Brussels Schaerbeek load 1400 - 1700 (1600 - 1700
on ⑤), depart 1811, Avignon Ville arrive 0525.
Train **1375/6** or **1389/90**: 🛏 1,2 cl., 🛏 1,2 cl. (T2), 🛏 2 cl.
and ✕.

BIARRITZ: ③ June 21 - Aug. 30, 1995.
Brussels Schaerbeek load 1400 - 1930, depart 2034,
Biarritz arrive 0837.
Train **1486/5**: 🛏 1,2 cl., 🛏 1,2 cl. (T2) and 🛏 2 cl.

BOLOGNA: ⑤ June 2 - Sept. 22, 1995.
Brussels Schaerbeek load 1400 - 1615, depart 1726,
Bologna arrive 0800.
Train **1291**: 🛏 1,2 cl., 🛏 1,2 cl. (T2), 🛏 2 cl. and ⏲.

BORDEAUX: ③ June 21 - Aug. 30, 1995.
Brussels Schaerbeek load 1400 - 1930, depart 2034,
Bordeaux St. Jean arrive 0629.
Train **1486/5**: 🛏 1,2 cl., 🛏 1,2 cl. (T2) and 🛏 2 cl.

BRIVE: ⑤ June 2 - Sept. 22, 1995.
Brussels Schaerbeek load 1745 - 1845, depart 2000,
Brive arrive 0527.
Train **1236/7**: 🛏 1,2 cl. (T2) and 🛏 2 cl.

LJUBLJANA: ⑦ June 18 - Sept. 3, 1995.
Brussels Schaerbeek load 1615 - 1645, depart 1854,
Ljubljana arrive 1205.
Train **1413**: 🛏 1,2 cl. (T2) and 🛏 2 cl.

NARBONNE: ⑤ Jan. 6 - Sept. 22; ①②④ July 3 - Aug. 24.
On ⑤ to May 26: Brussels Schaerbeek load 1500 - 1745,
depart 1852, Narbonne arrive 0811.
On ⑤ from June 2: Brussels Schaerbeek load 1400 - 1715,
depart 1834, Narbonne arrive 0842.
On ①②④: Brussels Schaerbeek load 1400 - 1715, depart
1826, Narbonne arrive 0725.
Train **1284/5, 1361/2** or **1482/1**: 🛏 1,2 cl. (T2), 🛏 2 cl.
and ⏲ (also 🛏 1,2 cl. (T2) on ⑤).

ST RAPHAËL: ⑦ throughout the year; ③ June 14 - Aug. 30;
⑤ June 23 - Sept. 1.
③: Brussels Schaerbeek load 1400 - 1715, depart 1811,
St Raphaël arrive 0930.
⑤⑦: Brussels Schaerbeek load 1400 - 1630 (1400 - 1700
on ⑤); depart 1811, St Raphaël arrive 0835.
Train **1375/6** or **1389/90**: 🛏 1,2 cl., 🛏 1,2 cl. (T2), 🛏 2 cl.
and ✕.

SALZBURG: ⑦ June 18 - Sept. 3, 1995.
Brussels Schaerbeek load 1715 - 1745, depart 1854,
Salzburg Hbf arrive 0644.
Train **1413**: 🛏 1,2 cl. (T2) and 🛏 2 cl.

TARBES: ⑦ July 2 - Aug. 20, 1995.
Brussels Schaerbeek load 1700 - 1745, depart 2000,
Tarbes arrive 0940.
Train **1236/7**: 🛏 1,2 cl. (T2) and 🛏 2 cl.

BRUSSELS (continued) to

TOULOUSE: ⑤ June 2 - Sept. 22; ⑦ July 2 - Aug. 20, 1995.
⑤ to May 26: Brussels Schaerbeek load 1500 - 1745,
depart 1852, Toulouse arrive 0650.
Other dates: Brussels Schaerbeek load 1700 - 1745 (1745 -
1845 on ⑦), depart 2000, Toulouse arrive 0755.
Train **1236/7** or **1361/2**: 🛏 1,2 cl. (T2) and 🛏 2 cl.

VILLACH: ⑦ June 18 - Sept. 3, 1995.
Brussels Schaerbeek load 1645 - 1715, depart 1854,
Villach Hbf arrive 0949.
Train **1413**: 🛏 1,2 cl. (T2) and 🛏 2 cl.

BUDAPEST to

THESSALONIKI: ⑤ June 30 - Sept. 22, 1995.
Budapest Keleti load 1120 - 1140, depart 1220,
Thessaloniki arrive 0950.
Train **11411/1411**: 🛏 2 cl.

CALAIS to

AVIGNON: Apr. 7,14,21, May 19,26; ②⑤⑦ May 28 - Sept.
22; ③④ July 6 - Sept. 7, 1995.
On ⑦ May 28 - July 16, Sept. 3-17: Calais auto/train load
1700 - 1900, depart 1930, Avignon Ville arrive 0713, 🚗
to Avignon Sud.
On ⑦ Sept. 5-19: load 1715 - 1915, depart 1955, Avignon
Ville arrive 0713, 🚗 to Avignon Sud.
On other dates: Calais auto/train load 1815 - 2015, depart
2100, Avignon Sud arrive 0917.
Train **1526, 1520** or **1556**: 🛏 1,2 cl., 🛏 1,2 cl. and ⏲.

BIARRITZ: ⑦ June 18 - Sept. 3, 1995.
Calais auto/train load 1600 - 1800, depart 1820,
Biarritz arrive 0837.
Train **1548/9**: 🛏 1,2 cl., 🛏 1,2 cl. and ⏲.

BOLOGNA: ② July 4 - Sept. 5; ⑤ May 26 - Sept. 22, 1995.
Calais auto/train load 1515 - 1715, depart 1745,
Bologna arrive 1133.
Train **1410/1**: 🛏 1,2 cl., 🛏 1,2 cl. and ⏲.

BORDEAUX: ⑦ June 18 - Sept. 3, 1995.
Calais auto/train load 1600 - 1800, depart 1820,
Bordeaux arrive 0629.
Train **1548/9**: 🛏 1,2 cl., 🛏 1,2 cl. and ⏲.

BRIVE: Apr. 7,14,21, May 19,26; ②⑤⑦ May 28 - July 4;
②④⑤⑥⑦ July 6 - Sept. 2; daily Sept. 7-10,15,22.
On ⑤ July 7 - Sept. 15: Calais auto/train load 1915 - 2115,
depart 2140, Brive arrive 0805.
On other dates: Calais auto/train load 1800 - 2000, depart
2030, Brive arrive 0624.
Train **1532/3** or **1536/7**: 🛏 1,2 cl., 🛏 1,2 cl. and ⏲.

LIVORNO: ⑥ July 1 - Sept. 2, 1995.
Calais auto/train load 1300 - 1430, depart 1520,
Livorno arrive 0806.
Train **1414/5**: 🛏 1,2 cl., 🛏 2 cl. and ⏲.

MILANO: ③ July 5 - Aug. 30; ⑥ June 24 - Sept. 2, 1995.
③: Calais auto/train load 1630 - 1800, depart 1840,
Milano San Cristoforo arrive 0927.
⑥: Calais auto/train load 1745 - 1915, depart 1950,
Milano San Cristoforo arrive 1018.
Train **1328/9**: 🛏 1,2 cl., 🛏 1,2 cl. and ⏲.

MOUTIERS-SALINS: ⑤ Jan. 6 - Mar. 31, 1995.
Calais auto/train load 1845 - 2015, depart 2121,
Moutiers-Salins arrive 0855.
Train **1562/3**: 🛏 1,2 cl.

NARBONNE: Apr. 7,14,21, May 19,26; ②⑤⑦ May 28 - July
2; ②④⑤⑥⑦ July 4 - Sept. 12; also Sept. 15,19,22, 1995.
On ⑤ Sept. 5 - 19: Calais auto/train load 1715 - 1915,
depart 1955, Narbonne arrive 0919, 🚗 to auto/train.
On other dates: Calais auto/train load 1800 - 2000, depart
2030, Narbonne arrive 1014, 🚗 to Narbonne auto/train.
Train **1536/7**: 🛏 1,2 cl. and 🛏 1,2 cl.

NICE: Apr. 1, daily Apr. 3 - May 27; ①③⑤⑥ May 29 - Sept.
22 (daily July 2 - Sept. 2), 1995.
Calais auto/train load 1730 - 1900, depart 1941,
Nice arrive 1006.
Train **6206/7** or **2046/7**: 🛏 1,2 cl. (T2) and 🛏 2 cl.

ROMA: ⑥ July 1 - Sept. 2, 1995.
Calais auto/train load 1300 - 1430, depart 1520,
Roma Tuscolana arrive 1129.
Train **1414/5**: 🛏 1,2 cl., 🛏 2 cl. and ⏲.

ST. RAPHAËL: ⑦ May 28 - Sept. 17, 1995.
Calais auto/train load 1700 - 1900, depart 1930,
Fréjus-St-Raphäel arrive 1037.
Train **1520/1**: 🛏 1,2 cl., 🛏 1,2 cl. and ⏲.

TOULOUSE: Apr. 7,14,21, May 19 - June 30; ④⑤⑥ July
6 - Aug. 9; also Sept. 15,22, 1995.
Calais auto/train load 1800 - 2000, depart 2030,
Toulouse arrive 0852.
Train **1536/7**: 🛏 1,2 cl., 🛏 1,2 cl. and ⏲.

CHUR to

HAMBURG: ⑥ Jan. 7 - Apr. 22, 1995, also Jan. 2,4.
Chur load 1730 - 1845, depart 2045,
Hamburg Altona arrive 1119.
Train **13308**: 🛏 1,2 cl. and 🛏 2 cl.

HANNOVER: ⑥ Jan. 7 - Apr. 22, 1995, also Jan. 2,4.
Chur load 1845 - 1930, depart 2045,
Hannover Hbf arrive 0859.
Train **13308**: 🛏 1,2 cl. and 🛏 2 cl.

KÖLN: ⑥ Jan. 7 - Apr. 22, 1995, also Jan. 2,4.
Chur load 1930 - 1945, depart 2045, Köln Deutz arrive 0851.
Train **13308**: 🛏 1,2 cl. and 🛏 2 cl.

DÜSSELDORF to

BIARRITZ: ⑦ May 28 - Sept. 17, 1995.
Düsseldorf Hbf load 1545 - 1615, depart 1532,
Biarritz arrive 1050.
Train **13354**: 🛏 1,2 cl. and 🛏 2 cl.

NANTES: ⑤ June 2 - Sept. 22, 1995.
Düsseldorf Hbf load 1545 - 1615, depart 1632,
Nantes arrive 0848.
Train **13352**: 🛏 1,2 cl. and 🛏 2 cl.

NARBONNE: ⑤ June 2 - Sept. 22; ⑦ May 28 - Sept. 17,
1995.
Düsseldorf Hbf load 1500 - 1530, depart 1549,
Narbonne arrive 0953.
Train **13301**: 🛏 1,2 cl. and 🛏 2 cl.

SALZBURG: ③ Apr. 5 - May 24; ③ June 14 - Oct. 25, 1995.
Düsseldorf Hbf. load 0720 - 0750, depart 0807,
Salzburg Hbf arrive 1800.
Train **1529**: 🛏 and ✕.

VILLACH: ⑤ June 3 - Sept. 30; ⑦ May 29 - Sept. 25, 1994.
⑤: Düsseldorf Hbf load 1655 - 1725, depart 1738,
Villach Hbf arrive 0659.
⑦: Düsseldorf Hbf load 1850 - 1920, depart 1938,
Villach Hbf arrive 0932.
Train **13321** or **13323**: 🛏 1,2 cl., 🛏 2 cl. and ⏲.

FRANKFURT (MAIN) to

AVIGNON: ⑦ May 28 - Sept. 17, 1995.
Frankfurt Neu Isenburg load 1730 - 1845, depart 1920,
Avignon Ville arrive 0745, 🚗 to Avignon Sud.
Train **13301**: 🛏 1,2 cl. and 🛏 2 cl.

BIARRITZ: ⑦ May 28 - Sept. 17, 1995.
Frankfurt Neu Isenburg load 1830 - 1845, depart 1853,
Biarritz arrive 1050.
Train **13354**: 🛏 1,2 cl. and 🛏 2 cl.

BOLOGNA: ⑦ May 29 - Sept. 25, 1994.
Frankfurt Neu Isenburg load 1830 - 1905, depart 1930,
Bologna arrive 0955.
Train **13317**: 🛏 1,2 cl., 🛏 2 cl. and ⏲.

BOLZANO: ⑤ June 3 - Oct. 28, 1994; ⑤ Jan. 6 - May 26,
1995, also Sept. 22,25, Jan. 1.
May 5 - 26: Frankfurt Neu Isenburg load 2050 - 2110, depart
2122, Bolzano arrive 1058.
Other dates: load 2200 - 2220, depart 2242, arrive 1058.
Train **13313**: 🛏 1,2 cl., 🛏 2 cl. and ⏲.

BORDEAUX: ⑤⑦ May 28 - Sept. 22, 1995.
⑤: Frankfurt Neu Isenburg load 1800 - 1830, depart 1944,
Bordeaux arrive 1043.
⑦: Frankfurt Neu Isenburg load 1730 - 1800, depart 1853,
Bordeaux arrive 0850.
Train **13352** or **13354**: 🛏 1,2 cl. and 🛏 2 cl.

BORDEAUX: ⑦ May 28 - Sept. 17, 1995.
Frankfurt Neu Isenburg load 1730 - 1800, depart 1853,
Bordeaux arrive 0850.
Train **13352**: 🛏 1,2 cl. and 🛏 2 cl.

LIVORNO: ③ June 1 - Oct. 5, 1994; ③ May 3 - 24, 1995.
Frankfurt/Main Neu Isenburg depart 1818,
Livorno arrive 1109.
Train **13173**: 🛏 1,2 cl., 🛏 2 cl. and ⏲.
Loading at Neu Isenburg 1730 - 1800.

NANTES: ⑤ June 2 - Sept. 22, 1995.
Frankfurt Neu Isenburg load 1830 - 1845, depart 1944,
Nantes arrive 0848.
Train **13352**: 🛏 1,2 cl. and 🛏 2 cl.

FRANKFURT/MAIN (continued) to

NARBONNE: ⑤ Mar. 17 - May 26, ③ May 3-24; ③⑤⑦
May 28 - Sept. 22, 1995.
③: Frankfurt Neu Isenburg load 1810 - 1900, depart 1944,
Narbonne arrive 1000.
⑤ to May 26: load 1730 - 1815, depart 1855, arrive 0953.
⑤⑦ from May 28: load 1730 - 1845, depart 1920, arr. 0953.
Train **13301** or **13303**: 🚗 1,2 cl. and ➡ 2 cl.

SALZBURG: ③ Apr. 5 - May 24; ⑤ June 14 - Oct. 25, 1995.
Frankfurt Neu Isenburg load 1030 - 1100, depart 1129,
Salzburg arrive 1800.
Train **1529**: 🚙 and ✕.

VILLACH: ⑦ May 29 - Sept. 25, 1994; ⑤ Apr. 7 - May 26,
1995.
⑤: Frankfurt Neu Isenburg load 2200 - 2220 (2050 - 2110 in
May), depart 2242 (2122 in May), Villach Hbf arrive 1053.
⑦: Frankfurt Neu Isenburg load 2230 - 2300, depart 2312,
Villach Hbf arrive 0932.
Train **13321/3/83**: 🚗 1,2 cl., ➡ 2 cl. and 🍴.

FRÉJUS ST. RAPHAEL
see St. Raphael

HAMBURG to

AVIGNON: ③ May 3 - 24, 1995. No summer service.
Hamburg Altona load 1230 - 1300, depart 1308,
Avignon Sud arrive 0750.
Train **13373**: 🚗 1,2 cl. and ➡ 2 cl.

BOLZANO: ⑤ June 3 - Oct. 28, 1994.
Hamburg Altona load 1710 - 1800, depart 1819,
Bolzano arrive 1058.
Train **13315**: 🚗 1,2 cl., ➡ 2 cl. and 🍴.

BORDEAUX: ⑤ June 2 - Sept. 22, 1995.
Hamburg Altona load 1150 - 1220, depart 1228,
Bordeaux arrive 1043.
Train **13350**: 🚗 1,2 cl. and ➡ 2 cl.

CHUR: ⑤ Jan. 6 - Mar. 31, 1995.
Hamburg Altona load 1550 - 1655, depart 1713,
Chur arrive 0809.
Train **13309**: 🚗 1,2 cl. and ➡ 2 cl.

INNSBRUCK: ⑤ Jan. 6 - Mar. 31, 1995.
Hamburg Altona load 1710 - 1825, depart 1843,
Innsbruck Hbf arrive 0810.
Train **13313**: 🚗 1,2 cl., ➡ 2 cl. and 🍴.

NANTES: ⑤ June 2 - Sept. 22, 1995.
Hamburg Altona load 1150 - 1220, depart 1228,
Nantes arrive 0848.
Train **13350**: 🚗 1,2 cl. and ➡ 2 cl.

NARBONNE: ③ May 3 - 24; ③⑤ May 31 - Sept. 22, 1995.
Hamburg Altona load 1230 - 1315, depart 1343,
Narbonne arrive 1000.
Train **13371** or **13373**: 🚗 1,2 cl. and ➡ 2 cl.

VERONA: ⑤ June 3 - Sept. 30, 1994.
Hamburg Altona load 1550 - 1655, depart 1713,
Verona arrive 0922.
Train **13315**: 🚗 1,2 cl., ➡ 2 cl. and 🍴.

VILLACH: ⑤ June 3 - Oct. 28, 1994; ⑤ Apr. 7 - May 26,
1995; ⑦ May 29 - Sept. 25, 1994.
⑤: Hamburg Altona load 1710 - 1800 (1550 - 1655 in May),
depart 1819 (1713 in May), Villach Hbf arrive 1053.
⑦: load 1710 - 1800, depart 1819, arrive 0932.
Train **13383** or **13393**: 🚗 1,2 cl., ➡ 2 cl. and 🍴.

HANNOVER to

ALESSANDRIA: ③ June 1 - Oct. 5, 1994; ③ May 3-24,
1995.
Hannover Hbf load 1300 - 1400, depart 1500,
Alessandria arrive 0615.
Train **13303**: ➡ 2 cl. and 🍴.

AVIGNON: ③ May 3 - 24; ③⑦ May 28 - Sept. 20, 1995.
Hannover Hbf load 1400 - 1500, depart 1605,
Avignon Ville arrive 0751; 🚌 to Avignon Sud.
Train **13371** or **13373**: 🚗 1,2 cl. and ➡ 2 cl.

BOLOGNA: ⑦ May 29 - Sept. 25, 1994; ⑦ May 7-21, 1995.
Hannover Hbf load 1515 - 1615, depart 1717,
Bologna arrive 0955.
Train **13317**: 🚗 1,2 cl., ➡ 2 cl. and 🍴.

BOLZANO: ⑤ June 3 - Oct. 28, 1994; ⑤ Jan. 6 - May 26,
1995, also Dec. 22,25, Jan. 1.
Hannover Hbf load 1930 - 2000, depart 2043,
Bolzano arrive 1058.
Train **13313**: 🚗 1,2 cl., ➡ 2 cl. and 🍴.

HANNOVER (continued) to

BORDEAUX: ⑤ June 2 - Sept. 22, 1995.
Hannover Hbf load 1300 - 1330, depart 1432,
Bordeaux arrive 1043.
Train **13350**: 🚗 1,2 cl. and ➡ 2 cl.

BRIG: ⑤ Jan. 6 - Mar. 31, 1995, also Dec. 22,25, Jan. 1.
Hannover Hbf load 1830 - 1900, depart 2000,
Brig arrive 0838.
Train **13309**: 🚗 1,2 cl. and ➡ 2 cl.

CHUR: ⑤ Jan. 6 - Mar. 31, 1995, also Dec. 22,25, Jan. 1.
Hannover Hbf load 1800 - 1830, depart 2000,
Chur arrive 0809.
Train **13309**: 🚗 1,2 cl. and ➡ 2 cl.

INNSBRUCK: ⑤ Jan. 6 - Mar. 31, 1995.
Hannover Hbf load 1930 - 2100, depart 2152,
Innsbruck Hbf arrive 0810.
Train **13313**: 🚗 1,2 cl., ➡ 2 cl. and 🍴.

LIVORNO: ③ June 1 - Oct. 5, 1994; ③ May 3 - 24, 1995.
Hannover Hbf load 1300 - 1400, depart 1500,
Livorno arrive 1109.
Train **13173**: 🚗 1,2 cl., ➡ 2 cl. and 🍴.

NANTES: ⑤ June 2 - Sept. 22, 1995.
Hannover Hbf load 1300 - 1330, depart 1432,
Nantes arrive 0848.
Train **13350**: 🚗 1,2 cl. and ➡ 2 cl.

NARBONNE: ③ May 3 - 24; ③⑤⑦ May 28 - Sept. 22, 1995.
Hannover Hbf load 1400 - 1500, depart 1605,
Narbonne arrive 1000.
Train **13371** or **13373**: 🚗 1,2 cl. and ➡ 2 cl.

SIOFOK: ⑦ May 29 - Sept. 25, 1994; ⑦ May 7 - 21, 1995.
Hannover Hbf load 1515 - 1615, depart 1717,
Siofok arrive 1105.
Train **13317**: ➡ 2 cl. and 🍴.

VERONA: ⑤ June 3 - Sept. 30, 1994; ⑤ May 5 - 26, 1995.
Hannover Hbf load 1800 - 1900, depart 1949,
Verona arrive 0922.
Train **13315**: 🚗 1,2 cl., ➡ 2 cl. and 🍴.

VILLACH: ⑤ June 3 - Oct. 28, 1994; ⑤ Apr. 7 - May 26,
1995; ⑦ May 29 - Sept. 25, 1994.
Hannover Hbf load 1930 - 2000, depart 2043 (1949 on ⑤ in
May), Villach Hbf arrive 1053 (0932 on ①).
Train **13393** or **13383**: 🚗 1,2 cl., ➡ 2 cl. and 🍴.

HELSINKI to

MOSKVA: ③.
Helsinki load 1400 - 1500, depart 1708,
Moskva Leningradski arrive 0910.
Train **31**: 🚗 1,2 cl.

's-HERTOGENBOSCH to

AVIGNON: ① June 19 - Aug. 28; ③ Apr. 26 - May 24; ③
June 14 - Aug. 30 (also Sept. 13,20); ⑤ Mar. 24 - Sept. 22;
⑥ June 3 - Sept. 9, 1995.
③ June 14 - Aug. 30: 's-Hertogenbosch load 1300 - 1500,
depart 1612, Avignon Ville arrive 0808.
Other dates: 's-Hertogenbosch load 1230 - 1430, depart
1524, Avignon Ville arrive 0626 (0648 on ④⑦), 🚌 to
Avignon Sud.
Train **1371/85/96**: 🚗 1,2 cl., ➡ 2 cl. and ✕.

BIARRITZ: ④ May 25 - Sept. 7, 1995.
's-Hertogenbosch load 1330 - 1530, depart 1707,
Biarritz arrive 0837.
Train **1331/2**: 🚗 1,2 cl., ➡ 2 cl. and ✕.

BIASCA: ⑥ May 6 - Sept. 23, 1995.
's-Hertogenbosch load 1600 - 1815, depart 1929,
Biasca arrive 0653.
Train **1305**: 🚗 1,2 cl., ➡ 2 cl. and 🍴.

BORDEAUX: ④ May 25 - Sept. 7, 1995.
's-Hertogenbosch load 1330 - 1530, depart 1707,
Bordeaux St. Jean arrive 0629.
Train **1331/2**: 🚗 1,2 cl., ➡ 2 cl. and ✕.

BRIVE: ⑦ May 21 - Sept. 3; ② June 27 - Aug. 8, 1995.
's-Hertogenbosch load 1400 - 1600, depart 1707,
Brive arrive 0559.
Train **1335/6**: 🚗 1,2 cl., ➡ 2 cl. and ✕.

LJUBLJANA: ④ May 4 - Sept. 21, 1995.
's-Hertogenbosch load 1600 - 1815, depart 1929,
Ljubljana arrive 1205.
Train **1317**: 🚗 1,2 cl., ➡ 2 cl. and 🍴.

MILANO: ⑥ May 6 - Sept. 23, 1995.
's-Hertogenbosch load 1600 - 1815, depart 1929,
Milano S. Cristoforo arrive 0925.
Train **1305**: 🚗 1,2 cl., ➡ 2 cl. and 🍴.

's-HERTOGENBOSCH (continued) to

NARBONNE: ① June 19 - Aug. 28; ② June 27 - Aug. 8;
⑤ Mar. 24 - Sept. 28, also Sept. 22; ⑦ May 21 - Sept. 3.
①⑤: 's-Hertogenbosch load 1230 - 1430, depart 1524,
Narbonne arrive 0907.
②⑦: load 1400 - 1600, depart 1707, arrive 0942.
Train **1335/6** or **1371/2**: 🚗 1,2 cl., ➡ 2 cl. and ✕.

ST. RAPHAËL: ③ Apr. 26 - May 24; ③ June 14 - Aug. 30,
also Sept. 13,20; ⑥ June 3 - Sept. 9, 1995.
③ June 14 - Aug. 30: 's-Hertogenbosch load 1300 - 1500,
depart 1612, St.-Raphaël-Fréjus arrive 0930.
Other dates: load 1230 - 1430, depart 1524, arrive 0943.
Train **1385/6** or **1396/7**: 🚗 1,2 cl., ➡ 2 cl. and ✕.

SALZBURG: ④ May 4 - Sept. 21, 1995.
's-Hertogenbosch load 1600 - 1815, depart 1929,
Salzburg Hbf arrive 0644.
Train **1317**: 🚗 1,2 cl., ➡ 2 cl. and 🍴.

TOULOUSE: ⑦ May 21 - Sept. 3; ② June 27 - Aug. 8, 1995.
's-Hertogenbosch load 1400 - 1600, depart 1707,
Toulouse arrive 0819.
Train **1335/6**: 🚗 1,2 cl., ➡ 2 cl. and ✕.

VILLACH: ④ May 4 - Sept. 21, 1995.
's-Hertogenbosch load 1600 - 1815, depart 1929,
Villach Hbf arrive 0949.
Train **1317**: 🚗 1,2 cl., ➡ 2 cl. and 🍴.

INNSBRUCK to

BERLIN: ⑥ Jan. 7 - Apr. 8, 1995, also Apr. 17,22.
Innsbruck Hbf load 1900 - 1945, depart 2040,
Berlin Wannsee arrive 0833.
Train **1182**: 🚗 1,2 cl., ➡ 2 cl., 🚙 and 🍴.

HAMBURG: ⑥ Jan. 7 - Apr. 1, 1995, also Jan. 2,4.
Innsbruck load 1800 - 1845, depart 2018,
Hamburg Altona arrive 0958.
Train **13088**: 🚗 1,2 cl., ➡ 2 cl. and 🍴.

HANNOVER: ⑥ Jan. 7 - Apr. 1, 1995, also Jan. 2,4.
Innsbruck Hbf load 1800 - 1845, depart 2018,
Hannover Hbf arrive 0740.
Train **13088**: 🚗 1,2 cl., ➡ 2 cl. and 🍴.

KÖLN: ⑥ Jan. 7 - Apr. 1, 1995, also Jan. 2,4.
Innsbruck Hbf load 1800 - 1845, depart 2018,
Köln Deutz arrive 0824.
Train **13088**: 🚗 1,2 cl., ➡ 2 cl. and 🍴.

ISTANBUL to

LÉBÉNY (Hungary): May 29, June 5,12,19,25,26; ①②⑦
July 2 - Aug. 1; ③④⑤ Aug. 3 - Sept. 8; also Sept.
12,16,20,24,28, 1995.
Istanbul depart 2230, Lébény arrive 0759 (two days later).
Operated by Optima Tours, München - see under Lébény.

KÖLN to

ALESSANDRIA: ③ June 1 - Oct. 5, 1994; ③ May 3-24,
1995.
Köln Deutz load 1430 - 1500, depart 1530,
Alessandria arrive 0615.
Train **13373**: ➡ 2 cl. and 🍴.

AVIGNON: ③ May 3 - 24; ③⑦ May 28 - Sept. 20, 1995.
③: Köln Deutz load 1500 - 1530, depart 1610,
Avignon Ville arrive 0751; 🚌 to Avignon Sud.
⑦: load 1530 - 1600, depart 1627, arrive 0745.
Train **13301** or **13303**: 🚗 1,2 cl. and ➡ 2 cl.

BOLOGNA: ⑦ May 29 - Sept. 25, 1994; ⑦ May 7-21, 1995.
Köln Deutz load 1520 - 1550, depart 1625,
Bologna arrive 0955.
Train **13317**: 🚗 1,2 cl., ➡ 2 cl. and 🍴.

BOLZANO: ⑤ June 3 - Oct. 28, 1994; ⑤ Jan. 6 - May 26,
1995, also Dec. 22,25, Jan. 1.
May 5-26: Köln Deutz load 1725 - 1745, depart 1828,
Bolzano arrive 1058.
Other dates: load 1830 - 1900, depart 1927, arrive 1058.
Train **13313**: 🚗 1,2 cl., ➡ 2 cl. and 🍴.

BORDEAUX: ⑤⑦ May 28 - Sept. 22, 1995.
⑤: Köln Deutz load 1615 - 1645, depart 1710,
Bordeaux St. Jean arrive 1043.
⑦: load 1430 - 1530, depart 1610, arrive 0850.
Train **13352** or **13354**: 🚗 1,2 cl. and ➡ 2 cl.

Table 1   **INTERNATIONAL CAR SLEEPER TRAINS**

KÖLN (continued) to

BRIG: ⑤ Feb. 17 - Mar. 31, 1995, also Dec. 22,25, Jan. 1,6.
Köln Deutz load 1900 - 1930, depart 1958, Brig arrive 0838.
Train **13309**: 🛏 1,2 cl. and 🚗 2 cl.

CHUR: ⑤ Jan. 6 - Mar. 31, 1995, also Dec. 22,25, Jan. 1.
Köln Deutz load 1900 -1930, depart 1958, Chur arrive 0809.
Train **13309**: 🛏 1,2 cl. and 🚗 2 cl.

INNSBRUCK: ⑤ Jan. 6 - Mar. 31, 1995, also Dec. 22,25,
Jan. 1.
Köln Deutz load 1830 - 1900, depart 1927,
Innsbruck Hbf arrive 0810.
Train **13717**: 🛏 1,2 cl., 🚗 2 cl. and 🍴.

NARBONNE: ③ May 3 - Sept. 20, 1995.
Köln Deutz load 1510 - 1530, depart 1610,
Narbonne arrive 1000.
Train **13303**: 🛏 1,2 cl. and 🚗 2 cl.

SALZBURG: ③ Apr. 5 -May 24; ③ June 14 - Oct. 25, 1995.
Köln Deutz load 0745 - 0815, depart 0844,
Salzburg arrive 1800.
Train **1529**: 🚗 and 🍴.

SIOFOK: ⑦ May 29 - Sept. 25, 1994; ⑦ May 7 - 21, 1995.
Köln Deutz load 1520 - 1550, depart 1625,
Siofok arrive 1105.
Train **13317**: 🚗 2 cl. and 🍴.

VERONA: ⑤ June 3 - Sept. 30, 1994; ⑤ May 5 - 26, 1995.
Köln Deutz load 1725 - 1745, depart 1828,
Verona arrive 0922.
Train **13315**: 🛏 1,2 cl., 🚗 2 cl. and 🍴.

VILLACH: ⑤⑦ May 29 - Sept. 30, 1994; ⑤ Jan. 6 - May 26,
1995.
⑤ to May 26: Köln Deutz load 1830 - 1900 (1725 - 1745 in
May), depart 1927 (1828 in May), Villach Hbf arrive 1053.
⑤ June 3 - Sept. 30: load 1720 - 1750, depart 1824,
Villach arrive 0659.
⑦: load 1910 - 1940, depart 2022, arrive 0932.
Train **13313/21/93**: 🛏 1,2 cl., 🚗 2 cl. and 🍴.

LAUSANNE to

NARBONNE: ⑦ June 25 - Aug. 27, 1995.
Lausanne Renens load 1930 - 2130, depart 2219,
Narbonne arrive 0700, 🚌 to Narbonne auto/train.
Train **1300/1**: 🛏 1,2 cl. and 🚗 2 cl.

LÉBÉNY (HUNGARY) to

Lébény is situated north-west of Györ, close to
the borders with Austria and Slovakia.
These services are organised by Optima Tours,
Karlstrasse 56, D-80333 München ☎ (89) 592272,
fax (89) 595655. Apply to operator for further details.

ISTANBUL: May 27, June 3,10,17,23,24; ⑤⑥⑦ June 30 -
July 30; ①②③ Aug. 1 - Sept. 6, also Sept. 10,14,18,22,26.
Lébény depart 1325, Istanbul arrive 0100 (2 days later).

SOFIJA: ②③④ June 21 - July 27; ⑤⑥⑦ Aug. 5 - Sept. 3,
also Aug. 3, 1995.
Lébény depart 1325, Sofija arrive 1125.

SVILENGRAD: May 31, June 7,14; daily June 30 - Sept. 8,
also 10,16,22, 1995.
Lébény depart 1225, Svilengrad arrive 1445 next day.

LIÈGE to

AVIGNON: ① June 19 - Aug. 28; ③ Apr. 26 - May 24 and
Sept. 13,20; ⑤ Mar. 24 - Sept. 22; ⑥ June 3 - Sept. 9.
Liège Bressoux load 1530 - 1700, depart 1834, Avignon
Ville arrive 0626 (0648 on ⑦), 🚌 to Avignon Sud.
Train **1396/7 or 1371/2**: 🛏 1,2 cl., 🚗 2 cl. and 🚿.

BIARRITZ: ④ May 25 - Sept. 7, 1995.
Liège Bressoux load 1700 - 1830, depart 1953,
Biarritz arrive 0837.
Train **1331/2**: 🛏 1,2 cl., 🚗 2 cl. and 🚿.

BORDEAUX: ④ May 25 - Sept. 7, 1995.
Liège Bressoux load 1700 - 1830, depart 1953,
Bordeaux St. Jean arrive 0629.
Train **1331/2**: 🛏 1,2 cl., 🚗 2 cl. and 🚿.

BRIVE: ⑦ May 21 - Sept. 3, 1995.
Liège Bressoux load 1700 - 1830, depart 1953,
Brive arrive 0559.
Train **1335/6**: 🛏 1,2 cl., 🚗 2 cl. and 🚿.

NARBONNE: ⑤ Mar. 24 - Sept. 8, also Sept. 22;
① June 19 - Aug. 28, 1995.
①⑤: Liège Bressoux load 1530 - 1700, depart 1834,
Narbonne arrive 0907.
②⑦: Liège Bressoux load 1700 - 1830, depart 1953,
Narbonne arrive 0942.
Train **1335/6 or 1371/2**: 🛏 1,2 cl., 🚗 2 cl. and 🚿.

LIÈGE (continued) to

ST. RAPHAËL: ③ Apr. 26 - May 24 and Sept. 13,20;
⑥ June 3 - Sept. 9, 1995.
Liège Bressoux load 1530 - 1700, depart 1834,
Fréjus-St.-Raphaël arrive 0943.
Train **1396/7**: 🛏 1,2 cl., 🚗 2 cl. and 🚿.

TOULOUSE: ② June 27 - Aug. 8, 1995.
Liège Bressoux load 1700 - 1830, depart 1953,
Toulouse arrive 0819.
Train **1335/6**: 🛏 1,2 cl., 🚗 2 cl. and 🚿.

LIVORNO to

CALAIS: ⑦ July 2 - Sept. 3, 1995.
Livorno load 1730 - 1930, depart 2035,
Calais auto/train arrive 1302.
Train **1416/7**: 🛏 1,2 cl., 🚗 2 cl. and 🍴.

FRANKFURT: ④ June 2 - Oct. 6, 1994; ④ May 4 - 25, 1995.
Livorno load 1400 - 1530, depart 1555,
Frankfurt Neu Isenburg arrive 0839.
Train **13102**: 🛏 1,2 cl., 🚗 2 cl. and 🍴.

HANNOVER: ④ June 2 - Oct. 6, 1994; ④ May 4 - 25, 1995.
Livorno load 1400 - 1530, depart 1555,
Hannover Hbf arrive 1251.
Train **13102**: 🛏 1,2 cl., 🚗 2 cl. and 🍴.

LJUBLJANA to

BRUSSELS: ① June 19 - Sept. 4, 1995.
Ljubljana load 1400 - 1630, depart 1700,
Brussels Schaerbeek arrive 0949.
Train **1412**: 🛏 1,2 cl. (T2) and 🚗 2 cl.

's-HERTOGENBOSCH: ⑤ May 5 - Sept. 22, 1995.
Ljubljana load 1400 - 1630, depart 1700,
's-Hertogenbosch arrive 0944.
Train **1316**: 🛏 1,2 cl., 🚗 2 cl. and 🍴.

MADRID to

PARIS: Daily.
Madrid Chamartin load 0900 - 1600.
Train **301/0** (🚗 2 cl. and 🍴): Madrid Chamartin depart
1815, Paris Austerlitz arrive 1034.
Train **407/6** (Talgo, 🛏 1,2 cl. and 🚿): Mardid Chamartin
depart 1930, Paris Austerlitz arrive 0830.
Unload Paris Tolbiac (🚌 connection from Austerlitz).

MILANO to

CALAIS: ④ July 6 - Aug. 31; ⑦ June 25 - Sept. 3, 1995.
Milano San Cristoforo load 1530 - 1700, depart 1820,
Calais auto/train arrive 0930.
Train **1322/3**: 🛏 1,2 cl., 🚗 1,2 cl. and 🍴.

's-HERTOGENBOSCH: ⑦ May 7 - Sept. 24, 1995.
Milano San Cristoforo load 1630 - 1800, depart 1914,
's-Hertogenbosch arrive 1021.
Train **1304**: 🛏 1,2 cl., 🚗 2 cl. and 🍴.

PARIS: ⑤ July 7 - Sept. 1; ⑦ June 18 - Sept. 17, 1995.
Milano San Cristoforo load 1930 - 2100, depart 2225,
Paris Bercy arrive 0904 (0920 ① June 19 - Sept. 18).
Train **1324**: 🛏 1,2 cl. (T2) and 🚗 2 cl.

MOSKVA to

HELSINKI: ②.
Moskva Leningradski load 110 - 1500, depart 1817,
Helsinki arrive 0902.
Train **32**: 🛏 1,2 cl.

MOUTIERS-SALINS to

CALAIS: ⑥ Jan. 7 - Apr. 1, 1995; also Dec. 31, 1994.
Moutiers load 1000 - 1830, depart 1955,
Calais auto/train arrive 0658.
Train **1564/5**: 🚗 1,2 cl.

MÜNCHEN to

AVIGNON: ⑦ May 28 - Sept. 17, 1995.
München Ost load 1450 - 1505, depart 1605,
Avignon Ville arrive 0745, 🚌 to Avignon Sud.
Train **13360**: 🚗 2 cl.

NARBONNE: ⑤ Mar. 17 - May 26; ⑤⑦ May 28 - Sept. 22.
München Ost load 1500 - 1525, depart 1605,
Narbonne arrive 0953.
Train **13360**: 🚗 2 cl.

RIMINI: daily May 28 - Sept. 22.
München Ost load 2100 - 2130, depart 2150,
Rimini arrive 0655.
Train **1289**: 🚗 2 cl. (also 🛏 1,2 cl. on ⑤ to Sept. 15).

NANTES to

DÜSSELDORF: ⑥ June 3 - Sept. 23, 1995.
Nantes load 1400 - 1545, depart 1654,
Düsseldorf Hbf arrive 0922.
Train **19036/7**: 🛏 1,2 cl. and 🚗 2 cl.

FRANKFURT: ⑥ June 3 - Sept. 23, 1995.
Nantes load 1400 - 1545, depart 1654,
Frankfurt Neu Isenburg arrive 0606.
Train **19036/7**: 🛏 1,2 cl. and 🚗 2 cl.

HAMBURG: ⑥ June 3 - Sept. 23, 1995.
Nantes load 1400 - 1545, depart 1654,
Hamburg Altona arrive 1211.
Train **19036/7**: 🛏 1,2 cl. and 🚗 2 cl.

HANNOVER: ⑥ June 3 - Sept. 23, 1995.
Nantes load 1400 - 1545, depart 1654,
Hannover Hbf arrive 0952.
Train **19036/7**: 🛏 1,2 cl. and 🚗 2 cl.

NAPOLI to

ZÜRICH: ⑥ June 24 - Aug. 26, 1995.
Napoli Campi Flegrei load 1600 - 1800, depart 1908,
Zürich Altstetten arrive 0934.
Train **1384**: 🛏 1,2 cl. and 🚗 2 cl.

NARBONNE to

Loading takes place at the Gare auto/train
(🚌 connection to passenger station)

BRUSSELS: ②③⑤ July 4 - Aug. 25; ⑤ Jan. 7 - Sept. 23,
1995.
⑥: Narbonne load 1630 - 1800, depart 1900,
Brussels Schaerbeek arrive 0833.
②③⑤: load 1630 - 1800, depart 1927, arrive 0718.
⑥: Train **1483/4**: 🛏 1,2 cl., 🛏 1,2 cl. (T2), 🚗 2 cl. and 🍴.
②③⑤: Train **1281/0**: 🛏 1,2 cl. (T2), 🚗 2 cl. and 🍴.

CALAIS: Apr. 8,15,22, May 20,27; ①③⑥ May 29 - July 5;
①③⑤⑥⑦ July 7 - Sept. 13; also Sept. 16,23, 1995.
On ③ Sept. 6 - 20: Narbonne load 1300 - 1645, depart
1745, Calais auto/train arrive 0650.
On other dates: Narbonne load 1300 - 1715, depart 1825,
Calais auto/train arrive 0828.
Train **1540/1**: 🛏 1,2 cl., 🚗 2 cl. and 🍴.

DÜSSELDORF: ① May 29 - Sept. 18; ⑥ Mar. 18 - Sept. 23.
Narbonne load 1515 - 1630, depart 1740,
Düsseldorf arrive 1107.
Train **19004/5**: 🛏 1,2 cl. and 🚗 2 cl.

FRANKFURT: ① May 29 - Sept. 18; ④ May 4 - Sept. 21;
⑥ Mar. 18 - Sept. 23, 1995.
①⑥: Narbonne load 1515 - 1630, depart 1740,
Frankfurt Neu Isenburg arrive 0748.
④: load 1400 - 1500, depart 1639, arrive 0631.
Train **19004/5 or 19018/9**: 🛏 1,2 cl. and 🚗 2 cl.

HAMBURG: ④ May 4 - 25; ④⑥ June 1 - Sept. 23, 1995.
④: Narbonne load 1400 - 1500, depart 1639,
Hamburg Altona arrive 1211.
⑥: load 1515 - 1630, depart 1745, arrive 1331.
Train **19004/5 or 19018/9**: 🛏 1,2 cl. and 🚗 2 cl.

HANNOVER: ④ May 4 - 25; ①④⑥ May 29 - Sept. 23, 1995.
①⑥: Narbonne load 1515 - 1630, depart 1740,
Hannover Hbf arrive 1128.
④: load 1400 - 1500, depart 1639, arrive 0952.
Train **19004/5 or 19018/9**: 🛏 1,2 cl. and 🚗 2 cl.

's-HERTOGENBOSCH: ① May 22 - Sept. 4; ② June 20 -
Aug. 29; ④ June 28 - Aug. 9; ⑥ Mar. 25 - Sept. 9, also
Sept. 23, 1995.
Narbonne load 1400 - 1515, depart 1639,
's-Hertogenbosch arrive 0921 (0951 on ②④).
Train **1338/7 or 1374/3**: 🛏 1,2 cl., 🚗 2 cl. and 🚿.

KÖLN: ④ May 4 - Sept. 21, 1995.
Narbonne load 1400 - 1500, depart 1639,
Köln Deutz arrive 1011.
Train **19018/9**: 🛏 1,2 cl. and 🚗 2 cl.

LAUSANNE: ① June 26 - Aug. 28, 1995.
Narbonne load 1800 - 1930, depart 2200,
Lausanne Renens arrive 0703.
Train **1302/3**: 🛏 1,2 cl. and 🚗 2 cl.
Loading at Narbonne 1800 - 1930.

LIÈGE: ① May 22 - Sept. 4; ② June 20 - Aug. 29; ③ June 28
- Aug. 9; ⑥ Mar. 25 - Sept. 9, also Sept. 23, 1995.
Narbonne load 1400 - 1515, depart 1639,
Liège Bressoux arrive 0616 (0702 on ②④).
Train **1338/7 or 1374/3**: 🛏 1,2 cl., 🚗 2 cl. and 🚿.

MÜNCHEN: ⑥ Mar. 18 - May 27; ①⑥ May 29 - Sept. 23.
Narbonne load 1515, depart 1740,
München Ost arrive 1015 (1049 on ②).
Train **19004/5**: 🚗 2 cl.

Table 1 — INTERNATIONAL CAR SLEEPER TRAINS

NARBONNE (continued) to

ZÜRICH: ① June 26 - Aug. 28, 1995.
Narbonne load 1800 - 1930, depart 2200,
Zürich Altstetten arrive 1004.
Train **1302/3**: 🛏 1,2 cl. and ➤ 2 cl.

NICE to

CALAIS: Apr. 1, daily Apr. 3 - May 27; ①②④⑥ May 29 -
Sept. 23 (daily July 2 - Sept. 2), 1995.
Nice load 1100 - 1730 (1400 - 1730 to May 27), depart
1834, Calais auto/train arrive 0900.
Train **6704/5** or **6708/9**: 🛏 1,2 cl. (T2) and ➤ 2 cl.

PARIS to

BOLOGNA: ④ July 6 - Aug. 31, 1995.
Paris Bercy load 1600 - 1900, depart 1947,
Bologna arrive 0958.
Train **1325**: 🛏 1,2 cl. (T2) and ➤ 2 cl.

MADRID: daily.
Paris Tolbiac load 0900 - 1600, 🚌 connection to Austerlitz.
Train **303/2** (➤ 2 cl. and 🍴): Paris Austerlitz depart 1805,
Madrid Chamartin arrive 0950.
Train **409/8** (Talgo, 🛏 1,2 cl. and 🍴): Paris Austerlitz
depart 2000, Madrid Chamartin arrive 0832.

MILANO: ④ July 6 - Aug. 31; ⑥ June 17 - Sept. 16, 1995.
Paris Bercy load 1600 - 1900, depart 1925 (1947 on ④),
Milano San Cristoforo arrive 0641.
Train **1325**: 🛏 1,2 cl. (T2) and ➤ 2 cl.

RIMINI: ⑥ June 17 - Sept. 16, 1995.
Paris Bercy load 1600 - 1900, depart 1925,
Rimini arrive 1120.
Train **1325**: 🛏 1,2 cl. (T2) and ➤ 2 cl.

RIMINI to

MÜNCHEN: daily May 28 - Sept. 23.
Rimini load 2000 - 2200, depart 2245,
München Ost arrive 0815.
Train **1288**: ➤ 2 cl. (also 🛏 1,2 cl. ⑥ June 3 - Sept. 16).

PARIS: ⑦ June 18 - Sept. 17, 1995.
Rimini load 1500 - 1700, depart 1755,
Paris Bercy arrive 0920.
Train **1324**: 🛏 1,2 cl. (T2) and ➤ 2 cl.

WIEN: ⑥ June 10 - Sept. 9, 1995.
Rimini load 1500 - 1700, depart 1856,
Wien Süd arrive 0811.
Train **1134**: 🛏 1,2 cl. and ➤ 2 cl.

ROMA to

CALAIS: ⑦ July 2 - Sept. 3, 1995.
Roma Tuscolana load 1430 - 1600, depart 1708,
Calais auto/train arrive 1302.
Train **1416/7**: 🛏 1,2 cl., ➤ 2 cl. and 🍴.

ST RAPHAËL to

BRUSSELS: ① throughout the year; ④ June 15 - Aug. 31;
⑥ June 24 - Sept. 2, 1995.
①⑥: Fréjus-St-Raphaël load 1500 - 1800, depart 1920,
Brussels Schaerbeek arrive 0934.
④: load 1300 - 1500, depart 1543, arrive 0752.
Train **1378/7** or **1391/2**: 🛏 1,2 cl., 🛏 1,2 cl. (T2), ➤ 2 cl.
and 🍴.

CALAIS: ① May 29 - Sept. 18, 1995.
Fréjus-St-Raphaël load 1500 - 1715, depart 1800,
Calais auto/train arrive 0930.
Train **1524**: 🛏 1,2 cl., 🛏 1,2 cl. and 🍴.

's-HERTOGENBOSCH: ④ Apr. 27 - May 25 and June 15 -
Aug. 31, also Sept. 14,21; ⑦ June 4 - Sept. 10, 1995.
Fréjus-St-Raphaël load 1300 - 1500, depart 1543,
's-Hertogenbosch arrive 0921 (0951 on ⑤).
Train **1398/91**: 🛏 1,2 cl., ➤ 2 cl. and 🍴.

LIÈGE: ④ Apr. 27 - May 25 and Sept. 14,21; ⑦ June 4 -
Sept. 10, 1995.
Fréjus-St-Raphaël load 1300 - 1500, depart 1543,
Liège Bressoux arrive 0616.
Train **1398/9**: 🛏 1,2 cl., ➤ 2 cl. and 🍴.

SALZBURG to

BRUSSELS: ① June 19 - Sept. 4, 1995.
Salzburg Hbf load 2110 - 2150, depart 2232,
Brussels Schaerbeek arrive 0949.
Train **1412**: 🛏 1,2 cl. (T2) and ➤ 2 cl.

SALZBURG (continued) to

DÜSSELDORF: ④ Mar. 30 - May 25; ④ June 15 - Oct. 26.
Salzburg Hbf load 0920 - 0950, depart 1114,
Düsseldorf Hbf arrive 2051.
Train **1528**: 🚟 and 🍴.

FRANKFURT: ④ Mar. 30 - May 25; ④ June 15 - Oct. 26.
Salzburg Hbf load 1020 - 1045, depart 1114,
Frankfurt Neu Isenburg arrive 1742.
Train **1528**: 🚟 and 🍴.

's-HERTOGENBOSCH: ⑤ May 5 - Sept. 22, 1995.
Salzburg Hbf load 2110 - 2150, depart 2232,
's-Hertogenbosch arrive 0944.
Train **1316**: 🛏 1,2 cl., ➤ 2 cl. and 🍴.

KÖLN: ④ Mar. 30 - May 25; ④ June 15 - Oct. 26, 1995.
Salzburg Hbf load 0950 - 1020, depart 1114,
Köln Deutz arrive 2017.
Train **1528**: 🚟 and 🍴.

SIOFOK to

HANNOVER: ① May 30 - Sept. 26, 1994; ① May 8-22,
1995.
Siofok load 1500 - 1600, depart 1710,
Hannover Hbf arrive 1051.
Train **13386**: ➤ 2 cl. and 🍴.

KÖLN: ① May 30 - Sept. 26, 1994; ① May 8-22, 1995.
Siofok load 1500 - 1600, depart 1710,
Köln Deutz arrive 1249.
Train **13386**: ➤ 2 cl. and 🍴.

SOFIJA to

LÉBÉNY (Hungary): June 23; ④⑤⑥ June 29 - July 29;
①②⑦ Aug. 6 - Sept. 5, 1995.
Sofija depart 1150, Lébény 0759 next day.
Organised by Optima Tours, München - see under Lébény.

SVILENGRAD to

LÉBÉNY (Hungary): June 26,29; daily July 2 - Sept. 10,
1995.
Svilengrad depart 1345, Lébény arrive 1655 next day.
Organised by Optima Tours, München - see under Lébény.

TARBES to

BRUSSELS: ① July 3 - Aug. 21, 1995.
Tarbes load 1700 - 1745, depart 1844,
Brussels Schaerbeek arrive 1015.
Train **1230/1**: 🛏 1,2 cl. (T2) and ➤ 2 cl.

THESSALONIKI to

BUDAPEST: ⑥ July 1 - Sept. 23, 1995.
Thessaloniki load 1800 - 1900, depart 2000,
Budapest Keleti arrive 1458.
Train **1410/11410**: ➤ 2 cl.

WIEN: ⑥ July 1 - Sept. 23, 1995.
Thessaloniki load 1800 - 1900, depart 2000,
Wien Süd arrive 1805.
Train **1410**: 🛏 1,2 cl., ➤ 2 cl. and 🍴.

TOULOUSE to

BRUSSELS: ⑥ Apr. 1 - Sept. 23; ① July 3 - Aug. 21, 1995.
Toulouse load 1500 - 1900, depart 2047 (2026 to May 27),
Brussels Schaerbeek arrive 1015 (0822 to May 27).
Train **1230/1** or **1364/3**: 🛏 1,2 cl. (T2) and ➤ 2 cl.

CALAIS: Apr. 8,15,22; ⑥ May 20 - July 1; ⑤⑥⑦ July 7 -
Sept. 10; also Sept. 16,23, 1995.
Toulouse load 1500 - 1830, depart 2013,
Calais auto/train arrive 0845.
Train **1540/1**: 🛏 1,2 cl., 🛏 1,2 cl. and 🍴.

's-HERTOGENBOSCH: ① May 22 - Sept. 4, ③ June 28 -
Aug. 9, 1995.
Toulouse load 1630 - 1730, depart 1830,
's-Hertogenbosch arrive 0951.
Train **1338/7**: 🛏 1,2 cl., ➤ 2 cl. and 🍴.

LIÈGE: ③ June 28 - Aug. 9, 1995.
Toulouse load 1500 - 1630, depart 1830,
Liège Bressoux arrive 0702.
Train **1338/7**: 🛏 1,2 cl., ➤ 2 cl. and 🍴.

VENEZIA to

WIEN: ⑥ June 10 - Sept. 9, 1995.
Venezia Mestre load 2030 - 2215, depart 2306,
Wien Süd arrive 0811.
Train **1134**: 🛏 1,2 cl. and ➤ 2 cl.

VERONA

HAMBURG: ⑥ June 4 - Oct. 1, 1994.
Verona load 1400 - 1645, depart 1728,
Hamburg Altona arrive 1119.
Train **13384**: 🛏 1,2 cl., ➤ 2 cl. and 🍴.

HANNOVER: ⑥ June 4 - Oct. 1, 1994; ⑥ May 6-27, 1995.
Verona load 1400 - 1645, depart 1728,
Hannover Hbf arrive 0859.
Train **13384**: 🛏 1,2 cl., ➤ 2 cl. and 🍴.

KÖLN: ⑥ June 4 - Oct. 1, 1994; ⑥ May 6-27, 1995.
Verona load 1400 - 1645, depart 1728,
Köln Deutz arrive 0930.
Train **13384**: 🛏 1,2 cl., ➤ 2 cl. and 🍴.

VILLACH to

BERLIN: ⑥ Jan. 7 - Apr. 8; ⑥ June 3 - Oct. 7, 1995.
To Apr. 8: Villach Hbf load 1600 - 1645, depart 1720,
Berlin Wannsee arrive 0700.
From June 3: Villach Hbf load 1900 - 1945, depart 2025,
Berlin Wannsee arrive 0824.
Train **1208**: 🛏 1,2 cl., ➤ 2 cl., 🚟 and 🍴.

BRUSSELS: ① June 19 - Sept. 4, 1995.
Villach Hbf load 1745 - 1845, depart 1928,
Brussels Schaerbeek arrive 0949.
Train **1412**: 🛏 1,2 cl. (T2) and ➤ 2 cl.

DÜSSELDORF: ① May 30 - Sept. 26; ⑥ June 4 - Oct. 1,
1994.
①: Villach Hbf load 1700 - 1800, depart 1917,
Düsseldorf Hbf arrive 1016.
⑥: oad 1900 - 1930, depart 2008, arrive 1016.
Train **13320** or **13322**: 🛏 1,2 cl., ➤ 2 cl. and 🍴.

FRANKFURT/MAIN: ① May 30 - Sept. 26; ⑥ June 4 - Oct.
1, 1994; ⑥ Apr. 1 - May 27, 1995.
①: Villach Hbf load 1700 - 1800, depart 1917,
Frankfurt Neu Isenburg arrive 0600.
⑥ to May 27: load 1700 - 1750, depart 1830, arrive 0503.
Train **13320/2/80**: 🛏 1,2 cl., ➤ 2 cl. and 🍴.

HAMBURG: ① May 30 - Sept. 26, 1994; ⑥ Apr. 1 - May 27,
1995.
①: Villach Hbf load 1700 - 1800, depart 1917,
Hamburg Altona arrive 0935.
⑥: load 1700 - 1750, depart 1830, arrive 0958.
Train **13380** or **13392**: 🛏 1,2 cl., ➤ 2 cl. and 🍴.

HANNOVER: ① May 30 - Sept. 26, 1994; ⑥ Apr. 1 - May
27, 1995.
①: Villach Hbf load 1700 - 1800, depart 1917,
Hannover Hbf arrive 0745.
⑥: load 1700 - 1750, depart 1830, arrive 0740.
Train **13380** or **13392**: 🛏 1,2 cl., ➤ 2 cl. and 🍴.

s'HERTOGENBOSCH: ⑤ May 5 - Sept. 22, 1995.
Villach Hbf load 1745 - 1845, depart 1928,
s'Hertogenbosch arrive 0944.
Train **1316**: 🛏 1,2 cl., ➤ 2 cl. and 🍴.

KÖLN: ① May 30 - Sept. 26, 1994; ⑥ Apr. 1 - May 27, 1995.
①: Villach Hbf load 1700 - 1800, depart 1917,
Köln Deutz arrive 0934.
⑥: load 1700 - 1750, depart 1830, arrive 0824.
Train **13322** or **13380**: 🛏 1,2 cl., ➤ 2 cl. and 🍴.

WIEN to

RIMINI: ⑤ June 9 - Sept. 1, 1995.
Wien Süd load 1905 - 2005, depart 2102,
Rimini arrive 0910.
Train **1135**: 🛏 1,2 cl. and ➤ 2 cl.

THESSALONIKI: ⑤ June 30 - Sept. 22, 1995.
Wien Süd load 0800 - 0840, depart 0913,
Thessaloniki arrive 0950 next day..
Train **1411**: 🛏 1,2 cl., ➤ 2 cl. and 🍴.

VENEZIA: ⑤ June 9 - Sept. 1, 1995.
Wien Süd load 1905 - 2005, depart 2102,
Venezia Mestre arrive 0526.
Train **1135**: 🛏 1,2 cl. and ➤ 2 cl.

ZÜRICH to

NAPOLI: ⑤ June 23 - Aug. 25, 1995.
Zürich Altstetten load 1700 - 1800, depart 1845,
Napoli Campi Flegre arrive 0933.
Train **1385**: 🛏 1,2 cl. and ➤ 2 cl.

NARBONNE: ⑦ June 25 - Aug. 27, 1995.
Zürich Altstetten load 1630 - 1800, depart 1913,
Narbonne arrive 0700, 🚌 to Narbonne auto/train.
Train **1300/1**: 🛏 1,2 cl. and ➤ 2 cl.

Table 2

INTERNAL CAR TRAINS

AUSTRIA
to 27/5/95

Bischofshofen - Wien (day train): ⑥ May 29 - Sept. 24; ⑥ Dec. 17 - Apr. 15 (also Apr. 17, May 20,27).

Feldkirch - Graz: daily (day and overnight trains).
Feldkirch - Linz: daily.
Feldkirch - Wien: daily (day and overnight trains).
Feldkirch - Villach: daily.
Graz - Feldkirch: daily (day and overnight trains).

Innsbruck - Wien: daily (2 day trains).

Lienz - Wien (day train): ⑥⑦ May 29 - Sept. 24; ⑥ Dec. 17 - Apr. 15, also June 2, Aug. 15, Dec. 23,25,26, Jan. 6,8, Apr. 17,18,29, May 25,27.

Linz - Feldkirch: daily.

Salzburg - Wien: daily (day train).

Wien - Bischofshofen (day train): ⑥ May 29 - Sept. 24; ⑥ Dec. 17 - Apr. 15 (also May 20,27).

Wien - Feldkirch: daily (day and overnight trains).
Wien - Innsbruck: daily (2 day trains).
Wien - Lienz (day train): ⑥⑦ May 29 - Sept. 24; ⑥ Dec. 17 - Apr. 15, also June 2, Aug. 15, Dec. 23,25,26, Jan. 6,8, Apr. 17,18,29, May 25,27.
Wien - Salzburg: daily (2 day trains).
Wien - Villach: daily (day train).

Villach - Feldkirch: daily.
Villach - Wien: daily (day and overnight trains).

FINLAND
to 27/5/95

Helsinki - Kontiomäki: daily (not Dec. 24).
Helsinki - Oulu: daily (not Dec. 24).
Helsinki - Rovaniemi: daily (not Dec. 24).
Kontiomäki - Helsinki: daily (not Dec. 24).
Oulu - Helsinki: daily (not Dec. 24).

Oulu - Tampere: daily except ⑥ (①②③④ Feb. 13 - May 1). Not Apr. 12,13,17,18, May 1.
Oulu - Turku: daily except ⑥ (①②③④ Feb. 13 - May 1). Not Apr. 12,13,17,18.

Rovaniemi - Helsinki: daily (not Dec. 24).
Rovaniemi - Tampere: daily (not Dec. 24).
Rovaniemi - Turku: daily (not Dec. 24).

Tampere - Rovaniemi: daily (not Dec. 24).
Tampere - Oulu: daily except ⑥ (①②③⑦ Feb. 12 - Apr. 30). Not Apr. 12,13,17,18, May 1.
Turku - Rovaniemi: daily (not Dec. 24).
Turku - Oulu: daily except ⑥ (①②③⑦ Feb. 13 - May 1). Not Apr. 11,12,16,17,30.

FRANCE
to 23/9/95

For services from Calais, see Table 1.

Auray - Lyon: ⑥ June 3 - Sept. 23 (daily July 1 - Sept. 3).
Auray - Metz: ⑥ June 9 - Sept. 8.
Auray - Paris: Apr. 17,23, May 1,8,14,21,28, June 5; ⑦ June 11 - Sept. 17 (daily July 1 - Sept. 3).
Auray - Strasbourg: ⑥ June 9 - Sept. 8.
Avignon - Lille: ①⑤⑥⑦ Apr. 14 - May 1, also May 6,7,13,14, 20,21,25-27. For summer service see Avignon - Seclin.
Avignon - Metz: ①; also ⑦ June 4 - Sept. 17.
Avignon - Mulhouse: ⑦ June 4 - Sept. 17.
Avignon - Paris: daily (day train). Also overnight train daily May 28 - Sept. 23.
Avignon - Seclin (Lille): ① July 24 - Aug. 28; ③ May 31 - Aug. 30; ⑤ July 7 - Sept. 8; ⑥ June 3 - July 1 and Sept. 2,9,23.
Avignon - Strasbourg: ① to May 22; ⑦ June 4 - Sept. 17.
Biarritz - Lille: ⑥ July 1 - Sept. 2.
Biarritz - Metz: ② June 13 - Sept. 5.
Biarritz - Paris: ①④⑥ (daily Mar. 25 - Sept. 23).
Biarritz - Strasbourg: ② June 13 - Sept. 5.
Bordeaux - Lille: ⑥ July 1 - Sept. 2.
Bordeaux - Lyon: Apr. 14,21, May 26 and daily May 28 - Sept. 23.
Bordeaux - Marseille: ⑦ to July 2 and from Sept. 10 (also May 1,8, June 5, July 14; not Apr. 16,30, May 7, June 4, July 13); ②④⑥ July 8 - Sept. 2.
Bordeaux - Metz: ② June 13 - Sept. 5.
Bordeaux - Paris: daily except Dec. 24,31.
Bordeaux - St. Raphaël: ⑤ (also May 24, July 13; not May 26, July 14); ⑦ May 28 - Sept. 17 (also June 5; not June 4); ①③ July 10 - Aug. 30 (not Aug. 14).
Bordeaux - Strasbourg: ② June 13 - Sept. 5.
Briançon - Paris: ④⑥⑦ (daily Dec. 19 - Mar. 26 and June 29 - Sept. 3).
Brive - Paris: ⑥ Feb. 18 - May 27 (not Apr. 15); ⑦ Nov. 6 - Apr. 23, also Apr. 13,17,20,27, May 1,4,8,11,16,18,21, 23,25; daily May 28 - Sept. 23.
Évian les Bains - Paris: ⑥ Dec. 17 - Apr. 29; daily July 1 - Sept. 3;
Fréjus-St. Raphaël - see St. Raphaël.
Lille - Avignon: ④⑤⑥⑦ Apr. 13-30; also May 5-7,12,13,19, 20,24-27. For summer service see Seclin - Avignon.
Lille - Biarritz: ⑤ June 30 - Sept. 1.
Lille - Bordeaux: ⑤ June 30 - Sept. 1.
Lille - Narbonne: ⑤ Mar. 31 - May 26; ①⑤ May 29 - Sept. 22; ③ June 21 - Aug. 23.
Lille - Nice: daily.
Lyon - Auray: ⑤ June 2 - Sept. 22 (daily June 30 - Sept. 2).
Lyon - Bordeaux: Apr. 22,29 and daily May 28 - Sept. 23.
Lyon - Nantes: daily.
Lyon - Paris: daily (day train).
Marseille - Bordeaux: ⑤ (also May 24; not May 26, July 7); also ③⑦ July 9 - Sept. 3.
Marseille - Nancy: ⑤ July 7 - Sept. 1.
Marseille - Nantes: ⑤ July 9 - Sept. 3.

Marseille - Paris: daily (day and overnight trains).
Marseille - Strasbourg: ②⑥ June 24 - Sept. 5.

Metz - Auray: ④ June 8 - Sept. 7.
Metz - Avignon: ⑦ June 3 - Sept. 16).
Metz - Biarritz: ① June 12 - Sept. 4.
Metz - Bordeaux: ① June 12 - Sept. 4.
Metz - Nantes: ④ June 8 - Sept. 7.
Metz - Narbonne: ⑤ to June 23 and from Sept. 8 (also May 24; not May 26); ④⑥ July 1 - Sept. 2.
Metz - Nice: ⑤ to June 23 and from Sept. 1 (also May 24; not May 26).
Metz - St. Raphaël: ⑦; also ④ June 24 - Sept. 1.
Moutiers-Salins - Paris: ⑥⑦ Dec. 25 - Apr. 2, also Jan. 4, Feb. 24, Mar. 3, Apr. 23,30.
Mulhouse - Avignon: ⑥ June 3 - Sept. 16.
Mulhouse - Narbonne: ⑥ June 3 - Sept. 16.
Mulhouse - St. Raphaël: ⑤ June 23 - Aug. 25.
Nancy - Marseille: ④ July 6 - Aug. 31.
Nancy - Narbonne: ⑤ (also May 24; not May 26); also ⑦ July 2 - Aug. 27.
Nancy - Nice: ⑤ to June 23 and from Sept. 8 (also May 24; not May 26); ①③⑥ July 1 - Sept. 2.
Nantes - Lyon: daily.
Nantes - Marseille: ⑤ July 7 - Sept. 1 (also July 13; not July 14).
Nantes - Metz: ⑤ June 9 - Sept. 8.
Nantes - Nice: ①③ to July 5 and from Sept. 4 (not Apr. 17, May 1,8,24).
Nantes - Paris (day train): Apr. 17,23, May 1,8,14,21,28, June 5; ⑦ June 11 - Sept. 17 (daily July 1 - Sept. 3).
Nantes - St. Raphaël: ⑤⑦ (also Apr 17, May 1,8,24, June 5; not Apr. 16,30, May 7,26, June 4); daily July 7 - Sept. 3 (not Aug. 14).
Nantes - Strasbourg: ⑤ June 9 - Sept. 8; ② July 4 - Aug.22.
Nantes - Toulouse: ①⑥ May 29 - Sept. 23 (also June 6, Aug. 16; not June 5).
Narbonne - Lille: ⑥ Apr. 1 - May 27; ②⑥ May 30 - Sept. 23; ④ June 22 - Aug. 24.
Narbonne - Metz: ⑦ (also Apr. 17, May 1,8; not Apr. 16,30, May 7); also ⑤ July 7 - Sept. 1.
Narbonne - Mulhouse: ⑦ June 4 - Sept. 17.
Narbonne - Nancy: ⑦ to June 25 and from Sept. 3 (also Apr. 17, May 1,8; not May 7); ①⑤ July 1 - Aug. 28.
Narbonne - Paris: daily except ⑦ (daily May 28 - Sept. 23), also runs Dec. 25, Jan. 1, Apr. 16.
Narbonne - Strasbourg: ④⑦ June 1 - Sept. 21 (also July 5,12; not July 6,13).
Nice - Lille: daily.
Nice - Metz: ⑤ to June 25 and from Sept. 3 (also Apr. 17, May 1,8; not Apr. 16,30, May 7).
Nice - Nancy: ② (also Apr. 17, May 1,8; not Apr. 16,30, May 7); also ②④ July 4 - Aug. 31.
Nice - Nantes: ②④ to July 6 and from Sept. 5 (not Apr. 18, May 2, 9,25).
Nice - Paris: daily.
Nice - Strasbourg: ③⑦ June 25 - Sept. 3.
Nice - Toulouse: ④ June 22 - Sept. 7.

Paris - Auray: ⑤ Apr. 14 - Sept. 22 (daily June 30 - Sept. 2); also May 24, not May 26.
Paris - Avignon: daily (day train). Also overnight train daily May 28 - Sept. 23.
Paris - Biarritz: ③⑤⑦ (daily Mar. 24 - Sept. 23).
Paris - Bordeaux: daily except Dec. 24,31.
Paris - Briançon: ③⑤⑥ (daily Dec. 18 - Mar. 25 and June 28 - Sept. 2).
Paris - Brive: ⑤; also ③ Apr. 12 - May 24; also Apr. 30, May 7,15,22; daily May 27 - Sept. 23.
Paris - Évian les Bains: ⑤ Dec. 16 - Apr. 28; daily June 30 - Sept. 2;
Paris - Lyon: daily (day train).
Paris - Marseille: daily (day and overnight trains).
Paris - Moutiers-Salins: ⑤⑥ Jan. 6 - Apr. 22, also Dec. 16,17,21,23,30.
Paris - Nantes: daily except ⑥ (daily May 28 - Sept. 23).
Paris - Nantes (day train): ⑤ Apr. 14 - Sept. 22 (daily June 30 - Sept. 2); also May 24, not May 26.
Paris - Narbonne: daily except ⑥ (daily May 28 - Sept. 23).
Paris - Nice: daily.
Paris - St. Gervais: ①③④⑤⑥ Sept. 25 - May 27 (also Apr. 16,30, May 7); May 28 - Sept. 23.
Paris - St. Raphaël: daily.
Paris - Tarbes: ③⑤⑦ (daily May 28 - Sept. 23).
Paris - Toulon: daily.
Paris - Toulouse: daily except Dec. 24,31.

St. Gervais - Paris: ②④⑤⑥⑦ Sept. 25 - May 27 (also Apr. 17, May 1,8); daily May 28 - Sept. 23.

St. Raphaël - Bordeaux: ⑦ to July 2 and from Sept. 10 (also Apr. 17, May 1,8, June 5; not Apr. 16,30, May 7, June 4); ⑤ June 2 - 30 and Sept. 8 - 22; ①②④⑥ July 8 - Sept. 2 (not Aug. 14).
St. Raphaël - Metz: ①; also ⑥ June 24 - Sept. 2.
St. Raphaël - Mulhouse: ⑤ June 24 - Aug. 26.
St. Raphaël - Nantes: ⑤⑦ (also Apr. 17, May 1,8,24, June 5; not Apr. 16,30, May 7,26, June 4); daily July 7 - Sept. 3 (not Aug. 14).
St. Raphaël - Paris: daily.
St. Raphaël - Strasbourg: ① to June 19 and from Sept. 4; ⑥ June 24 - Aug. 26.

Seclin (Lille) - Avignon: ② May 30 - Aug. 29; ④ July 6 - Aug. 31; ⑤ June 2 - 30 and Sept. 1,8,22; ⑦ July 23 - Aug. 27.
Strasbourg - Auray: ④ June 8 - Sept. 7.
Strasbourg - Avignon: ⑦ to May 21; ⑥ June 3 - Sept. 16.
Strasbourg - Biarritz: ① June 12 - Sept. 4.
Strasbourg - Bordeaux: ① June 12 - Sept. 4.
Strasbourg - Marseille: ①⑤ June 23 - Sept. 4.
Strasbourg - Nantes: ④ June 8 - Sept. 7; ① July 3 - Aug. 21.
Strasbourg - Narbonne: ③⑥ May 31 - Sept. 20 (also July 4,11; not July 5,12).
Strasbourg - Nice: ⑥ June 24 - Sept. 2.
Strasbourg - St. Raphaël: ⑦ to June 18 and from Sept. 3; ⑤ June 23 - Aug. 25.

Tarbes - Paris: ①④⑥ (daily May 28 - Sept. 23).

Toulon - Paris: daily.

Toulouse - Nantes: ⑤⑦ May 28 - Sept. 22 (also June 5, July 13, Aug. 15; not June 4, July 14, Aug. 13).
Toulouse - Nice: ③ June 21 - Sept. 6.
Toulouse - Paris: daily except Dec. 24,31.

GERMANY
to 27/5/95

Basel (Lörrach) - Berlin Wannsee: ⑥ Sept. 3 - Oct. 29; ⑥ Jan. 28 - May 27, also Dec. 25, Jan. 1,3.
Basel (Lörrach) - Düsseldorf: ⑤ Sept. 2 - Oct. 21; ⑤ Mar. 31 - Apr. 21 (day train).
Basel (Lörrach) - Hamburg Altona: ②④ Oct. 24-26,31; ②④ Dec. 6 - May 25 (not Dec. 20,22); ③ May 3 - 24.
Basel (Lörrach) - Hamburg Sternschanze: daily Sept. 1 - Oct. 30), also May 16,19-23,25,30, Jan. 2-6, Mar. 5, Apr. 2,9 and ⑤ Feb. 3 - May 26; not Dec. 24,31.
Basel (Lörrach) - Hannover: ⑤ daily Sept. 1 - Oct. 30), also Nov. 1, Dec. 16,19-23,25,30, Jan. 2-6, Mar. 5, Apr. 2,9 and ⑤ Feb. 3 - May 26, not Dec. 24,31.
Basel (Lörrach) - Köln Deutz: ⑤ Sept. 2 - Oct. 21; ⑤ Mar. 31 - Apr. 21 (day train).
Berlin Wannsee - Basel (Lörrach): ⑤ Sept. 2 - Oct. 28, also Dec. 23,30, Jan. 2; ⑤ Jan. 27 - May 26.

Berlin Wannsee - Düsseldorf: daily except Dec. 24,31.
Berlin Wannsee - Frankfurt Neu Isenburg: ④ Sept. 1 - Oct. 27, also Nov. 5,19, Dec. 3,17, Jan. 5,14,28, Feb. 11,25, Mar. 4,18,30; ④ Apr. 13 - May 25.
Berlin Wannsee - München Ost: daily.
Berlin Wannsee - Stuttgart Kornwestheim: ④ Sept. 1 - Oct. 27, also Nov. 5,19, Dec. 3,17, Jan. 5,14,28, Feb. 11,25, Mar. 4,18,30; ④ Apr. 13 - May 25.
Düsseldorf - Basel (Lörrach): ⑤ Sept. 2 - Oct. 21; ⑤ Mar. 31 - Apr. 21 (day train).
Düsseldorf - Berlin Wannsee: daily except Dec. 24,31.
Düsseldorf - Lindau: ⑤ Sept. 2 - Oct. 27, also Dec. 17,23,25, Jan. 7,21, Feb. 4,18, Mar. 4,18; ⑥ Apr. 1 - May 27 (day train).
Düsseldorf - München Ost: daily except Dec. 24,31. Also day train (see Köln - München for dates).

Frankfurt Neu Isenburg - Berlin Wannsee: ③ Sept. 7 - Oct. 26, also Nov. 4,18, Dec. 2,16, Jan. 4,13,27, Feb. 10,24, Mar. 3,17,29; ③ Apr. 12 - May 24.
Frankfurt Neu Isenburg - Niebüll: ⑤ Sept. 2 - Oct. 28; ⑤ Mar. 31 - May 26.
Frankfurt Neu Isenburg - Westerland: ⑤ Sept. 2 - Oct. 28; ⑤ Mar. 31 - May 26.
Hamburg Altona - Basel (Lörrach): Oct. 24-26,31; ①③ Dec. 5 - May 24 (not Dec. 19,21); ③ May 2 - 23.
Hamburg Sternschanze - Basel (Lörrach): ⑤ (daily Sept. 1 - Oct. 30), also Nov. 1, Dec. 17,19-22,25, Jan. 2-7, Mar. 5, Apr. 2,9 and ⑥ Feb. 4 - May 27.
Hamburg Altona - München Ost: daily Sept. 1 - Oct. 22, also Oct. 24-28,30,31, Nov. 4,11,18,25, Dec. 5,7,12,14,17-22,25,26, Jan. 1-5; ①③④⑤⑥ Jan. 7 - Mar 31 (also Mar. 5); ①③⑤⑥ Apr. 1-29 (also Apr. 13,30); ① - ⑥ May 1-27.
Hamburg Altona - Sonthofen: ⑤ Sept. 2 - Oct. 7, also Dec. 16,22,25, Jan. 4; ⑤ Jan. 6 - Apr. 7.

Table 2

INTERNAL CAR TRAINS

GERMANY continued

Hannover - Basel (Lörrach): ⑤ (daily Sept. 1 - Oct. 30), also Nov. 1, Dec. 17,19-22,25, Jan. 2-7, Mar. 5, Apr. 2,9 and ⑥ Feb. 4 - May 27.

Hannover - München Ost: daily Sept. 1 - Oct. 22, also Oct. 28,30, Dec. 17-23,25,26,30, Jan. 1-7; ⑤⑥ Jan. 13 - May 27, also Mar. 5, Apr. 13,30.

Köln Deutz - Basel (Lörrach): ⑤ Sept. 2 - Oct. 21; ⑤ Mar. 31 - Apr. 21 (day train).

Köln Deutz - Lindau: ⑥ Sept. 3 - Oct. 29, also Dec. 17,23,25, Jan. 7,21, Feb. 4,18, Mar. 4,18; ⑥ Apr. 1 - May 27 (day train).

Köln Deutz - München Ost (day train): ①③⑤⑥ Sept. 2-30; ①③⑥ Oct. 1-31; ⑥ Nov. 5 - Dec. 17 (also Dec. 5,12,19-23,25,26,30); ⑥ Jan. 7 - May 27 (also Jan. 1-6,9,16,23, 25,30, Feb. 8,13,22,27, Mar. 8,13,22,27,31, Apr. 3,10, 14,21, May 1,8,15,22).

Köln Deutz - Niebüll: ⑤ Sept. 2 - Oct. 28; ⑤ Mar. 31 - May 26.

Köln Deutz - Westerland: ⑤ Sept. 2 - Oct. 28; ⑤ Mar. 31 - May 26.

Lindau - Düsseldorf (day train): ⑥ Sept. 3 - Oct. 29, also Dec. 17,23,25, Jan. 7,21, Feb. 4,18, Mar. 4,18; ⑥ Apr. 1 - May 27.

Lindau - Köln Deutz (day train): ⑥ Sept. 3 - Oct. 29, also Dec. 17,23,25, Jan. 7,21, Feb. 4,18, Mar. 4,18; ⑥ Apr. 1 - May 27.

München Ost - Berlin Wannsee: daily.

München Ost - Düsseldorf: daily except Dec. 24,31. Also day train (see München - Köln for dates).

München Ost - Hamburg Altona: daily Sept. 1 - Oct. 22, also Oct. 24-27,29-31, Nov. 4,11,18,25, Dec. 2,5,7,9,12,14, 16-23,25,26,30, Jan. 1-7; ①③④⑤⑥ Jan. 9 - Mar. 30 (also Mar. 5); ①③⑤⑥ Apr. 1 - 29 (also Apr. 13, 30); ① - ⑥ May 1-27.

München Ost - Hannover: daily Sept. 1 - Oct. 22, also Oct. 29,30, Dec. 17-23,25,26,30, Jan. 1-7; ⑤⑥ Jan. 13 - May 27, also Mar. 5, Apr. 13,30.

München Ost - Köln Deutz (day train): ①③⑤⑥ Sept. 2-30; ①③⑥ Oct. 1-31; ⑥ Nov. 5 - Dec. 17 (also Dec. 5,12,19-23,25,26,30); ⑥ Jan. 7 - May 27 (also Jan. 1-6,9,16,23, 25,30, Feb. 8,13,22,27, Mar. 8,13,22,27,31, Apr. 3,10, 14,21, May 1,8,15,22).

Niebüll - Frankfurt Neu Isenburg: ⑥ Sept. 3 - Oct. 29; ⑥ Apr. 1 - May 27.

Niebüll - Köln Deutz: ⑥ Sept. 3 - Oct. 29; ⑥ Apr. 1 - May 27.

Niebüll - Stuttgart Kornwestheim: ⑥ Sept. 3 - Oct. 29; ⑥ Apr. 1 - May 27.

Sonthofen - Hamburg: ⑥ Sept. 3 - Oct. 8, also Dec. 23, Jan. 1,5; ⑥ Jan. 7 - Apr. 8.

Stuttgart Kornwestheim - Berlin Wannsee: ③ Sept. 7 - Oct. 26, also Nov. 4,18, Dec. 2,16, Jan. 4,13,27, Feb. 10,24, Mar. 3,17,29; ③ Apr. 12 - May 24.

Stuttgart Kornwestheim - Niebüll: ⑤ Sept. 2 - Oct. 28; ⑤ Mar. 31 - May 26.

Stuttgart Kornwestheim - Westerland: ⑤ Sept. 2 - Oct. 28; ⑤ Mar. 31 - May 26.

Westerland - Frankfurt Neu Isenburg: ⑥ Sept. 3 - Oct. 29; ⑥ Apr. 1 - May 27.

Westerland - Köln Deutz: ⑥ Sept. 3 - Oct. 29; ⑥ Apr. 1 - May 27.

Westerland - Stuttgart Kornwestheim: ⑥ Sept. 3 - Oct. 29; ⑥ Apr. 1 - May 27.

GREAT BRITAIN to 27/5/95

Enquiries: InterCity Motorail Office, P.O. Box 44, Edinburgh EH1 1BA. ☎ 0345 090700.
All services are expected to cease on May 27.

Aberdeen - London Euston: ⑧ (daily July 2 - Sept. 17).
Bristol - Edinburgh: ⑧.
Carlisle - London Euston (day train): daily.

Edinburgh - Bristol: ⑧.
Edinburgh - London Euston: ⑧ (daily July 2 - Sept. 17).

Fort William - London Euston: ⑧ (daily July 16 - Sept. 3).

Glasgow - London Euston: ⑧ (daily July 2 - Sept. 17).
Glasgow - London Euston (day train): daily.
Inverness - London Euston: ⑧ (daily July 2 - Sept. 17).

London Euston - Aberdeen: ⑧ (daily July 2 - Sept. 17).
London Euston - Carlisle (day train): daily except ⑦.
London Euston - Edinburgh: ⑧ (daily July 2 - Sept. 17).
London Euston - Fort William: ⑧ (daily July 16 - Sept. 3).
London Euston - Glasgow: ⑧ (daily July 2 - Sept. 17).
London Euston - Glasgow (day train): daily.
London Euston - Inverness: ⑧ (daily July 2 - Sept. 17).

ITALY to 27/5/95

Bari - Bologna: ② - ⑦ June 25 - Sept. 1.
Bari - Bolzano: ⑤ (not Dec. 23,30).
Bari - Milano: ③⑤⑦ June 26 - Aug. 31.
Bari - Torino: daily Sept. 1-24, Dec. 18-20,27-29; ⑤⑥ Sept. 30 - Dec. 17 and Jan. 6 - May 27.

Bologna - Bari: ② - ⑦ June 24 - Aug. 31.
Bologna - Brindisi: ③⑤⑦ June 24 - Aug. 31, also Sept. 2,4.
Bologna - Catania: daily.
Bologna - Villa S. Giovanni: daily.

Bolzano - Bari: ⑥ (not Dec. 24,31).
Bolzano - Roma: Sept. 1,3, Dec. 17-31, Jan. 1-4,7,8,14,15, Jan. 21 - Apr. 15, also Apr. 17.
Bolzano - Villa S. Giovanni: ⑤ July 22 - Sept. 2.

Brindisi - Bologna: ①③⑤ June 24 - Aug. 31, also Sept. 2,5,7,9.
Brindisi - Milano: ①③⑤ June 24 - Aug. 31, also Sept. 2,5,7,9.

Brunico - Roma: Sept. 1,3, Dec. 17-31, Jan. 1-4,7,8,14,15, Jan. 21 - Apr. 15, also Apr. 17.

Calalzo - Roma: Sept. 1,3, Dec. 17-31, Jan. 1-4,7,8,14,15, Jan. 21 - Apr. 15, also Apr. 17.

Catania - Bologna: daily.
Catania - Milano: ①④⑥ June 16 - Sept. 24, Dec. 15 - Jan. 7 and Apr. 13 - 22 (not Dec. 24,31).
Catania - Roma: daily.
Catania - Torino: ②⑤⑦ June 17 - Sept. 23, Dec. 16 - Jan. 8 and Apr. 11 - 23 (not Dec. 25, Jan. 1).

Firenze - Villa S. Giovanni: ⑤⑥ May 29 - Sept. 24.

Genova - Villa S. Giovanni: ①②④⑤⑥⑦ June 16 - Sept. 24, Dec. 15 - Jan. 8 and Apr. 11 - 23 (not Dec. 24,25,31, Jan. 1).

Lamezia - Milano: ②⑤⑦ June 17 - Sept. 23, Dec. 16 - Jan. 8 and Apr. 11 - 23 (not Dec. 25, Jan. 1).
Lamezia - Torino: ①④⑥ June 16 - Sept. 24, Dec. 15 - Jan. 7 and Apr. 13 - 22 (not Dec. 24,31).

Milano - Bari: ①③⑤ June 24 - Aug. 29.
Milano - Brindisi: ②④⑥ June 23 - Aug. 30, also Sept. 1,3.
Milano - Catania: ①④⑥ June 16 - Sept. 24, Dec. 15 - Jan. 7 and Apr. 13 - 22 (not Dec. 24,31).
Milano - Lamezia: ②⑤⑦ June 17 - Sept. 23, Dec. 16 - Jan. 8 and Apr. 11 - 23 (not Dec. 25, Jan. 1).
Milano - Napoli: ②⑤⑦ June 17 - Sept. 23, Dec. 16 - Jan. 8 and Apr. 11 - 23 (not Dec. 25, Jan. 1).
Milano - Palermo: ①④⑥ June 16 - Sept. 24, Dec. 15 - Jan. 7 and Apr. 13 - 22 (not Dec. 24,31).
Milano - Roma: daily.
Milano - Villa S. Giovanni: ②⑤⑦ June 17 - Sept. 23, Dec. 16 - Jan. 8 and Apr. 11 - 23 (not Dec. 25, Jan. 1).

Napoli - Milano: ②⑤⑦ June 17 - Sept. 23, Dec. 16 - Jan. 8 and Apr. 11 - 23 (not Dec. 25, Jan. 1).
Napoli - Torino: ①④⑥ June 16 - Sept. 24, Dec. 15 - Jan. 7 and Apr. 13 - 22 (not Dec. 24,31).

Palermo - Milano: ①④⑥ June 16 - Sept. 24, Dec. 15 - Jan. 7 and Apr. 13 - 22 (not Dec. 24,31).
Palermo - Roma: daily June 25 - Sept. 11, Dec. 7 - Jan. 8 and Apr. 14 - May 7.
Palermo - Torino: ②⑤⑦ June 17 - Sept. 23, Dec. 16 - Jan. 8 and Apr. 11 - 23 (not Dec. 25, Jan. 1).

Roma - Bolzano: Sept. 2, Dec. 16-31, Jan. 1-3,6,7,13,14, Jan. 20 - Apr. 15.

Roma - Brunico: Sept. 2, Dec. 16-31, Jan. 1-3,6,7,13,14, Jan. 20 - Apr. 15.
Roma - Calalzo: Sept. 2, Dec. 16-31, Jan. 1-3,6,7,13,14, Jan. 20 - Apr. 15.
Roma - Catania: daily.
Roma - Milano: daily.
Roma - Palermo: daily June 25 - Sept. 11, Dec. 7 - Jan. 8 and Apr. 14 - May 7.
Roma - Torino: ①④⑥ (also Sept. 1,2; not Dec. 24,31).
Roma - Villa S. Giovanni: daily.

Torino - Bari: daily Sept. 1-24, Dec. 18-20,27-29; ⑤⑥ Sept. 30 - Dec. 17 and Jan. 6 - May 27.
Torino - Catania: ②⑤⑦ June 17 - Sept. 23, Dec. 16 - Jan. 8 and Apr. 11 - 23 (not Dec. 25, Jan. 1).
Torino - Lamezia: ①④⑥ June 16 - Sept. 24, Dec. 15 - Jan. 7 and Apr. 13 - 22 (not Dec. 24,31).
Torino - Napoli: ①④⑥ June 16 - Sept. 24, Dec. 15 - Jan. 7 and Apr. 13 - 22 (not Dec. 24,31).
Torino - Palermo: ②⑤⑦ June 17 - Sept. 23, Dec. 16 - Jan. 8 and Apr. 11 - 23 (not Dec. 25, Jan. 1).
Torino - Roma: ②⑤⑦ (also Sept. 1-3, not Dec. 24, Jan. 1).
Torino - Villa S. Giovanni: ①④⑥ June 16 - Sept. 24, Dec. 15 - Jan. 7 and Apr. 13 - 22 (not Dec. 24,31).

Villa S. Giovanni - Bologna: daily.
Villa S. Giovanni - Bolzano: ⑥ July 23 - Aug. 6; ⑥ Aug. 20 - Sept. 10.
Villa S. Giovanni - Firenze: ⑥⑦ May 29 - Sept. 24.
Villa S. Giovanni - Genova: ①②④⑤⑥⑦ June 16 - Sept. 24, Dec. 15 - Jan. 8 and Apr. 11 - 23 (not Dec. 24,25,31, Jan. 1).
Villa S. Giovanni - Milano: ②⑤⑦ June 17 - Sept. 23, Dec. 16 - Jan. 8 and Apr. 11 - 23 (not Dec. 25, Jan. 1).
Villa S. Giovanni - Roma: daily.
Villa S. Giovanni - Torino: ①④⑥ June 16 - Sept. 24, Dec. 15 - Jan. 7 and Apr. 13 - 22 (not Dec. 24,31).

PORTUGAL to 27/5/95

Castelo Branco - Lisboa: daily (day train).
Faro - Porto: summer only.

Guarda - Lisboa: daily (day train).
Lisboa - Castelo Branco: daily (day train).
Lisboa - Guarda: daily (day train).
Lisboa - Porto: daily (day and overnight trains).

Porto - Faro: summer only.
Porto - Lisboa: daily (day and overnight trains).

SPAIN to 27/5/95 *

Algeciras - Madrid: daily (train 347).

Alicante - Bilbao: ⑤⑦ also daily June 2 - Sept. 23 (train 953).
Alicante - Madrid: daily (day service, train 11025).

Almería - Madrid: daily except Dec. 24, 31 (train 773).

Barcelona - Coruña: daily except Dec. 24, 31 (train 923).
Barcelona - Madrid: daily except Dec. 24, 31 (train 875).
Barcelona - Málaga: daily (train 997).
Barcelona - Sevilla: daily (train 997).
Barcelona - Vigo: daily June 26 - Sept. 10 (train 923).

Bilbao - Alicante: ⑤⑦, also daily June 2 - Sept. 23 (train 950).
Bilbao - Cádiz: ⑤, also daily June 26 - Sept. 23 (train 940).
Bilbao - Málaga: ⑤, also daily June 26 - Sept. 23. (train 940).

Cádiz - Bilbao: ⑦, also daily June 26 - Sept. 23.
Cádiz - Madrid: daily except Dec. 24, 31 (train 813).

Coruña - Barcelona: daily except Dec. 24, 31 (train 920).
Coruña - Madrid: ①③⑤; daily July 16 - Aug. 3, Aug. 13 - Sept. 6 (train 852).

Madrid - Algeciras: daily (train 344).
Madrid - Alicante: daily (day service, train 22).
Madrid - Almería: daily except Dec. 24, 31 (train 770).
Madrid - Barcelona: daily except Dec. 24, 31 (train 874).
Madrid - Cádiz: daily except Dec. 24, 31 (train 810).
Madrid - Coruña: ②④⑦; daily July 15 - Aug. 2, Aug. 12 - Sept. 5 (train 851).
Madrid - Málaga: daily except Dec. 24, 31 (train 840).
Madrid - Santander: daily except Dec. 24, 31 (train 831).
Madrid - Sevilla: daily except Dec. 24, 31 (train 810).

Madrid - Vigo: ①③⑤, also June 24 - July 4, July 15 - Aug. 2, Aug. 12 - Sept. 5 (train 851/5).

Málaga - Barcelona: daily (train 994).
Málaga - Bilbao: ⑦; also daily June 26 - Sept. 23 (train 941).
Málaga - Madrid: daily (train 843).

Santander - Madrid: daily except Dec. 24, 31 (train 830).

Sevilla - Barcelona: daily (train 994).
Sevilla - Madrid: daily except Dec. 24, 31 (813).

Vigo - Barcelona: daily June 23 - Sept. 11 (train 920).
Vigo - Madrid: ②④⑦, also June 25 - July 5, July 16 - Aug. 3, Aug. 13 - Sept. 6 (train 852/6).

* – All services are subject to confirmation

Table 3

CRUISE TRAINS

The services shown in the European Timetable are the regular scheduled services of the railway companies concerned. However, a number of specialised operators also run luxurious cruise trains taking several days to complete their journey. Overnight accommodation is provided either on the train or in hotels, and meals and excursions are included in the price.

These additional services are marketed by, and bookable through, the operating company and appointed agents only and **normal rail tickets are not valid on these trains**. A selection of operators is shown below:

Venice-Simplon-Orient-Express (London - Paris - Venezia): VSOE Ltd., 20 Upper Ground, London, SE1 9PF, ☎ 0171 928 6000.

Premier Land Cruises (various cruises and days out within Great Britain): Waterman Railways, P.O. Box 4472, Lichfield, Staffs. WS13 6RU, ☎ 01543 419472.

Al Andalus Express (luxury train journeys through Andalucia, Spain): UK agents: Cox & Kings Travel Ltd, 4th floor, Gordon House, 10 Greencoat Place, London SW1P 1PH, ☎ 0171 873 5002, fax 0171 630 6038.

Transcantabrico (northern coast of Spain): Transcantabrico-FEVE, Avda. Santander s/n, 33001 Oviedo, Asturias, Spain, ☎ (+34) 985 529 0104.

Table 5

AIRPORT – CITY CENTRE LINKS

Principal gateways only

City	Airport ✈	Distance	Transport ‡	City Terminal	Table
Aberdeen	Dyce ✈	10 km	🚌 27, every 30/40 mins. ✗, (on ⑦ 70/125).	Guild Street.	
Alicante	Alicante ✈	12 km	🚌 13/14 services daily.	Plaza Chapi.	
Amsterdam	Schiphol ✈	15 km	Train, every 15 mins.	Centraal Station.	238
Athinai	Hellenikon ✈	14 km	🚌 A&B every 20 mins.	Syntagma Square/Amalias Avenue.	
Barcelona	Prat ✈	14 km	Train, every 30 mins.	Barcelona Sants.	414
Basel	Basel/Mulhouse ✈	8 km	🚌 50, every 20 – 30 mins.	SBB Station/Kannenfeldplatz.	
Belfast	Belfast International ✈	22 km	🚌 300 ('Airbus') every 30 (on ⑦ 60) mins.	Europa Buscentre, Glengall Street ◊	
Beograd	Beograd ✈	20 km	🚌 every 15 – 20 mins.	Bulevar Revolucije.	
Berlin	Schönefeld ✈	18 km	S–Bahn train, every 20 mins.	Bahnhof Zoo/Hbf.	
Berlin	Tegel ✈	7 km	🚌 109, every 5 - 10 mins.	Bahnhof Zoo.	
Birmingham	Birmingham ✈	11 km	Train, every 20 mins.	New Street Station.	540
Bonn	Köln – Bonn ✈	27 km	🚌 670, every 20 mins.	Hauptbahnhof.	
Bordeaux	Merignac ✈	12 km	🚌 15 services daily.	Gare St. Jean.	
Bristol	Bristol ✈	13 km	🚌 820, every 2 hours until 1956.	Bus Station, also Temple Meads Station.	
Brussels	Nationaal ✈	12 km	Train, every 20 mins.	Central Station.	201
Bucureşti	Otopeni ✈	16 km	🚌 783 every 30 mins ✗, 60 mins. ⑦.	Piata Unirii.	
Budapest	Ferihegy ✈	16 km	🚌 every 15 mins.	Bus Stn., Engels - ter.	
Cardiff	Cardiff – Wales ✈	20 km	🚌 X91, hourly on weekdays.	Cardiff Bus Station.	
Derby	East Midlands ✈	19 km	🚌 hourly ✗, every 2 hours on ⑦.	Bus Station.	
Douglas, IoM	Ronaldsway/Isle of Man ✈	14 km	🚌 20½/10 ⑦ times daily.	Douglas Bus Station.	
Dublin	Dublin ✈	9 km	🚌 'Airlink' every 20-30 minutes	Heuston Station/Central Bus Station.	
Düsseldorf	Düsseldorf ✈	8 km	Train (S–Bahn) every 20 mins.	Hauptbahnhof.	704
Edinburgh	Edinburgh ✈	11 km	🚌 100, every 30 mins. Ⓐ, hourly ⑦.	Waverley Bridge.	
Frankfurt/Main ✈	Frankfurt/Main ✈	10 km	Train (S–Bahn) 6 times hourly.	Hauptbahnhof.	715
Genève	Cointrin ✈	4 km	Train, 6 times hourly.	Cornavin Station.	
Genova	Cristoforo Colombo ✈	7 km	'Volabus' 12/14 sevices daily.	Brignole & Principe stations; Piazza de Ferari.	
Glasgow	Glasgow ✈	14 km	🚌 500 every 15 – 20 mins.	Buchanan Bus Station.	■
Göteborg	Landvetter ✈	25 km	🚌 every 15 mins. Ⓐ, 20/30 mins. Ⓒ.	City Air Terminal/Central Station.	
Grenoble	Lyon Satolas ✈	85 km	🚌 (Cars Faure) 9 -11 times daily.	Gare routière (bus station).	
Hamburg	Fuhlsbüttel ✈	8 km	🚌 (Jasper) every 20 mins.	Hauptbahnhof/Kirchenallee.	
Hannover	Langenhagen ✈	11 km	🚌 60, every 30 mins.	Bus Stn. at Hbf.	
Helsinki	Vantaa ✈	19 km	🚌 every 15 – 20 mins.	City Air Terminal/Rail Station.	
Istanbul	Ataturk (Yesilkoy) ✈	24 km	🚌 every 60 mins.	City Terminal, Sishane.	
København	Kastrup ✈	10 km	🚌 every 10 – 15 mins.	Central Station.	▼
Köln	Köln/Bonn ✈	18 km	🚌 170, every 15 – 20 mins.	Dom/Hauptbahnhof.	
Leicester	East Midlands ✈	35 km	🚌 hourly ✗, every 2 hours ⑦.	Bus Station.	
Lisboa	Portela ✈	7 km	🚌 90, (Linha Verde), every 15 – 20 mins.	S. Apolonia & Rossio.	
London	City ✈	10 km	🚌 Ⓐ every 20 minutes, 0700 - 2140	Liverpool Street Station.	537
London	Gatwick ✈	43 km	Train, every 15 mins.	Victoria Station.	537
London	Heathrow ✈	25 km	LT train, every 5 – 10 mins.	See map, page 34.	
London	Stansted ✈	55 km	Train every 30 mins.	Liverpool Street Station.	537
London	Luton ✈	50 km	Bus/train 'Luton Flyer'	St. Pancras or Kings Cross Thameslink	537
Luxembourg	Findel ✈	7 km	🚌 9, every 15 – 30 mins.	Gare Centrale.	
Lyon	Satolas ✈	25 km	🚌 ('Satobus'), every 20 mins.	Perrache Station, via Part Dieu Station	
Madrid	Barajas ✈	16 km	🚌 approx every 10 mins.	Plaza Colon.	
Malaga	Malaga ✈	10 km	Train, every 30 mins.	Malaga Station.	427
Manchester	Manchester ✈	26 km	Train, every 15 - 20 minutes.	Piccadilly Station.	545
Marseille	Marseille – Provence ✈	28 km	🚌 every 20 mins.	Gare St. Charles.	
Milano	Linate ✈	10 km	🚌 approx every 20 mins.	Piazza S. Babila/Milano Centrale Station.	
Milano	Milano – Malpensa ✈	45 km	🚌 ('Airpullman') for each scheduled flight.	Centrale & Garibaldi Stations.	
Moskva	Sheremetyevo 1 ✈	26 km	🚌 every 30 mins.	37 Leningradski Prospekt.	
Moskva	Sheremetyevo 2 ✈	26 km	🚌 N517/N551, every 10 mins.	Plaernaia & Rechnoi Vokzal Metro Stations.	
München	Strauss ✈	37 km	S–Bahn Train, every 20 mins.	Hauptbahnhof.	757
Napoli	Capodichino ✈	7 km	🚌 14, every 20 mins.	Piazza Garibaldi (Central Station).	
Newcastle	Newcastle ✈	9 km	Metro train, every 10 – 12 mins.	Central Station.	
Nice	Nice – Côte d' Azur ✈	7 km	🚌 every 20 mins.	Gare Routière Départmentale.	
Nottingham	East Midlands ✈	24 km	🚌 hourly ✗, every 2 hours ⑦.	Broad Marsh Bus Station.	
Oslo	Fornebu ✈	10 km	🚌 every 15/30 mins.	Central Station. * *	
Palma	Palma ✈	11 km	🚌 every 30 mins.	Plaza España.	
Paris	Charles de Gaulle ✈	26 km	RER train every 15 mins.	Gare du Nord/Châtelet les Halles.	100
Paris	Orly ✈	16 km	RER train every 15 mins.	Gare du Nord/Châtelet les Halles.	100
Piraeus	Hellinikon ✈	20 km	🚌 19, am. every 30 mins./pm. every 90 mins.	Central Passenger Terminal & Akti Tzelepi.	
Pisa	Pisa (Galileo) ✈	2 km	1 per hour.	Pisa Centrale.	369
Porto	Pedras Rubras ✈	17 km	🚌 every 15 – 30 mins.	Praça do Carmo.	
Praha	Ruzyně ✈	17 km	🚌 (ČSA) every 30 mins.	Vltava Terminal/25 Ul. Revolučni.	
Roma	Leonardo da Vinci (Fiumicino) ✈	32 km	Train every 20 – 30 mins.	Roma Tiburtina/Ostiense/Termini.	389
Salzburg	Maxglan ✈	5 km	🚌 77, every 15 mins.	Salzburg Bahnhof.	
Sofija	Sofija ✈	10 km	🚌 approx. every 20 mins.	University.	
Stavanger	Sola ✈	14 km	🚌 every 15 – 30 mins.	Sentrum/Hotel Atlantic.	
Stockholm	Arlanda ✈	40 km	🚌 1, every 10 – 15 mins.	Cityterminalen (close to Central Station)	
Strasbourg	Entzheim ✈	12 km	🚌 every 30 mins.	Place de la Gare (Grand Hôtel).	
Stuttgart	Echterdingen ✈	14 km	Train – see Table 739.	Hauptbahnhof.	739
Torino	Caselle ✈	16 km	🚌 every 45 mins.	Corso Inghilterra 3.	
Toulouse	Blagnac ✈	8 km	🚌 every 30 mins. whilst airport open.	Gare Routière.	
Valencia	Manises ✈	9 km	Train 17 times daily (14 on ⑦).	Valencia Termino Station.	
Venezia	Marco Polo ✈	13 km	🚌 5, every 30/60 mins. (Summer/Winter).	Piazzale Roma.	✗
Warszawa	Okecie ✈	10 km	🚌 144, approx. every 10 – 15 mins.	Dluga/Pl. Krasinkich & Pl. Trzech Krzyzy.	
Wien	Schwechat ✈	18 km	Train every 30 mins.	Wien Mitte & Wien Nord Stations.	835
Zagreb	Zagreb ✈	17 km	🚌 every 30 mins.	JAT Terminal, Hotel Esplanade.	
Zürich	Zürich (Kloten) ✈	12 km	Train 5 times hourly.	Zürich Hauptbahnhof.	

‡ – The service frequency shown applies during daytime on weekdays. There are fewer journeys in the evening and in some cases at weekends and during winter months.

▼ – Table 1217 for SAS Hovercraft service Kastrup ✈ – Malmö.

■ – And for Prestwick ✈; also refer to Table 591.

◊ – Also calls at Oxford Street Bus Station and Central Rail Station.

* * – The Braathens S.A.F.E. terminal is at Vaterlandsenteret.

✗ – See also Table 1480 for waterbus service.

04

HOLIDAYS BY RAIL

FROM BRITAIN
TO EUROPE AND BEYOND

Escorted ————— Unescorted ————— Tailor – made
Scenic routes a speciality. 147 centres in 23 countries

Please ask for our coloured brochure of package holidays or a quotation for your personal requirements. We also offer a comprehensive continental rail ticket and reservations service.

 **Ffestiniog Travel**

Porthmadog, Gwynedd,
Wales, LL49 9NF
(Telephone 01766 – 512340)
(Fax 01766 – 514715)

CRAC
CONTINENTAL
RAIL AGENTS
CONSORTIUM

ATOL
CAA
3047

9925

2950

ASCUTNEY TRAVEL, Inc.

38 Tremont Square

Claremont NH 03743-2610

★ Specialists in World Wide rail travel.
★ Well traveled staff familiar with remote places.
★ Full service travel agency, hotels, rental cars, bus, air, ship and rail reservations tickets.

800-TRAINS-4   phone 603-542-8782
Toll Free in U.S.   FAX–603-542-0103

Bodensee Ferries

Navigation on Lake Constance

From Easter until mid October there are daily excursions with scheduled or special ships running between Germany, Austria and Switzerland. The car ferry Germany – Switzerland (between Friedrichshafen and Romanshorn) runs all year round.

For more information contact:
Deutsche Bahn AG
Bodensee-Schiffsbetriebe
Hafenstraße 6 · D-78462 Konstanz
Tel. 07531/281389 · Fax 281373

Die Erlebnis-Flotte

 Deutsche Bahn

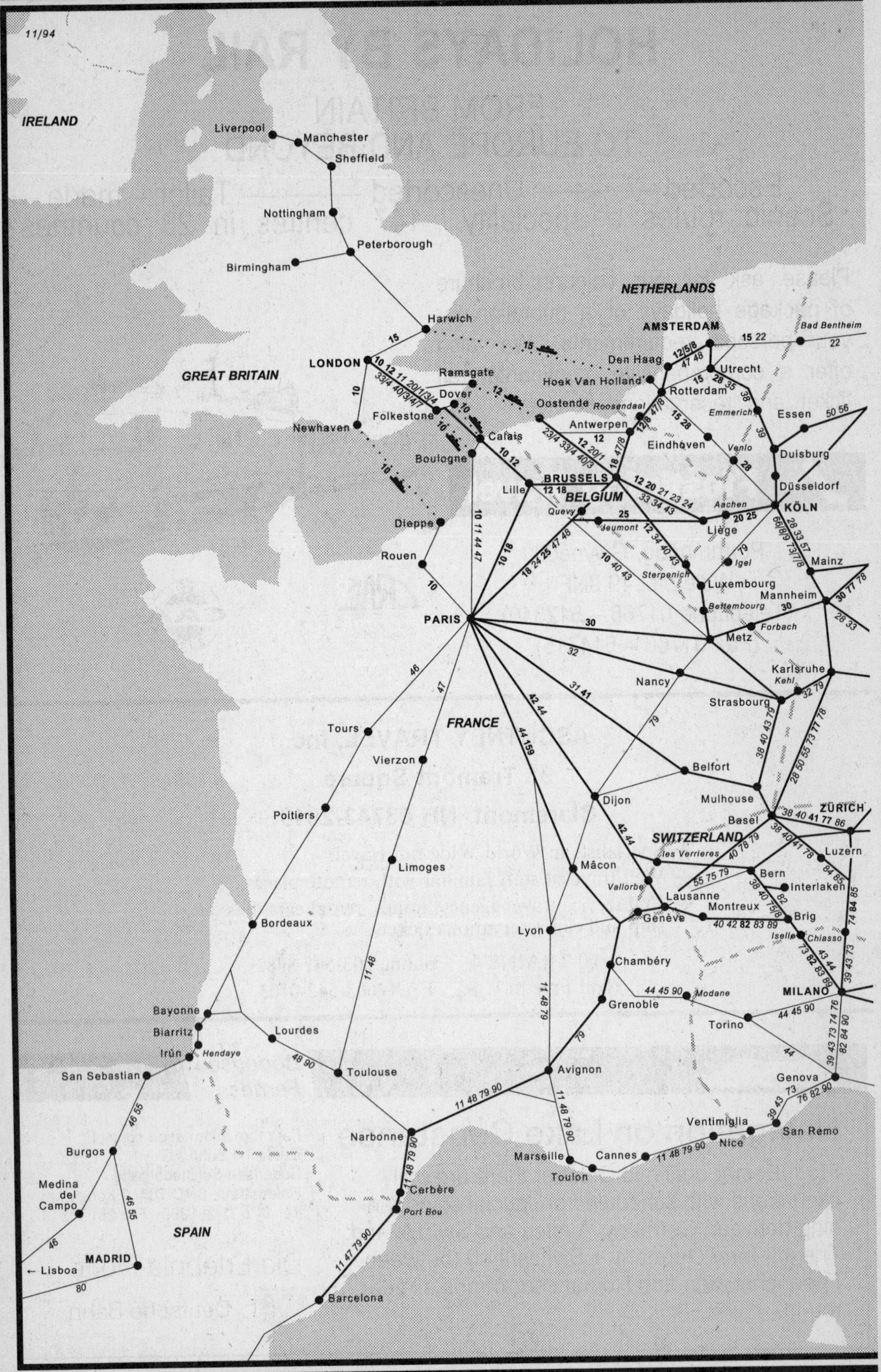

11/94

IRELAND

GREAT BRITAIN

Liverpool
Manchester
Sheffield
Nottingham
Peterborough
Birmingham
Harwich

LONDON
Ramsgate
Dover
Folkestone
Newhaven
Calais
Boulogne
Dieppe
Rouen

NETHERLANDS

AMSTERDAM
Den Haag
Hoek Van Holland
Rotterdam
Utrecht
Bad Bentheim
Oostende
Roosendaal
Antwerpen
Eindhoven
Emmerich
Venlo
Essen
Duisburg
Düsseldorf

BRUSSELS
BELGIUM
Lille
Quevy
Seumont
Aachen
Liège
KÖLN
Mainz
Luxembourg
Igel
Bettembourg
Sterpenich
Mannheim
Forbach
Metz
Karlsruhe
Kehl.

PARIS

Nancy
Strasbourg

FRANCE

Tours
Vierzon
Poitiers
Limoges
Bordeaux
Belfort
Mulhouse
ZÜRICH
Basel
Luzern
Dijon
les Verrieres
Bern
Interlaken
Mâcon
Vallorbe
Lausanne
Montreux
Brig
Genève
Iselle
Chiasso
Lyon
Chambéry
Modane
MILANO
Grenoble
Torino
Bayonne
Biarritz
Irún
Hendaye
Lourdes
San Sebastian
Toulouse
Avignon
Genova
Burgos
Narbonne
Ventimiglia
San Remo
Nice
Marseille
Cannes
Toulon
Medina
del
Campo
Cerbère
Port Bou

SPAIN

← Lisboa
MADRID
Barcelona

SWITZERLAND

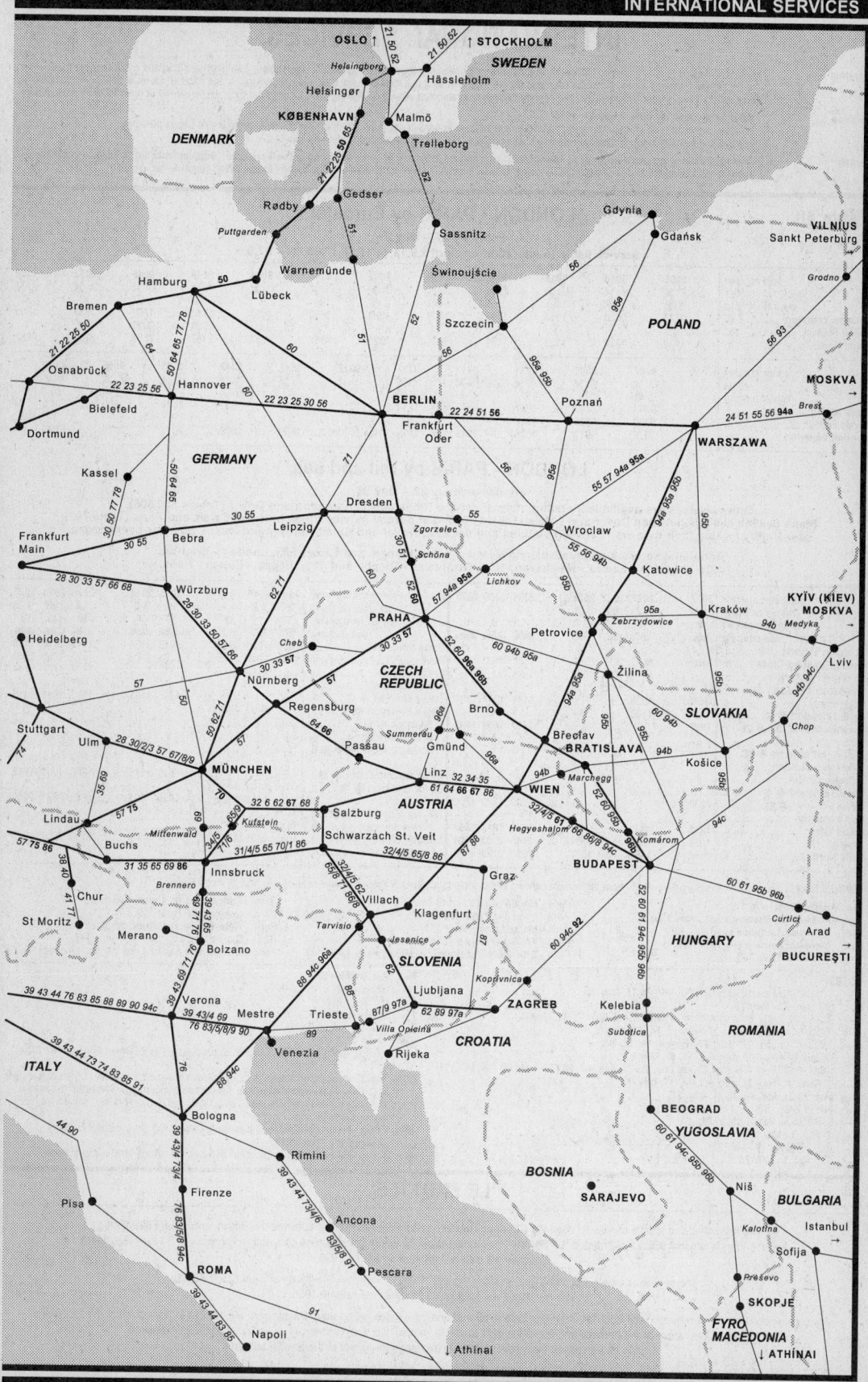

INTERNATIONAL SERVICES

Services	Trains conveying First and Second classes of seating accommodation are shown as "1" and "2" in the Tables. Sleeping cars (🛏) and couchettes (🛏) are usually of the normal European types, but some countries (former U.S.S.R. etc.) use their own stock for international trains, see page 10 for more details. Restaurant (✕) and buffet (♀) cars vary considerably from country to country in standard of service offered. The catering car may not be carried or open for the whole journey.
Timings	**Valid September 25, 1994 – May 27, 1995.** Services can change at short notice and passengers are advised to consult the latest Thomas Cook European Timetable before travelling. International trains are not normally affected by public holidays, but can be affected at Christmas and Easter.
Tickets	**Seat reservations** are available for most international trains and are advisable as some trains can get very crowded. **Supplements** are payable on EuroCity (EC) trains in most countries and on most InterCity trains, consult the introduction at the start of each country to see which supplements apply.

Table 10

LONDON - PARIS by Eurostar

February 27 – May 27
Service liable to alteration on April 2,9,13,14,15,16,17,30 May 1,7,8.

train number	9006	9010	9018	9028	9038	9042	9044	9044	9048	9048	9052	9052
notes	Ⓡ✕	Ⓡ✕	Ⓡ✕	Ⓡ✕	Ⓡ✕	Ⓡ✕	Ⓡ✕	Ⓡ✕	Ⓡ✕	Ⓡ✕	Ⓡ✕	Ⓡ✕
days of running	①–⑥	①–⑥	⑦	⑦	W	①–⑦	⑤	⑦	①–⑤	⑥⑦	⑦	Z
London Waterloo..............d.	0723	0823	1010	1253	1523	1623	1648	1653	1748	1753	1853	1853
Calais Fréthun................a.	...	...	...	...	...	...	...	...	2026	2026	...	...
Paris Nord........................a.	1124	1224	1422	1654	1924	2023	2057	2057	2157	2157	2252	2252

train number	9007	9007	9011	9011	9027	9027	9043	9047	9051	9055	9059
notes	Ⓡ✕	Ⓡ✕	Ⓡ✕	Ⓡ✕	Ⓡ✕	Ⓡ✕	Ⓡ✕	Ⓡ✕	Ⓡ✕	Ⓡ✕	Ⓡ✕
days of running	①–⑤	⑥	⑦	①–⑥	①–⑥	①–⑥	X	①–⑦	Y	①–⑥	⑦
Paris Nord..........................d.	0713	0713	0807	0810	1212	1212	1606	1709	1818	1908	2011
Calais Fréthun................d.	0839	0839	0936								
London Waterloo.............a.	0920	0913	1026	1013	1413	1413	1809	1909	2013	2113	2209

LONDON - PARIS by rail and sea

Service January 22 – May 27.
Other services are available by taking normal service trains between London and Dover (Tables 500,506),
Stena Sealink sailings between Dover and Calais (Tables 1025) and normal service trains between Calais and Paris (Table 102),
passengers making their own way between stations and docks at Dover and Calais, allowing at least 1 hour for connections.

Additional services are available via Newhaven and Dieppe, see Tables 505, London - Brighton;
507, Brighton - Lewes - Newhaven; 1025, Newhaven - Dieppe and 115, Dieppe - Rouen - Paris.

French train number	2027	2027	2027	2027	2031	2039	2039
classes on trains	1,2	1,2	1,2	1,2	1,2	1,2	1,2
notes (see below)	A	N	R	S	C	D	E
sea crossing		SC	SC	SC			
London Victoria ....d.	...	...	...	...	...	...	...
London Charing Cross ......d.	0700	0830	0855	0900	1000	1100	1130
Folkestone Harbour..........a.			1053	1053			
Folkestone Harbour 🚇.....d.			1115	1115			
Dover Priory ....a.	0858b	1028			1144	1244	1328
Dover Hoverport ♣ 🚇.......d.		1100					
Dover Eastern Docks ♣ 🚇..d.	1000				1230	1430	1430
Boulogne Maritime ♣ ......a.			1315	1315			
Boulogne Maritime...........d.			1411	1411			
Boulogne Ville...................d.		1250					
Calais Hoverport ♣ 🚇.......a.					1500	1700	1700
Calais Maritime ♣ 🚇.........a.	1230						
Calais Maritime ....d.					1550	1814	1808
Calais Ville ....d.	1341	1341	1532	1532	1749	2003	2000
Amiens...............................a.	1532	1532	1657	1657	1921	2123	2123
Paris Nord..........................a.	1657	1657					

French train number	2015	2015	2015	2025	2025	2025	2025	2025
classes on trains	1,2	1,2	1,2	1,2	1,2	1,2	1,2	1,2
notes (see below)	T	P	Q	G	J	K	L	M
sea crossing	SC	SC	SC					
Paris Nord............................d.	0928	0928	0928	0928	0928	1418	1418	1418
Amiens...............................a.	1105	1105	1105	1105	1105	1535	1535	1552
Calais Ville ....a.		1312	1312	1312	1312	1727	1727	1744
Calais Maritime ....a.				1445	1445	1830	1830	1915
Calais Maritime ♣ 🚇.........d.		1400	1400					
Calais Hoverport ♣ 🚇......d.	1232							
Boulogne Ville...................a.								
Boulogne Maritime...........a.								
Boulogne Maritime ♣ 🚇 d.	1400							
Dover Eastern Docks ♣ 🚇..a.				1515	1515	1900	1900	1945
Dover Hoverport ♣ 🚇........a.		1400	1400					
Dover Priory ....d.		1451	1521	1605	1621	1949	2021	2049
Folkestone Harbour 🚇......a.	1405							
Folkestone Harbour ....d.	1440							
London Charing Cross ......a.	1635	1635	1707	1804	1807	2135	2207	2235
London Victoria ....a.	...	...	...	...	...	...	...	...

CONNECTIONS: Connections are available in Paris from the services shown in this table to all parts of France. Allow at least one hour to cross Paris.

Paris - **Nantes** see Table **123**.
Paris - **Poitiers** and **Bordeaux** see Table **136**.
Paris - **Brive** and **Toulouse** see Table **138**.
Paris - **Clermont Ferrand** see Table **145**.
Paris - **Dijon** see Table **155**.

Paris - **Mâcon** see Table **149**.
Paris - **Lyon** see Table **150**.
Paris - **Marseille** see Table **151**.
Paris - **Toulon** and **Nice** see Table **164**.
Paris - **Chambéry** and **Bourg St Maurice** see Table **152**.

Paris - **Annecy** and **St. Gervais** see Table **167**.
Paris - **Genève** see Table **159**.
Paris - **Metz, Nancy** and **Strasbourg** see Table **173**.
Paris - **Biarritz** and **Lourdes** see Table **137**.
For other French destinations see the map on pages **98/99**.

NOTES

A – ①②③④⑤⑥ Feb. 10 - May 27, not Apr. 14,17, May 8.
C – ⑥⑦ Jan. 22 - May 27.
D – ⑦ Jan. 22 - May 27, also Apr. 14,17, May 8; not Apr. 16, 30, May 7.
E – ①②③④⑤ Jan. 22 - May 27, not Apr. 14, 17, May 8.
G – ①②③④⑤⑥ Jan. 22 - May 27, not Apr. 14, 17, May 8.
J – ⑦ Jan. 22 - May 27, also Apr. 14, 17, May 8.
K – ①②③④⑤⑥ Feb. 10 - May 27, not May 27, Apr. 20-24, Apr. 4-6,14,17-21, May 3-5,8.
L – ⑦ Feb. 10 - May 27, also Apr. 14, 17, May 8.
M – Mar. 20-24, Apr. 4-6,18-21, May 3-5.
N – Feb. 1 - Mar. 31.
P – ①②③④⑤⑥ Feb. 1 - Mar. 31.
Q – ⑦ Feb. 1 - Mar. 31.
R – ①②③④⑤ Apr. 1 - May 27.
S – ⑥⑦ Apr. 1 - May 27.

T – Apr. 1 - May 27.
W – ⑦ from Apr. 9.
X – ⑤⑦ from Apr. 7.
Y – ⑤⑦, daily from Apr. 3.
Z – Daily from April 3.
b – Arrive 0904 on ⑥.
c – On ⑥ London depart 0835; on ⑦ London depart 0855, Dover Priory arrive 1034.

SC – Seacat service (Hoverspeed). Ⓡ, supplement payable, one class only on catamaran, ♀. When bad weather interrupts sailings. passengers are transferred to the next available car-ferry service, see Table **1025**, and arrival at destination will be correspondingly later.
🚢 – Ship service (Sealink), one class only on ship, ✕, for additional car-ferry services see Table **1025**.
♣ – A free 🚌 connection is provided between the railway station and the port.

'LE SHUTTLE'

The first scheduled shuttle service through the **Channel Tunnel** has commenced running between the British terminal at Folkestone and the French terminal at Calais. Branded **'Le Shuttle'** the journey takes 35 minutes and carries cars and motorcycles with their passengers.
Coaches will also be carried from Spring 1995.

The service is initially operating hourly during the day (0700 - 2300) and two-hourly at night (2300 - 0700).
The frequency will increase to four per hour later in 1995.

Advance reservation will be required until April 1st. After that date a 'turn up and go' service will operate. Passengers will be able to buy tickets at the toll booths when they arrive at the terminal and board the next available shuttle. No reservations will be necessary although vouchers can be purchased from travel agents to exchange for tickets at the Shuttle terminal.

For explanation of standard symbols see page 4

Table 11

LONDON - SOUTHERN FRANCE AND BARCELONA
Other services are available by changing in Paris.

	2046 / 6208 (B)	11401 / 6214 (S)	11401 / 6212 (S)	6210 / 6211 (R)
London Charing Cross .... d.	▲	▲	▲	▲
Dover Eastern Docks .... d.	▲	▲	▲	▲
Calais Auto/train .... d.	1941	1946	1946	2039
Boulogne Ville .... d.	2013	2027	2027	
Lyon Perrache .... a.				
Aix les Bains .... a.				
Chambéry .... a.			0816	
Albertville .... a.			0858	
Moutiers Salins .... a.			0939	
Aime-la-Plagne .... a.			1007	
Bourg St Maurice .... a.			1029	
Annecy .... a.				
La Roche-sur-Foron .... a.		0912		
Cluses .... a.		0945		
Sallanches .... a.		1002		
St. Gervais .... a.		1011		
Chamonix .... a.		*1201*		
Valence .... a.	0504			0559
Avignon .... a.	0604			0707
Nîmes .... a.				0739
Montpellier .... a.				0814
Sète .... a.				0831
Agde .... a.				0847
Béziers .... a.				0900
Narbonne .... a.				0916
Perpignan .... a.				1006
Argèles sur Mer .... a.				1024
Port Vendres .... a.				1037
Port Bou .... a.				1102
Girona .... a.				
Barcelona Saints .... a.				
Arles .... a.	0628			
Marseille St Charles .... a.	0716			
Toulon .... a.	0808			
St. Raphaël .... a.	0904			
Cannes .... a.	0931			
Juan les Pains .... a.	0942			
Antibes .... a.	0948			
Nice .... a.	1005			
Beaulieu .... a.	1022			
Monaco-Monte Carlo .... a.	1033			
Menton .... a.	1045			
Ventimiglia .... a.	1059			

	6710 / 6711 (N)	6708§ / 6709§ (C)	6714 / 12001 (T)	6712 / 12001 (T)
Ventimiglia .... d.		1734		
Menton .... d.		1748		
Monaco-Monte Carlo .... d.		1758		
Beaulieu .... d.		1809		
Nice .... d.		1834		
Antibes .... d.		1849		
Juan les Pains .... d.		1854		
Cannes .... d.		1905		
St. Raphaël .... d.		1938		
Toulon .... d.		2029		
Marseille St. Charles .... d.		2121		
Arles .... d.				
Barcelona Saints .... d.				
Girona .... d.				
Cerbère .... d.	1855			
Port Vendres .... d.	1910			
Argèles sur Mer .... d.	1921			
Perpignan .... d.	1939			
Narbonne .... d.	2028			
Béziers .... d.	2044			
Agde .... d.	2058			
Sète .... d.	2116			
Montpellier .... d.	2134			
Nîmes .... d.	2202			
Avignon .... d.	2234	2228		
Valence .... d.	2331	2326		
Chamonix .... d.			1826	
St. Gervais .... d.			2010	
Sallanches .... d.			2018	
Cluses .... d.			2045	
La Roche-sur-Foron .... d.			2120	
Annecy .... d.			2210	
Bourg St Maurice .... d.				2048
Aime-la-Plagne .... d.				2110
Moutiers Salins .... d.				2132
Albertville .... d.				2214
Chambéry .... d.				2251
Aix les Bains .... d.			2317	2325
Lyon Perrache .... d.		0103		
Boulogne Ville .... a.		0830	0857	0857
Calais Auto/train .... a.	0858	0901	0930	0930
Dover Eastern Docks .... a.				
London Victoria .... a.			▲	▲

NOTES

B – FLANDRES RIVIERA – ①③⑤⑥ from Jan. 22, also ④⑦ Feb. 23 - Mar. 12 and daily Apr. 3 - May 27: 1,2 cl. (T2) and 2 cl. Calais auto/train - Ventimiglia.

C – RIVIERA FLANDRES – ①②④⑥ from Jan. 22, also ⑤⑦ Feb. 24 - Mar. 12 and daily Apr. 3 - May 27: 1,2 cl. (T2) and 2 cl. Ventimiglia - Calais auto/train.

N – ROUSSILLON FLANDRES – ⑤ Apr. 1 - May 27: 1,2 cl. (T2) and 2 cl. Cerbère - Calais auto/train.

R – FLANDRES ROUSSILLON – ⑤ Mar. 31 - May 26: 1,2 cl. (T2) and 2 cl. Calais auto/train - Port Bou.

S – ⑤ Jan. 13 - Mar. 24, also Dec. 23; not Feb. 17: 1,2 cl. Calais auto/train - Bourg St Maurice and St Gervais.

T – ⑥ Jan. 21 - Apr. 1, also Jan. 1; not Feb. 25: 1,2 cl. Bourg St Maurice and St Gervais - Calais auto/train.

§ – Train number 6706/7 on Feb. 24-27, Mar. 3-6, 10-12, Apr. 14-17, 21-30, May 1, 6-8, 13, 14, 20, 21, 25-27.

▲ – For service London - Calais see the following tables: Table 500 London Victoria - Dover Priory or Table 506 London Charing Cross - Dover Priory; Table 1025 Dover Eastern Docks - Calais. Passengers must make their own way between Calais Port and the auto/train terminal and **connections are not guaranteed.**

INTERNATIONAL SERVICES FROM PARIS

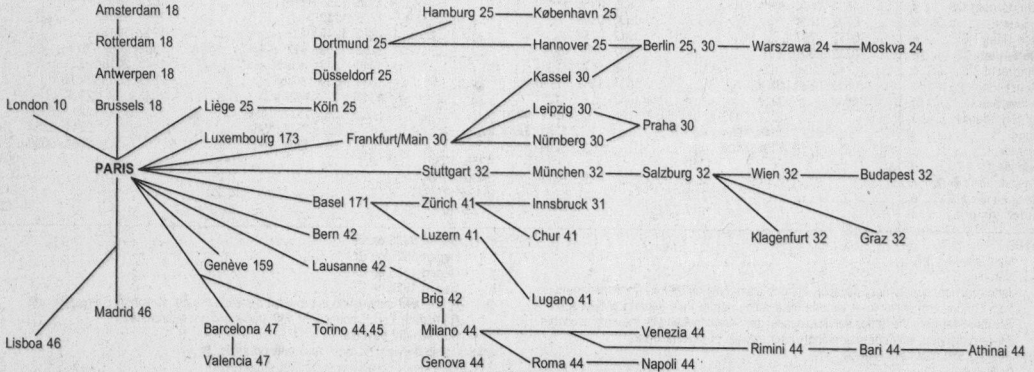

 For service from May 28 see page 510

Table 12

LONDON - BRUSSELS by Eurostar

February 27 – May 27

Service liable to alteration on April 2,9,13,14,15,16,17, May 1,8.

train number		**9110**	**9116**	**9132**	**9136**		**9152**		**9152**	
notes		Ⓡ✕	Ⓡ✕	Ⓡ✕	Ⓡ✕		Ⓡ✕		Ⓡ✕	
days of running		①-⑥	⑦	①-⑥	⑦		①-⑤		⑥⑦	
London Waterloo d.	...	0657	0814	1227	1310	...	1715	...	1727	...
Lille Europe a.	...	0955	1125	│	│	...	2026	...	2026	...
Brussels Midi a.	...	1108	1238	1644	1738	...	2139	...	2139	...

train number		**9113**	**9121**	**9133**		**9141**		**9157**	**9161**
notes		Ⓡ✕	Ⓡ✕	Ⓡ✕		Ⓡ✕		Ⓡ✕	Ⓡ✕
days of running		①-⑥	⑦	①-⑥		⑦		①-⑥	⑦
Brussels Midi d.	...	0731	0928	1231	...	1426	...	1826	1928
Lille Europe d.	...	0844	1041	│	...	│	...	1939	2041
London Waterloo a.	...	0943	1143	1443	...	1639	...	2039	2139

LONDON - BRUSSELS by rail and sea

September 25 – May 27

train number			**512**	**637**	**2152**	**2487**				**515**	**640**	**2164**	**2490**			**517**	**642**	**2172**	**2492**			**439**	**643**	**2176**	**2493**
classes on trains		1,2⫽	1,2	1,2	1,2	1,2		1,2	1,2⫽	1,2	1,2	1,2	1,2		1,2⫽	1,2	1,2	1,2	1,2		1,2	1,2	1,2	1,2	1,2
notes (see below)		Ⓡ			①-⑤	⑥⑦		Ⓡ	Ⓡ N			①-⑤	⑥⑦		Ⓡ			①-⑤	⑥⑦		Ⓡ			①-⑤	⑥⑦
sea crossing		J						🚢	J						J						🚢				
London Victoria d.	...	0805	...	...	...	...	...	0805	1105	...	...	...	...	...	1305	...	...	...	...	...	1105	...	...	...	...
Ramsgate ♣ a.	...	0947	...	...	...	...	...	0947	1247	...	...	...	...	...	1447	...	...	...	...	...	1247	...	...	...	...
Ramsgate Port ♣ 🏛 d.	...	1025	...	...	...	...	...	1030	1325	...	...	...	...	...	1525	...	...	...	...	...	1345	...	...	...	...
Oostende 🏛 a.	...	1300	...	...	...	...	...	1545	1600	...	...	...	...	...	1800	...	...	...	...	...	1830	...	...	...	...
Oostende d.	...	...	1334	1348	...	...	...	...	...	1634	1648	...	...	...	...	1834	1848	...	...	...	...	1934	1948	...	...
Brugge a.	...	...	1348	1401	...	...	...	...	...	1648	1701	...	...	...	...	1848	1901	...	...	...	...	1948	2001	...	...
Gent Sint Pieters a.	...	...	1412	1425	...	...	...	...	...	1712	1725	...	...	...	...	1912	1925	...	...	...	...	2012	2025	...	...
Antwerpen C a.	...	...	│	1515	...	1554	...	...	...	│	1815	...	1854	...	...	│	2015	...	2057	...	...	│	2115	...	2200
Roosendaal 🏛 a.	...	...	│	1549b	1552	1621	...	...	...	│	1849b	1852	1921	...	...	│	2049b	2052	2124	...	...	│	2149b	2152	2226
Dordrecht a.	...	...	│	▬	1614	1645	...	...	...	│	▬	1914	1945	...	...	│	▬	2114	2148	...	...	│	▬	2214	2249
Rotterdam CS a.	...	...	│	...	1631	1701	...	...	...	│	...	1931	2001	...	...	│	...	2131	2203	...	...	│	...	2231	2305
Den Haag HS a.	...	...	│	...	1651	1720	...	...	...	│	**109**	1951	2021	...	...	│	...	2151	2220	...	...	│	...	2251	2323
Leiden a.	...	...	│	**962**	1703	1733	...	...	...	│	12	2003	2033	...	...	│	**968**	2203	2233	...	...	│	...	2303	2334
Amsterdam CS a.	...	...	│	1,2	1738	1808	...	...	...	│	Ⓐ	2038	2108	...	...	│	1,2	2238	2308	...	...	│	...	2338	0010
Brussels Midi a.	...	...	1443	1521	▬	...	...	...	...	1743	1753	▬	...	...	...	1943	2021	▬	...	...	...	2043	...	...	...
Brussels Nord a.	...	...	1455	1530	...	...	...	...	...	1755	1803	...	...	...	...	1955	2030	...	...	...	...	2055	...	...	...
Namur a.	...	...	│	1620	...	...	...	...	...	│	1845	...	...	...	...	│	2118	...	...	...	...	│	...	...	...
Luxembourg 🏛 a.	...	...	│	1815	...	...	...	...	...	│	2025	...	...	...	...	│	2311	...	...	...	...	│	...	...	...
Leuven a.	...	...	1515	...	1,2	...	...	...	...	1815	...	1,2	...	...	...	2015	...	1,2	...	...	...	2115	1,2	...	...
Liège Guillemins a.	...	...	1556	...	1748	...	...	...	...	1856	...	1948	...	...	...	2056	...	2148	...	...	...	2156	2248	...	...
Maastricht 🏛 a.	...	...	...	...	1817	...	...	...	...	...	...	2017	...	...	...	...	...	2217	...	...	...	...	2317	...	...

train number		**520**	**645**				**413**	**630**	**2124**	**2480**	
classes on trains	1,2⫽	1,2	1,2			1,2	1,2	1,2	1,2	1,2	
notes (see below)	Ⓡ B					Ⓡ			①-⑤	⑥⑦	
sea crossing	J					🚢					
London Victoria d.	1605	...	...	...	...	2205	...	...	...	...	...
Ramsgate ♣ a.	1751	...	...	...	...	2358	...	...	...	...	...
Ramsgate Port ♣ 🏛 d.	1825	...	...	...	...	0045	...	...	...	...	...
Oostende 🏛 a.	2100	...	...	...	...	0530	...	...	...	...	...
Oostende d.	...	2134	2148	...	...	...	0634	0646	...	...	...
Brugge a.	...	2148	2201	...	...	...	0648	0700	...	...	...
Gent Sint Pieters a.	...	2212	2225	...	...	...	0712	0725	...	...	...
Antwerpen C a.	...	│	2315	...	...	...	│	0815	...	0854	...
Roosendaal 🏛 a.	...	│	...	...	...	...	│	0849b	0852	0921	...
Dordrecht a.	...	│	...	...	...	...	│	▬	0914	0945	...
Rotterdam CS a.	...	│	...	...	...	...	│	...	0931	1001	...
Den Haag HS a.	...	│	...	...	...	...	│	...	0951	1020	...
Leiden a.	...	│	...	...	...	...	│	**966**	1003	1033	...
Amsterdam CS a.	...	│	...	...	...	...	│	1,2	1038	1108	...
Brussels Midi a.	...	2243	...	...	...	...	0743	0821	▬	...	...
Brussels Nord a.	...	2257	...	...	...	...	0755	0830	...	...	...
Namur a.	...	│	...	...	...	...	│	0918	...	...	...
Luxembourg 🏛 a.	...	│	...	...	...	...	│	1111	...	...	...
Leuven a.	...	2317	...	...	...	...	0815	...	1,2	...	...
Liège Guillemins a.	...	2358	...	...	...	...	0856	...	0948	...	...
Maastricht 🏛 a.	...	...	...	...	...	...	...	...	1018	...	...

train number		**604**	**529**			**605**	**530**		
classes on trains		1,2	1,2	1,2⫽		1,2	1,2	1,2	
notes (see below)				Ⓡ				Ⓡ	
sea crossing				J				🚢	
Maastricht 🏛 d.	...	...	...	...	...	...	...	...	...
Liège Guillemins d.	...	...	0546	...	...	...	0646	...	...
Leuven d.	...	...	0626	...	...	...	0726	...	...
Luxembourg 🏛 d.	...	...	│	...	...	...	│	...	...
Namur d.	...	...	│	...	...	...	│	...	...
Brussels Nord d.	...	...	0647	...	...	...	0747	...	...
Brussels Midi d.	...	...	0659	...	...	...	0759	...	...
Amsterdam CS d.	...	...	│	...	...	...	│	...	...
Leiden d.	...	...	│	...	...	...	│	...	...
Den Haag HS d.	...	...	│	...	...	...	│	...	...
Rotterdam CS d.	...	...	│	...	...	...	│	...	...
Dordrecht d.	...	...	│	...	...	...	│	...	...
Roosendaal 🏛 d.	...	...	│	...	...	...	│	...	...
Antwerpen C d.	...	0627	│	...	...	0727	│	...	...
Gent Sint Pieters d.	...	0717	0730	...	...	0817	0830	...	...
Brugge d.	...	0741	0754	...	...	0841	0854	...	...
Oostende a.	...	0754	0809	...	...	0854	0909	...	...
Oostende 🏛 d.	...	...	...	0825	...	...	...	0945	...
Ramsgate Port ♣ 🏛 a.	...	...	...	0900	...	...	...	1245	...
Ramsgate ♣ d.	...	...	...	0932c	...	...	...	1332f	...
London Victoria a.	...	...	...	1117	...	...	...	1517	...

train number		**2456**	**683**	**982**	**412**			**2458**	**685**	**984**	**534**				**2461**	**688**	**296**	**422**			**2468**	**695**	**994**	**438**	
classes on trains		1,2	1,2	1,2	1,2	1,2⫽		1,2	1,2	1,2	1,2	1,2⫽	1,2		1,2	1,2	1,2	1,2	1,2⫽		1,2	1,2	1,2	1,2	1,2
notes (see below)		⑥⑦				Ⓡ N		⑥⑦				Ⓡ	Ⓡ		⑥⑦				Ⓡ B		⑥⑦				Ⓡ C
sea crossing						J						J	🚢						J						🚢
Maastricht 🏛 d.	...	...	0724	...	...	...	...	...	0924	...	...	...	...	...	...	1224	...	...	...	...	...	1924	...	...	...
Liège Guillemins d.	...	...	0755	...	0846	...	...	...	0955	...	1046	...	...	...	...	1255	...	1346	...	...	...	1955	...	2146	...
Leuven d.	...	...	▬	...	0926	...	...	...	▬	...	1126	...	...	...	...	▬	...	1426	...	...	...	▬	...	2226	...
Luxembourg 🏛 d.	...	...	...	0627	│	...	...	...	...	0827	│	...	...	...	...	...	1206	│	...	...	...	...	1827	│	...
Namur d.	...	...	**2127**	0822	│	...	...	...	**2135**	1022	│	...	...	...	...	**2147**	1345	│	...	...	...	**2175**	2022	│	...
Brussels Nord d.	...	...	1,2	0912	0947	...	...	...	1,2	1112	1147	...	...	...	...	1,2	1427	1447	...	...	...	1,2	2112	2247	...
Brussels Midi d.	...	...	①-⑤	0921	0959	...	...	...	①-⑤	1121	1159	...	...	...	...	①-⑤	1434	1459	...	...	...	①-⑤	2121	2259	...
Amsterdam CS d.	...	0623	0646	▬	│	...	...	0825	0855	▬	│	...	...	...	1125	1155	▬	│	...	...	1825	1855	▬	│	...
Leiden d.	...	0700	0724	...	│	...	...	0900	0930	...	│	...	...	...	1200	1230	...	│	...	...	1900	1930	...	│	...
Den Haag HS d.	...	0712	0737	...	│	...	...	0912	0942	...	│	...	...	...	1212	1242	...	│	...	...	1912	1942	...	│	...
Rotterdam CS d.	...	0732	0801	**607**	│	...	...	0932	1003	**609**	│	...	...	...	1232	1302	**612**	│	...	...	1932	2002	**619**	│	...
Dordrecht d.	...	0748	0818	1,2	│	...	...	0948	1022	1,2	│	...	...	...	1248	1318	1,2	│	...	...	1948	2018	12	│	...
Roosendaal 🏛 d.	...	0814	0839	0853b	│	...	...	1014	1043	1053b	│	...	...	...	1314	1339	1353b	│	...	...	2014	2039	2053b	│	...
Antwerpen C d.	...	0843	...	0927	│	...	...	1043	...	1127	│	...	...	...	1343	...	1427	│	...	...	2043	...	2127	│	...
Gent Sint Pieters d.	...	...	...	1017	1030	...	...	...	...	1217	1230	...	...	...	...	...	1517	1530	...	...	...	...	2217	2330	...
Brugge d.	...	...	...	1041	1054	...	...	...	...	1241	1254	...	...	...	...	...	1541	1554	...	...	...	...	2241	2354	...
Oostende a.	...	...	...	1054	1109	...	...	...	...	1254	1309	...	...	...	...	...	1554	1609	...	...	...	...	2254	0009	...
Oostende 🏛 d.	...	...	...	...	...	1150	...	...	...	...	...	1355	1350	...	...	...	...	...	1655	...	...	...	...	...	0030
Ramsgate Port ♣ 🏛 a.	...	...	...	...	...	1225	...	...	...	...	...	1430	1650	...	...	...	...	...	1730	...	...	...	...	...	0330
Ramsgate ♣ d.	...	...	...	...	...	1332f	...	...	...	...	...	1532g	1732	...	...	...	...	...	1832h	...	...	...	...	...	0437
London Victoria a.	...	...	...	...	...	1517	...	...	...	...	...	1723	1917	...	...	...	...	...	2019	...	...	...	...	...	0630

NOTES

- **B** – Mar. 26 - May 27.
- **C** – Not Jan. 1.
- **J** – Jetfoil service, supplement payable, Ⓡ, one class only on Jetfoil, 🍸. Passengers from London can check-in at Victoria 60 minutes before train departs. When bad weather interrupts the Jetfoil service, passengers are conveyed by the next available car-ferry service, with correspondingly later arrivals at destinations.
- **N** – Jan. 1,2 and Mar. 26 - May 27.
- **b** – ①-⑤ only.
- **c** – Depart 0925 on ⑦.
- **f** – Depart 1325 on ⑦.
- **g** – Depart 1525 on ⑦.
- **h** – Depart 1825 on ⑦.
- ♣ – A free 🚌 connection is provided between the rail station at Ramsgate and Ramsgate Port. Connections with trains are not guaranteed.
- ⫽ – Supplement payable.
- 🚢 – Ship service, Ⓡ, one class only on ships, ✕.

 For explanation of standard symbols see page 4.

Table 15

LONDON - NETHERLANDS AND KÖLN

train type train number	4177	366	1977	4177	577	577	3377	6283	215	1981	881			362	529	529	3329	6235	EC 3	2343	7531	1531	833
classes on trains	1,2	1,2	1,2	1,2	1,2	1,2	1,2	1,2	1,2	1,2	1,2		1,2	1,2	1,2	1,2	1,2	1,2	1,2	1,2	1,2	1,2	1,2
notes (see below)	A	E	♀		⑤f								ℝ A	♀					✕	✕			
sea crossing	⛴												⛴										
London Liverpool Street..... d.	0925c	...	...	...	...	...	...	...	...	...	...		1900c	...	...	...	...	...	...	...	...	...	...
Peterborough..................... d.	...	...	...	...	...	...	...	...	...	...	...		...	...	...	...	...	...	...	...	...	...	...
Ely.................................. d.	...	...	...	...	...	...	...	...	...	...	...		...	...	...	...	...	...	...	...	...	...	...
Ipswich............................ d.	...	...	...	...	...	...	...	...	...	...	...		...	...	...	...	...	...	...	...	...	...	...
Harwich Parkeston Quay...... a.	1045	...	...	...	...	...	...	...	...	...	...		2020	...	...	...	...	...	...	...	...	...	...
Harwich Parkeston Quay 🚢.. d.	1130	...	...	...	...	...	...	...	...	...	...		2130	...	...	...	...	...	...	...	...	...	...
Hoek van Holland 🚢.......... a.	1900	...	...	...	...	...	...	...	...	...	...		0700	...	...	...	...	...	...	...	...	...	...
Hoek van Holland................. d.	...	1948	1958	...	2001	...	...	...	...	...	...		...	0803	...	...	...	...	...	...	...	...	...
Schiedam-Rotterdam West ... a.	...	2014	2017	...	2028	...	...	...	...	...	...		...	...	...	...	...	...	...	...	...	...	...
Rotterdam CS................ a.	...	2018		2034	2032	2037	...	...	...	2134	...		...	0830	0837	...	...	...	...	...	0912	...	...
Den Haag HS..................... a.	...	...	2039				...	...	...	...	...		...	0855		...	...	...	...	...	...	...	...
Leiden 220........................ a.	...	...	2051				...	...	...	...	...		...	...	...	...	...	...	...	...	...	...	...
Haarlem............................. a.	...	...	2113				...	...	...	...	...		...	0933	...	...	...	...	...	...	...	...	...
Amsterdam Centraal .... a.	...	...	2132				...	...	...	...	...		...	0949	...	...	...	...	...	...	...	...	...
Dordrecht........................... a.	...	...		2051			...	...	...	2151	...		...	...	...	...	...	...	...	...	...	...	...
Breda................................ a.	...	...		2115	877		...	...	...	2215	...		...	...	...	...	...	...	...	...	0926	...	...
Tilburg............................... a.	...	...		2130	1,2		...	...	...	2230	...		...	...	...	...	...	...	...	...	0945	...	...
Eindhoven.......................... a.	...	...		2154	2159		...	...	...	2254	2259		...	...	...	...	...	...	...	...	1000	...	...
Maastricht.......................... a.	...	...			2304		...	...	...		0005		...	...	...	...	...	...	...	...	1024	1059	...
Venlo 🚊............................. a.	...	...		2244			...	...	...	2344			...	...	...	...	...	...	...	...	1204		
Utrecht CS..................... a.	...	...				2113	2122	2120	2130				...	0913	0922	0920	0930		...	...	1102	...	...
Arnhem.............................. a.	...	...						2155	2206	2204			...	...	...	0955	1006	1003	...	...	...	...	...
Nijmegen............................ a.	...	...							2222				...	...	...	1022			...	...	...	...	...
Emmerich 🚊....................... a.	...	...								2235			...	...	...		1023		...	...	...	...	...
Duisburg............................ a.	...	...								2335			...	...	...		1110		...	...	...	...	...
Düsseldorf Hbf.................... a.	...	...								2352			...	...	...		1132		...	...	...	...	...
Mönchengladbach................ a.	...	...								**1677**			...	...	...				...	...	...	...	...
Köln Hbf........................ a.	...	...								0022	1,2		...	...	...		1157		...	...	...	...	...
Amersfoort.......................... a.	...	...				2137	2137		2141				...	0937	0937				...	...	...	...	...
Groningen........................... a.	...	...					2314						...	...	1114				...	0941	...	...	...
Hengelo.............................. a.	...	...							2255				...	...	...				...	1055	1101	...	...
Enschede............................ a.	...	...							2304				...	...	...				...	1108		...	...

train number	826	1802	726	367	6222	3326	1726	4128			766	866	1820	6262	3366	1766	4168	363		
classes on trains	1,2	1,2	1,2	1,2	1,2	1,2	1,2	1,2		1,2	1,2	1,2	1,2	1,2	1,2	1,2	1,2	1,2		1,2
notes (see below)				♀				A A										♀	ℝ A	B
sea crossing							⛴													
Enschede.......................... d.	...	...	...	...	...	...	0758	...		...	...	...	...	...	1758	...	...	...	...	...
Hengelo............................ d.	...	...	...	...	...	...	0806	...		...	...	...	...	...	1806	...	...	...	...	...
Groningen......................... d.	...	...	0737	...	...	...		...		1737	...	...	...	...		...	...	...	...	...
Amersfoort........................ d.	...	...	0924	...	...	...	0927	...		1924	...	...	...	...	1927	...	...	...	...	...
Köln Hbf....................... d.	...	0717		...	...	...		...			1717	...	...	...		...	...	...	...	...
Mönchengladbach............... d.	...	0758		...	...	...		...			1758	...	...	...		...	...	...	...	...
Düsseldorf Hbf.................. d.	...			...	...	...		...				...	...	...		...	...	...	...	...
Duisburg........................... d.	...			...	...	...		...				...	...	...		...	...	...	...	...
Emmerich 🚊...................... d.	...			...	...	...		...				...	...	...		...	...	...	...	...
Nijmegen.......................... d.	...			...	0842			...				1842		...		...	...	...	...	...
Arnhem............................ d.	...			...	0859	0909		...				1859	1909	...		...	...	...	...	...
Utrecht CS.................... d.	...			...		0943	0947	...					1944	1947		...	...	...	...	...
Venlo 🚊........................... d.	...	0831		...	...			...			1831			...		...	...	...	...	...
Maastricht........................ d.	0731			...	...			...		1731				...		...	...	...	...	...
Eindhoven........................ d.	0835	0909		...	...			...		1835	1909			...		...	...	...	...	...
Tilburg............................. d.	...	0933		...	...			...			1933			...		...	...	...	...	...
Breda.............................. d.	...	0947		...	...			...			1947			...		...	...	...	...	...
Dordrecht......................... d.	...	1005		...	...			...			2005			...		...	...	...	...	...
Amsterdam Centraal .... d.	...	...		0932	...			...						...		1948	...	...	...	...
Haarlem........................... d.	...	...		0948	...			...						...		2003	...	...	...	...
Leiden............................. d.	...	...		1007	...			...						...		2024	...	...	...	...
Den Haag HS.................... d.	...	...		1021	...			...						...		2037	...	...	...	...
Rotterdam CS................ d.	...	...	1020		...		1025	1042				2020		...	2025	2040	...	...	...	...
Schiedam-Rotterdam West ... d.	...	...			...		1042	1046						...	2044	2044	2055	...	...	...
Hoek van Holland 🚊........... d.	...	...			...		1059	1110						...	2109	2109	2113	...	...	...
Hoek van Holland 🚢........... a.	...	...			...		1200							...		2200	...	...	...	...
Harwich Parkeston Quay 🚢.. a.	...	...			...		1800							...		0700	...	...	...	...
Harwich Parkeston Quay...... d.	...	...			...			1845						...				0750	...	...
Ipswich............................ a.	...	...			...									...					...	...
Ely.................................. a.	...	...			...									...					...	...
Peterborough..................... a.	...	...			...									...					...	...
London Liverpool Street..... a.	...	...			...			2000						...				0905	...	...

NOTES

A – Not Dec. 25,26,31.
B – Not Dec. 26,27, Jan. 1.

E – Daily except ⑤ (not Apr. 13, May 24).
c – Service by 🚌 on ⑦.
f – Also Apr. 13, May 24.

INTERNATIONAL SERVICES FROM AMSTERDAM

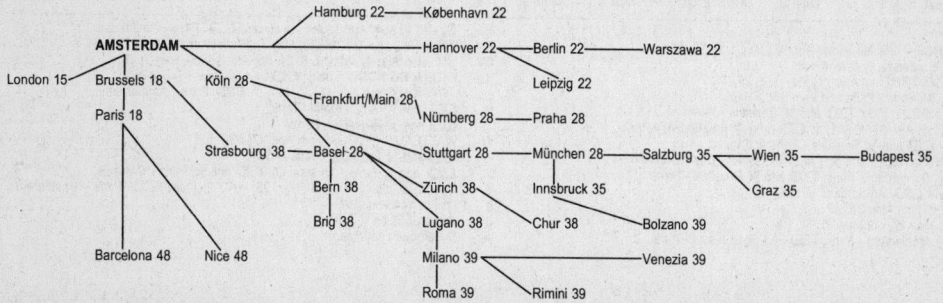

For service from May 28 see page 512

Table 18

AMSTERDAM - BRUSSELS - PARIS

Block 1

train type / number	TGV 80	2454	482	482	2455	2455	2456	282	2457	2458	EC 82	2459	2460	284	2461	TEE 88	2462	EC 38
classes / notes	1,2 A[R] ⚒	1,2	1,2✗ ☒	1,2 H	1,2 J	⑥⑦	①–⑤	1,2 S	1,2	1,2	1,2 C[R]	1,2	1,2	1,2 F	1,2	1,2 W	1,2	1,2✗ E
Amsterdam Centraal d.	…	…	…	…	…	…	0623	0657	0725	0825	0853	0925	1025	1052	1125	…	1225	…
A'dam Schiphol ✈ d.	…	…	…	…	…	…	0643		0743	0843		0943	1043		1143	…	1243	…
Leiden d.	…	…	…	…	…	…	0700		0800	0900		1000	1100		1200	…	1300	…
Den Haag HS d.	…	…	…	…	…	…	0712	0741	0812	0912	0933	1012	1112	1136	1212	…	1312	…
Rotterdam CS d.	…	0527	…	…	0624	0624	0732	0804	0832	0932	0953	1032	1132	1204	1232	…	1332	…
Dordrecht d.	…	0543	…	…	0639	0639	0748		0848	0948		1048	1148		1248	…	1348	…
Roosendaal 🚃 d.	…	0614	…	…	0714	0714	0814	0848	0914	1014	1032	1114	1214	1247	1314	…	1414	…
Antwerpen Centraal d.	…	0649	…	…	0749	0749	0849		0949	1049		1149	1249	1315	1349	…	1449	…
Antwerpen Berchem d.	…	0653	…	…	0753	0753	0853	0914	0953	1053	1059	1153	1253	1315	1353	…	1453	1550
Brussels Nord a.	…	0723	0744	0744	0823	0828	0923	0945	1023	1123	1132	1223	1323	1346	1423	…	1523	1556
Brussels Midi a.	…	0730	0750	0750	0830	0835	0930	0951	1030	1130	1138	1230	1352	1352	1430	…	1530	1600
Brussels Midi d.	0704	…	0800	0800	…	…	…	1006	…		1154	…	…	…	1413	1504	…	1600
Mons (🚃 = Quévy) d.		…	0841	0841	…	…	…	1044	…	…	…	…	…	…	1450	…	…	1639
Aulnoye a.		…	0900	0900	…	…	…	1104	…	…	…	…	…	…	1510	…	…	1717
St Quentin d.		…	…	0952	…	…	…	1143	…	…	…	…	…	…	1553	…	…	1748
Paris Nord a.	0938	…	1055	1115	…	…	…	1258	…	1426	…	…	…	…	1708	1741	…	1859

Block 2

train type / number	2463	TGV 84	2464	TGV 86	2465	286	2466	280	2467	2468	2469	2470	2471	288
classes / notes	1,2	1,2✗ B[R]	1,2	1,2✗ D[R]	1,2	1,2 M	1,2	1,2 ☕	1,2	1,2	1,2	1,2	1,2	1,2 G
Amsterdam Centraal d.	1325	…	1425	…	1525	1552	1625	…	1724	1825	1925	2025	2125	2215
A'dam Schiphol ✈ d.	1343	…	1443	…	1543		1643	…	1743	1843	1943	2043	2143	…
Leiden d.	1400	…	1500	…	1600		1700	…	1800	1900	2000	2100	2200	…
Den Haag HS d.	1412	…	1512	…	1612	1636	1712	…	1812	1912	2012	2112	2212	2307
Rotterdam CS d.	1432	…	1532	…	1632	1658	1732	…	1832	1932	2032	2132	2232	2334
Dordrecht d.	1448	…	1548	…	1648		1748	…	1848	1948	2048	2148	2248	…
Roosendaal 🚃 d.	1514	…	1614	…	1714	1743	1814	…	1914	2014	2114	2214	2314	0025
Antwerpen Centraal d.	1549	…	1649	…	1749		1849	…	1949	2049	2149	2249	2343	…
Antwerpen Berchem d.	1553	…	1653	…	1753	1812	1853	…	1953	2053	2153	2253	…	0054
Brussels Nord a.	1623	…	1723	…	1823	1845	1923	…	2026	2123	2223	2326	…	0127
Brussels Midi a.	1630	…	1730	…	1830	1851	1930	…	2030	2130	2230	2330	…	0134
Brussels Midi d.	…	1704	…	1834	…	1907	…	2004	…	…	…	…	…	0153
Mons (🚃 = Quévy) d.	…		…		…	1946	…	2042	…	…	…	…	…	0232
Aulnoye a.	…		…		…	2007	…		…	…	…	…	…	0300
St Quentin d.	…		…		…	2048	…		…	…	…	…	…	
Paris Nord a.	…	1930	…	2106	…	2206	…	2259	…	…	…	…	…	0623c

Block 3

train type / number	2478	2479	2480	2481	TGV 81	2482	281	2483	2484	2485	283	TGV 83	2486	TGV 89	2487	2488
classes / notes	1,2 ⚒	1,2	1,2	1,2	1,2✗ B[R]	1,2	1,2 ☕	1,2	1,2	1,2	1,2 X	1,2✗ D[R]	1,2	1,2✗ W[R]	1,2	1,2
Paris Nord d.	…	…	…	…	0707	…	0752	…	…	…	1023	1049	…	1152	…	…
St Quentin d.	…	…	…	…		…	0908	…	…	…	1136		…		…	…
Aulnoye d.	…	…	…	…		…	0949	…	…	…	1216		…		…	…
Mons (🚃 = Quévy) d.	…	…	…	…		…	1010	…	…	…	1238		…		…	…
Brussels Midi a.	…	…	…	…	0934	…	1049	…	…	…	1317	1312	…	1415	…	…
Brussels Midi d.	0610	0710	0810	0910	…	1010	1104	1110	1210	1310	1329	…	1410	…	1510	1610
Brussels Nord d.	0619	0719	0819	0919	…	1019	1112	1119	1219	1319	1337	…	1419	…	1519	1619
Antwerpen Berchem d.	0646	0746	0846	0946	…	1046	1147	1146	1246	1346		…	1446	…	1546	1646
Antwerpen Centraal d.	0654	0754	0854	0954	…	1054	1154	1154	1254	1354		…	1454	…	1554	1654
Roosendaal 🚃 d.	0723	0824	0923	1023	…	1123	1215	1224	1323	1423	1442	…	1523	…	1623	1723
Dordrecht a.	0745	0845	0945	1045	…	1145	1246		1345	1445		…	1545	…	1645	1745
Rotterdam CS a.	0804	0901	1001	1101	…	1201	1256	1302	1401	1501	1526	…	1601	…	1701	1801
Den Haag HS a.	0823	0920	1020	1120	…	1220	1317	1321	1420	1520	1550	…	1620	…	1720	1820
Leiden a.	0833	0933	1033	1133	…	1233		1334	1433	1533		…	1633	…	1733	1833
A'dam Schiphol ✈ a.	0849	0949	1049	1149	…	1249		1350	1449	1549		…	1649	…	1749	1849
Amsterdam Centraal a.	0908	1008	1108	1208	…	1308	1402	1408	1508	1608	1634	…	1708	…	1808	…

Block 4

train type / number	EC 39	2489	285	2490	2491	287	TEE 85	2492	2493	EC 87	2494	487	487	2495	231 289	1289 289
classes / notes	1,2✗ E	1,2	1,2	1,2	1,2	1,2	1,2 A	1,2	1,2	1,2 R[R]	1,2	1,2 PX	1,2 QX	1,2	1,2 Y	1,2 N
Paris Nord d.	…	1346	1433b	…	…	1636	1725	…	…	1839	…	1926	1941	…	2316	2322
St Quentin d.	…	1458	1604	…	…	1751		…	…		…	2048		…	0103	0125
Aulnoye d.	…	1542	1640	…	…	1822		…	…		…	2127		…	0202	0202
Mons (🚃 = Quévy) d.	…	1606	1702	…	…	1903		…	…	2110	…	2151	2151	…	0353	0353
Brussels Midi a.	…	1645	1742	…	…	1942	2001	…	…	2120	…	2230	2230	…	0432	0449
Brussels Midi d.	…	1655	1710	1753	1810	1910	1956	2010	2110	2120	2210	2239	2239	2310	0449	0449
Brussels Nord d.	…	1701	1719	1801	1819	1919	2004	2019	2119	2127	2157	2246	2246	2346	0531	0531
Antwerpen Berchem d.	…		1746	1832	1846	1946	2035	2046	2146	2157	2246			2354	0602	0602
Antwerpen Centraal d.	…		1754		1854	1954		2057	2126	2200	2254			0023	0602	0602
Roosendaal 🚃 d.	…		1823	1911	1923	2023	2102	2126	2228	2225	2323			0045	0602	0602
Dordrecht a.	…		1845		1945	2045		2148	2249		2345	0001		0107	0647	0647
Rotterdam CS a.	…		1901	1950	2001	2101	2138	2203	2305	2301					0707	0707
Den Haag HS a.	…		1920	2009	2021	2120	2156	2220	2323	2319					0707	0707
Leiden a.	…		1933		2033	2133		2233	2334						0802	0802
A'dam Schiphol ✈ a.	…		1949		2049	2149		2249	2350						0802	0802
Amsterdam Centraal a.	…	2008		2102	2108	2208	2248	2308	0010	2359					0802	0802

NOTES:

A – ÎLE DE FRANCE – ①②③④⑤, not Apr. 17, May 1, 8, 25, 26: ☒ and ✗ Brussels - Paris and v.v.

B – RUBENS – ①②③④⑤, not Apr. 17, May 1, 8, 25, 26: ☒ and ✗ Brussels - Paris and v.v.

C – ÉTOILE DU NORD – daily: ☒ and ✗ Brussels - Paris; ①②③④⑤⑥, not Apr. 17, May 1, 8: ☒ and ☕ Amsterdam - Paris.

D – BRABANT – ☒ and ✗ Brussels - Paris and v.v.

E – JACQUES BREL – ☒ and ✗ Paris - Brussels - (Dortmund) and v.v.

F – ☒ and ☕ Amsterdam - Paris; ☒ and ✗ Brussels - Paris.

G – 1,2 cl. and ☒ Amsterdam - Paris.

H – ⑥, also May 25; not May 27.

J – ①②③④⑤⑦, May 27; not May 25.

M – ☒ and ☕ Amsterdam - Paris; ☒ and ✗ Brussels - Paris.

N – ⑤, also ⑦ from Apr. 2: ➡ 1,2 cl. and ☒ Paris - Amsterdam.

P – ①②③④⑥, also Apr. 16, 30, May 7, 26; not Apr. 17, May 1, 8, 24.

Q – ⑤⑦, also Apr. 17, May 1, 8, 24; not Apr. 16, 30, May 7, 26.

R – ÉTOILE DU NORD – daily: ☒ and ✗ Paris - Brussels; ①②③④⑤⑦, not Apr. 16, 30, May 7: ☒ Paris - Amsterdam.

S – ☒ and ☕ Amsterdam - Paris; ☒ and ✗ Brussels - Paris.

W – WATTEAU – ①②③④⑤, not Apr. 17, May 1, 8: ☒ and ✗ Brussels - Paris and v.v.

X – ☒ and ☕ Paris - Amsterdam; ☒ and ✗ Paris - Brussels.

Y – ①②③④⑥, also ⑦ Nov. 6 - Mar. 26: ➡ 1,2 cl. and ☒ Paris - Amsterdam.

b – Depart 1445 on ⑥⑦.

c – Arrive 0655 on ①⑥.

✗ – Supplement payable.

For explanation of standard symbols see page 4.

Table 20

LONDON AND BRUSSELS - KÖLN
For Eurostar connections between London and Brussels see Table 12.

train type					EC				EC	EC			EC		
train number	411	413	417	419	47	425	429	514	39	49	233	517	37	439	225
classes on trains	1,2	1,2	1,2	1,2	1,2✗	1,2	1,2✗	1,2	1,2✗	1,2✗	2	1,2	1,2✗	1,2	2
notes (see below)		Ⓡ M			A		Ⓡ N		B	Ⓡ L / Ⓡ P / C	2	Ⓡ M	D	Ⓡ G	
sea crossing							J		⛴	J		J		⛴	
London Victoria 12 ....d.	...	2205	...	...	...	...	0805	...	0805	1105	...	1305	...	1105	...
Ramsgate Port 🚌 ♣ ...d.	...	0045	...	...	...	...	1025	...	1030	1325	...	1525	...	1345	...
Oostende ⛴ ....a.	...	0530	...	...	...	...	1300	...	1545	1600	...	1800	...	1830	...
Oostende ⛴ ....d.	0532	0634	0834	0934	...	1234	...	1434	...	...	...	1657	...	1934	2013
Brugge ....d.	0548	0650	0850	0950	...	1250	...	1450	...	1712	1750	1850	...	1950	2028
Gent Sint Pieters ...d.	0617	0715	0915	1015	...	1315	...	1515	1615	1736	1815	1915	...	2015	2054
Brussels Midi ......d.	0647	0748	0948	1048	1203	1348	...	1548	...	1655	1808	1847	1947	2048	2126
Brussels Nord ......d.	0657	0757	0957	1057	1212	1357	...	1557	...	1703	1817	1857	1957	2057	2134
Leuven ....d.	0717	0817	1017	1117	...	1417	...	1617	...	...	1917	2017	...	2117	...
Liège Guillemins ...d.	0800	0900	1100	1200	1313	1500	...	1700	1756	1803	1913	2000	2056	2113	2117
Aachen 🚌 ....a.	0843	0943	1143	1243	1351	1543	...	1743	1845	...	1955	2043	2151	2200	2243
Düren ....a.	0913	1013	1213	1313	...	1613	...	1813	...	...	2016	2132	...	2243	2318
Köln ....a.	0942	1042	1242	1342	1442	1642	...	1842	1942	2042	2155	...	2242	2342	0017
Düsseldorf ....a.	...	...	...	...	1531	...	...	...	2016	2116	2224	...	...	...	...
Duisburg ....a.	...	...	...	...	1544	...	...	...	2031	2132	2240	...	...	...	...
Essen ....a.	...	...	...	...	1557	...	...	...	2046	2145	2253	...	...	...	...
Dortmund ....a.	...	...	...	...	1620	...	...	...	2111	2209	...	...	...	...	...

train type		EC	EC			EC			EC		EC			
train number	224	113	36	412	232	48	420	422	38	426	46	430	434	438
classes on trains	2	1,2✗	1,2✗	1,2	1,2✗	1,2	1,2	1,2	1,2✗	1,2	1,2✗	1,2	1,2	1,2
notes (see below)	Ⓡ G		D		Ⓡ P	C			Ⓡ E	B	A			Ⓡ Q
sea crossing	⛴				J				J		A			⛴
Dortmund 700 .....d.	...	...	0511	...	...	0748	...	...	1146	...	1338	...	...	...
Essen 700 ....d.	...	...	0535	...	0654	0812	...	...	1210	...	1404	...	...	...
Duisburg ....d.	...	...	0549	...	0708	0825	...	...	1224	...	1414	...	...	...
Düsseldorf 700 ...d.	...	...	0604	...	0732	0840	...	...	1239	...	1428	...	...	...
Köln Hbf ....d.	0508	0626	0630	0714	0802	0914	1114	1214	1314	1414	1514	1614	1814	2014
Düren ....d.	...	...	...	0739	...	...	1139	1239	...	1439	...	...	...	...
Aachen 🚌 ....d.	0606	...	0710	0805	0905	1001	1205	1305	1410	1505	...	1639	1839	2039
Liège Guillemins ..a.	0647	...	0749	0843	0943	1036	1243	1343	1449	1543	1607	1705	1905	2105
Leuven ....a.	...	...	...	0924	...	1024	1324	1424	...	1624	...	1824	2024	2224
Brussels Nord .....a.	0755	...	0850	0944	1044	1132	1344	1444	1548	1644	1749	1844	2044	2244
Brussels Midi .....a.	0804	...	0901	0955	1055	1142	1355	1455	1556	1655	1801	1855	2055	2255
Gent Sint Pieters .a.	0838	...	...	1027	1127	1212	1427	1527	...	1727	...	1927	2127	2327
Brugge ....a.	0903	...	...	1052	1152	1234	1452	1552	...	1752	...	1952	2152	2352
Oostende ⛴ ....a.	0918	...	...	1109	1209	1248	1509	1609	...	1809	...	2009	2209	0009
Oostende ⛴ ....d.	...	0945	...	...	...	1150	1355	1350	...	1655	...	...	...	0030
Ramsgate Port 🚌 ...a.	...	1245	...	...	...	1225	1430	1650	...	1730	...	...	...	0330
London Victoria 12 .a.	...	1517	...	...	...	1517	1723	1917	...	2019	...	...	...	0630

NOTES

A – ALEXANDER VON HUMBOLDT – [12] and ✗ Brussels - Berlin and v.v., supplement payable in Germany.
B – JACQUES BREL – [12] and ✗ (Paris) - Brussels - Dortmund and v.v., supplement payable in Germany.
C – MEMLING – [12] and ✗ Oostende - Dortmund and v.v., supplement payable in Germany.
D – FELIX TIMMERMANS – [12] and ✗ Brussels - Köln and v.v., supplement payable in Germany.

E – Mar. 26 - May 27.
G – Oct. 23 - May 27, not Dec. 25.
L – Oct. 23 - May 27, not Dec. 25,26.
M – Not Dec. 24,25,26,31.
N – Not Dec. 25,26.
P – Daily to Jan. 2 and from Mar. 26, not Dec. 25.
Q – Not Dec. 25,26,27, Jan. 1.
J – Jetfoil service, see Table 12.
⛴ – Ship service, see Table 12.
✗ – Supplement payable.

INTERNATIONAL SERVICES FROM LONDON AND BRUSSELS

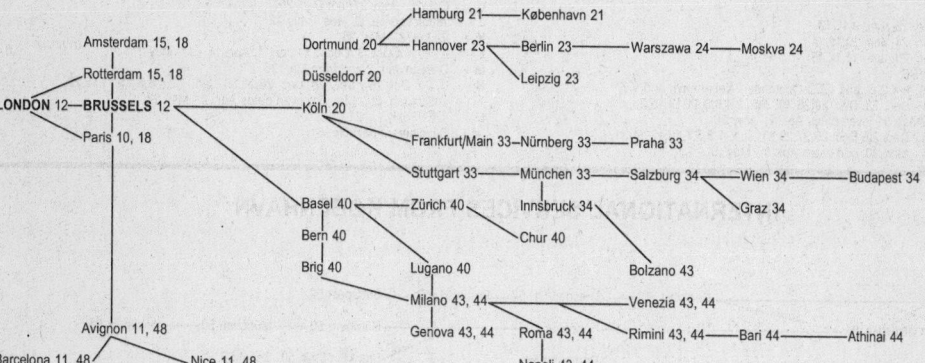

 For service from May 28 see page 514

Table 21

LONDON AND BRUSSELS - HAMBURG AND KØBENHAVN

For Eurostar connections between London and Brussels see Table 12.

train type		IC		IC			IC		IC		EC	IC		IC		IC	EC	EC				IN	IN	
train number	411	826	413	526		417	524	419	522		47	620	425	520	429	724	39	26			233	384	288	
classes on trains	1,2	1,2⚡	1,2	1,2⚡		1,2	1,2⚡	1,2	1,2⚡		1,2⚡	1,2⚡	1,2	1,2⚡	1,2	1,2⚡	1,2⚡	1,2⚡	1,2	1,2⚡	2	1,2	1,2	
notes (see below)		🍴		🍴			🍴		🍴		🍴	🍴		🍴		🍴	🍴	🍴	⛴	J M	D	🅁 🍴	🅁 🍴	
London Victoria 12 d.	...	...	...	...	...	...	...	...	...	...	...	...	...	...	...	...	...	...	0805	1105	...	...	...	...
Ramsgate Port 🏛 **12** d.	...	...	...	...	...	...	...	...	...	...	...	...	...	...	...	...	...	...	1030	1325	...	...	...	...
Oostende 🏛 **12** d.	0532	...	0634	...	...	0834	...	0934	...	...	...	...	1234	...	1434	...	...	...	1545	1600	1734	...	...	...
Brugge d.	0548	...	0650	...	...	0850	...	0950	...	...	...	...	1250	...	1450	...	...	...	...	...	1750	...	...	...
Gent St. Pieters d.	0617	...	0715	...	...	0915	...	1015	...	...	...	...	1315	...	1515	...	...	...	...	...	1815	...	...	...
Brussels Midi d.	0647	...	0748	...	...	0947	...	1047	...	...	1203	...	1347	...	1547	...	1655	...	...	...	1847	...	...	...
Brussels Nord d.	0657	...	0757	...	...	0957	...	1057	...	...	1212	...	1357	...	1557	...	1703	...	...	...	1857	...	...	...
Liège Guillemins d.	0800	...	0900	...	...	1100	...	1200	...	...	1313	...	1500	...	1700	...	1803	...	...	...	2000	...	...	...
Aachen 🏛 d.	0843	...	0943	...	...	1143	...	1243	...	...	1354	...	1543	...	1743	...	1845	...	...	...	2106	...	...	...
Köln d.	0942	1010	1042	1110	...	1242	1310	1342	1409	...	1442	1510	1642	1709	1842	1909	1942	2010	...	...	2200	...	...	...
Münster a.	...	1154	...	1254	...	...	1454	...	1554	...	...	1654	...	1854	...	2054	...	2154	...	...	2350	...	...	...
Osnabruck a.	...	1219	...	1319	...	...	1519	...	1619	...	...	1719	...	1919	...	2119	...	2219	...	...	0020	...	...	...
Bremen Hbf a.	...	1314	...	1414	...	...	1614	...	1714	...	...	1814	...	2014	...	2214	...	2314	...	...	0127	...	...	...
Hamburg Hbf 50 a.	...	1411	...	1511	...	...	1711	...	1811	...	...	1911	...	2111	...	2311	...	0011	...	...	0235	...	...	...
Hamburg Altona a.	...	1424	...	1524	...	...	1724	...	1824	...	...	1924	...	2124	...	2324	...	0024	...	...	|	...	...	...
Lübeck a.	...	...	...	...	...	...	...	...	...	...	...	...	...	...	...	...	...	...	...	...	0330	...	...	...
Rødby 🏛 a.	...	...	...	...	...	...	...	...	...	...	...	...	...	...	...	...	...	...	...	...	0600	...	...	...
Nykøbing a.	...	...	...	...	...	...	...	...	...	...	...	...	...	...	...	...	...	...	...	...	0649	...	...	...
København 50 a.	...	...	...	...	...	...	...	...	...	...	...	...	...	...	...	...	...	...	...	...	0825	0948	0948	...
Stockholm C a.	...	...	...	...	...	...	...	...	...	...	...	...	...	...	...	...	...	...	...	...	...	|	1747	...
Göteborg C a.	...	...	...	...	...	...	...	...	...	...	...	...	...	...	...	...	...	...	...	...	...	1435	...	...
Oslo S a.	...	...	...	...	...	...	...	...	...	...	...	...	...	...	...	...	...	...	...	...	...	1937**b**	...	...

train type	IC	EC	IC		EC		IC	EC	EC		IC	EC	IC		IC		IC		IN	IN				
train number	725	48	727	420	29	422	621	38	729	426	521	46	823	430	625	434	827	438	385	33	232			
classes on trains	1,2⚡	1,2⚡	1,2⚡	1,2	1,2⚡	1,2	1,2⚡	1,2⚡	1,2⚡	1,2	1,2⚡	1,2⚡	1,2⚡	1,2	1,2⚡	1,2	1,2⚡	1,2	1,2	1,2	2	1,2⚡	1,2	
notes (see below)	🍴	🍴	🍴		🍴		🍴	🍴	🍴		🍴	🍴	🍴		🍴		🍴		🅁 🍴	🅁 🍴	D	J 🅁	G ⛴	
Oslo S d.	...	...	L	...	...	...	...	...	...	...	...	...	...	...	...	...	...	...	1015**b**	...	...	...		...
Göteborg C d.	...	...	...	...	...	...	...	...	...	...	...	...	...	...	...	...	...	...	1525	...	...	...	...	...
Stockholm C d.	...	...	...	...	...	...	...	...	...	...	...	...	...	...	...	...	...	...	|	1212	...	...	...	...
København 50 d.	...	...	...	...	...	...	...	...	...	...	...	...	...	...	...	...	...	...	2016	2058	2105	...	...	...
Nykøbing d.	...	...	...	...	...	...	...	...	...	...	...	...	...	...	...	...	...	...	...	...	2245	...	...	...
Rødby 🏛 d.	...	...	...	...	...	...	...	...	...	...	...	...	...	...	...	...	...	...	...	...	2330	...	...	...
Lübeck d.	...	...	...	...	...	...	...	...	...	...	...	...	...	...	...	...	...	...	...	...	0212	...	...	...
Hamburg Altona d.	0433	...	0633	...	0733	...	0833	...	0933	...	1033	...	1133	...	1333	...	1533	...	...	...	|	...	...	...
Hamburg Hbf 50 d.	0447	...	0647	...	0747	...	0847	...	0947	...	1047	...	1147	...	1347	...	1547	...	...	...	0312	...	...	...
Bremen d.	0545	...	0745	...	0845	...	0945	...	1045	...	1145	...	1245	...	1445	...	1645	...	...	...	0420	...	...	...
Osnabruck d.	0639	...	0839	...	0939	...	1039	...	1139	...	1239	...	1339	...	1539	...	1739	...	...	...	0532	...	...	...
Münster d.	0705	...	0905	...	1005	...	1105	...	1205	...	1305	...	1405	...	1605	...	1805	...	...	...	0604	...	...	...
Köln Hbf a.	0850	0914	1050	1114	1150	1214	1250	1314	1350	1414	1450	1514	1550	1614	1750	1814	1950	2014	...	...	0757	...	...	...
Aachen 🏛 a.	...	1001	...	1205	...	1305	...	1410	...	1505	...	1600	...	1705	...	1905	...	2105	...	...	0848	...	...	...
Liège Guillemins a.	...	1036	...	1243	...	1343	...	1449	...	1543	...	1648	...	1743	...	1943	...	2143	...	...	0943	...	...	...
Brussels Nord a.	...	1132	...	1344	...	1444	...	1548	...	1644	...	1749	...	1844	...	2044	...	2244	...	...	1044	...	...	...
Brussels Midi a.	...	1142	...	1355	...	1455	...	1556	...	1655	...	1801	...	1855	...	2055	...	2255	...	...	1055	...	...	...
Gent St. Pieters a.	...	1212	...	1427	...	1527	...	...	...	1728	...	...	...	1927	...	2127	...	2327	...	...	1127	...	...	...
Brugge a.	...	1234	...	1452	...	1552	...	...	...	1752	...	...	...	1952	...	2152	...	2352	...	...	1152	...	...	...
Oostende 🏛 a.	...	1248	...	1509	...	1609	...	...	...	1809	...	...	...	2009	...	2209	...	0009	...	...	1209	1355	1350	...
Ramsgate Port 🏛 a.	...	...	...	...	...	...	...	...	...	...	...	...	...	...	...	...	...	...	...	...	...	1430	1650	...
London Victoria a.	...	...	...	...	...	...	...	...	...	...	...	...	...	...	...	...	...	...	...	...	...	1723	1917	...

LONDON - HAMBURG AND KØBENHAVN by Sea

			446							
	1,2	⛴	1,2		1,2	⛴		1,2	⛴	
	B	B 🅁	C 🅁		E	E 🅁		K	K	
London Liverpool Street d.	1425	...	...	...	1325	...	...	1525	...	...
Harwich Parkeston Quay a.	1545	...	...	...	1445	...	...	1645	...	...
Harwich Parkeston Quay d.	...	1700	...	...	...	1530	...	...	1730	...
Hamburg Fischereihafen a.	...	|	...	...	...	1300	...	...	1500	...
Hamburg Altona a.	...	|	...	...	...	...	...	...	...	...
Esbjerg Havn a.	...	1345	...	...	...	...	...	...	...	...
Esbjerg Havn d.	...	...	1420	...	...	...	...	...	...	...
Odense a.	...	...	1608	...	...	...	...	...	...	...
København a.	...	...	1848	...	...	...	...	...	...	...

		445							
		1,2	⛴	1,2			⛴	1,2	
		A 🅁	A 🅁	B			F 🅁	N	
København d.	...	1255	...	...	...	...	...	...	...
Odense d.	...	1535	...	...	...	...	...	...	...
Esbjerg Havn a.	...	1725	...	...	...	...	...	...	...
Esbjerg Havn d.	...	...	1800	...	...	...	...	...	...
Hamburg Altona d.	...	...	|	...	...	...	...	...	...
Hamburg Fischereihfn d.	...	...	|	...	...	...	1630	...	...
Harwich Parkeston Quay a.	...	...	1230	...	...	...	1200	...	...
Harwich Parkeston Quay d.	...	...	...	1305	...	...	...	1305	...
London Liverpool Street a.	...	...	...	1430	...	...	...	1430	...

NOTES

- **A** – ①③⑤, not Dec. 23, Jan. 9,11,13.
- **B** – ②④⑥, not Dec. 24, Jan. 10,12,14.
- **C** – ③⑤⑦, not Dec. 25, Jan. 11,12,15.
- **D** – NORD EXPRESS – 🛏 1,2 cl. (T2), 🛏 2 cl. and 🚃(2) Oostende - København and v.v.
- **E** – ③⑤⑦ Oct. 26 - Dec. 23, Dec. 26,28,30, Jan. 2,4,6,8,11,13,15,22, ③⑤ Jan. 25 - Mar. 31, even dates Apr. 2 - May 26.
- **F** – ②④⑥ Oct. 25 - Dec. 22, Dec. 25,27,29,31, Jan. 1,3,5,7,10,12,14,21, ②④⑥ Jan. 24 - Mar. 30, odd dates Apr. 1 - May 27.
- **G** – Oct. 23 - May 27, not Dec. 25.
- **J** – Jetfoil service, 🅁, see Table **12**.
- **K** – ⑦ Jan. 8 - Mar. 26.
- **L** – ①-⑥, not Oct. 3, Dec. 25 - Jan. 1, Apr. 15 - 17, May 1.
- **M** – Daily to Jan. 2 and from Mar. 26.
- **N** – ③⑤⑦ Oct. 26 - Dec. 23, Dec. 26,28,30, Jan. 1,2,4,6,8,11,13,15,22, ③⑤⑦ Jan. 25 - Mar. 31, even dates Apr. 2 - May 28.
- **b** – ⑤⑥⑦ only.
- ⚡ – Supplement payable.

INTERNATIONAL SERVICES FROM KØBENHAVN

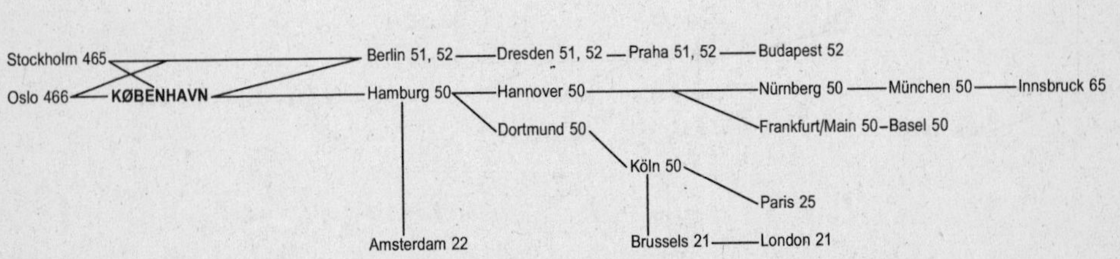

For standard symbols see page 4.

Table 22 — AMSTERDAM - HAMBURG AND BERLIN

Section 1

train number	521	2341	IC737	IC508	EC43	2449	529	2343	2243	IC826	IC504	2743	545	2345	2245	IC522	EC47	561	2347	EC28
classes	1,2	1,2	1,2	1,2	1,2	1,2	1,2	1,2	1,2	1,2	1,2	1,2	1,2	1,2	1,2	1,2	1,2	1,2	1,2	1,2
notes	Ⓐ	✕	✕	✕	✕Ⓡ	🍴		Ⓑ	Ⓒ	✕	🍴	🍴		Ⓑ	Ⓒ	✕	🍴		✕	✕
Amsterdam Schiphol d.	…	0635	…	…	…	…	…	0831	0831	…	…	…	…	1235	1235	…	…	…	1635	…
Amsterdam Centraal d.	…	0702	…	…	…	…	…	0902	0902	…	…	…	…	1302	1302	…	…	…	1702	…
Rotterdam CS d.	0637		…	…	…	…	0837	…	…	…	…	…	1237	…	…	…	…	1637	…	…
Utrecht CS d.	0722		…	…	…	…	0922	…	…	…	…	…	1322	…	…	…	…	1719	…	…
Amersfoort d.	0737	0741	…	…	…	…	0937	0941	0941	…	…	…	1337	1341	1341	…	…	1737	1741	…
Duisburg d.	…	…	…	…	…	…	…	…	…	…	…	…	…	…	…	…	…	…	…	…
Hengelo d.	…	0858	…	…	…	…	…	1058	1058	…	…	…	…	1458	1458	…	…	…	1858	…
Bad Bentheim a.	…	0916	…	…	…	…	…	1116	1116	…	…	…	…	1516	1516	…	…	…	1916	…
Rheine a.	…	0937	…	…	…	…	…	1137	1137	…	…	…	…	1537	1537	…	…	…	1937	…
Osnabrück a.	…	1003	1021	…	…	…	…	1203	1203	1221	…	…	…	1603	1603	1621	…	…	2003	2021
Bremen Hbf a.	…	…	1114	…	…	…	…	…	…	1314	…	…	…	…	…	1714	…	…	…	2114
Hamburg Hbf a.	…	…	1211	…	…	…	…	…	…	1411	…	…	…	…	…	1811	…	…	…	2211
Hamburg Altona a.	…	…	…	…	…	…	…	…	…	1424	…	…	…	…	…	1824	…	…	…	2224
Rødby 50 a.	…	…	…	…	…	…	…	…	…	…	…	…	…	…	…	…	…	…	…	…
København 50 a.	…	…	…	…	…	…	…	…	…	…	…	…	…	…	…	…	…	…	…	…
Hannover Hbf a.	…	1119	…	1204	…	…	…	1319	1319	…	1404	…	…	1719	1719	…	1804	…	2119	…
Braunschweig a.	…	…	…	1245	…	…	…	…	1415	…	1447	…	…	…	…	…	1841	…	…	…
Magdeburg a.	…	…	…	1332	…	1421	…	…	1514	…	1532	1621	…	…	…	…	1932	…	…	…
Halle a.	…	…	…	…	…	1516	…	…	…	…	1716	…	…	…	…	…	…	…	…	…
Leipzig a.	…	…	…	…	…	1549	…	…	…	…	1749	…	…	…	…	…	…	…	…	…
Dresden Hbf a.	…	…	…	…	…	…	…	…	…	…	…	…	…	…	…	…	…	…	…	…
Potsdam Stadt a.	…	…	…	…	…	…	…	…	…	…	…	…	…	…	…	…	…	…	…	…
Berlin Zoo a.	…	…	…	1454	…	…	…	…	1715	…	…	1726	…	…	…	2115	…	…	…	…
Berlin Hbf a.	…	…	…	…	1632	…	…	…	…	…	…	…	…	…	…	…	…	…	…	…
Warszawa Centralna 56 a.	…	…	…	…	2240	…	…	…	…	…	…	…	…	…	…	…	…	…	…	…

Section 2 (westbound — left block)

train number	569	EC153	233	1783	341	EC41
classes	1,2	1,2	2	1,2	2	1,2
notes		✕	M	B		✕Ⓡ
Amsterdam Schiphol d.	…	…	…	…	…	…
Amsterdam Centraal d.	…	1906	…	…	…	…
Rotterdam CS d.	1837		…	2207	2238	…
Utrecht CS d.	1913	1935	…	…	2252	…
Amersfoort d.	…	…	…	…	2307	2320
Duisburg d.	…	2106	2242	…	…	…
Hengelo d.	…	…	…	…	0037	…
Bad Bentheim a.	…	…	…	…	0056	…
Rheine a.	…	…	…	…	0125	…
Osnabrück a.	…	…	0020	…	0157	…
Bremen Hbf a.	…	…	0127	…	…	…
Hamburg Hbf a.	…	…	0235	…	…	…
Hamburg Altona a.	…	…	…	…	…	…
Rødby a.	…	…	0600	…	…	…
København 50 a.	…	…	0825	…	…	…
Hannover Hbf a.	…	…	…	…	0325	…
Braunschweig a.	…	…	…	…	0434	…
Magdeburg a.	…	…	…	…	0532	…
Berlin Zoo a.	…	…	…	…	0706	…
Berlin Hbf a.	…	…	…	…	…	0810
Warszawa Centralna 56 a.	…	…	…	…	…	1430

Section 2 (eastbound — right block)

train number	EC27	2346	1730	2738	EC109	IC729	2344	2244	1746
classes	1,2	1,2	1,2	1,2	1,2	1,2	1,2	1,2	1,2
notes	✕	✕	🍴	✕	✕	①–⑥	⑦		
Warszawa Centralna 56 d.	…	…	…	…	…	…	…	…	…
Berlin Hbf d.	…	…	…	…	…	…	…	…	…
Berlin Zoo d.	…	…	…	0638	…	…	…	…	…
Potsdam Stadt d.	…	…	…	…	…	…	…	…	…
Dresden Hbf d.	…	…	…	…	…	…	…	…	…
Leipzig d.	…	…	…	…	0653	…	…	…	…
Halle d.	…	…	…	…	0722	…	…	…	…
Magdeburg d.	…	…	…	…	0816	0830	…	…	…
Braunschweig d.	…	…	…	…	…	0915	…	…	…
Hannover Hbf d.	…	0638	…	…	…	0955	1038	1038	…
København 50 d.	…	…	…	…	…	…	…	…	…
Rødby d.	…	…	…	…	…	…	…	…	…
Hamburg Altona d.	0533	…	0933	…	…	…	…	…	…
Hamburg Hbf d.	0547	…	0947	…	…	…	…	…	…
Bremen Hbf d.	0645	…	1045	…	…	…	…	…	…
Osnabrück d.	0737	0755	1137	…	…	…	1155	1155	…
Rheine d.	…	0819	…	…	…	…	1219	1219	…
Bad Bentheim d.	…	0841	…	…	…	…	1241	1241	…
Hengelo d.	…	0858	…	…	…	…	1300	1300	…
Duisburg d.	…	…	…	…	…	…	…	…	…
Amersfoort a.	1011	1027	…	…	…	…	1412	1412	1427
Utrecht CS a.	…	1043	…	…	…	…	…	…	1443
Rotterdam CS a.	…	1125	…	…	…	…	…	…	1525
Amsterdam Centraal a.	1053	…	…	…	…	…	1453	1453	…
Amsterdam Schiphol a.	1116	…	…	…	…	…	1516	1516	…

Section 3 (eastbound)

train number	2736	IC503	IC625	2342	2242	1762	EC42	2634	IC509	IC736	2340	2240	1778	EC40	340	524	232	EC140	1726
classes	1,2	1,2	1,2	1,2	1,2	1,2	1,2	1,2	1,2	1,2	1,2	1,2	1,2	1,2	2	1,2	1,2	1,2	1,2
notes		✕	✕	①–⑤	⑥⑦		✕Ⓡ	🍴	✕	✕	Ⓑ	⑥		✕	B		M	✕	
Warszawa Centralna 56 d.	…	…	…	…	…	…	0615	…	…	…	…	…	…	1650	…	…	…	…	…
Berlin Hbf d.	…	…	…	…	…	…	1218	…	…	…	…	…	…	2254	…	…	…	…	…
Berlin Zoo d.	…	1038	…	1034	…	…	…	…	…	…	1438	1424	…	…	…	2340	…	…	…
Potsdam Stadt d.	…	…	…	1055	…	…	…	…	…	…	…	1455	…	…	…	…	…	…	…
Dresden Hbf d.	0911	…	…	…	…	…	…	…	…	1311	…	…	…	…	…	…	…	…	…
Leipzig d.	1053	…	…	…	…	…	…	…	…	1453	…	…	…	…	…	…	…	…	…
Halle d.	1122	…	…	…	…	…	…	…	…	1522	…	…	…	…	…	…	…	…	…
Magdeburg d.	1216	1230	…	1256	…	…	…	…	…	1616	1630	1656	…	…	0110	…	…	…	…
Braunschweig d.	…	1315	…	1346	…	…	…	…	…	…	1715	1746	…	…	0205	…	…	…	…
Hannover Hbf d.	…	1355	…	1438	1438	…	…	…	…	…	1755	1838	1838	…	0402	…	…	…	…
København 50 d.	…	…	…	…	…	…	…	…	…	…	…	…	…	…	2105	…	…	…	…
Rødby d.	…	…	…	…	…	…	…	…	…	…	…	…	…	…	2330	…	…	…	…
Hamburg Altona d.	…	…	1333	…	…	…	…	…	…	…	…	…	…	…	…	…	…	…	…
Hamburg Hbf d.	…	…	1347	…	…	…	…	1747	…	…	…	…	…	…	0312	…	…	…	…
Bremen Hbf d.	…	…	1445	…	…	…	…	1845	…	…	…	…	…	…	0420	…	…	…	…
Osnabrück d.	…	…	1537	1555	1555	…	…	1937	…	…	1955	1955	…	0538	0532	…	…	…	…
Rheine d.	…	…	…	1619	1619	…	…	2019	…	…	2019	2019	…	0610	…	…	…	…	…
Bad Bentheim d.	…	…	…	1641	1641	…	…	2041	…	…	2041	2041	…	0653	…	…	…	…	…
Hengelo d.	…	…	…	1700	1700	…	…	2100	…	…	2100	2100	…	0713	…	…	…	…	…
Duisburg d.	…	…	…	…	…	…	…	…	…	…	…	…	…	…	…	…	…	…	…
Amersfoort a.	…	…	…	1811	1811	1827	…	2212	2212	…	…	…	2227	0833	0857	…	…	0706	0752
Utrecht a.	…	…	…	…	…	1843	…	2243	…	…	…	…	…	…	0913	…	…	…	…
Rotterdam CS a.	…	…	…	…	…	1925	…	2325	…	…	…	…	…	…	0955	…	0923	0947	…
Amsterdam Centraal a.	…	…	…	1853	1853	…	…	2253	2253	…	…	…	…	0923	…	…	0954	…	1025
Amsterdam Schiphol a.	…	…	…	1916	1916	…	…	2316	2316	…	…	…	…	0954	…	…	…	…	…

NOTES
A – Not Dec. 25, Jan. 1.
B – 🛏 1,2 cl., 🛌 2 cl. and 🚗 Amsterdam - Berlin and v.v.
C – Not Dec. 24,31.

M – NORD EXPRESS – 🛏 1,2 cl. (T2), 🛏 1,2 cl., 🛌 2 cl. and 🚗
    (Oostende/Paris) - Duisburg - København and v.v.
✕ – Supplement payable.

Table 23 — LONDON and BRUSSELS - HANNOVER and BERLIN
For Eurostar connections between London and Brussels see Table 12.

	411	IC 506	413	IC 504	2743	IC 417	502	2645	419	IC 500	ICE 594	2637	EC 47	425	EC 108	IC 547	[ship]	[ship]	520/243	2443
classes	1,2	1,2✓	1,2	1,2	1,2	1,2	1,2	1,2	1,2	1,2✓	1,2✓	1,2	1,2	1,2✓	1,2	1,2✓	1,2 [R]	1,2 [R]	2	1,2
notes	X	X		X	Y	X	Y			X	X		N		X	X		J	M	Y
London Victoria 12 d.	…	…	…	…	…	…	…	…	…	…	…	…	…	…	…	…	1105	1305	…	…
Ramsgate Port 12 d.	…	…	…	…	…	…	…	…	…	…	…	…	…	…	…	…	1345	1525	…	…
Oostende 12 d.	0532	…	0634	…	…	0834	…	…	…	0934	…	…	…	…	1234	…	1830	1800	2134	…
Brugge d.	0548	…	0650	…	…	0850	…	…	…	0950	…	…	…	…	1250	…	…	…	2150	…
Gent St. Pieters d.	0617	…	0715	…	…	0915	…	…	…	1015	…	…	…	…	1315	…	…	…	2215	…
Brussels Midi d.	0647	…	0748	…	…	0947	…	…	…	1047	…	…	1203	1347	…	…	…	…	2250	…
Brussels Nord d.	0657	…	0757	…	…	0957	…	…	…	1057	…	…	1212	1357	…	…	…	…	2259	…
Liège Guillemins d.	0800	…	0900	…	…	1100	…	…	…	1200	…	…	1313	1500	…	…	…	…	0048	…
Aachen d.	0849	…	0949	…	…	1149	…	…	…	1249	…	…	1358	1549	…	…	…	…	0142	…
Köln a.	0942	1009	1042	1109	…	1242	1309	…	1342	1410	…	…	1509	1642	1710	1810	…	…	0428	…
Bielefeld a.	…	1211	…	1311	…	…	1511	…	…	1611	…	…	…	1711	1911	2013	…	…	0556	…
Hannover Hbf a.	…	1302	…	1402	…	…	1602	…	…	1702	…	…	…	1802	2002	2102	…	…	0638	…
Braunschweig a.	…	1347	…	1447	…	…	1647	…	…	…	1745	1803	1845	1932	2047	2147	…	…	0729	…
Magdeburg a.	…	1432	1500	1532	1621	1732	1821	…	…	…	1850	1921	1932	…	2132	2232	…	…	0821	…
Halle a.	…	…	…	…	1716	…	1916	…	…	…	…	2016	…	…	2336	…	…	…	…	0916
Leipzig a.	…	…	1644	…	1749	…	1949	…	…	…	…	2049	…	…	0005	…	…	…	…	0949
Dresden Hbf a.	…	…	…	…	…	…	2135	…	…	…	…	2242	…	…	…	…	…	…	…	1135
Potsdam Stadt a.	…	1616	…	…	…	…	…	…	…	…	…	…	…	…	…	…	…	…	0858	…
Berlin Zoo a.	…	1640	…	1654	…	1854	…	…	…	2010	…	…	2054	…	…	2254	…	…	…	…
Berlin Hbf a.	…	…	…	…	…	…	…	…	…	…	…	…	…	…	…	…	…	…	…	…

	ICE 591	IC 546	422	2738	EC 109	38	IC 501	426	2636	EC 46	ICE 595	IC 605	430	2736	IC 505	434	2734	IC 507	438	2440	242
classes	1,2	1,2✓	1,2	1,2	1,2✓	1,2✓	1,2✓	1,2	1,2	1,2✓	1,2✓	1,2	1,2	1,2✓	1,2	1,2	1,2✓	1,2✓	1,2	1,2	1,2
notes	X	X L			Y	X	Y		X	N	X			Y	X		Y	Y		M	J [R] / [R]
Berlin Hbf d.	…	…	…	0707	…	0723	…	…	0907	0948	…	…	1123	…	…	1307	…	…	…	2049	…
Berlin Zoo d.	0548	…	…	…	0707	…	0745	…	…	…	…	…	1145	…	…	…	…	…	…	…	…
Potsdam Stadt d.	…	…	…	…	…	…	…	…	…	…	…	…	…	…	…	…	…	…	…	…	…
Dresden Hbf d.	…	…	…	…	…	…	0711	…	0853	0922	0911	…	…	1053	…	1253	…	…	1811	2013	…
Leipzig d.	…	0555	…	0653	…	0722	…	…	…	…	1053?	…	…	…	…	…	1322	…	2013	2042	…
Halle d.	…	0623	…	0722	…	…	…	…	0922	…	1122	…	…	…	…	1322	…	…	2042	…	…
Magdeburg d.	0707	0730	…	0816	0830	…	0930	1016	1030	1109	1216	1330	1416	1430	…	…	…	…	2137	2223	…
Braunschweig d.	0815	…	…	0915	1015	…	1057?	1115	1154	1215	…	1415	1515	…	…	…	…	…	2312	…	…
Hannover Hbf d.	0857	0957	…	1057	1157	…	1246	…	1257	1346	…	1457	1557	1646	…	…	…	…	2359	…	0054
Bielefeld d.	0946	1046	…	1146	1246	…	1346	…	…	1446	…	1546	1646	…	…	…	1850	…	2014	…	…
Köln d.	1150	1214	1250	1314	1350	1414	1514	1550	1614	1705	1750	1814	1850	…	1905	…	…	…	2105	…	0413
Aachen d.	1305	…	1343	1410	1444	1505	1543	1607	1648	1705	1743	1844	1943	…	2044	2143	2244	…	0452	…	0644
Liège Guillemins a.	1343	…	…	1449	1543	…	1648	1743	1844	…	2044	…	2244	…	…	0452	…	0644	…	…	…
Brussels Nord a.	1444	1305	…	1548	1644	…	1749	1855	2055	…	2255	…	…	…	…	0655	…	…	…	…	…
Brussels Midi a.	1455	…	…	1556	1655	…	1801	1927	2127	…	2327	…	…	…	0727	…	…	…	…	…	…
Gent St. Pieters a.	1527	…	…	…	1728	…	1952	…	2152	…	2352	…	…	…	0752	…	…	…	…	…	…
Brugge a.	1552	…	…	…	1809	…	2009	…	2209	…	0009	…	…	…	0809	0825	0945	…	…	…	…
Oostende 12 a.	1609	…	…	…	1809	…	2009	…	…	…	…	…	…	…	…	0900	1245	…	…	…	…
Ramsgate Port 12 a.	…	…	…	…	…	…	…	…	…	…	…	…	…	…	…	0900	1245	…	…	…	…
London Victoria 12 a.	…	…	…	…	…	…	…	…	…	…	…	…	…	…	…	1117	1517	…	…	…	…

LONDON - BERLIN by Sea

	1,2 E	[ship] E [R]	1,2 P	[ship] P [R]	IC539 1,2 X	IC877 1,2 X			IC876 1,2 X	IC538 1,2 X	[ship] F [R]	1,2 R
London Liverpool Street d.	1325	…	1525	…	…	…	Dresden Hbf d.	…	0736	…	…	…
Harwich Parkeston Quay a.	1445	…	1645	…	…	…	Berlin Zoo d.	…	…	1000	…	…
Harwich Parkeston Quay d.	…	1530	…	1730	…	…	Nauen d.	…	1023	1036	…	…
Hamburg Fischereihafen ♣ a.	…	1300	…	1500	…	…	Hamburg Altona ♣ d.	…	…	1315	…	…
Hamburg Altona ♣ d.	…	…	…	…	1638	…	Hamburg Fischereihafen d.	…	…	…	1630	1200
Nauen a.	…	…	…	…	1913	1924	Harwich Parkeston Quay a.	…	…	…	…	1305
Berlin Zoo a.	…	…	…	…	1950	…	Harwich Parkeston Quay d.	…	…	…	1630	…
Dresden Hbf a.	…	…	…	…	…	2212	London Liverpool Street a.	…	…	…	…	1430

NOTES

E – ③⑤⑦ Oct. 26 - Dec. 23, Dec. 26,28,30, Jan. 2,4,6,8,11,13,15,22,
   ③⑤ Jan. 25 - Mar. 31, even dates Apr. 2 - May 26.

F – ②④⑥ Oct. 25 - Dec. 22, Dec. 25,27,29,31, Jan. 1,3,5,7,10,12,14,21,
   ②④⑥ Jan. 24 - Mar. 30, odd dates Apr. 1 - May 27.

J – Jetfoil service see Table 12.

K – ①②③④⑤⑦, not Oct. 2, Dec. 24-31, Apr. 14-16,30.

L – ①-⑥, not Oct. 3, Dec. 25-Jan. 1, Apr. 15-17, May 1.

M – ⊏ 2 cl. Oostende - Berlin and v.v.;
   ⊏ 1,2 cl. and [couchette] (Paris) - Liège - Berlin and v.v.

N – ALEXANDER VON HUMBOLDT – [couchette] and X Brussels - Berlin and v.v.

P – ⑦ Jan. 8 - Mar. 26.

R – ③⑤⑦ Oct. 26 - Dec. 23, Dec. 26,28,30, Jan. 1,2,4,6,8,11,13,15,22,
   ③⑤⑦ Jan. 25 - Mar. 31, even dates Apr. 2 - May 28.

✓ – Supplement payable.

♣ – [bus] service Hamburg Fischereihafen - Hamburg Altona and v.v.

NOTES for Table 25.

B – ①②③④⑥ also Oct. 30, Nov. 11, Apr. 16,30, May 7,26;
   not Nov. 1,10, Apr. 17, May 1,8,24.

C – ⑤⑦ also Nov. 1,10, Apr. 17, May 1,8,24;
   not Oct. 30, Nov. 11, Apr. 16,30, May 7,26.

D – JACQUES BREL – [couchette] and X Paris - Dortmund and v.v.

E – MOLIERE – [couchette] and X Paris - Dortmund and v.v.

F – PARSIFAL – [couchette] and X Paris - Köln and v.v.

G – ⊏ 1,2 cl., ⊏ 2 cl., [couchette] and Y Paris - Dortmund and v.v.

J – ⊏ 1,2 cl., ⊏ 2 cl. and [couchette] Paris - Hamburg and v.v.; [couchette] Paris - Liège and v.v.

K – ⊏ 1,2 cl. Paris - København and v.v.

N – ⊏ 1,2 cl., ⊏ 2 cl., [couchette] and Y Paris - Berlin and v.v.

P – ①-⑥, not Oct. 3, Dec. 25 - Jan. 1, Apr. 15-17, May 1.

Q – ①②③④⑤⑦, not Oct. 2, Dec. 24 - 31, Apr. 14-16,30.

✓ – Supplement payable.

Table 24 — LONDON, BRUSSELS AND PARIS - WARSZAWA AND MOSKVA

For Eurostar connections between London and Brussels see Table 12.

	TEE							Moskva/Kyïv/St. P. train no.	15	683	49		
train number	83		512	241	241	241		Warszawa train number	240	240	240	420	284
classes	1,2✗	1,2✗	1,2	2	2	2		classes	2			1,2	1,2
notes (see below)	✗	J⃞R		A	B	C		notes (see below)	A	D	E	JF⃞R	⃝
London Victoria 12 .... d.	...	0805	...	...	...	...		Moskva Smolenskaya .... d.	2015	...	...	...	...
Ramsgate Port 🚢 12 .... d.	...	1025	...	...	...	...		Smolensk .... d.	0326	...	...	...	...
Oostende 🚢 12 .... d.	...	1300	1334	...	...	...		Sankt Peterburg Vitebski d.	...	...	1510	...	...
Brugge .... d.	...	...	1350	...	...	...		Minsk .... d.	0736	...	...	...	...
Gent Sint Pieters.............. d.	...	...	1415	...	...	...		Kyïv (Kiev) .... d.	...	1805	...	...	...
Paris Nord .... d.	1134	...	...	...	...	...		Brest 🚢 .... d.	1436	1436	1436	...	...
Brussels Midi .... d.	1404	...	1443	1555	1555	1555		Terespol .... d.	1500	1500	1500	...	...
Brussels Nord .... d.	...	...	...	1603	1603	1603		**Warszawa Wschodnia** .... d.	1910	1910	1910	...	...
Liège Guillemins.............. d.	...	...	...	1703	1703	1703		**Warszawa Centralna** ...... d.	1925	1925	1925	...	...
Aachen 🚢 .... d.	...	...	...	1808	1808	1808		Poznań Glówny .... d.	2250	2250	2250	...	...
Frankfurt/Oder 🚢 .... a.	...	...	...	0310	0310	0310		Rzepin .... d.	0100	0100	0100	...	...
Kunowice .... a.	...	...	...	0354	0354	0354		Kunowice .... d.	0115	0115	0115	...	...
Rzepin .... a.	...	...	...	0409	0409	0409		Frankfurt/Oder 🚢 .... d.	0147	0147	0147	...	...
Poznań Glówny .... a.	...	...	...	0625	0625	0625		Aachen 🚢 .... a.	1055	1055	1055	...	...
Warszawa Centralna ...... a.	...	...	...	1015	1015	1015		Liège Guillemins.......... a.	1158	1158	1158	...	...
Warszawa Wschodnia ...... a.	...	...	...	1029	1029	1029		**Brussels Nord** .... a.	1314	1314	1314	...	...
Terespol .... a.	...	...	...	1338	1338	1338		**Brussels Midi** .... a.	1322	1322	1322	1359	1413
Brest 🚢 .... a.	...	...	...	1616	1616	1616		**Paris Nord** .... a.	...	...	...	...	1708
Kyïv (Kiev).................... a.	...	...	...	...	1120	...		Gent Sint Pieters.......... a.	...	...	...	1427	...
Minsk .... a.	...	...	...	2227	...	...		Brugge .... a.	...	...	...	1452	...
Sankt Peterburg Vitebski ... a.	...	...	...	...	...	1742		Oostende 🚢 12 .... a.	...	...	...	1509	1655
Smolensk .... a.	...	...	...	0418	...	...		Ramsgate Port 🚢 12 ...... a.	...	...	...	1730	...
Moskva Smolenskaya ...... a.	...	...	...	1206	...	...		**London Victoria** 12 ...... a.	...	...	...	2019	...

NOTES

A – OST WEST EXPRESS – 🛏 1,2 cl. Brussels - Moskva and v.v. (journey 2 nights);
🛏 1,2 cl., 🍴 2 cl. and 🛋 Brussels - Warszawa and v.v. (journey 1 night).
B – ⑦ 🛏 1,2 cl. Brussels - Kyïv (journey 2 nights).
C – ①⑤ 🛏 1,2 cl. Brussels - Sankt Peterburg (journey 2 nights).

D – ⑤ 🛏 1,2 cl. Kyïv - Brussels (journey 2 nights).
E – ③⑥ 🛏 1,2 cl. Sankt Peterburg - Brussels (journey 2 nights).
F – Mar. 26 - May 27.
J – Jetfoil service see Table 12.
✗ – Supplement payable.

Table 25 — PARIS - LIÈGE, KÖLN, HAMBURG and BERLIN

	EC	IC	IC	EC	EC	EC	EC	EC	487			EC	ICE	ICE
train number	33	502	524	39	8	26	31	31	331	331	243	243	180	231	641	639
classes	1,2✗	1,2✗	1,2✗	1,2✗	1,2✗	1,2✗	1,2✗		1,2	1,2	2	1,2	1,2✗	1,2	1,2✗	1,2✗
notes (see below)	F	✗	✗	D	✗	✗	E	K	B	C	N	J	✗	G	P	✗
Paris Nord.................... d.	0737	✗	✗	1346	✗	✗	1632	1632	1926	1945	2101	2101	2316	...	...	
St. Quentin .... d.	0846			1458					2053	2101	2215	2215	0103			
Jeumont 🚢 .... d.	...								2210	2210			0224			
Charleroi Sud .... d.	0954						1853	1853	2234	2234	2326	2326	0248			
Namur .... d.	1023						1922	1922	2302	2302	2355	2355	0317			
Liège Guillemins............ a.	1059			1759			1959	1959	2343	2343	0033	0033	0405			
Aachen 🚢 .... a.	1150			1845			2050	2050			0130	0130	0448			
Köln Hbf .... a.	1248	1309	1310	1942	2009	2010	2149	2149						0550	0605	0626
Düsseldorf .... a.	...	1331		2016	2031		2216	2224						0621		
Duisburg .... a.	...	1344		2031	2044		2232	2240						0642		
Essen .... a.	...	1357		2046	2057		2244	2253						0656		
Dortmund .... a.	...	1420	1420	2111	2120	2120	2308				0321	0321		0722		
Münster .... a.	...		1454			2154		2350								0752
Osnabrück .... a.	...		1519			2219		0020								
Bremen Hbf .... a.	...		1614			2314		0127				0600				
Hamburg Hbf .... a.	...		1711			0011		0235				0711	0719			0946
Hamburg Altona .... a.	...		1724			0024						0724				0959
Rødby F 🚢 .... a.	...							0600					1000			
København 50 .... a.	...							0825					1208			
Bielefeld .... a.	...	1511		2211							0428			0748		
Hannover Hbf .... a.	...	1602		2305							0556			0837		
Braunschweig .... a.	...	1647									0638					
Magdeburg .... a.	...	1732									0729					
Berlin Zoo .... a.	...	1854									0858					
Berlin Hbf .... a.	...	...												1108		

		EC			EC	IC	EC		IC	IC	EC		IC	ICE		EC		
train number	330	30	232		109	621	38		503	523	32		830	640	230	181	234	242
classes	1,2	1,2✗	🛏		1,2✗	1,2✗	1,2✗		1,2✗	1,2✗	1,2✗		1,2✗	1,2✗	1,2	1,2✗	1,2	2
notes (see below)		E	K		✗	✗	D		✗	✗	F		✗	✗ Q	G	✗	J	N
Berlin Hbf.................... d.	...	...	...		...	...	...		...	...	...		...	...	...	...	...	...
Berlin Zoo .... d.	...	...	...		0707	...	...		1107	...	...		...	1847	...	...	...	2049
Magdeburg .... d.	...	...	...		0830	...	...		1230	...	...		...	...	...	...	...	2223
Braunschweig .... d.	...	...	...		0915	...	...		1315	...	...		...	...	...	...	...	2312
Hannover Hbf .... d.	...	...	...		0957	...	...		1357	...	...		2120	...	...	...	...	2359
Bielefeld .... d.	...	...	...		1046	...	...		1446	...	...		2207	...	...	...	...	0054
København 50 .... d.	...	...	2105		...	...	...		...	...	...		...	...	1730	...	...	...
Rødby F 🚢 .... d.	...	...	2330		...	...	...		...	...	...		...	...	1925	...	...	...
Hamburg Altona .... d.	...	...	...		0833	...	...		1233	...	1933		...	...	2223	...	...	...
Hamburg Hbf .... d.	...	...	0312		0847	...	...		1247	...	1947		...	...	2215	2242	...	...
Bremen Hbf .... d.	...	...	0420		0945	...	...		1345	...	2045		...	...	...	2353	...	...
Osnabrück .... d.	...	...	0532		1039	...	...		1439	...	2139		...	...	...	...	...	...
Münster .... d.	...	...	0604		1105	...	...		1505	...	2205		...	...	...	...	...	...
Dortmund .... d.	...	0648	...		1138	1140	1146		1538	1540	2240		...	2237	0213	...	0213	...
Essen .... d.	...	0712	0654		1201		1210		1601		...		...	2300	...	...	...	...
Duisburg .... d.	...	0725	0708		1214		1224		1614		...		2317	2321	...	...	...	...
Düsseldorf .... d.	...	0740	0732		1228		1239		1628		...		2330	2338	...	...	...	...
Köln Hbf .... d.	...	0814	0814		1250	1250	1314		1650	1650	1708		2350	2352	0007	...	...	...
Aachen 🚢 .... d.	...	0909	0909		...	...	1410		...	...	1800		...	...	0100	0413	0413	...
Liège Guillemins............ d.	0700	0959	0959		...	...	1452		...	...	1847		...	...	0155	0509	0509	...
Namur .... d.	0740	1039	1039		...	...	...		...	...	1925		...	...	0234	0548	0548	...
Charleroi Sud .... d.	0810	1108	1106		...	...	...		...	...	1954		...	...	0304	0617	0617	...
Jeumont 🚢 .... d.	0837	...	...		...	...	...		...	...	...		...	...	0328	...	...	...
St. Quentin .... d.	0952	1215	1215		...	...	1750		...	...	2057		...	...	0444	...	...	...
Paris Nord .... a.	1115	1330	1330		...	...	1859		...	...	2209		...	...	0623	0840	0840	...

FOR NOTES see previous page.

Table 28

AMSTERDAM AND ROTTERDAM – KÖLN AND FRANKFURT/MAIN

	EC	IC	EC	ICE		EC	EC	EC	EC	ICE	EC	IC	ICE		IC	EC	EC	ICE		EC	EC	IC	IC	ICE
train number	141	725	103	591	1803	115	143	27	9	793	105	727	593	1807	513	3	29	895	1811	19	145	729	501	897
classes	1,2	1,2✔	1,2✔	1,2✔		1,2✔	1,2✔	1,2✔	1,2✔	1,2✔	1,2✔	1,2	1,2✔		1,2	1,2✔	1,2✔	1,2✔	1,2	1,2✔	1,2✔	1,2	1,2	1,2✔
notes (see below)	Ac	✗	✗	✗	①-⑥	✗	B	✗	✗	✗	✗C	Z✗	✗		✗	✗D	✗	✗		✗	E	✗	✗	✗
Amsterdam Centraal d.	0602					0706					0800					0900					1106			
Utrecht CS d.	0633					0735					0830					1005					1135			
Arnhem d.	0705					0806					0905					1034					1206			
Emmerich a.	0732					0832					0934					1102					1232			
Oberhausen a.	0759					0859					1002					1110					1259			
Duisburg a.	0806	0814				0906		0914			1010	1014				1110	1114				1306	1314		
Düsseldorf a.	0819	0828				0919		0928			1032	1028		0745		1132	1128			0945	1319	1328		
Den Haag C.S. d.														0750						0950				
Den Haag H.S. d.														0756						0957				
Delft d.														0812						1012				
Rotterdam C.S. d.					0553									0827						1027				
Dordrecht d.					0611									0847						1047				
Breda d.					0637									0901						1101				
Tilburg d.					0656									0929						1129				
Eindhoven d.					0729									1012						1212				
Venlo d.					0812									1030						1230				
Viersen a.					0830									1037						1237				
Mönchengladbach a.					0837																			
Köln Hbf a.	0842	0854	0900	0919		0930	0942	0954	1000		1057	1054		1119		1130	1157	1154		1319	1330	1342	1354	1400
Bonn a.		0912	0919			0948	1012	1018			1118	1112		1148		1218	1212			1348	1421	1444	1451	
Koblenz a.		0944	0951			1021	1044	1051			1150	1145		1221		1250	1245			1512	1534	1542		
Mainz a.		1034	1042			1112	1134	1142			1240	1236		1312		1340	1336			1406	1608			
Frankfurt/Main a.		1106					1206				1306						1526				1726			
Würzburg a.		1226					1326				1426					1625					1825			
Nürnberg a.		1328					1425				1525						1929							
Praha Hlavni 57 a.																1729								
Regensburg 740 a.							1529																	
Mannheim a.			1123	1127	1153	1205	1223	1227	1323	1327		1353	1423		1427		1553	1605			1623		1627	
Heidelberg a.						1208	1251		1308		1406	1451		1506		1651	1708							
Stuttgart a.				1208	1251				1308		1403	1503		1554		1603	1754			1803				
Ulm a.				1303	1354				1403		1445	1544		1636		1644	1836			1845				
Augsburg a.				1345	1436									1700			1900							
München Pasing a.					1500				1515								1910							
München Hbf a.				1415	1510				1515		1615			1710		1715	1910			1654				1915
Karlsruhe a.		1154				1254			1254	1354					1454		1510							
Baden Baden a.						1310																	1728	
Offenburg a.		1228																			1759			
Freiberg im Breisgau a.		1259				1359			1359	1459					1559						1843			
Basel SBB a.		1343				1443			1443	1543					1643									

	IC	IC	EC	IC	IC	ICE	IC	IC	EC	IC	IC	ICE	IC		EC	IC	IC	IC		EC		EC	EN	EN
train number	1815	617	147	823	605	899	1819	517	149	625	505	795	1823	151	827	607	223	353	1827	153	1829	203	215	215
classes	1,2	1,2✔	1,2✔	1,2✔	1,2✔	1,2✔	1,2	1,2✔	1,2✔	1,2✔	1,2✔	1,2✔	1,2	1,2	1,2✔	1,2	1,2✔	1,2	1,2	1,2	1,2	2	2	2
notes (see below)		F	✗	✗	✗	✗		✗®	G	✗	✗	✗		H	✗®		T	N		J		K	L	M
Amsterdam Centraal d.		1306						1506					1700							1906		2005	2056	2056
Utrecht CS d.		1335						1535					1729							1935		2047	2130	2130
Arnhem d.		1406						1606					1805							2006		2127	2214	2214
Emmerich a.		1432						1632					1832							2032		2157	2250	2250
Oberhausen a.		1459						1659					1859							2059		2233	2326	2326
Duisburg a.		1506	1514					1706	1714				1906		1914	1947				2106		2242	2335	2335
Düsseldorf a.		1519	1528					1719	1728				1919		1928	2005				2119		2318	2352	2352
Den Haag C.S. d.	1145					1345						1545							1745		1945			
Den Haag H.S. d.	1150					1350						1550							1750		1950			
Delft d.	1157					1357						1557							1757		1957			
Rotterdam C.S. d.	1212					1412						1612							1812		2012			
Dordrecht d.	1227					1427						1628							1827		2027			
Breda d.	1247					1447						1647							1847		2047			
Tilburg d.	1301					1501						1701							1901		2101			
Eindhoven d.	1329					1529						1729							1929		2129			
Venlo d.	1412					1612						1812							2012		2212			
Viersen a.	1430					1630						1830							2030		2230			
Mönchengladbach a.						1637						1837							2037		2237			
Köln Hbf a.	1519	1530	1542	1554	1600		1719	1730	1742	1754	1800		1919	1942	1954	2000	2037	2111	2119	2142	2319	2347	0022	0022
Bonn a.		1548		1612	1618			1748		1812	1818			2012	2018	2059	2131					0019		0109
Koblenz a.		1621		1644	1651			1821		1844	1851			2044	2051	2135	2207					0055		0144
Mainz a.		1712		1734	1742			1912		1934	1942			2134	2142	2302	2302							
Frankfurt/Main a.				1806						2006				2206		2300	2330			0054	0115			
Würzburg a.				1926						2126b										0200	0222			
Nürnberg a.				2025						2227b										0838	0838		0514	
Praha Hlavni 57 a.																							0618	
Regensburg 740 a.					2129																			
Mannheim a.		1753			1823	1827		1953			2023	2027						2223				0313		0335
Heidelberg a.		1805				2005						2108										0454		0454
Stuttgart a.		1851			1908	2051					2203											0603		0603
Ulm a.		1954			2003						2245											0652		0652
Augsburg a.		2036			2045						2308													
München Pasing a.		2100									2318												0736	
München Hbf a.		2110			2115						2254											0349		
Karlsruhe a.				1854						2054							2254					0414		
Baden Baden a.				1910						2110												0437		
Offenburg a.																						0515		
Freiberg im Breisgau a.				1959						2159												0626		
Basel SBB a.				2043						2243														

NOTES

A – BONIFACIUS – 🛏 and ✗ Amsterdam – Köln.
B – ERASMUS – 🛏 and ✗ Amsterdam – Köln.
C – BERNER OBERLAND – 🛏 and ✗ Amsterdam – Basel – (Interlaken).
D – REMBRANDT – 🛏 and ✗ Amsterdam – Basel – (Chur).
E – FRANZ HALS – 🛏 and ✗ Amsterdam – Köln.
F – PIET MONDRIAAN – 🛏 and ✗ Amsterdam – Köln.
G – JOHANNES VERMEER – 🛏 and ✗ Amsterdam – Köln.
H – JAN PIETERSZ. SWEELINCK – 🛏 and ✗ Amsterdam – Köln.
J – HIERONYMUS BOSCH – 🛏 and ✗ Amsterdam – Köln.

K – SCHWEIZ EXPRESS – 🛏 2 cl. and 🛌 Amsterdam – Basel;
    also 🛌 1,2 cl. on ⑤ Dec. 23 – Mar. 24.
L – 🛌 1,2 cl., 🛏 2 cl. and 🛌 Amsterdam – Regensburg – (Wien).
M – 🛌 1,2 cl., 🛏 2 cl. and 🛌 Amsterdam – München.
N – Sept. 25 – Oct. 31, Dec. 16 – Jan. 8 and Mar. 31 – May 27:
    🛌 1,2 cl., 🛏 2 cl. and 🛌 Köln – Praha.
T – Nov. 1 – Dec. 15 and Jan. 9 – Mar. 30:
    🛌 1,2 cl., 🛏 2 cl. and 🛌 (Dortmund) – Duisburg – Praha.
Z – ①②③④⑤⑥, not Oct. 3, Dec. 25 – Jan. 1, Apr. 15,16,17, May 1.
b – Not ⑥.
c – Not Dec. 25, Jan. 1.
✔ – Supplement payable.

Table 28 KÖLN AND FRANKFURT/MAIN - AMSTERDAM AND ROTTERDAM

train type	EC			IC	EC		352	IC	ICE	IC	IC	EC		IC	ICE	IC	IC	EC		IC	ICE	IC	IC	EC	
train number	140	1802	352	739	142	1804	222	618	694	504	526	144	1808	616	598	502	524	146	1812	614	596	602	620	148	1816
classes	1,2⁄	1,2	1,2	1,2⁄	1,2⁄	1,2	1,2	1,2⁄	1,2⁄	1,2⁄	1,2⁄	1,2⁄	1,2	1,2⁄	1,2⁄	1,2⁄	1,2⁄	1,2⁄	1,2	1,2⁄	1,2⁄	1,2⁄	1,2⁄	1,2⁄	1,2
notes (see below)	A		P	🍷	B		T	🍷	✕	✕	✕	C		✕	✕	✕	✕	D		✕	✕	✕	✕	E	
Basel SBB d.	...	...	...	...	...	...	...	...	...	...	...	...	...	...	...	0817	...	...	...	...	...	1017	...	...	...
Freiberg im Breisgau d.	...	...	...	...	...	...	...	...	...	0654	...	...	...	...	...	0858	...	...	...	...	...	1058	...	...	...
Offenburg d.	...	...	...	...	...	...	...	...	...	0725	...	...	...	...	...	0928	...	...	...	...	...	1128	...	...	...
Baden Baden d.	...	...	...	...	...	...	...	...	...	0744	...	...	...	...	...	|	...	...	...	...	...	|	...	...	...
Karlsruhe d.	...	...	...	...	...	...	...	...	...	0802	...	...	...	...	...	1002	...	...	...	...	...	1202	...	...	...
München Hbf d.	...	...	...	...	...	...	...	...	0542f	|	...	...	...	0650	0746	|	...	...	...	0850	0946	|	...	...	...
München Pasing d.	...	...	...	...	...	...	...	...	0550f	|	...	...	...	0656	|	|	...	...	...	0856	|	|	...	...	...
Augsburg d.	...	...	...	...	...	...	...	...	0614f	|	...	...	...	0720	0812	|	...	...	...	0920	1012	|	...	...	...
Ulm d.	...	...	...	...	...	...	...	...	0654f	|	...	...	...	0805	0854	|	...	...	...	1005	1054	|	...	...	...
Stuttgart d.	...	...	...	...	...	...	...	0711	0753	|	...	...	...	0911	0953	|	...	...	...	1111	1153	|	...	...	...
Heidelberg d.	...	...	...	...	...	...	...	0754	|	|	...	...	...	0954	|	|	...	...	...	1154	|	|	...	...	...
Mannheim d.	...	...	...	...	...	...	...	0807	0832	0837	...	...	...	1007	1032	1037	...	...	...	1207	1232	1237	...	...	...
Regensburg **740** d.	...	...	...	...	...	...	...	|	...	|	...	...	...	|	...	|	...	...	...	|	...	|	...	...	...
Praha Hlavni **57** d.	...	...	2050	...	...	...	2050	|	...	|	...	...	...	|	...	|	...	...	...	|	...	|	...	...	...
Nürnberg d.	...	...	0304	...	...	...	0406	|	...	|	0629b	...	...	|	...	|	0832	...	...	|	...	|	1032	...	...
Würzburg d.	...	...	0414	...	...	...	0510	|	...	|	0730b	...	...	|	...	|	0930	...	...	|	...	|	1130	...	...
Frankfurt/Main Hbf d.	...	...	0544	0651	...	...	0658	|	...	|	0851	...	...	|	...	|	1051	...	...	|	...	|	1251	...	...
Mainz d.	...	...	0610	0724	...	...	0728	0848	...	0918	0924	...	...	1048	...	1118	1124	...	...	1248	...	1318	1324	...	...
Koblenz d.	...	...	0705	0813	...	...	0823	0937	...	1007	1013	...	...	1137	...	1207	1213	...	...	1337	...	1407	1413	...	...
Bonn d.	...	...	0739	0845	...	...	0859	1009	...	1039	1045	...	...	1209	...	1239	1245	...	...	1409	...	1439	1445	...	...
Köln Hbf d.	0717	0717	0801	0905	0917	0917	0921	1029	...	1059	1105	1117	1117	1229	...	1259	1305	1317	1317	1429	...	1459	1505	1517	1517
Mönchengladbach d.	|	0758	...	...	|	0958	|	...	...	|	...	|	1158	...	...	|	...	|	1358	...	...	...	...	|	1558
Kaldenkirchen d.	|	0816	...	...	|	1016	|	...	...	|	...	|	1216	...	...	|	...	|	1416	...	...	...	...	|	1616
Venlo ▥ a.	|	0821	...	...	|	1021	|	...	...	|	...	|	1221	...	...	|	...	|	1421	...	...	...	...	|	1621
Eindhoven a.	|	0905	...	...	|	1105	|	...	...	|	...	|	1305	...	...	|	...	|	1505	...	...	...	...	|	1705
Tilburg a.	|	0932	...	...	|	1132	|	...	...	|	...	|	1332	...	...	|	...	|	1532	...	...	...	...	|	1732
Breda a.	|	0946	...	...	|	1146	|	...	...	|	...	|	1346	...	...	|	...	|	1546	...	...	...	...	|	1746
Dordrecht a.	|	1004	...	...	|	1205	|	...	...	|	...	|	1404	...	...	|	...	|	1604	...	...	...	...	|	1804
Rotterdam C.S. a.	|	1020	...	...	|	1220	|	...	...	|	...	|	1420	...	...	|	...	|	1620	...	...	...	...	|	1820
Delft a.	|	1033	...	...	|	1233	|	...	...	|	...	|	1433	...	...	|	...	|	1633	...	...	...	...	|	1833
Den Haag H.S. a.	|	1043	...	...	|	1243	|	...	...	|	...	|	1443	...	...	|	...	|	1643	...	...	...	...	|	1843
Den Haag C.S. a.	|	1049	...	...	|	1249	|	...	...	|	...	|	1449	...	...	|	...	|	1649	...	...	...	...	|	1849
Düsseldorf d.	0739	...	...	...	0939	...	0951	...	...	1133	...	1139	...	...	...	1333	...	1339	...	...	...	...	...	1539	...
Duisburg d.	0752	...	...	...	0952	...	1015	...	...	1144	...	1152	...	...	...	1344	...	1352	...	...	...	...	...	1552	...
Oberhausen d.	0758	...	...	...	0958	...	...	...	...	...	...	1158	...	...	...	...	...	1358	...	...	...	...	...	1558	...
Emmerich ▥ a.	0826	...	...	...	1026	...	...	...	...	...	...	1226	...	...	...	...	...	1426	...	...	...	...	...	1626	...
Arnhem a.	0852	...	...	...	1052	...	...	...	...	...	...	1252	...	...	...	...	...	1452	...	...	...	...	...	1652	...
Utrecht a.	0923	...	...	...	1123	...	...	...	...	...	...	1323	...	...	...	...	...	1523	...	...	...	...	...	1723	...
Amsterdam Centraal a.	0954	...	...	...	1151	...	...	...	...	...	...	1351	...	...	...	...	...	1551	...	...	...	...	...	1751	...

train type	IC	ICE	EC	IC	EC		EC	ICE	EC	EC	IC	ICE	IC	EC			EC	ICE	EC	IC	EC		EN	
train number	612	594	108	520	150	1820	112	894	28	104	118	592	724	2	1824	1826	114	590	106	726	152	214	224	202
classes	1,2⁄	1,2⁄	1,2⁄	1,2⁄	1,2⁄	1,2	1,2⁄	1,2⁄	1,2⁄	1,2⁄	1,2⁄	1,2⁄	1,2⁄	1,2⁄	1,2	1,2	1,2⁄	1,2⁄	1,2⁄	1,2⁄	1,2⁄	2	2	1,2
notes (see below)	🍷	✕	✕	✕	F		✕	✕	✕	M	✕	✕	🍷	N		e	✕	✕	✕	Y ✕	G c	H	J	K
Basel SBB d.	...	...	1217	...	...	...	...	...	...	1317	...	...	...	1417	...	...	...	...	1617	...	...	...	...	2325
Freiberg im Breisgau d.	...	...	1258	...	...	...	...	...	...	1358	...	...	...	1458	...	...	...	...	1658	...	...	...	...	0033
Offenburg d.	...	...	1328	...	...	...	...	...	...	|	...	...	...	1528	...	...	...	...	1728	...	...	...	...	0112
Baden Baden d.	...	...	|	...	...	...	...	...	...	1444	...	...	...	|	...	...	...	...	|	...	...	...	...	0134
Karlsruhe d.	...	...	1402	...	...	...	...	...	...	1502	...	...	...	1602	...	...	...	...	1802	...	...	...	...	0158
München Hbf d.	1050	1146	|	...	...	...	1150	1246	...	|	1250	1346	...	|	...	...	1450	1546	|	...	...	2211	...	|
München Pasing d.	1056	|	|	...	...	...	1156	|	...	|	1256	|	...	|	...	...	1456	|	|	...	...	|	...	|
Augsburg d.	1120	1212	|	...	...	...	1220	1314	...	|	1320	1414	...	|	...	...	1520	1612	|	...	...	2246	...	|
Ulm d.	1205	1254	|	...	...	...	1305	1354	...	|	1405	1454	...	|	...	...	1605	1654	|	...	...	2334	...	|
Stuttgart d.	1311	1353	|	...	...	...	1411	1453	...	|	1511	1553	...	|	...	...	1711	1753	|	...	...	0041	...	|
Heidelberg d.	1354	|	|	...	...	...	1454	|	...	|	1554	|	...	|	...	...	1754	|	|	...	...	0157	...	0235
Mannheim d.	1407	1432	1437	...	...	...	1507	1532	...	1537	1607	1632	...	1637	...	...	1807	1832	1837	...	...	|	...	|
Regensburg **740** d.	|	...	|	...	...	...	|	...	...	|	|	...	...	|	...	...	|	...	|	...	...	|	2320	|
Praha Hlavni **57** d.	|	...	|	...	...	...	|	...	1228	|	|	...	...	|	...	...	|	...	|	...	...	|	|	|
Nürnberg d.	|	...	|	1232	...	...	|	...	1332	|	|	...	1432	|	...	...	|	...	|	1632	...	|	0024	|
Würzburg d.	|	...	|	1330	...	...	|	...	1430	|	|	...	1530	|	...	...	|	...	|	1730	...	|	|	|
Frankfurt/Main Hbf d.	|	...	|	1451	...	...	|	...	1551	|	|	...	1651	|	...	...	|	...	|	1851	...	|	|	|
Mainz d.	1448	...	1518	1524	...	...	1548	...	1624	1618	1648	...	1724	1718	...	...	1848	...	1918	1924	...	|	|	|
Koblenz d.	1537	...	1607	1613	...	...	1637	...	1713	1707	1737	...	1813	1807	...	...	1937	...	2007	2013	...	0350	|	0449
Bonn d.	1609	...	1639	1645	...	...	1709	...	1745	1739	1809	...	1845	1839	...	...	2009	...	2039	2045	...	0425	|	0523
Köln Hbf d.	1629	...	1659	1709	1717	1717	1729	...	1805	1802	1829	...	1909	1902	1917	2017	2029	...	2109	2105	2117	0510	0510	0550
Mönchengladbach d.	...	...	...	|	|	1758	...	...	|	|	...	...	|	|	1958	2058	...	...	|	...	|	|	|	|
Kaldenkirchen d.	...	...	...	|	|	1816	...	...	|	|	...	...	|	|	2016	2116	...	...	|	...	|	|	|	|
Venlo ▥ a.	...	...	...	|	|	1821	...	...	|	|	...	...	|	|	2021	2121	...	...	|	...	|	|	|	|
Eindhoven a.	...	...	...	|	|	1905	...	...	|	|	...	...	|	|	2105	2205	...	...	|	...	|	|	|	|
Tilburg a.	...	...	...	|	|	1932	...	...	|	|	...	...	|	|	2132	2232	...	...	|	...	|	|	|	|
Breda a.	...	...	...	|	|	1946	...	...	|	|	...	...	|	|	2146	2246	...	...	|	...	|	|	|	|
Dordrecht a.	...	...	...	|	|	2004	...	...	|	|	...	...	|	|	2204	2307	...	...	|	...	|	|	|	|
Rotterdam C.S. a.	...	...	...	|	|	2020	...	...	|	|	...	...	|	|	2220	2324	...	...	|	...	|	|	|	|
Delft a.	...	...	...	|	|	2035	...	...	|	|	...	...	|	|	2233	2337	...	...	|	...	|	|	|	|
Den Haag H.S. a.	...	...	...	|	|	2044	...	...	|	|	...	...	|	|	2243	2346	...	...	|	...	|	|	|	|
Den Haag C.S. a.	...	...	...	|	|	2049	...	...	|	|	...	...	|	|	2249	2350	...	...	|	...	|	|	|	|
Düsseldorf d.	...	...	...	1733	1739	...	...	...	1833	1826	...	...	1933	1926	...	...	...	...	2133	...	2139	0545	0545	0620
Duisburg d.	...	...	...	1744	1752	...	...	...	1844	1848	...	...	1944	1948	...	...	...	...	2144	...	2152	0613	0613	0655
Oberhausen d.	...	...	...	...	1758	...	...	...	...	1855	...	...	...	1955	...	...	...	...	...	...	2158	0626	0626	0703
Emmerich ▥ a.	...	...	...	...	1826	...	...	...	...	1924	...	...	...	2024	...	...	...	...	...	...	2226	0704	0704	0740
Arnhem a.	...	...	...	...	1852	...	...	...	...	1952	...	...	...	2052	...	...	...	...	...	...	2252	0741	0741	0825
Utrecht a.	...	...	...	...	1923	...	...	...	...	2023	...	...	...	2123	...	...	...	...	...	...	2323	0823	0823	0906
Amsterdam Centraal a.	...	...	...	...	1951	...	...	...	...	2051	...	...	...	2151	...	...	...	...	...	...	2351	0857	0857	0940

NOTES

- A – HIERONYMUS BOSCH – [12] and ✕ Köln - Amsterdam.
- B – JAN PIETERSZ. SWEELINCK – [12] and ✕ Köln - Amsterdam.
- C – JOHANNES VERMEER – [12] and ✕ Köln - Amsterdam.
- D – PIET MONDRIAAN – [12] and ✕ Köln - Amsterdam.
- E – FRANS HALS – [12] and ✕ Köln - Amsterdam.
- F – ERASMUS – [12] and ✕ Köln - Amsterdam.
- G – BONIFACIUS – [12] and ✕ Köln - Amsterdam.
- H – 🛏 1,2 cl., ▬ 2 cl. and [2] München - Amsterdam.
- J – 🛏 1,2 cl., ▬ 2 cl. and [2] (Wien) - Regensburg - Amsterdam.
- K – SCHWEIZ EXPRESS – ▬ 2 cl. and [12] Basel - Amsterdam, also 🛏 1,2 cl. on Dec. 26, Jan. 1 and ⑥ Jan. 7 - Mar. 25.
- M – BERNER OBERLAND – [12] and ✕ (Interlaken) - Basel - Amsterdam.
- N – REMBRANDT – [12] and ✕ (Chur) - Basel - Amsterdam.
- P – Sept. 25 - Oct. 30, Dec. 15 - Jan. 7 and Mar. 30 - May 27: 🛏 1,2 cl., ▬ 2 cl. and [12] Praha - Köln.
- T – Oct. 31 - Dec. 14 and Jan. 8 - Mar. 29: 🛏 1,2 cl., ▬ 2 cl. and [2] Praha - Duisburg - (Dortmund).
- Y – ①②③④⑤⑦, not Oct. 2, Dec. 24-31, Apr. 14,15,16,30.
- b – Not ⑦.
- c – Not Dec. 24,31.
- e – Not Dec. 31.
- f – Not ⑥.
- ⁄ – Supplement payable.

Table 30 — PARIS - FRANKFURT/MAIN, LEIPZIG AND PRAHA

train type	EC	IC	ICE		EC	IC	ICE	IC		EC	D	D	D	D			IC	IC
train number	57	621	594		55	523	590	555		53	1955	353	451	223			261	721	655
classes	1,2✗	1,2✓	1,2✓		1,2✓	1,2✓	1,2✓	1,2✓		1,2✓	1,2	1,2	1,2	1,2			2	1,2✗	1,2✓
notes (see below)	C	✗	✗		B			K		G	W	N	P	S			L	H	✗
Paris Est .... d.	0854			...	1301				...	1716					...	...	2230		...
Metz .... d.	1154	...		...	1555	...			...	2006							0205		...
Forbach ⑭ .... d.	1240	...		...	1640	...			...	2049									...
Saarbrücken .... a.	1249	...		...	1648	...			...	2056									...
Kaiserlautern .... a.	1328	...		...	1728	...			...	2136									...
Mannheim 742 .... a.	1411	1435		...	1811	1835			...	2219									...
Heidelberg 742 .... a.				...	1845				...	2253							0548		...
Darmstadt .... a.	1444			...	1845				...	2315	2323	2343	2359	2327			0624		...
Frankfurt/Main .... a.	1506	1514	1518	...	1906	1914	1918	1922	...	2315	2323	2343	2359	2327			0652	0714	0722
Würzburg .... a.		1626		...		2026			...		0115		0054					0826	
Nürnberg .... a.		1725		...		2127			...		0222		0200					0925	
Fulda .... a.	1618		1613	...			2013	2008	...			0119							0808
Bebra .... a.	1651			...				2051	...			0156							0841
Erfurt .... a.	1824			...				2224	...			0345							1016
Leipzig .... a.	1955			...				2355	...			0457							1155
Dresden Hbf .... a.	2140			...					...			0638b							1340
Děčín ⑭ .... a.				...					...			0455		0455					
Cheb ⑭ .... a.				...					...			0650		0650					
Plzeň Hlavni .... a.				...					...										
Praha Holešovice .... a.				...					...			0839		0839					
Praha Hlavni .... a.				...					...										
Kassel Wilhelmshöhe .... a.		1644		...			2044		...										
Magdeburg .... a.		1850		...			2250		...										
Berlin Zoo .... a.		2010		...			0010		...	0641									
Berlin Hbf .... a.				...					...										

train type	D	D		EC		IC	ICE	IC	EC		ICE	IC	EC		IC	IC	
train number	352	352	450	1954	52		554	591	524	54		595	520	56		654	722	401
classes	1,2	1,2	1,2	1,2	1,2✓		1,2✓	1,2✓	1,2✓	1,2✓		1,2✓	1,2✓	1,2✓		1,2✓	1,2✓	2
notes (see below)	M	T	P	W	G		✗	✗	✗	B		✗	✗	C		✗	✗Q	R
							Y											
Berlin Hbf .... d.																		
Berlin Zoo .... d.				2349			0548					0948						
Magdeburg .... d.							0709					1109						
Kassel Wilhelmshöhe .... d.							0913					1313						
Praha Hlavni .... d.	2050	2050																
Praha Holešovice .... d.																		
Plzeň Hlavni .... d.	2241	2241																
Cheb ⑭ .... d.	0053	0053																
Děčín ⑭ .... d.												0822				1622		
Dresden Hbf .... d.			2243b				0604					1004				1804		
Leipzig .... d.			0035				0734					1134				1944		
Erfurt .... d.			0207				0915					1305				2105		
Bebra .... d.			0350	0510			0950	0945				1345		1339		2137		
Fulda .... d.			0430	0548									1232			2032		
Nürnberg .... d.	0304	0406							0832				1330				2130	
Würzburg .... d.	0414	0510							0930							2235	2243	2255
Frankfurt/Main .... d.	0536	0643	0600	0703	0727		1035	1039	1043	1051		1439	1443	1451		2235	2243	2255
Darmstadt .... d.					0747					1111				1511			2314	
Heidelberg 742 .... d.																	0010	
Mannheim .... d.					0822			1124		1146		1524		1546				
Kaiserlautern .... d.					0904					1228				1628				
Saarbrücken .... d.					0946					1309				1709				
Forbach ⑭ .... d.					0954					1318				1718				
Metz .... a.					1039					1402				1806			0337	
Paris Est .... a.					1337					1709				1709			0704	

NOTES

B – GUSTAVE EIFFEL – ⬜ and ✗ Paris - Frankfurt/Main and v.v.
C – HEINRICH HEINE – ⬜ and ✗ Paris - Dresden and v.v.
G – GOETHE – ⬜ and ✗ Paris - Frankfurt/Main and v.v.
H – ①–⑥, not Oct. 3, Dec. 25-Jan. 1, Apr. 15-17, May 1.
K – Not Nov. 19, Dec. 24,31.
L – ⬛ 2 cl. and ⬜ Paris - Frankfurt/Main;
  daily except ⑥ to Dec. 22 and from Jan. 2: 1,2 cl. (T2) Paris - Frankfurt/Main.
M – Sept. 25 - Oct. 30, Dec. 15 - Jan. 7 and Mar. 30 - May 27:
  🛏 1,2 cl., ⬛ 2 cl., ⬜ and ⚏ Praha - Frankfurt/Main - (Köln).
N – Sept. 25 - Oct. 30, Dec. 15 - Jan. 7 and Mar. 30 - May 27:
  🛏 1,2 cl., ⬛ 2 cl., ⬜ and ⚏ (Köln) - Frankfurt/Main - Praha.

P – 🛏 1,2 cl., ⬛ 2 cl. and ⬜ Frankfurt/Main - Dresden - (Warszawa) and v.v.
Q – ①②③④⑤⑥⑦, not Oct. 2, Dec. 24-31, Apr. 14-16,30.
R – ⬛ 2 cl. and ⬜ Frankfurt/Main - Paris;
  daily except ⑥ to Dec. 22 and from Jan. 2: 1,2 cl. (T2) Frankfurt/Main - Paris.
S – Nov. 1 - Dec. 15 and Jan. 9 - Mar. 30:
  🛏 1,2 cl., ⬛ 2 cl. and ⬜ (Dortmund) - Frankfurt/Main - Praha.
T – Oct. 31 - Dec. 14 and Jan. 8 - Mar. 29:
  🛏 1,2 cl., ⬛ 2 cl. and ⬜ Praha - Frankfurt/Main - (Dortmund).
W – 🛏 1,2 cl., ⬛ 2 cl., ⬜ and ⚏ Berlin - Frankfurt/Main and v.v.
Y – Not Dec. 25, Jan. 1.
b – Dresden Neustadt.
✓ – Supplement payable.

Table 31 — PARIS - INNSBRUCK

train type					IC		train type	IC				
train number	1169		469	365	517		train number	516	364	468		1168
classes	2		2	1,2	1,2		classes	1,2	1,2	2		2
notes (see below)	A		B		⚏		notes (see below)	⚏		B		D
Paris Est .... d.	... 2214	...	2240	...	...		Zell am See .... d.	... 1646	...	...	...	1852 ...
Mulhouse .... d.	... 0307	...	0504	...	...		Saalfelden .... d.	... 1656	...	...	...	1902 ...
Basel SBB ⑭ .... d.	... 0350	...	0549	...	...		St. Johann in Tirol .... d.	... 1726	...	...	...	1930 ...
Zürich Hbf .... d.		...	0700	0735	...		Kitzbühel .... d.	... 1735	...	...	...	1939 ...
Buchs ⑭ .... a.	... 0602	...	...	0845	...		Kirchberg in Tirol .... d.		...	...	...	1948 ...
Feldkirch .... a.	... 0644	...	...	0908	...		Innsbruck .... d.	... 1840	1844	...	...	2110 ...
Bludenz .... a.	... 0707	...	...	0925	...		Ötztal .... d.		1909	...	...	2141 ...
Langen am Arlberg .... a.	... 0741	...	...	0953	...		Landeck .... d.		1932	...	...	2214 ...
St. Anton am Arlberg .... a.	... 0807	...	...	1003	...		St. Anton am Arlberg .... d.		1959	...	...	2247 ...
Landeck .... a.	... 0836	...	...	1028	...		Langen am Arlberg .... d.		2008	...	...	2301 ...
Ötztal .... a.	... 0912	...	...	1051	...		Bludenz .... d.		2034	...	...	2333 ...
Innsbruck .... a.	... 0940	...	...	1116 1120		Feldkirch .... d.		2052	...	...	2349 ...
Kirchberg in Tirol .... a.	... 1046	...	...	1218		Buchs ⑭ .... d.		2115	...	...	0014 ...
Kitzbühel .... a.	... 1055	...	...	1227		Zürich Hbf .... d.		2226	2300	...	
St. Johann in Tirol .... a.	... 1103	...	...	1235		Basel SBB ⑭ .... a.			0006	...	0230 ...
Saalfelden .... a.	... 1131	...	...	1304		Mulhouse .... a.			0054	...	0313 ...
Zell am See .... a.	... 1142	...	...	1313		Paris Est .... a.			0648	...	0807 ...

NOTES

A – ARLBERG EXPRESS – ⑤ Feb. 3 - Mar. 24, also Dec. 16, 23, 30:
  🛏 1,2 cl. and ⬛ 2 cl. Paris - Zell am See.
B – 🛏 1,2 cl., ⬛ 2 cl. and ⬜ Paris - Zürich - (Chur) and v.v.

D – ARLBERG EXPRESS – ⑥ Feb. 4 - Mar. 25, also Dec. 17,24,31:
  🛏 1,2 cl. and ⬛ 2 cl. Zell am See - Paris.
✓ – Supplement payable.

For explanation of standard signs see page 4.

Table 32 — PARIS - MÜNCHEN AND WIEN

train type	EC	EC	IC		EC			EC		IC	IC	IC	IR
train number	65	65	890		67	269	269	69	263	590	511	503	261	2191
notes	B	C			D	E	H	F	A				G	
Paris Est .... d.	0751	0751			1345			1719	1943				2230	
Nancy .... d.	1031	1031			1632			2007	2227					
Strasbourg .... d.	1155	1155			1757			2144	2359					
Kehl .... a.	1205	1205			1805			2153	0009				0351	
Baden Baden .... a.	1231	1231			1831			2219					0402	
Karlsruhe .... a.	1251	1251			1851			2240	0056				0444	
Stuttgart .... a.	1346	1346			1946			2349	0157				0504	
Ulm .... a.	1454	1454			2055								0620	
Augsburg .... a.	1535	1535			2135								0726	
München Pasing .... a.	1559	1559			2159								0811	
München Hbf .... a.	1610	1610			2210	2319	2319						0850	0951
Salzburg .... a.	1753	1753	1908			0101	0101		0553	0708				1140
Bischofshofen ..... a.		1848	1950							0750	0801			
Schwarzach St. Veit a.			2004							0804				
Badgastein .... a.			2037							0835				
Villach Hbf .... a.			2151	2213						0943				
Klagenfurt .... a.			2249							1014				
Linz .... a.	1912					0231	0425		0725			0840		
Radstadt .... a.		1918									0822			
Stainach Irding ... a.		2006									0909			
Selzthal .... a.		2024									0928	1016		
Graz .... a.		2205									1120	1210		
Wien Westbahnhof .. a.	2105						0632		0925					
Hegyeshalom .... a.						0519			1103					
Györ .... a.						0621			1141					
Budapest Keleti ... a.						0808			1328					

train type	EC			EC	IC	EC	EC	EC		IC	IC	IC	
train number	68	268	248	66	791	64	116	62	260	602	612	691	262
notes	F	E	H	D		B	C	X	G				A
Budapest Keleti ... d.		2120						1225					1530
Györ .... d.		2259						1404					1714
Hegyeshalom .... d.		2347						1445					1755
Wien Westbahnhof .. d.			2330			0900		1600					1940
Graz .... d.							0757			1750		1840	
Selzthal .... d.							0937			1944		2031	
Stainach Irding ... d.							0955					2049	
Radstadt .... d.							1043					2137	
Linz .... d.		0213	0127			1046		1748					2134
Klagenfurt .... d.					0746						1946		
Villach Hbf .... d.					0819						2019		
Badgastein .... d.					0928						2129		
Schwarzach St. Veit d.					0957						2157		
Bischofshofen ..... d.					1011						2211		
Salzburg .... d.			0408	0408	1053	1209	1209	1905		2159	2248	2253	2307
München Hbf .... d.		0603	0603	0750		1350	1350	2036	2106				
München Pasing .... d.				0758		1358	1358						
Augsburg .... d.				0822		1422	1422		2142				
Ulm .... d.				0902		1505	1505		2229				
Stuttgart .... d.	0612			1015		1615	1615						0303
Karlsruhe .... d.	0704			1107		1707	1707		2335				0402
Baden Baden .... d.	0719			1125		1725	1725		0049				
Kehl .... d.	0745			1155		1757	1757		0143				0452
Strasbourg .... d.	0753			1204		1806	1806		0152				0501
Nancy .... a.	0928			1335		1934	1934						0643
Paris Est .... a.	1215			1622		2220	2220		0704				0933

NOTES

A – ORIENT EXPRESS – ▭1,2 cl., ▭2 cl. and ✕ Paris - Wien and v.v.; ▭ 2 cl. and ▭ Paris - Budapest and v.v.; ▭ and ✕ Salzburg - Budapest and v.v.; ▭ and ⚐ Bischofshofen - Graz and v.v.

B – MOZART – ▭ and ✕ Paris - Wien and v.v.

C – ▭ Paris - Graz and v.v.; ✕ Paris - Salzburg and v.v.; ⚐ Bischofshofen - Graz and v.v.

D – MAURICE RAVEL – ▭ and ✕ Paris - München and v.v.

E – KÁLMÁN IMRE – ▭ 1,2 cl., ▭ 2 cl. and ▭ München - Budapest and v.v.

F – MARIE CURIE – ▭ and ✕ Paris - Stuttgart and v.v.

G – ▭1,2 cl., ▭ 2 cl. and ⚐ Paris - München and v.v.

H – ▭ 2 cl. and ▭ München - Wien and v.v.

✗ – Supplement payable.

Table 33 — LONDON AND BRUSSELS - FRANKFURT/MAIN AND MÜNCHEN

For Eurostar connections between London and Brussels see Table 12.

train type		EC	IC		IC	IC	ICE		IC	EC	ICE		IC	IC	ICE		EC	IC	IC	ICE
train number	411	27	715	413	727	105	593	417	621	109	595	419	729	501	897	47	521	603	597
London Victoria 12 ... d.				2205															
Ramsgate Port 12 ...... d.				0045															
Oostende .... d.	0532			0530	0634			0834				0934							
Brussels Midi/Zuid .... d.	0647			0748				0947				1047				1203			
Brussels Nord/Noord ... d.	0657			0757				0957				1057				1212			
Liège Guillemins ...... d.	0800			0900				1100				1200							
Aachen .... a.	0843			0943				1143				1243				1313			
Köln .... a.	0942	0954	1030	1042	1054	1100		1242	1254	1300		1342	1354	1400		1442	1454	1500	
Bonn .... a.		1012	1048		1112	1118			1312	1318			1412	1418			1512	1518	
Koblenz .... a.		1045	1121		1145	1151			1345	1351			1445	1451			1545	1551	
Mainz .... a.		1136	1212		1236	1242			1436	1442			1536	1542			1636	1642	
Frankfurt/Main .... a.				1206			1306				1506				1606				1706
Würzburg .... a.				1343			1443				1643				1743				1843
Nürnberg .... a.				1425			1525				1725				1825				1925
Praha Hlavni 57 .... a.																			
Regensburg 740 .... a.				1542											1942				
Mannheim .... a.		1253			1323	1327			1523	1527			1623	1627			1723	1727	
Stuttgart .... a.		1351				1408				1608				1708				1808	
Ulm .... a.		1459				1503				1703				1803				1903	
Augsburg .... a.		1545								1745				1845				1944	
München Hbf .... a.		1615								1815				1915				2015	

NOTES

✗ – Supplement payable.

For service from May 28 see page 522

Table 33 LONDON AND BRUSSELS - FRANKFURT/MAIN AND MÜNCHEN

For Eurostar connections between London and Brussels see Table 12.

train type			IC	IC	ICE	IC			IC	IC	ICE		EC	IC				EC	IC				EN	
train number		425	523	503	599	517		429	527	507	695		39	827	223			49	738	353			225	225
classes		1,2	1,2⁄	1,2⁄	1,2⁄	1,2⁄	J	1,2	1,2⁄	1,2⁄	1,2⁄		1,2⁄	1,2⁄	2	⛴	J	1,2⁄	1,2⁄	1,2	⛴	J	2	2
notes (see below)			🍷	✕	✕	✕ W	C		🍷	✕	✕		✕	🍷	N	C	E	✕	✕	M	D	D	A	B
London Victoria 12 d.	...	...	...	...	...	...	0805	...	...	...	...	...	...	...	...	0805	1105	...	...	...	1105	1305	...	...
Ramsgate Port 🚢 **12** d.	...	...	...	...	...	...	1025	...	...	...	...	...	...	...	...	1030	1325	...	...	...	1345	1447	...	...
Oostende 🚢 d.	...	1234	...	...	...	...	1300	1434	...	...	...	...	...	...	...	1545	1600	1657	...	...	1830	1800	2013	2013
Brussels Midi d.	...	1347	...	...	...	...	...	1547	...	...	...	...	1655	...	...	...	...	1808	...	...	...	...	2126	2126
Brussels Nord d.	...	1357	...	...	...	...	...	1557	...	...	...	...	1703	...	...	...	...	1818	...	...	...	...	2134	2134
Liège Guillemins d.	...	1500	...	...	...	...	...	1700	...	...	...	...	1803	...	...	...	...	1917	...	...	...	...	2235	2235
Aachen 🚢 a.	...	1543	...	...	...	...	...	1743	...	...	...	...	1845	...	...	...	...	1955	...	...	...	...	2318	2318
Köln a.	...	1642	1654	1700	...	1730	...	1842	1854	1900	...	...	1942	1954	2037	...	...	2042	2054	2111	...	...	0017	0017
Bonn a.	...	...	1712	1718	...	1748	...	...	1912	1918	...	...	...	2012	2059	...	...	...	2112	2131	...	...	|	0109
Koblenz a.	...	...	1745	1751	...	1821	...	...	1945	1951	...	...	...	2045	2135	...	...	...	2145	2207	...	...	|	0144
Mainz a.	...	...	1836	1842	...	1912	...	...	2036	2042	...	...	...	2136	2228	...	...	...	2236	2302	...	...	|	|
Mannheim a.	...	...	|	1923	1927	1953	...	...	|	2123	2127	...	...	|	|	...	...	...	|	|	...	...	|	|
Frankfurt/Main a.	...	...	1906	...	|	|	...	...	2106	...	|	...	...	2208	2300	...	...	...	2308	2330	...	...	|	|
Würzburg a.	...	...	2043	...	|	|	...	...	2243	...	|	...	...	...	0054	...	...	...	...	0115	...	...	|	|
Nürnberg a.	...	...	2127	...	|	|	...	...	2327	...	|	...	...	...	0200	...	...	...	...	0222	...	...	0514	|
Praha Hlavni **57** a.	...	...	...	...	|	|	...	...	...	...	|	...	...	...	0839	...	...	...	...	0839	...	...	|	|
Regensburg **740** a.	...	...	...	...	|	|	...	...	...	...	|	...	...	...	...	...	...	...	...	...	...	...	0618	|
Heidelberg a.	...	...	...	...	|	2005	...	...	...	...	|	...	...	...	...	...	...	...	...	...	...	...	...	0335
Stuttgart a.	...	...	...	...	2008	2051	...	...	...	...	2208	...	...	...	...	...	...	...	...	...	...	...	...	0454
Ulm a.	...	...	...	...	2105	...	...	...	...	...	...	...	...	...	...	...	...	...	...	...	...	...	...	0603
Augsburg a.	...	...	...	...	2144	...	...	...	...	...	...	...	...	...	...	...	...	...	...	...	...	...	...	0652
München Pasing a.	...	...	...	...	|	...	...	...	...	...	...	...	...	...	...	...	...	...	...	...	...	...	...	|
München Hbf a.	...	...	...	...	2215	...	...	...	...	...	...	...	...	...	...	...	...	...	...	...	...	...	...	0736

train type		IC	EC			352	IC		IC	ICE	IC	IC			IC	ICE	IC	IC	EC	IC	ICE	IC	IC	
train number	352	739	48			222	526	420	516	898	604	822	422		616	598	502	524	38	718	896	500	522	426
classes	1,2	1,2⁄	1,2⁄	⛴	J	2	1,2⁄	1,2	1,2⁄	1,2⁄	1,2⁄	1,2⁄	1,2	J	1,2⁄	1,2⁄	1,2⁄	1,2⁄	1,2⁄	1,2⁄	1,2⁄	1,2⁄	1,2⁄	1,2
notes (see below)	P	✕	✕	D	D	Q	✕		Z	✕	🍷	✕		F	✕	✕	✕	✕	✕	✕	✕	✕	✕	
München Hbf d.	...	...	...	...	...	...	...	...	...	0646	...	...	...	...	0650	0746	...	...	...	...	0846	...	...	...
München Pasing d.	...	...	...	...	...	...	...	...	...	|	...	...	...	...	0656	|	...	...	...	...	|	...	...	...
Augsburg d.	...	...	...	...	...	...	...	...	...	0712	...	...	...	...	0720	0812	...	...	...	...	0912	...	...	...
Ulm d.	...	...	...	...	...	...	...	...	...	0754	...	...	...	...	0805	0854	...	...	...	...	0954	...	...	...
Stuttgart d.	...	...	...	...	...	...	...	...	0811	0853	...	...	...	...	0911	0953	...	...	...	1011	1053	...	...	...
Heidelberg d.	...	...	...	...	...	...	...	...	0854	|	...	...	...	...	0954	|	...	...	...	1054	|	...	...	...
Regensburg **740** d.	...	...	...	...	...	...	...	...	|	|	...	...	...	...	|	|	...	...	...	|	|	...	0828	...
Praha Hlavni **57** d.	2050	...	...	...	...	2050	...	...	|	|	...	...	...	...	|	|	...	...	...	|	|	...	|	...
Nürnberg d.	0304	...	...	...	...	0406	...	...	|	|	...	...	...	...	|	|	...	0832	...	|	|	...	0932	...
Würzburg d.	0414	...	...	...	...	0510	...	...	|	|	...	...	...	...	|	|	...	0930	...	|	|	...	1015	...
Frankfurt/Main d.	0544	0651	...	...	...	0658	0851	...	|	|	...	0951	...	...	|	|	...	1051	...	|	|	...	1151	...
Mannheim d.	|	|	...	...	...	|	|	...	0907	0932	0937	|	...	...	1007	1032	1037	|	...	1107	1132	1137	|	...
Mainz d.	0610	0724	...	...	...	0728	0924	...	0948	...	1018	1024	...	...	1048	...	1118	1124	...	1148	...	1218	1224	...
Koblenz d.	0705	0813	...	...	...	0823	1013	...	1037	...	1107	1113	...	...	1137	...	1207	1213	...	1237	...	1307	1313	...
Bonn d.	0739	0845	...	...	...	0859	1045	...	1109	...	1139	1145	...	...	1209	...	1239	1245	...	1309	...	1339	1345	...
Köln d.	0801	0905	0914	...	...	0921	1105	1114	1129	...	1159	1205	1214	...	1229	...	1259	1305	1314	1329	...	1359	1405	1414
Aachen 🚢 d.	...	...	1001	...	...	...	...	1205	...	...	...	...	1305	...	...	...	...	...	1410	...	...	...	...	1505
Liège Guillemins a.	...	...	1036	...	...	...	...	1243	...	...	...	...	1343	...	...	...	...	...	1449	...	...	...	...	1543
Brussels Nord a.	...	...	1132	...	...	...	...	1344	...	...	...	...	1444	...	...	...	...	...	1548	...	...	...	...	1644
Brussels Midi a.	...	...	1142	...	...	...	...	1355	...	...	...	...	1455	...	...	...	...	...	1556	...	...	...	...	1655
Oostende 🚢 a.	...	...	1248	1350	1355	...	...	1509	...	...	...	...	1609	1655	...	...	...	...	...	...	...	...	...	1809
Ramsgate Port 🚢**12** a.	...	...	...	1650	1430	...	...	...	...	...	...	...	...	1730	...	...	...	...	...	...	...	...	...	...
London Victoria 12 a.	...	...	...	1917	1723	...	...	...	...	...	...	...	...	2019	...	...	...	...	...	...	...	...	...	...

train type	IC	ICE	IC	IC	EC	EC	ICE	EC	IC		EC	ICE	EC	EC		IC	ICE	EC	EC		EN			
train number	614	596	602	620	46	18	896	102	728	430	112	894	104	28	434	714	792	8	26	438	224	214		
classes	1,2⁄	1,2⁄	1,2⁄	1,2⁄	1,2⁄	1,2⁄	1,2⁄	1,2⁄	1,2⁄	1,2	1,2⁄	1,2⁄	1,2⁄	1,2⁄	1,2	1,2⁄	1,2⁄	1,2⁄	1,2⁄	1,2	2	2	⛴	J
notes (see below)	✕	✕	✕	✕	✕	✕	✕	✕	✕		✕	✕	✕	✕		✕	✕	✕	✕		A	B	G	E
München Hbf d.	0850	0946	...	...	...	0950	1046	...	...	...	1150	1246	...	...	...	...	1446	...	...	...	...	2211	...	...
München Pasing d.	0856	|	...	...	...	0956	|	...	...	...	1156	|	...	...	...	...	|	...	...	...	...	|	...	...
Augsburg d.	0920	1012	...	...	...	1020	1112	...	...	...	1220	1312	...	...	...	...	1512	...	...	...	...	2246	...	...
Ulm d.	1005	1054	...	...	...	1105	1154	...	...	...	1305	1354	...	...	...	1500	1554	...	...	...	...	2334	...	...
Stuttgart d.	1111	1153	...	...	...	1211	1253	...	...	...	1411	1453	...	...	...	1611	1653	...	...	...	...	0041	...	...
Heidelberg d.	1154	|	...	...	...	1254	|	...	...	...	1454	|	...	...	...	1654	|	...	...	...	...	0157	...	...
Regensburg **740** d.	|	|	...	...	...	|	|	...	1028	...	|	|	...	1228	...	|	|	...	1428	...	2320	|	...	...
Praha Hlavni **57** d.	|	|	...	...	...	|	|	...	|	...	|	|	...	|	...	|	|	...	|	...	|	|	...	...
Nürnberg d.	|	|	...	1032	...	|	|	...	1132	...	|	|	...	1332	...	|	|	...	1532	...	0024	|	...	...
Würzburg d.	|	|	...	1130	...	|	|	...	1215	...	|	|	...	1415	...	|	|	...	1615	...	|	|	...	...
Frankfurt/Main d.	|	|	...	1251	...	|	|	...	1351	...	|	|	...	1551	...	|	|	...	1751	...	|	|	...	...
Mannheim d.	1207	1232	1237	|	...	1307	1332	1337	|	...	1507	1532	1537	|	...	1707	1732	1737	|	...	|	|	...	...
Mainz d.	1248	...	1318	1324	...	1348	...	1418	1424	...	1548	...	1618	1624	...	1748	...	1818	1824	...	|	|	...	...
Koblenz d.	1337	...	1407	1413	...	1437	...	1507	1513	...	1637	...	1707	1713	...	1837	...	1907	1913	...	|	0350	...	...
Bonn d.	1409	...	1439	1445	...	1509	...	1539	1545	...	1709	...	1739	1745	...	1909	...	1939	1945	...	|	0425	...	...
Köln d.	1429	...	1459	1505	1514	1529	...	1559	1605	1614	1729	...	1759	1805	1814	1929	...	1959	2005	2014	0508	0508	...	...
Aachen 🚢 d.	...	...	...	...	1607	...	...	...	...	1705	...	...	...	...	1905	...	...	...	...	2105	0606	0606	...	...
Liège Guillemins a.	...	...	...	...	1648	...	...	...	...	1743	...	...	...	...	1943	...	...	...	...	2143	0647	0647	...	...
Brussels Nord a.	...	...	...	...	1749	...	...	...	...	1844	...	...	...	...	2044	...	...	...	...	2244	0755	0755	...	...
Brussels Midi a.	...	...	...	...	1801	...	...	...	...	1855	...	...	...	...	2055	...	...	...	...	2255	0804	0804	...	...
Oostende 🚢 a.	...	...	...	...	...	...	...	...	...	2009	...	...	...	...	2209	...	...	...	...	0009	0918	0918	0945	1150
Ramsgate Port 🚢 **12** a.	...	...	...	...	...	...	...	...	...	...	...	...	...	...	...	...	...	...	...	...	...	...	1245	1225
London Victoria 12 a.	...	...	...	...	...	...	...	...	...	...	...	...	...	...	...	...	...	...	...	...	...	...	1517	1517

NOTES

A – 🛏 1,2 cl., ━ 2 cl. and (2) Oostende - Regensburg - (Wien) and v.v.

B – 🛏 1,2 cl., ━ 2 cl. and (2) Oostende - München and v.v.

C – Not Dec. 25,26.

D – Not Dec. 25.

E – Sept. 25 - Jan. 2 and Mar. 26 - May 27 (not Dec. 25).

F – Mar. 26 - May 27.

G – Oct. 23 - May 27, not Dec. 25.

J – Jetfoil service, see Table **12**.

M – Dec. 16 - Jan. 8 and Mar. 31 - May 27:
🛏 1,2 cl., ━ 2 cl., (12) and 🍷 Köln - Praha.

N – Nov. 1 - Dec. 15 and Jan. 9 - Mar. 30:
🛏 1,2 cl., ━ 2 cl. and (2) (Dortmund) - Köln - Praha.

P – Dec. 15 - Jan. 7 and Mar. 30 - May 27:
🛏 1,2 cl., ━ 2 cl., (12) and 🍷 Praha - Köln.

Q – Oct. 31 - Dec. 14 and Jan. 8 - Mar. 29:
🛏 1,2 cl., ━ 2 cl. and (2) Praha - Köln - Dortmund.

W – ①②③④⑤⑦, not Oct.2, Dec. 24-31, Apr. 14,15,16,30.

Z – ①②③④⑤⑥, not Oct. 3, Dec. 25-Jan. 1, Apr. 15,16,17, May 1.

⛴ – Ship service, see Table 12.

⁄ – Supplement payable.

For explanation of standard symbols see page 4

Table 34 — LONDON AND BRUSSELS - WIEN AND INNSBRUCK

For Eurostar connections between London and Brussels see Table 12.

train number	299	1219	1117	1117		EN225	499	365
classes	K	1,2	2	2	2	2	2	1,2
notes (see below)	(F)		(B)	(D)		J	A	H
sea crossing								
London Victoria 12 ..... d.	...	0805	...	...		1105	1305	...
Ramsgate Port ..... d.	...	1030	...	...		1345	1525	...
Oostende ..... d.	...	1545	1807	...	1830	1800	2013	2053
Brussels Midi ..... d.	1913	...	1923	2008	2008	...	2125	2218
Brussels Nord ..... d.	1921	...	1932	2018	2018	...	2134	2226
Liège Guillemins ..... a.		...	2034	2121	2121	...	2235	...
Aachen ..... a.		...	2118			...	2318	...
Köln Hbf ..... a.		...	2227			...	0017	...
Namur ..... d.	2008	...				...	2316	...
Luxembourg ..... d.	2201	...				...	0118	...
Metz ..... d.	2252	...				...	0215	...
Strasbourg ..... d.	0018	...				...	0353	...
Basel ..... d.	0350	...				...	0516	...
Sargans ..... d.		...				...	0819	0835
Buchs ..... a.	0602	...				...		0852
Feldkirch ..... a.	0644	...				...		0908
Bludenz ..... a.	0707	...				...		0925
Langen am A. ..... a.	0737	...				...		0953
St. Anton am A. ..... a.	0752	...				...		1001
Landeck ..... a.	0836	...				...		1028
Ötztal ..... a.	0909	...				...		1051
Kufstein ..... a.		...	0657	0657		...		
Wörgl ..... a.		...	0723	0723		...		
Innsbruck ..... a.	0940	...	0803	...		...		1116
Lienz ..... a.		...		0753		...		
Kirchberg in Tirol ..... a.		...				...		
Kitzbühel ..... a.		...		0802		...		
St. Johann in Tirol ..... a.		...		0813		...		
Saalfelden ..... a.		...		0845		...		
Zell am See ..... a.		...		0856		...	IC505	
Passau ..... a.		...				0730	EC63 1,2	
Linz ..... a.		...				0900	X 1040	
Wien Westbahnhof ..... a.	IC513	...				1058	1320	
Budapest Keleti ..... a.	1,2	...				1643		
Salzburg ..... a.	Y 0733	...						
Bischofshofen ..... a.	1001	0840						
Graz ..... a.	1320	...						1414
Schwarzach St. Veit ..... a.		0859		0930				
Badgastein ..... a.		0938						
Villach Hbf ..... a.		1054						
Klagenfurt ..... a.		...						

train number	EC62	600	EN224		1616	IC610	1214		1168
classes	1,2	1,2	2	1,2	1,2	2	1,2		1,2
notes (see below)	X	Y	A	P	J N	C	G		L
sea crossing									
Klagenfurt ..... d.									
Villach Hbf ..... d.							1849		
Badgastein ..... d.							2002		
Schwarzach St. Veit ..... d.							2030		
Graz ..... d.		1550			1958	1640			
Bischofshofen ..... d.						1959	2047		
Salzburg ..... d.							2143		
Budapest Keleti ..... d.	1225								
Wien Westbahnhof ..... d.	1550		1844						
Linz ..... d.		1920	2039						
Passau ..... d.			2211						
Zell am See ..... d.					2035				
Saalfelden ..... d.					2046				
St. Johann in Tirol ..... d.	EC				2116	1116			
Kitzbühel ..... d.	168				2127	2			
Kirchberg in Tirol ..... d.	1,2				2137	E			
Lienz ..... d.	X								
Innsbruck ..... d.	1653					2134			2110
Wörgl ..... a.					2220	2220			
Kufstein ..... a.					2241	2241			
Ötztal ..... d.	1717								2141
Landeck ..... a.	1740								2214
St. Anton am A. ..... a.	1807								2247
Langen am Arlberg ..... a.	1817								2301
Bludenz ..... a.	1843	1794							2333
Feldkirch ..... a.	1901								2349
Buchs ..... a.	1917	H							0014
Sargans ..... d.	1934	2039							
Basel ..... a.	2359								
Strasbourg ..... a.	0125								0420
Metz ..... a.	0302								0550
Luxembourg ..... a.	0357								0647
Namur ..... a.	0552								0836
Köln Hbf ..... a.		0450					0622		
Aachen ..... a.		0555					0732		
Liège Guillemins ..... a.		0647			0813	0813			
Brussels Nord ..... a.	0640	0755			0917	0917	0923		0921
Brussels Midi ..... a.	0649	0804			0927	0927	0933		0930
Oostende ..... a.	0802	0918	0945	1150			1045	1350	
Ramsgate Port ..... a.			1245	1225				1650	
London Victoria 12 ..... a.	1517	1517					1917		

NOTES

A – DONAUWALZER – [symbol]1,2 cl., [symbol]2 cl. and [symbol]Oostende - Wien and v.v.
B – ⑤ Jan. 6 - Apr. 7: [symbol]1,2 cl., [symbol]2 cl. and [symbol]Brussels-Schwarzach St. Veit.
C – ⑥ Jan. 7 - Apr. 15: [symbol]1,2 cl., [symbol]2 cl. and [symbol]Schwarzach St Veit-Brussels.
D – ⑤ Jan. 6 - Apr. 7: [symbol]1,2 cl., [symbol]2 cl. and [symbol]Brussels - San Candido.
E – ⑥ Jan. 7 - Apr. 15: [symbol]1,2 cl., [symbol]2 cl. and [symbol]San Candido - Brussels.
F – ⑤ Jan. 6 - Mar. 24, also Dec. 23: [symbol]2 cl. and [symbol]Oostende - Villach.
G – ⑥ Jan. 7 - Mar. 25, also Jan. 1: [symbol]2 cl. and [symbol]Villach - Oostende.
H – [symbol]2 cl. Oostende - Chur and v.v. (also [symbol]1,2 cl. Dec. 8 - Apr. 16).
J – Jetfoil service, see Table 12.
K – ⑤ Dec. 16 - 30 and Feb. 3 - Mar. 24: [symbol]2 cl. Brussels - Innsbruck.
L – ⑥ Dec. 17 - 31 and Feb. 4 - Mar. 25: [symbol]2 cl. Innsbruck - Brussels.
N – Sept. 27 - Jan. 2 and Mar. 26 - May 27, not Dec. 25.
P – Oct. 23 - May 27, not Dec. 25.
[ship symbol] – Ship service, see Table 12.

Table 35 — AMSTERDAM - WIEN AND INNSBRUCK

train number	1215	IC513	EN215	EC63	IC505	EN215	D489	IC545
classes	2	1,2	2	1,2	1,2	2	1,2	1,2
notes (see below)	D	Y	B	X	X	C		X
Amsterdam Centraal ..... d.	1939	...	2056			2056		
Utrecht ..... d.	2028	...	2130			2130		
Arnhem ..... d.	2105	...	2214			2214		
Emmerich ..... d.	2134	...	2250			2250		
Friedrichshafen Stadt ..... a.								
Lindau ..... a.								
Bregenz ..... a.								
Feldkirch ..... a.								
Bludenz ..... a.								
Langen ..... a.								
St. Anton ..... a.								
Landeck ..... a.								
Ötztal ..... a.								
München Hbf ..... d.						0736	0820	
Kufstein ..... a.							0920	
Wörgl ..... a.							0943	1057
Innsbruck ..... a.							1020	
Kirchberg in Tirol ..... a.								1120
Kitzbühel ..... a.								1129
St. Johann in Tirol ..... a.								1137
Saalfelden ..... a.								1207
Zell am See ..... a.								1218
Salzburg ..... a.		0733						
Bischofshofen ..... a.		0840	1001					
Schwarzach St. Veit ..... a.		0859						
Badgastein ..... a.		0938						
Villach Hbf ..... a.		1054						
Klagenfurt ..... a.		...						
Passau ..... a.		...		0730				
Linz ..... a.		...		0900	1040			
Graz ..... a.		1320			1414			
Wien Westbahnhof ..... a.		...		1058	1320			
Budapest Keleti ..... a.		...			1643			

train number	IC600	EC62	EN224	546	488	EN214	IC610	1214
classes	1,2	1,2	2	2	1,2	2	1,2	1,2
notes (see below)	Y	X	B	X		C	Y	G
Budapest Keleti ..... d.		1225						
Wien Westbahnhof ..... d.		1550	1844					
Graz ..... d.	1550						1640	
Linz ..... d.	1920		2039					
Passau ..... d.			2211					
Klagenfurt ..... d.								
Villach Hbf ..... d.								1849
Badgastein ..... d.								2002
Schwarzach St. Veit ..... d.								2030
Bischofshofen ..... d.							1959	2047
Salzburg ..... d.								2143
Zell am See ..... d.				1741				
Saalfelden ..... d.				1751				
St. Johann ..... d.				1821				
Kitzbühel ..... d.				1831				
Kirchberg ..... d.				1840				
Innsbruck ..... d.					1837			
Wörgl a.				1903	1916			
Kufstein ..... a.					1928			
München Hbf ..... a.				2030	2210			
Ötztal ..... a.								
Landeck ..... a.								
St. Anton ..... a.								
Langen ..... a.								
Bludenz ..... a.								
Feldkirch ..... a.								
Bregenz ..... a.								
Lindau ..... a.								
Friedrichshafen Stadt ..... a.								
Emmerich ..... a.		0704			0704			0806
Arnhem ..... a.		0741			0741			0845
Utrecht ..... a.		0823			0823			0935
Amsterdam Centraal ..... a.		0857			0857			1011

NOTES

B – DONAUWALZER – [symbol]1,2 cl., [symbol]2 cl. and [symbol]Amsterdam - Wien and v.v.
C – [symbol]1,2 cl., [symbol]2 cl. and [symbol]Amsterdam - München and v.v..
D – ⑤ Jan. 6 - Mar. 24, also Dec. 23: [symbol]1,2 cl., [symbol]2 cl. and [symbol]Amsterdam - Villach.
G – ⑥ Jan. 7 - Mar. 25, also Jan. 1: [symbol]1,2 cl., [symbol]2 cl. and [symbol]Villach - Amsterdam.

Table 38 — AMSTERDAM - STRASBOURG, ZÜRICH AND INTERLAKEN

	EC105	1685	IC337	983	EC3			IC839	IC257	1736	203	1663	1706	203		
classes	1,2∕	1,2	1,2	1,2	1,2∕	1,2	1,2	1,2	1,2	1,2	1,2	1,2	1,2	1,2	1,2	1,2
notes	B	⚓	⚓	⚓	A			✗	⚓		E	⚓	⚓	F		
Amsterdam Centraal ...d.	0800				0900						2005			2005		
Utrecht ...d.	0830				0930						2047			2047		
Arnhem ...d.	0905				1005						2127			2127		
Emmerich ...d.	0934				1034						2157			2157		
Basel SBB ...a.	1543	1551		1625	1643			1701	1720			0626	0651	0815		
Zürich Hbf ...a.				1723	1803									0937		
Sargans ...a.					1913										0951	1040
Landquart ...a.					1925	1935										1146
Davos Platz ...a.						2050									1004	
Chur ...a.					1937	1952										1052
St. Moritz ...a.						2158										1258
Olten ...a.		1627	1621					1727	1747			0727	0721			
Luzern ...a.		1704						1827				0804				
Arth Goldau ...a.		1740						1858				0840				
Bellinzona ...a.		1951						2047				1051				
Lugano ...a.		2021						2117								
Chiasso ...a.		2056						2142								
Bern ...a.	1712		1722						1812	1828			0812			0828
Thun ...a.	1748		1741						1841	1848			0841			0848
Spiez ...a.	1759		1752						1852	1859			0852			0859
Interlaken West ...a.	1816								1916				0916			
Interlaken Ost ...a.	1821								1921				0921			
Brig ...a.			1859							1959						0959

			EC96	250	1821	EC104		1723	IC820	1670	EC2			472	IC890	IC254	844
classes	1,2	1,2	1,2	1,2	1,2	1,2∕	1,2	1,2∕	1,2	1,2	1,2∕	1,2	1,2	H	1,2∕	1,2	498
notes			✗		⚓	B		⚓	✗		A			H	✗	⚓	G
Brig ...d.						1001				1101							1949
Interlaken Ost ...d.						1039				1139				1939	1944		2055
Interlaken West ...d.						1044				1144					2001		2055
Spiez ...d.					1107	1101		1201	1207						2012		2106
Thun ...d.					1118	1112		1212	1218						2032		2148
Bern ...d.					1138	1148		1232	1248							1830	
Chiasso ...d.			0827							0906						1857	
Lugano ...d.			0854							0941						1927	
Bellinzona ...d.			0923							1009						2114	
Arth Goldau ...d.			1120							1256						2146	
Luzern ...d.			1156													2227	2232
Olten ...d.			1239			1232				1332	1339						
St. Moritz ...d.		0805									1107	1115		1800	2007	2028	
Chur ...d.		1007	1023							1005						2040	
Davos Platz ...d.	0905		1034							1117				1905	2017		
Landquart ...d.	1017		1045							1139					2055		
Sargans ...d.			1200							1257					2215		
Zürich Hbf ...d.			1306	1309		1317		1359	1409		1417				2253	2325	
Basel SBB ...d.														v	0740		0740
Emmerich ...a.				1924					2024						0825		0825
Arnhem ...a.				1952					2052						0906		0906
Utrecht ...a.				2023					2123						0906		0906
Amsterdam Centraal ...a.				2051					2151						0940		0940

Table 39 — AMSTERDAM - MILANO AND ROMA

	EC151	201	IC533	2093	2183
classes	1,2∕	2	1,2∕	1,2	1,2
notes	✗	C	✗		
Amsterdam Centraal ...d.	1700				
Utrecht ...d.	1729				
Arnhem ...d.	1805				
Emmerich ...d.	1832				
Duisburg ...d.	1906	2019			
Basel SBB ...d.		v			
Chiasso ...a.		0637			
Como ...a.		0700			
Milano Centrale ...a.		0745	0800	0810	0815
Brennero ...a.					
Fortezza ...a.					
Bolzano ...a.					
Verona ...a.					0951
Venezia Santa Lucia ...a.					1125
Genova P. Principe ...a.			1005		
Ventimiglia ...a.			1250		
Bologna ...a.				0944	
Firenze SMN ...a.				1053	
Roma Termini ...a.				1255	
Napoli Centrale ...a.				1500	
Ravenna ...a.					
Rimini ...a.					

	IC688	IC658	IC544	200	EC142
classes	1,2∕	1,2∕	1,2∕	2	1,2∕
notes	⚓	⚓	✗	C	✗
Rimini ...d.					
Ravenna ...d.					
Napoli Centrale ...d.					
Roma Termini ...d.			1605		
Firenze SMN ...d.			1807		
Bologna ...d.			1916		
Ventimiglia ...d.					
Genova P. Principe ...d.	1913				
Venezia Mestre ...d.		1817			
Verona ...d.		1934			
Bolzano ...d.					
Fortezza ...d.					
Brennero ...d.					
Milano Centrale ...d.	2050	2055	2100		2125
Como ...d.				2205	
Chiasso ...d.				2230	
Basel SBB ...a.					v
Duisburg ...a.				0908	0952
Emmerich ...a.					1026
Arnhem ...a.					1052
Utrecht ...a.					1123
Amsterdam Centraal ...a.					1151

NOTES for Tables 38 and 39.

A – REMBRANDT – 🛏 and ✗ Amsterdam - Chur and v.v.

B – BERNER OBERLAND – 🛏 and ✗ Amsterdam - Interlaken and v.v.

C – 🛋 1,2 cl., ⊸ 2 cl. and 🛏 (Dortmund) - Duisburg - Milano and v.v.

E – SCHWEIZ EXPRESS – 🛋 1,2 cl., ⊸ 2 cl. and 🛏 Amsterdam - Basel; conveys ⑤ Dec. 23 - Mar. 24: 🛋 1,2 cl. and ⊸ 2 cl. Amsterdam - Brig.

F – SCHWEIZ EXPRESS – 🛏 and ⚓ Amsterdam - Basel; 🛋 1,2 cl. and ⊸ 2 cl. Amsterdam - Zürich; ⑤ to Oct. 21 and daily Dec. 16 - Apr. 21: 🛋 1,2 cl. and ⊸ 2 cl. Amsterdam - Chur.

G – SCHWEIZ EXPRESS – 🛋 1,2 cl., ⊸ 2 cl. and 🛏 Basel - Amsterdam; conveys ⑥ Jan. 7 - Mar. 25, also Dec. 26, Jan. 1: 🛋 1,2 cl. and ⊸ 2 cl. Brig - Amsterdam.

H – SCHWEIZ EXPRESS – 🛏 and ⚓ Basel - Amsterdam; 🛋 1,2 cl. and ⊸ 2 cl. Zürich - Amsterdam; ⑥ to Oct. 22 and daily Dec. 17 - Apr. 22: 🛋 1,2 cl. and ⊸ 2 cl. Chur - Amsterdam.

v – Via Basel Bad.

∕ – Supplement payable.

Table 40 — LONDON AND BRUSSELS - BASEL, ZÜRICH AND INTERLAKEN

train type		EC			EC		EC					EC					EC					
train number	2125	91	1728	1679	103		97	1789		2691	893	2443	295	115	299	⛴	J	499	1661	2405	499		499
notes (see page 4)			🍴	🍴	✕			🍴						✕					🍴				
notes (see below)		G ✐					H ✐						K		D			A			B		C
London Victoria 12 . d.	...	...	...	...	...		...	...		...	...	...	...	...	1105	1305		...	...	...	...		...
Ramsgate Port 12 ..... d.	...	...	...	...	...		...	...		...	...	...	...	...	1345	1525		...	...	...	...		...
Oostende 🚢 .... d.	...	...	...	...	...		...	...		...	...	...	...	...	1830	1800	2053	...	...	2053		2053
Brussels Midi/Zuid .... d.	...	0715	...	...	...		1219	...		...	...	1513	1913				2217			2217		2217
Brussels Nord/Noord d.	...	0723	...	...	...		1227	...		...	...	1521	1921				2226			2226		2226
Brussels QL .... d.	...	0733	...	...	...		1238	...		...	...	1531	1931				2238			2238		2238
Namur .... d.	...	0808	...	...	...		1312	...		...	...	1608	2008				2316			2316		2316
Luxembourg 🚆 .... d.	...	1001	...	...	...		1459	...		...	...	1802	2201				0118			0118		0118
Lille Flandres .... d.	0650		...	...	...			...		...	...											
Metz .... d.	1038	1046	...	...	...		1544	...		...	...	1847	2252				0215			0215		0215
Strasbourg .... d.	...	1211	...	...	...		1708	...		...	...	2008	0018				0353			0353		0353
Mulhouse .... d.	...	1315	...	...	...		1803	...		...	...	2106	0117				0453			0453		0453
Basel SBB .... a.	...	1339	1351	1354	...		1825	...		1851	1901	2130	2148	0140			0516			0516		0516
Zürich Hbf .... a.	...		...	1500	...		1945	2010		...	...		2247					0600				
Sargans .... a.	...		...	1613	...			2119		...	...											
Landquart .... a.	...		...	1625	...	1640		2135	2145	...	...								0819			
Davos Platz .... a.	...		...		...	1746			2259	...	...							0833	0852			
Chur .... a.	...		1637	1652	...			2149		...	...								1002			
St. Moritz .... a.	...		...	1858	...					...	...							0845		0900		
Olten .... a.	...	1427	...	1421	...					1921	1927						0621	0630			1118	
Luzern .... a.	...		...	1504	...					2004								0712				
Arth Goldau .... a.	...		...	1540	...					...	...							0744				
Bellinzona .... a.	...		...	1751	...					...	...							0951				
Lugano .... a.	...		...	1821	...					...	...		0505					1021				
Chiasso .... a.	...		...	1856	...					...	...		0535					1056				
Bern .... a.	...	1512	1528	...	...					...	...	2012	2028	0602								
Thun .... a.	...	1541	1548	...	...					...	...		2048				0712	0728				
Spiez .... a.	...	1552	1559	...	...					...	...	2059					0741	0748				
Interlaken West .... a.	...		1616	...	...					...	...	2119					0752	0759				
Interlaken Ost ...... a.	...		1621	...	...					...	...	2123						0816				
Biel .... a.	...		...	...	...					...	...							0821				
Neuchâtel .... a.	...		...	...	...					...	...										0730	
Lausanne .... a.	...		...	...	...					...	...										0759	
Vevey .... a.	...		...	...	...					...	...										0848	
Montreux .... a.	...		...	...	...					...	...										0914	
Aigle .... a.	...		...	...	...					...	...										0919	
Bex .... a.	...		...	...	...					...	...										0931	
Martigny .... a.	...		...	...	...					...	...										0937	
Sion .... a.	...		...	...	...					...	...										0952	
Sierre .... a.	...		...	...	...					...	...										1008	
Visp .... a.	...		...	...	...					...	...										1020	
Brig .... a.	...	1659	...	...	...					...	...							0859			1046	
																					1053	

train type	IC		IC	EC			EC						EC	IC					
train number	952	296	1821	104	250		96	2146	1676		1780	1727	90	254	498		1794	1647	J	🚆	298
notes (see page 4)	🍴		🍴	✕	🍴			🍴			✕									
notes (see below)		K					L ✐						G ✐		A		M	E		D
Brig .... d.	...	...	1001	...	...		...	...	...		...	...	1301		2001		...	1907		
Visp .... d.	...	...		...	...		...	...	...		...	...					...	1913		
Sierre .... d.	...	...		...	...		...	...	...		...	...					...	1940		
Sion .... d.	...	...		...	...		...	...	...		...	...					...	1952		
Martigny .... d.	...	...		...	...		...	...	...		...	...					...	2008		
Bex .... d.	...	...		...	...		...	...	...		...	...					...	2023		
Aigle .... d.	...	...		...	...		...	...	...		...	...					...	2030		
Montreux .... d.	...	...		...	...		...	...	...		...	...					...	2043		
Vevey .... d.	...	...		...	...		...	...	...		...	...					...	2049		
Lausanne .... d.	...	...		...	...		...	...	...		...	...					...	2121		
Neuchâtel .... d.	...	...		...	...		...	...	...		...	...					...	2209		
Biel .... d.	...	...		...	...		...	...	...		...	...					...	2230		
Interlaken Ost ...... d.	...	...		1039	...		...	...	...		1339			2040			...			
Interlaken West .... d.	...	...		1044	...		...	...	...		1344			2044			...			
Spiez .... d.	...	...	1107	1101	...		...	...	...		1401	1408		2102	2107		...			
Thun .... d.	...	...	1118	1112	...		...	...	...		1412	1418			2118		...			
Bern .... d.	...	...	1138	1148	...		...	...	...		1432	1448			2148		...			
Chiasso .... d.	...	...		0827	...		1106	...	...		...	...	1830				...			2240
Lugano .... d.	...	...		0854	...		1141	...	...		...	...	1857				...			2307
Bellinzona .... d.	...	...		0923	...		1209	...	...		...	...	1927				...			2335
Arth Goldau .... d.	...	...		1120	...		1420	...	...		...	...	2114				...			
Luzern .... d.	...	...		1156	...		1456	...	...		...	...	2146				...			
Olten .... d.	...	...	1230	1239	...		1539	...	...		1532	2225			2232		...			
St. Moritz .... d.	...	...			0805				1100							1800	...			
Chur .... d.	...	...			1007			1023	1307	1315						2007	2013			
Davos Platz .... d.	...	...			0905			1034	1205	1326							1905			
Landquart .... d.	...	...			1017			1045	1317	1339							2017	2024		
Sargans .... d.	...	...			1200			1200		1500							2039			
Zürich Hbf .... d.	0635	...															2200			
Basel SBB 🚆 .... d.	0735	0814	1259	1309			1330	1609		1611	1626	2253		2359			2359	2359		0300
Mulhouse .... d.	0840						1353				1650			0026			0026	0026		0324
Strasbourg .... d.	0943						1444	1716			1748			0125			0125	0125		0423
Metz .... d.	1117						1605	1844			1913			0302			0302	0302		0553
Lille Flandres .... a.								2235												
Luxembourg 🚆 ...... a.	1200						1649				1956			0357			0357	0357		0647
Namur .... a.	1343						1837				2143			0552			0552	0552		0836
Brussels QL .... a.	1417						1910				2218			0630			0630	0630		0911
Brussels Nord .... a.	1427						1920				2228			0640			0640	0640		0921
Brussels Midi .... a.	1435						1928				2237			0649			0649	0649		0930
Oostende 🚆 .... a.	...	...					...	...	...		...	...		0802			...			
Ramsgate Port 12 🚆 a.	...	...					...	...	...		...	...		0802	0802	0825	0945		
London Victoria 12 . a.	...	...					...	...	...		...	...				0900	1245		...
																	1117	1517		...

NOTES

A – 🚢 1,2 cl. and 🚢 2 cl. Oostende - Brig and v.v.
B – 🚆 2 cl. Oostende - Chur
(also 🚢 1,2 cl. Dec. 8 - Apr. 16);
🚆 Oostende - Basel; 🚆 Basel - Chur.
C – ⑤ Dec. 23 - Apr. 7: 🚢 1,2 cl. Oostende - Brig;
⑥ Dec. 17 - Apr. 15: 🚆 2 cl. Oostende - Brig.

D – 🚢 1,2 cl., 🚢 1,2 cl. (T2), and 🚢 2 cl. Brussels - Chiasso - (Milano) and v.v.
E – ⑥ Dec. 31 - Apr. 15: 🚢 1,2 cl. Brig - Oostende;
⑦ Dec. 18 - Apr. 16: 🚆 2 cl. Brig - Oostende.
G – VAUBAN -
🚆 and ✕ Brussels - Chiasso - (Milano) and v.v.
H – IRIS - 🚆 and ✕ Brussels - Zürich.

J – Jetfoil service, see Table 12.
K – EDELWEISS - 🚆 and ✕ Brussels - Basel and v.v.
L – IRIS - 🚆 and ✕ Chur - Brussels.
M – 🚆 2 cl. Chur - Oostende
(also 🚢 1,2 cl. Dec. 7 - Apr. 15);
🚆 Basel - Oostende; 🚆 Chur - Basel.
✐ – Supplement payable.

Table 41 — PARIS - ZÜRICH AND LUZERN

train type	EC		EC	IC				IC	EC								EC					
train number	113	2677	57	769			1743	977	9	1745	1783	2687	1847	1747	1789	2691	115	2697		469		1661
classes	1,2✗	1,2	1,2✗	1,2	1,2	1,2	1,2	1,2	1,2	1,2	1,2	1,2	⑥	Ⓐ	Ⓟ	1,2	1,2✗	1,2		2	1,2	1,2
notes (see below)	A		✕	✕				Ⓖ	Ⓟ	Ⓟ	Ⓟ	Ⓟ			Ⓟ		B			C		
Paris Est .... d.	0730	...	...	...	...	...	0842b	...	1152	...	...	...	1330	1341	...	...	1700	...	...	2240	...	...
Belfort .... d.	1114	...	...	...	...	...	1309	...	1544	...	...	...	1733	1734	...	...	2045	...	...	0413	...	...
Mulhouse .... d.	1145	...	...	...	...	...	1342	...	1612	...	...	...	1811	1811	...	...	2117	...	...	0504	...	...
Basel SBB/SNCF ▥ .. a.	1211	1251	...	...	...	...	1408	1425	1507	1637	1649	1651	1836	1836	1849	1851	2140	2202	...	0530	...	0600
Zürich Hbf .... a.	1323		1333	1410	...	...		1523		1800						2000	2247		...	0700	...	
Sargans 310 .... a.	...			1513	...	...													...	0819	...	
Landquart 310 ...... a.	...			1525	1540	...													...	0833	0852	
Davos Platz .... a.	...				1646	...													...	0845	1002	
Chur 310 .... a.	...			1537		1550													...		1118	
St. Moritz .... a.	...					1758													...			0630
Olten .... a.	...	1321	...	...	...	...		1533			1721				1921			2228	...		...	0712
Luzern .... a.	...	1404	...	...	...	...		1612			1804				2004			2310	...		...	0744
Arth Goldau 290 ... a.	...		...	1559	...	...		1644											...		...	0951
Bellinzona 290 ..... a.	...		...	1629	...	...		1832											...		...	1021
Lugano 290 .... a.	...		...		...	...		1903											...		...	
Chiasso 290 .... a.	...		...		...	...		1930											...		...	1056

train type		5204	EC		IC	IC							EC								
train number		2656	114		302	966	1744		1676			1780	116		1680	1784	1748		256		468
classes		1,2	1,2✗		1,2	1,2	1,2		1,2	1,2	1,2	1,2	1,2✗		1,2	1,2	1,2		1,2	1,2	2
notes (see below)		Ⓟ	B		Ⓟ	Ⓟ			Ⓟ			✕	F		Ⓟ	Ⓟ					C
Chiasso .... d.	...	...	...	...	0730	...		1106		...	...	...		...		...		1930	...	...
Lugano 290 .... d.	...	...	...	...	0757	...		1141		...	...	...		...		...		1957	...	...
Bellinzona .... d.	...	...	...	...	0827	...		1209		...	...	...		1409		...		2027	...	...
Arth Goldau .... d.	...	0600	...	...	1020	...		1420		...	...	...		1620		...		2214	...	...
Luzern .... d.	...	0635	...	...	1056	...		1456		...	...	...		1656		...		2246	...	...
Olten .... d.	...	0717	...	...	1139	...		1539		...	...	...		1739		...		2331	...	...
St. Moritz .... d.	...	...	...	...	...	...			1100	...	...	...				...			1900	...
Chur 310 .... d.	...	...	...	...	...	...			1307	1315	...	...				...		2107		2113
Davos Platz .... d.	...	...	...	...	...	...					1205	...				...			2000	2115	2124
Landquart 310 .... d.	...	...	...	...	...	...			1317	1326	...	...				...			2115	2139
Sargans .... d.	...	...	...	...	...	...				1339	...	...				...				2300
Zürich Hbf .... d.	...	...	0712	...	...	1137			1450	1537	...	...		1700		...		2359		0028
Basel SBB/SNCF ▥ d.	...	0749	0823	...	1209	1235	1248	1609		1648	1809	1811	1830		2359		0054
Mulhouse .... a.	...	...	0846	...	...	...	1313			1710			1854			0141
Belfort .... a.	...	...	0918	...	...	...	1355			1736			1935			0648
Paris Est .... a.	...	...	1314	...	...	...	1806			2132			2343			

NOTES

A — LE CORBUSIER – ①②③④⑤⑥, not Oct. 31, Nov. 1,12, Apr. 17, May 1,8:
   🍴 Paris - Zürich; ♀ Paris - Basel.

B — L'ARBALETE - 🍴 and ✕ Paris - Zürich and v.v.

C — 🛏 1,2 cl., 🛏 2 cl. and 🍴 Paris - Chur and v.v.; 🍴 Paris - Basel and v.v.

F — LE CORBUSIER – ①②③④⑤⑥⑦, not Oct. 30,31, Nov. 11, Apr. 16,30, May 7:
   🍴 Zürich - Paris; ✕ Basel - Paris.

G — ⑤⑥, also Oct. 31, Nov. 10, May 24; not Nov. 12, May 26.

b — Depart 0839 on ⑦.

✗ — Supplement payable.

Table 42 — PARIS - LAUSANNE AND BERN

train type	TGV	IC			TGV	IC				TGV	IC		TGV		TGV			
train number	EC21	323	1923		EC23	335	1937	423		EC29	329	1536	EC429		EC27	2147	427	
classes	1,2✗	1,2	1,2	1,2	1,2✗	1,2	1,2	1,2		1,2✗	1,2	1,2	1,2✗		1,2✗	1,2	1,2	
notes (see below)	A	✕			B	Ⓟ	Ⓟ			C	Ⓟ		C		D			
Paris Lyon .... d.	...	0714	...	...	1225	...	...	...	...	1553	...	...	1553	...	1807	...	...	
Dijon .... d.	...	0853	...	...	1403	...	...	...	...	1731	...	...	1731	...	1946	...	...	
Frasne .... d.	...	1015	...	...	1518	...	...	1521	...	1851	...	...	1855	...	2106	...	2110	
Pontarlier ▥ ...... d.	...		...	...		...	...	1534	...		...	...	1908	...		...	2123	
Neuchâtel .... a.	...		...	...		...	...	1614	...		...	...	1949	...		...	2204	
Bern .... a.	...		...	...		...	...	1647	...		...	...	2022	...		...	2239	
Vallorbe ▥ .... d.	...	1034	...	...	1534	...	...	...	...	1909	...	...		...	2125	...	...	
Lausanne .... a.	...	1106	1113	1132	1607	1613	1632	...	...	1945	1953	1956		...	2157	2202	...	
Vevey .... a.	...		1146	...		1646	...	...	...		2015	...		...	2216	...	
Montreux .... a.	...		1151	...		1651	...	...	...		2028	...		...	2221	...	
Aigle .... a.	...		1203	...		1703	...	...	...		2034	...		...	2223	...	
Bex .... a.	...		1209	...		1709	...	...	...		2038	...		...	2239	...	
St. Maurice .... a.	...		1214	...		1714	...	...	...		2047	2104		...	2244	...	
Martigny .... a.	...		1225	...		1725	...	...	...			2116		...	2255	...	
Sion .... a.	...	1207	1241	...		1707	1741	...	...			2116		...	2310	...	
Sierre .... a.	...		1255	...			1755	...	...			2126		...	2322	...	
Leuk .... a.	...		1304	...			1804	...	...			2145		...	2331	...	
Visp .... a.	...		1316	1336			1816	1836	...			2152		...	2348	...	
Zermatt .... a.	...			1445				1945	...					...		...	
Brig .... a.	...	1236	1323	...		1736	1823	...	...	2116	2152			...	2355	...	

train type	TGV		TGV			TGV			IC	TGV			IC	TGV		TGV	
train number	EC422	1904	EC22		420	1521	EC20		1918	330	EC24		426	1930	322	EC26	2136	EC28
classes	1,2✗	1,2	1,2✗	1,2	1,2	1,2	1,2✗	1,2	1,2	1,2	1,2✗	1,2	1,2	1,2	1,2✗	1,2	1,2✗
notes (see below)	C	Ⓟ	C			Ⓟ	D			Ⓟ	A			Ⓟ	B			E
Brig .... d.	...	...	0525	...	...	0807	...	...	1036	1116	...	...		1536	1615		1807	
Zermatt .... d.	...	...	...	...	0600	...	...	0910	...	...	...	...	1410			1610		
Visp .... d.	...	...	0532	0709	...	0813	1021	1042	...	...	...	...	1521	1542		1721	1813	
Leuk .... d.	...	...	0551	...	...	0830	...	1054	...	...	...	...		1554			1830	
Sierre .... d.	...	...	0601	...	...	0840	...	1104	...	...	...	...		1604			1840	
Sion .... d.	...	...	0613	...	...	0852	...	1117	1147	...	...	...	1617	1645			1852	
Martigny .... d.	...	...	0629	...	...	0908	...	1134	...	...	...	...		1634			1908	
St. Maurice .... d.	...	...	0640	...	...	0918	...	1145	...	...	...	...		1645			1918	
Bex .... d.	...	...	0645	...	...	0923	...	1150	...	...	...	...		1650			1923	
Aigle .... d.	...	...	0652	...	...	0930	...	1156	...	...	...	...		1656			1930	
Montreux .... d.	...	...	0703	...	...	0943	...	1207	...	...	...	...		1707			1943	
Vevey .... d.	...	...	0710	...	...	0949	...	1213	...	...	...	...		1713			1949	
Lausanne .... d.	...	...	0725	0731	...	1003	1015	1227	1240	1246	...	...	1727	1740	1754	2003	2015
Vallorbe ▥ .... d.	...	...		0804	...		1047			1318	...	...		1827			
Bern .... d.	...	0700		...	...	0922	...	...			...	...	1705			2105	
Neuchâtel .... d.	...	0733		...	...	1004	...	...			...	...	1740				
Pontarlier ▥ .... d.	...	0814		...	...	1047	...	...			...	...	1823				
Frasne .... a.	...	0828		0823	...	1059	1106	...			1444	...	1835	1845		2105	2216
Dijon .... a.	...	0943		0939	...		1216	...				...		1957		2216	2356
Paris Lyon .... a.	...	1124		1124	...		1357	...			1628	...		2137		2356	

NOTES see next page.

Table 43 — LONDON AND BRUSSELS - MILANO AND ROMA

	EC 91	P 515	IC 687	2113	⛴	⛴	EC 49	P 299	P 505	2093	2183	1117
classes	1,2	1,2	1,2	1,2			2	1,2	1,2	1,2	1,2	
notes (see below)	E	[B]X	Y		T	Y	G	[B]X	Y			A
London Victoria 12 ..... d.					0805	1105						
Ramsgate Port ⛴ 12 .... d.					1030	1325						
Oostende ⛴ .... d.					1545	1600	1657					
Brussels Midi .... d.		0715					1804					
Brussels Nord .... d.		0723					1913					2008
Liège Guillemins ...... d.							1921					2018
Aachen ⋒ .... d.												2121
Namur ⋒ .... d.		0808						2008				
Luxembourg ⋒ .... d.		1001						2201				
Lille Flandres ⋒ ...... d.	0650											
Metz .... d.	1038	1045						1644				
Strasbourg .... d.		1211						2031	2252			
Mulhouse .... d.		1315						0018				
Basel SBB ⋒ .... a.		1401						0117				
.... d.								0200				
Domodossola ⋒ .... a.		1732										
Stresa .... a.		1811										
Arona .... a.		1825										
Chiasso ⋒ .... a.								0602				
Como .... a.								0625				
Milano Centrale .... a.		1915	1940	2010			0710	0750	0810	0815		
Brennero ⋒ .... a.												0850
Fortezza .... a.												0950
Dobbiaco .... a.												1116
San Candido .... a.												
Bolzano 380 .... a.												1124
Verona .... a.												
Venezia Santa Lucia ... a.				2151				0903f	0951			
Genova P. Principe .... a.			2147	2325				1032f	1125			
Ventimiglia 355 .... a.										1005	1250	
Bologna .... a.		2115							0928			
Firenze SMN .... a.		2212r										
Roma Termini .... a.		2353							1025r			
Napoli Centrale 405 ... a.									1205			
Ravenna 388 .... a.												
Rimini 390 .... a.												
Ancona 390 .... a.												

	IC 674	IC 532	2094	EC 90	IC 544	IC 688	2110	298	412	⛴	1116
classes	1,2	1,2	1,2	1,2	1,2	1,2	1,2	2	1,2		
notes (see below)		Y		E	X	Y	Y	R		W V	M
Ancona 390 .... d.											
Rimini 390 .... d.											
Ravenna 388 .... d.											
Napoli Centrale 405 ... d.											
Roma Termini .... d.					1605						
Firenze SMN .... d.		0700			1807						
Bologna .... d.		0816			1916						
Ventimiglia 388 .... d.											
Genova P. Principe .... d.	0813										
Venezia Santa Lucia ... d.			0625			1913					
Verona .... d.			0801			1725	1742f				
Bolzano 390 .... d.						1901	1934f				
San Candido .... d.											
Dobbiaco .... d.											1750
Fortezza .... d.											1757
Brennero ⋒ .... d.											1944
Milano Centrale .... d.	0950	1000	0945	1025	2100	2050	2045	2135			2049
Como .... d.								2216			
Chiasso ⋒ .... d.								2240			
Arona .... d.			1116								
Stresa .... d.			1129								
Domodossola ⋒ .... d.			1213								
Basel SBB ⋒ .... a.			1559					0240			
Mulhouse .... a.			1648					0322			
Strasbourg .... a.			1745					0420			
Metz .... a.			1911					0550			
Lille Flandres ⋒ ...... a.									0758		
Luxembourg ⋒ .... a.			1956					0647	1142		
Namur ⋒ .... a.			2143					0836			
Aachen ⋒ .... a.											
Liège Guillemins ...... a.											
Brussels Nord .... a.			2228					0921			0813
Brussels Midi .... a.			2237								0917
Oostende ⛴ .... a.								0930	0959		0927
Ramsgate Port ⛴ 12 .... a.					1109	1150	1350				
London Victoria 12 .... a.					1225	1517	1650			1917	
						1917					

NOTES

A – SKI EXPRESS – ⑤ Jan. 6 - Apr. 7:
  ⛌ 1,2 cl., ⛌ 2 cl. and ⛌ Brussels - San Candido.
E – VAUBAN – ⛟ and ✕ Brussels - Milano and v.v.
G – ⛌ 1,2 cl., ⛌ 1,2 cl. (T2), ⛌ 2 cl. and ⛌ Brussels - Milano;
  ⑤⑥: ⛌ 1,2 cl., ⛌ 1,2 cl. (T2), ⛌ 2 cl. and ⛌ Brussels - Venezia.
J – Jetfoil service, see Table 12.
M – SKI EXPRESS – ⑥ Jan. 7 - Apr. 15:
  ⛌ 1,2 cl., ⛌ 2 cl. and ⛌ San Candido - Brussels.
R – ⛌ 1,2 cl., ⛌ 1,2 cl. (T2), ⛌ 2 cl. and ⛌ Milano - Brussels;
  ⑥⑦: ⛌ 1,2 cl., ⛌ 1,2 cl. (T2), ⛌ 2 cl. and ⛌ Venezia - Brussels.

T – Not Dec. 25,26.
V – Not Dec. 25.
W – Oct. 23 - Jan. 2 and Mar. 26 - May 27, not Dec. 25.
Y – Daily to Jan. 2 and from Mar. 26, not Dec. 25.
e – Roma Tuscolana.
f – ⑥⑦ only.
r – Firenze Rifredi.
t – Roma Tiburtina.
∕ – Supplement payable.

NOTES for Table 42.

A – LUTETIA – ⛟ and ✕ Paris - Lausanne and v.v.
B – CISALPIN – ⛟ and ✕ Paris - Lausanne and v.v.
C – CHAMPS ELYSEES – ⛟ and ✕ Paris - Lausanne and Bern and v.v.
D – VALAIS – ⛟ and ✕ Paris - Lausanne and v.v.
E – LEMANO – ⑤⑦, also Nov. 10, May 24; not Oct. 30, Nov. 11, Apr. 16,30, May 7: ⛟ and ✕ Lausanne - Paris.
∕ – Supplement payable.

For summer service from May 28 see page 528

Table 44 — PARIS - MILANO AND ROMA

train type	TGV	IC	IC	IC	IC	TGV	IC		IC	TGV	IC	EN	EN	EN	EN	IC				EN
train number	EC21	323	543	655	679	EC23	335	2113	687	EC29	329	213	223	223 227	227	565	211	1211	1211	217
classes	1,2 A	1,2 ✗	1,2 ☕	1,2 ☕	1,2 ☕	1,2 C	1,2	1,2	1,2 ☕	1,2 E	1,2	→ N	→ K	→ Q	→ L	1,2 ✗ H	1,2 P	1,2 T	2 X	2 M
London Victoria 10 ... d.																				
Dover Eastern Docks ... d.																				
Folkestone Harbour ... a.																				
Paris Nord ... a.										1553		1847	2006	2006	2009		2056	2213	2213	2222
Paris Lyon ... d.	0714					1225				1731		2118	2236	2236	2242		2348	0102	0102	0118
Dijon ... d.	0853					1403				1909			0030	0030	0049					
Vallorbe ... d.	1034					1534				1945										
Lausanne ... d.	1106	1113				1607	1613			1953	2147									
Domodossola (= Iselle) ... a.		1307					1807					2352	0248					0350	0350	
Chambéry ... d.												0435		0535	0540		0540			
Modane ... d.											0248	0610		0655	0706p		0706p			
Torino Porta Nuova ... a.																	0845	0845		
Milano Centrale ... a.		1445	1500	1505	1510		1945	2010	2010			0439	0443g			0443g	0827	0854		
Genova P. Principe ... a.				1647					2147			0910								
Rapallo 360 ... a.												0955								
La Spezia 360 ... a.												1035								
Viareggio 360 ... a.												1051								
Pisa Centrale ... a.												1110								
Livorno 360 ... a.												0630								
Verona ... a.			1624					2151					0640			0805				
Padova ... a.			1719					2250								0833				
Venezia Mestre ... a.			1740					2313								0845				
Venezia Santa Lucia ... a.			1752					2325					0710	0710		0859				
Bologna ... a.			1648										1005							
Rimini 390 ... a.													1100							
Ancona 390 ... a.													1220							
Pescara 390 ... a.													1521							
Bari 390 ... a.													1654b	2000						
Brindisi Marittima 390 ... a.													1330							
Patras ... a.													1745							
Athinai by 1525 ... a.													0826	0826						
Firenze SMN ... a.		1802														0945	1429r			
Roma Termini ... a.		1855															1700			
Napoli Centrale 405 ... a.																				

train type	IC	IC	TGV	EC			IC	TGV		EN	EN	EN	EN		EN
train number	672	330	EC24	52	2098	2162	322	EC26	1210 216	216	226	226 222	222	210	212
classes	1,2 ✗	1,2 ✗	1,2 A	1,2 ✗	1,2 ☕	1,2	1,2 ☕	1,2 C	1,2 W	2 Y	→ R	→ S	→ K	1,2 V	2 N
Napoli Centrale 405 ... d.														1355	1910
Roma Termini ... d.				0805							1943	1943		1622r	
Firenze SMN ... d.				1007											
Athinai by 1525 ... d.															
Patras ... d.															
Brindisi Marittima 390 ... d.															
Bari 390 ... d.															
Pescara 390 ... d.															
Ancona 390 ... d.															
Rimini 390 ... d.											2100	2100			
Bologna ... d.				1116											
Venezia Santa Lucia ... d.					1025									2010	
Venezia Mestre ... d.					1037									2019	
Padova ... d.					1100									2046	
Verona ... d.					1201									2142	
Livorno 360 ... d.														1926	
Pisa Centrale ... d.														1943	2226
Viareggio 360 ... d.														1959	
La Spezia 360 ... d.														2035	
Rapallo 360 ... d.							1154							2121	
Genova P. Principe ... d.	0713								2010					2204	0018
Milano Centrale ... d.	0850	0905		1300	1345	1345	1400			2100	2213	2240p		0015	0213
Torino Porta Nuova ... d.											2345	0018		0143	0333
Modane ... a.											0145	0145			
Chambéry ... a.															
Domodossola (= Iselle) ... d.		1046					1544							0312	0455
Lausanne ... a.		1240	1246				1740	1754			0325	0342	0342	0601	0737
Vallorbe ... a.			1318					1827			0530	0537	0537		
Dijon ... a.			1444					1957	0432	0432	0825	0838	0838	0855	1006
Paris Lyon ... a.			1628					2137	0722	0722					
Paris Nord ... d.															
Folkestone Harbour ... a.															
Dover Eastern Docks ... a.															
London Victoria ... a.															

NOTES

A – LUTETIA – 🛏 and ✗ Paris - Lausanne and v.v.
C – CISALPIN – 🛏 and ✗ Paris - Lausanne and v.v.
E – CHAMPS ELYSEES – 🛏 and ✗ Paris - Lausanne.
H – Hellenic Mediterranean Lines, for days of running see Table **1525**.
K – RIALTO – 🛏 1,2 cl., 🛏 1,2 cl. (T2), ⬅ 2 cl. and ☕ Paris - Venezia and v.v.
L – GALILEI– ⑤⑥, daily Oct. 21-Nov. 1, Dec. 16-Jan. 7, Feb. 17-Mar. 11, Apr. 7-May 27, also Nov. 10: 🛏 1,2 cl., 🛏 1,2 cl. (T2) and ⬅ 2 cl. Paris - Firenze.
M – STENDHAL – Oct. 20-Nov. 1, Dec. 15-Jan. 7, Feb. 23-Mar. 25 and Apr. 6-May 27: 🛏 1,2 cl., 🛏 1,2 cl. (T2), ⬅ 2 cl. and ☕ Paris - Roma and v.v.
N – PALATINO – 🛏 1,2 cl., 🛏 1,2 cl. (T2), ⬅ 2 cl. and ☕ Paris - Roma and v.v.
P – NAPOLI EXPRESS– Oct. 21-Nov. 1, Dec. 16-Jan. 7, Feb. 24-Mar. 25, Apr. 7-May 27: 🛏 1,2 cl., 🛏 1,2 cl. (T2) and ⬅ 2 cl. Paris - Torino - Napoli.
Q – GALILEI– ①②③④⑦ Sept. 25-Oct. 20, Nov. 2-Dec. 15, Jan. 8-Feb. 16, and Mar. 12-Apr. 6, not Nov. 10: 🛏 1,2 cl., 🛏 1,2 cl. (T2) and ⬅ 2 cl. Paris - Firenze.
R – GALILEI– ⑥⑦, daily Oct. 22-Nov. 2, Dec. 17-Jan. 8, Feb. 18-Mar. 12, Apr. 8-May 27, also Nov. 11: 🛏 1,2 cl., 🛏 1,2 cl. (T2) and ⬅ 2 cl. Firenze - Paris.

S – GALILEI– ①②③④⑤ Sept. 25-Oct. 21, Nov. 3-Dec. 16, Jan. 9-Feb. 17, and Mar. 13-Apr. 7, not Nov. 11: 🛏 1,2 cl., 🛏 1,2 cl. (T2) and ⬅ 2 cl. Firenze - Paris.
SC – SeaCat service.
T – Sept. 25-Oct. 20, Nov. 2-Dec. 15, Jan. 8-Feb. 23, Mar. 26-Apr. 6: 🛏 1,2 cl., ⬅ 2 cl. and ☕ Paris - Torino - Genova.
V – NAPOLI EXPRESS– Oct. 22-Nov. 2, Dec. 17-Jan. 8, Feb. 25-Mar. 26, Apr. 8-May 27, also Sept. 25: 🛏 1,2 cl., ⬅ 2 cl. and ☕ Napoli - Torino - Paris.
W – Sept. 25-Oct. 21, Nov. 3-Dec. 16, Jan. 9-Feb. 24, Mar. 27-Apr. 7: 🛏 1,2 cl., ⬅ 2 cl. and ☕ Genova - Torino - Paris.
X – STENDHAL – Sept. 25-Oct. 19, Nov. 2-Dec. 14, Jan. 8-Feb. 22, Mar. 26-Apr. 5: 🛏 1,2 cl., 🛏 1,2 cl. (T2), ⬅ 2 cl. and ☕ Paris - Milano.
Y – STENDHAL – 🛏 1,2 cl., 🛏 1,2 cl. (T2), ⬅ 2 cl. and ☕ Milano - Paris.

b – Brindisi Centrale.
g – Milano Porta Garibaldi.
p – Torino Porta Susa.
r – Roma Ostiense.
t – Roma Tiburtina.
∕ – Supplement payable.

Table 45 — LYON - TORINO

	410	TGV 925	416	TGV 943	218
classes	1,2	1,2✔	1,2	1,2✔	1,2
notes	ⓠ	1024		1432	ⓠB
Paris Lyon .... d.	...	...	...	...	...
Lyon Perrache .... d.	0704	...	1232	...	1703
Lyon Part Dieu .... d.	0715	...	1243	...	1714
Aix les Bains .... d.	0830	...	1352	...	1826
Chambéry .... d.	0844	1318	1408	1726	1838
Modane 🚻 .... d.	1004	...	1538	...	2001
Torino Porta Nuova .... a.	1130	...	1700	...	2122
Milano Centrale .... a.	...	...	...	...	2305

	214	TGV 932	414	TGV 922	418	TGV 936
classes	1,2	1,2✔	1,2	1,2✔	1,2	1,2✔
notes	ⓠB	ⓠ		ⓠ		⑥ⓡ
Milano Centrale .... d.	0710	...	...	...	...	...
Torino Porta Nuova ..... d.	0855	...	1225	...	1645	...
Modane 🚻 .... a.	1025	...	1348	...	1807	...
Chambéry .... a.	1147	...	1511	1542	1925	...
Aix les Bains .... a.	1201	1315	1524		1939	1957
Lyon Part Dieu .... a.	1316		1638		2104	...
Lyon Perrache .... a.	1326		1648		2115	...
Paris Lyon .... a.	...	1616	...	1839	...	2254

NOTES   B –   MONT CENIS – 🛏 and ⓠ Lyon - Milano and v.v.   ✔ – Supplement payable.

Table 46 — PARIS - MADRID AND LISBOA

train number	TGV 8515	200	1202	TGV 8543	313	313	204		303 302		409 408
classes	1,2✔	1,2✔	2	1,2✔	1,2	2	2		🛏		🛏
notes (see below)	ⓡⓠ	⑧ⓠ	⑥ⓠ	ⓡⓠ	✗A	ⓠB	Mn		E		D
Paris Montparnasse ...... d.	1000	...	...	1555	...	...	...	...	...	...	...
Paris Austerlitz .... d.	...	...	...	...	...	...	...	...	...	...	...
Bordeaux St. Jean .... d.	...	1259	...	1901	...	...	...	...	1805	...	2000
Hendaye 🚻 .... d.	...	1510	...	2121	...	...	...	...	0157	...	0237
Irún 🚻 .... d.	...	1522	1545	1545	2126	2200	2200	2215	0203	...	0253
San Sebastián/Donostia ..... a.	...	...	1601	1601	...	2218	2218	2245	0219	...		
Burgos .... a.	...	...	1903	1903	...	0158	0158	0242	0521	...	0541
Valladolid .... a.	...	...		2003	...	0327	0327	0410	0645	...		
Medina del Campo .... a.	...	...		2025	...	0359	0359	0451	...	...	...
Salamanca .... a.	...	...	...	...	...	0453	0453	...	...	...	...
Pampilhosa .... a.	...	...	...	...	...	1015	1015	...	...	...	...
Lisboa Santa Apolónia ... a.	...	...	...	...	...	1305		...	...	...	...
Porto Campanhã .... a.	...	...	...	...	...		1145	...	...	...	...
Madrid Chamartín .... a.	...	2224	2240	...	...	...	...	0740	0950	...	0850

train number	203	TGV 8596	TGV 8598		301 300	407 406		205	311	316	TGV 8530
classes	1,2✔	1,2✔	1,2✔		🛏	🛏		2	1,2	1,2	1,2✔
notes (see below)	ⓠ	✗ⓡ	ⓣⓡ		E	D		Mn	✗A	ⓠB	ⓠⓡ
Madrid Chamartín .... d.	...	1000	...	...	1815	1915	...	2300	...	...	...
Porto Campanhã .... d.	...		...	...	...	...	...	...	...	1805	...
Lisboa Santa Apolónia ... d.	...		...	...	...	...	...	...	1703		...
Pampilhosa .... d.	...		...	...	...	...	...	...	2000	2000	...
Salamanca .... d.	...		...	...	...	...	...	...	0205	0205	...
Medina del Campo .... d.	...	1210	...	...	...	...	...	0127	0254	0254	...
Valladolid .... d.	...	1232	...	...	2049	...	...	0215	0323	0323	...
Burgos .... d.	...	1333	...	...	2158	2209	...	0343	0445	0445	...
San Sebastián/Donostia ..... d.	...	1623	...	...	0135	...	...	0755	0832	0832	...
Irún 🚻 .... a.	...	1645	...	...	0203	0123	...	0825	0900	0900	...
Hendaye 🚻 .... a.	...	1650	1723	1826	0208	0139	...	0830	0904	0904	0936
Bordeaux St. Jean .... a.	...		1933	2035	0550	0355	...	...	...	...	1157
Paris Austerlitz .... a.	...				1040	0830	...	...	...	...	...
Paris Montparnasse ...... a.	...		2300	2345	...	...	...	...	...	...	1505

NOTES
A –   SUD EXPRESS – 🛏 1,2 cl., 🛌 2 cl., 🛏 and ✗ Irún - Lisboa and Lisboa - Hendaye.
B –   🛌 2 cl. and 🛏 Irún - Porto and Porto - Hendaye.

D –   FRANCISCO DE GOYA – 🛏 1,2 cl. and ✗ Paris - Madrid and v.v.
E –   PUERTA DEL SOL – 🛌 2 cl. and ⓠ Paris - Madrid and v.v.
M –   🛌 1,2 cl., 🛌 2 cl. and 🛏 Irún - Madrid and Madrid - Hendaye.
n –   Not Dec. 24, 31.   ✔ – Supplement payable.

Table 47 — PARIS - BARCELONA

train number	147 471			TGV 524	TGV 853	71		477		473	463
classes	1,2		2	1,2✔	1,2✔	1,2✔		🛏		🛏	1,2✔ 2
notes (see below)	ⓠ			ⓡⓠ	ⓡⓠ	J		H		W	ⓠ
Paris Austerlitz .... d.	1006	...	...	...	...	...	...	2115	...	2145	...
Paris Lyon .... d.		...	...	...	1049	...	...		...		...
Lille Europe .... d.		...	...	0834	...	...	...		...		...
Montpellier .... d.		...	...	1452	1459	1510	...		...		...
Limoges .... d.	1309	...	...			...	...	0021	...	0122	...
Cerbère .... d.	2041	...	...			1701	...	0846	...	0846	...
Port Bou 🚻 .... a.	2045	2110	...			1718	...	0850	...	0850	1030 1035
Figueres .... a.		2132	...			1740	...	0645	...		1050 1057
Girona .... a.		2201	...			1806	...	0710	...		1116 1126
Barcelona França .... a.			...			1920	...	0820	...		...
Barcelona Sants .... a.		2327	...			...	...		...	1225	1247
València Término .... a.			...			...	...		...	1615	...
Alicante Término .... a.			...			...	...		...	1829	...

train number	370	470		73	TGV 862	TGV 862	TGV 582		460	472		475 474
classes	2	1,2		1,2✔	1,2✔	1,2✔	1,2✔		1,2✔	2		🛏
notes (see below)	⑤⑥⑦			J	ⓡⓠ	ⓡⓠ	ⓡⓠ		ⓠ	V		H
Alicante Término .... d.					②③④	⑤			1100	...	...	...
València Término .... d.						⑥⑦			1357	...	...	...
Barcelona Sants .... d.	0710								1707	...	...	...
Barcelona França .... d.				0855						1720	...	2100
Girona .... d.	0835			1001					1816	1849	...	2210
Figueres .... d.	0907			1027					1842	1930	...	2237
Port Bou 🚻 .... d.	0940			1055					1910	1958	...		
Cerbère .... a.	0945	1027		1123					1915	2003	2035	0459
Limoges .... a.		1654									0342	...
Montpellier .... a.					1315	1354	1404	1556			...	...
Lille Europe .... a.								2212			...	...
Paris Lyon .... a.					1814	1818					...	...
Paris Austerlitz .... a.		2032								0745	...	0815

NOTES
H –   JOAN MIRÓ – 🛏 and ✗ Paris - Barcelona and v.v.
J –   CATALAN TALGO – 🛏 and ✗ Montpellier - Barcelona and v.v.

V –   🛌 2 cl. and 🛏 Cerbère - Paris (also 🛏 1,2 cl. (T2) on ①②③④⑥).
W –   🛌 2 cl. and 🛏 Paris - Port Bou (also 🛏 1,2 cl. (T2) on ①②③④⑥).
✔ – Supplement payable.

Table 48   AMSTERDAM AND BRUSSELS - SOUTHERN FRANCE AND BARCELONA

train number notes (see below)	1199 A	1199 B	1199 C	286 L	1184 D
Amsterdam Centraal d.					
Den Haag HS d.					
Rotterdam CS d.					
Roosendaal d.					
Antwerpen Berchem d.					2034
Brussels Nord d.					
Brussels Midi d.	1859	1859	1859	1907	2052
Brussels Nord d.	1908	1908	1908		
Mons d.				1946	2135
Namur d.	1954	1954	1954		
Luxembourg d.	2143	2143	2143		
Tournai d.					
Lille Flandres d.					
Brive a.					
Montauban a.					
Toulouse a.					
Tarbes a.					
Lourdes a.					
Lyon Perrache a.				0349	
Aix les Bains a.	0430	0435			0628
Chambéry a.	0454				0651
Albertville a.	0532				0741
Moutiers Salins a.	0607				0820
Aime a.	0635				0840
Bourg St. Maurice a.	0658				0902
Annecy a.		0517			
La Roche sur Foron a.		0557			
Cluses a.		0630			
Sallanches a.		0649			
St. Gervais a.		0658			
Chamonix a.					
Gap a.			0732		
Embrun a.			0826		
Montdauphin a.			0847		
Briançon a.			0925		
Valence a.				0504	
Avignon a.				0604	
Nîmes a.					
Montpellier a.					
Sète a.					
Agde a.					
Béziers a.					
Narbonne a.					
Perpignan a.					
Argelès sur Mer a.					
Port Vendres a.					
Port Bou a.					
Port Bou d.					
Girona a.					
Barcelona Sants a.					
València Término a.					
Arles a.				0628	
Marseille a.				0716	
Toulon a.				0808	
St. Raphaël a.				0904	
Cannes a.				0931	
Juan les Pins a.				0942	
Antibes a.				0948	
Nice a.				1005	
Beaulieu a.				1022	
Monaco-Monte Carlo a.				1033	
Menton a.				1045	
Ventimiglia a.				1059	

train number		6708			
train number notes (see below)	1282 E	6709 L	6626 P	6628 Q	6622 R
Ventimiglia d.		1734			
Menton d.		1748			
Monaco-Monte Carlo d.		1758			
Beaulieu d.		1809			
Nice d.		1834			
Antibes d.		1849			
Juan les Pins d.		1854			
Cannes d.		1905			
St. Raphaël d.		1938			
Toulon d.		2029			
Marseille d.		2121			
Arles d.		2206			
València Término d.					
Barcelona Sants d.					
Girona d.					
Cerbère a.					
Cerbère d.					
Port Vendres d.					
Argelès sur Mer d.					
Perpignan d.					
Narbonne d.					
Béziers d.					
Agde d.					
Sète d.					
Montpellier d.					
Nîmes d.					
Avignon d.		2228			
Valence d.		2326			
Briançon d.					1744
Montdauphin d.					1813
Embrun d.					1831
Gap d.					1907
Chamonix d.					
St. Gervais d.				2000	
Sallanches d.				2009	
Cluses d.				2029	
La Roche sur Foron d.				2102	
Annecy d.				2152	
Bourg St Maurice d.	1920		2030		
Aime d.	1942		2050		
Moutiers Salins d.	2015		2114		
Albertville d.	2055		2153		
Chambéry d.	2133		2239		
Aix les Bains d.	2149				2239
Lyon Perrache d.		0103			
Lourdes d.					
Tarbes d.					
Toulouse d.					
Montauban d.					
Brive d.					
Lille Flandres d.					
Tournai a.					
Luxembourg a.			0750	0750	0750
Namur a.			0953	0953	0953
Mons a.	0715	0824	1040	1040	1040
Brussels Nord a.					
Brussels Midi a.	0801	0903	1048	1048	1048
Brussels Nord a.	0816				
Antwerpen Berchem a.					
Roosendaal a.					
Rotterdam CS a.					
Den Haag HS a.					
Amsterdam Centraal a.					

NOTES

A – ⑤ Jan. 20 - Mar. 17, also Dec. 23: ⊨ 2 cl. Brussels - Bourg St. Maurice.
B – ⑤ Jan. 20 - Mar. 17, also Dec. 23: ⊨ 2 cl. Brussels - St. Gervais.
C – ⑤ Jan. 20 - Mar. 17, also Dec. 23: ⊨ 2 cl. Brussels - Briançon.
D – FRANCE-ALP EXPRESS – ⑤ Jan. 6 - Apr. 7:
    ⊨ 1,2 cl. and ⊨ 2 cl. Brussels - Bourg St. Maurice.
E – FRANCE-ALP EXPRESS – ⑥ Jan. 7 - Apr. 15:
    ⊨ 1,2 cl. and ⊨ 2 cl. Bourg St Maurice - Brussels.

L – FLANDRES RIVIERA –
    ⊨ 1,2 cl., ⊨ 1,2 cl. (T2) and ⊨ 2 cl. Brussels - Ventimiglia and v.v..
P – ⑥ Jan. 28 - Apr. 1: ⊨ 2 cl. Bourg St. Maurice - Brussels.
Q – ⑥ Jan. 28 - Apr. 1: ⊨ 2 cl. St. Gervais - Brussels.
R – ⑥ Jan. 28 - Apr. 1: ⊨ 2 cl. Briançon - Brussels.

INTERNATIONAL SERVICES FROM MADRID AND BARCELONA

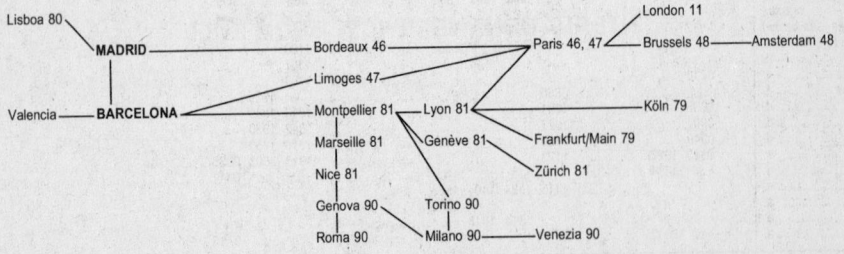

Table 50 KØBENHAVN - HAMBURG AND KÖLN

train type	IN	IN	EC	ICE	IC	ICE	IC	EC	ICE	IC	ICE	IC	EC	ICE	IC	ICE
train number	381	293	189	77	523	589	621	187	775	527	681	521	185	677	736	989
classes	▬	▬	1,2⁄	1,2⁄	1,2⁄	1,2⁄	1,2⁄	1,2⁄	1,2⁄	1,2⁄	1,2⁄	1,2⁄	1,2⁄	1,2⁄	1,2⁄	1,2⁄
notes (see below)	[R]	[R]		✗	✗	✗	✗		✗	✗	✗	✗		✗	🍷	✗
notes (see below)	C	J	H					G					F	V		
Oslo S d.	2137	...	...	...	...	...	...	...	...	...	...	...	...	...	...	...
Göteborg C d.	0220	...	...	...	...	...	...	...	...	...	...	...	...	...	...	...
Stockholm C d.	|	2224	...	...	...	...	...	...	...	...	...	...	...	...	...	...
København H d.	0700	0700	0730	...	...	...	...	0920	...	...	...	...	1230	...	...	...
Nykøbing F d.	...	...	0901	...	...	...	...	1052	...	...	...	...	1401	...	...	...
Rødby F ⛴ d.	...	...	0925	...	...	...	...	1130	...	...	...	...	1425	...	...	...
Puttgarden ⛴ a.	...	...	1035	...	...	...	...	1235	...	...	...	...	1535	...	...	...
Lübeck Hbf a.	...	...	1148	...	...	...	...	1348	...	...	...	...	1642	...	...	...
Hamburg Hbf a.	...	...	1225	...	...	...	...	1429	...	...	...	...	1722	...	...	...
Hamburg Hbf d.	...	...	...	1237	1247	1307	...	...	1437	1447	1507	...	...	1737	1747	1902
Bremen a.	...	...	...	|	1343	|	...	...	|	1543	|	...	...	|	1843	|
Osnabrück a.	...	...	...	|	1437	|	...	...	|	1637	|	...	...	|	1937	|
Münster a.	...	...	...	|	1503	|	...	...	|	1703	|	...	...	|	2003	|
Dortmund a.	...	...	...	|	1533	|	...	...	|	1733	|	...	...	|	2033	|
Essen a.	...	...	...	|	|	|	...	...	|	1759	|	...	...	|	2059	|
Duisburg a.	...	...	...	|	|	|	...	...	|	1812	|	...	...	|	2112	|
Düsseldorf a.	...	...	...	|	|	|	...	...	|	1826	|	...	...	|	2126	|
Köln Hbf a.	...	...	...	|	1650	|	...	...	|	1850	|	...	...	|	2150	|
Hannover Hbf a.	...	...	...	1349	...	1421	...	...	1549	...	1621	...	...	1849	...	2021
Frankfurt/Main a.	...	...	...	1605	...	|	...	...	1805	...	|	...	...	2105	...	|
Mannheim a.	...	...	...	1650	...	|	...	...	1850	...	|	...	...	2150	...	|
Heidelberg a.	...	...	...	|	...	|	...	...	|	...	|	...	...	|	...	|
Karlsruhe a.	...	...	...	1721	...	|	...	...	1921	...	|	...	...	2215	...	|
Offenburg a.	...	...	...	1756	...	|	...	...	1956	...	|	...	...	...	...	|
Freiburg im Breisgau a.	...	...	...	1827	...	|	...	...	2027	...	|	...	...	...	...	|
Basel SBB a.	...	...	...	1910	...	|	...	...	2110	...	|	...	...	...	...	|
Würzburg a.	...	...	...	...	...	1621	1628	...	...	...	1821	1828	...	...	...	2221
Nürnberg a.	...	...	...	...	...	|	1725	...	...	...	|	1925	...	...	...	2320
München Hbf a.	...	...	...	...	...	1838	...	...	...	...	2041	...	...	...	...	...

train type	EC	IC25	ICE	IN	EC			IC33	IN	
train number	183	IN285	91	393	181	483	483	IN289	385	232
classes	1,2⁄	1,2	1,2	1,2	1,2⁄	▬	2	1,2	1,2	2
notes (see below)		✗	Y	✗				✗	✗	
notes (see below)	D	[R]	[R]	[R]	B	R	S	[R]	[R]	A
Oslo S d.	...	...	0810	...	...	...	...	...	1015e	...
Göteborg C d.	...	...	1215	1227	...	...	...	...	1525	...
Stockholm C d.	...	0812	...	|	...	...	...	1212	|	...
København H d.	1520	1658	...	1658	1730	1905	1905	2058	2018	2105
Nykøbing F d.	1652	...	...	...	1901	2048	2048	...	...	2245b
Rødby F ⛴ d.	1730	...	...	...	1925	2130	2130	...	...	2330
Puttgarden ⛴ a.	1835	...	...	...	2035	2235	2235	...	...	0035
Lübeck Hbf a.	1946	...	...	...	2137	2358	2358	...	...	0210
Hamburg Hbf a.	2027	...	...	...	2215	0040	0040	...	...	0300
Hamburg Hbf d.	...	...	...	...	...	0057	0057	...	...	0312
Bremen a.	...	...	...	...	...	|	|	...	...	0418
Osnabrück a.	...	...	...	...	...	|	|	...	...	0530
Münster a.	...	...	...	...	...	|	|	...	...	0600
Dortmund a.	...	...	...	...	...	|	|	...	...	|
Essen a.	...	...	...	...	...	|	|	...	...	0652
Duisburg a.	...	...	...	...	...	|	|	...	...	0706
Düsseldorf a.	...	...	...	...	...	|	|	...	...	0722
Köln Hbf a.	...	...	...	...	...	|	|	...	...	0757
Hannover Hbf a.	...	...	...	...	...	0227	0227	...	...	...
Frankfurt/Main a.	...	...	...	...	...	0620	|	...	...	...
Mannheim a.	...	...	...	...	...	|	|	...	...	...
Heidelberg a.	...	...	...	...	...	0722	|	...	...	...
Karlsruhe a.	...	...	...	...	...	0759	|	...	...	...
Offenburg a.	...	...	...	...	...	0842	|	...	...	...
Freiburg im Breisgau a.	...	...	...	...	...	0917	|	...	...	...
Basel SBB a.	...	...	...	...	...	1023	|	...	...	...
Würzburg a.	...	...	...	...	...	...	0619	...	...	...
Nürnberg a.	...	...	...	...	...	...	0723	...	...	...
München Hbf a.	...	...	...	...	...	...	0921	...	...	...

NOTES

A – NORD EXPRESS –
🛏 1,2 cl., 🛏 1,2 cl. (T2), ▬ 2 cl. and [2] København - Köln - (Oostende/Paris).
B – CHRISTIAN MORGENSTERN – [12] and 🍷 København - Hamburg.
C – 🛏 1,2 cl. and ▬ 2 cl. Oslo - København; not Dec. 24, 31.
D – THOMAS MANN – [12] and 🍷 København - Hamburg.
F – BERTEL THORVALDSEN – [12] and 🍷 København - Hamburg.
G – KAREN BLIXEN.– [12] and 🍷 København - Hamburg.
H – HAMLET – [12] and 🍷 København - Hamburg.
J – 🛏 1,2 cl., ▬ 2 cl. and [2] Stockholm - København; not Dec. 24,31.
R – 🛏 1,2 cl. and ▬ 2 cl. København - Basel.
S – 🛏 1,2 cl., ▬ 2 cl. and [2] København - München.
V – Daily except ⑥; not Oct. 2, Dec. 24-31, Apr. 14,15,16,30.
Y – Not Dec. 25, Jan. 1.
b – Depart 2252, Sept. 25 - Dec. 15.
e – ⑤⑥⑦ only.
⁄ – Supplement payable.

INTERNATIONAL SERVICES FROM KÖLN

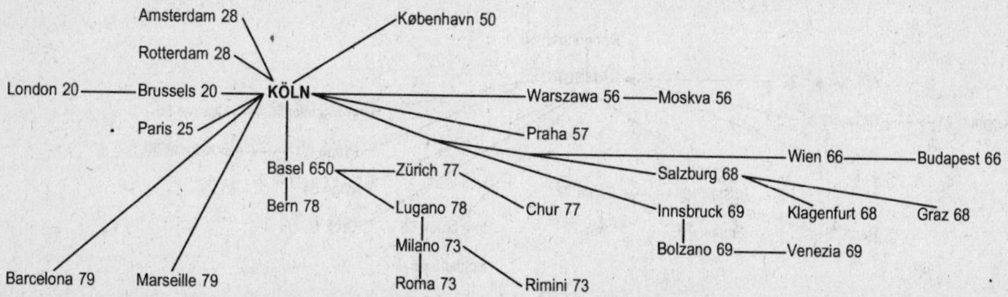

For summer service from May 28 see page 532

Table 50 — KÖLN AND HAMBURG - KØBENHAVN

	EC 180	IN 392	ICE 94	IN 284	EC 182	ICE 776	IC 524	ICE 682	IC 739	EC 184	ICE 76	IC 620	ICE 680	IC 526	EC 186
classes	1,2✗	1,2	1,2	1,2	1,2✗	1,2✗	1,2✗	1,2✗	1,2✗	1,2✗	1,2✗	1,2✗	1,2✗	1,2✗	1,2✗
notes	B		✗ Z R	R Z	D	✗ V	✗	✗ V	✗	F	✗	Y	✗	Y	G
München Hbf d								0720					0920		
Nürnberg d							0832					1128	1032	1136	
Wurzburg d							0928	0936				0752	1128	1136	
Basel SBB d						0633					0833				
Freiburg im Breisgau d						0702					0902				
Offenburg d						0737					0937				
Karlsruhe d															
Heidelberg d						0808					1008				
Mannheim d						0851					1051				
Frankfurt/Main d						1108	1137				1308	1337			
Hannover Hbf d									0909					1110	
Köln Hbf d									0933						
Düsseldorf d									0946						
Duisburg d									0959						
Essen d									1025						1225
Dortmund d									1056						1256
Münster d									1121						1321
Osnabrück d									1216						1416
Bremen d						1221	1251		1311		1421	1451			1511
Hamburg Hbf a									1326						1519
Hamburg Hbf d	0719				0919					1402					1557
Lübeck Hbf d	0758				0957					1505					1705
Puttgarden d	0905				1105					1600					1800
Rødby F a	1000				1200					1633					1841
Nykøbing F a	1033				1241					1808					2020
København H a	1208	1228		1315	1420										
Stockholm C a				2141											
Göteborg C a		1734	1800												
Oslo S a			2219												

	ICE 576	IC 520	ICE 794	IC 522	EC 188	IN 380	IN 292	233	482	351 / 482	IN 384	IN 288
classes	1,2✗	1,2✗	1,2✗	1,2✗	1,2✗		1,2	2	2		✗	1,2
notes	✗	Y	✗	✗	H	N	C	A	S	R	R	R
München Hbf d		1156							1928			
Nürnberg d		1338							2133			
Wurzburg d		1436								1749		
Basel SBB d										1838		
Freiburg im Breisgau d										1913		
Offenburg d										2009		
Karlsruhe d	1237									2045		
Heidelberg d												
Mannheim d	1308									2216		
Frankfurt/Main d	1351								0224	0224		
Hannover Hbf d	1606	1631	1643					2200				
Köln Hbf d				1409				2226				
Düsseldorf d				1433				2242				
Duisburg d				1446				2256				
Essen d				1459								
Dortmund d				1525				2353				
Münster d				1556				0024				
Osnabrück d				1621				0130				
Bremen d				1716				0235				
Hamburg Hbf a	1721		1810	1811				0245	0355	0355		
Hamburg Hbf d					1826				0405	0405		
Lübeck Hbf d					1902			0332	0445	0445		
Puttgarden d					2005			0505	0605	0605		
Rødby F a					2100			0600	0700	0700		
Nykøbing F a					2133			0649	0749	0749		
København H a					2308	2315	2315	0825	0925	0925	0948	0948
Stockholm C a							0747				1747	
Göteborg C a						0340						1435
Oslo S a						0837						1937b

NOTES

A – NORD EXPRESS – [sleeper] 1,2 cl., [couchette] 1,2 cl. (T2), [couchette] 2 cl. and [restaurant] (Oostende/Paris) - Köln - København.
B – CHRISTIAN MORGENSTERN – [restaurant] and ♀ Hamburg - København.
C – [sleeper] 1,2 cl., [couchette] 2 cl. and [restaurant] København - Stockholm.
D – THOMAS MANN – [restaurant] and ♀ Hamburg - København.
F – BERTEL THORVALDSEN – [restaurant] and ♀ Hamburg - København.
G – KAREN BLIXEN – [restaurant] and ♀ Hamburg - København.

H – HAMLET – [restaurant] and ♀ Hamburg - København.
N – [sleeper] 1,2 cl. and [couchette] 2 cl. København - Oslo.
R – [sleeper] 1,2 cl. and [couchette] 2 cl. Basel - København.
S – [sleeper] 1,2 cl., [couchette] 2 cl. and [restaurant] München - København.
V – ①-⑥, not Dec. 25 - Jan. 1, Apr. 15,16,17, June 1.
Z – Not Dec. 24.
b – ⑤⑥⑦ only.
✗ – Supplement payable.

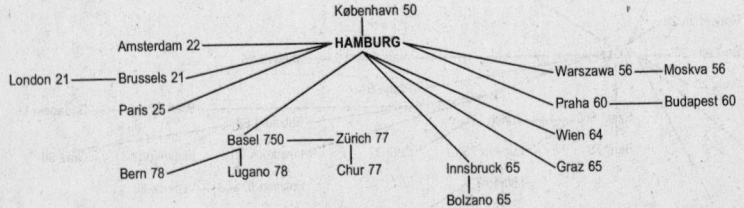

INTERNATIONAL SERVICES FROM HAMBURG

København 50 — HAMBURG
Amsterdam 22 — HAMBURG
London 21 — Brussels 21 — HAMBURG
Paris 25 — HAMBURG
Warszawa 56 — Moskva 56
Praha 60 — Budapest 60
Wien 64
Basel 750 — Zürich 77
Bern 78 — Lugano 78 — Chur 77
Innsbruck 65 — Graz 65
Bolzano 65

Table 51 — KØBENHAVN - BERLIN AND PRAHA

train number		EC							EC
train number	305	179	2245	2379	345	309	309	173
classes	1,2	1,2✗	1,2	2	2	2	2	1,2✗
notes (see below)		A	✗	c	🚢c	🍴c	D	E	B	✗
København .... d.	0720	...	1241	...	...	2105	2230	
Nykøbing .... d.	0852	...	1434	...	...	2300	0018	
Gedser .... d.	0925	...	1455	1525	...	0125	0125	
Warnemünde 🚢 .... a.	1120	...	...	1720	1817	0320	0320	
Rostock .... a.	1221	...	...	...	1821	0422	0422	
Berlin Lichtenberg ...... a.	1513	1621	...	2107	2207	0704	0704	0821
Poznań Glówny 🚻 .... a.			...	...	0200	...	...	
Warszawa Centralna..... a.			...	...	0615	...	...	
Dresden Hbf .... a.	...	1812	...	...	...	...	...	1012
Děčín 🚻 .... a.	...	1918	...	...	...	...	...	1118
Praha Holešovice .... a.	...	2059	...	...	...	...	...	1259
Praha Hlavni .... a.	...	2113	...	...	...	...	...	

train number				EC		EC		
train number	344	2278	2242	178	304	170	308	308
classes	2	1,2	1,2	1,2✗	1,2	1,2✗	2	2
notes (see below)	D	🍴e	e	✗	C	✗	G	F
Praha Hlavni .... d.	...	...	...	...	1833	...	...	...
Praha Holešovice .... d.	...	...	0847	...	1847	...	...	...
Děčín 🚻 .... d.	...	...	1033	...	2033	...	...	...
Dresden Hbf .... d.	...	...	1136	1246	2136	...	...	...
Warszawa Centralna.... d.	2355	...	...	...	...	...	...	...
Poznań Glówny 🚻 .... d.	0405	...	...	...	...	...	...	...
Berlin Lichtenberg ...... d.	0802	0851	...	1329	1451	2329	2352	2352
Rostock .... d.	...	1128	...	...	1728	...	0231	0231
Warnemünde 🚢 .... d.	...	1145	1205	...	1805	...	0330	0405
Gedser 🚻 .... a.	...	...	1410	1440	2010	...	0530	0610
Nykøbing .... a.	...	...	1458	...	2058	...	0654	0654
København .... a.	...	1655	...	2255	...	0833	0855	

NOTES

A – NEPTUN – 🛏 København - Berlin - (Chemnitz).
B – OSTSEE EXPRESS – Dec. 16 - May 27, not Dec. 24, 31:
    🛏 1,2 cl., 🛏 2 cl. and 🛏 København - Berlin.
C – NEPTUN – 🛏 Dresden - København.
D – 🛏 1,2 cl., 🛏 2 cl. and 🛏 Berlin - Warszawa and v.v.
E – OSTSEE EXPRESS – Sept. 25 - Dec. 15:
    🛏 1,2 cl., 🛏 2 cl. and 🛏 København - Berlin.

F – OSTSEE EXPRESS – Sept. 25 - Dec. 14:
    🛏 1,2 cl., 🛏 2 cl. and 🛏 Berlin - København.
G – OSTSEE EXPRESS – Dec. 15 - May 27, not Dec. 24,31:
    🛏 1,2 cl., 🛏 2 cl. and 🛏 Berlin - København.
b – Berlin Hbf.
c – Not Dec. 24,31.
e – Not Dec. 25, Jan. 1.
✗ – Supplement payable.

Table 52 — STOCKHOLM - BERLIN AND PRAHA

train type		IN		ICE	IN	IC		IN	IC	
train number	205	383	317	91	393	29	1011	385	37	319
classes	2	2	2	1,2	1,2	1,2	1,2	1,2	1,2	2🆁
notes (see below)	R	🆁 Lb	🆁 c	🆁 c	✗🆁	P	✗🆁	✗🆁	🆁	M b
Oslo Sentral .... d.	...	2137	...	0810	...	...	1015f	e	...	...
Göteborg C .... d.	...	0220	...	1215	1227	...	1525	...	...	...
Stockholm .... d.	2312	...	...	...	1012	...	...	1412	...	...
Malmö .... d.	0645	0632	0747	...	1614	1640	1712	1913	2045	2120
Trelleborg 🚢 .... d.	...	...	0830	...	...	1800	...	...	...	2230
Sassnitz Hafen 🚢 ...... a.	...	...	1200	...	...	2215	...	...	...	0230
Berlin Lichtenberg ..... a.	...	...	1716	...	...	0211	...	...	...	...
Berlin Hbf .... a.	...	...	...	...	...	...	...	...	...	0701
Dresden Hbf .... a.	...	...	...	...	...	0412	...	...	...	...
Děčín .... a.	...	...	...	...	...	0519	...	...	...	...
Praha Holešovice .... a.	...	...	...	...	...	0714	...	...	...	...
Bratislava Hlavni .... a.	...	...	...	...	...	1248	...	...	...	...
Budapest Keleti .... a.	...	...	...	...	...	1628	...	...	...	...
Beograd .... a.	...	...	...	...	...	...	...	...	...	...

train type		IN		IC	IC			IC	IN	ICE
train number	316	682	206	318	34	606	1010	42	692	94
classes	2	2	2	1,2	1,2	1,2	1,2	1,2	1,2	1,2
notes (see below)	b	Lb 🆁	R	M b	🆁✗	✗🆁	T	✗🆁	✗🆁	
Beograd .... d.	...	...	...	...	...	...	...	...	...	...
Budapest Keleti .... d.	...	...	...	...	...	...	1320	...	...	...
Bratislava Hlavni .... d.	...	...	...	...	...	...	1718	...	...	...
Praha Holešovice .. d.	...	...	...	...	...	...	2249	...	...	...
Děčín .... d.	...	...	...	...	...	...	0046	...	...	...
Dresden Hbf .... d.	...	...	...	...	...	...	0150	...	...	...
Berlin Hbf .... d.	...	...	...	2320	...	...	...	...	...	...
Berlin Lichtenberg .. d.	1300	...	...	...	...	...	0354	...	...	...
Sassnitz Hafen 🚢 ..... a.	1800	...	...	0330	...	...	0830	...	...	...
Trelleborg 🚢 .... a.	2130	...	...	0715	...	...	1200	...	...	...
Malmö .... a.	2230	2247	2300	0812	0917	0845	1256	1320	1317	...
Stockholm .... a.	...	0641	...	1541	...	...	1941	...	...	...
Göteborg C .... a.	...	0340	...	...	1245	...	...	1734	1800	
Oslo Sentral .... a.	...	0837	...	...	...	...	...	...	2219	

NOTES

L – 🛏 2 cl. and 🛏 Oslo - Malmö and v.v.
M – SASSNITZ EXPRESS – 🛏 1,2 cl., 🛏 2 cl., 🛏 and 🍴 Malmö - Berlin and v.v.
P – CSÁRDÁS – Daily to Nov. 6 and from Apr. 7:
    🛏 1,2 cl., 🛏 2 cl. and 🛏 Malmö - Budapest;
    🛏 Sassnitz - Budapest; ✗ Dresden - Budapest.
Q – Service to Jan. 8 only.
R – ①②③④⑤⑥⑦, not Nov. 5, Dec. 25, Jan. 6:
    🛏 1,2 cl., 🛏 2 cl. and 🛏 Stockholm - Malmö and v.v.

T – CSÁRDÁS – Daily to Nov. 6 and from Apr. 7:
    🛏 1,2 cl., 🛏 2 cl. and 🍴 Budapest - Malmö;
    🛏 Budapest - Sassnitz; ✗ Budapest - Dresden.
b – Not Dec. 24,31.
c – Not Dec. 25, Jan. 1.
e – Not Dec. 24.
f – ⑤⑥⑦ only.

Table 55 — FRANKFURT AND DRESDEN - WARSZAWA AND MOSKVA

train number		451	451	IC651	457	IC559	453	453
classes		1,2	2	1,2✗	1,2	1,2✗	1,2	2
notes (see below)		T	V	✗	🍴	✗	W	Y
Frankfurt/Main .... d.	...	2359	2359	1122	...	1322	...	...
Fulda .... d.	...	0113	0113	1220	...	1420	...	...
Bebra .... d.	...	0156	0156	1301	...	1501	...	...
Erfurt .... d.	...	0340	0340	1437	...	1637	...	...
Leipzig .... d.	...	0507	0507	1555	...	1755	1905	1905
Dresden Hbf .... d.	...	...	...	...	1740	...	...	...
Dresden Neustadt .... d.	...	0654	0654	1732	1748	...	2048	2048
Görlitz .... a.	...	0900	0900	...	1935	...	2255	2255
Zgorzelec 🚻 .... a.	...	0905	0905	...	1940	...	2300	2300
Jelenia Góra .... a.	...	...	1100	...	...	...	...	...
Legnica .... a.	...	1041	...	...	2103	...	0029	0029
Wroclaw Glówny .... a.	...	1137	1309	...	2156	...	0122	0122
Opole .... a.	...	...	1422	...	...	...	...	0254
Katowice .... a.	...	...	1607	...	...	...	...	0437
Kraków Glówny .... a.	...	...	1732	...	...	...	...	0614
Warszawa Centralna..... a.	...	1725	...	...	...	...	0735	...
Warszawa Wschodnia.... a.	...	1744	...	...	...	...	0748	...
Terespol 🚻 .... a.	...	2335	...	...	...	...	...	...
Brest 🚻 .... a.	...	0151	...	...	...	...	...	...
Kyïv (Kiev) .... a.	...	...	...	...	...	...	...	...
Minsk .... a.	...	0830	...	...	...	...	...	...
Moskva Smolenskaya .... a.	...	2210	...	...	...	...	...	...

Moskva train number					13				
Polish train number	456		450	36000		452	36006	IC556
classes	1,2		1,2	2		1,2	2	1,2✗
notes (see below)	🍴		T	V		W	Y	✗
Moskva Smolenskaya ... d.	...	...	1310	...	...	...	...	...
Minsk .... d.	...	...	0044	...	...	...	...	...
Kyïv (Kiev) .... d.	...	...	...	...	...	...	...	...
Brest .... d.	...	...	0800	...	...	...	...	...
Terespol .... d.	...	...	0743	...	...	...	...	...
Warszawa Wschodnia ... a.	...	...	1205	...	...	1810	...	...
Warszawa Centralna ...... a.	...	...	1220	...	...	1825	...	...
Kraków Glówny .... d.	...	...	...	1200	...	...	1942	...
Katowice .... d.	...	...	...	1327	...	...	2107	...
Opole .... d.	...	...	...	1512	...	...	2256	...
Wroclaw Glówny .... d.	0642	...	1750	1615	...	0012	0012	...
Legnica .... d.	0734	...	1845	...	...	0108	0108	...
Jelenia Góra .... d.	...	...	...	1823	...	...	...	...
Zgorzelec 🚻 .... d.	0902	...	2033	2033	...	0247	0247	...
Görlitz .... d.	0908	...	2038	2038	...	0252	0252	...
Dresden Neustadt .... a.	1054	...	2231	2231	...	0453	0453	...
Dresden Hbf .... a.	1102	...	...	...	...	0501	0501	...
Leipzig .... a.	...	...	0025	0025	...	0645	0645	0804
Erfurt .... a.	...	...	0155	0155	...	...	...	0922
Bebra .... a.	...	...	0338	0338	...	...	...	1055
Fulda .... a.	...	...	0428	0428	...	...	...	1137
Frankfurt/Main .... a.	...	...	0600	0600	...	...	...	1235

NOTES

T – 🛏 1,2 cl., 🛏 2 cl., 🛏 and 🍴 Frankfurt/Main-Warszawa and v.v. (journey 1 night);
    🛏 1,2 cl. Frankfurt/Main - Moskva and v.v. (journey 2 nights).
V – 🛏 2 cl. and 🛏 Frankfurt/Main - Kraków and v.v. (journey 1 night)

W – 🛏 1,2 cl., 🛏 2 cl., 🛏 and 🍴 Leipzig - Warszawa and v.v.
Y – 🛏 1,2 cl., 🛏 and 🍴 Leipzig - Kraków and v.v.
✗ – Supplement payable.

Table 56 — BERLIN - WARSZAWA AND MOSKVA

train number	328	EC 41	247	247	IC 508	IC 537	EC 43	449	345	320	299	299	241	241	241
classes / notes	1,2 S	1,2✗ Vb	🛏 K	🛏 L	1,2✗ ✗	1,2✗ ✗	1,2✗ Bc	1,2 N	1,2 P	1,2 E	🛏 Q	🛏 T	🛏 D	🛏 W	🛏 G
Köln Hbf d.					0910								1916	1916	1916
Düsseldorf d.													2001	2001	2001
Duisburg d.													2016	2016	2016
Essen d.													2040	2040	2040
Dortmund d.					1027								2148	2148	2148
Bielefeld d.					1113								2307	2307	2307
Hannover d.					1204	1251									
Hamburg Hbf d.					1454	1550									
Berlin Zoo d.							1632								
Berlin Hbf d.		0810													
Berlin Lichtenberg d.	0632		1140	1140			1722	2024	2207	2225	2300	2300	0341	0341	0341
Frankfurt/Oder d.		0900	1320	1320				2145	2319		0024	0024			
Szczecin Główny a.	0844									0047					
Gdynia Główna a.	1315									0604					
Gdańsk Główny a.										0655					
Kaliningrad a.										1330					
Kunowice a.			1333	1333				2158	2332		0037	0037			
Rzepin a.		0918	1352	1352			1740	2225	2349		0057	0057	0409	0409	0409
Wrocław Główny a.								0158							
Katowice a.								0507							
Kraków Główny a.								0636							
Poznań Główny a.		1109	1605	1605			1928		0200		0315	0315	0625	0625	0625
Warszawa Centralna a.		1430	2010	2010			2240		0615				1015	1015	1015
Warszawa Wschodnia a.		1449	2024	2024			2254		0629		0720g	0720g	1029	1029	1029
Grodno a.											1649	1649			
Vilnius a.											2038	2038			
Riga a.												0810			
Terespol a.			2335	0036									1338	1338	1338
Brest a.			0151	0256									1616	1616	1616
Kyïv (Kiev) a.				1805											1120
Minsk a.			0830								1250			1742p	
St Peterburg Varshavski a.													0418		
Smolensk a.			1430										1206		
Moskva Smolenskaya a.			2210												

train number	EC 42	IC 507	EC 536	67 248	13 246	329	EC 40	49 240	15 240	683 240	222 298	25 298	448	7 321	344
classes / notes	1,2 Bb	1,2✗ ✗	1,2✗ ✗	🛏 L	🛏 K	1,2 S	1,2✗ Vc	🛏 Y	🛏 D	🛏 H	🛏 T	🛏 Q	1,2 N	1,2 F	1,2 P
Moskva Smolenskaya d.					1309				2015						
Smolensk d.					2027				0326						
St Peterburg Varshavski d.								1510p				2025			
Minsk d.					0044				0736						
Kyïv (Kiev) d.				1110						1805					
Brest d.				0305	0800			1436	1436	1436					
Riga d.											2205				
Vilnius d.											1022	1022			
Grodno d.											1434	1434			
Terespol d.				0300	0743			1500	1500	1500					
Warszawa Wschodnia d.	0600			1038	1038		1635	1910	1910	1910	2206g	2206g			2340
Warszawa Centralna d.	0615			1050	1050		1650	1925	1925	1925					2355
Kraków Główny d.													2102		
Katowice d.													2232		
Wrocław Główny d.													0132		
Poznań Główny d.	0918			1445	1445		1953	2250	2250	2250	0215	0215			0405
Rzepin d.	1108			1653	1653		2144	0100	0100	0100	0430	0430	0503		0615
Kaliningrad d.														1712	
Gdańsk Główny d.						1530								2211	
Gdynia Główna d.						1942								2330	
Szczecin Główny d.													0531	0450	
Kunowice a.				1711	1711			0115	0115	0115	0450	0450			0637
Frankfurt/Oder a.	1128			1723	1723	2200	2204	0127	0127	0127	0627	0627	0704	0728	0649
Berlin Lichtenberg a.	1218			1847	1847		2254								0802
Berlin Hbf a.															
Berlin Zoo a.		1307	1400												
Hamburg Hbf a.			1715												
Hannover a.		1555						0547	0547	0547					
Bielefeld a.		1644						0709	0709	0709					
Dortmund a.		1733						0824	0824	0824					
Essen a.								0900	0900	0900					
Duisburg a.								0917	0917	0917					
Düsseldorf a.								0933	0933	0933					
Köln Hbf a.			1850					1000	1000	1000					

NOTES

B – BEROLINA – 🍴 and 🍷 Berlin - Warszawa and v.v.
D – 🛏1,2 cl., 🛏 2 cl. and 🍴 (Brussels) - Köln - Warszawa and v.v. (journey 1 night);
   🛏 1,2 cl. (Brussels) - Köln - Moskva and v.v. (journey 2 nights).
E – GEDANIA – 🛏 1,2 cl., 🛏 2 cl. and 🍴 Berlin - Gdynia (1 night);
   🛏 1,2 cl. Berlin - Kaliningrad (1 night, not Dec. 23,24,25,30,31, Apr. 15,16).
F – GEDANIA 🛏 1,2 cl., 🛏 2 cl. and 🍴 Gdynia - Berlin (1 night);
   🛏 1,2 cl. Kaliningrad - Berlin (1 night, not Dec. 24,25,26,31, Jan. 1, Apr. 16,17).
G – ⑦: 🛏 1,2 cl. (Brussels) - Köln - Kyïv (2 nights).
H – ⑤: 🛏 1,2 cl. Kyïv - Köln - (Brussels) (2 nights).
K – MOSKWA EXPRESS – 🛏 1,2 cl. Berlin - Moskva and v.v.
L – KIEW EXPRESS – 🛏 2 cl. Berlin - Kyïv and v.v. (1 night).
N – 🛏 1,2 cl., 🛏 2 cl., 🍴 and 🍷 Berlin - Krakow and v.v. (1 night).

P – 🛏1,2 cl., 🛏 2 cl. and 🍴 Berlin - Warszawa and v.v. (1 night).
Q – ST. PETERSBURG EXPRESS – 🛏 1,2 cl. Berlin - St Peterburg and v.v. (2 nights).
S – MARE BALTICUM – 🍴 and 🍷 Berlin - Gdynia and v.v.
T – 🛏 2 cl. Berlin - Riga and v.v. (2 nights).
V – VARSOVIA – 🍴 and 🍷 Berlin - Warszawa and v.v.
W – ①⑤: 🛏 2 cl. (Brussels) - Köln - Sankt Peterburg (journey 2 nights).
Y – ③⑥: 🛏 2 cl. Sankt Peterburg - Köln - (Brussels) (journey 2 nights).
b – Not Dec. 25, Jan. 1.
c – Not Dec. 24,31.
g – Warszawa Gdańska.
p – Sankt Peterburg Vitebski.
✗ – Supplement payable.

INTERNATIONAL SERVICES FROM BERLIN

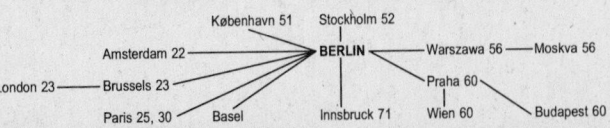

København 51   Stockholm 52
Amsterdam 22 — BERLIN — Warszawa 56 — Moskva 56
London 23 — Brussels 23   Praha 60
Paris 25, 30   Basel   Innsbruck 71   Wien 60   Budapest 60

Table 57 — KÖLN, FRANKFURT/MAIN AND MÜNCHEN - PRAHA

train type / number / classes	2606 IR 1,2	169 IC 1,2 E	107 IC 1,2 ✗	2663 IR 1,2	259 1,2	2063 IR 1,2	2465 1,2	51 EC 1,2✗ A	7009 2	27 EC 1,2 ✗	3521 1,2	2195 IR 1,2	167 EC 1,2 F	201 1,2 H	154 EC 1,2✗ Ⓡb	357 1,2 D	223 1,2 L	353 1,2 B	1980 1,2 C
Dortmund Hbf d.								0540		0840									
Hagen Hbf d.								0601		0901									
Wuppertal Hbf d.								0620		0920									
Düsseldorf Hbf d.																	2005		
Köln Hbf d.								0654		0954							2037	2111	
Bonn d.								0714		1014							2059	2133	
Koblenz d.								0746		1046							2135	2209	
Mainz d.								0838		1136							2228	2305	
Frankfurt/Main Hbf d.								0914		1214							2327	2343	
Würzburg d.								1028		1328							0054	0119	
Bern d.													0814						
Zürich Hbf d.													0940			1811			
St. Gallen d.													1040						
Bregenz d.													1121						
Lindau d.													1137						
Stuttgart d.				0607			0807												
München Hbf d.	0657						0857						1116	1335	1408	2100	2144		
Regensburg d.	0831						1031			1529				1538					2312
Nürnberg d.		0755		0834			1016	1135				1444		1615		0025	0240	0240	0240
Schwandorf d.	0858	0904					1049					1541		1715					
Fürth im Wald d.		1002																	
Marktredwitz d.	1006			0955	1011	1206		1254							0200	0426	0426	0426	
Schirnding a.					1024										0214	0440	0440	0440	
Cheb a.					1037			1321	1350						0229	0455	0455	0455	
Karlovy Vary a.					1203				1459										
Plzeň a.								1503											
Praha Hlavni a.		1136	1326	1340						1645			1848		0425	0650	0650	0650	
Warszawa Centralna a.			2245										2039	2116	0611	0839	0839	0839	

train number / classes / notes	200 EC 1,2 H	166 EC 1,2✗ G	3518 IR 1,2	2192 EC 1,2✗	28 EC 1,2 ✗	258 1,2	2603 1,2	2668 IR 1,2	7044 1,2	50 EC 1,2✗ A	2607 1,2	2662 1,2	106 IC 1,2 ✗	168 IC 1,2 E	2160 Ⓡ 1,2	2162 1,2 ⑥	352 1,2 J	352 1,2 C	352 1,2 K	356 1,2 D	481 1,2
Warszawa Centralna d.	2005												0610								
Praha Hlavni d.	0612	0723								1308			1459	1623			2050	2050	2050	2352	
Plzeň d.		0913								1446				1811			2241	2241	2241	0148	
Karlovy Vary d.									1423												
Cheb d.						1008				1536		1632									
Schirnding a.						1113											0053	0053	0053	0347	
Marktredwitz a.						1126	1140	1201		1659		1748					0108	0108	0108	0402	
Fürth im Wald a.		1045						1148							1953		0124	0124	0124	0420	
Schwandorf a.		1143	1211								1906		2110		2050	2055					
Nürnberg a.			1314					1324		1819	1945		2203								
Regensburg a.		1221			1228		1325			1925					2125	2140	0250	0250	0250	0547	
München Hbf a.		1351		1426			1501			2101					2301	2312		0607			
Stuttgart a.					1644			1553		2153											
Lindau a.		1622																		0831	0942
Bregenz a.		1638																			
St. Gallen a.		1718																			
Zürich Hbf a.		1823																			
Bern a.		1945																			1247
Würzburg a.				1428						1928							0404				
Frankfurt/Main Hbf a.				1543						2043							0536		0506		
Mainz a.				1624						2122							0608		0643		
Koblenz a.				1713						2211							0701		0728		
Bonn a.				1745						2243							0737		0823		
Köln Hbf a.				1805						2305							0801		0859		
Düsseldorf Hbf a.				1831															0921		
Wuppertal Hbf a.										2340									0951		
Hagen Hbf a.										2357											
Dortmund Hbf a.				1920						0020									1056		

NOTES

A – KARLSTEIN – [sleeper] and ✗ Dortmund - Praha and v.v.
B – Sept. 25 - Oct. 31, Dec. 16 - Jan. 8 and Mar. 31 - May 27:
    [1,2 cl., 2 cl.] and tray Köln - Praha and v.v.
C – [1,2 cl., 2 cl. and sleeper] München - Praha and v.v.
D – [1,2 cl., 2 cl., sleeper] and tray Stuttgart - Praha and v.v.
E – FRANZ KAFKA – [sleeper] and ✗ Nürnberg - Praha and v.v.
F – ALBERT EINSTEIN – [sleeper] and ✗ (Interlaken) - Bern - Praha.
G – ALBERT EINSTEIN – [sleeper] and ✗ Praha - Bern.
H – SILESIA – [sleeper] 1,2 cl., 2 cl. and [sleeper] Praha - Warszawa and v.v.
J – Sept. 25 - Oct. 30, Dec. 15 - Jan. 7 and Mar. 30 - May 27:
    [sleeper] 1,2 cl., 2 cl., [sleeper] and tray Praha - Köln.
K – Oct. 31 - Dec. 14 and Jan. 8 - Mar. 29:
    [sleeper] 1,2 cl., 2 cl. and [sleeper] Dortmund - Praha.
L – Nov. 1 - Dec. 15 and Jan. 9 - Mar. 30:
    [1,2 cl., 2 cl. and sleeper] Praha - Dortmund.
b – Not Oct. 2, Dec. 24-31, Apr. 14-16,30.
✗ – Supplement payable.

INTERNATIONAL SERVICES FROM FRANKFURT/MAIN

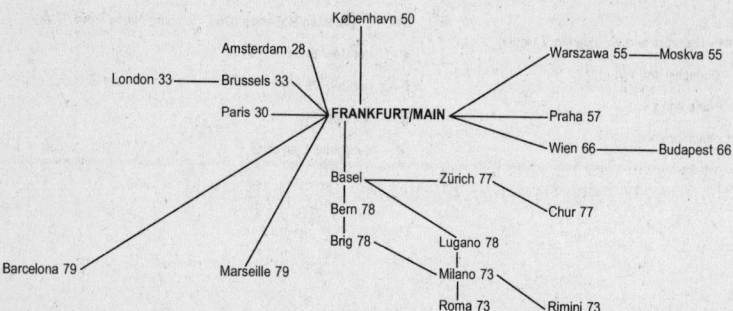

INTERNATIONAL – 60 For summer service from May 28 see page 536

Table 60 HAMBURG AND BERLIN - PRAHA AND WIEN

train type		EC	EC	IC	EC	IC	EC	EC	IC	EC	D	D	D	D	D
train number	2603	171	173	531	175	533	177	9	537	179	371	379	377	373	477
classes	2	1,2/	1,2/	1,2/	1,2/	1,2/	1,2/	1,2	1,2/	1,2/	1,2	1,2	2	1,2	1,2
notes (see below)		G b	H	f 🍷	F	✕	C	✕	✕	J	N	K	A	E	B
Hamburg Altona d.	...	...	...	0638	...	0838	...	...	1238	...	...	...	...	...	2153
Hamburg Hbf d.	...	...	...	0651	...	0851	...	...	1251	...	...	...	...	...	2221
Nauen d.	...	...	...	0913	0924	1113	1124	...	1513	1524	...	...	...	...	|
Berlin Hbf d.	...	...	...	...	|	...	|	...	...	|	...	...	...	...	|
Berlin Lichtenberg d.	0612	0621	0821	...	1021	...	1221	...	...	1621	...	1848	2224	2348	|
Leipzig d.	0833	|	|	...	|	...	|	...	...	|	...	|	|	|	0324
Bad Brambach d.	1215	|	|	...	|	...	|	...	...	|	...	|	|	|	|
Karlovy Vary a.	1343	|	|	...	|	...	|	...	...	|	...	|	|	|	|
Dresden Hbf d.	...	0825	1025	...	1225	...	1425	...	...	1825	1955	2109	0028	0153	0525
Bad Schandau d.	...	0857	1057	...	1257	...	1457	...	...	1857	2030	2150	0103	0253	0605
Děčín a.	...	0918	1118	...	1318	...	1518	...	...	1918	2051	2211	0122	0314	0626
Praha Holešovice a.	...	1059	1259	...	1459	...	1659	1711	...	2059	2309	0007	0314	0514	0815
Praha Hlavni a.	...	1113	|	...	|	...	...	|	...	2113	|	|	|	|	0831
Pardubice a.	...	...	|	...	|	...	...	|	...	...	0038	|	|	|	...
Olomouc a.	...	...	|	...	|	...	...	|	...	...	0228	|	|	|	...
Poprad Tatry a.	...	...	|	...	|	...	...	|	...	...	0741	|	|	|	...
Košice a.	...	...	|	...	|	...	...	|	...	...	0903	|	|	|	...
Brno hlavni a.	...	...	1617	...	1817	...	...	2017	...	...	...	0340	0634	0917	...
Břeclav a.	...	...	1657	...	1857	...	...	2057	...	...	...	0427	0717	1014	...
Wien Süd a.	...	...	1804	...	|	...	...	2203	...	...	...	|	0852	|	...
Bratislava hlavni a.	...	...	...	...	2000	...	...	...	...	...	...	0539	...	1130	...
Stúrovo a.	...	...	...	...	2127	...	...	...	...	...	...	0738	...	1310	...
Budapest Nyugati a.	...	...	...	...	|	...	...	...	...	...	...	0858	...	|	...
Budapest Keleti a.	...	...	...	...	2242	...	...	...	...	...	...	...	...	1442	...
Komárom a.	...	...	...	...	...	...	...	...	...	...	...	...	...	|	...
Siofok a.	...	...	...	...	...	...	...	...	...	...	...	...	...	|	...
Fonyód a.	...	...	...	...	...	...	...	...	...	...	...	...	...	|	...
Lököshaza a.	...	...	...	...	...	...	...	...	...	...	...	...	...	1840	...
Curtici a.	...	...	...	...	...	...	...	...	...	...	...	...	...	2025	...
Bucureşti Nord a.	...	...	...	...	...	...	...	...	...	...	...	...	...	0559	...
Beograd a.	...	...	...	...	...	...	...	...	...	...	...	...	...	...	...
Sofija a.	...	...	...	...	...	...	...	...	...	...	...	...	...	...	...

train number		EC	IC	EC	EC	IC	EC	IC	EC		EC				
train number	226	178	536	8	176	532	174	530	172	366	170	476	372	376	378
classes	1,2	1,2/	1,2/	1,2/	1,2/	1,2/	1,2/	1,2/	1,2/	2	1,2/	1,2	1,2	2	1,2
notes (see below)	N	J	✕	✕	C	✕	F	🍷 g	H		G e	B	E	A	K
Sofija d.	...	...	...	...	...	...	...	...	...	...	...	...	...	...	...
Beograd d.	...	...	...	...	...	...	...	...	...	...	...	...	...	...	...
Bucureşti Nord d.	...	...	...	...	...	...	...	...	...	...	...	...	0110	...	...
Curtici d.	...	...	...	...	...	...	...	...	...	...	...	...	1100	...	...
Lököshaza d.	...	...	...	...	...	...	...	...	...	...	...	...	1040	...	...
Fonyód d.	...	...	...	...	...	...	...	...	...	...	...	...	|	...	...
Siofok d.	...	...	...	...	...	...	...	...	...	...	...	...	|	...	...
Komárom d.	...	...	...	...	...	...	...	...	...	...	...	...	|	...	...
Budapest Keleti d.	...	...	...	...	...	...	0655	...	...	...	...	...	1500	...	...
Budapest Nyugati d.	...	...	...	...	...	...	|	...	...	...	...	...	|	...	1825
Stúrovo d.	...	...	...	...	...	...	0811	...	...	...	...	...	1630	...	1945
Bratislava hlavni d.	...	...	...	...	...	...	0943	...	...	...	...	...	1818	...	2145
Wien Süd d.	...	...	...	0739	...	...	|	...	1139	...	...	...	|	2025	|
Břeclav d.	...	...	...	0845	...	...	1047	...	1247	...	...	...	1931	2154	2258
Brno hlavni d.	...	...	...	0925	...	...	1128	...	1328	...	...	...	2017	2237	2341
Košice d.	2007	...	...	|	...	...	|	...	|	...	...	...	|	|	|
Poprad Tatry d.	2134	...	...	|	...	...	|	...	|	...	...	...	|	|	|
Olomouc d.	0249	...	...	|	...	...	|	...	|	...	...	...	|	|	|
Pardubice d.	0440	...	...	|	...	...	|	...	|	...	...	...	|	|	|
Praha Hlavni d.	|	...	...	|	1233	...	|	...	|	...	1833	1945	|	|	|
Praha Holešovice d.	0612	0847	...	1232	1247	...	1447	...	1647	...	1847	1958	0035	0205	0312
Děčín d.	0831	1033	...	...	1433	...	1633	...	1833	...	2033	2202	0241	0411	0509
Bad Schandau a.	0850	1055	...	...	1452	...	1655	...	1852	...	2052	2220	0307	0430	0528
Dresden Hbf a.	0925	1136	...	...	1525	...	1736	...	1925	...	2125	2255	0347	0505	0603
Karlovy Vary d.	...	|	...	...	|	...	|	...	|	1430	|	|	|	|	|
Bad Brambach a.	...	|	...	...	|	...	|	...	|	1555	|	|	|	|	|
Leipzig a.	...	|	...	...	|	...	|	...	|	1915	|	0045	|	|	|
Berlin Lichtenberg a.	...	1329	...	...	1729	...	1929	...	2129	2150	2329	|	0544	0714	0814
Berlin Hbf a.	...	|	...	...	|	...	|	...	...	...	...	|	...	...	...
Nauen a.	...	1423	1436	...	1823	1836	2023	2036	...	...	...	|	...	...	...
Hamburg Hbf a.	...	...	1659	...	...	2059	...	2259	...	...	...	0604c	...	...	...
Hamburg Altona a.	...	...	1715	...	...	2117	...	2315	...	...	...	0630c	...	...	...

NOTES

A – SANSSOUCI – 1,2 cl., 2 cl. and [2] Berlin - Wien and v.v.

B – 1,2 cl., 2 cl. and [12] Hamburg - Praha and v.v.

C – PORTA BOHEMICA – [12] and ✕ Nauen - Praha and v.v.

E – BALT ORIENT EXPRESS – 1,2 cl., 2 cl. and [12] Berlin - Bucureşti and v.v. (journey 2 nights).

F – HUNGARIA – [12] and ✕ Nauen - Budapest and v.v.

G – COMENIUS – [12] and ✕ Berlin - Praha and v.v.

H – VINDOBONA – [12] and ✕ Berlin - Wien and v.v.

J – CARL MARIA VON WEBER – [12] and ✕ Nauen - Praha and v.v.

K – METROPOL – 1,2 cl., 2 cl. and [12] Berlin - Budapest and v.v.

N – [12] Dresden - Košice and v.v.

b – Not Dec. 25, Jan. 1.

c – ⑦: Hamburg Hbf arrive 0708, Hamburg Altona arrive 0730.

e – Not Dec. 24,31.

f – Not Dec. 25.

g – Not Dec. 24.

/ – Supplement payable.

76 For explanation of standard symbols see page 4 03

Table 61 — MÜNCHEN AND WIEN - BUDAPEST AND BEOGRAD

Travel to or from Beograd/Serbia is dangerous, passengers are strongly recommended to use an alternative route.

train type	EC			EN				EC		EC						
train number	41	345	467	263	491	63	343	25	347	347	341	341	269
classes	1,2✗	1,2	1,2	1,2	1,2	1,2✗	1,2	1,2✗	2	1,2	2	2	2
notes (see below)	H	M	F	A	J	C	P	E	L	K	R	Z	B
Stuttgart Hbf.............d.	...	...	...	...	...	0600	...	...	...	...	...	...	...
München Hbf.............d.	...	...	...	...	...	0825	...	...	...	...	...	...	2319
Salzburg.............d.	...	...	0453	0605	...	1000	...	...	...	...	...	...	0116
Linz.............d.	...	...	0612	0727	...	1114	...	1614	...	...	...	...	0233
Wien West.............d.	...	...	0830	1005	...	1320	...	1820	...	...	...	...	...
Wien Süd.............d.	0711	0803	...	...	...	...	1505	...	1905	1905	2300	2300	...
Hegyeshalom ▥.............a.	0755	0848	0928	1103	...	1423	1603	1923	2008	2008	0005	0005	0519
Györ.............a.	0825	0927	1006	1141	...	1501	1643	2001	2051	2051	0056	0056	0621
Budapest Keleti.............a.	...	1108	1153	1328	1510	1638	1833	2138	2238	2238	...	...	0808
Budapest Déli.............a.	1003	...	...	...	...	...	...	...	...	...	...	...	...
Záhony 898.............a.	...	...	...	...	...	...	2300	...	...	...	...	...	...
Szeged 895.............a.	...	...	...	...	...	...	...	...	...	...	...	0552	...
Curtici ▥.............a.	...	...	...	...	...	...	...	...	0350	...	...	...	1335
Arad.............a.	...	...	...	...	...	...	...	...	0452	...	...	...	1425
Brașov.............a.	...	...	...	...	...	...	...	...	1056	...	...	...	2016
București Nord ▥.............a.	...	...	...	...	...	...	...	...	1339	...	...	...	2257
Kelebia ▥.............a.	...	1350	...	1745	...	...	...	...	0310	0520	...	...	...
Beograd.............a.	...	1710	...	2128	...	...	...	...	0709	0907	...	...	...
Niš.............a.	...	...	...	0205	...	...	...	...	1140	1452	...	...	...
Skopje.............a.	...	...	...	...	...	...	...	...	1614	1757	...	...	...
Thessaloniki.............a.	...	...	...	...	...	...	...	...	2138	...	...	...	...
Athínai.............a.	...	...	...	...	...	...	...	...	0633	...	...	...	...
Dimitrovgrad.............a.	...	...	...	0416	...	...	...	...	...	...	...	...	...
Sofija.............a.	...	...	...	0738	...	...	...	...	...	...	...	...	...
Svilengrad.............a.	...	...	...	1250	...	...	...	...	...	...	...	...	...
Kapikule ▥.............a.	...	...	...	1345	...	...	...	...	...	...	...	...	...
Istanbul.............a.	...	...	...	1959	...	...	...	...	...	...	...	...	...

train number			EC		EC		EN		EC			
train number	23	334	24	342	62	490	262	466	344	40	21	7059	212
train number	346										268	340	340
classes	1,2	2	1,2✗	1,2	1,2✗	1,2	2	1,2	1,2	1,2✗	2	2	2
notes (see below)	K	L	E	P	C	J	A	F	M	H	B	Z	R
Istanbul.............d.	...	...	...	...	...	1000	...	...	...	...	...	...	...
Kapikule ▥.............d.	...	...	...	...	...	1620	...	...	...	...	...	...	...
Svilengrad.............d.	...	...	...	...	...	1715	...	...	...	...	...	...	...
Sofija.............d.	...	...	...	...	...	2255	...	...	...	...	...	...	...
Dimitrovgrad.............d.	...	...	...	...	...	0010	...	...	...	...	...	...	...
Athínai.............d.	...	2330	...	...	...	...	...	...	...	...	...	...	...
Thessaloniki.............d.	...	0826	...	...	...	...	...	...	...	...	...	...	...
Skopje.............d.	...	1220	...	...	...	...	...	...	...	...	...	...	...
Niš.............d.	...	1730	...	...	...	0201	...	...	...	...	...	0925
Beograd.............d.	...	2145	...	...	...	0650	...	1155	...	...	1315
Kelebia ▥.............d.	...	0205	...	...	...	1140	...	1545	...	...	1920
București Nord.............d.	1625	...	...	...	...	...	...	...	...	0821	...	2305
Brașov.............d.	1904	...	...	...	...	...	...	...	...	1105	...	...
Arad.............d.	0053	...	...	...	...	...	...	...	...	1655	...	...
Curtici ▥.............d.	0150	...	...	...	...	...	...	...	...	1750	...	...
Szeged 895.............d.	...	...	...	...	...	...	...	...	...	...	...	2240
Záhony 898.............d.	...	...	...	0525	...	...	...	...	...	...	...	...
Budapest Déli.............d.	...	...	...	...	...	...	...	...	...	1905	...	...
Budapest Keleti.............d.	0555	0555	0825	0955	1230	1413	1530	1725	1830	...	2120
Györ.............d.	0734	0734	0959	1145	1404	...	1714	1904	2014	2038	2259	0342	0342
Hegyeshalom ▥.............d.	0815	0815	1040	1229	1445	...	1755	1945	2055	2112	2347	0425	0425
Wien Süd.............a.	...	...	...	...	...	...	...	...	2145	2156	...	...	...
Wien West.............a.	0920	0920	1146	1334	1550	...	1900	2050	...	...	...	...	...
Linz.............a.	...	...	...	...	1746	...	2131	2313	...	0228	...	0530	0530
Salzburg ▥.............a.	...	...	1346	...	1900	...	2255	0033	...	0353	...	...	...
München Hbf.............a.	...	...	...	...	2036	...	...	...	...	0603	...	...	...
Stuttgart Hbf.............a.	...	...	...	...	2311	...	...	...	...	...	...	...	...

NOTES

A – ORIENT EXPRESS – ▭ and ✕ Salzburg - Budapest and v.v.
B – KÁLMÁN IMRE – ▱ 1,2 cl., ▰ 2 cl. and ▭ Budapest - București and v.v.; ▭ München - București and v.v.; ▭ Budapest - București and v.v.
C – BARTÓK BÉLA – ▭ and ✕ Stuttgart - Budapest and v.v.
E – FRANZ LISZT – ▭ (Dortmund) - Linz - Budapest and v.v.
F – WIENER WALZER – ▰ 2 cl. and ▭ (Basel) - Salzburg - Budapest and v.v.;
▭ Wien - Budapest and v.v.
H – LEHÁR – ▭ and ✕ Wien - Budapest and v.v.
J – BALKAN EXPRESS – ▱ 1,2 cl., ▰ 2 cl. and ▭ Budapest - Sofija and v.v.; ▰ 1,2 cl. and ▭ Budapest - Istanbul and v.v.; ▭ Sofija - Istanbul and v.v.

K – DACIA EXPRESS – ▱ 1,2 cl., ▰ 2 cl. and ▭ Wien - București and v.v.; ▭ and ✕ Wien - Budapest and v.v.
L – ▭ Wien - Athínai and v.v. (journey 2 nights); ▱ 1,2 cl., ▰ 2 cl. and ▭ Budapest - Athínai and v.v.
M – AVALA – ▭ and ✕ Wien - Budapest and v.v.
P – ARRABONA – ▭ and ✕ Wien - Záhony and v.v.
R – BEOGRAD EXPRESS – ▱ 1,2 cl., ▰ 2 cl. and ▭ Wien - Beograd and v.v.; ▰ 2 cl. Wien - Skopje and v.v.
Z – ▭ Wien - Szeged and v.v.
✗ – Supplement payable.

Table 62 — MÜNCHEN AND VILLACH - LJUBLJANA AND ZAGREB

train number	IC		EC	EC					train number		EC	EC		IC		
train number	590	311	11	115	315	297	297		train number	310	114	10	314	691	296	480
classes	1,2 ☕	2	1,2✗	1,2✗	1,2	2	2		classes	2	1,2✗	1,2✗	1,2	1,2	2	2
notes (see below)			C	✕		A	B		notes (see below)	✕	C				A	B
Leipzig.............d.	...	...	0715	...	...	...	...		Zagreb.............d.	...	0810	...	...	2100	...
Nürnberg.............d.	...	...	1124	...	...	...	...		Zidani Most ▥.............d.	...	...	...	...	2223	...
München Hbf.............d.	...	...	1325	1525	...	2246	2246		Rijeka.............d.	...	...	...	...	...	...	2035
Salzburg.............d.	0708	...	1508	1708	...	0045	0045		Ljubljana.............d.	0825	1020	1725	2335	2335
Bischofshofen.............d.	0752	...	1552	1752	...	0128	0128		Jesenice ▥.............d.	0930	1129	1840	0057	0057
Schwarzach St Veit.............d.	0807	...	1607	1807	...	0145	0145		Villach Hbf.............a.	1005	1019	1206	1918	2019	0134e	0134e
Klagenfurt.............d.	...	...	...	...	...	...	...		Klagenfurt.............d.	...	...	...	...	...	...	...
Villach Hbf.............d.	0943	1040	1753	1944	1956	0327e	0327e		Schwarzach St Veit.............a.	...	1155	1355	...	2155	0318	0318
Jesenice ▥.............a.	...	1114	1830	...	2033	0405	0405		Bischofshofen.............a.	...	1209	1409	...	2209	0332	0332
Ljubljana.............a.	...	1220	1937	...	2140	0525	0525		Salzburg.............a.	...	1253	1453	...	2253	0415	0415
Rijeka.............a.	...	...	...	...	...	...	0810		München Hbf.............a.	...	1435	1635	...	...	0613	0613
Zidani Most ▥.............a.	...	...	...	2241	0635	...		Nürnberg.............a.	...	...	1834	...	...	...	...
Zagreb.............a.	...	...	2150	...	0004	0800	...		Leipzig.............a.	...	...	2240	...	...	...	...

NOTES

A – ▱ 1,2 cl., ▰ 2 cl. and ▭ München - Zagreb and v.v.
B – ▰ 2 cl. and ▭ München - Rijeka and v.v.

C – MIMARA – ▭ and ✕ Leipzig - Zagreb and v.v.
e – Villach West.
✗ – Supplement payable.

Table 64 — HAMBURG - WIEN

train type	ICE	ICE	EC	ICE	ICE	EC	ICE	ICE	EC	ICE	ICE	EC	IR	EN
train number	791	881	23	793	883	25	895	785	27	897	787	29	2489	491
classes	1,2	1,2	1,2	1,2	1,2	1,2	1,2	1,2	1,2	1,2	1,2	1,2	1,2	2
notes (see below)	D	D			B				B			C		A
Hamburg Altona .... d.	0546	...	...	0748	...	...	0948	...	0533	1148	...	0733	...	2023
Hamburg Hbf .... d.	0600	...	...	0802	...	...	1002	...	0547	1202	...	0747	...	2037
Bremen Hbf .... d.		0617	...	...	0817	...	...	1017	0645	...	1217	0845	2110	...
Hannover Hbf .... d.	0715	0727	...	0915	0927	...	1115	1127	...	1315	1327	...	2215	2224
Nürnberg .... d.		1020	1028	...	1220	1228	...	1420	1428	...	1620	1628	...	0253
Passau .... d.			1254	...	...	1454	...	...	1644	...	...	1844	...	0520
Linz .... a.			1411	...	...	1611	...	...	1811	...	...	2011	...	0630
Wien Westbahnhof ...... a.			1605	...	...	1805	...	...	2005	...	...	2205	...	0830

train type	EC	ICE	ICE	EC	ICE	ICE	EC	ICE	ICE	EC	ICE	ICE	EN	IR
train number	28	882	794	26	784	894	24	880	792	22	782	892	490	2588
classes	1,2	1,2	1,2	1,2	1,2	1,2	1,2	1,2	1,2	1,2	1,2	1,2	2	1,2
notes (see below)	C			B									A	
Wien Westbahnhof ...... d.	0800	...	...	1000	...	...	1200	...	...	1400	...	...	2000	...
Linz .... d.	0949	...	...	1149	...	...	1349	...	...	1549	...	...	2150	...
Passau .... a.	1108	...	...	1308	...	...	1508	...	...	1708	...	...	2305	...
Nürnberg .... a.		1329	1338	...	1529	1538	...	1729	1738	...	1929	1938	0123	...
Hannover Hbf .... a.		1631	1643	...	1831	1843	...	2031	2043	...	2231	2243	0602	0643
Bremen Hbf .... a.	2114	1743	...	2314	...	1943	2143	...	...	...	2343	...	0751	0748
Hamburg Hbf .... a.	2211	...	1756	0011	...	1956	2158	...	...	...	...	2358	0804	...
Hamburg Altona .... a.	2224	...	1810	0024	...	2010	2212	...	...	...	...	0012	...	...

NOTES

A – HANS ALBERS – [symbol] 1,2 cl., [symbol] 2 cl. and [symbol] Hamburg - Wien and v.v.
B – JOSEPH HAYDN – [symbol] and [symbol] Hamburg - (Köln) - Wien and v.v.
C – PRINZ EUGEN – [symbol] and [symbol] (Kiel) - Hamburg - (Köln) - Wien and v.v.
D – ①②③④⑤⑥, not Oct. 3, Dec. 25 - Jan. 1, Apr. 15,16,17, May 1.
✗ – Supplement payable.

Table 65 — HAMBURG - INNSBRUCK AND KLAGENFURT

train number	1299	1299	1299	1299	1089	483	1883
classes	2	1,2	2	2	[bed]	2	2
notes (see below)	L	K	J	G	A	C	D
København 50 .... d.	...	...	...	...	...	1905	...
Kiel 663 .... d.	...	...	...	...	...	...	2245
Hamburg Altona ...... d.	1938	1938	1938	1938	...	2053	0033
Hamburg Hbf .... d.	1952	1952	1952	1952	2107	0057	0057
Hannover .... d.	2202	2202	2202	2202	2251	0229	0229
Lindau .... a.					0823		
Bregenz .... a.					0832		
Feldkirch .... a.					0903		
Bludenz .... a.					0932		
Langen am Arlberg ... a.					1014		
St. Anton am Arlberg . a.					1026		
Landeck .... a.					1055		
Ötztal .... a.					1128		
Kufstein .... a.	0525	...	...	0525	...	1037	1037
Wörgl .... a.	0550	...	...	0550	...	1055	1055
Kitzbühel .... a.	0742						
St. Johann .... a.	0753						
Saalfelden .... a.	0823						
Zell am See .... a.	0836						
Innsbruck .... a.	...	...	...	0629	1153	1136	1136
Brennero .... a.	...	...	...	0720	...		
Bolzano .... a.	...	...	...	0908	...		
Merano .... a.							
Salzburg .... a.		0607	0607				
Bischofshofen .... a.		0705	0705				
Radstadt .... a.		0738					
Selzthal .... a.		0845					
Graz .... a.		1050					
Schwarzach St Veit ... a.	0912	...	0724	...			
Badgastein .... a.	...	...	0802	...			
Villach .... a.	...	...	0914	...			
Klagenfurt .... a.	...	...	0948b	...			

train number	482	482	1018	1614	1298	818	1122
classes	2	2	[bed]	2	2	1,2	2
notes (see below)	E	F	B	M	N	P	H
Klagenfurt .... d.	...	...	...	...	1950b	...	...
Villach .... d.	...	...	...	...	2026	...	...
Badgastein .... d.	...	...	...	...	2148	...	...
Schwarzach St Veit ... d.	...	...	...	1828	2223	...	...
Graz .... d.	...	...	...	...	...	1900	...
Selzthal .... d.	...	...	...	...	...	2113	...
Radstadt .... d.	...	...	...	...	...	2219	...
Bischofshofen .... d.	...	...	...	...	2257	2257	...
Salzburg .... d.	...	...	...	...	2358	2358	...
Merano .... d.	...	...	...	...	...	...	2016
Bolzano .... d.	...	...	...	...	...	...	2200
Brennero .... d.	...	...	...	...	...	...	2248
Innsbruck .... d.	1705	1705	1805	...	...	...	...
Zell am See .... d.	...	...	...	1905	...	...	...
Saalfelden .... d.	...	...	...	1918	...	...	...
St. Johann .... d.	...	...	...	1950	...	...	...
Kitzbühel .... d.	...	...	...	2005	...	...	...
Wörgl .... d.	1744	1744	...	2325	...	...	2325
Kufstein .... d.	1802	1802	...	2356	...	...	2356
Ötztal .... d.	...	...	1833				
Landeck .... d.	...	...	1904				
St. Anton am Arlberg . d.	...	...	1935				
Langen am Arlberg .... d.	...	...	1947				
Bludenz .... d.	...	...	2020				
Feldkirch .... d.	...	...	2054				
Bregenz .... d.	...	...	2126				
Lindau .... a.	...	...	2136				
Hannover .... a.	0222	0222	0658	0757	0757	0757	0757
Hamburg Hbf .... a.	0355	0355	0847	0956	0956	0956	0956
Hamburg Altona ...... a.	0416	0416	0900	1014	1014	1014	1014
Kiel 663 .... a.		0656					
København 50 .... a.	0925						

NOTES

A – ⑤ to Oct. 7 and Jan. 6 - Apr. 7, also Dec. 16,22,25, Jan. 4: [symbol] 2 cl. Hamburg - Innsbruck, also [symbol] 1,2 cl. on ⑤ Jan. 6 - Mar. 24 and Dec. 16,22,25, Jan. 4.

B – ⑥ to Oct. 8 and Jan. 7 - Apr. 8: [symbol] 2 cl. Innsbruck - Hamburg, also [symbol] 1,2 cl. on ⑥ Jan. 7 - Mar. 25..

C – ⑤ Jan. 6 - Mar. 24: [symbol] 1,2 cl., [symbol] 2 cl., [symbol] and [symbol] København - Innsbruck.

D – ⑤ Jan. 6 - Mar. 24: [symbol] 1,2 cl., [symbol] 2 cl. and [symbol] Kiel - Innsbruck.

E – ⑥ Jan. 7 - Mar. 25: [symbol] 1,2 cl., [symbol] 2 cl., [symbol] and [symbol] Innsbruck - København.

F – ⑥ Jan. 7 - Mar. 25: [symbol] 1,2 cl., [symbol] 2 cl. and [symbol] Innsbruck - Kiel.

G – Daily to Oct. 28 and from Mar. 31, ⑤ Jan. 6 - Mar. 24, also Dec. 16,20,22,25, Jan. 4: [symbol] 2 cl. Hamburg - Bolzano; also [symbol] daily to Oct. 28 and from Mar. 31; conveys ⑤ to Oct. 21 and ⑤ Jan. 6 - Mar. 24, also Dec. 16,20,22,25, Jan. 4: [symbol] 1,2 cl. Hamburg - Bolzano.

H – Daily to Oct. 29 and from Apr. 1, ⑥ Jan. 7 - Mar. 25, also Dec. 17,21,23, Jan. 1,5: [symbol] 2 cl. Bolzano - Hamburg; also [symbol] daily to Oct. 29 and from Apr. 1; conveys ⑥ to Oct. 22 and ⑥ Jan. 7 - Mar. 25, also Dec. 17,21,23, Jan. 1,5: [symbol] 1,2 cl. Hamburg - Bolzano.

J – KÄRNTEN EXPRESS – Daily to Oct. 28 and from Mar. 31, ⑤ Jan. 6 - Mar. 24, also Dec. 16,20,22,25, Jan. 4: [symbol] 2 cl., [symbol] and [symbol] Hamburg - Villach (Klagenfurt to Oct. 28 and from Mar. 31); conveys daily to Oct. 28 and ⑤ Jan. 6 - Mar. 24, also Dec. 16,20,22,25, Jan. 4: [symbol] 1,2 cl. Hamburg - Klagenfurt/Villach.

K – Daily to Oct. 28 and from Mar. 31, ⑤ Jan. 6 - Mar. 24, also Dec. 16,20,22,25, Jan. 4: [symbol] 2 cl. and [symbol] Hamburg - Graz.

L – ⑤ Jan. 6 - Mar. 17, also Dec. 16,22,25, Jan. 4: [symbol] 1,2 cl. and [symbol] 2 cl. Hamburg - Schwarzach St Veit.

M – ⑤ Jan. 7 - Mar. 18, also Dec. 23, Jan. 1,5: [symbol] 2 cl. Schwarzach St Veit - Hamburg; also [symbol] 1,2 cl. Schwarzach St Veit - Hamburg, not Dec. 23, Jan. 1,5.

N – KÄRNTEN EXPRESS – Daily to Oct. 29 and from Apr. 1, ⑥ Jan. 7 - Mar. 25, also Dec. 17,21,23, Jan. 1,5: [symbol] 2 cl., [symbol] and [symbol] Villach (Klagenfurt to Oct. 28 and from Mar. 31) - Hamburg; conveys daily to Oct. 29 and ⑥ Jan. 7 - Mar. 25, also Dec. 17,21,23, Jan. 1,5: [symbol] 1,2 cl. Klagenfurt/Villach - Hamburg.

P – Daily to Oct. 29 and from Apr. 1, ⑥ Jan. 7 - Mar. 25, also Dec. 17,21,23, Jan. 1,5: [symbol] 2 cl. and [symbol] Graz - Hamburg.

b – Daily to Oct. 29 and from Apr. 1.

Table 66 — KÖLN AND FRANKFURT/MAIN - WIEN AND BUDAPEST

train type / train number / classes / notes (see below)	EC 23 1,2✗ J	EC 25 1,2✗ F	EC 27 1,2✗ G	EC 29 1,2✗ H	223 2 B
Dortmund............d.	...	...	0638	0840	1038 ... 1905
Essen.................d.	...	...	0701		1101 ... 1931
Duisburg.............d.	...	...	0714		1114 ... 1947
Düsseldorf...........d.	...	...	0728		1128 ... 2005
Köln Hbf.............d.	0554	0754	0954	1154	2037
Bonn.................d.	0614	0814	1014	1214	2059
Koblenz..............d.	0646	0846	1046	1246	2135
Mainz................d.	0736	0936	1138	1338	2228
Frankfurt/Main.......d.	0814	1014	1214	1414	2327
Würzburg.............d.	0928	1128	1328	1528	0057
Nürnberg.............d.	1028	1228	1428	1628	0205
Regensburg...........d.	1131	1331	1531	1731	0311
Passau...............d.	1244	1444	1644	1844	0433
Linz.................a.	1411	1611	1811	2011	0544
Wien West............a.	1605	1805	2005	2205	0740
Hegyeshalom..........a.	...	...	1923		0928
Györ.................a.	...	...	2001		1006
Budapest Keleti......a.	...	...	2143		1153

train type / train number / classes / notes (see below)	EC 28 1,2✗ H	EC 26 1,2✗ G	EC 24 1,2✗ F	EC 22 1,2✗ J	466 222 2 B
Budapest Keleti......d.	...	...	0820	...	1725
Györ.................d.	...	...	0959	...	1904
Hegyeshalom..........d.	...	...	1040	...	1945
Wien West............d.	0800	1000	1200	1400	2218
Linz.................a.	0949	1149	1349	1549	0010
Passau...............a.	1108	1308	1508	1708	0122
Regensburg...........a.	1226	1426	1626	1826	0247
Nürnberg.............a.	1329	1529	1729	1929	0354
Würzburg.............a.	1428	1628	1828	2028	0506
Frankfurt/Main.......a.	1543	1743	1943	2143	0643
Mainz................a.	1622	1822	2022	2222	0726
Koblenz..............a.	1711	1911	2111	2311	0820
Bonn.................a.	1743	1943	2143	2344	0857
Köln Hbf.............a.	1805	2005	2205	0007	0921
Düsseldorf...........a.	1831		2231		0951
Duisburg.............a.	1844		2244		1015
Essen.................a.	1857		2257		1031
Dortmund.............a.	1920	2120	2320		1056

NOTES

B – DONAU KURIER – ⚏ 1,2 cl., ⚏ 2 cl. and ⚏ Dortmund - Wien and v.v.;
   ⚏ 1,2 cl., ⚏ 2 cl. and ⚏ Dortmund - Budapest and v.v.
F – FRANZ LISZT – ⚏ and ✗ Dortmund - Budapest and v.v.

G – JOSEPH HAYDN – ⚏ and ✗ (Hamburg) Dortmund - Wien and v.v.
H – PRINZ EUGEN – ⚏ and ✗ (Kiel) - Dortmund - Wien and v.v.
J – JOHANN STRAUSS – ⚏ and ✗ Köln - Wien and v.v.
✗ – Supplement payable.

Table 67 — MÜNCHEN - WIEN

train type / train number / classes / notes	E 3501 1,2	IC 561 1,2 ✗	EC 63 1,2✗ E	IR 2191 1,2 ⚏	IC 543 1,2	E 3513 1,2	IC 565 1,2✗	EC 113 1,2✗ ⚏	IC 545 1,2	EC 11 1,2✗ ✗	IC 567 1,2 ✗	IR 2195 1,2 ⚏	IC 547 1,2 ✗	EC 115 1,2✗ ✗	IC 569 1,2 ✗	EC 65 1,2✗ A	3533 3535 1,2 ✗	IC 661 1,2✗ D	EC 17 1,2✗ C	269 1,2
Stuttgart............d.	...	...	0600	...	...	...	...	...	...	...	...	...	...	...	...	1357	...	...	...	...
Ulm..................d.	...	...	0658	...	...	...	...	...	...	...	...	...	...	...	...	1456	...	...	...	...
Augsburg.............d.	...	...	0739	...	...	...	...	...	...	...	...	...	...	...	...	1537	...	...	...	...
München Hbf..........d.	0650	...	0825	0951	...	1050	...	1225	...	1325	...	1351	...	1525	...	1625	1650	...	1825	2319
Salzburg ⛟............a.	0845	0905	0955	1140	1205	1245	1305	1355	1405	1455	1505	1540	1605	1655	1705	1753	1845	1905	1955	0101
Linz.................a.	...	1025	1112	1325	...	...	1425	...	1525	...	1625	...	1725	1825b	...	1912	...	2025	2112	0425
Wien West............a.	...	1225	1305	1525	...	...	1625	...	1725	...	1825	...	1925	2025b	...	2105	...	2225	2305	0632

train type / train number / classes / notes	EC 16 1,2✗ D	IC 562 1,2 ✗	3522 1,2	EC 64 1,2✗ A	IC 564 1,2 ✗	EC 114 1,2✗ ✗	IR 544 1,2	IR 2190 1,2 ⚏	EC 566 1,2✗ ✗	IC 10 1,2✗ ✗	IR 546 1,2	IC 2098 1,2 ⚏	IC 568 1,2 ✗	3540 1,2	EC 62 1,2✗ E	IC 640 1,2 ✗	IR 2094 1,2 ⚏	740 1,2 ✗	IC 2092 1,2 c	248 1,2 c
Wien West............d.	0600	0740	...	0900	...	0940	...	1040	...	1140	...	1240	...	1340	...	1600	1640	...	1840	...
Linz.................d.	0748	0934	...	1046	...	1134	...	1234	...	1334	...	1434	...	1534	...	1748	1834	...	2034	2330
Salzburg ⛟............d.	0905	1055	1118	1209	1255	1305	1355	1418	1455	1505	1555	1618	1655	1718	1905	1955	2018	2155	2215	0127
München Hbf..........a.	1035	...	1310	1338	1435	...	1607	...	1635	...	1807	...	1910	...	2036	...	2200	...	2400	0408
Augsburg.............a.	...	...	...	1420	...	...	...	...	...	...	...	...	...	...	2122	...	...	...	...	0603
Ulm..................a.	...	...	...	1503	...	...	...	...	...	...	...	...	...	...	2203	...	...	...	...	...
Stuttgart............a.	...	...	...	1603	...	...	...	...	...	...	...	...	...	...	2311	...	...	...	...	...

NOTES

A – MOZART – ⚏ and ✗ (Paris) - Stuttgart - Wien and v.v.
C – ⚏ 2 cl. and ⚏ München - Wien and v.v.
D – MAX REINHARDT – ⚏ and ✗ München - Wien and v.v.

E – BARTÓK BÉLA – ⚏ and ✗ Stuttgart - Wien - (Budapest) and v.v.
b – ⑦: Linz arrive 1830, Wien arrive 2030.
c – Not Dec. 24,31.
✗ – Supplement payable.

Table 68 — KÖLN AND MÜNCHEN - VILLACH AND GRAZ

train type / train number / classes / notes (see below)	EC 113 1,2✗ R	EC 11 1,2✗ T	EC 115 1,2✗ S	EC 65 1,2✗ W	1125 1123 2 ⚏ M	1125 1123 2 ⚏ N
Dortmund............d.	0511	...	0811	...	1954	1954
Essen.................d.	0535	...	0835	...	2030	2030
Duisburg.............d.	0549	...	0849	...	2037	2037
Düsseldorf...........d.	0604	...	0904	...	2101	2101
Köln Hbf.............d.	0630	...	0930	...	2130	2130
Bonn.................d.	0650	...	0950	...	2152	2152
Koblenz..............d.	0722	...	1022	...	2232	2232
Mainz................d.	0812	...	1112	...	2326	2326
Frankfurt/Main.......d.					0002	0002
Mannheim.............d.	0855	...	1155	...		
Heidelberg...........d.	0907	...	1207	...		
Stuttgart............d.	0957	...	1257	1357		
Ulm..................d.	1056	...	1356	1456		
Augsburg.............d.	1137	...	1437	1537		
München Hbf..........d.	1225	1325	1525	1625		
Salzburg ⛟...........a.	1355	1455	1655	1753	0607	0607
Bischofshofen........a.	1442	1550	1750	1848	0705	0705
Selzthal.............a.					2024	
Graz.................a.					2205	1050
Schwarzach St Veit...a.	1457	1604	1804		0724	...
Villach Hbf..........a.	1649	1744	1944		0914	...
Klagenfurt...........a.	1723		2014		0948e	...

train type / train number / classes / notes (see below)	EC 112 1,2✗ R	EC 116 1,2✗ W	EC 114 1,2✗ S	EC 10 1,2✗ T	1298 2 ⚏ P	818 ⚏ Q
Klagenfurt...........d.	0645	...	0952	...	1950e	
Villach Hbf..........d.	0723	...	1019	1218	2026	
Schwarzach St Veit...d.	0907	...	1157	1357	2223	
Graz.................d.		0757	...	...		1900
Selzthal.............d.		0938	...	...		2113
Bischofshofen........d.	0921	1116	1211	1411	2257	2257
Salzburg ⛟...........d.	1005	1209	1305	1505	2358	2358
München Hbf..........a.	1138	1338	1435	1635		
Augsburg.............a.	1220	1420	1520	...		
Ulm..................a.	1303	1503	1603	...		
Stuttgart............a.	1403	1603	1703	...		
Heidelberg...........a.	1452		1752	...		
Mannheim.............a.	1504		1804	...		
Frankfurt/Main.......a.					0601	0601
Mainz................a.	1546		1846	...	0636	0636
Koblenz..............a.	1635		1935	...	0729	0729
Bonn.................a.	1707		2007	...		
Köln Hbf.............a.	1729		2029	...	0833	0833
Düsseldorf...........a.	1755		2055	...	0910	0910
Duisburg.............a.	1809		2109	...	0931	0931
Essen.................a.	1822		2122	...	0945	0945
Dortmund.............a.	1848		2148	...	1010	1010

NOTES

M – Daily to Oct. 28 and from Mar. 31, ⑤ Jan. 6 - Mar. 24, also Dec. 16,20,22, Jan. 4:
   ⚏ 1,2 cl., ⚏ 2 cl. and ⚏ Dortmund - Villach (Klagenfurt to Oct. 28 and from Mar. 31).
N – Daily to Oct. 28 and from Mar. 31, ⑤ Jan. 6 - Mar. 24, also Dec. 16,20,22, Jan. 4:
   ⚏ 2 cl. Dortmund - Graz and v.v.
P – Daily to Oct. 29 and from Apr. 1, ⑥ Jan. 7 - Mar. 25, also Dec. 17,21,23, Jan. 1,5:
   ⚏ 1,2 cl., ⚏ 2 cl. and ⚏ Villach (Klagenfurt to Oct. 29 and from Apr. 1) - Dortmund.

Q – Daily to Oct. 29 and from Apr. 1, ⑥ Jan. 7 - Mar. 25, also Dec. 17,21,23, Jan. 1,5:
   ⚏ 2 cl. Graz - Dortmund and v.v.
R – WÖRTHERSEE – ⚏ and ✗ Dortmund - Klagenfurt and v.v.
S – BLAUER ENZIAN – ⚏ and ✗ Dortmund - Klagenfurt and v.v.
T – MIMARA – ⚏ and ✗ (Leipzig) - München - Villach - (Zagreb) and v.v.
W – MOZART – ⚏ (Paris) - Stuttgart - Graz and v.v.;
   ✗ Stuttgart - Salzburg and v.v.; ⚏ Salzburg - Graz and v.v.
e – Daily to Oct. 29 and from Apr. 1.
✗ – Supplement payable.

Table 69 KÖLN AND STUTTGART - INNSBRUCK AND VENEZIA

train type	IR	EC		EC	IC	IR	EC						
train number	361	15		13	119	461	19		1123	1125	1015	1015	1015	1019
classes	1,2	1,2✗		1,2✗	1,2✗	1,2	1,2✗		2	2	2	2	2	2
notes (see below)	⟐	G		D	F		E		H	K	L	R	T	A
Dortmund .... d.	...	...	...	0611	...	...	1211	...	1954	1954	2000	2000	2000	2222
Essen .... d.	...	...	...	0635	0735	...	1235	...	2020	2020	2025	2025	2025	2251
Duisburg .... d.	...	...	...	0649	0749	...	1249	...	2037	2037	2042	2042	2042	2307
Düsseldorf .... d.	...	...	...	0704	0804	...	1304	...	2101	2101	2113	2113	2113	2324
Köln Hbf .... d.	...	...	...	0730	0830	...	1330	...	2130	2130	2156	2156	2156	2359
Bonn .... d.	...	...	...	0750	0850	...	1350	...	2152	2152	...	...	...	...
Koblenz .... d.	...	...	...	0822	0922	...	1422	...	2232	2232	2300	2300	2300	0104
Mainz .... d.	...	...	...	0912	1012	...	1512	...	2326	2326	2352	2352	2352	...
Frankfurt/Main ...... d.	...	...	...	...	...	0950	...	...	0002	0002	...	...	...	...
Saarbrücken .... d.	0548	0626	...	...	...	...	...	...	...	...	...	...	...	...
Mannheim .... d.	0713	0755	...	0955	1055	1113	1555	...	...	...	...	...	...	0358
Heidelberg .... d.	...	0807	...	1007	1107	...	1607	...	...	...	...	...	...	...
Stuttgart .... d.	0816	0857	...	1057	1157	1216	1657	...	...	...	...	...	...	0626
Ulm .... d.	0927	0956	...	1156	1256	1327	1756	...	...	...	...	...	...	0823
Lindau ⋒ .... d.	1108	...	...	...	...	1508	...	...	...	...	...	...	...	0832
Bregenz .... a.	1118	...	...	...	...	1518	...	...	...	...	...	...	...	0932
Bludenz .... a.	...	...	...	...	...	1605	...	...	...	...	...	...	...	1014
Langen am Arlberg ... a.	...	...	...	...	...	1648	...	...	...	...	...	...	...	1026
St. Anton am Arlberg ... a.	...	...	...	...	...	1658	...	...	...	...	...	...	...	1055
Landeck .... a.	...	...	...	...	...	1725	...	...	...	...	...	...	...	...
Augsburg .... d.	...	1037	...	1237	1337	...	1837	...	...	...	0400	0400	0400	...
München Hbf .... d.	...	1130	...	1330	1421	...	1930	...	...	...	0512	0512	0512	...
Seefeld in Tirol ⋒ ... a.	...	...	...	...	1703	...	...	...	...	...	...	...	0723	...
Kufstein ⋒ .... a.	...	1231	...	1431	...	...	2031	...	0525	0600	0627	0627	...	...
Wörgl .... a.	...	1243	...	1443	...	...	2043	...	0550	0627	0650	0650	...	...
Kitzbühel .... a.	...	...	...	...	...	...	...	...	...	...	0742	...	...	...
St Johann in Tirol ... a.	...	...	...	...	...	...	...	...	...	...	0753	...	...	...
Saalfelden .... a.	...	...	...	...	...	...	...	...	...	...	0823	...	...	...
Zell am See .... a.	...	...	...	...	...	...	...	...	...	...	0836	...	...	...
Schwarzach St Veit ... a.	...	...	...	...	...	...	...	...	...	...	0912	...	...	...
Innsbruck ⋒ .... a.	...	1320	...	1520	1746	...	2118	...	0629	0709	0730	...	0801	1153
Brennero ⋒ .... a.	...	...	...	1559	...	...	...	...	0720	0802	...	...	...	...
Bolzano .... a.	...	...	...	1729	...	...	...	...	0908	0939	...	...	...	...
Trento .... a.	...	...	...	1800	...	...	...	...	...	...	...	...	...	...
Verona .... a.	...	...	...	1905	...	...	...	...	...	...	...	...	...	...
Padova .... a.	...	...	...	2002	...	...	...	...	...	...	...	...	...	...
Venezia Mestre ...... a.	...	...	...	2024	...	...	...	...	...	...	...	...	...	...
Venezia S. Lucia ..... a.	...	...	...	2035	...	...	...	...	...	...	...	...	...	...

train type	EC	IR	IC	IR	EC	EC						
train number	18	460	118	360	12	14		1018	1114	1614	1014	1122	1124
classes	1,2	1,2	1,2✗	1,2	1,2✗	1,2✗		2	2	2	2	2	2
notes (see below)	E	⟐	C	⟐	D	G		B	M	S	V	P	N
Venezia S. Lucia ..... d.	...	...	...	...	0855	...	...	...	...	...	...	...	...
Venezia Mestre ...... d.	...	...	...	...	0906	...	...	...	...	...	...	...	...
Padova .... d.	...	...	...	...	0927	...	...	...	...	...	...	...	...
Verona .... d.	...	...	...	...	1054	...	...	...	...	...	...	...	...
Trento .... d.	...	...	...	...	1152	...	...	...	...	...	...	2016	2016
Bolzano .... d.	...	...	...	...	1233	...	...	...	...	...	...	2200	2200
Brennero ⋒ .... d.	...	...	...	...	1404	...	...	...	...	...	...	2248	2248
Innsbruck ⋒ .... d.	...	0739	...	0943	1441	1539	...	1805	2008	...	1949	2248	2248
Schwarzach St Veit ... d.	...	...	...	...	...	...	...	...	1828	...	...	...	...
Zell am See .... d.	...	...	...	...	...	...	...	...	1905	...	...	...	...
Saalfelden .... d.	...	...	...	...	...	...	...	...	1918	...	...	...	...
St Johann in Tirol ... d.	...	...	...	...	...	...	...	...	1950	...	...	...	...
Kitzbühel .... d.	...	...	...	...	1516	1616	...	...	2053	2053	...	2325	2325
Wörgl .... d.	...	0816	...	...	1528	1628	...	...	2114	2114	...	2356	2356
Kufstein ⋒ .... d.	...	0828	1021	...	...	...	...	...	...	...	2023	...	...
Seefeld in Tirol ⋒ ... d.	...	...	1239	...	1630	1730	...	...	2224	2224	2224	...	...
München Hbf .... a.	...	0930	1320	...	1720	1820	...	...	2356	2356	2356	...	...
Augsburg .... a.	...	1020	...	...	...	...	...	1904	...	...	...	...	...
Landeck .... d.	...	...	0850	...	...	...	...	1935	...	...	...	...	...
St. Anton am Arlberg ... d.	...	...	0917	...	...	...	...	1947	...	...	...	...	...
Langen am Arlberg ... d.	...	...	0927	...	...	...	...	2020	...	...	...	...	...
Bludenz .... d.	...	...	0958	...	1227	...	...	2126	...	...	...	...	...
Bregenz .... d.	...	...	1040	...	1238	...	...	2136	...	...	...	...	...
Lindau ⋒ .... d.	...	...	1050	...	...	...	...	2334	...	...	...	...	...
Ulm .... a.	1103	1230	1403	1430	1803	1903	...	...	0042	0042	0042	...	...
Stuttgart .... a.	1203	1344	1503	1544	1903	2003	...	...	...	...	...	...	...
Heidelberg .... a.	1252	...	1552	...	1952	2052	...	...	...	...	...	...	...
Mannheim .... a.	1304	1446	1604	1646	2004	2104	...	...	...	...	...	...	...
Saarbrücken .... a.	...	1608	...	1808	...	2230	...	...	...	...	...	0601	0601
Frankfurt/Main ...... a.	...	...	...	...	...	...	...	...	...	...	...	0636	0636
Mainz .... a.	1346	...	1646	...	2046	...	...	...	...	...	...	0729	0729
Koblenz .... a.	1435	...	1735	...	2135	...	...	0431	0459	0459	0459	...	...
Bonn .... a.	1507	...	1807	...	2207	...	...	0509	...	...	...	0833	0833
Köln Hbf .... a.	1529	...	1829	...	2229	...	...	0535	0559	0559	0559	0910	0910
Düsseldorf .... a.	1555	...	1855	...	2255	...	...	0606	0637	0637	0637	0931	0931
Duisburg .... a.	1609	...	1909	...	2309	...	...	0625	...	...	...	0945	0945
Essen .... a.	1622	...	1922	...	2322	...	...	0640	0654	0654	0654	...	...
Dortmund .... a.	1648	...	1948	...	2348	...	...	0705	0745	0745	0745	1010	1010

NOTES

A – VORARLBERG EXPRESS – ⑤ to Oct. 7 and Jan. 6 - Apr. 7, also Dec. 16,22,25, Jan. 4: ⛌ 2 cl. and ⊏▭⊐ Dortmund - Innsbruck (also ⛌ 1,2 cl. from Dec. 16).

B – VORARLBERG EXPRESS – ⑥ to Oct. 8 and Jan. 7 - Apr. 8, also Dec. 23, Jan. 1,5: ⛌ 2 cl. and ⊏▭⊐ Innsbruck - Dortmund (also ⛌ 1,2 cl. from Dec. 23).

C – KARWENDEL - ⊏▭⊐ and ✗ Innsbruck - Dortmund.

D – PAGANINI - ⊏▭⊐ and ✗ Dortmund - Venezia and v.v.

E – ANDREAS HOFER – ⊏▭⊐ and ✗ Dortmund - Innsbruck and v.v.

F – KARWENDEL - ⊏▭⊐ and ✗ (Munster) - Essen - Innsbruck.

G – PATSCHERKOFEL - ⊏▭⊐ and ✗ Saarbrücken - Innsbruck and v.v.

H – DOLOMITEN EXPRESS – Daily to Oct. 28 and from Mar. 31: ⛌ 1,2 cl., ⛌ 2 cl. and ⊏▭⊐ Dortmund - Bolzano.

K – DOLOMITEN EXPRESS – ⑤ Jan. 6 - Mar. 24, also Dec. 16,20,22,25, Jan. 4: ⛌ 1,2 cl., ⛌ 2 cl. and ⊏▭⊐ Dortmund - Bolzano.

L – ⑤ Jan. 6 - Apr. 7 also Dec. 16,22,25, Jan. 4: ⛌ 1,2 cl., ⛌ 2 cl. and ⊏▭⊐ Dortmund - Innsbruck.

M – ⑥ Jan. 7 - Apr. 8, also Dec. 23, Jan. 1,5: ⛌ 1,2 cl., ⛌ 2 cl. and ⊏▭⊐ Innsbruck - Dortmund.

N – DOLOMITEN EXPRESS – ⑥ Jan. 7 - Mar. 25, also Dec. 17,21,23, Jan. 1,5: ⛌ 1,2 cl., ⛌ 2 cl. and ⊏▭⊐ Bolzano - Dortmund.

P – DOLOMITEN EXPRESS – Daily to Oct. 29 and from Apr. 1: ⛌ 1,2 cl., ⛌ 2 cl. and ⊏▭⊐ Bolzano - Dortmund.

R – ⑤ Jan. 6 - Apr. 7, also Dec. 16,22,25, Jan. 4: ⛌ 2 cl. and ⊏▭⊐ Dortmund - Schwarzach St Veit (also ⛌ 1,2 cl. to Mar. 17).

S – ⑥ Jan. 7 - Apr. 8, also Dec. 23, Jan. 1,5: ⛌ 2 cl. and ⊏▭⊐ Schwarzach St Veit - Dortmund (also ⛌ 1,2 cl. to Mar. 18).

T – ⑤ Jan. 6 - Apr. 7, also Dec. 16,22,25, Jan. 4: ⛌ 2 cl. and ⊏▭⊐ Dortmund - Innsbruck.

V – ⑥ Jan. 7 - Apr. 8, also Dec. 23, Jan. 1,5: ⛌ 2 cl. and ⊏▭⊐ Innsbruck - Dortmund.

✗ – Supplement payable.

Table 70 — MÜNCHEN - INNSBRUCK AND ZELL AM SEE

train type	EC	D	IC	EC	IC	EC	IC	EC	IC	D	EC	EC	IC	IC
train number	81	489	515	85	545	15	547	13	549	283	169	87	641	801
classes	1,2✗	1,2	1,2	1,2✗	1,2	1,2✗	1,2	1,2✗	1,2	1,2	1,2	1,2✗	1,2✗	1,2✗
notes (see below)	C	♟	♟	D	✗	A	✗	B	✗		♟	E	✗	H
München Hbf .... d.	...	0700	0830	...	0930	...	1130	...	1330	...	1430	...	1530	1537
Kufstein ▩ .... a.	...	0756	0931	...	1031	...	1231	...	1431	...	1531	...	1631	1706
Wörgl .... a.	...	...	0943	0956	1043	1057	1243	1257	1443	1457	1543	1558	1643	1657	1718
Kirchberg in Tirol ...... a.	...			1025		1120		1320		1520		1619		1720	1756
Kitzbühel .... a.	...			1025		1129		1329		1529		1628		1729	1806
St. Johann in Tirol ..... a.	...			1033		1137		1337		1537		1636		1739	1814
Saalfelden .... a.	...			1103		1207		1407		1607		1703		1807	1849
Zell am See .... a.	...			1113		1218		1418		1618		1713		1818	1903
Jenbach .... a.	...	0959				1259		1459		1559				...
Innsbruck Hbf .... a.	...	0836	1020	...	1118	...	1320		1520		1620	...	1718	...

train type	D	IC	EC	D	D			train type	D	D	IC	EC		D
train number	285	715	19	5031	287			train number	288	286	712	18		282
classes	1,2	1,2	1,2✗	2	2			classes	2	2	1,2	1,2✗		1,2
notes (see below)		♟	G					notes (see below)			♟	G		
München Hbf .... d.	...	1730	...	1930	...	2030	...		Innsbruck Hbf .... d.	0437	...	0641	...	...	0739	...	0839
Kufstein ▩ .... a.	...	1831	...	2031	...	2131	...		Jenbach .... d.				0800		0900
Wörgl .... a.	...	1843	1956	2043	2056	2143	...		Zell am See .... d.			0637			
Kirchberg in Tirol ..... a.	...	2018		2121	...			Saalfelden .... d.			0647			
Kitzbühel .... a.	...	2028		2131	...			St. Johann in Tirol .... d.			0716			
St. Johann in Tirol .... a.	...	2036		2138	...			Kitzbühel .... d.			0725			
Saalfelden .... a.	...	2103		2145	...			Kirchberg in Tirol ..... d.			0734			
Zell am See .... a.	...	2113						Wörgl .... d.	0514	...	0716	0756	0816	...	0916
Jenbach .... a.	1859							Kufstein ▩ .... d.	0530	...	0728	...	0828	...	0928
Innsbruck Hbf .... a.	1920	...	2118	...	2218	...		München Hbf .... a.	0635	...	0830	...	0930	...	1030

train type	IC	IC	D	IC	EC	IC	EC	EC	EC	IC	EC	IC	D	EC
train number	800	844	284	540	86	542	12	168	14	544	84	546	488	80
classes	1,2✗	1,2	1,2	1,2	1,2✗	1,2	1,2✗	1,2	1,2✗	1,2	1,2✗	1,2	1,2	1,2✗
notes (see below)	F	✗		✗	B	✗	B	♟	A	✗	D	✗	♟	C
Innsbruck Hbf .... d.	...	...	1039	...	1241	...	1441	...	1539	...	1641	...	1837	2103
Jenbach .... d.	...	...	1100	...		...		...	1600	...		...	1859	
Zell am See .... d.	0855	0941		1141		1341		1453		1541		1741		
Saalfelden .... d.	0909	0951		1151		1351		1503		1551		1751		
St. Johann in Tirol .... d.	0942	1021		1221		1421		1530		1621		1821		
Kitzbühel .... d.	0952	1031		1231		1431		1539		1631		1831		
Kirchberg in Tirol ..... d.	1001	1040		1240		1440		1547		1640		1840		
Wörgl .... d.	1040	1103	1116	1303	1316	1503	1516	1609	1616	1703	1716	1903	1916	
Kufstein ▩ .... d.	1052		1128		1328		1528		1628		1728		1928	2143
München Hbf .... a.	1218		1230		1430		1630		1730		1830		2030	2240

NOTES
A – PATSCHERKOFEL – 🛏 and ✗ (Saarbrücken) - München - Innsbruck and v.v.
B – PAGANINI – 🛏 and ✗ (Dortmund) - München - Innsbruck - (Venezia) and v.v.

C – GARDA – 🛏 and ✗ München - Innsbruck - (Milano) and v.v.
D – MICHELANGELO – 🛏 and ✗ München - Innsbruck - (Roma) and v.v.
E – LEONARDO DA VINCI – 🛏 and ✗ München - Innsbruck - (Milano) and v.v.

F – THERESE GIEHSE – ⑥⑦ to Oct. 30, Jan. 7-Apr. 9 and from May 20:
🛏 and ✗ Zell am See - Berlin.
G – ANDREAS HOFER – 🛏 and ✗ (Dortmund) - München - Innsbruck and v.v.

H – THERESE GIEHSE – ⑥ to Oct. 29, Jan. 7-Apr. 8 and from May 20:
🛏 and ✗ Berlin - Zell am See.
✗ – Supplement payable.

Table 71 — BERLIN - INNSBRUCK AND VILLACH

train type	EC	IC	IC	1209	1183			train type	E	IC	EC	1208	1282
train number	11	801	813	1209	1283			train number	812	800	10	1208	1282
classes	1,2✗	1,2✗	1,2✗	2	2			classes	1,2✗	1,2✗	1,2✗	2	2
notes (see below)	G	C	H	E	A			notes (see below)	N	D	G	F	
Berlin Hbf .... d.	...	...	0706	...	0906			Verona .... d.	...	...	...	...	1540b
Berlin Zoo .... d.	...					2058		Trento .... d.	...				1642
Berlin Wannsee ...... d.	...			2022	2125			Bolzano .... d.	...				1756
Halle .... d.	...			2200	2340			Brennero .... d.	...				1948
Leipzig .... d.	0715	0915	1115					Innsbruck .... d.	...				2040
Nürnberg Hbf .... d.	1124	1324	1524					Seefeld in Tirol ...... d.	0825				
München Hbf .... d.	1325	1537	1718					Zell am See .... d.	...	0855			
Salzburg .... d.	1455			0642				Saalfelden .... d.	...	0909			
Bischofshofen .... d.	1550	1955e		0741				St. Johann .... d.	...	0942			
Schwarzach St Veit .. d.	1604	1938e		0757				Kitzbühel .... d.	...	0952			
Villach Hbf .... d.	1744			0954				Wörgl .... d.	...	1040			2122
Klagenfurt .... d.	...			1034c				Kufstein ▩ .... d.	...	1052			2208
Kufstein ▩ .... a.	...	1706			0741			Klagenfurt .... d.	...			1634c	
Wörgl .... a.	...	1718			0803			Villach Hbf .... d.	...		1218	1720	
Kitzbühel .... a.	...	1804						Schwarzach St Veit .. d.	...	0821e	1357	1913	
St. Johann .... a.	...	1813						Bischofshofen .... d.	...	0804e	1411	1935	
Saalfelden .... a.	...	1849						Salzburg .... d.	...	1505	2039		
Zell am See .... a.	...	1903						München Hbf .... a.	1038	1218	1635		
Seefeld in Tirol ...... a.	...		2003					Nürnberg Hbf .... a.	1234	1434	1834		
Innsbruck .... a.	...				0849			Leipzig .... a.	1640	1840	2240		
Brennero .... a.	...				0938			Halle .... a.	...			0505	0641
Bolzano .... a.	...				1120			Berlin Wannsee ...... a.	...			0832	
Trento .... a.	...				1219			Berlin Zoo .... a.	...			0700	
Verona .... a.	...				1330			Berlin Hbf .... a.	1849	2049			

NOTES
A – SPREE ALPEN EXPRESS – ⑤ to Oct. 28, and from Jan. 6, also Apr. 13, not Apr. 14:
🛏 2 cl. and 🛏 Berlin - Verona;
🛏 1,2 cl. Berlin - innsbruck (Bolzano to Oct. 28 and from Apr. 28).

B – SPREE ALPEN EXPRESS – ⑥ to Oct. 29, and from Jan. 7, also Apr. 17, not Apr. 15:
🛏 2 cl., 🛏 2 cl., Verona - Berlin;
🛏 1,2 cl. Innsbruck (Bolzano to Oct. 29 and from Apr. 29) - Berlin.

C – THERESE GIEHSE – ⑥ to Oct. 29, Jan. 7-Apr. 8 and from May 20:
🛏 and ✗ Berlin - Zell am See - Bischofshofen.

D – THERESE GIEHSE – ⑥⑦ to Oct. 30, Jan. 7-Apr. 9 and from May 20:
🛏 and ✗ Bischofshofen - Zell am See - Berlin.

E – ⑤ to Oct. 7 and Jan. 6-Apr. 7:
🛏 1,2 cl., 🛏 2 cl., 🛏 and ♟ Berlin - Villach (Klagenfurt to Oct. 7).

F – ⑥ to Oct. 8 and Jan. 7-Apr. 8:
🛏 1,2 cl., 🛏 2 cl., 🛏 and ♟ Villach (Klagenfurt to Oct. 8) - Berlin.

G – MIMARA – 🛏 and ✗ Leipzig - Villach - (Zagreb) and v.v.

H – WETTERSTEIN – ⑥ Jan. 7-Apr. 8, also Dec. 17,21,22,23,26:
🛏 and ✗ Berlin - Seefeld in Tirol.

N – WETTERSTEIN – ⑥ Jan. 7-Apr. 8, also Jan. 2-6,8:
🛏 and ✗ Seefeld in Tirol - Berlin.

b – Depart 1600 Jan. 7 - Apr. 22.
c – To Oct. 8 only.

e – Via Zell am See.
✗ – Supplement payable.

For summer service from May 28 see page 542

Table 73 KÖLN AND FRANKFURT/MAIN - MILANO AND ROMA

train number		EC	IC	P				EC	IC													IC		
train number		5	685	515				9	689			1205	1005							201	401	533	2183	
classes		1,2⚡	1,2⚡	1,2⚡				1,2⚡	1,2⚡			2	2							2	2	1,2⚡	1,2	
notes (see below)		R	🍷	[R] 🍴				S	🍷			D	E							A	B	🍷		
Dortmund d.	...	0640	...	...	...	...	...	0838	...	...	...	1755	...	...	...	...	...	...	...	1909	...	...	...	...
Essen d.	...	|	...	...	...	...	...	0901	...	...	...	1821	...	...	...	...	...	...	...	1935	...	...	...	...
Duisburg d.	...	|	...	...	...	...	...	0914	...	...	...	1836	...	...	...	...	...	...	...	2019	...	...	...	...
Düsseldorf d.	...	|	...	...	...	...	...	0928	...	...	...	1853	...	...	...	...	...	...	...	2036	...	...	...	...
Köln Hbf d.	...	0800	...	...	...	...	...	1000	...	...	...	1929	...	...	...	...	...	...	...	2106	...	...	...	...
Bonn d.	...	0820	...	...	...	...	...	1020	...	...	...	1950	...	...	...	...	...	...	...	2127	...	...	...	...
Koblenz d.	...	0852	...	...	...	...	...	1052	...	...	...	2027	...	...	...	...	...	...	...	2203	...	...	...	...
Mainz d.	...	0942	...	...	...	...	...	1142	...	...	...	2123	...	...	...	...	...	...	...	2258	...	...	...	...
Frankfurt/Main d.	...	|	...	...	...	...	...	|	...	...	...	|	2115	...	...	...	...	...	...	|	2255	...	...	...
Mannheim d.	...	1031	...	...	...	...	...	1231	...	...	...	2211	|	...	...	...	...	...	...	2341	|	...	...	...
Heidelberg d.	...	|	...	...	...	...	...	|	...	...	...	|	2211	...	...	...	...	...	...	0006	0006	...	...	...
Karlsruhe d.	...	1056	...	...	...	...	...	1256	...	...	...	2302	2302	...	...	...	...	...	...	0038	0038	...	...	...
Offenburg d.	...	|	...	...	...	...	...	|	...	...	...	2345	2345	...	...	...	...	...	...	|	|	...	...	...
Freiburg im Breisgau d.	...	1201	...	...	...	...	...	1401	...	...	...	0021	0021	...	...	...	...	...	...	|	|	...	...	...
Basel SBB 🏛 d.	...	1307	...	...	...	...	...	1507	...	...	...	v	v	...	...	...	...	...	...	v	v	...	...	...
Domodossola 🏛 a.	...	|	...	...	...	...	...	|	...	...	...	0420	0420	...	...	...	...	...	...	|	|	...	...	...
Arona a.	...	|	...	...	...	...	...	|	...	...	...	|	|	...	...	...	...	...	...	|	|	...	...	...
Chiasso 🏛 a.	...	1730	...	...	...	...	...	1930	...	...	...	|	|	...	...	...	...	...	...	0637	0637	...	...	...
Como a.	...	1754	...	...	...	...	...	1954	...	...	...	|	|	...	...	...	...	...	...	0700	0700	...	...	...
Milano Centrale a.	...	1835	1910	1940	...	...	...	2035	2110	...	...	|	|	...	...	...	...	...	...	0745	0745	0800	0815	...
Alessandria a.	...	...	|	|	...	...	...	...	|	...	...	|	|	...	...	...	...	...	...	...	...	|	|	...
Genova P. Principe a.	...	...	2047	|	...	...	...	...	2247	...	...	|	|	...	...	...	...	...	...	...	...	|	1005	...
San Remo a.	...	...	2302	|	...	...	...	...	...	...	...	|	|	...	...	...	...	...	...	...	...	|	1228	...
Ventimiglia a.	...	...	2320	|	...	...	...	...	...	...	...	|	|	...	...	...	...	...	...	...	...	|	1250	...
Bologna a.	...	...	...	2115	...	...	...	...	...	...	...	0806	0806	...	...	...	...	...	...	...	...	0944	...	...
Firenze SMN a.	...	...	...	2212r	...	...	...	...	...	...	...	0926	0926	...	...	...	...	...	...	...	...	1053	...	...
Roma Termini a.	...	...	...	2353	...	...	...	...	...	...	...	1145	1145	...	...	...	...	...	...	...	...	1255	...	...
Napoli Centrale a.	...	...	...	...	...	...	...	...	...	...	...	...	...	...	...	...	...	...	...	...	...	1500	...	...
Ravenna a.	...	...	...	...	...	...	...	...	...	...	...	...	...	...	...	...	...	...	...	...	...	...	...	...
Rimini a.	...	...	...	...	...	...	...	...	...	...	...	...	...	...	...	...	...	...	...	...	...	...	...	...

train number		IC	EC			IC675	P		EC				IC	IC										
train number		672	8			IC676	500		4				688	544	200	200							1204	1204
classes		1,2⚡	1,2⚡			1,2⚡	1,2⚡		1,2⚡				1,2⚡	1,2⚡	2	2							2	2
notes (see below)		🍷	S			🍷	Ⓐ 🍴		R				🍷	🍴	A	B							F	G
Rimini d.	...	...	...	...	...	...	...	...	...	...	...	...	...	...	...	...	...	...	...	...	...	...	...	...
Ravenna d.	...	...	...	...	...	...	...	...	...	...	...	...	...	...	...	...	...	...	...	...	...	...	...	...
Napoli Centrale d.	...	...	...	...	...	...	...	...	...	...	...	...	...	...	...	...	...	...	...	...	...	...	...	...
Roma Termini d.	...	...	...	...	...	...	0655	...	...	...	...	...	...	1605	...	...	...	...	...	...	...	...	1710	1710
Firenze SMN d.	...	...	...	...	...	...	0832r	...	...	...	...	...	...	1807	...	...	...	...	...	...	...	...	2025	2025
Bologna d.	...	...	...	...	...	...	0930	...	...	...	...	...	...	1916	...	...	...	...	...	...	...	...	2150	2150
Ventimiglia d.	...	...	...	...	...	0650	|	...	...	...	...	...	...	|	...	...	...	...	...	...	...	...	|	|
San Remo d.	...	...	...	...	...	0709	|	...	...	...	...	...	...	|	...	...	...	...	...	...	...	...	|	|
Genova P. Principe d.	...	0713	...	...	...	0913	|	...	...	...	...	...	1913	|	...	...	...	...	...	...	...	...	|	|
Alessandria d.	...	|	...	...	...	|	|	...	...	...	...	...	|	|	...	...	...	...	...	...	...	...	|	|
Milano Centrale d.	...	0850	0920	...	...	1050	1105	...	1125	...	...	...	2050	2100	2125	2125	...	...	...	...	...	...	|	|
Como d.	...	...	1004	...	...	...	...	...	1205	...	...	...	...	...	2205	2205	...	...	...	...	...	...	|	|
Chiasso d.	...	...	1030	...	...	...	...	...	1230	...	...	...	...	...	2230	2230	...	...	...	...	...	...	|	|
Arona d.	...	...	|	...	...	...	...	...	|	...	...	...	...	...	|	|	...	...	...	...	...	...	|	|
Domodossola d.	...	...	|	...	...	...	...	...	|	...	...	...	...	...	|	|	...	...	...	...	...	...	0144	0144
Basel SBB a.	...	...	1453	...	...	...	...	...	1653	...	...	...	...	...	v	v	...	...	...	...	...	...	v	v
Freiburg im Breisgau a.	...	...	1556	...	...	...	...	...	1756	...	...	...	...	...	|	|	...	...	...	...	...	...	0536	0536
Offenburg a.	...	...	|	...	...	...	...	...	|	...	...	...	...	...	|	|	...	...	...	...	...	...	0610	0610
Karlsruhe a.	...	...	1700	...	...	...	...	...	1900	...	...	...	...	...	0456	0456	...	...	...	...	...	...	0659	0659
Heidelberg a.	...	...	|	...	...	...	...	...	|	...	...	...	...	...	0529	0529	...	...	...	...	...	...	|	0757
Mannheim a.	...	...	1727	...	...	...	...	...	1927	...	...	...	...	...	0546	|	...	...	...	...	...	...	0740	|
Frankfurt/Main a.	...	...	|	...	...	...	...	...	|	...	...	...	...	...	|	0652	...	...	...	...	...	...	|	0859
Mainz a.	...	...	1816	...	...	...	...	...	2016	...	...	...	...	...	0630	...	...	...	...	...	...	...	0830	...
Koblenz a.	...	...	1905	...	...	...	...	...	2105	...	...	...	...	...	0723	...	...	...	...	...	...	...	0923	...
Bonn a.	...	...	1937	...	...	...	...	...	2137	...	...	...	...	...	0757	...	...	...	...	...	...	...	0957	...
Köln Hbf a.	...	...	1959	...	...	...	...	...	2159	...	...	...	...	...	0821	...	...	...	...	...	...	...	1021	...
Düsseldorf a.	...	...	2031	...	...	...	...	...	|	...	...	...	...	...	0851	...	...	...	...	...	...	...	1103	...
Duisburg a.	...	...	2044	...	...	...	...	...	|	...	...	...	...	...	0908	...	...	...	...	...	...	...	1120	...
Essen a.	...	...	2057	...	...	...	...	...	|	...	...	...	...	...	0921	...	...	...	...	...	...	...	1137	...
Dortmund a.	...	...	2120	...	...	...	...	...	2320	...	...	...	...	...	0948	...	...	...	...	...	...	...	1203	...

NOTES

A – 🛏 1,2 cl., couchette 2 cl. and [2] Dortmund - Milano and v.v.
B – 🛏 1,2 cl., couchette 2 cl. and [2] Frankfurt/Main - Milano and v.v.
D – ITALIA EXPRESS – Daily to Nov. 4 and from Mar. 31: couchette 2 cl. and [2] Dortmund - Roma (also 🛏 1,2 cl., not Mar. 31, Apr. 1).
E – ITALIA EXPRESS – Daily to Nov. 4 and from Mar. 31: 🛏 1,2 cl., couchette 2 cl. and [2] Frankfurt/Main - Roma.
F – ITALIA EXPRESS – Daily to Nov. 5 and from Apr. 1: couchette 2 cl. and [2] Roma - Dortmund (also 🛏 1,2 cl., not Nov. 4,5).
G – ITALIA EXPRESS – Daily to Nov. 5 and from Apr. 1: 🛏 1,2 cl., couchette 2 cl. and [2] Roma - Frankfurt/Main.
R – VERDI – [12] and 🍷 Dortmund - Milano and v.v.; 🍴 Dortmund - Chiasso and v.v.
S – TIZIANO – [12] and 🍷 (Hannover) - Dortmund - Milano and v.v.; 🍴 (Hannover) - Dortmund - Chiasso and v.v.
r – Firenze Rifredi
v – Via Basel Bad.
⚡ – Supplement payable.

INTERNATIONAL SERVICES FROM MILANO

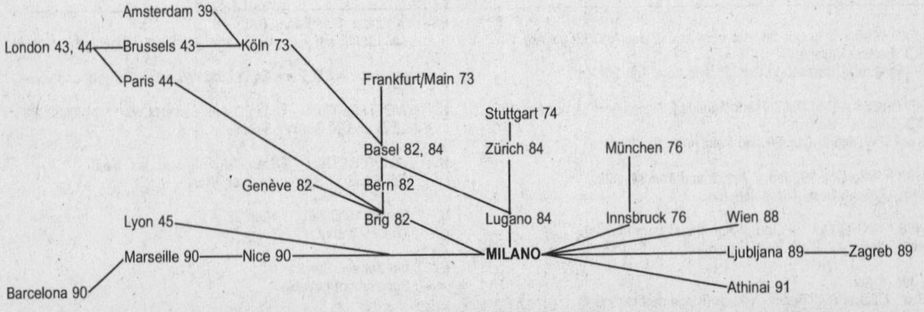

For explanation of standard symbols see page 4

Table 74 — STUTTGART - ZÜRICH AND MILANO

train type	EC		IC		EC	P	IC			IC						EC			
train number	155	383	545		481	57	515	683		387	687	381	2201	823		389	159	485	487
classes	1,2✗	1,2	1,2✗		1,2	1,2✗	1,2✗	1,2✗		1,2	1,2✗	1,2	1,2	1,2		1,2	1,2✗	1,2	1,2
notes (see below)	G		⚐			⚐	✗	⚐		A			K		E		J		
Nürnberg .... d.	...	...	...	...	0719	...	...			...	...	...	...	...		...	...	...	...
Stuttgart .... d.	0656	...	0742	...	0942	...	...			1142	...	1342	...	...		1542	1652	1742	1942
Singen 🔄 .... d.	0854	...	0952	...	1152	...	...			1352	...	1552	...	...		1752	1854	1952	2152
Schaffhausen .... a.	0908	...	1005	...	1205	...	...			1405	...	1605	...	...		1805	1909	2005	2205
Winterthur .... a.	0934	...															1934		
Zürich Hbf .... a.	0955	...	1047	...	1247	1333	...			1447	...	1647	...	...		1847	1955	2047	2247
Zürich Flughafen .... a.	...	...	...	...															
Zug .... a.	...	...	1129	...	1331					1529	...	1731	...	...		1929	...	2129	...
Arth Goldau .... a.	...	...	1145	...	1345					1545	...	1745	...	...		1945	...	2145	...
Bellinzona .... a.	...	...	1332	...	1532	1559				1732	...	1932	...	...		2132	...	2334	...
Locarno .... a.	...	...			1556														
Lugano .... a.	...	...	1403	...		1629				1803	...	2003	...	...		2203	...	0004	...
Chiasso 🔄 .... a.	...	...	1430	...		1700				1830	...	2030	...	...		2230	...	0038	...
Como .... a.	...	...	1454	...		1700				1854	...	2054	...	...		2254	...		...
Milano Centrale .... a.	...	...	1535	1600		1735	1940	1805		1935	2010	2135	2215	2215		2335	...		...
Genova P. Principe .... a.	...	...	1805				...	1947		...	2147	...	0005				...		...
Bologna .... a.	...	...		1744			2015							0048		0220	...		...
Ancona .... a.	...	...														0428	...		...
Pescara .... a.	...	...														0608	...		...
Bari .... a.	...	...														0949	...		...
Brindisi C. .... a.	...	...														1141	...		...
Lecce .... a.	...	...														1218	...		...
Firenze SMN .... a.	...	...	1853				2212r										...		...
Roma Termini .... a.	...	...	2055				2353							0524t			...		...
Napoli Centrale .... a.	...	...	2300				...							0816			...		...

train number	EC					IC	IC		IC		P	IC		EC	P	
train number	158	480	484		486	820	2156	386	674	388	500	676	380	154	504	382
classes	1,2✗	1,2	1,2		1,2	1,2	1,2	1,2	1,2✗	1,2	1,2✗	1,2✗	1,2	1,2✗	1,2✗	1,2
notes (see below)	J				⚐	K		D	⚐	F	Ⓡ✗Ⓐ	⚐		H	Ⓡ✗	
Napoli Centrale .... d.	...	...	...	...	...	1947	...	...	...	...	...	...	...	...	...	...
Roma Termini .... d.	...	...	...	...	...	2244t	...	...	...	...	0655	...	...	0955	...	...
Firenze SMN .... d.	...	...	...	...	...		...	...	...	...	0832r	...	...	1132r	...	...
Lecce .... d.	...	...	...	...	...		...	...	2106	...		...	...		...	...
Brindisi C. .... d.	...	...	...	...	...		...	...	2152	...		...	...		...	...
Bari .... d.	...	...	...	...	...		...	...	2352	...		...	...		...	...
Pescara .... d.	...	...	...	...	...		...	...	0326	...		...	...		...	...
Ancona .... d.	...	...	...	...	...		...	...	0501	...		...	...		...	...
Bologna .... d.	...	...	...	...	...	0345	...	...	0746	...	0930	...	...	1230	...	...
Genova P. Principe .... d.	...	...	...	...	...	0548	...	0813	...	...	0913	...	...		1223	...
Milano Centrale .... d.	...	...	...	...	...	0620	0740	0825	0950	1025	1105	1050	1225	1405	1425	...
Como .... d.	...	...	...	...	...		0905	...	...	1105	...	...	1305	...	1505	...
Chiasso 🔄 .... d.	...	...	...	...	0730		0930	...	...	1130	...	...	1330	...	1530	...
Lugano .... d.	...	...	...	...	0757		0957	...	...	1157	...	...	1357	...	1557	...
Locarno .... d.	...	...	...	...	...		...	...	...	...	...	...	...	...	...	...
Bellinzona .... d.	...	...	...	...	0827		1027	...	...	1227	...	...	1427	...	1627	...
Arth Goldau .... d.	...	...	...	...	1015		1215	...	...	1415	...	...	1615	...	1815	...
Zug .... d.	...	...	...	...	1031		1232	...	...	1431	...	...	1631	...	1832	...
Zürich Flughafen .... d.	...	...	...	...	...		...	...	...	...	...	...	...	...	...	...
Zürich Hbf .... d.	0630	0713	...	0913	1113		...	1313	...	1513	...	...	1713	1811	1913	...
Winterthur .... d.	...	...	...	...	...		...	...	...	...	...	...	...	1828	...	...
Schaffhausen .... d.	0705	0755	...	0955	1155		...	1355	...	1555	...	...	1755	1850	1955	...
Singen 🔄 .... a.	0718	0808	...	1008	1208		...	1408	...	1608	...	...	1808	1903	2008	...
Stuttgart .... a.	0913	1022	...	1222	1422		...	1622	...	1822	...	...	2022	2100	2222	...
Nürnberg .... a.	...	...	...	...	...		...	1913	...	...	...	...	...	...	...	...

NOTES

A – 🔄 Stuttgart - Milano; ⚐ Singen - Chiasso.

D – 🔄 Milano - Nürnberg; ✗ Chiasso - Singen.

E – ➡ 2 cl. and 🔄 Stuttgart - Lecce; ✗ Singen - Chiasso.

F – ➡ 2 cl. and 🔄 Lecce - Stuttgart.

G – KILLESBERG – ①-⑥ not Oct. 3, Dec. 25-31, Jan. 1, Apr. 15,16,17, May 1:
🔄 and ✗ Stuttgart - Zürich.

H – KILLESBERG – ①-⑤,⑦ not Oct. 2, Dec. 24-31, Apr. 14,15,16,30:
🔄 and ✗ Zürich - Stuttgart.

J – UETLIBERG – ①-⑤ not Oct. 3, Dec. 24-31, Jan. 1, Apr. 14,15,16,17, May 1:
🔄 and ✗ Stuttgart - Zürich and v.v.

K – ➡ 1,2 cl. and 🔄 Napoli - Milano and v.v.

r – Firenze Rifredi.

t – Roma Tiburtina.

✗ – Supplement payable.

Table 75 — MÜNCHEN - ZÜRICH

train type	EC	IC	IC	EC	IC	IC	EC	EC	EC	IC	EC
train number	92	924	726	94	934	1736	736	166	740	2443	98
classes	1,2✗	1,2	1,2	1,2✗	1,2	1,2	1,2	1,2✗	1,2	1,2	1,2✗
notes (see below)			⚐	✗	D		⚐	✗	B	✗	E
München Hbf .... d.	0810	...	...	1210	...	...	1402	...	...	...	1837
Kempten .... d.	...	...	...	...	...	...	1520	...	...	...	...
Lindau 🔄 .... a.	1029	...	...	1429	...	...	1629	...	...	...	2104
Bregenz 🔄 .... a.	1040	...	...	1440	...	...	1640	...	...	...	2115
St. Margrethen 🔄 .... a.	1054	...	...	1454	...	...	1654	...	...	...	2128
St. Gallen .... a.	1118	...	...	1518	...	...	1718	...	...	...	2153
Winterthur .... a.	1158	...	...	1558	...	...	1758	...	...	...	2233
Zürich Hbf .... a.	1221	1233	1303	1621	1633	...	1703	1823	1903	...	2256
Olten .... a.	...	...	...	...	...	...	...	...	...	...	...
Bern .... a.	...	1345	1415	...	1745	1828	1815	1945	2015	2028	...
Interlaken West .... a.	...	1444		...	1916					2119	...
Interlaken Ost .... a.	...	1449		...	1921					2123	...
Lausanne .... a.	...	...	1526	...	...	1926		2126			...
Genève .... a.	...	...	1602	...	...	2002		2202			...

train type	EC	IC	EC	EC	IC	EC	IC		EC
train number	99	711	167	104	721	95	729	1729	93
classes	1,2✗	1,2	1,2✗	1,2✗	1,2	1,2✗	1,2	1,2	1,2✗
notes (see below)	E		A	✗	D		⚐		C
Genève .... d.	...	0558	...	...	0958	...	1358	...	...
Lausanne .... d.	...	0634	...	...	1034	...	1434	...	...
Interlaken Ost .... d.	...		0711	1039		...		1439	...
Interlaken West .... d.	...		0716	1044		...		1444	...
Bern .... d.	...	0745	0814	1132	1145	...	1545	1551	...
Olten .... d.	...					...		1642	...
Zürich Hbf .... d.	0740	0857	0940	...	1257	1340	1657	1730	1740
Winterthur .... d.	0802		1002	...		1402		...	1802
St. Gallen .... d.	0840		1040	...		1440		...	1840
St. Margrethen 🔄 .... d.	0906		1106	...		1506		...	1906
Bregenz 🔄 .... d.	0921		1121	...		1521		...	1921
Lindau 🔄 .... d.	0930		1130	...		1530		...	1930
Kempten .... a.	...		1240	...				...	...
München Hbf .... a.	1155		1357	...		1751		...	2148

NOTES

A – ALBERT EINSTEIN – 🔄 and ✗ Interlaken - München - (Praha).

B – ALBERT EINSTEIN – 🔄 and ✗ (Praha) - München - Bern.

C – ANGELIKA KAUFFMANN – 🔄 and ✗ Zürich - München and v.v.

D – GOTTFRIED KELLER – 🔄 and ✗ Zürich - München and v.v.

E – BAVARIA – 🔄 and ✗ Zürich - München and v.v.

✗ – Supplement payable.

For summer service from May 28 see page 544

Table 76 MÜNCHEN AND INNSBRUCK - MILANO AND VENEZIA

train type	EC	IC						EC	EC			EC	IC		EC									
train number	81	649	2191		489	2099	2102	85	40	2101		13	658		87	2113	285		287		289	289	289	
classes	1,2 ⁄	1,2	1,2		1,2	1,2	1,2	1,2 ⁄	1,2 ⁄	1,2		1,2 ⁄	1,2 ⁄		1,2 ⁄	1,2	1,2		2		1,2	1,2	1,2	
notes (see below)	J	🍷					🍷	K	🍴	🍷		H	🍷		L				N		S	D	C	
München Hbf d.	0700	...	...	...	0830	...	...	0930	...	...	...	1330	...	...	1530	...	1730	...	2030	...	2330	2330	2330	...
Kufstein 🏛 d.	0759	...	...	...	0934	...	...	1034	...	...	...	1434	...	...	1634	...	1834	...	2134	...	0040	0040	0040	...
Wörgl d.	|	...	...	...	0945	...	...	1045	...	...	...	1445	...	...	1645	...	1845	...	2145	...	0053	0053	0053	...
Innsbruck d.	0839	...	...	...	1026	...	...	1122	...	...	...	1522	...	...	1722	...	1924	...	2222	...	0138	0138	0138	...
Brennero 🏛 d.	0925	...	...	...	1128	...	...	1214	...	...	...	1614	...	...	1814	...	2026	...	2319	...	0235	0235	0235	...
Bolzano a.	1038	...	...	...	1258	...	...	1329	...	...	...	1729	...	...	1931	...	2155	...	0034	...	0354	0354	0354	...
Trento a.	1107	...	...	...	1335	...	...	1400	...	...	...	1800	...	...	2006	...	...	...	0106	...	0432	0432	0432	...
Verona a.	1210	1227	...	...	1440	1454	1501	1504	1534	1554	...	1905	1934	...	2108	2154	...	...	0208	...	0540	0540	0540	...
Padova a.	|	1321	...	...	...	1550	|	|	|	1650	...	2002	|	...	|	2250	...	...	|	...	|	0805	|	...
Venezia Mestre a.	|	1346	...	...	...	1613	|	|	|	1713	...	2024	|	...	|	2313	...	...	|	...	|	0833	|	...
Venezia Santa Lucia a.	|	1359	...	...	...	1625	|	|	|	1725	...	2035	|	...	|	2325	...	...	|	...	|	0845	|	...
Milano Centrale a.	1355	...	1415	...	...	...	1645	|	1655	...	...	...	2055	...	2250	...	...	...	|	...	0830	...	|	...
Genova Porta Principe a.	...	...	1605	...	...	...	...	|	...	...	...	...	2247	...	...	...	...	...	|	...	1047	...	|	...
San Remo a.	...	...	...	...	...	...	...	|	...	...	...	...	...	...	...	...	...	...	|	...	...	...	|	...
Ventimiglia a.	...	...	...	...	...	...	...	|	...	...	...	...	...	...	...	...	...	...	|	...	...	...	|	...
Bologna a.	...	...	...	...	...	...	...	1706	...	...	...	...	...	...	...	...	...	...	0408	...	...	...	0755	...
Firenze SMN a.	...	...	...	...	...	...	...	1826	...	...	...	...	...	...	...	...	...	...	|	...	...	...	0912	...
Roma Termini a.	...	...	...	...	...	...	...	2030	...	...	...	...	...	...	...	...	...	...	0815	...	...	...	...	...
Napoli Centrale a.	...	...	...	...	...	...	...	...	...	...	...	...	...	...	...	...	...	...	1038	...	...	...	...	...
Rimini a.	...	...	...	...	...	...	...	...	...	...	...	...	...	...	...	...	...	...	...	...	...	...	...	...
Pesaro a.	...	...	...	...	...	...	...	...	...	...	...	...	...	...	...	...	...	...	...	...	...	...	...	...
Ancona a.	...	...	...	...	...	...	...	...	...	...	...	...	...	...	...	...	...	...	...	...	...	...	...	...
Pescara a.	...	...	...	...	...	...	...	...	...	...	...	...	...	...	...	...	...	...	...	...	...	...	...	...

train number				EC89	IC672	EC	IC		EC	IC				IC		EC83			220	2172				
train number	282	284	2096	EC86	IC647	12	649	2098	84	652	351	488		680	2106	EC80		288	288	2117				286
classes	1,2	1,2	1,2	1,2 ⁄	1,2 ⁄	1,2 ⁄	1,2 ⁄	1,2	1,2 ⁄	1,2 ⁄	1,2	1,2		1,2 ⁄	1,2	1,2 ⁄		1,2	1,2	1,2				2
notes (see below)	F	W		L	🍷	H	🍷	🍷	K	🍷	🍴			🍷	🍷	J		C	D	S				N
Pescara d.	...	...	...	...	...	...	...	...	...	...	...	...	...	...	...	...	...	...	...	...	...	...	...	...
Ancona d.	...	...	...	...	...	...	...	...	...	...	...	...	...	...	...	...	...	...	...	...	...	...	...	...
Pesaro d.	...	...	...	...	...	...	...	...	...	...	...	...	...	...	...	...	...	...	...	...	...	...	...	...
Rimini d.	...	...	...	...	...	...	...	...	...	...	...	...	...	...	...	...	...	...	...	...	...	...	...	...
Napoli Centrale d.	...	...	...	...	...	...	...	...	...	...	...	...	...	...	...	...	...	...	...	...	...	...	...	1815
Roma Termini d.	...	...	...	...	...	...	...	...	0725	...	...	...	...	...	...	...	...	...	...	...	...	...	...	2035
Firenze SMN d.	...	...	...	...	...	...	...	...	0927	...	...	...	...	...	...	...	...	2125	...	...	...	...	...	|
Bologna d.	...	...	...	...	...	...	...	...	1038	...	...	...	...	...	...	...	...	2240	...	...	...	...	...	0050
Ventimiglia d.	...	...	...	...	...	...	...	...	|	...	...	...	...	...	...	...	...	|	...	...	...	...	...	|
San Remo d.	...	...	...	...	...	...	...	...	|	...	...	...	...	...	...	...	...	|	...	...	...	...	...	|
Genova P. Principe d.	...	...	...	...	0713	...	...	...	|	...	...	...	...	1313	...	...	...	|	...	1954	...	...	...	|
Milano Centrale d.	...	...	...	0700	0905	...	1105	...	|	...	1210	...	...	1450	...	1530	...	|	...	2210	...	...	...	|
Venezia Santa Lucia d.	...	...	0625	|	|	0855	|	1025	|	1205	|	...	...	...	1525	|	...	|	2205	|	...	...	...	|
Venezia Mestre d.	...	...	0637	|	|	0906	|	1034	|	1217	|	...	...	...	1537	|	...	|	2242	|	...	...	...	|
Padova d.	...	...	0700	|	|	0927	|	1110	|	1239	|	...	...	...	1600	|	...	|	2307	|	...	...	...	|
Verona d.	...	...	0758	0832	1024	1054	1224	1158	1255	1331	1351	1406	...	...	1658	1721	...	0030	0030	0030	...	...	...	0255
Trento d.	...	...	...	0932	...	1152	...	...	1352	...	...	1504	...	...	...	1820	...	0128	0128	0128	...	...	...	0350
Bolzano d.	0600	0800	...	1030	...	1233	...	...	1433	...	...	1600	...	...	...	1854	...	0212	0212	0212	...	...	...	0426
Brennero 🏛 d.	0756	0956	...	1204	...	1404	...	...	1604	...	...	1750	...	...	...	2025	...	0351	0351	0351	...	...	...	0604
Innsbruck a.	0834	1034	...	1237	...	1437	...	...	1637	...	...	1828	...	...	...	2058	...	0424	0424	0424	...	...	...	0637
Wörgl a.	0914	1114	...	1314	...	1514	...	...	1714	...	...	1913	...	...	...	|	...	0510	0510	0510	...	...	...	0714
Kufstein 🏛 a.	0925	1125	...	1325	...	1525	...	...	1725	...	...	1925	...	...	...	2140	...	0523	0523	0523	...	...	...	0725
München Hbf a.	1030	1230	...	1430	...	1630	...	...	1830	...	...	2030	...	...	...	2240	...	0635	0635	0635	...	...	...	0830

NOTES

C – BRENNER EXPRESS – 🛏 1,2 cl., 🛏 2 cl. and [2] München - Firenze and v.v.
D – 🛏 2 cl. and [2] München - Venezia and v.v.
F – ①②③④⑤, not Dec. 19-Jan. 6 and Apr. 14,17.
H – PAGANINI – [12] and 🍴 (Dortmund) - München - Venezia and v.v.
J – GARDA – [12] and 🍴 München - Milano and v.v.
K – MICHELANGELO – [12] and 🍴 München - Roma and v.v.
L – LEONARDO DA VINCI – [12] and 🍴 München - Milano and v.v.
N – 🛏 1,2 cl., 🛏 2 cl. and [2] München - Napoli and v.v.
S – 🛏 1,2 cl., 🛏 2 cl. and [2] München - Genova and v.v.
W – ⑥⑦, daily Dec. 17-Jan. 8 and Apr. 14-17.
⁄ – Supplement payable.

Table 77 KÖLN, HAMBURG AND FRANKFURT/MAIN - ZÜRICH AND CHUR

train type	ICE		ICE	EC	IC	ICE	EC		ICE	EC	IC	ICE	ICE	EC	ICE	EC	IC		ICE	EC		ICE	EC	
train number	271	1765	997	101	767	999	107	1769	791	5	769	771	591	103	793	9	777		593	105	1781	895	3	
classes	1,2 ⁄	1,2	1,2 ⁄	1,2 ⁄	1,2	1,2 ⁄	1,2 ⁄	1,2	1,2 ⁄	1,2 ⁄	1,2	1,2 ⁄	1,2 ⁄	1,2 ⁄	1,2 ⁄	1,2 ⁄	1,2		1,2 ⁄	1,2 ⁄	1,2	1,2 ⁄	1,2 ⁄	
notes (see below)	B	🍴	🍴	🍴	🍷	🍴	🍴	🍷	🍴	🍴	🍴	🍴	🍴	C	🍴	🍴	🍴		🍴	🍴	🍷	🍴	A	
Dortmund d.	...	...	①-⑥	...	...	...	0538	...	①-⑥	0640	...	...	...	0740	...	0838	...	...	...	...	...	...	...	...
Essen d.	...	...	b	...	...	...	0601	...	b	|	...	...	...	|	...	0901	...	...	...	...	...	...	...	...
Duisburg d.	...	...	...	...	...	...	0614	...	...	|	...	...	...	|	...	0914	...	...	...	1019	...	...	1119	...
Düsseldorf d.	...	...	...	...	...	...	0628	...	...	|	...	...	...	|	...	0928	...	...	...	1034	...	...	1134	...
Köln Hbf d.	...	...	...	...	...	...	0700	...	...	0800	...	...	...	0900	...	1000	...	...	...	1100	...	...	1200	...
Bonn d.	...	...	...	...	...	...	0720	...	...	0820	...	...	...	0920	...	1020	...	...	...	1120	...	...	1220	...
Koblenz d.	...	...	...	...	...	...	0753	...	...	0853	...	...	...	0953	...	1053	...	...	...	1153	...	...	1253	...
Mainz d.	...	...	...	0742	...	...	0842	...	...	0942	...	...	...	1042	...	1142	...	...	...	1242	...	...	1342	...
Hamburg Altona d.	...	...	...	|	...	0446	|	...	0546	|	...	0623	...	|	0748	|	...	...	...	|	...	...	|	...
Hamburg Hbf d.	...	...	...	|	...	0500	|	...	0600	|	...	0637	...	|	0802	|	...	...	...	|	...	...	|	...
Bremen Hbf d.	...	...	...	|	...	|	|	...	|	|	...	|	...	|	|	|	...	...	...	|	...	...	|	...
Hannover Hbf d.	...	...	0520	|	...	0620	|	...	0720	|	...	0751	...	|	0920	|	...	...	...	|	...	1120	|	...
Kassel Wilhelmshöhe d.	...	...	0613	|	...	0713	|	...	0813	|	...	0845	0913	|	1013	|	...	...	1113	|	...	1213	|	...
Frankfurt/Main Hbf d.	0640	...	0743	|	...	0843	|	...	0943	|	...	1009	1043	|	1143	|	...	...	1243	|	...	1343	|	...
Mannheim d.	0731	...	0824	0831	...	0924	0931	...	1024	1031	...	1058	1124	1131	1224	1231	...	...	1324	1331	...	1424	1431	...
Karlsruhe d.	0756	...	...	0856	...	...	0956	...	...	1056	...	1121	...	1156	...	1256	...	...	...	1356	...	...	1456	...
Freiburg im Breisgau d.	0901	...	...	1001	...	...	1101	...	...	1201	...	1227	...	1301	...	1401	...	...	...	1501	...	...	1601	...
Basel SBB 🏛 a.	0941	...	...	1043	1049	...	1143	1149	...	1243	1249	1310	...	1343	...	1443	1449	...	...	1543	1549	...	1643	...
Zurich Hbf a.	1045	1110	...	...	1200	...	...	1300	...	...	1400	...	...	1500	...	...	1600	...	...	...	1700	...	1803	...
Sargans a.	...	1219	...	...	1313	...	...	1419	...	...	1513	...	...	1613	...	...	1713	...	...	...	1819	...	1913	...
Landquart a.	...	1233	...	...	1325	...	...	1433	...	...	1525	...	...	1625	...	...	1725	...	...	...	1833	...	1925	...
Landquart d.	...	*1240*	...	...	*1340*	...	...	*1440*	...	...	*1540*	...	...	*1640*	...	...	*1740*	...	...	...	*1840*	...	*1935*	...
Davos Platz a.	...	*1346*	...	...	*1446*	...	...	*1546*	...	...	*1646*	...	...	*1746*	...	...	*1846*	...	...	...	*1946*	...	*2050*	...
Chur a.	...	1245	...	...	1337	...	...	1445	...	...	1537	...	...	1637	...	...	1737	...	...	...	1845	...	1937	...
Chur d.	...	*1252*	...	...	*1352*	...	...	*1452*	...	...	*1550*	...	...	*1652*	...	...	*1752*	...	...	...	*1852*	...	*1952*	...
St. Moritz a.	...	*1458*	...	...	*1558*	...	...	*1658*	...	...	*1758*	...	...	*1858*	...	...	*1958*	...	...	...	*2058*	...	*2158*	...

NOTES

A – REMBRANDT – [12] and 🍴 (Amsterdam) - Duisburg - Chur.
B – JOHANNA SPYRI – [12] and 🍴 Frankfurt/Main - Zürich.
C – RÄTIA – [12] and 🍴 Dortmund - Chur.
b – Not Oct. 3, Dec. 25-31, Jan. 1, Apr. 15,16,17, May 1.
⁄ – Supplement payable.

For explanation of standard symbols see page 4

Table 77   KÖLN AND FRANKFURT/MAIN - ZÜRICH

train number	IC 613	ICE 71	ICE 595	EC 109	1787	ICE 897	IC 501	1789	IC 615	ICE 77	ICE 597	IC 603	1791	IC 899	ICE 605	1793	ICE 775	ICE 599	IC 503	EC 115	403 203	471	1,2	1,2
classes	1,2	1,2	1,2	1,2	1,2	1,2	1,2	1,2	1,2	1,2	1,2	1,2	1,2	1,2	1,2	1,2	1,2	1,2	1,2	1,2			1,2	1,2
notes (see below)	✕	R	✕	✕		✕	✕		✕	S	✕	✕		✕	✕		✕	✕	✕	✕	N P			
Dortmund......d.				1138				1240							1440						2205			
Essen......d.	1135			1201						1335									1538					
Duisburg......d.	1149			1214						1349									1601		2231			
Düsseldorf......d.	1204			1228						1404									1614		2304			
Köln Hbf......d.	1230			1300			1400		1430			1500			1600				1700		2321			
Bonn......d.	1250			1320			1420		1450			1520			1620				1720		2359			
Koblenz......d.	1323			1353			1453		1523			1553			1653				1753		0021			
Mainz......d.	1414			1444			1544		1614			1644			1744				1844		0057			
Hamburg Altona......d.		1023								1223								1423			0150			
Hamburg Hbf......d.		1037								1237								1437			2112			
Bremen Hbf......d.					1217								1417								2132			
Hannover Hbf......d.		1151			1320				1351				1520				1551				2244			
Kassel Wilhelmshöhe......d.		1246	1313		1413				1446	1513			1613			1645	1713				2355			
Frankfurt/Main Hbf......d.		1409	1443		1543				1609	1643			1743			1809	1843							
Mannheim......d.	1453	1458	1524	1531		1624	1631		1653	1724	1731		1824	1831		1858	1924	1931						
Karlsruhe......d.		1523		1556			1656			1723	1756			1856			1956							
Freiburg im Breisgau......d.		1629		1701			1801			1829	1901			2001			2101			0357				
Basel SBB ▥......a.		1710		1743	1749		1843	1849		1910	1943	1949		2043	2049	2110		2143	2148		0520	0550		
Zürich Hbf......a.		1815			1900		2000			2015		2100			2200			2247			0815	0815		
Sargans......a.					2019		2119					2219									0937	0937		
Landquart......a.					2035		2135					2235									0951	0951		
Landquart......d.					2045		2145																1040	
Davos Platz......a.					2159		2259																1146	
Chur......a.					2049		2149					2249									1004	1004		
Chur......d.					2057																			1052
St. Moritz......a.					2301																			1258

train type	ICE 76	IC 616	EC 114	IC 502	ICE 598	ICE 774	1756	ICE 500	ICE 896	1760	IC 602	ICE 596	EC 102	ICE 794		1764	ICE 108	ICE 594	EC 70	EC 96	EC 104	ICE 894	EC 2	ICE 592
classes	1,2	1,2	1,2	1,2	1,2	1,2	1,2	1,2	1,2	1,2	1,2	1,2	1,2	1,2		1,2	1,2	1,2	1,2	1,2	1,2	1,2	1,2	1,2
notes (see below)	S	✕	✕	✕	✕	✕	✕	✕	✕	✕	✕	✕	T	✕		☕	✕	✕	R	☕	✕	M	✕	
St. Moritz......d.																0705				0805			0900	
Chur......a.																0907				1007			1107	
Chur......d.							0613			0715			0823			0915				1015			1115	
Davos Platz......d.										0600			0700			0805				0905			1005	
Landquart......a.										0714			0817			0917				1017			1117	
Landquart......d.							0624			0726			0834			0926				1026			1126	
Sargans......d.							0639			0739			0845			0939				1039			1139	
Zürich Hbf......d.	0645		0712				0800			0900			1000			1100			1145	1200			1257	
Basel SBB ▥......a.	0752		0812	0817		0852	0911	0917		1011	1017		1117			1211	1217		1251	1306	1317		1417	
Freiburg im Breisgau......a.	0832			0856		0932		0956			1056		1156				1256		1330		1356		1456	
Karlsruhe......a.	0935			1000		1035		1100			1200		1300				1400		1435		1500		1600	
Mannheim......a.	1002	1007		1027	1035	1102		1127	1135		1227	1235	1327	1335		1427	1435	1502		1527	1535	1627	1635
Frankfurt/Main Hbf......a.	1047				1114	1147			1214			1314		1414										
Kassel Wilhelmshöhe......a.	1211				1244	1311			1344			1444		1544			1514	1547			1614		1714	
Hannover Hbf......a.	1305					1405			1438				1544			1638		1644	1711			1744		1844
Bremen Hbf......a.							1543															1838		
Hamburg Hbf......a.	1421					1521								1756				1921				1943		
Hamburg Altona......a.	1434					1534								1810				1934						
Mainz......a.		1046		1116					1216			1316		1416				1516			1616		1716	
Koblenz......a.		1135		1205					1305			1405		1505				1605			1705		1805	
Bonn......a.		1207		1237					1337			1437		1537				1637			1737		1837	
Köln Hbf......a.		1229		1259					1359			1459		1559				1659			1759		1859	
Düsseldorf......a.		1255		1331										1631							1824		1924	
Duisburg......a.		1309		1344										1644							1838		1938	
Essen......a.		1322		1357										1657										
Dortmund......a.				1420					1520					1720			1820							

train type	ICE 770	IC 778	EC 8	IC 792	1780	EC 106	ICE 590		IC 782	EC 4	ICE 892	1784	EC 100	ICE 790	IC 788	IC 600	ICE 996	1788	ICE 270		1,2	1,2	472	472
classes	1,2	1,2	1,2	1,2	1,2	1,2	1,2		1,2	1,2	1,2	1,2	1,2	1,2	1,2	1,2	1,2	1,2	1,2		1,2	1,2		
notes (see below)	✕	☕	✕	✕	✕	✕	✕		✕	✕	✕	✕	✕	⑥	c	✕	✕	Q					W	X
St. Moritz......d.		1000			1100				1200			1300		1400			1500				1800			
Chur......a.		1207			1307				1407			1507		1607	c		1707				2007			
Chur......d.		1223			1315				1423			1515		1623			1715							
Davos Platz......d.		1105			1205				1305			1405		1438			1605				1905		2028	2028
Landquart......a.		1217			1317				1417			1517		1607			1717				2017			
Sargans......d.		1234			1326				1434			1526		1634			1726						2040	2040
Zürich Hbf......d.		1245			1339				1445			1539		1645			1739						2055	2055
Basel SBB ▥......d.	1452	1400	1517		1500	1611	1617		1600	1717		1700	1811	1800		1850	1911	1917					2215	2215
Freiburg im Breisgau......a.	1532	1511			1611	1617	1656		1711	1717		1811	1817		1911	1917		2020					v	v
Karlsruhe......a.	1635	1556				1656				1756		1900		1856		2100		2059					0018	0029
Mannheim......a.	1702	1700	1727	1735		1827	1835		1900	1927	1935	2000		2027	2035	2127	2135	2227						0153
Frankfurt/Main Hbf......a.	1747		1814				1914			2014		2114		2214		2316								
Kassel Wilhelmshöhe......a.	1911		1944				2044			2144		2244												
Hannover Hbf......a.	2005		2038							2238		2338												
Bremen Hbf......a.																					0608			
Hamburg Hbf......a.	2121		2158																		0721			
Hamburg Altona......a.	2134		2212																		0831			
Mainz......a.		1816			1916				2016		2116		2218										0353	
Koblenz......a.		1905			2005				2105														0446	
Bonn......a.		1937			2037				2137														0521	
Köln Hbf......a.		1959			2059				2159														0545	
Düsseldorf......a.		2031			2131																		0617	
Duisburg......a.		2044			2144																		0633	
Dortmund......a.		2057			2157				2320														0723	
			2120			2220																	0749	

NOTES

M – REMBRANDT – 🍴 and ✕ Chur - Duisburg - (Amsterdam).
N – 2 cl. Dortmund - Zürich (Chur on ⑤ to Oct. 21, daily Dec. 16-Apr. 21);
   ☕ Dortmund - Basel;
   conveys Dec. 16-Apr. 13, not Dec. 24,31; ◄ 1,2 cl Dortmund - Chur.
P – 1,2 cl. and ◄ 2 cl Hamburg-Zürich (Chur on ⑤ to Oct. 21, daily Dec. 16-Apr. 21);
   1,2 cl. (T2) and ☕ Hamburg - Basel.
Q – JOHANNA SPYRI – 🍴 and ✕ Zürich - Mainz - Frankfurt/Main.
R – HELVETIA – 🍴 and ✕ Hamburg - Zürich and v.v.

S – PANDA – 🍴 and ✕ Hamburg - Zürich and v.v.
T – RÄTIA – 🍴 and ✕ Chur - Dortmund - (Berlin).
W – ◄ 1,2 cl. and ◄ 2 cl Zürich (Chur on ⑥ to Oct. 22, daily Dec. 17-Apr. 22)-Hamburg;
   1,2 cl. (T2) and ☕ Basel - Hamburg.
X – ◄ 2 cl Zürich (Chur on ⑥ to Oct. 22, daily Dec. 17-Apr. 22) - Dortmund;
   ☕ Dortmund - Basel; conveys Dec. 18-Apr. 14: ◄ 1,2 cl. Chur - Dortmund.
c – Not Oct. 2, Dec. 24-31, Apr. 14,15,16,30.
v – Via Basel Bad.
✗ – Supplement payable.

Table 78 — KÖLN AND FRANKFURT/MAIN - BERN AND LUZERN

train number	ICE 997	EC 101	1720	ICE 999	EC 107	ICE 791	EC 5	ICE 793	EC 9	ICE 593	EC 105	ICE 595	EC 109	201	401	403 / 203	471	1706
classes	1,2✓	1,2✓	1,2	1,2✓	1,2✓	1,2✓	1,2✓	1,2✓	1,2✓	1,2✓	1,2✓	1,2✓	1,2✓	2	2	2	2	1,2
notes (see below)	✕	K	♟	✕	N	✕	F	✕	G	✕	A	✕	M	C	B	D	H	♟
Dortmund d.	①-⑥				0538	①-⑥	0640		0838				1138		1909	2205		
Essen d.	b				0601	b			0901		1019		1214		2019	2231		
Duisburg d.					0614				0914		1034		1228		2036	2304		
Düsseldorf d.					0628				0928		1034		1300		2106	2321		
Köln Hbf d.					0700		0800		1000		1100		1300		2106	2359		
Bonn d.					0720		0820		1020		1120		1320		2127	0021		
Koblenz d.					0752		0852		1052		1152		1352		2203	0057		
Mainz d.		0742			0842		0942		1142		1242		1442		2258	0150		
Hamburg Altona d.			0446			0546		0748										2112
Hamburg Hbf d.			0500			0600		0802										2132
Bremen Hbf d.																		2245
Hannover Hbf d.	0520			0620		0720		0920		1115		1315						2355
Kassel Wilhelmshöhe d.	0615			0713		0815		1015		1115		1443			2255			
Frankfurt/Main Hbf d.	0743			0843		0944		1143		1243		1443			2341			
Mannheim d.	0824	0831		0924	0931	1024	1031	1224	1231	1324	1331	1524	1531			0357		
Karlsruhe d.	0856				0956		1056		1256		1356		1556		0038 0038	0520 0550		
Freiburg im Breisgau d.	1001				1101		1201		1401		1501		1701					
Basel SBB ⬛ a.	1043	1043		1143			1243		1443		1543		1743	v	v	0626 0651		
Biel a.				1304														
Neuchâtel a.				1325														
Lausanne a.				1412														
Genève a.				1455												0727 0727		
Olten a.		1127					1333		1533		1627		1827			0812 0812	0828	
Bern a.		1212	1228								1712		1912			0852 0852	0859	
Spiez a.		1252	1259								1801		2001			0854 0854	0901	
Spiez d.			1301								1816		2016				0916	
Interlaken West a.			1316															
Interlaken Ost a.			1321								1821		2021			0959 0959	0921	
Brig a.		1359																
Luzern a.							1412		1612						0543 0543			
Bellinzona a.							1632		1832						0612 0612			
Lugano a.							1703		1903						0637 0637			
Chiasso a.							1730		1930									

train number	EC 108	ICE 594	EC 104	ICE 592	EC 8	ICE 792	EC 106	ICE 590	EC 4	ICE 892	1733	EC 100	ICE 790	IC 890	1845 498	1845 498	200	200
classes	1,2✓	1,2	1,2✓	1,2✓	1,2✓	1,2✓	1,2✓	1,2✓	1,2✓	1,2✓	1,2	1,2✓	1,2✓	1,2	🛏	🛏	2	2
notes (see below)	M	✕	A	✕	G	✕	N	✕	F	✕	♟	K	✕⑧	✕	P	J	C	B
Chiasso d.					1030				1230								2230	2230
Lugano d.					1057				1257								2257	2257
Bellinzona d.					1127				1327								2327	2327
Luzern d.					1346				1546			1501			1949	1949		
Brig d.											1539			1939				
Interlaken Ost d.	0939		1039								1544			1944				
Interlaken West d.	0944		1044								1559	1605		1959	2053	2053		
Spiez d.	0959		1059								1601	1607		2001	2055	2055		
Spiez d.	1001		1101								1632	1648		2032	2148	2148		
Bern d.	1048		1148		1232				1627			1732			2232	2232		
Olten d.	1132		1232															
Genève d.							1308											
Lausanne d.							1348											
Neuchâtel d.							1436											
Biel d.							1457											
Basel SBB ⬛ d.	1217		1317		1517		1617		1717			1817			2325	2318	v	v
Freiburg im Breisgau a.	1256		1356		1556		1656		1756			1856			0029	0018	0456	0456
Karlsruhe a.	1400		1500		1700		1800		1900			2000		0153			0546	
Mannheim a.	1427	1435	1527	1635	1727	1735	1827	1835	1927	1935		2027	2035					0652
Frankfurt/Main Hbf a.		1514		1714		1814		1914		2014			2114					
Kassel Wilhelmshöhe a.		1642		1842		1942		2042		2142			2238		0608			
Hannover Hbf a.						2038				2238			2338		0721			
Bremen Hbf a.															0831			
Hamburg Hbf a.						2158									0850			
Hamburg Altona a.						2212												
Mainz a.	1516		1616		1816		1916		2016			2118		0353		0630		
Koblenz a.	1605		1705		1905		2005		2105					0446		0723		
Bonn a.	1637		1737		1937		2037		2137					0521		0757		
Köln Hbf a.	1659		1759		1959		2059		2159					0545		0821		
Düsseldorf a.			1824		2031		2131							0617		0851		
Duisburg a.			1838		2044		2144							0633		0908		
Essen a.					2057		2157							0723		0921		
Dortmund a.	1820				2120		2220		2320					0749		0948		

NOTES

A – BERNER OBERLAND – [couchette] and ✕ (Amsterdam) - Duisburg - Interlaken and v.v.

B – [bed] 1,2 cl., [couchette] 2 cl. and [sleeper] Frankfurt/Main - Chiasso - (Milano) and v.v.

C – [bed] 1,2 cl., [couchette] 2 cl. and [sleeper] Dortmund - Chiasso - (Milano) and v.v.

D – [bed] 1,2 cl., [couchette] 2 cl. and [sleeper] Dortmund - Basel; ♟ Duisburg - Basel;
⑤⑥ also Oct.2, Dec. 20,22,25-29, Jan. 2-5, Apr. 13,30; not Dec. 24,31:
[bed] 1,2 cl. and [couchette] 2 cl. Dortmund - Brig.

F – VERDI – [sleeper] and ✕ Dortmund - Chiasso - (Milano) and v.v.

G – TIZIANO – [sleeper] and ✕ (Hannover) - Dortmund - Chiasso - (Milano) and v.v.

H – [bed] 1,2 cl., [bed] 1,2 cl. (T2), [couchette] 2 cl. and ♟ Hamburg - Basel;
Daily Dec. 16-30, ⑤ Jan. 6-Apr. 7, also Apr. 13, not Dec. 24:
[bed] 1,2 cl. and [couchette] 2 cl. Hamburg - Brig.

J – [bed] 1,2 cl., [bed] 1,2 cl. (T2), [couchette] 2 cl. and ♟ Basel - Hamburg;
Daily Dec. 17-31, ⑥ Jan. 7-Apr. 8, also Apr. 14, not Dec. 25:
[bed] 1,2 cl. and [couchette] 2 cl. Brig - Hamburg.

K – MATTERHORN – [sleeper] and ✕ (Wiesbaden) - Mainz - Brig and v.v.

M – THUNERSEE – [sleeper] and ✕ (Berlin) - Dortmund - Interlaken and v.v.

N – MONT BLANC – [sleeper] and ✕ Dortmund - Genève and v.v.

P – [bed] 1,2 cl., [couchette] 2 cl. and [sleeper] Basel - Dortmund; ♟ Basel - Duisburg;
⑥⑦ also Oct. 3, Dec. 21,23,26-30, Jan. 3-6, Apr. 14, May 1; not Dec. 25, Jan. 1:
[bed] 1,2 cl. and [couchette] 2 cl. Brig - Dortmund.

b – Not Oct.3, Dec. 25-31, Jan.1, Apr. 15,16,17, May 1.

c – Not Oct.2, Dec. 24-31, Apr. 14,15,16,30.

v – Via Basel Bad.

✓ – Supplement payable.

Table 79 — KÖLN AND FRANKFURT/MAIN - MARSEILLE AND BARCELONA

train number	1173			train number	6694
train number				train number	6695
classes	2			classes	2
notes (see below)	F			notes (see below)	J
Köln Hbf .... d.	...		Ventimiglia .... d.		1847
Koblenz .... d.	...		Menton .... d.		1900
Trier .... d.	...		Monaco .... d.		1911
Luxembourg ▥ .... d.	...		Beaulieu .... d.		1922
Metz .... d.	...		**Nice** .... d.		1946
Nancy .... d.	...		Antibes .... d.		2008
Frankfurt/Main .... d.	1717		Cannes .... d.		2021
Mannheim .... d.	1807		St. Raphaël .... d.		2046
Karlsruhe .... d.	1842		Les Arcs .... d.		2105
Kehl ▥ .... d.	1937		Toulon .... d.		2154
Strasbourg .... d.	2024		**Marseille St. Charles** . d.		2259
Mulhouse .... d.	2140		Barcelona Sants .... d.		
Dijon .... d.	0026		Girona .... d.		
Avignon .... a.	0500		Figueres .... d.		
Nîmes .... a.	...		Port Bou .... d.		
Montpellier .... a.	...		Cerbère .... d.		
Béziers .... a.	...		Perpignan .... d.		
Narbonne .... a.	...		Narbonne .... d.		
Perpignan .... a.	...		Béziers .... d.		
Cerbère .... a.	...		Montpellier .... d.		
Port Bou .... a.	...		Nîmes .... d.		
Figueres .... a.	...		Avignon .... d.		0010
Girona .... a.	...		Dijon .... d.		0435
Barcelona Sants .... a.	...		Mulhouse .... d.		0739
Marseille St. Charles . a.	0613		Strasbourg .... d.		0908
Toulon .... a.	0715		Kehl ▥ .... a.		0918
Les Arcs .... a.	0756		Karlsruhe .... a.		1013
St. Raphaël .... a.	0815		Mannheim .... a.		1053
Cannes .... a.	0840		**Frankfurt/Main** .... a.		1201
Antibes .... a.	0855		Nancy .... a.		
Nice .... a.	0916		Metz .... a.		
Beaulieu .... a.	0934		Luxembourg ▥ .... a.		
Monaco .... a.	0944		Trier .... a.		
Menton .... a.	0954		Koblenz .... a.		
Ventimiglia .... a.	1007		**Köln** .... a.		

NOTES

F – Daily to Oct. 30 and from Mar. 31: 2 cl. and ⟨⟩ Frankfurt/Main - Ventimiglia; ♀ Frankfurt/Main - Strasbourg.

J – Daily to Oct. 30 and from Mar. 31: 2 cl. and ⟨⟩ Ventimiglia - Frankfurt/Main; ♀ Strasbourg - Frankfurt/Main.

Table 80 — MADRID - LISBOA

	30	332			31	335
	1,2✗	1,2✗			1,2✗	1,2✗
	B	A			B	A
Madrid Chamartín .... d.	...	2230	**Lisboa Santa Apolónia** ... d.		1155	2205
Madrid Puerta de Atocha d.	1405	...	Entroncamento .... d.		1259	2325
Valencia de Alcántara ▥ ... d.	1850	0500	Marvão Beirã ▥ .... d.		1445	0120
Marvão Beirã ▥ .... a.	1904	0517	Valencia de Alcántara ▥ .. a.		1500	0150
Entroncamento .... a.	2044	0703	**Madrid Puerta de Atocha** a.		1953	...
Lisboa Santa Apolónia ...... a.	2145	0833	**Madrid Chamartín** .... a.		...	0837

NOTES

A – LUSITANIA – 🛏 1,2 cl., ⟨⟩ 2 cl., ⟨⟩ and ✗ Madrid - Lisboa and v.v.

B – LUIS DE CAMOENS – ①②③④⑤⑦: ⟨⟩ and ♀ Madrid - Lisboa and v.v.

✗ – Supplement payable.

Table 81 — BARCELONA – LYON, GENÈVE AND MARSEILLE

Train number	73	TGV 860/1	6464 6465	EN 272		471	376 375	364 365
classes	1,2✗	1,2✗	1,2	L	2	2	1,2	1,2
notes (see below)	N	X R		L		⑤⑥⑦	P	R
Barcelona França ..... d.	0855			2015				
Barcelona Sants .... d.					1923	2000		
Girona .... d.	1001			2126	2052	2134		
Figueres .... d.	1027			2153	2133	2201		
Port Bou .... d.	1055				2159	2227		
Cerbère ▥ .... d.	1126				2204	2232	2305	2355
Perpignan .... a.	1151						2353	0030
Narbonne .... a.	1225						0036	0118
Montpellier .... a.	1315	1330	1349				0157	0253
Nîmes .... a.		1357	1415				0228	0325
Avignon .... a.		1423					0300	|
Marseille .... a.			1533					0450
Nice .... a.			1835					0742
Ventimiglia .... a.								0853
Valence .... a.		1520					0426	
Lyon Part Dieu .... a.		1603					0600	
Grenoble .... a.								
Chambéry .... a.								
Genève ▥ .... a.			1745	0552			0820	
Lausanne .... a.				0640				
Bern .... a.				0751				
Basel SBB .... a.								
Zürich .... a.				0915				

Train number	164 165	TGV 868/9	71	6950	5511		378	362 363	471	EN 274
classes	1,2✗	1,2✗	1,2✗	1,2	1,2	2	1,2	1,2	2	M
notes (see below)	X	R	X	N			P	R	⑤⑥⑦	M
Zürich .... d.										1933
Basel SBB .... d.										
Bern .... d.										2048
Lausanne .... d.										2158
Genève ▥ .... d.		1044						2154		2250
Chambéry .... d.										
Grenoble .... d.										
Lyon Part Dieu .... d.		1226					1403	2357		
Valence .... d.		1315					1507	0108		
Ventimiglia .... d.								2120		
Nice .... d.	1030		1148					2220		
Marseille .... d.	1302		1442					0120		
Avignon .... d.		1411					1607	0207		
Nîmes .... d.		1437		1552			1638	0236	0242	
Montpellier .... d.	1426	1502	1510	1636	1714			0306	0315	
Narbonne .... d.			1600		1817		1735	0410	0436	
Perpignan .... d.			1633		1858			0450	0514	
Cerbère ▥ .... d.			1656		1951			0538	0548	
Port Bou ▥ .... a.			1718		2110		1955	0552		0645
Figueres .... a.			1740		2132				0708	0729
Girona .... a.			1806		2202			0735	0756	
Barcelona Sants .... a.					2327			0902		
Barcelona França ..... a.			1920							0910

NOTES

– PABLO CASALS – ②④⑦, daily Sept. 25-Oct. 23, Dec. 20-Jan. 10 and Apr. 6-18: 🛏 1,2 cl., ⟨⟩ and ✗ Barcelona - Zürich.

M – PABLO CASALS – ①③⑤, daily Sept. 25-Oct. 24, Dec. 21-Jan. 11 and Apr. 7-19: 🛏 1,2 cl., ⟨⟩ and ✗ Zürich - Barcelona.

N – CATALAN TALGO – ⟨⟩ and ✗ Barcelona - Montpellier and v.v.

P – HISPANIA – 🛏 1,2 cl. and ⟨⟩ Genève - Port Bou/Cerbère and v.v.

R – 🛏 2 cl. and ⟨⟩ Cerbère/Port Bou - Ventimiglia and v.v.

✗ – Supplement payable.

 For summer service from May 28 see page 548

Table 82 GENÈVE AND BERN - MILANO

train type		IC		IC	IC		EC	IC	IC	IC	IC	IC		IC		IC	IC		EC	IC	IC		IC		IC
train number	2109	331	499	321	321	1808	39	813	677	819	323	679	1925	333	1822	327	683	1929	91	335	687	1628	337	1838	329
classes	1,2	1,2	1,2	1,2	1,2	1,2	1,2⚡	1,2⚡	1,2⚡	1,2	1,2	1,2⚡	1,2	1,2	1,2	1,2	1,2⚡	1,2	1,2⚡	1,2	1,2⚡	1,2	1,2	1,2	1,2
notes (see below)		🍷	🍷	🍷	C	D	Q		🍷	🍷	✕	🍷	🍷	✕	🍷	🍷	🍷	🍷	S		🍷		🍷		🍷
Genève d.	...	...	...	0731	0731	...	0820	...	...	...	1034	...	1148	...	...	1248	...	1348	...	1535	...	...	...	...	1916
Lausanne d.	0637	...	...	0809	0809	...	0857	...	...	...	1113	...	1232	...	...	1332	...	1432	...	1613	...	1656	...	...	1953
Montreux d.	0657	...	...	|	|	...	|	...	...	...	|	...	1253	...	...	1353	...	1453	...	|	...	1717	...	...	|
Martigny d.	0726	...	...	|	|	...	|	...	...	...	|	...	1325	...	...	1421	...	1525	...	|	...	1749	...	...	|
Sion d.	0744	...	...	0904	0904	...	0951	...	...	...	1208	...	1343	...	...	1438	...	1543	...	1708	...	1806	...	...	2048
Basel d.	|	...	0550	|	|	...	|	0723	...	0901	|	...	|	...	...	|	...	|	1401	|	...	|	...	...	|
Bern d.	|	0650	0722	|	|	0756	|	0851	...	1022	|	...	|	1256	1322	|	...	|	1522	|	...	|	1722	1922	|
Spiez d.	|	0722	0754	|	|	0828	|	0923	...	1054	|	...	|	1328	1354	|	...	|	1554	|	...	|	1754	1954	|
Brig d.	0817	0822	0859	0934	0945	0945	1031	1031	...	1159	1238	...	1423	1431	1459	1517	...	1623	1702	1738	...	1852	1902	2059	2118
Domodossola 🏛 a.	...	0850	...	1002	1017	1017	1100	1100	...	...	1307	...	...	1500	...	1547	...	...	1732	1807	...	...	1932	...	2147
Stresa a.	...	0938	...	1045	1107	1107	1140	1140	...	...	1344	...	...	1542	...	1632	...	...	1813	|	...	...	2013	...	2233
Arona a.	...	0950	...	1057	1123	1123	1152	1152	...	...	|	...	...	1554	...	1645	...	...	1825	1854	...	...	2025	...	2246
Milano Centrale a.	...	1045	...	1145	|	|	1240	1240	1315	...	1445	1510	...	1645	...	1745	1805	...	1915	1945	2010	...	2115	...	2345
Genova P.P. a.	...	...	...	...	1332	1332	...	...	1451	...	...	1647	...	...	...	...	1947	...	...	...	2147	...	...	...	...
Ventimiglia a.	...	...	...	...	1640	1640	...	...	...	...	...	...	...	...	...	...	...	...	...	...	...	...	...	...	...

train number				IC	IC	IC	IC	EC		IC		IC		IC	IC					1021	1021	IC	EC	EC	IC
train number			320	1821	332	330	674	90	1922	334	1639	322	1839	680	336	2136	344	326	1843	1022	1022	682	40	40	328
classes			1,2	1,2	1,2	1,2	1,2⚡	1,2⚡	1,2	1,2	1,2	1,2	1,2	1,2⚡	1,2	1,2	1,2	1,2	1,2	1,2	1,2	1,2⚡	1,2⚡	1,2⚡	1,2
notes (see below)				🍷	✕		🍷	S		🍷			🍷	🍷	🍷		🍷	✕	🍷	E	F	🍷	Q		
Ventimiglia d.	...	...	...	...	...	...	...	...	...	...	...	...	...	...	...	...	...	...	...	1225	1225	...	...	...	...
Genova P. Principe d.	...	...	...	...	...	...	0805	...	...	...	...	...	...	1313	...	...	1354	...	...	1520	1520	1513	...	...	...
Milano Centrale d.	...	...	0725	...	0825	0905	0950	1025	...	1225	...	1400	...	1450	1525	...	1545	1625	...	|	|	1650	1725	1725	1905
Arona d.	...	...	0816	...	0915	0953	...	1116	...	1316	...	1442	...	...	1617	...	...	1716	...	1741	1741	...	1815	1816	1952
Stresa d.	...	...	0830	...	0929	1006	...	1129	...	1329	...	1458	...	...	1630	...	...	1729	...	1758	1758	...	1828	1828	2000
Domodossola 🏛 d.	...	...	0915	...	1011	1046	...	1213	...	1411	...	1544	...	...	1713	...	...	1813	...	1850	1850	...	1913	1913	2100
Brig a.	...	...	0945	1001	1040	1114	...	1243	1248	1440	1507	1613	1622	...	1743	1807	...	1843	1901	1920	1920	...	1943	1943	2130
Spiez a.	...	...	|	1105	1140	|	...	1405	|	1540	|	|	1731	...	1905	|	...	|	2005	|	2053	...	|	2105	|
Bern a.	...	...	|	1138	1212	|	...	1438	|	1612	|	|	1804	...	1938	|	...	|	2038	|	2126	...	|	2138	|
Basel a.	...	...	|	...	...	|	...	1559	|	...	|	|	...	...	2059	|	...	|	...	|	...	...	|	2259	|
Sion a.	...	...	1023	...	...	1146	...	...	1321	...	1550	1644	...	...	...	1850	...	1921	...	2010	...	...	2017	...	2202
Martigny a.	...	...	1040	...	...	|	...	...	1338	...	1608	|	...	...	...	1908	...	1938	...	2037	...	...	|	...	|
Montreux a.	...	...	1105	...	...	|	...	...	1405	...	1641	|	...	...	...	1941	...	2005	...	2106	...	...	|	...	|
Lausanne a.	...	...	1127	...	...	1240	...	...	1427	...	1703	1740	...	...	...	2003	...	2027	...	2127	...	...	2111	...	2255
Genève a.	...	...	1212	...	...	1316	...	...	1512	...	...	1817	...	...	...	...	...	2112	...	2212	...	...	2148	...	2332

Table 83 GENÈVE - ROMA AND VENEZIA

train number	EC	IC	P					IC	IC	IC	IC			IC	IC	EC			EN	EN				
train number	39	813	509					819	323	543	655		1925	333	657	53		311	311	313				221
classes	1,2⚡	1,2	1,2⚡					1,2	1,2	1,2⚡	1,2⚡		1,2	1,2	1,2⚡	1,2⚡		1,2	━	━				1,2
notes (see below)	Q		[R] ✕					🍷	✕	🍷	🍷		🍷	✕	🍷	✕			V	W				A
Genève d.	0820	...	...	...	...	...	...	...	1034	...	...	...	1148	...	...	...	...	2025	2025	...	...	...	...	2302
Lausanne d.	0857	...	...	...	...	...	...	...	1113	...	...	...	1232	...	...	...	...	2110	2110	...	...	...	...	2345
Sion d.	0951	...	...	...	...	...	...	...	1208	...	...	...	1343	...	...	...	...	2216	2216	...	...	...	...	0052
Basel d.	|	0723	...	...	...	...	...	0901	|	...	...	...	|	...	...	...	...	|	|	2001	...	...	...	|
Bern d.	|	0851	...	...	...	...	...	1022	|	...	...	...	|	1256	...	...	...	|	|	2122	...	...	...	|
Brig d.	1031	1031	...	...	...	...	...	1159	1238	...	...	...	1423	1431	...	...	...	2305	2332	2332	...	...	...	0130
Domodossola 🏛 a.	1100	1100	...	...	...	...	...	...	1307	...	...	...	...	1500	...	...	...	2335	|	|	...	...	...	0200
Milano Centrale a.	1240	1240	1255	...	...	...	...	...	1445	1500	1505	...	...	1645	1705	1700	...	|	|	|	...	...	...	|
Verona a.	1424	1424	|	...	...	...	...	...	...	|	1624	...	...	...	1824	|	...	|	|	|	...	...	...	0512
Padova a.	1519	1519	|	...	...	...	...	...	...	|	1719	...	...	...	1919	|	...	|	|	|	...	...	...	0613
Venezia Mestre a.	1540	1540	|	...	...	...	...	...	...	|	1740	...	...	...	1940	|	...	|	|	|	...	...	...	0640
Venezia Santa Lucia a.	1552	1552	|	...	...	...	...	...	...	|	1752	...	...	...	...	|	...	|	|	|	...	...	...	0700
Bologna a.	...	...	1442	...	...	...	...	...	...	1644	...	...	...	...	...	1844	...	0350	|	|	...	...	...	...
Rimini a.	...	...	|	...	...	...	...	...	...	|	...	...	...	...	...	|	...	|	|	|	...	...	...	...
Ancona a.	...	...	|	...	...	...	...	...	...	|	...	...	...	...	...	|	...	|	|	|	...	...	...	...
Pescara a.	...	...	|	...	...	...	...	...	...	|	...	...	...	...	...	|	...	|	|	|	...	...	...	...
Firenze SMN a.	...	...	1527r	...	...	...	...	...	...	1753	...	...	...	...	...	1953	...	0514	0631	0631	...	...	...	...
Roma Termini a.	...	...	1705	...	...	...	...	...	...	1955t	...	...	...	...	...	2155	...	0800t	0923	0923	...	...	...	...
Napoli Centrale a.	...	...	...	...	...	...	...	...	...	...	...	...	...	...	...	...	...	1031	...	...	...	...	...	...

train type	EC		IC				IC	P					IC			EC	EC	EC	9720			EN	EN	
train number	52	2098	322	1839			652	504	336	2136		354	536	326	1843	54	40	40	220			314	314	312
classes	1,2⚡	1,2	1,2	1,2			1,2⚡	1,2⚡	1,2	1,2		1,2	1,2⚡	1,2	1,2	1,2⚡	1,2⚡	1,2⚡	1,2			━	━	1,2
notes (see below)	✕	🍷		🍷			🍷	[R] ✕	✕			✕	✕	✕	🍷	✕	Q		A			V	W	
Napoli Centrale d.	...	...	...	...	...	...	...	...	...	...	...	...	0857	...	...	...	...	...	...	...	...	...	...	1915
Roma Termini d.	0805	...	...	...	...	...	...	0955	...	...	...	...	1105	...	...	1205	...	...	...	...	...	2100	2100	2155t
Firenze SMN d.	1007	...	...	...	...	...	...	1132	...	...	...	...	1307	...	...	1407	...	...	...	...	...	2346	2346	0117
Pescara d.	|	...	...	...	...	...	...	|	...	...	...	...	|	...	...	|	...	...	...	...	...	|	|	|
Ancona d.	|	...	...	...	...	...	...	|	...	...	...	...	|	...	...	|	...	...	...	...	...	|	|	|
Rimini d.	|	...	...	...	...	...	...	|	...	...	...	...	|	...	...	|	...	...	...	...	...	|	|	|
Bologna d.	1116	...	...	...	...	...	...	1227	...	...	...	...	1416	...	...	1516	...	...	...	...	...	|	|	0301
Venezia Santa Lucia d.	|	1025	...	...	...	...	1205	|	...	...	...	1225	|	...	...	|	1405	1405	2205	...	...	|	|	|
Venezia Mestre d.	|	1037	...	...	...	...	1217	|	...	...	...	1237	|	...	...	|	1417	1417	2242	...	...	|	|	|
Padova d.	|	1100	...	...	...	...	1239	|	...	...	...	1300	|	...	...	|	1439	1439	2307	...	...	|	|	|
Verona d.	|	1201	...	...	...	...	1334	|	...	...	...	1401	|	...	...	|	1534	1534	0010	...	...	|	|	|
Milano Centrale d.	1300	1345	1400	...	...	...	1455	1405	1525	...	...	1545	1600	1625	...	1700	1725	1725	|	...	...	|	|	0625
Domodossola 🏛 d.	...	...	1544	...	...	...	...	...	1713	...	...	...	...	1813	...	...	1913	1913	0325	...	...	0609	0609	0813
Brig a.	...	...	1613	1622	...	...	...	...	1743	1807	...	...	...	1843	1901	...	1943	1943	0355	...	...	0639	0639	0843
Bern a.	...	...	|	1804	...	...	...	...	1938	|	...	...	...	|	2038	...	|	2138	|	...	...	|	0838	|
Basel a.	...	...	|	...	...	...	...	...	2059	|	...	...	...	|	...	...	|	2259	|	...	...	|	0959	|
Sion a.	...	...	1644	...	...	...	...	...	...	1850	...	...	...	1921	...	...	2017	...	0448	...	...	0721	...	0921
Lausanne a.	...	...	1740	...	...	...	...	...	...	2003	...	...	...	2027	...	...	2111	...	0555	...	...	0827	...	1027
Genève a.	...	...	1817	...	...	...	...	...	...	...	...	...	...	2112	...	...	2148	...	0639	...	...	0912	...	1112

NOTES for Tables 82 and 83

A – SIMPLON EXPRESS – ━ 2 cl. and [2] Genève - Venezia Santa Lucia and v.v.; 🛏 1,2 cl., ━ 2 cl. and [12] Genève - Venezia Mestre - (Zagreb) and v.v.

C – ⑤⑥, June 4 - Oct. 15: [12] Genève - Ventimiglia.

D – ⑤⑥, June 4 - Oct. 15: [12] Bern - Ventimiglia.

E – ⑥⑦ June 5 - Oct. 16: [12] Ventimiglia - Genève.

F – ⑥⑦ June 5 - Oct. 16: [12] Ventimiglia - Bern.

Q – MONTEVERDI – [12] and ✕ Genève - Venezia and v.v.

S – VAUBAN – [12] and ✕ (Brussels) - Basel - Milano and v.v.

V – ROMA – 🛏 1,2 cl., 🛏 1,2 cl. (T2) and ━ 2 cl. Genève - Roma and v.v.

W – ROMA – 🛏 1,2 cl. and ━ 2 cl. Basel - Roma and v.v.

r – Firenze Rifredi.
t – Roma Tiburtina.
⚡ – Supplement payable.

 For explanation of standard symbols see page 4

Table 84 ZÜRICH - MILANO

train type	IC		IC	EC	IC	EC		IC	IC	IC	EC	IC	EC	IC	EC	IC	IC	IC	EC	IC	IC	IC	IC	
train number	351	2187	251	55	677	51	2189	255	679	383	53	681	57	683	5	685	387	687	9	689	381	257	389	1087
classes	1,2	1,2	1,2	1,2⁄	1,2⁄	1,2⁄	1,2	1,2	1,2⁄	1,2	1,2⁄	1,2⁄	1,2	1,2⁄	1,2⁄	1,2⁄	1,2	1,2⁄	1,2⁄	1,2⁄	1,2	1,2	2	1,2
notes (see below)	S		🍷	P	🍷	X		🍷	🍷	G	R	🍷	T	🍷	A	🍷	D	🍷	B	🍷	C	🍷	J	V
Zürich Hbf d.	0703	...	...	0803	...	0903	...	...	...	1103	...	...	1333	...	...	...	1503	...	...	...	1703	...	1903	0006
Zug d.	0731	...	...	0831	...	0931	...	...	...	1131	...	...	1359	...	...	...	1531	...	...	...	1731	...	1931	|
Basel d.	|	...	0707	|	...	|	...	0907	...	|	1107	...	|	...	1307	...	|	...	1507	...	|	1720	|	|
Luzern d.	|	...	0819	|	...	|	...	1019	...	|	1219	...	|	...	1419	...	|	...	1619	...	|	1834	|	|
Arth Goldau d.	0749	...	|	0849	...	0949	...	1049	...	1149	1249	...	|	...	1449	...	1549	...	1649	...	1749	1900	1949	|
Bellinzona d.	0935	...	1028	1035	...	1135	...	1235	...	1335	1435	...	1602	...	1635	...	1735	...	1835	...	1935	2049	2135	|
Lugano d.	1006	...	1059	1106	...	1206	...	1306	...	1406	1506	...	1632	...	1706	...	1806	...	1906	...	2006	2119	2206	|
Chiasso 🏛 d.	1048	...	1141	1148	...	1248	...	1348	...	1448	1548	...	|	...	1748	...	1848	...	1948	...	2048	2200	2248	0355
Como a.	1054	...	1146	1154	...	1254	...	1354	...	1454	1554	...	1700	...	1754	...	1854	...	1954	...	2054	2205	2254	0400
Milano Centrale a.	1135	1215	1230	1235	1315	1335	1405	1435	1510	1535	1635	1710	1735	1805	1835	1910	1935	2010	2035	2110	2135	2240	2335	0440
Genova Porta Principe a.	...	1405	...	...	1451	...	1559	...	1647	1805	...	1847	...	1947	...	2047	...	2147	...	2247	...	...	...	0652
Ventimiglia a.	...	...	...	...	...	...	...	...	...	...	...	...	...	...	...	...	...	...	...	...	...	...	...	1005

train number			IC	EC	IC		IC	EC		IC	EC		IC	EC			IC	EC		1089			IC	EC
train number	250	386	672	8	674	388	676	4	380	678	52	382	680	56	252	354	682	54	254	1086	2164	256	684	58
classes	1,2	1,2	1,2⁄	1,2⁄	1,2⁄	1,2	1,2⁄	1,2⁄	1,2	1,2⁄	1,2⁄	1,2	1,2⁄	1,2⁄	1,2	1,2	1,2⁄	1,2⁄	1,2	1,2	1,2	1,2	1,2⁄	1,2⁄
notes (see below)	🍷	H	🍷	B	🍷	K	🍷	A	D	🍷	R	G	🍷	X	🍴	S	🍷	P	🍷	V	🍷	🍷	🍷	T
Ventimiglia d.	...	...	...	...	...	...	...	...	...	...	...	...	...	...	...	...	...	...	...	1255	...	...	...	...
Genova Porta Principe d.	...	...	0713	...	0813	...	0913	...	...	1113	...	1223	1313	...	...	...	1513	...	...	1602	1554	...	1713	...
Milano Centrale d.	0725	0825	0850	0920	0950	1025	1050	1125	1225	1305	1325	1425	1450	1500	1525	1625	1650	1720	1725	|	1745	1825	1850	1925
Como d.	0804	0905	...	1004	...	1105	...	1205	1305	...	1405	1505	...	1538	1605	1705	...	1755	1806	1839	...	1905	...	1959
Chiasso 🏛 a.	0812	0912	...	1012	...	1112	...	1212	1312	...	1412	1512	...	1545	1612	1712	...	1802	1812	1845	...	1912	...	|
Lugano a.	0851	0954	...	1054	...	1154	...	1254	1354	...	1454	1554'	...	1630	1654	1754	...	1844	1854	1925	...	1954	...	2028
Bellinzona a.	0920	1024	...	1124	...	1224	...	1324	1424	...	1524	1624	...	1659	1724	1824	...	1915	1924	1954	...	2024	...	2058
Arth Goldau a.	1111	1211	...	1311	...	1411	...	1511	1611	...	1711	1811	...	1845	1911	2011	...	2101	2111	2140	...	2211	...	|
Luzern a.	1146	|	...	1339	...	|	...	1539	|	...	1739	|	...	|	1939	|	...	|	2139	|	...	2239	...	|
Basel a.	1309	|	...	1453	...	|	...	1653	|	...	1853	|	...	|	2053	|	...	|	2253	|	...	2359	...	|
Zug a.	...	1231	...	...	...	1431	...	...	1631	...	...	1831	...	1901	...	2031	...	2120	...	2159	...	...	...	2300
Zürich Hbf a.	...	1257	...	...	...	1457	...	...	1657	...	...	1857	...	1928	...	2057	...	2148	...	2226	...	...	...	2324

Table 85 ZÜRICH - ROMA AND VENEZIA

train type	IC	EC	EC	EC	IC			IC	IC			EC	IC	EC	IC			IC		IC			EN	
train number	351	55	39	51	541	2101		383	545	2105	1571	53	657	57	559	2109		387	2113	389	301	1593	303	
classes	1,2	1,2⁄	1,2⁄	1,2⁄	1,2⁄	1,2		1,2	1,2⁄	1,2	1,2	1,2⁄	1,2⁄	1,2⁄	1,2⁄	1,2		1,2	1,2	1,2	1,2	1,2	▬	
notes (see below)	S	P	🍴	X	🍴	🍷		G	🍷	🍷		R	🍷	T	🍷	🍷	-	D		J	N	M	L	
Zürich Hbf d.	0703	0803	...	0903	...	...	...	1103	...	...	1203	...	...	1333	...	...	...	1503	...	1903	...	2003	2203	...
Basel d.	|	|	...	|	...	...	...	|	...	...	|	1107	...	|	...	...	...	|	...	|	1920	|	|	...
Luzern d.	|	|	...	|	...	...	...	|	...	...	|	1219	...	|	...	...	...	|	...	|	2034	|	|	...
Arth Goldau d.	0749	0849	...	0949	...	...	...	1149	...	...	1245	1249	...	|	...	...	...	1549	...	1949	2108	2108	2247	...
Bellinzona d.	0935	1035	...	1135	...	...	...	1335	...	...	...	1435	...	1602	...	...	...	1735	...	2135	2302	2302	0030	...
Lugano d.	1006	1106	...	1206	...	...	...	1406	...	...	...	1506	...	1632	...	...	...	1806	...	2206	2333	2333	0059	...
Chiasso 🏛 d.	1048	1148	...	1248	...	...	...	1448	...	...	...	1548	...	|	...	...	...	1848	...	2248	0015	0015	0140	...
Milano Centrale a.	1135	1235	1305	1335	1400	1410	...	1535	1600	1610	...	1635	1705	1735	1755	1810	...	1935	2010	2335	|	|	|	...
Verona a.	1351	|	1424	...	|	1551	...	...	|	1751	...	|	1824	...	|	1951	...	...	2151	|	|	|	|	...
Padova a.	1450	|	1519	...	|	1650	...	...	|	1850	...	|	1919	...	|	2050	...	...	2250	|	|	|	|	...
Venezia Mestre a.	1513	|	1540	...	|	1713	...	...	|	1913	...	|	1940	...	|	2113	...	...	2313	|	|	|	|	...
Venezia Santa Lucia a.	1525	|	1552	...	|	1725	...	...	|	1925	...	|	...	...	|	2125	...	...	2325	|	|	|	|	...
Bologna a.	...	1444	...	...	1544	...	...	...	1744	...	...	1844	...	...	1958	...	...	...	...	0220	0350	0350	|	...
Ancona a.	...	|	...	...	|	...	...	...	|	...	...	|	...	...	|	...	...	...	...	0428	|	|	|	...
Pescara a.	...	|	...	...	|	...	...	...	|	...	...	|	...	...	|	...	...	...	...	0608	|	|	|	...
Bari a.	...	|	...	...	|	...	...	...	|	...	...	|	...	...	|	...	...	...	...	0949	|	|	|	...
Brindisi Centrale a.	...	|	...	...	|	...	...	...	|	...	...	|	...	...	|	...	...	...	...	1141	|	|	|	...
Lecce a.	...	|	...	...	|	...	...	...	|	...	...	|	...	...	|	...	...	...	...	1218	|	|	|	...
Firenze SMN a.	...	1553	...	...	1653	...	...	...	1853	...	...	1953	...	...	2110	...	...	...	...	...	0514	0514	0631	...
Roma Termini a.	...	1755	...	...	1855	...	...	...	2055	...	...	2155	...	...	...	...	...	...	...	...	0800t	0800t	0923	...
Napoli Centrale a.	...	...	...	...	2100	...	...	...	2307	...	...	...	...	...	...	...	...	...	...	...	1031	1031	...	...

train type		EC		P		EC		IC		EC	EC			P		IC	IC	EC		EN				
train number		52	1582	504	2100	56		536	354	40	54		2104	506	256	540	656	58		314		312	312	388
classes		1,2⁄	1,2	1,2⁄	1,2	1,2⁄		1,2⁄	1,2	1,2⁄	1,2⁄		1,2	1,2⁄	1,2	1,2⁄	1,2⁄	1,2⁄		▬		1,2	1,2	1,2
notes (see below)		R		[R] 🍴		X		🍴	S	🍴	P			[R] 🍴		🍴	🍷	T		L		N	M	K
Napoli Centrale d.	...	...	...	...	...	...	...	0857	...	...	...	...	...	...	...	...	...	...	...	...	...	1915	1915	...
Roma Termini d.	...	0805	...	0955	...	...	...	1105	...	...	1205	...	...	1355	...	1405	...	...	...	2100	...	2155t	2155t	...
Firenze SMN d.	...	1007	...	1132r	...	...	...	1307	...	...	1407	...	...	1532r	...	1607	...	...	...	2346	...	0117	0117	...
Lecce d.	...	|	...	|	...	...	...	|	...	...	|	...	...	|	...	|	...	...	...	|	...	|	|	2106
Brindisi Centrale d.	...	|	...	|	...	...	...	|	...	...	|	...	...	|	...	|	...	...	...	|	...	|	|	2152
Bari d.	...	|	...	|	...	...	...	|	...	...	|	...	...	|	...	|	...	...	...	|	...	|	|	2352
Pescara d.	...	|	...	|	...	...	...	|	...	...	|	...	...	|	...	|	...	...	...	|	...	|	|	0326
Ancona d.	...	|	...	|	...	...	...	|	...	...	|	...	...	|	...	|	...	...	...	|	...	|	|	0501
Bologna d.	...	1116	...	1230	...	...	...	1416	...	...	1516	...	...	1630	...	1716	...	...	...	|	...	0301	0301	0746
Venezia Santa Lucia d.	...	|	...	|	1125	...	...	|	1225	1405	|	...	1425	|	...	|	1605	...	...	|	...	|	|	|
Venezia Mestre d.	...	|	...	|	1137	...	...	|	1237	1417	|	...	1437	|	...	|	1617	...	...	|	...	|	|	|
Padova d.	...	|	...	|	1200	...	...	|	1300	1439	|	...	1500	|	...	|	1639	...	...	|	...	|	|	|
Verona d.	...	|	...	|	1301	...	...	|	1401	1534	|	...	1601	|	...	|	1734	...	...	|	...	|	|	|
Milano Centrale d.	...	1325	...	1405	1445	1500	...	1600	1625	1655	1720	...	1745	1805	1825	1900	1855	1925	...	|	...	|	|	1025
Chiasso 🏛 a.	...	1412	...	...	...	1545	...	...	1712	...	1802	...	...	...	1912	...	...	|	...	0455	...	0712	0712	1112
Lugano a.	...	1454	...	...	...	1630	...	...	1754	...	1844	...	...	...	1954	...	...	2028	...	0554	...	0754	0754	1154
Bellinzona a.	...	1524	...	...	...	1659	...	...	1824	...	1915	...	...	...	2024	...	...	2058	...	0624	...	0824	0824	1224
Arth Goldau a.	...	1711	1715	...	...	1845	...	...	2011	...	2101	...	...	...	2211	...	...	|	...	0811	...	1011	1011	1411
Luzern a.	...	1739	|	...	...	|	...	...	|	...	|	...	...	...	2239	...	...	|	...	|	...	1046	|	|
Basel a.	...	1853	|	...	...	|	...	...	|	...	|	...	...	...	2359	...	...	|	...	|	...	1209	|	|
Zürich Hbf a.	...	...	1757	...	...	1928	...	...	2057	...	2148	...	...	...	...	...	...	2324	...	0857	...	...	1057	1457

NOTES for Tables 84 and 85

- A – VERDI – [12] (Dortmund) - Basel - Milano and v.v.; 🍴 Basel - Chiasso and v.v.
- B – TIZIANO – [12] (Hannover) - Basel - Milano and v.v.; 🍴 Basel - Chiasso and v.v.
- C – [12] (Stuttgart) - Zürich - Milano; 🍴 Zürich - Chiasso.
- D – [12] Milano - Zürich - (Stuttgart) and v.v.
- G – [12] Stuttgart - Zürich - Genova and v.v.
- H – [12] Milano - Zürich - (Nürnberg); 🍴 Chiasso - Zürich.
- J – ▬ 2 cl. and [12] (Stuttgart) - Zürich - Lecce; [12] and 🍴 Zürich - Chiasso.
- K – ▬ 2 cl. and [12] Lecce - Zürich - (Stuttgart).
- L – ROMA – 🛏 1,2 cl. and ▬ 2 cl. Zürich - Roma and v.v.
- M – [12] Zürich - Napoli and v.v.
- N – [12] Basel - Napoli and v.v.
- P – RAFFAELLO – [12] and 🍴 Zürich - Roma and v.v.
- R – COLOSSEUM – [12] and 🍴 Basel - Roma and v.v.
- S – CANALETTO – [12] and 🍴 Zürich - Venezia and v.v.
- T – GOTTARDO – [12] and 🍷 Zürich - Milano and v.v.
- V – ⑥ June 4 - Oct. 15: [12] Zürich - Ventimiglia and v.v.
- X – TICINO – [12] and 🍴 Zürich - Milano and v.v.
- r – Firenze Rifredi.
- t – Roma Tiburtina.
- ⁄ – Supplement payable.

Table 86 — ZÜRICH - INNSBRUCK AND WIEN

train type			IC	EC	IC	EC	EC	EC	IC	IC	IC	IC	IC		EN
train number	365	517	163	519	169	169	161	613	777	449	863	349	865	465	465	467
classes	1,2	1,2	1,2	1,2	1,2	1,2	1,2	1,2	1,2	1,2	1,2	2	1,2	1,2	2
notes			B			E	D	F			X			H	J	A
Basel SBB .... d.			0825						1542		1809	2105		2025	2025	2117
Zürich Flughafen + ... d.	0713		0905	1042			1316		1553		1821	2118		2123	2123	2223
Zürich Hbf .... a.	0723		0918	1053			1326							2123	2123	2223
Zürich Hbf .... d.		0735		0933	1120	1120	1335			1610		1835		2133	2133	2339
Sargans .... d.		0835		1034	1224	1224	1434	1713	1725			1950		2234	2234	
Buchs .... d.		0852		1052	1244	1244	1452		1750			2018		2253	2253	0007
Feldkirch .... a.		0908		1108	1259	1259	1509		1812	1844		2034	2044	2308	2308	0023
Bludenz .... a.		0925		1125	1323	1323	1525			1858			2058	2339	2352	
Langen am Arlberg ...... a.		0952		1152	1349	1349	1552			1926			2126	0014	0029	
St. Anton am Arlberg ... a.		1001		1201	1358	1358	1601			1937			2135	0025	0040	
Landeck .... a.		1028		1228	1425	1425	1628			2007			2207	0050	0106	
Ötztal .... a.		1050		1250	1447	1447	1650			2032			2232			
Innsbruck Hbf .... a.	1116	1120	1316	1316	1513	1513	1716	1720				2058	2258	0137	0155	0246
Kitzbühel .... a.		1227		1427	1626	1626		1827								
Zell am See .... a.		1313		1513	1713	1713		1913						0348	0402	
Schwarzach St. Veit .... a.		1345		1545	1744	1744		1945						0405		
Bischofshofen .... a.		1359		1559	1759			1959						0732		
Graz .... a.		1720		1920	2120			2320							0545	0550
Villach Hbf .... a.						1935									0550	
Klagenfurt .... a.						2006									0614	
Salzburg .... a.			1522				1922									0445c
Linz .... a.			1637				2037									0610
St. Pölten .... a.			1743				2143									0718
Wien West .... a.			1830				2230									0805
Hegyeshalom .... a.																0928
Györ .... a.																1006
Budapest Keleti .... a.																1153

train type	IC		IC	IC			IC	EC		IC	EC		EC	EC		IC		EN			IC		
train number	860	348	712	862	448		510	160		512	162		168	198		516	364	466			894	464	
classes	1,2	1,2	1,2	1,2	1,2		1,2	1,2		1,2	1,2		1,2	1,2		1,2	1,2	A			1,2	2	1,2
notes	X			X				F			B		E	D				A			J	H	
Budapest Keleti .... d.																		1725					
Györ .... d.																		1904					
Hegyeshalom .... d.																		1945					
Wien West .... d.								0735			0935							2125					
St. Pölten .... d.								0816			1016							2207					
Linz .... d.								0923			1123							2315					
Salzburg .... d.				0534				1038			1238							0043c					
Klagenfurt .... d.				0700									1203								2146		
Villach Hbf .... d.													1235								2210	0008	
Graz .... d.							0640			0840			1040			1240					2200		
Bischofshofen .... d.			0553				1001			1201			1401			1601						0141	
Schwarzach St. Veit .... d.			0607				1015			1215			1423	1423		1615					0157	0212	
Zell am See .... d.			0637				1046			1246			1453	1453		1646							
Kitzbühel .... d.			0725				1133			1333			1539	1539		1735							
Innsbruck Hbf .... d.	0702		0832	0902			1240	1244		1440	1444		1653	1653		1840	1844	0240			0415	0430	
Ötztal .... d.	0729			0930				1309			1509		1717	1717		1909					0506	0516	
Landeck .... d.	0755			0954				1331			1531		1740	1740		1932					0533	0559	
St Anton am Arlberg .... d.	0825			1025				1359			1559		1807	1807		1959					0543	0615	
Langen am Arlberg ...... d.	0835			1035				1408			1608		1817	1817		2008					0615	0625	
Bludenz .... d.	0901			1101				1434			1634		1843	1843		2034					0652	0652	
Feldkirch .... d.	0917	0931		1117	1134			1452			1652		1901	1901		2052		0501			0708	0708	
Buchs .... a.		0947			1150			1508			1708		1917	1917		2108		0518			0726	0726	
Sargans .... a.		1013			1209			1526			1726		1934	1934		2126		0547			0826	0826	
Zürich Hbf .... a.		1126		1,2	1326			1626			1826		2041	2041		2226		0651			0837	0837	
Zürich Hbf .... d.			1139				1345			1639	1837		1845			2107		2315	0700	0710	0837	0837	0839
Zürich Flughafen + ... a.			1151				1356			1651	1856					2116		2325	0720		0832		0850
Basel SBB .... a.													1935					0832			0935	0935	

NOTES

A – WIENER WALZER – 🛏 1,2 cl., ⊢ 2 cl. and 🍴 Basel - Wien and v.v.; ⊢ 2 cl. and 🍴 Basel - Budapest and v.v.

B – TRANSALPIN – 🍴 and ✕ Basel - Wien and v.v.

D – ROBERT STOLZ – 🍴 Zürich - Klagenfurt and v.v.; ✕ Zürich - Schwarzach St Veit and v.v.; 🍵 Schwarzach St Veit - Klagenfurt and v.v.

E – ROBERT STOLZ – 🍴 and ✕ Zürich - Graz and v.v.

F – MARIA THERESIA – 🍴 and ✕ Zürich - Wien and v.v.

H – 🛏 1,2 cl., ⊢ 2 cl. and 🍴 Basel - Graz and v.v.

J – ⊢ 2 cl. and 🍴 Basel - Villach and v.v.

c – Subject to confirmation.

/ – Supplement payable.

Table 87 — WIEN - LJUBLJANA AND ZAGREB

train number	IC 151	221	IC 159	IC 159		train number	IC 158	IC 512	220	IC482 IC150
classes	1,2	1,2	1,2	1,2		classes	1,2	1,2	1,2	1,2
notes	A		C	D		notes	C	D		A
Wien Süd .... d.	0822		1622	1622		Trieste .... d.				1255
Graz .... d.	1058		1858	1858		Rijeka .... d.				1540
Maribor .... a.	1159		1956	1956		Ljubljana .... d.		0715	1410	1540
Zidani Most ...... a.	1321	1326		2131		Zagreb .... d.	0715		1531	1635
Zagreb .... a.		1450	2235			Zidani Most ...... d.	0814		1531	1635
Ljubljana .... a.	1418			2230		Maribor .... d.	0955	0955		1758
Rijeka .... a.	1725					Graz .... a.	1055	1055		1855
Trieste .... a.						Wien Süd .... a.	1340	1340		2140

NOTES

A – EMONA – 🍴 and ✕ Wien - Ljubljana and v.v.; 🍴 Wien - Rijeka and v.v.

C – CROATIA – 🍴 and ✕ Wien - Zagreb and v.v.

D – 🍴 Wien - Ljubljana and v.v.; ✕ Wien - Maribor and v.v.

Table 88 — WIEN - VENEZIA AND MILANO

train number		EC 31	IC 592	2847	2106		IC597 233	2855		IC 892	235	235		1235	1235		EN 237	2841	EC 12
classes		1,2✗ D	1,2✗ E	2 ①-⑥	1,2 ⚲		1,2	1,2		1,2 ⚲	1,2 H	1,2 J		2 L	1,2 N		2 A	1,2 ①-⑥	1,2✗ ✕
notes (see below)																			
Budapest Keleti .... d.		...	...	...	...		...	...		...	...	...		...	...		...	...	...
Wien Süd .... d.		...	0718	...	...		1322	...		...	1945	1945		2015	2015		2222	...	...
Bruck an der Mur .... d.		...	0914	...	...		1524	...		...	2136	2136		2206	2206		0041	...	...
Klagenfurt .... d.		...	1121	...	...		1746	...		...	2347	2347		0012	0012		0257	...	...
Salzburg Hbf .... d.		...	...	0908	...		...	...		2108	...	...		...	...		...	...	...
Villach Hbf .... d.		...	1200	1200	...		1827	...		2343	0014	0014		0054	0054		0332	...	...
Tarvisio 🚊 .... a.		...	1225	1225	...		1852	...		...	0042	0042		0118	0118		0420	...	...
Udine .... a.		...	1358	1358	1430		2040	2047		...	0219	0219		0256	0256		0612	0646	...
Trieste .... a.		...			1539			2156		...	...	...		...	...			0754	...
Venezia Mestre .... a.		...	1518	1518	1537	1546	2216			...	0344	0344		0423	0423		0821		0906
Venezia Santa Lucia .... a.						1555	2228			...		0405			0442		0832		
Padova .... a.		...	1552	1552						...	0420	0557		0502	0557				0927
Verona .... a.		...			1658					...		0658			0658				1050
Milano Centrale .... a.		...			1845					...		0850			0850				
Bologna .... a.		...	1706	1706						...	0540			0627					
Firenze SMN .... a.		...	1816	1816						...	0656			0753					
Roma Termini .... a.		...	2020	2020						...	0930								
Ravenna .... a.		...	...	...	...		...	...		...	...	...		...	...		...	...	...
Rimini .... a.		...	...	...	...		...	...		...	...	...		...	...		...	...	...
Pesaro .... a.		...	...	...	...		...	...		...	...	...		...	...		...	...	...
Ancona .... a.		...	...	...	...		...	...		...	...	...		...	...		...	...	...

train type	2842	232		2846	IC 647		2	EC 30	EC 30		2107	872	EN 236		1234	2113		234	2113
train number																			
classes	1,2 ①-⑥	1,2		1,2	1,2 ⚲		2	1,2✗ D	1,2✗ E		1,2	1,2	2 A		2 M	1,2 P		1,2 H	1,2 K
notes (see below)																			
Ancona .... d.	...	...		...	...		...	...	...		...	...	...		...	...		...	...
Pesaro .... d.	...	...		...	...		...	...	...		...	...	...		...	...		...	...
Rimini .... d.	...	...		...	...		...	...	...		...	...	...		...	...		...	...
Ravenna .... d.	...	...		...	...		...	...	...		...	...	...		...	...		...	...
Roma Termini .... d.	...	...		...	...		...	0745	0745		...	...	...		...	1920		...	...
Firenze SMN .... d.	...	...		...	...		...	0947	0947		...	...	...		1953	2148		...	...
Bologna .... d.	...	...		...	...		...	1058	1058		...	...	...		2115	2300		...	...
Milano Centrale .... d.	...	...		0905			...				1710	...	...			2010			2010
Verona .... d.	...	...		1027			...				1854	...	...			2154			2154
Padova .... d.	...	...		1122			...	1208	1208			...	2050		2300	2253		0022	2253
Venezia Santa Lucia .... d.	...	0730			1147		...					...			2355	2355			2355
Venezia Mestre .... d.	...	0742		1140	1157		1241	1241			2013	...	2101		0006	0006		0102	0102
Trieste .... d.	0735			1224								2118							
Udine .... d.	0848	0923		1336			1403	1403				2230	2254		0132	0132		0222	0222
Tarvisio 🚊 .... a.		1109					1535	1535					0043		0328	0328		0358	0358
Villach Hbf .... a.		1133					1600	1600					0111		0351	0351		0420	0420
Salzburg Hbf .... a.								1853											
Klagenfurt .... a.		1214					1637						0150		0435	0435		0447	0447
Bruck an der Mur .... a.		1436					1847						0401		0644	0644		0655	0655
Wien Süd .... a.		1640					2046						0623		0850	0850		0857	0857
Budapest Keleti .... a.	...	...		...	...		...	...	...		...	...	...		...	...		...	...

NOTES

A — SAN MARCO – 🛏 1,2 cl. (T2), 🛏 2 cl. and 🍴 Wien - Venezia and v.v.

D — ROMULUS – 🍴 and ✕ Wien - Roma and v.v.

E — 🍴 Salzburg - Roma and v.v.; ⚲ Salzburg - Villach and v.v.;
✕ Villach - Roma and v.v.

H — REMUS – 🛏 1,2 cl., 🛏 2 cl. and 🍴 Wien - Roma and v.v.

J — Daily to Dec. 26, Jan. 10-Apr. 7 and Apr. 25-May 19:
🛏 1,2 cl., 🛏 2 cl. and 🍴 Wien - Milano.

K — Daily to Dec. 25, Jan. 9-Apr. 6 and Apr. 24-May 18:
🛏 1,2 cl., 🛏 2 cl. and 🍴 Milano - Wien.

L — Dec. 27-Jan. 9, Apr. 8-24 and May 20-27: 🛏 2 cl. and 🍴 Wien - Firenze.

M — Dec. 26-Jan. 8, Apr. 7-23 and May 19-27: 🛏 2 cl. and 🍴 Firenze - Wien.

N — Dec. 27-Jan. 9, Apr. 8-24 and May 20-27:
🛏 1,2 cl., 🛏 2 cl. and 🍴 Wien - Milano.

P — Dec. 26-Jan. 8, Apr. 7-23 and May 19-27:
🛏 1,2 cl., 🛏 2 cl. and 🍴 Milano - Wien.

✗ — Supplement payable.

Table 89 — VENEZIA - LJUBLJANA, ZAGREB AND BUDAPEST

train type / train number	221	IC 641	243		2215	265		2109	241
classes	1,2 A	1,2✗ ⚲	1,2 C		1,2	1,2 D		1,2 ⚲	1,2 B
notes (see below)									
Genève .... d.	2302	...	...		...	...		...	...
Lausanne .... d.	2345	...	...		...	...		...	...
Brig ◉ .... d.	0130	...	...		...	...		...	...
Milano Centrale .... d.		0705	...		1810	...		...	...
Verona .... d.	0516	0827	...		1954	...		...	...
Roma Termini .... d.			...			...		...	...
Firenze S.M.N. .... d.			...			...		...	...
Padova .... d.	0616	0922	...			...		2053	...
Venezia Santa Lucia .... d.			0940		1540				2122
Venezia Mestre .... d.	0708	0940	0951		1551			2113	2134
Trieste .... d.	0916		1204		1747	1758			2343
Villa Opicina 🚊 .... d.	1005		1300			1840			0031
Ljubljana .... a.	1215		1500			2044			0240
Zagreb .... a.	1450					2255			0505
Budapest Keleti .... a.	...		2258						1158

train type / train number	240	IC 648		264	2212		242	2114	220
classes	1,2 B	1,2✗ ⚲		1,2 D	1,2		1,2 C	1,2	1,2 A
notes (see below)									
Budapest Keleti .... d.	1730	...		...	0600		...	...	...
Zagreb .... d.	0020	...		0540			...	...	1410
Ljubljana .... d.	0320	...		0800			1355	...	1645
Villa Opicina 🚊 .... d.	0540	...		1014			1555	...	1854
Trieste .... d.	0638	...		1057	1212		1650	...	1949
Venezia Mestre .... a.	0907	1017		...	1407		1907	1937	2219
Venezia Santa Lucia .... a.	0918			...	1418		1918		
Padova .... a.		1036		...				1957	2304
Firenze S.M.N. .... a.				...					
Roma Termini .... a.				...					
Verona .... a.		1131		...				2058	0002
Milano Centrale .... a.		1300		...				2245	
Brig ◉ .... a.				...					0355
Lausanne .... a.				...					0555
Genève .... a.				...					0639

NOTES

A — SIMPLON EXPRESS – 🛏 1,2 cl., 🛏 2 cl. and 🍴 Genève - Zagreb and v.v.

B — VENEZIA EXPRESS – 🛏 1,2 cl., 🛏 2 cl. and 🍴 Venezia - Budapest and v.v.

C — DRAVA – 🍴 and ✕ Venezia - Budapest and v.v.

D — KRAS – 🍴 Trieste - Zagreb and v.v.

◉ — 🚊 is at Domodossola/Iselle.

✗ — Supplement payable.

Table 90   BARCELONA AND MARSEILLE - MILANO

train number		6464	162		6173		6453	6132			EN			364	6478		342
train number	73	6465	163	349	6172	367	6452	6133	359		273		471	365	365		343
classes	1,2✗	1,2	1,2	1,2	1,2	1,2	1,2	1,2	1,2		⛴	2	2	1,2	1,2		1,2
notes (see below)	M	⚊	⛐	J	⛐	H	⛐	⛐	F		E			⑤⑥⑦ G	N		L
Hendaye................. d.	...	0632	...	...	...	...	1147	...	...	...	...	...	...	...	1810		2244
Bordeaux................ d.	...	...	1102	...	...	...	1412	...	...	...	...	...	...	...	2259		0126
Toulouse................. d.	...	1129	1306	...	...	...	...	...	...	...	...	...	...	...	...		
Barcelona França....... d.	0855				...	...	...	...	...	...	2015	...	1923	2000	...		
Barcelona Sants........ d.	1001				...	...	...	...	...	...	2126	...	2052	2133	...		
Girona.................. d.	1001				...	...	...	...	...	...		...	2204	2232	2355		
Cerbère ⛢............. d.	1126				...	...	...	...	...	...		...	0151	0151	...		0258
Narbonne............... d.	1227	1250			...	...	1537	...	...	...		...	0257	0257	...		0409
Montpellier............. d.	1315	1349	1458		...	...	1648	...	...	...		...	0502	0502	...		0615
Marseille.............. d.	...	1552	1636	...	1743	...	1847	2021	...	...		...	0553	0553	...		0700
Toulon................. d.	...	1638	1720	...	1832	...	1932	2103	...	...		...	0709	0709	...		0833
Cannes................. d.	...	1803	1835	...	1952	...	2058	2218	...	...		...	0811	0811	...		0910
Nice................... d.	...	1835	1900	1911	2019	2029	2133	2245	2312	...		...	0830	0830	...		0933
Monaco Monte Carlo..... d.	...	...	...	1927	...	2048	...	...	2342	...		...	0853	0853	...		1000
Ventimiglia ⛢.......... a.	...	...	...	1950	...	2109	...	...	0015	...		...	1008	1008	...		1132
San Remo............... d.	...	...	...	2025	...	2207	...	...	0132	...		...	1213	1213	...		1340
Genova P. Principe....... a.	...	...	...	2212	...	0024	...	...	0340	...		...	1333	1333	...		
La Spezia.............. a.	...	...	...		...	0210	...	...		...		...	1430	1430	...		
Pisa................... a.	...	...	...		...	0305	...	...		...		...	1805	1805	...		
Roma Termini........... a.	...	...	...		...	0655	...	...		...		...			...		
Chambéry.............. d.	...	...	...		...		...	...		...	0706	...			...		
Torino Porta Susa........ a.	...	...	...		...		...	0540		...	0845	...			...		1545
Milano Centrale......... a.	...	...	...	2355	...		...	0751		...		...			...		
Verona................. a.	...	...	...		...		...	0925		...		...			...		
Venezia Santa Lucia...... a.	...	...	...		...		...			...		...			...		

train number	IC347	6950			2191						EN		356	5682		164	
train number	IC346	6951			2192		362	362	362	472	276		357	5683		366	165	71
classes	1,2	1,2	1,2		1,2		1,2	1,2	1,2	2	⛴		1,2	1,2		1,2	1,2	1,2✗
notes (see below)	J	⛐			L		Q	K	G	⑤⑥⑦	R		F	⛐		H	⛐	M
Venezia Santa Lucia...... d.	...	...	...		...		...	...	...	...		...	2025					
Verona................. d.	...	...	...		...		...	...	...	...	2000		2201					
Milano Centrale......... d.	0640	...	...		1415		...	...	...	...	2132		0015					
Torino Porta Susa........ d.	...	...	...				...	...	...	...	2132							
Chambéry.............. d.	...	...	...				1225	1225	1225	...						2330		
Roma Termini........... d.	...	...	...				1559	1559	1559	...						0311		
Pisa................... d.	...	...	...				1658	1658	1658	...						0410		
La Spezia.............. d.	...	...	...		1620		1816	1816	1816	...			0300			0558		
Genova P. Principe....... d.	0822	...	...		1825		2009	2009	2009	...			0626			0817		
San Remo............... d.	1008	...	...		1905		2120	2120	2120	...			0740			0925		
Ventimiglia ⛢.......... d.	1044	...	...		1926		2143	2143	2143	...			0803			0947		
Monaco Monte Carlo..... a.	1107	...	...		1946		2200	2200	2200	...			0825	0905		1010	1030	
Nice................... a.	1120	1148	...		2030		2245	2245	2245	...				0929			1059	
Cannes................. a.	...	1219	...		2153		0007	0007	0007	...				1048			1209	
Toulon................. a.	...	1342	...		2240		0056	0056	0056	...				1132			1250	
Marseille.............. a.	...	1425	...		0038		0311	0311	0311	...						1426	1510	
Montpellier............. a.	...	1618	...		0151		0416	0416	0416	...							1558	
Narbonne............... a.	...	1735	1817						0552	0645							1718	
Port Bou ⛢............ a.	...		1955						0735								1806	
Girona................. a.	...								0902		0756							
Barcelona Sants......... a.	...										0910						1920	
Barcelona França....... a.	...															1619		
Toulouse............... a.	...	1904	...		0329		0549	0648	...	...						1823		
Bordeaux............... a.	...	2153	...		0625				...	...								
Irún................... a.	...		...				1050	1149	...	...								

NOTES

E –   SALVADOR DALI – ②④⑦, daily to Oct. 23, Dec. 20-Jan. 10 and Apr. 6-18: ⛴ 1,2 cl., ⛖ and ✗ Barcelona - Milano; Special fares apply.

F –   ROBERT SCHUMANN – ⛴ 1,2 cl., ⛏ 1,2 cl. and ⛖ Nice - Venezia and v.v.

G –   ⛏ 2 cl. and ⛖ Cerbère/Port Bou - Roma and v.v.

H –   ⛴ 1,2 cl., ⛴ 1,2 cl. (T2), ⛏ 2 cl. and ⛖ Nice - Roma and v.v.

J –   LIGURE – ⛖ and ✗ Marseille - Milano and v.v.

K –   ⑤⑦; also Apr. 17, May 1,8,24; not Apr. 16,30, May 7,26: ⛖ Roma - Irún.

L –   ⛏ 2 cl. and ⛖ Bordeaux - Milano and v.v.

M –   CATALAN TALGO – ⛖ and ✗ Montpellier - Barcelona and v.v.

N –   ⛖ Hendaye - Roma.

Q –   ①②③④⑥; also Apr. 16,30, May 7,26; not Apr. 17, May 1,8,24: ⛖ Roma - Irún.

R –   SALVADOR DALI – ①③⑤, daily to Oct. 24, Dec. 21-Jan. 11 and Apr. 7-19: ⛴ 1,2 cl., ⛖ and ✗ Milano - Barcelona; Special fares apply.

✓ –   Supplement payable.

Table 91   ROMA - ATHÍNAI

train type		IC		E					train type			E	E	E
train number		565		969					train number			1950	950	956
classes		1,2✓	2	1,2					classes			1,2	1,2	1,2
notes (see below)		✗		⛐	HM	AD			notes (see below)	AD	HM	B	B	C
Milano Centrale..... d.	...	0705	...	...					**Athínai** (by ⛟)........... d.	1300	1530	...	...	...
Bologna.............. d.	...	0859	...	...					Patras.................... d.	2200	2100	...	...	...
Rimini............... d.	...	1005	...	...					**Brindisi Marittima**....... a.	1700	1600	...	...	...
Ancona.............. d.	...	1100	...	...					**Brindisi Centrale**........ d.	...	...	2002	2059	2241
Pescara.............. d.	...	1220	...	...					Bari Centrale............. a.	...	...	2137	2231	0022
Roma Termini........ d.	...	...	...	1310					Foggia................... a.	...	...	2318	0052	0214
Napoli Centrale........ d.	...	...	1430						Caserta.................. a.	...	...		0420	0537
Caserta.............. d.	...	...	1503	1531					Napoli Centrale.......... a.	...	...		0500	
Foggia............... a.	...	1413	...	1802					**Roma Termini**.......... a.	...	...			0750
Bari Centrale.......... a.	...	1540	...	1927					Pescara.................. a.	...	...	0126		
Brindisi Centrale..... a.	...	1654	...	2054					Ancona.................. a.	...	...	0259		
Brindisi Marittima.... a.	...	...	...	...	2200	2230			Rimini................... a.	...	...			
Patras............... a.	...	...	...	...	1700	1800			Bologna.................. a.	...	...	0523		
Athínai (by ⛟)....... a.	...	...	...	...	2115	2200			**Milano Centrale**........ a.	...	...	0900		

NOTES

B –   ⛴ 1,2 cl., ⛴ 1,2 cl. (T2) and ⛏ 2 cl. Brindisi - Milano.

C –   ⛴ 1,2 cl., ⛏ 2 cl. and ⛖ Brindisi - Roma.

✓ –   Supplement payable.

AD –   ADRIATICA DI NAVIGACIONE SPA, for days of running see **Table 1490**.

HM –   HELLENIC MEDITERRANEAN LINES, for days of running see **Table 1525**.

Table 92 — BUDAPEST - ZAGREB AND LJUBLJANA

train number	897	242	200	202	204	240	208
classes	1,2	1,2	1,2	1,2	1,2	1,2	1,2
notes (see below)		R	T	V	P	S	M
Miskolc .... d.	...	...	...	0730	...	...	...
Budapest Keleti .... d.	...	...	...	1015	...	1730	...
Budapest Déli .... d.	...	0600	0635		1425		1935
Székesfehérvár .... d.	...	0703		1127	1528	1835	2039
Nagykanizsa .... d.	...	0933		1413	1811	2126	2324
Pécs .... d.	0540						
Gyékényes .... d.	0805		1040	1450		2205	0012
Kotoriba 🚉 .... a.		1007			1843		
Koprivnica 🚉 .... d.	0828		1053	1518		2218	0025
Zagreb .... a.	0931		1206	1619	2125	2332	0145
Rijeka .... a.	...	...	...	...	...	...	0618
Ljubljana .... a.	...	1350	...	...	...	0250	
Trieste .... a.	...	1645	...	...	...	0638	
Venezia Santa Lucia ... a.	...	1918	...	...	...	0918	

train number	205	203	201	207	243	209	241
classes	1,2	1,2	1,2	1,2	1,2	1,2	1,2
notes (see below)	P	V	T		R	M	S
Venezia Santa Lucia ...... d.	...	...	...	0940	...	...	2122
Trieste .... d.	...	...	...	1204	...	...	2343
Ljubljana .... d.	...	...	...	1505	...	...	0253
Rijeka .... d.	...	...	...	...	...	2050	
Zagreb .... d.	0835	1350	1605	1735	...	0115	0554
Koprivnica 🚉 .... d.		1505	1720	1850	...	0235	0717
Kotoriba 🚉 .... d.	1101				1852		
Gyékényes .... a.		1518	1733	1848		0248	0730
Pécs .... a.			2150				
Nagykanizsa .... a.	1138	1558			0927	0345	0814
Székesfehérvár .... a.	1431	1842		2156		0627	1055
Budapest Déli .... a.	1529		2143	2258		0728	
Budapest Keleti .... a.		1953					1158
Miskolc .... a.		2340					

NOTES

M – ADRIATICA – 🛏 1,2 cl. and 🍴 Budapest - Rijeka and v.v.
P – MAESTRAL – 🍴 Budapest - Zagreb and v.v.

R – DRAVA – 🍴 and 🍴 Budapest - Venezia and v.v.
S – VENEZIA EXPRESS – 🛏 1,2 cl., 🛏 2 cl. and 🍴 Budapest - Venezia and v.v.
T – AGRAM – 🍴 and 🍴 Budapest - Zagreb and v.v.
V – AVAS – 🍴 Budapest - Zagreb and v.v.

Table 93 — SANKT PETERBURG, RIGA AND VILNIUS - WARSZAWA

train number	2/14	79014	57	57	25	222	27
classes	2	1,2	🛏	🛏	🛏	🛏	🛏
notes (see below)	Y	T	B	A	Z	S	W
St Peterburg Vars..... d.	...	...	1210	1210	...	2025	...
Tallinn .... d.	1710	...			...		...
Riga .... d.	0025	...			...	2205	
Kaunas .... d.	0625	...			...		
Šeštokai .... d.	0805	0900			...		
Trakiszki 🚉 .... d.		0930			...		
Vilnius .... d.					1022	1022	1715
Grodno 🚉 .... d.			0855	0855	1434	1434	2136
Warszawa Gdańska a.			1501		2132	2132	
Warszawa Wschodnia a.	1525						0411
Warszawa Centralna a.	1537						0447
Gdynia Główna .... a.				2045			

train number	299	299	79011	14	11105	11113	15001
classes	🛏	🛏		1,2	🛏	🛏	
notes (see below)	Z	S	T	Y	W	B	A
Gdynia Główna .... d.	...	...	1437	...	2117	...	1925
Warszawa Centralna ...... d.	...	...	1447	...	2144	...	
Warszawa Wschodnia ..... d.	0758	0758				0043	
Warszawa Gdańska .... d.	1649	1649			0526	1106	1106
Grodno 🚉 .... a.	2038	2038			0950		
Vilnius .... a.			1950				
Trakiszki 🚉 .... a.			2200	2225			
Šeštokai .... a.				0002			
Kaunas .... a.			0810		0606		
Riga .... a.				1310			
Tallinn .... a.							
St Peterburg Varshavski . a.	1250					0910	0910

NOTES

A – 🛏 2 cl. Gdynia - Sankt Peterburg and v.v.
B – 🛏 1,2 cl. Warszawa - Sankt Peterburg and v.v.

S – 🛏 2 cl. Riga - Warszawa - (Berlin) and v.v.
T – BALTI – 🍴 Warszawa - Šeštokai and v.v.
W – 🛏 2 cl. Vilnius - Warszawa and v.v.

Y – BALTI EKSPRESS – 🛏 1,2 cl., 🍴 and 🍴 Šeštokai - Tallinn and v.v.
Z – 🛏 1,2 cl. Sankt Peterburg - Warszawa - (Berlin) and v.v.

Table 94a — MOSKVA - WARSZAWA, PRAHA AND WIEN

train number	67	103	13	9	21	15	15	49	683	39	109
classes	🛏	🛏	🛏	🛏	🛏	🛏	🛏	🛏	🛏	🛏	🛏
notes (see below)	C	P	A	L	G	N	S	V	X	D	B
Moskva Smolenskaya .... d.	...	...	1309	1517	1901	2015	2015	...	...	...	...
Smolensk .... d.	...	...	2027	2124	0208	0326	0326	...	...	...	...
Sankt Peterburg Vitebski ... d.	...	...						1510	...	...	...
Minsk .... d.	...	...	2125	0044	0632	0736	0736		...	...	...
Kyïv (Kiev) .... d.	...	1110						1806	...	0608	0850
Brest 🚉 .... d.	...	0305	0415	0800	1325	1436	1436	1436		2353	0105
Terespol .... d.	...	0223	0333	0718	1243	1354	1354	1354		2311	0023
Warszawa Wschodnia .... a.	...	0536	0727	1018	1615	1725	1725	1725		0238g	0454g
Warszawa Centralna .... a.	...	1045	0742	1045	1832	1917	1917	1917			
Wrocław Główny .... a.	...				2355						
Lichkov .... a.	...				0324						
Hradec Králové .... a.	...				0502						
Praha Hlavni .... a.	...				0703						
Poznań Główny .... a.	...	1425		1425		2245	2245	2245			
Katowice .... a.	...				2337						
Petrovice 🚉 .... a.	...				0115						
Breclav .... a.	...				0426						
Wien Süd .... a.	...				0652						

train number		253 11005	241	241	202 11005	241	10	110	104	247	249	40
classes		🛏	🛏	🛏	🛏	🛏	🛏	🛏	🛏	🛏	🛏	🛏
notes (see below)		G	O	Q	N	S	L	E	P	A	C	M
Wien Süd .... d.		...	...	...	2150	...	...	...	...	...	...	...
Breclav .... d.		...	...	...	2342	...	...	...	...	...	...	...
Petrovice 🚉 .... d.		...	...	...	0300	...	...	...	...	...	...	...
Katowice .... d.		...	...	...	0445	...	...	...	...	...	...	...
Poznań Główny .... d.		...	0630	0630		0630	...	...	...	1625	...	...
Praha Hlavni .... d.		1813					...	...	...		1625	...
Hradec Králové .... d.		2005					...	...	...			...
Lichkov .... d.		2204					...	...	...			...
Wrocław Główny .... d.		0130					...	...	...			...
Warszawa Centralna ... d.		0902	1022	1022	1022	1022	1454		1942	2017	2017	...
Warszawa Wschodnia .. d.		0937	1111	1111	1111	1111	1509	1630g	2010	2043	2158	0050g
Terespol .... d.		1248	1430	1430	1430	1430	1735	2023	2316	0005	0110	0513
Brest 🚉 .... d.		1434	1616	1616	1616	1616	1906	2209	0102	0151	0256	0652
Kyïv (Kiev) .... a.				1120				1346			1805	2152
Minsk .... a.		2047			2227	2227			0723	0830		
Sankt Peterburg Vitebski . a.			1742				0041					
Smolensk .... a.		0242			0418	0418	0550			1430		
Moskva Smolenskaya ... a.		1025			1206	1206	1217			2210		

NOTES

A – MOSKWA EXPRESS – 🛏 1,2 cl. Moskva - Poznań - (Berlin) and v.v.
   - ②⑥ not Dec. 23-Jan. 6, Apr. 14,18: 🛏 2 cl. Kyïv - Warszawa.
B – KIEW EXPRESS – 🛏 2 cl. Kyïv - Poznań - (Berlin) and v.v.
   - ①②⑥ not Dec. 24-Jan. 10, Apr. 11-18: 🛏 2 cl. Kyïv - Warszawa.
C – ③⑥, not Dec. 24, Jan. 4,7, Apr. 15,19: 🛏 2 cl. Warszawa - Kyïv.
D – 🛏 1,2 cl. Moskva - Praha and v.v. (journey 2 nights).
E – POLONEZ – 🛏 1,2 cl. Warszawa - Moskva and v.v.
   - ①③④; not Dec. 26-Jan. 12, Apr. 13-20: 🛏 2 cl. Warszawa - Kyïv.

N – 🛏 1,2 cl. Moskva - Wien and v.v. (journey 2 nights).
O – ①⑤: 🛏 1,2 cl. Brussels - Warszawa (②⑥) - Sankt Peterburg.
P – 🛏 2 cl. Minsk - Warszawa and v.v.
Q – ⑦: 🛏 1,2cl. Brussels - Poznań (①) - Kyïv.
S – 🛏 2 cl. Moskva - Poznań - (Brussels) and v.v.
V – ③⑥: 🛏 1,2 cl. St Peterburg - Warszawa - (Brussels).
X – ⑤: 🛏 1,2 cl. Kyïv - Poznań - (Brussels).
g – Warszawa Gdańska.

Table 94b — MOSKVA AND KYÏV - PRAHA AND WIEN

train number	44	51	7	183	183
notes (see below)	Z	H	J	K	U
Moskva Kievskaya............d.	...	...	1147	1300	...
Kyïv (Kiev)......................d.	1906	...	0229	0352	...
Sankt Peterburg Varshavski d.	...	...	...	2240	2240
Vilnius............................d.	...	...	...	1530	1530
Lviv.................................d.	0704	...	1407	1533	1533	1533
Chop ▣..........................d.	...	...	2115	2300	2300	2300
Kraków Główny.............a.	1502	...	...	...	...
Katowice.......................a.	1637	...	...	...	...
Wrocław Główny...........a.	1940	...	...	...	...
Košice...........................a.	...	...	2245	0020	0020	0020
Žilina.............................a.	...	...	0209	0349	0349	0349
Bratislava.....................a.	...	...	0446	...	1030
Wien Süd.......................a.	...	...	0713	...	...
Olomouc........................a.	...	...	...	0709	0709
Pardubice......................a.	...	...	...	0901	0901
Praha Hlavni..................a.	...	...	...	1026	1026

train number	221	221	907	404 223	63002
notes (see below)	J	K	V	H	Z
Praha Hlavni ....d.	1835	1835	...	...	...
Pardubice.........................d.	1948	1948	...	...	...
Olomouc...........................d.	2139	2139	...	...	...
Wien Süd..........................d.	...	...	1950	1600	...
Bratislava.........................d.	...	...	1950	1735	...
Žilina................................d.	0106	0106	0106	2017	...
Košice...............................d.	0453	0453	0453	2327	...
Wrocław Główny..............d.	...	...	...	...	0918
Katowice...........................d.	...	...	...	...	1215
Kraków Główny.................d.	...	...	...	...	1345
Chop ▣.............................d.	0813	0813	0813	0240	...
Lviv..................................a.	1613	1613	1613	1017	0018
Vilnius..............................d.	...	1022	1022	...	...
Sankt Peterburg Vars.......a.	...	0545	0545	...	...
Kyïv (Kiev).......................a.	0319	...	...	2134	1226
Moskva Kievskaya............a.	2028	...	...	1503	...

NOTES

H – SLOVAKIA – 🚉 1,2 cl. Moskva - Wien and v.v. (journey 2 nights).
J – DUKLA – 🚉 1,2 cl. Moskva - Praha and v.v. (journey 2 nights).
K – 🚉 2 cl. Sankt Peterburg - Praha and v.v. (journey 3 nights).

U – ⑤: 🚉 2 cl. Sankt Peterburg - Bratislava (journey 3 nights).
V – ①: 🚉 2 cl. Bratislava - Sankt Peterburg (journey 3 nights).
Z – 🚉 2 cl. Kyïv - Przemyśl - Wroclaw and v.v.

Table 94c — MOSKVA AND KYÏV - BUDAPEST, VENEZIA, BEOGRAD AND ATHÍNAI

Travel to or from Beograd/Serbia is dangerous, passengers are strongly recommended to use an alternative route.

train number	9	15	15	189	667
notes (see below)	N	K	Y	V	Z
Moskva Kievskaya............d.	0956	...	2033	2033	...
Sankt Peterburg Varshavski d.	...	...	...	1205	...
Vilnius............................d.	...	...	...	0338	...
Kyïv (Kiev)......................d.	0023	...	1155	1155	...
Minsk..............................d.	...	...	...	...	2342
Lviv.................................d.	1202	...	0002	0002	0002	0002
Chop ▣..........................d.	1920	...	0725	0725	0725	0725
Szolnok...........................a.	2257	...	1033	1033	1033	1033
Budapest Keleti...............a.	...	...	1202	1202	1202	1202
Siofok.............................a.	...	...	...	1913	...
Zagreb............................a.	...	...	...	2332	...
Ljubljana.........................a.	...	...	...	0250	...
Trieste............................a.	...	...	...	0628	...
Venezia Santa Lucia.......a.	...	...	...	0918	...
Subotica.........................a.	...	0340	...	...	...
Beograd..........................a.	...	0634	...	...	...
Niš..................................a.	...	1140	...	...	...
Skopje............................a.	...	1614	...	...	...
Thessaloniki....................a.	...	2211	...	...	...
Athínai............................a.	...	0628	...	...	...

train number	334 488	16	241	16	16
notes (see below)	A	K	M	R	V
Athínai..............................d.	2330	...	...	...	...
Thessaloniki......................d.	0836	...	...	...	...
Skopje...............................d.	1220	...	...	...	...
Niš....................................d.	1715	...	...	...	...
Beograd.............................d.	2145	...	...	...	...
Subotica............................d.	0112	...	...	...	...
Venezia Santa Lucia..........d.	...	...	2122	...	...
Trieste...............................d.	...	...	2343	...	...
Ljubljana............................d.	...	...	0253	...	...
Zagreb...............................d.	...	...	0554	...	...
Siofok................................d.	...	...	1016	...	...
Budapest Keleti..................d.	...	1615	1615	1615	1615
Szolnok..............................d.	0533	1745	1745	1745	1745
Chop ▣.............................a.	1010	2240	2240	2240	2240
Lviv...................................a.	1734	0608	0608	0608	0608
Minsk................................a.	...	...	...	2238	...
Kyïv (Kiev).........................a.	0433	1738	1738	...	...
Vilnius...............................a.	...	...	...	...	2158
Sankt Peterburg Var..........a.	...	...	...	...	1535
Moskva Kievskaya.............a.	2141	1121	1121	...	...

Table 94d — MOSKVA AND KYÏV - BUCUREŞTI AND SOFIJA

train number	59	5	13	85	53	621	195
notes (see below)	F	T	H	B	C	D	G
Moskva Kievskaya............d.	1444	...	1645	1645	...	...	...
Sankt Peterburg Varshavski d.	...	...	...	...	1610	...	...
Riga ▣.............................d.	...	...	...	...	2205	...	...
Vilnius............................d.	...	...	...	...	0856	0856	...
Minsk..............................d.	...	...	...	...	...	...	0930
Kyïv (Kiev)......................d.	0614	...	0800	0800	1853	...	...
Chişinău (Kishinev)..........d.	...	...	2130	2130	...	...	...
Ungheni ▣.......................d.	...	...	2355	2355	...	...	...
Vadul Siret ▣...................d.	2300	...	...	...	1240	1240	1240	1240
Bucureşti Nord................a.	0737	...	1049	1049	2102	2102	2102	2102
Ruse ▣............................a.	1105	...	...	...	0030	0030	0030	0030
Sofija..............................a.	1902	...	2235	...	0856	0856	0856	0856
Kapikule ▣......................a.	...	...	...	...	...	...	...
Istanbul...........................a.	...	...	...	...	...	...	...

train number	485 501	485 501	485 501	485 501	14	6	412 483 511
notes (see below)	B	C	E	G	J	S	F
Istanbul.............................d.	...	...	...	...	...	...	...
Kapikule ▣.......................d.	...	...	...	...	...	...	...
Sofija................................d.	2140	2140	2140	2140	1115	...	1300
Ruse ▣.............................d.	0530	0530	0530	0530	...	...	2020
Bucureşti Nord...................d.	0906	0906	0906	0906	2316	2316	2355
Vadul Siret ▣...................d.	1728	1728	1728	1728	...	...	0815
Ungheni ▣.......................d.	...	...	...	...	0610	0610	...
Chişinău (Kishinev)............d.	...	...	...	...	1255	1255	...
Kyïv (Kiev).........................d.	1126	...	...	2238	0306	0306	0113
Minsk................................a.	...	...	...	...	...	...	...
Vilnius...............................a.	...	2158	2158	...	...	...	...
Riga ▣............................a.	...	...	0810	...	...	...	...
Sankt Peterburg Vars........a.	1535	...	...	...	2114	2114	1933
Moskva Kievskaya.............a.	...	...	...	...	...	...	...

NOTES for Tables 94c and 94d

A – PUŠKIN – 🚉 1,2 cl. Beograd - Moskva (journey 2 nights);
   ②③⑤⑦: 🚉 1,2 cl. Athínai - Beograd - Moskva (journey 3 nights).
B – BULGARIA EXPRESS – 🚉 2 cl. and ✕ Kyïv - Sofija and v.v. (journey 2 nights).
C – 🚉 2 cl. Sankt Peterburg - Sofija and v.v. (journey 3 nights).
D – ③⑦: 🚉 2cl. Riga - Sofija (journey 3 nights).
E – ③⑥: 🚉 2 cl. Sofija - Riga (journey 3 nights).
F – SOFIJA EXPRESS – 🚉 1,2 cl. and ✕ Moskva - Sofija and v.v. (journey 2 nights).
G – 🚉 2 cl. Moskva - Sofija and v.v.
H – DANUBIUS EXPRESS – ①⑤: 🚉 1,2 cl. and ♀ Moskva - Sofija.
J – DANUBIUS EXPRESS – ①④: 🚉 1,2 cl. and ♀ Sofija - Moskva.
K – TISZA EXPRESS – 🚉 1,2 cl. Moskva - Budapest and v.v. (journey 2 nights).

M – 🚉 2 cl. Zagreb - Moskva (journey 2 nights);
   ③⑥: 🚉 2 cl. Venezia - Moskva (journey 3 nights).
N – PUŠKIN – 🚉 1,2 cl. Moskva - Beograd (journey 2 nights);
   ②④⑥⑦: 🚉 2 cl. Moskva - Beograd - Athínai (journey 3 nights);
   ①③⑤: 🚉 2 cl. Moskva - Beograd - Thessaloniki (journey 2 nights).
R – ②⑤: 🚉 2 cl. Budapest - Minsk (journey 2 nights).
S – ROMANIA EXPRESS - ②⑤⑥: 🚉 1,2 cl. Bucureşti - Moskva (journey 2 nights).
T – ROMANIA EXPRESS - ③④⑦: 🚉 1,2 cl. Moskva - Bucureşti (journey 2 nights).
V – 🚉 2 cl. Sankt Peterburg - Budapest and v.v. (journey 2 nights).
Y – 🚉 2 cl. Moskva - Zagreb (journey 2 nights);
   ③⑦: 🚉 2 cl. Moskva - Venezia (journey 3 nights).
Z – ③⑦: 🚉 2 cl. Minsk - Budapest (journey 2 nights).

Table 95a

WARSZAWA - PRAHA AND WIEN

train number	IC			EC								34004			57000	
train number	106		34102	105		490		252		200		203	203	254	254	
classes	1,2		1,2	1,2		1,2		1,2		1,2		1,2	2	1,2	1,2	
notes (see below)	G ®			H ®		⑤⑥⑦		C		F		A	B	D	E	
Warszawa Wschodnia .... d.	...	0555	...	...	0855	...	...	1805	...	1950	...	2020	...	...	...	
Warszawa Centralna .... d.	0610	...	...	0910	...	...	...	1820	...	2005	...	2045	...	...	...	
Gdynia Główna .... d.																
Gdańsk Główny .... d.														...	1800	
Szczecin Główny .... d.														...	1830	
Poznań Główny .... d.														2035		
Wrocław Główny .... d.														2340	2340	
Lichkov ⛟ .... d.								0020						0208	0208	
Kraków Główny .... d.			1017					0324						0501	0501	
Katowice .... d.	0853		1137	1153		1640		...		2320		2347		2235	...	
Petrovice ⛟ .... a.	1005			1258		1757				0038		0115	0115		...	
Bohumín .... a.	1034			1326		1831				0126		0152	0152		...	
Ostrava Hlavní .... a.	1047			1340		1847				0141		0208	0208		...	
Pardubice .... a.	1345									0450					...	
Praha Hlavní .... a.	1459							0703		0612					...	
Břeclav .... a.				1557								0426	0426	0843	0843	
Wien Süd .... a.				1704								0652	0652			

train number			EC		IC									
train number	491		104	42104	107		253		255	255		201	202	202
classes	1,2		1,2	1,2	1,2		1,2		1,2	1,2		1,2	1,2	2
notes (see below)	⑤⑥⑦		H ®		G ®		C		D	E		F	A	B
Wien Süd .... d.	...		0939		...		...		...	...		...	2150	2150
Břeclav .... d.	...		1053		...		...		...	...		...	2342	2342
Praha Hlavní .... d.	...				1340		1813		2012	2012		2116		
Pardubice .... d.	...				1453							2231		
Ostrava Hlavní .... d.	0701		1310		1756							0142	0206	0206
Bohumín .... d.	0717		1323		1811							0158	0222	0222
Petrovice ⛟ .... d.	0753		1352		1840							0230	0300	0300
Katowice .... a.	0912		1456	1515	1955							0348	0438	
Kraków Główny .... d.				1725										0535
Lichkov ⛟ .... d.							2204		0001	0001				
Wrocław Główny .... a.							0104		0240	0240				
Poznań Główny .... a.									0540	0540				
Szczecin Główny .... a.									0848					
Gdańsk Główny .... a.										1014				
Gdynia Główna .... a.										1044				
Warszawa Centralna .... a.			1740		2245		0643					0715	0750	
Warszawa Wschodnia .... a.			1754		2259		0657					0734	0804	

NOTES

A – CHOPIN – 🛏 1,2 cl., 🛏 2 cl. and ⛙ Warszawa - Wien and v.v.

B – 🛏 2 cl. and ⛙ Kraków - Wien and v.v.

C – BOHEMIA – 🛏 1,2 cl., 🛏 2 cl. and ⛙ Warszawa - Praha and v.v.

D – BALTIC – 🛏 2 cl. and ⛙ Szczecin - Praha and v.v.

E – BALTIC – 🛏 1,2 cl., 🛏 2 cl., ⛙ and ✕ Gdynia - Praha and v.v.

F – SILESIA – 🛏 1,2 cl., 🛏 2 cl. and ⛙ Warszawa - Praha and v.v.

G – PRAHA – ⛙ and ✕ Warszawa - Praha and v.v.

H – SOBIESKI – ⛙ and ✕ Warszawa - Wien and v.v.

Table 95b

WARSZAWA - BRATISLAVA, BUDAPEST AND BUCUREŞTI

train number	334	381	IC131	332	391		337	337	311
classes	1,2 ✗	1,2	1,2	1,2 ✗	1,2		1,2	2	1,2
notes (see below)	V	P	Q		N		M	T	R
Warszawa Wschodnia .... d.	...	0545	1055	...	...		1855	1855	...
Warszawa Centralna .... d.	...	0600	1110	...	...		1910	1910	...
Katowice .... d.	...		1353	...	...		2233	2233	...
Szczecin Główny .... d.	...								
Poznań Główny .... d.	...								
Wrocław Główny .... d.	...				1710				...
Chałupki ⛟ .... d.	...				1933				...
Bohumín .... d.	...				1941				...
Kraków Główny .... d.	0728	0905		1445					2105
Košice ⛟ .... a.		1638							0356
Petrovice ⛟ .... a.			1504				2350	2350	
Zwardoń ⛟ .... a.	1120			1827					
Žilina .... a.	1232	1648	1940	2205			0152	0152	
Bratislava hlavní .... a.	1530		2230					0540	
Zvolen osob .... a.	...			0032					
Filakovo ⛟ .... a.	...			0156					
Štúrovo ⛟ .... a.	...	1953					0521		
Komárom ⛟ .... a.	...		2112	0522			0647		0842
Budapest Keleti .... a.	...								
Szolnok .... a.	...	2146							
Curtici .... a.	...	0120							
Bucureşti Nord .... a.	...	1158							
Beograd .... a.	...								
Niš .... a.	...								
Sofija .... a.	...								
Istanbul .... a.	...								

train number		25						
train number	333	IC130	380	335	336	7125	310	390
classes	1,2 ✗	1,2	1,2	1,2 ✗	1,2	2	1,2	1,2
notes (see below)	V	Q	P		M	T	R	N
Istanbul .... d.	...							
Sofija .... d.	...							
Niš .... d.	...							
Beograd .... d.	...							
Bucureşti Nord .... d.	...		2008					
Curtici .... d.	...		0610					
Szolnok .... d.	...		0727					
Budapest Keleti .... d.	...	0920		1850			1905	1920
Komárom ⛟ .... d.	...	1040		2025				
Štúrovo ⛟ .... d.	...							
Filakovo ⛟ .... d.	...							2214
Zvolen osob .... d.	...							2344
Bratislava hlavní .... d.	0550			1450		2050		
Žilina .... d.	0844	1355		1750	0010	0010		0209
Zwardoń ⛟ .... a.	0955			1900				
Petrovice ⛟ .... d.	...	1540						
Košice ⛟ .... d.	...		1244				0005	
Kraków Główny .... a.	1347		1953	2245			0647	
Bohumín .... d.	...							0428
Chałupki ⛟ .... d.	...							0436
Wrocław Główny .... a.	...							0700
Poznań Główny .... a.	...							
Szczecin Główny .... a.	...							
Katowice .... a.	...	1655		0326	0326			
Warszawa Centralna .... a.	...	1940	2253	0647	0647			
Warszawa Wschodnia .... a.	...	1954	2314	0701	0701			

NOTES

P – BATHORY – 🛏 1,2 cl., 🛏 2 cl., ⛙ and ✕ Warszawa - Budapest and v.v.

– BEM – 🛏 1,2 cl. and ⛙ Wrocław - Budapest and v.v.

– KARPATY – ⛙ Warszawa - Bucureşti and v.v.; 🛏 1,2 cl. and 🛏 2 cl. Košice - Bucureşti and v.v.

Q – POLONIA – ⛙ and ✕ Warszawa - Budapest and v.v.

R – CRACOVIA – 🛏 1,2 cl., 🛏 2 cl., ⛙ and ✕ Kraków - Budapest and v.v.

T – 🛏 1,2 cl., 🛏 2 cl. and ⛙ Warszawa - Bratislava and v.v.

V – Not Sept. 25-Dec. 2, Mar. 26.

✗ – Supplement payable.

Table 96a — PRAHA - WIEN AND LINZ

train number	377	271	EC 173	1273	EC 9	833	273
classes	2	1,2	1,2	1,2	1,2	1,2	1,2
notes (see below)	A		B		C		①-⑥
Praha Holešovice ..... d.	0324	...	1311	...	1711	...	...
Praha Hlavní .... d.		0623	...	1503	...	1752	0011
Tábor .... d.		0803	...	1640	...	1932	0146
České Budějovice .... d.							
Summerau 🚂 .... a.							
Linz .... a.							
Villach Westbf .... a.							
Udine 🚂 .... a.							
Venezia Mestre .... a.							
Venezia Santa Lucia a.							
Brno .... d.	0639	...	1620	...	2020	...	...
Břeclav 🚂 .... d.	0730	...	1707	...	2105	...	...
Gmünd 🚂 .... d.		0946	...	1837	...	2107	0345
Wien Franz Josefs . a.							0606
Wien Südbf .... a.	0852	...	1804	...	2203	...	...

train type	972	1974	EC 8	EC 172	270	272	376
classes	1,2	1,2	1,2	1,2	1,2	1,2	2
notes (see below)			C	B		⑥	A
Wien Südbf .... d.	...	...	0739	1139	...	...	2025
Wien F. Josefs .... d.	...	...	...	...	1724	...	
Gmünd 🚂 .... d.	0700	1245	...	1632	1951		
Břeclav 🚂 .... a.	...	...	0837	1239	...	...	2139
Brno .... a.	...	...	0922	1325	...	...	2232
Venezia S. Lucia .. d.							
Venezia Mestre .... d.							
Udine 🚂 .... d.							
Villach Westbf .... d.							
Linz .... d.							
Summerau 🚂 .... a.							
České Budějovice .. a.							
Tábor .... a.	0837	1423	...	...	1759	2125	
Praha Hlavní .... a.	1014	1606	...	...	1935	2304	
Praha Holešovice .. a.	...	...	1232	1637	...	...	0148

NOTES

A – SANSSOUCI – 🚋 (Berlin) - Praha - Wien and v.v.

B – VINDOBONA – 🚋 and ✕ (Berlin) - Praha - Wien and v.v.

C – ANTONÍN DVOŘÁK – 🚋 and ✕ Praha - Wien and v.v.

Table 96b — PRAHA - BUDAPEST, BUCUREŞTI AND BEOGRAD

train number	373	1011	EC 175	375	379
classes	2	1,2	1,2	1,2	1,2
notes (see below)	R	V	S	M	T
Praha Holešovice ...... d.	0558	0739	1511	...	0028
Praha Hlavní .... d.	...	...	...	2222	...
Brno .... d.	0934	1055	1620	0211	0348
Břeclav .... d.	1019	1137	1900	0316	0431
Bratislava Hlavní ..... d.	1145	1306	2005	0442	0606
Rajka 🚂 .... d.		1400			
Štúrovo 🚂 .... d.	1325	...	2132	0630	0755
Györ .... a.		1442			
Budapest Nyugati ..... a.					0858
Budapest Keleti ...... a.	1442	1628	2242	0747	
Subotica 🚂 .... a.					
Beograd .... a.					
Niš .... a.					
Sofija .... a.					
Skopje .... a.					
Idomeni 🚂 .... a.					
Thessaloniki .... a.					
Athínai .... a.					
Curtici 🚂 .... a.	2025				1335
Arad .... a.	2121				1425
Braşov .... a.	0320				2016
Bucureşti Nord .... a.	0559				2257

train number	EC 174	1010	33 372	378	21 374
classes	1,2	1,2	2	1,2	1,2
notes (see below)	S	W	R	T	M
Bucureşti Nord .... d.	...	...	0110	...	0821
Braşov.................... d.	...	...	0354	...	1105
Arad .... d.	...	...	0953	...	1655
Curtici 🚂 .... d.	...	...	1100	...	1750
Athínai .... d.					
Thessaloniki .... d.					
Idomeni 🚂 .... d.					
Skopje .... d.					
Sofija .... d.					
Niš .... d.					
Beograd .... d.					
Subotica 🚂 .... d.					
Budapest Keleti .... d.	0655	1320	1500	...	2120
Budapest Nyugati .... d.		1503		1825	
Györ .... a.	0806	...	1615	1925	2235
Štúrovo 🚂 .... a.					
Rajka 🚂 .... a.		1550			
Bratislava Hlavní .... a.	0938	1703	1800	2120	0030
Břeclav .... a.	1043	1723	1929	2256	0153
Brno .... a.	1125	1908	2010	2337	0245
Praha Hlavní .... a.					0629
Praha Holešovice .... a.	1437	2228	2337	0253	

NOTES

M – PANNONIA EXPRESS – 🛏 1,2 cl., 🚃 2 cl. and 🚋 Praha - Bucureşti and v.v.

R – BALT ORIENT EXPRESS – 🛏 1,2 cl., 🚃 2 cl. and 🚋 (Berlin) - Praha - Bucureşti and v.v.

S – HUNGARIA – 🚋 and ✕ (Berlin) - Praha - Budapest and v.v.

T – METROPOL – 🛏 1,2 cl., 🚃 2 cl., 🚋 and ✕ (Berlin) - Praha - Budapest and v.v.

V – CSÁRDÁS – Sept. 25-Nov. 7 and Apr. 8-May 27: 🚋 (Malmö) - Praha - Budapest; ✕ Praha - Budapest.

W – CSÁRDÁS – Sept. 25-Nov. 5 and Apr. 6-May 27: 🚋 Budapest - Praha - (Malmö); ✕ Budapest - Praha.

Table 97 — BUDAPEST AND BEOGRAD - ATHÍNAI AND ISTANBUL

Travel to or from Beograd/Serbia is dangerous, passengers are strongly recommended to use an alternative route.

train number	335	291	491
classes	1,2	1,2	1,2
notes (see below)	A ⑧	C	B
Budapest Keleti .... d.	0030	...	1510
Kelebia 🚂 .... d.	0350	...	1800
Beograd .... d.	0740	1800	2200
Niš .... d.	1150	2210	0225
Preševo .... d.	...		
Skopje .... a.	1640	0225	
Idomeni 🚂 .... a.	1927	0555	
Thessaloniki .... a.	2138	0725	
Athínai .... a.	0633	...	
Dimitrovgrad .... a.	...	...	0419
Kalotina 🚂 .... a.	...	...	0558
Sofija .... a.	...	...	0738
Plovdiv .... a.	...	...	1005
Kapikule 🚂 .... a.	...	...	1345
Istanbul .... a.	...	...	1955

train number	490	290	334
classes	1,2	1,2	1,2
notes (see below)	B	C	A
Istanbul .... d.	1000	...	...
Kapikule 🚂 .... d.	1620	...	...
Plovdiv .... d.	2005	...	...
Sofija .... d.	2255	...	...
Kalotina 🚂 .... d.	0032	...	...
Dimitrovgrad .... d.	0012	...	...
Athínai .... d.	...	...	2330
Thessaloniki .... d.	...	2100	0826
Idomeni 🚂 .... d.	...	2235	1020
Skopje .... a.	...	0025	1200
Preševo 🚂 .... a.			
Niš .... a.	0151	0501	1650
Beograd .... a.	0619	0927	2115
Kelebia 🚂 .... a.	1120	...	0140
Budapest Keleti .... a.	1413	...	0513

NOTES

A – HELLAS EXPRESS – 🛏 1,2 cl., 🚃 2 cl. and 🚋 Budapest - Athínai and v.v.

B – BALKAN EXPRESS – 🚃 1,2 cl. and 🚋 Budapest - Istanbul and v.v.; 🛏 1,2 cl., 🚃 2 cl. and 🚋 Budapest - Sofija and v.v.; 🚋 Beograd - Istanbul and v.v.

C – 🛏 1,2 cl., 🚃 2 cl. and 🚋 Beograd - Thessaloniki and v.v.

FRANCE

Operator: Société Nationale des Chemins de Fer Français (SNCF), unless otherwise shown.

Services: Trains convey first and second classes of accommodation unless otherwise shown. **Sleeping** cars (🛏) and couchette cars (🛏) are of the normal European types, see page 10 for more details. 'Cabine 8' cars are second class carriages fitted with eight semi-reclined bunks per compartment, see below for a list of trains in which these cars operate. **Restaurant** cars (✕) offer full dining services at meal times either in a restaurant car or at first class seats, in addition to refreshment services at other times, and may be limited to first class only. Full dining services may not be available at weekends or on holidays even where a train is shown with ✕. **Refreshment** services (♇) consist of self-service buffet cars, bar cars or trolleys wheeled through the train. It is important in France to state whether meals may be required when booking first class travel, as some meals are served at your reserved seat.

Timings: **Valid September 25, 1994 - May 27, 1995.** Services are liable to change at short notice and passengers are advised to consult the latest Thomas Cook European Timetable before travelling. Amended services operate on and around **public holidays** and passengers are strongly advised to confirm their train times locally before travelling during these periods. Public holidays are Jan. 1, Easter Monday, May 1,8, Ascension Day, Whit Monday, July 14, Aug. 15, Nov. 1,11, Dec. 25 (see page 2).

Tickets: **Seat reservations** are available (for a small fee) on most long distance trains and are required for travel by all TGV trains and trains marked Ⓡ. Advance reservations are strongly recommended for travel to ski resorts during the season. **Supplements** (which include the cost of seat reservation) are payable for travel in sleeping cars and couchettes and for travel on all TGV trains and other trains marked ✗. Rail tickets purchased and used in France must be date-stamped by the holder before boarding the train, using the self-service validating machines (composteurs) at the platform entrances.

'CABINE 8' SEMI-COUCHETTES IN FRANCE

French Railways operate some twelve-compartment second class coaches in which each compartment is fitted with eight semi-reclined bunks, instead of seats. They are treated as seats for reservation purposes and no supplement is payable.

From *September 24 - May 27* they will run in the following trains:

234/5 Paris - Hamburg and v.v., **1611/2** Paris - Strasbourg and v.v.,
3626/7/8 Paris - Brest and v.v., **3726/7, 3744** Paris - Quimper and v.v., **4318/9** Paris - Bordeaux and v.v.

Table 100 — PARIS AÉROPORTS +

RATP/SNCF

CHARLES DE GAULLE + - PARIS
Roissyrail (RER line B)

RER line B : Aéroport Charles de Gaulle TGV/RER - Paris. Every 7 - 15 minutes. From airport 0455 - 2356 (0526 - 2356 on ©); from Châtelet les Halles 0526 - 2326 and 0011 (also 0456 from Gare du Nord).

Journey time from Charles de Gaulle + :

Gare du Nord	33 minutes
Châtelet les Halles	37 minutes
St. Michel Notre Dame	39 minutes
Antony (for Orly +)	58 minutes

🚌 connection: TGV/RER station (Terminal 2) - Terminal 1.

See page 32 for Paris map, page 34 for Paris Métro map.

ORLY + - PARIS
ORLY VAL + RER line B

VAL light rail : Orly Sud - Orly Ouest - Antony. Every 7 minutes (0630 - 2115 ✗, 0700 - 2255 ⑦). Journey 7 minutes. Cross platform interchange with RER line B :

RER line B : Antony - Paris. Every 7 - 15 minutes (0508 - 0011 from Antony, 0520 - 0039 from Gare du Nord).

Journey time from Antony :

St. Michel Notre Dame	23 minutes
Châtelet les Halles	25 minutes
Gare du Nord	28 minutes
Charles de Gaulle +	58 minutes

ORLY + - PARIS
Orlyrail (RER line C)

🚌 : Orly + (Ouest and Sud) - Pont de Rungis Aéroport d'Orly. Frequent shuttle service.

RER line C : Pont de Rungis Aéroport d'Orly - Paris. Every 15 minutes (0504 - 2334 from Pont de Rungis, 0536 - 0006 from Champ de Mars Tour Eiffel).

Journey time from Pont de Rungis Aéroport d'Orly :

Paris Austerlitz	24 minutes
St Michel Notre Dame	27 minutes
Musée d'Orsay	31 minutes
Champ de Mars Tour Eiffel	39 minutes

Table 100a — PARIS - DISNEYLAND

RATP/SNCF

RER LINE A:
Paris Châtelet les Halles - Paris Gare de Lyon - **Marne la Vallée Chessy** (for Disneyland). Trains run approximately every 15 minutes 0500 - 2400.

Journey time Châtelet les Halles - Marne la Valleé Chessy: 39 minutes. 32 km. For **TGV** services see Table **160.**

Table 101 — PARIS - ST. QUENTIN - MAUBEUGE

km		12303	33	281		283	12321		EC39	285		EC31	287	12333	2335	12337	12339	487	487	331		243	231	
				✕	✕				✕	✕		✕						L	K	K				
					♇					♇					Ⓐt	Ⓐ								
									Ⓐ															
0	Paris Nord .... d.	0710	0737	0752	...	1023	1216		1346	1433b		1632	1636	1609	1739	1756	1856	1926	1941	1945	...	2101	2316	...
51	Creil .... d.	0741			...		1243						1639		1923					...	2316	...		
84	Compiègne .... d.	0805		0835	...		1307					1704	1822	1846	1943	2013			2031	...		0003	...	
131	Tergnier .... d.	0846			...		1349			1612		1750		1923	2016					...		0044	...	
154	St. Quentin .... d.	0904	0846	0908	0918	1136	1142	1405	1458	1604	1628	1751	1808	1856	1937	2031	2048		2104	2111	2215	0103	...	
181	Busigny .... d.			0944		1208	1427	1443		1648		1834n	1917		2051				2135	...		0122	...	
207	Cambrai Ville 110 . a.			1009		1229	1509		1709			1856n	1939					2158		...				
217	Aulnoye .... a.		0939		1206	1457	1532	1638			1820			2119	2122	2122	2135	...		0144	...			
229	Maubeuge .... a.	0923				1512				1823				2133			2156	2222	...			0214		
239	Jeumont .... a.																2205		...		2254	0224		

		230		12304	12306	2308	242			330		282	EC30	12318			284	EC38		12336		12338		286	32	12340
							✕	†		✕			✕	✕				♇	✕	✗				✕	✕	
		Ⓐ		Ⓐ		Ⓐt												Ⓑ		⑦n	⑦n	Ⓐ				Ⓑ
	Jeumont .... d.	0328	...	...	...	...	...	...	0837		...	1222	1436										...	2206	2209	2242
	Maubeuge .... d.	0336	...	0605		0646			0847		1137	1231	1447			1711						Ⓐ	2021			
	Aulnoye .... d.	0406	...	0619			0919		1106		1254	1500	1520	1718		1726			2017							
	Cambrai Ville 110 .. d.		0535		0635	0849	0853		1041								1713	1826		1959			2020n			
	Busigny .... d.	0425	0602		0650	0912	0916		1103		1339						1744	1756	1848		2023			2045n		
	St. Quentin ..... d.	0444	0624	0632	0709	0714	0931	0938	0952	1126	1141	1215	1205	1401		1553	1750	1806	1816	1907	1916	2045	2050	2057	2107
	Tergnier .... d.	0501		0649	0734					1231									1830	1926	1931				2125
	Compiègne ...... d.	0538		0723	0809	0749		1028			1313								1910		2011				2157
	Creil .... a.			0832							1330								1931						2214
	Paris Nord .... a.	0623		0810	0900	0830	0840		1115			1258	1330	1403		1706	1859		1959		2052		2206	2209	2242

– ⑤⑦ (also Apr. 17, May 1,8,24; not Apr. 16,30, May 7,26).
– Daily except when train K runs.
– Depart 1445 on ©.

n – ⑦ (also Apr. 17, May 1,8; not Apr. 16,30, May 7).
t – Not May 25,26.
✗ – Supplement payable.

Table 101a — AMIENS - COMPIÈGNE

1,2 class

km			✕				⑦	✕		⑦						✕	✕	①⑦		⑥	Ⓐ	⑦	✕	⑦
0	Amiens .... d.		0608	0808	1225	1624	1728	1838	1840	2153	...		Compiègne .... d.		0606	0705	0803	1228	1628	1726	1840	1902	2004
5	Longueau .... d.		0613		1630	1735	1844		2159	...			Longueau .... d.		0728		0915	1348	1742	1844	1956	2006	2110
76	Compiègne .... a.		0740	0918	1349	1759	1849	2000	2015	2306			Amiens .... a.		0733	0820	0921	1353	1748	1850	2001	2012	2115

For explanation of standard symbols see page 4

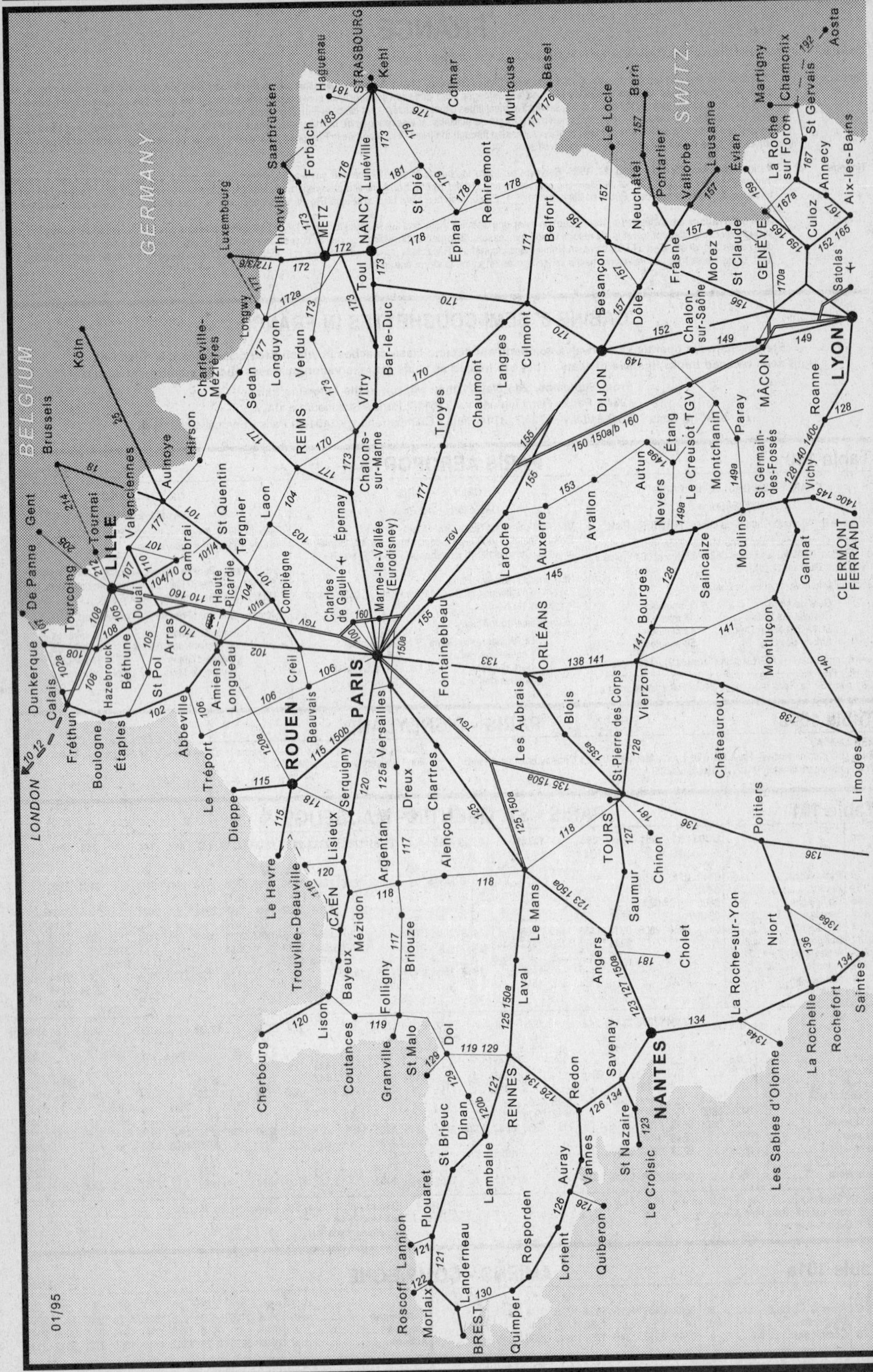

GERMANY

BELGIUM

SWITZ.

LONDON

Roscoff
Lannion
Plouaret
Landerneau
BREST
Morlaix
Quimper
Rosporden
Lorient
Auray
Quiberon
Vannes
St Nazaire
Le Croisic
Les Sables d'Olonne
La Rochelle
Rochefort
Saintes
La Roche-sur-Yon
Cholet
Niort
Poitiers
Limoges
CLERMONT FERRAND
Gannat
Vichy
Montluçon
Châteauroux
Bourges
Moulins
Nevers
Saincaize
Le Creusot TGV
Montchanin
Paray
St Germain-des-Fossés
Roanne
MÂCON
LYON
Aix-les-Bains
Culoz
Annecy
St Gervais
Chamonix
Martigny
Aosta
La Roche sur Foron
GENÈVE
Evian
Morez
St Claude
Frasne
Pontarlier
Vallorbe
Lausanne
Bern
Le Locle
Neuchâtel
Besançon
Dôle
DIJON
Chalon-sur-Saône
Autun
Avallon
Auxerre
Laroche
Culmont
Langres
Chaumont
Troyes
Chalons-sur-Marne
Épernay
REIMS
Laon
Tergnier
St Quentin
Compiègne
Charles de Gaulle
Marne-la-Vallée (Eurodisney)
PARIS
Creil
Beauvais
Versailles
Fontainebleau
Les Aubrais
ORLÉANS
Blois
Vierzon
St Pierre des Corps
TOURS
Saumur
Chinon
Le Mans
Angers
Laval
Redon
Savenay
NANTES
RENNES
Dol
Dinan
St Brieuc
Lamballe
Folligny
Granville
St Malo
Coutances
Lison
Bayeux
Mézidon
Briouze
CAEN
Argentan
Lisieux
Trouville-Deauville
Le Havre
ROUEN
Dieppe
Le Tréport
Abbeville
Amiens
Longueau
Arras
St Pol
Béthune
Hazebrouck
Boulogne
Étaples
Fréthun
Calais
Dunkerque
De Panne
Gent
Tourcoing
LILLE
Valenciennes
Aulnoye
Hirson
Charleville-Mézières
Sedan
Longuyon
Verdun
Vitry
Bar-le-Duc
Toul
NANCY
METZ
Thionville
Forbach
Saarbrücken
Haguenau
STRASBOURG
Kehl
Colmar
Mulhouse
Basel
Belfort
Remiremont
Épinal
St Dié
Lunéville
Luxembourg
Köln
Brussels
Tournai
Douai
Cambrai
Haute Picardie
Béthune
Aubrais
Chartres
Dreux
Alençon
Brussels

Quimperlé
Dol
Vannes
Savenay
St Nazaire
La Rochelle
Rochefort
Saintes
Les Sables d'Olonne

01/95

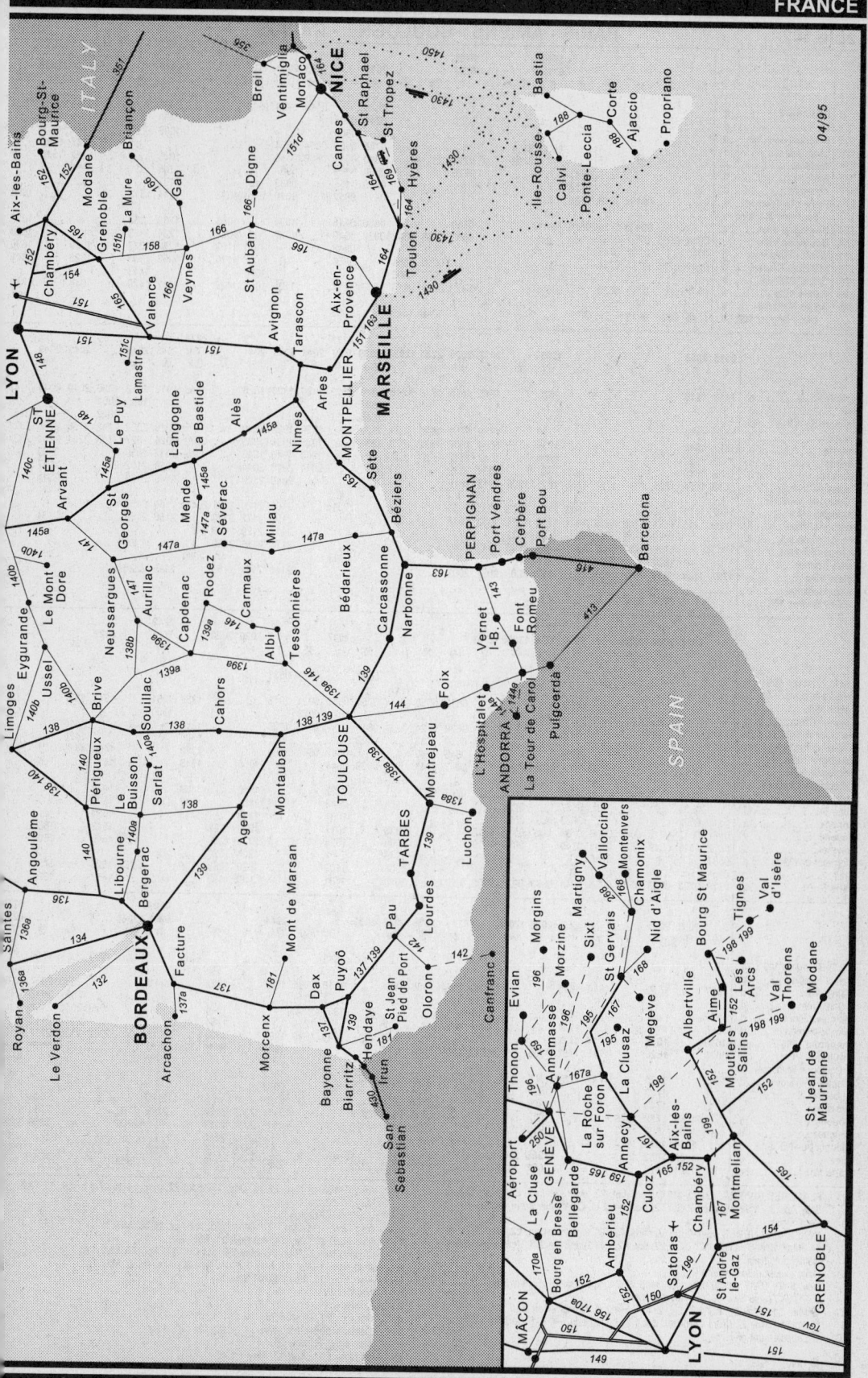

Table 102 — PARIS - AMIENS - BOULOGNE - CALAIS

1,2 class

Block 1

km		6710/6711 Ⓐ	6710/6711 Ⓐ	✗	✗	✗	6706/6708 S	Ⓑ	6706/6708 C	⑦z	2001 Ⓐ	2001 ✗Ⓡ	2003 Ⓐq	2003 ⑦e	7227 TGV ⑦Ⓡ	2015	✗	12019 ✗	⑦z
0	Paris Nord d.										0646	0714	0748	0749	0749 / 0915	0928		1103	1209
51	Creil d.				0609				0629			0805				0956		1139	1237
66	Clermont-de-l'Oise d.															1008		1154	
126	Longueau d.				0650	0654			0703 / 0711		0755	0906	0854	0854		1046		1247	1318
131	Amiens a.								0711		0800	0911	0859	0859	0907	1105		1252	1324
131	Amiens d.			0643	0718				0725		0808	0836 ✗	0907	0932	via Lille	1132		via	1600
176	Abbeville d.			0718	0758						0836	0911	0852	1016	1037	1214	1313	Arras	1627
227	Étaples-le-Touquet d.		0619a	0718	0758		via		0830		0911	0918	1034		1055	1232	1338	Ⓐ 1611	1628
	Boulogne Maritime a.		0643a	0736	0826		Arras		0830										
254	Boulogne Ville a.		0643a	0736	0826				0832	0838	0842	0932	0940	1036	1056	1234	1339	1611	1627
254	Boulogne Ville d.	0534	0653	0701	0737				0832	0838	0842	0932	0940		1102	1243	1347	1620	1636
261	Wimille-Wimereux d.	0540		0709	0745				0846			0948			1110	1253	1355	1628	1645
271	Marquise Rinxent d.	0549	0705	0717	0754				0855	0854		0956				1413			
288	Calais Fréthun a.								0907	0908					1045			1129	
296	Calais Ville a.	0607		0741	0820			0858t	0901t	0914	0916	1000	1017		1105 / 1054	1312	1420	1646	1710
299	Calais Maritime a.														1129				
	Lille Flandres 108 a.	0748	0838	0913						1048	1049				1155				

Block 2

	2025 E	2025 F	Ⓐ	⑦z	Ⓐ	⑥	12031 ⑤f	2033 J	2035 ⑤f	2235 Ⓐ	12037 ⑥	12039 Ⓐq	7273 TGV ⑦h	2041 Ⓐ	2041 ⑥	2041 ⑤f	7275 TGV Ⓐk	2043 Ⓐ	2043 ⑦e	2049 Ⓐ	2049 ⑤f
Paris Nord d.	1418	1418					1625		1655	1655	1718	1718	1810	1822	1826	1826	1826	1848	1912 / 1912	1930 / 2049	2049 / 2148
Creil d.													1837		1940	2004	2022				2221
Clermont-de-l'Oise d.													1849			2022					2237
Longueau d.	1522	1539					1729		1759	1759	1820	1823	1925	1930	1930	1930	via Lille	2019	2024 / 2118	2156 / 2201	2201 / 2321
Amiens a.	1527	1544					1735		1804	1804	1832	1829	1931	1935	1935	1935		2024	2035	2201	2327
Amiens d.	1535	1552		⑦z					1812	1812	1839	1839		1943	1943	1943		2032		2059	2237 / 2209
Abbeville d.	1603	1619			1752			1825	1906	1913	1919			2014	2010	2014		2046	2100 / 2101	2135 / 2138	2314
Étaples-le-Touquet d.	1638	1654	1705		1752																
Boulogne Maritime a.																					
Boulogne Ville a.	1657	1713	1730		1815	1823	1849		1923	1931	1935		2021c	2105	2120	2121	2048c	2154	2157		2334
Boulogne Ville d.	1659	1715	1731	1740	1816	1824	1850		1924	1933	1937			2107	2122	2122		2156	2159		
Wimille-Wimereux d.			1740	1746	1823	1832	1859		1932					2115	2129	2129					
Marquise Rinxent d.			1749	1754	1832	1840	1908		1940	1947	1949			2126	2139	2139	2030				
Calais Fréthun a.			1804		1848	1859						2003		2146	2159	2159		2225	2228		
Calais Ville a.	1727	1744	1813	1813	1856	1908	1859		1927	2000	2007	2007									
Calais Maritime a.																					
Lille Flandres 108 a.			1954	1948							2049										

Block 3

	2004 ①g	2004 Ⓐ	2202 Ⓐ	✗	2006 ✗	7211 TGV ✗Ⓡ	12008 Ⓐ	12008 C	①g	✗	2017 ✗	✗	†	2020 Ⓐ	2020 ⑥	7242 TGV ✗v	2027 ✗	†
Lille Flandres 108 d.							0632			0751	0833					1222		
Calais Maritime d.																		
Calais Ville d.				0528			0612	0658		0756	0815	0921	1018		1230	1251	1341	1357
Calais Fréthun d.					0653			0706			0928					1300		
Marquise Rinxent d.				0548			0630	0724		0814	0942	1038			1256		1416	
Wimille-Wimereux d.				0559			0639	0733		0822	1047				1304	1409	1430	
Boulogne Ville a.		0440		0601	0634c	0620g	0646	0740		0829	0844	1055		1058	1312	1411		
Boulogne Ville d.		0440		0601	0634c	0620g	0647	0741		0829	0844			1058	1313			
Boulogne Maritime d.																		
Étaples-le-Touquet d.		0457		0620		0641g	0707	0808		0902		1116	1333	via Lille	1412	1429		
Abbeville d.		0539		0657	0728	via	0943	1153		1412	1443					1505	1532	
Amiens a.		0602		0723	via	Lille	0802	1007		1219	1443						1532	
Amiens d.	0527	0612	0612	0640	0655	0733	0812	0812		0858	1017	1024		1229	1229		1542	1600
Longueau d.	0533	0619	0619	0651	0701	0740	0819	0819		0903	1024			1236	1236		1549	1606
Clermont-de-l'Oise d.					0745					0945	1102			1308	1320		1628	1708
Creil d.	0631				0757					1004	1131			1320	1333		1657	1727
Paris Nord a.	0651	0723	0723	0755	0836	0844	0833	0922	0922	1040	1131	1348b	1403	1433			1807	

Block 4

	2031 Ⓐ	2031 ①C	✗	†	2036 Ⓐk	12038 ✗	✗	2039 Ⓐ	2039 ⑦e	2039	Ⓐ	2044 ⑦h	✗	6206/6208 B	12048 ⑦h	Ⓐ	⑤n	Ⓒ	6210/6211 R
Lille Flandres 108 d.					1558				1658					1903		1856			
Calais Maritime d.																	2030	2037	2039
Calais Ville d.	1537		1550	1640	1645	1730	1754	1808	1814	1818	1835	1907	1922	1941t		2037	2046		
Calais Fréthun d.						1738				1844	1902			1945	2029	2050	2102		
Marquise Rinxent d.	1557			1701	1706	1756	1813	1837	1902	1911		1954		2057	2111				
Wimille-Wimereux d.	1606			1709	1714	1804	1822		1911		1954	2003	2011	2042	2103	2117			
Boulogne Ville a.	1613	1618		1717	1722	1811	1829	1837	1841	1848	1919	1932	2003	2011					via
Boulogne Ville d.	1614	1620		1718	1723	1736	1812	1830	1839	1843		1934		2013					Arras
Boulogne Maritime d.																			
Étaples-le-Touquet d.	1633	1638		1744	1750	1754	1838	1849	1857	1904		1952							
Abbeville d.	1718	1723		1838	1902	1934	1937	2000	2003		2101	2033		2120		⑮	2244		
Amiens a.	1749	1749			1902			2013	2013	2013	2111	2049	2122	2149	2159		2250		
Amiens d.		1759	1759	1828	1912	1912	1919	2020	2020	2020	2118	2055	2128		2206		2250		
Longueau d.	1806	1806	1833	1919	1919			2020	2020	2020	2142	2210						233	
Clermont-de-l'Oise d.	1841	1924			1958						2155	2225	2229						
Creil d.	1852	1852	1942	1958	2000		2123	2123	2123		2221	2228	2306	2309					
Paris Nord a.	1921	1921	2027	2013			2123	2123	2123		2221	2228	2306		2233				

Notes

B – FLANDRES RIVIERA, runs ①③⑤⑥ from Jan. 22, also ④⑦ Feb. 23 - Mar. 12 and daily Apr. 3 - May 27: 🛏 1,2 cl. (T2) and 🚗 auto/train - Nice - Ventimiglia.
C – RIVIERA FLANDRES, runs (from Ventimiglia) ①②④⑥ from Jan. 22, also ⑤⑦ Feb. 24 - Mar. 12 and daily Apr. 3 - May 27: 🛏 1,2 cl. (T2) and 🚗 2 cl. Ventimiglia - Nice - Calais auto/train.
E – Daily except dates in note F.
F – Nov. 8-10, 15-17, 28-30, Dec. 1,2, Mar. 20-24, Apr. 4-6,18-21, May 3-5.
J – ①②③④⑦ (also May 26; not Nov. 10, May 24).
R – ⑤ Mar. 31 - May 26: 🛏 1,2 cl. (T2) and 🚗 2 cl. Calais - Port Bou.
S – ⑥ Apr. 1 - May 27 (from Cerbère): 🛏 1,2 cl. (T2) and 🚗 2 cl. Cerbère - Calais.
TGV – Ⓡ, supplement payable.
a – Ⓐ only.

b – Arrive 1403 on Nov. 22-24, Dec. 13-15,20-22, Mar. 14-16,27-31, Apr. 11-13,25-27, May 10-12.
c – Via Calais Fréthun.
e – Also Nov. 1,11, Apr. 17, May 1,8,25; not Apr. 16,30, May 7.
f – Also Nov. 10, May 24; not Nov. 11, May 26.
g – ① (also Nov. 2, Apr. 18, May 2,9; not Oct. 31, Apr. 17, May 1,8).
h – Also Nov. 1, Apr. 17, May 1,8; not Oct. 30, Apr. 16,30, May 7.
j – Also Nov. 11, May 25; not Nov. 12.
k – Not Oct. 31.
n – Not Nov. 11.
q – Not Oct. 31, May 25,26.
t – Calais auto/train station.
v – Also Nov. 11, May 25.
z – Also Nov. 1,11, Apr. 17, May 1,8,25.

✗ – Daily except Sundays and holidays   † – Sundays and holidays

Table 102a
CALAIS - DUNKERQUE - DE PANNE

km		⊞	✕	§	✕		⊞	⊞	✕§	⑦§		⊞
0	Calais Ville........d.	0511	0637	...	1226	1228	1350	...	1722			
24	Gravelines........d.	0543	0701	0840	1249	1300	1445	1455	1743			
43	Dunkerque Gare........d.	0625	0730	0935	1316	1340	1540	1550	1810			
59	Bray Dunes........d.	...	...	1010	...	...	1615	1625	...			
69	De Panne Place Marché....a.	...	...	1040	...	...	1645	1710	...			

		✕	⊞	✕	⊞	⊞	⑦§	✕§	✕	✕	§
	De Panne Place Marché...d.	...	...	...	1105	1110	...	...	...	1710	
	Bray Dunes........d.	...	...	...	1145	1145	...	...	...	1745	
	Dunkerque Gare.........d.	0631	0731	1222	1225	1220	1220	1446	1712	1826	1820
	Gravelines........d.	0659	0813	1247	1303	1315	1255	1513	1742	1856	1855
	Calais Ville........a.	0718	0845	1308	1337	1400	1350	1530	1802	1917	1945

§ – Operated by Cariane Littoral, 10 Rue d'Amsterdam, 62100 Calais; ☎ 21.34.74.40, fax 21.97.73.33.
Other (infrequent) journeys operate Boulogne - Calais - Dunkerque and v.v. (serving the railway stations), operated by 'Autocars B.C.D.' ☎ 21.70.82.82.

Table 103
PARIS - LAON
1,2 class

km				12357	12361		12375						12389		12391	
				✕	ⓒ	⊞		⑦		✕	⊞		⊞			
0	Paris Nord........d.	...	0600	0708	0816	0829	...	1246	1246	...	1450	...	1635	...	1744	1839	...	2002
61	Crépy-en-Valois........d.	...	0654	0747	0915	0908	...	1325	1323	...	1535	...	1714	...	1830	...	2042
105	Soissons........d.	...	0732	0820	0952	0941	...	1359	1356	...	1612	...	1747	...	1906	1949	...	2117
140	Laon........a.	...	0800	0847	1020	1008	...	1424	1424	...	1647	...	1818	...	1935	2016	...	2144

		⊞	✕	⑦	12360	12362	12364			⑦	⑤f	G	⑦	⑦	⊞	⑥	12386	12394	
					✕	⊞											⑦g	✕	⑦
	Laon........d.	0529	0638	0657	...	0746	...	0847	...	0946	...	1220	1220	1540	1557	1604	1706	1707	1736	1807	...	2025	2025	...	2052
	Soissons........d.	0556	0708	0723	...	0815	...	0916	...	1015	...	1249	1246	1613	1626	1630	1733	1739	1803	1839	...	2056	2052	...	2121
	Crépy-en-Valois........d.	...	0743	0756	...	0850	...	0950	...	1049	...	1324	1327	1655	1701	1706	1813	1811	1843	1916	...	2131	2125	...	2159
	Paris Nord........a.	0708	0828	0847	...	0926	...	1026	...	1128	...	1408	1421	1755	1755	1753	1855	1855	1925	1953	...	2207	2213	...	2250

G – ①②③④⑥ (also Feb. 17,24, Apr. 14, May 26; not Nov. 1,10,11, Feb. 16,23, Apr. 13,17,24, May 1,8,25).
f – Also Nov. 10, Feb.16,23, Apr. 13,24; not Nov. 11, Feb. 17,24, Apr. 14, May 26.
g – Also Nov. 1, Apr. 17, May 1,8; not Apr. 16,30, May 7.

Table 104
LILLE and AMIENS - REIMS
1,2 class

km		⊞		✕	⊞	⑥	✕	⑦e	⊞	✕
0	Lille Flandres 110....d.	...	...	0800	1156	1647	1707	1736	1808	2139
34	Douai 110........d.	...	...	0825	1228	1731	1731	1801	1834	2217
66	Cambrai Ville 110....d.	...	...	0849	1303	1810	1810	1826	1904	2243
92	Busigny........d.	...	...	0912	...	1833	1833	1848		
119	St. Quentin........d.	...	...	0932	...	1852	1853	1907		
	Amiens........d.	0625	0824	...						
142	Tergnier........d.	0741	0930	0950	...		1910	1929		
170	Laon........d.	0808	...	1015	...		1942	1956		
222	Reims........a.	0844	...	1050	...			2032		

		⊞	†	✕	✕	⊞	⊞	†	⊞	✕	⊞
	Reims........d.	...	0621	...	1115	1508	...	...	...	1705	1727
	Laon........d.	...	0715	0753	1200	1547	...	...	...	1741	1825
	Tergnier........d.	...	0738	0819	1233	1612	...	1644	...	1804	1856
	Amiens........a.	...	...	0920	1338		...	...	...	...	2002
	St. Quentin........d.	0542	...	0759	...	1628	...	1716	1816c	1822	
	Busigny........d.	0603	...	0825	...	1648	1704	1741	1844	1848	
	Cambrai Ville 110....d.	0627	0809	0851	1313	1711	1730	1806	1907	1915	
	Douai 110........d.	0658	0841	0916	1348	1737	1800	1839	1934	1940	
	Lille Flandres 110....a.	0727	0905	0939	1413	1801	1832	1903	2008	2003	

⊞ – ⊞ only.
e – Also Apr. 17, May 1,8; not Apr. 16,30, May 7.

Table 105
BOULOGNE - ST. POL - ARRAS and LILLE
1,2 class

km		✕	⊞	⑥			✕	⊞	†	†			⊞		†			⊞	⊞	†	⊞	†
0	Boulogne Ville........d.	...	0530	...	...	...	0647	...	0830	0910	...	...	1226	...	1525	...	...	1718	1723	1830	...
27	Étaples-le-Touquet........d.	...	0555	0555	...	...	0708	...	0851	0931	...	...	1258	...	1546	...	...	1753	1753	1900	...
39	Montreuil sur Mer........d.	...	0605	0605	...	...	0718	...	0901	0942	...	...	1308	...	1556	...	...	1803	1803	1910	...
88	St. Pol........d.	0544	0653	0653	0656	...	0732	0809	0814	0946	1018	1024	...	1227	1356	...	1650	1830	1847	1847	1959	2010
127	Arras........a.	...	0739	0739	...	0814	...	0852	...	1053	...	1432	...	1725	...	1910			2050
120	Béthune........d.	0621	...	...	0733	0801	...	0844	...	0919	1018	...	1054	1230	1312	...	1453	...	1729	...	1920	1920	2031	...
162	Lille Flandres........a.	0709	...	...	0817	0845	...	0919	...	1002	1058	...	1138	1318	1358	...	1540	...	1814	...	2001	2001	2110	...

		✕	⊞	⊞	†	✕		⊞	⊞		⑥	⊞	⊞	⊞	⊞	†		⊞	⊞	⊞	✕z	
	Lille Flandres........d.	...	0645	0745	...	...	0838	0902	1210	...	...	1215	1215	1339	1341	...	1548	1557	1629	1713	...	1814	1818	...	2003
	Béthune........d.	...	0733	0851t	...	...	0914	0942	1258	...	...	1319	1319	1419	1424	...	1626	1633	1714	1808	...	1905	1922	1922	2054
	Arras........d.	...	...	...	0856	0856	...	...	...	1230	1307	...	...	...	...	1608	...	...	...	1826	...			
	St. Pol........d.	0713	0806	0925	0936	0935	0947	...	...	1304	1349	1358	1358	...	1453	1647	1657	1702	1747	1843	1909	...	1958	2006	...
	Montreuil sur Mer........d.	0811	...	...	1022	...	1022	...	...	1351	...	1440	1440	...	...	1740	1742	...	...	2001	...	2043	2043	...
	Étaples-le-Touquet........d.	0822	...	...	1032	...	1037	...	...	1400	...	1449	1450	...	...	1755	1752	...	...	2013	...	2053	2053	...
	Boulogne Ville........a.	0850	...	...	1058	...	1055	...	...	1418	...		1509	...	...	1823	1815	...	...	2037	...	2113	2114	...

– Arrive 0828.
v – † only.
z – On ⑤ depart Béthune 1933, arrive Boulogne 2128.

Table 106
PARIS - BEAUVAIS - LE TRÉPORT
1,2 class

km		⊞	⊞	⑥	†		✕	⊞	⑤f	ⓒ
0	Paris Nord ▲........d.	0615	...	0743	0836	1136	...	1719	...	1904	1906
38	Persan-Beaumont ▲....d.	0643	...	0815	0908	1206	...		...	1938	1940
78	Beauvais ▲........d.	0738	0752	0856	0949	1244	1315	1837	1900	2022	2022
127	Abancourt........d.	...	0836	0939	1033	...	1402	...	1946	2112	2107
181	Eu........d.	...	0921	1023	1117	...	1446	...	2030	2156	2150
184	Le Tréport........a.	...	0925	1027	1121	...	1450	...	2034	2200	2154

		⊞	⊞	⑥	†		†	✕	⑦e
	Le Tréport........d.	0618	...	0703	...	0747	1130	...	1658	1722	1843
	Eu........d.	0622	...	0707	...	0751	1134	...	1702	1726	1848
	Abancourt........d.	0708	...	0754	...	0831	1216	...	1751	1813	1934
	Beauvais ▲........d.	0747	0802	0835	0847	0915	1302	1310	1833	1855	2012
	Persan-Beaumont ▲....a.	...	0836	...	0918	0944	...	1345	1906	1949	2044
	Paris Nord ▲........a.	...	0910	...	0948	1014	...	1417	1935	...	2116

▲ – Also Apr. 17, May 1,8; not Apr. 16,30, May 7.
f – Also Nov. 10, May 24; not Nov. 11, May 26.
▲ – Additional trains Paris Nord - Beauvais : From Paris Nord 0634⑥, 0743✕, 1259†, 1305✕, 1635ⓒ, 1649⊞, 1749⊞, 1805ⓒ, 1819⊞, 1904⊞, 1937⑥, 1949⊞, 2120†.
From Beauvais 0617⊞, 0624⑥, 0644⊞, 0707†, 0709⊞, 0731⑥, 0808†, 0852⊞, 0915†, 1310, 1700†, 1818⊞, 1832⑥, 1906†, 2110ⓒ, 2115⊞. Journey 65-70 minutes.
Additional trains run Beauvais - Persan-Beaumont and Beauvais - Creil (suburban trains run Persan-Beaumont and Creil to/from Paris Nord).
ABBEVILLE - LE TRÉPORT : 25 km, journey 50 - 60 minutes. From Abbeville 0654🚌, 0840✕🚌, 0940†🚌, 1135🚌, 1310🚌, 1650, 1843✕, 2019✕.
From Le Tréport : 0605⊞🚌, 0633✕, 0740✕, 0827🚌, 1156🚌, 1600🚌, 1720🚌.

Table 107
LILLE AREA LOCAL SERVICES
1,2 class

LILLE - LENS : 38 km Journey 45 - 55 minutes.
Lille Flandres depart: 0655⊞, 1219✕, 1658⑥, 1704⊞, 1755⊞, 1818⊞, 1832⑥;   Lens depart: 0652⊞, 0655⑥, 0747✕, 1354✕, 1741✕.

LILLE - VALENCIENNES : 48 km Journey 45 minutes. Subject to alteration from Apr. 18.
Lille Flandres depart: 0608⑥, 0636✕, 0704✕, 0807✕, 0855⑥, 0911†, 1037†, 1140✕, 1225✕, 1345⊞, 1408, 1551†, 1558⊞, 1613✕, 1626⊞, 1644, 1704⊞, 1729, 1738, 1819✕, 1842†, 46⊞, 1925✕, 2017⊞, 2037ⓒ, 2133⊞, 2310⑤⑥⑦. Valenciennes depart: 0450⑤, 0556✕, 0622✕, 0644⊞, 0650⑥, 0701✕, 0712⊞, 0726⊞, 0738ⓒ, 0746⊞, 0823⊞, 0842⊞, 1048, 13, 1220✕, 1244✕, 1322, 1401⊞, 1628⊞, 1658⊞, 1721⊞, 1754ⓒ, 1822⊞, 1911⑦, 1914✕, 1925✕, 2006ⓒ, 2020①②③④, 2206, 2249⑤⑥⑦.

VALENCIENNES - CAMBRAI : 40 km Journey 40 - 45 minutes.
Valenciennes depart: 0538⊞, 0638✕, 0728⊞, 0803✕, 1010✕, 1223✕, 1319✕, 1714, 1747✕, 1822⊞, 1925⊞, 1930†.
Cambrai depart: 0621⊞, 0644✕, 0732✕, 0751✕, 1103✕, 1221✕, 1314✕, 1717✕, 1836, 1945⊞, 2204†.

⊞ – Mondays to Fridays, except holidays   ⑥ – Daily except Saturdays   ⓒ – Saturdays, Sundays and holidays

Table 108 ARRAS and LILLE - DUNKERQUE and CALAIS

1,2 class

km		⚒	⚒	⚒	Ⓐ	⑥	⚒	⚒	7305 TGV Ⓐk 🍷	7105 TGV ⑥t 🍷		7215 TGV Ⓐk 🍷	⚒	†		Ⓐ	7227 TGV ⚒d 🍷	7109 TGV ⑦y 🍷	⑥	†	⚒	⚒	⚒	⚒	
	Paris Nord **110** d.	...	...	...	...	...	...	...	0721	0721	...	0745	...	...	...	...	0915	0921	...	...	...	...	...	...	...
0	**Arras** d.	...	0607	0626	...	...	...	0734	0818	0815	...	|	0835	0841	...	0922	|	1015	1024	...	...	1209	...	1226	...
20	Lens d.	...	0624	0644	...	...	...	0800	0832	0828	...	|	0849	0854	...	0936	|	1028	1038	...	...	1223	...	1245	...
39	Béthune d.	...	0641	0706	...	...	...	0820	0846	0841	...	|	0901	0910	...	0952	|	1041	1050	...	...	1235	...	1306	...
	Lille Europe d.	...	|	|	...	...	...	|	|	|	...	0848	|	|	...	|	1018	|	|	...	...	|	...	|	...
	Lille Flandres d.	0632	|	|	0732	0732	0751	|	|	|	0833x	|	|	|	0930	|	|	|	|	1214	1222	|	1227	|	1315
	Armentières d.	0649	|	|	0750	0750	0810	|	|	|	0854x	|	|	|	0947	|	|	|	|	1231	|	|	1246	|	1334
73	Hazebrouck a.	0706	0714	0740	0809	0809	0829	0853	0907	0900	0914x	|	0926	0934	1006	1017	|	1100	1115	1251	1255	1300	1307	1330	1352
73	Hazebrouck d.	0708	0716	*0746*	0811	*0820*	0833	...	...	0902	0915	|	0927	0935	1007v	1018	|	1102	1116	1252	1256	1301	1308	1331	1354
113	**Dunkerque** a.	|	0743	|	0835	*0855*	|	...	...	0923	|	0918	0952	1006	1038v	1044	|	1123	1141	1326	|	1326	1341	1401	|
94	St. Omer d.	0722	...	*0805*	...	...	0848	...	...	...	0933	...	...	...	...	...	|	...	...	...	1314	...	...	...	1408
137	**Calais Ville** a.	0748	...	*0842*	...	...	0913	...	...	...	1010	...	...	...	...	...	1054	...	...	...	1349	...	...	...	1433
	Boulogne Ville **102** a.	0829	...	...	...	...	0954	...	...	...	1055v	...	...	...	...	...	...	...	...	...	1430	...	...	...	...

	7115 TGV ⚒d 🍷	Ⓐ	⚒	7119 TGV 🍷				Ⓐ	Ⓐ	Ⓐ		Ⓐ		Ⓐ	Ⓐ	7125 TGV Ⓐk 🍷	Ⓐ	Ⓐ	7127 TGV Ⓒn 🍷	Ⓒ	Ⓐ	7329 TGV ⑤f 🍷	7271 TGV Ⓑh 🍷	7273 TGV ⑦e 🍷	7275 TGV Ⓐk 🍷
Paris Nord **110** d.	1236	...	...	1436	...	...	...	...	...	...	...	...	...	...	...	1706	...	...	1733	...	...	1807	1822	1822	1848
Arras d.	1332	...	1339	1529	...	...	1540	...	...	1630	...	1701	...	...	...	1758	1803	...	1829	...	...	1858	|	|	|
Lens d.	1346	...	1353	1542	...	...	1556	...	...	1649	...	1716	...	...	...	1811	1818	...	1842	...	...	1911	|	|	|
Béthune d.	1359	...	1408	1555	...	...	1612	...	...	1707	...	1733	...	...	...	1825	1836	...	1855	...	...	1925	|	|	|
Lille Europe d.	|	...	|	|	...	...	|	...	...	|	...	|	...	...	...	|	|	...	|	...	...	|	1925	1928	1952
Lille Flandres d.	|	1352	|	|	1546	1558	|	1645	1658	|	1715	|	1738	...	1808	|	|	1836	|	1856	1903	|	|	|	|
Armentières d.	|	|	|	|	1605	|	|	1703	|	|	1737	|	1756	...	|	|	|	1856	|	1920	|	|	|	|	|
Hazebrouck a.	1418	1426	1433	1614	1623	1628	1637	1722	1729	1742	1755	1802	1814	...	1839	1845	1902	1913	1915	1939	1936	1944	|	|	|
Hazebrouck d.	1420	1438	1434	1616	1624	1630	1638	1723	1730	1744	1757	...	1815	1827	1840	1848	1903	1914	1917	1940	1937	1946	|	|	|
Dunkerque a.	1441	|	1459	1637	1701	|	1704	1758	|	1821	|	...	1848	|	1906	1910	1928	|	1938	|	|	|	1955	|	|
St. Omer d.	...	1454	...	...	...	1649	...	...	1744	...	1816	...	...	1842	...	...	...	1930	...	1956	1951	1959	...	|	|
Calais Ville a.	...	1519	...	...	...	1722	...	...	1809	...	1853	...	...	1913	...	...	...	2001	...	2029	|	...	...	2003c	2030c
Boulogne Ville **102** a.	...	...	...	...	...	1811	...	...	1848	...	...	...	...	2003	...	...	...	...	...	2117	2042	...	...	2021	2048

		Ⓑ	7331 TGV E 🍷	7131 TGV ⑤f 🍷		Ⓒ		7133 TGV ⑤f 🍷	Ⓑ	⚒
Paris Nord **110** d.	...	...	1851	1851	...	...	...	1951	...	...
Arras d.	...	1914	1945	1945	...	2010	...	2047	2051	2150
Lens d.	...	1929	1959	1958	...	2024	...	2101	2107	2204
Béthune d.	...	1945	2013	2012	...	2040	...	2114	2124	2220
Lille Europe d.	...	|	|	|	...	|	...	|	|	|
Lille Flandres d.	1920	|	|	|	2000	|	2036	|	|	|
Armentières d.	1937	|	|	|	2020	|	2056	|	|	|
Hazebrouck a.	1955	2010	2033	2031	2043	2104	2117	2133	2150	2244
Hazebrouck d.	1956	2011	2035j	2033	2044	2105	2118	2135	2151	2245z
Dunkerque a.	2029	2038	|	2053	2121	2132	|	2156	2218	2310z
St. Omer d.	...	...	2048j	...	...	...	2133	...	...	...
Calais Ville a.	...	...	...	...	...	...	2208	...	...	...
Boulogne Ville **102** a.	...	...	...	...	...	...	...	...	...	...

	Ⓐ	⚒	⚒	⚒	Ⓐ	⚒	7304 TGV Ⓐk 🍷		Ⓐ	7211 TGV ⚒p 🍷
Boulogne Ville **102** d.	...	...	...	...	...	...	...	...	...	0634
Calais Ville d.	0511	...	...	...	*0524*	...	...	...	...	0653c
St. Omer d.	0544	...	...	...	*0558*	...	0628	...	...	|
Dunkerque d.	|	0533	...	0551	|	0607	|	...	0638	|
Hazebrouck a.	0559	0604	...	0624	*0617*	0633	0640	...	0701	|
Hazebrouck d.	...	0607	0610	0626	0630	0640	0643	0646	0702	|
Armentières d.	...	0626	|	|	0649	0707	|	|	0724	|
Lille Flandres a.	...	0646	|	|	0707	0732	|	|	0740	|
Lille Europe a.	...	...	|	|	...	...	|	|	...	0728
Béthune d.	...	...	0641	0648	...	...	0705	0712	...	|
Lens d.	...	...	0654	0720	...	...	0716	0730	...	|
Arras a.	...	...	0708	0740	...	...	0730	0745	...	|
Paris Nord **110** a.	...	...	...	...	...	...	0827	...	...	0833

	7212 TGV Ⓐk 🍷	⚒	⚒	⚒	⚒	†	7108 TGV G 🍷	⚒	Ⓐ	Ⓐ	⚒	Ⓐ	⚒	†	Ⓑ	7112 TGV Ⓑg 🍷	⚒	⚒	7116 TGV ⚒d 🍷		⚒		7242 TGV ⚒d 🍷		7122 TGV Ⓑh 🍷
Boulogne Ville **102** d.	...	0534a	...	...	...	...	...	...	0653	...	0701	...	...	...	0838	...	0940	...	...	...	...	...	...	...	...
Calais Ville d.	...	0615	...	0633	...	...	...	...	|	...	0749	...	...	...	0922	...	1025	...	...	...	...	1218	1251	...	...
St. Omer d.	...	0648	...	0711	...	...	...	...	0749	...	0820	...	...	...	0954	...	1054	...	...	...	...	1257	|	...	...
Dunkerque d.	0654	|	...	|	0700	0716	0722	0727	|	0755	|	0905	...	0928	|	0959	|	1050	1152	1202	...	|	|	1424	1441
Hazebrouck a.	|	0705	...	0730	0736	0741	0743	0755	0803	0820	0832	0932	...	1001	1007	1020	1108	1115	1213	1229	...	1316	|	1450	1502
Hazebrouck d.	|	0707	0711	0731a	0737	0742	0745	0756	0805	0821	0833	0933	0942	1002	1008	1022	1120	1122	1215	1230	1237	1317	|	1451	1504
Armentières d.	|	0733	|	|	0756	0800	|	|	|	|	0856	0952	|	|	1027	|	1139	|	|	1248	|	1336	|	|	|
Lille Flandres a.	|	0748	|	0805a	0814	0817	|	|	0838	0852	0913	1009	|	|	1049	|	1155	|	|	1305	|	1355	|	|	|
Lille Europe a.	0724	...	|	...	...	...	|	|	...	...	...	...	|	|	...	|	...	|	|	...	|	...	1328	|	|
Béthune d.	|	...	0744	...	...	...	0807	0822	...	...	...	...	1008	1027	...	1043	...	1148	1237	...	1308	...	|	1516	1524
Lens d.	|	...	0801	...	...	...	0818	0839	...	...	...	...	1024	1045	...	1055	...	1205	1248	...	1327	...	|	1532	1538
Arras a.	|	...	0821	...	...	...	0833	0853	...	...	...	...	1039	1059	...	1108	...	1217	1303	...	1345	...	|	1544	1550
Paris Nord **110** a.	0833	...	...	...	...	...	0927	...	...	...	...	...	...	...	...	1200	...	...	1357	...	...	...	1433	...	1642

				⚒	†	7126 TGV 🍷	⚒		Ⓐ	Ⓐ	Ⓒ		†	⚒	7276 TGV Ⓑh 🍷	7332 TGV ⑦e 🍷	⚒	†		†	†	Ⓐ	†	7136 TGV ⑦e 🍷	7290 TGV ⑦e 🍷
Boulogne Ville **102** d.	1339r	...	...	...	...	...	...	...	1611	...	...	...	...	...	...	...	1731a	1740	...	...	...	...	1850	...	...
Calais Ville d.	1428	...	...	1546	...	...	...	...	1654	...	...	1735	...	...	...	...	1821	1821	...	...	...	1933	1935	...	...
St. Omer d.	1455	...	...	1618	...	...	...	...	1721	...	...	1811	...	...	...	1834	1900	1859	...	...	...	2004	2005	...	...
Dunkerque d.	|	1444	1544	|	1559	1619	1628	1709	|	1716	1741b	|	1801	1816	1828	|	*1831*	|	1856	1932	...	*1936*	|	2007	2128
Hazebrouck a.	1510	1517	1615	1632	1633	1640	1701	1734	1739	1749	1808b	1826	1836	1843	|	1846	1914	1911	1921	2005	...	2018	2018	2028	|
Hazebrouck d.	...	1518	1616	1634	1634	1642	1702	1735	...	1750	1809	1827	1838	1846	|	1849	1916	1912	1922	2006	2013	2019	2019	2030	|
Armentières d.	...	1536	|	1655	1653	|	1720	|	...	1807	1828	|	1900	1906	|	|	1935	1930	|	2024	|	2038	|	|	|
Lille Flandres a.	...	1551	|	1712	1712	|	1738	|	...	1824	1845	|	1920	1925	|	|	1954	1948	|	2043	|	2055	2049	|	|
Lille Europe a.	...	...	|	...	...	|	...	|	...	...	...	|	...	...	1858	|	...	...	|	...	|	...	...	|	2158
Béthune d.	...	...	1642	...	...	1704	...	1802	...	...	...	1855	...	...	|	1911	...	...	1947	...	2039	...	...	2052	|
Lens d.	...	...	1702	...	...	1715	...	1815	...	...	...	1913	...	...	|	1923	...	...	2003	...	2055	...	...	2103	|
Arras a.	...	...	1721	...	...	1730	...	1828	...	...	...	1927	...	...	|	1936	...	...	2016	...	2110	...	...	2118	|
Paris Nord **110** a.	...	...	...	...	...	1824	...	...	...	...	...	...	...	...	2003	2028	...	...	...	...	...	...	...	2212	2303

E – Daily except ⑤ (also runs Nov. 11, May 26; not Nov. 10, May 24).
G – ①⑥ (also Nov. 2,11, Apr. 18, May 2,9,25; not Apr. 17,May 1,8).

TGV – 🅁, supplement payable.

a – Ⓐ only.
b – ⑥ only.
c – Calais **Fréthun**.
d – Also Nov. 11, May 25.
e – Also Nov. 1, Apr. 17, May 1,8; not Oct. 30, Apr. 16,30, May 7.
f – Also Nov. 10, May 24; not Nov. 11, May 26.

g – Not Oct. 31, Nov. 11, May 25.
h – Not Oct. 30,31, Nov. 11, Apr. 16,30, May 7,25.
j – ①-④ (also May 26; not Oct. 31, Nov. 1,10, Apr. 17, May 1,8).
k – Not Oct. 31.
n – Also Oct. 31.
p – Also Nov. 11, May 25; not Nov. 12.
r – ⚒ only.
t – Also Oct. 31, Nov. 11, May 25.
v – ⑦ only (also Nov. 1,11, Apr. 17, May 1,8,25).
x – ①⑦ only (also Nov. 1,2,11,12, Apr. 18, May 2,9,25,26).
y – Also Nov. 1, Apr. 17, May 1,8.
z – ⑤⑥ (not Nov. 11) only.

 Ⓐ – Mondays to Fridays, except holidays Ⓑ – Daily except Saturdays Ⓒ – Saturdays, Sundays and holidays

Table 110   PARIS - LILLE - TOURCOING

1,2 class

km		Ⓐ	Ⓐ	7009 6710 6711 TGV Ⓐk ♦	✕	†	Ⓐ	6720 6721 ♦	✕	7155 TGV Ⓐk	7305 TGV ✕	7215 TGV Ⓐk	✕	2203 Ⓐq	✕	6708 6709 ♦	7219 TGV †	✕n	Ⓐ	7157 TGV ✕v	✕	7225 TGV ⑦x
0	Paris Nord 108 ..... d.			0700				0650		0721	0721	0745		0652			0815			0821		0900
	Longueau .... d.																					
	Amiens .... d.		0613				0721											0756	0818			
	Albert .... d.		0637				0752												0841			
199	Arras 108 .... a.	0623	0704				0812	0721		0812		0818		0827			0836		0904			0911
199	Arras .... d.		0706					0735 0716	0727					0753	0815		0819 0829		0838	0906		0914
224	Douai .... a.	0641	0724				0750	0742 0747		0809		0830		0836	0843		0852		0921			0928
224	Douai .... d.	0643	0655 0726				0752	0754 0754 0750		0812	0804	0825		0837	0837 0845	0851	0854	0900	0923	0935		0947
	Valenciennes .... a.		0727							0834		0901			0922		0929		1000			
	Cambrai Ville .... a.							0828		0852												1018
227	Lille Europe .... a.													0845								
*258	Lille Flandres ...... a.	0723	0750		0802			0814 0830	0828	0838		0900			0905		0914		0917	0943		1002
*258	Lille Flandres 205 .. d.				0841			0900				0918			0938				0926			1011
268	Roubaix 205 .... a.				0856			0916				0933			0952				0941			1026
271	Tourcoing 205 ...... a.				0900			0920				0937			0956				0944			1029

		7227 TGV ✕v	⑥	†	2205 TGV ⑥	7159 TGV ⑦x	562/3 TGV	7233 TGV ✕v	7313 TGV ✕	†	✕	7037 TGV Ⓐk	7165 TGV ✕v	✕	7241 TGV ⑥t	7241 TGV Ⓐk	†	7247 TGV †	7119 TGV	7169 TGV R
	Paris Nord 108 ..... d.	0915			0842	0921		1100	1107			1200	1236		1300	1300		1430	1436	1439
	Longueau .... d.																			
	Amiens .... d.		0916	0916				1122	1122				1215					1254		
	Albert .... d.		0938	0938				1142	1142				1247					1318		
	Arras 108 .... a.		1003	1014	1012			1157	1202	1205			1318	1326				1349	1526	1532
	Arras .... d.		1004	1016	1018		1049		1205	1206			1320	1329				1351	1500	1532
	Douai .... a.		1021	1031	1033		1103		1221	1224			1338	1343				1408	1518	1547
	Douai .... d.		1022	1033	1040	1048	1105		1223	1225	1228	1232	1340	1350	1357			1410	1419	1519
	Valenciennes .... a.				1105							1304			1415					
	Cambrai Ville .... a.					1119														
	Lille Europe .... a.	1015					1123				1303						1450			
	Lille Flandres ...... a.		1045	1053				1201	1244	1247			1302	1404		1402	1402	1437	1532	1541
	Lille Flandres 205 .. d.			1101				1210								1411		1541		
	Roubaix 205 .... a.			1116				1225								1426		1553		
	Tourcoing 205 ...... a.			1120				1228								1429		1556		

		7169 TGV ⑦x	†	✕	Ⓐ	Ⓐ	Ⓒ	7173 TGV ⑤f	✕	7055 TGV Ⓐk	7057 TGV ⑤f	7125 TGV Ⓐk	7263 TGV	Ⓒ	✕	7177 TGV	7267 TGV Ⓐk	2235 Ⓐ	7329 TGV ⑤f	7271 TGV	7275 TGV Ⓐk
	Paris Nord 108 ..... d.	1439						1615		1621		1645	1706	1721			1733	1745	1718	1807	1822	1848
	Longueau .... d.																		1822			
	Amiens .... d.					1606				1619				1724						1823		
	Albert .... d.					1631				1654				1746						1846		
	Arras 108 .... a.	1529				1658	1705			1725		1756		1808	1810		1823		1851	1856	1908
	Arras .... d.	1532	1535a			1649 1659	1707							1810	1810		1826		1853		Ⓐ
	Douai .... a.	1547	1554a			1706 1720	1720							1825	1827		1840		1907		†
	Douai .... d.	1554	1558	1602	1623	1708	1722	1727	1731	1736				1827	1828	1834	1847		1909	1919	1928 1939
	Valenciennes .... a.	1619		1629			1753			1808							1912		1952		1928 1939
	Cambrai Ville .... a.		1627		1700			1803								1904				1958 2010	
	Lille Europe .... a.																			1922	
	Lille Flandres ...... a.					1745	1759				1723		1747	1823	1847	1851		1846	1931			1949
	Lille Flandres 205 .. d.													1832c				1856	1939		
	Roubaix 205 .... a.													1847c				1911	1954		
	Tourcoing 205 ...... a.													1850c				1914	1958		

		578/9 TGV	7331 TGV Ⓐk	7381 TGV ✕	7181 TGV ⑥z	†	⑥	7279 TGV Ⓑ	⑥	Ⓐ	7183 TGV Ⓑh	7283 TGV Ⓐk	7283 TGV ⑦e	2241 2243 ⑤f	2043 G	†	582/3 TGV	7385 TGV G	7287 TGV ⑦e	7095 TGV ⑤f	2249
	Paris Nord 108 ..... d.	1851	1851		1851			1921			1951	2021	2021	1926	1912		2052		2121	2300	2300
	Longueau .... d.													2035	2044						0005
	Amiens .... d.			1851				1942						2034							
	Albert .... d.			1918				2004						2055							
	Arras 108 .... a.		1942	1942		1942	1947	2022			2041	2107	2108	2117			2141		2350	0038
	Arras .... d.	1937	1948	2003		1948	1949	2023	2023		2044	2109	2110	2118	2137	2143			2352	0040
	Douai .... a.	1952	2003	2008				2038	2040		2059	2124	2126	2134	2151	2158			0006	0055
	Douai .... d.	1954	2010	2014	2010	2010	2018	2039	2041	2044	2106	2114	2126	2128	2135	2153	2206y	2210	0008	0057
	Valenciennes .... a.			2046	2035					2112	2131						2240y	2243		
	Cambrai Ville .... a.				2033			2050				2145								
	Lille Europe .... a.	2013															2212			
	Lille Flandres ...... a.				2034			2023	2102	2105		2123	2123	2147	2148	2159			2223	0027	0117
	Lille Flandres 205 .. d.							2032r						2132					2232b	
	Roubaix 205 .... a.							2047r						2147					2247b	
	Tourcoing 205 ...... a.							2050r						2150					2250b	

♦ – NOTES (LISTED BY TRAIN NUMBER)

6708/9 – RIVIERA FLANDRES – runs (from Ventimiglia) except on dates when train 6720/1 runs: ⊨ 1,2 cl. (T2), ⊢ 2 cl. and 🛏 Ventimiglia - Nice - Lille - Tourcoing. Only conveys passengers joining south of Lyon.

6710/1 – ROUSSILLON FLANDRES – runs (from Cerbère) on ⑥ Apr. 1 - May 27: ⊢ 1,2 cl. Cerbère - Lille - Tourcoing.

6720/1 – RIVIERA FLANDRES – runs (from Nice) on Oct. 1,8,15,22,26-31, Nov. 1-7, Dec. 21 - Jan. 4, Feb. 24-27, Mar. 3-6, 10-12, Apr. 14-17, 21-24, 28-30, May 1,6-8,13,14,20,21,25-27: ⊨ 1,2 cl., ⊢ 1,2 cl. (T2), ⊢ 2 cl. and 🛏 Nice - Lille - Tourcoing. Only conveys passengers joining south of Arras.

a – Ⓐ only.
b – Ⓑ (not Oct. 30,31, Nov. 11, Apr. 16,30, May 7,25).
c – Ⓒ (also Oct. 31).
e – Also Nov. 1, Apr. 17, May 1,8; not Oct. 30, Apr. 16,30, May 7.
f – Also Nov. 10, May 24; not Nov. 11, May 26.
h – Not Oct. 31, Nov. 11, May 25.
k – Not Oct. 31.
n – Also Nov. 11, May 25; not Oct. 31, Nov. 12.
q – Not Oct. 31, May 25,26.
r – ✕ only (also Nov. 11, May 25).
t – Also Oct. 31, Nov. 11, May 25.
v – Also Nov. 11, May 25.
x – Also Nov. 1, Apr. 17, May 1,8.
y – 20 minutes later on ✕.
z – Also Oct. 30,31, Nov. 11, Apr. 16,30, May 7,25.

Ⓖ – ①②③④ (not Oct. 31, Nov. 1,10, Apr. 17, May 1,8,24,25).
Ⓡ – ⑤⑥ (also Oct. 31, Nov. 10, May 24,25; not May 26).
TGV – Ⓡ, supplement payable.

* – Paris - Lille by TGV is 227 km.

Table 110   TOURCOING - LILLE - PARIS

1,2 class

Block 1

	Ⓐ	✕	2202 Ⓐ	✕	7150 TGV Ⓐk	✕	7004 TGV Ⓐk	⑥	Ⓐ	7355 TGV Ⓐk	7208 TGV Ⓐk	7212 TGV ✕n	7156 TGV Ⓐk	7216 TGV Ⓐk	7158 TGV Ⓒt	7108 TGV †	✕	✕	7220 TGV Ⓐk
Tourcoing 205 d.			0513								0634			0734					
Roubaix 205 d.			0518								0639			0739					
Lille Flandres 205 a.			0532								0652			0752					
Lille Flandres d.			0540				0621		0630	0701	0718	0718		0801			0759	0812	0831
Lille Europe d.												0733			0702				
Cambrai Ville d.	0519			0547					0645			0721			0744	0753			
Valenciennes d.		0523			0600		0619	0629			0658		0742	0746		0808	0829	0829	0834
Douai a.	0550	0557	0600	0616	0625	0641		0649	0702	0707	0731	0738	0740	0753	0815	0830	0835		
Douai d.			0602		0634	0643					0716	0740	0741		0806	0830	0851	0851	
Arras a.			0616		0648	0657					0733	0755	0759			0851			
Arras 108 d.			0618		0651	0659					0738	0757	0800	0808	0838	0838	0852		0906
Albert d.					0720							0822	0826				0921		0933
Amiens a.					0739							0846	0851				0947		0957
Longueau a.			0651																
Paris Nord 108 a.			0755		0742		0732			0827	0803	0833	0857	0903	0927	0927			0933

Block 2

	7220 TGV Ⓒc	524/5 TGV †	7160 TGV ⑦x	✕	Ⓐ	Ⓒ	7112 TGV Ⓑq	7162 TGV Ⓒt	7232 TGV ✕	✕	⑤⑥	7166 TGV Ⓐk	7116 TGV ✕b	†	7238 TGV ✕	✕	Ⓐ	7242 TGV
Tourcoing 205 d.	0804								1035v							1204		
Roubaix 205 d.	0809								1040v							1209		
Lille Flandres 205 a.	0822								1052v							1222		
Lille Flandres d.	0831			0834			1009		1101		1150			1229	1231	1315		
Lille Europe d.						0933				1138						1333		
Cambrai Ville d.			0809										1313					
Valenciennes d.		0805		0820	0844	0914	0952	0947	0955	1023	1133	1150					1319	
Douai a.	0836	0840	0853	0844	0914	0952	1018	1024	1032	1047	1204	1208	1212	1214	1259	1336	1346	1350
Douai d.			0855	0851			1033		1054		1214	1221	1231	1235	1324	1338	1353	
Arras a.			0911	0905			1050		1108			1231			1324	1355		
Arras 108 d.				0907			1110	1110				1237	1308	1325	1355			
Albert d.																1350	1417	
Amiens a.																1420	1437	
Longueau a.						1033												
Paris Nord 108 a.	0933			0957		1033	1200	1200	1203			1327	1357		1333			1433

Block 3

	Ⓒ	7248 TGV †	7122 TGV Ⓐk	7052 TGV Ⓐ	7174 TGV Ⓑj	✕	Ⓐ	Ⓒ	7260 TGV Ⓒ	7126 TGV Ⓐ	⑥	Ⓐ	7264 TGV Ⓐk	7268 TGV ✕	7268 TGV Ⓒc	Ⓑ	7178 TGV ✕	2236 ⑧h
Tourcoing 205 d.		1438							1634				1704	1733				
Roubaix 205 d.		1443							1639				1709	1738				
Lille Flandres 205 a.		1452							1651				1721	1751				
Lille Flandres d.			1347	1501		1552	1601		1647	1647	1701		1729	1731	1801	1801		1805
Lille Europe d.								1630					1706	1711		1730		
Cambrai Ville d.	1324			1453		1550	1616		1640				1731			1747		
Douai a.	1357	1409		1519	1612	1614	1644	1702	1708	1709	1712	1735	1734	1754	1803	1808	1812	1825
Douai d.		1410		1527	1614	1621			1709	1711			1756		1813	1821	1827	
Arras a.		1427		1545	1629	1636			1725	1727					1835	1841		
Arras 108 d.		1428		1553		1638			1727	1729		1735			1838	1843		
Albert d.		1451							1748	1751								
Amiens a.		1511							1807	1809								
Longueau a.																		
Paris Nord 108 a.			1603		1642	1703	1727		1803	1824			1833	1903	1903		1927	2017

Block 4

	⑥	Ⓐ	Ⓐ	7276 TGV †	7332 TGV ⑦e	Ⓐ	✕	548/9 TGV ⑦e	7280 TGV Ⓑj	†	7182 TGV ◆	6208/6209 Ⓐk	6220/6221 ⑦e	7284 TGV †	7086 TGV †	7386 TGV ⑦e	6210/6211 ◆	7290 TGV † ⑦e
Tourcoing 205 d.								1934			1939	1939	1944	2001			2040	
Roubaix 205 d.								1939			1944	1944	1958	2006			2045	
Lille Flandres 205 a.								1951			1958	1958	2019	2019			2059	
Lille Flandres d.	1803			1850	1851			2001			2002	2009	2009	2031	2101		2120	2129
Lille Europe d.							1903		1916					2027				2203
Cambrai Ville d.			1806						1907		1915		1945			2026		
Valenciennes d.					1829				1915		1938	2010	2025	2030	2030	2056	2059	
Douai a.	1826	1838	1859	1912	1913	1933	1935	1938	2010	2025	2030	2030	2056	2059	2141	2153	
Douai d.	1827			1913	1915	1937			2019	2026	2032	2032			2111	2143	2155	
Arras a.	1844			1930	1932	1952			2034	2043	2047				2126	2200	2213	
Arras 108 d.	1845	1848		1931		1938	1940		2037		2049				2129	2220		
Albert d.		1910	1915	1954				2006										
Amiens a.		1932	1938					2025				2122				2258		
Longueau a.				2014														
Paris Nord 108 a.				2003	2028			2103			2126			2133	2203	2218		2303

◆ – NOTES (LISTED BY TRAIN NUMBER)

6208/9 – FLANDRES RIVIERA – runs except when train 6220/1 runs: ⊨ 1,2 cl. (T2), ⊨ 2 cl. and ⟐ Tourcoing - Lille - Nice - Ventimiglia. Only carries passengers travelling to Lyon or beyond.

6210/1 – FLANDRES ROUSSILLON – runs ⑤ Mar. 31 - May 26: ⊨ 1,2 cl. Tourcoing - Lille - Port Bou.

6220/1 – FLANDRES RIVIERA – runs Sept. 30, Oct. 7,14,21,25-31, Nov. 1-6, Dec. 20 - Jan. 3, Feb. 23-26, Mar. 2-5, 9-11, Apr. 13-16, 20-23, 27-30, May 5-7, 12,13,19,20,24-27: ⊨ 1,2 cl., ⊨ 1,2 cl. (T2), ⊨ 2 cl. and ⟐ Tourcoing - Lille - Nice. Only carries passengers travelling to Lyon or beyond.

TGV – ℝ, supplement payable.
b – Also Nov. 11, May 25.
c – Also Oct. 31.
e – Also Nov. 1, Apr. 17, May 1,8; not Oct. 30, Apr. 16,30, May 7.
g – Not Nov. 11.
h – Not Oct. 31, Nov. 11, Apr. 16,30, May 7.
j – Not Oct. 30,31, Nov. 11, Apr. 16,30, May 7,25.
k – Not Oct. 31.
n – Also Nov. 11, May 25; not Nov. 12.
q – Also Nov. 11, May 25.
t – Also Oct. 31, Nov. 11, May 25.
v – ⑦ only (also Nov. 1, Apr. 17, May 1,8).
x – Also Nov. 1, Apr. 17, May 1,8.

PUBLIC HOLIDAYS IN FRANCE: On the following holiday dates, train services in France are liable to alteration. Passengers travelling on these dates (or on days before or after holidays) are strongly recommended to reserve seats on trains and to recheck timings locally before travelling:

WINTER 1994/95: Nov. 1,11, Dec. 25, Jan. 1, Apr. 17, May 1,8,25.

Table 115

PARIS - ROUEN - DIEPPE and LE HAVRE

Service January 22 - May 27

1,2 class

km				3131	131		13161		13163	3139		3193	3193				13165	3141		3125		3145	13167
		Ⓐ	✕	Ⓐ	✕	✕q	✝	✕		✝	✕		✝		Ⓐ	⑥	Ⓒ	✕	✕	✕	⑥	⑥	✝	✕
0	Paris St. Lazare ...... d.	...	...	0643	0646	0755	...	0740	...	0819	0915	...	1041	1050	...	...	1200	1236	...	1346	...	1346	1422
57	Mantes-la-Jolie .... d.	...	...	...	0720	...	...	0812	...	0852	...	...	...	...	...	...	1232	...	...	...	...	1418	1456
79	Vernon (Eure) .... d.	...	...	0724	0741	...	...	0826	...	0907	...	...	1124	...	...	...	1247	...	...	1427	...	1432	1511
111	Val-de-Reuil .... d.	...	...	...	0806	...	...	0847	...	0925	...	...	1141	...	...	...	1311	...	...	...	...	1450	1529
126	Oissel .... d.	...	...	...	0819	...	...	0857	...	0937	...	...	...	...	...	...	1322	...	...	...	...	1500	1540
140	Rouen Rive-Droite ... a.	...	...	0755	0838	0902	...	0909	...	0950	1026	...	1201	1201	...	...	1335	1345	...	1451	...	1513	1553
140	Rouen Rive-Droite ... d.	0621	0627	0650	0757	...	0904	0912	0911	0917	...	1028	1032	1213	1213	1207	1218	1231	...	1347	1355	1506	1512	1515
154	Clères .... d.	...	0650	...	...	...	...	...	...	...	...	1055	...	...	...	...	...	...	1410	...	1530	...
179	Dieppe .... a.	...	0733	...	...	...	0953	...	0958	...	...	1133	1259	1259	...	...	...	...	1441	...	1602	...
178	Yvetot...................... d.	0649	...	0727	0818	...	0924	...	0936	...	...	1049	...	...	1231	1246	1308	...	1408	...	1527	...	1537	...
203	Bréauté-Beuzeville ... d.	0711	...	0747	0833	...	...	...	0951	...	...	1104	...	...	1245	1301	1331	...	1423	...	1542	...	1552	...
228	Le Havre.................. a.	0728	...	0815	0847	...	0949	...	1005	...	...	1119	...	...	1259	1317	1359	...	1438	...	1556	...	1607	...

	3147		3119		3149		3143	13171		3181	3181	3151		135		13175			3153		3153	3153
	✕	Ⓐ	✕	✕	⑤f	✝	Ⓐ	Ⓐ	⑥	Ⓐ	⑥	Ⓐq	⑤f	✝	⑦	✕	Ⓐ	⑥	Ⓒ	M	Ⓐ	⑤f	⑦e
Paris St. Lazare ...... d.	1513	...	...	1648	...	1700	...	1709	1720	1724	1740	1740	1748	...	...	1840	...	1848	...	1853	1931	...	1951	2004
Mantes-la-Jolie .... d.		...	...	...	...	...	...	...	1752	1802	...	...	...	...	...	...	...	...	...	1935	...	...	...
Vernon (Eure) .... d.		...	...	...	...	...	...	1751	1807	1824	...	...	...	...	...	1933	...	1956	2013	...	...	2045
Val-de-Reuil .... d.		...	...	...	...	...	...	1808	1825	1854	...	...	...	...	...	1954	...	2021	2029	...	...	...
Oissel .... d.		...	...	...	...	...	...	1818	1835	1907	...	...	...	...	...	2005	...	2033	...	...	...	...
Rouen Rive-Droite .... a.	1621	...	...	1802	...	1810	...	1831	1847	1925	1851	1851	1900	...	...	1950	...	2018	...	2051v	2048	...	2102	2115
Rouen Rive-Droite .... d.	1624	1648	1710	1715	1804	1805	1813	1827	1833	...	1853	1903	1911	1911	1952	2000	...	2025	...	2050	2059	2104	2117
Clères .... d.	...	...	1703	1738	...	...	1850	...	...	...	...	...	1924	...	...	...	...	...	...	...	...
Dieppe .... a.	...	...	1732	1817	...	...	1926	...	...	...	...	...	1952	1957	...	...	...	...	...	...	2138	...
Yvetot...................... d.	1645	...	1748	...	1825	1840	1834	...	1854	...	...	1914	1924	...	...	2031	...	2056	...	2111	...	2125	2138
Bréauté-Beuzeville ... d.	1700	...	1809	...	1840	1901	1849	...	1909	...	...	1929	1939	...	...	2046	...	2111	...	2125	...	2140	2153
Le Havre................... a.	1714	...	1835	...	1854	1928	1903	...	1923	...	...	1944	1953	...	2033	2106	...	2132	...	2139	...	2154	2207

	736/7 TGV	3135		3155	13155	3155	3155	3157	3159			13162	13140	3132	3132	3130	13164	13166
	⑦e Y	Ⓐ	⑥h	⑥h	M	⑤f	⑦e	⑤f	H	P			Ⓐ	Ⓐ	Ⓐq	✝	⑥	Ⓐ	Ⓐq	✝	Ⓐ
Paris St. Lazare ...... d.	...	2039	2120	2120	2136	2153	2314	2350		Le Havre...................... d.	...	...	...	0546	0550	...	...	...
Mantes-la-Jolie .... d.	2103	2152	2152	2209	2346		Bréauté-Beuzeville ..... d.	...	...	...	0601	0606	...	...	...
Vernon (Eure) .... d.	2121	2205	2207	2222	0000	0031		Yvetot........................... d.	...	...	...	0617	0621	...	...	...
Val-de-Reuil .... d.	2222	2226	2239	0017	0047		Dieppe .... d.	...	...	...	...	...	...	...	0603
Oissel .... d.	2231	2238	2248	0027	0057		Clères .... d.	...	...	...	...	...	...	...	0640
Rouen Rive-Droite .... a.	2148	2155	2243	2250	2300	2302	0040	0109		Rouen Rive-Droite .... a.	...	...	0637	0641	...	...	0702
Rouen Rive-Droite .... d.	2126	2157	2204	2246	2303	2305	0111		Rouen Rive-Droite .... d.	0538	0556	0625	0637	0639	0643	0646	0708	0706
Clères .... d.	2703	2243		Oissel .... d.	0548	0605	0637	0646	0649	...	0655	...	0719
Dieppe .... a.	2206		Val-de-Reuil .... d.	0558	0618	...	0656	0659	...	0705	0725	0730
Yvetot...................... d.	2218	2307	2324	2330	0132		Vernon (Eure) .... d.	0620	0645	0700	0715	0719	...	0730	0746	0754
Bréauté-Beuzeville ... d.	2233	2322	2339	2344	0147		Mantes-la-Jolie .... a.	...	0713	0718	0732	...	...	0751	0803	0816
Le Havre.................. a.	2248	2337	2354	2359	0201		Paris St. Lazare .... a.	0706	0746	0753	0803	0803	0755	0826	0835

	3134		130	704/5 TGV		3136			3138	3140	13172		3142		13174	3126	712/3 TGV	3144		13176	13180
	Ⓐ	Ⓐ	⑥	Ⓐq Y	✕	Ⓐ		✕	✕	⑦e	✕		✕	✕	✕	✕	✕ Y	✕		Ⓒ	⑤f	Ⓐ
Le Havre.................. d.	0629	...	0657	...	0700	...	0759	...	0842	1007	1109	...	1201	1220	...	1326	...	1402	...
Bréauté-Beuzeville ..... d.	0645	...	...	0726	...	...	0902	1022	1124	...	1217	1248	...	1340	...	1417	...
Yvetot....................... d.	0701	...	0723	...	0747	...	0920	1037	1139	...	1232	1309	...	1354	...	1431	...
Dieppe .... d.	0644	0644	...	0758	0843	...	1202	...	1301	...	...	1620
Clères .... d.	0720	0719	...	0924	...	1338	...
Rouen Rive-Droite .... a.	0725	0736	0740	0744	...	0823	0839	0846	0946	0951	1057	1202	...	1239	1252	1338	1400	...	1416	...	1453	...	1702
Rouen Rive-Droite .... d.	0728	...	0746	0754	...	0848	...	1059	1204	1207	...	1254	...	1412	1418	1431	1455	1643	1657	1713
Oissel .... d.	...	...	...	1214	1217	...	1423	...	1658	...	1723
Val-de-Reuil .... d.	...	...	...	1224	1227	...	1433	...	1710	...	1733
Vernon (Eure) .... d.	0801	...	1241	1250	...	1452	...	1736	...	1754
Mantes-la-Jolie .... d.	...	0837	...	1256	1308	...	1509	1516	1755	...
Paris St. Lazare .... a.	0846	...	0855	...	0957	...	1211	1329	1341	...	1402	...	1541	1529	...	1604	1829	1810	1845

	13180	3128		3148	3148	134		13178		3146	3150		13188	13152	3162	3154		3156	13186	13158	3158
	Ⓒ	⑦e	⑥	⑦e	⑥h	Ⓐq	Ⓐ		✝e	⑥	Ⓐq	⑦e	✕	✕		⑦e	⑥	⑦e	✝	Ⓐ	⑦e	⑦e	⑦e
Le Havre.................. d.	...	1640	1623	1701	1701	1709	1641	...	1818	1822	1823	...	1927	1938	...	2017	...	2113	...
Bréauté-Beuzeville ..... d.	...	1655	1651	1716	1716	1724	1710	...	1835	1838	1848	...	1943	1954	...	2032	...	2128	...
Yvetot....................... d.	...	1710	1712	1731	1731	1738	1731	...	1850	1853	1906	...	1956	2009	...	2046	...	2143	...
Dieppe .... d.	1620	...	1743	1836	...	2003	...
Clères .... d.	...	1821	1922	...	2042	...
Rouen Rive-Droite .... a.	1702	1730	1747	1751	1751	1758	1814	...	1835	1910	1913	1940	1946	...	2018	2029	2103	2108	...	2205	...
Rouen Rive-Droite .... d.	1715	1733	...	1754	1754	1801	...	1834	1830	...	1851	1912	1915	...	1952	2020	2020	2032	...	2110	2120	2157	2207
Oissel .... d.	1725	...	1803	...	1845	1840	...	1904	...	2002	2029	...	2129	...
Val-de-Reuil .... d.	1735	...	1812	...	1859	1850	...	1914	...	2012	2038	...	2139	...
Vernon (Eure) .... d.	1756	...	1831	...	1925	1910	...	1940	...	2034	2057	...	2143	2201	...
Mantes-la-Jolie .... a.	...	1848	...	1948	1927	...	2000	...	2113	...	2158	2218	...
Paris St. Lazare .... a.	1843	1845	...	1908	1919	1908	...	2022	2026	2028	...	2120	2133	2145	2141	...	2230	2252	2308	2321

H – ①②③④⑥ (also Apr. 16,30, May 7,25,26; not Apr. 17, May 1,8,24).

M – ①②③④ (not Apr. 17, May 1,8,24,25).

P – ⑤⑦ (also Apr. 17, May 1,8,24; not Apr. 16,30, May 7,25,26).

TGV –Ⓡ, supplement payable.

Y – ⌷⓵⓶ and ♈ Lyon - Rouen and v.v. (Table 150b).

e – Also Apr. 17, May 1,8; not Apr. 16,30, May 7.

f – Also May 24; not May 26.

h – Also Apr. 16,30, May 7.

q – Not May 26.

v – ✝ only.

✗ – Supplement payable.

Ⓐ – Mondays to Fridays, except holidays   Ⓑ – Daily except Saturdays   Ⓒ – Saturdays, Sundays and holidays

Table 116 LE HAVRE - CAEN 🚌

Service July 6 - Sept. 7, 1994

	⚒§	⚒	⑦§	⑦	⚒	⑦	§		
Le Havre Gare Maritime........ d.	0756	0756	0855	0855	...	...	...	...	...
Le Havre Gare Routière ...... d.	0806	0806	0906	0906	1035	1145	1701	1701	...
Pont Audemer...................... d.	0900	0900	1000	1000	1129	1239	1755	1755	...
Honfleur Gare Routière .... d.	|	0938	|	1038	1207	1317	|	1835	...
Deauville Gare SNCF............ d.	|	1007	|	1107	1240	1350	|	1908	...
Caen Gare Routière/SNCF .. a.	1025	1138	1125	1241	1411	1527	1922	2032	...

	⚒	⚒§	⑦	⑦§	⚒	⑦	⚒	⑦	§	
Caen Gare Routière......... d.	0640	0730	0740	0830	1232	1232	1501	1501	1622	...
Deauville Gare SNCF........... d.	0744	|	0847	|	1401	1412	1632	1634	|	...
Honfleur Gare Routière ..... d.	0814	|	0917	|	1436	1447	1706	1712	|	...
Pont Audemer.................. d.	0900	0900	1000	1000	1525	1530	1755	1755	1755	...
Le Havre Gare Routière .. a.	0949	0949	1049	1049	1615	1620	1844	1844	1844	...
Le Havre Gare Maritime.... a.	...	...	...	...	...	...	1852	1852	1852	...

Operated by Bus Verts du Calvados, 11 rue des Chanoines, 14000 Caen, ☎ 31.44.77.44 Fax: 31.46.17.09.

§ – Express service. Change at Pont Audemer.

Table 117 PARIS - GRANVILLE

1,2 class

On Ⓐ most journeys arrive and depart Paris Montparnasse 3 Vaugirard (allow 10 minutes walk from main concourse)

km		Ⓐ	⑥		3055 Ⓐ	3057 Ⓒ 🍷		†	Ⓐ	3061 ⚒ 🍷		3063 L	⑥	3069 G	3067 H 🍷		3071 ⑤f 🍷	Ⓐ	3065 Ⓒ		3073 G 🍷	3073 ⑤f		⑤f
0	**Paris Montparnasse 125** .. d.	...	...	...	0713	0818	...	0914	0919	1118	...	1412	1432	1637	1637	...	1735	1820	1921	...	1938	1938	...	1941
17	Versailles Chantiers **125** .... d.	...	...	...	|	0832	...	0926	0931	|	...	|	1445	|	1652	...	|	1836	1937	...	|	|	...	1955
82	Dreux.......................... d.	...	...	...	0802	0908	...	1013	1014	1207	...	|	1535	1727	1728	...	|	1921	2027	...	|	|	...	2053
118	Verneuil-sur-Avre .... d.	...	...	...	|	0930	...	1040	1039	1230	...	|	1605	|	1751	...	|	1949	2053	...	|	|	...	2124
142	L'Aigle.......................... d.	0618	...	...	0836	0945	...	1057	1053	1247	...	1539	1624	1802	1808	...	|	2008	2109	...	2059	|	...	2139
183	Surdon **118** .... d.	0653	...	...	|	1008	...	1129	1126	1311	...	1605	1659	1828	1833	...	1923	2038	2141	...	2124	2128	...	...
198	Argentan **118** .... d.	0708	0708	...	0909	1021	...	1141	1136	1323	...	1618	1709	1839	1845	...	1937	2050	2153	...	2135	2141	...	...
226	Briouze.......................... d.	0731	0731	...	0929	1040	...	...	...	1343	...	|	...	1900	1905	...	1958	...	2213	...	2155	2203	...	...
243	Flers.............................. d.	0744	0744	...	0942	1052	...	...	...	1356	...	1649	...	1913	1918	...	2012	...	2226	...	2208	2217	...	...
272	Vire................................ d.	0803	0803	...	1003	1112	...	...	...	1417	...	1711	...	1935	1940	...	2035	...	2248	...	2230	2239	...	...
298	Villedieu.......................... d.	0824	0824	...	1022	1131	...	...	...	1436	...	1731	...	1955	1959	...	2056	...	2308	...	2249	2300	...	...
313	Folligny **119** .... d.	0835	0835	...	1035	1143	...	...	...	|	...	1745	...	2007	2012	...	|	...	|	...	|	2313	...	...
328	**Granville**....................... a.	0845	0845	...	1046	1153	...	...	...	1457	...	1756	...	2018	2023	...	2116	...	2328	...	2310	2324	...	...

	Ⓐ	⑥	†	3052 Ⓐ	3054 Ⓒ 🍷		3056 Ⓐ 🍷	⑥	⑥	Ⓐ	3060 Ⓐ	3062 K	3062 ⑥ 🍷	3062 ⑦g	13266 K	Ⓐ	3068 K	13272 ⑦e	13276 K	3076 ⑦e 🍷	3074 ⚒h 🍷	†	3078 ⑦e 🍷	
Granville....................... d.	...	...	...	0605	0637	...	1005	...	1142	...	1410	1440	1451	1451	...	1623	1637	...	1741	1809	1813	...	1914	1111
Folligny **119** .... d.	...	...	...	0618	0651	...	1018	...	1154	...	|	1451	1502	1502	...	1635	1652	...	1755	1824	1826	...	1926	...
Villedieu.......................... d.	...	...	...	0629	0702	...	1029	...	1205	...	1431	1501	1512	1512	...	1646	1704	...	1807	1836	1837	...	1938	...
Vire................................ d.	...	...	...	0648	0721	...	1048	...	1225	...	1449	1518	1529	1529	...	1706	1724	...	1827	1855	1856	...	1956	...
Flers.............................. d.	...	...	...	0708	0743	...	1108	...	1246	...	1510	1537	1548	1548	1605	1727	1747	...	1850	1918	1916	...	2016	...
Briouze.......................... d.	...	...	...	0722	0757	...	1122	...	1259	...	1524	1550	1601	1601	1620	1739	|	...	1906	1933	1930	...	2030	...
Argentan **118** .... d.	0605	0615	0640	0744	0819	...	1143	1143	1320	1433	1547	1618	1624	1629	1641	1800	1822	1855	1931	1957	1952	...	2051	...
Surdon **118** .... d.	0615	0626	0651	0755	0830	...	1154	1154	...	1444	1558	|	1635	1640	1652	...	|	1907	|	2009	2003	...	|	...
L'Aigle.......................... d.	0648	0655	0721	0818	0856	...	1218	1228	...	1513	1622	|	1658	1703	1717	...	1904	1940	2006	|	2027	2054	2125	...
Verneuil-sur-Avre .... d.	0703	0709	0737	|	0911	...	1234	1247	...	1527	|	|	1712	1718	1732	...	1922	1956	|	|	|	2113	|	...
Dreux.............................. d.	0728	0734	0800	|	0933	...	1256	1317	...	1551	|	|	1734	1740	1754	...	1949	2022	|	|	2102	2203	2159	...
Versailles Chantiers **125** ...... a.	0813	0829	0853	|	|	...	|	1405	...	1633	|	|	|	|	|	...	2030	2103	|	|	|	2300	2236	...
Paris Montparnasse 125 .... a.	0828	0843	0907	0942	1028	...	1347	1419	...	1647	1746	1814	1820	1829	1844	...	2045	2118	2128	2157	2152	2314	2251	...

G – ①②③④ (not Apr. 17, May 1,8,24,25).
H – ⑤⑥⑦ (also Apr. 17, May 1,8,24,25).
K – Apr. 17, May 1,8 only.
L – Apr. 15, May 6 only.
e – Also Apr. 17, May 1,8; not Apr. 16,30, May 7.
f – Also May 24; not May 26.
g – Also May 25.
h – Also Apr. 16,30, May 7,25.

Table 118 ROUEN - CAEN - LE MANS - TOURS

1,2 class

Service January 22 - May 27

km		①g	Ⓐ	Ⓐ	Ⓐ	E	①g	13024	†	B	C	†	⑥	⑤f	⑤f	⚒	†	N	G	G	†	13020 ⑦e	⚒	13022 ⑤f	
0	**Rouen Rive-Droite**... d.	...	...	...	0548	0656	0656	...	0854	*1103*	1116	...	1308	...	1441	...	...	1625	1657	...	1742	...	1827	...	...
14	Oissel **115** .... d.	...	...	...	0558	|	|	...	0907	|	|	...	1327	...	|	...	...	|	|	...	1757	...	1842	...	...
23	Elbeuf St. Aubin .... d.	...	...	...	0606	0712	0712	...	0915	*1119*	1135	...	1335	...	1459	...	...	1642	1715	...	1806	...	1851	...	...
73	Serquigny **120** .... d.	...	...	...	0648	|	0748	...	|	1155	1207	...	1413	...	1529	...	...	|	|	...	1853	...	1930	...	...
83	Bernay **120** .... d.	...	...	...	0657	0748	0756	...	0950	1202	1215	...	1421	...	1537	...	...	1720	1749	...	1901	...	1939	...	...
114	Lisieux **120** .... d.	...	...	...	0719	0808	0816	...	1011	1220	1235	...	1442	...	1557	...	...	1742	1809	...	1922	...	2025r	...	...
	Caen .... d.	0505	...	0607	|	|	|	0836	|	|	|	...	|	...	|	...	...	|	|	1834	|	1942	|	2030	...
139	Mézidon **120** .... a.	0523	...	0626	0744	0831	0838	0855	1033	1241	1258	...	1505	...	1617	...	...	1802	1829	1852	1943	2001	2046	2049	...
139	Mézidon **120** .... d.	0524	...	0627	0745	0832	0839	0857	1034	1242	1259	...	1506	...	1618	...	...	1803	1830	1853	1944	2002	...	2051	...
162	**Caen 120** .... a.	|	...	|	0809	0850	0857	|	1053	1259	1316	...	1524	...	1637	...	...	1825	1847	|	2001	|	...	|	...
183	Argentan .... d.	0550	...	0657	...	...	...	0925	...	▬	...	...	...	...	...	...	...	...	...	1924	...	2037	...	2126	...
198	Surdon .... d.	0600	...	0707	...	...	...	|	...	...	...	...	...	...	...	...	...	...	...	|	...	2048	...	2137	...
227	Alençon.................... d.	0635	0635	0729	...	...	...	0952	...	...	...	...	...	...	...	...	...	...	...	1952	...	2110	...	2158	...
282	**Le Mans** .... a.	0727	0727	0813	...	...	...	1022	...	⚒	...	...	...	...	...	...	...	...	...	2021	...	2139	...	2227	...
282	**Le Mans** .... d.	0740	0740	...	...	...	...	1035	...	1215	...	1238	...	1656	...	1828	1857	...	...	...	...	2211	...	2244	...
331	Chateau du Loir .... d.	0808	0808	...	...	...	...	1105	...	1305	...	1326	...	1733	...	1919	1946	...	...	...	...	2249	...	2323	...
381	St. Pierre des Corps.. a.	|	|	...	...	...	...	1134	...	|	...	|	...	|	...	|	|	...	...	...	...	|	...	|	...
382	**Tours**..................... a.	0836	0836	...	...	...	...	*1150*	...	1355	...	1406	...	1805	...	2005	2022	...	...	...	...	2319	...	2353	...

	Ⓐ	①	E	Ⓐ	M	†	†	13033 ⚒	13033 †	F	D	B	Ⓐ	⑥			⑤	⑥	G	⑤f	N	13038 ⑦e	Ⓐ	13038 ⑤f	Ⓒ
Tours..................... d.	...	0357	...	...	0600	...	0905	0935	...	...	...	...	...	...	1221	...	...	...	1745	1758	1816	1957	2016	2016	2305
St. Pierre des Corps.... d.	...	|	...	...	|	...	|	0951	...	...	...	...	...	...	|	...	...	...	|	|	|	2008	|	|	|
Chateau du Loir .... d.	...	0427	...	...	0642	...	0940	1019	...	...	...	...	...	...	1311	...	...	...	1832	1838	1905	2037	2046	2046	2337
Le Mans .... a.	...	0459	...	...	0730	...	1024	1051	...	...	...	...	...	...	1400	...	...	...	1920	1914	1952	2106	2116	2116	0009
Le Mans .... d.	...	0502	...	0645	▬	...	...	1053	1053	...	...	...	1236	1236	▬	...	...	1758	▬	...	...	2107	...	2119	...
Alençon..................... d.	...	0533	...	0717	...	...	...	1124	1124	...	...	...	1327	1333	...	...	...	1848	...	...	...	2142	...	2151	...
Surdon .... d.	...	0554	...	0738	...	...	...	1145	1145	...	...	...	1350	1357	...	...	...	1909	...	...	...	|	...	|	...
Argentan .... d.	...	0606	...	0750	①g	...	...	1155	1155	...	...	...	1402	1411	...	...	...	1920	†	...	...	2211	...	2220	...
Caen 120 .... d.	0530	|	0642	|	0702	0813	...	|	|	1213	1222	1233	|	|	1649	1745	1843	|	2001	...	...	|	...	|	...
Mézidon **120** .... a.	0545	0638	0656	|	0716	0827	...	1224	1224	1228	1239	1248	1434	1445	1704	1800	1857	1948	2015	...	...	|	...	|	...
Mézidon **120** .... d.	0546	0639	0657	|	0717	0828	...	1225	1225	1229	1240	1249	1435	1446	1705	1801	1858	1949	2016	...	...	|	...	|	...
Caen .... a.	|	0658	|	0836	|	|	...	1244	1244	|	|	|	1454	1504	|	|	|	2008	|	...	...	2255	...	2305	...
Lisieux **120** .... d.	0609	...	0721	...	0753	0903	...	...	...	1253	1301	1311	...	...	1727	1826	1922	...	2041	...	...	...	...	...	...
Bernay **120** .... d.	0632	...	0742	...	0813	0922	...	...	...	1314	1321	1333	...	...	1747	1848	1943	...	2101	...	...	...	...	...	...
Serquigny **120** .... d.	0641	...	0750	...	0821	|	...	...	...	1322	1329	1340	...	...	1755	1856	|	...	|	...	...	...	...	...	...
Elbeuf St. Aubin .... d.	0718	...	0823	...	0853	0955	...	...	...	1352	1359	1411	...	...	1824	1936	2017	...	2134	...	...	...	...	...	...
Oissel **115** .... a.	|	...	|	...	|	1004	...	...	...	1400	1407	1419	...	...	|	1945	2026	...	2142	...	...	...	...	...	...
Rouen Rive-Droite..... a.	0737	...	0842	...	0915	1016	...	...	...	1413	1417	1429	...	...	1841	2000	2036	...	2155	...	...	...	...	...	...

B – Ⓐ Mar. 6 - Apr. 28.
C – Daily except when train **B** runs.
D – Ⓐ May 2 - 27.
E – ②-⑥ (not Apr. 18, May 2,9).
F – Ⓒ (daily Jan. 22 - Mar. 5).
G – ①②③④ (not Apr. 17, May 1,8).
M – ①⑥ (also Apr. 18, May 2,9,26; not Apr. 17, May 1,8).
N – ⑤⑥⑦ (also Apr. 17, May 1,8,24).
e – Also Apr. 17, May 1,8; not Apr. 16,30, May 7.
f – Also May 24; not May 26.
g – Also Apr. 18, May 2,9; not Apr. 17, May 1,8.
r – Arrive 1957.

For explanation of standard symbols see page 4

Table 119 — CAEN - RENNES

1,2 class

km			Ⓐ		B	Ⓐ		H	†		Ⓐ	⑥
0	Caen 120 .... d.		0733	...	1424	...	1718	1858	...	...	...	...
30	Bayeux .... d.		0751	...	1442	...	1736	1919	...	...	...	...
57	Lison .... d.		0810	...	1504	1553	1755	1940	2119	2143	2141	
75	St. Lô .... d.		0824	...	1520	1606	1808	1956	2136	2200	2201	
105	Coutances .... d.		0847	...	1542	1628	1829	2021	2158	2222	2229	
132	Folligny 117 .... d.		0912	...	1603	...	1851	2047	...	...	...	...
151	Avranches .... d.		0926	...	1618	...	1906	2103	...	...	...	...
173	Pontorson .... d.		0943	...	1634	...	1924	2120	...	...	...	...
194	Dol 129 .... d.		1001	...	1652	...	1943	2138	...	...	...	...
252	Rennes 129 .... a.		1033	...	1725	...	2015	2213	...	...	...	...

km			Ⓐ	✕	E	⑥	Ⓐ		F	J	H	⑦b
	Rennes 129 .... d.		...	0818	1305	...	...	...	1626	1719	1818	2046
	Dol 129 .... d.		...	0853	1340	...	...	...	1703	1755	1855	2120
	Pontorson .... d.		...	0910	1356	...	...	...	1720	1812	1914	2137
	Avranches .... d.		...	0932	1418	...	...	...	1745	1834	1938	2159
	Folligny 117 .... d.		...	0947	1434	...	...	...	1802	1852	1954	2214
	Coutances .... d.		0700	1011	1456	1650	1656	1831	1914	2022	2236	
	St. Lô .... d.		0726	1034	1519	1718	1720	1856	1938	2044	2300	
	Lison .... d.		0742	1049	1533	1738	1734	1914	1953	2059	2314	
	Bayeux .... d.		...	1106	1552	...	...	...	1934	2009	2115	...
	Caen 120 .... a.		...	1129	1610	...	...	...	1956	2027	2134	...

B – ①⑤⑥⑦ (also Apr. 17,18, May 1,2,8,9,24,25).
E – ⑤⑦ (also Apr. 17, May 1,8,24,25).
F – ⑤⑥⑦ (also Apr. 17, May 1,8,24,25).

H – ⑤⑦ (also Apr. 17, May 1,8,24,25; not Apr. 16,30, May 7).
J – ①②③④ (not Apr. 17, May 1,8,24,25).
b – Not Apr. 16,30, May 7. To Cherbourg (arrive 0012).

Table 120 — PARIS - CAEN - CHERBOURG

1,2 class

km		3919			3331	3301		3303	3933				3971	3305	3305	3305		3337	3337		3337	3307
		①g	✕	Ⓐ②	✕	①g	C	Ⓐ	①g		✕	†	D	X	Y	†z	⑤f	⑥	A	A	⑥	B	B	⑥	⑥
0	Paris St. Lazare .... d.	0027			0657	0657		0712	0806				0830	0858	0906	0906		1030	1030		1030	1129
57	Mantes-la-Jolie .... d.				0727																		
108	Evreux .... d.	0141		0602	0759	0755			0912									1132	1132		1132	...
150	Serqigny 118 .... d.			0637																		
160	Bernay 118 .... d.	0213		0646	0825	0821			0940									1155	1155		1155	...
191	Lisieux 118 .... d.	0237		0708	0755	0843	0838	0853		0959	1005	1014	1025			1040		1216	1217	1229	1220	1250	1303	1310
209	Pont l'Eveque .... d.			0812			0906			1021	1029	1040								1245		1306		1326
221	Trouville-Deauville ..... a.			0822			0916			1032	1039	1051								1255		1315		1335
245	Dives-Cabourg .... a.												1140											
216	Mézidon 118 .... d.			0731					1024														
239	Caen 118 .... a.	0320		0749		0918	0913		0921	1042				1104	1111	1114		1253		1259		1338
239	Caen 119 .... d.	0350	0719				0916		0924					1114	1114	1117	1220					1341
269	Bayeux 119 .... d.	0412	0738				0933		0940					1133	1130	1133	1239					1357
296	Lison 119 .... d.	0433	0756				0949		0956					1150	1147	1150	1258					1414
314	Carentan .... d.	0447	0808				1001		1007					1201	1158	1201	1311					1425
343	Valognes .... d.	0506	0828				1017		1023					1217	1214	1217	1328					1441
371	Cherbourg .... a.	0531	0850				1035		1042					1236	1233	1236	1349					1500

	3941	3341	3907	3909	3309	3931	3943		3399	3399	3319	3311	3311		3911			137	137	137	
	⑤f	L	⑥	Ⓐb	⑥h	N			P	E	⑤k	n	⑥n	n	R	R	⑥j	Ⓐ	G	⑤f	S	T	W	⑥
Paris St. Lazare .... d.	1151	1158	1227	1255	1334	1331	1408		1446	1452	1452	1500	1500		1500			1640	1640	1640		...
Mantes-la-Jolie .... d.																						
Evreux .... d.	1256	1256	1336	1353			1515														
Serqigny 118 .... d.			1405																		
Bernay 118 .... d.	1324	1322	1415				1543														
Lisieux 118 .... d.	1342	1340	1437	1432			1602		1621	1628		1636	1636	1643	1646	1653			1816	1816	1823
Pont l'Eveque .... d.													1700	1709							1840
Trouville-Deauville ..... a.									1647	1647			1710	1719							1851
Dives-Cabourg .... a.																					
Mézidon 118 .... d.																					
Caen 118 .... a.	1419	1415	1517	1507	1539	1604	1641		1658	1709	1709		1724					1847	1850	1850	
Caen 119 .... d.				1510	1541	1607			1701		1711		1726		1726	1819	1845			1853	1901
Bayeux 119 .... d.				1526	1557	1630			1717		1727		1744		1745	1838	1904			1910	1919
Lison 119 .... d.				1544	1614	1650			1734		1747		1803		1804	1856	1922			1927	1937
Carentan .... d.				1555	1625	1705					1758		1815		1817	1908	1934			1938	1949
Valognes .... d.				1611	1641	1725					1814		1832		1834	1927	1952			1954	2009
Cherbourg .... a.				1630	1700	1749			1813		1833		1853		1855	1949	2011			2013	2029

	3913		3945	3945	3947	3993	3917	3313	3315	3915	3915		133	3355	3353	3355	3355	3977	3923		3321	3921	3357
	⑤t	⑤t	K	⑤f	⑤v	†	⑤f	⑦x	†	⑥	Ⓐ		✕	⑤t	K	†	K	⑤t	⑤t	⑤f	F	V	⑤f
Paris St. Lazare .... d.	1642		1722	1722	1730	1745	1755	1822	1830	1829	1830		1903	1903	1903	1903	1905	1920	1953		2043	2043	2202
Mantes-la-Jolie .... d.				1830		1838	1854							2005	2001	2010		2031			2114	2117	...
Evreux .... d.				1859	1856	1909	1923			2001	2001			2032	2027	2031	2102			2145	2152	2300
Serqigny 118 .... d.					1901																	
Bernay 118 .... d.										2001	2001			2032	2027	2031	2102			2210	2219	2326
Lisieux 118 .... d.	1831	1837	1920	1916	1929	1945		2020	2020	2026			2044	2054	2049	2124			2228	2239	2343
Pont l'Eveque .... d.		1854			1958					2040	2051			2107		2138					
Trouville-Deauville ..... a.		1906			2009					2050	2102			2117		2149					
Dives-Cabourg .... a.																				
Mézidon 118 .... d.													2107							
Caen 118 .... a.	1910		1958	1954	2008		2016	2027	2035	2058	2058		2122	2124		2124		2213		2302	2316	0018
Caen 119 .... d.	1913						2019	2030	2038	2100	2100			2216						2305	2318
Bayeux 119 .... d.	1931						2037	2046	2054	2117	2117			2234						2321	2336
Lison 119 .... d.	1950						2057	2103	2112	2137	2137			2253						2338	2355
Carentan .... d.	2003						2109	2114	2123	2149	2149			2305						2350	0007
Valognes .... d.	2020						2126	2130	2139	2206	2206			2322						0006	0024
Cherbourg .... a.	2041						2147	2149	2158	2227	2227			2344						0024	0046

A – ⑧ (except when train B runs).
B – ④ Mar. 6 - Apr. 28.
C – ②-⑥ (not Apr. 18, May 2,9).
D – ⑥⑦ Apr. 15 - May 7 (also May 25; not Apr. 23).
E – Apr. 14,28, May 24 only.
F – ①②③④⑥ (also Apr. 16,30, May 7,25,26; not Apr. 17, May 1,8,24).
G – ⑤⑦ (also Apr. 17, May 1,8,24,25).
K – ①②③④⑥ (not Apr. 17, May 1,8,24,25).
L – ①②③④ (also May 26; not Apr. 17, May 1,8,24,25).
N – Apr. 15,29, May 6 only.
P – Apr. 15,29 only.
R – Apr. 14,15 only.
S – Daily except ⑤ (not Apr. 16,30, May 7,24,25).
T – ①②③④ (not Apr. 17, May 1,8,24,25).
V – ⑤⑦ (also Apr. 17, May 1,8,24; not Apr. 16,30, May 7).
W – Daily except ⑤.

X – Ⓐ Apr. 3 - May 27.
Y – ⑥ (✕ to Apr. 1). Runs 11-15 minutes later from Caen on Ⓐ Mar. 6-31 and ⑥ Apr. 15 - May 6.
b – Also Apr. 16,30, May 7,25.
f – Also May 24; not May 26.
g – Also Apr. 18, May 2,9; not Apr. 17, May 1,8.
h – Not Apr. 15,29, May 6.
j – Not Apr. 15.
k – Not Apr. 14,28.
n – Not when train R runs.
t – Also May 24.
v – Also May 24; not Apr. 14,28, May 5.
x – Not Feb. 12, Apr. 9,16,30, May 7,25.
z – Runs 12-25 minutes later from Lisieux on Apr. 16,23, May 25.
✎ – Supplement payable.

✕ – Daily except Sundays and holidays   † – Sundays and holidays

Table 120 — CHERBOURG - CAEN - PARIS
1,2 class

Table 120 (part 1)

Train	3328	3330	3936	3336	3334	3370	3334	3318	3970		3302						3300		3906	3310	3310	3312	3312		
Note	①g	✕	Ⓐ	Ⓐ	⑥	⑥	Ⓐ	C	C	†	①g	①g	✕	E	⑥	F	Ⓐ	†	†	⑥	✕b	A	B	Ⓐ	⑥
Cherbourg d.											0521		0553	0557	0614	0614	0659		0709	0851	0911	1029	1044		
Valognes d.											0537		0609	0615	0632	0632	0715			0907	0927	1045	1100		
Carentan d.											0552		0624	0634	0652	0652	0730			0922	0942	1100	1115		
Lison 119 d.											0606		0638	0648	0705	0705	0744		0752	0936	0956				
Bayeux 119 d.											0622		0708		0725	0725	0759		0810	0952	1012				
Caen 119 a.											0640		0708	0730	0749	0749	0818		0830	1010	1030	1140	1155		
Caen 118 d.	0450	0502		0550		0605		0631		0640	0648				0720	0731	0750	0805	0832	1018	1038	1145	1200		
Mézidon 118 d.						0619					0654						0747								
Dives-Cabourg d.			0554	0609			0632			0656							0827			0833	0837				
Trouville-Deauville d.			0604	0619			0642			0707							0839				0848				
Pont l'Eveque d.																									
Lisieux 118 d.	0522	0538	0619	0626	0634	0641		0713	0713	0716	0720		0725	0749		0805	0826	0852	0900	0853	0902	0909	1049	1109	
Bernay 118 d.		0556		0646	0659			0731	0731	0735			0747						0919		0929				
Serqigny 118 d.						0654													0948						
Evreux d.	0607	0623		0715		0726	0732	0759	0759	0802			0818						0948		0959	1133	1153		
Mantes-la-Jolie a.							0816	0831	0831		0831														
Paris St. Lazare a.	0713	0726		0833		0827	0853	0906	0906	0906	0927	0929							1049	1107	1234	1300	1359	1408	

Table 120 (part 2)

Train		3908	3908	3346	3346	3346		3348	3348	3952	3316	3916	3974	3954	3354	3354	3926
Note		M	M	N	N	W	T	†	†	U	D	V	G	G	H	L	P	R	Q	P	⑤f	J	K	⑦e	⑤h
Cherbourg d.				1115		1131		1201			1219		1234					1408	1407						1505
Valognes d.				1136		1152		1222			1241		1256					1424	1426						1524
Carentan d.				1153		1209		1239			1259		1314					1439	1443						1540
Lison 119 d.				1207		1223		1253			1311		1326					1453	1458						1555
Bayeux 119 d.				1228		1244		1314			1332		1347					1509	1515						1612
Caen 119 a.				1247		1303		1333			1351		1406					1527	1536						1633
Caen 118 d.			1206		1220		1304	1312				1340			1359		1414	1443	1532	1539		1556	1604	1611	1636
Mézidon 118 d.																			1501						
Dives-Cabourg d.							1316					1356			1408				1557						
Trouville-Deauville d.		1155		1218				1316				1347	1406		1418				1622						1648
Pont l'Eveque d.		1207		1228				1326											1717						1700
Lisieux 118 d.		1224	1241	1245	1256		1336	1338	1344		1405	1413	1425	1433	1437	1448	1524		1622		1652	1657	1702		1717
Bernay 118 d.			1300		1315				1402					1451		1506					1700	1706	1710		
Serqigny 118 d.														1518		1533	1619								
Evreux d.			1329		1344		1418		1429		1455			1518							1729	1734	1734	1755	
Mantes-la-Jolie a.									1501																1557
Paris St. Lazare a.			1437		1452		1522		1532		1557		1622	1634		1732	1740	1802	1827	1837	1837	1837		1903	

Table 120 (part 3)

Train	3986		3960	3960	3958	3920	136	136	3982		3902		3922		3366	3962	3962	3320	3386	3322	3326	3924	3928	
Note	S	⑥	⑥	①-④	Ⓐ	†	⑤f	⑦e	✕	P	⑦e	⑦e	Ⓐ	⑦e	✕k	①g	⑦e	X	⑤f	†	①g	Y	⑦e	⑦e	†
Cherbourg d.						1613		1703			1742	1800	1812			1829	1849		1910	1919	1933	2017	2229
Valognes d.								1719				1823	1831			1850	1905		1926	1935	1952	2036	2248
Carentan d.								1734				1844	1847			1907	1920		1941	1950	2009	2052	2305
Lison 119 d.						1659		1748			1830	1859	1902			1923	1935		1957	2004	2013	2038	2319
Bayeux 119 d.						1718		1804			1851	1918			1936	1942	1951		2013	2020	2031	2057	2138	2355
Caen 119 a.						1740		1822			1914	1939	1936			2004	2009		2031	2036	2043	2100	2141
Caen 118 d.			1724		1728	1729	1742	1830	1830		1916		1938	1953	1944	2007	2007	2017	2031		2057		
Mézidon 118 d.									1757						1953	1958		2031					
Dives-Cabourg d.														1946				2106					
Trouville-Deauville d.	1724	1724		1728				1854	1913				1956							2120		2215	
Pont l'Eveque d.	1735	1734	1800	1739				1924															
Lisieux 118 d.	1756	1752	1800	1757	1804	1808		1919	1944	1957		2019	2012		2020	2046	2046	2054		2120	2138		
Bernay 118 d.			1819		1823										2038	2109	2109	2112					
Serqigny 118 d.															2119	2119					2205		2301
Evreux d.			1848		1852	1856									2105	2145	2145	2140		2223	2223		2212
Mantes-la-Jolie a.																					2306	2323	
Paris St. Lazare a.	1955		1954		1958	2003	2010	2037	2037	2121		2159		2209	2206	2257	2257	2243	2305	2243	2306	2323	0009

Notes

A – Ⓒ (daily Sept. 25 - Apr. 2).
B – Ⓐ Apr. 3 - May 26.
C – ②-⑥ (not Apr. 18, May 2,9,25).
D – ⑤ Jan. 6 - Mar. 3.
E – ②③④⑤ Mar. 7 - Apr. 28 (not Apr. 18).
F – Ⓐ (except dates in note E).
G – Ⓐ Mar. 6 - May 26.
H – ⑥; also ①②③④ Jan. 30 - Mar. 4.
J – ①②③④ Mar. 6 - Apr. 27 (not Apr. 17).
K – ①②③④⑥ (except when train J runs). Also runs May 26; not May 1,8,24,25.
L – ⑥ (also ①-⑤ Jan. 30 - Mar. 3).
M – Daily except when train N runs.
N – Ⓐ Mar. 6 - Apr. 28.
P – Apr. 17, May 1,8 only.
Q – Apr. 17,23, May 1,8 only.

R – Daily except Apr. 17,23, May 1,8.
S – ⑦ to Apr. 9 (also May 14,21).
T – ⑤ Mar. 10 - May 26 (also May 24).
U – ⑤ Feb. 3 - Mar. 31.
V – ①②③④ Mar. 6 - May 23 (not Apr. 17, May 1,8).
W – ⑤ Apr. 7 - May 26 (also May 24).
X – Apr. 16,30, May 7,25 only.
Y – ②③④⑥ (also May 26; not Apr. 18, May 2,9,24,25).
b – Runs 8 minutes later Lisieux - Paris on Ⓐ Mar. 6 - Apr. 28.
e – Also Apr. 17, May 1,8; not Apr. 16,30, May 7.
f – Also May 24; not May 26.
g – Also Apr. 18, May 2,9; not Apr. 17, May 1,8.
h – Also May 24; not Apr. 14.
k – Not Apr. 14,28, May 5.
↗ – Supplement payable.

Table 120a — AMIENS - ROUEN
1,2 class

km		✕	†	✕	Ⓒ	Ⓐ	Ⓐ	†	⑥	†			Ⓐ	⑥	†	✕	Ⓐ	Ⓐ	⑥	Ⓐ	⑥
	Lille Flandres 110 d.	0621					1647				Rouen Rive-Droite d.		0646	0646	0917	1215	1629	1812	1812	1820	1921
0	Amiens d.	0742	0927	1227	1538	1613	1814	1845	1903	2011	Serqueux d.		0722	0727	0953	1300	1707	1844	1848	1849	2002
52	Abancourt d.	0814	1005	1310	1614	1649	1844	1944	1948	2047	Abancourt d.		0741	0758	1009	1317	1723	1858	1903	1903	2019
73	Serqueux d.	0828	1024	1326	1630	1706	1900	2001	2006	2102	Amiens a.		0816	0832	1040	1359	1755	1928	1936	1936	2052
121	Rouen Rive-Droite a.	0900	1100	1405	1707	1743	1934	2042	2042	2137	Lille Flandres 110 a.		0943					2101		2102	

Table 120b — ST. BRIEUC - DINAN
1,2 class

km		✕		✕					✕	J	K	
0	St Brieuc d.		0727		1236		1724	Dol 129 d.		1020	1020	
21	Lamballe d.		0745		1254		1741	Dinan d.	0638	1043	1043	1824
62	Dinan d.		0822		1331		1819	Lamballe d.	0719	1120	1130	1902
	Dol 129 a.				1408			St Brieuc a.	0738	1138	1148	1919

J – Ⓐ Sept. 25 - Dec. 16.   K – Ⓒ (daily Dec. 19 - May 27).

Ⓐ – Mondays to Fridays, except holidays   Ⓑ – Daily except Saturdays   Ⓒ – Saturdays, Sundays and holidays

Table 121 — (PARIS) - RENNES - BREST
1,2 class

km	Station	8705 TGV ⚒2	8707 Ⓐ	8709 TGV Ⓒ	13643 ⚒k ⑥	8617 TGV ⑥	89125 ⑥	8719 TGV C	8719 TGV E	8627 TGV ⑤f	13645 ⑤f	8737 TGV 5f	8641 TGV ⚒
	Paris Montparnasse 125 … d.	…	…	0725	0805	1020	0820	1120	1135	1300	…	1420	1520
	Le Mans 125 … d.	…	…	…	0917	…	…	…	…	1355	…	1516	…
	Rennes 125 … a.	…	…	0929	1009	1224	1036	1324	1339	1509	…	1630	1724
0	Rennes … d.	…	0634	0932	1012	1234	1046	1343	1328	1519	1633	1640 / 1643	1742
80	Lamballe … d.	…	0713	…	…	1312	1125	…	…	1559	…	1718 / 1743	1821
101	St. Brieuc … d.	0625	0731	1021	1058	1325	1139	1416 / 1423	1431 / 1439	1612	1724	1731 / 1750 / 1758	1835
132	Guingamp … d.	0649	0752	1039	…	1342	1156	1444	1456	1629	1741	1748 / 1820	1854
158	Plouaret … d.	0711	0807	…	1016	1357	1211	1504	1513	1645	1650	1802 / 1846	1908
175	Lannion … a.	0733	0828	…	…	…	1231 / 1215	1525	1534	…	1706	1902	…
189	Morlaix … d.	0740	0824	1107	1034	1415	1230	1522	1532	1703	…	1810 / 1820	1927
215	Landivisiau … d.	0807	0840	…	1049	1430	1246	…	…	1719	…	1844	1943
230	Landerneau … d.	0820	0850	…	1059	1440	1256	…	…	1729	…	1857	1953
248	Brest … a.	0839	0902	1138	1113 / 1206	1454	1308	1524	1539	1742	…	1842 / 1915	2007

km	Station	8753 TGV ⑤f	8647 TGV ⑧h	3617 ⑤f	8755 TGV ⚒n	13659 H	J †	8759 TGV ⑤f	8763 TGV J	8773 K	3647 ⑤f	8777 TGV L	M	8679 TGV ⑤f	3721 TGV ⑤f	8679 TGV ⑦e	3621 ⑦e	8799 TGV ①g	3627 K W	3727 ⑦e X
	Paris Montparnasse 125 … d.	…	…	…	1705	1620	1502 / 1720	1755	1810	1905	1741	1920	…	1955	1913	1955	…	0001	2300	2320
	Le Mans 125 … d.	…	…	…	1715	1653	…	…	…	…	…	2016	…	2052	…	2052	…	0115	…	0123
	Rennes 125 … a.	…	…	…	1833	1823	1924	1959	2013	…	2053	2130	2211	2217	2211	…	…	0215	0301	0307
0	Rennes … d.	…	1752	1815	1846	…	1934	2002	2015	2053	2056	2133	…	2230	2230	0218	0313	0323		
80	Lamballe … d.	…	1832	1920	1930	…	2014	2044	…	2137	2214	…	2311	2311	…	0358	0406			
101	St. Brieuc … d.	…	1846	1931 / 1953	2001	…	2026	2058	2102 / 2157	2205	2226	2324	2324	0307	0427	0420				
132	Guingamp … d.	…	1904	…	2021	…	2044	2115	…	2222	2244	2342	2342	…	0450	0439				
158	Plouaret … d.	1913	1919	1950	2038	2058	2103 / 2131	2237	2259 / 2304	2358	2358	…	0510	0456						
175	Lannion … a.	1929	…	2006	2059	…	2119 / 2152	…	2320	0021	0021	…	0536							
189	Morlaix … d.	…	1937	…	2058	…	2116	2150	…	2256	2316	0016	0016	…	0536	0517				
215	Landivisiau … d.	…	1953	…	…	2131	…	…	…	0032	0032	…	0556	0534						
230	Landerneau … d.	…	2003	2123	…	2141	…	2213	…	2339	0042	0042	…	0609	0546					
248	Brest … a.	…	2017	2101	2136	2153	2225 / 2210	2305	2329	2351	0055	0055	0418	0623	0600					

km	Station	8710 13640 N	8712 TGV ⚒	⑥	†	Ⓐ	8612 TGV ⚒	8714 TGV ⚒2	8722 TGV E	8722 E Q	8724 TGV U	13648 3634 ①g ①-⑥	8630 TGV E	8630 TGV C'	H	8738 TGV ⚒	8754 ⑧h
	Brest … d.	…	0454	…	…	0546	…	0644	0649	…	0855	0929	1032	…	…	1259	1514
	Landerneau … d.	…	…	…	…	0557	…	0656	0705	…	0906	…	1044	…	…		
	Landivisiau … d.	…	…	…	…	0607	…	…	0718	…	0916	…	1054	…	…		
	Morlaix … d.	…	0526	…	…	0623	…	0719	0743	…	0931	…	1109	…	…	1330	
	Lannion … d.	…	…	…	…	0613	…	0650	…	…	0923	1059	…	…		1330	
	Plouaret … d.	…	…	…	…	0641	…	0710	0737	…	0950	…	1116 / 1127	…	1301	1310	
	Guingamp … d.	…	0555	…	0643	0656	…	0730	0752	…	1005	1142	…	…	1319	1326	
	St. Brieuc … d.	0609	0613	0630	0700	0714	…	0757	0810	0934	0943	1023 / 1037	1201	…	…	1337 / 1342	1359
	Lamballe … d.	0620	0625	0641	0712	0726	…	0757	0934	0946	0955	1035	1213	…	…	1429	
	Rennes … a.	0700	0707	0744	0806	0806	…	0856	0904	1048	1058	1115 / 1122	1253	…	…	1509	1709
	Rennes 125 … a.	…	0710	0710	…	…	0816	0904	1058	1108	1125	1301 / 1304	…	…		1514	1714
	Le Mans 125 … a.	…	0822	0822	…	…	0934	…	1217	1227	1422 / 1427	…	…		1720	1920	
	Paris Montparnasse 125 … a.	…	0920	0920	…	…	1030	1110r	1315	1325	1520 / 1525	…	…		1720	1920	

km	Station	8664 13650 ⚒	8762 TGV ⚒	†	8770 TGV ⚒	3618 ⑦e	3618 ⑧x	8770 TGV ⚒2	13652 ⑦e	8784 TGV ⚒	8782 TGV P	8786 TGV †	8782 TGV ⚒	8798 TGV ⑦e	K	3626 ⑤f Y	3624 ⑦e Y	3628 ⑦e Y
	Brest … d.	1540	…	1600	1633	1633	…	1648	1729	…	1757	1814	1842 / 1851	1846 / 1856	1924	…	2240	2250	2300
	Landerneau … d.	1552	…	…	1646	1646	…	1709	1741	…	1834	…	1859	1908	…	2255	2304	2313
	Landivisiau … d.	1602	…	…	1657	1657	…	1722	1752	…	1848	…	1910	1918	…	2308	2304	2324
	Morlaix … d.	1617	…	1632	1714	1714	…	1747	1809	…	1829	1913	1923	1926 / 1934	1956	…	2331	2329	2342
	Lannion … d.	1602	…	1602	…	1706	…	1805	1805	…	1919	…	2325	…					
	Plouaret … d.	1636	…	1620	1734	1734	…	1817	1830	1823	…	1946	1955	…	2342	2355 / 2351	0001	
	Guingamp … d.	1650	…	1639	1701	1749	1749	…	1847	1858	1843	1952	2002 / 2012	2026	…	0016	0009	0018
	St. Brieuc … d.	1708	…	1708	1719	1731	1807	1807	…	1841	1906	1916	1951	2010 / 2025	2033 / 2044	…	0016	0046	0038
	Lamballe … d.	1722	…	1732	1746	1821	1821	…	1855	1921	2038 / 2046	…	0104	0052					
	Rennes … a.	1803	…	1810	1845	1901	1901	…	1950	2002	2003	2057 / 2119	2126	…	0154	0145	0135	
	Rennes 125 … d.	…	1818	1814	…	1917	1913	…	2014	2008	2102	…	0218	0210	0157				
	Le Mans 125 … a.	…	1941	…	2039	…	2122	…	2217	…	0353	0337							
	Paris Montparnasse 125 … a.	…	2040	2020	2229	2120	…	2225	2240	2315	2335	…	0620	0620	0610				

C – ⑥⑦ (daily Sept. 25 - Feb. 12 and Apr. 3 - May 27).
E – Ⓐ Feb. 13 - Mar. 31.
H – ①②③④⑥ (not Apr. 17, May 1,8).
J – ①②③④ (not Apr. 17, May 1,8,24,25).
K – ⑤⑦ (also Apr. 17, May 1,8,24; not Apr. 16,30, May 7).
L – Daily except ⑤ (not May 24).
M – ①②③④⑥ (also Apr. 16,30, May 7,25; not Apr. 17, May 1,8,24).
N – ②–⑥ (not Apr. 17,18, May 1,2,8,9,25).
P – ⑤⑥ (also Apr. 16,30, May 7,24).
Q – ⑥ (⚒ Sept. 25 - Feb. 11 and Apr. 3 - May 26).
TGV – Ⓡ, supplement payable.
U – ⑥⑦ (daily Sept. 25 - Feb. 12 and Apr. 3 - May 26).
W – ⚋⚋ and ⚒ Paris - Brest (also ⚋ 1,2 cl. on ⑤ and May 24; not May 26).
X – 1,2 cl. Paris - Brest and v.v.
Y – ⚋⚋ and ⚋ 1,2 cl. Brest - Paris.

e – Also Apr. 17, May 1,8; not Apr. 16,30, May 7.
f – Also May 24; not May 26.
g – Also Apr. 18, May 2,9; not Apr. 17, May 1,8.
h – Not Apr. 16,30, May 7,25,26.
k – Also May 25.
n – Also Apr. 16,30, May 7,25.
r – Arrive 1115 on †.
v – Also Apr. 16,30, May 7,24.
x – Not May 25.

Table 122 — MORLAIX - ROSCOFF
1,2 class

km	Station	⚒	†	⚒	🚌 J	🚌 K		†	🚌 A	🚌 ⑤f			Station	🚌 ⑥	🚌 Ⓐ	🚌	⚒		†	⚒	🚌
0	Morlaix 121 … d.	0753	0930	1115	1230	1315		1530	1815	1950	2155		Roscoff … d.	0625	0705	1030	1248		1637	1715	1910
21	St. Pol de Léon … a.	0814	0951	1136	1300	1315		1551	1850	2005	2210		St. Pol de Léon … d.	0635	0715	1038	1256		1645	1725	1920
28	Roscoff … a.	0821	0958	1143	1315	1330		1558	1905	2020	2225		Morlaix 121 … a.	0709	0750	1057	1315		1704	1759	1945

A – Daily except ⑤ (also runs Nov. 11; not Nov. 10, May 24).
J – ⑥ Sept. 25 - Dec. 17; ⚒ Dec. 19 - May 27.
K – Ⓐ Sept. 25 - Dec. 16.
f – Also Nov. 10, May 24; not Nov. 11.

① – Mondays ② – Tuesdays ③ – Wednesdays ④ – Thursdays ⑤ – Fridays ⑥ – Saturdays ⑦ – Sundays

Table 123 — (PARIS) - LE MANS - NANTES - LE CROISIC

Service January 23 - May 27

1,2 class

Southbound (Paris → Le Croisic) — part 1

km	Station	8899 TGV ①g	8901 TGV ✕	8805 TGV ✕	8807 TGV Ⓐk	8909 TGV †	8813 TGV Ⓐ	728/9 TGV ⑥ O	8823 TGV	730/1 TGV L	8929 TGV E L	8933 TGV G	8933 TGV H	8839 TGV Ⓐ F
0	Paris Montparnasse 125 d.	0005	…	…	0645	0715	0750	…	0850	0940	1130	1340	1350	1350	1450
211	Le Mans 125 d.	0101	0625	…	0811	0818	0846	0832	…	1037	1138	1226	1301	1307	…
260	Sablé d.	…	0654	…	…	…	…	…	…	…	…	…	…	…	…
308	Angers St. Laud 127 d.	0139	0749	0623	0853	0914	0919	0925	1021	1116	1216	1223	1304	1306	1621
362	Ancenis 127 d.	…	…	0712 0821	…	0958	…	…	…	…	…	…	…	…	…
396	Nantes 127 a.	0224	0840	0742	0853	0938	1004	1017	1106	1201	1300	1330	1349	1706	
396	Nantes 126 d.	…	0653 0759	…	0856	0932	1019	1109	1209	1356	1553	1613	1642	1704	
435	Savenay 126 d.	…	0721 0832	…	0958	1231	1432	1628							
460	St. Nazaire d.	…	0740 0857	…	0928	1012	1054	1145	1246	1450	1501v	1649	1727	1737	
475	Pornichet d.	…	0757c 0907	…	1023	1106	1259	1508v	1643	1705	1744				
479	La Baule Escoublac d.	…	0803c 0913	…	1030	1112	1200	1302	1521v	1652	1713	1757			
489	Le Croisic a.	…	0815c 0925	…	1043	1124	1209	1319							

Southbound (Paris → Le Croisic) — part 2

Station	8843 TGV ⑤q	8947 TGV ✕	⑥h	⑤f	✕	Ⓑ	†	8849 TGV ⑤q	ⓈV	8955 TGV ⑤f	8957 TGV V	3861 TGV Ⓐ	8859 TGV ⑤f	8863 TGV ⑤q	8967 TGV †	8869 TGV ⑤f N	8975 TGV ⑤q	3789 TGV ⑤f
Paris Montparnasse 125 d.	…	…	1540	…	1610	…	…	1650	1725 1730	…	1619	1750 1750	1815	1840	1845	1925	1810	
Le Mans 125 d.	1527	…	…	…	1714	1730	1746	1821 1846	1940	1956								
Sablé d.	1550	…	…	…	1750	1759	1845	2000	2021									
Angers St. Laud 127 d.	1626	1709	…	1751	1815	1818	1827	1824	1910	1924	1923	2021	2055					
Ancenis 127 d.	1658	1754	1818	1834	1858	1903	1929v	1909	1935	1938	1922v	2005 2009 2009	2025	2048	2110	2135	2149	
Nantes 127 a.	1718	…	…	1903	1906	1915	1938	1941	1922r	2015	2051	2138						
Nantes 126 d.	…	1723	1808	1830	1925	1946	2003r	2042	2103	2126	2214							
Savenay 126 d.	…	1745	1833	1907	1940	1941	2007	2014	2014	2024	2113	2126	2227					
St. Nazaire d.	…	1801	1847	1920	1951	1953	2034	2113	2227									
Pornichet d.	…	1819	1902	2030	2041	2120	2233											
La Baule Escoublac d.	…	1829	1910	1958	1959	2030	2041	2120	2141	2233	2245							
Le Croisic a.	…	1842	1924	2011	2011	2038	2054	2132	2150	2245								

Southbound (Paris → Le Croisic) — part 3

Station	8879 TGV P	8885 TGV ⑤f	3771 TGV ⑤f	8887 TGV V	738/9 TGV L	3787 TGV ⑦e	8889 TGV ⑤q	8895 TGV M	T
Paris Montparnasse 125 d.	1950	…	2020	1950	2050	…	2120	2240	…
Le Mans 125 d.	…	…	…	2137	2146	2153	…	…	…
Sablé d.	…	…	…	…	…	…	…	…	…
Angers St. Laud 127 d.	…	2150	2223	2224	2230	…	2250	0010	…
Ancenis 127 d.	…	…	…	…	…	…	…	…	…
Nantes 127 a.	2158	2236	2312	2309	2315	…	2336	0056	…
Nantes 126 d.	…	2203 2207	2333	2331	…	…	…	…	…
Savenay 126 d.	…	2228 2229	2355	2354	…	…	…	…	…
St. Nazaire d.	…	2244 2245	0011	0011	…	…	…	…	…
Pornichet d.	…	2256	0023	0022	…	…	…	…	…
La Baule Escoublac d.	…	2303	0031	0031	…	…	…	…	…
Le Croisic a.	…	2316	0046	0046	…	…	…	…	…

Northbound (Le Croisic → Paris) — part 1

Station	8800 TGV ①g	8802 TGV Q	8904 TGV ①g	8904 TGV Q	8806 TGV ①gn	Ⓐ	⑥	8812 TGV O	Ⓐ
Le Croisic d.	…	…	…	…	0458	…	0600	0616	…
La Baule Escoublac d.	…	…	…	…	0510	…	0612	0629	…
Pornichet d.	…	…	…	…	0517	…	0617	0636	…
St. Nazaire d.	…	…	0535	0539	0544	…	0628	0649	…
Savenay d.	…	…	0551	…	0558	…	0643	0704	…
Nantes 126 a.	0500	0527	0611 0611	0619	…	0705	0725	…	…
Nantes 127 d.	0500	0527	0615	0615	…	0629	0636	0708	0732
Ancenis 127 d.	0518	…	…	…	0647y	0657	…	…	…
Angers St Laud 127 d.	0550	0612	…	…	0719	0743	0752	0817	…
Sablé d.	0613	0634	…	…	0813	…	…	…	…
Le Mans 125 d.	0632	0654	…	…	0757	0842	…	…	…
Paris Montparnasse 125 a.	0730	0750	0825	0825	0855	…	…	0950	…

Northbound (Le Croisic → Paris) — part 2

Station	8814 TGV Ⓐ	706/7 TGV ✕	8920 TGV L	Ⓐ	⑥	8826 TGV ✕	Ⓐ	⑥	Ⓐ	8834 TGV ⑥x	710/1 TGV ✕ L	8938 TGV ⑥b	708/9 TGV ⑧p	Ⓐ	8848 TGV ⑧q	Ⓐ	Ⓐ
Le Croisic d.	…	0645	0735	0733	…	0833	0848	1010	…	1152	…	1326	…	1505	…	1548	…
La Baule Escoublac d.	…	0657	0748	0745	…	0843	0901	1022	…	1209	1337	…	1517	1601	…		
Pornichet d.	…	0705	0755	0753	…	0908	1028	…	1216	…	1523	1608	…				
St. Nazaire d.	0652	0715	0806	0804	…	0858	0920	1039	…	1227 1227	1352	…	1534	1620	1635		
Savenay d.	0712	0740	0821	0820	…	0936	1053	…	1245 1245	…	1551	1638	1653				
Nantes 126 a.	0746	0802	0843	0847	…	0932	1000	1114	…	1313 1313	1426	…	1612	1705	1717		
Nantes 127 d.	0737	…	…	0853	0903	0937	1122	1253	1328 1338	1431	1529	1532	1622	1625	1736		
Ancenis 127 d.	0757	…	…	…	…	1317	…	1549	…	1804							
Angers St Laud 127 d.	0842	…	0938	0948	1207	1232	1404	1413 1423	1517	1614	1622	1645	1708	1720	1756	1857	
Sablé d.	…	…	…	1310	…	1645	…	1756									
Le Mans 125 a.	…	1017	1026	1340	1452	1501	1652	1714	1747	1824							
Paris Montparnasse 125 a.	…	1115	1150	1340	1550	1650	1845										

Northbound (Le Croisic → Paris) — part 3

Station	8954 TGV Ⓐk	8858 TGV	8962 TGV ⑦e	8862 TGV ⑧q	†	8866 TGV ⑦e	Ⓐ	⑥	8968 TGV ⑦e	3866 TGV ⑦e	8970 TGV ✕z	8978 TGV ⑦e	Ⓐ	8886 TGV Ⓐk	8892 TGV ⑦e	8894 TGV ⑦e	8998 TGV ⑦e
Le Croisic d.	…	…	1634	…	…	1733	1757	1803	1814	1841	1853	1909	2016				
La Baule Escoublac d.	…	…	1648	…	…	1744	1807	1813	1828	1854	1909	1922	2029				
Pornichet d.	…	…	1701	…	…	1750	1834	1900	1916	1928	1939	2036					
St. Nazaire d.	1649	…	1704	1711	…	1803 1803	1827	1827	1846	1913	1916	1928	2047	2109			
Savenay d.	…	…	1729	1729	…	1820	1822	1906	1934	1943	2108						
Nantes 126 a.	1722	…	1800	1756	…	1844	1854	1859	1903	1936	1947	2003	2005	2013	2135	2142	
Nantes 127 d.	1725	1733 1736	…	1820	1820	1823	1833	1841	1903	1906	1908	1952	2008	2010	2018	2052	2145
Ancenis 127 d.	…	1801	…	…	1841	1852	1906	1926	…								
Angers St Laud 127 d.	…	1819 1849	…	1915	1923	1944	2001	1953	2117	2055	2104	2114					
Sablé d.	…	1841	…	1940	1947	2026	…	2201	2151								
Le Mans 125 a.	…	1902	…	2004	2006	2050	2032	2205									
Paris Montparnasse 125 a.	1935	2000	2035	2035	2105	2115	2242	2130	2350	2225	2250	2305	2355				

Notes

E – ⑥⑦ (also Apr. 17, May 1,8; not Apr. 16,30, May 7,14,21).
F – ⑤⑥ (also May 24,25).
G – ⑤⑥ (also May 24; not May 26).
H – ①②③④⑦ (also May 26; not May 24).
L – 🔄 Nantes - Lyon and v.v. (Table 150a).
M – ⑤⑦ (also Apr. 17, May 1,8,24; not Apr. 16,30, May 7,26).
N – ①②③④⑥ (also Apr. 16,30, May 7,25; not Apr. 17, May 1,8,24).
O – 🔄 Orléans - Nantes - Le Croisic and v.v.
P – ①②③④⑦ (not Apr. 16,30, May 7,24,25).
Q – ②③④⑤ (not Apr. 18, May 2,9,25,26).
S – ①②③④ (not Apr. 17, May 1,8, May 24,25).
T – ①②③④ (also May 26 and ⑥ Jan. 28 - Apr. 1; not May 1,8).

b – Not Apr. 16,30, May 7,25.
c – Ⓐ only.
e – Also Apr. 17, May 1,8; not Apr. 16,30, May 7.
f – Also May 24; not May 26.
g – Also Apr. 18, May 2,9; not Apr. 17, May 1,8.
h – Not May 25,26.
k – Not May 26.
n – Not Apr. 17, May 1,8,25.
p – Not May 25.
q – Not Apr. 16,30, May 7,25,26.
r – ⑤ only (also May 24).
v – ⑥ only.
x – Not May 13 - 27.
y – Not ① or Apr. 16,30, May 7,25.
z – Also Apr. 16,30, May 7,25.

TGV – Ⓡ, supplement payable.
V – Daily except ⑤ (not May 24).

✕ – Daily except Sundays and holidays   † – Sundays and holidays

Table 125

PARIS - LE MANS - RENNES

1, 2 class

km		8699 TGV ①g	8899 TGV ①g		8601 TGV ※ 2	13613 ※	Ⓐ	8805 TGV Ⓐ	8705 TGV †	8707 TGV Ⓐ	8709 TGV ⑥		8709 J	J	8613 TGV ※	K	Ⓐ		8813 TGV †	8617 TGV b	728/9 TGV ⑥	Ⓐ		8721 TGV E	8823 TGV
0	Paris Montparnasse 125a d.	0001	0005	...	0629	0650	0700	0700	0715	0725	0805	0820		0829	0835	0920	0929	0929	0940	1020	...	1114	1120	1130
	Lyon Part Dieu 150a d.			...																	0818			
17	Versailles Chantiers 125a d.			0642		0713	0712				0842				0942	0941				1127			
88	Chartres ▲ d.			0739		0756	0758				0938				1028	1039				1227			
*202	Le Mans d.		0059	0617c 0909n	0745	0910	0924	0809			0917		0932			1034			1141	1409		1224
292	Laval d.	0138		0729		0826					0959	1007	1014									
327	Vitré d.												1033									
365	Rennes a.	0215		0813		0903			0929	1009	1036		1051	1124			1224	1255q		1324		

		8721 TGV F	8623 TGV K	730/1 TGV M	8623 TGV J		※	†	8627 TGV ⑤f	8629 TGV ⑤	8933 TGV		8737 TGV G	†	13617 ⑤f	3617 ※	13617	8641 TGV ⑧h	8647 TGV ⑤f	3861 Ⓐ		3741 ⑤f	8849 TGV Ⓐ	Ⓐ	8755 TGV ※	Ⓐ
	Paris Montparnasse 125a d.	1135	1205		1220	1229	1259	1300	1340	1350	1355	1404	1420	1430	1502	1505	1520	1620	1619	1628	1643	1650	1658	1720	1728
	Lyon Part Dieu 150a d.			0944																					
	Versailles Chantiers 125a d.				1242	1312		1410	1417		1443		1518				1640		1711		1742
	Chartres ▲ d.				1338	1408		1449	1514		1530	1551	1606		1708	1733	1730		1808		1840
	Le Mans d.		1301	1310	1316		1355		1444	1552		1516	1702	1653	1740		1715	1808	1926	1830	1744	
	Laval d.		1343		1358					1637			1740					1756			
	Vitré d.		1402		1417					1658			1802								
	Rennes a.	1339	1423	1424	1438		1509		1520	1720		1630	1823		1724	1833			1954		1924

		8857 TGV ⑤t	3647 ⑤f	8861 TGV	8759 TGV A	8763 TGV ⑤f		8763 TGV G	3789 ⑤f	8663 TGV Ⓐ		8869 TGV	8771 TGV ⑤f	732/3 TGV B		3721 G	8777§ TGV ⑤t		3771 G	8679 TGV ⑤f	8683 TGV H		8887 TGV A	8689 TGV H	3627 Q
	Paris Montparnasse 125a d.	1740	1741	1750	1755	1758	1810	1810	1820	1828	1845	1855		1856	1913	1920	1928	1928	1950	1955	2020	2033	2050	2140	2300
	Lyon Part Dieu 150a d.											1651													
	Versailles Chantiers 125a d.				1811			1842						1911		1941	1942			2046		2317
	Chartres ▲ d.				1910			1940					2004		2029	2038			2142		2359
	Le Mans d.	1834		1844				1954		1938		2006	2128		2016	2203		2135	2052		2144	2236	0115
	Laval d.		2015				1954		2049								2134	2154			0213
	Vitré d.						2013			2156											0237
	Rennes a.		2053		1959		2034		2059	2125	2217	2130			2211	2231			2351	0301

		3628 ①g	3626 ⑥v			13610 Ⓐ	8800 TGV ①g	8802 TGV L	Ⓐ		8602 TGV Ⓒ	3632 ※	8604 TGV ※	8906 TGV ※	8710 TGV †		8612 TGV Ⓐ		8814 TGV	8714 TGV	13616 Ⓐ	706/7 TGV	8722 TGV F
	Rennes d.	0157	0218								0553	0600	0629		0710		0816				0904	0909	1058
	Vitré d.	0221	0241								0613	0621											
	Laval d.	0248	0306								0632	0641					0852				0924	0945	1135
	Le Mans d.	0347	0408		0538	0625a	0634	0656	0638	0651	0716	0742		0754	0824		0936		1004	1014	1013	1034	1219
	Chartres ▲ d.	0506	0521	0609	0636	0701	0730		0826	0804	0845											
	Versailles Chantiers 125a a.	0554	0604	0706	0736	0740	0810		0916	0848			0850		0945	1121						
	Lyon Part Dieu 150a a.														0946		1043	1204			
	Paris Montparnasse 125a a.	0610	0620	0720	0749	0753	0824	0730	0750	0900	0901	0810	0933	0835	0930	1000	1056	1217	1110	1110e		1315

		8722 TGV E	8724 TGV R		8630 TGV E	8630 TGV F	3734 F	8834 TGV Ⓐ			710/1 TGV N	8738 TGV ⑧h	708/9 Ⓐ	Ⓒ	⑥	Ⓑ		8746 TGV ⑧j	8948 TGV ⑧h	8754 TGV	13624
	Rennes d.	1108	1125			1301	1304	1308			1348	1514	1539					1603		1714	
	Vitré d.						1330														
	Laval d.	1145				1340	1344	1351										1640			
	Le Mans d.	1229				1421	1424	1429	1438	1454		1500		1509		1700		1658	1706	1724	1749	1810
	Chartres ▲ d.		1223	1404	1409		1543		1630	1645	1647		1725	1745	1841	1841		1936
	Versailles Chantiers 125a a.		1319	1453	1504			1733	1746		1821	1841	1938	1938		2009
	Lyon Part Dieu 150a a.									1832	2017					
	Paris Montparnasse 125a a.	1325	1330	1332	1507	1518	1520	1525	1638	1550		1747	1759	1720		1835	1855	1951	1951	1820	1845	1920	2022

		13624 Ⓒ	8856 TGV ⑤t	8858 TGV	8762 TGV †h		8664 TGV †	3716 ⑤f	8866 TGV †h	8770 TGV ⑧h	8970 TGV T		Ⓐ	†	3618 ⑤j	3866 †h		8678 TGV †h	8782 TGV S	8784 TGV †j	8892 TGV †h	3720 †j	8796 TGV †h
	Rennes d.				1814			1818	1821	1913					1917			1955	2008	2014		2025	2118
	Vitré d.							1838	1842						1938			2015					
	Laval d.							1858	1903						1959			2035				2111	
	Le Mans d.	1813	1845	1854		1836	1913	1943	1949	2009		2029		2041	2052	2059	2118	2124		2154	2157	
	Chartres ▲ a.	1937			1940	2024	2047	2049		2110	2133	2139	2148	2219		2257	
	Versailles Chantiers 125a a.	2019			2037	2122		2124		2206	2222	2226	2304		2332	
	Lyon Part Dieu 150a a.															
	Paris Montparnasse 125a a.	2033	1940	1950	2020	2051	2135	2040	2138	2105	2120	2125	2219	2236	2229	2242	2317	2215	2220	2250	2346	2325

A – Daily except ⑤ (not May 24).
B – Not Dec. 24, 31, Feb. 18, 25.
E – Daily Sept. 25 - Feb. 12, Apr. 3 - May 27; Ⓒ Feb. 18 - Apr. 2.
F – Ⓐ Feb. 13 - Mar. 31.
G – ①②③④ (not Apr. 17, May 1, 8, 25).
H – ⑤ and † (also May 24; not Apr. 16, 30, May 7, 25).
J – Ⓒ (daily from Dec. 19).
K – Ⓐ to Dec. 16.
L – ②③④⑤ (not Apr. 18, May 2, 9).
M – ⑥ (Ⓒ Dec. 24 - Apr. 15); also Apr. 17, 23, May 1, 8.
N – ⑥ Dec. 24 - May 6.
Q – ⑤ and † (also May 24; not Apr. 16, 30, May 7, 25, 26).
R – Daily except ⑦.
S – ⑤⑥; also May 16, 30, May 7, 24.
T – ※ (also Apr. 16, 30, May 7, 25). Runs 5 minutes later from Jan. 23.
TGV – Ⓡ, supplement payable.

a – ① (also Apr. 18, May 2, 9; not Apr. 17, May 1, 8)
b – Runs 10 minutes later Sept. 25 - Jan. 22.
c – Depart 0635 on ⑥.
e – Arrive 1115 on † from Jan. 29.
f – Also May 24; not May 26.
g – Also Apr. 18, May 2, 9; not Apr. 17, May 1, 8.
h – Not Apr. 16, 30, May 7, 25.
j – Not Apr. 16, 30, May 7.
n – ⑥ only.
p – Also May 25.
q – Arrive 1300 Feb. 13 - Mar. 31.
t – Also May 24.
v – Also May 25; not May 27.
▲ – Additional trains run during peak hours between Paris and Chartres.
* – Paris - Le Mans via Chartres is 211 km.
§ – Train number 8675 on ⑤ (also May 24; not May 26).

Table 125a

PARIS - VERSAILLES

RER (express Métro) Line C: **Paris Austerlitz** - St. Michel Notre Dame - **Versailles Rive Gauche** (for Château). Every 15 - 30 minutes, 0530 - 0030. Journey 37 minutes.

Alternative services:

RER Line C: Paris Austerlitz - St. Michel Notre Dame - Versailles Chantiers.
SNCF suburban service: Paris St. Lazare - Versailles Rive Droite.

Ⓐ – Mondays to Fridays, except holidays   Ⓑ – Daily except Saturdays   Ⓒ – Saturdays, Sundays and holidays

Table 126

(PARIS) - RENNES - QUIMPER

1,2 class

First section (Paris → Quimper)

km	Station	4378/4379 ◆	6848/6849 ⑥	Ⓐ	8705 TGV ①g	3701		8709 TGV A	8709 TGV B	4361 S	Ⓐ	⑥	8721 TGV J	R	8721 TGV K	K	4372	8623 TGV B	8623 TGV A	3713	8629 TGV 5f	89171 5f
0	Paris Montparnasse 125 d.	…	…	…	0725	…	…	0820	0835	…	…	…	1120	…	1135	…	…	1220	1220	1340	…	…
202	Le Mans 125 d.	…	…	…	…	…	…	0917	0932	…	…	…	1324	…	1339	…	…	1301	1316	1544	…	…
365	Rennes 125 a.	…	…	…	0929	…	…	1036	1051	1132	…	…	1331	…	1346	…	…	1423	1438	…	1450	1605
365	Rennes d.	0524	…	…	0632	0910	…	…	1022	…	…	…	1130	1224	…	…	1437	…	…	…	…	…
	Nantes 134 d.	…	…	…	0656	0933	…	…	1044	…	…	…	1154	1247	…	…	1521	…	1529	…	…	1643
	Savenay 134 d.	…	0624	0630	…	…	…	…	…	…	…	…	…	…	…	…	…	…	…	…	…	…
457	Redon 134 d.	0609	0709	0712	0726	1005	…	1017	1108	1115	1130	1211	1224	1316	…	…	1430	1438	1445	1453	1557	1710
492	Vannes d.	0642	…	…	0759	…	…	1045	…	1142	1157	…	1255	1348	…	…	1430	1438	1451	1506	1611	1723
511	Auray d.	0655	…	…	0816	…	…	1058	…	1155	1210	…	1308	1401	…	…	1457	…	…	…	1611	1723
539	Quiberon ▲ a.	…	…	…	…	…	…	…	…	…	…	…	…	…	…	…	1512	…	…	…	1630	…
545	Lorient d.	0715	…	…	0840	…	…	1117	…	1214	1229	…	1331	1424	…	…	1457	1512	…	…	1643	1756
565	Quimperlé d.	0728	…	…	0854	…	…	1129	…	1227	1242	…	1344	1437	…	…	…	…	…	…	1659	1813
591	Rosporden d.	0745	…	…	0912	…	…	1145	…	1244	1259	…	1400	1454	…	…	…	…	…	…	1711	1826
612	Quimper a.	0758	…	…	0925	…	…	1158	…	1256	1311	…	1413	1507	1532	…	1547	…	…	…	…	…

Second section (Paris → Quimper)

Station	8739 TGV H	L	89175 5h	®e	8641 TGV P	89231	8947 TGV Y	89177		6934/6935 ◆	8755 TGV A	8963 TGV X		8771 TGV 5f	3741 5h	5h	8775 TGV M	8775 TGV F	89179		3721 H	8679 TGV †	3725 N	3727 † W
Paris Montparnasse 125 d.	1420	…	…	…	1520	…	1610	…	…	…	1720	1810	…	1643	1855	…	1920	1920	…	…	1913	1955	…	2320
Le Mans 125 d.	1516	…	…	…	…	…	…	…	…	…	…	…	…	1830	…	…	2016	2016	…	…	2052	…	…	0115
Rennes 125 a.	1630	…	…	…	1724	…	…	…	…	…	1924	…	…	1954	2059	…	2130	2130	…	…	2217	2211	…	0307
Rennes d.	1637	…	1650	…	…	…	1736	…	1822	…	1927	…	…	2025	2102	…	2136	…	2144	…	2222	…	2226	0324
Nantes 134 d.	…	1617	…	…	1730	…	…	1821	…	1825	…	…	…	2022	…	2121	…	…	…	…	2203	…	2225	…
Savenay 134 d.	…	1639	…	…	…	…	…	…	…	1849	…	…	…	2043	…	2142	…	…	…	…	…	…	…	…
Redon 134 d.	…	1707	1729	1735	1811	…	1818	1904	1904	1918	2003	…	2109	2114	2140	2208	2213	…	2219	2252	2304	…	2305	0406
Vannes d.	1737	…	1757	1813	…	…	1851	1931	…	1951	2028	2124	…	2146	2204	…	2239	…	2249	…	2336	…	2333	0447
Auray d.	1750	…	1810	1829	…	…	1904	1944	…	2004	2040	2136	…	2159	…	…	2251	…	2302	…	2350	…	2345	0521
Quiberon ▲ a.	…	…	…	…	…	…	…	…	…	…	…	…	…	…	…	…	…	…	…	…	0009	…	0004	0546
Lorient d.	1809	…	1834	1900	…	…	1929	2002	…	2028	2058	2155	…	2223	…	…	2309	…	2320	…	0009	…	0016	0600
Quimperlé d.	1823	…	1851	…	…	…	1942	…	…	2041	…	…	…	2236	…	…	2322	…	2333	…	0022	…	0032	0617
Rosporden d.	1840	…	1911	…	…	…	1958	…	…	2058	…	…	…	2253	…	…	2339	…	2349	…	0038	…	0045	0630
Quimper a.	1852	…	1924	…	…	…	2011	2037	…	2111	2132	2230	…	2305	…	…	2351	…	0001	…	0051	…	…	…

Third section (Quimper → Paris)

Station	13718 E	8710 TGV	8710 TGV ①g	89166 Ⓐ	8612 TGV Ⓐ		8716 TGV	6434/6435	8722 TGV K	8722 TGV J	3734	8630 TGV K	8630 TGV J	4361 S	13506 T	13506 U	89168 Ⓐ	3716 G 5f
Quimper d.	…	…	…	0545	…	…	0608	0653	0728	0837	0847	1018z	…	…	1338	…	1512	…
Rosporden d.	…	…	…	0558	…	…	0622	…	0742	0850	0900	1031z	…	…	1352	…	1526	…
Quimperlé d.	…	…	…	0613	…	…	0640	…	0756	0905	0915	1046z	…	…	1407	…	1540	…
Lorient d.	0530	…	0530	0627	…	…	0657	0727	0810	0918	0928	1101	…	…	1420	1435	1554	1625
Quiberon ▲ d.	…	…	…	…	…	…	…	…	…	…	…	…	…	…	…	…	…	…
Auray d.	0547	…	0547	0645	…	…	0730	0745	0834	0936	0946	1126	…	…	1439	1452	1616	1644
Vannes d.	0559	…	0559	0658	0708	…	0745	0757	0847	0947	0957	1140	…	…	1452	1504	1629	1658
Redon 134 d.	0626	…	0626	0659	0731	0740	0746	0800	…	0920	1016	1026	1211	1229	1510	1530	1702	1712	1726
Savenay 134 d.	…	…	…	0744	…	0815	…	…	0949	…	…	…	…	1259	1555	1555	…	…
Nantes 134 a.	…	…	…	0821	…	0836	…	…	1011	…	…	…	…	1321	1617	1617	1746	…
Rennes 125 a.	0702	0710	0702	…	0807	…	0841	0859	1053	1103	1252	…	1558	…	1603	…	…	1807 1803
Le Mans 125 a.	…	0710	0710	…	0816	…	…	0904	1058	1108	1301	1304	1722	…	…	…	…	1821
Paris Montparnasse 125 a.	…	0822	0822	…	0934	…	1110k	…	1217	1227	1422	1427	1520	1525	1820	…	…	1947 2138

Fourth section (Quimper → Paris)

Station	8962 TGV †e	4304 Ⓐ	8770 TGV †j	®j	®j	®j Ⓐ	3720 †e	89176 5®f	8782 TGV 5®f V		8784 TGV †	8796 †j	6348/6349 †j	6348/6349 ®q	87578 †j	4365 ◆	3742 †j	3724 5h	3726 †j	3744
Quimper d.	1556	…	1603	…	…	1706	…	1726	1735	…	1753	1912	1842	1913	1940	…	2013	2245	2300	2300
Rosporden d.	…	…	1616	…	…	…	…	1740	1748	…	1806	…	1857	1928	1953	…	2027	2301	2316	2317
Quimperlé d.	…	…	1632	…	…	…	…	1756	1804	…	1821	…	1917	1949	2013	…	2042	2318	2336	2336
Lorient d.	1631	…	1646	…	1740	…	1745	1810	1818	…	1834	1947	1931	2004	2027	…	2057	2335	2354	2354
Quiberon ▲ d.	…	…	…	…	…	…	…	…	…	…	…	…	…	…	…	…	…	…	…	…
Auray d.	1649	…	1710	1743	…	1835	1818	1849	…	…	1852	…	2030t	2029	2050	…	2117	0006	0024	0026
Vannes d.	1701	…	1723	1755	1806	1812	1833	1848	1849	…	1903	2012	2043	2043	2103	…	2131	2357	0039	0044
Redon 134 d.	1731	…	1739	1757	…	…	1849	…	1921	1922y	1923	1926	1932	2119	2119	2137	2141	2201	0047	0121	0123
Savenay 134 d.	…	…	1806	1822	…	…	…	…	…	…	1953	1956	…	2148	2148	…	2210	…	…	0156
Nantes 134 a.	1815	…	1833	1844	…	…	…	2002	1957	…	2014	…	…	2210	2210	2231	2245	…	…	0222
Rennes 125 a.	…	…	…	1908	…	…	…	2025	…	2008	2009	2115	…	2215	…	…	0125	0133	0201	…
Le Mans 125 a.	…	…	…	1913	…	…	…	2155	…	2122	2014	2118	…	…	…	…	0157	0210	0218	…
Paris Montparnasse 125 a.	2035c	…	…	2120	…	…	…	2346	…	2220	2225	2325	…	…	…	…	0337	0353	0431	…
																	0610	0620	0620	0638

◆ – NOTES (LISTED BY TRAIN NUMBER):

3724 – ⟶ 1,2 cl. Quimper - Paris.
3726 – 🍴 and ⟶ 1,2 cl. Quimper - Paris.
3742 – 🍴 and ⟶ 1,2 cl. Auray - Paris.
4364/5 – ⑤ and † (also May 24; not Apr. 16, 30, May 5): ⟶ 1,2 cl. Quimper - Toulouse; 🍴 and 🍷 Quimper - Bordeaux.
4378/9 – Runs (from Toulouse) on ⑦ (also Apr. 17, May 1, 8): ⟶ 1,2 cl. Quimper - Bordeaux (depart next day) - Quimper.
6348/9 – RHÔNE OCÉAN – 🍴 and ⟶ 1,2 cl. Quimper - Lyon. Conveys (except when train 4364/5 runs) ⟶ 1,2 cl. Quimper - Toulouse; 🍴 Quimper - Bordeaux. Runs 6 minutes earlier Sept. 25 - Jan. 22.
6434/5 – 🍴 and 🍷 Quimper - Marseille.
6848/9 – RHÔNE OCÉAN – ⟶ 1,2 cl. and 🍴 Lyon - Quimper. Conveys (except when train 4378/9 runs) 1,2 cl. Toulouse - Quimper; 🍴 and 🍷 Bordeaux (depart next day) - Quimper.
6934/5 – 🍴 and 🍷 Marseille - Quimper.

A – ⑥ (daily Dec. 19 - May 27).
B – ⑥ Sept. 25 - Dec. 16.
C – ⑤ (also May 24). Runs 5 minutes earlier Sept. 30 - Jan. 20.
E – ②③④⑤ (not Apr. 18, May 2, 9, 25).
F – ⑤⑥ (also May 24).
G – ①②③④ (also May 26; not Apr. 17, May 1, 8).
H – ①②③④ (not Apr. 17, May 1, 8, 24, 25).
J – ⑥ (daily Sept. 25 - Feb. 12 and Apr. 3 - May 27).

K – ⑥ Feb. 13 - Mar. 31.
L – Runs 5 minutes earlier Sep. 25 - Jan. 22.
M – ①②③④⑥ (also May 26; not Apr. 17, May 1, 8, 24, 25). Runs 8 minutes earlier Sep. 25 - Jan. 21.
N – ⑤ (also May 24; not Apr. 16, 30, May 7, 25).
P – ⑤ (also May 24). Sept. 30 - Jan. 20 departs Paris 1615 and runs 3 minutes earlier Nantes - Quimper.
R – ⑥ Sept. 26 - Feb. 10 and Apr. 3 - May 26.
S – Runs 5 minutes later Sept. 25 - Jan. 22.
T – Runs 4 minutes later Sept. 25 - Jan. 22.
TGV – Ⓡ, supplement payable.
U – ⑥ (also May 24). Runs 4 minutes earlier Sept. 30 - Jan. 20.
V – 🍴 Runs 4 minutes earlier Sept. 26 - Jan. 21.
W – ⑤ and † (also May 24; not Apr. 16, May 7, 26): 🍴 and ⟶ 1,2 cl. Paris - Quimper.
X – ⑤ (also May 24). Sept. 30 - Jan. 20 runs 8 minutes earlier Vannes - Quimper.
Y – Runs 3 minutes earlier Sept. 25 - Jan. 22.

c – Arrive 2025 Sept. 25 - Jan. 21.
e – Not Apr. 16, 30, May 7.
f – Also May 24.
g – Also Apr. 18, May 2, 9; not Apr. 17, May 1, 8, 25.
h – Also May 24; not May 26.
j – Not Apr. 16, 30, May 7, 25.
k – Sept. 26 - Jan. 21 arrive 1115.
q – Also Apr. 16, 30, May 7, 25.
t – Arrive 1955.
y – Arrive 1916.
z – On ⑥ Jan. 30 - Mar. 10, depart Quimper 1003, Rosporden 1016, Quimperlé 1031.
▲ – No rail service in winter.

01

Table 127 — NANTES - ANGERS - TOURS

1,2 class

km			6302		6304		6306	3508	6308						4304		6348
			✕	Ⓐ		Ⓐ		⑤†	H	G	Ⓐ	†	⑥	⑥	ⒶJ	ⒶK	⑦e	†J	†K	R
0	**Nantes** 123 .... d.		0652z	0708		0827c	1016z	1130	1358z		1625z	1625z	1645z		1710y	1833	1833	1847z	2016	2018	2252y
88	Angers St. Laud **123** d.	0653	0745	0754	0920	1102	1105	1215	1223c	1448	1717	1759	1834	1914	1922	1937	2056	2106	2347
132	Saumur .... d.	0635	0718	0807	0817	0901	0946	1123	1127	1237	1255	1510	1622	1739	1739	1822	1822	1826	1908	1939	1943	1959	2120	2129	0013
196	St Pierre des Corps.. a.	0847	0938		1306		1859	1905		2012	2038	2152	2159	0048
199	**Tours** .... a.	0734	0759	0839	0857	0948	1025	1200	1200	1315	1348	1543	1704	1811	1811	1900	1908	1915	2023	2023	2048	2201	2201	0102
202	St Pierre des Corps... a.	0854		1217		1556	1826	1826			
	Orléans **135a** .... a.	0938		1400		2000	2103	2103	2246	2251
	Lyon Part Dieu **128** .. a.	1339		1703		2049		2316			0643

		Ⓐ	Ⓐ	†	⑥	Ⓐ	†	6803	Ⓐ	†	✕	F	⑥	6805	⑤⑥	Ⓐ	6817	B	†	✕	F	✕	6807	6809	6809	6849
								⑥t									⑤						✕	⑤f		R
	Lyon Part Dieu **128** . d.						0646			0912				1248			1507	1757	1757		2228
	Orléans **135a** .... d.	0645	0728		1103		1627			1725	1805			
	St Pierre des Corps.... d.		1135		1405		1748			1958	2249	2249	
	Tours .... d.	0642	0728	0757	0811	0852	1155	1145	1202	1228	1315	1418	1451	1610	1711	1729	1802	1822	1831	1808	1847	2011	2302	2302	0403
	St Pierre des Corps... d.	0738	0806	0821	0901	1115	1325	1459	1711		1818	1857		0413
	Saumur .... d.	0726	0809	0844	0859	0939	1228	1226	1248	1316	1400	1452	1543	1651	1752	1824	1835	1921	1930	1849	2043	2335	2335	
	Angers St. Laud **123** .. d.	0749	0832	0910	0925	1003	1251	1249	1348	1514	1718	1815	1849	1902	1912	1951	2106	2356	2358	0511
	Nantes 123 .... a.	0840b	0919	1002b	1017b	1340b	1336	1603a	1808b	1903a	1952b	2002b	2038	2155b	0048b	0606b

FOR NOTES SEE TABLE **128**.

Table 128 — TOURS - BOURGES - LYON

For TGVs Nantes - Lyon see Table 150a

km			3501	6302	6302		6304	6304		6306			6308	3508		6348	
			①g	6303	6303		6305	6305		6307				3509		6349	
		✕		✕	†		Ⓐ	Ⓐ					G	G	G	H	⑦e	R	Ⓐ
0	**Nantes** 127 .... d.		0708		0652z		1016z		1358z		1625z	1625z		2252y	
180	**Tours** .... d.	0607		0849	0849	1212	1212	1551	1641	1821	1821	1830	2325	
	St Pierre des Corps.... d.	0613	0847	0856	0856	1219	1219	1558	1648	1827	1827	1836	2331	0100
288	Vierzon .... d.	0742		0959	0959	1323	1323	1702		1823	1934	1934	2020	0036
320	Bourges .... d.	0802	0809	1019	1019	1342	1342	1721	1857r	1954	1953	2113	0101
	Nevers .... d.	0829	1038		1401		1740		2013	
378	Saincaize .... d.	0843	1047	1052	1052	1057	1410	1416	1416	1622	1749	1758	1804	2022	2027	2035	
	Nevers .... a.		1106		1429		1813		2044		0151	
427	Moulins .... d.	0910	1120	1120	1444	1444	1825		2055	0353	
468	St. Germain des Fossés.. d.	0934	✕n	1143	1143	✕n	1507	1507	1849		2118	⑤	⑦e	0433	
535	Roanne .... a.	1016	1117	1226	1226	1238	1550	1550	1602	1935	2005	2202	2240	2250	0520	0526	0722
	St. Étienne Châteaucreux a.	1229		1356		1724		2118		2354	2354	0652	0835
632	**Lyon Part Dieu** ...... a.	1129	1339	1339	1703	1703	2049		2316		0643	
632	**Lyon Perrache** ...... a.	1138	1349	1349	1837	1837	2059		2326		0654	
761	Grenoble 154 .... a.										

			6802	6802		6804			6816		6806		6808	6808	6848
			6803	6803		6805			6817		6807		6809	6809	6849
		✕	①g	✕	⑩⑥	⑥t	①g			Ⓐ	B	B			Ⓐ	†	Ⓐ	⑦e	R
								✕		n				✕			R
	Grenoble 154 .... d.				0721									
	Lyon Perrache ...... d.		0636	0636			1236	1455		1745	1745	2215
	Lyon Part Dieu ...... d.		0646	0646	0912	1248	1507	1757	1757	2228
	St. Étienne Châteaucreux.. d.	0630		0900	1217	1505	1737	1752	2118
	Roanne .... d.	0744	0802	0802	1012	1029	1326	1405	1612	1623	1847	1901	1915	1915	2240	2353
	St. Germain des Fossés... d.	0848	0848	1113	1453	1709	1959	1959	0043
	Moulins .... d.	0909	0909	1135	1517	1731	⑧	2022	2022	0114
	Nevers .... d.	0626	0634	0919	1149	1530	B	1740	2036	
	Saincaize .... d.	0928	0935	0935	0940	1158	1203	1207	1539	1546	1749	1757	1804	2044	2048	2048	2056
	Nevers .... a.	0949		1216		1559		1813		2105	
	Bourges .... d.	0616	0706	0736	E	1009	1008	1008	1056	1238	1621	Ⓐ	1832	2122	2122	
	Vierzon .... d.	0642	0729	0759	0813	1030	1030	1030	1123	1300	1642	1655	1854	2144	2144	0250
	St Pierre des Corps.. a.	0810	0833		0949	1133	1133	1133	1249	1403	1746	1822	1957	2247	2247	0401
	Tours .... a.	0817	0840		0956	1140	1140	1140	1255	1410	1753	1829	2003	2254	2254	0416
	Nantes 127 .... a.				1340b		1603a	1952b	2155b	0048b	0606b

B –	⑤⑦ (also Dec. 21,24,31, Feb. 11,18,25, Mar. 11, Apr. 15, 17,29, May 1,6,8,24; not Apr. 16,30, May 7,26).
E –	②③④⑤ (not Dec. 21,22, Apr. 18, May 2,9,25,26).
F –	①②③④ (not Apr. 17, May 1,8,24,25).
G –	⑤⑦ (also Dec. 20,21, Apr. 17, May 1,8,24,25; not Apr. 16,30, May 7).
H –	①②③④ (not Dec. 20,21, Apr. 17, May 1,8,24,25).
J –	Runs Sept. 25 - Jan. 22.
K –	RHÔNE OCÉAN – 🍴 and 🛏 1,2 cl. Quimper - Lyon and v.v.
R –	RHÔNE OCÉAN – 🍴 and 🛏 1,2 cl. Quimper - Lyon and v.v.
a –	Arrive 6 minutes earlier Sept. 25 - Jan. 22.
b –	Arrive 7 minutes earlier Sept. 25 - Jan. 22.
c –	✕ only.
e –	Also Nov. 1, Apr. 17, May 1,8; not Oct. 30, Apr. 16,30, May 7.
f –	Also Nov. 10, May 24; not Nov. 11, May 26.
g –	Also Apr. 18, May 2,9; not Apr. 17, May 1,8.
n –	By 🚌 Roanne - Balbigny and v.v. on Ⓐ Sept. 25 - Dec. 16 (departs earlier from Roanne).
r –	Ⓐ only.
t –	Also May 25; not May 27.
y –	Depart 6 minutes later Sept. 25 - Jan. 22.
z –	Depart 7 minutes later Sept. 25 - Jan. 22.

Table 129 — RENNES - ST. MALO

1,2 class

km										J	K	⑤f	Ⓐ					⑤g	H	H	⑤g	Ⓐ		
		✕2	✕2	✕	✕		✕	✕																
0	Rennes .... d.	0621		0743	0818		0937	0937		1134		1240	1336	1351	1522	1646		1734		1754	1801	1830	1849	1907	1913
58	Dol .... d.	0721	0724	0830	0852	0859	1014	1016	1020	1215	1220	1338	1419	1434	1556	1733	1738	1813	1817	1841	1846	1927	1941	2005	1959
86	Dinan .... d.	0745		1042		1242		1808	1846		
91	St. Malo .... a.	0739		0850		0915	1030	1034		1231		1358	1435	1450	1613	1751		1828		1901	1906	1947	2000	2026	2014

		H	H	⑤g	⑤g	⑤f	Hb	M	⑥t	N	N				Ⓐb	Ⓐ	Ⓐ		⑥	Ⓐ	⑥	Ⓐ	
Rennes .... d.	1941		2009		2117	2140	2140		2227		St. Malo .... d.		0600	0619	0619		0655	0658		0807	
Dol .... d.	2020	2025	2046	2051	2156		2215	2219	2304	2308	Dinan .... d.	0610		0640		0750		
Dinan .... a.		2047		2113		2230		2241		2330	Dol .... d.		0617	0640	0640	0708	0713	0718	0818	0823	
St. Malo .... a.	2035		2102		2212		2231		2320		Rennes .... a.		0700	0656	0725	0737		0759	0759		0858	

		H	H	⑤g		⑥	Ⓐ	†	⑧	⑥		⑧h	⑥	⑤	A	Ⓐ	⑦e		R	Ⓐ	⑦e	⑦e
St. Malo .... d.	0936	0935			1154			1404	1405		1601			1705	1724	1821	1828		1906		2002		2021
Dinan .... d.			1138		1342	1348		1620		1651		1850		2006	
Dol .... d.	0953	0951	1001	1210	1408	1410	1420		1617	1642	1652	1713	1723	1746	1820	1849	1913	1923		2018	2028	2037
Rennes .... a.	1032		1033	1248		1504	1504		1704	1725		1757	1841	1857	1945		1956		2052		2108

A –	Daily except ⑤ (not May 24).
H –	①②③④ (not Nov. 1,10, Apr. 17, May 1,8,24,25).
J –	✕ (except Ⓐ Feb. 13 - Mar. 31).
K –	Ⓐ Feb. 13 - Mar. 31.
M –	Daily except dates in note N.
N –	⑤⑦ (also Nov. 10, Apr. 17, May 1,8,24; not Nov. 11, Apr. 16,30, May 7,25).
R –	⑤⑥⑦ (also Nov. 10, Apr. 17, May 1,8,24,25).
b –	By 🚌.
e –	Also Apr. 17, May 1,8; not Apr. 16,30, May 7.
f –	Also Nov. 10, May 24; not Nov. 11, May 26.
g –	Also Nov. 10, May 24; not Nov. 11.
h –	Not Nov. 11, Apr. 16,30, May 7,25.
t –	Also Apr. 30, May 7.

Table 130 BREST - QUIMPER

1,2 class except where shown

km		Ⓐ	⚒				⑤f	2		Ⓑ	
0	**Brest** d.	0602	0703	0827	...	1152	1612	1717	1803	1950	...
18	Landerneau d.	0615	0716	0840	...	1205	1627	1733	1820	2009	...
72	Châteaulin d.	0658	0802	0917	...	1242	1705	1812	1904	2052	...
102	**Quimper** a.	0719	0823	0938	...	1303	1726	1832	1927	2113	...

	⚒	Ⓐ	2	⚒n	⑤f		Ⓐ	M	⑤f
Quimper d.	0635	0738	0940	1307	1523	1734	1840	2025	2117
Châteaulin d.	0657	0801	1002	1329	1546	1755	1904	2051	2139
Landerneau d.	0736	0839	1041	1406	1629	1840	1944	2132	2218
Brest a.	0754	0852	1053	1420	1643	1853	1957	2146	2231

M – ⑤⑦ (also Nov. 1,10,11). f – Also Nov. 10; not Nov. 11. n – Runs 10 minutes later on Ⓐ Sept. 25 - Dec. 16.

Table 132 BORDEAUX - LE VERDON - POINTE DE GRAVE

1,2 class

km		Ⓐ	🚌 Ⓐ	⑥	🚌 †		Ⓐ	🚌 Ⓐ	⑥	🚌 ⑥	⑤f	🚌 ⑤f	Ⓐ	🚌 Ⓐ	Ⓐ		🚌 ⑥	Ⓐ	🚌 Ⓐ	Ⓐ	🚌 Ⓐ		🚌 †	
0	**Bordeaux St. Jean** d.	0721	...	1038	1040	...	1210	...	1319	...	1429	...	1635	...	1710	...	1730	1758	...	1917	...	...	1915	...
23	Blanquefort d.	0747	...	1056	1107	...	1237	...	1336	...	1445	...	1702	...	1736	...	1757	1827	...	1934	...	...	1942	...
39	Margaux d.	0803	...	1106	1130	...	1254	...	1349	...	1458	...	1716	...	1752	...	1820	1845	...	1947	...	...	2005	...
61	Pauillac d.	0822	...	1123	1156	...	1313	...	1406	...	1514	...	1735	...	1817	...	1846	1903	...	2004	2009	...	2031	...
80	Lesparre d.	0837	0842	1139	1223	...	1328	1333	1421	1426	1529	1534	1751	1756	1833	...	1913	1918	1923	...	2039	...	2058	...
106	Soulac sur Mer d.	...	0912	1159	1251	...	...	1403	...	1456	...	1604	...	1826	1853	...	1943	...	1953	...	2109	...	2126	...
113	**Le Verdon** a.	...	0922	1206	1302	...	...	1413	...	1506	...	1614	...	1836	1900	...	1953	...	2003	...	2119	...	2137	...
116	Pointe de Grave § a.	...	0929	...	1309	...	...	...	...	...	...	...	...	1843	...	...	...	...	...	...	...	...	...	...

	Ⓐ	🚌 Ⓐ	Ⓐ	🚌 Ⓐ	Ⓐ		🚌 †	⚒		🚌 Ⓐ	Ⓐ	🚌 ⑥	⑥		⑤f	🚌 Ⓐ	Ⓐ		🚌 ⑥		🚌 †			
Pointe de Grave § d.	...	...	...	...	...	...	...	...	...	1121	...	...	...	...	...	1619	...	...	1646	...	1755	...	...	...
Le Verdon d.	...	0547	...	0628	...	...	0748	0836	...	1128	...	1142	...	...	...	1626	...	...	1653	...	1800	...	...	...
Soulac sur Mer d.	...	0557	...	0638	...	...	0759	0843	...	1138	...	1152	...	...	...	1636	...	...	1704	...	1811	...	...	...
Lesparre d.	...	0627	0637	0708	0718	...	0827	0903	...	1208	1218	1222	1232	...	1616	1706	1716	...	1732	...	1849	...	...	...
Pauillac d.	0620	...	0653	...	0733	...	0854	0920	...	...	1234	...	1247	...	1631	...	1734	...	1759	...	1916	...	...	...
Margaux d.	0637	...	0711	...	0751	...	0920	0937	...	...	1253	...	1303	...	1647	...	1753	...	1825	...	1940	...	...	...
Blanquefort d.	0652	...	0725	...	0806	...	0943	0948	...	...	1307	...	1316	...	1703	...	1809	...	1848	...	2003	...	...	...
Bordeaux St. Jean a.	0719	...	0754	...	0834	...	1010	1006	...	...	1333	...	1333	...	1721	...	1840	...	1915	...	2030	...	...	...

f – Also Nov. 10; not Nov. 11.

§ – A ferry service operates between Pointe de Grave and Royan (frequent service in summer; 6 - 8 departures per day in winter). ☎ 56.09.60.84.

Table 133 PARIS - LES AUBRAIS - ORLÉANS

Rail service **Paris - Les Aubrais** and v.v. Journey: 1 hour. 119 km. (Rail shuttle service **Les Aubrais - Orléans** and v.v. connects with all trains below. Journey: 4 minutes. 2 km.)

Departures from Paris Austerlitz: 0620⚒, 0645⚒, 0702⑦, 0732, 0910, 1108⚒, 1200, 1221, 1339, 1354⑤, 1539⑤, 1600 (not ⑤⑥); 1603⑤, 1632⑤, 1639⚒, 1715, 1750Ⓑ, 1817, 1830⑤, 1847, 1920⑤, 1931, 2030, 2218.

Departures from Les Aubrais: 0551, 0615Ⓐ, 0705Ⓐ, 0716⚒, 0747⚒, 0843, 1102, 1119, 1249, 1338⚒, 1412⚒, 1620, 1715, 1755, 1917⚒, 1920⑦, 2017⑦, 2032Ⓐ, 2052⑥, 2101⑤, 2125⑦, 2141⑦, 2207⑦.

Table 134 RENNES - NANTES - BORDEAUX

1,2 class

km		Ⓐ	4319 ⚒ ♦	4363 🍷	⚒	⑥	Ⓐ		6434 6435 D 🍷	4361 4360 🍷	⑤	3713 🍷	c	4399 ⑤f 🍷	6433 6432 ⑦e A	89233 Ⓐ	343 342 ♦	6425 ♦	⚒ z	†	G	6348 6349	⑦e	4364 4365 ♦
0	**Rennes** d.	...	...	...	...	*0624*	0644	0818	...	1132c	...	1450	...	...	...	1644	...	...	1822	1822	2021	...	2044	...
72	Redon a.	...	...	...	...	*0709*	0739	0915	...	1211c	...	1525	...	...	...	|	...	...	1904	1904	2111	...	2124	...
72	Redon d.	...	...	...	...	0746	0746	...	0920	1229c	...	...	1530	...	...	|	...	...	1920	1926	...	2119	2141	...
106	Savenay d.	...	...	...	...	0815	0815	...	0949	1259c	...	...	1555	...	...	|	...	...	1949	1956	...	2148	2210	...
145	**Nantes** a.	...	...	...	...	0836	0836	...	1011	1321c	...	...	1617	...	...	1804	...	...	2010	2018	...	2210	2231	...
145	**Nantes** d.	...	...	0649	...	...	...	...	1023	1354	...	...	...	1650	1707	...	1813	1940	...	...	...	...	...	2322r
222	La Roche sur Yon d.	...	...	0735	...	...	...	...	1112	1442	...	...	...	1741	1757	...	1901	2024	...	...	...	...	...	0020r
325	**La Rochelle** d.	...	0621	0842	1121	...	...	...	1221	1547	1744	...	...	1848	1907	...	2009	2125	...	...	...	...	...	0219
354	Rochefort d.	...	0646	0903	1146	...	...	...	1242	1610	1807	...	...	1912	1933	...	2030	2145	...	...	...	...	...	0244
398	Saintes d.	0610	0720	0932	1221	...	...	...	1313	1640	1846	...	...	1943	2003	...	2100	2215	...	...	...	...	...	0315
521	**Bordeaux St. Jean** a.	0750	0854	1048	1347	...	...	...	1428	1800	2028	...	...	2111	2138	...	2215	2326	...	...	...	...	...	0501
	Toulouse **139** a.	...	...	...	...	...	...	...	1706	...	...	...	...	2352	0026	...	0113	|	...	...	...	...	...	0857
	Marseille **163** a.	...	...	...	...	...	...	...	2107	...	...	...	...	...	0526	...	0600	0538	...	...	...	...	...	...
	Nice **164** a.	...	...	...	...	...	...	...	...	...	...	...	...	...	...	...	0900	0837	...	...	...	...	...	...

	4378 4379 ♦	6932 6933 ⑤f A	4398 ⑦e ♦	6848 6849 n	Ⓑ	⚒	6924 6925 ♦		340 341 ♦	89229 ⚒	4372 4373 🍷	⑥	Ⓐ	89231 Ⓑj	6934 6935 D	89176 🍷	⑤f	4374 ⚒ 🍷	E	4376 4377 † 🍷	4384 4385 ⑤f 🍷	Ⓑ	⑥	4318 Ⓑh ♦
Nice **164** d.	...	...	...	...	...	...	1824	...	2000	...	...	...	...	...	...	...	...	...	...	...	...	...	...	...
Marseille **163** d.	...	1855	...	...	...	...	2214	...	2252	...	...	...	...	...	0656	...	...	...	...	...	...	...	...	...
Toulouse **139** d.	2114	2328	2328	...	...	...	|	...	0348	...	...	...	...	...	1113x	...	...	...	...	...	...	...	...	...
Bordeaux St. Jean d.	0006	0207	0207	...	...	...	0530	...	0646b	...	1027	1223	1223	...	1404	...	...	1700	...	1737	1752	1755	1810	1923
Saintes d.	0134	0327	0327	...	...	...	0648	...	0819	...	1141	1355	1357	...	1525	...	...	1820	...	1853	1906	1932	1951	2110
Rochefort d.	0210	0359	0359	...	...	...	0719	...	0850	...	1212	▬	1432	...	1556	...	...	1850	...	1924	1938	...	...	2142
La Rochelle d.	0241	0422	0422	...	...	...	0741	...	0916	...	1234	...	1455	...	1617	...	...	1912	...	1947	2000	...	...	2208
La Roche sur Yon d.	0355	0527	0527	...	...	...	0850	...	1019	...	1336	...	▬	...	1723	...	...	2017	...	2051	2102	...	...	...
Nantes a.	0452	0622	0622	...	...	...	0938	...	1105	...	1421	n	...	...	1809	...	...	2104	...	2138	2147	...	...	...
Nantes d.	...	...	...	0627	...	0710	...	1022	...	1200	1437	1612	...	1730	1825	...	2022	...	2114	2203	2203	...	...	...
Savenay d.	...	...	...	0650	...	0732	...	1044	...	|	|	1634	...	|	1849	...	2043	...	2135	2225	2225	...	...	...
Redon a.	...	...	...	0718	...	0755	...	1108	...	|	1521	1703	H	1811	1916	...	2109	...	2200	2252	2252	...	...	...
Redon d.	...	...	...	...	0730	0800	...	1116	...	|	1539	...	1712	1821	...	1921	2127	...	2205	2310	2310	...	...	...
Rennes a.	...	...	...	...	0807	0841	...	1155	...	1320	1616	...	1807	1901	...	2003	2203	...	2245	2347	2347	...	...	...

♦ – **NOTES** (LISTED BY TRAIN NUMBERS)

340-3 – 🛌 1,2 cl., 🛏 1,2 cl. and (12) Ventimiglia - Nice - Nantes and v.v.; 🍷 Bordeaux - Nantes and v.v.

4318 – Conveys on ⑤⑦, also Apr. 17, May 1,8,24; not Apr. 16,30, May 7,26: (12) and 🛏 1,2 cl. Bordeaux - La Rochelle - Paris.

4319 – Conveys on ⑤⑦, also Apr. 17, May 1,8,24; not Apr. 16,30, May 7,26 (from Paris): (12) and 🛏 1,2 cl. Paris - La Rochelle - Bordeaux.

4364/5 – (12) Quimper - Bordeaux; 🛏 1,2 cl. Quimper - Toulouse.

4378/9 – (12) and 🍷 Bordeaux - Quimper; 🛏 1,2 cl. Toulouse - Quimper.

4398 – 🛏 2 cl. and (12) Toulouse - Nantes.

6425 – ⑤⑦ (also Apr. 17, May 1,8,24; not Apr. 16,30, May 7,26): 🛌 1,2 cl. (T2), 🛏 1,2 cl. and (12) Nantes - Nice.

6924/5 – ⑤⑦ (also Apr. 17, May 1,8,24; not Apr. 16,30, May 7,26): 🛌 1,2 cl. (T2), 🛏 1,2 cl. and (12) Nice - Nantes; 🍷 Bordeaux - Nantes.

A – (12) and 🛏 2 cl. Nantes - Marseille - Les Arcs and v.v.; 🍷 Nantes - Agen and v.v.

D – (12) and 🍷 Quimper - Marseille and v.v.

E – ①②③④⑥ (not Apr. 17, May 1,8,24). Runs 7 minutes later Jan. 23 - May 27.

G – ①②③④⑥ (also Apr. 16,30, May 7,25,26; not Apr. 17, May 1,8). On ⑥ (also Apr. 16,30, May 7,25) depart Rennes 2030, arrive Redon 2108.

H – ①②③④⑦ (also May 26; not Apr. 16,30, May 7).

b – Depart 0653 on ⚒.

c – 5 minutes later Sept. 25 - Jan. 22.

e – Also Apr. 17, May 1,8; not Apr. 16,30, May 7.

f – Also Nov. 10, May 24; not Nov. 11, May 26.

h – Not Apr. 16,30, May 7,25,26.

j – Not Apr. 16,30, May 7.

n – Runs 5 minutes later Jan. 23 - May 27.

q – Depart 1726 on ⑤.

r – On ⑤ (also May 24; not May 26), depart Nantes 2341, La Roche 0045.

x – Depart 1108 on Ⓐ Feb. 21 - Mar. 24.

z – 3/4 minutes later Jan. 23 - May 27.

Table 134a — NANTES - LES SABLES D'OLONNE

1,2 class

km		Ⓐh	Ⓐ	✗		Ⓐ	†				⑤g	Ⓐ	⑤f		⑥		⑥	†		⑥	C		†	⑤f
0	Nantes 134 .... d.		0620	0723		0858	0924	...	1223	1354	...	1615	1650	...	1720	...	1731	1823	...	1914	1944	...	2014	2019
77	La Roche sur Yon 134 ..... d.	0645	0725	0830	0857	0949	1034	...	1327	1440	1448	1713	1739	1752	1824	1831	1831	1931	...	2015	2040	...	2108	2119
114	Les Sables d'Olonne .... a.	0721	0800	...	0929	1017	1106	...	1359	...	1518	1741	...	1829	...	1903	2004	...	2045	2108	...	2140	2148

		Ⓐ	✗	⑦	Ⓐ		⑥		Ⓐ		⑥		Ⓐ	Ⓐ	Ⓐ		⑦e		⑥	Ⓐ	⑤f	Ⓐ		
	Les Sables d'Olonne.......... d.	0537	0649	0724	0726	...	0936	...	1142	...	1251	...	1554	1623	1636	...	1714	...	1731	1756	1803	2108	...	
	La Roche sur Yon 134 .... d.	0608	0727	0744	0803	...	1009	1124	1215	1223	1324	1336	...	1625	1656	1708	1723	1745	...	1802	1833	1838	2141	...	
	Nantes 134 .... a.	0717	0820	0858	0858	...	1105	...	1320	...	1421	...	1718	1804	1809	1840	...	1901	1932	1945	2228	...	

C – ①②③④ Jan. 2 - May 23, also May 26; not Apr. 17, May 1, 8.
e – ⑦, also Apr. 17, May 1, 8, not Apr. 16, 30, May 7, 25.
f – Also May 24, not May 26.
g – Also May 24.
h – Ⓐ, not Apr. 17, May 1, 8, 25.

Table 135 — PARIS - TOURS

km		8501 TGV J	8501 TGV K	8307 TGV ✗	8311 TGV J	8311 TGV K	8417 TGV K	8417 TGV J	8323 TGV	8433 TGV	8441 TGV ⑤g	8347 TGV	8453 TGV	8363 TGV ⑧b	8367 TGV ⑤f	8469 TGV A	8375 TGV M	8377 TGV ⑦e	8379 TGV ⑤g	8383 TGV ⑦e	8387 TGV Ⓐ	8489 TGV ⑤f	8489 TGV ⑦e'	8499 TGV
0	Paris Montparnasse .... d.	0655	0705	0745	0900	0915	1035	1045	1215	1355	1525	1645	1710	1805	1835	1850	1930	1935	1935	2015	2045	2130	2130	2355
14	Massy .... d.	0705	0715																					
162	Vendôme .... d.			0830					1259				1849	1918		2012		2057						
221	St. Pierre des Corps .... a.	0755	0810	0850	0954	1014	1131	1140	1318	1451	1621	1740	1807	1908	1936	1945	2031	2031	2031	2116	2140	2226	2226	0051
221	St. Pierre des Corps .... d.	0800	0815	0852	1002	1019	1138	1145	1320	1457	1626	1742	1812	1910	1938	1951	2033	2038	2038	2118	2147	2231	2231	0056
224	Tours .... a.	0805	0820	0857	1007	1024	1143	1150	1325	1502	1631	1747	1817	1915	1943	1956	2038	2043	2043	2123	2152	2236	2236	0101

		8300 TGV Ⓐk	8302 TGV	8308 TGV	8414 TGV R	8414 TGV S	8420 TGV Ⓐk	8322 TGV	8328 TGV	8434 TGV	8538 TGV b	8346 TGV ⑧h	8448 TGV	8358 TGV ⑤f	8362 TGV	8466 TGV ⑦e	8472 TGV ✗n	8374 TGV M	8378 TGV ⑦e	8596 TGV ✗n	8492 TGV
	Tours .... d.	0626	0704	0807		0938	0954	1040	1209	1303	1443		1607	1714	1747	1841		1909	1949		2026	2038	2059	2154	2207
	St. Pierre des Corps .... a.	0630	0708	0812		0943	0954	1045	1214	1308	1448		1612	1718	1752	1846		1914	1954		2031	2043	2104	2159	2212
	St. Pierre des Corps .... d.	0632	0710	0818		0948	0958	1050	1216	1313	1454		1617	1720	1758	1848		1919	1959		2036	2048	2107	2204	2217
	Vendôme .... d.	0653	0732						1236				1742									2128			
	Massy .... a.																				2130			2311	
	Paris Montparnasse .... a.	0735	0815	0915		1045	1055	1145	1320	1410	1555		1715	1825	1855	1945		2015	2055		2140	2145	2210	2300	2320

A – Daily except ⑤ (also runs May 24).
J – Daily except when train K runs.
K – Ⓐ Mar. 27 - May 4.
M – ①②③④⑥ (also Apr. 16,30, May 7,25; not May 24).
R – Daily except when train S runs.
S – Ⓐ Mar. 13-27 and Ⓐ May 3-24.
TGV –Ⓡ, supplement payable.
b – Runs 10 minutes later on Mar. 17,24,31, May 5,12,19.
e – ⑦, also Apr. 17, May 1, 8, not Apr. 16, 30, May 7, 25.
f – Also May 24; not May 26.
g – Also May 24.
h – Not Apr. 16,30, May 7,25.
k – Not May 26.
n – Also Apr. 16,30, May 7,25.

Table 135a — ORLÉANS - TOURS

For TGV services Paris - Tours and v.v. see Table 135.

km		Ⓐ	Ⓐ	Ⓐ	⑥	4085	†	x	4011 LⓎ	4011 KⓎ	Ⓐ	4059	†	4057 A	4005 ⑤f		4061	⑤f	4007 ⑤f		Ⓐ	E
0	Paris Austerlitz 133 .... d.					0620			0721	0732		1108		1200	1200		1339		1354			
121	Orléans .... d.	0645	0629	0653	0728	0738	0803	0812			1014	1103	1224	1224	1251		1321	1454	1444		1600	1627
119	Les Aubrais-Orléans ..... d.						0811	0816	0821	0833	1022				1255	1300	1300	1329		1448	1453		
173	Blois .... d.	0712	0718	0741	0755	0820	0847		0849	0901	1056	1129	1306	1306		1331	1331	1409	1537		1639	1653
210	Amboise .... d.		0739	0803		0841	0905			1115		1327	1327			1430	1600			1657		
232	St. Pierre des Corps ...... a.	0736	0750	0818	0819	0855	0916		0917	0929	1126	1153	1342	1342		1400	1400	1440	1441	1613	1539		1708	1719
235	Tours .... a.	0746	0756	0824	0830	0901	0923		0927	0938	1133	1203	1349	1349		1407	1410	1448	1620		1549		1714	1720
	Nantes 127 .... a.	0915				1017					1336											1903

		4023 ⑤f	4053 Ⓐ	F	G	14067 †	✗	Ⓐ	⑦	4069	4071 F	F	4091 ⑤f	✗	4083 ⑤f	Ⓐ	4073 L	4073 Ⓐ	†	307		Ⓐ
	Paris Austerlitz 133 .... d.	1539	1600			1639				1715		1747		1750		1920		1931	1931		2224		
	Orléans .... d.	1629		1725	1715	1728	1755	1805	1806		1836		1841		1911	2012		2025			2128	2317	
	Les Aubrais-Orléans .... d.	1633	1637	1701					1812	1817	1840	1845	1850	1920	2016	2021	2029	2034	2034	2136	2321	2326	
	Blois .... d.		1703	1728	1752	1804	1818	1838	1832		1847		1911		1919	1952		2053		2112	2112	2211		2355
	Amboise .... d.		1749		1813	1847			1909										2134	2134	2228		0014
	St. Pierre des Corps .... a.	1728	1801	1816	1846	1908		1855		1922		1934		1947	2017		2120		2146	2146	2239		0027
	Tours .... a.	1738	1808	1826	1852	1908		1905		1929		1941		1957	2023		2127		2152	2157	2245		0037
	Nantes 127 .... a.			2002			2038															

		304	4054 ✗	4058 ✗	4060 Ⓐ	†	✗	4062 N	N	4062 N	M	4066 Ⓐ		✗	Ⓐ	Ⓐ	4068 ⑥	4070 Ⓐ		Ⓐ	Ⓐ
	Nantes 127 .... d.					0708							1130								
	Tours .... d.	0517		0642n	0709	0745	0817	0840		0946		0957		1049	1140		1217	1258		1258	1457		1557	1632
	St. Pierre des Corps ...... d.	0527		0648	0716	0752	0824	0845	0849	0952		1004		1056	1147		1223	1303	1308	1305	1503		1603	1639
	Amboise .... d.			0701		0728	0837		1004		1016		1108	1159		1237		1317	1515		1614	1651
	Blois .... d.	0555		0719		0749	0820	0905		0912	1021		1033		1129		1306		1333	1340	1536		1632	1710
	Les Aubrais-Orléans .... a.	0625	0633	0745	0750				1100	1105	1113	1118		1247	1252		1410	1618	1623	1707	1749	
	Orléans .... a.		0637		0754	0829	0849	0947		0938		1109		1122	1211		1256	1346		1400	1419		1627	1715	1758
	Paris Austerlitz 133 ...... a.	0736		0848		0948		1104		1203		1216		1346				1516	1725		

		4010 Ⓨ		G	H	J	⑥	⑥	14088 ⑤f	⑥	4002 Ⓐ	4072 ⑦e	⑦e	Ⓐ	4304 ⑦e	⑦e	†	†	†	⑤f	†
	Nantes 127 .... d.							1710							1833				2018		
	Tours .... d.	1635		1733	1733	1824	1857		1915	1929	1952	2000	2004		2026		2047	2054	2151		2200	2221
	St. Pierre des Corps ...... d.	1645		1739	1739	1831	1902	1907	1922	1935	2002	2007	2009	2014	2040		2053	2100	2156	2201	2207	2228
	Amboise .... d.			1754	1755	1843		1938	1948			2053		2104	2112			2218	2240	
	Blois .... d.	1723		1813	1822	1904	1932	1959	2010		2028		2034		2037	2110		2120	2127		2224	2237	2259
	Les Aubrais-Orléans .... a.	1753	1759		1908		2044	2050	2059	2105	2103	2108		2139	2144		2159		2313	
	Orléans .... a.		1803	1902	1902	1915	1946		2000	2048		2059	2109		2112		2103		2148	2152	2207		2251	2321	2337
	Paris Austerlitz 133 ...... a.	1855				2103			2152		2201	2204		2243				

A – Daily except ⑤ (runs May 26; not May 24).
E – ⑤⑥ (also May 24).
E – ①②③④⑦ (not Apr. 16, 30, May 7, 24).
G – ①②③④ (not Apr. 17, May 1, 8, 25).
H – ⑤⑥⑦ also Apr. 17, May 1, 8, 24, 25.
H – ①②③④⑥ (not Apr. 17, May 1, 8, 24, 25).
K – Ⓒ Mar. 18 - May 27, also May 26.
L – ✗, also Apr. 17, May 1, 8, not Apr. 16, 30, May 7, 25.
M – Ⓐ Mar. 13 - 27, May 3 - 24.
N – Daily Jan. 2 - Mar. 12, Mar. 28 - Apr. 2; also Mar. 18, 19, 25, 26, May 6, 7, 13, 14, 20, May 21, 26, 27.
e – ⑦, also Apr. 17, May 1, 8, not Apr. 16, 30, May 7, 25.
f – Also May 24, not May 26.
n – Depart 0639 on ① (also Apr. 18, May 2, 9, not Apr. 17, May 1, 8, and change at St Pierre des Corps).
x – 12 minutes later on Ⓒ, also May 26.

Ⓐ – Mondays to Fridays, except holidays   Ⓑ – Daily except Saturdays   Ⓒ – Saturdays, Sundays and holidays

Table 136 — PARIS - POITIERS - LA ROCHELLE and BORDEAUX

1,2 class

km				8501 TGV J	8501 TGV K	8503 TGV K	8503 TGV K	8305 TGV ✗F	8305 TGV K	8507 TGV ✗F	8507 TGV K	8409 TGV J	8409 TGV K	4011 C	4011 B	8311 TGV J	3879 N	8311 TGV K	13879 K	8515 TGV J	8417 TGV J	8417 TGV K	8319 TGV J	8319 TGV J
		⑥	Ⓐ																					
0	Paris Montparnasse .... d.	...	...	0655	0705	0705	0705	0720	0720	0735	0810	0825	0815	0830			0900		0915	...	1000	1035	1045	1050	1100
	Paris Austerlitz 135a ...... d.	...	...												0721	0732									
14	Massy .... d.	...	...	0705	0715																				
	Tours .... d.	...	...	0748	0802									0909	0921	0946		1007			1123	1133		
287	St. Pierre des Corps .... d.	...	...	0757	0812									0919	0931	0956		1016			1133	1142		
	Châtellerault .... d.	...	...	0832	0857									1007	1018									
320	Poitiers .... a.	...	...	0848	0911			0856	0915			0949	1007	1023	1034	1045		1105			1221	1229	1226	1236
320	Poitiers .... d.	...	0625	0850	0913			0859	0918			0951	1009	1030	1040		1054		1115			1223	1231	1223	1238
400	Niort .... a.	...	...					0941	1003							1142		1208					1310	1320
467	La Rochelle .... a.	...	...					1026	1044							1228		1253					1348	1358
432	Angoulême .... d.	0629	0728	0937	0959			...	...			1035	1052	1128	1139		1230			1308	1316		
515	Coutras .... d.	0717	0816					...	...					1206	1219		1316						
531	Libourne .... d.	0730	0825					...	...			1115	1131	1218	1230		1328			1349	1358		
568	Bordeaux St. Jean .... a.	0805	0846	1032	1051	1001	1026	...	...	1106	1124	1133	1148	1237	1250		1350			1256r	1406	1415		
	Irún 137 .... a.	...	...			1254	1315														1515r			
	Tarbes 137 .... a.	...	...									1350	1411				1612	1612y						
	Toulouse 139 .... a.	...	...			1210q	1236																	

		8519 TGV K	8519 TGV J	8423 TGV ✗b	8525 TGV	4005 ⑤f	8433 TGV ⑤g	8433 TGV A	8535 TGV	4007 ⑤f		8441 TGV		8543 TGV ⑦e	8545 TGV ⑤g	4023 ✗	8549 TGV ⑤f	8453 TGV ⑥h	8353 TGV ⑤g	8557 TGV H	8559 TGV E	8361 TGV ⑥h
Paris Montparnasse .... d.		1055	1115*	1140	1245	...	1355	1355	1400		...	1525		1555	1600		...	1700	1710	1710	1740	1745	1800
Paris Austerlitz 135a ...... d.						1200				1354						1539	1539						
Massy .... d.																							
Tours .... d.						1352	1443	1443		1531	1613					1720	1720		1759	1759			
St. Pierre des Corps .... d.						1402	1454	1454		1541	1623					1730	1730		1809	1809			
Châtellerault .... d.							1533	1533								1807	1807		1844	1844			
Poitiers .... a.				1314	1419	1458	1550	1550		1633	1710					1826	1826		1901	1901			1935
Poitiers .... d.				1316	1421	1459	1553	1553	1559	1635	1640	1714	1717	1719		1835	1845		1906	1909			1938
Niort .... a.									1644		1728	1815	1816			1931			1955			2020
La Rochelle .... a.									1729		1809	1900	1905z			2016			2036			2058
Angoulême .... d.				1401	1506	1552		1639		1723	1801					1927			1951		1957	
Coutras .... d.										1806	1838				2009						
Libourne .... d.										1806	1838				2009						
Bordeaux St. Jean .... a.		1409	1419	1455	1559	1654		1731		1659q	1825	1855		1858	1904	2031		2004	2047v		2050	2053
Irún 137 .... a.											2105			2126								
Tarbes 137 .... a.											1944q	2223			2147					2339	2342	
Toulouse 139 .... a.		1620	1630													2214						

		8565 TGV ⑥h	8471 4015 ⑤f	8469 TGV ⑤g	8369 TGV ⑤g	4091 A	8369 TGV H	303 302 ♇	4315 ⑤f	8477 TGV ✗	8379 TGV ⑤g	8377 TGV ⑦e	8481 TGV H t	8387 TGV Ⓐ	4073 ⑦e	8489 TGV E	8499 TGV ⑦e	307 ◆	4319 ⑦e W	4047 ⑦e W	4045 ⑦e W	4319 ⑦e W
Paris Montparnasse .... d.		1830	1850	1850	1850					1930	1935	1935	2000		2045	1931	2130	2355		2224	2356	2359	2359	2359
Paris Austerlitz 135a ...... d.			1747			1750	1805	1832															
Massy .... d.																						
Tours .... d.		1920	1938	1938	1944	2012	2023	2023			2132	2141	2218	0043	0021	0210	0216	0216	0216
St. Pierre des Corps .... d.		1930	1947	1947	1955	2022	2033	2033			2142	2151	2228	0053	0032	0220	0226	0226	0226
Châtellerault .... d.			2022	2022	2040	2102	2109			2217	2237		0111	0303	0308	0308	0308
Poitiers .... a.		2019	2025	2039	2039	2100		2124		2127	2120	2135	2233	2256	2315	0137	0131	0326	0329	0329	0329
Poitiers .... d.		2021	2027	2033	2042	2045	2055		2142	2130	2123	2137	2142	2317	0139	0141	0345	0333	0333	0345
Niort .... a.			2121	2130	2148		2229		2215	2210	2229				0439		0439
La Rochelle .... a.			2204	2212	2229		2311		2257	2251	2311				0554		0554
Angoulême .... d.		2109	2118		2127				2224			0002	0224	0236	0454	0454
Coutras .... d.												0539	0539
Libourne .... d.		2153	2201	2209			2304f					0552	0552
Bordeaux St. Jean .... a.		2134	2212	2218	2226		2236	2239	2317		0057	0316	0339	0614	0614	0854
Irún 137 .... a.					0202						0717	
Tarbes 137 .... a.										0734	
Toulouse 139 .... a.											

◆ – NOTES (LISTED BY TRAIN NUMBERS)

302/3 – LA PUERTA DEL SOL – ⇌ 2 cl. Paris - Madrid; 🛏 Paris - Hendaye; 🍴 Paris - Bordeaux.

307 – 🛏 and ⇌ 2 cl. Paris - Irún; 🛏 and ⇌ 2 cl. Paris - Tarbes.

A – Daily except ⑤ (not May 24).
B – Daily except dates in note C.
C – Ⓐ Mar. 13 - May 24.
E – ⑤⑦ (also Apr. 17, May 1,8,24; not Apr. 16,30, May 7).
F – Will not run on Ⓐ Mar. 27 - May 4.
G – ②③④⑤ (not Apr. 18, May 2,9,25).
H – ①②③④⑥ (also Apr. 16,30, May 7; not Apr. 17, May 1,8,24).
J – Daily except dates in note K.
K – Ⓐ Mar. 27 - May 4.
N – Conveys 🛏 Paris Austerlitz - La Rochelle from train 4011.
P – ①②③④ (also Apr. 16,30, May 7; not Apr. 17, May 1,8,24).

TGV – Ⓡ, supplement payable.
W – 🛏 and ⇌ 1,2 cl. Paris - Bordeaux.

b – Runs 15 minutes later on ✗ Mar. 27 - Apr. 27.
c – Also Apr. 18, May 2,9; not Apr. 17, May 1,8.
e – Also Apr. 17, May 1,8; not Apr. 16,30, May 7.
f – ⑤ (also May 24; not May 26).
g – Also May 24.
h – Not Apr. 16,30, May 7,25.
n – Apr. 16,30, May 7,25.
q – 5 minutes later Mar. 13 - May 27.
r – From Mar. 13, arrive Bordeaux 1303, Irún 1522.
t – Runs 13 minutes later on Dec. 24,31, Feb. 25, Mar. 4,11.
v – ⑦ (also Apr. 17, May 1,8; not Apr. 16,30, May 7).
x – ⑤⑦ (also Apr. 17, May 1,8,24; not Apr. 16,30, May 7).
y – Arrive 1622 on Ⓐ Sept. 25 - Jan. 30.
z – Arrive 1914 on ⑤.

Table 136a — ANGOULÊME - SAINTES - ROYAN

1,2 class

km		①c	G		✗F	K	K	✗F	†	✗	⑧	⑦e	⑦n	⑤f	✗	⑤f	A	⑤f	E	P	E	⑤f
0	Angoulême 136 ...... d.	0622	0643	...	1045	1058		1322	1424		1647		1647		1816		1908	2004	2004		2124	223
49	Cognac .... d.	0704	0728	...	1125	1137		1403	1501		1726		1726		1857		1950	2043	2043		2206	231
75	Niort 136 .... d.			0818			1318	1328		1507			1735		1821			2028		
75	Saintes .... a.	0726	0750	...	0922	1145	1156	1411	1423	1423	1520	1608	1746	1746	1837	1916	1928	2009	2102	2102	2124	2226	232
75	Saintes .... d.	0732	...	0823	...	1152	1203	1413	1423	1434	1532	...	1756	1825		1922		2023		2114	2127	2237	234
111	Royan .... a.	0759	...	0850	...	1220	1231	1441	1451	1502	1602	...	1829	1858		1954		2056		2142	2154	2307	000

FOR NOTES SEE TABLE 136 ABOVE

Table 136 — BORDEAUX and LA ROCHELLE - POITIERS - PARIS

1,2 class

km		304 ♦	4054 ①g	Ⓐ	8402 TGV Ⓐk ⍾	8404 TGV Ⓐk ⍾	300 ♦	8308 TGV ⑦ ⍾	8308 TGV ⍄ ⍾	8410 TGV ⍄ ⍾	8412 TGV ①g ⍾	Ⓐ	⑥	†	8414 TGV z ⍾	8516 TGV ①g ⍾	8518 TGV ⍄ ⍾	Ⓐ	8420 TGV Ⓐk ⍾	8527 TGV ⍾	8426 TGV ⍾	8326 TGV ⍾
	Toulouse 139 .... d.	...	...	...	...	...	...	...	...	...	...	...	...	...	...	...	...	...	...	...	...	...
	Tarbes 137 .... d.	2234	...	...	...	...	...	...	...	...	...	...	...	...	...	0611	...	...	...	...	...	...
	Hendaye 137 .... d.	2255	...	...	...	...	0336	...	...	...	...	...	...	...	...	0607	...	...	0735	...	...	...
0	Bordeaux St. Jean .... d.	0212	...	...	...	0534	0553	...	...	0612	0633	...	...	...	0713	...	0825	0825	...	1024	1024	...
37	Libourne .... d.		...	...	...	...	...	...	...	0631	...	...	...	...	0732	...	...	...	...	...	...	...
53	Coutras .... d.		...	...	...	...	...	...	...	...	...	...	...	...	...	...	...	...	...	...	...	...
136	Angoulême .... d.	0328	...	...	0553	...	...	...	0708	...	...	...	...	...	0812	...	...	...	0916	1119	1119	...
	La Rochelle .... d.		...	...		...	...	0548	...	...	0640	0707	0715	...	...	...	0805	...	...	...	...	1052
	Niort .... d.		...	...		...	...	0628	...	...	0730	0752	0758	...	...	...	0851	...	...	...	...	1128
249	Poitiers .... a.	0419	...	...	0637	...	...	0716	0750	...	0826	0845	0845	0855	...	...	0944	0959	1204	1204	1211
249	Poitiers .... d.	0423	0548	0632	0639	...	...	0721	0721	0752	...	...	...	0857	...	...	...	1001	1207	1207	1214
281	Châtellerault .... d.	0445	0606	0658	0655	...	...	0738	0738	...	...	...	...	...	...	...	...	...	...	...	...
349	St. Pierre-des-Corps .... a.	0522	0646		...	...	...	0815	0815	...	...	...	...	0946	...	...	1048	...	...	...	...
	Tours .... a.	0532	0656	0744	...	...	...	0824	0824	...	...	...	...	0956	...	...	1059	...	...	...	...
	Massy .... a.		...	...	...	...	...	...	...	...	...	...	...	...	...	...	...	...	...	...	...
581	Paris Austerlitz 135a .... a.	0736	0851		...	1034	...	...	...	...	...	...	...	...	...	...	...	...	...	...	...
	Paris Montparnasse .... a.		...	...	0820	0840	...	0915	0915	0930	0940	...	...	...	1045	1125y	1125y	...	1145	1345x	1345x	1350x

		8328 TGV ⍾	8530 TGV ⍺	8434 TGV ⍾	8536 TGV S ⍾	3884 4010 ⍾	4010	8539 TGV m ⍾	·⍾	8448 5f ⍾	8552 TGV ⍾	⑧ ⍾	⍺q ⍾	8560 TGV ⍾	8362 TGV E ⍾	8362 TGV 5f ⍾	4002	8563 TGV ⍾	⑦e ⍾	8466 TGV ⑦e ⍾	8470 TGV ⑦e ⍾
	Toulouse 139 .... d.	...	...	...	...	...	...	...	...	1348	...	...	...	...	...	...	...	...	...	...	...
	Tarbes 137 .... d.	...	...	...	...	1002	...	1059	...	...	...	...	...	...	...	...	1445	...	...	...	...
	Hendaye 137 .... d.	...	...	0936	...	1041	...	...	...	...	...	...	...	1421	...	...	...	...	...	...	...
	Bordeaux St. Jean .... d.	...	...	1159	1210	1216	1306	...	1320	...	1345	...	1524	1601b	1636	...	...	1650	1731	1734	1800
	Libourne .... d.	...	...	...	1230	1246	...	...	1340	...	...	...	...	...	...	...	1712	...	...	1819
	Coutras .... d.	...	...	...		1259	...	...	1350	...	...	...	...	...	...	...	...	...	...	...
	Angoulême .... d.	...	...	1310	1346	...	...	...	1426	...	1440	...	1617	...	1731	...	1758	...	1826	1859
	La Rochelle .... d.	...	...	...	...	1339	...	...	...	...	...	...	1635	1652	...	...	...	...	...
	Niort .... d.	...	...	...	...	1427	...	...	1559	...	...	1718	1733	...	1759	...	...
	Poitiers .... a.	...	...	1353	...	1514	1521	1523	1657	1701	...	1806	1814	1819	1823	1903	1909	1943
	Poitiers .... d.	1217	1220	1356	...	1540	1540	1526	...	1706	...	1816	1823	1823	1858	...	1911	1945
	Châtellerault .... d.	1235	1248	1413	...	1603	1603	...	...	1807	...	1845	1845	1919	...	...	...
	St. Pierre-des-Corps .... a.	1311	...	1452	...	1643	1643	1614	1755	...	...	1916	1916	2000	...	1957	...
	Tours .... a.	1321	1339	1502	...	1653	1653	1625	1804	1900	...	1926	1926	2010	...	2007	...
	Massy .... a.	...	...	...	...	...	...	...	...	...	...	...	...	2201	...	...	...
	Paris Austerlitz 135a .... a.	...	...	...	1855	1855	...	...	...	...	...	...	...	...	...	...	...
	Paris Montparnasse .... a.	1410	...	1500x	1555	...	1615	...	1715	...	1855	1900j	...	1955	2015	2015	...	2030	...	2055	2125

		3886 ①-④ 5f ⍾	8472 TGV ⍺q ⍾	8574 TGV ⍺ ⍾	4312 ⑦e ⍾	⑦e ⍾	8374 TGV H ⍾	E ⍾	8384 TGV E ⍾	8586 TGV ⑧h ⍾	8492 TGV ⑦e ⍾	8596 TGV ⍺q ⍾	⑦e ⍾	8594 TGV ⑦e ⍾	8598 TGV ⑦e ⍾	4318 E W	4026 ⑦e ♦	4034 E W
	Toulouse 139 .... d.	...	...	...	...	...	...	...	1715	...	...	...	...	1720	...	...	...	...
	Tarbes 137 .... d.	...	...	...	...	...	...	...	...	...	...	...	...	...	...	1921	...	...
	Hendaye 137 .... d.	...	...	...	1609	...	...	...	...	1723	...	...	...	1826	...	1956	...	...
	Bordeaux St. Jean .... d.	...	...	1800	1806	1824	...	1907	1928	1932	1938	...	2006	2040	1923	2250	2345
	Libourne .... d.	...	...	1819	1833		...	1947	...	...	...	...	2025	...	2315	0011
	Coutras .... d.	...	...	...	1846		...	2002	...	...	...	...	...	2328	0025
	Angoulême .... d.	...	...	1859	1935	...	2050	...	2029	2030	...	2105	...	0014	0145
	La Rochelle .... d.	...	1755	...	1803	1822	1930	...	...	2014	...	2231	...
	Niort .... d.	1823	1838	...	1847	1902	2006	...	...	2058	...	2332	...
	Poitiers .... a.	1927	1936	1943	...	1939	1950	2049	2118	2113	2144	2148	0023	0130	0248
	Poitiers .... d.	...	...	1945	...	1957	1955	2052	2120	2115	...	2151	0057	0134	0255
	Châtellerault .... d.	...	...	...	2018	...	2140	...	...	0120	0159	...
	St. Pierre-des-Corps .... a.	...	2034	2054	2045	...	2215	2202	...	0203	0241	0356
	Tours .... a.	...	2043	2104	2057	...	2224	2212	...	0212	0252	0406
	Massy .... a.	...	2130	...	...	...	2311	...	...	...	...
	Paris Austerlitz 135a .... a.	...	...	2239	...	...	...	...	0558	0547	0610
	Paris Montparnasse .... a.	...	2140	2130	...	2145	2230	2235	2320	2300	...	2330	2345	...	...	...

NOTES (LISTED BY TRAIN NUMBERS):

♦ —

300 — LA PUERTA DEL SOL — ⊨ 2 cl. Madrid - Paris; ⟠ Hendaye - Paris; ⟀ Bordeaux - Paris.

304 — ⟠ and ⊨ 2 cl. Hendaye and Tarbes - Paris.

4026 — ⟠ and ⊨ 1,2 cl. Hendaye and Tarbes - Paris.

E — ⑤⑦ (also Apr. 17, May 1,8,24; not Apr. 16,30, May 7).
G — ①②③④ (not Apr. 17, May 1,8).
H — ①②③④⑥ (also Apr. 16,30, May 7; not May 1,8,24).
S — Apr. 17,23,29,30, May 1,8 only.

TGV — ℝ, supplement payable.

W — ⟠ and ⊨ 1,2 cl. Bordeaux - Paris.

b — Depart 1609 on Ⓐ Feb. 21 - Mar. 10.
e — Also Apr. 17, May 1,8; not Apr. 16,30, May 7.
f — ⑤ (also May 24; not May 26).
g — Also Apr. 18, May 2,9; not Apr. 17, May 1,8.
h — Not Apr. 16,30, May 7,25.
j — Arrive 1907 on Ⓐ Feb. 21 - May 24.
k — Not May 26.
m — Runs 10 minutes later throughout on Mar. 17,24,31, May 5,12,19.
q — Also Apr. 16,30, May 7,25.
x — 5 minutes later from Mar. 13.
y — 10 minutes later from Mar. 13.
z — Runs 10 minutes later throughout on Ⓐ Mar. 13-27 and Ⓐ May 3-24.

Table 136a — ROYAN - SAINTES - ANGOULÊME

1,2 class

	Ⓐ	⍺	Ⓐ	⍺		⍺	⑦					⑥					E	G	E			⑦	
Royan .... d.	...	0605	0647	...	...	0857	...	0953	...	1235	...	...	1544	...	1708	...	1750	1819	1915	...	2019	2019	...
Saintes .... a.	...	0632	0714	...	...	0925	...	1020	...	1305	...	...	1612	...	1735	...	1823	1852	1946	...	2048	2048	...
Saintes .... d.	0618	0643	...	0838	...	0952	0952	1023	...	1318	...	1612	1643	...	1746	...	1844	1844	1907	1958	...	2107	...
Niort 136 .... a.	0724	...	...	0943	...	...	...	1117	...	...	...	1707	...	...	...	1951	1951	...	...	...	...
Cognac .... d.	...	0703	...	...	1011	1011	...	1338	...	1702	...	1808	...	1926	2017	...	2126	...
Angoulême 136 .... a.	...	0742	...	...	1050	1050	...	1420	...	1744	...	1851	...	2008	2100	...	2207	...

FOR NOTES SEE TABLE 136 ABOVE

Table 137 — (PARIS) - BORDEAUX - TARBES/IRÚN — 1,2 class

km	409 408 D	307 4830 C	307 ◆	179 ◆	179 172 B	Ⓐ	4541	4516	99733 ✕	8501 TGV F 🍴	Ⓐ	8501 TGV G 🍴	8507 TGV J 🍴	8507 TGV K 🍴	8507 TGV G 🍴	8515 TGV L 🍴	4011 4810 14013	Ⓐ
Paris Montparnasse 136 d	...	...	...	...	...	...	...	...	...	0655	...	0705	0810	0810	0825	1000	...	...
Paris Austerlitz 136 d	2000	2224	2224	2258	2258	...	...	...	...	0850	...	0913	...	...	...	...	0732y	...
Poitiers 136 d	...	0141	0141	...	...	...	...	...	...	...	...	...	...	...	...	...	1040y	...
0 Bordeaux St Jean d	0031	0403	0403	...	...	...	0710	...	0810	1035	...	1054	1109	1112	1127	1259	1309 1426	...
109 Morcenx a	...	0457	0457	0538	0538	...	0811	...	...	...	...	...	...	...	...	...	1404	...
148 Dax a	...	0519	0519	0601	0601	...	0830	...	0915	1141	...	1200	1214	1219	1236	...	1424 1533	...
148 Dax d	...	0533	0546	0618	0624	0630	0834	0837	0918	1143	1147	1202	1217	1222	1238	...	1427 1535	...
Pau 139 d	...	0646	0547	...	0722	...	0932	...	...	...	1237	...	1309	1314	1330	...	1528	...
Lourdes 139 d	...	0719	...	...	0749	...	1001z	...	...	...	...	...	1335	1340	1356	...	1556	...
Tarbes 139 a	...	0734	...	...	0805	...	1015z	...	...	...	...	...	1350	1355	1411	...	1612	...
199 Bayonne 139 d	...	...	0627	0650	...	0711	0909	...	0945	1214	...	1234	1419	...	...	1435	1607 1729	...
209 Biarritz 139 d	...	...	0639	0704	...	0720	0918	...	...	1224	...	1245	1428	...	...	1445	1618 1738	...
222 St Jean-de-Luz 139 d	...	...	0656	0718	...	0732	0932	...	...	1237	...	1257	1441	...	...	1458	1632 1751	...
235 Hendaye 139 d	...	...	0707	0730	...	0744	0941	...	...	1247	...	1307	1453	...	...	1508	1642 1803	...
237 Irún 139 a	0251	...	0717	0740	...	...	0949	...	...	1254	...	1315	1459	...	...	1515	1649 1809	...

	8525 TGV ⑥	8535 TGV 🍴	⑥	Ⓐ	†	4545 ⑤f	4037	4007 14804 A 🍴	4007 4006 ⑤f 🍴	8543 TGV ⑤f 🍴	8545 TGV 🍴	8557 TGV H	8559 TGV E	Ⓐ	8565 TGV E	303 302 ◆	⑤f
Paris Montparnasse 136 d	1245	1400	...	...	...	...	...	...	...	1555	1600	...	1740	1745	1830	...	...
Paris Austerlitz 136 d	...	...	...	...	...	...	...	...	...	...	...	...	...	...	...	1805	...
Poitiers 136 d	1421	...	...	...	...	1354	...	1354	...	1635	...	1635	...	...	...	...	...
Bordeaux St Jean d	1602	1702	1646	1646	...	1742	1830	1830	1830	1901	1907	2053	2056	...	2137	2240	2245
Morcenx d	...	1744	1744	...	...	1832	1926	1926	1926	...	...	...	...	...	...	...	...
Dax a	1706	1808t	1804	1804	...	1852	1946	1946	1946	2008	2011	2159	2202	...	2346	...	2357
Dax d	1708	1811t	1823	1823	1823	1854	1950	2014	2006	2011	2013	2202	2205	2210	2348	2359	0056
Pau 139 d	...	1903t	...	...	...	1948	...	2118	2136	...	2105	2258	2301	...	...	...	0121
Lourdes 139 d	...	1929t	...	...	...	...	...	2148	2207	...	2131	2324	2327	...	...	...	0136
Tarbes 139 a	...	1944t	...	...	...	...	...	2204	2223	...	2147	2339	2342	...	...	...	...
Bayonne 139 d	1740	...	1908	1910	1910	...	2023	...	...	2041	...	...	...	2246	2313	0019	...
Biarritz 139 d	1750	...	1919	1919	...	...	2034	...	...	2052	...	...	...	2255	2323	...	...
St Jean-de-Luz 139 d	1802	...	1933	1933	...	...	2047	...	...	2105	...	...	...	2305	2335	...	...
Hendaye 139 a	1812	...	1946	1946	...	...	2057	...	...	2116	...	...	...	2315	2345	0046	...
Irún 139 a	...	...	1953	1953	...	...	2105	...	...	2126	...	...	...	...	...	0202	...

	407 D	300 301 ◆	Ⓐ	4801 4800 🍴 S	8516 TGV 🍴	✕ S	Ⓐ	97290 ✕ M	8527 TGV 🍴	8530 TGV 🍴	8536 TGV 🍴 S R	4811 14010 🍴	8539 4010 TGV N	8539 TGV O	✕	8560 TGV 🍴	8563 TGV 🍴	97270 Ⓐ	8574 TGV ⑦e 🍴
Hendaye 139 d	0123x	0336	0533	...	0607	...	0750	...	0936	1041	1041	...	1312	1421	...	1525	1609	...	...
St. Jean-de-Luz 139 d	...	...	0545	...	0619	0708	0802	...	0949	1055	1055	...	1324	1433	...	1537	1621	...	...
Biarritz 139 d	...	...	0558	...	0631	0721	0815	...	1001	1107	1107	...	1337	1445	...	1550	1633	...	...
Bayonne 139 d	...	0410	0607	...	0641	0655	0730	0742	0824	1012	1118	1118	1345	1455	1535	1558	1643	...	...
Tarbes 139 d	...	...	...	0501g	...	...	...	0735	...	1002	1059	1110	...	1445	...	...	...	...	...
Lourdes 139 d	...	...	...	0517g	...	...	...	0752	...	1019	1116	1127	...	1502	...	...	...	...	...
Pau 139 d	...	...	...	0545	...	...	...	0818	...	1048	1142	1153	...	1528	...	...	...	...	...
Dax a	...	0439	0640	0644	...	0735	...	0807	0855	0909	1042	1149	1149	1146	1229	1240	1607	1615	...
Dax d	...	0441	...	0647	...	...	...	0809	...	0912	1045	1152	...	1159	1231	1242	...	1617	...
Morcenx d	...	...	...	0709	...	...	...	...	...	...	...	1222	...	...	...	...	...	...	...
Bordeaux St. Jean a	0355	0550	0808	0817	...	0916	...	1019	1157	1301	1316	1340	1351	...	1631	1727	...	1819	...
Poitiers 136 a	...	...	1034	...	...	...	...	1204	...	...	1521	1523	1534	...	1814	...	...	...	...
Paris Austerlitz 136 a	...	...	...	1125h	...	...	...	...	...	...	...	1855	...	...	...	...	...	...	...
Paris Montparnasse 136 a	0833	...	...	...	1350	1505	...	1615	...	1715	1725	...	1955	...	2030	...	2130	...	...

	14803 E	14040 E	14805 H	8596 TGV ✕c 🍴	8594 TGV ⑦e 🍴	4540 P	4540 †	4521 T	4521 ✕	4540 ⑦e	8598 TGV E	4547 †	4546 99730	4827 ⑦e ◆	4026 ⑦e ◆	4026 W	171 178 ◆	178 U	304 ◆	4831 304 Y
Hendaye 139 d	...	1639	...	1723	...	...	1733	...	...	1818	1826	...	1936	...	1956	...	2240	...	2255	...
St. Jean-de-Luz 139 d	...	1652	...	1735	...	...	1747	...	...	1832	1838	...	1947	...	2010	...	2254	...	2312	...
Biarritz 139 d	...	1705	...	1746	...	...	1803	...	...	1844	1849	...	1959	...	2023	...	2315	...	2330	...
Bayonne 139 d	...	1717	...	1756	...	...	1813	...	...	1855	1859	...	2009	...	2035	...	2326	...	2345	...
Tarbes 139 d	1606	...	1626	...	1720	...	1756	...	...	1844	...	1900	...	1921	...	2212	...	2234		
Lourdes 139 d	1622	...	1642	...	1737	...	1812	...	...	1900	...	1940	...	2232	...	2252				
Pau 139 d	1651	...	1710	...	1803	...	1839	1839	...	1929	...	2008	...	2305	...	2330				
Dax a	1747	1746	1805	1824	1850	1846	1932	1932	1927	2028	2042	2106	2105	2355	0000	...	0015	0026		
Dax d	...	1802	...	1826	1852	1902	1936	...	2034	2046	2120	2120	0018	0018	0039	0039				
Morcenx d	...	1824	...	...	1928	1957	2107	2145	2145	2246	2246	0044	0044	0105	0105	0157	0157			
Bordeaux St. Jean a	1916	1933	2001	2030	2056	2035	2146	2202	2246	2246	0130	0130	0419	0419						
Poitiers 136 a	...	2113	...	2148	...	0130	0130	0419	0419											
Paris Austerlitz 136 a	...	1855	0547	0547	0715	0715	0736	0736												
Paris Montparnasse 136 a	...	2300	...	2330	...	2345	0547	0547												

NOTES (LISTED BY TRAIN NUMBER):

◆ –

178/9 – LA PALOMBE BLEUE – 🛏1,2 cl. (T2) and 🍴1,2 cl. Paris - Irún and Hendaye - Paris.

300-303 – LA PUERTA DEL SOL – 🛏2 cl. Paris - Madrid and v.v.; 🍴 Paris - Hendaye and v.v.; 🍴 Paris - Bordeaux and v.v.

304 – 🍴 and 🍴2 cl. Hendaye - Paris.

307 – 🍴 and 🍴2 cl. Paris - Irún.

4026 – 🍴 and 🍴1,2 cl. Hendaye - Paris.

A – Daily except May 24.

B – 🛏1,2 cl. (T2) and 🍴1,2 cl. Paris - Tarbes.

C – 🍴 and 🍴2 cl. Paris - Tarbes.

D – FRANCISCO DE GOYA – Special fares apply. Inter-Rail cards cannot be used on this service: 🛏1,2 cl. and 🍴 Paris - Madrid and v.v. International passengers only.

E – ⑤⑦ (also Apr. 18, 24; not Apr. 16, May 7, 25).

F – Daily to Mar. 26, May 9 - 27; ⑥⑦ Apr. 1 - 30, also Apr. 17, May 1, 5, 6, 7.

G – ④ Mar. 27 - May 4.

H – ①②③④⑤ (also Apr. 16, 30, May 7; not Apr. 17, May 1, 8).

J – ✕ Feb. 1 - 18, daily Feb. 19 - Mar. 11.

K – Mar. 13 - 17, 20 - 24, Apr. 1 - 4, 8, 15, 16, 22, 23, 29, 30, May 5, 6, 9 - 13, 15 - 20, 22 - 24, 26, 27 only.

L – Daily except May 25.

M – ②③④⑤ (not May 25).

N – Daily Jan. 2 - Mar. 16, Apr. 7 - May 4, May 20 - 27; daily except ⑤ Mar. 18 - Apr. 6, May 6 - 18.

O – Mar. 17, 24, 31, May 5, 12, 19 only.

P – ⑤ Jan. 2 - Mar. 18; ⑤⑥ Mar. 24 - May 27.

R – Daily except Apr. 17, 23, 29, 30, May 1, 8.

S – ① (also Apr. 18, May 2, 9, not Apr. 17, May 1, 8).

T – ①②③④ Mar. 20 - May 24, not Apr. 17, May 1, 8.

TGV – 🅁 supplement payable.

U – 🛏1,2 cl. (T2) and 🍴1,2 cl. Tarbes - Paris.

W – 🍴 and 🍴1,2 cl. Tarbes - Paris.

Y – 🍴 and 🍴2 cl. Tarbes - Paris.

c – ⑤⑥ (also Apr. 16, 30, May 7, 25).

e – Also Apr. 17, May 1, 8, not Apr. 16, 30, May 7, 25.

f – Also May 24, not May 26.

g – ①⑦ (also Apr. 18, May 2, 9, not Apr. 17, May 1, 8).

h – Mar. 13 - May 27 arrive Paris 1135.

t – 5 minutes later Mar. 13 - May 27.

x – Irún timing.

y – ④ Mar. 13 - May 24 depart Paris 0721, Poitiers 1030.

z – ⑤⑥⑦ Mar. 24 - May 27 also Apr. 17, May 1, 8, 25 (daily Jan. 2 - Mar. 19).

Table 137a — BORDEAUX - ARCACHON

km		凸		凸	†	†	凸		Ⓐ	†	Ⓐ	凸		Ⓑ		Ⓑ	Ⓑ	C	⑤f		
0	Bordeaux St Jean.....d.	0624	0650	0751	0838	0908	1040	1158	1235	1433	1610	1649	1710	1714	1717	1801	1838	1935	2014	2141	2248	2345	...	...
40	Facture.....d.	0653	0719	0823	0859	0938	1101	1228	1307	1455	1640	1712	1735	1751	1837	1907	2006	2034	2208	2313	0007	...	...
56	La Teste.....a.	0709	0735	0842	0916	0953	1119	1245	1325	1513	1657	1727	1750	1748	1809	1857	1925	2024	2048	2225	2329	0021	...	...
59	Arcachon.....a.	0713	0739	0847	0920	0957	1123	1249	1329	1517	1701	1731	1754	1752	1813	1901	1930	2028	2052	2229	2333	0025	...	...

		Ⓑ	Ⓐ	Ⓐ	Ⓐ		Ⓐ		凸			Ⓐ	†	Ⓐ		凸		凸	†	凸	凸	⑦e	
	Arcachon.....d.	...	0610	0627	0654	0723	0758	0932	1047	1238	1255	1540	1622	1708	1725	1737	1811	1819	1906	1934	2107	2153	...
	La Teste.....d.	...	0614	0631	0658	0728	0802	0936	1051	1242	1259	1545	1626	1712	1729	1741	1816	1823	1910	1938	2112	2157	...
	Facture.....d.	...	0630	0649	0717	0743	0819	0953	1108	1258	1316	1558	1644	1727	1746	1758	1833	1839	1927	1956	2130	2211	...
	Bordeaux St Jean.....a.	...	0700	0726	0750	0805	0849	1014	1134	1330	1336	1619	1707	1751	1815	1826	1855	1907	1957	2026	2156	2232	...

C – ⑤⑦ (also Apr. 17, May 1, 8, 25; not Apr. 16, 30, May 7).   **e** – Also Apr. 17, May 1, 8; not Apr. 16, 30, May 7, 25.   **f** – Also May 24; not May 26.

Table 138 — PARIS - LIMOGES - TOULOUSE
For faster TGV services Paris - Toulouse see Table 139
1, 2 class

km		4501		4403		75		4403	4451	4451 4503	147 471		4407	4409			151	4471
		Ⓐ	⑥	Ⓐ	凸🍷	🗲🍴		凸🍷	🍷	C	🍷		🍷	🍷	凸	⑤⑦	⑤f🍷	⑤🍷
0	Paris Montparnasse.....d.	...	...	...	...	...		...	...	...	...		...	...	...	...	...	...
	Paris Austerlitz 141.....d.	...	...	0632	...	0718		0702	0910	0910	1006		1303	1345	...	...	1603	1632
	Orléans.....d.	...	...	0720	...	...		0754	1005	1005	...		1355	...	...	...	1651	1725
119	Les Aubrais 141.....d.	...	...	0733	...	...		0803	1014	1014	...		1404	...	...	...	1700	1733
200	Vierzon 141.....d.	...	0625	0639	0819	0845		0853	1054	1054	...		1445	...	...	...	1737	1818
236	Issoudun.....d.	...	0653	0703	0837	...		0911	...	...	...		1503	...	...	...	...	...
263	Châteauroux.....d.	...	0713	0721	0854	0905		0927	1125	1125	...		1520	...	...	...	1809	1852
341	La Souterraine.....d.	...	0810	0810	0937	...		1015	1205	1205	...		1607	...	...	...	...	1927
400	Limoges.....a.	...	0848	0850	1014	1020		1047	1238	1238	1305		1643	1651	...	...	1913	1959
400	Limoges 140.....d.	0623	...	...	1022	1022v	1030	...	1241	1253	1305		1647	1655	...	1659	1915	2003
499	Périgueux 140.....d.	...	...	...	1033	...	1127	...	1403	1437	...		1723	1814	1855		...	...
539	Les Eyzies.....d.	...	...	...	1101	...	...	...	1506	...	...		1755	...	1929		...	...
556	Le Buisson.....d.	...	...	...	1120	...	...	...	1522	...	...		1811	...	1946		...	...
651	Agen.....a.	...	...	...	1235	...	...	...	1645	...	...		1932	...	2104		...	...
459	Uzerche.....d.	...	0700	...	...	1103v	...	1320	...	...	...		1727	...	...		1953	2042
499	Brive la Gaillarde.....a.	...	0730	...	...	1121	1131v	1349	...	...	1410		1752	1756	...		2019	2110
499	Brive la Gaillarde.....d.	0618	0732	...	...	1133	...	...	...	...	1425		...	1804	...		2021	...
536	Souillac.....d.	0643	0756	...	...	1157	...	...	...	...	1452		...	1832	...		2045	...
559	Gourdon.....d.	0700	0811	...	...	1212	...	...	...	...	1508		...	1849	...		2100	...
600	Cahors.....d.	0735	0837	...	...	1239	...	...	...	...	1537		...	1916	...		2128	...
639	Caussade.....d.	0803	0903	...	...	1304	...	...	...	...	1606		...	1946	...		2154	...
662	Montauban 139.....d.	0822	0920	...	...	1321	...	...	...	...	1624		...	2004	...		2210	...
713	Toulouse Matabiau 139.....a.	0852	0950	...	...	1348	...	...	...	...	1655		...	2035	...		2241	...
	Narbonne 139.....a.	...	...	...	...	...	...	...	...	...	1843		...	...	...		...	...
	Port Bou 139.....a.	...	...	...	...	...	...	...	...	...	2045		...	...	...		...	...
	La Tour de Carol 144.....a.	...	...	...	...	...	...	...	...	...	...		...	...	...		...	...

		153 4747	153	155	4479	4433	77	4411	4443	4613	157		157	4459	4459	1117	4415	473	4417	4417 4435	175	4425	4425 4423
		H🍷	⑤🍷	⑤f🍷	⑥t🍷	H🍷	⑥h🍴	⑤f🍷	⑤f🍷	⑧h🍷	Ⓑ🍷		⑥t🍷	A	⑤f🍷	♦	♦	♦	♦	W	♦	Q
	Paris Montparnasse.....d.	...	...	...	...	...	...	...	...	...	...		...	...	...	...	...	...	...	...	...	...
	Paris Austerlitz 141.....d.	...	1700	1700	1745	1745	1750	1800	1815	1830	1847	1909		1909	2030	2030	2054	2106	2145	2218	2218	2236	2256	2256
	Orléans.....d.	...	...	...	...	1847	1856	...	...	1918	1939	...		...	2122	2122	...	2203	2241	2317	2317	2351	2351	...
	Les Aubrais 141.....d.	...	...	...	...	1856	...	...	...	1929	1948	...		...	2132	2132	...	2213	2250u	2328	2328	2359	0004	0004
	Vierzon 141.....d.	...	1829	1829	...	1940	...	...	2014	2032	...	2038		2038	2215	2215	...	2258	2333	0017	0017	...	0055	0055
	Issoudun.....d.	...	...	...	...	2000	...	...	2034	...	...	2056		2056	2234	2234	...	...	...	...	...	...	...	...
	Châteauroux.....d.	...	1900	1900	...	1951	2017	...	2018	2049	...	2109		2113	2250	2250	2315	2337	0007	0053	0053	...	0132	0132
	La Souterraine.....d.	...	...	...	...	2059	...	...	2055	2136	...	2146		2156	2333	...	...	...	...	...	...	...	...	...
	Limoges.....a.	...	2005	2005	2044	2057	2134	2058	2128	2212	...	2217		2221	2230	2232	...	0006	0027	0053	0118	0208	0208	...	0254	0254
	Limoges 140.....d.	...	2008	2025	2046	2100	...	2100	2105	...	...	2221		2221	2230	2236	...	0008	0029	0057	0122	0212	0212	...	0259	0312
	Périgueux 140.....d.	...	...	...	2133	...	...	2205	...	...	...	...		2334	...	...	...	...	...	...	...	...	0450
	Les Eyzies.....d.	...	...	...	...	...	...	...	...	...	...	...		...	...	...	...	...	...	...	...	0519
	Le Buisson.....d.	...	...	...	...	...	...	...	...	...	...	...		...	...	...	...	...	...	...	...	0537
	Agen.....a.	...	...	...	...	...	...	...	...	...	...	...		...	...	...	...	...	...	...	...	0705
	Uzerche.....d.	...	2045	...	...	...	...	...	...	2258	...	2313		...	0045	...	...	...	...	...	...	...
	Brive la Gaillarde.....a.	...	2111	...	2146	2200	...	2200	...	...	2323	...	2338		...	0111	...	0200	0226	0320	0320	...	0408	...
	Brive la Gaillarde.....d.	...	...	...	2150	2202	...	2202	...	...	...	...		...	...	...	0204	0229	...	0421	0421	...
	Souillac.....d.	...	...	...	...	2228	...	2228	...	...	...	...		...	...	...	...	...	0449	0449	...
	Gourdon.....d.	...	...	...	...	2245	...	2245	...	...	...	...		...	...	...	0507	...	0507	...
	Cahors.....d.	...	...	...	2251	2312	...	2312	...	...	...	...		...	...	0538	0523	0538	...
	Caussade.....d.	...	...	...	...	...	...	...	...	...	...	...		...	...	0607	...	0607	...
	Montauban 139.....d.	...	...	...	2331	2350	...	2350	...	...	...	...		...	0352	0414	...	0628	0622	0628	...
	Toulouse Matabiau 139.....a.	...	...	...	0002	0021	...	0021	...	...	...	...		...	0359	0424	0445	...	0700	0656	0700	...
	Narbonne 139.....a.	...	...	...	...	...	...	...	...	...	...	...		...	0543	...	0644	...
	Port Bou 139.....a.	...	...	...	...	...	...	...	...	...	...	...		...	0755	...	0850	...
	La Tour de Carol 144.....a.	...	...	...	...	...	...	...	...	...	...	...		...	...	0800	0800	...

OR FASTER TGV SERVICES PARIS - TOULOUSE SEE TABLE 139

♦ – NOTES (LISTED BY TRAIN NUMBER):

75 – L'OCCITAN – 🛏 1,2 cl. (T2) and 🍴 1,2 cl. Paris - Toulouse.

73 – PARIS – CÔTE VERMEILLE – 🛏 1,2 cl. (T2), 🍴 1,2 cl. and 🚗 Paris - Port Bou. Conveys, except when train 4415 runs, 🚗 and 🍴 1,2 cl. Paris - La Tour de Carol.

117 – Apr. 14, 21, May 24 only: 🚗 and 🍴 2 cl. Paris - Port Bou.

415 – ⑤ (also Apr. 15, 22, May 24; not May 26): 🚗 and 🍴 1,2 cl. Paris - La Tour de Carol; 🚗 and 🍴 1,2 cl. Paris - Luchon.

417 – 🚗 and 🍴 1,2 cl. Paris - Carmaux. For other cars see Table 139a.

425 – ⑤⑦ (also Apr. 17, May 1, 8; not Apr. 16, 30, May 7, 25): 🚗 and 🍴 2 cl. Paris - Toulouse.

A – Daily except ⑤ (not Apr. 16, 30, May 7, 24).
C – ⑤⑦ (also Apr. 17, May 1, 8, 24, 25).
H – ①②③④⑦ (not Apr. 16, 30, May 7, 24).
Q – ⑤ (also May 24, not May 26): 🚗 and 🍴 1,2 cl. Paris - Agen; 🍴 2 cl. Paris - Périgueux.
TGV – 🅁, supplement payable. Via Bordeaux (Table 136).
W – ①②③④⑥ (also Apr. 16, 30, May 7, 25, 26; not Apr. 17, May 1, 8, 24): 🚗 Paris - Toulouse. Conveys on ⑥ Dec. 17 - Apr. 1: 🚗 and 🍴 1,2 cl. Paris - Luchon.
f – Also May 24, not May 26.
h – Not Apr. 16, 30, May 7.
t – Also Apr. 16, 30, May 7.
u – Stops to pick up only.
v – ⑦ only.
♦ – Supplement payable.

TRAIN NAMES: **75** LE TURENNE, **77** LE CAPITOLE DU SOIR, **4409** LE VALENTRÉ.

Table 138

TOULOUSE - LIMOGES - PARIS
For faster TGV services Toulouse - Paris see Table 139

1,2 class

	472	4462	152	154	154		4404	4404		156	4444		74	4406	4480	4466			470	470	4402	4442	4442
	◆	Ⓐ	Ⓐ Ⓨ	⑥ Ⓨ	⑦p Ⓨ		⑦p Ⓨ	✕ Ⓨ		Ⓐ Ⓨ	Ⓨ	①g Ⓨ	⑦t Ⓨ	✕ Ⓨ	Ⓨ	G Ⓨ			⑥h Ⓨ	⑥k Ⓨ	⑦e Ⓨ	⑤f Ⓨ	H Ⓨ
La Tour de Carol 144 .... d.	...	...	...	...	...		...	...		...	...	...	...	...	...	...			1027	1027	...	...	...
Cerbère 139 .... d.	2035	...	...	...	...		...	...		...	...	...	...	...	...	...			1204	1204	...	...	...
Narbonne 139 .... d.	2217	...	...	...	...		...	...		0623	0729	0729	1029y	...	...	...			1340	1340	1400	1400	...
Toulouse Matabiau 139 ..... d.	0009	...	...	...	...		...	...		0653	0759	0800	1100	...	...	...			1410	1410	1430	1430	...
Montauban 139 .... d.	0042	...	...	...	...		...	...		0708	0817		1115	...	...	...					1446	1446	...
Caussade .... d.							0615			0736	0846	0838	1143	...	...	...			1450	1450	1513	1513	...
Cahors .... d.							0643			0802	0912	0905	1210	...	...	...			1540	1540			
Gourdon .... d.							0658			0818	0929	0922	1227	...	...	...			1556	1556			
Souillac .... d.							0725			0846	0954	0948	1255	...	...	...			1552	1552	1625	1625	...
Brive la Gaillarde............. a.	0232													...	...	...			1554	1554	1627	1627	1627
Brive la Gaillarde............. d.	0238	0509	0509		0718				➡ 0741	0848		➡ 0950	1313	1316	...					1658	1658	1658
Uzerche .... d.		0535	0535		0743				0807	0914				1343	...							
Agen .... d.															1238							
Le Buisson .... d.															1356							
Les Eyzies .... d.															1411							
Périgueux 140 .... d.					0736					0933				1316	1442	1531						
Limoges 140 .... a.	0342	0613	0613		0821			0837	0845	0952	1041	1049	1413	1421	1426			1650	1654	1654	1736	1736	1736
Limoges .... d.	0347	0615	0615	0615	0823	0823		0847	0954		1051	1417	1425	1441				1659	1659	1739	1739	1739
La Souterraine.............. d.		0647	0647	0647	0900	0900							1514							1812	1815	1815
Châteauroux .... d.		0609	0726	0726	0945	0945		0953			1157		1533	1558				1807	1807	1900	1852	1852
Issoudun .... d.		0626		0743	1000	1000								1614						1917	1910	1910
Vierzon 141 .... d.	0538	0647	0758	0804	1034	1034		1130			1210		1608	1634				1841	1841	1944	1944	1944
Les Aubrais 141 .... a.	0622	0727		0841	1117	1117					1218		1649	1713					1918	2015	2023	2023
Orléans .... a.	0631	0735		0849	1126	1126					1218		1655	1723					1926	2024	2033	2033
Paris Austerlitz 141 .... a.	0733	0833	0928	0939	0939			1219		1155			1355	1728	1755	1816			2014	2022	2117	2134	2134
Paris Montparnasse .... a.	...	...	...	...	...		...	...		...	...	...	...	...	...	...			...	...	...	...	...

	78	4400		4460		4758 4460		4458	158	158	4502		4504	4422 4420 4434	4434	4424	4424 4416	4416	174	1116
	⑧	⑥k ✕		⑦e Ⓨ	⑦e	⑦e ⑤⑦ ⑦e	Ⓐ	H Ⓨ	G ✕	⑥ Ⓨ	⑤f Ⓨ		Ⓐ	◆	Y	⑦e Ⓨ	⑦e ◆	W ◆	◆	◆
La Tour de Carol 144 .... d.	...	...		...	...	...	...	...	...	...	...		...	...	...	1917	... 1917	...	...	...
Cerbère 139 .... d.	...	...		...	...	...	...	...	...	...	...		...	...	...	...	...	...	1936
Narbonne 139 .... d.	...	...		...	...	1731 1737		1803	1859	1927	2108		2204	2245		2245	2300	2311	2128
Toulouse Matabiau 139 ..... d.	...	...		...	...	1800 1807		1832	1947	1959	2139		2238	2317		2317	2337	2346	
Montauban 139 .... d.	...	...		...	...	1817		1846	2005	2014	2157		2255	2334		2334		
Caussade .... d.	...	...		1651		1844 1844		1914	2033	2040	2233		2324	0004		0004	0023	0035
Cahors .... d.	...	...		1720		1910 1910		1941		➡ 2107	2307		2351	0031		0031		
Gourdon .... d.	...	...		1737		1925 1926		1959		2123	2326		0007	0049		0049		
Souillac .... d.	...	...		1803		1952 1952		2024		2148	2355		0032	0114		0114		0200
Brive la Gaillarde............. a.	...	...				1954 1954 1954		2026		2152	0007		0102	0121	0147	0147		0218
Brive la Gaillarde............. d.	1725			1827		2019				2052	2218		0033	0129			
Uzerche .... d.				1852									2113				
Agen .... d.				1534							1819		2237				
Le Buisson .... d.				1652							1945		2255				
Les Eyzies .... d.				1708							2000						
Périgueux 140 .... d.	1659			1739	1756 1835						2030		2343				
Limoges 140 .... a.	1801	1823		1930		1927 2001		2056	2052	2052	2130		2257	0112	0100	0208	0224 0249	0249	0335
Limoges .... d.		1825	1837	1946		1946		2058	2054	2054				0130	0222	0222	0242 0308	0308	0340
La Souterraine.............. d.			1914											0206			
Châteauroux .... d.			2003	2058		2058		2202	2157	2157				0247	0339	0338	0405 0426	0426	0454
Issoudun .... d.			2020											0305			
Vierzon 141 .... d.			2043											0333	0430	0430	0446 0503	0503
Les Aubrais 141 .... a.			2123	2205		2205								0418	0512	0513	0535 0548	0548	0555
Orléans .... a.			2131	2214		2214								0426	0521	0522	0545 0556	0556	0605
Paris Austerlitz 141 .... a.		2123	2226	2308		2308		0004	2351	2351				0541	0628	0628	0648 0700	0700	0706 0730
Paris Montparnasse .... a.	...	...		...	...	...	...	...	...	...	...		...	...	...	...	...	...	...

◆ ━ NOTES (LISTED BY TRAIN NUMBER):
174 – L'OCCITAN – 🚃 1,2 cl. (T2) and ━ 1,2 cl. Toulouse - Paris.
472 – CÔTE VERMEILLE - PARIS – 🚃 1,2 cl. (T2), ━ 1,2 cl. and 🚃 Cerbère - Paris.
1116 – Apr. 17, May 1,8: 🚃 and ━ 2 cl Cerbère - Paris.
4416 – 🚃 and ━ 1,2 cl. Carmaux - Paris. For other cars see Table 139a.
4420 – ⑤⑦ (also Apr. 17, May 1, 8, 24, 25; not Apr. 16, 30, May 7): 🚃 and ━ 1,2 cl. Toulouse - Paris.
4424 – 🚃 and ━ 1,2 cl. La Tour de Carol - Paris; 🚃 and ━ 1,2 cl. Luchon - Paris.
4434 – 🚃 and ━ 1,2 cl. Toulouse - Paris.
G – ⑤⑦ (also Apr. 17, May 1, 8, 24, 25; not Apr. 16, 30, May 7).
H – ①-④ (also May 26; not Apr. 17, May 1,8,24).
TGV –Ⓡ, supplement payable. Via Bordeaux (Table 136).
W – Daily except when train 4424 runs: 🚃 and ━ 1,2 cl. La Tour de Carol - Paris. Conveys on ⑥ Dec. 17 - Apr. 8 (not Mar. 4): 🚃 and ━ 1,2 cl. Luchon - Paris.

Y – ⑦ (not Apr. 16,30, May 7): 🚃 and ━ 1,2 cl. Agen - Paris; ━ 2 cl. Périgueux - Paris.
d – ⑦ Feb. 25 - May 27 (also Apr. 17, May 1, 8; not Apr. 16, 30, May 7).
e – Also Apr. 17, May 1, 8; not Apr. 16, 30, May 7.
f – Also May 24; not May 26.
g – Also Apr. 18, May 2, 9; not Apr. 17, May 1, 8.
h – Also Feb. 26, Mar. 5; not Apr. 16, 30, May 7, 25.
k – Also Apr. 16, 30, May 7, 25.
p – Also Apr. 17, May 1, 8. 25.
t – Also Apr. 17, May 1, 8.
y – Depart 1021 on Ⓐ Feb. 21 - Mar. 24.
↗ – Supplement payable.

TRAIN NAMES: 74 LE CAPITOLE DU MATIN, 78 LE TURENNE, 4406 LE VALENTRÉ

Table 138a

TOULOUSE - LUCHON

1,2 clas

km				🚌					🚌			🚌 🚌			🚌 🚌	
		T	Ⓐ		N	P			✕	✕	✕	V			⑤⑦ C	H H
	Paris Austerlitz 138 .... d.	2106	...	...	...	2218	...	...	...	...	...	...	...	...	...
0	Toulouse Matabiau 139 ... d.	0515	...	0614	...	0730	0724	1005	1229	1418	1639	1713	1916	... 1916	...
66	Boussens 139 .... d.	0557	...	0704	...	0821	0816	1045	1318	1507	1733	...	1955	... 2007	...
104	Montréjeau 139 .... d.	0637	...	0736	0741	0852	0859	1111	1121 1341 1346 1534 1539	1810	1816	1823 2021 2027 2033 2039	
139	Luchon .... a.	0725	...		0837	...	0928	0943	1216	1441	1634	1846	...	1918	... 2117	... 2129

		🚌					✕	✕	†				R W	
	Luchon .... d.	0625	...	0906	...	1127	1355	1613	...	1731	1753		2018 2018 2018	
	Montréjeau 139 .... d.	0716 0728	...	1001 1013	1206	1449	1708 1718	1819	1848 1901		2111 2111 2111	
	Boussens 139 .... d.	... 0751	...	1038	1230		1742	1849		1928	2137 2137 2137	
	Toulouse Matabiau 139 .. a.	... 0839	...	1114	1318		1831	1939		2007	2221 2221 2221	
	Paris Austerlitz 138 .... a.											0648 0700	

C – ⑤⑦ (also Apr. 17, May 1, 8; not Apr. 16, 30, May 7).
H – ①②③④⑥ (also Apr. 16, May 7, 25).
N – Daily except when train P runs.
P – Feb. 4, 11, Mar. 4, 11, 18, 25 only.
R – ⑦ (also Feb. 25, Mar. 4, Apr. 17, May 1, 8; not Apr. 16, May 7, 25).
T – ⑤ (also Feb. 18, 25, May 24; not May 26.
V – ① - ⑤ (also ⑥ Apr. 8 - May 27).
W – ⑥ Feb. 4 - 18, Mar. 11 - Apr. 8.

① – Mondays ② – Tuesdays ③ – Wednesdays ④ – Thursdays ⑤ – Fridays ⑥ – Saturdays ⑦ – Sundays

Table 138b — BRIVE - AURILLAC

1,2 class

km		P	✕					A				✕		⑦e		B	
	Paris Austerlitz 138 ......d.							2218	...	Aurillac............d.	0522	0757		1110	1528		1806	2258
0	Brive la Gaillarde............d.	0740	...	1131	1427	...	1823	2214	0451	Brive la Gaillarde............a.	0713	0941		1302	1708		1944	0052
102	Aurillac............................a.	0918	...	1310	1617	...	2003	2350	0657	Paris Austerlitz 138 ......a.	...	...		...	...		...	0700

A – ⑤ (also Nov. 10, May 24; not Nov. 11, May 26): 🛏 and 🍴 1,2 cl. Paris - Brive - Aurillac (train 4417/6491).

B – ⑦ (also Nov. 1, Apr. 17, May 1,8,25; not Oct. 30, Apr. 16,30, May 7): 🛏 and 🍴 1,2 cl. Aurillac - Brive - Paris (train 6999/4416).

P – ②③④⑤⑥⑦ Dec. 17 - Mar. 19 (also Feb. 27, Mar. 3,6,10).

e – Also Nov. 1, Apr. 17, May 1,8,25; not Apr. 16,30, May 7.

Table 139 — BORDEAUX and HENDAYE - TOULOUSE - NARBONNE

1,2 class

km		6460 6461	6460 6461		98500	6451 6450	4514	4531	6464 6465	6466 6467	8503 TGV	8503 TGV	162 163				6452 6453	6452 6453	8519 TGV	8519 TGV	4820
		✕		Ⓐ	⚐	✕	♦	✕		⚐	⚐	L	M	♦	✝	✕	J	K	✕	K	J
					⚐									✕			⚐	⚐			
	Paris Montparnasse 136 .d.	...	...	...	...	...	...	...	...	...	0705	0720		...	...	...	...	...	1055	1115	...
	Paris Austerlitz 136/8 ......d.	...	...	...	...	...	...	...	...	...	...	...		...	...	...	...	...	...	...	...
	Nantes 134 ......d.	...	...	...	...	2322g	...	...	...	...	...	...		...	...	...	...	...	...	...	...
0	Bordeaux St. Jean..........d.	...	...	0554	0639		0824		1004	1029	1102		...	...	...	1147	1155	1413	1423	...
79	Marmande ......d.	...	...	0657	0719		0912		...	...	...		...	...	...	1226	1235	...	...	...
136	Agen ......d.	...	...	0733	0749		0949		1105	1130	...		...	...	...	1257	1306	1515	1525	...
206	Montauban ......d.	...	...	0815	0826		1036		1140	1206	...		...	...	...	1333	1342	1551	1601	...
	Hendaye 137 ......d.	...	...	...	...	0632			...	...	...		...	...	...	...	...	...	...	1137
	St. Jean de Luz 137 ......d.	...	...	...	...	0644			...	...	...		...	...	...	...	...	...	...	1149
	Biarritz 137 ......d.	...	...	...	...	0657			...	...	...		...	...	...	...	...	...	...	1203
	Bayonne 137 ......d.	...	...	...	0545t	0720			...	...	...		...	...	...	...	...	...	...	1226
	Puyoô ......d.	...	...	...	0620t	0758			...	...	...		...	...	...	...	...	...	...	1304
	Pau 137 ......d.	...	0604t		0702	0836			...	...	...		1047	1116	...	...	...	...	...	1345
	Lourdes 137 ......d.	0552	0633r		0729	0906			...	...	...		1115	1144	...	...	...	...	...	1415
	Tarbes 137 ......d.	0608	0649		0746	0923			...	...	...		1129	1200	...	...	...	...	...	1431
	Lannemezan ......d.	0632	0716		0823	0959			...	...	...		1155	1227	...	...	...	...	...	1508
	Montréjeau ......d.	0644	0728		0835	1013			...	...	...		1206	1240	...	...	...	...	...	1522
	Boussens ......d.	0708	0751		0900	1038			...	...	...		1230		...	...	...	...	...	1547
257	Toulouse Matabiau ....a.	0757	0839	0849	0857	0954	1107	1114		1210	1236	1302	1318	1338	...	1620	1630	1635
257	Toulouse Matabiau ....d.	0618	0704	0704	0711		0902			1129	1200		1306	...	...	1412	1421	1541	...
312	Castelnaudary ......d.	0707			0748		0929			1158				...	...	1440	1449	1614	...
348	Carcassonne ......d.	0734			0809		0950			1219	1246			...	...	1501	1510	1637	...
385	Lézignan ......d.	0754									1306			...	...			1656	...
407	Narbonne ......a.	0808	0814	0814			1018			1247	1319			...	...	1529	1537	1709	...
	Marseille 163 ......a.	...	1109x				1312			1533				...	...	1827	1842	...	...
	Nice 164 ......a.	...								1830				...	...	2128	2133	...	...
	Lyon Part Dieu 151 ......a.	...		1210b							1735			...	...			...	...
	Genève 159 ......a.	...												...	...			...	...
	Perpignan 163 ......a.	...												...	...			...	...
	Port Bou 163 ......a.	...												...	...			...	...

		147 471	6434 6435		6455 6454	4518	4513	4513		6456 6457		4515	8549 TGV	6478 6479	6478 364/5	6484 6485	4399	6432 6433	342 343	1117	473	6425
		⚐		✕	⚐	⑦e	⑥	Ⓐ	Ⓐ		Ⓐ		⑦e	⑧h	Ⓑ	♦	C	♦	⑤f	⑦e	♦	♦	♦
					⚐								1700						⚐				
	Paris Montparnasse 136 ...d.												1700							2054	2145		
	Paris Austerlitz 136/8 ......d.	1006																					
	Nantes 134 ......d.		1023											1650	1707	1813						1940	
	Bordeaux St. Jean..........d.		1447		1635		1715	1717		1833		1914	2007	2100		2140	2156	2244				2344
	Marmande ......d.		1527				1802	1802		1913		1958		2147		2218	2241	2326				
	Agen ......d.		1558		1742		1840	1842		1943		2037	2109	2221		2247	2314	2359				
	Montauban ......d.	1624	1635		1820			1928		2025		2121	2144			2322	2355	0040		0414		
	Hendaye 137 ......d.								1525						1810	1810	1850					
	St. Jean de Luz 137 ......d.								1537						1823	1823	1903					
	Biarritz 137 ......d.								1550						1836	1836	1916					
	Bayonne 137 ......d.							1558	1610		1718				1859	1859	1939					
	Puyoô ......d.								1644		1758											
	Pau 137 ......d.		1557n					1724		1834					2012	2012	2047					
	Lourdes 137 ......d.		1626		1736			1754		1906					2039	2039	2115					
	Tarbes 137 ......d.		1642		1753			1811		1922					2058	2058	2136					
	Lannemezan ......d.		1707		1830			1841							2137	2137	2220					
	Montréjeau ......d.		1718		1843			1901							2151	2151	2235					
	Boussens ......d.		1742		1909			1928														
	Toulouse Matabiau ....a.	1655	1706	1831	1851	1950		1958		2007	2056		2153	2214		2248	2248	2332	2352	0026	0113	0359	0445
	Toulouse Matabiau ....d.	1716	1713		1856						2104					2259	2259	2347		0034	0126	0409	0508
	Castelnaudary ......a.	1746	1741		1925						2133					2329	2329	0017		0105		0440	0540
	Carcassonne ......a.	1811	1803		1946						2154					2350	2350	0039		0127	0216	0509	0605
	Lézignan ......a.	1830			2006						2214									0152		0529	0629
	Narbonne ......a.	1843	1831		2019						2227					0020	0020	0108		0209	0249	0543	0644
	Marseille 163 ......a.		2107		2259											0450	0450		0524	0600			0538
	Nice 164 ......a.															0742	0742			0900			0837
	Lyon Part Dieu 151 ......a.													0600									
	Genève 159 ......a.													0820									
	Perpignan 163 ......a.	1947																		0658	0740		
	Port Bou 163 ......a.	2045																		0755	0850		

♦ – NOTES (LISTED BY TRAIN NUMBER):

162/3 – LE GRAND SUD – 🛏 and ✕ Bordeaux - Nice.

342/3 – 🛏 1,2 cl., 🍴 1,2 cl. and 🛌 Nantes - Ventimiglia; 🛌 and 🍴 2 cl. Bordeaux - Milano.

473 – PARIS - CÔTE VERMEILLE – 🛏 1,2 cl. (T2), 🍴 1,2 cl. and 🛌 Paris - Port Bou.

1117 – Oct. 28, Nov. 10, Dec. 20,21,23,29, Apr. 14,21, May 24: 🛌 and 🍴 1,2 cl. Paris - Port Bou.

6425 – ⑤⑦ (also Apr. 17, May 1,8,24; not Apr. 16,30, May 7,26): 🛏 1,2 cl. (T2), 🛌 and 🍴 1,2 cl. Nantes - Nice.

6432/3 – 🛌 and 🍴 2 cl. Nantes - Les Arcs; ♀ Nantes - Agen.

6434/5 – 🛌 and ♀ Quimper - Marseille.

3450/1 – 🛌 and ♀ Bordeaux - Marseille; 🍴 1,2 cl. Quimper - Toulouse.

6478/9 – 🛌 and ✕ 1,2 cl. Hendaye - Genève.

6484/5 – ⑤⑦ (also Apr. 17, May 1,8,24; not Apr. 16,30, May 7,26): 🛏 1,2 cl., 🍴 1,2 cl. and 🛌 Hendaye - Nice - Ventimiglia; 🛌 Hendaye - Roma; 🍴 1,2 cl. and ♀ Hendaye - Grenoble - Annecy.

C – Conveys (except when train 6484/5 runs), 🛏 1,2 cl., 🍴 1,2 cl. and 🛌 Hendaye - Nice - Ventimiglia; 🛌 Hendaye - Roma.

J – Daily except dates in note K.

K – Ⓐ Mar. 27 - May 4.

L – ✕ (except when train M runs). Runs 5 minutes later Bordeaux - Toulouse Mar. 13 - May 27.

M – Ⓐ Mar. 27 - May 4.

TGV – 🅁, supplement payable.

b – Arrive 1223 on Ⓐ Apr. 10 - May 12.

e – Also Apr. 17, May 1,8; not Apr. 16,30, May 7.

f – Also Nov. 10, May 24; not Nov. 11, May 26.

g – Depart 2341 on ⑤ and dates in Table 134.

h – Not Oct. 30,31, Nov. 11, Apr. 16,30, May 7,25.

n – ⑤⑥ (daily Dec. 10, May 24; not Nov. 11).

r – Daily except ⑥ (not Nov. 11, May 25).

t – ① only (also Apr. 18, May 2,9; not Apr. 17, May 1,8).

x – Arrive 1126 on Ⓐ Jan. 3 - Feb. 24.

Table 139 — NARBONNE - TOULOUSE - IRUN and BORDEAUX

1,2 class

	6924 6925 ♦	340 341 ♦	Ⓐ	⑥	6978 6979 ♦	362 6978 C	8518 TGV ☒⚲	†	Ⓐ	6984 6985 ♦	4702 Ⓐ	☒	6956 6957 Ⓐ z	6956 6957 Ⓒ	4807 ⚲	6934 6935 ♦⚲	☒	6964 6965 z	4704 z	470 ⚲ z	8552 TGV z
Cerbère 163 .... d.																				1027	
Perpignan 163 .... d.																				1112	
Genève 159 .... d.					2154																
Lyon Part Dieu 151 .... d.					2357																
Nice 164 .... d.	1824	2000					2220			2220									0550k		
Marseille 163 .... d.	2214	2252					0120			0120					0547g	0656			0906k		
Narbonne .... d.		0200			0433	0433				0532	0651		0745	0824	0824	0944			1158	1204	
Lézignan .... d.											0705			0759	0837					1220	
Carcassonne .... d.		0236			0505	0505				0604	0727		0820	0854	0857	1016			1228	1243	
Castelnaudary .... d.		0258									0749		0842			1037			1247		
Toulouse Matabiau .... a.		0329			0549	0549				0648	0825		0912	0938	0940	1105			1315	1326	
Toulouse Matabiau .... d.		0348			0609	0609	0611			0709		0747	0944	0944	1005	1113y	1229		1323	1340	1348
Boussens .... d.					0708	0708				0810					1045		1318				
Montréjeau .... d.															1113		1343				
Lannemezan .... d.					0724	0724									1127		1355				
Tarbes 137 .... d.					0753	0753				0855					1208		1425				
Lourdes 137 .... d.					0811	0811				0914					1224		1439				
Pau 137 .... d.					0839	0839				0943					1254		1508n				
Puyoô .... d.															1332						
Bayonne 137 .... a.					0952	0952				1052					1405						
Biarritz 137 .... a.					1017	1017				1117					1428						
St. Jean de Luz 137 .. a.					1030	1030				1129					1441						
Hendaye 137 .... a.					1041	1041				1140					1453						
Irún 137 .... a.					1050	1050				1149					1459						
Montauban .... d.		0422	0508	0602			0641		0718		0817		1013	1013		1142y		1220y	1353	1408	1418
Agen .... d.		0508	0602	0630			0718	0726	0749		0905		1049	1049		1220y		1250	1439		1512
Marmande .... d.		0541	0639	0707				0759	0824		0934		1119	1119		1250					1512
Bordeaux St. Jean .... a.	0530	0625	0737	0809			0820	0857	0910		1014		1158	1158		1329			1550		1556
Nantes 134 .... a.	0938	1105														1809					
Paris Austerlitz 136/8 .. a.																			2014q		
Paris Montparnasse 136 .. a.							1125j														1900d

	6964 6965 m	6961 6960 ⑤ ⚲		164 165 ☒	6952 6953 ⚲	4825 ⚲	8586 TGV ⑧h	Ⓐ	6950 6951 ⚲	4517 F	4517 G	15470 ⑤f		6954 6955 ⚲	6967 6966 ⚲	1116 ♦	6932 6933 ⑤f	6962 6963 ⚲	4398	F	472 ♦
Cerbère 163 .... d.															1936						2035
Perpignan 163 .... d.															2027						2125
Genève 159 .... d.																					
Lyon Part Dieu 151 .... d.		0900										1717									
Nice 164 .... d.	0550k			1030c					1153b					1713			1855	1919			
Marseille 163 .... d.	0906k			1302	1246				1442		1606			1713			1855	1919			
Narbonne .... d.	1158	1318			1521				1741		1859			1946	2106	2128	2145	2158			2217
Lézignan .... d.									1756												2233
Carcassonne .... d.	1228	1350			1552				1817		1933			2017	2208	2217	2231	2253			2257
Castelnaudary .... d.	1247								1837		1953				2230						2320
Toulouse Matabiau .... a.	1315	1434			1619	1636			1904		2021			2100	2218	2300	2304	2320			2350
Toulouse Matabiau .... d.	1355v			1609	1623	1648	1713	1715	1813	1915	1916	1916		2109	2114	2311	2328		2328	2335	0009
Boussens .... d.					1708				1902					2156					0014		
Montréjeau .... d.						1818			1925			2023		2220					0042		
Lannemezan .... d.				1720		1833			1936			2037		2231							
Tarbes 137 .... d.				1745		1903			2002			2109		2257					0123		
Lourdes 137 .... d.						1920						2126		2312					0140		
Pau 137 .... d.						1952			2155			2206		2343n					0205		
Puyoô .... d.						2030															
Bayonne 137 .... a.						2103			2308												
Biarritz 137 .... a.						2127															
St. Jean de Luz 137 .. a.						2140															
Hendaye 137 .... a.						2151															
Irún 137 .... a.						2159															
Montauban .... d.				1718			1745		1944	2032				2226		2344	2359	2359	0039		
Agen .... d.		1511		1754			1822		2032	2105				2255		0038	0037		0037		
Marmande .... d.		1546		1825					2105					2255		0146		0146			
Bordeaux St. Jean .... a.		1627		1823			1904		1923					2153		2335	0146		0146		
Nantes 134 .... a.														0452			0622		0622		
Paris Austerlitz 136/8 .. a.																	0730				0733x
Paris Montparnasse 136 .. a.							2235														

♦ – NOTES (LISTED BY TRAIN NUMBERS)

164/5 – LE GRAND SUD – [12] and ☒ Nice - Bordeaux and v.v.

340/1 – ☕1,2 cl., ⊨ 2 cl. and [12] Ventimiglia - Nantes; [12] and ⊨ 2 cl. Milano - Bordeaux.

472 – CÔTE VERMEILLE - PARIS - ☕1,2 cl. (T2), ⊨ 1,2 cl. and [12] Cerbère - Paris.

1116 – Nov. 1,6, Dec. 25, Jan. 1,3, Apr. 17, May 1,8: [12] and ⊨ 2 cl. Cerbère - Paris.

4398 – ⑦ (also Apr. 17, May 1,8; not Apr. 16, 30, May 7): [12] and ⊨ 2 cl. Toulouse - Nantes.

6924/5 – ⑤⑦ (also Apr. 17, May 1,8,24; not Apr.16,30, May 7,26): ☕1,2 cl. (T2), [12] and ⊨ 1,2 cl. Nice - Nantes.

6932/3 – [12] and ⊨ 2 cl. Les Arcs - Nantes; ⚲ Montauban - Nantes.

6934/5 – [12] and ⚲ Marseille - Quimper.

6954/5 – [12] and ⚲ Marseille - Bordeaux; ⊨ 1,2 cl. Toulouse - Nantes - Quimper.

6978/9 – [12] and ⊨ 1,2 cl. Genève - Irún.

6984/5 – ⑤⑦ (also Apr. 17, May 1,8,24; not Apr.16,30, May 7,26): ☕1,2 cl., ⊨ 1,2 cl. and [12] Ventimiglia - Nice - Irún; [12] Roma - Irún; [12] and ⊨ 1,2 cl. Annecy - Grenoble - Irún.

C – Conveys (except when train 6984/5 runs): ☕1,2 cl., ⊨ 1,2 cl. and [12] Ventimiglia - Nice - Irún; [12] Roma - Irún.

F – ⑤⑦ (also Apr. 17, May 1,8; not Apr. 16,30, May 7).

G – Daily except dates in note F.

TGV – ℝ, supplement payable.

b – Depart 1200 on ⑥ (not Dec. 3,17, Jan. 28) and daily Mar. 6 - May 27.

c – Depart 1036 on ⑥ (not Dec. 3,17, Jan. 28) and daily Mar. 6 - May 27.

d – Arrive 1907 on Ⓐ Feb. 21 - May 24.

f – Also Nov. 10, May 24; not Nov. 11, May 26.

g – ① (also Apr. 18, May 2,9; not Apr. 17, May 1,8).

h – Not Apr. 16,30, May 7,25.

j – Arrive 1135 Mar. 13 - May 24.

k – Depart Nice 0600 on ⑥ (not Dec. 3,17, Jan. 28) and daily Mar. 6 - May 27. Marseille 0852 on Ⓐ Jan. 3 - Feb. 24 (also Jan. 28).

m – Runs 7 minutes later Narbonne - Toulouse Nov. 28 - Apr. 7 and Ⓐ Apr. 10 - May 12.

n – ⑤⑥ (also Nov. 10, May 24).

q – Arrive 2019 Nov. 14 - Dec. 22. On ⑥ arrive 2022 (2032 Nov. 19 - Dec. 17).

v – Depart 1358 on ①②③④⑦ (not Apr. 16,30, May 7,24).

x – Arrive 0745 Nov. 15 - Dec. 22.

y – On Ⓐ Feb. 21 - Mar. 24, depart Toulouse 1108, Montauban 1150, Agen 1226.

z – Runs approximately 10 minutes later from Montauban on Ⓐ Feb. 21 - Mar. 10.

Table 139a BRIVE and AURILLAC - FIGEAC - TOULOUSE

1,2 class

km		Ⓐ	⚒	†	⚒	⚒	51551 ⚒	†	⑦e	⚒	51553	147 4527 G	4527 ⑤f	51555 ⑤q	98903	⚒	⑤p	†	H		M	155 4959 ⑤f ⁄	4417 4916 C	4417 4951 R
	Paris Austerlitz **138** d.	...	...	...	...	...	...	...	...	...	...	1006	...	...	...	...	...	...	...	...	...	1745	2218	2218
	Limoges **138** d.	...	...	...	...	...	...	...	...	...	...	1309	...	...	...	...	...	...	...	...	...	2046	0212	0212
0	**Brive la Gaillarde** d.	...	0541	...	...	...	...	0914	...	1136	...	1438	1438	...	...	...	...	...	1813	1813	2208	2208	0340	0340
45	Rocamadour d.	...	0623	...	...	...	...	0954	...	1216	...	|	|	...	...	...	...	...	1903	1903	|	2249	0430	0430
	Clermont Ferrand **147** d.	...	|	...	...	...	0655	|	...	|	0933	|	|	...	...	...	...	...	|	|	|	|	|	|
	Aurillac d.	0548	|	...	...	...	0921	|	...	|	1231	|	|	1537	1643	1821	1821	1850	|	|	|	|	|	|
88	Figeac d.	0654	0702	0702	...	...	1026	1030	...	1252	1341	1555	1555	1643	1745	1936	1936	1951	1945	1945	2318	2328	0513	0513
94	Capdenac a.	0701	0709	0709	...	...	1033	1036	...	1258	1348	1602	1602	1650	1752	1944	1944	1958	1952	1952	2325	2335	0521	0521
94	Capdenac d.	...	0714	0714	0726	...	1038	1037	1054	1259	1353	1603	1603	1654	1757	2005	2005	...	2005	2010	2327	2337	0527	0557
161	**Rodez** a.	...	|	|	0836	...	|	|	1203	1403	|	1711	1711	|	|	|	|	...	|	2120	0030	0045	|	0708
123	Villefranche de Rouergue d.	...	0742	0742	...	...	1107	1107	...	...	1422	...	...	1720	1826	2034	2037	...	2037	▬	...	...	0556	...
140	Najac d.	...	0756	0756	...	...	1123	1123	...	...	|	...	...	1735	1840	...	2054	...	2054	...	...	...	0614	...
189	Tessonnières d.	...	0841	0841	...	0912	|	|	...	...	|	...	...	|	|	...	2140	...	2140	2153	...	...	0728	...
	Albi Ville **146** a.	...	|	|	...	0923	|	|	...	...	|	...	...	|	|	...	|	...	|	2210	...	...	0744	...
	Carmaux **146** a.	...	|	|	...	0939	|	|	...	...	|	...	...	|	|	...	|	...	|	2227	...	...	0808	...
193	Gaillac d.	...	0845	0845	...	...	1210	1209	...	...	1521	...	...	1822	1925	...	2147	...	2147	...	...	...	...	...
247	**Toulouse Matabiau** a.	...	0930	0930	...	...	1257	1257	...	...	1602	...	...	1906	2019	...	2234	...	2234	...	...	...	...	...

	⚒	E		⚒		Ⓐ	⑦	4524 4406		51554	Ⓑh		⑤q		Ⓐ				Ⓒe		4950 4416 R	4917 4416 C	🚌 ⑤f	
Toulouse Matabiau d.	...	0536	...	...	...	0905	0905	...	...	1232	...	...	1536	...	1649	...	...	1740	...	...	...	...	...	...
Gaillac d.	...	0624	...	...	...	0940	0940	...	...	1315	...	...	1618	...	1724	...	...	1824	...	...	...	...	...	...
Carmaux **146** d.	...	|	...	...	...	|	|	...	1213	|	...	...	|	...	|	1705	...	|	...	...	...	2050	...	...
Albi Ville **146** d.	...	|	...	...	...	|	|	...	1229	|	...	...	|	...	|	1723	...	|	...	...	...	2112	...	...
Tessonnières d.	...	0630	...	...	...	|	|	...	1242	1320	...	...	|	...	|	1737	...	1829	...	...	...	2204	...	...
Najac d.	...	0715	...	...	...	1024	1024	...	...	1403	...	...	1704	...	1810	...	...	1917	...	...	...	2251	...	...
Villefranche de Rouergue d.	...	0731	0741	...	...	1039	1039	...	...	1420	...	...	1720	...	1828	...	...	1934	...	...	...	2307	...	...
Rodez d.	...	...	|	0715	...	|	|	1022	...	|	1439	...	|	1715	|	...	1835	|	1835	...	2220	|	...	...
Capdenac a.	...	...	0810	0816	...	1104	1104	1125	...	1447	1545	...	1749	1814	1853	...	1942	2003	1942	...	2324	2332	...	...
Capdenac d.	0603	...	0823	0817	...	1105	1105	1126	...	1450	1546	...	1754	1815	1859	...	...	2008	2000	...	2327r	2348	2340	...
Figeac d.	0611	...	0833	0824	...	1116	1115	1135	...	1459	1555	...	1804	1823	1908	...	...	2017	2020	...	2337r	2358	|	...
Aurillac a.	0723	...	0949	|	...	1217b	...	|	...	1605	|	...	1915	|	|	...	...	2123	|	...	|	|	0100	...
Clermont Ferrand **147** a.	...	...	...	|	...	...	...	|	...	1851	|	...	...	|	|	...	...	...	|	...	|	|	...	...
Rocamadour d.	...	...	...	0859	...	...	...	|	...	...	1635	...	...	1902	1950	...	...	...	2059	...	|	0041	...	...
Brive la Gaillarde a.	...	...	...	0936	...	...	...	1253	...	...	1716	...	...	1940	2033	...	...	...	2143	...	0101r	0127	...	...
Limoges **138** a.	...	...	...	...	...	...	...	1413	...	...	...	...	...	...	...	...	...	...	...	...	0249	0249	...	...
Paris Austerlitz **138** a.	...	...	...	...	...	...	...	1728x	...	...	...	...	...	...	...	...	...	...	...	...	0700	0700	...	...

C – [2] and 🛏 1,2 cl. Paris - Carmaux and v.v.
E – ①⑥ (also Jan. 4, Apr. 18, May 2,9; not Apr. 17, May 1,8).
G – Daily except ⑤ (also Nov. 11, May 26; not Nov. 10, May 24).
H – ⑤⑦ (also Apr. 17, May 1,8; not Apr. 16,30, May 7).
M – ①②③④⑦ (also May 26; not Apr. 16,30, May 7,24).
R – [2] and 🛏 1,2 cl. Paris - Rodez and v.v.

b – By 🚌 (arrive 1235) on ①, also Apr. 18, May 2,9,26; not Apr. 17, May 1,8.
e – Also Apr. 17, May 1,8,25; not Apr. 16,30, May 7.
f – Also Nov. 10, May 24; not Nov. 11, May 26.
h – Not Apr. 16,30, May 7.
p – Not Nov. 11.

q – Also Nov. 10, Dec. 20, May 24; not Nov. 11, Dec. 23,30, Apr. 14,21.
r – 20 minutes later on ⚒.
x – Arrive 1737 Nov. 14 - Dec. 22.
⁄ – Supplement payable.

Table 140 BORDEAUX - LIMOGES - LYON

1,2 class

km		⚒	Ⓐ	⚒	6390 V		⚒	6380	U	⚒		6382 E🍷	F	H	Ⓐ	⑤f		⑦e	⑦e	Ⓐq	Ⓐq	⚒	⑤⑦	6386 N
0	**Bordeaux St. Jean** d.	...	0618	0647	0747	0747	...	1057	...	1228	1354x	1546	...	...	1654	...	1740	1810	1810	1815	1815	1849	1953	2225
37	Libourne d.	...	0638	0723	0809	0809	...	1118	...	1251	1417	1606	...	...	1718	...	1804	1831	1831	1837	1837	1911	2015	2249
53	Coutras d.	...	|	0734	0821	0821	...	|	...	1303	1430	|	...	...	1729	...	1816	|	|	|	|	1926	2027	2302
129	Périgueux a.	...	0732	0836	0910	0910	...	1207	...	1357	1520	1655	...	...	1827	...	1912	1932	1932	1932	1932	2020	2122	2353
129	Périgueux d.	0620	0736	...	0912	0912	0933	1211	1214	▬	1531	1659	1703	1804	*1835*	1844	*1925*c	1940	1945	1940	1945	...	2138	0013
	Brive la Gaillarde a.	0725	|	...	1005	1005	|	|	1303	...	|	|	1756	1907	|	1949	*2020*c	|	2040	|	2040	...	|	|
	Clermont Ferrand **140b** a.	▬	|	...	1344	...	|	|	...	...	|	|	...	...	|	...	...	|	...	|	...	...	|	|
228	**Limoges** a.	⑥t	0837	...	|	...	1041	1311	...	...	1650	1801	...	...	*2001*	...	...	2045	...	2045	...	...	2253	0117
228	**Limoges** d.	0805	▬	...	|	...	...	1313	...	1533	...	1805	...	...	...	...	...	...	...	...	...	...	...	0121
306	Guéret d.	0908	...	...	|	...	...	1410	...	1653	...	1909	...	...	...	...	...	...	...	...	...	...	...	0250
384	Montluçon d.	1008	...	...	|	...	...	1505	...	1803	...	2012	...	...	...	...	...	...	...	...	...	...	...	0359
452	Gannat d.	1114	...	...	|	...	...	1608	...	...	...	2118	...	...	...	...	...	...	...	...	...	...	...	0530
475	St. Germain des Fossés d.	1129	1143	...	1447	...	...	1627	...	...	...	2138	...	...	...	...	...	...	...	...	...	...	...	0607
542	Roanne d.	...	1227	...	1530	...	...	1707	...	...	...	2222	...	...	...	...	...	...	...	...	...	...	...	0653
	Lyon Part Dieu a.	...	1339	...	1646	...	...	1821	...	...	...	2332	...	...	...	...	...	...	...	...	...	...	...	0808
639	**Lyon Perrache** a.	...	1349	...	1655	...	...	1834	...	...	...	2342	...	...	...	...	...	...	...	...	...	...	...	0818

	⚒	Ⓐ	⚒			⚒	⚒	⚒				⑤f	†	⚒	Ⓐ		6890 V	⑦	UZ	6880	⑦e	†	6882 E🍷	6886 N
Lyon Perrache d.	...	...	...	...	...	...	...	...	...	...	...	...	...	...	...	...	1109	...	...	1255	...	...	1540	2125
Lyon Part Dieu d.	...	...	...	...	...	...	...	...	...	...	...	...	...	...	...	...	1119	...	...	1305	...	...	1552	2138
Roanne d.	...	...	...	...	...	...	...	...	...	...	...	...	...	...	...	...	1235	...	...	1422	...	...	1702	2256
St. Germain des Fossés d.	...	...	...	...	...	...	...	...	...	...	...	...	...	...	...	...	1327	...	...	1509	...	...	1746	2353
Gannat d.	...	...	...	...	...	...	...	...	...	...	...	...	...	...	...	...	|	...	...	1528	...	...	1805	0026
Montluçon d.	...	...	...	...	...	...	0810	...	...	...	...	...	...	...	...	...	|	...	...	1631	...	...	1905	0144
Guéret d.	...	...	...	...	...	...	0909	...	...	...	...	...	...	...	...	...	|	...	...	1724	...	...	2007	0244
Limoges a.	...	...	...	...	...	...	1006	...	...	...	...	...	...	...	...	...	|	...	...	1756	...	...	2103	0354
Limoges d.	...	0612	...	0713	...	...	...	1030	...	1253	...	...	*1423*	1447	...	1659	|	...	...	1823	...	...	2105	0405
Clermont Ferrand **140b** d.	...	|	...	|	...	0657	...	|	...	|	...	...	|	|	...	|	1418	...	...	|	...	...	|	|
Brive la Gaillarde d.	...	|	0615r	|	0728	1028	...	|	...	|	1310	...	|	|	...	|	1803	1803	1803	|	...	2105	|	|
Périgueux a.	...	0723	0717r	0820	0820	1121	...	1127	...	1403	1409	...	*1528*	1555	...	1814	1859	1859	1859	1919	...	2155	2205	0505
Périgueux d.	0609	0730	0730	...	0830	...	...	1131	1218	...	...	1455	1550	1605	1705	1828	1901	1901	...	1923	2022	...	2209	0519
Coutras d.	0706	0822	0822	...	0922	...	...	|	1309	...	...	1549	1645	1655	1800	1932	1946	1945	...	|	2115	...	2256	|
Libourne d.	0718	0833	0833	...	0933	...	...	1221	1320	...	...	1601	1656	1706	1811	1944	1958	1958	...	2012	2126	...	2308	0615
Bordeaux St. Jean a.	0745	0859	0859	...	0957	...	...	1243	1342	...	...	1625	1719	1728	1839	2013	2021	2021	...	2034	2150	...	2329	0637

– ⑤⑦ (also Dec. 20,21, Jan. 3,4, Feb. 25, Mar. 4, Apr. 17, May 1,8,24; not Apr. 16,30, May 7,26).
– ⑤⑦ (also Apr. 17, May 1,8,24,25).
– ①②③④ (also May 26; not Apr. 17, May 1,8,24,25).
– ⑧ (also Feb. 11,18, Apr. 8,15; not Apr. 16,30, May 7): [12] and 🛏 1,2 cl. Bordeaux - Lyon and v.v.; 🍷 St. Germain des Fossés - Lyon and v.v.
– [12] Périgueux - Ussel and v.v.
– LE VENTADOUR, ⑤ (also Dec. 20 - Jan. 3, Feb. 11,12,18,19,25,26, Apr. 8,9,15,17, 22,23, May 1,8,24; not Nov. 11, May 26): [12] Bordeaux - Clermont Ferrand - Lyon and v.v.; 🍷 Bordeaux - Clermont Ferrand and v.v.; 🍷 St. Germain des Fossés - Lyon and v.v.

Z – ①②③④ Sept. 25 - Dec. 15 and Jan. 4 - May 23 (also May 26; not Apr. 17, May 1,8).

c – ⑥ only.
e – Also Apr. 17, May 1,8; not Apr. 16,30, May 7.
f – Also Nov. 10, May 24; not Nov. 11, May 26.
q – Also Apr. 16,30, May 7,25.
t – Also Nov. 11, May 25; not Nov. 12, May 27.
r – Ⓐ only.
x – Depart 1347 on Mar. 17,24,31, May 5,12,19.

Table 140a — BORDEAUX - BERGERAC - SARLAT - SOUILLAC

1,2 class

km			R		S			†		J	K	⑦e			⑤	⑦e	Ⓐ		†		Ⓐ								
0	Bordeaux St. Jean d.	...	0604	0604	0717	0717	0840	...	1100	1108	...	1334	1334	...	...	...	1613	1704	1744	1819	1849	...	...	1918	2145
37	Libourne d.	...	0632	0632	0739	0739	0912	...	1122	1137	...	1404	1404	...	...	...	1640	1727	1809	1843	1909	1917	1942	2213
99	Bergerac d.	...	0727	0724	0857	0849	1012	...	1209	1226	...	1503	1505	...	...	...	1736	1817	1902	1936	...	2016	2042	2259
135	Le Buisson d.	...	0820	...	0944	...	...	...	1241	1258	...	...	1605	...	...	...	1821	...	1955	...	...	...	...	...
168	Sarlat d.	0834	0846	...	1010	...	...	1136	1307	1324	1513	...	1633	1647	1808	1830	1848	...	2021	...	...	...	...	...
198	Souillac a.	0911	...	...	...	...	...	1217	...	...	1546	...	1728	1850	1915	...	...	...	...	...	...	...	...	...

			Ⓐ	Ⓐ			①g			†		Ⓐ				†		⑦e	⑦e	⑤†	⑤†	⑦e	⑤f	Ⓑ
	Souillac d.	...	...	...	0650	...	0804	...	...	...	...	1454	...	...	...	1840	...	...	...	2054	2232
	Sarlat d.	...	0607	...	0732	0742	0845	1023	...	1550	1550	1536	...	...	...	1922	1928	...	2131	2309
	Le Buisson d.	...	0647	...	...	0818	...	1051	...	1619	1619	...	...	...	...	1958	...	...	...	...
	Bergerac d.	0614	0700	0728	...	0900	...	1123	1227	1653	1653	...	1735	1735	1901	1928	...	2045	2226
	Libourne d.	0715	0756	0816	...	0948	...	1249n	1313	1757	1754	1814	...	1845	1845z	1954	2014	2020	2132	2312
	Bordeaux St. Jean a.	0741	0819	0838	...	1011	...	1328	1336	1820	...	1909	1936z	2017	...	2042	2156	2334

J – Daily except dates in note K.
K – Ⓐ Mar. 27 - May 4.
R – ① (also Nov. 8, Jan. 5, May 9,15,22; not Oct. 31, Nov. 7, Dec. 26, Jan. 2, Feb. 20,27).
S – ✗ (except when train R runs).
e – Also Nov. 1, Apr. 17, May 1,8; not Oct. 30, Apr. 16,30, May 7.

f – Also Nov. 10, Nov. 24; Nov. 11, May 26.
g – Also Apr. 18, May 2,9,26; not Apr. 17, May 1,8.
n – Arrive 1221.
z – On ⑤ (also May 24) Libourne arrive 1841/depart 1901, Bordeaux arrive 1936.
🚌 – By bus. Rail tickets not valid.

Table 140b — BRIVE and LE MONT DORE - CLERMONT FERRAND

1,2 class

km			Z	✗	✗n	✗	▲	6390	W	V	⑥		W	P	✗	⑦e	A		⑤q	⑤f	✗	⑤q		†	†	✗
0	Bordeaux 140 d.	...	...	...	...	...	...	0747	...	...	...	...	...	...	...	...	...	...	...	...	...	...	...	...	...
203	Brive la Gaillarde d.	...	...	0623	...	...	1007	...	...	1306	...	...	...	...	...	1534	1608	1733	...	...	1808	1830	...
229	Tulle d.	...	...	0652	...	...	1040	...	...	1340	...	...	...	...	...	1607	1640	1804	...	...	1836	1854	...
	Limoges d.	0548	...	...	...	1035	...	...	1318	...	...	...	...	...	...	...	...	1725	...	...	2112	
282	Meymac d.	0733	...	0749	...	1135	1204	...	1433	1457	...	...	...	...	1705	1744	1853	1909	...	1942	2008b	2249
295	Ussel a.	0746	...	0802	...	1149	1216	...	1446	1510	...	...	...	...	1717	1757	1906	1922	...	1954	2030b	2303
295	Ussel d.	▬	...	0805	...	1150	...	...	1512	...	1700	...	...	1718	1801	...	1927r	...	1957	...	
313	Eygurande d.	...	...	0827	...	1209	...	✗	1529	...	1722	...	1738	1820	...	1945r	...	2014	
	Le Mont Dore d.	0600	0729	0829		1119	1206	...	1453	1532		1555		1740		...	1933		2003	
	La Bourboule d.	0607	0738	0837		1128	1212	...	1502	1539		1602		1747		...	1942		2012	
335	Laqueuille d.	0618	0754	0847	0854	1141	1224	1234	1518	1550	1600	1614	1755	1805	1805	1847	1958	2008r	2028	2038
395	Royat d.	0723	...	...	0954	1242	...	1337	...	1659	1714	...	1908	1908	1944	...	2108r	...	2135
400	Clermont Ferrand a.	0730	...	1000	1249	...	1344	...	1706	1720	...	1915	1915	1950	...	2114r	...	2141
	Lyon Perrache 140c a.	...	...	1655															

			✗	†	✗	✗	Ⓐ	†	⑥		W			6890		†	V	W	✗	Ⓐ		E	F	Ⓐ	⑦e	⑦e
	Lyon Perrache 140c d.	...	...	...	...	...	...	...	...	...	...	1109	...	...	...	...	...	...	...	...	...	...	...	...
	Clermont Ferrand d.	...	0657	...	...	0744	...	1034	...	1305	...	1418	...	...	1727	1727	...	1954	2108
	Royat d.	...	0704	...	...	0751	...	1041	...	1312	...	1427	...	...	1734	1734	...	2001	2115
	Laqueuille d.	...	0804	0808	0857	0857	1144	1145	1238	1419	1423	1528	1532	...	1604	1850z	1846	1849	2115	2217	2221
	La Bourboule a.	...	0822	0908	0908	0911	...	1157	1250	1431	...	1546	...	1615	1901	...	2128	2235
	Le Mont Dore a.	...	0833	0915	0915	0922	...	1203	1256	1438	...	1557	...	1622	1908	...	2135	2246
	Eygurande d.	...	0826	...	...	1211	...	1450	1553	...	▬	1908	1914	...	2239
	Ussel a.	...	0843	...	1228	...	1513	1611	...	†	1925	1930	...	2258
	Ussel d.	0625	0844	0844	0859	...	1229	1246	...	1544	1613	...	1613	1801	1854	1926	...	2305
	Meymac d.	0639	0857	0857	0913	...	1243	1300	...	1558	1628	...	1628	1814	1911	1940	...	2318
	Limoges a.	0816	...	1041	...	1434	...	1729	...	1955	2046	...	
	Tulle d.	...	1001	1001	...	1349	...	1731	1731	...	2039	...	0018
	Brive la Gaillarde d.	...	1025	1025	...	1414	...	1753	1753	...	2102	...	0039
	Bordeaux 140 a.	...	...	...	...	2021	...	...	...	...	

A – Daily except ⑤ (also runs May 26; not Oct. 25, Nov. 10, Dec. 20, May 24).
E – ⑤⑦ (also Dec. 20, Apr. 17, May 1,8; not Apr. 16,30, May 7,26). Change at Laqueuille on Dec. 20, May 24.
F – Daily except when train E runs.
P – 🚌 Périgueux - Ussel.
V – LE VENTADOUR, ⑤ (also Dec. 20 - Jan. 3, Feb. 11,12,18,19,25,26, Apr. 8,9,15,17, 22,23, May 1,8,24; not Nov. 11, May 26): 🚌 Bordeaux - Clermont Ferrand - Lyon and v.v.; ♀ Bordeaux - Clermont Ferrand and v.v.; ♀ St. Germain des Fossés - Lyon and v.v.

W – Runs on dates of train V.
Z – Ⓐ (daily Dec. 17 - Mar. 17).
b – Connection by 🚌.
e – Also Apr. 17, May 1,8; not Apr. 16,30, May 7.
f – Also Nov. 10, May 24; not Nov. 11, May 26.
n – By 🚌 on ⑥ (depart 8 minutes earlier).
q – Also Oct. 25, Nov. 10, Dec. 20, May 24; not Nov. 26.
r – ① only.   z – Arrive 1844.
▲ – Extended to Paris Gare de Lyon (arrive 1657) on Jan. 3,4, Mar. 4,5, May 1.

Table 140c — CLERMONT FERRAND - LYON

1,2 class

km				5900	3501	59574	6302		6390	6304		6380		6306			6308	
			①g	✗	✗	✗	①g	P		V	A			⑤f			⑦e	F	⑦e
0	Clermont Ferrand d.	0508	...	0612	0743	0836	...	0848	1020	...	1110	1354	1402	...	1533	...	1623	1755	...	1819	1939	2024	...	2056
55	Vichy d.	...	...	0644	...	0910	...	0922	1055	...	1430	1439	...	1608	...	1830	...	2014	2100	...	2131
65	St. Germain des Fossés 128 d.	...	...	0700	...	0918	0934	0935	1103	1143	1447	1447	1507	1617	1627	1839	1849	2037	2108	2118	2153
132	Roanne 128 d.	...	...	0742	...	1016	1019	...	1226	1530	...	1550	...	1709	...	1935	...	2126	...	2202	2240
	Montbrison d.	0652	...	0917	...	1245	...	1805	...	2002	...	
	St. Étienne Châteaucreux d.	0736	...	0950	...	1312	...	1842	...	2031	...	
	Lyon Part Dieu 128 a.	...	0850	...	1129	1129	1339	...	1646	...	1703	...	1821	...	2049	2240	...	2316	2357
229	Lyon Perrache 128 a.	0836	...	0859	1039	1138	1138	1349	1358	1655	...	1834	1939	...	2059	2123	2250	2326	0008

			6802		6804	5957		6890	5812	6816		6880	5901	6806			6882			6808		59580	6886	5907
			✗	G	E	E	♀	V	H	H	⑤f	♀	✗	H			⑤x	F♀					R	R
	Lyon Perrache 128 d.	0632	0636	0636	...	...	1050	1109	1236	...	1255	...	1455	...	1510	1540	...	1610	1745	...	1935	2125	...
	Lyon Part Dieu 128 d.	0646	0646	...	0912	...	1119	1130	1249	...	1305	...	1523	1552	...	1757	...	1945	2138	...
	St. Étienne Châteaucreux d.	0728	...	...	1151	...	...	1705	...	1737	...	
	Montbrison d.	0758	...	...	1217	...	...	1737	...	
	Roanne 128 d.	...	0757	0802	1029	...	1235	1241	1405	...	1422	...	1623	...	1642	1702	...	1915	...	2058	2256	...
	St. Germain des Fossés 128 d.	...	0841	0846	0854	1111	1146	1327	1327	1446	1454	1505	1525	1707	1712n	1737	1741	1810q	...	1957	2003	2124	2338	2344
	Vichy d.	...	0850	...	0904	...	1156	...	1337	1337	...	1504	...	1721n	1747	...	1810q	...	2013	2151	...	2355
	Clermont Ferrand a.	0934	0923	...	0942	1229	1354	1413	1413	...	1542	...	1611	1759	1824	...	1853	1915	...	2046	2224	...	0034

A – Daily except when train V runs. Runs 10 minutes later on ①②③④⑥.
E – ①⑥ (also Dec. 21,22, Apr. 18, May 2,9,25; not Apr. 17, May 1,8).
F – ⑤⑦ (also Dec. 20,21, Apr. 17, May 1,8,24; not Apr. 16,30, May 7,26).
G – ✗ (except when train E runs).
H – ①②③④⑥ (except when train V runs). Not May 25.
P – Daily except ① (runs Apr. 17, May 1,8; not Apr. 18, May 2,9).
R – ⑧ (also Feb. 11,18, Apr. 8,15; not Nov. 11, Apr. 16,30, May 7).

V – LE VENTADOUR, runs on ⑤, also dates in Table 140b (note V).
e – Also Apr. 17, May 1,8; not Apr. 16,30, May 7.
f – Also Nov. 10, May 24; not Nov. 11, May 26.
g – Also Apr. 18, May 2,9; not Apr. 17, May 1,8.
n – 5 minutes later on ✗.
q – 5 minutes later on ⑥.
x – Also Nov. 10, Feb. 18,25, Mar. 4,11; not May 26.

Table 141

PARIS - BOURGES - MONTLUÇON

1,2 class

km		4403 ✕✕	4403 ✕✕	⑦q	4607	14635 ⑥		Ⓐ	Ⓐ	⑤	153 Ⓑh	Ⓐ	Ⓒ	4433 G	†	4613	157	4459 h	4615 ⑦e	4459 ⑤f
0	**Paris Austerlitz 138** .... d.	0632	0718	0702	0910	...	1221	...	...	...	1700	...	...	1750	...	1847	1909	2030	...	2030
119	Les Aubrais 138 .... d.	0733		0803	1014	...	1322	...	1446	...		...	...	1856	...	1948		2132	...	2132
200	Vierzon 138 .... a.	0815	0843	0848	1052	...	1538	...	...	...	1826	...	...	1936	...	2032	2036	2211	...	2211
200	Vierzon 128 .... d.	0829	0850	0857	0903	1059	...	1215	1412	1416	1540	1646	...	1838	1833	1907	1951	2045	2049	2225	2225
	Bourges 128 .... a.	0849	0911		0923	1125	1220	1244	...	1445	1604	1710	1743	1838	1857	1936	2012	2020	2113	2240	
291	St. Amand Montrond .... d.			0958			1306	1504	...	...	...	...	1834	1929	1930			2106	2141		2318	2318
341	**Montluçon** .... a.			1033			1352	1540	...	...	...	...	1916	2013	2005			2151	2219		2353	2353

		4638 Ⓐ	✕✕	✕✕	152	154	✕✕	4604	4636		Ⓐ		4466 ⑥t	4600 ⑦e	4632 Ⓒ	4600 Ⓐ		4606 Ⓐ	4608 ⑦e
	Montluçon .... d.			0626				0845		1221		1450		1648	1648	...	1722		1757	1853
	St. Amand Montrond .... d.			0658				0922		1305		1531		1724	1724	...	1807		1833	1931
	Bourges 128 .... d.	0630	0710			0733		0943	1008	1224	1320	1348	1556		1726		1749	1853	1858	1915		
	Vierzon 128 .... a.	0651	0742	0750		0759		1012	1034	1244	1349		1620	1626		1757	1817	1809	1817	1922		1939	1925	2024
	Vierzon 138 .... d.	0703			0758	0804		1034	1256				1634			1828	1833			1944	2036
	Les Aubrais 138 .... d.	0747				0841		1117	1336				1713			1915	1915			2023	2116
	Paris Austerlitz .... a.	0851x			0928x	0939x		1219x	1443x				1816x			2022x	2022x			2134x	2219x

G – ①②③④⑦ (also May 26; not Apr. 16,30, May 7,24).
e – Also Apr. 17, May 1,8; not Apr. 16,30, May 7.
f – Also May 24; not May 26.

h – Not Apr. 16,30, May 7.
q – Also Apr. 17, May 1,8.

t – Also Apr. 16,30, May 7,25.
x – 6 - 12 minutes later Nov. 14 - Dec. 22.

Table 142

PAU - CANFRANC

Subject to alteration during the currency of the winter timetable

1,2 class

km		Ⓒ		Ⓐ	Ⓐ					
0	**Pau** .... d.	0642		0741	0800	0950	1355	1644	1825	1912
36	Oloron .... a.	0717		0816	0835	1025	1430	1720	1902	1947
36	Oloron 🚌 .... d.			0821	0840	1030	1435			
90	**Canfranc** 🚌 .... a.			1002	1021	1206	1616			

		Ⓐ	Ⓒ	Ⓐ				✕✕	†	⑤⑦
Canfranc 🚌 .... d.					1113	1254		1645	1727	
Oloron 🚌 .... a.					1251	1432		1823	1905	
Oloron .... d.	0652	0720	0828	1301	1442	1730	1833	1916	2210
Pau .... a.	0728	0756	0903	1336	1517	1805	1908	1955	2243

🚌 – By bus, Oloron - Canfranc and v.v.

Table 143

PERPIGNAN - LA TOUR DE CAROL

1,2 class ▲

km		🚌			E 🚌	🚌		✕✕	⑦v	H	⑦v	J				Ⓑ
0	**Perpignan** .... d.	...		0750			1206	...					1714		1819		1914
40	Prades .... d.	...		0834			1247	...					1759		1905		1955
46	Villefranche Vernet les Bains .d.	...		0841	0910		1254	1305	1340				1806	1820	1912		2002
	Mont Louis la Cabanasse ... d.	0912			1028	1210		1358	1421	1600	1730	1734		1933			
81	Font Romeu .... d.	0942			1049	1240		1431	1435	1630	1747	1804		1949			
102	Bourg Madame .... d.	1014			1141						1833	1836		2034			
109	**La Tour de Carol** .... a.	1025			1154	1310				1700	1847	1847		2050			

		✕✕	①x		🚌	E			H		Ⓑ		†	J
La Tour de Carol .... d.		0549			0810	0910	1036		1315		1547		2025
Bourg Madame .... d.		0555					1049				1600		2031
Font Romeu .... d.		0629		0829		0840	0940	1138		1345		1650		2105
Mont Louis la Cabanasse ... d.		0648		0900		0911	1011	1155		1416		1707		2133
Villefranche Vernet les Bains .d.	0630	0737	0747	1000	1014		1252	1302		1711		1805	1818	2019	
Prades .... d.	0638		0755		1022		1310		1719		1826	2027	
Perpignan .... a.	0718		0835		1102		1350		1800		1906	2107	

E – ⑥ Dec. 17 - Mar. 25.
H – ⑥⑦ Dec. 17 - Mar. 25.
J – ⑤⑥ (also Oct. 25, Nov. 10, Dec. 20, Jan. 3,4, May 24; not Nov. 11, May 26).

v – Also Nov. 1, Apr. 17, May 1,8.
x – Also Nov. 2, Apr. 18, May 2,9; not Apr. 17, May 1,8.
▲ – Villefranche - La Tour de Carol is 2 class only, narrow gauge.

Table 144

TOULOUSE - LA TOUR DE CAROL

1,2 class

km		4871 A	J	K	⑥	🚌			🚌	4880 E	†	⑤f	4874 A
	Paris Austerlitz 138 .... d.	2145b											
0	**Toulouse** .... d.	0502	0719	0752	1014	1221	1425	...	1725	2110			
65	Pamiers .... d.	0544	0804	0837	1058	1310	1513	...	1813	2220			
83	Foix .... d.	0606	0818	0854	1113	1325	1531	...	1830	2240			
123	Ax les Thermes .... d.	0656	0903	0935	1155	1405	1612	1640	1911	2335			
144	L'Hospitalet .... d.	0727	0932	1003	1222			1707	1944				
163	**La Tour de Carol** .... a.	0800	1000	1028	1249			1747	2015				

		🚌	4880 E	†	⑤f	4874 A
La Tour de Carol .... d.	0700	1040	1335	1517	...	1710	1735	...	1916
L'Hospitalet .... d.	0734	1104	1403	1605	...	1742	1811	...	1949
Ax les Thermes .... d.	0806	1134	1433	1637	1655	1815	1845	1845	2020
Foix .... d.	0852	1214	1513	...	1735	1900	1930	1930	2113
Pamiers .... d.	0905	1227	1529	...	1753	1919	1947	1947	2128
Toulouse .... a.	0945	1311	1612	...	1844	2004	2035	2035	2217
Paris Austerlitz 138 .... a.									0700r

A – 🛏 1,2 cl. and 🛌 Paris - La Tour de Carol and v.v.
E – ⑥ Dec. 17 - Mar. 25.
J – ⑦ Dec. 18 - Mar. 26.
K – Daily except when train J runs.

b – Train 473 (on ⑤ and dates in Table **138** depart 2106 in train **4415**).
f – Also Nov. 10, May 24; not Nov. 11, May 26.
r – Arrive 0648 on ① and dates in Table **138**.

Table 144a

ANDORRA 🚌

Subject to cancellation when mountain passes are closed by snow.

km		S A	P D	S K	P C	S E	S B	P H		S C	P K	S H	S E	S B
	Ax les Thermes Gare ...... d.			1200	1615	...	...				1400			...
	L'Hospitalet Gare ...... d.	0740		1235	1645	1720	1830							...
0	**La Tour de Carol Gare** .. d.		1115	1200					1835					
	Pas de la Casa .... d.		0810	1215	1300	1300	1715	1750	1900	1935				
	Soldeu .... d.		0840	1240	1325	1330	1745	1820	1930	2000				
63	**Andorra la Vella** .... a.		0920	1325	1400	1405	1825	1900	2010	2045				
69	Sant Julia de Loria .... a.			1345	1420				2115					

		S	P	S C		P K	S H	S E	S B
Sant Julia de Loria .... d.		0730							
Andorra la Vella .... d.	0545	0745	0815	1100	1430	1530	1630	...
Soldeu .... d.	0620	0830	0900	1135	1515	1610	1725	...
Pas de la Casa .... d.	0650	0915	0935	1245	1600	1650	1800	...
La Tour de Carol Gare .. a.		1000	1000		1700			
L'Hospitalet Gare .... a.	0715		1000	1325		1740	1900	...
Ax les Thermes Gare ...... a.			1045	1415				...

A – May 29 - Sept. 24, 1994.
P – Sept. 25 - Dec. 14, 1994 and May 1 - 27, 1995.
P – To Oct. 31, 1994 and from May 1, 1995.

D – Sept. 25, 1994 - May 28, 1995.
E – Dec. 15, 1994 - Apr. 30, 1995.
H – July 1 - Sept. 24, 1994.

K – July 15 - Sept. 15, 1994.

🚌 service operated by Autos Pujol Huguet, Place Major 7, Sant Julia de Loria, ☎ 41019.
🚌 service operated by Societe Franco-Andorrane de Transports (SFAT), Carrer la Llacuna 12, Andorra la Vella, ☎ 21372, fax 61408.

Table 145 — PARIS - NEVERS - CLERMONT FERRAND
1,2 class

Train numbers (southbound): 191 (Ⓐ, G, 2) · 56071 (Ⓐ) · 5957 (⑥, C) · 5935 (†) · 5901 · 5911 (✗) · 5911 (Ⓐk) · 193 (⑤⑥, D, t) · 5913 (⑥h) · 59330 (⑥n) · 195 (♀) · 5909 (✗) · 5903 (Ⓒ) · 5915 (⑤f) · 5917 · 5907 (⑤f) · 5945 (A) · 5947 (H)

km	Station	Times (as printed, left→right)
0	Paris Lyon d.	0702 0711 0854 · 1124 1231 1403 1403 1608 1650 · 1730 1752 1856 1903 2015 2043 2242 2312
119	Montargis d.	0830 · 1228 · 1504 1502 · 1759 · 1908 · 2015 2120 · 2353
155	Gien d.	0853 · 1248 · 1522 1522 · 1823 · 1933 · 2036 2141 2157 0017
196	Cosne d.	0931 · 1309 · 1547 1547 · 1844 · 1954 · 2058 2204 2219 0044 0106
228	La Charité d.	0954 · 1326 · 1604 1604 · 1901 · 2012 · 2117 2222 2236 0105 0125
254	Nevers d.	0642 · 0625 0855 1015 1054 · 1344 1431 1618 1622 1801 1917 · 1924 2028 2056 2131 2237 2252 0128 0148
314	Moulins d.	0708 0708 0800 0925 1125 · 1502 · 1651 1831 · 1932 1953 · 2126 · 2321 0209 0230
355	St. Germain des Fossés d.	0717 0738 0738 0829 · 1146 · 1525 · 1717 · 2003 · 2147 · 2344 0241 0255
365	Vichy d.	0726 0748 0748 0839 0954 1156 · 1535 · 1726 1900 2013 2021 2158 · 2353 0252 0306
406	Riom d.	0754 0815 0815 0907 1018 1220 · 1601 · 1750 · 2037 2045 2222 · 0016 0318 0333
420	Clermont Ferrand a.	0804 0827 0827 0917 1027 1229 · 1611 · 1759 1929 2046 2054 2231 · 0025 0328 0343

Train numbers (northbound): 5910 (✗) · 190 (D) · 59328 (♀) · 5906 (†) · 5922 · 5900 (†) · 5900 · 5912 (✗) · 5912 (⑥) · 5936 (J) · 5936 (K) · 5902 (♀) · 5928 (L) · 5908 (℗) · 192 (R, 2) · 5914 · 194 (✗, 2) · 5916 (⑦e) · 196 (C) · 5958 (M) · 5924 · 5944 (B)

Station	Times (as printed, left→right)
Clermont Ferrand d.	0535 0618 0628 · 0650 · 0836 · 1311 1328 · 1611 · 1715 1744 · 1856 1927 0133 0157
Riom d.	0627 0638 · 0700 0757 0846 · 1322 1338 · 1725 · 1906 1937 0145 0208
Vichy d.	0604 0651 0700 · 0726 0820 0910 · 1345 1402 1641 · 1747 1814 · 1929 2000 0224 0233
St. Germain des Fossés d.	0659 0709 · 0734 0809 0919 · 1354 1411 · 1756 · 1821 1840 · 1955 2030 0252 0314
Moulins d.	0630 0725 0730 · 0806 0851 0941 · 1416 1434 1707 · 1822 · 2025 2101 0326 0400
Nevers d.	0604 0659 · 0800 0821 0854 0922 1012 1034 1046 1316 1320 1447 1506 1641 1737 1822 1909 1943 · 0416
La Charité d.	0624 · 0842 · 1053 1105 1334 1338 · 1655 · 1842 · 2005 · 0416
Cosne d.	0641 · 0900 · 1111 1123 1352 1356 · 1713 · 1900 · 2026 0357 0436
Gien d.	0702 · 0920 · 1133 1143 1413 1417 · 1734 · 1926 · 2051 · 0500
Montargis d.	0723 · 0940 · 1154 1204 1433 1439 · 1754 · 1947 · 2123 0438 0523
Paris Lyon a.	0831 0852 · 0958 1043 1120 1212 1304 1304 1537 1547 1646 1712 1907 1933 2057 2103 2233 2219 2302 2057 0557 0639

A – Ⓑ (also Feb. 25, Mar. 4, Apr. 22; not Nov. 11, Apr. 16,30, May 7): [couchette] and [bed] 1,2 cl. Paris - Millau; also (except when train H runs) [couchette] and [bed] 1,2 cl. Paris - Aurillac. Conveys on ⑤ (see Table 145a), [couchette] and [bed] Paris - Nimes.
B – Runs (from Millau) on Ⓑ (also Feb. 25, Mar. 4, Apr. 22; not Nov. 11, Apr. 16,30, May 7): [couchette] and [bed] 1,2 cl. Millau - Paris; also (except when train M runs) [couchette] and [bed] 1,2 cl. Aurillac - Paris. Conveys from Nimes on ⑦, [couchette] and [bed] 1,2 cl. Nimes - Paris.
C – LE CÉVENOL – [couchette] Paris - Nimes - Marseille and v.v.
D – [couchette] Clermont Ferrand - Dijon and v.v.
H – Oct. 27, Dec. 21, Feb. 17, Apr. 14 only: [couchette] and [bed] 1,2 cl. Paris - Aurillac.
J – Jan. 17 - Feb. 9.
K – Daily except Jan. 17 - Feb. 9.

L – Jan. 3,4, Mar. 4,5, May 1 only.
M – Runs (from Aurillac) Nov. 6, Mar. 5, May 1 only: [couchette] and [bed] 1,2 cl. Aurillac - Paris.
R – Daily except Nov. 6, Mar. 5, May 17.
e – Also Nov. 1, Apr. 17, May 1,8; not Oct. 30, Apr. 16,30, May 7.
f – Also Nov. 10, May 24; not Nov. 11, May 26.
h – Not Nov. 11, Apr. 16,30, May 7,25.
k – Not Oct. 31, May 25,26.
n – Not Oct. 30, Apr. 16,30, May 7,25.
q – Not Oct. 30, Apr. 16,30, May 7.25.
t – Also Oct. 31, Nov. 10, May 24; not Nov. 11.
↗ – Supplement payable.

Table 145a — CLERMONT FERRAND - NIMES - MONTPELLIER
1,2 class

Train numbers: 5919 (H) · [bus] (⑥q) · 59561 (①g) · [bus] · [bus] · 5957 (C) · [bus] · 59563

km	Station	Times (as printed, left→right)
	Paris Lyon 145 d.	2242 · 0854
0	Clermont Ferrand d.	0602 · 0620 0647 · 0933 · 1122 1158 · 1254 · 1646 · 1840 1925
36	Issoire 147 d.	0630 0647 0713 · 1005 · 1150 1225 · 1322 · 1712 · 1910 1952
61	Arvant 147 d.	0712 0737 · 1023 1028 · 1214 1246 · 1345 · 1732 · 1934 2013
71	Brioude d.	0703 0724 0747 · 1040 · 1224 1256 1356 1400 1746 · 1944 2024
95	St. Georges d'Aurac d.	0745 · 1102 · 1808 1813 2004 2047
103	Langeac d.	0730 0734 0813 0817 · 1112 · 1424 · 1817 · 1903 2055 2137
	Le Puy a.	0817 0836 0900 · 1155 · 1335 1408 · 1505 · 1528
170	Langogne d.	0844 · 0915 · 1925
	Mende a.	0538 · 0831 · 1116 · 1339 · 1659
188	La Bastide d.	0641 0734t 0904 0934 0934 · 1219 · 1435 1552 1643 1802 1956
241	Grand Combe la Pise d.	0732 0833 1003 1029 1029 · 1312 · 1643 1857 2049
254	Alès a.	0716 0747 0848 1020 1044 1044 · 1329 1329 1536 1659 1912 2104
303	Nimes 163 a.	0754 0822 1057 · 1123 1123 · 1408 1408 1613 1737 1949 2144
	Marseille 163 a.	1910
353	Montpellier 163 a.	0858 · 1156 · 1440 1440 · 2023

Train numbers: 59562 · 5958 (C) · 58338 · 5924 (N)

Station	Times (as printed, left→right)
Montpellier 163 d.	0707 · 1202x · 1622 1628 · 1733 1733
Marseille 163 d.	1221
Nimes 163 d.	0635 0707 0737 0822 1029 · 1244 1350 · 1608 1657 1703 1804 1804 1839 1950 1950
Alès d.	0713 0748 0817 0859 1110 · 1328 1430 · 1652 1744 1750 1841 1841 1926 2033 2032
Grand Combe la Pise d.	0801 0834 0914 · 1342 1446 · 1801 1816 1856 1856 2050 2054
La Bastide d.	0910 0939 1017 · 1447 1550 1556 · 1959 1959 2159 2206
Mende d.	1007 1036 · 1544 · 1652 · 2056
Langogne d.	1036 · 1612 · 2017 · 2226
Le Puy d.	0553 0615 1049 1152 1226 1623 1735 1758 1954 2022 2106 2116 2336
Langeac d.	1138 · 1715 1819 1842
St. Georges d'Aurac d.	0642 0704 1243 1316 1713 1724 1829 1852 2045
Brioude d.	0705 0726 1154 1204 1302 1335 1745 1905 1914 1934 2106 2141 0004
Arvant 147 d.	0714 0738 1312 1344 1755 1920 1924 2115 2150
Issoire 147 d.	0734 0758 1231 1335 1411 1816 1953 2136 2210 0033
Clermont Ferrand a.	0807 0825 1258 1405 1440 1843 2019 2203 2237 0100
Paris Lyon 145 a.	2302 0639

C – LE CÉVENOL – [couchette] and ♀ Paris - Nimes - Marseille and v.v.
H – ⑤ (also Nov. 10, May 24; not Nov. 11, Feb. 17, Apr. 14, May 26): [couchette] and [bed] 1,2 cl. Paris - Nimes.
N – ⑦ (also Nov. 1, Jan. 4, Apr. 17, May 8; not Oct. 30, Nov. 6, Mar. 5, Apr. 16,30, May 7): [couchette] and [bed] 1,2 cl. Nimes - Paris.
e – Also Nov. 1, Apr. 17, May 1,8; not Oct. 30, Apr. 16,30, May 7.
f – Also Nov. 10, May 24; not Nov. 11, May 26.
g – Also Nov. 2, Apr. 18, May 2,9; not Oct. 31, Apr. 17, May 1,8.
h – Not Apr. 16,30, May 7.
q – Also Nov. 11, May 26; not Nov. 12, May 27.
t – Ⓑ (also Nov. 11, Jan. 4, May 25; not Nov. 12).
x – Not Apr. 10 - May 12.
z – 16 minutes later on Ⓐ Feb. 13 - Mar. 3.

Table 146 — TOULOUSE - ALBI - RODEZ
1,2 class

km	Station	Times (Toulouse → Rodez)
0	Toulouse Matabiau d.	0718 0819 1004 1220 1354 1722 1800 1918 2107 2235
54	Gaillac d.	0759 0906 1053 1305 1438 · 1849 2003 2148 2320
58	Tessonnières d.	0804 0912 · 1310 · 2008 2153
75	Albi Ville d.	0817 0924 1111 1328 1454 1813 1911 2024 2212 2339
92	Carmaux d.	0837 0939 1126 1348 1515 1830 1928 2041 2227
158	Rodez a.	0940 · 1237 1455t 1623 1939 · 2145

Station	Times (Rodez → Toulouse)
Rodez d.	0730 0856 · 1213v 1408x · 1720r 1820h 2032
Carmaux d.	0646b 0834 0957 1213 1316 1512 1705 1831 1934 2133
Albi Ville d.	0703 0850 1012 1229 1336 1529 1723 1849 1955 2151
Tessonnières d.	0717 · 1243 · 1738
Gaillac d.	0721 0905 1027 1247 1351 1548 1743 1911 2013 2212
Toulouse Matabiau a.	0813 1013 1103 1332 1433 1636 1833 2000 2054 2253

b – Ⓑ only.
e – Also Nov. 1, Apr. 17, May 1,8,25; not Apr. 16,30, May 7.
h – ⑤⑥⑦ only.
r – Ⓐ only.
t – Ⓑ only.
v – Depart 1155 (by [bus] to Carmaux) on Ⓐ Sept. 25 - Oct. 31, Nov. 2-4 and Ⓐ Mar. 13 - May 24.
x – Depart 1350 (by [bus] to Carmaux) on Ⓐ Mar. 13 - May 24.

Ⓐ – Mondays to Fridays only, except holidays   Ⓑ – Daily except Saturdays   Ⓒ – Saturdays, Sundays and holidays

Table 147 CLERMONT FERRAND - AURILLAC

1,2 class

km		51551	51553	5957		5901					5945
			⚒				⚒	E	G	⑤f	A
	Paris Lyon **145** ..... d.	...	...	0854	...	1231	...	...	...	...	2242r
0	**Clermont Ferrand** .... d.	0655	0933	1243	...	1626	1809	1936	2107	2240	0348
26	Issoire .... d.	0723	1005	1310	...	1653	1836	|	2135	|	0416
61	Arvant .... d.	0742	1024	1332	...	1714	1853	2020	2155	|	0438
111	Neussargues .... d.	0825	1111	1418	1428	1803	1939	2110	2239	0004	0600
120	Murat (Cantal) .... d.	0835	1122	...	1438	1814	1949	2120	2249	0013	0612
131	Le Lioran .... d.	0848	1135	...	1452	1831	2002	2134	2303	0024	0631
168	**Aurillac** .... a.	0918	1205	...	1523	1903	2032	2205	2332	0054	0703
476	*Toulouse* **139a** ..... a.	1257	1602	...	1906v	...	...	...	...	...	...

			5962		5950	51554				5964
	⚒	①g	H				Ⓑh	⑦e	⑤f	Az
Toulouse **139a** .... d.	...	...	...	...	...	1232	...	...	...	...
Aurillac .... d.	0552	0747	1003	1318	...	1610	1750	2011	2136	2220
Le Lioran .... d.	0628	|	1046	1354	...	1646	1830	2048	2211	2304
Murat (Cantal) .... d.	|	|	1058	1405	...	1659	1841	2059	2222	2316
Neussargues .... d.	0649	0846	1110	1414	1423	1715	1851	2109	2238	0003
Arvant .... d.	0730	|	1157	...	1508	1804	1934	2158	2319	0049
Issoire .... a.	0749	0943	1218	...	1528	1823	1952	2216	2337	0111
Clermont Ferrand .. a.	0818	1010	1246	...	1554	1851	2019	2243	0003	0140
Paris Lyon **145** ... a.	...	...	1646	...	1933	...	...	...	...	0639

A – Ⓑ (also Feb. 25, Mar. 4, Apr. 22; not Nov. 11, Apr. 16,30, May 7): (2) and 🛏 1,2 cl. Paris - Aurillac and v.v.
E – ⑤⑦ (also Oct. 25, Nov. 1,10, Dec. 20, Apr. 17, May 1,8,24; not Nov. 11, Apr. 16,30, May 7,26).
G – ⑤⑦ (also Nov. 1,10, Apr. 17, May 1,8,24,25; not Oct. 30, Apr. 16,30, May 7).
H – Runs 5-30 minutes later on Jan. 3,4, Mar. 4,5, May 1 (Aurillac 1008, Paris 1712).
e – Also Nov. 1, Apr. 17, May 1,8; not Oct. 30, Apr. 16,30, May 7.
f – Also Nov. 10, May 24; not Nov. 11, May 26.
g – Also Nov. 2, Apr. 18, May 2,9; not Oct. 31, Apr. 17, May 1,8.
h – Not Apr. 16,30, May 7.
r – Depart 2312 on Oct. 27, Dec. 21, Feb. 17, Apr. 14.
v – ⑤ (also Oct. 25, Nov. 10, Dec. 20, May 24; not Nov. 11, Dec. 23,30, Apr. 14,21, May 26).
z – On Nov. 6, Mar. 5, May 1, depart Neussargues 2332 and runs earlier to Paris (arrive 0557).

Table 147a CLERMONT FERRAND - BÉZIERS

1,2 class

km			5945				5949	🚌	🚌		🚌
		⚒	A	⚒	Ⓐ			⚒		H	Ⓑh
	Paris Lyon **145** ..... d.	...	2242	...	...	...	0854	...	...	...	...
0	**Clermont Ferrand** .... d.	...	0348	...	...	...	1243	...	1620	...	2100
26	Issoire **147** .... d.	...	0416	...	...	...	1310	...	|	...	|
61	Arvant **147** .... d.	...	0438	...	...	...	1332	...	|	...	|
111	Neussargues **147** ...... d.	...	0548	...	...	...	1427	...	|	1740	|
130	St Flour .... d.	...	0611	...	...	...	1445	...	|	1758	2210
168	St Chély d'Apcher ..... d.	...	0647	...	1210	...	1518	...	1750	|	2236
201	Marvejols .... d.	...	0720	0726	1240	1249	1548	...	1826	1906	2312
236	**Mende** .... a.	...	|	0806	|	1329	|	...	1905	|	2351
243	Sévérac .... d.	...	0759	...	1317	...	1624	...	...	1945	...
273	Millau .... d.	0722	0826	...	1348	...	1650	1700	...	2014	...
352	Bédarieux .... d.	0841	...	...	1508	...	1808	|	...	2133	...
394	**Béziers** .... a.	0917	...	...	1544	...	1843	|	...	2216	...
	Montpellier **163** ..... a.	1003	...	...	...	...	...	1835	...	...	...

	🚌	🚌		5950					5944	
	Ⓐ		⚒		Ⓐ	Ⓐ	⚒	Ⓑh	A	⑦e
Montpellier **163** ... d.	...	...	...	...	...	1645c	...	...	...	1832
Béziers .... d.	...	...	...	0939	1150	|	1730	...	...	1927
Bédarieux .... d.	...	...	...	1017	1224	|	1809	...	...	2003
Millau .... d.	...	...	...	1136	1341	1830	1929	...	2101	2131
Sévérac .... d.	...	...	...	1203	...	1857	...	...	2129	2157
Mende .... d.	0721	1006	1150	|	...	|	...	2119	|	|
Marvejols .... d.	0803	1048	1230	1240	...	1933	...	2200	2209	2236
St Chély d'Apcher ... d.	0831	1124	...	1311	...	2003	...	...	2242	2305
St Flour .... d.	|	|	...	1347	...	...	...	...	2318	...
Neussargues **147** .... d.	|	|	...	1423	...	...	...	...	0003	...
Arvant **147** .... d.	|	|	...	1508	...	...	...	...	0049	...
Issoire **147** .... d.	|	|	...	1529	...	...	...	...	0112	...
Clermont Ferrand .. a.	1005	1250	...	1554	...	...	...	...	0140	...
Paris Lyon **145** ... a.	...	...	...	1933	...	...	...	...	0639	...

A – Ⓑ (also Feb. 25, Mar. 4, Apr. 22; not Nov. 11, Apr. 16,30, May 7): (2) and 🛏 1,2 cl. Paris - Millau and v.v.
H – ⑤⑦ (also Nov. 1,10, Dec. 20, Apr. 17, May 1,8,24,25; not Apr. 16,30, May 7,26).
c – By 🚌 Montpellier - Millau, arrive 1820 (bus runs ⚒).
e – Also Jan. 3, May 1,8; not Oct. 30, Dec. 25, Feb. 1,12,19, Apr. 9,16,30, May 7.
h – Not Nov. 11, Apr. 16,30, May 7,25.

Table 148 LYON - ST ÉTIENNE - LE PUY

1,2 class

km												681 TGV									685 TGV			
			⚒	Ⓐ	Ⓐ		Ⓐ	©	Ⓐ		⚒	⚒🍷			⚒		⚒		©		🍷		J	K
	Paris Lyon **150** .... d.	...	...	...	...	...	...	...	...	...	...	0700	...	...	...	...	...	...	...	...	1300	...	...	...
0	**Lyon Part-Dieu** .... d.	...	...	0550	0615	...	0650	...	...	...	0800	0906	0915	...	...	1212	...	1308	...	1412	1504	...	1515	1522
	Lyon Perrache .... d.	0515	...	|	|	0632	|	0653	0714	0748	|	|	0926	1050	...	1224	1233	1321	...	1423	|	...	1526	1533
22	Givors Ville .... d.	0533	...	0609	0633	0651	0709	0724	0733	|	0818	|	0943	1109	...	1243	1301	1339	...	1441	|	...	1546	1551
47	St Chamond .... d.	0554	...	0630	0654	0714	0734	0751	0759	|	0839	|	1004	1134	...	1304	1331	1401	...	1504	|	...	1607	1612
59	**St Étienne Châteaucreux** .. a.	0604	...	0639	0704	0725	0743	0800	0808	0840	0849	0949	1015	1147	...	1314	1344	1410	...	1514	1547	...	1617	1621
59	**St Étienne Châteaucreux** .. d.	...	0618	...	...	...	...	...	...	0848	...	...	...	...	1220	...	...	...	1422	...	...	1604	...	...
74	Firminy .... d.	...	0634	...	...	...	...	...	...	0908	...	...	...	...	1236	...	...	...	1443	...	...	1620	...	...
147	**Le Puy** .... a.	...	0744	...	...	...	...	...	...	1012	...	...	...	...	1339	...	...	...	1552	...	...	1725	...	...

															687 TGV			689 TGV						
	Ⓐ		Ⓑ	Ⓐ		Ⓐ	Ⓐ		⚒	Ⓐ		Ⓑh			Ⓐn	Ⓐ		🍷		M	⚒	†	⑤f	T
Paris Lyon **150** .... d.	...	...	...	...	...	...	...	...	...	...	...	...	...	...	1724	...	...	1900	...	...	...	...	...	...
yon Part-Dieu .... d.	...	...	...	1620	...	...	1710	...	...	...	1752	...	1856	...	1932	...	...	2107	...	...	2223	...	...	...
yon Perrache .... d.	1552	1610	...	1631	1645	1702	|	...	1725	1743	1803	1828	|	1921	|	...	2026	|	2049	2130	2235	2238	2309	2323
ivors Ville .... d.	1620	|	...	1650	|	1718	1729	...	1744	1802	1824	1846	1916	1938	|	...	2051	|	2107	2148	2252	2311	2326	2352
t Chamond .... d.	1642	1650	...	1717	1730	1741	1751	...	1808	1823	1845	1910	1940	2002	|	...	2113	|	2132	2210	2314	2333	2347	0013
Étienne Châteaucreux .... a.	1652	1703	...	1726	1742	1751	1801	...	1818	1833	1855	1919	1953	2014	2017	...	2123	2150	2145	2220	2324	2342	2357	0023
Étienne Châteaucreux .... d.	...	...	1723	...	...	...	...	1817	...	...	...	...	...	...	...	2027	...	...	2157	...	...	...	...	...
rminy .... d.	...	...	1740	...	...	...	...	1833	...	...	...	...	...	...	...	2042	...	...	2211	...	...	...	...	...
e Puy .... a.	...	...	1848	...	...	...	...	1948	...	...	...	...	...	...	...	2143	...	...	2313	...	...	...	...	...

						691 TGV									693 TGV									
	Ⓐ	©	Ⓐ		Ⓐ	⚒🍷	Ⓐ	†	Ⓐ	⚒	⚒	Ⓐ	⚒		⚒n		©	Ⓐ						
e Puy .... d.	...	...	...	...	0453	...	...	...	...	...	...	...	0609	...	...	...	0746	0750	...	...	...	...	...	1130
rminy .... d.	...	...	...	...	0554	...	...	...	...	...	...	...	0719	...	...	...	0848	0848	...	...	...	...	...	1233
Étienne Châteaucreux .... d.	...	...	...	...	0609	...	...	...	...	...	...	...	0740	...	...	...	0901	0901	...	...	...	...	...	1250
Étienne Châteaucreux .... d.	0517	0545	0546	0605	...	0619	0637	0637	0652	0658	0715	0732	0744	0800	0812	0842	0904	0904	0953	1038	...	1205	1235	...
Chamond .... d.	0526	0554	0555	0614	...	|	0646	0646	0701	0707	0724	0741	0753	0809	|	0852	|	|	1003	1047	...	1214	1244	...
vors Ville .... d.	0546	0614	0616	0638	...	|	0708	0708	0724	0729	0747	0804	0816	0832	|	0915	|	|	|	1110	...	1237	1308	...
yon Perrache .... a.	|	0632	|	0656	...	|	0726	0726	0745	|	0807	0821	0836	0850	|	0934	|	|	1039	1138	...	|	1326	...
yon Part-Dieu .... a.	0605	...	0635	...	...	0702	...	0740	...	0750	0818	...	...	0902	0855	...	0950	0950	...	1149	...	1255	1337	...
Paris Lyon **150** .... a.	...	...	...	...	...	0908	...	...	...	...	...	...	...	...	1102	...	...	...	...	...	...	...	...	...

	695 TGV											699 TGV												
	🍷		⚒				Ⓐ		Ⓐ			🍷	©	Ⓐ	Ⓑh		Ⓑ	Ⓐ		†	Ⓐ	†	⚒	
Puy .... d.	...	...	...	1303	...	...	...	...	...	...	1625	...	...	...	...	1745	...	1908	...	1958	...	...	...	...
miny .... d.	...	...	...	1412	...	...	...	...	...	...	1733	...	...	...	...	1855	...	2010	...	2104	...	...	...	...
Étienne Châteaucreux .... d.	...	...	...	1430	...	...	...	...	...	...	1751	...	...	...	...	1912	...	2025	...	2122	...	...	...	...
Étienne Châteaucreux .... d.	1309	1315	1345	1434	...	1559	1625	1644	1718	1741	...	1800	1814	1818	1849	1915	2000	...	2034	2125	2130	2230	2250	...
Chamond .... d.	|	|	1354	1446	...	1608	1634	1653	1727	1751	...	|	1823	1827	1858	|	2009	...	2043	2135	2139	2239	2259	...
vors Ville .... d.	|	|	1416	|	...	1629	1656	1714	1750	1811	...	|	1849	1853	1920	|	2030	...	2105	2157	2200	2301	2320	...
on Perrache .... a.	|	1358	|	1528	...	|	1714	|	1808	|	...	|	1914	1911	1939	2000	|	...	2123	2215	2219	2332	2339	...
on Part-Dieu .... a.	1352	...	1434	...	...	1647	...	1732	...	1830	...	1842	...	...	...	...	2050	...	...	...	...	...	...	...
Paris Lyon **150** .... a.	1602	...	...	...	...	...	...	...	...	...	...	2053	...	...	...	...	...	...	...	...	...	...	...	...

– Oct. 24 - Nov. 4.
– Daily except Oct. 24 - Nov. 4.
– ⑤⑦ (also Nov. 1,10, Apr. 17, May 1,8,24; not Oct. 30, May 26).
– ①②③④⑥ (also May 26; not Nov. 1,10,11, Apr. 17, May 1,8,24,25).

TGV – Ⓡ, supplement payable, 🍷.
f – Also Nov. 10, May 24; not Nov. 11, May 26.
h – Not Apr. 16,30, May 7.
n – Not Oct. 31.

⚒ – Daily except Sundays and holidays † – Sundays and holidays

Table 149 — DIJON - CHALON SUR SAÔNE - LYON

1,2 class

km					931 TGV	5001	59303 6131	6130 59305	973 TGV		5511	753 TGV				6175 6174	6132 6133	5053	975 TGV
		Ⓐ	Ⓐ	Ⓐ	⑥	Ⓐ						Ⓐ		✕					
0	Paris Lyon 155 .... d.	...	...	...	0709	...	...	...	...	1028	...	1032		...	...	...	1240r	1440
315	Dijon 149a .... d.	...	0518	0640	0635	0702	0734	0809	0904	1053	1128	1215	1219	1230	1439	1535	1605	
352	Beaune 149a .... d.	...	0542	0700	0659		0759		0926		1153	1239	1256	1503		1627		
367	Chagny 149a .... d.	...	0552		0710		0810		0937		1206		1310	1516		1638		
382	Chalon sur Saône .... d.	...	0604	0717	0725	0736	0823	0845	0948	1128	1157	1253	1255			1649		
440	Mâcon Ville .... a.	0513	0647	0715	0749	0801	0803	0858	0914	1019	1158	1229	1323		1617		1724	
	Mâcon Loché TGV .... a.					0848					1208	1215		1255				1620
478	Villefranche sur Saône ... a.	0536	0723	0738	0812	0804		0935c		1041	1254		1255			1748	1710c
512	Lyon Part Dieu .... a.	...		0800	0833	0845	0838	0950	1104	1233	1313		1358		1653	1707	1806	
512	Lyon Perrache .... a.	0602	0749	0810	0842	0855	0849		1113		1322				1702		

		6134 6135	977 TGV				5742	6144 5515	5073	763 TGV		913 TGV		6106 6107	765		5047				5079
		5009 Ⓐ	Ⓐ	⑥f	Ⓐ	Ⓑ	⑤q	Ⓐ B 2	Ⓐ	Ⓑ	Ⓐ H	Ⓔ		Ⓐ ⑥t	M	⑤f	⑦e	P	R	
	Paris Lyon 155 .... d.				1728			1556	1811		1924		1920		1853				2356
	Dijon 149a .... d.	1630	1706	1706		...	1726	1812	1821	1830	1910	1926	1955	2001	2015	2044	2103	2106	2146	2151	2258	0327
	Beaune 149a .... d.	1655					1800	1832		1904		1952	2016	2024	2039		2123	2138	2209	2210	2250	2322	0352
	Chagny 149a .... d.	1705					1817	1845		1917		2002		2033	2049			2151	2219		2300	2332	0403
	Chalon sur Saône .... d.	1719	1743	1743		...	1834		1901	1931	1948	2014	2031	2043	2100	2118	2139		2229	2229	2310	2343	0422
	Mâcon Ville .... d.	...	1812	1812	1815		1914		1934		2050	2051			2133	2147		2300	2300		0458
	Mâcon Loché TGV .... d.					1910	1917					2104								
	Villefranche sur Saône ... a.	...		1845		1957			2117		2152c	2155			2322	2322		
	Lyon Part Dieu .... a.	...	1846	1846				2014		2057	2141		2218	2225	2341	2341		0540
	Lyon Perrache .... a.	1859		1913							2227	2236	2351	2351		

		602 TGV	750 TGV				970 TGV	646 TGV	6606 6607				616 TGV		6634 6635		6674 6675		758 TGV	976 TGV
		✕	Ⓐ	Ⓐn	Ⓐ		Ⓐ	Ⓒ	Ⓐn		Ⓐ	Ⓒg		Ⓐ		✕ J	†		Ⓐ	
	Lyon Perrache .... d.		0542				0700	0643	0640	0743	0743		0914		1049			1300		
	Lyon Part Dieu .... d.		0553				0711	0652					0924		1100		1223	1311		
	Villefranche sur Saône ... d.				0640			0715	0804	0804		1030							1340c
	Mâcon Loché TGV .... d.		0619		0720	0734	0737					1110	1125		1302		1345		1431
	Mâcon Ville .... d.			0616			0731	0747	0828	0828	1002		1221	1332	1337			1404
	Chalon sur Saône .... d.	0540		0610	0655		0801	0826	0900	0900	1030		1241		1348			1422
	Chagny 149a .... d.	0549			0750		0837		0911	0928			1256		1400			1441
	Beaune 149a .... d.	0558		0628	0711	0802		0848		0921	0940		1334	1405	1424			1632	1611
	Dijon 149a .... a.	0620		0647	0730	0827		0835	0914	0940	0946	1000	1102					
	Paris Lyon 155 .... a.		0807	0840			0915	0924					1312					

		5052	5510		5090		6638 6639		978 TGV				5008		5012		674 TGV	6688 6689
						Ⓐ	Ⓐ		Ⓐ	Ⓒ	Ⓐ	Ⓐ		Ⓐ	⑦e	⑦e F	N
	Lyon Perrache .... d.				1607		1643	1713		1743	1752	1821		1928		2052	2135	2138	2148
	Lyon Part Dieu .... d.	1403	1456		1617		1654	1740	1745		1802		1844	1937	2025		2103	2145	2150	2200
	Villefranche sur Saône ... d.	1424			1638		1727		1750		1822	1825	1858	1905	2009		2120	2125		2210	2220
	Mâcon Loché TGV .... d.							1830	1845						2200		2211	
	Mâcon Ville .... d.	1448	1533		1701		1749	1825	1822		1847	1848	1920	1930	2032	2102	2146	2232	2243
	Chalon sur Saône .... d.	1521	1603	1614	1736	1815		1906	1851	1900		1928		1959	2007	2132		2301	2315
	Chagny 149a .... d.	1532		1631	1703	1746	1832		1911					2018				2310	2326
	Beaune 149a .... d.	1543		1715	1755	1842		1922					2028				2319	2335
	Dijon 149a .... a.	1602	1636	1739	1817	1907		1924	1947		2031	2052		2204		2350	2354
	Paris Lyon 155 .... a.	1930			2132b				2027							

A – Daily except ⑤ (runs May 26; not May 24).
B – ⑤⑦ (also Feb. 16, 23, Apr. 17, 23, May 1, 8, 24; not Apr. 16, 30, May 7, 25, 26).
E – ①②③④ (also Apr. 16, 30, May 7; not Apr. 17, May 1, 8, 24, 25).
F – Also Apr. 16, 17, 30, May 7, 24, 25.
H – ⑤⑦ (also Apr. 17, May 1, 8, 24, 25; not Apr. 16, 30, May 7).

J – Daily to Apr. 9, May 15 - 24, 26; Ⓒ Apr. 15 - May 14. 12 - 15 minutes later on Apr. 10 - 12.
M – ①②③④⑥ (also Apr. 16, 30, May 7, 25; not May 24).
N – ⑦ (also Apr. 18, May 1, 8; not Apr. 16, 17, 30, May 7, 25).
P – ①②③④ (not Apr. 17, May 1, 8, 25).
R – ⑤⑦ (also Apr. 17, May 1, 8; not Apr. 16, 30, May 7).
TGV – Ⓡ, supplement payable.
b – Ⓐ only.   c – Connection by 🚌

e – Also Apr. 17, May 1, 8; not Apr. 16, 30, May 7, 25.
f – Also May 24; not May 26.
g – Also Apr. 17, May 1, 8, 25.
n – Not Apr. 17, May 1, 8.
q – Also Feb. 16, 23, Apr. 13, May 24; not Feb. 17, 24, Apr. 14.
r – Feb. 1 - 9 depart Paris 1234.
t – Not Apr. 16, 30, May 7.

Table 149a — DIJON - MOULINS and NEVERS

1,2 clas

km			✕		Ⓐ			⑤⑥		✕	Ⓐ	A	Ⓐ		Ⓐ	Ⓐb	Ⓐ		A		🚌
0	Dijon 149 .... d.	0548		0734		0904		1128	1230	1439r		1605		1658	1720			1812		h	2106
37	Beaune 149 .... d.	0614		0759		0926		1153	1256	1503r		1627		1720			1832			2138
	Chalon sur Saône .... d.											1614			1740				2038
52	Chagny 149 .... d.	0633		0809	0845	0945		1211	1315	1521		1636	1643		1756	1809		1745		2027	2102	2155
81	Montchanin ▲ .... d.	0655	0658		0913	1015	1019	1237	1548		1649		1714	1720	1751	1808		1830	1909	1915	2058	2123
96	Montceau les Mines ▲ .. d.		0711			1026						1728		1803			1931	2111	
198	Moulins .... a.												1926			2056		
	Clermont Ferrand 145 .... a.												2046				
89	Le Creusot ▲ .... d.	0703	✕		0920		1029	1241	1344	1556		1659		1729		1816	1825	1838	1917		2233
111	Étang ▲ .... d.	0720	0726			1052	1255		1612	1700	1722		1755		1831		1901	1932		1941	
	Autun ▲ .... d.		0743				1121		1718			1820			1905		1958	2213	
216	Nevers .... d.	0843					1409		1730				1935			2049		

		Ⓐ		Ⓒ	Ⓒ	Ⓒ	Ⓐ		Ⓐb		✕			⑤⑦g	Ⓐ	Ⓐ			⑦e	⑦h
	Nevers .... d.			0554	0645	0700			1108		1209		1459			1836		193?
	Autun ▲ .... d.		0640				0745		0909		1545		1723		1933		
	Étang ▲ .... d.	0606	0658	0705	0749	0810	0809		1227	1303	1417	1603	1616		1741	1753	1950	2000	
	Le Creusot ▲ .... a.	0632	—	0719	0804	0824	0834		1243	1329	1432	1631	1710		1809		2015	205?
	Clermont Ferrand 145 ... d.					0618											
	Moulins .... d.					0733											
	Montceau les Mines ▲ .. d.		0636			0822		1430		1616			1807		2018	
	Montchanin ▲ .... d.	0641	0657	0726	0812	0832	0838	0846	0904	1250	1336	1445	1455	1631	1639	1718		1818	1828	2029	2043	210?
	Chagny 149 .... d.		0729	0750		0854		0920	0928		1515	1532	1703		1852	1911	2056	2107
	Chalon sur Saône .... a.		0742			0937		1020										
	Beaune 149 .... d.		0801	0804		0939		1329		1543		1716		1922	2108	
	Dijon 149 .... d.		0827	0900	0904	1000		1354		1602	1739	1812		1947	2141	2141	215?

A – Daily except ⑤ (also Mar. 3, 10, Apr. 28, May 5, 26; not May 24).
b – By 🚌.   e – Also Apr. 17, May 1, 8; not Apr. 16, 30, May 7, 25.
g – Also May 24; not Apr. 16, 30, May 7.

h – ⑦ (also May 1, 8; not Apr. 16, 30, May 7).   r – ✕ only.
▲ – 🚌 services run between these places and Le Creusot TGV station connecting with TGV trains to and from Paris (Table 150). Rail tickets not valid.

Table 150 — PARIS - LYON

1,2 class

km		601 TGV	641 TGV	681 TGV	643 TGV	605 TGV	645 TGV	607 TGV	905 TGV	609 TGV	611 TGV	613 TGV	685 TGV	819 TGV	615 TGV	907 TGV	617 TGV	657 TGV
		Ⓐk ✕	Ⓐk ✕	✕n	✕	Ⓐk ✕	✕n	☐	☐	☐	✕n ☐	☐	☐	☐	☐	☐	☐	⑤q ☐
0	Paris Lyon .... d.	0615	0645	0700	0735	0800	0815	1000	1005	1100	1200	1300	1300	1320	1400	1436	1500	1525
303	Le Creusot TGV .... a.	0740	...	...	0900	...	...	...	...	1204	...	...	...	1445	...	...	...	...
	Lyon Satolas TGV ✈ .. a.	...	...	...	...	...	...	...	...	...	...	...	...	...	...	1633	...	...
427	Lyon Part-Dieu .... a.	0823	0845	0900	0943	1000	1016	1200	...	1301	1401	1501	1501	...	1601	...	1700	1725
431	Lyon Perrache .... a.	0833	0855	...	...	1010	1026	1210	...	1311	1411	1515	...	...	1611	...	1710	1735

	619 TGV	659 TGV	661 TGV	623 TGV	947 TGV	663 TGV	687 TGV	625 TGV	627 TGV	665 TGV	629 TGV	689 TGV	669 TGV	631 TGV	671 TGV	633 TGV	635 TGV
	Ⓐk ☐	⑤f ☐	☐	N ☐	☐	Ⓐk ☐	Ⓐk ☐	H ☐	G ☐	⑧h ♣ ☐	☐	☐	Ⓐk ☐	☐	⑦e ☐	⑧h ☐	E ☐
Paris Lyon .... d.	1600	1620	1648	1700	1708	1724	1724	1800	1800	1821	1900	1900	1928	2000	2036	2100	2149
Le Creusot TGV .... a.	...	1745	...	...	...	...	...	...	1925	...	...	...	2054	...	...	...	...
Lyon Satolas TGV ✈ .. a.	...	...	...	1906	...	...	...	...	...	...	...	...	...	...	...	...	...
Lyon Part-Dieu .... a.	1801	1828	1849	1901	...	1926	1926	2001	2008	2022	2101	2101	2137	2201	2237	2301	2350
Lyon Perrache .... a.	1811	1838	1859	1911	1936	...	...	2011	2018	2032	2111	...	2147	2211	2247	2311	0000

	640 TGV	602 TGV	642 TGV	604 TGV	920 TGV	644 TGV	691 TGV	646 TGV	648 TGV	610 TGV	693 TGV	612 TGV	614 TGV	616 TGV	904 TGV	618 TGV	658 TGV
	①g ☐	Ⓐk ✕	Ⓐk ✕	♥ ☐	Ⓐk ✕	✕	☐	Ⓒp ☐	H ☐	R ☐	✕ ☐	✕ ☐	☐	☐	♣ ☐	☐	☐
Lyon Perrache .... d.	0517	0542	0621	0646	...	0651	...	0700	0720	0749	...	0845	0949	1049	...	1149	1319
Lyon Part-Dieu .... d.	0528	0553	0632	0657	0705	0707	0707	0711	0730	0800	0900	0900	1000	1100	1200	1330	...
Lyon Satolas TGV ✈ .. d.	...	...	...	...	...	...	...	...	...	...	...	...	1141	...	1200	...	...
Le Creusot TGV .... d.	...	0640	...	...	...	0757	...	0840	...	...	...	1145	...	...	...	...	...
Paris Lyon .... a.	0730	0807	0834	0859	0905	0908	0908	0924	0930	1009	1102	1102	1200	1312	1340	1402	1532

	620 TGV	695 TGV	622 TGV	906 TGV	624 TGV	664 TGV	626 TGV	666 TGV	628 TGV	699 TGV	668 TGV	630 TGV	632 TGV	672 TGV	634 TGV	838 TGV	878 TGV	878 TGV	674 TGV
	☐	☐	☐	⑤f ☐	☐	☐	☐	Ⓐk ⬆ ☐	☐	☐	E ☐	⑧h ☐	☐	⑦e ☐	⑧h ☐	⑧h ☐	Ⓐk ☐	⑦e ☐	⑦e ☐
Lyon Perrache .... d.	1348	...	1449	...	1549	1612	1649	1714	1749	...	1831	...	1949	2013	2049	...	...	...	...
Lyon Part-Dieu .... d.	1400	1400	1500	...	1600	1622	1700	1724	1800	1847	1847	1900	2000	2023	2100	...	...	...	2135
Lyon Satolas TGV ✈ .. d.	...	...	...	1520	...	...	...	...	...	...	...	...	...	...	...	...	...	...	2145
Le Creusot TGV .... d.	...	...	...	...	1702	1740	...	...	...	1926	1926	...	...	...	...	2150	2150	2157	...
Paris Lyon .... a.	1602	1602	1702	1718	1800	1830	1908	1926	2002	2053	2053	2100	2202	2225	2305	2316	2316	2323	2352

E – ⑤⑦ (also Nov. 1,10, Apr. 17, May 1,8,24; not Oct. 30, Nov.11, Apr. 16,30, May 7,26).
G – ⑤⑥⑦ (also Oct. 31, Nov. 1,10,11, Apr. 17, May 1,8,24,25).
H – ①②③④ (not Oct. 31, Nov. 1,10, Apr. 17, May 1,8,24,25).
Q – Ⓐ (not Oct. 31); also ⑦ Dec. 18 - Apr. 2.
R – Daily except Oct. 30, Apr. 16,30, May 7.
TGV –Ⓡ, supplement payable.

e – Also Nov. 1, Apr. 17, May 1,8; not Oct. 30, Apr. 16,30, May 7.
e – Also Nov. 10, May 24; not Nov. 11, May 26.

g – Also Nov. 2, Apr. 18, May 2,9; not Oct. 31, Apr. 17, May 1,8.
h – Not Oct. 30,31, Nov. 11, Apr. 16,30, May 7,25.
k – Not Oct. 31.
n – Also Nov. 1, May 25.
p – Also Oct. 31; not Nov. 12.
q – Also Nov. 10, May 24; not Nov.11.
♣ – 1 class only on ① (also Nov. 2, Apr. 18, May 2,9; not Oct. 31, Apr. 17, May 1,8).
♥ – 1 class only on ②③④⑤ (not Nov. 2, Apr. 18, May 2,9).
♣ – 1 class only on ①②③④ (not Nov. 10, May 24).

Table 150a — LYON - MASSY - TOURS, RENNES and NANTES

For service Lyon - Tours and Nantes via Bourges see Table 128.

1,2 class

	724/5 TGV ①g ☐	728/9 TGV Ⓐ ☐	728/9 TGV Ⓐ ☐	726/7 TGV ⑥t ☐	730/1 TGV N ☐	730/1 TGV N ☐	732/3 TGV J ☐	734/5 TGV K ☐	738/9 TGV ☐	738/9 TGV ☐
Chambéry .... d.							1605			
Grenoble .... d.							1529r			1705r
Lyon Perrache .... d.	0603	0807	0807	0807	0933	0933	1638v			1818
Lyon Part Dieu .... d.	0616	0818	0818	0818	0944	0944	1651	1725	1830	1830
Massy .... a.	0847	1045	1045	1045	1214	1214	1916	1956	2107	2103
St. Pierre des Corps .. a.	0937			1136			2046	2157		
Tours .... a.	0945			1143			2054n	2204		
							2145q			
Le Mans 125 .... a.		1134	1134		1303	1303	2003			2150
Rennes 125 .... a.		1255x			1424		2125			
Angers St Laud 123 .. a.			1216			1345				2230
Nantes 123 .... a.			1252y			1422y				2307y

	702/3 TGV J ☐	700/1 TGV K ☐	706/7 TGV ☐	706/7 TGV E ☐	710/1 TGV E ☐	710/1 TGV ☐	708/9 TGV ⑧h ☐	708/9 TGV ⑧h ☐	714/5 TGV P ☐
Nantes 123 .... d.			0903z		1338z		1529c		
Angers St Laud 123 .. d.			0948		1423		1611		
Rennes 125 .... d.		0909		1348		1539			
Le Mans 125 .... d.		1034	1034	1509	1509	1700	1700		
Poitiers 136 .... d.	0738q								
Tours .... d.	0829n	0829							1941
St. Pierre des Corps .... d.	0836	0836							1949
Massy .... d.	0931	0931	1125	1125	1602	1602	1752	1752	2045
Lyon Part Dieu .... a.	1155	1155	1350	1350	1832	1832	2017	2017	2313
Lyon Perrache .... a.		1206	1401v	1401v	1842	1842	2028	2028	2323
Grenoble .... a.			1512r	1512r					
Chambéry .... a.	1326								

E – ⑥ Dec. 24 - May 6.
J – ⑥ Dec. 24 - Mar. 11.
K – Daily except when train J runs.
N – ⑥ (not Nov. 12); ⑦ Dec. 25 - Apr. 9, Apr. 23; also Nov 11, Apr. 17, May 1, 8.
P – ⑤⑦ (also Nov. 1, 10, Apr. 17, May 1, 8, 24; not Nov. 11, Apr. 30, May 7).
TGV –Ⓡ, supplement payable.

t – Depart 1536 Sept. 25 - Jan. 22.
v – Also Nov. 2, Apr. 18, May 2, 9; not Oct. 31, Apr. 17, May 1,8.

h – Not Oct. 31, Nov. 11, Apr. 16, 30, May 7, 25.
n – ⑥ Jan. 7 - Feb. 18.
q – ⑥ Dec. 24, 31, Feb. 25 - Mar. 11
r – Dec. 24, 31, Feb. 11, 18, 25 only.
t – Also Oct. 31, Nov. 11, May 25.
v – Not Dec. 24, 31, Feb. 11, 18, 25.
x – Arrive 1300 Feb. 13 - Mar. 31.
y – 8 minutes later Jan. 23 - May 27.
z – 8 minutes later Sept. 25 - Jan. 22.

Table 150b — LYON - MASSY - ROUEN

1,2 class

	736/7 TGV
Lyon Perrache .... d.	1741
Lyon Part Dieu .... d.	1753
Massy Palaiseau §.......... d.	2020
Versailles Chantiers §.......... d.	2034
Mantes la Jolie .... d.	2103
Rouen Rive Droite .... a.	2148

	704/5 TGV ✕n ☐	712/3 TGV ⑦p ☐
Rouen Rive Droite .... d.	0751	1431
Mantes la Jolie .... d.	0839	1518
Versailles Chantiers §...... d.	0907	1546
Massy Palaiseau §.......... d.	0922	1604
Lyon Part Dieu .... a.	1151	1832
Lyon Perrache .... a.	1202	1842

TGV –Ⓡ, supplement payable.
§ – Local journeys by these trains not permitted between Massy and Versailles.

n – Also Nov. 11, May 25.
p – Also Nov. 1, Apr. 17, May 1, 8.

Table 151 — (PARIS) - LYON - MARSEILLE

1,2 class except where shown

km		6206 6208 ♦	Ⓐ	✗	G	801 TGV H 🍴	5501 G	5501 H	✗	803 TGV J	803 TGV H	5357	6960 6961	851 TGV 🍴	Ⓐ	807 TGV Ⓒ	807 TGV Ⓐ	5001	809 TGV	5680 5681 ♦
	Paris Gare de Lyon ... d.									0656	0656			0810		0822	0822		1017	
	Lille Europe 160 ... d.																			
	Charles de Gaulle + 160 d.																			
	Metz 170 ... d.																			
	Strasbourg 156 ... d.																	0809		
	Dijon 149 ... d.																			
	Genève 165 ... d.																			0930
	Lyon Perrache ... d.	0349			0558	0558				0701		0756		0834		0920	0923		0956	
0	Lyon Part-Dieu ... d.					0645	0725	0725							0900					
	Lyon Satolas TGV + ... d.																			
32	Vienne ... d.				0623	0623		0731		0823		0857				0951				
105	Valence ... a.	0504			0722	0722	0727	0826	0835	0835	0913	0921	0921	0934	1012	1035	1043	1043	1105	1241 1245
105	Valence ... d.	0507		0610	0652	0735	0735	0729		0838	0838	0923	0923	0937	1018	1037			1109	1308
150	Montélimar ... d.			0633	0721	0801	0833							1033						
202	Orange ... d.			0705	0754	0833														
230	Avignon ... a.	0604		0727	0816	0849	0855	0822	0940	1000	1021	1048	1053	1116		1140	1145	1205	1344	1353
230	Avignon ... d.	0607	0657				0824		0942	1010	1023	1053	1056	1120		1142	1147	1208		1356
	Montpellier 163 ... a.								1047	1113				1226	1230					
	Béziers 163 ... a.								1131	1204				1309						
	Narbonne 163 ... a.								1150	1221				1324						
	Toulouse 139 ... a.								1225	1259				1434						
	Perpignan 163 ... a.													1115						
	Port Bou 163 ... a.																			
265	Arles ... d.	0630	0717					0917						1115						
351	Marseille St. Charles ... a.	0716	0809						1117	1146	1200					1235	1240	1305		1453
	Toulon 164 ... a.	0808									1250					1323	1328	1357		1545
	Nice 164 ... a.	1005									1445						1555			1735

		524/5 TGV 🍴	526/7 TGV 🍴	868/9 TGV	811 TGV	6130 6131 TGV	813 TGV 🍴	5005 ✗	855 TGV 🍴	815 TGV 🍴	6172 6173 5511	534/5 TGV ⑧n 🍴	534/5 TGV ⑥t 🍴	819 TGV Ⓐ	857 TGV Ⓐ	823 TGV	⑥	⑥q	⑥
	Paris Gare de Lyon ... d.				1112		1128		1212	1212r		1217	1217	1320	1334	1427			
	Lille Europe 160 ... d.	0834	0834									1313c	1313c						
	Charles de Gaulle + 160 d.	1005c	1005c			0734													
	Metz 170 ... d.						1053				0800								
	Strasbourg 156 ... d.										1215								
	Dijon 149 ... d.			1044															1621
	Lyon Perrache ... d.					1221		1308			1419						1622	1622	
	Lyon Part-Dieu ... d.	1217	1217	1226		1239	1326	1318		1403	1411	1510	1510				1646	1646	1650
	Lyon Satolas TGV + ... d.				1243		1355				1444						1725	1725	1740
	Vienne ... a.	1258	1258	1309	1333	1340	1353	1423	1449	1504	1510	1537	1543	1543	1559		1730		
	Valence ... a.	1300	1300	1315	1343	1355	1425		1507	1513	1545	1545	1601	1621	1648	1755			
	Valence ... d.				1408				1537		1605			1723	1824				
	Montélimar ... d.				1444				1605										
	Orange ... d.								1529	1529	1616	1621	1639	1639	1644	1739		1839	
	Avignon ... a.	1356	1356	1409	1500	1519	1533	1536	1607	1624	1643	1643	1646	1700		1842			
	Avignon ... d.	1400	1403	1411	1504	1521	1624	1711			1743								
	Montpellier 163 ... a.	1452		1500				1759											
	Béziers 163 ... a.							1815											
	Narbonne 163 ... a.							1854											
	Toulouse 139 ... a.							1955											
	Perpignan 163 ... a.							1645		1720							1902		
	Port Bou 163 ... a.				1524														
	Arles ... d.															1836	1942		
	Marseille St. Charles ... a.	1456	1520	1605	1542	1617	1629	1731	1736	1736	1739	1821		1924					
	Toulon 164 ... a.		1607	1654				1829	1818		2000								
	Nice 164 ... a.			1846				2019											

		5634 5635 ⑥	827 TGV ⑤f ♦	867 TGV b	6174 6175 Ⓐ	6132 6133 🍴	6967 6966 🍴	831 TGV	871 TGV m	5053	6134 6135 ⑤f	6134 6135 5535 ⑤f	542/3 TGV 🍴	544/5 TGV 🍴	835 TGV	873 TGV ⑤
	Paris Gare de Lyon ... d.		1534	1534				1636	1636		1610	1610			1745	1749
	Lille Europe 160 ... d.										1705c	1705c				
	Charles de Gaulle + 160 d.				1223					1345	1345					
	Metz 170 ... d.				1153											
	Strasbourg 156 ... d.					1535			1605	1706	1706					
	Dijon 149 ... d.															192_
	Genève 165 ... d.	1621		1643				1721		1812	1821					195_
	Lyon Perrache ... d.				1653	1713	1717				1851	1851	1917	1917		204_
	Lyon Part-Dieu ... d.	1650		1713				1800	1840	1849					2015	
	Lyon Satolas TGV + ... d.	1740	1759	1759	1807	1815		1854	1901	1901	1917	1940	1949	1949	1957	1957
	Vienne ... a.	1743	1748	1801	1801	1818	1822	1903	1903	1920	1952	1952	1959	1959	2017	2022
	Valence ... a.	1814				1843	1854			1944					2039	2049
	Valence ... d.					1930				2018					2122	
	Montélimar ... d.						1954	1957	1957	2033	2050	2050	2053	2053	2103	2137
	Orange ... d.		1847	1855	1855	1908		2001	2004	2036	2053	2117	2057	2100	2105	2206
	Avignon ... a.	1850	1859	1902		1911		2051		2221		2307	2153			
	Avignon ... d.			1953		2013		2132		2322						
	Montpellier 163 ... a.					2104				0002						
	Béziers 163 ... a.					2218										
	Narbonne 163 ... a.															
	Toulouse 139 ... a.									2056						
	Perpignan 163 ... a.							2054		2144	2150	2153		2158		
	Port Bou 163 ... a.		1946	1952	2009						2251			2247		
	Arles ... d.		2041			2100										
	Marseille St. Charles ... a.		2230			2245					0038					

◆ — **NOTES** (LISTED BY TRAIN NUMBER)

189 – LE PHOCÉEN – ⚟ 1,2 cl., ⚟ 1,2 cl. (T2) and ⚟ 1,2 cl. Paris - Toulon (Paris - Nice on ④⑥, also Oct. 31, Nov. 9, Apr. 16, 30, May 7, 23; not Oct. 29, Nov. 10, Apr. 15, 29, May 6, 25).

377/8 – HISPANIA – ⚟ and ⚟ 1,2 cl. Genève - Port Bou; ⚟ and ⚟ 1,2 cl. Genève - Toulouse - Irún; 🍴 Genève - Valence.

5059 – ⚟ 2 cl., ⚟ and 🍴 Paris - Nice.
5065 – ⚟ 2 cl. and ⚟ Paris - Toulon - Les Arcs.
5521 – ⑤⑥⑦ (daily Dec. 19 - Apr. 2; also Oct. 27, 31, Nov. 1, 10): ⚟ 1,2 cl. (T2) ⚟ 1,2 cl. and ⚟ Paris - Béziers.

NOTES CONTINUED ON NEXT PAGE

Table 151 — (PARIS) - LYON - MARSEILLE

1,2 class except where shown

	837 TGV Ⓐk ⊗	877 TGV Ⓐk ⊗b	Ⓐ	5742 5743 ⑤f	5515	Ⓑ	839 TGV Ⓑh ⊗	5515 5015 ⑦e	E	377 378 ◆	377 378 ◆	E	5065 ⑦e	5059 ◆	5696 5697 ◆	5795 ⑦e	6196 6197 Ⓡ	6196 5521 ◆	5799 5525 D	6136 5137 ◆	5799 5525 B	5521 ◆	189 ◆
Paris Gare de Lyon .... d.	1832	1832	...	...	...	...	1951	...	...	...	...	...	2029	2117	...	2130	...	...	2210	2210	...	2239	2236
Lille Europe 160 .... d.			...	...	...	...	...	...	...	...	...	...	...	...	...	...	...	...	...	...	...		
Charles de Gaulle + 160 .. d.			...	...	...	...	...	...	...	...	...	...	...	...	...	...	...	...	...	...	...		
Metz 170 .... d.			...	...	...	...	...	...	...	...	...	...	...	...	...	...	2024	2024	...	...	...		
Strasbourg 156 .... d.			...	...	...	...	...	...	...	...	...	...	...	...	...	...	2024	2024	...	2048	...		
Dijon 149 .... d.			...	1821	...	1910	...	1910	...	...	...	...	2324	...	2312	...	0030	0047	0047	0113	0113	0050	0138
Genève 165 .... d.			...	...	...	...	...	...	...	2154	2154	...	...	...	...	...	...	...	...	...	...		
Lyon Perrache .... d.				...	...	...	...	...	...	...	...	2352	0109	...	...	...	0218	0245	0245	0307	0307	0250	0322
Lyon Part-Dieu .... d.			...	2018	2038	2101	...	2101	...	2357	2357	0007	...	...	...	...	0218	0245	0245	0307	0307	0250	0322
Lyon Satolas TGV + ... d.			...	...	...	...	...	...	...	...	...	0034	...	...	...	...	...	...	...	...	...		
Vienne .... d.			...	2043	2103	2125	...	2125	...	...	...	...	...	...	...	...	...	...	...	...	...		
Valence .... a.	2057	2057	...	2122	2152	2203	2224	2203	...	0105	0105	0121	0210	...	0258	0331	0351	0351	0409	0409	0359	0425	
Valence .... d.	2059	2059	...	2124	...	2208	2226	2208	...	0108	0108	...	0219	...	0317	...	0357	0357	...	0442	0402	0442	
Montélimar .... d.			...	...	...	2233	2249	2233	...	...	...	...	0246	...	...	...	...	...	...	...	...		
Orange .... d.			...	...	...	2306	...	2306	...	...	...	...	0318	...	...	...	...	...	...	...	...		
Avignon .... a.	2153	2153	...	2228	...	2322	2325	2322	...	0205	0205	...	0333	...	0420	...	0500	0500	...	0546	0504	0546	0551
Avignon .... d.	2157	2200	2207	...	...	2326	...	2326	2342	2342	0207	0207	...	0343	...	0446	...	0512	0551	...	0551	0513	0551	0554
Montpellier 163 .... a.		2251	...	...	...	0025	...	...	...	0304	0304	...	...	...	...	...	...	0700	...	0700	...	0700	
Béziers 163 .... a.			...	...	...	0115	...	...	...	0349	0349	...	...	...	...	...	...	0758	...	0758	...	0758	
Narbonne 163 .... a.			...	...	...	...	...	...	...	0405	0405	...	...	...	...	...	...	...	...	...	...		
Toulouse 139 .... a.			...	...	...	...	...	...	...	...	0549	...	...	...	...	...	...	...	...	...	...		
Perpignan 163 .... a.			...	...	...	...	...	...	...	0447	...	...	...	...	...	...	...	...	...	...	...		
Port Bou 163 .... a.			...	...	...	...	...	...	...	0542	...	...	...	...	...	...	...	...	...	...	...		
Arles .... d.			2227	...	...	...	...	0002	0002	...	...	...	0507	...	...	...	...	...	...	...	...		0619
Marseille St. Charles .... a.	2250		...	...	...	...	...	0049	0049	...	...	...	0453	0510	0557	...	0613	...	...	0616	...		0710
Toulon 164 .... a.			...	...	...	...	...	0155	0155	...	...	...	0553	0615	0702	...	0715	...	...	0719	...		0804
Nice 164 .... a.			...	...	...	...	...	...	...	...	...	...	0818	0911	0916	...	0916	...	...	0920	...		0955

◆ – NOTES (LISTED BY TRAIN NUMBER)

89-5521 – SEE PAGE 130.
634/5 – ⬜ Annecy - Nice.
680/1 – ⬜ Genève - Nice; ⬜ St. Gervais - Nice.
696/7 – ━ 1,2 cl. and ⬜ Genève - Nice (also ⇤ 1,2 cl. (T2) on ①③⑤); ⬜ and ━ 1,2 cl. St. Gervais - Nice.
795 – ⇤ 1,2 cl. (T2), ━ 1,2 cl. and ⬜ Paris - Briançon.
799 – ⇤ 1,2 cl. (T2), ━ 1,2 cl. and ⬜ Paris - Briançon.
136/7 – ━ 1,2 cl. Metz - Nice (also ⇤ 1,2 cl. (T2), replaced by ⬜ when LORAZUR runs, see Table 164); ⬜ and ━ 1,2 cl. Reims - Nice.
196/7 – ━ 1,2 cl. (T2), ━ 1,2 cl. and ⬜ Strasbourg - Nice (- Ventimiglia Sept. 25 - Oct. 30 and Mar. 31 - May 27). Conveys Sept. 25 - Oct. 30 and Mar. 31 - May 27, ⬜ and ━ 2 cl. Frankfurt - Nice - Ventimiglia.
206/8 – FLANDRES RIVIERA – for composition see Table 164.

⬜ – ①②③④ Sept. 25 - Dec. 15 and Apr. 3 - May 23 (not Oct. 27, 31, Nov. 1, 10, Apr. 17, May 1, 8): ━ 1,2 cl. and ⬜ Paris - Béziers.
⬜ – Daily except ⑤: ━ 2 cl. and ⬜ Strasbourg - Béziers.

E – ⑤⑦ (also Nov. 1,10, Apr. 17, May 1,8,24; not Oct. 30, Nov. 11, Apr. 16,30, May 7,26).
G – Daily except dates in note **H**.
H – Ⓐ Feb. 13 - Mar. 3.
J – Ⓐ Sept. 26 - Feb. 10 and Mar. 6 - May 26 (not Oct. 31).
TGV – Ⓡ, supplement payable.

b – Runs 4 minutes later Paris - Avignon on ⑤ (also Nov. 10, May 24; not Nov. 11, May 26).
c – Calls from Nov. 13.
e – Also Nov. 1; not Oct. 30.
f – Also Nov. 10, May 24; not Nov. 11, May 26.
h – Not Oct. 30, 31, Nov. 11, Apr. 16, 30, May 7, 25.
k – Not Oct. 31.
m – Runs 4 minutes later Paris - Avignon on ⑦ (also Nov. 1; not Oct. 30).
n – Also Nov. 12; not Nov. 11.
p – Not Apr. 16, 30, May 7.
q – Not Nov. 11, Apr. 16, 30, May 7.
r – Depart 1216 on ⑤ (also Nov. 10, May 24; not Nov. 11, May 26).
t – Also Nov. 11; not Nov. 12.

Ⓐ – Mondays to Fridays, except holidays   Ⓑ – Daily except Saturdays   Ⓒ – Saturdays, Sundays and holidays

Table 151 — MARSEILLE - LYON - (PARIS)

1,2 class except where shown

Section 1

Station	800 TGV	5920	59202	802 TGV	566/7 TGV	564/5 TGV	59204	804 TGV	852 TGV	854 TGV	812 TGV	6634/6635 K	6634/6635 J
(symbols)	Ⓐ	⑦ Ⓐ	⑥ Ⓐk ⓨ	Ⓐ ⤬	⤬ ①g	Ⓐk	⤬	ⓨ	ⓨ	ⓨ	ⓨ	K	J
Nice 164 .... d.	...	...	...	...	...	...	...	...	...	...	0814	0820	0644
Toulon 164 .... d.	...	...	...	...	...	...	...	...	...	...	0903	0910	0921
Marseille St. Charles .... d.	...	...	0520	0622	...	0635	...	0642	0745	...	...	...	...
Arles .... d.	...	...	0603	...	...	...	...	0734	...	...	...	...	...
Cerbère 163 .... d.	...	...	...	...	...	...	...	...	...	...	...	...	...
Perpignan 163 .... d.	...	...	...	...	...	...	...	...	...	...	...	...	...
Toulouse 139 .... d.	...	...	...	...	...	...	...	...	...	...	...	...	...
Narbonne 163 .... d.	...	...	...	...	...	...	...	...	0653	...	...	...	...
Béziers 163 .... d.	...	...	...	...	...	...	0632	...	0733	0839	...	...	...
Montpellier 163 .... d.	...	...	0620	0715	...	0632	0728	0724	0753	0934	0936	1007	1017
Avignon .... a.	...	0528	0533x	0622	0622	0717	0728	0733	0755	0828	...	1010	1020
Avignon .... d.	...	...	0549x	0637	0637	0717	0733	0733	0811	0828	...	...	...
Orange .... d.	...	...	0604	0622x	0711	0711	...	...	0843	...	1034	...	...
Montélimar .... d.	...	...	0624	0644	0735	0735	0810	0828	0906y	0920	1055	...	...
Valence .... a.	0532	0609	0613	0626	0646	0712	0737	0830	0911y	0923	1057	...	...
Valence .... d.	0630	0700	0708	0708	0736	0737	0812	0815y	0830	...	...	...	...
Vienne .... d.	...	...	0805	...	...	0909	...	...	...	...	...	...	...
Lyon Satolas TGV ✈ .... a.	...	...	...	...	...	...	...	1020	...	...	...	...	...
Lyon Part-Dieu .... a.	...	...	0845	0845	...	0911	0911	...	...	...	...	1215	1230
Lyon Perrache .... a.	0710	0735	0738	0738	0803	0830	0938	...	...	...	...	...	...
Genève 165 .... a.	...	...	...	...	...	...	...	...	...	...	...	1405	1418
Dijon 149 .... a.	...	0934	0946	...	...	...	...	...	...	...	...	...	...
Strasbourg 156 .... a.	...	...	...	...	...	...	...	...	...	...	...	1739	1739
Metz 170 .... a.	...	...	...	...	...	...	...	...	...	...	...	...	...
Charles de Gaulle ✈ 160 .... a.	...	...	...	...	1126c	1126c	...	...	...	...	...	...	...
Lille Europe 160 .... a.	...	...	...	...	1216	1216	...	...	...	...	...	...	...
Paris Gare de Lyon .... a.	...	...	0905	...	...	1039	...	1155	1151	1255	1324	...	...

Section 2

Station	6460/6461 K	6460/6461 J	5052	6676/6677	814 TGV	5510	5682/5683 ♦	5004	818 TGV	856 TGV	576/7 TGV	576/7 TGV	860/1 TGV	822 TGV	862 TGV m	6466/6567
(symbols)	K	J	⤬	⤬	ⓨ	ⓨ	♦	Ⓐ	⤬ ⓨ	⑦e ⓨ	ⓨ	ⓨ	ⓨ	ⓨ	m	
Nice 164 .... d.	...	...	...	0820	...	...	0905	...	...	...	1057	...	...	...	...	...
Toulon 164 .... d.	...	...	...	1008	...	...	1051	...	1154	1243	1236	1324	...	1356	...	...
Marseille St. Charles .... d.	...	...	...	1106	1125	...	1143	1212	1215	1243	1335	1324	1324	...	...	...
Arles .... d.	...	...	...	1154	...	...	...	...	...	...	...	...	...	...	...	...
Cerbère 163 .... d.	...	...	...	...	...	...	0825	...	...	...	...	...	...	...	...	...
Perpignan 163 .... d.	...	...	...	...	...	...	0916	...	...	...	...	...	...	...	...	...
Toulouse 139 .... d.	...	...	...	...	...	...	...	...	...	...	...	...	...	...	...	1200
Narbonne 163 .... d.	0704	0704	...	...	...	...	1003	...	...	...	...	...	...	...	...	1321
Béziers 163 .... d.	0816	0816	...	...	...	...	1019	...	...	...	...	...	...	...	...	1338
Montpellier 163 .... d.	0906	0906	...	...	...	...	1107	...	...	1230	...	...	1330	...	1354	1420
Avignon .... a.	...	...	...	1212	1218	1228	1244	1308	1355	...	1417	1417	1423	1449	1445	1514
Avignon .... d.	...	...	...	1223	1220	1232	1248	1310	...	1422	1422	1426	1454	1454	...	1517
Orange .... d.	...	...	...	1240	...	...	...	1308	...	...	...	...	...	...	...	...
Montélimar .... d.	...	...	...	1308	...	...	...	...	1400	1508	...	...	...	...	...	1619
Valence .... a.	1058	1109	...	1329	...	1332	1348	1408	1421	1540	1517	1517	1520	...	...	1600
Valence .... d.	1101	1112	1122	1211	1247	1303	1332	1335	1402	1411	1423	1519	1519	1523	1600	1622
Vienne .... d.	...	...	1211	1307	1325	1402	...	...	...	...	1553	1553	...	...	1655	...
Lyon Satolas TGV ✈ .... a.	...	...	...	...	...	...	...	...	...	...	...	...	...	...	...	...
Lyon Part-Dieu .... a.	1210	1223	1311	1348	1431	1438	1451	1512	...	...	...	...	1603	1729	...	1735
Lyon Perrache .... a.	...	...	1245	1340	...	1442	...	...	1715	...	...	...	1745	...	...	...
Genève 165 .... a.	...	...	...	...	...	...	...	...	...	...	...	...	...	...	...	...
Dijon 149 .... a.	...	...	...	1602	...	...	1636	...	...	...	...	...	...	...	...	...
Strasbourg 156 .... a.	...	1826	...	2045	...	...	...	...	...	...	...	...	...	...	...	...
Metz 170 .... a.	...	...	...	...	...	...	...	...	...	...	1757c	1757c	...	...	...	...
Charles de Gaulle ✈ 160 .... a.	...	...	...	...	...	...	...	...	...	...	1848	1848	...	...	...	...
Lille Europe 160 .... a.	...	...	...	...	...	1539	...	...	...	1653	...	...	...	1814	1814	...
Paris Gare de Lyon .... a.	...	...	...	...	...	1539	...	...	1649	1653	...	...	...	1814	1814	...

Section 3

Station	6638/6639	824 TGV	826 TGV	866 TGV	584/5 TGV	582/3 TGV	828 TGV	832 TGV	872 TGV	5012	834 TGV	874 TGV	836 TGV	550
(symbols)		ⓨ	Ⓐ ⓨ	⑦ ⓨ	B ⓨ	ⓨ	ⓨ	Ⓓj ⓨ	Ⓓj ⓨ		B ⓨ	Ⓐ ⓨ	ⓨ	⑦
Nice 164 .... d.	1135	1409	...	...	...	...	...	1413n	1615	...	1642	...	1804	...
Toulon 164 .... d.	1330	1409	...	...	...	...	...	1615	1706	...	1731	...	1804	...
Marseille St. Charles .... d.	1419	1458	...	1548	...	1558	...	1658	1749	...	1731	1804	...	...
Arles .... d.	1502	...	...	...	...	...	...	...	...	...	...	...	...	...
Cerbère 163 .... d.	...	...	...	...	...	...	...	...	...	...	...	...	...	164
Perpignan 163 .... d.	...	...	...	...	...	...	...	...	...	...	...	...	...	172
Toulouse 139 .... d.	...	...	...	...	...	...	...	...	...	...	...	...	...	173
Narbonne 163 .... d.	...	...	...	...	...	...	...	...	...	...	...	...	...	182
Béziers 163 .... d.	...	...	...	...	...	...	...	...	1657	...	...	1732	...	182
Montpellier 163 .... d.	...	...	1548	...	...	1556	...	...	1657	...	...	1732	...	193
Avignon .... a.	1520	...	1641	1637	1651	1647	1705	1751	1807	...	1824	1820	1857	1914
Avignon .... d.	1523	1600	1646	1646	1656	1656	1731	1756	1756	1810	1813	1829	1859	1936
Orange .... d.	1540	1617	...	...	...	...	1726	...	1810	...	1848	...	...	2008
Montélimar .... d.	1608	1650	...	...	...	...	1759	1810	1831	...	1922	1922	1953	2031
Valence .... a.	1630	1642	1714	...	1751	1751	1823	...	1907	...	1944	1922	1955	2053
Valence .... d.	1633	1646	1716	1716	1725	1753	1753	1836	1833	1910	1920	1924	1955	2141
Vienne .... d.	...	...	1807	1807	...	...	1924	...	...	2008	...	...	...	...
Lyon Satolas TGV ✈ .... a.	...	...	...	...	1838	1833	1950	...	...	2020	...	2038	...	21..
Lyon Part-Dieu .... a.	1741	...	...	...	1838	1833	1950	...	...	2020	2039	...	...	2205
Lyon Perrache .... a.	...	...	1837	1837	...	...	...	...	...	...	...	...	...	...
Genève 165 .... a.	...	...	...	...	2031	...	...	...	...	...	...	...	...	...
Dijon 149 .... a.	1924	...	...	...	...	...	...	...	...	2008	...	...	...	...
Strasbourg 156 .... a.	2248	...	...	...	...	...	...	...	...	...	...	...	...	...
Metz 170 .... a.	...	...	...	...	...	...	...	...	...	...	...	...	...	...
Charles de Gaulle ✈ 160 .... a.	...	...	...	...	2049c	2049c	...	...	...	...	...	...	...	...
Lille Europe 160 .... a.	...	...	...	...	2212	2212	...	...	...	...	...	...	...	...
Paris Gare de Lyon .... a.	...	1912	2006	2006	...	...	2106	2115	2115	...	2150	2150	...	...

FOR NOTES SEE NEXT PAGE

Table 151

MARSEILLE - LYON - (PARIS)

1,2 class except where shown

	838 TGV ⑨h ♥	878 TGV ⑥k ♥	878 TGV ⑦e ♥	5636 5637 ⑦e	5356 ✕	5356 ⑦e	5504 ⑤f		5016 ⑦e	6706 6708	5064 ⑦e ◆	5058	5792 B	5792 5520 ♥	5520 6694 ✕ D		5520	188	6694 6695 ◆	5698 5699	375 376 ◆	375 376 ◆
Nice 164 .... d.	...	...	...	1610	1600	...	...	...	1731	1834	...	1923	...	...	...		...	...	1942	1946	2045	...
Toulon 164 .... d.	...	...	...	1802	1802	...	...	...	1921	2029	...	2120	...	...	...		...	...	2143	2154	2258	...
Marseille St. Charles .... d.	1852	...	...	1855	1858	1858	...	...	2010	2121	2140	2211	...	...	...		...	...	2236	2256	2349	...
Arles .... d.	...	...	...	...	1946	1946	...	...	2206	2229	...	...	...	...	...		...	2327	...	0035	...	...
Cerbère 163 .... d.	...	...	...	...	...	...	...	...	...	...	...	...	...	...	...		...	...	...	...	...	...
Perpignan 163 .... d.	...	...	...	...	...	...	1727	...	...	...	...	...	...	...	...		...	...	...	...	2305	...
Toulouse 139 .... d.	...	...	...	...	...	...	...	...	...	...	...	...	...	...	...		...	...	...	...	2357	...
Narbonne 163 .... d.	...	...	...	...	...	...	1820	...	...	...	...	...	...	...	...		...	...	...	...	...	2259
Béziers 163 .... d.	...	...	...	...	...	...	1836	...	...	...	...	...	...	...	...		...	...	...	...	0100	0100
Montpellier 163 .... d.	...	1849	1858	...	...	...	1938	...	...	...	...	...	...	2126	2126		...	...	...	...	0117	0117
Avignon .... a.	1945	1945	1950	1954	2003	2003	2041	...	2106	2223	2247	...	...	2217	2217		...	...	...	...	0202	0202
Avignon .... d.	1950	1950	1953	1957	2006	2006	2044	...	2108	2228	2254	...	...	2321	2321		2321	2347	2359	0055	0300	0300
Orange .... d.	...	...	...	2023	2023	...	...	...	...	...	2312	...	...	2324	2324		2324	2358	0004	0131	0305	0305
Montélimar .... d.	...	...	...	2038	2057	2057	2124	...	...	...	2347	...	...	...	...		...	...	...	...	0323	0323
Valence .... a.	2043	2043	2047	2100	2118	2118	2146	...	2205	2324	0009	...	...	0022	...		0022	...	0108	0243	0357	0357
Valence .... d.	2045	2045	2049	...	2121	2121	2150	...	2207	2326	0015	0018	0049	0120	...		0049	...	0120	0316	0426	0426
Vienne .... d.	...	...	...	2157	2157	...	...	...	...	...	0055	...	...	...	...		...	...	...	...	0434	0434
Lyon Satolas TGV ✈ .... a.	...	...	...	...	...	...	...	...	...	...	...	...	...	...	...		...	...	...	...	0537	0537
Lyon Part-Dieu .... a.	...	...	...	...	...	...	...	...	2305	...	...	...	...	...	...		...	...	...	...	0600	0600
Lyon Perrache .... a.	...	...	...	2225	2225	2250	...	...	...	0026	0119	...	0132	0204	0230		0204	...	0230	...	...	...
Genève 165 .... a.	...	...	...	...	...	...	...	...	...	...	...	...	...	...	...		...	0743	...	0820	0820	...
Dijon 149 .... a.	...	...	...	...	...	...	...	...	...	0318	...	0326	0400	0416	...		0400	...	0416	...	...	...
Strasbourg 156 .... a.	...	...	...	...	...	...	...	...	...	...	...	...	...	0846	...		...	...	0846	...	...	...
Metz 170 .... a.	...	...	...	...	...	...	...	...	...	...	...	...	...	...	...		...	...	...	...	...	...
Charles de Gaulle ✈ 160 .... a.	...	...	...	...	...	...	...	...	...	...	...	...	...	...	...		...	...	...	...	...	...
Lille Europe 160 .... a.	...	...	...	...	...	...	...	...	...	...	...	...	...	...	...		...	...	...	...	...	...
Paris Gare de Lyon .... a.	2316	2316	2323	...	...	...	...	...	0624	0620	0629	0658	...	...	...		0658	0715	...	...	...	...

◆ – NOTES (LISTED BY TRAIN NUMBER)

88 – LE PHOCÉEN – 1,2 cl., 1,2 cl. (T2) and 1,2 cl. Toulon - Paris (Nice - Paris on ⑤⑦); also Nov.1,10, Apr. 17, May 1,8,24; not Oct. 30, Nov.11, Apr. 16,30, May 7,26).

75/6 – HISPANIA – and 1,2 cl. Cerbère - Genève; and 1,2 cl. Hendaye - Toulouse - Genève.

058 – 2 cl., and ♀ Nice - Paris.
064 – 2 cl. and Marseille - Paris.
520 – 1,2 cl. and Béziers - Paris (also 1,2 cl. (T2) on ⑤⑦ and daily Dec. 19 - Apr. 2).

636/7 – Nice - Annecy.
682/3 – Nice - Genève; Nice - St. Gervais.
698/9 – and 1,2 cl. Nice - Genève (also 1,2 cl. (T2) on ②④⑦); and 1,2 cl. Nice - St. Gervais.

694/5 – 1,2 cl. (T2), 1,2 cl. and Nice - Strasbourg (Ventimiglia - Nice - Strasbourg Sept. 25 -Oct. 29 and Mar. 30 - May 27). Conveys Sept. 25 - Oct. 29 and Mar. 30 - May 27, and 2 cl. Ventimiglia - Nice - Strasbourg - Frankfurt.

706/8 – RIVIERA FLANDRES – for composition see Table **164**.

B – ⑤⑥⑦ (daily Dec. 19 - Apr. 2; also Oct. 27,31, Nov. 1,10): 1,2 cl. (T2), 1,2 cl. and Briançon - Paris.
C – Daily except when train B runs: 1,2 cl. (T2), 1,2 cl. and Briançon - Paris.
D – 2 cl. and Béziers - Strasbourg.
J – Ⓐ Apr. 10 - May 12.
K – Daily (except Ⓐ Oct. 10 - 21).

TGV – Ⓡ, supplement payable.

c – Calls from Nov. 13.
e – Also Nov. 17, May 1,8; not Oct. 30, Apr. 16,30, May 7.
f – Also Nov. 10, May 24; not Nov. 11, May 26.
g – Also Nov. 2, Apr. 18, May 2,9,26; not Apr. 17, May 1,8.
h – Not Oct. 30,31, Nov. 11, Apr. 16,30, May 7,25.

j – Not Oct. 31, Nov. 11, May 25.
k – Not Oct. 31.
m – On ①⑤⑥⑦ (also Nov. 1,2,10; not Oct. 30) departs Montpellier 1404 and runs 4 minutes later Avignon - Paris.

n – Depart 1429 on Ⓒ (not Dec. 3,17, Jan. 28) and daily Mar. 6 - May 27.
x – 8 minutes earlier from Avignon Oct 10 - 21 (not calling at Orange or Montpellier).
y – On Ⓐ Jan. 30 - Feb. 10, calls at St. Peray with ➡ connection for Valence, arrive 0930.

Table 151b LA MURE

2 class

Scenic electric railway. 1994 service

Days of running: ⑥⑦ Apr. 16 - Oct. 9 (daily May 12 - Sept. 18), also Sept. 21,28.

km			B		C		D
0	St. Georges de Commiers... d.	0945	...	1200	...	1430	...	1700
30	La Mure Gare.......... a.	1130	...	1330	...	1615	...	1830

		D		F		E		C	
La Mure Gare.......... d.	0945	...	1200	...	1430	...	1700	
St. Georges de Commiers.. a.	1115	...	1330	...	1600	...	1830	

Operated by Chemin de fer de la Mure, 38450 St. Georges de Commiers, ☎ 76.72.57.11. Fax 76.72.47.43.

– Daily Aug. 2 - 18.
– ⑥⑦ Apr. 16 - Oct. 9 (daily June 4 - Sept. 4), also May 12,13,23.
– Daily June 4 - Sept. 4.
– Daily May 30 - Sept. 9 (also May 16-20, 24-27, Sept. 12-16,21,28).
– ⑥⑦ Apr. 16 - May 29 (also May 12,13,23); daily Aug. 2-18; ⑥⑦ Sept. 10 - Oct. 9.

Table 151c VIVARAIS RAILWAY

2 class

Scenic steam and diesel railway. 1994 Service

Days of running: ⑥⑦ Mar. 27 - May 1; daily except ①, May 7 - June 30; daily July 1 - Aug. 31; daily except ①, Sept. 1 - 18; also Sept. 21, 24, 25, Oct. 2, 9, 16, 23, 30, Nov. 11.

km			🚂			
			Ⓒ	ⒸD	Ⓐ	Ⓒ
0	Tournon.......... d.	...	1000	1045	1430	1800	1810	...
33	Lamastre.......... a.	...	1200	1200	1530	1905	1915	...

			🚂	🚂		
			ⒸD	Ⓐ	Ⓒ	Ⓒ
Lamastre.......... d.	...	0800	1210	1530	1600	...	1700	...
Tournon.......... a.	...	0900	1410	1730	1755	...	1800	...

Operated by CFTM, 2 Quai Jean Moulin, 69001 LYON. ☎ 78.28.83.34. Fax 72.00.97.67.

D – Does not run in Mar., Apr, Oct.

🚂 – Steam train.

Nearest rail station to Tournon is Tain-Hermitage-Tournon between Valence and Vienne, served by most local Valence - Lyon trains.

Table 151d NICE - ANNOT - DIGNE

2 class only

Through service suspended due to storm damage

An appeal to assist in reconstruction has been launched by the Newspaper *Nice Matin*, 214 Route de Grenoble, 06290 Nice.

km											
0	Nice (CFP, Gare du Sud) ... d.	...	...	...	...	...	Digne 166.......... d.	...	...	...	...	...
58	Puget Théniers.......... d.	...	...	...	...	...	St. André les Alpes .... d.	...	...	...	...	...
78	Annot.......... d.	...	...	...	...	...	Thoramé Haute .... d.	...	...	...	...	...
95	Thoramé Haute .... d.	...	...	...	...	...	Annot.......... d.	...	...	...	...	...
106	St. André les Alpes .... d.	...	...	...	...	...	Puget Théniers.......... d.	...	...	...	...	...
150	Digne 166.......... a.	...	...	...	...	...	Nice (CFP, Gare du Sud) . a.	...	...	...	...	...

Narrow gauge railway, operated by Chemins de Fer de la Provence (CFP). Only CFP tickets are valid.

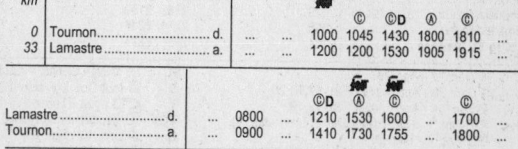

Table 152 — PARIS and LYON - CHAMBÉRY - BOURG ST. MAURICE

1,2 class

km				412 413 T	5430 5431 A	5406	951 B	931 TGV	953 TGV C	5432 5433 E	5432 5433 G	556/7 TGV F	991 TGV D ♣	955 TGV	957 TGV H	993 TGV J	925/4 TGV K
	⑦	✕	⑦	✕/🍴2	✕		Ⓐ							✕			✕
0	Paris Lyon d.						0655	0709	0719				0834	0845	0937	0941	1024
315	Dijon 155 d.																1135v
440	Mâcon Loché TGV d.			0651v	0753v			0850									1159
477	Bourg-en-Bresse d.			0728	0825			0910							1137		
	Lyon Perrache d.	0550	0640	0704			0803	0857						0930			
	Lyon Part Dieu d.	0600	0650	0715		0819								0941			
	Lyon Satolas + d.																1224
508	Ambérieu d.	0631	0723	0740	0751												1259
560	Culoz d.	0710	0803														1314
582	Aix-les-Bains 167 d.	0730	0823	0830			0928	1012			1019		1052	1215	1255	1313	1318
596	Chambéry 167 a.	0742	0834	0840			0940	1024			1031	1104	1106 1106 1154	1218	1219	1300	1325
596	Chambéry d.	0717		0844			0945				1033	1106	1106 1154	1218	1230	1344	
667	St. Jean-de-Maurienne a.										1204	1204	1230			1410	
695	Modane a.			0952							1230	1230	1257				
646	Albertville a.	0759					1017	1024			1049	1111		1242	1219	1258	1324
646	Albertville d.	0812					1026	1033			1057	1124		1252	1228		1332
674	Moutiers-Salins a.	0845					1046	1053			1118	1147		1320	1250		1355
689	Aime-la-Plagne a.	0905					1104				1140	1204		1343	1310		1423
702	Bourg St. Maurice a.	0922					1121				1158	1221		1359	1323		1436

km		959 TGV L	416 417 M	552/3 TGV T	5434 5435	5408 5409 O	933 TGV	5436 5437	5436 5437 O	943 TGV P	961 TGV	218 219 R
			✕		⑥n				✕ Ⓐ		C	Ⓐ 2
	Paris Lyon d.		1117				1244			1432	1515	1716v
	Dijon 155 d.											
	Mâcon Loché TGV d.			1135v	1259v	1159 1332	1441					1750
	Bourg-en-Bresse d.					1232	1252		1424		1703	1717 1800
	Lyon Perrache d.					1243	1311 1417		1435		1714	1728
	Lyon Part Dieu d.	1214								1600r		
	Lyon Satolas + d.											1800
	Ambérieu d.		1236								1731	1843
	Culoz d.		1318							1751	1826 1831a	1903
	Aix-les-Bains 167 d.	1323	1339 1343			1352	1428 1534	1543 1550 1550	1726 1728r	1802	1835 1843a	1914 1937
	Chambéry 167 a.	1352 1355				1403	1428 1534	1602 1602	1655 1704	1743	1930 1930	1838 1848
	Chambéry d.	1355				1408 1411 1430		1605 1605	1753		1924	
	St. Jean-de-Maurienne a.					1453 1502		1753			1958 1958	
	Modane a.					1523 1530		1817			1949	
	Albertville a.	1439	1454			1510	1637 1637	1746	1826 1908		1926	
	Albertville d.	1452	1509			1524	1650 1650	1752	1841 1916		1933	
	Moutiers-Salins a.	1520	1538			1551	1713 1713	1821	1918 1938		1954	
	Aime-la-Plagne a.	1539	1600			1621	1736 1736		1940 2002		2012	
	Bourg St. Maurice a.	1557	1617			1637	1754 1754		1956 2020		2028	

km		963 TGV Q	947 TGV S	5412 5413	58793 56456	935 TGV U	⑥h	⑦	965 TGV V	979 TGV	929 TGV	⑤⑦ b	⑤	211 W	1211 W	5117 Y	5109 Z	5107 X	5111 AA	5119 CC	5119 BB	323 TGV N
	Paris Lyon d.	1612	1708			1716			1842	1910	1914			2056 2348	2213 0102	2256	2230	2300	0221	2305	0255	2324
	Dijon 155 d.																					
	Mâcon Loché TGV d.					1916	2005	2108									0403		0417			
	Bourg-en-Bresse d.		1905			1902					2120											
	Lyon Perrache d.																					
	Lyon Part Dieu d.	1909																				
	Lyon Satolas + d.							2031										0526		0530		
	Ambérieu d.							2109	2153													1843
	Culoz d.			2013 2017	2026 2124					2228c							0526		0530			
	Aix-les-Bains 167 d.	2011 2031		2025	2038 2135	2140		2209 2229		0228 0338 0458 0505			0537 0537 0537									
	Chambéry 167 a.			2037 2040 2040		2142			2235	0248 0350 0510 0517			0612 0622 0622 0623									
	Chambéry d.			2129						0345 0442 0613			0722 0722 0722									
	St. Jean-de-Maurienne a.			2152						0412 0507 0645			0751 0751 0751									
	Modane a.					2118 2118			2213	2345			0552 0513 0649							0356		
	Albertville a.	1952				2131 2131			2224	2345			0605 0526 0702							0408		
	Albertville d.	2002				2152 2152			2244	0010			0631 0548 0729							0432		
	Moutiers-Salins a.	2023				2211 2211			2304				0625 0759							0457		
	Aime-la-Plagne a.	2048				2227 2227			2317				0645 0818							0517		
	Bourg St. Maurice a.	2104																				

A – ⑥ Dec. 17 - Apr. 29.
B – ⑥ Jan. 8 - Apr. 1, also Feb. 12,19,26.
C – ⑥ Jan. 14 - Apr. 1, also Feb. 12,19.
D – ⑥⑦ Jan. 1 - Apr. 2 (also Dec. 17; not Jan. 1).
E – ⑥⑦ Feb. 4 - Mar. 26.
F – ⑥⑦ Dec. 24 - Apr. 2.
G – ⑥ Dec. 24 - Mar. 25; 🚗 Lille Flandres (depart 0649) - Bourg St. Maurice.
H – ⑥⑦ Jan. 4 - Apr. 30 (also Dec. 17).
J – ⑥⑦ Dec. 17 - Apr. 2.
K – Daily except dates in note L.
L – Ⓐ Mar. 27 - Apr. 21.
M – ⑥⑦ Jan. 14 - Apr. 16 (also Dec. 17,18).
N – Feb. 17,18,24,25 only.
O – Dec. 21,23,24, Feb. 11,18,25, Mar. 4 only.
P – Ⓐ Jan. 28 - Apr. 1.
Q – ⑤ Dec. 16 - Apr. 21, also ⑥ Feb. 18 - Mar. 11.

R – LE MONT CENIS – 🍴 and 💺 Lyon - Milano.
S – Ⓐ (not Oct. 31); also ⑦ Dec. 18 - Apr. 2.
T – 🚗 Lyon - Torino.
TGV – Ⓡ supplement payable.
U – ⑤ Dec. 16 - Apr. 28.
V – ⑤ Feb. 4 - Apr. 26.
W – For days of running and composition see Table 44.
X – ⑤⑥ Jan. 27 - Apr. 21 (also Dec. 16,21,23; not Apr. 1,8).
Y – ⑤⑥ Jan. 20 - Mar. 25 (also Dec. 23): 🚻 2 cl. Paris - Modane.
Z – ⑤⑥ Dec. 16 - Apr. 22 (also Dec. 21; not Dec. 24,31): 🚻 1,2 cl. Paris - Moutiers.
AA – 🚻 1,2 cl. and 🚗 Paris - Bourg St. Maurice.
BB – ⑤⑥⑦ Dec. 16 - Apr. 30 (also Dec. 21, Apr. 17, May 1; not Dec. 24,31): 🚻 1,2 cl. and 🚗 Paris - Modane.
CC – ⑤⑦ Sept. 25 - Dec. 11 and Apr. 5 - 21 (also Nov. 30, Nov. 1, May 7; not Oct. 30, Nov. 1, May 7): ①②③④ Dec. 19 - Apr. 27 (also Dec. 24,31; not Dec. 21, Apr. 17): 🚻 1,2 cl. and 🚗 Paris - Modane.

a – Ⓐ only.
b – Also Nov. 1,10, Apr. 17, May 1,8,24; not Apr. 16,30, May 7.
c – Via Chambéry.
h – Not Oct. 31, Nov. 11, May 25.
n – From Lille Europe (depart 0911).
r – ⑤ (also Nov. 10, May 24; not Nov. 11, May 26).
v – Mâcon Ville.
♣ – First class only.

Table 153 — LAROCHE MIGENNES - AUXERRE - AUTUN

1,2 class

km		©	⑦	✕	✕	⑦		6t		✕	Ⓐ	Ⓑ	✕	6t	Ⓐ	Ⓐ	✕	⑦
	Paris Lyon 155 d.					0705		0912					1644		1733			
0	Laroche Migennes d.	0615	0615	0642	0742	0818	0838		0920 1043 1150	1407 1407	1558	1723		1810 1819	1906	2022 2209 230		
19	Auxerre d.	0633	0634	0704	0704	0803	0837 0855	0900	0939 1100 1209	1426 1427	1619	1738		1829 1836 1840	1922 1927	2040 2228 232		
36	Cravant Bazarnes d.		0655					0918		1448	✕	1751 1753			1903	1946			
60	Sermizelles-Vézelay a.		0723					0950		1514	✕	1819			1933	2012			
74	Avallon a.		0737					1003		1527	1724	1833			1947	2034			
161	Autun a.										1909	2026v							

t – Also Nov. 11, May 25; not Nov. 12, May 27.
v – ⑦ only.

Table 152 — BOURG ST. MAURICE - CHAMBÉRY - LYON and PARIS

1,2 class

	210 W	(A)	920/1 TGV 2	970 TGV (A)k	✗	✗	5414 5415	✗	930 TGV (A)		⚲		5416 TGV A	950 TGV A	214 R
Bourg St. Maurice ... d.							0529			0607		0826			0925	
Aime-la-Plagne ... d.							0545			0624		0844			0946	
Moutiers-Salins ... d.							0600			0639	0711	0905			1005	
Albertville ... a.							0628			0702	0738	0929			1025	
Albertville ... d.							0634			0715	0744	0942			1034	
Modane ... d.	0205			0540		0620							0859			1040
St. Jean-de-Maurienne ... d.	0233			0605		0647						0927			1106
Chambéry ... a.	0312				0712	0715	0746			0756		0826	1015	1023	1147
Chambéry 167 ... d.	0325	0537	0558		0631	0723	0720 0751	0803		0812					
Aix-les-Bains 167 ... d.		0550	0542c			0735	0804		0824	0838			1032	1050	1150 1217
Culoz ... d.		0607					0819		0854						1203r
Ambérieu ... d.		0654			0707		0904	0907							
Lyon Satolas + ... a.			0700												
Lyon Part Dieu ... a.		0732					0920	0940				1142			1316r
Lyon Perrache ... a.		0741			0812		0844	0949							1326r 1408
Bourg-en-Bresse ... d.		0644		0714	0737		0927		0944			1217			
Mâcon Loché TGV ... d.		0720v		0734			0947v					1251v			
Dijon 155 ... d.	0601				0934										
Paris Lyon ... a.	0855		0905	0915					1140				1349	1420	

	932 TGV	952 🚌	952 TGV B	10414 10415	414 415 C	954 TGV D	992 TGV E	922/3 TGV F	5438 5439 G♣	956 TGV (A)	2	5420 5421 Hn	592/3 TGV	978 TGV	(A)	(C)	994 TGV J	958 TGV K	(A)
Bourg St. Maurice ... d.	1048					1308	1342		1402	1445		1500					1538		
Aime-la-Plagne ... d.	1105					1329	1400		1422	1501		1521					1559		
Moutiers-Salins ... d.	1122		1152			1347	1419		1441	1521		1552					1622		
Albertville ... a.	1153		1212			1407	1442		1508	1542		1614					1645		
Albertville ... d.	1206		1220	1309		1415	1455		1521	1550		1622					1654		
Modane ... d.		1133			1340	1403		1420					1553	1600					
St. Jean-de-Maurienne ... d.		1208			1409	1431		1449					1618	1629					
Chambéry ... a.	1247	1345		1353	1448	1511		1531	1554			1702	1711	1708					
Chambéry 167 ... d.	1222 1249			1458	1514		1542	1604		1646	1651		1716	1716	1713				
Aix-les-Bains 167 ... d.	1238 1259	1315		1511	1526		1524c	1618		1659			1732	1732					
Culoz ... d.	1256								1714				1754	1754					
Ambérieu ... d.													1837	1837					1857
Lyon Satolas + ... a.																			
Lyon Part Dieu ... a.				1619	1638			1732			1812		1912	1912					
Lyon Perrache ... a.				1631	1648			1741					1921	1921					
Bourg-en-Bresse ... d.	1420							1621					1824						1926
Mâcon Loché TGV ... d.								1652v					1845						1958v
Dijon 155 ... d.																			
Paris Lyon ... a.	1616	1557			1804	1847		1839	1936				2027	2031	2053				

	5422 5423	944 TGV	326 TGV CC		L	M	N		418 419 T	960 TGV O	936 TGV P	10948 Q	5426 5427 S	948 TGV Q	5118 U	5118 V		5110 X	5106 Y	5108 Z		5116 AA	5104 BB
Bourg St. Maurice ... d.	1600		1619		1715	1715	1721		1739		1830							2108	2127				2245
Aime-la-Plagne ... d.	1619		1639		1734	1734	1738		1755		1851							2132	2148				2306
Moutiers-Salins ... d.	1635		1704		1751	1751	1758		1815		1910							2157	2226	2246			2326
Albertville ... a.	1705		1730		1814	1814	1830		1836		1947							2223	2248	2308			2350
Albertville ... d.	1718		1744		1827	1827	1843		1845		2005							2240	2301	2322			0006
Modane ... d.				1725					1822						2140	2140						2305	
St. Jean-de-Maurienne ... d.				1756					1846						2214	2214						2347	
Chambéry ... a.	1800		1857	1907	1907	1922	1925			2043			2307	2307	2320	2335	0001			0035		
Chambéry 167 ... d.		1805	1814		1912	1912	1925	1928		2049	2055	2330	2337	2337	2346	0010			0040		
Aix-les-Bains 167 ... d.					1923	1927	1936	1953	1957			0022	2351	2351							
Culoz ... d.															0051						
Ambérieu ... d.																					
Lyon Satolas + ... a.																					
Lyon Part Dieu ... a.	1922				2038		2104														
Lyon Perrache ... a.					2049		2115														
Bourg-en-Bresse ... d.												2200									
Mâcon Loché TGV ... d.													0131	0205			0205				
Dijon 155 ... d.													0250	0340			0340	0231		0403	
Paris Lyon ... a.		2111	2130							2230	2254	2359	0600	0652	0709			0732		0804	

– ⑥ Dec. 17 - Apr. 22, also Apr. 17 and ⑦ Jan. 29 - Mar. 26.
– ⑥ Jan. 28 - Apr. 1; also ⑦ Feb. 12 - 26.
– ⑥⑦ Feb. 4 - Mar. 26.
– ⑥ Jan. 14 - Apr. 1, also Feb. 19,26.
– ⑥⑦ Dec. 24 - Apr. 2.
– ⑥⑦ Dec. 17 - Apr. 30.
– ⑥⑦ Jan. 1 - Apr. 2; not Jan. 7.
– ⑥ Dec. 24 - Mar. 25.
– ⑥⑦ Dec. 17 - Apr. 2.
– ⑥⑦ Jan. 7 - Apr. 30 (also Dec. 17).
– ⑥ Dec. 17 - Apr. 29.
– ⑦ Dec. 18 - Apr. 23 (also Apr. 17, May 1; not Apr. 16).
– Daily except when trains L and M run.
– ⑥⑦ Jan. 14 - Apr. 30.
– ⑧ (daily Dec. 17 - Apr. 7); not Oct. 31, Nov. 11, Apr. 30, May 7,25.

Q – ⑦ Dec. 18 - Apr. 2, also ⑥ Feb. 11 - Apr. 1.
R – LE MONT CENIS – 🚗 and ⚲ Milano - Lyon.
S – ⑦ Dec. 18 - Apr. 2.
T – 🚗 Torino - Lyon.
TGV – Ⓡ, supplement payable.
U – ⑤⑥⑦ Dec. 16 - Apr. 30 (also Dec. 21, Apr. 17, May 1; not Dec. 24,31): ⊷ 1,2 cl. and 🚗 Modane - Paris.
V – ⑤⑥⑦ Sept. 25 - Dec. 11 and Apr. 5 - 21 (also Nov. 1,10, May 8,24; not Oct. 30, Nov. 11, May 7), also ①②③④ Dec. 19 - Apr. 27 (also Dec. 24,31; not Dec. 21, Apr. 17): ⊷ 1,2 cl. and 🚗 Modane. - Paris.
W – For days of running and composition see Table 44.
X – ⊷ 1,2 cl. and 🚗 Bourg St. Maurice - Paris.
Y – ⑦ Jan. 29 - Mar. 26 (also Jan. 1,4): ⊷ 1,2 cl., ⊷ 1,2 cl. (T2) and ⊷ 2 cl. Bourg St. Maurice - Paris.
Z – ⑥⑦ Dec. 25 - Apr. 30 (also Jan. 4, Feb. 24, Mar. 3; not Apr. 9,16): ⊷ 1,2 cl. Moutiers - Paris.

AA – ⑥ Feb. 4 - Mar. 25 (also Jan. 1,4, Feb. 24, Apr. 3): ⊷ 2 cl. Modane - Paris.
BB – ⑥ Jan. 28 - Apr. 29 (also Dec. 31): ⊷ 1,2 cl., ⊷ 1,2 cl. (T2) and ⊷ 1,2 cl. Bourg St Maurice - Paris.
CC – Feb. 18,25, Mar. 4 only.
c – Via Chambéry.
k – Not Oct. 31.
n – To Lille Europe (arrive 2150).
r – On ⑥ Apr. 24 - May 12, arrive Lyon Perrache 1259, not calling at Aix les Bains or Lyon Part Dieu.
v – Mâcon Ville.
♣ – First class only.

Table 153 — AUTUN - AUXERRE - LAROCHE MIGENNES

1,2 class

	✗	(A)	✗	⑦	(A)	(A)	(C)	✗		✗				✗	⑦e	✗	✗	⑦	⑦e	⑥	(A)	⑥	⑤⑥
Autun ... d.																							
Avallon ... d.		0609		0706		1016				1636				1658		1724	1724						
Sermizelles-Vézelay ... d.		0623		0720		1030				1650				1839	1847	1906	1907	1916					
Avant Bazarnes ... d.		0655		0752		1055	1102			1719	1719	1803			1901		1921	1930					
Auxerre ... d.	0428	0605	0714	0714	0806	0838	0846		1120	1323	1533	1653	1737	1738	1817	1846	1929	1928	1943	1947	1956		
Laroche Migennes ... a.	0447	0624	0733	0733	0820	0906	0906		1341	1554	1713	1757	1833	1908	1947	1958	2000	2009	2041	2134			
Paris Lyon 155 ... a.													2018		2135	1958				2059	2152		

– Also Nov. 1, Apr. 17, May 1,8; not Oct. 30, Apr. 16,30, May 7.

Table 154

PARIS and LYON – GRENOBLE

1,2 class

km			6348 6349	5455	901 TGV	903 TGV	5456		915 TGV	905 TGV	5459	5461	5463		907 TGV	5465	6304 6305		5469	909 TGV
			⚒	Ⓐ G	Ⓐk ⚒	Ⓒn ⚒	⚒		H	Ⓐ	🍷				🍷		C	Ⓑ		Ⓐk 🍷
0	Paris Lyon 150 .... d.		...	...	0650	0800	...		0925	1005	...	...	...		1436	...	...	...	...	1704
439	Lyon Satolas TGV ✈ ... d.		...	...	...	...	...			1207	...	...	...		1636	...	...	...	...		
	Lyon Perrache .... d.	0518	0620	...	0712	...	1027			...	...	...	...		...	1630	1720	1723	1818	
	Lyon Part-Dieu .... d.		0710	0818	0922	1040			1222	1315	1414		1743	...	1847	1926				
528	Voiron .... d.	0701	0758	0922	1035				1327		1513		...	...	...				
553	Grenoble .... a.	0725	0820	0828	0831	0938	0946	1053	1059	1154	1223	1311	1343	1425	1529	1741	1759	1837	1910	1943	2003

		5471	911 TGV	5473		913 TGV				km				900 TGV	5450	902 TGV	6804 6805
			Ⓐk ⚒	Ⓑ		🍷		⑤⑦ z						Ⓐ	Ⓒ	Ⓐk 🍷	Ⓐ	⚒h	B
	Paris Lyon 150 .... d.	...	1828	...	1924	...	...		0	Grenoble .... d.	0505	0529	0546	0615	0701	0712	0721
	Lyon Satolas TGV ✈ ... d.	...							25	Voiron .... d.	0524	0551		0630			0739
	Lyon Perrache .... d.				2112				129	Lyon Part-Dieu .... a.			0745	0815			0850
	Lyon Part-Dieu .... d.	1926		2052	2124	2250				Lyon Perrache .... a.	0700	0732					
	Voiron .... d.	2033		2156	2250	2353				Lyon Satolas TGV ✈ ... a.							
	Grenoble .... a.	2049	2127	2212	2230	2306	0009			Paris Lyon 150 .... a.			0845			1015	

		5454	5458	904 TGV	914 TGV	5460	5462	906 TGV	5464	5466	908 TGV	5468	5470	596/7 TGV	910 TGV	5472	5474	912 TGV		6848 6849
		⚒			H								Ⓑ	L			⑤⑦	⑦q z		F
	Grenoble .... d.	0819	1015	1030	1042	1212	1224	1305	1409	1428	1600	1617	1700	1723	1818	1818	1822	1916	2012	2024	2038	2106
	Voiron .... d.		1030	1059		1321		1616			1743	1833		1931		2130					
	Lyon Part-Dieu .... a.	0933	1135	1226	1338	1428	1542	1724	1817	1934	1939		2044	2128	2155	2259				
	Lyon Perrache .... a.		1237		1517				1906									
	Lyon Satolas TGV ✈ ... a.	1138			1920				2127		2327							
	Paris Lyon 150 .... a.	1340	1516	1718														

B – 🚃 and 🍷 Grenoble - Nantes.
C – 🚃 Tours - Grenoble (Nantes - Grenoble on ⑥⑦).
F – ⑥ Dec. 17 - Mar. 25: 🛏 1,2 cl. and 🚃 Grenoble - Nantes - Quimper.
G – ⑤ Dec. 16 - Mar. 24 (from Quimper): 🛏 1,2 cl., 🚃 and 🍷 Quimper - Nantes - Grenoble.
H – ⑥ Dec. 17 - Apr. 1.
L – ⑥ Dec. 24 - Mar. 25: 🚃 Lille Europe - Grenoble.

TGV – Ⓡ, supplement payable.

h – Also Nov. 11, May 25.
k – Not Oct. 31.
n – Also Oct. 31.
q – Also Nov. 1, Apr. 17, May 1,8.
z – Also Nov. 1,10,11, Apr. 17, May 1,8,24,25; not Apr. 16,30, May 7,26.

Table 155

PARIS – DIJON

1,2 class

km		⑥	Ⓐ	⚒	⑦	5881	EC21 TGV	751 TGV	5041		753 TGV		5053		EC23 TGV	773 TGV	5097	755 TGV		EC29 TGV	5073		5043
							🍷	🍷		⚒	🍷				⚒	Ⓐh		🍷		Ⓑb	Ⓐ		⑤f
0	Paris Lyon .... d.	...	0602	0620	0705	0714	0804	0756	0829	1032	1043	1134	1225	1228	1240x	1248	1347	1419	1450	1553	1556	1614	1644
45	Melun § .... d.	...	0635	0647	0730		0854				1111	1200				1315	1411		1516		1646		
60	Fontainebleau-Avon § .. d.	...	0648	0700			0907				1128	1212				1329	1425		1528		1658		
79	Montereau § .... d.	...	0708	0717			0927				1147	1232				1348	1448		1547		1718		
113	Sens .... d.	0553	0735	0743	0804		0852	0951			1256			1336	1516		1651					
156	Laroche Migennes .. d.	0623	0630	0808	0813	0828	0915	1023			1323			1400	1548		1724					
197	Tonnerre .... d.	0648	0654			0939					1422				1750						
243	Montbard .... d.	0717	0720			0911	1002	1139			1449				1819						
315	Dijon .... d.	0759	0759			0851	0946	1040	1214		1401	1406	1525		1556		1729	1859	1906		

		775 TGV	759 TGV			EC27 TGV	763 TGV		5045	5047	777 TGV		767 TGV	5065	5095	211		767 TGV	5795	5799		5079
		Ⓒ	Ⓐ	Ⓒ	Ⓐ		Ⓐ	E	⑤f				H	⑦e	⚒	N		E	⑦e	⚒ 2		⑦e
						🍷	🍷				🍷		🍷					🍷		2		
	Paris Lyon .... d.	1655	1655	1720	1720	1733	1755	1807	1811	1824	1844	1853	1920	1935	2036	2029	2029	2056	2104	2108	2210	2245	2356
	Melun § .... d.	1727					1820		1850			2001			2151			2312				
	Fontainebleau-Avon § .. d.	1739	1728				1831		1903			2013			2102	2203		2325				
	Montereau § .... d.	1757	1744				1848		1921			2030			2120	2220		2340				
	Sens .... d.		1809		1831	1916		1954	1949		2055		2135	2139			0003	0059				
	Laroche Migennes .. d.		1839		1857			2017				2159	2202		2259	2334	0131				
	Tonnerre .... d.							2043							2324	2357					
	Montbard .... d.			1828	1828			2107				2216	2319		2347	0023					
	Dijon .... d.			1903	1903		1944	1949		2106	2141	2057			2343	2246	0027	0110	0304			

		5520	Ⓐ	Ⓒ	Ⓐ	Ⓒ	Ⓐ	Ⓒ	5042	770 TGV	772 TGV	774 TGV		EC22 TGV	752 TGV		776 TGV	EC20 TGV	5092		Ⓑ	⑥t	⑥	⑤f
		2								Ⓐk	⚒	Ⓐv		🍷	🍷		⑨g	D	⚒					
	Dijon .... d.	0403	...	...	...	...	...	...	0610	0633	0656	0756		0945	0950		0956	1124	1218		1225	...	1401
	Montbard .... d.								0649		0731					1043	1200		1305	1441		
	Tonnerre .... d.								0712						1114		1332	151				
	Laroche Migennes . d.	0532	0526	0531		0639	0652		0739		0828	1053	1141		1231	1350	1400	1408	151			
	Sens .... d.	0557	0600	0604	0632	0712	0724	0757	0805	0902	1123	1213r		1301	1419		1437	160				
	Montereau § .... d.		0625	0629	0701	0708	0734	0746	0826	0929		1148		1321	1444		1502	...			
	Fontainebleau-Avon § . d.		0639	0646	0715	0727	0750	0806	0847	0948		1205		1341	1500		1517	...			
	Melun § .... d.		0649	0705	0724	0739	0801	0820	0901	1001		1218		1352	1512		1529	...			
	Paris Lyon .... a.	0706	0718	0731	0753	0827	0830	0849	0902	0813	0840	0936		1029	1124	1129	1246	1307	1357	1418	1537	1554

CONTINUED ON NEXT PAGE

D – Daily except Jan. 17 - Feb. 9.
E – ⑤⑦ (also Nov. 1,10, Apr. 17, May 1,8,24; not Oct 30, Nov. 11, Apr. 16,30, May 7,26).
G – ①②③④ (not Nov. 1, Apr. 17, May 1,8,24,25).
H – ①②③④ (not Oct. 31, Nov. 1,10, Apr. 17, May 1,8,24,25).
N – For days of running see Table 152.

TGV – Ⓡ, supplement payable.

b – Not Apr. 16,30, May 7.
e – Also Nov. 1, Apr. 17, May 1,8; not Oct. 30, Apr. 16,30, May 7.

f – Also Nov. 10, May 24; not Nov. 11, May 26.
g – Also Nov. 2, Apr. 18, May 2,9; not Oct. 31, Apr. 17, May 1,8.
h – Not Oct. 31, Nov. 11, Apr. 16,30, May 7,25.
k – Not Oct. 31.
t – ⚒ only.
t – Not Oct. 29, Nov. 5, Dec. 24,31, Mar. 4,11, Apr. 29, May 6,27.
v – Not Oct. 31, May 25,26.
x – Depart 1234 Jan. 17 - Feb. 9.

§ – Additional suburban trains operate between Paris Gare de Lyon and Montereau.

∗ – Train number 762 on Ⓒ.

Table 155 — DIJON - PARIS

1,2 class

		EC24 TGV	758* TGV	5096	5052	760 TGV				5090	778 TGV	764 TGV			766 TGV E	5046	5744	EC26 TGV	5098		5746	768 TGV	EC28 TGV
		✕	⚲			⚲	Ⓑ	✕	⑦e	Ⓐ	⚲	⚲	⑦e	✕	⚲	⑥	⑤f	⚲		Ⓖ	⑦	⑦e	⚲
Dijon	d.	1449	1452	...	...	1646	1720	...	1723	...	...	1823	1823	1836	1859	...	1940	1934	1940	1959	...	2042	2042	2108	2218
Montbard	d.			...	...	1723		...	1817	...	...	1904	1904	1912	1935	...		2012	2019		...	2116	2116		
Tonnerre	d.			...	...	1748		...	1854	...	...	1931	1931			...		2038	2045		...	2140	2140		
Laroche Migennes	d.			...	1602	1811		1807	1931	...	...	1956	1956			...		2104	2110		...	2114	2202	2202		
Sens	d.			...	1635	1835		1842		...	...	2023	2025			...		2134	2135		...	2148	2222	2224		
Montereau §	d.			1629	1703			1909		...	2024					2100	2130		2157		...	2217				
Fontainebleau-Avon §	d.			1651	1721			1926		...	2044					2117	2147				...	2237				
Melun §	d.			1703	1736			1946		...	2057					2129	2201				...	2252	2258			
Paris Lyon	a.	1628	1632	1732	1808	1930	1902	2016		2124		2132	2021	2044	2159	2229	2118	2235	2235	2137	2320		2323	2248	2356

FOR **NOTES** SEE FOOT OF PREVIOUS PAGE

Table 156 — (STRASBOURG) - BELFORT - LYON

1,2 class

km			D	G	✕	H	✕	G	6162 6163 R	6162 6163 S	6171 6170 ✕		6173 6172 ⚲			5320 ✕	6175 6174 ⚲	6191 6190 ⑤q		6187 6186 Ⓐ	6177 6176 ⑦v	6183 6182 C		6158 ⑥		6159 6158 ⑤n
													⚲							⚲	C ⑤n			Ⓑ ⚲	⑥	⚲
0	Strasbourg 176	d.	...	...	...	...	0627	...	0627	...	...	0800	...	...	1153	1357	...	1513	1523	1557	...	...	...	1629
106	Mulhouse 176	d.	...	...	...	...	0732	...	0732	...	...	0906	...	...	1255	1501	...	1620	1628	1654	...	...	...	1747
155	Belfort	d.	...	...	0530	...	0600	0700	0803	...	0803	...	...	0941	1216	1305	1327	1540	1610	1655	1659	...	1736	1748	1802	1828
173	Montbéliard	d.	...	...	0545	...	0614	0714	0816	...	0816	...	...	0954	1230	1320	1340	1552	1625	1708	1711	...	1750	1802	1816	1843
252	Besançon Viotte	d.	0502	0615	0646	0709	0729	0820	0907	0907	0912	...	...	1051	1328	1444	1436	1649	1725	1803	1803	1819	1905	1914	1914	1939
	Dôle 157	d.			0716									1117	1358	1509	1458	1712							2005
	Dijon 157	a.			0743						0937					1430	1541	1736							2029
	Mâcon Ville 149	d.									1055					1616								
292	Mouchard	d.	0529	0650		0747			0934	0934									1837	1837				
341	Lons-le-Saunier	d.	0607	0758		0847			1006	1006									1911	1908	1919			
405	Bourg-en-Bresse	d.	0659	0846		0948			1052	1052		1304			1909			1957	1949				
448	Lyon Part-Dieu	a.	0748	0929		1032			1139	1139	1132	1353			1653	1953	2046	2032	2046			
	Lyon Perrache	a.	0755	0936		1039			1146	1146	1142				1702	2003	2053	2039	2053			
	Marseille 151	a.	...	...								1731								
	Nice 164	a.	...	...								2019								
	Montpellier 163	a.	...	...																
	Port Bou 163	a.	...	...																

		6189 6188 ⑦ 2	6179 6178 ⑦	6181 6180 M		6197 6196 6196 N ⑨n	6196 5521 B Ⓡ					6692 6693 A	5520 6694 P	6694 6695	✕	✕	Ⓐ		6670 6671 ✕
		⚲	⚲									⚲							⚲
Strasbourg 176	d.	...	1820	1820	...	1910	...	2024	2024	...		Cerbère 163	d.	...	...	...	...	...	...
Mulhouse 176	d.	...	1924	1924	...	2014	...	2140	2140	...		Montpellier 163	d.	...	2216	...	...	...	...
Belfort	d.	1830	1955	1955	1958	2045	...	2219	2219	...		Nice 164	d.	...		1946	...	...	...
Montbéliard	d.	1845	2007	2007	2013	2058	...	2234	2234	...		Marseille 151	d.	...		2256	...	...	...
Besançon Viotte	d.	1945	2059	2101	2112	2150	...	2332	2332	...		Lyon Perrache	d.	0015	0234	0234	...	...	0626
Dôle 157	d.							2359	2359	...		Lyon Part-Dieu	d.	0027			...	...	0636
Dijon 157	a.							0026	0026	...		Bourg-en-Bresse	d.	0150			...	...	0718
Mâcon Ville 149	d.											Lons-le-Saunier	d.	0236			...	...	0757
Mouchard	d.		2127									Mouchard	d.	0315			...	...	0827
Lons-le-Saunier	d.		2157	2157	...	2301						Mâcon Ville 149	d.						
Bourg-en-Bresse	d.		2248	2247	...	2344						Dijon 157	d.		0436	0436			
Lyon Part-Dieu	a.		2328	2325	...	0021						Dôle 157	d.		0508	0508			
Lyon Perrache	a.		2335	2332	...	0028						Besançon Viotte	d.	0422	0538	0538	0604	0649	0845	0909
Marseille 151	a.							0237	0237	...		Montbéliard	d.	0520	0633	0633	0721	0748	0940	1000
Nice 164	a.							0613				Belfort	a.	0535	0646	0646	0736	0802	0954	1012
Montpellier 163	a.					0916			0700	...		Mulhouse 176	a.	0618	0724	0724				1042
Port Bou 163	a.											Strasbourg 176	a.	0741	0846	0846				1143

		6672 6673 ⚲		6674 6675 ⚲	6676 6677 ⚲						6668 6669 ⑦e ⚲	6678 6679 ✕	6678 6679 W ⚲		6688 6689 E ⑦b	6698 6699 ⑦b
			✕	⑦	⑥	Ⓐ	Ⓐ 2	Ⓐ	Ⓒ	Ⓐ	Ⓑ	⑤f				
Cerbère 163	d.	...	...	...	...	...	...	...	...	...	...	...	...	...	...	1633	...
Montpellier 163	d.	...	...	...	...	...	...	...	...	...	...	...	...	...	...	1938	...
Nice 164	d.	...	...	...	0820	...	...	...	...	...	...	...	...	...	...		...
Marseille 151	d.	...	...	...	1106	...	...	...	...	...	...	...	...	...	...		...
Lyon Perrache	d.	0911	...	1300	...	...	...	1545	...	1758	1828	1836	1836	2108	2148	2307
Lyon Part-Dieu	d.	0921	...	1311	1503	...	...	1555	...	1808	1841	1848	1848	2118	2200	2317
Bourg-en-Bresse	d.				1542			1652		1855	1926	1930	1930	2214		0012
Lons-le-Saunier	d.							1740		1948	2006	2010	2010	2302		0055
Mouchard	d.							1851		2023	2039	2041	2041	2340		0130
Mâcon Ville 149	d.	0957		1347											2243	
Dijon 157	d.		1230	1230				1738	1738	1915					0009	
Dôle 157	d.	1116	1300	1301	1509		1730	1811	1817	1945					0033	
Besançon Viotte	d.	1145	1208	1329	1334	1403	1536	1700	1756	1818	1842	1855	1934	2019	2057	2118	2119	2122	0012	0100	0213
Montbéliard	d.	1240	1329	1428	1433	1520	1634	1818	1851	1930	1947	2019		2117		2212		2211		0154	0310
Belfort	a.	1252	1344	1443	1448	1534	1646	1833	1903	1945	2002	2034		2132		2224		2224		0206	0324
Mulhouse 176	a.	1322			1716		1939									2258		2254		0248	0404
Strasbourg 176	a.	1426			1826		2045									0006		0002		0359	0520

A – Daily except ⑦: ✕ 2 cl. and ⟂ Béziers - Strasbourg.
B – Daily except ⑤: ✕ 2 cl. and ⟂ Strasbourg - Béziers.
C – ①②③④⑥ (also Nov. 11, Apr. 16,30, May 7; not Nov. 10, Dec. 21, Feb. 16,23, Apr. 13, May 24).
D – ①⑥ (also Nov. 2, Apr. 18, May 2,9,26; not Nov. 12, Apr. 17, May 1,8).
E – ⑤⑦ (also Nov. 1,10, Apr. 17, May 1,8,24,25; not Nov. 11, Apr. 16,30, May 7).
G – ②③④⑤ (not Nov. 1,2,11, Apr. 18, May 2,9,25).
H – ①⑥ (also Nov. 1,2,11, Apr. 18, May 2,9,25,26; not Apr. 17, May 1,8).
M – ①②③④ (also Apr. 22, May 26; not Oct. 31, Nov. 1,10, Feb. 16,23, Apr. 13,17, May 18,25).
N – ⟂ 1,2 cl. (T2), ⟂ 1,2 cl. and ⟂ Strasbourg - Nice (- Ventimiglia Sept. 25 - Oct. 30 and Mar. 31 - May 27). Conveys Sept. 25 - Oct. 30 and Mar. 31 - May 27, ⟂ and ⟂ 2 cl. Frankfurt - Nice - Ventimiglia.
P – ⟂ 1,2 cl. (T2), ⟂ 1,2 cl. and ⟂ Nice - Strasbourg (Ventimiglia - Nice - Strasbourg Sept. 25 - Oct. 29 and Mar. 30 - May 27). Conveys Sept. 25 - Oct. 29 and Mar. 30 - May 27, ⟂ and ⟂ 2 cl. Ventimiglia - Nice - Strasbourg - Frankfurt.

R – ⑦ Dec. 11 - Mar. 12.
S – ⑦ Sept. 25 - Dec. 4 and Mar. 19 - May 21 (also Apr. 17, May 1,8).
W – Ⓐ (✕ Dec. 10 - Mar. 17).
b – Also Nov. 1, Dec. 26, Jan. 2, Apr. 18, May 1,8; not Oct. 30, Dec. 25, Jan. 1, Apr. 16,30, May 7.
e – Also Nov. 1, Apr. 17, May 1,8; not Apr. 16,30, May 7.
f – Also Nov. 10, Apr. 17, May 1,8; not May 24, May 26.
n – Also Nov. 10, Feb. 16,23, Apr. 13, May 24; not Nov. 11, Feb. 17,24, Apr. 14.
q – Also Nov. 10, Feb. 16,23, Apr. 13, May 24; not Nov. 11.
v – Also Apr. 17, May 1,8; not Apr. 16,30, May 7.

Table 157   DIJON - BESANÇON, ST. CLAUDE and LAUSANNE   1,2 class

km										EC21 TGV	771 TGV										EC23 TGV	423
		Ⓐ	✕	✕	✕	✕		⑦	Ⓐ		Ⓐk		Ⓒ		⑥	⑥		✕	✕	⑦	Ⓐ	✕	
0	*Paris Lyon* 155 ....d.	...	...	...	...	...	...	...	0714	0714r	...	...	...	...	...	...	...	...	...	...	1225	...
315	**Dijon**.................d.	...	0604c	...	0633	...	0739	...	0823	0853	0853r	0835v	0902	1006	...	...	...	1140	1230	1230	1348	1403	...
361	Dôle........................a.	...	0637c	...	0706	...	0808	...	0851	0917	0917	0908v	0930	1037	...	...	...	1211	1259	1300	1422		...
361	Dôle 156 ....d.	0604	0648	0643	0707	...	0810	...	0852	0920	0924	0927	0933	1039	1134	...	...	1213	1300	1301	1438		...
406	**Besançon Viotte** 156 ...d.	0640	0729			0802	0843	0903	0923		0950		1001	1104		...	1218	1250	1327	1332	1515		...
486	Le Locle................d.	...	...	...	...	1000		1100								1408							...
393	Mouchard..............d.	...	0702	0743					0940		0955			1218									...
417	Andelot.................d.	...	0720	0804							1019		1238	1250									...
466	Morez....................a.	...		0904							1120			1350									...
489	**St. Claude**..........a.	...		0934							1149			1417									...
438	Frasne....................d.	...	0739						1015	1020												1518	1521
	Pontarlier...............a.	...	0754							1042													1532
	Bern 255 ....a.	...																					1647
462	Vallorbe..................a.	...							1032													1533	1607
508	**Lausanne**.............a.	...							1106														

	773 TGV ⑥t 🍴	773 TGV ⑧ ✕	5053 5321 ⑥		EC29 TGV Ⓐ 🍴	EC429 TGV Ⓒ	Ⓐ	Ⓐ		775 TGV Ⓐk 🍴	EC27 TGV	427 🍴	n	⑥	⑥		777 TGV 🍴	EN 223 F R	EN 227 G E	
Paris Lyon 155 ....d.	1225	1228	1240x		1553	1553				1720	1807			...	...		1920	2006	2009	
Dijon..................d.	1408	1408	1611	1643	1654	1731	1731	1738	1738	1813	1905	1915	1946	...	2000	2012	2100	2151	2236	2239	2256
Dôle......................a.	1431	1431	1643	1717	1720			1809	1815	1842	1929	1944		...	2032	2044	2123	2218	2302	2242	2324
Dôle 156 ....a.	1433	1433	1645	1725	1733			1811	1817	1843	1931	1945		2001v	2033	2045	2125	2221	2304	2314	2325
Besançon Viotte 156 ...a.	1459	1459	1707		1810			1840	1858	1914	1921	1957	2017		2101	2113	2152	2255			2349
Le Locle.................a.	...	...	...	...	...	...	...	...	...	2107											
Mouchard...............d.	...	...	1750								2029		2048								
Andelot..................d.	...	...	1825										2114								
Morez....................d.	...	...	1926										2214								
St. Claude..........a.	...	...	2003										2242								
Frasne.....................d.	...	...	...		1851	1855					2106	2110									
Pontarlier................a.	...	...	...			1906						2121									
Bern 255 ....a.	...	...	...			2022						2239									
Vallorbe...................a.	...	...	...		1906						2123							0010	0030		
Lausanne..............a.	...	...	...		1945						2157										

	EN 226 G	EN 222 R	772 TGV ✕ 🍴	⑦	774 TGV Ⓐq 🍴	✕	Ⓐ		✕		EC22 TGV	EC422 TGV	776 TGV		420	EC20 TGV	⑥	Ⓐ	⑥	
Lausanne.............d.											0731					1015				
Vallorbe...................d.	0340	0410									0806					1049				
Bern 255 ....d.												0700			0922			1215		
Pontarlier.................d.					0651							0816			1047			1230		
Frasne......................d.					0704						0825	0833			1059	1108				
St. Claude............d.							0623						0829				1058			
Morez.......................d.							0653						0905				1140			
Andelot....................d.					0720		0758						1012				1240	1245		
Mouchard.................d.					0742		0834		0856	0903			1030					1325		
Besançon Viotte 156 ...d.			0602	0644	0646	0702	0705	0625 0817		0830			0923	1040	1058		1215	1219		1328
Dôle 156 ....d.	0502	0510	0625	0712	0714		0747	0806	0859			0956	1053	1049	1130		1249	1259		1357
Dôle.........................d.	0504	0512	0627	0713	0716		0749	0808	0854	0900		0957	1055	1100	1131		1250	1300	1349	1358
Dijon...................a.	0530	0537	0651	0743	0743		0750	0829	0833		0931	0939	0943	1035	1119	1134	1201	1216	1326	1346	1430
Paris Lyon 155 ....a.	0825	0838	0840		0936			1124	1124			1307			1357					

	EC24 TGV ✕	5052	✕	778 TGV 🍴	⑦	⑦	5744 ⑤f	✕	426 🍴	EC26 TGV	✕	⑦	M	⑥	⑦	⑦	EC28 TGV H	N	⑤f	6197 6196
Lausanne.............d.	1246								1754								2015			
Vallorbe...................d.	1320								1829								2049			
Bern 255 ....d.									1705											
Pontarlier.................d.					1715		1735		1823								2107			
Frasne......................d.					1731		1752		1835	1847										
St. Claude............d.			1526			1632		1653												
Morez.......................d.			1554			1702		1723												
Andelot....................d.			1659	1747	1807		1808	1828									2137			
Mouchard.................d.		1200	1725		1809	1833		1832	1855											
Besançon Viotte 156 ...d.		1346	1444	1541		1742		1823	1842		1908	1913	1930	1930	1955	2119		2132	2156	2332
Dôle 156 ....d.			1507	1604	1751	1805		1901	1906		1947	1953	2003	2028	2144		2157	2223	2357
Dôle.........................d.			1509	1605		1807	1836	1852		1908		1915		1934		1955	2004	2029	2145		2158	2223	2359
Dijon...................a.	1444		1541	1642		1831	1906	1927		1937		1949		1957		2026	2035	2059	2211	2216	2224	2248	0026
Paris Lyon 155 ....a.	1628		1930			2021		2235				2323v					2356			

E – ⑤⑦ (also Nov. 10, Apr. 17, May 1,2,24,25).
F – ⑤⑦ (also Nov. 10, Apr. 17, May 1,8,24,25).
G – GALILEI – for days of running see Table 44. International journeys only.
H – ⑤⑦ (also Nov. 1,10, Apr. 17, May 1,8; not Oct. 30, Nov. 11, Apr. 16,30, May 7,26).
M – ①②③④⑦.
N – ①②③④ (not Nov. 1, Apr. 1,8,25).
R – RIALTO – see Table 44. International journeys only.
TGV – ℍ, supplement payable.
c – Ⓐ only.

f – Also Nov. 10, May 24; not Nov. 11, May 26.
h – Not Oct. 31, Nov. 11, Apr. 16,30, May 7,25.
k – Not Oct. 31.
n – Runs 9 minutes later on ⑤.
q – Not Oct. 31, May 25.
r – Depart Paris 0719, Dijon 0859 on ① (also Nov. 2, Apr. 18, May 2,9, Apr. 17, May 1,8).
t – Also Oct. 31, Nov. 11, Apr. 16,30, May 7,25.
v – ⑦ only.
x – Depart 1234 Jan. 21 - Feb. 4.

Table 158   GRENOBLE - VEYNES   1,2 class

km			Ⓒ		⑥	⑧	⑧					Ⓐ		⑤-⑦	①-④	①-④	⑤-⑦	
	Lyon Perrache 154 ....d.	...	0620	...	...	1750	1750	1843	...		*Briançon* 166 ....d.	...	0630r	...	1405	...	1635	...
0	**Grenoble**.................d.	...	0842	1215	1350	...	1810	1810	1903	...		*Gap* 166 ....d.	...	0754	...	1522	...	1800	...
19	St. Georges de Commiers ▲ d.	...	0902	1239	1413	...	1945	1945	2052	...		**Veynes**......................d.	0500	0819	1054	1604	1604	1848	1848
110	**Veynes**.....................a.	...	1042	1415	1601	...	2015	2015	...			St. Georges de Commiers ▲ a.	0630	...	1743	1743	2039	2039	...
	Gap 166 ....a.	...	1105	...	...	2130						**Grenoble**....................a.	0650	1018	1245	1808	1808	2101	2101
	Briançon 166 ....a.	...	1219	...	...	2130						*Lyon Perrache* 154 ....a.	...						...

r – ①-⑥ only.

▲ – Station for *Chemin de Fer de la Mur* (scenic tourist railway) – see Table 151b.

Table 159 — PARIS and LYON - CULOZ - GENÈVE

1,2 class

km			376 375	5750 5751 K	EC971 TGV	5752 5753	5752 5443	5656 5657	967	EC973 TGV R	5754 5755		5682 5683	860/1 TGV C	EC975 TGV
		Ⓐ		z	z							Ⓐ W			
0	Paris Lyon .... d.	...	...	...	...	...	0725	...	...	0858	1028	...	...	...	...
	Lyon Perrache .... d.	...	...	0730	...	0924	0924	...	...	...	...	1213	...	...	...
	Lyon Part-Dieu ...... d.	...	0607c	0739	...	0933	0933	...	...	...	...	1225	...	1607	...
508	Ambérieu .... d.	...	...	0803	...	0957	0957	...	...	...	...	1249	...	...	...
560	Culoz .... d.	...	0717c	0842	...	1027	1027	...	...	...	...	1325	...	...	...
593	Bellegarde .... a.	...	0747	0906	...	1026	1047	1047	...	...	...	1348	...	...	1745
593	Bellegarde 165 ...... d.	0615	0702	0751	0910	0917	1029	1059	1053	1142	1149	1336	1351	1358	1650	1659	1747	1800
	Annemasse .... d.	0745			1006				1128		1235	1251			1436	1720	1751	1850
	Thonon-les-Bains ... d.	0820			1032				1153			1319			1502	1754	1822	1929
	Évian-les-Bains ..... a.	0828			1041				1201			1328			1511	1802	1830	1938
626	Genève 165 .... a.	0642		0820	0940		1054	1126		1208		1401	1416		1715		1745	1812

		5756 5757	5656 5447	EC977 TGV	5758 5759	EC979 TGV	5760 5761 ⑤f	5115 5597 Y				970 TGV Ⓐ	5440 5764 Ⓐk W	5764 5765 Ⓐ		EC972 TGV	Ⓐ W
	Paris Lyon .... d.	...	...	1728	...	1910	...	2333r	Genève 165 .... d.	...	0540	...	...	...	...	...	...
	Lyon Perrache .... d.	1710	1710	1921	...	2122	...	Évian-les-Bains ...... d.	...	0515	0547	...	0624	...	0707
	Lyon Part-Dieu ...... d.	1720	1720	1932	...	2132	...	Thonon-les-Bains .... d.	...	0523	0557	...	0634	...	0715
	Ambérieu .... d.	...	...	1956	...	...	Annemasse .... d.	0521	0555	0624	...	0713	...	0743
	Culoz .... d.	1817	1817	2034	2155	2231	Bellegarde 165 .... a.	0555	0604	0710	0733	0750	0809
	Bellegarde .... a.	1840	1840	2035	2058	2215	2256	Bellegarde .... d.	0606	0737	0737	...	0811
	Bellegarde 165 ...... d.	1842	1847	2037	2101	2108	2217	2224	2259	Culoz .... d.	...	...	...	...	...
	Annemasse .... d.	1936			2145	2301	0812	Ambérieu .... d.	...	...	...	...	...
	Thonon-les-Bains ... d.	2003			2211	2325	0846	Lyon Part-Dieu .... a.	...	0828	0828	...	0853	0853
	Évian-les-Bains ..... a.	2011			2220	2333	0854	Lyon Perrache .... a.	...	0903	0903	...	...
	Genève 165 .... a.	1909		2102	2129	2245	2325	Paris Lyon .... a.	0915				1112

		5680 5681	EC974 TGV	5766 5767 C	868/9 TGV	EC976 TGV	5768 5769	🚌	966 TGV S		5770 5771	EC978 TGV		5446 5772	EC980 TGV	5772 5773	5596 5118 Y	378 377 H
	Genève 165 .... d.	...	0930	1003	1022	1044	1237	1255	...	1630	1650	1746	...	1910	1929	...	2154
	Évian-les-Bains ...... d.	0835					1140	1203	1415	1531		1700		1812		2042
	Thonon-les-Bains .... d.	0845					1152	1215	1429	1541		1710		1821		2052
	Annemasse .... d.	0911					1219	1315	1508	1609		1748		1852		2122
	Bellegarde 165 .... a.	0946	0956	1027	1046	1253	1301	1319	1646	1654	1714	1815	1830	1927	1936	1954	2219
	Bellegarde .... d.		1030	1048		1304	1323	1658	1717		1957	1937	1957	2221
	Culoz .... d.		1109		1346	1720	2022	2022	2244
	Ambérieu .... d.		1147		1423	1754	2058	2058
	Lyon Part-Dieu .... a.		1212	1222	1445	1818	2125	2125	2350
	Lyon Perrache .... a.		1222		1455	1827	2134	2134
	Paris Lyon .... a.		1332		1611	1859	2027	2240	0642

C – 🚟 Genève - Lyon - Montpellier and v.v.
H – HISPANIA – 🚟 and ➤ 1,2 cl. Genève - Narbonne - Port Bou and Irún.
K – HISPANIA – 🚟 and ➤ 1,2 cl. Cerbère and Hendaye - Narbonne - Genève.
R – ⑥⑦ Dec. 17 - Apr. 16.
S – ⑥⑦ Dec. 24 - Apr. 16.
TGV – Ⓡ, supplement payable.
W – 🚟 Évian les Bains - Genève Eaux Vives and v.v.

Y – ⑤⑦ (daily Dec. 16 - May 1), also Nov. 1,10, May 8,24,25; not Oct. 30, Nov. 11, May 7,26; ➤ 1,2 cl. and 🚟 Paris - Évian les Bains and v.v.
c – On ②③④⑤ Oct. 11 - Nov. 18 (not Nov. 2), depart Lyon Part Dieu 0546, Culoz 0658.
f – Also Nov. 10, May 24; not Nov. 11, May 26.
k – Not Oct. 31.
r – Depart 2339 (in train 5119) on ⑤⑥⑦ Dec. 16 - Apr. 30 (not Dec. 24,31).
z – Runs 5-10 minutes later Bellegarde - Genève on ②③④⑤ Oct. 11 - Nov. 18.

Table 160 — LILLE - CHARLES DE GAULLE ✈ - LYON

1,2 class

km			520 TGV	🚌	524/5 TGV	524/5 TGV	532/3 TGV	534/5 TGV E	534/5 TGV	542/3 TGV	542/3 TGV	546 TGV	🚌	548/9 TGV
0	Lille Europe 110 .... d.	...	0605	...	0834	0834	1029	1217	1217	1610	1610	1750	...	1916
	Douai 110 .... d.	...			0855	0855	...						...	1937
	Arras 110 .... d.	...			0913	0913	...						...	1954
	Amiens .... d.	...	0830				...						1910	...
99	TGV Haute Picardie .... d.	...	0920		0932	0932	...						2000	2014
204	Paris Charles de Gaulle ✈ .. d.	0659		1005	1005	1125	1313	1313	1705	1705	1846	...	2048
228	Marne la Vallée Chessy § ... d.	0711		1020	1020	1140			1719	1719	1900	...	2103
657	Lyon Part Dieu .... a.	0905		1212	1212	1332	1913	1913	2053	...	2256
661	Lyon Perrache .... a.					1343				...	2307
	Satolas TGV ✈ .... a.						1510	1510			...
	Grenoble 154 .... a.						1620			...
	Valence 151 .... a.		1258	1258		1543	1957	1957	...
	Avignon 151 .... a.		1356	1356		1639	2053	2053	...
	Montpellier 163 .... a.			1452				2153	...
	Marseille 151 .... a.		1456			1736	2153	...
	Nice 164 .... a.					2000t		...

			560/1 TGV	🚌	562/3 TGV	564/5 TGV	566/7 TGV	576/7 TGV	578/9 TGV	582/3 TGV	584/5 TGV	🚌	586 TGV	596/7 TGV E
	Nice 164 .... d.	...					1057v	...				...	...
	Marseille 151 .... d.	...				0635	1324		1558		...	...
	Montpellier 163 .... d.	...			0632			1556			...	...
	Avignon 151 .... d.	...			0733	0733	1422	1656	1656	...	...
	Valence 151 .... d.	...			0830	0830	1519	1753	1753	...	...
	Grenoble 154 .... d.	...								1818	...
	Satolas TGV ✈ .... d.	...					1553			...	...
	Lyon Perrache .... d.	...	0613							...	...
	Lyon Part Dieu .... d.	...	0624		0755	0915	0915	1643	1838	1838	...	...
	Marne la Vallée Chessy § ... d.	...	0821		0951	1110	1110	1839	2033	2033	1944	1944
	Paris Charles de Gaulle ✈ .. d.	...	0837		1007	1126	1126	1757	1856	2049	2049	2151	2151
	TGV Haute Picardie .... d.	...	0907	0915					2118	2118	2125	...
	Amiens .... a.	...		1005						2215	...
	Arras 110 .... a.	...			1049			1937	2137	2137	...
	Douai 110 .... a.	...			1105			1954	2153	2153	...
	Lille Europe 110 .... a.	0933		1123	1216	1216	1848	2013	2212	2212	2241	2241

E – ⑥ Dec. 24 - Mar. 25.
TGV – Ⓡ, supplement payable.

t – ⑥ (also Nov. 11; not Nov. 12).
v – ⑦ only (also Apr. 17, May 1,8; not Apr. 16,30, May 7).
§ – Station for Disneyland.

Table 163   AVIGNON and MARSEILLE - NARBONNE - PORT BOU

1,2 class

km		1117	473	Ⓐ	6146/6147 ⑦e P	6146/6147 ⑤f Q	6196/5521 D	5799/5525 B	5521	6956/6957	6956/6957 ✗	6956/6957 ①g	6210/6211	6934/6935	✗	5501 R	5501 S
	Paris Lyon 151 .... d.							2210	2239								
	Paris Austerlitz 138 ...... d.	2054	2145														
	Lille Europe 160 ...... d.												2120b				
	Charles de Gaulle + 160 d.																
	Metz 170 ...... d.				2048	2048											
	Strasbourg 156 ...... d.						2024										
	Dijon 149 ...... d.				0105	0105		0113	0138								
	Genève 159 ...... d.				0309p	0309p	0245p	0307p	0322p							0725	0725
	Lyon Part Dieu 151 ...... d.				0532	0532	0551	0551	0551				0645	0711	0735	0942	1010
0	Avignon ...... d.																
	Nice 164 ...... d.									0547				0656			
	Marseille St. Charles ...... d.									0630				0740			
	Arles ...... d.									0658					0747	0751	
21	Tarascon				0600	0600	0622	0605	0605								
49	Nimes ...... a.				0600	0600	0622	0622	0622	0653	0720	0739	0802		0806	1008	1037
49	Nimes ...... d.				0613	0613	0629	0629	0629	0700	0700		0810	0722	0741	1011	1039
99	Montpellier ...... a.				0643	0643	0700	0700	0700	0729	0729		0811	0814	0838	1047	1113
99	Montpellier ...... d.			0544		0646	0707	0707	0707	0731	0731		0817	0842	0857	1049	1116
126	Sète			0601		0706	0730	0730	0730	0746	0746		0833	0900	0918	1105	1134
149	Agde			0616		0724	0746	0746	0746				0849	0934		1120	1151
170	Béziers			0630		0741	0758	0758	0758	0809	0809	0809	0902	0926	0948	1133	1206
196	Narbonne ...... a.		0543	0646		0757		0757		0822	0822	0822	0916	0940	1004	1150	1221
196	Narbonne ...... d.	0605	0608	0703		0740		0805		0824	0824	0824	0932	0944	0849	1153	1224
	Toulouse 139 ...... a.			0825						0938	0938	0938		1105			
	Irún 139 ...... a.																
	Bordeaux 139 ...... a.									1158	1158	1158		1329			
	Nantes 134 ...... a.													1809			
259	Perpignan ...... a.	0647	0658	0740		0823		0839					0933	1006		1225	1259
259	Perpignan ...... d.	0650	0703	0754		0843							0936	1009		1241	
281	Argelès sur Mer	0707	0719	0816		0902							0952	1026		1246	
286	Collioure	0712	0726										0957	1033		1250	
289	Port Vendres	0716	0732	0827		0912							1001	1039		1255	
294	Banyuls sur Mer	0721	0739	0834									1006	1046		1301	
301	Cerbère ...... a.	0727	0746	0841		0923							1012	1053			
303	Port Bou ...... a.		0755	0850		0935							1021	1102			

		6964/6965	58125	58129	6960/6961 M	6960/6961 J	851 TGV K	851 TGV J K	✗ q	5958/5959	6952/6953	164	165	524/5 TGV	853 TGV	868/9 TGV	71	Ⓐ	58139	58141
	Paris Lyon 151 ...... d.						0810	0810									1049			
	Paris Austerlitz 138 ...... d.														0834					
	Lille Europe 160 ...... d.														1005					
	Charles de Gaulle + 160 d.																			
	Metz 170 ...... d.																			
	Strasbourg 156 ...... d.															1044				
	Dijon 149 ...... d.																			
	Genève 159 ...... d.													1217	1226					
	Lyon Part Dieu 151 ...... d.				1100	1100	1120	1120						1400	1411					1510
	Avignon ...... d.									1215			1030y							
	Nice 164 ...... d.	0550c									1221	1246	1302							
	Marseille St. Charles ...... d.	0852c									1221	1246	1311							1523
	Arles ...... d.	0954v									1226	1321								1523
	Tarascon				1113	1113					1226	1321								
	Nimes ...... a.	1019v	1128	1128	1147	1147	1156	1156		1245	1338	1348		1424	1431	1435			1442	1538
	Nimes ...... d.	1022v		1129	1149	1151	1158	1158		1246	1350		1426	1426	1433	1437			1510	1539
	Montpellier ...... a.	1054		1201	1216	1226	1222	1230		1314	1416	1426	1420	1452	1459	1502			1513	1608
	Montpellier ...... d.	1058		1203	1219	1229			1240	1315	1420	1429					1510		1531	1610
	Sète	1115		1223	1237	1246			1303	1332	1437								1545	1628
	Agde			1238					1319	1344									1558	1641
	Béziers	1140		1251	1302	1311			1334	1356	1504						1558		1611	1653
	Narbonne ...... a.	1154		1305	1316	1324			1354	1409	1519						1600		1615	1713
	Narbonne ...... d.	1158	1214	1307	1318	1326				1410	1521						1600		1615	1725
	Toulouse 139 ...... a.	1315			1434	1441					1636	1619								
	Irún 139 ...... a.	1846																		
	Bordeaux 139 ...... a.										1904	1823								
	Nantes 134 ...... a.																			
	Perpignan ...... a.		1256	1347						1441							1631		1659	1809
	Perpignan ...... d.		1301														1633	1647	1718	1812
	Argelès sur Mer ...... d.		1317															1703	1736	1828
	Collioure ...... d.		1323															1708	1741	1833
	Port Vendres ...... d.		1327															1714	1745	1837
	Banyuls sur Mer ...... d.		1332															1719	1750	1842
	Cerbère ...... d.		1338														1657	1725	1756	1848
	Port Bou ...... a.																1723		1805	

◆ – NOTES (LISTED BY TRAIN NUMBER)

71 – CATALAN TALGO – ⊡ and ✗ Montpellier - Barcelona and v.v.
164/5 – LE GRAND SUD – ⊡ and ✗ Nice - Bordeaux.
473 – PARIS-CÔTE VERMEILLE – ⊟ 1,2 cl. (T2), 1,2 cl. and ⊡ Paris - Port Bou.
1117 – Dec. 20,21,23,29, Apr. 14,21, May 24: ⊡ and ◄ 1,2 cl. Paris - Port Bou.
5521 – ⑤⑥⑦ (daily Dec. 19 - Apr. 2, also Apr. 13,17, May 1,8,24,25): ◄ 1,2 cl. and ⊡ Paris - Béziers (also ⊟ 1,2 cl. (T2) on ⑤⑦ and Apr. 17, May 1,8,24; not Apr. 16,30, May 7,26).

5958/9 – LE CÉVENOL ⊡ and ☕ Marseille - Nimes - Clermont Ferrand - (Paris).
6210/1 – FLANDRES ROUSSILLON, runs ⑤ Mar. 31 - May 26: ⊟ 1,2 cl. (T2) and ◄ 2 cl. Calais auto/train - Port Bou; ◄ 1,2 cl. Tourcoing - Lille - Port Bou; ☕ Valence - Montpellier.
6934/5 – ⊡ Marseille - Nantes - Quimper.

B – ①②③④ Sept. 25 - Dec. 15 and Apr. 3 - May 23 (not Oct. 27,31, Nov. 1,10, Apr. 17, May 1,8): ◄ 1,2 cl. and ⊡ Paris - Béziers.
D – Daily except ⑤ (also runs May 26): ◄ 2 cl. and ⊡ Strasbourg - Béziers.
J – Daily except dates in note K.
K – Daily Nov. 21 - Apr. 7 (not Nov. 25-27); Ⓐ Apr. 10 - May 12.

M – On Ⓐ Apr. 10 - May 12 runs Avignon - Nimes and Montpellier - Perpignan only.
P – ⊡ and ◄ 1,2 cl. Metz - Montpellier.
Q – ⊡ and ◄ 1,2 cl. Metz - Port Bou; ◄ 1,2 cl. Reims - Port Bou.
R – Daily except when train S runs.
S – Ⓐ Feb. 13 - Mar. 3.

TGV –Ⓡ, supplement payable.

b – Lille Flandres.
c – On Ⓒ (not Dec. 3,17, Jan. 28) and daily Mar. 6 - May 27, Nice depart 0600, Marseille depart 0906.
e – Also Apr. 17, May 1,8; not Apr. 16,30, May 7.
f – Also May 24; not May 26.
g – Also Apr. 18, May 2,9; not Apr. 17, May 1,8.
p – Lyon Perrache.
q – On Ⓐ Apr. 10 - May 12, runs 7-14 minutes later Nimes - Perpignan.
v – On Ⓐ Jan. 3 - Feb. 24 (also Jan. 28) depart Arles 0936, Nimes 1014.
y – Depart 1036 on Ⓒ (also Dec. 3,17, Jan. 28) and daily Mar. 6 - May 27.

↗ – Supplement payable.

Table 163 — AVIGNON and MARSEILLE - NARBONNE - PORT BOU

1,2 class

	855 TGV	6950 6951	5511	857 TGV	534/5 TGV	819 TGV	15740 58147 15741 A	147 58147 471 ⑤f	15740 15741 ⑤f	6954 59248	6955	58151	59234 Ⓐ	867 TGV ✕	6966 6967 Ⓑ
Paris Lyon 151 ...... d.	1212			1334		1320								1534n	
Paris Austerlitz 138 ... d.								1006							
Lille Europe 160 ...... d.				1217											
Charles de Gaulle + 160 . d.				1313											
Metz 170 ...... d.															
Strasbourg 156 ...... d.															
Dijon 149 ...... d.			1215												
Genève 159 ...... d.															
Lyon Part Dieu 151 ... d.			1403												
Avignon ...... d.	1533		1607	1639	1644		1657	1657		1756	1845			1902	1717
Nice 164 ...... d.		1153z													
Marseille St. Charles ... d.		1442					1606			1619	1713		1807		
Arles ...... d.		1526								1715	1756		1854		
Tarascon ...... a.			1621		1710	1711		1725				1808	1903		
Nîmes ...... a.	1558	1549	1636		1724	1730	1724			1740	1820	1824	1913	1917	1945
Nîmes ...... d.	1600	1552	1638		1726	1735	1726			1743	1822	1827	1915	1919	1947
Montpellier ...... a.	1624	1618	1711	1743	1757	1806	1757			1817	1848	1908	1945	1949	2013
Montpellier ...... d.		1636	1714				1759		1759	1819	1850	1951		1953	2022
Sète ...... d.		1653	1731				1815		1815	1844	1906	2007			2040
Agde ...... d.		1707	1747				1829		1829	1902		2021			2054
Béziers ...... d.		1721	1801				1843		1843	1916	1929	2032			2106
Narbonne ...... a.		1735	1815				1857		1857	1944		2104			2104
Narbonne ...... d.		1741	1817				1859		1902	1946	1958	2106			2106
Toulouse 139 ...... a.		1904							2021	2100		2218			2218
Irún 139 ...... a.															
Bordeaux 139 ...... a.		2153							2335	2335					
Nantes 134 ...... a.															
Perpignan ...... a.			1854					1947					2041		
Perpignan ...... d.			1858					1952					2046		
Argelès sur Mer ...... d.			1920					2011					2102		
Collioure ...... d.			1927					2018					2108		
Port Vendres ...... d.			1932					2023					2111		
Banyuls sur Mer ...... d.			1939					2030					2116		
Cerbère ...... a.			1946					2036					2122		
Port Bou ...... a.			1955					2045							

	6932 6933 ⑤f ♦	871 TGV	6962 6963	543/4 TGV	873 TGV	6134 5535 ⑤f	877 TGV Ⓐ ✕	6924 6925 ♦	6144 6145 ⑤f	340 341 ⑦e ♦	5515	378 379 ♦	378/9 6978 G	362 363 ♦	362 6978 F W	362 6984 E W	6984 6985 ♦
Paris Lyon 151 ...... d.			1636r		1749		1832n										
Paris Austerlitz 138 ... d.																	
Lille Europe 160 ...... d.				1610													
Charles de Gaulle + 160 . d.				1705													
Metz 170 ...... d.									1542								
Strasbourg 156 ...... d.																	
Dijon 149 ...... d.					1706												
Genève 159 ...... d.								1910		1910		2154	2154				
Lyon Part Dieu 151 ... d.			2004	1917	1851			2103		2103		2357	2357				
Avignon ...... d.	1922		2004	2100	2117		2200	2326		2326		0207	0207				0254
Nice 164 ...... d.		1855												2220	2220	2220	
Marseille St. Charles ... d.			1919				2214			2252				0120	0120	0120	
Arles ...... d.	1941		2002											0213	0213	0213	
Tarascon ...... a.	1955					2131											
Nîmes ...... a.	2005		2025	2125	2140	2147	2225	2322	2353	2353	0000	0234	0234	0239	0239	0239	0323
Nîmes ...... d.	2007		2031	2127	2142	2151	2227	2327	2355	2355	0010	0236	0236	0242	0242	0242	0327
Montpellier ...... a.	2036		2051	2153	2206	2221	2253	0001	0025	0025	0050	0304	0304	0311	0311	0311	0356
Montpellier ...... d.	2039		2054	2059		2224		0028	0028	0050		0306	0306	0315	0315	0315	0400
Sète ...... d.	2058		2111	2116		2241		0046	0046	0109		0324	0324				0418
Agde ...... d.						2255		0102	0102								
Béziers ...... d.	2126		2132	2140	2150	2309		0115	0115	0136		0351	0351	0401	0401	0401	0443
Narbonne ...... a.	2143		2155	2203		2322				0151		0405	0405	0416	0416	0416	0500
Narbonne ...... d.	2145		2158	2204		2324				0200		0410	0433	0436	0433	0532	0532
Toulouse 139 ...... a.	2304		2320							0329			0549		0549	0648	0648
Irún 139 ...... a.													1050		1050	1149	1149
Bordeaux 139 ...... a.	0146					0530				0625							
Nantes 134 ...... a.	0622					0938				1105							
Perpignan ...... a.					2242	0002						0447		0510			
Perpignan ...... d.												0450		0514			
Argelès sur Mer ...... d.																	
Collioure ...... d.																	
Port Vendres ...... d.												0519		0533			
Banyuls sur Mer ...... d.																	
Cerbère ...... a.												0533		0543			
Port Bou ...... a.												0542		0552			

♦ — NOTES (LISTED BY TRAIN NUMBER)

340/1 — 1,2 cl., 1,2 cl. and Ventimiglia - Nice - Nantes; 1,2 cl. Ventimiglia - Nice - Bordeaux; and 2 cl. Milano - Ventimiglia - Bordeaux.

362/3 — and 1,2 cl. Ventimiglia - Nice - Port Bou; and 2 cl. Roma - Ventimiglia - Port Bou.

377/8 — HISPANIA – and 1,2 cl. Genève - Port Bou; ♀ Genève - Valence.

6924/5 — ⑤⑦ (also Nov. 1,10, Apr. 17, May 1,8,24; not Oct. 30, Nov. 11, Apr. 16,30, May 7,26): 1,2 cl. (T2), 1,2 cl. and Nice - Nantes.

6932/3 — and 2 cl. Les Arcs - Toulon - Nantes.

6984/5 — ⑤⑦ (also Apr. 17, May 1,8,24; not Apr. 16,30, May 7,26): and 1,2 cl. Annecy - Grenoble - Toulouse - Irún.

A – Daily except ⑤ (also runs Nov. 11, May 26; not Nov. 10, May 24).
E – ⑤⑦ (also Nov. 1,10, Apr. 17, May 1,8,24; not Oct. 30, Nov.11, Apr. 16,30, May 7,26).
F – Daily except dates in note E.
G – and 1,2 cl. Genève - Irún.

TGV – Ⓡ, supplement payable.

W – 1,2 cl., 1,2 cl. and Ventimiglia - Irún; Roma - Irún.

e – Also Nov. 1, Apr. 17, May 1,8; not Oct. 30, Apr. 16, May 7.
f – Also Nov. 10, May 24; not Nov. 11, May 26.
n – Depart 4 minutes later on ⑤ (also Nov. 10, May 24; not Nov. 11, May 26).
r – Depart 1640 on ⑦ (also Apr. 17, May 1,8; not Apr. 16,30, May 7.
z – Depart 1200 on Ⓒ (also Dec. 3,17, Jan. 28) and daily Mar. 6 - May 27.

Table 163 — CERBÈRE - NARBONNE - AVIGNON and MARSEILLE

1,2 class

		342 343 ♦	59236 ✗	564/5 TGV ⒜	⒜ ♟	58112 58114 ✗	852 TGV P ♟	58114 58114 Q R	✗	854 TGV ♟	58120 ⒜	6460 6461 ✗	6461 5560
Cerbère ....d.	...	...	...	...	...	...	...	...	...	0605	...	0650	... 0743
Banyuls sur Mer..................d.	...	...	...	...	...	...	...	...	...	0612	...	0657	... 0749
Port Vendres.....................d.	...	...	...	...	...	...	...	...	...	0617	...	0702	... 0754
Collioure ....d.	...	...	...	...	...	...	...	...	...	0620	...	0705	... 0757
Argelès sur Mer ....d.	...	...	...	...	...	...	...	...	...	0626	...	0710	... 0802
Perpignan ....a.	...	...	...	...	...	...	...	...	...	0641	...	0725	... 0816
Perpignan ....d.	...	...	...	...	...	0537	...	0551 0601	...	0644	...	0721 0728	... 0818
Nantes 134 ....d.	...	1813	...	...	...	...	...	...	...	...	...	...	...
Bordeaux 139 ....d.	...	2244	...	...	...	...	...	...	...	...	...	...	...
Hendaye 139 ....d.	...			...	...	...	...	...	...	...	...	0704 0704	...
Toulouse 139 ....d.	...	0126	...	...	...	0624	...	0638 0648	...	0727	...	0759 0810	0814 0814 0852
Narbonne ....a.	...	0249	...	...	...	0604 0626	...	0640 0650 0659	...	0728	...	0801	0816 0816 ...
Narbonne ....d.	...	0258	...	...	...	0619 0642 0653	...	0656 0706 0715	...	0750	...	0816	0816 0816 ...
Béziers ....d.	...	0317	0459 0538	...	...	0635 0655	...	0709 0719 0731	...	0802	...	0828	...
Agde ....d.	...			0513 0551	...	0652 0709 0716	...	0723 0733 0749	...	0815	...	0841	...
Sète ....d.	...	0343	0528 0606	...	...	0717 0727 0730	...	0741 0751 0813	...	0833	...	0858	0903 0903
Montpellier ....a.	...	0400	0547 0624	...	...	0719 0736 0733	...	0743 0753	...	...	0839	0900	0906 0906
Montpellier ....d.	...	0408	0550	0632	...	0750 0813 0758	...	0822 0826	...	...	0907	0930	0935 0935
Nîmes ....a.	...	0437	0620	0658	...	0752 0832 0800	...	0832 0832	...	...	0909	...	0939 1000
Nîmes ....d.	...	0443 0449	0622	0700 0704	...	0806 0848	...	0848 0848	...	...	...	...	1017
Tarascon ....d.	...	0502 0505	0638		0730	0816	...		...	...	...	...	1109q
Arles ....d.	...		0648	...	...	0900	...		...	...	...	...	...
Marseille St. Charles......a.	...	0600	0740	...	...		...		...	...	...	...	...
Nice 164 ....a.	...	0900		...	...	0901 0826	...	0901 0901	...	0934	...	...	...
Avignon ....a.	...	...	0518	0724 0745	...		...		...	...	...	1210j	...
Lyon Part Dieu 151 ....a.	...	...	...	0911	...	...	...	...	...	...	...	...	...
Genève 165 ....a.	...	...	...	...	...	...	...	...	...	...	...	...	...
Dijon 149 ....a.	...	...	...	...	...	...	...	...	...	...	...	...	...
Strasbourg 156 ....a.	...	...	...	...	...	...	...	...	...	...	...	...	...
Metz 170 ....a.	...	...	...	...	...	...	...	...	...	...	...	...	...
Charles de Gaulle ✈ 160 ..a.	...	...	...	1126	...	...	...	...	...	...	...	...	...
Lille Europe 160 ....a.	...	...	...	1216	...	...	...	...	...	...	...	...	...
Paris Austerlitz 138 ....a.	...	...	...	...	...	1151	...	...	...	...	...	...	...
Paris Lyon 151 ....a.	...	...	...	...	...	...	...	...	...	1255	...	...	...

			5510 J ✗	5510 K	6450 6451 K	6450 6451 J	856 TGV ♟	470 ♟	58127 ♟	576/7 TGV ✗	72 ♦⚡ ✗	860/1 TGV ♟	6464 6465 ♟	862 TGV E ♟	862 TGV F ♟	6466 6467 ♟	162 163 ♦⚡ ✗
Cerbère ....d.	...	...	0825	0825	...	...	1027	...	...	1126	...	...	...	...	...	...
Banyuls sur Mer..................d.	...	...	0834	0834	...	...	1035	...	...	...	...	...	...	...	...	...
Port Vendres.....................d.	...	...	0842	0842	...	...	1042	...	...	...	...	...	...	...	...	...
Collioure ....d.	...	...	0847	0847	...	...	1046	...	...	...	...	...	...	...	...	...
Argelès sur Mer ....d.	...	...	0854	0854	...	...	1052	...	...	...	...	...	...	...	...	...
Perpignan ....a.	...	...	0913	0913	...	...	1110	...	...	1151	...	...	...	...	...	...
Perpignan ....d.	...	...	0916	0916	...	...	1112	...	...	1153	...	...	...	...	1102	...
Nantes 134 ....d.	...	...	...	...	2322b	2322b	...	...	...	...	...	...	...	...	...	...
Bordeaux 139 ....d.	...	...	...	...	0639	0639	...	...	...	...	0632	...	...	...	...	...
Hendaye 139 ....d.	...	...	...	...	...	...	...	...	...	...	...	...	...	...	...	...
Toulouse 139 ....d.	...	...	...	...	0902	0902	...	...	...	1225	1129	1247	⟋	1319	1306	...
Narbonne ....a.	...	1000	1000	...	1018	1018	1150	...	...	1204 1211c	1250	1321	...	...	...	...
Narbonne ....d.	...	1003	1003	...	1020	1020	...	...	...	1226c	1227	1306	1338	...	...	...
Béziers ....d.	0922	1019	1019	...	1036	1036	...	...	...	1239c	...	...	...	...	...	...
Agde ....d.	0934	1033	1033	...	...	...	...	...	...	1253c	...	1330	...	1401	...	...
Sète ....d.	0946	1048	1048	...	1059	1059	...	...	...	1311c	1315	1345	...	1416	1456	...
Montpellier ....a.	1003	1105	1105	...	1113	1113	...	...	...	1312c	...	1349 1354	1404	1420	1458	...
Montpellier ....d.	...	1107	1123	...	1117	1116	1230	...	1330	...	1415 1419	1429	1446	...	...	...
Nîmes ....a.	...	1145	1155	...	1145	1150	1257	1340	...	1357	1425 1421	1431	1449	...	...	...
Nîmes ....d.	...	1158	1158	...	1148	1155	1259	1341	...	1359	...	...	...	...	...	...
Tarascon ....d.	...	1215	1215	...	1203	1212	...	1356	...	...	1449	...	...	...	...	...
Arles ....d.	...	...	...	...	1211	1221	...	...	...	...	1533	...	...	1620	...	...
Marseille St. Charles......a.	...	...	...	...	1259	1312	...	...	...	...	1830	...	...	1900	...	...
Nice 164 ....a.	...	...	...	...	...	...	1409	1422	...	1423	...	1445 1456	1514	...	...	...
Avignon ....a.	...	1228	1228	...	...	...	...	...	...	1603	...	...	...	1735	...	...
Lyon Part Dieu 151 ....a.	...	1451	1451	...	...	...	...	...	...	1745	...	...	...	...	...	...
Genève 165 ....a.	...			...	...	...	...	...	...	...	...	...	...	...	...	...
Dijon 149 ....a.	...	1636	1636	...	...	...	...	...	...	...	...	...	...	...	...	...
Strasbourg 156 ....a.	...	...	...	...	...	...	...	...	...	...	...	...	...	...	...	...
Metz 170 ....a.	...	...	...	...	...	...	...	...	...	...	...	...	...	...	...	...
Charles de Gaulle ✈ 160 ..a.	...	...	...	...	...	...	...	1757	...	...	...	...	...	...	...	...
Lille Europe 160 ....a.	...	...	...	...	...	...	...	1848	...	...	...	...	...	...	...	...
Paris Austerlitz 138 ....a.	...	...	...	...	...	...	...	2014x	...	...	...	...	1814 1818	...	...	...
Paris Lyon 151 ....a.	...	...	...	...	...	...	1649	...	...	...	...	...	...	...	...	...

♦ — **NOTES** (LISTED BY TRAIN NUMBER)

72 – CATALAN TALGO – 🛏 and ✗ Barcelona - Montpellier.

162/3 – LE GRAND SUD – 🍴 and ✗ Bordeaux - Nice.

342/3 – 🛏 1,2 cl., 🛏 1,2 cl. and 🍴 Nantes - Bordeaux - Nice - Ventimiglia.; 🛏 1,2 cl. Bordeaux - Nice - Ventimiglia; 🍴 and 🛏 2 cl. Bordeaux - Milano.

E – ②③④ (also Oct. 30, Apr. 16,30, May 7,26; not Nov. 1,2,10, Apr. 18, May 2,9,24,25.

F – Daily except dates in note E.

J – ⒶOct. 10 - May 12 (daily Dec. 3 - Apr. 7); not Nov. 25.

K – Daily except dates in note J.

P – ⒶApr. 10 - May 12.

Q – ⒶNov. 21 - Apr. 7.

R – ⒶSept. 25 - Nov. 18 and May 15 - 27.

TGV – Ⓡ, supplement payable.

b – Depart 2341 on ⑤ and dates in Table 134.

c – Runs 5 minutes earlier on ⒶApr. 10 - May 12.

j – Arrive 1223 on ⒶApr. 10 - May 12.

q – Arrive 1126 on ⒶJan. 3 - Feb. 24.

x – Arrive 2019 Nov. 14 - Dec. 22. On ⑥ arrive 2022 (2032 Nov. 19 - Dec. 17).

⚡ – Supplement payable.

Table 163 — CERBÈRE - NARBONNE - AVIGNON and MARSEILLE

1,2 class

	58128	866 TGV	582/3 TGV	6452 6453 TGV	872	6452 6453	58130	5956 5957	58132	874 TGV	Ⓐ	5500	878 TGV	878 TGV	Ⓐ	6698 6699	5504	6434 6435
	M	Ⓑh		N	Ⓑh	Ⓐ		♦		Ⓐ			Ⓐ	Ⓐ ⑦e	Ⓐ	⑦v	5f	♦
Cerbère d.	1322										1600					1633		
Banyuls sur Mer d.	1328										1607					1642		
Port Vendres d.	1333										1612					1650		
Collioure d.	1337										1616					1655		
Argelès sur Mer d.	1342										1622					1702		
Perpignan a.	1357										1640					1721		
Perpignan d.	1400									1602		1647		1715		1726	1727	
Nantes 134 d.																		
Bordeaux 139 d.				1147		1155												1023
Hendaye 139 d.																		1447
Toulouse 139 d.					1412	1421												1713
Narbonne a.	1442				1529	1537				1644		1721		1758		1816	1816	1831
Narbonne d.	1443				1537	1545		1605		1647		1723		1801		1820	1820	1833
Béziers d.	1457				1554	1601		1620		1707		1739		1825		1836	1836	1850
Agde d.	1509				1609	1616		1633		1721		1754		1838		1851	1851	1914
Sète d.	1521				1625	1631		1647		1736		1809		1854		1907	1907	
Montpellier a.	1538				1640	1646		1705		1757		1824		1910		1922	1922	1929
Montpellier d.	1600	1548	1556	1648	1657	1659	1702	1709	1732	1759		1827	1849	1858		1938	1938	1931
Nîmes a.	1626		1621		1714	1719	1725	1733	1751			1859	1914	1923		2010	2010	1957
Nîmes d.	1628		1623		1717	1721	1730	1735	1758	1801		1901	1916	1925		2012	2012	1959
Tarascon d.	1642						1800	1815	1822			1919				2028	2028	
Arles d.					1740		1753		1824									2022
Marseille St. Charles a.					1827		1842		1910									2107
Nice 164 a.					2128		2133											
Avignon a.	1654	1637	1647		1747		1813		1834	1820		1932	1941	1950		2041	2041	
Lyon Part Dieu 151 a.			1833									2140y				2250p	2250p	
Genève 165 a.																		
Dijon 149 a.																		
Strasbourg 156 a.																0520		
Metz 170 a.																		
Charles de Gaulle + 160 a.			2049															
Lille Europe 160 a.			2212															
Paris Austerlitz 138 a.																		
Paris Lyon 151 a.		2006			2115				2150n			2316	2323					

	Ⓑ	Ⓑ	6455 6454 ⑦e	6710 6711	5546 5520 ⑦e	5520	6694 D	1116 Q	6646 6647 ⑦e P	6646 6647 5f	472	6456 6457 Ⓑt	6456 6457 G	6456 6457 H	6478 375/6	375 376	6484 6485 W	6478 364/5	364 365	6432 6433 ⑦e	6425
Cerbère d.	1733		1840		1855		1936		2030		2035				2305				2355		
Banyuls sur Mer d.	1740		1847		1903		1945				2043										
Port Vendres d.	1745		1852		1910		1952				2050				2320				0008		
Collioure d.	1748		1856		1914		1957														
Argelès sur Mer d.	1754		1901		1921		2005		2053		2057										
Perpignan a.	1809		1918		1935		2024		2113		2116				2353				0030		
Perpignan d.	1811		1920	1935	1939		2027		2117		2125				2357				0035		
Nantes 134 d.																				1707	1940
Bordeaux 139 d.				1635								1833	1833	1833	1810		1850	1810r		2156	2344
Hendaye 139 d.																					
Toulouse 139 d.				1856								2104	2104	2104	2259		2347	2259r		0034	
Narbonne a.	1855		2007	2013	2019	2011		2114	2151		2201	2227	2227	2227	0020	0036	0108	0118		0209	
Narbonne d.	1857		2017	2021	2028			2208			2217	2234	2234	2234	0100	0100	0116	0151	0151	0214	
Béziers d.	1911		2037					2208			2224	2248	2250	2250	0117	0117	0132	0211	0211	0237	
Agde d.	1924			2050	2058		2140	2140			2239		2305	2305							
Sète d.	1937				2105		2116	2156	2156		2255		2320	2320	0142	0142	0200				
Montpellier a.	1955			2112	2120		2131	2131			2310	2335	2335	2335	0157	0157	0216	0253	0253	0307	
Montpellier d.		2005		2112	2115	2125	2134	2217	2217		2310	2337	2337		0202	0202	0219	0257	0257	0326	
Nîmes a.		2035		2141			2153	2202	2252		2313				0228	0228	0250	0325	0325	0402	
Nîmes d.					2153	2202	2252	2252			2341	2341		0011	0009	0232	0232	0253	0329	0329	0408
Tarascon d.							2308	2308			2343	2343						0253			0429
Arles d.			2217														0355	0355			
Marseille St. Charles a.			2259														0450	0450		0524	0538
Nice 164 a.																	0742	0742			0837
Avignon a.				2229	2321	2321		0111	0111				0038	0300	0300	0325					
Lyon Part Dieu 151 a.				0204p	0230p		0239p	0239p					0600	0600							
Genève 165 a.					0400	0416		0425	0425					0820	0820						
Dijon 149 a.						0846															
Strasbourg 156 a.																					
Metz 170 a.								0816	0816												
Charles de Gaulle + 160 a.																					
Lille Europe 160 a.																					
Paris Austerlitz 138 a.							0730		0733z												
Paris Lyon 151 a.					0658																

♦ — NOTES (LISTED BY TRAIN NUMBER)

364/5 — [couchette] and [sleeper] 1,2 cl. Cerbère - Nice - Ventimiglia; [couchette] and ➝ 2 cl. Cerbère - Ventimiglia - Roma.
375/6 — HISPANIA – [couchette] and ➝ 1,2 cl. Cerbère - Genève.
472 — CÔTE VERMEILLE-PARIS – [car] 1,2 cl. (T2), ➝ 1,2 cl. and [couchette] Cerbère - Paris Austerlitz.
1116 — Nov. 1,6, Dec. 25, Jan. 1,3, Apr. 17, May 1,8 only: [couchette] and ➝ 2 cl. Cerbère - Paris Austerlitz.
5520 — [sleeper] 1,2 cl. Barcelona - Paris (also [car] 1,2 cl. (T2) on ⑤⑦ and Apr. 17, May 1,8,24; not Apr. 16,30, May 7,26).
5956/7 — LE CÉVENOL – [couchette] and Y (Paris) - Clermont Ferrand - Nîmes - Marseille.
6425 — ⑤⑦ (also Nov. 1,10, Apr. 17, May 1,8,24; not Oct. 30, Nov. 11, Apr. 16,30, May 7,26): [car] 1,2 cl. (T2), [couchette] and ➝ 1,2 cl. Nantes - Nice.
6432/3 — [couchette] and ➝ 2 cl. Nantes - Les Arcs.
6434/5 — [couchette] and Y Quimper - Nantes - Bordeaux - Marseille.
6484/5 — ⑤⑦ (also Apr. 17, May 1,8,24; not Apr. 16,30, May 7,26): [sleeper] 1,2 cl., ➝ 1,2 cl. and [couchette] Hendaye - Nice - Ventimiglia; [couchette] Hendaye - Roma; [couchette], ➝ 1,2 cl. and Y Hendaye - Grenoble - Annecy.
6710/1 — ROUSSILLON FLANDRES, runs ⑥ Apr. 1 - May 27: [car] 1,2 cl. (T2) and ➝ 2 cl. Cerbère - Calais auto/train; ➝ 1,2 cl. Cerbère - Lille - Tourcoing.

D – ①-⑥ (also Apr. 16,30, May 7; not Apr. 7, May 1,8): ➝ 2 cl. and [couchette] Béziers - Strasbourg.
G – ⑤⑦ (also Nov. 1,10, Apr. 17, May 1,8,24; not Oct. 30, Nov. 11, Apr. 16,30, May 7,26).
H – [couchette] and ➝ 1,2 cl. Hendaye - Genève.
M – Daily except dates in note N.
N – Ⓐ Mar. 27 - May 4.
P – [couchette] and ➝ 1,2 cl. Montpellier - Metz.
Q – [couchette] and ➝ 1,2 cl. Cerbère - Metz; ➝ 1,2 cl. Cerbère - Reims.
TGV – [R], supplement payable.
W – [car] 1,2 cl. and [couchette] Hendaye - Nice - Ventimiglia; [couchette] Hendaye - Ventimiglia - Roma.
e – Also Apr. 17, May 1,8; not Apr. 16,30, May 7.
f – Also Nov. 10, May 24; not Apr. 17, Nov. 11, May 26.
h – Not Oct. 31, Nov. 11, May 25.
n – Arrive 2154 on ⑤⑦.
p – Lyon Perrache.
r – On ⑤⑦ (also Apr. 17, May 1,8,24; not Apr. 16,30, May 7,26) Hendaye depart 1850, Toulouse depart 2347, Narbonne arrive 0108 in train 6484/5.
t – Not Ap[r. 16,30, May 7,25,26.
v – Also Jan. 2, Apr. 18, May 1,8; not Dec. 25, Jan. 1, Apr. 16,30, May 7.
y – Arrive 2150 on ⑤⑦ (also Apr. 17, May 1,8,24; not Apr. 16,30, May 7,26).
z – Arrive 0745 Nov. 15 - Dec. 22.

Table 164 — MARSEILLE - NICE - VENTIMIGLIA

1,2 class

Table (part 1)

km	364 365 ◆	6478 364/5 C	5065 ⑦e	183	◆	5059 ①-⑥	6138 6139 ⑤f	6433 6432 ⑦e	6425 ◆	◆	343 342 ◆Ⓡ	5696 5697 ◆	◆	6197 6196 ✕	6136 6137	◆	189 ◆	◆	6208 6209 ◆	6220 6221 ◆
Paris Lyon 151 d.			2029	2143		2117											2236			
Lille Europe 160 d.															2048				2009b	2009b
Metz 170 d.								2110							2024					
Strasbourg 156 d.														2024			0047	0050		
Dijon 149 d.			2324																	
Genève 165 d.												2312n								
Lyon Part-Dieu 151 d.																				
Lyon Perrache 151 d.			0109					1707	1940		1813				0245	0250			0349	0332
Nantes 134 d.								2156	2344		2244									
Bordeaux 139 d.																				
Hendaye 139 d.		1810r							0032		0126									
Toulouse 139 d.		2259r																		
Cerbère 163 d.		2355																		
Narbonne 163 d.		0151	0151								0258									
Montpellier 163 d.		0257	0257								0408									
0 Marseille St. Charles d.		0502	0502	0506		0534	0538	0543	0552		0615	0620		0634	0639		0644	0721	0728	0731
37 La Ciotat d.													0647		0659			0714	0726	0753
51 Bandol d.																				
67 Toulon d.			0553	0553	0557	0614	0620	0625	0631	0638	0649	0700	0706	0711	0718	0724	0740	0806	0811	0815
Hyères a.											0710									
135 Les Arcs d.				0633		0700	0704	0710	0717			0752		0758	0803		0844			
161 St. Raphaël d.		0644	0644		0704		0718	0722	0740	0725	0805	0813		0818	0824		0901	0906	0911	
194 Cannes d.	0522	0612	0640	0657	0709	0709	0728	0737	0744	0750	0810	0801	0833	0839	0844	0851	0911	0927	0934	0940
203 Juan les Pins d.	0533	0623	0650	0708			0746		0800		0811		0849				0922		0944	0950
205 Antibes d.	0536	0626	0653	0712	0724	0724		0740	0749	0758	0805	0821	0814	0845	0854		0857	0906	0925	0938	0950	0955
216 Cagnes sur Mer d.	0546	0638	0704	0723					0800	0808	0830			0906			0936			
225 Nice Ville a.	0600	0652	0717	0738	0742	0742	0756	0813	0818	0822	0837	0843	0900	0911	0916	0920	0950	0955	1005	1011
225 Nice Ville d.	0605	0655	0722	0741	0811	0811	0800		0835		0847	0910			0928		0952		1015	
230 Villefranche sur Mer d.	0612	0702	0730	0748							0854				0936		0959			
232 Beaulieu sur Mer d.	0615	0706	0734	0752		0808			0843		0858	0920			0936		1002		1024	
241 Monaco-Monte Carlo d.	0628	0719	0747	0804	0830	0830		0818	0852		0912	0933			0946		1014		1135	
245 Cap Martin-Roquebrune d.	0633	0725	0752	0809							0918						1019			
248 Menton d.	0640	0725	0759	0816	0842	0842		0830	0901		0926	0946			0957		1026		1047	
258 Ventimiglia a.	0653	0745	0812	0828	0853	0853		0840			0940	1000			1007		1038		1059	

Table (part 2)

	59253 J	59253 K					5357 J	5357 L	5359 M	807 TGV © Ⓡ	807 TGV © Ⓡ	5001 J	5001 K		①-⑤			J
Paris Lyon 151 d.										0822	0822							
Lille Europe 160 d.																		
Metz 170 d.																		
Strasbourg 156 d.																		
Dijon 149 d.												0809	0809					
Genève 165 d.												0956	0956					
Lyon Perrache 151 d.							0834	0834	0834									
Marseille St. Charles d.	0734	0930		0940	0945	1100	1212	1212	1230	1215	1242	1247	1317	1317			1442	
La Ciotat d.		0806			1015	1136				1249							1512	
Bandol d.		0819			1028	1149				1301							1524	
Toulon d.	0827	0833	1012		1022	1043	1203	1253	1253	1311	1315	1323	1328	1400	1400		1539	
Hyères a.	0847																	
Les Arcs d.			1049	1100				1330	1330	1347				1437	1437			
St. Raphaël d.			1106	1125				1346	1352	1404				1455	1455			
Cannes d.	1008		1133	1138	1157		1214	1255	1327	1413	1422	1435		1523	1530	1534	1556	1604	1629	1656
Juan les Pins d.	1018				1149		1225	1307	1337							1543		1614	1640	1657
Antibes d.	1022		1143	1153	1207		1229	1311	1340	1422	1432	1442		1534	1541	1547	1605	1617	1643	1701
Cagnes sur Mer a.	1033		1151	1205	1216		1241	1324	1353							1559	1615	1628	1656	1711
Nice Ville a.	1047		1200	1219		1255	1340	1406	1436	1445	1458		1547	1555	1612	1624	1641	1711	1726
Nice Ville d.		1049	1150	1222		1300	1343	1409					1616	1628	1643	1715		
Villefranche sur Mer d.		1056	1157	1230		1307	1350	1416					1623		1650	1722		
Beaulieu sur Mer d.		1100	1201	1234		1311	1353	1420					1627	1633	1653	1726		
Monaco-Monte Carlo d.		1112	1213	1247		1324	1406	1432					1638	1646	1705	1739		
Cap Martin-Roquebrune d.		1117	1218	1252		1331	1411	1437					1643		1710	1745		
Menton d.		1123	1225	1258		1337	1417	1444					1650	1655	1716	1752		
Ventimiglia a.		1135	1237	1311		1351	1430	1456					1702		1728	1805		

Notes

◆ — NOTES (LISTED BY TRAIN NUMBER)

183 — LE TRAIN BLEU – 🛏1,2 cl., 🛏1,2 cl. (T2) and ⊐1,2 cl. Paris - Ventimiglia.

189 — LE PHOCÉEN – 🛏1,2 cl., 🛏1,2 cl. and ⊐1,2 cl. Paris - Toulon (- Nice on ④⑥), also Oct. 31, Nov. 9, Apr. 16, 30, May 7, 23; not Oct. 29, Nov. 10, Apr. 15, 29, May 6, 25).

342/3 — 🛏1,2 cl., ⊐1,2 cl. and ⊏⊐ Nantes - Bordeaux - Nice - Ventimiglia.; 🛏1,2 cl. Bordeaux - Nice - Ventimiglia; ⊏⊐ and ⊐ 2 cl. Bordeaux - Milano.

364/5 — ⊏⊐ and ⊐1,2 cl. Cerbère - Nice - Ventimiglia; ⊏⊐ and ⊐ 2 cl. Cerbère - Ventimiglia - Roma.

5059 — ⊐ 2 cl., and ♀ Paris - Nice.

5065 — ⊐ 2 cl. and ⊏⊐ Paris - Les Arcs.

5696/7 — ⊏⊐ and ⊐1,2 cl. St Gervais - Nice; ⊏⊐ and ⊐1,2 cl. Genève - Nice. Also conveys on ①③⑤ and Sep. 25, Apr. 13 (not Nov. 11, Apr. 17, May 1, 8) ⊐1,2 cl. (T2) Genève - Nice.

6136/7 — ⊏⊐ and ⊐1,2 cl. Metz - Nice (also 🛏1,2 cl. (T2), replaced by ⊏⊐ on ⑤ and Nov. 11, May 26, not Nov. 10, May 24); ⊏⊐ and ⊐1,2 cl. Reims - Nice and v.v.

6196/7 — ⊏⊐1,2 cl. (T2), ⊐1,2 cl. and ⊏⊐ Strasbourg - Nice (- Ventimiglia Sept. 25 - Oct. 30 and Mar. 31 - May 27). Conveys Sept. 25 - Oct. 30 and Mar. 31 - May 27 ⊏⊐ and ⊐ 2 cl. Frankfurt - Strasbourg - Nice - Ventimiglia.

6208/9 — FLANDRES RIVIERA – (Train 6207/6 when train 6220/1 runs). 🛏1,2 cl. (T2), ⊐1,2 cl. and ⊏⊐ Tourcoing - Lille - Nice - Ventimiglia (except when train 6220/1 runs); ⊏⊐1,2 cl. (T2) and ⊐ 2 cl. Brussels - Nice - Ventimiglia; daily Sept. 25 - Jan. 21 and Apr. 3 - May 27, ①③⑤⑥ Jan. 23 - Apr. 1, also ④⑦ Feb. 23 - Mar. 12 🛏1,2 cl. (T2) and ⊐ 2 cl. Calais - Nice - Ventimiglia.

6220/1 — FLANDRES RIVIERA – Runs Sept. 30, Oct. 7,14, 21, 25-31, Nov. 1-6, Dec. 20 - Jan. 3, Feb. 23-26, Mar. 2-5, 9-11, Apr. 13-16, 20-23, 27-30, May 5-7, 12, 13, 19, 20, 24-27; 🛏1,2 cl. (T2), ⊐1,2 cl. and ⊏⊐ Tourcoing - Lille - Nice.

6425 — ⑤⑦ (also Nov. 1, 10, Apr. 17, May 1, 8, 24; not Oct. 30, Nov. 11, Apr. 16, 30, May 7, 26). ⊐1,2 cl. Nantes - Nice.

6432/3 — ⊏⊐ and ⊐ 2 cl. Nantes - Les Arcs.

C — ⊏⊐1,2 cl., ⊐1,2 cl. and ⊏⊐ Hendaye - Nice - Ventimiglia; ⊏⊐ Hendaye - Ventimiglia - Roma.

J — © to Mar. 5 (not Dec. 3, 17, Jan. 28); daily from Mar. 6.

K — Ⓐ to Mar. 3 (also Dec. 3, 17, Jan. 28).

L — Ⓐ to Feb. 10 (also Dec. 3, 17, Jan. 28).

M — Ⓐ Feb. 13 - Mar. 3.

TGV — Ⓡ, supplement payable.

b — Lille Flandres.

e — Also Nov. 1, Apr. 17, May 1, 8; not Oct. 30, Apr. 16, 30, May 7.

f — Also Nov. 10, May 24; not Nov. 11, May 26.

n — Depart 2225 on Mar. 27-30, Apr. 3-6, 10-13, 18-20.

r — On ⑤⑦ (also Apr. 17, May 1,8,24; not Apr. 16,30, May 7,26) depart Hendaye 1850 Toulouse 2347 in train 6484/5.

Table 164 — MARSEILLE - NICE - VENTIMIGLIA

1,2 class

	5680/5681 K ◆	5680/5681 J ◆	845 TGV K ✕	845 TGV J ✕	811 TGV K 🍴	6464/6465 🍴	6130/6131 J 🍴	6130/6131 K 🍴	162/163 J ✕	348/349 K	Ⓐ	Ⓐ	Ⓐ	534/5 TGV ⑥t 🍴
Paris Lyon 151 …d.			1107	1107	1112									
Lille Europe 160 …d.														1217
Metz 170 …d.							0734	0734						
Strasbourg 156 …d.														
Dijon 149 …d.							1053	1053						
Genève 165 …d.	0930	0930												
Lyon Part-Dieu 151 …d.							1239	1239						
Lyon Perrache 151 …d.														
Nantes 134 …d.														
Bordeaux 139 …d.									1102					
Hendaye 139 …d.						0632								
Toulouse 139 …d.						1129			1306					
Cerbère 163 …d.						1250								
Narbonne 163 …d.						1349			1458					
Montpellier 163 …d.														
Marseille St. Charles …d.	1504	1504		1527	1530	1552	1615	1615	1618	1636	1645	1700	1712	1740
La Ciotat …d.					1558				1647	1659	1720	1730	1737	
Bandol …d.					1610					1659	1733	1742	1750	
Toulon …d.	1548	1548		1607	1626	1638	1657	1657	1714	1720	1730	1750	1758	1821
Hyères …a.					1645							1812	1904	
Les Arcs …d.							1734	1733				1833		
St. Raphaël …d.		1638	1643	1643		1710	1751	1750	1811			1820		1909
Cannes …d.	1652	1705	1713	1705s	1715s	1722	1816	1824	1835	1827		1857	1916	1935
Juan les Pins …d.	1702					1733				1837		1907	1926	
Antibes …d.	1706	1715	1723	1717s	1726s	1736	1828	1834	1846	1847b		1910	1929	1946
Cagnes sur Mer …d.	1717					1749				1859		1922	1942	
Nice Ville …a.	1731	1731	1735	1737	1741	1803	1843	1848	1900	1913		1936	1955	2000
Nice Ville …d.				1745	1750	1810	1829			1911	1915	1938		
Villefranche sur Mer …d.				1752	1757	1817	1837			1922		1946		
Beaulieu sur Mer …d.				1756	1801	1821	1841			1926		1950		
Monaco-Monte Carlo …d.				1809	1813	1832	1857			1927	1939	2003		
Cap Martin-Roquebrune …d.				1815	1820	1838	1903				1943	2008		
Menton …d.				1822	1826	1844	1910			1937	1950	2014		
Ventimiglia …a.				1836	1840	1857	1926			1950	2003	2027		

	534/5 TGV 🍴	6173/6172 Ⓐ 🍴	847 TGV 🍴	367 ◆	823 TGV Ⓑ 🍴	6453/6452 M 🍴	6453/6452 M 🍴	N 🍴	N	827 TGV ⑤f 🍴	5634/5635 ◆ 🍴	6132/6133	835 TGV ◆	6134/6135 ⑤f 🍴	59259 A	5515/5015 ⑦e 🍴
Paris Lyon 151 …d.			1356		1427					1534			1745			
Lille Europe 160 …d.	1217															
Metz 170 …d.												1223		1345		
Strasbourg 156 …d.		0800														
Dijon 149 …d.												1535	1706			1910
Genève 165 …d.																
Lyon Part-Dieu 151 …d.		1411										1713	1851			2101
Nantes 134 …d.																
Bordeaux 139 …d.						1147	1155									
Hendaye 139 …d.																
Toulouse 139 …d.						1412	1421									
Cerbère 163 …d.																
Narbonne 163 …d.						1537	1545									
Montpellier 163 …d.						1648	1659									
Marseille St. Charles …d.	1736	1743	1753		1815	1843	1847	1850	1854	1900	1952	2002 2021	2025	2205 2208	2208 2211	2332 0101
La Ciotat …d.		1807	1828		1849	1925	1934					2056			2242 0002	0132
Bandol …d.		1819	1839		1901	1937	1946					2109			2254 0014	0143
Toulon …d.	1832	1850	1900		1915	1924	1932	1951	1938	2000	2044	2103 2124	2247	2254 2254	2310 0030	0155
Hyères …a.			1920													
Les Arcs …d.		1910				2011	2017			2121				2330	2330	
St. Raphaël …d.		1927	1934	1940		2032	2038			2138	2153			2348	2348	
Cannes …d.		1952	1957s	2017		2058	2103			2203	2218	2224		0012	0012	
Juan les Pins …d.				2027								2234				
Antibes …d.		2002	2009s	2030		2109	2114			2216	2231	2237		0023	0023	
Cagnes sur Mer …d.				2042		2118	2123					2250				
Nice Ville …a.		2019	2026	2056		2128	2133			2230	2245	2303		0038	0038	
Nice Ville …d.				2036								2138	2312		0045	
Villefranche sur Mer …d.				2044								2145	2321		0052	
Beaulieu sur Mer …d.												2148	2325		0056	
Monaco-Monte Carlo …d.				2054								2200	2342		0108	
Cap Martin-Roquebrune …d.												2205	2350		0113	
Menton …d.				2104								2211	2358		0120	
Ventimiglia …a.				2115								2223	0015		0132	

◆ – NOTES (LISTED BY TRAIN NUMBER)

162/3 – LE GRAND SUD – 🛏 and ✕ Bordeaux - Nice.

348/9 – 🛏 Nice - Milano.

359 – 🛏 1,2 cl., ◄ 1,2 cl. and 🛏 Nice - Venezia.

367 – 🛏 1,2 cl., ◄ 2 cl. and 🛏 Nice - Roma.

5634/5 – 🛏 Annecy - Nice.

5680/1 – 🛏 Genève - Nice; 🛏 St. Gervais - Nice.

A – Daily except ⑤ (also Nov. 11, May 26; not Nov. 10, May 24).

J – ⓒ to Mar. 5 (not Dec. 3,17, Jan. 21); daily from Mar. 6.

K – Ⓐ to Mar. 3 (also Dec. 3,17, Jan. 28).

M – Daily except dates in note N.

N – Ⓐ Mar. 27 - May 4.

TGV – 🅁, supplement payable.

b – Arrive 1840.

e – Also Nov. 1; not Oct. 30.

f – Also Nov. 10, May 24; not Nov. 11, May 26.

s – Stops to set down only.

t – Also Nov. 11; not Nov. 12.

Table 164 VENTIMIGLIA - NICE - MARSEILLE

1,2 class

	⚒		①-⑥	Ⓐ	J		6964 6965 K 🍷	K		6964 6965 J 🍷		⚒ b	812 TGV 🍷	6634 6635 F	6634 6635 E		①-⑥	①-⑤		6676 6677 🍷	358 ♦ Ⓡ			5682 5683 ♦
Ventimiglia d.	...	...	...	...	0500	...	...	0510	...	...	...	0530	...	...	...	0615	0647	0707	0712	...	0740	...	0808	...
Menton d.	...	...	...	...	0511	...	...	0521	...	...	...	0542	...	...	...	0627	0659	0719	0724	...	0754	...	0820	...
Cap Martin-Roquebrune d.	...	...	...	...	0517	...	...	0527	...	...	...	0547	...	...	...	0632	0705	|	0729	...	|	...	0826	...
Monaco-Monte Carlo d.	...	...	...	...	0523	...	...	0533	...	...	...	0553	...	...	...	0639	0712	0730	0736	...	0806	...	0833	...
Beaulieu sur Mer d.	...	...	...	...	0534	...	...	0544	...	...	...	0604	...	...	...	0650	0724	0741	0748	...	0817	...	0845	...
Villefranche sur Mer d.	...	...	...	...	0537	...	...	0547	...	...	...	0608	...	...	...	0654	0728	|	0752	...	|	...	0848	...
Nice Ville a.	...	...	...	...	0543	...	...	0553	...	...	...	0614	...	...	...	0700	0735	0750	0758	...	0825	...	0855	...
Nice Ville d.	...	...	0505	...	0545	...	0550	0555	...	0600	...	0616	...	0634	0644	0702	0737	0754	0800	0820	▬	0845	...	0905
Cagnes sur Mer d.	...	...	0520	...	0558	...	0600	0608	...	0610	...	0630	...	|	|	0717	0752	0803	0815	|	...	0854	...	|
Antibes d.	...	...	0531	...	0608	...	0608	0618	...	0619	...	0640	...	0649	0659	0728	0803	0813	0825	0835	...	0904	...	0920
Juan les Pins d.	...	...	0534	...	0611	...	|	0621	...	|	...	0643	...	|	|	0732	0806	|	0828	|	...	|	...	|
Cannes d.	...	...	0544	...	0620	...	0618	0630	...	0630	...	0652	...	0700	0711	0741	0816	0821	0838	0846	...	0916	...	0931
St. Raphaël d.	...	...	...	...	...	...	0644	...	...	0653	...	▬	...	0728	0740	...	...	...	...	0914	...	0951	...	0958
Les Arcs d.	...	...	...	...	...	...	0700	...	...	0709	...	...	...	|	|	...	...	...	...	0931	...	...	...	|
Hyères d.	...	...	...	0628	...	...	|	...	0720	|	...	...	...	|	|	...	...	...	...	|	0921	...	...	|
Toulon d.	0510	0625	...	0650	...	0725	0736	...	0739	0746	...	0749	0814	0820	0831	...	...	...	...	1008	1017	...	...	1051
Bandol d.	0525	0641	...	0703	...	0740	0748	...	...	0757	...	0803	|	|	|	...	...	...	...	1021	1032	...	...	|
La Ciotat d.	0537	0655	...	0713	...	0752	0758	...	...	0808	...	0814	|	|	|	...	...	...	...	1033	1044	...	...	|
Marseille St. Charles a.	0605	0730	...	0742	...	0821	0825	...	...	0835	...	0847	0856	0859	0909	...	...	...	...	1056	1115	...	...	1132
Montpellier **163** a.	...	...	...	...	...	...	1054	...	...	1054	...	...	|	|	|	...	...	...	...	|	...	...	...	|
Narbonne **163** a.	...	...	...	...	...	...	1154	...	...	1154	...	...	|	|	|	...	...	...	...	|	...	...	...	|
Port Bou **163** a.	...	...	...	...	...	...	|	...	...	|	...	...	|	|	|	...	...	...	...	|	...	...	...	|
Toulouse **139** a.	...	...	...	...	...	...	1315	...	...	1315	...	...	|	|	|	...	...	...	...	|	...	...	...	|
Irún **139** a.	...	...	...	...	...	...	1846	...	...	1846	...	...	|	|	|	...	...	...	...	|	...	...	...	|
Bordeaux **139** a.	...	...	...	...	...	...	...	...	...	...	...	...	|	|	|	...	...	...	...	|	...	...	...	|
Nantes **134** a.	...	...	...	...	...	...	...	...	...	...	...	...	|	|	|	...	...	...	...	|	...	...	...	|
Lyon Perrache **151** a.	...	...	...	...	...	...	...	...	...	...	...	...	|	|	|	...	...	...	...	|	...	...	...	|
Lyon Part-Dieu **151** a.	...	...	...	...	...	...	...	...	...	...	...	...	|	1223	1238	...	...	...	...	1438	...	...	...	|
Genève **165** a.	...	...	...	...	...	...	...	...	...	...	...	...	|	|	|	...	...	...	...	|	...	...	...	1715
Dijon **149** a.	...	...	...	...	...	...	...	...	...	...	...	...	|	1405	1418	...	...	...	...	|	...	...	...	...
Strasbourg **156** a.	...	...	...	...	...	...	...	...	...	...	...	...	|	|	|	...	...	...	...	2045	...	...	...	...
Metz **170** a.	...	...	...	...	...	...	...	...	...	...	...	...	|	1739	1739	...	...	...	...	...	...	...	...	...
Lille Europe **160** a.	...	...	...	...	...	...	...	...	...	...	...	...	|	...	...	...	...	...	...	...	...	...	...	...
Paris Lyon **151** a.	...	...	...	...	...	...	...	...	...	...	...	...	1324	...	...	...	...	...	...	...	...	...	...	...

	Ⓐ		844 TGV K 🍴	844 TGV J 🍴			818 TGV 🍷	366 ♦		164 165 ♦K 🍴	164 165 ♦J 🍴		576/7 TGV ⑦q 🍷	576/7 TGV 🍷			346 347 ♦ 🍷	6638 6639 K 🍷	6638 6639 J 🍷	6950 6951 K 🍷	6950 6951 J 🍷			846 TGV K 🍷
Ventimiglia d.	0808	0842	...	...	...	...	...	0920	0935	...	...	...	...	...	1017	...	1044	...	...	...	...	...	1140	...
Menton d.	0820	0856	...	...	...	...	...	0933	0947	...	...	...	...	...	1028	...	1057	...	...	...	...	...	1153	...
Cap Martin-Roquebrune d.	0826	0902	...	...	...	...	...	|	0952	...	...	...	...	...	1034	...	|	...	...	...	...	...	1159	...
Monaco-Monte Carlo d.	0833	0909	...	...	...	...	...	0945	0959	...	...	...	...	...	1040	...	1107	...	...	...	...	...	1206	...
Beaulieu sur Mer d.	0845	0921	...	...	...	...	...	0956	1011	...	...	...	...	...	1051	...	|	...	...	...	...	...	1219	...
Villefranche sur Mer d.	0848	0925	...	...	...	...	...	|	1014	...	...	...	...	...	1054	...	|	...	...	...	...	...	1222	...
Nice Ville a.	0855	0932	...	...	...	...	...	1005	1020	...	...	...	...	...	1100	...	1120	...	...	...	...	...	1229	...
Nice Ville d.	0908	...	0943	0948	0955	...	...	...	...	1030	1036	1039	1057	...	1103	...	▬	1135	1143	1153	1200	1216	...	1239
Cagnes sur Mer d.	0922	...	|	|	1010	...	...	...	...	|	|	1053	|	...	1117	...	...	|	|	|	|	1230	...	|
Antibes d.	0933	...	0958u	1002u	1021	...	...	...	...	1044	1051	1103	1112	...	1128	...	...	1150	1158	1208	1215	1242	...	1253u
Juan les Pins d.	0936	...	|	|	1024	...	...	...	...	|	|	1107	|	...	1131	...	...	|	|	|	|	1245	...	|
Cannes d.	0946	...	1009u	1013u	1035	...	...	...	...	1055	1102	1116	1123	...	1139	...	...	1201	1208	1218	1225	1254	...	1304u
St. Raphaël d.	...	...	1041	1041	...	...	...	...	...	1124	1125	...	1149	...	...	...	...	1235	1235	1252	1252	...	...	1336
Les Arcs d.	...	...	|	|	...	...	...	...	...	|	|	...	|	...	...	...	...	|	|	|	|	...	...	|
Hyères d.	...	...	|	|	...	...	...	...	...	|	|	...	|	...	...	...	⚒	1252	1252	|	|	...	...	|
Toulon d.	...	...	|	|	...	1135	1154	...	...	1212	1212	...	1236	...	...	1239	1306	1330	1330	1344	1344	...	...	|
Bandol d.	...	...	|	|	...	1151	|	...	...	|	|	...	|	...	...	1253	1323	|	|	|	|	...	...	|
La Ciotat d.	...	...	|	|	...	1202	|	...	...	|	|	...	|	...	...	1304	1336	|	|	|	|	...	...	|
Marseille St. Charles a.	...	...	|	|	...	1230	1236	...	...	1250	1250	...	1316	1324	...	1340	1406	1409	1409	1425	1425	...	...	|
Montpellier **163** a.	...	...	|	|	...	...	|	...	...	1426	1426	...	|	|	...	...	...	|	|	1618	1618	...	...	|
Narbonne **163** a.	...	...	|	|	...	...	|	...	...	|	|	...	|	|	...	...	...	|	|	1735	1735	...	...	|
Port Bou **163** a.	...	...	|	|	...	...	|	...	...	|	|	...	|	|	...	...	...	|	|	|	|	...	...	|
Toulouse **139** a.	...	...	|	|	...	...	|	...	...	1619	1619	...	|	|	...	...	...	|	|	1904	1904	...	...	|
Irún **139** a.	...	...	|	|	...	...	|	...	...	|	|	...	|	|	...	...	...	|	|	|	|	...	...	|
Bordeaux **139** a.	...	...	|	|	...	...	|	...	...	1823	1823	...	|	|	...	...	...	|	|	2153	2153	...	...	|
Nantes **134** a.	...	...	|	|	...	...	|	...	...	...	...	...	|	|	...	...	...	|	|	...	...	...	...	|
Lyon Perrache **151** a.	...	...	|	|	...	...	|	...	...	...	...	...	|	|	...	...	...	|	|	...	...	...	...	|
Lyon Part-Dieu **151** a.	...	...	|	|	...	...	|	...	...	...	...	...	|	|	...	...	...	1745	1745	...	...	...	...	|
Genève **165** a.	...	...	|	|	...	...	|	...	...	...	...	...	|	|	...	...	...	|	|	...	...	...	...	|
Dijon **149** a.	...	...	|	|	...	...	|	...	...	...	...	...	|	|	...	...	...	1924	1924	...	...	...	...	|
Strasbourg **156** a.	...	...	|	|	...	...	|	...	...	...	...	...	|	|	...	...	...	|	|	...	...	...	...	|
Metz **170** a.	...	...	|	|	...	...	|	...	...	...	...	...	|	|	...	...	...	2248	2248	...	...	...	...	|
Lille Europe **160** a.	...	...	|	|	...	...	|	...	...	...	...	...	1848	1848	...	...	...	...	...	...	...	...	...	|
Paris Lyon **151** a.	...	...	1620	1620	...	...	1653	...	...	...	...	...	...	...	...	...	...	...	...	...	...	...	...	1916

♦ – **NOTES** (LISTED BY TRAIN NUMBER)

164/5 – LE GRAND SUD – [12] and 🍴 Nice - Bordeaux.

346/7 – LIGURE – [12] Milano - Nice.

358 – 🛏 1,2 cl., ▬ 1,2 cl. and [12] Venezia - Genova - Nice.

366 – 🛏 1,2 cl., ▬ 2 cl. and [12] Roma - Nice.

5682/3 – [12] Nice - Genève; [12] Nice - St. Gervais.

E – Ⓐ Apr. 10 - May 12.

F – Daily except dates in note **E**.

J – © to Mar. 5 (not Dec. 3,17, Jan. 28); daily from Mar. 6.

K – Ⓐ to Mar. 3 (also Dec. 3,17, Jan. 28).

TGV – Ⓡ, supplement payable.

b – Runs 12 minutes later Nice - Cannes on Ⓐ Oct. 10 - 21.

q – Also Apr. 17, May 1,8; not Apr. 16,30, May 7.

u – Stops to pick up only.

Table 164 — VENTIMIGLIA - NICE - MARSEILLE

1,2 class

	824 TGV (A) ♀	59256 K	846 TGV J ♀		59256 J	15470 ⑤f	5012 K ♀	5012 J ♀	834 TGV ✕	6932/6933 ⑤f ◆	5356 K	5356 R	(A)
Ventimiglia .... d	...	...	...	...	1208	...	1250	...	1330	...	1507	1612	...
Menton .... d	...	...	...	...	1220	...	1302	...	1342	...	1519	1626	...
Cap Martin-Roquebrune .... d					1226		1308		1349		1525	1632	
Monaco-Monte Carlo .... d					1233		1315		1355		1531	1639	
Beaulieu sur Mer .... d					1245		1327		1407		1543	1652	
Villefranche sur Mer .... d					1248		1331		1411		1546	1655	
Nice Ville .... a					1255		1338		1417		1553	1702	
Nice Ville .... d		1242	1245	1250	1305	1310	1352	1413 1429	1433	1600 1610	1614 1645	1705	
Cagnes sur Mer .... d		1252		1304	1326	1315	1407	1448			1629 1700	1719	
Antibes .... d		1301	1259u	1315	1338	1324	1420	1428 1444	1459	1617 1627	1641 1712	1731	
Juan les Pins .... d					1318	1342	1423		1502				
Cannes .... d		1311	1310u	1327	1352	1334	1433	1440 1455	1511	1628 1638	1654 1725	1745	
St. Raphaël .... d		1342	1339		1401			1527 1523			1712	1706	
Les Arcs .... d		1400			1418					1710	1728	1723	
Hyères .... d						1440			1708				1820
Toulon .... d	1350	1409	1440		1455	1506	1545	1616 1615	1642	1655 1730 1750	1805	1802	1830 1840
Bandol .... d	1405					1601				1710 1745			1847
La Ciotat .... d	1417					1613				1722 1757			1900
Marseille St. Charles .... a	1446	1451	1523		1537	1554	1643	1654 1653	1724	1751 1826 1838	1844	1842	1935
Montpellier 163 .... a					1757					2036			
Narbonne 163 .... a					1857					2143			
Port Bou 163 .... a													
Toulouse 139 .... a					2021					2304			
Irún 139 .... a													
Bordeaux 139 .... a										0146			
Nantes 134 .... a										0622			
Lyon Perrache 151 .... a											2225	2225z	
Lyon Part-Dieu 151 .... a							2025 2025						
Genève 165 .... a													
Dijon 149 .... a							2204 2204						
Strasbourg 156 .... a													
Metz 170 .... a													
Lille Europe 160 .... a													
Paris Lyon 151 .... a		1912		1916					2150				

	5016 ⑦e	59258 ①-⑤ ✕	59258	6924/6925 ◆	6708/6709	6720/6721	5058 ◆	188 ◆	6694/6695	340/341 ◆ ⑦e	6630/6631	6632/6633 ◆	182 ◆	5698/5699	362/363 ◆
Ventimiglia .... d	...	1640	...	1714	...	1734	1754	1825	1847	1852 1905	...	1921 1955	...	2100 2120	2300
Menton .... d		1654	1715	1726		1748	1806	1839	1859 1905	1917		1934 2010		2112 2133	2315
Cap Martin-Roquebrune .... d		1700		1732			1813	1845	1911			1940		2117	2320
Monaco-Monte Carlo .... d		1707	1725	1738		1758	1820	1852	1909 1917	1929		1947 2019		2124 2146	2327
Beaulieu sur Mer .... d		1720	1735	1750		1809	1832	1904	1919 1939	1959		2029		2136	2338
Villefranche sur Mer .... d		1723		1753			1836	1908	1932			2003		2140	2342
Nice Ville .... a		1730	1745	1800		1816	1842	1915	1926 1938	1946		2010 2035		2146 2200	2348
Nice Ville .... d	1731	1735		1800	1803	1824 1834 1840	1844	1923 1927	1942 1946		2000 2017	2022 2026	2040 2045	2150 2220	2350
Cagnes sur Mer .... d		1749			1817		1858	1934 1941	1957					2205	0003
Antibes .... d	1746	1800		1815	1829	1840 1849 1855	1910	1942 1953	1959 2007		2016 2036	2042 2052	2059 2104	2217 2235	0015
Juan les Pins .... d		1804			1833	1854 1900	1914	1956			2021 2041	2055		2109 2220	0018
Cannes .... d	1757	1813		1826	1843	1852 1905 1912	1923	1954 2006	2014 2018		2032 2051	2057 2104	2113 2125	2231 2247	0027
St. Raphaël .... d	1824			1853	1917	1923 1938 1945	2022	2041 2046	2058		2119 2126		2142 2153	2314	
Les Arcs .... d	1840			1910		2007	2040	2059 2105	2116		2139 2145		2215		
Hyères .... d							2030								
Toulon .... d	1921		1951	2011	2050	2029 2038	2054 2120	2143 2154	2158 2221		2228	2236 2258			0011
Bandol .... d				2025	2104		2111	2155							
La Ciotat .... d				2037	2117		2124								
Marseille St. Charles .... a	1959		2029	2107	2142	2109 2118	2155 2200	2225 2236	2240 2302		2309	2338			0056
Montpellier 163 .... a				0001					0039					0311	
Narbonne 163 .... a									0151					0416	
Port Bou 163 .... a															
Toulouse 139 .... a									0329					0552	
Irún 139 .... a															
Bordeaux 139 .... a				0530					0625						
Nantes 134 .... a				0938					1105						
Lyon Perrache 151 .... a					0026 0036			0234			0247				
Lyon Part-Dieu 151 .... a	2305														
Genève 165 .... a													0743		
Dijon 149 .... a								0416			0428				
Strasbourg 156 .... a								0846			0719 0816				
Metz 170 .... a															
Lille Europe 160 .... a					0914b	0838b									
Paris Lyon 151 .... a							0620	0715					0743		

NOTES (LISTED BY TRAIN NUMBER)

82 – LE TRAIN BLEU – 1,2 cl., 1,2 cl. (T2) and 1,2 cl. Ventimiglia - Nice - Paris.

88 – LE PHOCÉEN – 1,2 cl., 1,2 cl. (T2) and 1,2 cl. Toulon - Paris (Nice - Paris on ⑤⑦, also Nov. 1, 10, Apr. 17, May 1, 8, 24; not Oct. 30, Nov.11, Apr. 16, 30, May 7, 26).

340/1 – 1,2 cl., 1,2 cl. and Ventimiglia - Nice - Nantes; 1,2 cl. Ventimiglia - Nice - Bordeaux; and 2 cl. Milano - Ventimiglia - Bordeaux.

362/3 – 1,2 cl., 1,2 cl. Ventimiglia - Nice - Port Bou; and 2 cl. Roma - Ventimiglia - Port Bou.

5058 – 2 cl., and ♀ Nice - Paris.

5698/9 – 1,2 cl. Nice - Genève (also 1,2 cl. (T2) on ②④⑦); and 1,2 cl. Nice - St. Gervais.

6630/1 – LORAZUR – 1,2 cl. (T2), 1,2 cl. and Nice - Metz.

6632/3 – and 1,2 cl. Nice - Metz (also 1,2 cl. (T2), replaced by when train 6630/1 runs); and 1,2 cl. Reims - Nice and v.v.

6694/5 – 1,2 cl. (T2), 1,2 cl. and Nice - Strasbourg (Ventimiglia - Strasbourg Sept. 25 - Oct. 29 and Mar. 30 - May 27). Conveys Sept. 25 - Oct. 29 and Mar. 30 - May 27, and 2 cl. Ventimiglia - Nice - Strasbourg - Frankfurt.

6708/9 – RIVIERA FLANDRES – (Train 6706/7 when train 6720/1 runs). 1,2 cl. (T2), 2 cl. and Lille - Tourcoing (except when train 6720/1 runs); 1,2 cl., 1,2 cl. (T2) and 2 cl. Ventimiglia - Brussels; daily Sept. 25 - Jan. 21 and Apr. 3 - May 27, ①②④⑥ Jan. 22 - Apr. 2 (also ⑤⑦ Feb. 24 - Mar.12) 1,2 cl. (T2) and 2 cl. Ventimiglia - Calais.

6720/1 – RIVIERA FLANDRES. Runs Oct. 1, 8, 15, 22, 26-31, Nov. 1-7, Dec. 21 - Jan. 4, Feb. 24-27, Mar. 3-6, 10-12, Apr. 14-17, 21-30, May 1, 6-8, 13, 14, 20, 21, 25-27. 1,2 cl., 1,2 cl. (T2), 2 cl. and Nice - Lille - Tourcoing.

6924/5 – ⑤⑦ (also Nov. 1, 10, Apr. 17, May 1, 8, 24; not Oct. 30, Nov. 11, Apr. 16, 30, May 7, 26): 1,2 cl. (T2), 1,2 cl. and Nice - Nantes.

6932/3 – and 2 cl. Les Arcs - Toulon - Nantes.

J – Ⓒ to Mar. 5 (also Dec. 3, 17, Jan. 28); daily from Mar. 6.

K – Ⓐ to Mar. 3 (also Dec. 3, 17, Jan. 28).

R – Ⓒ to Mar. 5 (also Dec. 3, 17, Jan. 28); daily from Mar. 6.
On ⑦ (also Nov. 1, Apr. 17, May 1, 8; not Oct. 30, Apr. 16, 30, May 7), runs Nice - Annecy as train **5636/1**, not calling at Lyon.

TGV – Ⓡ, supplement payable.

b – Lille Flandres
e – Also Apr. 17, May 1, 8; not Apr. 16, 30, May 7.
f – Also Nov. 10, May 24; not Nov. 11; May 26.
u – Stops to pick up only.
z – Not on ⑦ (see note **R**).

Table 165 GENÈVE - GRENOBLE - VALENCE

1,2 class

km				5600			5684 5685		5680 5681	5630 5680	868/9 TGV		5607	5608 5609	5610 5611	5634 5635		5612 5613	5614 5615	5616 5617		6984 6985	5646 5697	5696 5697	5696 5697
		⚒	⚒	⚒			M	⚒A			V			Ⓐ	B	⑤f			⑧h	E	Ⓒ	W	P	RY	RX
0	**Genève** d.	...	...	...	...	...	0655	...	0930	...	1044	...	...	...	...	...	...	1532	...	1838	...	...	...	2225	2312
33	Bellegarde d.	...	...	...	...	...	0722	...	0958	...	|	...	...	...	...	...	...	1559	...	1905	...	...	...	2250	2340
	St. Gervais **167** d.	...	...	...	...	...	|	...	|	0824	|	...	...	...	1307	*1307*	...	|	...	|	...	...	2051	|	|
	Annecy 167 d.	...	...	...	0628**c**	0721	|	0808	|	0957	|	...	...	1256	1459	1459	...	|	1725	|	1934	2155	2242	|	|
88	Aix les Bains **167** d.	...	...	0646	0710**c**	0750	0759	0846	1048	1048	via	...	1156	1326	1531	1531	...	1637	1755	1944	2011	2228	2324	2334	0022
102	Chambéry a.	...	...	0658	0728**c**	0803	0810	0858	1100	1100	Lyon	...	1209	1339	1542	1542	...	1648	1808	1956	2025	2240	2336	2345	0034
102	Chambéry d.	...	0625	0700	0730	0806	0820	0900	1102	1102	|	...	1212	1341	1545	1545	...	1700	1810	2006	2027	2254	0052**r**	0020	0052
165	**Grenoble** a.	...	0735	0746	0833	0853	0900	0941	1143	1143	|	...	1257	1422	1625	1625	...	1745	1855	2051	2117	2350	0135**r**	|	0135
165	**Grenoble** d.	0600	...	0748	...	0903**z**	0903	...	1146	1146	|	1218	1300	...	1628	1628	1714	1749	1858	2054	...	0008	0145**r**	|	0145
242	Romans-Bourg de Péage d.	0705	...	0849	...	0955**z**	0955	...	|	|	|	1329	1352	...	1721	1721	1830	1844	1951	2143	...	0125	|	|	|
262	**Valence** a.	0718	...	0903	...	1008**z**	1008	...	1245	1245	1309	1344	1406	...	1735	1735	1844	1857	2005	2157	...	0140	0258	0258	0258
	Avignon **151** a.	...	...	...	...	...	1120	...	1353	1353	1409	...	...	...	...	1847	...	...	...	...	...	0250	0420	0420	0420
	Marseille **151** a.	...	...	...	...	...	1222	...	1453	1453	...	...	...	...	...	1946	...	...	...	...	...	...	0557	0557	0557
	Nice **164** a.	...	...	...	...	...	1518	...	1735	1735	...	...	...	...	...	2230	...	...	...	...	...	...	0911	0911	0911

			5650 5651		5652 5653		5656 5657	5658 5659		5682 5683	5682 5632	860/1 TGV	5660 5661	5662 5663			5664 5665	5636 5637			5698 5649	5698 15649	5698 5699	5698 5699	6484 6485
	⚒	H	Ⓐ	⚒	⚒	Ⓐ		🍷				V				⑤f	⑧h	⑦e	F	E	PX	PY	SX	SY	W
Nice **164** d.	...	...	...	...	...	...	...	...	...	0905	0905	...	...	...	...	...	...	1610	...	...	2045	2045	2045	2045	...
Marseille **151** d.	...	...	...	...	...	...	...	...	...	1143	1143	...	...	...	...	...	...	1855	...	...	2349	2349	2349	2349	...
Avignon **151** d.	...	...	...	...	...	...	...	...	...	1248	1248	1426	...	...	...	...	...	1957	...	...	0131	0131	0131	0131	0329
Valence d.	...	...	0607	...	0620	0729	0840	1119	1225	1402	1402	1523	1553	1707	1729	1830	1917	2112	2131	2215	0316	0246	0316	0246	0450
Romans-Bourg de Péage d.	...	...	0623	...	0636	0744	0856	1136	1241	|	|	|	1609	1722	1744	1846	1933	|	2147	2231	|	|	|	|	0508
Grenoble a.	...	...	0718	...	0758	0837	0957	1241	1358	1506	1506	|	1708	1810	1855	1958	2034	2225	2254	2338	0420	|	0420	|	0600
Grenoble d.	0633	0633	0720	0732	0801	...	1000	1251	...	1509	1509	|	1716	1813	1900	...	2037	2228	...	...	0426	|	0426	|	0604
Chambéry a.	0730	0730	0804	0836	0843	...	1042	1335	...	1550	1550	|	1804	1900	2002	...	2121	2310	...	...	0507	0546	0507	0546	0645
Chambéry d.	...	0740	0806	...	0845	...	1052	1337	...	1600	1612	via	1806	1902	...	...	...	2312	...	...	0521	0554	0540	0607	0655
Aix les Bains **167** d.	...	0753	0818	...	0858	...	1104	1351	...	1612	1627	Lyon	1819	1915	...	...	...	2325	...	...	0604	0625	0615	0619	0709
Annecy 167 a.	...	|	0856	...	0928	...	|	1422	...	|	1657	|	1853	1955	...	...	...	2354	...	...	0644	0705	|	|	0759
St. Gervais **167** a.	...	|	...	...	...	...	|	1613	...	|	1835	|	...	...	...	...	...	...	...	...	0857	0913	|	|	...
Bellegarde a.	...	0830	...	...	...	...	1140	...	...	1648	...	|	...	...	...	...	...	...	...	...	...	...	0656	0656	...
Genève a.	...	0859	...	...	...	...	1208	...	...	1715	...	1745	...	...	...	...	...	...	...	...	...	...	0743	0743	...

A – (12) Annemasse - Grenoble.
B – Daily except ⑤ (also runs Nov. 11, May 26; not Nov. 10, May 24).
E – ⑤⑦ (also Nov. 1,10, Apr. 17, May 1,8,24; not Nov. 11, Apr. 16,30, May 7).
F – ①②③④ (also Apr. 16,30, May 7; not Dec. 26, Jan. 2, Apr. 17,18, May 1,8,24).
H – ①⑥ (also Nov. 2,11, Apr. 18, May 2,9,25; not Nov. 12, Apr. 17, May 1,8).
M – Oct. 29, Nov. 11, Apr. 15,29, May 6,25 only.
P – (12) and 🛏 1,2 cl. St. Gervais - Nice and v.v.
R – (12) and 🛏 1,2 cl. Genève - Nice (also 🛌 1,2 cl. (T2) on ①③⑤ and Apr. 13; not Nov. 11, Apr. 17, May 1,8).
S – (12) and 🛏 1,2 cl. Nice - Genève (also 🛌 1,2 cl. (T2) on ②④⑦ and Apr. 17).
TGV – Ⓡ, supplement payable.

V – (12) and 🍷 Genève - Lyon - Montpellier and v.v.
W – Runs (from Annecy and Hendaye) on ⑤⑦, also Apr. 17, May 1,8,24; not Apr. 16,30, May 7,26: (12) and 🛏 1,2 cl. Annecy - Toulouse - Irún and Hendaye - Toulouse - Annecy.
X – Daily except when train **Y** runs.
Y – ①②③④ Mar. 27 - Apr. 20 (not Apr. 17).
c – ⚒ only.
e – Also Nov. 1, Apr. 17, May 1,8; not Oct. 30, Apr. 16,30, May 7.
f – Also Nov. 10, May 24; not Nov. 11, May 26.
h – Not Apr. 16,30, May 7.
r – On dates in note **Y**, departs Chambéry 0020 and does not call at Grenoble.
z – Change at Grenoble on Oct. 29, Nov. 11, Apr. 15,29, May 6,25.

Table 166 BRIANÇON - VALENCE and MARSEILLE

1,2 class

km		🚌	5370	🚌		5372	🚌	🚌	5382	5384	5374	🚌	5386	🚌		5388		🚌		2	5376	🚌	5792	5790
		⚒	⚒	⚒	⚒				M	E			N🍷		F	G🍷	⑦e	⑧h	H	⑤f			P	R
0	**Briançon** d.	...	...	...	0630	0750	...	...	1032	1225	1250**r**	...	1320	...	1405	1437	...	...	1635	1635	1713**v**	...	2000	2035
28	Montdauphin d.	...	...	...	0655	0814	...	...	1109	1250	1314**r**	...	1351	...	1429	1508	...	...	1707	1707	1736**v**	...	2030	2105
45	Embrun d.	...	...	...	0712	0832	...	...	1140	1306	1328**r**	...	1410	...	1444	1527	...	...	1725	1725	1751**v**	...	2050	2127
82	**Gap** d.	...	0545	...	0754	0907	...	...	1218	1339	1405	...	1447	...	1522	1627	1705	...	1800	1800	1821	...	2138	2215
109	Veynes **154** d.	...	0606	...	0819	0931	...	1048	1246	1406	1427	...	1523	1532	1604	1658	1725	...	1848	1826	1842	...	2206	2300
	Grenoble **158** a.	...	|	...	1018	|	...	|	|	|	|	...	|	|	1808	|	|	...	2101	|	|	...	|	|
172	Die d.	...	|	...	▬	|	...	|	|	1507	|	...	1624	|	...	1756	|	...	...	1921	|	...	2305	|
244	**Valence** a.	...	|	...	...	|	...	|	1449	1613	|	...	1728	|	...	1900	|	...	...	2023	|	...	0006	|
	Paris Lyon **151** a.	...	|	...	...	|	...	|	...	▬	|	...	...	|	...	...	|	...	...	▬	|	...	0629**x**	0804
	St. Auban a.	...	0657	0703	...	1025	1030	|	...	...	1520	1525	...	|	...	...	1816	1848	...	...	1934	2027	...	...
	Digne a.	...	|	0738	🚌	|	1105	1230	...	🚌	|	1559	...	1659	...	...	|	1922	...	🚌	|	2102	...	...
	Digne d.	0612	|	...	0941	|	...	...	...	1436	|	...	...	...	...	...	|	...	...	1850	|	...	...	...
	St. Auban d.	0647	0658	...	1016	1026	...	...	...	1511	1521	...	...	...	...	...	1816	...	...	1925	1935	...	...	...
	Manosque d.	...	0722	...	...	1050	...	...	...	...	1545	...	...	...	...	...	1843	...	...	...	2001	...	...	...
	Aix en Provence ♣ d.	...	0805	...	...	1133	...	...	...	...	1623	...	...	...	...	...	1922	...	...	...	2045	...	...	...
	Marseille St. Charles ♣ a.	...	0835	...	...	1203	...	...	...	...	1658	...	...	...	...	...	1957	...	...	...	2113	...	...	...

	5791	5795	5799	🚌	5360	🚌		5383	🚌	5385	🚌	5362	🚌	5387	🚌	🚌	🚌	5364	🚌		🚌	5366	🚌	🚌
	S	JP	KP				L	T🍷		N🍷				🍷		⑦e	W	⑧h	Ⓑ	Ⓑ				
Marseille St. Charles ♣ d.	...	...	...	...	0749	...	...	...	...	...	...	1223	...	...	...	...	...	1710	...	...	...	1850	...	...
Aix en Provence ♣ d.	...	...	...	...	0824	...	...	...	...	...	...	1256	...	...	...	...	...	1743	...	...	...	1920	...	...
Manosque d.	...	...	...	...	0906	...	...	...	...	...	...	1336	...	...	...	...	...	1821	...	...	...	2000	...	...
St. Auban a.	...	...	...	...	0930	0935	...	...	...	...	...	1400	1406	...	...	...	...	1843	1850	...	...	2022	...	2027
Digne a.	...	...	...	...	|	1010	...	...	...	...	...	|	1441	...	...	...	...	|	1925	...	...	|	...	2102
Digne d.	...	...	...	0846	|	...	...	...	1217	...	1316	|	...	...	1628	1731	1759	|	▬	...	1850	|	2025	...
St. Auban d.	...	...	...	0921	0931	...	...	...	|	...	1351	1401	...	...	|	1806	1834	1844	...	...	1925	2023	|	...
Paris Lyon **151** d.	2053	2130	2210	...	|	...	...	...	|	...	...	|	...	...	|	...	...	|	...	...	...	|	|	...
Valence d.	|	0345	0425	...	|	...	...	1049	|	1152	...	|	...	1319	|	...	...	|	...	...	...	|	|	...
Die d.	|	0452	0536	...	|	...	...	1149	|	|	...	|	...	1426	|	...	...	|	⑥	...	...	|	|	...
Grenoble **158** d.	|	|	|	...	|	...	0842	|	|	|	...	|	...	|	|	...	...	|	1750	1750	...	|	|	...
Veynes **154** d.	0518	0607	0643	...	1028	...	1046	1253	1350	1408	...	1457	...	1528	1816	...	...	1935	1952	1952	...	2117	2155	...
Gap d.	0548	0634	0712	...	1048	...	1106	1319	...	1446	...	1519	...	1551	...	...	...	1958	2015	2016	...	2139	...	...
Embrun d.	0631	0715	0755	...	1122**r**	...	1140	1412	...	1528	...	1553**v**	...	1627	...	...	...	...	...	2050	...	2214	...	...
Montdauphin d.	0655	0740	0815	...	1137**r**	...	1154	1433	...	1545	...	1608**v**	...	1642	...	...	...	...	...	2104	...	2229	...	...
Briançon a.	0727	0823	0848	...	1200**r**	...	1219	1511	...	1618	...	1633**v**	...	1712	...	...	...	...	...	2130	...	2255	...	...

E – Daily (not ① Sept. 26 - Dec. 12 or ① Apr. 10 - May 22).
F – ⑤⑥⑦ (also Nov. 1,10, Apr. 17, May 1,8,24,25; not Nov. 11, May 26).
G – ⑦ Jan. 29 - Apr. 23 (also Dec. 31, Jan. 1, Feb. 25, Mar. 4, Apr. 17, May 1,8; not Apr. 16).
H – ①②③④ (also Nov. 11, May 26; not Nov. 1,10, Apr. 17, May 1,8,24,25).
J – Daily except when train **K** runs.
K – ⚒ (also Oct. 30, Nov. 11, Apr. 16,30, May 7,25).
L – (12) Lyon - Briançon.
M – ⑥⑦ Feb. 18 - Mar. 11 (also Oct. 31, Jan. 1).
N – ⑥ Dec. 17 - Apr. 1.
P – 🛌 1,2 cl. (T2), 🛏 1,2 cl. and (2) Paris - Briançon and v.v.
R – ⑥⑦ Jan. 1 - Mar. 26 (also Jan. 4; not Jan. 7): 🛏 1,2 cl. Briançon - Paris.
S – ⑤⑥ Jan. 7 - Mar. 25 (also Dec. 21,23): 🛏 1,2 cl. Paris - Briançon.
T – ⑥ Jan. 28 - May 6 (also Dec. 31, Jan. 1).

W – ① - ⑤ (not Oct. 31, Apr. 17, May 1,8).
e – Also Apr. 17, May 1,8; not Apr. 16,30, May 7.
f – Also Nov. 10, May 24; not Nov. 11, May 26.
h – Not Oct. 31, Apr. 16,30, May 7.
r – ⑥ Dec. 24 - Mar. 11, also Oct. 26,29, Nov. 2,6,10, Dec. 21,22,23,26,30, Jan. 1, Apr. 22, May 8 (also Apr. 23 from Marseille, Apr. 24 from Briançon).
v – ⑤⑥⑦ (also Nov. 1,10,11, Dec. 21,22, Jan. 2,3, Apr. 17, May 1,8,24,25).
x – Arrive 0658 on ②③④⑤ Sept. 26 - Dec. 16 and Apr. 4 - May 24 (not Oct. 28, Nov. 1,2,11, Apr. 18, May 2,10).
♣ – Additional trains Aix en Provence - Marseille and v.v. (journey 40 minutes):
Aix en Provence depart: 0604⚒, 0655, 0720Ⓐ, 0740, 0830Ⓐ, 0944, 1025, 1215⚒, 1310, 1355⚒, 1500, 1542, 1700, 1747, 1835, 1922, 2120.
Marseille depart: 0611, 0638⚒, 0701, 0835Ⓐ, 0925, 1117⚒, 1203, 1330⚒, 1417 1522, 1602, 1644Ⓐ, 1725, 1751Ⓐ, 1814, 1923Ⓐ, 1959, 2118, 2210, 2310.

Table 167
PARIS and LYON - ANNECY - ST GERVAIS
1,2 class

km		5649 DR	15649 DS	✗	412/3 5405	931 TGV	5406 5407	983 TGV M	985 TGV N	925/4 TGV V	5658 5659	933 TGV	5409 5408	5632 5633 G	Ⓐ B	Ⓑ U	✗	5660 5661	218/9 5411
	Paris Gare de Lyon 152 . d.	...	...	...		0709		0826	0918	1024	...	1244						...	...
	Lyon Perrache ...... d.	...	...	0704		0900			1214			1417					...	1703
0	Lyon Part-Dieu ...... d.	...	...	0715		0918											...	1714
107	Chambéry 165 ...... a.	0521	0554	0627		1035			1326	1337		1547	1612			1657	1806	
121	Aix les Bains 165 ...... a.	0532	0606	0639	0826	1012	1045			1323	1338 1349	1543	1558	1624		1708	1817	1822
121	Aix les Bains 165 ...... d.	0604	0625	0640	0845	1020	1047			1330	1340 1351	1551	1600	1627	1636	1710	1819	1833
160	Annecy 165 ...... a.	0644	0705	0736	0912	1049	1118			1401	1409 1422	1622	1633	1657	1711	1757	1853	1904
160	Annecy 167a ...... d.	0649	0711		0914		1122			1440		1638	1701	1730				1907
199	La Roche sur Foron 167a .. a.	0739	0755		1005		1155			1515		1710	1735	1812				1949
199	La Roche sur Foron ...... d.	0759	0816		1019		1202			1528		1723	1748		1818			2003
221	Cluses ...... d.	0829	0850		1046		1225	1259	1350	1552		1746	1814		1843			2025
240	Sallanches Megève ...... d.	0851	0906		1102		1239	1314	1405	1607		1800	1829		1858			2039
246	St Gervais ...... d.	0857	0913		1110		1246	1320	1411	1613		1806	1835		1904			2046
	Chamonix 268 ...... a.	0946	0954		1201		1335	1428	1501	1656		1856	1948		1948			2145

		935 TGV ⑧h	5412 5413	929 TGV	389 TGV E	P	W	Ⓐ	5113 X	5115	5115 Y
	Paris Gare de Lyon 152 ... d.	1716		1914	2355		2233			2333	2305x
	Lyon Perrache ...... d.		1905								
	Lyon Part-Dieu ...... d.		1923	2120							
	Chambéry 165 ...... d.		2038	2217	2234						
	Aix les Bains 165 ...... a.	2017	2049	2228	2244		0415		0502		0510
	Aix les Bains 165 ...... d.	2025	2051	2230	2246		0425		0521		0604
	Annecy 165 ...... a.	2054	2120	2259	2318		0418	0455	0607		0644
	Annecy 167a ...... a.		2124				0423	0500	0618		0649
	La Roche sur Foron 167a ... a.		2156					0534	0710		0739
	La Roche sur Foron ...... d.		2203			0552	0635		0726		0759
	Cluses ...... d.		2225			0550	0623	0703	0756		0829
	Sallanches Megève ...... d.		2239			0606	0639	0719	0815		0851
	St Gervais ...... a.		2245			0612	0645	0725	0822		0857
	Chamonix 268 ...... a.		2326r			0728			0946		

		920/1 TGV Ⓐ	5414 5415	5604 5605	930 TGV	5416 5417	940 TGV	5630 G	938 TGV J
	Chamonix 268 ...... d.						0658		0824
	St Gervais ...... d.		0527	0809			0824		0918
	Sallanches Megève ...... d.		0533	0815			0832		0927
	Cluses ...... d.		0549	0830			0849		0943
	La Roche sur Foron ...... a.		0616	0854			0909		1002
	La Roche sur Foron 167a ... d.		0629 0653	0902			0922		1010
	Annecy 167a ...... a.	0517	0705 0739	0808 0807	0801	0938	0941	0957	1055
	Aix les Bains 165 ...... d.	0543	0708 0740	0844 0830	1011		1024	1030	1132
	Aix les Bains 165 ...... a.	0545	0710 0741	0846 0838	1013		1048	1100	1140
	Chambéry 165 ...... a.	0553	0728 0753	0858	1024	1050			
	Lyon Part-Dieu ...... a.		0920			1142			
	Lyon Perrache ...... a.	0905							
	Paris Gare de Lyon 152 a.			1140		1349			1440

		938 10938 K	938 K	5418	932 TGV	5610 5611	922/3 TGV	414 415	5610 5611	986 TGV	5420 5421	988 TGV	5422 5423	944 TGV	934 TGV	5424 5425	5424 418/9	418 419	936 TGV	5426 5427	5646	5646 5114	5114 Y	5112 Z
	Chamonix 268 ...... d.	0824		1000		1211			1211	1304	1339 1510n					1626 1626			1735	1955	1955	2025		
	St Gervais ...... d.	0924		1055		1307			1307 1414	1428	1557					1723 1723			1819	2051	2051	2134	2230
	Sallanches Megève ...... d.	0932		1104		1315			1315 1422	1435	1608					1730 1730			1828	2100	2100	2142	2241
	Cluses ...... d.	0952		1120		1330			1330 1440	1449	1625					1747 1747			1844	2116	2116	2158	2259
	La Roche sur Foron ...... a.	1010		1142		1353			1353	1511						1809 1809			1904	2139	2139	2223	2317
	La Roche sur Foron 167a ... a.	1018		1156		1406			1406	1518						1823 1823			1916	2157	2157	2237	2331
	Annecy 167a ...... a.	1049		1230		1439			1439	1549						1858 1858			1953	2231	2231	2311	0004
	Annecy 165 ...... d.		1055	1248	1240		1455		1459	1552		1712		1758	1816	1905 1905		1920	1956	2242	2242	2320	0045
	Aix les Bains 165 ...... a.		1132	1319	1307		1522		1529	1626		1744		1830	1907	1938 1938		1949	2024	2319	2319	2357	0050
	Aix les Bains 165 ...... d.		1140	1329	1315		1524 1526	1531		1628		1746		1838	1910	1940 1953	1953	1957	2026	2324	0026	0026	0102
	Chambéry 165 ...... d.						1534		1542			1757 1814		1922	1951			2038	2336			
	Lyon Part-Dieu ...... a.			1438				1638			1812		1922				2104 2104			2200			
	Lyon Perrache ...... a.							1648									2115 2115			2254		0652 0642	0727
	Paris Gare de Lyon 152 ... a.		1440		1616		1839			1926		2100		2111	2141								

— Daily except ⑤ (also runs May 26; not May 24).
▯ Ⓡ12 Aix les Bains - Annemasse.
▯ Ⓡ12 Annemasse - Aix les Bains - Grenoble.
▯ ▯ and ⚊ 1,2 cl. St Gervais - Nice and v.v.
⑤⑦ (also Nov. 1,10,11, Apr. 17, May 1,8,24,25; not Apr. 16,30, May 7).
⑦ Dec. 18 - Apr. 2.
▯ Ⓡ12 St Gervais - Nice and v.v.
✗ (daily Sept. 25 - Dec. 18 and Apr. 2 - May 27).
⑥ Feb. 11 - Mar. 11 (also Dec. 31, Feb. 19,26).
⑥ Dec. 17 - Feb. 4 (also Mar. 18,25, Apr. 1; not Dec. 31).
⑥⑦ Dec. 24 - Apr. 22 (not Apr. 9,16).
⑥⑦ Dec. 17 - Apr. 15 (not Apr. 9).
⑥ Dec. 17 - Apr. 1.
⑦ Dec. 18 - Apr. 2.
Feb. 17,18,24,25 only.
⑧ (daily Dec. 17 - Apr. 7); not Oct. 31, Nov. 11, Apr. 30, May 7,25.

R – Runs daily except when train S runs.
S – Runs (from Nice) on ①②③④ Mar. 27 - Apr. 20 (not Apr. 17).
TGV –Ⓡ, supplement payable.
U – Ⓡ12 Genève Eaux-Vives - St. Gervais.
V – Ⓡ12 Valence - St. Gervais.
W – ⑤⑥ Jan. 20 - Mar. 25 (also Dec. 23): ⚊ 1,2 cl., ⚊ 1,2 cl. (T2) and ⚊ 1,2 cl. Paris - St. Gervais.
X – Dec. 16 - May 1: ⚊ 1,2 cl. and ⚊ 1,2 cl. Paris - St. Gervais and v.v. (also ⚊ 1,2 cl. (T2) except on ⑤ or Dec. 21,22, Feb. 18,25 from Paris and except when train Z runs from St. Gervais).
Y – Sept. 25 - Dec. 15 and May 2-27: ⚊ 1,2 cl. and Ⓡ12 Paris - St. Gervais and v.v.
Z – ⑥⑦ Feb. 25 - Mar. 26 (also Jan. 1,4, Feb. 24, Mar. 3): ⚊ 1,2 cl., ⚊ 1,2 cl. (T2) and 1,2 cl. St. Gervais - Paris.
e – Also Nov. 1,10, Apr. 17, May 1,8,24; not Apr. 16,30, May 7.
h – Not Oct. 31, Nov. 11, May 25.
n – Dec. 17 - Apr. 23.
r – ⑤⑥† (also May 24).
x – Depart 2333 on ⑤⑦ (also May 24; not May 7,26).

Table 167a
GENÈVE - LA ROCHE SUR FORON - ANNECY
1,2 class

km		Ⓐ	✗	Ⓐ	Ⓒ			Ⓐ						Ⓐ						
0	Genève Eaux-Vives ...... d.	0611		0707		0827	1110	1110			1215	1320	1411	1436		1644	1709	1735	1832	1920
6	Annemasse ...... a.	0621		0717		0836	1120	1120			1225	1330	1421	1446		1654	1719	1745	1842	1930
6	Annemasse 159 ...... d.		0626	0723		0840		1131		1128	1230	1339	1436	1455		1720	1751	1751 1850	1854	1936
	Thonon-les-Bains 159 ...... a.								1153			1502			1754		1822	1929		2003
	Évian-les-Bains 159 ...... a.								1201			1511			1802		1830	1938		2011
23	La Roche sur Foron ...... a.		0648	0741		0857		1147		1250	1356		1513		1812			1912		
23	La Roche sur Foron 167 ...... d.		0653		0759	0902		1156	1202		1406	1518	1528		1818r	1823				
62	Annecy 167 ...... a.		0739			0938		1230			1439	1549			1858					
	St Gervais 167 ...... a.			0857				1246				1613		1904r						
	Chamonix 268 ...... a.			0946				1335				1656		1948r						

		Ⓐ	Ⓐ		Ⓐ	✗			Ⓒ				Ⓐ		✗				✗	Ⓐ
	Chamonix 268 ...... d.					1000		1211	1339			1626						
	St Gervais 167 ...... d.		0527			1055		1307	1428			1723						
	Annecy 167 ...... d.		0616		0914	1005		1122	1242		1440			1730c		1907
	La Roche sur Foron 167 ...... d.		0630		1005	1010		1142 1317	1353		1511	1515		1809	1812c	1949
	La Roche sur Foron ...... d.							1200	1321	1400	1523		1816		1955
	Évian-les-Bains 159 ...... d.	0515	0547	0624	0707		1140			1531	1700		1812	
	Thonon-les-Bains 159 ...... d.	0523	0557	0634	0715		1152			1541	1710		1821	
	Annemasse 159 ...... a.	0555	0620	0650	0711	0743	1026	1217	1218	1338	1417	1540	1606	1745	1837	1849	2012
	Annemasse ...... d.	0557	0627	0654	0721	0746	0813	1030	1030	1145	1227	1347	1422	1545	1655	1750	1818	1856
	Genève Eaux-Vives ...... a.	0607	0637	0703	0731	0756	0823	1030	1040	1155	1237	1352	1432	1555	1705	1800	1828	1906

Ⓐ only.   r – Daily except ⑥.   Additional holiday variations: Ⓐ or ✗ journeys may not operate on Jan. 2 or Apr. 14.

Table 168   MONT BLANC and MER DE GLACE   Rack Railways

St. Gervais - Nid d'Aigle (altitude 2372 metres): 2 to 5 journeys daily mid-June to end September (11 journeys mid July to late August). Also operates 2/3 journeys daily December to April to Bellevue only, altitude 1800 metres). Departs from opposite the SNCF station. Journey 70 minutes in each direction. *Tramway du Mont Blanc* ☎ 50.53.30.80, fax 50.55.99.76.

Chamonix - Montenvers "Mer de Glace" (altitude 1913 metres): Hourly service early May to late September (every 20 minutes in July and August). Limited winter service (closed mid-November to mid-December). Station is 200 metres from SNCF station. Journey 20 minutes in each direction. *Chemin de Fer Chamonix - Montenvers* ☎ 50.53.12.54, fax 50.55.80.94.

Table 169   🚐 TOULON - ST TROPEZ - ST RAPHAËL   🚐 service
Service January 2 - July 2, 1995

km		A	A	A	E	A	A		A	E	A				A	E	F	A	A	A		A		A
0	Toulon Gare .... d.	0630	0800	0910	0930	1135	1220	1445	1640	1700	1900	St Tropez .... d.		0540	0710	0730	0900	1035	1200	1400	1500	1725	1920
23	Hyères .... d.	0705	0835	0945	1005	1210	1255	1525	1725	1735	1930	Cavalaire .... d.		0605	0740	0800	0930	1105	1230	1430	1530	1755	1950
46	Le Lavandou .... d.	0740	0910	1020	1040	1245	1330	1600	1810	1810	2005	Aiguebelle .... d.		0612	0747	0807	0937	1112	1237	1437	1537	1802	1957
51	Aiguebelle .... d.	0747	0917	1027	1047	1252	1337	1607	1807	1817	2012	Le Lavandou .... d.		0635	0810	0830	1000	1135	1305	1500	1600	1825	2020
67	Cavalaire .... d.	0810	0940	1050	1110	1315	1400	1630	1830	1840	2035	Hyères .... d.		0710	0845	0905	1035	1210	1340	1535	1635	1900	2050
84	St Tropez .... a.	0840	1015	1120	1140	1345	1430	1700	1900	1910	2105	Toulon Gare .... a.		0750	0915	0940	1110	1245	1415	1610	1715	1935	2115

km			A	A	A	A	A	A	A	A	A				E	A	A	A	A	A	A	A	A
0	St Tropez .... d.	...	0620	0840	1020	1200	1400	1540	1730	1915	...	St Raphaël .... d.	...	0645	0835	1020	1215	1350	1550	1740	1945	...
4	Ste Maxime .... d.	...	0705	0925	1105	1245	1445	1625	1815	2000	...	Fréjus .... d.	...	0650	0845	1030	1225	1400	1600	1750	1950	...
18	St Aygulf .... d.	...	0725	0945	1125	1305	1505	1645	1835	2020	...	St Aygulf .... d.	...	0655	0855	1040	1235	1410	1610	1800	2000	...
24	Fréjus .... d.	...	0735	0955	1135	1315	1515	1655	1845	2030	...	Ste Maxime .... d.	...	0715	0915	1100	1255	1430	1630	1820	2020	...
27	St Raphaël .... a.	...	0745	1005	1145	1325	1525	1705	1855	2040	...	St Tropez .... a.	...	0800	1000	1145	1340	1515	1715	1905	2100	...

A – 🕱 (daily Mar. 20 - July 2).　　E – ⑦ Oct. 10 - Mar. 19.　　F – ⑦ Mar. 20 - July 2.

Service by 🚐, operated by SODETRAV, 47 Avenue Alphonse Denis, BP 711, 83412 Hyères. ☎ 94.65.21.00.　Fax 94.65.40.26.

Table 170   REIMS and METZ - DIJON   1,2 class

km		3560 3561		6130 6131 11961	6132 6133		3566 3567	6134 6135	6144 6145		3562 3563	6106 6107		1967 11965	6136 R	M		1967 6146	6136 6146	6136 6146	6138 6139
				🕱 N	🍴	Ⓐ		Ⓐ 5f	5f		Ⓑq	Ⓑq		Ⓑh	R	M		5f P	5f T	⑦e S	5f L
0	Reims .... d.	0618	...	0710	...	...	1209	1244	...	...	1652	...	1840	...	2041	...	...	2041	...	...	...
	Paris Est 173 .... d.	...	...	...	0659	...	...	...	...	...	...	...	1802	...	...	...	...	...	...	...	...
58	Châlons sur Marne .... d.	0657	...	0751	0840	...	1249	1325	...	...	1732	...	1934	1952	2120	...	...	2120	...	...	...
91	Vitry le François .... d.	0717	...	0808	0857	...	...	1346	...	...	1752	...	...	2010	2141	...	...	2141	...	...	...
120	St. Dizier .... d.	0739	...	...	0917	...	...	1407	...	...	1813	...	...	2032	2202	...	...	2202	...	...	...
193	Chaumont .... d.	0824	...	...	...	...	...	1454	...	...	1858	...	...	...	2248	...	...	2248	...	...	...
227	Langres .... d.	0846	...	...	...	...	...	1517	...	...	1919	...	...	...	2310	...	...	2310	...	...	...
	Luxembourg 173 .... d.	...	...	...	...	...	...	...	...	...	...	...	...	...	...	...	...	...	...	...	...
	Saarbrücken 173 .... d.	...	...	...	...	...	...	...	...	...	...	...	...	...	...	...	...	...	...	...	...
	Metz 172 .... d.	...	...	0734	1223	...	1345	1542	...	1721	...	...	...	2048	...	...	2048	2048	2110		
	Nancy 172 .... d.	...	...	0818	1307	...	1426	1632	...	1806	...	...	...	2142	...	...	2142	2142	2200		
	Toul .... d.	...	...	0838	1328	...	1446	1652	...	1826	...	...	...	2203	...	...	2203	2203			
	Neufchâteau .... d.	...	...	0904	1355	...	1512	1718	...	1851	...	...	...	2230	...	...	2230	2230			
238	Culmont Chalindrey .... a.	0855	...	...	...	...	1527	...	...	1929	1938	...	...	2323	2317	...	2323	2317	2317		
238	Culmont Chalindrey .... d.	0901	...	...	...	...	1541	...	...	1947	...	...	...	2348	2348	...	0005	0005	0005		
315	Dijon .... a.	0947	...	1040	1523	...	1630	1639	1849	2032	...	...	0033	0033	...	0049	0049	0049			
	Lyon Part-Dieu 149 .... d.	...	...	1233	1707	...	...	1846	2057	2225	...	...	...	...	...	...	...	...	...		
	Lyon Perrache 149 .... d.	...	...	...	...	...	...	...	...	2236	...	...	0240	0240	...	0255	0255	0255			
	Montpellier 163 .... a.	...	...	...	...	...	...	...	0025	...	...	...	...	...	...	0643	0643	0643			
	Port Bou 163 .... a.	...	...	...	...	...	...	...	...	...	...	...	...	...	...	0935	0935				
	Marseille 151 .... a.	...	...	1605	2009	...	...	2150	...	...	...	...	0616	0616	...	...	...	0518			
	Nice 164 .... a.	...	...	1848	2245	...	...	0038	...	...	...	...	0920	0920	...	...	...	0822			

		6630 11962	6631	6632 6633	6632 1960		6646 1960	6646 6632	6646 6632		6606 6607	3584		6636 6637	6636 6637	1966			3586 11968 3587	6638 3588 3589
		🕱 L	⑦e	V	R		⑦e P	⑦e T	5f S		🕱	Ⓐ		W	🕱	Ⓐ C	B	Ⓐ	⑦j N	⑦e	🍴
Nice 164 .... d.		...	2017	...	2022	2022	...	...	...	...	...	0634	0644	...	...	...	...	1135b		
Marseille 151 .... d.		...	2314	...	2321	2321	...	...	...	...	...	0910	0921	...	...	...	...	1419		
Cerbère 163 .... d.		...	...	...	...	...	2030	2030	...	...	...	...	...	...	...	...	...	...		
Montpellier 163 .... d.		...	...	...	...	...	2313	2313	2313	...	...	...	...	...	...	...	...	...		
Lyon Perrache 149 .... d.		...	0240	...	0247	0247	0243	0243	0243	...	0643	...	...	...	...	...	...	...		
Lyon Part-Dieu 149 .... d.		...	...	...	...	...	...	...	...	...	0652	...	...	1223	1238	...	...	1745		
Dijon .... d.		...	...	...	0445	0445	0439	0439	0439	...	0846	...	...	1433	1433	...	...	1651	1942	1958
Culmont Chalindrey .... a.		...	...	...	0533	0533	0527	0527	0527	...	0935	...	...	...	...	...	...	1735		2046
Culmont Chalindrey .... d.		...	...	...	0552	0557	0557	0552	0552	0628	0945	0946	...	...	...	...	...	1742		2048
Neufchâteau .... d.		...	...	...	0640	...	...	0640	0640	0752	1032	...	...	1610	1610	...	...	2114		
Toul .... d.		...	...	...	0707	...	...	0707	0707	0814	1058	...	...	1638	1638	...	...	2140		
Nancy 172 .... a.		...	0629	...	0727	...	...	0727	0727	0841	1116	...	...	1657	1657	...	...	2158		
Metz 172 .... a.		...	0719	...	0816	...	...	0816	0816	...	1201	...	...	1739	1739	...	...	2248		
Saarbrücken 173 .... a.		...	...	...	...	...	...	...	...	...	...	...	...	...	...	...	...	...		
Luxembourg 173 .... a.		...	...	...	...	...	...	...	...	...	...	...	...	...	...	...	...	...		
Langres .... d.		...	...	...	0608	...	0608	...	...	0638	...	0957	...	...	...	...	...	1753		2058
Chaumont .... d.		...	...	...	0632	...	0632	...	...	0726	...	1018	...	...	...	...	...	1814		2120
St. Dizier .... d.		0558	...	...	0720	...	0720	...	...	0845	...	1105	...	...	1718	1841	1859	2206		
Vitry le François .... d.		0619	...	...	0742	...	0742	...	...	...	...	1126	...	...	1738	1849	1902	1920		2226
Châlons sur Marne .... d.		0651	...	...	0803	...	0803	...	...	...	0850	1147	1307	...	1756	1907	1921	1942		2246
Paris Est 173 .... a.		0838	...	...	...	...	...	...	...	...	...	...	...	1933	...	2058	...	...		
Reims .... a.		...	...	...	0840	...	0840	...	...	...	0931	1226	1347	...	1949	...	2017	2324		

B – Ⓐ Apr. 10 - May 12.
C – Not Ⓐ Apr. 10 - May 12.
L – LORAZUR - 🛏 1,2 cl. (T2), 🛏 1,2 cl. and 🍴 Metz - Nice and v.v.
M – 🛏 1,2 cl. Metz - Nice (also 🛏 1,2 cl. (T2), replaced by 🍴 on ⑤ and Nov. 11, May 26, not Nov. 10, May 24).
N – 🍴 Reims - Nancy and v.v.
P – 🛏 1,2 cl. Reims - Port Bou and Cerbère - Reims.
R – 🍴 and 🛏 1,2 cl. Reims - Nice and v.v.
S – 🍴 and 🛏 1,2 cl. Metz - Montpellier and v.v.
T – 🍴 and 🛏 1,2 cl. Metz - Port Bou and Cerbère - Metz.
V – 🍴 and 🛏 1,2 cl. Nice - Metz (also 🛏 1,2 cl. (T2), replaced by 🍴 on ⑦ and Apr. 17, May 1,8, not Apr. 16,30, May 7).
W – ①-⑥ (not Apr. 17, May 1,8).

b – Depart 1143 on Ⓒ (not Dec. 3,17, Jan. 28) and daily Mar. 6 - May 27.
e – Also Apr. 17, May 1,8; not Apr. 16,30, May 7.
f – Also Nov. 10, May 24; not Nov. 11, May 26.
h – Not Oct. 31, Nov. 11, Apr. 16,30, May 7,25.
j – Not Nov. 1,11, Apr. 16,30, May 7,25.
q – Not Apr. 16,30, May 17.

Table 170a

LYON - LA CLUSE - ST. CLAUDE

1,2 class

km		⚒	🚌 †	†	†	⚒	🚌 ⚒	Ⓐ		🚌 Ⓑ
	Lyon Perrache 156 d.	0610	0745	...	1053	1135	...	...	1653	...
0	**Lyon Part Dieu 156** d.	0619	0800	...	1103	1145	...	*1503*	1703	...
65	Bourg en Bresse **156** d.	0736	0919	0931	1202	1251	...	1555	1813	...
101	La Cluse a.	0827	...	1016	1247	1341	...	1637	1903	...
101	La Cluse d.	0835	...	1019	1254	1351	1350	1640	1907	1911
	Nantua a.	|	...	|	|	|	1356	|	|	1917
	Bellegarde a.	|	...	|	|	|	1434	|	|	1955
114	Oyonnax d.	0854	...	1039	1313	1410	...	1653	1928	...
147	**St. Claude 157** a.	0930	...	1114	1349	1447	...	...	2008	...
170	**Morez 157** a.	...	...	...	...	...	...	...	2036	...

	🚌 Ⓐ		Ⓐ	🚌 ⚒		Ⓑ		🚌 Ⓑ	
Morez 157 d.	...	0555	...	...	...	...	...	...	...
St. Claude 157 d.	...	0637	...	...	1157	...	...	...	1746
Oyonnax d.	...	0717	0817	...	1233	1532	...	...	1831
Bellegarde d.	0640	|	|	1156	|	|	...	1732	|
Nantua d.	0718	|	|	1234	|	|	...	1810	|
La Cluse a.	0724	0731	0829	1240	1248	1550	...	1816	1846
La Cluse d.	...	0736	0839	...	1251	1553	...	...	1849
Bourg en Bresse **156** d.	...	0842	0920	...	1341	1638	1710	...	1932
Lyon Part Dieu 156 a.	...	0940	...	...	1424	...	1815	...	...
Lyon Perrache 156 a.	...	0949	...	...	1433	...	1824	...	...

Table 171

PARIS - BASEL

1,2 class

km				1641 ⚒	EC 113 D 🍷	1743 ⑦ 🍷	1743 ⚒ 🍷	1745 G 🍷	1643	1847 Ⓒ 🍷	1747 Ⓐ 🍷		1945 ⑤f 🍷	1645 ⚒	EC 115 L ✕⚡	1947 E 🍷	117 E 🍷	1749 F 🍷	1849 ⑤f	1649	1169 A	469 C	1949 ⑦q	
0	**Paris Est** d.	...	...	0708	0730	0839	0842	1152	1240	1330	1341	...	1610	1632	1700	1809	1857	1857	1901	2010	2214	2240	2329	...
167	Troyes d.	0658	...	0837	|	1014	1015	|	1411	1454	|	...	1737	1831	|	1939	2024	2024	2045	2203	|	0020	0113	...
222	Bar sur Aube d.	0738	...	0910	|	1048	|	|	1439	|	|	...	|	1910	|	|	|	|	2116	2236	|	0056	0146	...
263	Chaumont d.	0809	0824	0943	|	1111	1107	|	1501	1543	|	...	1831	1936	|	2034	|	2116	2141	2301	|	0130	0213	...
297	Langres d.	...	0846	1004	|	1131	|	|	1521	|	|	...	|	...	|	|	|	|	2202	2322	|	0156	0237	...
308	Culmont Chalindrey d.	...	0855	1016	|	1143	1134	|	1533	|	|	...	|	...	|	|	|	|	2215	2334	|	0211	0251	...
381	Vesoul d.	...	...	...	1036	1220	1215	1454	...	1648	1652	...	1938	...	2008	2143	2218	2221	...	...	|	0301	0333	...
443	**Belfort** d.	...	...	...	1114	1309	1309	1544	...	1733	1734	...	2022	...	2045	2236	2259	2310	...	...	0238	0413	0435	...
492	Mulhouse a.	...	...	...	1140	1334	1334	1610	...	1801	1801	...	2050	...	2112	2304	2326	2336	...	...	0305	0444	0510	...
526	**Basel** a.	...	...	...	1211	1408	1408	1637	...	1836	1836	...	...	...	2140	...	...	...	...	...	0330	0530	...	...

	468 B	1168 A	1640 ⚒	112 Ⓐ 🍷	1642 ⚒	1940 ⑥ 🍷		1942 † 🍷	EC 114 L ✕⚡		1644 Ⓐ	1844 ⑥	1742 G 🍷		1744 ⚡ 🍷	1746 †		1946 ⑤f 🍷	1846 ⑥t	1646 Ⓐ 🍷	EC 116 R ✕⚡	1948 ⑦e	118 ⑦e 🍷	1748 🍷
Basel d.	0028	0250	...	...	...	...	...	...	0823	...	...	...	...	...	1248	...	...	...	...	...	1648	...	...	1830
Mulhouse d.	0114	0320	...	0510	...	0628	...	0633	0848	...	...	...	1143	...	1325	...	...	1525	...	...	1712	...	1804	1905
Belfort d.	0152	0403	...	0542	...	0700	...	0707	0920	...	...	...	1217	...	1358	...	...	1602	...	...	1745	...	1833	1937
Vesoul d.	0236	|	...	0615	...	0734	...	0748	0954	...	...	...	1258	...	1440	...	...	1641	...	...	1819	...	1906	2016
Culmont Chalindrey d.	0327	|	0620	|	...	|	...	0834	|	...	1042	1114	|	...	|	1626	...	1727	1755	1801	|	1905	|	2101
Langres d.	0339	|	0631	|	...	|	...	0844	|	...	1052	1124	|	...	|	1638	...	|	1805	1811	|	1916	|	|
Chaumont d.	0404	|	0652	|	0756	|	...	0906	|	...	1113	1145	|	...	1550	1659	...	|	1826	1833	|	1937	2013	2129
Bar sur Aube d.	0428	|	0714	|	0817	|	...	0928	|	...	1135	1206	|	...	|	1723	...	|	1846	1855	|	1959	|	|
Troyes d.	0503	|	0744	|	0852	|	...	1003	1145	...	1208	1240	|	...	1636	1753	...	1841	1919	1928	|	2033	2058	2215
Paris Est a.	0648	0807	0916	0926	1030	1043	...	1143	1314	...	1341	1411	1614	...	1806	1937	...	2020	2107	2107	2132	2217	2223	2343

A – ARLBERG EXPRESS – for composition and days of running see Table **31**.
B – (12) and ▬ 2 cl. Basel - Paris; ▬ 1,2 cl., ▬ 2 cl. and (2) Chur - Paris; ▬ 1,2 cl. Strasbourg - Belfort - Paris.
C – (12) and ▬ 2 cl. Paris - Basel; ▬ 1,2 cl., ▬ 2 cl., (2) and 🍷 Paris - Chur; ▬ 1,2 cl. Paris - Belfort - Strasbourg.
D – LE CORBUSIER – ⚒ (also Nov. 11, May 25; not Oct. 31, Nov. 12): (12) Paris - Basel - Zürich; (12) and 🍷 Paris - Basel.
E – ⑤⑦ (also Nov. 1,10, Apr. 17, May 1,8,24; not Nov. 11, Apr. 16,30, May 7,26).
F – Daily except when train **E** runs.
G – ⑤⑥ (also Oct. 31, Nov. 10, May 24; not Nov. 12, May 26).
L – L'ARBALETE – (12) and ✕ Paris - Basel - Zürich and v.v.
R – LE CORBUSIER – daily except ⑥, not Oct. 30,31, Nov. 11, Apr. 16,30, May 7: (12) Zürich - Paris; ✕ Basel - Paris.
e – Also Nov. 1, Apr. 17, May 1,8; not Apr. 16,30, May 7.
f – Also Nov. 10, May 24; not Nov. 11, May 26.
q – Also Nov. 1, Dec. 26, Jan. 2, Apr. 17,18, May 1,8; not Apr. 16,30, May 7.
t – Also Nov. 11, Apr. 16,30, May 7,25.
⚡ – Supplement payable.

Table 172

LUXEMBOURG - METZ - NANCY

1,2 class

km		⚒	Ⓐ	⚒	⚒	⚒	Ⓐ		†	⚒		⚒	†	⚒	Ⓐ		Ⓒ	Ⓐ	⚒	⚒	†	Ⓐ		Ⓐ
0	**Luxembourg 173 176** d.	...	...	...	0627	...	...	0750r	...	...	...	...	...	...	...	...	...	...	...	...	1558	1620	...	1714
34	Thionville **173 176** d.	...	0513	0621	0652	0722	0747	0820	...	0921	1027	1120	...	1220	...	1312	1420	1420	1525	1621	1621	1647	1723	1741
46	Hagondange **173** d.	...	0523	0630	0701	0731	0756	0829	...	0930	1035	1129	...	1229	...	1323	1429	1429	1533	1630	1630	1659	1731	1750
64	**Metz 170 173 176** d.	0513	0543	0643	0715	0745	0809	0844	0930	0943	1049	1143	1156	1243	1315	1336	1442	1451	1545	1643	1643	1712	1745	1805
93	Pont-à-Mousson d.	0533	0607	0704	0733	0806	0827	0904	0959	1003	1109	1203	1225	1303	1333	1356	1503	1512	1605	1703	1703	1730	1806	1825
121	**Nancy 170** a.	0600	0635	0721	0752	0824	0845	0922	1024	1021	1126	1221	1254	1320	1352	1414	1521	1529	1622	1720	1720	1748	1824	1843

	⑥	†		Ⓐ	⚒	†	⑤f	†	†	
Luxembourg 173 176 d.	...	...	...	1825	...	1851	1925	...	...	...
Thionville **173 176** d.	...	...	1821	1850	1921	1921	1948	2021	...	...
Hagondange **173** d.	...	...	1830	1859	1930	1930	1956	2030	...	...
Metz 170 173 176 d.	1810	1830	1843	1913	1944	1944	2011	2043	2130	2313
Pont-à-Mousson d.	1838	1911	1904	1931	2004	2004	2032	2103	2154	2337
Nancy 170 a.	1901	1943	1922	1950	2022	2022	2049	2121	2213	2358

	⚒	Ⓐ	Ⓐ	⚒	Ⓐ	⚒	†		⑥
Nancy 170 d.	0558	0620	0653	0658	0731	0758	...	0900	0958
Pont-à-Mousson d.	0616	0637	|	0718	0749	0815	...	0917	1015
Metz 170 173 176 d.	0636	0657	0726	0740	0809	0836	0845	0937	1035
Hagondange **173** d.	0648	0709	...	0752	0822	0849	0857	0950	1047
Thionville **173 176** a.	0658	0717	...	0801	0832	0859	0905	1003	1057
Luxembourg 173 176 a.	...	0743	...	0827	...	...	0931	...	...

	Ⓐ	†	⚒	⑥	Ⓐ	⑥	Ⓒ	⚒		⚒	⑤f		Ⓐ	⚒		Ⓐ		Ⓐ			Ⓐ		⚒	
Nancy 170 d.	0958	1058	1058	1158	1158	1217	1240	1258	1358	1458	1531	1558	1624	1658	1705	1725	1758	1823	1902	1908	1941	2022	2135	2206
Pont-à-Mousson d.	1015	1115	1115	1216	1216	1238	1307	1315	1415	1515	1550	1616	1642	1715	|	1744	1815	1843	1920	1940	1959	2039	2201	2228
Metz 170 173 176 d.	1038	1134	1136	1237	1237	1256	1340	1336	1436	1536	1609	1637	1701	1736	1739	1805	1836	1902	1942	2015	2017	2100	2222	2248
Hagondange **173** d.	1057	...	1148	1250	1250	...	...	1349	1449	1549	1620	1649	1713	1748	...	1818	1848	1914	1954	2028	...	2112	...	...
Thionville **173 176** a.	1108	...	1158	1259	1259	...	...	1359	1459	1559	1631	1658	1724	1758	...	1831	1905	1925	2004	2039	...	2123	...	...
Luxembourg 173 176 a.	...	...	...	...	1324	...	...	...	...	...	...	...	1745	...	...	1852	...	1946	...	2100	...	...	...	...

– Also Nov. 10, May 24; not Nov. 11, May 26.
r – ⚒ only.

Table 172a

NANCY and METZ - LONGWY

1,2 class

km				⑤⑥	⚒	⚒	†			⚒	⑦e
0	**Nancy** d.	...	0753	1233	1404	...	...	1714	...	1829	2220
28	Pont-à-Mousson d.	...	0811	1252	1424	...	...	1739	...	|	2240
71	Conflans-Jarny d.	...	0844	1327	1455	...	...	1822	...	1918	2314
	Metz d.	0758	|	|	|	1714	1736	|	1844	|	|
112	Longuyon d.	0849	0912	1358	1524	1814	1841	1854	1933	1948	2345
128	**Longwy** a.	...	0924	1411	1536	1826	...	1907	...	2000	2357

	⚒	†	⚒	⚒	⚒		†	h		†
Longwy d.	0521	0532	0628	0656	1010	1225	1632	1840	...	1930
Longuyon d.	0534	0545	0641	0709	1023	1238	1646	1854	1937	1944
Metz a.	|	|	0738	|	|	|	|	|	2031	|
Conflans-Jarny d.	0604	0613	...	0742	1054	1307	1714	1925	...	2013
Pont-à-Mousson d.	0635	0642	...	0815	1123	1338	1744	1958	...	2043
Nancy a.	0654	0700	...	0834	1142	1356	1801	2018	...	2100

– Also Apr. 17, May 1,8; not Apr. 16,30, May 7.
h – On ⚒ runs 2 minutes later (change at Pagny-sur-Moselle, arrive 1947/depart 1957).

Table 173 PARIS - METZ, NANCY, LUXEMBOURG and STRASBOURG

1,2 class

km				11711 ①v	1611 ♦	Ⓐ	⑥	⚒		†	†	60207 ⚒ B	⚒ R	105 Ⓐk 🍴↯		EC 203 ♦ ↯	⚒p	⚒	11961 ⚒	EC 65 ♦ ↯	1903 †	1701 ⚒		EC57 1832 † ↯	EC 57 ♦
0	**Paris Est**	d.	...	0005	0017	...	...	...	...	...	...	...	...	0652	...	0656	...	...	0659	0751	0806	0806	...	0854	0854
95	Château Thierry	d.	...	0059	0110	...	...	...	...	...	...	...	...	|	...	|	...	...	0751	|	0854	0854	...	|	|
142	Épernay	d.	...	0125	0137	...	...	...	...	...	...	...	...	|	...	|	...	...	0819	|	0922	0922	...	|	|
172	Châlons sur Marne	d.	...	0145	0206	...	...	...	...	...	...	...	0751	0812	...	0818	...	0825	0840	|	0940	0943	...	|	|
	Verdun	a.	...	|	|	...	...	...	...	...	...	...	|	|	...	|	...	0956	|	|	|	|	...	|	|
205	Vitry le François	d.	...	0205	0227	...	...	...	...	...	...	...	0809	|	...	|	...	|	0855	|	0958	1001	...	|	|
255	Bar le Duc	d.	...	0232	0304	...	...	...	...	...	...	...	0837	|	...	0857	...	|	...	|	1022	1028	...	1049	1049
354	**Metz**	a.	...	|	|	...	...	...	...	...	...	...	|	|	...	0951	...	1153	...	|	|	|	...	1146	1146
354	**Metz 172/6**	d.	...	|	|	0642	0642	0751	...	0846	...	...	|	|	...	0954	1000	...	...	|	|	|	...	1150	1154
404	St. Avold	d.	...	|	|	0715	0715	0827	...	0916	...	...	|	|	...	|	1030	...	...	|	|	|	...	|	1221
424	Forbach	d.	...	|	|	0733	0731	0843	...	0934	0939	...	|	|	...	|	1046	...	...	|	|	|	...	|	1240
434	**Saarbrücken**	a.	...	|	|	0741	...	0851	...	...	0948	...	|	|	...	|	1054	...	...	|	|	|	...	|	1249
	Hagondange **172**	d.	...	|	|	...	...	...	...	...	...	...	|	|	...	1007	...	...	...	|	|	|	...	1202	...
	Thionville **172/6**	a.	...	|	|	...	...	...	...	...	...	...	|	|	...	1020	...	...	...	|	|	|	...	1210	...
	Luxembourg 172/6	a.	...	|	|	...	...	...	...	...	...	...	|	|	...	1041	...	...	...	|	|	|	...	1233	...
320	Toul	d.	...	0312	0348	...	...	...	...	...	...	...	0914	|	...	...	...	...	...	|	1103	1109	...	...	...
353	**Nancy**	a.	...	0333	0408	...	...	...	...	...	...	...	0932	0937	...	...	...	...	...	1029	1122	1130	...	...	...
353	**Nancy**	d.	...	0336	0426	...	...	...	...	...	...	0704	...	0940	...	...	...	...	...	1031	1125	...	...	...	...
386	Lunéville	d.	...	0358	0445	...	...	...	...	...	...	0722	...	|	...	...	...	...	...	|	1144	...	...	...	...
433	Sarrebourg	d.	...	0428	0511	...	...	...	...	...	...	0749	...	1017	...	...	...	...	...	|	1208	...	...	...	...
459	Saverne	a.	...	|	0531	...	...	...	...	...	...	0806	...	1033	...	...	...	...	...	|	1224	...	...	...	...
504	**Strasbourg**	a.	...	0517	0600	...	...	...	...	...	...	0832	...	1100	...	...	...	...	...	1141	1251	...	...	...	...

		†	1603 ⚒ 🍷	EC 357 ⚒ 🍷	⚒	Ⓐ		1905 ⑤f 🍷	EC 55 ♦ ↯	EC 96 🍴	1605 🍷	EC 67 ♦ ↯	Ⓐ	⑥	Ⓐ	1807 ⑤f 🍷	1607 Ⓑh 🍷		1917 ⑤f 🍷	EC 90 🍴 ↯			1707	Ⓐ	
Paris Est	d.	...	0901	1053	...	...	...	1256	1301	...	1320	1345	...	...	...	1522	1556	...	1600	...	...	...	1622	...	...
Château Thierry	d.	...	|	|	...	...	...	|	|	...	|	|	...	...	...	|	|	...	|	...	...	...	|	...	...
Épernay	d.	...	|	|	...	...	...	|	|	...	1428	|	...	...	...	1631	|	...	1709	...	...	...	1731	...	...
Châlons sur Marne	d.	0946	|	1212	...	1233	...	|	|	...	1446	|	...	...	...	1649	|	...	1727	...	...	...	1750	1829	...
Verdun	a.	1118	|	|	...	1406	...	|	|	...	|	|	...	...	...	|	|	...	|	...	...	...	|	2018	...
Vitry le François	d.	|	|	|	...	...	...	|	|	...	1503	|	...	...	...	1706	|	...	1745	...	...	...	1808	...	...
Bar le Duc	d.	|	|	1249	...	...	...	|	|	...	1527	|	...	...	...	1730	|	...	1809	...	...	...	1833	...	...
Metz	a.	1250	|	1344	...	...	...	|	1547	...	|	|	...	...	...	|	|	...	1908	...	...	...	|	...	...
Metz 172/6	d.	...	|	1348	1355	...	...	|	1555	1605	|	|	1641	1701	1752	|	|	...	...	1913	1920	...	|	...	...
St. Avold	d.	...	|	|	1428	...	...	|	1621	|	|	|	1729	1743	1822	|	|	...	...	|	2003	...	|	...	...
Forbach	d.	...	|	|	1444	...	...	|	1640	|	|	|	1755	1804	1837	|	|	...	...	|	2020	...	|	...	...
Saarbrücken	a.	...	|	|	1452	...	...	|	1648	|	|	|	1804	1813	1845	|	|	...	...	|	...	...	|	...	...
Hagondange **172**	d.	...	|	1402	...	...	...	|	...	|	|	|	...	...	...	|	|	...	...	|	...	...	|	...	...
Thionville **172/6**	a.	...	|	1411	...	...	...	|	...	1626	|	|	...	...	...	|	|	...	...	1932	...	...	|	...	...
Luxembourg 172/6	a.	...	|	1435	...	...	...	|	...	1649	|	|	...	...	...	|	|	...	...	1956	...	...	|	...	...
Toul	d.	...	|	...	...	...	...	|	...	...	1606	|	...	...	...	1812	|	...	...	...	...	...	1913	...	...
Nancy	a.	...	1147	...	...	...	...	1540	...	...	1626	1629	...	...	...	1832	1838	...	...	...	...	...	1931	...	...
Nancy	d.	...	1212	...	...	...	...	1543	...	...	1647	1632	...	...	...	...	1841	1846	...	...	...	...	...	...	...
Lunéville	d.	...	1232	...	...	...	...	1602	...	...	1705	|	...	...	...	...	|	1909	...	...	...	...	...	...	...
Sarrebourg	d.	...	1254	...	...	...	...	1627	...	...	1727	|	...	...	...	...	|	1940	...	...	...	...	...	...	...
Saverne	a.	...	1310	...	...	...	...	1646	...	...	1745	|	...	...	...	...	|	...	...	...	...	...	...	...	...
Strasbourg	a.	...	1338	...	...	...	...	1711	...	...	1811	1744	...	...	...	...	1952	...	...	...	...	...	...	...	...

		EC53 1834 ↯	EC 53 ♦ ↯	EC 69 ♦ ↯		1909 ⑤f 🍷	11965 Ⓑh		EC 207 Ⓑh ↯	1719 Ⓑh	109 🍷 ↯		11609 T			263 ♦		1709 🍷	1836 ⚒	1836 ⑦e			261 ♦	469 ♦	
Paris Est	d.	1716	1716	1719	...	1756	1802	...	1845	...	1848	...	1854	...	...	1943	...	1948	...	1955	...	...	2230	2240	...
Château Thierry	d.	|	|	|	...	|	1904	...	|	...	|	...	1949	...	...	|	...	|	...	|	...	...	|	|	...
Épernay	d.	|	|	|	...	|	1933	...	|	...	|	...	2016	...	...	|	...	2056	...	|	...	...	|	|	...
Châlons sur Marne	d.	|	|	|	...	|	1952	...	|	...	2010	...	2034	2042	...	|	...	2114	...	|	...	...	0004	|	...
Verdun	a.	|	|	|	...	|	|	...	|	...	|	...	...	2215	...	|	...	|	...	|	...	...	|	|	...
Vitry le François	d.	|	|	|	...	|	2009	...	|	...	|	...	...	...	...	|	...	2132	...	|	...	...	|	|	...
Bar le Duc	d.	|	|	|	...	|	...	...	2041	...	|	...	...	...	...	|	...	2159	2210	2210	...	...	0045	|	...
Metz	a.	1959	1959	|	...	|	...	...	2136	...	|	...	...	...	...	|	...	|	2305	2305	...	...	0141	|	...
Metz 172/6	d.	2004	2006	|	...	|	...	...	2140	2149	|	...	...	...	...	|	...	|	2309	2309	2313	...	0205	|	...
St. Avold	d.	|	2032	|	...	|	...	...	|	2223	|	...	...	...	...	|	...	|	|	|	2345	...	|	|	...
Forbach	d.	|	2049	|	...	|	...	...	|	2243	|	...	...	...	...	|	...	|	|	|	0002	...	|	|	...
Saarbrücken	a.	|	2056	|	...	|	...	...	|	2252	|	...	...	...	...	|	...	|	|	|	0010	...	|	|	...
Hagondange **172**	d.	2016	...	|	...	|	...	...	2154	...	|	...	...	...	...	|	...	|	2321	2321	...	...	|	|	...
Thionville **172/6**	a.	2025	...	|	...	|	...	...	2204	...	|	...	...	...	...	|	...	|	2330	2330	...	...	|	|	...
Luxembourg 172/6	a.	2048	...	|	...	|	...	...	2229	...	|	...	...	...	...	|	...	|	2354	2354	...	...	|	|	...
Toul	d.	...	...	|	...	|	...	...	...	...	|	...	...	...	...	|	...	2240	...	...	...	...	|	|	...
Nancy	a.	...	...	2004	...	2044	...	...	...	...	2135	...	...	...	...	2225	...	2258	...	...	...	...	|	|	...
Nancy	d.	...	...	2007	...	2047	...	...	...	...	2138	2144	...	...	...	2227	...	...	...	...	...	...	|	|	...
Lunéville	d.	...	...	2026	...	|	...	...	...	...	|	2206	...	...	...	2246	...	...	...	...	...	...	|	|	...
Sarrebourg	d.	...	...	2049	...	2125	...	...	...	...	|	...	...	...	...	2308	...	...	...	...	...	...	|	|	...
Saverne	a.	...	...	2105	...	|	...	...	...	...	|	...	...	...	...	2325	...	...	...	...	...	...	|	|	...
Strasbourg	a.	...	...	2131	...	2204	...	...	...	...	2250	...	...	...	...	2350	...	...	...	...	...	...	0332	0741	...

♦ – **NOTES** (LISTED BY TRAIN NUMBER)

EC53 – GOETHE – [12] and 🍴 Paris - Frankfurt/Main.
EC55 – GUSTAVE EIFFEL – [12] and 🍴 Paris - Frankfurt/Main.
EC57 – HEINRICH HEINE – [12] and 🍴 Paris - Dresden.
EC65 – MOZART – [12] and 🍴 Paris - Wien; [12] Paris - Graz.
EC67 – MAURICE RAVEL – [12] and 🍴 Paris - München.
EC69 – MARIE CURIE – [12] and 🍴 Paris - Stuttgart.
EC203 – VICTOR HUGO – ⚒ (also Nov. 11, May 25; not Nov. 12): [12] and 🍷 Paris - Luxembourg.
261 – 🛏 1,2 cl., 🛌 2 cl. and [2] Paris - München; 🛌 2 cl. and [2] Paris - Frankfurt (also 🛏 1,2 cl. (T2) except on ⑥); 🍷 Paris - Strasbourg.
263 – ORIENT EXPRESS – 🛏 1,2 cl., 🛌 2 cl. and [2] Paris - Wien; 🛌 2 cl. and [2] Paris - Budapest; 🍴 Paris - Strasbourg.
469 – 🛌 1,2 cl. Paris - Belfort (Table **171**) - Strasbourg.
1611 – 🛌 1,2 cl. and [12] Paris - Strasbourg.

B – [12] Nancy - Basel.
R – [12] Reims - Nancy.
T – [12] Paris - Épernay daily;
[12] Paris - Châlons sur Marne ① and † (also Apr. 18, May 2, 9; not May 25).

e – Also Nov. 1, Apr. 17, May 1, 8; not Apr. 16, 30, May 7.
f – Also Nov. 10, May 24; not Nov. 11, May 26.
h – Not Oct. 31, Nov. 11, Apr. 16, 30, May 7.
k – Not Oct. 31, May 25,26.
p – Also Nov. 11, May 25; not Nov. 12.
v – Also Nov. 2, Dec. 27, Jan. 3, Apr. 18, 19, May 2, 9; not Oct. 31, Dec. 26, Jan. 2, Apr. 17, May 1, 8.

↯ – Supplement payable.

Table 173 — STRASBOURG, LUXEMBOURG, NANCY and METZ - PARIS

1,2 class

Section 1

	1612 ◆	260 ◆	11962	1600 ※Ⓐt	209 208 ※⑦g	262 ※	1702	⑦q	Ⓐ	1814 ⑦q	351 350 ※⑦g	1714	353 352 ※p	1704 ◆	EC 68 ⑦v	1802 Ⓐ	EC 91 ※	EC 52 ◆
Strasbourg.........d.	...	0015	0210	...	0446	...	0527	...	...	...	...	...	...	0650	...	0806	...	...
Saverne...........d.	...	0042		...	0509	...	...	...	...	...	...	...	...	0715	...	0829	...	...
Sarrebourg........d.	...	0105		...	0530	...	...	...	...	...	...	...	...	0739	...	0852	...	...
Lunéville.........d.	...	0129		...	0553	...	...	...	...	...	...	...	...	0805b	...	...	...	...
Nancy.............a.	...	0157		...	0612	...	0643	...	...	...	...	...	...	0824b	...	0928	...	...
Nancy.............d.	...	0218		...	0616	...	0646	0702	...	...	...	...	...	...	0856	0930	0937	...
Toul..............d.	...	0242		...	...	...	...	0722	...	...	...	...	...	0915	...	...	0956	...
Luxembourg 172/6 ...d.					...	0526	...	...	...	0710	...	0759	...	...	...	...	...	1001
Thionville 172/6 ...d.					...	0550	...	...	...	0735	...	0824	...	...	...	...	...	1024
Hagondange 172 ...d.					...	0600	...	...	...	0745	...	0834	...	...	...	...	...	...
Saarbrücken........d.					...	...	...	...	...	0638	0653	...	0742	...	...	...	0832	0946
Forbach............d.					...	...	...	...	...	0649	0702	...	0753	...	...	...	0842	0959
St. Avold..........d.					...	...	...	...	...	0704	0717	...	0809	...	...	...	0856	1013
Metz 172/6 ....a.	...	0337		...	...	0611	...	...	...	0738	0749	0758	0839	0847	...	...	0927	1042
Metz...............d.	...	0355		...	...	0615	...	...	...	0802	0850	...	...	...	...	...	...	1054
Bar le Duc.........d.	0330			...	...	0709	0758	...	...	...	0854	...	...	0950	...	1031	...	...
Vitry le François...d.	0359		0619	0723	...	...	0824	...	...	...	...	...	...	1014	...	1054	...	...
Verdun.............d.	...			...	0610	...	...	...	0756	...	...	...	...	...	...	...	...	...
Châlons sur Marne..d.	0421	0532	0651	...	...	0736	0746	...	0842	...	0924	...	0932	...	1015	1031	1111	...
Épernay............d.	0441		0708	...	...	...	0859	...	...	...	0948	...	...	1048	...	1128	...	...
Château Thierry....d.	0507		0736	...	...	...	0923	...	...	...	1013	...	...	1113	...	1151	...	...
Paris Est...........a.	0603	0704	0838	0907	...	0910	0933	1014	...	...	1104	...	1140	1204	...	1215	1242	1337

Section 2

	104 Ⓐ	1904 ⑤f	EC 66 ◆	1835 EC54 ◆	54 ◆	U	1804 1706 ⑤f	1806 ⑤f F	1906 G	1906	EC 97 Ⓐ	1966 J	1606 K	1606 Ⓐ	205/4 ◆ ⑥h R	11968 ⑦e
Strasbourg.........d.	...	1015	1154	1219	...	...	1245	...	1418	1450	...	1556	1556	...	...	...
Saverne...........d.	...		1236		...	...	1313	...	...	...	...	1639	1639	...	...	...
Sarrebourg........d.	...				...	...	1331	...	...	...	...			...	...	...
Lunéville.........d.	...		1300		...	...	1357	...	...	...	...			...	...	...
Nancy.............a.	...	1131	1317	1335	...	...	1415	...	1535	1609	...	1718	1718	...	...	...
Nancy.............d.	...	1134	1320	1337	...	...	1433	...	1537	1611	...	1721	1721	...	...	1729
Toul..............d.	...				...	...	1453	...	1556	1630	...			...	...	1747
Luxembourg 172/6 ...d.	...			1307	...	...	...	...	...	...	1459			...	1634	...
Thionville 172/6 ...d.	...			1332	...	...	...	...	...	...	1522			...	1658	...
Hagondange 172 ...d.	...			1342	...	...	...	...	...	...				...		...
Saarbrücken........d.	...				1219	1310	...	...	...	...	...			1553		...
Forbach............d.	...				1229	1323	...	...	...	...	...			1603		...
St. Avold..........d.	...				1248	1336	...	...	...	...	...			1617		...
Metz 172/6 ....a.	...			1331	1355	1402	...	...	...	...	1540			1652	1718	...
Metz...............d.	...				1415	1415	...	...	...	...	...				1724	...
Bar le Duc.........d.	...	1221	1407		1508	1508	1532	...	1632	1706	...			1816	1822	...
Vitry le François...d.	1056						1558	...			...	1738		1841	1849	1902
Verdun.............d.	...							1441	1455		...					...
Châlons sur Marne..d.	1225	1300			1546	1546	1610	1619	1633	1651	...	1756		1859	1907	1921
Épernay............d.	...						1636	1714	1722	1800	...	1813			1922	1938
Château Thierry....d.	...						1700	1745			...	1840				2005
Paris Est...........a.	1426		1608	1622	1709	1709	1752	1843	1839	1911	...	1933	2006	2012	2023	2058

Section 3

	EC 56 ◆	1839 EC56 ❋	108 ⑥k	2	1908 1708 ⑤c M	M	1912 ⑦e	295 ❋	EC 64 Ⓐ	※	†	⑦e	⑤f	※	†	Ⓐn	1610 E	6192 468 S
Strasbourg.........d.	...	...	1706	...	1724	...	1758	...	1819	...	...	...	...	...	...	1822	1906	2300
Saverne...........d.	...	...	1729	...	1750	...	1822	...	...	...	...	...	...	...	...	1848	1931	...
Sarrebourg........d.	...	...	1751	...	1810	...	1843	...	...	...	...	...	...	...	...	1907	1952	...
Lunéville.........d.	...	...	1813	...	1834	...	1906	...	...	...	...	...	...	...	...	1933		...
Nancy.............a.	...	...	1832	...	1852	...	1924	...	1934	...	...	...	...	...	...	1954	2029	...
Nancy.............d.	...	...	1835	...	1855	1855	1927	...	1937	...	...	...	...	...	...		2032	...
Toul..............d.	...	...		...	1915	1915		...		...	...	...	...	...	...			...
Luxembourg 172/6 ...d.	...	1725		...	...	...		1802	1825	1851	...	...	...	...	...			...
Thionville 172/6 ...d.	...	1749		...	...	...		1827	1850	1921	...	...	...	...	...			...
Hagondange 172 ...d.	...			...	...	...			1859	1930	...	...	...	...	...			...
Saarbrücken........d.	1709			...	...	...					1818	...	...	1925	...			...
Forbach............d.	1723			...	...	...					1828	1844	...	1935	2037			...
St. Avold..........d.	1737			...	...	...					1849	1901	...	1949	2054			...
Metz 172/6 ....a.	1806	1806		...	...	...		1845	1911	1925	1942	1935	...	2021	2123			...
Metz...............d.	1819	1819		1718	...	...				1948	1948		...					...
Bar le Duc.........d.				1952	1952		2024			2044	2044		...			2121		...
Vitry le François...d.				2019	2019								...					...
Verdun.............d.				1856									...					...
Châlons sur Marne..d.				2023	2037	2037	2103			2123	2123		...		2159			...
Épernay............d.				2054	2054					2140	2140		...					...
Château Thierry....d.				2118	2118								...					...
Paris Est...........a.	2105	2105	2114		2208	2208	2227		2220			2251	2251		2324		0648	...

NOTES (LISTED BY TRAIN NUMBER)

◆ –

EC52 – GOETHE – 🍴 and ✕ Frankfurt/Main - Paris.
EC54 – GUSTAVE EIFFEL – 🍴 and ✕ Frankfurt/Main - Paris.
EC56 – HEINRICH HEINE – 🍴 and ✕ Dresden - Paris.
EC64 – MOZART – 🍴 and ✕ Wien - Paris; 🍴 Graz - Paris.
EC66 – MAURICE RAVEL – 🍴 and ✕ München - Paris.
EC68 – MARIE CURIE – 🍴 and ✕ Stuttgart - Paris.
EC204/5 – VICTOR HUGO – ⑥ (not Oct. 31, Nov. 11, Apr. 16, 30, May 7):
          🍴 Luxembourg - Paris.
260 – 🛏 1,2 cl., 🍴 2 cl. and 🍴 München - Paris; 🍴 2 cl. and 🍴 Frankfurt/
      Main - Paris (also 🛏 1,2 cl. (T2) except on ⑥ or Dec. 23 - Jan. 1).
262 – ORIENT EXPRESS – 🛏 1,2 cl., 🍴 2 cl. and 🍴 Wien - Paris;
      🍴 2 cl. and 🍴 Budapest - Paris; 🍴 and ✕ Strasbourg - Paris.
1612 – 🍴 1,2 cl. and 🍴 Strasbourg - Paris.

K – ⑤ (also Nov. 10, Feb. 16, 23, Apr. 13, May 24; not Nov. 11, Feb. 17, 24, Apr. 14).
M – ①②③④⑦ (not Oct. 31, Nov. 10, Feb. 16, 23, Apr. 13, 16, 30, May 7, 24, 25).
R – 🍴 Nancy - Reims.
S – 🛏 1,2 cl. Strasbourg - Belfort (Table 171) - Paris.
U – ①②③④ (not Nov. 1, 11, Feb. 16, 23, Apr. 13, 17, May 1, 8, 24, 25).
b – Change at Sarrebourg on ① and Nov. 2, 12, Dec. 27, Apr. 15, 18, May 2, 9, 26.
c – Also Nov. 10, Feb. 16, 23, Apr. 13, May 24.
e – Also Nov. 1, Apr. 17, May 1, 8; not Apr. 16, 30, May 7.
f – Also Nov. 1, May 24; not Nov. 11, May 26.
g – Also Nov. 11, May 25; not Nov. 12.
h – Not Nov. 1, 11, Apr. 16, 30, May 7.
k – Not Oct. 31, Nov. 11, Apr. 16, 30, May 7, 25, 26.
n – Not Dec. 26, Apr. 14.
p – Also Nov. 11, May 25.
q – Also Nov. 1, 12, Apr. 17, May 1, 8.
t – Not Oct. 31, May 25.
v – Also Nov. 1, Apr. 17, May 1, 8.

E – ⑤⑦ (also Nov. 1, 10, Apr. 17, May 1, 8, 24; not Nov. 11, Apr. 16, 30, May 7, 26).
F – ⑤ Nov. 25 - May 19 (also Feb. 16, 23, Apr. 13, May 24; not Feb. 17, 24, Apr. 14).
G – ⑤ Sept. 30 - Nov. 18 (also Nov. 10; not Nov. 11).
J – ①②③④⑦ (not Oct. 31, Nov. 10, Feb. 16, 23, Apr. 13, 16, 30, May 7, 24;
    not Feb. 17, 24, Apr. 14).

✗ – Supplement payable,

Table 176 — LUXEMBOURG - METZ - STRASBOURG - BASEL

1,2 class

For additional weekend trains Strasbourg - Lyon and v.v., see Table **156**.

Southbound (Part 1)

km		499 ♦	2123 ⑦t	6171/6170 ✗g	6162/6163 ⑦x	Ⓐk	Ⓒn	Ⓐk	6173/6172 B	69031 ①-⑥	60207 ✗v N	Ⓐk	6175/60211 Q	6174 🍷	2125 🍷	EC 91 ♦	T	6191/69037/6190 ⑤v 🍷	Ⓐk
0	Luxembourg 173 … d.	0118													1001				
	Lille Flandres 177 … d.		2229												0647q				
33	Thionville 173 … d.	0149	0250												1024				
63	Metz 173 … a.	0209	0311												1038				
63	Metz … d.	0215	0340						0627		0853				1042	1045		1221	
177	Saverne … d.								0742		1000							1325	
222	Strasbourg … a.	0343	0522						0807		1025				1208			1352	
222	Strasbourg … d.	0353	0530	0627	0627		0700	0733	0747	0800		0834	1031	1153	1211	1300	1300	1354	1403
265	Sélestat … d.			0650	0650		0720	0800	0806			0853	1050			1320	1324		1423
287	Colmar … d.	0426	0610	0704	0704		0731	0816	0818	0833		0905	1102	1226	1247	1331	1339	1427	1434
328	Mulhouse … a.	0449	0638	0727	0727		0750	0843	0837	0903		0924	1121	1248	1312	1351	1401	1450	1454
328	Mulhouse 171 … d.	0453		0732	0732	0743		0851	0839	0906		0926	1123	1255	1254	1315		1408	1459
	Belfort … a.			0758	0758					0932			1321					1529	
	Paris Est 173 … a.			1132	1139					1353			1653					1956	
	Lyon Part-Dieu 156 … a.					0810		0921	0904			0951							
362	Basel 171 … a.	0516											1148		1329	1339		1444	

Southbound (Part 2)

	6187/6186 Ⓒn	6177/6176 Q	⑦b 🍷	C	Q	Ⓐk	Q	Ⓐk	EC 97	60225	6179/6178 D	6189/6188 ⑦b	Ⓐk	69035 Ⓑ	295/6197/6196 ♦ E	✗	†	2129 🍷	6192/6193 R	6192/6193 R	299
Luxembourg 173 … d.									1459						1802						2201
Lille Flandres 177 … d.																			1641q		2227
Thionville 173 … d.									1522						1827						2247
Metz 173 … a.									1540						1845			2031			2247
Metz … d.									1542					1715	1847			2034			2252
Saverne … d.														1819		2013	2012				
Strasbourg … a.									1704					1844	2005	2038	2037	2153			0015
Strasbourg … d.	1403		1452	1513	1523		1618		1704	1708	1740	1820	1820	1833	1922	2008	2024		2300	2300	
Sélestat … d.	1425		1522				1638		1724		1800			1903	1942		2049		2325	2325	
Colmar … d.	1444		1539	1547	1556		1649		1735		1812	1854	1854	1921	1953	2042	2105		2340	2340	0051
Mulhouse … a.	1509		1602	1612	1623		1709		1755	1800	1831	1919	1919	1953	2013	2103	2130		0012	0012	0114
Mulhouse 171 … d.		1520		1620	1628	1629		1726		1803	1833	1924	1924		2015	2106	2140		0032	0114	0117
Belfort … a.				1646	1654							1950	1950				2210		0105	0141	
Paris Est 173 … a.				2046	2032							2325	2328			0237p			0550		
Lyon Part-Dieu 156 … a.							1705													0648	
Basel 171 … a.		1550						1705		1802		1825	1858		2040	2130					0140

Northbound (Part 1)

	298 ♦ E	6698/6699 ⑦ 🍷	2140	✗	✗k	✗k		6692/6693 R	469/6692 Ⓐk	Ⓐk	6694/6695 E	Q	Ⓐk	296 ✗k	✗g	6670/6671 Ⓐk	†n	60210 ⑥	†n	✗k 🍷	6672/6673
Basel 171 … d.	0300			0538			0635	0705		0728		0814	0933	1003		0636		1048		1233	
Lyon Part-Dieu 156 … d.		2317			0027					0234						0636					0921
Paris Est 173 … d.					2240		0545	0545			0655					1017					1257
Belfort … d.		0331			0545	0545										1017					
Mulhouse 171 … a.	0322	0404		0613	0618	0618	0700	0729	0724	0755		0836	0958	1037	1042		1113		1258	1322	
Mulhouse … d.	0324	0407	0600	0628	0628	0702	0732	0739	0807	0840	1000	1047	1052	1115	1230	1300	1322				
Colmar … d.	0348	0441	0630	0702	0702	0721	0754	0806	0825	0906	1019	1031	1110	1117	1134	1301	1319	1351			
Sélestat … d.	0456		0645	0716	0716	0733	0808	0821	0838	1031	1131	1145	1316	1330	1404						
Strasbourg … a.	0420	0520	0714	0741	0741	0753	0837	0846	0857	0940	1050	1143	1157	1205	1347	1350	1426				
Strasbourg … d.	0423		0634	0650					0943			1200	1240								
Saverne … d.			0712									1224	1305								
Metz … a.	0550		0755	0831					1114r			1337	1418								
Metz 173 … d.	0553		0758						1117r												
Thionville 173 … a.	0613								1137r												
Lille Flandres 177 … a.			1142h																		
Luxembourg 173 … a.	0647								1200												

Northbound (Part 2)

	EC 96 ♦	Ⓒn	Ⓒn	Ⓐk	Ⓐk	2146 ⑤c	2146	2148 ⑤c	S	EC 90 Ⓐk P	6674/6675	Q	†n	Ⓐk	✗	†	6676/6677 B	Ⓒn	69036 Ⓑ	69036	6668/6669 ⑦e	6678/6679 Ⓐj 🍷	498
Basel 171 … d.	1330	1508		1518						1626		1715	1731		1753	1753		1940	2054	2215			2359
Lyon Part-Dieu 156 … d.											1311						1503				1841	1848	
Paris Est 173 … d.											1651						1912				2232	2229	
Belfort … d.	1351	1540		1550						1648	1716	1746	1756		1818	1818	1939	2010	2119	2245	2258	2254	0022
Mulhouse 171 … a.	1353		1550			1600	1606		1618	1626	1650	1720	1721		1807	1807	1822	1942	2013	2122	2300	2259	0049
Mulhouse … d.			1613			1619	1629		1640	1645	1714	1739	1747		1826	1826	1851	1907	2013	2043	2141	2330	2324
Colmar … d.			1626			1631	1642		1654	1657		1751	1801		1838	1838	1907	1907		2100	2153	2344	2339	0121
Sélestat … d.	1442	1656		1650	1712	1716	1716	1720		1745	1811	1826		1858	1858	1935	1935	2045	2128	2212	0006	0002	
Strasbourg … a.	1444					1716	1716	1720		1748								1950	1950				0125
Strasbourg … d.						1746									2014	2016							
Saverne … d.						1841	1841	1851		1911		2119	2131										0258
Metz … a.	1603					1844	1844	1855		1913													0302
Metz 173 … d.	1605									1932													0322
Thionville 173 … a.	1626				2235	2235	2259																
Lille Flandres 177 … a.										1956													
Luxembourg 173 … a.	1649																						0357

NOTES (LISTED BY TRAIN NUMBER)

♦ —

EC90/1 — VAUBAN – 🛏 and ✗ Brussels - Milano and v.v.

EC96 — IRIS – 🛏 and ✗ Chur - Zürich - Brussels and v.v.

EC97 — IRIS – 🛏 and ✗ Brussels - Zürich - Chur and v.v.

295/6 — EDELWEISS – 🛏 and ✗ Brussels - Basel and v.v.

298 — 🛏 1,2 cl., 🛌 1,2 cl. (T2), 🍴 2 cl. and 🍷 Milano - Brussels (Venezia - Milano - Brussels on ⑥⑦).

299 — 🛏 1,2 cl., 🛌 1,2 cl. (T2), 🍴 2 cl. and 🍷 Brussels - Milano (Brussels - Milano - Venezia on ⑤⑥).

498 — 🛏 1,2 cl. and 🍴 2 cl. Brig - Basel - Oostende; 🛌 Basel - Oostende; 🍴 2 cl. Chur - Oostende (also 🛏 1,2 cl. Dec. 7 - Apr. 15). Conveys on dates in Table 40 🛏 1,2 cl. and 🍴 2 cl. (Brig) - Sierre - Oostende.

499 — 🛏 1,2 cl. and 🍴 2 cl. Oostende - Brig; 🛌 Oostende - Basel; 🍴 2 cl. Oostende - Chur (also 🛏 1,2 cl. Dec. 8 - Apr. 16). Conveys on dates in Table 40 🛏 1,2 cl. and 🍴 2 cl. Oostende - Sierre (- Brig).

B — LE ROUGET DE L'ISLE – 🛌 and 🍷 Strasbourg - Nice and v.v.

C — ①②③④⑥ (also Apr. 16,30, May 7; not Brussels Dec. 21, Feb. 16,23, Apr. 13, May 24).

D — ①②③④ (also Feb. 22, Apr. 22, May 26; Feb. 16,23, Apr. 13,17, May 1,8,25).

E — For days of running and composition see Table 156.

N — 🛌 Nancy - Strasbourg - Basel.

Q — ①-⑤ (not Dec. 26, Apr. 14,17, May 25).

S — ①-④ (not Dec. 26, Feb. 16,23, Apr. 13,17, May 1,8,24,25).

T — ①②③④⑥ (not Dec. 26, Feb. 16,23, Apr. 13,17, May 1,8,24,25).

b — Also Apr. 17, May 1,8; not Apr. 16,30, May 7.

c — Also Feb. 16,23, Apr. 13, May 24; not May 26.

e — Also Apr. 17, May 1,8; not Apr. 16,30, May 7.

g — Also May 25.

j — Also ⑥ Dec. 10 - Mar. 11.

n — Also Dec. 26, Apr. 14.

P — 🛌 Mulhouse - Strasbourg - Nancy.

Q — 🛌 1,2 cl. Paris - Strasbourg and v.v.

h — Arrive 1157 from Apr. 18.

k — Not Dec. 26, Apr. 14.

p — Lyon Perrache.

q — Depart 3 mins later Sep. 25 - Apr. 17.

r — 10 - 12 minutes earlier on ⑦ Oct 2 - Dec. 11.

t — Also Dec. 26, Jan. 2, Apr. 17,18, May 1,8; not Dec. 25, Jan. 1, Apr. 16,30, May 7.

v — Also Feb. 16,23, Apr. 13, May 24.

x — Dec. 11 - Mar. 12 only.

y — Not Apr. 14.

Table 177 — PARIS - REIMS - SEDAN - LUXEMBOURG

1,2 class

km		Ⓐ	Ⓐ	✗p	2125 Ⓨ	1621	69301 ✗	1701 1721 ✗	1903 1923 ✗⑦n	1623 ✗	1625	69305	1925 Ⓑ		2129 Ⓨ	🚌	1627 Ⓑh	1629 Ⓨ	1727 Ⓑh	69339	1729	2123 ⑦q
0	Paris Est ...... d.	...	...	...	...	0713	...	0806	0806	1100	1218	...	1517	...	...	...	1625	1800	1851	...	2146	...
95	Château Thierry ...... d.	...	...	...	...	0854	...	0854	1148	1306	...	...	...	...	...	1719	...	...	...	2235	...
142	Epernay ...... d.	...	...	...	0825	0933	...	0933	1211	1335	...	...	...	...	...	1743	1913	...	2302	...
173	Reims ...... d.	...	...	...	0848	0954	1004	0957	1231	1358	...	1647	...	...	...	1808	1937	...	2324	...
	Lille Flandres 107 ...... d.	...	...	0647y											1641y				2229
	Valenciennes 107 ...... d.	...	...	0722										1716					2302
	Hirson ...... d.	...	...	0803															2355
256	Charleville-Mézières ...... d.	0605	...	0851	0940	0948	...	1100	1100	...	1450	1500	1738	1748	1844	...	1859	1907	2029	2037	0048
274	Sedan ...... d.	0619	...	0906	...	1002	...	1115	...	1514	...	1805	...	...	1935	...	2054	0105
324	Montmédy ...... d.	0650	...	1035	...	1148	...	1546	1835	...	...	...	2127	0137
345	Longuyon ...... d.	0703	0726	0946	...	1050	...	1211	...	1602	1851	1937	...	...	2142	0154
	Hayange ...... d.											2009	2012				
	Thionville ...... a.											2024					
	Metz 176 ...... a.			1038								2031				0235
	Strasbourg 176 ...... a.	✗p										2153				0311
361	Longwy ...... d.	0647	0738	0754	...	1108	...	1223	...	1614	1903					2154	0522
369	Rodange ...... d.	0657	0803	...	1115k	1134								
392	Luxembourg ...... a.	0727	0828	...	1201								

		1720 Ⓐ	1620 ✗	✗p	1920 †	69302	1622	🚌	2140 Ⓨ		1722 ✗		1924 ✗⑤f	1724 Ⓐ			1626 E	69836	1726 G	Ⓑj	✗p	†g	✗b		2146 ✗p
	Luxembourg ...... d.	...	...	0600	...	...	...	...	0905	...	...	...	...	...	1718	...	...	...	1810
	Rodange ...... d.	...	...	0627	...	...	...	0931	...	...	...	1740	...	1830
	Longwy ...... d.	...	...	0634	0744	...	0938	...	1502	...	1619	...	1747	1756	1810	...	1837
	Strasbourg 176 ...... d.	...	0634	...	...	...	...	1716
	Metz 176 ...... d.	...	0758	...	...	...	...	1844
	Thionville ...... d.	...	0757	...	...	...	...	
	Hayange ...... d.	...	0810	0822	...	...	...	
	Longuyon ...... d.	...	0759	...	0851	...	1517	1634	...	1820	1825	...	1935
	Montmédy ...... d.	...	0813	...	...	1531	1649	...	1834	1839	...	
	Sedan ...... d.	...	0845	...	1054	...	1603	1603	1722	...	1907	1911	...	2019
	Charleville-Mézières ...... d.	0610	0720	0900	0908	...	0953	1120	1128	...	1620	1630c	1743	...	1934	1926	1934	2041
	Hirson ...... d.																	2121
	Valenciennes 107 ...... d.						1113											2206
	Lille Flandres 107 ...... d.						1142x											2235
	Reims ...... d.	0616	0704	0812	...	1001	...	1231	1533	1624	...	1724	1859	...	2028	2028
	Epernay ...... d.	0638	0834	...	1252	1555	1645	...	1746	1921	...	2050	2050
	Château Thierry ...... d.	0701	0901	...	1813	...	
	Paris Est ...... a.	0755	0841	0952	1132	...	1409	1705	1759	...	1905	2033	...	2202	2202

E – ⑤⑦ (also Nov. 1, 10, 11, Apr. 17, May 1, 8, 24, 25).
G – ①②③④ (not Nov. 1, Apr. 17, May 1, 8, 25).
b – Also Apr. 16, 30, May 7.   c – Daily except ⑥.
f – Also Nov. 10, May 24; not Nov. 11, May 26.
g – Not Apr. 16, 30, May 7.   h – Not Nov. 11.
j – Not Nov. 11, Apr. 16, 30, May 7.
k – Not Dec. 26, 27, Jan. 2, Feb. 27.
n – Also Nov. 1, 11, Apr. 17, May 1, 8, 25; not Apr. 16, 39, May 7.
p – Also Nov. 11, May 8; not Dec. 26, 27, Jan. 2, Feb. 27.
q – Also Nov. 1, Dec. 26, Jan. 2, Apr. 17, 18; not Dec. 25, Jan. 1, Apr. 16, 30, May 7.
x – Arrive 1157 from Apr. 18.
y – Depart 3 minutes later Sep. 25 - Apr. 17.

Table 178 — NANCY - ÉPINAL - BELFORT

1,2 class

km		✗	✗	✗2	Ⓐ	✗	Ⓐ		✗	✗	✗	Ⓐ	Ⓐ	Ⓐ		Ⓐ	Ⓑh	⑥	Ⓐ	⑤⑦
	Paris Est 173 ...... d.																1622			
0	Nancy ...... d.	0609	...	0640	0741	0850	0945	...	1040	1140	...	1216	1240	1342	1610	1643	1737	...	1813	1850	1944	1949	2011	2148	2148
74	Épinal ...... d.	0712	0717	0734	0832	0949	1037	1122	1138	1234	1248	1318	1348	1439	1706	1738	1833	1840	1913	2006	2032	2041	2116	2243	2339
	Remiremont ...... a.	0752	...	0856	...	1204	...	1317	...	1502	1731	1807	...	1905	...	2100	2106
182	Belfort ...... a.	0844	...	1240	...	1350r	...	...	...	1949

		Ⓐ	⑥	Ⓐ	✗	Ⓐ		Ⓐ		✗	✗	Ⓐ		✗	✗	Ⓐ	†	Ⓐ		G		⑤f	†
	Belfort ...... d.	...	...	...	0608	...	...	1130	...	1316r	...	...	...	1702	...	...	1911	1911
	Remiremont ...... d.	...	0615	0641	...	0718	...	1231	1328	1407	...	1544	1604	1657	...	1810	1918	...
	Épinal ...... d.	0506	0527	0544	0640	0710	0735	0748	0748	0841	1004	...	1248	1255	1356	1450	1540	1608	1629	1731	1821	1836	1943	2032	2047
	Nancy ...... a.	0601	0633	0650	0734	0801	...	0841	0841	0935	1124	1230	1328	...	1351	1451	1526	1634	1702	1733	1821	...	1929	2036	2125	2147
	Paris Est 173 ...... a.							1204													

G – ①②③④⑥ (also May 26; not Apr. 17, May 1,8,24,25).
f – Also Nov. 10, May 24; not Nov. 11, May 26.
h – Not Apr. 16,30, May 7.
r – ⑥ only.

Table 179 — ÉPINAL - ST DIÉ - STRASBOURG

1,2 class

km		✗2	Ⓒ		✗	⑥	Ⓒ		†	Ⓐ	Ⓐ				✗n	✗	†		Ⓐ	Ⓒ	⑥		
0	Épinal ...... d.	0740r	1100	...	1238	...	1642	...	1748	1821	1907	Strasbourg ...... d.	...	0535	0642	0830	...	1210	1240	...	1740
60	St Dié ...... d.	0840	1200	1215	1344	1537	1545	1746	1808	1852	1919	2010	St Dié ...... d.	0628	0735	0830	1011	1242	1420	1416	1645	1750	1820	1905
147	Strasbourg ...... a.	0958	...	1354c	...	1727	1730	...	1955	...	2132	Épinal ...... a.	0730	0840	...	1344	...	1745	1852	1922	2006f

Service on Dec. 26, Apr. 14 is as on †.   c – Arrive 1404 on ⑥, 1411 on †.   f – Ⓒ only.   r – ✗ only (from Nancy, depart 0640).   n – To Nancy, arrive 0935.

Table 181 — OTHER LOCAL SERVICES

1,2 class

ANGERS - CHOLET: *60 km* Journey 60 minutes. **Service Jan. 23 - May 27** (timings vary by up to 10 minutes Sept. 25 - Jan. 22).   b – Subject to alteration on Ⓐ Mar. 24 - Apr. 6.
Angers depart: 0639Ⓐ, 0857Ⓐ, 0931⑥, 1121Ⓐ, 1130†, 1150⑥, 1312✗, 1534Ⓐ, 1631⑤, 1725†, 1735Ⓐ, 1739Ⓐ, 1831Ⓐ, 1937 (not ⑤), 1947⑤, 2031, 2120†, 2238Ⓑ.
Cholet depart: 0613Ⓐ, 0630✗, 0657✗, 0815Ⓐ, 0842†, 1102b, 1253b, 1655✗, 1824Ⓐ, 1825†, 1845⑥, 1937⑤, 1954①②③④, 1954†, 2219†.

BAYONNE - ST-JEAN-PIED-DE-PORT: *50 km* Journey 60 minutes.
Bayonne depart: 0925, 1448, 1846✗, 2054⑤†.   St-Jean-Pied-de-Port depart: 0630Ⓐ, 0823Ⓒ, 1332, 1655✗, 1754⑦ (also Apr. 17, May 1,8; not Apr. 16,30, May 7); 1904†.

BORDEAUX - MORCENX - MONT-DE-MARSAN: *147 km* Journey 90 - 100 minutes.   c – Change at Morcenx (25 - 30 minutes from Bordeaux).
Bordeaux depart: 0710c, 1116†, 1153✗, 1436✗, 1646Ⓐc, 1830c, 2059Ⓑ.   Mont de Marsan depart: 0623✗c, 0843✗, 1005✗, 1141c, 1543†, 1613✗, 1840c (arrive 2056 on ✗), 2032†.

NANCY - LUNEVILLE - ST DIÉ: *84 km* Journey 62 - 72 minutes. Trains call at Lunéville approximately 20 minutes after leaving Nancy and 40 minutes after leaving St Dié.
Nancy depart: 0605✗, 0735✗, 0815†, 1045, 1235✗, 1424Ⓒ, 1540⑥, 1636, 1745†, 1750⑥, 1752Ⓐ, 1910Ⓐ, 2016✗, 2032†, 2144.
St Dié depart: 0458✗, 0625✗, 0742, 0930✗, 0935†, 1015✗, 1216, 1541Ⓐ, 1546Ⓒ, 1717Ⓒ, 1721Ⓐ, 1810Ⓐ, 1813†, 1906Ⓐ, 1913Ⓒ, 2012†, 2227†.

STRASBOURG - HAGUENAU: *34 km* Journey 30 - 40 minutes. Service on Dec. 26, Apr. 14 is as on †.
Strasbourg depart: 0559✗, 0655✗, 0810Ⓑ, 1112✗, 1120†, 1211✗, 1438✗, 1620Ⓐ, 1632†, 1635✗, 1711Ⓐ, 1738⑥, 1740Ⓐ, 1825Ⓐ, 1832†, 1844✗, 1912✗, 2015Ⓐ, 2019†, 2141†.
Haguenau depart: 0537✗, 0614Ⓐ, 0640✗, 0704Ⓐ, 0709†, 0722✗, 0757Ⓐ, 0805✗, 0852✗, 1051Ⓑ, 1306✗, 1410†, 1417✗, 1715✗, 1726†, 1741Ⓐ, 1812†, 1822✗, 2051✗, 2058†.

TOURS - CHINON: *49 km* Journey 55 - 60 minutes.
Tours depart: 0640Ⓐ🚌, 0842Ⓐ🚌, 0930†🚌, 1312✗🚌, 1720Ⓐ, 1835, 1959⑤.   Chinon depart: 0624✗, 0700Ⓐ🚌, 0702Ⓐ, 1100†🚌, 1105✗🚌, 1228Ⓐ🚌, 1745✗🚌, 1949†.

Table 183

STRASBOURG - SAARBRÜCKEN

1,2 class

Services shown as ✕ and Ⓐ do not run on Dec. 26, Apr. 14.

km			✕	⑥	✕		✕	Ⓐ		⑧				✕	Ⓐ	✕	✕			⑧	⑦
0	Strasbourg	d.	...	0755	1100	1231	...	1640	...	1838		Saarbrücken	d.	...	0704	1132	...	...	1710	1732	...
71	Diemeringen	d.	...	0859	1157	1334	...	1743	...	1938	...	Forbach	d.	...	0717		...	...			1750
97	Sarreguemines	a.	...	0920	1218	1359	...	1806	...	2001		Sarreguemines	a.	...	0751	1156	...	...	1728	1756	1829
97	Sarreguemines	d.	...	0922	1220		1402	...	1811	...	2006	Sarreguemines	d.	0705	0753	...	1211	...	1735	...	1832
	Forbach	a.	...									Diemeringen	d.	0729	0816	...	1246	...	1759	...	1857
139	Saarbrücken	a.	...	0941	1240		1425	...	1830	...	2025	Strasbourg	a.	0828	0913	...	1351	...	1859	...	1958

Table 188

BASTIA - AJACCIO AND CALVI

timings valid to May 20

2 class only

km				A	✕		A			A	A	✕		A				✕	
0	Bastia	d.	...	...	0655	...	0815	...	0920	...	...	1505	...	...	...	1615	...	1645	...
47	Ponte Leccia	d.	...	...	0751	...	0917	...	1030	...	...	1606	...	...	...	1728	...	1747	...
99	Ile Rousse	d.	0915	...		1105	...	...	1148	1350	1600		...	1755	...	1846	...		...
120	Calvi	a.	1000	...		1150	...	...	1221	1435	1645		...	1840	...	1918	...		...
74	Corté	d.	...	...	0823	...	...	0951	...	...		1645	...	...	...	...	...	1820	...
152	Ajaccio Gare	a.	...	...	1004	...	...	1140	...	...		1838	...	...	...	...	...	2005	...

		✕		⑦			A		A		A				A		A
Ajaccio Gare	d.	...	0635	...	...	0755	...	...	...	...	1450	...	...	...	1630	...	...
Corté	d.	...	0823	...	...	0951	...	...	...	...	1646	...	...	...	1820	...	...
Calvi	d.	0600		0720		...	0820	1010	1200	...	1415	...	1500	...		1700	...
Ile Rousse	d.	0634		0755		...	0905	1055	1245	...	1450	...	1545	...		1745	...
Ponte Leccia	d.	0751	0854	0916	1027	...	...	...	...	1608	1723	...	...	1852		...	...
Bastia	a.	0847	0949	1015	1128	...	...	...	...	1712	1830	...	...	1947		...	...

A – ✕ Apr. 18 - May 20.

Table 192

🚌 CHAMONIX - AOSTA

🚌 SAT/SAVDA

		K	E	E		E			E	H		H	E		G		E		E		E
Chamonix	d.	0900	0915	1005	...	1330	...	...	1500	1500	...	1615	1615	...	1730	...	1745	...	1815	...	1930
Courmayeur	a.	0940	0955	1045	...	1410	...	...	1540	1540	...	1655	1655	...	1810	...	1825	...	1855	...	2010
Aosta ‡	a.			1140			...	...	1700	1700	...		1800	...	1930		1930	...			2135

		E		J		E		E		H		H		E		E		G		E		E		E
Aosta ‡	d.	...	0745	...	0940	...	1130	...	1215	...	1305	...	...	1425	...	1425	...	...	...	1745	...	
Courmayeur	d.	...	0900	...	1050	...	1230	...	1415	...	1500	...	1540	...	1530	...	1645	...	1710	...	1845	...	1905
Chamonix	a.	...	0940	...	1130	...	1310	...	1455	...	1540	...	1620	...	1610	...	1725	...	1750	...	1925	...	1945

E – July 1 - Sept. 11, 1995.
G – Sept. 12, 1994 - June 30, 1995.
H – Dec. 26 - Jan. 8 and Feb. 1 - Apr. 25, 1995.

J – Daily (not ⑦ or holidays, Sept. 18 - Dec. 11 or Apr. 30 - June 25).
K – Daily Sept. 12 - June 30 (not ⑦ or holidays, Sept. 18 - Dec. 11 or Apr. 30 - June 25).
‡ – Change buses at Courmayeur (timings subject to confirmation).

Table 195

🚌 GENÈVE ✈ - ST GERVAIS

🚌 Ski Buses

Service December 27, 1994 - April 2, 1995 (not Dec. 25), also April 8,9,15-17,22,23.

one way fare FF	🚌 operator (see below) service number days of running (see also above) reservations (see below)	G 48 daily	S 50	B/T 61 daily	C 52 A	G 52 ⑥	B/T 62 ⑥⑦	C 54 A	S 54 ⑦	B/T 63 ①-⑤	S 56 ①-⑤	S 64 E	C 58 ⑥⑦	S 58 H	C daily	S daily
0	Genève ✈, Secteur France d.	...	1040	...	1045	1130	...	1400	1430	1445	...	1600	1630	...	1810	1800	1830	...	...
0	Genève ✈, Secteur International d.	...	1050	...	1055	1145	1350	1410	1445	1455	...	1610	1640	...	1820	1815	1840	...	...
0	Genève, gare routière d.	0830	1100	...	1110	1200	1405	1425	1500	1510	...	1630	1655	...	1835	1830	1855	...	...
160	Le Grand-Bornand a.				1300			1600							1930			...	...
160	St Jean de Sixt a.				1310			1610							1940			...	...
160	La Clusaz a.				1320			1620							1950			...	...
180	Saint Gervais a.		1205					1520							1930			...	...
180	Combloux a.		1220					1535				1840			1945			...	...
180	Megève a.		1230					1545				1850			1950			...	...
200	Praz-sur-Arly a.		1245 →					1600				→			2010			...	...
180	Le Fayet Gare a.	0930	1200	1200		1505			1610	1610	...	1755	1755	...		1955	1955	...	...
212	Les Contamines a.			1245						1655	...		1840	...			2040	...	...
188	Les Houches a.	0950	1220			1525			1630		...	1815		...		2015		...	...
188	Chamonix Gare a.	1005	1235			1540			1645		...	1830		...		2030		...	...

	🚌 operator (see below) service number days of running (see also above) reservations (see below)	C 49 ⑥⑦ Ⓡ	S 49 daily Ⓡ	S 65 daily Ⓡ	B/T 65 E Ⓡ	B/T 66 H Ⓡ	S 66 ⑦ Ⓡ	S 51 ⑥⑦ Ⓡ	S 53 ①-⑤ Ⓡ	S 55 ①-⑤	G 55 ⑥⑦ Ⓡ	C 67 A Ⓡ	S 57 daily Ⓡ	S 68 daily Ⓡ	C 68 ⑥ Ⓡ	B/T 59 A Ⓡ	G 59 daily Ⓡ
Chamonix Gare	d.	...	0700				...	1015	...	1050	1100	...	1400				1630
Les Houches	d.	...	0715				...	1030	...	1105	1115	...	1415				1645
Les Contamines	d.	...	0705				1000	1000				1350					
Le Fayet Gare	d.	...	0735	0735			1050	1050	1125	1125	1135	...	1435	1435	...		1705
Praz-sur-Arly	d.	...										1345				1615	
Megève	d.	...			0700	0930						1355				1625	
Combloux	d.	...			0710	0940						1410				1640	
Saint Gervais	d.	...				0955											
La Clusaz	d.	0700											1500				
St Jean de Sixt	d.	0710											1510				
Le Grand-Bornand	d.	0720											1520				
Genève, gare routière	a.	0820	0835	0930	1050		1150		1225	1235	1505		1535	1620	1735		1805
Genève ✈, Secteur International	a.	0835	0850	0945	1105		1205		1240	1250	1520		1555	1635	1750		1820
Genève ✈, Secteur France	a.	0850	0900	0955	1115		1220		1250		1530		1605	1650	1800		

A – Dec. 27 - Apr. 2, also Apr. 8, 9,15 - 17, 22, 23 (not Dec. 25).
E – ✕ Dec. 21 - May 14.
H – Dec. 21 - Apr. 2, also Apr. 9, 16, 17, 23.

FF – French Francs.
* – Departure timings given when reservations made.

Ⓡ – Advance reservations are not required for **outward** journeys from the airport (except for groups of 10 or more people), but are compulsory for **all** return journeys to the airport. Reservations should be made through local Offices du Tourismes or Gares Routières 24 hours before travelling and may be made by ☎ on the following numbers:

Chamonix 50.53.01.15
Le Fayet 50.78.05.33, Fax 50.78.07.62.
Megève 50.21.27.28, Fax 50.93.03.09.

Combloux 50.58.60.49, Fax 50.93.33.55.
Le Grand Bornand 50.02.20.58.
Praz-sur-Arly 50.21.90.57.

Genève 732.02.30.
Les Contamines 50.47.01.58.
Saint Gervais 50.47.76.08

La Clusaz 50.02.40.11.
Les Houches 50.55.50.62.
St Jean-de-Sixt 50.02.70.14.

Operators - B- Autocars Borini, F74120, Megève. C- Autocars Crolard, BP81-74002 Annecy. G- Genève Excursions, 12 rue Chantepoulet, CH1201, Genève.
S- SAT, 2 Place de la Gare, F 74100 Annemasse. T- Transports Touriscar, F 74160 Collonges-sous-Salève.

Table 196

GENÈVE ✈ - MORZINE

Ski Buses

Service December 21, 1994 - April 9, 1995 (not Dec. 25), also April 15-17, 22, 23.

single fare FF	service number / days of running (see dates above) / reservations (see below)	71 ⑥	J	73	75 ⑥	77	K	79
0	**Genève** ✈, Secteur France d.	....	1035	1100	1240	1415	1700	1815
0	**Genève** ✈, Secteur International d.	....	1045	1110	1250	1430	1710	1830
0	**Genève**, Gare Routière d.	0850	1105	1130	1310	1445	1730	1845
40	Annemasse d.	0915	|	1155	1335	1510	|	1910
80	Thonon-les-Bains a.	|	1145	|	|	|	1815	|
170	Abondance ♥ a.	|	1255	|	|	|	1900	|
170	La Chapelle-d'Abondance ♥ a.	|	1305	|	|	|	1910	|
185	Châtel ♥ a.	|	1315	|	|	|	1915	|
215	Morgins ♥ a.	|	1325	|	|	|	1930	|
170	Saint-Jean-d'Aulps ♥ a.	|	1210	|	|	|	1900	|
125	Taninges a.	0940	|	1220	1405	1535	|	1935
210	Morillon-les Esserts ▲ a.	0950	|	1230	1410	1545	|	1945
210	Samoëns ▲ a.	0955	|	1235	1415	1550	|	1950
210	Sixt-Fer à Cheval ▲ a.	1005	|	1245	1425	1600	|	2000
210	Les Carroz ▲ a.	1005	|	1245	1425	1600	|	2000
230	Flaine ▲ a.	1035	|	1315	1455	1630	|	2030
170	Les Gets a.	1000	|	1240	1420	1555	|	1955
185	**Morzine**, autogare SAT a.	1015	1225	1255	1435	1610	1915	2010
215	Avoriaz a.	...	1315	...	...	...	1945	...

service number / days of running (see dates above) / reservations (see below)	70 Ⓡ	72 ⑥ Ⓡ	74 Ⓡ	J Ⓡ	76 ⑥ Ⓡ	78 Ⓡ
Avoriaz d.	...	...	...	1330	...	...
Morzine, autogare SAT d.	0825	1130	1410	1410	1530	1710
Les Gets d.	0840	1145	1425	|	1535	1725
Flaine ▲ d.	0750	1055	1335	|	1455	1635
Les Carroz ▲ d.	0820	1125	1405	|	1525	1705
Sixt-Fer à Cheval ▲ d.	0835	1140	1420	|	1540	1720
Samoëns ▲ d.	0845	1150	1430	|	1550	1730
Morillon-les Esserts ▲ d.	0850	1155	1435	|	1555	1735
Taninges d.	0900	1205	1445	|	1605	1745
Saint-Jean-d'Aulps ♥ d.	|	|	|	1425	|	|
Morgins ♥ d.	|	|	|	1330	|	|
Châtel ♥ d.	|	|	|	1340	|	|
La Chapelle-d'Abondance ♥ d.	|	|	|	1350	|	|
Abondance ♥ d.	|	|	|	1400	|	|
Thonon-les-Bains d.	|	|	|	1500	|	|
Annemasse a.	0930	1235	1515	|	1635	1815
Genève, gare routière a.	0955	1300	1540	1550	1700	1840
Genève ✈, Secteur International a.	1010	1315	1555	1610	1715	1855
Genève ✈, Secteur France a.	1025	1330	1610	1620	1730	1910

J – ⑥⑦ Dec. 24 - Apr. 23 (not Dec. 25, Jan. 1).
K – ⑥ Dec. 24 - Apr. 22.
FF – French Francs.
♥ – Change at Thonon les Bains.
▲ – Connection by taxi (Ⓡ) to or from Taninges.

Ⓡ – Advance reservations are not required for **outward** journeys from the airport (except for groups of 10 or more people), but are compulsory for **all** return journeys to the airport. Reservations should be made through local *Offices du Tourismes* or *Gares Routières* 24 hours before travelling and may be made by ☎ on the following numbers:

Annemasse 50.37.22.13, Fax 50.92.74.96
Genève 732.02.30
Morzine 50.79.03.45, Fax 50.79.03.48
Avoriaz 50.74.02.11, Fax 50.74.18.25
Les Carroz 50.90.00.04, Fax 50.90.07.00
Samoëns 50.34.40.09, Fax 50.34.95.82
Chatel 50.73.22.44
Les Gets 50.75.80.80, Fax 50.79.76.90
Thonon-les-Bains 50.71.00.88, Fax 50.71.89.85.
Flaine 50.90.80.01, Fax 50.90.86.26
Morgins 77.23.61

Operated by SAT, 2 Place de la Gare, F 74100 Annemasse.

Table 198

GENÈVE ✈ - BOURG ST MAURICE

Ski Buses

Service December 10, 1994 - April 23, 1995. No service Dec. 25.

single fare FF	service number / days of running (see dates above) / reservations (see below)	1 daily	2 ⑥⑦	3 ⑥	4a ⑥	4b K	5 daily
0	**Genève**, Gare routière d.	0940	1050	1245	1400	1430	1745
0	**Genève** ✈, Secteur France d.	1000	1110	1310	1425	1455	1805
0	**Genève** ✈, Secteur International d.	1015	1125	1325	1440	1515	1820
	Annecy d.	1105	1215	1420	1530	1605	1910
200	Albertville d.	1135	1245	1510	1600	1645	1940
240	Moutiers Gare a.	1205	1315	1540	1630	1715	2010
350	Courchevel-Valmorel ♣ a.	1300	1405	1635	1730	1805	2110
350	Méribel ♣ a.	1245	1345	1615	1710	1745	2050
350	Pralognan ♣ a.	1245	1345	1615	1710	1745	2050
350	Les Menuires ♣ a.	1300	1405	1635	1730	1805	2110
350	Val Thorens ♣ a.	1315	1405	1635	1730	1805	2110
250	Aime Gare a.	1225	1335	1600	1650	1735	2030
350	La Plagne ♥ a.	1320	1425	1655	1800	1825	2130
250	**Bourg St Maurice** Gare a.	1245	1355	1620	1710	1755	2050
350	Les Arcs 1800 ♠ a.	1320	1425	1700	1800	1830	2130
350	La Rosière ♠ a.	1335	1445	1705	1800	1830	2130
270	Tignes a.	1330	1440	1655	1755	1840	2140
270	Val d'Isère a.	1400	1515	1730	1830	1915	2155

service number / days of running (see dates above) / reservations (see below)	6 ⑥⑦ Ⓡ	7 ⑥⑦ Ⓡ	8 J Ⓡ	9 ①-⑤ Ⓡ	10 daily Ⓡ	11 ⑤⑥⑦ Ⓡ
Val d'Isère d.	0600	0730	0815	1020	1500	1600
Tignes d.	0625	0755	0840	1045	1520	1630
La Rosière ♠ d.	⊙	⊙	⊙	⊙	⊙	⊙
Les Arcs 1800 ♠ d.	⊙	⊙	⊙	⊙	⊙	⊙
Bourg St Maurice Gare d.	0705	0835	0920	1125	1600	1720
La Plagne ♥ d.	⊙	⊙	⊙	⊙	⊙	⊙
Aime Gare d.	0725	0855	0940	1145	1620	1740
Val Thorens ♣ d.	⊙	⊙	⊙	⊙	⊙	⊙
Les Menuires ♣ d.	⊙	⊙	⊙	⊙	⊙	⊙
Pralognan ♣ d.	⊙	⊙	⊙	⊙	⊙	⊙
Méribel ♣ d.	⊙	⊙	⊙	⊙	⊙	⊙
Courchevel-Valmorel ♣ d.	⊙	⊙	⊙	⊙	⊙	⊙
Moutiers Gare d.	0750	0920	1010	1215	1640	1805
Albertville d.	0820	0950	1040	1245	1710	1835
Annecy a.	0855	1025	1120	1320	1745	1910
Genève ✈, Secteur International a.	0945	1115	1210	1415	1835	1955
Genève ✈, Secteur France a.	|	|	|	|	|	|
Genève, Gare routière a.	1005	1135	1230	1435	1855	2015

J – Daily Dec. 3 - Apr. 30.
K – ①②③④⑤⑦ Dec. 3 - Apr. 30.
FF – French Francs. ♣ – Change at Moutiers. ♥ – Change at Aime. ♠ – Change at Bourg St Maurice. ⊙ – Departure timings given when reservation made.

Ⓡ – Advance reservations are not required for **outward** journeys from the airport (except for groups of 10 or more people), but are compulsory for **all** return journeys to the airport. Reservations should be made through local *Offices du Tourismes* or *Gares Routières* 24 hours before travelling and may be made by ☎ on the following numbers:

Bourg St Maurice 79.07.04.49.
Les Arcs 79.07.04.49.
Tignes 79.06.30.75.
Courchevel 79.08.01.17.
Les Menuires 79.00.61.38
Val d'Isere 79.06.00.42.
Genève 732.44.16, Fax 731.05.75.
Méribel 79.08.54.90.
Valmorel 79.09.85.55.
La Plagne 79.09.03.44.
Moutiers 79.24.24.46.
Val Thorens 79.00.06.83.
La Rosière 79.06.80.51.
Pralognan 79.08.71.68.

Operators : Autocars Martin, F73700 Bourg St Maurice. Touriscar, F74160 Collonges-sous-Salève. Transavoie, faubourg de la Madeleine, F73600 Moutiers.

Table 199

LYON ✈ - BOURG ST MAURICE - VAL D'ISÈRE

'Skiroute' Buses

Service December 16, 1994 - April 9, 1995.

single fare FF	days of running (see dates above)	⑥	⑥	⑤	⑥	⑤
0	**Lyon Satolas** ✈ d.	0830	1230	1315	1630	1815
240	Moutiers a.	1015	1415	1500	1815	2000
290	Valmorel ♣ a.	1250	1620	1620	|	|
290	Courchevel 1850 ♣ a.	1255	1625	1625	2125	2125
290	Méribel ♣ a.	1240	1610	1610	2110	2110
290	Les Menuires ♣ a.	1120	1550	1625	2120	2120
290	Val Thorens ♣ a.	1150	1620	1655	2150	2150
240	Aime a.	1035	1435	1520	1835	2015
290	La Plagne ♥ a.	1230	1630	1630	2050	2130
240	**Bourg St Maurice** a.	1055	1455	1540	1855	2040
290	Les Arcs 1800 ♠ a.	1215	1700	1900	2130	2200
290	Tignes le Lac a.	1140	1540	1625	1940	2125
290	**Val d'Isère** a.	1200	1600	1645	2000	2145

days of running (see dates above) / reservations (see below)	⑥§ Ⓡ	⑦ Ⓡ	⑥ Ⓡ	⑥ Ⓡ	⑦ Ⓡ
Val d'Isère d.	0715	0715	0915	1245	1400
Tignes le Lac d.	0735	0735	0915	1245	1400
Les Arcs 1800 ♠ d.	0715	|	0815	1145	1030
Bourg St Maurice d.	0820	0820	1030	1400	1505
La Plagne ♥ d.	0745	0745	1000	1300	1300
Aime d.	0840	0840	1100	1430	1525
Val Thoprens ♣ d.	0720	0720	0930	1230	1400
Les Menuires ♣ d.	0745	0745	0955	1255	1425
Méribel ♣ d.	0810	0810	1015	1415	1315
Courchevel 1850 ♣ d.	0755	0755	1000	1400	1300
Valmorel ♣ d.	0750	|	1000	1400	1300
Moutiers d.	0900	0900	1130	1500	1545
Lyon Satolas ✈ a.	1045	1045	1400	1715	1730

§ – Also Dec. 23,30. FF – French Francs. ♣ – Change at Moutiers. ♥ – Change at Aime. ♠ – Change at Bourg St Maurice.

Reservation recommended (compulsory for journeys to the airport). Operated by Cars Philibert, BP16, 69641 Caluire. ☎ 78.98.56.98 (Français), 78.98.56.62 (English), Fax 72.27.00.97.

Regular bus services operate between Lyon Satolas ✈ and Grenoble (Journey 1 hour) and Chambéry (Journey 1 hour), throughout the year.

THOMAS COOK SNOWLINE ☎ 0839 168350
FOR ACCURATE UNBIASED SNOW REPORTS, UPDATED DAILY, PLUS WEATHER FORECASTS FOR THE NEXT 4 DAYS:
CALLS CHARGED (UK ONLY) AT 39p PER MINUTE CHEAP RATE, 49p PER MINUTE AT OTHER TIMES.

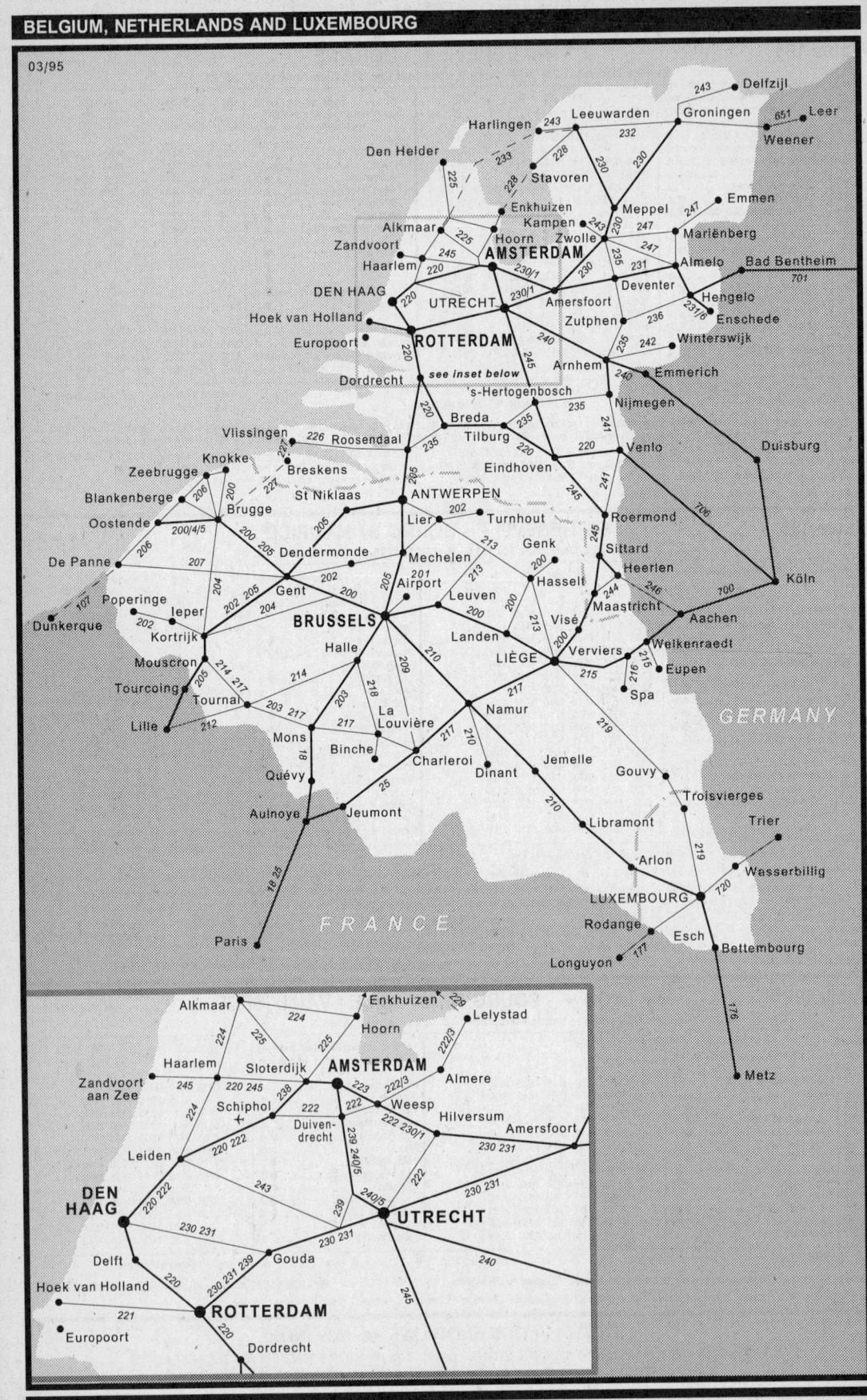

BELGIUM

Operator: Société Nationale des Chemins de fer Belges (SNCB); Nationale Maatschappij der Belgische Spoorwegen (NMBS)

Services: All trains convey first and second classes of travel unless otherwise shown by a figure '2' at the top of the column, or in a note situated to the right of the table heading. Overnight trains may only convey second class seats in addition to sleeping accommodation - see individual footnotes. Sleeping cars (🛏) and couchettes (🛌) are of the normal European types - see page 10 for more details. Supplements are not payable in Belgium except for International journeys on EC trains. Many trains convey portions for two or more destinations and are linked together for some distance. Passengers should be careful to join the correct part of the train.

Timings: Valid September 25, 1994 - May 27, 1995. Passengers are advised to consult the latest Thomas Cook European Timetable before travelling. Local trains may be amended at public holidays and passengers are advised to confirm their train times locally, before travelling at these periods. For details of public holidays see page 2..

Tickets: Seat reservations are not available in Belgium, except for international journeys to, from or via France, Germany and Luxembourg. Reservations can be made at most SNCB/NMBS stations or appointed agents.

Table 200 — OOSTENDE - BRUSSELS - LIÈGE - MAASTRICHT
1, 2 class except where shown

First block

km	Station	654 Ⓐ	654 Ⓐ	1805 Ⓐ	503	655	655	411 Y	656	656	413 Y	657	657	506	658	658	417 Y	659	659	419 Y	660	660	509	EC47 ✕◆
0	Oostende 204 205 d			0354				0532			0634			0734			0834			0934			1034	
	Knokke d								0601b			0701			0801			0901			1001			
	Blankenberge d							0605b				0705			0805			0905			1005			
22	Brugge 204 205 d			0407		0521	0521	0548	0625	0625	0650	0725	0725	0750	0825	0815	0850	0925	0915	0950	1025	1025	1050	
63	Gent Sint-Pieters d			0447		0548	0548	0617	0648	0648	0715	0748	0748	0815	0848	0848	0915	0948	0948	1015	1048	1048	1115	
115	Brussels Midi/Zuid a			0540		0615	0615	0645	0715	0715	0743	0815	0815	0843	0915	0915	0943	1015	1015	1043	1115	1115	1143	
115	Brussels Midi/Zuid d	0518	0518	0547	0555	0618	0618	0647	0718	0718	0747	0818	0818	0847	0918	0918	0947	1018	1018	1047	1118	1118	1147	1203
118	Brussels Central a	0522	0522	0547	0552	0622	0622	0652	0722	0722	0752	0822	0822	0852	0922	0922	0952	1022	1022	1052	1122	1122	1152	
121	Brussels Nord d	0529	0529	0551	0559	0629	0629	0657	0729	0729	0757	0829	0829	0857	0929	0929	0957	1029	1029	1057	1129	1129	1157	1212
150	Leuven a	0547	0547		0617	0647	0647	0717	0747	0747	0817	0847	0847	0917	0947	0947	1017	1047	1047	1117	1147	1147	1217	
169	Tienen a	0558	0558			0658	0658		0758	0758		0858	0858		0958	0958		1058	1058		1158	1158		
182	Landen a	0606	0606			0706	0706		0806	0806		0906	0906		1006	1006		1106	1106		1206	1206		
182	Landen d	0611	0614			0711	0714		0811	0814		0911	0914		1011	1014		1111	1114		1211	1214		
193	Sint-Truiden d	0622				0722			0822			0922			1022			1122			1222			
210	Hasselt d	0638				0738			0838			0938			1038			1138			1238			
226	Genk a	0652				0752			0852			0952			1052			1152			1252			
221	Liège Guillemins a		0640	©	0656			0740	0756		0840	0856		0940	0956		1040	1056		1140	1156	1256	1240	1311
221	Liège Guillemins d		0648		0648			0748	0800		0848	0900		0948			1048	1100		1148	1200		1248	1313
274	Aachen Hbf 215 a								0843			0943			1043			1143			1243			1351
	Köln Hbf 215 a								0942			1042									1242		1342	1442
236	Visé a			0703	0703				0803			0903			1003			1103			1203		1303	
255	Maastricht a			0717	0717				0817			0917			1017			1117			1217		1317	

Second block

Station	661	661	510	662	662	425 Y	663	663	512	664	664	429 Y	241 ◆	665	665	514	EC39 ✕◆	666	666	515 Y	EC49	667	667
Oostende 204 205 d			1134			1234			1334			1434				1534				1634		1657	
Knokke d		1101			1201			1301			1401				1501				1601				1701
Blankenberge d	1105			1205			1305			1405				1505				1605			1705		
Brugge 204 205 d	1125	1125	1150	1225	1225	1250	1325	1325	1350	1425	1425	1450		1525	1525	1550		1625	1625	1650	1725	1712	1725
Gent Sint-Pieters d	1148	1148	1215	1248	1248	1315	1348	1348	1415	1448	1448	1515		1548	1548	1615		1648	1648	1715	1748	1736	1748
Brussels Midi/Zuid a	1215	1215	1247	1315	1315	1343	1415	1415	1443	1515	1515	1543		1615	1615	1643		1715	1715	1743	1815	1804	1815
Brussels Midi/Zuid d	1218	1218	1247	1318	1318	1347	1418	1418	1447	1518	1518	1547	1555	1618	1618	1647	1655	1718	1718	1747	1818	1808	1818
Brussels Central a	1222	1222	1252	1322	1322	1352	1422	1422	1452	1522	1522	1552		1622	1622	1652		1722	1722	1752	1822	1812	1822
Brussels Nord d	1229	1229	1257	1329	1329	1357	1429	1429	1457	1529	1529	1557	1603	1629	1629	1657	1703	1729	1729	1757	1829	1817	1829
Leuven a	1247	1247	1317	1347	1347	1417	1447	1447	1517	1547	1547	1617		1647	1647	1717		1747	1747	1817	1847		1847
Tienen a	1258	1258		1358	1358		1458	1458		1558	1558			1658	1658			1758	1758			1858	1858
Landen a	1306	1306		1406	1406		1506	1506		1606	1606			1706	1706			1806	1806			1906	1906
Landen d	1311	1314		1411	1414		1511	1514		1611	1614			1711	1714			1811	1814			1911	1914
Sint-Truiden d		1322			1422			1522			1622				1722				1822				1922
Hasselt d		1338			1438			1538			1638				1738				1838				1938
Genk a		1352			1452			1552			1652				1752				1852				1952
Liège Guillemins a		1340	1356		1440	1456		1540	1556		1640	1656	1659		1740	1756	1759		1840		1856	1911	1940
Liège Guillemins d		1348			1448	1500		1548			1648	1700	1703		1748		1803		1848		1913		1948
Aachen Hbf 215 a					1543						1743	1747			1845				1955				
Köln Hbf 215 a					1642						1842	1902			1942				2042				
Visé a	1403			1503			1603			1703				1803				1903				2003	
Maastricht a	1417			1517			1617			1717				1817				1917				2017	

Third block

Station	233 ◆	1219 ◆	668	668	517	EC37 ✕◆	1117	669	669	439 Y	670	670	EN225	519	499 ◆	671	671	520	672 Ⓐ	672 Ⓐ	672 Ⓒ	672 Ⓒ	521 Ⓑ	521 ⑥
Oostende 204 205 d	1734	1807		1834						1934			2013	2034	2053			2134					2234	2234
Knokke d				1801					1901			2001					2101			2201		2201		
Blankenberge d			1805					1905			2005					2105			2205		2205			
Brugge 204 205 d	1750	1822	1825	1825	1850		1925	1925	1950	2025	2025	2028	2050	2109	2125	2125	2150	2215	2215	2225	2225		2250	2250
Gent Sint-Pieters d	1815	1844	1848	1848	1915		1948	1948	1950	2048	2048	2054	2115	2135	2148	2148	2215	2248	2248	2314			2314	2314
Brussels Midi/Zuid a	1843	1923	1918	1918	1947	2003	2008	2018	2018	2047	2118	2118	2125	2147	2208	2215	2215	2243	2315	2315	2345	2345	2314	2314
Brussels Central a	1852	1922	1922	1952				2022	2022	2052	2122	2122		2152		2218	2218	2250	2322	2322	2352	2352	2347	2347
Brussels Nord d	1857	1932	1929	1929	1957	2012	2018	2029	2029	2057	2129	2129	2134	2157		2229	2229	2259	2329	2329	2357	2357	2355	2355
Leuven a	1917		1947	1947	2017			2047	2047	2117	2147	2147		2217		2247	2247	2319	2347	2347	0023			
Tienen a			1958	1958				2058	2058		2158	2158				2258	2258		2358	2358	0035			
Landen a			2006	2006				2106	2106		2206	2206				2306	2306		0006	0006	0043			
Landen d			2011	2014				2111	2114		2211	2214				2311	2314		0014	0014	0044			
Sint-Truiden d			2022					2122			2222					2322								
Hasselt d			2038					2138			2238					2338								
Genk a			2052					2152			2252					2352								
Liège Guillemins a	1956	2031		2040	2056	2111	2118		2140	2156		2240	2233	2256			2340	2358			0040	0040	0114	
Liège Guillemins d	2000	2034		2048		2113				2240		2248	2235				2348							
Aachen Hbf 215 a	2043	2118			2151				2243			2318												
Köln Hbf 215 a	2155	2227			2242				2342			0017												
Visé a			2103					2203			2303					0003								
Maastricht a			2117					2217d			2317d					0017d								

NOTES (LISTED BY TRAIN NUMBERS)

37 – FELIX TIMMERMANS – 🛌2 and ✕ Brussels - Köln.
39 – JACQUES BREL – 🛌2 and ✕ Paris Nord - Brussels - Dortmund.
47 – ALEXANDER VON HUMBOLDT – 🛌2 and ✕ Brussels - Berlin Zoo.
49 – MEMLING – 🛌2 and Y Oostende - Dortmund.
225 – DONAUWALZER – 🛏 1,2 cl., ✕ 2 cl. and 🛌2 Oostende - Wien Westbahnhof; 🛏 1,2 cl., ✕ 2 cl. and 🛌2 Oostende - München Hbf.
3 – NORD EXPRESS – 🛏 1,2 cl. (T2), ✕ 2 cl. and 🛌2 Oostende - København; 🛌2 Oostende - Aachen.
OST-WEST EXPRESS, Brussels - Moskva – see Table 24. Not for local journeys.

499 – 🛌2 Oostende - Basel SBB; 🛏 1,2 cl. and ✕ 2 cl. Oostende - Basel - Brig; 🛌 2 cl. Oostende - Basel - Chur (also 🛏 1,2 cl. Dec. 8 - Apr. 16); conveys on dates in Table 40, 🛏 1,2 cl. and ✕ 2 cl. Oostende - Basel - Lausanne - Sierre (- Brig).
520 – 🛌2 Oostende - Liège; ✕ 2 cl. Oostende - Liège (243) - Berlin.
1117 – SKI EXPRESS – ⑤ Dec. 23 - Apr. 7; 🛏 1,2 cl., ✕ 2 cl. and 🛌2 Brussels - Lienz and Schwarzach St. Veit. Not for local journeys.
1219 – ⑤ Jan. 6 - Mar. 24 (also Dec. 23): ✕ 2 cl. and 🛌2 Oostende - Salzburg - Villach.
b – Ⓐ only.
d – Not Dec. 31.

Table 200 — MAASTRICHT - LIÈGE - BRUSSELS - OOSTENDE

1, 2 class except where shown

	679	679	528	528	680	680	680	680	498	529	681	681	530	EN224	682	682	531	EC36	683	683	1116	1118	412	684
			✗	⑦	Ⓐ	Ⓐ	Ⓒ	Ⓒ	◆	◆				◆				✗			◆	◆	Ⓨ	
Maastricht d.															0624				0724					0824
Visé d.															0638				0738					0838
Köln Hbf 215 d.													0508	0606				0630			0638		0714	
Aachen Hbf 215 d.													0647	0655			0710	0749	0755		0743	0803	0843	0855
Liège Guillemins a.										0546	0602		0646	0650	0702		0746	0752	0802		0817	0827	0846	0902
Liège Guillemins d.			0424	0502						0550b	0607				0707				0750					
Genk d.					0450	0607	0707	0807																
Hasselt d.					0507	0622	0722	0822																
Sint-Truiden d.					0522																			
Landen a.			0451		0528	0628	0728	0829			0531	0631			0728	0731			0829	0831				0929
Landen d.			0452	0536	0536	0636	0636	0736			0736				0836	0836								0936
Tienen d.			0506	0545	0545	0645	0645	0745			0745				0845	0845								0945
Leuven d.			0524	0557	0557	0617	0617	0643	0626	0657	0657	0717	0726	0757		0826	0847	0850	0857	0857	0917	0927	0926	0957
Brussels Nord d.	0547	0547			0617	0617	0617	0643	0652	0717	0717	0721		0752	0817	0817	0847	0850	0901	0921	0921	0927	0952	1017
Brussels Central d.	0552	0552	0621	0621	0621	0621			0649	0655	0724	0724	0724	0759	0804	0824	0855	0901	0907	0927	0927	0933	0959	1024
Brussels Midi/Zuid a.	0555	0555	0624	0624	0624	0624			0655	0724	0724	0724	0759	0809	0827	0827	0859		0927	0927		0938	0959	1056
Brussels Midi/Zuid d.	0559	0559	0627	0627	0627	0627			0649	0655	0724	0724	0759		0827	0827	0859		0927	0927	0938	0959	1030	1056
Gent Sint-Pieters d.	0630	0630	0658	0658	0658	0658			0724	0730	0756	0756	0830	0841	0856	0856	0930		0956	0956		1007	1030	1056
Brugge 204 205 d.	0624	0627	0654	0654	0724	0724	0724	0727	0749	0754	0824	0827	0854	0905	0924	0924	0954		1024		1027	1054		1124
Blankenberge a.	0637			0737			0737				0837				0937				1041					1141
Knokke a.	0641		0709	0709		0741		0741			0841				0941							1045	1109	
Oostende 204 205 a.			0709	0709					0802	0809					0909	0918			1009				1045	1109

	684	232	685	685	EC48	534		686	686	535	687		240	420	688	688	422	689	689	538	EC38	690	690	426
		◆			Ⓨ								◆	Ⓨ			Ⓨ				✗			Ⓨ
Maastricht d.			0924					1024			1124				1224			1324				1424		
Visé d.			0938					1038			1138				1238			1338				1438		
Köln Hbf 215 d.		0802		0914									1006	1114			1214				1314			1414
Aachen Hbf 215 d.		0905		1001									1115	1205			1305				1410			1505
Liège Guillemins a.		0943	0955	1036		1046		1055			1155		1158	1243	1255		1343	1355			1449	1455	1502	1543
Liège Guillemins d.		0946	1002	1039	1046			1102		1146	1202		1206	1246	1302		1346	1402			1446	1452	1502	1546
Genk d.	0850		0950						1050		1150				1250			1350				1450		
Hasselt d.	0907		1007						1107		1207				1307			1407				1507		
Sint-Truiden d.	0922		1022						1122		1222				1322			1422				1522		
Landen a.	0931		1028	1031				1128	1131		1228	1231			1328	1331		1428	1431			1528	1531	
Landen d.	0936		1036	1036				1136	1136		1236	1236			1336	1336		1436	1436			1536	1536	
Tienen d.	0945		1045	1045				1145	1145		1245	1245			1345	1345		1445	1445			1545	1545	
Leuven d.	0957	1026	1057	1057		1126		1157	1157	1226	1257	1257		1326	1357	1357	1426	1457	1457	1526	1548	1617	1557	1626
Brussels Nord d.	1017	1026	1057	1117	1135	1147		1217	1217	1247	1317	1317	1315	1347	1417	1447	1447	1517	1517	1547	1548	1617	1621	1656
Brussels Central d.	1021	1052	1121	1121	1139	1152		1221	1221	1252	1321	1321		1352	1421	1421	1454	1521	1521	1552	1556	1621	1624	1658
Brussels Midi/Zuid a.	1024	1055	1124	1124	1142	1155		1224	1224	1255	1324	1324	1322	1355	1424	1424	1455	1524	1524	1555	1556	1627	1627	1701
Brussels Midi/Zuid d.	1027	1059	1127	1127	1145	1159		1227	1227	1259	1327	1327		1359	1424	1427	1455	1527	1527	1556	1630	1656	1627	1730
Gent Sint-Pieters d.	1056	1130	1156	1156	1213	1230		1256	1256	1330	1356	1356		1430	1454	1456	1456	1530	1556	1556	1630	1656	1727	1754
Brugge 204 205 d.	1127	1154	1224	1227	1235	1254		1324	1327	1354	1424	1427		1454	1527	1554	1556	1624	1627	1654		1724	1727	1754
Blankenberge a.	1137			1237					1337			1437			1537				1637			1741		
Knokke a.		1209	1241		1248	1309		1341		1409	1441			1509	1541			1609		1641		1709		1801
Oostende 204 205 a.		1209			1248	1309				1409				1509				1609				1709		1801

	691	691	540	EC46	692	692	430	693	693	542	694	694	434	695	695	544	696	696	438	697	697	4015	698	699
				✗		Ⓨ							Ⓨ						Ⓨ			Ⓐ		
Maastricht d.	1524				1624			1724			1824			1924			2024			2124d			2224d	2324
Visé d.	1538				1638			1738			1838			1938			2038			2138			2238	2334
Köln Hbf 215 d.			1514	1607			1614	1705					1814	1905				2055		2014	2105			
Aachen Hbf 215 d.	1555		1607	1647	1655		1743	1755			1855		1943	1955			2046	2102		2143	2155		2255	2351
Liège Guillemins a.	1602		1646	1651	1702		1746	1802		1846	1902		1946	2002		2046	2102		2146	2202		2312		
Liège Guillemins d.																								
Genk d.		1550				1650			1750			1850			1950			2007		2107			2207	
Hasselt d.		1607				1707			1807			1907			2007			2022		2122			2222	
Sint-Truiden d.		1622				1722			1822			1922			2022									
Landen a.	1628	1631			1728	1731		1828	1831		1928	1931		2028	2031		2128	2131		2228	2231		2338	
Landen d.	1636	1636			1736	1736		1836	1836		1936	1936		2036	2036		2136	2136		2236	2236		2339	
Tienen d.	1645	1645			1745	1745		1845	1845		1945	1945		2045	2045		2145	2145		2245	2245		2348	
Leuven d.	1657	1657	1726		1757	1757	1826	1857	1857	1926	1957	1957	2017	2117	2117	2147	2157	2157	2247	2313	2313	2320	2359	0015
Brussels Nord d.	1717	1717	1747	1749	1817	1817	1847	1917	1917	1947	2017	2017	2117	2117	2117	2147	2217	2217	2247	2313	2313	2320	0001	0021
Brussels Central d.	1721	1721	1752		1821	1821	1852	1921	1921	1952	2021	2021	2052	2121	2121	2152	2221	2221	2252	2321	2321	2324	0021	
Brussels Midi/Zuid a.	1724	1724	1755	1801	1824	1824	1855	1924	1924	1955	2024	2024	2055	2124	2124	2155	2224	2224	2259	2329c	2329c	2329	0024	
Brussels Midi/Zuid d.	1727	1727	1759		1827	1827	1859	1924	1927	1959	2027	2027	2059	2127	2127	2159	2227	2227	2259	2329c	2329c	2329		
Gent Sint-Pieters d.	1756	1756	1830		1856	1856	1930	1956	2030	2056	2130	2156	2130	2156	2224	2227	2254	2317	2317	2354	0037c	0037c	0039	
Brugge 204 205 d.	1824	1827	1854		1924	1927	1954	2024	2027	2054	2124	2127	2130	2156	2224	2227	2137	2237						
Blankenberge a.		1837				1937			2037			2137			2241									
Knokke a.	1841				1941			2009		2041			2141		2209			2309			0009		0053	
Oostende 204 205 a.			1909				2009			2109			2209			2309					0009		0053	

◆ – NOTES (LISTED BY TRAIN NUMBERS)

EC36 – FELIX TIMMERMANS – 🍴 and ✗ Köln - Brussels.
EC38 – JACQUES BREL – 🍴 and ✗ Dortmund - Brussels - Paris Nord.
EC46 – ALEXANDER VON HUMBOLDT – 🍴 and ✗ Berlin - Brussels.
EC48 – MEMLING – 🍴 and Ⓨ Dortmund - Oostende.
EN224 – DONAUWALZER – 🛏 1,2 cl., ➡ 2 cl. and 🍴 Wien Westbahnhof - Oostende; 🛏 1,2 cl., ➡ 2 cl. and 🍴 München - Oostende.
232 – NORD EXPRESS – 🛏 1,2 cl. (T2), ➡ 2 cl. and 🍴 København - Oostende; 🍴 Aachen - Oostende.
240 – OST-WEST EXPRESS, Moskva - Brussels - see Table 24. Not for local journeys.
498 – 🍴 Basel SBB - Oostende; 🛏 1,2 cl. and ➡ 2 cl. Brig - Basel - Oostende; ➡ 2 cl. Chur - Basel - Oostende (also 🛏 1,2 cl. Dec. 7 - Apr. 15). Conveys on dates in Table 40: 🛏 1,2 cl. and ➡ 2 cl. (Brig -) Sierre - Lausanne - Basel - Oostende.

529 – 🍴 Welkenraedt - Oostende; ➡ 2 cl. Berlin (242) - Liège - Oostende.
1116 – SKI EXPRESS – ⑥ Dec. 31 - Apr. 15 (from Lienz): 🛏 1,2 cl. and ➡ 2 cl. Lienz and Schwarzach St. Veit - Brussels. Not for local journeys.
1118 – ⑥ Jan. 7 - Mar. 25, also Jan. 1 (from Villach): ➡ 2 cl. and 🍴 Villach - Salzburg - Oostende.
b – ⑧ only.
c – ⑥ (from Brussels) only.
d – Not Dec. 31.

Table 201 — BRUSSELS - BRUSSELS NATIONAAL AIRPORT ✈

1, 2 cla...

0	Brussels Central d.	0539	0556	0614	0639	0656	and at the	2256	2314	
3	Brussels Nord d.	0543	0602	0618	0643	0702	same mins.	2302	2318	
6	Schaerbeek d.		0607			0707	past each	2307		
17	Brussels Nationaal ✈ a.	0557	0618	0633	0657	0718	hour until	2318	2333	

Brussels Nationaal ✈ d.	0524	0609	0624	0646	and at the	2309	2324	23..
Schaerbeek a.	0536		0636		same mins.		2336	
Brussels Nord a.	0541	0624	0641	0700	past each	2324	2341	24..
Brussels Central a.	0547	0628	0648	0704	hour until	2329	2346	00..

Table 202 — TURNHOUT - MECHELEN - GENT - KORTRIJK - POPERINGE

1,2 class

km			©	Ⓐ		Ⓐ	Ⓒ		Ⓐ	Ⓒ	Ⓐ	Ⓒ
0	Turnhout	d.	...	0624r	0631	0724	0731		2024	2031	2124	2131
18	Herentals	d.	...	0638r	0645	0738	0745	and	2038	2045	2138	2145
48	Lier	d.	...	0656r	0659	0756	0759	at	2056	2059	2156	2159
64	Mechelen	d.	...	0714r	0718	0814	0818	the	2114	2118	2214	2218
91	Dendermonde	d.	...	0739	0737	0839	0837	same	2139	2137	2239	2237
121	Gent Sint-Pieters	a.	0703	0802	0800	0902	0900	mins.	2202	2200	2302	2300
121	Gent Sint-Pieters	d.	0703	0804	0803	0904	0903	past	2204	2203	2304	2303
163	Kortrijk	a.	0734	0836	0834	0936	0934	each	2236	2234	2336	2334
163	Kortrijk	d.	0738	0838	0840	0938	0940	hour	2238	2240	...	...
174	Menen	d.	0753	0853	0853	0953	0953	until	2253	2253	...	...
196	Ieper/Ypres	d.	0810	0910	0910	1010	1010		2310	2310	...	...
206	Poperinge	a.	0818	0918	0918	1018	1018		2318	2318	...	...

			Ⓐ	Ⓒ		Ⓒ	Ⓐ		Ⓐ	Ⓒ		Ⓐ	Ⓒ
	Poperinge	d.	0524	...	0620	0624		0724	0724		2024	2024	2124
	Ieper/Ypres	d.	0532	...	0628	0632	and	0732	0732		2032	2032	2132
	Menen	d.	0550	...	0647	0650	at	0750	0750		2050	2050	2150
	Kortrijk	a.	0602	...	0701	0704	the	0802	0804		2102	2104	2202
	Kortrijk	d.	0608	0606	0708	0706	same	0808	0806		2108	2106	2206
	Gent Sint-Pieters	a.	0639	0638	0739	0738	mins.	0839	0838		2139	2138	2238
	Gent Sint-Pieters	d.	0642	0640	0742	0740	past	0842	0840		2142	2140	2240
	Dendermonde	d.	0707	0704	0807	0804	each	0907	0904		2207	2204	2305
	Mechelen	d.	0727	0729	0827	0829	hour	0927	0929		2227	2229v	
	Lier	d.	0745	0746	0845	0846	until	0945	0946		2245	2246v	
	Herentals	d.	0758	0805	0858	0905		0958	1005		2258	2305v	
	Turnhout	a.	0811	0818	0911	0918		1011	1018		2311	2318v	

r – ⑥ only. v – ⑦ only.

Table 203 — BRUSSELS - MONS - TOURNAI

1,2 class

km			Ⓐ	Ⓒ		Ⓐ	Ⓒ		Ⓐ	Ⓒ		Ⓐ	Ⓒ		Ⓐ	Ⓒ			Ⓐ	Ⓒ		Ⓐ	Ⓒ
0	Brussels Nord	d.	0535	0540	...	0635	0640	...	0735	0740	...	0833	0840	...	0935	0940	...	and at	2135	2140	...	2235	2240
3	Brussels Central	d.	0539	0544	...	0639	0644	...	0740	0744	...	0839	0844	...	0939	0944	...	the	2139	2144	...	2239	2244
6	Brussels Midi/Zuid	d.	0545	0549	...	0645	0649	...	0745	0749	...	0845	0849	...	0945	0949	...	same	2145	2149	...	2248	2248
37	Braine-le-Comte	d.	0611	0611	...	0707	0711	...	0807	0811	...	0907	0911	...	1007	1011	...	minutes	2207	2211	...	2313	2313
43	Soignies	d.	0616	0616	...	0712	0716	...	0812	0816	...	0912	0916	...	1012	1016	...	past	2212	2216	...	2318	2318
67	Mons	a.	0632	0632	...	0726	0732	...	0826	0832	...	0926	0932	...	1026	1032	...	each	2226	2232	...	2333	2333
67	Mons 217	d.	0634	0634	0643	0732	0734	0743	0832	0834	0844	0932	0934	0943	1032	1034	1043	hour	2232	2234	2243	2345	2345
76	Saint-Ghislain	a.	0645	0645	0654	0743	0745	0755	0843	0845	0856	0943	0945	0955	1043	1045	1055	until	2243	2245	2255	2356	2346
115	Tournai 217	a.	...	...	0724	...	...	0824	...	...	0924	...	...	1024	...	...	1124		...	...	2324		

			⚒	Ⓐ	Ⓒ		Ⓐ	Ⓒ	Ⓐ		Ⓐ	Ⓒ	Ⓐ		Ⓐ		Ⓒ	Ⓐ			Ⓐ		Ⓒ	Ⓐ			Ⓒ	Ⓐ
	Tournai 217	d.	...	...	...	0618	...	...	0718	...	...	0818		...	0918		and at	2018		...	2118			2218
	Saint-Ghislain	d.	0453	0557	0559	0647	0657	0659	0747	0757	0759	0847	0857	0859	0947	0957	0959	the	2047	2057	2059	2147	2156	2159	2247
	Mons 217	a.	0504	0608	0610	0659	0708	0710	0758	0808	0810	0901	0908	0910	0959	1008	1010	same	2059	2108	2110	2159	2207	2210	2259
	Mons	d.	0506	0610	0613	...	0710	0712	...	0810	0813	...	0910	0916	...	1010	1016	minutes	...	2110	2116	...	2209	2212	
	Soignies	d.	0523	0627	0628	...	0727	0727	...	0827	0828	...	0927	0931	...	1027	1031	past	...	2127	2131	...	2226	2227	
	Braine-le-Comte	d.	0529	0633	0633	...	0733	0733	...	0833	0833	...	0933	0937	...	1033	1037	each	...	2133	2137	...	2232	2233	
	Brussels Midi/Zuid	a.	0553	0653	0657	...	0753	0757	...	0853	0857	...	0953	0958	...	1053	1057	hour	...	2153	2157	...	2253	2257	
	Brussels Central	a.	0558	0658	0702	...	0758	0804	...	0858	0902	...	0958	1003	...	1058	1102	until	...	2158	2202	...	2258	2302	
	Brussels Nord	a.	0606	0702	0706	...	0802	0809	...	0902	0906	...	1002	1007	...	1102	1106		...	2202	2206	...	2302	2306	

Table 204 — BRUSSELS - OUDENAARDE - KORTRIJK - OOSTENDE

1,2 class

km			Ⓐ	Ⓐ	Ⓒ		Ⓐ	Ⓒ		Ⓐ	Ⓒ		Ⓐ	Ⓒ		Ⓐ	Ⓐ	Ⓐ	Ⓐ
	Brussels Nord	d.	...	...	0519	...	0619	0619	...	1819	1819	...	1919	1919	...	2019	2019	2119	2219
	Brussels Central	d.	...	...	0523	...	0623	0623	and	1823	1823	...	1923	1923	...	2023	2023	2123	2223
0	Brussels Midi/Zuid	d.	...	...	0530	...	0630	0630	at	1830	1830	...	1930	1930	...	2030	2030	2130	2230
56	Zottegem	d.	...	...	0601	...	0701	0705	the	1901	1905	...	2001	2005	...	2101	2105	2201	2302
73	Oudenaarde	d.	...	...	0613	...	0713	0717	same	1913	1917	...	2013	2017	...	2113	2117	2213	2314
98	Kortrijk	a.	...	...	0630	...	0730	0734	minutes	1930	1934	...	2030	2034	...	2130	2134	2234	2334
98	Kortrijk	d.	0538	0553		0638	0653	0653	0738 0740 0753 past	1938 1940 1953	2038 2040 2053	2138							
119	Roeselare	d.	0556	0611		0656	0711	0711	0756 0757 0811 each	1956 1957 2011	2056 2057 2111	2156							
149	Brugge	a.	0619	0644		0719	0744	0744	0819 0819 0844 hour	2019 2019 2044	2119 2119 2144	2219							
149	Brugge 200	d.	0545	0622	0659 0659	0722	0759 0745	0822 0822 0859v until	2022 2022 2059v	2122 2122 2156	2222								
164	Zeebrugge	a.	0600	|	0714 0714	|	0814	| 0914v	| 2114v |	2211 |									
172	Oostende 200	a.	0636		0736		0757 0836 0836		2036 2036	2136 2136	2236								

			Ⓒ	Ⓐ	Ⓐ		Ⓐ	Ⓒ		Ⓐ	Ⓒ		Ⓒ	Ⓐ		Ⓐ	Ⓒ		Ⓐ	Ⓒ	t	Ⓐ	Ⓐ
	Oostende 200	d.	...	...	0504	...	0604	...	...	0704	...	...	0804	0804	...	2004	2004	...	2104	...	...		
	Zeebrugge	d.	...	...	|	0554	|	0628	...	|	0728	...	|	0828k	and	|	2028	...	|	...	2128	2214
	Brugge 200	d.	...	...	0518	0612	0618	0643	...	0718	0743	0818	0818	0843k	at	2018	2018	2043	2118	...	2143	2228
	Brugge	d.	...	0458	0523	...	0623	0658	...	0723	0758	0823	0823	0858	the	2023	2023	2058	2123	...	2158t	2230
	Roeselare	d.	...	0532	0547	...	0647	0658	...	0747	0832	0847	0846	0932	same	2047	2046	2132	2146	...	2232t	2256
	Kortrijk	a.	...	0549	0605	...	0705	0749	...	0805	0849	0905	0902	0949	minutes	2105	2102	2149	2205	...	2249t	2312
	Oudenaarde	d.	0508	0510	0608	0610	0708	...	0710	...	0808	0812	...	0912	0908	past	2112	2108	...	2212	...		
	Zottegem	d.	0526	0528	0626	0629	0726	...	0729	...	0826	0830	...	0930	0926	each	2130	2126	...	2230	...		
	Brussels Midi/Zuid	a.	0538	0541	0638	0643	0738	...	0743	...	0838	0843	...	0943	0938	hour	2143	2138	...	2243	...		
	Brussels Central	a.	0612	0612	0712	0712	0812	...	0812	...	0912	0912	...	1012	1012	until	2212	2212	...	2312	...		
	Brussels Nord	a.	0619	0618	0719	0719	0819	...	0820	...	0919	0918	...	1018	1019		2218	2219	...	2318	...		
			0624	0622		0724	0725	0824		0825			0924	0922		1022	1024		2222	2224		2322		

– Journeys from Zeebrugge to Brugge at 0828, 1028, 1228, 1428, 1628 and 1828 run on dates in note t only.
– Runs on Ⓐ (daily May 29 - Sept. 25), also Apr. 15-17, May 25-27.
v – Journeys from Brugge to Zeebrugge at 0959, 1159, 1359, 1559, 1759 and 1959 run on dates in note t only.

S264B

Table 205 — LILLE and BRUSSELS - ANTWERPEN - ROOSENDAAL

For International trains Paris - Brussels - Amsterdam and v.v., see Table 18.

1, 2 class

First panel

km		ⓐ	ⓒ	ⓐ	✕				✕	⑦			✕	⑦						
0	Lille Flandres d.								0655				0755				0856			
10	Roubaix d.								0706				0808				0907h			
13	Tourcoing d.								0711				0812	0812			0912h			
18	Mouscron d.						0619		0719	0719			0819	0819			0919			
30	Kortrijk d.		0506	0531			0631		0731	0731			0831	0831			0931			0948
	Oostende d.				0548			0646			0748				0848		0902	0948		1002
	Brugge d.				0602			0702			0802									
72	Gent Sint-Pieters d.		0555	0555	0627		0655	0727	0755	0755	0827		0855	0855	0927		0955	1027		
99	Lokeren d.		0615	0615	0646		0715	0746	0815	0825	0846		0915	0915	0946		1015	1046		
113	Sint-Niklaas d.		0625	0625	0656		0725	0756	0825	0825	0856		0925	0925	0956		1025	1056		
	Brussels Midi/Zuid d.	0542			0610	0642	0710	0742		0810	0842		0910		0942	1010				
	Brussels Central d.	0546			0614	0646	0714	0746		0814	0846		0914		0946	1014				
	Brussels Nord d.	0552			0619	0652	0719	0752		0819	0852		0919		0952	1019				
	Mechelen d.	0605			0632	0705	0732	0805		0832	0905		0932		1005	1032				
135	Antwerpen Berchem d.	0620	0641	0641	0646	0712	0720	0741	0746	0812	0820	0841	0841	0849	0912	0923	0944	0941	0946	1112
137	Antwerpen Central a.	0623	0644	0644	0649	0715	0723	0744	0749	0815	0823	0844	0844	0849	0915	0923	0944	0949	1044	1115
137	Antwerpen Central d.				0654	0720c			0754	0820c				0854	0920c			0954	1020c	
182	Roosendaal a.				0721	0749c			0821	0849c				0921	0949c			1021	1049c	
240	Rotterdam CS 220 a.				0804				0901					1001				1101		
326	Amsterdam CS 220 a.				0908				1008					1108				1208		

Second panel

		✕				✕	⑧	⑥											
Lille Flandres d.			0913	0958		1032					1155			1322		1357			
Roubaix d.			0924			1043					1208			1333		1410			
Tourcoing d.			0929			1048	1112				1212			1338		1414			
Mouscron d.			0936	1019		1054	1119	1119			1219		1319	1345		1420			
Kortrijk d.			0945	1031		1103	1131	1131			1231		1331	1356		1431			1448
Oostende d.					1048				1148			1248		1348					1502
Brugge d.					1102				1202			1302		1402					
Gent Sint-Pieters d.		1039	1055		1127	1139	1155	1155	1227		1255	1327	1355	1417	1427	1455			1527
Lokeren d.			1115		1146		1215	1215	1246		1315	1346	1415		1446	1515			1546
Sint-Niklaas d.			1125		1156		1225	1225	1256		1325	1356	1425		1456	1525			1556
Brussels Midi/Zuid d.	1042			1110	1142		1210	1242		1310	1342	1410		1442		1510			
Brussels Central d.	1046			1114	1146		1214	1246		1314	1346	1414		1446		1514			
Brussels Nord d.	1052			1119	1152		1219	1252		1319	1352	1419		1452		1519			
Mechelen d.	1105			1132	1205		1232	1305		1332	1405	1432		1505		1532			
Antwerpen Berchem d.	1120	1141	1146	1212	1220	1241	1246	1312	1320	1341	1346	1412	1423	1444	1512	1523	1544	1549	1612
Antwerpen Central a.	1123	1144	1149	1215	1223	1244	1249	1315	1323	1344	1349	1415	1423	1446	1515	1523	1549	1615	1615
Antwerpen Central d.			1154	1220c			1254	1320c			1354	1420c		1454	1520c			1554	1620c
Roosendaal a.			1221	1249c			1321	1349c			1421	1449c		1521	1549c			1621	1649c
Rotterdam CS 220 a.			1302				1401				1501			1601				1701	
Amsterdam CS 220 a.			1408				1508				1608			1708				1808	

Third panel

		ⓒ	ⓐ														
Lille Flandres d.		1501			1554			1654			1755		1852		1955		
Roubaix d.					1608			1708			1808		1903		2008		
Tourcoing d.					1612			1712			1812		1908		2012		
Mouscron d.		1519	1519		1619			1719			1819		1919		2020		
Kortrijk d.		1531	1531		1631			1731			1831		1931		2031		
Oostende d.				1548			1648			1748		1848		1948			
Brugge d.				1602			1702			1802		1902		2002			
Gent Sint-Pieters d.		1555	1555	1627	1655		1727	1755	1827	1855	1927	1955	2027		2055		
Lokeren d.		1615	1615	1646	1715		1746	1815	1846	1915	1946	2015	2046		2115		
Sint-Niklaas d.		1625	1625	1656	1725		1756	1825	1856	1925	1956	2025	2056		2125		
Brussels Midi/Zuid d.	1542			1610	1642	1710	1742	1810	1842	1910	1942	2010	2042		2110	
Brussels Central d.	1546			1614	1646	1714	1746	1814	1846	1914	1946	2014	2046		2114	
Brussels Nord d.	1552			1619	1652	1719	1752	1819	1852	1919	1952	2019	2052		2119	
Mechelen d.	1605			1632	1705	1732	1805	1832	1905	1932	2005	2032	2105		2132	
Antwerpen Berchem d.	1620	1641	1641	1646	1712	1720	1741	1746	1812	1820	1841	1846	1912	1920	1941	1946	2012
Antwerpen Central a.	1623	1644	1644	1649	1715	1723	1744	1749	1815	1823	1844	1849	1915	1923	1944	1949	2015
Antwerpen Central d.			1654	1720c			1754	1820c			1854	1920c			1954	2020c	
Roosendaal a.			1721	1749c			1821	1849c			1921	1949c			2021	2049c	
Rotterdam CS 220 a.			1801				1901				2001				2101		
Amsterdam CS 220 a.			1908				2008				2108				2208		

Fourth panel — southbound

		✕	⑦				ⓒ		Amsterdam CS 220 d.	⑥	ⓐ	ⓐ	✕	✕	✕	⑦	
Lille Flandres d.			2103			2201		Rotterdam CS 220 d.									
Roubaix d.								Roosendaal d.									
Tourcoing d.								Antwerpen Central a.	0458	0500		0549	0558	0558	0619	0627
Mouscron d.			2120	2120		2219		Antwerpen Central d.	0502	0504		0553	0602	0602	0623	0627
Kortrijk d.			2131	2131		2231		Antwerpen Berchem d.		0522		0609			0638	
Oostende d.	2048				2148		2248	Mechelen d.	0538			0621			0650	
Brugge d.	2102				2202		2302	Brussels Nord a.	0542			0626			0656	
Gent Sint-Pieters d.	2127	2155	2155	2227	2255	2327	Brussels Central a.	0546			0630			0700	
Lokeren d.	2146	2215	2215	2246	2315	2346	Brussels Midi/Zuid a.								
Sint-Niklaas d.	2156	2225	2225	2256	2325	2356	Sint-Niklaas d.	0519			0619	0619		0648	
Brussels Midi/Zuid d.		2142		2210	2242	2310	Lokeren d.	0528			0628	0628		0657	
Brussels Central d.		2146		2214	2246	2314	Gent Sint-Pieters d.	0539	0550		0619	0650	0650	0740	
Brussels Nord d.		2152		2219	2252	2319	Brugge d.								0754
Mechelen d.		2205		2232	2305	2332	Oostende d.								
Antwerpen Berchem d.	2212	2220	2241	2241	2246	2312	2320	2341	2346	0012	Kortrijk d.	0611	0611		0640	0711	0713	
Antwerpen Central a.	2215	2223	2244	2244	2249	2315	2323	2344	2349	0015	Mouscron d.	0621	0621		0649	0721	0722	
Antwerpen Central d.			2254			2354		Tourcoing d.	0628	0628		0656	0728	0731	
Roosendaal a.			2321			0021		Roubaix d.	0632	0632		0700	0732		
Rotterdam CS 220 a.			0001			0107		Lille Flandres a.	0643	0643		0712	0744		
Amsterdam CS 220 a.																	

c – ⓐ only.
h – ⑦ only.

Table 205 — ROOSENDAAL - ANTWERPEN - BRUSSELS and LILLE

1, 2 class

	⑥															✕				
Amsterdam CS 220 ....d.	...	...	...	...	...	0623	...	...	0725	...	...	0825	...	...	0925	...				
Rotterdam CS 220 ....d.	0527e	...	...	0623	...	0732	...	...	0832	...	0932	...	...	1032	...					
Roosendaal ▓ ....d.	0614e	...	0653c 0714	...	0753c 0814	...	0853c 0914	...	0953c 1014	...	1053c 1114	...								
Antwerpen Central ....a.	0643e	...	0723c 0743	...	0822c 0843	...	0922c 0943	...	1022c 1043	...	1122c 1143	...								
Antwerpen Central ....d.	0649 0658 0719 0727 0749 0758 0819	0827 0849 0858 0919 0927 0949 0958	1019 1027 1049	1058 1119 1127 1149 1158																
Antwerpen Berchem ....d.	0653 0702 0723 0732 0753 0802 0823	0832 0853 0902 0923 0932 0953 1002	1023 1032 1053	1102 1123 1132 1153 1202																
Mechelen ....d.	0709	0738	0809	0838	0909	0938	1009	1038	1109	1138	1209									
Brussels Nord ....a.	0721	0753	0826	0850	0921	0950	1021	1050	1121	1150	1221									
Brussels Central ....a.	0726	0758	0831	0856	0926	0957	1026	1056	1126	1156	1226									
Brussels Midi/Zuid ....a.	0730	0802	0835	0900	0930	1000	1030	1100	1130	1200	1230									
Sint-Niklaas ....d.	...	0719	...	0748	...	0819	...	0848	...	0919	...	0948	...	1019	...	1048	...	1119	...	1148	...	1219
Lokeren ....d.	...	0728	...	0757	...	0828	...	0857	...	0928	...	0957	...	1028	...	1057	...	1128	...	1157	...	1228
Gent Sint-Pieters ....d.	...	0750	...	0815	...	0850	...	0915	...	0950	...	1015	...	1050	...	1115	...	1150	...	1215	...	1250
Brugge ....a.				0840				0940				1040				1140				1240	
Oostende ....a.				0854				0954				1054				1154				1254	
Kortrijk ....d.	0813	...	0913	...	1013	...	1113	...	1208 1213	...	1313										
Mouscron ....d.	0823	...	0923	1006	1022	...	1123	...	1218 1222	...	1323										
Tourcoing ▓ ....d.	0830	...	0930	...	1029h	...	1130	...	1225	...	1330										
Roubaix ....d.	0834	...	0934	...	1134	...	1229	...	1334												
Lille Flandres ....a.	0846	...	0945	1023	1146	...	1240	...	1346												

												Ⓐ		Ⓒ		
Amsterdam CS 220 ....d.	...	1025	...	1125	...	1225	...	1325	...	1425	...	1525				
Rotterdam CS 220 ....d.	...	1132	...	1232	...	1332	...	1432	...	1532	...	1632				
Roosendaal ▓ ....d.	...	1153c 1214	...	1253c 1314	...	1353c 1414	...	1453c 1514	...	1553c 1614	...	1653c 1714				
Antwerpen Central ....a.	...	1222c 1243	...	1322c 1343	...	1422c 1443	...	1522c 1543	...	1622c 1643	...	1723c 1743				
Antwerpen Central ....d.	1219 1227 1249 1258 1319 1327 1349 1358 1419 1427 1449 1458 1519 1527 1549 1558 1619 1627 1649 1658 1719 1727 1749															
Antwerpen Berchem ....d.	1223 1232 1253 1302 1323 1332 1353 1402 1423 1432 1453 1502 1523 1532 1553 1602 1623 1632 1653 1702 1723 1732 1753															
Mechelen ....d.	1238	1309	1338	1409	1438	1509	1538	1609	1638	1709	1738	1809				
Brussels Nord ....a.	1250	1321	1350	1421	1450	1521	1550	1621	1650	1721	1750	1821				
Brussels Central ....a.	1256	1326	1356	1426	1456	1526	1556	1626	1656	1721	1750	1821				
Brussels Midi/Zuid ....a.	1300	1330	1400	1430	1500	1530	1600	1630	1700	1730	1800	1830				
Sint-Niklaas ....d.	...	1248	...	1319	...	1346	...	1419	...	1448	...	1519	...	1548	...	1619	...	1648	...	1719	...	1748
Lokeren ....d.	...	1257	...	1328	...	1357	...	1428	...	1457	...	1528	...	1557	...	1628	...	1657	...	1728	...	1757
Gent Sint-Pieters ....d.	...	1315	...	1350	...	1415	...	1450	...	1515	...	1550	...	1615	...	1650	...	1715 1734	...	1750	...	1815
Brugge ....a.		1340				1440				1540				1640		1740				1840	
Oostende ....a.		1354				1454				1554				1654		1754				1854	
Kortrijk ....d.	...	1413	...	1513	...	1613	...	1713	...	1811	1811v					
Mouscron ....d.	...	1422	...	1523	...	1623	...	1722	...	1821	1821v					
Tourcoing ▓ ....d.	...	...	1530	...	1629	...	1729	...	1827	1827t						
Roubaix ....d.	...	...	1534	...	1633	...	1732	...	1831	1831t						
Lille Flandres ....a.	...	1440t	1546	...	1644	...	1746	...	1842	1842t						

Amsterdam CS 220 ....d.	...	1625	...	1724	...	1825	...	1925	...	2025	...	2125 2215						
Rotterdam CS 220 ....d.	...	1732	...	1732	...	1932	...	2032	...	2132	...	2232 2234						
Roosendaal ▓ ....d.	...	1753c 1814	...	1853c 1914	...	1953c 2014	...	2053c 2114	...	2153c 2214	...	2314 0025						
Antwerpen Central ....a.	...	1822c 1843	...	1922c 1943	...	2022c 2043	...	2122c 2143	...	2222c 2243	...	2343						
Antwerpen Central ....d.	1758 1819 1827 1849 1858 1919 1927 1949 1958 2019 2027 2049 2058 2119 2127 2149 2158 2219 2227 2249 2258 2319																		
Antwerpen Berchem ....d.	1802 1823 1832 1853 1902 1923 1932 1953 2002 2023 2032 2053 2102 2123 2132 2153 2202 2223 2232 2253 2302 2323	0054																
Mechelen ....d.	1838	1909	1938	2009	2038	2109	2138	2209	2238	2309	2338							
Brussels Nord ....a.	1850	1921	1950	2021	2050	2121	2150	2221	2250	2321	2350							
Brussels Central ....a.	1856	1926	1956	2026	2056	2126	2156	2226	2256	2321	2350	0125						
Brussels Midi/Zuid ....a.	1900	1930	2000	2030	2100	2130	2200	2230	2300	2330	2400	0134						
Sint-Niklaas ....d.	1819	...	1848	...	1919	...	1948	...	2019	...	2048	...	2119	...	2148	...	2219	...	2248	...	2319
Lokeren ....d.	1828	...	1857	...	1928	...	1957	...	2028	...	2057	...	2128	...	2157	...	2228	...	2257	...	2328
Gent Sint-Pieters ....d.	1850	...	1915	...	1950	...	2015	...	2050	...	2115	...	2150	...	2215	...	2250	...	2315	...	2352
Brugge ....a.		1940				2040				2140				2240							
Oostende ....a.		1954				2054				2154				2254							
Kortrijk ....d.	1911	...	2012	...	2113	...	2213	...	2310	...	0025							
Mouscron ....d.	1923	...	2022	...	2123	...	2222	...	...									
Tourcoing ▓ ....d.	1929	...	...	...	...	...	...	...										
Roubaix ....d.	1933	...	...	...	...	...	...	...										
Lille Flandres ....a.	1944	...	2042e	...	2140	...	...	...										

Ⓐ – Ⓐ only.
✕ – ✕ only.
h – ⑦ only.
t – Ⓒ only.
v – Five minutes later on Ⓐ.

Table 206 — OOSTENDE - KNOKKE and DE PANNE

VVM/De Lijn

Oostende - Knokke	🚋 service (Line 1) via Blankenberge, Zeebrugge, Heist.	Every 30 minutes (every 15 minutes July 1 - Aug. 31, except early morning and late evening).
Oostende - De Panne	🚋 service (Line 2) via Middelkerke, Nieuwpoort, Koksijde.	Every 30 minutes (every 15 minutes July 1 - Aug. 31, except early morning and late evening).

Table 207 — GENT - DE PANNE

1, 2 class

km		Ⓐ					Ⓐ						Ⓐ Ⓐ						
0	Gent Sint-Pieters ....d.	0540 0640 0740			1940 2040 2140	...	De Panne-Adinkerke § ....d.	0444 0544 0641 0741			1941 2041	...
30	Tielt ....d.	0608 0708 0808	and	2008 2108 2208	...	Veurne ....d.	0452 0552 0652 0752	and	1952 2052	...
47	Lichtervelde ....d.	0622 0722 0822	hourly	2022 2122 2222	...	Diksmuide ....d.	0504 0604 0704 0804	hourly	2004 2104	...
65	Diksmuide ....d.	0639 0739 0839	until	2039 2139 2239	...	Lichtervelde ....d.	0522 0622 0722 0822	until	2022 2122	...
81	Veurne ....d.	0652 0752 0852		2052 2152 2252	...	Tielt ....d.	0535 0635 0735 0835		2035 2135	...
86	De Panne-Adinkerke § ....a.	0659 0759 0859		2059 2159 2259	...	Gent Sint-Pieters ....a.	0602 0702 0802 0902		2102 2202	...

§ – De Panne-Adinkerke station is 2 km from De Panne tramway.

Table 209 — BRUSSELS - CHARLEROI

1, 2 class

km		Ⓐ	Ⓒ		Ⓐ	Ⓒ						Ⓒ	Ⓐ	Ⓒ	Ⓐ	Ⓒ	Ⓐ			Ⓐ	Ⓒ	Ⓐ
	Antwerpen 205 ....d.	...	...	0619	...	...	and at	2119	...	2319		Charleroi Sud ....d.	0520 0538 0600 0600 0638	and at	2200 2220 2238	
0	Brussels Nord ....d.	0553 0628 0653 0709 0728	the	2153 2228 2353		Marchienne-au-Pont d.	0525 0543 0605 0625 0643	the	2205 2225 2243	
3	Brussels Central ....d.	0557 0632 0657 0713 0732	same	2157 2232 2357		Nivelles ....d.	0544 0602 0620 0644 0701	same	2220 2244 2302	
6	Brussels Midi/Zuid ....d.	0603 0637 0703 0719 0737	minutes	2203 2237 0002		Brussels Midi/Zuid ....d.	0605 0623 0639 0705 0722	minutes	2239 2305 2323	
36	Nivelles ....d.	0623 0700 0723 0742 0800	past	2223 2300 0038		Brussels Central ....a.	0610 0629 0645 0710 0729	past	2245 2310 2329	
59	Marchienne-au-Pont..d.	0638 0718 0738 0800 0818	each hour	2238 2318 0100		Brussels Nord ....a.	0614 0633 0649 0714 0733	each hour	2249 2314 2333	
63	Charleroi Sud ....a.	0642 0722 0742 0804 0822	until	2242 2322 0104		Antwerpen 205 ....d.	... ... 0723	until	2323	

Table 210 — BRUSSELS - NAMUR - DINANT and LUXEMBOURG

1, 2 class

(Brussels → Luxembourg / Dinant)

km	Station	952	1955	1804	953	1956	1805	954	1957	1806	EC91	955	1958	1807	956	1959	1808	957	1960	1809	958	1961	1810
		④	K	L							✕◆		K	L		K	L		K	L		K	L
0	Brussels Midi/Zuid d.				0521		0544v	0621		0644v	0715	0721		0744v	0821		0844v	0921		0944v	1021		1044v
3	Brussels Central d.				0525		0548v	0625		0648v		0725		0748v	0825		0848v	0925		0948v	1025		1048v
6	Brussels Nord d.				0530		0553	0630		0653	0723u	0730		0753	0830		0853	0930		0953	1030		1053
10	Brussels Quartier Leopold d.				0542		0605	0642		0705	0733u	0742		0805	0842		0905	0942		1005	1042		1105
36	Ottignies d.				0601		0621	0658		0721		0758		0821	0858		0921	0958		1021	1058		1121
51	Gembloux d.				0609		0631	0709		0731		0809		0831	0909		0931	1009		1031	1109		1131
68	Namur a.	0524	0538	0547	0624	0638	0647	0720	0738	0747	0808u	0824	0838	0847	0924	0938	0947	1024	1038	1047	1124	1138	1147
68	Namur d.		0548	0557		0648	0657		0748	0757			0848	0857		0948	0957		1048	1057		1148	1157
96	Dinant a.		0606	0615		0706	0715		0806	0815			0906	0915		1006	1015		1106	1115		1206	1215
97	Ciney d.	0544			0644			0744				0844			0944			1044			1144		
120	Marloie d.	0558			0658			0758				0858			0958			1058			1158		
126	Jemelle d.	0604			0704			0804				0904			1004			1104			1204		
159	Libramont d.	0626			0726			0826				0926			1026			1126			1226		
205	Arlon d.	0658			0758			0858			0930	0958			1058			1158			1258		
234	Luxembourg a.	0715			0815			0915			0949	1015			1115			1215			1315		

Station	959	1962	1811	EC97	960	1963	1812	961	1964	1813	962	1965	1814	295	963	1966	1815	964	1967	1816	965
	K	L		✕◆		K	L		K	L		K	L	✕◆		K	L		K	L	
Brussels Midi/Zuid d.	1121		1144v	1219	1221		1244v	1321		1344v	1421		1444v	1513	1521		1544v	1621		1644v	1721
Brussels Central d.	1125		1148v		1225		1248v	1325		1348v	1425		1448v		1525		1548v	1625		1648v	1725
Brussels Nord d.	1130		1153	1227	1230		1253	1330		1353	1430		1453	1521	1530		1553	1630		1653	1730
Brussels Quartier Leopold d.	1142		1205	1238	1242		1305	1342		1405	1442		1505	1531	1542		1605	1642		1705	1742
Ottignies d.	1158		1221		1258		1321	1358		1421	1458		1521		1558		1621	1658		1721	1758
Gembloux d.	1209		1231		1309		1331	1409		1431	1509		1531		1609		1631	1709		1731	1809
Namur a.	1220	1238	1247	1310	1324	1338	1347	1424	1438	1447	1524	1538	1547	1608	1624	1638	1647	1724	1738	1747	1824
Namur d.		1248	1257			1348	1357		1448	1457		1548	1557			1648	1657		1748	1757	
Dinant a.		1306	1315			1406	1415		1506	1515		1606	1615			1706	1715		1806	1815	
Ciney d.	1244				1344			1444			1544				1644			1744			1844
Marloie d.	1258				1358			1458			1558				1658			1758			1858
Jemelle d.	1304				1404			1504			1604				1704			1804			1904
Libramont d.	1326				1426			1526			1626				1726			1826			1926
Arlon d.	1358			1430	1458			1558			1658			1730	1758			1858			1915
Luxembourg a.	1415			1449	1515			1615			1715			1749	1815			1915			2015

Station	1968	1817	109	966	1969	1818	299	967	1970	1819	968	1971	1820	969	969	1821	1821	499	970	970	971
	K	L	④		K	L	◆			L		K	L	⑧	⑥	④	M	◆	④	©	
Brussels Midi/Zuid d.		1744v	1753	1821		1844v	1913	1921		1944v	2021		2044v	2121	2121	2144	2142	2217	2247	2247	2321
Brussels Central d.		1748v	1757	1825		1848v	1921	1925		1948v	2025		2048v	2125	2125	2148	2146	2226	2255	2255	2330
Brussels Nord d.		1753	1803	1830		1853	1931	1930		1953	2030		2053	2130	2130	2153	2153	2238	2305	2305	2342
Brussels Quartier Leopold d.		1805	1815	1842		1905		1958		2021	2042		2105	2158	2158	2221	2221		2321	2321	0007
Ottignies d.		1821	1831	1858		1921		2009		2031	2109		2131	2209	2209	2231	2231		2321	2331	0017
Gembloux d.		1831	1845	1909		1931		2020		2042	2120		2142	2220	2220	2242	2242	2312	2342	2342	0028
Namur a.	1838	1847	1847	1920		1942	2008	2024	2038	2047	2124	2138	2147	2224		2247		2316	2347		
Namur d.	1906	1915		1924	1938	1947						2206	2215								
Dinant a.				1944	2006	2015		2106	2115												
Ciney d.			1920	1944				2044			2144			2244					0007		
Marloie d.			1941	1958				2058			2158			2258					0021		
Jemelle d.				2004				2104			2204			2304					0026		
Libramont d.			2007	2026				2126			2226			2326							
Arlon d.			2058	2058			2130	2158			2258			2354				0046			
Luxembourg a.			2025	2115			2149	2215			2315							0106			

(Luxembourg → Brussels)

Station	978	979	498	1830	1830	980	980	1831	1977	981	981	1832	1978	982	298	102	1833	1979	983	1834	1980	984
	©	④	◆	④	M	④	©	L	K	④	©	L	K	④	◆	④	L	K		L	K	
Luxembourg d.			0409						0527						0627	0656	0707			0727		0827
Arlon d.			0432						0548						0648	0716	0726			0748		0848
Libramont d.			0517						0617						0717	0752				0817		0917
Jemelle d.	0439					0539			0639	0639					0739	0814				0845		0945
Marloie d.	0445					0545			0645	0645					0745		0800			0900		1000
Ciney d.	0500			0525		0600			0625	0636					0725	0736		0825	0836	0925	0936	
Dinant d.				0555			0617			0655	0704	0717	0717		0755	0804	0817	0836	0855	0904	0917	1017
Namur a.	0517	0552		0600	0600	0622	0622	0700		0722	0722			0800	0822	0839	0848	0900	0922	0935	1012	1035
Namur d.	0449	0522	0556	0600	0600	0622	0622	0700		0722	0722			0812	0835		0912		0946	1012?		1046
Gembloux d.	0501	0535		0612	0612	0635	0635	0712		0735	0735			0823	0846		0923		0946	1023		1046
Ottignies d.	0511	0546		0623	0623	0646	0646	0723		0746	0746			0837	0900	0911	0920	0937	1000	1037		1100
Brussels Quartier Leopold a.	0532	0600	0630	0637	0637	0700	0700	0737		0800	0800			0849	0912	0921	0932	0949	1012	1049		1112
Brussels Nord a.	0543	0612	0640	0649	0649	0712	0712	0749		0812	0812			0854	0917		0937	0954z	1017	1054z		1117
Brussels Central a.	0547	0617		0654	0656	0717	0717	0754z		0817	0817			0858	0921	0930	0941	0958z	1021	1058z		1121
Brussels Midi/Zuid a.	0551	0621	0649	0658	0700	0721	0721	0758z		0821	0821			0858	0921	0930	0941	0958z	1021	1058z		1121

◆ – NOTES (LISTED BY TRAIN NUMBERS)

EC91 – VAUBAN – 🍽 and ✕ Brussels - Basel SBB - Brig - Milano.

EC97 – IRIS – 🍽 and ✕ Brussels - Basel SBB - Zürich Hbf.

295 – EDELWEISS – 🍽 and ✕ Brussels - Basel SBB.

298 – 🛏 Luxembourg - Brussels; 🛌 1,2 cl., ◄ 2 cl. and 🛏 (Venezia Santa Lucia on ⑥⑦) - Milano Centrale - Chiasso - Basel SBB - Brussels. Conveys on ⑥ Dec. 17-31 and ⑤ Feb. 4 - Mar. 25 (from Innsbruck), ◄ 2 cl. Innsbruck (train 1168) - Brussels.

299 – 🛏 Brussels - Luxembourg; 🛌 1,2 cl., ◄ 2 cl. and 🛏 Brussels - Basel SBB - Chiasso - Milano Centrale - (Venezia Santa Lucia on ⑤⑥ from Brussels). Conveys on ⑤ Dec. 16-30 and ⑤ Feb. 3 - Mar. 24, ◄ 2 cl. Brussels - Innsbruck.

498 – 🛏 Basel SBB - Oostende; 🛌 1,2 cl. and ◄ 2 cl. Brig - Basel - Oostende; ◄ 2 cl. Chur - Basel - Oostende (also 🛌 1,2 cl. Dec. 7 - Apr. 15). Conveys on dates in Table 40: 🛌 1,2 cl. and ◄ 2 cl. (Brig -) Sierre - Lausanne - Basel - Oostende.

499 – 🛏 Oostende - Basel SBB; 🛌 1,2 cl. and ◄ 2 cl. Oostende - Basel - Brig; ◄ 2 cl. Oostende - Basel - Chur (also 🛌 1,2 cl. Dec. 8 - Apr. 16); conveys on dates in Table 40, 🛌 1,2 cl. and ◄ 2 cl. Oostende - Basel - Lausanne - Sierre (- Brig).

K – © Oct. 1 - May 27 (not Apr. 15-17, May 25-27).

L – Ⓐ (daily May 29 - Sept. 25). Also runs Apr. 15-17, May 25-27.

M – ⑥⑦ May 29 - Sept. 25 (also Apr. 15-17, May 25,27).

s – Stops to set down only.

u – Stops to pick up only.

v – Departs 2 minutes earlier on ©.

z – Arrives 2 minutes later on ©.

Table 210 LUXEMBOURG and DINANT - NAMUR - BRUSSELS

1,2 class

	1835	1981	985	1836	1982	986	1837	1983	987	296		1838	1984	988	1839	1985	989	1840	1986	990		1841	1987	991
	L	K		L	K		L	K		🍴 ♦		L	K		L	K		L	K			L	K	
Luxembourg d.	...	...	0927	...	...	1027	...	...	1127	1206	...	...	...	1227	...	...	1327	...	...	1427	...	...	...	1527
Arlon d.	...	...	0948	...	...	1048	...	...	1148	1226	...	...	...	1248	...	...	1348	...	...	1448	...	...	...	1548
Libramont d.	...	...	1017	...	...	1117	...	...	1217	|	...	...	...	1317	...	...	1417	...	...	1517	...	...	...	1617
Jemelle d.	...	...	1039	...	...	1139	...	...	1239	|	...	...	...	1339	...	...	1439	...	...	1539	...	...	...	1639
Marloie d.	...	...	1045	...	...	1145	...	...	1245	|	...	...	...	1345	...	...	1445	...	...	1545	...	...	...	1645
Ciney d.	...	...	1100	...	...	1200	...	...	1300	|	...	...	...	1400	...	...	1500	...	...	1600	...	...	...	1700
Dinant d.	1025	1036	|	1125	1136	|	1225	1236	|	|	...	1325	1336	|	1425	1436	|	1525	1536	|	...	1625	1636	|
Namur a.	1055	1104	1117	1155	1204	1217	1255	1304	1317	1343	...	1355	1404	1417	1455	1504	1517	1555	1604	1617	...	1655	1704	1717
Namur d.	1100	...	1122	1200	...	1222	1300	...	1322	1345	...	1400	...	1422	1500	...	1522	1600	...	1622	...	1700	...	1722
Gembloux d.	1112	...	1135	1212	...	1235	1312	...	1335	|	...	1412	...	1435	1512	...	1535	1612	...	1635	...	1712	...	1735
Ottignies d.	1123	...	1146	1223	...	1246	1323	...	1346	|	...	1423	...	1446	1523	...	1546	1623	...	1646	...	1723	...	1746
Brussels Quartier Leopold a.	1137	...	1200	1237	...	1300	1337	...	1400	1417	...	1437	...	1500	1537	...	1600	1637	...	1701	...	1737	...	1800
Brussels Nord a.	1149	...	1212	1249	...	1312	1349	...	1412	1427	...	1449	...	1512	1549	...	1612	1649	...	1712	...	1749	...	1812
Brussels Central a.	1154z	...	1217	1254z	...	1317	1354z	...	1417	|	...	1454z	...	1517	1554z	...	1617	1654z	...	1717	...	1754z	...	1817
Brussels Midi/Zuid a.	1158z	...	1221	1258z	...	1321	1358z	...	1421	1435	...	1458z	...	1521	1558z	...	1621	1658z	...	1721	...	1758z	...	1821

	1842	1988	992		EC96	1843	1989	993	1844	1990		994	1845	1991	995	EC90	1846	1992	996			997	997	
	L	K			🍴 ♦	L	K		L	K			L	K		🍴 ♦	L	K		L	K	Ⓐ	Ⓒ	
Luxembourg d.	...	...	1627	...	1659	...	...	1727	...	...	...	1827	...	...	1927	2006	...	...	2027	...	...	2127	2127	...
Arlon d.	...	...	1648	...	1720	...	...	1748	...	...	...	1848	...	...	1948	2027	...	...	2048	...	...	2148	2148	...
Libramont d.	...	...	1717	...	|	...	...	1817	...	...	...	1917	...	...	2017	|	...	...	2117	...	...	2217	2217	...
Jemelle d.	...	...	1739	...	|	...	...	1839	...	...	...	1939	...	...	2039	|	...	...	2139	...	...	2239	2239	...
Marloie d.	...	...	1745	...	|	...	...	1845	...	...	...	1945	...	...	2045	|	...	...	2145	...	...	2245	...	...
Ciney d.	...	...	1800	...	|	...	...	1900	...	...	...	2000	...	...	2100	|	...	...	2200	...	...	2300	...	...
Dinant d.	1725	1736	|	...	|	1825	1836	|	1925	1936	...	|	2025	2036	|	|	2125	2136	|	2225	2236	|	...	...
Namur a.	1755	1804	1817	...	1837	1855	1904	1917	1955	2004	...	2017	2055	2104	2117	2143	2155	2204	2217	2255	2304	2317	...	...
Namur d.	1800	...	1822	...	1839	1900	...	1922	2000	...	...	2022	2100	...	2122	2145	2200	...	2222	...	...	...	...	...
Gembloux d.	1812	...	1835	...	|	1912	...	1935	2012	...	...	2035	2112	...	2135	|	2212	...	2235	...	...	...	...	...
Ottignies d.	1823	...	1846	...	|	1923	...	1946	2023	...	...	2046	2123	...	2146	|	2223	...	2246	...	...	...	...	...
Brussels Quartier Leopold a.	1837	...	1900	...	1910	1937	...	2000	2037	...	...	2100	2137	...	2200	2218	2237	...	2300	...	...	...	...	...
Brussels Nord a.	1849	...	1912	...	1920	1949	...	2012	2049	...	...	2112	2149	...	2212	2228	2249	...	2312	...	...	...	...	...
Brussels Central a.	1854z	...	1917	...	|	1954z	...	2017	2054z	...	...	2117	2154z	...	2217	2233	2255z	...	2317	...	...	...	...	...
Brussels Midi/Zuid a.	1858z	...	1921	...	1928	1958z	...	2021	2058z	...	...	2121	2158z	...	2221	2237	2258z	...	2321	...	...	...	...	...

♦ – NOTES (LISTED BY TRAIN NUMBERS)

EC90 – VAUBAN - [12] and 🍴 Milano - Brig - Basel SBB - Brussels.
EC96 – IRIS - [12] and 🍴 Chur - Zürich - Basel SBB - Brussels.
296 – EDELWEISS - [12] and 🍴 Basel SBB - Brussels.

K – Ⓒ Oct. 1 - May 27 (not Apr. 15-17, May 25-27).
L – Ⓐ (daily May 29 - Sept. 25). Also runs Apr. 15-17, May 25-27.
z – Arrives 2 minutes **later** on Ⓒ.

Table 212 TOURNAI - LILLE

Service Sept. 25 - May 27 1,2 class

km		Ⓐ	⑥	Ⓐ	⑥	⑦	Ⓐ			⚒	Ⓐ	Ⓒ	Ⓐ	Ⓐ	⑥	Ⓐ	⑦	Ⓐ	⑥		⚒	⚒		
	Brussels Midi **214** d.	...	...	*0607*	*0607*	*0607*	*0707*	*0707*v	*0810*t	*1010*h	*1110*	*1114*	...	*1210*	...	*1410*	*1410*	...	...	*1510*t	*1610*h	*1707*x	*1810*	*2010*
0	**Tournai** § d.	0619	0622	0707	0710	0732	0807	0844	0947	1131	1211	1223	1251	1307	1311	1512	1529	1539	1542	1629	1728	1820	1929	2129
25	**Lille Flandres** a.	0649	0650	0737	0740	0750	0834	0909	1006	1150	1240	1250	1311	1339	1339	1532	1547	1610	1610	1654	1752	1847	1953	2147

	⚒	Ⓐ	⚒	⑦	⚒	⑥	⑦	Ⓒ	Ⓐ	⑥	Ⓐ	Ⓒ	Ⓐ	⑤	Ⓐ	⚒	⑦	⚒	⚒	⚒	⑦	⚒	⑦	
Lille Flandres d.	0628	0654	0741	0758	0811	0903	0919	1039	1039	1210	1210	1307	1311	1411	1508	1551	1555	1641	1708	1809	1838	1953	2041	2156
Tournai § a.	0659	0724	0810	0821	0838	0922	0937	1107	1109	1238	1241	1326	1329	1429	1527	1620	1620	1710	1737	1838	1906	2015	2104	2214
Brussels Midi **214** a.	*0828*	*0828*	*0928*	*0928*	*1028*	*1028*	...	*1228*	*1228*	...	...	*1428*	*1428*	*1528*	*1628*	*1730*	*1728*	*1828*	...	*1935*	*2028*	*2128*	*2227*	*2330*

– Depart 4 minutes later on ⑥.
– Depart 4 minutes later on Ⓒ.
v – Depart 0714 on Ⓒ.
x – Depart 1710 on Ⓒ.
§ – 🏛 between Tournai and Lille is Blandain.

Table 213 ANTWERPEN - HASSELT - LIÈGE

1,2 class

km		Ⓐ			ⒶK						
0	**Antwerpen Central** d.	0524	...	0624	...	and	1924	...	2024	2124	2224
3	Antwerpen Berchem d.	0529	...	0629	...	at	1929	...	2029	2129	2229
15	Lier d.	0540	...	0640	...	the	1940	...	2040	2140	2240
	Leuven d.	|	0624	|	0724	same	|	2024	|	|	|
42	Aarschot d.	0604	0637	0704	0737	mins.	2004	2037	2104	2204	2304
59	Diest d.	0616	0654	0716	0754	past	2016	2054	2116	2216	2316
80	**Hasselt** a.	0629	0710	0729	0810	each	2029	2110	2129	2229	2329
80	**Hasselt** d.	0641	...	0741	...	hour	2041	...	2141	...	...
106	Tongeren d.	0705	...	0805	...	until	2105	...	2202	...	...
133	**Liège Guillemins** a.	0736	...	0836	...		2136	...	...	...	...

	Ⓐ		Ⓐ		ⒶN					Ⓐ
Liège Guillemins d.	...	...	...	0606	...	0706	and	...	2106	2206
Tongeren d.	...	0538a	...	0638	...	0738	at	...	2138	2238
Hasselt a.	...	0559a	...	0659	...	0759	the	...	2159	2259
Hasselt d.	0513	0611	0632	0712	0732	0813	same	2132	2213	...
Diest d.	0527	0627	0649	0727	0749	0827	mins.	2149	2227	...
Aarschot d.	0543	0643	0707	0743	0807	0843	past	2207	2243	...
Leuven a.	|	|	0718	|	0818	|	each	2218	|	...
Lier d.	0603	0703	...	0803	...	0903	hour	...	2303	...
Antwerpen Berchem a.	0615	0715	...	0813	...	0913	until	...	2313	...
Antwerpen Central a.	0618	0718	...	0818	...	0918		...	2318	...

– Departures at 0824, 1024, 1224, 1424, 1624 and 1824 run daily.
N – Departures at 0732, 0932, 1132, 1332, 1532, 1732 and 1932 run daily.
a – Ⓐ only.

Table 214 BRUSSELS - TOURNAI - MOUSCRON

1, 2 class

km		755	853	756	756		757	757		758	758		759	759	760	760		761	761	762	762		763	763
		Ⓐ	Ⓒ	Ⓐ	Ⓒ		Ⓐ	Ⓒ		Ⓐ	Ⓒ		Ⓐ	Ⓒ	Ⓐ	Ⓒ		Ⓐ	Ⓒ	Ⓐ	Ⓒ		Ⓐ	Ⓒ
0	**Brussels Nord** d.	...	...	0557	0557	...	0657	0705	...	0801	0805	...	0901	0905	1001	1005	...	1101	1105	1201	1205	...	1301	1305
3	Brussels Central d.	...	...	0601	0601	...	0701	0709	...	0805	0809	...	0905	0909	1005	1009	...	1105	1109	1205	1209	...	1305	1309
6	**Brussels Midi/Zuid** d.	...	...	0607	0607	...	0707	0714	...	0810	0814	...	0910	0914	1010	1014	...	1110	1114	1210	1214	...	1310	1314
61	Ath d.	...	...	0643	0648	...	0743	0755	...	0846	0855	...	0946	0955	1046	1055	...	1146	1155	1244	1255	...	1346	1355
73	Leuze d.	...	...	0652	0656	...	0752	0803	...	0855	0903	...	0955	1003	1055	1103	...	1155	1203	1253	1303	...	1355	1403
89	**Tournai** a.	...	...	0703	0707	...	0803	0813	...	0906	0913	...	1006	1013	1106	1113	...	1206	1213	1303	1313	...	1406	1413
89	**Tournai 217** d.	0555	0626	0705	*0726*	...	0805	*0827*	...	0908	*0925*	...	1008	*1026*	1108	*1128*	...	1208	*1226*	1305	*1328*	...	1408	*1428*
108	**Mouscron 217** a.	0609	0640	0720	*0740*	...	0820	*0841*	...	0922	*0939*	...	1022	*1040*	1122	*1142*	...	1222	*1240*	1319	*1342*	...	1422	*1442*

	764	764		765	765	766	766		767	767	768	768		769	769	770	770		771	771	772	772	773	773
	Ⓐ	Ⓒ		Ⓐ	Ⓒ	Ⓐ	Ⓒ		Ⓐ	Ⓒ	Ⓐ	Ⓒ		Ⓐ	Ⓒ	Ⓐ	Ⓒ		Ⓐ	Ⓒ	Ⓐ	Ⓒ	Ⓐ	Ⓒ
Brussels Nord d.	1401	1401	...	1501	1505	1558	1605	...	1657	1701	1801	1801	...	1901	1905	2001	2001	...	2101	2105	2201	2205	2301	2305
Brussels Central d.	1405	1405	...	1505	1509	1603	1609	...	1701	1705	1805	1805	...	1905	1909	2005	2005	...	2105	2109	2205	2209	2305	2309
Brussels Midi/Zuid d.	1410	1410	...	1510	1514	1610	1614	...	1707	1710	1810	1810	...	1910	1914	2010	2010	...	2110	2114	2210	2214	2310	2314
Ath d.	1446	1451	...	1546	1555	1646	1655	...	1743	1751	1846	1851	...	1946	1955	2046	2051	...	2146	2155	2246	2255	2347	2355
Leuze d.	1455	1459	...	1555	1603	1655	1703	...	1752	1759	1855	1859	...	1955	2003	2055	2059	...	2155	2203	2255	2303	2356	0003
Tournai a.	1506	1509	...	1606	1613	1706	1713	...	1804	1809	1906	1909	...	2006	2013	2106	2109	...	2206	2213	2306	2313	0006	0013
Tournai 217 d.	1508	*1526*	...	1608	*1626*	1708	*1726*	...	1806	*1826*	1908	*1926*	...	2008	*2029*	2108	*2126*	...	2208	*2226*	2308	...	...	...
Mouscron 217 a.	1522	*1540*	...	1622	*1640*	1722	*1740*	...	1820	*1840*	1922	*1940*	...	2022	*2043*	2122	*2140*	...	2222	*2240*	2322	...	...	...

Table 214 — MOUSCRON - TOURNAI - BRUSSELS
1,2 class

	776 ©	776 Ⓐ	777 ©	777 Ⓐ	778 ©	778 Ⓐ	779 ©	779 Ⓐ	780 ©	780 Ⓐ	781 ©	781 Ⓐ	782 ©	782 Ⓐ	783 ©	783 Ⓐ	784 ©	784 Ⓐ	784
Mouscron 217 ... d.	...	...	0515	0602	0615	0702	0715	0802	0815	0902	0915	1002	1015	1102	1115	1202	1215	1302	1311
Tournai 217 ... a.	...	...	0530	0616	0630	0716	0730	0816	0830	0916	0930	1016	1030	1116	1130	1216	1230	1316	1326
Tournai ... d.	0427	0529	0532	0629	0632	0729	0732	0829	0832	0929	0932	1029	1032	1129	1132	1229	1232	1329	1332
Leuze ... d.	0439	0539	0544	0640	0644	0740	0744	0840	0844	0940	0944	1040	1044	1140	1144	1240	1244	1340	1344
Ath ... d.	0449	0549	0554	0649	0654	0749	0754	0849	0854	0949	0954	1049	1054	1149	1154	1249	1254	1349	1354
Brussels Midi/Zuid ... a.	0530	0628	0634	0728	0728	0828	0828	0928	0928	1028	1028	1128	1128	1228	1228	1328	1328	1428	1428
Brussels Central ... a.	0535	0634	0634	0734	0734	0834	0834	0934	0934	1034	1034	1134	1134	1234	1234	1334	1334	1434	1434
Brussels Nord ... a.	0539	0638	0638	0738	0738	0838	0838	0938	0938	1038	1038	1138	1138	1238	1238	1338	1338	1438	1438

	785 ©	785 Ⓐ	786 ©	786 Ⓐ	787 ©	787 Ⓐ	788 ©	788 Ⓐ	789 ©	789 Ⓐ	790 ©	790 Ⓐ	791 ©	791 Ⓐ	792 ©	792 Ⓐ	793 ©	793 Ⓐ
Mouscron 217 ... d.	1402	1411	1502	1515	1602	1615	1702	1715	1802	1817	1902	1915	2004	2015	2102	2115	2203	2215
Tournai 217 ... a.	1416	1426	1516	1530	1616	1630	1716	1730	1816	1832	1916	1930	2018	2030	2116	2130	2217	2230
Tournai ... d.	1429	1432	1529	1532	1629	1632	1729	1732	1840	1853	1929	1932	2040	2044	2140	2144	2240	2244
Leuze ... d.	1440	1444	1540	1544	1640	1644	1740	1744	1849	1901	1949	1954	2049	2054	2148	2154	2249	2254
Ath ... d.	1449	1454	1549	1554	1649	1654	1749	1754	1858	1911	1958	2004	2058	2104	2158	2204	2258	2304
Brussels Midi/Zuid ... a.	1528	1528	1628	1628	1728	1730	1828	1828	1928	1935	2028	2028	2128	2128	2227	2227	2328	2328
Brussels Central ... a.	1534	1534	1634	1634	1734	1735	1834	1834	1934	1940	2034	2034	2134	2134	2234	2234	2334	2334
Brussels Nord ... a.	1538	1538	1638	1638	1738	1739	1838	1838	1938	1944	2038	2038	2138	2138	2238	2238	2338	2338

Table 215 — CHARLEROI - NAMUR - LIÈGE - AACHEN
1, 2 class except where shown

km	7178 Ⓐ	503	7179	411 🍴	7180	413 🍴	7181	506	417 🍴	EC 33 ✗	7183	419 🍴	7184	509	EC 47 ✗	510	7186	425 🍴	7187	512	429 ◆	241 ◆	7189
0 Charleroi Sud 217 d.									0954														
37 Namur 217 d.									1023														
68 Huy 217 d.																							
Oostende 200 d.		0547		0647		0747		0847	0947			0934	1034			1134		1234		1334	1434		
Brussels Midi/Zuid 200 d.								0856	0956	1056	1059	1156	1256			1356		1456	1556	1656	1659		
97 Liège Guillemins 217 a.		0656		0756		0856		0956	1000			1200		1300	1313	1400		1500		1600	1700	1703	
97 Liège Guillemins d.		0700		0800		0900		1000	1100	1109		1200		1300		1400	1420	1425	1520	1525	1620	1720	1725
124 Verviers Central d.	0625	0720	0725	0820	0825	0920	0925	1020	1120	1128	1130	1220	1225	1320		1420	1425	1520		1620	1720	1723	1740
135 Welkenraedt d.	0641	0731	0742	0842		0940	1033			1144	1151	1240	1247	1333	1340		1447	1543	1547	1640			1747
140 Eupen a.	0648	0749		0849		0947	1040																
150 Aachen Hbf a.				0843		0943			1143	1150		1243		1351			1543				1743	1747	
Köln Hbf 700 a.				0942		1042			1242	1248		1342		1442			1642				1842	1902	

	514	EC 39 ✗	7190	515	EC 49 🍴	233 ◆	EC 31 ✗	7192	1219 🍴	517	7193	EC 37 ✗	439 🍴	7194	EN 225 ◆	7819	519	331	520	243	521 ⑥	231
Charleroi Sud 217 d.						1853												2234		2326		0248
Namur 217 d.						1922												2302		2355		0317
Huy 217 d.																		2325				
Oostende 200 d.	1534			1634	1657	1734			1807	1834			1934		2013		2034		2134	2234		0248
Brussels Midi/Zuid 200 d.	1647	1655		1747	1808	1847			1923	1947		2003	2047		2125		2147		2250	2347		0317
Liège Guillemins 217 a.	1756	1759		1856	1911	1956	1959		2031	2056		2111	2156		2233		2256	2343	2358	0033	0114	0355
Liège Guillemins d.	1800	1803		1900	1913	2000	2009		2034	2100		2113	2200		2235	2230	2300			0048	0116	0405
Verviers Central d.	1820	1823	1825	1920	1933	2020	2028	2030	2054	2120	2125		2220	2225	2254	2300	2320				0140	0425
Welkenraedt d.	1833		1839	1933			2044	2051			2131	2140	2239		2313	2331					0151	
Eupen a.	1840		1940								2147											
Aachen Hbf a.		1845			1955	2043	2050		2118			2151	2243		2318						0448	
Köln Hbf 700 a.		1942			2042	2155	2149		2227			2242	2342		0017							0550

	230 ◆	528 🍴	242 ◆	529 ◆	530	EN 224	330	531	EC 36 ✗	1118 🍴	7156	412 🍴	7157	232	EC 30 ✗	EC 48 🍴	7158	534	535
Köln Hbf 700 d.	0007					0508		0630	0638			0714		0802	0814	0914			
Aachen Hbf d.	0104				0604	0606		0710	0743		0805			0905	0909	1001			
Eupen d.					0507			0704		0755			0855				0955	1003	1104
Welkenraedt d.		0349			0519	0613		0713		0806	0817	0803	0903	0806	0917	0926	1017	1013 1017	1113 1126
Verviers Central d.	0127	0400	0453	0519	0536	0626	0647	0726	0743	0823		0826	0917	0926	0932	0943	1036	1043	1143
Liège Guillemins a.	0144	0421	0510	0536	0546	0643	0647	0743	0749	0827	0843	0846	0943	0949	0949	0959	1039	1046	1146
Liège Guillemins 217 d.	0155	0424	0526	0546	0546	0646	0650 0700	0746	0752	0827	0846	0846	0946	0955	0955	1055	1142	1155	1155
Brussels Midi/Zuid 200 a.		0555			0655	0755	0804	0855	0901	0933		0955		1055	1209		1248	1309	1409
Oostende 200 a.		0709			0809	0909	0918	1009		1045		1109		1209					
Huy 217 d.	0234		0608			0719	0740							1039		1106			
Namur 217 a.	0302		0636			0740	0807							1106					
Charleroi Sud 217 a.	0302		0636				0807												

♦ — NOTES (LISTED BY TRAIN NUMBERS)

EC30 — MOLIÈRE – 🛏 and ✗ Dortmund - Paris Nord; conveys Sept. 12 - May 27, 🛏 1,2 cl. København - Aachen - Paris Nord.

EC31 — MOLIÈRE – 🛏 and ✗ Paris Nord - Dortmund; conveys Sept. 11 - May 27, 🛏 1,2 cl. Paris Nord - Aachen (233) - København.

EC33 — PARSIFAL – 🛏 and ✗ Paris Nord - Köln.

EC36/7 — FELIX TIMMERMANS – 🛏 and ✗ Brussels - Köln and v.v.

EC39 — JACQUES BREL – 🛏 and ✗ Paris Nord - Dortmund. Supplement payable throughout.

EC47 — ALEXANDER VON HUMBOLDT – 🛏 and ✗ Brussels - Berlin.

EC48/9 — MEMLING – 🛏 and 🍴 Oostende - Dortmund and v.v.

EN224/5 — 🛏 1,2 cl., 🛏 2 cl. and 🛌 Oostende - Wien Westbahnhof and v.v. 🛏 1,2 cl., 🛏 2 cl. and 🛌 Oostende - München Hbf and v.v.

230/1 — 🛏 1,2 cl., 🛏 2 cl. and 🛌 Paris Nord - Dortmund and v.v.

232/3 — NORD EXPRESS – 🛌 1,2 cl. (T2), 🛏 2 cl. and 🛌 Oostende - København and v.v.; 🛌 Oostende - Aachen and v.v.

241 — OST-WEST EXPRESS, Brussels - Moskva – see Table 24. Not for local journeys.

242 — 🛏1,2 cl., 🛏 2 cl. and 🛌 Berlin - Paris Nord; 🛏 2 cl. Berlin - Liège (529) Oostende. Conveys Sept. 25 - May 27, 🛏 1,2 cl. and 🛏 2 cl. Hamburg - Paris Nord (also 🛌 Cabine 8 – see page 97); 🛌 Liège - Paris.

243 — 🛏 1,2 cl., 🛏 2 cl. and 🛌 Paris Nord - Berlin; conveys from Liège: 🛏 2 cl. Oostende - Berlin. Conveys Sept. 24 - May 27, 🛏 1,2 cl. and 🛏 2 cl. Paris - Hamburg (also 🛌 Cabine 8 – see page 97); 🛌 Paris - Liège.

330/1 — 🛌 Paris Nord - Liège and v.v.

520 — 🛌 Oostende - Liège; 🛏 2 cl. Oostende - Liège (243)- Berlin.

529 — 🛌 Welkenraedt - Oostende; conveys from Liège: 🛏 2 cl. Berlin (242)- Liège - Oostende.

1118 — ⑥ Jan. 7 - Mar. 25, also Jan. 1 (from Villach): 🛏 2 cl. and 🛌 Villach - Salzburg - Oostende.

1219 — ⑤ Jan. 6 - Mar. 24 (also Dec. 23): 🛏 2 cl. and 🛌 Oostende - Salzburg - Villach.

1

Table 215 AACHEN - LIÈGE - NAMUR - CHARLEROI

1, 2 class unless otherwise shown

	240	7160	420	7161	422	538	EC 38		7163	426	7164	540	EC 46	7165	430		7166	EC 32	542	7167	434	544	7169	438
	♦		🍷		🍷		🍴 ♦			🍷			🍴 ♦		🍷			🍴 ♦			🍷			🍷
Köln Hbf **700** d.	1006	...	1114	...	1214	...	1314	...	...	1414	...	...	1514	...	1614	...	...	1708	...	...	1814	...	...	2014
Aachen Hbf d.	1115	...	1205	...	1305	...	1410	...	...	1505	...	...	1607	...	1705	...	...	1800	...	...	1905	...	...	2105
Eupen d.	|	1155	|	1255	|	1404	|	...	1455	|	1555	...	|	1655	|	...	...	|	1805	1855	|	2004	2055	|
Welkenraedt d.	|	1203	|	1303	|	1413	1422	...	1503	|	1603	1613	|	1703	|	...	1803	|	1813	1903	|	2013	2103	|
Verviers Central d.	1138	1217	1226	1317	1326	1426	1433	...	1517	1526	1617	1626	|	1717	1726	...	1817	1821	1826	1917	1926	2026	2117	2126
Liège Guillemins a.	1158	...	1243	...	1343	1443	1449	...	...	1543	...	1643	1647	...	1743	...	...	1837	1843	...	1943	2043	...	2143
Liège Guillemins 217 d.	1206	...	1246	...	1346	1446	1452	...	...	1546	...	1646	1651	...	1746	...	...	1847	1846	...	1946	2046	...	2146
Brussels Midi/Zuid **200** a.	1322	...	1355	...	1455	1555	1556	...	...	1655	...	1755	1801	...	1855	...	...	|	1955	...	2055	2155	...	2255
Oostende **200** a.	...	...	1509	...	1609	1709	...	...	...	1809	...	1909	...	...	2009	...	...	|	2109	...	2209	2309	...	0009
Huy **217** d.	...	...	...	...	...	...	...	...	...	...	...	...	...	...	...	...	...	|	...	...	...	...	...	...
Namur 217 d.	...	...	...	...	...	...	...	...	...	...	...	...	...	...	...	...	...	1925	...	...	...	...	...	...
Charleroi Sud 217 a.	...	...	...	...	...	...	...	...	...	...	...	...	...	...	...	...	...	1952	...	...	...	...	...	...

♦ – **NOTES** (LISTED BY TRAIN NUMBERS)

EC32 – PARSIFAL – [12] and 🍴 Köln - Paris Nord.

EC38 – JACQUES BREL – [12] and 🍴 Dortmund - Paris Nord. Supplement payable throughout.

EC46 – ALEXANDER VON HUMBOLDT – [12] and 🍴 Berlin - Brussels.

240 – OST-WEST EXPRESS, Moskva - Brussels – see Table **24**. For international journeys **only**.

Table 216 VERVIERS - SPA

1, 2 class

Rail service Verviers Central - Spa. 16 km. Journey time: 21 minutes.

From Verviers: 0529Ⓐ, 0629Ⓐ, 0729 and hourly until 2129.

From Spa: 0552Ⓐ, 0652, 0734Ⓐ, 0752 and hourly until 1852, 1953, 2053, 2155.

Table 217 LIÈGE - NAMUR - CHARLEROI - TOURNAI - MOUSCRON

1, 2 class

km		Ⓐ	Ⓒ	Ⓐ	Ⓐ	Ⓒ	Ⓐ		Ⓐ	Ⓒ	Ⓐ	Ⓐ	Ⓒ	Ⓐ	Ⓐ	Ⓒ	Ⓐ	Ⓐ	Ⓒ	Ⓐ	Ⓐ	Ⓒ	Ⓐ	Ⓒ
0	**Liège Guillemins** d.	0549	...	0607	0649	0649	0707		1749	1749	1807	1849	1849	1907	1949	1949	2007	2049	2049	2107	2149	2149	2207	2301
29	Huy d.	0608	...	0628	0708	0710	0728	and	1808	1810	1828	1908	1910	1928	2008	2010	2028	2108	2110	2128	2208	2210	2228	2322
40	Andenne d.	|	...	0639	|	0719	0739	at	|	1820	1839	|	1920	1939	|	2020	2039	|	2120	2139	|	2220	2239	2332
60	**Namur** d.	0629	0634	0654	0729	0733	0754	the	1829	1834	1854	1929	1934	1954	2029	2034	2054	2129	2134	2154	2229	2234	2252	2344
77	Jemeppe-sur-Sambre d.	|	0647	0707	|	0746	0807	same	|	1847	1907	|	1947	2007	|	2047	2107	|	2147	2207	|	2247	...	...
82	Tamines d.	|	0655	0715	|	0753	0815	minutes	|	1855	1915	|	1955	2015	|	2055	2115	|	2155	2215	|	2255	...	...
96	**Charleroi Sud** d.	0658	0710	0728	0758	0810	0828	past	1858	1910	1928	1958	2010	2028	2058	2110	2128	2158	2210	2228	2258	2308	...	...
118	La Louviére-Sud d.	0714	0729	...	0814	0829	...	each	1914	1929	...	2014	2029	...	2114	2129	...	2214	2219	...	2314	...	...	...
137	**Mons** d.	0728	0744	...	0828	0844	...	hour	1928	1948	...	2028	2044	...	2128	2144	...	2226	2244	...	2326	...	...	...
185	**Tournai 214** d.	0759	0827	...	0859	0925	...	until	2000	2029	...	2100	2126	...	2157	2226	...	...	2324	...	...	...	...	...
204	**Mouscron 214** a.	0813	0841	...	0913	0940	...		2014	2043	...	2114	2140	...	...	2240	...	...	...	...	...	...	...	...

	Ⓐ	Ⓐ	Ⓐ	Ⓒ	Ⓐ	Ⓐ	Ⓒ	Ⓐ	Ⓐ	Ⓒ	Ⓐ	Ⓐ		Ⓒ	Ⓐ	Ⓐ	Ⓒ	Ⓐ	Ⓐ	Ⓒ	Ⓐ	Ⓐ	Ⓒ	Ⓐ
Mouscron 214 d.	...	...	...	...	...	...	0602	...	...	0702	0727**n**	...		1802	1829	...	1902	1929	...	2004	2029	...	2102	2126
Tournai 214 d.	...	...	...	...	...	...	0618	0645	...	0718	0745	...	and	1818	1845	...	1918	1945	...	2019	2045	...	2118	2145
Mons d.	...	...	...	0600	0615	...	0700	0715	...	0800	0815	...	at	1900	1915	...	2000	2015	...	2100	2115	...	2200	2215
La Louviére-Sud d.	...	...	...	0615	0628	...	0715	0728	...	0815	0828	...	the	1915	1928	...	2015	2028	...	2115	2128	...	2215	2228
Charleroi Sud d.	...	0502	0614	0634	0647	0714	0734	0747	0814	0834	0847	0914	same	1934	1947	2014	2034	2047	2114	2134	2147	2214	2237	2247
Tamines d.	...	0523	0628	0648	|	0728	0748	|	0828	0848	|	0928	minutes	1948	|	2028	2048	|	2128	2148	|	2228	2251	2301
Jemeppe-sur-Sambre d.	...	0530	0636	0656	|	0736	0756	|	0836	0856	|	0936	past	1956	|	2036	2056	|	2136	2156	|	2236	2259	2308
Namur d.	0550	0550	0650	0710	0715	0750	0810	0815	0850	0910	0915	0950	each	2010	2015	2050	2110	2115	2150	2210	2215	2248	2311	2324
Andenne d.	0604	...	0704	0723	|	0804	0823	|	0904	0923	|	1004	hour	2023	|	2104	2123	|	2204	2223	|	...	...	2338
Huy d.	0615	...	0715	0733	0735	0815	0845	0835	0915	0933	0935	1015	until	2033	2035	2115	2133	2135	2215	2233	2235	...	...	2348
Liège Guillemins a.	0635	...	0735	0753	0753	0835	0853	0853	0935	0953	0953	1035		2053	2053	2135	2153	2153	2235	2253	2253	...	...	0008

n – Trains depart Mouscron on Ⓐ at 0727, 0829, 0929, 1029, 1126, 1224, 1326, 1429, 1529, 1626, and 1726.

Table 218 BRUSSELS - LA LOUVIÈRE - BINCHE

1, 2 class

km		Ⓐ	⑥	Ⓐ	Ⓒ	Ⓒ		Ⓐ	Ⓒ	Ⓒ	Ⓐ
0	**Brussels Nord** d.	0607	0622	0707	0740	0715**r**	and	2107	2140	2122**r**	2207
3	Brussels Central d.	0611	0626	0711	0744	0719**r**	at	2111	2144	2126**r**	2211
6	**Brussels Midi/Zuid** d.	0617	0631	0717	0749	0724**r**	the	2117	2149	2131**r**	2217
18	Halle d.	0632	0651	0732	|	0744**r**	same	2132	|	2151**r**	2232
34	Braine-le-Comte a.	0645	0705	0745	0809	0758**r**	mins.	2145	2209	2205**r**	2245
34	Braine-le-Comte d.	0647	0715	0747	...	0815	past	2147	...	2215	2246
55	**La Louvière Centre** a.	0703	0732	0803	...	0832	each	2203	...	2232	2313
57	La Louvière Sud a.	0707	0736	0807	...	0836	hour	2207	...	2236	2318
76	**Binche** a.	0719	0747	0819	...	0847	until	2219	...	2247	2328

	Ⓐ	Ⓒ	Ⓒ		Ⓐ	Ⓒ	Ⓒ	Ⓐ	⑦	⑦
Binche d.	0521	0555	...	and	2021	2055	...	2121	2155	...
La Louvière Sud d.	0532	0606	...	at	2032	2106	...	2132	2206	...
La Louvière Centre d.	0537	0610	...	the	2037	2110	...	2137	2210	...
Braine-le-Comte a.	0554	0627	...	same	2054	2127	...	2154	2227	...
Braine-le-Comte d.	0556	0637**c**	0633	mins.	2056	2137**c**	2133	2156	2237**c**	2232
Halle d.	0609	0652**c**	|	past	2109	2152**c**	|	2209	2252**c**	|
Brussels Midi/Zuid a.	0624	0714**c**	0653	each	2124	2211**c**	2153	2224	2311**c**	2253
Brussels Central a.	0631	0719**c**	0658	hour	2131	2216**c**	2158	2231	2316**c**	2258
Brussels Nord a.	0635	0723**c**	0702	until	2135	2220**c**	2202	2235	2320**c**	2302

c – For faster journey change at Braine-le-Comte to train in next column.

r – For faster journey use train in previous column and change at Braine-le-Comte.

Table 219 LIÈGE - LUXEMBOURG

1, 2 class

km		111	113	115	117	2288	119	121	123	4445
0	**Liège Guillemins** d.	0708	0908	1108	1308	1508	1608	1748	1908	2245
23	Rivage d.	0729	0929	1129	1329	1529	1629	1811	1929	2306
31	Aywaille d.	0737	0937	1137	1337	1537	1637	1820	1937	2314
57	Trois-Ponts d.	0806	1006	1206	1406	1606	1700	1844	2006	2336
69	Vielsalm d.	0817	1017	1217	1417	1618	1711	1856	2017	2347
81	**Gouvy** 🏛 d.	0831	1031	1231	1431	1628	1731	1918	2031	2357
91	Troisvierges d.	0844	1044	1244	1444	...	1744	1929	2044	...
99	Clervaux d.	0851	1051	1251	1451	...	1751	1936	2051	...
115	Kautenbach d.	0903	1103	1303	1503	...	1803	1948	2103	...
130	Ettelbruck d.	0916	1116	1316	1516	...	1816	2001	2116	...
142	Mersch d.	0926	1126	1326	1526	...	1826	2011	2126	...
160	**Luxembourg** a.	0939	1139	1339	1539	...	1839	2024	2139	...

	2254	110	112	114	116	118	120	122	
Luxembourg d.	...	0810	1010	1210	1410	1610	1810	2048	...
Mersch d.	...	0823	1023	1223	1423	1623	1823	2101	...
Ettelbruck d.	...	0835	1035	1235	1435	1635	1835	2113	...
Kautenbach d.	...	0847	1047	1247	1447	1647	1847	2125	...
Clervaux d.	...	0900	1100	1300	1500	1700	1900	2138	...
Troisvierges d.	...	0908	1108	1308	1508	1708	1908	2146	...
Gouvy 🏛 d.	0718	0918	1118	1318	1518	1722	1918	2156	...
Vielsalm d.	0728	0928	1128	1328	1528	1732	1928	2206	...
Trois-Ponts d.	0739	0939	1139	1339	1539	1743	1939	2217	...
Aywaille d.	0802	1002	1202	1402	1602	1805	2002	2239	...
Rivage d.	0811	1011	1211	1411	1611	1813	2011	2247	...
Liège Guillemins a.	0834	1036	1234	1434	1634	1836	2034	2308	...

NETHERLANDS

Operator: Nederlandse Spoorwegen (NS).

Services: Trains convey First and Second classes of accommodation, unless otherwise indicated in the Tables. International trains may convey sleeping accommodation as indicated by footnote. Sleeping cars (🛏) and couchettes (▬) are of the normal European types – see page **10** for more details. **Supplements** are payable for travel by **EC** trains in the **Netherlands**. Many trains convey portions for two or more destinations – passengers should be careful to join the correct part of the train.

Timings: **Valid until May 27, 1995.** A reduced service operates on Dec. 25, 26, Jan. 1, Apr. 17. On Ascension Day (May 25) a Saturday service will operate. On Dec. 31, there will be no services from about 2000, except dedicated night trains which continue until 0200. International services are not affected.

Tickets: Seat reservations are not available in the **Netherlands**, except for international journeys to, from or via **France, Germany and Luxembourg.** Reservations can be made at most **NS** stations or appointed agents.

Table 220 AMSTERDAM - DEN HAAG - ROTTERDAM - EINDHOVEN - VENLO

1,2 class

For international trains Amsterdam - Brussels - Paris and v.v., see Table 18.

km		5497	31801	5499	31805	31809	31813	15415 Ⓐ	2454 ⚒	1803 ⚒	31817 ⑦	31817 ⚒	15419 ⚒	2455	1523 ⑥	1523 Ⓐ	2123 Ⓐ	15423	1925 ⑦	5425 ⚒	2456	1925 Ⓐ	1925 ⑥	5427 ⚒
0	**Amsterdam CS** d.	0018	0043	0046	0144	0245	0345	...	...	...	0445	0445	...	...	...	...	...	0531	...	0607	0623	...	...	0635
4	Amsterdam Sloterdijk d.	0024	0048	0051	|	|	|	...	...	...	|	|	...	...	...	...	...	0537	...	0612	0629	...	...	0640
	Haarlem d.	0038	|	0102	|	|	|	...	...	...	|	|	...	...	...	...	...	|	...	0625	|	...	...	0654
19	**Schiphol** ✈ **222** d.	|	0100	|	0200	0300	0400	...	...	...	0500	0500	...	...	...	...	...	0559	...	|	0643	...	...	|
48	Leiden **222** d.	0102	0116	0121	0216	0316	0416	...	...	...	0516	0516	...	...	...	...	...	0623	...	0644	0700	...	...	0714
	Den Haag CS d.	|	0133	0141	0232	0332	0432	...	...	...	0528	0528	0538	...	...	0620	...	|	...	|	|	0659	...	|
63	**Den Haag HS** d.	0113	|	...	|	|	|	...	...	...	0542	...	0542	...	...	0624	...	0643	...	0656	0712	0703	...	0725
72	Delft d.	0121	0144	...	0240	0340	0440	...	...	...	0550	...	0550	...	...	0634	...	0651	...	0704	|	0713	...	0734
82	Schiedam Rotterdam West d.	0131	|	...	|	|	|	...	...	...	0600	...	0600	...	...	0644	...	0701	...	0714	|	|	...	0742
86	**Rotterdam CS** a.	0136	0155	...	0254	0354	0454	...	...	...	0605	...	0605	...	...	0650	...	0706	...	0719	0729	0725	...	0746
86	**Rotterdam CS** d.	...	...	...	...	...	...	0500	0527	0553	...	...	0613	0623	0641	0652	0701	0713g	0717	...	0732	0734	0734	0748
106	Dordrecht d.	...	...	...	...	...	...	0528	0543	0611	...	...	0642	0639	0710	0710	0717	0736g	0752	...	0747	0752	0752	0814
144	**Roosendaal** 🏛 a.	...	...	...	...	...	...	|	0611	|	...	...	|	0707	|	|	0739	...	|	...	0811	|	|	|
	Brussels Midi/Zuid **205** a.	...	...	...	...	...	...	|	0730	|	...	...	|	0835	|	|	...	...	|	...	0930	|	|	|
136	Breda **235** d.	...	...	...	...	...	...	0554	...	0637	...	...	0706	...	0737	0737	...	...	0817	...	...	0817	0817	0836
157	Tilburg **235** d.	...	...	...	...	...	...	0613	...	0656	...	...	0723	...	0756	0756	...	...	0830	...	...	0830	0830	...
194	**Eindhoven** a.	...	...	...	...	...	...	0645	...	0724	...	...	0754	...	0824	0824	...	...	0854	...	...	0854	0854	...
194	**Eindhoven** d.	...	...	...	...	...	...	0649	...	0729	...	...	0759	...	0829	0829	...	...	0859	...	...	0859	0859	...
246	**Venlo** 🏛 a.	...	...	...	...	...	...	0734	...	0802	...	...	0840	...	0902	0902	...	...	0944	...	...	0944	0944	...
276	*Viersen* **706** a.	...	...	...	...	...	...	...	...	0830	...	...	...	...	...	...	...	...	...	...	...	...	...	...
283	*Mönchengladbach* **706** a.	...	...	...	...	...	...	...	...	0838	...	...	...	...	...	...	...	...	...	...	...	...	...	...
340	*Köln Hbf* **706** a.	...	...	...	...	...	...	...	...	0919	...	...	...	...	...	...	...	...	...	...	...	...	...	...

	2127	1807	5429	1929	2457	5431	2131	1531	5433	2458	1933	5435	2135	1811	5437	1937	2459	367 D	5439	2139	1539	5441	1941	2460
Amsterdam CS d.	0646	...	0709	...	0725	0739	0755	...	0809	0825	...	0838	0855	...	0909	...	0925	0932	0939	0955	...	1009	...	1025
Amsterdam Sloterdijk d.	0653	...	0714	...	|	0744	0801	...	0814	|	...	0843	|	...	0914	...	|	|	0944	|	...	1014	...	|
Haarlem d.	|	...	0725	...	|	0755	|	...	0825	|	...	0855	|	...	0925	...	|	0948	0956	|	...	1025	...	|
Schiphol ✈ **222** d.	0707	...	|	...	0743	|	0813	...	|	0843	...	|	0913	...	|	...	0943	|	|	1013	...	|	...	1043
Leiden **222** d.	0724	...	0744	...	0800	0814	0830	...	0844	0900	...	0914	0930	...	0944	...	1000	1007	1015	1030	...	1044	...	1100
Den Haag CS d.	|	0745	|	0759	|	|	|	0845	|	|	0859	|	|	0945	|	0959	|	|	|	|	1045	|	1059	|
Den Haag HS d.	0737	0750	0756	0803	0812	0825	0842	0850	0856	0912	0903	0926	0942	0950	0956	1003	1012	1021	1026	1042	1050	1056	1103	1112
Delft d.	|	0757	0803	0813	|	0834	|	0857	0903	|	0913	0933	|	0957	1003	1013	|	|	1033	|	1057	1103	1113	|
Schiedam Rotterdam West d.	|	|	0811	|	|	0842	|	|	0911	|	|	0941	|	|	1011	|	|	1042	1041	|	|	1111	|	|
Rotterdam CS a.	0754	0810	0816	0825	0829	0846	0859	0910	0916	0929	0926	0946	0959	1010	1016	1025	1029	...	1046	1059	1110	1116	1125	1129
Rotterdam CS d.	0801	0812	0818	0834	0832	0848	0902	0912	0918	0932	0934	0955	1003	1012	1018	1034	1032	...	1048	1102	1112	1118	1134	1132
Dordrecht d.	0818	0828	0841	0852	0848	0914	0918	0927	0941	0948	0952	1019	1022	1027	1041	1052	1048	...	1114	1118	1127	1140	1152	1147
Roosendaal 🏛 a.	0839	|	...	|	0911	|	0939	|	...	1011	|	|	1043	|	...	|	1111	...	|	1139	|	...	|	1211
Brussels Midi/Zuid **205** a.	...	|	...	|	1030	|	...	|	...	1130	|	|	...	|	...	|	1230	...	|	...	|	...	|	1330
Breda **235** d.	...	0847	...	0917	...	0936	...	0947	...	...	1017	1040	...	1047	...	1117	...	...	1136	...	1147	...	1217	...
Tilburg **235** d.	...	0901	...	0931	...	...	...	1001	...	...	1031	...	...	1101	...	1131	...	...	...	...	1201	...	1231	...
Eindhoven a.	...	0924	...	0954	...	...	...	1024	...	...	1054	...	...	1124	...	1154	...	...	...	...	1224	...	1254	...
Eindhoven d.	...	0929	...	0959	...	...	...	1029	...	...	1059	...	...	1129	...	1159	...	...	...	...	1229	...	1259	...
Venlo 🏛 a.	...	1002	...	1044	...	...	...	1102	...	...	1144	...	...	1202	...	1244	...	...	...	...	1302	...	1344	...
Viersen **706** a.	...	1030	...	...	...	...	...	...	...	...	...	...	...	1230	...	...	...	...	...	...	...	...	...	...
Mönchengladbach **706** a.	...	1038	...	...	...	...	...	...	...	...	...	...	...	1238	...	...	...	...	...	...	...	...	...	...
Köln Hbf **706** a.	...	1119	...	...	...	...	...	...	...	...	...	...	...	1319	...	...	...	...	...	...	...	...	...	...

	5443	2143	1815	5445	2461	1945	5447	2147	1547	5449	1949	2462	5451	2151	1819	5453	1953	2463	5455	2155	1555	5457	1957	2464
Amsterdam CS d.	1039	1055	...	1109	1125	...	1139	1155	...	1209	...	1225	1239	1255	...	1309	...	1325	1339	1355	...	1409	...	1425
Amsterdam Sloterdijk d.	1044	|	...	1114	|	...	1144	|	...	1214	...	|	1244	|	...	1314	...	|	1344	|	...	1414	...	|
Haarlem d.	1055	|	...	1125	|	...	1155	|	...	1225	...	|	1255	|	...	1325	...	|	1355	|	...	1425	...	|
Schiphol ✈ **222** d.	|	1113	...	|	1143	...	|	1213	...	|	...	1243	|	1313	...	|	...	1343	|	1413	...	|	...	1443
Leiden **222** d.	1114	1130	...	1144	1200	...	1214	1230	...	1244	...	1300	1314	1330	...	1344	...	1400	1414	1430	...	1444	...	1500
Den Haag CS d.	|	|	1145	|	|	1159	|	|	1245	|	1259	|	|	|	1345	|	1359	|	|	|	1445	|	1459	|
Den Haag HS d.	1126	1142	1150	1156	1212	1203	1226	1242	1250	1256	1303	1312	1326	1342	1350	1356	1403	1412	1426	1442	1450	1456	1503	1512
Delft d.	1133	|	1157	1203	|	1213	1233	|	1257	1303	1313	|	1333	|	1357	1403	1413	|	1433	|	1457	1503	1513	|
Schiedam Rotterdam West d.	1141	|	|	1211	|	|	1241	|	|	1311	|	|	1341	|	|	1411	|	|	1441	|	|	1511	|	|
Rotterdam CS a.	1146	1159	1210	1216	1229	1225	1246	1259	1310	1316	1325	1329	1346	1359	1410	1416	1425	1429	1446	1459	1510	1516	1525	1529
Rotterdam CS d.	1148	1202	1212	1218	1232	1234	1248	1302	1312	1318	1334	1332	1348	1402	1412	1418	1434	1432	1448	1502	1512	1518	1534	1532
Dordrecht d.	1214	1218	1227	1241	1248	1252	1314	1318	1327	1341	1352	1348	1414	1418	1427	1441	1452	1448	1514	1518	1527	1541	1552	1548
Roosendaal 🏛 a.	|	1239	|	...	1311	|	|	1339	|	...	|	1411	|	1439	|	...	|	1511	|	1539	|	...	|	1611
Brussels Midi/Zuid **205** a.	|	...	|	...	1430	|	|	...	|	...	|	1530	|	...	|	...	|	1630	|	...	|	...	|	1730
Breda **235** d.	1236	...	1247	...	...	1317	1336	...	1347	...	1417	...	1436	...	1447	...	1517	...	1536	...	1547	...	1617	...
Tilburg **235** d.	...	...	1301	...	...	1331	...	...	1401	...	1431	...	...	...	1501	...	1531	...	...	...	1601	...	1631	...
Eindhoven a.	...	...	1324	...	...	1354	...	...	1424	...	1454	...	...	...	1524	...	1554	...	...	...	1624	...	1654	...
Eindhoven d.	...	...	1329	...	...	1359	...	...	1429	...	1459	...	...	...	1529	...	1559	...	...	...	1629	...	1659	...
Venlo 🏛 a.	...	...	1402	...	...	1444	...	...	1502	...	1544	...	...	...	1602	...	1644	...	...	...	1702	...	1744	...
Viersen **706** a.	...	...	1430	...	...	...	...	...	...	...	...	...	...	...	1630	...	...	...	...	...	...	...	...	...
Mönchengladbach **706** a.	...	...	1438	...	...	...	...	...	...	...	...	...	...	...	1638	...	...	...	...	...	...	...	...	...
Köln Hbf **706** a.	...	...	1519	...	...	...	...	...	...	...	...	...	...	...	1719	...	...	...	...	...	...	...	...	...

D – (12) Amsterdam - Hoek van Holland (arrive 1059). Not Dec. 25, 26, 31.

g – ⚒ only.

3271A

Advertisement

THOMAS COOK TRAVELLERS – AMSTERDAM

See the order form at the back of this book for details.

For explanation of standard symbols see page 4

Table 220 AMSTERDAM - DEN HAAG - ROTTERDAM - EINDHOVEN - VENLO

1,2 class

	5459	2159	1823	5461	1961	2465	5463	2163	1563 Ⓐ	1563 Ⓒ	5465	1965	2466	5467 Ⓐ	5467 Ⓒ	2167	1827	5469	1969	2467	5471	2171	1571	5473
Amsterdam CS d.	1439	1455	...	1509	...	1525	1539	1555	...	...	1609	...	1625	1639	1639	1655	...	1709	...	1725	1739	1755	...	1809
Amsterdam Sloterdijk d.	1444	|	...	1514	...	|	1544	|	...	...	1614	...	|	1644	1644	|	...	1714	...	|	1744	|	...	1814
Haarlem d.	1455	|	...	1525	...	|	1555	|	...	...	1625	...	|	1655	1655	|	...	1725	...	|	1755	|	...	1825
Schiphol ✈ **222** d.	|	1513	...	|	...	1543	|	1613	...	...	|	...	1643	|	|	1713	...	|	...	1743	|	1813	...	|
Leiden **222** d.	1514	1530	...	1544	...	1600	1614	1630	...	...	1644	...	1700	1714	1714	1730	...	1744	...	1800	1814	1830	...	1844
Den Haag CS d.	|	|	1545	|	1559	|	|	|	1640	1645	|	1659	|	|	|	|	1745	|	1759	|	|	|	1845	|
Den Haag HS d.	1525	1542	1550	1556	1603	1612	1625	1642	1644	1650	1656	1703	1712	1725	1725	1742	1750	1756	1803	1812	1825	1842	1850	1856
Delft d.	1534	|	1557	1603	1613	|	1634	|	1651	1657	1703	1713	|	1734	1734	|	1757	1803	1813	|	1834	|	1857	1903
Schiedam Rotterdam West d.	1542	|	|	1611	|	|	1642	|	|	|	1712	|	|	1742	1742	|	|	1811	|	|	1842	|	|	1911
Rotterdam CS a.	1546	1559	1610	1616	1625	1629	1646	1659	1704	1710	1717	1725	1729	1746	1746	1759	1810	1816	1825	1829	1846	1859	1910	1916
Rotterdam CS d.	1548	1601	1612	1618	1628b	1632	1648	1702	1706	1712	1719	1734	1732	1748	1753	1801	1812	1818	1834	1832	1848	1902	1912	1918
Dordrecht d.	1617	1620	1628	1641	1651	1648	1716	1722	1727	1727	1742	1752	1748	1807	1817	1820	1827	1841	1852	1848	1914	1918	1927	1941
Roosendaal 🏛 a.	|	1643	|	...	1652	1711	|	1743	|	|	|	|	1811	|	|	1841	|	...	|	1911	|	1939	|	...
Brussels Midi/Zuid **205** a.	|	...	|	...	|	1830	|	...	|	|	|	|	1930	|	|	...	|	...	|	2030	|	...	|	...
Breda **235** d.	1638	...	1647	...	1717	...	1739	...	1747	1747	1808c	1817	...	1830	1839	...	1847	...	1917	...	1936	...	1947	...
Tilburg **235** d.	...	...	1701	...	1731	...	1757c	...	1801	1801	1825c	1831	...	1847	...	...	1901	...	1931	...	...	...	2001	...
Eindhoven a.	...	...	1724	...	1754	...	...	...	1824	1824	...	1854	...	1917	...	...	1924	...	1954	...	...	...	2024	...
Eindhoven d.	...	...	1729	...	1759	...	...	...	1829	1829	...	1859	...	...	...	...	1929	...	1959	...	...	...	2029	...
Venlo 🏛 a.	...	...	1802	...	1844	...	...	...	1902	1902	...	1944	...	...	...	...	2002	...	2044	...	...	...	2104	...
Viersen **706** a.	...	...	1830	...	...	...	...	...	...	...	...	...	...	...	...	...	2030	...	...	...	...	...	...	...
Mönchengladbach **706** a.	...	...	1838	...	...	...	...	...	...	...	...	...	...	...	...	...	2038	...	...	...	...	...	...	...
Köln Hbf **706** a.	...	...	1919	...	...	...	...	...	...	...	...	...	...	...	...	...	2119	...	...	...	...	...	...	...

	1973	2468	5475	2175	1829	5477	1977	2469	5479	363 K	2179	1579 Ⓒ	5481	1981	2470	5483	2183	1583 Ⓒ	5485	1985	2471	5487	2187	1587 ⑦
Amsterdam CS d.	...	1825	1839	1855	...	1909	...	1925	1939	1948	1955	...	2009	...	2025	2039	2055	...	2109	...	2125	2139	2155	...
Amsterdam Sloterdijk d.	...	|	1844	|	...	1914	...	|	1944	|	|	...	2014	...	|	2044	|	...	2114	...	|	2144	|	...
Haarlem d.	...	|	1855	|	...	1925	...	|	1955	2003	|	...	2025	...	|	2055	|	...	2125	...	|	2155	|	...
Schiphol ✈ **222** d.	...	1843	|	1913	...	|	...	1943	|	|	2013	...	|	...	2043	|	2113	...	|	...	2143	|	2213	...
Leiden **222** d.	...	1900	1914	1930	...	1944	...	2000	2014	2024	2030	...	2044	...	2100	2114	2130	...	2144	...	2200	2214	2230	...
Den Haag CS d.	1859	|	|	|	1945	|	1959	|	|	|	|	2045	|	2059	|	|	|	2145	|	2159	|	|	|	2245
Den Haag HS d.	1903	1912	1926	1942	1950	1956	2003	2012	2026	2037	2042	2050	2056	2103	2112	2126	2142	2150	2156	2203	2212	2226	2242	2250
Delft d.	1913	|	1933	|	1957	2003	2013	|	2033	|	|	2057	2103	2113	|	2133	|	2157	2203	2213	|	2233	|	2257
Schiedam Rotterdam West d.	|	|	1941	|	|	2011	|	|	2041	2055	|	|	2111	|	|	2141	|	|	2211	|	|	2241	|	|
Rotterdam CS a.	1925	1929	1946	1959	2010	2016	2025	2029	2046	...	2059	2110	2116	2125	2129	2146	2159	2210	2216	2225	2229	2246	2259	2310
Rotterdam CS d.	1934	1932	1948	2002	2012	2018	2034	2032	2048	...	2102	2112	2118	2134	2132	2148	2202	2212	2218	2234	2232	2252	2302	2312
Dordrecht d.	1952	1948	2014	2018	2027	2041	2052	2048	2114	...	2118	2127	2141	2151	2147	2214	2218	2227	2241	2252	2248	2315	2320	2327
Roosendaal 🏛 a.	|	2011	|	2039	|	...	|	2111	|	...	2139	|	...	|	2211	|	2239	|	...	|	2311	|	2353	|
Brussels Midi/Zuid **205** a.	|	2130	|	...	|	...	|	2230	|	...	...	|	...	|	2330	|	...	|	...	|	...	|	...	|
Breda **235** d.	2017	...	2036	...	2047	...	2117	...	2136	...	...	2147	...	2217	...	2236	...	2247	...	2317	...	2336	...	2347
Tilburg **235** d.	2031	...	...	...	2101	...	2131	...	...	...	...	2201	...	2231	...	...	...	2301	...	2331	...	...	...	0001
Eindhoven a.	2054	...	...	...	2124	...	2154	...	...	...	...	2224	...	2254	...	...	...	2324	...	2354	...	...	...	0024
Eindhoven d.	2059	...	...	...	2129	...	2159	...	...	...	...	2229h	...	2259	...	...	...	2329h	...	...	...	...	...	...
Venlo 🏛 a.	2144	...	...	...	2202	...	2244	...	...	...	...	2302h	...	2344	...	...	...	0003h	...	...	...	...	...	...
Viersen **706** a.	...	...	...	...	2230	...	...	...	...	...	...	...	...	...	...	...	...	...	...	...	...	...	...	...
Mönchengladbach **706** a.	...	...	...	...	2238	...	...	...	...	...	...	...	...	...	...	...	...	...	...	...	...	...	...	...
Köln Hbf **706** a.	...	...	...	...	2319	...	...	...	...	...	...	...	...	...	...	...	...	...	...	...	...	...	...	...

	5489	288	1989	2189	5491	2191	5493	2473	5495	
Amsterdam CS d.	2209	2215	...	2225	2239	2255	2309	2325	2345	...
Amsterdam Sloterdijk d.	2214	|	...	|	2244	|	2314	|	2350	...
Haarlem d.	2225	2232	...	|	2255	|	2325	|	0000	...
Schiphol ✈ **222** d.	|	|	...	2243	|	2313	|	2343	|	...
Leiden **222** d.	2244	|	...	2300	2314	2330	2345	0000	0022	...
Den Haag CS d.	|	|	...	|	|	|	|	|	|	...
Den Haag HS d.	2256	2307	...	2312	2326	2342	2356	0012	0039	...
Delft d.	2303	|	...	|	2333	|	0003	0021	0047	...
Schiedam Rotterdam West d.	2311	|	...	|	2341	|	0011	0031	0057	...
Rotterdam CS a.	2316	2326	...	2329	2346	2359	0016	0036	0102	...
Rotterdam CS d.	...	2334	2319	2331	...	...	0020	...	0104	...
Dordrecht d.	...	|	2355	2348	...	...	0044	...	0127	...
Roosendaal 🏛 a.	...	0019	|	0014	...	...	|	...	...	...
Brussels Midi/Zuid **205** a.	...	0134	|	...	...	...	|	...	...	...
Breda **235** d.	...	...	0020	...	...	...	0107	...	...	...
Tilburg **235** d.	...	...	0038	...	...	...	...	...	...	...
Eindhoven a.	...	...	0109	...	...	...	...	...	...	...
Eindhoven d.	...	...	...	...	...	...	...	...	...	...
Venlo 🏛 a.	...	...	...	...	...	...	...	...	...	...
Viersen **706** a.	...	...	...	...	...	...	...	...	...	...
Mönchengladbach **706** a.	...	...	...	...	...	...	...	...	...	...
Köln Hbf **706** a.	...	...	...	...	...	...	...	...	...	...

	31810	31814	31818	15404	15406 Ⓒ	2108 Ⓐ	2476 ⑥	2476 Ⓐ	5410
Köln Hbf **706** d.	...	...	...	...	...	...	...	...	...
Mönchengladbach **706** d.	...	...	...	...	...	...	...	...	...
Viersen **706** d.	...	...	...	...	...	...	...	...	...
Venlo 🏛 d.	...	...	...	...	...	...	...	...	...
Eindhoven a.	...	...	...	...	...	...	...	...	...
Eindhoven d.	...	...	...	...	...	...	...	...	...
Tilburg **235** d.	...	...	...	...	...	...	...	...	...
Breda **235** d.	...	...	...	...	...	...	...	...	...
Brussels Midi/Zuid **205** d.	...	...	...	...	...	...	...	...	...
Roosendaal 🏛 d.	...	...	...	...	...	...	...	...	...
Dordrecht d.	...	...	...	...	...	...	0515	0527	...
Rotterdam CS a.	...	...	...	...	...	...	0539	0549	...
Rotterdam CS d.	0202	0302	0402	0440	0506	0531	0542	0600	0609
Schiedam Rotterdam West d.	|	|	|	0445	0511	|	0547	|	0613
Delft d.	0213	0313	0413	0454	0520	|	0556	|	0623
Den Haag HS d.	|	|	|	0504	0530	0549	0606	0617	0635
Den Haag CS a.	0229	0329	0429	0511	0538	|	0615	|	|
Leiden **222** d.	0242	0342	0442	0530	0558	0601	0628	0628	0647
Schiphol ✈ **222** d.	0300	0400	0500	0550	0619	0618	0645	0645	|
Haarlem d.	|	|	|	|	|	|	|	|	0706
Amsterdam Sloterdijk d.	|	|	|	0601	0632	0631	0656	0656	0715
Amsterdam CS a.	0314	0414	0514	0607	0638	0637	0702	0702	0721

	2112	5412 Ⓐ	15414 Ⓐ	2477	5116	1516	2116	5416 Ⓒ	5416 Ⓐ	5118 Ⓐ	5220 Ⓐ	1918 Ⓐ	2478	5418 Ⓐ	5418 ⑥	5418 ⑦	1520 ⑦	1520 ⚒	2120	362 J	5420	2479	1922	5422
Köln Hbf **706** d.	...	...	...	...	...	...	...	...	...	...	...	...	...	...	...	...	...	...	...	...	...	...	...	...
Mönchengladbach **706** d.	...	...	...	...	...	...	...	...	...	...	...	...	...	...	...	...	...	...	...	...	...	...	...	...
Viersen **706** d.	...	...	...	...	...	...	...	...	...	...	...	...	...	...	...	...	...	...	...	...	...	...	...	...
Venlo 🏛 d.	...	...	...	...	...	...	...	...	...	...	0547	...	...	...	...	...	...	0619	...	...	...	...	0650g	...
Eindhoven a.	...	...	...	...	...	...	...	...	...	...	0626	...	...	...	...	...	...	0704	...	...	...	...	0735g	...
Eindhoven d.	...	...	0523	...	...	0557	...	...	...	...	...	0629	...	...	...	...	0658	0708	...	...	...	...	0739	...
Tilburg **235** d.	...	...	0554	...	...	0631	...	...	...	...	...	0654	...	...	...	...	0730	0733	...	...	...	...	0803	...
Breda **235** d.	...	0555	0613	...	...	0646	...	...	0658	...	...	0708	...	...	0727	...	0747	0747	...	...	0756g	...	0817	...
Brussels Midi/Zuid **205** d.	...	|	|	...	...	|	...	...	|	...	...	|	0610g	...	|	...	|	|	...	...	|	0710	|	...
Roosendaal 🏛 d.	0530c	|	|	...	0625c	|	0647g	...	|	0656	...	|	0723g	0716	|	...	|	|	0752	...	|	0824	|	...
Dordrecht d.	0603	0618	0637	...	0658	0707	0710g	0721	0726	0729	...	0732	0746g	0740	0752	...	0807	0807	0815	...	0820	0846	0840	0850
Rotterdam CS a.	0628	0641	0701	...	0721	0726	0731g	0744	0743	0749	...	0757	0804g	0801	0814	...	0824	0824	0832	...	0843	0901	0858	0913
Rotterdam CS d.	0629	0644	...	0703	0722	0728	0734	0745	0745	0753	...	0800	0806	0810	0816	0816	0826	0826	0834	0836	0845	0903	0906	0916
Schiedam Rotterdam West d.	0634	0648	...	|	0727	|	|	0749	0749	0758	...	|	|	0815	0821	0821	|	|	|	0842	0849	|	|	0921
Delft d.	0643	0655	...	|	0736	0740	|	0756	0756	0807	...	0812	|	0825	0828	0828	0839	0839	|	|	0856	|	0917	0928
Den Haag HS d.	0652	0705	...	0722	0746	0749	0752	0806	0806	0817	...	0822	0823	0835	0835	0835	0849	0849	0852	0857	0906	0922	0931	0935
Den Haag CS a.	|	|	...	|	0749	0752	|	|	|	0820	...	0823	|	|	|	|	0852	0852	|	|	|	|	0934	|
Leiden **222** d.	0704	0717	...	0734	...	...	0804	0818	0818	...	...	...	0834	0847	0847	0847	...	...	0904	|	0918	0934	...	0947
Schiphol ✈ **222** d.	0721	|	...	0751	...	...	0821	|	|	...	...	...	0851	|	|	|	...	...	0920	|	|	0951	...	|
Haarlem d.	|	0736	...	|	...	...	|	0837	0837	...	...	...	|	0906	0906	0906	...	...	|	0934	0938	|	...	1006
Amsterdam Sloterdijk d.	|	0745	...	|	...	...	|	0847	0847	...	...	...	|	0915	0915	0915	...	...	|	|	0947	|	...	1015
Amsterdam CS a.	0738	0751	...	0808	...	...	0838	0853	0853	...	...	...	0908	0921	0921	0921	...	...	0938	0949	0953	1008	...	1021

J – [12] Hoek van Holland (depart 0803) - Amsterdam. **Not** Dec. 26, 27, Jan. 1.
K – [12] Amsterdam - Hoek van Holland (arrive 2113). **Not** Dec. 25, 26, 31.
b – Depart 1634 on Ⓐ.

c – Ⓐ only.
g – ⚒ only.
h – ⑦ only.

For explanation of standard symbols see page 4

Table 220 VENLO - EINDHOVEN - ROTTERDAM - DEN HAAG - AMSTERDAM

1, 2 class

	1524	2124	5424	2480	1926	5426	1802	2128	5428	2481	1930	5430	1532	2132	5432	2482	1934	5434	1804	2136	5436	2483	1938	5438
Köln Hbf **706** d.	...	...	...	...	...	...	0717	...	...	...	...	...	...	...	...	...	...	...	0917	...	...	...	...	...
Mönchengladbach **706** d.	...	...	...	...	...	...	0758	...	...	...	...	...	...	...	...	...	...	...	0958	...	...	...	...	...
Viersen **706** d.	...	...	...	...	...	...	0805	...	...	...	...	...	...	...	...	...	...	...	1005	...	...	...	...	...
Venlo d.	0728	...	...	...	0750	...	0831	...	...	...	0850	...	0931	...	...	...	0950	...	1031	...	...	...	1050	...
Eindhoven a.	0805	...	...	...	0835	...	0905	...	...	...	0935	...	1005	...	...	...	1035	...	1105	...	...	...	1135	...
Eindhoven d.	0809	...	...	...	0839	...	0909	...	...	...	0939	...	1009	...	...	...	1039	...	1109	...	...	...	1139	...
Tilburg **235** d.	0833	...	...	...	0903	...	0933	...	...	...	1003	...	1033	...	...	...	1103	...	1133	...	...	...	1203	...
Breda **235** d.	0847	...	0856	...	0917	...	0947	...	0957	...	1017	...	1047	...	1057	...	1117	...	1147	...	1157	...	1221	...
Brussels Midi/Zuid **205** d.	|	...	|	0810	|	...	|	...	|	0910	|	...	|	...	|	1010	|	...	|	...	|	1110	|	...
Roosendaal d.	|	0852	|	0923	|	...	|	0952	|	1023	|	...	|	1052	|	1123	|	...	|	1152	|	1224	|	...
Dordrecht d.	0905	0915	0920	0946	0940	0950	1005	1015	1020	1046	1040	1050	1106	1115	1120	1146	1140	1150	1206	1215	1220	1247	1244	1250
Rotterdam CS a.	0920	0931	0943	1001	0958	1013	1020	1031	1043	1101	1058	1113	1120	1131	1143	1201	1158	1213	1220	1231	1243	1302	1259	1313
Rotterdam CS d.	0922	0934	0945	1003	1006	1016	1022	1034	1046	1103	1106	1116	1122	1134	1146	1203	1206	1216	1222	1234	1246	1305	1308	1316
Schiedam Rotterdam West d.	|	|	0949	|	|	1021	|	|	1051	|	|	1121	|	|	1151	|	|	1221	|	|	1251	|	|	1321
Delft d.	0934	|	0956	|	1017	1028	1034	|	1058	|	1117	1128	1134	|	1158	|	1217	1228	1234	|	1258	|	1319	1328
Den Haag HS d.	0945	0952	1006	1022	1029	1035	1045	1052	1105	1122	1129	1135	1145	1152	1205	1222	1229	1235	1245	1252	1305	1323	1330	1335
Den Haag CS a.	0949	|	|	|	1032	|	1049	|	|	|	1132	|	1149	|	|	|	1232	|	1249	|	|	|	1333	|
Leiden **222** d.	...	1004	1018	1034	...	1047	...	1104	1117	1134	...	1147	...	1204	1217	1234	...	1247	...	1304	1317	1335	...	1347
Schiphol ✈ 222 d.	...	1021	|	1051	...	|	...	1121	|	1151	...	|	...	1221	|	1251	...	|	...	1321	|	1351	...	|
Haarlem d.	...	|	1037	|	...	1106	...	|	1136	|	...	1206	...	|	1236	|	...	1306	...	|	1336	|	...	1406
Amsterdam Sloterdijk d.	...	|	1045	|	...	1115	...	|	1145	|	...	1215	...	|	1245	|	...	1315	...	|	1345	|	...	1415
Amsterdam CS a.	...	1038	1052	1108	...	1121	...	1138	1151	1208	...	1221	...	1238	1251	1308	...	1321	...	1338	1351	1408	...	1421

	1540	2140	5440	2484	1942	5442	1808	2144	5444	2485	1946	5446	1548	2148	5448	2486	1950	5450	1812	2152	5452	2487	1954	5454
Köln Hbf **706** d.	...	...	...	...	...	...	1117	...	...	...	...	...	...	...	...	...	...	...	1317	...	...	...	...	...
Mönchengladbach **706** d.	...	...	...	...	...	...	1158	...	...	...	...	...	...	...	...	...	...	...	1358	...	...	...	...	...
Viersen **706** d.	...	...	...	...	...	...	1205	...	...	...	...	...	...	...	...	...	...	...	1405	...	...	...	...	...
Venlo d.	1131	...	...	...	1150	...	1231	...	...	...	1250	...	1331	...	...	...	1350	...	1431	...	...	...	1450	...
Eindhoven a.	1205	...	...	...	1235	...	1305	...	...	...	1335	...	1405	...	...	...	1435	...	1505	...	...	...	1535	...
Eindhoven d.	1209	...	...	...	1239	...	1309	...	...	...	1339	...	1409	...	...	...	1439	...	1509	...	...	...	1539	...
Tilburg **235** d.	1233	...	...	...	1303	...	1333	...	...	...	1403	...	1433	...	...	...	1503	...	1533	...	...	...	1603	...
Breda **235** d.	1247	...	1257	...	1317	...	1347	...	1357	...	1417	...	1447	...	1457	...	1517	...	1547	...	1557	...	1617	...
Brussels Midi/Zuid **205** d.	|	...	|	1210	|	...	|	...	|	1310	|	...	|	...	|	1410	|	...	|	...	|	1510	|	...
Roosendaal d.	|	1252	|	1323	|	...	|	1352	|	1423	|	...	|	1452	|	1523	|	...	|	1552	|	1623	|	...
Dordrecht d.	1305	1315	1320	1346	1340	1350	1405	1415	1420	1446	1440	1450	1507	1515	1520	1546	1540	1550	1605	1615	1620	1646	1640	1650
Rotterdam CS a.	1320	1331	1343	1401	1358	1413	1420	1431	1443	1501	1458	1513	1521	1531	1543	1601	1558	1613	1620	1631	1643	1701	1658	1713
Rotterdam CS d.	1322	1334	1346	1403	1406	1416	1422	1434	1445	1503	1506	1516	1522	1534	1545	1603	1606	1616	1622	1634	1645	1703	1706	1716
Schiedam Rotterdam West d.	|	|	1351	|	|	1421	|	|	1449	|	|	1521	|	|	1549	|	|	1621	|	|	1649	|	|	1721
Delft d.	1334	|	1358	|	1417	1428	1434	|	1456	|	1517	1528	1534	|	1556	|	1617	1628	1634	|	1656	|	1717	1728
Den Haag HS d.	1345	1352	1405	1422	1429	1435	1445	1452	1506	1522	1529	1535	1545	1555	1606	1622	1629	1635	1645	1652	1706	1722	1729	1735
Den Haag CS a.	1349	|	|	|	1432	|	1449	|	|	|	1532	|	1549	|	|	|	1632	|	1649	|	|	|	1732	|
Leiden **222** d.	...	1404	1417	1434	...	1447	...	1504	1518	1534	...	1547	...	1607	1618	1634	...	1647	...	1704	1718	1734	...	1747
Schiphol ✈ 222 d.	...	1421	|	1451	...	|	...	1521	|	1551	...	|	...	1624	|	1651	...	|	...	1721	|	1751	...	|
Haarlem d.	...	|	1437	|	...	1506	...	|	1537	|	...	1606	...	|	1637	|	...	1706	...	|	1737	|	...	1806
Amsterdam Sloterdijk d.	...	|	1447	|	...	1515	...	|	1547	|	...	1615	...	|	1645	|	...	1715	...	|	1745	|	...	1815
Amsterdam CS a.	...	1438	1453	1508	...	1521	...	1538	1553	1608	...	1621	...	1640	1652	1708	...	1721	...	1738	1752	1808	...	1821

	1556	2156	5456	2488	1958	5458	1816	2160	5460	2489	1962	5462	1564	2164	5464	2490	1966	5466	366 D	1820	2168	5468	2491	1970
Köln Hbf **706** d.	...	...	...	...	...	...	1517	...	...	...	...	...	...	...	...	...	...	...	...	1717	...	...	...	...
Mönchengladbach **706** d.	...	...	...	...	...	...	1558	...	...	...	...	...	...	...	...	...	...	...	...	1758	...	...	...	...
Viersen **706** d.	...	...	...	...	...	...	1605	...	...	...	...	...	...	...	...	...	...	...	...	1805	...	...	...	...
Venlo d.	1531	...	...	...	1550	...	1631	...	...	...	1650	...	1731	...	...	...	1750	...	...	1831	...	...	...	1850
Eindhoven a.	1605	...	...	...	1635	...	1705	...	...	...	1735	...	1805	...	...	...	1835	...	...	1905	...	...	...	1935
Eindhoven d.	1609	...	...	...	1639	...	1709	...	...	...	1739	...	1809	...	...	...	1839	...	...	1909	...	...	...	1939
Tilburg **235** d.	1633	...	...	...	1703	...	1733	...	...	...	1803	...	1833	...	...	...	1903	...	...	1933	...	...	...	2003
Breda **235** d.	1647	...	1657	...	1717	...	1747	...	1757	...	1817	...	1847	...	1856	...	1917	...	...	1947	...	1957	...	2017
Brussels Midi/Zuid **205** d.	|	...	|	1610	|	...	|	...	|	1710	|	...	|	...	|	1810	|	...	...	|	...	|	1910	|
Roosendaal d.	|	1652	|	1723	|	...	|	1752	|	1823	|	...	|	1852	|	1923	|	...	...	|	1952	|	2023	|
Dordrecht d.	1705	1715	1720	1746	1740	1750	1805	1815	1820	1846	1840	1850	1906	1915	1920	1946	1940	1950	...	2005	2015	2020	2046	2040
Rotterdam CS a.	1720	1732	1743	1801	1758	1813	1820	1831	1843	1901	1858	1913	1920	1931	1943	2001	1958	2013	...	2020	2031	2043	2101	2058
Rotterdam CS d.	1722	1735	1745	1803	1806	1816	1822	1834	1846	1903	1906	1916	1922	1934	1946	2003	2006	2016	...	2024	2034	2046	2103	2106
Schiedam Rotterdam West d.	|	|	1749	|	|	1821	|	|	1851	|	|	1921	|	|	1951	|	|	2021	2025	|	|	2051	|	|
Delft d.	1734	|	1756	|	1817	1828	1834	|	1858	|	1917	1928	1934	|	1958	|	2017	2028	|	2036	|	2058	|	2117
Den Haag HS d.	1745	1752	1806	1822	1829	1835	1845	1852	1905	1922	1929	1935	1945	1952	2005	2022	2029	2035	2040	2045	2052	2105	2122	2129
Den Haag CS a.	1749	|	|	|	1832	|	1849	|	|	|	1932	|	1949	|	|	|	2032	|	|	2049	|	|	|	2132
Leiden **222** d.	...	1804	1818	1834	...	1847	...	1904	1917	1934	...	1947	...	2004	2017	2034	...	2047	2052	...	2104	2117	2134	...
Schiphol ✈ 222 d.	...	1821	|	1851	...	|	...	1921	|	1951	...	|	...	2021	|	2051	...	|	|	...	2121	|	2151	...
Haarlem d.	...	|	1837	|	...	1906	...	|	1936	|	...	2006	...	|	2036	|	...	2106	2115	...	|	2136	|	...
Amsterdam Sloterdijk d.	...	|	1845	|	...	1915	...	|	1945	|	...	2015	...	|	2045	|	...	2115	|	...	|	2145	|	...
Amsterdam CS a.	...	1838	1852	1908	...	1921	...	1938	1951	2008	...	2021	...	2038	2051	2108	...	2121	2132	...	2138	2151	2208	...

	5470	1572	2172	5472	2492	1974	5474	1824	2176	5476	1978	2493	5478	1826	2180 ⑦	5480	2494	5482	1982	1584 ©	31806	2495	1986	
Köln Hbf **706** d.	...	...	...	...	...	...	...	1917	...	...	...	...	...	2017	...	...	...	...	...	...	...	...	...	...
Mönchengladbach **706** d.	...	...	...	...	...	...	...	1958	...	...	...	...	...	2058	...	...	...	...	...	...	...	...	...	...
Viersen **706** d.	...	...	...	...	...	...	...	2005	...	...	...	...	...	|	...	...	...	...	...	...	...	...	...	...
Venlo d.	...	1931	...	...	...	1950	...	2031	...	...	2050	...	...	2131	...	...	...	...	2150	2231h	...	...	2250	...
Eindhoven a.	...	2005	...	...	...	2035	...	2105	...	...	2135	...	...	2205	...	...	...	...	2235	2305h	...	...	2335	...
Eindhoven d.	...	2009	...	...	...	2039	...	2109	...	...	2139	...	...	2209	...	...	...	...	2239	2309	...	...	2338	...
Tilburg **235** d.	...	2033	...	...	...	2103	...	2133	...	...	2203	...	...	2233	...	...	...	...	2303	2333	...	...	0011	...
Breda **235** d.	...	2047	...	2057	...	2117	...	2147	...	2156	2217	...	...	2249	...	2257	...	...	2317	2347	...	...	0031	...
Brussels Midi/Zuid **205** d.	...	|	...	|	2010	|	...	|	...	|	|	2110	...	|	...	|	2210	...	|	|	...	2310	|	...
Roosendaal d.	...	|	2052	|	2126	|	...	|	2152	|	|	2228	...	|	2252	|	2323	...	|	|	...	0023	|	...
Dordrecht d.	2050	2105	2115	2125	2149	2140	2151	2205	2215	2220	2240	2250	2253	2309	2315	2320	2346	...	2349	0007	...	0046	0056	...
Rotterdam CS a.	2113	2120	2131	2147	2203	2158	2214	2220	2231	2243	2258	2305	2316	2324	2331	2343	0001	...	0014	0025	...	0107	0122	...
Rotterdam CS d.	2116	2122	2134	2148	2204	2207	2216	2222	2234	2244	...	2307	2317	2326	2334	2344	...	0013	...	0027	0102	...	...	...
Schiedam Rotterdam West d.	2121	|	|	2152	|	|	2221	|	|	2249	...	|	2322	|	|	2349	...	0018	...	|	|	...	...	...
Delft d.	2128	2134	|	2159	|	2218	2228	2234	|	2258	...	|	2331	2338	|	2358	...	0027	...	0039	0111	...	...	...
Den Haag HS d.	2135	2145	2152	2206	2222	2230	2235	2245	2252	2308	...	2324	2341	2346	2352	0008	...	0037	...	0048	|	...	...	...
Den Haag CS a.	|	2149	|	|	|	2233	|	2249	|	|	...	|	|	2350	|	|	...	|	...	0051	0129	...	...	...
Leiden **222** d.	2147	...	2204	2218	2234	...	2247	...	2304	2321	...	2335	2354	...	0004	0019	...	0057	...	...	0142	...	...	...
Schiphol ✈ 222 d.	|	...	2221	|	2251	...	|	...	2321	|	...	2351	|	...	0021	|	...	|	...	...	0200	...	...	...
Haarlem d.	2206	...	|	2237	|	...	2306	...	|	2340	...	|	0013	...	|	0040	...	0116	...	...	|	...	...	...
Amsterdam Sloterdijk d.	2215	...	|	2247	|	...	2315	...	|	2349	...	0004	0022	...	|	0051	...	0125	...	...	|	...	...	...
Amsterdam CS a.	2221	...	2238	2254	2308	...	2321	...	2338	2354	...	0010	0027	...	0038	0056	...	0130	...	...	0214	...	...	...

D – (12) Hoek van Holland (depart 1958) - Amsterdam. **Not** Dec. 25, 26, 31.

h – ⑦ only.

170

For explanation of standard sysmbols see page 4

03

Table 221 ROTTERDAM - HOEK VAN HOLLAND LOCAL SERVICES

1, 2 class

Rail service Rotterdam CS - Hoek van Holland Haven. 28 km. Journey time 28 minutes. 1, 2 class. All trains call at Schiedam-Rotterdam West 4 minutes before/after Rotterdam CS.
From Rotterdam CS and **Hoek van Holland Haven**: approximately half-hourly 0500-2348 (less frequently in early mornings (especially on ⑥⑦).

The following trains provide useful connections into and out of the ⛴ sailings to and from Harwich Parkeston Quay:
From Rotterdam CS: 1012 and 1042, (also 1042 from Schiedam-Rotterdam West (**not** Dec. 25, 26, 31) are connections for the day sailing to Harwich; 2012, 2040, also 2055 from Schiedam-Rotterdam West (**not** Dec. 25, 26, 31) are connections for the night sailing to Harwich.
From Hoek van Holland Haven: the 0736⚒, 0748⑦ and 0803 (**not** Dec. 26, 27, Jan. 1) services are connections off the night sailing from Harwich; similarly the 1931⚒, 1948 (**not** ⑤ or Apr. 13, May 24), 1958 to Schiedam-Rotterdam West (**not** Dec. 25, 26, 31) and 2001 (⑤ also Apr. 13, May 24) services are connections off the day sailing from Harwich.

Table 222 DEN HAAG - SCHIPHOL ✈ - UTRECHT and LELYSTAD

1, 2 class

A faster service between Schiphol ✈ and Utrecht is available by changing at Duivendrecht. See Table 240.

km			Ⓐ	Ⓐ	⚒		Ⓐ	⚒	⚒		⚒													
0	**Den Haag CS 224**	d.	...	...	...	...	...	0554	...	0627	...	...	0657	...	0727	...	and	2227	...	2300	...	...	2330
15	Leiden **224**	d.	...	...	...	...	...	0613	...	0649	...	...	0719	...	0749	...	at	2249	...	2323	...	...	2355
44	**Schiphol ✈**	d.	...	0554	0610	...	0623	0640	0654	0711	0724	...	0741	0754	0811	0824	the	2311	2324	2344	2354	...	0015
55	Amsterdam RAI	d.	...	0603	0619	...	0632	0649	0703	0720	0733	...	0750	0803	0820	0833	same	2320	2333	2353	0003	...	0024
59	Duivendrecht	d.	...	0607	0623	...	0636	0653	0707	0724	0737	...	0754	0807	0824	0837	minutes	2324	2337	2357	0007	...	0028
68	Weesp ▲	d.	...	0617	0633	...	0646	0703	0717	0735	0747	...	0805	0817	0835	0847	past	2335	2347	0009	0017	...	0038
	Hilversum	d.	0602	0632	|	...	0701	|	0732	|	0802	...	|	0832	|	0902	each	|	0002	|	0032	...	|
	Utrecht CS	a.	0622	0652	|	...	0720	|	0751	|	0822	...	|	0852	|	0922	hour	|	0022	|	0052	...	|
83	Almere CS	d.	...	...	0645	...	...	0715	...	0747	...	...	0817	...	0847	...	until:	2347	...	0021	...	...	0050
107	**Lelystad Centrum**	a.	...	...	0702	...	...	0732	...	0803	...	...	0833	...	0903	...		0003	...	0038	...	...	0107

km			Ⓐ	Ⓐ		Ⓐ	⚒	⚒		⚒													
	Lelystad Centrum	d.	0528	...	0558	...	0628	...	0658	...	...	0728	...	0758	...	and	2228	...	2258	...	2328	...	0026
	Almere CS	d.	0545	...	0615	...	0645	...	0715	...	...	0745	...	0815	...	at	2245	...	2315	...	2345	...	0044
0	**Utrecht CS**	d.	|	...	|	0605	|	0642	|	0712	...	|	0742	|	0812	the	|	2242	|	2312	|	2343	|
18	Hilversum	d.	|	0559	|	0624	|	0701	|	0731	...	|	0801	|	0831	same	|	2301	|	2331	|	0001	|
33	Weesp ▲	d.	0557	0613	0627	0639	0657	0715	0727	0745	...	0757	0815	0827	0845	minutes	2257	2315	2327	2345	2357	0017	0100
42	Duivendrecht	d.	0606	0622	0637	0648	0707	0724	0737	0754	...	0807	0824	0837	0854	past	2307	2324	2337	2354	0007	0026	0109
46	Amsterdam RAI	d.	0610	0626	0641	0652	0711	0728	0741	0758	...	0811	0828	0841	0858	each	2311	2328	2341	2358	0011	0030	0113
57	**Schiphol ✈**	d.	0619	0636	0652	0702	0722	0738	0752	0808	...	0822	0838	0852	0908	hour	2322	2338	2352	0008	0020	0039	0123
86	Leiden **224**	d.	...	...	0716	...	0746	...	0816	...	...	0846	...	0922	...	until:	2347	...	0013	...	...	...	...
101	**Den Haag CS 224**	a.	...	...	0734	...	0804	...	0834	...	...	0904	...	0940	...		0004	...	0031	...	...	...	...

▲ – Local trains run between Amsterdam CS and Weesp and v.v. approximately every 15 minutes (30 minutes on ⑦) for most of the day.
For additional trains between Den Haag and Schiphol see Table **220**.

Table 223 AMSTERDAM - LELYSTAD

1, 2 class

km			Ⓐ	Ⓐ	⚒	⚒				
0	**Amsterdam CS**	d.	0619	0649	0719	0749	0819	0849	and every	2349
29	Almere CS	d.	0639	0709	0739	0809	0839	0909	30 minutes	0009
53	**Lelystad Centrum**	a.	0654	0724	0754	0824	0854	0924	until:	0023

		Ⓐ	Ⓐ	⚒	⚒				
Lelystad Centrum	d.	0607	0637	0707	0737	0807	0837	and every	2307
Almere CS	d.	0622	0652	0722	0752	0822	0852	30 minutes	2322
Amsterdam CS	a.	0644	0714	0744	0814	0844	0914	until:	2344

Table 224 DEN HAAG - HOORN

1, 2 class

km			Ⓐ	⚒	⚒		⚒	⑦		⚒	⑦		⚒	⑦						⑦d			
0	**Den Haag CS 222**	d.	0606h	0642c	0712c	0742r	0812	0812	0842	0912	0912	and at	1412	1412	1442	1512	1542		1842	1912	1942	and at	2242
15	Leiden **222**	a.	0625	0700c	0730c	0800r	0830	0830	0900	0930	0930	the	1430	1430	1500	1530	1600	and	1900	1930	2000	the	2300
15	Leiden	d.	0629	0705c	0735c	0805r	0835	0835	0905	0935	0935	same	1435	1435	1505	1535	1605	every	1905	1935	2005	same	2305
44	Haarlem	d.	0659	0729	0800	0829	0859	0854	0929	0959	0954	minutes	1459	1454	1529	1559	1629	30	1929	1959	2029	minutes	2329
57	Beverwijk	d.	0709	0739	0809	0839	0909	...	0939	1009	...	past	1509	...	1539	1609	1639	minutes	1939	2009	2039	past	2339
79	**Alkmaar**	a.	0726	0756	0826	0856	0926	...	0956	1026	...	each	1526	...	1556	1626	1656	until	1956	2026	2056	each	2356
79	**Alkmaar**	d.	0732	0802	0832	0902	0932	...	1002	1032	...	hour	1532	...	1602	1632	1702		2002	2032	2102	hour	0002
103	**Hoorn**	a.	0755	0825	0855	0925	0955	...	1025	1055	...	until	1555	...	1625	1655	1725		2025	2055	2125	until	0025

		Ⓐ	⚒	⚒	⚒d	⚒d		⚒	⑦			⚒	⑦						⑦d		⑦		⑦	
Hoorn	d.	0601	0631	0701	0735	0805	0835	0905	...	and at	1535	1605	...	1635	1705	1735		2005	2035	2105	2135	2205	2235	2305
Alkmaar	a.	0625	0655	0725	0800	0830	0900	0930	...	the	1600	1630	...	1700	1730	1800	and	2030	2100	2130	2200	2230	2300	2330
Alkmaar	d.	0628	0658	0731	0805	0835	0905	0935	...	same	1605	1635	...	1705	1735	1805	every	2035	2105	2135	2205	2235	2305	2335
Beverwijk	d.	0648	0722	0752	0823	0852	0922	0952	...	minutes	1622	1652	...	1722	1752	1822	30	2052	2122	2152	2222	2252	2322	2352
Haarlem	d.	0703	0739	0809	0839	0909	0939	1009	1009	past	1639	1709	1709	1739	1809	1839	minutes	2109	2139	2209	2239	2309	2339	0005
Leiden	a.	0721	0757	0827	0857	0927	0957	1027	1027	each	1657	1727	1727	1757	1827	1857	until	2127	2157	2227	2257	2327	2357	...
Leiden **222**	d.	0729	0802	0832	0902	0932	1002	1032	1032	hour	1702	1732	1732	1802	1832	1902		2132	2202	2232	2302	2332	0002	...
Den Haag CS 222	a.	0747	0820	0850	0920	0950	1020	1050	1050	until	1720	1750	1750	1820	1850	1918		2150	2220	2250	2320	2350	0021	...

c – Ⓐ only. **d** – Daily Den Haag - Haarlem and v.v. **h** – Den Haag **HS**. **r** – ⚒ only.

Table 225 AMSTERDAM - DEN HELDER and ENKHUIZEN

1,2 class

km			⚒	⚒							
	Arnhem **240**	d.	...	...	...	...	0707c	0735	0808	and at	2208
	Utrecht **240**	d.	...	0616	0646c	0715	0746	0816	0846	the same	2246
0	**Amsterdam CS**	d.	0605	0652	0722	0752	0822	0852	0922	minutes	2322
4	Amsterdam Sloterdijk	d.	0610	0657	0727	0757	0827	0857	0927	past	2327
39	**Alkmaar**	a.	0649	0722	0753	0823	0853	0923	0953	each hour	2353
39	**Alkmaar**	d.	0652	0728	0758	0828	0858	0928	0958	▲	2358
81	**Den Helder**	a.	0726	0805	0835	0905	0935	1005	1035	until	0034

		Ⓐ	⚒	⚒						
Den Helder	d.	0547	0613	0649	0726	0756	and at	2226	2256	2326
Alkmaar	a.	0622	0652	0729	0803	0833	the same	2303	2333	0003
Alkmaar	d.	0632	0702	0734	0808	0838	minutes	2308	2338	0005
Amsterdam Sloterdijk	d.	0704	0735	0805	0835	0905	past	2335	0016	0036
Amsterdam CS	a.	0710	0741	0811	0841	0911	each	2341	0021	0041
Utrecht **240**	a.	0747	0817	0847	0917	0947	hour	0017	...	...
Arnhem **240**	a.	0826	0855	0926	0955	1026	until	0106	...	...

km			Ⓐ	Ⓐ		⚒					
0	**Amsterdam CS**	d.	0619	0649	0719	0749	0819	0849	and	2319	2352
4	Amsterdam Sloterdijk	d.	0624	0654	0724	0754	0824	0854	every	2324	2357
10	Zaandam	d.	0631	0701	0731	0801	0831	0901	30	2331	0004
42	Hoorn	a.	0658	0728	0758	0828	0858	0928	minutes	2358	0029
60	**Enkhuizen**	a.	0729	0759	0824	0851	0921	0951	until	0021	0050

		Ⓐ	⚒		⚒					
Enkhuizen	d.	0511	0606	0635c	0706	0737	0809	0839	and	2309
Hoorn	d.	0534	0633	0703	0735	0805	0835	0905	every	2335
Zaandam	d.	0559	0701	0731	0801	0831	0901	0931	30	0001
Amsterdam Sloterdijk	a.	0604	0707	0737	0807	0837	0907	0937	minutes	0007
Amsterdam CS	a.	0610	0713	0744	0814	0844	0914	0944	until	0014

c – ⚒ only. ▲ – However: Amsterdam CS 1718 (not 1722), Sloterdijk 1723 (not 1727).

⛴ **DEN HELDER - TEXEL** Sailing time 20 minutes. Operator: *TESO* (☎ 02220 69691).

From Den Helder Havenhoofd : 0635⚒, 0735⚒, 0835 and hourly until 2135. **From Texel 't Horntje** : 0605⚒, 0705⚒, 0805 and hourly until 2105.

Connecting 🚌 (service **3**): Den Helder Station - Havenhoofd (departs 19 minutes before sailings) and v.v. (departs 4 minutes after boat arrives). Journey time: 6 minutes.

Table 226 ROOSENDAAL - VLISSINGEN

1, 2 class

km		14611	14613	14615	14617	14617	2123		14619	2127	14623	2131	14627	2135	14631	2139		14635	2143	14639	2147		14643	2151
		Ⓐ	Ⓐ	Ⓐ	Ⓐ	⑥	Ⓐ			⚒		Y		⚒		⚒			⚒		⚒			⚒
	Amsterdam CS **220** d.	...	...	...	...	...	...	...	*0623*	0646	*0725*	0755	*0825*	0855	*0925*	0955	...	*1025*	1055	*1125*	1155	...	*1225*	1255
	Den Haag HS **220** d.	...	...	...	...	...	...	...	*0712*	0737	*0812*	0842	*0912*	0942	*1012*	1042	...	*1112*	1142	*1212*	1242	...	*1312*	1342
	Rotterdam CS **220** d.	...	...	*0623*	...	...	0701	...	*0732*	0801	*0832*	0902	*0932*	1003	*1032*	1102	...	*1132*	1202	*1232*	1302	...	*1332*	1402
0	**Roosendaal** d.	0600	0638	0714	0730	0738	0742	...	0814	0842	0914	0941	1014	1045	1114	1141	...	1214	1243	1314	1341	...	1414	1441
13	Bergen op Zoom d.	0609	0647	0723	0739	0747	0753	...	0823	0853	0923	0953	1023	1056	1123	1153	...	1223	1254	1323	1353	...	1423	1453
50	Goes d.	0637	0715	0751	0807	0815	0815	...	0851	0917	0952	1015	1052	1120	1151	1215	...	1251	1318	1351	1415	...	1451	1515
69	Middelburg d.	0652	0730	0806	0822	0830	0827	...	0906	0929	1006	1027	1106	1132	1206	1227	...	1306	1330	1406	1427	...	1506	1527
75	**Vlissingen** a.	0700	0738	0814	0830	0838	0834	...	0914	0937	1013	1034	1113	1140	1214	1234	...	1314	1338	1414	1434	...	1514	1534

		14647	2155		14651	2159	14655	2163	14659	2167	14663	2171		14667	2175		14671	2179		14675	2183		14679	2187
			⚒			H		H		H		H			T			H			J			J
Amsterdam CS **220** d.	...	*1325*	1355	...	*1425*	1455	*1525*	1555	*1625*	1655	*1724*	1755	...	*1825*	1855	...	*1925*	1955	...	*2025*	2055	...	*2125*	2155
Den Haag HS **220** d.	...	*1412*	1442	...	*1512*	1542	*1612*	1642	*1712*	1742	*1812*	1842	...	*1912*	1942	...	*2012*	2042	...	*2112*	2142	...	*2212*	2242
Rotterdam CS **220** d.	...	*1432*	1502	...	*1532*	1601	*1632*	1702	*1732*	1801	*1832*	1902	...	*1932*	2002	...	*2032*	2102	...	*2132*	2202	...	*2232*	2302
Roosendaal d.	...	1514	1541	...	1614	1645	1714	1745	1814	1843	1914	1941	...	2014	2041	...	2114	2141	...	2214	2241	...	2314	2355
Bergen op Zoom d.	...	1523	1553	...	1623	1655	1723	1755	1823	1854	1923	1953	...	2023	2053	...	2123	2153	...	2223	2253	...	2324	0006
Goes d.	...	1551	1615	...	1651	1717	1751	1817	1851	1916	1951	2015	...	2051	2115	...	2151	2215	...	2251	2315	...	2355	0030
Middelburg d.	...	1606	1627	...	1706	1729	1806	1829	1906	1928	2006	2027	...	2106	2127	...	2206	2227	...	2306	2327	...	0010	0042
Vlissingen a.	...	1614	1634	...	1714	1736	1814	1836	1914	1935	2014	2034	...	2114	2134	...	2214	2234	...	2314	2334	...	0018	0050

	2116	14624		2120	14628	14628	14630	2124	14632		2128	14636		2132	14640		2136	14644	2140	14648		2144	14652	
	Ⓐ	Ⓐ		⚒	Ⓐ	Ⓒ	Ⓐ	Y			⚒			⚒			⚒		⚒			⚒		
Vlissingen d.	0543	0607	...	0658	0708	0720	0726	0759	0820	...	0859	0920	...	0959	1020	...	1059	1120	1159	1220	...	1259	1320	...
Middelburg d.	0550	0614	...	0706	0715	0727	0733	0807	0827	...	0907	0927	...	1007	1027	...	1107	1127	1207	1227	...	1307	1327	...
Goes d.	0604	0627	...	0717	0728	0740	0745	0818	0840	...	0918	0940	...	1018	1040	...	1118	1140	1218	1240	...	1318	1340	...
Bergen op Zoom d.	0634	0657	...	0739	0757	0808	0808	0840	0908	...	0940	1008	...	1040	1108	...	1140	1208	1240	1308	...	1340	1408	...
Roosendaal a.	0643	0708	...	0749	0807	0818	0818	0849	0918	...	0949	1018	...	1049	1118	...	1149	1218	1249	1318	...	1349	1418	...
Rotterdam CS **220** a.	0731	*0804*	...	0832	...	*0901*	*0901*	0931	*1001*	...	1031	*1101*	...	1131	*1201*	...	1231	*1302*	1331	*1401*	...	1431	*1501*	...
Den Haag HS **220** a.	0751	*0822*	...	0851	...	*0920*	*0920*	0951	*1020*	...	1051	*1120*	...	1151	*1220*	...	1251	*1321*	1351	*1420*	...	1451	*1520*	...
Amsterdam CS **220** a.	0838	*0908*	...	0938	...	*1008*	*1008*	1038	*1108*	...	1138	*1208*	...	1238	*1308*	...	1338	*1408*	1438	*1508*	...	1538	*1608*	...

	2148	14656	2152	14660		2156	14664	2160	14668	2164	14672		2168	14676		2172	14680	2176	14684		2180	14688		14692
	⚒		H			H		H		H			H			T		J			J			
Vlissingen d.	1359	1420	1459	1520	...	1559	1620	1655	1720	1759	1820	...	1859	1920	...	1959	2020	2059	2120	...	2159	2220	...	2320
Middelburg d.	1407	1427	1507	1527	...	1607	1627	1702	1727	1807	1827	...	1907	1927	...	2007	2027	2107	2127	...	2207	2227	...	2327
Goes d.	1418	1440	1518	1540	...	1618	1640	1713	1740	1818	1840	...	1918	1940	...	2018	2040	2118	2140	...	2218	2240	...	2340
Bergen op Zoom d.	1440	1508	1540	1608	...	1640	1708	1740	1808	1840	1908	...	1940	2008	...	2040	2108	2140	2208	...	2240	2308	...	0008
Roosendaal a.	1449	1518	1549	1618	...	1649	1718	1749	1818	1849	1918	...	1949	2018	...	2049	2118	2149	2218	...	2249	2318	...	0018
Rotterdam CS **220** a.	1531	*1601*	1631	*1701*	...	1732	*1801*	1831	*1901*	1931	*2001*	...	2031	*2101*	...	2131	*2203*	2231	*2305*	...	2331	*0001*	...	*0107*
Den Haag HS **220** a.	1553	*1620*	1651	*1720*	...	1751	*1820*	1851	*1920*	1951	*2021*	...	2051	*2120*	...	2151	*2220*	2251	*2323*	...	2351	*0036*b	...	...
Amsterdam CS **220** a.	1640	*1708*	1738	*1808*	...	1838	*1908*	1938	*2008*	2038	*2108*	...	2138	*2208*	...	2238	*2308*	2338	*0010*	...	0038	...	...	...

H – Not Dec. 25, Apr. 16.
J – ⑦ (also Dec. 26, Apr. 17; not Dec. 25, Apr. 16).
T – Not Dec. 24, 25, 31.
Y – Not Dec. 25, 26, Jan. 1.
b – Change at Roosendaal **and** Rotterdam.

Table 227 VLISSINGEN - BRESKENS - BRUGGE

VLISSINGEN - BRESKENS Car Ferry (PSD) Journey time 20 minutes

From Vlissingen: 0450⚒, 0550⚒, 0650, 0720Ⓐ, 0750, 0820Ⓐ, 0850 and every 30 minutes (every 60 minutes on ⑥⑦ Oct. to May) until 1850, 1950, 2050, 2150, 2250, 2350.
From Breskens: 0520⚒, 0620⚒, 0720, 0750Ⓐ, 0820, 0850Ⓐ, 0920 and every 30 minutes (every 60 minutes on ⑥⑦ Oct. to May) until 1920, 2020, 2120, 2220, 2320, 0020.

BRESKENS - BRUGGE (ZWN service 2) Journey time 74 - 77 minutes

From Breskens Ferry: 0724Ⓐ, 0824⚒, 0924⚒, 1024, 1124⚒, 1222⑦, 1224⚒, 1324⚒, 1424, 1524⚒, 1622⑦, 1624⚒, 1722⚒, 1824, 1922⚒, 2022⑦, 2024⚒.
From Brugge Station: 0657⚒, 0757⚒, 0857⚒, 0957, 1057⚒, 1157, 1257⚒, 1357, 1457⚒, 1557, 1657⚒, 1757, 1857⚒, 1957, 2057⚒, 2157⚒.

Table 228 LEEUWARDEN - STAVOREN - ENKHUIZEN

2 class

km			ferry A			ferry B			ferry A				ferry A			ferry B			ferry A		
0	**Leeuwarden** d.	0921	...	...	1322	...	...	1722	...	...	Enkhuizen d.	0845	...	...	1245	...	...	1645	...	...
22	Sneek ▲ d.	0943	...	...	1343	...	...	1743	...	...	**Stavoren** d.	1005	1014	...	1405	1414	...	1805	1814	...
51	**Stavoren** d.	1011	1015	...	1411	1415	...	1811	1815	...	Sneek § d.	...	1014	...	...	1444	...	...	1845	...
	Enkhuizen a.	...	1200	...	...	1600	...	...	1935	...	**Leeuwarden** a.	...	1044	...	...	1505	...	...	1905	...

A – May 29 - Oct. 31. B – May 29 - Oct. 1. (ferry) – Sailings by NACO (☎ 020 6262466). ▲ – Additional trains run hourly between Leeuwarden and Sneek (2 per hour on ⚒).

Table 229 LELYSTAD - ENKHUIZEN

Midnet service **150**

Journey time: 35 minutes

From Lelystad: Ⓐ : 0648, 0818, 1218, 1448, 1618, 1718 ⑥ : 1018, 1418, 1618, 1918 ⑦ : 1118, 1718, 2118
From Enkhuizen: Ⓐ : 0734, 0902, 1302, 1532, 1702, 1802 ⑥ : 1102, 1502, 1702, 2002 ⑦ : 1202, 1802, 2202

Table 230 AMSTERDAM / ROTTERDAM / DEN HAAG - LEEUWARDEN / GRONINGEN

1, 2 class

km		Ⓐ	Ⓐ	Ⓐ	Ⓐ	Ⓐ	Ⓐ	⑦	⚒		⑥	⑥	Ⓐ	Ⓐ										
0	**Amsterdam Schiphol** ✈ d.	...	...	...	...	...	...	...	...	...	...	...	...	...	0705	0705	...	...	0803	0803	...	...	0905	0905
15	Amsterdam Sloterdijk d.	...	...	...	...	...	...	...	...	...	...	...	...	...	0720	0720	...	...	0817	0817	...	...	0920	0920
19	**Amsterdam CS** d.	...	0543	...	...	...	...	...	0632	...	...	...	...	...	0732	0732	...	...	0832	0832	...	...	0932	0953
48	Hilversum d.	...	0615	...	...	...	...	...	0653	...	...	...	...	...	0753	0753	...	...	0853	0853	...	...	0953	|
	Rotterdam CS d.	...	|	...	0528	...	...	...	|	...	...	0631	0637	...	|	|	0737	...	|	|	...	0837	|	|
	Den Haag CS d.	...	|	0526	|	...	...	...	|	...	0628	|	|	0634	|	|	|	0736	|	|	0836	|	|	|
	Utrecht a.	...	|	0618	0618	...	...	...	|	...	0714	0717	0714	0717	|	|	0816	0813	|	|	0916	0913	|	|
	Utrecht d.	...	|	▬	▬	0622	...	...	|	...	0722	0722	0722	0722	|	|	0823	0823	|	|	0922	0922	|	|
64	Amersfoort a.	...	0628	...	...	0636	...	...	0706	...	0737	0737	0737	0737	0806	0806	0837	0837	0906	0906	0937	0937	1006	1006
64	Amersfoort d.	...	▬	...	...	0639	...	...	0710	...	0739	0739	0739	0739	0809	0809	0839	0839	0910	0910	0939	0939	1010	1010
130	**Zwolle** a.	...	Ⓐ	⚒	⚒	0714	...	...	0746	...	0814	0814	0814	0814	0846	0846	0914	0914	0946	0946	1014	1014	1046	1046
130	**Zwolle** d.	0619	0622	0648	0651	0716	0719	0749	0749	0752	0817	0817	0820	0817	0849	*0852*e	0916	0919	0949	*0952*e	1016	1019	1049	*1052*e
158	Meppel d.	0636	0639	0704	0707	|	|	0804	0804	0808	|	|	|	|	0904	*0909*e	|	|	1004	*1009*e	|	|	1104	*1109*e
196	Heerenveen d.	|	0703	|	0732	|	0759	|	|	0833	|	0856	0856	|	|	*0933*e	|	0956	|	*1033*e	|	1056	|	*1133*e
225	**Leeuwarden** a.	|	0725	|	0756	|	0816	|	|	0857	|	0913	0913	|	|	*0955*e	|	1013	|	*1055*e	|	1113	|	*1155*e
178	Hoogeveen d.	0648	...	0717	...	|	...	0816	0816	...	|	...	...	|	0916	...	|	...	1016	...	|	...	1116	...
208	Assen d.	0708	...	0737	...	0757	...	0835	0835	...	0857	...	...	0857	0935	...	0957	...	1035	...	1057	...	1135	...
236	**Groningen** a.	0727	...	0756	...	0814	...	0854	0854	...	0914	...	...	0914	0954	...	1014	...	1054	...	1114	...	1154	...

e – On Ⓒ (also Dec. 27–30, Apr. 14, May 26), (12) Amsterdam Schiphol - Leeuwarden; on other dates, change at Zwolle.

For other services Amsterdam / Rotterdam / Den Haag to Amersfoort and v.v., see Table 231.

For explanation of symbols used see page 4

Table 230 AMSTERDAM / ROTTERDAM / DEN HAAG - LEEUWARDEN / GRONINGEN

1, 2 class

	▲	▲			△	△				△					F	G	H					Ⓐ	Ⓒ		
Amsterdam Schiphol ✈ d	…	…	1005	1005	△	△			…	1505	1505				1605	1605			Ⓐ	Ⓒ	1705	1705			
Amsterdam Sloterdijk d	…	…	1020	1020					…	1520	1520				1620	1620					1720	1720			
Amsterdam CS d	…	…	1032	1032	and at				…	1532	1532				1632	1632					1732	1732			
Hilversum d	…	…	1053	1053	the				…	1553	1553				1653	1653					1753	1753			
Rotterdam CS d	0937				1037	same	1437								1637	1637						1737			
Den Haag CS d		0936			1036	minutes	1436		1536	1536				1634								1736			
Utrecht a	1016	1013			1116	1113	past	1516	1513	1613	1613				1713	1715	1715			1816	1813				
Utrecht d	1022	1022			1122	1122	each	1522	1522	1622	1622					1719	1722			1822					
Amersfoort a	1037	1037	1106	1106	1137	1137	hour	1537	1537	1606	1606	1637	1637	1706	1706	1732	1737	1806	1806	1837	1837				
Amersfoort d	1039	1039	1110	1110	1139	1139	until	1539	1539	1610	1610	1639	1639	1710	1710	1734	1739	1810	1810	1839	1839				
Zwolle a	1114	1114	1146	1146	1214	1214		1614	1614	1646	1646	1714	1714	1746	1746	1811	1814	1846	1846	1914	1914				
Zwolle d	1116	1119	1149	1152	1216	1219		1616	1619	1649	1652	1717	1720	1728	1749	1752	1820	1820	1849	1852	1916	1919			
Meppel d			1204	1209						1704	1709			1745	1804	1809			1904	1909					
Heerenveen		1156			1233		1256							1757			1833	1856	1856			1935			
Leeuwarden a		1213			1255		1313		1656					1814			1855	1913	1913			1957		1956	
Hoogeveen			1216						1713					1816										2013	
Assen d	1157		1235		1257			1657		1735		1757		1817	1835			1916			1935		1957		
Groningen a	1214		1254		1314			1714		1754		1814		1836	1854			1954					2014		

																								K	
Amsterdam Schiphol ✈ d	1805	1805			1905	1905			2005	2005			2105	2105			2205				2305				
Amsterdam Sloterdijk d	1820	1820			1920	1920			2020	2020			2120	2120			2220				2320				
Amsterdam CS d	1832	1832			1932	1932			2032	2032			2132	2132			2232				2332				
Hilversum d	1853	1853			1953	1953			2053	2053			2153	2153			2253				2353				
Rotterdam CS d			1837		1937			2037			2137			2237											
Den Haag CS d		1836			1936		2036			2136			2236												
Utrecht a	1906	1913			2016	2013			2116	2113		2216	2213			2313	2316								
Utrecht d	1922	1922			2022	2022			2122	2122		2222	2222			2322	2322			2355					
Amersfoort a	1906	1906	1937	1937	2006	2006	2037	2037	2106	2106	2137	2137	2206	2206	2237	2237	2306	2337	2337	0007	0016				
Amersfoort d	1910	1910	1939	1939	2010	2010	2039	2039	2110	2110	2139	2139	2210	2210	2239	2239	2310	2339	2339	0010	0017				
Zwolle a	1946	1946	2014	2014	2046	2046	2114	2114	2146	2146	2214	2214	2246	2246	2314	2314	2346	0033	0033	0046	0108				
Zwolle d	1949	1952	2016	2019	2049	2052	2116	2119	2149	2152	2216	2219	2249	2252	2316	2319	2349			0048	0051				
Meppel d	2004	2009			2104	2109			2204	2209			2304	2309			2335	0004	0010	0103	0109				
Heerenveen		2034			2056		2133		2156			2233		2256		2333	2357		0034	0133					
Leeuwarden a		2056			2113		2155		2213			2256		2313		2357			0056	0157					
Hoogeveen	2016				2116				2216				2316					0015							
Assen d	2035		2057		2135		2157		2235		2257		2335		2357		0016		0115	0132					
Groningen a	2054		2114		2154		2214		2254		2314		2354		0014		0035		0153						

km		Ⓐ	Ⓐ		Ⓐ	✗	⑥	Ⓐ	Ⓐ	✗	Ⓐ	⑥	✗	✗	Ⓐ	✗	Ⓐ	⑥	✗
0	Groningen d									0531			0613			0637	0657	0709	0715
28	Assen d									0550			0629			0656	0717	0729	0731
58	Hoogeveen d									0609						0715	0736		
	Leeuwarden d								0530					0613	0634				0718
	Heerenveen d								0551					0629	0655				0735
78	Meppel d								0618	0622				0724	0728	0749			0800
106	Zwolle a				0521		0616		0635	0638				0710	0707	0740	0744	0805	0811	0812	0816
106	Zwolle d					0613		0651		0642	0642	0642		0713	0713	0748	0748		0813	0819	0820
172	Amersfoort a								0717	0717	0717		0749	0749	0824	0824	0849	0853	0854
172	Amersfoort d	0510	0536	0545	0606	0615	0624	0646	0656	0656	0658	0724	0724	0724	0722p	0727	0757	0757	0828	0828	0851	0857	0857
193	Utrecht a			0608		0638		0708	0712	0712		0740q	0743	0813	0813				0910	0913	0913
193	Utrecht d			0620		0647		0716	0716	0718		0749	0747	0817	0819				0919	0919	0917
253	Den Haag CS a				0734			0758			0828			0859					
249	Rotterdam CS a		0709			0755	0755					0825	0855				0956	0956	
	Hilversum d	0523	0549		0619		0636		0710	0738	0738	0738			0840	0840			0955
	Amsterdam CS a		0620		0650		0656		0732	0801	0801	0801			0902	0902			
	Amsterdam Sloterdijk a								0744	0814	0814	0814			0914	0914			
	Amsterdam Schiphol ✈ a	0601				0715			0758	0828	0828	0828			0928	0928			

	⑦	⑦					△			▲							⑦H		
Groningen d			0737		0818		0837		0918			1618		1637		1718		1737 1757	1818
Assen d			0756		0834		0856		0934		1634		1656		1734		1756 1817	1834
Hoogeveen d			0815				0915						1715				1815 1836	
Leeuwarden d				0735		0818		0836		0918	and at	1618		1636		1716	1736		1818	1836
Heerenveen d				0756		0834		0857		0934	the	1634		1657		1732	1757		1834	1857
Meppel d			0824	0828			0924	0928			same		1724	1728			1824	1828 1849	1924
Zwolle a			0840	0844	0912	0915	0940	0944	1012	1015	minutes	1712	1715	1740	1744	1812	1815	1840 1845	1904 1905	1912 1915	1940
Zwolle d	0819	0819	0849	0849	0919	0919	0949	0949	1019	1019	past	1719	1719	1749	1749	1819	1819	1849 1849	1910	1919 1919	1949
Amersfoort a	0854	0854	0924	0924	0954	0954	1024	1024	1054	1054	each	1754	1754	1824	1824	1854	1854	1924 1924	1949	1954 1954	2024
Amersfoort d	0857	0857	0928	0928	0957	0957	1028	1028	1057	1057	hour	1757	1757	1828	1828	1857	1857				2028
Utrecht a	0913	0913			1013	1013			1113	1113		1813	1813			1913	1913			1957 1957	2028
Utrecht d	0917	0919			1019	1017			1117	1119		1819	1817			1917	1919			2013 2013	
Den Haag CS a		0956			1056				1156			1856				1956				2019 2017	
Rotterdam CS a	0955				1055				1155		until		1855			1955				2056	2055
Hilversum d			0940	0940			1040	1040					1840	1840							2040
Amsterdam CS a			1002	1002			1102	1102					1902	1902							2102
Amsterdam Sloterdijk a			1014	1014			1114	1114					1914	1914							2114
Amsterdam Schiphol ✈ a			1028	1028			1128	1128					1928	1928							2128

			⑦H	✗J			K				L	K					✗	⑦		
Groningen d	1837		1918			1937		2018		2037		2118		2137		2218			2242		2315
Assen d	1856		1934			1956		2034		2056		2134		2156		2234			2301		2335
Hoogeveen d	1915					2015												2320		2354
Leeuwarden d		1918		1936	1936		2018		2036		2118		2136	2136		2218		2240 2242		2316	
Heerenveen d		1934		1957	1957		2034		2057		2134		2157	2157		2234		2302 2302		2337	
Meppel d	1928		2024	2024	2028		2124	2128				2224	2228				2329 2329	2333	0002	0008
Zwolle a	1944	2012	2015	2040	2040	2044	2112	2115	2140	2144	2212	2215	2240	2240	2244	2312	2315	2346 2346	2349	
Zwolle d	1949	2019	2019	2041	2041	2049	2119	2119	2149	2149	2219	2219	2248	2248	2319	2319			2354	0045 0025
Amersfoort a	2024	2054	2054	2117	2124	2124	2154	2154	2224	2224	2254	2254	2324	2324	2354	2354				
Amersfoort d	2028	2057	2057	2118	2128	2128	2157	2157	2228	2228	2257	2257	2328	2328	2357	2357				
Utrecht a		2113	2113				2213	2213			2313	2313			0013	0013				
Utrecht d		2117	2119				2219	2217			2317	2319			0021					
Den Haag CS a			2156				2256				2356							0116		
Rotterdam CS a		2155					2255			2355			2340 2340							
Hilversum d	2040				2140	2140			2240	2240			2340							
Amsterdam CS a	2102		2153	2202	2202			2302	2302			0002	0002							
Amsterdam Sloterdijk a	2114			2214	2214			2314	2314			0021	0021							
Amsterdam Schiphol ✈ a	2128			2228	2228			2328	2328			0034	0034							

F – ⑤ (also Apr. 13, May 24; not Dec. 30, Apr. 14, May 26).
G – Not on days when train F runs.
H – Not Dec. 25, Apr. 16.
J – Also Dec. 25, Apr. 16.
K – ⑤⑦, also Apr. 13, May 24.
L – Not on days when train K runs.
p – Departs 0727 on ⑥.
q – Arrives 0743 on ⑥.
▲ – 2 hourly (🚈 Rotterdam - Groningen, Den Haag - Leeuwarden and v.v.)
△ – 2 hourly (🚈 Den Haag - Groningen, Rotterdam - Leeuwarden and v.v.)

Table 231 — AMSTERDAM / ROTTERDAM / DEN HAAG - HENGELO - ENSCHEDE

1, 2 class

km		7015 Ⓐ	1617 Ⓐ	1719 Ⓐ	1719 Ⓐ	2341 C	7523	1723 ⑦	1723 ⑦	1723 ※	1723 ※	1625	1727	1727	2243 B	2343 H	7531	1731	1731	1633	1735	1735	1637	1739
0	Amsterdam Schiphol ✈ d.	…	…	…	…	0635	…	…	…	…	…	0731	…	…	0831	0831	…	…	…	…	0935	…	1035	…
15	Amsterdam Sloterdijk d.	…	…	…	…	0650	…	…	…	…	…	0746	…	…	0846	0846	…	…	…	…	0950	…	1050	…
19	Amsterdam CS a.	…	…	…	…	0657	…	…	…	…	…	0753	…	…	0853	0853	…	…	…	…	0957	…	1057	…
19	Amsterdam CS d.	…	…	0602	…	0702	…	…	…	…	…	0802	…	…	0902	0902	…	…	…	…	1002	…	1102	…
48	Hilversum d.	…	0623	…	…	0723	…	…	…	…	…	0823	…	…	0923	0923	…	…	…	…	1023	…	1123	…
	Rotterdam CS d.	…	…	…	0610	…	…	0701	…	0707	…	…	0808	…	…	…	…	0904	0907	…	…	1007	…	1104
	Den Haag CS d.	…	…	0600	…	…	…	0700	…	0704	…	…	0804	…	…	…	…	0924	…	…	1004	…	…	1124
	Gouda d.	…	…	0623	0646	…	…	0743	0746	0746	0746	…	0843	0846	…	…	…	0943	0946	…	1043	1046	…	1143
	Utrecht a.	…	…	0652	0652	…	…	0752	0752	0752	0752	…	0852	0852	…	…	…	0952	0952	…	1052	1052	…	1152
	Utrecht d.	…	…	0652	0652	…	…	0752	0752	0752	0752	…	0852	0852	…	…	…	0952	0952	…	1052	1052	…	1152
64	Amersfoort a.	…	0636	0707	0707	0736	…	0807	0807	0807	0807	0836	0907	0907	0936	0936	…	1007	1007	1036	1107	1107	1136	1207
64	Amersfoort d.	…	0641	0712	0712	0741	…	0811	0811	0811	0811	0841	0912	0912	0941	0941	…	1012	1012	1041	1112	1112	1141	1212
107	Apeldoorn d.	…	0706	0737	0737	0806	…	0837	0837	0837	0837	0906	0937	0937	1006	1006	…	1037	1037	1106	1137	1137	1206	1237
122	Deventer d.	0652	0719	0751	0751	0819	…	0851	0851	0851	0851	0919	0951	0951	1019	1019	…	1051	1051	1119	1151	1151	1219	1251
161	Almelo d.	0725	0745	0815	0815	0845	…	0915	0915	0915	0915	0945	1015	1015	1045	1045	…	1115	1115	1145	1215	1215	1245	1315
175	Hengelo 236 701 d.	0740	0756	0826	0826	0855	0901	0926	0926	0926	0926	0956	1026	1026	1055	1055	1101	1126	1126	1156	1226	1226	1256	1326
183	Enschede 236 a.	0748	0804	0834	0834	…	0908	0934	0934	0934	0934	1004	1034	1034	…	…	1108	1134	1134	1204	1234	1234	1304	1334

	1739	1641	1743	1743	2345 J	7545	1747	1747	1649	1751	1751	1653	1755	1755	1657	1759	1759	2347 K	7561	17063	1763 ©	1763	1665
Amsterdam Schiphol ✈ d.	…	1135	…	…	1235	…	…	…	1335	…	…	1435	…	…	1535	…	…	…	…	1635	…	…	1735
Amsterdam Sloterdijk d.	…	1150	…	…	1250	…	…	…	1350	…	…	1450	…	…	1550	…	…	…	…	1650	…	…	1750
Amsterdam CS a.	…	1157	…	…	1257	…	…	…	1357	…	…	1457	…	…	1557	…	…	…	…	1657	…	…	1757
Amsterdam CS d.	…	1202	…	…	1302	…	…	…	1402	…	…	1502	…	…	1602	…	…	…	…	1702	…	…	1802
Hilversum d.	…	1223	…	…	1323	…	…	…	1423	…	…	1523	…	…	1623	…	…	…	…	1723	…	…	1823
Rotterdam CS d.	1107	…	1204	…	…	…	1307	…	…	1404	…	…	1507	…	…	1603	…	…	1607	…	1704	1704	…
Den Haag CS d.	…	…	1204	…	…	…	1304	…	…	1404	…	…	1504	1524	…	1624	…	…	…	…	1724	1724	…
Gouda d.	1146	…	1224	1246	…	…	1343	1346	…	1443	1446	…	1543	1546	…	1643	1646	…	…	…	1745	1743	1746
Utrecht a.	1152	…	1243	1252	…	…	1352	1352	…	1452	1452	…	1552	1552	…	1652	1652	…	…	…	1749	1752	1752
Utrecht d.	1207	1236	1307	1307	1336	…	1407	1407	1436	1507	1507	1536	1607	1607	1636	1707	1707	1736	…	1607	1802	1807	1807
Amersfoort a.	1207	1236	1307	1307	1336	…	1407	1407	1436	1507	1507	1536	1607	1607	1636	1707	1707	1736	…	1712	1803	1812	1812
Amersfoort d.	1212	1241	1312	1312	1341	…	1412	1412	1441	1512	1512	1541	1612	1612	1641	1712	1712	1741	…	1717	1827	1837	1837
Apeldoorn d.	1237	1306	1337	1337	1406	…	1437	1437	1506	1537	1537	1606	1637	1637	1706	1737	1737	1806	…	…	1839	1851	1851
Deventer d.	1251	1319	1351	1351	1419	…	1451	1451	1519	1551	1551	1619	1651	1651	1719	1751	1751	1819	…	1904h	1915	1915	1945
Almelo d.	1315	1345	1415	1415	1445	…	1515	1515	1545	1615	1615	1645	1715	1715	1745	1815	1815	1845	…	…	…	…	…
Hengelo 236 701 d.	1326	1356	1426	1426	1455	1501	1526	1526	1556	1626	1626	1656	1726	1726	1756	1826	1826	1855	1901	1917h	1926	1926	1956
Enschede 236 a.	1334	1404	1434	1434	…	1508	1534	1534	1604	1634	1634	1704	1734	1734	1804	1834	1834	…	1908	1925h	1934	1934	2004

	1767	1767	1669	1771	1771	1673	1775	1775	1677	1779	1779	1681	1783 ⑦	1783 ⑦	1783 ※	1783 ※	7083 A	341 ⑦	7083	787	587	1787	589
Amsterdam Schiphol ✈ d.	…	…	1835	…	…	1935	…	…	2035	…	…	2135	…	…	…	…	2205	…	2305	…	…	…	…
Amsterdam Sloterdijk d.	…	…	1850	…	…	1950	…	…	2050	…	…	2150	…	…	…	…	2220	…	2320	…	…	…	…
Amsterdam CS a.	…	…	1857	…	…	1957	…	…	2057	…	…	2157	…	…	…	…	2227	…	2327	…	…	…	…
Amsterdam CS d.	…	…	1902	…	…	2002	…	…	2102	…	…	2202	…	…	…	…	2238	…	2332	…	…	…	…
Hilversum d.	…	…	1923	…	…	2023	…	…	2123	…	…	2223	…	…	…	…	…	…	2353	…	…	2311	…
Rotterdam CS d.	…	1807	…	1907	…	…	2007	…	…	2107	…	…	2207	…	2207	…	…	…	…	2304	…	…	2332
Den Haag CS d.	1804	…	1904	…	…	2004	…	…	2104	…	…	2204	…	2204	…	…	…	…	…	2326	…	…	2353
Gouda d.	1824	…	1924	…	…	2024	…	…	2124	…	…	2224	…	2224	…	…	…	…	…	2345	2348	…	0014
Utrecht a.	1843	1846	1943	1946	…	2043	2046	…	2143	2146	…	2243	2246	2243	2246	…	…	…	…	2352	0025	…	…
Utrecht d.	1852	1852	1952	1952	…	2052	2052	…	2152	2152	…	2252	2252	2252	2252	…	…	…	…	…	2352	0025	0048
Amersfoort a.	1907	1907	1936	2007	2007	2036	2107	2107	2136	2207	2207	2236	2307	2307	2307	2307	…	2317	…	0007	…	0007	0048
Amersfoort d.	1912	1912	1941	2012	2012	2041	2112	2112	2141	2212	2212	2241	2312	2312	2312	2337	…	2320	…	…	…	0012	…
Apeldoorn d.	1937	1937	2006	2037	2037	2106	2137	2137	2206	2237	2237	2306	2337	2337	2337	2337	…	…	…	…	…	0037	…
Deventer d.	1951	1951	2019	2051	2051	2119	2151	2151	2219	2251	2251	2319	2351	2351	2348	2348	2351	2356	2359	…	…	0048	…
Almelo d.	2015	2015	2045	2115	2115	2145	2215	2215	2245	2315	2315	2345	0015	0015	…	…	0017	…	0031	…	…	0112	…
Hengelo 236 701 d.	2026	2026	2056	2126	2126	2156	2226	2226	2256	2326	2326	2356	0026	0026	…	…	0042	0035	0046	…	…	0125	…
Enschede 236 a.	2034	2034	2104	2134	2134	2204	2234	2234	2304	2334	2334	0004	0034	0034	…	…	0050	…	0054	…	…	0133	…

km		31914 ※	1616 ※	516 Ⓐ	516 Ⓐ	17018 Ⓐ	1718 ⑥	1718 ⑥	1718 ⑥	1620 ※	1722 ※	1722 ※	340 A	1624		1726	1726	1628	7030	2346 K	1730	1730	1632	1734
0	Enschede 236 d.	…	0528t	…	…	…	0543	…	0602	0627	0658	0658	…	0728v		0758	0758	0828	0840	…	0858	0858	0928	0958
8	Hengelo 236 701 d.	…	0536t	…	0551	0551	…	0610	0635	0706	0706	0716	0736v	0747v		0806	0806	0836	0848	0901	0906	0906	0936	1006
22	Almelo d.	…	0548t	0605	0605	…	0622	0646	0717	0717	…	0745	0745	0754	0814v	0826v	0845	0845	0914	0934	0938	0945	0945	1014	1044
61	Deventer d.	0547t	0615t	0640	0640	0648	0714	0745	0745	0759	0726	0758	0758	0826v		0858	0858	0926	…	0958	0958	1026	1058
76	Apeldoorn d.	0558t	0627t	0653	0653	0659	0726	0758	0758	0833	0852v					0924	0924	0952	1011	1024	1024	1052	1124
119	Amersfoort a.	0623t	0653t	0719	0719	0725	0752	0824	0824	0833	0858		0927	0927	0958	1019	1027	1027	1058	1127
119	Amersfoort d.	0624	0658	0656	0656	0727	0727	0727	0758	0827	0827	0839	0858		0943	0943		1047	1043	1043	1143
140	Utrecht a.		0712	0712	0740	0743	0743	0743	0847	0849		0947	0949	1009	1047	1109	1147
140	Utrecht d.		0716	0718	0747	0747	0747	0843	0849	0909		0947	0949	1009		1109	1147
172	Gouda d.		0809	0809		0909	0928		1009	1028		1128
200	Den Haag CS a.	0758	0828	0828	0925		1025		1125
196	Rotterdam CS a.	0755	0825	0825	0810	0910	1010	1110	1225
	Hilversum d.	0636	0710		0810	0832	0923	0932	1032	1053	1132
	Amsterdam CS a.	0656	0732	0838	0923	0938	1038	1058	1138
	Amsterdam CS d.	0659	0738	0844	0944	1044	1116	1144
	Amsterdam Sloterdijk d.		0744	0844	0944	1044	1144
	Amsterdam Schiphol ✈ a.	0715	0758	0858	0959	1058	1116	1158

Footnotes

A – 🚋 1,2 cl., 🚋 2 cl., 🍴 and 🍽 Amsterdam CS - Hannover - Magdeburg - Berlin Zoo and v.v.
B – ⑥ (not Dec. 24, 31, Apr. 15). 🚋 and 🍽 Schiphol ✈ - Hannover - Magdeburg - Berlin Zoo.
C – Daily except Dec. 25, Jan. 1. 🚋 and 🍽 Schiphol ✈ - Hannover.
H – ⑧ (also Dec. 24, 31, Apr. 15). 🚋 and 🍽 Schiphol ✈ - Hannover - Stendal - Berlin Zoo.
J – ⑥. 🚋 and 🍽 Schiphol ✈ - Hannover - Stendal - Berlin Zoo; ⑥: 🚋 and 🍽 Schiphol ✈ - Hannover.
K – 🚋 and 🍽 Schiphol ✈ - Hannover and v.v.
h – ⑤ (also Apr. 13, May 24).
t – ⑤ only.
v – ※ only.

For other services Amsterdam / Rotterdam / Den Haag to Amersfoort and v.v., see Table 230.

Table 231 ENSCHEDE - HENGELO - DEN HAAG / ROTTERDAM / AMSTERDAM

1, 2 class

	1636	1738	1738	1640	1742	1742	1644	7046		2344 A	1746	1746	1648	1750	1750	1652	1754	1754	1656	1758	1758	1660	7062	2242 E
Enschede 236 d.	1028	1058	1058	1128	1158	1158	1228	1240	...	...	1258	1258	1328	1358	1358	1428	1458	1458	1528	1558	1558	1628	1640	...
Hengelo 236 701 d.	1036	1106	1106	1136	1206	1206	1236	1248	...	1302	1306	1306	1336	1406	1406	1436	1506	1506	1536	1606	1606	1636	1648	1702
Almelo d.	1047	1117	1117	1147	1217	1217	1247	1302	...	|	1317	1317	1347	1417	1417	1447	1517	1517	1547	1617	1617	1647	1702	|
Deventer d.	1114	1145	1145	1214	1245	1245	1314	1334	...	1338	1345	1345	1414	1445	1445	1514	1545	1545	1614	1645	1645	1714	1734	1738
Apeldoorn d.	1126	1158	1158	1226	1258	1258	1326	...	...	|	1358	1358	1426	1458	1458	1526	1558	1558	1626	1657	1657	1726	...	|
Amersfoort a.	1152	1224	1224	1252	1324	1324	1352	...	...	1412	1424	1424	1452	1524	1524	1552	1624	1624	1652	1722	1722	1752	...	1811
Amersfoort d.	1158	1227	1227	1258	1327	1327	1358	...	...	1414	1427	1427	1458	1527	1527	1558	1627	1627	1658	1727	1727	1758	...	1814
Utrecht a.	|	1243	1243	|	1343	1343	|	...	...	|	1443	1443	|	1543	1543	|	1643	1643	|	1743	1743	|	...	|
Utrecht d.	|	1247	1249	|	1347	1349	|	...	...	|	1447	1449	|	1547	1549	|	1647	1649	|	1747	1749	|	...	|
Gouda d.	|	|	1309	|	|	1409	|	...	...	|	|	1509	|	|	1609	|	|	1709	|	|	1809	|	...	|
Den Haag CS a.	|	|	1328	|	|	1428	|	...	...	|	|	1528	|	|	1628	|	|	1728	|	|	1828	|	...	|
Rotterdam CS a.	|	1325	...	|	1425	...	|	...	...	|	1525	...	|	1625	...	|	1725	...	|	1825	...	|	...	|
Hilversum d.	1210	...	...	1310	...	...	1410	...	...	1426	...	...	1510	...	...	1610	...	...	1710	...	...	1810	...	1826
Amsterdam CS a.	1232	...	...	1332	...	...	1432	...	...	1453	...	...	1532	...	...	1632	...	...	1732	...	...	1832	...	1853
Amsterdam CS d.	1238	...	...	1338	...	...	1438	...	...	1458	...	...	1538	...	...	1638	...	...	1738	...	...	1838	...	1858
Amsterdam Sloterdijk d.	1244	...	...	1344	...	...	1444	...	...	1516	...	...	1544	...	...	1644	...	...	1744	...	...	1844	...	|
Amsterdam Schiphol ✈ a.	1258	...	...	1358	...	...	1458	...	...	...	...	...	1558	...	...	1658	...	...	1758	...	...	1858	...	1916

	2342 L	1762	1762	1664	1766	1766	1668	17070 N	1770	1770 N	1672	17074 N	1774	1774 N	1676	7078	2240 B	2340 F	1778	1778	1680	1782	1782	1684
Enschede 236 d.	...	1658	1658	1728	1758	1758	1828	1840	1858	1858	1928	1940	1958	1958	2028	2040	...	...	2058	2058	2128	2158	2158	2228
Hengelo 236 701 d.	1702	1706	1706	1736	1806	1806	1836	1848	1906	1906	1936	1948	2006	2006	2036	2048	2102	2102	2106	2106	2136	2206	2206	2236
Almelo d.	|	1717	1717	1747	1817	1817	1847	1902	1917	1917	1947	2002	2017	2017	2047	2102	|	|	2117	2117	2147	2217	2217	2247
Deventer d.	1738	1745	1745	1814	1845	1845	1914	1938	1945	1945	2014	2038	2045	2045	2114	2134	2138	2138	2145	2145	2214	2245	2245	2314
Apeldoorn d.	|	1758	1758	1826	1858	1858	1926	1952	1958	1958	2026	2052	2058	2058	2126	...	|	|	2158	2158	2226	2257	2257	2326
Amersfoort a.	1811	1824	1824	1852	1924	1924	1952	2019	2024	2024	2052	2119	2124	2124	2152	...	2212	2212	2224	2224	2252	2322	2322	2352
Amersfoort d.	1814	1827	1827	1858	1927	1927	1958	2021	2027	2027	2058	2121	2127	2127	2158	...	2214	2214	2227	2227	2258	2327	2327	2359
Utrecht a.	|	1843	1843	|	1943	1943	|	2040	2043	2043	|	2140	2143	2143	|	...	|	|	2243	2243	|	2343	2343	|
Utrecht d.	|	1847	1849	|	1947	1949	|	2049	2047	2049	|	2149	2147	2149	|	...	|	|	2247	2249	|	2349	2349	|
Gouda d.	|	|	1909	|	|	2009	|	2109	|	2109	|	2209	|	2209	|	...	|	|	|	2309	|	0010	0011	|
Den Haag CS a.	|	|	1928	|	|	2028	|	2128	|	2128	|	2228	|	2228	|	...	|	|	|	2328	|	|	0035	|
Rotterdam CS a.	|	1925	...	|	2025	...	|	...	2125	...	|	...	2225	...	|	...	|	|	2325	...	|	0034	...	|
Hilversum d.	1826	...	...	1910	...	...	2010	...	...	...	2110	...	...	...	2210	...	2226	2226	...	...	2310	...	...	0014
Amsterdam CS a.	1853	...	...	1932	...	...	2032	...	...	...	2132	...	...	...	2232	...	2253	2253	...	...	2332	...	...	0037
Amsterdam CS d.	1858	...	...	1938	...	...	2038	...	...	...	2138	...	...	...	2238	...	2258	2258	...	...	2338	...	...	*0043*
Amsterdam Sloterdijk d.	|	...	...	1944	...	...	2044	...	...	...	2144	...	...	...	2244	...	|	|	...	...	2344	...	...	*0048*
Amsterdam Schiphol ✈ a.	1916	...	...	1958	...	...	2058	...	...	...	2158	...	...	...	2258	...	2316	2316	...	...	2358	...	...	*0058*

A – ①–⑥ (not Apr. 17): [12] and 🍷 Berlin Zoo - Stendal - Hannover - Schiphol ✈. ⑦: [12] and 🍷 Hannover - Schiphol ✈.

B – ⑥ (not Dec. 24, 31, Apr. 15). [12] and 🍷 Berlin Zoo - Magdeburg - Hannover - Schiphol ✈.

E – ⑥⑦ (not Dec. 24, 25, 31, Jan. 1, Apr. 15, 16). [12] and 🍷 Berlin Zoo - Hannover - Magdeburg - Schiphol ✈.

F – Ⓑ (also Apr. 15), [12] and 🍷 Berlin Zoo - Stendal - Hannover - Schiphol ✈.

L – ①–⑤ (also Dec. 24, 25, 31, Jan. 1, Apr. 15, 16). [12] and 🍷 Berlin Zoo - Stendal - Hannover - Schiphol ✈.

N – ⑦ (also Dec. 26, Apr. 17; not Dec. 25, Apr. 16).

Table 232 GRONINGEN - LEEUWARDEN

2 class

From Groningen: 54 km

0538Ⓐ, 0610⚒, 0642Ⓐ, 0714⚒, 0752⚒, 0820, 0852⚒, then at 20/52⚒ minutes past each hour until 1620, 1652**H**, 1720, 1752**H**, 1820, 1852**H**, 1920, 1952**N**, 2020, 2052**N**, 2120, 2152**N**, 2220, 2341.

H – Not Dec. 25, Apr. 16.

From Leeuwarden: Journey time: 54 minutes

0538Ⓐ, 0609⚒, 0641Ⓐ, 0716⚒, 0751⚒, 0819, 0851⚒, then at 19/51⚒ minutes past each hour until 1551⚒, 1618, 1649⚒, 1719, 1751**H**, 1819, 1851**H**, 1919, 1951**N**, 2019, 2051**N**, 2119, 2151**N**, 2219, 2321.

N – ⑦ (also Dec. 26, Apr. 17; not Dec. 25, Apr. 16).

Table 233 🚌 LEEUWARDEN – HARLINGEN – ALKMAAR

Revised service from Nov. 6, 1994

FRAM / NZH *Interliner* service **350: Leeuwarden** to **Alkmaar** via Harlingen and North Sea Dyke. Journey time : 1 hour 50 minutes.

From Leeuwarden: 0615Ⓐ, 0710⚒, 0810 and hourly to 1710, 1814, 1914, 2014, 2114, 2214Ⓑ. **From Alkmaar**: 0630Ⓐ, 0732⚒, 0832 and hourly to 1732, 1835, 1935, 2035, 2135, 2235Ⓑ.

Table 235 ZWOLLE - ARNHEM - 's-HERTOGENBOSCH - ROOSENDAAL

1, 2 class

km		Ⓐ	Ⓐ	Ⓐ	⑦	⚒	Ⓐ	⑥	⑦	⑦	Ⓐ	⑥	⚒	⑦										
0	**Zwolle** d.	...	...	...	...	...	0615	...	...	...	0647	...	0718	...	0749	0823		2049	2123	2149	2223	2249	...	2354
31	Deventer a.	...	...	...	...	...	0638	...	...	...	0711	...	0742	...	0812	0842		2112	2142	2212	2242	2312	...	0017
31	Deventer d.	...	...	...	...	...	0639	...	...	...	0712	...	0744	...	0813	0844	and at	2113	2144	2213	2244	2313	...	0018
47	Zutphen d.	...	...	0550	...	...	0654	0654	...	...	0726	0726	0758	0758	0828	0858	the	2128	2158	2228	2258	2328	...	0032
60	Dieren d.	...	...	0600	...	...	0703	0703	...	...	0735	0735	0807	0807	0837	0907	same	2137	2207	2237	2307	2337	...	0043
76	**Arnhem** d.	...	...	0621	0645	0651	0722	0722	...	...	0752	0752	0821	0821	0851	0921	minutes	2151	2221	2251	2321	2350	...	0101
95	Nijmegen d.	0530	0608	0638	0700	0708	0738	0738	...	0746	0808	0808	0838	0838	0908	0938	past	2208	2238	2308	2338	0005	...	...
119	Oss d.	0549	0625	0655	0719	0725	0755	0755	...	0807	0825	0825	0855	0855	0925	0955	each	2225	2255	2325	2355	0026	...	...
138	**'s-Hertogenbosch** d.	0608	0647	0709	0739	0739	0809	0809	...	0839	0839f	0839	0909	0909	0939	1009	hour	2239	2309	2339	0009	0044	...	...
160	Tilburg **220** d.	0624	0703	0725	0756	0756	0825	0825	0825	0855	0855	0855	0925	0925	0955	1025	▲	2255	2325	2355	0024	...	...	...
181	**Breda 220** a.	0642	0721	0743	0814	0814	0843	0843	0843	0913	0913	0913	0943	0943	1013	1043	until	2313	2343	0013	...	...	...	...
181	**Breda** d.	0647	0722	0749	0819	0819	0849	0849	0849	0919	0919	0919	0949	0949	1019	1049		2319	2349	0014	...	...	...	...
205	**Roosendaal** a.	0705	0740	0807	0837	0837	0907	0907	0907	0937	0937	0937	1007	1007	1037	1107		2337	0007	0032	...	...	...	...

	Ⓐ	Ⓐ	Ⓐ	Ⓐ	⑥	Ⓐ	⑥	⑦	⑥	Ⓐ	⚒	⑦	⑦	⚒										
Roosendaal d.	...	...	...	...	...	0512	...	...	...	0552	0625	...	0648	0658	0725	0755		2025	2055	2125	2155	2228	2255	2326
Breda a.	...	...	...	...	...	0530	...	...	...	0610	0643	...	0705	0716	0743	0813		2043	2113	2143	2213	2245	2313	2344
Breda 220 d.	...	...	...	...	...	0531	...	...	...	0613	0647	...	0706	0717	0750	0820	and at	2050	2120	2150	2220	2250	2320	2350
Tilburg **220** d.	...	...	...	...	...	0550	...	...	...	0634	0706	...	0723	0736	0809	0839	the	2109	2139	2209	2239	2309	2339	0009
's-Hertogenbosch d.	...	...	...	0537	...	0606	...	...	0641	0654	0723	...	0745	0753	0825	0855	same	2125	2155	2225	2255	2325	0007e	0024
Oss d.	...	...	...	0554	...	0626	...	...	0659	0706	0735	...	0802	0806	0837	0907	minutes	2137	2207	2237	2307	2337	0026	...
Nijmegen d.	...	...	0558	0616	...	0656	...	...	0726	0726	0757	...	0827	0827	0857	0927	past	2157	2227	2257	2327	2357	0054	...
Arnhem d.	...	0545	0617	0641b	...	0711	0711	0734	0740	0740	0812	...	0842	0842	0912	0942	each	2212	2242	2312	2342	0013	0109	...
Dieren d.	...	0605	0635	0652	...	0723	0723	0751	0753	0753	0823	...	0853	0853	0923	0953	hour	2223	2253	2323	2353	...	...	...
Zutphen d.	0557	0631c	0646	0705	0705	0735	0735	0805	0805	0805	0835	0835	0905	0905	0935	1005	until	2235	2305	2335	0005	...	...	...
Deventer a.	0609	0643	...	0717	0717	0748	0748	0817	0817	0817	0848	0848	0917	0917	0948	1017		2248	2317	2348	...	...	...	...
Deventer d.	0614	0644	...	0719	0719	0749	0749	0819	0819	0819	0850	0850	0919	0919	0950	1019		2250	2319	2350	...	...	...	...
Zwolle a.	0638	0708	...	0743	0743	0813	0813	0843	0843	0843	0910	0910	0943	0943	1010	1043		2310	2343	0013	...	...	...	...

b – Arrives 0632. c – Arrives 0618. e – Arrives 2354. f – Arrives 0826. ▲ – However: Zwolle depart 1620 (not 1623) and 1720 (not 1723).

Table 236 ZUTPHEN - ENSCHEDE

1, 2 class

km		Ⓐ	Ⓐ	⚒				
0	**Zutphen** d.	0620	0737	0807	0907	and	2207	2307
45	Hengelo **231** d.	0655	0816	0845	0945	hourly	2245	2345
53	**Enschede 231** a.	0703	0824	0853	0953	until	2253	...

	Ⓐ	Ⓐ	⚒	⑦			
Enschede 231 d.	...	...	0735	...	0835	and	2235
Hengelo **231** d.	0606	0713	0744	0744	0844	hourly	2244
Zutphen a.	0646	0753	0823	0823	0923	until	2323

Table 238 AMSTERDAM - AMSTERDAM SCHIPHOL ✈

19 km — 1, 2 class

International trains to / from Hannover and Berlin are shown in Table 231

							⚒						⚒										
Amsterdam CS d.	0014	0043	0144	0245	0345	0445	0503	0531	0602	0623	0638	0646	0659	0708	0725	0738	0755	0808	0825	0838	0855	and at the same	2338
Amsterdam Sloterdijk d.	0021	0048	|	|	|	|	|	0537	0609	0629	0644	0653	|	0714	|	0744	0801	0814	|	0844	|	minutes past each	2344
Schiphol ✈ a.	0034	0058	0158	0258	0358	0458	0518	0549	0622	0641	0658	0705	0715	0728	0741	0758	0812	0828	0841	0858	0911	hour until:	2358

Schiphol ✈ d.	0007	0041	0100	0200	0300	0400	0500	0550	0618	0645	0705	0721	0731	0751	0803	0821	0831	0851	0905	0921	0935	and at the same	2351
Amsterdam Sloterdijk d.	0019	0053	|	|	|	|	|	0601	0631	0656	0720	|	0746	|	0817	|	0846	|	0920	|	0950	minutes past each	0004
Amsterdam CS a.	0027	0059	0114	0214	0314	0414	0514	0607	0638	0702	0727	0738	0753	0808	0824	0838	0853	0908	0927	0938	0957	hour until:	0010

Table 239 AMSTERDAM - GOUDA - ROTTERDAM

1, 2 class

km		Ⓐ	Ⓐ	Ⓐ	⚒				
0	**Amsterdam CS** d.	...	0605	0651	0722	0822	and	2222	...
8	Duivendrecht d.	...	0616	0703	0733	0833		2233	...
46	Woerden d.	0606	0640	0732	0802	0902	hourly	2302	2345
62	Gouda d.	0621	0656	0745	0813	0913	until:	2313	0001
86	**Rotterdam CS** a.	0646	0722	...	0836	0936		2336	0024

	Ⓐ	⚒	Ⓐ	⚒				
Rotterdam CS d.	0554	0654	0720	0754	0854	and	2154	2254
Gouda d.	0617	0717	0746	0817	0917		2217	2317
Woerden d.	0629	0729	0757	0829	0929	hourly	2229	2331
Duivendrecht d.	0657	0757	0828	0857	0956	until:	2257	2357
Amsterdam CS a.	0711	0810	0841	0910	1011		2310	0010

Table 240 AMSTERDAM - UTRECHT - ARNHEM - EMMERICH

1, 2 class except where shown

For connections at Utrecht to/from Rotterdam and Den Haag see Table 231
For additional connections to/from Schiphol ✈ changing at Duivendrecht, see Table 222

km		7391	7393	31802		31806	31810	31814		19817 Ⓐ	31818	7317 Ⓐ	EC 141 ❖🍷	3019 Ⓐ	3019 ⑥	19821 ⚒	3321 ⚒	EC 143 🍷	3023	3325	EC 105 ♦	IC 727 ✕	3027	
	Amsterdam Schiphol ✈ 238 d.	...	...	0100	...	0200	0300	0400	...	...	0500	...	*0500*	...	...	...	...	*0618*	...	...	0738	...	...	...
0	**Amsterdam CS 245** d.	0005	0035	0117	...	0217	0317	0417	...	...	0517	0544	0602	0618	...	...	0648	0706	0719	0749	0800	...	0819	...
8	Duivendrecht 245 d.	0016	0049	|	...	|	|	|	...	...	|	0557	|	0628	...	...	0658	|	0729	0759	|	...	0829	...
39	**Utrecht 245** a.	0045	0116	0150	...	0250	0350	0450	...	...	0550	0625	0631	0647	...	...	0717	0733	0747	0817	0828	...	0847	...
39	**Utrecht** d.	...	...	...	...	...	...	...	...	0549	...	...	0633	0650	0650	0706	0720	0735	0749	0820	0830	...	0850	...
51	Driebergen-Zeist d.	...	...	...	...	...	...	...	...	0600	...	...	|	0658	0658	0717	|	|	0758	|	|	...	0858	...
80	Ede-Wageningen d.	...	...	...	...	...	...	...	...	0620	...	...	|	0715	0715	0736	0743	|	0815	0843	|	...	0915	...
97	**Arnhem** a.	...	...	...	...	...	...	...	...	0635	...	...	0703	0726	0726	0752	0755	0804	0826	0855	0903	...	0926	...
97	**Arnhem 235 241** d.	...	...	...	...	...	...	...	...	...	...	...	0705	0737	0737	...	...	0806	0835	...	0905	...	0935	...
116	*Nijmegen 235 241* a.	...	...	...	...	...	...	...	...	...	...	...	|	0751	0751	...	...	|	0851	...	|	...	0950	...
127	**Emmerich** 🏛 a.	...	...	...	...	...	...	...	...	...	...	...	0723	...	...	...	...	0823	...	...	0923	...	...	...
	Duisburg Hbf 650 a.	...	...	...	...	...	...	...	...	...	...	...	0806v	...	...	...	...	0906v	...	...	1010t	1014	...	...
	Köln Hbf 650 a.	...	...	...	...	...	...	...	...	...	...	...	0842	...	...	...	...	0942	...	...	1057	1050	...	...

	3329	EC 3 ♦	EC 29 ✕	3031	3333	3035		2937	EC 145 🍷	3039	3341	3043		3345	EC 147 🍷	3047	3349	3051		3353	EC 149 🍷	3055	3357	3059
Amsterdam Schiphol ✈ 238 d.	...	0838	...	...	...	...	...	...	*1035*	...	...	...	...	...	*1235*	...	...	...	...	...	*1435*	...	...	...
Amsterdam CS 245 d.	0849	0900	...	0919	0949	1019	...	1049	1106	1119	1149	1219	...	1249	1306	1319	1349	1419	...	1449	1506	1519	1549	1619
Duivendrecht 245 d.	0859	|	...	0929	0959	1029	...	1059	|	1129	1159	1229	...	1259	|	1329	1359	1429	...	1459	|	1529	1559	1629
Utrecht 245 a.	0917	0928	...	0947	1017	1047	...	1117	1133	1147	1217	1247	...	1317	1333	1347	1417	1447	...	1517	1533	1547	1617	1647
Utrecht d.	0920	0930	...	0950	1020	1050	...	1120	1135	1150	1220	1250	...	1320	1335	1350	1420	1450	...	1520	1535	1550	1620	1650
Driebergen-Zeist d.	|	|	...	0958	|	1058	...	|	|	1158	|	1258	...	|	|	1358	|	1458	...	|	|	1558	|	1658
Ede-Wageningen d.	0943	|	...	1015	1043	1115	...	1143	|	1215	1243	1315	...	1343	|	1415	1443	1515	...	1543	|	1615	1643	1715
Arnhem a.	0955	1003	...	1026	1055	1126	...	1155	1204	1226	1255	1326	...	1355	1404	1426	1455	1526	...	1555	1604	1626	1655	1726
Arnhem 235 241 d.	...	1005	...	1035	...	1135	...	...	1206	1235	...	1335	...	...	1406	1435	...	1535	...	...	1606	1635	...	1735
Nijmegen 235 241 a.	...	|	...	1049	...	1149	...	...	|	1249	...	1350	...	...	|	1450	...	1550	...	...	|	1649	...	1749
Emmerich 🏛 a.	...	1023	...	...	...	...	...	...	1223	...	...	...	...	...	1423	...	...	...	...	...	1623	...	...	...
Duisburg Hbf 650 a.	...	1110e	1114	...	...	...	...	...	1306v	...	...	...	...	...	1506v	...	...	...	...	...	1706v	...	...	...
Köln Hbf 650 a.	...	1157	1150	...	...	...	...	...	1342	...	...	...	...	...	1542	...	...	...	...	...	1742	...	...	...

		3361	EC 151 🍷	3063	3365		3067	3369	EC 153 🍷	3071	2973	1215 ♦	203 ♦	3075		3377	EN 215 ♦	3079	3381	3083		3385	3087	3089
Amsterdam Schiphol ✈ 238 d.	...	...	*1624*	...	...	...	...	...	*1835*	...	...	*1905*	*1921*	...	...	...	*2021*	...	...	...	...	...	...	...
Amsterdam CS 245 d.	...	1648	1700	1719	1748	...	1819	1849	1906	1919	1949	1939	2005	2019	...	2049	2056	2119	2149	2219	...	2249	2319	2349
Duivendrecht 245 d.	...	1659	|	1729	1759	...	1829	1859	|	1929	1959	|	|	2029	...	2059	|	2129	2159	2229	...	2259	2329	2359
Utrecht 245 a.	...	1717	1728	1747	1817	...	1847	1917	1933	1947	2017	2010	2040	2047	...	2117	2125	2147	2217	2247	...	2317	2347	0017
Utrecht d.	...	1720	1730	1750	1820	...	1850	1920	1935	1950	2020	2028	2047	2050	...	2120	2130	2150	2220	2250	...	2320	2351	0020
Driebergen-Zeist d.	...	|	|	1758	|	...	1858	|	|	1958	|	|	|	2058	...	|	|	2158	|	2258	...	|	2359	0031
Ede-Wageningen d.	...	1743	|	1815	1843	...	1915	1943	|	2015	2043	|	|	2115	...	2143	|	2215	2243	2315	...	2343	0015	0051
Arnhem a.	...	1755	1803	1826	1855	...	1926	1955	2004	2026	2055	2102	2123	2126	...	2155	2204	2226	2255	2326	...	2355	0027	0106
Arnhem 235 241 d.	...	...	1805	1835	...	...	1935	...	2006	2035	...	2105	2127	2135	...	...	2214	2235	...	2335	...	...	0034	0110
Nijmegen 235 241 a.	...	...	|	1849	...	...	1949	...	|	2049	...	|	|	2149	...	...	|	2250	...	2349	...	...	0048	0125
Emmerich 🏛 a.	...	...	1823	...	...	...	...	...	2023	...	...	2125	2147	...	...	...	2235	...	...	...	...	...	...	...
Duisburg Hbf 650 a.	...	...	1906v	...	...	...	...	...	2106v	...	...	2216	2242	...	...	...	2335	...	...	...	...	...	...	...
Köln Hbf 650 a.	...	...	1942	...	...	...	...	...	2142	...	...	2300	2347	...	...	...	0022	...	...	...	...	...	...	...

	19888	31805	31809		31813	31817	7308		3012 Ⓐ	3012 ⑥	3014 ⚒	916 Ⓐ	30165 ⑥	3316 Ⓐ	3016 ⑦	3018 ⚒	3018 ⑦	3020 Ⓐ	3020 ⑥	EN 214 ♦	3022		202 ♦	3024
Köln Hbf 650 d.	...	...	...	...	...	...	...	...	...	...	...	...	...	...	...	...	...	...	...	0510	...	...	0550	...
Duisburg Hbf 650 d.	...	...	...	...	...	...	...	...	...	...	...	...	...	...	...	...	...	...	...	0613	...	...	0655	...
Emmerich 🏛 d.	...	...	...	...	...	...	...	...	...	...	...	...	...	...	...	...	...	...	...	0716	...	...	0802	...
Nijmegen 235 241 d.	...	...	...	...	...	...	...	...	...	...	...	...	0616	...	...	0644	...	0713	...	|	0743	...	|	0816
Arnhem 235 241 a.	...	...	...	...	...	...	...	...	...	...	...	...	0632	...	...	0700	...	0729	...	0741	0800	...	0825	0831
Arnhem d.	0012	...	...	...	...	...	...	...	0530	...	...	...	0637	0637	...	0707	...	0735	0735	0745	0808	...	0829	0837
Ede-Wageningen d.	0026	...	...	...	...	...	...	...	0545	...	...	...	0647	0647	...	0717	...	0747	0747	|	0819	...	|	0847
Driebergen-Zeist d.	0045	...	...	...	...	...	...	...	0604	...	...	...	0703	0703	...	0733	...	0803	0803	|	|	...	|	0903
Utrecht a.	0057	...	...	...	...	...	...	...	0615	...	...	...	0713	0713	...	0744	...	0813	0813	0823	0843	...	0906	0913
Utrecht 245 d.	...	0110	0209	...	0309	0409	0510	...	0616	0616	0646	0702	0715	0715	0715	0746	0746	0816	0816	0826	0846	...	0910	0916
Duivendrecht 245 d.	...	|	|	...	|	|	0536	...	0632	0632	0702	|	0732	0732	0732	0802	0802	0832	0832	|	0902	...	|	0933
Amsterdam CS 245 a.	...	0142	0242	...	0342	0442	0550	...	0643	0643	0714	0730	0744	0744	0744	0814	0814	0844	0844	0857	0914	...	0940	0945
Amsterdam Schiphol ✈ 238 a.	...	0158	0258	...	0358	0458	...	...	...	...	...	...	...	...	...	...	...	...	...	*0928*	...	...	*1011*	...

♦ – **NOTES** (LISTED BY TRAIN NUMBERS)

EC3 – REMBRANDT – [12] and ✕ Amsterdam Schiphol ✈ - Chur.

EC105 – BERNER OBERLAND – [12] and ✕ Amsterdam Schiphol ✈ - Interlaken Ost.

202/3 – SCHWEIZ EXPRESS – see Table **28**.

EN214/5 – DONAUWALZER – 1,2 cl., 2 cl. and [2] Amsterdam CS - Wien West and v.v; 1,2 cl., 2 cl. and [2] Amsterdam CS - München Hbf and v.v.

1215 – ⑤ Jan. 6 - Mar. 24, also Dec. 23: 1,2 cl., 2 cl., [2] and 🍷 Amsterdam CS - Villach.

e – Change here for train **EC29** and **not** at Köln Hbf. See also note **v**.

t – Change here for train **IC727** and **not** at Köln Hbf. See also note **v**.

v – Easy cross-platform interchange here for passengers travelling beyond Köln.

❖ – **Not** Dec. 25, Jan. 1.

✕ – ① - ⑥ (**not** Oct. 3, Dec. 25 - Jan. 1, Apr. 15 - 17, May 1, **1995**).

For explanation of standard symbols see page 4

Table 240
EMMERICH - ARNHEM - UTRECHT - AMSTERDAM

1, 2 class

		EC 140	3326	3028		3330	3032	EC 142	3334	3036	3338		3040	EC 144	3342	3044	3346	3048	EC 146	3350	3052	3354		3056
	1214																							
Köln Hbf 650 .... d.	0632	0717			...		0917					...		1117					1317				...	
Duisburg Hbf 650 ..... d.	0721	0752			...		0952					...		1152					1352				...	
Emmerich ▥ .... d.	0824	0834			...		1034					...		1234					1434				...	
Nijmegen 235 241 ..... d.			0916		...	1016			1116			1216			1316		1416			1516			...	1616
Arnhem 235 241 ...... a.	0845	0852	0931		...	1031	1052		1131			1231	1252		1331		1431	1452		1531			...	1631
Arnhem .... d.	0857	0854	0909	0937	1008	1037	1054	1109	1137	1209		1237	1254	1309	1337	1409	1437	1454	1509	1537	1609		...	1637
Ede-Wageningen .... d.			0920	0947	1020	1047		1120	1147	1220		1247		1320	1347	1420	1447		1520	1547	1620		...	1647
Driebergen-Zeist .... d.				1003		1103			1203			1303			1403		1503			1603			...	1703
Utrecht .... a.	0935	0923	0943	1013	1043	1113	1123	1144	1213	1243		1313	1323	1344	1413	1443	1513	1523	1544	1613	1643		...	1713
Utrecht 245 .... d.	0940	0925	0946	1016	1046	1116	1125	1146	1216	1246		1316	1325	1346	1416	1446	1516	1525	1546	1616	1646		...	1716
Duivendrecht 245 ...... d.			1002	1032	1102	1132		1202	1232	1302		1332		1402	1432	1502	1532		1602	1632	1702		...	1732
Amsterdam CS 245 .... a.	1011	0954	1004	1044	1114	1144	1151	1214	1244	1314		1344	1351	1414	1444	1514	1544	1551	1602	1614	1644	1714		1744
Amsterdam Schiphol ✛ 238 a.	*1041*	*1028*			...		*1228*					...		*1428*					*1628*				...	

	EC 148	3358	3060	3362	3064		EC 150	2966	3068		EC 104	3370	3072		EC 2	3374		3076	3378	3080	EC 152	3382		3084
Köln Hbf 650 .... d.	1517				...		1717				1802				1902					2117			...	
Duisburg Hbf 650 ..... d.	1552				...		1752				1848				1948					2152			...	
Emmerich ▥ .... d.	1634				...		1834				1934				2034					2234			...	
Nijmegen 235 241 ..... d.			1713		1816			1916					2016				2116		2216			...	2316
Arnhem 235 241 ...... a.	1652		1729		1831		1852		1931		1952		2031		2052			2131		2231	2252		...	2331
Arnhem .... d.	1654	1708	1737	1809	1837		1854	1909	1937		1954	2009	2037		2054	2109		2137	2209	2237	2254	2309		2340
Ede-Wageningen .... d.			1720	1747	1823	1847		1920	1947			2020	2047			2120		2147	2220	2247		2320		2350
Driebergen-Zeist .... d.			1803		1903				2003				2103					2203		2303			...	0007
Utrecht .... a.	1723	1743	1813	1843	1913		1923	1944	2013		2023	2044	2113		2123	2143		2213	2243	2313	2323	2343		0016
Utrecht 245 .... d.	1725	1746	1816	1846	1916		1925	1946	2016		2025	2046	2116		2125	2146		2216	2246	2316	2325	2346		0020
Duivendrecht 245 ...... d.			1802	1832	1902	1932			2002	2032		2102	2132			2202		2232	2302	2332		0002		0047
Amsterdam CS 245 .... a.	1751	1814	1844	1914	1944		1951	2014	2044		2051	2114	2144		2151	2214		2232	2302	2332	2344	0002		0101
Amsterdam Schiphol ✛ 238 a.	*1828*				...		*1951*	*2014*	*2044*		*2116*				*2228*					*2344*	*2351*	*0014*		*0101*

◆ – NOTES (LISTED BY TRAIN NUMBERS)
EC2 – REMBRANDT – 🔲 and ✗ Chur - Amsterdam CS.

EC104 – BERNER OBERLAND – 🔲 and ✗ Interlaken Ost - Schiphol ✛.
1214 – ⑥ Jan. 7 - Mar. 25: 🛏 1,2 cl., 🛏 2 cl., 🔲 and 🍴 Villach - Amsterdam CS.

Table 241
ARNHEM - ROERMOND

1, 2 class

km		Ⓐ	Ⓐ	Ⓐ	Ⓐ		Ⓐ				Ⓐ		Ⓐ	✗	†e								
0	Arnhem .... d.	...	...	0607	...	0707k	...	0806	...	0906		...	1506	...	1606	...	1706	...	1806	1906	2006	2106	2206	2306
19	Nijmegen .... d.	...	...	0624	0654	0724	0754	0824	0854	0924	and	1524	1554	1624	1654	1724	1754	1754	1824	1924	2024	2124	2224	2324
57	Venray .... d.	...	...	0702	0732	0802	0832	0902	0932	1002	hourly	1602	1632	1702	1732	1802	1832	1832	1902	2002	2102	2202	2302	0002
80	Venlo .... a.	...	...	0720	0750	0820	0850	0920	0950	1020	until	1620	1650	1720	1750	1820	1850q	1850q	1902	2002	2120	2220	2320	0020
80	Venlo .... d.	0625	0655	0725	0755	0825	0855	0925	0951	1025		1625	1655	1725	1755	1825	...	1855	1925	2025	2125	2225	2325	...
103	Roermond .... a.	0650	0721	0751	0821	0851	0921	0951	1021	1051		1651	1721	1751	1821	1851	...	1921	1951	2051	2151	2251	2351	...

		Ⓐ	Ⓐ	Ⓐ	✗	Ⓐ	Ⓐ				Ⓐ		Ⓐ		†e								
Roermond ...... d.		...	0611	0640	0711	0741	0811	0841	0911		...	1511	1541	1611	1641	1711	1741	1811	1911	2011	2111	2211	2311
Venlo .... a.		...	0638	0708	0738	0808	0838	0908	0938	and	...	1538	1608	1638	1708	1738	1808	1838	1938	2038	2108	2138	2238	2338
Venlo .... d.	0544	0644	0714	0744	0814	0844	0914	0944	hourly	1544	1614	1644	1714	1744	1814	1844	1944	2044	2108	2138	2238	2338	...
Venray .... d.	0601	0702	0733	0802	0833	0902	0933	1002	until	1602	1633	1702	1733	1802	1833	1902	2002	2102	2133	2202	2302	0002	...
Nijmegen .... d.	0637	0738	0808	0842	0908	0942	1008	1042		1642	1708	1742	1808	1842	1908	1942	2042	2142	2208	2242	2342	0038	0054
Arnhem .... a.		...	0859	...	0959	...	1059			1659	...	1859	...	1959	2059	2159	...	2259	2359	...	0109		

e – Not Dec. 25, Apr. 16.　　　　　k – ✗ only.　　　　　q – Ⓐ only.

Table 242
ARNHEM - WINTERSWIJK

1, 2 class

km		Ⓐ	Ⓐ	✗	Ⓐ						Ⓐ		✗	Ⓐ				
0	Arnhem .... d.	0537	0608	0637	0708	0737	and	2237	Winterswijk ...... d.	0622	...	0653	0722	0753	and	2253
30	Doetinchem ..... d.	0611	0642	0711	0742	0812	hourly	2312	Doetinchem ...... d.	0654	...	0725	0754	0825	hourly	2325
63	Winterswijk ..... a.	0644	0715	0744	0815	0844	until	2344	Arnhem .... a.	0730	...	0801	0830	0901	until	0001

Table 243
OTHER BRANCH LINES

LEIDEN - UTRECHT

50 km.　Journey time: ± 41 minutes.

1, 2 class

From Leiden:　(Trains call at **Alphen aan den Rijn**, 15 km, 13 mins from Leiden) 0550Ⓐ, 0625✗, 0644Ⓐ, 0702Ⓐ H, 0720, 0735Ⓐ H, 0751, 0821 and half-hourly until 2251; then 2324, 0026✗. 　　H – Not Dec. 27–30, Apr. 14, May 26.

From Utrecht:　(Trains call at **Alphen aan den Rijn**, 35 km, 25 mins from Utrecht) 0615✗, 0650✗, 0710✗, 0740✗, 0810, 0840 and half-hourly until 0010.

ZWOLLE - KAMPEN

13 km.　Journey time: 10 minutes.

1, 2 class

From Zwolle: 0547Ⓐ, 0614Ⓐ, 0646Ⓐ, 0721✗, 0752✗, 0821, 0852✗ and at 21 and 52✗ minutes past each hour until 1521; then 1552, 1621E, 1652 and at 21E and 52 minutes past until 2252; then 2321†E, 2355, 0050K.　　E – Not Dec. 25, Apr. 16.

From Kampen: 0600Ⓐ, 0627Ⓐ, 0659Ⓐ, 0734✗, 0805✗, 0834 and at 05✗ and 34 minutes past each hour until 1534; then 1605E, 1634 and at 05E and 34 minutes past each hour until 2305E; then 2334†, 0014, 0103K.　　K – ⑤⑥ (also May 13, 24).

GRONINGEN - DELFZIJL

38 km.　Journey time: 40 minutes.

2 class

From Groningen: 0528Ⓐ, 0624✗, 0702✗, 0732✗, 0805, 0835✗ and at 05 and 35✗ minutes past each hour until 1805; then 1835Ⓐ, 1905, 2005, 2105, 2135Ⓐ, 2205, 2305, 0005.

From Delfzijl: 0519①Q, 0614Ⓐ, 0642✗, 0713✗, 0746, 0817✗, 0847 and at 17✗ and 47 minutes past each hour until 1847; then 1947, 2047, 2147, 2247, 2347.　　Q – Also Dec. 27, Apr. 18.

LEEUWARDEN - HARLINGEN

26 km.　Journey time: 25 minutes.

2 class

From Leeuwarden: 0610✗, 0640Ⓐ, 0710✗, 0749✗, 0819Ⓐ, 0850, 0919, 1019, 1050✗, 1119, 1150⑥, 1219, 1250, 1319, 1350, 1419, 1450✗, 1519, 1550✗, 1619, 1650✗, 1719, 1750, 1819, 1850, 1919, 2019, 2119, 2219, 2330Y.　　Y – ②-⑦ (not Dec. 27, Apr. 18).

From Harlingen: 0541Ⓐ, 0638✗, 0707Ⓐ, 0747✗, 0817✗, 0847✗, 0917Ⓐ, 0947, 1017, 1047, 1117✗, 1147, 1217✗, 1247, 1317✗, 1347, 1417, 1447, 1517, 1547, 1617✗, 1647, 1717✗, 1747, 1817✗, 1847, 1917, 1947, 2017†, 2047, 2147, 2247, 0000Y.

Certain services continue to/start from Harlingen Haven in connection with boats to/from Vlieland and Terschelling.　　There are minor reductions in service levels on Dec. 25, 26, Jan. 1.

Table 244
MAASTRICHT - KERKRADE

1, 2 class

km		Ⓐ	✗	Ⓐ	⑦								Ⓐ	Ⓐ	✗	✗	⑦				
0	Maastricht .... d.	...	0709	0744	...	0809	and	2309	2344	Kerkrade Centrum . d.	...	0704	...	0734	...	0834	and	2234
11	Valkenburg .... d.	...	0722	0757	...	0822	hourly	2322	2357	Heerlen .... d.	0620	0717	0720	0751	0751	0851	hourly	2251
24	Heerlen .... d.	0617	0739	0817	0817	0839	until	2339	0013	Valkenburg .... d.	0636	...	0736	0807	0807	0907	until	2307
33	Kerkrade Centrum . a.	0630	0753	0830	0830	0853		2353	...	Maastricht .... a.	0649	...	0749	0820	0820	0920		2320

THOMAS COOK TRAVELLERS

This series of 192-page compact (192mm x 130mm) guides, each fully illustrated in colour and with completely new research and mapping, has been created for the holidaymaker of the 1990s by Thomas Cook Publishing and leading guidebook publishers AA Publishing.

Features include:

★ Facts at your fingertips

★ Background information on history, politics and culture

★ Descriptions of major sights plus snippets about lesser known places

★ A 'get-away-from-it-all' section

★ A street-by-street shopping and entertainment guide

★ An A-Z help list packed with practical information

★ Tips on 'finding your feet'

★ Up to 10 city walks or excursions with full-colour maps

These books contain not only a conventional guide to the sights of the cities and countries, but everything the traveller needs to know, and are presented in a way that is accessible, concise and innovative. The series reflects on every page Thomas Cook's depth of expertise on the destinations and on the subjects that are of most interest and concern to today's travellers.

Titles in the series:

The following titles are available at £6.99 each from all good UK high-street bookshops or from many Thomas Cook outlets in the UK. Also available by post at £7.99 (UK), £9.50 (Europe), £10.70 (overseas air mail) from the address below.

☐ ALGARVE ☐ AMSTERDAM ☐ BELGIUM ☐ BOSTON & NEW ENGLAND ☐ CALIFORNIA ☐ CYPRUS ☐ EASTERN CARIBBEAN ☐ EGYPT ☐ FLORENCE & TUSCANY ☐ FLORIDA ☐ IRELAND ☐ KENYA ☐ LONDON ☐ MALTA ☐ MUNICH & BAVARIA ☐ NEW YORK ☐ PARIS ☐ PRAGUE ☐ SINGAPORE & MALAYSIA ☐ SYDNEY & NEW SOUTH WALES ☐ THAILAND ☐ TURKEY ☐ VANCOUVER & BRITISH COLUMBIA ☐ VIENNA

NEW FOR '95

The following titles are new for 1995 and are available at £7.99 each from all good UK high-street bookshops or from many Thomas Cook outlets in the UK. Also available by post at £8.99 (UK), £9.99 (Europe), £11.79 (overseas air mail) from the address below.

☐ BERLIN ☐ BUDAPEST ☐ GREECE (Mainland) ☐ JAVA & BALI ☐ MADEIRA ☐ MALLORCA ☐ MEXICO ☐ MOROCCO ☐ NORMANDY ☐ PROVENCE ☐ ROME ☐ VENICE

Send your mail order request to Thomas Cook Publishing (TPO/FE), P.O. Box 227, PETERBOROUGH PE3 8BQ, UK.
☎ (01733) 505821/268943.

Thomas Cook

Table 245 — ZANDVOORT AAN ZEE - AMSTERDAM - UTRECHT - MAASTRICHT
1, 2 class

km			Ⓐ	Ⓐ	✕		✕		✕					⑦					
0	Zandvoort-aan-Zee	d.	…	…	…	…	…	…	…	0655t	0724	…	0754	…	0824b	…			
8	Haarlem	d.	…	…	…	…	…	…	…	0712t	0742	…	0812	…	0842	…			
23	Amsterdam Sloterdijk	d.	…	…	…	…	…	…	…	0723t	0753	…	0823	…	0853	…			
27	Amsterdam CS	a.	…	…	…	…	…	…	…	0729t	0759	…	0829	…	0859	…	and at
27	Amsterdam CS 240	d.	…	…	…	0559h	…	0632h	…	0702t	0732	0803 0803	0832	…	0903	…	the same
66	Utrecht 240	a.	…	…	…	0628h	…	0700h	…	0730t	0800	0831 0831	0900	…	0931	…	minutes
66	Utrecht	d.	…	0525h	…	0604 0634h	…	0704h	…	0734t	0804	0834 0834	0904	…	0934	…	past
114	's-Hertogenbosch	d.	…	0611h	…	0643 0705h	…	0735h	…	0805t	0835	0905 0905	0935	…	1005	…	each
146	Eindhoven	a.	…	0641h	…	0714 0727h	…	0757h	…	0827t	0857	0927 0927	0957	…	1027	…	hour
146	Eindhoven	d.	0617	0659h	…	0729	…	0759	…	0829	0859	0929 0929	0959	…	1029	…	until:
174	Weert	d.	0638	0717h	…	0747	…	0817	…	0847	0917	0947 0947	1017	…	1047	…	
198	Roermond	d.	0653	0732	…	0802	…	0832	…	0902	0932	1002 1002	1032	…	1102	…	
223	Sittard	d.	0721 0740	0749 0751	…	0819 0821	0849 0851	0919 0921	0949 0951	1019 1019 1021	1049 1051 1119 1121						
242	Heerlen	a.	…	0759	…	0815	…	0837	…	0913	0937	1013 1037 1037	…	1113 1137	…	
244	Maastricht	a.	0741	0804	…	…	0841 0905	…	0941 1004	…	1041	1104	…	1141			

												✕	Ⓐ	Ⓐ	✕	✕		✕	✕	
Zandvoort-aan-Zee	d.	2025	…	2055	…	2125	2155 2225 2255	Maastricht	d.	…	0521 0545	…	…	0627t 0654	…					
Haarlem	d.	2042	…	2112	…	2142	2212 2242 2312	Heerlen	d.	…	…	0558h 0612	…	0659t 0720						
Amsterdam Sloterdijk	d.	2053	…	2123	…	2153	2223 2253 2323	Sittard	d.	…	0537 0609 0617h 0636	0644t 0718 0742							
Amsterdam CS	a.	2059	…	2129	…	2159	2229 2259 2329	Roermond	d.	…	0552 0628 0632h	…	0659t	0733t						
Amsterdam CS 240	d.	2102	…	2132	…	2202	2232 2302 2332	Weert	d.	…	0607	…	0647h	…	0714t	0748t				
Utrecht 240	a.	2130	…	2200	…	2230	2300 2330 0001	Eindhoven	a.	…	0626	…	0704h	…	0734t	0805t				
Utrecht	d.	2134	…	2204	…	2234	2304 2334 …	Eindhoven	d.	0607h 0637	…	0706	…	0737	…	0807				
's-Hertogenbosch	d.	2205	…	2235	…	2305	2335 0005 …	's-Hertogenbosch	d.	0630h 0700	…	0730	…	0800	…	0830				
Eindhoven	a.	2227	…	2257	…	2327	2357 0027 …	Utrecht	d.	0659h 0729	…	0759	…	0829	…	0859				
Eindhoven	d.	2229	…	2259	…	2329	… … …	Utrecht 240	a.	0702h 0732	…	0802	…	0832	…	0902				
Weert	d.	2247	…	2317	…	2347	… … …	Amsterdam CS 240	d.	0730h 0800	…	0830	…	0900	…	0930				
Roermond	d.	2302	•	2332	…	0002	… … …	Amsterdam CS	d.	0733 0803	…	0833	…	0903	…	0935				
Sittard	d.	2319 2321	2349 2351	0021 0029	…	Amsterdam Sloterdijk	d.	0739 0809	…	0839	…	0909	…	0941						
Heerlen	a.	2337	│	│	0014	0052	Haarlem	d.	0753 0823	…	0850	…	0920	…	0952				
Maastricht	a.	…	2341 0005	…	0038	Zandvoort-aan-Zee	a.	0805 0835	…	0905c	…	0935c	…	1005c						

Maastricht	d.	0731 0754	…	0831			…	1931 1954	…	2031 2054	…	…	2131 2154	…	2231 2254					
Heerlen	d.	…	0759 0820	│	1859 1920	│	1959 2020	│	2059 2120	│	2159 2220	│	2254						
Sittard	d.	0748 0814	0817 0842 0848	1918 1942	1948 2014	2018 2042	2048 2114	2118 2142	2148 2214	2218 2242	2248 2254							
Roermond	d.	0803	0833	0903	and at	1933	2003	2033	2103	2133	2203	2233	2303 2343							
Weert	d.	0818	0848	0918	the same	1948	2018	2048	2118	2148	2218	2248	2318 2356							
Eindhoven	a.	0835	0905	0935	minutes	2005	2035	2105	2135	2205	2235	2305	2335 0017							
Eindhoven	d.	0837	0907	0937	past	2007	2037	2107	2137	2207	2237	2307	…							
's-Hertogenbosch	d.	0900	0930	1000	each	2030	2100	2130	2200	2230	2300	2330	…							
Utrecht	a.	0929	0959	1029	hour	2059	2129	2159	2229	2259	2329	2359	…							
Utrecht 240	d.	0932	1002	1032	until:	2102	2132	2202	2232	2302	2332	0002	…							
Amsterdam CS 240	a.	1000	1030	1100		2130	2200	2230	2300	2330	0001	0030	…							
Amsterdam CS	a.	1003	1033	1103		2133	2203	2233	2309n	…										
Amsterdam Sloterdijk	a.	1009	1039	1109		2139	2209	2239	2320n	…										
Haarlem	a.	1020	1050	1120		2150	2220	2250	…											
Zandvoort-aan-Zee	a.	1035c	…	1105	1135k	2205c	…	…												

b – Change at Haarlem on Ⓐ (except trains departing 0824, 1054 to 1454 and 1724 to 2024 inclusive).
c – Change at Haarlem on Ⓐ.
h – Ⓐ only.
k – Change at Haarlem on Ⓐ (except trains arriving 1135 to 1505 and 1735 to 2135 inclusive).
n – Ⓑ only.
t – ✕ only.

Table 246 — HEERLEN - AACHEN
Rail service Heerlen - Aachen Hbf. 24 km. Journey time: 33 minutes. 1, 2 class. 🚇 – Customs/ticket point is at Herzogenrath, 14 minutes from Heerlen, 16 minutes from Aachen.

From Heerlen: 0724 ✥, 0854, 1024, 1154, 1324, 1454, 1624, 1754, 1924, 2054 S, 2224 S.
From Aachen: 0807 ✥, 0940, 1109, 1240, 1409, 1540, 1709, 1840, 2009, 2140 S, 2309 S.

S – Not Dec. 24, 31.   ✥ – Not Dec. 25, Jan. 1.

Table 247 — ZWOLLE and ALMELO - EMMEN
1, 2 class

km			Ⓐ	Ⓐ	Ⓐ	✕		✕		Ⓐ		Ⓐ		✕				
0	Zwolle	d.	0556	…	0656	…	0718	…	0756	…	0822	…	0856 0922	…	0956 1022	…	1056 1122	and at
23	Ommen	d.	0616	…	0716	…	0732	…	0816	…	0837	…	0916 0937	…	1016 1037	…	1116 1137	the same
	Almelo	d.	…	0649	│	…	0750	│	…	0850	│	…	0950	│	1050	│	…	minutes
34	Mariënberg	d.	0624 0713 0724	│	0814 0824	…	0914 0924	│	1014 1024	│	1114 1124	…	past each	2050					
55	Coevorden	d.	0645	0745	0800	0845	0900	0945 1000	1045 1100	1145 1200	hour (Z)	2114							
75	Emmen	a.	0706	0806	0813	0906	0913	1006 1013	1106 1113	1206 1213	until:	…							

				J	G		J								Ⓐ	Ⓐ	Ⓐ		✕	Ⓐ		
Zwolle	d.	2056	…	2122	…	2156 2222	…	2256	…	2356	Emmen	d.	0524	…	0610	…	0624	…	0715	…	0724
Ommen	d.	2116	…	2137	…	2216 2237	…	2316	…	0015	Coevorden	d.	0546	…	0623	…	0646	…	0728	…	0746
Almelo	d.	…	…	2150	│	…	│	…	Mariënberg	d.	0605 0656	…	0705 0716	…	…	0805					
Mariënberg	d.	2124	…	2214 2224	…	2324	…	0023	Almelo	a.	…	0723	│	0741	│	…					
Coevorden	d.	2145	2200	2245 2300	2345	0045	Ommen	d.	0615	…	0646	…	0716	…	0751	…	0816				
Emmen	a.	2206	2213	2306 2313	0006	0106	Zwolle	a.	0632	…	0703	…	0733	…	0808	…	0833				

		✕			✕	✕	✕		✕					✕		J		J		G	J	
Emmen	d.	…	0817 0824	…	0917 0924	…	1017 1024	…	and at	1917 1924	…	2016 2024	…	2117 2124	…	2217 2224						
Coevorden	d.	…	0830 0846	…	0930 0946	…	1030 1046	…	the same	1930 1946	…	2029 2046	…	2130 2146	…	2230 2246						
Mariënberg	d.	0817	│	0905 0917	…	1005 1017	…	1105 1117	minutes	2005 2017	…	2105 2117	…	2205 2217	…	2305						
Almelo	a.	0842	│	0942	│	1042	past each	2042	│	2142	│	2242	…								
Ommen	d.	…	0853 0916	…	0953 1016	…	1053 1116	…	hour (Z)	1953 2016	…	2051 2116	…	2153 2216	…	2253 2316						
Zwolle	a.	…	0908 0933	…	1008 1033	…	1108 1133	…	until:	2008 2033	…	2108 2133	…	2208 2233	…	2308 2333						

G – ⑤⑥⑦ and holidays, also Apr. 13, May 24 only.
J – ⑦ and holidays, not Dec. 25, Apr. 16.
Z – The 1622, 1722, 1822, 1922, and 2022 trains from Zwolle, and the 1517, 1617, 1717, and 1817 trains from Emmen do not run on Dec. 25, Apr. 16.

Local rail service Zwolle - Almelo. 1, 2 class 45 km. Journey 43 minutes.
From Zwolle: 0615Ⓐ, 0641Ⓐ, 0727✕, 0827 and hourly until 2327.
From Almelo: 0528Ⓐ, 0556Ⓐ, 0630Ⓐ, 0720✕, 0741Ⓐ, 0820 and hourly until 2320.

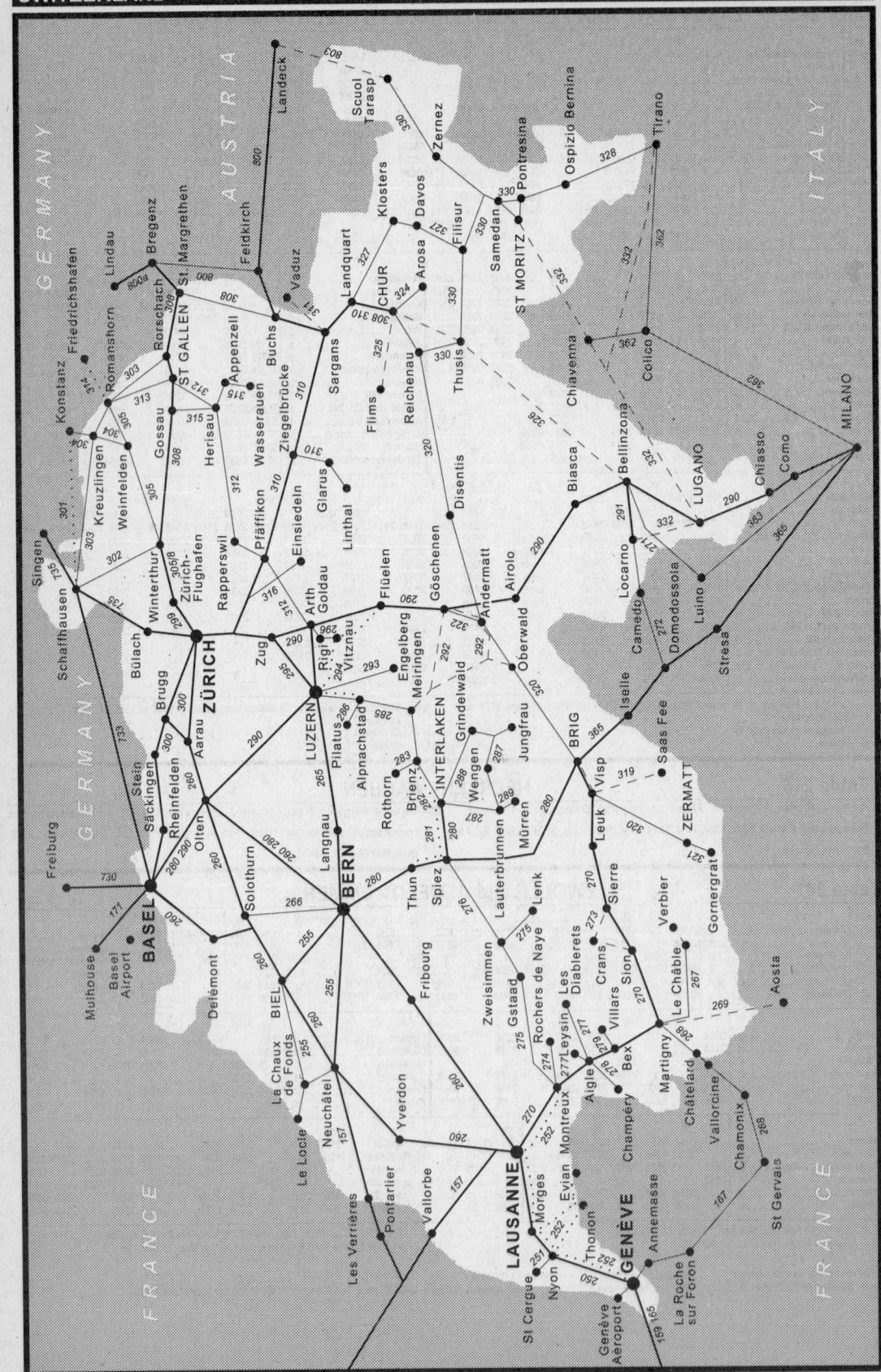

For list of Scenic Rail Routes in Switzerland see Page 27

SWITZERLAND

Operators: The principal operator is Schweizerische Bundesbahnen (SBB)/Chemins de fer Fédéraux (CFF)/Ferrovie Federali Svizzere (FFS). Bus services are provided by Post Telefon und Telegraphie (PTT). In addition there are many private railways operating mainly regional or mountain railways. These usually have a convenient interchange with the SBB network, often operating out of separate platforms in the station forecourt. Each table therefore shows the operator, to the right of the table heading.

Services: Trains convey first and second class seats, as shown by '1' and '2' or 🚃 in the tables. Faster trains are indicated by the codes **EC** (International EuroCity train), **IC** (Internal InterCity train) and **ICE** (German high-speed InterCity Express). Some international trains convey sleeping cars (🛏) and/or couchette cars (➤) of the normal European types – see page 10 for further details. **Restaurant** cars (✗) offer full dining services at meal times in addition to refreshment services at other times. **Buffet** cars (🍷) vary depending on the service concerned, and may consist of full buffet facilities, a bar car, or a trolley wheeled through the train.

Timings: Valid **September 25, 1994** to **May 27, 1995** unless stated otherwise in the table concerned. Local services are subject to alteration on **public holidays**.

Supplements: In general, no supplements are charged in Switzerland (including internal journeys on most EuroCity trains). Exceptions, which are indicated in the tables, are as follows: EuroCity supplements **are** payable on **EC57/8** (Zürich - Milano and v.v.), **EC154/5/8/9** (Zürich - Stuttgart and v.v.) and **ICE** services to/from Germany (via Basel).

Reservations: Seat reservations may be made on all EuroCity and InterCity trains. Reservations (inclusive of a supplement) are required for travel on the Crystal Panoramic, Panoramic, Glacier and Bernina Expresses. Details are given in the relevant table footnotes.

Table 250   GENÈVE - LAUSANNE   1, 2 class. SBB

km		IC 707 ✗	1511 ✗	3011	IC 711 ✗	1613	1913	IC 713 ✗	2009	IC 321 ✗	1915	IC 715 ✗	EC 39 ✗	2017	IC 1917 ✗	IC 717 ✗	1875	IC 1921 ✗	IC 721 ✗	2023	IC 323 ✗	1923	IC 723 ✗	1879	1925
0	Genève Aéroport ✈▲ d.	...	...	0539	...	...	0638	0648	0704	0721	0738	0748	0808	0815	0838	0848	0915	0938	0948	1015	1024	1038	1048	1115	1138
6	Genève ▲ a.	...	...	0546	...	...	0645	0655	0711	0728	0745	0755	0815	0822	0845	0855	0922	0945	0955	1022	1031	1045	1055	1122	1145
6	Genève d.	0447	0525	...	0558	0625	0648	0658	0714	0731	0748	0758	0820	0825	0848	0858	0925	0948	0958	1025	1034	1048	1058	1125	1148
27	Nyon d.	0501	0539			0639	0701		0729		0801			0839	0901		0939	1001		1039		1101		1139	1201
53	Morges d.	0517	0555			0655	0717		0744		0816			0855	0916		0955	1016		1055		1116		1155	1217
66	Lausanne a.	0527	0605		0632	0705	0727	0732	0755	0805	0827	0832	0854	0905	0927	0932	1005	1027	1032	1105	1108	1127	1132	1205	1227

	IC 725 ✗	1627	327	IC 727 ✗	EC 106	1885	1929	IC 729 🍷	1633	1933	IC 733 🍷	1891	335	IC 1937 🍷	737	1622	1893	IC 1939 🍷	739	1870	2037	2039	1941 ④	741 ✗	2041 ④
Genève Aéroport ✈▲ d.	1148	1215	1238	1248	...	1315	1338	1348	1415	1438	1448	1515	1525	1538	1548	1603	1615	1638	1648	1702	1713	...	1738	1748	...
Genève ▲ a.	1155	1225	1245	1255	...	1322	1345	1355	1422	1445	1455	1522	1532	1545	1555	1610	1622	1645	1655	1709	1720	...	1745	1755	...
Genève d.	1158	1225	1248	1258	1308	1325	1348	1358	1426	1448	1458	1525	1535	1548	1558		1625	1648	1658		1722	1735	1745	1758	1802
Nyon d.		1239	1301			1339	1401		1439	1501		1539		1601			1639	1701			1736	1748	1801		1815
Morges d.		1255	1316			1355	1416		1455	1516		1555		1616			1655	1716			1755		1816		...
Lausanne a.	1232	1305	1327	1332	1342	1405	1427	1432	1505	1527	1532	1605	1609	1627	1632		1705	1727	1732		1805	1810	1827	1832	...

	2028	2043	1943	IC 743 ✗	1876	IC 329 🍷	1545	1945	IC 745 🍷	2032	311	1936	2047	IC 747 🍷	1880	1649	1947	1749	1638	1549	740	221	1540	1942	2049
Genève Aéroport ✈▲ d.	1802	1815	1838	1848	1902	1906	1915	1938	1947	2002	2015	2038		2048	2102	2115	2138	2148	2202	2215	2230	2252	2302	2336	...
Genève ▲ d.	1809	1822	1845	1855	1909	1913	1922	1945	1954	2009	2022	2045		2055	2109	2122	2145	2155	2209	2222	2237	2259	2309	2343	...
Nyon d.		1825	1848		1916		1925	1948	1958		2025		2048	2058		2125	2148	2158		2225		2302	2315	...	0001
Morges d.		1839	1901			1939	2001		2039		2101			2139	2201			2239		2315	2345	...	0014
Morges d.		1855	1916			1955	2016		2055		2116			2155	2216			2255		2330	...	...	0033
Lausanne a.	1905	1927	1932		1950	2005	2027	2032		2105		2127	2132		2205	2227	2232		2305		2341	...	...	0044

	3011	2000	220	3004	1900	3006	1502	1902	1702	1904	2004	1704	706	1906	2006	IC 708 🍷	1908	1856	IC 712 🍷	312	1925	IC 1612 🍷	716	320	1860
Lausanne d.	...	0536	0600		0635		0652	0709	0728	0732	...	0755	0828	0832	0855	0928	0932	0955	1028	1032		1055	1128	1132	1155
Morges d.	...	0545	0610		0644		0718		0743		0804		0843	0904		0943	1004		1043		1104		1143	1204
Nyon d.	...	0600	0625	0627	0658	0701	0726	0734		0758	0807	0820		0858	0920		0958	1020		1058		1120		1158	1220
Genève ▲ a.	...	0614	0639	0658	0712	0734	0742	0748	0802	0812	0823	0834	0902	0912	0934	1002	1012	1034	1102	1112		1134	1202	1212	1234
Genève ▲ d.	0521	0617	0642	0701	0715	0737	...	0751	0805	0815		0837	0905	0915	0937	1005	1015	1037	1105		1117	1137	1205	1215	1237
Genève Aéroport ✈▲ a.	0528	0626	0649	0708	0724	0744	...	0758	0813	0824		0844	0913	0924	0944	1013	1024	1044	1113		1124	1144	1213	1224	1244

	IC 718 ✗	1918	330	2018	IC 720 ✗	1920	1866	1891	EC 107	722 ✗	1922	1622	1893	IC 726 ✗	1926	1870	2037	IC 728 ✗	1928	2028	2043	IC 730 ✗	1930	IC 322 🍷	1876
Lausanne d.	1228	1232	1243	1255	1328	1332	1355		1421	1428	1432	1455		1528	1532	1555		1628	1632	1655		1728	1732	1743	1755
Morges d.		1243		1304		1343	1404				1443	1504			1543	1604			1643	1704			1742		1805
Nyon d.		1258		1320		1358	1420				1458	1520			1558	1620			1658	1720			1800		1821
Genève ▲ a.	1302	1312	1316	1334	1402	1412	1434		1455	1502	1512	1534		1602	1612	1634		1702	1712	1734		1802	1814	1817	1834
Genève ▲ d.	1305	1315	1319	1337	1405	1415	1437	1451		1505	1515	1537	1551	1605	1615	1637	1647	1705	1715	1737	1751	1805	1817		1837
Genève Aéroport ✈▲ a.	1313	1322	1326	1344	1413	1424	1444	1458		1513	1524	1544	1558	1613	1624	1644	1654	1713	1724	1744	1758	1814	1824		1844

	1545	732 ✗	1932	2032	311	IC 736 ✗	1936	1880	1649	IC 738 ✗	326	1947	1638	EC 40 ✗	IC 740 ✗	1940	1540	IC 742 ✗	1942	690 ⑦n	328	IC 1642 🍷	744 ✗	1544	1898
Lausanne d.	...	1828	1832	1855		1928	1932	1955		2028	2032		2055	2114	2128	2132	2158	2228	2232	2241	2258	2258	2335	2355	0042
Morges d.	...		1843	1904			1943	2004			2043		2104		2143	2208		2243				2308		0004	0051
Nyon d.	...		1858	1920			1958	2020			2058		2120		2158	2223		2258				2323		0020	0106
Genève ▲ a.	...	1902	1912	1934		2002	2012	2034		2102	2112		2134	2148	2202	2212	2237	2302	2312	2315	2332	2337	0009	0034	0120
Genève ▲ d.	1851	1905	1915	1937	1951	2005	2017	2037	2051	2105		2117	2137	2151	2205	2215	2240	2305	2315		...	...	...	...	...
Genève Aéroport ✈▲ a.	1858	1914	1924	1944	1958	2013	2024	2044	2058	2112		2124	2144	2158	2212	2224	2247	2312	2322		...	...	...	...	...

– Not Dec. 25, Jan. 1, Apr. 14, 16, May 25.

④ – Additional services operate: Genève - Genève Aéroport at the following times: (Journey time 7 minutes):

From Genève: 0605, 0626, 0656, 0720, 0731, 0809, 0851, 0909, 1000, 1009, 1023, 1109, 1223, 1309, 1409, 1509, 1523, 1609, 1623, 1709, 1723, 1810, 1823, 1845, 1909, 1923, 2009, 2109, 2123, 2147.

From Genève Aéroport: 0656④, 0715④, 0819, 0844, 0902✗, 0944, 1030, 1044, 1130, 1144, 1244, 1344, 1444, 1502④, 1530, 1544, 1630, 1644, 1730, 1744, 1831, 1844, 1930, 1944, 2030, 2126, 2130, 2212, 2326.

Table 251   NYON - ST. CERGUE   (155) 2 class only. Narrow gauge. NStCM

Rail service **Nyon - St Cergue**. 18 km. Journey time: 35 minutes.

From Nyon: 0544④, 0635✗, 0708, 0735④, 0805, 0905, 1005, 1105, 1135④, 1205, 1305, 1408, 1435④, 1505, 1535④, 1605, 1635④, 1705, 1740④, 1805, 1825④, 1905, 2005, 2125, 2243.

From St. Cergue: 0547④, 0620, 0651④, 0720✗, 0752④, 0820, 0852④, 0920, 1020, 1120, 1220, 1252④, 1320, 1420, 1520, 1551④, 1620, 1651④, 1720, 1748④, 1820, 1920, 2011, 2042, 2203.

Operator: NStCM – NStCM, Nyon.

Table 252

⛴ LAC LÉMAN
Winter Service valid: September 20, 1994 - May 27, 1995

⛴ CGN

Period of operation:	SEPT. to MAR. ▲				APRIL 1995 ▲							MAY 1995 ▲											
	E				⑦		⑦	⑦	⑦	⑦		⑦	⑦	Ⓒ	Ⓐ	⑦		Ⓒ	⑦	⑥	Ⓒ	
Genève Mont-Blanc .... d.	...	...	...	...	...	...	...	...	...	...	...	...	...	...	...	...	...	...	...	1500	1500	...
Genève Jardin-Anglais ... d.	...	...	...	...	1030		1430						1030			1430						
Genève Pâquis .... d.	...	...	...	...	1035		1435						1035			1435						
Genève Eaux-Vives .... d.	...	...	...	...							0920b							1505	1505			
Nyon .... d.	...	...	...	...	1152		1545				1035b	1152			1545							
Yvoire .... d.	...	...	...	...	1210		1605				1055b	1212			1425	1605	1610	1610				
Thonon-les-Bains .... d.	...	...	...	...				1030		1115				1500							1735	
Evian-les-Bains ▲ .... d.	1100			1100			1550		1100	1145	1155		1240		1550		1540		1640	1640		
Rolle .... d.													1320				1620		1720	1720		
Morges .... d.													1352				1625	1655	1755	1755	1830	
Lausanne Ouchy ▲ .... a.	1135			1135			1625		1125	1135	1220	1228	1352		1625	1655			1755	1755	1830	
Lausanne Ouchy .... d.		1230	1000	1230	1400			1000		1230	1230		1400				1805					
Vevey-Marché .... d.		1325	1055	1325	1503			1055		1325	1325		1503				1900					
Montreux .... d.		1350	1120	1350	1530			1120		1350	1350		1530				1925					
St. Gingolph .... d.																						
Bouveret .... d.		1430	1202	1430	1611			1202		1430	1430		1611				2005					
St. Gingolph .... a.		1440	1215	1440	1623			1215		1440	1440		1623				2015					

Period of operation:	SEPT. to MAR. ▲			APRIL 1995 ▲							MAY 1995 ▲										
	E			⑦	⑦	⑦	🎿		⑦	Ⓒ	⑦		Ⓒ	Ⓐ	⑦e	🎿	⑦	Ⓒe	Ⓐe	⑦	
St. Gingolph .... d.	1547					1547	...	1640			0850		1202				1547	1640	...	
Bouveret .... d.	1600			1202	1430	1600		1652					1216				1430	1600	1652	2005	
St. Gingolph .... d.				1216	1500						0930		1240				1500			2015	
Montreux .... d.	1645			1240		1645		1735			0930		1240				1645	1735		2035	
Vevey-Marché .... d.	1710			1305		1710		1800			0957		1305				1710	1800		2035	
Lausanne Ouchy .... a.	1810			1402	1625f	1810		1900			1057		1402				1625f	1810	1900	2120	
Lausanne Ouchy ▲ .... d.	1015		1845	1015				1845	0915	0915	1015	1105	1115	1410		1515	1630	1845d		
Morges .... d.										0950		1135		1440						
Rolle .... d.										1040		1217		1521						
Evian-les-Bains ▲ .... d.	1050		1920	1050				1920	0952		1050		1150			1552	1702	1920d		
Thonon-les-Bains .... d.									1028	1115			1150			1625	1734			
Yvoire .... d.				1215	1650						1150		1245		1615	1650	1700			
Nyon .... a.				1235	1710								1305		1552	1710	1720			
Genève Eaux-Vives .... a.													1650							
Genève Pâquis .... a.				1350	1820										1725	1820	1832			
Genève Jardin-Anglais ... a.				1358	1825										1730	1825	1840			
Genève Mont-Blanc .... a.													1405		1700					

E – Daily Sept. 21 - Oct. 31; ⑦ Nov. 6 - Mar. 26.
b – ⑦ and holidays only.
d – Runs daily.
e – Change at Lausanne-Ouchy.
f – Via Evian-les-Bains (calls at 1550).

▲ – Additional sailings operate (September 20 - May 27): **EVIAN-LES-BAINS – LAUSANNE OUCHY** and v.v. Journey: 35 minutes.
  From Evian-les-Bains: 0540Ⓐ, 0700🎿, 1315, 1455, 1630, 1800, 1925, 0015.
  From Lausanne Ouchy: 0455Ⓐ, 0622🎿, 1230, 1415, 1545, 1715, 2045.

Operator: CGN – Compagnie Générale de Navigation, Genève. ☎ Genève (022) 311 25 21 or Lausanne (021) 617 06 66.

Table 255

BERN - BIEL/NEUCHATEL - LE LOCLE

1, 2 class. SBB, BN

km		Ⓐ			A				F													
0	Bern.............................. d.	0523	0605	0615	0654	0700	0715	0754	0822	0854	0922	0954	1022	1054	1122	1154	1222	1254	...	1322	1354	1422	1454	1522
33	Biel............................... a.			0652	0721		0821		0921		1021		1121		1221		1321		...		1421		1521	
33	Biel............................... d.			0737				0937				1137				1337			...				1537	
	Neuchâtel .... a.	0631	0655		0731	0752		0857		0957		1057		1157		1257		1357		1457		1557
	Neuchâtel .... d.		0702			0808	0908		1008		1108		1208		1308		1408		1508		1608	
77	La Chaux de Fonds......... a.	0742		0816		0838	0945	1016	1038		1145	1216	1238		1345	1416		1438		1545	1616	1641
77	La Chaux de Fonds......... d.	0748		0819		0841	0948	1019	1041		1148	1219	1241		1348	1419		1441		1548	1619	1641
84	Le Locle........................ a.	0758		0826		0850	0958	1026	1048		1158	1226	1248		1358	1426		1448		1558	1626	1651

		F			Ⓐ																
Bern.............................. d.	1554	1622	1654	1705	1722	1729	1754	1822	1854	...	1922	1954	2022		2054	2055		2154	...	2154	2254	2350
Biel............................... a.	1621		1721		1756	1821		1921		2021		2121			2221			2321			
Biel............................... d.			1737				1937				2137			2242			2245		0037		
Neuchâtel .... a.	1657		1736	1757		1857		1957		2057		2144			2245		0037		
Neuchâtel .... d.	1708		1808		1908		2008	2108	2108		2210		2322		
La Chaux de Fonds......... a.	1745	1816	1838		1945	2016	2038	2146	2146	2216		2240	2329	2356		
La Chaux de Fonds......... d.	1748	1819	1841		1948	2019	2041		2148	2219	2245		2358		
Le Locle........................ a.	1758	1826	1851		1958	2026	2048		2158	2226	2252		0008		

km		K	ⒶN	Ⓐ				⑦													
0	Le Locle......................... d.				0553b	0622		0700		0811	0833	0902	...	1011	1033	1102	...	1207	1233	1302	...	...
7	La Chaux de Fonds .... a.				0603	0629		0710		0818	0840	0912		1018	1040	1112		1218	1240	1312		
7	La Chaux de Fonds .... d.				0611	0631	0652	0715		0820	0843	0915		1020	1043	1115		1220	1243	1315		
36	Neuchâtel .... a.				0649		0726	0751		0851		0951		1051		1151		1251		1351		
36	Neuchâtel .... d.			0619	0702		0732	0730	0802		0902		1002		1102		1202		1302		1402	
	Biel............................... a.				0713				0923		1123		1323						
	Biel............................... d.	0617		0649	0718	0739		0839		0939		1139		1239		1339		1439	
90	Bern.............................. a.	0644	0702	0718	0742	0745	0806	0816	0816	0838	0906	0938	1006	1038	1106	1138	1206	1238	1306	1338	1406	1438	1506

		F							A									F				
Le Locle......................... d.	1411	1433	1502		1611	1633	1702		1811	1833		1902		2011		2033	2110		2211		2302
La Chaux de Fonds......... a.	1418	1440	1512		1618	1640	1712		1818	1840		1912		2018		2040	2119		2218		2312
La Chaux de Fonds......... d.	1420	1443	1515		1620	1643	1715		1820	1843		1915		2020		2043	2120		2222	2244	2317
Neuchâtel .... a.	1451		1551		1651		1751		1851		1951		2051		2154			2253		2353
Neuchâtel .... d.	1502		1602	1616		1702		1802		1902		1951	2016		2108		2206	2218	2310		
Biel............................... a.		1523			1723			1923				2123			2333	
Biel............................... d.		1539		1639	1739		1839	1939		2039		2139		2242		
Bern.............................. a.	1538	1606	1638	1647	1706	1738	1806	1838	1906	1938	2006	2022	2107	2106		2157	2206	2237	2306	2317	2359	

A – EuroCity TGV Paris - Bern and v.v. (see Table 42). Ⓡ with supplement payable.
  Internal journeys within Switzerland **not** permitted.

K – 🍴 Biel - Bern - Interlaken Ost.
N – Runs Ⓐ only: 🍴 Neuchâtel - Bern - Interlaken Ost.
b – 🎿 only.

F – 🍴 Bern - Frasne and v.v. (connection to/from Paris, see Table 42).

Operator: BN – Bern Neuenburg Bahn, Bern.

Table 260
LAUSANNE - BASEL and ZÜRICH

1, 2 class. SBB

Panel 1

km	Station	1703	1803	1503	1705	907	1507	1607	707	1807	IC 909	1511	1611	711	1811	EN 273	EC 167	2005	1613	513	713	1713	913	1515
		⚟			⚟	R		R	✗		Ⓐ R	R		✗	V	®♦	♦			✗	K	K		⚟ H
	Genève Aéroport + 250 d.													0539		0607s			0625	0638	0648			0721
	Genève 250 d.							0447		0529	0525	0612		0558	0634	0643s		0625	0625	0654	0658			0731
0	Lausanne d.							0507	0507	0529	0612		0634			0643s			0710	0712	0734			0812
	Yverdon d.									0534		0636								0736	0742			0836
	Neuchâtel d.								0601		0636		0701							0801	0806			0901
	Biel a.								0621				0721							0821	0825			0921
	Biel d.			0521				0625	0630				0727	0730						0830	0827			0927
	Moutier d.								0649				0749							0849				
	Delémont d.								0704				0804							0904				
	Basel SBB a.								0737				0837							0937				
41	Romont d.						0559							0718		0727s			0741					
66	Fribourg d.						0618							0718		0727s			0759			0819		
97	Bern a.						0641							0742		0751s	0814		0822			0842		
97	Bern d.	0451	0528		0551	0610	0644	0651	0714					0745	0751	0757s	0814				0845	0851	0914	
119	Burgdorf d.	0509			0609			0709							0809		0825				0909		0927	
144	Langenthal d.	0527		0541	0627		0646	0727					0748		0825						0927			
	Solothurn a.			0541																	0848			0948
164	Olten a.	0539	0609	0607	0639	0653	0713					0739	0813			0839				0913		0939	1013
164	Olten d.	0542	0611	0616	0642	0655	0715					0742	0816			0842				0916		0942	1016
177	Aarau d.	0553	0620	0626	0653		0725				0732	0753	0826			0853				0926		0953	1026
	Lenzburg d.			0633			0733						0833							0933			1033
195	Brugg d.	0607			0707							0807				0907				1007			
204	Baden d.	0615			0715							0815				0915				1015			
226	Zürich Hbf a.	0630		0653	0730	0726	0753		0757			0830	0826			0853	0857	0926		0953	0957	1030	1026	1053
243	Zürich Flughafen + a.		0656	0720	0756		0820				0816	0856				0920	0916	0956	0938		1020	1016	1045	1120
	St Gallen 308 a.								0917							1017			1039			1117		

Panel 2

Station	IC 615	IC 715	1815	1617	517	IC 717	1817	1875	1521	621	721	IC 1821	1623	IC 523	IC 723	1723	1879	1525	625	IC 725	1825	IC 927	1627	IC 527
	⚟	✗	⚟	⚟		✗	⚟	⚟ H				✗ V		⚟ B	✗	⚟	⚟ H	⚟	✗	⚟	✗	⑥♦		⚟ R
Genève Aéroport + 250 d.	0738	0748		0815	0844	0848		0915		0944	0948		1015	1044	1048		1115		1144	1148		1215		1254
Genève 250 d.	0754	0758		0825	0854	0858		0925		0954	0958		1025	1054	1058		1125		1154	1158		1225		1254
Lausanne d.		0834		0912		0934		1010	1012		1034		1112		1134		1210	1212	1234		1312			
Yverdon d.	0842			0936	0942			1036	1042			1136	1142			1236	1242			1336	1342			
Neuchâtel d.	0906		1001	1006			1101	1106			1201	1206			1301	1306			1401	1406				
Biel a.	0925		1021	1025			1121	1125			1221	1225			1321	1325			1421	1425				
Biel d.	0930		1030	1027			1127	1130			1230	1227			1327	1330			1430	1427				
Moutier d.	0949		1049				1149				1249				1349				1449					
Delémont d.	1004		1104				1204				1304				1404				1504					
Basel SBB a.	1037		1137				1237				1337				1437				1537					
Romont d.						1041						1241												
Fribourg d.		0919		1018		1059			1118			1241		1259				1318						
Bern a.		0942		1042		1122			1142			1242		1322				1342						
Bern d.		0945	0951	1045	1051				1145	1151		1245	1251					1345	1351	1414				
Burgdorf d.			1009		1109				1209			1309						1409						
Langenthal d.			1027		1127				1227			1327						1427						
Solothurn a.			1048			1148						1248						1348						1448
Olten a.			1039	1113	1139				1213		1239	1313					1339	1413		1439				1513
Olten d.			1042	1116	1142				1216		1242	1316					1342	1416		1442				1516
Aarau d.			1053	1126	1153				1226		1253	1326					1353	1426		1453				1526
Lenzburg d.				1133					1233			1333						1433						1533
Brugg d.			1107		1207						1307						1407			1507				
Baden d.			1115		1215						1315						1415			1515				
Zürich Hbf a.		1057	1130	1153	1157	1230			1253		1257	1330		1353	1357	1430		1453	1457	1530	1526			1553
Zürich Flughafen + a.		1116	1151	1220	1216	1256			1320		1316	1356		1420	1416	1456		1520		1516	1556			1620
St Gallen 308 a.		1217			1317				1417			1517						1617						2117

Panel 3

Station	IC 727	1727	EC 106	1885	IC 1529	629	IC 729	1729 EC93	IC931 EC93	1633	IC 533	733	1733	935	1891	1537	637	737	1837	IC 939	1893	1639	IC 539	739
	✗		✗		⚟	✗	⚟	⚟			⚟ R	✗		Ⓑ	⚟	⚟ H	✗	✗	⚟	⑥♦	⚟	⚟ B	✗	✗ D
Genève Aéroport + 250 d.	1248		1315			1344	1348			1415	1444	1448			1515		1544	1548			1615		1644	1648
Genève 250 d.	1258		1308	1325		1354	1358			1426	1454	1458			1525		1554	1558			1625		1654	1658
Lausanne d.	1334		1348	1410	1412		1434			1512		1534			1610	1612		1634			1710	1712		1734
Yverdon d.				1436	1442					1542					1636	1642					1736	1742		
Neuchâtel d.			1436		1501	1506				1601	1606				1701	1706					1801	1806		
Biel a.			1455		1521	1525				1621	1625				1721	1725					1821	1825		
Biel d.			1457		1527	1530				1630	1627				1727	1730					1830	1827		
Moutier d.					1549					1649					1749						1849			
Delémont d.			1529		1604					1704					1804						1904			
Basel SBB a.			1601		1637					1737					1837						1937			
Romont d.							1518				1618			1641				1718		1741				1818
Fribourg d.	1418		1459				1542				1618			1659			1718	1742		1759				1842
Bern a.	1442		1522				1542				1642			1722			1742			1822				1845
Bern d.	1445	1451			1545	1551	1614			1645	1651	1714			1745	1751	1814							
Burgdorf d.		1509				1609					1709					1809		1814						
Langenthal d.		1527				1627					1727					1827								
Solothurn a.				1548			1648					1748				1827						1848		
Olten a.		1539		1613		1639	1713			1739		1813				1839						1913		
Olten d.		1542		1616		1642	1716			1742		1816				1842						1916		
Aarau d.		1553		1626		1653	1726			1753		1826				1853						1926		
Lenzburg d.				1633			1733					1833										1933		
Brugg d.		1607				1707					1807					1907								
Baden d.		1615				1715					1815					1915								
Zürich Hbf a.	1557	1630		1653		1657	1730	1726		1753	1757	1830	1826			1853		1857	1930	1926			1953	1957
Zürich Flughafen + a.	1616	1656		1720		1716	1756	1851		1820	1816	1856	1851			1920		1916	1956	1950c			2020	2016
St Gallen 308 a.	1717					1817	1900	1839			1917		1956					2017		2056c				2117

Notes

NOTES (LISTED BY TRAIN NUMBER)

C106 – MONT BLANC – 🚃 and ✗ Genève - Basel - Köln - Dortmund.
C167 – ALBERT EINSTEIN – 🚃 and ✗ Interlaken Ost - München - Praha.
N273 – PABLO CASALS – Spanish Talgo train for International passengers only – For days of running see Table 81. Special fares payable.
927 – Runs ⑥ Jan. 7 - Mar. 25 only; 🚃 Brig - Bern - Zürich.
939 – Runs ⑦; conveys on ⑦ Sept. 25 - Oct. 16 and Dec. 18 - Mar. 26: 🚃 Brig (train 1839) - Bern - St Gallen.
675 – 🚃 Genève Aéroport - Bern - Luzern (train 1675) - Chiasso.
691 – 🚃 Genève Aéroport - Luzern; Conveys on ⑤, also Apr. 13, May 24, not Apr. 14, May 26: 🚃 Genève Aéroport - Luzern (train IC691) - Chiasso.

B – 🚃 Brig - Lausanne - Biel - Basel.
C – 🚃 Interlaken Ost - Bern - St Gallen - Chur.
D – 🚃 Genève Aéroport - St Gallen - Rorschach.
H – 🚃 Brig - Lausanne - Zürich - Winterthur - Romanshorn.
L – From Interlaken Ost (Table 280).
R – To Romanshorn (Table 305).
V – 🚃 Brig - Bern - Zürich Flughafen.
c – ⑦ Sept. 25 - Oct. 16 and Dec. 18 - Mar. 26 only.
s – Stops to set down only.

Ⓑ – Daily except Saturdays   ♦ – See Footnote   🚃 – Through carriage (1 and 2 class)

Table 260 — LAUSANNE - BASEL and ZÜRICH

1, 2 class. SBB

Table 260 (1)

		IC				IC				IC	IC			IC					IC		IC					1649 IC		
	1739	941	2037	1541	641	741	1741	2043	1643	543	743	1843	1545	645	745	1745	2045	1647	1547	747	1747	4899	1649	1749	1549
	K	V	Ⓐ	H	🍴	🍴	D	K		B	R	D	V	🍴	🍴			♦							
Genève Aéroport ✈ 250 ... d.			1713	1713	1744	1748		1815		1844	1848		1915	1944	1947		2015			2048		2115	2148	2215	
Genève 250 ... d.			1722	1722	1754	1758		1825		1854	1858		1925	1954	1958		2025			2058		2125	2158	2225	
Lausanne ... d.			1810	1812		1834		1910	1912		1934		2012		2034		2110	2121		2134		2212	2234	2312	
Yverdon ... d.				1836	1842			1936	1942				2036	2042				2145				2236		2337	
Neuchâtel ... d.				1901	1906			2001	2006				2101	2106				2209				2301		0001	
Biel ... a.				1921	1925			2021	2025				2121	2125				2228				2321		0023	
Biel ... d.				1927	1930			2030	2027				2127	2130				2230	2235			2340			
Moutier ... d.				1949				2049					2149					2249				0004			
Delémont ... d.				2004				2104					2204					2304				0018			
Basel SBB ... a.				2037				2137					2237					2337							
Romont ... d.			1840				1941					2018						2141	2159		2218			2320	1849
Fribourg ... d.					1918		1959				2018		2042					2142	2222		2242			2320	2344
Bern ... a.					1942						2042							2142			2242			2344	
Bern ... d.	1851	1914			1945	1951					2045	2051			2145	2148			2245	2251		2309		2350	
Burgdorf ... d.	1909					2009					2109								2309			2327		0008	0025
Langenthal ... d.	1927					2027					2127														
Solothurn ... d.				1948				2048					2148					2256						0036	
Olten ... a.	1939		2013			2039				2113	2139	2213				2230		2321	2327	2339				0036	
Olten ... d.	1942		2016			2042				2116	2142	2216			2243			2329						0037	0046
Aarau ... d.	1953		2026			2053				2126	2153	2226			2253			2338						0046	
Lenzburg ... d.			2033								2133														0053
Brugg ... d.	2007					2107					2207				2307										
Baden ... d.	2015					2115					2215				2315									0111	
Zürich Hbf ... a.	2030	2026	2053		2057	2130			2153	2157	2230	2253			2257			2303			0006				
Zürich Flughafen ✈ ... a.	2056		2120		2116				2220	2216					2325	2348					0032				
St Gallen 308 ... a.			2217						2323						0032										

Table 260 (2)

km			IC				IC	IC				IC				IC		IC	IC		IC		IC
	1502	1702	504	1604	1704	1704	706	506	2513	1606	1706	708	608	1508	1856	910	1812	712	512	1612	914	1716	716
	X	🍴	🍴	Y	X	⑦	🍴	🍴	X	♦	K	H	L	R🍴	V		D	🍴	R	🍴	Ⓐc	K	D
St Gallen 308 ... d.												0541					0641				0711		
0 — Zürich Flughafen ✈ ... d.												0642		0637		0708		0742	0739		0813	0805	0842
Zürich Hbf ... d.			0445				0600	0606			0625	0703	0706			0733	0730	0803	0806		0833	0830	0903
Baden ... d.			0502									0641				0745					0845		
Brugg ... d.			0511									0650				0754					0854		
37 — Lenzburg ... d.				0527				0625				0704		0725		0808		0825			0908		
Aarau ... d.				0537			0624	0633	0644			0713		0735		0817		0844			0917		
62 — Olten ... a.				0546	0546		0634	0647	0654			0715		0744		0820		0847			0920		
62 — Olten ... d.							0600							0747									
97 — Solothurn ... d.									0713								0813				0932		
Langenthal ... d.					0600	0600					0706	0728				0832					0932		
Burgdorf ... d.					0618	0618					0724	0749				0850					0950		
Bern ... a.					0635	0635	0715			0706	0742	0809	0815			0909	0915				0945	1009	1015
Bern ... d.		0610			0638		0718					0818		0838		0901		0918					1018
Fribourg ... d.		0634			0701		0741					0841				0901		0941					1041
Romont ... d.		0654			0719							0919											
Basel SBB ... d.										0623			0723					0823					
Delémont ... d.				0558b						0701			0801					0901					
Moutier ... d.				0609b						0712			0812					0912					
123 — Biel ... a.				0627b					0733	0730			0830	0833				0933	0930				
123 — Biel ... d.	0539		0635	0639					0735	0739			0835	0839				0935	0939				
152 — Neuchâtel ... d.	0601		0655	0701					0755	0801			0855	0901				0955	1001				
188 — Yverdon ... d.	0624		0718	0724					0818	0824			0918	0924				1018	1024				
227 — Lausanne ... a.	0647	0726		0748	0750		0826		0848		0926		0948	0950				1026		1048			1126
Genève 250 ... a.	0742	0802	0806		0834		0902	0906		0934		1002	1006		1034			1102	1106	1134			1202
Genève Aéroport ✈ 250 ... a.		0813	0816		0844		0913	0916		0944		1013	1016		1044			1113	1116	1144			

Table 260 (3)

					IC	IC		IC	IC	IC	IC			EC	IC	IC		IC	IC	IC		IC		
	616	1516	1860	1818	718	518	1618	1720	720	620	1520	1866	1822	107	722	522	1622	924	1726	726	626	1526	1870	1728
	X	🍴	🍴	X	D	X	B	K	X	🍴	🍴	🍴	V	♦	X	R	🍴	X	K	K	X	🍴	L	D
St Gallen 308 ... d.					0841				0941					1041					1141					
Zürich Flughafen ✈ ... d.		0839		0905	0942	0939		1005	1042	1039			1105	1142	1139			1205	1242			1239		1305
Zürich Hbf ... d.		0906		0930	1003	1006		1030	1103	1106			1130	1203	1206		1233	1230	1303		1306		1330
Baden ... d.					0945			1045						1245					1345					
Brugg ... d.					0954			1054						1254					1354					
Lenzburg ... d.		0925		1008					1025				1125	1208			1225		1308			1335		1408
Aarau ... d.		0935		1008				1035	1108				1135	1208			1235		1308			1335		1408
Olten ... a.		0944		1017	1044			1117	1144				1217	1244			1247		1317			1344		1412
Olten ... d.		0947		1020	1047			1120	1147				1220	1247					1320			1347		1420
Solothurn ... d.		1013			1113								1213					1313				1413		
Langenthal ... d.				1032				1132					1232											
Burgdorf ... d.				1050				1150					1250					1309						
Bern ... a.			1109	1115				1209			1215		1309	1315			1345	1409	1415			1438		
Bern ... d.		1038		1118						1218			1301	1318				1441			1501		
Fribourg ... d.		1101		1141						1241			1319	1341								1519		
Romont ... d.		1119																					
Basel SBB ... d.	0923							1023			1123			1159			1223			1323			
Delémont ... d.	1001							1101			1201			1239			1301			1401			
Moutier ... d.	1012							1112			1212						1312			1412			
Biel ... a.	1030	1033					1133	1130		1230	1230		1304	1333	1330			1430	1433			
Biel ... d.	1035	1039					1135	1139		1235	1239		1306	1335	1339			1435	1439			
Neuchâtel ... d.	1055	1101					1155	1201		1255	1301		1326	1355	1401			1455	1501			
Yverdon ... d.	1118	1124					1218	1224		1318	1324			1418	1424			1518	1524			
Lausanne ... a.			1148	1150		1226		1248		1326		1348	1350	1412	1426		1448			1526	1606	1634
Genève 250 ... a.		1206	1234		1302	1306	1334		1402	1406	1434		1455	1502	1506	1534		1602	1606		1634
Genève Aéroport ✈ 250 ... a.		1224	1244		1313	1316	1344		1413	1418	1444		1513	1516	1544		1613	1616		1644

♦ — NOTES (LISTED BY TRAIN NUMBER)

EC107 — MONT BLANC – 🚐 and 🍴 Dortmund - Köln - Basel - Genève.
IC708 — 🚐 and 🍴 (Rorschach Ⓐ -) St Gallen - Genève Aéroport.
1606 — 🚐 Basel - Lausanne - Brig; conveys 🛏 1, 2 cl. (on ⑤ Dec. 23 - Apr. 7 from Oostende) and 🛏 2 cl. (on ⑥ Dec. 17 - Apr. 15 from Oostende (train 499).
1647 — 🚐 Brig - Lausanne - Basel; conveys 🛏 1, 2 cl. (on ⑥ Dec. 31 - Apr. 15) and 🛏 2 cl. (on ⑦ Dec. 18 - Apr. 16) Brig - Basel (train 498) - Oostende.
B — 🚐 Brig - Lausanne - Basel and v.v.
D — 🚐 Genève Aéroport - St Gallen - Rorschach and v.v.
H — 🚐 Brig - Lausanne - Zürich - Winterthur - Romanshorn and v.v.

K – From/to Interlaken Ost (Table 280).
L – 🚐 Luzern - Bern - Genève Aéroport.
R – To/from Romanshorn (Table 305).
V – 🚐 Brig - Bern - Zürich/Zürich Flughafen and v.v.
Y – (Delémont 🍴 -) Biel - Lausanne - Brig.
b – 🍴 only.
c – Also runs ⑥ Oct. 1 - 15 and Jan. 28 - Mar. 25, also Apr. 14: 🚐 St Gallen - Zürich - Bern - Interlaken Ost.

Table 260 — ZÜRICH and BASEL - LAUSANNE

1, 2 class. SBB

	IC 728 ✗R	IC 528 ✗R	1628 B	1730 K	IC 730 ⚑	IC 630 ✗	1530 ◆	1876 ◆	1832	IC 732 ✗	IC 532 ✗R	1632 B	IC 934	IC 1736 K	IC 736	636	1536 H	1880 L	IC 936 Ⓐ	1838 V	IC 738 ✗	IC 538 ✗R	1638	EC 166 ◆
St Gallen 308 ... d	1241	...	...	...	1341	...	...	...	...	1441	...	...	*1520*	...	1541	...	...	...	*1611*	...	1641	...	...	1720
Zürich Flughafen + d	1342	1339	...	1405	1442	...	1439	...	...	1505	1542	1539	...	1605	1642	...	1639	...	*1713*	1705	1742	1739	...	...
Zürich Hbf ... d	1403	1406	...	1430	1503	...	1506	...	1530	1603	1606	...	1633	1630	1703	...	1706	...	1733	...	1803	1806	...	1833
Baden ... d				1445					1545						1645						1745			
Brugg ... d				1454					1554						1654						1754			
Lenzburg ... d		1425					1525				1625								1725			1825		
Aarau ... d		1435		1508			1535			1608	1635			1708					1735		1808	1835		
Olten ... a		1444		1517			1544			1617	1644			1717					1744		1817	1844		
Olten ... d		1447		1520			1547			1620	1647			1720					1747		1820	1847		
Solothurn ... d		1513					1613				1713								1813			1913		
Langenthal ... d				1532						1632				1732					1832					
Burgdorf ... d				1550						1650				1750					1850					
Bern ... a	1515			1609	1615					1709	1715			1745	1809	1815			1845	1909	1915			1945
Bern ... d	1518				1618			1638		1718				1818			1838		1918					
Fribourg ... d	1541				1641			1701	1741				1841			1901		1941						
Romont ... d								1719								1919								
Basel SBB ... d		1423			1523					1623			1723				1823							
Delémont ... d		1501			1601					1701			1801				1901							
Moutier ... d		1512			1612					1712			1812				1912							
Biel ... a		1533	1530			1630	1633			1733	1730			1830	1833			1933	1930					
Biel ... d		1535	1539			1635	1639			1735	1739			1835	1839			1935	1939					
Neuchâtel ... d		1555	1601			1655	1701			1755	1801			1855	1901			1955	2001					
Yverdon ... d		1618	1624			1718	1724			1818	1824			1918	1924			2018	2024					
Lausanne ... a	1626		1648		1726		1748	1750		1826		1848		1926		1948	1950		2026		2048			
Genève 250 ... a	1702	1706	*1734*		1802	1806		1834		1902	1906	*1934*		2002	2006		2034		2102	2106	2134			
Genève Aéroport + 250 ... a	1713	1716	*1744*		1814	1817		1844		1914	1917	*1944*		2013	2016		2044		2112	2116	2144			

	IC 1740 C	IC 740 ✗R	1640	1540 ✗R	1886 ◆	EN 274 ®◆	1742 ⚑	IC 742 ✗	IC 690 ⑦	1542 R	1744 ✗	744 R	1644	1544	1844	2549	IC 746 L	1898	1646 R	1546	1746 ⚑	1500	1848
St Gallen 308 ... d	1701	1741	...	...	...	...	1841	...	...	1941	...	...	...	...	2041	...	...	...	2101	2141	...	...	2241
Zürich Flughafen + d	1809	1842	...	1839	...	*1905*	1905	1942	...	1939	2005	2042	...	2039	2105	...	2142	...	2139	2212	2242	...	2341
Zürich Hbf ... d	1830	1903	...	1906	...	1933	1930	2003	...	2006	2030	2103	...	2106	2130	...	2203	...	2206	2230	2303	...	0003
Baden ... d	1845						1945			2045			2145				2245						
Brugg ... d	1854						1954			2054			2154				2254						
Lenzburg ... d				1925						2025				2125				2225		2322			0022
Aarau ... d	1908	1935		1935			2008			2035	2108			2135	2208			2235	2308	2330			0038
Olten ... a	1917	1944		1944			2017			2044	2117			2144	2217			2244	2317	2338			0038
Olten ... d	1920			1947			2020			2047	2120			2147	2224			2247		2339	2347		0039
Solothurn ... d				2013						2113				2213				2313				0013	
Langenthal ... d	1932						2032			2132				2236						2350			0050
Burgdorf ... d	1950						2050			2150				2254						0008			0108
Bern ... a	2009	2015				2045u	2109	2115		2209	2215			2312	2315					0025			0125
Bern ... d		2018			2038	2048u	2132	2132		2221						2326							
Fribourg ... d		2041			2101	2111u	2141	2154		*1642*	2245					2349							
Romont ... d					2119											0007							
Basel SBB ... d			1923							2023	2123						2223						
Delémont ... d			2001							2101	2201						2301						
Moutier ... d			2012							2112	2212						2312						
Biel ... a			2030	2033						2133	2130			2230	2233			2330	2333			0033	
Biel ... d				2039							2139				2239				*2342*				
Neuchâtel ... d				2101							2201				2301				*0013*				
Yverdon ... d				2124							2224				2324								
Lausanne ... a		2126		2148	2150	2156u		2226	2239		2248	2331			2348			0038					
Genève 250 ... a		2202		2237	2237	2231u		2302	2315		2337	0009			0034			0120					
Genève Aéroport + 250 ... a		2213		2247	2247			2312															

♦ – NOTES (LISTED BY TRAIN NUMBER)

EC166 – ALBERT EINSTEIN – 🍴 and ✗ Praha - München - Bern.
EN274 – PABLO CASALS – Spanish Talgo train for International passengers only – For days of running see Table 81. Special fares payable.
IC690 – Runs ⑦ only, not Dec. 25, Jan. 1, Apr. 14, 16, May 25.
1530 – 🍴 Romanshorn - Lausanne - Brig (train 4943) - Domodossola.
1876 – 🍴 Chiasso (train 1676) - Luzern - Bern - Genève Aéroport.
1886 – 🍴 Luzern - Bern - Lausanne; Conveys on Ⓐ: 🍴 Zürich (train 1985) - Luzern - Lausanne.

B – 🍴 Basel - Lausanne - Brig.
C – 🍴 Chur - St Gallen - Bern.
H – 🍴 Romanshorn - Winterthur - Zürich - Lausanne - Brig.
K – 🍴 Zürich Flughafen - Bern - Interlaken Ost.
L – From Luzern (Table 265).
R – From Romanshorn (Table 305).
V – 🍴 Zürich Flughafen - Bern - Brig.
u – Stops to **pick up** only.

Table 265 — BERN - LUZERN

1, 2 class. SBB

km		1803	1863	852	1865	IC314	1869	EC108	1875	IC820	1879	EC90	1885	1889	1733	1891	1893	1739	1895	6277	1843	1899	6285	IC747	6295
	Genève Aéroport + d	...	...	...	...	0915	...	1115	...	1315	...	...	1515	1615	...	...	...	...	...	...	...	...	...	2048	...
	Genève 250 ... d	...	...	...	...	0925	...	1125	...	1325	...	...	1525	1625	...	...	...	...	...	...	...	...	...	2058	...
	Lausanne 250 ... d	...	...	...	...	1010	...	1210	...	1410	...	...	1610	1710	...	...	...	...	...	...	...	...	...	2134	...
0	Bern ... d	0528	0629	0648	0731	0848	0931	1048	1131	1248	1331	1448	1531	1631	1651	1731	1831	1851	1931	1951	2051	2148	2221	2245	2323
37	Langnau ... d	...	0700	...	0800	...	1000	...	1200	...	1400	...	1600	1700	...	1800	1900	...	2000	2032	...	2215	2259		0004
	Olten ... a	0609	...	0730	...	0930	...	1130	...	1330	...	1530	...	...	1739	...	...	1939	...	2139	...	...	2327	...	
		1661		**IC251**		**IC255**		**EC53**		**EC5**		**EC9**			**IC257**			**301**		**5187**			**2699**		
		🍴		🍴		✗		C🍴		🍴		✗			🍴			🍴		🍴			🍴		
	Olten ... d	0632	...	0735	...	0935	...	1135	...	1335	...	1535	...	...	1749	...	...	1949	...	2149	...	...	2336	...	
95	Luzern ... a	0712	0746	0812	0846	1012	1046	1212	1246	1412	1446	1612	1646	1746	1827	1846	1946	2027	2046	2141	2252	2259	2357	0016	

		2654	1854	2656	1856	2658	1858	660	1860	1660	1866	250	1870	EC8	1876	EC4	1880	EC52	1882	1886	IC252	IC690	1890	1898	256	6292
	Luzern ... d	0531	0608	0635c	0713	0756	0813	0846	0913	0956	1113	1156	1313	1346	1513	1546	1714	1746	1813	1913	1946	2013	2101	2201	2246	2317
	Olten ... d	0611	...	0715c	...	0837	...	0925	...	1037	...	1237	...	1425	...	1625	...	1825	...	2025	...	...	...	2325	0014	
			499		**IC811**		**2515**		**IC819**		**2521**		**2525**		**EC91**		**EC105**		**EC109**		**IC313**			**1846**	**1848**	
	Olten ... d	0623	...	0729	...	0848	...	0929	...	1048	...	1248	...	1429	...	1629	...	1829	...	2029	...	...	...	2339	0039	
	Langnau ... d	0701	...	0801	...	0901	...	1001	...	1201	...	1401	...	1601	...	1801	...	1901	2001	...	2148	2252	...			
	Bern ... a	0712	0729	0812	0829	0936	0929	1012	1029	1136	1229	1336	1429	1512	1629	1712	1829	1912	1929	2029	2112	2129	2215	2320	0025	0125
	Lausanne 250 ... a	...	0950	...	1150	...	1350	...	1550	...	1750	...	1950	...	2150	...	2239	0038								
	Genève 250 ... a	...	1034	...	1234	...	1434	...	1634	...	1834	...	2034	...	2315	...	0120									
	Genève Aéroport + a	...	1044	...	1244	...	1444	...	1644	...	1844	...	2044													

B – Runs daily; conveys on dates in Table 290: 🍴 to Chiasso (train IC691).
C – 🍴 Genève Aéroport - Bern - Luzern (trains 1675/6) - Chiasso and v.v.
? – Runs daily; Conveys on Ⓐ: 🍴 Zürich (train 1985) - Luzern - Lausanne.

Z – Runs daily; Conveys on ©: 🍴 Zürich Flughafen (train 1981) - Luzern - Bern.
c – On Ⓐ depart Luzern 0646, arrive Olten 0725 (train IC650).
d – Runs ⑦, not Dec. 25, Jan. 1, Apr. 14, 16, May 25: 🍴 Chiasso - Luzern - Genève.

Table 266 — BERN - SOLOTHURN

1, 2 class except where shown. Narrow gauge. RBS

Rail service. 33km. Journey time: 37-45 minutes. **Operator:** RBS – Regionalbahn Bern Solothurn.

From Bern RBS: 0614⑧, 0644✗, 0714, 0746, 0816, 0846, 0916, 0946, 1016, 1046, 1116, 1146, 1216, 1246, 1316, 1346, 1416, 1446, 1516, 1546, 1616, 1646, 1716, 1746, 1816, 1846, 1916, 1946, 2022, 2048⑦, 2122, 2222, 2322, 2352✗b.

From Solothurn: 0555✗, 0628Ⓐ, 0631, 0658Ⓐ, 0701, 0731, 0801, 0831, 0901, 0931, 1001, 1031, 1101, 1131, 1201, 1231, 1301, 1331, 1401, 1431, 1501, 1531, 1601, 1631, 1701, 1731, 1801, 1831, 1901, 1931, 2017, 2117, 2217, 2317.

b – 2 class only.

Table 267 — MARTIGNY - LE CHÂBLE - VERBIER

MO, 🚌 PTT

	✗n	✗n	✗			Ⓑ🆁					Ⓑ🆁					Ⓓ🆁			
Martigny .... d.	...	...	0714	0755	...	0858	1010	1055	1055	1155	...	1255	1355	1530	1536	1636	1736	...	1836	1955	2055
Le Châble .... d.	...	...	0741	0823	...	0927	1038		1124	1224	...	1324	1424		1604	1704	1804	...	1904	2020	2114p
Le Châble (by 🚌) ▲ d.	0655	0730	...	0830	...	0930		1130	1230	...	1330	1435		1610	1710	1810	...	1910	2114p
Verbier (by 🚌) ...... ▲ d.	0720	0755	...	0855	...	0955	...	1140	1155	1255	...	1355	1500	1615	1635	1735	1835	...	1935	2140

	✗	✗n		✗	✗n		Ⓑ🚌					Ⓑ🆁					Ⓓ🆁			
Verbier (by 🚌) ...... ▲ d.	...	0620	...	0720	0820	...	0915	0900	...	1100	...	1205	1300	1400	1430	1550	1650	1745	...	1845	1915
Le Châble (by 🚌) ▲ d.	...	0645	...	0745	0845	...		0925	...	1125	...	1230	1325	1425		1615	1715	1810	...	1910	1926p
Le Châble .... d.	0553	...	0651	0801	...	0853		0937	1049	1135	...	1249	1336	1436		1630	1730	1815	...	1915	1926p
Martigny .... a.	0620	...	0722	0829	...	0921	1000	1003	1118	1203	...	1318	1403	1503	1515	1658	1758	1844	...	1944	2000

B – Runs ⑥ Dec. 24 - Apr. 22. Supplement (SFr 5,-) applies.
D – Runs ⑤⑥ Dec. 23 - Apr. 22. Supplement (SFr 5,-) applies.
▲ – An alternative service by cable car (🚠) operates Nov. 4 - Apr. 23: Le Châble - Verbier and v.v. Journey time 15 minutes. **Operator:** TV, Verbier.
Departures from Le Châble and Verbier: 0845, 0945, 1045, 1145, 1245E, 1345, 1445, 1545, 1645, 1745E, 1845E, 2015E.
E – Dec. 10 - Apr. 23. **p –** Le Châble **Poste**.
Operator: MO – Martigny Orsières, Martigny. For reservations: ☎ MO Martigny (026) 31 10 45.

Table 268 — MARTIGNY - CHAMONIX - ST. GERVAIS

Narrow gauge rack railway. MC, SNCF

km		12 Ⓐ	12 W	12 Ⓐ	2	2 U	2 X	12	2 N	2 W		12	2 X	2 U		12 Ⓒ		2		12		12 X	12 Q
0	**Martigny** .... d.	...	...	...	0702	0809	0859	...	1009	1057	...	1146	1330	...	1438	...	...	1547	...	1638	...	1809	1939
10	Salvan .... d.	...	...	...	0722	0829	0919	...	1029	1117	...	1206	1350	...	1458	...	...	1607	...	1658	...	1829	1957
11	Les Marécottes .... d.	...	...	...	0727	0834	0924	...	1033	1122	...	1211	1355	...	1503	...	...	1612	...	1703	...	1834	2002
20	Le Châtelard-Giétroz ... d.	...	...	...	0748	0855	0945	...	1055	1143	...	1232	1416	...	1524	...	...	1633	...	1724	...	1855	2023x
21	Le Châtelard-Frontière 🚩 a.	...	...	...	0751	0858	0948	...	1058	1146	...	1235	1419	...	1527	...	...	1636	...	1727	...	1858	2026x
						12							12										
21	Le Châtelard-Frontière ..... d.	...	...	...	0911	...	0959	1107	...	1214	1240	...	1428	1532	...	1641	...	1732	...	1900		
24	Vallorcine .... a.	...	...	...	0917	...	1005	1113	...	1220	1246	...	1434	1538	...	1647	...	1738	...	1906		
													12								12		
24	Vallorcine .... d.	...	0714		0917	...	1005	1113	...	1220	1300	...	1434	...	1548	...	1659	...	1743	1913	...	1950v
31	Argentière .... d.	0639	0729	0757	0934	...	1020	1128	...	1235	1315	...	1449	...	1603	...	1716	...	1759	1930	...	2005v
35	Les Tines .... d.	0648	0740	0808	0943	...	1029	1140	...	1244	1324	...	1458	...	1614	...	1725	...	1808	1939	...	2014v
39	**Chamonix** .... a.	0655	0747	0815	0950	...	1036	1147	...	1251	1331	...	1505	...	1621	...	1732	...	1815	1946	...	2021v
39	**Chamonix** .... d.	0658	0750	0824	1000	...	1039	1211	...	1304	1339	...	1510	...	1626	...	1735	...	1826	1955	...	2025	2150
59	**St. Gervais** .... a.	0739	0831	0905	1039	...	...	1118	1250	...	1345	1418	...	1549	...	1707	...	1814	...	1907	2034	...	2104	2229

	2	12 L	12 M	12 X	2 U	12		12	2	12	12 W	2 X	12 U	12 Ⓒ		2		12		2		12 Q
St. Gervais .... d.	...	0652	0711	0744	0837	...	0910	...	1125	...	1258	1350	1425	...	1520	...	1620	...	1727	...	1820	1912	2109	2250
Chamonix .... a.	...	0728	0749	0820	0913	...	0954	...	1201	...	1335	1428	1501	...	1559	...	1656	...	1805	...	1856	1948	2145	2326
Chamonix .... d.	...	0732	0800	...	0917	...	1003	...	1218	...	1340	1432	1506	...	1606	...	1659	...	1816	...	1901	...	...	
Les Tines .... d.	...	0739	0807	...	0924	...	1010	...	1225	...	1347	1439	1513	...	1613	...	1706	...	1823	...	1908	...	...	
Argentière .... d.	...	0748	0816	...	0933	...	1021	...	1236	...	1356	1450	1522	...	1622	...	1717	...	1832	...	1917	...	...	
Vallorcine .... a.	...	▬	0831	...	0948	...	1036	...	1251	...	1412	1505	1538	...	1637	...	1732	...	1847	...	1932	...	...	
Vallorcine .... d.	...		0831	...	0948	...	1036	...	...	1310	1412	...	...	1547	...	1654	...	1749	...	1916	...		
Le Châtelard-Frontière ..... a.	...		0837	...	0954	...	1042	...	...	1316	1418	...	...	1553	...	1700	...	1755	...	1922	...		
		2Ⓐ	2				2	2N		2												
Le Châtelard-Frontière 🚩 d.	0653	0759	0909	...	0959	1108	1213	...	1321	1429	...	1558	...	1705	...	1800	...	1927	...		
Le Châtelard-Giétroz .... d.	0656	0802	0912	...	1002	1111	1216	...	1324	1432	...	1601	...	1708	...	1803	...	1930	...		
Les Marécottes .... d.	0717	0823	0933	...	1023	1133	1237	...	1345	1453	...	1623	...	1729	...	1824	...	1951	...		
Salvan .... d.	0722	0828	0938	...	1029	1137	1242	...	1350	1458	...	1628	...	1734	...	1830	...	1957	...		
Martigny .... a.	0744	0850	1000	...	1051	1159	1304	...	1412	1520	...	1652	...	1756	...	1852	...	2019	...		

L – ⑥⑦ Dec. 17 - Apr. 23.
M – ①, also Jan. 4, May 2, 9, **not** Oct. 31, Dec. 26, Jan. 2, Feb. 13, 20, Apr. 10, 17, May 1, 8.
N – Daily Dec. 17 - Apr. 17, also Ⓐ Sept. 26 - Dec. 16 and Apr. 18 - May 26.
Q – ⑤⑥⑦, also Oct. 31, Nov. 10, May 24.
U – Dec. 17 - Apr. 17.
W – Ⓒ Dec. 17 - Apr. 23.
X – Dec. 17 - Apr. 23.
v – Not ⑤⑥.
x – Will only run beyond **Les Marécottes** on request.

Table 269 — 🚌 MARTIGNY - AOSTA

Winter Service valid: October 10 - May 27

🚌 MO, SAVDA

		A			A					A				A	R
Martigny Gare .... d.	...	0755	...	...	1630		Aosta Place Narbonne .... d.	...	...	0900	...	...	1625	...
Orsières Gare .... d.	...	0825	...	...	1700		Le Grand St Bernard .... d.	...	...		...	...	1730	...
Bourg St. Bernard 🚩 .... d.	...	0900	...	...	1735		Bourg St Bernard 🚩 .... d.	...	...	1005	...	...	1803	1815
Le Grand St. Bernard .... d.	...		...	...			Orsières Gare .... d.	...	...	1038	...	...		...
Aosta Place Narbonne ...... a.	...	1000	...	...	1835		Martigny Gare .... a.	...	...	1110	...	...		1844

A – Daily. Service operates via St Bernard Tunnel.
R – Rail service (MO).
Operators: MO – Martigny Orsières, Martigny; SAVDA – SAVDA, Aosta.

E2006

Will the times be the same in the next edition?

They may be, but many of the services in this timetable are likely to change frequently, and without advance notice.

For details of subscription rates, see the order form at the back of this book.

Table 270
LAUSANNE - MONTREUX - BRIG
1, 2 class. SBB

km		2109	2111	2111	1913	1604	IC 321	1915	EC 39	1606	1917	1508	1921	IC 323	1923	1516	1925	1618
		♦	Ⓐ	Ⓒ	🍴	♦	🍴	🍴	✕	🍴	🍴	🍴R	🍴	✕	🍴	🍴R	🍴	🍴B
	Genève Aéroport + 250 ... d.	...	...	...	...	0638	0721	0738	0808	...	0838	...	0938	1024	1038	...	1138	...
	Genève 250 ... d.	...	...	...	...	0648	0731	0748	0820	...	0848	...	0948	1034	1048	...	1148	...
0	Lausanne ... d.	0637	0656	0656	0732	0756	0809	0832	0857	0900	0932	0956	1032	1113	1132	1156	1232	1256
18	Vevey ... d.	0651	0710	0710	0746	0810		0846		0914	0946	1010	1046		1146	1210	1246	1310
25	Montreux ... d.	0657	0717	0717	0753	0817		0853		0921	0953	1017	1053		1153	1217	1253	1317
39	Aigle ... d.	0707	0727	0727	0803	0827		0903		0931	1003	1027	1103		1203	1227	1303	1327
48	Bex ... d.		0733	0733	0809	0839		0909		0937	1009	1033	1109		1209	1233	1309	1333
52	St. Maurice ... d.		0738	0738	0814	0844		0914		0941	1014	1038	1114		1214	1238	1314	1338
67	Martigny ... d.	0726	0749	0749	0825	0855		0925		0952	1025	1049	1125		1225	1249	1325	1349
92	Sion ... d.	0744	0806	0806	0843	0910	0904	0942	0951	1010	1043	1106	1143	1208	1243	1306	1343	1406
108	Sierre ... d.	0756	0816	0816	0855	0920		0952		1020	1055	1116	1155		1255	1316	1355	1416
117	Leuk ... d.		0823	0826	0904	0929		1000		1029	1104	1126	1204		1304	1326	1404	1426
137	Visp 320 ... d.		0835	0845	0916	0946		1011		1046	1116	1145	1216		1316	1345	1416	1445
146	Brig 320 ... a.	0817	0842	0852	0923	0953	0932	1018	1022	1053	1123	1152	1223	1236	1323	1352	1423	1452

	327	1520	1929	1933	1526	IC 335	1937	1628	1939	1530	1941	1632	1943	329	1536	1945	311	EN 311	2147	1947	221
	♦	🍴R		🍴R	♦	🍴	🍴	🍴B	🍴D	🍴	🍴B	🍴	🍴	🍴R	🍴				♦		♦
Genève Aéroport + 250 ... d.	1238	...	1338	1438	...	1525	1538	...	1638	...	1738	...	1838	1906	...	1938	2015	2015	...	2138	2252
Genève 250 ... d.	1248	...	1348	1448	...	1535	1548	...	1648	...	1748	...	1848	1916	...	1948	2025	2025u	...	2148	2302
Lausanne ... d.	1332	1356	1432	1532	1556	1613	1632	1656	1732	1756	1832	1856	1932	1953	1956	2032	2110	2110u	2202	2232	2345
Vevey ... d.	1346	1410	1446	1546	1610		1646	1710	1746	1810	1846	1910	1946		2010	2046	2124	2124u	2216	2246	2359
Montreux ... d.	1353	1417	1453	1553	1617		1653	1717	1753	1817	1853	1917	1953		2018	2053	2131	2131u	2223	2253	0006
Aigle ... d.	1403	...	1503	1603	1627		1703	1727	1803	1827	1903	1927	2003		2028	2103	2141	2141u	2233	2303	0016
Bex ... d.		1433	1509	1609	1633		1709	1733	1809	1833	1909	1933	2009		2034	2109			2239	2309	
St. Maurice ... d.		1438	1514	1614	1638		1714	1738	1814	1838	1914	1938	2014		2038	2114			2244	2314	
Martigny ... d.	1421	1449	1525	1625	1649		1725	1749	1825	1849	1925	1949	2025		2049	2125	2159	2159u	2255	2325	0034
Sion ... d.	1438	1506	1543	1643	1711	1708	1743	1806	1843	1906	1943	2006	2051	2048	2106	2143	2159	2216u	2312	2343	0052
Sierre ... d.	1449	1516	1555	1655	1722		1755	1816	1855	1916	1954	2016	2103		2116	2155	2227	2227u	2322	2353	0103
Leuk ... d.		1526	1604	1704	1731		1804	1826	1904	1926	2002	2026	2110		2126	2204			2331	0002	
Visp 320 ... d.		1545	1616	1716	1748		1816	1845	1916	1945	2014	2045	2122		2145	2221			2348	0019	
Brig 320 ... a.	1512	1552	1623	1723	1755	1736	1823	1852	1923	1952	2021	2052	2129	2116	2152	2228	2250	2250u	2355	0026	0127

	220	3106 / 1900	1900	M23092 / 1902	1904	1515	EN 1906	1617	1908	1521	312	1623	320	1525	1918	IC 330	1920	1529	1922
	♦	Ⓒ	Ⓐ			🍴R		🍴B	♦	🍴R	🍴B	🍴R	🍴	🍴R	🍴				
Brig 320 ... d.	...	0415	...	0431h	0525	0605	0648s	0707	0736	0807	0848	0907	0948	1007	1036	1116	1133	1207	1248
Visp 320 ... d.	...	...	...	0439h	0532	0611		0713	0742	0813		0913		1013	1042		1139	1213	...
Leuk ... d.	...	...	...	0458h	0551	0629		0730	0754	0830		0930		1030	1054		1156	1230	...
Sierre ... d.	0438	...	...	0510h	0601	0639	0711	0711s	0740	0804	0840	0911	0940	1014	1040	1104	1204	1240	1311
Sion ... d.	0450	...	...	0534	0613	0651	0723	0723s	0752	0817	0852	0923	0952	1025	1052	1117	1147	1217	1252	1323
Martigny ... d.	0505	...	...	0603	0629	0707	0738	0738s	0808	0834	0908	0938	1008	1040	1108	1134	1234	1308	1338
St. Maurice ... d.	...	0507	0538	0620	0640	0718		0818	0845	0918		1018		1118	1145	1245	1318	...
Bex ... d.	...	0512	0543	0625	0645	0723		0823	0850	0923		1023		1123	1150	1250	1323	...
Aigle ... d.	0523	0531	0550	0632	0652	0729	0756	0756s	0830	0856	0930	0956	1030	1056	1130	1156	1256	1356
Montreux ... d.	0535	0547	0607	0644	0707	0742	0807	0807s	0843	0907	0943	1007	1043	1107	1143	1207	1307	1343	1407
Vevey ... d.	0541	0558	0613	0651	0710	0749	0813	0813s	0849	0913	0949	1013	1049	1113	1149	1213	1313	1349	1413
Lausanne ... a.	0555	0622	0627	0705	0725	0803	0827	0827s	0903	0927	1003	1027	1103	1127	1203	1227	1327	1403	1427
Genève 250 ... a.	...	0639	0712	0712	0748	0812		0912	0912		1012		1112		1212	1312	1316	1412	1512
Genève Aéroport + 250 ... a.	...	0649	0724	0724	0758	0824		0924		1024		1124		1224	1322	1324	1424	1524

	1926	1537	1928	1639	1930	IC 322	1541	1932	1643	1228	1936	2136	EC 326	1647	1940	EC 40	1942	328	2144
	♦	🍴R		🍴B	♦	🍴R	🍴	🍴R	♦	🍴			✕	🍴	♦	✕	🍴	♦	♦
Brig 320 ... d.	1336	1407	1436	1507	1536	1615	1618	1632	1707	1730	1736	1807	1848	1907	1932	1948	2034	2133	2136
Visp 320 ... d.	1342	1413	1442	1513	1542		1624	1638	1713		1742	1813		1913	1939		2041	2143	2143
Leuk ... d.	1354	1430	1454	1530	1554		1635	1654	1730		1754	1830		1930	1951		2053	2155	2155
Sierre ... d.	1404	1440	1504	1540	1604		1642	1704	1740		1804	1840	1911	1940	2000		2104	2204	2204
Sion ... d.	1417	1452	1517	1552	1617	1645	1652	1717	1752	1800	1817	1852	1923	1952	2021	2018	2117	2203	2217
Martigny ... d.	1434	1508	1534	1608	1634		1708	1734	1808		1834	1908	1938	2008	2037		2134		2234
St. Maurice ... d.	1445	1518	1545	1618	1645		1718	1745	1818		1845	1918		2018	2045		2145		2245
Bex ... d.	1450	1523	1550	1623	1650		1723	1750	1823		1850	1923		2023	2050		2150		2250
Aigle ... d.	1456	1530	1556	1630	1658		1730	1756	1830		1856	1930	1956	2030	2056		2156		2256
Montreux ... d.	1507	1543	1607	1643	1707		1743	1807	1843		1907	1943	2007	2043	2107		2207		2307
Vevey ... d.	1513	1549	1613	1649	1713		1749	1813	1849		1913	1949	2013	2049	2113		2213		2313
Lausanne ... a.	1527	1603	1627	1703	1727	1740	1803	1827	1903	1852	1927	2003	2027	2103	2127	2111	2227	2255	2327
Genève 250 ... a.	1612	...	1712		1814	1817		1912		1929	2012	2112			2212	2148	2312	2332	...
Genève Aéroport + 250 ... a.	1624	...	1724		1824			1924			2024				2224	2158	2322		...

♦ – **NOTES** (LISTED BY TRAIN NUMBERS)

C39 – MONTEVERDI – Supplement payable in Italy: 🍴 and ✕ Genève Aéroport - Milano - Venezia Santa Lucia.

C40 – MONTEVERDI – Supplement payable in Italy: 🍴 and ✕ Venezia Santa Lucia - Milano - Genève Aéroport.

20/1 – SIMPLON EXPRESS – 🛏 1, 2 cl., 🛌 2 cl. and 🍴 Zagreb - Trieste - Genève Aéroport and v.v.; 🛌 2 cl. and 🍴 Venezia Santa Lucia - Genève Aéroport and v.v.

N311 – ROMA – 🛏 1, 2 cl. and 🍴 Genève Aéroport - Brig (train EN313) - Roma.

11/2 – 🛏 Genève (Aéroport) - Milano Porta Garibaldi - Firenze SMN - Roma Tiburtina - Napoli and v.v.

20 – 🍴 Milano - Genève Aéroport.

C321 – 🍴 Genève Aéroport - Milano; 🍴 Genève Aéroport - Brig; Conveys on ⑤⑥ Sept. 30 - Oct. 15: 🍴 Genève Aéroport - Brig (train 1023) - Genova (train 1024) - Ventimiglia.

C322 – CISALPIN – ® with supplement payable in Italy: 🍴 Milano - Genève.

C323 – LUTETIA – ® with supplement payable in Italy: 🍴 and ✕ Genève Aéroport - Milano.

26 – 🍴 and ✕ Milano - Genève.

27 – 🍴 Genève Aéroport - Milano.

328 – 🍴 Milano - Genève.

329 – CHAMPS ELYSEES – 🍴 Genève Aéroport - Milano.

330 – LUTETIA – 🍴 Milano - Genève Aéroport.

335 – CISALPIN – 🍴 Genève Aéroport - Milano.

1228 – Runs © Sept. 25 - Oct. 16 only: 🍴 Brig - Genève.

1604 – 🍴 (Delémont ✕ -) Biel - Lausanne - Brig.

1606 – 🍴 Basel - Delémont - Biel - Lausanne - Brig; Conveys on ⑥ Dec. 17 - Apr. 15 (from Oostende): 🛌 2 cl. Oostende (train 499) - Basel - Brig.

1647 – 🍴 Brig - Lausanne - Biel - Delémont - Basel; Conveys 🛏 1, 2 cl. (⑥ Dec. 18 - Apr. 15) and 🛌 2 cl. (⑦ Dec. 18 - Apr. 16) Brig - Basel (train 498) - Oostende.

EN1906 – ROMA – 🛏 1, 2 cl. and 🍴 Roma (train EN314) - Brig - Genève.

1940 – 🍴 Brig - Genève Aéroport; Conveys on © Sept. 25 - Oct. 16: 🍴 Ventimiglia (train 1021) - Arona (train 1022) - Brig - Genève.

2109 – 🍴 Lausanne - Brig; Conveys on ⑤ Jan. 20 - Mar. 17 (from Paris): 🛏 1, 2 cl. and 🛌 2 cl. Paris Gare de Lyon (train 1125) - Lausanne - Brig.

2144 – 🍴 Lausanne - Brig; Conveys on ⑥ Jan. 24 - Mar. 18: 🛏 1, 2 cl. and 🛌 2 cl. Brig - Lausanne (train 1124) - Paris Gare de Lyon.

B – 🍴 Basel - Delémont - Biel - Lausanne - Brig and v.v.

D – 🍴 Romanshorn - Zürich - Biel - Lausanne - Brig (train 4943) - Domodossola.

h – ✕ only.

s – Stops to set down only.

u – Stops to pick up only.

WE HAVE A VERY WIDE RANGE
of travel-related publications. See the list and order form at the back of this book.

® – Reservation obligatory   ♦ – See footnote   🚌 – Bus or coach service

Table 288 (Summer) INTERLAKEN - GRINDELWALD - KLEINE SCHEIDEGG

Narrow gauge rack railway

Summer Service valid Apr. 24 - May 27, **1995**. For Winter Service to Apr. 23 see Page **193**

BOB, WAB, JB

km		12	12	12	12	12	12	12	12	12	12	12	12	12	12	12	12	12	12	12	12	12	12	12	12
0	Interlaken Ost .... d.	0635	0738	0832	0902	0932	1002	1032	1132	1232	1332	1432	1502	1532	1602	1632	1702	1732	1802	1832	1932	2032	2132	2232	2332
4	Wilderswil ▲ .... d.	0640	0743	0837	0907	0937	1007	1037	1137	1237	1337	1437	1507	1537	1607	1637	1707	1737	1807	1837	1937	2037	2137	2237	2337
9	Zweilütschinen..... d.	0651	0752	0846	0916	0946	1016	1046	1146	1246	1346	1446	1516	1546	1616	1646	1716	1746	1816	1846	2046	2146	2246	2346	...
19	Grindelwald .... a.	0714	0814	0908	0938	1008	1038	1108	1208	1308	1408	1508	1538	1608	1638	1708	1738	1808	1838	1908	2008	2108	2208	2308	0008
		2	2	2	12	2	2	2	2	2	2	2	2v	2	2	2	2	2	2	2					
19	Grindelwald .... d.	0719	0819	0919	0949	1019	1049	1119	1219	1319	1419	1519	1549	1619	1649	1719	1749	1819	1849	1945	...				
20	Grindelwald Grund .... d.	0726	0826	0926	0956	1026	1056	1126	1226	1326	1426	1526	1556	1626	1656	1726	1756	1824	1854	1950	...				
27	Kleine Scheidegg ...... a.	0754	0854	0954	1024	1054	1124	1154	1254	1354	1454	1554	1630	1654	1730	1754	1830	...	...	...					

		12	12	2	12	2	2	2	2	2	2	2	2	2	2	2	2	2	2	2	2		12	12
	Kleine Scheidegg .... d.	...	...	...	...	...	0800	...	0900	1000	1100	1200	1300	1400	1432	1500	1532	1600	1632	1700	1732	1800	1900	...	
	Grindelwald Grund ...... d.	...	...	0710	...	0805	0841	0910	0941	1041	1141	1241	1341	1441	1511	1541	1611	1641	1711	1741	1811	1841	1939	...	
	Grindelwald .... a.	...	...	0715	...	0810	0845	0915	0945	1045	1145	1245	1345	1445	1515	1545	1615	1645	1715	1745	1815	1845	1943	...	
				12v				12v	12	12	12	12	12	12	12	12v	12	12v	12	12v	12	12			
	Grindelwald .... d.	0550	0643	0726	0754	...	0850	0920	0950	1050	1150	1250	1350	1450	1520	1550	1620	1650	1720	1750	1820	1850	1950	2050	2150
	Zweilütschinen........... d.	0615	0708	0751	0818	...	0915	0945	1015	1115	1215	1315	1415	1515	1545	1615	1645	1715	1745	1815	1845	1915	2015	2115	2215
	Wilderswil ▲ .... d.	0622	0715	0758	0825	...	0922	0952	1022	1122	1222	1322	1422	1522	1552	1622	1652	1722	1752	1822	1852	1922	2022	2122	2222
	Interlaken Ost......... a.	0627	0720	0803	0830	...	0927	0957	1027	1127	1227	1327	1427	1527	1557	1627	1657	1727	1757	1827	1857	1927	2027	2127	2227

v – Runs June 11 - Oct. 16 only.   ▲ – Rack railway (SPB) connection to/from **Schynige Platte**: 15 journeys each way daily.

Operators: BOB – Berner Oberland Bahnen; JB – Jungfraubahn; SPB – Schynige Platte Bahn; WAB – Wengernalpbahn, Interlaken.

WE HAVE A VERY WIDE RANGE

of travel-related publications. See the list and order form at the back of this book.

Table 271 — BELLINZONA - LUINO

2 class only. SBB, FS

km		Ⓐb		⑦			✕b			✕c				Ⓐb				Ⓐb
0	Bellinzona...................... d.	0520	0555	...	0755	...	0851	...	0955	...	1055	...	1155	...	1355	...	1455	...	1555	...	1655	...
10	Cadenazzo .... a.	0529	0606	...	0805	...	0900	...	1005	...	1105	...	1205	...	1405	...	1505	...	1605	...	1705	...
29	Cadenazzo .... d.	0600	...	0611	0811	...	0911	...	1011	...	1111	...	1211	...	1411	...	1511	...	1611	...	1711
29	Pino-Tronzano ⋒ ...... d.	0536	...	0635	0836	...	0936	...	1036	...	1136	...	1236	...	1436	...	1536	...	1636	...	1736
37	Luino .... a.	0551	...	0649	0851	...	0951	...	1051	...	1158	...	1251	...	1451	...	1551	...	1651	...	1751

							✕								✕b						Ⓐb
Bellinzona................... d.	1755	...	...	1955	...	2155	...		Luino .... d.	0557	...	0656	...	...	0907	...	1007	...
Cadenazzo .... a.	1805	...	...	2005	...	2205	...		Pino-Tronzano ⋒ .... d.	0612	...	0712	...	...	0923	...	1023	...
Cadenazzo .... d.	...	1811	...	2011	...	2211			Cadenazzo .... a.	0635	...	0734	...	...	0946	...	1046	...
Pino-Tronzano ⋒ ...... d.	...	1836	...	2036	...	2236			Cadenazzo .... d.	...	0650	...	0739	...	...	0952	...	1052
Luino .... a.	...	1851	...	2051	...	2251			Bellinzona............... a.	...	0702	...	0748	...	...	1002	...	1102

			✕b					Ⓐb				Ⓐb							⑦		✕
Luino .... d.	1107	...	1207	...	1307	...	1507	...	1602	...	1707	...	1807	...	1907	...	2107	...	...	2304
Pino-Tronzano ⋒ ...... d.	1123	...	1223	...	1323	...	1523	...	1617	...	1723	...	1823	...	1923	...	2123	...	...	2319
Cadenazzo .... a.	1146	...	1245	...	1346	...	1546	...	1639	...	1746	...	1846	...	1946	...	2146	...	...	2341
Cadenazzo .... d.	...	1152	1246	1252	...	1352	...	1552	...	1643	...	1752	...	1852	1952	...	2152	...	2304	2342
Bellinzona................... a.	...	1202	1255	1302	...	1402	...	1602	...	1654	...	1802	...	1902	2002	...	2202	...	2315	2352

b – Also Jan. 2, Apr. 14, **not** May 1.   c – **Not** Dec. 26, Jan. 2, Apr. 14, 17, May 25.   **Operator:** FS – Ferrovie dello Stato, Italy.

Table 272 — DOMODOSSOLA - LOCARNO

Centovalli Line (Line of One Hundred Valleys)

1, 2 class. Narrow gauge. FART

km																				
0	Domodossola .... d.	0902	1018	1112	1216	1318	1516	1600	1820	1940	...	Locarno................... d.	...	0728	0854	1028	1222	1350	1528	1628	1728	1905
33	Camedo ⋒............... d.	1005	1122	1214	1320	1423	1622	1702	1924	2042	...	Camedo ⋒............... d.	...	0801	0927	1101	1257	1423	1601	1701	1801	1940
54	Locarno .... a.	1040	1155	1248	1355	1455	1655	1737	1957	2116	...	Domodossola .... a.	...	0900	1034	1200	1400	1530	1700	1800	1900	2046

Operator: FART – Ferrovie Autolinee Regionali Ticinesi, Locarno.

Table 273 — 🚌 SIERRE and SION - CRANS - MONTANA

Sunday service operates on Nov. 1, Dec. 8, Apr. 17, May 25.

🚌 PTT

Journey time: Sierre - Crans 35-40 minutes, Sierre - Montana 45-50 minutes (See below for direct service). There is also a funicular railway **Sierre - Montana**.

From Sierre Station to **Crans-sur-Sierre** and **Montana:** 0704✕, 0800✕, 0820, 0900, 0958✕, 1050✕, 1120, 1201✕, 1227, 1245✕, 1400, 1455✕, 1600, 1700✕, 1730, 1800, 1825✕, 1900✕, 1930, 2020, 2125.

From Montana (Les Vignettes) to **Sierre Station:** 0615✕, 0630✕, 0650, 0755, 0855✕, 1009, 1058✕, 1130, 1237, 1340✕, 1503, 1550, 1600✕, 1655, 1715✕, 1755✕, 1835, 1914, 2020. Buses call at **Crans-sur-Sierre (Scandia)** 6 minutes later.

Journey time: Sierre - Montana 35-40 minutes by direct service. There is also a funicular railway **Sierre - Montana**.

From Sierre Station to **Montana direct:** 0653✕, 0745, 1000, 1140, 1235, 1322, 1410✕, 1525, 1610✕, 1730, 1900.

From Montana (Forum d'Ycoor) to **Sierre Station direct:** 0605✕, 0635, 0905, 0955✕, 1050, 1140, 1238, 1251✕, 1335, 1500✕, 1615, 1817.

Journey time: Sion - Crans 40 minutes.

From Sion Station to **Crans-sur-Sierre:** 0655✕, 0750, 0850✕, 0950, 1050✕, 1150, 1250✕, 1350✕, 1450, 1550, 1650, 1750, 1850.

From Crans-sur-Sierre (Poste) to **Sion Station:** 0655, 0755✕, 0855, 0955✕, 1055, 1155✕, 1255, 1355Ⓐ, 1455✕, 1555, 1655, 1755, 1855.

Table 274 — MONTREUX - CAUX - ROCHERS DE NAYE

No service between **Caux** and **Rochers de Naye** during bad weather.

2 class only. MOB
Narrow gauge Rack Railway

Rail service **Montreux - Caux - Rochers de Naye**. All trains call at **Glion** 12 minutes from Montreux, 11 minutes from Caux. Journey time: 25 minutes **Montreux** to **Caux**.
Operator: MOB – Montreux Oberland Bernois.

From Montreux to **Caux:** 0600, 0700, 0800, 0900b, 1000b, 1100b, 1208, 1300b, 1400b, 1500b, 1605d, 1700, 1800, 1900, 2000, 2100.

From Caux to **Montreux:** 0630, 0730, 0830, 0930, 1030c, 1130c, 1230, 1330c, 1430c, 1530c, 1630c, 1730e, 1830, 1930, 2030, 2130.

b – Daily Sept. 25 - Oct. 30, Dec. 19 - May 27, also ⓒ Nov. 5 - Dec. 18 service continues to **Rochers de Naye** (Journey time 55 minutes from Montreux).

c – Daily Sept. 25 - Oct. 30, Dec. 19 - May 27, also ⓒ Nov. 5 - Dec. 18 service starts from **Rochers de Naye** 30 minutes earlier.

d – Daily Sept. 25 - Oct. 30 and ⓒ Feb. 25 - May 27 service continues to **Rochers de Naye**.

e – Daily Sept. 25 - Oct. 30 and ⓒ Feb. 25 - May 27 service starts from **Rochers de Naye**.

🚂 STEAM TRAIN operates on ⓒ Sept. 25 - Oct. 30: **Caux - Rochers de Naye** and v.v. Operates in good weather **only**, or by prior arrangement for groups ☎ Montreux (021) 964 5511
From **Caux:** 1045, 1245, 1445.   From **Rochers-de-Naye:** 1135, 1335, 1535.

Table 275 — MONTREUX - GSTAAD - ZWEISIMMEN - LENK

1, 2 class except where shown. Narrow gauge. MOB

	211	415	213	419	117	1 C🅁🍴	217	19 P🍴	423	121	221	427	125	225	3 C🅁🍴	431	29 P🍴	229	435	133	233	439	137	237	241
Montreux 270 .... d.	0519	...	0700	...	0821	0900	0854	1000	...	...	1100	...	1221	1300	1400	...	1421	1500	...	1621	1700	...	1821	1900	2110
Les Avants .... d.	0539	...	0724	...	0844		0924	1024	...	...	1124	...	1244	1324		...	1444	1524	...	1644	1724	...	1844	1924	2136
Montbovon .... d.	0600	...	0746	...	0904		0946		...	...	1146	...	1304	1346		...	1504	1546	...	1704	1746	...	1904	1946	2158
Chateau d'Oex ...... d.	0628	...	0806	...	0921	0954	1006	1100	...	1118	1206	...	1321	1406	1459	...	1521	1606	...	1721	1806	...	1921	2006	2221
Rougemont .... d.	0640	...	0818	...	0931		1018		...	1131	1218	...	1331	1418		...	1531	1618	...	1731	1818	...	1931	2018	2231
Saanen .... d.	0645	0725	0824	...	0937		1024		...	1137	1224	...	1337	1424		...	1537	1624	...	1737	1824	1924	1937	2024	2237
Gstaad .... d.	0651	0730	0830	0930	0942	1011	1030	1118	1130	1142	1230	1330	1342	1430	1518	1530	1542	1630	1730	1742	1830	1930	1942	2030	2242
Schönried .... d.	0701	0739	0839	0939	0951		1039		1139	1151	1239	1339	1351	1439		1539	1551	1639	1739	1751	1839	1939	1951	2039	2251
Saanenmöser .... d.	0705	0743	0843	0943	0955		1043		1143	1155	1243	1343	1355	1443		1543	1555	1643	1743	1755	1843	1943	1955	2043	2255
Zweisimmen 276 ..... a.	0718	0758	0900	0958	1010	1036	1100	1145	1158	1210	1300	1358	1410	1500	1545	1558	1610	1700	1758	1810	1900	1958	2010	2058	2310

	315		169		321			325	327		329		333	335	337			343
Zweisimmen ▲ ..... d.	0720	0805	0942	1012		1049	...	1150	1205	1249	1332	1405	1449	...	1553	1605	1649	1732	1805	1849	...	2005	...	343
Lenk ▲ .... d.	0738	0823	0958	1030		1107	...	1208	1223	1307	1350	1423	1507	...	1608	1623	1707	1750	1823	1907	...	2023	...	2123

	310	312	316	116	418	318	218	320	120	422	222	324	426	326	28 C🅁🍴	430	230	332	434	4 C🅁🍴	334	438	340	442	444
Lenk ▲ .... d.	0540b	0627b	0740	...	0830	0910	...	1000	...	1037	...	1153	1237	1310	1425	1437	...	1553	1637	1653	1710	1827	1937	2037	2137
Zweisimmen ▲ ...... a.	0558b	0645b	0758	...	0848	0928	...	1018	...	1055	...	1211	1255	1328	1440	1455	...	1611	1655	1708	1728	1845	1955	2055	2155

	208	112	214		20 P🍴	2 C🅁🍴		124		226			132		234		238	
Zweisimmen 276 .... d.	0600	0650	0800	0850	0900	0950	1000	1043	1050	1100	1200	1250	1300	1400	1450	1500	1600	1650	1700	1715	1800	1850	2000	2100	2200
Saanenmöser .... d.	0614x	0706	0816	0906	0914		1016		1106	1114	1216	1306	1314	1416		1514	1616	1706	1714		1816	1906	2016	2114	2214
Schönried .... d.	0618x	0710	0821	0910	0918		1021		1110	1118	1221	1310	1318	1421		1518	1621	1710	1718		1821	1910	2021	2118	2218
Gstaad .... d.	0630	0720	0832	0920	0926	1020	1032	1114	1120	1126	1232	1320	1326	1432	1520	1526	1632	1720	1726	1744	1832	1918	2032	2126	2226
Saanen .... d.	0635	0724	0837	0924		1037		1124		1237	1324		1437	1524		1637	1724		1837	1922	2037	...	2229
Rougemont .... d.	0641	0730	0843	0930		1029	1043		1130		1243	1330		1443	1530		1643	1730		1843	...	2043	...
Chateau d'Oex ...... d.	0655	0741	0857	0941		1039	1055	1135	1141		1257	1341		1457	1541		1657	1741		1804	1857	...	2057	...
Montbovon .... d.	0716	0756	0916	0956				1156			1316	1356		1516			1716	1756		1916	...	2116	...
Les Avants .... d.	0738	0816	0938	1016				1216			1338	1416		1538	1618		1738	1816		1938	...	2138	...
Montreux 270 .... d.	0800	0838	1000	1038		1136		1230	1238		1400	1438		1600	1638		1800	1838		1900	2000	2200	

C — CRYSTAL PANORAMIC EXPRESS – Runs daily Sept. 25 - Oct. 30, also Ⓒ Nov. 5 - May 27; 🚃 (observation cars) only. Reservation is inclusive of supplement.
P — PANORAMIC EXPRESS – 🚃 (observation cars) only; 🅁 in first class, reservation recommended in second class). Reservation is inclusive of supplement.

b — Ⓐ only.
▲ – Additional trains Zweisimmen - Lenk: 0515Ⓐ, 0605Ⓐ, 0625, 0849, 2205.
Additional trains Lenk - Zweisimmen: 0657, 1353, 1753, 2237.

x — Stops on request.

Operator: MOB – Montreux Oberland Bernois, Montreux.

Table 276 — ZWEISIMMEN - SPIEZ

1, 2 class. SEZ

km		3507 Ⓐ	2307 K	3509	3513	3515	2315 K	2417	3517	3519 K	2319	3523	3525	2325 K	3529	3531	2331 C	3533	2333 D	3537	2337 K	3541	3543	2343 Ⓑ	3545
0	Zweisimmen 275 .... d.	0705	0721	0805	0905	1005	1021	1059	1105	1205	1221	1305	1405	1421	1505	1605	1621	1705	1731	1805	1821	1905	2005	2021	2105
13	Boltigen .... d.	0716	0731	0816	0916	1016	1031		1116	1216	1231	1316	1416	1431	1516	1616	1631	1716	1731	1816	1831	1916	2016	2031	2116
34	Erlenbach im Simmental d.	0736		0836	0936	1036		1136	1236		1336	1436		1536	1636		1736		1836		1936	2036		2136
49	Spiez 280 .... a.	0751	0757	0851	0951	1051	1057	1134	1151	1251	1257	1351	1451	1457	1551	1651	1657	1751	1757	1851	1857	1951	2051	2057	2151

		3502 Ⓐ	2502 Ⓐ	3506	2308 J	3508	2312 F	3512	2314 G	3514	3516	2318 K	3518	3522	2324 K	3524	3528	2330 E	3530	2332 K	3532	2336 K	3536	3540	3542	3544
	Spiez 280 .... d.	0558	0608	0708	0803	0808	0903	0908	1003	1008	1108	1203	1208	1308	1403	1408	1508	1603	1608	1703	1708	1803	1808	1908	2008	2108
	Erlenbach im Simmental d.	0623		0723		0823		0923		1023	1123		1223	1323		1423	1523		1623		1723		1823	1923	2023	2123
	Boltigen .... d.	0646	0644	0744	0830	0844	0930	0944	1030	1044	1144	1230	1244	1344	1430	1444	1544	1630	1644	1730	1744	1830	1844	1944	2044	2144
	Zweisimmen 275 .... a.	0657	0655	0755	0839	0855	0939	0955	1039	1055	1155	1239	1255	1355	1439	1455	1555	1639	1655	1739	1755	1839	1855	1955	2055	2155

– 🚃 Zweisimmen - Spiez - Bern and v.v.
B – Note B applies Sept. 25 - Oct. 16, ⑦ Jan. 15 - Mar. 12, also ⓐ Apr. 29 - May 27.
– Note B applies Ⓒ Dec. 17 - Mar. 26. Note K applies daily Sept. 25 - Dec. 18 and Mar. 25 - May 27, also ⓐ Dec. 19 - Mar. 24.
– Note K applies daily Sept. 25 - Dec. 18 and Mar. 25 - May 27, also ⓐ Dec. 19 - Mar. 24.
– Note B applies Ⓒ Sept. 25 - Oct. 16, Dec. 17 - Mar. 26 and Apr. 29 - May 27, also ① Jan. 16 - Mar. 13.
– GOLDEN PASS – 🚃 Interlaken Ost - Spiez - Zweisimmen; 🚃 Bern - Spiez - Zweisimmen.

H – GOLDEN PASS – Runs daily Sept. 25 - Oct. 30 and Ⓒ Nov. 5 - May 27 only: 🚃 Zweisimmen - Interlaken Ost.
J – Note B applies Ⓒ Jan. 21 - Mar. 26.
K – 🚃 Zweisimmen - Spiez - Interlaken Ost and v.v.

Operator: SEZ – Spiez Erlenbach Zweisimmen Bahn, Bern.

Table 277 — AIGLE - LEYSIN and LES DIABLERETS

2 class only. Narrow gauge. ASD, AL

Rail service Aigle (station forecourt) - Leysin Grand Hotel. Journey time: 32 minutes.
Operator: AL – Aigle Leysin (TPC), Aigle.
From Aigle: 0708, 0812 and hourly until 1212, 1310, 1412 and hourly until 2212.
From Leysin: 0603, 0807 and hourly until 1207, 1246, 1407 and hourly until 2107, 2146.

Rail service Aigle (station forecourt) - Les Diablerets. Journey time: 43-53 minutes.
Operator: ASD – Aigle Sépey Diablerets (TPC), Aigle.
From Aigle: 0626🍴, 0712⑦, 0808 and hourly until 1908, 2108.
From Les Diablerets: 0629, 0803, 0858, 1003, 1103, 1203, 1258, 1403 and hourly until 1803, 1858, 2058.

Table 278 — AIGLE - CHAMPÉRY

2 class only. Narrow gauge. AOMC

Rail service Aigle (SBB station forecourt) - Champéry. 35 km. Journey time: 62 minutes. All trains call at Monthey Ville, 16 km, 20 minutes from Aigle, 37 minutes from Champéry.
Operator: AOMC – Aigle Ollon Monthey Champéry (TPC), Aigle.
From Aigle: 0553🍴, 0620, 0735, 0835, 0935, 1035, 1107, 1207, 1307, 1407, 1507Ⓒ, 1607, 1707, 1807, 1907, 2007⑦, 2107.
From Champéry: 0615, 0715🍴, 0747, 0847, 0947, 1047, 1147, 1247, 1347⑦, 1447, 1547, 1651, 1747, 1847, 1947, 2047, 2147⑦.

Table 279 — BEX - VILLARS

2 class only. Narrow gauge. BVB

Rail service Bex (SBB station forecourt) - Villars. Journey time: 45 minutes. Operator: BVB – Bex Villars Bretaye (TPC), Aigle.
From Bex: 0540Ⓐ, 0602Ⓒ, 0735, 0832 and hourly until 1232, 1432 and hourly until 1932, 2102.
From Villars: 0540Ⓐ, 0602Ⓒ, 0735, 0832 and hourly until 1232, 1432 and hourly until 1932, 2102.

mountain rack railway (BVB) runs from Villars to Col de Bretaye. Journey time: 20 minutes. Operator: BVB – Bex Villars Bretaye (TPC), Aigle.

AUTUMN and SPRING SERVICE Sept. 25 - Dec. 16 and Apr. 18 - May 27:
From Villars: 0746, 0930, 1130, 1330, 1630.
From Col de Bretaye: 0810, 0955, 1155, 1355, 1655.

WINTER SERVICE Dec. 17 - Apr. 17:
From Villars: 0746, 0830 and half-hourly until 1700, 1740.
From Col de Bretaye: 0810, 0855, 0925, and half-hourly until 1725, 1800.

🚃 – Through carriage (1 and 2 class)   🅁 – Reservation obligatory

Table 280 BASEL - BERN - INTERLAKEN and BRIG

All trains 1, 2 class. SBB, BLS

For additional services Zürich - Bern see Table **260**; Basel - Olten see Table **290**.

km		1804	IC 331	IC 859	499	2405	3707	2513	1808	IC 811	2407	1706	3709	IC 813		1812	IC 865	2515	IC 914		IC 819	1716	3713	2417
			✕	🍷	🍷	🍷		🍷		✕		🍷		🍷		🍷	✕					🍷		
				♦	♦	♦	Z	Ⓐ	♦		♦			V		♦			♦				Z	G
	Zürich Flughafen ✈ **260** d.	...	...	...	...	...	...	...	...	...	...	...	...	...	...	...	...	...	0813	...	...	0805	...	...
	Zürich Hbf **260** d.	...	...	...	...	...	...	...	...	...	...	0625	...	...	...	0730	...	...	0833	...	...	0830	...	...
0	**Basel SBB** d.	...	...	...	0550	...	...	0620	...	0701	...	|	...	0723	...	|	0801	0811	|	...	0901	|	...	...
14	Liestal d.	...	...	...	0601	...	...	0630	...	|	...	|	...	|	...	|	|	0821	|	...	|	|	...	...
39	**Olten** a.	...	...	...	0621	...	...	0649	...	0727	...	0713	...	0749	...	0817	0827	0843	|	...	0927	0917	...	...
39	**Olten** d.	...	...	...	0623	...	...	0654	...	0729	...	0715	...	0751	...	0820	0829	0848	|	...	0929	0920	...	...
59	Langenthal d.	...	...	...	0635	...	...	0706	...	|	...	0728	...	|	...	0832	|	0900	|	...	|	0932	...	...
84	Burgdorf d.	...	...	...	0653	...	...	0724	...	|	...	0749	...	|	...	0850	|	0918	|	...	|	0950	...	...
106	**Bern** a.	...	...	...	0712	...	...	0742	...	0812	...	0809	...	0836	...	0909	0912	0936	0945	...	1012	1009	...	...
106	**Bern** d.	0622	0650	0656	0722	0728	...	...	0756	0822	0825	0828	...	0851	...	0922	0928	...	0956	...	1022	1028	...	...
137	Thun d.	0643	0711	0718	0743	0750	...	...	0817	0843	0846	0850	...	0912	...	0943	0950	...	1018	...	1043	1050	...	...
152	**Spiez** a.	0652	0720	0727	0752	0759	...	...	0826	0852	0855	0859	...	0921	...	0952	0959	...	1027	...	1052	1059	...	...
152	**Spiez** d.	0654	0722	0729	0754	0801	0804	...	0828	0854	...	0901	0908	0923	...	0954	1001	...	1029	...	1054	1101	1104	1135
	Interlaken West d.	|	|	0746	|	0818	0823	...	|	|	...	0918	0927	|	...	|	1018	...	1046	...	|	1118	1123	1154
	Interlaken Ost a.	|	|	0749	|	0821	0827	...	|	|	...	0921	0929	|	...	|	1021	...	1049	...	|	1121	1126	1157
169	Frutigen d.	0706	|	...	0806	...	...	...	0840	0906	...	...	...	|	...	1006	...	...	...	...	1106	...	...	...
194	Kandersteg d.	0724	|	...	0824	...	...	...	|	0924	...	...	...	|	...	1024	...	...	...	...	1124	...	...	...
218	Goppenstein d.	0736	|	...	0836	...	...	...	|	0936	...	...	...	|	...	1036	...	...	...	...	1136	...	...	...
253	**Brig** d.	0759	0820	...	0859	...	...	...	0929	0959	...	...	...	1021	...	1059	...	...	...	...	1159	...	...	...
	Milano Centrale **365** a.	...	1045	...	...	...	...	...	...	...	...	...	...	1240	...	...	...	...	...	...	...	...	...	...

	1818	IC 871	2521	EC 101	1720	3717	IC 333		1822	IC 875	2525	IC 924		IC 829	1726	3721	EC 91	1728	2529		IC 831	1730	1832	IC 337
	✕	🍷	🍷	✕	🍷		🍷		🍷					🍷	🍷		✕	🍷			✕	🍷	🍷	🍷
				♦		Z										Z	♦							
Zürich Flughafen ✈ **260** d.	0905	...	...	...	1005	...	...	...	1105	...	...	1205	...	...	...	...	...	1305	...	...	...	1405	1505	...
Zürich Hbf **260** d.	0930	...	...	...	1030	...	...	...	1130	...	...	1233	...	...	1230	...	...	1330	...	...	...	1430	1530	...
Basel SBB d.	|	1001	1011	1101	|	...	...	...	|	1201	1211	|	...	1301	|	...	1401	|	1411	...	1501	|	|	...
Liestal d.	|	|	1021	|	|	...	...	...	|	|	1221	|	...	|	|	...	|	|	1421	...	|	|	|	...
Olten a.	1017	1027	1043	1127	1117	...	...	...	1217	1227	1243	|	...	1327	1317	...	1427	1417	1443	...	1527	1517	1617	...
Olten d.	1020	1029	1048	1129	1120	...	...	...	1220	1229	1248	|	...	1329	1320	...	1429	1420	1448	...	1529	1520	1620	...
Langenthal d.	1032	|	1100	|	1132	...	...	...	1232	|	1300	|	...	|	1332	...	|	1432	1500	...	|	1532	1632	...
Burgdorf d.	1050	|	1118	|	1150	...	...	...	1250	|	1318	|	...	|	1350	...	|	1450	1518	...	|	1550	1650	...
Bern a.	1109	1112	1136	1212	1209	...	...	...	1309	1312	1336	1345	...	1412	1409	...	1512	1509	1536	...	1612	1609	1709	...
Bern d.	1122	1128	...	1222	1228	...	1256	...	1322	1328	...	1356	...	1422	1428	...	1522	1528	...	...	1622	1628	...	1722
Thun d.	1143	1150	...	1243	1250	...	1317	...	1343	1350	...	1418	...	1443	1450	...	1543	1550	...	...	1643	1650	...	1743
Spiez a.	1152	1159	...	1252	1259	...	1326	...	1352	1359	...	1427	...	1452	1459	...	1552	1559	...	...	1652	1659	...	1752
Spiez d.	1154	1201	...	1254	1301	1304	1328	...	1354	1401	...	1429	...	1454	1501	1504	1554	1601	...	...	1654	1701	...	1754
Interlaken West d.	|	1218	...	|	1318	1323	|	...	|	1418	...	1446	...	|	1518	1523	|	1618	...	...	|	1718	...	|
Interlaken Ost a.	|	1221	...	|	1321	1326	|	...	|	1421	...	1449	...	|	1521	1526	|	1621	...	...	|	1721	...	|
Frutigen d.	1206	...	...	1306	...	...	1340	...	1406	...	...	...	...	1506	...	...	1606	...	...	...	1706	...	...	1806
Kandersteg d.	1224	...	...	1324	...	...	|	...	1424	...	...	...	...	1524	...	...	1624	...	...	...	1724	...	...	1824
Goppenstein d.	1236	...	...	1336	...	...	|	...	1436	...	...	...	...	1536	...	...	1636	...	...	...	1736	...	...	1836
Brig d.	1259	...	...	1359	...	...	1429	...	1459	...	...	...	...	1559	...	...	1659	...	...	...	1759	...	...	1859
Milano Centrale **365** a.	...	...	...	...	...	...	1645	...	...	...	...	...	...	...	...	...	1915	...	...	...	...	...	...	2115

	EC 105	3727	2537	2439	IC 839	1736	3729	1838	EC 109	2541	IC 893	IC 740	2443	1742	EN 313	IC 313	3733	2545	IC 895	1744	1844	2549	2449	3551
	✕		🍷		✕				✕		✕			🍷	🍷	🍷		🍷	🍷					
	♦	♦		Ⓐ			Z		♦						♦									
Zürich Flughafen ✈ **260** d.	...	...	...	...	...	1605	...	1705	...	...	...	1842	...	1905	...	...	...	...	...	2005	2105	...	...	...
Zürich Hbf **260** d.	...	...	...	...	...	1630	...	1730	...	...	...	1903	...	1930	...	...	...	...	...	2030	2130	...	...	...
Basel SBB d.	1601	...	1611	...	1701	|	...	|	1801	1811	1901	|	...	|	2001	2001	...	2011	2101	|	|	2152	...	...
Liestal d.	|	...	1621	...	|	|	...	|	|	1821	|	|	...	|	|	|	...	2021	|	|	|	2202	...	...
Olten a.	1627	...	1643	...	1727	1717	...	1817	1827	1843	1927	|	...	2017	2027**u**	2027	...	2043	2127	2117	2217	2222	...	...
Olten d.	1629	...	1648	...	1729	1720	...	1820	1829	1848	1929	|	...	2020	2029**u**	2029	...	2048	2129	2120	...	2224	...	...
Langenthal d.	|	...	1700	...	|	1732	...	1832	|	1900	|	|	...	2032	|	|	...	2100	|	2132	...	2236	...	...
Burgdorf d.	|	...	1718	...	|	1750	...	1850	|	1918	|	|	...	2050	|	|	...	2118	|	2150	...	2254	...	...
Bern a.	1712	...	1736	...	1812	1809	...	1909	1912	1936	2012	2015	...	2109	2112**u**	2112	...	2136	2212	2209	...	2312	...	...
Bern d.	1728	...	...	1756	1822	1828	...	1922	1928	▬	...	...	2028	...	2122**u**	2122	...	...	...	2228	...	...	2328	...
Thun d.	1750	...	...	1821	1843	1850	...	1943	1950	**3731**	...	...	2050	...	2143**u**	2143	...	...	...	2250	...	...	2350	...
Spiez a.	1759	...	...	1830	1852	1859	...	1952	1959	...	...	...	2059	...	2152**u**	2152	...	...	...	2259	...	...	2359	...
Spiez d.	1801	1808	...	1834	1854	1901	1908	1954	2001	2008	...	...	2101	...	2154**u**	2154	2157	...	...	2301	...	...	0003	0006
Interlaken West d.	1818	1827	...	1901	|	1918	1927	|	2018	2027	...	...	2120	...	|	|	2216	...	...	2320	...	...	0021	|
Interlaken Ost a.	1821	1829	...	1904	|	1921	1929	|	2021	2029	...	...	2123	...	|	|	2219	...	...	2323	...	...	...	|
Frutigen d.	...	...	...	...	1906	...	...	2006	...	...	...	...	...	...	2206**u**	2206	...	...	...	...	...	...	...	0018
Kandersteg d.	...	...	...	...	1924	...	...	2024	...	...	...	...	...	...	2224**u**	2224	...	...	...	...	...	...	...	0035
Goppenstein d.	...	...	...	...	1936	...	...	2036	...	...	...	...	...	...	2236**u**	2236	...	...	...	...	...	...	...	0046
Brig d.	...	...	...	...	1959	...	...	2059	...	...	...	...	...	...	2259**u**	2259	...	...	...	...	...	...	...	0111
Milano Centrale **365** a.	...	...	...	...	...	...	...	...	...	...	...	...	...	...	...	...	...	...	...	...	...	...	...	...

♦ – **NOTES** (LISTED BY TRAIN NUMBERS)

EC91 – VAUBAN – [12] and ✕ Brussels - Luxembourg - Metz - Basel - Milano.
EC101 – MATTERHORN – [12] and ✕ Wiesbaden - Basel - Brig.
EC105 – BERNER OBERLAND – [12] and ✕ Amsterdam - Köln - Interlaken Ost.
EC109 – THUNERSEE – [12] and ✕ Berlin Zoo - Köln - Interlaken Ost.
EN313 – ROMA – 🛏 1, 2 cl., ▬ 2 cl. Basel - Brig - Roma Termini.
499 – 🛏 1, 2 cl. and ▬ 2 cl. Oostende - Brussels - Brig; [12] Basel - Brig; Conveys on ⓒ Jan. 21 - Mar. 26: [12] Bern - Spiez (train **2308**) - Zweisimmen.
IC859 – [12] Biel - Bern - Interlaken Ost.
IC914 – Runs ⑥ Oct. 1 - 15 and Jan. 28 - Mar. 25, also Apr. 14 **only**: [12] St Gallen - Interlaken Ost.
1808 – Runs Sept. 25 - Oct. 30 and Apr. 1 - May 27 **only**: [12] Bern - Brig; Conveys on ⓒ Sept. 30 - Oct. 15: [12] Bern - Brig (train **1023**) - Genova (train **1024**) - Ventimiglia.
1812 – [12] Zürich - Brig; [12] Bern - Spiez (train **2314**) - Zweisimmen.
2405 – [12] Bern - Interlaken Ost; Conveys on Ⓐ: [12] Neuchâtel - Bern - Interlaken Ost
2407 – Runs ⓒ Sept. 25 - Oct. 16, Dec. 17 - Mar. 26 and Apr. 29 - May 27, also ① Jan 16 - Mar. 13 **only**: [12] Bern - Spiez (train **2312**) - Zweisimmen.
3727 – Note **Z** applies daily Sept. 25 - Dec. 18 and Mar. 25 - May 27, also Ⓐ Dec. 19 Mar. 24.
G – GOLDENPASS – Runs Sept. 25 - Oct. 30, also ⓒ Nov. 5 - May 27: [12] Zweisimmen - Spiez - Interlaken Ost.
V – MONTEVERDI – [12] Basel - Brig (train **EC39**) - Milano - Venezia Santa Lucia
Z – [12] Zweisimmen - Spiez - Interlaken Ost.
u – Stops to **pick up** only.

Operator: Bern to Interlaken and Brig: BLS – Bern Lötschberg Simplon Bahn, Bern.

Table 280 — BRIG and INTERLAKEN - BERN - BASEL

For additional services Bern - Zürich see Table 260; Olten - Basel see Table 290.

All trains 1, 2 class. BLS, SBB

First section

Station	IC 852	IC 2404	IC 909	IC 2506	1811	IC 854	EC 167	1713	EN 314	IC 314	IC 913	2514	IC 864	1815	3710	EC 108	1817	2520	EC 104	IC 1821	IC 332	3714
symbol		Ⓐ	Ⓐ		◆		✕	◆	✕	⊔	⊔		⊔		G	✕	⊔	⊔	◆	⊔	⊔	Z
Milano Centrale 365 d.																					0825	
Brig d.				0538					0701	0701s			0801			0901			1001		1042	
Goppenstein d.				0608					0724	0724s			0824			0924			1024			
Kandersteg d.				0620					0737	0737s			0837			0937			1037			
Frutigen d.				0638					0754	0754s			0854			0954			1054			
Interlaken Ost d.	0531	0605				0639	0711	0739			0811			0839	0930		0939			1039		1131
Interlaken West d.	0536	0609				0644	0716	0744			0816			0844	0934		0944			1044		1135
Spiez a.	0556	0629		0651		0704	0731	0759	0805	0805s	0831		0859		0952	0905	0959	1005	1059	1105	1142	1155
Spiez d.	0558	0631		0657	0707		0733	0801	0807	0807s	0833		0901			0907		1007	1101	1107	1142	
Thun a.	0609	0642		0708	0718		0744	0812	0818	0818s	0844		0912			0918		1018	1112	1118	1153	
Bern a.	0632	0705		0732	0738		0804	0832	0838	0838s	0904		0932			0938		1038	1132	1138	1212	
Bern d.	0648		0714	0724	0748		0814	0851	0848	0848s	0914		0948			0951		1048	1148	1151		
Burgdorf d.					0742		0809		0909		0927					1009			1109	1209		
Langenthal d.					0800		0825									1027			1127	1227		
Olten a.		0730			0812	0839	0830		0939		0942	1000				1030		1139	1139	1239		
Olten d.		0732			0817	0842	0832		0942					1017		1032		1042	1217	1242		
Liestal d.					0838							1038							1238			
Basel SBB a.		0759			0849	0859			0959	0959		1049				1059			1249	1259		
Zürich Hbf 260 a.			0826			0930		0926		1030			1026			1130			1230		1330	
Zürich Flughafen + 260 a.						0956				1045						1151			1256		1356	

Second section

Station	IC 1723	IC 820	2524	IC 872	1825	IC 927	3718	1727	EC 90	2528	1729	IC 828	IC 334	3722	1733	EC 100	IC 935	2532	3724	IC 882	2428	1837
symbol	⊔	✕	⊔	⊔	⊔	◆	Z	✕	⊔ C	⊔	◆	✕	⊔	◆	✕	✕	◆	Z	⊔	◆	⊔	⊔
Milano Centrale 365 d.									1025				1225									
Brig d.		1101	1126c	1201				1226	1301			1401	1442			1501					1601	
Goppenstein d.		1124	1149c	1224				1249	1324			1424				1524					1624	
Kandersteg d.		1137	1202c	1237				1302	1337			1437				1537					1637	
Frutigen d.		1154	1219c	1254				1319	1354			1454				1554					1654	
Interlaken Ost d.	1139				1239	1330	1339				1439			1534	1539		1611		1630	1639		
Interlaken West d.	1144				1244	1334	1344				1444			1538	1544		1616		1634	1644		
Spiez a.	1159	1205	1230c	1259	1305	1330	1352	1359	1405		1459	1505	1540	1556	1559	1605	1631		1652	1659		1705
Spiez d.	1201	1207	1233c	1301	1307	1333		1401	1407		1501	1507	1542		1601	1607	1633			1701	1704	1707
Thun a.	1212	1218	1244c	1312	1318	1344		1412	1418		1512	1518	1553		1612	1618	1644			1712	1716	1718
Bern a.	1232	1238	1304c	1332	1338	1414		1432	1438		1532	1538	1612		1632	1638	1704			1732	1736	1738
Bern d.	1251	1248		1324	1348	1351	1414		1451	1448	1524	1551	1548		1651	1648	1714	1724		1748		1751
Burgdorf d.	1309			1342		1409			1509		1542	1609			1709			1742		1809		
Langenthal d.	1327			1400		1427			1527		1600	1627			1727			1800		1827		
Olten a.	1339	1330		1412	1430	1439			1539	1530	1612	1639	1630		1739	1730		1812		1830		1839
Olten d.	1342	1332		1417	1432	1442			1542	1532	1617	1642	1632		1742	1732		1817		1832		1842
Liestal d.				1438							1638							1838				
Basel SBB a.		1359		1449	1459				1559	1559	1649		1659			1759		1849		1859		
Zürich Hbf 260 a.	1430				1530	1526			1630			1730				1830	1826					1930
Zürich Flughafen + 260 a.	1456				1556				1656			1756				1856						1956

Third section

Station	1839	939	2534	3726	1739	2430	IC 834	941	1741	IC 336	890	1843	844	3732	IC 498	2544	2447	IC 747	256	1747	5090	1847	3734	3736
symbol	⊔	Ⓑ		Z	⊔		✕	⑦	⊔	⊔	✕	⊔	Ⓒ		◆			✕				⊔		
Milano Centrale 365 d.											1525				1725							1905		
Brig d.	1622						1701	1733		1801	1901	1949	2001									2135		
Goppenstein d.	1647						1724			1824	1924	2012	2024									2200		
Kandersteg d.	1700						1737			1837	1937	2025	2037									2212		
Frutigen d.	1717						1754			1854	1954	2042	2054									2228		
Interlaken Ost d.				1730	1739				1839		1939			2040				2137					2232	2332
Interlaken West d.				1734	1744				1844		1944			2044				2141					2236	2336
Spiez a.	1731			1752	1759		1805	1831	1859	1905	1959	2005	2053	2102	2105		2159					2239	2254	2354
Spiez d.	1733				1801	1804	1807	1833	1901	1907	2001	2007	2055		2107		2201					2241	2256	
Thun a.	1744				1812	1816	1818	1844	1912	1918	2012	2018	2106		2118		2212					2251	2312	
Bern a.	1804				1832	1836	1838	1904	1932	1938	2032	2038	2126		2138		2212					2310	2343	
Bern d.		1814	1824		1851		1848	1914	1951	1948	2048	2051		2148	2151			2245	2251					
Burgdorf d.		1842			1909				2009		2109			2209				2309						
Langenthal d.		1900			1927				2027		2127			2227				2327						
Olten a.		1912			1939	1930			2039	2030	2130	2139		2230	2239			2327	2339					
Olten d.		1917			1942	1932			2042	2032	2132	2142		2232	2241		2329	2331		2349				
Liestal d.		1938													2300			2348		0014				
Basel SBB a.		1949			1959				2059	2159				2259	2311			2359		0030				
Zürich Hbf 260 a.		1926			2030	2130				2230								0006						
Zürich Flughafen + 260 a.					2056																			

NOTES (LISTED BY TRAIN NUMBERS)

- **C90** – VAUBAN – ⊔ and ✕ Milano - Basel - Brussels.
- **C100** – MATTERHORN – ⊔ and ✕ Brig - Basel - Wiesbaden.
- **C104** – BERNER OBERLAND – ⊔ and ✕ Interlaken Ost - Köln - Amsterdam.
- **C108** – THUNERSEE – ⊔ and ✕ Interlaken Ost - Köln - Berlin Zoo.
- **C167** – ALBERT EINSTEIN – ⊔ and ✕ Interlaken Ost - München - Praha.
- **N314** – ROMA – 🛏 1, 2 cl., 🛌 2 cl. Roma Termini - Brig - Basel.
- **C498** – MONTEVERDI – ⊔ Venezia Santa Lucia - Milano (train EC40) - Brig - Basel; ⊔ Brig - Basel; 🛏 1, 2 cl. and 🛌 2 cl. Brig - Oostende; For Amsterdam cars see Table 38 and for Hamburg/Dortmund cars see Table 78.
- **4** – Runs Ⓒ only: ⊔ Brig - Bern; Conveys Ⓒ Sept. 24 - Oct. 16 (from Ventimiglia): ⊔ Ventimiglia (train 1021) - Arona (train 1022) - Bern; For Amsterdam cars see Table 38 and for Hamburg/Dortmund cars see Table 78.
- **927** – Runs Ⓖ Jan. 7 - Mar. 25 only: ⊔ Brig - Bern - Zürich.
- **935** – Runs Ⓖ Sept. 25 - Oct. 16 and Jan. 26, also Apr. 17.
- **939** – Runs Ⓑ: ⊔ Bern - Zürich (- St Gallen Ⓖ Sept. 25 - Oct. 16 and Dec. 18 - Mar 26); Conveys on Ⓖ Sept. 25 - Oct. 16 and Dec. 18 - Mar. 26: ⊔ Brig (train 1839) - Bern - Zürich - St Gallen.
- **11** – ⊔ Brig - Bern; ⊔ Spiez - Zürich Flughafen.
- **39** – Runs Sept. 25 - Oct. 16, also Ⓒ Dec. 18 - Mar. 26: ⊔ Brig - Bern; Conveys on Ⓖ Sept. 25 - Oct. 16 and Dec. 18 - Mar. 26: ⊔ Brig - Bern (train IC939) - Zürich - St Gallen.
- **28** – Runs Sept. 25 - Oct. 16, Ⓖ Jan. 15 - Mar. 12, Ⓒ Apr. 29 - May 27: ⊔ Zweisimmen - Spiez - Bern.
- **30** – Runs Ⓒ Dec. 17 - Mar. 26 only: ⊔ Zweisimmen - Spiez - Bern.

- **3722** – Note Z applies: daily Sept. 25 - Dec. 18 and Mar. 25 - May 27, also Ⓐ Dec. 19 - Mar. 24.
- **C** – ⊔ Interlaken Ost - Zürich - St Gallen - Rorschach - Chur.
- **G** – GOLDEN PASS – ⊔ Interlaken Ost - Spiez - Zweisimmen.
- **Z** – ⊔ Interlaken Ost - Spiez - Zweisimmen.
- **c** – Ⓖ Jan. 7 - Mar. 25 only.
- **s** – Stops to set down only.

Operator: Brig and Interlaken to Bern: BLS – Bern Lötschberg Simplon Bahn, Bern.

◆ – See footnote

Table 281 — THUN - SPIEZ - INTERLAKEN (THUNERSEE)

BLS

Winter Service September 26, **1994** - May 27, **1995**

(No Service Nov. 21 - Mar. 11)

			A🍷		B‡		C✕	P✕		E🍷	D✕		C🍷		G🍷	B🍷	C🍷			B🍷				
Thun △ d.	...	...	0854	...	0954	...	1054	1114	...	1154	1154	...	1330	...	1422	1422	1508	...	...	1612	...	...	...	...
Hilterfingen d.	...	...	0910	...	1010	...	1110	1131	...	1210	1210	...	1347	...	1438	1438	1525	...	...	1629	...	...	...	...
Oberhofen am Thunersee d.	...	...	0915	...	1015	...	1115	1137	...	1215	1215	...	1352	...	1443	1443	1530	...	...	1634	...	...	...	...
Gunten d.	...	...	0928	...	1028	...	1130	1150	...	1228	1228	...	1407	...	1458	1458	1544	...	...	1647	...	...	...	...
Spiez Schiffstation ▲ d.	...	...	0939	...	1040	...	1141	1203	...	1238	1240	...	1419	...	1510	1510	1553	...	...	1657	...	...	...	...
Merligen d.	...	...	1003	...	1104	...	1205	1229	...	1252	1304	...	1443	...	1550b	1534	...	...	...	1720	...	...	...	...
Beatenbucht d.	...	...	1009	...	1110	...	1211	1236	...	1258	1310	...	1450	...	1535	1540	...	...	...	1726	...	...	...	...
Interlaken West △ a.	...	...	1048	...	1150	...	1255	1320	...	...	1354	...	1534	...	...	1624	...	...	...	1822	...	...	...	...

		B🍷				A🍷	B‡		E🍷			C✕	D✕	P✕		G🍷	C🍷		C🍷		B🍷		F✕	
Interlaken West △ d.	...	0938	...	...	...	1054	1200	...	...	...	...	1300	1400	1435	...	...	...	...	1547	...	1647	...	1833	...
Beatenbucht d.	...	1016	...	...	...	1134	1240	...	1259	...	...	1344	1444	1517	...	1544	...	...	1631	...	1731	...	1908	...
Merligen d.	...	1022	...	...	...	1140	1246	...	1252b	...	...	1350	1450	1524	...	1550	...	...	1637	...	1737	...	1914	...
Spiez Schiffstation ▲ d.	...	1047	...	...	...	1155	1310	...	1323	...	...	1414	1514	1552	...	1614	1614	...	1704	...	1803	...	1928	...
Gunten d.	...	1057	...	...	...	1205	1319	...	1333	...	...	1424	1524	1603	...	1624	1624	...	1714	...	1813	...	1937	...
Oberhofen am Thunersee d.	...	1111	...	...	...	1218	1333	...	1346	...	...	1437	1538	1617	...	1637	1637	...	1728	...	1827	...	1950	...
Hilterfingen d.	...	1116	...	...	...	1223	1338	...	1351	...	...	1442	1543	1623	...	1642	1642	...	1733	...	1832	...	1955	...
Thun △ a.	...	1133	...	...	...	1239	1355	...	1407	...	...	1500	1600	1642	...	1700	1700	...	1753	...	1852	...	2011	...

A – Runs Sept. 26 - Oct. 23, also ⑦ Apr. 30 - May 25.
B – Runs Sept. 26 - Oct. 23 and Apr. 2 - May 27.
C – Runs Sept. 26 - Oct. 23 and May 7 - 27, also ⑦ Apr. 2 - 30.
D – Runs Sept. 26 - Nov. 20 and Apr. 2 - May 27.
E – Runs ⑦ Mar 12 - 26.
F – Runs ⑦ Apr. 30 - May 25.
G – Runs Mar. 12 - Apr. 1.
P – Runs ⑦ and holidays Oct. 2 - 23 and May 7 - 25 **only**. Service normally operated by Paddlesteamer 'BLÜMLISALP' – supplement payable.
b – Via Beatenbucht.
‡ – Conveys ✕ Sept. 26 - Oct. 23, May 7 - 27, also ⑦ Apr. 2 - 30; 🍷 on ⚒ Apr. 3 - May 6.
△ – Rail station 50 metres.
▲ – Rail station 1100 metres - steep hill. No bus service during winter.
Operator: BLS – Bern Lötschberg Simplon Bahn, Bern.

Table 282 — INTERLAKEN - BRIENZ (BRIENZERSEE)

BLS

Winter Service September 26, **1994** - May 27, **1995**

(No Service Oct. 24 - Apr. 13)

		N🍷		R🍷		N🍷	R🍷		S🍷	
Interlaken Ost △ d.	...	0934	...	1134	...	1334	1434	...	1638	...
Brienz △ a.	...	1053	...	1250	...	1453	1549	...	1751	...

		N🍷		R🍷		N🍷	R🍷		S🍷	
Brienz △ d.	...	1105	...	1305	...	1505	1605	...	1805	...
Interlaken Ost △ a.	...	1222	...	1412	...	1629	1722	...	1912	...

N – Runs Sept. 26 - Oct. 23 and May 7 - 27, also ⑦ Apr. 14 - 30.
R – Runs Sept. 26 - Oct. 23, Apr. 14 - May 27. Paddlesteamer 'LÖTSCHBERG' on Oct. 2, also ⑦ May 7 - 25; conveys ✕ Sept. 26 - Oct. 23, May 7 - 27, also ⑦ Apr. 14 - 30.
S – Runs ⑦ Oct. 2 - 23 and Apr. 14 - May 25.
△ – Rail station 50 metres.
Operator: BLS – Bern Lötschberg Simplon Bahn, Bern.

Table 283 — BRIENZ - ROTHORN

Summer service only. **NO WINTER SERVICE**

Narrow gauge rack railway. BRB
Most services operated by steam train

	S	S	J	S	S	S	S	S	K
Brienz Bf d.	0805	0905	0935	1015	1115	1305	1415	1515	1615
Rothorn Kulm a.	0855	1000	1035	1110	1215	1405	1510	1610	1710

		S	S	S	S	S	S	S	S	K
Rothorn Kulm d.	...	0905	1010	1120	1300	1340	1445	1545	1645	1720
Brienz Bf a.	...	1005	1112	1220	1400n	1445	1545	1645	1745	1816

J – Runs July 1 - Aug. 31.
K – Runs June 4 - Sept. 25.
S – Runs June 4 - Oct. 23.
n – Does not connect with train **2472** at Brienz SBB.
Extra trains operate at busy times.
Operator: BRB – Brienz Rothorn Bahn, ☎ Brienz (036) 51 12 32.

Table 285 — INTERLAKEN - BRIENZ - BRÜNIG - LUZERN

Due to engineering work trains between Meiringen and Giswil are replaced by buses Nov. 2 - Dec. 16

Narrow gauge rack railway. SBB
1, 2 class

km		6307	6309	2455	6313	2459	6315	2461	6321	2463	6325	2467	6331	2471	6335	2475	6341	2477	6345	2481	6351	2483	6357	2485
										🍷		P🍷		🍷		🍷				G🍷		🍷		S
0	**Interlaken Ost** d.	...	...	0632	...	0737	...	0844	...	0937	...	1044	...	1137	...	1244	...	1337	...	1444	...	1537	...	1613
17	**Brienz** d.	...	...	0656	...	0800	...	0902	...	1000	...	1102	...	1200	...	1302	...	1400	...	1502	...	1600	...	1635
29	Meiringen d.	...	0624	0717	...	0817	...	0917	...	1017	...	1117	...	1217	...	1317	...	1417	...	1517	...	1617	...	1650
34	Brünig Hasliberg d.	...	0635	0729	...	0829	...	0929	...	1029	...	1129	...	1229	...	1329	...	1429	...	1529	...	1629	...	1701
38	Lungern d.	...	0646	0740	...	0840	...	0940	...	1040	...	1140	...	1240	...	1340	...	1440	...	1540	...	1640	...	1714
45	Giswil d.	0621	0706	0758	0806	0858	0906	0958	1006	1058	1106	1158	1206	1258	1306	1358	1406	1458	1506	1558	1606	1658	1706	1728
54	Sarnen d.	0633	0718	0810	0818	0910	0918	1010	1018	1110	1118	1210	1218	1310	1318	1410	1418	1510	1518	1610	1618	1710	1718	|
62	Alpnachstad d.	0642	0730	|	0830	|	0930	|	1030	|	1130	|	1230	|	1330	|	1430	|	1530	|	1630	|	1730	|
66	Hergiswil **293** d.	0647	0737	0824	0837	0924	0937	1024	1037	1124	1137	1224	1237	1324	1337	1424	1437	1524	1537	1624	1637	1724	1737	|
74	**Luzern 293** a.	0659	0750	0836	0850	0936	0950	1036	1050	1136	1150	1236	1250	1336	1350	1436	1450	1536	1550	1636	1650	1736	1750	1758

		2487	6361	2489	6365	2491	6371	6375	6385	6393	6395
		R🍷		🍷						⑦	
Interlaken Ost d.	...	1644	...	1737	...	1844	...	1937	2037	2135	2235
Brienz d.	...	1702	...	1800	...	1902	...	2000	2100	2200	2300
Meiringen d.	...	1717	...	1817	...	1917	...	2017	2117	2213	2313
Brünig Hasliberg d.	...	1729	...	1829	...	1929	...	2032	2132	...	...
Lungern d.	...	1740	...	1840	...	1940	...	2043	2143	...	...
Giswil d.	...	1758	1806	1858	1906	1958	2006	2106	2206	...	...
Sarnen d.	...	1810	1818	1910	1918	2010	2018	2118	2218	...	...
Alpnachstad d.	...	|	1830	|	1930	|	2030	2130	2230	...	...
Hergiswil **293** d.	...	1824	1837	1924	1937	2024	2037	2137	2237	...	...
Luzern 293 a.	...	1836	1850	1936	1950	2036	2050	2150	2250	...	...

	6304	6306	6308	6310	6310	2452	6320	2458	2462	6324
				⚒	⑦	G🍷		P🍷	C	
Luzern 293 d.	...	...	...	0603	0619	0724	0809	0824	0905	0909
Hergiswil **293** d.	...	...	...	0617	0632	0736	0822	0836	|	0922
Alpnachstad d.	...	...	...	0624	0637	|	0829	|	|	0929
Sarnen d.	...	...	...	0640	0648	0748	0840	0848	0925	0940
Giswil d.	...	...	...	0700	0700	0800	0851	0900	0937	0951
Lungern d.	...	...	...	0715	0715	0815	...	0915	0952	...
Brünig Hasliberg d.	...	...	...	0727	0727	0827	...	0927	1003	...
Meiringen d.	0547	0642	0721	0746	0746	0846	...	0946	1022	...
Brienz d.	0602	0658	0736	0802	0802	0900	...	1002	1035	...
Interlaken Ost a.	0624	0720	0759	0823	0823	0916	...	1023	1103	...

	2464	6330	2468	6336	2470	6340	2472	6342	2474	6350	2478	6354	2480	6360	2482	6366	2484	6370	2488	6380	6380	6390	6392	6394	6396
	🍷		🍷		🍷		🍷		R🍷		🍷		🍷								⑦				
Luzern 293 d.	0924	1009	1024	1109	1124	1209	1224	1309	1324	1409	1424	1509	1524	1609	1624	1709	1724	1809	1824	1909	...	2009	2109	2223	2323
Hergiswil **293** d.	0936	1022	1036	1122	1136	1222	1236	1322	1336	1422	1436	1522	1536	1622	1636	1722	1736	1822	1836	1922	...	2022	2122	2236	2336
Alpnachstad d.	|	1029	|	1129	|	1229	|	1329	|	1429	|	1529	|	1629	|	1729	|	1829	|	1929	...	2029	2129	2240	2340
Sarnen d.	0948	1040	1048	1140	1148	1240	1248	1340	1348	1440	1448	1540	1548	1640	1648	1740	1748	1840	1848	1940	...	2040	2140	2250	2350
Giswil d.	1000	1051	1100	1151	1200	1251	1300	1351	1400	1451	1500	1551	1600	1651	1700	1751	1800	1851	1900	2000	...	2100	2200	2301	0001
Lungern d.	1015	...	1115	...	1215	...	1315	...	1415	...	1515	...	1615	...	1715	...	1815	...	1915	2015	...	2115	2215	...	...
Brünig Hasliberg d.	1027	...	1127	...	1227	...	1327	...	1427	...	1527	...	1627	...	1727	...	1827	...	1927	2027	...	2127	2227	...	...
Meiringen d.	1046	...	1146	...	1246	...	1346	...	1446	...	1546	...	1646	...	1746	...	1846	...	1946	2041	2046	2146	2241	...	...
Brienz d.	1100	...	1202	...	1300	...	1402	...	1500	...	1602	...	1700	...	1802	...	1900	...	2002	...	2102	2202	...	...	...
Interlaken Ost a.	1116	...	1223	...	1316	...	1423	...	1516	...	1623	...	1716	...	1823	...	1920	...	2023	...	2125	2225	...	...	...

C – © Sept. 25 - Oct. 30 only.
G – 12 Luzern - Interlaken Ost and v.v.; Sept. 25 - Oct. 30 and © Dec. 17 - May 27 conveys GOLDENPASS saloon cars – Reservation recommended.
P – Conveys 1 (observation car) and 12 ; ✕ Sept. 25 - Nov. 1 and Dec. 17 - May 27; 🍷 Nov. 2 - Dec. 16.
R – ✕ Sept. 25 - Nov. 1 and Dec. 17 - May 27; 🍷 Nov. 2 - Dec. 16.
S – ⑦ Sept. 25 - Oct. 30 only.

For explanation of standard symbols see page 4

Table 286

ALPNACHSTAD - PILATUS KULM

Summer service only

2 class only
Narrow gauge rack railway. PB

Rail service (mid-May - November) **Alpnachstad - Pilatus Kulm**. Journey time: 30 minutes uphill, 40 minutes downhill. For Luzern connections see Table **285**. **Operator**: PB – Pilatus Bahn, Luzern.
From Alpnachstad: 0850, 0930, 1010, 1050, 1130, 1210, 1310, 1350, 1430, 1510, 1550. **From Pilatus Kulm**: 0925, 1005, 1045, 1125, 1205, 1305, 1345, 1425, 1505, 1545, 1625.
A round trip ticket is available which covers train or boat from Luzern (Tables **285/294**), rack railway to Pilatus Kulm, cablecar and gondolas to Kriens and trolleybus route **1** back to Luzern.

Table 287

INTERLAKEN - LAUTERBRUNNEN - JUNGFRAUJOCH

At times of heavy snowfall (November 1 - April 30) the Eigergletscher – Jungfraujoch service is subject to cancellation.

Narrow gauge rack railway
BOB, WAB, JB

km		12	12	12	12	2	12	12	12	12	2	12	12	2	12	2	2	12	2	12	2	12	12	12
				v			v		t			t					t					t		t
0	**Interlaken Ost** d.	0635	0738	0805	0832	...	0902	0932	1002	1032	...	1102	1132	...	1232	...	...	1332	...	1432	...	1502	1532	1602
4	Wilderswil ▲ d.	0640	0743	0810	0837	...	0907	0937	1007	1037	...	1107	1137	...	1237	...	...	1337	...	1437	...	1507	1537	1607
9	Zweilütschinen d.	0648	0751	0818	0845	...	0915	0945	1015	1045	...	1115	1145	...	1245	...	...	1345	...	1445	...	1515	1545	1615
12	**Lauterbrunnen** a.	0657	0800	0827	0854	...	0924	0954	1024	1054	...	1124	1154	...	1254	...	...	1354	...	1454	...	1524	1554	1624
		2	2	2	2		2t	2	2	2		2t	2		2			2		2		2t	2	2
12	**Lauterbrunnen** d.	0705	0810	0835	0900	0925	0945	1010	1035	1100	1125	1145	1210	1235	1300	1325	1345	1410	1435	1500	1525	1545	1610	1635
16	Wengen a.	0719	0824	0849	0914	0939	0959	1024	1049	1114	1139	1159	1224	1249	1314	1339	1359	1424	1449	1514	1539	1559	1624	1649
16	Wengen d.	0724	0830	0855t	0920	0945t	1008	1030	1055t	1120	1145t	1208	1230	1255t	1320	1345t	1408	1430	1455t	1520	1545t	1609	1630r	...
27	**Kleine Scheidegg** a.	0749	0855	0920t	0945	1010t	1033	1055	1120t	1145	1210t	1233	1255	1320t	1345	1410t	1433	1455	1520t	1545	1612t	1633	1658r	...
		2	2	2	2	2		2	2	2	2		2	2	2	2		2	2x	2			2	
27	**Kleine Scheidegg** d.	0802	0902	0930t	1002	1030t	...	1102	1130t	1202	1230t	...	1302	1330t	1402	1430t	...	1500	1526	1556	...	...	1700	...
31	Eigergletscher d.	0812	0912	0940t	1012	1040t	...	1112	1140t	1212	1240t	...	1312	1340t	1412	1440t	...	1510	1536	1608	...	...	1710	...
37	**Jungfraujoch** a.	0853	0953	1022v	1053	1122v	...	1153	1222v	1253	1322v	...	1353	1422v	1453	1522v	...	1552	...	1646z	...	...	1746v	...

	12	12	12	12	12	12	12	12	12	12
		t								v
nterlaken Ost d.	1632	1702	1732	1802	1832	1932	2032	2132	2232	2332
Vilderswil ▲ d.	1637	1707	1737	1807	1837	1937	2037	2137	2237	2337
Zweilütschinen d.	1645	1715	1745	1815	1845	1945	2045	2145	2245	2345
.auterbrunnen a.	1654	1724	1754	1824	1854	1954	2054	2154	2254	2354
	2	2t	2	2	2	2	2	2	2	2
.auterbrunnen d.	1700	1745	1805	1835	1900	2000	2100	2200	2300	0000
Vengen a.	1714	1759	1819	1849	1914	2014	2114	2214	2314	0014
Vengen d.	1720	...	1823t	...	...	...	...	...	...	...
Kleine Scheidegg a.	1745	...	1846t	...	...	...	...	...	...	...
	2		2v							
Kleine Scheidegg d.	1800	...	1900	...	...	...	...	...	...	...
Eigergletscher d.	1810	...	1910	...	...	...	...	...	...	...
ungfraujoch a.	...	...	...	...	...	...	...	...	...	...

	2	2	2	2	2	2	2	2	2
								v	
Jungfraujoch d.	...	...	...	...	...	...	...	...	0900
Eigergletscher d.	...	...	...	...	...	...	...	0815	0940
Kleine Scheidegg a.	...	...	...	...	...	...	...	0824	0949
								2	2
Kleine Scheidegg d.	...	...	...	...	...	0757v	...	0902	0953
Wengen a.	...	...	...	...	...	0826v	...	0935	1023
Wengen d.	0541	0633	0720	0743	0807	0833	0857	0943	1033
Lauterbrunnen a.	0558	0650	0737	0800	0825	0850	0915	1000	1050
	12	12	12	12	12v	12	12v	12	12
Lauterbrunnen d.	0605	0658	0741	0808	0835	0905	0935	1005	1105
Zweilütschinen d.	0615	0708	0751	0818	0845	0915	0945	1015	1115
Wilderswil ▲ d.	0622	0715	0758	0825	0852	0922	0952	1022	1122
Interlaken Ost a.	0627	0720	0803	0830	0857	0927	0957	1027	1127

	2	2	2	2	2	2	2	2	2	2	2	2	2	2	2	2	2	2	2	2	2	2	2	2
	t		v			v		v			v		v		v	t				v				
ungfraujoch d.	...	1000	1030	1100	...	1130	1200	1230	1300	...	1330	1400	1430	1500	1530	...	1600	...	...	1800	...	...	...	...
igergletscher d.	...	1040	1112	1140	...	1212	1240	1312	1340	...	1412	1440	1510	1536	1605	...	1634	...	1741	1841	...	...	...	...
leine Scheidegg a.	...	1049	1121	1149	...	1221	1249	1321	1349	...	1421	1449	1519	1545	1614	...	1643	...	1750	1850	...	...	...	...
		2	2	2		2t	2	2	2		2t	2	2	2	2		2		2	2				
leine Scheidegg d.	1038	1102	1127t	1153	1215t	1238	1302	1327t	1353	1415t	1438	1502	1527t	1555	1619t	1640	1702	1727t	1756	1900t	...	...	...	...
Vengen a.	1110	1135	1200t	1223	1245t	1310	1335	1400t	1423	1445t	1510	1535	1600t	1624	1648t	1710	1735	1757t	1823	1929t	...	...	...	...
Vengen d.	1123	1143	1207	1233	1257	1323	1343	1407	1433	1457	1523	1543	1607	1633	1657	1723	1743	1802	1833	1933	2033	2133	2233	2333
auterbrunnen a.	1140	1200	1225	1250	1315	1340	1400	1425	1450	1515	1540	1600	1625	1650	1715	1740	1800	1820	1850	1950	2050	2150	2250	2350
		12		12			12		12	12t		12	12t	12	12t		12	12v	12	12	12	12	12v	
auterbrunnen d.	...	1205	...	1305	...	...	1405	...	1505	1535	...	1605	1635	1705	1735	...	1805	1835	1905	2005	2105	2205	2305	...
weilütschinen d.	...	1215	...	1315	...	...	1415	...	1515	1545	...	1615	1645	1715	1745	...	1815	1845	1915	2015	2115	2215	2315	...
Vilderswil ▲ d.	...	1222	...	1322	...	...	1422	...	1522	1552	...	1622	1652	1722	1752	...	1822	1852	1922	2022	2122	2222	2322	...
terlaken Ost a.	...	1227	...	1327	...	...	1427	...	1527	1557	...	1627	1657	1727	1757	...	1827	1857	1927	2027	2127	2227	2327	...

– Sept. 25 - Dec. 16, Feb. 5 - May 27.
– Sept. 25 - Oct. 2, Dec. 17 - Apr. 23.
v – Sept. 25 - Oct. 2.
z – Will **not** run: Oct. 3 - Dec. 16, Feb. 5 - May 27.
x – Dec. 17 - Apr. 23.
▲ – Rack railway (SPB) connection to/from **Schynige Platte**: 15 journeys each way daily.
perators: BOB – Berner Oberland Bahnen; JB – Jungfraubahn; SPB – Schynige Platte Bahn; WAB – Wengernalpbahn, Interlaken.

'able 288

INTERLAKEN - GRINDELWALD - KLEINE SCHEIDEGG

Winter Service valid December 17, **1994** - April 23, **1995**. For Summer Service valid April 24 - May 27, **1995** see Page **188**

Narrow gauge rack railway
BOB, WAB, JB

km		12	12	12	2	12	2	12	2	12	12	12	12	12	12	12	12	12	12	12	12	12	12	12	12
0	**Interlaken Ost** d.	0635	0738	0832	...	0932	...	1032	...	1132	1232	1332	1432	1502	1532	1602	1632	1702	1732	1802	1832	1932	2032	2132	2232
4	Wilderswil ▲ d.	0640	0743	0837	...	0937	...	1037	...	1137	1237	1337	1437	1507	1537	1607	1637	1707	1737	1807	1837	1937	2037	2137	2237
9	Zweilütschinen d.	0651	0752	0846	...	0946	...	1046	...	1146	1246	1346	1446	1516	1546	1616	1646	1716	1746	1816	1846	1946	2046	2146	2246
19	**Grindelwald** a.	0714	0814	0908	...	1008	...	1108	...	1208	1308	1408	1508	1538	1608	1638	1708	1738	1808	1838	1908	2008	2108	2208	2308
		2	2	2		2		2		2	2	2	2	2	2		2		2	2					
19	**Grindelwald** d.	0718	0818	0918	0950	1025	1100	1130	1203	1235	1310	1415	1520	1555	1630	...	1719	...	1819	1849	...	...	...	...	...
20	Grindelwald Grund d.	0725	0825	0928	1001	1034	1107	1140	1213	1246	1319	1425	1531	1604	1637	...	1726	...	1824	1854	...	...	...	...	...
27	**Kleine Scheidegg** a.	0754	0854	0957	1030	1100	1136	1209	1242	1315	1348	1454	1554	1633	1710	...	1754	...	...	...	...	...	...	...	...

	12	12	2	2	2	2	2	2	2	2	2	2	2	2	2	2	2	2	2	2	2	2	12	12	12
eine Scheidegg d.	...	...	...	0759	0902	0935	1008	1041	1114	1147	1220	1253	1326	1359	1432	1505	...	1538	1611	1648	1732	1800	...	...	...
indelwald Grund d.	...	...	0710	0840	0942	1016	1050	1121	1155	1227	1301	1333	1407	1440	1512	1545	1600	1621	1655	1735	1811	1841	...	...	...
indelwald a.	...	...	0715	0844	0946	1020	1054	1125	1159	1231	1305	1337	1411	1444	1516	1548	1604	1625	1659	1739	1815	1845	...	...	...
			12	12	12	12		12		12		12		12	12	12	12	12	12	12	12	12			
indelwald d.	0550	0643	0754	0850	0950	1050	...	1150	...	1250	...	1350	...	1450	1520	1550	1620	1650	1720	1750	1820	1850	1950	2050	2150
eilütschinen d.	0615x	0708	0818	0915	1015	1115	...	1215	...	1315	...	1415	...	1515	1545	1615	1645	1715	1745	1815	1844	1915	2015	2115	2215
lderswil ▲ d.	0622x	0715	0825	0922	1022	1122	...	1222	...	1322	...	1422	...	1522	1552	1622	1652	1722	1752	1822	...	1922	2022	2122	2222
erlaken Ost a.	0627	0720	0830	0927	1027	1127	...	1227	...	1327	...	1427	...	1527	1557	1627	1657	1727	1757	1827	...	1927	2027	2127	2227

– Stops on request.
▲ – Rack railway (SPB) connection to/from **Schynige Platte**: 15 journeys each way daily.
erators: BOB – Berner Oberland Bahnen; JB – Jungfraubahn; SPB – Schynige Platte Bahn; WAB – Wengernalpbahn, Interlaken.

able 289

LAUTERBRUNNEN - MÜRREN

Service valid throughout: May 29, **1994** - May 27, **1995**

Funicular with train connection. BLM

unicular operates from **Lauterbrunnen** (opposite side of road to main station) to **Grütschalp**, where passengers change into a connecting rail service to **Mürren**. Total distance is *7 km*. ırney time: approximately 30 minutes allowing for the connection. **Operator**: BLM – Lauterbrunnen Mürren Bahn, Interlaken.

om Lauterbrunnen: 0642, 0717, 0747, 0817, 0832**c**, 0847, 0902, 0917**c**, 0932**c**, 0947,)2, 1017**c**, 1032**c**, 1047, 1102, 1117**c**, 1132**c**, 1147, 1202, 1217**c**, 1247, 1302, 1317**c**, 32**c**, 1347, 1402, 1417**c**, 1432**c**, 1447, 1502, 1517**c**, 1532**c**, 1547, 1602, 1617**c**, 1632**c**, 47, 1702, 1717**c**, 1732**c**, 1802, 1832, 1900, 2000, 2100**d**.

From Mürren: 0625, 0700, 0730, 0800, 0830, 0845, 0900**c**, 0915**c**, 0930, 0945, 1000**c**, 1015**c**, 1030, 1045, 1100**c**, 1115**c**, 1130, 1145, 1200**c**, 1230, 1300**c**, 1315**c**, 1330, 1345, 1400**c**, 1415**c**, 1430, 1445, 1500**c**, 1515**c**, 1530, 1545, 1600**c**, 1615**c**, 1630, 1645, 1700**c**, 1715**c**, 1730, 1745, 1815**c**, 1830, 1900, 1930, 2030**d**.

June 4 - Oct. 2 and Dec. 17 - Apr. 23 **only**.
d – June 18 - Sept. 18 and Dec. 17 - Apr. 23 **only**.

Services run daily unless denoted otherwise by a standard symbol or stated in Table footnotes

193

Table 290 — BASEL and ZÜRICH - LUGANO - CHIASSO - MILANO

1, 2 class. SBB, FS

km	Station	299	201	1551 IC561	1553 IC563	5315	5211	1555	IC 351	1661	1561	1561	1663	IC 251	EC 55	1663	1665	EC 51	1665	IC 718	1567	IC 255	1567
			◆®	§	§				✕◆		Y(A)	Y(B)	Y	✕↗	Y	Y		✕↗	Y		Y	Y	
0	Basel SBB .... d	0200							0600				0651	0707			0751					0907	
14	Liestal .... d								0610					0701			0801						
39	Olten .... d								0632					0723	0735		0823					0935	
48	Zofingen .... d								0639					0730			0830						
70	Sursee .... d								0652					0744			0844						
96	Luzern .... a								0712					0804	0812		0904					1012	
96	Luzern .... d						0627		0719					0814	0819		0914					1019	
	Schaffhausen 735 .... d									0642	0713	0713				0742		0842			0942		
	Zürich Flughafen ✈ 299 d									0653	0723	0723				0753		0853			0953	0947	
	Zürich Hbf .... a								0630	0703	0730	0730				0803		0903				1003	
	Zürich Hbf .... d									0641	0741	0741						0831			0931	1014	
	Thalwil .... d																	0931			1031	←	
	Zug .... d								0659	0731	0759	0759											
124	Arth Goldau ...... a						0657		0715	0745	0744	0813	0813	0840	0845	0840	0940	0945	0940		1045	1044	1045
124	Arth Goldau ...... d								0717	0749	0752	0815	0815	0852	0849	0852	0952	0949	0952		1052	1049	1052
132	Schwyz .... d								0725	0800	0823	0823	→			0900					1000		1104
136	Brunnen .... d								0729	0804	0827	0827				0904					1004		1114
148	Flüelen .... d								0739	0814	0837	0837				0914					1014		1121
157	Erstfeld .... d								0746	0821	0844	0844				0921					1021		1147
185	Göschenen .... d								0812	0847	0910	0908				0947					1047		1159
201	Airolo .... d					0657				0824	0859		0923			0959					1138		1238
247	Biasca .... d					0738				0903	0938	1002				1038							
266	Bellinzona .... a	0505		0638		0751			0915	0932	0951	1015		1025	1032	1051		1132	1151			1232	1251
266	Bellinzona .... d	0507	0546	0654		0754		0812	0919	0935	0954			1028	1035			1135	1154			1235	
295	Lugano .... d	0538	0615	0723	0823	0846		0947	1006	1024				1059	1106			1206	1224			1306	1324
321	Chiasso .... a	0602	0637	0747	0847	0916		1019	1030	1056				1123	1130			1230	1256			1330	1356
321	Chiasso 🚐 .... d	0620	0655	0802	0902			1048						1141	1148			1248				1348	
326	Como San Giovanni .. a	0626	0702	0809	0909			1056						1148	1156			1256				1356	
372	Milano Centrale .. a	0710	0745	0852	1000			1135						1230	1235			1335				1435	

Station	IC 720	IC 383	1669	IC 722	EC 53	1571	IC 726	IC 481	1675	EC 113	EC 57	IC 728	EC 5	1577	IC 730	IC 387	1679	IC 732	EC 9	1583	IC 736	IC 381	1685
		✕	Y	✕↗	Y		Y	Y		Y	Y ®		✕↗		Y§			Y	Y		Y§		
Basel SBB .... d			0951	1107						1151		1225	1307		1351			1507					1551
Liestal .... d			1001							1201		1235			1401								1601
Olten .... d			1023		1135					1223			1335		1423			1535					1630
Zofingen .... d			1030							1230					1430								1644
Sursee .... d			1044							1244					1444								1704
Luzern .... a			1104			1212				1304			1412		1504			1612					1714
Luzern .... d			1114			1219				1314			1419		1514			1619					1714
Schaffhausen 735 .... d			1009				1109		1209					1309			1409			1509			1609
Zürich Flughafen ✈ 299 d	1042			1142			1242						1316	1342			1442			1542			1642
Zürich Hbf .... a	1053	1047		1153			1147		1253	1247			1323	1326	1353	1347	1453	1447	1547	1653	1647		1703
Zürich Hbf .... d			1103				1203							1303	1333		1403			1503	1603		1614
Thalwil .... d									1214														1731
Zug .... d	1131						1231							1331	1359		1431			1531	1631		1731
Arth Goldau ...... a	1145	1140		1244	1245			1345	1340				1444	1445	1545	1540		1644	1645		1745	1740	1740
Arth Goldau ...... d	1149	1152		1249	1252			1349	1352				1449	1452	1549	1552		1649	1652		1749	1752	1752
Schwyz .... d				1200				1300					1400		1500			1600			1700		1800
Brunnen .... d				1204				1304					1404		1504			1604			1704		1804
Flüelen .... d				1214				1314					1414		1514			1614			1714		1821
Erstfeld .... d				1221				1321					1421		1521			1621			1721		1847
Göschenen .... d				1247				1347					1447		1547			1647			1747		1859
Airolo .... d				1259				1359					1459		1559			1659			1759		1938
Biasca .... d				1338				1438					1538		1638			1738			1838		
Bellinzona .... a		1332	1351	1432	1451			1532	1551			1559	1632	1651	1732	1751		1832	1851		1932	1951	1951
Bellinzona .... d		1335	1354	1435	1454			1554				1602	1635	1654	1735	1754		1835	1854		1954	1954	
Lugano .... d		1406	1424	1506	1524			1624				1632	1706	1724	1806	1824		1906	1924		2006	2024	
Chiasso .... a		1430	1456	1530	1556			1649				1730	1756		1830	1856		1930	1956		2030	2056	
Chiasso 🚐 .... d		1448		1548								1702	1748		1848			1948			2048		
Como San Giovanni .. a		1456		1556								1702	1756		1856			1956			2056		
Milano Centrale .. a		1535		1635								1735	1835		1935			2035			2135		

◆ — NOTES (LISTED BY TRAIN NUMBERS)

EC5 — VERDI – [sleeper] Dortmund - Milano; ✕ Dortmund - Chiasso.
EC9 — TIZIANO – [couchette] (Braunschweig ✕ (not Oct. 3, Dec. 25 - Jan. 1, Apr. 15 - 17, May 1) -) Hannover - Köln - Basel - Milano; ✕ Dortmund - Chiasso.
EC51 — TICINO – [couchette] (also [obs] observation car) and ✕ Zürich - Milano.
EC53 — COLOSSEUM – [couchette] and ✕ Basel - Milano - Bologna - Firenze SMN - Roma.
EC55 — RAFFAELLO – [couchette] and ✕ Zürich - Milano - Bologna - Firenze SMN - Roma.
EC57 — GOTTARDO – [couchette] and ✕ Zürich - Milano. Supplement payable.
201 — Dortmund and Frankfurt (Main) - Milano: For composition see Table 73.
IC255 — [couchette] Basel - Milano - Genova - Sestri Levante; ✕ (Sept. 25 - Oct. 30 and Apr. 1 - May 27 only) and Y Basel - Chiasso.
299 — [sleeper] 1, 2 cl. (T2), [couchette] 2 cl. and [couchette] Brussels - Luxembourg - Metz - Basel - Milano (- Venezia Santa Lucia on ⑤⑥ only from Brussels).
IC351 — CANALETTO – [couchette] (also [obs] observation car) and ✕ Zürich - Milano - Venezia Santa Lucia.

IC381 — [couchette] Stuttgart - Schaffhausen - Zürich - Milano; ✕ Singen - Chiasso.
IC383 — [couchette] Stuttgart - Schaffhausen - Zürich - Milano - Genova; ✕ Zürich - Chiasso.
IC387 — [couchette] Stuttgart - Schaffhausen - Zürich - Milano.
IC481 — [couchette] Nürnberg - Stuttgart - Schaffhausen - Zürich - Locarno.
1661 — [couchette] Basel - Chiasso; Y Luzern - Bellinzona.
1663 — [couchette] Basel - Luzern - Bellinzona - Locarno.
1675 — [couchette] Basel - Chiasso; [couchette] Genève Aéroport (train 1875) - Bern - Luzern - Chiasso.
A — Runs Sept. 25 - Oct. 31 and Apr. 1 - May 27 only: [couchette] Zürich - Bellinzona - Locarno.
B — Runs ⓒ Dec. 17 - Mar. 26 only: [couchette] Zürich - Göschenen.
✕↗ — Supplement payable in Italy.
§ — Supplement payable in Italy (except for passengers with international tickets).
Operator: FS – Ferrovie dello Stato (Italian State Railways).

2144

Table 290 — BASEL and ZÜRICH - LUGANO - CHIASSO - MILANO

1, 2 class except where shown. SBB, FS

	IC 738	IC 587 ⑤ L	1589	IC 257	IC 691 ⑤	IC 740	IC 389	1691	IC 742	1593 301	301	IC 744	1693	485	1695	EN 303	IC 303	2697 Q	5295 Q	1085 ⑤	1087 ⑥	2699
Basel SBB .... d.	...	...	...	1720	...	...	...	1751	...	...	1920	...	1951	...	2051	...	...	2202	...	...	...	2302
Liestal .... d.	...	...	...		...	...	...	1801	...	...		...	2001	...	2101	...	...		...	...	...	2312
Olten .... d.	...	...	...	1749	...	...	...	1823	...	...	1949	...	2023	...	2123	...	...	2230	...	...	...	2336
Zofingen .... d.	...	...	...		...	...	...	1830	...	...		...	2030	...	2130	...	...	2237	...	...	...	2343
Sursee .... d.	...	...	...		...	...	...	1844	...	...		...	2044	...	2144	...	...	2250	...	...	...	2356
Luzern .... a.	...	...	...	1827	...	...	...	1904	...	...	2027	...	2104	...	2204	...	...	2310	...	...	...	0016
Luzern .... d.	...	...	...	1834	1859	...	...	1914	...	...	2034	...	2114	...	2211	...	...		2330	...	...	
Schaffhausen 735 .... d.	...	1709	1709			...	1809		...	1909		...		2009		...	...			2209	...	
Zürich Flughafen + 299.d.	1742				1842	...	1942		...			2042				2142	2142	...	...		...	
Zürich Hbf .... a.	1753	1747	1747		1853	1847	1953		1947			2053		2047		2153	2153	...	...	2247	...	
Zürich Hbf .... d.	1757	1800			1903				2003					2103	2203	2203	...	...		2322	0006	
Thalwil .... d.	1814							2014						2114			...	...				
Zug .... d.	1831				1931			2031						2131	2231u	2231	...	...		2355	0034	
Arth Goldau .... a.	1845	1858			1945	1940		2045	2058			2140	2145	2235	2245u	2245	...	2358				
Arth Goldau .... d.	1849	1900			1949	1952		2108	2108			2147		2247u	2247	...	2359				
Schwyz .... d.	1857							2000								...	0007				
Brunnen .... d.	1901							2004								...	0011				
Flüelen .... d.	1911							2014								...					
Erstfeld .... d.	1918							2021								...	0021				
Göschenen .... d.	1942	1948						2047	2157	2157			2235			...	0038				
Airolo .... d.		1959						2059	2208	2208			2246			...					
Biasca .... d.								2138								...					
Bellinzona .... a.		2032			2047	2103		2132	2151	2259	2259		2334		0028u	0028	...			0252	0337	
Bellinzona .... d.					2049	2105		2135	2154	2302	2302		2336		0030u	0030	...					
Lugano .... d.					2119	2135		2206	2224	2333	2333		0006		0059u	0059	...			0310	0355	
Chiasso .... a.					2142	2159		2230	2256	2357	2357		0038		0123u	0123	...					
Chiasso ▨ .... d.					2200			2248		0015	0015				0140u		...			0252	0337	
Como San Giovanni ... d.					2207			2256		0022	0022						...			0310	0355	
Milano Centrale .... a.					2335					0100g	0100g				0220g		...			0352t	0440	

km		2654	5204 2656 Ⓐ	IC 650	5220 2658 Ⓐ	660	EN 304	IC 304	IC 711	2660	1660	560	1560	1084	1664	IC302 1664 P	IC302 IC486 M	IC 715	1568	IC 250	IC 717	1670	IC 386	IC 721
0	Milano Centrale ..... d.					...	0410g								0515t		0625g	0625g			0725	...		0825
46	Como San Giovanni .. d.					...									0611		0705	0705			0804	...		0905
51	Chiasso ▨ .... a.					...	0455s								0617s		0712	0712			0810	...		0912
51	Chiasso .... d.			0506	0530	0530		0630						0640s	0706	0730	0730			0827	...	0906	0930
77	Lugano .... d.			0541	0557s	0557		0658						0707s	0741	0757	0757			0854	...	0941	0957
106	Bellinzona .... a.			0606	0624s	0624		0725						0733s	0806	0824	0824			0920	...	1006	1024
106	Bellinzona .... d.			0609	0627s	0627		0727						0736s	0809	0827	0827			0923	...	1009	1027
125	Biasca .... d.				0622										0822							1022	...
171	Airolo .... d.				0701				0814						0901							1101	...
187	Göschenen .... d.				0713					0813					0913				1013	1023		1113	...
215	Erstfeld .... d.		0531	0624	0738					0838					0938				1038			1138	...
224	Flüelen .... d.		0539	0632	0746					0846					0946				1046			1146	...
236	Brunnen .... d.		0551	0644	0757					0857					0957				1057			1157	...
240	Schwyz .... d.		0555	0648	0801					0901					1001				1101			1201	...
248	Arth Goldau .... a.		0603	0656	0808	0811s	0811			0908	0913		0919s	1008	1011	1011		1108	1111	1208	1211	
248	Arth Goldau .... d.		0600	0612	0700	0815	0815s	0815			0920	0915		0922s	1020	1020	1015		1115	1120	1220	1215	
264	Zug .... d.						0832s	0832				0932			1032				1132		1232		
281	Thalwil .... d.															1145							
293	Zürich Hbf .... a.					0857	0857				0957		1015s		1057				1157		1257		
293	Zürich Hbf .... d.					0913	0913	0907				1016	1013	1028s		1113	1107	1213		1207	1313	1307	
310	Zürich Flughafen + 299.a.							0916				1026				1116		1216			1316		
	Schaffhausen 735 .... a.					0951	0951				1051	1121s				1151		1251			1351		
	Luzern .... a.		0628	0639	0730	0839				0946				1046	1046				1146	1246			
	Luzern .... d.	0531	0635	0646	0756	0846			0856	0956				1056	1056				1156	1256			
	Sursee .... d.	0551	0655		0816				0916	1016				1116	1116				1216	1316			
	Zofingen .... d.	0604	0708		0829				0929	1029				1129	1129				1229	1329			
	Olten .... d.	0617	0717	0727	0839	0927			0939	1039				1139	1139				1239	1339			
	Liestal .... d.	0638	0738		0858				0958	1058				1158	1158				1258	1358			
	Basel SBB .... a.	0649	0749	0753	0909	0953			1009	1109				1209	1209				1309	1409			

NOTES (LISTED BY TRAIN NUMBERS)

301 – 🛏 Basel - Milano Porta Garibaldi (train 311) - Roma - Tiburtina - Napoli.

EN303/4 – ROMA - 🛏 1, 2 cl. and 🛏 2 cl. Zürich - Milano Porta Garibaldi (trains EN313/4) - Roma Termini and v.v.

386 – 🛏 Milano - Zürich - Stuttgart - Nürnberg; ✗ Chiasso - Singen.

389 – 🛏 2 cl. and 🛏 Stuttgart - Schaffhausen - Zürich - Milano - Ancona - Lecce; 🛏 Stuttgart - Chiasso; 🛏 Zürich - Milano - Lecce; ✗ Singen - Chiasso.

485 – 🛏 Stuttgart - Schaffhausen - Zürich - Chiasso.

691 – Runs ⑤ also Apr. 13, May 24, **not** Apr. 14, May 26: 🛏 Genève Aéroport (train 1891) - Luzern - Chiasso.

1084 – Runs Dec. 17, Jan. 1, Apr. 16 (from Napoli): 🛏 2 cl. and 🛏 Napoli - Roma Tiburtina - Firenze SMN - Zürich - Singen (train 486) - Stuttgart.

1085 – Runs ⑤ Dec. 16 - 24; also Apr. 13 (from Stuttgart): 🛏 2 cl. and 🛏 Stuttgart (train 487) - Zürich - Roma Tiburtina - Napoli.

1087 – Runs ⑥ Oct. 1 - 15, also Apr. 8, 14, and May 25: 🛏 2 cl. and 🛏 Zürich - Genova - Ventimiglia.

L – Runs ⑤ also Apr. 13, May 24, **not** Apr. 14, May 26: 🛏 Schaffhausen - Zürich - Bellinzona - Locarno.

M – 🛏 Napoli (train 312) - Roma Tiburtina - Milano Porta Garibaldi (train IC302) - Arth Goldau (train IC486) - Zürich; 🛏 Chiasso - Arth Goldau (train IC486) - Stuttgart.

N – 🛏 Schaffhausen - Zürich - Arth Goldau - Milano Porta Garibaldi (train 311) - Roma Tiburtina - Napoli.

P – 🛏 Napoli (train 312) - Roma Tiburtina - Milano - Arth Goldau - Basel.

Q – Runs daily; Conveys on Ⓐ: 🛏 Basel - Luzern - Erstfeld.

g – Milano **Porta Garibaldi**.

t – Milano **Lambrate**.

s – Stops to **set down** only.

u – Stops to **pick up** only.

✗ – Supplement payable in Italy.

§ – Supplement payable in Italy (except for passengers with international tickets).

Operator: FS – Ferrovie dello Stato (Italian State Railways).

Table 291 — LOCARNO - BELLINZONA

All trains 1, 2 class. SBB

km								B♀		Zp♀		S♀		⑦n		Zn					
0	Locarno .... d.	0634	...	0703	0803	0858	1003	1103	1203	1303	1335	1403	1503	1514	1603	1644	1703	1727	1803	1845	1903	2003	2135	2232	2335
20	Bellinzona 290 .... a.	0702	...	0721	0821	0916	1021	1121	1221	1321	1402	1421	1521	1539	1621	1707	1721	1745	1821	1907	1921	2021	2202	2259	2359

					Zp♀		B♀		Zt♀		N♀					⑤L	T♀			
Bellinzona 290 .... d.	0637	0734	0755	0827	0937	...	1018	1037	1055	1116	1137	1237	1337	1437	1537	1637	1737	...	1837	1937	2035	2055	2107	2155	2304
Locarno .... a.	0656	0758	0823	0846	0956	...	1043	1056	1123	1135	1156	1256	1356	1456	1556	1656	1756	...	1856	1956	2056	2123	2131	2223	2328

B – 🛏 Locarno - Bellinzona - Basel and v.v.

L – Runs ⑤, also Apr. 13, May 24, **not** Apr. 14, May 26: 🛏 Schaffhausen - Locarno.

P – 🛏 Nürnberg - Schaffhausen - Zürich - Locarno.

S – 🛏 Locarno - Zürich - Schaffhausen.

T – On ⑤ (also Apr. 13, May 24, **not** Apr. 14, May 26) depart Bellinzona 2107, arrive Locarno 2131.

Z – 🛏 Locarno - Zürich and v.v.

n – Will **not** run Dec. 25, Jan. 1, Apr. 14, 16, May 25.

p – Will **not** run Nov. 1 - Mar. 31.

t – Runs ⑥ Oct. 1 - 29 only.

Table 290 — MILANO - CHIASSO - LUGANO - ZÜRICH and BASEL

1, 2 class. FS, SBB

	1572	EC 8 ✕◆	IC 723 Y	2672 Y	1676 ◆	IC 388 ✕	IC 725 Y	1576	EC 4 ✕◆	IC 727	2678	1680 L	IC 380 Y	IC 729 Y	1582	EC 52 ✕◆	IC 733 Y	1584 C	1584 D	1686	IC 382 ✕	IC 737 ✕	EC 56 ✕◆	IC 990 ✕
Milano Centrale .... d.		0920				1025			1125				1225			1325					1425		1500	
Como San Giovanni ...... d.		1004				1105			1205				1305			1405					1505		1538	
Chiasso ▦ .... a.		1012				1112			1212				1312			1412					1512		1545	
Chiasso .... d.	1006	1030			1106	1130		1206	1230			1306	1330		1406	1430				1506	1530		1557	1603
Lugano .... a.	1041	1057			1141	1157		1241	1257			1341	1357		1441	1457				1541	1557		1624	1659
Bellinzona .... a.	1106	1124			1206	1224		1306	1324			1405	1424		1506	1524				1606	1624		1659	
Bellinzona .... d.	1109	1127			1209	1227		1309	1327			1409	1427		1509	1527		1542		1609	1627		1702	
Biasca .... d.	1122				1222			1322				1422			1522			1601	1634	1701				
Airolo .... d.	1201				1301			1401				1501			1601			1613		1713				
Göschenen .... d.	1213				1313			1413				1513			1613			1647	1647	1713		1738		
Erstfeld .... d.	1238				1338			1438				1538			1638			1713	1713	1738				
Flüelen .... d.	1246				1346			1446				1546			1646			1721	1721	1746				
Brunnen .... d.	1257				1357			1457				1557			1657			1732	1732	1757				
Schwyz .... d.	1301				1401			1501				1601			1701			1736	1736	1801				
Arth Goldau .... a.	1308		1311		1408		1411	1508		1511		1608		1611	1708		1711	1743	1743	1808	1815	1811	1820	1845/1847
Arth Goldau .... d.	1315		1314		1420		1415	1515		1514		1620		1615	1715		1714	1803	1803		1832		1902	
Zug .... a.	1332				1432			1532				1632			1532		1745	1817	1817					
Thalwil .... a.	1345							1545									1657	1830	1830		1857	1907	1928	
Zürich Hbf .... a.	1357				1457			1557				1657			1757						1913	1916	1945	1937
Zürich Hbf .... d.	1413		1407		1513	1507		1613	1607			1713	1707		1813	1807	1839	1839				1945	1956	
Zürich Flughafen + 299 . a.	1451		1416				1516		1616			1716				1816	1851	1851			1951			
Schaffhausen 735 ...... a.			1339		1446			1539		1646			1739	2682		1846							
Luzern .... a.		1339			1446			1539			1556	1656			1746	1756			1816		1856			
Luzern .... d.		1346		1356	1456			1546			1616	1716			1816						1916			
Sursee .... d.				1416	1516						1629	1729			1829						1929			
Zofingen .... d.				1429	1529						1639	1739					1827	1839			1939			
Olten .... d.		1427		1439	1558			1627			1658	1758						1858			1958			2023
Liestal .... d.				1458	1609											1853	1909				2009			2035
Basel SBB .... a.		1453		1509	1609			1653			1709	1809				1853	1909				2009			2035

	1588 M	IC 252 Y	IC 739 Y	2688	IC 690 Y⑦◆	1690	IC 354 ✕⑦◆	IC 592 Y	EC 54 ✕	IC 254 Y	2692	1594 Y	256	5384	EC 58 ✕ R	1796	5292	1596 ⑦	IC562 1598 §	1997 R	200 ◆	298 ◆	1294
Milano Centrale .... d.		1525			1625		1720	1725				1825		1925				2025			2125	2135	2258t
Como San Giovanni ...... d.		1605			1705		1755	1806				1905		1959				2106			2205	2216	2340
Chiasso ▦ .... a.		1612			1712		1802	1812				1912						2112			2230	2240	2358
Chiasso .... d.		1630		1658	1706	1730	1820	1830				1906	1930	1944	2031			2053	2157		2257	2307	
Lugano .... a.		1657		1725	1741	1757	1847	1857				1941	1957	2047	2058			2118	2224		2324	2333	
Bellinzona .... a.		1724		1751	1806	1824	1915	1924				2006	2024		2100			2120				2335	
Bellinzona .... d.	1709	1727		1754	1809	1827	1910	1918	1927			2009	2027		2100			2133					
Biasca .... d.	1722				1822		1901					2101						2211					
Airolo .... d.	1801				1901		1913					2113											
Göschenen .... d.	1813				1913		1938					2138											
Erstfeld .... d.	1838				1938		1946					2146					2239						
Flüelen .... d.	1846				1946		1957					2157					2251						
Brunnen .... d.	1857				1957		2001					2201					2255						
Schwyz .... d.	1901				2001		2011					2208	2211				2304	2308					
Arth Goldau .... a.	1908	1911			2008	2011	2101	2111				2215	2214				2306h	2311					
Arth Goldau .... d.	1915	1914			2020	2015	2104	2114				2232			2301			2328		2334			
Zug .... a.	1932						2032	2113	2122			2245			2341			2353					
Thalwil .... a.	1945						2057	2142	2148			2257			2324								
Zürich Hbf .... a.	1957						2107	2116	2207			2315			2325							2358	
Zürich Hbf .... d.	2013		2007				2116	2216	2207			2315			2325								
Zürich Flughafen + 299 . a.	2051		2016											2337									
Schaffhausen 735 ...... a.					2006	2046						2139			2334h			2358					
Luzern .... a.		1939		1956		2056				2146	2156			2239	2246								
Luzern .... d.		1946				2116				2216													
Sursee .... d.			2016			2129				2229				2318									
Zofingen .... d.			2029			2139						2236		2331					2227				
Olten .... d.		2027	2039			2158								2348								0240	0353
Liestal .... d.			2058			2209								2359						0050			
Basel SBB .... a.		2053	2109			2209						2253	2311		2359					0050		0240	0353

◆ — NOTES (LISTED BY TRAIN NUMBERS)

EC4 – VERDI – [Through carriage] Milano - Basel - Köln - Dortmund; ✕ Chiasso - Dortmund.
EC8 – TIZIANO – [Through carriage] Milano - Basel - Köln - Hannover; ✕ Chiasso - Hannover.
EC52 – COLOSSEUM – [Through carriage] and ✕ Roma - Firenze SMN - Milano - Basel.
EC54 – RAFFAELLO – [Through carriage] and ✕ Roma - Firenze SMN - Milano - Basel.
EC56 – TICINO – [Through carriage] (also [observation car]) and ✕ Milano - Zürich.
EC58 – GOTTARDO – [Through carriage] and ✕ Milano - Zürich. Supplement payable.
200 – Milano - Dortmund and Frankfurt (Main) – For composition see Table 73.
IC254 – [Through carriage] Sestri Levante (train 682) - Milano - Basel.
298 – 🛏 1, 2 cl., 🛋 2 cl. and [Through carriage] (Venezia Santa Lucia ⓒ -) Milano - Basel - Luxembourg - Brussels.
IC354 – CANALETTO – [Through carriage] (also [observation car]) and ✕ Venezia Santa Lucia - Verona - Milano - Zürich.
IC380 – [Through carriage] Milano - Zürich - Schaffhausen - Stuttgart.
IC382 – Genova Brignole - Milano - Zürich - Stuttgart; ✕ Chiasso - Zürich.
IC388 – 🛋 2 cl. and [Through carriage] Lecce - Ancona - Milano - Zürich - Stuttgart; [Through carriage] Lecce - Zürich; [Through carriage] Chiasso - Stuttgart; ✕ Chiasso - Schaffhausen.

IC592 – Runs ⑦, not Dec. 25, Jan. 1, Apr. 14, 16, May 25: [Through carriage] Locarno - Bellinzona - Zürich.
IC690 – Runs ⑦, not Dec. 25, Jan. 1, Apr. 14, 16, May 25: [Through carriage] Chiasso - Luzern - Bern - Genève.
1294 – Runs June 30 - Sept. 3 (from Roma): 🛏 1, 2 cl. (not June 30, July 1), 🛋 2 cl. and [Through carriage] Roma - Firenze SMN - Milano Lambrate - Basel - Luxembourg - Brussels.
1596 – Runs ⑦, not Dec. 25, Jan. 1, Apr. 14, 16, May 25: [Through carriage] Chiasso - Zürich.
1676 – [Through carriage] Chiasso - Basel; [Through carriage] Chiasso - Luzern (train 1876) - Genève Aéroport ⓒ Dec. 17 - Mar. 26.
C – Runs Sept. 25 - Oct. 31 and Apr. 1 - May 28 only: [Through carriage] Locarno - Zürich.
D – [Through carriage] Locarno - Basel.
L – [Through carriage] Locarno - Schaffhausen.
M – [Through carriage] Locarno - Schaffhausen.
h – 7 minutes later when train 1596 runs.
t – Milano Lambrate.
⚋ – Supplement payable in Italy.
§ – Supplement payable in Italy (except for passengers with international tickets).
Operator: FS - Ferrovie dello Stato (Italian State Railways).

For Table 291 see Page 195.

Table 292 — 🚐 MEIRINGEN - ANDERMATT

No Winter Service   🚐 P1

Meiringen Bahnhof 285 .... d.	...	...	...	...	...	Andermatt Bahnhof 320 322 ...... d.	...	...	...	...	...	...	...	...
Susten Passhöhe .... d.	...	...	...	...	...	Realp Post .... d.	...	...	...	...	...	...	...	...
Göschenen Bahnhof 290 .. a.	...	...	...	...	...	Furka Passhöhe .... d.	...	...	...	...	...	...	...	...
Göschenen Bahnhof 290 322 d.	...	...	...	...	...	Oberwald Bahnhof 320.......... a.	...	...	...	...	...	...	...	...
Grimsel Passhöhe Post........ d.	...	...	...	...	...	Oberwald Bahnhof 320.......... d.	...	...	...	...	...	...	...	...
Oberwald Bahnhof 320......... a.	...	...	...	...	...	Grimsel Passhöhe Post.......... d.	...	...	...	...	...	...	...	...
Oberwald Bahnhof 320......... d.	...	...	...	...	...	Göschenen Bahnhof 290 322 . a.	...	...	...	...	...	...	...	...
Furka Passhöhe .... d.	...	...	...	...	...	Göschenen Bahnhof 290...... d.	...	...	...	...	...	...	...	...
Realp Post .... d.	...	...	...	...	...	Susten Passhöhe .... d.	...	...	...	...	...	...	...	...
Andermatt Bahnhof 320 322 a.	...	...	...	...	...	Meiringen Bahnhof 320.......... a.	...	...	...	...	...	...	...	...

🚃 – Through carriage (1 and 2 class)   ◆ – See footnote   R – Reservation obligatory

Table 293 LUZERN - STANS - ENGELBERG

1, 2 class. Narrow gauge rack railway. LSE

	Ⓐ	⑦	⑦	⚒	⚒			T	⚒					⚒						🚌			🚌
Luzern 285 d.	...	0619	...	0632	0700	0724	...	0801	0801	...	0814		1514	1536	1614	1714	1814	1914	2014	...	2123	2323	...
Hergiswil **285** d.	0547	0631	0647	0647	0713	0736	0738	|	0813	...	0825	and	1525	1549	1625	1725	1825	1925	2025	...	2136	2335	2336
Stansstad d.	0550	...	0650	0650	0717	...	0742	|	0817	...	0829	hourly	1529	1553	1629	1729	1829	1929	2029	...	2140	...	2340
Stans d.	0554	...	0654	0654	0720	...	0747	|	0820	...	0834	until	1534	1556	1634	1734	1834	1934	2033	2035	2144	...	2344
Engelberg a.	0635	...	0725	0725	...	...	0820	0844	...	...	0912		1612	...	1712	1812	1912	2012	...	2102	2215	...	0015

	⚒	Ⓐ						T	Ⓐ			Ⓒ	Ⓐ							🚌			🚌
Engelberg d.	...	0625	0650	...	0745		1645	1705	...	...	1745	1845	1845	...	1945	...	2050	...	...	2150	...	...	...
Stans d.	0607	0705	0725	...	0825	and	1725	|	1802	...	1825	1925	1925	...	2025	...	2125	...	...	2222	...	...	2322
Stansstad d.	0611	0709	0729	...	0829	hourly	1729	|	1805	...	1829	1929	1932	...	2029	...	2129	...	...	2227	...	...	2327
Hergiswil **285** d.	0615	0713	0734	...	0834	until	1734	|	1809	...	1834	1934	1935	...	2034	...	2132	2137	...	2232	2237	...	2332
Luzern 285 a.	0625	0724	0745	...	0845		1745	1754	1824	...	1845	1945	*1950*	...	2045	...	...	2150	...	...	2250	...	...

T – TITLIS EXPRESS – Runs ⑦ Jan. 1 - Apr. 16, also Dec. 26, Apr. 17.

Operator: LSE – Luzern Stans Engelberg, Stansstad.

Table 294 ⛴ LUZERN - KÜSSNACHT, ALPNACHSTAD and FLÜELEN

Winter service valid: September 26 - October 23, **1994**, and April 9 - May 27, **1995**

1, 2 class ships ⛴ SGV

	3	5	9	59	65	153	11	13	71	15	415	73	17	17	157	77	19	21	79	81	159		25		27
	⚒🍷	D🍷	🍴	H🍷	🍷	⑦🍷	E🍴	G🍴	J🍷	🍴	D🍷	J🍷	🍴	E🍴	⑦🍷	🍷	🍷	🍷	L🍷	H🍷	⑦🍷		🍷		Ⓐ🍷
Luzern Bahnhofquai d.	0753	0825	0915	0915	1005	1020	1025	1125	1130	1200	...	1300	1315	...	1330	1405	1420	1515	1525	1525	1550	...	1715	...	1815
Verkehrshaus Lido d.	|	|	|	0925	1016	1030	1035	1135	1140	1210	...	1310	1325	...	1341	|	|	1525	1536	1536	1601	...	1725	...	|
Kehrsiten Bürgenstock d.	|	|	|	0948	1052	|	1102	|	1217	|	...	1341	|	...	|	1447	|	1548	|	1632	|	...	|	...	|
Hertenstein d.	|	|	0943	|	|	|	1113	1157	|	|	...	|	1345	...	|	|	1448	1601	|	|	1625	...	1743	...	1843
Küssnacht am Rigi a.	|	|	|	|	|	1116	|	|	|	|	...	|	|	...	1426	|	|	|	|	|	1657	...	|	...	|
Stansstad d.	|	|	|	1010	1117	...	|	|	1241	|	...	1403	|	...	...	1509	|	|	1618	1651	...	...	|	...	|
Alpnachstad a.	|	|	|	1045	1153H	...	|	|	1300H	|	...	1424H	|	...	...	1545H	|	|	...	...	...	...	|	...	|
Weggis d.	|	0901	0952	...	...	...	1123	1207	...	1237	...	...	1356	...	...	...	1458	1612	...	...	...	...	1753	...	1853
Vitznau d.	0836	0918	1009	...	...	...	1140	1226	...	1251	...	...	1415	...	...	...	1513	1630	...	...	...	...	1812	...	1909
Beckenried d.	...	0935	1026	...	...	...	1157	1313	...	...	...	...	1433	...	...	...	...	1648	...	...	...	...	1846	...	...
Gersau d.	...	|	1042	...	...	...	1213	1330	...	...	...	...	1451	...	...	...	...	1705	...	...	...	...	1902	...	...
Treib d.	...	1003	1058	...	...	...	1229	1347	...	...	1429	...	1508	...	...	...	...	1723	...	...	...	...	1918	...	...
Brunnen d.	...	1015	1107	...	...	...	1240	1357	...	...	1440	...	1515	1518	...	...	...	1733	...	...	...	...	1926	...	...
Rütli d.	...	1026	1118	...	...	...	1251	1409	...	...	1451	...	...	1530	...	...	...	1744	...	...	...	...	...	...	...
Tellsplatte d.	...	1045	|	...	...	...	1310	1436	...	...	1510	...	...	|	...	...	...	1802	...	...	...	...	...	...	...
Bauen d.	...	1057	1133	...	...	...	1321	1425	...	...	|	...	...	1546	...	...	...	1812	...	...	...	...	...	...	...
Flüelen a.	...	1115	1152	...	...	...	1340	1452	...	...	1525	...	...	1607	...	...	...	1830	...	...	...	...	...	...	...

	4	8	10	70	68	12	416	72	16	74	18	76	160	78	20	22	22	80	162	82	26	1026	28	30	
	⚒🍷	⚒🍷	🍷	H🍷	L🍷	🍷	D🍷	J🍷	🍴	H🍷	🍴	N🍷	⑦🍷	🍷	🍷	E🍴	🍴	🍷	⑦🍷	H🍷	G🍴	D🍷	E🍷	Ⓐ🍷	
Flüelen d.	...	...	...	...	...	0925	1120	...	...	...	1155	...	...	...	...	1351	...	...	...	...	1500	1530	1620	...	...
Bauen d.	...	...	...	...	...	0945	1140	...	...	...	1216	...	...	...	...	1413	...	...	...	...	1525	1550	1642	...	...
Tellsplatte d.	...	...	...	...	...	0956	1152	...	...	...	|	...	...	...	...	|	...	...	...	...	|	1602	1652	...	...
Rütli d.	...	...	...	...	...	1015	1211	...	...	...	1232	...	...	...	...	1429	...	...	...	...	1543	1621	1712	...	...
Brunnen d.	...	...	0900	...	...	1030	1225	...	...	...	1246	...	...	...	...	1445	...	...	...	...	1600	1634	1726	...	...
Treib d.	...	...	0908	...	...	1039	1232	...	...	...	1254	...	...	...	...	1454	...	...	...	...	1608	1642	1734	...	...
Gersau d.	...	...	0924	...	...	1057	▬	...	...	...	1311	...	...	...	...	1511	1512	...	...	...	1625	|	1751	...	...
Beckenried d.	...	...	0940	...	...	1115	...	...	...	...	1328	...	...	...	...	...	1530	...	...	...	1643	|	1808	...	...
Vitznau d.	0655	0838	1015	...	...	1133	...	...	1252	...	1347	...	...	...	1511	...	1550	...	...	...	1730	|	1845	1911	...
Weggis d.	0710	0855	1030	...	...	1150	...	...	1307	...	1404	...	...	...	1530	...	1607	...	...	...	1748	|	1902	1929	...
Alpnachstad d.	|	|	|	1050	...	|	**154**	1215H	|	1305	|	...	...	1445H	|	...	|	1555H	...	...	|	|	|	|	...
Stansstad d.	|	|	|	1122	1117	|	⑦🍷	1238	|	1343	|	1410	...	1512	|	...	|	1620	...	1653	|	|	|	|	...
Küssnacht am Rigi d.	|	|	|	|	|	|	1123	|	|	|	|	|	1430	|	|	...	|	|	1705	|	|	|	|	|	...
Hertenstein d.	0718	0905	|	1153b	|	1200	1154	|	|	1416b	|	|	|	|	1540	...	1617e	|	|	1738b	1758	|	1912	1939	...
Kehrsiten Bürgenstock d.	|	0917	1050e	1142	1150	1212e	|	1258	|	1403	1422e	1431	|	1534	1553	...	|	1642	|	1726	|	|	|	|	...
Verkehrshaus Lido d.	|	|	1108	1215	1227	1233	1238	1320f	1336	|	1442	|	1520	1608	1613	...	|	1717f	1757	1819	1824	|	1934	|	...
Luzern Bahnhofquai a.	0746	0946	1120	1225	1240	1246	1250	1332	1346	1446	1454	1500	1532	1620	1625	...	1646	1730	1810	1830	1836	1746	1946	2007	...

D – Daily Sept. 26 - Oct. 23 also May 1 - 27.
E – Daily Sept. 26 - Oct. 23, May 1 - 27, also ⑦ Apr. 9 - 30.
G – Paddlesteamer on dates in note **E**.
H – Daily Sept. 26 - Oct. 23 and May 7 - 27.
J – Daily Sept. 26 - Oct. 23 and May 7 - 27, also ⑦ Apr. 9 - 30.
L – Daily Apr. 9 - May 6. N – ⑦ Apr. 9 - 30.

b – Via Kehrsiten Bürgenstock. Change boats for Vitznau direction.
e – Change boats for Alpnachstad direction.
f – Change boats for Flüelen.
A skeleton service operates **Luzern - Flüelen** and v.v. Oct. 24, **1994** - Apr. 8, **1995**.

Operator: SGV – Schiffahrtsgesellschaft Vierwaldstättersee, ☎ Luzern (041) 40 45 40.

Table 295 LUZERN - ZÜRICH

All trains 1, 2 class. SBB

km		1952	1954	1956	1956	1958	1960	1962	1966	1968	1970	1972	1974	1976	1976	1980	1980	1982	1984	1986	1990	1992	1994	1996
		G🍷	Ⓐ🍷	Ⓒ🍷	Ⓐ🍷	Ⓐ	🍷	🍷	🍷	🍷	🍷	🍷	🍷	Ⓐ🍷	Ⓒ🍷	Ⓐ🍷	Ⓒ	🍷	🍷	c	A	c		
0	**Luzern** d.	0604	0642	0704	0704	0738	0804	0904	1004	1104	1204	1304	1404	1504	1504	1604	1604	1704	1804	1904	2004	2104	2204	2308
28	Zug d.	0628	0705	0728	0728	0805	0828	0928	1028	1128	1228	1328	1428	1528	1528	1628	1628	1728	1828	1928	2028	2128	2228	2332
45	Thalwil d.	0642	0724	0742	0742	|	0842	0942	1042	1142	1242	1342	1442	1542	1542	1642	1642	1742	1842	1942	2042	2142	2242	2346
57	**Zürich Hbf** a.	0656	0738	0753	0757	0834	0853	0953	1053	1153	1253	1353	1453	1553	1553	1653	1653	1753	1853	1953	2053	2153	2253	2357
	Zürich Flughafen ✈ **299** a.	0716	...	0810	...	...	0910	1010	1110	1210	1310	1410	1510	...	1610	...	1710	1812	...	...	...	...	...	...

	1955	1957	1961	1961	1963	1965	1967	1971	1973	1975	1977	1979	1981	1981	1983	1985	1985	1987	1989	1991	1993	1995	1997	1951
	🍷	H🍷	Ⓐ🍷	Ⓒ🍷	🍷	🍷	🍷	🍷	🍷	🍷	🍷	Ⓐ🍷	Ⓐ🍷	LⒸ🍷	Ⓐ	LⒶ	Ⓒ🍷	Ⓐ🍷	🍷	🍷	c	🍷		
Zürich Flughafen ✈ **299** d.	...	...	...	0833	0933	1033	1133	1233	1333	1433	1533	...	...	1633	...	...	1733	...	1833	...	...	...	...	...
Zürich Hbf d.	0707	0807	0907	0907	1007	1107	1207	1307	1407	1507	1607	1630	1705	1707	1730	1805	1807	1830	1907	2007	2107	2207	2307	0013
Thalwil d.	0718	0818	0918	0918	1018	1118	1218	1318	1418	1518	1618	1643	|	1718	1743	|	1818	1843	1918	2018	2118	2218	2318	0024
Zug d.	0734	0834	0934	0934	1034	1134	1234	1334	1434	1534	1634	1702	1734	1734	1802	1834	1834	1902	1934	2034	2134	2234	2334	0038
Luzern a.	0756	0856	0956	0956	1056	1156	1256	1356	1456	1556	1656	1732	1756	1756	1829	1856	1856	1932	1956	2056	2156	2256	2358	0100

A – Conveys on Ⓐ: [12] and 🍷 Genève Aéroport - Luzern - Zürich.
G – [12] Luzern - Zürich - St Gallen.
H – Conveys on Ⓐ: [12] St Gallen - Zürich - Luzern.

L – [12] Zürich (Flughafen) - Luzern - Bern - Lausanne.
c – 🍷 on Ⓒ only.

Table 296 VITZNAU and ARTH GOLDAU - RIGI KULM

2 class only. Narrow gauge rack railways. RB

Rail service **Vitznau - Rigi Kulm** and **Arth Goldau - Rigi Kulm**. Journey times 30 minutes uphill, 40 minutes downhill. **Operator**: RB – Rigi Bahn. Additional services run: **Vitznau - Rigi Kaltbad** and v.v., **Arth Goldau - Rigi Kulm** and v.v. at busy times. A cable car operates daily (**except** the last two weeks in November or April) between Weggis on Lake Luzern (Table **294**) and Rigi Kaltbad.

Vitznau to Rigi Kulm (**Sept. 26 - Oct. 23** and **Apr. 9 - May 27**) at: 0840, 0920, 1010, 1045, 1145, 1240, 1330, 1420, 1515, 1610, 1700.
Vitznau to Rigi Kulm (**Oct. 24 - Apr. 8**) at: 0915, 1015, 1145, 1255, 1420, 1515, 1620.

Arth Goldau to Rigi Kulm (**Sept. 26 - Oct. 23** and **Apr. 9 - May 27**) at: 0755, 1003, 1103, 1303, 1503, 1603, 1833.
Arth Goldau to Rigi Kulm (**Oct. 24 - Apr. 8**) at: 0755, 1015, 1115, 1315, 1515, 1615, 1833.

Rigi Kulm to Vitznau (**Sept. 26 - Oct. 23** and **Apr. 9 - May 27**) at: 0915, 0955, 1045, 1140, 1240, 1330, 1415, 1500, 1600, 1645, 1745.
Rigi Kulm to Vitznau (**Oct. 24 - Apr. 8**) at: 1000, 1145, 1245, 1330, 1500, 1620, 1700.

Rigi Kulm to Arth Goldau (**Sept. 26 - Oct. 23** and **Apr. 9 - May 27**) at: 0910, 1110, 1210, 1410, 1610, 1710, 1910.
Rigi Kulm to Arth Goldau (**Oct. 24 - Apr. 8**) at: 0910, 1110, 1210, 1410, 1610, 1710, 1910.

Table 299 ZÜRICH HBF - ZÜRICH FLUGHAFEN ✈

1, 2 class. SBB

Rail service **Zürich Hbf - Zürich Flughafen** ✈. *17 km.* Journey time: 10 - 12 minutes.

From **Zürich Hbf** : 0526, 0603, 0626, 0631, 0639, 0707, 0710, 0726, 0745, 0800Ⓒ, 0807, 0810, 0826, 0839, 0845, 0900, 0907, 0910, 0926, 0945, 1000, 1007, 1010, 1016, 1026, 1033, 1039, 1100, 1107, 1110, 1126, 1139, 1200, 1207, 1210, 1226, 1239, 1245, 1300, 1307, 1310, 1326, 1345, 1400, 1407, 1410, 1426, 1439, 1445, 1500, 1507, 1510, 1526, 1545, 1600Ⓒ, 1607, 1610, 1626, 1639, 1645, 1700Ⓒ, 1707, 1710, 1726, 1733Ⓐ, 1745, 1800, 1807, 1810, 1826, 1839, 1845, 1907, 1910, 1926, 1939⑦, 1945, 2007, 2010, 2026, 2039Ⓑ, 2045, 2107, 2110, 2126, 2207, 2210, 2226, 2315, 2326, 2339.

From **Zürich Flughafen** ✈ : 0611, 0621, 0637, 0642, 0702Ⓐ (**not** May 1), 0708⚒, 0713, 0721, 0739, 0742, 0805, 0813Ⓐ, 0821, 0833Ⓒ, 0839, 0842, 0905, 0921, 0933, 0939, 0942, 1005, 1012, 1021, 1033, 1039, 1042, 1105, 1121, 1133, 1139, 1142, 1205, 1212, 1221, 1233, 1239, 1242, 1305, 1316, 1321, 1333, 1339, 1342, 1405, 1412, 1421, 1433, 1439, 1442, 1505, 1521, 1533, 1539, 1542, 1605, 1612, 1621, 1633Ⓒ, 1639, 1642, 1705, 1713Ⓐ, 1721, 1733Ⓒ, 1739, 1742, 1809, 1821, 1833, 1839, 1842, 1905, 1921, 1939, 1942, 2005, 2012, 2021, 2039, 2042, 2105, 2121, 2139, 2142, 2212, 2221, 2239, 2242, 2321, 2341, 0021.

Table 300 BASEL - ZÜRICH

1, 2 class. SBB

km		2853	469	IC 753	1757	IC 757		959	1759	IC 759	EC 163	IC 763	963	7933	ICE 271	1765	IC 967	IC 767	969	7941	1769	EC 113		IC 769
		R	🍷 ◆	🍴 C		🍴 C		🍷 R	🍷 C	🍷 Ⓐv	🍴 ◆	🍴 C	🍷 R		🍴 ◆	🍴 C	🍴	🍷 C	🍷 R		🍷 C	🍴 ◆		🍴 C
0	**Basel SBB** d.	0523	0549	0625	0634	0704	...	0725	0749	0804	0825	0849	0925	0934	0947	0949	1025	1049	1125	1134	1149	1225	...	1249
16	Rheinfelden d.	|	0601	|	0647	|	...	|	0801	|	|	0901	|	0950	|	1001	|	1101	|	1150	1201	|	...	1301
29	Stein Säckingen d.	|	|	|	0659	|	...	|	|	|	|	|	|	1002	|	|	|	|	|	1202	|	|	...	|
57	Brugg d.	|	0635	|	0723	|	...	|	0835	|	|	0935	|	1025	|	1035	|	1135	|	1225	1235	|	...	1335
66	Baden d.	|	0644	|	0732	|	...	|	0844	|	|	0944	|	...	|	1044	|	1144	|	...	1244	|	...	1344
	Liestal d.	0533	|	0635	|	|	...	0735	|	|	0835	|	0935	...	|	|	1035	|	1135	...	|	1235	...	|
	Aarau d.	0557	|	0658	|	|	...	0758	|	|	0858	|	0958	...	|	|	1058	|	1158	...	|	1258	...	|
88	**Zürich Hbf** a.	0623	0700	0723	0749	0800	...	0823	0900	0903	0923	1000	1023	...	1045	1100	1123	1200	1223	...	1300	1323	...	1400
	Zürich Flughafen ✈ **299** a.	0650	*0716*	*0756*	...	*0816*	...	0850	*0916*	*0920*	*0956*	*1016*	1050	...	*1110*	*1116*	*1151*	*1216*	1250	...	*1316*	*1356*	...	*1416*

	975		7953	EC 103	IC 977		IC 777	979		1781	983	983	1783	EC 3	ICE 71	985	1787	IC 787	IC 989	EC 97	1789	ICE 77	991	991
	🍷 R			🍴 ◆	🍷		🍴 C	🍷 R		🍷 C	🍷 ◆Ⓐ	🍷 Ⓒ	🍷	🍴 ◆	🍴 ◆	◆	🍴 C	Ⓐy	🍷	🍴 ◆	🍷 C	🍴 ◆	ⒷG	⑥
Basel SBB d.	1325	...	1334	1354	1425	...	1449	1525	...	1549	1625	1625	1649	1704	1715	1725	1749	1804	1825	1847	1849	1915	1925	1925
Rheinfelden d.	|	...	1350	|	|	...	1501	|	...	1601	|	|	1701	|	|	|	1801	|	|	|	1901	|	|	|
Stein Säckingen d.	|	...	1402	|	|	...	|	|	...	|	|	|	|	|	|	|	|	|	|	|	|	|	|	|
Brugg d.	|	...	1425	1435	|	...	1535	|	...	1635	|	|	1735	|	|	|	1835	|	|	|	1935	|	|	|
Baden d.	|	...	...	1444	|	...	1544	|	...	1644	|	|	1744	|	|	|	1844	|	|	|	1944	|	|	|
Liestal d.	1335	...	...	|	1435	...	|	1535	...	|	1635	1635	|	|	|	1735	|	|	1835	|	|	|	1935	1935
Aarau d.	1358	...	...	|	1458	...	|	1558	...	|	1658	1658	|	|	|	1758	|	|	1858	|	|	|	1958	1958
Zürich Hbf a.	1423	...	...	1500	1523	...	1600	1623	...	1700	1723	1723	1800	1803	1815	1823	1900	1903	1923	1945	2000	2015	2023	2023
Zürich Flughafen ✈ **299** a.	1450	...	...	*1516*	*1556*	...	*1616*	1651	...	*1716*	1742	*1756*	*1816*	*1820*	*1838*	1851	*1916*	*1920*	*1956*	...	*2016*	*2038*	2050	*2056*

	1791	465	1793	EN 467		EC 115	1795	1797	1799	2651 1849
	🍴 C	◆		◆		🍴 ◆	H	🍷		
Basel SBB d.	1949	2025	2049	2117	...	2148	2150	2254	2332	0002
Rheinfelden d.	2001	|	2101	|	...	|	2202	2305	2345	|
Stein Säckingen d.	|	|	|	|	...	|	2211	2314	2356	|
Brugg d.	2035	|	2135	2157	...	|	2235	2337	0020	|
Baden d.	2044	|	2144	2206	...	|	2244	2345	0028	|
Liestal d.	|	2035	|	|	...	|	|	|	|	0011
Aarau d.	|	2058	|	|	...	|	|	|	|	0046t
Zürich Hbf a.	2100	2123	2200	2223	...	2247	2300	0003	0048	0111t
Zürich Flughafen ✈ **299** a.	*2116*	...	*2216*	...	...	...	*2325*	...	...	...

	1704 2652	1750	1752	952	952	ICE 76	1754	EC 114	EN 466
	Ⓐ	Ⓐ	🍷	🍷 ⚒G	🍷 ⑦	🍴 ◆	H	🍴 ◆	◆
Zürich Flughafen ✈ **299** d.	...	...	*0611*	0611	*0611*	*0621*	*0642*	*0642*	...
Zürich Hbf d.	0445	0555	0630	0635	0635	0645	0700	0712	0715s
Aarau d.	0527	|	|	0659	0659	|	|	|	|
Liestal d.	0606t	|	|	0723	0723	|	|	|	|
Baden d.	|	0614	0648	|	|	|	0716	|	0733s
Brugg d.	|	0623	0657	|	|	|	0725	|	0744s
Stein Säckingen d.	|	0643	0719	|	|	|	|	|	|
Rheinfelden d.	|	0654	0728	|	|	|	0758	|	|
Basel SBB a.	0618t	0708	0741	0735	0735	0747	0810	0812	0832

	954	1756	IC 758	464	1760	IC 960	EC 102	7938	964	1764	IC 966	ICE 70		EC 96	7946	970	EC 2	1772	IC 974	IC 778	7956	978	1780	
	🍷 ◆	🍴 C	🍷 Ⓐv	🍷 ◆	🍴 C	🍷	🍴 ◆		🍷 R	🍷 C	🍴	🍴 ◆		🍴 ◆		🍷 R	🍴 ◆	🍷 C	🍴	🍷 C		🍷 R	🍴 C	
Zürich Flughafen ✈ **299** d.	0713	*0742*	...	*0805*	*0842*	*0905*	*0942*	...	1012	*1042*	*1105*	*1121*	...	*1142*	...	1212	*1239*	*1242*	*1316*	*1342*	...	1412	*1442*	...
Zürich Hbf d.	0737	0800	0817	0837	0900	0937	1000	...	1037	1100	1137	1145	...	1200	...	1237	1257	1300	1337	1400	...	1437	1500	...
Aarau d.	0801	|	|	0901	|	1001	|	...	1101	|	1201	|	...	|	...	1301	|	|	1401	|	...	1501	|	...
Liestal d.	0823	|	|	0923	|	1023	|	...	1123	|	1223	|	...	|	...	1323	|	|	1423	|	...	1523	|	...
Baden d.	|	0816	|	|	0916	|	1016	...	|	1116	|	|	...	1216	...	|	|	1316	|	1416	...	|	1516	...
Brugg d.	|	0825	|	|	0925	|	1025	1031	|	1125	|	|	...	1225	1231	|	|	1325	|	1425	1431	|	1525	...
Stein Säckingen d.	|	|	|	|	|	|	|	1055	|	|	|	|	...	|	1255	|	|	|	|	|	1455	|	|	...
Rheinfelden d.	|	0858	|	|	0958	|	|	1108	|	1158	|	|	...	|	1308	|	|	1358	|	1458	1508	|	1558	...
Basel SBB a.	0835	0911	0914	0935	1011	1035	1106	1124	1135	1211	1235	1247	...	1306	1324	1335	1356	1411	1435	1511	1524	1535	1611	...

	EC 116	IC 782	982	1784	7972	IC 784	984	984	IC 786	IC 788	IC 790	EC 162	1788	ICE 270	IC 990	IC 792	992	1792	1794		2896	468	1796	1848 2650
	🍷 ◆	🍷 C	🍷 R	🍷 C	Ⓐz	🍷 Ⓐy	🍷 Ⓒ	🍷 ⒶG	🍷 Ⓐy	🍴 C	🍷 Ⓐy	🍴 ◆	🍷 C	🍴 ◆	🍴	🍴 C	R	🍷 C	🍴 ◆		R	◆		
Zürich Flughafen ✈ **299** d.	*1505*	*1542*	1612	*1642*	...	...	*1705*	1713	*1721*	*1742*	...	*1809*	*1842*	...	*1905*	*1942*	2012	*2042*	*2142*	...	2212	*2239*	...	*2341*
Zürich Hbf d.	1537	1600	1637	1700	1708	1717	1737	1737	1745	1800	1817	1837	1900	1917	1937	2000	2037	2100	2200	...	2237	2300	2337	0003
Aarau d.	1601	|	1701	|	|	|	1801	1801	|	|	|	1901	|	|	2001	|	2101	|	|	...	2301	|	|	0029
Liestal d.	1623	|	1723	|	|	|	1823	1823	|	|	|	1923	|	|	2023	|	2123	|	|	...	2323	|	|	0100t
Baden d.	|	1616	|	1716	1730	|	|	|	|	1816	|	|	1916	|	|	2016	|	2116	2216	...	|	2316	2355	|
Brugg d.	|	1625	|	1725	1741	|	|	|	|	1825	|	|	1925	|	|	2025	|	2125	2225	...	|	2325	0003	|
Stein Säckingen d.	|	|	|	|	1806	|	|	|	|	|	|	|	|	|	|	|	|	2149	2249	...	|	|	0025	|
Rheinfelden d.	|	1658	|	1758	1817	|	|	|	|	1858	|	|	1958	|	|	2058	|	2200	2300	...	|	|	0036	|
Basel SBB a.	1635	1711	1735	1811	1832	1814	1835	1835	1847	1911	1914	1935	2011	2014	2035	2111	2135	2213	2313	...	2336	0006	0050	0111t

◆ – **NOTES** (LISTED BY TRAIN NUMBERS)

- **EC2/3** – REMBRANDT – [12] and 🍴 Chur - Köln - Amsterdam and v.v.
- **ICE70/1** – HELVETIA – [12] and 🍴 Zürich - Basel - Frankfurt (Main) - Hamburg and v.v. Supplement payable.
- **ICE76/7** – PANDA – [12] and 🍴 Zürich - Basel - Frankfurt (Main) - Hamburg and v.v. Supplement payable.
- **EC96** – IRIS – [12] and 🍴 Chur - Zürich - Basel - Metz - Luxembourg - Brussels.
- **EC97** – IRIS – [12] and 🍴 Brussels - Luxembourg - Metz - Basel - Zürich.
- **EC102** – RÄTIA – [12] and 🍴 Chur - Basel - Köln - Dortmund - Hannover - Berlin Zoo.
- **EC103** – RÄTIA – [12] and 🍴 Dortmund - Köln - Basel - Chur.
- **EC113** – LE CORBUSIER – [12] and 🍴 Basel - Zürich; Conveys on ⚒ (**not** Aug. 15): [12] Paris Est - Basel - Zürich.
- **EC114/5** – L'ARBALÈTE – [12] and 🍴 Zürich - Basel - Paris Est.
- **EC116** – LE CORBUSIER – [12] and 🍷 Zürich - Basel; Conveys on Ⓑ (**not** Aug. 14): [12] Zürich - Basel - Paris Est.
- **EC162/3** – TRANSALPIN – [12] (also [1] observation car) and 🍴 Wien - Innsbruck - Basel - Zürich - and v.v.
- **ICE270/1** – JOHANNA SPYRI – [12] and 🍴 Zürich - Basel - Frankfurt (Main) and v.v. Supplement payable.
- **464/5** – 🛏 1, 2 cl., ▬ 2 cl. and [2] Graz - Innsbruck - Basel and v.v.; ▬ 2 cl. and [12] Villach - Innsbruck - Basel and v.v.
- **EN466** – WIENER WALZER – ▬ 2 cl. and [2] (sleeperette with supplement) Budapest - Wien - Zürich - Basel; 🛏 1, 2 cl. Wien - Basel.
- **EN467** – WIENER WALZER – ▬ 2 cl. and [2] (sleeperette with supplement) Basel - Zürich - Wien - Budapest; 🛏 1, 2 cl. Basel - Wien; [12] Basel - Buchs.
- **468** – 🛏 1, 2 cl., ▬ 2 cl. and [2] Chur - Paris Est; [12] Chur - Basel.
- **469** – 🛏 1, 2 cl., ▬ 2 cl. and [2] Paris Est - Chur; [12] Basel - Chur; ▬ 2 cl. (also 🛏 1, 2 cl. Dec. 8 - Apr. 16 from Oostende) Oostende - (train **499**) - Basel - Chur
- **954** – [12] (Altstätten Ⓐ -) Rorschach (train **8710**) - St Gallen - Zürich - Basel.
- **983** – [12] Basel - Zürich - Romanshorn.
- **985** – [12] Basel - Zürich - St Gallen - Rorschach.
- **1794** – [12] and 🍴 Chur - Basel; ▬ 2 cl. (also 🛏 1, 2 cl. Dec. 7 - Apr. 15) Chur - Basel (train **498**) - Oostende.
- **C** – [12] Basel - Zürich - Chur and v.v.
- **G** – [12] Basel - Zürich - St Gallen and v.v.
- **H** – [12] Basel - Zürich - Schaffhausen and v.v.
- **R** – [12] Basel - Zürich - St Gallen - Rorschach - Chur and v.v.
- **s** – Stops to **set down** only.
- **t** – Change at **Olten**.
- **v** – Will **not** run Dec. 27 - 30, May 1.
- **y** – Will **not** run Dec. 27 - 30, Apr. 13, May 1, 24.
- **z** – Will **not** run Apr. 13, May 1, 24.

198 IC – Internal **InterCity** train ICE – German high-speed **InterCity Express** EC – International **EuroCity** train

Table 301   ⛴ SCHAFFHAUSEN - KONSTANZ (BODENSEE)   SBB

		N ☕				N ☕				N ☕					N ☕				N ☕				N ☕
Schaffhausen.......... d.	...	0915	...	...	...	1340	...	...	...	1540		Kreuzlingen .... d.	...		0905	...	...	1140	...	...	1505
Stein am Rhein .... d.	...	1115	...	...	...	1540	...	...	...	1740		Konstanz 🚋 .... d.	...		0915	...	...	1155	...	...	1515
Konstanz 🚋.......... d.	...	1330	...	...	...	1805	...	...	...	1955		Stein am Rhein ...... d.	...		1130	...	...	1410	...	...	1730
Kreuzlingen........ a.	...	1345	...	...	...	1818	...	...	...	2010		Schaffhausen...... a.	...		1245	...	...	1525	...	...	1845

N – Daily Sept. 25 - Oct. 9 and May 1 - 27, also ⓒ Apr. 9 - 30.   **NO WINTER SERVICE:** Oct. 10 - Apr. 8.

Table 302   SCHAFFHAUSEN - WINTERTHUR   1, 2 class except where shown. SBB

km			Ⓐn		Ⓐn			EC														EC								
0	Schaffhausen.......... d.	0544	0613	0645	0713	0747	0847	0912	0947	1047	1147	1247	1347	1447	1547	1647	1747	1847	1912	1947	2047	2147	2247	...	...
30	Winterthur.............. a.	0618	0648	0721	0748	0821	0921	0934	1021	1121	1221	1321	1421	1521	1621	1721	1821	1921	1934	2021	2121	2221	2321	...	...

		Ⓐn													Ⓐn		Ⓐn	EC						
Winterthur.............. d.	0536	0636	0736	0839	0939	...	1039	1139	1239	1339	1439	1539	1639	1711	1739	1811	1828	1839	1939	2039	2139	2239	2344	...
Schaffhausen...... a.	0610	0710	0813	0914	1014	...	1114	1214	1314	1414	1514	1614	1714	1747	1814	1847	1849	1913	2013	2113	2213	2313	0016	...

EC – Stuttgart - Zürich and v.v. EuroCity service. For days of running see Table **735**.   **n –** Will **not** run May 1.

Table 303   SCHAFFHAUSEN - KREUZLINGEN - RORSCHACH   1, 2 class. SBB

km		Ⓐ	✗									Ⓐ	✗					
0	Schaffhausen.......... d.	0501	0552	0801		2001	2101	...	2201	Rorschach .... d.	0609	0712	0812		1912	2012	...	2112	2212
20	Stein am Rhein .... d.	0533	0629	0824	and	2024	2123	...	2224	Rorschach Hafen .... d.	0611	0714	0814	and	1914	2014	...	2114	2214
46	Kreuzlingen .... a.	0616	0703	0855		2055		...	2255	Arbon .... d.	0618	0721	0821		1921	2021	...	2121	2221
46	Kreuzlingen .... d.	0626	0706	0857	hourly	2057	...	2157	2257	Romanshorn .... d.	0631	0732	0833	hourly	1933	2033	...	2133	2233
65	Romanshorn .... d.	0655	0740	0925		2125	...	2225	2325	Kreuzlingen .... a.	0655	0758	0857		1957	2057	...	2157	2257
73	Arbon .... d.	0704	0750	0934	until	2134	...	2234	2334	Kreuzlingen .... d.	0656	0759	0859	until	1959	...	2159	...
80	Rorschach Hafen ... d.	0712	0757	0941		2141	...	2241	2341	Stein am Rhein .... d.	0730	0830	0930		2030	...	2130	2230	...
81	Rorschach............. a.	0714	0800	0944		2144	...	2244	2344	Schaffhausen................. a.	0754	0854	0954		2054	...	2154	2254	...

Table 304   KONSTANZ - WEINFELDEN   1, 2 class. Mittel Thurgau Bahn

km			✗		✗			✗					Ⓐ										
0	Konstanz 🚋.......... d.	0500	0549	0620	0650	0725	0749	0821	...	0920	and	1620	1649	1720	1745	1820	1920	2020	2120	2150	2248	2352
1	Kreuzlingen .... d.	0505	0555	0624	0706	0730	0802	0825	...	0925	hourly	1625	1701	1725	1751	1825	1925	2025	2125	2203	2259	2356
30	Weinfelden 305....... a.	0528	0621	0651	0730	0751	0827	0851	...	0951	until	1651	1728	1751	1820	1851	1951	2051	2151	2227	2319	0017

			✗		✗		✗					Ⓐ									
Weinfelden 305........ d.	0417	0515	0541	0608	0626	0701	0739	0810	...	0910	and	1610	1627	1710	1734	1810	1910	...	2010	2110	2210	2310
Kreuzlingen .... d.	0439	0543	0609	0640	0706	0732	0815	0838	...	0938	hourly	1638	1703	1738	1805	1838	1938	...	2038	2138	2238	2338
Konstanz 🚋 .... a.	0442	0545	0613	0643	0709	0735	0818	0842	...	0942	until	1642	1707	1742	1809	1842	1941	...	2041	2141	2241	2341

Table 305   ZÜRICH - ROMANSHORN   1, 2 class except where shown. SBB

km		19215	8121	1503	IC 1507	1511	IC 513	1515	IC 517	1521	IC 523	1525	IC 527	1529	983	IC 533	1537	IC 539	1541	IC 543	19291	8195	19295	8199
					☕	✗	☕		☕		B		✗		Ⓐ S		B	✗	B	✗		2		
					L	L		B		B		B												
	Genève Aéroport 250 ✈ .. d.	...	...	...	...	...	0844	...	1044	...	1244	...	...	1444	...	...	1644	...	1844	...	...	...	...
	Genève 250 .... d.	...	...	...	0525	0654	...	0854	...	1054	...	1254	...	...	1454	...	...	1654	...	1854	...	...	...	...
	Lausanne 250 .... d.	...	...	...	0612		0812		1012		1212		1412			1612		1812						
0	Zürich Hbf 299 .... d.	0619	...	0710	0810	0910	1010	1110	1210	1310	1410	1510	1610	1710	1733	1810	1910	2010	2110	2210	2219	...	2319	...
17	Zürich Flughafen ✈ 299 .. d.		...	0722	0822	0922	1022	1122	1222	1322	1422	1522	1622	1722	1744	1822	1922	2022	2122	2222		...		...
26	Winterthur .... d.	0639	0644	0738	0838	0938	1038	1138	1238	1338	1438	1538	1638	1738	1800	1838	1938	2038	2138	2238	2239	2244	2339	2347
42	Frauenfeld .... d.		...	0703	0750	0850	0950	1050	1150	1250	1350	1450	1550	1650	1750	1820	1850	1950	2050	2150	2250	...	2303		0005
59	Weinfelden .... d.		...	0723	0803	0903	1003	1103	1203	1303	1403	1503	1603	1703	1803	1832	1903	2003	2103	2203	2303	...	2323		0021b
82	Romanshorn .... a.		...	0747	0821	0921	1021	1121	1221	1321	1421	1521	1621	1721	1821	1856	1921	2021	2121	2221	2322	...	2347		0043b

		8112 952	IC 1508	910		IC 512	1516	IC 518	1520	IC 522	1526	IC 528		IC 1530	532	IC 1536	538	IC 1540	1542		1544	1546	1548	8192	18899
		☕				✗		B		✗		✗		D		B	☕	✗					L		L
			B	E✗		B		B																	
Romanshorn .... d.	...	0516	0605	...	0635	0739	0839	0939	1039	1139	1239	...	1339	1439	1539	1639	1739	1839	...	1939	2039	2139	2236	...
Weinfelden .... d.	...	0540	0626	...	0657	0757	0857	0957	1057	1157	1257	...	1357	1457	1557	1657	1757	1857	...	1957	2057	2157	2259	...
Frauenfeld .... d.	...	0559	0640	...	0710	0810	0910	1010	1110	1210	1310	...	1410	1510	1610	1710	1810	1910	...	2010	2110	2210	2318	...
Winterthur .... d.	0552	0623	0653	...	0724	0824	0924	1024	1124	1224	1324	...	1424	1524	1624	1724	1824	1924	...	2024	2124	2224	2335	2343
Zürich Flughafen ✈ 299 .. a.	0609	0636	0706	...	0737	0837	0937	1037	1137	1237	1337	...	1437	1537	1637	1737	1837	1937	...	2037	2137	2237		...
Zürich Hbf 299 .... a.	0623	0650	0720	...	0750	0850	0950	1050	1150	1250	1350	...	1450	1550	1650	1750	1850	1950	...	2050	2150	2250		0008
Lausanne 250 .... a.	...	...	0948	...		1148		1348		1548		...		1748		1948		2148		...	2348	...		
Genève 250 .... a.	...	...		...	1106		1306		1506		1706	...		1906		2106	2237			...	0034	...		
Genève Aéroport 250 ✈ .. a.	...	...		...	1116		1316		1516		1716	...		1917		2126	2247			...		...		

B – 🚆 Brig - Lausanne - Biel - Zürich - Romanshorn and v.v.   **E –** 🚆 Romanshorn - Zürich - Bern.   **S –** 🚆 Basel - Bern - Romanshorn.
D – 🚆 Romanshorn - Biel - Brig (train **4943**) - Domodossola.   **L –** 🚆 Biel - Zürich - Romanshorn and v.v.   **b –** ①⑥⑦ only (**not** May 26).

Table 308 ZÜRICH - ST GALLEN - BUCHS - CHUR

For direct service between Zürich and Chur see Table 310

1, 2 class. SBB

km		8713 Ⓐ	2705	2707 Ⓐ	2853	2709 L	IC 753 ✕	EC 99 ✕ ♦	IC 707 ✕	959 🍷	IC 711 ✕	EC 167 ✕ ♦		IC 713 ✕		963 🍷	IC 715 ✕		IC 717 ✕	969 🍷		IC 721 ✕	EC 113 ✕	EC 95 ✕ ♦
	Genève Aéroport **250** ✈ d.	...	...	...	...	...	...	...	...	...	...	...	...	0648	...	...	0748	...	0848	...	...	0948	...	...
	Genève **250** d.	...	...	...	...	...	...	...	0447	...	0558	...	...	0658	...	...	0758	...	0858	...	...	0958	...	...
	Lausanne **250** d.	...	...	...	...	...	...	...	0529	...	0634	...	...	0734	...	...	0834	...	0934	...	...	1034	...	...
	Bern **250** d.	...	...	...	*0451*	...	...	*0610*	0644	...	0745	0814	...	0845	...	...	0945	...	1045	...	...	1145	...	*1151*
	Basel SBB **300** d.	...	...	...	0523	...	0625	|	|	0725	|	|	...	|	...	0925	|	...	|	1125	...	|	1225	|
0	**Zürich Hbf 299** d.	...	...	0603	0639	0707	0723	0740	0807	0839	0907	0940	...	1007	...	1039	1107	...	1207	1239	...	1307	1323	1340
17	**Zürich Flughafen ✈ 299** d.	...	...	0616	0653	0718	...	|	0818	0853	0918	|	...	1018	...	1053	1118	...	1218	1253	...	1318	...	|
26	Winterthur d.	...	...	0634	0708	0734	...	0802	0834	0908	0934	1002	...	1034	...	1108	1134	...	1234	1308	...	1334	...	1402
54	Wil d.	...	0624	0654	0729	0754	...	|	0854	0929	0954	|	...	1054	...	1129	1154	...	1254	1329	...	1354	...	|
74	Gossau d.	...	0646	0714	0749	0809	...	|	0909	0949	1009	|	...	1109	...	1149	1209	...	1309	1349	...	1409	...	|
84	**St Gallen** a.	...	0658	0722	0756	0817	...	0839	0917	0956	1017	1039	...	1117	...	1156	1217	...	1317	1356	...	1417	...	1439
84	**St Gallen** d.	...	0702	0729	0802	...	...	0840	...	1002	...	1040	...	...	...	1202	...	...	...	1402	...	...	...	1440
99	Rorschach d.	0524	0721	0751	0822	...	...	|	...	1022	...	|	...	...	...	1222	...	...	...	1422	...	...	...	|
110	**St. Margrethen** d.	0535	0731	0803	0832	...	...	0904	...	1032	...	1104	...	...	...	1232	...	...	...	1432	...	...	...	1504
123	Altstätten d.	0551	0743	0820	0844	...	...	...	...	1044	...	...	...	...	...	1244	...	...	...	1444	...	...	...	...
148	**Buchs** d.	0617	0800	0844	0903	...	...	...	...	1103	...	...	...	...	...	1303	...	...	...	1503	...	...	...	...
164	Sargans d.	0641	0812	...	0917	...	...	...	...	1117	...	...	...	...	...	1317	...	...	...	1517	...	...	...	...
177	Landquart d.	0654	0827	...	0932	...	...	...	...	1132	...	...	...	...	...	1332	...	...	...	1532	...	...	...	...
191	**Chur** a.	0702	0836	...	0941	...	...	...	...	1141	...	...	...	...	...	1341	...	...	...	1541	...	...	...	...

	IC 723 ✕	975 🍷	IC 725 ✕	2727 Ⓐ	IC 727 ✕	979	IC 729 ✕	983 🍷	EC 93 ✕ ♦	1729 🍷 K	IC 733 ✕	985		IC 737 ✕	8787	IC 939 🍷 ⑦	IC 739 ✕	8791	991 ⑧	IC 741 ✕	8795	IC 743 ✕		IC 745 ✕
Genève Aéroport **250** ✈ d.	1048	...	1148	...	1248	...	1348	...	...	...	1448	...	...	1548	...	...	1648	...	...	1748	...	1848	...	1946
Genève **250** d.	1058	...	1158	...	1258	...	1358	...	...	...	1458	...	...	1558	...	...	1658	...	...	1758	...	1858	...	1958
Lausanne **250** d.	1134	...	1234	...	1334	...	1434	...	...	...	1534	...	...	1634	...	...	1734	...	...	1834	...	1934	...	2034
Bern **250** d.	1245	...	1345	...	1445	...	1545	...	1614a	1551	1645	...	...	1745	...	1814	1845	...	...	1945	...	2045	...	2145
Basel SBB **300** d.	|	1325	|	...	|	1525	|	1625	|	|	|	1725	...	|	...	|	|	...	1925	|	...	|	...	|
Zürich Hbf 299 d.	1407	1439	1507	...	1607	1639	1707	1723	1740	1745	1807	1839	...	1907	...	1939	2007	...	2039	2107	...	2207	...	2315
Zürich Flughafen ✈ 299 d.	1418	1453	1518	...	1618	1653	1718	...	|	1758	1818	1853	...	1918	...	1953	2018	...	2053	2118	...	2218	...	2327
Winterthur d.	1434	1508	1534	...	1634	1708	1734	...	1802	1814	1834	1908	...	1934	...	2008	2034	...	2108	2134	...	2234	...	2343
Wil d.	1454	1529	1554	...	1654	1729	1754	...	|	1832	1854	1929	...	1954	...	2029	2054	...	2129	2154	...	2254	...	0002
Gossau d.	1509	1549	1609	...	1709	1749	1809	...	|	1851	1909	1949	...	2009	...	2049	2109	...	2149	2209	...	2314	...	0023
St Gallen a.	1517	1556	1617	...	1717	1756	1817	...	1839	1900	1917	1956	...	2017	...	2056	2117	...	2156	2217	...	2323	...	0032
St Gallen d.	...	1602	...	1702	...	1802	...	...	1840	1902	...	2002	...	...	2025	...	2125	...	...	2225	...	2325	...	...
Rorschach d.	...	1622	...	1721	...	1822	...	...	|	1921	...	2020	...	...	2047	...	2145	2150	...	2245	2250	2345	...	...
St. Margrethen d.	...	1632	...	1731	...	1832	...	...	1904	1931	...	...	...	...	2059	...	...	2201	...	...	2301	...	0007	...
Altstätten d.	...	1644	...	1743	...	1844	...	...	...	1943	...	...	...	...	2114	...	...	2216	...	...	2320	...	...	...
Buchs d.	...	1703	...	1800	...	1903	...	...	...	2000	...	...	...	...	2137	...	...	2245	...	...	2355	...	...	...
Sargans d.	...	1717	...	1811	...	1917	...	...	...	2012	...	...	...	...	2154	...	...	2302	...	...	0011	...	...	...
Landquart d.	...	1732	...	*1833*	...	1932	...	...	...	2027	...	...	...	...	*2235*	...	...	*2353*	...	...	...	...	...	...
Chur a.	...	1741	...	*1845*	...	1941	...	...	...	2036	...	...	...	...	*2249*	...	...	*0004*	...	...	...	...	...	...

	952 🍷 ⚒	IC 708 ✕	8710 954 🍷	IC 712 ✕	2714 ⒶL	IC 914 🍷 Ⓐ♦	8718 ⚒	IC 716 ✕	2718 Ⓐ	IC 718 ✕	964 🍷	IC 720 ✕	8732	IC 722 ✕	970 🍷	EC 92 ✕ ♦	970 🍷	IC 726 ✕	IC 728 ✕	978 g	IC 730 ✕	IC 732 ✕	982 🍷	
Chur d.	...	...	...	...	...	...	0520	...	*0613*	...	0720	...	...	...	0920	...	...	...	...	1120	...	...	1320	...
Landquart d.	...	...	...	...	...	...	0529	...	*0624*	...	0730	...	...	...	0930	...	...	...	...	1130	...	...	1330	...
Sargans d.	...	...	...	...	...	...	0555	...	0639	...	0747	...	...	...	0947	...	...	...	...	1147	...	...	1347	...
Buchs d.	...	...	...	...	...	...	0615	...	0650	...	0759	...	0918	...	0959	...	...	...	*1118*	1159	...	*1318*	1359	...
Altstätten d.	...	...	0517a	...	...	...	0638	...	0707	...	0815	...	0941	...	1015	...	...	...	*1141*	1215	...	*1341*	1415	...
St Margrethen d.	...	...	0532a	...	...	...	0654	...	0719	...	0827	...	0956	...	1027	1056	...	...	*1156*	1227	...	*1356*	1427	...
Rorschach d.	...	0515a	0548	0621	...	...	0709	0721	0730	0823	0838	...	1013	...	1038	|	...	...	*1213*	1238	...	*1413*	1438	...
St Gallen a.	...	0537a	0608	0638	...	...	0729	0738	0746	0839	0854	...	1032	...	1054	1118	...	...	*1232*	1254	...	*1432*	1454	...
St Gallen d.	0501	0541	0611	0641	0647	0711	...	0741	...	0841	0901	0941	...	1041	1101	1120	...	1141	1241	1301	1341	1441	1501	...
Gossau d.	0510	0550	0619	0650	0655	0719	...	0750	...	0850	0910	0950	...	1050	1110	|	...	1150	1250	1310	1350	1450	1510	...
Wil d.	0532	0606	0639	0706	0714	0739	...	0806	...	0906	0932	1006	...	1106	1132	|	...	1206	1306	1332	1406	1506	1532	...
Winterthur d.	0552	0627	0659	0727	0733	0759	...	0827	...	0927	0954	1027	...	1127	1154	1159	...	1227	1327	1354	1427	1527	1554	...
Zürich Flughafen ✈ 299 a.	0609	0640	0711	0740	|	0811	...	0840	...	0940	1009	1040	...	1140	1209	|	...	1240	1340	1409	1440	1540	1609	...
Zürich Hbf 299 a.	0623	0653	0723	0753	0756	0823	...	0853	...	0953	1023	1053	...	1153	1223	1221	1237	1253	1353	1423	1453	1553	1623	...
Basel SBB **300** a.	0735	|	0835	|	...	|	...	|	...	|	1135	|	...	|	1335	|	1335	|	|	1535	|	|	1735	...
Bern **250** a.	...	0815	...	0915	...	0945	...	1015	...	1115	...	1215	...	1315	...	*1345*	...	1415	1515	...	1615	1715	...	...
Lausanne **250** a.	...	0926	...	1026	...	...	...	1126	...	1226	...	1326	...	1426	...	...	...	1526	1626	...	1726	1826	...	...
Genève **250** a.	...	1002	...	1102	...	...	...	1202	...	1302	...	1402	...	1502	...	...	...	1602	1702	...	1802	1902	...	...
Genève Aéroport **250** ✈ a.	...	1013	...	1113	...	...	...	1213	...	1313	...	1413	...	1513	...	...	...	1613	1713	...	1814	1914	...	...

	EC 94 ✕ ♦	982 🍷	IC 736 ✕	984 🍷 Ⓐ	IC 738 ✕	1740	EC 166 ✕ ♦	EC 162 ✕	8764	IC 740 ✕	IC 742 ✕	992 🍷	IC 744 ✕	8780	IC 746 ✕	2896	1846	EC 98 ✕ ♦	1794	8790	2748	1848	2998 🍷	8794
Chur d.	...	...	...	...	...	1520	...	...	...	...	...	1720	...	...	...	1920	...	...	2013	...	...	...	2213	...
Landquart d.	...	...	...	...	...	1530	...	...	...	...	...	1730	...	...	...	1930	...	...	2024	...	...	...	2224	...
Sargans d.	...	...	*1400*	...	...	1547	...	...	1600	...	...	1747	...	...	...	1947	...	...	2037	2050	...	...	2237	2241
Buchs d.	...	...	*1418*	...	*1518*	1559	...	...	1618	...	*1718*	1759	...	1918	...	1959	...	...	...	2118	...	...	...	2259
Altstätten d.	...	...	*1443*	...	*1541*	1615	...	...	1643	...	*1741*	1815	...	1941	...	2015	...	...	...	2141	...	...	...	2321
St Margrethen d.	1456	...	*1459*	...	*1556*	1627	1656	...	1659	...	*1756*	1827	...	1956	...	2027	...	2130	...	2156	...	...	...	2335
Rorschach d.	|	...	*1513*	...	*1613*	1638	|	...	1713	...	*1813*	1838	...	2013	...	2038	...	|	...	2213	...	...	...	2348
St Gallen a.	1518	...	*1532*	...	*1632*	1654	1718	...	1732	...	*1832*	1854	...	2032	...	2054	...	2153	...	2232	...	...	...	0006
St Gallen d.	1520	...	1541	1611	1641	1701	1720	...	...	1741	1841	1901	1941	...	2041	2101	2141	2155	...	...	2241	...	...	...
Gossau d.	|	...	1550	1619	1650	1710	|	...	...	1750	1850	1910	1950	...	2050	2110	2150	|	...	...	2249	...	...	...
Wil d.	|	...	1606	1639	1706	1732	|	...	...	1806	1906	1932	2006	...	2106	2132	2206	|	...	...	2308	...	...	...
Winterthur d.	1559	...	1627	1659	1727	1754	1759	...	...	1827	1927	1954	2027	...	2127	2154	2227	2235	...	...	2327	...	...	...
Zürich Flughafen ✈ 299 a.	|	...	1640	1711	1740	1807	|	...	...	1840	1940	2009	2040	...	2140	2209	2240	|	...	...	2340	...	...	...
Zürich Hbf 299 a.	1621	1637	1653	1723	1753	1821	1823	1837	...	1853	1953	2023	2053	...	2153	2223	2253	2256	...	...	2353	0003	...	...
Basel SBB **300** a.	|	1735	|	1835	|	|	|	1935	...	|	|	2135	|	...	|	2336	|	*0050*	...	...	...	|	...	...
Bern **250** a.	*1745*	...	1815	...	1915	2009	1945	...	...	2015	2115	...	2215	...	2315	...	0025	...	...	...	...	0125	...	...
Lausanne **250** a.	...	...	1926	...	2026	...	...	...	...	2126	2226	...	2331	...	*0038*	...	...	...	...	...	...	...	...	...
Genève **250** a.	...	...	2002	...	2102	...	...	...	...	2202	2302	...	0009	...	*0120*	...	...	...	...	...	...	...	...	...
Genève Aéroport **250** ✈ a.	...	...	2013	...	2112	...	...	...	...	2212	2312	...	...	...	...	...	...	...	...	...	...	...	...	...

♦ – **NOTES** (LISTED BY TRAIN NUMBERS)

EC92/3 – ANGELIKA KAUFFMANN – 12 and ✕ München - Bregenz - Zürich and v.v.; **EC93** conveys on Ⓐ: 12 Bern (train **IC931**) - Zürich - St Gallen.

EC94/5 – GOTTFRIED KELLER – 12 and ✕ München - Bregenz - Zürich and v.v.

EC98/9 – BAVARIA – 12 and ✕ München - Bregenz - Zürich and v.v.

EC166/7 – ALBERT EINSTEIN – 12 and ✕ Praha - Bern and Interlaken Ost - Praha.

IC914 – Runs Ⓐ: 12 St Gallen - Zürich - Bern; Also runs ⑥ Oct. 1 - 15, Jan. 28 - Mar. 25, and Apr. 14: 12 St Gallen - Zürich - Bern - Interlaken Ost.

L – 12 Luzern - Zürich - St Gallen and v.v.

K – 12 Interlaken Ost - Bern - Zürich - St Gallen - Chur.

a – Ⓐ only.

g – 🍷 Chur - St Gallen.

♦ – See footnote

Table 310 ZÜRICH - SARGANS - BUCHS and CHUR

1, 2 class. SBB

km		7317	1751	469	IC 753	365		IC 757	473		1759	EC 163		IC 763		1765	EC 169		IC 767		1769	EC 161		IC 769
		⚒	🍷	🍷 ◆	✕	🍷		✕	◆		🍷	✕ ◆		🍷		✕	✕ ◆		🍷		🍷	✕ ◆		✕
	Basel SBB **300** d.	...	...	0549	0625	...	...	0704	0706b	...	0749	0825	...	0849	...	0949	...	...	1049	...	1149	1225	...	1249
	Zürich Flughafen ✈ **299** d.	...	0611	0642	0713	...	0721	0742	|	0821	0842	0905	0921	0942	1021	1042	...	1121	1142	1221	1242	1316	1321	1342
0	**Zürich Hbf** d.	...	0633	0710	0733	0735	0738	0810	0828s	0838	0910	0933	0938	1010	1038	1110	1120	1138	1210	1238	1310	1335	1338	1410
12	Thalwil d.	...	0644	0721	|	|	0752	|	|	0852	0921	|	0952	|	1052	1121	|	1152	|	1252	1321	|	1352	|
24	Wädenswil d.	...	0653	0731	|	|	0803	|	|	0903	0931	|	1003	|	1103	1131	|	1203	|	1303	1331	|	1403	|
34	Pfäffikon d.	...	0701	0740	|	|	0818	|	|	0918	0940	|	1018	|	1118	1140	|	1218	|	1318	1340	|	1418	|
57	Ziegelbrücke ▲ d.	0622	0717	0757	|	|	0842	0851	|	0942	0957	|	1042	1051	1142	1157	|	1242	1251	1342	1357	|	1442	1451
90	**Sargans 308** d.	0704	0740	0821	|	0835	...	0914	0938s	...	1021	1034	...	1114	...	1221	1224	...	1314	...	1421	1434	...	1514
106	**Buchs** 🏛 **308** a.	|	|	|	|	0845	...	|	|	...	|	1045	...	|	...	|	1236	...	|	...	|	1445	...	|
	Innsbruck **73** a.	|	|	|	|	1116	...	|	|	...	|	1316	...	|	...	|	1513	...	|	...	|	1716	...	|
103	Landquart d.	0718	0754	0835	0841	...	...	0927	0953s	...	1035	...	...	1127	...	1235	...	...	1327	...	1435	...	...	1527
117	**Chur** a.	0727	0803	0845	0851	...	...	0937	1004	...	1045	...	...	1137	...	1245	...	...	1337	...	1445	...	...	1537
	St Moritz **330** a.	...	1018d	...	1118	...	...	1158	...	...	1258	...	...	1358	...	1458	...	...	1558	...	1658	...	...	1758

		EC 103	1777		IC 777	449	7369		1781		EC 3	349		1787		1789		1791	465		7395	EN 467		
		✕ ◆			✕	◆	Ⓐa		🍷		✕ ◆	◆		✕		🍷		✕	🍷 ◆			🍷 ◆		
Basel SBB **300** d.	...	1354	...	...	1449	...	...	...	1549	...	1704	1725	...	1749	...	1849	...	1949	2025	...	2049	2117	...	...
Zürich Flughafen ✈ **299** d.	1421	1442	...	1521	1542	...	1612	1621	1642	1721	1742	1809	1821	1842	1921	1942	2021	2042	2105	2121	2142	2212	2221	2321
Zürich Hbf d.	1438	1509	1510	1538	1610	...	1633	1638	1710	1738	1810	1835	1838	1910	1938	2010	2038	2110	2133	2138	2210	2233	2238	2338
Thalwil d.	1452	|	1523	1552	|	...	|	1652	1721	1752	|	1846	1852	1921	1952	2021	2052	2121	|	2152	2223	|	2252	2352
Wädenswil d.	1503	|	1533	1603	|	...	1654	1703	1731	1803	|	1856	1903	1931	2003	2031	2103	2131	|	2203	2232	|	2303	0003
Pfäffikon d.	1518	|	1542	1618	|	...	1701	1718	1740	1818	|	1908	1918	1940	2018	2040	2118	2140	|	2218	2240	|	2318	0013
Ziegelbrücke ▲ d.	1542	1551	1559	1642	1651	...	1717	1742	1757	1842	1851	1927	1942	1957	2042	2057	2142	2157	|	2242	2300	2314	2342	0037
Sargans 308 d.	...	1615	1630	...	1714	1715	1743	...	1821	...	1914	1950	...	2021	...	2121	...	2221	2234	...	2341	2339	...	...
Buchs 🏛 **308** a.	...	|	1642	...	|	1732	|	...	|	...	|	2008	...	|	...	|	...	|	2245	...	|	2352	...	...
Innsbruck **73** a.	...	|	...	...	|	...	|	...	|	...	|	...	...	|	...	|	...	|	0137	...	|	0246	...	...
Landquart d.	...	1627	...	...	1727	...	1756	...	1835	...	1927	...	...	2037	...	2137	...	2237	...	...	2355	...	...	...
Chur a.	...	1637	...	...	1737	...	1805	...	1845	...	1937	...	...	2049	...	2149	...	2249	...	...	0004	...	...	...
St Moritz **330** a.	...	1858	...	...	1958	...	...	...	2058	...	2158	...	...	2301	...	...	...	...	...	...	...	...	...	...

		8718	EN 466		1756		464	1760		EC 102			1764		348	EC 96		EC 2		448	IC 778			1780
		⚒	🍷 ◆		✕		◆	✕		✕ ◆			🍷		◆	✕ ◆		✕ ◆		◆	🍷			✕
St Moritz **330** d.	...	...	...	...	...	...	...	...	...	...	...	...	0705	...	...	0805	...	0900	...	...	1000d	...	...	1100
Chur d.	...	0520	...	...	0613	...	...	0715	...	0823	...	...	0915	...	...	1023	...	1115	...	...	1223	...	...	1315
Landquart d.	...	0529	...	...	0624	...	...	0726	...	0834	...	...	0926	...	...	1034	...	1126	...	...	1234	...	...	1326
Innsbruck **73** d.	...	|	0240	...	|	...	0430	|	...	|	...	...	|	...	...	|	...	|	...	...	|	...	...	|
Buchs 🏛 **308** d.	...	|	0535	...	|	...	0715	|	...	|	...	...	|	...	0957	|	...	|	...	1157	|	...	...	|
Sargans 308 d.	...	0543	0549	...	0639	...	0728	0739	...	0845	...	...	0939	...	1015	1045	...	1139	...	1211	1245	...	...	1339
Ziegelbrücke ▲ d.	0518	...	|	0618	0703	0718	|	0803	0818	0909	0918	...	1003	1018	1038	1109	1118	1203	1218	1238	1309	1318	...	1403
Pfäffikon d.	0548	...	|	0648	0718	0748	|	0819	0848	|	0948	...	1019	1048	1056	|	1148	1219	1248	1256	|	1348	...	1419
Wädenswil d.	0557	...	|	0657	0728	0757	|	0829	0857	|	0957	...	1029	1057	1105	|	1157	1229	1257	1305	|	1357	...	1429
Thalwil d.	0608	...	|	0708	0739	0808	|	0839	0908	|	1008	...	1039	1108	1115	|	1208	1239	1308	1315	|	1408	...	1439
Zürich Hbf a.	0622	...	0651	0722	0751	0822	0826	0850	0922	0950	1022	...	1050	1122	1126	1150	1222	1250	1322	1326	1350	1422	...	1450
Zürich Flughafen ✈ **299** a.	0638	...	0716	0738	0816	0838	0850	0910	0938	1010	1038	...	1110	1138	1151	1210	1238	1310	1338	1356	1410	1438	...	1510
Basel SBB **300** a.	...	...	0832e	...	0911	...	0935	1011	...	1106	...	...	1211	...	1235	1306	...	1356	...	1435	1511	...	...	1611

		IC 782		EC 160	1784			IC 788		EC 162	1788		IC 792		EC 168	1792		1794	472		364	468		2998
		🍷		✕ ◆	🍷			✕		✕ ◆	🍷		🍷		✕ ◆	🍷		✕ ◆	◆			◆		🍷
St Moritz **330** d.	...	1200	...	...	1300	...	...	1400	...	...	1500	...	1600	...	...	1700	...	1800	...	...	...	1900	...	2000
Chur d.	...	1423	...	...	1515	...	...	1623	...	...	1715	...	1823	...	...	1915	...	2013	2028	...	...	2113	...	2213
Landquart d.	...	1434	...	...	1526	...	...	1634	...	...	1726	...	1834	...	...	1926	...	2024	2040u	...	...	2124	...	2224
Innsbruck **73** d.	...	|	...	1244	|	...	...	|	...	1444	|	...	|	...	1653	|	...	|	|	...	1844	|	...	|
Buchs 🏛 **308** d.	...	|	...	1515	|	...	...	|	...	1715	|	...	|	...	1924	|	...	|	|	...	2115	|	...	|
Sargans 308 d.	...	1445	...	1528	1539	...	...	1645	...	1728	1739	...	1845	...	1936	1939	...	2039	2055u	...	2128	2139	...	2239
Ziegelbrücke ▲ d.	1418	1509	1518	|	1603	1618	...	1709	1718	|	1803	1818	1909	1918	|	2003	2018	2103	|	2118	|	2203	2222	2303
Pfäffikon d.	1448	|	1548	|	1619	1648	...	|	1748	|	1819	1848	|	1948	|	2019	2048	2119	|	2148	|	2219	2248	2319
Wädenswil d.	1457	|	1557	|	1629	1657	...	|	1757	|	1829	1857	|	1957	|	2029	2057	2129	|	2157	|	2229	2257	2329
Thalwil d.	1508	|	1608	|	1639	1708	...	|	1808	|	1839	1908	|	2008	|	2039	2108	2139	|	2208	|	2239	2308	2339
Zürich Hbf a.	1522	1550	1622	1626	1650	1722	...	1750	1822	1826	1850	1922	1950	2022	2041	2050	2122	2150	2202u	2222	2226	2250	2322	2350
Zürich Flughafen ✈ **299** a.	1538	1616	1638	1651	1716	1738	...	1812	1838	1851	1916	1938	2016	2038	...	2116	2138	2216	|	2238	|	2325	2338	...
Basel SBB **300** a.	...	1711	...	1735	1811	...	...	1911	...	1935	2011	...	2111	...	...	2213	...	2313	2319b	...	2336	0006	...	...

◆ – **NOTES** (LISTED BY TRAIN NUMBERS)

EC2/3 – REMBRANDT – [12] and ✕ Chur - Basel - Köln - Amsterdam and v.v.
EC96 – IRIS – [12] and ✕ Chur - Basel - Metz - Luxembourg - Brussels.
EC102 – RÄTIA – [12] and ✕ Chur - Basel - Köln - Dortmund - Hannover - Berlin Zoo.
EC103 – RÄTIA – [12] and ✕ Dortmund - Köln - Basel - Chur.
EC160/1 – MARIA THERESIA – [12] and ✕ Wien - Innsbruck - Zürich and v.v.
EC162/3 – TRANSALPIN – [12] (also [1] observation car) and ✕ Wien - Innsbruck - Zürich - Basel and v.v.
EC168/9 – ROBERT STOLZ – [12] (also [1] observation car) and ✕ Graz - Innsbruck - Zürich and v.v; [12] Klagenfurt (trains **EC198/9**) - Schwarzach St Veit - Innsbruck - Zürich and v.v.
348/9 – [12] Feldkirch - Buchs - Sargans - Zürich and v.v.
448/9 – [12] Feldkirch - Buchs - Sargans - Zürich and Sargans - Buchs - Feldkirch.
464/5 – 🛏 1, 2 cl., couchette 2 cl. and [2] Graz - Innsbruck - Zürich - Basel and v.v.; couchette 2 cl. and [12] Villach (trains **894/5**) - Schwarzach St Veit - Basel and v.v.
EN466 – WIENER WALZER – couchette 2 cl. and [2] (sleeperette with supplement) Budapest - Wien - Basel; 🛏 1, 2 cl. Wien - Basel; [12] Buchs - Zürich.
EN467 – WIENER WALZER – couchette 2 cl. and [2] (sleeperette with supplement) Basel - Wien - Budapest; 🛏 1, 2 cl. Basel - Wien; [12] Basel - Zürich - Buchs.
468 – 🛏 1, 2 cl., couchette 2 cl. and [2] Chur - Paris Est; [12] Chur - Basel.
469 – 🛏 1, 2 cl., couchette 2 cl. and [2] Paris Est - Chur; [12] Basel - Chur; couchette 2 cl. (and 🛏 1, 2 cl. Dec. 8 - Apr. 16 from Oostende) Oostende (train **499**) - Basel - Chur.
472/3 – 🛏 1, 2 cl. and couchette 2 cl. for international journeys **only**: For days of running to Hamburg and Dortmund see Table **77**, to Amsterdam see Table **38**.
1794 – [12] and ✕ Chur - Basel; couchette 2 cl. (also 🛏 1, 2 cl. Dec. 7 - Apr. 15) Chur - Basel (train **498**) - Oostende.
a – Will **not** run May 1.
b – Basel **Bad Bf**.
c – 🚌 Schwanden - Linthal and v.v.
d – Sept. 25 - Oct. 16, Dec. 17 - Apr. 9 and May 20 - 27 **only**.
e – Arrive 0810 by changing at Zürich Hbf (See Table **300**).
s – Stops to **set down** only.
u – Stops to **pick up** only.

▲ – Rail service **Ziegelbrücke - Glarus - Schwanden - Linthal**. *27 km*. Journey time: 41 minutes (14 minutes to **Glarus**, 22 minutes to **Schwanden**):

From **Ziegelbrücke**: 0623⚒, 0720, 0804, 0852, 1004, 1052, 1204, 1252, 1404, 1452, 1604, 1652, 1720Ⓐ, 1804, 1852, 2004, 2104**c**, 2204**c**, 2316⑤⑥⑦**c**.

From **Linthal**: 0526Ⓐ, 0610⚒, 0712, 0825, 0912, 1025, 1112, 1225, 1312, 1425, 1512, 1625, 1712, 1800⑦, 1809Ⓐ, 1825Ⓒ, 1912, 2012, 2112, 2203**c**.

Table 311 🚌 BUCHS - VADUZ - SARGANS

🚌 PTT

Bus service **Buchs** (Station) **- Vaduz** (Post) **- Sargans** (Station). Journey time: 17 minutes (Buchs - Vaduz), 29 minutes (Vaduz - Sargans).

From Buchs to Vaduz: 0545, 0622⚒**n**, 0640⚒**p**, 0655Ⓐ**n**, 0708, 0725, 0745, 0805, 0825, 0845 and every 20 minutes until 1945, 2015, 2045, 2115, 2145, 2220, 2300.

From Sargans to Vaduz: 0633⚒**p**, 0653, 0733, 0745Ⓐ**n**, 0755⚒**p**, 0833, 0853, 0933, 1013, 1033, 1053⚒**n**, 1128, 1153⚒**n**, 1213⚒**n**, 1233, 1253⚒**n**, 1313, 1353, 1433, 1453, 1533, 1613⚒**p**, 1633, 1653, 1713⚒**p**, 1733, 1753, 1813Ⓐ**n**, 1833, 1853, 1935, 1953, 2035, 2135, 2235.

n – Also runs Jan. 2, will **not** run Nov. 1, Dec. 8, Jan. 6, Feb. 2, May 1.
p – Will **not** run Dec. 26, Apr. 17, May 25.

From Vaduz to Buchs: 0530⚒**n**, 0555⚒**n**, 0620⚒**p**, 0630Ⓐ**n**, 0640⚒**p**, 0705, 0724, 0725, 0805 and every 20 minutes until 1605, 1645 and every 20 minutes until 1925, 2005, 2030, 2100, 2130, 2200, 2240.

From Vaduz to Sargans: 0601⚒**p**, 0640⚒**n**, 0656, 0710Ⓐ**n**, 0725⚒**p**, 0745, 0805, 0845⚒**n**, 0905, 0945, 1005, 1045, 1105⚒**n**, 1125⚒**n**, 1145, 1205, 1245, 1305, 1345, 1405, 1445, 1505, 1525⚒**p**, 1545, 1605, 1625⚒**p**, 1645, 1705, 1725Ⓐ**n**, 1745, 1805, 1825, 1900, 1925, 2000, 2100, 2200.

🚌 – Bus or coach service

Table 312 LUZERN - ARTH GOLDAU - ST GALLEN

All trains 1, 2 class. SBB, SOB, BT

km		8609	8609	8619	3910	8623	2561	8629	8633	2565	5227	8639	8643	2569	5237	8649	8653	2575	5251	8659	8663	2579	5257	8669	8673
		Ⓐ					🍷			🍷				🍷				🍷				🍷			
0	**Luzern 290** .... d.	...	...	...	...	...	0659	...	...	0909	0927	...	...	1109	1127	...	...	1309	1327	...	...	1509	1527	...	...
16	Küssnacht am Rigi .... d.	...	...	...	...	...	0714	...	...	0924	0944	...	...	1124	1144	...	...	1324	1344	...	...	1524	1544	...	...
28	**Arth Goldau 290** ..... d.	...	...	...	0631	...	0732	0818	...	0937	0957	1018	...	1137	1157	1218	...	1337	1357	1418	...	1537	1557	1618	...
57	Biberbrugg **316**......... d.	*0453*	...	*0552*	0707	...	0753	0844	0907	0958	...	1044	...	1158	...	1244	...	1358	...	1444	...	1558	...	1644	...
77	Pfäffikon **316**........... d.	*0516*	...	*0649*	0728	...	0816	0904	0929	1016	...	1104	...	1216	...	1304	...	1416	...	1504	...	1616	...	1704	...
83	Rapperswil .... d.	0546	...	0707	0733	0752	0822	0910	0952	1022	...	1110	1152	1222	...	1310	1352	1422	...	1510	1552	1622	...	1710	1752
110	Wattwil .... d.	0618	0621	0741	...	0821	0845	0941	1021	1045	...	1141	1221	1245	...	1341	1421	1445	...	1541	1621	1645	...	1741	1821
143	Herisau.................... d.	...	0648	0808	...	0848	0908	1008	1048	1108	...	1208	1248	1308	...	1408	1448	1508	...	1608	1648	1708	...	1808	1848
155	**St Gallen** .... a.	...	0659	0817	...	0857	0916	1017	1057	1116	...	1217	1257	1316	...	1417	1457	1516	...	1617	1657	1716	...	1817	1857
	Romanshorn **313** .. a.	...	0726	...	...	0926	0948	...	1126	1148	...	...	1326	*1426*	...	1448	1526	1548	...	...	1726	1748	...	...	1926

	2585	5265	8679	8683	2591	5275	3978	8689	3986	8695	3988
	🍷				🍷						
Luzern 290 .... d.	1709	1727	...	...	1909	1927	...	...	*2027*	...	*2127*
Küssnacht am Rigi ...... d.	1724	1744	...	...	1924	1944	...	...	*2044*	...	*2144*
Arth Goldau 290 .... d.	1737	1757	1818	...	1937	1957	2018	...	2114	...	2217
Biberbrugg **316**........... d.	1758	...	1844	...	1958	...	2045	...	2140	...	2243
Pfäffikon **316**.............. d.	1816	...	1904	...	2016	...	2105	...	2200	...	2303
Rapperswil .... d.	1822	...	1910	1952	2022	...	2109	2111	2204	2210	2308
Wattwil .... d.	1845	...	1941	2021	2045	...	...	2141	...	2237	...
Herisau....................... d.	1908	...	2008	2048	2108	...	...	2208	...	2306	...
St Gallen .... a.	1916	...	2017	2057	2116	...	...	2217	...	2314	...
Romanshorn **313** .... a.	1948	...	2048	...	2148	...	...	2248	...	2354	...

	3907	3911	2562	8620	5234	2568	8626	8630	5240
			🍷			🍷			
Romanshorn **313** .... d.	...	...	0608	0708	...	0808	0832	...	...
St Gallen .... d.	...	...	0645	0743	...	0845	0900	0943	...
Herisau.............................. d.	...	...	0653	0753	...	0853	0910	0953	...
Wattwil .... d.	...	...	0716	0819	...	0916	0938	1019	...
Rapperswil .... d.	0600	0639	0741	0850	...	0941	1005	1050	...
Pfäffikon **316**..................... d.	0605	0646	0747	0856	...	0947	*1014*	1056	...
Biberbrugg **316**.................. d.	0626	0707	0806	0918	...	1006	...	1118	...
Arth Goldau 290 .... d.	0652	0731	0830	0944	1000	1030	...	1144	1200
Küssnacht am Rigi .... d.	*0713*	*0753*	0843	...	1012	1043	...	...	1212
Luzern 290 .... a.	*0730*	*0808*	0856	...	1030	1056	...	...	1230

	2572	8636	8640	5254	2578	8646	8650	5264	2582	8656	8660	5272	2588	8666	8670	5280	2592	8676	8680	5288	8686	3987	5292	8694	8698
	🍷				🍷				🍷				🍷				🍷								
Romanshorn **313** .... d.	1008	1032	...	...	1208	1232	...	...	*1332*	1432	...	...	1608	1632	...	...	1808	1832	...	...	2032	...	...	2132	2254
St Gallen .... d.	1045	1100	1143	...	1245	1300	1343	...	1445	1500	1543	...	1645	1700	1743	...	1845	1900	1943	...	2100	...	...	2223	2326
Herisau....................... d.	1053	1110	1153	...	1253	1310	1353	...	1453	1510	1553	...	1653	1710	1753	...	1853	1910	1953	...	2110	...	...	2232	2336
Wattwil .... d.	1116	1138	1219	...	1316	1338	1419	...	1516	1538	1619	...	1716	1738	1819	...	1916	1938	2019	...	2138	...	...	2255	2400
Rapperswil .... d.	1141	1205	1250	...	1341	1405	1450	...	1541	1610	1650	...	1741	1806	1850	...	1941	2005	2046	...	2205	2210	...	*2326*	...
Pfäffikon **316**.............. d.	1147	*1214*	1256	...	1347	*1414*	1456	...	1547	1621	1656	...	1747	*1815*	1856	...	1947	*2014*	*2100*	...	...	2216	...	*0003*	...
Biberbrugg **316**........... d.	1206	...	1318	...	1406	...	1518	...	1606	1643	1718	...	1806	*1843*	1918	...	2006	*2043*	*2121*	...	...	2235	...	*0021*	...
Arth Goldau 290 .... d.	1230	...	1344	1400	1430	...	1544	1600	1630	...	1744	1800	1830	...	1944	2000	2030	*2107*	*2144*	2219	...	2259	2306n	...	...
Küssnacht am Rigi ...... d.	1243	...	...	1412	1443	...	...	1612	1643	...	...	1812	1843	...	...	2012	2043	...	...	2231	...	...	2318n	...	...
Luzern 290 .... a.	1256	...	...	1430	1456	...	...	1630	1656	...	...	1830	1856 •	...	...	2030	2056	...	...	2249	...	...	2334n	...	...

n – On ⑦ (**not** Dec. 25, Jan. 1, Apr. 14, 16, May 25) runs 7 minutes later.

Operators: SOB – Schweizerische Süd Ost Bahn, Wädenswil; BT – Bodensee Toggenburg, St Gallen.

Table 313 ST GALLEN - ROMANSHORN

All trains 1, 2 class. BT

Rail service **St Gallen - Romanshorn**. *20 km*. Journey time: 27 minutes. **Operator**: BT – Bodensee Toggenburg, St Gallen.

From **St Gallen**: 0601⚒, 0659, 0759, 0859, 0921, 0959, 1059, 1121, 1159, 1221Ⓐ, 1259, 1359, 1459, 1521, 1559, 1659, 1721, 1759, 1821Ⓐ, 1859, 1921, 2021, 2121, 2221, 2328.

From **Romanshorn**: 0608, 0632⚒, 0708, 0808, 0832, 0932, 1008, 1032, 1132, 1208, 1232, 1308Ⓐ, 1332, 1432, 1532, 1608, 1632, 1732, 1808, 1832, 1908Ⓐ, 1932, 2032, 2132, 2254.

Table 314 🚢 ROMANSHORN - FRIEDRICHSHAFEN car ferry service

Service valid throughout: May 29, **1994** - May 27, **1995**

🚢 SBB, DB

		A✕		C§		A✕		✕	A✕		✕	A✕		✕		A✕		✕	A✕		✕	A✕		B✕
Romanshorn Hafen .... d.	...	0636	...	0736	...	0836	...	0936	1036	...	1136	1236	...	1336	...	1436	...	1536	1636	...	1736	1836	...	1936
Friedrichshafen Hafen .... a.	...	0717	...	0817	...	0917	...	1017	1117	...	1217	1317	...	1417	...	1517	...	1617	1717	...	1817	1917	...	2017

		C§		A✕	✕		A✕	✕		A✕	✕		A✕		✕		A✕	✕		A✕		B✕		A✕
Friedrichshafen Hafen .... d.	...	0643	...	0743	0843	...	0943	1043	...	1143	1243	...	1343	...	1443	...	1543	1643	...	1743	...	1843	...	1943
Romanshorn Hafen .... a.	...	0724	...	0824	0924	...	1024	1124	...	1224	1324	...	1424	...	1524	...	1624	1724	...	1824	...	1924	...	2024

A – May 29 - Nov. 4, **1994** and Mar. 18 - May 27, **1995**.
B – **Not** Dec. 24, 31.
C – **Not** Dec. 25, Jan. 1.
§ – Conveys ✕ on dates shown in Note **A**.

Table 315 GOSSAU - APPENZELL - WASSERAUEN

All trains 1, 2 class. Narrow gauge. AB

km		⚒	⚒	⑦		b																			
0	**Gossau 308**............. d.	0548	0623	0653	0717	0753	0814	0914	0953	1014	1114	1214	1243	1314	1414	1514	1553	1614	1653	1714	1814	1914	2014	2114	2316
8	Herisau **312**............. d.	0558	0635	0700	0725	0800	0822	0922	1000	1022	1122	1222	1250	1322	1422	1522	1600	1622	1700	1722	1822	1922	2022	2122	2337
32	Appenzell .... d.	0633	0726	0733	0758	0833	0858	0958	1035	1058	1158	1256	1325	1358	1458	1558	1635	1658	1735	1758	1858	1956	2054	2154	0008
41	**Wasserauen**............ a.	0644	0737	0744	0809	0844	0909**c**	1009	1046**b**	1109	1209	1307	1336	1409	1509	1609	1646	1709	1746	1809	1909	2007	...	*2207*	...

		⚒						b						b		b								
Wasserauen .... d.	...	0619	0647	0747	0847	0947	1047	1120	1147	1245	1347	...	1447	1507	1547	1607	1647	1707	1747	1807	1847	1940	2047	...
Appenzell .... d.	0600	0632	0701	0801	0901	1001	1101	1132	1159	1301	1401	1421	1501	1521	1601	1621	1701	1721	1759	1821	1901	2001	2101	2200
Herisau **312**...................... d.	0637	0704	0740	0837	0937	1037	1137	1206	1237	1337	1437	1459	1537	1559	1637	1659	1737	1759	1837	1859	1937	2037	2137	2237
Gossau 308....................... a.	0643	0710	0746	0843	0943	1043	1143	...	1243	1343	1443	1505	1543	1605	1643	1705	1743	1805	1843	1905	1943	2043	2143	2243

b – Sept. 25 - Oct. 16.
c – Oct. 17 - May 27.

Operator: AB – Appenzeller Bahn, Herisau.

Table 316 WÄDENSWIL/PFÄFFIKON - EINSIEDELN

All trains 1, 2 class. SOB

Rail service **Wädenswil** (Table **310**) - **Biberbrugg** (Table **312**) (15 - 20 minutes) - **Einsiedeln** (23 - 25 minutes). *24 km*. **Operator**: SOB – Schweizerische Süd Ost Bahn, Wädenswil.

From **Wädenswil**: 0005, 0514Ⓐ, 0617, 0737, 0805, 0905, 0937, 1005, 1105, 1137, 1205, 1305, 1337, 1405, 1505, 1537, 1605, 1705, 1737, 1805, 1905, 1935, 2005, 2035, 2105, 2135, 2235, 2305.

From **Einsiedeln**: 0446Ⓐ, 0545, 0617⚒, 0658, 0730, 0758, 0830, 0930, 0958, 1030, 1130, 1158, 1230, 1330, 1358, 1430, 1530, 1558, 1630, 1730, 1758, 1830, 1930, 1958, 2030, 2130, 2201, 2314.

Rail service **Arth Goldau** (Tables **290, 312**) - **Biberbrugg** (Table **312**) (27 - 35 minutes) - **Einsiedeln** (33 - 40 minutes). *38 km*. **Operator**: SOB – Schweizerische Süd Ost Bahn, Wädenswil.

From **Arth Goldau**: 0709, 0903, 1103⑦, 1111⚒, 1303, 1503, 1703, 1903.

From **Einsiedeln**: 0813, 1013, 1213, 1413, 1613, 1813.

Rail service **Pfäffikon** (Table **310, 312**) - **Biberbrugg** (Table **312**) (21 - 23 minutes) - **Einsiedeln** (28 - 31 minutes). *28 km*. **Operator**: SOB – Schweizerische Süd Ost Bahn, Wädenswil.

From **Pfäffikon**: 0532Ⓐ, 0610Ⓐ, 0722⚒, 0821, 1021, 1221, 1421, 1621, 1821.

From **Einsiedeln**: 0639Ⓐ, 0900, 1100, 1300, 1500, 1700, 1900, 2106.

Table 319 🚌 BRIG - SAAS FEE

🚌 PTT

🚌 service Brig Station - Saas Fee. Journey time: 65 minutes. All services call at **Visp** (Post) 14 minutes from Brig, and **Saas Grund** 10 minutes from Saas Fee.

From **Brig**: 0615, 0645, 0715 and hourly to 1615, 1645, 1715, 1815, 1915.

From **Saas Fee**: 0535🅁 and hourly to 1935🅁.

Reservation of seats at least two hours before departure is obligatory on journeys from **Saas Fee/Grund**. Reservations: ☎ 028 57 19 45 (Saas Fee), ☎ 028 57 23 14 (Saas Grund).

🚢 – Shipping service   🅁 – Reservation obligatory   🚌 – Bus or coach service

Table 320

ZERMATT - BRIG - ANDERMATT - DISENTIS - CHUR

Winter Service valid: December 17, **1994** - April 17, **1995**

1, 2 class except where shown
Narrow gauge. BVZ, FO, RhB

km		⚒	⑦	⚒	⚒															904 ⁄C🍷					
0	**Zermatt** d.	...	...	...	...	...	...	...	...	0600	...	...	0710	...	...	0810	...	0910	...	1010	...	1110	...	1210	...
8	Täsch d.	...	...	...	...	...	...	...	...	0612	...	...	0723	...	...	0823x	...	0923	...	|	...	1123	...	1223x	...
21	St Niklaus d.	...	...	...	...	...	...	...	...	0636	...	...	0747	...	...	0847	...	0947	...	1047	...	1147	...	1247	...
29	Stalden-Saas d.	...	...	...	...	...	...	...	...	0657	...	...	0808	...	...	0908	...	1008	...	1108	...	1208	...	1308	...
36	Visp d.	...	...	...	...	...	...	...	...	0710	...	...	0822	...	...	0922	...	1022	...	1122	...	1222	...	1322	...
45	**Brig** a.	...	...	...	...	...	...	...	...	0722	...	...	0836	...	...	0936	...	1035	...	1136	...	1236	...	1336	...
										▬			▬			▬		Z		|		▬		Z	
45	**Brig** d.	...	...	...	...	...	...	...	0627	...	0736	0827	...	0917	...	...	1032	1117	...	1146	1217	...	1317	1417	...
52	Mörel d.	...	...	...	...	...	...	...	0639	...	0747	0838	...	0930	...	...	1045	1130	...	|	1230	...	1330	1430	...
55	Betten d.	...	...	...	...	...	...	...	0647	...	0753	0844	...	0936	...	...	1051	1136	...	|	1236	...	1336	1436	...
62	Fiesch d.	...	...	...	...	...	...	...	0707	...	0811	0900	...	0953	...	...	1112	1155	...	|	1255	...	1355	1455	...
86	Oberwald d.	...	...	...	...	...	...	...	0754	...	0852	0940	...	1040	...	...	1152	1240	...	1252	1340	...	1440	1540	...
102	Realp d.	...	...	...	...	...	...	...	0811x	...	0910	1000	...	1100	...	...	1212	1300	...	|	1400	...	1500	1600	...
	Göschenen **322** d.	...	...	...	...	...	...	*0716*	|	*0814*	|	|	0955	|	*1055*	*1155*	|	|	1316	|	|	1355	|	|	*1555*
113	**Andermatt 322** a.	...	...	...	...	...	...	*0726*	0825	*0824*	0925	1012	1006	1112	*1106*	*1206*	1224	1312	1332	1322	1412	1406	1512	1612	*1606*
113	**Andermatt 322** d.	...	...	...	...	...	...	0805	0850	0900	0927	1027	1018	1127	1118	1218	1227	1316	...	1334	1427	1418	1527	1627	1618
117	Göschenen **322** a.	...	...	...	...	...	...	|	0905	|	0942	1042	|	1142	|	|	1242	1331	...	|	1442	|	1542	1642	|
123	Oberalppasshöhe d.	...	...	...	...	...	...	0830	▬	0930	▬	...	1045	▬	1145	1245	▬	...	...	|	...	1445	▬	▬	1645
132	Sedrun d.	...	...	...	0617	0717	0817	0908	...	1004	...	...	1118	...	1218	1318	...	...	...	1419	...	1518	...	...	1718
142	**Disentis/Mustér** a.	...	...	...	0635	0735	0835	0926	...	1022	...	...	1136	...	1236	1336	...	...	...	1437	...	1536	...	...	1736
					Y⚒	Y	Y								Y					|					Y
142	**Disentis/Mustér** d.	0450	0550	0610	0642	0740	0840	...	0940	...	1050	...	...	1140	1250	...	1340	...	...	1500	...	...	1540	1652	1740
181	Ilanz d.	0530	0630	0652	0730	0825	0925	...	1025	...	1135	...	...	1225	1333	...	1425	...	...	1534	...	...	1625	1733	1825
192	Reichenau-Tamins d.	0555	0658	0719	0755	0851	0951	...	1051	...	1201	...	...	1251	1401	...	1451	...	...	1600	...	...	1651	1801	1851
271	*St Moritz* **330** a.	*0900*	|	|	|	*1118*	*1158*	...	*1258*	...	*1358*	...	...	*1458*	*1558*	...	*1658*	...	...	*1758*	...	...	*1858*	*1958*	*2058*
202	**Chur** a.	0606	0709	0734	0806	0903	1003	...	1103	...	1213	...	...	1303	1414	...	1503	...	...	1610	...	...	1703	1814	1903

										2	🚌
Zermatt d.	1310	1410	...	1510	1610	1710	...	1810	1910	2111	...
Täsch d.	1323	1423	...	1522x	1623	1722x	...	1823	1923	2123	2130
St Niklaus d.	1347	1447	...	1547	1647	1747	...	1847	1947	...	2146
Stalden-Saas d.	1408	1508	...	1608	1708	1808	...	1908	2008	...	2203
Visp d.	1422	1522	...	1622	1722	1822	...	1922	2022	...	2215
Brig a.	1435	1536	...	1636	1736	1836	...	1936	2036	...	2228
	Z	▬		Z	Z2⚒	Z		▬			
Brig d.	1519	...	1617	1717	1808	1838	1908	...	...	...	...
Mörel d.	1530	...	1629	1730	1822	1849	1922	🚌	...	...	...
Betten d.	1536	...	1635	1736	1828	1855	1928	...	...	...	...
Fiesch d.	1555	...	1655	1755	1844	1912	1944	1948	...	...	...
Oberwald d.	1640	...	1740	1840	▬	1952	...	2023	...	...	...
Realp d.	1700	...	1758	1858x	...	2011	...	...	...	...	...
Göschenen **322** d.	|	*1655*	|	|	...	|	...	...	...	...	...
Andermatt 322 a.	1712	*1706*	1812	1912	...	2025	...	...	...	...	...
Andermatt 322 d.	1727	1718	1827	▬	...	*2027*	...	...	...	...	...
Göschenen **322** a.	1742	|	1842	...	...	*2042*	...	...	...	...	...
Oberalppasshöhe d.	...	1741	▬	...	...	...	...	...	...	...	...
Sedrun d.	...	1810	...	1848	...	...	...	...	...	...	...
Disentis/Mustér a.	...	1828	...	1905	...	...	...	...	...	...	...
Disentis/Mustér d.	...	...	1835	...	1940	...	...	...	...	...	...
Ilanz d.	...	...	1919	...	2025	...	...	...	...	...	...
Reichenau-Tamins d.	...	...	1946	...	2051	...	...	...	...	...	...
St Moritz **330** a.	...	...	*2158*	...	*2301*	...	...	...	...	...	...
Chur a.	...	...	1958	...	2103	...	...	...	...	...	...

						⚒				
Chur d.	...	...	...	...	...	0545	...	...	...	0648
St Moritz **330** d.	...	...	...	...	...	|	...	...	...	|
Reichenau-Tamins d.	...	...	...	...	...	0559	...	...	...	0704
Ilanz d.	...	...	...	...	...	0629	...	...	...	0732
Disentis/Mustér a.	...	...	...	...	...	0717	...	...	...	0815
						▬				▬
Disentis/Mustér d.	...	...	...	...	0642	...	0720	...	...	...
Sedrun d.	...	...	...	...	0659	...	0743	...	...	...
Oberalppasshöhe d.	...	...	...	...	▬	...	0805	...	...	...
Göschenen **322** d.	...	...	...	...	...	0716	|	0814	...	0916
Andermatt 322 a.	...	...	...	...	...	0726	0829	0824	...	0926
Andermatt 322 d.	...	...	...	...	...	0732	*0850*	0832	...	0932
Göschenen **322** a.	...	...	...	...	...	|	*0905*	|	...	|
Realp d.	...	...	...	...	...	0745	...	0845	...	0945
Oberwald d.	...	...	0614c	...	...	0814	...	0906	...	1008
Fiesch d.	...	...	0656	0744	...	0900	...	0950	...	1100
Betten d.	...	...	0712	0800	...	0920	...	1009	...	1120
Mörel d.	...	...	0718	0807	...	0928	...	1016	...	1128
Brig a.	...	...	0729	0818	...	0940	...	1028	...	1140
				Z		Z		Z⑥		Z
Brig d.	0610	0723	...	0823	0923	1023	...	1039	1123	1223
Visp d.	0624	0736	...	0836	0936	1036	...	1051	1136	1236
Stalden-Saas d.	0639	0749	...	0849	0949	1049	...	1107	1149	1249
St Niklaus d.	0704	0810	...	0910	1010	1110	...	1128	1210	1310
Täsch d.	0733	0834	...	0932x	1034	1132x	...	1152x	1234	1334
Zermatt a.	0744	0847	...	0945	1047	1145	...	1203	1247	1347

								903 ⁄G🍷																	Ⓑn
Chur d.	0811	...	0903	...	...	0945	...	1055	...	...	1145	...	1255	...	1355	...	1455	1545	...	1645	1745	...	1855	1945	2215
St Moritz **330** d.	|	...	*0705*	...	...	*0805*	...	*0900*	...	...	|	...	*1100*	...	|	...	*1300*	*1400*	...	*1500*	*1600*	...	*1700*	*1800*	*2000*
Reichenau-Tamins d.	0825	...	0915	...	...	0959	...	1113	...	...	1159	...	1309	...	1409	...	1509	1559	...	1659	1759	...	1909	1959	2227
Ilanz d.	0853	...	0940	...	...	1028	...	1139	...	...	1228	...	1337	...	1443	...	1537	1628	...	1728	1828	...	1937	2028	2249
Disentis/Mustér a.	0932	...	1017	...	...	1108	...	1215	...	...	1308	...	1417	...	1523	...	1617	1708	...	1808	1908	...	2017	2108	2323
	▬		▬			Y		|			▬		▬		▬		Y	▬		Y	▬		▬		
Disentis/Mustér d.	...	0940	...	1022	...	1122	...	1220	...	1243	...	1322	...	1422	...	1528	1622	...	1722	1815	...	...	...	...	...
Sedrun d.	...	1003	...	1043	...	1143	...	1242	...	1305	...	1343	...	1443	...	1550	1643	...	1741	1832	...	...	...	...	...
Oberalppasshöhe d.	...	1041	...	1115	...	1215	...	|	...	1330	...	1420	...	1515	...	1620	1715	...	▬	▬	...	...	...	...	...
Göschenen **322** d.	1016	|	1116r	|	1216	|	1316	|	←	▬	1416	|	1455	|	1616	|	|	1714			...	1855	*1950*	...	...
Andermatt 322 a.	1026	1107	1126r	1146	1226	1246	1332	1325	1332	...	1426	1446	1506	1546	1626	1646	1746	1724	...	...	...	1906	*2000*	...	...
Andermatt 322 d.	1032	*1127*	1132	*1150*	1232	1250	→	1335	1345	...	1432	*1450*	1508	*1550*	1632	*1650*	1750	1748	...	...	...	1908	2002	...	...
Göschenen **322** a.	|	*1142*	|	*1205*	|	1305	...	|	|	...	|	*1505*	|	*1605*	|	*1705*	1805	|	...	...	...	|	|	...	...
Realp d.	1045	▬	1145	▬	1245	...	...	|	1358	...	1445	▬	1522	▬	1643	▬	...	1759	...	...	...	1920x	2013	...	...
Oberwald d.	1108	...	1208	...	1308	...	...	1405	1420	...	1508	...	1547	...	1711	...	...	1819	...	...	...	1944	2038	...	...
Fiesch d.	1200	...	1302	...	1400	...	...	1440s	1509	...	1600	...	1640	...	1758	...	...	1900	1949	...	...	2026	...	...	...
Betten d.	1220	...	1320	...	1420	...	...	|	1525	...	1620	...	1658	...	1814	...	...	1916	2004	...	...	2041	...	...	...
Mörel d.	1228	...	1328	...	1428	...	...	|	1531	...	1628	...	1705	...	1824	...	...	1924	2011	...	...	2047	...	...	...
Brig a.	1240	...	1340	...	1440	...	...	1511	1542	...	1640	...	1716	...	1835	...	...	1935	2021	...	...	2058	...	...	...
								|												🚌	2				
Brig d.	...	1323	...	1423	...	...	...	1523	...	1623	...	1723	...	1823	...	1923	...	...	...	2023	...	...	...	...	...
Visp d.	...	1336	...	1436	...	...	...	1536	...	1636	...	1736	...	1836	...	1936	...	...	...	2034	...	...	...	...	...
Stalden-Saas d.	...	1349	...	1449	...	...	...	1549	...	1649	...	1749	...	1849	...	1949	...	...	...	2045	...	...	...	...	...
St Niklaus d.	...	1410	...	1510	...	...	...	1610	...	1710	...	1810	...	1910	...	2010	...	...	...	2102	...	...	...	...	...
Täsch d.	...	1432x	...	1534	...	...	...	|	...	1734	...	1834	...	|	...	2034	...	...	...	2120	2135	...	...	...	...
Zermatt a.	...	1445	...	1547	...	...	...	1645	...	1747	...	1847	...	1945	...	2047	...	...	...	...	2146	...	...	...	...

C – GLACIER EXPRESS C – [12] Zermatt - Chur; [12] (also [12] observation cars) Zermatt - Reichenau Tamins - St Moritz; ✕ Andermatt - Chur; 🍷 Brig - Disentis.
G – GLACIER EXPRESS G – [12] Chur - Zermatt; [12] (also [12] observation cars) St Moritz - Reichenau Tamins - Zermatt; ✕ Chur - Andermatt; 🍷 Disentis - Brig.
Y – Change trains at Disentis.
Z – Change trains at Brig.

c – ⚒ only.
n – Will **not** run Dec. 25, Jan. 1, Apr. 16.
r – © only.
s – Stops on request to **set down** only.
x – Stops on request.

⁄ – GLACIER EXPRESS – Ⓡ with supplement (SFr 7,-) except for local journeys on the Brig - Zermatt and Disentis - Chur/St Moritz sections. ✕ reservations are necessary – ☎ (Chur) 081 22 14 25.

Operators: BVZ – Brig Visp Zermatt (Rack Railway), Brig; FO – Furka Oberalp Bahn (Rack railway), Brig; RhB – Rhaetische Bahn, Chur.

Table 320 ZERMATT - BRIG - ANDERMATT - DISENTIS - CHUR

Summer Service valid from April 18, **1995**

1, 2 class except where shown
Narrow gauge. BVZ, FO, RhB

km									900 N🍷			1902 ⁄A🍷		902 ⁄B🍷					904 ⁄C🍷				906 ⁄D🍷	f	
0	**Zermatt** d.	...	...	0600	...	...	...	0710	...	...	0810	0810	...	0854	...	...	0910	...	1010	...	1110	...	1210	1210	1310
8	Täsch d.	...	...	0612	...	...	...	0723	...	...	0823x	0823x	...	|	...	...	0923	...	|	...	1123	...	1223x	1223x	1323
21	St Niklaus d.	...	...	0636	...	...	...	0747	...	...	0847	0847	...	0929	...	...	0947	...	1047	...	1147	...	1247	1247	1347
29	Stalden-Saas d.	...	...	0657	...	...	...	0808	...	...	0908	0908	...	|	...	...	1008	...	1108	...	1208	...	1308	1308	1408
36	Visp d.	...	...	0710	...	...	...	0822	...	...	0922	0922	...	1003	...	...	1022	...	1122	...	1222	...	1322	1322	1422
45	**Brig** a.	...	...	0722	...	...	...	0836	...	...	0936	0936	...	1015	...	...	1035	...	1136	...	1236	...	1336	1336	1435
												|		|					|			|	N	
45	**Brig** d.	...	0627	...	0736	...	0827	...	0849	0910	...	0946	...	1030	...	1032	...	1115	1146	1207	...	1311	1346	1418	...
52	Mörel d.	...	0639	...	0747	...	0838	←	0859	0923	...	|	...	|	...	1045	...	1128	|	1220	...	1325	1355	1429	...
55	Betten d.	...	0647	...	0753	...	0844	0844	0904	0929	...	|	...	|	...	1051	...	1134	|	1225	...	1331	1401	1435	...
62	Fiesch d.	...	0707	←	0811	...	→	0900	0920	0947	...	1017	...	|	...	1112	...	1153	|	1243	...	1351	1416	1450	...
86	Oberwald d.	...	0754	0754	0852	...		0946	0954	1027	...	1052	...	|	...	1152	...	1235	1252	1335	...	1442	1452	1536	...
102	Realp d.	...	→	0811x	0910	...	...	1004	|	1058f	...	|	...	|	...	1210	...	1258f	|	1358	...	1505f	|	1558	...
	Göschenen **322** d.	...		|	|	0916	0955	|	|	|	...	|	...	|	1155	|	...	|	|	|	1355	|	|	|	1555
113	**Andermatt 322** a.	...	...	0825	0925	0926	1006	1018	1024	1112f	...	1122	...	1158	1206	1224	N	1312f	1322	1412	1406	1519f	1519	1614	1606
113	**Andermatt 322** d.	...	...	0829	0927	0934h	1010k	1027	1030	1127f	...	1134	...	1200	1218	1227	1300	1327f	1334	1427	1418	1527f	1527	1627	1618g
117	Göschenen **322** a.	...	...	|	0942	|	|	1042	|	1142f	...	|	...	|	|	1242	|	1342f	|	1442	|	1542f	|	1642	|
123	Oberalppasshöhe d.	...	...	0849		0955h	1033	...	1050		...	1155	...	|	1240		1322		|	...	1440		1546		1640g
132	Sedrun d.	0717	...	0917	...	1022h	1108	...	1117	...	...	1222	...	|	1315	...	1359	...	1419	...	1511	...	1611	...	1710g
142	**Disentis/Mustér** a.	0735	...	0935	...	1040h	1126	...	1134	...	...	1240	...	1300	1333	...	1417	...	1437	...	1528	...	1628	...	1726g
		Y		Y		Y								|				N	|				|	f	Y
142	**Disentis/Mustér** d.	0740	0840	0940	...	1050	...	...	...	1140	...	...	1250	1310	...	1340	...	1430	1500	...	...	1540	1652	1652	1740
181	Ilanz d.	0825	0925	1025	...	1135	...	...	...	1225	...	...	1333	1349	...	1425	...	1514	1534	...	...	1625	1733	1733	1825
192	Reichenau-Tamins d.	0851	0951	1051	...	1201	...	...	...	1251	...	...	1401	|	...	1451	...	1542	1600	...	...	1651	1800	1801	1851
271	*St Moritz* **330** a.	*1118*	*1158*	*1258*	...	*1358*	...	...	...	*1458*	...	...	*1558*	1658e	...	*1658*	...	*1758*	1758	...	...	*1858*	*1958*	*1958*	*2058*
202	**Chur** a.	0903	1003	1103	...	1213	...	...	...	1303	...	...	1414	1418	...	1503	...	1554	1610	...	...	1703	1813	1814	1903

Zermatt d.	...	1410	...	1510	...	1610	1710	...	1810	1910	...
Täsch d.	...	1423	...	1522x	...	1623	1722x	...	1823	1923	...
St Niklaus d.	...	1447	...	1547	...	1647	1747	...	1847	1947	...
Stalden-Saas d.	...	1508	...	1608	...	1708	1808	...	1908	2008	...
Visp d.	...	1522	...	1622	...	1722	1822	...	1922	2022	...
Brig a.	...	1536	...	1636	...	1736	1836	...	1936	2036	...
Brig d.	1530	...	1617	...	1717	...	...	1838	...	...	...
Mörel d.	1544	...	1629	...	1729	...	...	1849	...	...	...
Betten d.	1550	...	1635	...	1735	...	...	1855	...	...	...
Fiesch d.	1610	...	1655	...	1755	...	...	1912	...	...	...
Oberwald d.	1651	...	1740	...	1840	...	...	1952	...	...	...
Realp d.	1709	...	1758	...	1858x	...	...	2011	...	...	...
Göschenen **322** d.	|	...	|	1755	|	...	...	|	...	...	...
Andermatt 322 a.	1722	...	1812	1806	1912	...	...	2025	...	...	...
Andermatt 322 d.	1724	...	1827g	1818g		...	...	2027	...	...	...
Göschenen **322** a.	|	...	1842g	|	...	...	...	2042	...	...	...
Oberalppasshöhe d.	1744	...	...	1840g	...	...	...	...	...	...	...
Sedrun d.	1810	...	...	1908g	...	...	...	...	...	...	...
Disentis/Mustér a.	1826	...	...	1926g	...	...	...	...	...	...	...
Disentis/Mustér d.	...	1835	...	...	1940	...	...	...	...	...	...
Ilanz d.	...	1919	...	...	2025	...	...	...	...	...	...
Reichenau-Tamins d.	...	1946	...	...	2051	...	...	...	...	...	...
St Moritz **330** a.	...	*2158*	...	...	*2301*	...	...	...	...	...	...
Chur a.	...	1958	...	...	2103	...	...	...	...	...	...

	2						⚒			
Chur d.	...	...	...	...	...	...	0545	...	...	...
St Moritz **330** d.	...	...	...	...	...	...	|	...	...	...
Reichenau-Tamins d.	...	...	...	...	...	...	0559	...	...	...
Ilanz d.	...	...	...	...	...	...	0629	...	...	...
Disentis/Mustér a.	...	...	...	...	...	...	0717	...	...	...
Disentis/Mustér d.	...	...	...	...	...	...	...	0722	...	...
Sedrun d.	...	...	...	...	...	...	...	0743	...	...
Oberalppasshöhe d.	...	...	...	...	...	...	...	0805	...	...
Göschenen **322** d.	...	...	...	...	...	...	0716	|	...	0916
Andermatt 322 a.	...	...	...	...	...	...	0726	0829	...	0926
Andermatt 322 d.	...	...	...	...	...	...	0732	0832	...	0937
Göschenen **322** a.	...	...	...	...	...	...	|	|	...	|
Realp d.	...	...	...	...	...	...	0745	0845	...	0948
Oberwald d.	...	...	...	0614r	...	...	0808	0906	...	1014
Fiesch d.	...	...	...	0656	0744	...	0850	0950	...	1100
Betten d.	...	...	...	0712	0800	...	0905	1005	...	1116
Mörel d.	...	...	...	0718	0807	...	0921	1017	...	1126
Brig a.	...	...	...	0729	0818	...	0932	1028	...	1137
					Z		Z	Z⑥		Z
Brig d.	0510	0610	0723	...	0823	0923	1023	1039	1123	1223
Visp d.	0530	0624	0736	...	0836	0936	1036	1051	1136	1236
Stalden-Saas d.	0548	0639	0749	...	0849	0949	1049	1107	1149	1249
St Niklaus d.	0616	0704	0810	...	0910	1010	1110	1128	1210	1310
Täsch d.	0642	0733	0834	...	0932x	1034	1132x	1152x	1234	1334
Zermatt a.	0654	0744	0847	...	0945	1047	1145	1203	1247	1347

				901 ⁄F🍷		h	N		903 ⁄G🍷			2903 ⁄H🍷		905 ⁄K🍷	N										Ⓑp
Chur d.	0648	...	0811	0903	...	...	...	0945	1055	...	...	...	1145	1216	...	...	1255	1355	1455	1545	1645	1745	1855	1945	2215
St Moritz **330** d.	|	...	|	*0705*	...	...	...	*0805*	0900	...	...	0925	|	1000e	...	...	*1100*	*1200*	*1300*	*1400*	*1500*	*1600*	*1700*	*1800*	*2000*
Reichenau-Tamins d.	0704	...	0825	0915	...	...	...	0959	1105	...	...	1125	1159	|	...	...	1309	1409	1509	1559	1659	1759	1909	1959	2227
Ilanz d.	0732	...	0853	0940	...	...	...	1028	1130	...	...	1150	1228	1252	...	...	1337	1443	1537	1628	1728	1828	1937	2028	2249
Disentis/Mustér a.	0815	...	0932	1017	...	...	...	1108	1205	...	...	1230	1308	1326	...	...	1417	1523	1617	1708	1808	1908	2017	2108	2323
	YN		YN	|				Y	|			|		|				Y	Y	Y	Y				
Disentis/Mustér d.	0822	...	0935	1028	1020f	1048	...	1135	1220	...	...	1240	...	1340	...	1403	...	1540	1635	1735g	1830g	...	...	...	...
Sedrun d.	0842	...	0954	1048	1040f	1107	...	1155	1242	...	...	|	...	|	...	1425	...	1559	1657	1755g	1848g	...	...	...	...
Oberalppasshöhe d.	0908	...	1031	|	1103f	1132	...	1220	|	...	...	|	...	|	...	1446	...	1621g	1720	1820g	...	...	...	...	...
Göschenen **322** d.	|	1016g	|	|	|	|	1216	|	|	1255f	1314	|	1355	|	...	|	1616g	|	|	|	...	...	1855	1950	...
Andermatt 322 a.	0934	1026g	1058	1134	1129f	1200	1226	1246	1325	1306f	1324	1357	1406	1443	...	1513	1626g	1646g	1746	1846g	...	...	1906	2000	...
Andermatt 322 d.	...	1032	1127	1136	1132f		1232	1250	1335	1322f	1345f	1403	1425f	1445	...	1515	1632	1650g	1748	1850	...	...	1908	2002	...
Göschenen **322** a.	...	|	1142	|	|	...	|	1305	|	|	|	|	|	|	...	|	|	1705g	|	1905	...	...	|	|	...
Realp d.	...	1045		|	1145f	...	1245	...	|	1333f	1359f	|	1436f	|	...	1529	1643		1759	...	...	...	1920x	2013	...
Oberwald d.	...	1108	...	1205	1221	...	1306	...	1405	1408	1420f	|	1500f	|	1520	1553	1711	...	1819	...	...	...	1944	2038	...
Fiesch d.	...	1151	...	1240s	1302	...	1348	...	1440s	1452	1503f	|	1542f	|	1600	1639	1758	←	1900	...	...	1949	2026	...	...
Betten d.	...	1209	...	1256s	1317	...	1408	...	|	1508	1520f	|	1558f	|	1616	1656	1814	1814	1916	...	...	2004	2041	...	...
Mörel d.	...	1219	...	1301s	1324	...	1413	...	|	1516	1527f	|	1608f	|	1628	1704	→	1824	1924	...	...	2011	2047	...	...
Brig a.	...	1231	...	1311	1335	...	1425	...	1511	1527	1538f	1532	1621f	1616	1639	1715		1835	1935	...	...	2021	2058	...	...
			f	|				...	|			|	Z	|		Z		Z							
Brig d.	...	...	1323	1323	...	1423	...	...	1523	...	...	1539	1623	1639	...	1723	1823	1923	...	...	...	...	...	...	...
Visp d.	...	...	1336	1336	...	1436	...	...	1536	...	...	1551	1636	1651	...	1736	1836	1936	...	...	...	...	...	...	...
Stalden-Saas d.	...	...	1349	1349	...	1449	...	...	1549	...	...	1607	1649	|	...	1749	1849	1949	...	...	...	...	...	...	...
St Niklaus d.	...	...	1410	1410	...	1510	...	...	1610	...	...	1628	1710	1728	...	1810	1910	2010	...	...	...	...	...	...	...
Täsch d.	...	...	1432x	1432x	...	1534	...	...	|	...	...	|	1734	|	...	1834	1932x	2034	...	...	...	...	...	...	...
Zermatt a.	...	...	1445	1445	...	1547	...	...	1645	...	...	1703	1747	1804	...	1847	1945	2047	...	...	...	...	...	...	...

A – GLACIER EXPRESS A – Runs May 29 - Oct. 16: Relief train for prebooked groups only.
B – GLACIER EXPRESS B – Runs May 29 - Oct. 16: [1] Zermatt - Chur - St Moritz; ✕ Brig - St Moritz.
C – GLACIER EXPRESS C – [12] Zermatt - Chur (- Davos Platz, May 29 - Oct. 16 **only**); [12] Zermatt - Reichenau-Tamins - St Moritz; ✕ Andermatt - Chur.
D – GLACIER EXPRESS D – Runs May 29 - Oct. 16: [12] Zermatt - Chur; ✕ Brig - Chur.
F – GLACIER EXPRESS F – Runs May 29 - Oct. 16: [12] Chur - Zermatt; ✕ Chur - Brig.
G – GLACIER EXPRESS G – [12] Davos Platz (May 29 - Oct. 16 **only**) - Chur - Zermatt; [12] St Moritz - Reichenau-Tamins - Zermatt; ✕ Chur - Andermatt.
H – GLACIER EXPRESS H – Runs May 29 - Oct. 16: [12] St Moritz - Reichenau-Tamins - Zermatt; ✕ St Moritz - Disentis.
K – GLACIER EXPRESS K – Runs May 29 - Oct. 16: [12] St Moritz - Chur - Zermatt; ✕ St Moritz - Brig.

N – May 14 - Oct. 16.
Y – Change trains at Disentis.
Z – Change trains at Brig.
e – Via Chur.
f – Oct. 17 - Dec. 16 **only**.
g – May 14 - Oct. 16 **only**.
h – June 11 - Oct. 16 **only**.

k – Oct. 17 - Dec. 16 departs 12 minutes later with connection available from train in the following column.
p – **Not** July 31.
r – ⚒ only.
s – Stops on request to set down only.
x – Stops on request.

⁄ – GLACIER EXPRESS – Ⓡ with supplement (SFr 7,-) except for local journeys on the Brig - Zermatt and Disentis - Chur/St Moritz sections. ✕ reservations are necessary – ☎ (Chur) 081 22 14 25.

Operators: BVZ – Brig Visp Zermatt (Rack Railway), Brig; FO – Furka Oberalp Bahn (Rack railway), Brig; RhB – Rhaetische Bahn, Chur.

🚂 *STEAM RAILWAY:* REALP to FURKA operates June 25 - Oct. 9: **From Realp** (DFB station): 1100 and 1440 on ©, 1000 and 1305 on ⑤⑥⑦ (daily July 15 - Aug. 14). Round trip 2 - 2 ¾ hours.

Table 321 — ZERMATT - GORNERGRAT

2 class only. Narrow gauge rack railway. GGG

Rail service **Zermatt - Gornergrat**. Journey time: 44 minutes. Service liable to be suspended in bad weather. **Operator**: GGB – GGB, Brig.

From Zermatt: 0705A, 0800, 0824B, 0848B, 0912A, 0936B, 1000, 1024B, 1048B, 1112A, 1136B, 1200, 1224B, 1248B, 1312A, 1336B, 1400, 1424B, 1448B, 1512A, 1536B, 1600, 1624B, 1712A, 1800A.

From Gornergrat: 0755A, 0843B, 0907, 0931B, 0955A, 1019B, 1043B, 1107, 1131B, 1155A, 1219B, 1243B, 1307, 1331B, 1355A, 1419B, 1443B, 1507, 1531B, 1555A, 1619B, 1643B, 1707, 1755A, 1907A.

A – Daily Sept. 25 - Oct. 30 and Nov. 26 - May 27. B – Daily Sept. 25 - Oct. 8 and Dec. 17 - Apr. 30.

Table 322 — GÖSCHENEN - ANDERMATT

Certain services continue beyond Andermatt to/from Disentis or Brig - see Table 320.

1, 2 class. Narrow gauge rack railway. FO

Rail service **Göschenen - Andermatt**. Journey time 10 - 15 minutes. **Operator**: FO – Furka Oberalp, Brig.

From Göschenen: 0621bg, 0716, 0814, 0855c, 0916, 0955, 1016t, 1055, 1116c, 1155, 1216t, 1255, 1314h, 1316d, 1355, 1416d, 1455, 1516d, 1555, 1616t, 1655, 1714t, 1755, 1816t, 1855, 1921⑦, 1950, 2050b, 2200b.

From Andermatt: 0605bg, 0650, 0750, 0833c, 0850, 0927, 0950t, 1027, 1050c, 1127, 1150t, 1227, 1250, 1316d, 1327h, 1350d, 1427, 1450d, 1527, 1550, 1627t, 1650, 1727t, 1750, 1827t, 1850, 1915⑦, 2027b, 2104⑦b, 2115 ✕ b.

b – By 🚌. c – Runs ⒸDec. 17 - Apr. 17. d – Runs Dec. 17 - Apr. 17. g – Runs Ⓐ, not Nov. 1, Dec. 8. h – Not Dec. 17 - Apr. 17. t – Not Oct. 17 - Dec. 16, Apr. 18 - May 19.

Table 324 — CHUR - AROSA

1, 2 class. Narrow gauge. RhB

Rail service **Chur - Arosa**. Journey time: 58-66 minutes. **Operator**: RhB – Rhaetische Bahn, Chur.

From Chur: 0531Ⓐ, 0631, 0813 (**Not** Oct. 17 - Dec. 16, Apr. 10 - May 19) and hourly until 1755, 1855 (Oct. 17 - May 19 only), 1955, 2105, 2300.

From Arosa: 0600Ⓐ, 0645 ✕, 0700⑦, 0745, 0905, 1005 (**Not** Oct. 17 - Dec. 16, Apr. 10 - May 19), 1105 and hourly until 2105.

Table 325 — 🚌 CHUR - FLIMS

🚌 PTT

Bus service **Chur** (Station) - **Flims** Waldhaus (Post). Journey time: 36 minutes to **Flims Dorf**, 41 minutes to **Flims Waldhaus**.

From Chur: 0615 ✕, 0715, 0815, 0900, 0955, 1055, 1115, 1155 ✕, 1205, 1255, 1310 ✕, 1355, 1455, 1605, 1700, 1710 ✕, 1745⑥, 1810, 1855, 1955, 2100, 2200⑤⑥, 2300.
From Flims Waldhaus: 0555 ✕, 0628, 0700 ✕, 0720, 0820, 0930, 1020, 1130, 1215, 1300 ✕, 1320, 1420, 1520, 1615, 1620, 1715Ⓐ, 1720, 1820, 1835Ⓐ, 1913, 2000, 2100, 2200, 2240⑤⑥.

Table 326 — 🚌 CHUR - BELLINZONA

🚌 PTT

km		N Ⓡ		Ⓡ	N Ⓡ		Ⓡ			Ⓡ	N Ⓡ		Ⓡ	N Ⓡ	Ⓡ
0	Chur Station .... d.	0810	...	0910	1010	...	1210		1610	...	Bellinzona Station ..... d.	0825	...	0935	...	1435	...	1535	1635
40	Thusis Station .... d.	0840	...	0940	1040	...	1240		1640	...	Thusis Station .... a.	1015	...	1110	...	1613	...	1716	1816
179	Bellinzona Station ...... a.	1025	...	1125	1225	...	1425		1825	...	Chur Station .... a.	1045	...	1135	...	1640	...	1744	1844

N – Will **not** run Oct. 17 - May 27.

For reservations ☎ 081 26 31 84 (Chur), ☎ 092 25 77 55 (Bellinzona).

Table 327 — LANDQUART - DAVOS - FILISUR

1, 2 class. Narrow gauge. RhB

km		✕	H																					
0	Landquart 310 ...... d.	0535	...	0722	0852	0856	0940	1040	1047	1140	1240	1243	1340	1440	1447	1540	1640	1647	1740	1840	1847	1935	2045	2145
43	Klosters Dorf .... d.	0641	...	0813	0930	0947	1015		1137	1215		1337	1415		1537	1615		1737	1815		1937	2019	2129	2229
46	Klosters .... d.	0649	...	0820	0936	0952	1020	1120	1143	1220	1343	1343	1420	1520	1543	1620	1720	1743	1820	1920	1941	2024	2133	2233
65	Davos Dorf .... d.	0717	0825	0842	0958	1020	1042	1142	1209	1242	1342	1409	1442	1542	1609	1642	1742	1809	1842	1942	2004	2046	2155	2255
69	Davos Platz .... a.	0721	0828	0846	1002	1024	1046	1146	1213	1246	1346	1346	1446	1546	1613	1646	1746	1813	1846	1946	2008	2050	2159	2259
69	Davos Platz .... d.	0730	0832	0925	...	1025H	1125	...	1225H	1325	...	1425H	1525	...	1625H	1725	...	1825	...	2027b	...			
96	Filisur 330 .... a.	0757	0859	0952	...	1052H	1152	...	1252H	1352	...	1452H	1552	...	1652H	1752	...	1852	...	2052b	...			

		✕		G					H		H					
Filisur 330 .... d.	...	0645	...	0806	...	0918	...	1018	1106H	1206	...	1306H	1406	...	1506H	1606	...	1706H	1806	...	1906	...
Davos Platz .... a.	...	0712	...	0832	...	0945	...	1045	1134H	1234	...	1334H	1434	...	1534H	1634	...	1734H	1834	...	1932	...
Davos Platz .... d.	...	0700	0713	0805	0835	0905	...	1005	1038	1105	1205	1238	1305	1405	1438	1505	1605	1638	1705	1838	1905	2000	2100
Davos Dorf .... d.	...	0704	0717	0810	0841	0910	...	1010	1043	1110	1210	1243	1310	1410	1443	1510	1610	1643	1710	1810	1910	2005	2105
Klosters .... d.	0625	0727	...	0834	0905	0934	...	1034	1109	1134	1234	1309	1334	1434	1509	1534	1634	1709	1734	1834	1909	1934	2025	2125
Klosters Dorf .... d.	0628	0731	...	0837	0908	...	...	1037	1115	...	1237	1315	...	1437	1515	1537	1637	1715	...	1837	1915	...	2029	2129
Landquart 310 ...... a.	0714	0817	...	0917	0958	1017	...	1117	1207	1217	1317	1407	1417	1517	1607	1617	1717	1807	1817	1917	2007	2017	2115	2215

G – Conveys May 29 - Oct. 16, **1994**, also May 20 - 27, **1995**:
GLACIER EXPRESS – 🚃 Zermatt - Chur - Davos Platz and v.v.
H – Sept. 25 - Oct. 16, Dec. 17 - Apr. 9 and May 20 - 27.
b – ⑥ only.
Operator: RhB – Rhaetische Bahn, Chur.

Table 328 — ST. MORITZ - POSCHIAVO - TIRANO

1, 2 class. Narrow gauge. RhB

km		401	403	405 Ⓐ	405 Ⓒ	409	411 J	415	417 J	421 J	421 K	501 B Ⓨ	425 C	431	4435 ✕	441	445		451	455	459 J	459	471	473
0	St Moritz .... d.	...	...	...	...	0745	0835	0905	0930	1000	1010	...	1105	1200	1240	1400	1500	...	1600	1700	1800	1827	1935	2010
6	Pontresina .... d.	...	...	0650	...	0810	0852	0920	0943	1024	1024	1053	1125	1218	1305	1418	1518	...	1618	1718	1811	1838	1945	2020
12	Morteratsch .... d.	...	...	0659x	...	0821	0903	0931		1035	1035		1136	1229	1316	1430	1529	...	1629	1729		1905x	2015x	
18	Bernina Diavolezza .. d.	...	...	0708x	...	0831	0912	0941	1002	1045	1045		1147	1240	1327	1440	1540	...	1640	1740		1924vx	2024x	
19	Bernina Lagalb ..... d.	...	...	0710x	...	0833	0914	0944		1048		1150	1242	1330	1442	1542	...	1642	1742		1927vx	2026x	
23	Ospizio Bernina ..... d.	...	...	0721	...	0842	0925	0953	1014	1057	1057		1158	1252	1341	1452	1552	...	1652	1752		1936vx	2035x	
28	Alp Grüm .... d.	...	...	0731	...	0852	0933	1003	1029	1108	1107	1130	1212	1303	1356	1501	1601	...	1701	1801		1946vx	2044x	
44	**Poschiavo** .... d.	...	0600	0705	0818	0818	0940	...	1045	1104	1142	...	1203	1250	1345	1441	1549	1645	...	1745	1845		2025v	2119	
54	Brusio .... d.	...	0618	0729	0840	0840	1001	...	1107		1205	...		1311	1407	1523v	1611	1707	...	1807	1907				
57	Campocologno ...... d.	...	0629	0742	0855	0855	1014	...	1120	1138	1216	...	1232	1322	1420	1542v	1624	1720	...	1820	1920				
61	Tirano 🏛 .... a.	...	0637	0750	0903	0903	1022	...	1128	1146	1224	...	1240	1330	1428	1550v	1632	1728	...	1828	1928				

		424 ✕	426	430 Ⓐ	434	440	444		450 J	450 K	454	460 ✕		464		470 J	474 M	472 B Ⓨ	500 CN	478	480 Ⓐ	484	490	494	496	498
Tirano 🏛 .... d.	...	...	...	...	0730	0840	...	0930	...	1030	1130	...	1224	...	1305t	1405	...	1440	1505	1530	1610	1730	1830	1900	1950
Campocologno ...... d.	...	...	...	0650v	0744	0853	...	0942	...	1042	1142	...	1243	...	1322t	1417	...	1451	1517	1545	1640	1742	1842	1917	2002
Brusio .... d.	...	...	...	0700v	0754	0903	...	0952	...	1052	1152	...	1252	...	1334t	1427	...		1555	1651	1752	1852	1927x	2012x	
Poschiavo .... d.	...	...	0640	0725	0817	0930	...	1020	...	1120	1220	...	1320	...	1420	1450	...	1520	1552	1620	1720	1820	1914	1946	2031
Alp Grüm .... d.	...	...	0712x	0803	0853	1004	...	1100	1112	1155	1300	...	1400	...	1500	1526	...		1640	1700	1800	1900			
Ospizio Bernina ..... d.	...	...	0722	0814	0903	1013	...	1120	1122	1207	1309	...	1409	...	1509	1534	...		1651	1709	1810	1900			
Bernina Lagalb ..... d.	...	...	0732x	0824	0915	1022x	...	1131	1133	1218	1318	...	1418	...	1518	1543	1555		1701	1718	1820x	1918x			
Bernina Diavolezza .. d.	...	...	0734x	0826	0918	1025	...	1135	1137	1220	1320	...	1420	...	1520	1546	1558		1704	1720	1822x	1920x			
Morteratsch .... d.	...	...	0743x	0837	0931	1036	...	1149	1149	1231	1331	...	1431	...	1531	1557	1608		1715	1731	1831x	1931x			
Pontresina .... d.	0700	0725	0755	0851	0945	1047	...	1211	1211d	1251	1345	...	1445	...	1545	1611	1620	1637	1728	1745	1843	1945			
St Moritz .... a.	0710	0735	0806	0902	0956	1058	...	1222	1222d	1302	1356	...	1456	...	1556	1622	1631	1650	1739	1756	1853	1956			

B – BERNINA EXPRESS – Runs Sept. 25 - Oct. 16 and May 20 - 27 **only**: 🚃 and ⓨ Chur - Tirano and v.v. Ⓡ with supplement payable (SFr 7,-).
C – BERNINA EXPRESS (Winter) – 🚃 St Moritz - Tirano and v.v.
J – Sept. 25 - Oct. 16 and May 20 - 27.
K – Dec. 17 - Apr. 9.
M – Feb. 1 - Apr. 17.
N – Oct. 17 - May 19.
d – Daily Oct. 17 - May 19.
t – ✕ only.
v – Ⓐ only.
x – Stops on request.
Operator: RhB – Rhaetische Bahn, Chur.

🚃 – Through carriage (1 and 2 class)   2 – 2 class only   Ⓡ – Reservation obligatory

Table 330 — CHUR and SCUOL TARASP - ST. MORITZ

1, 2 class. Narrow gauge. RhB

km		305	224	307	311	515	234	315	240 R	521 T♈	321 U	501 B♈	1244 K	244 L	525 C♈	325	531 S	331	250	535	335	254	541 V✕	341 V
0	Chur d.					0640				0808		0857			0900		0952			1052			1152	
10	Reichenau-Tamins d.					0654				0818					0911		1003			1103			1203	
27	Thusis d.					0724				0840					0934		1025			1125			1225	
41	Tiefencastel d.					0743				0859					0954		1047			1147			1247	
51	Filisur d.					0802				0917		1002			1016		1102			1202			1302	
59	Bergün/Bravuogn d.					0815				0930					1030		1115			1215			1315	
	Scuol Tarasp d.		0600				0750		0837				0920	0937			1050			1150				
	Susch d.		0627				0814		0902				0945	1002			1114			1214				
	Zernez d.		0637				0825		0913				1000	1013			1125			1225				
	Zuoz d.		0658				0849		0940				1027	1040			1149			1249				
81	Bever a.		0709			0845	0902		0952			1041	1052				1202			1302				
84	Samedan a.		0712			0848	0905		0955		1004	1044	1055		1104		1145			1205		1305	1345	
84	Samedan d.	0638	0715	0714	0830	0852	0912	0908	1002	1010	1007	1102	1110	1112	1150	1152	1210	1250	1252	1310	1350	1352		
89	Pontresina a.	0645		0721	0837			0915			1014	1047					1119		1159		1259			
87	Celerina d.	0720				0856			1006			1106	1114			1154		1214		1314		1358		
89	St Moritz a.	0724				0900		0920		1010	1018		1110	1118			1158		1218	1258	1318		1358	

		260	545 S	345 S	264	347 J	551	351	270	555 G♈	355	274	561 H	361	280	565	365	571	371	290	575	375	294 ⑥e	581	585
	Chur d.		1252			1352				1452		1552	1610			1652		1752			1852			1952	2057
	Reichenau-Tamins d.		1303			1403				1503		1610				1703		1803			1903			2003	2110
	Thusis d.		1325			1425				1525		1633				1725		1825			1925			2028	2138
	Tiefencastel d.		1347			1447				1547		1649				1747		1847			1947			2047	2154
	Filisur d.		1402			1502				1602		1702				1802		1902			2002			2102	2115
	Bergün/Bravuogn d.		1415			1515				1615		1715				1815		1915			2015			2115	2221
	Scuol Tarasp d.	1250			1350			1450				1550		1650					1850			2024			
	Susch d.	1314			1414			1514				1614		1714					1914			2047			
	Zernez d.	1325			1425			1525				1625		1725					1929			2055			
	Zuoz d.	1349			1449			1549				1649		1749					1949			2116			
	Bever a.	1402			1502			1602		1645		1702		1802					2002			2126	2142		2248
	Samedan a.	1405	1445		1505		1545	1605	1645			1705	1710	1805	1845		1945		2005	2045		2129	2145	2251	
	Samedan d.	1410	1450	1452	1510	1518	1550	1552	1610	1650	1652	1710	1750	1752	1810	1850	1854	1950	1952	2010	2048	2052	2130	2150	2253
	Pontresina a.			1459		1525		1559			1659			1759			1901		1959			2059				
	Celerina d.	1414	1454		1514		1554		1614	1654		1714	1754		1814	1854		1954		2014	2054		2134	2154	2257
	St Moritz a.	1418	1458		1518		1558		1618	1658		1718	1758		1818	1858		1958		2018	2058		2138	2158	2301

		520 ✕	205 ✕	324	524	326	211	330	530	215	334	534	2903 HJ✕	340 R	221	540 GR	1544 K	344	225	544 L	231 S	350	550 ♈	235	354 V
	St Moritz d.	0545			0705		0717		0805		0840		0900	0925		0952	1000		1052	1100	1140		1200	1240	
	Celerina d.	0549			0709		0721		0809		0844		0904			0956	1000		1056	1105	1144		1204	1244	
	Pontresina d.			0701		0705		0808							0949			1059				1201			1301
	Samedan a.	0553		0708	0713	0732	0724	0815	0813		0848	0906	0908	0933	1006	1000	1009	1106	1100	1109	1148	1208	1208	1248	1308
	Samedan d.	0555	0610		0718		0734		0820		0855		0901	0915	0935	1012	1015	1056	1112	1115	1155	1215	1215	1255	1301
	Bever d.	0558	0614				0738					0901		0913		1028	1016		1128		1213			1313	
	Zuoz d.		0626				0754					0913				1053			1153		1238			1338	
	Zernez d.		0651				0822					0938													
	Susch d.		0658				0831					0946				1102			1202		1246			1346	
	Scuol Tarasp a.		0722				0856					1010				1128			1228		1310			1410	
	Bergün/Bravuogn d.				0626				0750			0850		0950			1050	1133		1150			1250		
	Filisur d.				0639				0804			0904		1004	1016		1104	1148		1204			1304		
	Tiefencastel d.				0655				0818			0918		1016	1029		1118	1204		1218			1318		1337
	Thusis d.				0716				0837			0937		1037	1057	1116	1137		1157			1247		1357	
	Reichenau-Tamins a.								0857			0957				1207	1256					1307		1407	
	Chur a.				0744				0907			1007		1107		1207	1256					1307		1407	

		554 V	241	360	560	245	364	564	251	370	570 ♈	500 B♈	255	374	574 CE♈	261	380	580 ⑤⑦d	382 J	265	584	271	390	590	275	283
	St Moritz d.	1300	1340		1400	1440		1500	1540		1600		1640		1700	1740		1800		1840	1900			2000	2040	2220
	Celerina d.	1304	1344		1404	1444		1504	1544		1604		1644		1704	1744		1804	1843	1844	1904		2005	2004	2044	2224
	Pontresina d.			1401			1501			1601		1646		1701			1801		1801		1908		2012	2008	2048	2228
	Samedan a.	1308	1348	1408	1408	1448	1508	1508	1548	1608	1608		1648	1708	1708	1748	1808	1808	1850	1848	1915	1915	1955	2015	2055	
	Samedan d.	1315	1355		1415	1455		1515	1555		1615		1655	1715	1755	1815		1855	1915	1918	2001		2018	2059		
	Bever d.		1401			1501			1601				1701	1713		1813			1910		2011			2110		
	Zuoz d.		1413			1513			1613				1713	1738		1836			1930		2030			2129		
	Zernez d.		1438			1538							1738	1746		1844			1938		2038			2138		
	Susch d.		1446			1546							1746	1810		1910			2002		2102			2202		
	Scuol Tarasp a.		1510			1610							1810			1910			2050							
	Bergün/Bravuogn d.	1350			1450			1550			1650			1750			1850			1950				2050		
	Filisur d.	1404			1504			1604			1704	1747		1804			1904			2004				2104		
	Tiefencastel d.	1418			1518			1618			1718	1804		1818			1918			2018				2118		
	Thusis d.	1437			1537			1637			1737	1820		1837			1937			2037				2137		
	Reichenau-Tamins a.	1457			1557			1657			1757			1857			1957			2057				2157		
	Chur a.	1507			1607			1707			1807	1855		1907			2007			2107				2207		

B – BERNINA EXPRESS (Summer) – Runs Sept. 25 – Oct. 16 and May 20 – 27: [12] and ♈ Chur – Samedan – Pontresina – Tirano. [R] with supplement (SFr 7,-) payable.
C – BERNINA EXPRESS (Winter) – [12] and ♈ Chur – St Moritz and v.v.
E – Conveys [12] Tirano – St Moritz – Chur (composition subject to confirmation).
G – Conveys [12] Zermatt – St Moritz and v.v. ▲
H – Conveys [12] Zermatt – Reichenau Tamins – St Moritz and v.v. ▲
J – Runs Sept. 25 – Oct. 16 and May 20 – 27 only.
K – Runs ⑥ Oct. 1 – 15, Jan. 2, ⑥ Jan. 7 – Apr. 8: [12] Scuol Tarasp – Samedan – Chur.
L – Conveys on ⑥ except when train K runs: [12] Scuol Tarasp – Samedan – Chur.
R – Runs May 29 – Oct. 16, Dec. 17 – Apr. 9 and May 20 – 27 only.

S – Conveys on ⑥: [12]. Chur – Samedan – Scuol Tarasp and v.v.
T – Runs Sept. 25 – Oct. 16, Dec. 17 – Apr. 9 and May 20 – 27: [12] and ♈ Chur – Samedan; [12] Chur – Samedan – Pontresina – Tirano (composition subject to confirmation).
U – Conveys on dates in note T: [12]. Chur – Samedan – Pontresina – Tirano.
V – Conveys on ⑥: [12]. Chur – Samedan – Pontresina – Tirano and v.v. (composition subject to confirmation).
d – Also Dec. 26, Jan. 2, Apr. 13, 17, May 24, 25, not Dec. 25, Jan. 1, Apr. 14, 16, May 26.
e – Will not run Dec. 25, Jan. 1, Apr. 16.
▲ – GLACIER EXPRESS – see Table 320.
Operator: RhB – Rhaetische Bahn, Chur.

Table 332 — 🚌 ST. MORITZ and TIRANO - LUGANO

🚌 PTT

	J[R]	M	J[R]
St Moritz Hauptpost d.	0810		1420
St Moritz Station [I] d.	0815		1425
Tirano Station d.		1415	
Chiavenna Station d.	1010		1610
Menaggio [O] d.	1115		1716
Lugano Station [O] a.	1220	1715	1817
Lugano Via S. Balestra a.	1230	1730	1825

	J[R]	M	K[R]	L[R]
Lugano Via S. Balestra d.	0810	1000	1340	1415
Lugano Station [O] d.	0815	1015	1350	1437
Menaggio [O] d.	0920		1450	1530
Chiavenna Station a.	1035		1610	1700
Tirano Station a.		1300		
St Moritz Station [I] a.	1200		1735	1825
St Moritz Hauptpost a.	1205		1740	1830

J – Daily Sept. 25 – Oct. 16, ⑤⑥⑦ Oct. 21 – May 27.
K – ⑤⑥⑦ Oct. 21 – May 27.
L – Sept. 25 – Oct. 16.
M – Sept. 25 – Oct. 16 and May 20 – 27.
[I] – 🚌 is at Castasegna.
[O] – 🚌 is at Gandria.

For reservations: ☎ St Moritz (082) 3 30 72 or ☎ Lugano (091) 21 95 20.

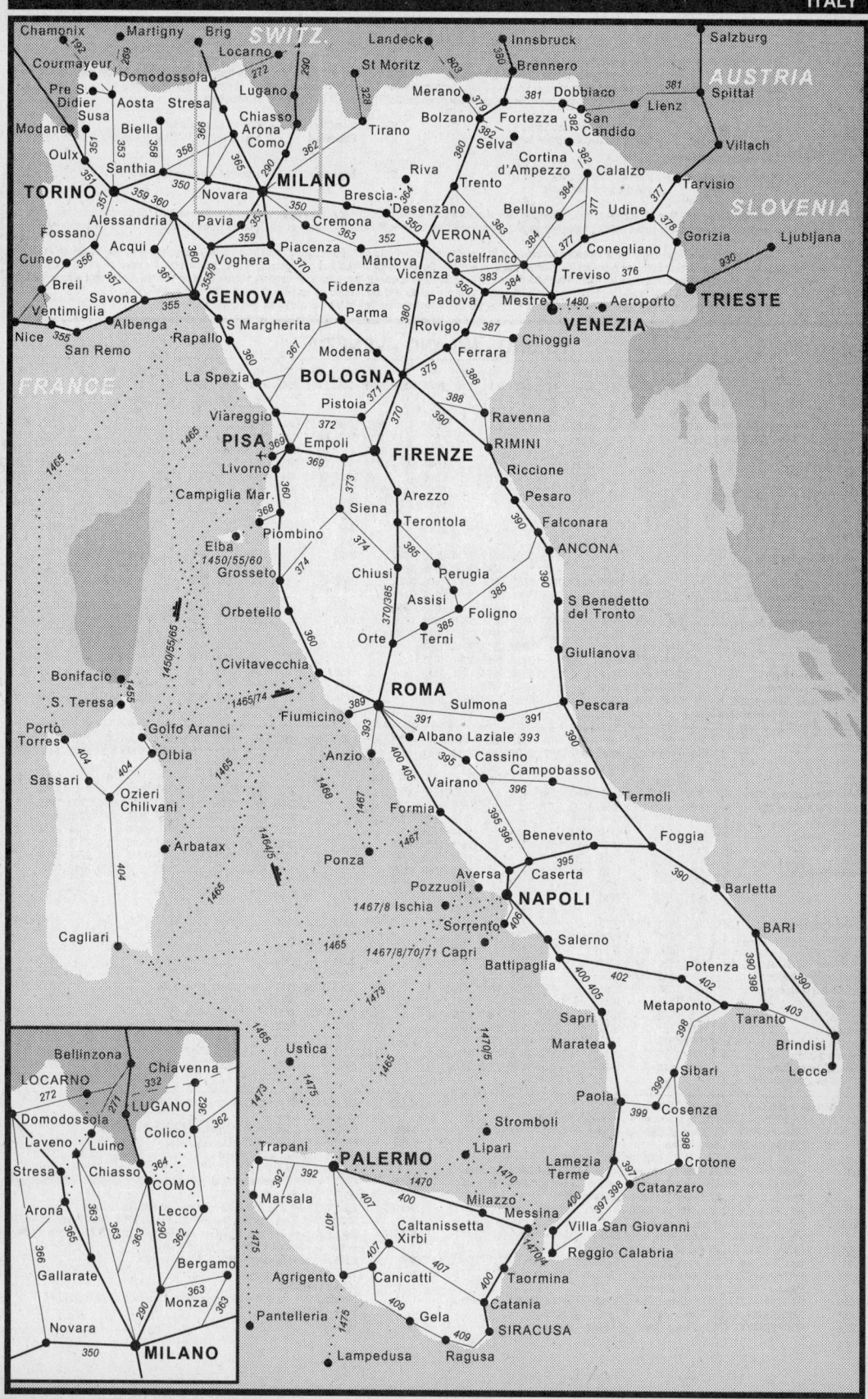

ITALY

Operator: Ente Ferrovie dello Stato (FS), unless otherwise noted.

Services: All trains convey first and second class seats unless otherwise shown by "2" in the train column or by a note in the top right hand corner of the Table heading. Overnight trains may only convey second class seats in addition to any sleeping accommodation - see individual footnotes.
Sleeping cars (🛏) are of the normal European types. See page **10** for more details. There are 4 categories of express train:

EC:	**EuroCity**	international express trains.	**IC:**	**InterCity**	internal express trains.
EN:	**EuroNight**	quality overnight express trains.	**P:**	**Pendolino**	high speed (ETR450/460) services at premium fare.

Other trains are classified:

IR:	**Interregionale**	internal cross-country trains.	**E:**	**Espresso**	semi-fast international trains.
D:	**Diretto**	internal semi-fast trains.			

Timings: **Valid September 25 - May 27**, subject to minor alteration. Some trains are cancelled or altered at holiday times - **express trains** which do not run during these periods are indicated in the tables. For public holiday dates see page 2. Passengers should consult the latest edition of the **Thomas Cook European Timetable** before travelling.

Tickets: **Seat reservations are strongly recommended** for travel on all long distance trains especially EuroCity (**EC**) and InterCity (**IC**) trains, and are **compulsory** on Pendolino trains and other services which are indicated by [R] under the train number. **Supplements**, which vary considerably in cost, are payable for travel on **all EC** and **IC** trains. A higher fare is payable for travel by **ETR 450/460** Pendolino trains (indicated by the letter **P** above the train number), but this does include the cost of seat reservations and meals. Some trains are only available to passengers holding long distance tickets and the restrictions applying to these are noted in the tables.
Refreshment services on other services (shown with 🍴 or 🍷 at the top of the column) may only be available for part of the journey.

Table 350 TORINO - MILANO - VENEZIA

1, 2 class except where shown

km		223	D 2705	E 361	IR 2001	EC 89	IC 641	IR 2091	E 299	IR 2003	IR 2095	IR 2005	IC 645	IR 2007	IR 2009	IC 649	IR 2097	E 351	IC 651	EC 39	IR 2099	E 863	IR 2011	IR 2013
		♦	2	♦	❖	🍴 M	🍷	❖	♦		🍷					🍷	🍷	🍴 ♦	🍷	🍴 ♦		🍷 ♦	🍷	
0	**Torino Porta Nuova 353** d.	...	...	...	0450	...	...	...	...	0550	...	0650	0708	0750	0850	0908	...	...	1108	...	...	...	1150	1250
6	**Torino Porta Susa 353** d.	...	...	...	0500	...	...	...	...	0600	...	0700	0718	0800	0900	0918	...	...	1118	...	...	...	1200	1300
29	Chivasso **353** d.	...	...	...	0516	...	...	...	...	0616	...	0716	|	0816	0916	|	...	...	|	...	...	...	1216	1316
60	Santhia d.	...	...	...	0534	...	...	...	...	0634	...	0734	|	0834	0934	|	...	...	|	...	...	...	1234	1334
79	Vercelli d.	...	...	...	0546	...	...	...	...	0646	...	0746	0802	0846	0946	1002	...	...	1202	...	...	...	1246	1346
101	Novara d.	...	...	...	0601	...	...	...	...	0701	...	0801	0818	0901	1001	1018	...	...	1218	...	...	...	1301	1401
153	**Milano Centrale** a.	...	...	...	0640	...	...	...	...	0740	...	0840	0850	0940	1040	1050	...	...	1250	...	...	...	1340	1440
										IR 2093 🍷			IC 647 ♦🍷			|							IR 2101 🍷	
153	**Milano Centrale** d.	...	...	0610	...	0700	0705	0710	0730	0810	0835	...	0905	...	...	1105	1110	1210	...	1305	1310	1320	1410	...
187	Treviglio d.	...	...	0635	...	|	|	0735	0800	0835	0901	...	|	...	...	|	1135	1235	...	|	1335	|	1435	...
236	Brescia d.	...	0616	0706	...	0747	0752	0806	0827	0906	0931	...	0952	...	...	1152	1206	1306	...	1352	1406	1413	1506	...
263	Desenzano del Garda d.	...	0637	0724	...	|	|	0824	|	0924	0949	...	|	...	...	|	1224	1324	...	|	1424	1431	1524	...
278	Peschiera del Garda d.	...	0647	0735	...	|	|	0835	|	0935	1000	...	|	...	...	|	1235	1335	...	|	1435	1441	1535	...
300	**Verona Porta Nuova** d.	0658	0709	0754	...	0820	0827	0854	0906	0954	1016	...	1027	...	...	1227	1254	1354	...	1427	1454	1500	1554	...
325	San Bonifacio d.	|	0729	0811	...	...	|	0911	|	1011	...	...	|	...	...	|	1311	1411	...	|	1511	1518	1611	...
351	Vicenza d.	0741	0750	0832	...	...	0900	0932	0940	1032	...	...	1100	...	...	1300	1332	1432	...	1500	1532	1540	1632	...
382	Padova d.	0808	0815	0853	...	...	0922	0953	1001	1053	...	...	1122	...	...	1323	1353	1453	...	1522	1553	...	1653	...
411	**Venezia Mestre** a.	0833	0838	0913	...	...	0940	1013	1021	1113	...	...	1140	...	...	1346	1413	1513	...	1540	1613	...	1713	...
411	**Venezia Mestre** d.	0836	0840	0916	...	...	0943	1016	1023	1116	...	...	1144	...	...	1349	1416	1516	...	1543	1616	...	1716	...
420	**Venezia Santa Lucia** a.	0845	0850	0925	...	...	0952	1025	1032	1125	...	...	1154	...	...	1359	1425	1525	...	1552	1625	...	1725	...
	Trieste Centrale **376** a.	...	...	...	...	...	...	...	...	...	...	...	1409	...	...	...	...	...	...	...	...	...	...	...

	IC 653	IR 2103	EC 83	IR 2015	IR 2017	IC 657	IR 2107	EC 13	IR 2019	IR 2021	IC 661	IC 663	IR 2111	IC 659	IR 2023	IR 2025	IC 665	IR 2115	IR 2027	IR 2029	IC 219	IR 2031	E 869	E 221
	🍷	❖	🍴 M	🍷		🍷 ♦		🍴 ♦	🍷		🍷	🍷 ♦	🍷	🍷 ♦			🍷 ♦		🍷		🍷 ♦		♦	♦
Torino Porta Nuova 353 d.	1308	...	...	1350	1450	1508	...	...	1550	1650	1708	...	...	...	1750	1850	1908	...	1950	2050	2132	2150	2250	...
Torino Porta Susa 353 d.	1318	...	...	1400	1500	1518	...	...	1600	1700	1718	...	...	...	1800	1900	1918	...	2000	2100	2140	2200	2300	...
Chivasso **353** d.	|	...	...	1416	1516	|	...	...	1616	1716	|	...	...	...	1816	1916	|	...	2016	2116	|	2216	2316	...
Santhia d.	|	...	...	1434	1534	|	...	...	1634	1734	|	...	...	...	1834	1934	|	...	2034	2134	|	2234	2334	...
Vercelli d.	1402	...	...	1446	1546	1602	...	...	1646	1746	1802	...	...	...	1846	1946	2002	...	2046	2146	|	2246	2346	...
Novara d.	1418	...	...	1501	1601	1618	...	...	1701	1801	1818	...	...	...	1901	2001	2018	...	2101	2201	2233	2301	0001	...
Milano Centrale a.	1450	...	...	1540	1640	1650	...	...	1740	1840	1850	...	...	...	1940	2040	2050	...	2140	2240	2305	2340	0040	...
	IC 655 ♦🍷			IR 2105 🍷		|			IR 2109 🍷❖						IR 2113 ♦		|		IR 2117 ♦				|	
Milano Centrale d.	1505	1510	1530	1610	...	1705	1710	...	1810	...	...	1905	1910	1930	2010	...	2105	2110	2210	...	...	...	0110	0342n
Treviglio d.	|	1535	|	1635	...	|	1735	...	1835	...	...	|	1935	|	2035	...	|	2135	2235	...	...	...	0150	|
Brescia d.	|	1606	1623	1706	...	1752	1806	...	1906	...	...	1952	2006	2027	2106	...	2152	2206	2306	...	...	...	0239	|
Desenzano del Garda d.	1552	1624	1640	1724	...	|	1824	...	1924	...	...	|	2024	|	2124	...	|	2224	2324	...	...	...	0257	|
Peschiera del Garda d.	|	1635	1649	1735	...	|	1835	...	1935	...	...	|	2035	|	2135	...	|	2235	2335	...	...	...	0309	|
Verona Porta Nuova d.	1627	1654	1707	1754	...	1827	1854	1910	1954	...	...	2027	2054	2104	2154	...	2227	2254	2351	...	...	...	0331	0516
San Bonifacio d.	|	1711	...	1811	...	|	1911	|	2011	...	...	|	2111	|	2211	...	|	2311	...	...	...	...	0347	|
Vicenza d.	1700	1732	...	1832	...	1900	1932	1945	2032	...	...	2100	2132	2136	2232	...	2300	2332	...	...	...	...	0410	0553
Padova d.	1722	1753	...	1853	...	1922	1953	2004	2053	...	...	2122	2153	...	2253	...	2322	2353	...	...	...	...	0433	0616
Venezia Mestre a.	1740	1813	...	1913	...	1940	2013	2024	2113	...	...	2140	2213	...	2313	...	2340	0013	...	...	...	...	0454	0640
Venezia Mestre d.	1743	1816	...	1916	...	1955	2016	2026	2116	...	...	2143	2216	...	2316	...	2343	0016	...	...	...	...	0459	0651
Venezia Santa Lucia a.	1752	1825	...	1925	...	|	2025	2035	2125	...	...	2152	2225	...	2325	...	2352	0025	...	...	...	...	0508	0700t
Trieste Centrale **376** a.	...	...	...	...	...	2145	...	...	...	...	...	...	...	...	...	...	...	...	...	...	...	...	0910b	0855

♦ – **NOTES** (LISTED BY TRAIN NUMBERS)

EC13 – PAGANINI – [12] and 🍴 Dortmund - Innsbruck - Venezia.
EC39 – MONTEVERDI – [12] and 🍴 Genève Aéroport ✈ - Brig - Venezia [12] Basel SBB - Bern - Venezia.
IC219 – MONT CENIS – [12] and 🍷 Lyon Perrache - Torino.
E221 – SIMPLON EXPRESS – 🛏 1,2 cl., ▬ 2 cl. and [12] Genève Aéroport ✈ - Brig - Milano - Trieste - Zagreb; ▬ 2 cl. and [2] Genève Aéroport ✈ - Venezia Santa Lucia. Zagreb cars depart **Mestre** 0708.
223 – ▬ 2 cl. and [2] München Hbf (**289**) - Verona - Venezia.
E299 – ⑤⑥ (from Brussels): 🛏 1,2 cl., 🛏 1,2 cl. (T2), ▬ 2 cl. and [2] Brussels Midi - Luxembourg - Strasbourg - Basel SBB - Chiasso - Venezia.
E351 – CANALETTO – [12] and 🍴 Zürich Hbf - Chiasso - Venezia.
E361 – 🛏 1,2 cl., ▬ 1, 2 cl. and [12] Nice - Ventimiglia - Venezia.
IC647 – SVEVO – [12] Sestri Levante (**IC672**) - Genova Porta Principe - Milano - Trieste; 🍷 Milano - Venezia.
IC655 – MAZZINI – [12] and 🍷 Genova Porta Principe (**IC680**) - Milano - Venezia.
IC657 – TERGESTE – [12] Torino - Trieste; 🍷 Torino - Venezia.
IC659 – FOGAZZARO – [12] Milano - Udine; 🍷 Milano - Verona.
IC663 – ANDREA DORIA – [12] Genova Porta Principe - Venezia; 🍷 Genova - Verona.
IC665 – FOSCARI – [12] Torino - Venezia; 🍷 Vercelli - Verona.
E863 – FRECCIA DELLE DOLOMITI – [12] Milano - Castelfranco Veneto - Calalzo (Cortina); [12] Milano - Castelfranco Veneto - Treviso - Udine; 🍷 Milano - Vicenza.
E869 – [12] Torino - Trieste; 🛏 1,2 cl. (T2) and ▬ 2 cl. Genova Porta Principe (**2176**) - Milano - Trieste.
IR2113 – 🛏 1,2 cl., ▬ 2 cl. and [12] Milano - Venezia Santa Lucia - Wien Südbahnhof. Train number from Santa Lucia is **9734**, from Mestre **234/1234**.
IR2117 – 🛏 1,2 cl., ▬ 2 cl. and [2] Genova Porta Principe (**2172**) - Verona (**288**) - Innsbruck - München Hbf.
M – [12] and 🍴 Milano - Innsbruck - München Hbf.
b – Via Udine.
n – Milano **Lambrate**.
t – Sleeping cars are in the Zagreb portion of the train and run only to **Venezia Mestre.**
❖ – **Not** Dec. 25, Jan. 1.

Table 350 — VENEZIA - MILANO - TORINO

1, 2 class except where shown

Venezia → Milano (first group)

Station	IR 2002	IC 214	IR 2004	D 2088	IR 2090	IR 2092	IC 640	IC 642	IC 644	IR 2094	IR 2096	IC 646	IR 2008	EC 12	IC 648	IC 650	IR 2012	IR 2098	EC 82	IR 2100	IC 652	IR 2016	E 354	IR 2018
Trieste Centrale 376 d.														0610										
Venezia Santa Lucia d.						0525	0605	0625		0725				0855	1005			1025		1125	1205		1225	
Venezia Mestre d.						0534	0614	0634	0802	0734				0904	1014			1034		1134	1214		1234	
Venezia Mestre d.						0537	0617	0637	0817	0737				0906	1017			1037		1137	1217		1237	
Padova d.						0600	0639	0713	0720	0820	0839			1000	1059			1100		1200	1239		1300	
Vicenza d.						0620	0659		0713	0720	0820	0839		0859				1120		1220	1259		1320	
San Bonifacio d.						0637			0737		0837							1137		1237			1337	
Verona d.			0525	0640	0701	0734	0751	0801	0901	0934				1050	1134			1201	1223	1301	1334		1401	
Peschiera del Garda d.			0540	0656	0716				0816	0916				1216	1237			1316						
Desenzano del Garda d.			0549	0709	0728				0828	0928				1228	1248			1328						
Brescia d.			0616	0732	0751	0808			0828	0851	0951	1008		1208				1251	1308	1351	1408		1451	
Treviglio d.			0705	0823					0918	1017				1317				1417		1417			1517	
Milano Centrale a.			0740	0830	0850	0855	0915	0945	1045	1055				1300				1345	1355	1445	1455		1545	

Milano → Torino (first group)

Continuation train numbers: D 2088 → IR 2006; EC 12 → IR 2010; IR 2098 → IR 2014.

Station	IR 2002	IC 214	IR 2004	IR 2006	IC 646	IR 2010	IC 648	IC 650	IR 2012	IR 2014	IR 2100	IC 652	IR 2016	IR 2018
Milano Centrale d.	0610	0710	0720	0820	0910	1110	1120	1220	1310	1320	1420	1510	1520	1620
Novara d.	0649	0742	0759	0859	0943	1143	1159	1259	1343	1359	1459	1543	1559	1659
Vercelli d.	0704	0755	0814	0914	0959	1157	1214	1314		1359 1414	1514	1559	1614	1714
Santhia d.	0716		0826	0926			1226	1326		1426	1526		1626	1726
Chivasso 353 d.	0733		0843	0943			1243	1343		1443	1543		1643	1743
Torino Porta Susa 353 a.	0749	0834	0900	1000	1042	1243	1300	1400		1443 1500	1600	1643	1700	1800
Torino Porta Nuova 353 a.	0800	0845	0913	1013	1055	1255	1313	1413		1455 1513	1613	1655	1713	1813

Venezia → Milano (second group)

Station	IR 2102	EC 40	IC 654	IR 2020	IR 2104	IR 2106	IC 656	IR 2024	IR 2108	IR 2110	E 298	IC 658	IC 662	IR 2028	IR 2112	IR 2114	EC 88	IC 664	E 356	E 866	IR 2000	9720 / E 220	E 874
Trieste Centrale 376 d.											1610												
Venezia Santa Lucia d.	1325	1405			1425	1525	1605		1625	1725	1742			1825	1925			2005	2025			2028	2118b
Venezia Mestre d.	1334	1414		1434	1534	1614		1634	1734	1751	1802			1834	1934			2014	2034			2205t	0036
Venezia Mestre d.	1337	1417		1437	1537	1617		1637	1737	1754	1817			1837	1937			2017	2037			2214	0045
Padova d.	1400	1439		1500	1600	1639		1700	1800	1822	1839			1900	2000			2039	2100			2242	0047
Vicenza d.	1420	1459		1520	1620	1659		1720	1820	1843	1859			1920	2020			2059	2120	2138		2307	0112
San Bonifacio d.	1437			1537	1637			1737	1837					1937	2037			2137	2155				0154
Verona d.	1501	1534		1601	1701	1734		1801	1901	1919	1934			2001	2101	2121	2134	2201	2219		0010		0220
Peschiera del Garda d.	1516			1616	1716			1816	1916					2016	2116			2216	2234				0235
Desenzano del Garda d.	1528			1628	1728			1828	1928					2028	2128			2228	2246				0250
Brescia d.	1551	1608		1651	1751	1808		1851	1951	1959	2008			2051	2151	2156	2208	2251	2308				0314
Treviglio d.	1617			1717	1817			1917	2017	2034				2117	2217		2317						0339
Milano Centrale a.	1645	1655		1745	1845	1855		1945	2045	2105	2055			2145	2245	2250	2255	2345	2358		0134n		0405

Milano → Torino (second group)

Continuation train numbers: IR 2020 → IR 2022; IR 2106 → IR 2026; IR 2114 → IR 2030.

Station	IC 654	IR 2022	IR 2104	IC 656	IR 2024	IR 2026	IC 658	IC 662	IR 2028	IR 2000	E 874
Milano Centrale d.	1710	1720	1820	1910	1920	2020	2110	2120	2220	0020	0450
Novara d.	1743	1759	1859	1943	1959	2059	2143	2159	2259	0059	0526
Vercelli d.	1759	1814	1914	1959	2014	2114	2159	2214	2314	0114	0540
Santhia d.		1826	1926		2026	2126		2226	2326	0126	0552
Chivasso 353 d.		1843	1943		2043	2143		2243	2343	0143	0609
Torino Porta Susa 353 a.	1842	1900	2000	2043	2100	2200	2243	2300	2400	0200	0626
Torino Porta Nuova 353 a.	1855	1913	2013	2055	2113	2213	2255	2313	0013	0213	0637

Notes

♦ — NOTES (LISTED BY TRAIN NUMBERS)

EC12 — PAGANINI – [12] and ✗ Venezia Santa Lucia – Innsbruck – Dortmund.
EC40 — MONTEVERDI – [12] and ✗ Venezia Santa Lucia – Brig – Genève Aéroport ✈; [12] Venezia – Bern – Basel SBB.
IC214 — MONT CENIS – [12] and ♀ Torino – Lyon Perrache.
E298 — ⑥⑦: ⇄ 1,2 cl., ⇄ 1,2 cl. (T2), ⇄ 2 cl. and [12] Venezia – Chiasso – Basel SBB – Strasbourg – Luxembourg – Brussels Midi.
E354 — CANALETTO – [12] and ✗ Venezia – Milano – Chiasso – Zürich Hbf.
E356 — 1,2 cl., ⇄ 2 cl. and [12] Venezia – Ventimiglia – Nice; ♀ Venezia -Verona.
IC640 — ANDREA DORIA – [12] Venezia – Milano (IC671) – Genova Porta Principe.
IC644 — FOGAZZARO – [12] Udine – Treviso – Castelfranco Veneto – Milano.
IC646 — TERGESTE – [12] Trieste – Torino; ♀ Venezia – Torino.
IC648 — MAZZINI – [12] Venezia – Milano (IC677) – Genova Porta Principe; ♀ Verona – Genova.
IC652 — FOSCARI – [12] Venezia – Torino; ♀ Venezia – Torino.
IC658 — SVEVO – [12] Trieste – Milano (IC689) – Genova Porta Principe; ♀ Venezia – Milano.
IC664 — [12] Venezia – Milano; ♀ Verona – Milano.

E866 — FRECCIA DELLE DOLOMITI – [12] Calalzo (Cortina) – Milano.
E874 — [12] Trieste – Torino; ⇄ 1,2 cl. (T2) and ⇄ 2 cl. Venezia – Milano (2179) – Genova Porta Principe.
IR2090 — [12], ⇄ 2 cl. and [12] München Hbf (289) – Verona – Milano (2185) – Genova Porta Principe.
IR2092 — [12], ⇄ 2 cl. and [12] Wien Südbahnhof (235/1235) – Venezia Santa Lucia – Milano.
A — SIMPLON EXPRESS – ⇄ 1,2 cl., ⇄ 1,2 cl. Zagreb – Trieste – Milano – Brig – Genève Aéroport ✈; ⇄ 2 cl. and [12] Venezia Santa Lucia – Verona (288) – München Hbf. Zagreb cars arrive Mestre 2219.
M — [12] and ✗ München Hbf – Innsbruck – Milano.
b — Via Udine. Train number E872 from Trieste.
n — Milano Lambrate.
t — Sleeping cars are in the Zagreb portion of the train and depart from Venezia Mestre, not Santa Lucia.
❖ — Not Dec. 25, Jan. 1.

Table 351 — MODANE and SUSA - TORINO

1, 2 class except where shown

km	Station	D 4049 (2)	9101	10007 (2)	9103	10009	4043 (2O)	411 (L♀)	10025	10011	4039 (2)	10013	417 (L♀)	1801 (2)	10029 (✗)	10015	1805 (⑦)	10017	4047 (2✗)	1841 (2⑦)	10019	219 (M♀)	10005
0	Modane ⊞ d.				0620		1004			1256	1538										1903	2001	
20	Bardonecchia d.	0517		0643	0718		1022		1132		1315	1557	1604			1743	1744	1840	1853	1924	2019	2041	
31	Oulx ▲ d.	0527		0654	0730		1031		1142		1326	1606	1613			1757	1757	1852	1902	1936	2029	2051	
61	Bussoleno d.	0558	0644	0658	0726	0811	0843	1056	1103	1213	1339	1406	1620	1640	1646	1740	1826	1832	1916	1928	2011		2118
100	Torino Porta Nuova a.	0643	0723	0748	0805	0850	0930	1130	1152	1305	1425	1500	1700	1719	1738	1830	1905	1930	2000	2000	2105	2122	2200

Station	D 10002 (2)	4042 (2O)	9102	10006 (2⑦)	1802 (M♀)	214 (2)	10022 (⑦)	1842 (L♀)	4054	414 (✗)	10008	10010	10012	10024 (⑦)	418 (L♀)	4244 (2)	10014 (✗)	1796 (2)	9104 (⑦)	10016	1798 (2)	10018	4048
Torino Porta Nuova d.		0600	0717	0743	0805	0852	0855	0918	1020	1200	1330	1400	1518	1600	1645	1710p	1745	1800	1808	1845	1900	1925	2108
Bussoleno d.		0700	0803	0819	0858	0912		1007	1059	1247	1255	1405e	1456	1610	1650	1715	1755	1836	1851	1853	1940	1952	2014 2204t
Oulx ▲ d.		0732		0846	0931	0939	0951		1126	1318	1437	1530		1738	1824		1923	1926		2023	2043	2229	
Bardonecchia d.		0745		0854	0942	0952	1003		1138	1327	1451	1542		1747	1835		1934	1938		2035	2054	2240	
Modane ⊞ a.		0806				1025			1348	1510				1807				2054	2113				

Notes (Table 351):

⎵ — [12] and ♀ Lyon Perrache – Torino and v.v.
M — [12] and ♀ Lyon Perrache – Milano Centrale and v.v.
⎵ — [12] Torino – Susa and v.v.
▲ — Arrives 1354.

p — Torino Porta Susa.
▲ — Station for the resorts of Cesana, Claviere and Sestriere.
For trains 210/1, 212/3, 216/7, 276/7, 1210/1, 1212/3, see International tables 44, 45, 90.

t — Arrives 2155.

Local trains Susa – Bussoleno: 0630✗, 0714✗, 0748✗, 0835O, 1020✗, 1044, 1201, 1240✗, 1323, 1350, 1444, 1604✗, 1628✗, 1705, 1729, 1813, 1853✗, 1917, 1957, 2103, 2135✗, 2212.
Bussoleno – Susa: 0617✗, 0702✗, 0733✗, 0804O, 0902✗, 1032, 1133, 1217✗, 1304, 1337, 1404, 1500✗, 1616, 1653✗, 1717, 1800, 1841✗, 1905, 1945, 2020, 2121✗, 2200.
2 class only. Journey time: 7 minutes.

Table 352 — VERONA - MANTOVA

Rail service Verona - Mantova and v.v. 37 km. Journey time 35 - 40 minutes. 2 class only. ✤ – **Not** Dec. 25, Jan. 1.

From Verona: 0642 ⚒, 0715 ✤, 0752 ⚒, 0752 ⚒, 0922, 1007 ⚒, 1151, 1237 ⚒, 1336, 1417, 1551, 1704, 1803, 1904, 2003, 2106, 2205.

From Mantova: 0635 ⚒, 0700, 0729 ⚒, 0808, 0919, 1153, 1240 ⚒, 1330 ⚒, 1443, 1527, 1624 ⚒, 1731, 1829, 1930, 2119, 2219 ✤.

Table 353 — TORINO - AOSTA

km		9141 ⚒	4213 ⑦	9143	4217 2	9145	9147	9149	9151	9153
0	Torino Porta Nuova 350 .. d.	0630	...	...	...	1120	1320	1420	1720	1920
6	Torino Porta Susa 350 .... d.	0640	...	0910	...	1130	1330	1430	1730	1930
29	Chivasso **350** .... a.	0701	...	0928	...	1152	1351	1450	1750	1950
29	Chivasso .... d.	0706	...	0947	...	1200	1359	1500	1755	1958
62	Ivrea .... d.	0746	...	1018	...	1226	1422	1525	1818	2029
79	Pont Saint Martin ...... d.	0802	...	1033	...	1239	1435	1544	1832	2045
91	Verrès .... d.	0817	...	1046	...	1250	1446	1554	1842	2058
104	Chatillon .... d.	0832	...	1104	...	1305	1502	1606	1901	2118
129	**Aosta** .... a.	0858	...	1124	...	1332	1520	1624	1920	2136
		2		2			2	2	2	
129	**Aosta** .... d.	0903	0945	1129	1305	...	1525	1735	1937	...
161	**Prè Saint Didier** .... a.	0946	1030	1211	1350	...	1610	1820	2026	...

Additional trains Aosta - Prè St. Didier: 0557 arriving 0642, 1837 arriving 1926;

	4208 2	9146 ⚒	4210 2⚒	4212 2⑦	4216 2	4218 2⚒	4220 2⑦	4222 2	4224 2	4226 2
Prè Saint Didier .... d.	0648	...	0953	1040	1355	1616	1640	1835	1935	2031
Aosta .... a.	0732	...	1037	1124	1436	1700	1724	1920	2020	2115
	12		2⚒	12	12	2⚒	12	12	12	
Aosta .... d.	0742	0842	1042	1242	1442	1715	1826	1932	2042	...
Chatillon .... d.	0804	0903	1103	1304	1501	1744	1845	1951	2101	...
Verrès .... d.	0816	0916	1115	1316	1514	1757	1857	2003	2113	...
Pont Saint Martin .... d.	0826	0926	1125	1326	1525	1810	1907	2013	2123	...
Ivrea .... d.	0838	0938	1136	1338	1538	1834	1920	2027	2136	...
Chivasso .... a.	0900	0958	1158	1358	1558	1906	1958	2050	2158	...
Chivasso **350** .... d.	0905	1003	...	...	1603	...	2003	2058	2203	...
Torino Porta Susa 350 ... a.	0924	1024	...	...	1623	...	2023	2124	2220	...
Torino Porta Nuova 350 ... a.	0935	1035	...	...	1634	...	2035	2135	2229	...

Additional trains Prè St. Didier - Aosta: 1216 arriving 1300.

Table 355 — VENTIMIGLIA - GENOVA - MILANO

1, 2 class except where shown

km		IR 2156	P523 524 525 ✕🅁 A⚡	IC 670	IC672 IC647 L		IR 2159 2160	IC 674 ♦	D 2881	IC 675 676 🍷 ♦	4391 ⚒ G	IC 678 🍷	D 1873 ⑦ G	IR 2161 2162 🍷	E 382 ♦	E 365 🍷 ♦	IR 1605 Ⓒ ♦	IC 680 655 🍷	IR 2077 Ⓐ R	E 343 344 🍷 M	D 2883	IR 2081 R		IC 682 🍷 ♦
0	**Ventimiglia** 🏛 .... d.	...	...	...	...	...	0457	...	0524	0650	0731	...	0853	0905	...	0950	1016	...	1045	1115	1145	1205	...	...
5	Bordighera .... d.	...	...	...	...	...	0505	...	0531	0657	0738	...	0859	0913	...	|	1023	...	1052	1123	1153	1213	...	...
16	**San Remo** .... d.	...	...	...	...	...	0515	...	0543	0709	0753	...	0912	0925	...	1010	1034	...	1109	1134	1207	1229	...	...
24	Taggia-Arma .... d.	...	...	...	...	...	0525	...	0552	|	...	...	...	0934	...	|	...	...	1120	1143	1219	1238	...	...
39	Imperia Porto Maurizio ... d.	...	...	...	...	...	0541	...	0613	0731	...	...	...	|	...	1045	...	...	1139	|	1238	1259	...	...
41	Imperia Oneglia .... d.	...	...	...	...	...	0546	...	0618	|	...	...	...	1001	...	|	...	...	1143	1201	1242	1303	...	...
46	Diano Marina .... d.	...	...	...	...	...	0553	...	0625	|	...	...	...	1008	...	|	...	...	...	1208	1248	...	...	...
61	Alassio .... d.	...	...	...	...	...	0607	...	0647	0750	...	...	...	1022	...	|	...	...	...	1222	1309	...	...	...
67	**Albenga** .... d.	...	...	...	...	...	0614	...	0656	0757	...	...	...	1029	...	|	...	...	...	1229	1316	...	...	...
76	Loano .... d.	...	...	...	...	...	0623	...	0710	|	...	...	...	1038	...	|	...	...	...	1238	1329	...	...	...
79	Pietra Ligure .... d.	...	...	...	...	...	0628	...	0715	|	...	...	...	|	...	|	...	...	...	1243	1334	...	...	...
85	Finale Ligure Marina ..... d.	...	...	...	...	...	0635	...	0725	|	...	...	...	1047	...	|	...	...	...	1250	1344	...	...	...
108	**Savona** .... d.	...	0547	...	...	...	0652	...	0752	0825	...	...	...	1105	...	1142	...	...	...	1305	1407	...	...	...
120	Varazze .... d.	...	|	...	...	...	0701	...	0800	|	...	...	...	1114	...	|	...	...	...	1314	1415	...	...	...
151	**Genova Piazza Principe** .... a.	...	0615	...	...	...	0730	...	0835	0855	...	...	...	1140	...	1213	...	...	...	1340	1447	...	...	...
151	**Genova Piazza Principe 359**. d.	0548	0617	0645	0713	...	0754	0813	...	0913	...	1113	...	1154	1223	1216	...	1313	...	1354	...	...	...	1513
219	Tortona **359** .... d.	0639	|	|	|	...	0844	|	...	|	...	|	...	1244	|	|	...	|	...	1444	...	...	...	|
236	Voghera **359** .... d.	0652	|	0739	0807	...	0857	0907	...	1007	...	1207	...	1257	1319	|	...	1407	...	1457	...	...	...	1607
263	Pavia .... d.	0709	|	0756	0823	...	0914	0923	...	1023	...	1223	...	1314	1334	|	...	1423	...	1514	...	...	...	1623
302	**Milano Centrale** .... a.	0740	|	0830	0850	...	0945	0950	...	1050	...	1305	...	1345	1405	|	...	1450	...	1545	...	...	...	1650
	Pisa Centrale **360** .... a.	...	0811	...	|	...	...	...	...	...	...	...	...	...	...	1430	...	|	...	...	...	...	...	...
	Roma Termini **360** .... a.	...	1035	...	|	...	...	...	...	...	...	...	...	...	...	1805	...	|	...	...	...	...	...	...
	Venezia Santa Lucia **350** a.	...	...	...	1154	...	...	...	...	...	...	...	...	...	...	...	...	1752	...	...	...	...	...	...

	E 1089 1086 F	IR 2163 2164		D 2885	IC 684 663 🍷	E 837 838 T	IR 2165 2166 🍷		D 2535 T	IR 2167 2168 🍷	4399 G	IR 1627 1626 2O	IC 688 🍷	IR 2170 ♦	IR 2171 2172 2117 H		IR 2174	D 2887	IR 2075 T	IR 2175 2176 N	IC 349 348 🍷 J		E 367 ♦	E359 360 361 K
Ventimiglia 🏛 .... d.	1255	1315	...	1350	...	1430	1515	...	1530	1558	1607	1615	...	...	1715	...	...	1738	1835	1905	2010	...	2150	0115
Bordighera .... d.	1302	1323	...	1358	...	1437	1523	...	1537	1606	1614	1623	...	...	1723	...	...	1745	1844	1913	|	...	2158	0123
San Remo .... d.	1315	1334	...	1410	...	1446	1534	...	1548	1617	1625	1636	...	...	1734	...	...	1757	1855	1925	2028	...	2210	0134
Taggia-Arma .... d.	1324	1343	...	1419	...	1455	1543	...	1556	1626	...	1645	...	...	1743	...	...	1806	1904	1935	|	...	2219	0143
Imperia Porto Maurizio ... d.	1340	|	...	1438	...	1509	|	...	1618	|	...	1700	...	...	|	...	...	1830	1919	|	2051	...	2238	|
Imperia Oneglia .... d.	1345	1401	...	1443	...	|	1601	...	1622	1644	...	1705	...	...	1801	...	...	1836	|	2001	|	...	|	0201
Diano Marina .... d.	1352	1408	...	1449	...	1518	1608	...	1628	1650	...	1711	...	...	1808	...	...	1843	1931	2008	|	...	2248	0208
Alassio .... d.	1406	1422	...	1512	...	1537	1622	...	1647	1710	...	1724	...	...	1822	...	...	1905	1952	2022	2110	...	2302	0222
Albenga .... d.	1415	1429	...	1522	...	1545	1629	...	1654	1717	...	1731	...	...	1829	...	...	1912	2001	2029	|	...	2309	0229
Loano .... d.	1425	1438	...	1531	...	1554	1638	...	1706	1726	...	1740	...	...	1838	...	...	1921	2009	2038	|	...	2318	0238
Pietra Ligure .... d.	1430	1443	...	1536	...	|	1643	...	1713	1731	...	1747	...	...	1843	...	...	1926	|	2043	|	...	|	0243
Finale Ligure Marina ..... d.	1437	1450	...	1546	...	1604	1650	...	1724	1741	...	1755	...	...	1850	...	...	1935	2018	2050	|	...	2328	0250
Savona .... d.	1500	1505	...	1606	...	1617	1705	...	1745	1758	...	1811	...	...	1905	...	...	1953	2032	2105	2143	...	2355	0305
Varazze .... d.	1509	1514	...	1615	...	...	1714	...	...	|	...	1821	...	...	1914	...	...	2007	...	2114	|	...	|	0314
Genova Piazza Principe ...... a.	1535	1540	...	1647	...	...	1740	...	...	1835	...	1851	...	...	1940	...	...	2050	...	2140	2212	...	0024	0340
Genova Piazza Principe 359. d.	1602	1554	...	...	1713	...	1754	...	...	1848	...	1909	1913	1930	1954	...	2050	...	...	2154	2225	...	0042	0354
Tortona **359** .... d.	1653	1644	...	...	|	...	1844	...	...	1939	...	2009	|	2019	2044	...	2144	...	...	2244	|	...	|	0444
Voghera **359** .... d.	1709	1657	...	...	1807	...	1857	...	...	1952	...	2021	2007	2032	2056	...	2156	...	...	2257	2315	...	|	0456
Pavia .... d.	1724	1714	...	...	1823	...	1914	...	...	2009	...	2037	2024	2049	2113	...	2213	...	...	2314	2330	...	|	0513
Milano Centrale .... a.	1753n	1745	...	...	1850	...	1945	...	...	2040	...	2105	2050	2120	2145	...	2245	...	...	2345	2355	...	|	0540
Pisa Centrale **360** .... a.	...	...	...	...	|	...	...	...	...	...	...	...	...	...	...	...	...	...	...	|	...	...	0305	|
Roma Termini **360** .... a.	...	...	...	...	|	...	...	...	...	...	...	...	...	...	...	...	...	...	...	|	...	...	0655	|
Venezia Santa Lucia **350** .. a.	...	...	...	...	2152	...	...	...	...	...	...	...	...	...	...	...	...	...	...	0508	...	...	...	0925

♦ – **NOTES** (LISTED BY TRAIN NUMBERS)

- **E365** – 🛏 2 cl. and (12) Cerbère - Roma; (12) Hendaye - Roma; 🍷 Ventimiglia - Roma. Only takes passengers holding tickets valid for over 200 kms.
- **E367** – 🛌 1,2 cl., 🛏 2 cl. and (12) Nice - Roma; 🛌 1,2 cl. Torino (**817**) - Savona - Roma.
- **E382** – (12) Genova - Milano - Chiasso - Zürich Hbf - Stuttgart.
- **IC674** – TIGULLIO – (12) La Spezia - Milano.
- **IC675** – CYCNUS – (12) Ventimiglia - Milano; 🍷 Genova - Milano.
- **IC682** – CATTANEO – (12) Sestri Levante - Milano; (12) Sestri Levante - Milano (**254**) - Chiasso - Basel SBB; 🍷 Genova - Milano.
- **IR1605** – (12) Torino Porta Nuova - Cuneo - San Remo.
- **IR2170** – (12) Genova (Sestri Levante ⚒) - Milano.
- **A** – CIMABUE – ⚒ Sept. 25 - Dec. 24, Jan. 9 - May 27: (12) and ✕ Savona - Pisa - Firenze - Roma. **ETR450**.
- **F** – Apr. 8, 17 only: (12) Ventimiglia - Chiasso - Zürich Hbf.
- **G** – (12) Cuneo - San Remo.
- **H** – (12) Ventimiglia - Verona; 🛌 1,2 cl., 🛏 2 cl. and (2) Genova - Verona (**288**) - München Hbf.
- **J** – LIGURE – (12) Nice - Milano; 🍷 Genova - Milano.
- **K** – 🛌 1,2 cl., 🛏 1, 2 cl. and (12) Nice - Venezia.
- **L** – SVEVO – (12) Sestri Levante - Trieste.
- **M** – 🛏 2 cl. and (12) Bordeaux - Marseille - Milano; 🍷 Ventimiglia - Milano.
- **N** – (12) Ventimiglia - Milano; 🛌 1,2 cl. (T2) and 🛏 2 cl. Genova - Venezia - Udine - Trieste.
- **O** – ⑦ Apr. 23 - May 27, also Dec. 26, Jan. 6, Apr. 17, 25, May 1: (12) Ventimiglia - Milano.
- **R** – (12) Torino Porta Nuova - Cuneo - Ventimiglia - Imperia Oneglia.
- **T** – (12) Ventimiglia - Savona - Fossano - Torino Porta Nuova.
- **h** – Venezia **Mestre**.
- **n** – Milano **Lambrate**.
- 🅁 – Reservation **compulsory**.
- ⚡ – **ETR450** Pendolino supplement payable.

Table 355 — MILANO - GENOVA - VENTIMIGLIA

1, 2 class except where shown

	E 366	4398	D 2880	E 1087 1088	4394	IR 2179 2180	IC 347 346	IR 2179 2180	D 2524	E 836	IR 2181	IR 2183 2184	IR 2185 2186	IC 640 671	IC 673	D 2882	IR 2187 2188	IR 2078	IC 1606	IC 648 677	IR 2068	D 2884
	◆	⚒		F	V	⑦	J	N	T	T	M	⚍	H	⚍				⚍	Ⓐ W	Ⓒ W		T
Venezia Santa Lucia 350 .. d.					0036									0605						1005		
Roma Termini 360 d.	2330																					
Pisa Centrale 360 d.	0311																					
Milano Centrale d.			0515			0605	0640				0720	0815	0850	0910	1110		1215	1244		1315		
Pavia d.			0540			0634	0704				0749	0844	0915	0935	1135		1244			1340		
Voghera 359 d.			0556			0653	0720				0808	0902	0934	0952	1152		1302			1357		
Tortona 359 d.			0609			0705					0820	0915	0946				1315					
Genova Piazza Principe 359 a.	0543		0652			0754	0810				0908	1005	1047	1047	1302		1405			1451		
Genova Piazza Principe d.	0558	0646	0715			0812	0822				0908	1020		1205		1306	1420					1506
Varazze d.	0623	0720		0746			0840	0853				1045		1236		1343	1445					1543
Savona c.	0636	0736		0758		0856c		0856	0900	1000		1054		1244		1355	1454			1535	1555	
Finale Ligure Marina d.	0651	0749		0816		→		0910	0920	1014		1107		1301		1411	1507			1549	1611	
Pietra Ligure d.				0823				0917	0933			1114		1308		1421	1514				1621	
Loano d.	0700	0800		0828				0922	0938	1022		1119		1313		1426	1519			1603	1626	
Albenga d.	0709	0809		0842				0929	0953	1031		1128		1321		1438	1528			1611	1636	
Alassio d.	0720	0816		0850			0923	0937	1001	1038		1136		1328		1445	1536			1623	1646	
Diano Marina d.	0739	0833		0905				0951	1026	1054		1151		1350		1519	1551			1649	1709	
Imperia Oneglia d.	0748	0839		0911				1002	1033			1202		1400		1526	1602				1717	
Imperia Porto Maurizio d.		0844		0915			0944		1040	1107				1406		1531				1658	1722	
Taggia-Arma d.	0807		0901	0935				1023	1101	1121		1220		1432		1555	1627			1712	1744	
San Remo d.	0817	0900	0910	0946	0950		1008	1033	1110	1132		1230		1447		1604	1638	1650	1705	1721	1758	
Bordighera d.	0828	0913	0923	0959	1003			1043	1123	1144		1242		1502		1617	1649	1703	1718	1731	1813	
Ventimiglia a.	0835	0921	0930	1005	1011		1025	1050	1130	1150		1250		1510		1623	1656	1710	1725	1737	1820	

	IR 2189	IR 2191 2192	IR 2082	IC 679		IR 2193 2194	E 362	IR 2193 2194	IC 681	D 2886		IC 683	IR 2197 2198	IC 685 686		IC 687	IR 2199 2200	IC 658 689	P526 527 528		IR 2201	E356 357 358
	S	X	◆	⚍		G	◆	G	⚍			M	⚍			⚍			L A✗			K
Venezia Santa Lucia 350 .. d.																		1817h				2025
Roma Termini 360 d.							1225												1905			
Pisa Centrale 360 d.							1602												2127			
Milano Centrale d.	1405	1415		1510		1615		1710				1805	1815	1910		2010	2015	2110			2215	0015
Pavia d.	1436	1444		1535		1644		1735				1830	1844	1935		2035	2044	2135			2244	0039
Voghera 359 d.	1454	1502		1552		1702		1752				1848	1902	1953		2052	2102	2152			2302	0057
Tortona 359 d.	1508	1515				1715						1915				2115					2315	0116
Genova Piazza Principe 359 a.	1559	1605		1647		1805	1811	1805	1847			1947	2005	2047		2147	2205	2247	2323		0005	0218
Genova Piazza Principe d.		1620				1820	1816	1820	1906			2020		2110		2220			2326			0300
Varazze d.		1645				→		1845	1939			2045				2245						0346
Savona d.		1654				1847		1854	1948			2054	2141			2254		2351				0405
Finale Ligure Marina d.		1707				1907			2007			2107				2312						0425
Pietra Ligure d.		1714				1914			2020			2114				2322						0435
Loano d.		1719				1919			2025			2119				2328						0440
Albenga d.		1728				1928			2033			2128	2207			2337						0508
Alassio d.		1736				1936			2040			2136	2215			2344						0518
Diano Marina d.		1751				1951			2106			2151				2359						0536
Imperia Oneglia d.		1800	1805			2002			2112			2157				0006						0547
Imperia Porto Maurizio d.			1810						2117				2239			0554						
Taggia-Arma d.		1833				1941			2020	2136			2218			0023						0614
San Remo d.		1825	1842			2009		2030	2145			2228	2303			0033						0626
Bordighera d.		1855						2041	2158			2238	2314			0044						0639
Ventimiglia a.		1840				2030	2048		2205			2245	2320			0050						0645

◆ — NOTES (LISTED BY TRAIN NUMBERS)

E362 – ▭ 2 cl. and ▭ Roma - Port Bou; ▭ Roma - Irún; ⚍ Roma - Ventimiglia.
E366 – ▭ 2 cl. and ▭ Roma - Nice; ⚑ 1,2 cl. Roma - Savona (818) - Torino Porta Nuova.
IC679 – CATTANEO – ▭ Milano - Sestri Levante; ▭ Basel SBB (255) - Chiasso - Milano - Sestri Levante; ⚍ Milano - Genova.
IR2082 – ▭ Imperia Oneglia - Ventimiglia - Cuneo - Torino Porta Nuova.
A – CIMABUE – ⚒ Sept. 25 - Dec. 24, Jan. 8 - May 26, also Apr. 16, 30: ▭ and ⚔ Roma - Firenze - Pisa - Savona. ETR450 supplement payable.
F – Apr. 8, 14, May 25 only: ⚍ and ▭ Zürich Hbf - Chiasso - Ventimiglia; ⚍ Milano - Genova.
G – ▭ Milano - Ventimiglia; ▭ Stuttgart - Zürich Hbf - Chiasso - Milano - Genova; ⚍ Milano - Genova.
H – ▭ Milano - Ventimiglia; ⚑ 1,2 cl., ⚑ 2 cl. and ▭ München Hbf (289) - Verona - Genova; ⚍ Milano - Genova.
J – LIGURE – ▭ Milano - Nice; ⚍ Milano - Genova.

K – ⚑ 1,2 cl., ⚑ 1, 2 cl. and ▭ Venezia - Nice.
L – SVEVO – ▭ Trieste - Sestri Levante.
M – ▭ Milano - La Spezia.
N – ▭ Milano - Ventimiglia; ⚑ 1,2 cl. (T2) and ⚑ 2 cl. Trieste (872) - Udine - Venezia - Genova.
S – ▭ and ⚍ Milano - Sestri Levante.
T – ▭ Torino Porta Nuova - Fossano - Savona - Ventimiglia.
V – ⚍ San Remo - Cuneo.
W – ▭ San Remo - Cuneo - Torino Porta Nuova.
X – ▭ Milano - Ventimiglia; ⚑ 2 cl. and ▭ Milano - Ventimiglia (340/1) - Bordeaux.
c – Arrives 0848.
h – Venezia Mestre.
Ⓡ – Reservation compulsory.
✗ – ETR450 Pendolino supplement payable.

Table 356 — CUNEO - NICE and VENTIMIGLIA

1, 2 class except where shown

km		4389	4391	56852	D 1873	4393	56854	IR 1605	IR 2077	D 5354	2907	IR 2081	4395	56860	D 1871	4397	4399	4401 56864	4403	4405	4407	4409	4377
		2	⚒	⚒	⑦		©	H	H©		G	H			②	②⚒		2				2	2
	Torino Porta Nuova 357 . d.							0723	0745	0745		0859			1010								
0	Cuneo d.		0525		0650	0727		0834	0844	0844	0913	1013	1032		1115	1314	1400	1616		1740	1923	2028	2156
29	Limone a.		0558		0723	0801		0900	0912	0912	0943	1047	1106		1136	1342	1438	1700		1817	1957	2059	2224
29	Limone d.		0603		0728	0806		0902	0918	0918		1050	1111			1444	1705			1839	2006		
49	Tende d.	0555	0620			0822						1128				1501	1727			1857	2027		
164	Breil sur Roya a.	0629	0654		0822	0856		0949	1007	1007		1138	1203			1532	1803			1927	2059		
164	Breil sur Roya d.	0631	0704	0700	0830	0901	0907	0954	1013	1016		1139	1208	1245		1535	1805	1815	1934	2102			
	Nice Ville a.	0730		0800			1010			1110				1343			1905						
187	Ventimiglia a.		0728		0850	0925		1013	1034			1201	1231			1558		1842	1957		2125		
203	San Remo 355 a.		0751			0912		1034	1105			1226				1625							

G – ▭ Savona - Fossano - Cuneo - Limone.
H – ▭ Torino - San Remo - Imperia Oneglia.

Table 356 VENTIMIGLIA and NICE - CUNEO

1, 2 class except where shown

km		4390 2⚒	10168 2⚒	4392	4396	56853	56855 ⑦	4398 ⚒	4094 ⑦	4400	4402	4384 2⚒	56859 4404 2	D 2908 G	4406	IR 1872 2⑦	5355 2078	IR 2078 Ⓐ	IR 1606 Ⓒ	56863 4388 2	IR 2082	56867 Ⓐ	56869 ⑦	4412
	San Remo 355 d.	...	...	...	...	...	...	0900	0950	...	...	...	...	...	1532	...	...	1650	1705	...	1842	...	...	...
	Ventimiglia d.	...	...	0624	0802	...	...	0927	1014	1110	1313	...	...	...	1559	...	...	1716	1732	...	1904	...	...	2004
0	**Nice Ville** d.	...	...	|	|	0725	0855	|	|	|	|	...	1228	...	|	...	1635	|	|	1747	|	1855	1925	|
44	Breil sur Roya a.	...	...	0650	0827	0829	0956	0953	1039	1135	1338	...	1341	...	1624	...	1736	1739	1756	1857	1929	2002	2026	2029
	Breil sur Roya d.	...	...	0656	0834	...	...	1008	1044	1140	...	...	1343	...	1629	...	1744	1744	1804	1908	1930	...	...	2034
	Tende d.	...	...	0732	0917	...	...	1048	1129	1218	...	...	1421	...	1707	...	1818	1818	|	1943	|	...	...	2116
	Limone 🏛 a.	...	...	0752	0939	...	...	1110	1148	1237	...	...	1443	...	1727	...	1838	1838	1900	...	2030	...	...	2136
	Limone 🏛 d.	0606	0642	0802	0944	...	...	1115	1153	1242	...	1349	1448	1638	1732	1742	1844	1844	1902	...	2032	...	...	2140
	Cuneo a.	0636	0713	0830	1012	...	...	1144	1222	1311	...	1420	1521	1710	1800	1812	1912	1912	1923	...	2056	...	...	2214
	Torino Porta Nuova 357 a.	...	...	...	...	...	...	...	...	...	...	...	...	...	...	1918	2016	2016	2043	...	2213	...	...	...

G – [12] Limone - Cuneo - Savona.

Table 357 TORINO - CUNEO and SAVONA

1, 2 class except where shown

km		D 2523	10185 2	10145 2	D 9181 Ⓐ	IR 1605 Ⓒ	IR 2077	E 835	D 2907 G	IR 2063	IR 2081	D 9183 2	D 1871 2⑦	D 9185 ⚒	10153 2	D 2529	D 9187 2	IR 2067	4359 2	D 9191 2	10159 2	D 9193 ⚒	D 2909 G	E 813
0	**Torino Porta Nuova** d.	0616	...	0653	0723	0723	0745	0805	...	0837	0859	0923	1010	1123	...	1210	1233	1342	1405	1523	1545	1623	...	1723
64	Fossano a.	0709	...	0752	0803	0814	0825	0847	...	0926	0947	1003	1055	1203	...	1302	1317	1422	1455	1603	1646	1704	...	1801
64	Fossano d.	0722	0718	0803	0804	0815	0826	0848	0853	0927	0949	1004	1056	1204	1210	1303	1318	1423	1456	1604	1649	1705	1740	1803
80	**Cuneo** d.	|	0741	|	0820	0833	0843	|	0912	|	1010	1020	1114	1220	|	|	1338	|	1514	1620	|	1728	|	|
83	Mondovi d.	0738	...	0803	...	|	|	0900	...	0939	|	...	...	...	1232	1320	...	1435	...	...	1707	...	1751	1816
103	Ceva d.	0755	...	0839	...	|	|	0916	...	0953	|	...	...	...	1251	1336	...	1450	...	...	1728	...	1810	1830
153	**Savona** a.	0845	...	0820	...	|	|	0957	...	1035	|	...	...	...	1350	1428	...	1532	...	...	1825	...	1902	1915
	Ventimiglia 355 a.	1130	...	0941	...	1013	1034f	1150	...	...	1159	...	...	...	...	...	...	1737	...	...	...	...	...	...

	4383 2⚒	D 9195	D 2531	10169	D 2905	4377 2	E 817 F	D 9199	10157	10187
Torino Porta Nuova d.	...	1805	1855	1938	2033	...	2055	2123	2215	2345
Fossano a.	...	1850	1948	2046	2126	...	2150	2203	2316	0043
Fossano d.	1810	1851	1949	2047	2127	2137	2154	2204	2317	0044
Cuneo d.	1828	1909	|	2110	|	2155	|	2220	2336	0106
Mondovi d.	...	...	2007	...	2139	...	2214	...	...	...
Ceva d.	...	...	2026	...	2159	...	2229	...	...	...
Savona a.	...	...	2123	...	2245	...	2313	...	...	...
Ventimiglia 355 a.	...	...	...	...	...	...	...	...	...	...

	D 9180	10156 2	D 9182	10172 2⚒	D 9184 2⚒	E 818 F	D 2906 G	D 9186 2	IR 2074
Ventimiglia 355 d.	...	...	...	...	...	...	...	...	...
Savona d.	...	...	...	0605	...	0644	0732	...	0836
Ceva d.	...	...	...	0700	...	0735	0820	...	0916
Mondovi d.	...	...	...	0713	...	0751	0835	...	0929
Cuneo d.	0530	0612	0700	|	0742	|	|	0857	|
Fossano a.	0547	0634	0717	0724	0758	0803	0846	0919	0940
Fossano d.	0548	0635	0718	0725	0759	0804	...	0920	0941
Torino Porta Nuova a.	0630	0735	0800	0818	0840	0905	...	1005	1028

	E 812	D 9188 ⚒	10164 2	10146 2	D 9190 2	D 2534	D 9192 2	4372 2	E 838	D 2908 G	D 9196 2	10178 2⚒	D 1872 2⑦	4368 2	D 2536	IR 2078	IR 1606 Ⓒ	D 9198 Ⓐ	D 2540	IR 2082	IR 2076	4410 2	4374 2	D 2904 2
Ventimiglia 355 d.	...	...	...	...	...	...	...	...	1430	...	...	...	...	...	1530	1716f	1732	...	...	1904	1835	...	...	...
Savona d.	1015	...	...	1144	...	1313	...	1525	1620	...	...	...	...	...	1750	|	|	...	1908	|	2035	...	2108	2300
Ceva d.	1101	...	...	1302	...	1410	...	1616	1704	...	...	...	...	...	1845	|	|	...	1952	|	2117	...	2158	2342
Mondovi d.	1115	...	...	1321	...	1427	...	1634	1718	...	...	...	...	...	1858	|	|	...	2007	|	2131	...	2211	2356
Cuneo d.	|	1142	1203	|	1342	|	1542	|	|	1711	1742	1756	1814	1832	|	1914	1926	1947	|	2058	|	2158	|	|
Fossano a.	1125	1201	1231	1337	1358	1443	1558	1646	1729	1732	1758	1820	1834	1850	1909	1934	1950	2002	2024	2116	2142	2219	2223	0007
Fossano d.	1126	1202	1238	1338	1359	1445	1559	...	1730	...	1759	1821	1835	1900	1911	1935	1952	2003	2026	2118	2143	...	2224	0008
Torino Porta Nuova a.	1206	1243	1338	1450	1440	1538	1640	...	1815	...	1840	1915	1918	1955	2004	2016	2043	2044	2120	2213	2225	...	2318	0058

F – [12] Torino - Savona and v.v; 🛏 1,2 cl. Torino - Roma and v.v.   G – [12] Savona - Fossano - Cuneo - Limone and v.v.   f – Ⓐ only.

Table 358 SANTHIA - ARONA and BIELLA

2 class only

Rail service Santhia - Arona. 65 km. Journey time: 63 minutes. Trains call at Borgomanero, 49 km, 49 minutes from Santhia.
From Santhia: 0638⚒, 0840, 0906⑦, 1240, 1440⚒, 1740, 1840, 1940⚒, 2040⑦. **From Arona**: 0710, 1120⑦, 1210⚒, 1410, 1710⚒, 1723⑦, 1810⚒, 1929⑦, 2010⚒, 2112.

The Santhia - Arona route shown above avoids Milano Centrale and provides a useful connecting service for passengers travelling from Torino to Domodossola and into Switzerland.

Rail service Santhia - Biella. 27 km. Journey time: 30 - 35 minutes. 2 class only.
From Santhia: 0620⚒, 0709⚒, 0745⑦, 0802⚒, 0844, 0940, 1244, 1348⚒, 1444, 1544⚒, 1648⚒, 1744, 1847⚒, 1919⚒, 1948, 2043.
From Biella: 0533⚒, 0610⚒, 0640⑦, 0659⚒, 0740⑦, 0840, 1150, 1235⚒, 1344, 1435⚒, 1538⚒, 1643, 1736⚒, 1842, 1947, 2038.

Table 359 TORINO and GENOVA - PIACENZA

1, 2 class except where shown

km		IR 2033 ♦	P〆 507 ✕Ⓡ ♦	IR 2284 2285	5283 2	IC 674	IR 2035	5285 2	IC 567 🍷 ♦	IR 2162 🍷	IC 33027	E 344 🍷	IR 2037 🍷	IC 615 🍷	5291 2	IR 2286 2287	IR 2053	10493 2	IR 2288 2289	D 2899	IR 2172	IR 2039 ❖	E 901 ♦	IR 2174	E 903 ♦
0	**Torino Porta Nuova 360** d.	0550	0648	...	...	...	0750	...	0845	...	1318	...	1350	1528	...	...	1628	...	...	1810	...	1950	2010	...	2100
56	Asti **360** d.	0626	0716	...	...	...	0826	...	0918	...	1351	...	1426	1558	...	...	1704	...	...	1848	...	2026	2048	...	2137
91	Alessandria **360** d.	0649	0736	...	0740	...	0849	0912	0940	...	1414	...	1449	1616	1622	...	1725	1813	...	1913	...	2049	2112	...	2203
	Genova Piazza Principe d.	|	|	0704	|	0813	|	|	|	1154	|	1354	|	...	|	1623	...	|	1823	|	1954	|	|	2050	|
113	Tortona d.	0704	|	0751	0804	|	0902	0936	|	1244	1435	1444	1502	...	1648	1704	...	1849	1904	1933	2044	2102	2128	2144	2220
130	Voghera d.	0716	0757	0804	0820	0906	0914	0950	1003	1255	1449	1455	1514	...	1703	1715	...	1905	1915	1945	2054	2114	2141	2155	2235
188	**Piacenza** a.	0749	0828	0839	0926	...	0948	...	1038	...	1520	...	1548	...	...	1748	...	...	1950	*2112*	...	2148	2218	...	2310
	Bologna Centrale 370 a.	0922	0936	1008	*1108*	...	1120	...	1155	...	1636	...	1720	...	...	1920	...	...	2136	...	...	2320	0003	...	0118

	E 902 ♦	IR 2179	IR 2181	IR 2034	IR 2183 🍷	IR 2276 2277	10488 2	IC 604 🍷	10490 2	IR 2036 🍷 ❖	IC 677 🍷	IR 2278 2279	IR 2038	IC 681 🍷	IC 33900	IC 612 🍷	IR 2280 2281 🍷	5296	IC 574 🍷 ♦	IC 687	IR 2199	P 508 ✕Ⓡ ♦	IR 2040 🍷 ♦	IC 689 🍷	E 900 ♦
Bologna Centrale 370 d.	0405	...	...	0620	...	0738	...	...	...	1138	...	1338	1538	...	1723	...	1738	...	1858	...	...	1935	1943	...	0204
Piacenza d.	0550	...	...	0753	...	0908	...	...	1137	1307	...	1507	1708	...	1835	...	1907	...	2014	...	...	2038	2112	...	0409
Voghera d.	0632	0653	0808	0828	0902	0942	1000	...	1320	1343	1357	1541	1743	1752	1910	...	1941	1958	2046	2052	2102	2108	2146	2152	0446
Tortona d.	|	0705	0820	0839	0915	0953	1015	...	1337	1354	|	1552	1754	|	1924	...	1952	2016	|	|	2115	|	2158	|	0500
Genova Piazza Principe a.	|	0754	0908	|	1005	1035	|	...	|	|	1451	1635	|	1847	|	...	2035	|	|	2147	2205	|	|	2247	|
Alessandria **360** d.	0707	...	...	0855	...	...	1036	1146	1403	1410	...	...	1810	...	1938	1943	...	2040	2112	...	...	2131	2215	...	0520
Asti **360** d.	0731	...	...	0914	...	...	...	1204	...	1429	...	...	1829	...	1956	2001	...	...	2132	...	...	2148	2235	...	0544
Torino Porta Nuova 360 a.	0813	...	...	0953	...	...	...	1238	...	1508	...	...	1908	...	2033p	2035	...	...	2208	...	...	2220	2313	...	0625

♦ – **NOTES** (LISTED BY TRAIN NUMBERS)
P507/8 – GUIDO RENI – Ⓐ, **not** Dec. 23 - Jan. 9: [12] and ✕ Torino - Roma Termini and v.v. Pendolino supplement payable.
IC567/74 – ROSSINI – [12] and 🍷 Torino - Bari Centrale.
E900/1 – ▬ 2 cl. and [12] Torino - Bari Centrale and v.v. **Not** Dec. 24, 31 from Torino or Bari.
E902/3 – 🛏 1,2 cl. (T2), ▬ 1, 2 cl. and [12] Torino - Lecce and v.v; ▬ 2 cl. and [12] Torino - Taranto and v.v; 🛏 1,2 cl. Torino - Bari Centrale and v.v.
IR2033/40 – [12] Torino - Rimini and v.v. **Not** Dec. 25, Jan. 1 from Torino or Dec. 24, 31 from Rimini.
p – Torino **Porta Susa**.
❖ – **Not** Dec. 25, Jan. 1.
〆 – **Pendolino** supplement payable.

Table 360 TORINO - GENOVA - PISA - ROMA

1, 2 class except where shown

km		D	IR	IC	D	IR	P523	IR	IC605	IR	IR	E	P↯	E	IC	IR	D	P↯	IR	IC	IR	E	IC		D
		3257	2441	601	3101	2443	524	2291	626	2041	2043	211	507	1211	607	2181	2893	1509	2045	609	2447	365	611		2895
					2		🍴Ⓡ		🍷			🍷	🍴Ⓡ		🍷			🍷Ⓡ		🍷	🍷	🍷	🍷		
				⚒	F		G↯	◆	H			◆	◆	◆	◆			◆				◆			
0	**Torino Porta Nuova 359** .. d.	...	...	...	...	...	...	...	...	...	0622	0633	0648	0713	0728	...	...	0818	0828	0928	...	...	1128	...	...
56	Asti **359** .... d.	...	...	...	...	...	...	...	...	...	0704	0708	0716	0747	0758	...	...	0848	0904	0958	...	...	1158	...	...
91	Alessandria **359** .... d.	...	...	...	...	...	...	...	...	...	0727	0733	0736	0808	0817	...	0823	0908	0927	1017	...	...	1217	...	1225
112	Novi Ligure .... d.	...	...	...	...	...	...	...	...	...	0741	|	|	|	|	...	0837	|	0941	|	...	...	|	...	1242
	Milano Centrale **355** .. d.	...	...	...	...	...	...	...	...	...	|	|	|	|	|	0720	|	|	|	|	...	...	|	...	|
138	Ronco Scrivia .... d.	...	...	...	...	...	...	...	...	...	0758	|	|	|	|	|	0901	|	0958	|	...	...	|	...	1306
166	**Genova Piazza Principe**. a.	...	...	...	...	...	...	...	...	...	0818	0827	|	0854	0858	0908	0922	0953	1018	1058	...	...	1258	...	1334
166	**Genova Piazza Principe**. d.	...	...	...	...	...	0617	0621	0654	0705	0821	0834	|	...	0901	0910	0924	0956	1021	1101	...	1216	1301	...	1337
169	**Genova Brignole** ..... d.	...	...	...	...	...	0625	0629	0702	0713	0829	0842	|	...	0909	0918	0929	1004	1026	1109	...	1224	1309	...	1345
194	Santa Margherita-Portofino . d.	...	...	...	...	...	|	0658	|	0739	0852	0904	|	...	|	0953	—	1024	—	|	...	|	|	...	1411
196	Rapallo .... d.	...	...	...	...	...	0645	0702	0726	0743	0856	0910	|	...	|	0958	...	|	...	1133	...	|	|	...	1415
205	Chiavari .... d.	...	...	...	...	...	0653	0709	0734	0752	0905	|	|	...	0940	1008	...	|	...	|	...	|	1339	...	1423
212	Sestri-Levante .... d.	...	...	...	...	...	|	0717	|	0800	0913	|	|	...	|	1024	...	|	...	|	...	|	|	...	1431
235	Levanto .... d.	...	...	...	...	...	|	0735	|	0816	0929	|	|	...	|	1058	...	|	IR	|	...	|	|	...	—
256	**La Spezia Centrale** .. a.	...	...	...	...	...	0723	0753	0809	0833	0948	0955	|	...	1013	1132	...	1107	**2151**	1213	...	1333	1413	...	...
256	**La Spezia Centrale** .. d.	...	...	0600	...	...	0725	...	0811	0835	0950	0957	|	...	1015	...	...	1109	❖	1215	...	1335	1415	...	...
272	Sarzana .... d.	...	...	|	0647	...	|	...	|	0849	1004	|	|	...	|	...	...	|	1104	|	...	|	|	...	...
282	Carrara-Avenza .... d.	...	...	|	0655	...	|	...	|	0857	1012	1018	|	...	|	...	...	|	1115	|	...	1354	|	...	...
289	Massa Centro .... d.	...	...	0621	0701	...	0745	...	0832	0903	1018	|	|	...	|	...	IR	|	1124	1236	...	1401	|	...	IR
310	Viareggio .... d.	...	...	0634	0716	...	0758	...	0846	0923	1030	1036	|	...	1046	...	**2445**	1140	1148	|	...	1414	1446	...	**2451**
331	**Pisa Centrale** .... a.	...	...	0649	0735	...	0811	...	0901	0938	1044	1051	|	...	1101	...	...	1154	1212	1301	...	1430	1501	...	...
331	**Pisa Centrale** .... d.	...	0515	0652	...	0745	0814	...	0904	0944	1047	1054	|	...	1104	...	1145	1157	1215	1304	1345	1435	1504	...	1545
351	**Livorno Centrale**...... a.	...	0528	0705	...	0758	|	...	|	0957	1100	1110	|	...	1117	...	1158	1210	1230	1317	1358	1449	1517	...	1558
351	**Livorno Centrale**...... d.	...	0531	0708	...	0801	|	...	|	...	...	1125	|	...	1120	...	1201	1213	...	1320	1401	1452	1520	...	1601
374	Rosignano .... d.	...	0549	|	...	0819	|	...	|	...	...	|	|	...	|	...	1219	|	...	|	1419	|	|	...	1619
385	Cecina .... d.	...	0559	|	...	0829	|	...	|	...	...	|	|	...	|	...	1229	|	...	|	1429	|	|	...	1629
420	Campiglia Marittima... d.	...	0623	0748	...	0854	|	...	|	...	...	|	|	...	|	...	1254	|	...	|	1454	1532	|	...	1654
437	Follonica .... d.	...	0636	|	...	0906	|	...	|	...	...	|	|	...	|	...	1306	|	...	|	1506	|	|	...	1706
479	Grosseto .... d.	0600	0703	0825	...	0933	|	...	|	...	...	|	|	...	1233	...	1333	1333	...	1433	1533	1612	1633	...	1733
517	Orbetello .... d.	0628	0724	|	...	0954	|	...	|	...	...	|	|	...	|	...	1355	|	...	|	1554	|	|	...	1755
556	Tarquinia .... d.	0700	0754	|	...	1024	|	...	|	...	...	|	|	...	|	...	1424	|	...	|	1624	|	|	...	1824
586	**Civitavecchia** .... d.	0713	0807	0921	...	1037	|	...	|	...	...	|	|	...	1329	...	1437	|	...	1529	1637	1712	1729	...	1837
595	Santa Marinella .... d.	0721	0815	|	...	1045	|	...	|	...	...	|	|	...	|	...	1445	|	...	|	1645	|	|	...	1845
617	Cerveteri .... d.	0734	0830	|	...	1100	|	...	|	...	...	|	|	...	|	...	1500	|	...	|	1700	|	|	...	1900
660	**Roma Ostiense** .... a.	0804	0858	0957	...	1128	|	...	|	...	...	1429	|	...	1405	...	1528	|	...	1605	1728	|	1805	...	1928
667	**Roma Termini** .... a.	0815	0910	1010	...	1140	1035	...	1230	...	...	|	1215	...	|	...	1540	1510	...	1620	1740	1805	1820	...	1940
	Napoli Centrale **370** .. a.	...	...	...	...	...	...	...	...	...	...	1700	...	...	1605	...	...	...	...	...	...	...	...	...	...

	IR	IC	IR	IR	D	IR	IC	IC	D	IR	IR	IC	IR	E	IC	IR	IC	E	IC	IR	E	E	IR	E	E
	2049	613	2453	2189	3131	2051	679	615	2493	2053	2297	617	2149	1941	683	2055	619	801	687	2057	805	809	2059	367	811
		🍷			2	🍷	🍷	🍷							🍷		🍷								
					F		◆				◆	F		◆				◆			◆	◆		◆	◆
orino Porta Nuova 359 .. d.	1228	1328	...	...	...	1428	...	1528	...	1628	...	1728	...	1735	...	1828	1928	1933	...	2028	2050	2200	2220	...	2305
sti **359** .... d.	1304	1358	...	...	...	1504	...	1558	...	1704	...	1758	...	1815	...	1904	1958	2010	...	2104	2127	2235	2304	...	2340
lessandria **359** .... d.	1327	1417	...	...	...	1527	...	1617	...	1727	...	1817	...	1838	...	1927	2017	2035	...	2127	2152	2300	2327	...	0005
lovi Ligure .... d.	1341	|	...	...	...	1541	...	|	...	1741	...	|	...	|	...	1941	|	2050	...	2141	|	2316	2341	...	0021
Milano Centrale **355** ... d.	|	|	...	1405	...	|	1510	|	...	|	...	|	1715	|	1805	|	|	|	2010	|	|	|	|	2215v	|
onco Scrivia .... d.	1358	|	...	1538	...	1558	|	|	...	1758	...	|	|	|	|	1958	|	|	|	2158	|	|	2358	|	|
enova Piazza Principe . a.	1418	1458	...	1559	...	1618	1647	1658	...	1818	...	1858	|	1927	1947	2018	2058	2127	2147	2218	2239	2353	0025	0005v	0056
enova Piazza Principe . d.	1421	1501	...	1600	...	1621	1650	1701	1722	1821	1832	1901	|	1930	1950	2021	2101	2131	2150	2221	2242	0010	0028	0042	0102
enova Brignole .... d.	1429	1509	...	1608	...	1629	1658	1709	1730	1829	1840	1909	|	1938	1958	2029	2109	2140	2158	2226	2250	|	0033	0050	0110
anta Margherita-Portofino ... d.	1454	|	...	1642	...	1652	1721	|	1752	1854	1907	|	|	|	2021	2054	|	|	2221	...	|	|	...	0113	0133
apallo .... d.	1458	1533	...	1647	...	1656	1726	1733	1757	1858	1911	1933	|	|	2026	2058	2133	|	2226	...	|	|	...	0119	0138
hiavari .... d.	1507	|	...	1659	...	1705	1734	|	1805	1907	1919	|	|	|	2034	2107	|	|	2234	...	|	|	...	0129	0147
estri-Levante .... d.	1515	|	...	1708	...	1713	1740	|	1814	1915	1927	|	|	|	2040	2115	|	|	2240	...	|	|	...	0138	0156
evanto .... d.	1531	|	...	—	...	1729	...	|	1830	1931	1944	|	|	|	2056	2131	|	|	...	...	|	|	...	0153	|
a Spezia Centrale .... a.	1548	1613	...	...	...	1748	...	1813	1847	1948	2005	2013	|	2040	2113	2148	2213	2250	...	...	2355	0128	...	0210	0234
a Spezia Centrale .... d.	1550	1615	...	...	1735	1750	...	1815	—	1950	...	2015	|	2043	...	...	2215	2253	...	...	2358	0131	...	0213	0237
arzana .... d.	1604	|	...	...	1752	1804	...	|	...	2004	...	|	2030	|	...	...	|	|	...	...	|	|	...	|	|
arrara-Avenza .... d.	1612	|	...	...	1800	1812	...	|	...	2012	...	|	2039	|	...	...	|	|	...	...	|	|	...	|	|
lassa Centro .... d.	1618	1636	...	**11727**	1806	1818	...	|	IR	2018	...	|	2045	|	...	...	2234	|	...	...	|	|	...	|	0259
iareggio .... d.	1630	|	...	F	1834	1830	...	1846	**2455**	2030	...	2046	2105	|	...	...	2249	|	...	...	|	|	...	0247	|
isa Centrale .... a.	1644	1701	...	...	1850	1844	...	1901	...	2044	...	2101	2122	2130	...	...	2304	2338	...	...	0046	0215	...	0305	0323
isa Centrale .... d.	1647	1704	1745	1828	...	1847	...	1904	1945	2047	...	...	2125	2133	...	...	2307	2341	...	...	0049	0220	...	0308	0328
ivorno Centrale........ a.	1700	1717	1758	1843	...	1900	...	1917	1958	2100	...	...	2140	2147	...	...	2320	2356	...	...	0104	0234	...	0322	0342
ivorno Centrale........ d.	...	1720	1801	1846	...	...	...	1920	2001	...	...	...	...	...	...	...	...	2359	...	...	0107	0239	...	0325	0347
osignano .... d.	...	|	1819	1912	...	...	...	|	2019	...	...	...	...	...	...	...	...	|	...	...	|	|	...	|	|
ecina .... d.	...	|	1829	1920	...	...	...	|	2029	...	...	...	...	...	...	...	...	|	...	...	|	|	...	|	|
ampiglia Marittima..... d.	...	|	1854	2002	...	...	...	|	2054	...	...	...	...	...	...	...	...	|	...	...	|	|	...	|	|
ollonica .... d.	...	|	1906	2015	...	...	...	|	2106	...	...	...	...	...	...	...	...	|	...	...	|	|	...	|	|
rosseto .... d.	...	1833	1933	2053	...	...	...	2033	2133	...	...	...	...	...	...	...	...	0125	...	...	|	0400	...	0445	0505
rbetello .... d.	...	|	1954	...	...	...	...	|	2154	...	...	...	...	...	...	...	...	|	...	...	|	|	...	|	0527
arquinia .... d.	...	|	2024	...	...	...	...	|	2224	...	...	...	...	...	...	...	...	|	...	...	|	|	...	|	0600
ivitavecchia .... d.	...	1929	2037	...	...	...	...	2129	2237	...	...	...	...	...	...	...	...	0231	...	...	|	0509	...	0555	0615
anta Marinella .... d.	...	|	2045	...	...	...	...	|	2245	...	...	...	...	...	...	...	...	|	...	...	|	|	...	|	|
erveteri .... d.	...	|	2100	...	...	...	...	|	2300	...	...	...	...	...	...	...	...	|	...	...	|	|	...	|	|
oma Ostiense .... a.	...	2005	2128	...	...	...	...	2205	2328	...	...	...	...	...	...	...	...	0323	...	...	0416	0554	...	0642	0702
oma Termini .... a.	...	|	2140	...	...	...	...	2220	2340	...	...	...	...	...	...	...	...	|	...	...	|	|	...	0655	0710
Napoli Centrale **370** .. a.	...	2203	...	...	...	...	...	...	...	...	...	...	...	...	...	...	...	0541c	...	...	0650	0904	...	...	...

– **NOTES** (LISTED BY TRAIN NUMBERS)

211 – NAPOLI EXPRESS – Dec. 16 - Jan. 7, Feb. 24 - Mar. 25, Apr. 7 - May 26 (from Paris): 🛏 1,2 cl., ▬ 2 cl. and [12] Paris Lyon - Modane - Napoli; 🍷 Genova - Napoli. On other dates see train **E1211**.

365 – ▬ 2 cl. and [12] Cerbère - Roma; [12] Hendaye - Roma; 🍷 Ventimiglia - Roma; only takes passengers holding tickets valid for over 200 km.

367 – 🛏 1,2 cl., ▬ 2 cl. and [12] Nice - Roma; 🛏 1,2 cl. Torino (**817**) - Savona - Roma; 🛏 1,2 cl. Milano (**IR2201**) - Genova - Roma.

507 – GUIDO RENI – Ⓐ (**not** Dec. 27 - Jan. 5): [12] and 🍴 Torino - Roma.

607 – CARIGNANO – [12] and 🍷 Torino - Salerno.

679 – CATTANEO – [12] Milano - Sestri Levante; [12] Basel (**255**) - Sestri Levante; 🍷 Milano - Genova.

801 – ▬ 2 cl. and [12] Torino - Reggio; ▬ 2 cl. and [12] Torino - Catanzaro - Reggio; ▬ 2 cl. and [12] Torino - Crotone.

805 – TRENO DELL' ETNA – [12] Torino - Palermo; [12] Torino - Siracusa; conveys Dec. 24, 26 - 30, Jan. 1, Jan. 9 - Apr. 11, 15, 16, 20: 🛏 1,2 cl. and [2] Torino - Reggio. Only takes passengers for Paola and beyond.

809 – 🛏 1,2 cl., 🛏 1,2 cl. (T2), ▬ 2 cl. and [12] Torino - Napoli.

811 – 🛏 1,2 cl., 🛏 1,2 cl. (T2), ▬ 2 cl. and [12] Torino - Roma.

E1211 – Jan. 8 - Feb. 23, Mar. 26 - Apr. 6 (from Paris): 🛏 1,2 cl., ▬ 2 cl. and [12] Paris Lyon (**217**) - Modane - Genova.

P1509 – ⑦ and holidays, **not** Dec. 25, Jan. 1: [12] and 🍴 Torino - Roma.

E1941 – TRENO DEL SOLE – 🛏 1,2 cl. (T2) and ▬ 2 cl. (also 🛏 1,2 cl. on ④⑤⑥) Torino - Palermo; 🛏 1,2 cl., and ▬ 2 cl. Torino - Siracusa; 🛏 1,2 cl. (T2) (also ▬ 2 cl. Dec. 7 - Jan. 8, Apr. 14 - May 7) Torino - Catania; ▬ 2 cl. Torino - Reggio.

IR2291 – [12] Genova - Aulla - Parma - Bologna.

IR2297 – [12] Genova - Aulla - Parma. **Not** Dec. 24, 31.

F – To or from Firenze.

G – CIMABUE – ⚒, **not** Dec. 25 - Jan. 8: [12] and 🍴 Savona (**523**) - Pisa (**524**) - Firenze (**525**) - Roma.

H – CRISTOFORO COLOMBO – [12] and 🍷 Genova (**605**) - Pisa (**626**) - Firenze (**627**) - Roma.

c – Napoli **Campi Flegrei**.

v – 🛏 1,2 cl. only from Milano (Train number **IR2201**).

❖ – **Not** Dec. 25, Jan. 1.

↯ – **ETR450** Pendolino supplement payable.

Table 360 — ROMA - PISA - GENOVA - TORINO

1, 2 class except where shown

	E 806	D 2888	IC 672	E 810	IR 2044	E 1940	IC 674	E 816	IR 2146	IC 602	11716	11856	3104	IC 604	11864	IR 2440	IC 606	IR 2048	IC622 608	IC 682	IR 2050	IR 2442	IC 610	IR 2052
	♦		♦	♦		♦		♦			F	F	F	Y	2		Y		G	♦	Y		Y	Y
Napoli Centrale 370 ... d.	2130																		0747					
Roma Termini d.														0630			0740		1000				1030	1140
Roma Ostiense d.	0013			0106				0236						0639			0749						1039	1149
Cerveteri d.														0707									1107	
Santa Marinella d.														0721									1121	
Civitavecchia d.	0056							0321						0728			0826						1128	1226
Tarquinia d.														0742									1142	
Orbetello d.														0812									1212	
Grosseto d.	0204							0424		0525		0630	0745	0839			0925						1239	1325
Follonica d.										0555			0657				0903						1303	
Campiglia Marittima d.										0606	0620		0709				0930	0940					1315	1340
Cecina d.										0634	0649		0733				0854	0940					1340	
Rosignano d.										0645	0700		0742				0901	0950					1350	
Livorno Centrale a.	0321			0416						0712	0726		0802				0921	1010	1037				1410	1437
Livorno Centrale d.	0326			0419		0506				0715	0729		0805				0923	1013	1040	1100		1300	1413	1440	1500
Pisa Centrale a.	0340			0433	0520					0730	0742		0819				0940	1026	1053	1113	1253	1313	1453	1513
Pisa Centrale d.	0345			0436	0525					0744				0856					1056	1116	1256	1316	1456	1516
Viareggio d.						0601	0615			0632	0701			0802			0911		1111	1131	1320	1331	1511	1531
Massa Centro d.							0651	0716			0820					IR			1143		1343		1543	
Carrara-Avenza d.							0658				0827					2296			1149		1349		1549	
Sarzana d.							0710				0835								1157		1357		1557	
La Spezia Centrale a.	0430			0529		0616		0647		0739				0850		0942			1142	1211	1342		1542	1613
La Spezia Centrale d.	0433	0436		0534	0558	0619	0644	0650		0741				0944	0957		1144	1213	1344		1413		1544	1613
Levanto d.		0505			0623		0702							1022				1231			1431			1633
Sestri-Levante d.		0535	0615		0645		0717			0811				1043			1248		1417	1448			1650	
Chiavari d.		0546	0624		0654		0725			0819				1052	IR		1256		1425	1456				
Rapallo d.		0557	0633		0702		0734			0827				1025	1101	2046	1225	1304	1429	1504			1625	1706
Santa Margherita-Portofino d.		0601	0638		0707		0738								1105			1308	1438	1508				1710
Genova Brignole d.	0547	0632	0705		0715	0733	0749	0805	0805	0852				1052	1136	1133	1252	1338	1452	1505	1533		1652	1733
Genova Piazza Principe a.	0552	0637	0710	0715	0738		0754	0810	0815	0857				1057	1141	1138	1257	1338	1457	1510	1538		1657	1738
Genova Piazza Principe d.	0610	0639	0713	0720	0741		0800	0813	0820	0900				1100		1141	1300	1341	1500	1513	1541		1700	1740
Ronco Scrivia d.		0700		0850				0800								1200		1400		1600			1650	1800
Milano Centrale 355 ... a.				0816		0950		1025		0900				1216		1416			1616					1816
Novi Ligure d.	0656	0725												1146		1232	1343	1432	1543		1632		1743	1832
Alessandria 359 d.	0720	0747		0813	0832	0900		0917		0943				1204		1252	1401	1452	1601		1652		1801	1832
Asti 359 d.	0749	0808		0835	0852	0924		0940		1001				1238		1333	1435	1533	1635		1733		1835	1933
Torino Porta Nuova 359 a.	0828	0850		0910	0933	1000		1015		1035				1333		1433	1533	1635						

	D 3122	E 362	IR 2444	IR 2170	IC 612	IR 2054	11724	IR 2152	IC 2448	E 1210	IC 614	D 3024	P 1510	IR 2056	E 210	IR 2148	IC 2450	P 508	IR 2452	IC616 33810	P526 528	IR 2454	IC 620	E 800	E 366
	2 F	♦	✗	Y	Y	2	F	♦	♦	♦	♦	2	✗ R	♦	Y	♦	♦	✗ R	♦	Y J	H	♦		♦	♦
Napoli Centrale 370 ... d.											1347				1355										
Roma Termini d.		1225	1230		1340			1430			1600					1630	1700	1710	1740	1905	1830		1940	2250	2330
Roma Ostiense d.			1239	1349				1439		1549						1639		1719	1747			1839	1949		2341
Cerveteri d.			1307					1507								1707		1747				1907	1921		
Santa Marinella d.			1321					1521								1721						1921			
Civitavecchia d.		1315	1328		1426			1528		1626						1728	1808	1826		1928	2026	2338		0025	
Tarquinia d.			1342					1542								1742	1821			1942		2012			
Orbetello d.			1412					1612								1812	1908			2012					
Grosseto d.	1345	1421	1439		1525			1639		1725	1713	1741				1839	1939	1925		2039	2125	0050	0132		
Follonica d.	1418		1503					1703		1737						1903	2003			2103					
Campiglia Marittima d.	1432		1515					1715		1800						1915	2015			2115	2159				
Cecina d.	1457		1540					1740		1823						1940	2040			2152					
Rosignano d.	1507		1550					1750		1831						1950	2050			2202					
Livorno Centrale a.	1530	1538	1610		1637			1810		1837	1854	1903		1923		2010	2110	2037		2222	2240	0230	0249		
Livorno Centrale d.	1533	1541	1613		1640	1700		1755	1840	1854	1900	1926	1935	2013		2113	2040		2225	2243	0235	0242		
Pisa Centrale a.	1548	1555	1626		1653	1713		1809	1826	1853	1908	1919	1913	1940	1948	2026	2126	2053	2124	2238	2256	0250	0306		
Pisa Centrale d.			1559		1656	1716	1745	1812		1856		1922	1916	1943	1951			2056	2127		2259	0255	0310		
Viareggio d.			1615		1711	1731	1807	1832			1936	1931	1959	2008				2111	2141		2314	0314	0329		
Massa Centro d.			1629			1743	1826	1853		1920		1943		2027	2034	2302			2154		2326	0331			
Carrara-Avenza d.			1636			1749	1832	1900				1949	2016	2034	2042										
Sarzana d.						1757	1843	1909				1957							2142	2216		2350	0359	0407	
La Spezia Centrale a.		1655	D		1742	1811	1900			1942	2006	2011	2033						2144	2218			0404	0410	
La Spezia Centrale d.		1658	2902	1702	1744	1813	1906			1944	2007	2013	2035		2106				2144	2218				0427	
Levanto d.				1735		1831	1939					2031		2126										0448	
Sestri-Levante d.			1732	1806		1848	2009				2019	2048		2143					2220	2249				0456	
Chiavari d.			1739	1824		1856				2019		2056		2151					2228	2257				0505	
Rapallo d.			1748	1840	1825	1904					2050	2104	2121		2159				2203					051	
Santa Margherita-Portofino d.			1752	1844		1908						2108	2127		2203										
Genova Brignole d.		1806	1828	1922	1852	1933				2052	2113	2133	2153		2233				2253	2318			0509	
Genova Piazza Principe a.		1811	1833	1927	1857	1938				2057	2118	2138	2158		2238				2258	2323			0514	054
Genova Piazza Principe d.			1835	1930	1900	1941			2010	2100	2121	2141	2204						2301				0519	0713
Ronco Scrivia d.			1857			2000							2200		2350									085
Milano Centrale 355 ... a.			2120			2016							2216											
Novi Ligure d.		1920												2131						2343			0610	
Alessandria 359 d.		1937		1943	2032				2059	2143		2208	2232	2300			2131		2343	0001			0634	
Asti 359 d.				2001	2052				2120	2201		2226	2252	2322			2148		2220	0035			0713	
Torino Porta Nuova 359 a.				2035	2133				2155	2235		2300	2333	2359			2220							

Table 361 — GENOVA and ALESSANDRIA - ACQUI TERME

Most trains 2 class only

Rail service Genova - Acqui Terme.　　61 km.　　Journey time: 65-80 minutes.

From Genova Piazza Principe: 0626, 0717, 0806, 1015, 1230, 1321, 1423, 1551, 1700 Ⓐ, 1733, 1811, 1915, 2013, 2206 Ⓑ, 2340.
From Acqui Terme: 0423, 0510 ✕, 0538 ✕, 0618 ✕, 0703, 0744 ✕, 0842, 1032, 1209, 1317, 1502, 1721, 1810, 1944, 2046.

Rail service Alessandria - Acqui Terme.　　34 km.　　Journey time: 30-35 minutes.　　2 class only.

From Alessandria: 0654, 0800, 1130 ✕, 1234, 1331, 1421 ✕, 1738, 1905, 1955.　　**From Acqui Terme:** 0554, 0636 ✕, 0711, 0741, 0935, 1318, 1502, 1732, 1840, 2032.

Table 362 — MILANO - COLICO - CHIAVENNA and TIRANO

1, 2 class except where shown

km		10614 2✕	5202 2✕	1748 ⑦	1856 ⑦	2588 ⑦	2590	2592	5206 2	1750 ⑦	5214 2✕	2594	2596	5218 2	2598	5220 2✕	2600 ✕	5224 2✕	2602	5226 2✕	9062 2⑦	2604	5228 2⑦	2606	2608
0	Milano Centrale ...... d.	0504	...	0615	0629	0715	0815	0915	...	1015	...	1215	1415	...	1615	...	1705	...	1800	...	...	1910	...	2015	2115
12	Monza .... d.	0521	...	0628	0640	0726	0828	0928	...	1028	...	1228	1426	...	1628	...	1721	...	1812	...	...	1921	...	2028	2128
50	Lecco .... d.	0607	...	0655	0712	0755	0855	0955	...	1055	...	1255	1455	...	1655	...	1755	...	1852	...	...	1953	...	2055	2158
72	Varenna .... d.	0635	...	0716	...	0816	0916	1016	...	1116	...	1316	1516	...	1716	...	...	...	1916	...	...	2016	...	2116	2223
75	Bellano .... d.	0643	...	0721	...	0821	0921	1021	...	1121	...	1321	1521	...	1721	...	...	...	1921	...	...	2021	...	2121	2229
89	Colico ▲ .... d.	0706	0709	0737	0802	0837	0937	1037	1042	1137	1331	1337	1537	1620	1737	1809	1837	1848	1937	1942	...	2037	2042	2137	2245
116	Chiavenna ▲ .... a.	...	0744	...	0825	...	...	...	1113	...	1405	...	...	1651	...	1840	...	1924	...	2013	...	...	2113	...	...
130	Sondrio................... d.	0753	...	0813	...	0912	1011	1110	...	1211	...	1411	1611	...	1811	...	1910	...	2010	...	...	2015	2111	...	2210 2333b
156	Tirano .... d.	0830	...	0845	...	0945	1040	1148	...	1240	...	1440	1640	...	1842	...	1945	...	...	...	...	2046	2140	...	...

	2585 2✕	5199	2589 2✕	5201 2⑦	5227	2591	2593 ⑦	5207 2✕	5209	2595	2597	5215 2✕	5217 2	2599	1745 2⑦	5219 2	2603 ⑦	1853 ⑦	1747 ⑦	2605 2✕	5225 ⑦	2607	1749 ⑦	9049	2609
Tirano .... d.	...	...	0550	...	...	0650	0902	...	0954	1250	...	1502	...	...	1702	...	1757	1902	...	...	...	2002	2054	...	
Sondrio .... d.	0522	...	0630	...	...	0732	0930	...	1130	1330	...	1530	1630	...	1730	...	1831	1930	...	...	2012	2030	2128	2130	
Chiavenna .... d.	...	0619	...	0705	0725			1120	1125		1430	1525	...	1725	...	1800	...	...	1934	...	...	...	...		
Colico .... d.	0600	0657	0705	0740	0800	0805	1005	1154	1200	1205	1405	1507	1600	1605	1705	1800	1805	1825	1905	2005	2008	2049	2105	...	2211
Bellano .... d.	0614	...	0722	...	...	0822	1022	...	...	1222	1422	...	...	1622	1722	...	1822	...	1922	2022	...	2107	2122	...	2230
Varenna .... d.	0619	...	0727	...	...	0827	1027	...	...	1227	1427	...	...	1627	1727	...	1827	1845	1927	2027	...	2117	2127	...	2235
Lecco .... d.	0644	...	0747	...	...	0847	1047	...	...	1247	1447	...	...	1647	1747	...	1847	1915	1947	2047	...	2147	2147	...	2301
Monza .... d.	0714	...	0817	...	...	0917	1117	...	...	1317	1517	...	...	1717	1816	...	1917	1955	2017	2117	...	2217	2217	...	2344
Milano Centrale ...... a.	0730	...	0830	...	...	0930	1130	...	...	1330	1530	...	...	1730	1830	...	1930	2008	2030	2130	...	2230	2230	...	2357

🚌 – By 🚌.　▲ – Additional services Colico - Chiavenna at: 0627✕, 0712⑦ 🚌, 0842, 1131✕, 1200⑦, 1237✕, 1345, 1437, 1530✕, 1745 🚌, 1826⑦, 1945⑦ 🚌, 2045✕ 🚌.
Additional services Chiavenna - Colico at: 0510✕ 🚌, 0616⑦ 🚌, 0753✕, 0925, 1234✕, 1325, 1611✕, 1847✕, 1925⑦.

Table 363 — MILANO LOCAL SERVICES

Rail service Milano - Mantova.　1, 2 class

km		2651	2653	2665	2655	2657	2667	10793	2661	2663			2650	2652	2654	4920	2646	2656	2662	2612	2664
0	Milano Centrale .... d.	0630	0820	1024n	1220	1420	1610	...	1720	1835	Mantova .... d.	0525	0655	0846	1000	...	1150	1450	1715	1842
60	Codogno .... d.	0720	0903	1103	1304	1505	1655	...	1758	1927	Cremona .... d.	0628	0742	0932	1112	...	1237	1542	1758	1934
88	Cremona .... d.	0744	0934	1126	1333	1527	1726	1740	1822	1952	Codogno .... d.	0649	0803	1000	1145	1201	1301	1603	1834	2001
151	Mantova .... a.	0833	1020	1219	1437	1608	...	1900	1921	2042	Milano Centrale .... a.	0745	0845	1049	...	1245	1350	1645	1922n	2045

Rail service Milano - Luino.　　91 km.　　Journey time: 1 hour 25 - 1 hour 45.　　2 class only.

From Milano Porta Garibaldi : 0530, 0708, 0835c, 1035e, 1225✕e, 1300c, 1425, 1614✕c, 1725e, 1755✕, 1835✕, 1925, 2100✕, 2220⑦.
From Luino: 0522, 0605✕, 0644✕, 0730, 0906e, 1238✕c, 1357✕, 1514e, 1558c, 1700✕c, 1812c, 1944, 2116✕c.

– Change at **Gallarate**. e – To or from Milano **Centrale**. Change at **Gallarate**.

Rail service Milano - Bergamo.　　43 km.　　Journey time: 50 - 70 minutes.　　2 class only.

From Milano Porta Garibaldi : 0510, 0530✕, 0620✕, 0720Ⓐ, 0735h, 0845h, 0853 ✕, 1140n, 1155c, 1233, 1336✕, 1412Ⓐ, 1437, 1540, 1618✕, 1650h, 1718Ⓐ, 1732✕n, 1748✕, 1800, 1814Ⓐ, 1845✕, 1850Ⓐ, 1930, 2037, 2210, 2223✕, 2315h.

From Bergamo : 0430✕, 0517, 0551Ⓐ, 0600, 0614✕, 0630Ⓐn, 0633Ⓐ, 0652✕, 0657h, 0718✕, 0730Ⓐ, 0748✕n, 0753✕, 0825Ⓐ, 0917, 1055, 1215✕, 1255✕, 1315h, 1450, 1515h, 1555✕, 1655Ⓐ, 1718h, 1755Ⓐ, 1819h, 1921, 2045h, 2230h.　　h – Milano **Centrale**.　　n – Milano **Lambrate**.

Rail service Milano - Laveno.　　Operator: see below.　　72 km.　　Journey time: 1 hour 15 - 1 hour 30.　　1, 2 class.

From Milano Nord: 0610⑦, 0625 ✕, 0730, 0803, 0905, 0942, 1047, 1150, 1238 ✕, 1244, 1405, 1505, 1600, 1645, 1703 ✕, 1739⑦, 1803 Ⓐ, 1817, 1905, 1940 ✕, 2018, 2114✕ 🚌, 2117 ⑦.
From Laveno : 0500✕ 🚌, 0545✕, 0610, 0640Ⓐ, 0707, 0732✕, 0743, 0814✕, 0918, 1012, 1105, 1204, 1258, 1349, 1421, 1524, 1613, 1700, 1730, 1800, 1905, 1950⑦, 2015, 2213⑦ 🚌.
All trains call at Varese Nord, approximately 50 minutes after leaving Milano, and 30 minutes after leaving Laveno.

Rail service Milano - Como.　　Operator: see below.　　46 km.　　Journey time: 50 - 60 minutes.　　1, 2 class.

From Milano Nord: 0508✕, 0533⑦, 0630✕, 0657, 0730✕, 0742, 0830, 0900, 0942, 1047, 1150, 1205✕, 1227, 1310✕, 1314, 1355, 1410, 1505, 1529, 1610✕, 1640, 1710✕, 1725, 1800✕, 1809, 1833Ⓐ, 1837, 1900, 1921, 1955Ⓐ, 2015Ⓐ, 2027, 2114, 2220⑦.
From Como Nord: 0529, 0551✕, 0618, 0641✕, 0651, 0714✕, 0734, 0800✕, 0819, 0844✕, 0923, 0956✕, 1027, 1120, 1242, 1308, 1326✕, 1354✕, 1424, 1519, 1619, 1707✕, 1710⑦, 1733, 1758, 1821, 1855, 1950, 2035, 2130, 2230 ⑦.

Operator of services between **Milano, Laveno and Como: Ferrovie Nord Milano**, Piazzale Cadorna 14, 20123 Milano.　　☎ 02 85 111, fax: 02 85 11 708.

Table 364 — ITALIAN LAKES - (LAGO MAGGIORE, GARDA, COMO)

Lago Maggiore: 🚢 services link Arona, Stresa, Baveno, Laveno, Luino and Locarno throughout the year on an irregular schedule. For details contact the operator below:
Operator: Navigazione Lago Maggiore, Viale F. Baracca, 28041 Arona, Italy. ☎ 322 46 651　Fax: 322 25 95 30

Lago di Garda: 🚢 services link Desenzano, Peschiera, Garda, Salo, Gardone and Riva, (April to September only), on an irregular schedule. For details contact the operator below:
Operator: Navigazione sul Lago di Garda, Piazza Matteotti, 25015 Desenzano, Italy.　☎ 30 91 41 321, 30 91 41 323　Fax: 30 91 44 640

Lago Di Como: 🚢 services link Como, Lecco, Bellagio, Menaggio, Varenna, Bellano and Colico, (April to September only), on an irregular schedule. For details contact the operator below:
Hydrofoil service: **March 27 - September 25, 1994**

		E	C	C		C		Ⓑ		
Como .... d.		0735	0840	1100	1215	1330	1430	1615	1710	1755 1905
Tremezzo .... d.		0806	0910	1139	1252	1410	1500	1653	1748	1833 1943
Bellagio .... d.		0812	0917	1146	1259	1417	1507	1700	1755	1840 1950
Menaggio .... d.		0819	0924	1153	1306	1424	1514	1707	1802	1847 1957
Tremezzo .... d.		0838	0932	1202	1318	1437	1522	1715	1811	1900 2005
Colico .... a.		0855	1000	1229	1345	1511	1556	1742	...	1927 2032

		G	E	E		E	C		Ⓑ	⑥
Colico .... d.		0605	0605	0723	...	0940	1005	1346	1557	1744	... 1927
Bellano .... d.		0633	0633	0751	...	1015	1038	1414	1632	1809	...	
Menaggio .... d.		0641	0800	0813	1024	1047	1422	1641	1817	1842 1950
Bellagio .... d.		0647	0807	0806	1031	1054	1429	1648	1824	1849 1956
Tremezzo .... d.		0653	0813	0820	1038	1101	1435	1655	1830	1855 2002
Como .... a.		0726	0730	0850	0852	1110	1130	1511	1730	1900 1927 2030

– ⑦ and holidays.　　G – Mar. 27 - June 18, Sept. 11 - 25, 1994
– June 19 - Sept. 11, 1994
Operator: Navigazione Lago di Como, Via Rubini 22, 22100 Como, Italy. ☎ 31 27 33 24,　31 26 02 34　Fax: 31 27 03 05

Table 365 — BRIG - ARONA - MILANO

1, 2 class except where shown

Southbound (part 1)

km	station	D 10601 2	9163 2	D 10605 2	D 2579 2 ✗	4907	D 2551 2	4913	E 331 ⚲	4915 2	9091 2	E 321 ⚲ J	4917	IC813 EC39	EC 39 ✗ M	10609 2 ✗	IC 323 ✗	10611	4923
	Genève Aéroport 270 d.											0721			0808		1024		
	Genève 270 d.											0731			0820		1034		
	Lausanne 270 d.											0809			0857		1113		
	Bern 280 d.						0650						0851						
0	Brig d.				0701		0755		0822		0905	0934	1008	1031	1031		1238		1341
22	Iselle di Trasquera ⛰ d.				0718		0814				0923		1025				1307		1400
42	Domodossola a.				0735		0831		0850		0940	1002	1042	1100	1100		1320		1418
42	Domodossola d.	0500	0555	0603	0655	0740			0905		0948	1015		1113	1113	1215	1320	1357	
72	Verbania-Pallanza d.	0522	0614	0627	0716	0758			0928		1019	1037		1132	1132	1257		1436	1442
77	Baveno d.	0528	0619	0632		0803			0932		1024			1140	1140	1302			1447
81	Stresa d.	0533	0625	0637	0727	0808			0938		1029	1045		1153	1153	1302	1344		1447
98	Arona d.	0552	0645	0658	0739	0824			0952		1047	1058		1211	1211	1323	1355		1510
124	Gallarate d.	0623		0730	0806	0853			1015		1122	1119				1433		1546	
	Milano Porta Garibaldi a.	0717		0815	0843	0926													
166	Milano Centrale a.								1045			1145		1240	1240		1445		
	Roma Termini 370 a.																		

Southbound (part 2)

station	E 333 ⚲	4927 ⚲	E 327	10613 2	4831 Ⓐ	EC 91 ✗	4933	10615 2	IC 335 ⚲	10615	4939	E 337 / 1530	4943	9097 2	IC 329	4947	E 311 ◆ C	EN311 EN313	EN 313 ◆	E 221
Genève Aéroport 270 d.			1238						1525						1906		2015	2015		2252
Genève 270 d.			1248						1535						1916		2025	2025		2302
Lausanne 270 d.			1332						1613			1756			1953		2110	2110		2345
Bern 280 d.	1256				1522							1722							2122	
Brig d.	1431	1504	1517		1650	1702	1719		1738		1815	1902		2003	2118	2138	2304	2332	2332	0130
Iselle di Trasquera ⛰ d.		1522				1708	1737				1835			2021		2157				
Domodossola a.	1500	1541	1547		1725	1732	1755		1807		1853	1932		2038	2147	2214	2334	0004	0004	0200
Domodossola d.	1515		1602	1640	1745		1802	1820			1945			2055	2202		2347		0030	0215
Verbania-Pallanza d.	1534		1624	1717	1804			1850							2126	2224			0005	
Baveno d.				1722				1856		←					2131					
Stresa d.	1542		1632	1727	1813			1902		1902					2136	2233			0013	
Arona d.	1555		1646	1748	1826		→		1856	1923					2155	2247			0025	
Gallarate d.	1616		1709	1821	1844						2000				2224	2311	0043			0337n
Milano Porta Garibaldi a.			1856								2044				2252		0108			
Milano Centrale a.	1645	1745							1915		1945				2115		2345			
Roma Termini 370 a.															0800t				0923	0923

Northbound (part 3)

station	EN 314 ◆	EN314 1906 C	4910	10600 ✗	E 312 ⚲	9086 2	IC 320 ⚲	4916	E 332	IC 330	4920	10602 2	EC 90 ✗	4926 ⚲	E 334 ⚲	D 2552 2	10604	IC 322 ⚲	4932	10604 2
Roma Termini 370 d.	2100	2100			2155t															
Milano Centrale d.							0725		0825	0905			1025		1225			1400		
Milano Porta Garibaldi d.				0455	0625	0650	0726	0756	0856			0920		1056		1238	1322			
Gallarate d.				0549	0652		0756	0816	0915	0953	1002	1031	1116	1116	1316	1308	1356		1430	
Arona d.				0621	0711		0755	0816	0929	1006	1052	1129	1330	1330	1402	1402			1504	1430
Stresa d.				0645	0724			0817			1057				1407				1509	1504
Baveno d.				0650				0822											1516	1509
Verbania-Pallanza d.				0656	0733		0822	0839	0938		1104	1138	1138	1338	1413		1506		1531	1555
Domodossola a.	0550	0550		0733	0758	0854	0900		0958	1033	1158	1158	1213	1341	1358	1411	1544	1612	1548	1555
Domodossola d.	0609	0609	0650		0813		0915	0921		1046	1138		1213	1341	1418	1440				
Iselle di Trasquera ⛰ d.			0713					0944			1201			1405						
Brig a.	0639	0639	0729		0843		0945	0957	1040	1114	1216		1243	1418	1613	1612	1628			
Bern 280 a.	0838				1027		1127			1201		1240	1438		1740					
Lausanne 270 a.			0827		1112		1212			1316					1817					
Genève 270 a.			0912		1112		1212			1326					1817					
Genève Aéroport 270 a.			0924		1124		1224			1326					1830					

Northbound (part 4)

station	E 336 ⚲	4936	E 326 ⚲	4938 Ⓐ	9092 2	EC40 40 IC498 ✗	D 9166 M	4940 ✗	10606 2	E 328 ⚲	10610 2	D 2560 2	4948	10612 2	E 220 ◆
Roma Termini 370 d.					1725	1725									
Milano Centrale d.	1525		1625							1905					0138n
Milano Porta Garibaldi d.				1650				1730				2250			
Gallarate d.	1556		1656		1724	1754	1754	1813	1940	2047	2144	2356			
Arona d.	1617		1716		1750	1815	1815	1832	1845	2000 2120	2205	0025			
Stresa d.	1630		1729		1807	1828	1828	1854	1900	2013 2142	2217	0045			
Baveno d.					1811			1900	1912	2018 2147	2222	0050			
Verbania-Pallanza d.	1639		1738		1816	1837	1837	1925	1918	2024 2153	2228	0056			0305
Domodossola a.	1658		1758		1848	1858	1858	1925	1952	2045 2218	2251	0127			0325
Domodossola d.	1713	1718	1813	1835	1913	1913	1938		2100			2255			0325
Iselle di Trasquera ⛰ d.		1742		1857			2001		2016			2316			0355
Brig a.	1743	1755	1843	1911	1943	1943	2016		2130			2330			0355
Bern 280 a.	1938					2138									0555
Lausanne 270 a.			2027		2111				2255						0555
Genève 270 a.			2112		2148				2332						0639
Genève Aéroport 270 a.			2124		2158										0649

◆ – NOTES (LISTED BY TRAIN NUMBERS)

EC39/40 – MONTEVERDI – 🛏 and ✗ Genève Aéroport ✈ - Venezia Santa Lucia.
EC90/1 – VAUBAN – 🛏 and ✗ Brussels Midi - Milano and v.v.
E220/1 – SIMPLON EXPRESS – 🛏 1,2 cl., 🛏 2 cl. and 🛏 Genève Aéroport ✈ - Zagreb and v.v.; 🛏 2 cl. and 🛏 Genève Aéroport ✈ - Venezia Santa Lucia and v.v. Sleeping cars in the Zagreb portion run to/from Venezia Mestre.
E311/2 – 🛏 Genève - Napoli Centrale and v.v.

EN313/4 – ROMA – 🛏 1,2 cl. and ➞ 2 cl. Basel SBB - Roma and v.v.
C – ROMA – 🛏 1,2 cl., 🛏 1,2 cl. (T2) and ➞ 2 cl. Genève Aéroport ✈ - Roma and v.v.
J – May 29 - Jan. 2. From Jan. 3 runs 7 minutes earlier.
M – 🛏 Basel SBB - Venezia Santa Lucia and v.v.
n – Milano Lambrate.
t – Roma Tiburtina.

Table 366 DOMODOSSOLA and ARONA - ALESSANDRIA

2 class only

km		10257	10253	10315	D9131	D9163	D2893	4607	10281	10273	D9133	4611	10285		10277	10259	10317	4615	10295	10287	10267	10269	4749	4659
			⚒	⚒					⚒		⑦		⑦				⚒		⑦	⚒			⚒	
0	**Domodossola** d.	...	...	0442	0530	0555	...	...	0642	...	0812	...	0927	...	...	...	1240	...	1255	1350	...	...	...	1606
38	Omegna d.	...	...	0533	0623	|	...	...	0742	...	0848	...	1028	...	...	...	1328	...	1340	1436	...	...	...	1654
60	Borgomanero d.	...	...	0554	0658	|	...	...	0811	...	0912	...	1056	...	...	...	1353	...	1411	1505	...	...	...	1721
	Arona d.	...	0552	|	|	0645	...	0755	|	...	|	1005	|	...	1205	...	|	1400	|	|	...	1603	...	|
	Oleggio d.	...	0616	|	|	0709	...	0817	|	...	|	1026	|	...	1231	...	|	1422	|	|	...	1632	...	|
90	**Novara** d.	...	0635	0640	0728	0724	...	0834	0847	...	0936	1044	1135	...	1251	...	1425	1441	1449	1544	...	1649	...	1754
90	**Novara** d.	0605	...	*0707*	...	...	0731	...	...	0915	...	...	...	...	...	1310	...	...	...	...	1605	...	1705	...
157	**Alessandria** a.	0726	...	*0848*	...	...	0817	...	...	1020	...	...	...	...	...	1427	...	...	...	...	1707	...	1812	...
	Genova Piazza Principe **360** a.	...	...	...	...	...	0922	...	...	...	...	...	...	...	...	...	...	...	...	...	...	...	...	...

	4599	10289	10275	D9125	10291	4619	D9135	10293	4601	D9127
	⑦	⚒		⑦	⚒		⑦	⚒		⑦
Domodossola d.	...	1722	...	1823	1832	...	1930	1930	...	2028
Omegna d.	...	1811	...	1854	1932	...	2003	2021	...	2105
Borgomanero d.	...	1846	...	1918	1956	...	2025	2050	...	2127
Arona d.	...	|	1836	|	|	2015	|	|	2112	|
Oleggio d.	...	|	1908	|	|	2040	|	|	2133	|
Novara d.	...	1925	1932	1949	2031	2055	2049	2125	2153	2149
Novara d.	1910	...	...	*2028*	...	...	...	...	...	...
Alessandria a.	2016	...	...	*2132*	...	...	...	...	...	...
Genova Piazza Principe **360** a.	...	...	...	...	...	...	...	...	...	...

	10282	10250	10316	4604	D9132	4654	4606	10284	10278
	⚒	⚒	⚒		⑦	⚒		⑦	
Genova Piazza Principe **360** d.	...	...	...	...	...	...	...	...	...
Alessandria d.	...	...	...	...	...	...	...	...	*0845*
Novara a.	...	...	...	...	...	...	...	...	*0956*
Novara d.	0534	0554	0618	0705	0822	0824	0905	0918	1006
Oleggio d.	|	0617	|	0728	|	|	0922	|	1024
Arona a.	|	0639	|	0750	|	|	0943	|	1050
Borgomanero d.	0612	...	0714	...	0847	0907	...	1000	...
Omegna d.	0647	...	0741	...	0909	0933	...	1027	...
Domodossola a.	0732	...	0827	...	0941	1015	...	1110	...

	D9134	10286	4610	10288	10260	10290	10258	10262	10292		10294	10268	4618	D9166	10314	10318	10276	10270	D2900	10296	10280	D2522	4612	10274
	⑦	⚒				⚒	⚒								⑦	⚒								
Genova Piazza Principe **360** d.	...	...	...	...	...	...	...	...	...	...	...	...	...	...	...	...	...	...	1717	...	...	...	...	...
Alessandria d.	...	...	...	...	*1244*	...	1350	1445	...	...	...	...	1644	...	...	...	1740	...	1821	...	1922	...	...	2045
Novara a.	...	...	...	...	*1347*	...	1505	1554	...	...	...	...	1747	...	...	...	1842	...	1917	...	2015	...	...	2147
Novara d.	1022	1022	1255	1322	1415	1422	...	...	1605	...	1718	1740	...	1803	1810	1824	...	1908	...	1926	...	2020	2115	...
Oleggio d.	|	|	1311	|	1438	|	...	...	|	...	|	1757	...	1819	|	|	...	1927	...	|	...	2039	2134	...
Arona a.	|	|	1331	|	1504	|	...	...	|	...	|	1818	...	1831	|	|	...	1950	...	|	...	2101	2156	...
Borgomanero d.	1058	1059	...	1409	...	1507	...	...	1645	...	1803	...	...	|	1848	1904	...	...	...	2013	...	...	...	...
Omegna d.	1122	1127	...	1438	...	1535	...	...	1717	...	1836	...	...	|	1917	1931	...	...	...	2045	...	...	...	...
Domodossola a.	1155	1213	...	1524	...	1620	...	...	1810	...	1926	...	...	1925	2005	2014	...	...	...	2136	...	...	...	...

Table 367 PARMA and FIDENZA - SARZANA and LA SPEZIA

1, 2 class except where shown

km		3101	11905	11907	2295	6775	2147	2271	2151	🚌	11911	6755	11915	6759	11917	6761	11921	6763	6789	11923	2149	🚌	2301	6765	11925
		2	2	2	G❖	2⚒		❖	❖		2	2⚒	2	2⚒	2	2⚒	2	2	2⚒	2⚒	M	...	B	2⚒	2
0	**Parma** d.	...	0517	0618	0731	0805	...	0913	...	...	1035	...	1255	...	1455	...	1630	...	1725	1755	...	...	1900	...	2045
	Fidenza d.	...	|	|	|	|	0835	|	0910	...	|	1248	|	1454	|	1613	|	1719	|	|	1833	...	|	2019	|
23	Fornovo d.	...	0539	0641	0757	0827	0851	0928	0938	...	1056	1312	1318	1515	1520	1638	1654	1744	1749	1820	1850	...	1919	2039	2105
61	Borgo Val di Taro d.	0550	0616	0729	0840	...	0923	...	1008	...	1131	...	1402	...	1556	...	1736	...	1831	1905	1919	...	2000	...	2144
79	Pontremoli d.	0606	0632	0748	0859	...	0945	...	1026	...	1148	...	1421	...	1612	...	1754	...	1848	1923	1937	...	2017	...	2205
100	Aulla d.	0627	0658	0816	0926	...	1002	...	1045	...	1213	...	1451	...	*1712*	...	1822	...	...	...	2002	2016	2037	...	2223t
108	San Stefano di Magra d.	0636	0708	0824	0932	...	1010	...	1053	1100	1222	...	1500	...	*1720*	...	1834	...	...	...	2012	|	2049	...	2231t
116	**Sarzana** a.	0644	|	|	|	...	1018	...	1101	|	|	...	|	...	|	...	|	...	...	...	2021	2042	|	...	|
120	**La Spezia Centrale** a.	...	0725	0840	0944	...	...	...	...	1120	1239	...	1515	...	*1738*	...	1852	...	...	...	...		2103	...	2245t

	6772	11906	2146	6774	2292	11910	11912	6756	11914	6758	11916	6760	11918	🚌	6764	11922	11924	🚌	2152	2272	6794	2298	2148	🚌	3140
	2⚒	2	M	2⚒	B	2	2	2⚒	2	2⚒	2	2⚒	2	⑦	2⚒	2⚒	2		❖	❖	2	G	M		2
La Spezia Centrale d.	...	0628	...	...	0756	0900	1002	...	1220	...	1324	...	1520	...	...	1727	1820	1855	...	...	...	2007	...	2045	...
Sarzana d.	...	|	0710	...	|	|	|	...	|	...	|	...	|	...	...	|	|	|	1912	...	...	|	2045	|	2107
San Stefano di Magra d.	...	0645	0718	...	0807	0915	1021	...	1236	...	1345	...	1536	...	...	1744	1835	1915	1925	...	...	2022	2053	2100	2114
Aulla d.	...	0659	0727	...	0815	0923	1046	...	1246	...	1353	...	1553	...	...	1754	1843	...	1933	...	...	2038	2101	...	2123
Pontremoli d.	0630	0726	0750	...	0836	0943	1112	...	1312	...	1419	...	1619	...	...	1822	1909	...	1952	...	...	2058	2123	...	2142
Borgo Val di Taro d.	0646	0745	0810	...	0855	1002	1131	...	1329	...	1442	...	1636	...	...	...	1928	...	2011	...	2038	2114	2145	...	...
Fornovo d.	0729	0830	0852	0900	0931	...	1208	1321	1417	1421	1522	1525	1714	1720	1753	...	2005	...	2040	2048	2106	2151	2215	...	...
Fidenza a.	|	|	0909	|	|	...	|	1344	|	1444	|	1550	|	1800	1815	...	|	...	2101	|	|	|	2230	...	...
Parma a.	0757	0854	...	0926	0949	...	1229	...	1440	...	1544	...	1738	...	...	...	2025	...	...	2106	2126	2212	...	...	...

– (12) Genova - Bologna and v.v. G – (12) Genova - Parma and v.v. M – (12) Milano - Livorno and v.v. t – ⚒ only. ❖ – **Not** Dec. 25., Jan. 1.

Table 368 CAMPIGLIA MARITTIMA - PIOMBINO MARITTIMA

16 km — 2 class only

From Campiglia: 0610⚒, 0627 🚌, 0730⚒, 1300⚒, 1357⚒, 1445⚒, 1536, 1720 🚌, 1837⚒ 🚌, 1920 🚌, 2000⚒, 2020 🚌, 2105⚒, 2205 🚌.

From Piombino Marittima: 0638⚒, 0710 🚌, 0802⚒, 0840, 1330⚒, 1438⚒, 1512⚒, 1618, 2027⚒, 2133⚒. Additional services operate between Oct. 10 and Mar. 27. Details locally.

Table 369 FIRENZE - PISA - LIVORNO

1, 2 class except where shown

km		11703	D3103	11707	D3105	D3107	IC603	D3109	D3111	11709	D3161	D3113	D3115	D3117	D3119	D3121	IC623	11713	D3123	D3125	D3127	D3129	D3133	D3135
		⚒	⚒	2			M	⚒		2	2						N							
0	**Firenze SMN** d.	0440	0553	0648	0705	0735	0755	0805	0835	0845	...	0935	1005	1035	1105	1135	1205	...	1235	1305	1335	1405	1435	1505
34	Empoli d.	0516	0621	0721	0731	0802	0820	0837	0902	0923	...	1002	1032	1102	1132	1202	|	...	1302	1332	1402	1432	1502	1532
81	**Pisa Centrale** d.	0610	0659	0810	0803	0833	0853	0912	0933	1015	1030	1033	1103	1133	1203	1233	1253	1258	1333	1403	1433	1503	1533	1603
	Pisa Aeroporto ✈ a.	|	|	...	|	|	...	0917	|	...	1035	|	1108	|	1208	|	...	1303	|	1408	|	1508	|	1608
101	**Livorno** a.	0626	0713	...	0817	0847	...	...	0947	...	...	1047	...	1147	...	1247	...	...	1347	...	1454	...	1547	...

	D3137	D3139	D3141	D3143	D3145	D3147	D3149	P527	11735	11737
								R⚡		
Firenze SMN d.	1535	1605	1635	1705	1735	1835	1935	2042t	2135	2235
Empoli d.	1602	1632	1702	1732	1802	1902	2002	|	2210	2308
Pisa Centrale d.	1633	1703	1733	1803	1833	1933	2033	2124	2259	2348
Pisa Aeroporto ✈ a.	|	1708	|	1808	|	|	|	...	|	|
Livorno a.	1647	...	1747	...	1847	1947	2047	...	2315	0003

	11700	11702	D3100	11716	11856	P524	D3104	IC626	D3106
	⚒					R⚡		L	
Livorno d.	0445	0530	0630	0715	0729	...	0805	...	0905
Pisa Aeroporto ✈ d.	|	|	|	|	|	...	|	...	|
Pisa Centrale d.	0510	0549	0648	0732	0750	0814	0821	0904	0921
Empoli d.	0603	0629	0722	0802	0840	|	0854	|	0951
Firenze SMN a.	0640	0700	0752	0834	0913	0856t	0920	0949t	1017

	11864	D3108	D3110	D3114	D3116	D3118	D3120	D3124	D3126	D3128	D3130	11726	D3122	D3136	D3138	D3142	11740	D3144	D3132	D3146	D3170	IC618	11738	11742
	2																		2	⚒	2	M	2	
Livorno d.	0923	...	1105	...	1205	...	1305	...	1405	...	1505	...	1533	1605	...	1705	...	1805	...	1905	...	...	2145	...
Pisa Aeroporto ✈ d.	|	1044	|	1144	|	1244	|	1344	|	1444	|	1541	|	|	1644	|	1753	|	...	|	2025	...	|	2350
Pisa Centrale d.	0943	1051	1121	1151	1221	1251	1321	1351	1421	1451	1521	1546	1551	1621	1651	1721	1758	1821	1852	1921	2030	2104	2212	2357
Empoli d.	1031	1121	1151	1221	1251	1321	1351	1421	1451	1521	1551	...	1621	1651	1721	1751	...	1851	1922	1951	...	2136	2301	0035
Firenze SMN a.	1110	1147	1217	1247	1317	1347	1417	1447	1517	1547	1617	...	1647	1717	1747	1817	...	1917	1952	2017	...	2202	2330	0110

– (12) and 🍷 Genova Porta Principe - Roma Termini.
– (12) Firenze - Torino Porto Nuova and v.v.
– (12) and 🍷 Napoli Centrale - Torino Porto Nuova.

R – (12) and ✕ Roma Termini - Genova - Savona and v.v.
t – Firenze **Rifredi**.
⚡ – **ETR450** Pendolino supplement payable.

Table 370
MILANO - BOLOGNA - FIRENZE - ROMA
For additional (slower) trains between Firenze and Roma see Table 385

1, 2 class except where shown

km		IC 551	IC 729	E 235	IC 553	E 1085	IC 731	E 1235	P 501	P 525	IC 555	E 289	IR 2123	IR 1711	P 503	IC 713	IC 565	IR 2033	IR 2147	P 505	P 507	IC 533	IR 2285
0	Milano Centrale d.					0357n							0605	0625	0655	0705	0710			0750		0800	0842
72	Piacenza d.										0618		0651	0721	0751	0811	0830			0831			0904
107	Fidenza d.										0638		0712	0749	0812	0830				0855			0917
129	Parma d.					0510					0651		0726	0806	0826								0932
157	Reggio Emilia d.					0527					0707		0742	0828	0842								0945
182	Modena d.					0542					0722		0756	0845	0856								1008
219	Bologna Centrale a.					0605			0747		0822	0912	0830		0855	0922	0928		0936	0944			1008
219	Bologna Centrale d.			0545	0600	0610	0634	0741	0751			0801	0842		0833	0848	IC 627		0931	0939	0948		IC 733
300	Prato d.					0653						0842				0952				1024			
313	Firenze Rifredi d.					0729c			0839	0859			0930										
316	Firenze SMN a.			0656	0709			0753			0856	0912			0953					1028	1040	1053	1110
316	Firenze SMN d.	0605	0630	0705	0718		0735				0905				1002					1102			
404	Arezzo d.	0711				0817																	1151
438	Terontola-Cortona d.	0731				0839																	
467	Chiusi d.	0750				0859			1015														1222
632	Roma Tiburtina a.					0948									1105								
632	Roma Termini a.	0855	0830	0930	0910	1007			1035	1055					1155				1230	1205	1215	1255	1330
	Napoli Centrale 405 a.					1218					1300												1500

		IR 2125	IC 715	IC 535	IR 2293	IC 557	IR 2035	IC 537	IC 567	IR 2127	P 1503	IC 717	IC 569	D 2919	IC 539	IR 2129	P 509	IR 735	EC 55	IC 573	IR 2131	IC 541	IR 2133	P 511	IC 33027
	Milano Centrale d.	0805		0900		0905		1000	1005		1055		1105			1200	1205	1255		1300	1305	1320	1400	1405		1522
	Piacenza d.	0851				0944	0951	1041	1051				1148		1251						1406		1451			1522
	Fidenza d.	0912				1002	1012		1112				1209		1312						1427		1512			1551
	Parma d.	0926			0952	1015	1026		1126				1222		1326						1440		1526			
	Reggio Emilia d.	0942			1011	1031	1042		1142				1240		1342						1457		1542			
	Modena d.	0956			1030	1046	1056		1156				1256		1356						1515		1556			
	Bologna Centrale a.	1020	1044	1055	1108	1120		1144	1155	1220	1230		1255	1324	1344	1422	1430		1444		1555	1544	1620			1636
	Bologna Centrale d.		1039	1048		1112			1148		1233	1248		1348		1433	1448		1530		1548		1633			1730
	Prato d.					1204						1330						1530								1730
	Firenze Rifredi d.										1330					1453		1530								
	Firenze SMN a.		1144	1153		1220		1253			1353				1453	1502			1510	1553		1653				
	Firenze SMN d.		1153	1202		1229		1302			1402				1502				1551	1602		1702				
	Arezzo d.					1307														1551						
	Terontola-Cortona d.														1626											
	Chiusi d.					1335																				
	Roma Tiburtina a.																									
	Roma Termini a.		1345	1355		1440		1455			1505	1605			1655	1705	1740	1755			1855		1905			
	Napoli Centrale 405 a.														1900						2100					

		IC 543	IC 1575	EC 31	EC 85	IR 2037	IC 545	IR 2135	IC 53	IC 737	E 1995	IC 577	P 1505	IC 2287	IC 831	IR 2149	IC 559	IR 2137	IR 2139	P 513	P 515	IR 2289	IC 723	IC 547	E 1981
	Milano Centrale d.	1500	1454p			1600	1605	1700			1635	1705	1750		1645	1715	1755	1800	1845	1930	1940			2000	1945
	Piacenza d.					1551	1651	1712				1744	1751		1802	1842	1851	1940		1952			2020		2050
	Fidenza d.					1612	1712	1726				1811	1826		1907	1926	2001			2033			2054		
	Parma d.					1626	1726	1742				1827	1829		1922	1942	2031			2054					
	Reggio Emilia d.					1642	1742	1756				1843	1856	IC 719	1936	1956	2048			2108					
	Modena d.					1656	1756					1908	1920	1932	1958	2020	2125			2115	2136			2145	2158
	Bologna Centrale a.	1644	1658			1720	1820	1844	1855		1900	1929	1920	1932	1958	2002	2125			2118		2139	2149		2203
	Bologna Centrale d.	1648		1710	1720	1748		1848			1900	1932	1938	1948	2002		2054					2232	2242		2335
	Prato d.	1739											2030	2055c						2215					2335
	Firenze Rifredi d.																								
	Firenze SMN a.	1753		1816	1826			1853	1953	2028			2053	2110						2248	2258				
	Firenze SMN d.	1802		1825	1835			1902	2002	2010	2037			2102	2119					2307					2350
	Arezzo d.										2051			2133	2157		2218								
	Terontola-Cortona d.									2126	2152			2210											0055
	Chiusi d.										2311			2318											0209
	Roma Tiburtina a.																								
	Roma Termini a.	1955		2020	2030			2055	2155	2245			2205		2255					2330	2353				0422
	Napoli Centrale 405 a.							2300																	0422

◆ – NOTES (LISTED BY TRAIN NUMBERS)

EC31 – ROMULUS – 🚃 and ✗ Wien Südbahnhof - Roma; ✗ Salzburg - Roma.
EC53 – COLOSSEUM – 🚃 and ✗ Basel SBB - Roma.
EC55 – RAFFAELLO – 🚃 and ✗ Zürich Hbf - Roma.
EC85 – MICHELANGELO – 🚃 and ✗ München Hbf - Roma.
E235 – REMUS – 🛏 1,2 cl., 🛋 2 cl. and 🚃 Wien Südbahnhof - Roma.
E289 – BRENNER EXPRESS – 🛏 1,2 cl., 🛋 2 cl. and 🚃 München Hbf - Firenze.
P501 – VERONESE – ✗ 🚃 and ✗ Venezia Santa Lucia - Roma.
P503 – BOTTICELLI – 🚃 and ✗ Milano - Roma.
P507 – GUIDO RENI – Ⓐ, not Dec. 24 - Jan. 8: 🚃 and ✗ Torino Porta Nuova - Roma.
P511 – CARACCI – ✗, also Dec. 25, Apr. 16, 30: 🚃 and ✗ Venezia Santa Lucia - Roma.
P513 – TINTORETTO – Ⓐ, not Dec. 25 - Jan. 8: 🚃 and ✗ Milano - Roma.
P525 – CIMABUE – Ⓐ, not Dec. 25 - Jan. 8: 🚃 and ✗ Savona (P523) - Genova Piazza Principe - Pisa (P524) - Firenze - Roma.
IC539 – PARTENOPE – 🚃 Milano - Salerno; ✗ Milano - Napoli.
IC559 – TACITO – 🚃 Milano - Arezzo - Perugia - Terni; ♈ Milano - Bologna.
IC565 – ADRIATICO – 🚃 Milano - Lecce; ✗ Milano - Bari Centrale.
IC567 – ROSSINI – 🚃 and ♈ Torino Porta Nuova - Ancona - Bari Centrale.
IC569 – MURGE – 🚃 Milano - Lecce; 🚃 Milano - Bari Centrale - Taranto; ✗ Milano - Bari.
IC573 – BRERA – 🚃 and ✗ Milano - Ancona - Bari Centrale.
IC577 – D'ANNUNZIO – 🚃 Milano - Pescara Centrale; ♈ Milano - Ancona.
IC627 – CRISTOFORO COLOMBO – 🚃 and ♈ Genova Piazza Principe (IC605) - Pisa (IC626) - Firenze - Roma.
IC713 – PALLADIO – 🚃 and ✗ Venezia Santa Lucia - Roma.
IC715 – MIRAMARE – 🚃 and ♈ Trieste Centrale - Roma.

IC717 – MARCO POLO – 🚃 Udine - Roma; 🚃 Bolzano - Roma; ✗ Venezia Mestre - Roma.
IC719 – BRENTA – 🚃 and ♈ Venezia Santa Lucia - Roma.
IC723 – DANTE – 🚃 Venezia Santa Lucia - Firenze; ♈ Rovigo - Firenze.
E1085 – Dec. 17, 24 and Apr. 14 only (from Stuttgart): ← 2 cl. and 🚃 Stuttgart - Napoli; 🚃 Zürich Hbf - Napoli.
E1235 – Dec. 26 - Jan. 8, Apr. 7 - 23, May 19 - 27 (from Wien): ← 2 cl. and 🚃 Wien Südbahnhof - Firenze.
P1505 – ⑦: 🚃 and ✗ Milano - Roma.
IC1575 – ① - ⑤, not Dec. 10 - Jan. 9, Apr. 13 - 20: 🚃 Milano - Pescara.
IR1711 – ⑥⑦, also Apr. 17, 25, not Dec. 25, Jan. 1, Apr. 16, 23, 30: 🚃 Milano - Pescara Centrale.
IR2033 – 🚃 Torino Porta Nuova - Bologna - Rimini. Not Dec. 25, Jan. 1.
IR2125 – ✗: 🚃 Milano - Bologna; ⑦ 🚃 Milano - Ancona.
IR2127 – 🚃 Milano - Ancona.
IC33027 – 🚃 Torino - Alessandria - Piacenza - Bologna.
A – 🚃 Milano - Ancona.
G – 🚃 Genova Piazza Principe - Voghera - Piacenza - Bologna.
H – 🚃 Genova Piazza Principe - Aulla - Parma - Bologna.
L – 🚃 Milano - Aulla - Livorno.
T – 🚃 Torino Porta Nuova - Bologna.
c – Firenze Campo di Marte.
n – Milano Lambrate.
p – Milano Porta Garibaldi.
✔ – Pendolino supplement payable.
◆ – Long distance express service - not available for local journeys. For days of running and composition see Table 400.

Table 370

MILANO - BOLOGNA - FIRENZE - ROMA

For additional (slower) trains between Firenze and Roma see Table 385

1, 2 class except where shown

	IR 2141	E 1771	E 1997	IR 2039	E 923	IC 33321	E 901	E 1951	IR 2143	E 925	E 823	E 1983	E 903	E 1757	E 1911	E 845	E 1913	E 1763	E 825	E 841		E 311		E 287
		♦	♣	✤ T			♦	♦			♦	♣	♦	♦	♦	♦	♦	♦	♦	♦		♦		♦
Milano Centrale d.	2005	...	2015	...	2105	2115	...	2200	2205	2210	2215	2220	...	...	2255	...	2330	...	0015	...	...	0139n	...	...
Piacenza d.	2052	...	|	2151	|	2200	2221	|	2251	|	2302	2307	2317	...	2345	...	0018	...	0104	...	...	0221	...	...
Fidenza d.	2113	...	|	2212	|	2223	2243	2305	2312	|	2324	2330	2344	...	0009	...	|	...	0126	...	...	|	...	...
Parma d.	2126	...	|	2226	|	2239	2258	|	2326	|	2339	2346	0003	...	0027	...	|	...	0142	...	...	0255	...	...
Reggio Emilia d.	2142	...	|	2242	|	2256	2317	|	2342	|	2358	0008	0026	...	0048	...	|	...	|	...	...	|	...	...
Modena d.	2156	...	|	2256	|	2312	2334	|	2356	|	0015	0027	0045	...	0107	...	|	...	|	...	...	|	...	...
Bologna Centrale a.	2220	...	2230	2320	2330	2338	0003	0013	0020	0030	0048	0102	0118	...	0138	...	0200	...	0239	...	...	0350	...	...
Bologna Centrale d.	...	2224	2236	...	...	2342	...	...	...	...	0053	0107	...	0135	0145	0155	0205	0215	0259	0310	...	0355	...	0415
Prato d.	...	|	|	...	...	0038	...	...	...	...	|	|	...	|	|	|	|	|	|	0412	...	|	...	|
Firenze Rifredi d.	...	2355c	0008c	...	...	|	...	...	...	...	0228c	0238c	...	|	0340c	0350c	0400c	0405c	0423c	0440c	...	|	...	0538c
Firenze SMN a.	...	|	|	...	...	0059	...	...	...	...	|	|	...	|	|	|	|	|	|	|	...	0514	...	|
Firenze SMN d.	...	|	|	...	...	...	...	...	...	...	|	|	...	|	|	|	|	|	|	|	...	0523	...	|
Arezzo d.	...	|	|	...	...	...	...	...	...	...	0330	|	...	|	|	|	|	0455	0507	0530	...	|	...	0619
Terontola-Cortona d.	...	|	|	...	...	...	...	...	...	...	|	|	...	|	|	|	0550	0521	|	0602	...	|	...	|
Chiusi d.	...	|	0127	...	...	...	...	...	...	...	|	|	...	|	|	|	|	0546	0539	0640	...	0637	...	0655
Roma Tiburtina a.	...	0220	|	...	...	...	...	...	...	...	0524	0542	...	0654	0610	|	|	0716	|	|	...	0800	...	|
Roma Termini a.	...	|	|	...	...	...	...	...	...	...	|	|	...	...	|	0625	0835	...	0710	0825	...	|	...	0815
Napoli Centrale **405** a.	...	0433v	0506	...	...	...	...	...	...	...	0816	0830	...	...	0850	0915v	...	...	...	...	...	1031	...	1038

	IR 2120	E 1910	E 1912	IR 2122	E 1770	E 1950	E 922	IR 2034	E 924	IR 2124	E 1982	IC 1574	IR 2276	E 388	IC 532	IC 712	IR 2126	IC 566	E 834	P⚡ 500	IC 550	E 1996	E 1980	E 832
	⚒	♦	♦		♦	♦	♦	T	♣		♣	♦	G	♦	🍷		A	🍷 ♦	♣	✕ Ⓡ ♦	♦	♣	♣	♣
Napoli Centrale **405** d.	...	...	...	...	...	...	...	...	...	...	...	...	...	...	...	...	...	...	0240	...	...	0259	0311	0356
Roma Termini d.	...	2330	...	...	...	...	...	...	...	...	0225	...	...	...	...	...	...	...	|	0655	...	|	|	|
Roma Tiburtina d.	...	|	2347	...	0123	...	...	...	...	...	|	...	...	...	...	...	...	...	0456	|	...	0530	0540	0618
Chiusi d.	...	|	0156	...	|	...	...	...	...	...	|	...	...	...	...	...	...	...	0613	|	...	0652	0702	0747
Terontola-Cortona d.	...	0218	|	...	|	...	...	...	...	...	|	...	...	...	...	...	...	...	|	|	0725	|	|	|
Arezzo d.	...	|	|	...	|	...	...	...	...	...	|	...	...	...	0615	...	...	...	|	|	0746	|	|	|
Firenze SMN a.	...	|	|	...	|	...	...	...	...	...	|	...	...	...	0651	...	...	...	|	|	0823	|	|	0856
Firenze SMN d.	...	|	|	...	|	...	...	...	...	...	|	...	...	...	0700	0715	...	...	|	|	0835	|	|	0905
Firenze Rifredi d.	...	0335c	0348c	...	0425c	...	...	...	...	...	0502c	...	...	...	|	|	...	...	0737c	0832	|	0808c	0907c	|
Prato d.	...	|	|	...	|	...	...	...	...	...	|	...	...	...	0718	0732	...	...	|	|	0852	|	|	|
Bologna Centrale a.	...	0457	0513	...	0534	...	...	...	...	...	0643	...	...	...	0812	0823	...	...	0911	0927	0944	0955	1025	1014
Bologna Centrale d.	0451	0502	0518	0528	...	0542	0600	0620	0630	0638	0655	0708	0738	0746	0816	▬	0838	0904	0916	0930	0948	1000	1030	1020
Modena d.	0521	|	0543	0553	...	|	|	0642	|	0659	0732	|	0759	|	|	IR	0859	|	|	|	1008	|	|	|
Reggio Emilia d.	0539	|	0600	0609	...	|	|	0657	|	0714	0753	|	0814	|	|	2146	0913	|	|	|	1023	|	|	|
Parma d.	0600	|	0620	0627	...	|	|	0715	|	0731	0812	|	0831	|	|	L	0930	|	|	|	1038	|	|	|
Fidenza d.	0617	|	0639	0643	...	0654	|	0728	|	0743	0834	|	0843	|	|	0914	0943	|	|	|	1051	|	|	|
Piacenza d.	0647	0702	0718	0713	...	0730	0744	0749	0800	0807	0901	|	0905	|	|	0940	1007	|	|	|	1110	|	1224	|
Milano Centrale a.	0750	0815	0825	0820	...	0900	0840	...	0920	0855	1005	0921p	...	0950	1000	1025	1055	1100	1120	1105	1150	1205	1310	1215

	IC 730	EC 84	EC 30	P⚡ 1504	EC 52	P⚡ 502	IR 2036	IC 534	P⚡ 504	IR 2130	IC 552	IC 622	IC 568	IC 536	IR 2132	EC 54	IC 716	IR 2038		IC 732	IC 538	IC 590	P⚡ 506	IR 2134
	2 Ⓡ	✕ ♦	✕ ♦	✕ Ⓡ ♦	✕ ♦	✕ Ⓡ ♦	✤ T	🍷 ♦	✕ Ⓡ	🍷 A	🍷	🍷 ♦	✕ ♦	✕ ♦	🍷 A	✕ ♦	♦	🍷 T		2 Ⓡ	✕	Ⓡ ♦	✕ Ⓡ	🍷 A
Napoli Centrale **405** d.	...	...	...	...	...	...	...	0657	...	...	...	0747	...	0857	...	...	...	...	...	...	...	...	...	...
Roma Termini d.	0635	0725	0745	0800	0805	0855	...	0905	0955	...	0920	1000	...	1105	...	1205	1215	...	...	1225	1305	1335	1355	...
Roma Tiburtina d.	|	|	|	|	|	|	...	|	|	...	|	|	...	|	...	|	|	...	...	|	|	|	|	...
Chiusi d.	0804	|	|	|	|	|	...	|	|	...	1027	|	...	|	...	|	|	...	...	1336	|	1501	|	...
Terontola-Cortona d.	|	|	|	|	|	|	...	|	|	...	|	|	...	|	...	|	|	...	...	|	|	1519	|	...
Arezzo d.	0832	|	|	|	|	|	...	|	|	...	1057	|	...	|	...	|	|	...	...	1406	|	...	|	...
Firenze SMN a.	0909	0918	0938	|	0958	|	...	1058	|	...	1137	1151	...	1258	...	1358	1408	...	...	1441	1458	...	|	...
Firenze SMN d.	▬	0927	0947	|	1007	|	...	1107	|	...	1146	▬	...	1307	...	1407	1417	...	...	▬	1507	...	|	...
Firenze Rifredi d.	IR	|	|	0950	|	1032	...	|	1132	...	|	IR	...	|	...	|	|	...	...	IC	|	...	1532	...
Prato d.	2128	|	|	|	|	|	...	|	|	...	1203	2278	...	|	...	|	|	...	...	570	|	...	|	...
Bologna Centrale a.	A	1034	1054	1046	1112	1127	...	1212	1227	...	1254	G	...	1412	...	1512	1523	...	...	♦	1612	...	1627	...
Bologna Centrale d.	1038	...	...	1049	1116	...	1138	1216	1230	1238	1258	1338	1404	1416	1438	1516	...	1538	...	1604	1616	...	1630	1638
Modena d.	1059	...	...	|	|	...	1159	|	|	1259	1319	1359	|	|	1459	|	...	1559	...	|	|	...	|	1659
Reggio Emilia d.	1114	...	...	|	|	...	1214	|	|	1314	1333	1414	|	|	1514	|	...	1614	...	|	|	...	|	1714
Parma d.	1131	...	...	|	|	...	1231	|	|	1331	1348	1431	|	|	1531	|	...	1631	...	|	|	...	|	1731
Fidenza d.	1143	...	...	|	|	...	1243	|	|	1343	1401	1443	|	|	1543	|	...	1643	...	|	|	...	|	1743
Piacenza d.	1207	...	...	|	|	...	1305	|	|	1407	1421	1505	|	|	1607	|	...	1705	...	|	|	...	|	1807
Milano Centrale a.	1255	...	...	1230	1300	...	...	1400	1405	1455	1505	...	1555	1600	1655	1700	...	...	...	1755	1800	...	1805	1855

– **NOTES** (LISTED BY TRAIN NUMBERS)

- C30 – ROMULUS – [12] and ✕ Roma - Wien Südbahnhof; [12] Roma - Salzburg.
- C52 – COLOSSEUM – [12] and ✕ Roma - Basel SBB.
- C54 – RAFFAELLO – [12] and ✕ Roma - Zürich Hbf.
- C84 – MICHELANGELO – [12] and ✕ Roma - München Hbf.
- 287 – 🛏 1,2 cl., ▬ 2 cl. and [2] München Hbf - Napoli.
- 311 – [12] Genève Aéroport ✈ - Brig - Milano - Napoli; [12] Basel SBB - Chiasso - Milano - Napoli; [12] Schaffhausen - Zürich Hbf - Chiasso - Milano - Napoli.
- 388 – ▬ 2 cl. and [2] Lecce - Zürich Hbf - Stuttgart; [12] Bari Centrale - Milano.
- 500 – GIOTTO – Ⓐ: [12] and ✕ Roma - Milano.
- 502 – CARRACCI – ⚒: [12] and ✕ Roma - Venezia Santa Lucia.
- 534 – VESUVIO – [12] Salerno - Milano; 🍷 Napoli Centrale - Milano.
- 536 – PARTENOPE – [12] and ✕ Salerno - Milano.
- 550 – TACITO – [12] Terni - Perugia - Milano; 🍷 Bologna - Milano.
- 566 – D'ANNUNZIO – [12] and 🍷 Milano.
- 568 – BRERA – [12] and ✕ Bari Centrale - Milano.
- 570 – MURGE – [12] Lecce - Milano; [12] Taranto - Bari Centrale - Milano; [12] Bari - Milano.
- 622 – CAPODIMONTE – [12] and 🍷 Napoli - Firenze (**623**) - Pisa (**608**) - Torino Porta Nuova.
- 716 – BRENTA – [12] and 🍷 Roma - Venezia Santa Lucia.
- 23 – ▬ 1,2 cl. and [12] Milano - Napoli. **Not** Dec. 25, Jan. 1.
- 25 – ▬ 2 cl. and [12] Milano - Roma; 🛏 1,2 cl., 🛏 1,2 cl. (T2), ▬ 2 cl. and [12] Bolzano (**E847**) - Verona - Roma; conveys from Bologna: 🛏 1,2 cl. and 🛏 1,2 cl. (T2) Venezia Santa Lucia - Roma.
- 41 – 🛏 1,2 cl. (T2), ▬ 2 cl. and [12] Trieste Centrale - Roma.
- 45 – 🛏 1,2 cl., ▬ 2 cl. and [12] Udine - Napoli; 🛏 1,2 cl. (T2), ▬ 2 cl. and [12] Venezia Santa Lucia - Napoli.
- 01 – [12] Torino Porta Nuova - Bari Centrale. **Not** Dec. 24, 31.
- 03 – 🛏 1,2 cl. (T2), ▬ 2 cl. and [12] Torino Porta Nuova - Lecce; ▬ 2 cl. and [12] Torino - Taranto; 🛏 1,2 cl. Torino - Bari Centrale.
- **E922** – ESPRESSO DEL LEVANTE – [12] Lecce - Milano. **Not** Dec. 24, 31 from Lecce.
- **P1504** – ⑦: [12] and ✕ Roma - Milano.
- **IC1574** – ① - ⑤, **not** Dec. 10 - Jan. 9, Apr. 13 - 20: [12] Pescara - Milano.
- **E1757** – Dec. 17 - Jan. 4, Jan. 7, 8, 14, 15, Jan. 21 - Apr. 15, 17 (from San Candido): 🛏 1,2 cl., 🛏 1,2 cl. (T2), ▬ 2 cl. and [12] San Candido - Roma; ▬ 2 cl. and [12] Bolzano - Roma.
- **E1763** – Dec. 17 - Jan. 4, Jan. 7, 8, 14, 15, Jan. 21 - Apr. 15, 17 (from Calalzo): 🛏 1,2 cl., 🛏 1,2 cl. (T2), ▬ 2 cl. and [12] Calalzo - Roma.
- **E1770** – ⑤ Jan. 6 - Mar. 17, also Dec. 21, 22, 23, 28, 29, 30, Jan. 2, 3, 4, Apr. 13, 14, 18 (from Reggio): 🛏 1,2 cl. (T2), ▬ 2 cl. and [12] Reggio - Bolzano.
- **E1771** – ⑤ Jan. 6 - Mar. 17, also Dec. 20, 21, 22, 27, 28, 29, Jan. 1, 2, 3, Apr. 12, 13, 17 (from Bolzano): 🛏 1,2 cl. (T2), ▬ 2 cl. and [12] Bolzano - Reggio.
- **E1910/3** – ⑧, **not** Dec. 24 - Jan. 2, Apr. 15 - 17 (from Milano or Roma): 🛏 1,2 cl. and 🛏 1,2 cl. (T2) Milano - Roma and v.v; 🛏 1,2 cl. (T2) Milano - Perugia - Terni and v.v.
- **E1911/2** – 🛏 1,2 cl., 🛏 1,2 cl. (T2) and ▬ 2 cl. Milano - Napoli and v.v.
- **E1950/1** – SALENTINO – 🛏 1,2 cl., 🛏 1,2 cl. (T2) and ▬ 2 cl. Milano - Lecce and v.v.
- **A** – [12] Ancona - Bologna - Milano.
- **G** – [12] Genova Piazza Principe - Voghera - Piacenza - Bologna and v.v.
- **L** – [12] Livorno - Aulla - Milano.
- **M** – [12] Bologna (Ancona ⑦) - Milano.
- **T** – [12] Torino Porta Nuova - Bologna and v.v.
- **c** – Firenze **Campo di Marte**.
- **n** – Milano **Lambrate**.
- **v** – Napoli **Campi Flegrei**.
- ✤ – **Not** Dec. 25, Jan. 1.
- ⚡ – **Pendolino** supplement payable.
- ♣ – Long distance express service - not available for local journeys. For days of running and composition see Table **400**.

Table 370 ROMA - FIRENZE - BOLOGNA - MILANO   *1, 2 class except where shown*

For additional (slower) trains between Roma and Firenze see Table 385

First section

Station	IC 540 ✗	IC 33900 ♦	IC 718 ✗	IR 2280 ♦ G	IR 2300 H	IC 542 ✗	IC 34122 ♦	IR 2136 A	IC 734 2	IC 574 ✗	IC 544 ✗	IC 720 ⟡	P✗ 1506 ♦ ✗R	P✗ 508 ♦ ✗R	IR 2040 ♦	IC 546 ♦	P✗ 510 ♦ ✗R	IR 2138 A	E 1710 ♦	E 1234 ♦	IC 578 ✗	IC 554 ✗ ⟡	IC 722 ✗ ♦
Napoli Centrale 405 ... d.						1257										1457						1557	
Roma Termini ... d.	1405		1415			1505				1515	1605	1615	1700	1700		1705	1750					1805	1815
Roma Tiburtina ... d.																							
Chiusi ... d.								1630															
Terontola-Cortona ... d.								1657															
Arezzo ... d.								1732															
Firenze SMN ... a.	1558		1612			1658					1758	1808				1858						1958	2008
Firenze SMN ... d.	1607		1621					1707	1718		1807	1817	1837	1837				1932		1953		2007	2017
Firenze Rifredi ... d.											1823											2024	
Prato ... d.								1735			1823								2024		2105	2115	2123
Bologna Centrale ... a.	1712		1727					1812	1824		1912	1923	1932	1932		2012	2027		2105			2115	2123
Bologna Centrale ... d.	1716	1723		1738	1754	1816	1824	1838	1838		1858	1916	1935	1935	1943	2016	2030	2038	2054			2116	2128
Modena ... d.				1759	1817		1848	1859						2005			2059	2118				2149	IR
Reggio Emilia ... d.				1814	1832		1902	1914						2020			2114	2136				2204	2148
Parma ... d.			1806	1831	1848		1918	1931				2012	2012	2037			2143	2211	2131	2156		2220	L
Fidenza ... d.				1843			1931	1943						2050			2207	2242				2233	
Piacenza ... d.		1833		1905			1952	2007		2014		2038	2037	2111			2252	2302				2236	
Milano Centrale ... a.	1900					2000	2036	2055		2100		2115	2200	2205			2255	2330		2315			2350

Second section

Station	IC 558	IC 736 2	P✗ 526 ✗R	P✗ 512 ✗R	P✗ 514 ✗R	IR 2140 A	E 288 ♦	E 234 ♦	IC 556 ⟡	E 286 ♦	E 900 ♦	E 1762 ♦	E 1084	E 312 ♦	E 1758 ♦	E 842 ♦	E 920 ♦	E 820 ♦	E 822 ♦	E 902 ♦	E 844 ♦
Napoli Centrale 405 ... d.										1815	1857	1915					1947			2230	2030v
Roma Termini ... d.	1755	1830	1905	1915	1945			1920	2005	2035	2112	2143	2155	2202			2215		2244		2305
Roma Tiburtina ... d.								2110		2208				2320				0019	0006		0043
Chiusi ... d.	1901	1942																	0028		0103
Terontola-Cortona ... d.	1922	1959																	0056		0130
Arezzo ... d.	1944	2022						2139	2213	2243				0001				0108	0056		
Firenze SMN ... a.	2025	2108						2125	2148	2222				0117				0108			
Firenze SMN ... d.			2039	2052	2122					2325c	0025c	0103c		0123c	0138c			0213c	0203c		0235c
Firenze Rifredi ... d.											0058	0145			0200						
Prato ... d.				2148	2217		2235	2255	2335	0045	0204	0240	0256	0310	0320			0340	0330	0405	
Bologna Centrale ... a.					2220	2238	2259				0204	0245	0301			0335	0345	0355	0405		
Bologna Centrale ... d.						2259	2313				0237	0310	0331			0410	0420	0430			
Modena ... d.						2313	2330				0300	0328	0350			0428	0437	0448			
Reggio Emilia ... d.						2330	2343				0320	0353	0410			0447	0456	0509			
Parma ... d.						2343	0010				0337		0426			0503	0514				
Fidenza ... d.						0010	0100				0406	0429	0449			0530	0543	0547			
Piacenza ... d.					2359																
Milano Centrale ... a.					0100						0509n	0535n				0605	0620	0650			

NOTES (LISTED BY TRAIN NUMBERS)

E234 – REMUS – ⟡1,2 cl., ⟡ 2 cl. and ⟡ Roma - Wien Südbahnhof.
E286 – ⟡1,2 cl., ⟡ 2 cl. and ⟡ Napoli - München Hbf.
E288 – BRENNER EXPRESS – ⟡1,2 cl., ⟡ 2 cl. and ⟡ Firenze - München Hbf.
E312 – ⟡ Napoli - Milano - Brig - Genève Aéroport ✈; ⟡ Napoli - Milano - Chiasso - Basel SBB; ⟡ Napoli - Milano - Chiasso - Zürich Hbf.
P508 – GUIDO RENI – Ⓐ, not Dec. 24 - Jan. 8: ⟡ and ⟡ Roma - Torino Porta Nuova.
P510 – BRUNELLESCHI – Ⓐ, not Dec. 25 - Jan. 8: ⟡ and ✗ Roma - Milano.
P512 – VERONESE – ✗, also Dec. 25, Apr. 16, 30, not May 27: ⟡ and ✗ Roma - Venezia Santa Lucia.
P526 – CIMABUE – ✗ Sept. 25 - Dec. 23, Jan. 8 - May 26, also Apr. 16, 30: ⟡ and ✗ Roma - Firenze (P527) - Pisa (P528) - Genova Piazza Principe - Savona.
IC556 – IL VIGNOLA – ✗, also Dec. 25, Apr. 16, 30: ⟡ Roma - Bologna; ⟡ Roma - Firenze.
IC574 – ROSSINI – ⟡ and ⟡ Bari Centrale - Torino Porta Nuova.
IC578 – ADRIATICO – ⟡ Lecce - Milano; ✗ Bari Centrale - Milano.
IC590 – TRASIMENO – ⟡ Roma - Terontola - Perugia.
IC718 – MARCO POLO – ⟡ Roma - Udine; ⟡ Roma - Bolzano; ✗ Roma - Venezia Mestre.
IC722 – PALLADIO – ⟡ and ✗ Roma - Venezia Santa Lucia.
E820 – ⟡ 2 cl. and ⟡ Napoli - Milano.
E822 – ⟡ 2 cl. and ⟡ Roma - Milano; conveys to Bologna: ⟡ and ⟡1,2 cl. (T2) Roma - Venezia Santa Lucia and ⟡1,2 cl., ⟡1,2 cl. (T2), ⟡ 2 cl. and ⟡ Roma - Bolzano.
E842 – ⟡1,2 cl. (T2), ⟡ 2 cl. and ⟡ Roma - Trieste Centrale.
E844 – ⟡1,2 cl., ⟡ 2 cl. and ⟡ Napoli - Udine; ⟡1,2 cl. (T2), ⟡ 2 cl. and ⟡ Napoli - Venezia Santa Lucia. Not Dec. 24, 31.

E900 – ⟡ 2 cl. and ⟡ Bari Centrale - Torino Porta Nuova.
E902 – ⟡ 2 cl. and ⟡ Taranto - Bari Centrale - Torino Porta Nuova; ⟡1,2 cl. Bari - Torino; ⟡1,2 cl. (T2), ⟡1,2 cl. and ⟡ Lecce - Torino.
E1084 – Dec. 17, Jan. 1, Apr. 16 only: ⟡ 2 cl. and ⟡ Napoli - Stuttgart; ⟡ Napoli - Zürich Hbf.
E1234 – Dec. 25 - Jan. 7, Apr. 6 - 22, May 18 - 27: ⟡ 2 cl. and ⟡ Firenze - Wien Südbahnhof.
P1506 – ⑦: ⟡ and ✗ Roma - Milano.
E1710 – ⑥⑦, also Apr. 17, 25, May 1, not Dec. 25, Jan. 1, Apr. 16, 23, Apr. 30: ⟡ Pescara - Milano.
E1758 – Dec. 16 - Jan. 3, Jan. 20 - Apr. 15, also Jan. 6, 7, 13, 14: ⟡1,2 cl., ⟡1,2 cl. (T2), ⟡ 2 cl. and ⟡ Roma - San Candido; ⟡ 2 cl. and ⟡ Roma - Bolzano.
E1762 – Dec. 16 - Jan. 3, Jan. 20 - Apr. 15, also Jan. 6, 7, 13, 14: ⟡1,2 cl., ⟡1,2 cl. (T2), ⟡ 2 cl. and ⟡ Roma - Calalzo.
IR2040 – ⟡ Rimini - Bologna - Torino Porta Nuova. Not Dec. 24, 31.
IC33900 – ⟡ Bologna - Piacenza - Alessandria - Torino Porta Susa.
A – ⟡ Ancona - Bologna - Torino.
G – ⟡ Bologna - Piacenza - Voghera - Genova Piazza Principe.
H – ⟡ Bologna - Parma - Aulla - Genova Piazza Principe.
L – ⟡ Livorno - Aulla - Milano.
c – Firenze **Campo di Marte**.
n – Milano **Lambrate**.
v – Napoli **Campi Flegrei**.
✗ – **Pendolino** supplement payable.

4T

Table 371 — BOLOGNA - PISTOIA

2 class only

km		6339	6375 ✗	6341	6377	6343	6379	6345	6381	6347 ✗	6349	6351	6385	6353	6355	6387	6357	6359	6389	6361	6391	11437	6365	6395	6367
0	Bologna Centrale .... d.	0608	...	0708	...	0808	...	0908	...	1008	1108	1208	...	1308	1408	...	1508	1608	...	1708	...	1808	1908	...	2008
58	Porretta Terme .... d.	0713	0723	0813	0820	0913	0920	1013	1020	1113	1213	1313	1320	1413	1513	1520	1613	1713	1720	1813	1820	1915	2013	2025	2110
99	Pistoia .... a.	...	0810	...	0912	...	1013	...	1108	...	...	...	1413	...	...	1609	...	...	1812	...	1916	...	...	2113	...

		11430 ✗	6370	6340	6372	6342	6374	6344	6376	6346	6348 ✗	6350	6380	6352	6382	6354	6384	6356	6358	6386	6360	6390	6362	6364	6394	6366
	Pistoia .... d.	...	0617	...	0712	...	0817	...	0920	...	...	1217	...	1317	...	1420	...	...	1620	...	1718	...	...	1924	...	...
	Porretta Terme .... d.	0618	0711	0720	0807	0821	0905	0921	1008	1021	1121	1221	1305	1321	1406	1421	1510	1521	1621	1708	1721	1808	1819	1921	2014	2042
	Bologna Centrale ...... a.	0729	...	0822	...	0921	...	1026	...	1126	1226	1326	...	1422	...	1526	...	1626	1726	...	1826	...	1926	2026	...	2151

Table 372 — FIRENZE - PISTOIA - VIAREGGIO

2 class only

km		6606	6833	D 3080	D3161	6610	D 3082	6967	D 3084	D3165	6612	D 3086	D3169	6616	D 3088	6973	D 3090	6975	D 3092	6937	D 3094	6979	D 3096	6981	6630
0	Firenze SMN .... d.	0615	...	0740	0845	...	0940	...	1140	1230	...	1340	1445	...	1542	...	1640	...	1745	...	1845	...	1935	...	2030
17	Prato .... d.	0640	...	0800	0903	...	1003	...	1200	1248	...	1402	1506	...	1603	...	1701	...	1806	...	1905	...	1956	...	2058
34	Pistoia .... d.	0655	...	0815	0917	...	1018	...	1213	1300	...	1416	1518	...	1616	...	1715	...	1819	...	1921	...	2010	...	2114
47	Montecatini Terme .... a.	0706	...	0827	0928	...	1030	...	1228	1310	...	1429	1528	...	1629	...	1729	...	1829	...	1930	...	2019	...	2127
78	Lucca .... a.	0745	...	0852	0955	...	1056	...	1254	1342	...	1457	1555	...	1657	...	1755	...	1855	...	1950	...	2050	...	2200
78	Lucca .... d.	0800	0750	0853	1000	...	1057	1144	1255	1343	1400	1458	1600	1600	1658	1707	1800	1814	1856	1900	2000	2000	2055	2110	2201
	Pisa Centrale ...... a.		0820	...	1021		...	1208	...	1400		...	1617		1735	...	1836		1925	...	2024	2135			
	Pisa Aeroporto ✈ .. a.		0910	...	1035		...	1309	...	1429		...	1631		1759	...	1859		1959	...	2059				
101	Viareggio .... a.	0820	...	0910	...	1020	1113	...	1312	1420	1515	...	1620	1715	...	1820	...	1915	...	2017	...	2112	...	2220	

km		D 3077	6958	D 3079	6609	6934 Ⓐ	D 3081	3083	3085	6946	D 3087	6617	D3162 D3163 ⑦	3089	6621	D3166 D3167	6852 Ⓐ	D 3091	6978	3095	6627	D3170 D3171	6629
0	Viareggio .... d.	0630	...	0740	...	0831	...	0940	1140	...	1338	1434	...	1540	1634	...	1740	...	1940	2034	...	2120	
2	Pisa Aeroporto ✈ .. d.					0845			1240	1440			1640	1840			2025							
2	Pisa Centrale ...... d.		0710		0900			1310		1440	1525		1631	1705		1934			2039					
24	Lucca .... d.	0649	0738	0757	...	0850	0925	...	0957	1157	1338	1359	1454	1459	1550	1558	1653	1650	1732	1758	1955	1958	2053 2068	2138
	Lucca .... d.	0650	...	0800	...		0900	1000	1200	...	1400	...	1500	...	1600	...	1700	...	1800	...	2000	...	2100	2139
	Montecatini Terme ... d.	0720	...	0826	...		0929	1029	1227	...	1428	...	1529	...	1628	...	1728	...	1830	...	2033	...	2126	2221
	Pistoia .... d.	0730	...	0840	...		0940	1038	1237	...	1437	...	1539	...	1637	...	1737	...	1839	...	2042	...	2136	2221
	Prato .... d.	0745	...	0855	...		0954	1050	1250	...	1450	...	1552	...	1650	...	1750	...	1852	...	2056	...	2149	2237
	Firenze SMN .... a.	0800	...	0918	...		1015	1110	1310	...	1510	...	1610	...	1710	...	1810	...	1910	...	2117	...	2210	2305

Table 373 — FIRENZE - SIENA

2 class only

km										✗				✗						✗							
0	Firenze SMN .... d.	0553	...	0635	0810	...	0915	1000	...	1145	1225	...	1325	1413	1500	...	1545	1710	1724	1820	1925	2025	2230	...
34	Empoli .... d.	0619	0624	0705	0845	...	0945	1023	1040	1220	1257	1310	1400	1443	1523	1528	1619	1739	1800	1855	2000	2056	2302	2310
72	Poggibonsi .... d.	...	0658	0730	0924	...	1021	...	1120	1300	...	1358	1438	1513	...	1608	1657	1808	1839	1930	2047	2138	...	2346
97	Siena .... d.	...	0727	0800	0948	...	1042	...	1145	1325	...	1425	1505	1533	...	1630	1720	1831	1906	1954	2113	2200	...	0010

		✗									✗													
	Siena .... d.	0500	...	0550	0635	0712	...	0810	0900	1055	1155	...	1235	...	1335	1438	...	1545	1633	...	1737	...	1838	1956	2115
	Poggibonsi .... d.	0522	...	0614	0659	0740	...	0832	0923	1119	1218	...	1305	...	1357	1501	...	1607	1656	...	1759	...	1903	2019	2137
	Empoli .... d.	0555	0603	0651	0730	0815	0840	0903	0956	1202	1253	1315	1346	1356	1430	1550	1615	1649	1733	1749	1845	1850	1933	2058	2208
	Firenze SMN .... a.	...	0640	0725	0800	...	0913	0933	1029	1232	...	1339	...	1430	1505	...	1639	1727	...	1823	...	1925	2000	2130	2236

Table 374 — SIENA - CHIUSI and GROSSETO

2 class only

Rail service Siena - Chiusi. 89 km. Journey time 1 hour 15 minutes.

From Siena: 0455✗, 0623, 0810, 1010, 1210, 1333, 1402✗, 1430✗, 1510, 1650, 1810, 2010.   **From Chiusi:** 0450✗, 0605✗, 0708✗, 0810, 1033, 1426, 1505, 1705✗, 1835, 2035, 2130.

- -

Rail service Siena - Grosseto. 101 km. Journey time 1 hour 17 - 1 hour 35 minutes.

From Siena: 0615✗, 0804, 1215, 1315✗, 1535, 1730, 1835, 1850Ⓐ, 1932⑦.   **From Grosseto:** 0620✗, 0728, 0913, 1355, 1537✗, 1702, 1755, 1951.

Table 375 — BOLOGNA - VENEZIA

1, 2 class except where shown

km		E 1762	E 842	E844 9844	E 844	E 940	IR 2224	E 1930	IR 2226	IC 712	IR 2228	EC 30	P✗ 502	IR 2230	IR 2232	IR 2234	IR 2236	IC 716	IR 2238	IR 2240	IC 718	IR 2242	IR 2244
		♦	♦	J	♦	♦		♦		✗		✗	✗ R					✗			✗ R		
	Napoli Campi Flegrei 405 d.	...	...	2030	2030	...																	
	Roma Termini 370 ...... d.	2112t	2215	2305	2305	...		...	...	0745	0855	...	...	...	...	1215	...	...	1415	...			
	Firenze SMN 370 ...... d.	0025c	0138c	0235c	0235c	...	0518c	...	0715	...	0947	1032r	...	...	...	1417	...	...	1621	...			
0	Bologna Centrale .... d.	0222	0355	0420	0420	0437	0602	0640	0647	0740	0827	0840	1058	1130	1140	1240	1340	.1527	1540	1640	1736	1746	1840
47	Ferrara .... d.	...	0424	0452	0452	0515	0634	0717	0813	0855	0913	...	1156	1213	1213	1413	1513	1556	1613	...	1713	...	1820	1913
80	Rovigo .... d.	...	0448	0516	0516	0539	0655	0740	0832	0916	0932	...	1218	1232	1332	1432	1532	1616	1632	...	1732	...	1838	1933
123	Padova .... d.	0352	0526	0552	0552	0630	0736	0822	0911	0946	1011	1028	1250	1311	1311	1511	1611	1646	1711	...	1811	1846	1914	2011
152	Venezia Mestre .... a.	...	0550	0613	0613	0656	0758	0849	0931	1004	1031	1227	1307	1331	1431	1531	1631	1704	1731	...	1831	1904	1934	2031
152	Venezia Mestre .... d.	...	0604	0620	0630	0700	0800	0900	0942	1006	1033	1241	1309	1333	1433	1533	1633	1706	1733	...	1833	1914	1936	2033
160	Venezia Santa Lucia .... a.	...		0629		0710	0810	0900	0942	1015	1042	...	1318	1342	1442	1542	1642	1715	1742	...	1842	...	1945	2042
	Trieste Centrale 376 ... a.	...	0801	...	1007																		
	Udine 377 .... a.	...	...	0817	...				1358												2035		

NOTES (LISTED BY TRAIN NUMBERS)

♦ —

EC30 – ROMULUS – 🛏 and ✗ Roma - Wien Südbahnhof; 🛏 Roma - Salzburg.

P502 – CARACCI – ✗ 🛏 and ✗ Roma - Venezia. ETR450 supplement payable.

C718 – MARCO POLO – 🛏 Roma - Udine; ✗ Roma - Venezia Mestre.

E842 – 1,2 cl. (T2), 2 cl. and 🛏 Roma - Trieste.

E844 – 1,2 cl., 2 cl. and 🛏 Napoli - Udine. Not Dec. 25, Jan. 1.

E940 – 2 cl. and 🛏 Lecce - Trieste; 1,2 cl. (T2) Lecce - Venezia; 1,2 cl. and 🛏 Bari Centrale - Venezia.

E1762 – Dec. 16 - Jan. 3, 6, 7, 13, 14, Jan. 20 - Apr. 15: 1,2 cl., 1,2 cl. (T2), 2 cl. and 🛏 Roma - Calalzo.

E1930 – 🛏 1,2 cl. and 2 cl. Reggio - Venezia; 🛏 1,2 cl. and 2 cl. Catania - Venezia; 🛏 1,2 cl. (T2) and 2 cl. (also 1,2 cl. on ①⑥⑦) Palermo - Venezia; 🛏 1,2 cl. (T2) and 2 cl. Siracusa - Venezia.

J – 🛏 1,2 cl. (T2), 🛏 2 cl. and 2 cl. Napoli - Venezia. Not Dec. 25, Jan. 1.

c – Firenze Campo di Marte.

r – Firenze Rifredi.

t – Roma Tiburtina.

❖ – Not Dec. 25, Jan. 1.

✗ – ETR450 Pendolino supplement payable.

Table 375 — BOLOGNA - VENEZIA

1, 2 class except where shown

Station	IC 720	IR 2246	IR 2248	IC 722	E 1234	P 512	D 2966	E 234
	🍴		T	X		X (R)	♦	♦
Napoli Campi Flegrei 405 ... d.	...	...	...	...	...	...	...	...
Roma Termini 370 ... d.	1615	...	...	1815	...	1915	...	1920
Firenze SMN 370 ... d.	1817	...	...	2017	1953	2052r	...	2148
Bologna Centrale ... d.	1927	1940	2040	2127	2115	2151	2215	2300
Ferrara ... d.	1956	2013	2113	2156	2146	2218	2247	2330
Rovigo ... d.	2017	2032	2132	2217	2224	2238	2308	|
Padova ... d.	2046	2111	2211	2246	2300	2310	2341	0022
Venezia Mestre ... a.	2104	2131	2231	2304	2320	2327	...	0042
Venezia Mestre ... d.	2120	2133	2233	2306	2322	2329	...	0102
Venezia Santa Lucia ... a.	|	2142	2242	2315	2331	2338	...	|
Trieste Centrale 376 ... a.	2312	...	...					
Udine 377 ... a.						0127		0219

Station	D 2951	P 501	IR 2225	IC 713	IR 2227	IR 2229	IC 715	IC 717
		X (R)	Y	X				🍴 X (R)
Udine 377 ... d.	...	...	...	...	...	...	0648	0925
Trieste Centrale 376 ... d.	...	...	...	...	...	...	...	...
Venezia Santa Lucia ... d.	...	0550	0620	0655	0720	0820	|	...
Venezia Mestre ... a.	...	0559	0629	0704	0729	0829	0840	1045
Venezia Mestre ... d.	...	0601	0631	0706	0731	0831	0855	1055
Padova ... d.	0546	0620	0658	0727	0758	0858	0916	1116
Rovigo ... d.	0617	0647	0728	0754	0828	0928	0943	|
Ferrara ... d.	0638	0705	0748	0814	0848	0948	1004	|
Bologna ... a.	0715	0738	0822	0844	0922	1022	1035	1230
Firenze SMN 370 ... a.	...	0836r	...	0953	...	...	1144	1356
Roma Termini 370 ... a.	...	1015	...	1155	...	...	1345	1605
Napoli Campi Flegrei 405 ... a.	...	...	...	...	...	...	...	...

Station	IR 2231	IR 2233	IR 2235	IR 2237	P 511	IR 2239	EC 31	IR 2241	IR 2243	IC 719	IR 2245	E 1931	IC 2247	E 723	IR 2249	E942 E943	E 845	9845 E845	E 1763	E840 E841	E 235	E 1235
	🍴	🍴			X (R)					X		♦	🍴	🍴		H		M	♦	J		
Udine 377 ... d.												1812				2105			2210		0219	0219
Trieste Centrale 376 ... d.	...	...					1401															
Venezia Santa Lucia ... d.	1120	1220	1320	...	1420	1442	1510	...	1620	1720	1755	...	1905	1920	1942	2020	2054	2250	...	...	...	...
Venezia Mestre ... a.	1129	1229	1329	...	1429	1451	1519	1518	1629	1729	1804	1829	1914	1929	1951	2029	2103	2251	2259	0004	0344	0344
Venezia Mestre ... d.	1131	1231	1331	...	1431	1453	1521	1531	1631	1731	1806	1831	1917	1931	1953	2031	2108	2303	2330	0037	0359	0440
Padova ... d.	1158	1258	1358	...	1458	1512	1543	1555	1658	1758	1827	1858	1940	1958	2016	2058	2134	2359	2359	0114	0422	0504
Rovigo ... d.	1228	1328	1428	...	1528	1538	1622	|	1728	1828	1853	1928	2013	2028	2044	2128	2211	0036	0055	0146	0449	0531
Ferrara ... d.	1248	1348	1448	...	1548	1557	1648	|	1748	1848	1914	1948	2037	2048	2104	2148	2234	0100	0100	0212	0507	0552
Bologna ... a.	1322	1422	1522	...	1622	1630	1722	1706	1822	1922	1944	2022	2110	2122	2135	2222	2310	0140	0140	0300	0540	0627
Firenze SMN 370 ... a.	...	...	...	...	1727r	...	1816	...	...	...	2053	2241c	...	2248	...	...	0342c	0342c	0358c	0435c	0656	0753
Roma Termini 370 ... a.	...	...	...	...	1905	...	2020	...	...	...	2255	...	...	...	...	0625	0625	0716t	...	...	0825	0930
Napoli Campi Flegrei 405 ... a.	...	...	...	...								...	...			0915	0915				0915	0915

♦ — NOTES (LISTED BY TRAIN NUMBERS)

EC31 – ROMULUS – (couchette) and X Wien Südbahnhof - Roma; (sleeper) Salzburg - Roma.
E234/5 – REMUS – (sleeper) 1,2 cl., (couchette) 2 cl. and (restaurant) Roma - Wien Südbahnhof and v.v.
P501 – VERONESE – X; (restaurant) and X Roma - Venezia.
P511 – CARACCI – X, also Dec. 25, Apr. 16, 30: (restaurant) and X Roma - Venezia.
P512 – VERONESE – X, also Dec. 25, Apr. 16, 30: (restaurant) and X Venezia - Roma.
IC717 – MARCO POLO – (restaurant) Udine - Roma; X Venezia - Roma.
E845 – (sleeper) 1,2 cl., (couchette) 2 cl. and (restaurant) Udine - Napoli. Not Dec. 24, 31 from Udine.
E1234 – Dec. 25 - Jan. 7, Apr. 6 - 22, May 18 - 27: (couchette) 2 cl. and (restaurant) Firenze - Wien Südbahnhof.
E1235 – Dec. 26 - Jan. 8, Apr. 7 - 23, May 19 - 27 (from Wien): (couchette) 2 cl. and (restaurant) Wien Südbahnhof - Firenze.
E1763 – Dec. 17 - Jan. 4, 7, 8, 14, 15, Jan. 21 - Apr. 15, 17 (from Calazo): (sleeper) 1,2 cl., (couchette) 1,2 cl. (T2), (couchette) 2 cl. and (restaurant) Calazo - Roma.

E1931 – (sleeper) 1,2 cl. (T2) and (couchette) 2 cl. Venezia - Siracusa; (couchette) 1,2 cl. and (couchette) 2 cl. Venezia - Catania; (sleeper) 1,2 cl. and (couchette) 2 cl. Venezia - Reggio; (sleeper) 1,2 cl. and (couchette) 2 cl. (also (sleeper) 1,2 cl. on ④⑤⑥) Venezia - Palermo.
H – (couchette) 2 cl. and (restaurant) Venezia - Lecce; (couchette) 1,2 cl. and (restaurant) Venezia - Bari Centrale.
J – (couchette) 1,2 cl. (T2), (couchette) 2 cl. and (restaurant) Venezia - Lecce; (sleeper) 1,2 cl. and (restaurant) Trieste - Lecce; (sleeper) 1,2 cl. and (restaurant) Venezia - Napoli.
M – (sleeper) 1,2 cl. (T2), (couchette) 2 cl. and (restaurant) Venezia - Napoli.
T – Not Dec. 24, 25, 31.
Y – Not Dec. 25, 26, Jan. 1.
c – Firenze Campo di Marte.
r – Firenze Rifredi.
t – Roma Tiburtina.
✧ – Not Dec. 25, Jan. 1.
✐ – ETR450 Pendolino supplement payable.

Table 376 — VENEZIA - TRIESTE

1, 2 class except where shown

km	Station	E842 11101 E843	5901	E 221	5963	E940 E941	IR 2209	E 243	IC 647	IR 2211	IR 2213	D 2869	IR 2215	IR 2217	11113	IR 2219	5917	IC 657	11115 IC721	E 241	IR 2221
		2 ❌ L	2		2	2 J		X	♦								2		♦		
	Roma Termini 370 ... d.	2215																1615			
	Firenze SMN 370 ... d.	0138d																1817			
	Bologna Centrale 370 ... d.	0355			0437													1927			
0	Venezia Santa Lucia ... d.	0450	0628			0800	0840	0940	1210	1240	1340	1417	1540	1640	1734	1840	1913	2028		2122	2240
9	Venezia Mestre ... a.	0459	0550	0638		0810	0849	0949	1219	1249	1349	1426	1549	1649	1745	1849	1922	2037	2104	2131	2249
9	Venezia Mestre ... d.	0500	0604	0639	0708	0851	0951		1221	1251	1351	1428	1551	1651	1746	1851	1924	1955	2039	2120 2134	2251
42	Santa Dona di Piave ... d.	0528	0630	0713	0731	0834	0912	1014	1243	1316	1413	1453	1616	1712	1820	1912	1959	2018	2114	2144 2156	2316
69	Portogruaro ... d.	0550	0649	0737	0750		0800	0935	1035	1301	1335	1435	1515	1635	1735	1845	1935	2022	2135	2204 2215	2335
83	Latisana ... d.	0607	0700			0813	0906	0946	1046		1346	1446	1538	1656	1746	1857	1914	1958	2146	2226	2346
101	San Giorgio di Nogaro ... d.	0623	0712			0831	0918	0958	1058		1358	1458	1538	1648	1759	1914	1958	2158	2239		2009
112	Cervignano ... d.	0634	0723			0843	0929	1009	1109	1332	1409	1509	1549	1709	1809	1926	2009	2108	2209	2235 2248	0009
129	Monfalcone ... d.	0647	0737	0832	0903	0943	1023	1123	1345	1423	1523	1603	1723	1823	1943	2023	2121	2223	2248	2303	0023
157	Trieste Centrale ... a.	0710	0801	0855	0931	1007	1047	1147	1409	1447	1547	1627	1747	1847	2010	2047	2145	2247	2312	2327	0047

Station	D 11100	IC 2860	646	2801	5960	IC714 IC715	5809	E 240	IR 2208	IR 2210	IR 2212	D 2864	IR 2214	IR 2216	IC 658	11063	E 242	11114	942	IR 2218	E 220	D 2765	IR 2220	E840 E841
	♦		2	2	2	🍴	X	X				♦						J	2					L
Trieste Centrale ... d.	0412	0536	0610		0616	0648		0712	0812	1012	1212	1312	1412	1512	1610		1712	1718	1812	1912	2028		2112	2210
Monfalcone ... d.	0436	0600	0635		0643	0713		0736	0836	1036	1236	1336	1436	1536	1635		1736	1746	1836	1936	2053		2136	2234
Cervignano ... d.	0449	0614	0649		0657	0727		0749	0849	1049	1249	1349	1449	1549	1649		1749	1800	1816	1900	2000		2149	2249
San Giorgio di Nogaro ... d.	0500	0625			0709			0800	0900	1100	1300	1400	1500	1600			1800	1816	1900	2000			2200	2311
Latisana ... d.	0513	0637			0728			0813	0913	1113	1313	1413	1513	1613			1813	1833	1913	2013			2213	2322
Portogruaro ... d.	0524	0648	0720		0741	0758		0824	0924	1124	1324	1424	1524	1624	1720		1842	1911	1924	2024	2135		2245	2340
Santa Dona di Piave ... d.	0546	0712	0738			0815		0843	0945	1145	1345	1441	1541	1644	1738		1907	1940	1942	2041	2154		2307	0004
Venezia Mestre ... a.	0620	0736	0802		0840			0907	1007	1207	1407	1507	1607	1707	1802		1909	1950	2009	2109	2219		2307	0037
Venezia Mestre ... d.	0621	0737		0816		0855	0848	0909	1009	1209	1409	1509	1609	1709	1809		1909	1950	2009	2109	2228		2237	0037
Venezia Santa Lucia ... a.	0632	0747		0825			0857	0918	1018	1218	1418	1518	1618	1718	1818		1918	1959	2018	2118	2310		2318	0300
Bologna Centrale 370 ... a.	...	...			1035																			0435c
Firenze SMN 370 ... a.					1144																			0825
Roma Termini 370 ... a.					1345																			

♦ — NOTES (LISTED BY TRAIN NUMBERS)

E220/1 – SIMPLON EXPRESS – (sleeper) 1,2 cl., (couchette) 2 cl. and (restaurant) Genève Aéroport + - Zagreb and v.v.
E240/1 – VENEZIA EXPRESS – (sleeper) 1,2 cl. and (restaurant) Venezia - Zagreb and v.v.; (sleeper) 1,2 cl., (couchette) 2 cl. and (restaurant) Venezia - Budapest Keleti and v.v; conveys (twice-weekly) (sleeper) 1,2 cl. Venezia - Moskva and v.v (see Table 94c).
E242/3 – DRAVA – (restaurant) and X Venezia - Budapest Keleti.
IC647 – SVEVO – (restaurant) Sestri Levante (IC672) - Milano - Trieste.
IC646/57 – TERGESTE – (restaurant) Torino Porta Nuova - Trieste and v.v.
IC658 – SVEVO – (restaurant) Trieste - Milano Centrale (IC689) - Genova Piazza Principe.
J – (couchette) 2 cl. and (restaurant) Lecce - Trieste and v.v.
L – (sleeper) 1,2 cl. (T2), (couchette) 2 cl. and (restaurant) Roma - Trieste and v.v.
d – Firenze Campo di Marte.

Table 377 VENEZIA - CALALZO, UDINE and VILLACH

1, 2 class except where shown

km		11002 2 ⚒	E 870 ◆	D 2742	E 844 ◆	11004	E 232 ◆	D 2748	5673 2	D 2776 2	5812 2 Ⓐ	5676 5677	D 2778	11014 2	5682 2 ⚒	11138	5714	EC 30 ✕ ◆	11018 2	2756 2757	D 2754 2 ⚒	D 2782	11022 2	D 2758
	Roma Termini **375** d.	...	...	...	2305	...	...	...	...	...	...	...	...	...	...	...	...	0745	...	...	...	...	...	...
	Firenze SMN **375** d.	...	...	...	0235c	...	...	...	...	...	...	...	...	...	...	...	...	0947	...	...	...	...	...	...
0	**Venezia Santa Lucia** d.	0521	0545	0556	|	0634	0730	0750	...	0910	0952	...	1110	1147	...	...	1214	|	1310	1345	...	1410	1428	1458
9	**Venezia Mestre** a.	0531	0554	0605	0613	0643	0739	0759	...	0919	1001	...	1119	1157	...	...	1224	1227	1319	1354	...	1419	1438	1507
9	**Venezia Mestre** d.	0533	0557	0607	0630	0644	0742	0802	...	0921	1002	...	1121	1200	...	...	...	1241	1321	1356	...	1421	1439	1509
30	Treviso d.	0559	0615	0624	0648	0706	0759	0822	...	0941	1028	...	1141	1221	...	...	...	|	1344	1416	...	1443	1500	1529
57	Conegliano d.	0622	0636	0644	0709	0733	0819	0842	...	0958	1058	1115	1159	1247	1241	...	...	|	1409	1438	...	1503	1523	1550
	Vittorio Veneto d.	|	|	0700	|	|	|	0855	...	|	...	1127	|	|	1255	...	...	|	|	1450	...	|	|	1603
	Ponte nelle Alpi d.	|	|	0744	|	|	|	0933e	0932	|	...	1158	|	|	1330	1348	...	|	|	1522	1555	|	|	1641
	Belluno a.	|	|	|	|	|	|	|	0940	|	...	1205	|	|	*1420*	|	...	|	|	1530	|	|	|	|
	Calalzo ▲ a.	|	|	0831	|	|	|	1015	...	|	...	...	|	|	...	1438	...	|	|	...	1647	|	|	1725
87	Pordenone d.	0651	0705	...	0736	0801	0844	...	...	1019	...	...	1224	1316	...	...	...	1328	1438	...	...	1527	1551	...
136	**Udine** a.	0730	0746	...	0817	0840	0918	...	...	1054	...	...	1305	1350	...	...	...	1358	1516	...	...	1600	1630	...
136	**Udine** d.	...	...	...	...	...	0923	...	...	...	...	...	...	...	...	...	...	1403	...	...	...	...	...	...
230	Tarvisio Centrale 🏛 a.	...	...	...	...	...	1049	...	...	...	...	...	...	...	...	...	...	1520	...	...	...	...	...	...
258	**Villach Hbf** a.	...	...	...	...	...	1133	...	...	...	...	...	...	...	...	...	...	1600	...	...	...	...	...	...

	5689 2	D 2784	5818 2 ⚒	E 864 ◆	11024	5692 5693 2	D 2760	11026 2	2762 2763	5694 2	IR 2206	11062	IC 718 Ⓡ ◆	E 1274 ◆	11034 2	11036 2 Ⓑ	EN 236 ◆	D 2790	IC 660 A	D 2792		E 1234 ◆	9734 E234 J	E 234 ◆
Roma Termini **375** d.	...	...	...	...	...	...	...	...	...	...	...	...	1415	...	...	...	...	...	...	...	...	...	...	1920
Firenze SMN **375** d.	...	...	...	...	...	...	...	...	...	...	...	...	1621	...	...	...	...	...	...	...	...	1953	...	2148
Venezia Santa Lucia d.	...	1516	1535	...	1615	...	...	1708	1746	...	1758	1845	|	1908	1936	2015	2050	2112	...	2228	...	2355	2355	|
Venezia Mestre a.	...	1525	1544	...	1624	...	...	1719	1755	...	1807	1854	1904	1917	1945	2024	2059	2121	...	2239	...	0004	0004	0042
Venezia Mestre d.	...	1527	1546	...	1626	...	...	1721	1757	...	1809	...	1914	1920	1947	2026	2101	2123	...	2241	...	0006	0102	0102
Treviso d.	...	1547	1607	1635	1648	...	...	1744	1816	...	1828	...	1931	1938	2009	2049	2118	2142	2222	2303	...	|	0118	0118
Conegliano d.	...	1605	1632	1655	1712	1730	...	1810	1838	...	1846	...	1948	1959	2033	2114	2138	2200	2240	2326	...	|	|	|
Vittorio Veneto d.	...	|	...	|	|	1742	...	|	1852	...	|	...	|	|	|	|	|	|	|	|	...	|	|	|
Ponte nelle Alpi d.	1643	|	...	|	|	1818	1906	|	1926	1928	|	...	|	|	|	|	|	|	|	|	...	|	|	|
Belluno a.	1650	|	...	|	|	1825	|	|	1934	|	|	...	|	|	|	|	|	|	|	|	...	|	|	|
Calalzo ▲ a.	...	|	...	|	|	...	1952	|	...	2014	|	...	|	|	|	|	|	|	|	|	...	|	|	|
Pordenone d.	...	1630	...	1721	1741	...	...	1841	...	...	1907	...	2008	2022	2102	2137	2204	2222	2301	2348	...	0056	0150	0150
Udine a.	...	1705	...	1758	1820	...	...	1920	...	...	1938	...	2035	2056	*2150*	2212	2239	2256	2328	0025	...	0127	0219	0219
Udine d.	...	...	...	...	...	...	...	...	...	...	...	...	...	2059	...	...	2254	...	...	...	...	0132	0222	0222
Tarvisio Centrale 🏛 a.	...	...	...	...	...	...	...	...	...	...	...	...	...	2225	...	...	0023	...	...	...	...	0308	0338	0338
Villach Hbf a.	...	...	...	...	...	...	...	...	...	...	...	...	...	2308v	...	...	0111	...	...	...	...	0351	0420	0420

km		D 2771	IC643 IC644 A	11003	11005 2	2740 2741 ⚒	EN 237 ◆	D 2775	🚌 ⑦	D 2743 2 ⚒	2744 2745	E 1275 ◆	D 2777 2	11011 2	IC 717 Ⓡ ◆	5709 2	D 2779 ⑦	D 2755 Ⓒ	D 2749 Ⓐ	11015 2	5680 5681 2	11017	5745	5685 2 ⚒
	Villach Hbf d.	...	...	...	...	...	0352	...	...	...	...	0534v	...	...	...	...	...	...	...	...	...	...	...	...
	Tarvisio Centrale 🏛 d.	...	...	...	...	...	0445	...	...	...	...	0620	...	...	...	...	...	...	...	...	...	...	...	...
	Udine a.	...	...	...	...	...	0612	...	...	...	...	0745	...	...	...	...	...	...	...	...	...	...	...	...
	Udine d.	0415	0520	...	0532	...	0643	0730	...	...	...	0750	0817	0852	0925	...	0950	...	...	1130	...	1215	...	...
	Pordenone d.	0448	0548	...	0605	...	0716	0807	...	...	...	0823	0850	0929	0952	...	1021	...	...	1205	...	1252	...	...
0	**Calalzo ▲** d.	|	|	...	|	...	|	|	0635	0640	...	|	|	|	|	...	|	0945	0945	|	...	|	1245	...
	Belluno d.	|	|	...	|	0624	|	|	|	|	0746	|	|	|	|	...	|	|	|	|	1215	|	|	...
37	Ponte nelle Alpi d.	|	|	...	|	0632	|	|	0725	0732	0757	|	|	|	|	...	|	1034	1034	|	1224	|	1327	1340
64	Vittorio Veneto d.	|	|	...	|	0701	|	|	...	...	0826	|	|	|	|	...	|	1059	1059	|	1255	|	...	1406
78	Conegliano d.	0509	0608	...	0633	0717	0741	0829	...	...	0841	0849	0911	0956	1010	...	1042	1110	1110	1230	1308	1320	...	1418
105	Treviso d.	0531	0625	0633	0700	0737	0805	0848	...	...	0901	0910	0939	1032	1028	...	1059	1130	1135	1258		1348	...	...
126	**Venezia Mestre** a.	0551	...	0655	0721	0755	0821	0911	...	...	0921	0928	1001	1055	1045	...	1117	1147	1201	1321	...	1411	...	...
126	**Venezia Mestre** d.	0553	...	0656	0723	0756	0823	0913	...	...	0923	0930	1002	1057	1055	1108	1119	1149	1203	1322	...	1413	...	...
135	**Venezia Santa Lucia** a.	0602	...	0707	0734	0806	0832	0922	...	...	0932	0939	1011	1106	|	1117	1128	1158	1212	1332	...	1422	...	...
	Firenze SMN **375** a.	...	...	...	...	...	...	...	...	...	...	...	...	...	1356	...	...	...	...	...	...	...	...	...
	Roma Termini **375** a.	...	...	...	...	...	...	...	...	...	...	...	...	...	1605	...	...	...	...	...	...	...	...	...

	11019 2	EC 31 ✕ ◆	5912	11139	D 2783 2	IR 2205 ⚒	11029 2	11143	5690 5691 2	D 2787	11033 2	E 865 ◆	E 867	5697	D 2789	E 233 ◆	D 2765	E 845 ◆	IR 2220	E 873 ◆	E235 9735 W	E 235 ◆		E1235 9731 T
Villach Hbf d.	...	1200	...	...	...	...	...	...	...	...	...	...	...	...	...	1827	...	...	...	...	0014	0014	...	0054
Tarvisio Centrale 🏛 d.	...	1240	...	...	...	...	...	...	...	...	...	...	...	...	...	1912	...	...	...	...	0103	0103	...	0138
Udine a.	...	1358	...	...	...	...	...	...	...	...	...	...	...	...	...	2040	...	...	...	...	0219	0219	...	0256
Udine d.	1315	1401	...	...	1420	1532	1615	...	...	1730	1835	1900	...	...	1930	2045	...	2105	...	2235	0225	0225	...	0302
Pordenone d.	1353	1429	...	...	1456	1602	1652	...	...	1808	1913	1936	...	...	2006	2116	...	2143	...	2310	0252	0252	...	0331
Calalzo ▲ d.	|	|	...	1327	|	|	|	1615	...	|	|	|	1816	...	|	|	2020	|	...	|	|	|	...	|
Belluno d.	|	|	...	|	|	|	|	|	1700	|	|	|	|	*1856*	|	|	|	|	...	|	|	|	...	|
Ponte nelle Alpi d.	|	|	...	1422	|	|	|	1705	1712	|	|	|	1903	1938	|	|	2110	|	...	|	|	|	...	|
Vittorio Veneto d.	|	|	...	1450	|	|	|	...	1742	|	|	|	...	2007	|	|	2136	|	...	|	|	|	...	|
Conegliano d.	1423	|	...	1502	1522	1623	1722	...	1755	1831	1940	2002	...	2018	2029	2139	2150	2208	...	2334	|	|	...	|
Treviso d.	1449	|	...	1522	1541	1640	1747	...	1820	1850	2004	2021	...	...	2048	2158	2209	2229	...	2354	0327	0327	...	|
Venezia Mestre a.	1511	1518	...	1544	1601	1657	1810	...	1844	1911	2016	...	...	...	2111	2216	2226	2251	...	0010	0344	0344	...	0423
Venezia Mestre d.	1513	1531	1524	1546	1603	1659	1812	...	1846	1913	2029	...	...	...	2113	2218	2228	2330	2309	0012	0356	0359	...	0433
Venezia Santa Lucia a.	1522	|	1533	1555	1612	1708	1821	...	1855	1922	2038	...	...	...	2122	2228	2237	|	2318	0021	0405	|	...	0442
Firenze SMN **375** a.	...	1816	...	...	...	...	...	...	...	...	...	...	...	...	...	...	...	0342c	...	...	...	0656	...	0753
Roma Termini **375** a.	...	2020	...	...	...	...	...	...	...	...	...	...	...	...	...	...	...	0625	...	...	...	0930	...	...

◆ – **NOTES** (LISTED BY TRAIN NUMBERS)

- **EC30/1** – ROMULUS – [12] and ✕ Roma - Wien Südbahnhof and v.v; [12] Roma - Salzburg and v.v.
- **E232/3** – GONDOLIERE – [12] Venezia - Villach and v.v; [12] Venezia - Villach (**IC592/597**) - Wien Südbahnhof and v.v.
- **E234/5** – REMUS – 🛏 1,2 cl., ▬ 2 cl. and [12] Roma - Wien Südbahnhof and v.v.
- **EN236/7** – SAN MARCO – 🛏 1,2 cl. (T2), ▬ 2 cl. and [2] Venezia - Wien Südbahnhof and v.v; [12] Venezia - Udine and v.v
- **IC717/8** – MARCO POLO – [1] Roma - Udine and v.v.
- **E844/5** – 🛏 1,2 cl., ▬ 2 cl. and [12] Napoli Campi Flegrei - Udine and v.v.
- **E864/5** – FRECCIA DELLE DOLOMITI – [12] Milano Centrale - Castelfranco Veneto - Treviso - Udine and v.v.
- **E870/3** – [12] Torino Porta Nuova - Venezia - Udine - Trieste and v.v; 🛏 1,2 cl. (T2) and ▬ 2 cl. Genova Piazza Principe - Venezia - Udine - Trieste and v.v.
- **E1234** – Apr. 6 - 22, May 18 - 27: ▬ 2 cl. and [2] Firenze SMN - Wien Südbahnhof; 🛏 1,2 cl., ▬ 2 cl. and [12] Milano - Wien.
- **E1274** – ⑥ Apr. 8 - May 27: 🛏 1,2 cl., ▬ 2 cl. and [12] Venezia - Salzburg - Linz - Summerau - Praha Hlavni.
- **E1275** – ⑤ Apr. 7 - May 28: (from Praha): 🛏 1,2 cl., ▬ 2 cl. and [12] Praha Hlavni - Summerau - Linz - Salzburg - Venezia.
- **A** – FOGAZZARO – [12] Milano - Castelfranco Veneto - Treviso - Udine and v.v.
- **J** – Jan. 8 - Apr. 5, Apr. 23 - May 17: 🛏 1,2 cl., ▬ 2 cl. and [12] Milano - Wien Südbahnhof.
- **T** – Apr. 7 - 23, May 19 - 27 (from Wien): ▬ 2 cl. and [2] Wien Südbahnhof - Firenze SMN; 🛏 1,2 cl., ▬ 2 cl. and [12] Wien - Milano.
- **W** – Jan. 9 - Apr. 6, Apr. 24 - May 18 (from Wien): 🛏 1,2 cl., ▬ 2 cl. and [12] Wien Südbahnhof - Milano.
- **c** – Firenze **Campo di Marte**.
- **e** – Arrives 0926. Connects with 0932 to Belluno.
- **v** – Villach **Westbahnhof**.
- **▲** – Full name of station is Calalzo-Pieve di Cadore-Cortina.

Table 378 UDINE - TRIESTE

1, 2 class except where shown

km		11151	11181	11153	2841	11183	E871	2843	11155	11157	11159	2845	11161	5953	2847	11163	11165	11167	2853	5955	2207	11169	2855	5957
		2⚒	2⚒	⑦	①-⑥	⚒	V		⚒	2⑦		⚒	2⚒	2⑦	①-⑥	2⑦	2⚒	2⚒	2	2⚒	⚒	2⑦		2
0	**Udine** d.	0528	0610	0625	0646	0708	0750	0845	0950	1102	1237	1323	1330	1410	1430	1632	1701	1740	1850	1913	1945	2000	2047	2310
33	Gorizia Centrale d.	0559	0633	0701	0711	0746	0825	0909	1014	1138	1308	1348	1406	1446	1455	1708	1732	1816	1914	1948	2010	2036	2112	2345
55	Monfalcone **376** d.	0622	0700	0725	0731	0811	0846	0930	1036	1202	1329	1412	1430	1511	1516	1732	1754	1840	1935	2011	2031	2100	2133	0009
83	**Trieste Centrale 376** a.	0650	0728	0754	0754	0841	0910	0953	1103	1230	1356	1435	1457	1539	1539	1800	1821	1907	1958	2039	2054	2128	2156	*0047*

	11180	2840	11154	2842		2844	11156	11158		11182	2846	11160		2204	5954	2848	11184	5956	2866	2850	11164	2852	5958	E872
	⚒	⚒	2	⚒		⑦	2⚒	2⑦		2		2⚒		⚒	2	2	⚒	2	2⚒	⚒	2	2	2⚒	V
Trieste Centrale 376 d.	0525	0629	0654	0735	...	0752	0842	0935	...	1046	1224	1320	...	1420	1440	1616	1704	1728	1745	1805	1830	1925	2000	2118
Monfalcone **376** d.	0549	0653	0721	0759	...	0816	0910	1001	...	1114	1248	1348	...	1444	1509	1640	1728	1753	1809	1831	1858	1949	2026	2142
Gorizia Centrale d.	0610	0719	0746	0820	...	0837	0935	1026	...	1138	1309	1413	...	1506	1532	1701	1749	1818	|	1853	1921	2010	2049	2204
Udine a.	0643	0743	0810	0848	...	0901	1010	1101	...	1209	1336	1448	...	1530	1606	1725	1823	1855	1849	1917	1954	2034	2115	2230

V – (12) Torino Porta Nuova - Venezia Santa Lucia - Udine - Trieste and v.v; 🛏 1,2 cl. (T2) and ━ 2 cl. Genova Piazza Principe - Trieste and v.v.

Table 379 MERANO - BOLZANO

2 class only

Rail service Merano - Bolzano. 32 km. Journey time: 40 minutes.

From Merano: 0625, 0644 ⚒, 0710, 0740 ⚒, 0840, 0940, 1040 ⚒, 1140, 1240, 1340, 1440, 1540, 1640, 1740, 1816 Ⓐ, 1840, 1940, 2200 ⑦.

From Bolzano: 0648 ⚒, 0736, 0844, 0944 ⚒, 1044, 1144 ⚒, 1244, 1344, 1444, 1544, 1644, 1722 Ⓐ, 1744, 1844, 1922, 1944, 2050, 2305 ⑦.

Table 380 INNSBRUCK - BOLZANO - VERONA - BOLOGNA

1, 2 class except where shown

km		IC 709	IR 2251	IR 2253	IR 2255	5209		IC711 717	IR 2257		E 1125	5213	E 1117	EC81 EC82	11451	IR 2259	E 1183	5215	E 489	EC 85	IR 2261	5221	E 433	2677
				①-⑥		2		🍷 A			♦	2	2 ♦	✕ K	2		2 ♦	2	🍷 ♦	✕ ♦	❖	2 ⚒	♦	2H
0	**Innsbruck** d.	...	...	...	...	0604	...	...	...	...	0719	0804	0810	0839	...	...	0856	0904	1026	1122	...	1204	1248	...
23	Steinach in Tirol d.	...	...	...	...	0627	...	...	...	...	0746	0827	0834	|	...	...	0922	0927	1052	|	...	1227	|	...
37	**Brennero** 🏛 a.	...	...	...	...	0645	...	...	...	...	0802	0845	0850	0915	...	...	0938	0945	1108	1159	...	1245	1320	...
37	**Brennero** 🏛 d.	...	...	...	0542	...	...	...	...	...	0822	...	0910	0925	...	...	0958	...	1128	1214	...	...	1330	...
60	Vipiteno d.	...	...	...	0602	...	...	...	...	...	|	...	0931	|	...	...	1016	...	1146	|	...	...	1350	...
78	Fortezza d.	...	...	...	0620	...	...	...	...	...	0856	...	0950	0957	...	...	1033	...	1202	1248	...	...	1408	1413
89	Bressanone d.	...	...	...	0630	...	...	...	...	...	0905	...	...	1006	...	...	1043	...	1212	1257	...	...	...	1422
99	Chiusa d.	...	...	...	0639	...	...	...	...	...	0914	...	...	|	...	...	1053	...	|	|	...	...	...	1431
127	**Bolzano** a.	...	...	...	0707	...	...	...	...	...	0939	...	...	1038	...	...	1120	...	1258	1329	...	...	...	1456
127	**Bolzano** d.	0548	0600	0635	0710	...	...	0930	0936	...	...	...	...	1040	...	1136	1140	...	1301	1332	1336	...	...	...
143	Ora d.	|	0610	0646	0721	...	...	|	0947	...	...	...	...	|	...	1147	1151	...	1311	|	1347	...	...	...
165	Mezzocorona d.	|	0623	0658	0736	...	...	|	0959	...	...	...	...	|	...	1159	1206	...	1324	|	1359	...	...	...
182	**Trento** d.	0618	0634	0710	0748	...	...	1000	1011	...	...	...	...	1108	...	1211	1221	...	1337	1402	1411	...	...	...
206	Rovereto d.	0631	0647	0724	0851	...	...	1013	1024	...	...	...	...	1121	...	1224	1237	...	1350	1415	1424	...	...	...
274	**Verona** a.	0720	0741	0815	0904**e**	...	...	1102	1118	...	...	...	...	1210	...	1318	1330	...	1440	1504	1518	...	...	...
274	**Verona** d.	0734	...	...	0942**e**	...	...	1108	1130	...	...	...	...	1223	1247	1330	...	...	...	1518	1530	...	...	...
304	Nogara d.	0810	...	...	1055**e**	...	...	|	1205	...	...	...	...	|	1329	1405	...	...	...	|	1604	...	...	...
388	**Bologna** a.	0902	...	...	...	...	...	1234	1314	...	...	...	...	|	1450	1514	...	...	...	1706	1714	...	...	...
	Milano Centrale **350** a.	...	...	...	...	...	...	|	...	...	...	...	...	1355	...	...	...	...	...	|	...	...	...	...
	Venezia Santa Lucia **350** a.	...	...	...	...	...	...	|	...	...	...	...	...	...	...	...	...	...	...	|	...	...	...	...
	Firenze SMN **370** a.	...	...	...	...	...	...	1356	...	...	...	...	...	...	...	...	...	...	...	1826	...	...	...	...
	Roma Termini **370** a.	...	...	...	...	...	...	1605	...	...	...	...	...	...	...	...	...	...	...	2030	...	...	...	...
	Napoli Centrale **370** a.	...	...	...	...	...	...	...	...	...	...	...	...	...	...	...	...	...	...	...	...	...	...	...

	IR 2263	5223	5225	5227	EC 13	IR 2265	5229	E 1771	D 2941	4607	EC87 EC88	IR 2267	5235	5237	E 1757	E 285	E847 825	5241	E 287	5245	E 1289	E 289	E289 2090 2185	E289 E223
		2	2 ⚒	2	✕ ♦		2 Ⓐ	♦	2	2 ♦	✕ M	🍷	2 Ⓐ	2	♦	♦	B	2	♦	2	♦	♦	F	C
Innsbruck d.	...	1304	1404	1504	1522	...	1604	...	...	1704	1722	...	1830	1904	...	1924	...	2104	2222	2317	2345	0138	0138	0138
Steinach in Tirol d.	...	1327	1427	1527	|	...	1627	...	...	1727	|	...	1853	1927	...	1950	...	2127	|	2340	|	|	|	|
Brennero 🏛 a.	...	1345	1445	1545	1559	...	1645	...	...	1745	1759	...	1911	1945	...	2006	...	2145	2259	2358	0022	0215	0215	0215
Brennero 🏛 d.	...	...	▬	...	1614	...	...	...	...	...	1814	...	...	...	...	2026	...	...	2319	...	0042	0235	0235	0235
Vipiteno d.	...	...	...	...	|	...	...	...	...	...	|	...	...	...	...	2047	...	...	|	...	|	|	|	|
Fortezza d.	...	...	...	...	1648	...	...	...	...	...	1848	...	...	...	2022	2104	...	...	2353	...	|	|	|	|
Bressanone d.	...	...	...	...	1657	...	...	...	...	...	1857	...	...	...	2033	2114	...	...	0003	...	0125	0318	0318	0318
Chiusa d.	...	...	**10915**	...	|	...	...	...	...	...	|	...	...	...	2043	2124	...	...	|	...	|	|	|	|
Bolzano a.	...	...	2	...	1729	...	...	...	...	...	1931	...	...	...	2110	2155	...	...	0034	...	0155	0354	0354	0354
Bolzano d.	1536	...	1626	...	1732	1736	...	1820	...	...	1934	1958	...	...	2137	...	2245	...	0037	...	0158	0359	0359	0359
Ora d.	1547	...	1641	...	|	1747	...	1831	...	...	|	2009	...	...	2150	...	2258	...	|	...	|	|	|	|
Mezzocorona d.	1559	...	1700	...	|	1759	...	1844	...	...	|	2022	...	...	2206	...	2312	...	|	...	|	0420	0420	0420
Trento d.	1611	...	1715	...	1802	1811	...	1858	...	...	2007	2036	...	...	2223	...	2327	...	0108	...	0228	0435	0435	0435
Rovereto d.	1624	...	1729	...	1815	1824	...	1913	...	...	2020	2049	...	...	2240	...	2342	...	|	...	0242	0449	0449	0449
Verona a.	1718	...	1830	...	1905	1918	...	2001	...	...	2108	2142	...	...	2332	...	0035	...	0208	...	0335	0540	0540	0540
Verona d.	1730	...	...	...	1910	1930	...	2015	2050	...	2121	2156	...	...	2346	...	0055	...	0226	...	0350	0600	0640	0658
Nogara d.	1808	...	...	...	|	2006	...	|	2132	...	|	2239	...	...	|	...	|	...	|	...	|	0636	|	|
Bologna a.	1914	...	...	...	|	2114	...	2215	2246	...	|	2350	...	...	0128	...	0232	...	0408	...	0532	0755	|	|
Milano Centrale **350** a.	...	...	...	...	|	...	...	|	...	...	2250	...	...	...	|	...	|	...	|	...	...	|	0830	|
Venezia Santa Lucia **350** a.	...	...	...	...	2035	...	...	|	...	...	...	...	...	...	|	...	|	...	|	...	...	|	...	0845
Firenze SMN **370** a.	...	...	...	...	...	...	...	2350**c**	...	...	...	...	...	...	|	...	0418**c**	...	0533**c**	...	...	0912	...	...
Roma Termini **370** a.	...	...	...	...	...	...	...	0220**t**	...	...	...	...	...	...	0654**t**	...	0710	...	0815	...	...	...	...	...
Napoli Centrale **370** a.	...	...	...	...	...	...	...	0433**v**	...	...	...	...	...	...	...	...	...	...	1038	...	...	...	...	...

♦ – **NOTES** (LISTED BY TRAIN NUMBERS)

EC13 – PAGANINI – (12) and ✕ Dortmund - Venezia.
EC85 – MICHELANGELO – (12) and ✕ München Hbf - Roma.
E285 – (12) München Hbf - Bolzano.
E287 – 🛏 1,2 cl., ━ 2 cl. and (2) München Hbf - Napoli.
E289 – BRENNER EXPRESS – 🛏 1,2 cl., ━ 2 cl. and (2) München Hbf - Firenze.
E433 – VAL PUSTERIA – (12) Innsbruck - Lienz - Villach - Wien Westbahnhof.
E489 – (12) München Hbf - Ancona; 🍷 Verona - Bologna.
E1117 – SKI-EXPRESS – ⑤ Dec. 23 - Apr. 7 (from Brussels): 🛏 1,2 cl. (T2), ━ 2 cl., (2) and 🍷 Brussels - San Candido.
E1125 – DOLOMITEN EXPRESS – ⑤ Jan. 6 - Mar. 24, also Dec. 20, 22, 25, Jan. 4 (from Dortmund/Hamburg): 🛏 1,2 cl., ━ 2 cl. and (2) Dortmund - Bolzano; 🛏 1,2 cl. and ━ 2 cl. Hamburg - Bolzano.
E1183 – SPREE-ALPEN EXPRESS – ⑤ Jan. 6 - Apr. 21, also Dec. 22, 25, Apr. 13, **not** Apr. 14 (from Berlin): ━ 2 cl. and (2) Berlin - Verona.
E1289 – May 19 - 26 (from München): ━ 2 cl. and (2) München - Pescara.
E1757 – Dec. 17 - Jan. 4, Jan. 7, 8, 14, 15, Jan. 21 - Apr. 15, 17: 🛏 1,2 cl., 🛏 1,2 cl. (T2), ━ 2 cl. and (12) San Candido - Roma; ━ 2 cl. and (12) Bolzano - Roma.
E1771 – ⑤ Jan. 6 - Mar. 17, also Dec. 20, 21, 22, 27, 28, 29, Jan. 1, 2, 3, Apr. 12, 13, 17: 🛏 1,2 cl. (T2), ━ 2 cl. and (12) Bolzano - Reggio.

IR2267 – (12) Bolzano - Bologna; ━ 2 cl. and (12) (also 🛏 1,2 cl. on ⑦ Jan. 15 - Apr. 9 and Dec. 21 - 24, 26 - 31, Jan. 2 - 9, Apr. 14, 15, 18, 19) Bolzano - Bologna (**925**) - Lecce; 🍷 Trento - Bologna.
4607 – (2) Innsbruck - Brennero; also conveys through carriages for Lienz. Passengers in these may not alight in Italy.

A – MARCO POLO – (1) Bolzano - Roma.
B – 🛏 1,2 cl., 🛏 1,2 cl. (T2), ━ 2 cl. and (12) Bolzano - Roma.
C – BRENNER EXPRESS - ━ 2 cl. and (2) München - Verona (**223**) - Venezia
F – BRENNER EXPRESS – 🛏 1,2 cl., ━ 2 cl. and (2) München - Milano - Genova Piazza Principe.
H – (2) San Candido - Bolzano.
K – GARDA – (12) and ✕ München Hbf - Milano.
M – LEONARDO DA VINCI – (12) and ✕ München Hbf - Milano.
c – Firenze **Campo di Marte**.
e – Ⓒ only.
t – Roma **Tiburtina**.
v – Napoli **Campi Flegrei**.
❖ – **Not** Dec. 25, Jan. 1.

Table 380 BOLOGNA - VERONA - BOLZANO - INNSBRUCK

1, 2 class except where shown

	5210	5214	E 282	5400	5402	2674	5218	E 1758	E 284	E822 E848	11444	10924	10922	E 1770	EC89 EC86	IR 2250	2692	5226	EC 12	10910	IR 2256	EC 84	IC 432	5234
	2	2		2	2	2	2				2	2	2		✕		2	2	✕	2		✕		2
			♦	⚒	H			♦	♦	B		⑦	Ⓐ	♦	M	❖		⚒	♦	⚒		♦	♦	Ⓐ
Napoli Centrale **370** d.	...	...	...	...	...	...	...	...	...	...	...	...	...	2308v	...	...	...	...	...	...	...	...	...	...
Roma Termini **370** d.	...	...	...	...	...	...	...	2202t	...	2230b	...	...	...	0123t	...	...	...	...	...	...	...	0725	...	...
Firenze SMN **370** d.	...	...	...	...	...	...	...	0123c	...	0203b	...	...	...	0425c	...	...	...	...	...	...	...	0827	...	...
Venezia Santa Lucia **350** d.	...	...	...	...	...	...	...	|	...	|	...	...	...	|	...	...	...	...	0855	...	...	|	...	...
Milano Centrale **350** d.	...	...	...	...	...	...	...	|	...	|	...	...	...	|	0700	...	...	...	|	...	...	|	...	...
Bologna d.	...	...	...	...	...	...	...	0315	...	0425	0524	...	...	0539	|	0643	...	...	|	...	...	1038	...	...
Nogara d.	...	...	...	...	...	...	...	0429	...	0529	0705	...	...	0711	|	0752	...	...	|	...	...	|	...	...
Verona a.	...	...	...	...	...	...	...	0504	...	0604	0730	...	...	0748	0820	0825	...	...	1050	...	...	1241	...	...
Verona d.	...	...	...	...	...	...	...	0522	...	0630	▬	0740	...	0802	0832	0840	...	...	1054	...	1240	1255	...	...
Rovereto d.	...	...	...	...	...	...	...	0609	...	0724	...	0831	...	0844	0915	0928	...	...	1137	...	1328	1338	...	...
Trento d.	...	...	...	0610	...	...	...	0627	...	0743	...	0847	0848	0902	0932	0942	...	...	1152	1238	1342	1352	...	...
Mezzocorona d.	...	...	...	0621	...	...	...	0641	...	0755	...	0858	0859	0913	|	0954	...	...	|	1250	1354	|	...	...
Ora d.	...	...	...	0642	...	...	...	0658	...	0810	...	0910	0914	0928	|	1011	...	...	|	1310	1411	|	...	...
Bolzano a.	...	...	...	0700	...	...	...	0714	...	0826	...	0924	0928	0942	1015	1024	...	...	1230	1325	1424	1430	...	...
Bolzano d.	...	...	0600	...	0710	...	...	0730	0800	...	...	...	...	...	1030	▬	1204	...	1233	1327	▬	1433	...	...
Chiusa d.	...	...	0627	...	0733	...	...	0756	0827	...	...	...	...	...	|	...	1225	...	1300	1348	...	|	...	...
Bressanone d.	...	...	0637	...	0742	...	...	0808	0837	...	...	...	...	...	1059	...	1236	...	1311	1352	...	1500	...	...
Fortezza d.	...	...	0648	...	0752	0809	...	0825	0850	...	...	...	...	...	1110	...	1247	...	|	1407	...	1511	1537	...
Vipiteno d.	...	...	0711	...	...	0826	...	...	0911	...	**5220**	...	...	...	|	**5224**	...	...	|	1426	**5230**	|	1554	...
Brennero 🏛 a.	...	...	0741	...	...	0850	...	...	0941	...	2	...	...	...	1149	2	...	...	1349	1448	2	1549	1613	...
Brennero 🏛 d.	0614	0729	0756	...	...	...	0904	...	0956	...	1014	...	...	...	1204	1214	...	1314	1404	...	1514	1604	1623	1721
Steinach in Tirol d.	0632	0747	0817	...	...	...	0922	...	1017	...	1032	...	...	...	|	1232	...	1332	|	...	1532	|	1643	1739
Innsbruck a.	0655	0810	0834	...	...	...	0945	...	1034	...	1055	...	...	...	1227	...	...	1355	1437	...	1555	1637	1659	1802

	E 488	IR 2258	2696	10914	5406	5238	E 1182	IR 2260	EC83 EC80	E 1116	10916	5464	E 1124	IR 2262	IC718 IC708	11456	IR 2264	IC 710	IR 2266	2172 2117 E288	9720 E220 E288	E 288	E 1288	E 286
	🍷		2	2	2	2			✕	🍷	2	2				2								
	♦		J	⚒	Ⓑ	Ⓐ	♦		K	♦	⚒	Ⓑ	♦		A		♦			F	C	♦	♦	
Napoli Centrale **370** d.	...	...	...	...	...	...	...	...	...	...	...	...	...	...	...	...	...	...	...	...	...	...	...	1815
Roma Termini **370** d.	...	...	...	...	...	...	...	...	...	...	...	...	...	...	1415	...	...	...	...	...	...	...	...	2035
Firenze SMN **370** d.	...	...	...	...	...	...	...	...	...	...	...	...	...	...	1621	...	...	...	...	...	...	2125	...	2325c
Venezia Santa Lucia **350** d.	...	...	...	...	...	...	...	...	...	...	...	...	...	...	|	...	...	...	...	...	2205	|	...	|
Milano Centrale **350** d.	...	...	...	...	...	...	...	...	1530	...	...	...	...	...	|	...	...	...	...	2210	|	|	...	|
Bologna d.	*1050*	1245	...	...	...	...	...	1445	|	...	...	...	...	1645	1742	1751	1845	1948	2045	|	|	2240	0008	0050
Nogara d.	*1216*	1357	...	...	...	...	...	1557	|	...	...	...	...	1756	|	1917	1957	2043	2157	|	|	2331	|	|
Verona a.	*1251*	1428	...	...	...	...	...	1628	1707	...	...	...	...	1828	1906	2000	2028	2114	2228	2351	0002	0010	0145	0232
Verona d.	1406	1440	...	1549	...	...	1600	1640	1721	...	...	...	...	1840	1912	...	2040	2129	2240	0030	0030	0030	0208	0255
Rovereto d.	1449	1528	...	1639	...	...	1645	1728	1804	...	...	...	...	1928	1954	...	2128	2211	2328	0113	0113	0113	0252	|
Trento d.	1504	1542	...	1654	...	...	1702	1742	1820	...	1828	...	...	1942	2009	...	2142	2225	2342	0128	0128	0128	0309	0350
Mezzocorona d.	1515	1554	...	1706	...	...	1713	1754	|	...	1839	...	...	1954	|	...	2154	|	2354	|	|	|	|	|
Ora d.	1529	1611	...	1723	...	...	1731	1811	|	...	1901	...	...	2011	|	...	2211	|	0011	|	|	|	|	|
Bolzano a.	1546	1624	...	1739	...	...	1749	1824	1852	...	1916	...	...	2024	2042	...	2224	2300	0024	0202	0202	0202	0345	0423
Bolzano d.	1600	▬	1712	...	1750	...	1756	▬	1854	...	...	1925	2016	2048	▬	...	2305h	...	...	0212	0212	0212	0355	0426
Chiusa d.	1621	...	1734	...	1813	...	1824	...	|	...	...	1949	2038	2109	...	...	2327h	...	...	|	|	|	|	|
Bressanone d.	1632	...	1743	...	1822	...	1834	...	1924	...	...	1958	2047	2117	...	...	2336h	...	...	0239	0239	0239	0424	0456
Fortezza d.	1650	...	1755	...	1831	...	1846	...	1935	1944	...	2009	2101	2126	...	...	2345h	...	...	0252	0252	0252	|	0509
Vipiteno d.	1707	**5236**	...	...	1847	...	1903	**5240**	|	2002	...	2028	|	2143	**5242**	...	...	...	...	|	|	|	|	|
Brennero 🏛 a.	1730	2	...	...	1911	...	1928	2	2015	2029	...	2051	2140	2206	2	...	...	...	...	0331	0331	0331	0520	0548
Brennero 🏛 d.	1750	1814	...	...	...	1920	1948	2003	2025	2049	...	...	2200	...	2216	...	...	...	...	0351	0351	0351	0540	0604
Steinach in Tirol d.	1806	1832	...	...	...	1938	2004	2021	|	2105	...	...	2216	...	2234	...	...	...	...	|	|	|	|	|
Innsbruck a.	1828	1855	...	...	...	2001	2026	2044	2058	2125	...	...	2238	...	2257	...	...	...	...	0424	0424	0424	0613	0637

NOTES (LISTED BY TRAIN NUMBERS)

C12 – PAGANINI – [12] and ✕ Venezia Santa Lucia - Dortmund.
C84 – MICHELANGELO – [12] and ✕ Roma - München Hbf.
282 – ① - ⑤, **not** Dec. 17 - Jan. 8, Apr. 14 - 17): [12] Bolzano - München Hbf.
284 – ⑥⑦ (daily Dec. 17 - Jan. 8, Apr. 14 - 17): [12] Bolzano - München Hbf.
286 – 🛏 1,2 cl., ▬ 2 cl. and [12] Napoli - München Hbf.
288 – BRENNER EXPRESS – 🛏 1,2 cl., ▬ 2 cl. and [12] Firenze - München.
432 – VAL PUSTERIA – [12] Wien Südbahnhof - Lienz - Innsbruck.
88 – [12] Ancona - München; 🍷 Bologna - Verona.
116 – SKI-EXPRESS – ⑥ Dec. 31 - Apr. 15: 🛏 1,2 cl. (T2), ▬ 2 cl., [2] and 🍷 San Candido - Brussels.
124 – DOLOMITEN EXPRESS – ⑥ Jan. 7 - Mar. 25, also Dec. 17, 21, 23, Jan. 1, 5: 🛏 1,2 cl., ▬ 2 cl. and [2] Bolzano - Dortmund; 🛏 1,2 cl. and ▬ 2 cl. Bolzano - Hamburg.
182 – SPREE ALPEN EXPRESS – ⑥ Jan. 7 - Apr. 8, also Dec. 17, 23, 26, Apr. 17, Apr. 22: ▬ 2 cl. and [2] Verona - Berlin.
288 – May 21 - 27 only: ▬ 2 cl. and [2] Pescara - München.
758 – Dec. 16 - Jan. 3, Jan. 20 - Apr. 15, also Jan. 6, 7, 13, 14 (from Roma): 🛏 1,2 cl., 🛏 1,2 cl. (T2), ▬ 2 cl. and [12] Roma - San Candido; ▬ 2 cl. and [12] Roma - Bolzano.
770 – ⑤ Jan. 6 - Mar. 17, also Dec. 21, 22, 23, 28, 29, 30, Jan. 2, 3, 4, Apr. 13, 14, 18 (from Reggio): 🛏 1,2 cl. (T2), ▬ 2 cl. and [12] Reggio - Bolzano.

IR2250 – **Not** Dec. 25, Jan.1 (from Bologna): [12] Bologna - Bolzano; ▬ 2 cl. and [12] (also 🛏 1,2 cl. on ⑤ Jan. 13 - Apr. 7 and Dec. 19 - 23, 25 - 30, Jan. 1 - 7, Apr. 13, 14, 17, 18 from Lecce) Lecce - Bolzano.
IR2264 – [12] Verona Ⓑ, Bologna ⑥ - Bolzano. Extended to Fortezza on ⑦. **Not** Dec. 25, Jan. 1.
A – MARCO POLO – [1] Roma - Bolzano.
B – 🛏 1,2 cl., 🛏 1,2 cl. (T2), ▬ 2 cl. and [12] Roma - Bolzano.
C – BRENNER EXPRESS – ▬ 2 cl. and [2] Venezia Santa Lucia - München Hbf.
F – BRENNER EXPRESS – 🛏 1,2 cl., ▬ 2 cl. and [12] Genova Piazza Principe - Milano - München Hbf.
H – [2] Bolzano - San Candido.
J – [2] Bolzano - Fortezza (San Candido on Ⓑ).
K – GARDA – [12] and ✕ Milano - München Hbf.
M – LEONARDO DA VINCI – [12] and ✕ Milano - München Hbf.
b – Train number **E822**.
c – Firenze **Campo di Marte**.
h – ⑦ only, **not** Dec. 25, Jan. 1.
t – Roma **Tiburtina**.
v – Napoli **Campi Flegrei**.
❖ – **Not** Dec. 25, Jan. 1.

able 381 FORTEZZA - LIENZ

2 class only except where shown

km		4611	2681	4613	4601	5401	E 1759	4615	2683	D/E 1117	2685	4617	2687	IC/E 433	4619	4603	2689	2691	4605	2693	4621	2695	4607	2697	2699
			⚒				♦		B	♦				♦		⑥	Ⓑ	⑥	⑤			Ⓑ			K
	Innsbruck **380** d.	...	...	...	0710	...	...	...	...	0810	...	...	...	1248	...	1357	...	...	1448	...	...	...	1704	...	...
	Steinach in Tirol d.	...	...	...	0736	...	...	...	...	0834	...	...	...	|	...	1421	...	...	1512	...	...	...	1727	...	...
	Bolzano **380** d.	...	...	...	|	0710	0730	...	...	|	...	...	...	|	...	|	...	...	|	...	...	1712	|	...	...
0	**Fortezza** d.	...	0652	...	|	0808	0845	...	1002	1000	1126	...	1252	1410	...	|	1518	1543	|	1707	...	1802	|	1940	2130
33	Brunico d.	...	0733	...	|	0840	0935	...	1037	1042	1202	...	1326	1439	...	|	1601	1620	|	1739	...	1837	|	2016	2202
61	Dobbiaco d.	...	0804	...	|	0914	1013	...	1108	1118	1234	...	1358	1514	...	|	1632	1650	|	1810	...	1908	|	2047	2233
65	**San Candido** 🏛 a.	...	0810	...	0940u	0920	1018	...	1114	1124	1239	...	1404	1520	...	1633u	1637	1655	1733u	1815	...	1913	1939u	2053	2239
65	**San Candido** 🏛 d.	0645	...	0832	0940u	...	...	1033	...	...	...	1242	...	1532	1555	1633u	...	...	1733u	...	1823	...	1939u	...	...
78	Sillian d.	0702	...	0849	0957	...	...	1051	...	...	...	1258	...	1552	1615	1646	...	...	1748	...	1840	...	1956	...	...
08	**Lienz** a.	0733	...	0920	1027	...	...	1123	...	...	...	1328	...	1612	1648	1715	...	...	1815	...	1914	...	2026	...	...

NOTES (LISTED BY TRAIN NUMBERS)

E433 – VAL PUSTERIA/PUSTERTAL – [12] Innsbruck (**IC**) - Brennero (**E**) - Lienz - Villach - Wien Südbahnhof.
17 – SKI-EXPRESS – ⑥ Dec. 31 - Apr. 15: 🛏 1,2 cl. (T2), ▬ 2 cl., [2] and 🍷 San Candido - Brussels.

E1759 – Dec. 16 - Jan. 3, Jan. 20 - Apr. 15, also Jan. 6, 7, 13, 14 (from Roma): 🛏 1,2 cl., 🛏 1,2 cl. (T2), ▬ 2 cl. and [12] Roma Tiburtina - San Candido.
B – **Not** ⑥ Dec. 24 - Apr. 15.
K – ⑦, **not** Dec. 25, Apr. 16, 30.
u – Stops to pick up only.

Table 381 FORTEZZA - LIENZ

2 class only except where shown

	2672 ①-⑥	4600	2674		4612	2676 ⚒	2678	4614		2680	4632	4602 ⑤⑥	2682 ⚒		E 432 ♦	4616	2684		2686	E 1116 ♦		4618	E 1756 ♦	4604	2694
Lienz d.	...	0530	...	...	0739	...	...	0922	...	...	1105	1137	...	...	1336	1409	...	...	...	...	...	1715	...	1828	...
Sillian d.	...	0603	...	...	0811	...	...	0955	...	...	1139	1212	...	...	1405	1443	...	...	...	...	...	1748	...	1859	...
San Candido 🏨 a.	...	0619s	...	...	0825	...	...	1011	...	...	1153	1227s	...	...	1418	1459	...	...	...	...	...	1805	...	1914s	...
San Candido 🏨 d.	0528	0619s	0655	...	...	0828	0944	...	...	1126	...	1227s	1250	...	1430	...	1525	...	1702	1750	...	...	1820	1914s	1940
Dobbiaco d.	0533	|	0700	...	...	0833	0949	...	...	1131	...	|	1255	...	1435	...	1530	...	1707	1757	...	...	1825	|	1945
Brunico d.	0603	|	0732	...	...	0904	1018	...	...	1201	...	|	1327	...	1504	...	1600	...	1740	1843	...	...	1916	|	2015
Fortezza a.	0638	|	0806	...	...	0937	1053	...	...	1235	...	|	1402	...	1536	...	1634	...	1819	1923	...	...	2000	|	2049
Bolzano **380** a.	0728	|	...	...	...	...	...	...	...	...	...	|	1456	...	|	...	...	...	...	|	...	...	2110	|	...
Steinach in Tirol **380** a.	...	0819	...	...	...	...	...	...	...	...	...	1441	...	...	1638	...	...	...	...	2105	...	...	...	2128	...
Innsbruck **380** a.	...	0840	...	...	...	...	...	...	...	...	...	1502	...	...	1659	...	...	...	...	2125	...	...	...	2149	...

♦ – **NOTES** (LISTED BY TRAIN NUMBERS)

E432 – VAL PUSTERIA – [12] Wien Südbahnhof - Lienz - Innsbruck.

E1116 – SKI-EXPRESS – ⑥ Dec. 31 - Apr. 15: 🛏 1,2 cl. (T2), ━ 2 cl., [2] and 🍸 San Candido - Brussels.

E1756 – Dec. 17 - Jan. 4, Jan. 7, 8, 14, 15, Jan. 21 - Apr. 15, 17: 🛏 1,2 cl., 🛏 1,2 cl. (T2), ━ 1, 2 cl. and [2] San Candido - Roma Tiburtina.

s – Stops to **set down** only.

Table 382 VAL GARDENA and CORTINA 🚌 services

	B	B	B	B	B⚒	B⚒	B⚒	BⒶ	B⑥	B	B
Bolzano d.	0740	1040	1215	*1320*	1415	1510	1615	1715	1735	*1810*	1915
Ponte Gardena d.	0810	1110	1245	1353	1445	|	1645	1745	1805	1852	1945
Ortisei d.	0840	1140	1315	1425	1515	1635	1715	1815	1835	1925	2015
Santa Cristina d.	0852	1152	1327	1437	1527	1647	1727	1827	1847	1937	2027
Selva a.	0902	1202	1337	1447	1537	1657	1737	1837	1857	1947	2037

	B⚒	B	B	B⚒			B	BⒶ	B
Selva d.	0613	0723	0908	1123	...	...	1323	1543	1743
Santa Cristina d.	0623	0733	0918	1133	...	...	1333	1553	1753
Ortisei d.	0635	0745	0930	1145	...	...	1345	1605	1805
Ponte Gardena d.	0705	0813	1000	1215	...	...	1415	1635	1835
Bolzano a.	0735	0845	1030	1245	...	...	1445	1705	1905

Bus service **120**. B – Sept. 12 - June 24, 1995. Operator: Servici Autobus Dolomiti, via Conciapelli 60, 39100, Bolzano, Italy. ☎ – (471) 971259. Fax: (471) 970042.

🚌 service **112** from Dobbiaco - Cortina d'Ampezzo and v.v. *33 km.* Journey time: 40 minutes.

From Dobbiaco Stazione: 0710⚒, 0810⑦, 1018, 1410**M**, 1515, 1812⚒.

From Cortina d'Ampezzo: 0850, 1245, 1600, 1655**M**, 1855⚒.

M – Dec. 26 - Apr. 1.

Operator: Servizi Autobus Dolomiti, via Conciapelli 60, 39100, Bolzano, Italy. ☎ – (471) 971259. Fax: (471) 970042.

🚌 service Cortina d'Ampezzo - Calalzo-Pieve di Cadore-Cortina. *35 km.* Journey time: 55 - 60 minutes. **Subject to confirmation.**

From Cortina d'Ampezzo: 0535 ⚒, 0625 ⚒, 0650 **H**, 0750, 0830, 0910, 1010 ⚒, 1130, 1215, 1240 ⚒, 1350, 1500, 1600 ⚒, 1640, 1700 **H**, 1805, 1900, 1940 ⚒.

From Calalzo Stazione: 0635 ⚒, 0700 ⚒, 0740 ⚒, 0810, 0840, 0930, 1030, 1115 ⚒, 1215 ⚒, 1245, 1405 ⚒, 1450, 1545, 1700, 1745, 1915, 2030.

H – ⑦ and holidays.

Operator: Dolomitibus, via Col Da Ren, 32100, Belluno, Italy. ☎ – (437) 940000. Fax: (437) 940522

Table 383 TRENTO - VENEZIA and TREVISO

2 class only except where shown

km		5633 ⚒	5635 ⚒	5637 ⚒	2803	2823 ⚒	5709	2825 ⑦	5643 ⚒	5713	🚌 ⑦	5649 ⚒	5651 ⚒	E863 A	2805	5653	5655 ⚒	5657	2807 C	2835 ⚒	2837 ⑦	5661 ⚒	IC659 B
0	**Trento** d.	...	...	...	0638	...	0808	...	...	1014	...	...	...	...	1414	...	...	...	1726	...	...	...	...
97	Bassano del Grappa d.	...	...	...	0833	...	1014	...	...	1221	...	...	...	...	1609	...	...	...	1922	...	...	...	...
	Milano Centrale **350** d.	...	...	...	|	...	|	...	...	|	...	...	...	1320	|	...	...	...	|	...	...	...	1930
	Vicenza d.	0615	0635	0713	|	0918	|	1115	1123	|	1205	1327	1417	1540	|	1635	1715	1836	|	1913	1940	2045	2138
116	Castelfranco Veneto d.	0655	0711	0751	0850	1001	1033	1145	1202	1242	1300	1408	1500	1613	1627	1713	1753	1915	1941	1943	2009	2125	2205
148	**Venezia Mestre 350** a.	|	|	|	0917	|	1106	|	|	1317	|	|	|	|	1700	|	|	|	2017	|	|	|	|
157	**Venezia Santa Lucia 350** a.	|	|	|	0928	|	1117	|	|	1328	|	|	|	|	1711	|	|	|	2028	|	|	|	|
	Treviso Centrale a.	0718	0732	0815	...	1020	...	1202	1226	...	1325	1432	1524	1632	...	1737	1817	1940	...	2000	2027	2148	2220
	Udine **377** a.	...	...	...	...	...	...	...	...	...	...	...	...	1758	...	...	...	...	...	...	...	...	2328

	5630 ⚒	IC644 B	🚌 ⑦	2802 C	5634 ⚒	2818 ⑦	2804 C	2824	2826 ⑦	5714	5644 ⚒	2828 ⑦	5648 ⚒	2830 ⑦	5650 ⚒	5722	5652	5654 ⚒	🚌 ⑦	5658 ⚒	2838	2808 C	E866 A
Udine **377** d.	...	0520	...	...	...	...	...	...	...	...	...	...	...	...	...	...	...	...	...	...	...	...	1900
Treviso Centrale d.	0555	0627	0630	...	0709	0755	...	0952	1155	...	1320	1355	1446	1555	1612	...	1751	1822	1825	1913	1956	...	2023
Venezia Santa Lucia 350 d.	|	|	|	0614	|	|	0736	|	|	1214	|	|	|	|	|	1628	|	|	|	|	|	1933	|
Venezia Mestre 350 d.	|	|	|	0625	|	|	0747	|	|	1226	|	|	|	|	|	1641	|	|	|	|	|	1944	|
Castelfranco Veneto d.	0620	0644	0655	0704	0733	0814	0816	1020	1214	1312	1345	1414	1510	1614	1635	1720	1814	1850	1858	1937	2016	2020	2100
Vicenza a.	0700	0711	0745	|	0812	0842	|	1050	1242	|	1425	1443	1552	1642	1715	|	1852	1930	1950	2013	2045	|	2136
Milano Centrale **350** a.	...	0915	...	|	...	...	|	...	...	|	...	...	...	...	...	|	...	...	...	...	...	|	2358
Bassano del Grappa d.	...	...	...	0727	...	...	0835	...	...	1339	...	...	...	...	...	1742	...	...	...	...	...	2040	...
Trento a.	...	...	...	0922	...	...	1032	...	...	1532	...	...	...	...	...	1952	...	...	...	...	...	2230	...

A – FRECCIA DELLE DOLOMITI - [12] Milano - Udine and v.v; [12] Milano - Castelfranco Veneto - Calalzo and v.v.

B – FOGAZZARO - [12] Milano - Udine and v.v.

C – Conveys [12].

Table 384 PADOVA and TREVISO - CALALZO

1, 2 class except where shown

km		5732 ⚒	2746	5736 ⚒	5672	5878 2⚒	2750	11138	11134 ⚒	11140	5882 ⑦	5884 ⚒	2754 ⚒	5746 2	5890 2	E862 M	5892 2	2760	5896 2	11144	2764	11148	2768 ⑦	E176 A
0	**Padova** d.	...	0620	0650	...	...	0928	1130	...	1233	...	...	1327	...	...	1532	...	1658	...	1740	1905	2030	2200	035
31	Castelfranco Veneto d.	...	0647	0722	...	...	0959	1208	...	1303	...	...	1401	...	...	1625	...	1724	...	1817	1935	2103	2226	|
	Treviso d.	0544	|	|	...	0944	|	|	1240	|	1315	1350	|	1452	1550	|	1700	|	1805	|	|	|	|	050
48	Montebelluna d.	0607	0700	0742	...	0958	1018	1223	1300	1317	1337	1410	1416	1521	1609	1640	1722	1737	1827	1836	1949	2124	2239	052
83	Feltre d.	0648	0738	0823	...	...	1052	1258	...	1359	...	...	1456	1553	...	1719	...	1821	...	1916	2032	2202	2314	061
114	Belluno d.	0722	0812	0853	0914	...	1126	1339	...	1440	...	...	1541	1627	...	1752	...	1856	...	1952	2102	2238	2342	065
121	Ponte nelle Alpi **377** d.	0730	...	...	0922	...	*1141*	1348	...	1449	...	...	1555	1635	...	1801	...	1906	...	*2100*	...	...	...	070
158	**Calalzo 377** ▲ a.	*0831*	...	...	*1015*	...	*1225*	1438	...	1540	...	...	1647	*1725*	...	1853	...	1952	...	...	...	...	...	075

	11125 2	5871 2⚒	11133 2	5875 2⚒	2743 2	5877 2⚒	2747	5879 2⚒	2751	5885 2⚒	11137	5887 2	5745	588 2⑦	11141	5895 2	1143	5897 2	E867 M	5899 2⑦	2759	2765	11147	E17 B
Calalzo 377 ▲ d.	...	...	...	...	0640t	...	0800	...	0845v	...	1105v	...	1245	...	1510	...	1615	...	1816	...	1903z	2020	...	204
Ponte nelle Alpi **377** d.	...	...	...	...	0737	...	0847	...	0937v	...	1157v	...	1328	...	1554	...	1710	...	1906	...	1953z	2102	2112	213
Belluno d.	0515	...	0615	...	0747	...	0857	...	1100	...	1245	...	1340	...	1602	...	1720	...	1915	...	2001	...	2119	214
Feltre d.	0543	...	0648	...	0823	...	0925	...	1131	...	1320	...	1416	...	1636	...	1756	...	1947	...	2032	...	...	222
Montebelluna d.	0625	0635	0740c	0743	0859	0910	1001	1008	1205	1318	1359	1418	1458	1516	1719	1734	1835	1842	2023	2026	2106	...	...	225
Treviso a.	|	0655	|	0800	|	0930	|	1025	|	1338	|	1438	|	1535	|	1755	|	1900	|	2042	|	...	...	231
Castelfranco Veneto d.	0648	...	0800	...	0912	...	1016	...	1223	...	1417	...	1514	...	1741	...	1848	...	2043	...	2119	...	...	|
Padova a.	0725	...	0833	...	0942	...	1045	...	1250	...	1448	...	1545	...	1810	...	1920	...	2112	...	2146	...	...	00

A – Dec. 16 - Jan. 3, Jan. 20 - Apr. 15, also Jan. 6, 7, 13, 14: (from Roma): 🛏 1,2 cl., 🛏 1,2 cl. (T2), ━ 2 cl. and [12] Roma Tiburtina (depart 2112) - Calalzo.

B – Dec. 17 - Jan. 4, Jan. 7, 8, 14, 15, Jan. 21 - Apr. 15, 17: 🛏 1,2 cl., 🛏 1,2 cl. (T2), ━ 2 cl. and [12] Calalzo - Roma Tiburtina, arrive 0735.

M – FRECCIA DELLE DOLOMITI - [12] Padova - Calalzo and v.v; [12] Milano - Calalzo and v.v.

c – Arrive 0732. Connects with 0743 to Treviso.

t – ⚒ only. On ⑦ is connection by 🚌, Calalzo depart 0635.

v – By 🚌.

z – ⑦ only.

▲ – Full name of station is Calalzo-Pieve di Cadore-Cortina.

Table 385 — ROMA - PERUGIA, FIRENZE and ANCONA

1, 2 class except where shown

km		D 3232 (2)	D 3054	D 3150	IC 550 ♦	12070 (2)	12104 (2)	IR 2304	12082	IC 586 ✿R	12108	IR 2322 ♀	12110 (2)	IR 2306	12112 (2)	IC 588 ♀R	2308	D 3152	12114	12088	12116 (2❊)	IR 2310	IC 590 ♦	D 3154
0	Roma Termini d.	…	…	…	…	…	…	0620	…	0700	…	0730	…	0815	…	1015	…	1040	…	…	…	1240	1335	…
	Roma Tiburtina d.	…	…	…	…	…	…	0628	…	0738	…			0823	…			1048	…	…	…	1248	1335	…
	Orte d.	…	…	…	…	…	…	0703	0610	0738	…	0812	…	0858	…	1055	1123	…	…	1208	…	1323	1417	…
	Orvieto d.	…	…	…	…	…	…	0737	…					0930	…		1155	…	…		…	1355		…
	Chiusi d.	…	0545	…	…	…	…	0812	…					0957	…		1222	…	…		…	1422	1501	…
112	Terni d.	…	…	…	…	0526	…	…	0650	0759	…	0839	…	…		1117		…	…	1235	…	1422	1501	…
141	Spoleto d.	…	…	…	…	0558	…	…	0725	0903	…	0903	…	…		1140		…	…	1307	…			…
167	Foligno a.	…	…	0614	…	…	…	…	0746	0839	…	0922	…	…		1155		…	…	1328	…			…
167	Foligno d.	…	…	0543	0617	0636	0652v	…	0753	0842	0845	0925	0934	…	1050	1157		1200	1304	1333	1335			1409
	Assisi d.	…	…	0601	0631		0712v	…	0810	0900		0949		…	1105			1213	1324		1354			1422
	Perugia a.	…	…	0624	0651		0736v	…	0836	0922		1015		…	1127			1232	1352	1416				1440
	Perugia d.	…	…	0627	0653		0738	…	0838					…	1128			1234	1356					1442
	Passignano sul Trasimeno d.	…	…	0657				0810	0905					…	1157			1302	1425					
	Terontola-Cortona d.	…	0609	0712	0725		0822	0832	0915					…	1016	1208		1241	1317	1436		1441	1519	1528
	Arezzo d.	…	0644	0750	0746		0902							…	1040			1305	1344			1505		1553
	Firenze SMN a.	…	0740	0850	0823		1005							…	1120			1345	1447					
224	Fabriano d.	0646	…	…	0752	…	…	0928			1020		…	…		1241		…	…	1454	…	1545		1648
268	Jesi d.	0731	…	…	0838	…	…	1000			1056		…	…		1312		…	…	1544	…			
286	Falconara Marittima 390 d.	0748	…	…	0854	…	…	1014			1109		…	…		1323		…	…	1544	…	1601		
295	Ancona a.	0800	…	…	0903	…	…	1022			1119		…	…		1330		…	…	1610	…			

		IR 12090 (2)	IR 2312 ✿	D 3156	IR 2326	IC 592 ♀	12118	IR 2328	IR 2314	D 3246 (2❊)	12092 Ⓐ	11690 (2)	12120	IR 2330	IR 2316	12122	IC 594 ♀R	12124	IR 2332	IC 596 ♀	IR 2318 ♦	D 3248 ♦	IR 2334 K	IR 2336 L
	Roma Termini d.	…	1325	1440	…	1420	1455	…	1525	1640	…	…	…	1725	1840	…	1835	…	1925	2030	2040	…	2130	2310
	Roma Tiburtina d.	…	1333	1448	…	1428		1533	1648		…	…	…	1733	1848	…		…	1933		2048	…	2137	2323
	Orte d.	1328v	1407	1523	…	1502	1536		1608	1723	…	1648	…	1808	1923	…	1915	…	2007	2110	2123	…	2218	0017
	Orvieto d.			1555	…			1755		1910	…		…		1955	…		…	2155			…		
	Chiusi d.			1622	…			1822			…	1910	…		2022	…		…	2222			…		
	Terni d.	1407v	1435		…	1528	1558		1639		…	1725	…	1836		…	1938	…	2036	2131		…	2207	2245 0044
	Spoleto d.	1438v			…	1555	1619		1707		…	1753	…	1900		…	2000	…	2101	2154		…	2236	2308 0108
	Foligno a.	1500v	1515		…	1616	1634		1723		…	1816	…	1914		…	2016	…	2129	2210		…	2255	2325 0127
	Foligno d.	1502	1520	1600	…	1636	1644	1725		1742	1830	…	1833	1918	…	1953	2018	2040	2122	2214	…	2257	2334 0130
	Assisi d.	1516		1613	…		1700		1759		…	1852	…			2013		2058		2227	…	2313		
	Perugia a.	1543		1632	…		1723		1822		…	1914	…			2039		2119		2243	…	2334		
	Perugia d.	1553		1634	…		1730		1830v		…	1928	…			2040		2120			…	2336		
	Passignano sul Trasimeno d.	1621		1702	…		1759		1900v		…	1956	…			2108		2145			…	0002		
	Terontola-Cortona d.	1634	1641	1724	…		1811		1841	1910v	1931	2008	…	2041	2118	2156		2223		2241	…	0012		
	Arezzo d.		1705	1748	…				1905		2000	…	2105			2305	…							
	Firenze SMN a.		1745	1842	…				1945		2125	…	2150			2345	…							
	Fabriano d.	1620	…	…	1720	1817	…	1940		…	…	…	2023	…	…	2104	…	2217	…	…	…	0024	0225
	Jesi d.	1656	…	…	1750	1858	…			…	…	…	2101	…	…	2135	…	2255	…	…	…	0057	0309
	Falconara Marittima 390 d.	1711	…	…	1801	1910	…			…	…	…	2117	…	…	2148	…	2310	…	…	…	0109	0324
	Ancona a.	1718	…	…	1810	1918	…			…	…	…	2125	…	…	2156	…	2318	…	…	…	0116	0332

km		IR 2321 L	D 3277 ✗	IR 2323	12103 (2✗)	IR 2325	IC 585 ✗R	IC 587	12105 ♦	12107 (2)	IC 551	12109	2305	IC 589 ♀R	12111 (2)	IR 2307 ♀	IR 2327 M	12113	12115	IR 2309 ♀	IR 2329	12117	D 3151
0	Ancona d.	0230	…	…	0440	…	0610	…	…	…	…	…	…	0715	…	…	…	…	1030	…	…	…	…
	Falconara Marittima 390 d.	0240	…	…	0450	…	0619	…	…	…	…	…	…	0726	…	…	0845	…	1043	…	…	…	…
	Jesi d.	0255	…	…	0503	…	0632	…	…	…	…	…	…	0739	…	…	0856	…	1056	…	…	…	…
	Fabriano d.	0338	…	…	0537	…	0703	…	…	…	…	…	…	0809	…	…	0908	…	1134	…	…	…	…
88	Firenze SMN d.		…	…				0630		0650					0815	…	0945	…			…	…	1115
122	Arezzo d.		…	…				0700		0800					0856	…		…	1015	…	1056	…	1215
134	Terontola-Cortona d.		…	…		0608	0642	0731	0738	0828		0850		0920	…	…	1045	1120	…	1248	…	…	1248
165	Passignano sul Trasimeno d.		…	…		0619	0658		0750			0906			…	…		…			…	…	1301
165	Perugia a.		…	0455	0537	0647	0730		0815			0934			…	…		…	1057	…	…	…	1326
189	Perugia d.		…	0517	0600	0658	0739		0816			0936			…	…	1048	1128	1151	…	1240	…	1330
205	Assisi d.		…				0723	0811		0839		1001			…	…	1151	…	…	…	1302	1318	1353
	Foligno a.	0430	…	0530	0615	0629	0704	0748	0740	0825		0857		0901	1016	…	1045	1130	1210	…	1230	1318	1406
	Foligno d.	0435	…	0533		0631	0706	0750	0756					0904		…	1049			…	1232	…	
	Spoleto d.	0456	…	0557		0650	0724	0807	0823					0921		…	1111			…	1252	…	
	Terni d.	0527	…	0628		0725	0746	0837	0900					0945		…	1138			…	1317	…	
	Chiusi d.		0542									0750		0849		…		…	0939	…	…	…	
	Orvieto d.		0612									0916				…		…	1006	…	…	…	
	Orte d.	0556	0647	0656		0756	0807	0859				0948	1008			…	1139	…	1206	…	…	…	
	Roma Tiburtina a.	0632	0725	0732		0832						1022				…	1238	1201	…	…	1346	…	
	Roma Termini a.	0640	…	0740		0840	0845	0938				0855	1030	1047		1120	1240	1311	1423	…	1320	1430	

		IR 2311	IR 2331 ♀✿	12119 (2)	D 3153	IR 2313	IC 593 ♀	IC 591 ♀R	12121 (2✗)	IC 595 R	3155	IR 2315	12123 (2)	IR 2333 ♀	3057 Ⓐ	12125 (2)	IR 2317 ♀	D 3157	IC 597 ♀R	D 3065	12127	12081	IR 2319	12083	IC 559 ♦
	Ancona d.	…	1230	…	…	1448	…	…	…	…	…	1740	…	…	…	1930	…	…	…	2035	…	2235	…		♦
	Falconara Marittima 390 d.	…	1241	…	…	1457	…	…	…	…	…	1750	…	…	…	1939	…	…	…	2048	…	2246	…		
	Jesi d.	…	1256	…	…	1510	…	…	…	…	…	1805	…	…	…	1952	…	…	…	2105	…	2301	…		
	Fabriano d.	…	1344	…	…	1538	…	…	…	…	…	1847	…	…	…	2022	…	…	…	2153	…	2345	…		
	Firenze SMN d.	1215	…	1310	1415							1515	1615	…	1707	…	1815	1807	…	1915	…	2025	…	2119	
	Arezzo d.	1256	…	1415	1456							1614	1656	…	1755	…	1856	1915	…	2026	…	2107	…	2157	
	Terontola-Cortona d.	1320	…	1333	1445	1520		1524				1648	1720	1744	1820	1846	1920	1944	…	2050	2056	2130	…	2229	
	Passignano sul Trasimeno d.		…	1344	1456							1701	1801	…	1859	…	1955	…	…	2107	…		…		
	Perugia a.		…	1414	1520			1552				1728	1828	…	1927	…	2018	…	…	2137	…		…	2256	
	Perugia d.		…	1419	1522							1733	1829	…	1929	…	2020	…	…	2138	…		…	2257	
	Assisi d.		…	1444	1541			1701	1741	1752		1851		…	1951	…	2038	…	…	2200	…		…	2316	
	Foligno a.	1436	1459	1553		1621		1715	1753	1814		1907	1938	…	2008	…	2050	2117	…	2213	2253		…	2324	
	Foligno d.	1438	…			1623		1756					1940	…	…	…	2120	…	…		…		…	2326	
	Spoleto d.	1501	…			1639		1814					2001	…	…	…	2140	…	…		…		…	2344	
	Terni d.	1525	…			1702		1837					2028	…	…	…	2208	…	…		…		…	0014	
	Chiusi d.	1339	…			1539					1739		…	1840	…	1939	…	…	…	2110	…	2149	…		
	Orvieto d.	1406	…			1606					1806		…		…	2006	…	…	…	2216	…		…		
	Orte d.	1438	1556			1638	1726			1901		1838	…	2056	…	2038	2231	…	…	2248	…	2248	…		
	Roma Tiburtina a.	1511	1632			1711						1911	2132	…	2111	…		…	…	2342	…		…		
	Roma Termini a.	1520	1640			1720	1805			1940		1940	2120	…	2120	…	2310	…	…		…		…		

NOTES (LISTED BY TRAIN NUMBERS)

- **550/9** – TACITO – 🍽 Terni - Milano Centrale and v.v.
- **590/1** – TRASIMENO – 🍽 Roma - Terontola - Perugia.
- **586** – IL PERUGINO – ✗, also Dec. 25, Apr. 16, 30: 🍽 Roma - Perugia.
- **2348** – 🛏 Terni - Terontola; 🛌 1,2 cl. (T2) Terni - Terontola (E1910) - Milano Centrale.
- **12105** – 🛏 Terontola - Terni; 🛌 1,2 cl. (T2) Milano Centrale (E1913) - Terontola - Terni.
- **v** – ✗ only.
- **✿** – Not Dec. 25, Jan. 1.

Table 387 — ROVIGO - CHIOGGIA

Rail service Rovigo - Chioggia. 57 km. Journey time 60 minutes (96 by 🚌). 2 class only. All trains/buses call at Adria, 25/45 minutes from Rovigo, 28/50 minutes from Chioggia.
From Rovigo: 0648🅇, 0839🅇, 0840⑦ 🚌, 1236🅇, 1340⑦ 🚌, 1348E, 1620🅇, 1740⑦ 🚌, 1843🅇, 1940⑦ 🚌, 2005 🅇.
From Chioggia: 0620🅇, 0649🅇, 0730⑦ 🚌, 0810🅇, 1228E, 1344⑦ 🚌, 1423🅇, 1544⑦ 🚌, 1723🅇, 1944⑦ 🚌, 2020.

E – 🅇, not Dec. 24 - Jan. 6, Apr. 13 - 19..

Table 388 — BOLOGNA - RAVENNA - RIMINI

2 class only

km		11585	3003	11587		6519	11559	1727 🅇	6521 ⑦		6525 🅇	6527 🅇	11589	11561	6529	11593	6531 🅇	3009	3015	11595	11563	6535	6483	6485
0	Bologna ....d.	...	0613	...	...	...	0821	...	...	...	...	...	1412	...	...	...	...	1720	1818	...	1941	...	2138	2240
42	Castel Bolognese ...d.	...	0647	...	...	...	0858	...	...	...	...	...	1440	...	...	...	...	1756	1852	...	2019	...	2211	2314
56	Lugo ....d.	...	0703	...	...	...	0911	...	...	...	...	...	1457	...	...	...	...	1813	1908	...	2032	...	2226	2327
	Ferrara ....d.	...		0620	...	0720		0820	0920	...	1220	1320		1420	1620	1720		...		1820		2020		
84	Ravenna ....a.	...	0733	0728	...	0831	0933	0929	1019	...	1330	1428	1523	1532	1725	1828	1838	1932	1935	2100	2120	2252	2352
84	Ravenna ....d.	0638	...	0738	...	0838	...	0938	1024	1238	1340	1438	...	1538	1738	...	1840	...	1938	...	2128	...	
105	Cervia ....d.	0701	...	0805	...	0857	...	0959	1040	1258	1401	1501	...	1557	1759	...	1902	...	2001	...	2145	...	
113	Cesenatico ....d.	0708	...	0814	...	0904	...	1007	1047	1305	1408	1508	...	1604	1807	...	1909	...	2008	...	2152	...	
134	Rimini ....a.	0737	...	0850	...	0934	...	1028	1115	1334	1436	1536	...	1635	1835	...	1935	...	2038	...	2216	...	

km		11584	3002 🅇	11586	3004 🅇	6470	6518 🅇	3006	6520	11560	6526	11562	11590	11592	3010	6528 🅇		1832	3014		6530	6480	6532		6842 🅇	6534 🅇
	Rimini ....d.	0520	...	0620	0655	...	...	0820	0920	...	...	1220	1320	...	1420	...	...	1620	...	...	1720	...	1820	...	...	2020
	Cesenatico ....d.	0543	...	0652	0729	...	...	0848	0948	...	...	1249	1353	...	1451	...	...	1655	...	...	1752	...	1853	...	...	2054
	Cervia ....d.	0550	...	0700	0736	...	...	0858	1000	...	...	1259	1400	...	1502	...	...	1702	...	...	1759	...	1901	...	...	2102
	Ravenna ....a.	0611	...	0721	0754	...	...	0917	1023	...	...	1321	1420	...	1525	...	...	1724	...	...	1820	...	1922	...	...	2124
	Ravenna ....d.	0628	0632	0731	0756	0822	0833	0935	1032	1120	1232	1339	1432	1431	...	1727	1730	...	1831	1840	1950	...	2006	2130
	Ferrara ....a.	0742	...	0845	...		0937		1137		1352		1504	1545	...		1840			1940		2102	...		2229
	Lugo ....d.	...	0704	...	0814	0846	...	0956	...	1147	...	1340	...	...	1456	...	...	1758	...	...	1909	...	...	2033	...	
	Castel Bolognese ....d.	...	0720	...	0900		1012	...	1206	...	1358	...	...	1511	...	...	1812	...	...	1922	...	...	2054	...	
	Bologna ....a.	...	0752	...	0852	0935	...	1100	...	1244	...	1435	...	...	1544	...	...	1845	...	...	2012	...	...	2126	...	

Table 389 — ROMA FIUMICINO AIRPORT ✈

Rail service (2 class only) Roma Tiburtina **and** Roma Ostiense - Roma Fiumicino ✈. 26 km. Journey times: to or from Tiburtina 40 minutes; to or from Ostiense 28 minutes
From Tiburtina: 0600, 0620 and every 20 minutes until 2200. **From Fiumicino** ✈: 0655, 0715 and every 20 minutes until 2255. All trains call at **Ostiense** 12 minutes from **Tiburtina.**

Rail service (1 class only) Roma Termini - Roma Fiumicino ✈. Journey time 30 minutes. 26km
From Roma Termini: 0700, 0730, 0810, 0915, and hourly to 2115 (also at 1535, 1735, 1935). **From Roma Fiumicino:** 0750, 0825, 0905, and hourly to 2205, (also at 1625, 1825, 2025)

A special rail service is operated by FS on behalf of Alitalia to or from Roma Fiumicino ✈, Firenze SMN and Napoli Mergellina. These services are available only to passengers holdin
international tickets booked through Alitalia. There are currently 2 services daily between Fiumicino ✈ and both Napoli and Firenze. Journey time is two and a half hours.
Timings of services vary with airline schedules and details should be obtained from Alitalia offices in major cities or direct from Alitalia at Roma Fiumicino Airport ✈ on ☎ (Rome) 6563244

Table 390 — BOLOGNA - ANCONA - BRINDISI - LECCE

1, 2 class except where show

km		12033 2 🅇	12001 2	12003 2	E 961 ⋄	D 3181 2	IC 761 Ⓡ ⚑⋄	IC 785 2 ◆	3511 2	11525 2	E 1289 ◆	IR 2121		E 911 ⚑	IR 2123	IC 565 🅇 2	12635 2 L	E963 E964	IR 2123 2	12035 2	IR 1711 ◆		D 3515 2	1263 2 🅇
	Torino Porta Nuova 400 .d.	...	...	...	...	...	...	...	...	...	...	...		...	0605	0705	...	...	...	...	0625		...	...
	Venezia Santa Lucia 375 .d.	...	...	...	...	...	...	...	...	...	...	...		...	0838	0859	...	...	...	...	0917		...	...
	Milano Centrale 370 ...d.	...	...	...	...	...	...	...	0455	0537	0638	0759		0828	0913		...	...	...	...	0953		...	...
0	**Bologna Centrale** ...d.	...	...	...	...	...	...	...	0536		0713			0841	0924	0934	...	...	...	1005		...	...
50	Faenza ....d.	...	...	...	...	...	...	...	0549	0617	0724	0841		0854	0937		...	...	...	1018		...	...
65	Forlì ....d.	...	...	...	...	...	...	...	0607	0632	0737	0854		0917	0958	1005	...	0958	...	1036		...	...
83	Cesena ....d.	...	...	...	...	...	...	...	0640	0654	0758	0917		0919	1010	1007	...	1010	1039		...	...
112	**Rimini** ....a.	...	...	...	...	...	...	...	0726	0659	0800	0919			1018		...			...	...
112	Rimini ....d.	...	0448	0555	...	...	...	...	0736	0709	0808			1025		...			...	...
121	Riccione ....d.	...	0456	0604	...	...	...	...	0746	0718	0815			→		...			...	...
130	Cattolica ....d.	...	0503	0613	...	...	...	...	0758	0732	0827	0942		1029		...	1037	1107		...	...
145	Pesaro ....d.	...	0515	0625	0653	...	...	0807	0742	0836			1046		...			...	...
157	Fano ....d.	...	0524	0633	0702	...	...	0823	0757	0836			1102		...			...	...
179	Senigallia ....d.	...	0540	0648	0717	...	...	0839		0904			1114		...			...	...
196	Falconara Marittima 385 .d.	...	0556	0704	0731	...	...	0849	0816	0913	1016		1100		...	1123		1144		...	...
204	**Ancona 385** ....a.	...	0604	0713	0738	...	...		0820		1019		1104		...		1130	1148	...	...
204	Ancona ....d.	0614	...	...	0743	...	...		0850		1049				...	1205	1220	...	...
247	Civitanova Marche ...d.	0657	...	...	0816	...	...		0918		1119				...	1239	1252	...	...
288	San Benedetto del Tronto .d.	0741	...	...	0842	...	...		1000		1158				...	1328	1334	...	...
350	**Pescara Centrale** ....a.	0844	...	...	0918	...	...					E 965	1220		...	1240		...	...
350	**Pescara Centrale** ....d.	0850	...	...		...	...					1223		...	1349		...	...
440	Termoli ....d.	1015	...	...		0700	...					1326			...		...	...
	Roma Termini 395 ..d.	...	...	...	0733	...	...					0910			...	1800		...	...
	Napoli P. Garibaldi 395 .d.	...	...	...	1053	1118	...							1405	1415		1456		...	...
527	Foggia ....d.	...	...	...	1127	1150	12629 2	12633 D 3513 2				1439	1447		...	...
595	Barletta ....d.	...	...	...	1200	1223						1512	1522		...	...
650	**Bari Centrale** ....a.	...	...	...			1235	1237	1303	1357	1418		1540	1532		1633	17
654	**Bari Centrale** ....d.	...	...	...			1308		1359	1512			1613		...	17
	Gioia del Colle ......d.	...	...	...			1351		1500	1611			1709		...	...
	Taranto ....a.	...	...	...			1705								...	...
	Crotone 398 .....a.	...	...	...											1709	...
691	Monopoli ....d.	...	...	...			1315		1436						1721	...
704	Fasano ....d.	...	...	...			1327		1447						1738	...
724	Ostuni ....d.	...	...	...			1342		1500				1655		1806	...
761	**Brindisi Centrale** ...d.	...	...	...			1408		1525							...
763	Brindisi Marittima ...a.	...	...	...									1727		1848	...
799	Lecce ....a.	...	...	...			1447		1552							...

◆ – **NOTES** (LISTED BY TRAIN NUMBERS)
IC785 – PITAGORA – 🚃 Bari - Villa San Giovanni. **Not** Dec. 25, 26, Jan. 1.
E1289 – May 19 - 26 (from München): 🛏 2 cl. and 🚃 München - Pescara.
E1711 – ⑥⑦, also Apr. 17, 25, **not** Dec. 25, Jan. 1, Apr. 16, 23, 30: 🚃 Milano - Pescara.

D3513 – Ⓐ, not Dec. 23, 24, 31.
L – 🚃 Pescara - Foggia - Napoli.
⋄ – Not Dec. 25, Jan. 1.

Table 390 BOLOGNA - ANCONA - BRINDISI - LECCE

1, 2 class except where shown

	IR 2125	12639	E 967	12483	IC 567	E 969	IR 2127	IC 569	IC569/IC571	IR 2127	E 981	D 2991	IR 2129	IC 573	IR 2129	E 913	IC766/IC767	IR 2133	IC 575	P 521	IC 763	IR 2133	IC 1575
	⑦	2	◆	2	⏢	✧	◆	✕	H	◆	◆			✕ Q	◆	⏢	®	⏢	✧	✕®	⏢		⏢
Torino Porta Nuova 400 .. d.																							
Venezia Santa Lucia 375 . d.					0845																		
Milano Centrale 370 ... d.	0805					1005v	1105	1105				1205	1305						1405				1454p
Bologna Centrale ...... d.	1038				1159	1238	1259	1259				1402	1438	1459			1559	1638	1659				1707
Faenza .... d.	1115					1313						1435	1513				1628	1713					1742
Forli .... d.	1126					1324	1335	1335				1447	1524				1641	1724					1752
Cesena .... d.	1139					1337						1500	1537				1654	1737					
Rimini .... a.	1158				1307	1400	1407	1407		1400		1528	1558	1605	1558		1717	1758	1805			1758	1823
Rimini .... d.	1200				1309	1412	1409	1409		1412		1530	1610	1607	1610		1719	1810	1807			1810	1826
Riccione .... d.	1208				→	1420						1538	→	1618			1727	→					1818
Cattolica .... d.	1215					1427						1545		1625									1825
Pesaro .... d.	1227				1329	1439						1557	1628	1637			1743		1837				1850
Fano .... d.	1236					1448						1606		1646					1846				
Senigallia .... d.	1252					1504						1622		1702					1902				
Falconara Marittima 385 .. d.	1304					1516						1634		1714					1914				
Ancona 385 .... a.	1313				1403	1502	1502	1525				1643	1658	1723			1818		1859			1923	1926
Ancona .... d.					1407		1506	1506					1702				1821		1903				1930
Civitanova Marche ...... d.					1431								1728				1847						1956
San Benedetto del Tronto . d.					1458								1752				1915		1948				2020
Pescara Centrale ...... d.					1537					1623	1623		1825				1955		2023				2057
Pescara Centrale ...... d.					1540					1626	1626		1828						2026				
Termoli .... d.					1650					1735	1735		1934						2133				
Roma Termini 395 .. d.			1338							1310													
Napoli P. Garibaldi 395 . d.																1847					1905		
Foggia .... d.	12515		1642		1745		1702			1802	12641	12519	1826		1826	2027		2123	D3517		2227	2247	
Barletta .... d.			1752		1820		1837			1900	1900 2					2100		2155			2304	2318	
Bari Centrale .... a.			1840		1905		1911			1932	1932					2134		2228			2338	2351	
Bari Centrale .... d.	1746	1804					1927			1925	1955		1958		2028	2047			2237				0005
Gioia del Colle .... a.		1848					2005						2034			2128							
Taranto .... a.		1951					2103						2116			2231							
Crotone 398 .... d.																0234							
Monopoli .... d.	1827				2000								2123						2321			0047	
Fasano .... d.	1839				2014								2137						2342			0058	
Ostuni .... d.	1857				2030								2156						0001			0111	
Brindisi Centrale ...... d.	1929				2055			2111					2230						0030			0134	
Brindisi Marittima ..... a.																							
Lecce .... a.	2017				2127			2141					2306						0108			0159	

	E 915	IR 2135	IC 577	D 2999	IR 2137	E951/E953	E958/E951/E953	E 951	E 1715	12621	E 921	E1975/E1979	E 955	E955/12625	E 943	E 923	E 901	E 1951	IC 773	E 925	E903/E905	E 903	E 389
	⏢	⏢	⏢			◆	⑤		◆	2	F	◆	C	◆	◆	◆	◆	◆	◆	◆	G		⏢
Torino Porta Nuova 400 .. d.																	2010				2100	2100	
Venezia Santa Lucia 375 . d.												2054											
Milano Centrale 370 ... d.		1605	1705		1800				1950e	2045	2045				2105		2200		2210				0225
Bologna Centrale ...... d.	1759	1838	1912	1959	2038			2148	2213	2300	2300	2324	2335	0008	0027			0052	0123	0123		0005	0225
Faenza .... d.	1828	1913		2037	2113			2219	2245						0008				0052	0123			0225
Forli .... d.	1841	1924	1949	2048	2124			2231	2259				0002										
Cesena .... d.	1854	1937		2101	2137			2245	2314				0017										
Rimini .... a.	1917	1958	2018	2121	2158			2310	2336	0008	0008		0041	0055	0121				0203	0235		0235	
Rimini .... d.	1919	2000	2020		2200			2312	2338	0012	0012		0044	0058	0124				0206	0238		0238	
Riccione .... d.		2008			2208				2215														
Cattolica .... d.		2015			2215																		
Pesaro .... d.	1941	2027	2043		2227				2336				0003						0302	0302			
Fano .... d.		2036			2236																		
Senigallia .... d.		2052			2252																		
Falconara Marittima 385 .. d.	2009	2104			2304																		
Ancona 385 .... a.	2018	2113	2117		2313				0010		0038	0113	0113		0139	0153	0219	0232		0302	0336	0336	0428
Ancona .... d.	2021		2120						0014		0042	0118	0118		0144	0157	0240	0236		0306	0341	0341	0432
Civitanova Marche ...... d.	2047		2145						0042		0112										0432	0432	0501
San Benedetto del Tronto . d.	2115		2208						0108		0139												0528
Pescara Centrale ...... d.	2154		2245						0150		0220	0240	0240		0306	0319	0404	0358		0428	0512	0512	0608
Pescara Centrale ...... d.	2159								0154		0226	0244	0244		0312	0323	0410	0402		0432	0516	0516	0612
Termoli .... d.	2311														0425		0523			0544	0626	0626	0737
Roma Termini 395 .. d.					2125t		2125t																
Napoli P. Garibaldi 395 . d.					2328n																		
Foggia .... d.	0023				0335	0335	0335	0354			0428	0450	0450	0500	0500	0524	0533	0639	0609		0648	0726	0835
Barletta .... d.					0410	0410	0410	0428			0505			0601	0717	0646		0725	0807	0807			0912
Bari Centrale .... a.					0444	0444	0444	0516			0553	0559	0559	0614	0614	0636	0642	0800	0726		0725	0846	0949
Bari Centrale .... d.					0500	0500	0510		0532		0624	0636	0649	0642	0741	0702	0708		0751	0825	0844	0912	1010
Gioia del Colle .... a.					0545				0612				0727		0823	0757			0859				1014
Taranto .... a.					0639				0713				0829		0917	0849		0943					1106
Crotone 398 .... d.													1207					1230					1253
Monopoli .... d.					0537	0537			0706		0735	0724				0754		0829			0924	0956	1045
Fasano .... d.					0553	0553			0721		0756	0739				0808		0852			0940	1009	1059
Ostuni .... d.					0609	0609			0738		0813	0756				0825		0909			0957	1026	1115
Brindisi Centrale ...... d.					0633	0633			0805		0842	0824				0853		0937			1027	1053	1142
Brindisi Marittima ..... a.																							
Lecce .... a.					0705	0705			0846		0924	0857				0934		1014			1058	1124	1218

– **NOTES** (LISTED BY TRAIN NUMBERS)

89 – ⊨ 2 cl. and ⊏⊐ Stuttgart - Lecce; ⊏⊐ Zürich Hbf - Lecce; ⏢ (except on ⑦) Foggia - Lecce.

21 – BORROMINI – ✕, also Dec. 25, Apr. 16, 30: ⊏⊐ and ✕ Roma - Bari.

73 – MAGNA GRECIA – ⊏⊐ Bari - Taranto - Reggio; ⊏⊐ Bari - Taranto - Cosenza - Lamezia Terme - Villa San Giovanni - Reggio.

01 – ⊨ 2 cl. and ⊏⊐ Torino - Bari. **Not** Dec. 24, 31 from Torino.

03 – ⊨ 1,2 cl. (T2), ⊨ 2 cl. and ⊏⊐ Torino - Lecce; ⊨ 1,2 cl. Torino - Bari.

23 – ⊏⊐ Milano - Crotone; conveys except when train **E1975** runs: ⊨ 1,2 cl. (T2), and ⊨ 2 cl. Milano - Taranto and ⊨ 2 cl. Milano - Crotone.

25 – ⊏⊐ Milano - Lecce; conveys except on Dec. 25, Jan. 1: ⊨ 2 cl. and ⊏⊐ (also ⊨ 1,2 cl. on ⑦ Jan. 15 - Apr. 9 and on Dec. 21 - 24, 26 - 31, Jan. 2 - 9, Apr. 14, 15, 18, 19) Bolzano - Lecce; conveys except when train **E1975** runs: ⊨ 2 cl. Milano - Bari.

43 – ⊨ 2 cl. and ⊏⊐ Trieste Centrale - Lecce; ⊨ 1,2 cl. (T2) Venezia - Lecce; ⊨ 1,2 cl. Venezia - Bari.

51 – ⊨ 2 cl. and ⊏⊐ Roma Tiburtina - Taranto.

55 – ⊨ 1,2 cl., ⊨ 2 cl. and ⊏⊐ Roma - Lecce.

67 – ⊏⊐ Napoli - Foggia - Pescara.

E981 – ⊨ 2 cl. and ⊏⊐ Bari - Villa San Giovanni.

E1951 – SALENTINO – ⊨ 1,2 cl., ⊨ 1,2 cl. (T2) and ⊨ 2 cl. Milano - Lecce.

E1975 – Dec. 16 - 23, Jan. 2 - 8, Apr. 12 - 14, 17 - 19 (from Milano): ⊨ 1,2 cl., ⊨ 1,2 cl. (T2), ⊨ 2 cl. Milano - Taranto; ⊨ 2 cl. Milano - Crotone.

IR2127 – ⊏⊐ Bologna (Milano Centrale ✕) - Ancona.

C – ⊏⊐ Bari - Taranto; conveys except Dec. 24, 31 from Roma): ⊨ 1,2 cl. Roma - Taranto.

F – Dec. 16 - 23, Jan. 2 - 8, Apr. 12 - 14, 17 - 19 (from Milano): ⊨ 2 cl. Milano - Lecce.

G – ⊨ 2 cl. and ⊏⊐ Torino - Taranto.

H – MURGE – ⊏⊐ Milano - Taranto; ✕ Milano - Bari.

Q – Not Dec. 25.

e – Only takes passengers for Rimini or beyond.

n – Napoli Centrale.

p – Milano Porta Garibaldi.

t – Roma Tiburtina.

v – ✕ only.

✧ – Not Dec. 25, Jan. 1.

✗∕ – ETR450 Pendolino supplement payable.

Table 390   LECCE - BRINDISI - ANCONA - BOLOGNA

1, 2 class except where shown

	D 3192	IC 566	E 910	IR 2128	D 3180		IR 2130		E 912	IR 2132	IC 764	D 3500	12502	P 520	12622	12504	D 3586	IC 568	E 962		E986 E988	12508		IR 2134	IC572 IC570
							⑦				ℝ	2	2	✕ℝ	2	2	C	Q	◆		G				A
Lecce........d.	...	...	...	...	...		...		...	...	...	...	...	...	...	0455		...	0620		...	0634		...	...
Brindisi Marittima ....d.	...	...	...	...	...		...		...	...	...	...	...	...	...	...		...	...		...	...		...	...
Brindisi Centrale......d.	...	...	...	...	...		...		...	...	0450	...	...	0538	...	...		0652			...	0723		...	...
Ostuni ....d.	...	...	...	...	...		...		...	...	0517	...	...	0600	...	...		0721			...	0757		...	...
Fasano ....d.	...	...	...	...	...		...		...	...	0536	...	...	0612	...	...		0740			...	0813		...	...
Monopoli ....d.	...	...	...	...	...		...		...	...	0554	...	...	0627	...	...		0755			...	0828		...	...
Crotone 398 ....d.	...	...	...	...	...		...		...	...	...	...	0511	0609	...	...		...			0248	...		...	0755
Taranto ....d.	...	...	...	...	...		...		...	...	...	...	0613	0655	...	...		0724			...	...		...	0839
Gioia del Colle ... d.	...	...	...	...	...		...		...	...	0644	...	0705	0721	0730	...		0826			0905	0913		...	0913
Bari Centrale.........a.	...	...	...	...	...		...		0604	...	...	0655	...	0727	0730	...		0837			...	...		...	0938
Bari Centrale..........d.	...	...	...	...	...		...		0634	...	...	0727	...	...	...	0735	0902				...	...		...	1009
Barletta ....d.	...	...	...	...	...		0638		0714	0735	...	0804	...	...	...	0804	0935				...	...		...	1046
Foggia ....d.	...	...	...	...	...		...		0958		...	...	...	...	...	0842	1028				...	...		...	...
Napoli P. Garibaldi 395 ..a.	...	...	...	...	...		...		...		...	...	1130	...	...	D	1520				...	...		...	...
Roma Termini 395 ..a.	...	...	...	...	...		0758		...	0847	...	...	...	...	...	3184	0934				...	...		...	1135
Termoli ....d.	...	...	...	...	...		0911		...	1015	...	...	...	...	...	2	1038				...	...		...	1235
Pescara Centrale ....a.	...	...	...	...	...		0914		...	...	...	...	...	...	0958	1041					...	...		...	1238
Pescara Centrale ....d.	...	0532	0605	0657	...		0952		...	...	...	...	...	...	1043						...	...		...	1310
San Benedetto del Tronto. d.	...	0608	0643	0744	...		1021		...	...	...	...	...	1111	1133						...	...		...	...
Civitanova Marche.....d.	...	0633	0711	0819	...		1050		...	...	...	...	...	1143	1200						...	...		...	1359
Ancona ....a.	...	0700	0739	0855	...		...		...	...	...	...	...	1204							1335	1403		...	...
Ancona ....d.	0633	0704	0742	0747	...		0947	1135	...	1053	...	...	...	...							1343			...	...
Falconara Marittima ..d.	0641	...	...	0755	...		0955	1143	...	...	...	...	...	...							1353			...	...
Senegallia ....d.	0655	...	...	0805	...		1005	1153	...	...	...	...	...	...							1408			...	...
Fano ....d.	0710	...	...	0820	...		1020	1208	...	...	...	...	...	...							1417			...	...
Pesaro ....d.	0719	0734	0816	0829	...		1029	1131	1217	...	...	...	...	1234	IR						1429			...	...
Cattolica ....d.	0731	...	...	0841	...		1041	1229	...	...	...	...	...	...	2132						1437			...	...
Riccione ....d.	0739	...	0834	0849	...		1049	1237	...	...	...	...	...	...							1448	1451b		...	...
Rimini ....a.	0750	0753	0841	0900	...		1100	1153	1248	...	...	...	...	1254	1248						1502	1453b		...	...
Rimini ....d.	...	0755	0843	0902	...		1102	1155	1302	...	...	...	...	1256	1302						→			...	...
Cesena ....d.	...	...	0902	0919	...		1119	1214	←	...	...	...	...	...	1319						...	1521		...	...
Forlì ....d.	...	0822	0915	0933	...		1133	1227	...	...	...	...	...	...	1333						...	...		...	...
Faenza ....d.	...	...	0923	0943	...		1143	1238	...	...	...	...	...	1400	1423						...	1600		...	...
Bologna Centrale ..a.	...	0900	0958	1023	...		1223	1312	...	...	...	...	...	1555	1655						...	1755		...	...
Milano Centrale 370 ..a.	...	1100	...	1255	...		1455	...	...	...	...	...	...	...	...						...	...		...	...
Venezia Santa Lucia 375 ..a.																									
Torino Porta Nuova 400 ..a.																									

	IC 570	E 12628	IR 914	IR 2136	12040	D 3512	IC 574	IR 2138	IC 576	E 964	IR 1710	12510		12632	12512	IC 578	IC790 IC792	E 1576	E 966	E 968		E 1288	12634	D 3516
	✕ ◆	2	⚥	⚥	2		⚥		✕	◆				2	2	✕ ◆	H	◆	◆	◆			2	✕
Lecce........d.	0733	...	...	...	0903		...		...		1103			...	1244			...	...					1422
Brindisi Marittima ....d.	...	...	...	...	...		...		...		...			...	...			...	...					1505
Brindisi Centrale ......d.	0801	...	...	...	0945		...		...		1147			1237	1313			...	...					1529
Ostuni ....d.		...	...	...	1012		...		...		1217			1310	1329			...	...					1543
Fasano ....d.		...	...	...	1029		...		...		1233			1329	1342			...	...					1554
Monopoli ....d.		...	...	...	1045		...		...		1243			1342	...		0956	...	...					...
Crotone 398 ....d.		0856	...	...	...		...		...		...			1210	...		1309	...	...		1332			...
Taranto ....d.		0953	...	...	...		...		...		...			1309	...		1358	...	...		1445			...
Gioia del Colle ... d.		...	...	...	...		...		...		1339			1358	1436	1429	1431	...	...		1530	1639		...
Bari Centrale.........a.	0918	1036	...	...	1127		...		...		...			1448				...	1520					...
Bari Centrale..........d.	0938	...	...	...	...		1153	1313	...		...			1519				...	1553					...
Barletta ....d.	1009	...	...	...	...		1236	1350	...		...			1557				...	1642	1649				...
Foggia ....d.	1046	...	...	...	...		1315	1430	1503		...			...				...	...	...				...
Napoli P. Garibaldi 395 ..a.		...	...	...	...		...		1800	D	...			...				...	2125					...
Roma Termini 395 ..a.	1135	...	...	...	...		1416	1525	...	3188	...			1645				...	1802					...
Termoli ....a.	1235	...	...	...	...		1517	1628	...	2	...			1744				...	1913					...
Pescara Centrale ....a.	1238	1303	...	1410	...		1520	1631	1638	1712	...			1748				1910	...	...		1945		...
Pescara Centrale ....d.	1310	1340	...	1500	...		1557	1707	1716	1751	...			1820			IR 2140	1947 2011	D 3196	...		2024		...
San Benedetto del Tronto. d.		1409	...	1535	...		1621	1730	1744	1816	...			...				2039	...	...		2050		...
Civitanova Marche.....d.	1359	1440	...	1610	...		1648	1758	1814	1849	...			1906			1947	2044	2047			2119		...
Ancona ....a.	1403	1443	1547	...	...		1652	1735	1802	1818	...			1910			1955	2055	...		2123		...
Ancona ....d.		...	1555	...	...		...	1743	...		...			...			2005	2105	...		2142		...
Falconara Marittima ..d.		...	1605	...	...		...	1753	...		...			...			2020	2120	...		2156		...
Senegallia ....d.		IR	1620	...	...		...	1808	...		...			...			2029	2117	2129		2208		...
Fano ....d.		2134	1518	1629	...		1723	1817	...	1852	...			1940			2041	2141	2141		2222		...
Pesaro ....d.		⚥		1641	...		1829		IR 2138		...			...			2049	2149	2149		2232		...
Cattolica ....d.				1649	...		1837		←		...			...			2100	2140	2200		2240		...
Riccione ....d.	1451b	1448	1543	1700	...		1746	1848	1854	1848	1918			2002			2102	2142	2202		2245		...
Rimini ....a.	1453b	1502	1543	1702	...		1748	1902	1856	1902	1920			2004			2119	2200	2219		2305		...
Rimini ....d.	1521	1533	1519	1604	1719		→		1920	1940				2032			2133	2214	2233		2321		...
Cesena ....d.			1618	1733					1933	1954				...			2143		2243					...
Forlì ....d.	1543	1629	1743						1943	2005				2112			2223	2255	2323		0003		...
Faenza ....d.	1600	1623	1702	1823	...		1854		2002	2023	2045			2315			0100		...					...
Bologna Centrale ..a.	1755	1855	...	2055					2255	2330				...					...					...
Milano Centrale 370 ..a.																								
Venezia Santa Lucia 375 ..a.					2208																			
Torino Porta Nuova 400 ..a.																								

◆ – NOTES (LISTED BY TRAIN NUMBERS)

P520 –	BORROMINI – ✕ 🍴 and ✕ Bari - Roma.
IC570 –	MURGE – 🍴 Lecce - Milano; ✕ Bari - Milano.
IC578 –	ADRIATICO – 🍴 Lecce - Milano; ✕ Bari - Milano.
E962 –	🍴 Lecce - Roma; ⚥ Bari - Roma. **Not** Dec. 25, Jan. 1.
E964/8 –	🍴 Pescara - Foggia - Napoli and v.v. **Not** Dec. 24, 31 from Napoli or Dec. 25, Jan. 1 from Pescara.
E1288 –	May 20 - 27 only: ⊢ 2 cl. and ✕ 🍴 Pescara - München Hbf.
E1576 –	⑦ Jan. 15 - Apr. 9, Apr. 23 - May 27: 🍴 Pescara - Bologna.
IR1710 –	⑥⑦, also Apr. 17, 25, May 1, **not** Dec. 25, Jan. 1, Apr. 16, 23, 30: 🍴 Pescara - Milano.

A – MURGE – 🍴 Taranto - Milano; ✕ Bari - Milano.
Ⓐ, also Dec. 23, 24, 31.
C – ⊢ 2 cl. and 🍴 Villa San Giovanni - Bari.
G – PITAGORA – 🍴 Villa San Giovanni - Bari.
H – **Not** Dec. 25.
Q – **Not** Dec. 25.
b – Only takes passengers for Milano.
✥ – **Not** Dec. 25, Jan. 1.
✗ – ETR450 Pendolino supplement payable.

Table 390 LECCE - BRINDISI - ANCONA - BOLOGNA

1, 2 class except where shown

	E 970 🍷 S	12640 2 ⚒	12518 2	IC 760 R S	E 900 ◆	12642 2	12520 E920 M	E 902 ◆	E904 E902 B	E 940 ◆	12644	E 1950 ◆	E 922 ◆	E 952 ◆	E950 E952	E950 E952 E954	IC770 IC772 J	E926 E924 K	IC 1574 ◆	E 388 🍷 ◆	E1978 E1974 F	E 1974 ◆	IR 2126	E 956 ◆
Lecce d.	...	...	1510	...	...	...	1613	1803	...	1814	...	1925	1945	...	2030	2030	...	...	...	2106	2152	...	...	2210
Brindisi Marittima d.	...	...	|	...	...	...	|	|	...	|	...	|	|	...	|	|	...	...	...	|	|	...	...	|
Brindisi Centrale d.	...	...	1554	...	...	...	1657	1835	...	1852	...	2002	2022	...	2059	2059	...	...	...	2152	2224	...	...	2241
Ostuni d.	...	...	1625	...	...	...	1727	|	...	1922	...	2031	2053	...	2128	2128	...	...	...	2223	2251	...	...	2310
Fasano d.	...	...	1641	...	...	...	1744	|	...	1938	...	2047	2109	...	2143	2143	...	...	...	2239	2305	...	...	2326
Monopoli d.	...	...	1651	...	...	...	1754	|	...	2001	...	2059	2122	...	2154	2154	...	...	...	2252	2322	...	...	2337
Crotone **398** d.	...		|	...	...	...	|	|	...	|	...	|	|	...	|	|	1812	1707	...	|	|	1838	...	|
Taranto d.	...	1541	|	...	...	1718	|	|	1825	|	1932	|	|	2043	|	|	2123	2140	...	|	|	2237	...	|
Gioia del Colle d.	...	1637	|	...	...	1815	|	|	1912	|	2035	|	|	2143	|	|	2206	2229	...	|	|	2321	...	|
Bari Centrale a.	...	1727	1738	...	...	1857	1844	1953	1954	2045	2118	2137	2200	2217	2231	2231	2241	2304	...	2327	2354	2356	...	0022
Bari Centrale d.	1706	▬	...	1757	1808	▬	1946	2023	2023	2107	...	2159	2222	2255	2255	2255	...	2323	...	2352	0018	0018	...	0050
Barletta d.	1738	...	...	1826	1842	...	2020	2100	2100	2149	...	2232	2304	2339	2339	2339	...	|	...	0025	0051	0051	...	0135
Foggia d.	1825	...	...	1907	1946	...	2105	2146	2146	2233	...	2318	2349	0052	0052	0052	...	0035	...	0107	0138	0138	...	0214
Napoli P. Garibaldi **395** a.	2120	...	...	|	|	...	|	|	|	|	...	|	|	|	|	0500	...	|	...	|	|	|	...	|
Roma Termini **395** a.	...	...	...	2325	|	E	|	|	|	|	...	|	|	0630t	0630t	...	...	|	...	|	|	|	...	0750
Termoli d.	...	**12046**	...	...	2043	**1716**	2210	2248	2248	2329	...	0018	0046	...	...	...	...	|	...	0203	|	|	...	...
Pescara Centrale a.	...	...	...	...	2159	⑦	2320	2358	2358	0036	...	0126	0150	...	...	...	...	0229	...	0321	0350	0350	...	...
Pescara Centrale d.	...	2110	...	...	2203	2313	2326	0002	0002	0040	...	0129	0154	...	...	...	...	0234	...	0326	0400	0400	...	...
San Benedetto del Tronto d.	...	2201	...	...	2242	2352	0004	|	|	|	...	|	|	...	...	...	...	0313	...	|	|	|	...	...
Civitanova Marche d.	...	2236	...	...	2308	0017	0036	|	|	|	...	|	|	...	...	...	...	0339	...	|	|	|	...	...
Ancona a.	...	2311	...	...	2337	0046	0106	0125	0125	0205	...	0259	0317	...	...	...	...	0407	...	0457	0522	0522	...	...
Ancona d.	...	...	...	...	2341	0050	0110	0131	0131	0210	...	0303	0321	...	...	...	...	0411	0455	0501	0526	0526	0530	...
Falconara Marittima d.	...	...	...	...	2350	|	|	|	|	|	...	|	|	...	...	...	...	|	|	|	|	|	0538	...
Senegallia d.	...	...	...	...	|	|	|	|	|	|	...	|	|	...	...	...	...	|	|	|	|	|	0548	...
Fano d.	...	...	...	...	|	|	|	|	|	|	...	|	|	...	...	...	...	|	|	|	|	|	0603	...
Pesaro d.	...	...	...	...	0020	|	|	|	|	|	...	|	|	...	...	...	...	|	0527	0542	|	|	0612	...
Cattolica d.	...	...	...	...	|	|	|	|	|	|	...	|	|	...	...	...	...	|	|	|	|	|	0624	...
Riccione d.	...	...	...	...	|	|	|	|	|	|	...	|	|	...	...	...	...	|	|	|	|	|	0632	...
Rimini a.	...	...	...	...	0044	0145	0206	0229	0229	0308	...	|	0415	...	...	...	...	0508	0548	0610	0622	0622	0643	...
Rimini d.	...	...	...	...	0046	0147	0209	0231	0231	0310	...	|	0417	...	...	...	...	0510	0550	0614	0625	0625	0645	...
Cesena d.	...	...	...	...	|	0208	|	|	|	|	...	|	0437	...	...	...	...	|	|	|	|	|	0704	...
Forli d.	...	...	...	...	|	0222	|	|	|	|	...	|	0452	...	...	...	...	|	0619	|	|	|	0721	...
Faenza d.	...	...	...	...	|	|	|	|	|	|	...	|	0505	...	...	...	...	|	0630	|	|	|	0734	...
Bologna Centrale a.	...	...	...	...	0154	0305	0330	0350	0350	0422	...	0523	0543	...	...	...	...	0625	0704	0736	0745	0745	0814	...
Milano Centrale **370** a.	...	...	...	...	|	0600	0605	|	|	|	...	0900	0840	...	...	...	...	0920	0911n	0950	1020	1020	1055	...
Venezia Santa Lucia **375** a.	...	...	...	...	|	...	...	|	|	0710	...	...	...	...	...	...	...	...	...	...	...	...	...	...
Torino Porta Nuova **400** a.	...	...	...	...	0625	...	...	0813	0813	...	...	...	...	...	...	...	...	...	...	...	...	...	...	...

◆ – **NOTES** (LISTED BY TRAIN NUMBERS)

E388 – ▬ 2 cl. and (2) Lecce - Stuttgart; (12) Lecce - Zürich Hbf.
E900 – ▬ 2 cl. and (12) Bari - Torino. **Not** Dec. 24, 31.
E902 – 🛏 1,2 cl. (T2), ▬ 2 cl. and (12) Lecce - Torino; 🛏 1,2 cl. Bari - Torino.
E922 – ESPRESSO DEL LEVANTE – **not** Dec. 24, 31: (12) Lecce - Milano; ▬ 2 cl. and (12) (also 🛏 1,2 cl. on ⑤ Jan. 13 - Apr. 17 and on Dec. 19 - 23, 25 - 30, Jan. 1 - 7, Apr. 13, 14, 17, 18) Lecce - Bologna - (**IR2250**) - Bolzano.
E940 – ▬ 2 cl. and (12) Lecce - Trieste Centrale; 🛏 1,2 cl. (T2) Lecce - Venezia; 🛏 1,2 cl. Bari - Venezia.
E952 – ▬ 2 cl. and (12) Taranto - Roma; 🛏 1,2 cl. Taranto - Roma do not run Dec. 24, 31 and are transferred to train **E956** at Bari.
E956 – 🛏 1,2 cl., ▬ 2 cl. and (12) Lecce - Roma; conveys except on Dec. 24, 31: 🛏 1,2 cl. Taranto (**E952**) - Roma.
IC1574 – ① - ⑤, **not** Dec. 10 - Jan. 9, Apr. 13 - 20: (12) Ancona - Milano Lambrate.
E1950 – SALENTINO – 🛏 1,2 cl., 🛏 1,2 cl. (T2) and ▬ 2 cl. Lecce - Milano.
E1974 – Dec. 7, 8, 16 - 23, Jan. 2 - 8, Apr. 12 - 14, 17 - 19: 🛏 1,2 cl., 🛏 1,2 cl. (T2) and ▬ 2 cl. Taranto - Milano; ▬ 2 cl. Crotone - Milano.
B – ▬ 2 cl. and (12) Taranto - Torino.
F – Dec. 16 - 23, Jan. 2 - 8, Apr. 12 - 14, 17 - 19: ▬ 2 cl. Lecce - Milano.
J – MAGNA GRECIA – (12) Reggio - Bari.
K – (12) (also ▬ 2 cl. except when train **E1974** runs) Crotone - Milano; (12) (also 🛏 1,2 cl., 🛏 1,2 cl. (T2) and ▬ 2 cl. except when train **E1974** runs) Taranto - Milano.
M – (12) Lecce - Milano; (12) (also ▬ 2 cl. except when train **F** runs) Bari - Milano.
S – **Not** Dec. 24, 31.
n – Milano **Lambrate**.
t – Roma **Tiburtina**.

Table 391 ROMA - PESCARA

1, 2 class except where shown

km		7042	D 3340 2	D 3342		IR 2342		12136 2	12266 2⚒	12268 2	IC 580 N R	IC 1580 T R		IR 2344	12140 2⚒	D 3344 2⚒	7044	IC 582 R	12142 2	12276 2	7334 2	IR 2346	7336 2⚒	12280 2
0	**Roma Termini** d.	...	...	0505t	...	0745	...	...	...	1142t	1300	1300	...	1355	...	1410	...	1620	...	1643t	1725	1835	1927t	2055t
108	Avezzano d.	...	0548	0651	...	0925	...	...	1255	1340	1421	1423	...	1523	...	1616	...	1744	...	1902	1944	2017	2135	2304
172	Sulmona d.	0450	0701	0801	...	1027	...	1220	1413	1450	1514	1520	...	1628	1705	1726	1755	1835	1903	...	2055	2120	...	...
226	Chieti d.	0540	0754	0902	...	1108	...	1321	1518	...	1554	1600	...	1712	1807	...	1905	1915	2005	...	...	2201	...	...
240	**Pescara Centrale** a.	0555	0809	0918	...	1123	...	1337	1534	...	1608	1615	...	1729	1822	...	1920	1929	2020	...	...	2217	...	...

	D 3343	D 3345 2⚒	IR 2341	IC 581 R	7043	12133 ⚒	7331 2	IR 2343	7335 2	12135 2	12137 2⚒	12265 2⚒	IR 2345	7337 2⚒	12267 2	D 3347 2	12143 2	IC 583 N R	IC 1581 T R	12145 2⚒		IR 2347	12147 2	9939
escara Centrale d.	...	...	0510	0618	0633	0715	...	1014	...	1135	1230	...	1400	...	...	...	1655	1738	1738	1749	...	1835	1947	2120
hieti d.	...	...	0526	0634	0648	0737	...	1030	...	1152	1246	...	1416	...	...	...	1711	1752	1753	1808	...	1851	2006	2136
ulmona d.	...	...	0609	0716	0744	0840	...	1117	...	1300	1344	1351	1458	...	...	1702	1810	1836	1836	1918	...	1938	2103	2226
vezzano d.	0500	0549	0708	0808	...	...	1055	1215	1303	1425	...	1516	1603	...	1727	1819	...	1927	1930	...	...	2036	...	...
oma Termini a.	0705	0735	0845	0935	...	...	1246t	1352	1519t	1648t	...	...	1740	1836t	1945t	2025t	...	2048	2100	...	...	2210t	...	...

– ① - ⑥, also Jan. 1, Apr. 16, 23, **not** Apr. 17, 25. T – ⑦ also Apr. 17, 25, **not** Jan. 1, Apr. 16, 23. t – Roma **Tiburtina**.

able 392 PALERMO - TRAPANI

1, 2 class

km		3847 ⚒	3847 ⚒	8657	8657 ⚒	3857	3857	3881	3881	12783 ⚒	3845 ⚒	3845 ⚒	3861	3861	8687 ⚒	8737 ⚒	12779	12887 ⑦	3867	3867	8685	8685	3869	🚌
0	**Palermo** d.	0515	0515	0650n	0650n	0900	0900	1055	1055	1120	1300	1300	1350	1350	1455	...	1555	...	1720	1720	1850	1850	1945	...
73	Castellammare del Golfo d.	0646	0646	0828	0828	1018	1018	1209	1209	1307	|	|	1504	1504	1620	...	1738	...	1843	1843	2016	2016	2109	...
79	**Alcamo Diramazione** d.	0700	0657	0838	0840	1028	1032	1219	1222	1317	1418	1420	1513	1516	1630	1634	1746	1752	1853	1855	2025	2030	2116	2123
121	Castelvetrano d.	|	0740	|	0919	|	1121	|	1308	1402	|	1459	|	1557	|	1715	|	1840	|	1935	|	2105	|	2202
144	Mazara del Vallo d.	|	0810	|	0940	|	1144	|	1334	1426	|	1521	|	1619	|	1740	|	1903	|	2000	|	...	|	2240
165	Marsala d.	|	0821	|	1007	|	1207	|	1400	1454	|	1540	|	1640	|	1800	|	1922	|	2017	|	...	|	2315
26*	**Trapani** a.	0745	0850	0915	1030	1110	1238	1305	1430	1530	1455	1610	1550	1715	1712	1830	1840	1955	1935	2050	2100	...	2150	2340

	8652 ⚒	3854	8570 ⑦	3882 ⑦	8662 ⚒	3858 ⚒	3858 ⚒	3884 ⑦	3884 ⑦	8682	8682	3862	3862	3864 ⑦	3864 ⑦	12784 ⚒	8572 ⑦	3886	3866	3866	8624	3942	8628	8680 ⚒
rapani d.	0425	0700	...	0800	0615	0753	0930	0753	0935	0940	1055	1120	1235	1240	1410	1325	1350	1700	1635	1755	1750	1910	1913	2015
Marsala d.	|	|	...	|	0642	0824	|	0824	|	1006	|	1148	|	1310	|	1359	1424	|	1706	|	1821	|	1940	2043
Mazara del Vallo d.	|	|	0700	|	0710	0851	|	0851	|	1025	|	1207	|	1332	|	1427	1443	|	1723	|	1840	|	1959	2100
Castelvetrano d.	|	|	0720	|	0739	0920	|	0920	|	1048	|	1230	|	1403	|	1500	1503	|	1746	|	1900	|	2018	2120
camo Diramazione d.	0508	0735	0800	0836	0818	1008	1008	1012	1012	1138	1138	1319	1319	1455	1455	1552	1548	1732	1835	1835	1942	1948	...	...
astellammare del Golfo d.	0516	0743	0807	|	0829	1019	1019	1020	1020	1146	1146	1326	1326	1505	1505	1600	1555	|	1842	1842	...	1955	...	...
alermo a.	0648	0858	0920	0955	1002	1140	1140	1132	1132	1320	1320	1450	1450	1626	1626	1753	1715	1845	2005	2005	...	2115	...	...

– Depart 0710 on ⑦, train number **8643**. * – By direct route; kilometres via Castelvetrano and Marsala = 196.

Table 393 ROMA - ANZIO and ALBANO LAZIALE

2 class only

Rail service Roma - Anzio and v.v. 57 km Journey time: 60 - 65 minutes.

From Roma Termini: 0447⚒o, 0645⚒o, 0755, 0955⚒, 1135, 1255, 1350, 1435, 1535⚒, 1645, 1745, 1855, 2015, 2130.
From Anzio: 0459⚒, 0632, 0651⚒, 0722⑥, 0824, 1004, 1314, 1412⚒, 1510, 1608, 1658⑦, 1814, 1918, 2020o, 2159.

o – To or from Roma **Ostiense**, not Termini.

Rail service Roma - Marino Laziale - Castel Gandolfo - Albano Laziale and v.v. 29 km. Journey time: 40 - 47 minutes (87 minutes by 🚌).

From Roma Termini: 0550⚒, 0550⑦ 🚌, 0720, 0830, 0955, 1235, 1345⚒, 1425, 1600⚒, 1700, 1810, 1930.
From Albano Laziale: 0610⚒, 0640⚒, 0640⑦ 🚌, 0704⚒, 0704⑦ 🚌, 0813, 1040, 1118, 1324, 1441⚒, 1540, 1650, 1754, 1903, 2025.

All trains/buses call at Marino Laziale and Castel Gandolfo 30/45 and 40/55 minutes from Roma and 5/10 and 12/15 minutes from Albano Laziale respectively.

Table 395 ROMA and NAPOLI - TERMOLI and FOGGIA

1, 2 class except where shown

km		8153	8032	8034	D 3470	D 3472	12411	8210	IR 2353 2354	E 961	IC 761	D 3357	8224	8040	E 965	D 3480	12415	IR 2364	12157	E 967	8213	D 3359	D 3484	12436
						2				❖	🍷🅁	2	2				2		2		2	2		2
		⚒	⚒				⚒	⚒	❖	K	♦		⑦		♦		⚒	⚒		♦	⚒		⚒	
0	**Roma Termini** d.	...	...	...	...	...	...	...	0605	...	0700	0725	...	...	0910	...	...	...	1005'	...	...	1215	...	...
86	Frosinone d.	...	...	...	...	...	...	...	0703	...	|	0836	...	...	1001	...	...	...	1121	...	...	1312	...	...
138	Cassino d.	...	...	...	...	...	...	...	0741	...	|	0927	...	...	1039	...	...	...	1212	...	1300	1405	...	...
	Napoli Centrale d.	...	...	...	0545	...	0550	0610	|	0733p	|	|	0838	...	|	1200	1215	1248	...	1338p	|	|	1400	1430
	Caserta d.	...	...	...	0616	...	0648	0652	|	0816	0900	|	0915	...	1133	1230	1301	|	...	1421	1420	|	1434	1503
170	Vairano-Caianello d.	...	0542	...	0654	...	|	0736	0813	|	|	0951	0959	1115	|	1310	|	|	...	|	...	1440	1514	1550
	Isernia d.	...	0636	0722	0743	...	|	...	0854	|	|	...	...	1203	|	1402	|	|	...	|	...	...	1600	...
	Carpinone d.	...	0651	0735	0758	0805	|	...	0909	|	|	...	...	1217	|	1415	|	|	...	|	...	...	...	...
	Campobasso a.	...	0750	0829	...	0857	|	...	0954	|	|	...	...	1310	|	1513	|	1550	...	|	...	...	...	...
288	Benevento d.	0558	...	...	...	...	0812	...	...	0925	1000	...	...	...	1236	...	1418	...	...	1518	...	...	...	...
389	**Foggia** a.	0745	...	...	...	...	1008	...	...	1040	1113	...	...	...	1353	...	1608	...	...	1642	...	...	...	...

	E 969	IR 2361 2362	D 3361	8146	12423	D 3486	D 3488	IC 749	IR 2363	IC 767	D 3490	8163	8147	D 3363	D 3365	D 3367	P⚡ 521	IR 2367 2368	12425	12169	D 3369	E 951	E958 E951	E 955
	🍷		2		2			🅁		🅁			2	2	2	2	✕🅁		2	2	2			
	♦	❖		⚒	⚒		⚒	❖	❖	K❖		⚒	⚒				♦		⚒	⚒		♦	M	♦
Roma Termini d.	1310	1350	1415	...	...	...	...	1620	1625	...	...	...	...	1630	1735	1825	1905	1905	...	1940	2020	2125t	...	2330
Frosinone d.	1405	|	1521	...	...	...	...	1711	|	...	...	...	...	1746	1854	1937	|	|	...	2100	2141	2222	...	0029
Cassino d.	1440	1528	1617	...	...	...	...	1746	|	...	...	...	...	1840	1945	2027	|	2045	...	2152	2232	2303	...	0110
Napoli Centrale d.	|	|	|	...	1630	1710	1740	|	|	1847	1900	...	...	|	...	...	|	|	2042	...	|	|	2328	|
Caserta d.	1531	|	|	...	1721	1740	1810	1838	1847	1914	1930	1931	...	1944	...	...	2051	|	2132	...	2345	0030	0030	0204
Vairano-Caianello d.	|	1558	1655	1713	|	1812	1847	|	...	|	2018	|	...	...	...	...	|	2115	|	...	...	|	|	|
Isernia d.	|	1636	...	1802	|	1858	1928	|	...	|	2106	|	...	...	...	...	|	2153	|	...	...	|	|	|
Carpinone d.	|	1648	...	1816	|	1910	1941	|	...	|	2119	|	...	...	...	...	|	2206	|	...	...	|	|	|
Campobasso a.	|	1735	...	1910	|	...	2038	|	...	|	2204	|	...	...	...	...	|	2253	|	...	...	|	|	|
Benevento d.	1626	...	...	...	1847	...	...	1924	...	2003	...	2050	2055	...	...	...	2137	...	2236	...	...	0146	0146	0303
Foggia a.	1749	...	...	...	2040	...	...	...	...	2118	...	...	2232	...	...	...	2241	...	...	...	...	0323	0323	0446

km		D 3360	IC 750	IR 2351	IR 2351 2350	IR 2352	8150	IR 2355	IR 2357 2358	12307	IC 764	P⚡ 520	12158	D 3297	8109	12160	D 3225	12162	E 962	12326	D 3362	8035	12164	8214
		2	🅁				2			2	🅁	✕🅁	2			2		2	🍷	2	2		2	2
			❖	❖	❖	❖	⚒	⚒			K❖	♦		⚒	⑦	⚒	⑦		♦			⚒		
	Foggia d.	...	...	...	...	...	0521	...	...	...	0714	0804	...	...	...	...	...	...	1028	...	...	...	...	...
	Benevento d.	...	0600	...	...	...	0648	...	...	...	0830	0906	...	...	...	...	...	...	1153	...	...	...	...	...
0	**Campobasso** d.	...	|	0520	0520	...	|	0544	0710	...	|	|	...	...	0835	...	...	...	|	...	...	1200	...	...
48	Carpinone d.	...	|	0603	0603	...	|	|	0759	...	|	|	...	0841	0932	...	1011	...	|	...	...	1258	...	...
59	Isernia d.	...	|	0614	0614	...	|	|	0810	...	|	|	...	0855	0943	...	1023	...	|	...	...	1317	...	...
95	Vairano-Caianello d.	...	|	0657	0659	...	|	|	0851	...	|	|	...	0933	1020	...	1105	...	|	...	...	1408	...	...
140	Caserta d.	0548	0647	0727	|	0730	0747	|	|	0812	0925	0948	...	1000	...	...	1137	...	1247	1257	1300	...	...	1421
175	**Napoli Centrale** a.	|	|	0759	|	|	...	0857	|	0850	0958p	|	...	1032	...	...	1205	...	|	1343	|	...	...	|
	Cassino d.	0656	0735	...	|	|	...	...	0916	...	...	|	0954	...	...	1205	...	1305	1337	...	1412	...	1505	1540
	Frosinone d.	0743	0813	...	|	|	...	...	0951	...	...	|	1047	...	...	1257	...	1357	1413	...	1458	...	1556	...
	Roma Termini a.	0850	0920	...	0905	1010	...	...	1050	...	...	1130	1210	...	...	1415	...	1510	1520	...	1605	...	1710	...

	8039	IR 2359 2360	D 3364	12166	12438	12426	D 3366	E 964	8043	12168	E 966	7877	12170	8045	E 970	IR 2365 2366	IC 760	D 3299		8047	E 952	E952 E954	D 3356	E 956
			2	2	2		2			2			2	2	🍷		🍷🅁						2	
						⚒		♦	⚒		♦			⚒	KS	S	♦				♦	M		♦
Foggia d.	...	...	...	...	...	1354	...	1503	...	...	1642	...	...	...	1825	...	1907	...	...	...	0052	0052	...	0235
Benevento d.	...	...	...	...	...	1550	...	1626	...	...	1806	...	...	...	1943	...	2022	...	...	...	0254	0254	...	0440
Campobasso d.	1315	1410	...	...	...	|	...	|	1610	...	|	...	...	1740	|	1915	|	...	...	2015	|	|	...	|
Carpinone d.	1416	1458	...	...	...	|	...	|	1710	...	|	...	...	1839	|	2003	|	...	...	2120	|	|	...	|
Isernia d.	1428	1511	...	...	...	|	...	|	1723	...	|	...	...	1852	|	2017	|	...	...	2131	|	|	...	|
Vairano-Caianello d.	1512	1555	1602	...	...	|	1730	|	1807	...	|	...	...	1939	|	2101	|	2142	...	...	|	|	...	|
Caserta d.	1556	|	|	...	1615	1705	|	1721	...	...	1908	1921	...	2014	2046	|	2118	2210	...	...	0404	0420	0435	053
Napoli Centrale a.	1628	|	|	...	|	...	|	1800p	...	...	|	1953	...	2047	2120p	|	|	2240	...	...	|	0500	|	|
Cassino d.	...	|	1630	1730	1740	...	1804	...	...	1854	1954	...	2045	...	...	2127	|	...	...	...	|	...	0558	|
Frosinone d.	...	|	1720	1824	...	...	1856	...	...	1939	2028	...	2129	...	...	2202	|	...	...	...	|	...	0644	|
Roma Termini a.	...	1750	1830	1950	...	...	1955	...	...	2100	2125	...	2245	...	...	2300	2325	...	...	...	0630t	...	0750	075

♦ – **NOTES** (LISTED BY TRAIN NUMBERS)

P520 – BORROMINI – ⚒: [12] and ✕ Bari Centrale - Roma.
P521 – BORROMINI – ⚒, also Dec. 25, Apr. 16, 30: [12] and ✕ Roma - Bari Centrale.
IC760 – MERCADANTE – [12] Bari Centrale - Roma; 🍷 Foggia - Caserta. **Not** Dec. 24, 31.
IC761 – MERCADANTE – [12] Roma - Bari Centrale; 🍷 Roma - Foggia. **Not** Dec. 25, Jan. 1.
E951/2 – ━ 2 cl. and [12] Roma - Bari Centrale - Taranto and v.v; [12] Roma - Lecce and v.v. **Not** Dec. 24, 31 from Roma or Lecce.
E955/6 – 🛏 1,2 cl., ━ 1, 2 cl. and [12] Roma - Bari Centrale - Lecce and v.v; 🛏 1,2 cl. Roma - Taranto and v.v.
E965/6 – [12] Roma - Bari Centrale and v.v.
E964/7 – [12] Napoli - Foggia - Pescara Centrale and v.v. **Not** Dec. 25, Jan. 1 from Napoli or Pescara.
E962/9 – [12] Roma - Lecce and v.v; 🍷 Roma - Bari Centrale and v.v. **Not** Dec. 25, Jan. 1 from Roma or Lecce.
K – [12] Napoli - Bari Centrale and v.v.
M – [12] Napoli - Bari Centrale - Lecce and v.v.
S – **Not** Dec. 24, 31.
t – Roma **Tiburtina**.
p – Napoli **Piazza Garibaldi**.
❖ – **Not** Dec. 25, Jan. 1.
⚡ – **ETR450** Pendolino supplement payable.

Table 396 CAMPOBASSO - TERMOLI

1, 2 cla

km		8124	8126	D3474	8112	D3482	8130	8186	8188	8220	8222
		⚒		⚒	⑦	⚒	⚒				
0	**Campobasso** d.	0535	0657	0752	0845	1210	1301	1406	1620	1831	1950
51	Larino d.	0644	0808	0852	0953	1315	1410	1511	1724	1935	2056
88	**Termoli** a.	0719	0842	0925	1025	...	1447	1546	...	...	...

	8125	8127	D3477	8133	8135	8185	8207	8187	8219	822
	⚒	⚒			⚒	⚒	⑦	⚒		
Termoli d.	...	0600	0723	1200	...	1326	1430	1451	...	...
Larino d.	0540	0642	0806	1241	1320	1408	1513	1539	1750	20
Campobasso a.	0648	0747	0915	1351	1436	1518	1616	1649	1901	21

Table 397

LAMEZIA TERME - CATANZARO - REGGIO DI CALABRIA

1, 2 class except where shown

km		E891 E893	E891 E894	D 3773	D 12707	D 3747	8459	D 3755	D 3753	E821 E829 E828	E821 E829	E801 E803 E802	E801 E803	D 3757	D 3763	E 1983	E1983 E1984	D 3765	8467	E 973	D 3781	8479	D 3777	D 3779
		G ✕	M ✕							A	B	C				H	J							
	Roma Termini 405 ...... d.	2220	2220							0322t	0322t	0335t	0335t			0554t	0554t				0915			
	Napoli Centrale 405 ..... d.	0057	0057							0539	0539	0553c	0553c			0842	0842				1138			
0	Lamezia Terme Centrale ... d.	0442	0442	0635		0700	0753		0840	1006	1006	1045	1045	1135	1235	1243	1243		1430	1530	1730	1830	1930	2140
38	Catanzaro .... d.	0524	0524	0712		0742	0838		0918	1050	1050	1137	1137	1220	1320	1340	1340	1409	1516	1620	1806	1920	2014	2218
47	Catanzaro Lido .... d.	0532	0532	0721		0752	0850		0927	1100	1100	1146	1146	1230	1330	1350	1350	1419	1531	1630	1818	1930	2025	2227
47	Catanzaro Lido 398 .... a.	0545	0555	0726	0742					1123	1131	1205	1210		1352	1431	1432	1425		1633			2028	2236
	Crotone .... a.		0642	0806						1215		1250				1520								
113	Roccella Jonica 398 .... d.	0644			0850			1130			1234		1318			1509	1542		1517		1730		2122	2345
214	Reggio di Calabria 398 ..... a.	0853			1314			1314			1447		1523			1755		1725		1958h			2305	

		D 3746	6748	8452	D 3750	D 3754	D 3756	E 12718	972	D3769 D3770	D 3760	D 3764	8462	🚌	E814 E816	E815 E814	E1985 E1982	E 1982	8466	E827 E824	E826 E824	8468	D 3780	E886 E888	E885 E886 E888
		✕		Z		Z				✕	⑦				F	C	N	O		P	R			G	G
																								M	M
	Reggio di Calabria 398 .... d.			0440		0900				1215					1355			1448		1655	1815		1940		
	Roccella Jonica 398 .... d.		0520	0630		1108	1145	1253		1423					1603			1658		1853	2025		2154		
	Crotone .... d.								1414						1618	1655			1900					2205	
	Catanzaro Lido 398 .... d.		0633		0727		1223	1237	1351	1500	1520				1705	1710	1752	1755		1952	1955		2250	2252	
	Catanzaro Lido .... d.	0510	0638	0730	0930	1125		1240	1354	1505		1720	1720	1750	1750	1819	1819	1835	2026	2026		2205	2315	2315
	Catanzaro .... d.	0525	0649	0741	0944	1136		1250	1408	1515		1732	1740	1807	1807	1830	1830	1846	2039	2039		2219	2330	2330
	Lamezia Terme Centrale ... a.	0605	0740	0818	1022	1215		1336	1455	1602		1819	1830	1853	1853	1914	1914	1928	2120	2120		2255	0012	0012
	Napoli Centrale 405 .... a.							1723							0141	0141				0141	0141		0410	0410	
	Roma Termini 405 .... a.							1945				0226o	0226o	0214t	0214t				0403t	0403t			0650	0650	

A – 🚃 (also ⊨ 2 cl. except when train J runs) Milano - Crotone.
B – 🚃 (also ⊨ 2 cl. except when train H runs) Roma - Reggio.
C – ⊨ 2 cl. and 🚃 Torino Porta Nuova - Crotone and v.v.
F – ⊨ 2 cl. and 🚃 Torino Porta Nuova - Reggio and v.v.
G – ⊨ 2 cl. and 🚃 (also 🛏 1,2 cl. (T2) on ⑤ from Roma and ⑦ from Reggio) Roma - Reggio and v.v. **Not** Dec. 24, 31 from Roma or Reggio.
H – Dec. 16 - 23, 30, Jan. 2 - 7, Apr. 12 - 14, 17 - 19, 22 (from Milano): ⊨ 2 cl. Milano - Reggio.
J – Dec. 16 - 23, 30, Jan. 2 - 7, Apr. 12 - 14, 17 - 19, 22 (from Milano): ⊨ 2 cl. Milano - Crotone.

M – ⊨ 1,2 cl. and 🚃 Roma - Crotone and v.v.
N – Dec. 16 - 23, Jan. 2 - 8, Apr. 12 - 14, 17 - 19, 25: ⊨ 2 cl. Crotone - Milano.
O – Dec. 16 - 23, Jan. 2 - 8, Apr. 12 - 14, 17 - 19, 25: ⊨ 2 cl. Reggio - Milano.
P – 🚃 (also ⊨ 2 cl. except when train N runs) Crotone - Milano.
R – 🚃 (also ⊨ 2 cl. except when train O runs) Reggio - Milano.
Z – By 🚌 on ⑦.
c – Napoli **Campi Flegrei.**
h – ⑦ only.
o – Roma **Ostiense.**
t – Roma **Tiburtina.**

Table 398

VILLA SAN GIOVANNI - SIBARI - TARANTO

1, 2 class except where shown

km		IR 2460 2461	IR 2462 2463	IC790 IC792	IR 2464 2465	IR 2466 2467	E926 E927 E924	IC770 E1972 E972	E985 E986	E985 E986 E987
		Z	Z		Z	Z	S	T	V	V
0	Villa San Giovanni... d.			0642c		1457		2250	2250	
15	Reggio di Calabria 397 .. d.		0700			1524		2315	2315	
127	Roccella Jonica 397 .. d.		0824			1646		0057	0057	
193	Catanzaro Lido 397 .. a.		0910			1730		0150	0150	
193	Catanzaro Lido .... d.		0913			1733		0155	0155	
253	Crotone .... d.	0455	0732	0956	1255	1615b	1735	1812	1840	0248	0248
340	Rossano .... d.	0602	0850	1100	1412	1732b	1840	1938	1940	0402	0402
366	Sibari .... a.	0625	0912	1120	1425	1754b	1902	1929	2001	0423	0423
366	Sibari .... d.	0647	1047	1132	1447	1822	1914	2013	0435	0435
445	Metaponto .... d.	0756	1156	1221	1556	1931	2024	2035	2134	0543	0543h
488	Taranto .... a.	0838	1238	1253	1638	2014	2057	2108	2204	0634	0634h
	Bari Centrale 390 ... a.		1431			2304	2241	2356		0905h
	Brindisi Centrale .... a.								0816	

		IR 2468 2469	E1975 E1977	E923 E929	E925 E925	IR 2470 2471	IC773 IC775	IR 2472 2473	IC785 IC787	IR 2474 2475	E982 E984	E982 E983 E984
		Z	W	X	Z	Y	Z	L	Z	V	V
	Brindisi Centrale .. d.								2129		
	Bari Centrale 390 .. d.		0636	0708		0825		1235		2047n
	Taranto .... d.	0523	0844	0905	0923	0959	1323	1408	1723	2305	2305
	Metaponto .... d.	0605	0925	0935	1005	1030	1405	1437	1805	2342	2342
	Sibari .... a.	0713	1028	1042	1113	1127	1513	1532	1913	0042	0042
	Sibari .... d.	0735	1040	1054		1139		1544	1935	0054	0054
	Rossano .... d.	0755	1102	1123		1158		1606	1955	0121	0121
	Crotone .... a.	0905	1207	1230		1256		1708	2105	0241	0241
	Catanzaro Lido 397 .. a.					1336		1801		0325	0325
	Catanzaro Lido 397 .. d.					1339		1804		0330	0330
	Roccella Jonica 397 .. d.					1425		1851		0425	0425
	Reggio di Calabria 397 .. a.					1552		2013		0610	0610
	Villa San Giovanni .... a.					1624		2030		0630	0630

L – **Not** Dec. 25, 26, Jan. 1.
S – 🚃 (also ⊨ 2 cl. except when train T runs) Crotone - Milano Centrale.
T – Dec. 16 - 23, Jan. 2 - 8, Apr. 12 - 14, 17 - 19: ⊨ 2 cl. Crotone - Milano Centrale.
V – ⊨ 2 cl. and 🚃 Villa San Giovanni - Bari and v.v. **Not** Dec. 24, 31 from Villa San Giovanni or Bari.
X – 🚃 (also ⊨ 2 cl. except when train W runs) Milano Centrale - Crotone.

W – Dec. 16 - 23, Jan. 2 - 8, Apr. 12 - 14, 17 - 19 (from Milano): ⊨ 2 cl. Milano Centrale - Crotone.
Y – 🚃 Reggio - Bari and v.v.; 🚃 Cosenza - Bari and v.v.
Z – 🚃 Cosenza - Taranto and v.v.
b – ✕ only.
c – Train number **IC789.**
h – Train number **E988.**
n – Train number **E981.**

Table 399

PAOLA - COSENZA - SIBARI

1, 2 class except where shown

km		IR 2460 2461	E895 E897	E 898	9883	IR 2462 2463	IR 2417	9885	3802	IR 2419	IR 2464 2465	9889	3804	9893	IR 2466 2467	IR 2421	8484	IC 778	IR 2423	8486	8488	IR 2421	3808	IC 757	IR 2427
			A	B		2		2				2				M	C					✕		S	
	Roma Termini 405 ... d.		2320																					1810	
	Napoli Centrale 405 .. d.		0545		0905		0720			0920				1320			1520			1720		2012p	1920
0	Paola .... d.		0545		0905		1105	1200		1305		1425			1622		1705		1905			1720	2012p	1920
	Cosenza .... d.	0530		0620		0930			1220		1330		1450		1705		1750	1826		1925	2025	2105	2130	2303	2310
15	Castiglione Cosentino .. d.	0535	0601	0626	0921	0935	1123	1216	1225	1323	1335	1441	1455	1645	1710	1755		1923	1930	2035	2123	2135	2319	2328
20	Cosenza .... a.		0608		0926		1130	1221		1330		1446		1650	1730		1930			2130		2325	2335
67	Sibari .... a.	0635	0742	0742		1035		1320		1435		1552		1810	1905	1924		2042	2130		2231	
	Taranto 398 ...... a.	0838			1238			1638			2014			2108							

		IR 2416	IC 752	3749	IR 2468 2469	IR 2418	8485	IR 2470 2471	IC 774 779	IR 2472 2473	8489	9894	3801	IR 2472 2473	12680	12735	IR 2426	8491	IR 2474 2475	9894	8493	9896	E880 E881	E 882
			M				✕		C						M	2	✕		✕		2	✕	F	G
	Taranto 398 .... d.			0523				0923	0959				1323				1723			
Sibari .... d.		0636	0725		0752		1125	1145	1338		1436	1525		1710		1843	1925		2012	2202	
Cosenza .... d.	0440	0635		0840		1040		1240	1440		1515		1620	1820		1945		2030	2140	2324
Castiglione Cosentino .. d.	0446	0639	0735	0824	0846	0857	1046	1224	1238	1246	1446	1447	1521	1536	1624	1821	1826	1945	2028	2115	2145	2330
Cosenza .... a.			0750	0830		0902		1230	1243		1455		1541	1630		1826		2030	2120	2312
Paola .... a.	0503	0654		0903		1103		1303	1503		1543		1640		1843		2044		2201	2345	2345
Napoli Centrale 405 .. a.	0838	0949p		1238		1438		1638	1838				2218						0335
Roma Termini 405 ... a.	1150																	0615

A – ⊨ 2 cl. and 🚃 Roma - Cosenza (depart 0620 as train **E898**) - Sibari - Crotone (arrive 0930).
B – 🚃 Cosenza - Crotone. From Roma as train **E895** – see note **A**.
C – MAGNA GRECIA – 🚃 Cosenza - Bari Centrale and v.v.
 – ⊨ 2 cl. and 🚃 Crotone (depart 2025) - Sibari - Cosenza (depart 2324 as train **E882**) - Paola - Roma.

G – ⊨ 2 cl. and 🚃 Cosenza - Roma. From Crotone as train **E880** – see note **F**.
M – By 🚌 on ⑦.
p – Napoli **Piazza Garibaldi.**
Additional services from Paola - Cosenza: 0425, 0518, 0620, 0705✕, 0745, 0845, 1345, 1525, 1725, 1805, 2000, 2205. Additional services from Cosenza to Paola: 0515✕, 0615, 0705⑦, 0715✕, 0820, 1115✕, 1215, 1315, 1415✕, 1715, 1845, 1915.

Table 400 — EXPRESS TRAINS TO SOUTHERN ITALY AND SICILY

1, 2 class except where shown

First section

km	Station	E 1925 ◆	D 3853	E 1939 S	E851 E853 ◆	E 851	E1921 12755 L	E1923 1921	D 3661	D 3889 ⑥⑦	E 891 ◆	E891 E831 B	E 1773	E 1995 ◆	IC 789 N	E 831	E831 E839 M	E831 E9791 C	D 3669 🍴	E 895	E 1941 ◆
	Torino Porta Nuova d.																				1735
	Genova Piazza Principe d.																				1930
	Pisa Centrale d.																				2133
	Milano Centrale d.						1550	1550													
	Venezia Santa Lucia d.																				
	Bologna Centrale d.						1807	1807													
	Firenze SMN d.						1927	1927													
0	Roma Termini d.	1935		2040	2115	2115	2153t	2153t			2220	2220	2230t	2323t		2335t	2335t	2335t		2320	
214	Napoli Centrale d.	2151		2255	2330	2330	0005c	0005c			0057	0057	0046c		0145	0300	0300	0300		0233	0417
268	Salerno d.	2232		2335	0008	0008					0347	0347	0358	0451		0505	0505	0505	0540	0528	0624
489	Paola d.	0034		0141	0214	0214	0301	0301			0443	0443	0432			0539	0539	0539	0612	0607	0658
546	Lamezia Terme Centrale d.				0247	0247															
674	Villa San Giovanni a.	0210		0320	0355	0355	0445	0445	0500		0556	0556	0551	0620	0642	0645	0645	0645	0724	0823	0800
688	Reggio di Calabria a.									0515	0615				0620			0657	0706	0740	0856
680	Messina Centrale a.	0355		0520	0550	0550	0640	0640				0830				0800	0830	0830			0945
680	Messina Centrale d.	0410	0530	0545	0610	0615	0650	0700	0707	0810					0905		0922	0922			1005
	Taormina-Giardini d.			0627		0700	0747	0801							1000z		1010	1020z			
	Catania Centrale d.			0738z			0815z	0833	0850z						1052			1114			
	Augusta d.			0835			0918	0944													
	Siracusa a.			0900			0945	1010							1120			1145			
715	Milazzo d.	0444	0600		0644		0747		0841												1042
844	Cefalu d.	0647	0807		0857				1040												1245
911	Palermo a.	0750	0900		0945		1030		1135												1335

Second section

Station	E1941 E1945 F	E1941 E1943 G	E1931 E1933 ◆	E 1931 G	E1931 E1935 ◆	D 3675	E 1771 J	E 1981 ◆	E1997 E1999 H	E 1997 T	E1997 E9771 T	E 833 ◆	E833 E9773 ◆	E 821 🍴	E 801 ◆	E 805	E805 E807 T	E805 E9799 T	D 3875	IC 12805 🍴	IC 517 ⑥⑦ N🍴	IC 517 NⒶ	E 1983 ◆
Torino Porta Nuova d.	1735	1735													1933	2050	2050	2050					
Genova Piazza Principe d.	1930	1930													2131	2242	2242	2242					
Pisa Centrale d.	2133	2133													2341	0049	0049	0049					2220
Milano Centrale d.							1945		2015	2015	2015	2100	2100	2025									
Venezia Santa Lucia d.			1905	1905	1905																		0107
Bologna Centrale d.			2127	2127	2127				2224	2203	2236	2236	2236	2305	2305	2245							0238v
Firenze SMN d.			2246v	2246v	2246v				2355v	2335v	0008v	0008v	0008v	0037v	0037v	0017v							0554t
Roma Termini d.									0232t	0218t		0330t	0330t	0322t	0335o	0429o	0429o	0429o			0615	0615	0554t
Napoli Centrale d.																					0817p	0817	0842
Salerno d.	0417	0417							0536	0514	0556	0556	0556	0633	0633	0619	0650	0702	0702		0851	0851	0933
Paola d.	0624	0624		0709	0709	0709			0753	0817	0806	0806	0806	0845	0845	0808	0840	0854	0950		1103	1103	1145
Lamezia Terme Centrale d.	0658	0658		0744	0744	0755			0830	0851	0841	0841	0841	0918	0918	0940	1012	1024	1024		1133	1133	1217
Villa San Giovanni a.	0800	0800		0850	0850	0914			0945	1053	1005	1005	1005	1025	1057	1122	1130	1130	1130		1240	1240	
Reggio di Calabria a.			0827		0920	0930			1010	1110				1025	1055	1115	1140		1150		1255	1255	
Messina Centrale a.	0945		1040	1040					1200	1200		1220					1315	1315					
Messina Centrale d.	1010		1100	1105					1220	1225		1235					1335	1340		1407	1422		
Taormina-Giardini d.	1056			1144					1316								1414			1528			
Catania Centrale d.	1150z			1250z					1415								1514z			1620			
Augusta d.	1238			1344													1615						
Siracusa a.	1310			1410													1645						
Milazzo d.						1132				1255		1308							1414	1439			
Cefalu d.						1332				1501		1534							1638	1650			
Palermo a.						1425				1600		1625							1730	1745			

Third section

Station	D 3681 🍴	D 3871 🍴	IC 693 ⟡	IC693 IC695 ⟡	IC693 IC697 ⟡	12765 12763 🍴	3887 ⑦	12807 🍴	D 973	D 3893	D 3883	IC699 IC703 ⟡	IC 699 ⟡	IC699 IC701 2	12679	D 3885	IC 753 ⟡	3685	IC 755 ⟡
Torino Porta Nuova d.																			
Genova Piazza Principe d.																			
Pisa Centrale d.																			
Milano Centrale d.																			
Venezia Santa Lucia d.																			
Bologna Centrale d.																			
Firenze SMN d.																			
Roma Termini d.			0810	0810	0810				0915			1210	1210	1210			1410		1610
Napoli Centrale d.			1012	1012	1012				1138			1412	1412	1412		1612p	1644		1812p
Salerno d.			1053	1053	1053				1219			1448	1448	1448		1853	1905		2053
Paola d.			1250	1250	1250				1444			1645	1645	1645		1923	2007		2127
Lamezia Terme Centrale d.	1308		1322	1322	1322				1518			1717	1717	1717	1725	2030	2109		2235
Villa San Giovanni a.	1428		1420	1420	1420							1815	1815	1815	1958	2022	2209		2330
Reggio di Calabria a.	1452				1440							1835		2022		2045	2230		2250
Messina Centrale a.			1555	1555								1950	1950						
Messina Centrale d.		1532	1610	1615		1622	1720	1735		1815	1830	2005	2010			2140	2223		
Taormina-Giardini d.		1614	1652			1727	1840	1918				2046				2310			
Catania Centrale d.		1705	1737			1815	1900	1925		2000		2132				2310			
Augusta d.		1755				1938	1947					2221							
Siracusa a.		1830	1850			2005	2010					2250							
Milazzo d.		1640								1852						2050			
Cefalu d.										2050						2223			
Palermo a.		1910								2140						2310			

NOTES (LISTED BY TRAIN NUMBERS) ◆

E801 – 🍴 2 cl. and 🛏 Torino - Reggio.

E821 – 🛏 1,2 cl. and 🛏 1,2 cl. (T2), 🍴 2 cl. and 🛏 Milano - Reggio.

E831 – FRECCIA DEL SUD – 🍴 2 cl. and 🛏 Milano - Agrigento; 🛏 Milano - Siracusa.

E851 – 🍴 2 cl. and 🛏 Roma - Agrigento; 🛏 1,2 cl. Roma - Siracusa; 🛏 Roma - Siracusa (12788) - Ragusa. Not Dec. 24, 31 from Roma.

E891 – 🛏 1,2 cl., 🍴 2 cl. and 🛏 Roma - Reggio; 🛏 1,2 cl. Roma - Villa SG (E831) - Messina.

E895 – 🛏 1,2 cl. (T2), 🍴 2 cl. and 🛏 Roma - Reggio.

E1771 – ⑥ Jan. 7 - Mar. 18, also Dec. 21 - 23, 28 - 30, Jan. 2 - 4, Apr. 13, 14, 18: 🛏 1,2 cl. (T2) and 🛏 Bolzano - Reggio.

E1773 – ⑤⑥, also Dec. 21, 22, 29, Apr. 13, not Dec. 24, 31, Apr. 15 (from Bologna): 🛏 2 cl. and 🛏 Bologna - Reggio.

E1921 – TRINACRIA – 🛏 1,2 cl., 🛏 1,2 cl. (T2), 🍴 2 cl. Milano - Palermo; 🛏 Messina - Palermo.

E1925 – 🛏 1,2 cl., 🛏 1,2 cl. (T2) and 🍴 2 cl. Roma - Palermo.

E1931 – 🛏 1,2 cl., 🛏 1,2 cl. (T2) and 🛏 1,2 cl. Venezia - Siracusa; 🛏 1,2 cl. Venezia - Catania; 🛏 Messina - Siracusa.

E1939 – 🛏 1,2 cl., 🛏 1,2 cl. (T2) and 🍴 2 cl. Roma - Siracusa.

E1941 – TRENO DEL SOLE – 🛏 1,2 cl. (T2) and 🍴 2 cl. (also 🛏 1,2 cl. ④⑤⑥) Torino - Palermo.

E1981 – Jan. 13, 20, 27, Feb. 2 also Dec. 22, 23, Jan. 5, 7, Apr. 12, 14, 21: 🛏 1,2 cl. (T2) and 🍴 2 cl. Milano - Reggio.

E1983 – Dec.16 - 23, 30, Jan. 2 - 7, Apr. 12 - 14, 17 - 19, 22: 🛏 2 cl. Milano - Roccella Jonica and Crotone – see Table 397.

E1995 – TRINACRIA – Dec. 10 - 23, 26 - 29, Jan. 2 - 8, Apr. 12 - 15, 17 - 19: 🛏 1,2 cl. and 🛏 2 cl. Milano - Catania; 🛏 Messina - Siracusa.

E1997 – Dec. 15 - 22, Jan. 1 - 7, Apr. 11 - 13, 16 - 18, 20: 🛏 1,2 cl. (T2) and 🛏 2 cl. Milano - Catania; 🛏 Messina - Catania.

B – 🛏 1,2 cl. Roma - Messina. Not Dec. 25, Jan. 1.

C – FRECCIA DEL SUD – 🛏 1,2 cl. and 🛏 Milano - Reggio.

F – TRENO DEL SOLE – 🛏 1,2 cl. and 🛏 2 cl. Torino - Siracusa; 🛏 Messina - Catania; 🛏 1,2 cl. (T2) (also 🛏 Dec. 7 - Jan. 8, Apr. 14 - May 7) Torino - Catania; 🛏 2 cl. Torino - Reggio.

G – 🛏 1,2 cl. (T2) and 🛏 2 cl. (also 🛏 1,2 cl. on ④⑤⑥) Venezia - Palermo; 🛏 1,2 cl. and 🛏 2 cl. Venezia - Reggio.

H – Dec. 15 - 22, Jan. 1 - 7, Apr. 11 - 13, 16 - 18: 🛏 1,2 cl. (T2) and 🛏 2 cl. Milano - Reggio.

J – Dec. 15 - 22, Jan. 1 - 7, Apr. 11 - 13, 16 - 18, 20: 🛏 1,2 cl. and 🛏 2 cl. Milano - Palermo.

K – Jan. 9 - Apr. 11, Apr. 20 - May 27, also Dec. 24, 26 - 30, Jan. 1, Apr. 15, 16, Apr. 20 - May 27: 🛏 1,2 cl. and 🛏 2 cl. Torino - Reggio.

L – Not when train E1995 runs: 🛏 1,2 cl. and 🛏 2 cl. Milano - Siracusa; 🛏 1,2 cl. (T2) Milano - Catania.

M – 🛏 2 cl. and 🛏 Milano - Agrigento.   N – Not Dec. 25, 26, Jan. 1, Apr. 16.

S – Not Dec. 24, 31.   T – Not Dec. 25, 31.   c – Napoli Campi Flegrei.

o – Roma Ostiense.   p – Napoli Piazza Garibaldi.   t – Roma Tiburtina.

v – Firenze Campo di Marte.   z – Arrive 10 - 20 minutes earlier.   ✤ – Not Dec. 25, Jan.

Table 400 — EXPRESS TRAINS FROM SICILY AND SOUTHERN ITALY

1, 2 class except where shown

Block 1

km	Station	IC 3674	D 754	D 3876	D 3840	12898 ⑦	12758	D 3904	D 3842	IC696 12776	IC694 694	IC 698	IC 12678	756	12842 12760	IC700 700	IC702 700	IC704 700	D 3888	12894 ⑦
	Palermo … d.				0420			0620				0800		0840					1035	1120
	Cefalu … d.				0510			0709				0840		0943					1118	1222
	Milazzo … d.				0718			0902				1015		1205					1256	1437
0	Siracusa … d.			0510					0700			0815			1205					
31	Augusta … d.			0535					0723						1050					
87	Catania Centrale … d.			0630		0640	0700		0810	0820	0925		1100	1113	1210			1300		
135	Taormina-Giardini … d.			0712		0732	0800		0812	0906	1002			1155	1252			1342		
182	Messina Centrale … a.			0755	0805	0833	0840	0935	0940	1000	1048	1050	1255	1258	1337 1340			1430		1530
	Messina Centrale … a.										1105	1105				1355	1355			
	Reggio di Calabria … d.	0600	0715																	
	Villa San Giovanni … d.	0623	0730							1205	1230		1415			1505				
	Lamezia Terme Centrale … d.	0753	0831							1240	1240	1240	1255	1430		1540	1540	1540		
	Paola … d.	0847	0903							1335	1335	1335	1520	1531		1635	1635	1635		
	Salerno … d.		1114							1406	1406	1406	1603			1706	1706	1706		
	Napoli Centrale … a.		1149p							1645	1645	1645	1814			1910	1910	1910	1945	1945
	Roma Termini … a.		1350							1850	1850	1850	2050			2150	2150	2150		
	Firenze SMN … a.																			
	Bologna Centrale … a.																			
	Venezia Santa Lucia … a.																			
	Milano Centrale … a.																			
	Pisa Centrale … a.																			
	Genova Piazza Principe … a.																			
	Torino Porta Nuova … a.																			

Block 2

Station	D 3850	IC 516 ⑥⑦	IC 516 Ⓐ	E9798 E810 A	E810 T	E808 E810 T	E1770 ◆	816 ◆	E1944 E1940 B	E1942 E1940 B	E1940 B	E1982 E1930 C	E1934 E1930	E1932 E1930 C	E1930 C	D 3852	D 3892	E1774 ◆	824 ◆	E1994 ◆	IC 788
Palermo … d.	1130	N✕	N✕		1200				1330			1350				1405					
Cefalu … d.	1222			1246					1418			1439				1500					
Milazzo … d.	1437			1500					1605			1638				1710					
Siracusa … d.				1230					1330											1515	
Augusta … d.				1257					1402											1542	
Catania Centrale … d.				1405z					1438											1650z	
Taormina-Giardini … d.				1449					1505z			1550z							1625	1712	1730
Messina Centrale … a.	1515			1538	1540				1555 1555	1548		1640 1645	1705 1705	1720 1720	1740 1740	1750	1800			1815	1830
Reggio di Calabria … d.		1605	1605	1705																	
Villa San Giovanni … d.		1640	1640	1740	1740	1740	1757	1802	1850 1850 1850			1830				1930	1940				2016
Lamezia Terme Centrale … d.		1740	1740	1842	1842	1842	1910	1942	1952 1952 1952			1925 1925 1925				2005	1958			2015	2030
Paola … d.		1810	1810	1917	1917	1917	1948	2022	2028 2028 2028			2001 2107 2107 2107				2127	2150				
Salerno … d.		2014	2014	2136	2136	2136	2159	2307	2241 2241 2241			2234 2321 2321 2321				2203	2231			2146	
Napoli Centrale … a.		2049p	2049				2256c					2322				0019	0103			2354	
Roma Termini … a.		2250	2250	0106o	0106o	0106o	0111t	0236o				0214t				0334t	0403t			0308t	
Firenze SMN … a.							0420c					0457v	0513v	0513v	0513v	0619	0631v			0537	
Bologna Centrale … a.								0534				0643	0633		0633	0834	0801			0700	
Venezia Santa Lucia … a.												0900	0900		0900						
Milano Centrale … a.												1005									
Pisa Centrale … a.				0433	0433	0433	0558	0520	0520 0520											1010	0905
Genova Piazza Principe … a.				0715	0715	0715	0815	0754	0754 0754												
Torino Porta Nuova … a.				0910	0910	0910	1015	1000	1000 1000												

Block 3

Station	E1922 E1920 K	E1920	E884 ◆	E1980 ◆	E9770 E1996 F	E1998 E1996 G	D 3890	E9772 E834 T	E834 T	888 ◆	E9790 E832 H	E830 E832 J	D 3898	12766 12792	D 3660	E1924 ◆	E1938 ◆	852 ◆	E850 E852 S
Palermo … d.		1540				1605			1630			1810				1920			2040
Cefalu … d.						1657			1716			1858				2007			2130
Milazzo … d.		1814				1857			1915			2105				2202			2325
Siracusa … d.	1550										1810		1910				2020	2045	
Augusta … d.	1616						1728				1837		1939				2046	2113	
Catania Centrale … d.	1725z						1800		1835		1900	1948z	2030	2030			2250	2200z 2225z	
Taormina-Giardini … d.	1805					1846	1917				2003	2033		2135			2250	2310	
Messina Centrale … a.	1850	1850				1935 1940	2005		2005	2020	2115	2125 2140	2235			2250 2340	2355	2359	
Reggio di Calabria … d.			2027	2042	2105			2130		2250	2255	2145				2305 2355	0015	0015	
Villa San Giovanni … d.	2050	2050	2105	2100	2140 2140	2145 2145		2250	2307	2330 2330					0015	0030 0050	0140	0200	0200
Lamezia Terme Centrale … d.	2221	2221	2314	2300	2250 2250	2307 2307		0046	0032	0032					0030	0050	0140	0200	0200
Paola … d.			2314	2335	2326 2326		2343 2343	0121		0108 0108					0223	0311	0331	0331	
Salerno … d.	0028	0028	0253				0150 0150	0331											
Napoli Centrale … a.			0335	0311	0259 0259	0259		0228 0228	0410		0356 0356				0223	0518	0553	0553	
Roma Termini … a.	0353t	0353t	0615	0530t	0530t 0530t		0442t 0442t	0650		0618t 0618t					0524	0558	0632	0632	
Firenze SMN … a.	0559	0559	0857v	0803v	0803v 0803v		0722v 0722v	0856		0856					0810	0845	0920	0920	
Bologna Centrale … a.	0720	0720	1025	0955	0955 0955		0911 0911	1014		1014									
Venezia Santa Lucia … a.																			
Milano Centrale … a.	0940	0940	1310	1205	1205 1205		1120 1120	1215		1215									
Pisa Centrale … a.																			
Genova Piazza Principe … a.																			
Torino Porta Nuova … a.																			

◆ – NOTES (LISTED BY TRAIN NUMBERS)

E816 – 🚋 2 cl. and (T2) Reggio - Torino.

E824 – 🚋1,2 cl. (T2), 🚋 2 cl. and (T2) Reggio - Milano.

E852 – 🚋 2 cl. and (T2) Agrigento - Roma; (T2) Ragusa (12789) - Siracusa - Roma; (T2) Siracusa - Roma. **Not** Dec. 24, 31.

E884 – 🚋1,2 cl., 🚋 2 cl. and (T2) Reggio - Roma.

E888 – 🚋1,2 cl., 🚋 2 cl. and (T2) Reggio - Roma.

E1770 – ⑤ Jan. 6 - Mar. 17, also Dec. 23, Jan. 2 - 8, Apr. 12 - 14, 17 - 19: 🚋1,2 cl. (T2), 🚋 2 cl. Reggio - Bolzano.

E1774 – ⑥⑦, also Dec. 22, 23, 26, Jan. 2, 3, Apr. 17, 18, 25, **not** Dec. 24, 25, 31, Jan. 1, Apr. 15, 16, 23: 🚋1,2 cl. Reggio - Bologna.

E1920 – TRINACRIA – 🚋1,2 cl., 🚋1,2 cl. Palermo - Milano.

E1924 – 🚋1,2 cl., 🚋1,2 cl. (T2) and 🚋 2 cl. Palermo - Roma; 🚋1,2 cl. Messina - Roma (**not** Dec. 24, 31).

E1930 – 🚋1,2 cl. (T2) and 🚋 2 cl. Siracusa - Venezia; 🚋1,2 cl. Catania - Venezia; (T2) Siracusa - Messina.

E1938 – 🚋1,2 cl., 🚋1,2 cl. (T2) and 🚋 2 cl. Siracusa - Roma.

E1940 – TRENO DEL SOLE – 🚋1,2 cl. (T2) and 🚋 2 cl. (also 🚋1,2 cl. on ①⑥⑦) Palermo - Torino; (T2) Palermo - Messina.

E1980 – Dec. 22, Jan. 1, 6, 7, 14, 21, 28, Feb. 4, Apr. 13 - 15, Apr. 17, 25: 🚋1,2 cl. (T2) and 🚋 2 cl. Reggio - Milano.

E1982 – Dec. 16 - 23, Jan. 2 - 8, Apr. 12 - 14, 17 - 19, 25: 🚋 2 cl. Crotone and Roccella Jonica - Milano. See Table 397.

E1994 – TRINACRIA – Dec. 10 - 23, 26 - 29, Jan. 1 - 8, Apr. 12 - 15, 17 - 19: 🚋1,2 cl. 🚋 2 cl. Siracusa - Milano; 🚋1,2 cl. (T2) Catania - Milano; (T2) Siracusa - Messina.

E1996 – Dec. 16 - 23, Jan. 2 - 8, Apr. 12 - 14, 17 - 19, 22: 🚋1,2 cl. (T2) and 🚋 2 cl. Catania - Milano.

A – Dec. 24, 26 - 30, Jan. 1, Jan. 9 - Apr. 11, 15, 16, Apr. 20 - May 27: 🚋1,2 cl. and (T2) Reggio - Torino.

B – TRENO DEL SOLE – 🚋 2 cl. Reggio - Torino; 🚋1,2 cl. and 🚋 2 cl. Siracusa - Torino; 🚋1,2 cl. (T2) (also 🚋1,2 cl. Dec. 7 - Jan. 8, Apr. 14 - May 7) Siracusa - Torino.

C – 🚋1,2 cl. and 🚋 2 cl. Reggio - Venezia; 🚋1,2 cl. (T2) and 🚋 2 cl. (also 🚋1,2 cl. on ①⑥⑦) Palermo - Venezia; (T2) Palermo - Messina.

F – Dec. 16 - 23, Jan. 2 - 8, Apr. 12 - 14, 17 - 19, 22: 🚋1,2 cl. and 🚋 2 cl. Reggio - Milano.

G – Dec. 16 - 23, Jan. 2 - 8, Apr. 12 - 14, 17 - 19, 22: 🚋1,2 cl. and 🚋 2 cl. Palermo - Milano.

H – 🚋 2 cl. and (T2) Reggio - Milano.

J – FRECCIA DEL SUD – 🚋1,2 cl. and (T2) Agrigento - Milano; (T2) Siracusa - Milano.

K – TRINACRIA – **not** when train E1994 runs: 🚋1,2 cl. and 🚋 2 cl. Milano - Siracusa; (T2) Milano - Catania.

N – Not Dec. 25, 26, Jan. 1, Apr. 16.

S – Not Dec. 24, 31.

T – Not Dec. 25, 31.

c – Napoli Campi Flegrei.

o – Roma Ostiense.

p – Napoli Piazza Garibaldi.

v – Firenze Campo di Marte.

❖ – Not Dec. 25, Jan. 1.

t – Roma Tiburtina.

z – Arrive 10 - 20 minutes earlier.

Table 402 NAPOLI - POTENZA - TARANTO

1, 2 class except where shown

km		12581	12583	12395	E945	2417	12397	D3455	IC741	E1663	8339	8343	D3457	12399	8067	12401	12599	2467	D3441	2431	34357	12603	IC755	12403
		2	2						①-⑥	⑥⑦	2⚒	2				2	2V				R	2		2
0	**Napoli Centrale 405** d.	...	...	...	0600	0720	...	0820	0912p	...	...	...	1150	...	...	...	...	...	1450	1550	1713p	...	1812p	...
26	Pompei **405** d.	...	...	...	|	0748	...	0848	|	...	...	...	1218	...	...	...	...	...	1519	1615	|	...	|	...
54	Salerno **405** d.	...	...	0500	0640	0810	0818	0918	0945	1000	...	...	1240	1320	1334	...	...	...	1543	1649	1750	...	1845	...
74	Battipaglia **405** d.	...	...	0530	0700	0830	0838	0942	...	1015	...	...	1303	1340	1354	1440	...	...	1605	1710	1805	...	1903	1915
80	Eboli d.	...	...	0537	0707	...	0845	...	...	1023	...	...	...	1347	1400	1448	...	...	1613	1717	1812	...	...	1922
166	**Potenza Inferiore** d.	0702	...	0740	0841e	...	1058	...	...	1150	1230	1433	...	1552	...	1646	1717	...	1750	1858	1939	2030	...	2127
273	Metaponto **398** d.	0845	0906	...	1007	...	...	...	...	1331	1408	1611	...	...	...	...	1850	1931	...	2017	2056	2206	...	...
316	**Taranto 398** a.	...	0953	...	1050	...	...	...	...	1406	1453	1651	...	...	...	...	...	2014	...	2048	2129	2244	...	...

	D3440	12396	IC752	2468	8332	34660	34676	2430	12398	2422	8340	12400	2424	12580	E948	12402		E1662	2426	2474	12404	12588	12592	12594
		2			2⚒	R⚒	⑦				2			2				⑥⑦				2	2	2
Taranto 398 d.	...	...	...	0523	...	0650	0800	1021	...	...	1133	...	...	1340	1505	...	...	1700	...	1723	...	...	1922	...
Metaponto **398** d.	...	...	...	0604	0610	0719	0829	1103	...	...	1230	...	...	1426	1536	...	...	1737	...	1804	...	1810	2010	2018
Potenza Inferiore d.	0518	0615	...	...	0738	0840	0951	1230	1315	...	1401	1425	...	1609	1649	1728	...	1919	...	...	2006	2007	...	2203
Eboli d.	0649	0815	...	...	...	0954	1106	1402	1508	...	...	1633	...	...	1814	1943	...	2052	...	...	2202	...	...	...
Battipaglia **405** d.	0655	0828	0859	...	...	1001	1113	1410	1515	1532	...	1640	1732	...	1821	1952	...	2100	2112	...	2212	...	...	...
Salerno **405** d.	0713	0844	0914	...	...	1013	1126	1426	...	1549	...	...	1749	...	1838	2015	...	2116	2130	...	2230	...	...	...
Pompei **405** d.	0734	...	|	...	...	|	|	1446	...	1610	...	...	1810	...	|	...	...	...	2151	...	...	...	...	...
Napoli Centrale 405 a.	0805	...	0949p	...	...	1055p	1158p	1515	...	1638	...	...	1838	...	1916	...	...	...	2218	...	...	...	...	...

R – Inter-City service: [12] Roma Termini - Taranto and v.v. V – 14 - 22 minutes later on ⑥⑦ as train **34653**. e – Arrive 0830. p – Napoli **Piazza Garibaldi**.

Table 403 TARANTO - BRINDISI

70 km Journey time: 60 - 75 minutes 2 class only

From Taranto: 0420 ⚒, 0613 ⚒, 0625 ⚒, 0653 ⚒, 0703 **E**, 0843 , 1144 ⚒, 1329 , 1435 , 1643 , 1745 , 1900 , 2138 , 2256.
From Brindisi: 0400 ⚒, 0503 ⚒, 0614, 0828, 1029 ⚒, 1151 ⚒, 1336, 1416 ⚒, 1618, 1727, 1933, 2033, 2129 **E**. **E** – Conveys [12] Villa San Giovanni - Brindisi and v.v – see Table **398**.

Table 404 CAGLIARI - SASSARI, PORTO TORRES and OLBIA

1, 2 class

km		3950	3980	3952	12908	3964	3994	3966	3970	8928	12928
		⚒	⚒				B				
0	**Cagliari** d.	0420	...	0610	1010	1425	...	1600	1820	...	1930
95	Oristano d.	0535	...	0716	1137	1548	...	1654	1925	...	2107
154	Macomer d.	0637	...	0803	▬	1650	...	1743	2019	...	2220
214	Ozieri - Chilivani d.	0738	0735	0903	0905	1748	1750	1832	2122	2124	...
281	**Sassari** a.	|	0815	0945	|	1829	|	1914	|	2205	...
300	**Porto Torres** a.	|	...	...	|	1847	|	...	|	...	...
284	**Olbia** a.	0838	...	...	1000	...	1852	...	2225	...	...

	3951	3955	3957	8887	3961	8891	3967	1293	8895	3971
	⚒		B							
Olbia d.	...	...	0705	0900	...	1345	...	...	1815	...
Porto Torres d.	...	...	|	|	0906	|	...	...	|	...
Sassari d.	...	0650	|	|	0924	|	1420	...	|	1845
Ozieri - Chilivani d.	...	0734	0820	1009	1018	1452	1507	...	1925	1938
Macomer d.	0550	0823	0926	...	1115	...	1606	...	...	2039
Oristano d.	0650	0907	1012	...	1203	...	1655	1927	...	2128
Cagliari a.	0754	1000	1116	...	1310	...	1800	2106	...	2230

Other services: **Olbia - Olbia Marittima**: 0600, 1853, 2226 **B**; **Olbia Marittima - Olbia**: 0655 **B**, 1910, 2255. 3 km. Journey time: 7 minutes. **B** – [12] Cagliari - Olbia Marittima.
Olbia to **Golfo Aranci**: 0706⚒, 0800⚒, 1310⑦ 🚌, 1348, 1625; **Golfo Aranci** to **Olbia**: 0735⚒, 0828⚒, 1515⑦ 🚌, 1525, 1745 ⚒, 2043⚒ 🚌.

Table 405 ROMA - NAPOLI - PAOLA

1, 2 class except where shown

km		E 801	D 3453	E 805	IR 2417	IC 517	E 823	E 1911	E 809	E 845	IC 741	D 2385	IC 693	E 311	E 287	D 2387	IC 1657	E 973	D 3457	IC 743	E 1085	D 2391	IC 555	D 2393
		♣		♣	C	♣	♦	♦	♦	♦		🍷	♣	♦	♦🍷		⑥	♦🍷		①-⑥	♦	①-⑥	♦🍷	🍷
0	**Roma Termini** d.	...	...	...	...	0615	...	...	...	0645	0710	0720	0810	...	0830	0820	0910	0915	...	1010	...	1020	1110	1120
0	**Roma Tiburtina** d.	0335o	...	0429o	...	|	0540	0623	0605o	|	|	|	|	0811	|	|	|	|	...	|	0958	|	|	|
62	Latina d.	|	...	|	...	|	0621	0659	0711	0721	|	0801	|	0854	|	0905	|	0949	...	|	1040	1108	|	1208
129	Formia d.	|	...	|	...	|	0707	0742	0755	0815	|	0848	|	|	|	0952	|	1030	...	|	1118	1148	|	1248
195	Aversa d.	|	...	0629	...	|	0752	0825	0843	|	|	0933	|	1010	|	1037	|	1107	...	|	1157	1233	|	1333
214	**Napoli Centrale** a.	0541c	...	0650	...	0809t	0813	0850	0904	0915c	0908p	0953	1000	1031	1038	1057	1112	1126	...	1203p	1218	1253	1300	1353
		|		|		|	D 3455				|	▬ 2419 C	|				|	|					IR 2421 C	
214	**Napoli Centrale 402** d.	0553c	0620	0702	0720	0817t	0820	...	...	...	0912p	0920	1012	...	...	...	1124	1138	1150	...	...	...	1320	...
240	Pompei **402** d.	|	0648	|	0748	|	0848	...	...	...	|	0948	|	...	...	...	|	1158	1218	...	...	...	1348	...
268	Salerno **402** d.	0650	0713	0742	0813	0851	0921	...	...	...	0945	1013	1053	...	...	...	1208	1219	1243	...	...	...	1413	...
288	Battipaglia **402** d.	0711	0731	|	0831	0908	0942	...	...	...	...	1031	|	...	...	...	...	1236	1304	...	...	...	1431	...
395	Sapri d.	0826	0850	0855	0945	1007	...	...	...	...	...	1145	|	...	...	...	...	1345	1420	...	...	...	1545	...
489	**Paola** d.	0920	...	0946	1057	1100	...	...	...	...	...	1300	1247	...	...	...	...	1440	...	...	...	...	1700	...

	IC 699	D 3463	IR 2371	IC 553	D 2397	IC 753	IC 607	IR 2373	E 211	IC 34357	IR 947	IC 755	IC 539	D 2403	P⚡ 519	D 2405	IC 757	IR 2375	IC 541	D 2409	IC 613	D 2411	IC 545	D 2413
	♣		Q🍷	♦		♦	♦	①-⑥	♦🍷	♦		♦🍷	♦✕		♦✕		♦	❖	♦✕		♦		♦🍷	🍷
Roma Termini d.	1210	...	1215	1310	1320	1410	...	1415	...	1500	1515	1610	1710	1620	1705	1720	1810	1815	1910	1920	...	2025	2110	2120
Roma Tiburtina d.	|	...	|	|	|	|	1409o	|	1437o	|	|	|	|	|	|	|	|	|	|	|	2009	|	|	|
Latina d.	|	...	1249	|	1401	|	|	1449	|	|	1549	|	|	1701	|	1801	|	1849	|	2000	|	2103	|	2201
Formia d.	|	...	1330	|	1448	|	|	1530	1559	|	1630	|	|	1748	|	1848	|	1930	|	2050	|	2154	|	2248
Aversa d.	|	...	1407	|	1533	|	|	1607	1640	|	1707	|	|	1833	|	1933	|	2007	|	2135	|	2239	|	2333
Napoli Centrale a.	1400	...	1426	1500	1553	1608p	1605	1630	1700	1708p	1726	1808p	1900	1853	1850h	1953	2008p	2026	2100	2155	2203	2306	2300	2353
	|			IR 2423 C		|	|		IR 2425 C	|		|	|	IR 2427 C			|	|	D 3467	12389 ⚒				
Napoli Centrale 402 d.	1412	1420	...	1520	...	1612p	1617	...	1720	1712p	...	1812p	1912	1920	...	...	2012p	2040	2120	2205	...	...	...	...
Pompei **402** d.	|	1452	...	1548	...	|	1636	...	1749	|	...	|	|	1948	...	...	|	2108	2153	2242	...	...	...	...
Salerno **402** d.	1448	1517	...	1613	...	1644	1658	...	1813	1747	...	1848	1945	2013	...	...	2048	2130	2236	2325	...	...	...	...
Battipaglia **402** d.	|	1535	...	1631	...	|	...	...	1831	...	...	1904	...	2031	...	...	2104	...	2258	...	...	...	...	...
Sapri d.	|	1652	...	1745	...	1757	...	...	1945	...	...	2000	...	2145	...	...	2204	...	0010	...	...	...	...	...
Paola d.	1642	*1841*	...	1900	...	1850	...	...	2100	...	...	2050	...	2257	...	...	2300	...	...	...	...	...	...	...

♦ – **NOTES** (LISTED BY TRAIN NUMBERS)
E211 – NAPOLI EXPRESS – Dec. 16 - Jan. 7, Feb. 24 - Mar. 25, Apr. 7 - May 27 (from Paris): 🛏 1,2 cl., ▬ 2 cl. and [12] Paris Lyon - Napoli; 🍷 Genova Piazza Principe - Napoli.
E287 – 🛏 1,2 cl., ▬ 2 cl. and [2] München Hbf - Napoli; 🍷 Chiusi - Napoli.
E311 – [12] Genève Aéroport ✈, Basel SBB and Schaffhausen - Napoli.
P519 – VANVITELLI – [12] and ✕ Roma - Napoli. **Not** Dec. 25, 26, Jan. 1, Apr. 16.
IC533 – CROCE – [12] and 🍷 Milano - Napoli.
IC539 – PARTENOPE – [12] Milano Centrale - Salerno; ✕ Milano - Napoli.
IC541 – AMBROSIANO – [12] and ✕ Milano Centrale - Napoli.
IC545 – VESUVIO – [12] and 🍷 Milano - Napoli.
IC555 – MARCONI – [12] and 🍷 Piacenza - Napoli.
IC607 – CARIGNANO – [12] Torino Porta Nuova - Salerno; 🍷 Torino - Napoli. **Not** Dec. 25.
IC613 – CAPODIMONTE – [12] and 🍷 Torino Porta Nuova - Napoli.
IC753 – VELIA – [12] Roma - Reggio.
IC755 – ASPROMONTE – [12] Roma - Reggio; 🍷 Roma - Villa San Giovanni.
IC757 – SILA – [12] Roma - Cosenza; 🍷 Roma - Paola. **Not** Dec. 24, 31.
E809 – 🛏 1,2 cl., 🛏 1,2 cl. (T2), ▬ 2 cl. and [12] Torino Porta Nuova - Napoli. **Not** Dec. 24, 31 from Torino.
E823 – ▬ 2 cl. and [12] Milano Centrale - Napoli. **Not** Dec. 24, 31 from Milano.
E845 – 🛏 1,2 cl., ▬ 2 cl. and [12] Udine - Napoli; 🛏 1,2 cl. (T2), ▬ 2 cl. and [12] Venezia Santa Lucia - Napoli. **Not** Dec. 24, 31 from Udine/Venezia.
E973 – [12] Roma - Catanzaro - Roccella Jonica; 🍷 Roma - Sapri.
E1085 – Dec. 16, 23, Apr. 13 only (from Stuttgart): ▬ 2 cl. and [2] Stuttgart - Napoli; [12] Zürich Hbf - Napoli.
E1911 – 🛏 1,2 cl., 🛏 1,2 cl. (T2) and ▬ 2 cl. Milano Centrale - Napoli.
IC34357 – [12] Roma - Battipaglia - Potenza Inferiore - Taranto.
C – [12] Napoli - Cosenza.
Q – **Not** Dec. 25.
c – Napoli **Campi Flegrei**.
h – Napoli **Mergellina**.
o – Roma **Ostiense**.
p – Napoli **Piazza Garibaldi**.
t – On ⑥⑦ departs from **Piazza Garibaldi**.
❖ – **Not** Dec. 25, Jan. 1.
♣ – Long distance express service – see Table **400**.
⚡ – **Pendolino** supplement payable. Ⓡ.

Table 405 PAOLA - NAPOLI - ROMA

1, 2 class except where shown

	D 2380	IC 740 ①-⑥	D 2382	E 852 ♣	IC 534 ♦	D 2384 🍷	P⚡ 518 ♦	D 3692	IR 2416 C	IC 536 ♦	12694 2	IC 752 ♦	D 2390 ①-⑥	IC 742 ①-⑥	IC 34660 ♦	IR 946	IC 754 ♦	IC 34676 ♦	D 2394 🍷	IR 2418 C	D 2396 🍷	IC 614 ♦	E 210 ♦	IR 2374	IR 2420 C
Paola d.	...	...	...	0331	...	...	...	...	0506	...	...	0657	...	...	...	...	0903	...	...	0906	...	...	...	...	1106
Sapri d.	...	...	...	0424	...	...	...	0505	0620	...	0630	0753	...	...	...	...	0956	...	...	1020	...	...	...	...	1220
Battipaglia **402** d.	...	...	...	0536	...	...	...	0625	0732	...	0823	0859	...	...	1001	...	1059	1113	...	1132	...	...	...	...	1332
Salerno **402** d.	...	...	...	0553	0558	...	...	0644	0749	0810	0840	0914	...	...	1016	...	1114	1126	...	1149	...	1250	...	...	1349
Pompei **402** d.	...	...	...	|	0620	...	...	0706	0810	|	0859	|	...	...	|	...	|	|	...	1210	...	1312	...	...	1410
Napoli Centrale 402 a.	...	...	...	0632	0645	...	...	0737	0838	0845	0932	0949p	...	...	1055p	...	1149p	1158p	...	1238	...	1335	...	...	1438
				|	|			IC 622 ♦	2370 ❖	|	D2388	|			|		|	|		IC 542 ✕		|			IC 546 E🍷
Napoli Centrale d.	0505	0600p	0605	0647	0657	0705	0725h	0747	0835	0857	0905	0953p	1005	1057	1059p	1135	1153p	1202p	1205	1257	1305	1347	1355	1435	1457
Aversa d.	0521	|	0621	|	|	0721	|	|	0851	|	0921	|	1021	|	|	1151	|	|	1221	|	1321	|	|	1451	|
Formia d.	0611	|	0712	|	|	0814	|	|	0931	|	1011	|	1111	|	|	1231	|	|	1311	|	1411	|	1458	1531	|
Latina d.	0659	|	0800	|	|	0859	|	|	1009	|	1059	|	1159	|	|	1309	|	|	1358	|	1459	|	|	1609	|
Roma Tiburtina a.	|	|	|	|	|	|	|	|	|	|	|	|	|	|	|	|	|	|	|	|	|	1545o	1617o	|	|
Roma Termini a.	0740	0800	0840	0920	0850	0940	0908	0945	1045	1050	1140	1150	1240	1250	1300	1345	1350	1405	1440	1450	1540	...	...	1645	1650

	D 2400 🍷	IC 1658 ⑥	D 3694	IR 2422 C	IC 694 ♣	E 972 ♦	D 2406	D 3462 ⚒	IR 2424 C	IC 756 ♦	E 1084 ♦	D 3696	E 312 ♦	E 820 ♦	IC 700 ♣	D 2410	E 844 ♦	E 1912 ♦	IC 516 ♣	D 3698	E 806 ♦	IR 2426 C	E 810 ♣	E 816 ♣	E 824 ♣
Paola d.	...	...	...	1306	1406	1424	...	...	1506	1603	...	...	...	...	1706	...	...	...	1810	...	...	1846	1917	2022	2231
Sapri d.	...	...	1305	1420	|	1518	...	...	1620	1656	...	1700	...	...	|	...	...	...	1900	1820	...	2000	2009	2127	2328
Battipaglia **402** d.	...	...	1432	1532	|	1628	...	...	1732	|	...	1832	...	...	|	...	...	...	1959	1932	...	2112	|	2246	|
Salerno **402** d.	...	1440	1449	1549	1610	1643	...	1705	1749	1814	...	1849	...	...	1910	...	...	...	2014	1949	...	2130	2136	2307	0103
Pompei **402** d.	...	|	1510	1610	|	1701	...	1737	1810	|	...	1910	...	...	|	...	...	...	|	2019	...	2151	|	|	|
Napoli Centrale 402 a.	...	1525	1538	1638	1645	1723	...	1805	1838	1849p	...	1935	...	...	1945	...	...	...	2049t	2045	...	2218	|	|	0141
		|	IC 554 ♦	D2402	|	|		E 286 ♦		|		D2408			|				|	D 2412			|	|	|
Napoli Centrale d.	1505	1537	1557	1605	1657	1735	1805	1815	...	1853p	1857	1905	1915	1947	1957	2005	2030c	2050	2057t	2105	2130	...	|	|	|
Aversa d.	1521	|	|	1621	|	1751	1821	|	...	|	1915	1921	1935	2007	|	2021	|	2114	|	2121	2148	...	|	|	|
Formia d.	1611	|	|	1711	|	1831	1913	|	...	|	2005	2011	2021	2102	|	2111	2125	2159	|	2216	2230	...	|	|	|
Latina d.	1659	|	|	1759	|	1909	2001	|	...	|	2050	2059	2104	2145	|	2159	2205	2241	|	2304	2309	...	|	|	|
Roma Tiburtina a.	|	|	|	|	|	|	|	|	...	|	2131	|	2145	2226	|	|	|	2320	|	2346	0008o	...	0055	0226o	0403
Roma Termini a.	1740	1745	1750	1845	1850	1945	2040	2020	...	2050	...	2140	...	...	2150	2240	2245	...	2250	...	...	...	...	...	...

♦ – **NOTES** (LISTED BY TRAIN NUMBERS)

E210 – NAPOLI EXPRESS – Dec. 17 - Jan. 8, Feb. 25 - Mar. 26, Apr. 8 - May 27: 🛏 1,2 cl., ▬ 2 cl. and [12] Napoli - Paris Lyon; 🍷 Napoli - Genova PP.
E286 – 🛏 1,2 cl., ▬ 2 cl. and [2] Napoli - München Hbf.
E312 – [12] Napoli - Genève Aéroport, Basel SBB and Zürich Hbf.
P518 – VANVITELLI – [12] and ✕ Napoli - Roma. **Not** Dec. 25, 26, Jan. 1, Apr. 16.
IC534 – VESUVIO – [12] Salerno - Milano; 🍷 Napoli - Milano.
IC536 – PARTENOPE – [12] Salerno - Milano Centrale; ✕ Napoli - Milano.
IC542 – AMBROSIANO – [12] and ✕ Napoli - Milano.
IC554 – MARCONI – [12] Napoli - Piacenza; 🍷 Napoli - Bologna.
IC614 – CARIGNANO – [12] Salerno - Torino PN; 🍷 Napoli - Torino. **Not** Dec. 25.
IC622 – CAPODIMONTE – [12] and 🍷 Napoli - Torino Porta Nuova.
IC752 – SILA – [12] Cosenza - Roma; 🍷 Battipaglia - Roma. **Not** Dec. 25, Jan. 1.
IC754 – ASPROMONTE – [12] Reggio - Roma; 🍷 Villa San Giovanni - Roma.
IC756 – VELIA – [12] Reggio - Roma.
E806 – 🛏 1,2 cl., 🛏 1,2 cl. (T2), ▬ 2 cl. and [12] Napoli - Torino Porta Nuova. **Not** Dec. 24, 31.
E820 – ▬ 2 cl. and [12] Napoli - Milano Centrale. **Not** Dec. 24, 31.
E844 – 🛏 1,2 cl., ▬ 2 cl. and [12] Napoli - Udine; 🛏 1,2 cl. (T2), ▬ 2 cl. and [12] Napoli - Venezia Santa Lucia. **Not** Dec. 24, 31.
E972 – [12] Roccella Jonica - Catanzaro - Roma; 🍷 Sapri - Roma.
E1084 – Jan. 1, Apr. 16: ▬ 2 cl. and [2] Napoli - Stuttgart; [12] Napoli - Zürich.
E1912 – 🛏 1,2 cl., 🛏 1,2 cl. (T2) and ▬ 2 cl. Napoli - Milano Centrale.
IC34660 – ①-⑥: [12] Taranto - Potenza Inferiore - Battipaglia - Roma.
IC34676 – ⑦: [12] Taranto - Potenza Inferiore - Battipaglia - Roma.
C – [12] Cosenza - Napoli.
c – Napoli **Campi Flegrei**.
h – Napoli **Mergellina**.
o – Roma **Ostiense**.
t – On ⑥⑦ departs from **Piazza Garibaldi**.
p – Napoli **Piazza Garibaldi**.
♣ – Long distance express service – see Table **400**.
⚡ – **Pendolino** supplement payable. Ⓡ.

Table 406 NAPOLI - SORRENTO

2 class only — Circumvesuviana Ferrovia

Rail service Napoli Circumvesuviana - Napoli FS ▲ – Pompei Villa di Misteri - Castellammare di Stabia - Vico Equense - Meta - Sorrento and v.v. Journey: 55-65 minutes. *45 km.*

From Napoli: 0451 ⚒, 0531, 0614, 0633 ⚒, 0654, 0734, 0814 then 2 or 3 times per hour until the last service at 2248. **From Sorrento**: 0413, 0501, 0541, 0601, 0641⚒, and 2 or 3 times per hour until 1721, 1801, 1841, 1901, 1921 ⚒, 1941, 2001, 2121, 2201, 2241. ▲ – This station is adjacent to **Napoli Centrale** main line station and is connected to it by a moving walkway.

Table 407 PALERMO - AGRIGENTO and CATANIA

1, 2 class except where shown

km		3934 ⚒	3880 ⚒	8702 ⑦	3920	3832	3848	3922	8706 2	3924 ❖	8636 ⚒	3926	3938 K	E832 H	8844 2	3834 ⚒	E854 M	3928	8726	3930	3838	3932 ⚒	3878	3936
0	**Palermo** d.	0555	...	...	0735	0810	...	1005	...	1105	1205	1302	1400	...	1420	1610	...	1620	...	1720	1820	1855	1950	2015
70	Roccapalumba-Alia d.	|	...	...	0827	0907	...	1055	...	1200	1304	1355	1451	...	1517	1705	...	1720	...	1813	1914	1953	2045	2106
139	**Agrigento** d.	|	0655	0755	0935	|	1000	1210	1300	1310	|	1500	|	1520	1620	|	1720	1835	1915	1925	|	2100	|	2210
	Canicatti d.	|	0750	0844	...	|	1048	...	1407	...	|	...	|	1625	...	|	1825	...	2009	...	|	...	|	...
	Caltanisetta Centrale d.	|	0825	0918	...	|	1125	...	1440	...	|	...	|	1700	...	|	1900	...	2046	...	|	...	|	...
	Caltanisetta Xirbi d.	0740	0835	0927	...	1001	1135	...	...	...	1412	...	1546	1710	...	1800	1910	...	2055	...	2008	...	2142	...
	Catania Centrale a.	0930	1030	1125	...	1154	1330	...	...	...	1602	...	1735	1922	...	2000	2122	...	...	...	2150	...	...	...

km		3902 ⚒	3941 ⚒	8842 ⚒	8699 ⚒	3841	3906	3841	3908	E855 M	3910	E831 H	3897	3891	3943 ⚒	8607 2⚒	3912	3914	8723 ⚒	3837	3873	3916	8631	3839	3833
0	**Catania Centrale** d.	...	0550	...	...	0805	...	0805	...	0827	...	1035	...	1310	1413	...	...	...	...	1614	...	...	1815	1910	2140
116	Caltanisetta Xirbi d.	...	0741	...	0745	1004	...	1006	...	1040	...	1240	1300	1510	1602	1605	...	...	*1720*	1817	1920	...	2010	2105	2342
123	Caltinasetta Centrale d.	...	|	...	0806	|	...	1015	...	1100	...	1251	|	1520	|	1614	...	...	1735	|	1935	...	2020	|	2350
	Canicatti d.	...	|	...	0835	|	...	1046	...	1146	...	1333	|	...	|	...	...	...	1816	|	2007	...	2058	|	...
	Agrigento d.	0645	|	0822	0920	|	1012	1130	1135	1245	1330	1440	|	...	|	...	1635	1750	1900	|	...	2000	2145	|	...
173	Roccapalumba-Alia d.	0755	0830	0930	...	1053	1118	...	1242	...	1432	...	1356	...	|	...	1739	1852	...	1913	...	2107	...	2158	...
243	**Palermo** a.	0850	0925	1020	...	1142	1215	...	1340	...	1530	...	1450	...	1740	...	1835	1950	...	2005	...	2200	...	2250	...

H – FRECCIA DEL SUD – ▬ 2 cl. and [12] Agrigento - Milano Centrale and v.v.
K – **Not** Dec. 25, 26, Jan. 1, 6, Apr. 16, 17, 23, 25, 30, May 1.
M – ▬ 2 cl. and [12] Agrigento - Roma Termini and v.v. **Not** Dec. 24, 31 from Agrigento or Roma.
❖ – **Not** Dec. 25, Jan. 1.

Table 409 SIRACUSA - RAGUSA - CANICATTI

1, 2 class except where shown

km		8698	8704	8824 2⚒	8712 ⚒	12788 A	3894 ⑦	12824 2	8690 2	8732 2	8738
0	**Siracusa** d.	...	0605	0815	...	1035	...	1235	1455	1738	1940
62	Pozzallo d.	...	0732	0920	...	1155	...	1345	1605	1847	2050
92	Modica d.	0537t	0810	0955	1145	1248	1410	1431	1650	1925	2125
112	**Ragusa** d.	0610t	0835	...	1212	1320	1435	1455	1718	...	...
182	Gela d.	0735	...	...	1331	...	1545	...	...	...	...
218	Licata d.	0810	...	...	1403	...	1618	...	...	...	...
264	**Canicatti** d.	0859	...	...	1452	...	1702	...	...	...	...

	8701	8703 ⚒	12809	12889 2⑦	3877	8713 ⚒	8715	8717	8637 ⚒	12789 A	8721	3873
Canicatti d.	...	...	...	0820	1011	...	1205	...	1456	...	...	2008
Licata d.	...	...	...	0907	1055	...	1255	...	1549	...	...	2055
Gela d.	0615	0740	...	0940	1130	1232	1328	1415	1620	...	1718	2125
Ragusa d.	0745	0855	0950	1050	...	1405	...	1533	...	1720	1834	*2326b*
Modica d.	0809	0915	1011	1110	...	1430	...	1554	...	1747	1858	*2344b*
Pozzallo d.	0840	...	1043	...	...	1510	...	1629	...	1823	1930	...
Siracusa a.	0950	...	1150	...	...	...	...	1730	...	2000	2032	...

A – [2] Roma Termini - Ragusa and v.v. **Not** Dec. 24, 31 from Roma or Ragusa.
b – By 🚌.
t – ⚒ only.

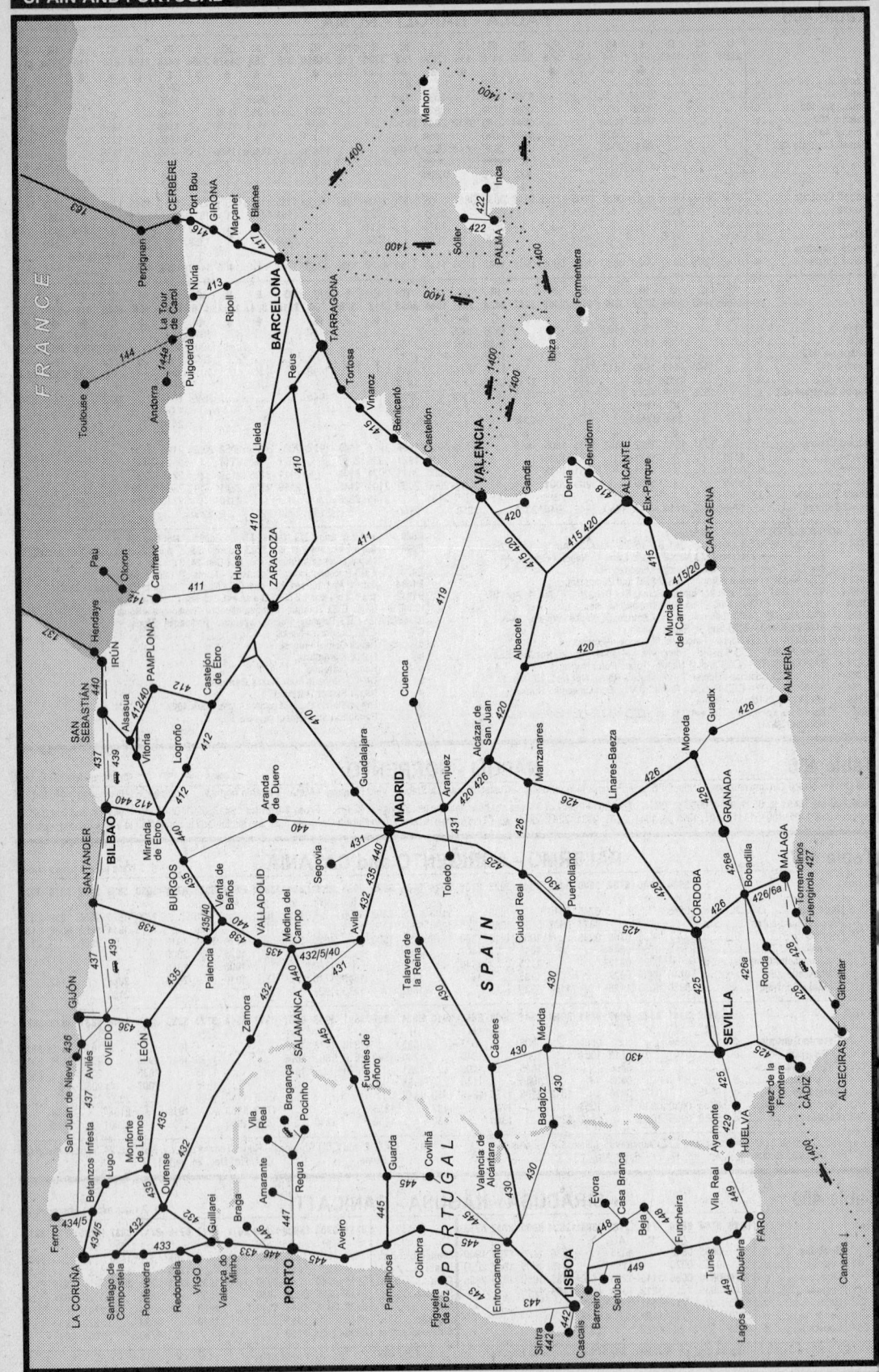

For list of scenic rail routes in Spain and Portugal see page 27

SPAIN

Operator: Red Nacional de Ferrocariles Españoles (**RENFE**) except where stated otherwise.

Services: Trains convey First and Second class seating accommodation, shown as '1' and '2' or ⬒ in the tables. All **AVE** and certain **TAL** (Talgo) trains carry a special fare structure with reservation obligatory, and instead convey 'Club', 'Preferente' and 'Turista' classes, shown as 'C', 'P' and 'T' in Tables 425/6. Sleeping cars (🛏) and couchette cars (▬) are of the normal European standard but have differing berth types. Many are fully air conditioned and some have showers. There is a luxury type of sleeper called 'Gran Clase', shown below as 🛏 (Gran Clase) which have showers and en-suite WC. See page 10 for more details.

Timings: Valid **May 29, 1994** to **May 27, 1995.** Services may be amended at and around Public Holidays. For dates of Public Holidays in Spain see page 2.

Supplements: Many trains, especially those designated **TAL** and **IC** carry a supplement which can be very expensive. The high speed **AVE** services carry a special fare structure depending on the class of travel and the time of day of the service. Special fares apply to the International Talgo trains *Francisco de Goya* (Paris - Madrid), *Joan Miro* (Paris - Barcelona), and the *Pablo Casals* (Zürich and Milano - Barcelona). The above three services can not be used by Inter-Rail cardholders.

Reservations: RENFE now requires passengers to hold reservations for **all** long distance journeys. The number in bold at the top of the train column (eg. **IC172**) is used for reservation purposes, and is called the **Numero Ordenador**. It may not be the same as the train number carried on timetable posters, electronic indicators and other literature. If no train number is shown at the top of the column in the following tables, reservation is **not** possible on that service.

Other Information: RENFE tracks are of broad gauge (1676 mm) with the exception of the new **AVE** line which has been built to the European standard gauge of 1435 mm. Only trains which have specially adjustable bogies fitted to the coaches can travel across the **French Frontier** or from the main Spanish network onto the **AVE** line.

Table 410 — MADRID - ZARAGOZA - BARCELONA

1, 2 class except where shown

km		IC 172 Ⓐ Ⓖ	IC 174 Ⓗ	IC 100	IC 180	2	IC 176 L🍴	IC 178 🍴f	2	2	IC 530 Ⓐ	TAL 374	IC 182	544 C	TAL 42 🍴 K	2	TAL 570 T Ⓑ	TAL 378 Ⓔe	620 F	IC 104 Vk	IC 142 Zr
0	Madrid Chamartin .... d.	...	...	0700	0715v	...	0900	0900	...	0940	...	1100	1115t	1200	1400	...	1500	1600	...	1700	1830
54	Guadalajara .... d.	...	0734			...	0932	0932	...	1020	...	1130		1232		...	1535	1631	...	1729	1903
242	Calatayud .... d.	...	0910			...	1113	1113	...		...	1306		1425		...	1727		...	1907	2046
338	Zaragoza El Portillo ... a.	...	1000			...	1207	1207	...		...	1400		1530	1655	...	1823	1855	...	2008	2150
338	Zaragoza El Portillo ... d.	0700	0915	h		...	1210	1220	1310	1405	h	1535	1700	1730		1900	1928		
530	Lerida/Lleida .... d.	0839	1105		1307				1544			1839		2035		2105			
618	Reus .... d.			1437		1501	1530	1617	1640	1830			2041					
636	Tarragona .... d.		1356	1451	1514	1545	1630	1653	1758	1843			2055					
661	Sant Vicenç de Calders .. d.	0945	1211		1517	1537	1611		1906			2118		2143	2213			
721	Barcelona Sants .... a.	1035	1300	1505	1605	1640	1705	1730	1800	1903	2000	1944	2118		2235	2304		
724	Barcelona Passeig de Gracia a.	1045	1307	1519	1610	1650	1705	1739	1808c	1910	2009	2035	2200		2245			
728	Barcelona Estació de França a.	1055	1315	1530	1620	1650	1715	1750		2020	2055	2215		2255			
	Cèrbere 416 .... a.								2015c	2130							

		IC 170 Ⓢn	950 E	370 Q	1370 Q	874 M	930 N	944 Up	1920 Bp	920 S	920 Pp			IC 171 Ⓢn	IC 141 Zr	IC 107 Vr	2	623 F	TAL 41 🍴 K	543 C	IC 179 Ⓐg
	Madrid Chamartin .... d.	2000		2200	2300	2300		0100t					Port Bou 416 .... d.	...	...	...	...	...	...	...	...
	Guadalajara .... d.			2241	2351	2351							Barcelona Estació de França d.	...	...	...	...	0810		0935	0935
	Calatayud .... d.	2206		0039	0144	0144							Barcelona Passeig de Gracia d.	...	0620		0821		0946	0946
	Zaragoza El Portillo ... a.	2300		0140	0245	0245		0432					Barcelona Sants .... d.	0625	0730	0830	1000	1000	
	Zaragoza El Portillo ... d.		0041	0145	0250	0250	0405	0433	0535	0608	0608		Sant Vicenç de Calders ... d.	0709	0809	0908	1040	1040	
	Lerida/Lleida .... d.		0247		0506	0506	0516	0627	0736	0758	0758		Tarragona .... d.	0734		1103	1103	
	Reus .... d.		0354	0440	0611	0611	0720			0906	0906		Reus .... d.	0748		1116	1116	
	Tarragona .... d.		0425	0520	0632	0632	0737			0930	0930		Lerida/Lleida .... d.	0925	1015		1355	1359
	Sant Vicenç de Calders ... d.		0558			0806							Zaragoza El Portillo ... a.	1110	1104	1151	1355	1359
	Barcelona Sants .... a.		0700	0800	0800	0905	0830	1005	1040	1040			Zaragoza El Portillo ... d.	0700	0830	1000	1200	1400	1400
	Barcelona Passeig de Gracia a.								0850				Calatayud .... d.	0751	0930	1051	1459	1459
	Barcelona Estació de França a.		0700	0800	0800	0905	0830	1005	1040	1040		Guadalajara .... d.	0930	1115	1302	1658	1643
	Cèrbere 416 .... a.		0945	1050									Madrid Chamartin .... a.	1005	1155	1305	1455	1740	1719

		IC 177 L Ⓑ	185	TAL 377	2	2	573 T Ⓑ	IC 533 A	IC 181	TAL 379 Ⓔe	IC 103 Rk	2		IC 175 Pp	923 S	923 Bp	1923		947 Up	373 Q	933 N	1373 Q	875 M	953 E
	Port Bou 416 .... d.	...	0850	0950d				...	...	...	...	...		...	...	...	...	1935		2020			
	Barcelona Estació de França d.	...	1051	1145d		1301		1340	1410	1510	1547		1715	1740		2015	2135					
	Barcelona Passeig de Gracia d.	...	1100	1200		1351	1421	1521	1557	1725	1751	2023						
	Barcelona Sants .... d.	1158		1400	1430	1530	1603	1733	1800	1900	1900	1933	2030	2200	2215	2230	2300	2300	
	Sant Vicenç de Calders ... d.		1403		1609	1645	1814	1837		2111	2308	2318				
	Tarragona .... d.	1158	1258	1429	1458	1528	1709	1839	2005	2005	2137	2338	2342	0017	0017	0137
	Reus .... d.		1311	1443	1511	1723	1853	2020	2020	2151	2352	2356	0031	0031	0151
	Lerida/Lleida .... d.		1405			1712		1950	2130	2130	2152	2350	0059	0132	0132	0254
	Zaragoza El Portillo ... a.		h	1552		1810	h	1855		2145	2315	2315	2345	0129	0305	0335	0335	0455
	Zaragoza El Portillo ... d.	1500	1600		1700		1900	2000		0130	0320	0340	0340	
	Calatayud .... d.	1551	1655		1833		2051		0431		0445	0445	
	Guadalajara .... d.	1732	1830	1931		2025		2124	2230		0540	0700	0700	
	Madrid Chamartin .... a.	1810	1855v	1905	2015	2100	2225t	2205	2310		0518t	0745		0800	0800

A – Irún and Bilbao - Barcelona and v.v. – For days of operation see Table 412.
B – Runs June 22 - Sept. 10, Dec. 22 - Jan. 8, Apr. 7 - 17 from Barcelona, one day later from La Coruña: 🛏 1, 2 cl., ▬ 2 cl., ⬒ and 🍴 Barcelona - La Coruña and v.v.
C – Runs May 29 - Sept. 24, Dec. Jan. 10 (not Dec. 25, 31), Apr. 7 - 19, also Dec. 2, 3, 8, 9 from Cáceres, May 29 - Sept. 24, Dec. 15 - Jan. 9 (not Dec. 25, 31), Apr. 6 - 18, also Dec. 1, 2, 3, 8 from Barcelona: ⬒ and 🍴 Cáceres - Barcelona and v.v.
E – Bilbao and Irún - Alicante and v.v. – For days of operation and composition see Table 415.
F – ⬒ Gijón - Barcelona and v.v.; conveys on ①③⑤⑦ (daily June 22 - Sept. 24, Dec. 23 - Jan. 9, Apr. 8 - 18) from La Coruña, ②④⑥⑦ (daily June 22 - Sept. 24, Dec. 22 - Jan. 8, Apr. 7 - 17) from Barcelona: ⬒ and 🍴 La Coruña - Barcelona and v.v.; conveys on ②④⑥ (daily June 22 - Sept. 24, Dec. 23 - Jan. 9, Apr. 8 - 18) from Vigo, ①③⑤ (daily June 23 - Sept. 24, Dec. 22 - Jan. 8, Apr. 7 - 17) from Barcelona: ⬒ and 🍴 Vigo - Barcelona and v.v.
G – Runs daily May 29 - Sept. 24, Ⓐ Sept. 25 - May 27; will not run Oct. 12, Nov. 1, Dec. 6, 8, Jan. 6, Apr. 14, May 1.
H – Runs Ⓒ Sept. 25 - May 27, also Oct. 12, Nov. 1, Dec. 6, 8, Jan. 6, Apr. 14, May 1; will not run Dec. 25, Jan. 1.
K – Runs 🍴 Sevilla - Madrid - Barcelona and v.v.; ⬒ and 🍴 Badajoz - Madrid - Barcelona and v.v.
L – Runs 🍴 May 30 - Sept. 24, Dec. 16 - Jan. 10, Apr. 7 - 19, also Dec. 2, 3, 8, 9 from Madrid, Ⓑ May 30 - Sept. 23, Dec. 15 - Jan. 9, Apr. 6 - 18, also Dec. 2, 3, 8, 24, 31 from Zaragoza: ⬒ and 🍴 Madrid - Zaragoza and v.v.
M – Runs Ⓑ only, daily May 29 - Sept. 24, Dec. Jan. 10 (not Dec. 24, 31), Apr. 6 - 18 (not Apr. 15): 🛏 1, 2 cl. (Gran Clase), 🛏 1, 2 cl., ⬒ and 🍴 Madrid - Barcelona and v.v.

N – Runs Ⓑ only from Barcelona, Irún and Bilbao: 🛏 1, 2 cl., ▬ 2 cl. and ⬒ and 🍴 Irún and Bilbao - Barcelona and v.v.
O – ⬒ Madrid - Castejón de Ebro - Pamplona and v.v.
P – 🛏 1, 2 cl., ▬ 2 cl. and ⬒ Vigo and Gijón - Barcelona and v.v.
Q – For days of running and composition see Table 416.
R – ⬒ and 🍴 Madrid - Pamplona and v.v.
S – Runs daily except June 22 - Sept. 10, Dec. 22 - Jan. 8, Apr. 7 - 17 from Barcelona, one day later from La Coruña: 🛏 1, 2 cl., ▬ 2 cl., ⬒ and 🍴 La Coruña - Barcelona and v.v.
T – Runs daily May 29 - Sept. 24, Ⓑ Sept. 25 - May 27, also Oct. 8, Dec. 3, 24, 31, Jan. 7: ⬒ and 🍴 Madrid - Jaca and v.v. and 🍴 Madrid - Logroño and v.v.
U – 🛏 1, 2 cl. (Gran Clase), 🛏 1, 2 cl. and 🍴 Sevilla - Barcelona and v.v.; ⬒ 1, 2 cl. (Gran Clase), 🛏 1, 2 cl. and 🍴 Málaga - Barcelona and v.v.
V – ⬒ and 🍴 Madrid - Pamplona and v.v.
Z – ⬒ and 🍴 Madrid - Málaga - Zaragoza and v.v.
c – June 24 - Sept. 24, Dec. 16 - Jan. 9, and Apr. 6 - 17 **only.**
d – Dec. 25 - Jan. 9. Daily June 24 - Sept. 24.
e – Daily July 28 - Sept. 3, also Oct. 8, Dec. 3, 24, 31, Jan. 7.
f – Will **not** run May 30 - Sept. 24, Dec. Jan. 10, Apr. 7 - 19.
g – Will **not** run May 29 - Sept. 24, Dec. 1, 2, 3, 8, Dec. 15 - Jan. 9, Apr. 6 - 18.
h – Via Valencia (Tables 415/420).
k – Will **not** run Apr. 15.
p – Will **not** run Dec. 24, 31 from point of origin.
r – Will **not** run Dec. 25, Jan. 1.
t – Madrid **Puerto de Atocha.**
v – Madrid **Puerto de Atocha.** For days of running see Table 420.

Table 411
VALENCIA - ZARAGOZA - CANFRANC
1, 2 class

km						570 M♥			⑧							570	573 ⑧t M♥
			⑧t												♨		
0	Valencia Término ....d.	...	...	...	...	0955	...	1545 1815		Canfranc 142 ....d.	...	...	0605	...	...	...	...	1750
10	Valencia Cabanyal ....d.	...	...	...	...	1005	...	1555 1825		Jaca ....d.	...	...	0638	...	...	1405	...	1823
170	Teruel ....d.	...	...	0705	...	1250	...	1837 2135		Sabiñánigo ....d.	...	...	0656	...	...	1427	...	1841
355	Zaragoza El Portillo ....a.	...	...	0956	...	1524	...	2130 ...		Ayerbe ....d.	...	...	0758	...	...	1531	...	1943
355	Zaragoza El Portillo ....d.	0715	...	...	1545	1840				Huesca ....d.	...	...	0833	...	...	1606	...	2024
438	Huesca ....d.	0828	...	...	1658	1947				Zaragoza El Portillo ....a.	...	...	0939	...	...	1703	...	2130
473	Ayerbe ....d.	0906	...	...	1732	2020				Zaragoza El Portillo ....d.	...	...	1005	1540	...	1825	...	...
532	Sabiñánigo ....d.	1010	...	...	1838	2125				Teruel ....d.	0710	...	1247	1832	...	2127	...	...
548	Jaca ....d.	1031	...	...	1905	2149				Valencia Cabanyal ....d.	0949	...	1510	2104	...	...	...	...
573	Canfranc 142 ....a.	1105	...	...	1940					Valencia Término ....a.	1000	...	1522	2115	...	...	...	...

M –   Runs ⑧ only, also Oct. 8, Dec. 3, 24, 31, Jan. 7: ⊡ and ♥ Madrid - Jaca and v.v.   t –   Will not run Nov. 1, Dec. 6, 8, Jan. 6.

Table 412
ZARAGOZA - PAMPLONA and LOGROÑO - BILBAO and IRÚN
1, 2 class except where shown

km		953 ♥ T	953 ♥ T	2 ♨	2 ⑧n	IC 100 ♥ r	623		2	2		2	IC 533 ♥ H	IC 533 ♥ G		570 L⑧	2	IC 104 ♥ k	923 ♥ Cp	923 ♥ D	1923 ♥ Kp	933 ⑧	933 B⑧
	Barcelona Sants 410 ......d.						0730						1400	1400					1900	1900	1933	2230	2230
	Madrid Chamartín 410 ....d.					0700		0940								1500	1700						
0	Zaragoza El Portillo ....d.	0458	0458	0630		1005	1107	1410		1450			1813	1813		1842	1930	2013	2325	2325	2350	0310	0310
91	Castejón de Ebro ....d.	0610	0625	0728	0730	1055	1203	1523	1433	1548			1903	1905			2038		0022	0022	0050	0433	0450
179	Pamplona........................d.		0736	0842		1148	1301		1550	1650	1925		2000					2203					0615
231	Altsasu/Alsasua Pueblo....d.		0811h	0916			1333			1726	2000		2040h										0654h
273	Gasteiz/Vitoria................d.			0950			1405			1755	2035												
	Logroño ....d.	0712			0830			1628				2000				2035	2139		0109	0109	0139	0543	
237	Miranda de Ebro ....a.	0816					1431	1730		1820	2103	2056										0645	
237	Miranda de Ebro 430 ....d.	0820										2057										0655	
	Zumárraga ....d.		0836									2109										0725	
	Donostia/San Sebastián a.		0935									2155										0835	
	Irún ....a.		1005									2218										0905	
	Hendaye........................a.																						
319	Bilbao Abando 430 ....a.	1005										2235									0835		

km			IC 107 ♥ r	2 ♨	IC 530 ♥ H	IC 530 ♥ M	2 bn	2	2	573 L⑧	2	620 ♥ F	IC 103 ♥ k	2	2	950 ♥ T	950 ♥ T	930 B⑧	930 A⑧	1920 ♥ Kp	920 ♥ D	920 ♥ Cp
0	Bilbao Abando 430 ....d.					0840												1900	2220				
	Irún ....d.					0900												1945	2205				
	Donostia/San Sebastián d.					0916												2005	2228				
	Zumárraga ....d.					1005												2106	2329				
82	Miranda de Ebro 430 ....a.					1019											2049	2112	2355				
82	Miranda de Ebro ....d.					1020	1240		1330			1606		1810	1900		2112	0010					
162	Logroño ....d.	0715				1115	1343			1515	1626		1913				2212		0110	0330	0400	0400	
	Gasteiz/Vitoria................d.				1045			1357			1627			1950									
	Altsasu/Alsasua Pueblo....d.				1117		1031h		1429			1651		2021	2135h	2359h							
	Pamplona........................d.		0800	1150		1102		1440	1506		1726	1807		2210	2210	0100							
242	Castejón de Ebro ....d.	0817	0855	1256		1215	1215	1443	1509		1731	1823		2024	2159	2336	2336	0245	0245	0424	0452	0452
333	Zaragoza El Portillo ....a.	0930	0955	1352		1307	1307	1552			1705	1845	1926	1955	2135	2255	0038	0038	0355	0355	0527 0558 0558
	Madrid Chamartín 410 ....a.			1305					2015			2100		2310									
	Barcelona Sants 410 ....a.					1730	1730						2304					0905	0905	1005	1040	1040	

A –   Runs ⑧ only: 🛏 1, 2 cl., 🛏 2 cl., ⊡ and ♥ Barcelona - Bilbao and v.v.
B –   Runs ⑧ only: 🛏 1, 2 cl., 🛏 2 cl., ⊡ and ♥ Barcelona - Irún and v.v.
C –   🛏 1, 2 cl., 🛏 2 cl., ⊡ and ♥ Barcelona - Vigo and Gijón and v.v.
D –   Runs daily except June 22 - Sept. 10, Dec. 22 - Jan. 8, Apr. 7 - 17 from Barcelona, one day later from La Coruña: 🛏 1, 2 cl., 🛏 2 cl., ⊡ and ♥ Barcelona - La Coruña and v.v.
F –   ⊡ Barcelona - Gijón and v.v.; conveys on dates in Table 410: ⊡ and ♥ Barcelona - Vigo/La Coruña and v.v.
F –   ⊡ Gijón - Barcelona; conveys on dates in Table 410: ⊡ and ♥ Vigo - Barcelona, and ⊡ and ♥ La Coruña - Barcelona.
G –   Runs ①③④⑦, (daily June 22 - Sept. 24, Dec. 22 - Jan. 8, Apr. 7 - 17): ⊡ and ♥ Barcelona - Irún.
H –   Runs ②④⑥ (daily June 22 - Sept. 24, Dec. 22 - Jan. 8, Apr. 7 - 17) from Barcelona, ③⑤⑦ (daily June 25 - Sept. 25, Dec. 22 - Jan. 8) from Bilbao: ⊡ and ♥ Barcelona - Bilbao and v.v.

K –   Runs June 22 - Sept. 10, Dec. 22 - Jan. 8, Apr. 7 - 17 from Barcelona, one day later from La Coruña: 🛏 1, 2 cl., 🛏 2 cl., ⊡ and ♥ Barcelona - La Coruña and v.v.
L –   Runs daily May 29 - Sept. 24, ⑧ Sept. 25 - May 27, also Oct 8 Dec. 3, 24, 31, Jan. 7: ⊡ and ♥ Madrid - Logroño and v.v.
M –   Runs ①②④⑥ (daily June 22 - Sept. 24, Dec. 22 - Jan. 8, Apr. 7 - 17): ⊡ and ♥ La Coruña - Barcelona.
T –   Bilbao and Irún - Alicante and v.v. - For days of operation and composition see Table 415.
b –   From Burgos.
h –   Alsasua main station, not Pueblo.
k –   Will not run Apr. 15.
n –   Will not run Oct. 12, Nov. 1, Dec. 6, 8, 25, Jan. 1, 6.
p –   Will not run Dec. 24, 31 from point of origin.
r – . Will not run Dec. 25, Jan. 1.

Table 413
BARCELONA - PUIGCERDÀ - LA TOUR DE CAROL
2 class only

km							c										c		
0	Barcelona Sants ....d.	0615	0715	0918	1206	1516	1616	1806	1906	2015		La Tour de Carol 🚂 ....d.	...	...	0815	...	1106	1323	...	1857
74	Vic................................d.	0733	0845	1034	1313	1625	1745	1919	2018	2127		Puigcerdà ....d.	...	0633	0821	...	1112	1329	1644	...	1903
110	Ripoll.............................d.	0820	0929	1121	1359	1712	1833	2009	2105	2208		La Molina ....d.	...	0650	0839	...	1130	1347	1702	...	1921
124	Ribes de Freser ▲ ....d.	0843	...	1138	1415	1730	...	2027	2123f			Ribes de Freser ▲ ....d.	...	0720	0913	...	1205	1417	1732	1834d	1951
142	La Molina ....d.	0923	...	1214	1447	1802	...	2059	2152f			Ripoll ....d.	0627	0743	0934	1024	1225	1440	1755	1854	2010
159	Puigcerdà ....d.	0945	...	1236	1508	1824	...	2120	2213f			Vic ....d.	0708	0827	1017	1111	1312	1525	1839	1939	2053
163	La Tour de Carol 🚂 ....a.	0952	...	1243	...	1831						Barcelona Sants ....a.	0816	0936	1127	1236	1418	1636	1948	2106	2209

b –   Will not run Aug. 15, Oct. 12, Nov. 1, Dec. 6, 8, 26, Jan. 6, 7, Apr. 14, 15, 17, May 1.
c –   Will not run Dec. 24, 25, 31, Jan. 6.
d –   ⑤⑦ only.
f –   Not Dec. 24, 25, 31.

▲ –   Vall de Núria FGC Rack Railway operates Ribes Enllaç to Queralbs (6 km) and Núria (12 km). Journey time Ribes Enllaç to Queralbs: 21-24 minutes, Núria: 40-43 minutes.
From Ribes Enllaç: 5 - 8 services operate daily 0915 - 1715.   From Núria: 6 - 10 services operate daily 0803 - 1815.   Winter Service subject to confirmation.
Operator: FGC – Ferrocarrils de la Generalitat de Catalunya.

Table 414
BARCELONA - BARCELONA AIRPORT ✈
Timings subject to confirmation
2 class only

Rail service Barcelona Sants to Barcelona Aeroport del Prat ✈. 15 km. Journey time 16 - 22 minutes.
From Barcelona Sants: 0544, 0614♨, 0644 and every 30 minutes to 2214.   **From Aeroport del Prat** ✈: 0612 and every 30 minutes to 2242.
Most trains run to or from Mataró, 50 km from Aeroport del Prat, 35 km from Barcelona Sants where connections can be made with Costa Brava trains - see Table 417.

Table 415 — BARCELONA - VALENCIA - ALICANTE - CARTAGENA
1, 2 class except where shown

km	Station	950	IC 83	2	IC 161	697	697	697	697	2	693	IC 163	2	2	185	2	TAL 463	IC 181	2	IC 165
		2	ⓎA	C	Ⅹp	Ⅹe	G		F		ⓎK	Ⓨ			Tn		L	S		k
0	Barcelona Estació de França d.					0640					0745		0910	0918	1045			1410		1540
4	Barcelona Passeig de Gracia d.				0601	0651					0756		0921	0928	1051	1055	1221	1421	1455	1550
7	Barcelona Sants 410 d.				0606	0700	0800	0800	0800	0800	0803	0900	0930	0933	1100	1103	1230	1430	1500	1600
67	Sant Vicenç de Calders 410 d.					0703					0843			1015		1141				1544
92	Tarragona 410 d.		0428		0730	0800	0858	0858	0858	0858	0907	0958	1029	1040	1158	1207	1328	1528	1609	1701
104	Salou d.		0439		0741	0908	0908	0908	0908		0916	1013		1050	1216		1337	1538	1620	
175	Tortosa d.		0523		0838	0853	0947	0947	0947	0947	1019	1048	1119	1148	1247	1318	1422	1622	1725	1750
220	Vinarós d.		0551	0655	0916	1013	1013	1013	1013			1148			1315			1647		1816
226	Benicarló d.		0557	0700		1019	1019	1019	1019			1154			1321					1822
298	Castelló/Castellón d.		0648	0755	0810	0955	1057	1057	1057	1057	1153	1231			1325	1406	1527	1733		1902
371	Valencia Término a.		0743	0905	0855	1045	1145	1145	1145	1145	1248	1320	1427		1450		1615	1822		1950
371	Valencia Término d.	0730	0800			1050	1200	1200	1200	1200	1300	1330			1445		1630			1955
521	Elda-Petrel d.	0925	0942			1216						1500			1700			1758		2139
562	Alicante Término a.	0958	1015			1250						1528			1733			1829		2205
562	Alicante Término d.	1005													1738			1834		
641	Murcia del Carmen 420 d.	1135													1901			1955		
706	Cartagena 420 a.														2005			2050		
	Córdoba 426 a.						1850		1850		1945									
	Granada 426 a.							2025												
	Almería 426 a.						2141													
	Málaga 426 a.					2140														
	Sevilla Santa Justa 425 a.								2035		2110									
	Cádiz 425 a.								2223		2302									

Second block (southbound, left — values in reading order)

Station	IC 167 ⑧	2	997 M	997 N	IC 63 ⑧k	1993 P	1993 Q	963 ⑧
Barcelona Estació de França d.	1710	1745			1915	1940		
Barcelona Passeig de Gracia d.	1721	1755			1925	1951		
Barcelona Sants 410 d.	1730	1803	1830	1830	1930	2000	1945	2245
Sant Vicenç de Calders 410 d.		1845			2009			2332
Tarragona 410 d.	1828	1910	1935	1935	2035	2058	2107	2355
Salou d.		1920	1946	1946	2045	2108	2118	0006
Tortosa d.	1922	2017	2028	2028	2141	2157	2211	0109
Vinarós d.	1953				2221	2241	2241	0140
Benicarló d.	1959							0146
Castelló/Castellón d.	2036		2142	2142	2306	2330	2330	0229
Valencia Término a.	2120		2235	2235	2355			0330
Valencia Término d.	2130		2255	2255		0012c	0012c	0350
Elda-Petrel d.	2257							0540
Alicante Término a.	2322							0611
Alicante Término d.								0630
Murcia del Carmen 420 d.								0805
Cartagena 420 a.								0914
Córdoba 426 a.			0555	0555		0808		
Granada 426 a.							1000	
Almería 426 a.			0922					
Málaga 426 a.				0755		0955		
Sevilla Santa Justa 425 a.				1028h		1200		
Cádiz 425 a.								

Second block (northbound, right — values in reading order)

Station	2 Ⅹp	994 M	994 N	IC 62 Ⅹe	1990 P	1990 Q	IC 260 f
Cádiz 425 d.			1850h	1850			
Sevilla Santa Justa 425 d.			2110	2115			
Málaga 426 d.		2005					
Almería 426 d.							
Granada 426 d.						2145	
Córdoba 426 d.		2300	2300	2250			
Cartagena 420 d.							
Murcia del Carmen 420 a.							
Alicante Término a.							0615d
Elda-Petrel d.							0639d
Valencia Término a.		0602	0602				0805d
Valencia Término d.		0625	0625	0705	0653c	0653c	0815
Castelló/Castellón d.		0715	0715	0755	0736	0736	0858
Benicarló d.				0830			
Vinarós d.							0936
Tortosa d.	0620	0745	0822	0822	0906	0851	0851 / 0910 / 1007
Salou d.	0718	0837	0936	0936	1000	1000	1000 / 1017
Tarragona 410 d.	0729	0847	0948	0948	0959	1022	1022 / 1028 / 1100
Sant Vicenç de Calders 410 d.	0759	0913					1059
Barcelona Sants 410 a.	0856	1000	1100	1100	1105	1140	1140 / 1156 / 1205
Barcelona Passeig de Gracia a.	0901	1005			1115		1201 / 1220
Barcelona Estació de França a.		1015			1130		1230

Third block (northbound — values in reading order)

Station	IC 262	IC 180 S	TAL 460 L	IC 182 T	690 K	IC 264 k	2	694 D	694	694	694 R	IC 266 ⑧	IC 84 C	953 A	960 ⑧
Cádiz 425 d.					0630						0700				
Sevilla Santa Justa 425 d.					0810						0845				
Málaga 426 d.									0800						
Almería 426 d.										0800					
Granada 426 d.										0905					
Córdoba 426 d.					0927			1034							
Cartagena 420 d.			0855									1615			2055
Murcia del Carmen 420 d.			0955			1355						1715			2215
Alicante Término a.			1055			1520						1834			2315
Alicante Término d.	0745		1100		1455	1523					1705	1837	1930		2335
Elda-Petrel d.	0809		1125		1517	1610					1730	1916	2004		0022
Valencia Término a.	0935		1305		1615	1659	1815	1746	1746	1746	1746	1905	2115	2150	0200
Valencia Término d.	0945	1115	1315	1515	1630	1705		1800	1800	1800	1800	1915	2045	2205	0220
Castelló/Castellón d.	1028	1201	1357	1556	1714	1752		1842	1842	1842	1842	1958	2130	2256	0312
Benicarló d.	1102	1237	1433	1633				1920	1920	1920	1920	2037		2343	0401
Vinarós d.	1108	1243		1639		1832		1926	1926	1926	1926			2350	0408
Tortosa d.	1134	1308	1320	1506	1550	1706	1831	1858	1838	1958	1958	1958	2106	0020	0104 / 0440
Salou d.		1411	1544	1642				1944	2045	2045	2045		0104	0543	
Tarragona 410 d.	1226	1356	1421	1544	1652	1758	1930	1957	2001	2056	2056	2056	2156	0115	0555
Sant Vicenç de Calders 410 d.		1440		1718					2026					0624	
Barcelona Sants 410 a.	1335	1505	1530	1703	1804	1903	2040	2103	2114	2205	2205	2205	2307		0730
Barcelona Passeig de Gracia a.	1350	1525	1510	1812		1910		2111					2315		
Barcelona Estació de França a.	1400	1530	1545	1822				2125					2328		

Notes

A – Runs ⑤ from Irún/Bilbao, ⑦ from Alicante, daily June 22 - Sept. 23, Apr. 8 - 16 from Irún/Bilbao and Alicante, also ①③ Dec. 5 - Jan. 4 from Irún/Bilbao, ②④ Dec. 6 - Jan. 5 from Alicante: 🛏 1, 2 cl., 🛌 2 cl. and 🍴 Bilbao - Alicante and v.v.; 🛏 1, 2 cl., 🛌 2 cl. and 🍴 Irún - Alicante and v.v.

B – Runs ⑧, daily June 25 - Sept. 10: 🛌 and 🍴 Barcelona - Cartagena and v.v.; conveys May 29 - Sept. 23, Dec. 22 - Jan. 8, and Apr. 7 - 17: 🛏 1, 2 cl., 🛏 1 cl.

C – 🛌 and 🍴 Castellón - Valencia - Madrid and v.v.

D – Runs ①③⑤ (daily June 24 - Sept. 25, Dec. 19 - Jan. 10, and Apr. 6 - 18): 🛌 and 🍴 Almería - Barcelona.

F – Runs May 29 - June 22, Sept. 25 - Dec. 20, Dec. 21, Jan. 3 - 6, Jan. 9 - Apr. 6, and Apr. 18 - May 27: 🛌 and 🍴 Barcelona - Cádiz; 🛌 and 🍴 Barcelona - Alcázar de San Juan - Badajoz.

G – Runs ②④⑦ (only daily June 23 - Sept. 24, Dec. 19 - Jan. 11, Apr. 6 - 18): 🛌 and 🍴 Barcelona - Almería.

K – For days of running see Table 420: 🛌 and 🍴 Barcelona - Cádiz and v.v.; 🛌 and 🍴 Barcelona - Alcázar de San Juan - Badajoz and v.v.

L – 🛌 and 🍴 Port Bou - Cartagena and Cartagena - Cerbère.

M – 🛏 1, 2 cl., 🛌 2 cl., 🛌 and 🍴 Barcelona - Málaga and v.v.

N – 🛌 2 cl., 🛌 and 🍴 Barcelona - Sevilla (- Cádiz) and v.v.

P – Runs June 23 - Sept. 24, Apr. 7 - 17 from Barcelona, returning one day later: 🛏 1, 2 cl., 🛌 2 cl., 🛌 and 🍴 Barcelona - Cádiz and v.v.

Q – Runs June 23 - Sept. 24, Apr. 7 - 17 from Barcelona, returning one day later: 🛏 1, 2 cl., 🛌 2 cl. and 🍴 Barcelona - Granada and v.v.

R – Runs May 29 - June 23, Sept. 26 - Dec. 21, Dec. 25 - 31, Jan. 3 - 6, Jan. 9 - Apr. 7, and Apr. 19 - May 27: 🛌 and 🍴 Cádiz - Barcelona; 🛌 and 🍴 Badajoz - Alcázar de San Juan - Barcelona.

S – 🛌 and 🍴 Barcelona - Valencia - Madrid and (Madrid ‡ -) Valencia - Barcelona.

T – 🛌 and 🍴 Port Bou - Valencia (- Madrid ‡) and Madrid - Valencia - Cerbère.

e – Valencia Cabanyal.   d – 🍴 only.

f – Will not run Oct. 23, Dec. 25, 26, Jan. 1.

k – Will not run Dec. 25.

Also Dec. 24, 31; will not run Apr. 30, May 1.

p – Will not run June 24, Aug. 15, Oct. 12, Nov. 1, Dec. 6, 8, 26, Jan. 6, 7, Apr. 14 - 17, May 1.

‡ – For days of running Valencia - Madrid and v.v. see Table 420.

🛏 – Sleeping car   🛌 – Couchette car   ⑧ – Daily except Saturdays

Table 416 PORT BOU - GIRONA - BARCELONA

1, 2 class except where shown

km				EC 477		472		EC 274					IC 185		TAL 377		TAL 463							
		2 Ⓐk	2 ⚒k	✕ B§	⚒n	2 E		✕ C§	⑦g	2 ⚒k	⚒n	2	🍷 R		🍷 U		🍷 P	2		2 M	2		2 M	2
0	**Port Bou** 🛃 **162** d.	...	0539	p	...	0645	...	r	...	0727	...	0815	0850	...	0950	...	1030	1035	...	...	1228	1345	...	1418
7	Llançà d.	...	0548	|	...	0653	...	|	...	0737	...	0825	0858	...	0958	...	|	1042	...	...	1238	1352	...	1428
28	Figueres d.	...	0604	0646s	0700	0708	...	0730	0735	0753	0810	0841	0912	...	1012	...	1050	1057	1200	...	1254	1406	...	1444
53	Flaça d.	...	0626	|	0713	0724	...	|	0749	0817	0824	0905	0928	...	|	...	|	1113	1214	...	1314	1422	...	1508
69	**Girona** d.	0616	0644	0711s	0726	0736	...	0757	0802	0842	0838	0923	0942	...	1038	...	1117	1127	1228	1300	1330	1436	1503	1526
99	Maçanet/Massanes d.	0638	0707	|	|	0756	...	|	|	0907	|	0948	1002	...	1058	...	|	1148	|	1325	1353	|	1524	1551
139	Granollers Centre d.	0708	0740	|	|	|	...	|	|	0936	|	1018	1026	...	|	...	|	1214	|	|	1422	1522	|	1621
167	**Barcelona Passeig de Gracia** a.	0742	0814	|	0839	0857	...	|	0914	1008	0949	1046	1050	...	1144	...	1220	1242	1339	|	1450	1553	|	1650
170	**Barcelona Sants** a.	0747	0819	|	0845	0902	...	|	0920	1013	0955	1051	1055	...	1149	...	1225	1247	1345	1501	1455	1558	1701	1655
	Barcelona Estació de França a.	...	...	0820	...	...	...	0910	...	...	...	...	...	...	...	...	...	...	...	...	...	...	...	...

		EC 70				373		1373	
	2	✕ H	2	2 M	2 M	🍷 L	2	🍷 K	2
Port Bou 🛃 **162** d.	...	1630	1722	1726	...	1830	1935	1945	2020	2110
Llançà d.	...	1640	|	1736	...	1838	1944	1955	2028	2117
Figueres d.	1600	1656	1741	1752	...	1852	2000	2011	2042	2132
Flaça d.	1615	1716	|	1814	...	1915	2017	2031	2059	2149
Girona d.	1627	1732	1807	1827	1830	1930	2035	2047	2115	2202
Maçanet/Massanes d.	1645	1753	|	1848	1854	1954	|	2112	|	2223
Granollers Centre d.	|	1821	|	1923	|	|	2122	2142	2158	2251
Barcelona Passeig de Gracia a.	1739	1850	|	1954	|	|	|	2211	|	2320
Barcelona Sants a.	1745	1855	|	1959	2031	2131	2155	2218	2225	2327
Barcelona Estació de França a.	...	...	1920	...	...	...	...	...	...	...

				370		1370	EC73		
	2 Ⓐk	2 ⚒k	2 ⚒k	🍷 L	2	🍷 K	✕ H	2 M	
Barcelona Estació de França d.	...	...	...	...	...	...	0855	...	...
Barcelona Sants d.	...	0600	0649	0710	0805	0810	|	0811	0910
Barcelona Passeig de Gracia d.	...	0605	0654	|	0810	|	|	|	0916
Granollers Centre d.	...	0633	0722	0740	0838	0843	|	|	|
Maçanet/Massanes d.	...	0705	0756	|	0908	|	|	0953	|
Girona d.	0610	0730	0822	0835	0934	0942	1001	1017	1027
Flaça d.	0623	0747	0835	0848	0951	0956	|	...	1038
Figueres d.	0645	0811	0853	0907	1011	1016	1027	...	1055
Llançà d.	0700	0826	0907	0924	1026	1032	|	...	...
Port Bou 🛃 a.	0709	0837	0916	0935	1037	1040	1045	...	...
Cerbère 🛃 **162** a.	0715	0846	0923	0945	...	1050	1123	...	...

										TAL 460			TAL 374		IC 182			471		EC 273		EC 475		
		2 M			2	2	2 M	2	2 M	🍷 P	2		🍷 T	Ⓑh	🍷 R	2		2 E	Ⓑh	✕ D§		✕ B§	2	
Barcelona Estació de França d.	...	...	...	...	...	...	...	...	...	...	...	...	...	...	...	...	...	...	...	2015	...	2100	...	...
Barcelona Sants d.	1020	1113	...	1220	1310	1420	1413	1550	1543	1707	1720	...	1804	1820	1907	1923	...	2000	2020	|	...	|	2120	...
Barcelona Passeig de Gracia d.	1026	|	...	1225	1315	1425	|	1555	|	1712	1725	...	1809	1825	1912	1928	...	2006	2025	|	...	|	2125	...
Granollers Centre d.	1051	|	...	|	1343	1454	|	1624	|	|	1754	...	|	|	1936	1957	...	|	|	|	...	|	2154	...
Maçanet/Massanes d.	|	1252	...	|	1412	1523	1553	1653	1723	|	1823	...	1859	|	2001	2026	...	2114	|	|	...	|	2223	...
Girona d.	1137	1316	...	1336	1437	1547	1618	1717	1748	1816	1849	...	1919	1938	2024	2052	...	2134	2138	2126u	...	2210u	2245	...
Flaça d.	1149	1333	...	1347	1450	1600	1635	1731	...	|	1906	...	|	1949	2037	2109	...	2146	2149	|	...	|	...	...
Figueres d.	1206	1356	...	1404	1510	1617	1658	1751	...	1842	1930	...	1945	2005	2055	2133	...	2201	2205	2153u	...	2237u	...	...
Llançà d.	1219	1411	...	...	1524	1631	1713	1806	...	|	1945	...	2000	...	2110	2148	...	2216	...	|	...	|	...	...
Port Bou 🛃 a.	1226	1421	...	...	1534	1639	1723	1817	...	1905	1956	...	2009	...	2120	2157	...	2225	...	|	...	|	...	...
Cerbère 🛃 **162** a.	1233	1428	...	...	1541	1646	1730	1824	...	1915	2003	...	2015	...	2130	2204	...	2232	...	r	...	p	...	...

B – JOAN MIRO – 🛏 1, 2 cl. and ✕ Paris - Barcelona and v.v.
C – PABLO CASALS – For days of running see Table **81**: 🛏 1, 2 cl. and ✕ Zürich - Barcelona.
SALVADOR DALI – For days of running see Table **90**: 🛏 1, 2 cl. and ✕ Milano - Barcelona.
D – PABLO CASALS – For days of running see Table **81**: 🛏 1, 2 cl. and ✕ Barcelona - Zürich.
SALVADOR DALI – For days of running see Table **90**: 🛏 1, 2 cl. and ✕ Barcelona - Milano.
E – HISPANIA EXPRES – Runs ⑤⑥⑦, also daily Apr. 6 - 18 from Port Bou, Apr. 7 - 19 from Barcelona: [2] Port Bou - Barcelona and Barcelona - Cerbère.
H – CATALÁN TALGO – [12] and ✕ Montpellier - Barcelona and v.v.
K – Runs ①②③④ **except** May 29 - Sept. 24, Dec. 5 - 10, Apr. 6 - 18 from Port Bou and Madrid: 🛏 1, 2 cl., ▬ 2 cl., [2] and 🍷 Port Bou - Madrid and Madrid - Cerbère.
L – Runs ⑤⑥⑦, daily May 29 - Sept. 24, Dec. 5 - Jan. 10, and Apr. 6 - 18 from Port Bou and Madrid: 🛏 1, 2 cl., ▬ 2 cl. and 🍷 (also [12] May 29 - Sept. 24) Port Bou - Madrid and Madrid - Cerbère.
M – Via Matáro (Table **417**).
P – [12] and 🍷 Port Bou - Cartagena and Cartagena - Cerbère.
R – [12] and 🍷 Port Bou - Valencia (- Madrid ‡) and Madrid - Valencia - Cerbère.
T – Runs June 24 - Sept. 24, Dec. 16 - Jan. 9, Apr. 6 - 17: [12] and 🍷 Madrid - Cerbère.
U – Runs June 25 - Sept. 25, Dec. 17 - Jan. 10, Apr. 7 - 18: [12] and 🍷 Port Bou - Madrid.
g – Also Jan. 6; will **not** run Dec. 25, Jan. 1.
h – Will **not** run Aug. 14, Dec. 24, 25, 31, Jan. 6, Apr. 14, 16, 30.
k – Will **not** run June 24, Aug. 15, Oct. 12, Nov. 1, Dec. 6, 8, 26, Jan. 6, Apr. 14, 17, May 1.
n – Will **not** run Aug. 15, Dec. 26, Jan. 6, 7, Apr. 15, 17, May 1.
p – To/from Paris Austerlitz.
r – To/from Zürich and Milano.
s – Stops to **set down** only.
u – Stops to **pick up** only.
‡ – For days of running Valencia - Madrid see Table **420**.
§ – Special fares are payable for travel by these trains. Inter-Rail cards are **not** valid.

Table 417 BARCELONA - COSTA BRAVA RESORTS

Timings subject to confirmation

2 class only

A rail service operates between **Barcelona** and **Blanes** and v.v. via the Costa Brava resorts of **Matáro, Arenys de Mar, Calella, Pineda de Mar, and Malgrat de Mar**.
Services run from **Barcelona** to **Blanes** every 30 minutes from 0612 - 2212, and from **Blanes** to **Barcelona** at 0603, 0632, 0701, 0730 and every 30 minutes to 2130.
Journey times (in minutes) from **Barcelona**: Mataro (45), Arenys de Mar (58), Calella (76), Pineda de Mar (80), Malgrat de Mar (86), Blanes (92).
Journey times (in minutes) from **Blanes**: Malgrat de Mar (6), Pineda de Mar (13), Calella (18), Arenys de Mar (34), Mataro (47), Barcelona (94).
Certain trains from Barcelona are extended to Cerbère; likewise certain trains from Blanes start from Port Bou – for details see note **M** in Table **416**.

Table 418 ALICANTE - BENIDORM - DENIA

Timings valid from March 14, **1994** until further notice

2 class only. FGV

																		B		C	C	C	C	
Alicante (FGV) d.	...	0600	0700	0800	0900	1000	1100	1200	1300	1400	1500	1600	1700	1800	1900	2000	...	2100	...	2300	0100	0300	0500	...
Benidorm d.	0607	0708	0807	0908	1007	1108	1207	1306	1408	1507	1608	1707	1808	1907	2008	2107	...	2207	...	0007	0207	0407	0607	...
Altea d.	0619	0721	0819	0921	1019	1121	1219	...	1421	1519	1621	1719	1821	1919	2021	2119	...	2219	...	0019	0219	0419	0619	...
Calpe d.	...	0737	...	0937	...	1137	...	...	1437	...	1637	...	1837	...	2037	...	...	...	...	...	...	...	...	...
Teulada d.	...	0754	...	0954	...	1154	...	...	1454	...	1654	...	1854	...	2054	...	...	...	...	...	...	...	...	...
Denia a.	...	0817	...	1017	...	1217	...	...	1517	...	1717	...	1917	...	2117	...	...	...	...	...	...	...	...	...

																		B	B		C	C	C	C
Denia d.	...	0625	...	0825	...	1025	...	...	1325	...	1525	...	1725	...	1925	...	...	...	...	...	...	...	...	...
Teulada d.	...	0650	...	0850	...	1050	...	...	1350	...	1550	...	1750	...	1950	...	...	...	...	...	...	...	...	...
Calpe d.	...	0707	...	0907	...	1107	...	...	1407	...	1607	...	1807	...	2007	...	...	...	...	...	...	...	...	...
Altea d.	0624	0722	0824	0922	1024	1122	1224	...	1422	1524	1622	1724	1822	1924	2022	2124	...	2124	2224	...	2224	0022	0222	0422
Benidorm d.	0636	0736	0836	0936	1036	1136	1236	1336	1436	1536	1636	1736	1836	1936	2036	2135	...	2136	2235	...	2236	0036	0236	0436
Alicante (FGV) a.	0742	0842	0942	1042	1142	1242	1342	1442	1542	1642	1742	1842	1942	2042	2142	...	...	2242	...	...	2342	0142	0342	0542

B – June 1 - Sept. 30.
C – July 1 - Aug. 27.
Operator: FGV – Ferrocarrils de la Generalitat Valenciana, ☎ Alicante (96) 526 27 31.

Table 419 MADRID - CUENCA - VALENCIA

2 class only

km										n
0	**Madrid Puerta de Atocha** d.	...	...	0850	...	...	...	1550	...	1950
53	Aranjuez d.	...	...	0923	...	...	...	1623	...	2023
193	Cuenca d.	...	...	1134	1511	...	...	1835	...	2227
408	**Valencia Termino** a.	...	...	1452	1822	...	...	2152	...	...

		Ⓐp						Ⓒv	
Valencia Termino d.	...	...	...	0810	...	1110	1510	...	...
Cuenca d.	...	0700	...	1136	...	1452	1839	2005	...
Aranjuez d.	...	0900	...	1331	...	1700	2022	2208	...
Madrid Puerta de Atocha a.	...	0938	...	1407	...	1740	2105	2250	...

g – Will **not** run Oct. 12, Nov. 1, Dec. 6, 8, 26, Jan. 6.
n – Will **not** run Dec. 24, 31.
v – Also Oct. 12, Nov. 1, Dec. 26, Jan. 5; will **not** run Dec. 24, 31.

Table 420 — MADRID - CARTAGENA, VALENCIA and ALICANTE

1, 2 class except where shown

km		IC 180	IC 20	TAL 220	IC 380	IC 22	IC 182	690	690	IC 24	IC 694	694	IC 80	TAL 76	IC 82	TAL 26	TAL 250	TAL 222	IC 84
		2 ⍟f					Y	K	A		2 L	B	⑥g	M	⑥	⑥r	⑥		H
0	Madrid Chamartín .... d	...	0800	...	0900	...	1000	...	...	...	1200	...	...	...	1330	1400	...	1600	1600	1605 ...
	Madrid Atocha Cercanias .. d	...	0715t	0815	...	0915	0915t	1015	1115t	...	...	1215	...	...	...	1315t	1345	1415	1515t	1615	1620	1645t
53	Aranjuez .... d	...	...	0842	...	0946	...	...	...	...	...	...	...	...	...	1414	1442	...	...	1648	...
	Badajoz 430 .... d	...	...	...	...	...	...	...	0630	...	...	...	0800	...	...	...	...	...	...	...
	Ciudad Real 426 ... d	...	...	...	0900	...	...	...	1120	...	...	...	1250	...	...	...	...	...	...	...
152	Alcázar de San Juan ... a	...	0823	0927	1007	1034	...	...	...	1223	1235	...	1405	...	...	1511	...	...	1733	...
152	Alcázar de San Juan ... d	0715	0823	0928	1010	1035	...	1223	1257	1315	...	1430	1430	...	1512	...	...	1734	...
287	Albacete .... d	0839	0918	1025	1130	1145	1118	1219	1318	1407	1421	1425	1543	1543	1518	1637	1625	1718	1825	1828	1833	1848
357	Hellín .... d	...	...	...	...	1224														1912
461	Alcantarilla .... d					1333														2019
469	Murcia del Carmen 415 ... d					1346														2030
534	Cartagena 415 ... d					1435														2116
422	Elda-Petrel .... d	...	1138	1249			1324			1543	1530				1732		1932	1943	...
463	Alicante Término .... a	...	1203	1315			1350			1612	1558				1758		1958	2014	...
494	Valencia Término .... a	1118	1105			1310			1505	1615			1746	1746	1710			1910			2040
557	Gandia ▲ .... a					1403														
	Barcelona Sants 415 ... a	...	1505					1903	2040				2205	2205						

	TAL 78	TAL 74	IC 384	TAL 224	IC 86	IC 28	820	994	1990
	N⑥	P⑥		⑥k	④v	⑥r	R⑥	C	X
Madrid Chamartín .... d	1800	1800	...	1835	1900	...	2000	2340	...
Madrid Atocha Cercanias ... d	1815	1815	1845t	1910	1915	2015t	2015	...	0045
Aranjuez .... d			1920						
Badajoz 430 .... d									
Ciudad Real 426 ... d									
Alcázar de San Juan .... a	1926	1926		2010		2129		0152	
Alcázar de San Juan .... d	1927	1927	2013		2130		0247	0245	0320
Albacete .... d	2025	2025	2048	2133	2119	2218	2228	0428	0350	0435
Hellín .... d								0531	
Alcantarilla .... d								0722	
Murcia del Carmen 415 ... d				2305				0745	
Cartagena 415 .... d				2351				0850	
Elda-Petrel .... d	2132	2132			2331				
Alicante Término .... a	2158	2158			2357				
Valencia Término .... a			2240		2400			0602	0650c
Gandia ▲ .... a			2330						
Barcelona Sants 415 ... a								1100	1140

	IC 225	IC 21	IC 81	IC 83		TAL 129	TAL 221	TAL 79
	④v	⑥d	⑥f	H		Q⑦		N⑦
Barcelona Sants 415 ... d	...	...	0700	...	0900	...	...
Gandia ▲ .... d							
Valencia Término .... d	...	...	0700	...	0900	...	...
Alicante Término .... d		0645				0945		1045
Elda-Petrel .... d		0706				1006		1106
Cartagena 415 .... d	0550					0855	
Murcia del Carmen 415 d	0630					0945	
Alcantarilla .... d						0954	
Hellín .... d							
Albacete .... d	0705	0810	0816	0842	1041	1115	1140	1215
Alcázar de San Juan .... a	0818					1213	1242	1313
Alcázar de San Juan .... a	0819					1214	1243	1314
Ciudad Real 426 .... a							
Badajoz 430 .... a							
Aranjuez .... d	0917					1328	
Madrid Atocha Cercanias a	0948	1026	1029	1055t	1250t	1329	1400	1429
Madrid Chamartín .... a	1002	1041	1043			1343	1414	1443

	IC 383	TAL 251	TAL 77	IC 697	697	IC 85	693	693	IC 23	IC 185	IC 25	IC 387	TAL 223	IC 27	TAL 181	IC 29	IC 87	997	1993	823
	⑦e	M	L	F	⑥h	A	K	Y⑥h						⑥r	⑥q		C	X	R⑥
Barcelona Sants 415 ... d	1000	...	...	0800	0800	...	0900	...	1100				1430			1830	1945
Gandia ▲ .... d	1000										1530						
Valencia Término .... d	1100			1200	1200	1300		1300		1500		1630		1830		2000	2255	0012c
Alicante Término .... d		1110	1215			1325		1415		1615		1715	1815		2000		2255
Elda-Petrel .... d		1137	1236			1356		1436		1636		1750	1836		2021
Cartagena 415 .... d										1540					2135
Murcia del Carmen 415 ... d										1625					2300
Alcantarilla .... d										1633					2311
Hellín .... d										1746					0049
Albacete .... d	1242	1254	1339	1355	1355	1442	1505	1511	1545	1642	1720	1745	1812	1830	1910	1946	2012	2130	2142	0100	0237	0230
Alcázar de San Juan .... a	1337			1507	1507		1608	1613		1835		1934	2020		2107		2227	0205	0357	0410
Alcázar de San Juan .... d	1337			1530			1638		1836		1935	2023	2107		2228		0435
Ciudad Real 426 .... a				1638			1744					2135
Badajoz 430 .... a				2135			2257				
Aranjuez .... a			1521														0540
Madrid Atocha Cercanias a	1455t	1508	1552		1655t		1759	1855t	2016	1959	2025t	2059	2159	2225t	2343	2355t
Madrid Chamartín .... a		1520	1606				1813		2033	2013		2113	2213	2355		0700

A – Runs June 24 - Sept. 5 from Alicante, June 25 - Sept. 6 from Cádiz. [box] Alicante - Cádiz and v.v.
B – [box] and Y Málaga - Barcelona; [box] and Y Granada - Barcelona; conveys on dates in Table 415: [box] Almería - Barcelona and [box] Cádiz - Barcelona.
C – 🛏 1, 2 cl., — 2 cl., [box] and Y Barcelona - Málaga and v.v.; — 2 cl. and [box] and Y Barcelona - Sevilla - (Cádiz on dates in Table 425) and v.v.
D – [box] and Y Barcelona - Málaga; [box] and Y Barcelona - Granada; conveys on dates in Table 415: [box] Almería and [box] Barcelona - Cádiz.
E – [box] and Y Madrid - Valencia - Castellón and v.v.
F – Runs June 23 - Sept 24, Dec. 21 - 24, Jan. 1, 2, 7, 8, Apr. 7 - 17 from Barcelona, June 24 - Sept. 6, Dec. 22 - 24, Jan. 1, 2, 7, 8, Apr. 8 - 18 from Cádiz and Badajoz. [box] and Y Barcelona - Alcázar de San Juan - Cádiz and v.v.; [box] and Y Barcelona - Badajoz and v.v.
G – Runs daily except when trains 690/3 (note K) run: [box] and Y Barcelona - Valencia - Badajoz and v.v.
H – [box] and Y Santander - Alicante and v.v.
K – [box] and Y Gijón - Alicante and v.v.
L – [box] and Y La Coruña and Vigo - Alicante and v.v.
M – [box] and Y Alicante - La Coruña and Vigo.
N – 🛏 1, 2 cl., — 2 cl. and [box] Madrid - Cartagena and v.v.
P – Runs June 23 - Sept. 24, Apr. 7 - 17 from Barcelona, returning one day later: 🛏 1, 2 cl., — 2 cl., [box] and Y Barcelona - Cádiz and v.v.; 🛏 1, 2 cl., — 2 cl. and [box] Barcelona - Granada and v.v.; [box] and Y Madrid - Valencia - Cerbère and Port Bou - Valencia (- Madrid ⑥h).

c – Valencia Cabanyal.
d – Will not run May 1.
e – Will not run Sept. 25.
f – Will not run Oct. 12, Nov. 1, Dec. 6, 8, Jan. 6, Apr. 14, May 1.
g – Also Dec. 24, 31, Mar. 18, Apr. 8, 29; will not run Apr. 30, May 1.
h – Also Dec. 24, 31; will not run Apr. 30, May 1.
k – Will not run Dec. 24, 31.
q – Will not run July 30, Apr. 30.
r – Will not run Apr. 30.
t – Madrid Puerta de Atocha.
v – Will not run July 25, Aug. 15, Oct. 12, Nov. 1, Dec. 6, 8.
▲ – Local service (2 class only) operates: Valencia - Gandia and v.v. Journey time 58 minutes. Timings subject to confirmation:
From Valencia Término: 0625④, 0655④, 0725, 0755④, and every 60 minutes (30 minutes on ④) until 1655, 1725, 1755, 1825, 1855, 1925, 1955, 2025, 2055④, 2125, 2155.
From Gandia: 0605④, 0635④, 0705④, 0735 and every 60 minutes (30 minutes on ④) until 1805, 1835, 1905, 1935, 2005, 2035, 2105, 2135.

Table 422 — MALLORCA

2 class only, except where shown. SFM, FS

Palma - Inca: Narrow gauge rail service (SFM). 29 km. Journey time: 36 minutes. Timings valid for Summer 1994. Operator: SFM – Serveis Ferroviaris de Mallorca, ☎ (971) 75 22 45.
From Palma and Inca at the following times: 0700, 0800, 0840④, 0900ⓒ, 0920④, 1000, 1100, 1200, 1240ⓒ, 1300ⓒ, 1320④, 1400, 1440④, 1500ⓒ, 1520④, 1600, 1700, 1800, 1900, 2000, 040④, 2100ⓒ, 2120④. There is an additional departure from Palma at 0600, and from Inca at 2200.

Palma - Sóller: Narrow gauge rail service (FS) 1, 2 class. 28 km. Journey time 55 minutes. Timings valid Jan. 1 - Dec. 31, 1994. Operator: FS – Ferrocarril de Sóller, ☎ Sóller 75 20 51.
From Palma: 0800, 1040, 1310, 1515, 1945w, 2005s.
ⓒ – Daily July 1 - Sept. 30, also ⓒ May 1 - June 30 and Oct. 1 - 31.
From Sóller: 0645, 0915, 1150, 1410, 1830w, 1900s, 1935h.
s – May 1 - Oct. 31.   w – Jan. 1 - Apr. 30 and Nov. 1 - Dec. 31.
Connecting tram service operates: Sóller - Puerto Sóller: 5 km. Journey time: 15 - 20 minutes.

① – Mondays   ② – Tuesdays   ③ – Wednesdays   ④ – Thursdays   ⑤ – Fridays   ⑥ – Saturdays   ⑦ – Sundays

Table 425 MADRID - SEVILLA, HUELVA and CÁDIZ
Via the **AVE** high speed line. Special fares apply

First section (Madrid → Cádiz / Huelva, morning)

km	station	3000	810	810	11810	997	947	947	940	AVE 9614 CPT	1993	AVE 9664 CPT	AVE 9616 CPT	3002	AVE 9618 CPT	AVE 9718 CT	TAL 9110 PT	TAL 9110 PT	TAL 9140 PT	AVE 9622 CPT	3004
	class / symbol	2 Ⓐb	Ⓐ	Ht	O	R	✕ Nt	♀ Mt	K	✕		B	Ⓐn	✕n	2	✕	♀	✕	✕	✕	2
	Barcelona Sants 420 d.	…	…	…	…	1830	2200	2200	…	…	1945										
	Madrid Chamartín d.	…	…	…	…				0255												
0	Madrid Puerta de Atocha d.	…	2240	2240	…		0523	0523		0700		0730	0800		0900	0915	1000	1000	1000		1100
171	Ciudad Real 430 d.						0629	0629		0751						1006	1101	1101	1101		
210	Puertollano 430 d.									0808						1025	1118	1118	1118		
343	Córdoba a.		0500	0500		0555	0738	0738	0735	0855	0808	0912				1042	1206	1206	1206		1242
343	Córdoba d.		0502	0502	0502	0615	0740	0740	0757	0857	0810	0914		0853		1044	1208	1208	1213		1244
	Málaga 426 a.								1020												1445
472	Sevilla Santa Justa a.		0706	0706	0843d	0840			0927	0940		0955	1010		1015	1027	1130	1325	1330		
472	Sevilla Santa Justa d.	0620	0735	0750	0750	0750	0820f	0845		0930					1035				1327		
587	Huelva Término a.				0925										1128				1435		
579	Jerez de la Frontera d.	0735	0850	0912	0912	0951f	1005			1046	1115					1142		1422			1456
593	Puerto de Santa Maria d.	0752	0901	0924	0924	1001f	1018			1104	1130					1153		1433			1507
613	San Fernando de Cádiz d.	0808	0913	0940	0940	1013f	1037			1117	1147					1207		1446			1521
628	Cádiz a.	0825	0925	0957	0957	1028f	1053			1132	1200					1219		1459			1535

Second section (Madrid → Cádiz / Huelva, afternoon / evening)

station	TAL 9144 PT	2	AVE 9726 CT	AVE 9628 CPT	AVE 9630 CPT	AVE 9730 CT	TAL 9142 PT	AVE 9632 CPT	TAL 41	AVE 9634 CPT	3006	AVE 9734 CPT	697	AVE 9638 CPT	AVE 9146 CT	693	AVE 9738 CPT	AVE 9640 CPT	AVE 9742 CT	AVE 9744 CPT
sym	✕♣		♀ r	✕ r	✕	♀5p	r	✕	♀Ⓑn	✕	2	✕	♀X	✕	♀5⑦p	W	♀Ⓐ♣	✕Ⓑ	t	✕5p
Barcelona Sants 420 d.	…	…	…	…	…	…	…	…	0830	…	…	…	…	…	…	0900				
Madrid Chamartín d.									1500											
Madrid Puerta de Atocha d.			1300	1315	1400	1500	1515	1530	1600	1605	1700		1715		1800		1900	1905	1930	2000 2100 2200 2200
Ciudad Real 430 d.			1401	1406			1606		1706		1806				1825			2006	2021	2149 2249 2249
Puertollano 430 d.			1418	1425			1625		1723		1825							2023	2040	2205 2310 2249
Córdoba a.			1506		1539	1642		1732	1742	1810	1842		1850	1942		1945	2042	2111	2142	2249 2355
Córdoba d.			1507		1541	1644		1734	1744	1812	1844		1915	1944	1925	1947	2044	2112	2144	2251 2357 0040
Málaga 426 a.				1735			2		2005		2							2335	2	
Sevilla Santa Justa a.					1625	1730		1830	1920	1930		2035	2030	2115	2110	2130		2230	2335	
Sevilla Santa Justa d.	1415	1515				1745		1925		1955		2040	2117e	2115				2145	2307	
Huelva Término a.	1557					1905		2027		2056		2139	2248e	2216						
Jerez de la Frontera d.		1626				1917		2038		2107		2150	2259e	2228						
Puerto de Santa Maria d.		1637				1934		2051		2121		2204	2313e	2302						
San Fernando de Cádiz d.		1703				1948		2105		2142		2221	2326e	2302						
Cádiz a.		1721																		

Third section (Cádiz → Madrid, morning)

station	AVE 9715 CT	AVE 9663 CPT	AVE 9615 CPT	2	AVE 9617 CPT	TAL 9147 PT	690	694	AVE 9619 CPT	TAL 42	3001	AVE 9623 CPT	AVE 9725 CPT	TAL 3013 PT	AVE 9629 CPT	AVE 9631 CPT	2	AVE 9733 CPT	AVE 3005 CT	AVE 9633 CPT
sym	✕g	Ⓐn	✕	b	✕	♀	Ⓐ♣ W	X	✕	✕	2	♀	♀	Ⓒ	Ⓑ	r	r	♀5p	r	Ⓑn
Cádiz d.			0540			0630	0700			0800		0900			1035d		1355			
San Fernando de Cádiz d.			0553			0641	0711			0811		0912			1048d		1406			
Puerto de Santa Maria d.			0607			0654	0723			0825		0925			1101d		1419			
Jerez de la Frontera d.			0620			0705	0734			0836		0936			1116d		1433			
Huelva Término d.									0725		0900				1221d					1420 1600
Sevilla Santa Justa a.			0734		0800	0805	0840	0847		0935	1020	1045			1222	1400	1541			
Sevilla Santa Justa d.		0630	0700		0800		0810	0845		0900	0940		1100			1400	1500		1600	
Málaga 426 d.				AVE 9717	0645								0930			1940		1940		
Córdoba a.		0711	0741	9717	0904	0925	1009		0941	1045		1141	1150	1352	1441	1541		1641		
Córdoba d.		0713	0743	♀	0906	0927	1034		0943	1047		1143	1152	1443	1543		1643			
Puertollano 430 d.	0700		0827	0845					1027	1139				1230 1241		1530		1715		
Ciudad Real 430 d.	0720		0843	0905					1043	1156				1250 1258		1550		1735		
Madrid Puerta de Atocha a.	0815	0855	0940	1000	1015	1105			1140	1259		1330 1345	1400		1625	1645	1730		1830 1830	
Madrid Chamartín a.										1337										
Barcelona Sants 420 a.					2040	2205				2035										

Fourth section (Cádiz → Madrid, afternoon / evening)

station	AVE 9635 CPT	2	AVE 9739 CT	TAL 9143 PT	AVE 9637 CPT	TAL 9111 PT	TAL 9111 PT	AVE 9639 CPT	3007	AVE 9641 CPT	AVE 9743 CT	941	AVE 9643 CPT	994	1990	2	TAL 9145 PT	944	944	2	AVE 9645 CPT	11813	813	813
sym	✕		Ⓑh	5⑦p	✕		♣			Ⓑ	Ⓒk	K	G	B			Ⓑ♣	Nt	Mt		✕	♀v	R	Ht
Cádiz d.		1505			1620			1755			1820		1850f	1850	1905						2125			2125
San Fernando de Cádiz d.		1518			1632			1807			1832		1903f	1903	1918						2136			2136
Puerto de Santa Maria d.		1538			1645			1820			1846		1917f	1917	1935						2151			2151
Jerez de la Frontera d.		1551			1656			1832			1857		1929f	1929	1948						2215		2145	2215
Huelva Término d.						1655												2000			2133			
Sevilla Santa Justa a.		1659			1750		1900	1935			1958		2040f	2040	2059						2320	2311	2320	
Sevilla Santa Justa d.	1700			1800	1755	1900	1900		2000		2000	2100	2110		2115			2115			2200	2345	2345	2345
Málaga 426 d.			1610														1940		1940					
Córdoba a.	1741		1828	1841	1908	1908	1943		2041		2130	2143	2238	2248			2204	2231	2231		2241	0128	0128	0128
Córdoba d.	1743		1830	1843	1910	1910	1943		2043		2150	2143	2300	2250			2205	2235	2235		2243		0130	0130
Puertollano 430 d.			1900		1958	1958			2126	2130							2254							
Ciudad Real 430 d.			1920		2015	2015			2142	2150							2311	2345	2345					
Madrid Puerta de Atocha a.	1930		2015	2035	2035	2125	2125	2130		2235	2245		2330				0015	0055	0055		0025		0810	0810
Madrid Chamartín a.														0230										
Barcelona Sants 420 a.													1100	1140				0830	0830					

B – Runs June 23 - Sept. 24, Apr. 7 - 17 from Barcelona, June 24 - Sept. 25, Apr. 8 - 18 from Cádiz: 🛏 1, 2 cl., 🛋 2 cl., �car and ♀ Barcelona - Cádiz and v.v.

CPT –Club, Preferente, Turista classes of travel.

CT – Club, Turista classes of travel.

G – 🛏 2 cl., �car and ♀ Barcelona - Valencia - Sevilla (- Cádiz) and v.v.

H – 🛏 1, 2 cl., 🛋 2 cl., �car and ♀ Madrid - Cádiz and v.v.

K – Runs ⑤ (daily June 26 - Sept. 23 and Apr. 7 - 16, ①③⑤ Dec. 2 - Jan. 7) from Bilbao, ⑦ (daily June 26 - Sept. 23 and Apr. 8 - 17, ②④⑦ Dec. 4 - Jan. 8) from Cádiz: 🛏 1, 2 cl., 🛋 2 cl., �car and ♀ Bilbao - Cádiz and v.v.

M – 🛏 1, 2 cl. (Gran Clase), 🛏 1, 2 cl. and ♀ Barcelona - Madrid - Málaga and v.v.

N – 🛏 1, 2 cl., 🛋 2 cl. and ✕ Barcelona - Madrid - Sevilla and v.v.

O – Runs May 29 - Sept. 24: 🛏 1, 2 cl., 🛋 2 cl. and �car Madrid - Huelva and v.v.

PT – Preferente, Turista classes of travel.

R – 🛏 only from Almería and Cádiz: 🛏 1, 2 cl., 🛋 2 cl. �car and ♀ Almería - Linares Baeza - Cádiz and v.v.

W – Runs June 23 - Sept. 24, Dec. 21 - 24, Jan. 1, 2, 7, 8, Apr. 7 - 17 from Barcelona, June 24 - Sept. 25, Dec. 22 - 24, Jan. 1, 2, 7, 8, Apr. 8 - 18 from Cádiz.

X – Runs daily except June 23 - Sept. 24, Dec. 21 - 24, Jan. 1, 2, 7, 8, Apr. 7 - 17 from Barcelona, June 24 - Sept. 25, Dec. 22 - 24, Jan. 1, 2, 7, 8, Apr. 8 - 18 from Cádiz.

b – Will not run Aug. 15.

d – ④ only.

e – ✕ only, will not run Aug. 15.

f – May 29 - June 23 and Dec. 22 - Jan. 9 only.

g – Will not run Oct. 12, Nov. 1, 9, Dec. 6, 8, 26, Jan. 2.

h – Also runs Dec. 24, 31.

k – Also Oct. 12, Nov. 1, 9, Dec. 6, 8, 26, Jan. 2; will not run Dec. 24, 25, 31, Jan. 1.

n – Will not run Oct. 12, Nov. 1, 9, Dec. 4 - 11, Dec. 24 - Jan. 7.

p – Will not run Dec. 4 - 11, Dec. 24 - Jan. 7.

r – Will not run Dec. 25, Jan. 1.

t – Will not run Dec. 24, 31 from point of origin.

v – Also Nov. 1; will not run Oct. 30, Dec. 4, Dec. 24 - Jan. 1.

♣ – Liable to alteration from Oct. 16.

*All **AVE** services are reservation obligatory with separate fare structure*

Table 426 — MADRID - ALCÁZAR - ALMERÍA, GRANADA and the COSTA del SOL

See Table 425 for Madrid - Córdoba AVE high speed services

1, 2 class except where shown

km		997 F	997 G	2	947 Mn	940 J	940 K	1993 B	1993 C	✕r	Y			TAL 278 ⑥	TAL 278 ⑥	TAL 9140 PT	2		TAL 9144 PT ✕♣	IC 141 Zp	TAL 9142 PT ♣		
	Barcelona Sants 415/20 .. d.	1830	1830	...	2200	...	...	1945	1945	...	...	...	...	...	...	...	...	...	...	...	...	...	...
	Valencia Término 415 .. d.	2255	2255	...		...	...	0012c	0012c	...	...	...	...	...	...	...	...	...	...	...	...	...	...
	Madrid Chamartín............ d.			...	0255	0255	...	...	...	...	...	0905	0905	...	...	...	...	...	1205	...	...	...	...
0	Madrid Atocha Cercanías .. d.			...			...	...	...	...	...	0920	0920	...	...	...	...	...	1220	...	...	...	...
0	Madrid Puerta de Atocha .. d.			...	0523		...	...	...	...	...			0945	0945	1000	...	1300		1530	...	...	...
53	Aranjuez 420 .... d.			...			...	...	...	...	...	0950	0950				...				...	...	...
152	Alcázar de San Juan 420 ..... d.	0222	0222	...			...	0417	0417	0715	...	1048	1055	1108	1108		...	1334			...	...	...
201	Manzanares .... d.			...	0454	0454	0450	0450	0747	...	...	1118	1123	1136	1136		...	1358			...	...	...
	Ciudad Real.................... a.			...			...	...	...	0826	...		1207				...				...	...	...
318	Linares-Baeza .... a.	0416	0416	...	0610	0610	0619	0619	...		1248	1307	1307		...	1519			...	...	...
318	Linares-Baeza .... d.	0417	0417	...	0611	0611	0639	0705	0720			1310	1310		...	1520			...	...	...
	Moreda .... d.			...			0900		0925	0929		1454	1505		...				...	...	...
	Granada .... d.			...		1000			1025	z	1335	1543		...				1835	...	...
	Guadix .... d.			...					0958		1449	1526		...				1949	...	...
	Almería .... a.			...					1131		1627	1645		...				2127	...	...
366	Andújar............................ d.	0453	0453	...					...					...	1552			...	...	...
444	Córdoba .... a.	0555	0555	...	0738	0735	0735	0808	...			1206		1506	1643	1732	...	...
444	Córdoba .... d.	0605		0650	0744	0745			...			1213	1315	1507	1645	1734	...	...
523	Puente Genil .... d.	0720		0754	0851	0908			...				1422	1609	1752	1845	...	...
570	Bobadilla-Antequera .... a.	0801		0831	0919	0944			...			1348	1458	1636	1819	1913	...	...
570	Bobadilla-Antequera .... d.	0802		0833	0920	0945		1030	...			1349	1500	1505	1637	1820	1914	1935
	Ronda .... d.			...				1138	...					1614			2038
	San Roque-La Linea .... d.			...				1313	...					1749			2210
	Algeciras .... a.			...				1330	...					1807			2227
639	Málaga .... a.	0922		0948	1020	1052			...			1445	1606	1735	1912	2005	2014

km		697 Y	697 X	697 S	697 V	697 b	2	693 W	693 V	TAL 270 ⑧h	TAL 270 ⑧h	2	⑧	TAL 9146 PT ④♣	N	340 U	344 A	840 Dn	11810 R	810 Hn	770 Ln	770 En	11813 R
	Barcelona Sants 415/20 d.	...	0800	0800	0800	0800	0800	...	0900	0900	...	...	...	...	...	...	...	...	...	...	...	...	...
	Valencia Término 415 d.	...	1200	1200	1200	1200	1200	...	1300	1300	...	...	...	...	...	...	...	...	...	...	...	...	...
	Madrid Chamartín............ d.	...						...			1635	1835	...	...	2205	2205	2240	...	2240	2315	2315	...	...
0	Madrid Atocha Cercanías .. d.	...						...			1650	1850	...	...				...				...	...
0	Madrid Puerta de Atocha .. d.	...				1420		...	1545	1545			1905	...				...				...	...
53	Aranjuez 420 .... d.	...				1452		...			1720	1920		...	2311	2311	2343	...	2343	0019	0019	...
152	Alcázar de San Juan 420 ..... d.	...	1525	1525	1525	1525	1530	1550	1628	1638	1708	1708	1818	2016	2023	0015	0015	0050	...	0050	0127	0127	...
201	Manzanares .... d.	...	1553	1553	1553	1553	1558	1620	1656	1705	1738	1738	1848	2044	2053	0046	0046	0123	...	0123	0159	0159	...
	Ciudad Real.................... a.	...				1638	1705		1744				2135				...				...
318	Linares-Baeza .... a.	...	1714	1714	1714	1714		1822		1910	1910	2013	2207		0215	0215	0245	...	0345	0330	0330	...
318	Linares-Baeza .... d.	...	1724	1724	1735	1735		1823		1912	1912				0218	0218	0252	0300	0300	0410	0410	0410
	Moreda .... d.	1921		1930	1950				2054	2105								0650	0620	0620
	Granada .... d.	2012		2025					2139									0800		
	Guadix .... d.	...			2013				2125									0649	0649
	Almería .... a.	...			2141				2239									0834	0834
366	Andújar............................ d.	...	1756	1756				1854						0259	0259	0345	0355	0355	...
444	Córdoba .... a.	...	1850	1850				1945				2111	0355	0355	0453	0500	0500	...
444	Córdoba .... d.	...	1900								2112	0400	0400	0455			...
523	Puente Genil .... d.	...	2001									0509	0509	0610			...
570	Bobadilla-Antequera .... a.	...	2032							2241	0545	0545	0646			...
570	Bobadilla-Antequera .... d.	...	2033							2242	0550	0550	0648			...
	Ronda .... d.	...									0703	0703				...
	San Roque-La Linea .... d.	...									0840	0840				...
	Algeciras .... a.	...									0900	0900				...
639	Málaga .... a.	...	2140							2335			0755			...

A – ◣ 1, 2 cl., ◣ 2 cl., ⊑⊐ and ♀ Madrid - Algeciras and v.v.
B – Runs June 23 – Sept. 24, Apr. 7 - 17 from Barcelona, one day later from Cádiz: ◣ 1, 2 cl., ◣ 2 cl., ⊑⊐ and ♀ Barcelona - Cádiz and v.v.
C – Runs June 23 – Sept. 24, Apr. 7 - 17 from Barcelona, one day later from Granada: ◣ 1, 2 cl., ◣ 2 cl., ⊑⊐ and ♀ Barcelona - Granada and v.v.
D – ◣ 1, 2 cl., ◣ 2 cl., ⊑⊐ and ♀ Madrid - Málaga and v.v.
E – ◣ 1, 2 cl., ◣ 2 cl., ⊑⊐ and ♀ Madrid - Almería and v.v.
F – ◣ 1, 2 cl., ◣ 2 cl., ⊑⊐ and ♀ Barcelona - Málaga and v.v.
G – ◣ 2 cl. and ⊑⊐ Barcelona - Sevilla (- Cádiz) and v.v.
H – ◣ 1, 2 cl., ◣ 2 cl. and ♀ Madrid - Cádiz and v.v.; ◣ 1, 2 cl., ◣ 2 cl. and ⊑⊐ Madrid - Huelva and v.v. (reservation recommended).
J – Runs ⑤ (daily June 26 - Sept. 23 and Apr. 7 - 16, ①③⑤ Dec. 2 - Jan. 7) from Bilbao, ⑦ (daily June 26 - Sept. 23 and Apr. 8 - 17, ②④⑦ Dec. 4 - Jan. 8) from Málaga: ◣ 1, 2 cl., ◣ 2 cl., ⊑⊐ and ♀ Bilbao - Málaga and v.v.
K – Runs ⑤ (daily June 26 - Sept. 23 and Apr. 7 - 16, ①③⑤ Dec. 2 - Jan. 7) from Bilbao, ⑦ (daily June 26 - Sept. 23 and Apr. 8 - 17, ②④⑦ Dec. 4 - Jan. 8) from Cádiz: ◣ 1, 2 cl., ◣ 2 cl., ⊑⊐ and ♀ Bilbao - Cádiz and v.v.
L – ◣ 1, 2 cl., ◣ 2 cl., ⊑⊐ and ♀ Madrid - Granada and v.v.
M – ◣ 1, 2 cl. (Gran Clase), ◣ 1, 2 cl. and ♀ Barcelona - Madrid - Málaga and v.v.
N – ⊑⊐ Alicante - Ciudad Real and v.v.
PT – Preferente, Turista classes of travel.
R – Runs ⑧ only from Almería and Cádiz: ◣ 1, 2 cl., ◣ 2 cl., ⊑⊐ and ♀ Almería - Linares Baeza - Cádiz and v.v.

S – Runs ②④⑦ (daily June 23 - Sept. 24, Dec. 19 - Jan. 11, and Apr. 6 - 18) from Barcelona, ①③⑤ (daily June 24 - Sept. 24, Dec. 19 - Jan. 10, and Apr. 6 - 18) from Almería: ⊑⊐ and ♀ Barcelona - Almería and v.v.
U – ◣ 2 cl., ⊑⊐ and ♀ Irún - Algeciras and Algeciras - Hendaye.
V – To/from Badajoz – For days of running see Table 430.
W – To/from Cádiz – For days of running see Table 425.
X – To/from Cádiz – For days of running see Table 425.
Y – ⊑⊐ Almería - Almería and v.v. via Moreda (for connections).
Z – ⊑⊐ and ♀ Zaragoza - Madrid - Málaga and v.v.

b – To/from Badajoz (Table 430).
c – Valencia Cabanyal.
g – Will not run July 25, Aug. 15, Nov. 1, Dec. 26.
h – Will not run Jan. 6, Apr. 13.
k – Will not run Oct. 12.
n – Will not run Dec. 24, 31 from point of origin.
p – Will not run Dec. 25, Jan. 1.
r – Will not run Oct. 12, Nov. 1, Dec. 6, 8, Jan. 6.
y – To Granada (arrive 2012).
z – From Granada (depart 0830).
♣ – Liable to alteration from Oct. 16.

Table 426a — GRANADA and MÁLAGA - SEVILLA

1, 2 class

km								km								
0	Granada .... d.		0815	1230	...	...	1720	...	0	Sevilla Santa Justa.......... d.		0800	0800	1220	...	1730	1730	...
	Málaga 426 .... d.	0820			1815			...	162	Bobadilla-Antequera ...... a.	1005	1005	1443	...	1925	1925	...
123	Bobadilla-Antequera ...... a.	0919	1007	1445		1911	1915	...	162	Bobadilla-Antequera ...... d.	1013	1015	...	1515	1933	1937	...
123	Bobadilla-Antequera ...... d.	0921	1012		1525	1926	1926	...	231	Málaga 426 .... a.	1105		...		2033		...
285	Sevilla Santa Justa.......... a.	1118	1212		1743	2122	2122	...		Granada .... a.		1215	...	1737		2140	...

Table 426 COSTA del SOL, GRANADA and ALMERÍA - ALCÁZAR - MADRID

See Table **425** for Córdoba - Madrid **AVE** high speed services

1, 2 class except where shown

km							TAL 9147 PT🍷 Ⓐ♣	690 2🍷 V	690 🍷 W	694 2🍷 V	694 2🍷 S	694 2🍷	694 🍷 X	694 🍷		TAL 9141 PT🍷 ♣		IC 142 🍷 Zp			2	TAL 271 🍷	TAL 271 🍷	TAL 9143 PT🍷 ♣
		⚒r	Ⓐ	Y	N	⑥																		
	Málaga d.	...	...	...	...	...	0645	...	...	...	...	...	...	0800	...	0930	...	1125	...	...	1350	...	...	1610
	Algeciras d.	...	...	...	...	...	|	...	...	...	...	...	...	|	0650	|	...	|	1130	...	|	...	...	|
	San Roque-La Linea d.	...	...	...	...	...	|	...	...	...	...	...	...	|	0704	|	...	|	1146	...	|	...	...	|
	Ronda d.	...	...	...	...	...	|	...	...	...	...	...	...	|	0855	|	...	|	1336	...	|	...	...	|
	Bobadilla-Antequera a.	...	...	...	...	...	0728	...	...	...	...	...	...	0847	0950	1013	...	1214	1435	...	1456	...	...	1653
	Bobadilla-Antequera d.	...	...	...	...	...	0729	...	...	...	...	...	...	0848	▬	1014	...	1215	...	...	1459	...	...	1654
	Puente Genil d.	...	...	...	...	...	|	...	...	...	...	...	...	0927	...	1042	...	1243	...	...	1534	...	...	1722
	Córdoba a.	...	...	...	...	...	0904	...	...	...	...	...	...	1017	...	1150	...	1341	...	...	1644	...	...	1828
	Córdoba d.	...	...	...	...	...	0906	...	0927	...	...	...	1034	1034	...	1152	...	1343	...	...	▬	...	...	1830
	Andújar d.	...	...	...	...	...	|	...	1018	...	...	...	1126	1126	...	|	...	1432	...	...	...	...	...	|
0	**Almería** d.	...	...	...	...	...	|	...	|	...	0800	...	|	|	0805	|	1340	|	...	...	...	...	1415	|
99	Guadix d.	...	...	...	...	...	|	...	|	...	0941	...	|	|	1000	|	1526	|	...	...	...	...	1530	|
	Granada d.	...	...	0830	...	...	|	...	|	...	|	0905	|	|	1119	|	1650	|	...	...	...	1510	|	|
124	Moreda d.	...	...	0926	...	...	|	...	|	...	1015	1015	|	|	...	|	▬	|	...	...	...	1605	1605	|
241	Linares-Baeza a.	...	...	...	...	...	|	...	1050	...	1157	1157	1202	1202	...	|	...	1502	...	...	...	1731	1731	|
241	Linares-Baeza d.	...	0712	...	...	1004	|	...	1051	...	1217	1217	1217	1217	...	|	...	1503	...	1624	...	1732	1732	|
	Ciudad Real d.	0700	|	...	0900	|	|	1120	|	1250	|	|	|	|	...	|	1405	|	...	|	1741	|	|	|
358	Manzanares d.	0742	0831	...	0940	1128	|	1204	1209	1334	1343	1343	1343	1343	...	|	1445	1612	...	1800	1830	1901	1901	|
407	Alcázar de San Juan **420** d.	0819	0900	...	1007	1157	|	1257	1257	1430	1430	1430	1430	1430	...	|	1516	1636	...	1829	1903	1930	1930	|
506	Aranjuez **420** d.	0917	|	...	...	|	|	|	|	|	|	|	|	|	...	|	1615	|	...	1922	2010	|	|	|
559	**Madrid Puerta de Atocha** a.	|	|	...	...	|	1105	|	|	|	|	|	|	|	...	1400	|	|	...	|	2048	2054	2054	2035
	Madrid Atocha Cercanias a.	0949	1022	...	...	1322	...	|	|	|	|	|	|	|	...	...	1649	1756	...	1950	...	...	...	...
	Madrid Chamartín a.	1002	1037	...	...	1336	...	|	|	|	|	|	|	|	...	...	1702	1810	...	2004	...	...	...	...
	Valencia Término **415** a.	...	...	...	...	...	...	1615	1615	1746	1746	1746	1746	1746	...	...	...	...	...	...	...	...	...	...
	Barcelona Sants **415/20** a.	...	...	...	...	...	...	2040	2040	2205	2205	2205	2205	2205	...	...	...	...	...	...	...	...	...	...

	2 Ⓑg	Y		2		941 🍷 J	941 🍷 K	TAL 9145 PT🍷 Ⓑ♣	944 🍷 M	994 🍷 G	994 🍷 F	1990 🍷 C	1990 🍷 B		11810 🍷 R	773 🍷 En	773 🍷 Ln	2	843 🍷 Dn	11813 🍷 R	813 🍷 Hn		347 🍷 A	343 🍷 U
Málaga d.	...	...	...	1700	...	1850	...	1940	1940	...	2005	...	...	...	...	...	...	2035	2235	...	...	...	...	...
Algeciras d.	...	...	...	|	1520	|	...	|	|	...	|	...	...	...	...	...	...	|	|	...	...	...	2100	2100
San Roque-La Linea d.	...	...	...	|	1535	|	...	|	|	...	|	...	...	...	...	...	...	|	|	...	...	...	2116	2116
Ronda d.	...	...	...	|	1727	|	...	|	|	...	|	...	...	...	...	...	...	|	|	...	...	...	2255	2255
Bobadilla-Antequera a.	...	...	...	1803	1824	1947	...	2034	2034	...	2058	...	...	...	...	...	...	2138	2333	...	...	...	2345	2345
Bobadilla-Antequera d.	...	...	...	...	...	1948	...	2035	2035	...	2059	...	...	...	...	...	...	2140	2334	...	...	...	0005	0005
Puente Genil d.	...	...	...	...	...	2022	...	|	|	...	2131	...	...	...	...	...	...	2214	0006	...	...	...	0041	0041
Córdoba a.	...	...	...	...	...	2125	...	2204	2231	...	2242	...	...	...	...	...	...	2323	0118	...	...	...	0155	0155
Córdoba d.	...	...	...	...	...	2150	2150	2205	2235	2300	2300	...	2250	...	...	...	...	...	0120	0130	0130	...	0200	0200
Andújar d.	...	...	...	...	...	|	|	|	|	2356	2356	...	|	...	...	...	...	...	0217	0228	0228	...	0311	0311
Almería d.	...	1705	...	...	...	|	|	|	|	|	|	...	|	...	2215	2215	...	...	|	|	|	...	|	|
Guadix d.	...	1849	...	...	...	|	|	|	|	|	|	...	|	...	2359	2359	...	...	|	|	|	...	|	|
Granada d.	...	y	1820	...	...	|	|	|	|	|	|	2145	|	...	|	|	2310	...	|	|	|	...	|	|
Moreda d.	...	1916	1921	...	...	|	|	|	|	|	|	2244	|	...	0050	0050	0050	...	|	|	|	...	|	|
Linares-Baeza a.	...	...	2119	...	...	2312	2312	|	|	0032	0032	0021	0027	...	0230	0230	0230	...	0258	0305	0305	...	0351	0351
Linares-Baeza d.	1805	...	...	...	...	2314	2314	|	|	0035	0035	0055	0055	...	...	0253	0253	...	0335	...	0335	...	0354	0354
Ciudad Real d.	|	...	...	...	...	|	|	|	|	|	|	|	|	...	...	|	|	...	|	...	|	...	|	|
Manzanares d.	1939	...	...	...	...	0030	0030	|	|	|	|	0231	0231	...	...	0445	0445	...	0508	...	0508	...	0532	0532
Alcázar de San Juan **420** d.	2010	...	...	...	...	|	|	|	|	0245	0245	0320	0320	...	...	0525	0525	...	0550	...	0550	...	0610	0610
Aranjuez **420** d.	2112	...	...	...	...	|	|	|	|	|	|	|	|	...	...	0633	0633	...	0650	...	0650	...	0709	0709
Madrid Puerta de Atocha a.	|	...	...	...	...	|	|	0015	0055	|	|	|	|	...	...	|	|	...	|	...	|	...	|	|
Madrid Atocha Cercanias a.	2147	...	...	...	...	|	|	...	|	|	|	|	|	...	...	|	|	...	|	...	|	...	|	|
Madrid Chamartín a.	2201	...	...	...	...	0230	0230	...	|	|	|	|	|	...	...	0755	0755	...	0810	...	0810	...	0830	0830
Valencia Término **415** a.	...	...	...	...	...	...	...	...	|	0602	0602	0652c	0652c	...	...	...	...	...	...	...	...	...	...	...
Barcelona Sants **415/20** a.	...	...	...	...	...	...	...	...	0830	1100	1100	1140	1140	...	...	...	...	...	...	...	...	...	...	...

← FOR NOTES SEE PREVIOUS PAGE ←

← SEE PREVIOUS PAGE ALSO FOR TABLE **426a** ←

Table 427 MÁLAGA - TORREMOLINOS - FUENGIROLA

Subject to confirmation

2 class only

km								
0	**Málaga Centro-Alameda** d.	...	0600	...	0630	and at	...	2230
1	**Málaga RENFE** d.	...	0602	...	0632	the same	...	2232
5	Aeropuerto ✈ d.	...	0611	...	0641	minutes	...	2241
11	**Torremolinos** d.	...	0620	...	0650	past each	...	2250
14	Benalmádena d.	...	0627	...	0657	hour until	...	2257
18	**Fuengirola** a.	...	0640	...	0710		...	2310

Fuengirola d.	...	0645	...	0715	and at	...	2315
Benalmádena d.	...	0657	...	0727	the same	...	2327
Torremolinos d.	...	0704	...	0734	minutes	...	2334
Aeropuerto ✈ d.	...	0711	...	0741	past each	...	2341
Málaga RENFE a.	...	0722	...	0752	hour until	...	2352
Málaga Centro-Alameda a.	...	0725	...	0755		...	2355

Table 428 GIBRALTAR

🚌 service

🚌 service **Algeciras - La Linea** bus station and v.v. (for **Gibraltar ▲**): every 30 minutes for most of the day. Journey time: 30 minutes. No definite timings are available.

🚌 service **Málaga - La Linea** bus station and v.v. (for **Gibraltar ▲**): 4 services per day. Journey time: 3½ hours. No definite timings are available.

▲ – Passengers must alight at **La Linea** and walk across the frontier (approximately 5 minutes) to reach local Gibraltar bus services. **THERE ARE NO THROUGH JOURNEYS.**

Table 429 HUELVA - AYAMONTE - VILA REAL

🚌 service for **1994.** DAMAS

🚌 service **Huelva - Ayamonte** and v.v. (for **Vila Real de Santa António** in Portugal). Journey time: 60-75 minutes. **Operator**: DAMAS – DAMAS S.A., Avenida de Portugal 9, 21001 Huelva, ☎ Huelva (955) 25 69 00, Fax: Huelva (955) 26 13 21. Adequate time should be allowed between Huelva rail station and the bus pick up/set down point (approximate distance *1km*).

From Huelva: 0900⚒, 1100⚒, 1230, 1330, 1500, 1700, 1830Ⓐ, 1930, 2030Ⓐ.

From Ayamonte: 0645, 0730Ⓐ, 0845⚒, 0930, 1145, 1330, 1545, 1645Ⓐ, 1900.

🚌 service **Ayamonte - Vila Real de Santa António (Portugal)** operates via a new road bridge. Journey time: 20 minutes. **Operator**: DAMAS – DAMAS S.A., address as above.

From Ayamonte: 0930, 1330, 1515, 2030.

From Vila Real de Santa António: 1000, 1115, 1400, 2000.

246 🛏 – Sleeping car ▬ – Couchette car 🚃 – Through carriage (1 and 2 class)

Table 430

MADRID - CÁCERES - BADAJOZ and LISBOA

See Table **425** for Madrid - Ciudad Real - Puertollano AVE services via the high speed line

1, 2 class except where shown
CP, RENFE

km									TAL 30 ⑥		TAL 41 Ⓨ Z	697 2Ⓨ B	2 z	693 2Ⓨ A		543 Ⓨ K	1543 M		332 ✕ E	11332 Ⓨ F
		2 ✕g	2			2	2	2												
	Madrid Chamartín............ d.	...	...	...	...	...	...	...	...		1515	...	...	...		1755	...		2230	2230
0	Madrid Puerta de Atocha.. d.	...	...	...	...	0905	1137	1405	...		1530c	...	1420	...		1810c	1810		...	...
	Ciudad Real 425 .... d.	...	...	...	...	...	...	...	...		1650	1708	1756							
	Puertollano 425 .... d.	...	...	...	...	...	...	...	1100		1724	1747	1832							
142	Talavera de la Reina .... d.	...	...	...	...	1038	1319	1514			1646					1940	1940		0009	0009
333	Cáceres.................... d.	...	0830	...	...	1345	1626	1718			1845					2225	2225		0254	0425
427	Valencia de Alcántara 🚇.. d.	...	...	...	...	...	...	1850											0500	
406	Mérida.................... d.	...	0656	0937	...	1440	1500	1724			1950	2047	2137	2210						0610
	Zafra...................... d.	...	...	1045	...	...	...	1830												
	Sevilla Santa Justa........ a.	...	...	1345	...	...	...	...												
	Badajoz.................... a.	...	0757	...	...	1535	1557	...			2037	2135	2228p	2257						0715
	Badajoz.................... d.	...	...	...	1435	...	...	...	1750											
	Elvas 🚇................... d.	0510	...	...	1454	...	...	...	1809											
	Portalegre................. d.	0603	...	...	1544	1557	...	...	1903											
434	Marvão Beirã 🚇........... d.	...	...	0810	...	...	...	...	1905s	1805v									0517	
539	Abrantes 445.............. d.	0749	...	0945	1121	1741	...	...	2020s	2054									0640	
567	Entroncamento 445......... a.	0826	...	...	1157	1819	...	...	2044s	2142									0703	
674	Lisboa Santa Apolónia 445 a.	0944	...	...	1345	1950	...	...	2145	2328									0833	

km		544 Ⓨ K	1544 N	690 2Ⓨ C	694 2Ⓨ D	TAL 42 Ⓨ Z		2	2		IR 841 Ⓨ	TAL 31 ✗	2			11335 ⑥h Ⓨ F	335 ✕ E
									z								
0	Lisboa Santa Apolónia 445 d.	...	...	...	...	...		0725	0725	0810	1155		...		...	...	2155
28	Entroncamento 445......... d.	...	...	...	...	...		0910	0910	0938	1259u	1315	...		1709	...	2325
	Abrantes 445.............. d.	...	...	...	...	...		0948	0948	1002	1323u	1354	...		1850	...	2350
	Marvão Beirã 🚇........... d.	...	...	...	...	...		...	...	1200	1445u		...		1931	...	0120
110	Portalegre................. d.	...	...	...	...	...		1141	1140v			1541	1600		2130v	...	
159	Elvas 🚇................... d.	...	...	...	...	...		1229	1227v				1650		2127	...	
169	Badajoz 🚇................ a.	...	...	...	...	...		1245	1245v				1705			...	
169	Badajoz.................... d.	...	...	0630	0800	0820	1215	...	...		1620				1940	2335	
	Sevilla Santa Justa........ d.	...	...	...	...	...		...	1230				1630				
	Zafra...................... d.	...	...	...	...	...		...	...				1931				
228	Mérida.................... d.	...	...	0712	0844	0916	1311	1329			1722		2030		2046	0056	
	Valencia de Alcántara 🚇... d.	...	...	...	...	...		...	...		1501						0150
	Cáceres................... d.	...	0710	0710	...	1012		1430			1625		2133		0335	0335	
	Talavera de la Reina .... d.	...	0939	0942	...	1207		1729			1825				0606	0606	
467	Puertollano 425 .... d.	...	...	1028	1200		1652	...				2048					
506	Ciudad Real 425 .... d.	...	...	1108	1238		1738	...									
772	Madrid Puerta de Atocha .. a.	...	1117c	1116	...	1320c	2048	1920			1953					0837	0837
	Madrid Chamartín......... a.	...	1130	...	...	1332											

A – Runs June 23 - Sept. 24, Dec. 21 - Jan. 1, 2, 7, 8, Apr. 7 - 17: 🛏 and Ⓨ Barcelona - Valencia - Badajoz.
B – Runs daily **except** when train 693 (note A) runs: 🛏 and Ⓨ Barcelona - Valencia - Badajoz.
C – Runs June 24 - Sept. 24, Dec. 22 - 24, Jan. 1, 2, 7, 8, Apr. 8 - 18: 🛏 and Ⓨ Badajoz - Valencia - Barcelona.
D – Runs daily **except** when train 690 (note C) runs: 🛏 and Ⓨ Badajoz - Valencia - Barcelona.
E – LUSITANIA – Supplement payable: 🛏 1, 2 cl., 🛏 2 cl., 🛏 and Ⓨ Madrid - Lisboa and v.v.
F – Runs ①③⑤ from Madrid, ②④⑦ from Badajoz: 🛏 1, 2 cl., 🛏 2 cl., 🛏 and Ⓨ Madrid - Badajoz and v.v.
K – Runs Dec. 1, 2, 3, 8, Dec. 15 - Jan. 9 (**not** Dec. 25, 31), Apr. 6 - 18: 🛏 and Ⓨ Barcelona - Madrid - Cáceres.
L – Runs Dec. 2, 3, 8, 9, Dec. 16 - Jan. 10 (**not** Dec. 25, 31), Apr. 7 - 19: 🛏 and Ⓨ Cáceres - Madrid - Barcelona.
M – Daily except Dec. 1, 2, 3, 8, Dec. 15 - Jan. 9, Apr. 6 - 18.
N – Daily except Dec. 2, 3, 8, 9, Dec. 16 - Jan. 10, Apr. 7 - 19.
Z – 🛏 and Ⓨ Barcelona - Madrid - Badajoz and v.v.

c – Madrid **Atocha Cercanias**.
g – Will **not** run Aug. 15, Sept. 8, Oct. 12, Nov. 1, Dec. 6, 8, 26, Jan. 6.
h – Will **not** run Aug. 14, Oct. 12, Nov. 1, Dec. 6, 8, 25, Jan. 6.
p – Will **not** run Dec. 24, 31.
s – Stops to **set down** only.
u – Stops to **pick up** only.
v – Change at Torre das Vargens.
z – Via Alcázar de San Juan (Table **426**).
✗ – Ⓡ with supplement payable.

Table 431

MADRID - TOLEDO, SEGOVIA and SALAMANCA

2 class only, except where shown

Rail service **Madrid Atocha Cercanias** - Toledo. 88 km. Journey time: 60 - 78 minutes.
From **Madrid**: 0720, 0825Ⓐn, 0939Ⓒ, 1055, 1225, 1425, 1625, 1755, 1955.
n – Will **not** run July 25, Aug. 15.

From **Toledo**: 0700Ⓐn, 0900, 1130, 1230, 1430, 1630, 1804Ⓐn, 1930, 2130.

Rail service **Madrid Chamartin** - Segovia. 106 km. Journey time: 94 - 112 minutes.
From **Madrid**: 0628✗, 0916, 1016, 1216✗n, 1416, 1516, 1616, 1716, 1910⑥b, 2016.
b – 1 and 2 class.   **n** – Will **not** run July 25, Aug. 15.

From **Segovia**: 0625✗, 0715✗b, 0940, 1155✗n, 1255, 1455, 1655, 1855, 1955, 2055.

Rail service **Madrid Chamartin** - Salamanca. 231 km. Journey time: 3 hours 25 minutes.
From **Madrid**: 0930, 1410⑤⑦q, 1610, 1915⑥.
n – Will **not** run July 25, Aug. 15.

From **Salamanca**: 0700Ⓐn, 0915, 1400⑤⑦q, 1735, 2025⑦q.
q – Runs also July 25, Aug. 15; will **not** run July 24, Aug. 14.

A reservation is now obligatory for all long-distance trains in Spain

Table 432 — MADRID - ZAMORA - VIGO and LA CORUÑA

1, 2 class except where shown

km		2 Ⓐp	2 Ⓐp	421 N	2	483 Ⓒ K♣	923 H	2	2	423 N	2	283 ✕ J	283 B	TAL 151 C	TAL 151 G	2 ⑦f	425 N	2	623 L	851 Dn	851 En	851 Fn
0	Madrid Chamartín 435 440 d.	...	...	...	...	...	...	...	...	...	...	1400	1400	...	...	...	...	...	2145	2145k	2145k
119	Avila 435 440 d.	...	...	...	...	...	...	...	...	...	...	1518	1518	...	...	...	...	...	2338	2338	2338
194	Medina del Campo 435 440 d.	...	...	...	...	...	...	...	1234	...	...	1608	1608	...	...	...	...	...	0048	0048	0048
284	Zamora d.	...	...	...	...	...	...	...	1335	...	...	1658	1658	...	...	...	...	...	0145	0145	0145
533	Ourense d.	0620	...	0720	...	0920	0931	1007	1325	1515	...	1730	1735	1834	1846	1955	2005	2005	2035	2130	0525	0555 0555
628	Guillarei 433 d.	0747		1023		1104	1145			1637	1753			1954		2120	2121	2214			0710	0710
653	Redondela 433 d.	0825		1050		1127	1212			1703	1821			2018		2141	2146	2242	2310		0757	0805
671	Pontevedra 433 a.																					0823
	Vigo 433 d.	0840		1105		1140	1225			1718	1842			2038		2155	2205	2255	2322			0825
663	Santiago de Compostela 433 d.	...		0925		1120		1515					1935	2028	2120		2150				0724	
737	La Coruña 433 a.	...												2138	2220						0855	

km		2 Ⓐp	620 L	420 N	280 R	280 J	TAL 74 M⑥	TAL 74 A⑥	422 N	2	TAL 152 ⑥	TAL 152 ⑥	2	2	2 P	920 H	480 S♣	2	424 N	856 Fv	856 Ev	852 Et	852 Ft	852 Dn
	La Coruña 433 d.	...	...	...	0805	...	...	0900	...	...	1250	...	...	...	...	...	...	...	...	...	...	...	...	2100
	Santiago de Compostela 433 d.	...	...	...	0904	...	...	0952	...	...	1343	...	...	1635	...	...	...	1947	...	...	...	...	...	2224
0	Vigo 433 d.	0630	0715	0720		0910	0925		1255	1320		1325			1615	1720	1915		2000		2120	2120		2115
	Pontevedra 433 d.																		2115					2115
12	Redondela 433 d.	0643	0728	0734		0923	0937		1307	1332		1338			1630	1733	1929		2013	2142	2142	2142	2142	
37	Guillarei 433 d.	0707		0801		0944	0957		1333	1352		1403			1654	1757	1953		2045	2217	2217	2217	2217	
132	Ourense d.	0840	0900		1051	1058	1135	1135		1532	1532	1535	1545	1835	1830	1916	2126	2152		2345	2345	0025	0025	0025
381	Zamora d.				1423	1423		1820	1820		1946									0352	0352	0420	0420	0420
471	Medina del Campo 435 440 d.				1508	1508		1908	1908		2055									0500	0500	0525	0525	0525
546	Avila 435 440 d.				1605	1605		2003	2003											0635	0635	0645	0645	0645
665	Madrid Chamartín 435 440 a.				1735	1735		2130	2130											0833	0833	0840	0840	0840

A – 🚉 and 🍴 La Coruña - Madrid - Alicante.
B – 🚉 and 🍴 Irún and Bilbao - La Coruña.
C – 🚉 and 🍴 (Alicante ⑦ -) Madrid - La Coruña (Train TAL129 on ⑦).
D – 🛏 1, 2 cl., ➡ 2 cl., 🚉 and 🍴 Madrid - La Coruña and v.v.
E – 🛏 1, 2 cl., ➡ 2 cl., 🚉 and 🍴 Madrid - Vigo and v.v.
F – 🛏 1, 2 cl., ➡ 2 cl., 🚉 and 🍴 Madrid - Pontevedra and v.v.
G – 🚉 and 🍴 (Alicante ⑦ -) Madrid - Vigo (Train TAL129 on ⑦).
H – 🛏 1, 2 cl., ➡ 2 cl., 🚉 and 🍴 Barcelona - Vigo and v.v.
J – 🚉 and ✕ Irún - Vigo and Vigo - Hendaye.
K – 🛏 1, 2 cl., ➡ 2 cl., 🚉 and 🍴 Irún - Vigo.
L – For days of running see Table 410. 🚉 and 🍴 Barcelona - Vigo and v.v.
M – 🚉 and 🍴 Vigo - Madrid - Alicante.
N – 🚉 Vigo - Porto and v.v.
P – 🚉 Vigo - Ponferrada.

R – 🚉 and 🍴 La Coruña - Bilbao and Hendaye.
S – 🛏 1, 2 cl., ➡ 2 cl., 🚉 and 🍴 Vigo - Hendaye.
b – 15 - 20 minutes later on ⑥.
f – Will not run Sept. 25, Oct. 2, Dec. 25, Jan. 1.
k – On June 24 - July 4, July 15 - Aug. 2, Aug. 12 - Sept. 5 and Dec. 2 - 10, Dec. 16 - Jan. 8 and Apr. 7 - 16 depart 2230 as Train 855.
n – Will not run Dec. 24, 31 from point of origin.
p – Will not run July 25, Aug. 15, Oct. 12, Nov. 1, Dec. 6, 8, Jan. 6.
t – Runs daily except June 25 - July 5, July 16 - Aug. 3, Aug. 13 - Sept. 6, Dec. 3 - 11, Dec. 17 - Jan. 9, Apr. 8 - 17.
v – Runs June 25 - July 5, July 16 - Aug. 3, Aug. 13 - Sept. 6, Dec. 3 - 11, Dec. 17 - Jan. 9, Apr. 8 - 17; will not run Jan. 24, 31.
♣ – For days of running see Table 440.

Table 433 — PORTO - VIGO - LA CORUÑA

1, 2 class except where shown. CP, RENFE

km		2	2	2	Int 421	IR 851	2	2	2	✕	2	Int 423		2g	🍴	2	2
0	Porto São Bento 446 d.	...	...	...	0552 0732 0821	...	1025	...	...	1308	...	1500 1756 1632	...	...	1915 2115 0035
3	Porto Campanhã 446 d.	...	...	...	0600 0739 0828	...	1032	...	...	1315	...	1509 1803 1639	...	1857 1921 2125 0041
42	Nine 446 d.	...	...	...	0709 0831 0951	...	1121	...	1245 1410	...	1557 1855 1740	...	1938 2026 2240c 0138
85	Viana do Castelo d.	...	...	...	0813 0918 1050	...	1204	...	1346 1513	...	1641 1958 1854	...	2017 2128b 2340 0237
133	Valença do Minho 🚉 a.	...	...	...	0930 1001	...	...	1501	...	1724	...	2020	2059
133	Valença do Minho 🚉 d.	...	...	...	1003	...	1735	2105
138	Tui d.	...	...	...	1015	...	1744	2114
141	Guillarei 432 d.	...	...	...	1023	...	1753	2121
166	Vigo d.	0640t	0800 0930	...	1225	1515	1655	...	1825	...	2005
	Redondela 432 d.	0652t	0944	1050	1238	1707	1821	2019 2146
178	Vigo 432 d.		1105	...	1842	2205
	Pontevedra 432 d.	0713t	0828 1010	1305	1543	1808	1852	2045
	Vilagarcia de Arousa d.	0745t	0859 1046	1338	1614	1808	1922	2125
	Santiago de Compostela 432 d.	0837	0936h 1143	1426	1651	1856	1959	2216
	La Coruña 432 a.	1005	1035h 1247	1540	1750	2028	2117	2320

km		⑧	✕	✕	⑦	🍴	Int 420	2Ⓐp 2	2	Int 422	2Ⓐp 🍴	2	2	2	Int 424	2	2	2	2
0	La Coruña 432 d.	...	...	...	...	...	0620 0730	...	0910	...	1100	...	1330 1500	...	1640	...	1915 1940
74	Santiago de Compostela 432 d.	...	...	...	...	...	0742 0835	...	1036	...	1220	...	1500 1606	...	1810	...	2029 2123
115	Vilagarcia de Arousa d.	...	...	...	...	...	0828 0917	...	1110	...	1307	...	1544 1644	...	1853	...	2101 2206
147	Pontevedra 432 d.	...	...	...	...	...	0908 0948	...	1142	...	1346	...	1623 1715	...	1934	...	2131 2243
	Vigo 432 a.	...	...	...	0720	...	1255	...	2000
165	Redondela 432 d.	...	...	...	0734 0929	...	1201 1307 1408	...	1641	...	1956 2013	...	2302
177	Vigo a.	...	...	...	0943 1015	...	1215	1422	...	1654 1745	...	2016	...	2158 2315
	Guillarei 432 d.	...	...	...	0801	...	1333	...	2045
	Tui d.	...	...	...	0806	...	1338	...	2049
	Valença do Minho 🚉 a.	...	...	...	0820	...	1350	...	2100
	Valença do Minho 🚉 d.	...	...	0545	0825	...	1357	1502	...	1738 1942 2105
	Viana do Castelo d.	0505 0600 0623	0705 0705 0816 0913	...	1207 1307	1441 1745	...	1856 2114 2157
	Nine 446 d.	0617 0709 0729	0811 0832 0832 0922 0954	...	1320 1412	1522	1717 1918	...	2008 2216 2244
	Porto Campanhã 446 a.	0728 0823	0857 0922 0922 1030 1038	...	1412 1504	...	1807 2026	...	2100 2313 2330
	Porto São Bento 446 a.	0732 0830	0905 0932 0932 1037 1045	...	1421	...	1817 2031	...	2107 2321 2335

b – Change at Nine (depart 2027).
c – Arrive 2214.
g – Daily except ①.
h – 12-15 minutes later on ⑥.
p – Will not run July 25, Aug. 15.
t – Ⓐ only; will not run July 25, Aug. 15.

Table 434 — FERROL - LA CORUÑA

Additional journeys are possible by changing at Betanzos Infesta. See Table 435

2 class only

km		Ⓐp								Ⓐp						
0	Ferrol d.	0720	...	1155	1430	...	2055		La Coruña d.	0710	0930	...	1500	...	1950	...	...
43	Betanzos Infesta d.	0752	...	1232	1502	...	2133		Betanzos Infesta d.	0812	1030	...	1604	...	2053	...	...
69	La Coruña a.	0846	...	1330	1600	...	2230		Ferrol a.	0843	1100	...	1635	...	2125	...	...

p – Will not run July 25, Aug. 15.

Table 435 — MADRID - OURENSE, FERROL and LA CORUÑA
1, 2 class except where shown

km		923 ⚟ X	923 ⚟ H	923 ⚟ G	1923 ⚟ X	2	IC 131 ⚟	283 ⚟ J	283 ⚟ B	2	623 2⚟	623 ⚟ L	623 ⚟ Y	2	TAL 79 ⚟ K	2	Ⓑ	751 M Ⓑ	751 ⚟ T	483 A♣	483 D♣	831 ⚟ N
	Barcelona Sants 412 .... d.	1900	1900	1900	1933	...					0730	0730	0730									
	Irún 440 .... d.					...		0845	0845											2220	2220	...
	Alicante Término 420 ...... d.														1045c							...
0	Madrid Chamartín 432 440 d.					...	0800			1130				1430	1500		1830	2000	2130	2130		2310
119	Avila 432 440 .... d.					...	0925			1258				1608	1621		1958	2126	2300	2300		0048
194	Medina del Campo 432/8/40 d.					...	1003			1324				1656	1703		2042	2210	2344	2344		0137
239	Valladolid Campo Grande 438/40 d.					...	1027			1407				1730	1727		2107	2234	0012	0012		0220
280	Venta de Baños 440 .... d.					...				1431				1759			2131	2256	0036	0036		0300
	Miranda de Ebro 440 .... d.					...	1122	1122			1432	1432	1432						0125	0125		...
	Burgos 440 .... d.	0312	0312	0312	0332	...	1220	1220			1523	1523	1523						0228	0228		...
292	Palencia 438 440 .... d.	0400	0400	0400		...	1056	1307	1307	1441	1610	1610	1610	1812	1800		2141	2305	0052	0052	0325	0325	0347
415	León .... d.	0507	0507	0530	0526	0805	1200	1423	1423	1600	1723	1738	1738	1929	1908	1945	2250	...	0202	0237	0441	0441	0515
	Gijón 436 .... a.				0842			1445				2005			2140								0820
465	Astorga .... d.	0544	0544		0851		▬	1456	1456	1632		1806	1806			2030			0237	0312	0518	0518	...
543	Ponferrada .... d.	0648	0648		1002		2	1602	1602	1737		1902	1902			2145			0348	0418	0610	0610	...
653	Monforte de Lemos .... a.	0834	0834		0838	1205		1734	1734	1915		2032	2032						0530	0600	0812	0812	...
653	Monforte de Lemos .... d.	0852	0903		0852	1210	1442	1748	1752	1802	1919		2047	2047					0555	0625	0830	0837	...
705	Ourense 432 .... a.			1007		1300		1834	1846	2017			2130							0931			...
	Vigo 432 .... a.			1225		1718		2038					2322							1140			...
723	Lugo .... d.	1025			1025		1558	1858					2148						0710	0740		0952	...
816	Betanzos Infesta 434 ...... d.	1152			1152		1736	2036					2303						0836	0921		1116	...
859	Ferrol 434 .... a.						2125												0925	1025			...
842	La Coruña 434 .... a.	1220			1220		1807		2138				2330							1150			...

		620 2⚟	620 ⚟ Y	620 ⚟ L	TAL 78 2 O	2 P	280 ⚟ J	280 ⚟ R	IC 130 ⚟	2	2	1920 ⚟ X	920 ⚟ X	920 ⚟ G	920 ⚟ H	830 ⚟ N	480 A♣	480 D♣	752 ⚟ T	752 M Ⓑ
La Coruña 434 .... d.		⚟		0700				0805		1345		1710	1710				1900			
Ferrol 434 .... d.						1030												1905	2045	
Betanzos Infesta 434 .... d.				0724		1117			1412			1737	1737				1924	2015	2137	
Lugo .... d.				0840		1252			1557			1857	1857				2105	2148	2315	
Vigo 432 .... d.				0715		0910		1325		1615				1720		1915				
Ourense .... d.				0901	0920	1100	1053	1545		1832				1920		2130				
Monforte de Lemos .... a.			0944	0947	1005	1146	1141	1358	1630	1704	1932	2008	2008	2009		2220	2225	2249	0015
Monforte de Lemos .... d.			1004	1004	1008	1204	1204		1634		1936	2018	2033	2033		2250	2250	2309	0036
Ponferrada .... d.			1130	1130	1142	1343	1343		1840	2135		2212		2212		0026	0026	0044	0211
Astorga .... d.			1228	1248	1252	1451	1451		2007			2321		2321		0130	0130	0152	0324
Gijón 436 .... d.		1045			1110			1255	1550			2048		2209					
León .... d.	0715	1310	1303	1303	1328	1332	1415	1535	1535	1600	1827	2055	2354	2350	2350	2350	0135	0220	0220	0230	0357
Palencia 438 440 .... d.	0705	0824	1428	1428	1428	1436	1547	1652	1652	1709	1925		0120	0120	0120	0120	0305	0335	0335	0358	0512
Burgos 440 .... d.			1513	1513	1513			1746	1746				0144	0208	0208	0208	0430	0430		
Miranda de Ebro 440 .... d.			1605	1605	1605			1840	1840								0528	0528		
Venta de Baños 440 .... d.	0715	0834				1559		1719					0332				0420	0523	
Valladolid Campo Grande 438/40 d.	0737	0857				1506	1635	1742	1955				0448				0448	0550	
Medina del Campo 432/8/40 d.	0758	0918				1528	1701	1806	2016				0526				0513	0617	
Avila 432 440 .... d.	0843	1003				1615	1750	1851	2057				0617				0605	0707	
Madrid Chamartín 432 440 .. a.	1010	1133				1742	1921	2025	2234				0810				0805	0855	
Alicante Término 420 .... a.					2158b														
Hendaye 440 .... a.						2130	2130										0845	0845	
Barcelona Sants 412 .... a.		2304	2304	2304							1005	1040	1040	1040					

A – ⬌ 1, 2 cl., ▬ 2 cl., 🛏 and ⚟ Irún - Vigo and Vigo - Hendaye; conveys in Summer **only**: ▬ 2 cl. and 🛏 Bilbao - Vigo and v.v.
B – ⬌ 1, 2 cl., ▬ 2 cl. and 🛏 Irún and Bilbao - La Coruña.
D – ⬌ 1, 2 cl., ▬ 2 cl. and 🛏 Bilbao - La Coruña and v.v.; ▬ 2 cl. and 🛏 Irún - La Coruña and La Coruña - Hendaye.
G – Runs daily **except** Dec. 24, 31 from Barcelona and Gijón: ⬌ 1, 2 cl., ▬ 2 cl., 🛏 and ⚟ Barcelona - Gijón and v.v.
H – ⬌ 1, 2 cl., ▬ 2 cl., 🛏 and ⚟ Barcelona - Vigo and v.v.
J – 🛏 and ✕ Irún - Vigo and Vigo - Hendaye.
K – 🛏 (Alicante ✕ -) Madrid - La Coruña.
L – For days of running see Table **410**: 🛏 and ⚟ Barcelona - Vigo and v.v.
M – Runs Ⓑ only during Winter: ⬌ 1, 2 cl., ▬ 2 cl., 🛏 and ⚟ Madrid - Ferrol and v.v.
M – Runs Ⓑ from Madrid and Gijón: ⬌ 1, 2 cl., ▬ 2 cl., and ⚟ Madrid - Gijón and v.v.

O – 🛏 Ourense - Gijón.
P – 🛏 and ⚟ Gijón - Madrid (- Alicante Ⓑ).
R – 🛏 Gijón - Madrid - Bilbao and Hendaye.
T – Runs in Summer **only**: ⬌ 1, 2 cl., ▬ 2 cl., 🛏 and ⚟ Madrid - Ferrol and v.v.
X – For days of running see Table **410**: ⬌ 1, 2 cl., ▬ 2 cl., 🛏 and ⚟ Barcelona - La Coruña and v.v.
Y – For days of running see Table **410**: 🛏 and ⚟ Barcelona - La Coruña and v.v.
b – Ⓑ only.
c – ✕ only.
♣ – For days of running see Table **440**.

Table 436 — LEÓN - OVIEDO - GIJÓN
1, 2 class except where shown

km		831 ⚟ N	923 ⚟ G	2 ⊠	2 ⊠	IC 131 ⚟	2 O	2	2 ⊠	623 2⚟ B	TAL 79 ⚟ K	2 Ⓑt
0	Madrid Chamartín 435 .... d.	2310	...	...	...	0800	...	...	...		1500	...
	León .... d.	0515	0530	...	...	1200	1340	...	...	1723	1908	1950
102	Pola de Lena .... d.	0703	0720	0925	1130		1523	1730	1900		2040	2140
129	Oviedo ▲ .... d.	0745	0810	1010	1215	1415	1557	1815	1945	1935	2112	2223
161	Gijón Jovellanos .... a.	0820	0842	1043	1248	1440	1624	1848	2018		2135	2256
161	Gijón Cercanías .... a.	...	...	1045	1250	1445	1628	1850	2020	2005	2140	2300

		2 Ⓐf	2 ⊠	2 ⊠	620 2⚟ B	TAL 78 ⚟ P	2	IC 130 ⚟	2	2 ⑦	920 ⚟ G	830 ⚟ N	2 ⊠
Gijón Cercanías .... d.	0530	0830	0935	1045	1110	1255		1550	1800	1820			2300
Gijón Jovellanos .... d.	0532	0832	0937		1113	1257		1554	1802	1822	2048	2209	2302
Oviedo ▲ .... d.	0558	0907	1011	1112	1138	1323		1621	1837	1850	2120	2305	...
Pola de Lena .... d.	0632	0951	1051	1204	1355				1920	1922	2156	2339	...
León .... a.	0837			1310	1330	1540		1825		2120	2348	0120	...
Madrid Chamartín 435 ...... a.					1742	2025		2234				0810	...

B – 🛏 and ⚟ Barcelona - Gijón and v.v.
G – Runs daily **except** Dec. 24, 31 from Barcelona and Gijón: ⬌ 1, 2 cl., ▬ 2 cl., 🛏 and ⚟ Barcelona - Gijón and v.v.
K – 🛏 and ✕ (Alicante ✕ -) Madrid - Gijón.
N – Runs Ⓑ from Madrid and Gijón: ⬌ 1, 2 cl., ▬ 2 cl., 🛏 and ⚟ Madrid - Gijón and v.v.
O – 🛏 Ourense - Gijón.
P – 🛏 and ⚟ Gijón - Madrid (- Alicante Ⓑ).

f – Will **not** run Aug. 15, Oct. 12, Nov. 1, Dec. 6, 8, Jan. 6.
t – Will **not** run Dec. 24, 31.
▲ – Local service (2 class only) operates: **Oviedo - Avilés - San Juan de Nieva** and v.v. 31km to Avilés, 34km to San Juan de Nieva. Journey time: 37-45 minutes. (10-12 trains daily) 0755-2215. Timings not available.
⊠ – Subject to confirmation.

For explanation of standard symbols see Page 4

Table 437 — SAN SEBASTIAN - OVIEDO - FERROL

2 class only. Narrow gauge. FEVE

	Ⓐ	Ⓐ	Ⓒ		Ⓐ		Ⓐ		Ⓐ
San Sebastián Amara ❍ ... d.	0550	0721	0900	1110	1328	1357c	1810	1910	2019
Bilbao Atxuri § ❍ .... a.	0850	0941	1205	1405	1543	1705	2105	2205	2226

	Ⓐ	Ⓒ	Ⓐ						
Bilbao Concordia § ... d.	...	...	...	0805	1335	...	...	...	1835
Treto ... d.	...	...	0730	0939	1512	...	...	...	2010
Santander ... d.	...	...	0827	1035	1604	...	...	...	2105
Santander ▲ ... d.	...	...	...	0835	...	...	1610	...	...
Torrelavega ▲ ... d.	...	...	...	0905	...	...	1641	...	...
San Vincente de la Barquera d.	...	...	...	1004	...	...	1731	...	...
Llanes ... d.	0645	0745	...	1051	...	...	1813	...	...
Ribadesella ... d.	0724	0824	...	1130	...	...	1848	...	...
Oviedo Económicos § ... a.	0930	1030	...	1330	...	...	2050	...	...

	Ⓐ	Ⓒ							
Oviedo Jovellanos § ▲ ... d.	...	...	...	0830	...	...	1515	...	1830
Gijón ▲ ... d.	...	...	0800		1500		1815		
Avilés ▲ ... d.	...	...	0843		1543		1900		
Pravia ▲ ... d.	...	...	0919	0932	1619	1620	1935	1937	
Navia ... d.	...	...	...	1130	...	1819	...	2134	
Ribadeo ... d.	...	...	...	1227	...	1916	...	...	
Vivero ... d.	0650	0748	...	1344	...	2033	...	...	
Ortigueira ▲ ... d.	0734	0835	...	1427	...	2116	...	...	
Ferrol ▲ ... a.	0850	0950	...	1542	...	2231	...	...	

		Ⓐ							
Ferrol ▲ ... d.	...	...	0715	...	1405	...	2000		
Ortigueira ▲ ... d.	...	...	0831	...	1521	...	2118		
Vivero ... d.	...	...	0914	...	1604	...	2200		
Ribadeo ... d.	...	...	1032	...	1722	...	...		
Navia ... d.	...	0650	1130	...	1820	...	...		
Pravia ▲ ... d.	0630	0848	1330z	1325	2018	2025	...		
Avilés ▲ ... d.				1402		2102	...		
Gijón ▲ ... d.				1445		2145	...		
Oviedo Jovellanos § ▲ ... a.	0730	0947		1430		2115	...		

			Ⓐ					
Oviedo Económicos § ... d.	...	...	0815	...	1535	1835		
Ribadesella ... d.	...	...	1010	...	1731	2032		
Llanes ... d.	...	...	1050	...	1811	2110		
San Vincente de la Barquera d.	...	...	1130	...	1854	...		
Torrelavega ▲ ... d.	...	...	1230	...	1947	...		
Santander ▲ ... a.	...	...	1300	...	2018	...		
Santander ... d.	...	0740	...	1355	1835	...		
Treto ... d.	...	0835	...	1453	1928	...		
Bilbao Concordia § ... a.	...	1008	...	1629	2107	...		

	Ⓐ	Ⓐ	Ⓒ	Ⓐ	Ⓐ	Ⓒ	Ⓐ	Ⓐ	Ⓐ
Bilbao Atxuri § ❍ ... d.	0620	0738	0815	1115	1115	1340	1515	1815	2035
San Sebastián Amara ❍ ... a.	0910	0958	1103	1426	1405	1555	1800	2118	2242

c – On Ⓒ depart 1410.
z – Connection available at 1325 to Gijón.
▲ – Additional local trains run: Santander - Torrelavega and v.v., Oviedo and Gijón - Pravia and v.v., also Ortigueira - Ferrol and v.v.
§ – Distance between Bilbao **Atxuri** and **Concordia** stations is 0.5 km; distance between Oviedo **Económicos** and **Jovellanos** is 1 km. **Connections are not guaranteed.**
❍ – Operator: ET/FV – Eusko Trenbideak / Ferrocarriles Vascos.

Table 438 — MEDINA DEL CAMPO - SANTANDER

1, 2 class except where shown

km		TAL 61 2 Ⓐ	⚇	2	TAL 77 ⚇ ⑤	831 Ⓑ	Y
	Alicante Término 420 ... d.	...	...	...	1215	...	...
	Madrid Chamartín 435 440 ... d.	...	0900	...	1630	1600	2310
0	Medina del Campo 435 440 ... d.	0835	1104	1115	1615	1836	1817	0137
45	Valladolid Campo Grande 435/40 d.	0912	1126	1142	1651	1857	1840	1945	0220
86	Venta de Baños 435 440 ... d.	0945		1210	1716		1904	2018	0300
98	Palencia 435 440 ... d.	0955	1156	1220	1727	1927	1937	2028	0317
196	Aguilar de Campoo ... d.	1110	1249	1332	1839	2019	2043	2139	0514
227	Reinosa ... d.	1138	1314	1401	1908	2044	2114	2210	0553
286	Torrelavega ... d.	1243	1402	1500	2005	2131	2208	...	0703
316	Santander ... a.	1322	1430	1535	2040	2155	2249	...	0755

		2 Ⓐp	TAL 76 2 ⚇	2	TAL 60 2 ⚇	2 ⑦q	830 Y
Santander ... d.	...	0630	0815	1345	1550	1445	1710	2300
Torrelavega ... d.	...	0706	0837	1425	1611	1523	1741	2329
Reinosa ... d.	0655	0814	0923	1532	1655	1641	1843	0046
Aguilar de Campoo ... d.	0724	0841	0944	1601	1718	1707	1916	0115
Palencia 435 440 ... d.	0837	0953	1041	1717	1814	1845	2030	0250
Venta de Baños 435 440 ... d.	0848	1003		1727		1855	2041	0332
Valladolid Campo Grande 435/40 d.	0920	1042	1113	1755	1845	1930	2105	0448
Medina del Campo 435 440 ... a.	0959		1134		1906	2010t	2147	0525
Madrid Chamartín 435/40 ... a.	...	...	1342	...	2120	...	2343	0610
Alicante Término 420 ... a.	...	...	1758	...	...	...	...	...

Y – Runs Ⓑ only from Madrid and Santander: 🚲 1, 2 cl., 🚲 2 cl. and 🛏 Madrid - Santander and v.v.
p – Will **not** run July 25, Aug. 15.
t – Ⓑ only.
q – Runs July 25, Aug. 15; will **not** run July 24, Aug. 14

Table 439 — 🚌 IRÚN - BILBAO - SANTANDER - GIJÓN

Service liable to alteration · 🚌 services (TURYTRANS)

km			✕			✕		✕		Ⓒ	✕			✕		⑦	
0	Irún ... d.	...	...	...	...	0815	...	0930	1030	...	...	1330	...	1630	...	1830	1930
20	Donostia/San Sebastián ... d.	...	...	...	...	0835	...	0955	1050	...	...	1350	...	1650	...	1850	1950
138	Bilbao ... a.	...	...	...	...	1025	...	1155	1225	...	...	1525	...	1825	...	2025	2125
138	Bilbao ... d.	...	0730	0830	0930	1030	1130	...	1230	1330	1430	1530	1630	1730	1830	1930	2030	2130
246	Santander ... a.	...	0920	1020	1135	1225	1320	...	1425	1520	1620	1725	1820	1855	2025	2120	2225	2300
246	Santander ... d.	0730	0930	...	...	1230	...	...	1430	...	...	1730	...	1900	2030	...	2230	...
272	Torrelavega ... d.	0750	0950	...	...	1250	...	...	1450	...	...	1750	...		2050	...	2250	...
310	San Vicente de la Barquera d.	0830	1030	...	...	1330	...	...	1530	...	...	1825	...		2130	...	...	...
345	Llanes ... d.	0900	1100	...	...	1400	...	...	1600	...	...	1900	...			...	...	...
377	Ribadesella ... d.		1120	...	...		...	...	1620	...	...		...			...	...	...
459	Oviedo ... d.	1030	1230	...	...	1520	...	...	1730	...	...	2120	2145			...	...	...
488	Gijón ... a.	1050	1250	...	...	1540	...	...	1750	...	...	2140	2205			...	...	...

			✕				✕		Ⓒ	✕			✕			✕	
Gijón ... d.	...	...	...	...	...	0800	...	0915	...	1030	...	1400	...	...	1600	1800
Oviedo ... d.	...	...	...	...	...	0825	...	0945	...	1055	...	1425	...	...	1625	1825
Ribadesella ... d.	...	...	...	...	...	...	...	1150	...	...	...	1720	...	...
Llanes ... d.	...	...	...	...	0950	...	...	1225	...	1545	...	...	1755	1950
San Vicente de la Barquera ... d.	...	...	...	0745	1020	...	...	1255	...	1615	...	...	1825	2020
Torrelavega ... d.	...	0710	...	0815	1100	...	...	1330	...	1655	...	...	1900	2120
Santander ... a.	...	0725	...	0845	1130	...	1230	1425	...	1725	...	...	1925	2120
Santander ... d.	0600	0730	0830	0900	1030	...	1130	1230	1330	1430	1530	1630	1730	1830	1930	2030
Bilbao ... a.	0725	0925	1020	1125	1220	...	1325	1400	1520	1625	1755	1820	1925	2045	2120	2220
Bilbao ... d.	0730	0930	...	1130	...	...	1330	...	1630	1800	...	1930	...	...	...	...
Donostia/San Sebastián ... d.	0840	1040	...	1240	...	...	1440	...	1740	2000	...	2040	...	...	...	...
Irún ... a.	0900	1100	...	1300	...	...	1500	...	1800	2020	...	2100	...	...	...	...

Ⓑ – Daily except Saturdays · 2 – 2 class only · Ⓐ – Mondays to Fridays only, except holidays

Table 440 — MADRID - BILBAO and IRÚN

1, 2 class except where shown

Block 1 — Madrid → Irún / Hendaye

km	Station	480 B	480 C	310 M	✗n	941 F	2	2	2	410 2☕	410 ☕	TAL61 Z	343 V	IC203 ☕	2	✗6r	280 D	280 W	280 A	TAL201 ☕	TAL201 2⑧	2
	Málaga 426 d.					1850																
	Algeciras 426 d.						2100															
0	Madrid Chamartín 432 435 d.					0235						0900	0920	1000	1010	1315				1530	1530	
	Avila 432 435 d.					0426						1021		1128		1440						
	Salamanca d.			0205						0930	0930											
	Medina del Campo 432/5/8 d.			0254		0519				1026	1026	1104		1210			1525	1529				
	Valladolid Campo Grande 435/8 d.			0323		0543				1110	1110	1126		1232			1550	1600				
	Venta de Baños 435 438 d.									1136	1136						1612	1642				
247	Aranda de Duero d.												1127							1726	1726	
	Palencia 435 438 d.	0335	0335									1155		1251		1626	1652	1652	1652			
364	Burgos 435 d.	0430	0430	0445		0658				1235	1235	1250	1333	1400	1420	1713	1746	1746	1746	1840	1840	
453	Miranda de Ebro 435 a.	0528	0528	0549		0756				1337	1337	1350	1424	1505		1812	1840	1840	1840	1937	1937	
453	Miranda de Ebro 412 d.	0538	0607	0550	0655	0757	0900			1400	1415	1415	1425	1506	2	1813	1900	1900	1848	1940	1940	2113
535	Bilbao Abando 412 a.		0755				0935			1545										2025	2125	
487	Gasteiz/Vitoria 412 d.	0603		0623	0721		0927	1015	1410		1437	1437	1447	1535	1545	1836	1845	1924	1924	2001		2140
530	Altsasu/Alsasua 412 d.	0631		0749			1050		1440		1503	1503	1509	1619		1912	1950	1950		2026		2212
562	Pamplona 412 a.																					
560	Zumárraga 412 d.	0700		0818			1118	1510			1530	1530	1535	1648		1939	2016	2016		2050		
618	Donostia/San Sebastián 412 d.	0806		0832	0925		1225	1617			1630	1630		1623	1755		2031	2105	2105	2137		
634	Irún ▲ 412 d.	0840		0900	0948		1248	1640			1655	1655		1645		2055	2125	2125		2156		
636	Hendaye ▲ 412 a.	0845		0904							1700	1700		1650			2130	2130		2200		

Block 2a — Madrid → Hendaye

Station	TAL77 2 Z⑤	301 Z	EC407 ⑧ K	1920 Q	205 H	205 Yt	205 St	831 T⑧ Z⑧
Madrid Chamartín 432 435 d.	1600	1630	1730	1815	1915	2300	2300	2310
Avila 432 435 d.	1730	1755	1856			0037	0037	0048
Salamanca d.				2200				
Medina del Campo 432/5/8 d.	1817	1836	1942	2255	0127	0127	0127	0137
Valladolid Campo Grande 435/8 d.	1840	1857	2006	2049 2335	0215	0215	0215	0220
Venta de Baños 435 438 d.	1904		2029	0001	0241	0241	0241	0300
Aranda de Duero d.			2042					
Palencia 435 438 d.	1913	1926	2042	0034				0312
Burgos 435 d.			2133	2158 2209	0140	0343	0343	0343
Miranda de Ebro 435 a.			2232	2251		0443	0443	0443
Miranda de Ebro 412 d.			2233	2252	0458	0550	0550	0755
Gasteiz/Vitoria 412 d.			2255	2341 2320	0530	0620		
Altsasu/Alsasua 412 d.						0605	0701p	0755
Pamplona 412 d.						0638		
Zumárraga 412 d.				0135				0755
Donostia/San Sebastián 412 d.				0203 0113				0825
Irún ▲ 412 d.				0208 0139				0830
Hendaye ▲ 412 a.								

Block 2b — Hendaye → Madrid

Station	830 Z✗	1923 H	302 K	EC409 ⑧ Q	TAL76 ✗ Z	IC202 2 ✗⑧	283 2 W
Hendaye ▲ 412 d.							
Irún ▲ 412 d.			0203	0253		0815	
Donostia/San Sebastián 412 d.			0219			0832	
Zumárraga 412 d.						0921	
Pamplona 412 d.							
Altsasu/Alsasua 412 d.					0720	0947	
Gasteiz/Vitoria 412 d.			0354	0436 0720	0801	1008	
Bilbao Abando 412 d.							0925
Miranda de Ebro 412 d.			0419	0741	0828	1029	1102
Miranda de Ebro 435 d.			0420	0742	0829	1029	1122
Burgos 435 d.		0332 0523	0544	0840	0940	1119	1220
Palencia 435 438 d.	0250				1041		1307
Aranda de Duero d.							
Venta de Baños 435 438 d.	0332	0452			0946		
Valladolid C.G. 435 438 d.	0448 0700	0645		1012	1113	1221	
Medina del Campo 432/5/8 d.	0526	0732		1034	1135	1243	
Salamanca d.		0850					
Avila 432 435 d.	0617				1120	1218	1326
Madrid Chamartín 432 435 a.	0810	0950	0850	1250	1342	1458	

Block 3 — Hendaye → Madrid

Station	283 ✗ D	283 2☕	TAL250 ☕⑥	TAL250 ⑥	2	340 V	413	413 2☕	2 b	TAL200	TAL200 ⑧	2 Z⑦q	940 G	2	313 ✗ M	204 J⑧	204 Pt	204 Yt	483 B	483 C
Hendaye ▲ 412 d.																				
Irún ▲ 412 d.	0845	0845		0915	0922	1152		1315	1315		1422	1545				1922	2200		2215	2220
Donostia/San Sebastián ▲ 412 d.	0904	0904	0931	0945	1215	1333	1333		1445	1601					1945	2218	2245		2340	2335
Zumárraga 412 d.	0946	0946	1014	1053	1323	1420	1420		1553	1644					2053				2340	2335
Pamplona 412 d.																	2245			
Altsasu/Alsasua 412 d.	1017	1017	1038	1124	1354	1449	1449		1624	1708					2124	2323p			0012	0005
Gasteiz/Vitoria 412 d.	1043	1043	1103	1155	1425	1430	1516	1516	1657	1732	1758		1900	2156		2156	0022		0001 0047	0032
Bilbao Abando 412 d.			0945						1400			1625								
Miranda de Ebro 412 d.	1104	1104	1115	1123	⑦qc	1459	1537	1537	1540	TAL60 1752	1755	1820	1929	2135	2222	0048 0040	0024	0115	0057	0100
Miranda de Ebro 435 d.	1122	1122	1136	1136			1552	1605	1605	1821		2136		2135		0049	0140	0140 0140	0125	0125
Burgos 435 d.	1220	1220	1233	1233		1550	1653	1705	1705	1903	1917		2237		0200	0252	0252	0252	0228	0228
Palencia 435 438 d.	1307	1307					1814			2002	2030								0325	0325
Aranda de Duero d.			1344	1344		1708	1839			2012d	2012									
Venta de Baños 435 438 d.		1336				1801	1801			2013	2041				0346	0346	0346			
Valladolid C.G. 435 438 d.		1402				1850	1850		1845	2002e	2035		2350		0328	0425	0425	0425		
Medina del Campo 432/5/8 d.		1432				1922	1922		1907	2101	2128		0015		0400	0453	0453	0453		
Salamanca a.		1535													0453					
Avila 432 435 d.						1951	2107e			2150	2214				0105	0547	0547	0547		
Madrid Chamartín 432 435 a.	1545	1545			2000	2100			2120	2224f	2224	2325	2343	0250	0740	0740	0740			
Algeciras 426 a.										0900										
Málaga 426 a.													1052							

Notes

A – On ✗ Madrid - Bilbao and Hendaye; on ⑦ runs as train TAL251: and Alicante - Madrid - Bilbao and Hendaye.

B – For days of running see note ♣: 1, 2 cl. and 2 cl. and Vigo - Hendaye and Irún - Vigo; 2 cl. and La Coruña - Hendaye and Irún - La Coruña.

C – For days of running see note ♣: 2 cl. and La Coruña - Bilbao and v.v.

D – and ✗ Vigo - Hendaye and Irún - Vigo; and La Coruña - Hendaye and Irún - La Coruña.

E – Runs ⑦, daily June 26 - Sept. 23 and Apr. 8 - 17, ②④⑦ Dec. 4 - Jan. 8 from Málaga and Cádiz: 1, 2 cl., 2 cl. and Málaga - Bilbao; 2 cl. and Cádiz - Bilbao.

F – Runs ⑤, daily June 26 - Sept. 23 and Apr. 7 - 16, ①③⑤ Dec. 2 - Jan. 7: 1, 2 cl., 2 cl. and Bilbao - Málaga; 2 cl., 2 cl. and Bilbao - Cádiz.

G – Runs June 23 - Sept. 11 from Salamanca, June 22 - Sept. 10 from Barcelona: 1, 2 cl., 2 cl. and Salamanca - Barcelona and v.v.

H – Runs ⑧ only: 1, 2 cl., 2 cl. and Bilbao - Madrid.

J – ⑧. Madrid - Paris and v.v.; and Hendaye and Irún - Madrid.

K – SUD EXPRESS – 1, 2 cl., 2 cl. and ✗ Lisboa - Hendaye and Irún - Lisboa; 2 cl. and Porto - Hendaye and Irún - Porto.

– 1, 2 cl. and 2 cl. Pamplona - Madrid.

M – FRANCISCO DE GOYA – Special fares apply. Inter-Rail cards can not be used on this service: 1, 2 cl. and ✗ Madrid - Paris and v.v.

P – Runs ⑧ only: 1, 2 cl., 2 cl. and Madrid - Bilbao.

– 2 cl., and Algeciras - Hendaye and Irún - Algeciras.

V – and La Coruña - Bilbao.

– 1, 2 cl., 2 cl., and Madrid - Hendaye and Irún - Madrid.

– To/from Santander – See Table 438.

b – On ⑥ train number 1202 (and only); arrive Madrid 2240.

d – ⑧ only.

e – ⑥ only.

f – On ⑧ arrive 2240.

n – Will not run July 25, Aug. 15, Oct. 12, Nov. 1, Dec. 6, 8, Jan. 6.

p – Altsasu/Alsasua Pueblo.

q – Runs July 25, Aug. 15; will not run July 24, Aug. 14.

r – Will not run Jan. 7.

t – Will not run Dec. 24, 31 from point of origin.

♣ – Daily June 25 - July 5, July 16 - 19, July 23 - Aug. 3, Aug. 13 - 18, Aug. 27 - Sept. 6, also ②④⑦ Dec. 1 - Jan. 8 and Apr. 6 - 18 from Vigo and La Coruña; daily June 24 - July 4, July 15 - 18, July 22 - Aug. 2, Aug. 12 - 17, Aug. 26 - Sept. 5, also ①③⑤ Dec. 2 - Jan. 9 and Apr. 7 - 19 from Irún and Bilbao.

▲ – Local service (ET/FV) Donostia/San Sebastián (Amara) - Irún - Hendaye and v.v. 22km. Journey time: 40 minutes.
Operator: ET/FV – Eusko Trenbideak / Ferrocarriles Vascos, Bilbao.
From Donostia/San Sebastián (Amara): 0715 and every 30 minutes until 2115.
From Hendaye (calling at Irún 5 minutes later): 0758 and every 30 minutes until 2158.

THE THOMAS COOK GUIDE TO
GREEK ISLAND HOPPING 1995
BY FREWIN POFFLEY

For the many thousands who appreciate the freedom of hopping around the Greek islands each year, this book is an essential guide, providing comprehensive, on-the-spot reference to every island and ferry service, including links to other Eastern Mediterranean areas. Detailed descriptions of islands include advice on accommodation, sightseeing and history, with useful town plans and maps illustrating island bus routes.

Now in its fifth year, *Greek Island Hopping* has established itself as the only really practical guide for independent travellers.

'The Island-hopper's bible'
The Independent

'. . . a remarkable compendium of all known Greek ferry timetables and services . . .'
The Bookseller

★ Covers all regular air and rail links to Greece.

★ Easy reference.

★ Descriptions and recommendations on every Greek island and ferry port.

★ Maps of every island chain and easy-to-use diagrams of every ferry route.

★ 46 street and accommodation maps (covering all the main island ports).

★ 78 island bus and beach boat maps.

★ Town plans for the most popular islands.

★ Ferry and Personal safety.

★ Historical background to Greece.

★ Budget accommodation for the independent traveller featured in every island description.

★ Suggested itineraries enable the independent traveller to plan a trouble-free visit around each major island group.

★ Expert advice on how to plan your own itinerary to avoid hold-ups and missed ferries.

★ Extensive introduction with advice on all practical details, from climate, food, drink and accommodation, to how to get there, currency, language, health, passports and visas.

★ Equally useful for the inclusive tourist based on one island – excursions and day trips covered.

Obtainable through Thomas Cook UK retail shops at £10.95, or by post at £12.45 (UK), £14.45 (Europe), £16.45 (overseas air mail) from:

Thomas Cook Publishing (TPO/FE), PO Box 227, PETERBOROUGH PE3 8SB, UK.

☎ (01733) 505821/268943.

PORTUGAL

SEE MAP PAGE 238

Operator:	Caminhos de Ferro Portugueses (CP).
Services:	Trains convey First and Second classes of accommodation, shown as '1' and '2' or ⟨2⟩ in the Tables. Certain trains convey sleeping cars (🛏) and couchette cars (▬) which are of normal European types – see page **10** for more details.
Timings:	Valid **May 29, 1994** to **May 27, 1995.** Times for local trains are subject to alteration without notice, as are all trains during public holiday periods – see page **2** for dates.
Tickets:	Certain trains may be available only to passengers travelling a specified minimum distance, or holding tickets with a fee paid for that distance. See individual tables for details. Seat reservations are obligatory on all **International, IC** and **Alfa** trains, and are recommended for travel on trains designated '**IR**'. If no train number is shown below, seat reservation is **not** possible. Supplements are payable on **Alfa** services between Lisboa and Porto and also on the **Talgo** and **Sud Express** services to or from Spain for international journeys. Reservations can be made at principal **CP** stations and appointed agents.

Table 442 — LISBOA - SINTRA and CASCAIS

2 class only

Rail service **Lisboa Rossio - Cacém** and **Sintra**. *28 km.* Journey time Lisboa - Cacém: 29 minutes; Lisboa - Sintra: 46 minutes.

From Lisboa Rossio: 0015, 0045, 0115, 0200, 0556, 0612, 0628, 0644, 0700 and every 15-20 minutes until 2232, 2315, 2345.

From Sintra ▲: 0015, 0115, 0515, 0531, 0547, 0607, 0623, 0639, 0655 and every 15-20 minutes until 2230, 2315, 2345. ▲ – 17 minutes later from Cacém.

Rail service **Lisboa Cais do Sodre - Estoril** and **Cascais**. *26 km.* Journey time Lisboa - Estoril: 37 minutes; Lisboa - Cascais: 40 minutes.

From Lisboa Cais do Sodre: 0030, 0100, 0130, 0200, 0230, 0530, 0600, 0620ⓐ, 0630ⓒ, 0643ⓐ, 0658ⓒ, 0700ⓒ, 0713ⓐ, 0725ⓒ, 0728ⓐ and every 15-20 minutes on ⓐ (every 20-30 minutes on ⓒ) until 2300, 2330, 2359.

From Cascais ▲: 0030, 0100, 0130, 0200, 0230, 0530, 0558ⓐ, 0600ⓒ, 0618ⓐ, 0630ⓒ, 0632ⓒ, 0647ⓒ, 0700ⓒ, 0702ⓐ and every 15-20 minutes on ⓐ (every 20-30 minutes on ⓒ) until 2238, 2300, 2330, 2359. ▲ – 3 minutes later from Estoril.

Table 443 — LISBOA - FIGUEIRA DA FOZ

1, 2 class except where shown

km		IR 801 ✕		IR 803 ✕	IC501 ⟨2⟩ⓑ						IC500 ⟨2⟩✕	IR 800	ⓐ	IR 802		IR 804 ⟨2⟩ⓑ
0	Lisboa Rossio ▲ .... d.	...	0736	...	1328	1730d	1816	...	...	Figueira da Foz .... d.	0710	...	1202	1355	...	1810	1913
18	Cacém ▲ .... d.	0543	0806u	0950	1358u	...	1816	1848u	...	2053	Leiria .... d.	0750	0910	1200	1316	1445	1710	1903	2031
65	Torres Vedras .... d.	0648	0852	1105	1305	1441	...	1900	1953	...	2202	Valado Nazaré .... d.	0813	0937	1231	1351	1511	1745	1930	2113
106	Caldas de Rainha .... d.	0737	0937	1230	1352	1518	1617	1939	2038	2050	2247	São Martinho do Porto ... d.	0824	0950	1246	1408	1527	1759	1948	2129
118	São Martinho do Porto ... d.	0752	0949	1247	1412	1527	1635	1950	...	2101	2257	Caldas de Rainha .... d.	0835	1002	1303	1435	1538	1815	2000	2148
132	Valado Nazaré .... d.	0814	1000	1304	1427	1538	1651	2001	...	2114	2308	Torres Vedras .... d.	0912	1040	1437	1527	1615	1927	2047	2236
162	Leiria .... d.	0845	1031	1340	1502	1606	1728	2029	...	2145	2333	Cacém ▲ .... d.	0946	1129	1547	...	1657	2042	2136	2334
218	Figueira da Foz .... a.	...	1118	1459	...	1650	1843	2110	...	2237	...	Lisboa Rossio ▲ .... a.	1023d	1200	...	...	1728	...	2203	...

d – Lisboa Santa Apolónia.
u – Stops to **pick up** only.

▲ – Additional trains (2 class only) operate **Lisboa Rossio - Cacém** – see Table **442.**

Table 445 — LISBOA - COIMBRA - GUARDA and PORTO

1, 2 class

km		3401				Alfa 121		IC 511	313 312	IC 541	IC 531		IR 811	IR 841		IR 823		
			✕	ⓐ		✕	⟨2⟩ ⓐ	⟨2⟩	⟨2⟩ S	⟨2⟩	⟨2⟩ B	ⓐ	⟨2⟩	⟨2⟩		✕ⓐ		
0	Lisboa Santa Apolónia .... d.	0020	...	...	...	0700	...	0722	...	0722 0725	0805	...	0810	0810	...	0900 0910	...	1025
31	Vila Franca de Xira ...... d.	0048	...	...	...	...	...	...	...	0754	...	...	0834	0834	...	0922 0950	...	1100
75	Santarém .... d.	0123	...	...	...	...	...	0807	...	0808 0836	0849	...	0904	0904	...	0950 1033	...	1150
107	Entroncamento .... d.	0150	...	...	...	...	...	0832	...	0842 0900	0908	...	0930	0938	...	1012 1056	...	1214
	Abrantes................ d.	...	...	...	...	...	...	...	...	0909	...	...	...	1006	...	...	...	...
	Castelo Branco .... d.	...	...	...	0530	...	...	...	...	1040	...	...	...	1155 1230	...	...	...	...
	Covilhã .... a.	...	...	...	0700	0705	...	...	...	1150	...	...	...	...	1400 1408	...	...	...
218	Coimbra B .... d.	0348	0555	0704	0743	...	...	0928	0942	...	1013	...	1049	1045	...	1132	...	1203
232	Pampilhosa .... d.	0414	0610	0723	0758	...	...	0940	1008	1032	...	...	1104	1110	...	1143	...	1218
	Guarda ▲ .... d.					0815	...	...	1245	...	...	...	...	1410	...	1520	...	...
	Salamanca ▲ .... a.																	
273	Aveiro .... d.	0505	0650	0801	0835	...	...	1017	...	1058	...	...	1047	1102	1142	...	1215	...	1256
318	Espinho .... d.	0555	0739	0850	0925	...	...	1048	...	1128	...	...	1113	1148	1228	...	1255	...	1344
334	Vila Nova de Gaia .... d.	0618	0804	0912	0948	...	0955	1101	...	1140	...	...	1125	1211	1251	...	1309	...	1410
337	Porto Campanhã .... a.	0625	0808	0916	1003	...	1000	1105	...	1145	...	...	1130	1222	1257	...	1315	...	1414
340	Porto São Bento .... a.	...	0820	0927	1009	...	1120	...	...	...	...	...	...	1227	...	...	...	...	1425

		IC 521 ✕	IR 825 ⑤⑥	TAL 31 ✕ Tⓑ	IR 813 ✕		Alfa 123 ⟨2⟩			IR 827 ⟨2⟩		Alfa 125 ⟨2⟩	310 311 ✕ P		IC 533 ⟨2⟩ B		Alfa 127 ⟨2⟩ ⓐ⓪⑷	Alfa 129 ⟨2⟩ ⑤⑦
	Lisboa Santa Apolónia ...... d.	1100	1135	1155	1230	...	1430	...	...	1535	...	1700	1703	...	1709 1800	1805 1809	1900	1900
	Vila Franca de Xira .... d.		1157	...	1254	...	...	...	...	1557	...	...	1733	1834	1844	...	...
	Santarém .... d.	1144	1224	...	1323	...	...	...	...	1625	...	...	1801	1904	1927	...	...
	Entroncamento .... d.	1203	1244	1259	1350	1405	...	...	...	1647	...	1807	1843	1923	1950	...	...
	Abrantes.................. d.	...	...	1323	...	1431	...	...	...	...	...	...	1913	...	...	...	...
	Castelo Branco .... d.	...	...	...	...	1622	...	...	...	...	...	...	2124	...	...	...	...
	Covilhã .... a.	...	...	...	...	1759	1810	...	...	...	...	...	2253	...	...	...	...
	Coimbra B .... d.	1308	1400	1442	...	1503	...	1631	1635	1716	1806	1821	1836	1901	1924	1931	...	2005	...	2101	2106
	Pampilhosa .... d.	...	1411	1458	...	1526	...	...	1650	1731	1818	1837	1851	...	2000	1947	...	...	2121
	Guarda ▲ .... d.				1824	...	1923	...	...	...	...	2229	...	2313	...	...	...	...
	Salamanca ▲ .... a.													0202				
	Aveiro .... d.	1342	1442	1535	...	...	1704	1728	...	1808	1850	1916	...	1934	...	2027	2037	...	2135	2157
	Espinho .... d.	1408	1518	1625	...	...	...	1817	...	1856	1930	2014	...	...	2123	2107	...	...	2245
	Vila Nova de Gaia .... d.	1420	1530	1648	...	...	1744	1840	...	1919	1944	2038	...	2014	...	2146	2120	...	2155 2215	2308
	Porto Campanhã .... a.	1425	1535	1656	...	...	1750	1844	...	1925	1950	2044	...	2020	...	2150	2125	...	2200 2220	2312
	Porto São Bento .... a.	...	...	1703	...	...	1855	...	...	...	2055	...	...	...	2203	...	...	...	2325

B – ⟨2⟩ and ⟨⟩ Lisboa - Porto - Braga.
P – SUD EXPRESS – 🛏 1, 2 cl., ▬ 2 cl., ⟨2⟩ and ✕ Lisboa - Hendaye; ▬ 2 cl. and ⟨2⟩ Porto - Hendaye.
S – SUD EXPRESS – ▬ 2 cl. and ⟨2⟩ Irún - Porto.

T – LUIS DE CAMOENS – Runs ⓑ: ⟨2⟩ and ✕ Lisboa - Madrid. Supplement payable. Only carries passengers for Spain - **Not** available for internal journeys within Portugal.
▲ – 🚂 is Vilar Formoso/Fuentes de Oñoro.

Alfa – Express train with supplement payable. Reservation obligatory

Table 445 — LISBOA - COIMBRA - GUARDA and PORTO

1, 2 class

	IC 513	IC 543		IC 523	IR 829		335				
	⚟	⚟		✕	✕ Ⓑ		✕ L	⚟	⚟		
Lisboa Santa Apolónia ...... d.	1904	1904		1915	2020	2025	2038	2205	...	2355	2355
Vila Franca de Xira .... d.		1946v			2047	2059	...	0019	0019
Santarém .... d.	1948	1948		2027v	2104	2115	2138	...	0050	0050
Entroncamento .... d.	2012	2022		2050v		2137	2203	2325	...	0116	0130
Abrantes .... d.		2053		...	...	...	...	2349	...	...	0206
Castelo Branco .... d.		2223		...	...	...	...	...	...	...	0345
Covilhã .... a.		2332		...	...	...	...	...	...	...	...
Coimbra B .... d.	2115	...		2226	2256	...	...	0238	...
Pampilhosa .... d.	2139	...			2308	...	...	0313	...
Guarda .... d.	0010	...		...	...	...	...	0649	...
Salamanca ▲ .... d.	...	...		...	...	...	...	...	...
Aveiro .... d.	...	...		2259	2340	...	...	...	...
Espinho .... d.	...	...		2325	0020	...	...	...	...
Vila Nova de Gaia .... d.	...	...		2340	0034	...	...	...	...
Porto Campanhã .... a.	...	...		2345	0040	...	...	...	...
Porto São Bento .... a.	...	...		...	...	...	...	...	...

	3400	5416	332			IC 520		Alfa 120
			⚟ L	✕	✕	⚟		Ⓐ
Porto São Bento .... d.						...	0616	...
Porto Campanhã .... d.	0025					0625	0631	0700
Vila Nova de Gaia .... d.	0033					0632	0638	0706
Espinho .... d.	0054					0644	0700	...
Aveiro .... d.	0145					0711	0756	...
Salamanca ▲ .... d.	...					...	...	...
Guarda .... d.	...	0044				...	...	...
Pampilhosa .... d.	0247	0354				...	0833	...
Coimbra B .... d.	0311	0409				0745	0847	...
Covilhã .... d.	...	...	0335			...	...	...
Castelo Branco .... d.	...	...	0505			...	...	...
Abrantes .... d.	...	...	0640	0650		...	...	...
Entroncamento .... d.	0510	0526	0718	0751	0833	...	...	...
Santarém .... d.	0533	0547		0813	0854	0906	...	...
Vila Franca de Xira .... d.	0608	0617		0844	0922		...	...
Lisboa Santa Apolónia ... a.	0635	0639	0833	0910	0944	0950		1000

	IR 820		IC 540	IC 510	IC 530	312 313		IR 822		IC 522						Alfa 122
	Ⓐ		⚟	⚟	⚟ B	S		⚟		✕			Ⓐ			⚟
Porto São Bento .... d.						0815		...		...		1020		1235		
Porto Campanhã .... d.	0735			0847		0827		0900		1100		1035		1244	1400	1430
Vila Nova de Gaia .... d.	0740			0855		0833		0907		1107		1041		1251	1407	1437
Espinho .... d.	0751			0907		0855		0920		1119		1104		1315	1430	
Aveiro .... d.	0823			0937		0952		0959		1146		1202		1406	1529	1514
Salamanca ▲ .... d.					0456			...		...		...		...	...	...
Guarda .... d.		0548		0705	0743			...		0820		...		...	...	...
Pampilhosa .... d.	0851			0945	1030	1040		1034		1233		1240		1445	1607	
Coimbra B .... d.	0900			0959	1010	1043	1054	1049		1219	1250	1254	1309	1500	1622	1549
Covilhã .... d.		0657	0730					0750		...		...		...	...	...
Castelo Branco .... d.			0837					0936		...		...		...	...	...
Abrantes .... d.			1003					1121		...		...		...	...	...
Entroncamento .... d.			1042		1110	1157		1204		1220	1324	1327	1452	1513	...	...
Santarém .... d.			1101	1117				1225		1246	1342	1350		1537	...	...
Vila Franca de Xira .... d.								1253		1318		1432		1620	...	...
Lisboa Santa Apolónia ...... a.			1145	1200	1212	1305		1315		1345	1425	1511		1700		1750

	IC 512	IC 542	IR 824	Alfa 124		IR 810	TAL 30	311 310	Alfa 126	Alfa 128		IR 840	IC 532		IR 812	IR 826
	Ⓐ	⚟	⚟	⚟		⚟	✕ T Ⓑ	P	✕ ①-④	✕ ⑤⑦		⚟	⚟ B	Ⓑ	⚟	⚟ Ⓑ
Porto São Bento .... d.				1625		...	...	...	...	1903		...	...		...	...
Porto Campanhã .... d.				1535	1634	1700		1805	1900	1900	1914		2010		2025
Vila Nova de Gaia .... d.				1542	1640	1707		1811	1906	1907	1922		2017		2032
Espinho .... d.				1555	1703			1824		1947			2030		2045
Aveiro .... d.				1638	1819	1745		1900	1940	2040		2056		2127
Salamanca ▲ .... d.								...		...		...		...	...
Guarda .... d.	1250		1412			1525			1645		1828	
Pampilhosa .... d.			1654	1709	1900	1852		1923	2129		2140	2158
Coimbra B .... d.			1706	1722	1913	1819	1906	1928	2015	2144		2129		2153	2212
Covilhã .... d.	1402		1505		1523			1757	1840	
Castelo Branco .... d.			1615		1708		2007	2010	
Abrantes .... d.			1731		1854	2020		2136	
Entroncamento .... d.		1742	1811	1840	1955	2024	2045	2105		2218	2234	2256	2308	2330
Santarém .... d.		1807	1827	1832	1900	2018	2045	2128		2240	2252	2320	2326	2350
Vila Franca de Xira .... d.		1842		1928	2046	2113	2213		2307		0004	2353	0018
Lisboa Santa Apolónia ...... a.		1908	1912	1920	1950	2110	2135	2145	2235		2200	2220	2328	2335	0035	0017	0040

B – 🚫 and ⚟ Braga - Porto - Lisboa.
L – LUSITANIA EXPRESS – Supplement payable: 🛏 1, 2 cl., 🛏 2 cl., 🚫 and ✕ Lisboa - Madrid and v.v.
P – SUD EXPRESS – 🛏 2 cl. and ⚟ Porto - Hendaye.
S – SUD EXPRESS – 🛏 1, 2 cl., 🛏 2 cl., 🚫 and ✕ Irún - Lisboa; 🛏 2 cl. and 🚫 Irún - Porto.

T – LUIS DE CAMOENS – Runs Ⓑ: 🚫 and ✕ Madrid - Lisboa. Supplement payable.
Only carries passengers from Spain – Not available for internal journeys within Portugal.
p – ① – ④ only.
t – ✕ only.
v – 6-10 minutes later on Ⓒ.
▲ – 🏛 is Fuentes de Oñoro/Vilar Formoso.

Table 446 — PORTO - BRAGA and VALENÇA DO MINHO

1, 2 class

km			Int 421		IR 851	IC 531			Int 423				Int 425		IC 533	
			✕	⚟			✕			⚟				⚟			1800
	Lisboa 445 .... d.		...	...	...	0805		...	...	...	...	...	...	...	...	...
0	Porto São Bento ...... d.	0552	0620	0732	0821	0927	1025	1105		1200	1308	1421	1500	1600	1632		1756	1814		1915	1957	2115		0035
3	Porto Campanhã ...... d.	0600	0627	0739	0828	0934	1032	1113	1145		1207	1315	1427	1509	1606	1639	1710	1803	1820	1857	1921	2004	2125	2152	0046
42	Nine ▲ .... d.	0709	0742	0831	0951	1047	1121	1154		1245	1256	1410	1523	1557	1649	1740	1827	1855	1920	1938	2026	2124	2240c		0138
57	Braga ▲ .... a.		0811		1114		1208	1245		1318		1543		1706		1905		1953	2152	2258	
85	Viana do Castelo ...... d.	0813		0918	1050	1204		1346		1513		1641	1854		1958		2017	2128b		2340		0237
133	Valença do Minho 🏛 a.	0930		1001			1501		1724	2020		2059		2205	
	Vigo 433 .... a.			1105					1842				

					IC 530			Int 420				Int 422			IC 532			Int 424
																		2000
	Vigo 433 .... d.							0720					1255						
	Valença do Minho 🏛 d.							0825				1357	1502			1738		1942	2105
	Viana do Castelo ...... d.			0505	0600	0625		0705	0705	0816	0913		1207	1307		1621		1745	1856		2114	2147
	Braga ▲ .... d.	0505				0725	0744			1030	1216		1429		1620		1726	1845		2102	
	Nine ▲ .... d.	0526	0617	0709	0729		0811	0832	0832	0922	0964	1244	1241	1320	1412	1449	1522	1635	1717	1741		1918	2008	2125	2216	2244
	Porto Campanhã ...... a.	0626	0728	0823		0832	0857	0922	0922	1030	1038	1123	1323	1412	1504	1553	1605	1718	1830	1947	2026	2100	2240	2313	2330
	Porto São Bento ...... a.	0633	0732	0830		0905	0932	0932	1037	1045	1128	1330	1421		1559		1724	1817	1840		2031	2107	2248	2321	2335
	Lisboa 445 .... a.					1212										2335			

b – Change at Nine (depart 2027).
c – Arrive 2214.

▲ – Additional connecting services operate Nine - Braga and v.v. Journey time: 19-31 minutes.
From Nine: 0142, 0713, 0837, 0955, 1125, 1419, 1608, 1743, 1908, 1941, 2220.
From Braga: 0030, 0547Ⓑ, 0617, 0634Ⓐ, 0811, 0844, 0917, 1245, 1334, 1453, 1644, 1819, 1933, 2127

Alfa – Express train with supplement payable. Reservation obligatory

Table 447 — PORTO - AMARANTE, VILA REAL and POCINHO
1, 2 class (Régua - Vila Real 2 class only)

Train services: IR861 · IR863 · Ⓐ · Ⓒ · ✕ · IR865 · Ⓐ · IR867 · IC561 (symbols ⚲/restaurant as printed)

km	Station																							
0	Porto São Bento d.	0045	0655	0744	…	0845	1048	…	1215	1319	1435	…	1615	…	1703	…	…	…	2028	…	2108			
3	Porto Campanhã d.	0052	0701	0751	…	0852	1056	…	1223	1326	1442	…	1623	…	1712	…	1830	…	2034	…	2115			
59	Livração d.	0212	0837	0907	0930	1025	1202	1225	…	1332	…	1459	1549	1555	1734	1735	1831	1832	…	1928	1940	2132	2220	2241
72	Amarante a.	…	…	…	0955	…	…	1250	…	…	…	…	…	…	1620	…	1800	…	1857	…	2005	…	2245	
64	Marco de Canaveses d.	0217	0842	0916	▬	1034	1209	…	…	1339	…	1504	1555	…	1740	…	1839	…	1934	…	2138	…	2248	
107	Régua a.	0310	0942	1012	1030	1121	1254	…	1313	1313	1429	1457	1602	1644	1649	1836	1844	1928	…	1937	2052	…	2220	2355
133	Vila Real a.	…	…	…	1126	…	…	…	…	1553	…	…	1940	…	…	…								
143	Tua ▲ a.	…	…	1106	…	…	1408	1408	1509	…	…	1739	…	…	2035	2135								
175	Pocinho a.	…	…	1201	…	…	1500	…	…	…	1830	…	…	2220										

Train services: IC560 · IR860 · IR862 · IR864 · IR866 (with Ⓐ, Ⓒ as printed)

Station																				
Pocinho d.	…	…	0630	0925	…	…	…	1402	…	…	1905	…								
Tua ▲ d.	…	…	0718	1023	1220	1400	1510	1510	1700	…	1955	…								
Vila Real d.	…	0721	0721	0918	1330	…	1637	…	1945	…										
Régua d.	0515	0638	0834	0845	1012	1122	1316	1425	1445	1450	1552	1552	1602	1732	1754	1907	…	2040	2051	2110
Marco de Canaveses d.	0622	0738	0917	0949	▬	1208	1408	…	1537	…	1656	1841	2012	2110	2207					
Amarante d.	…	0708	0839	…	1130	1335	…	…	1634	1804a	1900	2050	…							
Livração d.	0629	0733	0745	0904	0923	0955	1155	1216	1400	1413	1547	1659	1704	1847	1925	2019	2115	2118	2215	
Porto Campanhã a.	0747	0907	1018	1105	1331	1512	1638	1821	1955	2132	2306	2322								
Porto São Bento a.	0753	0914	1025	1112	1338	1518	1645	1830	2002	2141	2315	2330								

a – Ⓐ only.
▲ – Local trains operate: **Tua - Mirandela**, *38 km*, connecting with buses to/from Bragança. Journey time Tua - Mirandela: 1 hour 55 minutes, Tua - Bragança 4 - 5 hours.
From Tua: 0606✕, 1121, 1410Ⓐ, and 1753. **From Mirandela:** 0812, 1023, 1450, and 1752. Intending travellers to Bragança should check the times of buses locally.

Table 448 — LISBOA – ÉVORA, BEJA and TUNES
1, 2 class

km	Station								
0	Lisboa Terreiro do Paço ⛴ d.	0545	0725	0725	1515	1515	1920	…	2310
10	Barreiro Pier ⛴ a.	0615	0815	0815	1545	1545	1950	…	2340

Train services: IR891 · IR891 · IR893 · IR893 · IC591 · 4707

km	Station						
0	Barreiro d.	0620	0820	0820	1600	1600	2005 … 2350 …
16	Pinhal Novo d.	0642	0836	0836	1616	1616	2020 … 0007 …
91	Casa Branca a.	0829	0946	0952	1723	1732	2116 2125 0120 0125
117	Évora a.	…	1030	…	1810	…	2158 … 0158
154	Beja a.	0938	1035	…	1812	…	2200 … 0217 …
218	Funcheira 449 a.	1116	…		2150	…	0343 …
303	Tunes 449 a.	1300	…		2355	…	0508 …

Train services: 4706 V · IC590 · IR892 · IR892 · IR894 · IR894

Station									
Tunes 449 d.	0002	…		0813	…		1710		
Funcheira 449 d.	0135	…		0959	…		1933		
Beja d.	0300	…	0745		…	1250	1915	2125	
Évora d.	…	0505	0745		1257		1925	2203	
Casa Branca d.	0358	0555	0817	0832	1352	1352	2021	2021	2245
Pinhal Novo d.	0516	0732	…	0928	1453	1453	2124	2124	2349
Barreiro a.	0540	0800	…	0940	1510	1510	2141	2141	0012
Barreiro Pier ⛴ d.	0600	0825	…	0945	1520	1520	2150	2150	0040
Lisboa Terreiro do Paço ⛴ a.	0630	0855	…	1015	1550	1550	2220	2220	0110

B – Runs Ⓐ, also Ⓒ July 2 - Aug. 28.   **C** – Runs daily except Ⓒ July 2 - Aug. 28.   **V** – 🚲 Barreiro - Vila Real de St António Guadiana and v.v.
⛴ service operates **Lisboa Terreiro do Paço - Barreiro** and v.v. across the **Rio Tejo**. Journey time: 30 minutes. CP advertised connecting times shown in Tables. All ships convey ⚲.
From Lisboa Terreiro do Paço Pier: 0020, 0040, 0125, 0245, 0545, 0615, 0705, 0725B, 0745C, 0755, 0825, 0905, 0920, 0950, 1025, 1045, 1125, 1150, 1225, 1250, 1325, 1410, 1440, 1515, 1540, 1600, 1635, 1700, 1730, 1810, 1820, 1850, 1920, 1935, 1950, 2015, 2040, 2055, 2110, 2135, 2200, 2230, 2310, 2350. *Additional services run on Ⓐ during peak hours:* 0645 - 1010 and 1650 - 2030.
From Barreiro Pier: 0040, 0205, 0505, 0535, 0600, 0645, 0715, 0745, 0825, 0840, 0905, 0945, 1000, 1030, 1110, 1135, 1205, 1230, 1305, 1340, 1415, 1455, 1520, 1555, 1620, 1645, 1720, 1740, 1800, 1830, 1855, 1910, 1935, 2000, 2015, 2030, 2055, 2120, 2150, 2205, 2240, 2355. *Additional services run on Ⓐ during peak hours:* 0615 - 0925 and 1610 - 1950.

Table 449 — LISBOA - SETÚBAL, LAGOS, FARO and VILA REAL
1, 2 class except where shown

km	Station																
	Lisboa Terreiro do Paço ⛴ d.	…	…	0725	0755	0755	…	1325	1600	1730	…	1850	2310	…		
	Barreiro Pier ⛴ a.	…	…	0755	0825	0825	…	1355	1630	1800	…	1920	2340	…		

Train services: IR970 Ⓐ · IC20581 ✕ · IR871 H · IR2871 · IR974 Ⓐ · IC581 · 3801 · IR980 · IC571 · IR873 · 4707

km	Station																
0	Barreiro ▲ d.	…	…	0805	0835	0835	…	1405	1635	1815	…	1935	2350	…		
16	Pinhal Novo ▲ d.	…	…	0850	0850	…			1651			1950	0007			
29	Setúbal ▲ d.	…	…	0903	0903	…			1707			2006				
165	Funcheira d.	…	…	1106	1106	…			1919			2209	0343			
	Lagos d.	0610	0715	0755	0933	…	1215	1330	1415	1820	1912	2035	…		
	Portimão d.	0640	0731	0829	0957	…	1233	1352	1448	1836	1942	2053	…		
249	Tunes a.	0727	0808	0912	1037	1100	1217	1217	1310	1441	1536	1654	1910	2035	2124	2129 2316 0508
249	Tunes 🄳 d.	0655	0736	0810	0914	1105	1105	1223	1229	1312	1455	1540	1657	1918	2040	2127 2132 2322 0525
278	Portimão 🄳 d.	1305									2206					0614
295	Lagos 🄳 d.	1323									2222					0643
255	Albufeira d.	0703	0747	0816	0923	1046	1113	1319	1503	1549	1704	1925	2049	2134	2332	0521
288	Tunes d.	0800	0830	0855	1010	1015	1124	1140	1302	1348	1603	1645	1730	1742	1910	1956 2135 2200 0005 0615
344	Vila Real de St António d.	0934	0951	1145	1404	1450	1737	1850	2024	2052	2250	2312	0741			
345	Vila Real de SA Guadiana a.	0937	0954	1148	1407	1453	1740	1853	2027	2055	2253	2315	0106	0744		

Train services: 3800 · IC580 · IR870 · IR972 Ⓐ · IR976 · IC582 · IR2872/IR872 J · IC570 · IR978 · 4706

km	Station																
0	Vila Real de SA Guadiana d.	…	0530	…	0600	0635	0750	0855	1020	1240	1420	1615	1655	1755	1905	2140
1	Vila Real de St António d.	…	0533	…	0603	0638	0753	0858	1023	1242	1423	1618	1658	1757	1908	2143
57	Faro d.	…	0645	…	0720	0752	0857	1025	1151	1220 1346	1415 1553	1730 1745 1835	1845 1906 2050			2300
90	Albufeira d.	…	0727	…	0749	0833	0924	1111	1318 1412	1443 1649	1757 1838	1913 1940 2136				2335
	Lagos ◑ d.	0610							1330	1700		2230				
	Portimão ◑ d.	0640							1352	1719		2252				
96	Tunes ◑ d.	0734	0727	0755	0838	0929	1116	1325	1417 1441 1448 1656	1756 1802 1845	1918 1945 2143	2337 2340				
96	Tunes d.	0744		0800	0843	0930	1136	1328	1418	1452 1705	1816 1816 1847	1922 1946	0002 2342			
125	Portimão d.	0830				0959	1232	1419		1749	1940	2016	0017			
142	Lagos d.	0853				1015	1259	1444 1508		1809	2007	2030	0033			
180	Funcheira d.	0550				0956			1927 1927				0135			
316	Setúbal ▲ d.	0810				1149			2123 2123		2206					
329	Pinhal Novo ▲ d.	0829				1202			2137 2137				0516			
345	Barreiro a.	0857		1059	1217			1748	2153 2153		2229		0540			
	Barreiro Pier ⛴ d.	0905		1110	1230			1800	2205 2205		2240		0600			
	Lisboa Terreiro do Paço ⛴ a.	0935		1140	1300			1830	2235 2235		2310		0630			

▮ – Daily July 1 - Aug. 31.
– Daily July 1 - Aug. 31, also ⑦. Will **not** run on the day preceding a public holiday.
▲ – Local service (2 class only) operates **Barreiro - Pinhal Novo - Setúbal** and v.v. Journey time: Barreiro - Pinhal Novo 14-30 minutes, Barreiro - Setúbal 28-50 minutes.
🄳 – Additional trains between Tunes and Lagos appear in the lower frame of the table.
◑ – Additional trains between Lagos and Tunes appear in the upper frame of the table.
From Barreiro: 0030, 0205, 0500, 0625, 0652, 0845, 0925, 1035, 1205, 1300, 1412, 1640, 1735, 1820, 1905, 1940, 2028, 2120, 2235. *Additional services run on Ⓐ at peak times.*
From Setúbal: 0120, 0413, 0543, 0632, 0725, 0746, 0810, 0830, 1000, 1105, 1240, 1317, 1500, 1650, 1805, 1912, 1952, 2132, 2220, 2350. *Additional services run on Ⓐ at peak times.*

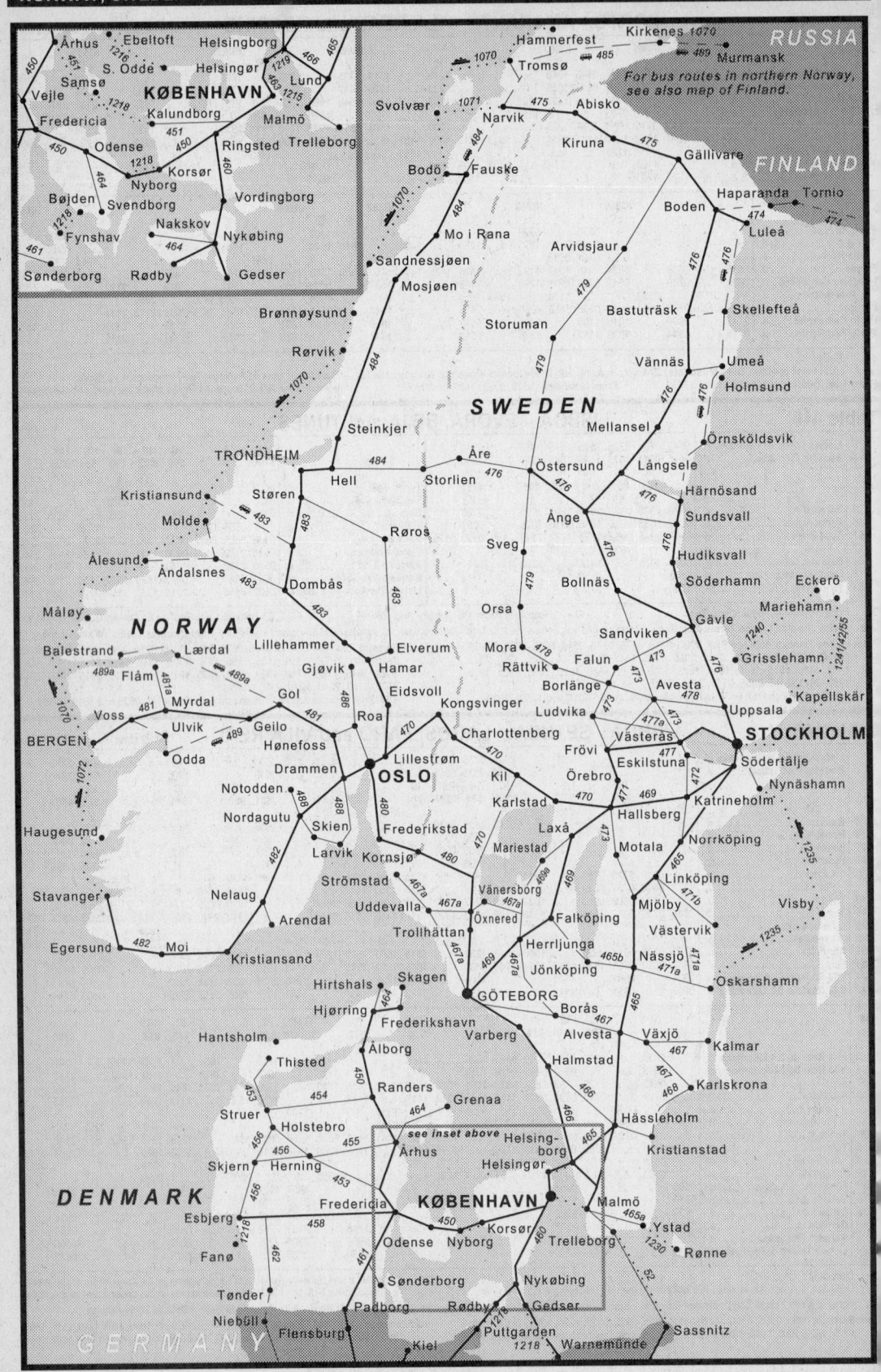

DENMARK

Operator: Danske Statsbaner (DSB).

Services: Trains convey first and second classes of accommodation unless otherwise shown. Intercity (**IC**) and Lyntog (**Lyn**) trains offer *Salon* (first class), *IC-Pladser* and *Hvilepladser* accommodation (also *Familiepladser* in **IC** trains). Sleeping cars (🛏) on internal services have one berth in first class, two berths in second class. Couchette cars (🛌) have six berths and are second class only. **IC** trains consist of two or more portions for different destinations and care should be taken to join the correct portion.

Timings: Valid **September 25, 1994 to May 27, 1995**. A ⑦ service is operated on public holidays (page **2**). Some local trains are cancelled on the evening of Dec. 24,31.

Reservations: Seat reservations are **compulsory** for trains travelling on the Great Belt ferries (Nyborg–Korsør), and in general are compulsory on Intercity and Lyntog trains travelling on the following sections: København–Aalborg/Herning/Esbjerg (also on the section København–Fredericia for trains continuing to Sønderborg and Flensburg). Seat reservations are also available on other **IC** trains and on EuroCity (**EC**) trains.

Supplements: Supplements are payable for international journeys on EuroCity (**EC**) trains.

Table 450 FREDERIKSHAVN - ÅRHUS - FREDERICIA - KØBENHAVN

1,2 class except where shown

Local trains run hourly Aalborg - Nyborg and Korsør - København, connecting with Nyborg - Korsør ferries.

	IC 108	IC 112	IC 116	IC 120	Lyn 122	IC 124	Lyn 126	IC 128	IC 132	IC 136	IC 140	IC 144	IC 148	IC 152	Lyn 154	IC 156	IC 2951	IC 160	IC 164	IC 168	IC 174	IC 176	IC 178	3188	594	590
	[R]	[R]	[R]	[R]	[R]	[R]	[R]	[R]	[R]	[R]	[R]	[R]	[R]	[R]	[R]	[R]	[R]	[R]	[R]	[R]	[R]			2	2	2
	⚒🍷	🍷	🍷	🍷	Ⓐ🍷	🍷	Ⓐ🍷	🍷	🍷	🍷	🍷	🍷	🍷	🍷	Ⓐ🍷	🍷	N	🍷	🍷	🍷	🍷d			⚒	⑦G	E
Frederikshavn § d.	...	...	...	0440n	...	0539c	...	*0638*	*0716*c	0847	*0936*	1047	*1136*	1247	...	*1336*	*1336*	1447	*1536*z	1647	*1736*r	1846	...	2040	2120	2207
Hjørring d.	...	...	...	0512n	...	0607c	...	*0711*	*0750*c	0912	*1010*	1112	*1210*	1312	...	*1410*	*1410*	1512	*1610*z	1712	*1810*r	1915	...	2112	2152	2234
Aalborg a.	...	...	...	0547n	...	0645c	...	*0747*	*0827*c	0947	*1047*	1147	*1247*	1347	...	*1447*	*1447*	1547	*1647*z	1747	*1847*r	1949	...	2147	2230	2308
Aalborg d.	...	...	0451n	0551c	0617	0651	...	0751	0851	0951	1051	1151	1251	1351	...	1451	1451	1551	1651	1751	1851	1951	2051	2210	2237	2315
Hobro d.	...	...	0523n	0623c	0645	0723	...	0823	0923	1023	1123	1223	1323	1423	...	1523	1523	1623	1723	1823	1923	2023	2123	2245	2311	2349
Randers d.	...	...	0542n	0642c	0703	0742	...	0842	0942	1042	1142	1242	1342	1442	...	1542	1542	1642	1742	1842	1942	2042	2142	2304	2331	0010
Langå d.	...	...	0553n	0653c	|	0753	...	0853	0953	1053	1153	1253	1353	1453	...	1553	1553	1653	1753	1853	1953	2053	2153	2314	2341	|
Århus a.	...	...	0623n	0723c	0735	0823	...	0923	1023	1123	1223	1323	1423	1523	...	1623	1623	1723	1823	1923	2023	2123	2223	2348	0010	0045
Århus d.	...	0526	0626	0726	0743	0826	...	0926	1026	1126	1226	1326	1426	1526	1543	1626	1636	1726	1826	1926	2026	2126	2226r	...	0022	0106
Skanderborg d.	...	0540	0640	0740	|	0840	...	0940	1040	1140	1240	1340	1440	1540	|	1640	1650	1740	1840	1940	2040	2140	2240r	...	0042	|
Horsens d.	...	0555	0655	0755	|	0855	...	0955	1055	1155	1255	1355	1455	1555	|	1655	1706	1755	1855	1955	2055	2155	2255r	...	0102	|
Vejle d.	...	0613	0713	0813	0826	0913	...	1013	1113	1213	1313	1413	1513	1613	1626	1713	1723	1813	1913	2013	2113	2213	2313r	...	0126	|
Fredericia a.	...	0630	0730	0830	|	0930	...	1030	1130	1230	1330	1430	1530	1630	|	1730	1738	1830	1930	2030	2130	2230	2328r	...	0145	|
Fredericia d.	0533	0633	0733	0833	|	0933	0939	1033	1133	1233	1333	1433	1533	1633	|	1733	...	1833	1933	2033	2133	2233	2329r	...	0205	0227
Odense d.	0608	0708	0808	0908	0911	1008	1011	1108	1208	1308	1408	1508	1608	1708	1711	1808	...	1908	2008	2108	2208	2308	0004r	...	0250	|
Nyborg d.	0625	0725	0825	0925	|	1025	|	1125	1225	1325	1425	1525	1625	1725	|	1825	...	1925	2025	2125	2225	2325	0021r	...	0310	|
Nyborg Ferry ▲ d.	0627	0727	0827	0927	|	1027	|	1127	1227	1327	1427	1527	1627	1727	|	1827	...	1927	2027	2127	2227	...	...	...	0345	|
Korsør ▲ a.	0735	0835	0935	1035	|	1135	|	1235	1335	1435	1535	1635	1735	1835	|	1935	...	2035	2135	2235	2335	...	...	...	0455	|
Slagelse d.	0753	0853	0953	1053	|	1153	|	1253	1353	1453	1553	1653	1753	1853	|	1953	...	2053	2153	2253	2400	...	...	...	0527	0548
Ringsted **460** d.	0809	0909	1009	1109	|	1209	|	1309	1409	1509	1609	1709	1809	1909	|	2009	...	2109	2209	2309	0018	...	...	...	0548	0610
Roskilde ‡ a.	0826	0926	1026	1126	|	1226	|	1326	1426	1526	1626	1726	1826	1926	|	2026	...	2126	2226	2326	0041	...	...	...	0609	0631
Høje Taastrup ‡ a.	0834	0934	1034	1134	1125	1234	1225	1334	1434	1534	1634	1734	1834	1934	1925	2034	...	2134	2234	2334	0049	...	...	...	0620	0641
København H. a.	0848	0948	1048	1148	1138	1248	1238	1348	1448	1548	1648	1748	1848	1948	1938	2048	...	2148	2248	2348	0105	...	...	...	0636	0700

km		3205	595	3207	3209	IC 113	IC 117	Lyn 123	IC 121	IC 125	IC 129	IC 2934	IC 133	IC 137	IC 141	IC 145	IC 149	Lyn 155	IC 153	Lyn 159	IC 157	IC 161	IC 165	IC 169	IC 173	591
		2	2			[R]	[R]	[R]	[R]	[R]	[R]	[R]	[R]	[R]	[R]	[R]	[R]	[R]	[R]	[R]	[R]	[R]	[R]	[R]	[R]	2
		Ⓐ	⑥H			🍷	🍷	Ⓐ🍷	🍷	🍷	🍷	N	🍷	🍷	🍷	🍷	🍷	Ⓐ🍷	🍷	Ⓐ🍷	🍷	🍷	🍷	🍷	🍷	E
0	**København H.** d.	...	0010	...	...	...	0552c	0702	0652	0752	0852	...	0952	1052	1152	1252	1352	1502	1452	1602	1552	1652	1752	1852	1952	2330
20	Høje Taastrup ‡ d.	...	0026	...	...	...	0605c	0716	0705	0805	0905	...	1005	1105	1205	1305	1405	1516	1505	1616	1605	1705	1805	1905	2005	2345
31	Roskilde ‡ d.	...	0036	...	...	...	0613c	|	0713	0813	0913	...	1013	1113	1213	1313	1413	|	1513	|	1613	1713	1813	1913	2013	2355
64	Ringsted **460** d.	...	0102	...	...	...	0630c	|	0730	0830	0930	...	1030	1130	1230	1330	1430	|	1530	|	1630	1730	1830	1930	2030	0015
93	Slagelse d.	...	0123	...	...	...	0646c	|	0746	0846	0946	...	1046	1146	1246	1346	1446	|	1546	|	1646	1746	1846	1946	2046	0033
110	Korsør ▲ d.	...	0136	...	...	...	0658c	|	0758	0858	0958	...	1058	1158	1258	1358	1458	|	1558	|	1658	1758	1858	1958	2058	0100
136	Nyborg Ferry ▲ a.	...	0315	...	...	...	0808c	|	0908	1008	1108	...	1208	1308	1408	1508	1608	|	1708	|	1808	1908	2008	2108	2206	|
136	Nyborg d.	...	0340	...	...	0716	0816	|	0916	1016	1116	...	1216	1316	1416	1516	1616	|	1716	|	1816	1916	2016	2116	2216	|
165	**Odense** d.	...	0406	...	...	0735	0835	0929	0935	1035	1135	...	1235	1335	1435	1535	1635	1729	1735	1829	1835	1935	2035	2135	2235	|
226	**Fredericia** a.	...	0444	...	...	0810	0910	|	1010	1110	1210	...	1310	1410	1510	1610	1710	|	1810	1902	1910	2010	2110	2210	2310	0324
226	**Fredericia** d.	...	0512	...	0654n	0813	0913	|	1013	1113	1213	1222	1313	1413	1513	1613	1713	|	1813	...	1913	2013	2113	2213	2313	|
251	Vejle d.	...	0528	...	0715n	0828	0928	1015	1028	1128	1228	1237	1328	1428	1528	1628	1728	1815	1828	...	1928	2028	2128	2228	2328	|
283	Horsens d.	...	0547	...	0735n	0845	0945	|	1045	1145	1245	1255	1345	1445	1545	1645	1745	|	1845	...	1945	2045	2145	2245	2345	|
311	Skanderborg d.	...	0603	...	0754n	0901	1001	|	1101	1201	1301	1311	1401	1501	1601	1701	1801	|	1901	...	2001	2101	2201	2301	0001	|
334	**Århus** a.	...	0618	...	0809n	0915	1015	1057	1115	1215	1315	1325	1415	1515	1615	1715	1815	1857	1915	...	2015	2115	2215	2315	0015	0448
334	**Århus** d.	0607	0645	0717	0814	0919	1019	...	1119	1219	1319	1331	1419	1519	1619	1719	1819	1902	1919	...	2019	2119	2219	2319r	0019t	0503
380	Langå d.	0635	0720	0746	0845	0946	1046	...	1146	1246	1346	1358	1446	1546	1646	1746	1846	|	1946	...	2046	2146	2246	2346r	0046t	|
393	Randers d.	0647	0730	0755	0855	0955	1055	...	1155	1255	1355	1414	1455	1555	1655	1755	1855	1934	1955	...	2055	2155	2255	2355r	0055t	0539
425	Hobro d.	0706	0750	0814	0915	1014	1114	...	1214	1314	1414	1433	1514	1614	1714	1814	1914	1951	2014	...	2114	2214	2314	0014r	0114t	0559
474	**Aalborg** a.	0740	0824	0846	0949	1046	1146	...	1246	1346	1446	1503	1546	1646	1746	1846	1946	2020	2046	...	2146	2246	2346	0046r	0146t	0634
474	**Aalborg** d.	0751	0831	0851	0951	1051	*1151*	...	1251	*1351*	1451	...	*1551*	1651	*1751*	1851	*1951*r	...	2051	...	*2153*	2258v	2351	0051t	...	0646
522	Hjørring d.	0830	0920	0939	1030	1130	*1230*	...	1330	*1430*	1530	...	*1630*	1730	*1832*	1932	*2030*r	...	2130	...	*2233*	2336v	0030	0130t	...	0745
559	**Frederikshavn** § a.	0900	0936	0953	1100	1153	*1300*	...	1353	*1500*	1553	...	*1700*	1753	*1905*	1955	*2059*r	...	2153	...	*2301*	2359v	0053	0153t	...	0812

E – 🛏 1,2 cl. and 🛌 2 cl. Frederikshavn - København and v.v.; 🛏 1,2 cl. and 🛌 2 cl. Århus - København and v.v.; 🛏 1,2 cl. and 🛌 2 cl. Esbjerg - København and v.v.; 🛌 2 cl. (not ⑥) Struer - Herning - København and v.v.; (2) Frederikshavn - Århus and v.v. Conveys on night of ⑥, 🛌 2 cl. Fredericia - København and v.v.

G – Runs ⑦ and holidays (also Dec. 23,30, Apr. 12; not Dec. 25, Apr. 13,14,16, May 12, 25): 🛌 2 cl. and (2) Frederikshavn - København; 🛌 2 cl. Fredericia - København. After Odense stops to set down only.

H – Runs ⑥ (also Apr. 13, May 12, 24; not Apr. 14, May 12, 26): 🛌 2 cl. and (2) København - Frederikshavn; 🛌 2 cl. København - Fredericia.

N – NORDPILEN – (12) and 🍷 Aalborg - Flensburg and Esbjerg.

c – Not ⑦ or holidays.

d – On ⑤ runs 7 - 17 minutes earlier Slagelse - København (arrive 0048) as train **IC172**.

n – Ⓐ only.

r – Daily except ⑥.

t – Night of ⑤⑦ only.

v – Night of ⑤⑦ only (also Apr. 12, May 5, 24; not Dec. 25, Apr. 14, May 12).

z – Ⓑ (not Dec. 25, Apr. 13,14, May 12,25).

‡ – Frequent local trains run between Roskilde and København.

§ – Certain journeys are extended to/from Frederikshavn Harbour.

▲ – Trains are conveyed on board train ferries between Nyborg and Korsør (⚒ available on board the ferries). **IC** trains do not pick up or set down at these points but passengers may join or leave the trains on board the ferries.

Table 451 ÅRHUS - KALUNDBORG - KØBENHAVN by sea/rail

1,2 class

km		Kat	IC514	⛴	2516	Kat	IC520	⛴	2528	Kat	IC528	2532	Kat	IC536	Kat	IC544	⛴	2550	Kat	IC552	⛴	2560	Kat	IC560	2564
			[R]				[R]				[R]			[R]		[R]				[R]				[R]	
		Ⓐ	Ⓐ	⚒		⑥	⑥		⚒	⑦	⑦		⚒	⚒	⑦	⑦	Ⓑ		Ⓐ	Ⓐ	Ⓑ	Ⓑ	⑦	⑦	
0	**Århus Harbour** d.	0640	...	0505	...	0840	...	0805	...	1040	...	...	1240	...	1440	...	1305	...	1640	...	1605	...	1840	...	...
118	Kalundborg § d.	0810	0820	0820	0837	1010	1022	1120	1132	1210	1222	1232	1410	1422	1610	1622	1620	1632	1810	1822	1920	1932	2010	2022	2032
197	Roskilde § a.	...	0920	...	0951	...	1120	...	1251	...	1320	1351	...	1520	...	1720	...	1751	...	1920	...	2051	...	2120	2151
229	**København H.** a.	...	0942	...	1017	...	1142	...	1317	...	1342	1417	...	1542	...	1742	...	1817	...	1942	...	2117	...	2142	2217

	IC521	Kat	4519	⛴	IC529	Kat	2531	⛴	IC537	Kat	IC545	Kat	IC553	Kat	2553	⛴	IC561	Kat	2567	⛴	IC569	Kat	2591	2593	⛴
	[R]				[R]				[R]		[R]		[R]				[R]				[R]				
	Ⓐ	Ⓐ	⚒	⚒	⑥	⑥			⑦	⑦	⚒	⚒	⑦	⑦	Ⓐ	Ⓑ	Ⓐ	Ⓐ		Ⓑ	⑦	⑦		⑦	⚒
København H. d.	0638	...	0656	...	0848	...	1015	...	1048	...	1248	...	1448	...	1514	...	1648	...	1815	...	1848	...	2215	2315	...
Roskilde § d.	0659	...	0722	...	0912	...	1040	...	1112	...	1312	...	1512	...	1541	...	1712	...	1840	...	1912	...	2240	2340	...
Kalundborg § d.	0812	0820	0837	0910	1012	1020	1159	1210	1212	1220	1412	1420	1612	1620	1659	1710	1812	1820	1959	2010	2012	2020	2359	0059	0115
Århus Harbour a.	...	0955	...	1220	...	1155	...	1520	...	1355	...	1555	...	1755	...	2020	...	1955	...	2320	...	2155	...	...	0425

Kat – Catamaran, operated by *IC Kat*, (DSO/DSB). ⛴ – Shipping service operated by DSB. § – Local trains run approximately hourly between Kalundborg and København.

Table 453 — THISTED - STRUER - FREDERICIA

1,2 class except where shown

km			IC 716 ✕	IC 724 ✕	IC 730	IC 740	IC 748 Ⓑ	IC 756 Ⓑ	IC 762	3776 2	3794 ⒷN
0	Thisted ▲	d.			0802c				1602t		
74	Struer 455	d.	0522	0722	0923	1123	1323	1523	1723	1932	2336
89	Holstebro 455	d.	0536	0736	0936	1136	1336	1536	1736	1948	2351
130	Herning 455	d.	0607	0807	1007	1207	1407	1607	1807	2035	0033
203	Vejle	d.	0706	0906	1106	1306	1506	1706	1906	2142	0130
229	Fredericia 450	a.	0722	0922	1122	1322	1522	1722	1922	2203	0147
455	København 450	a.	1048	1248	1448	1648	1848	2048	2248		0700

			3705 ✕N	IC 717 ✕	IC 725	IC 733 ✕	IC 741 Ⓑ	IC 749 Ⓑ	IC 757	IC 765 Ⓑ	IC 3769 2 Ⓑ
	København 450	d.	2330	0552	0752	0952	1152	1352	1552	1752	
	Fredericia	d.	0515	0913	1113	1313	1513	1713	1913	2113	2243
	Vejle	d.	0537	0930	1130	1330	1530	1730	1930	2130	2305
	Herning 455	d.	0647	1028	1228	1428	1628	1828	2028	2228	0022
	Holstebro 455	d.	0720	1059	1259	1459	1659	1859	2059	2259	0053
	Struer 455	a.	0736	1110	1310	1510	1710	1910	2110	2310	0107
	Thisted ▲	a.			1430				2220b		

N – 🚃 Struer - Fredericia and v.v.; conveys Ⓑ, ◼ 2 cl. Struer - København and v.v.
b – Arrive 2249 on Ⓖ.
c – Depart 0811 on Ⓐ (train number IC732 on Ⓐ).
t – Depart 1606 on Ⓐ (train number IC764 on Ⓑ).

▲ – THISTED - STRUER AND V.V. (complete service) :
Thisted to Struer 0552Ⓐ, 0601Ⓖ, 0735Ⓒ, 0811Ⓑ, 0956Ⓐ, 1058✕, 1134⑦, 1158Ⓐ, 1358Ⓐ, 1533Ⓐ, 1602Ⓒ, 1606Ⓐ, 1649Ⓐ, 1736⑦, 1900Ⓐ, 1939Ⓐ, 2223Ⓑ, 2254Ⓖ.
Struer to Thisted 0543Ⓑ, 0619Ⓐ, 0629Ⓖ, 0640⑦, 0804Ⓐ, 0939, 1025Ⓐ, 1224Ⓐ, 1314, 1352Ⓐ, 1431⑦, 1522Ⓐ, 1722Ⓐ, 1821Ⓑ, 1935⑦, 2111Ⓑ, 2133Ⓑ, 2334Ⓑ.

Reservation is compulsory on IC trains between Herning and København. Additional local trains run between Struer and Herning and between Herning and Fredericia.

Table 454 — STRUER - VIBORG - ÅRHUS

For direct services between Struer and København see Table 453.

2 class only (IC trains are 1,2 class)

km			3822 Ⓐ	IC824 ✕	3828 Ⓐ	3830 ⑦	3832 ✕	3836 Ⓐ	3840	3844	3848	3852 ⑤⑦	IC850 H	IC852 ⑤⑦	3856	3860	3864 ⑤⑦	IC862 ①-④	IC864 ⑤⑦	3868	IC868 Ⓒ	3872 ⑦	3876 Ⓑ	3878 Ⓒ	3888 Ⓒ	3890 Ⓒ
0	Struer 453	d.	0546	0620	0646	0720	0820	0920	1020	1120	1220	1320	1332	1420	1520	1620	1620	1629	1720	1732	1820	1920	2020	2120	2220
32	Skive	d.	0611	0646	0710	0743	0843	0943	1043	1143	1243	1343	1355	1443	1543	1643	1643	1655	1743	1755	1843	1943	2043	2143	2243
62	Viborg	d.	0637	0709	0749	0809	0909	1009	1109	1209	1309	1409	1417	1509	1609	1709	1709	1717	1809	1817	1909	2009	2109	2209	2309
102	Langå 450	d.	0714	0746	0829	0846	0946	1046	1146	1246	1346	1446		1546	1646	1746	1746	1753	1846	1853	1946	2046	2146	2246	2346
148	Århus 450	a.	0746	0818	0901	0918	1018	1118	1218	1318	1418	1518	1518	1523	1618	1718	1818	1823	1918	1923	2018	2118	2218	2318	0018
482	København 450 §	a.		1248								1948	1948					2248	2248		2348					

			3803 Ⓐ	3805 ✕	3807 Ⓐ	3809 ⑦	3813 ✕	3817 Ⓐ	IC821 ✕	3821 ⑦	3825	3829	3833	IC837 Ⓑ	C839 Ⓑ	3837 Ⓑ	3841	3845	3849 Ⓑ	3853	3857 ⑤⑦	IC861 ⑦	IC863 Ⓒ	3861 Ⓒ	3865 ⑦	3867 Ⓒ	3869 Ⓒ
	København 450 §	d.						0652						1052	1052						1652	1652					
	Århus 450	d.	0533	0622	0722	0822a	0922	1022	1122	1122	1222	1322	1422	1519	1522	1522	1622	1722	1822	1922	2022	2119	2122	2122	2222	2246	2322
	Langå 450	d.	0612	0658	0758	0858	0958	1058	1158	1158	1258	1358	1458	1549	1558	1558	1658	1758	1858	1958	2058	2149	2158	2158	2258	2323	2358
	Viborg	d.	0654	0732	0832	0932	1032	1132	1232	1232	1332	1432	1532	1621	1632	1632	1732	1832	1932	2032	2132	2221	2232	2232	2332	0000	0032
	Skive	d.	0724	0756	0856	0956	1056	1156	1256	1256	1356	1456	1556	1642	1656	1656	1756	1856	1956	2056	2156	2242	2256	2256	2356	0023	0056
	Struer 453	a.	0747	0819	0919	1019	1119	1219	1319	1319	1419	1519	1619	1702	1719	1719	1819	1919	2019	2119	2219	2302	2319	2319	0019	0046	0119

H – ①②③④⑥.
a – Ⓐ only.
§ – Reservation obligatory for journeys to or from København.

Table 455 — STRUER - HOLSTEBRO - HERNING - ÅRHUS

2 class only

km			Ⓐ	✕	Ⓐ	Ⓐ	✕		Ⓐ			Ⓐ		Ⓐ	Ⓑ	⑦		Ⓑ			
0	Struer 453	d.			0551r		0644	0725t	0827		1025r		1225r		1425		1536r		1625		1825t	1932	2025	2138
15	Holstebro 453	d.			0609r		0700	0740t	0845		1041r		1241r		1441		1553r		1641		1841t	1948	2041	2151
	Esbjerg 456	d.				0548			0841						1441				1641					
57	Herning 453	a.			0645r	0740	0738	0812t	0917	0957		1117r		1317r		1517	1559	1622r		1717	1757		1917t	2022	2117	2223
57	Herning	d.	0515	0621	0701r		0749	0822	0925	1000	1024	1124	1224	1324	1424	1524	1600	1623	1701	1724	1800	1824	1924	2024	2124	2224
98	Silkeborg	d.	0551	0658	0738		0838	0904	1004	1038	1104	1204	1304	1404	1504	1604	1640	1704	1740	1804	1838	1904	2004	2104	2204	2304
128	Skanderborg 450	d.	0619	0725	0806		0906	0933	1033	1100	1133	1233	1333	1433	1533	1633	1707	1733	1806	1833	1901	1933	2033	2133	2233	2333
151	Århus 453	a.	0637	0741	0824		0924	0949	1049	1119	1149	1249	1349	1449	1549	1649	1724	1749	1823	1849	1919	1949	2049	2149	2249	2349

			Ⓐ	Ⓐ		Ⓐ	✕		Ⓐ								Ⓐ		Ⓑ	⑦			⑦k	⑤⑦		
	Århus	d.	0515	0604	0641	0713	0750	0850	0915	0950	1050	1150	1250	1350	1450	1515	1550	1630	1650	1715	1750	1850	1950	2050	2150	2250
	Skanderborg 450	d.	0532	0621	0701	0731	0807	0907	0934	1007	1107	1207	1307	1407	1446	1507	1534	1607	1646	1707	1734	1807	1907	2007	2107	2207	2307
	Silkeborg	a.	0604	0658	0738	0801	0838	0938	1005	1038	1138	1238	1338	1438	1516	1538	1605	1638	1716	1738	1805	1838	1938	2038	2138	2238	2338
	Herning	a.	0643	0737	0814	0835	0914	1014	1035	1114	1214	1314	1414	1514		1614	1635	1714		1814	1835	1914	2014	2114	2214	2314	0014
	Herning 453	d.	0702		0815		0918		1036	1118r		1318r		1518b		1636	1718			1836	1918		2118	2234	2318		
	Esbjerg 456	a.						1153								1753				1953				0014			
	Holstebro 453	a.	0735		0846		0954		1154r		1354r		1554b			1754				1952			2152		2351		
	Struer 453	a.	0749		0900		1007		1207r		1407r		1607b			1807				2006			2206		0005		

b – Daily except ⑥.
k – Not Dec. 25, Apr. 13,14,16, May 12,25.
r – ✕ only.
t – ⑦ only.

Table 456 — STRUER - HOLSTEBRO - ESBJERG

2 class only (IC trains are 1,2 class)

km			Ⓐ	IC628 Ⓐ	4636 ▲✕				Ⓐ		Ⓐ		Ⓐ	Ⓑ	⑦	⑥	Ⓑ	Ⓑ	
0	Struer 453/5	d.	0537		0700		0900		1057k	1257		1414		1457			1712		1803	1857	2055
15	Holstebro 453/5	d.	0552	0646	0718		0918		1118	1318		1430		1518	1556		1725		1818	1918	2118
63	Ringkøbing	d.	0634	0726	0759		0959		1159	1359		1514		1559	1639		1759		1859	1959	2159
	Århus 455	d.				0915										1515		1715			
	Herning	d.	0611a		0740r	0930		1036	1130		1330		1530		1636	1730		1836	1830	1930	2130	2230
86	Skjern	d.	0653	0745	0819	1009	1019	1109	1225	1219	1405	1419	1527	1533	1611	1619	1658	1709	1809	1909	1919	2005	2109	2219	2319
129	Varde	d.	0734	0822	0857		1057	1140		1257		1457	1606			1657		1740		1857	1940	1957		2057	2257	2357
146	Esbjerg	a.	0752	0839	0914		1114	1153		1314		1514	1625			1714		1914	1953	2014			2114	2314	0014
235	Fredericia 458	a.		1001	1025		1225											2025							
460	København 450 §	a.		1348	1548													2348							

			Ⓐ	Ⓐ	Ⓐ	Ⓐ	✕	Ⓐ	IC621				Ⓐ			Ⓐ	⑦	Ⓑ	⑥	▲ IC661	
	København 450 §	d.						0527	0652							1444				1452	1652
	Fredericia 458	d.					0527		0744t	1015						1521				1815	2015
	Esbjerg	d.	0505	0521	0621	0641	0721c	0841	0921		1121	1121		1321		1441		1608	1641	1721		1821	1921	2121
	Varde	d.	0520	0537	0642	0702	0737c	0856	0937		1137	1137		1337		1456		1625	1656	1737		1837	1937	2137
	Skjern	d.	0615	0618	0724	0742	0808	0928	1018	1023	1218	1218	1228	1418	1529	1537	1618	1622	1708	1818	1822	1918	2018	2218	2228
	Herning	a.				0840	0903c	0957		1100			1303		1503	1559		1703		1757		1903	2003	2103		2303
	Århus 455	a.					1119									1724				1919					
	Ringkøbing	a.	0634	0637	0758		0837		1037		1237	1237		1437		1558	1637		1727		1837		1937	2037	2237
	Holstebro 453/5	a.	0717	0717	0838		0917		1117		1317	1317		1517		1656	1717		1917		2017	2117	2317
	Struer 453/5	a.	0736	0736	0900		0936		1136		1336	1336		1536		1656	1750f		1824		1932		2032	2132	2332

a – Ⓐ only.
c – Ⓒ only.
f – Arrive 1736 on Ⓖ.
k – Depart 1103 on ⑦.
r – ⑥ only.
t – ⑦ only.
§ – Reservation obligatory for journeys to or from København.
▲ – 🚃 Struer - København and v.v. (IC train Esbjerg - København and v.v.).

For explanation of standard symbols see page 4

Table 458   FREDERICIA - ESBJERG

2 class only (**IC** and **ICE** trains are 1,2 class).

km	IC/ICE trains are Ⓡ		IC 621	Lyn 127 Ⓐ	IC 629		IC 637		IC 645		IC 2951 N		IC 653		Lyn 159		IC 661		IC 669			591 E
		Køvenhavn 450 ..... d.		... 0652	...	... 0802t	0852		... 1052		... 1252		... 1452		... 1602		... 1652		... 1852	Ⓒ	...	2330
0	**Fredericia** d.	0639 0734n	0844 0944		1044 1107	1215	1244	1415	1444	1615	1644	1740	1744	1815	1844	1907	1944	2015	2144	2215	2244	
20	Kolding d.	0655 0800	0900 1000		1029 1100	1122	1229	1300	1429	1500	1629	1744	1755	1800	1829	1900	1921	2000	2029	2200	2229	2300	0424
33	Lunderskov 461 d.	0704 0809	0909 1009		1109		1309		1509		1709		1809		1909		2009		2209		2309	
72	Bramming 462 d.	0737 0842	0942 1042		1101 1142		1301	1342	1501	1542	1701	1827	1842	1901	1942		2042	2101	2242	2301	2342	
88	**Esbjerg** a.	0750 0855	0955 1055		1112 1155	1203	1312	1355	1512	1555	1712	1755	1838	1855	1912	1955	2003	2055	2112	2255	2312	2355	0515

	IC/ICE trains are Ⓡ		IC 612	IC 620	Lyn 126 Ⓐ	IC 628		IC 634 N	IC 636		IC 644 Ⓑ		IC 652 Ⓑ		ICE 158 Ⓑ		IC 660		IC 668 Ⓑ			3685 G
	Esbjerg d.	0515 0648	0728 0748	0841	0848 0928	0948	1048	1114 1128	1128	1248	1328	1348	1448	1528	1548	1641	1648	1748	1748	1848	1928	2148	0026
	Bramming 462 d.	0528 0702	0739 0802		0902 0939	1002	1102	1126	1302	1339	1402	1502	1539	1602		1702	1739	1802	1902	1939	2202	0040
	Lunderskov 461 d.	0558 0734	0834		0934	1034	1134		1334		1434	1534		1634		1734		1834	1934		2234	0113
	Kolding a.	0607 0745	0811 0845	0921	0945 1011	1045	1145	1158 1211	1345	1411	1445	1545	1611	1645	1721	1745	1811	1845	1945	2011	2245	0124
	Fredericia a.	0622 0801	0825 0901	0934	1001 1025	1101	1201	1210 1225	1401	1425	1501	1601	1625	1701	1734	1801	1825	1901	2001	2025	2301	0137
	Køvenhavn 450 ... a.	0948	1148	1238	1348			1548		1748		1948	2038v		2148		2348			0700

E – 🚂 1, 2 cl. and ⭤ 2 cl. København - Esbjerg.
G – 🚂 1, 2 cl. and ⭤ 2 cl. Esbjerg - København; ⊡ Esbjerg - Fredericia.
N – NORDPILEN – ⊡ and ⲟ Aalborg - Esbjerg and v.v.

n – Depart 0744 on ⑦.
t – Also calls at Høje Taastrup (0816) and Odense (1029).
v – Also calls at Odense (1811) and Høje Taastrup (2025).

ADDITIONAL TRAINS: Fredericia - Esbjerg at 0527ⵝ, 0600Ⓐ, 1144ⵝ, 1544, 2044⑤⑥⑦, 2244Ⓒ; Esbjerg - Fredericia at 0542Ⓐ, 0635Ⓐ, 1148ⵝ, 1818⑦, 1948Ⓑ, 2048Ⓒ, 2248Ⓒ.

Table 460   KØBENHAVN - RØDBY - PUTTGARDEN - (HAMBURG)

1,2 class except where shown

km		2221	305 K	EC 189	2223	2229	EC 187	2233	2237	4239 ⵝ	2241	EC 185 ⲟ	2245	2249	2253	4253 Ⓐ	EC 183 Ⓒ	2255 Ⓐ	4257	4261		2261	181 ⲟ N	2265	2269
0	**København H.** d.	0641	0720	0730	0741	0841	0920	0941	1041	...	1141	1230	1241	1341	1441	1456	1520	1541	1556	1620	...	1641	1730	1741	1841
19	Høje Taastrup d.	0656	0734	0743	0756	0856	0934	0956	1056	...	1156	1243	1256	1356	1456	1512	1534	1556	1612	1635	...	1656	1743	1756	1856
31	Roskilde d.	0706			0806	0906		1006	1106		1206		1306	1406	1506	1525		1606	1625			1706		1806	1906
64	Ringsted 450 d.	0726			0826	0926		1026	1126		1226		1326	1426	1526			1626				1726		1826	1926
91	Naestved d.	0745	0812	0820	0845	0945	1012	1045	1145		1245	1320	1345	1445	1545	1606	1612	1645	1703	1715		1745	1820	1845	1945
118	Vordingborg d.	0806						1030c	1010		1305c		1405	1505c	1605			1705e	1723	1733			1910b		2005
147	Nykøbing a.	0840	0850	0900	0940c	1044	1051	1133c	1233		1333c	1400	1434	1533c	1633		1651	1733e	1749	1756		1842	1900	1941b	2033
147	Nykøbing d.		0852	0901			1052			1248		1401	1434	1537c			1652		1757			1846	1901		
170	Gedser a.		0910									1455													
170	Gedser ▲ d.		0925									1525													
268	Warnemünde ▲ a.		1120									1720													
281	Rostock 669 a.		1221									1759													
183	Rødby a.			0925			1115			1318		1425			1607c		1715		1820			1911	1925		
183	Rødby ▲ d.						1130			1330					1630c		1730		1830						
202	Puttgarden ▲ a.			1035			1235			1435		1535			1735c		1835		1935			2035	2035		
291	*Lübeck 665* ... a.			1148			1348					1642					1946						2137		
353	*Hamburg Hbf 665* . a.			1225			1429					1722					2027						2215		

	483 M	2273	2277	232 A		2291	309 O	2293	2295			4204 ⵝ	4214 Ⓐ	4206 Ⓒ	4212 Ⓐ	4218 ⵝ	233	308 Ⓞ	308 Ⓞ	2210	482 L
København H. d.	1905	1941	2041	2105		2141	2230	2241	2341		*Hamburg Hbf 665* .... d.							0245			0405
Høje Taastrup ...... d.	1922	1956	2056	2122		2156	2245	2256	2356		*Lübeck 665* .... d.							0332			0445
Roskilde d.		2006	2106			2206		2306	0006		Puttgarden ▲ .... d.	*0305*		*0505*				0505			0605
Ringsted 450 d.		2026	2126			2226	2315	2326	0026		Rødby ▲ .... a.	*0400*		*0600*				0600			0700
Naestved d.	2004	2045	2145	2204		2244	2331	2345	0045		Rødby d.	0430						0622			0726
Vordingborg d.		2107b	2205					0010	0105		*Rostock 669* .... d.							0231	0231		
Nykøbing a.	2047	2133b	2233	2244			0017	0037c			Warnemünde ▲ .. d.							0330	0330		
Nykøbing d.	2048			2245			0018				Gedser ▲ ...... d.							0530	0530		
Gedser a.							0036				Gedser d.							0635	0635		
Gedser ▲ d.							0125				Nykøbing a.							0649s	0654	0654		0749
Warnemünde ▲ a.							0320				Nykøbing d.	0454	0553		0600	0627		0655	0655	0730	0750
Rostock 669 ... a.							0422				Vordingborg d.	0519	0619	0621	0626	0650		0715	0715	0730	
Rødby a.	2111			2308							Naestved d.	0539		0638	0646	0709	0726s	0733	0733	0751	0827
Rødby ▲ d.	2130			2330							Ringsted 450 d.	0558	0650	0656	0706	0728				0812	
Puttgarden ▲ a.	2235			0035							Roskilde d.	0616	0707	0715	0727	0746		0808		0830	
Lübeck 665 ... a.	2358			0210							Høje Taastrup d.	0625	0715	0722	0736	0757	0809	0816	0814	0839	0909
Hamburg Hbf 665 ... a.	0040			0300							**København H.** a.	0641	0732	0737	0754	0813	0825	0833	0830	0855	0925

	2212	2216	4230 ⵝ	5340 T	2220	EC 180 ⲟ	2224	2228	EC 182 ⲟ	2232	2234	4244 Ⓐ	4242	2244	EC 184 ⲟ	2250	2252	EC 186 ⲟ	2256	2260	304 N	188 ⲟ	2268	2272
Hamburg Hbf 665 d.						0719			0919						1326			1519				1826		
Lübeck 665 .... d.						0758			0957						1402			1557				1902		
Puttgarden ▲ .. d.			*0805*			0905			1105			*1305*			1505	*1505c*		1705		*1805r*		2005		
Rødby ▲ ...... d.			*0900*						1200			*1400*			1600	*1600c*		1800		*1900r*				2225
Rødby d.			*0923*			1005			1215			*1424*			1605	1617c		1815		1921r		2105		
Rostock 669 .. d.				0617									*1128*							1728				
Warnemünde ▲ .. d.				0700									*1200*							1800				
Gedser ▲ ...... d.				0900									*1400*							2000				
Gedser d.				0935									*1440*							2040				
Nykøbing d.	0800c	0900	0949	0953	1033			1241			1450	1500	1633	1650c		1841		1949r	2058	2133		2300	
Vordingborg d.	0830c	0900			1000c	1034	1102 1200c	1042 1402b		1502	1602b	1634	1700	1800b	1842	1900	2002b	2130	2100	2134	2202r	2302	
Naestved d.	0851	0900			1030c		1131 1231c		1331 1431b	1531	1631b		1730	1830b	1921	1951	2031b	2130		2230r	2331	
Ringsted 450 d.	0912	0951			1051 1116s	1151	1251	1328	1351	1451	1551	1651	1716s	1851	1926	1951	2051	2152	2216s	2251	2351	
Roskilde d.	0930	1030			1112		1212	1312		1412	1512		1612	1712		1812	1912	2012	2112		2312	0012	
Høje Taastrup d.	0939	1039			1130	1139	1230	1330		1430	1530		1630	1730		1830	1930	2030	2130	2230	2330	0030	
København H. a.	0955	1055			1139 1152	1139	1255	1355	1420	1455	1555		1655	1755	1808	1855	1955	2020	2055	2155	2255	2308	2355	0055

A – NORD EXPRESS – 🚂 1, 2 cl. (T2), ⭤ 2 cl. and ⊡ København - Oostende and v.v.; 🚂 1,2 cl. København - Aachen - Paris and v.v.
K – NEPTUN – ⊡ København - Berlin Lichtenberg - Chemnitz.
L – 🚂 1, 2 cl., ⭤ 2 cl., ⊡ and ⲟ München - København (from Innsbruck on ⑥ Jan. 7 - Mar. 25); 🚂 1, 2 cl. and ⭤ 2 cl. Basel - Frankfurt - København.
M – 🚂 1, 2 cl., ⭤ 2 cl., ⊡ and ⲟ København - München (- Innsbruck on ⑤ Jan. 6 - Mar. 24); 🚂 1, 2 cl. and ⭤ 2 cl. København - Frankfurt - Basel.
N – NEPTUN – ⊡ Dresden - Berlin Lichtenberg - København.
O – OSTSEE EXPRESS – 🚂 1, 2 cl., ⭤ 2 cl., ⊡ København - Berlin Lichtenberg and v.v.

T – Daily except ②.
b – Daily except ⑥.
c – Not ⑦ or holidays.
e – ⑦ only.
r – Ⓐ only.
s – Stops to set down passengers only.
▲ – Through trains are conveyed on board train-ferries between Rødby and Puttgarden or between Gedser and Warnemünde. ✗ available on board the ferries.

Table 461 FREDERICIA - FLENSBURG - (HAMBURG)

1,2 class except where shown

km		3303	4312	273	3311	4320	IC917	3317	4324		IC925	275	IC933	3333	4340	4344	IC941	277	4352	IC949	3349	4356	3351	2951
		2	2		2	2		2	2					2	2	2			2		2	2	2	
		Ⓐ	⚒			Ⓐ	⚒					b	⚒			Ⓐ			Ⓑ	Ⓑ	①-④	⑤-⑦	⑤-⑦	N
	København **450** § ... d.	...	...	...	...	...	0552	...	...	...	0752	...	0952	...	...	...	1152	...	...	1352	...	...	...	...
	Århus **450** ... d.	...	...	...	...	...	|	...	...	...	|	0958	|	...	...	...	|	1358	...	|	...	...	...	1636
0	**Fredericia 458** ... d.	...	0634	0725	...	0834	0915	...	0934	...	1115	1125	1315	...	1334	1434	1515	1525	1634	1715	...	1720	...	1740
20	Kolding **458** ... d.	...	0649	0740	...	0849	0929	...	0949	...	1129	1140	1329	...	1349	1449	1529	1540	1649	1729	...	1736	...	1753
33	Lunderskov **458** ... d.	...	0658	0748	...	0858	0937	...	0958	...	1137	1148	1337	...	1358	1458	1537	1548	1658	1737	...	1746	...	|
60	Vojens ... d.	...	0719	0809	...	0919	0957	...	1019	...	1157	1210	1357	...	1419	1519	1557	1608	1719	1757	...	1808	...	1819
95	Tinglev ... a.	0647	0746	0838	0842	0945	1028	1030	1050	...	1229	1238	1428	1430	1450	1546	1629	1639	1751	1828	1830	1836	1839	1848
136	**Sønderborg** ... a.	0727	|	|	0922	|	|	1110	|	...	1310	|	|	1511	|	|	1710	|	|	|	1910	|	1919	|
110	Padborg 🏛 ... a.	...	0758	0852	...	0957	1039	...	1107	...	...	1252	1439	...	1502	1559	...	1652	1803	1839	...	1851	...	1900
121	**Flensburg** 🏛 ... a.	...	0810	0905	...	1010	1105	...	1121	...	...	1305	1451	...	1513	1610	...	1705	1819	1851	...	1903	...	1911
302	*Hamburg Altona* **664** ... a.	...	...	1118	...	...	*1318*	...	...	...	...	1518	*1718*	...	...	...	...	1918	...	...	...	...	...	*2118*

	4360	IC957	4364	4368	3363	IC965	3365	4372	4376	IC973
	2		2	2	2		2	2	2	
	Ⓑ		⑤⑦		⑥	Ⓑ	Ⓑ	⑦	Ⓒ	Ⓑ
København **450** § ... d.	...	1552	...	...	...	1752	...	...	...	1952
Århus **450** ... d.	...	|	...	...	...	|	...	...	...	|
Fredericia 458 ... d.	1834	1915	1934	2034	...	2115	...	2134	2234	2315
Kolding **458** ... d.	1849	1929	1949	2049	...	2129	...	2149	2249	2329
Lunderskov **458** ... d.	1858	1937	1958	2058	...	2137	...	2158	2258	2337
Vojens ... d.	1919	1957	2019	2119	...	2157	...	2219	2326	2357c
Tinglev ... a.	1946	2029	2050	2150	2201	2228	2230	2247	2352	0024c
Sønderborg ... a.	|	2109	|	|	2241	|	2310	|	|	0105c
Padborg 🏛 ... a.	1958	...	2107	2202	...	2239	...	2302	0004	...
Flensburg 🏛 ... a.	2010	...	2119	2213	...	2251	...	2313	...	...
Hamburg Altona **664** ... a.	...	...	...	...	...	...	...	...	...	...

	IC916	4313	4317	3324	IC924	3328	4321	4327	IC932
		2	2	2		2	2	2	
	⚒	⚒		⚒	⚒	⑦			
Hamburg Altona **664** ... d.	...	...	...	...	...	...	...	...	...
Flensburg 🏛 ... d.	...	...	0724	...	0748	...	0826	...	...
Padborg 🏛 ... d.	...	0634	0735	...	0803	...	0837	1000	...
Sønderborg ... d.	0531	|	|	0731	|	0757	|	|	0931
Tinglev ... d.	0613	0649	0746	0811	0813	0837	0852	1010	1013
Vojens ... d.	0641	0719	0819	...	0841	...	0919	...	1041
Lunderskov **458** ... d.	0701	0740	0840	...	0901	...	0940	...	1101
Kolding **458** ... d.	0711	0751	0851	...	0911	...	0951	...	1111
Fredericia 458 ... a.	0725	0805	0905	...	0925	...	1005	...	1125
Århus **450** ... a.	|	...	...	...	|	...	...	...	|
København **450** § ... a.	1048	...	...	...	1248	...	...	...	1448

	4329	2934		3340	IC940	276	4341	IC948	3346	4345	4349	3354	3356	IC956	274	IC964	4361	4365	3372	IC972	IC972	272	3374	4373
	2			2			2		2	2	2	2	2				2	2	2				2	2
		N				d	Ⓑ	Ⓑ	⑥		Ⓑ	⑤t	E	Ⓑ				⑦		⑦	Ⓑ			⑦
Hamburg Altona **664** ... d.	...	*0839*	...	...	...	1039	...	...	...	...	...	...	...	...	1439	...	...	...	...	...	...	1839	...	...
Flensburg 🏛 ... d.	1028	1043	...	...	1148	1244	1324	...	...	1428	1524	...	...	1548	1644	...	1828	1924	...	1948	1948	2044	...	2127
Padborg 🏛 ... d.	1039	1056	...	...	1203	1255	1335	...	...	1439	1535	...	...	1603	1655	...	1839	1935	...	2003	2003	2055	...	2138
Sønderborg ... d.	|	|	...	1131	|	|	|	1331	1331	|	|	1517	1531	|	|	1731	|	|	1931	|	|	|	2115	|
Tinglev ... d.	1050	1107	...	1211	1213	1306	1346	1413	1411	1450	1546	1558	1611	1613	1706	1813	1850	1946	2011	2013	2013	2106	2154	2156
Vojens ... d.	1119	1133	...	...	1241	1333	1419	1441	...	1519	1619	1631	...	1641	1733	1841	1919	2019	...	2041	2041	2133	...	2222
Lunderskov **458** ... d.	1140	|	...	...	1301	1357	1440	1501	...	1540	1640	1650	...	1701	1757	1901	1940	2040	...	2101	2101	2157	...	2242
Kolding **458** ... d.	1151	1203	...	...	1311	1406	1451	1511	...	1551	1651	1700	...	1711	1806	1911	1951	2051	...	2111	2111	2206	...	2252
Fredericia 458 ... a.	1205	1216	...	...	1325	1420	1505	1525	...	1605	1705	1714	...	1725	1820	1925	2005	2105	...	2125	2125	2220	...	2306
Århus **450** ... a.	...	1325	...	...	|	1546	...	|	...	...	...	...	...	|	1946f	|	...	...	...	|	...	...	...	...
København **450** § ... a.	...	...	...	...	1648	...	...	1848	...	...	...	...	...	2048	...	2248	...	...	...	0105	...	...	...	...

E – Daily except ⑤ (also runs Apr. 14, May 12; not Apr. 12, May 11,24).
N – NORDPILEN - (12) and 🍷 Aalborg - Flensburg and v.v. (**IC** train).
b – From Frederikshavn (depart 0638) and Aalborg (depart 0810).
c – Night of ④⑤⑦ only.
d – To Aalborg (arrive 1730) and Frederikshavn (arrive 1905).
f – Arrive 1934 on ⑤⑦.
t – Also Apr. 12, May 11,24; not Apr. 14, May 12.
§ – Reservation obligatory for journeys to or from København.

Table 462 ESBJERG - RIBE - TØNDER

2 class only

km																								
		Ⓐ	Ⓐ		Ⓐ	Ⓒ	Ⓐ	⚒		⚒		⚒		Ⓐ	Ⓐ		Ⓑ	Ⓐ		Ⓐ	⑦			
0	**Esbjerg** ... d.	...	0500	...	0619	0701	0701	0755	0855	0955	1055	1155	1255	1334	1355	1455	1555	1630	1655	1755	1755	1855	2055	2303
16	Bramming **458** ... d.	0455	0515	...	0633	0716	0716	0809	0909	1009	1109	1209	1309	1349	1409	1509	1609	1645	1709	1809	1809	1909	2109	2316
33	Ribe ... d.	0512	0546	...	0655	0734	0734	0830	0930	1030	1130	1230	1330	1409	1430	1530	1630	1703	1730	1830	1830	1930	2131	2335
80	**Tønder** ... a.	0600	0642	...	0745	0821	...	0920	1020	1120	1220	1320	1420	...	1520	1620	1720	...	1820	...	1920	2019	2220	...

	Ⓐ	Ⓐ	Ⓐ	⑥	Ⓐ	Ⓐ		⚒		⚒		⚒	Ⓐ		Ⓐ		Ⓐ	Ⓑ	Ⓐ		⑦			
Tønder ... d.	...	0605	...	...	0650	...	0825	0925	1025	1125	1225	1325	...	1425	1525	1625	...	1725	...	1825	1944	2043	2225	...
Ribe ... d.	0544	0655	0714	0740	0740	0812	0912	1012	1112	1212	1312	1412	1437	1512	1612	1712	1737	1812	1837	1912	2035	2132	2312	...
Bramming **458** ... d.	0603	0716	0744	0803	0803	0833	0933	1033	1133	1233	1333	1433	1512	1533	1633	1733	1757	1833	1912	1933	2106	2151	2333	...
Esbjerg ... a.	0617	0730	0757	0816	0816	0846	0946	1046	1146	1246	1346	1446	1525	1546	1646	1746	1811	1846	1925	1946	2119	2204	2346	...

🚌 **connection Tønder - Niebüll:** From Tønder station 0823⚒, 1148Ⓐ, 1230⑥, 1437⑥, 1627Ⓐ, 1926Ⓐ. Buses start from bus station 2 minutes earlier. From Niebüll (station) 0753⚒, 1103Ⓐ, 1138⑥, 1338⚒, 1817Ⓐ. Buses start from bus station 3 minutes earlier. Operated by *Autokraft* (1505). *Timings are subject to confirmation.*

Table 463 KØBENHAVN - HELSINGØR - HELSINGBORG

Local trains 1,2 class

KØBENHAVN - HELSINGØR Journey 55 minutes (46 minutes by departures at 03, 23, and 43 minutes past the hour). *46* km.

Ⓐ : 0523, 0543, 0603, 0623, 0643 then every 20 minutes until 1823, 1831, 1851, 1911 then every 20 minutes until 0031.
⑥ : 0551, 0611, 0631, 0651 then every 20 minutes until 0811, 0843, 0903, 0923, 0943 then every 20 minutes until 1443, 1451, 1511, 1531 then every 20 minutes until 0031.
⑦ : 0651, 0711, 0731, 0751 then every 20 minutes until 0031.

HELSINGØR - KØBENHAVN Journey 54 minutes (45 minutes by departures at 18, 38 and 58 minutes past the hour). *46* km.

Ⓐ : 0441, 0501, 0521, 0541, 0558, 0618, 0638, 0658 then every 20 minutes until 1818, 1838, 1901, 1921 then every 20 minutes until 2341.
⑥ : 0441, 0501, 0521, 0541 then every 20 minutes until 0821, 0841, 0858, 0918, 0938 then every 20 minutes until 1458, 1521, 1541, 1601 then every 20 minutes until 2341.
⑦ : 0541, 0601, 0621, 0641 then every 20 minutes until 2341.

⛴ **HELSINGØR - HELSINGBORG**: Sailings every 20 - 40 minutes – for timings see Table **1219**. Sailing time approximately 25 minutes.

Table 464 BRANCH LINES IN DENMARK

2 class only

ÅRHUS - GRENAA *69 km* Journey 80-90 minutes. DSB (73).
Århus depart: 0507Ⓐ, 0610⑥, 0710Ⓑ, 0810⚒, 1010, 1210, 1410, 1610, 1710Ⓐ, 1810, 2010, 2210⑦, 2325Ⓐ, 0025①⑦.
Grenaa depart: 0459Ⓐ, 0631Ⓐ, 0640⑦, 0740⑥, 0837Ⓑ, 0940⑥, 1037Ⓐ, 1140, 1340, 1540, 1737, 1838Ⓐ, 1940, 2140, 2340⑦.

HJØRRING - HIRTSHALS Journey 25 minutes. Hjørring Privatbaner private railway (77).
Hjørring depart: 0535Ⓐ, 0613⚒, 0643Ⓐ, 0713, 0743Ⓐ, 0813, 0913, 1013, 1113, 1213, 1313, 1343Ⓐ, 1413, 1443Ⓐ, 1513, 1543Ⓐ, 1613, 1643Ⓐ, 1713, 1813, 1913, 2013, 2133, 2243.
Hirtshals depart: 0615Ⓐ, 0645⚒, 0712Ⓐ, 0745, 0815Ⓐ, 0845, 0945, 1045, 1145, 1245, 1345, 1415Ⓐ, 1445, 1515Ⓐ, 1545, 1615Ⓐ, 1645, 1715Ⓐ, 1745, 1845, 1945, 2045, 2200, 2335.
Certain journeys are extended to/from Hirtshals Havn in connection with sailings.

NYKØBING - NAKSKOV Journey 45 minutes. Lollandsbanen private railway (54).
Nykøbing depart: 0555Ⓐ, 0656Ⓐ, 0700Ⓒ, 0727Ⓐ, 0800⚒, 0905, 1000⚒, 1100, 1200Ⓐ, 1210⑥, 1253⑦, 1300⑥, 1310Ⓐ, 1405Ⓒ, 1410Ⓐ, 1500Ⓒ, 1510Ⓐ, 1540Ⓐ, 1610Ⓐ, 1700Ⓒ, 1710Ⓐ, 1740Ⓐ, 1746⑦, 1800⚒, 1905⑥, 1910Ⓐ, 1913⑦, 2000Ⓑ, 2100, 2200Ⓑ, 2250, 0028.
Nakskov depart: 0500Ⓐ, 0540Ⓐ, 0600, 0655Ⓐ, 0700⑥, 0728Ⓐ, 0800, 0905⚒, 1000, 1100⚒, 1200Ⓑ, 1210⑥, 1300⑥, 1310Ⓐ, 1405Ⓒ, 1410Ⓐ, 1437Ⓐ, 1510Ⓐ, 1513⑦, 1600Ⓒ, 1610Ⓐ, 1637Ⓐ, 1700Ⓒ, 1710Ⓐ, 1800, 1910Ⓐ, 1913⑦, 2000, 2100Ⓑ, 2200, 2338.

ODENSE - SVENDBORG *48 km* Journey 60 minutes. DSB (61).
Odense depart: 0515Ⓐ, 0615, 0630Ⓐ, 0715⚒, 0815, 0915⚒, 1015, 1115⚒, 1215, 1315, 1415, 1515, 1553Ⓐ, 1615Ⓑ, 1715, 1815Ⓑ, 1915, 2015⑤⑦, 2115, 2215⑦, 2315.
Svendborg depart: 0016, 0453Ⓐ, 0529Ⓐ, 0629⚒, 0645Ⓐ, 0729, 0829⚒, 0929, 1029⚒, 1129, 1229⚒, 1329, 1429, 1529, 1629, 1729Ⓑ, 1829, 1929Ⓑ, 2029, 2129⑤⑦, 2229, 2329⑦.

260 Ⓐ – Mondays to Fridays, except holidays Ⓑ – Daily except Saturdays ⚒ – Daily except Sundays and holidays 03

SWEDEN

SEE MAP PAGE 256

Operator: Statens Järnvägar (SJ). The regional transport authorities have responsibility for some local lines.

Services: Trains convey first and second classes of accommodation, unless otherwise shown. Sleeping cars (⬛) are of two basic types with a range of supplements: older cars (those without showers) have one berth in first class, two or three berths in second class. Newer cars either have compartments with shower and WC (one or two berth, first class only) or have shower and WC available in the car (one or two berths in first class, two berths in second class); these normally run as *Intercity Natt*, except on ⑤⑥ when the two-berth compartments are normally second class. Couchette cars (⬛) have six berths and are second class only.

Timings: Valid January 9 - June 11, 1995.
Services may be modified during **holiday periods** (particularly Apr. 14-17, 30, May 12, 25, June 4) and passengers are advised to check locally before travelling.

Reservations: Seat reservation is **compulsory** for many fast trains, as shown in the tables, except for certain local journeys. Reserved seats are not labelled and, if occupied, must be claimed by presenting the seat ticket on the train.

Supplements: Special supplements are payable for travel on the *X2000* high speed trains, and in first class this includes a tray meal, beverages and newspaper.

Table 465 STOCKHOLM - KØBENHAVN and MALMÖ

1,2 class

km		355 2	213	357	893 R	IC 17 R	3707	217	3647	IC 21 R	X2000 503 R	X2000 523 R	IN 25 R	IN25 285 R	365	IN 29 R	367	IN 33 R	IN33 289 R	X2000 535 R	3751 2	3755 2	IC 37 R	3767 2
			Ⓐ	✕	◆	✕	⑥	⑥	Ⓐ 2	✕	✕K	ⒶJ	✕	✕		✕		✕	✕	✕	Ⓐ	Ⓐ	✕	Ⓑ
0	Stockholm Central .... d.	...	...	...	...	...	...	...	...	0618	0718	0718	0812	0812	...	1012	...	1212	1212	1300	...	...	1412	...
15	S'holm Syd Flemingsberg ‡. d.	...	...	...	...	...	...	...	...	0629	0728	0728	0823	0823	...	1023	...	1223	1223	1310	...	...	1423	...
35	Södertälje Syd ‡ .... d.	...	...	...	...	...	...	...	...	0642	0740	0740	0836	0836	...	1036	...	1236	1236	1322	...	...	1436	...
	Flen 469 472 .... d.	...	...	...	...	...	...	...	...						...		...				...	...		1605a
	Katrineholm 469 472 ..... d.	...	...	...	...	...	...	...	...						...		...				...	...		1622
104	Nyköping .... d.	...	...	...	...	...	...	...	...	0724			0923	0923	...	1123	...	1323	1323		...	...	1523		
163	Norrköping 472 .... a.	...	...	...	...	...	...	...	...	0803	0841	0841s	1003	1003	...	1203	...	1403	1403	1428s	...	...	1603	1648
163	Norrköping 472 .... d.	...	...	...	0606	0606	...	...	...	0806	0843		1006	1006	...	1206	...	1406	1406		...	...	1606	1652
209	Linköping 472 .... d.	...	...	...	0638	0638	...	...	0705	0838	0908	0906	1038	1038	...	1238	...	1438	1438	1455	1540	1638	1722
242	Mjölby 472 .... d.	...	...	0625	0700	0700	...	...	0730	0900			1100	1100	...	1300	...	1500	1500		1520	1600	1700	1742
278	Tranås .... d.	...	...	0647	0723	0723	...	...	0757	0921			1121	1121	...	1321	...	1521	1521		...	1623	1721	1805
330	Nässjö .... a.	...	...	0720	0758	0758	...	...	0835	0956	1011		1156	1156	...	1356	...	1556	1556		...	1700	1756	1840
330	Nässjö .... d.	...	...	0725	0805	...	0805	...	1000	1013		1200	1200	...	1400	...	1600	1600		...	1800		1840
359	Sävsjö .... d.	...	...		0821		0821	...	1016			1216	1216	...	1416	...	1616	1616		...	1816	...	
417	Alvesta .... a.	...	...		0815	0857		0857	...	1052	1100		1252	1252	...	1452	...	1652	1652		...	1852	...	
417	Alvesta .... d.	0545	0653		0820	0900		0900	...	1105	1102		1255	1305	...	1455	...	1655	1655		...	1855	...	
464	Älmhult .... d.	0607	0715		0846	0922		0922	...	1128			1318		...	1518	...	1718	1718		...	1918	...	
515	Hässleholm .... a.	0636	0743		0920	0948		0948	...	1157	1142s		1347	1352	...	1547	...	1747	1747		...	1947	...	
515	Hässleholm 468 .... d.	0650	0745	0757	0924	0950		0950	1000	1157	1142s	1205	1350	1350	1415	1500	1600	1750	1758		...	1950	2005
594	Helsingborg .... a.	0747		0852					1054			1308		1448	1520	1655		1855		...		2100
598	Helsingør ▲ 1219 .... a.			0934r				1134r			1355r		1555		1734r		1955		...		2215r
644	København H. 463 .... a.			1043				1243v			1503v		1658		1843v		2058		...		2335
	Hamburg Hbf. 665 .... a.																				
565	Eslöv 468 § .... a.							1227												...		
582	Lund 468 § .... a.		0822		1005	1025		1025	1243	1222		1425			1625		1825		...	2030	
599	Malmö 468 .... a.		0835		1020	1040		1040	1256	1235		1440			1640		1840		...	2045	

		X2000 219 ⑤	X2000 507 R ⒶK	541 R Ⓑ	2343 Ⓑ	IC 41 R ⑥	221 R Ⓑ	IC 13 R F	IC 15 R ⑦K	3779 2	X2000 509 R ⑦K	245 R ⑦J	243 R Ⓐ	3781 2 R Ⓐ	X2000 543 R Ⓑ	IC 45 R Ⓐ		247 Ⓐ	253 Ⓐ	255 Ⓑ	293 R ◆	293 R M	683 R Ⓑ	205 R Ⓑ	355 R
			✕			✕	✕	✕	✕		✕		🍴		✕	✕		Ⓐ	Ⓐ	Ⓑ				Ⓑ	Ⓑ
	Stockholm Central .... d.	1512	1554	1630		1618	1618	1642	1642	...	1718	...	1712	...	1748	1812		1954	2124	2218	2224	2224	2224	2312	2312
	S'holm Syd Flemingsberg ‡.. d.	1523	1604	1640		1629	1629	1653	1653	...	1729	...	1723	...	1758	1823		2005	2135	2229	2236	2236	2236	2325	2325
	Södertälje Syd ‡ .... d.	1536		1652		1642	1642			...	...	...	1736	...	1810	1836		2018	2148	2242	2250	2250	2250	2340	2340
	Flen 469 472 .... d.									1830									2224		2327	2327	0022	0022
	Katrineholm 469 472 .... d.																		2238		2340	2340	0040	0040
	Nyköping .... d.	1618				1725	1725			...	...	...	1818	...		1923		2107		2325				
	Norrköping 472 .... a.	1705		1753		1805	1805	1817	1817	1858	...	1905		1911s	2003		2146	2306	0005			0010		0110	0110
	Norrköping 472 .... d.	1708	1720u	1755		1808	1808	1820	1820	1900	1843u		1917		2006		2202	2308	0008f	0015			0115	0115
	Linköping 472 .... a.	1738	1745u	1820		1840	1840	1850	1850	1930	1908u		1945	1938	2038		2232	2340	0040f	0050			0150	0150
	Mjölby 472 .... a.	1757			1854	1900	1859			1948					2100		2252	2359	0059f				
	Tranås .... a.			1917	1921		1928	1928							2121								
	Nässjö .... a.		1930	1954	1956		2000	2000						2158						0202		0300	0300
	Nässjö .... d.				2002		2002	2002		2010										0202		0302	0302
	Sävsjö .... d.				2018		2018	2018		2026												
	Alvesta .... a.		1935s		2053		2053	2053		2058	2100								0300		0412	0412
	Alvesta .... d.				2056		2056	2103		2100	2103								0305		0412	0545
	Älmhult .... d.				2118		2118	2126			2126										
	Hässleholm .... a.		2017s		2147		2147	2155		2140s	2155								0355		0512	0636
	Hässleholm 468 .... d.				2150		2150	2155		2142s	2155	2203							0400		0545	0650
	Helsingborg .... a.											2303							0455	0455		0747
	Helsingør ▲ 1219 .... a.																		0555	0555		
	København H. 463 .... a.																		0700	0700		
	Hamburg Hbf. 665 .... a.																				
	Eslöv 468 § .... a.									2227											
	Lund 468 § .... a.		2055			2225		2225	2242		2220	2242									0652	0630
	Malmö 468 .... a.		2108			2240		2240	2255		2233	2255									0706	0645

◆ – **NOTES** (LISTED BY TRAIN NUMBER)

205 – ⑧: ⬛ 1,2 cl., ⬛ 2 cl. and 🍴 Stockholm - Malmö.
293 – ⬛ 1,2 cl., ⬛ 2 cl. and 🍴 Stockholm - København. Conveys on ⑧, ⬛ 1,2 cl. Stockholm - Kalmar (also ⬛ 2 cl. on ①).
893 – 🍴 Hallsberg - Malmö; ⬛ 1,2 cl. and ⬛ 2 cl. Storlien - Östersund - Malmö; 🍴 Mjölby - Malmö.

F – Ⓐ (also ⑦ Jan. 15 - Mar. 5).
J – Runs Jan. 9 - Mar. 5.
K – Runs Mar. 6 - June 11.
M – ⑥: ⬛ 1,2 cl. and ⬛ 2 cl. Stockholm - Malmö.
R – ⑧: ⬛ 1 cl. and ⬛ 2 cl. Stockholm - Helsingborg (also ⬛ 1,2 cl. on ⑤).

a – Ⓐ only.
f – Night of ⑤ only.
r – By ⛴ Helsingborg - Helsingør (Scandlines, Table 1219).
s – Stops to set down only.
u – Stops to pick up only.
v – Arrive 12 minutes later on Ⓒ.
▲ – Through trains are conveyed aboard train ferries between Helsingborg and Helsingør.
‡ – Most trains on this table do not convey passengers for local journeys between Stockholm and Södertälje Syd. Local trains run every 30 minutes Stockholm Central - Södertälje Hamn - Södertälje Centrum and v.v. (journey 42 mins).
🚍 Södertälje Syd - Södertälje Centrum runs every 30 minutes.
§ – Stops to set down only. Frequent local trains run between Lund and Malmö.
X2000 - High speed train. Special supplement payable.

Göta Canal

Four day cruises on the Göta Canal operate between May and September from Stockholm to Göteborg or v.v.
There are also special six day cruises during July.
For further details contact the Göta Kanal Rederiaktiebolaget, P.O. Box 272, S-40124 Göteborg, Sweden.
☎ +46 31 806315 Fax +46 31 158311.

Table 465   KØBENHAVN and MALMÖ - STOCKHOLM   1,2 class

	216	218	IC 20	3704 2	520 X2000	IC 22	222	2308	522 X2000	524 X2000	IC 26	26 X2000	356	526 X2000	502	358	IC 30	504 X2000	360	IC 34	362	IN 38	IN288 IN38	538 X2000
	Ⓐ	Ⓐ	Ⓐ	Ⓐ			⑦		⑥		Ⓒ	Ⓐ		ⒶJ	ⒶK			⑥K						
Malmö 468 .... d.									0520				0627		0714	0733				0917			1117	
Lund 468 § .... d.									0533				0640		0728	0745				0930			1130	
Eslöv 468 § .... d.																								
Hamburg Hbf. 665 .... d.																	0651v		0851v				0948	
København H. 463 .... d.														0610r			0810r		1010r				1032	
Helsingør ▲ 1219 .... d.														0652					0900		1055		1130	
Helsingborg .... d.											0550													
Hässleholm 468 .... a.									0606			0645		0715u	0750	0803	0820u	0955	1006	1153	1206		1219s	
Hässleholm .... d.									0608					0715u		0805	0820u		1008		1208			
Älmhult .... d.									0636							0833			1036		1236			
Alvesta .... a.									0700				0755		0857	0900			1100		1300		1310	
Alvesta .... d.									0703				0757		0903	0902			1103		1318		1318	
Sävsjö .... d.									0735							0935			1135					
Nässjö .... a.									0755			⑥			0956				2⑥	1156		1405	1405	
Nässjö .... d.			0505		0600		0622	0640	0715	0802		0802			1000			1108	1200			1408	1408	
Tranås .... d.			0539		0632		0656			0833		0833			1032			1140	1232			1440	1440	
Mjölby 472 .... d.		0455	0555	0605	0613	0700	0700	0720	0810u	0900	0900	0915			1100			1210	1300			1505	1505	
Linköping 472 .... d.		0517	0615	0635	0630u	0722	0722	0755	0745	0827	0922	0922	0935	0950	0950			1122	1055	1227	1322	1525	1525	1605
Norrköping 472 .... a.		0545	0642	0703		0750	0750	0823	0808	0850	0950	0950	1003		1013			1150	1118	1257	1350	1552	1552	
Norrköping 472 .... d.	0527	0548	0645		0655u	0753		0825	0810	0852	0953	0953	1020	1015u	1015			1153	1120	1300	1353	1555	1555	1630u
Nyköping .... d.	0608		0726			0834	0834				1034	1034						1234			1434	1636	1636	
Katrineholm 469 472 .... d.		0617				0855					1050							1328						
Flen 469 472 .... d.		0630				0908					1103													
Södertälje Syd ‡ .... a.	0650	0708	0807		0754	0915	0915		0910	0952	1121	1121		1315				1515				1717	1717	1729
S'holm Syd Flemingsberg ‡ .. a.	0703	0722	0821		0805	0928	0928		0922	1004	1134	1134	1128	1128				1328	1233	1528		1731	1731	1740
Stockholm Central .... a.	0717	0735	0835		0817	0941	0941		0935	1017	1147	1147	1141	1141				1341	1247	1541		1747	1747	1753

	3648 2	3762	220	364	IC 42	224	352	IN 46	IN284 IN46	376	506 X2000	368	250	IC 50	508 X2000	894	370	252	372 2	372 206	682 206	292	292	292
	Ⓐ	W	⑤		⑦			Ⓐ	ⒶK		⑦J		⑦K	◆	Ⓑ	Ⓑ	Ⓑ			R	◆	M	◆	◆
Malmö 468 .... d.					1320		1500			1635		1655	1720	1730	1740		1922			2300	2247			
Lund 468 § .... d.					1333		1513			1647		1708	1733	1743	1753		1935			2315	2300			
Eslöv 468 § .... d.							1525					1720												
Hamburg Hbf. 665 .... d.																								
København H. 463 .... d.			1051v		1203v			1315t	1351x		1451x					1651v		1931		2315n	2315n			
Helsingør ▲ 1219 .... d.			1210r		1330r			1355	1510r		1610r					1810r		2050r		2355n	2355n			
Helsingborg .... d.			1248		1428			1450	1602		1700					1900		2205	2205	0100	0100			
Hässleholm 468 .... a.			1350	1406		1528	1555	1553	1659	1722u	1754	1818u	1827	1958	2008	2306	2306	2352	2352	0153				
Hässleholm .... d.				1408		1608	1608	1722u		1800	1808	1818u	1830	2010	2310	2310	2355	0156						
Älmhult .... d.				1436		1636	1636			1828	1836	1858	2038	2337	2337									
Alvesta .... a.				1500		1700	1700	1802		1852	1900	1858	1924	2103	0005	0005	0058	0250						
Alvesta .... d.				1503		1703	1703	1804		1855	1903	1900	1927	2107f	0125	0125	0300							
Sävsjö .... d.				1535		1735	1735			1958	2137f													
Nässjö .... a.				1556		2Ⓐ	1756	1756	1851	1944	1952	1947	2015	2158f				0358						
Nässjö .... d.	1453			1600		1712	1800	1800	1853	1957	1949	2019					0410							
Tranås .... d.	1527			1632		1745	1832	1832		2028	2051													
Mjölby 472 .... d.	1555		1610	1700	1755	1810	1900	1900		2052	2115					0350	0345	0527						
Linköping 472 .... d.	1615	1620	1630	1722	1815	1830	1922	1922	2000	2113	2055					0424	0424	0556						
Norrköping 472 .... a.	1641	1647	1657	1750	1842	1857	1950	1950	2023	2140	2118					0428	0424	0600						
Norrköping 472 .... d.	1650	1700		1753	1845	1900	1953	1953	2025	2143	2120													
Nyköping .... d.		1747		1834	1925		2034	2034		2212														
Katrineholm 469 472 .... d.		1720				1928																		
Flen 469 472 .... d.		1733																						
Södertälje Syd ‡ .... a.		1810	1833		1915	2006		2115	2115	2127			2301	2222					0614	0610	0720	0720	0720	
S'holm Syd Flemingsberg ‡ .. a.		1822	1846		1928	2020		2128	2128	2139			2315	2234					0632	0625	0734	0734	0734	
Stockholm Central .... a.		1835	1859		1941	2035		2141	2141	2153			2329	2247					0647	0641	0747	0747	0747	

◆ – NOTES (LISTED BY TRAIN NUMBER)

206 – 🛏 1,2 cl. and ━ 2 cl. Malmö - Stockholm.
292 – 🛏 1,2 cl., ━ 2 cl. and 🍴 København - Stockholm. Conveys on ⑧, 🛏 1,2 cl. Kalmar - Stockholm (also ━ 2 cl. on ⑦).
894 – 🍴 Malmö - Hallsberg; 🛏 1,2 cl. and ━ 2 cl. Malmö - Östersund - Storlien; ☕ Malmö - Mjölby.

J – Runs Jan. 9 - Mar. 5.
K – Runs Mar. 6 - June 11.
M – ⑥: 🛏 1,2 cl. and ━ 2 cl. Malmö - Stockholm.
R – ⑧: 🛏 1,2 cl. and ━ 2 cl. Helsingborg - Stockholm.
W – ①②③④ only.
f – ⑤ only.

n – From May 28 depart København 2308, Helsingør 2349.
r – By ⛴ Helsingør - Helsingborg (Scandlines. Table 1219).
s – Stops to set down only.
t – Depart 1307 from May 28.
u – Stops to pick up only.
v – Depart 12 minutes later on Ⓐ.
x – Depart 12 minutes later on ✕.
▲ – Through trains are conveyed aboard train ferries between Helsingør and Helsingborg.
‡ – Most trains on this table do not convey passengers for local journeys between Södertälje Syd and Stockholm. Local trains run every 30 minutes Stockholm Central - Södertälje Hamn - Södertälje Centrum and v.v. (journey 42 mins).
⛔ Södertälje Syd - Södertälje Centrum runs every 30 minutes.
§ – Stops to pick up only. Frequent local trains run between Malmö and Lund.
X2000 – High speed train. Special supplement payable.

Table 465a   MALMÖ - YSTAD   MLT (107)

Journey 55-60 minutes. 2 class only. 65 km.
From Malmö: 0627Ⓐ, 0806Ⓐ, 0844⑥, 0937⑥, 1051⑥, 1109Ⓐ, 1145Ⓐ, 1307✕, 1429⑥, 1515⑥, 1620Ⓐ, 1720⑧, 1849✕, 1952⑦, 2037Ⓐ, 2235.
From Ystad: 0520Ⓐ, 0639Ⓐ, 0752, 0949⑥, 0955Ⓐ, 1054⑧, 1155⑥, 1251⑧, 1534, 1745✕, 1834⑥, 2056.

Table 465b   FALKÖPING - NÄSSJÖ   2 class only

km		Ⓐ	Ⓐ	⑥	Ⓐ	⑥	Ⓐ	Ⓐ			Ⓐ	Ⓐ	Ⓐ		Ⓐ	Ⓐ	Ⓐ		Ⓐ	⑥X	Ⓐ		⑥	⑦
0	Skövde 469 .... d.		0601	0610	0642	0730	0755	0800			1000	1120	1200		1400	1520		1600	1720	1800	1912	1920		
30	Falköping 469 .... d.		0630	0630	0703	0750	0815	0820		0900	1026	1140	1227		1424	1540		1623	1749	1823	1937	1940	2040	2140	2150
100	Jönköping .... d.	0602	0725	0725	0758	0849	0918	0918	0948	1008	1116	1230	1318	1412	1514	1631	1649	1717	1845	1916	2008	2031	2135	2235	2257
143	Nässjö 465 .... a.	0635	0757	0757	0835	0923	0952	0952	1030	1047	1150	1318	1352	1453	1551	1704	1727	1753	1923	1953		2114	2208	2322	2310

	Ⓐ	ⒶX	Ⓐ	⑥	Ⓐ	⑥X		Ⓐ			Ⓐ		Ⓐ				Ⓐ					⑥	⑦	Ⓐ
Nässjö 465 .... d.	0443		0640	0646	0700		0810	1006		1105	1206		1254	1410	1500	1537	1606	1712		1806	1859	2006	2006	2215
Jönköping .... d.	0518	0615	0632	0718	0725	0740	0800	0847	1041		1142	1241	1332	1445	1542	1610	1645	1750		1842	1935	2041	2041	2250
Falköping 469 .... a.	0607	0654u	0722		0811	0835	0835u	0933	1130			1330	1415	1530	1638		1730	1840		1930	2028	2127	2127	2315
Skövde 469 .... a.	0635		0743			0900		0955	1150			1350	1458	1550	1700		1750	1915		1950	2050	2200	2205	

X – X2000 high speed train to/from Stockholm (1,2 class) – see Table 469. Special supplement payable.   u – Stops to pick up only.

Table 466 — GÖTEBORG - KØBENHAVN and MALMÖ
1,2 class

km		IN 381 R W Ⓐ	IN 1431 Ⓐ	381 X Ⓐ	1401 Ⓐ	671 ✕	1403 Ⓐ	1435 2	1405 2 Ⓒ Ⓐ	IC 71 R Ⓐ ✕	1407 2	1409 2	IC 605 R ✕ ✕	1411 2	IC 603 R ✕	1413 2	1415 2	IC 607 R ✕	1437 2 ✕
0	Oslo Sentral 480 d.	2137		2137															
0	Göteborg d.	0220		0220						0610			0710		0810			1030	
29	Kungsbacka d.									0628			0728		0828			1046	
78	Varberg d.									0705			0810		0905			1121	
109	Falkenberg d.									0723			0829		0923			1139	
152	Halmstad a.	0400		0400	0533					0757			0903		0958			1215	
	Hässleholm 465 a.									0858									
177	Laholm d.				0554								0924		1019			1245	
192	Båstad d.				0608								0938		1039			1258	
218	Ängelholm d.				0632								0959		1101			1319	
245	Helsingborg 1219 a.	0510		0510	0649								1015		1118			1335	
245	Helsingborg 1219 d.	0510	0538	0610	0632	0658	0710r	0708	0750	0805		0905	1005	1020	1030r	1105	1121	1130r	1205	1305	1340	1350r	1405
249	Helsingør 1219 ▲ d.	0555					0735r							1055r			1155r			1415r
249	Helsingør 463 d.						0758						1118c				1218e			1438f
293	København H. 463 a.	0700					0843						1203c				1303e			1523f
301	Lund a.		0616	0652	0712	0740		0748	0828	0842	0937	0941	1041	1106	1141	1200	1241	1341	1420	1441
317	Malmö a.		0632	0706	0728	0753		0800	0844	0855	0950	0953	1053	1120	1153	1217	1253	1353	1433	1453

	1417 2	IN 393 R	693 R	1419 2	IC 609 R Ⓐ	1433 2 ⑥	1421 2 ⑥	1423 2 ⑥	IN 385 R	685 R	1425 2	IC 73 R ⑥	1427 2	IC 679 R Ⓐ	1439 2	IC 619 R ⑧	667 ⑧	1429 2
Oslo Sentral 480 d.								1015b	1015b									
Göteborg d.		1227	1227		1325				1525	1525		1710		1825		1925	2125	
Kungsbacka d.					1343				1543	1543		1728		1843		1943	2143	
Varberg d.		1317	1317		1423				1619	1619		1803		1918		2026	2222	
Falkenberg d.					1441				1637	1637		1820		1940		2044	2240	
Halmstad d.		1403	1403		1515				1710	1710		1850		2013		2118	2310	
Hässleholm 465 a.												1946						
Laholm d.					1542				1731	1731				2035		2138		
Båstad d.					1555									2048		2152		
Ängelholm d.		1453	1453		1621				1802	1802				2109		2212		
Helsingborg a.		1510	1510		1638				1818	1818				2125		2228		
Helsingborg 1219 d.	1502	1510	1513	1615	1648	1650r	1702	1705	1812	1818	1822	1855	2000	2138	2210r	2232		2315
Helsingør 1219 ▲ d.		1555				1715r			1915							2235r		
Helsingør 463 d.						1738g										2301		
København H. 463 a.		1658				1823g			2018							2355		
Lund a.	1540		1557	1656	1724		1739	1750		1848		1900	1935	2025	2037	2215	2309	0001
Malmö a.	1553		1614	1708	1738		1755	1802		1900		1913	1950	2038	2052	2230	2322	0016

	660 Ⓐ	662 ✕	IC 670 R ✕	1400 2 ✕	IC 70 R ✕	666 ⑥	1402 2 Ⓐ	IC 604 R ✕	614 ⑦	1404 2	IC 606 R	1406 2	1436 ⑦	1408 2 ✕	684 R	IN 384 R	1410 2 ✕	1412 2	1414 2 ✕
Malmö d.				0544	0617		0641		0655	0705	0754		0845	0857	0950	0957	1028	1057	1157	1257
Lund d.				0556	0630		0657		0708	0718	0809		0858	0909	1002	1009	1042	1109	1209	1309
København H. 463 d.							0603					0703h						0948		
Helsingør 463 d.							0649					0749								
Helsingør 1219 ▲ d.							0710r					0810r						1033		
Helsingborg 1219 a.			0635					0738	0735r	0755	0755	0847	0835r	0934	0944	1037	1044	1127	1130	1144	1244	1345
Helsingborg d.		0542						0800	0800		0937					1140	1140		
Ängelholm d.		0602						0818	0818		1001					1158	1158		
Båstad d.		0627						0838	0838		1025					1218	1218		
Laholm d.		0642						0851	0851		1038								
Hässleholm 465 d.					0706														
Halmstad d.	0500	0543	0707		0805	0833			0913	0913		1100					1250	1250		
Falkenberg d.	0528	0611	0739		0832	0901			0941	0941		1127					1318	1318		
Varberg d.	0546	0628	0757		0848	0920			0959	0959		1145					1336	1336		
Kungsbacka d.	0623	0710	0831		0928	0955			1034	1034		1223					1410	1410		
Göteborg a.	0645	0730	0850		0948	1015			1053	1053		1245					1435	1435		
Oslo Sentral 480 a.																	1937v	1937v		

	692 R ✕	IN 392 R ✕	1416 2	IC 612 R 2 Ⓐ ✕	1418 2	1420 2	676 ⑥	1422 2 Ⓐ	IC 72 R ⑦ ✕	1432 2	1424 2	1426 2	IC 618 R	1438 2	678 ⑧	1428 2	682 R / 380 X	1430 ✕	IN 380 R W
Malmö d.	1317		1357		1428	1510	1600		1638	1700	1703	1710	1800		1900		1910	2000		2057	2142	2247	2328
Lund d.	1330		1409		1442	1522	1612		1651	1712	1716	1726	1815		1915		1923	2015		2110	2157	2300	2343
København H. 463 d.		1228		1343k				1543k							1823n		1931				2315t
Helsingør 463 d.				1429				1629							1909		2026				
Helsingør 1219 ▲ d.		1313		1450r				1650r					1930r				2050r				2355t
Helsingborg 1219 a.	1406	1410	1449	1515r	1531	1557	1650	1715r	1737	1754		1804	1852		1951	1955r	2000	2052	2115r	2142	2234	2334	0018	0045
Helsingborg d.	1415	1415		1534			1740								2005					2155		0050	0050
Ängelholm d.	1435	1435		1552			1800								2023					2213			
Båstad d.	1501	1501		1612			1820								2042					2233			
Laholm d.				1630			1833								2059					2246			
Hässleholm 465 d.								1757															
Halmstad d.	1543	1543		1658			1852	1900							2124					2306		0204	0204
Falkenberg d.	1611	1611		1726				1928							2153								
Varberg d.	1630	1630		1744				1946							2213								
Kungsbacka d.	1705	1705		1823				2021							2255								
Göteborg a.	1734	1734		1845				2039							2315								
Oslo Sentral 480 a.																					0340	0340 / 0837	0837

W – 🚄 1,2 cl. and 🚄 2 cl. and 🚃 Oslo - København and v.v.
X – 🚃 and 🚄 2 cl. Oslo - Malmö and v.v.

b – ⑤⑥⑦ only.
c – On ⑦ depart Helsingør 1101, arrive København 1155.
e – On ⑦ depart Helsingør 1201, arrive København 1255.
f – On Ⓒ depart Helsingør 1441, arrive København 1535.
g – On Ⓒ depart Helsingør 1741, arrive København 1835.

h – On Ⓒ depart København 0651.
k – On ⑦ depart København 12 minutes earlier.
n – On Ⓒ depart København 1811.
r – By 🚢 (Scandlines, Table 1219).
t – From May 28, depart København 2308, Helsingør 2349.
v – ⑤⑥⑦ only. Arrive 1952 from May 28.

▲ – Through trains are conveyed aboard Scandlines train ferries between Helsingborg and Helsingør.

Table 467 — GÖTEBORG - ALVESTA - KALMAR

1,2 class

km		321 N Ⓐ	341 P	323 ⒶⓎ⑥	325 Ⓐ	325 ⑥	1375	327 ⑥Ⓨ	327 ⑥Ⓨ	1377	329 Ⓨ	1379	331 Ⓨ	1381	343 ⒶⓎ	1391 Ⓐ	333	1383	335	1385 🚌	337 ⑥Ⓨ	1387 ⑥Ⓨ
0	Göteborg d.				0607			0805					1218				1404		1605		1812	
72	Borås ▲ d.				0717			0859					1309				1509		1711		1911	
111	Limmared d.				0745			0927					1337				1537		1739		1939	
172	Värnamo d.				0824			1012					1419				1620		1821		2023	
221	Alvesta a.				0854			1042					1449				1648		1848		2050	
	Stockholm 465 a.	2224	2224																			
221	Alvesta 465 d.	0610	0650	0707		0906	0906		1106	1106	1306		1507		1543		1709		1909		2105	2108
238	Växjö d.	0637	0718	0724		0922	0922		1121	1121	1322		1521		1558		1725		1925		2130	2124
295	Emmaboda a.	0714	0721	0752	0800	0805	0956	0956	1001	1155	1155	1203	1357	1405	1555	1601	1639	1700	1800 1805	1959	2004	2158 2203
352	Karlskrona a.		0804		0847	0847	1038	1038		1238	1238		1444		1640		1749		1844		2043	2239
323	Nybro a.	0740	0818			1017			1219	1419			1615		1701		1821		2017			2219
352	Kalmar a.	0759	0837			1035			1237	1438			1633		1720		1839		2035			2237

		1370 Ⓐ	320 Ⓐ	1372 Ⓐ	322 ⒶⓎ	1374 ✕	324 ✕Ⓨ	1376	326 Ⓒ	326 Ⓐ	1378	328	1380	330	1382	332	1390	344 Ⓐ	1384 ⑥	334 ⑥	1386 ⑤⑦	336 ⑧	1388 ⑧	338 ⑧R
	Kalmar d.	0522		0610	0722	0920			1119					1327	1516		1552			1724		1920		2119
	Nybro d.	0540		0628	0741	0938			1137					1345	1534		1614			1742		1939		2138
	Karlskrona d.		0515	0558	0708		0911	0911		1315		1119	1119		1513	1545		1715			1911		2113	
	Emmaboda d.	0556	0601	0641	0645	0753	0802	0953	1001	1001	1152	1200	1354	1402	1549	1557	1635	1641	1754	1801	1950	2000	2152	2200
	Växjö d.		0636		0725	0839		1037	1037		1235		1437		1635		1723	1825		1836	2015	2036		2243
	Alvesta 465 a.		0649		0738	0852		1050	1050		1248		1450		1648		1736	1850		1849	2040	2050		2257
	Stockholm 465 a.																							0747
	Alvesta d.		0707			0906			1106		1308		1507							1908				
	Värnamo d.		0741			0934			1137		1337		1538							1939				
	Limmared d.		0826			1015			1217		1421		1621							2023				
	Borås ▲ d.		0854			1043			1245		1449		1649							2051				
	Göteborg a.		0954			1135			1350		1543		1750							2145				

N – Ⓐ : 🍴 Alvesta - Kalmar. Conveys on ①②③④⑦ (from Stockholm), 🛏 1,2 cl. Stockholm - Kalmar (also 🚆 2 cl. on ①).

P – ⑥ : 🍴 Alvesta - Kalmar. Conveys on ⑤ (from Stockholm), 🛏 1,2 cl. Stockholm - Kalmar.

R – ⑧ : 🍴 Kalmar - Alvesta; 🛏 1,2 cl. Kalmar - Stockholm (also 🚆 2 cl. on ⑦).

▲ – Additional trains (2 cl.) Göteborg - Borås: 0642Ⓐ, 0750Ⓐ, 0955, 1305, 1520Ⓐ, 1634Ⓐ, 1720✕, 1850Ⓐ, 2330; Borås - Göteborg: 0530Ⓐ, 0630Ⓐ, 0656Ⓐ, 0730Ⓐ, 0856Ⓒ, 1105⑦, 1308Ⓐ, 1507, 1612, 1848.

Table 467a — BORÅS/GÖTEBORG - UDDEVALLA - STRÖMSTAD

Göteborg - Strömstad is 2 cl. only

km		Ⓐ	⑥	Ⓐ	Ⓐ	⑥		✕			F				⑥	⑥			⑧		⑧
0	Borås 467 d.			0610		0738	0745		0915		1100	1115		1300	1515	1515		1715		1920		2130
43	Herrljunga 469 a.			0645		0813	0820		0950		1135	1150		1337	1553	1553		1753		1955		2205
43	Herrljunga 469 d.			0713		0818		1032		1203			1403		1603		1811		2003		2210
107	Vänersborg a.			0802		0917		1127		1258			1453		1652		1900		2050		2258
111	Öxnered 470 a.			0807		0922		1132		1303			1501		1657		1905		2054		2302
	Göteborg d.	0635	0715		0800		1020		1220	1220		1420		1620		1820		2030	
133	Uddevalla a.	0758	0825	0824	0914	0945	1134	1150	1320	1334	1334	1518	1539	1714	1734	1922	1931	2111	2145	2319
133	Uddevalla d.	0800	0830			1140		1340		1543		1940	
224	Strömstad a.	0925	0955			1305		1513		1710		2105	

		Ⓐ	Ⓐ	✕	Ⓐ	Ⓐ	①-④	⑤	⑥		⑤⑥	⑦				Ⓐ	Ⓐ		Ⓐ		Ⓐ	⑤⑦
	Strömstad d.				0630	0700				1055			1410	1455		1605		1800	
	Uddevalla a.				0757	0824				1218			1533	1621		1733		1922	
	Uddevalla d.	0533	0605		0700	0800	0830	0843	0843	0830	1025	1030	1045	1225	1225	1425	1428	1540	1625	1635	1740 1740	1835	1932	1926
	Göteborg a.		0720			0920	0945			1140		1340		1540	1658	1740		1858 1858	2048	
	Öxnered 470 d.	0550			0717		0901	0901	0849		1048	1103	1242		1451		1654		1855		1946
	Vänersborg d.	0555			0722		0906	0906	0854		1053	1108	1247		1457		1702		1901		1951
	Herrljunga 469 a.	0641			0816		0954	0954	0942		1138	1156	1332		1547		1750		1949		2046
	Herrljunga 469 d.	0646		0825	0825		1000	1025	1025		1200	1400		1600	1600		1800		1958		2205
	Borås 467 a.	0724		0902	0902		1035	1059	1059		1235	1435		1635	1635		1835		2033		2240

F – ⑤⑥⑦ only.

Table 468 — MALMÖ - KRISTIANSTAD - KARLSKRONA

1,2 class

km		240 Ⓐ	356 Ⓐ	256 ⑥	256 Ⓐ	358	258 ✕	308 ⑦	230	260	262	264	232	352 Ⓐ	266	276 Ⓐ	368	268	234	270 Ⓐ	242 ⑥	236	238 ⑥	272 ⑥	310 ⑥
0	Malmö 465 d.				0607		0707		0737	0907	1107	1307	1407		1507	1610		1707	1807	1907	1907	2007	2107	2107
16	Lund 465 d.				0620		0720		0750	0920	1120	1320	1420		1520	1623		1720	1820	1920	1920	2020	2120	2120
34	Eslöv 465 d.				0631		0731		0801	0931	1131	1331	1431		1531	1634		1731	1831	1931	1931	2031	2131	2131
83	Hässleholm 465 a.				0700		0800		0829	1000	1200	1400	1500		1600	1703		1800	1903	2000	2000	2100	2200	2200
	Helsingborg 465 a.		0550			0652		0652		0900	1055	1248		1428	1450	1602	1700		1900	
83	Hässleholm 465 d.	0518	0655	0707	0707	0753	0804	0830		1005	1205	1405	1502	1554	1605	1707	1756	1805	1906	2005	2008	2102	2202	2202	2224
113	Kristianstad a.	0536	0715	0728	0728	0813c	0824	0831	0853	1025	1225	1425	1523	1614	1625	1726	1815c	1824	1927	2025	2029	2123	2222	2222	2243
113	Kristianstad d.			0540	0734	0734			1031	1231	1434			1631	1731		1831		2031		2227
144	Sölvesborg d.			0604	0801	0801			0858	1058	1258	1458			1658	1758		1858		2058		2254
175	Karlshamn d.			0633	0830	0830			0923	1123	1323	1523			1723	1828		1929		2123		2319
213	Ronneby d.			0705	0901	0901			0959	1159	1358	1559			1757	1900		2001		2157		2351
243	Karlskrona a.			0728	0924	0924			1022	1222	1422	1622			1820	1923		2024		2220		0014

		231 Ⓐ	257 Ⓐ	235 Ⓒ	357 ✕	259 Ⓐ	261 ✕	261 ⑦	361	233 Ⓐ	263	363	265	285 Ⓡ	365 ✕	267	353	237	269	239	271	273 ⑥	375 ⑥	275 ⑧	375 ⑧	241 ⑧
	Karlskrona d.		0538			0637	0736			0935			1135			1334			1535		1733	1832		1933		2129
	Ronneby d.		0602			0704	0800			1000			1200			1359			1600		1758	1859		2031		2156
	Karlshamn d.		0634			0734	0831			1031			1231			1429			1631		1831	1931		2031		2227
	Sölvesborg d.		0700			0802	0859			1059			1259			1458			1659		1859	1959		2059		2255
	Kristianstad a.		0724			0826	0925			1123			1323			1523			1723		1923	2023		2123		2319
	Kristianstad d.	0618	0730	0730		0830	0930	0930		1030	1130		1330			1630		1730	1825	1930	2028	2130		2325
	Hässleholm 465 a.	0642	0750	0750	0757	0850	0950	0950	1000	1050	1150	1205	1350	1355	1415	1550	1651	1750	1845	1950	2045	2141	2150	2203	2345
	Helsingborg 465 a.	0747			0852	0956		1054			1308	1448	1520		1655	1805	1855		2100	2303	2303
	Hässleholm 465 d.	0644	0754	0754		0833	0953	0951		1050	1153		1353			1553		1653	1753	1847	1953	2046		2153
	Eslöv 465 d.	0711	0822	0822		0919	1019	1020		1120	1220		1419			1619		1719	1819	1914	2019	2111		2219
	Lund 465 d.	0722	0837	0837		0934	1034	1034		1134	1234		1434			1634		1734	1834	1927	2034	2125		2234
	Malmö 465 a.	0735	0850	0850		0947	1047	1047		1147	1247		1447			1647		1747	1847	1940	2047	2140		2247

c – Ⓐ only.

Table 469 STOCKHOLM - HALLSBERG - GÖTEBORG

1,2 class

km		1605	873	119	1607	X2000 403	X2000 405	971	IC 121	IN 51	X2000 407	X2000 409	IC 125	IC 129	X2000 411	IC 133	633	X2000 417	IC 137	X2000 419	IN 53	X2000 421	IC 141	X2000 423
		2 Ⓐ	🅁 ♦ ♣	Ⓐ	⑥	🅁 Ⓐ ✕	🅁 ①-④ ✕	🅁 ♦ ♠	🅁 ⚒ ✕	🅁 ✕	🅁 Ⓐ ✕	🅁 ⑥ ✕	🅁 ✕	🅁 ✕	🅁 Ⓑ ✕	🅁 ✕	🅁 Ⓐ 🍸	🅁 ✕	🅁 ✕	🅁 ⑤ ✕	🅁 ✕	🅁 Ⓑ ✕	🅁 ✕	🅁 Ⓑ ✕
	Uppsala **476** d.	...	...	...	...	...	0610	...	...	...	...	...	...	...	...	...	...	...	...	...	...	...	...	...
0	**Stockholm** Central d.	...	...	...	...	0630	0700	...	0642	0742	0800	0800	0818	1018	1100	1218	1230	1400	1418	1500	1536	1600	1612	1700
15	S'holm Syd Flemingsberg ‡ d.	...	...	...	...	0640	0710	...	0653	0753	|	0810	0829	1029	1110	1229	1241	1410	1429	1510	1547	1610	1623	1710
35	Södertälje Syd ‡ d.	...	...	...	...	0652	|	...	0706	0806	|	|	0842	1042	1122	1242	1255	|	1442	|	1600	|	1636	|
109	Flen **465** d.	...	...	...	...	|	|	...	0742	|	|	|	0918	1118	|	1318	|	|	1518	|	|	|	1712	|
133	Katrineholm **465** d.	...	...	...	...	|	0801	...	0805	0901	|	0900	0935	1135	|	1335	|	|	1535	|	|	|	1725	|
198	**Hallsberg** a.	...	...	...	...	0755	|	...	0837	0933	|	|	1007	1207	|	1407	1418	|	1607	|	1720	|	1759	|
	Örebro **471** d.	...	0430	0550	...	|	|	0800	|	...	|	|	|	|	|	|	...	|	|	|	...	|	|	|
198	**Hallsberg** d.	...	0510	0613	...	0756	|	0830	0840	...	|	|	1010	1210	|	1410	...	|	1610	|	...	|	1802	|
228	Laxå d.	...	|	0630	...	|	|	0847n	0855	...	|	|	1027	1227	|	1427	...	|	1627	|	...	|	1819	|
273	Töreboda d.	...	|	0652	...	|	|	0908n	0918	...	|	|	1050	1250	|	1450	...	|	1650	|	...	|	1840	|
312	**Skövde** d.	0601	0615	0715	0808	0840	|	0931	0940	...	|	1010	1115	1315	1310	1515	...	1609	1715	1708	...	1807	1915	|
343	Falköping d.	0620	0639	0735	0828	|	|	0953	1000	...	|	|	1135	1335	|	1535	...	|	1735	|	...	|	1935	|
	Jönköping **465b** a.	|	|	|	|	|	|	|	|	...	|	|	|	|	|	|	...	|	|	|	...	|	|	|
376	Herrljunga d.	0639	0703	0755	0850	|	0935s	1015	1020	...	|	|	1155	1355	1339	1555	...	|	1755	|	...	|	1955	1932s
411	Alingsås a.	0656	0723	0813	0910	|	|	|	1040	...	|	1050s	1213	1413	|	1613	...	|	1813	|	...	1848s	2013	|
456	**Göteborg** a.	0729	0756	0845	0942	0945	1015	1102	1115	...	1108	1120	1245	1445	1420	1645	...	1715	1845	1812	...	1915	2045	2010

	X2000 443	703	X2000 425	IC 145	IC 67	IC 147	3793	X2000 429	177	109
	🅁 Ⓑ ✕	🅁 Ⓐ	🅁 V ✕	🅁 ✕	🅁 Ⓑ ✕	🅁 ⑤⑦ ✕	2 ①-④	🅁 V ✕	🅁 ⑦	Ⓑ ♦
Uppsala **476** d.	...	...	...	...	...	...	...	...	...	...
Stockholm Central d.	1706	1718	1800	1818	1848	1942	1942	2000	2124	2342
S'holm Syd Flemingsberg ‡ d.	1716	1729	|	1829	1859	1953	1953	2010	2135	2354
Södertälje Syd ‡ d.	|	1742	|	1842	|	2006	2006	2022	2148	|
Flen **465** d.	|	1818	|	1918	|	2042	2042	|	2224	|
Katrineholm **465** d.	|	1835	|	1935	|	2103	2103	|	2238	|
Hallsberg a.	|	1907	|	2008	2028	2135	2135	2124	2310	|
Örebro **471** d.	|	1940	|	|	...	|	...	|	...	|
Hallsberg d.	|	...	|	2012	...	2140	...	2125	...	|
Laxå d.	|	...	|	2029	...	|	...	|	...	|
Töreboda d.	|	...	|	2051	...	|	...	|	...	|
Skövde d.	1912	...	|	2115	...	2233	...	2210	...	|
Falköping d.	1927	...	|	2135	...	|	...	|	...	|
Jönköping **465b** a.	2008	...	|	|	...	|	...	|	...	|
Herrljunga d.	...	...	|	2155	...	|	...	|	...	|
Alingsås a.	...	...	|	2213	...	|	...	2250s	...	|
Göteborg a.	...	...	2059	2245	...	2350	...	2315	...	0550

	702	IC 122	X2000 402	X2000 442	IC 64	IC 120	IC 124	X2000 404	X2000 406
	🅁 Ⓐ	🅁 ① ✕	🅁 Ⓐ ✕	🅁 Ⓐ ✕	🅁 ⚒ ✕	🅁 Ⓐ ✕	🅁 ⑥ ✕	🅁 ①-④ ✕	🅁 Ⓐ ✕
Göteborg d.	...	0445	0600	...	...	0603	0620	0630	0700
Alingsås d.	...	0514	0624	...	...	0632	0650	|	|
Herrljunga d.	...	0532	|	...	...	0652	0710	0707u	|
Jönköping **465b** d.	...	|	|	0615	...	|	|	|	|
Falköping d.	...	0549	|	0654u	...	0712	0730	|	|
Skövde d.	...	0608	|	0710u	...	0735	0750	0737	|
Töreboda d.	...	0626	|	|	...	0800	0808	|	|
Laxå d.	...	0649	|	|	...	0825	0829	|	|
Hallsberg a.	...	0706	0744	|	...	0847	0847	|	|
Örebro **471** d.	0620	|	|	|	...	|	|	|	|
Hallsberg d.	0650	0708	0745	|	0803	0850	0850	|	|
Katrineholm **465** d.	0725	|	|	|	0840	0920	0920	|	|
Flen **465** d.	0740	|	|	|	0900t	0935	0935	|	|
Södertälje Syd ‡ a.	0815	0823	|	|	0934	1012	1012	0921	|
S'holm Syd Flemingsberg ‡ a.	0828	0835	0858	0904	0947	1026	1026	0933	|
Stockholm Central a.	0841	0847	0911	0917	0959	1041	1041	0947	1005
Uppsala **476** a.	...	...	...	...	...	...	...	...	...

	626	X2000 446	IC 126	X2000 408	IC 130	X2000 414	IN 57	IC 134	X2000 418	IC 138	X2000 422	IC 142	X2000 424	978	1614	X2000 426	IC 146	X2000 428	IN 59	IC 150	X2000 432	874	1618	110
	🅁 Ⓐ 🍸	🅁 ⑥ ✕	🅁 ✕	🅁 ⑥ ✕	🅁 ✕	🅁 Ⓑ ✕	🅁 ✕	🅁 ✕	🅁 ✕	🅁 ✕	🅁 ⑤ ✕	🅁 ✕	🅁 Ⓑ ✕	🅁 ♦	Ⓐ	🅁 V ✕	🅁 ✕	🅁 Ⓑ ✕	🅁 Ⓑ ✕	🅁 R ✕	🅁 V ✕	🅁 ♦	2 ⑦	Ⓑ ♦
Göteborg d.	...	...	0740	0800	0910	1105	...	1110	1305	1310	1505	1510	1605	1610	1628	1705	1710	1805	...	1910	2000	2005	2230	2355
Alingsås d.	...	...	0810	0824	0940	|	...	1140	|	1340	|	1540	|	|	1700	|	1740	|	...	1940	|	2035	2300	|
Herrljunga d.	...	...	0830	0840	1000	1143u	...	1200	1342u	1400	|	1600	|	1659	1720	|	1800	|	...	2000	|	2055	2320	|
Jönköping **465b** d.	...	0800	|	|	|	|	...	|	|	|	|	|	|	|	|	|	|	|	...	|	|	|	|	|
Falköping d.	...	0835u	0850	|	1020	|	...	1220	|	1420	|	1620	|	1720	1740	|	1820	|	...	2020	|	2116	2340	|
Skövde d.	...	0850u	0910	|	1040	1212	...	1240	1412	1440	1610	1640	1708	1742	1758	1805	1840	1908	...	2040	2102	2140	2359	|
Töreboda d.	...	|	0928	|	1058	|	...	1258	|	1458	|	1658	|	|	...	|	1858	|	...	2058	|	|	...	|
Laxå d.	...	|	0949	|	1119	|	...	1319	|	1519	|	1720	|	|	...	|	1919	|	...	2119	|	|	...	|
Hallsberg a.	...	0934	1007	|	1137	|	...	1337	|	1537	|	1740	|	1858	...	|	1937	|	...	2137	2145	2240	...	|
Örebro **471** d.	...	|	|	|	|	|	...	|	|	|	|	|	|	1928	...	|	|	|	...	|	|	2318	...	|
Hallsberg d.	0926	0935	1010	|	1140	|	1250	1340	|	1540	|	1750	|	...	...	|	1950	|	2048	2145	2146	...	...	|
Katrineholm **465** d.	1003	|	1043	1014s	1213	|	1325	1413	|	1613	|	1825	|	...	...	|	2025	2013s	2122	2220	|	...	...	|
Flen **465** d.	1018	|	1057e	|	1228	|	|	1428	|	1628	|	1840	|	...	...	|	2040	|	|	2235	|	...	...	|
Södertälje Syd ‡ a.	1055	|	1132	|	1306	1357	1412	1506	|	1706	|	1919	1850	...	...	|	2119	2051	2209	2312	2247	...	...	0538
S'holm Syd Flemingsberg ‡ a.	1110	1051	1146	1103	1320	1409	1426	1520	1609	1720	1803	1933	1902	...	...	1957	2133	2103	2222	2326	2258	...	...	0555
Stockholm Central a.	1123	1105	1159	1117	1335	1423	1441	1535	1623	1735	1817	1947	1917	...	...	2011	2147	2117	2235	2341	2311	...	...	0611
Uppsala **476** a.	...	...	...	...	...	...	...	...	...	...	...	...	...	...	...	2100r	...	...	...	...	...	...	...	...

♦ – **NOTES** (LISTED BY TRAIN NUMBER)

109/10 – 🛏 1,2 cl. and ▬ 2 cl. Stockholm - Göteborg and v.v.;

873/4 – 🛏 1,2 cl., ▬ 2 cl. and [2] Göteborg - Östersund - Storlien and v.v.

971/8 – 🛏 1,2 cl., ▬ 2 cl., [2] and ✕ Göteborg - Luleå and v.v.; also conveys cinema/bistro car (*Bio*).

R – ⑤⑦ only. Also runs Göteborg - Hallsberg on ①-④ as train **152** (🅁, 🍸).
V – Runs on ①②③④⑦.

e – Calls on ⑥⑦ only.
n – ⑦ only.

r – ①②③④ only.
s – Stops to set down only.
t – only.
u – Stops to pick up only.

X2000 – High speed train. Supplement payable.
♣ – On Ⓐ, stops to set down only.
♠ – On ①-⑥, stops to set down only.

‡ – Most trains on this table do not convey passengers for local journeys between Stockholm and Södertälje Syd or v.v. Local trains run every 30 minutes Stockholm Central - Södertälje Hamn - Södertälje Centrum and v.v. (journey 42 mins). 🚌 Södertälje Syd - Södertälje Centrum runs every 30 minutes.

Table 469a HALLSBERG - LIDKÖPING - HERRLJUNGA

2 class only

km		Ⓐ	Ⓐ		Ⓐ	⑥	Ⓐ		⑦	⚒	⚒	⑦v	Ⓐ	Ⓐ		Ⓐ		⑥	⑦		Ⓐ		⑦	
0	**Hallsberg 469** d.	...	...	...	...	...	...	...	...	...	...	...	...	1345	...	...	...	...	...	...	...	...	...	...
30	Laxå **469** d.	...	...	...	0636	...	...	...	...	1035	...	1241	...	1432	...	1510	...	1632	1632	...	1822	...	2032	...
92	Mariestad d.	...	0654	...	0732	...	0838	...	...	1135	1201	1359	1410	1535	...	1625	...	1731	1750	...	1922	...	2128	...
146	Lidköping d.	0533	0748	...	...	0913	0928	...	1050	...	1300	1452	1500	1635	...	1715	...	1822	1840	...	2014	...	2221	...
201	**Herrljunga 469** a.	0624	0840	...	...	1003	1015	...	1140	...	1350	1547	...	1727	...	...	...	...	1929	...	...	...	...	...

	Ⓐ	Ⓐ		Ⓐ	⑥	⑦		⑥	Ⓐ		Ⓐ	⑦	⚒	⑦		Ⓐ	Ⓐ	⑦v	Ⓐv	⑥		Ⓐ	Ⓑv	⑦
Herrljunga 469 d.	...	...	...	0655	...	...	...	1010	1015	...	1211	1219	...	...	...	1412	...	1603	1603	1606	...	1802	2003	2058
Lidköping d.	0511	0600	...	0748	0748	0920	...	1100	1111	...	1300	1310	1317	...	...	1505	1532	1700	1720	1658	...	1852	2105	2150
Mariestad d.	0602	0649	...	0840	0840	1010	...	...	1200	...	...	1358	1410	1410	...	...	1622	1810	1810	...	...	...	...	...
Laxå **469** a.	0654	...	...	0941	0941	1110	...	...	...	...	...	...	1505	1505	...	...	1717	1907	1907	...	...	...	...	...
Hallsberg 469 a.	0715	...	...	...	...	...	...	...	...	...	...	...	...	...	...	...	...	...	...	...	...	...	...	...

v – Change at Vara.

Table 470 (STOCKHOLM) - HALLSBERG - KARLSTAD - GÖTEBORG and OSLO   1,2 class

km		3001	627 3003	3003	IN 51	3007	629 3011	3129	633 3013	633	3115	637	3015	IN X2000 53	463	3095	3017	3163	645	IC 67	3167	3019	398
0	Stockholm 469 d.				0742		1018		1218	1230		1418	1418	1536	1654				1818	1848			2300
15	S'holm Syd F'berg 469 d.				0753		1029		1229	1241		1429	1429	1547	1704				1829	1859			
35	Södertälje Syd 469 d.				0806		1042		1242	1255		1442	1442	1600	1715				1842				
198	Hallsberg 469 a.				0933		1207		1407	1418		1607	1607	1720				2008	2028				v
198	Hallsberg d.		0615		0935		1215		1420	1420		1618	1618	1725				2020	2030			0225
263	Degerfors d.		0655		1010		1256		1457	1457		1656	1656	1804	1848s			2056	2103			0259
289	Kristinehamn d.		0714		1028		1313		1514	1514		1713	1713	1820	1903s			2113	2120			0318
329	Karlstad a.		0746		1053		1337		1538	1538		1742	1742	1850	1927			2138	2144			0344
329	Karlstad d.	0555	0752	0752	1058	1132	1346	1357	1546	1546	1700	1747	1757	1855	1947	1947	1952	2140	2150	2205	0400
349	Kil d.	0610	0808	0808	1113	1147	1401	1418	1607	1607	1715		1812	1913	2002	2002	2008	2153	2209	2226	
400	Säffle d.	0645	0844	0844		1222	1436		1643	1643		1840	1848		2037	2037			2301	
417	Åmål d.	0658	0857	0857		1235	1451		1656	1656		1900	1902		2050	2050			2315	
458	Mellerud d.	0725	0924	0924		1302	1519		1723	1723		1945	1930		2128			
499	Öxnered d.	0758	0958	0958		1328	1544		1749	1749			1956		2153			
509	Trollhättan d.	0810	1008	1008		1338	1600		1759	1759		2040	2008		2203			
581	Göteborg a.	0900	1054	1054		1428	1648		1855	1855		2145	2055		2248			
397	Arvika d.				1148			1459			1804			1948			2047		2250		0448
431	Charlottenberg d.				1215						1840			2016					2318		0525
473	Kongsvinger d.				1242									2044							0556
552	Lillestrøm a.				1345									2146							0710
573	Oslo Sentral a.				1405									2206							0740

	X2000 3162	462	IC 64	3136	3096 626	3164	X2000 464	634	3120	3130	630	630	IN 57	3006 638	3140	3142	642	3146	646	3014	IN 59	3016	3018	397
Oslo Sentral d.												0820						1620			2250
Lillestrøm d.												0842						1643			2312
Kongsvinger d.												0941						1743			0014
Charlottenberg d.				0611			0714	0821				1011		1357	1425		1618		1814			0048
Arvika d.	0505			0644		0700		0753	0855			1036		1432	1500		1650		1839			0113
Göteborg d.										0656			1040			1300		1500	1547		1717	1925
Trollhättan d.										0750			1128			1343		1543	1636		1801	2009
Öxnered d.										0803			1139			1400		1555	1646		1811	2019
Mellerud d.										0827			1205			1424		1621	1715		1838	2045
Åmål d.						0630				0854			1232			1454		1648	1748		1905	2112
Säffle d.						0642				0908			1246			1507		1707	1801		1918	2125
Kil d.	0546			0729	0725	0741		0805	0835s	0936	0949		1109	1327	1518	1541	1548	1735	1748	1842	1914	2007	2204
Karlstad a.	0607			0743	0738	0804		0819	0850	0950	1002		1125	1340	1532		1601	1749	1801	1855	1927	2020	2220	0203
Karlstad d.		0620	0643		0807		0820	0827			1010	1010	1130	1411	1540		1609		1810		1930			0215
Kristinehamn d.		0641u	0709		0833		0841u	0853			1041	1041	1156	1437	1605		1634		1837		1956			0240
Degerfors d.		0655u	0726		0849		0855u	0909			1057	1057	1212	1453			1652		1855		2012			
Hallsberg a.			0800		0924			0927	0945		1133	1133	1247	1532			1730		1933		2046			0335
Hallsberg 469 d.			0803		0926				1010		1140	1140	1250	1540			1750		1950		2048			v
Södertälje Syd 469 a.		0829	0934		1055			1029	1132		1306	1306	1412	1706			1919		2119		2209			
S'holm Syd F'berg 469 a.		0840	0947		1110			1041	1146		1320	1320	1426	1720			1933		2133		2222			
Stockholm 469 a.		0853	0959		1123			1053	1159		1335	1335	1441	1735			1947		2147		2235			0647

N – ⑧: 🍴 1,2 cl., 🍴 2 cl. and 🛏 Stockholm - Oslo and v.v.
s – Stops to set down only.
u – Stops to pick up only.

v – Via Västerås (Table 477).
X2000 – High speed train. Special supplement payable.

Table 471 HALLSBERG - ÖREBRO   Summary table. 1,2 class

Rail service Hallsberg - Örebro and v.v. (summary of day trains). Journey 20 minutes. 25 km. For through services see also Table 473.

From Hallsberg: 0440Ⓐ, 0500Ⓐ, 0530Ⓐ, 0540✗, 0550✗, 0600Ⓐ, 0650✗, 0720Ⓐ, 0750✗, 0810, 0855, 0945✗, 1000Ⓒ, 1015, 1025, 1200, 1215, 1235, 1350, 1430, 1520Ⓐ, 1550Ⓑ, 1610, 1615, 1640, 1735Ⓐ, 1750Ⓑ, 1800, 1810, 1830E, 1910 Ⓗ, 1920Ⓐ, 1950Ⓐ, 2020, 2055Ⓑ, 2150Ⓑ, 2255 Ⓗ, 2320⑦.

From Örebro: 0430 Ⓗ, 0550Ⓐ, 0620Ⓐ, 0700✗, 0710Ⓐ, 0720✗, 0750Ⓐ, 0800 Ⓗ, 0815✗, 0900, 0935, 1040, 1110, 1140, 1310, 1315⑤⑦, 1340, 1505Ⓑ, 1510, 1540, 1610Ⓐ, 1640Ⓐ, 1715, 1735, 1815Ⓐ, 1840Ⓐ, 1910, 1927, 1935, 1943, 2000E, 2020Ⓐ, 2055, 2120Ⓑ, 2220Ⓑ, 2330Ⓑ.

E – Ⓐ Mar. 3 - June 11.

Table 471a LINKÖPING and NASSJÖ - OSKARSHAMN   2 class only   Ötraf/KLT/JLT

km		⑥	✗	Ⓑ	Ⓐ	⑥	Ⓐ	Ⓑ	Ⓐ	Ⓒ	Ⓐb
	Linköping 465 d.		0842f		1042f	1405		1442f	1655	1725	
0	Nässjö 465 d.	0907		1010		1415	1510			1812	1812
83	Hultsfred d.	1024	1045	1125	1246	1605	1624	1647	1904	1933	1935
149	Oskarshamn a.		1136		1337	1656		1738	1955	2024	2035

		Ⓐ	✗	Ⓐ	⑥	Ⓐ	⑤	Ⓐ			
	Oskarshamn d.	0730		1144		1351	1506	1535		1700b	1756c
	Hultsfred d.	0823	0830	1236	1239	1445	1600	1627	1630	1814	1850
	Nässjö 465 a.		0950		1401				1750	1937	
	Linköping 465 a.	1042f		1443f		1650f	1807	1857			2105

b – By 🚌 Hultsfred - Oskarshamn.   c – Depart 1811 on Ⓐ.   f – By 🚌 on certain dates.

Table 471b LINKÖPING - VÄSTERVIK   2 class only   ÖTraf/KLT

Rail service Linköping - Västervik and v.v. Journey 1 hour 50 minutes (2 hours 10 minutes by 🚌). 116 km.

From Linköping: 0900Ⓐ, 0950Ⓒ, 1105Ⓐ, 1220⑥🚌, 1315Ⓑ, 1405⑤ (change at Bjärka-Säby), 1450Ⓐ, 1655Ⓑ, 1820⑦🚌, 1842⑥, 1950Ⓑ.

From Västervik: 0550Ⓐ, 0630⑥, 0825Ⓐ, 0915Ⓒ, 0940✗🚌, 1207Ⓐ, 1242⑦, 1330⑥, 1420Ⓐ, 1530⑦🚌, 1615⑦, 1733⑥, 1842Ⓐ, 1915⑦.

Table 472 MJÖLBY - NORRKÖPING - VÄSTERÅS   1,2 class

km		784	2308	2314	2320	2326	2338	2346	2346	2352	3794
		Ⓐ	✗	✗	E	⑦			Ⓐ	⑦	
0	Mjölby 465 d.		0720	0915	1115	1315	1715	1915			
32	Linköping 465 d.		0755	0935	1135	1335	1735	1935			
79	Norrköping 465 a.		0823	1003	1202	1402	1802	2002			
79	Norrköping 465 d.	0635	0834	1015	1205	1405	1805	2010	2010	2155	
127	Katrineholm 465 d.	0708	0855	1050	1235	1435	1835	2040	2040	2235	2235
150	Flen 465 d.	0726	0913	1105	1250	1450	1850	2055	2055	2250	2250
191	Eskilstuna d.	0811	0941	1139	1330	1530	1930	2130	2130	2323	2323
239	Västerås a.	0858	1018	1218	1409	1609	2009	2209	2209	2400	2400

		3713	2311	2317	8219	2329	2341	2345	2345	793	2351
		Ⓐ	⑦	Ⓐ	⑤	Ⓑ		⑤	⑦		
	Västerås d.		0550	0750	0950	1150	1550	1750	1750	1907	2150
	Eskilstuna d.	0555	0633	0828	1032	1235	1630	1828	1828	2000	2228
	Flen 465 d.	0630	0710	0902		1310	1705	1905	1905	2033	2305
	Katrineholm 465 d.	0645	0728	0925		1328	1720	1920	1920	2127	2320
	Norrköping 465 a.	0712	0756	0953		1356	1749	1948	1948	2155	2349
	Norrköping 465 d.	0725	0758	0955		1358	1800		1950		
	Linköping 465 d.	0753	0828	1025		1428	1827		2020		
	Mjölby 465 a.		0848	1045		1448	1849		2040		

E – ⑦ (also Ⓐ Mar. 6 - June 11).

Table 473

MJÖLBY - ÖREBRO - GÄVLE

1,2 class

km		3300	860	3302	3302	2312	3462	🚌	3304	3306	2318	866	3312	3312	868	2330	3308	3310	2336	978 Ⓡ	2342	874 Ⓡ	894 874 Ⓡ
		※	※	Ⓐ	⑥⑦		Ⓐ		⑥					⑦	※			Ⓑ	E	L		G	M
	Malmö 465 .... d.																						1740
0	Mjölby .... d.					0905					1105					1507			1710		1907		2117
27	Motala .... d.					0921					1121					1523			1725		1923		2135
	Göteborg 469 .... d.																			1610		2005	
96	Hallsberg .... a.					1010					1210					1612			1825	1858	2012	2240	2233
96	Hallsberg 471 .... d.		0540	0600		1015	1025				1200	1215	1235		1610	1615	1640	1750	1830	1910	2020	2255	2255
121	Örebro 471 .... a.		0600	0620		1035	1045				1220	1235	1255		1630	1635	1700	1810	1850	1928	2040	2318	2318
121	Örebro .... d.		0605	0623		1047					1240		1300		1640		1705	1812		1933		2320	2320
146	Frövi .... d.		0624	0640		1105					1257		1318		1658		1723	1828					
168	Lindesberg .... d.			0703							1317						1743	1849					
232	Grängesberg .... d.			0755							1407						1844	1939					
247	Ludvika .... d.			0810							1420						1856	1950					
293	Borlänge .... a.			0848							1450						1927	2020					
293	Borlänge 478 .... d.	0623		0850	0820			1200	1236	1456c		1608						2022					
317	Falun 478 .... d.	0641		0908	0908			1230	1254	1520c		1631	1631					2044					
	Fagersta .... d.		0720				1155							1750									
	Västerås 477 .... d.																		2055				
	Avesta Krylbo .... d.		0747				1222				1451			1824					2203				
385	Sandviken .... d.	0730	0850	0957	0957		1324	1330	1350		1553	1726	1726	1926		2137				0057	0057	
408	Gävle .... a.	0746	0906	1013	1013		1340	1355	1406		1612	1742	1742	1943		2153						
	Östersund 476 .... a.																			0606	0606	
	Umeå 476 .... a.																		0725				
	Luleå 476 .... a.																		1059				

		873 893 Ⓡ		3301	3461	2313	971 Ⓡ	2319	807	2325		863	2331	3309	3465	2337	2343	3317	2349	3313	867	2349	2355	3315
		G	M			※	L	※	F				⑥⑦		Ⓑ				⑦			⑦	E	Ⓑ
	Luleå 476 .... d.						1630																	
	Umeå 476 .... d.						2020																	
	Östersund 476 .... d.	2123	2123																					
	Gävle .... d.				0416				0627			1004		1150	1220					1615	1646		1914	
	Sandviken .... d.				0432				0645			1024		1206	1236					1632	1704		1937	
	Avesta Krylbo .... d.	0242	0242		0528		0521					1125			1330						1802			
	Västerås 477 .... d.						0613																	
	Fagersta .... d.				0555							1151			1357						1833			
	Falun 478 .... d.								0745			1256							1724			2030	
	Borlänge 478 .... a.								0802			1312							1746			2054	
	Borlänge .... d.				0444				0820				1312			1714								
	Ludvika .... d.				0516				0854				1348			1748								
	Grängesberg .... d.				0528				0907				1406			1759								
	Lindesberg .... d.				0618				0958				1456			1850								
	Frövi .... d.				0639	0644			1017			1244	1515	1445		1907			1923					
	Örebro .... a.	0430	0430		0656	0702		0752	1035			1302	1535	1502		1924			1941					
	Örebro 469 .... d.	0430	0430		0700	0710	0720	0800	0900	1040	1110	1310	1315	1540	1505	1510	1715	1927		1943	2000			
	Hallsberg 469 .... a.	0450	0450		0720	0730	0740	0820	0920	1100	1130	1330	1335	1600	1525	1530	1735	1947		2003	2020			
	Hallsberg 469 .... d.	0510	0515				0745	0830	0950		1140		1345		1540	1740		2010			2015	2050		
	Göteborg 469 .... a.	0756					1102											2010			2015	2050		
	Motala .... d.		0602					0832	1037		1232		1432			1634	1827		2057		2102	2136		
	Mjölby 465 .... a.		0622					0851	1055		1251		1451			1653	1845		2117		2120	2200		
	Malmö 465 .... a.		1020																					

E – Ⓐ Mar. 6 - June 11.
F – ⑦ (runs ⑧ Mar. 6 - June 11).
G – 🛏 1,2 cl., 🍴 2 cl. and 🚊 Göteborg - Östersund - Storlien and v.v.
L – 🍴 1,2 cl., 🍴 2 cl., 🚊 and ✕ Göteborg - Luleå and v.v.
     Also conveys cinema/bistro car (Bio).

M – 🚊 Malmö - Hallsberg and v.v.; 🛏 1,2 cl. and 🍴 2 cl. Malmö - Östersund -
     Storlien and v.v.; 🍸 Malmö - Mjölby and v.v.
c – ※ only.

Table 474

🚐 BODEN - TORNIO - KEMI

🚐 service

km	Timings in Sweden	Ⓒ	Ⓐ	Ⓐ	Ⓑ	Ⓐ		Ⓐ	Ⓐ	Ⓐ					Ⓐ		⑥	Ⓑ	Ⓐ		Ⓐ	Ⓐ	Ⓐ
0	Boden Railway Station 476 d.	0805	1055	1055	1335	1335	...	1645	1950	1950	Haparanda Bus Station .... d.		...	0720	0725	0820	...	1010	1425	1745	...
165	Haparanda Bus Station ...... a.	1020	1315	1325	1540	1550	...	1925	2155	2215	Boden Railway Station 476 a.		...	0955	0950	1040	...	1235	1645	1950	...

There is a walk of approximately 1500 metres from Haparanda Bus Station (Sweden) to Tornio Railway Station (Finland). Finnish time is one hour ahead of Swedish time.
Other local buses run from Haparanda Bus Station to Kemi Bus Station (200 metres from Kemi Station).

km	Timings in Finland	⑥	Ⓐ	※	Ⓑ		⑦	※	⑦				Ⓐ	※	※						
0	Tornio Railway Station .... d.	0702	0707	1317	1335	1617	1928	1936	2157	2203	Kemi Railway Station 495. d.	0600	0642	0923	0927	1132	1515	1535	1902	2128
26	Kemi Railway Station 495... a.	0742	0755	1352	1400	1700	1958	2000	2229	2233	Tornio Railway Station ...... a.	0650	0712	0955	0957	1200	1543	1622	1935	2155

Subject to alteration on holidays. Timings in Sweden are valid Jan. 9 - June 11, 1995 (☏ 020 470047). Timings in Finland are valid Jan. 1 - May 27, 1995 (☏ 9600 4000).

Table 475

LULEÅ - KIRUNA - NARVIK

2 class

km		3588 2 E	904 Ⓡ	994 2Ⓡ		980 2Ⓡ	3552 2Ⓡ			3551 2Ⓡ		981 2Ⓡ		903 2Ⓡ	903	3583 2 F
			N			🍸						🍸			N	
	Stockholm 476 .... d.		1740					Narvik .... d.			1030		1345	1345	1655
0	Luleå 476 .... d.		0648		1000	1728	Riksgränsen .... d.			1116		1434	1434	1753
36	Boden 476 .... a.	0713	0711	1031	1750	Vassijaure 🚡 .... d.			1127		1444	1444	1804
36	Boden .... d.	0732	0732	1043	1756	Björkliden .... d.			1147		1458	1458	1826
204	Gällivare .... d.	0940	0940	1247	1954	Abisko Östra .... d.			1203		1516	1516	1839
304	Kiruna .... a.	1055	1055	1410	2111	Kiruna .... a.			1326		1645	1645	2019
304	Kiruna .... d.	0715	1115	1115	1423	Kiruna .... d.	0600		1336		1705	1705	
398	Abisko Östra .... d.	0835	1227	1227	1534	Gällivare .... d.	0709		1448		1811	1811	
407	Björkliden .... d.	0850	1243	1243	1556	Boden .... a.	0906		1656		2011	2011	
427	Vassijaure 🚡 .... d.	0918	1306	1306	1618	Boden 476 .... d.	0909		1706		2023	2035	
433	Riksgränsen .... d.	0928	1314	1314	1630	Luleå 476 .... a.	0931		1736		2046		
473	Narvik .... a.	1022	1403	1403	1720	Stockholm 476 .... a.					1045		

E – Feb. 12 - May 15.
F – Feb. 11 - May 14.

N – NORDPILEN - 🛏 1,2 cl., 🍴 2 cl., 🚊 and ✕ Stockholm - Kiruna and v.v.;
     🛏 Stockholm - Narvik and v.v. Also conveys cinema/bistro car (Bio) Stockholm -
     Kiruna and v.v.

Table 476
STOCKHOLM - GÄVLE - STORLIEN and LULEÅ
1,2 class except where shown

km		956 IC Ⓐ	880	958 IC M	822 IC	960 Ⓐ	970 ⑤⑥	886 IC ①-④	882 IC ①-④	3472 ⑤-⑦	962 IC Ⓑ	964 IC Ⓐ	884 IC	966 IC Ⓐ	904 IC Ⓑ	968 IC ◆	902 IC ◆	978 ◆	952 IC ◆	874 IC ◆	954 IC Ⓑ◆	3470 Ⓐ	950 ⑦
	Malmö 465 ...d.																		1740	2005			
	Göteborg 469 ...d.																1610			2210			2343
0	Stockholm Central ...d.	0537	0713	0813	0940	1013	1013	1143	1213		1413	1513	1613	1713	1740	1813	2010		2210	2302			2343
66	Uppsala 478 ...d.	0630	0800	0900	1024	1045h	1100	1230	1300		1500	1600	1700	1800	1832	1900	2102		2302	2302			0027
181	Gävle ...a.	0751	0910	1015	—	1210h	1215	1315			1415		1618	1718	1807	1911f	1948	2007	2218	0016	0016	0500	0134
181	Gävle ...d.	0800	0912	1018	—	1220	1222k	1315			1418	1425		1705	1807		2002f	2055		0111	0111	0546	
264	Söderhamn ...d.	0850		1112		1325	1314k				1522		1600	1751	1910		2044f	2133		0156	0156	0632	
326	Hudiksvall ...d.	0937		1156		1410	1356k				1600		1751	1910		2146f		2231		0314	0314	0737	
414	Sundsvall ...a.	1045		1259	[bus]	1508k	[bus]				1704	1849	2012			2240				0314		0500	0745x
414	Sundsvall ...d.	1048		1307	1305		1520z				1720e	1900	2020										
279	Bollnäs ...d.		1021					1521	1521					1904		2052		2325	2349		0246		
342	Ljusdal ...d.		1109					1604	1604					1947		2138		0012	0037		0342		
448	Ånge ...d.		1217					1708	1708					2046		2246		0123	0146	0430	0454		
550	Östersund ...a.		1331					1815	1815					2149						0540	0606		
550	Östersund ...d.		1335					1842	1842											0551	0640		
656	Åre ...d.		1510					2026	2026											0737	0826		
712	Storlien 🚇 ...a.		1606					2122	2122											0849	0937		
818	Trondheim 484 ...a.		1900e					2325	2325											1200	1200	[bus]	
482	Härnösand ...a.	1146			1405	1345c		1600c			1805e	1959	2120				2339			0558	Ⓐ	0845	
482	Härnösand ...d.		1200		1355c			1610c			1815e	2001								0600	0620	0900	
584	Sollefteå ...d.									2133										0737			
610	Långsele ...d.									2150					0051		0316	0340		0755			
700	Mellansel ...a.																0433	0458					
	Örnsköldsvik ...a.		1340			1535			1745		2010e				0355		0530t	0550t				0755	1040
821	Vännäs ...d.																0616	0641					
852	Umeå § ...a.		1520			1715			1935		2200e			0511			0725	0725				0945	1210
932	Bastuträsk ...a.																0749	0808					
	Skellefteå [bus] § ...a.		1725			1925			2140					0620			0910	0910				1235	1410
1061	Älvsbyn ...d.																0918	0935					
	Piteå [bus] ...d.		1845			2045			2300					0815r			1100	1100					1530
1107	Boden ...d.														0713		1002	1015					
1143	Luleå § ...a.		1945			2145			2355					0753			1043	1059					1630
1375	Kiruna 475 ...a.														1055		1410q	1410q					
1544	Narvik 475 ...a.														1403		1720q	1720q					

		971 IC	901 IC	911 IC	955 IC	903 IC	957	881 IC	959 IC	[bus]	961 IC	[bus]	963 IC	883 IC	[bus]	965 IC	3477	885 IC M	969 IC ⑦	[bus]	873 IC Ⓑ	[bus]	953 IC ◆	951 IC ◆
	Narvik 475 ...d.	1030q	1030q		1345																			
	Kiruna 475 ...d.	1336q	1336q		1705															1255		1515		
	Luleå § ...d.	1630	1658		1946									0800						1350		1615		
	Boden ...d.	1715	1738		2035									0855										
	Piteå [bus] ...d.	1600	1600		1930b															1515		1740		
	Älvsbyn ...d.	1745	1815		2105									1015										
	Skellefteå [bus] § ...d.	1820	1820		2130									1215						1720		1950		
	Bastuträsk ...d.	1916	1943		2236																			
	Umeå § ...d.	2020	2020		2310v						0815			1215						1900		2130		
	Vännäs ...d.	2103	2125		2354									1350										
	Örnsköldsvik ...d.	2155t	2205t					0800	0800		0955					1350								
	Mellansel ...d.	2239	2300				0245														2150			
	Långsele ...d.	2355	0014					0620			0634										2300c		2336	
	Sollefteå ...a.							0806	0955	0955		1135		1520					2035		2305c	2339		
	Härnösand ...d.					0605		0808	0955		1005f	1135f	1205r	1530	1530			0945y		1600				1600
	Trondheim 484 ...d.															0747		1325		1810		1920		
	Storlien 🚇 ...d.															0952		1421		1913		2025		
	Åre ...d.															1049		1556		2102		2218		
	Östersund ...a.								0610							1222		1610		2123		2230		
	Östersund ...d.	0144	0203		0505				0711							1227		1715		2246		2338		
	Ånge ...d.		0316		0616				0812							1334		1820		2348				
	Ljusdal ...d.	0331	0412		0700				0854							1441		1906		0038				
	Bollnäs ...d.				0702				0905	1050	Ⓐ	1106f	1230f	1302r	1524	1615c	1628			2130		2350c	0035	0035
	Sundsvall ...a.			0504a	0719				0919		1113	1113f		1309		1631	1745	1800			0110	0110		
	Sundsvall ...d.			0614a	0817				1017		1217	1217f		1410		1732	1849	1915			0220	0220		
	Hudiksvall ...d.			0659a	0858				1058		1258	1258f		1455		1817	1930	2001			0306	0306		
	Söderhamn ...d.			0748a	0944			0952	1144		1344	1344f		1544	1640	1908	2022	2029	2056		0410	0410		
	Gävle ...a.	0521	0521	0811	0949			0955	1149		1349	1549	1647	1911		2034	2106			0410	0410		
	Gävle ...d.	0521	0649	0751	0811	1057		1110	1257		1457	1657	1757	2040		2140	2210			0526	0526		
	Uppsala 478 ...a.	0640	0757	0857	0946	1144		1200	1344		1544	1744	1844	2130		2227	2257			0615	0615		
	Stockholm Central ...a.	0733	0844	0944	1045	1144		1200	1344		1544	1744	1844	2130		2227	2257		0756					
	Göteborg 469 ...a.	1102																		1020				
	Malmö 465 ...a.																							

◆ – NOTES (LISTED BY TRAIN NUMBER)

873/4 – 🛏 1,2 cl., 🍴 2 cl. and [car] Göteborg - Storlien and v.v.; 🛏 1,2 cl., 🍴 2 cl. Malmö - Storlien and v.v.
901/2 – 🛏 1,2 cl., 🍴 2 cl. and [car] Stockholm - Luleå and v.v.; 🛏 1,2 cl., 🍴 2 cl., and [car] Stockholm - Umeå and v.v.; ✕ Stockholm - Gävle/Vännäs - Boden; ✕ Boden - Mellansel/Uppsala - Stockholm.
903/4 – NORDPILEN 🛏 1,2 cl., 🍴 2 cl. and [car] Stockholm - Luleå and v.v.; 🛏 1,2 cl. and 🍴 2 cl. Stockholm - Kiruna and v.v. (also Bio cinema/bistro car); [car] Stockholm - Narvik and v.v.; ✕ Stockholm - Ånge/Älvsbyn - Kiruna; ✕ Kiruna - Vännäs/Bollnäs - Stockholm.
951/2 – 🛏 1,2 cl., 🍴 2 cl. and [car] Stockholm - Storlien and v.v.
953/4 – 🍴 2 cl. and [car] Stockholm - Långsele and v.v.
971/8 – 🛏 1,2 cl., 🍴 2 cl., [car] and ✕ Göteborg - Luleå and v.v. (also Bio cinema/bistro car).

M – [car] and ✕ Stockholm - Östersund and v.v.; [car] Stockholm - Storlien and v.v.
a – Ⓐ only.
b – Ⓑ only.

c – Bus Station.
e – [bus].
f – ⑦ only.
h – Runs ①②③④.
k – ⑥ only.
q – Change at Boden (Table 475).
r – ⑦ only.
t – By taxi ([R] – [phone] 0660 84325).
v – ⑥ only (by [bus]).
x – On ⑥⑦ depart 0800 (from Bus Station).
y – ✕ only, by [bus]. Depart 0830 on ⑥.
z – From Bus Station on Ⓐ (depart 1515).

[bus] – Connection by [bus].
§ – Buses call at Bus Station (not railway station). Additional buses run as follows to connect with trains to and from northern Sweden:
Skellefteå - Bastuträsk: 0650, returning at 2000.
Umeå - Vännäs: 0500Ⓐ, returning at 2110Ⓐ, 2125.
♣ – Diverted via Avesta Krylbo.

LOCAL TRAINS SUNDSVALL – ÅNGE – ÖSTERSUND:
From Sundsvall: 0527①, 0800Ⓐ, 1400Ⓐ, 1530⑥, 1630⑧, 2136⑦. From Östersund: 0515①, 0804✕, 1405Ⓐ, 1632Ⓑ, 1855⑦. Journey 130 minutes.

Table 477 STOCKHOLM - VÄSTERÅS - ÖREBRO

1,2 class

km		721 Ⓐ	971 L R	725 ⚒	782 Ⓐ	🚌 Ⓐ	728 Ⓐ	🚌 Ⓐ	🚌 Ⓐ	🚌 Ⓐ	733 Ⓒ	737 Ⓒ	788 Ⓐ	🚌 Ⓐ	741	791 Ⓐ	745	793 Ⓐ	749	🚌 Ⓐ	753 Ⓑ	756 ⑦	799 ⑥	398 C
0	**Stockholm** Central d.	...	...	0619	0737	...	0837	...	1020	...	1037	1237	1337	...	1437	1537	1637	1737	1837	...	2037	2237	2300	2300
74	Enköping d.	...	...	0727	0832	...	0932	...	|	...	1132	1332	1432	...	1532	1632	1732	1832	1932	...	2132	2332	2357	2357
111	**Västerås** a.	...	...	0759	0859	...	0959	...	1150	...	1159	1359	1459	...	1559	1659	1759	1859	1959	...	2159	2359	0024	0024
111	**Västerås** d.	0545	0623	0802	...	0910	...	1010	...	1150	1202	...	...	1505	1602	1702	1802	...	...	2015	2205	...	0029	0029
146	Köping d.	0612	0647	0828	...	0945	...	1045	...	1225	1228	...	...	1538	1628	1728	1828	...	...	2105	2231	...	0054	0054
163	Arboga d.	0630	0707	0844	...	1015	...	1105	...	1250	1244	...	...	1610	1644	1749	1844	...	...	2125	2247	...	0109	0109
192	Frövi d.	0659	|	0912	...	...	...	...	...	|	1312	...	...	...	1712	1816	1912	...	...	...	2312	...	|	|
217	**Örebro** a.	0717	0752	0930	...	...	...	...	...	1325	1330	...	...	...	1730	1835	1930	...	...	...	2330	...	0150	0150
217	**Örebro 469** d.	...	0800	0935	...	...	...	...	...	...	1340	...	...	...	1735	1840	1935	...	...	...	2330	...	0150	0150
242	**Hallsberg 469** a.	...	0820	0955	...	...	...	...	...	...	1400	...	...	...	1755	1900	1955	...	...	...	2355	...	0210	0211

	397 E	715 Ⓐ	778 Ⓐ	781 Ⓐ	718 ⚒	718 ⑦	🚌 Ⓐ	784 ⚒	723 ⑥	🚌 Ⓐ	🚌 Ⓐ	726 Ⓒ	🚌 Ⓐ	🚌 Ⓐ	730	🚌 Ⓐ	789 Ⓐ	734	795 Ⓐ	738 Ⓑ	742	978 L R	746 Ⓐ	746 ⑦
Hallsberg 469 d.	0348	...	0440	...	0550	...	...	...	...	...	...	1000	...	...	...	...	...	1350	...	1550	1800	1910	1950	1950
Örebro 469 a.	0405	...	0500	...	0610	...	...	...	...	...	...	1020	...	...	...	...	...	1410	...	1610	1820	1928	2010	2010
Örebro d.	0408	...	0510	...	0615	...	...	...	...	...	1015	1030	...	...	...	...	...	1430	...	1630	1830	1933	2030	2030
Frövi d.	|	...	0528	...	0634	...	...	...	...	...	|	1048	...	...	...	...	...	1448	...	1648	1848	|	2048	2048
Arboga d.	|	...	0556	...	0703	...	0750	...	...	...	1045	1116	...	1250	...	1345	...	1516	...	1716	1916	|	2116	2116
Köping d.	|	...	0616	...	0723	...	0815	...	...	...	1110	1133	...	1315	...	1415	...	1533	...	1733	1933	|	2133	2133
Västerås a.	0521	...	0645	...	0751	...	0853	...	...	...	1145	1201	...	1353	...	1453	...	1601	...	1801	2001	2050	2201	2201
Västerås d.	0527	0554	...	0700	0800	0800	...	0904	1004	1020	...	1204	1220	...	1404	...	1504	1604	1704	1804	2004	...	...	2204
Enköping d.	|	0620	...	0725	0829	0829	...	0931	1031	1050	...	1231	|	...	1431	...	1531	1631	1731	1831	2031	...	...	2231
Stockholm Central a.	0647	0717	...	0827	0927	0927	...	1027	1127	1200	...	1327	1350	...	1527	...	1627	1727	1827	1927	2127	...	...	2327

C – Daily except ⑥ (not Apr. 14,16,30, June 4): 🛏 1,2 cl., ▬ 2 cl. and 🚃2 Stockholm - Västerås - Oslo; 🚃12 Stockholm - Hallsberg.

E – From Oslo daily except ⑥ (not Apr. 14,16,30, June 4): 🛏 1,2 cl., ▬ 2 cl., 🚃2 Oslo - Västerås - Stockholm.

L – 🛏 1,2 cl., ▬ 2 cl. and 🚃2 Göteborg - Luleå and v.v. – see Table **473**.

Table 477a VÄSTERÅS - LUDVIKA

2 class only VL (152)

km		Ⓐ	⚒			Ⓐ		Ⓐ	Ⓑ	Ⓐ		Ⓑ
0	**Västerås** d.	0715	0815	1215	1415	1515	1615	1715	1815	1915	2015	2215
80	Fagersta a.	0812	0912	1313	1512	1612	1712	1812	1912	2012	2112	2312
129	**Ludvika** a.	...	0956	1356	...	...	1756**b**	...	1956**n**	...	2156**r**	2356**c**

	Ⓐ	⚒	⚒	Ⓐ			Ⓐ			Ⓐ	Ⓑ
Ludvika d.	...	0601	...	...	1001	1401	...	...	1801**b**	...	2001**c**
Fagersta d.	0545	0645	0745	0845	1045	1445	1545	1645	1845	1945	2045
Västerås a.	0640	0745	0845	0945	1145	1545	1645	1745	1945	2045	2145

b – Daily except ⑥. c – ⑦ only. r – ⚒ only. n – ⑤⑦ only.

Table 478 STOCKHOLM - BORLÄNGE - MORA

1,2 class

km		3362 Ⓐ	IC 820 ⚒ 🍷R	3364 ⚒	X2000 552 ⚒ 🍷R	IC 822 ⚒ 🍷R	3368 ⚒	IC 842 ⑦ 🍷R	3342 ⑦	X2000 554 ⑦ 🍷R	3378 ⑦	3370 Ⓐ	IC 824 ⚒ 🍷R	3372 ⚒	IC 844 ⑦ 🍷R	3312 ⑦	IC 826 Ⓐ 🍷R	3374 Ⓐ	X2000 556 Ⓑ 🍷R	3376 Ⓑ	IC 828 F 🍷R	3308 F	IC 848 ⑤ 🍷R	X2000 558 C 🍷R	IC 830 Ⓑ 🍷R
0	**Stockholm** C. **476** ▲ d.	...	0605	...	0730	0940	...	0940	...	1200	...	...	1313	...	1313	...	1434	...	1630	...	1700	...	1700	1830	2043
66	Uppsala **476** ▲ d.	...	0652	...	0817**u**	1027	...	1027	...	|	...	...	1400	...	1400	...	1522	...	|	...	1747	...	1747	|	2130
128	Sala d.	...	0735	...	|	1105	...	1105	...	|	...	...	1438	...	1438	...	1607	...	|	...	1825	...	1825	|	2207
161	Avesta Krylbo d.	...	0808	...	0906**s**	1127	...	1127	...	1335**s**	...	...	1508	...	1508	...	1636	...	1805**s**	...	1847	...	1847	2005**s**	2229
226	**Borlänge** a.	...	0857	...	0943**s**	1216	...	1216	...	1422**s**	...	...	1603	...	1603	...	1731	...	1842**s**	...	1936	...	1936	2042**s**	2318
226	**Borlänge** d.	0616	0859	0912	|	1221	1221	1221	1221	|	1457	1517	1608	1608	1608	1608	1734	1746	|	1852	1944	1946	1946	|	2320
250	Falun **473** a.	|	0917	|	0959	1239	|	|	1239	1438	|	|	1626	|	|	1626	1752	|	1859	|	2002	|	*2002*	2058	2338
269	Leksand d.	0648	...	0946	...	...	1253	1257	...	...	1529	1549	...	1641	1644	...	...	1818	...	1925	...	2022	2022	...	...
289	Rättvik a.	0705	...	1003	...	...	1310	1316	...	...	1546	1608	...	1659	1704	...	...	1835	...	1942	...	2042	2042	...	...
329	**Mora 479** a.	0740	...	1035	...	...	1342	1351	...	...	1620	1640	...	1730	1737	...	...	1909	...	2013	...	2115	2115	...	...
330	Mora Strand a.	...	...	...	...	...	...	...	...	...	...	...	...	...	...	...	...	...	...	...	...	...	...	...	...

	X2000 551 Ⓐ 🍷R	IC 821 ⚒ 🍷R	3363 ⚒	X2000 553 ⚒ 🍷R	807	3365 Ⓑ	IC 823 Ⓑ 🍷R	IC 843 ⑥ 🍷R	3367 Ⓐ	IC 825 Ⓐ 🍷R	3371	IC 829 🍷R	3373 Ⓐ	X2000 557 Ⓑ 🍷R	3375 ⚒	IC 831 ⚒ 🍷R	3347 ⑦	IC 841 ⑦ 🍷R	3377 ⑦	X2000 559 ⑦ 🍷R	3379 Ⓐ	IC 833 Ⓐ 🍷R	3349 ⑦	IC 853 ⑦ 🍷R	3381 Ⓐ
Mora Strand d.	...	...	...	...	...	...	...	...	...	...	...	...	...	...	...	...	...	...	...	...	...	...	...	...	...
Mora 479 d.	...	...	0546	...	...	0638	...	0638	0834	...	1135	...	1348	...	1518	...	...	1518	1628	...	1808	...	...	1816	2128
Rättvik d.	...	...	0616	...	...	0709	...	0709	0904	...	1205	...	1418	...	1549	...	...	1549	1701	...	1838	...	...	1847	2158
Leksand d.	...	...	0633	...	...	0730	...	0730	0921	...	1222	...	1435	...	1609	...	...	1609	1720	...	1855	...	...	1907	2215
Falun **473** d.	0600	0606	|	0657	0745	|	0754	|	|	0930	|	1324	|	1456	|	1630	1630	|	|	1758	|	1926	1926	|	|
Borlänge a.	|	0623	0708	|	0802	0808	0812	0808	0954	0955	1301	1342	1508	|	1648	1648	1648	1648	1754	|	1932	1944	1944	1946	2248
Borlänge d.	0616**u**	0626	...	0713**u**	...	...	0815	0815	...	1000	...	1345	...	1513**u**	...	1653	...	1653	...	1814**u**	...	1949	...	1949	...
Avesta Krylbo d.	0653**u**	0714	...	0750**u**	...	...	0912	0912	...	1049	...	1437	...	1550**u**	...	1742	...	1742	...	1904**u**	...	2046	...	2046	...
Sala d.	|	0736	...	|	...	...	0935	0935	...	1122	...	1500	...	|	...	1822	...	1822	...	|	...	2106	...	2106	...
Uppsala **476** ▲ d.	|	0811	...	|	...	...	1010	1010	...	1157	...	1535	...	1640**s**	...	1857	...	1857	...	|	...	2151	...	2151	...
Stockholm C. **478** ▲ a.	0832	0902	...	0930	...	...	1057	1057	...	1244	...	1622	...	1732	...	1944	...	1944	...	2044	...	2244	...	2244	...

C – ①②③④⑦.
F – Daily except ⑤.
s – Stops to set down only.
u – Stops to pick up only.
▲ – Additional local trains run Stockholm - Uppsala and v.v.
X2000 – High speed train. Supplement payable.

Table 479 MORA - ÖSTERSUND - GÄLLIVARE

Service June 17 - August 20, 1995. No winter service.

INLANDSBANAN
Inlandståget AB

km			D		W			D		
0	**Mora 478** d.	...	...	...	...	...	...	1540	...	...
14	Orsa d.	...	...	...	...	...	...	1610	...	...
138	Sveg d.	...	...	...	...	...	...	1845	...	...
322	**Östersund 476** a.	...	...	...	...	...	...	2206	...	...
322	**Östersund 476** d.	...	0630	...	0840	...	...	...	...	...
437	Ulriksfors d.	...	0810	...	1105	...	...	...	...	...
566	Vilhelmina d.	...	1030	...	1515	...	...	...	...	...
634	Storuman d.	...	1200	...	1820	...	...	...	...	...
706	Sorsele d.	...	1315	...	2010	...	...	...	...	...
795	Arvidsjaur 🚂 d.	...	1500	...	2200	...	...	...	...	...
968	Jokkmokk d.	...	1925	...	...	...	...	...	...	...
1068	**Gällivare 476** a.	...	2120	...	...	...	...	...	...	...

		E				W		E	
Gällivare 476 d.	...	...	...	...	...	...	...	0715	...
Jokkmokk d.	...	...	...	...	...	...	...	0958	...
Arvidsjaur 🚂 d.	...	...	...	...	...	0820	...	1440	...
Sorsele d.	...	...	...	...	...	1020	...	1600	...
Storuman d.	...	...	...	...	...	1155	...	1730	...
Vilhelmina d.	...	...	...	...	...	1435	...	1845	...
Ulriksfors d.	...	...	...	...	...	1745	...	2042	...
Östersund 476 a.	...	...	...	...	...	2005	...	2220	...
Östersund 476 d.	...	0700	...	...	...	...	...	...	...
Sveg d.	...	1100	...	...	...	...	...	...	...
Orsa d.	...	1335	...	...	...	...	...	...	...
Mora 478 a.	...	1350	...	...	...	...	...	...	...

D – Daily June 17 - Aug. 12. Railbus, 2nd class only.
E – Daily June 18 - Aug. 13. Railbus, 2nd class only.
W – VILDMARKSTÅGET (WILDERNESS EXPRESS) - runs from Östersund ①④⑥ June 26 - Aug. 19; from Arvidsjaur ②⑤⑦ June 27 - Aug. 20. Conveys 🚃1 (historic carriages), 🚃2 and ✕.

🚂 – Steam excursions from Arvidsjaur (depart 1730) run on ⑤ July 14 - Aug. 12.

Information and reservations:
☎ +46 63 10 15 90 (within Sweden toll free 020 - 53 53 53), fax 063 - 11 99 80.

NORWAY

SEE MAP PAGE 256

Operator: Norges Statsbaner (NSB).

Services: All trains convey second class seating accommodation. Certain trains – as shown in the notes – also convey: first-class seating accommodation (🚃1); sleeping cars (🛏 1,2 cl.), with one berth per compartment in first class, two or three berths in second class; second class couchette cars (🛌 2 cl.), with six berths per compartment. Fast and express trains in Norway are classified **IN** (InterNord), **IC** (InterCity), **ICE** (InterCityExpress) and **Et** (Ekspresstog). Passengers on **ICE** trains require second class tickets only, but must pay a **supplement**, choosing between *Økonomiklasse* (currently kr. 20 – includes seat reservation), *IC Standard* (kr. 50 – further includes coffee and a newspaper), and *IC Kontor* (kr. 120 for journeys within Norway, kr. 200 for journeys to and from Sweden – further includes meals served at seats).

Timings: Valid **September 25, 1994 - May 27, 1995**. Most overnight trains and some day trains do not operate on December 24, 25, 31.

Reservations: Seat reservation is **compulsory** on **ICE** (see above), **IN**, **Et** and many other express trains (indicated [R] in the tables), except for certain local journeys. Passengers without seat tickets must pay a reservation fee to the conductor.

Table 480 OSLO - HALDEN - GÖTEBORG

2 class only unless otherwise shown

km		ICE 11 Ⓐ [R]	ICE 91 [R]	IN 393 R	IN 393 F	IC 103	IN 385 A [R]	IN 385 B [R]		ICE 93 [R]	ICE 17 Ⓐ [R]	IC 105	ICE 19 Ⓐ [R]	IC 107 Ⓐ	IC 95 Ⓐ	IC 109	ICE 97 Ⓑ [R]	ICE 25 [R]		IC 113	IN 381 D [R]	IN 381 E [R]		IC 117 ⑦c	ICE 29 [R]
0	**Oslo Sentral** d.	0710	0810	...	...	0910	1015	1015	...	1310	1410	1507	1538	1607	1637	1710	1810	1910	...	2110	2137	2137	...	2244	2340
60	Moss d.	0801	0856	...	...	1004	1108	1108	...	1357	1456	1601	1629	1703	1727	1804	1859	1956	...	2203	2232	2232	...	2333	0029
94	Fredrikstad d.	0826	0920	...	...	1036	1136	1136	...	1423	1523	1632	1651	1736	1750	1839	1922	2021	...	2235	2300	2300	...	0002	0054
109	Sarpsborg d.	0839	0934	...	...	1051	1151	1151	...	1437	1541	1647	1704	1751	1804	1854	1940	2035	...	2250	2317	2317	...	0017	0107
137	**Halden** d.	0857	0954	...	...	1111	1214	1214	...	1455	1559	1713	1722	1812	1822	1915	2000	2054	...	2310	2339	2339	...	0037	0125
169	Kornsjø 🏛 d.	...	|	...	...	...	1244	1244	...	...	...	...	...	...	...	...	|	...	...	...	0005	0005	...	...	...
275	Öxnered **470** d.	...	|	...	...	...	1400	1400	...	...	...	...	...	...	...	...	|	...	...	...	|	|	...	...	...
284	Trollhättan **470** d.	...	1131	...	...	...	1408	1408	...	...	...	...	...	...	...	...	2140	...	...	...	|	|	...	...	...
357	**Göteborg 470** a.	...	1215	1227	1227	...	1458	1458	...	...	...	...	...	...	...	...	2225	...	...	...	0207	0207	...	...	...
674	*Malmö* **466** a.	...	...	1614	|	...	1913	|	...	...	...	...	...	...	...	...	...	...	...	...	|	0706	...	...	...
650	*København H* **466** a.	...	...	...	1658	...	...	2018	...	...	...	...	...	...	...	...	...	...	...	...	0700	...	...	...	...

	IC 100 Ⓐ	IC 102 ⚒	IC 104 Ⓐ	IC 106 Ⓐ	IN 682 E	IN 380 D	ICE 12 [R]		ICE 90 Ⓐh [R]	ICE 96 ⑥p [R]	ICE 16 Ⓑ [R]		IC 110	ICE 92 [R]		ICE 24 [R]	IN 384 B [R]	IN 384 A [R]		ICE 26 [R]	IC 114 ⑦c	IN 392 R	IN 692 F	ICE 94 [R]	ICE 28 [R]
København H **466** d.	...	...	...	...	...	2315	...	...	...	..	...	...	...	...	...	...	0948	...	...	...	...	1228	...	...	...
Malmö **466** d.	...	...	...	...	2247	|	...	...	...	...	...	...	...	...	...	...	|	1028	...	...	...	|	1317	...	...
Göteborg 470 d.	...	...	...	...	0350	0350	...	...	0640	0730	...	...	...	...	...	...	1450	1450	...	...	...	1734	1734	1800	...
Trollhättan **470** d.	...	...	...	...	|	|	...	...	0722	0812	...	...	...	...	...	...	1536	1536	...	...	...	...	...	1842	...
Öxnered **470** d.	...	...	...	...	|	|	...	...	|	|	...	...	...	...	...	...	1547	1547	...	...	...	...	...	|	...
Kornsjø 🏛 d.	...	...	...	...	0605s	0605s	...	...	|	|	...	...	...	...	...	...	1705	1705	...	...	...	...	...	|	...
Halden d.	0450	0523	0554	0614	0636s	0636s	0705	...	0903	1005	1005	...	1252	1505	...	1655	1731	1731	...	1901	...	...	...	2026	2105
Sarpsborg d.	0512	0545	0615	0636	0659s	0659s	0724	...	0923	1024	1024	...	1313	1525	...	1719	1753	1753	...	1924	2015	...	...	2051	2124
Fredrikstad d.	0527	0600	0630	0651	0715s	0715s	0737	...	0941	1037	1037	...	1328	1539	...	1733	1812	1812	...	1937	2035	...	...	2104	2137
Moss d.	0600	0631	0701	0725	0743s	0743s	0805	...	1005	1105	1105	...	1400	1605	...	1805	1843	1843	...	2006	2103	...	...	2126	2206
Oslo Sentral a.	0652	0725	0752	0825	0837	0837	0852	...	1052	1152	1152	...	1452	1652	...	1852	1937	1937	...	2052	2152	...	...	2216	2252

A – ⑤⑥⑦ (also May 1, Apr. 13). 🚃12 Oslo - Malmö and v.v.
B – ⑤⑥⑦ (also May 1, Apr. 13). 🚃12 and 🍷 Oslo - København and v.v.
D – 🛏 1,2 cl. and 🛌 2 cl. Oslo - København and v.v.; 🚃2 Oslo - Helsingborg, Helsingør - København and v.v.
E – 🛏 1,2 cl. and 🚃2 Oslo - Malmö and v.v.
F – Also conveys 🚃1 .
R – Also conveys 🚃1 and 🍴.
c – Also Apr. 14, 17, May 1, 17, 25. Not Apr. 16.
h – Also Apr. 13, 14.
p – Not Apr. 15.
s – Stops to set down only.

Table 481 OSLO - VOSS - BERGEN

2 class only unless otherwise shown

km		611 Ⓐ	613 ⚒		615 Ⓐ	615 ⑥	617	619 Ⓐ	619 Ⓒ	ET61 H [R]	621	623	601 J [R]	625 ⚒	627	627 ⑦	1843 ⑤r	603 ⑤⑦ 🍷	ET63 H [R]	815	693 Ⓐ		607 G [R]	605 F [R]
0	**Oslo Sentral** § d.	...	...	...	...	...	...	...	...	0742	...	...	1048	...	...	...	...	1455	1609	1709	1721k	...	2230	2300
7	Lysaker / Fornebu § d.	...	...	...	...	...	...	...	...	0752u	...	...	1059u	...	...	...	...	|	1619u	1720u	|	...	2242u	2312u
40	Drammen § d.	...	...	...	...	...	...	...	...	0820u	...	...	1130u	...	...	...	...	|	1647u	1748	1811	...	2320u	2350u
90	Hønefoss d.	...	...	...	...	...	...	...	...	0915	...	...	1239	...	...	...	...	1621	1740	...	1912	...	0025	0055
203	Gol **489a** d.	...	...	...	...	...	...	...	...	1039	...	...	1410	...	...	...	...	1748	1905	...	2050	...	0214	0234
229	Ål d.	...	...	...	...	...	...	...	...	1058	...	...	1435	...	...	...	...	1811	1925	...	2115	...	0240	0307
254	Geilo d.	...	...	...	...	...	...	...	...	1118	...	...	1502	...	...	...	...	1842	1945	...	2137	...	0310	0335
266	Ustaoset d.	...	...	...	...	...	...	...	...	1129	...	...	1515	...	...	...	...	1854	1956	...	...	...	0324	0347
303	Finse d.	...	...	...	...	...	...	...	...	1203	...	...	1553	...	...	...	...	1928	2028	...	...	...	0405	0424
337	Myrdal a.	...	...	...	...	...	...	...	...	1228	...	...	1621	...	...	...	...	|	2053	...	...	...	0433	0450
337	Myrdal d.	...	...	...	0736	...	...	1125	1125	1231	...	...	1624	1656	...	1745	1830	|	2054	...	...	...	0435	0502
355	Mjølfjell d.	...	...	...	0753	...	...	1145	1145	|	...	...	|	1717	...	1805	1850	|	|	...	...	...	|	|
386	**Voss** a.	...	...	...	0830	...	...	1222	1222	1314	...	...	1715	1754	...	1840	1925	2034	2135	...	...	...	0520	0550
386	**Voss** d.	0515	0633	...	0842	0842	1030	1230	...	1316	1455	1600	1722	...	1846	1846	...	2036	2137	...	...	...	0523	0600
425	Dale d.	0543	0701	...	0910	0910	1102	1302	...	|	1528	1635	|	...	1918	1918	...	|	|	...	...	...	|	0631
441	Vaksdal d.	0559	0716	...	0928	0928	1118	1318	...	|	1549	1651	|	...	1936	1936	...	|	|	...	...	...	|	0648
462	Arna § a.	0617	0738	...	0945	0945	1139	1335	...	1415s	1609	1707	1824s	...	1953	1953	...	2132s	2233s	...	...	...	0626s	0706s
471	**Bergen** § a.	0625	0749	...	0953	0953	1146	1345	...	1424	1617	1715	1833	...	2001	2001	...	2141	2242	...	...	...	0635	0721

	694 Ⓐ	1609 ⚒	1840 Ⓐ	612 Ⓐ	ET62 H [R]		614	602 J [R]		616 Ⓐ		618	600 ⑦v	604 ⑤⑦ 🍷	620 Ⓐ	ET64 H [R]	622 Ⓐ	622 ⑤r	624		626		628 Ⓑ	606 [R] F
Bergen § d.	...	...	...	0705	0733	...	0900	1020	...	1200	...	1330	...	1507	1517	1545	1603	1603	1659	...	1909	...	2150	2300
Arna § d.	...	...	...	0714	0742u	...	0908	1029u	...	1208	...	1338	...	1515u	1525	1553u	1611	1611	1707	...	1917	...	2158	2309u
Vaksdal d.	...	...	...	0736	|	...	0928	|	...	1226	...	1357	...	|	1548	|	1631	1631	1724	...	1936	...	2217	2328
Dale d.	...	...	...	0752	|	...	0943	|	...	1242	...	1413	...	|	1603	|	1650	1650	1740	...	1954	...	2234	2344
Voss a.	...	...	...	0825	0838	...	1012	1130	...	1316	...	1444	...	1612	1633	1647	1722	1722	1809	...	2023	...	2304	0014
Voss d.	...	...	0620	...	0840	...	1017	1135	...	...	...	1450	...	1614	...	1649	...	1727	...	...	...	...	...	0020
Mjølfjell d.	...	...	0656	...	|	...	1051	|	...	...	...	1527	...	|	...	|	...	1805	...	...	...	...	...	|
Myrdal a.	...	...	0715	...	0921	...	1110	1220	...	...	...	1547	...	1656	...	1732	...	1823	...	...	...	...	...	0105
Myrdal d.	...	...	...	...	0923	...	...	1228	...	...	...	...	...	1658	...	1734	...	...	...	...	...	...	...	0117
Finse d.	...	...	...	...	0950	...	...	1304	...	...	...	...	...	1727	...	1800	...	...	...	...	...	...	...	0146
Ustaoset d.	...	...	...	...	1024	...	...	1341	...	...	...	...	...	1801	...	1831	...	...	...	...	...	...	...	0220
Geilo d.	0543	...	...	...	1036	...	...	1356	...	...	...	...	1727	1815	...	1844	...	...	...	...	...	...	...	0246
Ål d.	0605	...	...	...	1057	...	...	1417	...	...	...	...	1749	1837	...	1905	...	...	...	...	...	...	...	0314
Gol **489a** d.	0628	...	...	...	1116	...	...	1440	...	...	...	...	1812	1904	...	1928	...	...	...	...	...	...	...	0339
Hønefoss d.	0801	...	...	...	1241	...	...	1613	...	...	...	...	1945	2033	...	2054	...	...	...	...	...	...	...	0510
Drammen § a.	0908	0937	...	...	1331s	...	...	1714s	...	...	...	...	2040	|	...	2144s	...	...	...	...	...	...	...	0610s
Lysaker / Fornebu § a.	...	1005	...	...	1359s	...	...	1746s	...	...	...	...	2111s	|	...	2210s	...	...	...	...	...	...	...	0648s
Oslo Sentral § a.	...	1015	...	...	1409	...	...	1757	...	...	...	...	2121	2155	...	2221	...	...	...	...	...	...	...	0700

F – 🛏 2 cl. and 🚃2 Oslo - Bergen and v.v.; conveys (except on night of ⑥) 🛏 2 cl. Oslo - Flåm and v.v.
G – ⑦ only. 🛏 2 cl. and 🚃2 Oslo - Bergen.
H – 🚃12 and 🍷 Oslo - Bergen and v.v.
J – 🚃12 and 🍴 Oslo - Bergen and v.v.
k – ⑤ (not Apr. 14).
r – Not Apr. 14.
s – Stops to set down only.
u – Stops to pick up only.
v – Also Apr. 14, 17, May 1, 17, 25. Not Apr. 16.
§ – Frequent local service Oslo - Drammen, Bergen - Arna.

Skibladner

The *Skibladner* is the world's oldest paddle steamer. She will sail between Gjøvik and Hamar (also to Lillehammer on ②④⑥, Eidsvoll on ①③⑤) on Mondays to Saturdays June 19 - Aug. 19, 1995. Further information from Skibladner, Strandgata 23, 2300 Hamar, Norway. ☎ +47 62 527085 fax +47 62 533923.

For explanation of standard symbols see page 4

Table 481a
MYRDAL - FLÅM
2 class only

SUMMER SERVICE May 29 - Sept. 18, 1994: WINTER SERVICE Sept. 19, 1994 - May 27, 1995:

km				※	※N	Ⓐ							B				※	※N	Ⓐ			
0	Myrdal 481 .... d.	...		0120	0500	0735	0925	1015	1115	1232	1340	1700	1736	1920	2100	...		0120	0500	0735	0925	1236	1736	2100
1	Vatnahalsen .... d.	...		0124	0504	0739	0929	1019	1119	1236	1343	1704	1740	1924	2104	...		0124	0504	0739	0929	1240	1740	2104
30	Flåm .... a.	...		0205	0545	0820	1010	1103	1215	1330	1430	1758	1836	2005	2145	...		0205	0545	0820	1010	1328	1828	2145

			※N	※	Ⓐ								B				※N	※	Ⓐ			
Flåm .... d.	...		0010	0400	0640	0830	0925	1015	1125	1240	1510	1550	1836	2005	...		0010	0400	0640	0830	1125	1535	2000
Vatnahalsen .... d.	...		0048	0432	0718	0908	1008	1106	1221	1328	1602	1645	1913	2047	...		0048	0432	0718	0908	1203	1613	2038
Myrdal 481 .... a.	...		0051	0435	0721	0911	1011	1109	1224	1331	1605	1648	1916	2050	...		0051	0435	0721	0911	1206	1616	2041

B – Runs May 29 - Aug. 28.   N – Conveys (**except** on night of ⑥) 🛏 2 cl. Oslo - Flåm and v.v.

Table 482
OSLO - KRISTIANSAND - STAVANGER
2 class only unless otherwise shown

km		ET71 ® ※	701 ® R		ET73 ® R	703 ® R	1632 ® P	707 ® N	705 ® A	705 ® A
0	Oslo Sentral § .... d.		0718	1033	1539	1718	1945	2239	2248	2248
7	Lysaker/Fornebu §.... d.		0729	1043	1549	1728	1955	2250	2259	2259
40	Drammen §............... d.		0757	1114	1620	1759	2028	2324	2335	2335
86	Kongsberg .... d.		0829	1157	1653	1838	2109	0007	0018	0018
133	Nordagutu .... d.		0907	1238	1729	1922	2151	0051	0107	0107
150	Bø .... d.		0922	1254	1743	1938	2205	0108	0125	0125
164	Lunde .... d.			1307		1950		0123	0139	0139
208	Neslandsvatn .... d.		1004	1342	1828	2028		0158	0217	0217
269	Nelaug .... a.		1049	1431	1913	2115		0245	0305	0305
269	Nelaug .... d.	0830	1055	1440	1650	1920	2120			0315
305	**Arendal** .... a.	0910	1135	1521	1730	2000	2200			0405
269	Nelaug .... d.		1051	1434		1917	2117		0251	0311
352	**Kristiansand** .... a.		1152	1544		2016	2215		0358	0416
352	**Kristiansand** .... d.	0700	1202	1557		2026				0430
465	Moi .... d.	0837	1322	1730		2148				0606
513	Egersund § .... d.	0915	1358	1810		2226				0646
571	Sandnes § .... d.	1005	1436	1848		2303				0740
586	Stavanger § .... a.	1017	1448	1900		2315				0756

km		518 Ⓐ	704 ⚲	ET72 ® R		702 ® S	708 ® ※	ET74 ® R	710 ® N	706 ®	2500 ® T
0	Stavanger § .... d.		0700		1206		1522	1826	2200		
7	Sandnes § .... d.		0713		1220		1538	1846	2214		
40	Egersund § .... d.		0748		1305		1616	1935	2302		
86	Moi .... d.		0824		1346		1652	2014	2340		
133	**Kristiansand** .... a.		0940		1517		1808	2150	0120		
133	**Kristiansand** .... d.	0720	0950		1531	1630	1818		0140		
164	Nelaug .... d.	0823	1051		1638		1917		0251		
208	**Arendal** .... d.	0720	1005	1345	1550		1830			0135	
269	Nelaug .... d.		1049	1431	1631		1910			0225	
269	Nelaug .... a.	0825	1053	1425	1648		1919		0305	0305	
305	Neslandsvatn .... d.	0918	1139		1738	1826	2003		0355	0355	
352	Lunde .... d.	0956			1818	1904			0429	0429	
352	Bø .... d.	0637	1008	1223	1629	1830	1918	2045		0443	0443
465	Nordagutu .... d.	0703	1025	1239	1648	1846	1941	2059		0500	0500
513	Kongsberg .... d.	0750	1108	1316	1745	1926	2023	2136		0543	0543
571	Drammen §............... d.	0837	1146	1346	1837	2005	2103	2208		0625	0625
586	Lysaker/Fornebu §.... a.	0905	1216	1410	1905	2031	2132	2230		0700	0700
	Oslo Sentral § .... a.	0915	1227	1421	1915	2042	2142	2242		0712	0712

A – ⑥: 🛏 2 cl. Oslo - Arendal.   P – ⑦: 🛏 2 cl. and � 2 cl. Oslo - Kristiansand. T – ①-⑥: 🛏 2 cl. Arendal - Oslo.
N – ⑥: 🛏 2 cl., 🚋 2 cl. and 🚌 Oslo - Stavanger R – Also conveys 🚌 and ※. § – Additional local trains operate Oslo - Drammen and v.v.
and v.v.; 🛏 2 cl. Oslo - Kristiansand and v.v. S – ® (departures from Kristiansand); conveys ⚲. (approx. hourly), Stavanger - Egersund and v.v.

Table 483
OSLO - ÅNDALSNES and TRONDHEIM
2 class only unless otherwise shown

km		371 ※		ET41 S ®	351	301	c33	ICE35		403	403 T	315 Ⓐ	377		ET43 S ®	317	317 ⑤r	ICE37		319 ⑧	305 N	321 ⑦	405 R	405 A
0	Oslo Sentral .... d.			0805	0905	1005	1105	1305		1405	1405	1505	1532		1605	1705	1705	1905		2105	2230	2247	2300	2300
21	Lillestrøm .... d.			0824	0925	1026	1124	1324		1425	1425	1525	1554		1624	1725	1725	1924		2125	2250	2309	2322	2322
68	Eidsvoll .... d.			0857	1001	1103	1158	1359		1501	1501	1603	1636		1657	1803	1803	1958		2203	2337	2348	2358	2358
126	Hamar .... d.	0545		0940	1048	1200	1240	1442		1543	1543	1657	1735		1738	1853	1853	2040		2256	0030	0036	0048	0048
184	Lillehammer .... a.			1020	1135		1331	1527		1630	1630	1753			1818	1942	1942	2130		2345		0125	0136	0136
184	Lillehammer .... d.			1022	1137		1333			1633	1633				1820		1952	2132v				0149	0149	0149
	Elverum .... d.	0617				1227							1804							0102				
	Koppang .... d.	0747				1337							1916							0214				
	Røros .... d.	1007				1559							2130							0431				
242	Ringebu .... d.			1103	1228		1426			1720	1720							2052	2219v			0243	0243
266	Vinstra .... d.			1121	1246		1444			1738	1738			1915				2114	2237v			0311	0311
297	Otta .... d.			1143	1317		1507			1803	1803			1938				2139	2300v			0336	0336
343	Dombås .... a.			1212	1349					1838	1838			2008			2215					0412	0412
343	Dombås .... d.			1214	1358					1841	1848			2010								0426	0445
457	**Åndalsnes** .... a.				1525					2015													0620
521	Molde 🚌 .... a.				1655					2155													0755
583	Ålesund 🚌 .... a.				1800					2250													0855
430	Oppdal .... a.			1312						1937				2107								0534	
595	Kristiansund 🚌 ..... a.			1745										0045n								0915c	
501	Støren .... a.					1737				2035											0614	0633	
553	**Trondheim** .... a.			1445		1830				2120			2311p	2355g	2239						0710	0725	

	310 Ⓐ	312 ※	370 Ⓐ	ICE30 Ⓐ ®	ICE32 ⑥t	ICE32	372	344 ※	344	ET42 S ®	352 S ®	402 T Ⓐ	376	ICE34	ICE36	302 ⑦		348 Ⓐ	378	354	ET44 S ®	3162 ⑧	356 A ®	406 R ®	306 N ®
Trondheim .... d.	⚲	⚲							0745		0920	1010p				1320				1550			2245	2225	
Støren .... d.											1004	1056p				1414							2331	2323	
Kristiansund 🚌 ..... d.									0510c										1245			2020b			
Oppdal .... d.									0918		1100								1721			0030			
Ålesund 🚌 .... d.									0745									1400			2030				
Molde 🚌 .... d.									0835									1455			2130				
Åndalsnes .... d.									1020									1635			2315				
Dombås .... a.								0755		1013	1155	1202						1810	1817			0105	0133	
Dombås .... d.				0600	0710			0841		1015	1212	1212				1705			1819			0150	0150	
Otta .... d.				0623	0733			0906		1107	1306	1306				1713			1915			0236	0236	
Vinstra .... d.				0641	0751			0926		1130	1324	1324				1736			1933			0317	0317	
Ringebu .... d.								0545		1235							1602						0117	
Røros .... d.		0605					0749			1438							1814		1914				0322	
Koppang .... d.		0724					0901			1549							1930		2020				0437	
Elverum .... d.																								
Lillehammer .... a.				0723	0833			1017		1210	1410	1410				1827		1925		2013		0402	0402	
Lillehammer .... d.	0515	0613		0725	0835	0835		1020	1020	1212	1413	1413		1630		1829		1929		2015	2044	0415	0415	
Hamar .... d.	0607	0703	0750	0816	0920	0920	0938	1112	1112	1256	1509	1509	1626	1715	1917	2003	2023	2046		2058	2137	0510	0510	0529
Eidsvoll .... d.	0653	0753		0857	1001	1001	1026	1158	1158	1333	1555	1555	1721g	1759	1833	2044	2136	2150		2136	2225	0553	0553	0612
Lillestrøm .... a.	0735	0835		0936	1037	1037	1105	1235	1235	1407	1635	1635	1801g	1833	2034	2136	2150		2209	2308	0635	0635	0703
Oslo Sentral .... a.	0755	0855		0955	1055	1055	1128	1255	1255	1427	1655	1655	1825g	1855	2055	2156	2210		2228	2328	0655	0655	0728

A – 🚋 2 cl. and 🚌 Oslo - Åndalsnes and v.v. T – Also conveys 🚌 and ※.   r – Not Apr. 14.
N – 🛏 2 cl. and 🚌 Oslo - Trondheim and v.v. b – ⑧ only. c – ※ only.   t – Not Apr. 15.
R – 🛏 2 cl. and 🚌 Oslo - Trondheim and v.v.; g – ⑤⑦ (also Apr. 17, May 1, 17, 25; not Apr. 30). v – Ⓐ.only.
🛏 2 cl. Lillehammer - Trondheim and v.v. n – ⑧ (from Oppdal) only.   🚌 – Connection by bus. Reservations (not compulsory)
S – Also conveys 🚌 and ⚲. p – ⑦ (also Apr. 14, 17, May 1, 17, 25; not Apr. 30). may be made through the NSB reservation system.

Table 484 TRONDHEIM - BODØ - NARVIK

2 class only unless otherwise shown

km		459 Ⓐ	421	433 S	433 ⚒	451 P[R]	457 Q	457 R[R]	445	455 N[R]	🚌
0	**Trondheim** § d.	...	0747	0753	0753	0855	1505	1505	1850	2300	...
31	Hell § d.	...	0816x	0837x	0837x	|	|	|	1920x	|	...
34	Stjørdal § d.	...	0824	0842	0842	0929	1537	1537	1925	2337	...
106	Storlien **476** a.	...	0938	|	|	|	|	|	|	|	...
126	Steinkjer § d.	...	...	1005	1002	1050	1659	1701	2050	0100	...
220	Grong d.	...	...	1110	▬	1204	▬	1813	▬	0213	...
406	Mosjøen d.	0700	...	...	...	1426	...	2027	...	0502	...
498	Mo i Rana d.	0806	...	...	🚌	1538	...	2135	🚌	0625	...
	Bodø d.	|	...	...	1630	|	...	...	0715	|	...
674	Fauske a.	1018	...	...	1745	1755	🚌	...	0830	0846	0910
674	Fauske d.	1020	...	...	...	1800	1815	...	...	0850	|
729	**Bodø** a.	1100	...	...	...	1840	|	...	...	0930	1405
982	**Narvik** 🚌 a.	...	...	...	...	...	2300	...	...	...	

	422	436	458 ⚒🍷	458 S[R] 🍷	🚌	452 P	446	450 Ⓐ	🚌	456 N[R]
Narvik 🚌 d.	...	...	...		0645	...	...	...	1615	...
Bodø d.	...	...	...	...	|	1115	...	1515	|	2100
Fauske a.	...	...	...	...	1140	1154	...	1555	2120	2140
Fauske d.	...	...	...	...	1150	1200	...	1555	2140	2153
Bodø a.	...	...	...	...	1300	|	...	|	2250	|
Mo i Rana d.	...	...	...	0830	▬	1436	...	1824	▬	0029
Mosjøen d.	...	...	...	0940	...	1559	...	1935	...	0156
Grong d.	...	...	1206	1206	**442**	1815	...	...	...	0415
Steinkjer § d.	...	1108	1315	1315	1640	1921	2012	...	**428**	0524
Storlien **476** d.	1005	|	|	|	|	|	|	...	2135	|
Stjørdal § a.	1123	1232	1437	1437	1810	2037	2139	...	2248	0645
Hell d.	1131	1237x	|	|	1814x	|	2144x	...	2253x	|
Trondheim § a.	1200	1310	1513	1513	1844	2110	2214		2325	0720

N – 🛏 2 cl., (2) and 🍷 Trondheim - Bodø and v.v.; 🛏 2 cl. Trondheim - Mosjøen and v.v. Conveys (except night of ⑥) 🛏 2 cl. Trondheim - Mo i Rana and v.v.
P – (12) and ✕ Trondheim - Bodø and v.v..
Q – ⑥, also Apr. 13, 30. Conveys 🍷.
R – Not ⑥, not Apr. 13, 30. Conveys 🍷.
S – ⑦, also Apr. 13, 14, 17, May 1, 25.
x – Trains call on request.
🚌 – Operated by *Ofotens Bilruter* and *Saltens Bilruter*. Reservations (not compulsory) may be made through the NSB reservation system.
§ – Additional local trains run Trondheim - Steinkjer and v.v.

Table 485 🚌 NARVIK - TROMSØ - HAMMERFEST and KIRKENES

Jan. 1 - Mar. 25 1995

km		Ⓐ			Ⓑ	D	Ⓑ	D▲	⑦	
0	**Narvik** (Bus Station) d.	0515	...	...	1245	...	1200	1515t	1850	...
186	Nordkjosbotn d.	0825	...	...	1620	...	1620	1850	2205	...
259	**Tromsø** (Prostneset) d.	0935	...	...	|	1600	1730	1955	2305	...
246	Lyngseidet d.	...	...	...	1745	1750	...	...	...	...
473	**Alta** a.	...	...	...	*2300*	2300	...	...	...	...
		②④⑤	⑦	⚒	⚒	H	⑤⑦	D	D	
473	**Alta** d.		...	0715	...	...	...	1535	...	...
	Hammerfest d.	...	...	|	0750	...	...	|	1600	...
560	Skaidi d.	...	...	0905	0905	...	...	1720	1720	...
617	Hammerfest a.	...	...	1015	|	...	...	1830	|	...
647	Lakselv d.	...	...	...	1105	...	...	...	1905	...
722	Karasjok d.	...	...	...	1215	1225	1410	...	2030	...
900	Tana Bru d.	0840	1230	...	...	1540	1730	...	...	...
1044	**Kirkenes** a.	1115	1500	...	...	1800	1955	...	...	...

		⚒	⚒	D			L		
Kirkenes d.	...	...	...	0915	...	...	1530	...	...
Tana Bru d.	...	...	...	1140	...	...	1815	...	...
Karasjok d.	...	0630	...	1500	...	...	...	...	...
Lakselv d.	...	0810	...	1630	...	...	...	...	...
Hammerfest d.	...	|	0850	|	1705	...	...	...	...
Skaidi d.	...	1015	1015	1825	1825	...	...	...	...
Hammerfest a.	...	1115	|	1930	|	...	...	...	...
Alta a.	...	...	1145	...	1955	...	...	...	...
	Ⓐ	D▲	Ⓐ	Ⓐ	⑥	D	⑦	⑦	⑦
Alta d.	...	...	0900	*0900*	0900	...	1345	*1345*	...
Lyngseidet d.	...	...	1430	1430	1430	...	1935	1935	...
Tromsø (Prostneset) d.	0620	1015	1605	|	1635n	1600	2115	|	2025
Nordkjosbotn d.	0745	1125	...	1555	1555	1710	...	2140	2145
Narvik (Bus Station) a.	1110t	1455t	...	...	...	2035	...	...	0030

D – Daily.
H – ①②③④⑥.
L – ②④⑤⑦.
n – Via Nordkjosbotn.
t – Runs to / from railway station.
▲ – Reservations (not compulsory) may be made through the NSB reservation system.

Table 486 OSLO - GJØVIK

2 class only

km			🍷			Ⓐ🍷			Ⓑ	
0	**Oslo** Sentral d.	0710	0910	1210	1410	1610	1715	1910	2210	0000
70	Jaren d.	0819	1018	1319	1517	1727	1824	2020	2320	0118
99	Eina d.	0842	1041	1342	1540	1752	1847	2043	2343	0141
110	Raufoss a.	0851	1050	1351	1549	1803	1856	2052	2352	0150
122	**Gjøvik** a.	0901	1100	1401	1559	1815	1906	2102	0002	0200

	Ⓐ	Ⓐ	🍷					🍷	Ⓑ
Gjøvik d.	0450	0533	0705	0935	1137	1435	1645	1935	2139
Raufoss d.	0501	0545	0716	0946	1148	1446	1656	1946	2150
Eina d.	0510	0557	0725	0955	1157	1455	1705	1955	2159
Jaren d.	0533	0624	0748	1020	1221	1519	1729	2019	2223
Oslo Sentral a.	0638	0747	0856	1127	1329	1629	1842	2127	2334

Table 488 OSLO - LARVIK - SKIEN - NOTODDEN

2 class only

km	ICE trains: [R]	572 Ⓐ	574	IC 801	576	578	IC 803 🍷	IC 805 🍷	IC 807 🍷	582	IC 809 Ⓐ🍷	IC 811 🍷	ICE 81 🍷	584 Ⓑ	584 ⑥	IC 813 Ⓐ	ICE 83 Ⓐ🍷	IC 815 🍷	586 Ⓑ	IC 817 Ⓐ🍷	IC 819 🍷	ICE 85 🍷	ICE 87 Ⓑ🍷	IC 821 🍷
0	**Oslo** Sentral § d.	...	...	0621	...	...	0909	1109	1309	...	1418	1509	1551	...	...	1618	1648	1709	...	1818	1909	2109	2209	2339
7	Lysaker / Fornebu § d.	...	...	0632	...	...	0920	1120	1320	...	1429	1520	1601	...	...	1629	1659	1720	...	1829	1920	2120	2220	2350
40	Drammen § d.	...	...	0709	...	...	0950	1150	1350	...	1459	1550	|	...	...	1659	|	1750	...	1859	1950	2148	2250	0020
73	Holmestrand d.	...	...	0741	...	...	1021	1221	1421	...	1534	1621	|	...	...	1734	|	1823	...	1935	2021	2215	2318	0051
87	Skoppum d.	...	...	0755	...	...	1033	1233	1433	...	1546	1633	|	...	...	1746	|	1835	...	1947	2033	2226	2329	0103
103	Tønsberg d.	...	...	0809	...	...	1047	1247	1447	...	1600	1647	1712	...	...	1800	1819	1849	...	2001	2049	2239	2340	0117
127	Sandefjord d.	...	...	0830	...	...	1108	1308	1508	...	1622	1708	1727	...	...	1821	1840	1913	...	2023	2115	2255	2357	0138
146	**Larvik** d.	...	...	0846	...	...	1124	1324	1524	...	1644	1724	1739	...	...	1843	1854	1929	...	2037	2137	2308	0010	0154
169	Porsgrunn d.	0642	...	0920	...	...	1157	1358	1603	...	1718	1758	1816	...	...	1917	1927	2005	...	...	2211	2341	0043	0228
179	**Skien** d.	0657	0825	0928	0949	1158	1205	1406	1611	1641	1726	1806	1824	1836	...	1925	1935	2013	2020	...	2219	2349	0051	0236
214	Nordagutu **482** a.	0727	0855	...	1021	1230	...	...	...	1711	...	...	...	1910	...	...	...	...	2052	...	...	...	...	...
214	Nordagutu **482** d.	0730	0910	...	1035	1248	...	...	...	1733	...	...	...	1924	1924	...	...	...	2108	...	...	...	...	...
233	**Notodden** a.	0752	0932	...	1057	1310	...	...	...	1755	...	...	...	1946	1946	...	...	...	2130	...	...	...	...	...

ICE trains: [R]	IC 800 Ⓐ	IC 802 ⚒🍷	IC 804 Ⓐ	ICE 80 Ⓐ🍷	IC 806	ICE 82 Ⓐ🍷	IC 808 ⚒🍷	573 Ⓐ	IC 810 🍷	575 ⚒	ICE 84 🍷	577	IC 814 🍷	579	IC 816 🍷	IC 818 🍷	585	IC 820 🍷	IC 822 ⑦	587 ⑥	587 Ⓑ	ICE 86 🍷	IC 824	589
Notodden d.	...	...	...	...	...	...	...	0638	...	0828	...	0955	...	1200	...	...	1622	...	...	1820	1820	...	...	2028
Nordagutu **482** a.	...	...	...	...	...	...	...	0700	...	0850	...	1017	...	1222	...	...	1644	...	...	1842	1842	...	...	2050
Nordagutu **482** d.	...	...	...	...	...	...	...	0703	...	0908	...	1028	...	1242	...	...	1648	...	...	...	1850	...	...	2100
Skien d.	...	0438	0503	0540	0550	0630	0645	0737	0741	0940	0950	1100	1145	1314	1345	1542	1721	1735	1824	...	1920	1957	2053	2130
Porsgrunn d.	...	0448	0514	0550	0600	0639	0656	0755	0752	...	0959	...	1156	...	1356	1552	...	1746	1835	...	...	2008	2103	...
Larvik d.	0437	0523	0549	0625	0635	0712	0731	...	0827	...	1032	...	1231	...	1431	1628	...	1826	1911	...	...	2042	2142	...
Sandefjord d.	0452	0540	0606	0641	0652	0726	0750	...	0848	...	1047	...	1247	...	1447	1646	...	1842	1932	...	...	2056	2159	...
Tønsberg d.	0512	0602	0628	0658	0714	0742	0812	...	0910	...	1110	...	1310	...	1510	1710	...	1906	1954	...	...	2113	2222	...
Skoppum d.	0525	0618	0641	|	0727	|	0825	...	0923	...	1123	...	1323	...	1523	1723	...	1919	2007	...	...	2124	2241	...
Holmestrand d.	0537	0630	0653	|	0740	|	0837	...	0935	...	1135	...	1335	...	1535	1735	...	1935	2021	...	...	2135	2253	...
Drammen § a.	0606	0702	0729	|	0809	|	0907	...	1009	...	1209	...	1409	...	1609	1809	...	2009	2050	...	...	2207	2327	...
Lysaker / Fornebu § a.	0639	0730	0801	0809	0839	0858	0939	...	1039	...	1239	...	1439	...	1639	1839	...	2039	2128	...	...	2239	0000	...
Oslo Sentral § a.	0651	0742	0812	0821	0851	0909	0951	...	1051	...	1251	...	1451	...	1651	1851	...	2051	2139	...	...	2251	0012	...

§ – Local trains run approx. hourly between Oslo and Drammen.

Table 489 🚌 OTHER BUS SERVICES

BERGEN - ÅLESUND: Depart Bergen 0720 (arrive Ålesund 1745). Depart Ålesund 1050 (arrive Bergen 2030).
BERGEN - ODDA (🚌/⛴): Depart Bergen 0730, 1030, 1400⑥, 1515Ⓑ, 1715Ⓑ. Depart Odda 0630⚒, 1020Ⓐ, 1030⑦, 1410⚒, 1540⑦, 1705. Journey 3 hours - 3 hours 50 mins.
BERGEN - TRONDHEIM: Depart Bergen 1615 (arrive Trondheim 0650). Depart Trondheim 1830Ⓑ, 2030⑥ (arrive Bergen 0830⚒, 1015⑦).
GEILO - ODDA: Summer service (June - Sept.) only – 1995 times to be confirmed: Depart Geilo 1200 (arrive Odda 1600). Depart Odda 0720, 1410 (arrive Geilo 1115, 1745).
KIRKENES - MURMANSK: Depart Kirkenes (Rica Arctic) 1500③⑤⑦ (arrive Murmansk 2200③⑤⑦). Depart Murmansk (Hotel Arktika) 0900③⑤⑦ (arrive Kirkenes 1200③⑤⑦).
VOSS - ODDA - KRISTIANSAND: Depart Voss 0850, Odda 1125, arrive Kristiansand 1930. Depart Kristiansand 0900, Odda 1705, arrive Voss 2000.
VOSS - ULVIK: Dep. Voss 0745⑦, 0850⑦, 1140⚒, 1445⑦, 1535⚒, 1730Ⓑ, 2030⑦, 2140Ⓑ. Dep. Ulvik 0720⚒, 0745⑦, 0915⚒, 1355⚒, 1525Ⓑ, 1650Ⓑ, 1845⑦, 1945⑦. Jny 50-75 mins.

272 [R] Reservation obligatory Ⓑ Daily except Saturdays ⑦ Sundays *03*

Table 489a GOL and FLÅM - BALESTRAND - BERGEN

January 1 - April 18, 1995

	⚓	⚓	Ⓐ§	🚌	⚓	🚌		🚌	🚌						
	⚓	⚓		⑦		Ⓑ									
Gol 481 .... d.	⚓	⚓	Ⓐ§	...	1300	...	1850								
Lærdal .... d.	...	...	...	1525	1515	...	2100								
Årdalstangen .... d.	0610	...	...	1525	...	...	...								
Flåm 481a ...... d.		0620f	1335			1840									
Kaupanger .... d.	0640		1425	1600	1600	1550	2135								
Sogndal .... d.				1620		1615	2150								
Leikanger .... d.	0730	0730		1640	1635	1645	1940	2220							
Balestrand .... d.	0800	0800			1700	1730	2005	2300							
Bergen .... a.	1140	1140		2025	2045										

	Ⓐ§	🚌	🚌	🚌	⚓		⚓	⚓	
				§	⚓§		⑥	Ⓐ	Ⓑ§
Bergen .... d.	...	...	0810	...	...	...	1415	1630	...
Balestrand .... d.	...	1005	...	1355	...	...	1805	2020	2200
Leikanger .... d.	...	1050	1205	1435	...	...	1830	2045	2230
Sogndal .... d.	...	1130	1250	1505	...	...			
Kaupanger .... d.	0840	1150	1310	1525	1555	...	1855		...
Flåm 481a ...... a.	0950				1705				2345
Årdalstangen .... a.	...	...	...	...	...	...	1925	2150	...
Lærdal .... a.	...	1220	1340	1555	...	...	...	...	...
Gol 481 .... a.	...	1430	...	1755	...	...	...	...	...

f – Change ships in mid-fjord.

⚓ – Express ship (*Fylkesbaatane*, Strandkaiterminalen, Bergen).

§ – Reservations may be made through NSB reservation system.

FINLAND

Operator: Valtionrautatiet (VR).

Services: Trains convey first and second classes of accommodation as shown by '1, 2 class' or '2 class' (second class only) in the table headings. Exceptions are indicated in the footnotes or by a '2' in the train column. Sleeping cars (🛏) have one berth in first class, two or three berths in second class. There are no couchette car (🛏) services in Finland. ✗ indicates a train with full restaurant car service; trains marked ♀ convey a self-service restaurant or buffet car.

Timings: Valid **January 1 - May 27, 1995**. Services are subject to modification on Finnish public holiday dates (see page 2) **and on days preceding and following them.**

Reservations: Seats on long-distance trains may be reserved at stations and travel agencies. A **supplement** is payable for travel on **EP** (special express) and **IC** (Intercity) trains (and on others marked Ⓡ in the tables): this includes, **if paid in advance**, the fee for a reserved seat. A supplement paid on the train, however, does not guarantee the availability of a seat.

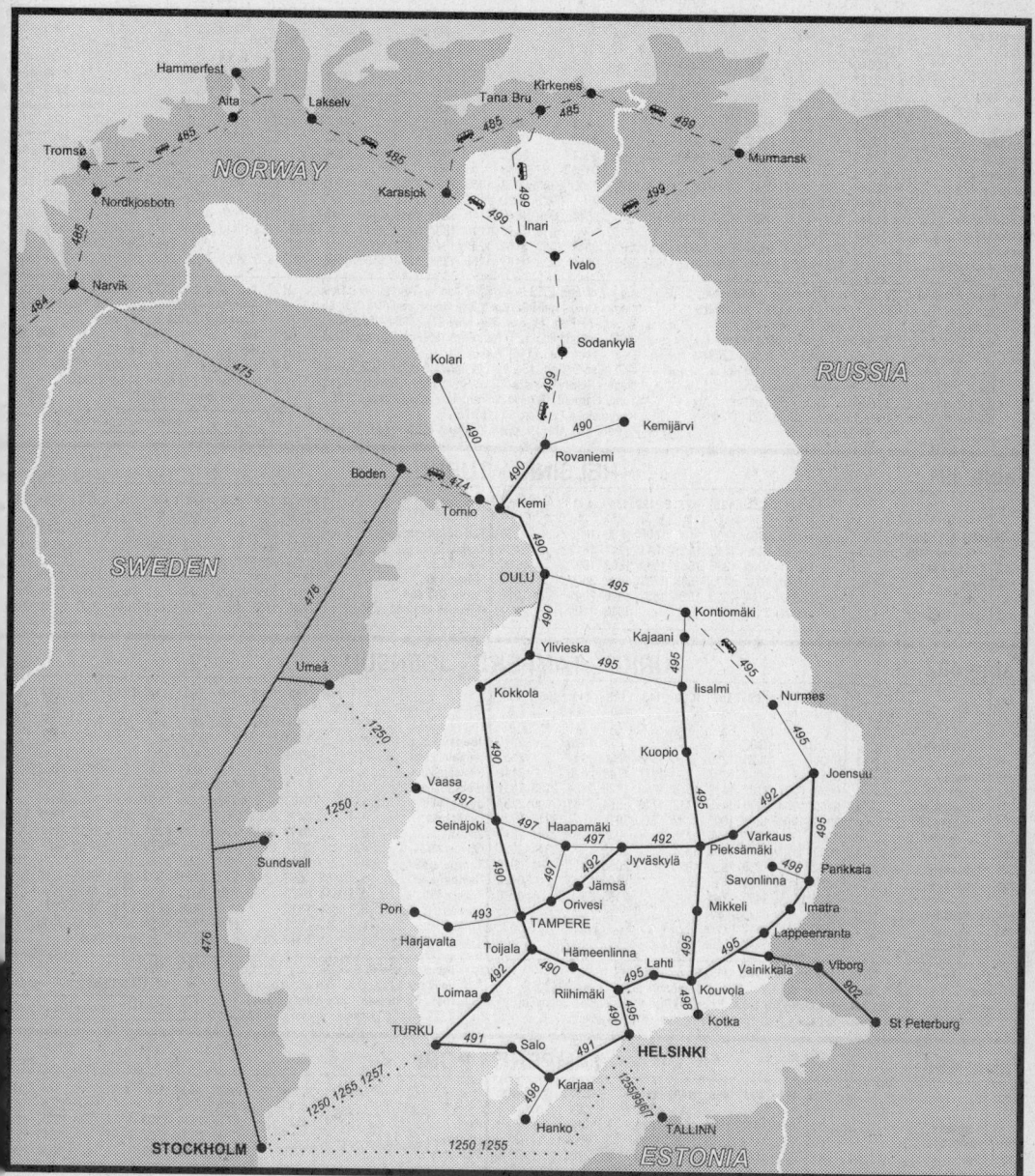

For explanation of standard symbols see page 4

Table 490 HELSINKI - TAMPERE - OULU - ROVANIEMI

1, 2 class

km		141	69	IC99	143	67	145	147	55	149	IC41	IC93	IC57	151	IC153	47	43	155	63	95	65	157	61	51	159
		⚒									IC53‡				Ⓑ	⑤	605‡	Ⓑ	A		B	Ⓑ	C	D	Ⓒ
		🍷	🍷	✕	🍷	🍷	🍷	🍷	✕	🍷	Ⓑ✕	✕	✕	🍷	✕		✕	🍷	🍷2	✕	🍷2	🍷	🍷2	🍷2	🍷
0	**Helsinki 491 495** d.	0606	0658	0758	0858	0958	1058	1158	1258	1358	1454	1524	1558	1602	1658	1726	1758	1858	1926	2002	2028	2102	2125	2202	2302
3	Pasila **491 495** d.	0611	0704	0804	0904	1004	1104	1204	1304	1404	1500	1530	1604	1608	1704	1732	1804	1904	1934	2008	2036	2108	2132	2209	2308
71	Riihimäki **495** d.	0700	0748	0848	0948	1048	1148	1248	1348	1448	1544	|	|	1651	|	1814	1848	1948	2020	2054	2124	2152	2218	2254	2353
108	Hämeenlinna d.	0725	0811	0910	1011	1111	1211	1311	1411	1511	|	1633	|	1713	1806	1834	1911	2011	2046	2116	2149	2214	2243	2319	0015
147	Toijala **492** d.	0748	|	0932	1036	|	1236	1336	|	1536	|	1655	|	1737	|	|	1936	2036	|	2138	2218	2238	|	2346	0039
187	**Tampere 492** a.	0814	0855	0954	1100	1155	1300	1400	1455	1600	1641	1718	1747	1802	1848	1917	2000	2100	2135	2200	2245	2300	2330	0012	0103
187	**Tampere 497** d.	—	0900	—	...	1200	—	...	1500	...	1643	...	1750	...	...	1920	2005	...	2200	...	2318	...	2355	0043	—
346	Seinäjoki **497** a.	**601**	1026	...	...	1327	...	...	1626	...	1804	...	1916	...	...	2054	2138	...	2342	...	0105	...	0138	0242	...
346	Seinäjoki d.	2	1032	...	...	1332	...	...	1633	...	1808	...	1919	...	...	...	2142	...	2347	...	0117	...	0152	0328	...
479	Kokkola d.	0735	1155	...	...	1455	...	...	1805	...	1931	...	2036	...	...	...	2310	...	0147	...	0305	...	0326	0500	...
558	Ylivieska **495** d.	0829	1242	...	...	1544	...	...	1852	...	2020q	...	2123	...	...	...	...	...	0300	...	0358	...	0415	0558	...
680	**Oulu 495** a.	0954	1352	...	...	1708	...	...	2005	...	2125q	...	2232	...	...	...	...	...	0420	...	0509	...	0533	0733	...
680	**Oulu** d.	1005	1404	...	...	1728	...	...	2018q	...	...	...	...	...	...	...	...	...	0440	...	0522	...	0547	0800	...
786	Kemi d.	1120	1512	...	...	1840	...	...	2125q	...	...	...	...	...	...	...	...	...	0605	...	0640	...	0720	0930	...
995	Kolari a.	|	|	...	...	|	🚌	...	|	...	...	...	...	...	...	...	...	...	|	...	0930	...	1025v	|	🚌
900	**Rovaniemi** a.	1241	1640	🚌	...	2005	Ⓑ	...	2300q	...	...	...	...	...	...	...	...	...	0742	...	...	...	0920	1109	Ⓑ
900	**Rovaniemi** d.	*1250*n	...	1650	...	...	2015	...	...	...	...	...	...	...	...	...	...	...	0810	...	...	...	...	...	1135
983	Kemijärvi a.	*1415*n	...	1840	...	...	2135	...	...	...	...	...	...	...	...	...	...	...	0930	...	...	...	...	...	1250

	52	140	66	60	142	64	IC144	IC96	IC604	146	606	148	IC58	150	152	68	IC100	154	56	158	48	160	50	70	602
	E	Ⓐ	F	G	Ⓐ	H	⚒	⚒	IC42‡		IC44‡									⚒	⑦		⑤⑦		
	🍷2		🍷2	🍷2	🍷	🍷2	✕	✕	⚒✕	🍷	✕	🍷	✕	🍷	🍷	✕	✕	🍷	✕	🍷	🍷	🍷	Ⓡ🍷	🍷	2
Kemijärvi d.	*1630*k	...	...	...	...	1910	...	...	...	...	...	...	...	...	...	...	...	...	*0705*h	...	...	...	...	*1120*e	*1400*h
Rovaniemi a.	*1750*k	...	...	...	...	2035	...	...	...	...	...	...	...	...	...	...	...	...	*0830*h	...	...	...	...	*1245*e	*1525*h
Rovaniemi d.	1805	...	2010	...	...	2105	...	...	...	...	...	...	...	...	...	0700	...	...	0945t	...	...	...	...	1300	1600
Kolari d.	1650y	...	|	1925	...	|	...	...	...	...	...	...	...	...	...	|	...	...	|	...	...	...	...	|	|
Kemi d.	2010	...	2148	2214	...	2243	...	...	...	...	...	...	...	...	...	0832	...	...	1122t	...	...	...	...	1422	1723
Oulu a.	2127	...	2300	2328	...	2357	...	...	...	...	...	...	...	...	...	0936	...	...	1232t	...	...	...	...	1539	1842
Oulu 495 d.	2210	...	2315	2343	...	0012	...	...	...	...	...	...	0715	...	...	0956	...	...	1252	...	...	...	1547	1603	1850
Ylivieska **495** d.	2350	...	0038	|	...	0127	...	...	...	...	...	...	0826	...	...	1109	...	...	1409	...	...	...	1648	1719	2030
Kokkola d.	0048	...	0135	0150	...	0228	...	...	0525	...	0610	...	0913	...	...	1156	...	...	1457	...	...	...	1729	1806	2124
Seinäjoki a.	0217	...	0315	0322	...	0401	...	...	0632	...	0740	...	1029	...	...	1314	...	...	1615	...	...	...	1838	1920	—
Seinäjoki **497** d.	0243	...	0330	0355	...	0423	...	...	0644	...	0815	...	1033	...	...	1328	...	...	1630	...	1746	...	1842	1925	**92**
Tampere 497 a.	0423	...	0506	0533	...	0602	...	...	0804	...	0953	...	1156	...	...	1454	...	...	1801	...	1911	...	2008	2052	✕
Tampere 492 d.	0448	0527	0535	0542	0605	0622	0707	0746	0806	0858	0958	1058	1200	1258	1358	1500	1600	1620	1804	1858	1914	1956	2010	2058	2210
Toijala **492** d.	0515	0550	0604	0611	0627	|	0729	|	|	0922	1022	1122	|	1322	1422	|	|	1644	|	1922	|	2018	|	2121	2235
Hämeenlinna d.	0542	0613	0632	0639	0650	0710	0751	|	0847	0946	1046	1146	1243	1346	1446	1546	|	1708	1848	1946	1956	2041	|	2146	2258
Riihimäki 495 d.	0609	0635	0702	0709	0711	0737	|	0850	|	1010	1110	1210	1307	1410	1510	1610	1703	1733	1913	2010	|	2104	|	2210	2320
Pasila 491 495 a.	0703	0722	0808	0804	0752	0820	0851	0930	0948	1052	1152	1252	1349	1452	1552	1652	1748	1820	1954	2052	2057	2146	2150	2254	0001
Helsinki 491 495 a.	0710	0728	0815	0810	0758	0827	0857	0936	0954	1058	1158	1258	1355	1458	1558	1658	1754	1826	2000	2058	2103	2152	2156	2300	0007

A – 🛏 1,2 cl. and [2] Helsinki - Rovaniemi - Kemijärvi; 🛏 1,2 cl. Turku Harbour (**111**) - Tampere - Rovaniemi.

B – ② Jan. 3 - Apr. 25 (also ⑤ Feb. 17 - Apr. 21): 🛏 1,2 cl. and [2] Helsinki - Kemi - (**665**) Kolari.

C – ⑤⑦ (also ⑥ Feb. 18 - Apr. 22): 🛏 1,2 cl. and [2] Helsinki - Rovaniemi and (⑤ Jan. 6 - Apr. 28) Kolari; 🛏 1,2 cl. Turku (**101**) - Tampere - Rovaniemi.

D – 🛏 1,2 cl. and [2] Helsinki - Oulu - Rovaniemi; 🛏 1,2 cl. Turku (**101**) - Tampere - Oulu and (①②③④, also ⑤ Feb. 17 - Apr. 21) Rovaniemi.

E – 🛏 1,2 cl. and [2] Kolari (③⑥ Jan. 4 - Apr. 26) and Rovaniemi - Oulu - Helsinki; 🛏 1,2 cl. Rovaniemi (①②③④, also ⑥ Jan. 7 - Feb. 11, Apr. 29 - May 27) - Oulu - Tampere - (**102**) Turku Harbour; ⑦ (not Feb. 19 - Apr. 23) 🛏 1,2 cl. Oulu - Tampere - (**116**) Turku.

F – ⑤⑦ (also ⑥ Feb. 18 - Apr. 22) 🛏 1,2 cl. and [2] Rovaniemi - Helsinki; ⑤ 🛏 1,2 cl. Rovaniemi - Tampere - (**102**) Turku Harbour; ⑦ (also ⑥ Feb. 18 - Apr. 22) 🛏 1,2 cl. Rovaniemi - Tampere - (**116**) Turku.

G – ⑥ Feb. 18 - Apr. 29: 🛏 1,2 cl. and [2] Kolari - Helsinki.

H – 🛏 1,2 cl. and [2] Kemijärvi - Rovaniemi - Tampere - Helsinki; 🛏 1,2 cl. Rovaniemi - Tampere - (**102**) Turku Harbour.

e – 🚌. h – 🚌; Ⓐ. k – 🚌; Ⓑ.
n – 🚌; ⚒. q – ⑤⑦ only. t – ①⑥ only.
v – Number **661** from Kemi (depart 0735).
y – Number **652** to Kemi (arrive 1936).
‡ – Number from Seinäjoki.

☛ **IC** trains: Ⓡ, supplement payable.

Table 491 HELSINKI - TURKU

1, 2 class

km		121	123	125	127	EP129	131	133		135
		🍷	🍷	🍷	🍷	✕Ⓡ	🍷	🍷		🍷
0	**Helsinki 490 495** d.	0650	0904	1138	1406	1606	1706	1838	...	2130
3	Pasila **491 495** d.	0655	0909	1143	1411	1611	1711	1843	...	2135
87	Karjaa **498** d.	0751	1003	1236	1503	1659	1802	1937	...	2230
144	Salo d.	0820	1032	1305	1535	1731	1832	2009	...	2259
200	**Turku** a.	0852	1104	1338	1614	1802	1906	2041	...	2330
203	Turku Harbour a.	0901	...	...	...	...	1916	2101	...	...

	EP122	124	126	128	130	132	398	134	136
	✕Ⓡ	🍷	🍷	🍷	🍷	🍷	⑦	🍷	🍷
Turku Harbour d.	...	0840	...	...	...	...	...	*1926*	2046
Turku d.	0650	0902	1134	1402	1548	1700	...	1938	2107
Salo d.	0725	0935	1208	1435	1626	1732	...	2010	2139
Karjaa **498** d.	0753	1004	1236	1504	1659	1803	1910	2040	2207
Pasila **490 495** d.	0841	1057	1329	1557	1757	1856	2028	2129	2304
Helsinki 490 495 a.	0846	1102	1334	1602	1802	1902	2033	2134	2310

Table 492 TURKU - TAMPERE - JOENSUU

1, 2 class

km		103	IC99	105	107	IC93	113	109	111	95	101
			⚒					Ⓑ	A		B
		🍷	H	🍷	🍷	H	🍷	🍷	🍷	H	🍷2
0	Turku Harbour d.	...	...	0902	...	...	...	...	1926	...	*2046*
3	**Turku** d.	0700	...	0925	1255	...	1533	1700	1937	...	2100
69	Loimaa d.	0742	...	1007	1337	...	1617	1745	2020	...	2142
131	Toijala **490** d.	0824	0932	1102	1419	1655	1659	1828	2104	2138	2231
171	**Tampere 490** a.	0850	0954	1130	1445	1718	1726	1854	2131	2200	2257
171	**Tampere 497** d.	0900	1005	1201	1500	1732	...	1910	...	2215	2320
213	Orivesi **497** d.	0926	|	1227	1526	1758	...	1936	...	2241	2347
269	Jämsä d.	1002	1101	1303	1602	1831	...	2012	...	2314	0024
326	**Jyväskylä** a.	1032	1133	1338	1634	1858	...	2050	...	2341	0058
326	**Jyväskylä** d.	1050	...	1355	1649	...	...	2100	...	...	0120
406	Pieksämäki a.	1145	...	1450	1744	...	...	2155	...	...	0210
406	Pieksämäki d.	1200	...	1525	1850e	...	...	...	...	...	0435
455	Varkaus d.	1247	...	1612	1937e	...	...	...	...	...	0527
589	**Joensuu** a.	1423	...	1747	2110e	...	...	...	...	...	0700

	116	102	IC96	110	106	114	IC100	104	108	92
	C	D	⚒						Ⓑ	
	2	🍷2	H	🍷	🍷	🍷	H	🍷	🍷	H
Joensuu d.	...	2220	...	...	0705	...	...	1250	1615	...
Varkaus d.	...	2354	...	...	0837	...	...	1424	1746	...
Pieksämäki a.	...	0045	...	...	0923	...	...	1510	1832	...
Pieksämäki d.	...	0310	...	*0640*v	0940	1205	...	1525	1850	...
Jyväskylä a.	...	0400	...	*0736*v	1035	1300	...	1620	1945	...
Jyväskylä d.	...	0415	0607	0813	1055	1320	1424	1644	—	2010
Jämsä d.	...	0450	0636	0847	1129	1351	1453	1715	**118**	2041
Orivesi **497** d.	...	0527	0710	0924	1206	1428	|	1752	Ⓑ	2117
Tampere 497 a.	...	0555	0735	0950	1232	1454	1549	1818	🍷	2142
Tampere 490 d.	0550	0655	0746	1000	1251	1503	*1630*	1828	2213	2210
Toijala **490** d.	0616	0723	...	1028	1318	1530	*1700*	1856	2240	2234
Loimaa d.	0654	0813	...	1115	1406	1615	*1746*	1942	2325	...
Turku a.	0742	0857	...	1156	1447	1656	*1827*	2032	0006	...
Turku Harbour a.	...	0917	...	...	...	...	*1842*	2041	...	...

A – Conveys 🛏 1.2 cl. Turku Harbour - Tampere - (**63**) Rovaniemi.

B – 🛏 1,2 cl. and 🛏 Turku - Joensuu; 🛏 1,2 cl. Turku - Tampere - (**51**) Oulu - (①②③④⑥, also ⑤ Feb. 17 - Apr. 21) Rovaniemi; 🛏 1,2 cl. Helsinki (**71**) - Pieksämaki - Joensuu; ⑤⑦ (also ⑥ Feb. 18 - Apr. 22) 🛏 1,2 cl. Turku - Tampere - (**61**) Rovaniemi.

C – Runs ① (also ⑦ Feb. 26 - Apr. 30). Conveys 🛏 1,2 cl. Oulu (**52**) and Rovaniemi (**66**) - Turku (see Table **490** for dates).

H – [12] and ✕ Helsinki - Jyväskylä and v.v.

e – Ⓑ.
v – ⚒; [2] Pieksämäki - Vaasa.

IC trains: Ⓡ, supplement payable.

Table 493 TAMPERE - PORI

1, 2 class

km		461	463	465	149	151		IC153		469
		⚒			A	⑤A		ⒷY		
0	**Tampere** d.	0818	1012	1305	1610	1821	...	1900	...	2208
109	Harjavalta d.	0936	1122	1415	1726	1930	...	2006	...	2320
135	**Pori** a.	0956	1142	1435	1746	1950	...	2025	...	2340

	IC144		146	462	464	466		160	468
	⚒Y		⚒A					⑦A	
Pori d.	0532	...	0715	1010	1303	1554	...	1800	1910
Harjavalta d.	0550	...	0734	1029	1322	1613	...	1819	1930
Tampere a.	0657	...	0845	1148	1440	1727	...	1936	2048

A – [12] and 🍷 Helsinki (Table **490**) - Pori and v.v.

Y – [12] and ✕ Helsinki (Table **490**) - Pori and v.v. Ⓡ.

☛ **IC** trains: Ⓡ, supplement payable.

Table 495 — HELSINKI - KOUVOLA - JOENSUU and OULU

1, 2 class

km		701	9413	35	3	81	9425	11	75	27	593	1	1 79‡	IC83	IC17	33	25	IC7	705	31	77	13	71	71	9491
		2		E	P		E					2	⑤⑦	®	®	P	Ⓐ	®	2	M	®		A	B	®
0	Helsinki 490 491 ..... d.		0600	0630	0702	0802	0910	1030	1122	1225	...	1332	1332	1500	1528	1532	1626	1702	...	1708	1802	1904	2130	2130	2310
3	Pasila 490 491 ..... d.		0605	0635	0708	0808	0914	1036	1128	1231	...	1338	1338	1506	1534	1538	1632	1708	...	1714	1808	1910	2137	2137	2315
71	Riihimäki 490 ..... d.		0657	0717	0753	0854	1014	1122	1213	1314	...	1425	1425	1550	1616	1624	1722	1752	...	1757	1853	1954	2224	2224	0015
130	Lahti ..... d.		0738	0750	0826	0927	1055	1159	1247	1348	...	1500	1500	1622	1651	1702	1756	1827	...	1834	1927	2027	2302	2302	0052
192	Kouvola 498 ..... a.		0818		0858	0959	1135	1233	1322	1423	...	1535	1535	1654	1723		1831	1902	...		2001	2100	2338	2338	0131
192	Kouvola ..... d.	0637		0824	0900	1008		1236	1331	...	1540	1544	1702	1725	1742		1904	1906	1912	2010	2102	2357	2357	0131
305	Mikkeli ..... d.	0800			1113			1437		...	1704	1803				2022		2114		0126	0126	...
376	Pieksämäki ..... d.	0844			1153			1518		...	1746	1840				2104		2154		0216	0216	...
376	Pieksämäki 492 ..... d.	0849			1155			1528		...	1749	1843				2106		2200		0310	0435	...
278	Lappeenranta ..... a.			0947		1323				1640		1808			1952			2154			
314	Imatra ..... d.			1013		1349				1709		1835			2016			2220			
378	Parikkala 498 ..... d.		☐	1052		⑦	1436			1759		1925k			2059						
508	Joensuu 492 ..... a.	0715		1204	1215	1550				1922		2034k			2210						
612	Lieksa ..... d.	0905		1326						2055									0700		
668	Nurmes ..... a.	0955		1405	1420					2140										591
465	Kuopio ..... d.	0952			1245			1619		...	1840	1933				2157		2249		0432		2
550	Iisalmi ..... d.		973		1355			1735		1745	1935	2028				2350			0554		0610
604	Ylivieska 490 ..... a.		2						h	1945										0810
633	Kajaani ..... d.			1126		1450	1610		1830	1835		2131						0707		
659	Kontiomäki ..... d.		1135	1149		1513		1853			2158							0736		
825	Oulu 490 ..... a.			1348		1704	1935		2106e	2120								0933		

		974	☐	594	72	26	32	IC18	IC78	9444	IC8	14	84	34	725	702	2	28	592	76	9488	6	36	80	4	82
		2		®	D		M				E				P	E	2	®			2 ⑦	⑦				
				2	2														2	⑦			P	®		
Oulu 490 ..... d.		1610		1855															0945						1256n
Kontiomäki ..... d.		1807	1810	2113						0550								1148					1510
Kajaani ..... d.		1826		2145						0625								1212					1532
Ylivieska 490 ..... d.				2124													1110						
Iisalmi ..... d.				2324	2330					0440			0742			1100		1310	1322		1630		1645
Kuopio ..... d.				0104						0541			0841					1430			1722		1749
Nurmes ..... d.		1950	102												0820			12			1420	
Lieksa ..... d.		2035	C												0905						1500	
Joensuu 492 ..... d.		2210	2220					0605						1037	1337		1625			1647	
Parikkala 498 ..... d.								0716						1210	1500		1730			1802	
Imatra ..... d.						0624		0758	0914					1256	1544		1727	1811		1850	
Lappeenranta ..... d.						0650		0821	0944			1155	1326	1613		1752	1837		1917	
Pieksämäki 492 ..... a.				0045	0205		0731	0626			0929		1201			1519		1837	
Pieksämäki ..... d.		9420		0300	0300			0628			0933		1245			1537		1845	
Mikkeli ..... d.		Ⓐ		0358	0358			0704			1017		1410			1624		1845	1930
Kouvola ..... d.		2		0516	0516		0626		0803		0903	1033	1124	1146			1418		1657	1740	1849		1932	1941	2003	2043
Kouvola 498 ..... a.		0435		0532	0532	0635		0733	0811	0803	0905	1035	1132		1324		1421	1555	1700	1755	1854		1950	2006	2055
Lahti ..... d.		0515		0612	0612	0712	0720	0808		0905	0940	1113	1207	1226	1405		1458	1631	1737	1831	1936	1953	2009		2041	2131
Riihimäki 490 ..... d.		0555		0651	0651	0746	0803	0842		0955	1015	1147	1243	1307	1455		1536	1709	1811	1906	2025		2041		2115	2205
Pasila 490 ..... a.		0644		0738	0738	0828	0855	0924	0954	1044	1057	1228	1326	1356	1544		1620	1752	1855	1950	2116	2104	2128	2134	2156	2250
Helsinki 490 ..... a.		0650		0745	0745	0834	0902	0930	1000	1050	1103	1234	1332	1403	1550		1626	1758	1901	1956	2122	2110	2134	2140	2202	2256

A – ☐ 1,2 cl. and ☐. Helsinki - Kuopio - Oulu; ☐ 1,2 cl. Turku (101) - Pieksämäki - Oulu.
B – ☐ 1,2 cl. Helsinki - Pieksämäki - (101) Joensuu.
C – ☐ 1,2 cl. Joensuu - Pieksämäki - (72) Helsinki.
D – ☐ 1,2 cl. and ☐. Oulu - Kuopio - Helsinki; ☐ 1,2 cl. Kontiomäki - Pieksämäki - (102) Turku Harbour.
E – ☐ Helsinki - Kotka and v.v.

M – To/from Moskva – for international journeys only (see Table 902).
P – To/from St Peterburg – for international journeys only (see Table 902).
e – ⑤⑦ only.   h – Not ⑤⑦.   k – ⑤ only.
n – ①⑥ only (☐ 1220②③④⑤, 1245⑦).   ‡ – Number from Kouvola.

⏵ IC trains: ®, supplement payable.

Table 497 — JYVÄSKYLÄ and TAMPERE - HAAPAMÄKI - VAASA

1, 2 class

km		565	422	443	523	421	569	☐	441	43
		☐C	2		2	2	®		®	B
0	Jyväskylä ..... d.	0740	1043			1630	1825			
	Tampere 490 492 ..... d.			1020	1625			1820		
	Orivesi 492 ..... d.			1047	1652			1847		
78	Haapamäki ..... d.	0844	1145	1149	1745	1747	1935	1944		
123	Ähtäri ..... d.	0923		1227		1822		2025		
151	Alavus ..... d.	0946		1250	IC41	1841	47	2048		
196	Seinäjoki 490 ..... a.	1018		1322	®A	1912	⑤B	2120		
196	Seinäjoki ..... d.	1035		1335	1630	1815	1928	2105		2152
238	Tervajoki ..... d.	1107		1407	1702	1841	2000			2224
270	Vaasa ..... a.	1130		1430	1725	1903	2023	2150		2247

		IC42	442	44	☐	560	522	444	48	566
		☐A	☐	B	☐	2	2		⑦B	®2
Vaasa ..... d.		0540		0650		0925	1225	1525	1638	1813
Tervajoki ..... d.		0603		0713		0948	1248	1548	1704	1843
Seinäjoki ..... a.		0630		0745		1020	1320	1620	1732	1915
Seinäjoki 490 ..... d.			0637			1038		1635		1930
Alavus ..... d.		0709	☐			1109	422	1706	421	2002
Ähtäri ..... d.		0733	①			1130	2	1727	2	2025
Haapamäki ..... d.		0810	0815	0820	1214	1220	1808	1810	2106
Orivesi 492 ..... a.		0905				1315	1919		
Tampere 490 492 ..... a.		0932				1343	1946		
Jyväskylä ..... a.				0925	1000	1315			1911	2207

A – ☐ and ✕ Helsinki (Table 490) - Vaasa and v.v. ®, supplement payable.   B – ☐ and ☐ Helsinki (Table 490) - Vaasa and v.v.   C – ☐ Pieksämäki (depart 0640) - Vaasa.

Table 498 — HANKO, KOTKA and SAVONLINNA BRANCH LINES

2 class

HANKO - KARJAA 50 km. Journey time: 42 minutes (☐ 60 minutes).
From Hanko: 0700✕, 0910, 1145, 1410, 1605, 1825⑦A, 1845✕, 1930☐, 2110.   From Karjaa: 0800, 1010, 1245, 1510, 1710, 1810☐, 1945, 2240.
A – ☐ Hanko - Karjaa – (398) Helsinki.

KOTKA - KOUVOLA 51 km. Journey time: 40 minutes.
From Kotka: 0725✕B, 0915, 1230A, 1610, 1915, 2150®.   From Kouvola: 0640✕, 0820A, 1140A, 1430, 1750, 2105®.
A – ☐ Kotka - Helsinki and v.v.   B – ☐ Kotka - Kouvola - (9444) Helsinki.

SAVONLINNA - PARIKKALA 59km. Journey time: 51 minutes (☐ 65–90 minutes).
From Savonlinna: 0618, 1030☐, 1632⑦, 1700✕.   From Parikkala: 1100, 1220④☐, 1450☐, 1805☐, 2105.

Table 499 — ☐ ROVANIEMI - NORTHERN NORWAY and MURMANSK

January 1 - May 27, 1995

Rovaniemi a	Sodankylä	Ivalo	Murmansk b	Inari	Karasjok c	Lakselv	Tana Bru		Tana Bru	Lakselv	Karasjok c	Inari	Murmansk b	Ivalo	Sodankylä	Rovaniemi a
0800④	1000④	1500④	2230④					✣	0310h	→		0715	→	0810	1040	1225
1120	1350	1630		1705	1805		✣		0930	→		1330	1610	1745
1655	1925	2145		2220		0025h				0730④	1605④r	1840	2030

– Railway station.   b – Hotel Arktika.   c – Turisthotel.   h – ①⑤⑥ (☐ from March 6).   r – Arrive 1300.

✣ – Arrive 1250.

▲ – Operated by the Finnish postal service (Postilinjat) ☎ (960) 326722/326407 and Murmanskautotrans (Murbus). Tickets, which must be purchased in advance, are available from post offices in Finland, not from the bus station or driver. Only Russians may purchase tickets in Murmansk. The Ivalo - Murmansk service is liable to cancellation due to road conditions – prospective passengers are advised to enquire at a post office before travelling.
✣ – Operated by J. M. Eskelisen Lapin Linjat Oy, Rovaniemi ☎ (960) 344152.

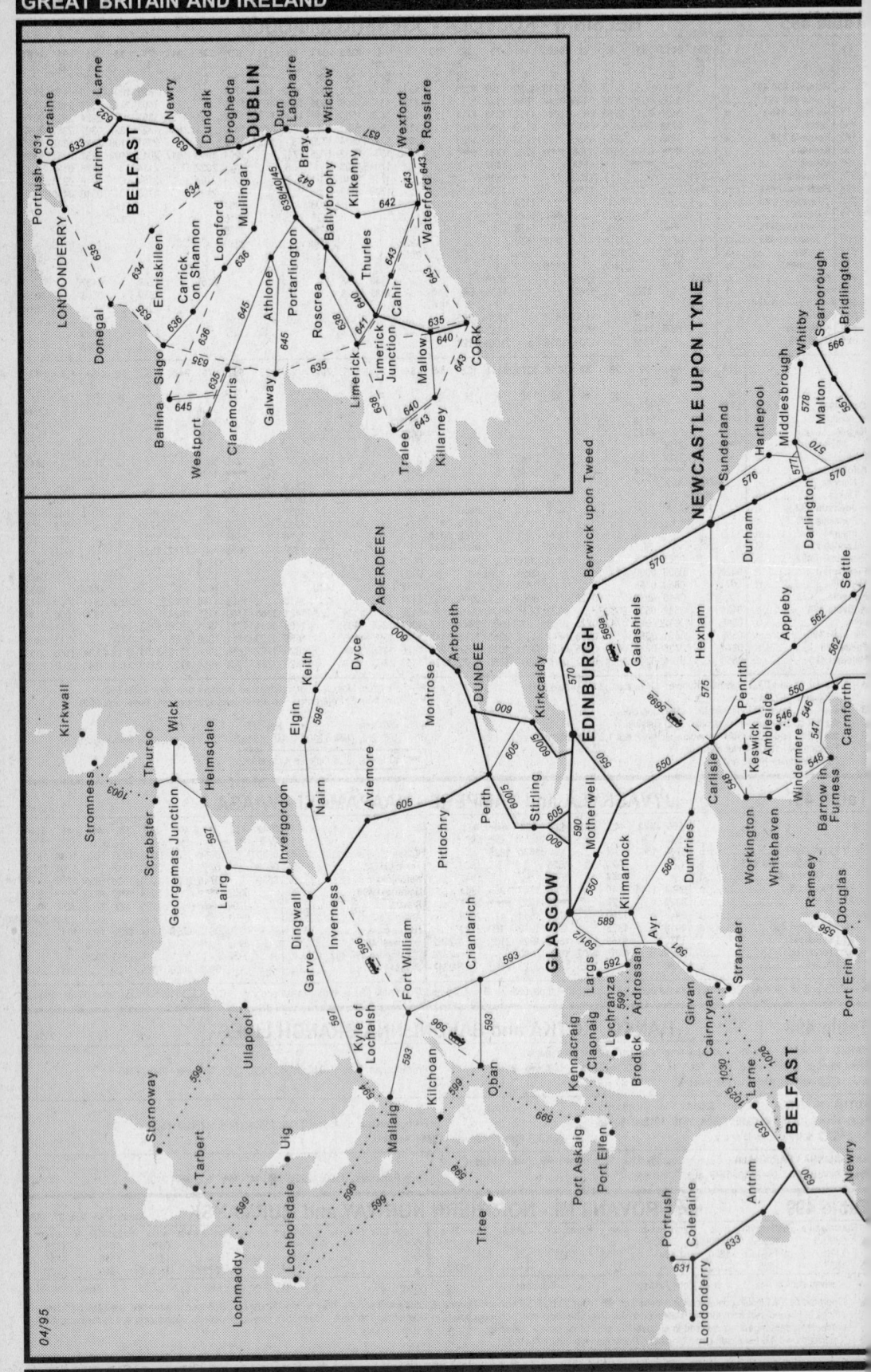

FOR CROSS CHANNEL SHIPPING SERVICES SEE MAP ON PAGE 481

PARIS
BRUSSELS

Margate, Ramsgate, Dover, Folkestone, Canterbury, Chatham, Ashford, Tonbridge, Hastings, Eastbourne, Newhaven, Brighton, Gatwick, Guildford, Woking, Portsmouth, Shanklin, Ryde, Bournemouth, Poole, Weymouth, Dorchester, Southampton, Winchester, Basingstoke, Salisbury, Westbury, Yeovil, Axminster, Exmouth, Torquay, Paignton, Exeter, Newton Abbot, Totnes, Plymouth, Looe, Par, Bodmin, Gunnislake, St Austell, Truro, Falmouth, St Erth, Penzance, St Ives, Newquay, St Mary's

LONDON, Reading, Didcot, Oxford, Banbury, Leamington, Stratford, Swindon, Bath, Bristol, Bristol Parkway, Newport, Weston-super-Mare, CARDIFF, SWANSEA, Tenby, Pembroke Dock, Milford Haven, Fishguard, Carmarthen, Llandindod, Hereford, Gloucester, Cheltenham, Worcester, WOLVERHAMPTON, BIRMINGHAM, Shrewsbury, Craven Arms, Ludlow, Newtown, Welshpool, Machynlleth, Aberystwyth, Barmouth, Harlech, Pwllheli, Porthmadog, Blaenau Ffestiniog, Bala, Ruabon, Wrexham, Chester, Crewe, Bangor, Caernarfon, Holyhead, Llandudno, Llandudno Junction, Rhyl, Prestatyn

Watford, Luton, Milton Keynes, Northampton, Kettering, Rugby, Coventry, Nuneaton, LEICESTER, Loughborough, Peterborough, Grantham, Newark, NOTTINGHAM, Derby, Matlock, Buxton, STOKE, Stafford, MANCHESTER, Stockport, Airport, Warrington, Wigan, LIVERPOOL, Southport, Blackpool, Preston, Blackburn, Fleetwood, Heysham, Lancaster

Cambridge, Stansted, Colchester, Harwich, Felixstowe, Lowestoft, Great Yarmouth, Cromer, Sheringham, NORWICH, Bury St Edmunds, IPSWICH, Ely, March, Spalding, Kings Lynn, Boston, Skegness, Sleaford, Lincoln, Cleethorpes, Grimsby, Hull, Doncaster, SHEFFIELD, Wakefield, Bradford, LEEDS, YORK, Harrogate, Huddersfield

DUBLIN, Dun Laoghaire, Bray, Wicklow, Wexford, Rosslare, Dundalk, Drogheda, Mullingar, Portarlington, Kilkenny, Waterford, Cork, Portlaoise

GREAT BRITAIN

Operators: 25 Train Operating Units (TOUs) provide rail services, currently under the overall control of the British Railways Board (British Rail - BR). Railway infrastructure (including stations) is the property of Railtrack. Under UK Government plans, Railtrack and the TOUs will eventually be privatized. International services via the Channel Tunnel (Eurostar) are operated by European Passenger Services.

Services: Trains convey **first** and **standard** classes of accommodation (shown as '1, 2 class' or [1.2] in the tables), except where '2' in the train column denotes standard class only. **Sleeping cars** (🛏) have one berth in first class and two berths in standard class. Sleeping car passengers may usually remain in their berths until 0730. **Couchette cars** (▬) are **not** operated in Great Britain. Restaurant cars (✕), where shown in the tables, usually operate **only** on ① - ⑤ in the most important services and **may be restricted to** first class passengers. InterCity Pullman trains (indicated by footnote) convey ✕ and in addition offer full meals to first class passengers at their seats, which should be reserved **in advance**. All catering facilities may be withdrawn or reduced on ⑥⑦ and, in addition, may not be available for the complete journey of the train.

Timings: Valid **Sept. 25, 1994** to **May 27, 1995**. **No services** operate on Dec. 25 or Dec. 26 in England and Wales (Jan. 1 in Scotland). Passengers are advised to recheck train times **locally** before travelling during holiday periods (see page **2** for dates) when a reduced service usually operates, and also at weekends (⑥⑦) when engineering work frequently necessitates alterations to the published service. Services on ⑦ shown are liable to change during the currency of the above period.

Tickets: **Reservations** for seats on long-distance journeys and sleeping cars may be made through most main rail stations and appointed agents by quoting the departure time of the train and destination. With the exception of Eurostar services, **train numbers** are not used in Great Britain.

Table 500 LONDON - CHATHAM - DOVER and RAMSGATE

1, 2 class

Timings may vary by up to 3 minutes earlier or later

km			Ⓐ	Ⓐ	⑥	⑥	Ⓐ	Ⓐ	✕ 🍷	✕	✕ 🍷	✕ 🍷	⑦	⑦	✕ 🍷	✕		✕ 🍷	⑥	Ⓐ	⑦ 🍷	⑦	Ⓐ 🍷	Ⓐ 🍷
0	**London Victoria**	d.	0530	...	0541	...	0612	...	0735	...	0805	0805	0805	...	0835	...	and at	1535	...	...	1605	...	1605	1605
55	**Chatham**	d.	0625	...	0639	...	0717	...	0818	...	0848	0848	0849	...	0919	...	the	1619	...	...	1649	...	1650	1650
58	Gillingham (Kent)	d.	0629	...	0643	...	0721	...	0821	...	0851	0851	0852	...	0922	...	same	1622	...	...	1652	...	1654	1654
84	Faversham	a.	0655	...	0708	...	0750	...	0844	...	0913	0913	0914	...	0944	...	minutes	1644	...	...	1714	...	1716	1716
84	Faversham	d.	0656	0702	0719	0714	0752	0753	0846	0847	0916	0918	0920	0917	0946	0947	past	1646	1647	1647	1720	1717	1719	1721
99	**Canterbury East**	d.	│	0717	│	0728	│	0808	│	0902	│	0931	│	0932	│	1002	each	│	1702	1702	│	1732	│	1736
124	**Dover Priory**	a.	│	0746	│	0755	│	0837	│	0920	│	0958	│	1000	│	1020	hour	│	1720	1730	│	1800	│	1804
119	**Margate**	d.	0728	...	0752	...	0824	...	0916	...	0938	...	0952	...	1016	...	until:	1719	...	...	1752	...	1741	...
128	**Ramsgate**	a.	0738	...	0802	...	0834	...	0926	...	0947	...	1002	...	1026	...		1730	...	...	1802	...	1751	...

		⑥ 🍷	⑥ 🍷	Ⓐ 🍷	Ⓐ 🍷	⑥ 🍷	⑥ 🍷	⑥ 🍷	⑦ 🍷	⑦	Ⓐ 🍷	Ⓐ 🍷	⑥ 🍷	Ⓐ 🍷	Ⓐ 🍷	⑥ 🍷	⑥ 🍷	⑦ 🍷	⑦	Ⓐ 🍷	⑥ 🍷	⑥	✕ 🍷	⑦ 🍷	A
London Victoria	d.	1605	1605	1620	1620	1635	1705	1705	1705	...	1707	1707	1735	1753	1753	1805	1805	1805	...	1835	1835	...	1905	1905	...
Chatham	d.	1648	1648	1705	1705	1719	1748	1748	1749	...	1752	1752	1819	1837	1837	1848	1848	1849	...	1917	1919	...	1948	1949	...
Gillingham (Kent)	d.	1651	1651	1709	1709	1722	1751	1751	1752	...	1756	1756	1822	1841	1841	1851	1851	1852	...	1921	1922	...	1951	1952	...
Faversham	a.	1713	1713	1735	1735	1744	1813	1813	1814	...	1822	1822	1844	1904	1904	1913	1913	1914	...	1944	1944	...	2014	2014	...
Faversham	d.	1716	1718	1738	1740	1746	1816	1818	1820	1817	1825	1827	1846	1907	1909	1916	1918	1916	1917	1946	1946	1947	2015	2016	2017
Canterbury East	d.	│	1731	│	1755	*1801*	│	1831	│	1832	│	1842	*1901*	│	1924	│	1931	│	1932	│	│	2002	│	│	2032
Dover Priory	a.	│	1758	│	1824	*1820*	│	1858	│	1900	│	1910	*1920*	│	1952	│	1958	│	2000	│	│	2020	│	│	2101
Margate	d.	1738	...	1810	...	1816	1838	...	1852	...	1855	...	1916	1939	...	1938	...	1948	...	2009	2016	...	2044	2048	...
Ramsgate	a.	1747	...	1822	...	1826	1847	...	1902	...	1906	...	1926	1951	...	1947	...	1958	...	2019	2026	...	2101	2058	...

		Ⓐ 🍷	A 🍷	A	Ⓐ	A 🍷	A	A	A	✕	②-⑦ n
London Victoria	d.	1935	2005	...	2035	2105	...	2205	...	2305	0005
Chatham	d.	2019	2050	...	2119	2150	...	2248	...	2348**k**	0046
Gillingham (Kent)	d.	2022	2054	...	2122	2154	...	2251	...	2351**k**	0049
Faversham	a.	2044	2116	...	2144	2216	...	2313	...	0013**n**	0113
Faversham	d.	2045	2117	2119	2145	2217	2219	2315	2316	0015**n**	0116
Canterbury East	d.	│	│	2133	│	│	2233	│	2328	│	│
Dover Priory	a.	│	│	2200	│	│	2300	│	2347	│	│
Margate	d.	2117	2146	...	2217	2249	...	2347	...	0047**n**	0148
Ramsgate	a.	2127	2201	...	2227	2301	...	2358	...	0058**n**	0158

		⑥	Ⓐ	Ⓐ	⑥	⑥	Ⓐ	Ⓐ	⑥	⑥ 🍷
Ramsgate	d.	0437	0437	...	...	0522	0531	...	...	0557
Margate	d.	0445	0447	...	...	0532	0541	...	...	0607
Dover Priory	d.	│	*0441*	0513	0521	│	│	0552	0603	│
Canterbury East	d.	│	*0506*	0541	0548	│	│	0619	0621	│
Faversham	a.	0510	0517	0554	0601	0604	0611	0632	0634	0635
Faversham	d.	0510	0520	...	0607	0607	0612	0633	...	0637
Gillingham (Kent)	d.	0531	0542	...	0629	0629	0635	0700	...	0658
Chatham	d.	0535	0546	...	0633	0633	0639	0704	...	0702
London Victoria	a.	0630	0630	...	0717	0717	0726	0749	...	0747

		⑥ 🍷	⑥ 🍷	⑦ 🍷	Ⓐ	Ⓐ 🍷	✕	⑥ 🍷	Ⓐ 🍷	⑥ 🍷	⑥ 🍷	⑦	⑦ 🍷	✕	✕ 🍷	Ⓐ 🍷	Ⓐ 🍷	⑥ 🍷	⑥ 🍷	⑦	⑦ 🍷	✕	✕ 🍷	⑦	⑦ 🍷
Ramsgate	d.	...	0622	0625	...	0631	...	0657	*0656*	...	0722	...	0725	...	0754	...	0815	...	0832	...	0825	...	0857	...	0925
Margate	d.	...	0632	0635	...	0641	...	0707	0709	...	0732	...	0735	...	0804	...	0826	...	0840	...	0835	...	0907	...	0935
Dover Priory	d.	0621	│	│	0629	│	0653**h**	│	│	0721	│	0723	│	0752**h**	│	0815	│	0821	│	0823	│	0903	│	0923	│
Canterbury East	d.	0649	│	│	0656	│	0720	│	│	0749	│	0751	│	0819	│	0842	│	0849	│	0851	│	0921	│	0951	│
Faversham	a.	0701	0704	0705	0709	0712	0734	0735	0744	0801	0804	0804	0805	0833	0834	0855	0857	0901	0903	0904	0905	0934	0935	1004	1005
Faversham	d.	0707	0707	0707	...	0713	...	0737	0745	0807	0807	...	0807	...	0835	0901	0901	0907	0907	...	0907	...	0937	...	1007
Gillingham (Kent)	d.	0729	0729	0728	...	0740	...	0758	0808	0829	0829	...	0828	...	0858	0924	0924	0929	0929	...	0928	...	0958	...	1028
Chatham	d.	0733	0733	0732	...	0744	...	0802	0812	0833	0833	...	0832	...	0902	0928	0928	0933	0933	...	0932	...	1002	...	1032
London Victoria	a.	0817	0817	0820	...	0833	...	0847	0900	0917	0917	...	0920	...	0947	1017	1017	1017	1017	...	1020	...	1047	...	1120

		✕ 🍷	✕ 🍷		✕ 🍷	✕ 🍷	Ⓐ	Ⓐ	⑦	⑦ 🍷	✕ 🍷	✕ 🍷	Ⓐ	Ⓐ 🍷	⑥	⑥ 🍷	⑦	⑦ 🍷	✕ 🍷	✕ 🍷	Ⓐ	Ⓐ 🍷
Ramsgate	d.	...	0932	and at	...	1532	...	1557	...	1625	...	1632	...	1652	...	1657	...	1720	...	1732	...	1752
Margate	d.	...	0940	the	...	1540	...	1608	...	1635	...	1640	...	1703	...	1707	...	1730	...	1740	...	1803
Dover Priory	d.	0921	│	same	1519	│	1559	│	1623	│	1619	│	1652	│	1703	│	1723	│	1719	│	1752	│
Canterbury East	d.	0949	│	minutes	1547	│	1626	│	1651	│	1647	│	1719	│	1721	│	1751	│	1747	│	1819	│
Faversham	a.	1001	1003	past	1600	1603	1639	1639	1704	1705	1700	1703	1732	1734	1734	1735	1804	1800	1800	1803	1832	1834
Faversham	d.	1007	1007	each	1607	1607	...	1641	...	1707	1707	1707	...	1737	...	1737	...	1807	1807	1807	...	1837
Gillingham (Kent)	d.	1029	1029	hour	1629	1629	...	1702	...	1728	1729	1729	...	1758	...	1758	...	1828	1829	1829	...	1858
Chatham	d.	1033	1033	until:	1633	1633	...	1706	...	1732	1733	1733	...	1802	...	1802	...	1832	1833	1833	...	1902
London Victoria	a.	1117	1117		1723**e**	1723**e**	...	1757	...	1820	1823**e**	1823**e**	...	1848	...	1847	...	1920	1917	1917	...	1947

		⑥	⑥ 🍷	⑦	⑦	✕	✕ 🍷	✕	✕ 🍷	⑦	⑦	✕	✕	⑦	⑦	✕	✕	⑦	⑦	A	A	✕	✕		
Ramsgate	d.	...	1757	...	1825	...	1832	...	1852	...	1925	...	1952	...	2025	...	2055	...	2125	...	2155	...	2255	...	...
Margate	d.	...	1807	...	1835	...	1840	...	1903	...	1935	...	2003	...	2035	...	2106	...	2135	...	2205	...	2306	...	...
Dover Priory	d.	1803	│	1823	│	1819	│	1852	│	1923	│	1952	│	2023	│	2052	│	2123	│	2152	│	2301	│	...	...
Canterbury East	d.	1821	│	1851	│	1847	│	1919	│	1951	│	2019	│	2051	│	2119	│	2151	│	2219	│	2318	│	...	...
Faversham	a.	1834	1835	1904	1905	1900	1903	1932	1934	2004	2005	2032	2034	2104	2105	2132	2137	2204	2205	2232	2237	2330	2337	...	...
Faversham	d.	...	1837	...	1907	1907**b**	1907	...	1935	...	2007	...	2035	...	2107	...	2138	...	2207	...	2238	...	2340	...	...
Gillingham (Kent)	d.	...	1858	...	1928	1929**b**	1929	...	1956	...	2028	...	2056	...	2128	...	2159	...	2228	...	2259	...	0002	...	...
Chatham	d.	...	1902	...	1932	1933**b**	1933	...	2000	...	2032	...	2100	...	2132	...	2203	...	2232	...	2303	...	0006	...	...
London Victoria	a.	...	1947	...	2020	2017**b**	2019	...	2047	...	2120	...	2147	...	2220	...	2247	...	2315	...	2349	...	0108	...	...

A – Daily service.
b – ⑥ only.
e – On ⑥ arrive 6 minutes earlier.
h – On ⑥ depart 10 minutes later.
k – On (evening of) ⑦ runs 18 minutes later.
n – Runs daily **except** (morning of) ①.

For explanation of standard symbols see page 4

Table 501

LONDON - TONBRIDGE - HASTINGS

Timings may vary by up to 3 minutes earlier or later

1, 2 class

km		⑥	Ⓐ 🍷	⑥⑦	Ⓐ 🍷	⑥ 🍷	Ⓐ 🍷	A 🍷	⚒ 🍷		⚒ 🍷	⑥ 🍷	Ⓑ 🍷	⑥ 🍷	Ⓐ 🍷	⑥⑦ 🍷	Ⓐ 🍷	⑥ 🍷	Ⓐ 🍷	⑥⑦ 🍷	Ⓐ 🍷	⑥ 🍷	Ⓐ 🍷
0	**London Charing Cross** d.	0740	0743**c**	0810	0815	0840	0843**c**	0910	0940	and at	1540	1610	1610	1640	1700**c**	1710	1716	1740	1800	1810	1823**c**	1840	1845
35	Sevenoaks d.	0812	0817	0843	0846	0912	0916	0947	1012	the same	1612	1643	1645	1712	1730	1743	|	1812	|	1843	|	1912	1917
47	**Tonbridge** d.	0823	0836	0852	0857	0923	0927	0956	1023	minutes past	1623	1652	1656	1723	1740	1752	|	1823	|	1852	|	1923	1926
55	Tunbridge Wells d.	0833	0846	0902	0907	0933	0936	1008	1033	each hour	1633	1702	1706	1733	1750	1802	1804	1833	1848	1902	1910	1933	1936
100	**Hastings** a.	0917	0930	0938**h**	0943	1017	1026	1038	1117	until:	1718	1738	1750	1817	1835	1838**h**	1849	1917	1933	1938**h**	2000	2017	2021

	Ⓐ 🍷	⑥ 🍷	Ⓑ 🍷	⚒ 🍷	Ⓑ 🍷	⑥ 🍷	Ⓐ 🍷	⑦	⚒ 🍷	A
London Charing Cross d.	1900**c**	1910	1910	1940	2010	2010	2040	2110	2110	2210
Sevenoaks d.	1932	1943	1941	2012	2043	2043	2112	2144	2142	2242
Tonbridge d.	1943	1952	1956	2023	2052	2055	2123	2155	2153	2253
Tunbridge Wells d.	1955	2002	2006	2033	2103	2106	2133	2205	2203	2303
Hastings a.	2040	2038	2044	2117	2142	2152	2217	2245	2251	2351

	Ⓐ	Ⓐ 🍷	⑥ 🍷	Ⓐ	Ⓐ 🍷	⑥⑦ 🍷	⑥ 🍷	Ⓐ 🍷	⑥⑦ 🍷	Ⓐ 🍷
Hastings d.	0553	0628	0652	0648	0707	0711	0752	0755	0811	0840
Tunbridge Wells d.	0640	0718	0729	0738	0758	0758	0829	0842	0858	0929
Tonbridge d.	0648	|	0737	|	|	0806	0837	0850	0906	0937
Sevenoaks d.	0702	|	0747	|	|	0818	0847	0906	0918	0947
London Charing Cross a.	0734**c**	0806	0821	0823**c**	0846	0851**h**	0921	0940	0951**h**	1022

	⑥ 🍷	A 🍷	⚒ 🍷		⚒ 🍷	⑥⑦ 🍷	Ⓐ 🍷	⚒ 🍷	⚒ 🍷	⑦ 🍷	⚒ 🍷	⑥⑦ 🍷	Ⓐ 🍷	⑥ 🍷	A 🍷	Ⓐ 🍷	⑥⑦	Ⓐ 🍷	A	Ⓐ	⑦	⑥	⚒
Hastings d.	0852	0911	0952	and at	1452	1511	1511	1552	1610	1611	1652	1711	1740	1752	1811	1842	1911	1915	2011	2053	2111	2111	2211
Tunbridge Wells d.	0929	0958	1029	the same	1529	1558	1601	1629	1657	1658	1729	1758	1826	1829	1858	1929	1958	2002	2058	2141	2159	2158	2258
Tonbridge d.	0937	1006	1038	minutes past	1537	1606	1609	1637	1706	1706	1737	1806	1837	1837	1906	1937	2006	2011	2106	2149	2204	2206	2307
Sevenoaks d.	0947	1018	1048	each hour	1547	1618	1622	1651	1721	1718	1747	1818	1847	1847	1918	1947	2018	2023	2118	*2233*	2218	*2233*	*2322*
London Charing Cross a.	1021	1051	1121	until:	1619**d**	1651**h**	1704	1730**d**	1755	1757	1822	1851**h**	1921	1921	1955	2021	2051**h**	2058	2151**h**	*2306*	2257	*2306*	*2358*

A – Daily service. Arrival time at destination may be 7 minutes later on ⑦.
c – London **Cannon Street**.
d – On Ⓐ arrive London **Cannon Street**, on ⑥ arrive London **Charing Cross**.
h – Arrive 7 minutes later on ⑦.

Table 502

LONDON - SOUTHAMPTON - WEYMOUTH

Timings may vary by up to 3 minutes earlier or later. For InterCity trains on this route see Table **520**

1, 2 class

km		Ⓐ	⚒		⚒ 🍷	⚒	⑦	Ⓐ	⑥ 🍷	⑦	⚒ 🍷		⚒ 🍷	⚒ 🍷	⑦ E	Ⓐ 🍷	⑥ 🍷	⑦ F 🍷		⚒ 🍷	⑦ 🍷	Ⓐ 🍷
0	**London Waterloo** d.	...	0535	...	0640	0705	0725	0745	0750	0825	0830	...	0850	0910	0925	0930	0930	1315	and at	1630	1630	1645
39	Woking d.	...	0604	...	0707	0736	0815	0812	0817	0915	|	...	0917	|	1015	|	|	|	the	|	|	1710
77	Basingstoke d.	...	0625	...	0727	0811	0839	0832	0836	0939	|	...	0936	0956	1039	|	|	1422	same	|	1716	1732
107	Winchester d.	...	0645	...	0743	0832	0855	0851	0854	0955	0922	...	0954	1013	1055	1022	1022	1438	minutes	1722	1731	1749
121	Southampton Airport ✈ d.	...	0658	...	0756	0848	0911	0904	0907	1011	0932	...	1007	1022	1111	1032	1032	1448	past	1732	1741	1801
128	**Southampton Central** d.	...	0710	...	0805	0859	0923	0915	0916	1023	0941	...	1016	1029	1123	1041	1041	1500	each	1743	1750	1812
174	**Bournemouth** d.	0700	0800	...	0854	...	1005	1000	0956	1105	1011	...	1056	...	1205	1111	1113	1535	hour	1813	1826	1852
183	Poole d.	0712	0811	...	0911	...	1016	1012	1008	1116	1020	...	1108	...	1216	1120	1122	1547	until:	1824	1838	1905
219	Dorchester South d.	0746	0846	...	0946	...	1044	...	...	1144	1056	...	...	...	1244	1154	1156	1620		1859	1911	...
230	**Weymouth** a.	0757	0857	...	0957	...	1053	...	...	1153	1106	...	...	...	1253	1204	1206	1630		1911	1923	...

	⑥ 🍷	⑥ 🍷	Ⓐ 🍷	⑥ 🍷	⑦ 🍷	Ⓐ 🍷	⑥ 🍷	⑥ 🍷	⚒ 🍷	⑦ 🍷	⑥ 🍷	Ⓐ 🍷	⚒ 🍷	⑦ 🍷	⑥ 🍷	Ⓐ 🍷	⚒ 🍷	⑦ 🍷	⑥ 🍷	Ⓐ 🍷	⑦ 🍷	⚒ 🍷	⑦	⚒ 🍷
London Waterloo d.	1650	1710	1715	1730	1730	1745	1750	1810	1830	1830	1850	1853	1930	1930	1950	1953	2030	2030	2050	2053	2130	2153	2245	2253
Woking d.	1717	|	|	|	|	|	1817	|	|	|	1917	1920	|	|	2017	2020	|	|	2117	2120	|	2220	2320	2320
Basingstoke d.	1736	1756	|	|	1816	1826	1836	1856	|	1916	1936	1939	|	2016	2036	2039	|	2116	2136	2139	2216	2242	2342	2342
Winchester d.	1754	1813	1808	1822	1831	1843	1854	1913	1922	1931	1954	1957	2022	2031	2057	2100	2122	2131	2154	2157	2231	2259	2359	0002
Southampton Airport ✈ d.	1807	1822	1818	1832	1841	1852	1907	1922	1932	1941	2007	2010	2032	2041	2110	2113	2132	2141	2207	2210	2241	2312	0015	0015
Southampton Central d.	1816	1829	1830	1841	1850	1903	1916	1929	1941	1950	2016	2019	2041	2050	2119	2122	2141	2150	2216	2219	2250	2321	0024	0026
Bournemouth d.	1856	...	1858	1913	1926	1931	2001	...	2013	2026	2059	2102	2127	2126	2205	2207	2217	2226	2303	2306	2326	0008	0100	0106
Poole d.	1908	...	1907	1923	1938	1943	2013	...	2023	2038	2111	2117	2139	2138	2217	2219	2227	2238	2315	2318	2337	0020	0109	0118
Dorchester South d.	...	...	1941	1956	2011	2015	...	...	2058	2111	...	...	2211	2211	...	...	2300	2311	...	...	...	...	...	...
Weymouth a.	...	...	1953	2006	2021	2028	...	...	2111	2121	...	...	2222	2221	...	...	2310	2321	...	...	...	...	...	...

	Ⓐ 🍷	⑥ 🍷	Ⓐ 🍷	Ⓐ 🍷	Ⓐ 🍷	⑥ 🍷	⑦	⑥ 🍷	Ⓐ 🍷	⑥ 🍷	⑥ 🍷	Ⓐ 🍷	⑦	⑥ 🍷	Ⓐ 🍷	⑥ 🍷	Ⓐ 🍷	⑦	⚒ 🍷	⑥ 🍷	Ⓐ 🍷			
Weymouth d.	...	...	...	...	0603	...	...	...	0642	0646	...	...	...	...	0742	0746	...	...	...	0846	0848	...	...	...
Dorchester South d.	...	...	...	...	0615	...	...	...	0652	0658	...	...	...	...	0755	0758	...	...	...	0858	0900	...	...	...
Poole d.	0509	0541	0545	0619	0648	0641	0648	...	0719	0732	0741	0738	0748	...	0829	0832	0836	0848	...	0932	0934	...	...	...
Bournemouth d.	0524	0555	0600	0633	0701	0655	0702	...	0730	0744	0755	0752	0802	...	0840	0844	0850	0858	...	0944	0944	...	...	...
Southampton d.	0602	0635	0645	0704	0732	0735	0742	0755	0801	0815	0835	0840	0842	0855	0915	0915	0935	0942	0955	1015	1015	...	...	...
Southampton Airport ✈ d.	0610	0643	0652	0712	0739	0743	0750	0803	0809	0822	0843	0847	0850	0903	0922	0922	0943	0950	1003	1022	1022	...	...	...
Winchester d.	0623	0657	0706	0722	0750	0757	0804	0813	0819	0832	0857	0901	0904	0913	0932	0932	0957	1004	1013	1032	1032	...	...	...
Basingstoke d.	0641	0715	|	|	|	0815	0823	0831	0837	|	0915	0919	0923	0931	|	|	1015	1023	1031	|	|	...	...	...
Woking a.	0659	0734	|	|	|	0834	0845	|	0855	|	0933	0938	0945	|	|	|	1033	1045	|	|	|	...	...	...
London Waterloo a.	0730	0803	0803	0820	0847	0903	0917	0918	0926	0928	1003	1008	1041	1018	1028	1028	1103	1141	1118	1128	1128	...	...	...

		⚒ 🍷	⑦ G	⚒ 🍷	⑥ 🍷	Ⓐ 🍷	⑦ H 🍷		⚒ 🍷	Ⓐ 🍷	⑥ 🍷	⑦ 🍷	⚒ 🍷	⑥ 🍷	Ⓐ 🍷	⑥ 🍷	⑦ 🍷	⑥ 🍷	Ⓐ 🍷	⑥ 🍷	Ⓐ 🍷	⑦
Weymouth d.	...	...	0910	...	0948	0950	1240	and at	...	...	...	1540	1548	...	...	...	1640	1648	1648	...	...	...
Dorchester South d.	...	...	0920	...	1000	1002	1252	the	...	...	...	1552	1600	...	...	...	1652	1700	1700	...	...	...
Poole d.	...	0941	0948	...	1032	1034	1324	same	1541	...	...	1624	1634	1641	1641	...	1724	1732	1734	1741	1741	...
Bournemouth d.	...	0955	1002	...	1044	1044	1340	minutes	1555	...	...	1640	1644	1655	1655	...	1740	1744	1744	1755	1755	1755
Southampton d.	...	1035	1042	1055	1115	1115	1415	past	1635	1655	1655	1715	1715	1735	1740	1755	1815	1815	1818	1835	1842	1842
Southampton Airport ✈ d.	...	1043	1050	1103	1122	1122	1423	each	1643	1703	1703	1723	1722	1743	1748	1803	1823	1822	1826	1843	1849	1852
Winchester d.	...	1057	1104	1113	1132	1132	1434	hour	1657	1713	1713	1734	1732	1757	1802	1813	1834	1832	1836	1857	1903	1911
Basingstoke d.	...	1115	1123	1131	|	|	1452	until:	1715	|	1731	1752	|	1815	1820	1831	1852	|	|	1915	1921	1931
Woking a.	...	1133	1145	|	|	|	|		1733	|	|	|	|	1833	1838	|	|	|	|	1933	1939	1951
London Waterloo a.	...	1203	1241	1218	1228	1228	1559		1803	1810	1818	1840	1829	1903	1910	1919	1940	1928	1931	2003	2009	2024

	⑥ 🍷	⑦ 🍷	⚒ 🍷	⑥ 🍷	Ⓐ 🍷	⑦	⑦ 🍷		⚒ 🍷	⑦	⑥ 🍷	⑦	Ⓐ 🍷	⑦	⑦	Ⓐ	Ⓐ	⑥	⑦	Ⓐ	⚒	⑥	⑦	
Weymouth d.	...	1740	1748	...	...	...	1840	...	1857	...	1957	2000	2005	2040	...	2100	...	2100	2140	...	2232	...	2240	...
Dorchester South d.	...	1752	1800	...	...	...	1852	...	1909	...	2009	2012	2019	2052	...	2112	...	2112	2152	...	2244	...	2252	...
Poole d.	...	1824	1834	1841	1841	...	1924	...	1941	...	2041	2044	2051	2124	...	2143	2150	2148	2224	2250	2316	...	2324	...
Bournemouth d.	...	1840	1844	1855	1855	1855	1940	...	1955	2000	2055	2100	2107	2138	2200	...	2202	2202	2237	2302	2329	2332	2333	...
Southampton d.	1855	1915	1915	1935	1942	1942	2015	...	2040	2042	2140	2142	2152	...	2242	...	2250	2250	...	2345	...	0014	...	...
Southampton Airport ✈ d.	1903	1923	1922	1943	1949	1952	2023	...	2047	2052	2147	2152	2159	...	2252	...	2259	2259	...	2354	...	0023	...	...
Winchester d.	1913	1934	1932	1957	2003	2011	2034	...	2101	2111	2201	2211	2213	...	2311	...	2314	2314	...	...	...	0050	...	...
Basingstoke d.	1931	1952	|	2015	2023	2031	2052	...	2119	2131	2219	2231	2231	...	2331	...	2335	2335	...	...	...	0111	...	...
Woking a.	|	|	|	2033	2041	2051	|	...	2137	2151	2240	2251	2249	...	2351	...	0007	0007	...	...	...	0133	...	...
London Waterloo a.	2018	2040	2028	2103	2113	2124	2140	...	2209	2225	2313	2325	2323	...	0022	...	0055	0055	...	...	...	0204	...	...

E – From London Waterloo up to 1125 **only**; for subsequent service see note **F**.
F – Runs 1315, 1415, 1515 from London Waterloo.
G – From Weymouth up to 1110 **only**; for subsequent service see note **H**.
H – Runs 1240, 1340, 1440 from Weymouth.

Service on ⑦ above valid Sept. 25 - Nov. 13 and Jan. 15 - Mar. 5. A revised service operates Nov. 20 - Jan. 8 and from Mar. 12. Please enquire **locally**.

0

For an explanation of standard symbols see page 4

279

Table 504 LONDON - PORTSMOUTH

1, 2 class

Timings may vary by up to 3 minutes earlier or later

km		Ⓐ	⑥	Ⓐ	Ⓐ	⑥	Ⓐ 🍷	⑦	⑥	⚒ 🍷	⑦	Ⓐ 🍷	⑥ 🍷			⚒ 🍷	⑦ 🍷	⚒ 🍷		Ⓐ 🍷	⑥	
0	**London Waterloo** d.	...	...	...	0610	0715	0723	...	0745	0815	0808k	0845	0845	...	...	0915	0908k	0945	and at	1545	1545	...
39	Woking d.	0556	0556	0626	0656	0739	0747	0753	0811	0839	0853	0911	0911	...	...	0939	0953	1011	the same	1609	1611	...
49	**Guildford** d.	0610	0619	0652	0715	0748	0756	0805	0819	0848	0905	0919	0919	...	...	0948	1005	1019	minutes	1618	1619	...
69	Haslemere d.	0632	0641	0714	0737	0802	0812	0827	0841	0902	0924	0941	0941	...	...	1002	1024	1041	past	1632	1641	...
107	Havant d.	0703	0712	0745	0808	0826	0833	0856	0912	0926	0953	1012	1012	...	...	1026	1053	1112	each	1656	1712	...
118	**Portsmouth and Southsea** a.	0718	0727	0800	0828	0842	0844	0908	0927	0939	1005	1027	1027	...	...	1039	1105	1127	hour	1709	1727	...
120	**Portsmouth Harbour** a.	0722	...	0805	...	0846	0849	0916	0936	0943	1009	1033	...	...	...	1045	1113	...	until:	1713	...	...

	⑥ 🍷	Ⓐ 🍷	⑦ 🍷	⑥	Ⓐ 🍷	⑦	⑥ 🍷	Ⓐ 🍷	⑦ 🍷	⑥	Ⓐ 🍷	⑦	⑥ 🍷	Ⓐ	⑦ 🍷	⑥	Ⓐ 🍷	⑦	⚒ 🍷	⑦ 🍷	⑥	Ⓐ	⑦	⚒ 🍷
London Waterloo d.	1615	1620	1625	1645	1650	1655	1715	1720	1725	1745	1752	1755	1815	1815	1825	1845	1850	1855	1915	1925	1945	1945	1955	2015
Woking d.	1639	1646	1653	1711	|	1723	1739	|	1751	1811	|	1823	1839	|	1851	1911	|	1923	1939	1951	2011	2011	2023	2039
Guildford d.	1648	1654	1705	1719	1722	1735	1748	1754	1803	1819	|	1835	1848	1848	1903	1919	1921	1935	1948	2003	2019	2019	2035	2048
Haslemere d.	1702	1717	1724	1741	1736	1756	1802	1813	1818	1841	1839	1856	1902	1905	1918	1941	1941	1956	2002	2018	2041	2041	2056	2102
Havant d.	1726	1748	1753	1812	1800	1827	1826	1838	1843	1912	1904	1927	1926	1935	1943	2012	2004	2027	2026	2043	2112	2110	2127	2126
Portsmouth and Southsea a.	1739	1807	1805	1827	1813	1844	1839	1849	1856	1927	1917	1944	1939	1950	1956	2027	2017	2044	2039	2056	2127	2126	2144	2139
Portsmouth Harbour a.	1743	...	1809	...	1820	...	1843	...	1900	...	1923	...	1943	1954	2000	...	2023	...	2046	2100	...	2130	...	2147

	⑦ 🍷	⚒ 🍷	⑦	⚒ 🍷	⑦ 🍷	⚒	⑦	⑦	⚒	⑦
London Waterloo d.	2025	2045	2055	2115	2125	2145	2155	2225	2245	2255
Woking d.	2051	2111	2123	2139	2151	2211	2223	2251	2315	2323
Guildford d.	2103	2119	2135	2148	2203	2219	2235	2303	2325	2335
Haslemere d.	2118	2141	2156	2205	2218	2241	2256	2318	2347	2356
Havant d.	2143	2210	2227	2226	2243	2310	2327	2344	0016	0027
Portsmouth and Southsea a.	2156	2226	2245	2242	2256	2326	2340	0001	0029	0040
Portsmouth Harbour a.	2200	2230v	...	2249	2300	2330v	...	0005	0033	0044

	Ⓐ	⑥	Ⓐ 🍷	⑥ 🍷	Ⓐ	⑥	Ⓐ 🍷		Ⓐ 🍷
Portsmouth Harbour d.	...	0459	0515	0525	...	...	0620	...	0650
Portsmouth and Southsea d.	0445	0505	0519	0531	0549	0622	0624	...	0654
Havant d.	0456	0519	0534	0547	0603	0636	0637	...	0705
Haslemere d.	0530	0545	0609	0615	0637	0708	0704	...	0736
Guildford d.	0551	0606	0633	0635	0658	0730	|	...	0752
Woking d.	0600	0615	0641	0643	0707	0737	|	...	|
London Waterloo a.	0630	0700	0711	0713	0735	0806	0751	...	0828

	⑥	⑦	⑥	Ⓐ 🍷			⚒ 🍷	⑦	⑥	Ⓐ			⚒ 🍷	⑦	⚒ 🍷		⑦ 🍷	Ⓐ	⑦	⚒ 🍷	Ⓐ	⑦ 🍷
Portsmouth Harbour d.	0701	0707	...	0725	...	...	0801	0813	...	0830	...	...	0901	0907	...	and at	1620	1636	...	1701	...	1720
Portsmouth and Southsea d.	0705	0711	0722	0729	...	...	0805	0817	0822	0834	...	...	0905	0911	0922	the same	1624	1640	1641	1705	1710	1724
Havant d.	0718	0722	0736	0740	...	...	0818	0828	0836	0847	...	...	0918	0922	0936	minutes	1636	1653	1654	1718	1724	1736
Haslemere d.	0744	0754	0808	0806	...	...	0844	0900	0908	0919	...	...	0944	0954	1008	past	1703	1727	1728	1743	1756	1803
Guildford d.	0800	0817	0830	0822	...	...	0900	0917	0930	0941	...	...	1000	1017	1030	each	1719	1748	1747	1800	1818	1819
Woking d.	0807	0826	0837	0831	...	...	0907	0926	0937	0949	...	...	1007	1026	1037	hour	1727	1800	1757	1807	1828	1827
London Waterloo a.	0832	0916p	0906	0859	...	...	0936	1016p	1006	1018	...	...	1033	1116p	1106	until:	1758	1830	1833	1832	1858	1858

	⑥	⑦	⚒ 🍷	⚒ 🍷	⑦ 🍷	⑦	⚒ 🍷	⚒	⑦ 🍷	⑦	Ⓐ 🍷	⑥	⑦ 🍷	⑦	Ⓐ		⑥	⑦ 🍷	⑦	⑥	⑥	⑦	Ⓐ	⚒
Portsmouth Harbour d.	...	...	1801	...	1820	...	1901	...	1920	...	1950	...	2020	...	2050	...	...	2120	...	2210	...	2210	2218	2333
Portsmouth and Southsea d.	1722	1741	1805	1820	1824	1841	1905	1922	1924	1941	1956	2022	2024	2041	2054	...	2122	2124	2141	2216	2222	2214	2222	2337
Havant d.	1736	1754	1818	1833	1836	1854	1918	1935	1936	1954	2010	2036	2036	2054	2108	...	2136	2136	2154	2232	2236	2227	2235	2350
Haslemere d.	1808	1828	1844	1905	1903	1928	1944	2007	2003	2028	2042	2108	2103	2128	2140	...	2208	2203	2228	2301	2308	2301	2308	0023
Guildford d.	1830	1847	1900	1928	1919	1947	2000	2025	2019	2047	2100	2130	2119	2147	2200	...	2230	2219	2247	2323	2330	2321	2330	0043
Woking d.	1837	1857	1910	1935	1927	1957	2008	2032	2027	2057	2107	2141	2127	2157	2208	...	2244	2227	2257	2331	2337	2330	2338	0051
London Waterloo a.	1906	1933	1935	2006	1958	2033	2033	2107	2058	2133	2136	2212	2158	2233	2244	...	2315	2258	2333	...	0007	...	0011	...

k – Nov. 20 - Jan. 8 and Mar. 12 - May 21 depart 17 minutes later.

p — Nov. 20 - Jan. 8 and Mar. 12 - May 21 arrive 13 minutes earlier.

v – **Not** ⑥.

Table 505 LONDON - GATWICK AIRPORT ✈ - BRIGHTON

1, 2 class

Timings may vary by up to 3 minutes earlier or later. For InterCity trains on this route see Table **520**

For Gatwick Express (London Victoria - Gatwick Airport ✈ non-stop) see Table **537**.

km		⑥	⚒	⑦	Ⓐ	Ⓐ	Ⓐ	⑦	⑥	Ⓐ	⑥⑦	Ⓐ	⑥	Ⓐ	⑥⑦	⑦	⚒ 🍷	⑥⑦	Ⓐ 🍷	⑥ 🍷	A 🍷	⑦	Ⓐ 🍷	⑥ 🍷
0	**London Victoria** d.	0502	0540	0547	...	...	0617	0632	...	0647	...	...	...	...	0732	...	0747	...	...	...	0832	...	...	0904
	London Blackfriars d.	|	|	|	0601	0612	|	|	0634	|	0704c	0707	0719	0731	|	0734c	|	0804c	0811	0819	|	0834c	0851	|
17	East Croydon d.	0522	0558	0607	0623	0636	0638	0650	0655	0703	0725	0731	0740	0756	0748	0757	0804	0825	0836	0840	0848	0857	0915	0925
34	Redhill d.	0539	0616	|	|	|	0656	0709	|	0716	|	|	|	|	0801	|	|	|	|	|	|	|	|	|
43	**Gatwick Airport** ✈ d.	0548	0628	0628	0640	0655	0709	0718	0711	0728	0741	0748	0756	0812	0810	0820	0821	0841	0856	0856	0906	0920	0941	0941
61	Haywards Heath d.	0604	0645	0642	0653	0709	0725	0736	0727	0747	0757	0804	0810	0828	0824	0834	0839	0857	0910	0910	0922	0934	0957	0957
82	**Brighton** a.	0618	0706	0703	0709	0729	0747	0757	0747	0808	0819	0826	0823	0848	0849	0852	0900	0919	0925	0923	0949	0952	1017	1017

	⚒ 🍷		⑥ 🍷	Ⓐ 🍷	A 🍷	⑦	⚒ 🍷	⚒ 🍷	⑦ 🍷		A 🍷	⑦	Ⓐ 🍷	⑥ 🍷	Ⓐ 🍷	⚒ 🍷	⑦	⑥ 🍷	Ⓐ 🍷	A 🍷	⑦	Ⓐ 🍷	⑦
London Victoria d.	0908	...	...	...	0932	...	1008	...	...	and at	1532	...	...	1608	1607	...	...	...	...	1631	...	...	1700
London Blackfriars d.	|	...	0919	0918	|	0934c	|	1004	1004c	the same	|	1534	1549	|	|	1604	1604	1619	1619	|	1634	1646	|
East Croydon d.	0922	...	0940	0946	0948	0957	1022	1025	1027	minutes	1548	1557	1610	1622	1622	1625	1627	1640	1640	1648	1657	1711	1720
Redhill d.	|	...	|	|	1001	|	|	|	|	past	1601	|	|	|	|	|	|	|	|	1701	|	1722	|
Gatwick Airport ✈ d.	|	...	0956	1003	1010	1020	|	1041	1050	each	1606	1620	1626	|	|	1641	1650	1656	1658	1710	1720	1733	|
Haywards Heath d.	|	...	1010	1015	1024	1034	|	1057	1104	hour	1622	1634	1640	|	1648	1657	1704	1710	1712	1726	1734	1749	|
Brighton a.	0959	...	1023	1028	1049	1052	1059	1117	1119	until:	1649	1652	1654	1659	1704	1717	1719	1723	1735	1751	1752	1813	1804

	⑥ 🍷	Ⓐ 🍷	⑥ 🍷	⑦	⑥ 🍷	⑥⑦ 🍷	Ⓐ 🍷	Ⓐ 🍷	⑦	⑦	⑥ 🍷	Ⓐ 🍷	⑥	⑦	Ⓐ	⑥	⑥⑦ 🍷	Ⓐ	⑦	⑦	⑥ 🍷	Ⓐ 🍷	⚒	⑦
London Victoria d.	1708	1706	...	...	...	1732	1736	...	...	1800	1808	1806	...	...	...	...	1832	...	...	1900	1908	1908	...	...
London Blackfriars d.	|	|	1704	1704	1719	|	|	1725	1734	|	|	|	1804	1804	1758	1819	|	1830	1834	|	|	|	1904	1904
East Croydon d.	1722	1723	1725	1727	1740	1748	1753	1750	1757	1820	1822	1823	1825	1827	1821	1840	1848	1852	1857	1920	1922	1922	1925	1927
Redhill d.	|	|	|	|	|	1801	|	1803	|	|	|	|	|	|	1833	|	1901	|	|	|	|	|	|	|
Gatwick Airport ✈ d.	|	|	1741	1750	1756	1810	|	1812	1820	|	|	|	1841	1850	1841	1856	1910	1909	1920	|	|	|	1941	1950
Haywards Heath d.	|	1753	1757	1804	1810	1824	1823	1829	1834	|	|	1853	1857	1904	1859	1910	1924	1928	1934	|	|	1948	1957	2004
Brighton a.	1759	1818	1817	1819	1823	1849	1848	1852	1852	1904	1859	1918	1917	1919	1924	1923	1949	1948	1952	2004	1959	2002	2017	2019

	⚒	A 🍷	⑦	⑦	⚒ 🍷	⚒	⑦	⚒	A 🍷	⑦	⚒ 🍷	⚒	A 🍷	⑦	⚒	⚒	⑦	A	⚒	⚒	⚒	⑦	⑦	⚒
London Victoria d.	...	1932	...	2000	2008	...	...	...	2032	...	2102	...	2132	...	2202	...	...	2232	...	2302	...	...	2332	2332
London Blackfriars d.	1919	|	1934	|	|	2004	2004	2019	|	2034	|	2104	|	2134	|	2204	2204	|	2234	|	2304	2304	|	|
East Croydon d.	1940	1948	1957	2020	2022	2025	2027	2040	2048	2057	2118	2125	2148	2157	2218	2225	2227	2248	2255	2318	2325	2327	2353	2351
Redhill d.	|	2001	|	|	|	|	|	|	2101	|	|	|	2201	|	|	|	|	2301	|	|	|	|	0006	0004
Gatwick Airport ✈ d.	1956	2010	2020	|	|	2041	2050	2056	2110	2120	2136	2141	2210	2220	2236	2241	2250	2310	2311	2336	2341	2350	0014	0012
Haywards Heath d.	2010	2024	2034	|	2048	2057	2104	2110	2124	2134	2148	2157	2224	2234	2248	2257	2304	2327	2324	2348	2357	0004	0028	0034
Brighton a.	2023	2049	2052	2104	2102	2117	2119	2123	2149	2152	2202	2217	2249	2252	2302	2317	2319	2349	2338	0002	0017	0019	0042	0055

A – Daily service.

c – Will **not** run on ⑦ Nov. 20 - Dec. 11 and Jan. 8 - Feb. 5 until 1004 departure.

280 *For an explanation of standard symbols see page 4* 0

Table 505

BRIGHTON - GATWICK AIRPORT ✈ - LONDON

For InterCity trains on this route see Table 520. For **Gatwick Express** (Gatwick Airport ✈ - London Victoria non-stop) see Table **537**.

1, 2 class

km		⚒	⑥	Ⓐ	⑥	Ⓑ	⑥	⑥	⑥		⑥⑦	Ⓐ	⑥	⑥	⑥	Ⓐ	⑥	Ⓐ	Ⓐ	⑥
0	Brighton........................d.	...	...	...	0545	...	0613	0615	0623	0625	0630	...	0647	0700	0705	0715	0715	0718	0730	0750	0745	0745
21	Haywards Heath.............d.	...	...	...	0612	...	0634	0636	0637	0645	0650	...	0708	0721	0722	0736	0729	0731	0750	...	0759	0807
39	Gatwick Airport ✈.........d.	0538	0600	0615	0630	0645	0653	0653	0653	0702	0715	0715	0722	0738	0737		0745	0745	0815		0815	
48	Redhill.........................d.	0548							0703	0710			0746								0822	0830
65	East Croydon..................d.	0607	0617	0632	0647	0702	0710	0712	0716	0724	0732	0731	0738	0759	0753	0804	0802	0832	0824	0831	0834	0839	0847
83	**London Blackfriars**.......a.	...	0637	0652	0707	0722			0745	0752	0753c		0815		0823c	0822	0852		0853c		0907	0907
	London Victoria............a.	0624				0726	0731	0734				0756	0818		0822		0841		0851			

		⑥⑦	Ⓐ	⑥⑦	Ⓐ	⑥	Ⓐ	⑥	Ⓐ	⑥	⑦	A	A	⑦	⚒	A	A			A	⚒	⑦	⚒	⚒	⑦
Brighton........................d.	0800	0803	0815	0818	0830	0839	0850	0845	0845	0900	0912	0930	0945	0950	1000	1015	and at	1400	1412	1415	1450	1430	1445
Haywards Heath.............d.	0821	0824	0829	0841	0850	0859		0859	0909	0921	0925	0950	0959		1021		the same	1421	1425	1429		1450	1459
Gatwick Airport ✈.........d.	0838	0842	0845	0845	0915	0916		0915	0923	0938	0940	1015	1015		1038	1045	minutes	1438	1440	1445		1515	1515
Redhill.........................d.	0846						0947							1047			✧	1446					
East Croydon..................d.	0859	0858	0902	0912	0932	0932	0924	0931	0942	1000	0957	1032	1031		1100	1101	past	1459	1457	1501	1524	1532	1531
London Blackfriars.......a.		0922	0923c		0952	0952		0953c			1023	1052	1053		1123	each hour	1522	1523			1552	1553
London Victoria............a.	0918			0931			0941		1001	1018			1041	1118			until	1518		1541			

		⚒	Ⓐ	⑥	⚒	Ⓐ	⚒	⑥	⑦	⑥	A	⑥	⑥	⑥⑦	⚒	Ⓐ	⚒	⑥⑦	⚒	⑦	⚒	⚒	⑦	A
Brighton........................d.	1500	1508	1515	1550	1530	1545	1550	1600	1608	1615	1645	1650	1652	1630	1700	1700	1713	1715	1728	1750	1745	1730	1752	1800
Haywards Heath.............d.	1521	1527	1529		1551	1559		1621	1625	1629	1659		1651	1720	1721	1735	1729	1745		1759	1750			1821
Gatwick Airport ✈.........d.	1538	1541	1545		1612	1615		1638	1641	1645	1715		1707	1738	1738		1745	1800		1815	1815			1838
Redhill.........................d.	1546												1746	1746										1846
East Croydon..................d.	1559	1559	1601	1624	1628	1631	1624	1659	1657	1701	1731	1724	1734	1728	1757	1759	1802	1801	1816	1824	1831	1832	1834	1859
London Blackfriars.......a.		1621	1623		1652	1653			1722	1723	1753			1750	1821			1823	1845		1853	1851		
London Victoria............a.	1618			1643			1641	1718				1743	1753			1818	1816			1841			1853	1918

		A	⚒	⚒	⑦	A	A	A	⚒	⑦	⚒	A	⚒	⑦	⚒	⑥⑦	Ⓐ	⑥⑦	Ⓐ	⚒	⚒	⑦	⑥	⑦
Brighton........................d.	1815	1850	1852	1830	1845	1900	1915	1930	1945	2000	2015	2030	2045	2100	2115	2130	2145	2200	2215	2230	2245	2345
Haywards Heath.............d.	1829			1850	1859	1921	1929		1950	1959	2021	2029		2050	2059	2121	2150	2159	2221	2250	2259	2359
Gatwick Airport ✈.........d.	1845			1915	1915	1938	1945		2015	2015	2038	2045		2115	2115	2138	2145	2215	2238	2245	2315	0015
Redhill.........................d.						1946					2046					2146			2246			0022
East Croydon..................d.	1901	1924	1934	1932	1931	1959	2001	2024e	2032	2031	2059	2101	2124	2132	2131	2159	2201	2232	2231	2259	2301	2332	2331	0034
London Blackfriars.......a.	1923			1952	1953		2023		2053		2123		2152	2153		2223	2252	2253		2323	2352	2353	0058
London Victoria............a.	...	1941	1953			2018		2041e		2118		2141			2218			2318				

A – Runs daily.   c – Not ⑦ Nov. 20 - Dec. 11, Jan. 8 - Feb. 5.   e – 10-12 minutes later on ⑦.   ✧ – Timings may vary by up to 3 minutes on certain journeys.

Table 506

LONDON - ASHFORD - DOVER
Timings may vary by up to 3 minutes earlier or later

1, 2 class

km		Ⓐ	⚒	Ⓐ	⚒	⚒	⚒	⑦		⚒	⚒	⑦			⚒	⑥⑦	Ⓐ	⚒	⑥⑦	Ⓐ	⚒	⑥⑦	Ⓐ	⑥
0	London Charing Cross d.	0625	0700	0730	0730	0755t	0830	0855t	0900		0930	1000	1000	and at	1430	1500	1500	1530	1600	1600	1629	1650	1700	1735	1730
90	Ashford......................d.	0757	0826	0846	0846	0915	0957	1014	1014	the same	1057	1114	1114	minutes	1557	1614	1614	1657	1714	1727	1744	1804	1814	1847	1857
113	Folkestone Central.... d.	0818	0847	0904	0904	0930	1016	1029	1033	past each	1116	1129	1133	1617	1629	1634	1717	1729	1744	1803	1824	1829	1905	1916
124	Dover Priory..............d.	0829	0904	0917	0928	0941	1028	1042	1044	hour until:	1128	1141	1144	1629	1641	1645	1728	1741	1756	1828	1836	1841	1916	1928

		⑥⑦	Ⓐ	⑥	⑥⑦	Ⓐ	A	A	⚒	⚒			Ⓐ	Ⓐ	⑥	Ⓐ	⑥	⑥	⑦	⑥	⑦	Ⓐ
London Charing Cross d.	1800	1814	1830	1900	1906	2000	2100	2200	2300	2330		**Dover Priory** ....d.	0456	0530	0612	0616	0652	0656	0707	0719	0752	0754
Ashford......................d.	1914	1957	2014	2016	2116	2216	2316	0021	0054			Folkestone Central ....d.	0508	0542	0624	0628	0704	0708	0719	0731	0804	0806
Folkestone Central ... d.	1929	1954	2016	2033	2046	2135	2235	2335	0040	0112		Ashford......................d.	0531	0609	0647	0649	0722	0729	0747	0753	0822	0825
Dover Priory ....d.	1941	2006	2028	2044	2058	2148	2248	2347	0052	0123		**London Charing Cross** ... a.	0652	0734	0806	0803	0835	0844	0906	0907	0935	0948

		⑥	⑦	⑥	⑥⑦	A	⚒	⚒			⚒	⑦	Ⓐ	⚒	⑦	⚒	⚒	⑦	⚒	⚒	⚒	⑥
Dover Priory ....d.	0807	0821	0848	0907	0921	0952	and at	1507	1521	1550	1605	1621	1651	1705	1721	1749	1821	1849	1921	1949	2021	2049	2107	2203
Folkestone Central ... d.	0819	0833	0902	0919	0933	1004	the same	1519	1533	1601	1617	1633	1703	1717	1733	1802	1833	1902	1933	2002	2033	2102	2120	2215
Ashford......................d.	0847	0853	0920	0947	0953	1022	minutes past each	1547	1553	1619	1647	1653	1721	1747	1753	1822	1853	1922	1953	2022	2053	2121	2147	2235
London Charing Cross a.	1006	1007	1035	1106	1107	1135	hour until:	1709	1607	1738	1804	1807	1833	1906	1907	1936	2007	2036	2107	2106	2207	2235	2311	2358

– Daily service.   t – 5 minutes later on ⑥.

Table 507

BRIGHTON and HASTINGS AREA SERVICES

1, 2 class

GATWICK ✈ - EASTBOURNE - HASTINGS Approximate journey time from Gatwick: **Lewes** (30km) 28 mins, **Eastbourne** (63km) 51 mins, **Bexhill** (81km) 77 mins, **Hastings** (88km) 87 mins.

From Gatwick ✈ :
Ⓐ : 0728, 0921 and hourly to 1721, then 1827, 1921 and hourly to 2321.
⑥ : 0615, 0821 and hourly to 2321.   ⑦ : 0926 and hourly to 2226.

From Hastings :
Ⓐ : 0746, 0823 and hourly to 1423, then 1520, 1623 and hourly to 2123.
⑥ : 0623 and hourly to 2123.   ⑦ : 0815 and hourly to 2015.

BRIGHTON - EASTBOURNE - HASTINGS Approximate journey time from Brighton: **Lewes** (13km) 15 mins, **Eastbourne** (38km) 40 mins, **Bexhill** (56km) 66 mins, **Hastings** (63km) 76 mins.

From Brighton :
Ⓐ : 0734, 0816, 0854 and hourly to 1854, then 1934L and hourly to 2334L.
⑥ : 0654 and hourly to 1854, then 1934L and hourly to 2334L.
⑦ : 0740, 0840, 0940L and hourly to 2240L.   L – Change at Lewes.

From Hastings :
Ⓐ : 0720, 0836, 0923L, 1000 and hourly to 1900, 1923L and hourly to 2123L, 2200, 2300.
⑥ : 0700 and hourly to 1900, 1923L and hourly to 2123L, then 2200, 2300.
⑦ : 0815L and hourly to 2015L, then 2115, 2215.

HASTINGS - ASHFORD Approximate journey time from Hastings: **Rye** (18km) 21 minutes, **Ashford** (42km) 47 minutes.

From Hastings :
Ⓐ : 0528, 0558, 0621, 0733, 0811, 0833, 0924 and hourly to 1624, then 1704, 1728, 1816, 1917, 2026, 2120.
⑥ : 0624 and hourly to 2124.   ⑦ : 1021, 1221, 1421, 1621, 1821, 2021.

From Ashford :
Ⓐ : 0618, 0651, 0730, 0829, 0922 and hourly to 1622, then 1725, 1806, 1856, 1935, 2023, 2118, 2227.
⑥ : 0722 and hourly to 2222.   ⑦ : 1117, 1317, 1517, 1717, 1917, 2117.

BRIGHTON - NEWHAVEN Approximate journey time from Brighton: **Lewes** (13km) 15 minutes, **Newhaven Town ▲** (23km) 31 minutes.

From Brighton :
Ⓐ : 0555, 0634, 0654, 0714, 0754, 0842, 0914, 0934 and hourly to 1434, then 1514, 1534, 1614, 1634, 1734, 1816, 1834, 1916, 1934 and hourly to 2334.
⑥ : 0555, 0634, 0714, 0734, 0814, 0834, 0914, 0934 and hourly to 2334.
⑦ : 0710, 0810, 0910, 0940 and hourly to 2240.

From Newhaven Town :
Ⓐ : 0516, 0552, 0638, 0723, 0740, 0806L, 0906 and hourly to 1506, then 1525, 1604, 1626, 1704, 1726, 1804, 1826, 1906, 1932, 2006, 2106, 2206, 2326.
⑥ : 0516, 0636, 0706, 0725, 0806, 0825, 0906 and hourly to 2206, then 2226, 2326.
⑦ : 0800 and hourly to 2100, then 2138, 2238.

– Change at Lewes.   ▲ – Most trains also run to and from **Newhaven Harbour**, approximately 500m from Newhaven Town station.

Table 508 GATWICK ✈ and BRIGHTON - SOUTHAMPTON

1, 2 class

km		⑥	Ⓐ	Ⓐ	⑥	Ⓐ	⑥	⑥	⚒B	⚒	⚒	⚒	⑦C	⚒	⚒	⚒	⚒	⑦	⑦C	⑦	⚒	⑦C	⑥C	ⒶC
	London Victoria **505 537** .. d.	...	...	0532	0532	...	0640	...	...	0817	0917	1017	...	1117	1217	1317	1417	1417	...	1517	1517	...	1532	1532
	Gatwick Airport ✈ 505 537 d.	0557	0603	0619	0619	0655	0728	...	0810	0851	0951	1051	1047y	1151	1251	1351	1451	1456	1450	1556	1551	1550	1610	1610
0	**Brighton 505** .... d.	|	|	0710f	0708g	0742	|	0815	0900	0902	1002	1102	1110	1202	1302	1402	1502	|	1550	|	1602	1650	1700	1700
2	Hove .... d.	|	|	0713	0711	0745	|	0819	|	0919	1019	1119	1114	1219	1319	1419	1519	1523	1554	1623	1619	1654	|	|
17	Worthing .... d.	|	|	0726	0724	0806	|	0835	0917	0935	1035	1135	1129	1235	1335	1435	1535	1537	1608	1637	1635	1708	1717	1717
36	Barnham .... d.	0704	0702	0743	0740	0829	0839	0850	0933	0950	1050	1150	1145	1250	1350	1450	1550	1552	1624	1652	1650	1724	1733	1733
46	**Chichester** .... d.	0712	0710	0751	0749	0837	0847	0858	0942	0958	1058	1158	1153	1258	1358	1458	1558	1601	1635	1701	1658	1735	1742	1742
60	Havant .... d.	0723	0721	0802	0809	0857	0901	0909	0953	1009	1111	1211	1203	1311	1411	1511	1619	...	1648	...	1709	1748	1753	1753
76	Fareham .... d.	0740	0737	0820	0826	0923	...	0926	1006	1026	1126	1226	1232	1326	1426	1526	1635	...	1701	...	1726	1801	1808	1808
100	**Southampton Central 502** a.	0803	0800	0850	0849	0946	...	0949	1031	1049	1149	1249	1253	1349	1454	1549	1657	...	1722	...	1751	1822	1831	1834
	Bournemouth **502** .... a.	0835	0833	0926	0931	1031	...	1031	1110	1131	1231	1331	1401	1431	1531	1631	1730	...	1816	...	1831v	1916	1910	1929

	⑥	Ⓐ	⑦E	⑥	Ⓐ	⑥	Ⓐ	⑥	Ⓐ	⑦
London Victoria **505 537** ... d.	1617	1616	...	1717	1722	1817	1831	1917	1917	...
Gatwick Airport ✈ 505 537 d.	1651	1651	1747z	1751	1756	1851	1906	1951	1951	2120
Brighton 505 .... d.	1702	1702	1810	1802	1816	1902	|	2014	2014	2213
Hove .... d.	1719	1719	1814	1819	1824	1919	1933	2019	2019	2217
Worthing .... d.	1735	1739	1829	1835	1843	1935	1952	2038	2038	2230
Barnham .... d.	1750	1754	1845	1850	1902	1950	2007	2050	2055	2245
Chichester .... d.	1758	1802	1853	1858	1910	1958	2015	2058	2103	2253
Havant .... d.	1811	1816	1903	1911	1924	2011	2026	2109	2115	2303
Fareham .... d.	1826	1831	1917	1926	1942	2026	2041	2126	2131	2317
Southampton Central 502 .. a.	1849	1853	1938	1949	2004	2049	2104	2149	2154	2338
Bournemouth **502** .... a.	1931	1937	2022	2031	2038	2131	2138	2302	2305	0058

	⑥	Ⓐ	⑥	ⒶA	⑥A	Ⓐ	⑥	⚒	⑦
Bournemouth **502** .... d.	...	0524	0545n	0554	0555	0633	0631	0730	0702
Southampton Central 502 d.	...	0606	0622	0638	0638	0710	0722	0822	0838
Fareham .... d.	...	0630	0645	0704	0704	0734	0745	0845	0902
Havant .... d.	...	0646	0700	0720	0722	0750	0800	0900	0916
Chichester .... d.	...	0659	0711	0730	0732	0810	0811	0911	0926
Barnham .... d.	0621	0711	0720	0738	0740	0819	0820	0920	0934
Worthing .... d.	0636	0745	0739	0800	0800	0837	0839	0939	0948
Hove .... d.	0653	0806	0753	0816	0816	0855	0853	0953	1000
Brighton 505 .... a.	0718	0810	0808	0820	0820	0908	0908	1008	1004
Gatwick Airport ✈ 505 537 a.	0721	0808	0821	0907p	0907q	0922	0921	1021	1043
London Victoria **505 537** a.	...	...	0856	...	...	0958	0956	1056	...

	⚒	⚒	⚒	⚒	⑦C	⚒	⑦C	⚒	⑥B	ⒶC	⚒	⚒	⑦	⚒	⚒	⚒	⚒	⑦E	⚒	⑦C	①-④	⑤⑥	⑥	Ⓐ
Bournemouth **502** .... d.	0845h	0950	1050	1150	1202	1250	1255	1350	1355	1355	...	1450	1440	1550	1650	1750	1850	1840	1950	1940	2050	2050	2150	2155
Southampton Central 502 .. d.	0922	1022	1122	1222	1300	1322	1400	1422	1448	1448	...	1522	1526	1622	1722	1822	1922	1936	2022	2021	2122	2122	2222	2228
Fareham .... d.	0945	1045	1145	1245	1327	1345	1427	1445	|	|	...	1545	1548	1645	1745	1845	1945	1957	2045	2045	2145	2145	2245	2251
Havant .... d.	1000	1100	1200	1300	1405	1400	1505	1500	1522	1522	1544	1600	1607	1700	1800	1900	2000	2044	2100	2105	2200	2200	2300	2307
Chichester .... d.	1011	1111	1211	1311	1420	1411	1520	1511	1532	1532	1559	1611	1620	1711	1811	1911	2011	2056	2111	2120	2214	2214	2317	2317
Barnham .... d.	1020	1120	1220	1320	1428	1420	1528	1520	1540	1540	1611	1620	1628	1720	1820	1920	2020	2108	2120	2127	2222	2222	2325	2325
Worthing .... d.	1039	1139	1239	1339	1446	1439	1546	1539	1555	1555	|	1639	1646	1739	1839	1939	2039	2125	2139	2142	2243	2243	2356	2356
Hove .... d.	1053	1153	1253	1353	1459	1453	1559	1553	1608	1608	|	1653	1659	1753	1853	1953	2053	2138	2153	2155	2304	2304	0017s	0017s
Brighton 505 .... a.	1108	1208	1308	1408	1503	1508	1603	1608	1612	1612	|	1708	1703	1808	1908	2006	2108	2142	2218	2159	2308	2308	0021	0021
Gatwick Airport ✈ 505 537 a.	1121	1221	1321	1421	1543	1521	1643	1621	1714	1706	1707	1721	1744	1821	1921	2021	2121	2237	2221	2243	0014	...	...	...
London Victoria **505 537** ... a.	1156	1256	1356	1456	...	1556	...	1657	...	...	1747	1756	...	1856	1956	2056	2156	...	2256	...	...	...	...	...

A – (2) and 🍷 Westbury - Brighton.
B – (2) and 🍷 Brighton - Milford Haven and v.v.
C – (2) and 🍷 Brighton - Cardiff and v.v.
E – (2) and 🍷 Brighton - Exeter and v.v.
f – Arrive 0657.
g – Arrive 0659.
h – Depart 0850 on ⑥.
n – Not Feb. 11 - Mar. 4.
p – From Barnham (depart 0806).
q – From Barnham (depart 0811).
s – Stops to set down only.
v – Arrive 1824 on Ⓐ.
y – Change at Barnham (arrive 1141).
z – Change at Barnham (arrive 1841).

Table 509 GATWICK ✈ and BRIGHTON - PORTSMOUTH

1, 2 class

km		⚒	⑥	Ⓐ	⑥	Ⓐ	⑥	Ⓐ	Ⓐ	⚒	Ⓐ	⑥	Ⓐ	⑥	Ⓐ	⚒	⚒		⚒	⚒	Ⓐ	⑥	Ⓐ
	London Victoria **505 537** .. d.		...	...	...	...	0532	...	0602	...	0717	...	...	0802	0806	...	0902		1502	...	1601	1602	...
0	**Gatwick Airport ✈ 505 537** d.		0557	0603	...	...	0619	...	0651	...	0759	...	...	0840	0843	0851v	0940	and	1540	1551v	1640	1640	...
18	Horsham .... d.		0625	0624	...	...	0655	...	0715	...	0822	...	...	0858	0900	|	0958	at	1558	|	1658	1658	...
	Brighton 505 .... d.		|	|	0612	0650	|	0652	|	0722	|	0822	0822	|	|	0922	|	the	|	1622	|	|	1642
	Hove .... d.		|	|	0615	|	|	0655	|	0725	|	0825	0825	|	|	0925	|	same	|	1625	|	|	1645
	Worthing .... d.		|	|	0636	0703	|	0716	|	0746	|	0846	0846	|	|	0946	|	mins	|	1646	|	|	1706
59	Barnham .... d.		0704	0702	0709h	0720	0734	0749	0751	0809	0909	0909	0913	0939	0941	1009	1039	past	1639	1709	1736	1739	1739
70	**Chichester** .... d.		0712	0710	0717	0730	0742	0757	...	0817	...	0917	0921	0947	0949	1017	1047	each	1647	1717	...	1747	1747
84	Havant .... d.		0723	0721	0737	0741	0756	0817	...	0837	...	0937	0941	1001	1003	1037	1101	hour	1701	1737	...	1801	1807
95	Portsmouth and Southsea ... a.		...	...	0751	0754	0808	0832	...	0854g	...	0951	0957	1015	1015	1051	1113	until	1713	1751	...	1813	1821
97	**Portsmouth Harbour** .... a.		...	...	0755	0758	0812	0836	...	0858g	...	0957	1005	1019	1019	1057	1119		1718	1755	...	1818	1828

	Ⓐ	⑥	Ⓐ	Ⓐ	⑥	⑥	Ⓐ	⑥	Ⓐ	⑥	Ⓐ	⚒	⚒	⚒	⚒	⚒	⑦	⑦	⑦		⑦	⑦	⑦
London Victoria **505 537** .... d.	...	...	1637	...	1702	...	...	1802	...	...	...	1902	...	2002	2017	2117		0802	0817		2017	2102	2117
Gatwick Airport ✈ 505 537 d.	1651v	1651v	1712u	...	1740	1751v	1756v	1840	...	1851v	1906v	1940	1951v	2040	2051	2151		0847	0856	and	2056	2147	2156
Horsham .... d.	|	|	1736	...	1758	|	|	1858	...	|	|	1958	|	2058	|	|		0905	|	at	|	2205	|
Brighton 505 .... d.	1702	1722	|	1742	|	1822	1835	|	1925	1922	1928	|	2022	|	|	|		|	0915	the	2115	|	|
Hove .... d.	1705	1725	|	1745	|	1825	1839	|	|	1925	1936b	|	2025	|	2119	2219		|	0923	same	2123	|	2223
Worthing .... d.	1726	1746	|	1806	|	1846	1900	|	1940	1946	1958	|	2046	|	2138	2235		|	0937	mins	2137	|	2237
Barnham .... d.	1808	1809	1813	1824	1839	1909	1923	1939	2000	2009	2020	2039	2109	2136	2155	2257		0941	0952	past	2152	2241	2252
Chichester .... d.	1816	1817	...	1832	1847	1917	1931	1947	2008	2017	2028	2047	2117	...	2203	2305		...	1001	each	2201	...	2301
Havant .... d.	1835	1837	...	1852	1901	1937	1950	2001	2022	2037	2048	2101	2137	...	2217	2325		...	1015	hour	2215	...	2315
Portsmouth and Southsea ..... a.	1846	1851	...	1904	1913	1951	2004	2013	2038	2051	2100	2113	2151	...	2230	2337		...	1026	until	2226	...	2326
Portsmouth Harbour .... a.	1850	1855	...	...	1918	1955	...	2018	2042	2055	2104	2118c	2155c	...	2236	2342		...	1031		2235	...	2330

	⚒	Ⓐ	Ⓐ	⑥	Ⓐ	⑥	⑥	Ⓐ	Ⓐ	⑥	Ⓐ	⑥	Ⓐ	Ⓐ	⑥	Ⓐ	⑥	Ⓐ	⚒	⚒		⚒	⚒
Portsmouth Harbour .... d.		0522	...	0540	0555	0614	0629	0638	0706	0714	...	0729	0740	...	0814	...	0829	0850	0914	0929		1614	1629
Portsmouth and Southsea ..... d.		0526	0533	0544	0601	0618	0633	0642	0710	0718	...	0733	0744	0758	0818	0825	0833	0854	0918	0933	and	1618	1633
Havant .... d.		0539	0547	0556	0614	0632	0644	0655	0725	0732	...	0744	0757	0812	0832	0838	0844	0907	0932	0944	at	1632	1644
Chichester .... d.		0552	0606	0606	0635	0652	0659	0715	0745	0752	...	0759	0817	0833	0852	0859	0859	0923	0952	0959	the	1652	1659
Barnham .... d.		0600	0614	0614	0645	0700	0711	0729	0753	0800	0806	0811	0829	0841	0900	0911	0911	0932	1000	1011	same	1700	1711
Worthing .... d.		0615	0636	0628	0710	0723	|	|	0814	0823	|	|	|	0903	0923	|	|	1003	1023	|	mins	1723	|
Hove .... d.		|	0656	0647	0731	0744	|	|	0830	0844	|	|	|	0924	0944	|	|	1024	1044	|	past	1744	|
Brighton 505 .... a.		0633	0700	0651	0736	0748	|	|	0834	0848	|	|	|	0928	0948	|	|	1028	1048	|	each	1748	|
Horsham .... d.		|	|	|	|	...	0749	0808	...	...	0846	0849	0905	...	...	0949	0949	...	...	1049	hour	...	1749
Gatwick Airport 505 537 .... a.		0720	0805	0721v	0808v	...	0807	0837	...	...	0907	0907	0926	...	...	1007	1007	...	...	1107	until	...	1807
London Victoria **505 537** ... a.		...	...	...	...	...	0846	...	...	...	0949	0946	1001	...	...	1046	1046	...	...	1146		...	1846

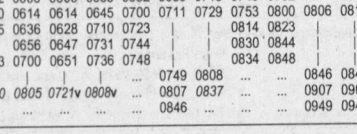

	Ⓐ	⚒	⚒	⑥	Ⓐ	⚒	⚒	⚒	⚒	⚒	⚒	⚒	⚒	⚒	⚒	⚒	⑦	⑦	⑦		⑦	⑦	⑦
Portsmouth Harbour .... d.	...	1714	1729	1744	1750	1805	...	1835	1905	...	1935c	2005c	...	2035c	2114	...		...	0744		1944	...	...
Portsmouth and Southsea ..... d.	1651	1718	1733	1748	1754	1809	...	1839	1909	...	1939	2009	...	2039	2118	2218		0720	0748	and	1948	2020	2120
Havant .... d.	1704	1732	1744	1805	1807	1822	...	1851	1922	...	1951	2022	...	2051	2132	2232		0732	0800	at	2000	2032	2132
Chichester .... d.	1724	1752	1759	1812	1818	1842	...	1905	1942	...	2005	2042	...	2105	2152	2252		0752	0814	the	2014	2052	2152
Barnham .... d.	1732	1800	1811	1818	1827	1900k	1856	1913	2000k	1956	2013	2100k	2056	2113	2200	2300		0808f	0822	same	2022	2108f	2208
Worthing .... d.	1803	1823	|	1845	1852	1923	|	1953	2023	|	2053	2123	|	2153	2223	2323		0830	0840	mins	2040	2130	2230
Hove .... d.	1824	1844	|	|	|	1944	|	2014	2044	|	2114	2144	|	2214	2244	2344		0851	0854	past	2054	2151	2251
Brighton 505 .... a.	1828	1848	|	1911	1911	1948	|	2018	2048	|	2118	2148	|	2218	2248	2348		0856	0900	each	2100	2156	2256
Horsham .... d.	...	...	1849	|	|	...	1932	|	|	2032	|	...	2132	|	|	...		0841p	|	hour	|	2141q	2241
Gatwick Airport 505 537 .... a.	...	...	1907	1921v	1921v	...	1956	2021v	2021v	2056	2121v	...	2156	2221v	2336	...		0858p	0922	until	2122	2158q	2258
London Victoria **505 537** ... a.	...	...	1946	...	...	...	2043	...	...	2143	...	...	2243	...	...	...		0946p	1001		2201	2246q	2346

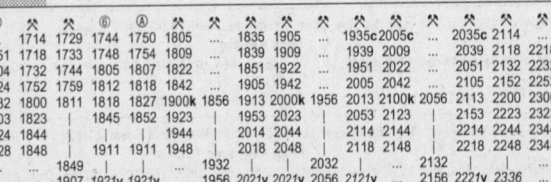

b – Arrive 1931.
c – ⑥ only.
f – Arrive 8 minutes earlier.
g – Arrive 3 minutes earlier on ⑥.
h – Arrive 0658.
k – Arrive 10 minutes earlier.
p – From Barnham (depart 0804).
q – From Barnham (depart 2104).
r – From Barnham (depart 2204).
u – Stops to pick up only.
v – To/from Barnham (see Table **508**).

For explanation of standard symbols see page 4

Table 510   LONDON, CARDIFF and BRISTOL - PAIGNTON and PLYMOUTH

1, 2 class

km		2	2	2	Ⓐ2	Ⓐ2	Y2	2	2	2♀	2	Ⓐ	2	⑥	✕U	2	B2	⑦2	2	⑦q
0	London Paddington 530 ... d.													0725	0740					0915
58	Reading 530 ... d.													0808	0805					0949
154	Westbury ... d.						0620f													1053
	Bath Spa 530/2 ... d.							0728												
	Cardiff 530/2 ... d.											0800								
	Newport 530/2 ... d.											0814								
189	Bristol Temple Meads 530/2 d.			0611		0612s	0650		0750		0845	0852	0916	0915	0903		1008	1006		
220	Weston-super-Mare 530 ... d.					0713			0811			0913		0939			1029	1041		
243	Bridgwater ... d.			0644			0732		0830			0929		0957				1100		
230	Taunton ... d.			0658		0723s	0746		0843		0922	0942	0949	0952	1012		1051	1122		
253	Tiverton Parkway ... d.			0712			0801		0857			1001	1027							1130
279	Exeter St Davids ... d.	0605	0635	0650	0710	0729	0752	0756s	0825	0915	0924	0954	1011	1019	1019	1046	1120	1124	1144	1208
299	Dawlish ... d.	0620	0650	0705	0727	0744	0814		0842	0928	0943		1024					1144	1159	
304	Teignmouth ... d.	0625	0655	0710	0732	0749	0819		0847	0933	0948		1029					1149	1204	
312	Newton Abbot ... d.	0635	0705	0718	0742	0756	0830		0855	0904	0941	0958	1015	1037	1040	1040	1048	1141	1157	1200	1229
321	Torquay ... a.	0645	0715		0752		0841			0914		1009	1046				1059		1208	1221
325	Paignton ... a.	0650	0720		0757		0846			0919		1014	1054				1104		1213	1226
326	Totnes ... a.			0730		0808			0908			0952	1053	1052			1153			1242
363	Plymouth ... a.			0802		0840	0903		0939			1023	1100	1121	1121		1225		1239	1314
	Penzance 515 ... a.			1010								1217		1320	1320				1438	1500

	2♀	2n	2	⑥	Ⓐ♀	V	✕	✕	⑦2	H	2	⑦R	2	⑦N	D	D	✕n	⑦2	2♀2	S	2	2n
London Paddington 530 ... d.	0925b		0932	0945		1025	1035	1015									1125b	1115				
Reading 530 ... d.	1003		1013	1015		1103	1103	1051									1203	1149				
Westbury ... d.	1056							1153									1248	1253				
Bath Spa 530/2 ... d.			1112	1112																		
Cardiff 530/2 ... d.		1000																1155				1300
Newport 530/2 ... d.		1014																1209				1314
Bristol Temple Meads 530/2 d.		1046	1127	1127	1108				1210				1234	1239				1250		1310		1347
Weston-super-Mare 530 ... d.		1114	1148	1148	1153p													1311		1342		1407
Bridgwater ... d.		1133			1212													1330		1401		1424
Taunton ... d.	1133	1146	1211	1211	1226				1230	1245			1311	1316	1328	1330	1343		1419		1436
Tiverton Parkway ... d.	1145	1200													1340	1343					
Exeter St Davids ... d.	1203	1218	1224	1235	1248		1242	1242	1305	1314		1314	1320	1342	1343	1348	1358	1408	1412	1420	1424	1450	1505
Dawlish ... d.		1232	1244		1300							1334	1337				1421	1425	1440	1437		1510	1518
Teignmouth ... d.		1237	1249		1305							1339	1342				1426	1430	1445	1442		1515	1523
Newton Abbot ... d.	1224	1246	1257		1313				1326	1335	1340	1348	1351	1404	1403	1409	1419	1433	1438	1454	1450	1524	1533
Torquay ... a.		1257	1308							1345		1358	1402	1412				1445		1505		1534	1542
Paignton ... a.		1302	1313							1400		1403	1407	1420				1455		1510		1539	1548
Totnes ... a.					1325					1351					1417	1423	1433		1449		1502		
Plymouth ... a.	1310				1400		1340	1340	1407	1421					1450	1500	1505		1518		1536		
Penzance 515 ... a.							1535	1535	1600									1716		1733		

	2	C	E	⑦2	⑦2♀	2	Ⓐ2	⑦2	⑥2	2	Q	M	⑦2	K	T	2	2	2n	G	2	⑦2
London Paddington 530 ... d.				1315	1325b							1415						1525b		1515
Reading 530 ... d.				1349	1406							1450						1603		1550
Westbury ... d.				1454														1648		
Bath Spa 530/2 ... d.															1558					1641
Cardiff 530/2 ... d.														1505k						
Newport 530/2 ... d.														1520k						
Bristol Temple Meads 530/2 d.		1405	1452			1445	1505	1510		1550			1604	1600	1620	1635		1658
Weston-super-Mare 530 ... d.						1509	1535	1540						1631	1640			
Bridgwater ... d.						1527	1553	1558						1648	1658			
Taunton ... d.		1442		1531	1534	1542	1607	1612		1627	1627		1640	1701		1712	1716	1725		1736
Tiverton Parkway ... d.		1459		1544	1546						1640	1653				1730	1737		1748
Exeter St Davids ... d.	1520	1518	1551	1609	1604	1620		1626	1637	1659	1701	1705	1711	1716	1730	1759e	1748	1755		1806
Dawlish ... d.	1535					1639		1646	1650	1711		1725	1736		1750			
Teignmouth ... d.	1540					1644		1651	1655	1718	1730		1741		1755	1819		
Newton Abbot ... d.	1550			1610	1630	1625	1632	1654		1701	1704	1720	1722		1732	1750	1804	1828	1809	1816	1821	1827
Torquay ... a.	1600			1619			1643	1705		1712	1714				1800	1815	1839		
Paignton ... a.	1606			1624			1648	1710		1717	1719				1805	1845		
Totnes ... a.					1643	1637				1733	1734	1744						1833		
Plymouth ... a.		1649		1715	1708					1805	1803	1820					1846	1859	1906	1904
Penzance 515 ... a.		1855		1910							1950						2045	2100		2055

	⑦M	2	⑦K	L	⑥2	Ⓐ2	F	2	✕2	2	2	⑦2	J	2n	⑦2♀P	2	2	⑤2	⑥2	⑦2	⑦2	F	2	⑥2♀
London Paddington 530 ... d.									1625b		1635				1735			1751	1735			1802
Reading 530 ... d.									1703		1710				1803			1830	1810			1839
Westbury ... d.									1757		1814											
Bath Spa 530/2 ... d.																		1858				1940
Cardiff 530/2 ... d.											1700											
Newport 530/2 ... d.											1714											
Bristol Temple Meads 530/2 d.	1708		1711	1711		1725			1735		1815	1800	1800		1835			1913		1932	1940	1954
Weston-super-Mare 530 ... d.				1733					1810		1831	1824		1909				2011	2023
Bridgwater ... d.									1828		1850	1843		1927				2030	2045
Taunton ... d.	1746		1748	1756		1801		1837		1844	1854	1851	1902	1859	1920	1941		1947	1951	2008	2044	2100
Tiverton Parkway ... d.			1802	1810				1849			1905						2003	2022		
Exeter St Davids ... d.	1816		1820	1825	1828	1830	1835	1907		1914k	1921	1923	1931	1928	1946		2014	2021	2026	2042
Dawlish ... d.					1848		1855	1919			1944	1948			2046		
Teignmouth ... d.					1853		1900	1924			1949	1953			2051		
Newton Abbot ... d.			1840	1841	1903		1910	1932	1935		1942	1943	1958	2002	2007	2013		2033	2035	2042	2106c	2103
Torquay ... a.			1851		1914		1921	1945			2009	2013			2042	2116		
Paignton ... a.			1857		1919		1926	1950			2014	2018			2047	2121		
Totnes ... a.		1853						1945			1954	1956		2025			2047	2054		
Plymouth ... a.	1915	1930			1925	2015				2023	2032		2044	2101		2047	2125		2140
Penzance 515 ... a.					2120					2215			2230			2310			2335

- 🚲 and ♀ Wolverhampton - Plymouth.
- 🚲 and ♀ Leeds - Plymouth.
- 🚲 and ♀ York - Exeter.
- 🚲 and ♀ Liverpool - Plymouth.
- 🚲 and ♀ (Dundee on Ⓐ -) Edinburgh - Penzance.
- 🚲 and ♀ Edinburgh - Penzance.
- 🚲 and ♀ Edinburgh - Glasgow - Penzance.
- 🚲 and ♀ Leeds - Paignton.
- 🚲 and ♀ Aberdeen - Plymouth.
- 🚲 and ♀ Newcastle - Plymouth.

L – 🚲 and ♀ Newcastle - Exeter.
M – 🚲 and ♀ Manchester - Plymouth.
N – 🚲 and ♀ London Waterloo - Paignton.
P – Pullman service and ✕ available in 1 cl.
Q – Conveys Feb. 12 - Mar. 5 🚲 and ♀
    Basingstoke - Paignton, Mar. 12 - May 21
R – 🚲 Exeter Central (d. 1308) - Paignton.
S – 🚲 Exmouth (Table 513) - Penzance.
T – 🚲 Exeter Central (d. 1710) - Paignton.

U – 🚲 Bristol - Exmouth.
V – Ⓖ Gloucester (d. 1012) - Taunton.
Y – Ⓑ from Edinburgh and Glasgow.
   🚲 1,2 cl. Edinburgh - Glasgow - Plymouth.
b – Depart 10 minutes later on Ⓐ.
c – Arrive 2058.   e – Arrive 1740.
f – ②③④⑤.   k – Arrive 1140.
n – ♀ on ⑥.   p – Arrive 1140.
q – Feb. 19, 26, Apr. 9, 23 only.
s – Stops to set down only.

For explanation of standard symbols see page 4

Table 510 — LONDON, CARDIFF and BRISTOL - PAIGNTON and PLYMOUTH

1, 2 class

	Ⓐ	⑤	①–④	Ⓐ	✕ K	B	⑦	⑤	⑦	2	Ⓐ	2	✕	J	2	2	Ⓐ	⑤	Ⓐ	✕ K	Ⓐ	2	⑦	Ⓐ	Ⓐ	⑤ R
London Paddington 530 d.	1815	1835	1835	1835			1850	1835		1851		1935			1935	2025	2035		2035		2115	2215	2355
Reading 530 d.	1840	1903	1903	1910			1919	1910		1933		2003			2010	2101	2103b		2110		2145	2249	0046z
Westbury d.			1957	1958			2015	2019		2026		2057			2152	2154		2214			2251	2355
Bath Spa 530/2 d.	1938												2106								2355
Cardiff 530/2 d.																					
Newport 530/2 d.																					
Bristol Temple Meads 530/2 d.	1956			2012	2007						2101		2110	2121			2208		2230	2306	0010
Weston-super-Mare 530 d.	2024				2026							2142	2142				2300		0029s
Bridgwater d.	2044											2200				2318
Taunton d.	2107		2037	2038	2047	2051	2056	2101		2109		2137	2137		2214	2207	2234	2244	2255	2334	2343	0054s	0355y
Tiverton Parkway d.			2049	2050	2101	2104	2108	2113		2121		2149	2151		2219	2246	2257s	2307		2356
Exeter St Davids d.			2045	2107	2108	2119	2121	2127	2131	2131	2139		2207	2209	2226	2237	2318	2304	2314	2325	0008	0015	0120s	0433g
Dawlish d.				2120				2143	2150				2245			2250
Teignmouth d.				2125				2148	2155				2250
Newton Abbot d.			2106	2128	2133	2140		2148	2156	2203	2200	2200	2228	2230	2300	2258		2325	2335	2346		0457
Torquay a.								2213		2211	2216		2310
Paignton a.								2218		2216		2315
Totnes d.			2118	2140	2145	2152		2208		2212	2241		2310		2337		2358
Plymouth a.			2148	2215	2214	2225	2225	2235	2237		2245		2315	2310	2340		0010	0020	0030		0220	0538
Penzance 515 a.			2340		0001			0025					2340		0001				0025		0819

km		Q	Ⓐ	⑥	Ⓐ	Ⓐ	⑥	Ⓐ	2	A	⑥	✕	K	C	2	⑦	✕P	✕	2	J	✕	⑦	⑥	S	2
	Penzance 515 d.	2215															0515							
0	Plymouth d.	0030				0538		0600	0620				0700	0700			0725	0735	0735
37	Totnes d.					0605		0626	0647							0752	0802	0802
	Paignton d.										0655			0723					0800
	Torquay d.										0700			0728					0805
51	Newton Abbot d.	0112				0618	0616		0638	0700	0713		0736	0736	0741	0805	0815	0815	0818
59	Teignmouth d.					0623				0720			0748			0825
64	Dawlish d.					0628				0725			0753			0830
84	Exeter St Davids d.	0139	0600	0603	0620	0640	0640	0645	0652		0659	0722	0734	0744	0757	0757	0812	0827	0837	0837	0840	0842	0846
110	Tiverton Parkway d.		0614	0619	0634	0654	0654			0713	0736	0750			0841	0851	0851	0854
133	Taunton d.	0210	0628	0636	0648	0710	0710		0720	0724	0726	0749	0807	0813	0820	0820	0854	0904	0904	0916	0909
152	Bridgwater d.				0648	0720	0720	0734			0809	0823		0920
176	Weston-super-Mare 530 d.		0710	0711	0740	0740			0840	0844		0939
205	Bristol Temple Meads 530/2 a.		0740	0741	0811	0811		0820	0827	0912	0912	0932	1001
248	Newport 530/2 a.		0817			0852	0949	1035
267	Cardiff Central 530/2 a.		0833			0908	1006	1052
224	Bath Spa 530/2 a.				0755	0825	0825			0802	0805			0925	0943	0943	0955
209	Westbury d.		0707																0943	0943	0955
305	Reading 530 a.	0517s	0800			0921	0923			0855	0857		1024		0939		1036	1036	1109
363	London Paddington 530 a.	0610	0835			0920	0952	1010		0940	0930		1110	1000	1025		1110	1119	1153

	✕ U	✕ 2	Ⓐ	⑥	✕ 2	G	Ⓐ	⑥	✕ 2	Ⓐ	⑥	⑦	V	✕	✕ 2	F	✕ 2	⑦	✕	⑥	⑦	Ⓐ	✕ D
Penzance 515 d.			0641	0645		0720				0750	0847	0847			0923				0941	0941	0934		1144
Plymouth d.		0818	0832	0835		0915		0935	0935		1000	1035	1035	1025	1044		1115			1135	1135	1130	1144
Totnes d.		0848					1002	1002		1030			1051									1156	1212
Paignton d.	0830				0857		0940		1017						1115				1140
Torquay d.	0836				0902		0945		1022						1120				1145
Newton Abbot d.	0848	0900	0909	0911	0915	0951	0957	1015	1015	1035	1044		1112	1104	1133		1155			1211	1209	1226
Teignmouth d.					0922		1004	1021	1021	1042			1110		1140						1215
Dawlish d.					0927		1009	1026	1026	1047			1115		1145						1220
Exeter St Davids d.	0910		0933	0933	0946	1014	1024	1041	1041	1107		1131	1134	1138	1143	1202	1211			1233	1243	1250
Tiverton Parkway d.						1028		1055	1055			1145	1148	1153							1317	1317
Taunton d.	0933		0959	0956		1041	1054	1108	1108			1158	1201	1215	1210		1234	1240	1250
Bridgwater d.			1010				1106									1252
Weston-super-Mare 530 d.			1028				1126				1251				1317
Bristol Temple Meads 530/2 a.	1009		1049			1118	1154				1251		1234	1240	1346							1358
Newport 530/2 a.			1127			1234p					1252p
Cardiff Central 530/2 a.			1142			1252p
Bath Spa 530/2 a.							1144	1151				1254				1327		1323	1331
Westbury d.							1232	1236		1313	1315	1407				1413		1416	1507
Reading 530 a.			1111				1232	1236		1313	1315	1407				1413		1416	1507
London Paddington 530 a.			1155				1305	1320		1350	1400	1447				1453		1455	1455	1547

	⑦ J	✕ 2	⑥	✕ W	✕ 2h	B	⑦ L	✕	⑦ N	⑦	✕ 2	✕ 2	V	✕ 2	U	✕	⑥ W	✕	✕	⑥n	⑦	✕ T	✕ Y
Penzance 515 d.					1025					1150	1145											
Plymouth d.	1155			1228		1300	1300	1315		1335	1343	1344		1353			1435		1435
Totnes d.	1221			1257			1326		1402				1420						1501
Paignton d.			1217		1241	1318			1332				1410		1410	1430		1457	1500				1514
Torquay d.			1222		1247	1323			1337				1415		1415	1436		1503	1506				1519
Newton Abbot d.	1234	1235		1259	1310	1334		1339	1350	1350	1415		1422	1427	1434	1440	1448		1518	1514			1531
Teignmouth d.			1242		1306	1317		1356	1357			1429	1434			1447		1519	1520				1541
Dawlish d.			1247		1311	1322		1401	1402			1434	1439			1452		1524	1525				1546
Exeter St Davids d.	1304	1306	1325	1324	1336		1354	1403	1418	1419	1437	1438	1448	1454	1500	1514	1510	1529	1539	1540	1550		1601
Tiverton Parkway d.	1319		1339				1433		1451							1557
Taunton d.	1335		1353		1403		1417	1437	1456	1449	1504	1512	1515		1538		1533	1552		1603	1618	1617	1622
Bridgwater d.					1414			1501	1526											1634
Weston-super-Mare 530 d.					1434	1442		1521									1641			1655
Bristol Temple Meads 530/2 a.	1422			1455		1501	1517		1543		1552	1602		1621		1611		1641		1658	1727
Newport 530/2 a.									1637
Cardiff Central 530/2 a.									1653
Bath Spa 530/2 a.				1515					1611f						1655		1703
Westbury d.			1432				1535	1543										1710	1753	1751
Reading 530 a.			1517				1622	1631										1745	1845	1835
London Paddington 530 a.			1610				1710	1705e										1745	1845	1835

A – 🚋 Exmouth (Table 513) - Carmarthen.
B – 🚋 and ♁ Leeds - Plymouth and v.v.
C – 🚋 Exeter Central (d. 0730) - Cardiff.
D – 🚋 and ♁ Plymouth - Liverpool.
F – 🚋 and ♁ Penzance - Edinburgh.
G – 🚋 and ♁ Penzance - Glasgow - Edinburgh.
J – 🚋 and ♁ Aberdeen - Plymouth and v.v.
K – 🚋 and ♁ Newcastle - Plymouth and v.v.
L – 🚋 and ♁ Plymouth - Edinburgh.
N – 🚋 Paignton - Bristol (- Swindon on Ⓐ).

P – Pullman service and ✕ available in 1 cl.
Q – Ⓐ from Penzance.
R – 🚲 1,2 cl. and 🚋 Penzance - London.
S – 🚋 and ♁ Exeter Central (d. 0838) - Cardiff.
T – 🚋 and ♁ Exeter - Sheffield.
U – 🚋 and ♁ Paignton - Newcastle.
V – 🚋 and ♁ Plymouth - Manchester.
W – 🚋 and ♁ Paignton - London Waterloo.
Y – 🚋 Taunton - Gloucester (a. 1825).

b – Depart 2110 on ⑦.
e – Arrive 1715 on ⑥.
f – Ⓐ only.
g – Arrive 0427.
h – on ⑥.
n – Feb. 18, 25, Apr. 8, 15, 22.
p – ⑥ only.
s – Stops to set down only.
y – ②–⑥ only.
z – Stops to take up 🚲 passengers only.

For an explanation of standard symbols see page 4

Table 510
PLYMOUTH and PAIGNTON - BRISTOL, CARDIFF and LONDON
1, 2 class

	⑦	Ⓐ	⑥	Ⓐ	⑦	✕	⑦	✕	⑦	⑦	⑦	Ⓐ	⑦	✕	Ⓐ	①-④	✕	⑦	Ⓐ	✕	⑦	⑦	⑦
	2	✕	♀	2	B	Y	♀	2	2	2	2	♀	♀	2n	2♀	♀	2	2	A	♀	2	♀	W
Penzance 515...........d.	...	...	...	...	...	...	...	...	...	...	1445	1449	...	...	...	...	...	...	1520	1545	...	...	...
Plymouth................d.	...	1535	1535	...	1540	1545	...	...	...	...	1620	1635	1640	...	1700	...	...	...	1735	1735	...	1755	...
Totnes...................d.	...	1602	1602	...	1606	1613	...	...	...	1651		1707	...	1729	...	...	...	1804		...	1822	...
Paignton................d.	1550	...	...	1600	...	...	1610	...	1612	1630	...	...	1655	...	1733	1752	1754	...	...	...	1812	...	1825
Torquay.................d.	1555	...	...	1605	...	...	1616	...	1617	1635	...	...	1701	...	1738	1758	1759	...	...	...	1817	...	1830
Newton Abbot...........d.	1606	1615	1615	1616	1619	1627	1627	...	1631	1648	1703	...	1714	1741	1745	1753	1811	1810	1817	...	1828	1835	1842
Teignmouth..............d.	...	...	...	...	...	1633	...	1638	1655	...	...	1721	...	1752	1800	1818	...	1824	...	...	1849
Dawlish..................d.	...	...	...	...	...	1638	...	1643	1700	...	...	1726	...	1757	1805	1823	...	1829	...	...	1854
Exeter St Davids........d.	...	1637	1637	...	1643	1651	1657	...	1704	1722	...	1729	1739	1747	1804	1813	1826	1842	...	1843	1829	...	1857	1907
Tiverton Parkway........d.	...	...	...	...	...	1659	1706	1711	...	...	1743	...	1802	...	...	...	...	...	1911
Taunton.................d.	...	1700	1700	...	1712	1721	1724	1735	...	1748	...	1756	...	1817	...	1907	...	1910	...	1924
Bridgwater..............d.	...	...	...	...	...	...	1747	1759	...	1828	...	1918	...	1921	...	...
Weston-super-Mare 530..d.	...	...	...	...	...	1810	1822	...	1853	...	1938	...	1938	...	...
Bristol Temple Meads 530/2 a.	...	1750	1801	1802	1844	...	1850	...	1921	1905	...	1959	...	2000q	...	...
Newport 530/2...........a.	...	...	...	...	...	1926	...	1959	...	2035	...	...
Cardiff Central 530/2...a.	...	...	...	...	...	1943	...	2016	...	2052	...	...
Bath Spa 530/2..........a.	...	1815	1920k	...	...	...	...
Westbury................d.	...	1739	1739	...	...	1832	...	...	2003
Reading 530.............a.	...	1828	1831	...	1911	...	1911	1922	...	...	2004	2053
London Paddington 530..a.	...	1905	1915	...	1950	...	1945p	2005	...	...	2046	2133

	✕	Ⓐ	⑥	✕	✕b	⑦	✕	⑦	⑥	Ⓐ	Ⓐ	⑦	⑧	⑦	⑦	⑦	✕	⑦	⑦	Ⓐ	⑦
	2	2	2	✕	2	2	✕	2	2	2	S	2	2	C	2	2	2	2	2	2	R
Penzance 515...........d.	...	...	...	1630	...	1716	...	...	1735	1735	...	1842	...	...	...	...	...	...	2115
Plymouth................d.	...	...	...	1835	...	1905	1915	...	1935	1935	...	2045	2055	...	2111	...	...	2330
Totnes...................d.	...	...	...	1902	...	1932	...	...	2004	2004	...	2125	...	2141	...	...	...
Paignton................d.	1826	1852	1852	...	1900	...	1930	1954	...	2035	2052	...	2135	...	2221	2225	2320
Torquay.................d.	1831	1857	1857	...	1905	...	1935	1959	...	2040	2057	...	2140	...	2226	2230	2325
Newton Abbot...........d.	1843	1908	1920f	1915	...	1918	1945	...	1946	2009	2016	2016	2053	2059	2125u	2138	...	2151	2154	2239	2243	2337	0012
Teignmouth..............d.	1850	...	1927	...	1925	...	2023	2023	2100	2116	2145	...	2201	2246	2250	2344
Dawlish..................d.	1855	...	1932	...	1930	...	2028	2028	2105	2121	2150	...	2206	2251	2255	2349
Exeter St Davids........d.	1911	...	1952	1937	...	1950	2007	2013	...	2041	2043	2125	2138	2150u	2204	...	2219	2308	2315	0005	0139e
Tiverton Parkway........d.	...	1951	...	2021	2027	...	2058	...	...
Taunton.................d.	...	2004	2008	...	2034	2040	...	2112	...	2219u	...	2225
Bridgwater..............d.	...	2020	...	...	2123	...	2237
Weston-super-Mare 530..d.	...	2041	...	...	2143	...	2258
Bristol Temple Meads 530/2 a.	...	2113	...	2120	...	2212	...	2320u	...	2330
Newport 530/2...........a.	...	...	...	...	...
Cardiff Central 530/2...a.	...	...	...	...	...
Bath Spa 530/2..........a.	...	...	...	2226	...
Westbury................d.	...	2043	...	2113	...	...
Reading 530.............a.	...	2131	...	2158	...	...	0517s
London Paddington 530..a.	...	2210r	...	2240	...	...	0610

- ⛐ and ♀ Penzance - Gloucester (arrives 2103).
  (Ⓐ - Birmingham International, arrives 2224).
- ⛐ and ♀ Plymouth - Leeds.
- ⛐ 1,2 cl. Plymouth - Edinburgh - Glasgow.
- ⛐ 1,2 cl. Penzance - London.
- ⛐ Penzance - Swindon.
- ⛐ and ♀ Paignton - London **Waterloo**.
- ⛐ and ♀ Plymouth - Derby.

b –	Not Jan. 7.		p –	Arrives 2000 on ⑥.
e –	Arrives 0034.		q –	Arrives 2011 on ⑥.
f –	Arrives 1908.		r –	Arrives 2215 on ⑥.
k –	⑥ only.		s –	Stops to set down only.
n –	♀ on ⑥.		u –	Stops to pick up only.

Table 511
LONDON - SALISBURY - EXETER
1, 2 class

km		⑥	Ⓐ		⑦	Ⓐ		✕	⑦		⑦	Ⓐ	Ⓐ	Ⓐ	⑦		Ⓐ	⑥	⑦	✕	⑦	⑥	Ⓐ
			D			♀		♀		C	C	♀		C		♀		♀		♀
0	London Waterloo.....d.	...	...	...	...	0605	...	0709	...	...	0754	0835	0835	0855	0935	...	1035	1035	1055	1135	1235	1255	1335	1335	1355
39	Woking..............d.	...	...	...	...	0636	...	0734	0735	...	0819	0858	0900	0929	1000	1058	1100	1129	1200	1300	1329	1400	1400	1429
77	Basingstoke..........d.	...	...	...	...	0709	0720	0754	0808	0825	0848	0919	0921	0952	1021	1119	1121	1152	1221	1321	1352	1421	1421	1452
107	Andover.............d.	...	...	...	...	0742	0816	...	0847	0902	0936	1008	1043	1138	1214	1243	1338	1409	1443	1443	1514
134	Salisbury............a.	...	...	...	...	0802	0837	...	0906	0921	0953	0954	1027	1102	1152	1154	1233	1302	1354	1431	1502	1502	1533
134	Salisbury............d.	0550	0556	...	0710	0725	0805	0837	...	0908	...	0956	0957	1039	1110	1155	1157	1238	...	1357	1409	...	1514	1540
169	Gillingham (Dorset)...d.	0614	0643	...	0741	0752	0835	0901	...	0932	...	1020	1018	1108	1138	1216	1221	1259	...	1421	1503	...	1537	1624
180	Templecombe.........d.	0621	0650	...	0749	0759	0842	0909	...	0939	...	1028	1026	1115	1224	1229	1306	...	1429	1510	...	1631
190	Sherborne...........d.	0629	0658	...	0756	0807	0850	0916	...	0947	...	1035	1033	1123	1231	1236	1314	...	1436	1518	...	1639
197	Yeovil Junction......d.	0644	0708	...	0802	0814	0855	0923	1002b	...	1042	1040	1130	1238	1243	1335f	...	1443	1525	...	1644
211	Crewkerne...........d.	0653	0717	...	...	0933	1011	...	1052	1050	1139	...	1248	1253	1344	...	1453	1534	...
233	Axminster...........d.	0724	0745	...	0834	0946	1025	...	1105	1103	1153	...	1301	1306	1358	...	1506	1556	...
249	Honiton.............d.	0736	0757	...	0849	1002	1037	...	1117	1115	1205	...	1313	1318	1410	...	1518	1608	...
276	Exeter Central 512..a.	0757	0821	...	0904	1023	1056	...	1134	1130	1224	...	1330	1335	1425	...	1537	1627	...
277	Exeter St Davids 512.a.	0801	0827	...	0908	1030	1100	...	1139	1138	1224	...	1336	1339	1429	...	1543	1631	...

	✕	⑦	⑦	✕	⑦	⑦	⑦	✕	⑦	⑦	⑥	⑦	Ⓐ	⑦	⑦	✕	⑦	⑦	✕
	♀	♀	B	♀	♀	♀	♀	♀	♀	♀	A	♀	♀	♀	♀	♀	♀
London Waterloo.....d.	1435	1455	...	1535	1605	1620	1635	1705	1720	1730	1735	1805	1820	1835	...	1905	1920	1935	2020	2035	2120	...	2230	2235	...
Woking..............d.	1458	1529	...	1600	1630	1647	1700	...	1748	...	1800	1831	1848	1858	...	1930	1948	2000	2048	2100	2148	...	2258	2303	...
Basingstoke..........d.	1519	1552	...	1621	1651	1709	1721	1746	1809	1812	1821	1852	1909	1920	...	1951	2009	2021	2109	2121	2209	...	2322	2325	...
Andover.............d.	1536	1609	...	1643	1714	1731	1743	1808	1826	1834	1843	1915	1926	1943	...	2013	2031	2038	2126	2143	2226	...	2344	2347	...
Salisbury............a.	1554	1629	...	1702	1736	1750	1802	1827	1846	1854	1902	1937	1942	2003	...	2032	2050	2054	2142	2202	2242	...	0003	0006	...
Salisbury............d.	1557	1642	1642	1717	...	1805	1830	1857	1858	1905	...	1947	2005	2014	...	2058	2057	2145	2205	...
Gillingham (Dorset)...d.	1621	...	1745	...	1826	1855	1919	1922	1929	...	2011	2029	2043	...	2122	2121	2210	2229	...
Templecombe.........d.	1627	...	1752	...	1832	1902	1926	1930	1937	...	2018	2037	...	2130	2129	2217	2237	...
Sherborne...........d.	1634	...	1800	...	1841	1910	1934	1937	1944	...	2026	2044	2057	...	2137	2136	2225	2244	...
Yeovil Junction......d.	1641	1720	1720	1805	...	1851	1917	1941	1944	1950	...	2031	2051r	2104	...	2144	2143	2230	2250	...
Crewkerne...........d.	1651	1729	1729	...	1901	...	1950	1954	...	2101v	2113	...	2154	2153	...
Axminster...........d.	1714	1743	1743	...	1914	...	2004	2007	...	2122	2136	...	2207	2206	...
Honiton.............d.	1727	1755	1755	...	1926	...	2016	2019	...	2134	2148	...	2219	2217	...
Exeter Central 512..a.	1751	1810	1810	...	1948	...	2031	2034	...	2153	2203	...	2238	...
Exeter St Davids 512.a.	1757	1814	1814	...	1954	...	2035	2038	...	2158	2208	...	2243	...

- ⛐ and ♀ Brighton - Exeter.
- ⛐ and ♀ Portsmouth - Exeter.
- ⛐ and ♀ London - Paignton.
- ⛐ Southampton - Yeovil.

b –	Arrives 0952.
f –	Arrives 1319.
r –	Departs 2057 on Ⓐ.
v –	Departs 2106 on Ⓐ.

For an explanation of standard symbols see page 4

Table 511 — EXETER - SALISBURY - LONDON (1, 2 class)

	Ⓐ	Ⓐ	⑥	Ⓐ	⑦	Ⓐ	⑦	Ⓐ	⑦	Ⓐ	⑦	Ⓐ	⑥	Ⓐ	⑦	⑥	⑦	Ⓐ	⑦	⑦	Ⓐ	Ⓐ	⑦	⑦	C
Exeter St Davids 512 d.	…	…	…	…	…	…	0641	0707	…	0808	…	…	0937	0937	0932	…	…	…	…	1135	…	…	1232	1330	
Exeter Central 512 d.	…	…	…	…	…	…	0649	0711	…	0813	…	…	0941	0941	0936	…	…	…	…	1139	…	…	1236	1334	
Honiton d.	…	…	…	0620	0650	…	0713	0737	…	0839	…	…	0958	1000	0955	…	…	…	…	1158	…	…	1301	1358	
Axminster d.	…	…	…	0631	0701	…	0725	0749	…	0850	…	…	1009	1011	1006	…	…	…	…	1209	…	…	1312	1409	
Crewkerne d.	…	…	…	0644	0714	…	0738	0802	…	0903	…	…	1022	1024	1030	…	…	…	…	1222	…	…	1325	1422	
Yeovil Junction d.	0513	0539	0615	0617	0654	0724	0730	0748	0812	0838	0913	0932n	0938	1032	1034	1046	…	…	…	1232	1257	…	1335	1432	
Sherborne d.	0519	0545	0621	0623	0700	0730	0736	0754	0818	0844	0919	0938n	0944	1039	1041	1052	…	…	…	1239	1303	…	1342	1439	
Templecombe d.	0527	0553	0629	0631	0708	0738	0744	0802	0826	0852	…	0946n	0952	…	1048	1100	…	…	…	1246	1311	…	1349	1446	
Gillingham (Dorset) d.	0534	0600	0636	0638	0715	0745	0751	0809	0833	0903	0932	0953	0959	1052	1056	1107	1150	1153	…	1254	1318	…	1357	1454	
Salisbury a.	0559	0625	0700	0703	0740	0810	0815	0834	0904	0927	0955	1023	1023	1115	1118	1131	1222	1224	…	1320	1340	…	1421	1529	
Salisbury d.	0608	0630	0715	0708	0745	0815	0829	0839	0915	0928	1000	1026	1029	1123	1123	1137	1225	1227	1237	1323	1345	1415	1429	1523	1615
Andover d.	0628	0650	0734	0728	0805	0834	0848	0856	0934	…	1010	1045	1048	1141	1140	1141	1244	1246	…	1341	1402	1434	1448	1557	1656
Basingstoke a.	0652	0714	0756	0752	0829	0856	0910	0913	0956	1010	1034	1107	1110	1157	1159	1211	1306	1308	1311	1358	1419	1456	1510	1557	1656
Woking d.	0712	…	0817	0812	…	0917	0942	0933	1017	…	1057	1127	1136	1217	1218	1236	1326	1328	1336	1418	1441	1517	1536	1617	1718
London Waterloo a.	0742	0801	0846	0841	0918	0946	1018	1003	1046	1052	1123	1156	1219	1242	1246	1318	1355	1355	1419	1446	1518	1546	1616	1646	1747

	⑦	⑦	⑦	Ⓐ	⑦	⑦	⑦	A	⑦	⑦	⑦	C	⑦	⑦	⑦	⑦	⑦	⑦	⑦
Exeter St Davids 512 d.	…	1509	1545	…	1618	1620	…	…	1725	…	1741	…	1822	1915	…	2028	…	2043	…	2105	…	…	2230	2230	2230
Exeter Central 512 d.	…	1513	1549	…	1622	1624	…	…	1729	…	1745	…	1826	1919	…	2032	…	2047	…	2109	…	…	2234	2234	2234
Honiton d.	…	1529	1605	…	1638	1648	…	…	1753	…	1809	…	1848	1935	…	2056	…	2109	…	2135	…	…	2250	2256	2300
Axminster d.	…	1540	1616	…	1649	1659	…	…	1805	…	1820	…	1859	1946	…	2107	…	2120	…	2146	…	…	2301	2307	2311
Crewkerne d.	…	1553	1629	…	1702	1712	…	…	1818	…	1833	…	1920	2010	…	2128	…	2133	…	2212	…	…	2314	2320	2324
Yeovil Junction d.	1527	1603	1639	…	1715	1722	1727	…	1828	1823	1855f	1856	1938	2020	…	2138	…	2144	…	2230	…	…	2324	2330	2334
Sherborne d.	1533	1610	1646	…	…	1729	1733	…	…	1829	1902	1902	1944	2026	…	2145	…	2150	…	…	…				
Templecombe d.	1541		1653	…	…	1736	1741	…	…	1838	1909	1910	1952	2034	…	2152	…	2158	…	…	…				
Gillingham (Dorset) d.	1548	1623	1701	1712	…	1744	1748	…	…	1845	1920	1920	1959	2041	…	2200	…	2210	…	…	…				
Salisbury a.	1612	1645	1722	1746	1750	1808	1812	…	1902	1911	1950	1945	2033	2103	…	2233	…	2234	…	2307	…	2358	0004	0004	
Salisbury d.	1619	1647	1725	1750	1800	1815	1818	…	1915	1953	1954	2045	2106	2240	…	2255	…	2236	…						
Andover a.	1636	1704	1743	1810	1817	1834	1837	…	1934	2011	2013	2104	2124	2259	…	2255	…								
Basingstoke a.	1656	1721	1759	1832	1834	1856	1859	…	1956	2027	2035	2126	2140	2321	2335	2317	2331								
Woking a.	1717	1741	1819	1852	…	1917	1920	…	2017	2048	2056	2147	2204	…	0007	…	2351								
London Waterloo a.	1744	1813	1852g	1916	1925	1948	1949	…	2046	2118	2130	2223h	2235	…	0055	…	0022								

A – 🚃 and 🍴 Exeter - Brighton.
C – 🚃 and 🍴 Paignton - London.
f – Arrives 1842.
g – Arrives 1845 on Ⓐ.
h – Arrives 2219 on ⑥.
n – Ⓐ only.

Table 512 — EXETER - EXMOUTH (2 class only)

From Exeter St Davids: Trains call at Exeter Central – 3 minutes from Exeter St Davids.
✕: 0555Ⓐ, 0650, 0716, 0747, 0821, 0850, 0920, 0950, 1020, 1050, 1116, 1151, 1215, 1247, 1320, 1350, 1420, 1450, 1520, 1545C, 1620C, 1719, 1744C, 1830, 1914, 2020, 2124Ⓐ, 2224.
⑦: 1124A, 1322, 1522, 1722, 1856, 2030, 2135, 2240.

From Exmouth: 18km Journey time: 24 - 34 minutes
✕: 0620Ⓐ, 0720, 0754, 0824, 0854, 0924, 0954, 1024, 1054, 1124, 1151, 1224, 1254, 1324, 1354, 1424, 1454, 1524, 1554C, 1624E, 1654, 1724C, 1754, 1834, 1904, 1954, 2054, 2154Ⓐ, 2254K.
⑦: 1054A, 1205A, 1354, 1554, 1754, 1930, 2105, 2205, 2310K.

A – Apr. 16 - May 21.   C – Change at Exeter Central.   E – To Exeter Central only.   K – Does not call at Exeter Central.

Table 513 — EXETER - BARNSTAPLE (2 class only)

km		Ⓧ	ⒶC	Ⓧ	Ⓧ	Ⓧ	Ⓐ	Ⓧ	⑦	Ⓧ	Ⓐ	Ⓧ	⑥	⑦P	Ⓧ	Ⓧ	⑦	Ⓐ	⑥	Ⓐ	⑦	Ⓐ	⑥
	Exmouth 512 d.	…	0620	…	0754	0824	0924	1024	…	…	…	1324	1354	1424	…	1554	1654	…	1754	…	1930	…	1954
	Exeter Central 511 d.	…	0648	…	0817	0848	0948	1048	1140	1206	1206	1344	1418	1454	1458	1618	1718	1803	1819	…	1954	2000	2018
0	Exeter St Davids 511 d.	0608	0651	0702	0821	0854	1002	1053	1144	1214	1214	1311	1349	1421	1458	1611	1625	1735	1807	1833	2000	2005	2323
1	Crediton d.	0618	…	0712	0831	0904	1012	1103	1155	1225	1226	1324	1400	…	1509	1621	1635	1735	1821	1843	2010	2015	2033
12																							
64	Barnstaple a.	0705	…	0829	…	0955	1102	1200	1248	…	1313	1417	…	1557	1715	1728	1829	1915	1939	2103	2108	2125

	Ⓐ	Ⓧ	Ⓐ	Ⓧ	Ⓐ	⑥	Ⓐ	⑦	Ⓐ	⑥	Ⓐ	Ⓧ	Ⓐ	Ⓐ	⑥	Ⓐ	⑦	Ⓐ	⑥
Barnstaple d.	…	0710	…	0900	…	1010	1107	…	1217	1253	1326	…	1423	…	1618	…	1732	1735	1845	1922	2015	2110	2115	2130
Crediton d.	0712	0802	0842	0948	…	1103	1151	1235	1306	1342	1412	1416	1508	…	1707	…	1822	1823	1948	2009	2100	2159	2202	2228
Exeter St Davids 511 a.	0722	0818	0853	0959	…	1114	1204	1247	1317	1354	1429	1429	1519	…	1718	…	1833	1835	1948	2020	2111	2211	2214	2228
Exeter Central 511 a.	0725	0824	0857	1003	…	1119	1218	1250	1323	1358	1433	1433	1523	…	1722	…	1837	1859	1951	2031	2127	2233	2227	
Exmouth 512 a.	…	0848	…	…	…	1144	1244	1318	1344	…	…	1544	…	1748	…	1923	…	2151	…	2251				

C – 🚃 Exmouth - Carmarthen.   P – 🚃 Exmouth - Penzance.

Table 514 — CORNISH BRANCH LINES (2 class only unless otherwise shown)

PLYMOUTH - GUNNISLAKE 24 km. Journey time: 44 - 47 minutes. NO SERVICE ON ⑦. Trains call at Calstock (32 minutes from Plymouth, 12 minutes from Gunnislake) on request.
From Plymouth:
✕: 0515Ⓐ (does not call at Calstock), 0650, 0930, 1135, 1345, 1625, 1810, 2100.
From Gunnislake:
✕: 0600 Ⓐ, 0740, 1020, 1230, 1435, 1715, 1900, 2150.

LISKEARD - LOOE 14 km. Journey time: 24 - 30 minutes. NO SERVICE ON ⑦.
From Liskeard:
✕: 0635, 0735, 0945, 1055, 1155, 1407, 1550, 1700, 1807.
From Looe:
✕: 0705, 0810, 1015, 1125, 1225, 1435, 1625, 1730, 1835.

PAR - NEWQUAY 33 km. Journey time: 50 - 54 minutes. NO SERVICE ON ⑦.
From Par:
✕: 0628 P, 0910, 1135, 1312, 1342 Q, 1745 R.
From Newquay:
✕: 0730 S, 1015, 1237, 1437 Q, 1515 P, 1845 Q, 1915 S.
P – May 27 only. 🚃 Leeds - Newquay and v.v.   Q – Not May 27.   R – Conveys 🚃 Edinburgh - Newquay on May 27.   S – May 27 only. 🚃 Newquay - Penzance

TRURO - FALMOUTH DOCKS 20 km. Journey time: 23 minutes. NO SERVICE ON ⑦. All trains call at Falmouth Town 2 minutes before / after Falmouth Dock
From Truro:
✕: 0626, 0730, 0855, 1005, 1130, 1240, 1415, 1505, 1605, 1715, 1825, 1921, 2020.
From Falmouth Docks:
✕: 0651, 0800, 0925, 1035, 1155, 1342, 1440, 1535, 1640, 1740, 1850, 1946, 2045.

(PENZANCE) - ST ERTH - ST IVES 6 km. Journey time: 10 - 13 minutes. NO SERVICE ON ⑦.
From St Erth:
✕: 0658T, 0731, 0802, 0848T, 0917, 1005T, 1110, 1211T, 1309T, 1356T, 1437, 1543T, 1711T, 1747, 1857, 2008T, 2050.
From St Ives:
✕: 0712, 0745, 0816U, 0902, 0931U, 1020, 1135U, 1227U, 1323U, 1410, 1455U, 1600U, 1725, 1821, 1920U, 2025, 2110.
T – 🚃 Penzance - St Ives. Depart Penzance 7 - 9 minutes earlier.
U – 🚃 St Ives - Penzance. Arrive Penzance 21 - 22 minutes later.

For an explanation of standard symbols see page 4

Table 515 PLYMOUTH - ST AUSTELL - TRURO - PENZANCE 1, 2 class

km		※ 2	A	④ 2	⑥	※ 2	④ 2	⑦n 2	※ 2❤		⑥ ❤	④ ❤		※	⑦h ❤	※	⑦j ❤	※ 2
	London Paddington 510...d.	...	2355	...		...		...			0725	0740			0915			...
0	Plymouth................d.	...	0555	...	0725	...	0806	0912	...	1020	1025	...	1125	1125	...	1242	1315	...	1025q	1015r	...	1340	1408	...	1510
7	Saltash................d.	...		...	0733	...	0817	0922	...	1030	1035	...			...	1252			1518
29	Liskeard................d.	...	0623	...	0754	...	0836	0941	...	1049	1051	...	1149	1149	...	1310	1341		1404	1434	...	1525
43	Bodmin Parkway........d.	...	0637	...	0807	...	0848	0952	...	1101	1102	...	1201	1201	...	1321		1416	1446	...	1547
49	Lostwithiel.............d.	...	0643	...	0812	...	0853	0957	...	1106	1107	...			...	1326			1552
56	Par....................d.	0635	0652	...	0818	0824	0906	1004	...	1113	1114	...	1211	1211	...	1333		1427		...	1600
	Newquay 518.........a.																		
64	St Austell..............d.	0642	0704	...	0825		0913	1011	...	1120	1121	...	1219	1219	...	1340		1435	1502	...	
87	Truro..................d.	0700	0724	...	0842	0844	0931	1029	...	1138	1138	...	1237	1237	...	1358	1419	1454	1521	...	
101	Redruth................d.	0713	0739	...	0854		0944	1041	...	1151	1150	...	1249	1249	...	1410		1506	1531	...	
107	Camborne..............d.	0719	0747	...	0900		0950	1048	...	1157	1156	...	1256	1256	...	1416		1513	1540	...	
117	Hayle..................d.	0726	0755	...	0908		0957	1055	...	1204	1204	...			...	1424				...	
119	St Erth 514.............d.	0729	0802	...	0911	0908	1000	1059	...		1207	...	1307	1307	...	1427		1524		...	
128	Penzance 514..........a.	0738	0819	...	0921	0919	1010	1108	...	1216	1217	...	1320	1320	...	1438	1500	1535	1600	...	

	※	⑦n	※	※	④	※	④	※	※	⑦	※	⑦y	⑦z		④	④	⑦n	④	⑦y	④	⑦z
		B	S	2	2	C	❤	2	2	F ❤	❤	E	❤	❤		❤ P	2	E	※	❤	2	❤
London Paddington 510....d.						1335q			1415v			1515			1735	1751			1835	1835		1835
Plymouth...................d.	1523	1540	1555	1630	1654	1711	1745	1745	1806	1850	1900	1907	1928	2012	2027		2047	2119	2125	2143	2151	2217	2240	2240
Saltash.....................d.	1531	1548	1603	1644		1800	1800											2135					2247x
Liskeard....................d.	1547	1607	1621	1705	1719	1735	1822	1822	1830	1914	1926	1931	1952	2036	2051		2111	2152	2207	2215	2241	2304	2304
Bodmin Parkway............d.	1559	1619	1634	1717	1731	1747	1834	1834	1842	1926	1938	1943	2004	2048	2103		2123	2155	2203	2219	2227	2253	2315x	2316
Lostwithiel.................d.	1604	1624	1638	1722			1839	1839											2207				2319x
Par........................d.	1611	1631	1645	1730	1742	1758	1846	1846		1936	1949								2215				2325x
Newquay 518..............a.																						
St Austell...................d.	1618	1638	1653	...	1750	1806	1853	1854	1858	1944	1957	1959	2020	2104	2119		2139	2211		2235	2243	2309	2332	2332
Truro......................d.	1636	1655	1710	...	1808	1823		1917	1916	2002	2015	2017	2038	2122	2137		2157	2229		2253	2310	2327	2349	2350
Redruth....................d.	1649	1708	1723	...	1820	1835		1930	1928	2014	2029	2029	2050	2134	2149		2209	2241		2305	2313	2339	0001	0002
Camborne..................d.	1656	1714	1729	...	1827	1842		1936		2021	2036	2036		2141	2156					2320		0008		
Hayle......................d.	1703	1721	1737	...		1849		1943															
St Erth 514.................d.	1707		1741	...	1838	1854		1946		2032	2047												
Penzance 514..............a.	1716	1733	1752	...	1855	1910		1957	1950	2045	2100	2055	2120	2200	2215		2230	2310		2335	2340	0001	0025	0025

	④	④	※	※	⑥	※	※	※		⑦	⑦j	⑥	※	⑦	※	⑦n	④
	❤ P	2		H	❤		F	2	※		E ❤	Q	❤			❤	H	E	2
Penzance 514...........d.	0515	...	...	0641	0645	...	0720	...	0750	...	0847	...	0923	0934	0941	...	1025	...	1119	1145	1150	...	1240
St Erth 514.............d.			...	0649		...	0729	...	0801	...			0932		0950	...	1035	...		1153		...	1248
Hayle..................d.			...	0652		...		...	0804	...						...	1038	...		1157		...	
Camborne..............d.			...	0701	0701	...	0739	...	0814	...	0903	...	0950	1000	...	1047	...	1135	1206	...	1258
Redruth................d.	0536		...	0707	0709	...	0747	...	0821	...	0911	...	0947	0958	1008	...	1053	...	1143	1213	1211	...	1304
Truro..................d.	0548		...	0719	0721	...	0759	...	0833	...	0923	...	0959	1010	1020	...	1104	...	1155	1225	1223	...	1315
St Austell..............d.	0605		...	0736	0738	...	0816	...	0850	...	0940	...	1016	1027	1037	...	1121	...	1212	1242	1240	...	1332
Newquay 518..........d.		0618		0715					0858				1024		1045		1128		1249			1339
Lostwithiel.............d.		0624		0721					0904								1134		1256			
Bodmin Parkway........d.	0621	0630		0727	0750	0753		0832	0910		0956		1035	1042	1056		1140		1227	1301	1255		1349
Liskeard...............d.	0632	0643		0745	0803	0805		0844	0923		1008		1047	1054	1107		1155		1239	1314	1307		1402
Saltash................d.		0703		0800					0942								1213		1330			1418
Plymouth...............d.	0658	0718		0815	0830	0830		0909	0954		1033		1112	1127	1132		1225		1312	1341	1340		1428
London Paddington 510.....a.	1000					1155					1400b			1547c	1455				1733e			

	⑦n	※	※	④	※	⑦	※	⑦		※	⑦	※	⑦n	⑥	※	⑦n	④
	2	2		2	❤				※ Q		❤	G	2	T	2	2	U	U
Penzance 514...........d.	1330	1330	...	...	1445	1449	1520	1545	...	1630	...	1716	1735	...	1840	1842	...	2010	...	2115	...	2215
St Erth 514.............d.	...	1339	...	...	1454		1529		...	1639	...		1743	...	1849		...	2018	...		...	
Hayle..................d.	...	1339	1342	...			1532		...	1643	...		1746	...	1852	1851	...	2021	...		...	
Camborne..............d.	...	1349	1351	...		1505	1542	1601	...	1652	...	1732	1755	...	1901	1901	...	2031	...		...	
Redruth................d.	...	1355	1357	...	1509	1513	1548	1609	...	1700	...	1740	1801	...	1907	1907	...	2037	...	2137	...	2237
Truro..................d.	...	1407	1410	...	1521	1525	1605	1621	...	1712	...	1752	1813	...	1918	1919	...	2048	2110	2150	...	2250
St Austell..............d.	...	1425	1427	...	1538	1542	1621	1638	...	1729	...	1809	1830	...	1935	1936	...	2105	2127	2210	...	2310
Newquay 518..........d.				1437			1529														
Par....................d.	...	1432	1435	1529			1629		...	1737	...		1837	...	1942	1943	...	2111	2135		...	
Lostwithiel.............d.	...	1438	1442				1635		...		...		1844	...	1949	1950	...				...	
Bodmin Parkway........d.	...	1444	1447		1554	1559	1641	1655	...	1748	...	1825	1849	...	1954	1956	...			2229	...	2329
Liskeard...............d.	...	1457	1503		1551	1606	1611	1657	1707	...	1800	...	1837	1903	...	2007	2009	...			2244	...	2344
Saltash................d.	...	1515	1519				1716		...		...		1920	...	2024	2025	...				...	
Plymouth...............d.	...	1525	1528		1617	1638	1732	1732	...	1825	...	1902	1931	...	2036	2035	...			2310	...	0010
London Paddington 510.....a.						2000	2025f		2109g		2215k		2305t							0610	...	0610

⑧ from London: ⟶ 1,2 cl. and ⤇ London - Penzance.

– ⤇ (and ❤ on ④) Cardiff - Penzance.
– ⤇ and ❤ (Dundee on ④ -) Edinburgh - Penzance.
– ⤇ and ❤ Edinburgh - Penzance and v.v.
– ⤇ and ❤ Edinburgh - Glasgow - Penzance and v.v.
– ⤇ Penzance - Exeter (- Swindon on ④).
– ⤇ and ❤ Penzance - Cardiff.
– ⤇ and ❤ Penzance - Gloucester (- Birmingham International on ④).
– Pullman service and ✕ available in 1 cl.

Q – Conveys ❤ (and ✕ on ④).
S – ⤇ Exmouth - Penzance.
T – ⤇ Penzance - Exeter.
U – ⟶ 1,2 cl. and ⤇ Penzance - London.
b – Arrive 1350 on ④.
c – Arrive 1526 Nov. 20 - Jan. 8.
e – Arrive 1710 Sept. 25 - Jan. 8.
f – Arrive 2005 Sept. 25 - Jan. 8.
g – Arrive 2046 Sept. 25 - Jan. 8.
h – Feb. 19 and 26, Apr. 9 and 23.

j – Nov. 20 - May 21.
k – Arrive 2210 on ④.
n – Not Jan. 1.
q – Depart 10 minutes later on ④.
r – Depart 1035 Nov. 20 - Jan. 8.
t – Arrive 2240 Sept. 25 - Jan. 8.
v – Depart 1435 Sept. 25 - Jan. 8.
x – Stops on request.
y – Sept. 25 - Jan. 8.
z – Jan. 15 - May 21.

3275A

Table 520 — CARDIFF and BRISTOL - BIRMINGHAM - SHEFFIELD - YORK

1, 2 class

First part

km	Station	⚔2	♉	⚔2	⚔2♉	♉	♉	⚔2	⑥2♉	Ⓐ2	⚔	♉	♉	⚔2♉	⚔2	♉	♉	⑥	Ⓐ	♉	⑦	⚔2	♉	⑥	Ⓐ	⚔2♉	⑦♉
	Penzance 510 d.																				0620						
	Plymouth 510 d.																										
	Paignton 510 d.																				0722						
	Exeter St. Davids 510 d.																					0715					
	Swansea 530 d.					0610						0710										0809				0900	
	Cardiff Central d.					0624						0724										0823				0915	
	Newport d.																										
	Chepstow d.					0643						0745															
0	Bristol Temple Meads d.				0504						0657										0830	0905					0857
9	Bristol Parkway d.				0514						0707										0840	0915					
63	Gloucester 529 d.				0549	0714					0742			0820								0950				1000	
71	Cheltenham 529 d.				0559	0724					0752			0830							0913	0959				1010	1036
107	Worcester Shrub Hill d.																										
	Brighton d.																										
	Gatwick Airport ✈ d.																	0634	0642								
	Poole d.								0545	0554								0650	0652								
	Bournemouth d.								0618	0627								0728	0736								
	Southampton Central d.								0626	0636								0736	0744								
	Southampton Airport ✈ d.								0637	0647								0751	0754								
	Winchester d.								0659	0706								0811	0812								
	Basingstoke d.																										
	London Paddington 530 d.							0557r						0738	0738			0846	0846								
	Reading d.							0635						0805	0805			0918	0918								1005
	Oxford d.							0651						0826	0826			0939	0939								
	Banbury d.							0703										0959	0959								
	Leamington Spa d.							0746						0846	0846			1015	1015								
	Coventry d.							0802						0903	0903			1015	1015					1027	1027		
	Birmingham International ✈ d.							0814						0915	0915			1027	1027								
145	Birmingham New Street a.			0640				0809	0829	0839				0913	0929	0929		0954				1040	1045	1048		1116	1116
145	Birmingham New Street d.			0635	0655	0755		0812	0812	0834	0844	0902		0934	0934	0955		1019	1044			1055	1055			1117	1135
165	Wolverhampton 550 d.								0852					0952	0952							1113	1113				
	Manchester Piccadilly 550 a.								1015					1122	1122							1240	1240				
	Liverpool Lime Street 550 a.																					1240	1240				
173	Tamworth d.			0659	0714	0814		0836	0837			0921										1043				1056	1121
193	Burton-on-Trent d.		0638	0712	0726	0827		0849	0850		0910	0934										1038	1043				
211	Derby 561 d.		0638	0736	0740	0843		0910	0915		0924	0954						1038	1043			1122	1124			1208	1228
237	Nottingham 561 a.			0801				0934	0937			1016							1149								1231v
250	Chesterfield d.	0648	0701	0735		0802	0907				0946							1100	1106			1146					1251
270	Sheffield a.	0706	0717	0753		0817	0924				1001							1115	1122			1201					1301
270	Sheffield d.	0713	0719	0800		0819	0927				1003							1119	1124			1203					1303
299	Doncaster 570 d.		0746			0842					1031							1142	1150			1231					1348
316	Wakefield Westgate a.	0812		0838		0958					1031											1248					
332	Leeds a.	0834		0901		1018					1048											1319					1411
344	York 570 a.		0819			0911	1053				1114							1207	1230			1313					1520
	Newcastle 570 a.					1020					1226							1313									
	Glasgow Central 550 a.																										
	Edinburgh 570 a.												1513	1513													

Second part

Station	⚔A	♉	⑥2♉	⑥♉	Ⓐ♉	⚔2♉	⑦♉	⚔G♉	⑦♉	♉	⚔2♉	⚔2♉	⚔♉	⚔	⑦2♉	⑥2♉	Ⓐ2	⑦♉
Penzance 510 d.										0720								
Plymouth 510 d.	0725									0915								
Paignton 510 d.			0830															
Exeter St. Davids 510 d.	0827		0910							1014								
Swansea 530 d.							0920	1015		1050						1215		
Cardiff Central d.				0915			1015	1029		1105						1229		
Newport d.				0928				1048								1248		
Chepstow d.				0950														1157
Bristol Temple Meads d.	0935	1012					1027			1123	1204							
Bristol Parkway d.	0945	1022					1120			1133	1214							
Gloucester 529 d.	1020						1120			1150	1249					1320		
Cheltenham 529 d.	1030	1058					1130			1208	1201	1259				1330		
Worcester Shrub Hill d.											1227							
Brighton d.							0920					0945						
Gatwick Airport ✈ d.																		
Poole d.							0900											
Bournemouth d.							0912											
Southampton Central d.							0947											
Southampton Airport ✈ d.							0956											
Winchester d.							1007											
Basingstoke d.							1025											
London Paddington 530 d.			0851	0905		0940						1133						
Reading d.			0934	0936		1019	1054					1200					1305	
Oxford d.			1005	1005		1045	1119	1135				1221						
Banbury d.			1026	1026		1104	1140					1246						
Leamington Spa d.			1046	1046		1126	1200					1303						
Coventry d.			1103	1103		1142	1216					1315						
Birmingham International ✈ d.			1115	1115		1153	1228											
Birmingham New Street a.	1124	1140	1129	1129		1208	1213	1243	1246	1255	1311	1329	1340		1413	1425		1445
Birmingham New Street d.	1134	1144	1155	1155	1216	1220		1255	1305	1305	1317	1334	1344	1403	1416	1416	1435	1450
Wolverhampton 550 d.	1152		1213	1213		1244				1322		1352					1522	
Manchester Piccadilly 550 a.			1336	1336								1522						
Liverpool Lime Street 550 a.															1441	1441		
Tamworth d.					1241	1254		1327	1342		1336	1349			1451	1454	1454	1510
Burton-on-Trent d.					1315			1342	1357	1407	1424				1515	1519		1527
Derby 561 d.			1224		1315	1340				1430		1424			1533	1537		1544
Nottingham 561 a.			1246		1340			1406	1421		1446					1550		
Chesterfield d.			1246					1406	1421		1501					1606		
Sheffield a.			1301					1424	1436		1503					1608		
Sheffield d.			1303					1427	1439		1530					1633		
Doncaster 570 d.			1331					1459	1509							1649		
Wakefield Westgate a.			1348					1518								1708		
Leeds a.			1414					1551	1541		1600t					1739		
York 570 a.			1414					1551	1541									
Newcastle 570 a.			1526				1800			1740		1912						
Glasgow Central 550 a.										1740								
Edinburgh 570 a.	1605									1855p								

A – 🚌 and ♉ Plymouth - Aberdeen.
G – 🚌 Milford Haven - Birmingham.
p – Arrives 1847 on Ⓐ.
r – Departs 0604 on ⑥.
t – Arrives 1555 on ⑥.
v – Arrives 1228 on ⑥.

Table 520 — CARDIFF and BRISTOL - BIRMINGHAM - SHEFFIELD - YORK

1, 2 class

Upper panel

Station																		
Penzance 510 .... d.			0923															
Plymouth 510 .... d.	1044	1115				1144			1155					1300		1300		
Paignton 510 .... d.																		
Exeter St Davids 510 .... d.	1143	1211				1250		1304		1220		1354		1403				
Swansea 530 .... d.				1115														
Cardiff Central .... d.				1255	1255					1405	1405	1340						1455
Newport .... d.				1310	1309					1419	1419	1354						1510
Chepstow .... d.					1331					1440	1440							
Bristol Temple Meads .... d.	1255	1323				1408	1405		1425			1449h	1504		1520			
Bristol Parkway .... d.	1307					1418	1415		1435			1459	1514		1530			
Gloucester 529 .... d.				1358	1413		1453			1510	1510		1535	1547		1606	1556	
Cheltenham 529 .... d.	1340			1408	1423	1455	1502		1508	1520	1520		1544	1557		1615	1606	1629
Worcester Shrub Hill .... d.				1430	1434													1629
Brighton .... d.																		
Gatwick Airport + ... d.																		
Poole .... d.																		
Bournemouth .... d.		1119				1219												
Southampton Central .... d.		1150				1250												
Southampton Airport + ... d.		1158				1258												
Winchester .... d.		1208				1308												
Basingstoke .... d.		1225				1325												
London Paddington 530 .... d.												1340			1418			
Reading .... d.		1253				1351						1420		1448	1449			
Oxford .... d.		1320				1418						1451		1516	1516			
Banbury .... d.		1341				1439						1512		1537	1537			
Leamington Spa .... d.		1400				1458						1536		1557	1557			
Coventry .... d.		1416				1514						1552		1613	1613			
Birmingham International + ... d.		1427				1525						1603		1625	1625			
Birmingham New Street .... a.	1429	1444	1445	1511	1514	1515	1540	1543	1556	1607	1612	1618	1625	1640	1640	1656	1710	
Birmingham New Street .... d.	1434	1444	1505	1515	1517	1555	1555	1549	1600	1605	1613	1626	1635	1655	1705	1705	1705	1717
Wolverhampton 550 .... d.	1452	1522				1613			1622			1643		1721	1721			1722
Manchester Piccadilly 550 .... a.	1619											1808						
Liverpool Lime Street 550 .... a.						1740												
Tamworth .... d.			1534	1536				1608	1621		1637			1714				1736
Burton-on-Trent .... d.			1547	1549			1626		1634		1650			1726				1749
Derby 561 .... d.		1524	1609	1607			1640	1637	1653		1710	1717		1740				1807
Nottingham 561 .... a.			1632	1631					1720		1734							1832
Chesterfield .... d.							1702	1700						1717	1740			
Sheffield .... a.	1559						1717	1715					1740	1749	1802			
Sheffield .... d.	1603						1719	1718					1757	1807	1817			
Doncaster 570 .... d.	1631						1742	1740					1758	1810	1819			
Wakefield Westgate .... d.													1827	1911	1847			
Leeds .... a.	1648												1849	1931	1909			
York 570 .... a.	1714						1807	1808										
Newcastle 570 .... a.	1822						1916	1916										
Glasgow Central 550 .... a.		1935															2148	
Edinburgh 570 .... a.	2005	2040				2055p	2100		2039								2138	2300

Lower panel

Station																			
Penzance 510 .... d.		1150						1353											
Plymouth 510 .... d.		1343															1540		
Paignton 510 .... d.					1430	1430													
Exeter St Davids 510 .... d.		1438			1510	1510		1500					1550				1643		
Swansea 530 .... d.									1520k										
Cardiff Central .... d.	1510						1605	1615										1703	
Newport .... d.	1524						1619	1629										1718	
Chepstow .... d.							1638	1648										1740	
Bristol Temple Meads .... d.		1555			1614	1614	1624						1709	1703			1800		
Bristol Parkway .... d.		1605			1624	1624	1635						1719	1713			1810		
Gloucester 529 .... d.	1616				1702	1702		1713	1720					1748				1810	
Cheltenham 529 .... d.	1626	1638			1712	1712	1710	1723	1730				1754	1757			1842	1822	
Worcester Shrub Hill .... d.																		1849	
Brighton .... d.										1420	1420	1420							
Gatwick Airport + ... d.										1448u	1445	1445							
Poole .... d.						1405													
Bournemouth .... d.				1421		1417										1505			
Southampton Central .... d.				1450		1449										1517			
Southampton Airport + ... d.				1458		1457										1549			
Winchester .... d.				1508		1508										1557			
Basingstoke .... d.				1525		1529										1608			
London Paddington 530 .... d.																1629			
Reading .... d.				1543	1550		1605						1653	1656					
Oxford .... d.				1611	1618		1632			1652	1700	1700t	1720	1724					
Banbury .... d.				1631	1639		1651			1713	1719	1719	1741	1745					
Leamington Spa .... d.				1653	1658		1711			1735	1743	1745	1801	1807					
Coventry .... d.				1708	1712		1726			1753	1757	1803	1817	1822					
Birmingham International + ... d.				1720	1725		1738			1808	1810	1816	1829	1834					
Birmingham New Street .... a.	1711	1725		1735	1740	1754	1754	1753	1801	1812	1813	1820	1829	1840	1840	1844	1849	1923	1929
Birmingham New Street .... d.		1735	1733	1743	1755	1746	1758	1758	1816	1805	1818	1825	1835	1834	1844	1844	1905	1905	1930	1931
Wolverhampton 550 .... d.					1811	1806		1822			1853	1852	1852			1922	1921		
Manchester Piccadilly 550 .... a.						1931		1958				2019	2020				2044		
Liverpool Lime Street 550 .... a.				1940												2044			
Tamworth .... d.		1758	1806				1817	1817			1842	1846				2044		1955	
Burton-on-Trent .... d.		1811	1817				1829	1829	1844		1855	1901				1958	2008		
Derby 561 .... d.		1817	1830	1830			1843	1843	1902		1921	1919		1925	1926	2014	2026		
Nottingham 561 .... a.			1857	1907							1947	1946				2048			
Chesterfield .... d.					1905	1905	1927						1949	1951		2037			
Sheffield .... a.		1854			1920	1920	1944						2010	2005		2052			
Sheffield .... d.		1856			1922	1922	1946							2007		2055			
Doncaster 570 .... d.					1945	1945	2009							2034					
Wakefield Westgate .... d.		1925											2103			2124			
Leeds .... a.		1944														2145			
York 570 .... a.		2009			2010	2013	2045									2124			
Newcastle 570 .... a.		2122			2120	2131							2215			2145			
Glasgow Central 550 .... a.																			
Edinburgh 570 .... a.		2305									2320								

⊏⊐ and ⊖ Carmarthen - Birmingham.

①–⑥, ⊏⊐ Fishguard (not Apr. 13, 14, 15, May 27) - Cardiff - Birmingham.

h – Arrives 1430.
k – Not Apr. 13, 14, 15, May 27.
p – Arrives 2045 on ⑥.
t – Arrives 1646.

For an explanation of standard symbols see page 4

Table 520 — CARDIFF and BRISTOL - BIRMINGHAM - SHEFFIELD - YORK

1, 2 class

	⑦ 2⏟	⏟	⏟	⑦ ⏟	2	⑦ 2⏟		⑦ ⏟	⏟	⑦ ⏟	⑦ ⏟		⑦ ⏟	⑦ 2⏟	Ⓐ 2⏟	⑥ 2⏟		⑦ ⏟	⑦	Ⓐ 2	Ⓐ 2	⑦ 2	⑥ A
Penzance 510 .... d.	...	...	...	...	...	...		...	...	...	...		...	...	...	...		...	...	...	...	...	2045
Plymouth 510 .... d.	...	1545	...	...	...	...		...	...	...	...		...	...	...	...		...	...	...	...	...	
Paignton 510 .... d.	...	...	...	...	...	...		...	...	...	...		...	...	...	...		...	...	...	...	...	2150u
Exeter St. Davids 510 ...... d.	...	1651	...	...	...	...		...	...	...	...		...	...	...	...		...	...	...	...	...	
Swansea 530 .... d.	...	...	...	...	...	...		...	...	...	...		...	1905	1903	1910		...	2000	2130	2225	...	
Cardiff Central.......... d.	1705		...	1803	1805	...		...	1920	1918	1925		...	2014	2145	2240			2014	2145	2240		
Newport.................. d.	1720		...	1817	1819	...		...	1940	1938	1945		...	2033	2207	2302			2033	2207	2302		
Chepstow................. d.	1740		...	1838	1839	...		...					2010			2320u							2320u
Bristol Temple Meads...... d.		1804	...			1915	1918					2020				2333u							2333u
Bristol Parkway .... d.		1817	...			1925	1928		2010	2010	2017	2055		2102		2240	2335k				2240	2335k	
Gloucester 529 .... d.	1813		...	1912	1910	2000		2010	2010	2017	2055		2102		2250	2345k				2250	2345k	
Cheltenham 529 .... d.	1823	1852	...	1922	1920	2009	2002		2020	2020	2027	2104				2312	0007k				2312	0007k	
Worcester Shrub Hill ...... d.	1854		...			2045	2047	2050															
Brighton .... d.			...																			
Gatwick Airport ✈....... d.			...			1705																
Poole .... d.			1616			1716	1717															
Bournemouth............. d.			1616			1716	1717															
Southampton Central .... d.			1648			1748	1749															
Southampton Airport ✈.. d.			1656			1756	1757															
Winchester .... d.			1706			1807	1808															
Basingstoke.............. d.			1725			1825	1829					1920										
London Paddington 530 .. d.				1720								1920										
Reading .... d.			1752	1756		1854	1859					2001										
Oxford.................... d.			1821	1827		1923	1927					2025										
Banbury .... d.			1842	1850		1944	1946	2010				2046										
Leamington Spa.......... d.			1901	1908		2003	2007					2107										
Coventry .... d.			1917	1923		2019	2022					2122										
Birmingham International ✈ d.			1928	1934		2030	2034					2134				⑦ 2						
Birmingham New Street.... a.	1931	1940	1942	1948	2010	2010	2043	2050	2047	2050	2118	2122	2124	2128	2150	2150			2225	2230	
Birmingham New Street.... d.	1935	1958	1955	2000	...	...	2105	2058	2105	2105	2125	2127	2128		2205	2210			2225	2230	
Wolverhampton 550 .... d.			2013	2018			2122		2121		2142				2222						
Manchester Piccadilly 550 .. a.			2140	2139			2244				2316				2347						
Liverpool Lime Street 550 .. a.								2249													
Tamworth .... d.	1957		...						2149	2149					2247	2251			2247	2251	
Burton-on-Trent .... d.	2008		...			2133		2200	2202					2258	2306			2258	2306	
Derby 561 .... d.	2034	2038	...			2138	2151	2224	2221			2257		2318	2325			2318	2325	
Nottingham 561 .... a.	2057		...			2200	2216	2246	2243					2342	2350			2342	2350	
Chesterfield .... d.			...			2215	2235													
Sheffield .... a.			...			2219														
Sheffield .... d.			...																	
Doncaster 570 .... d.			...			2247														
Wakefield Westgate ...... d.			...			2307														
Leeds..................... a.			...																	
York 570 .... a.			...																	
Newcastle 570 .... a.			...															0655s		
Edinburgh 570 .... a.			...															0830		
Glasgow Central 550 ... a.			...																	

km		B A	C A	⏟ 2	⏟ 2	⏟ 2	Ⓐ 2	⏟	⑥ 2⏟	Ⓐ 2⏟	⏟	G 2	Ⓐ ⏟	⑥ 2⏟	⏟	⏟	⑦ ⏟	Ⓐ ⏟	⑥ ⏟	Ⓐ ⏟
	Glasgow Central 550 ... d.	2110	2130	...	...	...	...	...	...	...	...	...	...	...	...	...	...	...	...	...
	Edinburgh 570 .... d.	2238	2255	...	...	...	...	...	...	...	0640	...	...	...	...	...	...	...	...	...
	Newcastle 570 .... d.			...	...	...	...	...	...	...	0741	...	...	...	...	...	...	...	...	...
0	**York 570** .... d.			...	...	...	...	...	...	...		...	...	...	0815	...	...	...	...	...
	Leeds..................... d.			...	...	...	0605	...	...	...		...	...	...	0815	...	...	...	...	...
	Wakefield Westgate ...... d.			...	...	...	0617	...	...	...		...	0809	...	0827	...	...	...	...	...
	Doncaster 570 .... d.			...	...	...	0635	...	...	...		0824	0833	...	0859	...	...	...	...	...
75	**Sheffield**................ a.			...	...	...	0659	...	...	...		0824	0835	...	0902	...	...	...	...	...
75	**Sheffield**................ d.			...	...	...	0702	...	...	0720					0914	...	...	...	...	...
94	Chesterfield............... d.			...	...	...	0715	...	...			0824				...	...	...	...	...
130	**Derby 561** .... d.			0600	...	...	0610	0645	0645	0720		0854	0910	...	0938	...	...	...	...	...
148	Burton-on-Trent............ d.			0612	...	...	0646	0713	0713	0739	0750	0906		...	0951	...	...	...	...	...
168	Tamworth.................. d.			0625	...	...	0700	0726	0726	0751	0805	0919		...		...	...	0910	0910	
	Liverpool Lime Street 550 .. d.				...	0517		0617								...	...			
	Manchester Piccadilly 550 .. d.				...	0630	0643	0734				0840	0840		0935	...	...	1030	1030	
196	**Birmingham New Street**.... a.			0647	0649	0700	0713	0737	0754	0806	0806	0824	0844	0900	0906	0944	0950	0954	1021	1025	1050	1050
196	**Birmingham New Street**.... d.				0706	0703		0806	0810	0810	0828	0858	0906	0906	0946	1000	1006	1028	1030	1045	1058	1058
209	Birmingham International ✈ d.				0716			0816					0916	0916		1016					
228	Coventry .... d.				0727			0827					0927	0927		1027					
243	Leamington Spa............ d.				0744			0844					0944	0944		1044					
276	Banbury .... a.				0803			0903					1005	1005		1103					
312	Oxford.................... a.				0828			0924					1027	1027		1124					
361	**Reading** .... a.				0901			1000					1054	1058		1154					
	London Paddington 530 .. a.															1228					
386	Basingstoke............... a.				0928			1029								1244					
418	Winchester .... a.				0944			1045								1253					
432	Southampton Airport ✈ a.				0953			1054								1301					
439	Southampton Central .... a.				1001			1102								1340					
485	Bournemouth.............. a.				1040			1140													
494	Poole .... a.																				
445	Gatwick Airport ✈........ a.												1224s	1243s							
484	Brighton .... a.												1257	1328							
0	Worcester Shrub Hill ...... d.				0628	⏟		0851	0855						1022						
19	**Cheltenham 529** .... d.				0649	2	0751	0914	0917	0907		0941			1047	1038		1109	1114	1125	1142	1142
29	**Gloucester 529** .... d.				0700	0733		0925	0929	0923		0952			1100			1125	1125	1137		
	Bristol Parkway .... d.	0600s	0600s				0827			0953	⑥				1113			1155			1219	1225
74	**Bristol Temple Meads** ..... a.	0612s	0612s	2			0839			1005	2				1127			1207	1257		1231	1236
101	Chepstow................. a.			0620	0729	0801				1008	1020						1205				
120	Newport.................. a.			0641	0751	0823		1007	1011	1031	1040	1147t				1229				
	Cardiff Central.......... a.			0658	0807	0839		1024	1028	1046	1056	1204t				1245				
	Swansea 530 .... a.			0806		0930					1158r									
	Exeter St. Davids 510 ...... a.	0756s	0756s			0951				1117					1311			1340	1345	
	Paignton 510 .... a.														1400				
	Plymouth 510 .... a.	0903	0903			1100			1225									1450	1500	
	Penzance 510 .... a.																			

A – 1,2 cl. Plymouth - Edinburgh - Glasgow and v.v.
B – Runs ⑦ from Glasgow and Edinburgh.
C – Runs Ⓐ from Glasgow and Edinburgh.

G – ①–⑥. Birmingham - Cardiff - (not Apr. 13, 14, 15, May 27) Fishguard.
k – Ⓐ only.

r – Not Apr. 13, 14, 15, May 27.
s – Stops to set down only.
u – Stops to pick up only.

For an explanation of standard symbols see page 4

Table 520   YORK - SHEFFIELD - BIRMINGHAM - BRISTOL and CARDIFF

1, 2 class

Upper table

Station																						
Edinburgh 570 .... d.						0655	0707			0650 M		0805 E			0910							
Glasgow Central 550 .... d.										0810												
Newcastle 570 .... d.						0828	0837					0940				1005						
York 570 .... d.						0933	0942	0943				1043				1115	1110					
Leeds.................. d.				0930				1015				1115										
Wakefield Westgate........ d.				0943				1029				1127										
Doncaster 570 .... d.						1009	1009									1147						
Sheffield .... a.						1016	1033	1033	1103		1159					1214						
Sheffield .... d.						1018	1035	1035	1105		1202					1218	1235					
Chesterfield .... d.						1031	1048	1048	1120							1231	1255					
Nottingham 561 .... d.		0957	1001		1025							1155	1202					1237	1242			
Derby 561 .... d.		1026	1029		1058	1054	1112	1112	1145		1237		1243		1254			1311	1313			
Burton-on-Trent........ d.		1040	1043		1110	1108	1124	1124				1236	1256		1308			1326	1325			
Tamworth .... d.		1053	1055		1122							1309						1338	1337			
Liverpool Lime Street 550 .. d.																						
Manchester Piccadilly 550 .. d.	0917													1217								
Wolverhampton 550 ..... d.	1040			1047					1235				1329	1341		1217	1336					1431
Birmingham New Street..... a.	1100	1117	1122	1112	1144	1150	1159	1159	1226	1259	1320	1320	1336	1349	1400	1351	1401	1406	1406			1450
Birmingham New Street..... d.	1106		1127	1146	1157	1206	1206	1228	1245	1306	1328	1337		1406	1404	1415	1417	1415	1415	1445	1458
Birmingham International + d.	1116		1137			1216	1216			1316				1416			1427				
Coventry .... d.	1127		1149			1227	1227			1327				1427			1437				
Leamington Spa......... d.	1144		1205			1244	1244			1344				1444			1454				
Banbury .... a.	1205		1233			1303	1303			1403				1505			1511				
Oxford .... a.	1227		1248		1311	1324	1324			1427				1527			1535				
Reading .... a.	1257		1332			1353	1353			1455				1605			1605				
London Paddington 530 .. a.	1335e																1644				
Basingstoke............ a.			1404s			1428	1428			1526											
Winchester .... a.			1422s			1444	1444			1542											
Southampton Airport + a.			1432s			1453	1453			1551											
Southampton Central .... a.			1440s			1501	1501			1559											
Bournemouth .... a.			1520s			1540	1540			1650											
Poole .... a.			1540																		
Gatwick Airport + ... a.																					
Brighton .... a.																					
Worcester Shrub Hill ...... d.				1237r							1412						1452	1451			
Cheltenham 529 .... d.				1300				1312	1325		1436			1452	1500		1514	1514	1525	1540	
Gloucester 529 .... d.				1311					1337		1452			1516			1526	1526	1537		
Bristol Parkway .... a.								1348						1531	1549					1614	
Bristol Temple Meads .... a.					1427			1400		1449				1546	1601					1630	
Chepstow............. a.								1405			1521							1605			
Newport.............. a.				1353				1427			1547						1608	1608	1627		
Cardiff Central......... a.				1410				1444			1607						1625	1625	1644		
Swansea 530 .... a.								1558											1810		
Exeter St. Davids 510 .... a.							1518			1548				1656	1709					1745	
Paignton 510 .... a.										1649				1805	1820					1846	
Plymouth 510 .... a.										1855										2045	

Lower table

Station																						
Edinburgh 570 .... d.							1035				1150											
Glasgow Central 550 .... d.									1040	1040												
Newcastle 570 .... d.			1203	1203			1228													1238		
York 570 .... d.	1143	1143	1305	1305			1331						1407		1418							
Leeds.................. d.	1215	1215																				
Wakefield Westgate........ d.	1229	1229																				
Doncaster 570 .... d.			1332	1332			1400						1450									
Sheffield .... a.	1304	1304	1359	1359			1425					1459	1518									
Sheffield .... d.	1313	1313	1402	1402			1427					1502	1520									
Chesterfield .... d.	1328	1328	1415	1415									1535									
Nottingham 561 .... d.			1352			1400		1442			1455				1546		1556					
Derby 561 .... d.	1353	1353	1418	1439	1439	1428	1501	1511		1539	1550	1559		1617	1624						
Burton-on-Trent........ d.	1406	1406	1430			1441	1522		1535	1602	1613		1629	1636							
Tamworth .... d.			1443				1535	1548		1615			1642	1649							
Liverpool Lime Street 550 .. d.								1410													
Manchester Piccadilly 550 .. d.				1335					1417	1417					1510	1510					
Wolverhampton 550 ..... d.				1502				1540	1539	1535	1558			1639	1639		1653				
Birmingham New Street..... a.	1442	1442	1512	1521	1521	1520	1524	1545	1559	1557	1606	1606	1613	1617	1624	1640	1647	1700	1700	1710	1712	1717
Birmingham New Street..... d.	1506	1506	1514	1528	1528	1527		1552	1600	1606	1606	1616	1616	1628	1629	1645	1700	1706	1706	1730	
Birmingham International + d.	1516	1516						1618	1616	1616						1710	1716	1716	1740		
Coventry .... d.	1527	1527						1630	1627	1627						1722	1727	1727	1752		
Leamington Spa......... d.	1544	1544						1646	1644	1644						1738	1744	1744	1809		
Banbury .... a.	1605	1605						1706	1705	1705							1805	1805	1835		
Oxford .... a.	1627	1631						1727	1727	1730						1816	1826	1827	1856		
Reading .... a.	1657	1705						1800	1758	1805						1857	1902	1902	1926		
London Paddington 530 .. a.								1841													
Basingstoke............ a.	1729	1734														1934s	1928	1932			
Winchester .... a.	1747	1752														1952s	1946	1950			
Southampton Airport + a.	1757	1805														2002s	1956	2000			
Southampton Central .... a.	1807	1815														2002s	1956	2000			
Bournemouth .... a.	1840s	1901s														2010s	2003	2007			
Poole .... a.	1856	1920														2041s	2020	2024			
Gatwick Airport + ... a.								1932s	1942s							2102	2055	2100			
Brighton .... a.								2011	2028										2058		
Worcester Shrub Hill ...... d.			1601z							1636		1657								2132	
Cheltenham 529 .... d.			1610	1610	1617				1700		1720	1707	1714	1727							
Gloucester 529 .... d.			1626	1626					1712		1731	1723									
Bristol Parkway .... a.			1655	1655			1710				1753	1748	1803								
Bristol Temple Meads .... a.			1708	1708	1705		1722				1805	1802	1815								
Chepstow............. a.								1741		1800											
Newport.............. a.								1803		1824											
Cardiff Central......... a.								1820		1843											
Exeter St. Davids 510 .... a.			1817	1825	1815		1827				1920										
Paignton 510 .... a.																					
Plymouth 510 .... a.			1930		1915		1925				2032										
Penzance 510 .... a.							2120														

E – [logo] and ♀ (Dundee on Ⓐ -) Edinburgh - Penzance.
L – [logo] and ♀ Aberdeen - Plymouth.
M – [logo] and ♀ Birmingham - Milford Haven.

e – Ⓐ only.
r – Arrives 1228.

s – Stops to set down only.
z – Worcester **Foregate** Street.

Table 520 YORK - SHEFFIELD - BIRMINGHAM - BRISTOL and CARDIFF

1, 2 class

	Ⓐ 🍷	⑥ 🍷	⑦ 🍷	⑦ 2	⚒ 2	⑦ 🍷	⑦ 🍷	⚒ 🍷	⑦ 🍷	⚒ 2🍷	⑦ 🍷	⚒ 🍷	⑦ 2	⑦ 🍷	⑥ 🍷	Ⓐ 🍷		Ⓐ 2	⑦ 2	⑥ 2🍷	Ⓐ 2🍷	⑦ 🍷	⚒ 🍷	⑦ L
Edinburgh **570** d.	...	...	1145	...	...	1305	...	...	1235	...	...	...	...	...	...	...	...	...	...	...	...	...	...	1450
Glasgow Central **550** d.	...	...	|	...	...	|	...	1230	|	...	...	...	...	1410	...	...	...	...	...	...	...	...	...	|
Newcastle **570** d.	1338	1338	1339	...	...	|	...	|	1435	...	...	1500	...	|	...	...	...	...	...	...	...	...	...	|
York 570 d.	1443	1443	1457	...	...	|	...	|	1552	...	...	1602	...	|	...	...	...	...	...	...	...	1635	1643	|
Leeds d.	1515	1515	|	...	...	|	...	|	|	...	1613	|	...	|	...	...	...	...	...	...	...	1659	1715	|
Wakefield Westgate d.	1527	1527	|	...	...	|	...	|	|	...	1625	|	...	|	...	...	...	...	...	...	...	1712	1727	|
Doncaster **570** d.	|	|	1530	...	...	|	...	|	1622	...	|	1631	...	|	...	...	...	...	...	...	...	1731	|	|
Sheffield a.	1600	1600	1553	...	...	|	...	|	1648	...	1658	1656	...	|	...	...	...	...	...	...	...	1757	1759	|
Sheffield d.	1602	1602	1555	...	...	|	...	|	1649	...	1700	1702	...	|	...	...	...	...	...	...	...	1759	1802	|
Chesterfield d.	1615	1615	1608	...	...	|	...	|	1703	...	1714	1715	...	|	...	...	...	...	...	...	...	1813	1815	|
Nottingham 561 d.	|	|	|	...	...	|	...	|	|	1659	|	|	1700	|	...	...	...	1746	1750	...	...	|	|	|
Derby 561 d.	1639	1639	1631	...	...	|	...	|	1727	1727	1737	1739	1743	|	...	...	...	1814	1817	...	...	1836	1838	|
Burton-on-Trent d.	1651	1651	|	...	...	|	...	|	|	1739	|	1751	1755	|	...	...	...	1828	1830	...	...	|	|	|
Tamworth d.	|	|	|	...	...	|	...	|	|	1751	|	|	1809	|	...	...	...	1840	1843	...	...	|	|	|
Liverpool Lime Street **550** d.	|	|	|	...	...	|	...	|	|	|	|	|	|	|	...	...	...	|	|	...	...	|	|	|
Manchester Piccadilly **550** d.	|	|	|	...	...	|	1617	1617	|	|	|	|	|	|	1710	1710	...	|	|	...	...	|	|	|
Wolverhampton **550** d.	|	|	|	...	...	1723	1742	1739	|	|	|	|	|	1828	1832	1835	...	|	|	...	...	|	|	1909
Birmingham New Street a.	1721	1721	1715	...	...	1743	1800	1806	1810	1815	1821	1824	1834	1846	1851	1854	...	1907	1914	...	...	1920	1921	1927
Birmingham New Street d.	1728	1728	1728	1737	1743	1748	1805	1806	1815	1817	1827	1828	1837	1905	1906	1912	...	...	...	1915	1915	1927	1935	1932
Birmingham International ✈ d.	|	|	|	|	|	|	1815	1816	1825	|	|	|	|	1915	1916	1922	...	...	...	|	|	|	|	|
Coventry d.	|	|	|	|	|	|	1827	1827	1835	|	|	|	|	1927	1928	1934	...	...	...	|	|	|	|	|
Leamington Spa d.	|	|	|	|	|	|	1842	1844	1851	|	|	|	|	1942	1944	1950	...	...	...	|	|	|	|	|
Banbury a.	|	|	|	|	|	|	1903	1905	1910	|	|	|	|	2003	2005	2011	...	...	...	|	|	|	|	|
Oxford a.	|	|	|	|	|	|	1924	1927	1932	|	|	|	|	2024	2028	2036	...	...	...	|	|	|	|	|
Reading a.	|	|	|	|	|	|	1954	2003	...	|	|	|	|	2055	2105s	2105	...	...	...	|	|	|	|	|
London Paddington **530** a.	|	|	|	|	|	|	|	|	...	|	|	|	|	|	2150	2145	...	...	...	|	|	|	|	|
Basingstoke a.	|	|	|	|	|	|	2027s	2032	...	|	|	|	|	2127s	...	...	...	...	...	|	|	|	|	|
Winchester a.	|	|	|	|	|	|	2045s	2050	...	|	|	|	|	2145s	...	...	...	...	...	|	|	|	|	|
Southampton Airport ✈ a.	|	|	|	|	|	|	2055s	2100	...	|	|	|	|	2155s	...	...	...	...	...	|	|	|	|	|
Southampton Central a.	|	|	|	|	|	|	2103s	2107	...	|	|	|	|	2203s	...	...	...	...	...	|	|	|	|	|
Bournemouth a.	|	|	|	|	|	|	2135s	2141	...	|	|	|	|	2235s	...	...	...	...	...	|	|	|	|	|
Poole a.	|	|	|	|	|	|	2157	2210	...	|	|	|	|	2257	...	...	...	...	...	|	|	|	|	|
Gatwick Airport ✈ a.	|	|	|	|	|	|	...	...	...	|	|	|	|	...	...	...	...	...	...	|	|	|	|	|
Brighton a.	|	|	|	|	|	|	...	...	...	|	|	|	|	...	...	...	...	...	...	|	|	|	|	|
Worcester Shrub Hill d.	|	|	|	1816	|	|	...	...	...	1855	|	|	1917	...	...	...	...	...	...	|	|	|	|	|
Cheltenham 529 d.	1809	1809	1809	1839	1829	1831	...	...	...	1917	1906	1909	1941	...	...	...	...	...	...	1955	2002	2006	2014	2012
Gloucester 529 d.	1825	1825	|	1849	1840	1847	...	...	...	1929	1922	1925	1951	...	...	...	...	...	...	2007	2014	2022	2030	|
Bristol Parkway a.	1856	1856	1844	|	|	1917	...	...	...	|	1952	1954	|	...	...	...	...	...	...	|	|	2052	2100	2046
Bristol Temple Meads a.	1909	1909	1900	|	|	1929	...	...	...	|	2004	2006	|	...	...	...	...	...	...	|	|	2104	2112	2058
Chepstow a.	|	|	...	1918	1909	|	...	...	...	|	|	|	|	...	...	...	...	...	...	2035	2042	|	...	|
Newport a.	1948	1953	...	1941	1925	|	...	...	...	2011e	|	|	|	...	...	...	...	...	...	2055	2106	2136	...	|
Cardiff Central a.	2004	2010	...	1958	1945h	|	...	...	...	2028e	|	|	2039s	...	...	...	...	...	...	2111	2122	2152	...	|
Swansea **530** a.	2100	2102	...	...	...	|	...	...	...	...	|	|	2057	...	...	...	...	...	...	2246	...	2243	...	|
Exeter St. Davids **510** a.	...	...	...	...	...	2037	...	...	...	...	2120	2116	...	...	...	...	...	...	...	...	...	...	...	2206
Paignton **510** a.	...	...	...	...	...	|	...	...	...	...	|	|	...	...	...	...	...	...	...	...	...	...	...	|
Plymouth **510** a.	...	...	...	...	...	2140	...	...	...	...	2225	2225	...	...	...	...	...	...	...	...	...	...	...	2310
Penzance **510** a.	...	...	...	...	...	2335	...	...	...	...	...	...	...	...	...	...	...	...	...	...	...	...	...	...

	⑦ 2	Ⓐ 🍷	⑥ 🍷	⑦ 🍷	⑦ 🍷	⚒ 🍷	Ⓐ 🍷	⑥ 🍷	⑦ 2	⚒ 🍷	⑦ 2	⑥ 2	Ⓐ 2	⑦ 🍷	⑦ 2	⚒ 2	⑦ 🍷		Ⓐ 2	⑦ 2	Ⓐ 2		⑦	
Edinburgh **570** d.	...	...	...	...	...	...	...	1603	...	...	...	...	...	1615	...	...	...	...	...	...	...	...	...	...
Glasgow Central **550** d.	...	...	...	...	...	...	1610	|	...	...	...	...	...	|	...	...	...	...	...	...	...	...	...	...
Newcastle **570** d.	...	...	...	...	1700	1700	|	|	...	...	...	...	...	|	...	...	...	...	...	...	...	...	...	...
York 570 d.	...	1727	1725	...	1801	1802	|	|	...	...	...	...	...	|	...	...	1918	...	...	...	...	...	2120	...
Leeds d.	...	|	|	...	|	|	|	|	...	...	...	...	...	|	...	...	|	...	...	...	...	...	|	...
Wakefield Westgate d.	...	|	|	...	|	|	|	|	...	...	...	...	...	|	...	...	|	...	...	...	...	...	|	...
Doncaster **570** d.	...	1755	1755	...	1831	1832	|	|	...	...	...	...	...	|	...	...	1944	...	...	...	...	...	2154	...
Sheffield a.	...	1821	1821	...	1858	1854	|	|	...	...	...	...	...	|	...	...	2011	...	...	...	...	...	2222	...
Sheffield d.	...	1823	1823	...	1900	1902	|	|	...	...	...	...	...	|	...	...	2013	...	...	...	...	...	2224	...
Chesterfield d.	...	1838	1838	...	1913	1915	|	|	...	...	...	...	...	|	...	...	2026	...	...	...	...	...	2239	...
Nottingham 561 d.	...	|	|	...	|	|	|	|	1910	1908	...	...	...	|	1958	2002	|	...	2123	2134	2144	...	|	...
Derby 561 d.	...	1905	1922	...	1937	1939	|	|	1942	1944	...	...	...	|	2030	2032	2050	...	2154	2203	2213	...	2305	...
Burton-on-Trent d.	...	...	...	...	1950	1951	|	|	1955	1959	...	...	...	|	2043	2046	2103	...	2206	2215	2225	...	...	...
Tamworth d.	...	...	...	...	|	2003	|	|	2008	2012	...	...	...	|	2056	2059	2115	...	2218	2227	2237	...	...	...
Liverpool Lime Street **550** d.	...	...	...	...	|	|	|	|	|	|	...	...	...	|	|	|	|	...	|	|	|	...	...	...
Manchester Piccadilly **550** d.	...	...	...	1817	|	|	|	|	|	|	...	...	...	|	|	|	|	...	|	|	|	...	...	...
Wolverhampton **550** d.	...	...	...	1942	|	|	2001	2001	|	|	...	...	...	2030	|	|	|	...	|	|	|	...	...	...
Birmingham New Street a.	...	...	...	2000	2023	2024	2020	2020	2033	2034	...	...	...	2055	2124	2124	2139	...	2248	2254	2306	...	...	...
Birmingham New Street d.	1940	...	...	2007	2028	2035	2042	2042	...	...	2040	2045	2045	2105	...	...	2147	...	...	...	...	...	...	...
Birmingham International ✈ d.	|	...	...	2017	|	|	2052	2052	...	...	|	|	|	2115	...	...	|	...	...	...	...	...	...	...
Coventry d.	|	...	...	2029	|	|	2104	2104	...	...	|	|	|	2127	...	...	|	...	...	...	...	...	...	...
Leamington Spa d.	|	...	...	2044	|	|	2120	2120	...	...	|	|	|	2143	...	...	|	...	...	...	...	...	...	...
Banbury a.	|	...	...	2105	|	|	2141	2141	...	...	|	|	|	2203	...	...	|	...	...	...	...	...	...	...
Oxford a.	|	...	...	2126	|	|	2202	2203	...	...	|	|	|	2224	...	...	|	...	...	...	...	...	...	...
Reading a.	|	...	...	2201	|	|	2234s	2238s	...	...	|	|	|	2256	...	...	|	...	...	...	...	...	...	...
London Paddington **530** a.	|	...	...	2245	|	|	2315	2327	...	...	|	|	|	2340	...	...	|	...	...	...	...	...	...	...
Basingstoke a.	|	...	...	...	|	|	...	...	...	...	|	|	|	...	...	...	|	...	...	...	...	...	...	...
Winchester a.	|	...	...	...	|	|	...	...	...	...	|	|	|	...	...	...	|	...	...	...	...	...	...	...
Southampton Airport ✈ a.	|	...	...	...	|	|	...	...	...	...	|	|	|	...	...	...	|	...	...	...	...	...	...	...
Southampton Central a.	|	...	...	...	|	|	...	...	...	...	|	|	|	...	...	...	|	...	...	...	...	...	...	...
Bournemouth a.	|	...	...	...	|	|	...	...	...	...	|	|	|	...	...	...	|	...	...	...	...	...	...	...
Poole a.	|	...	...	...	|	|	...	...	...	...	|	|	|	...	...	...	|	...	...	...	...	...	...	...
Gatwick Airport ✈ a.	|	...	...	...	|	|	...	...	...	...	|	|	|	...	...	...	|	...	...	...	...	...	...	...
Brighton a.	|	...	...	...	|	|	...	...	...	...	|	|	|	...	...	...	|	...	...	...	...	...	...	...
Worcester Shrub Hill d.	|	...	...	...	|	|	...	...	...	...	2118	|	2131	...	...	...	|	...	...	...	...	...	...	...
Cheltenham 529 d.	2024	...	...	...	2107	2114	...	...	...	...	2141	2129	2152	...	...	...	2223	...	...	...	...	...	...	...
Gloucester 529 d.	2035	...	...	...	2123	2130	...	...	...	...	2151	2140	2204	...	...	...	2239	...	...	...	...	...	...	...
Bristol Parkway a.	|	...	...	...	2153	2200	...	...	...	...	|	|	|	...	...	...	2311	...	...	...	...	...	...	...
Bristol Temple Meads a.	|	...	...	...	2205	2212	...	...	...	...	|	|	|	...	...	...	2324	...	...	...	...	...	...	...
Chepstow a.	2103	...	...	...	|	...	...	...	...	...	|	2209	2232	...	...	...	...	...	...	...	...	...	...	...
Newport a.	2123	...	...	...	|	...	...	...	...	...	2232	2231	2254	...	...	...	...	...	...	...	...	...	...	...
Cardiff Central a.	2140	...	...	...	|	...	...	...	...	...	2249	2248	2310	...	...	...	...	...	...	...	...	...	...	...
Swansea **530** a.	...	...	...	...	|	...	...	...	...	...	...	...	...	...	...	...	...	...	...	...	...	...	...	...
Exeter St. Davids **510** a.	...	...	...	...	2313	...	...	...	...	...	...	...	...	...	...	...	...	...	...	...	...	...	...	...
Paignton **510** a.	...	...	...	...	|	...	...	...	...	...	...	...	...	...	...	...	...	...	...	...	...	...	...	...
Plymouth **510** a.	...	...	...	...	0020	...	...	...	...	...	...	...	...	...	...	...	...	...	...	...	...	...	...	...
Penzance **510** a.	...	...	...	...	...	...	...	...	...	...	...	...	...	...	...	...	...	...	...	...	...	...	...	...

L – (12) and 🍷 Aberdeen - Plymouth.
e – Ⓐ only.
h – Arrives 1941 on Ⓐ.
s – Stops to set down only.

For an explanation of standard symbols see page 4

Table 523 — READING - GATWICK AIRPORT
1, 2 class

km			Ⓐ	Ⓐ	Ⓐ ⛾	Ⓐ	Ⓐ ⛾	Ⓐ ⛾	Ⓐ		Ⓐ	Ⓐ ⛾	Ⓐ	Ⓐ	Ⓐ	Ⓐ	Ⓐ	Ⓐ	Ⓐ	Ⓐ	Ⓐ			
0	Reading d.	Ⓐ	0439	0539	0619	0739	0839	0934	and at	1434	1534	1639	1734	1833	1934	2039	2139	2239	2339	...	...	...	
41	Guildford d.		0509	0615	0658	0821	0914	1009	the same	1509	1609	1714	1812	1909	2009	2114	2223	2329	0032	...	...	...	
71	Reigate d.		0534	0640	0723	0847	0939	1034	mins past	1534	1634	1739	1840	1934	2034	2139	2248	0005	0057	...	...	...	
74	Redhill a.		0538	0643	0727	0851	0943	1038	each hour	1538	1640	1749	1849	1938	2038	2143	2252	0009	0101	...	...	...	
84	Gatwick Airport ✈ a.		0549	0655	0741	0902	0958	1049	until	1549	1651	1802	1902	1949	2049	2158	2303	0020	0112	...	...	...	

		⑥	⑥	⑥	⑥		⑥	⑥	⑥	⑥	⑥		⑦	⑦		⑦	⑦	⑦	⑦	⑦
Reading d.	⑥	0439	0534	0634	0734	and at	1834	1934	2039	2139	2239	2339	⑦	0623	0723	and at	1823	1923	2023	2123	2223
Guildford d.		0509	0609	0709	0809	the same	1909	2009	2114	2224	2329	0032		0659	0759	the same	1859	1959	2059	2207	2259
Reigate d.		0534	0634	0734	0834	mins past	1934	2034	2139	2249	0005	0057		0724	0824	mins past	1924	2024	2124	2235	2324
Redhill a.		0538	0639	0739	0838	each hour	1938	2038	2143	2252	0009	0101		0729	0829	each hour	1929	2029	2129	2239	2329
Gatwick Airport ✈ a.		0552	0650	0751	0849	until	1949	2049	2158	2304	0020	0112		0743	0843	until	1943	2043	2143	2250	2343

		Ⓐ	Ⓐ	Ⓐ ⛾	Ⓐ	Ⓐ ⛾	Ⓐ		Ⓐ	Ⓐ	Ⓐ	Ⓐ	Ⓐ	Ⓐ	Ⓐ	Ⓐ	Ⓐ			
Gatwick Airport ✈ d.	Ⓐ	0527	0611	0649	0722	0811	0917	1003	and at	1603	1716	1818	1911	2003	2124	2224	2317	...	...	
Redhill d.		0539	0622	0700	0733	0824	0928	1014	the same	1614	1727	1829	1922	2014	2135	2235	2329	...	...	
Reigate d.		0543	0626	0704	0737	0828	0932	1018	mins past	1618	1731	1833	1926	2018	2139	2239	2333	...	...	
Guildford d.		0608	0653	0739	0805	0855	1000	1043	each hour	1643	1758	1903	1951	2043	2204	2315	2358	...	...	
Reading a.		0643	0728	0831	0848	0930	1028	1118	until	1718	1840	1940	2026	2121	2246	0003	0033	...	...	

		⑥	⑥		⑥	⑥	⑥	⑥	⑥	⑥	⑥		⑦	⑦		⑦	⑦	⑦	⑦	⑦	⑦
Gatwick Airport ✈ d.	⑥	0531	0603	and at	1803	1903	2003	2124	2224	2317		⑦	0611	0711	and at	1811	1911	2011	2111	2211	2311
Redhill d.		0543	0614	the same	1814	1914	2014	2135	2235	2329			0625	0725	the same	1825	1925	2025	2125	2225	2325
Reigate d.		0548	0618	mins past	1818	1918	2018	2139	2239	2333			0629	0729	mins past	1829	1929	2029	2129	2229	2329
Guildford d.		0613	0643	each hour	1843	1943	2043	2204	2315	2358			0654	0754	each hour	1854	1954	2054	2156	2256	2354
Reading a.		0658	0718	until	1918	2018	2119	2245	0001	0035			0729	0829	until	1929	2029	2130	2239	2340	0030

For InterCity through trains Scotland and northern England - **Reading - Gatwick** - Brighton and v.v., see **Table 520**.

Table 524 — BIRMINGHAM - STRATFORD-UPON-AVON
2 class only

km			Ⓐ	⑥	✕	✕	✕		✕		✕		✕		✕		✕		✕	✕	✕	✕	✕	✕
0	Birmingham Snow Hill d.		0640	0720	0730	0820	0922	...	1022	...	1122	...	1222	...	1322	...	1422	...	1522	1620	1710	1720	1740	1820	1850
2	Birmingham Moor Street d.		0643	0723	0733	0823	0925	...	1025	...	1125	...	1225	...	1325	...	1425	...	1525	1623	1713	1723	1743	1823	1853
28	Henley-in-Arden d.		0720	0800	0810	0900	1002	...	1100	...	1200	...	1300	...	1400	...	1500	...	1600	1700	1751	1758	1820	1900	1930
41	Stratford-upon-Avon a.		0732	0812	0822	0912	1014	...	1114	...	1213	...	1313	...	1413	...	1513	...	1613	1715	1803	1811	1832	1913	1942

		Ⓐ	⑥	Ⓐ	⑥	Ⓐ	⑥		✕		✕		✕		✕	Ⓐ	✕	Ⓐ	✕	✕	✕	✕	✕	Ⓐ
Stratford-upon-Avon d.		0705	0720	0742	0820	0830	0920	...	1020	...	1120	...	1220	...	1320	1420	1520	1545	1620	1720	1820	1850	1950	2305
Henley-in-Arden d.		0718	0733	0756	0833	0843	0933	...	1033	...	1133	...	1233	...	1333	1433	1533		1633	1733	1833	1903	2003	
Birmingham Moor Street a.		0757	0810	0835	0909	0920	1009	...	1109	...	1209	...	1309	...	1409	1509	1609	1622	1711	1811	1910	1941	2040	
Birmingham Snow Hill a.		0800	0814	0839	0912	0924	1012	...	1112	...	1212	...	1312	...	1412	1512	1612	1626	1714	1815	1914	1946	2001n	2044	2347n

n – Birmingham **New Street**.

Table 525 — LONDON - OXFORD
1, 2 class

From London Paddington: 102 km.
Ⓐ : 0020, 0535, 0604, 0720, 0750, 0820, 0848, 0905, 0918, 0948, 1005, 1048, 1107, 1148, 1207, 1248, 1307, 1348, 1418, 1448, 1520, 1548, 1620, 1650, 1710, 1720, 1723, 1750, 1820, 1848①-④, 1903⑤, 1920, 1948, 2007, 2048, 2107, 2148, 2207, 2248, 2307, 2348.
⑥ : 0020, 0557, 0625, 0707, 0745, 0807, 0845, 0907, 0945, 1007, 1045, 1107, 1145, 1207, 1245, 1307, 1345, 1407, 1445, 1507, 1545, 1607, 1645, 1707, 1745, 1805, 1807, 1845, 1907, 1945, 2007, 2045, 2107, 2145.
⑦ : 0918, 0940, 1020, 1120, 1220, 1340, 1420, 1520, 1620, 1720, 1820, 1840, 1920, 1940, 2040, 2140, 2203, 2243, 2348.

Trains call at Reading – 25 - 47 minutes from London, 24 - 43 minutes from Oxford.

From Oxford: Journey time: 53 - 92 minutes.
Ⓐ : 0018②-⑤, 0400, 0600, 0610, 0642, 0709, 0715, 0752, 0815, 0850, 0915, 0940, 1000, 1015, 1036, 1115, 1136, 1215, 1227, 1236, 1315, 1336, 1415, 1436, 1515, 1536, 1615, 1658, 1715, 1745, 1815, 1845, 1915, 1936, 2015, 2036, 2130, 2138, 2204, 2238.
⑥ : 0018, 0715, 0738, 0815, 0841, 0855, 0915, 0945, 1015, 1036, 1115, 1136, 1215, 1236, 1340, 1415, 1438, 1515, 1538, 1615, 1638, 1715, 1745, 1815, 1840, 1915, 1939, 2015, 2028, 2040, 2115, 2138, 2210.
⑦ : 1030, 1130, 1230, 1330, 1430, 1535, 1600, 1657, 1727, 1755, 1822, 1848, 1942, 2014, 2110, 2126, 2224, 2236.

Table 526 — LONDON - LEAMINGTON - STRATFORD-UPON-AVON and BIRMINGHAM
1, 2 class

km		✕	✕	✕	⑥	✕	Ⓐ	✕	✕	✕	✕	✕	✕	✕	✕	✕	✕	✕	Ⓐ	⑥
0	London Marylebone d.	...	0640	...	0740	0745	0840r	0918p	0922p	0940	1040	...	1140	1240	...	1340	1345p	1440	...	1540	...	1640r	1650p	1645p
45	High Wycombe d.	...	0715	...	0815	0817	0915			1015	1115	...	1215	1315	...	1415		1515	...	1615	...	1715		
	Oxford d.	...		...			1022					...			1449t				...		...	1750	1755	
111	Banbury d.	...	0808	...	0908	0915	1008		1046	1108	1208	...	1308	1409	...	1508	1518	1608	...	1708	...	1808	1819	1822
143	Leamington Spa d.	0729	0830	0900	0930	0937	1030	1105	1106	1130	1230	1300	1330	1430	1452	1526	1537	1629	1637	1730	1750	1829	1839	1843
146	Warwick d.	0733	0835	0904	0934	0941	1034	1110	1110	1134	1234	1304	1334	1434	1456	1534	1542	1633	1641	1734	1754	1833	1844	1847
167	Stratford-upon-Avon a.	0759		0930				1131	1133			1330			1522		1601		1707		1822		1902	1905
181	Birmingham Snow Hill a.		0916		1009	1004				1204	1304		1404	1504		1604e		1718		1820		1918		

		✕	✕	✕	✕	⑥	①-④	⑤	✕	✕	✕	✕
London Marylebone d.		1740r	1815	1840r		1848	1903p	1940	2040	2140	2240
High Wycombe d.		1815	1851	1915				2015	2115	2215	2317
Oxford d.					1946	2001					
Banbury d.		1907	1953	2008		2019	2031	2108	2207	2306	0008
Leamington Spa d.		1927		2030	2039	2041	2051	2130e	2229e		
Warwick d.		1931		2034	2043	2046	2056	2134e			
Stratford-upon-Avon a.					2109	2113	2123				
Birmingham Snow Hill a.		2010			2119			2219e			

		✕	✕	✕	✕	✕		⑥	✕	✕	✕	✕	⑥	⑥
Birmingham Snow Hill d.		1130		1230k	1330		1430k	1530		1630				
Stratford-upon-Avon d.			1155			1355			1555		1710	1731	1731	
Warwick d.		1157	1222	1257k	1357	1421	1457k	1557	1623	1657	1736	1752	1752
Leamington Spa d.		1207	1226	1301k	1407	1425	1504k	1607	1628	1704	1740	1758	1758
Banbury d.		1230	1248	1330	1430		1530	1630		1730			
Oxford d.			1315									1830	1930
High Wycombe d.		1320		1420	1520		1620	1720		1820			
London Marylebone a.		1356	1414p	1456	1556		1656	1756		1856		1953p	1953p

		✕	✕	✕		⑥	✕	✕	⑥	Ⓐ
Birmingham Snow Hill d.			1725	1830k		1930	1930		2030e	
Warwick d.			1803	1902k	1931	1951	1951	2004	2103e	2115	2315
Leamington Spa d.			1808	1908k	1935	1958	1955	2010	2107e	2141	2334
Banbury d.			1830	1930		2014	2030	2034	2049	2130	2230	2145	2338
Oxford d.		1840	1845				2040		2110		0018
High Wycombe d.		1920	2020			2124	2124		2221		
London Marylebone a.		1953p	1953p	1957	2056		2211p	2156	2200	2239p	2256	0001	0128p

For other trains **London Paddington - Leamington** and v.v., see **Table 520**.
Additional services **London Marylebone - Leamington** on ⑦ : 1631z, 1636v, 1840, 1940.
Additional services **Leamington - London Marylebone** on ⑦ : 1958, 2158.

e – Ⓐ only.	k – ⑥ only.	t – 5 minutes later on ⑥.
p – London Paddington.	v – Dec. 18 - Jan. 8, Mar. 26 - May 21.
r – 5 minutes later on Ⓐ.	z – Jan. 15 - Mar. 19.

For an explanation of standard symbols see page 4

Table 527 LONDON - OXFORD - WORCESTER - HEREFORD

1, 2 class

km		Ⓐ	⑥	Ⓐ	⚒	Ⓐ	⚒	Ⓐ	⑥	⑦	⑥	Ⓐ	⑦	⑦	⑥	Ⓐ	⑥	Ⓐ	⑦	Ⓐ	⑦	⑥	⑦	⚒
0	**London Paddington** d.	...	0625	...	0845h	1005	1045h	1248	1245	*1340*	1445	1520	1520	1620	...	1710	1805	1820	1820	1920	1940	1945	2040	2107
58	Reading d.	...	0703	...	0921p	1032	1121p	1321	1326	*1420*	1526	1552	1601	1702	...	|	1846	|	1855	1952	2023	2026	2123	2155
102	**Oxford** d.	0709	0731	0843	0959	1100	1155	1355	1355	1458	1555	1624	1643	1732	1800	1807	1918	1910	1921	2021	2055	2054	2157	2241
123	Charlbury d.	0725	0747	0900	1016	1113	1211	1411	1411	1514	1611	1640	1659	1748	1816	1820	1931	1923	1936	2037	2111	2110	2213	2257
136	Kingham d.	0734	0756	0912	1025	1122	1220	1420	1420	1523	1620	1649	1708	1757	1825	1829	1940	1932	1945	2046	2120	2119	2222	2306
147	Moreton-in-Marsh d.	0742	0804	0927c	1035	1129	1231h	1430	1435c	1531	1633	1657	1716	1805	1833	1836	1947	1939	1952	2057	2128	2139	2230	2314
172	Evesham d.	0800	0819	0942	1052	1144	1249	1444	1450	1552	1651	1715	1735	1823	1851	1851	2002	1954	2009	2115	2146	2157	2248	2332
194	**Worcester Shrub Hill 528** d.	0822	0841	1005	1113	1205	1310	1508	1511	1612	1712	1736	1755	1845	1912	1911	2024	2023	2032	2136	2206	2217	2308	2352
195	**Worcester Foregate Street** d.	0824	0844	1008	1116	1209	1313	1512	1514	...	1714	1738	...	1848	1915	1914	2030	2027	2035	2139	...	...	...	...
208	Great Malvern **528** d.	...	0854	1022	1127	1225	1326	1522	1524	...	...	...	...	1858	1926	1926	2045	2038	2046	2150	...	...	...	...
219	Ledbury **528** d.	...	...	1035	...	...	1338v	...	...	...	...	...	...	...	1936	1939	2057	2050	2058	2201	...	...	...	...
241	**Hereford 528** a.	...	...	1052	...	...	1355v	...	...	...	...	...	...	...	1955	2000	2115	2110	2115	2219	...	...	...	...

	Ⓐ	⚒	Ⓐ	2Ⓐ	Ⓐ	⑥	Ⓐ	⑥	⚒	⚒	2⑥	⑥	Ⓐ	⑦	Ⓐ	2⑦	⑥	2Ⓐ	⑦	⚒	⑦	⑦	Ⓐ	⑥
Hereford 528 d.	...	...	0556	...	0655	0703	...	0805	...	...	...	...	...	...	1409	...	...	...	1635	...	...	...	1920	2015
Ledbury **528** d.	...	...	0613	...	0710	0719	...	0821	...	...	...	...	...	...	1426	...	...	...	1651	...	...	...	1951	2031
Great Malvern **528** d.	...	...	0628	...	0722	0730	...	0833	0937y	1142	...	1342	1342	...	1446	...	1540	1554	1703	...	...	1932	2002	2040
Worcester Foregate Street d.	...	...	0643	0700	0743	0743	0845	0852	0948y	1153	...	1353	1354	...	1457	...	1551	1606	1715	1748	...	1943	2013	2053
Worcester Shrub Hill 528 d.	0511	0553	0649	0703	0749	0746	0848	0900	0957	1156	1325	1356	1358	1440	1501	1532	1554	1609	1719	1751	1856	1947	2016	2056
Evesham d.	0528	0610	0704	0721	0804	0819	0905	0916	1014	1216	1346	1413	1412	1457	1521	1549	1611	1627	1736	1810	1913	2009	2034	2122
Moreton-in-Marsh d.	0549	0631	0720	0738	0819	0837	0924	0933	1029	1231	1406	1432	1434z	1516	1536	1608	1630	1647	1753	1829	1932	2027	2052	2134
Kingham d.	0556	0638	0727	0746	0826	0845	0931	0940	1037	1238	1414	1439	1441	1524	1543	1616	1637	1655	1800	1836	1939	2035	2100	2142
Charlbury d.	0605	0647	0737	0758	0836	0854	0940	0950	1046	1247	1426	1448	1451	1533	1552	1625	1646	1707	1810	1845	1948	2044	2109	2151
Oxford a.	0620	0704	0751	0818	0848	0910	0957	1007	1105	1305	1446	1505	1511	1555	1610	1647	1709	1726	1822	1905	2008	2105	2126	2207
Reading a.	0710	0736	0817	...	|	0938	|	1038	1138	1338	...	1538	1538	1627	1638	1723	1738	...	1851	1938	2040	2136	2155	2233
London Paddington a.	0753	0809t	0850	...	0945	1019	1059	1125	1214p	1414p	...	1619	1620	1714	1717	1813	1819	...	1936	2014p	2128	2224	2239	2330

c – Arrives 7 minutes earlier.
h – Departs 3 minutes later on Ⓐ.
p – 5 minutes later on ⑥.
t – 10 minutes later on ⑥.
v – Not ⑥.
y – ⑥ only.
z – Arrive 1426.

Table 528 BIRMINGHAM - WORCESTER - HEREFORD

2 class

km		⚒	⚒	⚒	Ⓐ	Ⓐf	⑥f	⚒	⚒	⚒	⚒▲	Ⓐf	⚒	⑦	⚒	⚒	⑦	⚒	Ⓐf	⚒	⑦	⚒▲	⚒f	⑦	⚒
0	**Birmingham New Street** d.	0630	0804	0831	0901	...	0901	1001	1031	1131	1201	...	1301	1347	1431	1531	1530	1631	1710	1731	1730	1801	...	1830	1831
30	Kidderminster d.	0708	0847	0903	0931	...	0931	1030	1103	1203	1230	...	1330	|	1500	1603	1601	1704	|	1806	1801	1834	...	1901	1903
45	Droitwich Spa d.	0722	0900	0914	0941	...	0943	1041	1114	1214	1241	...	1341	1415	1511	1614	1614	1715	1742	1816	1814	1853	...	1914	1914
55	**Worcester Shrub Hill** d.	0733	|	|	0951	1005	1006	|	|	|	|	1310	|	1426	1523	|	1625	|	1754	|	1825	|	1911	1925	1925
55	**Worcester Foregate Street** d.	0736	0909	0924	...	1008	1009	1055	1126	1223	1253	1313	1359	1429	1526	1623	1628	1724	1757	1823	1828	1903	1914	1928	1928
68	Great Malvern d.	0755	0921	0935	...	1022	1021	1107	1138	1235	1305	1326	1411	1441	1538	1635	1640	1736	1808	1838	1840	1915	1926	1940	1940
79	Ledbury d.	0808g	0933	...	...	1035	1033	1120	...	1247	...	1338k	1428	1452	1549	1648	1651	1748	1820	1853	1851	...	1936	1951	1954
101	**Hereford** a.	0825g	0953	...	...	1052	1053	1138	...	1305	...	1355k	1445	1511	1606	1705	1708	1805	1837	1910	1908	...	2000r	2008	2011

	⑦	⚒▲	Ⓐf	⑥f	⑦f	⑥⑦	Ⓐ	Ⓐ	Ⓐ	⑦
Birmingham New Street d.	1930	1931	...	...	...	2030	2031	...	2113	2130
Kidderminster d.	2001	2003	...	...	...	2101	2103	...	2151	2201
Droitwich Spa d.	2014	2014	...	...	...	2114	2114	...	2203	2214
Worcester Shrub Hill d.	2021	|	2023	2024	2032	2125	2121	2136	2214	2225
Worcester Foregate Street d.	...	2023	2027	2030	2035	2128	...	2139	2218	2227
Great Malvern d.	...	2034k	2038	2045	2046	2140	...	2150	2229	...
Ledbury d.	...	...	2050	2057	2058	2151	...	2201	...	...
Hereford a.	...	...	2110	2115	2115	2208	...	2219	...	...

	⑥	Ⓐ	Ⓐf	⚒	Ⓐf	⑥f	Ⓐ	⚒	⑥f	⑥▲
Hereford d.	...	...	0556	...	0655	0703	0709	0732	0805	...
Ledbury d.	...	...	0613	...	0710	0719	0725	0747	0821	...
Great Malvern d.	...	...	0628	...	0722	0730	0736	0759	0833	0903
Worcester Foregate Street d.	...	...	0643	0700	0743	0743	0747	0810	0852	0915
Worcester Shrub Hill d.	0603	0626	0645	|	0745	0746	0754	|	0854	|
Droitwich Spa d.	0611	0636	...	0709	...	...	0802	0819	...	0924
Kidderminster d.	0621	0644	...	0719	...	...	|	0832	...	0934
Birmingham New Street a.	0706	0720	...	0757	...	...	0840	0909	...	1009

	⚒	⚒	⚒		⚒	⚒	⑦	Ⓐf	⚒▲	⚒	⑦	⚒	Ⓐ	⑥	⑦	⚒	⑦	⑥	Ⓐ	⑥▲	⑦	Ⓐf	⚒	⑦f	⚒f
Hereford d.	0855	1000	1103	...	1230	1318	...	1409	...	1502	1534	1629	1730	1730	1734	1835	1934	2002	2006	...	2134	2145	...	2225	2240
Ledbury d.	0910	1015	1120	...	1250	1345	...	1426	...	1518	1550	1650	1750	1750	1750	1852	1950	2018	2022	...	2150	2205	...	2241	2256
Great Malvern d.	0927	1027	1131	...	1302	1403	...	1446	1503	1530	1602	1702	1802	1802	1802	1903	2002	2029	2033	2144	2202	2216	2240	2252	2307
Worcester Foregate Street d.	0939	1039	1144	...	1315	1415	1413	1457	1515	1542	1613	1714	1813	1815	1813	1916	2013	2043	2047	2156	2213	2228	2251	2304	2319
Worcester Shrub Hill d.	0945	1045	|	...	|	|	1420	1500	|	|	1620	|	1816	|	1820	|	2020	2058	2056	2202	2220	2230	2257	2307	2322
Droitwich Spa d.	0953	1053	1153	...	1324	1424	1428	...	1525	1551	1628	1723	1826	1824	1828	1925	2028	2106	2104	2210	2228	...	2305	...	...
Kidderminster d.	1003	1103	1203	...	1334	1434	|	...	1534	1601	1638	1735	1837	1834	1838	1935	2038	2116	2114	2220	2238	...	2315	...	...
Birmingham New Street a.	1034	1139	1235	...	1409	1509	1457	...	1609	1635	1714	1822	1911	1911	1914	2009	2115	2157	2157	2302	2312	...	2351	...	...

f – Also conveys (1).
g – On ⑥ depart Ledbury 0823, arrive Hereford 0840.
k – Not ⑥.
r – Arrives 1955 on ⑥.
▲ – Passengers travelling to or from the Hereford line are advised to change trains at Great Malvern and not at Worcester Foregate Street.

Table 529 SWINDON - GLOUCESTER - WORCESTER

2 class

km		⑥f	⚒	⚒	Ⓐf	⑦j	⑦n	⚒	Ⓐ	⑦j	⑥	Ⓐf	⑦b	⑦j	⚒	Ⓐ	⑥	⑦j	Ⓐ	⑦n	⚒	⑦f	Ⓐ	⑥	Ⓐf
	London Paddington **530** d.	2340	...	...	0845	0900	...	...	...	1100	...	1125	...	1230	...	...	...	1330	...	...	...	1535	...	...	1703
0	**Swindon** d.	0057	0720	0845	0944	1003	1050	1054	1200	1203	1205	1224	1250	1333	1330	1420	1423	1433	1522	1550	1620	1643	1710	1722	1807
22	Kemble d.	0108s	0734	0859	0956	1016	1104	1108	1214	1216	1219	1236	1304	|	1344	1434	1437	1446	1536	1604	1634	1657	1724	1736	1820
40	Stroud d.	0122s	0749	0914	1010	1030	1119	1123	1229	1230	1234	1250	1319	|	1359	1449	1452	1500	1551	1619	1649	1711	1739	1751	1835
44	Stonehouse d.	|	0754	0919	1015	1035	1124	1128	1234	1235	1239	1255	1324	|	1404	1454	1457	1505	1556	1624	1654	1716	1744	1756	1840
59	**Gloucester** a.	0139	0807	0932	1028	1050	1141	1141	1251	1250	1252	1308	1341	1413	1421	1507	1510	1520	1609	1639	1709	1731	1800	1813	1857
70	**Cheltenham Spa** a.	...	0819	0944	1045	*1120b*	...	1153	...	*1320b*	*1328*	1322	...	*1502*	1432	1524	1525	*1544*	1621	1651	1721	1745	*1820*	*1920*	1915
105	**Worcester Shrub Hill** a.	...	0844e	*1032*	...	...	...	*1225*	...	...	*1429*	1348	...	...	...	*1627*	*1627*	...	...	...	*1800*	*1849*	*1845*	...	...

	⑦f	⑥f	Ⓐf	⑥	Ⓐ	⑦f	⚒	Ⓐ	⑦f	Ⓐ
London Paddington **530** d.	...	1725	1803	...	...	1910	...	...	...	...
Swindon d.	1830	1836	1902	1902	2005	2025	2105	2210	2215	2315
Kemble d.	1844	1850	1915	1916	2019	2039	2119	2224	2229	2329
Stroud d.	1859	1904	1930	1931	2034	2053	2134	2239	2244	2344
Stonehouse d.	1904	1909	1935	1936	2039	2058	2139	2244	2249	2349
Gloucester a.	1917	1924	1948	1949	2052	2111	2152	2257	2302	0006
Cheltenham Spa a.	1929	1940	2006	2001	2106	2125	2204	2309	2314	...
Worcester Shrub Hill a.	*2043*	*2049*	*2043*	*2049*	...	*2312*	...	*0007*	...	...

	Ⓐ	⚒	Ⓐf	⑥	⑥	⚒f		⚒f	⑦n	⑥
Worcester Shrub Hill d.	...	...	...	...	*0628*	0655	...	...	...	*0852*
Cheltenham Spa d.	...	...	0605	...	*0649*	0727	...	0830	...	0931
Gloucester d.	0522	0552	0625	0625	0710	0746	...	0851	0945	1000
Stonehouse d.	0533	0603	0635	0636	0721	0757	...	0901	0956	1011
Stroud d.	0538	0608	0640	0641	0726	0802	...	0906	1001	1016
Kemble d.	0553	0623	0654	0656	0741	0816	...	0920	1016	1031
Swindon a.	0608	0638	0707	0711	0756	0829	...	0933	1034	1046
London Paddington **530** a.	...	...	0815	...	...	0940p	...	1045q	...	...

	Ⓐ	⑦j	⚒	⑦n	⑦j	⚒				Ⓐ	⑦j	⑦n	⚒	Ⓐf	⑥	⑦f	⑦j	⚒		Ⓐ	⑦f	⑥	⑦f	Ⓐ	
Worcester Shrub Hill d.	0910	...	...	...	...	*1022*	...	*1237*	...	...	...	...	...	1537	*1452*	*1412*	...	*1636*	...	1820	*1816*	*1855*	*1917*	...	...
Cheltenham Spa d.	0931	*0955b*	1034	...	*1155b*	1218	...	*1300*	...	1403	*1355b*	...	1508	1557	1604	1610	1710	1736	...	1842	1846	*1917*	2000	2100	...
Gloucester d.	1000	1024	1100	1145	1224	1230	...	1322	...	1422	1424	1442	1522	1617	1616	1628	1724	1748	...	1900	1906	1935	2012	2112	...
Stonehouse d.	1011	1035	1111	1156	1235	1241	...	1333	...	1433	1435	1453	1533	1627	1628	1640	1736	1800	...	1911	1916	1946	2024	2123	...
Stroud d.	1016	1040	1116	1201	1240	1246	...	1338	...	1438	1440	1458	1538	1632	1633	1645	1741	1805	...	1916	1921	1951	2029	2128	...
Kemble d.	1031	1054	1131	1216	1250	1301	...	1353	...	1453	1454	1513	1553	1646	1647	1659	1755	1819	...	1931	1935	2006	2043	2143	...
Swindon a.	1046	1112	1146	1234	1349	1316	...	1408	...	1508	1512	1534	1608	1701	1703	1713	1812	1835	...	1946	1949	2021	2059	2158	...
London Paddington **530** a.	...	1232	...	...	1429	...	...	...	...	...	1629	...	...	1810	...	1829	...	...	...	...	2105	...	...	...	...

b – By 🚌.
e – Ⓐ only.
f – Conveys (12) and 🍸.
j – Runs Jan. 15 - Mar. 26. Conveys (12) and 🍸.
n – Runs Apr. 2 - May 21.
p – Arrives 10 minutes later on ⑥.
q – Arrives 5 minutes later on ⑥.
s – Stops to set down only.

Table 530 — LONDON - BRISTOL - CARDIFF - SWANSEA

1, 2 class

Ⓐ (weekdays) — part 1

km	Station	2	2	2	2	V	H	N	2	K★	L	M	Ⓨ	✕	✕P	✕	Ⓨ	A	✕	Q Ⓐn	Ⓐ
0	London Paddington 510 d.									0645	0715	0740	0800	0815	0830	0845	0900				0915
58	Reading 510 d.					0620b		0716			0740	0805	0825	0845	0900	0912	0925				0942
85	Didcot Parkway d.					0635		0731			0754					0914					
124	Swindon d.					0700	0728		0752		0815	0835		0915	0935	0942	0955				1014
151	Chippenham d.					0714	0744				0828			0928							1028
172	Bath Spa 510 532 d.					0728	0800				0828	0841		0941							1041
180	Bristol Parkway d.									0820				0917			1002			1022	
189	Bristol Temple Meads 510/32 a.						0744	0820			0845	0853	0911		0955						1055
189	Bristol Temple Meads 510/32 a.					0703	0750														
189	Weston-super-Mare 510 a.					0810					0823	0850									
215	Newport 510 532 a.				0643	0741	0825		0831	0842	0854	0920		0939			1024	1046	1040		
234	Cardiff Central 510 532 a.				0658	0755	0839		0846	0856	0908	0936		0953			1040	1100	1056		
234	Cardiff Central d.	0600	0619		0700	0733	0757	0841		0910	0940		0956				1103	1108	1108		2
266	Bridgend d.	0620	0645	0725	0759	0817	0900			0910	0929	0959		1016			1123				
286	Port Talbot Parkway d.	0635	0700	0740	0814	0828				0925	0941	1015		1027			1134				
295	Neath a.	0645	0710	0750	0824	0836				0935	0949	1025		1035			1142				
307	Swansea a.	0701	0728	0806	0840	0847	0930			0951	1002	1040		1050			1155	1158	1158		
	Pembroke Dock 531 a.	0908																	1409		
	Milford Haven 531 a.				1004							1235									
	Fishguard Harbour 531 a.																	1338			

Ⓐ (weekdays) — part 2

Station	Ⓐt	T	✕	Ⓨ	Q	Ⓨ	B	C	✕	✕	Ⓨ	R	D	S	Ⓨ	Ⓨ	Ⓨ	R	Ⓨ	Ⓨ	Ⓨ
London Paddington d.	0925	0945	1000	1015	1100		1115	1046y	1125	1200	1215	1300		1218y		1315	1400	1415	1500		1515 1545 1600 1615
Reading d.	0953	1015	1025	1040	1125		1140	1146	1152	1225	1240	1325			1340	1427	1440	1525		1540 1610 1642
Didcot Parkway d.			1029	1054			1154			1254					1354	1454			1554 1625
Swindon d.		1050	1056	1115	1155		1215	1223	1255	1315	1355		1415	1459	1515	1554			1615 1646 1653 1714
Chippenham d.				1128			1228			1328			1428	1528			1628 1728
Bath Spa 510 532 d.		1112		1141	1202	1241				1341	1422s		1441	1543			1641 1709 1741
Bristol Parkway d.			1122		1221		1252		1322	1422			1527	1620		1641 1720
Bristol Temple Meads a.		1124	1155		1220	1255			1355	1438s		1453	1600			1655 1725 1755
Bristol Temple Meads d.		1127			1227						1456				1720
Weston-super-Mare a.		1146								1525				
Newport 510 532 d.		1145		1244	1256		1314		1344	1444	1429	1509s	1531		1549		1644	1629		1743
Cardiff Central a.	1114	1159		1257	1311	1330		1358		1501	1444	1525	1545		1603	1658	1644		1757
Cardiff Central d.	1116	1202		1300	1314		1401		1501	1510		1600	1606	1701	1710		1800
Bridgend d.		1222		1320			1421		1521	1529		1619	1626	1721	1737		1820
Port Talbot Parkway d.		1233		1331			1432		1532			1631	1637	1732	1747		1831
Neath a.		1241		1339			1440		1540			1639	1645	1740	1757		1839
Swansea a.		1255		1355	1359		1455		1555	1558		1652	1655	1755	1810		1855
Pembroke Dock 531 a.					1536											
Milford Haven 531 a.										1749	1834			1957
Fishguard Harbour 531 a.	1329											1834			

Ⓐ (weekdays) — part 3

Station	Ⓐ Ⓨ	Ⓐ	A	Ⓨ	Ⓐ	✕	F	A	Ⓨ	Ⓐ	Ⓐ	Ⓐ	Ⓐ	G	U	U	Ⓐ	Ⓐ	Ⓐ	2-5
London Paddington d.	1645	1700	1703	1715	1730	1745	1800		1803	1815	1830	1845	1900	1915	2000	1918y	2015	2100	2115	2200 2230 2330 2340 0045
Reading d.	1710		1730	1742	1755			1830	1840	1857	1910	1927	1942	2027		2043	2127	2145	2232 2303 0003 0016 0120
Didcot Parkway d.	1725		1746			1821	1837			1913	1925	1957		2058		2204	2251	2322	2322 0022 0033 0141
Swindon d.	1746	1752	1805	1813	1825	1842		1900	1910	1934	1946	1959	2018	2059		2119	2200	2224	2311 2342 0043 0056 0206
Chippenham d.	1759		1826		1855				1923	1959			2133		2238		2356 0057
Bath Spa 510 532 d.	1812		1839		1908				1938	2012	2045		2129	2146		2251		0011 0110
Bristol Parkway d.		1819		1852		1919	1856			2002	2027	2127		2228	2339		0124
Bristol Temple Meads a.	1825		1851		1925		1909		1953	2025	2100		2143	2158	2303		0025 0125
Bristol Temple Meads d.			1855			1918			1956				2148	2201		
Weston-super-Mare a.			1925						2022				2235			
Newport 510 532 d.		1841		1914		1942	1950			2024		2049	2149	2215		2250		0001		0144s 0255
Cardiff Central a.		1855		1929		1956	2004		2038		2103	2203	2230		2304		0019		0205 0314
Cardiff Central d.		1858		1931		1959	2007		2041		2106	2206	2235		2309		0023
Bridgend d.		1918		1951		2019	2027		2101		2126	2226	2255		2329		0043
Port Talbot Parkway d.		1929		2002		2030	2038		2112		2137	2237	2307		2340		0054
Neath a.		1937		2010		2038	2046		2120		2145	2245	2316		2348		0102
Swansea a.		1950		2020		2050	2100		2135		2200	2300	2327		2359		0115
Pembroke Dock 531 a.																
Milford Haven 531 a.										0049				
Fishguard Harbour 531 a.														

⑥ (Saturdays)

Station	2	2		2	V		H	2	2Ⓨ	J	M				Q	2	X
London Paddington d.										0705	0725	0748	0805	0825	0848		0905 0932
Reading d.										0742	0808	0825	0842	0901	0924		0940 1013
Didcot Parkway d.										0757			0915				0955 1028
Swindon d.							0700			0816	0840	0857	0914	0936	0956		1016 1049
Chippenham d.							0714			0830			0928				1030
Bath Spa 510 532 d.							0728	0748	0828	0843			0941				1045 1112
Bristol Parkway d.											0925		1004	1024			
Bristol Temple Meads a.							0744	0807	0845	0855	0913		0955				1057 1120
Bristol Temple Meads d.					0703				0750	0823	0850		0956				1100p 1127q
Weston-super-Mare a.									0810				1022				1127p 1146q
Newport 510 532 d.					0741		0825			0854	0920		0947	1026	1046	1040	
Cardiff Central a.					0755		0839			0910	0936		1001	1040	1100	1056	
Cardiff Central d.	0600	0619		0700	0757		0841	0850		0912	0940		1004	1042	1103	1108	1108
Bridgend d.	0620	0645		0725	0817		0900	0910		0932	0959		1024	1102	1123		
Port Talbot Parkway d.	0635	0700		0740	0828			0915		0945	1015		1035	1113	1134		
Neath a.	0645	0710		0750	0836			0935		0954	1025		1043	1121	1142		
Swansea a.	0701	0728		0806	0847		0930	0951		1009	1040		1053	1135	1155	1158	1158
Pembroke Dock 531 a.	0908															1410
Milford Haven 531 a.				1004						1235			1235			
Fishguard Harbour 531 a.													1328z 1338		

A – ▭ and ♦ London - Cheltenham.
B – ▭ London Waterloo - Cardiff ★.
C – ▭ and ♦ London - Worcester.
D – ▭ and ♦ London Waterloo - Cardiff; ℝ ★.
E – ▭ and ♦ London - Carmarthen.
F – ▭ and ♦ Newcastle - Swansea.
G – ▭ London Waterloo - Carmarthen; ℝ ★.
H – ▭ Gloucester - Swansea.
J – ▭ Frome - Carmarthen.
K – Abergavenny - Swansea.

L – ▭ Exeter - Carmarthen.
M – ▭ and ♦ Brighton - Portsmouth - Milford Haven.
N – ▭ and ♦ (Reading ②③④⑤ -) Didcot - Penzance.
P – Pullman service and ✕ in 1 cl.
Q – ▭ and ♦ Birmingham - Fishguard Harbour.
R – ▭ Birmingham - Milford Haven.
S – ▭ and ♦ Manchester - Milford Haven.
T – ▭ and ♦ London - Plymouth.
U – ▭ and ♦ London - Exeter.
V – Runs via Bristol Parkway (dep. 0719).

X – Conveys (not May 27) ▭ and ♦ London - Exeter.
Y – ▭ and ♦ London - Taunton.

b – ②③④⑤.
k – Not Apr. 15, May 27.
n – Jan. 5 - Apr. 12 and Apr. 17 - May 26.
p – May 27 only.
q – Not May 27.
s – Stops to set down only.

t – Jan. 2, 3, 4 and Apr. 13, 14 only.
y – London Waterloo.
z – Apr. 15, May 27 only.
★ – Eurostar connecting service.

Table 530 — LONDON - BRISTOL - CARDIFF - SWANSEA

1,2 class

Block 1 (Saturdays ⑥)

Train codes: Q, R, D, S, R, E, A

Station																							
London Paddington 510 d.	0950	1005	1050		1105	1150	1205	1250		1218y	1305		1350	1405	1450		1505	1550	1605	1632	1650	1705	1725	1732
Reading 510 d.	1026	1040	1126		1140	1226	1240	1324			1339		1424	1439	1524		1559	1624	1659	1709	1724	1740	1801	1807
Didcot Parkway d.			1055		1155		1255				1358				1459						1726			1825
Swindon d.	1058	1116	1158		1216	1258	1316	1358		1419			1459	1519	1558		1619	1658	1719	1747	1758	1816	1836	1859
Chippenham d.		1130			1230		1330			1433			1533				1633		1733	1801		1830		
Bath Spa 510 532 d.		1145		1202	1245		1343		1422s	1446			1546				1646		1745	1814	1826	1845		1912
Bristol Parkway d.	1127		1226			1326		1424				1527		1626			1726		1800	1830		1856		1925
Bristol Temple Meads 510/32 a.		1158		1220	1256		1355		1438s	1459		1600				1700		1800	1830		1856			
Bristol Temple Meads 510/32 d.			1227							1502											1900			
Weston-super-Mare 510 a.										1525											1930			
Newport 510 532 d.	1150		1249	1256		1348		1448	1429	1509s		1531	1549		1648	1629		1748			1848			
Cardiff Central 510 532 a.	1203	1303	1311		1402		1502	1444	1525		1545	1603		1702	1644		1802		1902					
Cardiff Central d.	1205	1305	1314		1405		1505	1510			1600	1605		1705	1710		1805		1905					
Bridgend d.	1225		1325		1425		1525	1529			1619	1625		1737	1737		1836		1936					
Port Talbot Parkway d.	1236		1336		1436		1536				1631	1636		1736	1749		1844		1944					
Neath d.	1244		1344		1444		1544				1639	1644		1744	1757		1855		1954					
Swansea a.	1255	1355	1359		1455		1555	1558			1652	1655		1755	1810		1855							
Pembroke Dock 531 a.																								
Milford Haven 531 a.			1536				1749				1834				1957									
Fishguard Harbour 531 a.																								

Block 2 (Saturdays ⑥ / Sundays ⑦)

Train codes: F, J, H

Station																	⑦						
London Paddington 510 d.	1748	1802	1832	1848		1925	1932	1918y	2032	2130	2230	2330	2340			0800	0900		0900	0930
Reading 510 d.	1823	1839	1907	1923		2001	2107	2143	2115	2315	0015	0021				0833	0933		0933	1003
Didcot Parkway d.				1925			2025		2121	2229	2329	0030	0035							1019
Swindon d.	1857		1912	1946	1959		2036	2046	2143	2251	2351	0052	0057			0903	1003		1003	1052
Chippenham d.			1926	2000			2100	2157		0005	0106									1105
Bath Spa 510 532 d.			1940	2013			2117	2129	2212		0020	0121					1034			1122
Bristol Parkway d.	1925	1856			2027		2103			2130	2143	2236								
Bristol Temple Meads 510/32 a.		1909	1951	2025					2130	2143	2236	0044	0145			0850b	0850c		1045	
Bristol Temple Meads 510/32 d.		1918	1954					2148												
Weston-super-Mare 510 a.			2021																	
Newport 510 532 d.	1949	1955		2049	2056	2130			2215		0023s		0229s			0931	1029	1104	1135	1140
Cardiff Central 510 532 a.	2003	2010		2103	2111	2144			2230		0045s		0251s			0951	1035	1051	1205	1204
Cardiff Central d.	2005	2013		2105	2126	2146										0953	1051	1126		1211
Bridgend d.	2025	2033		2149	2214	2229					0128s		0334s			1038	1136	1215		1256
Port Talbot Parkway d.	2036	2044		2200	2226	2240					0139s		0345s			1050	1148	1226		1307
Neath d.	2044	2052		2208	2234	2248					0150s		0356s			1059	1157	1235		1316
Swansea a.	2055	2102		2230	2246	2300					0207		0412			1114	1212	1250		1331
Pembroke Dock 531 a.																1303				
Milford Haven 531 a.				0049																
Fishguard Harbour 531 a.																				

Block 3 (Sundays ⑦)

Train codes: A, X

Station																								
London Paddington 510 d.	1000	1000		1030	1100	1100	1130	1200		1230	1230	1300	1300	1330	1330	1400	1430	1500	1515	1530	1535	1600		1615
Reading 510 d.	1036	1036		1103	1133	1133	1203	1233		1303	1303	1333	1333	1403	1403	1433	1503	1533	1550	1603	1610	1633	1626	1649
Didcot Parkway d.			1119				1219			1319			1349		1419		1519							1706
Swindon d.	1107	1107		1137	1203	1203	1237	1303		1333	1337	1403	1410	1433	1437	1503	1537	1603	1630	1633	1643	1705		1726
Chippenham d.				1152			1252			1352		1425		1452		1552								1740
Bath Spa 510 532 d.				1205			1305			1405		1442		1505		1605		1641	1701	1733			1721	1753
Bristol Parkway d.	1138				1234			1334			1434			1534			1622	1655			1736	1805		
Bristol Temple Meads 510/32 a.			1153	1225		1322		1325	1353		1422		1456		1522	1554					⑦	1745		
Bristol Temple Meads 510/32 d.						1325					1502		1525		1531						K			
Weston-super-Mare 510 a.			1246			1354																		
Newport 510 532 d.	1208	1234	1253		1304	1340		1404	1458	1503		1503		1605		1605	1656		1725	1734	1755	1818		
Cardiff Central 510 532 a.	1230	1254	1323		1326	1404		1426	1528	1525		1525		1623		1623	1712		1739	1750	1809	1833		
Cardiff Central d.	1230	1256			1326	1413		1426		1525		1525		1623		1623			1741	1755	1811	1840		
Bridgend d.	1315	1345			1415	1500		1511		1610		1610		1643		1643			1801	1814	1831	1906		
Port Talbot Parkway d.	1326	1356			1426	1511		1522		1621		1621		1654		1654			1812		1842			
Neath d.	1335	1405			1435	1520		1531		1630		1630		1704		1704			1820		1850			
Swansea a.	1350	1420			1450	1536		1546		1647		1647		1722		1722			1830	1843	1900	1935		
Pembroke Dock 531 a.																			2046					
Milford Haven 531 a.																						2119		
Fishguard Harbour 531 a.																								

Block 4 (Sundays ⑦)

Train codes: X, U, A, Y, G

Station																									
London Paddington 510 d.	1700		1715	1735	1800		1815	1900	1910		1915	1935	2000	1915y	2015	2100	2115	2130	2200	2215	2240	2300	2330	2340
Reading 510 d.	1733		1751	1810	1833		1850	1934	1950		1957	2010	2033		2049	2134	2149	2203	2233	2249	2313	2333	0003	0018
Didcot Parkway d.	1750						1907		2007						2106	2151	2206		2251	2306				
Swindon d.	1809		1824		1905		1926	2005	2025		2030	2040	2105		2126	2209	2227	2239	2313	2328	2347s	0011s	0041s	0052s
Chippenham d.		1823	1838	1851	1858		1940		1953			2046			2140		2241			2342	0002s		0056s	
Bath Spa 510 532 d.											2058	2106		2124s	2153		2254			2355	0014s		0108s	
Bristol Parkway d.	1837		1841	1903	1910	1933		2005		2033		2052		2133		2205	2235	2306	2317		2305	2341	0039s	0125
Bristol Temple Meads 510/32 a.			1841	1903	1910		2005				2104	2110	2118		2140s	2205	2235	2306	2237		0007	0030		
Bristol Temple Meads 510/32 d.		1845									2109		2121								0010			
Weston-super-Mare 510 a.													2140								0029			
Newport 510 532 d.	1859	1915			1955	2012		2055		2138				2155	2213s		2259				0003		0101s	0142s
Cardiff Central 510 532 a.	1913	1930			2009	2028		2109		2152				2209	2230		2315				0019		0119s	0205
Cardiff Central d.	1915	1935			2011	2033		2111		2154				2211	2235		2317				0023			
Bridgend d.	1935	1954			2031	2053		2131		2214				2231	2301		2337				0043		0140s	
Port Talbot Parkway d.	1946				2042	2106		2142		2225				2242	2313		2348				0054		0151s	
Neath d.	1954				2050	2115		2150		2233				2250	2321		2356				0102		0159s	
Swansea a.	2004	2024			2100	2128		2200		2243				2300	2334		0006				0115		0215	
Pembroke Dock 531 a.																								
Milford Haven 531 a.		2209												0049										
Fishguard Harbour 531 a.																								

A – [IC] and [buffet] London - Cheltenham.
D – [IC] and [buffet] London Waterloo - Cardiff; [wheelchair] ★.
E – [IC] and [buffet] London - Carmarthen.
F – [IC] and [buffet] London - Newcastle - Swansea.
G – [IC] and [buffet] London Waterloo - Carmarthen; [wheelchair] ★.
H – [IC] London Waterloo - Cardiff; [wheelchair] ★.
J – [IC] Birmingham - Carmarthen.
K – [IC] Birmingham - Pembroke Dock.
L – [IC] and [buffet] London - Plymouth.
N – [IC] and [buffet] London - Penzance.

Q – [IC] and [buffet] Brighton - Miford Haven.
R – [IC] and [buffet] Birmingham - Milford Haven.
S – [IC] and [buffet] Manchester - Milford Haven.
T – [IC] and [buffet] London - Taunton.
U – [IC] and [buffet] Manchester - Swansea.
X – [IC] and [buffet] Portsmouth - Milford Haven.
Y – [IC] and [buffet] York - Swansea.
▯ – Train may be affected by engineering work. Passengers are advised to check at stations or ☎ (0171) 262 6767 before travelling.

b – From Apr. 2 only. Runs via Bristol Parkway (d. 0901).
c – Runs via Bristol Parkway (d. 0910).
q – To Mar. 26 only.
r – From Apr. 2 only.
s – Stops to set down only.
y – London Waterloo.

★ – Eurostar connecting service.

Services on Jan.1, 8 and evening of Jan. 7 are liable to alteration. Passengers are advised to check locally (see note ▯) if intending to travel on these dates.

Table 530

SWANSEA - CARDIFF - BRISTOL - LONDON

1, 2 class

(A) — Weekdays

km	Station	⚟	X	⚟	X	A	X	⚟	⚟	⚟	⚟	X	X	F	A	F	G	⚟	Y	H	E
	Fishguard Harbour 531 d.	0150																			
	Milford Haven 531 d.																				
	Pembroke Dock 531 d.																				
	Swansea d.	0332					0532		0602		0632			0650	0702	0715	0719				0732
	Neath d.	0343					0543		0613		0643			0701	0713	0726	0731				0743
	Port Talbot Parkway d.	0350					0550		0620		0650			0708	0720	0733	0738				0750
	Bridgend d.	0402					0602		0632		0702			0721	0728	0745	0751				0802
	Cardiff Central a.	0422					0622		0652		0722			0742	0752	0805	0818				0822
	Cardiff Central 510 532 d.	0425			0555		0625		0655	0715	0725			0747	0755	0809	0830				0825
	Newport 510 532 d.	0439			0609		0639		0709	0729	0739			0759	0809	0823	0844				0839
	Weston-super-Mare 510 d.				0535b		0603b			0642				0711		0740					
0	Bristol Temple Meads 510/32 a.		0535	0550	0606			0645		0700	0715			0741		0811	0830		0855	0916	
	Bristol Temple Meads 510/32 d.										0712			0741		0811	0830	0855	0916		
	Bristol Parkway d.	0505		0600		0630			0700			0730	0750	0800				0830	0913		0900
18	Bath Spa 510 532 d.		0547		0618			0657		0712	0727			0757		0827	0857		0933		
39	Chippenham d.		0558		0629			0708		0723	0738			0808		0838					
66	Swindon d.	0533	0615	0626	0645	0658	0709		0728	0739	0754	0816		0825	0830	0854		0900			0928
105	Didcot Parkway d.	0549		0641	0700	0713	0725	0734		0754		0815		0848							
133	Reading 510 a.	0606	0644	0659	0717	0730	0743		0754	0811	0823	0832			0906	0921		0927			0955
190	London Paddington 510 a.	0640	0720	0730	0750	0801	0815	0820	0830	0845	0855	0905	0910	0915	0920	0940	0952	1111y	0958		1030

(A) — Weekdays (continued)

Station	A	⚟	⚟	⚟	M	R	⚟	U	⚟	S	⚟	⚟P	⚟	K	X	B	⚟	X	D	M	⚟
Fishguard Harbour 531 d.					0635	0735															
Milford Haven 531 d.									0840											1240	
Pembroke Dock 531 d.																					
Swansea d.					0823	0920	0932	0952		1023		1132		1222	1232		1332			1420	1432
Neath d.					0834		0943			1034		1143		1233	1243		1343				1443
Port Talbot Parkway d.					0842		0950			1042		1150		1240	1250		1350				1450
Bridgend d.					0856	0947	1002	1019		1056		1202		1253	1302		1402			1447	1502
Cardiff Central a.					0917	1009	1022	1040		1117		1222		1314	1322		1422			1509	1522
Cardiff Central 510 532 d.			0925		0930	1015	1025	1045		1145	1125	1225		1330	1325		1410	1425		1530	1525
Newport 510 532 d.			0940		0944	1027	1039	1057		1157	1139	1239		1342	1339		1425	1439		1542	1539
Weston-super-Mare 510 d.					1016									1416						1521	1616
Bristol Temple Meads 510/32 a.		0915		1015	1022		1115			1215		1315		1422	1415		1515	1530		1622	
Bristol Temple Meads 510/32 d.			1000				1100		1200		1300		1400		1447	1500				1600	
Bristol Parkway d.		0927		1027	1033		1127		1227		1327		1433		1427		1527	1543u	1633		
Bath Spa 510 532 d.		0938		1038			1138		1238		1338		1438		1538						
Chippenham d.	0935	0954	1029	1054		1129		1154		1229	1254	1329	1354		1429	1454	1515	1528	1554		1629
Swindon d.	0951		1111					1209		1311		1409			1509		1609				
Didcot Parkway d.	1008	1021	1100	1128		1158		1226		1258	1328	1358	1426		1458	1526		1555	1625		1658
Reading 510 a.	1045	1055	1131	1205		1230		1300		1330	1400	1430	1500		1530	1600	1642y	1630	1700	1755y	1730
London Paddington 510 a.																					

(A) — Weekdays (continued)

Station	Q	At	N	X	C	⚟	⚟	2	⚟	⚟	⚟	M	⚟	⚟	⚟	⚟	2	⚟	2⚟	2⚟	⚟	Z	V
Fishguard Harbour 531 d.		1350	1343																				
Milford Haven 531 d.											1540							1840	1840				2010
Swansea d.			1520				1532			1632		1721	1732		1832		1922		2022	2022	2032		2224
Neath d.							1543			1643		1743			1843		1933		2033	2033	2043		2239k
Port Talbot Parkway d.							1550			1650		1738	1750		1941				2040	2040	2050		2248
Bridgend d.							1602			1702		1753	1802		1902		1955		2053	2053	2102		2304
Cardiff Central a.		1553	1612				1622			1722		1819	1822		1922		2016		2113	2113	2122		2325
Cardiff Central 510 532 d.		1555	1615				1625			1725		1830	1825		1925				2125		2125		2338
Newport 510 532 d.	1521		1627				1639			1739		1842	1839		1939				2139		2139		2351
Weston-super-Mare 510 d.	1521		1544				1613						1944								2143		
Bristol Temple Meads 510/32 a.	1543		1608				1646				1916		2012								2212		
Bristol Temple Meads 510/32 d.	1555		1615		1645	1650	1715	1745		1815	1922		2015		2125						2215		
Bristol Parkway d.					1700				1800		1900		2000				2200		2200				
Bath Spa 510 532 d.	1613		1627		1657	1708	1727	1757		1827	1936		1927	2027		2137					2228		
Chippenham d.	1627		1638		1708	1722	1738	1808		1838			1938	2038		2148					2241		
Swindon d.	1644		1655	1701	1724	1730	1740	1754		1824	1855		1928	1954	2029	2055		2205	2234		2229	2258	
Didcot Parkway d.				1719		1745			1839		1911		2009	2044		2221							
Reading 510 a.		1717		1725	1736	1750	1802		1821	1854	1900		1928	1955	2026	2102	2123		2238	2308		2258	
London Paddington 510 a.		1750		1800	1810	1825	1835		1855	1930	1935	2000		2030	2100	2140	2200		2320	2353		2340	

(6) — Saturdays

Station	⚟	⚟	⚟	⚟	⚟	⚟	⚟	⚟	A	J	G	⚟	Y	⚟	A	2	L	M
Fishguard Harbour 531 d.		0150																
Milford Haven 531 d.																		0635
Pembroke Dock 531 d.																		
Swansea d.		0332		0532			0632		0650	0702	0715	0732		0740				0823
Neath d.		0343		0543			0643		0701	0713	0726	0743		0751				0834
Port Talbot Parkway d.		0350		0550			0650		0708	0720	0733	0750		0804				0842
Bridgend d.		0402		0602			0702		0721	0728	0745	0802		0820				0856
Cardiff Central a.		0422		0622			0722		0742	0752	0805	0822		0844				0917
Cardiff Central 510 532 d.		0425		0625			0725		0745	0755	0809	0825						0930
Newport 510 532 d.		0439		0639			0739		0759	0809	0823	0839						0944
Weston-super-Mare 510 d.					0620			0740					0844					
Bristol Temple Meads 510/32 a.					0647			0811	0830		0855		0912					1016
Bristol Temple Meads 510/32 d.			0545	0615		0700	0735		0815	0840		0905		0915	0945	1022		
Bristol Parkway d.		0505			0700		0800		0830	0913	0900		0955				1033	
Bath Spa 510 532 d.			0557	0627		0712	0747		0827	0857		0927						
Chippenham d.			0608	0638		0723	0758		0838			0938						
Swindon d.	0345	0532	0625	0655	0728	0740	0815	0828	0830	0855	0901		0928	0935	0955	1022		
Didcot Parkway d.	0405	0549	0641	0701	0745		0849		0917			0951						
Reading 510 a.	0423	0606	0657	0729	0800	0809		0859	0906	0923	0933		0957	1008	1024	1050		
London Paddington 510 a.	0532		0647	0740	0808	0841	0855		0925	0945	0950	1010	1111y	1015	1040	1050	1110	1140

A – 🚃 and ⚟ Cheltenham - London.
B – 🚃 and ⚟ Cardiff - London **Waterloo** ★.
C – 🚃 and ⚟ Worcester - London.
D – 🚃 and ⚟ Cardiff - London **Waterloo**; ℝ ★.
E – 🚃 and ⚟ Carmarthen - London.
F – 🚃 and ⚟ Exeter - London.
G – 🚃 and ⚟ Haverfordwest - Portsmouth.
J – 🚃 and ⚟ Plymouth - London.
K – 🚃 and ⚟ Carmarthen - Portsmouth.
L – 🚃 and ⚟ Taunton - London.
M – 🚃 and ⚟ Milford Haven - Portsmouth.
N – 🚃 and ⚟ Fishguard Harbour - Birmingham.
P – Pullman service and X available in 1 cl.
Q – 🚃 and ⚟ Paignton - Swindon.
R – 🚃 and ⚟ Milford Haven - Birmingham.
S – 🚃 and ⚟ Milford Haven - Manchester.
U – 🚃 and ⚟ Swansea - Manchester.
V – 🚃 Pembroke Dock - Hereford.
Y – 🚃 and ⚟ Swansea - York.
Z – 🚃 Penzance - Swindon.
★ – Eurostar connecting service.

b – ① only.
k – Not ⑤.
n – Jan. 5 - Apr. 12 and Apr. 17 - May 26.
t – Jan. 2, 3, 4 and Apr. 13, 14 only.
u – Stops to pick up only.
y – London **Waterloo**.

For an explanation of standard symbols see page 4

Table 530 SWANSEA - CARDIFF - BRISTOL - LONDON

1, 2 class

Block 1 (⑥ Saturdays)

	⑥	⑥	⑥ U	⑥ E	⑥	⑥ M	⑥ 2	⑥	⑥	⑥	⑥	⑥	⑥ D	⑥ X	⑥	⑥	⑥k Q	⑥	⑥	⑥
Fishguard Harbour 531 ...... d.																	1343	1350z		
Milford Haven 531 .... d.						0915							1240							
Pembroke Dock 531 .... d.																				
Swansea .... d.	0832		0932	0952		1032		1056	1100	1132		1232		1332	1420	1432		1520	1532	1632
Neath .... d.	0843		0943			1043		1107	1115	1143		1243		1343		1443		1543	1643	1650
Port Talbot Parkway ...... d.	0850		0950			1050		1114	1124	1150		1250		1350		1450		1550	1650	
Bridgend .... d.	0902		1002	1019		1102		1127	1143	1202		1302		1402	1447	1502		1602	1702	
Cardiff Central .... a.	0922		1022	1040		1122		1148	1210	1222		1322		1422	1509	1522	1612	1622	1722	
Cardiff Central 510 532 .. d.	0925		1025	1045		1125		1203		1225		1325		1425	1435	1530	1525	1615	1625	1725
Newport 510 532 .... d.	0939		1039	1057		1139		1217		1239		1339		1439	1449	1542	1539	1627	1639	1739
Weston-super-Mare 510 .. d.				1050											1544					
Bristol Temple Meads 510/32 a.				1107			1246								1521	1616	1608			
Bristol Temple Meads 510/32 d.		1015		1115		1215	1258			1315		1415	1515	1530	1622		1615	1645		1715
Bristol Parkway .... d.	1001		1100		1200					1300		1400	1500	1527	1543u	1633	1600	1627	1657	1700
Bath Spa 510 532 .... d.		1027		1127		1227	1315			1327		1427		1438	1538		1638		1727	1738
Chippenham .... d.		1038		1138		1238				1338		1438							1738	
Swindon .... d.	1028	1055	1128	1155	1228	1255		1328	1355	1428	1455	1528		1555		1628	1655	1730	1755	1813
Didcot Parkway .... d.		1111		1211		1313			1413		1513		1613				1713			1813
Reading 510 .... a.	1056	1127	1157	1227	1257	1329		1400	1429	1500	1531	1600	1628		1700	1728	1753	1801	1829	1845
London Paddington 510 .. a.	1145	1210	1245	1310	1340	1410		1445	1515	1545	1615	1645	1710	1755y	1745	1810	1845	1845	1910	1945

Block 2 (⑥ Saturdays / ⑦ Sundays)

	⑥ X	⑥	⑥	⑥	⑥ 2	⑥ 2	⑥	⑥ 2	⑥ 2	⑦	⑦	⑦q	⑦	⑦r	⑦	⑦q	⑦r	⑦	⑦p🚌	⑦q	⑦r
Fishguard Harbour 531 ...... d.										0150											
Milford Haven 531 .... d.	1540					1840															
Pembroke Dock 531 .... d.				1713																	
Swansea .... d.	1721	1732		1832	1922	1933		2022	2035		0410		0640		0710	0740				0800	0840
Neath .... d.		1743		1843	1933	1948			2050		0421		0651		0721	0751				0811	0851
Port Talbot Parkway ...... d.	1738	1750		1850	1941	1957			2059		0428		0658		0728	0758				0818	0851
Bridgend .... d.	1753	1802		1902	1955	2014			2116		0441		0711		0741	0811				0831	0911
Cardiff Central .... a.	1819	1822		1922	2016	2036		2117	2138		0528		0759		0828	0859				0918	0929
Cardiff Central 510 532 .. d.		1830	1825	1925							0530		0800		0830	0900	0905		0920	1000	
Newport 510 532 .... d.		1844	1839	1925							0544		0814		0844	0914	0925		0934	1014	
Weston-super-Mare 510 .. d.																	0934		1002	1035	
Bristol Temple Meads 510/32 a.												0730	0805		0905			1005			
Bristol Temple Meads 510/32 d.	1815		1935			2125								0841		0941					1041
Bristol Parkway .... d.		1900		2000								0742	0817		0917			1017			
Bath Spa 510 532 .... d.	1827		1947			2137						0753	0828		0928			1028			
Chippenham .... d.	1838		1958																		
Swindon .... d.	1855	1928	2015	2028							0712	0809	0841	0921	0944	1012	1012	1044		1112	1112
Didcot Parkway .... d.	1913		2034									0829	0904		1004			1104			
Reading 510 .... a.	1929	2000	2056	2059		2251					0748	0851	0925	0949	1025	1049	1049	1125		1149	1149
London Paddington 510 .. a.	2010	2045	2140	2145		2340					0829	0932	1007	1030	1107	1132	1132	1209		1232	1232

Block 3 (⑦ Sundays)

	⑦	⑦p	⑦q	⑦r	⑦🚌	⑦q	⑦r	⑦	⑦p🚌	⑦r	⑦q	⑦	⑦ J	⑦ J	⑦	⑦	⑦ B	⑦	⑦ D	⑦ B	⑦ D	⑦	⑦ K
Fishguard Harbour 531 ...... d.																							
Milford Haven 531 .... d.																							
Pembroke Dock 531 .... d.																							
Swansea .... d.			0910	0940		1000	1040		1100	1115	1125	1140			1200	1220			1250		1310	1315
Neath .... d.			0921	0951		1011	1051		1111	1126	1136	1151			1211	1231			1301		1321	1326
Port Talbot Parkway ...... d.			0928	0958		1018	1058		1118	1133	1142	1158			1218	1238			1308		1328	1334
Bridgend .... d.			0941	1011		1031	1111		1131	1148	1158	1211			1231	1251			1321		1341	1350
Cardiff Central .... a.			1028	1059		1118	1159		1218	1235	1243	1259			1318	1338			1408		1428	1435
Cardiff Central 510 532 .. d.			1020	1030	1100		1105	1120	1200		1220	1230	1255	1255	1300		1320	1340	1400	1338	1420	1430	1430	1505
Newport 510 532 .... d.			1040	1044	1114		1125	1134	1214		1240	1244	1307	1307	1314		1334	1354	1414	1352	1432	1444	1444	1518
Weston-super-Mare 510 .. d.													1327			1437							
Bristol Temple Meads 510/32 a.		1135				1235				1335			1355		1430		1457	1524		1525			
Bristol Temple Meads 510/32 d.	1105			1205			1305						1405		1449		1500	1530		1530			
Bristol Parkway .... d.			1141				1241						1341		1457	1441							
Bath Spa 510 532 .... d.	1117			1217			1317						1417				1512	1543u		1543u			
Chippenham .... d.	1128			1228			1328						1428				1523						
Swindon .... d.	1144	1212	1212	1244		1312	1312	1344		1412	1444	1512		1512	1542			1609					
Didcot Parkway .... d.	1204		1304				1404				1504			1604								
Reading 510 .... a.	1225	1249	1249	1325		1349	1349	1431		1449	1526	1549		1549	1621			1642					
London Paddington 510 .. a.	1307	1329	1329	1407		1429	1429	1510		1529	1607	1629		1629	1707	1758y		1805y	1730				

Block 4 (⑦ Sundays)

	⑦r	⑦ K	⑦	⑦ A	⑦	⑦ L	⑦	⑦ E	⑦	⑦	⑦	⑦ Y	⑦ S	⑦ A	⑦	⑦	⑦ 2	⑦	⑦	⑦ 2
Fishguard Harbour 531 ...... d.												1505								
Milford Haven 531 .... d.													1518			1740				
Pembroke Dock 531 .... d.																				2051
Swansea .... d.	1340	1340		1425		1520	1530	1600		1630		1700	1710	1730		1830	1924		2030	2300
Neath .... d.	1351	1351		1436			1541	1611		1641		1711		1741		1841	1935		2041	
Port Talbot Parkway ...... d.	1358	1359		1443			1548	1618		1648		1718		1748		1848	1942		2048	
Bridgend .... d.	1411	1415		1456		1549	1602	1632		1702		1732	1741	1802		1902	1956		2102	2330
Cardiff Central .... a.	1459	1448		1543		1617	1623	1653		1723		1757	1804	1823		1923	2018		2123	2352
Cardiff Central 510 532 .. d.	1500	1505	1545		1630	1625	1655	1725	1755		1800	1810	1825	1925			2125			
Newport 510 532 .... d.	1514	1518	1559		1644	1639	1709	1739	1809		1814	1823	1839	1939			2139			
Weston-super-Mare 510 .. d.				1614							1846						⑦			
Bristol Temple Meads 510/32 a.				1642	1718				1830	1853			1935		2030	2130				
Bristol Temple Meads 510/32 d.		1555		1645	1725		1730		1805	1830	1853			1935		2030	2130			
Bristol Parkway .... d.	1541		1625		1705	1730		1800		1830		1900			2000		2200			
Bath Spa 510 532 .... d.		1607		1657	1736		1742		1817		1842	1904			1947		2042	2142		
Chippenham .... d.		1618			1708		1753				1853				1958		2053	2153		
Swindon .... d.	1609	1634	1654	1713	1724		1731	1809	1827	1839	1857	1911			1927	1949	2014	2027	2109	2228	2247
Didcot Parkway .... d.		1653			1749			1846		1931					2047	2126	2228	2247		
Reading 510 .... a.	1642	1710	1726	1745	1757		1806	1926	1841	1903	1911	1929	1948		1958	2021	2046	2102	2143	2245	2303
London Paddington 510 .. a.	1730	1752	1807	1829	1838		1844	1911	1925	1946	1950	2008	2028		2036	2105	2128	2150	2227	2323	2345

A – [train] and ☕ Cheltenham - London.
B – [train] and ☕ Swansea - Leeds.
C – Conveys on Feb. 18, 25, Apr. 8, 15, 22 and ☕ Paignton - London.
D – [train] and ☕ Cardiff - London **Waterloo** (Eurostar connecting service).
E – [train] and ☕ Carmarthen - London.
H – [train] and ☕ Paignton - London.
J – [train] and ☕ Carmarthen - Birmingham.
K – [train] and ☕ Carmarthen - Manchester.
L – [train] and ☕ Tenby - Portsmouth.
M – [train] and ☕ Milford Haven - Portsmouth.
Q – [train] and ☕ Fishguard Harbour - Birmingham.
S – [train] and ☕ Milford Haven - Portsmouth.
U – [train] and ☕ Swansea - Manchester.
X – [train] and ☕ Milford Haven - Portsmouth.
Y – [train] and ☕ Fishguard Harbour - Portsmouth.

k – Not Apr. 15, May 27.
p – Jan. 15 - Mar. 26.
q – To Mar. 26 only.
r – From Apr. 2 only.
u – Stops to pick up only.
y – London **Waterloo**.
z – Apr. 15, May 27 only.

Services on Jan. 1, 8 and evening of Jan. 7 are liable to alteration. Passengers are advised to check at stations or to telephone (0171) 262 6767 if intending to travel on these dates.

Table 531 — SWANSEA - MILFORD HAVEN and FISHGUARD
1, 2 class

Panel 1

km		✼2	✼2	✼2	Ⓐ2	✼2	⑥2	✼2	Ⓐ2	A	B	C	E2	Y♀	Z♀	✼cG	✼2	✼2	⑦2
	London Paddington 530 d.													0848	0925				
	Cardiff Central 530 d.				0600		0700			0910	0912	0940	0953	1103	1116	1108	1108z	1100g	
0	Swansea d.				0711		0813	0905		1019	1019	1105	1135	1203		1205	1210	1230	1305
18	Llanelli d.				0727		0829	0923		1038		1121	1135	1218	1217	1226	1245		1325
40	Ferryside d.				0745		0848	0942		1055	1059								1345
51	Carmarthen d.	0530	0553	0630		0735	0800	0809		0905	0958	1108	1112	1144	1206	1214	1246	1256	1316 1358 1420
72	Whitland d.	0545	0609	0645		0750	0815	0824		0921	1014	1159	1221	1231	1253	1254	1301	1312	1331 1435
99	Tenby d.		0637				0842			1042			1307			1341			
118	Pembroke Dock a.		0705				0908			1110						1409			
101	Haverfordwest d.			0608		0709	0813		0847	0946e			1221	1249					1458
115	Milford Haven a.	0621		0722			0826		0900	1004			1235	1303					1511
117	Fishguard Harbour a.														1328	1329	1338	1414	

Panel 2

		⑦2	✼H	✼2	⑦2	✼2		✼J	⑦2	✼K	✼2	⑦J	✼2	⑦2	✼C	Ⓐ		⑦C2	✼2		⑥2	❖	ⓐL	L
	London Paddington 530 d.		1314												1650	1730							1918y	1915y
	Cardiff Central 530 d.		1314			1510		1600		1705	1710	1755		1840	1905	1931	1935				2126		2235	2235
0	Swansea d.	1357	1405	1457	1505	1605	1624	1705	1725	1803	1822	1850	1905	1904	2005	2027	2035		2110	2121	2250	2307	2331	2338
18	Llanelli d.	1415	1420	1513	1523	1623	1642	1720	1743	1822	1837	1906	1923	1955	2021	2043	2050		2128	2139	2306	2323	2346	2354
40	Ferryside d.	1434			1541	1640		1802	1839		1942	2012			2147	2159			2323				0002x	0011
51	Carmarthen d.	1450	1446	1455	1543	1656	1712	1744	1818	1855	1906	1935	1958	2028	2047	2113	2119		2203	2214	2336	2354	0015	0024
72	Whitland d.	1506	1501b	1511	1558	1611	1713	1729	1759	1834	1910	1921	1950	2014	2043		2134s		2219				0011	
99	Tenby d.	1536		1540		1644				1900			2018	2042										
118	Pembroke Dock a.	1604		1608		1710				1930			2046	2109										
101	Haverfordwest d.		1522		1620		1735	1755	1821		1932	1944			2106				2155s	2244				
115	Milford Haven a.		1536		1635		1749	1810	1834		1946	1957			2119				2209	2302f				
117	Fishguard Harbour a.																						0049	

Panel 3

		✼♀	⑦♀		✼2	Ⓐ	✼2	✼2	✼2	⑦2	✼2	✼♀	⑦g♀	⑦g♀	✼2	✼2	✼2	⑦g2	✼2	⑥2	✼2	✼2	⑦2	✼2	✼G
		L	Q		C	2	J	K	♀	H	S	S	S	2				T	U		U	R	2	F	G
	Fishguard Harbour d.	0150	0150																						1343
	Milford Haven d.				0635		0735	0840		0915			1030				1240	1313							
	Haverfordwest d.			0547		0650	0749	0854		0929			1046				1254	1328							
	Pembroke Dock d.				0713							0916				1116	1116								
	Tenby d.				0743							0944				1144	1146				1315				
	Whitland d.	0223	0221		0605	0709	0810	0913		0948		1011	1108			1211	1214		1313	1348	1350				
	Carmarthen d.			0600	0625	0645	0729	0833	0933	0943	1018	1026	1030	1133	1133	1219	1231	1235	1244	1333		1410	1434		
	Ferryside d.			0609x		0738		0842			1027	1035	1042			1228	1240	1244	1253			1419			
	Llanelli d.	0300	0303	0625	0648	0708	0756	1858	0956	1007	1031	1044	1054	1101	1157h	1156	1245	1300	1304	1310	1355		1436	1455	
	Swansea d.	0318	0328	0650	0708	0725	0819	0914	1014	1025	1049	1109	1119	1121	1216h	1216	1310	1322	1322	1335	1412		1456	1512	
	Cardiff Central 530 a.	0422	0528	0742	0818	0822	0917		1009	1117	1122	1148	1235	1243		1314	1435		1500	1509		1611	1612		
	London Paddington 530 a.	0640	0829	1111y		1030			1340																

Panel 4

		Z♀	Y♀	✼2	⑦N	✼K	✼R	✼C	⑦2	✼2	✼2	✼♀	⑥2	⑦2	✼2		⑦2	✼2	✼2	✼2	⑦2
		Z	Y		N	K	R	C				♀			2		2	2	2	2	2
	Fishguard Harbour d.	1350	1350		1505																
	Milford Haven d.					1518	1540	1540			1740	1805	1825	1840	1840		1955	2010		2140	2305
	Haverfordwest d.					1533	1555	1554			1755	1820	1842	1853	1853		2010	2024		2156	2321
	Pembroke Dock d.			1413				1610	1613	1713							2010	2051	2116		
	Tenby d.			1443				1640	1643	1741							2042	2120	2146		
	Whitland d.	1422	1422	1511	1538	1553	1615	1613	1710	1711	1808	1818	1839	1904	1911	1911	2030	2104	2110	2148	2214 2215 2341
	Carmarthen d.		1506	1532	1559	1613	1637	1633	1734	1734	1838	1857	1925	1931	1931		2047	2101	2131	2207	2232 2232 0001
	Ferryside d.			1541		1622		1642x	1740	1743				1934	1940	1940x		2140	2217		
	Llanelli d.	1458	1458	1529	1601	1621	1639	1700	1658	1759	1802	1858	1902	1952	1957	1957		2200	2234		
	Swansea a.		1516	1547	1622	1639	1659	1718	1721	1821	1821	1914	1920	2013	2013		2221	2254			
	Cardiff Central 530 a.	1553	1622	1653		1757	1804	1819	1819		2016	2018		2113	2117		2325b	2352			
	London Paddington 530 a.	1750	1845	1911						2353r											

Table 531 notes

A – 🚃 Exmouth - Carmarthen.
B – 🚃 Frome - Carmarthen.
C – 🚃 and ♀ Portsmouth - Milford Haven and v.v.
E – 🚃 and ♀ Newport - Milford Haven.
F – 🚃 and ♀ Tenby - Portsmouth.
G – 🚃 and ♀ Birmingham - Fishguard and v.v.
H – 🚃 and ♀ Brighton - Milford Haven and v.v.
J – 🚃 and ♀ Birmingham - Milford Haven and v.v.
K – 🚃 and ♀ Manchester - Milford Haven and v.v.
L – 🚃 and ♀ London Waterloo - Carmarthen and v.v. ℝ Eurostar connecting service.
N – 🚃 and ♀ Fishguard Harbour - Portsmouth.
Q – 🚃 and ♀ Haverfordwest - Portsmouth.
S – 🚃 and ♀ Carmarthen - Birmingham.
T – 🚃 and ♀ Carmarthen - Portsmouth.
U – 🚃 and ♀ Carmarthen - Manchester.
Y – Apr. 15, May 27 only.
Z – Jan. 2-4, Apr. 13, 14 only.

b – Ⓐ only.
c – ① - ④ only.
e – Departs 0950 on ⑥.
f – Arrives 2258 on ⑥.
g – From Apr. 2.
h – ⑥ only.

j – To Mar. 26.
s – Stops to set down only.
x – Stops on request.
y – London Waterloo.
z – Jan. 2-4, Apr. 13, 14.

❖ – Runs daily.

Table 532 — CARDIFF - BRISTOL - WEYMOUTH and PORTSMOUTH
2 class

km		✼♀	⑥♀	Ⓐ♀	Ⓐ♀	⑦♀	✼♀	⑥♀	⑥♀	Ⓐ♀	Ⓐ♀	✼W♀	Ⓐ♀	✼♀	✼f♀	✼M♀	✼♀	⑦♀	✼♀	✼♀	⑦♀	⑦♀
	Swansea 530 d.								0650			0719e				0823						
0	Cardiff Central 530 535 d.		0500	0500		0605	0605	0630	0730		0745		0830			0930		0945▲	0945▲	1030		
19	Newport 530 535 d.		0515	0515		0620	0620	0644	0744		0759		0844			0944		0959▲	0959▲	1048		
61	Bristol Temple Meads a.		0550	0550		0653	0653	0716	0817		0830		0916			1016		1042▲	1042▲	1116		
61	Bristol Temple Meads 530 d.		0555	0555	0703	0703	0722	0727	0822	0833	0840	0900	0910▲	0922	0933	1022	1033	1048	1048	1105	1105	1135
80	Bath Spa 530 d.		0613	0613	0721	0721	0735	0745	0835	0851	0857	0918		0935		1035	1051	1105	1105	1125	1125	
100	Trowbridge d.		0630	0631	0710	0741	0741	0750	0805	0909	0915u	0938		1011		1050	1109	1125	1125			
107	Westbury d.	0535	0638	0642	0646	0717	0753	0755	0759	0814	0916	0950	1003	0956	1019	1057c	1116	1140	1140	1156		
116	Frome d.				0659			0804			0926	1002		1028								
157	Yeovil Pen Mill d.				0739			0840b			0957	1035		1100								
190	Dorchester West d.				0812			0915			1031	1113		1135								
202	Weymouth a.				0824			0927			1042	1123		1147								
114	Warminster d.		0542	0647	0650		0726		0802	0806	0823	0903	0927u			1004		1104	1126			1204
146	Salisbury d.		0604	0647	0714		0751		0826	0830	0846	0932		1037	1030	1118	1130	1148	1218	1218		1248
173	Romsey d.		0624	0734	0737		0810	0825	0850		0850	0910	0950		1048	1141	1148	1212				1248
184	Southampton Central a.		0635	0746	0747		0821	0837	0901		0900	0920	1001		1105	1059	1151	1159	1225	1247	1247	1259
208	Fareham a.		0704		0810			0859	0923		0923	1023		1127	1123	1227		1321	1321			1343
225	Portsmouth and Southsea a.				0828			0943	0943			1043		1143		1244	1243	1343				
226	Portsmouth Harbour a.				0834			0947	0947			1047		1152	1147	1248	1247	1348	1347			
	Brighton 509 a.	0820						1004											1503			

Table 532 notes

A – Runs May 13, 20, 27 only.
H – 🚃 and ♀ (Haverfordwest on Ⓐ -) Cardiff - Portsmouth.
M – 🚃 and ♀ Milford Haven - Portsmouth.
W – 🚃 and ♀ Carmarthen - London Waterloo (arrive 1111).
Eurostar connecting service. ℝ (except west of Bath).

b – Arrive 0834.
c – ⑥ only.
e – Also conveys 🚃.

▲ – Not Jan. 15 - Mar. 26. For substitute 🚃 service on these dates, see Table 530.
u – Stops to pick up only.

For an explanation of standard symbols see page 4

Table 532 **CARDIFF - BRISTOL - WEYMOUTH and PORTSMOUTH** 2 class

Times shown in reading order per row (day symbols: ⑦ = Sundays, ⑥ = Saturdays, Ⓐ, ⚒ = workdays symbol, ₸ = catering).

Section 1 (Cardiff → Portsmouth/Weymouth/Brighton)

Header symbols: ⑦ | ⑦ | ⚒ | ⚒ | ⑦n | N | ⚒ | Ⓐ | ⑦ | ⑥ | ⑦ | ⑦ | ⚒ | Ⓐ | ⑥ | ⑦ | ⚒(W) | ⚒(X) | ⑦ | ⚒(M)

Swansea 530 d.	1056c ... 1222e ... 1420
Cardiff Central 530 535 d.	1045▲ 1045▲ 1130 1145▲ 1203 1230 1245▲ 1245▲ 1330 1345r 1430 1435 1430z 1430z 1530
Newport 530 535 d.	1059▲ 1059▲ 1144 1200▲ 1217 1244 1300▲ 1300▲ 1344 1359r 1444 1449 1444z 1444z 1544
Bristol Temple Meads a.	1140▲ 1140▲ 1216 1241▲ 1246 1316 1344▲ 1344▲ 1416 1440 1516 1521 1540 1616
Bristol Temple Meads 530 d.	1148 1148 1158 1222 1248 1258 1322 1333 1333 1348 1348 1422 1433 1448 1522 1530u 1541h 1548 1616
Bath Spa 530 d.	1204 1204 1216 1235 1306 1315 1335 1351 1351 1402 1402 1435 1451 1451 1504 1535 1543u 1543u 1559 1601 1635
Trowbridge d.	1219 1219 1236 1250 1326 1333 1411 1411 1420 1420 1450 1511 1511 1519 1559u 1559u 1618 1626 1629 1650
Westbury d.	1235 1235 1252 1342 1345 1356 1419 1419 1437 1437 1537b 1519 1519 1532 1556 1626 1629 1658
Frome d.	1302 1428 1454 1500 1533 1608
Yeovil Pen Mill d.	1344b 1500 1533 1606 1642
Dorchester West d.	1416 1535 1606 1642
Weymouth a.	1428 1547 1618 1654
Warminster d.	1242 1242 1304 1352 1404 1428 1445 1510 1530 1504 1527 1539 1604 1612 1620 1635 1636 1705
Salisbury d.	1318 1318 1330 1424 1418 1430 1452 1455 1510 1530 1530 1605 1630 1658 1701 1730
Romsey d.	1348 1436v 1448 1516 1513 1528 1548 1623 1648 1722 1719 1748
Southampton Central a.	1352 1352 1400 1459 1448v 1459 1526 1524 1538 1600 1634 1659 1657 1723 1736 1729 1752 1800
Fareham a.	1421 1421 1423 1523 1547 1601 1623 1714 1740 1810 1843
Portsmouth and Southsea a.	1443 1543 1618 1643 1810 1843
Portsmouth Harbour a.	1448 1447 1547 1623 1647 1723 1747 1814 1847
Brighton 509 a.	1603 1612 1703

Section 2 (Cardiff → Portsmouth/Weymouth)

Header symbols: ⑦ ⚒ ⑦ ⚒ ⚒ ⑦ ⚒ ⑦ ⚒ ⑦ ⑦ ⚒ ⑦ ⚒ ⑦ ⑥ ⑦ ⑦ ⚒ Ⓐ ⑥ (letters: T, E, G/M, M, B, k)

Swansea 530 d.	1520t 1700 1721
Cardiff Central 530 535 d.	1415g 1429g 1630 1630 1700 1730 1730 1800 1830 1830 1900 1930 1930 1930 2000 2030 2030 2130 2130k
Newport 530 535 d.	1429g 1644 1645 1714 1744 1744 1814 1844 1914 1944 1944 1945 2014 2044 2044 2145 2145k
Bristol Temple Meads a.	1605g 1718 1716 1750 1817 1820 1846 1918 1916 1948 2017 2020 2015 2043 2118 2115 2220 2219k
Bristol Temple Meads 530 d.	1618 1633 1725 1722 1733 1753 1803 1822 1833 1833 1851 1923 1922 1953 2033 2051 2051 2106 2123 2133 2242 2310
Bath Spa 530 d.	1635 1651 1738 1737 1751 1811 1821 1835 1849 1851 1906 1936 1938 2006 2051 2106 2106 2136 2152 2258 2328
Trowbridge d.	1655 1711 1753 1753 1811 1831 1850 1907 1911 1951 1955 2023 2111 2111 2121 2130 2128 2202 2218 2329 2348s
Westbury d.	1710 1719 1802 1804 1819 1840 1847 1859 1919 1919 2004 2033 2120 2120 2128 2202 2218 2338 0008
Frome d.	1728 1829 1849 2130 2140
Yeovil Pen Mill d.	1809b 1900 1921 2203 2211
Dorchester West d.	1843 1933 1954 2235 2244
Weymouth a.	1855 1945 2006 2247 2256
Warminster d.	1719 1809 1811 1855 1906 1926 1927c 1933 2004 2011 2041 2128 2128 2136 2209 2226
Salisbury d.	1755 1833 1834 1904 1930 1950 2000 2034 2036 2110 2150 2150 2159 2239 2249
Romsey d.	1818 1851 1852 1922 1953 2008 2018 2052 2055 2128 2209 2209 2221 2257 2312
Southampton Central a.	1828 1901 1903 1934 2003 2018 2028 2102 2107 2138 2219 2223 2234 2307 2322
Fareham a.	1851 1925 1925 1957 2026 2044 2053 2127 2130 2203 2241 2250 2257 2336 2345
Portsmouth and Southsea a.	1908 1942 1944 2014 2045 2111 2144 2149 2220 2300 2308 2315 2357 0004
Portsmouth Harbour a.	1913 1949 1949 2018 2054j 2115 2148 2159p 2224 2304 2312 2319 0001 0008
Brighton 509 a.	2142 2159

Section 3 (Portsmouth/Weymouth → Cardiff)

Header symbols: ⑥ Ⓐ Ⓐ ⑥ ⚒ ⑥ ⑦ ⚒ ⑦ ⑦ ⑥ ⑦ ⑦ ⚒ ⑦ ⑦r ⑦q ⚒ ⚒ ⑦ ⑦ ⑦ (letters: f, H, M, B; 0900)

Brighton 509 d.	0900
Portsmouth Harbour d.	0603 0703e 0724 0824 0910 0910 0924 1024 1110 1124
Portsmouth and Southsea d.	0505n 0607 0707e 0728 0828 0914 0914 0928 1028 1114 1128
Fareham d.	0521n 0628 0725e 0745 0847 0932 0932 0947 1006 1047 1132 1147
Southampton Central d.	0556n 0630 0652 0755 0808 0824 0836 0909 0929 0955 0955 1009 1033 1109 1155 1209
Romsey d.	0608n 0641 0703 0806 0818 0835 0847 0929 0940 1005 1005 1020 1044 1120 1205 1220
Salisbury d.	0628 0705 0723 0830 0909 0909 0940 1003 1028 1028 1040 1107 1140 1228 1240
Warminster d.	0648 0743 0850 0929 0929 1000 1023 1048 1048 1100 1127 1200 1248 1300
Weymouth d.	0555 0656 0656 0840 1100
Dorchester West d.	0606 0708 0708 0853 1113
Yeovil Pen Mill d.	0638 0739 0739 0924 1144
Frome d.	0709 0709 0810 0810 0935 0957
Westbury d.	0636 0655 0719 0719 0756 0819 0819 0858 0938 0938 0944 1010 1031 1059 1059 1136 1207 1228 1259 1307r
Trowbridge d.	0642 0701 0725 0725 0802 0825 0825 0904 0944 0944 1011 1016 1037 1105 1105 1111 1142 1234 1305 1311
Bath Spa 530 a.	0702 0722 0747 0747 0825 0847 0850 0922 1002 1010 1027 1123 1123 1127 1201 1227 1254 1320 1329
Bristol Temple Meads 530 a.	0720 0739 0807 0807 0845 0907 0910 0938 1021 1021 1042 1034 1052d 1120 1141 1142 1220 1242 1313 1340 1342
Bristol Temple Meads 530 d.	0745 0823 0850 0950 1050 1045▲ 1153 1200▲ 1150 1227 1250 1353▲ 1350
Newport 530 535 a.	0817 0817 0853 0919 1016 1118 1116▲ 1236▲ 1218 1255 1318 1426▲ 1435
Cardiff Central 530 535 a.	0833 0833 0910 0936 1032 1135 1139▲ 1248 1258▲ 1235 1311 1335 1448▲ 1435
Swansea 530 a.	1009 1040 1359

Section 4 (Portsmouth/Weymouth → Cardiff, continued)

Header symbols: ⚒ ⚒ ⑦ ⑦ ⑥ ⑦ ⑥ ⑦ ⑦ ⑦ ⑦ ⑥ ⑦ ⑦ Ⓐ ⑦ ⑦ ⑦ (letters: Y, M, M, E, M)

Brighton 509 d.	1110 ... 1550
Portsmouth Harbour d.	1224 1310 1324 1410 1424 1510 1524 1610 1624
Portsmouth and Southsea d.	1228 1314 1328 1414 1428 1514 1528 1528 1614 1628
Fareham d.	1232 1247 1332 1347 1432 1447 1532 1544 1547 1632 1647 1725
Southampton Central d.	1233e 1255 1309 1333 1355 1409 1437 1455 1509 1555 1608 1609 1625 1629 1655 1709 1725
Romsey d.	1244e 1305 1320 1344 1405 1420 1448 1505 1520 1605 1620 1637 1640 1705 1720 1737
Salisbury d.	1310e 1328 1340 1410 1428 1440 1509 1528 1540 1628 1642 1640 1702 1706 1728 1740 1802
Warminster d.	1330e 1355 1348 1400 1430 1448 1500 1529 1540 1548 1600 1648 1700 1723 1726 1748 1800 1822
Weymouth d.	1300 1300 1448 1457 1630
Dorchester West d.	1313 1313 1501 1510 1642
Yeovil Pen Mill d.	1344 1344 1532 1541 1712
Frome d.	1415 1415 1603 1612 1740
Westbury d.	1339 1402 1407 1428 1433 1439 1459 1539 1548 1559 1607 1620 1625 1700 1732 1735 1750 1755 1830
Trowbridge d.	1345 1405s 1408 1434 1439 1445 1505 1511 1554 1605 1626 1631 1711 1738 1741 1757 1801 1811 1836
Bath Spa 530 a.	1404 1422 1428 1448 1454 1503 1523 1527 1602 1615 1620 1627 1647 1651 1720 1727 1759 1802 1816 1822 1828 1902
Bristol Temple Meads 530 a.	1422 1438s 1452 1444 1513 1520 1544 1542 1616 1630 1640 1642 1707 1711 1736 1745 1819 1822 1838 1841 1844 1902
Bristol Temple Meads 530 d.	1503 1450 1603 1550 1638 1645 1650 1713 1720c 1734 1750 1820 1845 1850 1935
Newport 530 535 a.	1509s 1536▼ 1520 1636 1618 1707 1718 1718 1742 1756c 1814 1914 1920 1937 2019
Cardiff Central 530 535 a.	1525 1559▼ 1537 1658 1635 1735 1735 1800 1811c 1833 1837 1930 1937 2019
Swansea 530 a.	1757 1935 2024

Notes

A – [train] and ₸ (Carmarthen on Ⓐ -) Cardiff - Portsmouth.
B – [train] and ₸ Brighton - Milford Haven.
E – [train] and ₸ Exeter - Portsmouth and v.v.
G – [train] and ₸ Fishguard Harbour - Portsmouth.
H – [train] and ₸ Frome - Carmarthen.
M – [train] and ₸ Milford Haven - Portsmouth and v.v.
N – [train] and ₸ (Milford Haven on ⑥ -) Cardiff - Brighton.
T – [train] and ₸ Tenby - Portsmouth.
W – [train] and ₸ Cardiff - London Waterloo (a. 1755). ★
X – [train] and ₸ Cardiff - London Waterloo (a. 1805). ★
Y – [train] and ₸ London Waterloo (d. 1218) - Cardiff. ★

a – Arrive 0943.
b – Arrive 9 minutes earlier.
c – ⑥ only.
d – On Ⓐ arrive 3 minutes earlier.
e – Ⓐ only.
f – Also conveys [train].
g – Jan. 15 - Mar. 26 only.
h – On Ⓐ depart 1545.
j – Arrive 2049 on Ⓐ.
k – Not Jan. 14 - Mar. 25.
n – ① only.

p – Arrive 2151 on ⑥.
q – To Mar. 26.
r – From Apr. 2.
s – Stops to set down only.
t – Jan. 1, 8 depart 1505.
u – Stops to pick up only.
v – On Ⓐ stops to pick up only.
y – Jan. 15 - Mar. 26 depart 55 minutes earlier.
z – Jan. 15 - Mar. 26 depart 52 minutes earlier.

★ – Eurostar connecting service. Ⓦ (except west of Bath).

▲ – Not Jan. 15 - Mar. 26. For substitute [train] service on these dates, see Table 530.
▼ – Jan. 15 - Mar. 26 arrive 54 minutes later.

Additional service:
Cardiff – Westbury at 2230 daily.

For an explanation of standard symbols see page 4

Table 532 PORTSMOUTH and WEYMOUTH - BRISTOL - CARDIFF

2 class

		⚒	⑦ 🍷	⚒ 🍷c	Ⓐ 🍷	⑦ 🍷	⚒ 🍷	⑦n 🍷	⚒ 🍷	⑦ R	⑦	⑦ Y	⚒ W	⑦ 🍷	⑥ 🍷	Ⓐ	⚒ 🍷	⑦	⑦ 🍷	⑥ 🍷	Ⓐ	⚒	Ⓐ f	⑦	⑦ f
Brighton **509**	d.	...	...	...	...	1650	1700	...	...	1810	...	...	...	...	...	...	...	...	...	...	...	...	...	...	2213
Portsmouth Harbour	d.	...	1710	...	1724	|	|	1810	1824	|	...	...	...	...	...	...	1924	1928	2010	2024	2024	2124	2232	2228	|
Portsmouth and Southsea	d.	...	1714	...	1728	|	|	1814	1828	|	...	...	...	1910	...	...	1928	1932	2014	2028	2028	2128	2236	2232	|
Fareham	d.	...	1732	...	1747	1801	1808	1832	1847	1917	...	...	...	1932	...	...	1947	1950	2032	2047	2047	2147	2256	2250	2316
Southampton Central	d.	1745	1755	...	1809	1825	1836	1855	1909	1940	...	...	...	1955	...	...	2011	2025	2055	2113	2113	2222	2328	2326	2339
Romsey	d.	1756	1807	...	1820	1838	1846	1907	1920	1951	...	...	...	2007	...	...	2022	2037	2107	2124	2124	2234	2339	2336	|
Salisbury	d.	1821	1828	...	1840	1902	1911	1928	1940	2008	...	...	...	2028	...	...	2044	2102	2128	2146	2146	2258	2356	0008	0006
Warminster	d.	1842	1848	...	1900	1922	1931	1948	2000	—	...	2055	2058	2048	...	...	2104	2122	2148	2206	2206	2318	...	0028	...
Weymouth	d.	|	|	1726	|	|	|	|	|	...	1920	|	|	|	1938	1938	|	|	|	|	|	|	...	|	...
Dorchester West	d.	|	|	1739	|	|	|	|	|	...	1933	|	|	|	1951	1951	|	|	|	|	|	|	...	|	...
Yeovil Pen Mill	d.	|	|	1810	|	|	|	|	|	...	2004	|	|	|	2022	2022	|	|	|	|	|	|	...	|	...
Frome	d.	|	|	1841	|	|	|	|	|	Ⓐ	2035	|	|	|	2053	2053	|	|	|	|	|	|	...	|	...
Westbury	d.	1849	|	1854	|	1930	1940	1956	2007	2030	2047	|	|	2104	2102	2113	2113	2129	2158	2213	2213	2325	...	0034	...
Trowbridge	d.	...	1859	1900	1911	1936	1946	2002	|	2036	2053	2105s	2108s	2110	...	2119	2119	...	2204	2219	2219	...	...	...	...
Bath Spa **530**	a.	...	1917	1920	1927	1955	2004	2020	2027	2056	2113	2124s	2127	2130	...	2138	2138	...	2223	2240	2240	...	...	...	...
Bristol Temple Meads 530	a.	...	1935	1940	1943	2013	2021	2037	2042	2119	2134	2140s	2143	2145	...	2154	2154	...	2241	2259	2259	...	...	...	...
Bristol Temple Meads	d.	...	1945	...	1950	2020	2029	2045	2050	2127	...	|	2148	2152	...	2200	2200	...	2246	2304	2304	...	...	...	...
Newport **530 535**	a.	...	2018	...	2018	2049	2100	2116	2118p	2157	...	2213s	2214v	2223	...	2226	2226v	...	2320	2334h	2339	...	...	...	...
Cardiff Central 530 535	a.	...	2035	...	2034	2105	2116	2133	2135p	2214	...	2230	2230v	2240	...	2244	2244v	...	2337	2354h	2359	...	...	...	...
Swansea **530**	a.	...	...	...	...	...	...	...	...	...	...	2334	2327e	...	...	...	...	...	...	...	...	...	...	...	...

R – [12] and 🍷 Brighton - Exeter.
W – [2] and 🍷 London **Waterloo** - Cardiff (- Carmarthen on Ⓐ). ★
Y – [2] and 🍷 London **Waterloo** - Carmarthen. ★
c – ⑥ only.
e – Ⓐ only.
f – Also conveys [1].
h – Not Jan. 14 - Mar. 25.
p – On ⑥ Jan. 14 - Mar. 25 arrive 50 minutes later.
s – Stops to set down only.
v – Not ⑥ Jan. 14 - Mar. 25.
★ – Eurostar connecting service. [R] (except west of Bath).

Table 533 STEVENAGE - LUTON, HEATHROW and GATWICK AIRPORTS

Jetlink 747 Speedlink Airport Services. Buses run daily unless shown otherwise.

				Ⓐ	Ⓒ																				
Stevenage Bus Station ⚡	d.	...	0630	...	...	...	0830	0920	...	1030	1120	...	1230	1320	...	1430	1520	...	1630	1720	...	1830	1920	...	2030
Luton ✈	d.	0605	0705	0725	0750	...	0905	0950	...	1105	1150	...	1305	1350	...	1505	1550	...	1705	1750	...	1905	1950	...	2105
Luton Bus Station ▲	d.	0615	0715	0735	0800	...	0915	1000	...	1115	1200	...	1315	1400	...	1515	1600	...	1715	1800	...	1915	2000	...	2115
Watford Junction ▲	d.	0655	0750	0835	0850	...	0950	1050	...	1150	1250	...	1350	1450	...	1550	1650	...	1750	1850	...	1950	2050	...	2150
Heathrow ✈ (Bus Station)	d.	0730	0830	0930	0930	...	1030	1130	...	1230	1330	...	1430	1530	...	1630	1730	...	1830	1930	...	2030	2130	...	2230
Heathrow ✈ (Terminal 4)	d.	0740	0840	0940	0940	...	1040	1140	...	1240	1340	...	1440	1540	...	1640	1740	...	1840	1940	...	2040	2140	...	2240
Gatwick ✈ (North Terminal)	d.	0830	0930	1030	1030	...	1130	1230	...	1330	1430	...	1530	1630	...	1730	1830	...	1930	2030	...	2130	2230	...	2330
Gatwick ✈ (South Terminal)	a.	0835	0935	1035	1035	...	1135	1235	...	1335	1435	...	1535	1635	...	1735	1835	...	1935	2035	...	2135	2235	...	2335

Gatwick ✈ (South Terminal)	d.	0530	0645	...	0745	0845	...	0945	1045	...	1145	1245	...	1345	1445	...	1545	1645	...	1745	1845	...	1945	...	2045
Gatwick ✈ (North Terminal)	d.	0535	0650	...	0750	0850	...	0950	1050	...	1150	1250	...	1350	1450	...	1550	1650	...	1750	1850	...	1950	...	2050
Heathrow ✈ (Terminal 4)	d.	0625	0740	...	0840	0940	...	1040	1140	...	1240	1340	...	1440	1540	...	1640	1740	...	1840	1940	...	2040	...	2140
Heathrow ✈ (Bus Station)	d.	0655	0755	...	0855	0955	...	1055	1155	...	1255	1355	...	1455	1555	...	1655	1755	...	1855	1955	...	2055	...	2155
Watford Junction ▲	d.	0730	0830	...	0930	1030	...	1130	1230	...	1330	1430	...	1530	1630	...	1730	1830	...	1930	2030	...	2130	...	2230
Luton Bus Station ▲	d.	0820	0905	...	1020	1105	...	1220	1305	...	1420	1505	...	1620	1705	...	1820	1905	...	2020	2105	...	...	...	2305
Luton ✈	d.	0830	0915	...	1030	1115	...	1230	1315	...	1430	1515	...	1630	1715	...	1830	1915	...	2030	2115	...	...	...	2315
Stevenage Bus Station ⚡	a.	0855	0945	...	1055	1145	...	1255	1345	...	1455	1545	...	1655	1745	...	1855	1945	...	...	2145	...	...	...	2345

▲ – Rail station nearby. ⚡ – Services call at Stevenage Rail Station 2 minutes before/after time shown. Buses arrive at Heathrow Bus Station 5 minutes earlier.

Table 534 SWANSEA - SHREWSBURY

2 class

km			⚒		⚒			⚒		⚒	
0	**Swansea 531**	d.	0613	...	1019	...	...	1417	...	1815	...
18	**Llanelli 531**	d.	0633	...	1040	...	...	1437	...	1833	...
37	Pantyffynnon	d.	0655	...	1102	...	...	1459	...	1855	...
39	Ammanford (**x**)	d.	0658	...	1105	...	...	1502	...	1858	...
50	**Llandeilo**	d.	0715	...	1122	...	...	1519	...	1915	...
68	Llandovery	d.	0737	...	1149	...	...	1544	...	1940	...
86	Llanwrtyd	d.	0808	...	1217	...	...	1610	...	2008	...
103	Builth Road (**x**)	d.	0826	...	1235	...	...	1628	...	2026	...
112	**Llandrindod**	d.	0840	...	1251	...	...	1644	...	2045	...
144	Knighton	d.	0919	...	1330	...	...	1723	...	2124	...
164	Craven Arms **535**	d.	0945	...	1356	...	...	1749	...	2153	...
176	Church Stretton **535**	d.	0956	...	1407	...	...	1800	...	2204	...
196	**Shrewsbury 535**	a.	1012	...	1423	...	...	1817	...	2220	...

		⚒			⚒		⚒		⚒	
Shrewsbury 535	d.	0557	...	...	1110	...	1501	...	1905	...
Church Stretton **535**	d.	0614	...	...	1127	...	1518	...	1923	...
Craven Arms **535**	d.	0625	...	...	1138	...	1529	...	1934	...
Knighton	d.	0654	...	...	1206	...	1600	...	2001	...
Llandrindod	d.	0736	...	...	1250	...	1644	...	2045	...
Builth Road (**x**)	d.	0745	...	...	1259	...	1653	...	2055	...
Llanwrtyd	d.	0808	...	...	1320	...	1714	...	2115	...
Llandovery	d.	0834	...	...	1349	...	1740	...	2144	...
Llandeilo	d.	0900	...	...	1417	...	1806	...	2212	...
Ammanford (**x**)	d.	0914	...	...	1430	...	1820	...	2225	...
Pantyffynnon	d.	0917	...	...	1434	...	1823	...	2229	...
Llanelli 531	d.	0940	...	...	1501	...	1846	...	2251	...
Swansea 531	a.	1005	...	...	1522	...	1911	...	2313	...

x – Trains stop on request.

Table 535 CARDIFF - SHREWSBURY - MANCHESTER

2 class

km			⚒ 🍷	⚒ 🍷	⚒ 🍷	⚒ 🍷	⑦p	⚒ 🍷	⚒ 🍷	⚒ S	⑦q 🍷	⚒ M	⚒ 🍷	⑦	⚒ 🍷	⑦g	⚒ 🍷	⑦h C	⑦j C	⚒ 🍷	⚒	⑦r 🍷	⑦t 🍷	⚒ 🍷	⑦
0	**Cardiff Central 530 532**	d.	...	0512	0620	0719	0830	0845	0945	1045	...	1145	1245	1305	1345	...	1445	1505	1505	1545	1600	1610	1610	1645	1710
19	**Newport 530 532**	d.	...	0527	0634	0733	0845	0859	0959	1059	1125	1159	1259	1319	1359	1449	1459	1520	1520	1559	1615	1625	1625	1659	1725
30	Cwmbran	d.	...	0537	0644	0743	0855	0909	1009	1109	1135	1209	1309	1329	1409	|	1509	1530	1530	1609u	1625	1635	1635	|	1735
35	Pontypool and New Inn	d.	...	|	0649	0748	0901	|	1014	|	1141	1214	|	|	1414	|	|	1536	1536	|	1631	1641	1641	|	1741
50	Abergavenny	d.	...	0552	0659	0758	0911	0922	1024	1122	1151	1224	1322	1343	1424	1512	1522	1546	1546	1622	1642	1651	1651	1721	1751
89	**Hereford**	d.	...	0623	0726	0824	0939	0948	1050	1148	1219	1250	1348	1412	1450	1539	1548	1613	1613	1648	...	1718	1718	1747	1818
109	Leominster	d.	...	0638	0739	0837	...	1002	|	1202	...	|	1402	1426	|	...	1602	1627	1627	1702	...	1732	1732	1801	...
127	Ludlow	d.	...	0650	0750	0848	...	1013	1111	1213	...	1311	1413	1438	1511	...	1613	1639	1639	1713	...	1744	1744	1813	...
139	Craven Arms	d.	...	0700	0759	0857	...	1021	1120	|	...	|	|	1447	1520	...	1621	1648	1648	1721	...	1753	1753	1823	...
151	Church Stretton	d.	...	0710	0808	0906	...	1030	|	1227	...	1326	1427	1457	|	...	|	1658	1658	1730	...	1803	1803	1833	...
171	**Shrewsbury**	d.	0659	0730	0823	0923	...	1046	1142	1243	...	1341	1443	1518	1542	...	1643	1717	1716	1746	...	1822	1822	1850	...
224	**Crewe 550**	a.	0738	0817	0855	0955	...	1120	1219	1319	...	1419	1519	1604	1615	...	1723	1753	1753	1817	...	1858	1858	1921	...
	Liverpool Lime Street 550	a.	0835	...	|	|	...	|	|	|	...	|	|	1656	1703	...	|	|	|	|	...	|	|	|	...
224	**Crewe**	d.	...	...	0855	0957	...	1121	1220	1320	...	1420	1520	...	...	...	1725	1754	1755	1819	...	1858	1858	1923	...
254	Wilmslow	d.	...	...	0915	1016	...	1141	1240	1340	...	1440	1540	...	...	...	1744	1829	|	1840	...	1926	|	1948	...
264	Stockport	d.	...	...	0926	1027	...	1149	1249	1349	...	1449	1549	...	...	...	1755	1842	1858	1852	...	1941	2014	1958	...
273	**Manchester Piccadilly**	a.	...	...	0938	1038	...	1202	1302	1402	...	1502	1602	...	...	...	1804	1852	1907	1904	...	1951	2023	2012	...

C – [2] and 🍷 Carmarthen - Manchester.
M – [2] and 🍷 (Milford Haven on Ⓐ -) Cardiff - Manchester.
S – [2] and 🍷 Swansea - Manchester.
g – Not Jan. 15 - Mar. 26. Also conveys [1].
h – Not Jan. 15 - Apr. 9.
j – Jan. 15 - Apr. 9.
p – Runs 3 minutes later Jan. 15 - Mar 26.
q – Runs 22 minutes later Jan. 15 - Mar. 26.
r – Not Jan. 15 - Mar. 26.
t – Jan. 15 - Mar. 26.
u – Stops to pick up only.

Additional services **Shrewsbury - Crewe** on ⚒ – 0930, 1150, 1350, 1550, 1755, 1955; on ⑦ – 1350.
Additional services **Crewe - Shrewsbury** on ⚒ – 0827, 1030, 1247, 1447, 1647, 1851, 2310.

‖ Services on ⑦ Jan. 1 and 8 are liable to alteration. Check locally if intending to travel on these dates.

For an explanation of standard symbols see page 4

Table 535 CARDIFF - SHREWSBURY - MANCHESTER

2 class

	⚒	⚒ H	⑦ L	⚒ 🍷	⚒ 🍷	⑦ 🍷	⚒	Ⓐ	⑥	Ⓐ P
Cardiff Central 530 532 d.	1715e	1745	1810	1845	1945c	2015	2045	2145	2150	2338
Newport 530 532 d.	1729	1759	1825	1859	2000	2030	2100	2159	2205	2352
Cwmbran d.	1740	1809	1835	1909	2010	2040	2110	2209	2215	0003
Pontypool and New Inn d.	1746	1815	1841	1914	2016	2046	2116	2214	2221	0008
Abergavenny d.	1757	1824	1851	1924	2026	2056	2126	2224	2231	0018
Hereford d.	...	1850	1918	1950	2053	2123	2153	2250	2258	0045
Leominster d.	...	1904	1932	2003	...	2137	2207	2303	...	...
Ludlow d.	...	1915	1944	2014	...	2149	2219	2314	...	...
Craven Arms d.	...	1923	1953	2023	...	2158	2228	2323	...	...
Church Stretton d.	...	1932	2003	|	...	2208	2238	2332	...	...
Shrewsbury d.	...	1948	2020	2045	...	2225	2258	2347	...	...
Crewe 550 a.	...	2019	2101	2116	...	2309	2347	0028	...	...
Liverpool Lime Street 550 a.	...	...	|	|	...	...	...	...	...	...
Crewe d.	...	...	2113	2121	...	...	...	...	...	...
Wilmslow d.	...	...	2139k	2141	...	...	...	...	...	...
Stockport d.	...	...	2150v	2150	...	...	...	...	...	...
Manchester Piccadilly a.	...	...	2159v	2202	...	...	...	...	...	...

	⚒	⚒ 🍷	Ⓐ A	⚒ 🍷	⑥ H	Ⓐ H	⑥	⑦p 🍷	⚒ 🍷
Manchester Piccadilly d.	...	...	...	...	...	...	...	...	0833
Stockport d.	...	...	...	...	...	...	...	...	0842
Wilmslow d.	...	...	...	...	...	...	...	...	0850
Crewe a.	...	...	...	...	...	...	...	...	0911
Liverpool Lime Street 550 d.	...	...	...	...	...	...	...	...	|
Crewe 550 d.	...	0539	...	0625	0727	0727	...	...	0913
Shrewsbury d.	...	0615	...	0725	0819	0819	...	...	0945
Church Stretton d.	...	0630	...	0740	0834	0834	...	...	|
Craven Arms d.	...	0638	...	0748	0842	0842	...	...	1006
Ludlow d.	...	0646	...	0756	0850	0850	...	...	1014
Leominster d.	...	0657	...	0807	0901	0901	...	...	1025
Hereford d.	0630	0713	...	0823	0917	0917	...	0950	1041
Abergavenny d.	0653	0736	0804	0846	|	0940	0952	1013	1104
Pontypool and New Inn d.	0702	0745	0814	0855	|	0949	1002	1023	|
Cwmbran d.	0707	0750	0819	0900	|	0954	1007	1028	1116
Newport 530 532 d.	0719	0801	0830	0911	0958	1005	1018	1044	1130
Cardiff Central 530 532 a.	0736	0817	0846	0927	1014	1021	...	...	1146

	⚒ 🍷	⚒ 🍷	⑦ 🍷	⚒ 🍷	⚒ L	Ⓐ	⑦	⚒ 🍷	Ⓐ	⚒ 🍷
Manchester Piccadilly d.	...	1033	...	1133	1233	...	...	1333	...	1433
Stockport d.	...	1042	...	1142	1242	...	...	1342	...	1442
Wilmslow d.	...	1050	...	1150	1250	...	...	1350	...	1450
Crewe a.	...	1113	...	1211	1311	...	...	1411	...	1511
Liverpool Lime Street 550 d.	0918	|	...	|	|	...	...	|	...	|
Crewe 550 d.	1013	1113	...	1213	1313	...	1332	1413	...	1513
Shrewsbury d.	1044	1145	...	1245	1345	...	1420	1445	...	1545
Church Stretton d.	1100	1201	...	|	1401	...	1438	|	...	1601
Craven Arms d.	|	|	...	|	1409	...	1447	|	...	1609
Ludlow d.	1113	1214	...	1312	1417	...	1456	1512	...	1617
Leominster d.	|	1225	...	|	1427	...	1507	|	...	1627
Hereford d.	1137	1241	1250	1335	1443	...	1530	1535	...	1643
Abergavenny d.	1200	1304	1313	1358	1506	...	1553	1558	...	1706
Pontypool and New Inn d.	1209	|	1323	1408	|	...	1603	1608	1707	|
Cwmbran d.	1214	1316	1328	1413	1519	1603	1608	1613	1712	1719
Newport 530 532 d.	1225	1327	1345	1423	1529	1612	1620	1623	1723	1729
Cardiff Central 530 532 a.	1241	1343	1408	1439	1545	1630	1645	1639	1740	1745

	⑦	⚒ 🍷	⑦	⑦	⚒	⚒ 🍷	⑦ S	⚒ 🍷	⑦ H	⑦	⚒ 🍷	⑦ 🍷	⚒ 🍷	Ⓐ 🍷
Manchester Piccadilly d.	...	1533	1540	...	...	1633	1620	...	...	1755g	1833	...	1933	...
Stockport d.	...	1542	1549	...	...	1642	1630	...	...	1805g	1842	...	1942	...
Wilmslow d.	...	1550	1558	...	...	1650	|	...	...	|	1852	...	1950	...
Crewe a.	...	1611	1626	...	...	1712	1729	...	...	1905	1911	...	2011	...
Liverpool Lime Street 550 d.	...	|	|	...	...	|	|	1714	...	|	|	1915	|	...
Crewe 550 d.	1541	1613	1633	...	...	1713	1739	1809	1828	1906	1915	2002	2020	2133
Shrewsbury d.	1626	1645	1720	...	...	1753	1816	1854	1902	1939	1947	2051	2052	2222
Church Stretton d.	1642	1701	...	...	...	1808	1835	|	|	1958	2002	2107	2107	2240
Craven Arms d.	1651	1709	...	...	...	1816	1844	1915	|	2006	|	2116	2115	2249
Ludlow d.	1700	1717	...	...	...	1824	1853	1923	|	2014	2016	2125	2123	2258
Leominster d.	1711	1727	...	⑦	...	1835	1904	1933	|	2025	2026	2136	2134	2311
Hereford d.	1728	1743	...	1830	...	1851	1921	1949	1949	2041	2042	2153	2150	2328
Abergavenny d.	1751	1806	...	1855	1900	1914	1944	2012	|	2104	2105	2217	2213	2352
Pontypool and New Inn d.	1801	|	...	1906	1910	|	1954	2022	|	2113	|	|	2222	0003
Cwmbran d.	1806	1819	...	1911	1915	1926	1959	2027	|	2118	2118	2230	2227	0008
Newport 530 532 d.	1820	1829	...	1921	1926	1937q	2010	2037	2031	2129	2128	2240	2238	0019
Cardiff Central 530 532 a.	1840	1845	...	1939	1942c	1952q	2028	2053	2048	2146	2144	2257	2254	0041

A – (2) Abergavenny - Swansea.
H – (2) and 🍷 Cardiff - Holyhead and v.v.
L – (2) and 🍷 Milford Haven - Manchester and v.v.
P – (2) Pembroke Dock - Hereford.
S – (2) and 🍷 Manchester - Swansea.
c – ⑥ only.
e – Ⓐ only.
g – Departs 25 minutes later from Apr. 16.
k – Not Jan. 15 - Apr. 9.
p – Runs 40 minutes later Jan. 15 - Mar. 26.
q – On ⑥ arrives Newport 1940, Cardiff 1956.
v – Jan. 15 - Apr. 9 arrives 16 minutes later.

Table 536 BANGOR - ABERYSTWYTH - CARDIFF

🚌

	701 D	202 ⚒	202 ⚒	202 ⚒	701 D	202 ⚒	202 ⚒	202 ⚒	202 ⚒	
Bangor Clock d.	...	...	...	...	1005	...	...	...	...	...
Caernarfon Castle Square d.	...	...	...	...	1030	...	...	...	...	...
Porthmadog d.	...	...	...	...	1110	...	...	...	...	...
Dolgellau d.	...	...	...	...	1200	...	...	...	...	...
Machynlleth d.	...	...	...	...	1235	...	...	...	...	...
Aberystwyth a.	...	...	...	...	1310	...	...	...	...	...
Aberystwyth d.	0740	*0905*e	*1105*e	*1305*e	1405	*1455*h	*1705*e	*1820*e	*1940*e	...
Aberaeron d.	0815	0945	1150	1350	1435	1550	1750	1905	2015	...
Lampeter d.	0845	1020	1220	1420	1500	1625	1825	1940	2045	...
Pencader d.	0910	1050	1250	1450	|	1655	1855	2010	2115	...
Carmarthen Bus Station ▲ d.	0930	1118	1318	1518	1545	1723	1921	2036	2136	...
Swansea Quadrant a.	1015	...	...	...	1635	...	...	...	...	...
Cardiff Bus Station a.	1130	...	...	...	1750	...	...	...	...	...

	202 ⚒	202 ⚒	202 ⚒	701 D	202 ⚒	202 ⚒	202 ⚒	202 ⚒	701 D
Cardiff Bus Station d.	...	...	...	0900	...	...	...	...	1710
Swansea Quadrant d.	...	...	...	1020	...	...	...	...	1820
Carmarthen Bus Station ▲ d.	...	0800	1010	1125	1210	1410	1715	1810	1910
Pencader d.	...	0830	1040	|	1240	1440	1745	1840	1930
Lampeter d.	0803	0900	1110	1210	1310	1510	1815	1910	1955
Aberaeron d.	0840	0936	1139	1235	1339	1539	1851	1939	2020
Aberystwyth a.	*0923*e	*1025*e	*1225*e	1305	*1420*y	*1620*e	*1930*e	*2015*e	2045
Aberystwyth d.	...	...	...	1400	...	...	...	...	...
Machynlleth d.	...	...	...	1436	...	...	...	...	...
Dolgellau d.	...	...	...	1510	...	...	...	...	...
Porthmadog d.	...	...	...	1611	...	...	...	...	...
Caernarfon Castle Square d.	...	...	...	1640	...	...	...	...	...
Bangor Clock a.	...	...	...	1705	...	...	...	...	...

D – Daily except Dec. 25, 26, Jan. 1.
e – Connecting service **550**.
h – Service **550**. Runs 10 minutes later on ⑥ and during school holidays.
y – Service **550**. Runs 5 minutes later on ⑥ and during school holidays.
▲ – Service **202** also calls at Carmarthen rail station.
Additional services Bangor - Caernarfon: see Table **544**.

Service **202** : Davies Bros, Pencader (☎ 01559 384209) / Service **550** : Crosville Cymru (☎ 01970 617951) and Richards Bros (☎ 01239 613756) / Service **701** : Crosville Cymru.

Table 537 AIRPORT LINKS

LUTON ✈ 🚌 connection every 10 – 30 minutes throughout the day to/from **Luton Station**.
InterCity express trains to/from **London** St. Pancras, **Leicester**, **Nottingham**, **Derby** and **Sheffield** are shown in Table **560**.

STANSTED ✈ Rail service by STANSTED EXPRESS to/from Tottenham Hale and **London**. Journey time to/from London is 41 minutes.
From London Liverpool Street : 0530Ⓐ, 0600Ⓐ, 0630⚒, 0700 and half-hourly to 2100, 2200, 2300. **From Stansted ✈** : 0600Ⓐ, 0630Ⓐ, 0700⚒, 0730 and half-hourly to 2200, 2300.

LONDON CITY ✈ Frequent 🚌 service London Liverpool Street - London City Airport ✈ and v.v. Operating hours are designed to coincide with flight times.
For details call the Airport Information Desk: ☎ (0171) 474 5555. Journey time is 25 minutes.
Docklands Light Railway trains run from Bank and Tower Gateway to Canary Wharf and v.v. on Ⓐ. A courtesy shuttle bus is operated between Canary Wharf and the airport.

GATWICK ✈ Daily rail service by non-stop GATWICK EXPRESS. Journey time 30 minutes (35 minutes on ⑦). Night services are less frequent and take 45 minutes.
From **London Victoria**: every 15 minutes 0430 – 2100 then 2130, 2200, 2230, 2300. From **Gatwick Airport ✈**: every 15 minutes 0520 – 2150 then 2220, 2250, 2320, 2350.
Additional night services: from **London Victoria** : 0015, 0100, 0200, 0300, 0400, 2321 ⚒, 2330 ⑦, 2359 ⚒. From **Gatwick Airport ✈**: 0010, 0105, 0205, 0305, 0405, 0505.
For other services London / Gatwick ✈ / south coast towns and v.v., see Tables **505, 507, 508, 509**; to/from Reading, Table **523**; to/from the Midlands and the North, Table **520**.

HEATHROW ✈ London Underground (PICCADILLY LINE) service: Kings Cross and Central London to Heathrow ✈ Terminals 1, 2 and 3 / Terminal 4 (separate stations) and v.v.
Frequent service (every 4 –10 mins) 0530 – 2300 ⚒, 0730 – 2330 ⑦, from **Kings Cross** and **Heathrow ✈**. Journey time to/from Central London is 50–58 minutes.

🚌 service Heathrow ✈ to/from Reading. Services call at Terminals 1, 2, 3 and 4 from Reading, and start from Terminal 4, then 3, 2 and 1 from Heathrow. Times shown below are those for Reading Station and Heathrow Terminal 4. Journey times vary between 45 and 70 minutes depending on Terminal. Allow at least 15 minutes for transfer between 🚌 and train at Reading.

From Reading :
Ⓐ 0530, 0600 and half-hourly to 0800, 0845, 0915 and half-hourly to 2045, then 2145.
Ⓒ 0545, 0615 and half-hourly to 2045, then 2145.

From Heathrow ✈ :
Ⓐ 0635, 0710, 0750, 0820 and half-hourly to 2150, then 2250.
Ⓒ 0650, 0720 and half-hourly to 2150, then 2250.

🚌 service Heathrow ✈ to/from Woking. Services call at Terminals 1, 2, 3 and 4 from Woking, and start from Terminal 4, then 3, 2 and 1 from Heathrow. Times shown below are those for Woking Station (use exit on Platform 4) and Heathrow Terminal 4. Journey times vary between 30 and 60 minutes depending on Terminal.
From Woking: 0610, 0650, 0720 and half-hourly to 1900, 2000, 2100, 2200. **From Heathrow ✈** : 0610, 0650, 0720, 0800, 0830 and half-hourly to 2000, 2100, 2200, 2300.

🚌 service Heathrow ✈ to/from Watford Junction. Services run from Stansted ✈ (🚌 724) and from Stevenage and Luton ✈ (🚌 747) to Heathrow Central Bus Station.
🚌 747 continues to Terminal 4 and then to Gatwick ✈. For full details see Table **533**.

302 *For an explanation of standard symbols see page 4* 04

Table 540 LONDON - BIRMINGHAM - WOLVERHAMPTON

1, 2 class

km		Ⓐ	Ⓐ	Ⓐ	Ⓐ		Ⓐ	Ⓐ	Ⓐ	Ⓐ	Ⓐ	Ⓐ	Ⓐ	Ⓐ	Ⓐ		Ⓐ	Ⓐ	Ⓐ	Ⓐ	Ⓐ	Ⓐ
0	**London Euston** d.		...	...	0534	...	0635	...	0715	0654	0745	0754	0815	0845	0854	▲	1354	1415	1445	1454	1515	1545
28	Watford Junction d.		...	...	0554	...	0652u	...	|	0711	0802u	0811	0832u	|	0911	and at	1411	1432u	1502u	1511	1532u	|
80	Milton Keynes Central d.		...	...	0637	...	0716	...	0752	0747	|	0847	|	0922	0947	the	1447	|	|	1547	|	1622u
106	**Northampton** a.		...	...	0656	...	|	...	|	0806	|	0906	|	|	1006	same	1506	|	|	1606	|	|
106	**Northampton** d.		0540	0614	0658	...	|	0733	|	0811	|	0912	|	|	1013	minutes	1513	|	|	1613	|	|
133	Rugby d.		0602	0636	0720	...	0744	0755	|	0833	|	0934	|	|	1034	past	1534	|	|	1634	|	|
151	**Coventry** d.		0613	0647	0734	...	0757	0808	0827	0846	0857	0946	0927	0957	1046	each	1546	1527	1557	1646	1627	1657
168	Birmingham International ✈ d.		0624	0657	0744	...	0809	0824	0839	0856	0926	0956	0939	1009	1056	hour	1556	1539	1609	1656	1639	1709
182	**Birmingham New Street** d.		...	0709	0759	...	0826	0842	0857	0913	0950	1013	0957	1026	1113	until	1613	1557	1626	1709	1657	1726
202	**Wolverhampton** a.		...	...	...	...	0850	...	...	...	...	...	...	1050	...		...	...	1650	...	...	1750

	Ⓐ	Ⓐ	Ⓐ	Ⓐ	Ⓐ	Ⓐ	Ⓐ	Ⓐ	Ⓐ	Ⓐ	Ⓐ	Ⓐ	Ⓐ	Ⓐ		Ⓐ	Ⓐ		Ⓐ	Ⓐ		Ⓐ	Ⓐ	Ⓐ
London Euston d.	1554	1615	1635	1655	1715	1650	1745	1750	1815	1845	1850	1915	1945	1954	...	2045	2054	...	2145	2154	...	2254	2310	2354
Watford Junction d.	1611	1632u	|	|	|	1707	1802u	1806	1832u	|	1907	1932u	|	2011	...	2102	2111	...	|	2211	...	2311	|	0011
Milton Keynes Central d.	1647	|	1713u	|	1752u	1744	|	1835	|	|	1945	|	2022	2047	...	2126	2147	...	2222	2248	...	2348	2351	0050
Northampton a.	1706	|	|	|	|	1801	|	1854	|	|	2002	|	|	2106	...	|	2206	...	|	2309	...	0009	|	0111
Northampton d.	1710	|	|	|	|	1817	|	1900	|	|	2013	|	|	2113	...	|	2213	...	|	2315	...	0015	|	...
Rugby d.	1732	|	|	|	|	1741	|	1922	|	1946	2035	2020	2050	2135	...	2154	2235	...	2300	2336	...	0036	0035	...
Coventry d.	1743	1727	1747	1803	1827	1852	1857	1946	1927	1958	2046	2032	2102	2146	...	2206	2246	...	2312	...	...	...	0047	...
Birmingham International ✈ d.	1755	1739	1800	1816	1839	1902	1909	1956	1939	2009	2056	2044	2114	2156	...	2218	2256	...	2323	...	...	...	0058	...
Birmingham New Street d.	1809	1757	1816	1837b	1857	1914	1926	2013	1959	2026	2113	2108c	2131	2213	...	2239	2312	...	2341	...	...	...	0119	...
Wolverhampton a.	...	...	1841	1900	1920	...	1950	...	2022	2050	...	2131	...	...	...	2258	...	...	0005	...	...	...	0139	...

	⑥	⑥	⑥	⑥	⑥	⑥	⑥		⑥	⑥	⑥	⑥	⑥	⑥	⑥	⑥	⑥	⑥	⑥	⑥	⑥	⑥
London Euston d.		...	...	0534	0705	0654	0735	■	1535	1605	1554	1635	1705	1654	1735	1754	1835	1854	1935	1954	2035	2054
Watford Junction d.		...	...	0554	0722u	0711	|	and at	|	1622u	1611	1652u	|	1711	|	1811	|	1911	|	2011	2052u	2111
Milton Keynes Central d.		...	...	0637	|	0747	0812	the	1612	|	1647	|	1742	1747	1812	1847	|	1947	2012	2047	2116	2151
Northampton a.		...	...	0700	|	0810	|	same	|	|	1710	|	|	1810	|	1910	|	2010	|	2110	|	2214
Northampton d.		0540	0613	0713	|	0813	|	minutes	|	|	1713	|	|	1813	|	1913	|	2013	|	2113	|	2217
Rugby d.		0602	0635	0735	|	0835	|	past	|	|	1735	|	|	1835	|	1935	1946	2035	2050	2135	2204	2239
Coventry d.		0613	0646	0746	0827	0846	0857	each	1657	1727	1746	1757	1827	1846	1857	1946	1958	2046	2102	2146	2216	2250
Birmingham International ✈ d.		0625	0656	0801	0839	0856	0909	hour	1709	1739	1756	1809	1839	1856	1909	1956	2009	2056	2114	2156	2227	2300f
Birmingham New Street d.		0643	0711	0814	0857	0913	0926	until	1726	1757	1813	1826	1857	1913	1926	2013	2026	2113	2131	2213	2245	2312f
Wolverhampton a.		...	...	...	...	...	0950		1750	...	...	...	1918	...	1950	...	2050	...	2154	...	2309	...

	⑥g	⑥f	⑥	⑥	⑥g	⑥f	⑥g	⑥f	⑦	⑦	⑦	⑦	⑦	⑦	⑦	⑦	⑦	⑦	⑦	⑦	⑦	⑦	⑦
London Euston d.	2135	2135	2154	2254	2300	2300	2354	2354		0654	0745	0754	0845	0854	0945	0954	1045	1054	1145	1154	1245	1254	1345
Watford Junction d.	2152u	2152u	2211	2311	|	|	0011	0011		0717	1902u	0814	|	0914	|	1014	1102u	1114	1202u	1214	|	1314	1402u
Milton Keynes Central d.	2216	2216	2251	2351	2345	2345	0049	0049		0759	0846	0857	|	0957	|	1057	1146	1157	|	1257	1342	1357	1446
Northampton a.	|	|	2314	0010	|	|	0108	0147r		0852r	|	0951r	|	1051r	|	1151r	|	1251r	|	1351r	|	1451r	|
Northampton d.	|	|	2317	...	|	|	...	|		|	0916	|	|	|	|	|	|	|	|	|	|	|	|
Rugby d.	2304	2304	2338	...	0029	0029	...	0128b		0833b	0931	0932b	1012	1032b	1112	1132b	|	1232b	|	1332b	1412	1432b	|
Coventry d.	2317	2317	...	...	0041	0041	...	...		...	0943	...	1027	...	1127	...	1227	...	1322	...	1427	...	1527
Birmingham International ✈ d.	2327	2327	...	...	0052	0052	...	...		...	1012h	...	1039	...	1139	...	1239	...	1334	...	1439	...	1539
Birmingham New Street d.	2344	2350	...	...	0108	0115b	...	...		...	...	...	1101b	...	1203k	...	1301b	...	1353b	...	1501b	...	1556
Wolverhampton a.	0005	0019	...	...	0140	0145	...	...		...	...	...	1131	...	1231	...	1331	...	1422	...	1531	...	1619

	⑦	⑦	⑦	⑦	⑦	⑦	⑦	⑦	⑦	⑦	⑦	⑦	⑦	⑦	⑦	⑦	⑦	⑦	⑦	⑦	⑦	⑦	⑦	⑦
London Euston d.	1354	1445	...	1454	1545	1554	1645	1654	1745	1754	1845	1854	1945	2015	1954	2045	2054	2115	2145	2154	2245	2254	2324	2345
Watford Junction d.	1414	1502u	...	1514	|	1614	1702u	1714	|	1814	1902u	1914	|	|	2014	2102u	2114	2132u	|	2214	|	2314	2348	|
Milton Keynes Central d.	1457	|	...	1557	1629	1657	|	1750	|	1850	|	1950	2024	|	2050	|	2150	2159	2222	2250	|	2350	0027	0022
Northampton a.	1551r	|	...	1651r	|	1720	|	1813	|	1913	|	2013	|	|	2113	|	2213	|	|	2313	|	0013	0050	|
Northampton d.	|	|	1618	|	|	1721	|	1814	|	1914	|	2014	|	|	2114	|	2214	|	|	2314	|	0014	...	|
Rugby d.	1532b	1612	1640	1632b	1659	1743	|	1835	|	1936	|	2036	|	2116	2136	2157	2236	2237	|	2335	2353	0035	...	0057
Coventry d.	...	1627	1651	...	1714	1754	1807	1847	1907	1947	2007	2047	2109	2139	2147	2212	2247	2251	2307	...	0008	...	...	0112
Birmingham International ✈ d.	...	1639	1701	...	1926	1804	1819	1857	1919	1957	2019	2057	2121	2151	2157	2224	2257	2303	2319	...	0020	...	...	0124
Birmingham New Street d.	...	1657	1713	...	1744	1816	1839	1909	1937	2009	2037	2109	2139	2208	2209	2242	2309	2320	2337	...	0038	...	...	0142
Wolverhampton a.	...	1720	...	...	1807	...	1902	...	2000	...	2100	...	2202	2231	...	2305	...	2343	2359	...	0101	...	...	0205

	Ⓐ	Ⓐj	Ⓐ	Ⓐ	Ⓐ	Ⓐ	Ⓐ	Ⓐ	Ⓐ	Ⓐ	Ⓐ	Ⓐ	Ⓐ	Ⓐ	Ⓐ	Ⓐ	Ⓐ	Ⓐ	Ⓐ	Ⓐ		Ⓐ
Wolverhampton d.		...	...	...	0519	0549	0619	...	0649	...	...	0719	0749	...	0819	...	...	0919	...	...	❖	1419
Birmingham New Street d.		0015	...	...	0545e	0615e	0645e	...	0715	0718	0733	0745e	0815e	0818	0845a	0915	0936	0945	1015	1036	and at	1445a
Birmingham International ✈ d.		0025	...	...	0556	0626	0656	...	0726	0734	0744	0756	0826	0834	0856	0926	0946	0956	1026	1046	the	1456
Coventry d.		0037	...	...	0607	0637	0707	0726	0737	0759n	|	0807	0837	0851	0907	0937	0956	1007	1037	1058	same	1507
Rugby d.		0048	0422	0540	0619	0649	0719	0737	0751	0811	|	|	0851	0909	|	|	1007	|	|	1112	minutes	|
Northampton a.		0108	0441	0601	|	|	|	0759	|	0832	|	|	|	0930	|	|	1031	|	|	1133	past	|
Northampton d.		0114	0444	0608	|	|	|	0808	|	0838	|	|	|	0938	|	|	1038	|	|	1138	each	|
Milton Keynes Central d.		0131	0501	0625	0644	|	|	0825	|	0855	|	0840	|	0955	0939	|	1055	1039	|	1155	hour	|
Watford Junction d.		0207	0543	0655	|	|	|	0857	|	0930	|	|	0941s	1030	|	1033s	1130	|	1133s	1230	until	1603s
London Euston a.		0233	0607	0716	0733	0758	0828	0916	0902	0950	0904	0928	1004	1051	1027	1057	1151	1127	1157	1251		1627

	Ⓐ	Ⓐ	Ⓐ	Ⓐ	Ⓐ	Ⓐ	Ⓐ	Ⓐ	Ⓐ	Ⓐ	Ⓐ	Ⓐ	Ⓐ	Ⓐ	Ⓐ	Ⓐ	⑥	⑥	⑥	⑥	⑥	⑥	⑥
Wolverhampton d.	...	...	...	1619	...	...	1719	...	...	1849	...	1949	...	2049	...	...		...	...	0519	...	...	0619
Birmingham New Street d.	1515	1536	1633	1645e	1715	1733	1745e	1815	1836	1915p	1936	2015	2036	2115e	2136	2250		0015	...	0545e	...	...	0645e
Birmingham International ✈ d.	1526	1546	1649	1656	1726	1749	1756	1826	1846	1926	1946	2026	2046	2126	2146	2300		0025	...	0556	...	...	0656
Coventry d.	1537	1558	1701	1707	1737	1759	1807	1937	1858	1937	1958	2037	2058	2137	2158	2312		0037	...	0607	...	...	0707
Rugby d.	|	1612	1715	|	1749	1811	|	|	1912	|	2012	2049	2112	2149	2212	2323		0048	0516	0619	0616	0646	0719
Northampton a.	|	1633	1737	|	|	1834	|	|	1933	|	2034	|	2133	|	2233	2345		0107	0537	|	0637	0707	|
Northampton d.	|	1638	1738	|	|	1838	|	|	1938	|	2038	|	2138	|	2238	2348		0114	0538	|	0638	0708	|
Milton Keynes Central d.	|	1655	1755	1739	|	1855	1841	1910	1955	2011	2055	|	2155	2215	2255	0005		0131	0555	0644	0655	0725	|
Watford Junction d.	1636s	1730	1830	|	|	1930	|	1937s	2030	|	2130	2138s	2230	2242s	2331	0041		0207	0630	|	0730	0757	|
London Euston a.	1659	1751	1851	1827	1902	1951	1929	2001	2051	2059	2151	2202	2252	2316	2356	0114		0237	0653	0743	0753	0820	0838

	⑥	⑥	⑥	⑥	⑥	⑥	⑥	⑥	⑥		⑥	⑥	⑥	⑥	⑥	⑥	⑥	⑥	⑥	⑥	⑥	⑥	⑥
Wolverhampton d.	...	...	0649	...	0719	0749	...	0819	...		...	...	1619	...	...	1719	...	...	...	1849	...	1949	...
Birmingham New Street d.	...	0712	0715	0736	0745e	0815e	0836	0845e	0915	and at	1615	1636	1645e	1715	1736	1745e	1815	1836	1845	1915p	1936	2015	2036
Birmingham International ✈ d.	...	0722	0726	0746	0756	0826	0846	0856	0926	the	1626	1646	1656	1726	1746	1756	1826	1846	1856	1926	1946	2026	2046
Coventry d.	...	0734	0737	0756	0807	0837	0856	0907	0937	same	1637	1656	1707	1737	1758	1807	1837	1858	1907	1937	1958	2037	2058
Rugby d.	0716	0745	0751	0814	|	0851	0909	|	|	minutes	|	1709	|	1749	1809	|	|	1913	|	|	2012	2049	2109
Northampton a.	0737	0807	|	0835	|	|	0931	|	|	past	|	1731	|	|	1831	|	|	1934	|	|	2033	|	2131
Northampton d.	0738	0808	|	0838	|	|	0938	|	|	each	|	1738	|	|	1838	|	|	1938	|	|	2038	|	2138
Milton Keynes Central d.	0755	0825	|	0855	0840	|	0955	0939	|	hour	|	1755	1739	|	1855	1841	1910	1955	1939	2009	2055	|	2155
Watford Junction d.	0830	0857	|	0930	|	0941s	1030	|	1033s	until	1733s	1830	|	1838	1930	|	1937s	2030	|	|	2130	2148s	2230
London Euston a.	0853	0920	0910	0953	0938	1014	1053	1037	1107		1807	1853	1837	1912	1953	1939	2011	2053	2037	2107	2157	2222	2257

b – Arrive 5 minutes earlier.
c – Arrive 2101.
e – Arrive 6 minutes earlier.
f – Not May 27.
g – May 27 only.
h – Arrive 1000.
j – Not Jan. 9.
k – Arrive 1153.
n – Arrive 0751.
p – Arrive 1908.
r – Via Rugby.
s – Stops to pick up only.
u – Stops to set down only.
■ – Departure from London at 1205 calls at Milton Keynes (d. 1242), does not call at Watford Junction.
▲ – Departures from London at 0845, 0945, 1045 and 1345 call at Milton Keynes; those at 1145, 1245 and 1445 call at Watford Junction (to pick up only).
❖ – Departures from Wolverhampton at 0819, 0919, 1119 and 1319 call at Milton Keynes; those at 1019, 1219 and 1419 call at Watford Junction (to set down only).

01 For an explanation of standard symbols see page 4 303

Table 540 — WOLVERHAMPTON - BIRMINGHAM - LONDON

1, 2 class

	⑥	⑥	⑥	⑥		⑦	⑦	⑦	⑦	⑦	⑦	⑦	⑦	⑦	⑦	⑦	⑦	⑦	⑦	⑦	⑦
Wolverhampton d.	2049	...	2149	...		...	0712	...	0812	...	...	0912	...	1012	...	1112	...	1212	...	1312	...
Birmingham New Street d.	2115e	2136	2215e	2250		0015	...	0742	...	0845	...	0943	...	1045	...	1145	...	1243	...	1345	...
Birmingham International ✦ d.	2126	2146	2226	2300		0024	...	0755	...	0856	...	0956	...	1058	...	1155	...	1256	...	1358	...
Coventry d.	2137	2158	2237	2312		0034	...	0806	...	0907	...	1007	...	1109	...	1207	...	1307	...	1409	...
Rugby d.	2149	2209	2249	2323		0049	0624b	0724b	0818	0824b	0918	0924b	0954b	1018	1024b		1124b	1218	1224b	1318	1324b		1424b
Northampton a.		2231		2345		0110															
Northampton d.		2238		2346		0115	0600r	0700r		0800r		0900r	0930r		1000r		1100r		1200r		1300r		1400r
Milton Keynes Central d.	2214	2255	2315s	0003		0207	0655	0755	0848	0855	0948	0955	1025	1048	1055	1144	1155		1255	1348	1355	1444	1455
Watford Junction d.	2252s	2331	2359s	0039		0243	0737	0837	0933s	0937	1033s	1037	1107	1133s	1137	1229s	1237	1329s	1337		1437	1529s	1537
London Euston a.	2326	0001	0030	0105		0305	0757	0857	0959	0957	1058	1057	1127	1158	1157	1254	1257	1354	1357	1454	1457	1554	1557

	⑦	⑦	⑦	⑦		⑦	⑦	⑦	⑦	⑦	⑦	⑦	⑦	⑦	⑦	⑦	⑦	⑦	⑦	⑦	⑦
Wolverhampton d.	1412	...	...	1530	...	1619	...	1719	...	...	1819	...	...	1919	...	...	2019	...	...	2149	...	...
Birmingham New Street d.	1445	...	...	1600	1635	1645	...	1745	1735	...	1845	1835	...	1945	1935	...	2035	2045	...	2135	...	2215	2250
Birmingham International ✦ d.	1456	...	...	1612	1644	1656	...	1756	1744	...	1856	1844	...	1956	1944	...	2044	2056	...	2144	...	2226	2259
Coventry d.	1507	...	...	1623	1654	1717	...	1807	1754	...	1907	1854	...	2007	1954	...	2054	2107	...	2154	...	2237	2309
Rugby d.	1519	1524b	1609	1635	1710		...	1819	1810	...	1919	1910	...	2019	2010	...	2110		...	2210	...	2249	2323
Northampton a.			1630		1731		...		1831			1931			2031			2131		2231	...		2345
Northampton d.			1500r	1638		1738	...		1838			1938			2038			2138		2238	...		2346
Milton Keynes Central d.	1555	1655	1700	1755			...	1844	1855		1944	1955		2044	2055		2155		...	2255	...	2314	0003
Watford Junction d.	1629s	1637	1730		1830	1813s	...	1910s	1930		2013s	2030		2113s	2130		2230	2209	...	2337	...	2343s	0039
London Euston a.	1655	1657	1753	1758	1853	1845	...	1946	1953		2046	2053		2146	2153		2253	2241	...	0001	...	0016	0105

b – From Northampton. Arrive 5 minutes earlier. r – Via Rugby.
e – Arrive 6 minutes earlier. s – Stops to set down only.

For other trains London–Birmingham–Wolverhampton and beyond and v.v., see Table 550.

Table 541 — BIRMINGHAM - SHREWSBURY - CHESTER

2 class only

km		✕		✕	✕		✕	✕	✕	✕	✕	✕	✕	✕	✕	⑦	✕	⑦	✕	✕	✕
					Y			C						Y	Y			Y	Y		
0	Birmingham New Street 540 d.	...	0620	...	...	0817	...	0917	1006	1017	1037	1117	1217	1237	...	1313r	1337	1417	1437	...	...
20	Wolverhampton 540 d.	...	0638	0648	...	0754	0838	0917	0938	1027	1038	1058	1138	1238	1300	...	1317	1343	1358	1438	1458	1500	1517
45	Telford Central d.	...	0655	0714	...	0820	0855	0943	0955	...	1055	1115	1155	1255	1317	...	1343	1400	1415	1455	1515	1526	1543
68	Shrewsbury d.	0600	0715	0740	...	0843	0916	1010	1015	...	1115	1135	1216	1315	1337	1400	1405	1432	1435	1515	1515	1550	1600
77	Gobowen d.	0619	...	0759	...	0904	...	1029	...	...		...	1237	...	1421	1425	...	...	...	...	1610	1625
88	Ruabon d.	0630	...	0810	...	0916	...	1040	...	...		...	1249	...	1433	1436	...	...	...	...	1621	1635
97	Wrexham General d.	0637	...	0817	...	0923	...	1047	...	...		...	1256	...	1440	1442	...	...	...	...	1637	1642
116	Chester a.	0655	...	0835	...	0945	...	1105	...	1146		...	1318	...	1459	1501	...	...	...	...	1656	1701

	⑦	✕	✕	⑦	✕	✕	⑦	✕		✕	✕	⑦		✕	✕	⑥	✕	⑦	✕	⑦	✕	✕
	Y				Y					Y					Y	C						C
Birmingham New Street 540 d.	...	1537	1617	1645	...	1717	1748	...	1806	...	1845	1917	...	...	1945	2017	2045	2057	...	2150	2150	2210	2300
Wolverhampton 540 d.	1545	1600	1638	1702	1719	1738	1807	...	1827	...	1903	1938	...	2003	2043	2102	2116	2135	...	2207	2207	2229	2318
Telford Central d.	1602	1626	1655	1728	1745	1755	1824	...	1853	...	1929	1955	...	2020	2100	2128	...	2201	...	2224	2224		2344
Shrewsbury d.	1621	1648	1715	1751	1809	1816	1845	1900	1915	1948	1951	2015	...	2055	2040	2123	2150	...	2227	...	2244	2244		0013
Gobowen d.	...	1708	...	...	1824	...	1906	1919	...		...		...	2114	...	...	2246	...	...			
Ruabon d.	...	1719	...	...	1840	...	1918	1930	...		...		...	2125	...	...		...	...			
Wrexham General d.	...	1731	...	...	1847	...	1925	1944	...		...	2110	2132	...	...	...		...	2237	...		
Chester a.	...	1750	...	...	1905	...	1942	2002	...	2044	...	2128	2150	...	...	...	2225	...	2255	...	2335		

	✕p	✕		⑥	Ⓐ	✕	✕	⑦	✕		✕	✕	⑦		✕		✕	⑦	✕	✕	⑦	✕
	C					Y			Y				P						Y			
Chester d.	0447	...	...	...	...	0710	...	...	0900	...	1000	...	...	1128	...	...	...	...	...	...	1328	...
Wrexham General d.		...	...	...	...	0727	...	...	0916	...	1016	...	...	1144	...	...	...	...	...	...	1344	...
Ruabon d.		...	...	...	...	0735	...	...	0923	...	1024	...	...	1151	...	...	...	...	...	...	1351	...
Gobowen d.		...	...	0630	0643	0747	...	...	0934	...	1037	...	...	1202	...	...	...	...	...	...	1402	...
Shrewsbury d.	...	0556	...	0652	0704	0715	0748	0809	0903	0922	0956	1024	1059	1124	1203	1224	1300	1303	1324	1403	1415	1424
Telford Central d.	...	0615	...	0710	0725	0735	0809	0827	0921	0942	1016	1042	1117	1142	1221	1244	1321	1321	1344	1421	1435	1444
Wolverhampton 540 a.	0605	0638	...	0730	0744	0806	0842	0846	0942	1003	1036	1103	1137	1203	1244	1304	1402	1346	1403	1444	1516	1504
Birmingham New Street 540 a.	0624	...	...	...	0812	...	...	0903	...	1000	1022	1054	1122	1200	1224	1305	1322	...	1405	1422	1505	1522

	⑦	✕		✕	✕		⑦	✕		⑦	✕		✕	⑦	✕	✕		✕	⑦	✕	⑦	✕	⑥
	Y	Y					Y	Y					C		Y	Y				Y			
Chester d.	...	...	...	1514	1523	...	...	1710	1714	...	1830	1814	...	...	1928	2002	2028	...	...	...	...	2205	2214
Wrexham General d.	...	...	...	1530	1539	...	...	1726	1730	...		1830	...	...	1944	2018	2044	...	...	...	...	2221	2230
Ruabon d.	...	...	...	1537	1547	...	...	1733	1737	...		1837	...	...	1951	2026	2051	...	...	...	...	2228	2237
Gobowen d.	...	...	...	1548	1600	...	...	1744	1748	...		1843	...	...	2002	2039	2102	...	...	...	...	2239	2248
Shrewsbury d.	1508	1524	...	1624h	1622	1705	1727	1736	1815	1816	1858		1910	1920	1926	2000	2023	2101	2122	2125	...	2300	2259	2308
Telford Central d.	1527	1542	...	1644	1643	1725	1746	1756	1837	1837	1918		1929	1939	1944	2021	2044	2120	...	2145	...	2320	...	...
Wolverhampton 540 a.	1559	1603	...	1704	1711	1746	1805	1826	1906	1905	1937	1940	1957	1958	2005	2049	2113	2139	...	2204	...	2348	...	...
Birmingham New Street 540 a.	1618	1623	...	...	1727	...	1821	1848	1924		2000	2004		2017	2024	2105	...	2155	...	2225	...	0004	...	...

C – 🚲 and ⚲ Birmingham International - Holyhead (via Crewe) and v.v.
P – To/from Pwllheli (Table 542).
Y – To/from Aberystwyth (Table 542).
h – Arrive 1609.
r – Jan. 1, 8 depart 1325.
p – Not May 27.

Table 542 SHREWSBURY - ABERYSTWYTH and PWLLHELI

2 class only

km		⚒	⚒	⚒	⚒	⚒		⚒	⑦	⚒	⚒	Ⓐ	⑦	⚒	⑥	⑦	⚒	⚒	⑦	⑦	⚒	⚒	⚒	⑦	⚒
	Birmingham New St **541** d.	...	...	...	...	...	...	0817	...	1017	...	...	...	1217	...	1313b	1417	...	...	...	1617	1806	...	1845	2017
	Wolverhampton **541** d.	...	...	...	...	...	...	0838	...	1038	...	...	...	1238	...	1343	1438	...	1545	...	1638	1827	...	1903	2043
0	**Shrewsbury** d.	...	...	...	...	...	...	0925	...	1123	...	...	...	1325	...	1439	1525	...	1629	...	1725	1925	...	2025	2131
32	Welshpool d.	...	...	...	...	...	...	0948	...	1147	...	...	...	1347	...	1501	1547	...	1654	...	1747	1947	...	2047	2154
54	Newtown d.	...	...	...	...	...	...	1004	...	1203	...	...	...	1403	...	1517	1603	...	1710	...	1803	2003	...	2103	2210
63	Caersws d.	...	...	...	...	...	...	1011	...	1210	...	...	...	1410	...	1524	1610	...	1716	...	1810	2010	...	2110	2217
98	Machynlleth d.	0530	0630	0641	0815	0906	...	1043	1210	1242	1250	1420	1431	1443	1458	1558	1643	1705	1748	1800	1843	2046	2105	2142	2249
104	Dovey Junction d.	0537	0637	0648	0822	0913	...	1050	|	1249	1257	1427	|	1450	1505	|	1650	1712	|	|	1850	2053	2112	|	2256
118	Borth d.	|	0647	|	0832	|	...	1101	1228	1259	|	|	1449	1500	|	1616	1700	|	1806	|	1900	2103	|	2159	2307
131	**Aberystwyth** a.	|	0659	|	0844	|	...	1112	1239	1311	|	|	1500	1512	|	1627	1712	|	1817	|	1912	2115	|	2211	2318
114	Aberdovey d.	0549	...	0700	...	0925	...	...	...	...	1309	1439	...	...	1517	...	...	1724	...	1819	...	...	2124	...	...
120	Tywyn d.	0555	...	0708	...	0933	...	...	...	...	1315	1454	...	...	1523	...	...	1730	...	1825	...	...	2130	...	...
135	Fairbourne d.	0612	...	0725	...	0950	...	...	...	...	1332	1511	...	...	1540	...	...	1748	...	1842	...	...	2147	...	...
139	**Barmouth** a.	0622	...	0735	...	1000	...	...	...	...	1342	1520	...	...	1550	...	...	1757	...	1852	...	...	2157	...	...
139	**Barmouth** d.	...	...	0819	...	1014	...	...	...	...	1342	1521	...	...	1602	...	...	1759	...	1853	...	...	2158	...	...
156	Harlech d.	...	...	0843	...	1036	...	...	...	...	1404	1539	...	...	1623	...	...	1820	...	1914	...	...	2219	...	...
165	Penrhyndeudraeth d.	...	...	0852	...	1046	...	...	...	...	1414	1550	...	...	1633	...	...	1830	...	1925	...	...	2229	...	...
167	Minffordd d.	...	...	0856	...	1049	...	...	...	...	1418	1553	...	...	1636	...	...	1833	...	1929	...	...	2232	...	...
170	Porthmadog d.	...	...	0901	...	1055	...	...	...	...	1423	1559	...	...	1642	...	...	1839	...	1934	...	...	2238	...	...
178	Criccieth d.	...	...	0909	...	1103	...	...	...	...	1431	1607	...	...	1650	...	...	1847	...	1942	...	...	2246	...	...
185	Butlins Penychain (**x**) d.	...	...	0916	...	1109	...	...	...	...	1438	1613	...	...	1656	...	...	1853	...	1949	...	...	2252	...	...
191	**Pwllheli** a.	...	...	0922	...	1117	...	...	...	...	1445	1620	...	...	1703	...	...	1900	...	1956	...	...	2301	...	...

	⚒	⚒	⚒	⚒	⚒	⚒	⚒	⚒	⑦	⚒	⚒	⑦	⑦	⚒	⚒	⑦	⚒	Ⓐ	⑦	⑥	⚒	⚒	⚒	⑦	⚒
Pwllheli d.	...	...	...	0648	...	0758	0952	...	...	1143	...	1353	...	...	1456	...	...	1650	...	1737	...	1910	...	...	...
Butlins Penychain (**x**) d.	...	...	...	0655	...	0806	1000	...	...	1150	...	1401	...	...	1503	...	...	1657	...	1744	...	1917	...	...	...
Criccieth d.	...	...	...	0702	...	0813	1007	...	...	1157	...	1408	...	...	1510	...	...	1704	...	1751	...	1924	...	...	...
Porthmadog d.	...	...	...	0712	...	0822	1016	...	...	1207	...	1417	...	...	1520	...	...	1713	...	1801	...	1934	...	...	...
Minffordd d.	...	...	...	0716	...	0826	1020	...	...	1211	...	1421	...	...	1524	...	...	1717	...	1805	...	1938	...	...	...
Penrhyndeudraeth d.	...	...	...	0719	...	0830	1023	...	...	1214	...	1425	...	...	1527	...	...	1721	...	1808	...	1941	...	...	...
Harlech d.	...	...	...	0730	...	0842	1037	...	...	1225	...	1437	...	...	1538	...	...	1731	...	1822	...	1951	...	...	...
Barmouth a.	...	...	...	0752	...	0903	1058	...	...	1247	...	1458	...	...	1600	...	...	1753	...	1844	...	2008	...	...	...
Barmouth d.	...	0642	...	0754	...	0905	1100	...	...	1248	...	1500	...	...	1602	...	...	1800	...	1853	...	2010	...	...	...
Fairbourne d.	...	0650	...	0802	...	0913	1108	...	...	1256	...	1508	...	...	1610	...	...	1808	...	1901	...	2018	...	...	...
Tywyn d.	...	0707	...	0820	...	0932	1126	...	...	1316	...	1525	...	...	1627	...	...	1826	...	1921	...	2034	...	...	...
Aberdovey d.	...	0713	...	0826	...	0938	1132	...	...	1322	...	1531	...	...	1633	...	...	1832	...	1927	...	2040	...	...	...
Aberystwyth d.	0524	|	0706	|	0931	|	|	1130	1251	|	1331	|	1526	1531	|	1713	1731	|	1835	|	1931	|	2135	2230	2335
Borth d.	0536	|	0718	|	0943	|	|	1142	1304	|	1343	|	1539	1543	|	1725	1743	|	1848	|	1943	|	2147	2243	2347
Dovey Junction d.	0547	0726	0729	0838	0954	0950	1144	1153	|	1335	1354	1544	|	1554	1651	|	1754	1850	|	1940	1954	2052	2158	|	2358
Machynlleth d.	0555	0732	0737	0845	1001	1002	1151	1201	1323	1341	1402	1550	1558	1602	1657	1748	1802	1856	1905	1948	2005	2058	2205	2300	0005
Caersws d.	0623	...	0805	...	...	1031	...	1229	1351	...	1430	...	1626	1630	...	1817	1830	...	...	...	2033	...	...	...	...
Newtown d.	0630	...	0812	...	...	1038	...	1236	1358	...	1437	...	1633	1637	...	1824	1837	...	...	...	2040	...	...	...	...
Welshpool d.	0646	...	0828	...	...	1054	...	1252	1414	...	1453	...	1649	1653	...	1840	1853	...	...	...	2056	...	...	...	...
Shrewsbury a.	0710	...	0852	...	...	1118	...	1318	1440	...	1519	...	1711	1719	...	1906	1919	...	...	...	2121	...	...	...	...
Wolverhampton **541** a.	0806	...	0942	...	...	1203	...	1403	1559	...	1603	...	1805	1826	...	1958	2005	...	...	...	2204	...	...	...	...
Birmingham New St **541** a.	...	...	1000	...	...	1224	...	1422	1618	...	1623	...	1821	1848	...	2017	2024	...	...	...	2225	...	...	...	...

b – Depart 1325 on Jan. 1, 8.

x – Trains stop on request.

Table 543 WREXHAM - RUABON - BALA - BARMOUTH

km		⚒	⚒	⑦	⚒	⚒	⑦	⑦	⚒	⚒	⚒
0	**Wrexham King Street** d.	...	0905	1015	1115	1405	1545	1700	1705	1820	2100
8	Ruabon Station Approach d.	...	0915	1025	1125	1415	1555	1710	1715	1830	2110
18	**Llangollen Market Street** d.	...	0930	1040	1140	1430	1610	1725	1725	1845	2125
35	Corwen d.	0745	0950	1100	1200	1450	1630	1745	1750	1905	2145
53	**Bala** d.	0820	1025	1120	1235	1525	1650	1820	1825	1940	2220
62	Llanuwchllyn d.	0830	1035	1130	1245	1535	1700	1830	1835	1950	2230
82	Dolgellau d.	0855	1105	1200	1315	1615	1735	1900	1905	2015	2255
98	**Barmouth** a.	...	1122	1222	1337	1637	1757	1922	1927	2037	...

	⚒	⚒	⚒	⑦	⚒	⑦	⚒	⚒	⑦	⚒
Barmouth d.	0620	0830	1035	1135	1235	1305	1545	1830	1830	*1930*
Dolgellau d.	0645	0905	1105	1205	1305	1335	1615	1900	1905	2000
Llanuwchllyn d.	0710	0930	1130	1230	1330	1400	1645	1925	1930	2025
Bala d.	0720	0940	1140	1240	1340	1410	1655	1935	1940	2035
Corwen d.	0755	1015	1215	1315	1415	1430	1730	2010	2000	2110
Llangollen Market Street d.	0815	1035	1235	1335	1435	1450	1750	2030	2020	...
Ruabon Station Approach d.	0830	1048	1248	1350	1448	1505	1806	2045	2035	...
Wrexham King Street a.	0845	1100	1300	1400	1500	1515	1815	2055	2045	...

Service **94** - operated by Crosville Cymru (☎ 01492 596969). Additional journeys (approximately 10 per day on ⚒, 6 per day on ⑦) are operated between Wrexham and Llangollen (Service **1**).

Table 544 CAERNARFON – BANGOR, LLANBERIS, and PORTHMADOG

CAERNARFON - BANGOR and v.v. — **Crosville Cymru** services **5** / **5A** — Journey time: 25 - 30 minutes

From Caernarfon: ⚒ : 0600, 0630, 0700, 0730, 0805, 0820, 0830, 0845, and at 00, 05, 15, 30, 35, and 45 mins. past each hour from 0900 to 1745, then 1815 and half-hourly to 2215.
⑦**p** : 0810, 1000, 1100 and hourly to 1900, then 1930, and half-hourly to 2200.

From Bangor Clock: ⚒ : 0630, 0700, 0730, 0745, 0800, 0820, 0830, 0855 and at 00, 15, 25, 30, 45, and 55 mins. past each hour from 0900 to 1755, then 1825, 1845 and half-hourly to 2315. Also at 1110**X**, 1430**X**, 1735**X**.
⑦**p** : 0855, 1130, 1230 and hourly to 1930, then 2000, and half-hourly to 2230.

CAERNARFON - LLANBERIS and v.v. — **KMP** service **88** — Journey time: 25 minutes

From Caernarfon: ⚒ : 0725**A**, 0805**A**, 0810**H**, 0835**A**, 0850**H**, 0905, 0935 and half-hourly to 1635, then 1650**A**, 1705**H**, 1710**A**, 1735, 1840, 1920, 2100, 2210, 2310⑤⑥.
⑦**p** : 1000, 1100 and hourly to 1800, then 1920, 2100, 2210.

From Llanberis: ⚒ : 0655**A**, 0710, 0730**A**, 0740**H**, 0800**A**, 0810**H**, 0830, 0900 and half-hourly to 1730, then 1810, 1850, 2020, 2140, 2245⑤⑥.
⑦**p** : 0930, 1030 and hourly to 1730, then 1850, 2020, 2140.

CAERNARFON - PORTHMADOG and v.v. — **Express Motors** service **1** / **Crosville Cymru** service **2** — Journey time: 43 - 55 minutes

From Caernarfon: ⚒ : 0700, 0705, 0725, 0745, 0900, 0925, 0950, 1050, 1115, 1120, 1150, 1250, 1345, 1425, 1450, 1550, 1635, 1650, 1735, 1805, 1835, 1945, 2115.
⑦**p** : 1140, 1710.

From Porthmadog Parc: ⚒ : 0745, 0755, 0900, 1000, 1007, 1100, 1200, 1207, 1300, 1330, 1400, 1407, 1520, 1600, 1700, 1707, 1800, 1857, 1945, 1947, 2047, 2117, 2207.
⑦**p** : 1305, 1825.

CAERNARFON - PWLLHELI and v.v. — **Clynnog & Trefor** service **12** / **Berwyn** service **222** — Journey time: 42 - 55 minutes

From Caernarfon: ⚒ : 0735, 0745, 0845, 0850, 0910, 0945, 0950, 1010, 1045, 1050, 1110, 1135, 1145, 1150, 1210, 1245, 1250, 1310, 1345, 1355, 1420, 1455, 1515, 1530, 1620, 1625, 1645, 1720, 1745, 1800, 2215. ⑦**p** : 1305, 1505, 1705.

From Pwllheli Maes: ⚒ : 0745, 0750, 0845, 0850, 0905**X**, 0945, 0950, 1015, 1045, 1050, 1115, 1145, 1150, 1215, 1245**X**, 1300, 1315, 1345, 1350, 1430, 1515, 1520, 1540, 1600**X**, 1620, 1625, 1640, 1720, 1740, 2125. ⑦**p** : 1205, 1405, 1555, 1755.

A – Ⓐ (schooldays only).
H – ⑥ (⚒ during school holidays).
X – Clynnog & Trefor service X12: Bangor - Caernarfon - Pwllheli and v.v.
p – Also public holidays (**not** Dec. 25, 26, Jan. 1).

Operators: Crosville Cymru ☎ 01492 596969; KMP ☎ 01286 870880; Express Motors ☎ 01286 674570; Clynnog & Trefor ☎ 01286 660208; Berwyn ☎ 01286 660315.

Table 545 MANCHESTER - MANCHESTER AIRPORT ✈

2 class only

From Manchester Piccadilly: *16 km.* Journey time 13 - 22 minutes.

⚒ : 0025, 0045, 0115, 0225, 0325, 0355, 0425, 0435, 0458, 0515, 0545, then five to six times hourly to 2206⑥, 2210, 2217, 2225, 2240, 2251Ⓐ, 2255, 2307Ⓐ, 2325.

⑦ : 0025, 0045, 0125, 0225, 0325, 0425, 0445, 0525, 0545, 0605, 0625, 0645, then four to five times hourly to 2205, 2225, 2237, 2245, 2300, 2305, 2325, 2337.

From Manchester Airport ✈ :

⚒ : 0002, 0010, 0110, 0125, 0213, 0310, 0410, 0513, 0533, 0548, 0556, then five to six times hourly to 2205, 2228, 2235, 2256, 2302, 2305, 2328, 2350.

⑦ : 0010, 0110, 0150, 0210, 0310, 0410, 0525, 0545, 0605, 0625, 0645, then four to five times hourly to 2202, 2205, 2225, 2235, 2245, 2305, 2325.

See also Tables **547**, **550**, **551** for through journeys to and from stations beyond Manchester.

Table 546 — WINDERMERE
2 class

km		⚒	⚒	⚒	⚒	A⚒	⚒	A⚒	⚒	A⚒	⑦	⑦	A⚒	⑦	⚒	⑦	A⚒	⑦	⚒	⑦	⑤
	Manchester Piccadilly 550 d.					0903		1103		1303			1503				1703				
0	Oxenholme Lake District d.	0630	0726	0826	0926	1037	1132	1237	1336	1441	1519	1536	1625	1637	1726	1744	1837	1843	1930	2003	2027	2201
3	Kendal d.	0634	0730	0830	0930	1041	1136	1241	1340	1445	1523	1540	1629	1641	1730	1748	1841	1847	1934	2007	2030	2205
17	Windermere a.	0647	0746	0846	0946	1059	1152	1259	1356	1503	1541	1556	1643	1702	1747	1804	1855	1908	1951	2023	2048	2221

		⚒	⚒	⚒	⚒		A⚒	A⚒	A⚒		⚒	⚒	A⚒	⑦	⑦	⑦	A⚒	⑦	⚒	⑦	⑦	B⑦
	Windermere d.	0655	0755	0855	0954		1107	1206	1307	1406		1511	1549	1606	1647	1711	1755	1814	1900	1930	1955	2040	2045	2052	2225
	Kendal d.	0709	0809	0909	1008		1121	1218	1321	1418		1525	1603	1618	1701	1725	1809	1826	1914	1944	2009	2054	2059		2239
	Oxenholme Lake District a.	0715	0815	0915	1014		1127	1224	1327	1424		1531	1609	1624	1707	1731	1815	1832	1920	1950	2015	2100	2104	2111	2245
	Manchester Piccadilly 550 a.				1203			1403		1603				1806					2003					2258c

A – [train] and [bus] Manchester Airport (Table 550) - Windermere and v.v.　　B – [train] Windermere - Lancaster.　　c – Change at Lancaster (arrive 2125 / depart 2137).

⛴ service Lakeside – Bowness Pier (40 minutes) – Ambleside (90 minutes).　Operator: **Windermere Iron Steamboat Company Limited**, Ulverston, Cumbria.　☎ : 015395 31188
From Lakeside – Bowness : 0905, 1010, 1120, 1230, 1335, 1440, 1545, 1655.
From Bowness – Lakeside : 1025, 1140, 1350, 1455, 1600, 1755.
From Bowness – Ambleside : 1000, 1050, 1120, 1325, 1430, 1540, 1640, 1755.
From Ambleside – Bowness : 0940, 1050, 1200, 1305, 1410, 1520, 1715.

The Lakeside and Haverthwaite Railway connects with most sailings in summer. For full details: ☎ 015395 31594.
Stagecoach Cumberland (☎ 01946 63222) [bus] service no. **W1** operates between Windermere Rail Station and Bowness Pier.

Table 547 — PRESTON - BARROW IN FURNESS
2 class

km		ⓐ	⚒	⚒	ⓐ	⑥		C	⚒		⚒	⚒	C		⚒	⑦	⚒	⑦	⚒	N
	Manchester Airport + 550 d.		0548		0746	0746		0948			1148				1348			1533	1548	
0	Preston 550 d.		0547	0657		0857	0857	1006	1057		1157	1310	1318		1457	1500	1518	1659	1657	1740
34	Lancaster 550 d.		0607	0718	0839	0918	0918	1035	1118		1227	1330	1350		1520	1521	1603	1720	1718	1800
44	Carnforth d.		0615	0736	0847	0927	0936	1043	1127		1235	1339	1358		1529	1539	1611	1728	1727	1809
53	Arnside d.		0626	0744	0857			1053	1135		1245		1408		1537	1539	1621	1738	1737	1820
58	Grange-over-Sands d.		0631	0752	0903	0939	0948	1059	1141		1251	1352	1414		1543	1545	1627	1744	1743	1825
74	Ulverston d.		0647	0807	0918	0953	1002	1114	1154		1306	1405	1429		1556	1600	1642	1759	1758	1841
90	Barrow-in-Furness a.		0707	0829	0939	1011	1020	1135	1212		1327	1423	1450		1614	1625	1703	1820	1819	1902

	⑦	⑦	⚒	ⓐ	ⓐ	⑦	⚒ R		⑦ T	
Manchester Airport + 550 d.		1748	1748		1848	1848	1933		2132	
Preston 550 d.		1859	1914	1932	1957	2005	2054	2122	2241	
Lancaster 550 d.	1828	1920	1935	1952	2018	2025	2115	2150	2213	2301
Carnforth d.	1836	1929	1943	2000	2027	2034	2123	2158	2221	2310
Arnside d.	1848		1954	2011	2035	2043	2132	2208	2231	2321
Grange-over-Sands d.	1853	1941	1959	2016	2041	2048	2137	2214	2237	2326
Ulverston d.	1910	1955	2015	2032	2054	2102	2151	2229	2252	2342
Barrow-in-Furness a.	1931	2016	2036	2053	2112	2125	2209	2250	2313	0003

	⑥	ⓐ	⑥	ⓐ	⑥	⚒	⑥	ⓐ
Barrow-in-Furness d.	0538	0546	0632	0638	0725	0725	0745	0750
Ulverston d.	0555	0603	0651	0657	0744	0744	0802	0810
Grange-over-Sands d.	0608	0616	0706	0712	0759	0759	0815	0823
Arnside d.	0613	0621	0711	0717	0804	0804		
Carnforth d.	0623	0631	0723	0729	0816	0816	0828	0836
Lancaster d.	0632	0640	0732	0740	0825	0826	0837	0845
Preston a.	0703	0703	0803	0803	0848		0908	0908
Manchester Airport + 550 a.	0824	0824	0920	0920			1020	1020

	⑥	ⓐ		⚒		⚒	⚒	⚒ C		⚒	⑦	⑦	⑦	C		⚒ S		⑦		
Barrow-in-Furness d.	0838	0846		0925		1053	1111	1221	1248	1333	1409	1451	1514	1534	1540	1645	1733	1745	1915	2035	2153
Ulverston d.	0855	0903		0944		1110	1130	1240	1305	1352	1428	1508	1531	1553	1559	1704	1752	1804	1934	2054	2214
Grange-over-Sands d.	0908	0916		0959		1123	1145	1255	1318	1407	1443	1521	1544	1608	1614	1719	1807	1819	1949	2109	2227
Arnside d.	0913	0921		1004			1150	1300		1412	1448		1613	1619	1724	1812	1824	1954	2114	2232
Carnforth d.	0923	0931		1016		1136	1202	1312	1331	1424	1503	1534	1600	1625	1634	1736	1822	1836	2006	2124	2244
Lancaster d.	0932	0940		1028		1145	1212	1322	1340	1434	1514	1545	1612	1637	1646	1745	1833	1845	2015	2135	2253
Preston a.	1003	1003		1059		1208	1247		1403	1508	1537	1608	1635	1708		1808	1856	1908	2038	2158	2316
Manchester Airport + 550 a.	1120	1120				1320			1520		1649	1722	1749			1920	2014		2315	

C – [train] Lancaster - Carlisle and v.v.
L – [train] Barrow-in-Furness - Liverpool Lime Street.
N – [train] Liverpool Lime Street - Millom.
R – [train] Manchester Victoria - Millom.
S – [train] Sellafield - Preston.
T – [train] and [food] Manchester Airport - Millom.

Table 548 — BARROW IN FURNESS - CARLISLE
2 class

km		⚒	⚒	⚒K	⚒	ⓐ	⑥	⚒	⑦	⚒	⚒	⚒	⑦	⚒	⚒	⑦	⚒N	ⓐR	⑥T
	Lancaster 547 d.																	1800	1952	2018
0	Barrow-in-Furness d.		0612	0655		1022	1030	1142		1350		1457	1540		1711	1753		1909	2055	2114
26	Millom d.		0638	0721		1045	1053	1208	1338	1405		1523	1606		1737	1820		1936	2122	2141
47	Ravenglass for Eskdale d.		0656	0739		1103	1111	1225				1541	1623		1755				
56	Sellafield d.		0708	0756		1114	1122	1235				1553	1633		1806				
74	Whitehaven d.	0647	0728	0816	0920	1015	1132	1140	1255	1341	1342		1520	1613	1635	1659	1826	1910	1931	1947
85	Workington d.	0704	0745	0833	0937	1032	1149	1157	1311	1358	1359		1537	1630	1652	1716	1843	1927	1949	2004
93	Maryport d.	0712	0753	0841	0945	1040	1157	1205	1319	1407	1407		1545	1638	1701	1724	1851	1935	1958	2012
138	Carlisle a.	0753	0834	0922	1026	1121	1246	1246	1407	1451	1448		1626	1719	1744	1805	1932	2016	2039	2053

	⚒	⚒	ⓐ		⚒	⚒	⚒	⚒	⚒	⚒	⚒		⚒	⚒	⚒	⚒	⚒	⚒		ⓐ	⑥
Carlisle d.		0758	0900		0940	1058	1213	1303	1346	1425	1513		1545	1635	1725	1757	1816	1835		2020	2104	2112
Maryport d.		0837	0939		1019	1137	1252	1342	1425	1504	1551		1624	1714	1804	1836	1856	1914		2059	2144	2151
Workington d.	0625	0846	0948		1028	1146	1305	1351	1434	1513	1602		1633	1723	1813	1845	1905	1923		2108	2154	2200
Whitehaven d.	0642	0905	1007		1045	1203	1320	1408	1453	1530	1624		1652	1740	1835	1904	1924	1942		2127	2213	2219
Sellafield d.	0715	0756			1108	1223	1431		1555		1640		1803							
Ravenglass for Eskdale d.	0725	0806			1119	1234	1442		1605		1650		1814				1955			ⓐ	⑥
Millom a.	0645	0743	0824	0925		1035	1137	1252	1416	1500		1623		1708		1832		2024		2131	2200
Barrow-in-Furness a.	0714	0813	0854	0954		1104	1214	1328	1445	1529		1653		1738		1901				2200	2214
Lancaster 547 d.						1212	1322			1635				1844						

K – Change of trains at Sellafield on ⓐ.　　N – [train] Liverpool Lime Street - Millom.　　R – [train] Manchester Victoria - Millom.　　T – [train] and [food] Manchester Airport - Millom.

Table 549 — PRESTON - LIVERPOOL
2 class

km		⚒	⚒	⚒	⑦	⚒		⚒	⚒	⚒	⚒	⚒	G	ⓐ	Gⓐ	⚒	⚒	⑦	⚒	⑦	⚒	⚒
0	Preston d.		0724		0812	0850		1012	1050	1212	1240		1412	1455	1604	1636	1657		1755	1836	1936	2025	2036
24	Wigan North Western d.	0615	0750	0830	0900	0913	1011	1110	1110	1300	1330	1330	1500	1513	1630	1700	1713	1800	1815	1900	1955	2045	2100	2145	2200
38	St. Helens Central d.	0633	0808	0848	0920	0929	1029	1120	1120	1320	1329	1348	1520	1529	1648	1720	1730	1833	1920	2013	2103	2120	2203	2220
57	Liverpool Lime Street a.	0704	0836	0919	0949	0954	1054	1149	1149	1349	1354	1419	1552	1719	1745	1755	1845	1904	1945	2040	2134	2145	2234	2245

	⚒	⚒	⑦	G⚒	⚒	⚒	⚒	⚒	⚒	⚒	⚒	⚒	⚒	⚒	⚒	⚒	⑦	⚒	⑦	⚒	⚒
Liverpool Lime Street d.	0542	0657	0732	0802	0937	1002	1037	1137	1202	1237	1402	1412	1437	1602	1637	1702	1712	1752	1802	1857	2002	2157	2202	2312
St. Helens Central d.	0610	0725	0800	0825	0915	0959	1025	1059	1159	1225	1259	1425	1440	1459	1625	1659	1725	1734	1817	1825	1925	2025	2225	2225	2340
Wigan North Western d.	0629	0742	0817	0844	0928	1017	1044	1113	1219	1244	1313	1444	1457	1513	1644	1714	1752	1811	1813	1901	1910	2044	2222	2242	2359
Preston a.		0807		0933	0948	1041	1133	1135		1333	1335	1524	1517	1710	1738	1811	1813	1901	1910	2008	2111	2331	2310

G – [train] and [food] Liverpool - Edinburgh and v.v.　　Additional trains run between Wigan and Liverpool and v.v. (approximately half-hourly).

Table 550 LONDON - CREWE - PRESTON - CARLISLE - GLASGOW

1, 2 class

Block 1

km	Station								⑥✕	Ⓐ✕	W			⑥	Ⓐ✕		⑥	⑥/ⒶP	⑥
0	**London Euston** d.								0610	0620				0645	0655		0700	0725	0730
28	Watford Junction d.								0626u	0636u				0701u	0711u		0716u	0741u	
80	Milton Keynes Central d.								0648	0658				0724	0734				
133	Rugby d.																		0805
156	Nuneaton d.								0725	0725							0811		0844
168	Birmingham International + d.								0739	0739									0814
182	**Birmingham New Street** d.				0521	0636	0655						0751		0800				0834
202	Wolverhampton d.				0535	0651	0712						0805		0816				0852
215	**Stafford** d.				0553	0709	0726		0816	0816			0823		0831		0848	0858	0908
253	Stoke-on-Trent d.													0844	0844	0850			0930
285	Macclesfield d.													0903	0903	0908			0948
254	**Crewe** d.				0617	0738	0751		0840	0840			0849				0912	0922	0942
295	Stockport d.													0918	0918	0923			1003
	Manchester Airport + d.	0548	0602				0746		0848										
304	**Manchester Piccadilly** d.	0603	0616				0803		0903					0932	0932	0934			1015
290	Runcorn d.					0642	0803						0911				0932	0941	
312	**Liverpool Lime Street** a.				0657	0707	0827						0850	0931					
322	Bolton d.	0621	0642				0821				0921						0937	0956	1005
293	Warrington Bank Quay d.						0810		0859	0859									1001
312	Wigan North Western d.	0637			0743		0823		0911	0911	0937		0928				1017		1013
336	**Preston** d.	0657	0708		0807		0838	0857	0928	0928	0957	1006					1041		1036
370	Lancaster d.	0718	0727				0856	0918	0946	0946	1018	1022							
	Barrow-in-Furness 547 a.	0829						1011t											
401	Oxenholme Lake District d.		0745				0912		1002	1002	1037	1041							
453	Penrith d.		0815						1028	1028	1106								
481	**Carlisle** d.		0848				1005		1048	1048	1126								
646	**Glasgow Central** a.		1039c						1212	1212									
646	**Edinburgh** a.		1032				1137				1255								
	Aberdeen 600 a.																		

Block 2

Station	Ⓐ			⑥	Ⓐ	⑥	Ⓐ✕	✕		W	B		⑥	H	E	⑥	Ⓐ	Ⓐ✕	⑥	⑥	Ⓐ	
London Euston d.	0740			0750	0800	0800	0810	0830	0840		W	B		0853	H	E	0850	0900	0900	0910		0930	0940
Watford Junction d.				0806u	0816u							0911u						0916u	0926u				
Milton Keynes Central d.	0815					0834	0844										0924	0936				1005	1015
Rugby d.	0844												1015					1011	1011			1020	
Nuneaton d.						0920	0920																1034
Birmingham International + d.											0915				0946								
Birmingham New Street d.		0851	0905								0934	0949		1006						1034			
Wolverhampton d.		0908	0922								0952	1008		1027						1052			
Stafford d.		0925	0936			0948	0948				1008	1025	1043	1043			1048	1048	1108			1113	
Stoke-on-Trent d.				0944							1031						1046	1046	1130				
Macclesfield d.				1003							1049						1105	1105	1152				
Crewe d.	0942	0949	1001			1012	1012				1049	1106	1109				1112	1112		1137	1137	1138	
Stockport d.				1018	1020						1105						1120	1120	1207				
Manchester Airport + d.				0948							1048									1219			
Manchester Piccadilly d.				1003	1034	1033					1103	1125					1133	1132					
Runcorn d.		1011				1031	1031				1109						1131	1131					
Liverpool Lime Street a.		1030				1056	1056		1037		1131						1156	1156					
Bolton d.			1021								1121	1144											
Warrington Bank Quay d.	1001	1020							1114	1137										1156	1156		
Wigan North Western d.	1013	1031	1037						1126	1126	1157	1218	1239							1208	1208		
Preston d.	1036		1048	1057				1107	1107	1136	1157	1219								1230	1230		
Lancaster d.			1106	1118				1126	1126	1157	1218	1239											
Barrow-in-Furness 547 a.				1212																			
Oxenholme Lake District d.			1122					1143	1143		1237	1256											
Penrith d.												1322											
Carlisle d.			1204					1230	1230		1345												
Glasgow Central a.			1330					1358	1358														
Edinburgh a.											1513												
Aberdeen 600 a.																							

Block 3

Station	L		⑥	Ⓐ	⑥	Ⓐ	Ⓐ	⑥	Ⓐ✕		F	❖	⑥	W	⑥	Ⓐ		⑥	Ⓐ		⑥	
London Euston d.	L		0950	1000	1000	1010	1020	1030	1040		F	1055g		1050	1100			1100	1110		1130	
Watford Junction d.			1006u	1016u			1037u							1125	1135			1116u	1126u		1146u	
Milton Keynes Central d.					1034	1044																
Rugby d.					1111	1111										1211	1211			1220	1244	
Nuneaton d.							1133														1234	
Birmingham International + d.	1027	1047											1115									
Birmingham New Street d.	1055	1105									1134				1151	1155			1234			
Wolverhampton d.	1113	1121									1152				1208	1213			1252			
Stafford d.	1128	1136			1148	1148								1225	1230	1248	1248	1309	1313			
Stoke-on-Trent d.			1144	1144									1244	1244	1251			1331				
Macclesfield d.			1203	1203									1303	1303	1311			1353				
Crewe d.	1155	1200			1212	1212	1222				1233			1249		1312	1312	1340	1342			
Stockport d.			1218	1218									1318	1318	1326			1408				
Manchester Airport + d.								1148	1248	1248												
Manchester Piccadilly d.			1234	1234	1231	1231		1203					1303	1303	1332	1332	1339	1419				
Runcorn d.	1216													1311	1331	1331						
Liverpool Lime Street a.	1240		1256	1256				1221					1330	1356	1356							
Bolton d.									1328	1321												
Warrington Bank Quay d.								1252	1300												1401	
Wigan North Western d.		1229						1237	1318	1337											1413	
Preston d.		1244					1301	1301	1310h	1318	1337	1352	1401								1436	
Lancaster d.		1304							1330	1336	1401	1422										
Barrow-in-Furness 547 a.									1423													
Oxenholme Lake District d.							1331	1331			1352	1417	1430	1441								
Penrith d.													1500									
Carlisle d.		1358					1413	1413			1435	1504	1520									
Glasgow Central a.		1530					1539	1539														
Edinburgh a.											1601	1714										
Aberdeen 600 a.											1907											

A – 🚲 and ♟ London **Paddington** (Table 520) - Manchester.
B – 🚲 and ♟ Bournemouth (Table 520) - Edinburgh.
E – 🚲 and ♟ Birmingham International - Holyhead.
F – 🚲 and ♟ Plymouth (Table 520) - Aberdeen.
H – 🚲 and ♟ London - Holyhead.

J – 🚲 and ✕ London - Holyhead.
L – 🚲 and ♟ Poole (Table 520) - Liverpool.
P – Pullman service and ✕ available in 1 cl.
W – 🚲 and ♟ Manchester Airport - Windermere.
❖ – Runs Jan. 2–5, Apr. 12–15, 17–19.

c – Change at **Carstairs** (a. 0955 / d. 1003).
g – Depart 1045 on Apr. 15.
h – Arrive 1256.
t – Arrive 1020 on ⑥.
u – Stops to pick up only.

☛ For trains on ⑦, see pages 309–310.

Table 550 LONDON - CREWE - PRESTON - CARLISLE - GLASGOW
1, 2 class

Panel 1

Station	Ⓐ✕	✕2	✕G	✕2🍴	⑥🍴	⑥🍴	⑥	⑥	Ⓐk	Ⓐ✕	⑥2	⑥2	W	J	⑥2	⑥🍴	⑥✕	⑥	⑥	Ⓐ	✕	⑥🍴	Ⓐ🍴
London Euston d.	1140				1150	1200	1200	1210	1230	1230	1240					1250	1300	1300	1310			1330	1340
Watford Junction d.	1156u				1206u	1216u						1324	1334				1316u	1326u				1405	1415
Milton Keynes Central d.							1234	1244	1304		1314					1411	1411				1420		
Rugby d.	1244				1301	1301	1320	1320														1434	1453 / 1453
Nuneaton d.												1315											
Birmingham International + d.												1334	1351							1434			
Birmingham New Street d.		1251	1305									1352	1408							1452			
Wolverhampton d.		1308	1322									1408	1425			1444	1444		1448	1448	1508	1516	
Stafford d.		1325	1337		1348	1348										1503	1503		1512	1512	1531		
Stoke-on-Trent d.																					1549		
Macclesfield d.												1434	1449			1504			1518	1518	1605		
Crewe d.	1342	1349	1402		1412	1412																1542	1542
Stockport d.																							
Manchester Airport + d.				1348								1448											
Manchester Piccadilly d.			1403	1437	1437							1503	1522			1532	1532			1619			
Runcorn d.		1411				1431	1431							1511		1531	1531						
Liverpool Lime Street a.		1431			1456	1456			1412	1437		1521	1543	1531		1556	1556						
Bolton d.				1421																	1601	1601	
Warrington Bank Quay d.	1401		1422									1458	1514	1537							1613	1613	
Wigan North Western d.	1413	1434	1437									1518	1537	1557	1618						1636	1636	
Preston d.	1436	1452	1457				1506	1508	1506	1518	1537	1557	1618	1636									
Lancaster d.			1510	1520			1523	1529	1523	1539		1618	1636										
Barrow-in-Furness 547 a.				1614																			
Oxenholme Lake District d.			1526				1539	1547	1539		1637	1652											
Penrith d.			1551				1605	1613	1605			1718											
Carlisle d.			1612				1625	1634	1625			1738											
Glasgow Central a.			1740				1755	1807	1755			1912											
Edinburgh a.			1855b																				
Aberdeen 600 a.																							

Panel 2

Station	✕2	N	🍴	⑥	Ⓐ	✕	Ⓐ	⑥	🍴	Ⓐ	E	🍴	🍴	W	🍴	✕2	Ⓐ	✕	Ⓐ	🍴	Ⓐ	✕	⑥	Ⓐ
London Euston d.				1350	1400	1400	1410	1430	1440		E						1450	1500	1500	1510			1530	1540
Watford Junction d.				1406u	1416u		1446u	1456u									1524	1534	1516u	1526u			1605u	1615u
Milton Keynes Central d.					1434	1444										1530			1644	1644				
Rugby d.					1511	1511										1544		1620	1620				1644	1644
Nuneaton d.																			1616				1634	
Birmingham International + d.		1427										1534							1634					
Birmingham New Street d.	1451	1505										1534	1555				1613		1652					
Wolverhampton d.	1508	1522										1551u	1613	1627	1632				1707					
Stafford d.	1525			1544	1544	1548	1548					1630		1644	1644		1648	1648	1727					
Stoke-on-Trent d.				1603	1603							1652		1703	1703				1745					
Macclesfield d.						1612	1612					1707		1712	1712									
Crewe d.	1549	1600		1618	1618							1652	1656			1718	1718	1802				1742	1742	
Stockport d.														1719				1813						
Manchester Airport + d.			1548						1648	1648	1648					1732	1732							
Manchester Piccadilly d.			1603	1634	1636			1703	1703	1703	1719					1732	1732					1731	1731	
Runcorn d.	1612					1631	1631					1714	1740					1731	1731					
Liverpool Lime Street a.	1631		1621			1656	1656	1637				1712	1740				1756	1756						
Bolton d.									1728	1728	1725											1801	1801	
Warrington Bank Quay d.		1619						1717				1743		1752				1813	1813					
Wigan North Western d.		1631	1637			1706	1706	1740	1752	1752	1803		1813				1831	1831						
Preston d.		1650	1657			1706	1706	1740	1752	1752	1803	1800	1810	1810	1824				1850	1850				
Lancaster d.		1707	1718			1723	1723					1800	1810	1810	1824									
Barrow-in-Furness 547 a.			1819				1902																	
Oxenholme Lake District d.		1723				1739	1739					1829	1829	1843										
Penrith d.		1749				1805	1805					1859	1859						1948	1944				
Carlisle d.		1809				1825	1825					1918	1919							2118				
Glasgow Central a.		1935				1952	1952																	
Edinburgh a.		2040										2110												
Aberdeen 600 a.																								

Panel 3

Station	✕2	R	T	✕2🍴	✕2	C	⑥	Ⓐ🍴P	⑥	Ⓐ🍴	⑥	Ⓐ🍴P	⑥	Ⓐ	✕	S	✕2	⑥	Ⓐ🍴	Ⓐ🍴P	⑥	Ⓐ	✕	✕	⑥	H	Ⓐ	Y	✕2🍴
London Euston d.							1550	1600	1600	1610	1630	1630	1640					1650	1700	1705	1700		1715		1725	1730		
Watford Junction d.							1606u	1616u	1617u	1627u	1646u	1646u	1657u				1706u			1734									
Milton Keynes Central d.																		1807	1811										
Rugby d.																	1821						1837						
Nuneaton d.														1725															
Birmingham International + d.		1631	1625	1625										1725															
Birmingham New Street d.		1648	1705	1705										1746	1750														
Wolverhampton d.	1706u	1721	1721								1744	1744		1806	1810	1821	1828		1833										
Stafford d.	1723	1736	1736				1744						1814			1842		1847											
Stoke-on-Trent d.							1803				1833					1901		1907											
Macclesfield d.																			1907		1915	1915			1932				
Crewe d.	1749	1801	1801					1808	1808	1808	1836	1836		1919		1852		1923	1923										
Stockport d.																											1848	1848	
Manchester Airport + d.				1748																							1903	1903	
Manchester Piccadilly d.			1803		1828v	1834	1834				1902			1931		1936	1936				1925	1930							
Runcorn d.	1817							1827	1828		1851			1915			1950	1955											
Liverpool Lime Street a.	1840					1853																				1921	1921		
Bolton d.					1821									1854				1933											
Warrington Bank Quay d.		1820	1820										1854	1854							1948				1937	1937			
Wigan North Western d.		1832	1832	1839	1836						1906	1906		1924	1924						2013	1955			1957	2005			
Preston d.		1848	1852	1859	1901	1932					1924	1924		1942	1942						2013	1955			1957	2018	2025		
Lancaster d.		1906		1920		1952					1958	1958									2016				2053	2112	2125		
Barrow-in-Furness 547 a.				2016		2053																							
Oxenholme Lake District d.		1922				1958	1958				2024	2024																	
Penrith d.		1948									2024	2024																	
Carlisle d.		2009									2047	2047									2103				2229				
Glasgow Central a.		2138																											
Edinburgh a.																													
Aberdeen 600 a.																													

C – [train] Manchester **Victoria** - Millom.
E – [train] Liverpool - Millom.
G – [train] and 🍴 Penzance (Table **520**) - Edinburgh.
H – [train] and ✕ London - Holyhead.
J – [train] and 🍴 Brighton (Table **520**) - Glasgow.
N – [train] and 🍴 Bournemouth (Table **520**) - Edinburgh.
P – Pullman service and ✕ available in 1 cl.
R – [train] and 🍴 London **Paddington** (Table **520**) - Edinburgh.
S – [train] and 🍴 Bournemouth (Table **520**) - Manchester.
T – [train] and 🍴 Poole (Feb. 11 - Mar. 4) - Reading - Preston (see Table **520**).
W – [train] and 🍴 Manchester Airport - Windermere.
Y – [train] and 🍴 Manchester Airport - Millom.
b – Arrive 1847 on Ⓐ.
k – Dec. 21 - Jan. 5, Apr. 12-19 only.
u – Stops to pick up only.
v – Manchester **Victoria**.

Table 550 — LONDON - CREWE - PRESTON - CARLISLE - GLASGOW

1, 2 class

(Mondays–Saturdays, part 1)

	☆☆2	⑥2	☆☆U	⑥	Ⓐ	☆☆Q	⑥	ⒶP	⑥	Ⓐ	⑤	Ⓐ	Ⓐ	☆☆	⑥	Ⓐ	☆☆U	Ⓐ	⑥	Ⓐ	Ⓐ	⑥H	☆☆2	☆🍴2
London Euston ... d.				1725	1735		1750	1800	1800	1805	1825	1820	1830		1850	1900		1910	1920	1930	1930			
Watford Junction ... d.								1816u	1816u	1822u	1841u	1836u	1846u					1928u	1938u					
Milton Keynes Central ... d.							1824				1845u							1950	2000	2005	2004u			
Rugby ... d.				1834						1912	1912													
Nuneaton ... d.			1842				1910	1910							2006	2006					2050			
Birmingham International + d.			1810n		1829												1928							
Birmingham New Street ... d.			1834		1905							1948			1955	2010								
Wolverhampton ... d.			1852		1922							2003			2013	2027								
Stafford ... d.			1908	1919	1916	1936			2002	2007	2007	2021			2030	2043					2111	2118		
Stoke-on-Trent ... d.			1930	1938			1950	1950							2045	2045	2052							
Macclesfield ... d.			1948	1957			2009	2009							2108	2108	2114							
Crewe ... d.			1944		2001				2008	2008	2027	2034	2034	2045				2110			2136	2141		
Stockport ... d.			2004	2018	2012		2024	2024							2123	2123	2127							
Manchester Airport + ... d.																								
Manchester Piccadilly ... d.			2020	2031	2025		2037	2037							2137	2137	2140				2132	2147		
Runcorn ... d.					2020				2027	2027				2108				2138	2138					
Liverpool Lime Street ... a.	1857				2044		2051	2051				2131						2202	2202					2157
Bolton ... d.																					2204			
Warrington Bank Quay ... d.							2046	2054	2052			2131								2156				
Wigan North Western ... d.	1947						2058	2104	2104			2145								2208				
Preston ... d.	2010	2023					2121	2127	2122			2145						2205		2208	2220		2220	2243
Lancaster ... d.	2030	2043							2215t	2140								2230			2241		2304	2301z
Barrow-in-Furness 547 ... a.		2144																						2301z
Oxenholme Lake District ... d.										2156														0003z
Penrith ... d.										2222														
Carlisle ... d.										2245														
Glasgow Central ... a.																								
Edinburgh ... a.																								
Aberdeen 600 ... a.																								

(Mondays–Saturdays, part 2)

	Ⓐ2	⑥S	Ⓐ✕	⑥	☆☆U	ⒶH	⑥	ⒶV	ⒶZ	ⒶC	Ⓐ	Ⓐ	☆☆🍴	⑥p	⑥v	⑥y	Ⓐ	ⒶW	🍴	⑥p	⑥q	ⒶX	ⒶY
London Euston ... d.			2000	1950		2010	2025	2025			2120	2045		2150	2150	2150	2200	2205		2300	2300	2330	2355
Watford Junction ... d.						2026u				2102u				2206u	2206u	2206u	2216u						0015u
Milton Keynes Central ... d.			2034	2025					2155			2126		2238	2238	2238	2239			2345	2345		
Rugby ... d.							2120					2154							V..		0029	0029	
Nuneaton ... d.														2329			2327					0051	
Birmingham International + d.		2040				2030			2152		2218										0052		
Birmingham New Street ... d.	2048	2057				2105			2210		2239										0115	0131	
Wolverhampton ... d.	2103	2116				2122			2229		2259										0145	0152	
Stafford ... d.	2121	2131				2137	2148		2244	2257	2314			2357	0020		2355						
Stoke-on-Trent ... d.			2144	2153v											0042								
Macclesfield ... d.			2203	2212v																			
Crewe ... d.	2145	2155			2201	2211	2242u	2242u	2310	2322	2340				0026		0044	0020					
Stockport ... d.			2218	2227	2231										0116s			0102					
Manchester Airport + ... d.														0002									
Manchester Piccadilly ... d.			2232	2240	2244									0016	0101s	0124s	0120s	0114					
Runcorn ... d.									2342														
Liverpool Lime Street ... a.	2208								0006						0146	0208	0213						
Bolton ... d.	2231													0034									
Warrington Bank Quay ... d.											0001												
Wigan North Western ... d.											0011			0049									
Preston ... d.											0033			0130								0251u	
Lancaster ... d.						2349u	2349u																
Barrow-in-Furness 547 ... a.																							
Oxenholme Lake District ... d.																							
Penrith ... d.																							
Carlisle ... d.														0253								0414s	
Glasgow Central ... a.																							0640
Edinburgh ... a.														0450				0433s					0636
Aberdeen 600 ... a.																		0750					

⑦ (Sundays)

	⑦k	⑦2	⑦J	⑦🍴	⑦2	⑦🍴	⑦2	⑦🍴	⑦2	⑦🍴	⑦2	⑦🍴	⑦	⑦🍴	⑦	⑦2	⑦A	⑦🍴	⑦
London Euston ... d.			0850			0935				1030	1110		1210	1215		1240		1310	1320
Watford Junction ... d.			0907u			0951u				1046u	1126u		1231u					1326u	1336u
Milton Keynes Central ... d.					1034					1129			1305			1335			
Rugby ... d.											1236					1406			
Nuneaton ... d.																			
Birmingham International + d.				1049			1123		1153		1218					1405			
Birmingham New Street ... d.					1042					1220		1336		1406		1425	1443h		
Wolverhampton ... d.					1112					1244		1401		1431		1452	1508		
Stafford ... d.			1125	1129		1200		1303		1257	1337	1421	1430	1437	1446	1504	1510	1527	
Stoke-on-Trent ... d.					1152		1221		1325		1359		1451					1548	
Macclesfield ... d.					1211		1240		1344		1417		1510					1607	
Crewe ... d.			1149			1226		1322		1447	1507	1512	1529	1536	1543			1605	
Stockport ... d.					1256s		1358		1434s		1531s							1623s	
Manchester Airport + ... d.											1546								
Manchester Piccadilly ... d.					1239		1308		1410		1446							1636	
Runcorn ... d.										1342		1510		1527		1600			
Liverpool Lime Street ... a.		0802	1002			1202				1402	1413		1533		1551		1622		
Bolton ... d.									1428										
Warrington Bank Quay ... d.																			
Wigan North Western ... d.		0846	1046			1246				1444		1532	1549		1603				
Preston ... d.		0908	1108			1308		1500	1510g	1510		1601	1627		1631			1647	
Lancaster ... d.								1521	1528			1619			1649			1705	
Barrow-in-Furness 547 ... a.								1625											
Oxenholme Lake District ... d.								1543				1635			1704			1721	
Penrith ... d.								1608				1700			1729			1747	
Carlisle ... d.								1632				1724			1753			1759	
Glasgow Central ... a.								1800											
Edinburgh ... a.												1855			1920			1935	
Aberdeen 600 ... a.																			

- 🚉 and 🍴 Poole (Table 520) - Glasgow.
- 🚉 and 🍴 Birmingham International + - Holyhead.
- 🚉 and ✕ London - Holyhead.
- 🚉 and 🍴 London - Holyhead.
- Pullman service and ✕ available in 1 cl.
- 🚉 and 🍴 Reading (Table 520) - Liverpool.
- 🚉 Birmingham International + - Chester.

T – 🚉 and 🍴 Bournemouth (Table 520) - Manchester.
U – 🚉 and 🍴 Brighton (Table 520) - Manchester.
V – ⛟ 1,2 cl. London - Fort William (arrive 0835).
W – ⛟ 1,2 cl. London - Inverness (arrive 0840).
X – ⛟ 1,2 cl. and 🚉 London - Glasgow;
    ⛟ 1,2 cl. and 🚉 London - Carlisle.
Y – ⛟ 1,2 cl. London - Edinburgh.

Z – ⛟ 1,2 cl. London - Inverness (arrive 0840).
g – Arrive 1500.
h – Arrive 1420.
k – To Apr. 9.
n – Depart 1816 on ⑥.
p – Jan. 7.
q – Jan. 14 - May 27.
s – Stops to set down only.
t – By connecting 🚌.
u – Stops to pick up only.
v – Jan. 14 - May 20.
y – May 27.
z – Ⓐ; also May 27.

Table 550 **LONDON - CREWE - PRESTON - CARLISLE - GLASGOW** 1, 2 class

	⑦2♉	⑦♉	⑦♉	⑦♉	⑦♉	⑦C	⑦♉	⑦2♉	⑦D	⑦♉	⑦2	⑦♉	⑦♉	⑦♉	⑦2	⑦2	⑦	⑦♉	⑦♉
London Euston d.				1340	1405		1440		1450		1510	1520	1540					1600	1610
Watford Junction d.				1356u	1425u								1556u					1616u	1626u
Milton Keynes Central d.							1534		1551		1605	1614	1656						
Rugby d.				1506	1532		1615											1720	
Nuneaton d.																			
Birmingham International + d.								1603											
Birmingham New Street d.			1450			1605		1626		1640						1705		1710	
Wolverhampton d.			1514			1622		1643		1655						1722		1726	
Stafford d.			1531	1606	1630			1659		1713	1723					1743	1806	1811	1802
Stoke-on-Trent d.			1554		1651			1710		1721	1734					1753	1806	1825	1831
Macclesfield d.			1613					1739	1726	1737	1751	1801					1806		1831
Crewe d.				1637	1702				1726		1751	1801				1806		1844	1849
Stockport d.			1630	1726s						1755	1808						1748		
Manchester Airport + d.	1533						1637												
Manchester Piccadilly d.	1547		1643		1738		1656				1808	1822				1804		1858	1902 / 1850
Runcorn d.									1745	1801									
Liverpool Lime Street a.		1602					1702					1810	1828			1802			1914
Bolton d.	1604						1716				1809	1828				1826			
Warrington Bank Quay d.				1656	1723							1821	1838	1846	1854				
Wigan North Western d.	1623	1646		1708				1735	1746			1843	1850	1857	1911	1914			
Preston d.	1659n	1710		1730				1748	1755	1802	1811			1908	1914				
Lancaster d.	1720			1748				1806	1813	1821					1935				2036
Barrow-in-Furness 547 a.	1820																		
Oxenholme Lake District d.				1805				1822	1829	1840				1911	1930				
Penrith d.				1831				1855	1910					1937	1956				
Carlisle d.				1852				1908	1915	1935			2001	2001	2020				
Glasgow Central a.				2017					2044				2127	2148					
Edinburgh a.								2039		2130					2300				
Aberdeen 600 a.								2322											

	R	⑦♉	⑦♉	⑦♉	F	⑦g	⑦k	⑦♉	⑦2	⑦2	⑦2	U	⑦♉	⑦♉	D	⑦♉	⑦♉	H	⑦g	⑦k
London Euston d.	1640		1700	1710	1730	1730	1740					1800	1810		1840	1900	1910	1920	1930	1930
Watford Junction d.				1726u								1817u	1845		1856u	1934	1926u	1956		
Milton Keynes Central d.	1714			1734			1812													
Rugby d.				1808		1837	1837	1900								1948	2015	2020	2036	2036
Nuneaton d.																				
Birmingham International + d.		1720			1804							1850	1905		1934					
Birmingham New Street d.		1755	1805		1835							1907	1921		2000	2018				
Wolverhampton d.		1811	1822		1853							1927	1936		2001	2033				
Stafford d.		1828	1838		1857	1908		1936				1957	2005		2033	2054	2102	2139		
Stoke-on-Trent d.			1903	1908			1941	2000				2015	2024		2054	2113	2131	2158		
Macclesfield d.		1921	1927			1926	1936		1951	1956		2015	2024	2031	2056	2131	2137	2149		
Crewe d.	1851	1856			1926	1936		1951	1956		2001	2030	2040		2128	2147s		2214s	2220s	
Stockport d.			1944	1949		2000		2018s	2022s		1933	2030			2139	2159		2226	2236	
Manchester Airport + d.				2000																
Manchester Piccadilly d.		1916	1958			1949			1947			2025	2050		2139	2154				
Runcorn d.										2002	2048		2112			2224				
Liverpool Lime Street a.		1940			2014					2002			2112			2224				
Bolton d.									2004							2115				
Warrington Bank Quay d.					1955			2006		2014						2127				
Wigan North Western d.					2006			2023	2026	2030	2046					2148				
Preston d.	1935				2041				2052	2054	2111					2206				
Lancaster d.	1953									2115	2209									
Barrow-in-Furness 547 a.																2222				
Oxenholme Lake District d.	2009				2057					2122						2248				
Penrith d.	2035				2122											2312				
Carlisle d.	2055				2146															
Glasgow Central a.	2225				2320															
Edinburgh a.																				
Aberdeen 600 a.																				

	⑦♉	P	V	⑦♉	⑦2	H	⑦♉	W	⑦♉	X	Y
London Euston d.	1940		1950	2000	2035	2040	2100	2105	2200	2250	2325
Watford Junction d.	1956u			2016u	2056u		2125v	2216u	2310v	2344v	
Milton Keynes Central d.					2111	2134					
Rugby d.	2103										
Nuneaton d.					2201						
Birmingham International + d.		2034									
Birmingham New Street d.		2105		2125	2205						
Wolverhampton d.		2121		2142	2222						
Stafford d.		2135		2157	2222	2234	2237	2258	2303	0024	
Stoke-on-Trent d.				2203	2219		2317	2322			
Macclesfield d.				2224	2242		2246	2301	2348v		
Crewe d.	2200	2205	2207v	2240	2304	2246	2301	2332s	2339s	0110s	
Stockport d.				2240	2304		2332s	2339s			
Manchester Airport + d.				2252	2316					0122	
Manchester Piccadilly d.				2252	2316		2347	2351		0122	
Runcorn d.		2225			2305						
Liverpool Lime Street a.		2249			2202	2329					
Bolton d.	2220										
Warrington Bank Quay d.	2232										
Wigan North Western d.	2232				2246				0035v	0229	
Preston d.	2254		2253v		2310				0035v	0229	
Lancaster d.											
Barrow-in-Furness 547 a.											
Oxenholme Lake District d.											
Penrith d.										0352s	
Carlisle d.										0640	
Glasgow Central a.							0433s			0635	
Edinburgh a.							0433s	0750			
Aberdeen 600 a.								0750			

C – [train] and ♉ Plymouth (Table 520) - Aberdeen.
D – [train] and ♉ London Paddington (Table 520) - Manchester.
F – [train] and ♉ Coventry (depart 1752) - Glasgow.
H – [train] and ♉ London - Holyhead.
P – [train] and ♉ Poole (Table 520) - Liverpool.
R – [train] and ♉ Reading (Table 520) - Liverpool.
U – [train] and ♉ Poole (Table 520) - Manchester.
V – 1,2 cl. London - Fort William (arrive 0835); 1,2 cl. London - Inverness (arrive 0840).
W – 1,2 cl. and [train] London - Aberdeen.
X – 1,2 cl. and [train] London - Glasgow; 1,2 cl. and ♉ London - Carlisle.
Y – 1,2 cl. London - Edinburgh.
Z – 1,2 cl. London - Inverness (arrive 0840).
g – To Apr. 9.
k – From Apr. 16.
n – Arrive 1643.
s – Stops to set down only.
u – Stops to pick up only.
v – Stops to pick up [train] passengers only.

Table 550 — GLASGOW - CARLISLE - PRESTON - CREWE - LONDON

1, 2 class

Panel 1

km	Station	E ✕ⓐ	J ⑥	S ✕ⓐ	⑥♀	ⓐ♀	✕	✕	✕	♀	S	♀	♀P	♀	2	2	H	♀	♀P	♀P	B
	Aberdeen 600 .... d.																				
	Edinburgh .... d.																				
0	Glasgow Central .... d.																				
165	Carlisle .... d.																				
193	Penrith .... d.																				
245	Oxenholme Lake District .... d.																				
	Barrow-in-Furness 547 d.																				
276	Lancaster .... d.																				
310	Preston .... d.						0615	0615													
334	Wigan North Western .... d.						0629	0629													
	Warrington Bank Quay .... d.						0641	0641													
349	Bolton .... d.																				
	Liverpool Lime Street d.							0600				0645	0627	0637					0710		
	Runcorn .... d.							0617				0702	0646	0657					0727		
367	Manchester Piccadilly .... d.			0517	0520	0530		0600			0617	0630	0645					0700	0710	0717	
383	Manchester Airport + a.																				
	Stockport .... d.			0524	0528	0538		0608			0624	0638	0654					0708	0718	0726	
	Crewe .... d.	0525	0545	0551	0557			0639	0705	0705		0723	0730e	0730	0736	0736			0751	
0	Macclesfield .... d.				0552		0622			0637	0652	0706							0740	
32	Stoke-on-Trent .... d.				0612		0642			0656	0712	0727							0801	
58	Stafford .... d.	0548	0605	0612	0617			0700			0717		0744	0753	0753	0756			0823	
83	Wolverhampton .... d.	0607		0630				0734					0814	0814					0840	
104	Birmingham New Street a.	0624		0648				0754					0832	0832					0900	
117	Birmingham International + a.	0643		0716				0816											0916	
	Nuneaton .... d.		0631		0652			0735									0824			
	Rugby .... d.						0730		0805	0808			0822							
	Milton Keynes Central .... d.								0820	0846										
	Watford Junction .... d.				0755s					0822							0923s	0921s	0927s	
	London Euston .... a.	0803			0813	0828		0840	0853	0911	0924		0917	0916	0943		0934	0956	0944	0950

Panel 2

Station	ⓐ✕	⑥♀	⑥2♀	ⓐ2♀	♀P	⑥♀	✕ⓐ2	ⓐ✕	⑥♀	✕ⓐ2	ⓐ✕	✕♀	S✕	✕2♀	⑥2♀	♀	✕2	ⓐD	⑥A
Aberdeen 600 .... d.																			
Edinburgh .... d.																			
Glasgow Central .... d.																			
Carlisle .... d.			0538	0538												0638			
Penrith .... d.			0555	0555												0655			
Oxenholme Lake District .... d.			0621	0621												0721			
Barrow-in-Furness 547 d.																			
Lancaster .... d.		0538	0546		0645	0637								0632	0638		0745		
Preston .... d.		0704	0704	0715	0715					0724	0745			0804	0804	0810			
Wigan North Western .... d.		0720	0720	0729	0729					0750	0759			0820	0820	0823	0834		
Warrington Bank Quay .... d.				0741	0741						0811					0836	0846		
Bolton .... d.		0737	0737											0837	0837				
Liverpool Lime Street .. d.					0727	0745	0745		0836		0810					0845			
Runcorn .... d.					0748	0802	0802				0827					0902			
Manchester Piccadilly .... d.	0730	0730			0803	0803				0817	0830	0903	0903					0917	0917
Manchester Airport + a.					0824	0824						0920	0920						
Stockport .... d.	0738	0738								0824	0838							0926	0926
Crewe .... d.					0829f		0823			0833	0853			0914	0925	0944			
Macclesfield .... d.	0752	0752								0837	0852							0940	0940
Stoke-on-Trent .... d.	0812	0812								0858	0912							1000	1000
Stafford .... d.					0852	0837	0844			0854	0912	0918						1023	1023
Wolverhampton .... d.					0914					0929	0935			0929	0935		1008	1040	1040
Birmingham New Street .. a.					0935					0949	0954			0948			1007	1100	1100
Birmingham International + a.										1012	1016							1116	1116
Nuneaton .... d.	0849	0849																
Rugby .... d.									0932							1008	1106	
Milton Keynes Central .... d.	0924	0924				0933	0944							1031	1049	1023	1120	
Watford Junction .... d.				0932s	0932s		1012s		1021s		1045s			1059s				
London Euston .... a.	1011	1021		0955	1005		1020	1045		1045		1118c		1132c	1146c			

Panel 3

Station	✕ⓐ	ⓐ♀	⑥♀	⑥♀	ⓐ♀	✕	✕2	✕♀	✕	✕♀	✕2♀	⑥2♀	K	✕	⑥2	✕2	✕♀	✕ⓐN	⑥N
Aberdeen 600 .... d.								0627											
Edinburgh .... d.																	0640	0650	
Glasgow Central .... d.				0610						0720							0810	0810	
Carlisle .... d.				0738				0818		0844							0939	0939	
Penrith .... d.				0755													0956	0956	
Oxenholme Lake District .... d.				0821				0906		0921							1022	1022	
Barrow-in-Furness 547 d.		0725		0745	0750			0838	0846									
Lancaster .... d.		0825		0837	0845	0848		0925k	0932	0940	0948					1022	1038	1038
Preston .... d.		0850	0850	0909	0909	0920		1009g	1009h	1009h	1020					1050	1100	1100
Wigan North Western .... d.		0913	0913	0925	0925	0934			1025	1025	1025					1110	1115	1115
Warrington Bank Quay .... d.						0946											1127	1127
Bolton .... d.				0943	0943			1043	1043	1043								
Liverpool Lime Street .. d.		0954	0954			0910		0945	0948			1045	1048	1154				
Runcorn .... d.						0927		1002	1006			1102	1106					
Manchester Piccadilly .... d.	0930			1003	1003			1017	1030	1103	1103	1103					1117	1130
Manchester Airport + a.				1020	1020					1120	1120	1120						
Stockport .... d.	0938							1026	1038								1124	1138
Crewe .... d.				0953	1008	1025	1034						1119	1125	1133	1148		1157	1157
Macclesfield .... d.	0952						1039							1137	1152			
Stoke-on-Trent .... d.	1012						1102							1155	1212			
Stafford .... d.				1013		1046	1056	1123					1146	1155	1212	1215		
Wolverhampton .... d.				1030			1114	1141						1214		1231	1235	1235
Birmingham New Street .. a.				1050			1130	1203						1230		1251	1259	1259
Birmingham International + a.																1310	1316	1316
Nuneaton .... d.														1306				
Rugby .... d.					1125								1223	1320				
Milton Keynes Central .... d.								1221					1247					
Watford Junction .... d.	1142s			1215s								1228s	1256s				1342s	
London Euston .... a.	1215c			1228c	1249c		1317c					1305c	1329c	1344c			1415c	

Footnotes

A - 🚋 and ♀ Manchester - Reading ☉.
B - 🚋 and ♀ Manchester - Brighton ☉.
D - 🚋 and ♀ Manchester - London **Paddington** ☉.
E - 🚋 and ♀ Holyhead - Birmingham International.
H - 🚋 and ♀ Holyhead - London.
    Pullman service and ✕ available in 1cl.
J - 🚋 and ♀ Holyhead - London.

K - 🚋 and ✕ (✕ on ⓐ) Holyhead - London.
N - 🚋 and ♀ Edinburgh - Bournemouth ☉.
P - Pullman service and ✕ available in 1 cl.
S - 🚋 and ♀ Manchester - Bournemouth ☉.
☉ - See Table 520.
c - Arrive 10 minutes earlier on ⓐ.

e - Arrive 0715.
f - Arrive 0818.
g - Arrive 0955.
h - Arrive 1003.
k - Depart 0934 on ⓐ.
s - Stops to set down only.

☞ For trains on ⑦, see pages 313–4

Table 550 GLASGOW - CARLISLE - PRESTON - CREWE - LONDON

1, 2 class

Block 1

Station	W✕✕	✕	✕	2	E	⚡	2⚡	✕	✕	✕	2	2	G	W✕✕	2	✕	⚡	✕	✕	⑥2	Ⓐ2
Aberdeen 600 .... d.																					
Edinburgh .... d.				0910			0950						1010								
Glasgow Central .... d.				1035			1107						1136								
Carlisle .... d.				1053									1152								
Penrith .... d.				1119									1218	1225							
Oxenholme Lake District . d.																					
Barrow-in-Furness 547 .. d.							1053														
Lancaster .... d.	1045			1135				1145	1157				1237	1245							
Preston .... d.	1109	1120		1157				1209	1220				1240	1259	1309		1320				
Wigan North Western ..... d.	1125	1134		1210				1225					1310	1313	1325		1334				
Warrington Bank Quay .... d.		1146		1222											1325		1346				
Bolton .... d.	1143						1243						1354								
Liverpool Lime Street .. d.		1145	1148							1245	1248							1345	1348		1406
Runcorn .... d.		1202	1206							1302	1306							1402	1406		1406
Manchester Piccadilly .. d.	1203			1217				1303		1230			1403			1317	1330				
Manchester Airport ✈ .. a.	1220							1320					1420			1326	1338				
Stockport .... d.		1208	1225	1233	1246			1226	1238				1325	1333	1352	1351	1408			1425	1433
Crewe .... d.				1240				1252								1339	1352				
Macclesfield .... d.								1312								1401	1412				
Stoke-on-Trent .... d.				1300																	
Stafford .... d.		1246	1255	1306	1322			1346	1355				1413		1417	1422				1446	1455
Wolverhampton .... d.			1314	1329	1341			1414					1431			1438				1515	1525
Birmingham New Street .. a.			1330	1349	1400			1430					1450			1500				1530	1548
Birmingham International ✈ a.				1416																	
Nuneaton .... d.		1254						1412							1507	1522	1505			1527	
Rugby .... d.			1325					1359								1530					
Milton Keynes Central ... d.		1330						1424	1447											1542s	1614s
Watford Junction .... d.			1412s													1618t				1605t	1637t
London Euston .... a.		1418t	1435t					1449t	1510t	1534t											

Block 2

Station	J✕✕	2	R⚡	✕✕2⚡	2⚡	✕⑥	⚡	✕	F✕✕	✕	⚡P	⚡	Q	ⒶP⚡	⚡	2	2	W	✕✕C	Ⓐ2
Aberdeen 600 .... d.									0910											
Edinburgh .... d.				1103					1150										1205	
Glasgow Central .... d.		1040		1100		1140	1140		1316										1328	
Carlisle .... d.		1208		1223		1242	1257	1257	1316										1344	
Penrith .... d.		1240		1301		1314	1314		1353										1409	
Oxenholme Lake District . d.		1245		1307		1330	1341	1341										1425	1409	
Barrow-in-Furness 547 .. d.				1248					1409							1431	1445		1424	
Lancaster .... d.		1300		1326	1340	1357	1357		1409							1455	1509	1520	1528n	1604
Preston .... d.		1328	1340	1352	1404	1408	1420	1420	1432							1513	1525	1534		1630
Wigan North Western ..... d.			1358		1420				1455									1546		
Warrington Bank Quay .... d.									1455									1543	1553	
Bolton .... d.		1353			1438	1434							1510	1545	1545	1548	1552			1719
Liverpool Lime Street .. d.			1438						1445		1502		1527	1602	1602	1607		1603	1617	
Runcorn .... d.		1417			1503	1503			1430			1517	1530	1530				1620		
Manchester Piccadilly .. d.					1520	1520			1438			1524	1538	1538		1552			1626	
Stockport .... d.		1426							1438			1524	1538	1538				1608		
Crewe .... d.		1458		1442					1518	1525		1552				1623	1633		1640	
Macclesfield .... d.									1452		1537	1552	1552						1700	
Stoke-on-Trent .... d.									1512		1556	1612	1612						1722	
Stafford .... d.		1522							1546	1616		1621	1637	1644	1655				1739	
Wolverhampton .... d.		1539							1558	1632		1639	1700		1714				1806	
Birmingham New Street .. a.		1606							1617	1651		1700			1730				1816	
Birmingham International ✈ a.		1616							1612			1716								
Nuneaton .... d.									1628						1722					
Rugby .... d.									1653											
Milton Keynes Central ... d.				1620s		1630s	1630s		1618				1742s	1742s		1758s	1812s		1753s	
Watford Junction .... d.			1644			1658	1708	1705t	1739t				1805	1815		1819	1845		1816t	
London Euston .... a.																				

Block 3

Station	Ⓐ2	✕	ⒶP⚡	H	✕⚡	2	⑥⚡	2	Ⓐ2	D✕	D⚡	✕	Ⓐ⚡	W	2	⚡	2	✕	2	S⚡
Aberdeen 600 .... d.																				
Edinburgh .... d.														1405			1445			
Glasgow Central .... d.		1338			1459							1525		1532			1607			1640
Carlisle .... d.		1459										1542		1548			1623			
Penrith .... d.												1608		1613	1625		1648			1720
Oxenholme Lake District . d.		1539							1451z					1613	1625		1648			
Barrow-in-Furness 547 .. d.														1628	1645		1703	1711		1738
Lancaster .... d.	1545z	1555										1640		1657	1709	1720	1725	1734	1755	1800
Preston .... d.	1609	1620										1653		1713	1725	1734	1738		1815	
Wigan North Western ..... d.	1625											1705		1746	1752					
Warrington Bank Quay .... d.														1743						
Bolton .... d.	1643													1755			1745	1748	1904	
Liverpool Lime Street .. d.					1645			1648									1802	1806	1800	
Runcorn .... d.					1702			1709												
Manchester Piccadilly .. d.	1706		1630	1630					1710	1710	1730		1806				1823	1838	1809	
Manchester Airport ✈ .. a.	1722												1822							
Stockport .... d.			1638	1638					1717	1717	1738				1802	1808	1815	1823		1849
Crewe .... d.			1717	1723	1720	1730	1740		1732	1735	1752				1823		1844	1859		
Macclesfield .... d.									1735	1751	1756	1812						1845		
Stoke-on-Trent .... d.			1744	1744					1802	1808	1811	1818		1834		1839	1844	1859	1905	
Stafford .... d.									1823	1832	1835			1852		1857			1919	1926
Wolverhampton .... d.									1857	1851	1851			1915		1919			1942	1948
Birmingham New Street .. a.				1759	1829				1916	1922				1935						
Birmingham International ✈ a.									1856						1905		1921			
Nuneaton .... d.					1823	1844	1839		1914				1918			1930				
Rugby .... d.			1820	1820	1858s	1847							1947s		1958s		2010s			
Milton Keynes Central ... d.														2022t				2010s		2048
Watford Junction .... d.		1848	1905	1915	1921t	1934t		1927s	1952		2010t			1805	1815		1819	1845		
London Euston .... a.		1848	1905	1915	1921t	1934t		1952		1739t	2010t						2022t		2033t	2048

Footnotes

C – 🛏 and ⚡ Glasgow - Poole ⊙.
D – 🛏 and ⚡ Manchester - London **Paddington** ⊙.
E – 🛏 and ⚡ Edinburgh - Reading ⊙.
F – 🛏 and ⚡ Aberdeen - Plymouth ⊙.
G – 🛏 and ⚡ Edinburgh - Glasgow - Penzance ⊙.
H – 🛏 and ✕ Holyhead - London.
J – 🛏 and ⚡ Glasgow - Brighton ⊙.
P – Pullman service and ✕ available in 1 cl.
Q – 🛏 and ⚡ Liverpool - Poole ⊙.
R – Runs Jan. 2–5, Apr. 12–14, 17–19.
S – Runs Apr. 14, 17, 18.
W – 🛏 and ⚡ Windermere - Manchester Airport.
⊙ – See Table 520.
n – Arrive 1514 on Ⓐ, 1516 on ⑥.
s – Stops to set down only.
t – Arrive 10 minutes later on ⑥.

Table 550 — GLASGOW - CARLISLE - PRESTON - CREWE - LONDON

1, 2 class

Block 1

Station	☆☆ E ✕	Ⓐ ✕	⑥ ☕	☆☆2 ☕	☆☆ ✕	⑥ ☕	⑥ R	⑥ F	⑥ 2	Ⓐ 2	☆☆ U	Ⓐ ✕	⑥ ✕	Ⓐ ☕	Ⓐ	⑥ ☕	Ⓐ ☕	☆☆	Ⓐ	☆☆ 2	☆☆ 2
Aberdeen 600 d.																					
Edinburgh d.								1603													
Glasgow Central d.					1530	1610								1700	1700				1710		
Carlisle d.					1704h	1729		1729						1822	1822				1838		
Penrith d.					1721	1743		1743											1854		
Oxenholme Lake District d.					1748	1810		1810					1833z						1920		
Barrow-in-Furness 547 d.				1645							1745										
Lancaster d.				1745	1804	1825		1825			1853z		1845						1936		
Preston d.				1809	1828	1846		1846	1908	1917				1928	1928	1936	1956		2009	2025	2032
Wigan North Western d.				1825	1842											1955	2009	2045	2021		
Warrington Bank Quay d.					1854												1943		2021		
Bolton d.				1843																	
Liverpool Lime Street d.					1845			1854						1945	1945			2040	2018		2134
Runcorn d.					1902			1913						2002	2002			2035			
Manchester Piccadilly d.		1830	1830	1903										2003							
Manchester Airport + a.				1920										2020							
Stockport d.		1838	1938											2008	2008						
Crewe d.	1856				1915	1923	1926		1926	1942				2010	2010	2026	2026			2045	2101
Macclesfield d.		1852	1852											2022	2022						
Stoke-on-Trent d.		1912	1912											2042	2042						
Stafford d.	1919				1944		2003							2049	2049					2112	2123
Wolverhampton d.	1940				2001	2001	2021							2102	2102					2128	2144
Birmingham New Street a.	2004				2020	2020	2037							2150							2207
Birmingham International + a.	2020				2052	2052															
Nuneaton d.							2010							2128	2128						
Rugby d.														2134	2134						
Milton Keynes Central d.		2018	2018		2048									2122	2122	2159	2159	2204	2204		
Watford Junction d.					2126s							2150s	2200s	2227s	2237s	2232s	2242s				
London Euston a.		2105	2115		2124n	2159						2218	2238	2250	2310	2305	2315				

Block 2

Station	☆☆ O	⑥e 2	⑥f 2	Ⓐ 2	⑥ T	Ⓐ T	Ⓐ ☕	Ⓐ ☕	Ⓐ 2	Ⓐ 2	⑥ 2	Ⓐ 2	Ⓐ 2	⑤ T	Ⓐ ☕ Y	Ⓐ X	Ⓐ W	Ⓐ V
Aberdeen 600 d.																	2130	
Edinburgh d.						1850									2325	2350	0042u	
Glasgow Central d.					1850c										2337		0208u	
Carlisle d.					2035	2035								0112				
Penrith d.					2053	2053												
Oxenholme Lake District d.				2048	2101	2122	2122							2246				
Barrow-in-Furness 547 d.	1915													2153				
Lancaster d.	2015				2109	2122	2139	2139				2221		2253	2307			
Preston d.	2044					2206	2206		2214	2214		2246		2316	0250	0330s	0343s	0436s
Wigan North Western d.									2245	2300					0305			
Warrington Bank Quay d.																		
Bolton d.	2109					2229	2229											
Liverpool Lime Street d.			2148	2148					2318	2334	2349							
Runcorn d.		2128	2205	2205					2335									
Manchester Piccadilly d.	2129v					2249	2249							0353				
Manchester Airport + a.						2308	2308							0430				
Stockport d.																		
Crewe d.		2157	2234	2235						0015					0440s		0526s	
Macclesfield d.																		
Stoke-on-Trent d.																		
Stafford d.		2219	2256	2257						0036								
Wolverhampton d.			2316	2317						0055								
Birmingham New Street a.		2328	2332	2332						0111								
Birmingham International + a.																		
Nuneaton d.		2256																
Rugby d.																		
Milton Keynes Central d.																		
Watford Junction d.															0546s	0620s	0649	
London Euston a.															0620	0655	0710	0747

Block 3 — ⑦ (Sundays)

Station	⑦ 2	⑦j 2	⑦j 2	⑦ ☕	⑦ ☕	⑦ ☕	⑦ 2	⑦j 2	⑦ ☕	⑦ 2	⑦ 2	⑦ ☕	⑦ 2	⑦ D	⑦ 2	⑦ ☕	⑦ 2	⑦ 2	⑦ ☕	⑦ S	⑦ 2
Aberdeen 600 d.																					
Edinburgh d.																					
Glasgow Central d.																					
Carlisle d.																					
Penrith d.																					
Oxenholme Lake District d.																					
Barrow-in-Furness 547 d.																					
Lancaster d.																					
Preston d.	0820	0836					0920			1020	1036		1120			1220	1236				1320
Wigan North Western d.	0839	0900					0939		1039	1100		1139			1239	1300					1339
Warrington Bank Quay d.																					
Bolton d.		0859					0959		1059			1159			1259						1359
Liverpool Lime Street d.			0949					1045			1149			1230		1349			1410		
Runcorn d.								1102						1247					1426		
Manchester Piccadilly d.	0923	0817	0830	0930	1017	1023	1030		1123	1130	1217	1223	1230		1323	1330	1335				1423
Manchester Airport + a.	0940						1040		1140				1240		1340						1440
Stockport d.		0825	0838u	0938u	1024		1038u		1138u	1224		1238u			1338u	1343					
Crewe d.							1132						1324					1455			
Macclesfield d.		0837	0852	0952	1037		1052		1152	1237		1252			1352	1357					
Stoke-on-Trent d.		0856	0912	1012	1056		1112		1212	1256		1312			1412	1417					
Stafford d.		0917	0931	1031	1117		1131	1159	1231	1317		1331	1346		1431	1440		1520			
Wolverhampton d.			0936		1135					1336						1500	1540				
Birmingham New Street a.		1002			1204					1401						1527	1557				
Birmingham International + a.			1010	1110						1309	1427						1618				
Nuneaton d.																					
Rugby d.													1426								
Milton Keynes Central d.				1127			1303									1558					
Watford Junction d.			1145	1244s			1357s			1445s					1545s	1550s					
London Euston a.			1211	1306			1407	1422		1501					1611	1612		1659			

🚃 and ☕ Manchester - London **Paddington** ⊙.
🚃 and ☕ Holyhead - Birmingham International.
🚃 and ☕ Edinburgh - London **Paddington** ⊙.
🚃 Barrow-in-Furness - Manchester **Victoria**.
🚃 and ☕ Glasgow - London **Paddington** ⊙.
🚃 and ☕ Liverpool - London **Paddington** ⊙.
🚃 Windermere - Lancaster.

U – 🚃 and ☕ Windermere - Manchester Airport.
V – 1,2 cl. Fort William (depart 1950) - London; 1,2 cl. Inverness (depart 2030) - London.
W – 1,2 cl. and 🚃 Aberdeen - London.
X – 1,2 cl. and 🚃 Carlisle - London.
Y – 1,2 cl. Edinburgh - London.
Z – 1,2 cl. Inverness (depart 2030) - London.
c – Change at **Carstairs** (a. 1923 / d. 1928).
e – Jan. 7.
f – From Jan. 14.
h – Arrive 1647.
j – To Apr. 9.
n – Arrive 2114 on Ⓐ
s – Stops to set down only.
u – Stops to pick up only.
v – Manchester **Victoria**.
⊙ – See Table 520.

Table 550 GLASGOW - CARLISLE - PRESTON - CREWE - LONDON
1, 2 class

Panel 1

Station	⑦♟	⑦2	⑦j 2	⑦♟	⑦H	⑦♟	⑦♟	⑦♟	⑦2	⑦B	⑦♟	⑦2	⑦♟	⑦♟	⑦A	⑦♟	⑦♟	⑦♟	⑦j 2	⑦2
Aberdeen 600 .....d.														1305						
Edinburgh .....d.						1230								1305						
Glasgow Central .....d.									1238						1338					
Carlisle .....d.					1404				1411				1430	1435	1505					
Penrith .....d.									1448											
Oxenholme Lake District .....d.													1513	1516						
Barrow-in-Furness 547 ..d.										1409										
Lancaster .....d.						1455			1503				1514			1532	1555			
Preston .....d.		1420	1436	1500		1520			1520	1525			1539	1550r	1555	1620			1620	1636
Wigan North Western .....d.		1450	1500	1512					1543				1556	1603	1609				1639	1700
Warrington Bank Quay .....d.				1524									1615	1621					1659	
Bolton .....d.		1506							1559				1612							
Liverpool Lime Street ..d.			1549			1510				1545						1617	1645			1745
Runcorn .....d.						1527					1602					1635	1702			
Manchester Piccadilly .....d.	1430	1529			1517		1530		1623		1632				1617	1630		1700	1723	
Manchester Airport ✈ .....a.		1545							1640		1651								1740	
Stockport .....d.	1438u				1526		1538u								1625	1638u		1708u		
Crewe .....d.	1452			1548	1555		1604		1614		1631		1643	1648	1703	1715		1727		
Macclesfield .....d.					1540		1552						1639	1652				1722		
Stoke-on-Trent .....d.	1512				1559		1612						1659	1712				1742		
Stafford .....d.	1531			1609	1620	1621	1630	1635					1722	1738						
Wolverhampton .....d.					1640					1653			1723	1742	1759					
Birmingham New Street ..a.					1701					1712			1743	1800	1818					
Birmingham International ✈ a.					1740									1815						
Nuneaton .....d.				1640								1723	1736							
Rugby .....d.			1644									1743	1757							
Milton Keynes Central .....d.						1725	1737								1828s		1838	1851		
Watford Junction .....d.	1707s					1753s	1802s	1807						1847s	1853s	1903s	1919s	1925s		
London Euston .....a.	1740			1801	1811	1827	1833	1841			1900		1920		1926	1930	1953	1958		

Panel 2

Station	⑦2	⑦♟	⑦C	⑦H	⑦♟	⑦j 2	⑦2	⑦♟	⑦♟	⑦2	⑦k 2	⑦♟	⑦♟	⑦D	⑦♟	⑦♟	⑦2	⑦2	⑦R	⑦2	⑦♟
Aberdeen 600 .....d.						1150													1615		
Edinburgh .....d.			1400			1450					1455								1615	1630	
Glasgow Central .....d.		1400																	1742	1750	
Carlisle .....d.			1530	1544							1629								1818		
Penrith .....d.			1546	1604							1646										
Oxenholme Lake District .....d.			1612	1633					1654		1712								1820	1840	
Barrow-in-Furness 547 ..d.	1514																		1733		
Lancaster .....d.	1612		1627	1650			1724		1710		1729			1820		1824	1836	1857	1903	1920	
Preston .....d.	1637	1650	1648	1714			1724	1738q		1741	1750		1820		1824	1843	1900	1910	1921	
Wigan North Western .....d.	1656	1702	1707				1743			1800	1804		1834		1843	1900	1910	1922	
Warrington Bank Quay .....d.		1714	1720					1800		1816		1846				1922	1937	
Bolton .....d.	1713			1738			1759							1859	1945	
Liverpool Lime Street ..d.						1726		1745		1805		1845	1945		
Runcorn .....d.						1744	1802		1821		1902	1957	
Manchester Piccadilly .....d.	1732		1744	1749	1758	1717	1730	1823		1817	1830		1923	1957	
Manchester Airport ✈ .....a.	1749		1838n		1840		1825	1838u		1940	2014	
Stockport .....d.					1724	1738u	1818	1828	1833		1843	1848	1914	1927	1949	2009	
Crewe .....d.		1744	1749	1752			1818	1828	1833		1843	1848	1914	1927	1949	2009	
Macclesfield .....d.				1738	1752				1839	1852	1953	2012	
Stoke-on-Trent .....d.				1756	1812				1859	1912		
Stafford .....d.				1818		1841	1900		1914	1922	1953	2012	
Wolverhampton .....d.		1828		1836		1902	1907		1928	1942	2030	
Birmingham New Street ..a.		1846		1854		1918	1925		1946	2000	2055	
Birmingham International ✈ a.		1915						2017	2115	
Nuneaton .....d.				1844	1853				2006	2026	2035	
Rugby .....d.		1853			1937				1946	2037	2051	2126	
Milton Keynes Central .....d.						2000			2034s	2101s	2119s	2125s	2158	
Watford Junction .....d.				1944s	2002s							
London Euston .....a.		2009		2017	2033			2051	2107		2132	2152	2158	2225	

Panel 3

Station	⑦♟	⑦2	⑦♟	⑦♟	⑦j 2	⑦2	⑦2	⑦2	⑦T	⑦2	⑦2	⑦2	⑦j 2	⑦♟	⑦Y	⑦X	⑦W	⑦V
Aberdeen 600 .....d.																	2025	
Edinburgh .....d.															2304	2320		2356u
Glasgow Central .....d.		1700														2315		
Carlisle .....d.		1825													0110	0208u		
Penrith .....d.		1841					2111											
Oxenholme Lake District .....d.		1907						2035										
Barrow-in-Furness 547 ..d.							2132	2137										
Lancaster .....d.		1922																
Preston .....d.		1924	1944		2024	2036	2124		2200	2224	2236	2324		0248		0330	0343s	0431
Wigan North Western .....d.		1943	1957		2043	2100	2143		2222	2243	2300	2343		0304				
Warrington Bank Quay .....d.		2009																
Bolton .....d.	1959				2059		2159		2238	2259		2159						
Liverpool Lime Street ..d.			1955			2117	2145				2345							
Runcorn .....d.			2014			2135												
Manchester Piccadilly .....d.	1930	2023		2030	2123		2223		2258	2323		0023		0353				
Manchester Airport ✈ .....a.	2043			2140		2243		2315	2340		0043		0430				
Stockport .....d.	1938u			2038u		2213										0440s		0521
Crewe .....d.		2036	2048		2213											0440s		0521
Macclesfield .....d.	1952			2052													
Stoke-on-Trent .....d.	2012			2112													
Stafford .....d.			2110		2236												
Wolverhampton .....d.		2114	2131		2257												
Birmingham New Street ..a.		2132	2147		2315												
Birmingham International ✈ a.																	
Nuneaton .....d.			2157														
Rugby .....d.	2114																
Milton Keynes Central .....d.	2139																
Watford Junction .....d.	2204s			2300s											0546		0620	0649s
London Euston .....a.	2236			2333											0620	0655	0710	07

A – 🚃 and ♟ Manchester - Poole ☉.
B – 🚃 and ♟ Glasgow - Brighton ☉.
C – 🚃 and ♟ Glasgow - Poole ☉.
D – 🚃 and ♟ Manchester - London **Paddington** ☉.
H – 🚃 and ♟ Holyhead - London.
R – 🚃 and ♟ Edinburgh - London **Paddington** ☉.
T – 🚃 Windermere - Lancaster.

V – 🚃 1,2 cl. Fort William (depart 1900) - London; 🚃 1,2 cl. Inverness (depart 2010) - London.
W – 🚃 1,2 cl. and 🚃 Aberdeen - London.
X – 🚃 1,2 cl. and 🚃 Glasgow - London; 🚃 1,2 cl. and 🚃 Carlisle - London.
Y – 🚃 1,2 cl. Edinburgh - London.
☉ – See Table 520.

j – To Apr. 9.
k – From Apr. 16.
n – From Apr. 16 arrive 1820.
q – Arrive 1733.
r – Arrive 1544.
s – Stops to set down only.
u – Stops to pick up only.

Table 551 LIVERPOOL - MANCHESTER - LEEDS - HULL and YORK

2 class only

Service on ⑦ valid to Jan. 8 only. Liverpool - Manchester, see also Table 585. Leeds - York, see also Table 552.

km		✕ 🍷	✕ 🍷	✕	⑦ 🍷	✕	✕	⑦ 🍷	✕ 🍷	⑥	✕ B	✕ 🍷	Ⓐ	✕ 🍷	⑦ 🍷	✕ 🍷	✕	✕ 🍷	⑦	✕ 🍷	⑦ 🍷	✕ 🍷	✕ P	⑦	✕
0	**Liverpool Lime Street** ... d.	...	...	...	...	...	...	...	...	...	...	0620	...	...	...	...	...	0715	...	...	...	...	...	...	...
30	Warrington Central .... d.	...	...	...	...	...	...	...	...	...	...	0644	...	...	...	...	...	0741	...	...	...	...	...	...	...
	Manchester Airport ✈ .. d.	...	0513	...	0525	...	...	0605	0623	...	...	|	...	...	0705	0723	...	|	...	...	0805	0826	...	...	...
56	Manchester Victoria .. d.	...	|	...	|	...	...	|	|	...	...	|	...	...	|	|	0745	|	...	...	|	|	...	...	0855
56	**Manchester Piccadilly** .. d.	...	0545	...	0539	...	...	0619	0645	...	...	0712	...	0723	0719	0745	|	0812	...	0834	0819	0850	...	...	|
62	Stalybridge .... d.	...	|	...	|	...	...	|	0700	...	...	0728	...	0738	|	0800	0805	0828	...	|	|	|	...	...	0910
91	**Huddersfield** .... d.	...	0619	...	|	0636	...	|	0724	0733	...	0749	0752	0803	|	0824	0833	0848	...	0908	|	0924	...	...	0938
	Wakefield Westgate .. a.	...	|	...	|	0707	...	|	|	0804	...	|	0824	|	|	|	0909	|	...	|	|	|	...	...	1009
118	**Leeds** .... d.	0620	0650	0657	0704	...	...	0746	0752	...	0807	0824	...	0843	0846	0852	...	0917	0920	0937	0946	0952	1007	1012	...
	Selby .... d.	|	|	0721	|	...	...	|	|	...	|	|	...	0906	|	|	...	|	|	1000	|	|	|	1036	...
	Hull .... a.	|	|	0813	|	...	...	|	|	...	|	|	...	0942	|	|	...	|	|	1038	|	|	|	1112	...
160	**York** .... a.	0657	0716	...	0734	...	...	0815	0818	...	0835	0849	...	...	0912	0918	...	0942	0946	...	1012	1018	1035	...	...
160	**York** .... d.	0705	0718	...	...	...	0742	0817	0823	...	0839	0852	...	...	...	0921	...	0945	0948	...	1014	1021	1038	...	...
194	Malton .... d.	|	|	...	...	...	0804	|	|	...	0901	|	...	...	...	|	...	1007	1011	...	|	|	1100	...	...
229	**Scarborough** .... a.	|	|	...	...	...	0828	|	|	...	0926	|	...	...	...	|	...	1032	1036	...	|	|	1125	...	...
	Middlesbrough **570** ... a.	|	0822	...	...	...	...	0946	0925	...	...	|	...	...	...	1024	...	...	...	...	1143	1122	...	...	...
	Newcastle **570** ...... a.	0827	...	...	...	...	...	...	...	...	...	1010	...	...	...	...	...	...	...	...	...	...	...	...	...

	✕ 🍷	✕ 🍷	⑦ 🍷	✕ 🍷	✕	✕ 🍷	⑦ 🍷	⑦ H	✕ 🍷	⑦ 🍷	✕ 🍷	✕ B	✕	⑦ 🍷	✕ 🍷	✕ 🍷	⑦ 🍷	✕ 🍷	✕	✕ 🍷	⑦ 🍷	✕ 🍷	⑦ 🍷	✕ 🍷	✕ B
verpool Lime Street ... d.	0822	...	...	...	...	0922	0921	...	...	...	...	...	...	...	1022	...	...	...	...	1122	1121	...	...	...	...
/arrington Central ...... d.	0845	...	...	...	...	0945	|	...	...	...	...	...	...	...	1045	...	...	...	...	1145	|	...	...	...	...
Manchester Airport ✈ .. d.	|	...	0905	0928	...	|	|	...	...	1005	1028	...	...	...	|	...	1105	1128	...	|	|	...	1205	1228	...
Manchester Victoria ... d.	|	...	|	|	0955	|	1009	...	...	|	|	...	1055	1109	|	...	|	|	1155	|	1209	...	|	|	...
anchester Piccadilly ... d.	0912	0934	0919	0950	|	1012	|	...	1034	1019	1050	...	|	|	1112	1134	1119	1150	|	1212	|	1234	1219	1250	...
alybridge .... d.	0928	|	|	|	1010	1028	|	...	|	|	|	...	1110	|	1128	|	|	|	1210	1228	|	|	|	|	...
uddersfield .... d.	0948	1008	|	1024	1038	1048	|	...	1108	|	1124	...	1138	|	1148	1209	|	1224	1238	1248	|	1308	|	1324	...
Wakefield Westgate ... a.	|	|	|	|	1109	|	|	...	|	|	|	...	1209	|	|	|	|	|	1309	|	|	|	|	|	...
eeds .... d.	1017	1037	1058	1054	...	1117	1116	1126	1137	1158	1152	1207	...	1216	1217	1238	1258	1254	...	1317	1323	1337	1358	1354	1407
Selby .... d.	|	1100	|	|	...	|	|	|	1200	|	|	|	...	1240	|	1301	|	|	...	|	|	1400	|	|	|
Hull .... a.	|	1136	|	|	...	|	|	|	1236	|	|	|	...	1316	|	1338	|	|	...	|	|	1436	|	|	|
ork .... a.	1042	...	1129	1123	...	1142	1142	1154	...	1225	1218	1235	...	...	1243	...	1325	1324	...	1343	1348	...	1424	1423	1436
ork .... d.	1045	...	...	1126	...	1145	1154	1200	...	1227	1221	1237	...	...	1245	...	...	1327	...	1345	1354	...	1427	1426	1441
alton .... d.	|	...	...	|	...	1207	|	1222	...	|	|	1300	...	...	|	...	...	|	...	1407	|	...	|	|	1503
carborough .... a.	|	...	...	|	...	1232	|	1247	...	|	|	1325	...	...	|	...	...	|	...	1432	|	...	|	|	1528
Middlesbrough **570** ... a.	|	...	...	1227	...	...	|	...	...	1352	1321	...	...	...	|	...	...	1432	...	...	|	...	1524	1526	...
Newcastle **570** .... a.	1211	...	...	...	...	...	1335	...	...	...	...	...	...	...	1410	...	...	...	...	...	1531	...	...	...	...

	✕	⑦ 🍷	✕ 🍷	✕ 🍷	⑦ 🍷	Ⓐ 🍷	⑥ 🍷	⑦ 🍷	✕	✕ 🍷	⑦ B	✕ 🍷	⑦ 🍷	✕ 🍷	✕ B	✕	⑦ 🍷	✕ 🍷	Ⓐ	✕ 🍷	⑦ 🍷	✕ 🍷	✕	⑦ 🍷	✕ 🍷
verpool Lime Street ... d.	...	...	1222	...	...	...	...	1321	...	1322	...	...	...	...	...	...	...	1422	...	...	...	...	...	1521	1522
arrington Central ...... d.	...	...	1245	...	...	...	...	|	...	1345	...	...	...	...	...	...	...	1445	...	...	...	...	...	|	1545
Manchester Airport ✈ .. d.	...	...	|	...	1305	1328	1328	|	...	|	...	...	1405	1428	...	...	...	|	...	...	1505	1528	...	|	|
Manchester Victoria ... d.	1255	1309	|	...	|	|	|	1409	1355	|	...	...	|	|	...	1455	1509	|	...	...	|	|	1555	1609	|
anchester Piccadilly ... d.	|	|	1312	1334	1319	1350	1350	|	|	1412	...	1434	1419	1450	...	|	|	1512	...	1534	1517	1550	|	|	1612
alybridge .... d.	1310	|	1328	|	|	|	|	|	1410	1428	...	|	1451	|	...	1510	|	1528	...	|	1551	|	1610	|	1628
uddersfield .... d.	1338	|	1348	1408	|	1424	1424	|	1438	1448	...	1508	1511	1524	...	1538	1541	1548	...	1608	1611	1624	1638	1641	1648
Wakefield Westgate ... a.	1409	|	|	|	|	|	|	|	1509	|	...	|	|	|	...	1609	|	|	...	|	|	|	1709	|	|
eeds .... d.	...	1414	1417	1437	1458	1452	1452	1523	...	1517	1526	1537	1541	1552	1607	...	1612	1617	...	1637	1641	1654	...	1718	1717
Selby .... d.	...	1438	|	1500	|	|	|	|	...	|	|	1600	|	|	|	...	1637	|	...	1700	|	|	...	|	|
Hull .... a.	...	1515	|	1536	|	|	|	|	...	|	|	1636	|	|	|	...	1713	|	...	1736	|	|	...	|	|
ork .... a.	...	...	1451	...	1525	1518	1524	1548	...	1542	1557	...	1611	1618	1635	...	...	1642	...	...	1712	1723	...	1745	1742
ork .... d.	...	...	1454	...	...	1521	1527	1554	...	1545	1602	...	1614	1621	1638	...	...	1645	1712	...	...	1726	...	1749	1745
alton .... d.	...	...	|	...	...	|	|	|	...	1607	1624	...	|	|	1700	...	...	|	1738	...	...	|	...	|	1807
carborough .... a.	...	...	|	...	...	|	|	|	...	1632	1649	...	|	|	1725	...	...	|	1803	...	...	|	...	|	1832
Middlesbrough **570** ... a.	...	...	|	...	...	1626	1626	|	...	...	...	...	1719	1723	...	...	...	|	...	...	...	1832e	...	|	...
Newcastle **570** .... a.	...	...	1621h	...	...	...	...	1716	...	...	...	...	...	...	...	...	...	1814	...	...	...	...	...	1911	...

	⑦ B	✕ 🍷	⑦ 🍷	⑥ 🍷	Ⓐ 🍷	✕ B	✕	⑦ 🍷	⑥ 🍷	Ⓐ 🍷	⑦ 🍷	✕ 🍷	⑦ 🍷	✕ 🍷	✕	⑦ 🍷	✕ 🍷	⑦ B	✕ 🍷	⑦ 🍷	✕ 🍷	✕ B	✕	⑦ 🍷	✕ 🍷
verpool Lime Street ... d.	...	...	...	...	...	...	...	1621	1622	1622	...	...	...	...	...	1721	1722	...	...	...	...	...	...	1821	1822
arrington Central ...... d.	...	...	...	...	...	...	...	|	1645	1645	...	...	...	...	...	|	1745	...	...	...	...	...	...	|	1845
Manchester Airport ✈ .. d.	...	...	1605	1628	1628	...	...	|	|	|	...	...	1705	1728	...	|	|	...	...	1805	1828	...	...	|	|
Manchester Victoria ... d.	...	...	|	|	|	...	1655	1709	|	|	1733	...	|	|	1755	1809	|	...	...	|	|	...	1855	1909	|
anchester Piccadilly ... d.	...	1634	1619	1649	1649	...	|	|	1712	1712	|	1733	1719	1747	|	|	1812	...	1834	1819	1850	...	|	|	1912
alybridge .... d.	...	|	1651	1704	1704	...	1710	|	1728	1728	|	1748	1751	1800	1810	|	1828	...	|	1851	|	...	1910	|	1928
uddersfield .... d.	...	1708	1711	1724	1724	...	1738	1741	1748	1748	1806	1808	1813	1824	1840	1841	1848	...	1908	1911	1924	...	1938	1941	1948
Wakefield Westgate ... a.	...	|	|	|	|	...	1812	|	|	|	|	|	|	|	1911	|	|	...	|	|	|	...	2009	|	|
eeds .... d.	1726	1740	1742	1752	1752	1807	...	1809	1820	1822	1831	1837	1846	1852	...	1913	1917	1926	1937	1939	1952	2010	...	2013	2017
Selby .... d.	|	1807	|	|	|	|	...	|	|	|	1855	1901	|	|	...	|	|	|	2001	|	|	|	...	|	|
Hull .... a.	|	1846	|	|	|	|	...	|	|	|	1932	1939	|	|	...	|	|	|	2037k	|	|	|	...	|	|
ork .... a.	1754	...	1812	1818	1822	1836	...	1837	1846	1852	...	...	1912	1917	...	1940	1943	1958	...	2005	2018	2040	...	2039	2044
ork .... d.	1800	...	1817	1821	1826	1839	...	...	1853	1853	...	...	...	1921	...	1945	1947	2003	...	2008	2021	2052	...	...	...
alton .... d.	1823	...	|	|	|	1901	...	...	|	|	...	...	...	|	...	|	2009	2025	...	|	|	2114	...	...	...
carborough .... a.	1848	...	|	|	|	1926	...	...	|	|	...	...	...	|	...	|	2034	2050	...	|	|	2138	...	...	...
Middlesbrough **570** ... a.	...	...	1919	1923	1926	...	...	...	|	|	...	...	...	|	...	|	...	...	...	2114	2120	...	...	...	...
Newcastle **570** .... a.	...	...	...	...	...	...	...	...	2016	2016	...	...	...	2151	...	2107	...	...	...	...	...	...	...	...	...

	⑦ 🍷	⑦ 🍷	✕ 🍷	✕	⑦ 🍷	⑥ 🍷	Ⓐ 🍷	⑥	⑦ J	Ⓐ	⑦ 🍷	✕ 🍷	⑦ 🍷	✕ 🍷	✕	⑦ 🍷	⑦ 🍷	Ⓐ 🍷	⑥ 🍷	⑦ 🍷	Ⓐ 🍷	⑦ 🍷	Ⓐ 🍷	✕ 🍷	⑦ 🍷
verpool Lime Street ... d.	...	...	...	...	1921	1922	1922	...	...	...	...	...	2021	2022	...	...	...	...	...	...	...	...	...	...	...
arrington Central ...... d.	...	...	...	...	|	1945	1945	...	...	...	...	...	|	2045	...	...	...	...	...	...	...	...	...	...	...
Manchester Airport ✈ .. d.	...	1905	1928	...	|	|	|	...	...	...	2005	...	|	|	...	...	2105	2128	2128	2205	2228	2305	2328	0213	0215
Manchester Victoria ... d.	1933	|	|	1955	2009	|	|	...	...	...	|	...	2109	|	...	2133	|	|	|	|	|	|	|	|	|
anchester Piccadilly ... d.	|	1919	1950	|	|	2012	2012	...	...	...	2019	2050	|	2112	...	|	2119	2150	2150	2219	2250	2319	2350	0240	0239
alybridge .... d.	|	1951	|	2010	|	2028	2028	...	...	...	2051	|	|	2128	...	|	2151	|	|	2251	2305	|	|	|	|
uddersfield .... d.	2006	2013	2024	2038	2041	2048	2048	...	...	...	2111	2124	2141	2148	2152	2206	2213	2224	2224	2311	2325	0009	0024	0319r	|
Wakefield Westgate ... a.	|	|	|	2109	|	|	|	...	...	...	|	|	|	|	2223	|	|	|	|	|	|	|	|	|	|
eds .... d.	2031	2048	2052	...	2113	2117	2117	...	2126	...	2139	2152	2210	2217	...	2231	2246	2252	2252	2337	2351	0038	0053	0344r	0414
Selby .... d.	2055	|	|	...	|	|	|	...	|	...	▬	2216	|	|	...	2255	|	|	|	...	...	|	|	|	|
Hull .... a.	2131	|	|	...	|	|	|	...	|	...	...	2255	|	|	...	2331	|	|	|	...	...	|	|	|	|
rk .... a.	...	2115	2120	...	2139	2142	2142	...	2155	...	⑦	...	2238	2246	...	...	2312	2322	2322	...	...	0127	0142	0431	0453
rk .... d.	...	...	...	...	2142	2145	2145	2156	...	2206	2225	...	...	...	...	...	*2324*	*2330*	...	...	...	...	...	0433	...
alton .... d.	...	...	...	...	|	|	|	2218	...	2228	2247	...	...	...	...	...	|	|	...	...	...	...	...	|	...
arborough .... a.	...	...	...	...	|	|	|	2242	...	2252	2311	...	...	...	...	...	|	|	...	...	...	...	...	|	...
Middlesbrough **570** ... a.	...	...	...	...	|	|	|	...	...	...	...	...	...	...	...	...	|	|	...	...	...	...	...	0536	...
Newcastle **570** .... a.	...	...	...	...	2304	2310	2320	...	...	...	...	...	...	...	...	...	*0100*	*0117*	...	...	...	...	...	...	...

– [2] and 🍷 Blackpool - Scarborough.
– [2] and 🍷 Halifax - Scarborough.
J – [2] and 🍷 Blackpool - York.
P – [2] and 🍷 Preston - Scarborough.
e – Arrive 1824 on ⑥.
h – Arrive 1612 on Ⓐ.
k – Arrive 2043 on ⑥ Jan. 14 - May 27.
r – Depart 14 minutes later on ① until Jan. 9.

For an explanation of standard symbols see page 4

315

Table 551 — YORK and HULL - LEEDS - MANCHESTER - LIVERPOOL

2 class only

Service on ⑦ valid to Jan. 8 only. York - Leeds, see also Table 552. Manchester - Liverpool, see also Table 585.

Block 1

Station																					
Newcastle 570 d.									0610								0705	0713			
Middlesbrough 570 d.							0621											0745			
Scarborough d.								0638		0638			0729								
Malton d.								0700		0700			0751								
York a.						0715	0724	0727	0724				0815	0822	0831	0835					
York d.	0500		0604	0618		0704	0718	0727	0736	0740			0804	0819	0836	0836	0843				0907
Hull d.			0602	0610							0717	0721		0818							
Selby d.			0643	0651							0749	0755		0849							
Leeds d.	0551	0608	0637	0651	0706	0723	0723	0737	0751	0800	0808	0809	0824	0824	0837	0851	0908	0908	0913	0924	0937
Wakefield Westgate d.		0623				0725								0823t						0925	
Huddersfield d.	0613	0628	0654	0713	0728	0746	0746	0754		0828		0847	0847	0854		0914	0928	0928		0947	0954
Stalybridge d.	0633	0649	0725	0733	0749	0808	0808	0825		0834		0849		0925			0949	0949			1025
Manchester Piccadilly d.	0655	0708		0800	0755	0807	0825	0825	0900	0855		0907	0923	0925		1000	0955	1007	1007	1023	1100
Manchester Victoria a.			0745							0846					0946						
Manchester Airport + a.	0710			0815	0811				0915	0909				0930		1015	1010		1030	1030	1115
Warrington Central d.					0830					0930									1059	1059	
Liverpool Lime Street a.					0859					0959											

Block 2

Station																						
Newcastle 570 d.								0855	0912												1112	1118
Middlesbrough 570 d.	0809	0814				0921							1018							1024	1118	
Scarborough d.			0848		0915		0937			0955				1035	1043					1202	1215	1226	1231
Malton d.			0910		0937					1017				1057	1105								
York a.	0906	0911	0934		1001	1015	1032	1026		1043		1115	1121	1128		1137				1202	1207	1219	1237	1231
York d.	0919	0919	0937		1004	1019	1037	1037		1046		1107	1118	1123		1137		1056	1118	1207	1219	1237	1231
Hull d.			0856		0916							1018						1056	1118				
Selby d.			0927		0948							1049						1127	1149				
Leeds d.	0951	0951	1000	1008	1024	1037	1051	1110	1108	1115	1124	1137	1151	1157	1200	1208	1224	1237	1251	1308	1308
Wakefield Westgate d.					1025						1124						1225				
Huddersfield d.	1014	1014	1028		1047	1054		1114		1128	1154		1147		1214		1228	1247	1254	1314	1328	1328
Stalybridge d.	1055	1055	1049		1125					1149	1225						1249		1325		1349	1349
Manchester Piccadilly d.	1055	1055	1107		1123		1200	1155		1207			1223	1300	1255		1307	1323		1346	1400	1355	1407	1407
Manchester Victoria a.			1119				1146				1215	1210								1415	1410	
Manchester Airport + a.	1110	1110						1215	1210					1315	1310					1430	1430	
Warrington Central d.			1130					1230									1330				
Liverpool Lime Street a.			1159					1259	1259								1359			1459	1459	

Block 3

Station																					
Newcastle 570 d.	1058												1300	1314							
Middlesbrough 570 d.				1213									1234	1321					1436	1448	
Scarborough d.		1157			1236		1243					1355							1436	1448	
Malton d.		1219		1258		1305						1417							1458	1510	
York a.	1235	1243		1311	1322	1329				1359	1415	1432	1427	1444					1522	1534	
York d.	1240	1246		1307	1315	1324	1333	1337		1407	1418	1440	1431	1444		1506			1524	1537	1540	1518
Hull d.			1218						1309	1318					1416		1446				1518
Selby d.			1249						1340	1349					1448		1517				1549
Leeds d.	1310	1315	1324		1337	1351e	1354	1403	1408	1418	1424	1437	1451	1510	1508	1515	1524	1537	1551	1557	1608	1610	1624
Wakefield Westgate d.			1325								1425						1523				
Huddersfield d.		1347	1354		1414			1428	1446	1447	1454	1514	1530	1528		1547	1554	1559	1611	1628	1630	1647
Stalybridge d.		1425						1449		1525	1521		1549			1625	1621		1649		
Manchester Piccadilly d.		1423		1500	1455		1516	1507	1519	1523		1554	1555	1607		1623	1646	1654	1647	1707	1723
Manchester Victoria a.	1416		1446								1546			1614			1710			1714	
Manchester Airport + a.				1515	1510							1610	1610			1630				1732	1759
Warrington Central d.							1530							1630						1802	1759
Liverpool Lime Street a.	1459				1559	1559						1659	1659							1802	1759

Block 4

Station																					
Newcastle 570 d.				1513	1500												1709	1713		1758	1820
Middlesbrough 570 d.		1503	1521					1603		1615							1718		1757		
Scarborough d.					1557			1636	1648									1757		1856	1914
Malton d.					1619			1658	1710									1819			
York a.		1602	1615	1626	1637	1643		1702		1712	1722	1734				1815	1831	1832	1844	1907	1914
York d.		1606	1619	1637	1640	1646		1707		1715	1724	1737	1740			1807	1817	1837	1838	1847	1907	1919
Hull d.				1618				1646				1711					1812				
Selby d.				1649				1717				1749					1849				
Leeds d.		1637	1651	1708	1710	1715	1724	1737	1751	1751e	1754	1805	1810	1824		1837	1851	1908	1910	1915	1924	1937	1946
Wakefield Westgate d.	1625						1723							1824					1925		
Huddersfield d.	1654	1659	1714	1730	1730		1747	1754	1759	1811	1814		1828	1830	1847	1854	1859	1914	1928	1930	1947	1954	1959
Stalybridge d.	1725	1721					1825	1821				1849			1925	1921	1949			2021
Manchester Piccadilly d.		1754	1755	1807		1825		1854	1847	1855	1907		1923	1946		1954	1955	2007		2023	2054
Manchester Victoria a.	1755				1814		1846					1914	1946				2010	2010		2014	2110
Manchester Airport + a.		1810	1812				1910		1910			1930				2010	2010				2110
Warrington Central d.				1830								1930					2030				
Liverpool Lime Street a.				1859	1859							1959	1959				2059	2059			

Block 5

Station																					
Newcastle 570 d.								1917										2153	2208		
Middlesbrough 570 d.					1920					2005	2019										0145n
Scarborough d.		1836	1846			1940						2045	2045								
Malton d.		1858	1908			2002				2107	2107										
York a.		1922	1932		2015	2026		2034		2101	2115	2131	2131				2306	2304			0325
York d.		1924	1934	1935		2004	2019	2028		2037		2121		2134				2308	2307	0249	0238	0349	0348	0648
Hull d.	1846						1959								2106	2117					
Selby d.	1917						2030								2137	2151					
Leeds d.	1951	1954	2005	2010		2037	2051	2055	2106	2110		2137	2151		2203	2207	2220	2341	2337	0322	0311	0422	0421	0522
Wakefield Westgate d.				2023							2125			2242						0441	
Huddersfield d.	2011		2028	2030	2052	2114		2126	2130	2154	2159	2214	2311			0001	2359		0331		0441
Stalybridge d.			2049		2121			2149		2225	2221	2235					0021				
Manchester Piccadilly d.	2047		2107		2154	2155		2207		2254	2255				0045	0055	0451	0435	0551	0545	0651
Manchester Victoria a.				2114								2214	2246				0110	0120	0516	0500	0610	0610	0710
Manchester Airport + a.			2130		2210	2210				2310	2311										
Warrington Central d.							2231														
Liverpool Lime Street a.			2159	2159			2300	2259													

B – 🚲 and 🍴 Scarborough - Blackpool.   M – 🚲 and 🍴 Middlesbrough - Blackpool.   e – Arrive 8 minutes **earlier**.   n – Depart 0200 on ①.   t – Depart 0830 on Ⓐ.

Table 552 MANCHESTER and BLACKPOOL - BRADFORD - LEEDS - YORK

2 class only

km		⚒	⚒	⚒	⚒🍷	⚒	⑦	⚒	⚒🍷	⚒	⑦	⚒	⚒🍷	⚒	⑦	⚒	⚒🍷	⚒	⑦	⚒	⚒🍷	⚒	⑦	⚒
0	**Manchester Victoria** d.	...	...	0617h	...	0640	...	0717	...	0740	...	0817	...	0847	0915	0919	...	0947	...	1019	...	1047	1115	1119
17	Rochdale d.	...	...	0639	...	0701	...	0738	...	0800	...	0840	...	0903	0938	0941	...	1003	...	1041	...	1103	1138	1141
31	Todmorden d.	...	0623	0655	...	0717	...	0756	...	0817	...	0856	...	0919	0955	0955	...	1019	...	1055	...	1119	1155	1155
	Blackpool North 553 d.	...	|	|	0547	|	...	|	0647	|	...	|	...	|	|	|	0847	|	...	|	0947	|	|	|
	Preston 553 d.	...	|	|	0612	|	...	|	0712	|	...	|	0812	|	|	|	0912	|	...	|	1012	|	|	|
	Blackburn d.	...	|	|	0631	|	...	|	0731	|	...	|	0831	|	|	|	0931	|	...	|	1031	|	|	|
	Accrington d.	...	|	|	0641	|	...	|	0741	|	...	|	0841	|	|	|	0941	|	...	|	1041	|	|	|
	Burnley Manchester Road d.	...	|	|	0652	|	...	|	0752	|	...	|	0854	|	|	|	0954	|	...	|	1052	|	|	|
38	Hebden Bridge d.	...	0629	0701	0712	0723	...	0802	0813	0823	...	0902	0914	0925	1001	1001	1014	1025	...	1101	1112	1125	1201	1201
52	Halifax d.	...	0644	0717	0725	0738	...	0817	0825	0838	0916	0917	0926	0941	1016	1016	1026	1041	1046	1116	1124	1141	1216	1216
65	**Bradford Interchange** d.	...	0700	0734	0741	0800	0832	0833	0841	0900	0932	0933	0942	1000	1032	1033	1042	1100	1102	1133	1141	1200	1232	1233
80	**Leeds** a.	...	0724	0755	0802	0822	0853	0855	0902	0922	0953	0955	1002	1022	1053	1055	1102	1122	1123	1155	1202	1222	1253	1255
80	**Leeds 551** d.	0620	0727	...	0807	0827	0856	...	0907	0925	0956	...	1007	1025	1102	...	1107	1125	1126	...	1207	1225	1302	...
122	**York 551** a.	0657	0806	...	0835	0902	0932	...	0936	1004	1035	...	1035	1100	1138	...	1136	1204	1154	...	1237	1300	1338	...
	Scarborough **551** a.	...	...	...	0926	...	...	...	...	...	...	...	1125	...	...	...	...	...	...	...	1325	...	...	...

	⚒🍷	⚒	E🍷	⑦	⚒	⚒🍷	⚒	⑦	⚒	⚒🍷	⚒	E🍷	⑦	⚒	⚒🍷	⚒	⑦	⚒	⚒🍷	⑥	Ⓐ	E🍷	⑦	⚒
Manchester Victoria d.	...	1147	...	1215	1219	...	1247	1315	1319	...	1347	...	1415	1419	...	1447	1515	1519	...	1547	1547	...	1615	1619
Rochdale d.	...	1203	...	1238	1241	...	1303	1338	1341	...	1403	...	1438	1441	...	1503	1538	1541	...	1603	1603	...	1638	1641
Todmorden d.	...	1219	...	1255	1255	...	1319	1355	1355	...	1419	...	1455	1455	...	1519	1555	1555	...	1619	1619	...	1655	1657
Blackpool North 553 d.	1047	|	1103	|	|	1147	|	|	|	1247	|	1303	|	|	1347	|	|	|	1447	|	|	1503	|	|
Preston 553 d.	1112	|	1131	|	|	1212	|	|	|	1312	|	1331	|	|	1412	|	|	|	1512	|	|	1531	|	|
Blackburn d.	1131	|	1149	|	|	1231	|	|	|	1331	|	1349	|	|	1431	|	|	|	1531	|	|	1549	|	|
Accrington d.	1141	|	1200	|	|	1241	|	|	|	1341	|	1400	|	|	1441	|	|	|	1541	|	|	1600	|	|
Burnley Manchester Road d.	1152	|	1214	|	|	1252	|	|	|	1352	|	1414	|	|	1452	|	|	|	1552	|	|	1614	|	|
Hebden Bridge d.	1212	1225	1234	1301	1301	1312	1325	1401	1401	1412	1425	1434	1501	1501	1512	1525	1601	1601	1612	1625	1625	1634	1701	1702
Halifax d.	1224	1241	1246	1316	1316	1324	1341	1416	1416	1424	1441	1446	1516	1516	1524	1541	1616	1616	1624	1641	1641	1646	1716	1718
Bradford Interchange d.	1241	1300	1302	1332	1333	1341	1400	1432	1433	1441	1500	1502	1532	1533	1541	1600	1632	1633	1641	1700	1700	1702	1732	1734
Leeds a.	1302	1322	1323	1353	1355	1402	1422	1453	1455	1502	1522	1523	1553	1555	1602	1623	1653	1655	1702	1722	1722	1723	1753	1755
Leeds 551 d.	1307	1325	1326	1402	...	1407	1425	1502	...	1507	1525	1526	1556	...	1607	1625	1656	...	1705	1725	1731	1726	1756	...
York 551 a.	1336	1406	1355	1440	...	1436	1500	1538	...	1536	1604	1557	1634	...	1635	1700	1734	...	1736	1807	1814	1754	1834	...
Scarborough **551** a.	...	...	1446	...	...	1528	...	...	...	...	...	1649	...	...	1725	...	...	...	...	...	...	1848	...	...

	⚒🍷	⚒	⑦	⚒	⚒🍷	Ⓐ	⑥	E🍷	⑦	⚒	⚒🍷	Ⓐ	⑦	⚒	⚒🍷	E🍷	⑦	⚒	⑦	⚒	⚒🍷	E🍷	⑦	⚒
Manchester Victoria d.	...	1647	1715	1719	...	1747	1747	...	1815	1819	...	1847	1915	1919	...	...	2015	2019	2115	2119	...	...	2215	2247
Rochdale d.	...	1703	1738	1741	...	1809	1809	...	1838	1841	...	1908	1938	1941	...	...	2038	2041	2138	2141	...	...	2238	2309
Todmorden d.	...	1719	1755	1757	...	1825	1825	...	1855	1857	...	1925	1955	1957	...	...	2055	2057	2155	2157	...	...	2255	2325
Blackpool North 553 d.	1547	|	|	|	1647	|	|	1710	|	|	1747	...	|	|	1847	1911	|	|	|	|	2047	2111	|	|
Preston 553 d.	1612	|	|	|	1712	|	|	1733	|	|	1812	...	|	|	1912	1935	|	|	|	|	2112	2135	|	|
Blackburn d.	1631	|	|	|	1740	|	|	1752	|	|	1831	...	|	|	1931	1953	|	|	|	|	2131	2153	|	|
Accrington d.	1641	|	|	|	1751	|	|	1802	|	|	1841	...	|	|	1941	2004	|	|	|	|	2141	2204	|	|
Burnley Manchester Road d.	1652	|	|	|	1801	|	|	1813	|	|	1852	...	|	|	1952	2014	|	|	|	|	2152	2214	|	|
Hebden Bridge d.	1714	1725	1801	1802	1821	1831	1831	1833	1901	1902	1914	...	2001	2002	2014	2034	2102	2102	2201	2202	2214	2234	2301	2330
Halifax d.	1726	1741	1816	1818	1833	1847	1847	1846	1916	1918	1926	...	2016	2018	2026	2046	2116	2118	2216	2218	2226	2246	2316	2346
Bradford Interchange d.	1742	1800	1832	1834	1849	1903	1903	1902	1932	1934	1942	...	2032	2034	2042	2102	2132	2134	2232	2234	2242	2302	2332	0002
Leeds a.	1802	1822	1853	1855	1910	1924	1924	1923	1953	1955	2005	...	2053	2055	2105	2123	2153	2157	2254	2256	2302	2323	2356	0024
Leeds 551 d.	1807	1825	1856	1858	...	...	1925	1926	1956	1958	2010	...	2056	2058	...	2126	2156	2159	...	...	2304	...	...	...
York 551 a.	1836	1904	1932	1934	...	...	2004	1958	2034	2034	2040	...	2132	2136	...	2155	2234	2238	...	...	2346	...	...	...
Scarborough **551** a.	1926	...	...	...	...	...	...	...	...	...	2138	...	...	...	...	...	...	...	...	...	...	...	...	...

km		⚒	⚒🍷	⚒	⚒	⚒🍷	⚒	⚒	⚒	⚒🍷	⑦	Ⓐ	⑥	⚒	⚒🍷	⑦	⚒	E🍷	⚒	⚒🍷	⑦	⚒	⚒	⚒🍷
	Scarborough **551** d.	...	...	...	...	...	...	...	...	0638	...	...	...	...	...	...	...	...	...	...	...	...	...	0955
0	**York 551** d.	...	0543	...	0625	...	...	0700b	...	0727r	...	...	0749	0823	0843	0844	...	0924	0913	0946	0948	...	1024	1046
41	**Leeds 551** a.	...	0615	...	0700	...	...	0743b	...	0800r	...	...	0829	0859	0913	0924	...	0953	0959	1015	1024	...	1059	1115
41	**Leeds** d.	0549	0618	0630	0703	0717	0728	0746	0802	0818	0827	0832	0832	0902	0918	0927	0932	0957	1002	1018	1027	1032	1102	1118
56	**Bradford Interchange** d.	0612	0638	0653	0725	0738	0752	0809	0824	0838	0850	0855	0855	0924	0938	0950	0955	1017	1024	1038	1050	1055	1124	1138
69	Halifax d.	0625	0650	0706	0738	0750	0805	0822	0837	0850	0903	0908	0908	0937	0950	1003	1008	1041	1037	1050	1103	1108	1137	1150
83	Hebden Bridge d.	0640	0701	0721	0753	0802	0820	...	0852	0902	0924	0923	0923	0952	1002	1024	1023	1100	1052	1102	1124	1123	1152	1202
104	Burnley Manchester Road d.	|	0702	|	|	0821	|	...	|	0921	|	|	|	|	1021	|	|	1111	|	1121	|	|	|	1221
113	Accrington d.	|	0721	|	|	0831	|	...	|	0931	|	|	|	|	1031	|	|	1119	|	1131	|	|	|	1231
122	Blackburn d.	|	0739	|	|	0839	|	...	|	0939	|	|	|	|	1039	|	|	1142	|	1139	|	|	|	1239
141	**Preston 553** a.	|	0802	|	|	0858	|	...	|	0958	|	|	|	|	1058	|	|	1210	|	1158	|	|	|	1258
170	**Blackpool North 553** a.	|	0828	|	|	0924	|	...	|	1024	|	|	|	|	1124	|	|	...	|	1224	|	|	|	1324
	Todmorden d.	0647	...	0728	0800	...	0827	...	0859	...	0930	0930	0930	0959	...	1030	1030	...	1059	...	1130	1130	1159	...
	Rochdale d.	0707	...	0747	0817	...	0843	...	0920	...	0946	0943	0943	1020	...	1046	1043	...	1120	...	1146	1143	1220	...
	Manchester Victoria a.	0729	...	0810	0841	...	0904	...	0937	...	1009	1007	1007	1037	...	1109	1107	...	1137	...	1209	1207	1237	...

	⑦	⚒	E🍷	⚒	⚒🍷	⑦	⚒	⚒	⚒🍷	⑦	⚒	E🍷	⚒	⚒🍷	⑦	⚒	⚒	⚒🍷	⑦	⚒	E🍷	⚒	⚒🍷	⑦
Scarborough **551** d.	...	...	...	...	...	...	...	...	1157	...	...	1236	...	...	...	...	...	1355	...	...	1436	...	...	...
York 551 d.	1044	...	1123	1115	1146	1148	...	1224	1246	1244	...	1324	1319	1346	1348	...	1424	1444	1444	...	1524	1513c	1546	1548
Leeds 551 a.	1124	...	1153	1159	1215	1224	...	1259	1315	1324	...	1354	1359	1415	1424	...	1459	1515	1524	...	1554	1559	1615	1624
Leeds d.	1127	1132	1157	1202	1218	1227	1232	1302	1318	1327	1332	1357	1402	1418	1427	1432	1502	1518	1527	1532	1557	1602	1618	1627
Bradford Interchange d.	1150	1155	1217	1224	1238	1250	1255	1324	1338	1350	1355	1417	1424	1438	1450	1455	1524	1538	1550	1555	1617	1624	1638	1650
Halifax d.	1203	1208	1229	1237	1250	1303	1308	1337	1350	1403	1408	1429	1437	1450	1503	1508	1537	1550	1603	1608	1629	1637	1650	1703
Hebden Bridge d.	1224	1223	1241	1252	1302	1324	1323	1352	1402	1424	1423	1444	1452	1502	1518	1523	1552	1602	1618	1623	1641	1652	1702	1718
Burnley Manchester Road d.	|	|	1300	|	1321	|	|	|	1421	|	|	1505	|	1521	|	|	|	1621	|	|	1700	|	1721	|
Accrington d.	|	|	1311	|	1331	|	|	|	1431	|	|	1515	|	1531	|	|	|	1631	|	|	1710	|	1731	|
Blackburn d.	|	|	1319	|	1339	|	|	|	1439	|	|	1523	|	1539	|	|	|	1639	|	|	1718	|	1739	|
Preston 553 a.	|	|	1342	|	1358	|	|	|	1458	|	|	1542	|	1558	|	|	|	1658	|	|	1744	|	1758	|
Blackpool North 553 a.	|	|	1410	|	1424	|	|	|	1524	|	|	1612	|	1624	|	|	|	1724	|	|	1808	|	1824	|
Todmorden d.	1230	1230	...	1259	...	1330	1330	1359	...	1430	1430	...	1459	...	1525	1530	1559	...	1625	1630	...	1659	...	1725
Rochdale d.	1246	1243	...	1320	...	1346	1343	1420	...	1446	1443	...	1520	...	1542	1543	1620	...	1642	1648	...	1720	...	1742
Manchester Victoria a.	1309	1307	...	1337	...	1409	1407	1437	...	1509	1507	...	1537	...	1605	1607	1637	...	1705	1712	...	1737	...	1805

	⚒	⚒	⚒🍷	⑦	⚒	E🍷	⚒	⚒🍷	⑦	⚒	⚒	⚒🍷	⑦	⚒	E🍷	⚒	⑦	⚒	⑦	⚒	⑦	⚒	⚒	⚒
Scarborough **551** d.	...	...	1557	...	...	1636	...	...	...	...	...	1757	...	...	1836	...	...	...	...	...	...	...	...	...
York 551 d.	...	1624	1646	1644	...	1724	1718	1746	1748	...	1823	1847	1844	...	1924	...	1948	1948	2044	2053	2148	2149	2249	2308
Leeds 551 a.	...	1659	1715	1724	...	1754	1759	1815	1827	...	1859	1915	1924	...	1954	...	2024	2029	2124	2129	2224	2229	2333	2338
Leeds d.	1632	1702	1718	1727	1732	1757	1802	1818	1848	1832	1902	1918	1927	1932	1957	2018	2027	2032	2127	2132	2227	2232	...	...
Bradford Interchange d.	1655	1724	1738	1750	1755	1817	1824	1838	1850	1856	1925	1938	1950	1955	2017	2038	2050	2055	2150	2155	2250	2255	...	...
Halifax d.	1708	1737	1750	1803	1808	1829	1837	1850	1903	1909	1938	1950	2003	2008	2029	2050	2103	2108	2203	2208	2302	2308	...	...
Hebden Bridge d.	1723	1752	1802	1818	1823	1841	1852	1902	1918	1924	...	2002	2018	2023	2041	2102	2118	2123	2218	2223	...	2323	...	...
Burnley Manchester Road d.	|	|	1821	|	|	1900	|	1921	|	|	...	2021	|	|	2100	2121	|	|	|	|	...	|	...	...
Accrington d.	|	|	1831	|	|	1910	|	1931	|	|	...	2031	|	|	2110	2131	|	|	|	|	...	|	...	...
Blackburn d.	|	|	1839	|	|	1918	|	1939	|	|	...	2039	|	|	2118	2139	|	|	|	|	...	|	...	...
Preston 553 a.	|	|	1858	|	|	1944	|	1958	|	|	...	2058	|	|	2138	2158	|	|	|	|	...	|	...	...
Blackpool North 553 a.	|	|	1924	|	|	2008	|	2024	|	|	...	2124	|	|	2202	2224	|	|	|	|	...	|	...	...
Todmorden d.	1730	1759	...	1825	1830	...	1859	...	1925	1931	...	...	2025	2030	...	...	2125	2130	2225	2230	...	2330	...	...
Rochdale d.	1749	1820	...	1842	1849	...	1920	...	1942	1949	...	...	2042	2049	...	...	2142	2149	2242	2249	...	2349	...	...
Manchester Victoria a.	1812	1837	...	1905	1912	...	1937	...	2005	2012	...	...	2105	2112	...	...	2205	2212	2305	2312	...	0006	...	...

– To or from Blackpool North (Preston from Nov. 13). **b** – **Not** ⑥. **c** – Depart 1519 on ⑥. **h** – Depart 0623 on ⑥. **r** – On ⑥ depart York 0740, arrive Leeds 0809.

2 *For an explanation of standard symbols see page 4* 317

Table 553 — STOCKPORT - MANCHESTER - SOUTHPORT and BLACKPOOL

2 class only

km																									
0	Stockport.......................d.	...	0640	0651	...	0740	...	...	0809	0815	0840	...	...	0910	0909	0939	0940	...	...	1010	1009	1040	1039	...
	Manchester Airport ✈.....d.	0556					0745	0749				0845	0856					0945	0956					1045
10	Manchester Piccadilly......d.	0612	0650	0701	0712	0750	0759	0812	0823	0825	0850	0859	0912	0920	0923	0952	0950	0959	1012	1020	1023	1050	1052	1059
28	Bolton.............................d.	0633	0711	0725	0733	0811	0821	0833	0845	0846	0911	0921	0933	0941	0945	1012	1015	1021	1033	1041	1045	1111	1112	1121
43	Wigan Wallgate...............d.			0752						0905					1000		1027				1100			1127	
71	Southport.......................a.			0830						0937					1038		1056				1132			1156	
60	Preston...........................d.	0708	0751			0808	0848	0851	0902	0921			0945	0954	1002		1020		1050	1051	1102		1120	1145	1151
88	Blackpool North ....a.	0736	0821			0836	0916	0920	0928	0948			1013	1023	1028		1046		1118	1120	1128		1146	1213	1220

Stockport.......................d.	❖ and at	1610	1609	1640	1639		1709	1740	1740	1739		1809	1839	1840			1909	1920	1939			
Manchester Airport ✈.....d.	the	1556				1645	1656				1745	1756			1845	1856				1945	1956
Manchester Piccadilly......d.	same	1612	1620	1623	1650	1652	1659	1712	1723	1750	1750	1752	1759	1812	1823	1852	1850	1859	1913	1923	1931	1952	1959	2012
Bolton.............................d.	mins.	1633	1641	1642	1711	1712	1721	1733	1742	1811	1811	1812	1821	1833	1842	1911	1911	1921	1933	1942	1952	2012	2021	2033
Wigan Wallgate...............d.	past	1705			1727				1829				1827			1927	1931				2010	2027	
Southport.......................a.	each	1743			1756				1901				1856			1956	2009				2042	2056	
Preston...........................d.	hour	1714		1718	1745		1751	1808	1818		1845		1854	1908	1918		1951	2008	2013			2048	2108
Blackpool North ....a.	until	1742		1743	1813		1816	1836	1843		1913		1920	1936	1943		2016	2036	2035			2114	2136

Stockport.......................d.	2009	2020	...	2039		2109						Blackpool North 553 ...... d.	0600		0721		0756	0800	0824	0827	0850
Manchester Airport ✈.....d.			2045		2056		2145	2156	2245	2256		Preston 553 .... d.	0627		0750		0826	0827	0851	0854	0925
Manchester Piccadilly......d.	2023	2031	2059	2052	2112	2123	2159	2212	2259	2312		Southport..................... d.		0702		0752					
Bolton.............................d.	2042	2052	2121	2112	2133	2142	2221	2233	2321	2333		Wigan Wallgate.......... d.		0735		0830					
Wigan Wallgate...............d.	2115		2127									Bolton.............................. d.	0700	0755	0825	0855	0900	0900	0924	0925	1000
Southport.......................a.	2153		2156									Manchester Piccadilly.... a.	0723	0819	0851	0919	0923	0923	0949	0949	1023
Preston...........................d.	2118		2154		2208	2215	2254	2309	2355	0008		Manchester Airport ✈..... a.	0742				0940	0942			1040
Blackpool North ....a.	2143		2219		2236	2237	2319	2340	0020	0036		Stockport..................... a.		0834	0904c	0929			1002	0959	

Blackpool North 553 ...... d.	0909		0924	0927		0956	1009	1024	1027	...	and at	1556	1603	1625	1630		1700	1705	1727	1730		
Preston 553 .... d.	0933		0951	0954		1026	1033	1051	1054	...	the	1626	1628	1654	1653		1728	1731	1754	1753	
Southport..................... d.		0957			1005					1102	1105	same		1657	1707						1757	1802
Wigan Wallgate.......... d.		1035			1035					1135	1135	mins.		1735	1737						1835	1837
Bolton.............................. d.	1000	1055	1024	1025	1054	1100	1100	1124	1125	1155	1154	past	1700	1755	1724	1755	1755	1800	1825	1824	1855	1854
Manchester Piccadilly........ d.	1023	1119	1049	1049	1119	1123	1123	1149	1149	1219	1219	each	1723	1724	1749	1749	1819	1819	1823	1823	1849	1849	1919
Manchester Airport ✈...... d.	1042							1140	1142			hour	1740	1747					1842	1840		
Stockport..................... a.		1129c	1102	1059	1134			1202	1159	1229	1234	until		1759	1829	1834				1859	1902	1929	1934

Blackpool North 553 ...... d.	1805	1809	1827	1830		1900	1905	1930		2000	2005	2030			2100	2105	2130	2200	2205	2300	2305
Preston 553 .... d.	1831	1833	1854	1853		1928	1931	1953		2027	2031	2053			2127	2131	2153	2227	2231	2327	2331
Southport..................... d.			1902	1907				2002	2007			2102	2107								
Wigan Wallgate.......... d.			1935	1937				2035	2037			2135	2137								
Bolton.............................. d.	1900	1900	1925	1924	1955	1954	2000	2000	2024	2055	2054	2100	2100	2124	2154	2200	2200	2224	2300	2300	0001	0001
Manchester Piccadilly........ d.	1923	1923	1949	1949	2019	2019	2023	2023	2049	2119	2119	2123	2123	2149	2219	2219	2223	2223	2249	2323	2323	0023	0023
Manchester Airport ✈...... d.	1940	1942					2042	2040				2142	2140				2242	2240		2342	2340	0050	0050
Stockport..................... a.			1959	2002	2029	2034			2102	2129	2134			2202	2232	2234			2302				

c – ⑥ only.

❖ – Timings may vary by a few minutes on some journeys.

Table 554 — LOCAL SERVICES IN MANCHESTER and LIVERPOOL AREAS

2 class only

MANCHESTER - BUXTON 42 km. Journey time: 54 - 58 minutes.

From Manchester Piccadilly:
✗: 0642, 0740, 0854, 0950 and hourly to 1550, then 1620Ⓐ, 1650, 1723Ⓐ, 1820, 1850, 1950, 2050, 2150, 2300.
⑦: 0950 and hourly to 2250.
Trains call at Stockport 9 and at New Mills Newtown 29 minutes later.

From Buxton:
✗: 0600, 0636, 0704, 0731, 0756, 0856, 0959, 1102, 1159, 1302, 1359, 1502, 1547, 1659, 1720Ⓐ, 1756, 1859, 1956, 2056, 2256.
⑦: 0922 (to Nov. 6), 1022 and hourly to 2222.
Trains call at New Mills Newtown 21 and at Stockport 40 minutes later.

MANCHESTER - BLACKBURN 41 km. Journey time: 46 - 61 minutes. NO SERVICE ON ⑦.

From Manchester Victoria:
✗: 0640, 0713, 0740, 0820, 0830, 0913 and hourly to 1613, then 1643Ⓐ, 1713, 1743Ⓐ, 1813 and hourly to 2313.

From Blackburn:
✗: 0647Ⓐ, 0720, 0747Ⓐ, 0822, 0847, 0920, 0944, 1020 and hourly to 1620, then 1715, 1743Ⓐ, 1820, 1843Ⓐ, 1910, 2012, 2112, 2210.

MANCHESTER - ALTRINCHAM - CHESTER 73 km. Journey time: 81 - 93 minutes. NO SERVICE ON ⑦.

From Manchester Piccadilly:
✗: 0650Ⓐ, 0750, 0920 and hourly to 1620, then 1647Ⓐ, 1720, 1747Ⓐ, 1820, 1920, 2020, 2120, 2220⑥, 2314Ⓐ.
Trains call at Stockport 11, at Altrincham 27, and at Northwich 50 minutes later.

From Chester:
✗: 0620, 0650Ⓐ, 0720, 0750Ⓐ, 0827Ⓐ, 0849⑥, 0950, 1100, 1150, 1300, 1350, 1450, 1550, 1720, 1800, 1900, 2000, 2100, 2250.
Trains call at Northwich 31, at Altrincham 55, and at Stockport 74 minutes later.

MANCHESTER - LIVERPOOL 51 km. Journey time: 48 - 64 minutes.

From Manchester Victoria (on ✗) / Oxford Road (on ⑦):
✗: 0552, 0619, 0649, 0729, 0801, 0850, 0901, 0934, 1001, 1050, 1101, 1201, 1250, 1301, 1401, 1450, 1501, 1601, 1650, 1733, 1850, 2001, 2050, 2201, 2301.
⑦: 0818, 0918 and hourly to 2218.
Trains call at St Helens Junction 25-33 minutes later.

From Liverpool Lime Street:
✗: 0557, 0652, 0712, 0753, 0827, 0927, 0953, 1027, 1127, 1153, 1227, 1327, 1353, 1427, 1527, 1553, 1627, 1717, 1737, 1842, 1952, 2027, 2152, 2327.
⑦: 0832, 0932 and hourly to 2232.
Trains call at St Helens Junction 19-26 minutes later.

LIVERPOOL - CHESTER 29 km. Journey time: 40 minutes.

From Liverpool Lime Street:
Ⓐ: 0614, 0637, 0659, 0714, 0729, 0759, 0814, 0844 and half-hourly to 1544, then 1607, 1629, 1652, 1707, 1722, 1744, 1759, 1822, 1844, 1914 and half-hourly to 2344.
⑥⑦: 0614⑥, 0644⑥, 0714⑥, 0744, 0814 and half-hourly to 2344.

From Chester:
Ⓐ: 0619, 0649, 0719, 0734, 0804, 0826, 0849, 0919 and half-hourly to 1719, then 1749, 1756, 1819, 1849 and half-hourly to 2319.
⑥⑦: 0619⑥, 0649⑥, 0719⑥, 0819 and half-houly to 2319 (service at 1719 not ⑥).

LIVERPOOL - SOUTHPORT 31 km. Journey time: 40 minutes.

From Liverpool Central:
✗: 0606, 0621 and every 15 minutes to 1651, then 1702⑥, 1706⑥, 1710Ⓐ, 1721, 1736, and every 15 minutes to 2306, 2336.
⑦: 0806, 0836 and half-hourly to 2306.

From Southport:
✗: 0549, 0604 and every 15 minutes to 0734, then 0744Ⓐ, 0749⑥, 0754Ⓐ, 0804, 0819⑥, 0824Ⓐ, 0834, 0849 and every 15 minutes to 2319.
⑦: 0819, 0849 and half-hourly to 2249, 2304.

LIVERPOOL - ORMSKIRK 21 km. Journey time: 27 minutes.

From Liverpool Central:
✗: 0600, 0630, 0700, 0715 and every 15 minutes to 1900, then 1930, 2000 and every 30 minutes to 2330.
⑦: 0800, 0830 and every 30 minutes to 2330.

From Ormskirk:
✗: 0612, 0642, 0712, 0727 and every 15 minutes to 1912, then 1942, 2012 and every 30 minutes to 2312.
⑦: 0812, 0842 and every 30 minutes to 2312.

For an explanation of standard symbols see page 4

Table 555 — CREWE and MANCHESTER - HOLYHEAD

2 class only (1, 2 class on London trains)

km											⑦q	⑦r		⑦					⑥	⑦	⑦r	B
	London Euston 550 ....d.	...	...	...	...	...	...	...	...	...	...	...	...	...	...	...	...	0853	...	...	...	
0	Crewe ....d.	0033	0643	0712	...	0817	0849	...	0932	0949	0950	0950	...	1024	...	...	1100	1107	...	...	1124
	Manchester Piccadilly ...d.	...	...	0720b	...	0820	...	...	0917	...	...	1012v	1017	...	...	...	1010				
	Warrington Bank Quay ▲ ..d.	...	...	0750	...	0854	...	...	0950	...	...	1042	1050								
34	Chester ....d.	0056	0706	0735	0822	0840	0912	0924	0955	1012	1011	1017	1022	1047	1111	1118	1123	1123	1130	1130k	1147
54	Flint ....d.	...	0722	0751	0835	0856	...	...	1032	1037			1138			1146					
76	Prestatyn ....d.	...	0736	0805	0849	0910	0949	...	1046	1051			1143	1152	1201	1200	1212				
82	Rhyl ....d.	...	0742	0811	0855	0916	0955	1024	1052	1057	1116	1142	1149	1158	1208	1206	1218				
89	Abergele and Pensarn ....d.	...	0748	0817	...	0922			1059	1104			1205		1212						
99	Colwyn Bay ....d.	...	0757	0826	0907	0931	1007	1036	1107	1112	1128	1154	1201	1213	1221	1221	1230				
106	Llandudno Junction 557 ...d.	0139	0810	0833	0914	0918	0938	1014	1043	1047	1106	1127	1120	1130	1135	1202	1209	1222	1229	1228	1237	1238
111	Llandudno 557 ....d.	...	...	0845	...	0926	0949	1055	1138			1146		1221			1245				
107	Conwy ....d.	...	0812x	0934					1108x		1122x	1133x									
114	Penmaenmawr ....d.	...	0818x						1114x		1128x	1139x									
130	Bangor ....d.	0157	0832			1034	1101		1128		1142	1203	1219		1247	1301	1255				
170	Holyhead ....a.	0236	0910			1130	1206		1218		1251		1323	1340	1335						

		⑦			⑦r	Ⓐ	⑥	⑦		⑦			⑦								⑦
	London Euston 550 ....d.	...	0850	...	...	1020	...	...	...	...	...	...	...	...	...	...	...	...	...	...	
	Crewe ....d.	1149	1149	...	1209	...	1224	1224	...	1249	...	1324	1344	1349	...	1415	1424	1449	...	1524	1524
	Manchester Piccadilly ....d.	...		1117	...				...	1217					1305	1317			1417	1421		
	Warrington Bank Quay ▲ ..d.	...		1150	...				...	1250					1350			1450				
	Chester ....d.	1212	1214	1218	...	1232	...	1249	1247	1307	1312	1318	...	1347	1407	1412	1415	1418	1436	1447	1512	1518	1534	1547	1546
	Flint ....d.	...			...	1248			1303	1322			1400				1500			1600	1601	
	Prestatyn ....d.	...	1243	...	1302		1317	1336	1345		1414				1445	1502	1514		1545		1614	1615
	Rhyl ....d.	...	1244	1249	...	1308	1320	1323	1342	1351		1420			1451	1508	1520		1551		1620	1621
	Abergele and Pensarn ....d.	...			1314		1329	1349			1427					1527				1627	1628
	Colwyn Bay ....d.	...	1256	1301	...	1323		1333	1338	1357		1403		1435		1503	1520	1535	⑦r	1603	1635	1636
	Llandudno Junction 557 ...d.	1259	1313	1308	1318	1330	1340	1343	1345	1405		1411	1415	1443		1511	1527	1543	1555	1615	1643	1644
	Llandudno 557 ....d.	1307		1319		1348						1423	1430			1524			1603	1624		
	Conwy ....d.	...		1320x					1407x											1647x
	Penmaenmawr ....d.	...		1326x					1413x		1450x										1653x
	Bangor ....d.	...	1331		1340	1350		1401	1405	1443		1506	1530		1600	1600		1703	1722
	Holyhead ....a.	...	1411		1418			1435		1531			1608		1630	1630			2128

			⑦		⑦		⑦					⑦			Ⓐ	⑦	⑥	Ⓐ	⑦		⑦
	London Euston 550 ....d.	1549	1553	...	1614	1624	1649	1653	...	1724	1737	1749	...	1824	...	...	1842	1849	1849	...	1904
	Crewe ....d.			1517					1617				1717		1720		1750v	1755		1805	1817	
	Manchester Piccadilly ....d.			1550					1650				1750			1823	1828		1850		
	Warrington Bank Quay ▲ ..d.																				
	Chester ....d.	1612	1616	1618	...	1636	1647	1712	1718	1722	1747	1800	1812	1822	1825	1831	1849	1857	1859	1907	1912	1912	1915	1918	1930
	Flint ....d.					1651			1737	1803			1844	1849		1910		1922		
	Prestatyn ....d.		1645		1705	1714		1743	1751	1817		1849	1858		1924	1936	1940	1940		1958
	Rhyl ....d.		1651		1711	1720		1749	1757	1823		1855	1904		1930	1942	1946	1946		2004
	Abergele and Pensarn ....d.			1718	1727			1804						⑦ 1936	1949		
	Colwyn Bay ....d.		1703		1726	1735		1801	1812	1835		1907	1916		1945	1957	1958	1958		2016
	Llandudno Junction 557 ...d.		1711	1714	1734	1743		1808	1823	1842		1915	1924	1935	1956	2005	2005	2005		2025
	Llandudno 557 ....d.		1724					1833			1927		1950						2025
	Conwy ....d.			1716x												2008x		
	Penmaenmawr ....d.			1722x												2014x		
	Bangor ....d.			1736	1806	1803		1838		1900			1956		2014		2043	2023	2025		2056
	Holyhead ....a.			1814	1836			1907		1938					2043			2052		2128

			Ⓐ	⑦	Ⓐ	⑦q	⑦r	G					⑦			⑥	⑦			⑦	⑦	Ⓐ	Ⓐ	⑥	⑥
	London Euston 550 ....d.	...	1730		...	...	...	...	...	...	...	...	...	1920	1930	2010	...	...	2040	...	B				
	Crewe ....d.	1927	1935	1938	...	2007	2007	2024	2042	2050	...	2108	...	2124	2137	2142	2212	2217	...	2301	...	2313	2315	2242
	Manchester Piccadilly ....d.				1917						2017		2020						2210		2217			2314
	Warrington Bank Quay ▲ ..d.				1950						2050								2250					2346
	Chester ....d.	1950	2003	2001	2018	2029	2040n	2046	2105	2113	2118	2129	2131	2147	2200	2205	2237	2239	2250	2321	2324	2322	2336	2338	2346
	Flint ....d.	2003				2044		2101							2254	2306				
	Prestatyn ....d.	2017	2028			2058	2109	2115							2308	2320				
	Rhyl ....d.	2023	2035			2104	2115	2121					2231	2235	2307	2314	2326		2355		0005
	Abergele and Pensarn ....d.					2111	2122	2128								2332			
	Colwyn Bay ....d.	2035	2048			2119	2130	2136					2244	2248	2320	2326	2341		0008		0017
	Llandudno Junction 557 ...d.	2043	2059			2127	2138	2144					2254	2259	2331	2334	2352		0018		0024
	Llandudno 557 ....d.	2053															2337x			
	Conwy ....d.					2130x	2141x	2146x											
	Penmaenmawr ....d.					2136x	2147x	2152x								2343x			
	Bangor ....d.		2117			2206	2217	2206					2312	2317	2349	2358			0036		0042
	Holyhead ....a.		2150			2235	2246	2244					2348	2352	0034	0029			0112		0125

km		B	⑥	⑦			G	P						⑥	⑦			⑦						⑦	
0	Holyhead ....d.	0315	0335	...	...	0507	0524	...	...	...	0635	...	...	...	0750	...	0804	...	...	...	
40	Bangor ....d.	0343	0404	...	0534	0602	...	...	0700	0710	0724	...	...	0822	...	0839				
56	Penmaenmawr ....d.									0722x						0852x				
63	Conwy ....d.									0728x						0857x				
	Llandudno 557 ....d.						0631				0750	0758		0850		0931			
64	Llandudno Junction 557 ..d.	0402				0605	0620	0641	0719	0734	0743	0759	0806	0841	0905			0941
71	Colwyn Bay ....d.					0611	0627	0647	0725		0749	0805		0847	0911		0947
81	Abergele and Pensarn ....d.						0655			0757			0855				0955
88	Rhyl ....d.				0622	0638	0702	0736		0804	0816		0902	0922		1002
94	Prestatyn ....d.				0628		0708	0742		0810	0822		0908	0928		1008
116	Flint ....d.				0642		0721	0756		0823				1021
136	Chester ....d.	0447	0502	0558	0630	0647	0703	0709	0725	0741	0755	0817	0819	0841	0855	0917	0941	0957	1017	1019	1042
165	Warrington Bank Quay ▼ ..d.				0718		0752	0822		0921			1021
200	Manchester Piccadilly ....a.				0754		0828v	0858		0958			1058
	Crewe ....a.	0522	0539	0621	0653		0724	0735		0805	0840	0840	0905	0940	1005	1040	1042
	London Euston 550 ....a.		0803			0934							

— [bicycle] and [restaurant] Birmingham International - Holyhead and v.v.
— [bicycle] and [restaurant] Cardiff Central - Shrewsbury - Crewe - Holyhead and v.v.
— [bicycle] and [restaurant] Holyhead - London. Pullman service and [knife/fork] available in 1 cl.

b – Manchester **Oxford Road**.
k – Arrives 1120.
n – Arrives 2027.

q – To Apr. 9.
v – Manchester **Victoria**.
x – Stops on request.

r – From Apr. 16.

— **Warrington Bank Quay - Chester** on ⑦:
Jan. 15 - Apr. 9: 1208, 1408, 1608, 1808, 2008 (journey time 59 mins);
Apr. 16 - May 21: 1201 [bus], 1439 [bus], 1709, 1939 (journey time 56-57 mins).

— ▼ **Chester - Warrington Bank Quay** on ⑦:
Jan. 15 - Apr. 9: 1132, 1332, 1532, 1732, 1932, 2132 (journey time 49-53 mins);
Apr. 16 - May 21: 1020 [bus], 1300 [bus], 1832, 2102 (journey time 48-58 mins).

Table 555 — HOLYHEAD - MANCHESTER and CREWE

2 class only (1, 2 class on London trains)

Holyhead d.	0905	…		…	0947										…	1155		…		1242	
Bangor d.	0934	…	0952	1022	1046					1213	1222			…	1311	1317	
Penmaenmawr d.	│		1004x	│	│					│	│			…	1324x	…	
Conwy d.	│		1009x	│	│					│	│			…	1330x	…	
Llandudno 557 d.		0956	│	1029	│	1043		1105	1120r	1127	1156	1215	1253	1320	1326	│	
Llandudno Junction 557 d.	0952	1005	1014	1036	1041	1050	1105	1125	1130	1135	1205	1223	1231	1241	1302	1328	1334	1336	1341
Colwyn Bay d.	0959	1011	──	1047	──	1111	1136	1141	1211	1237	1247	1308	──	1342	1347
Abergele and Pensarn d.			1055			1147		1245	1255		1350	1355
Rhyl d.	1010	1022	1102	1122	1147	1155	1222	1252	1302	1319	1357	1402
Prestatyn d.	1017	1028	1108	1128	1153	1202	1228	1258	1308	1325	1403	1408
Flint d.	│	│	1121	│	1207	1218	│	1321	│	1416	1421
Chester d.	1046	1050	1057	1117	1141	1145	1157	1217	1245	1241	1254	1257	1317	1342	1339	1357	1417	1418	1451	1439	1455
Warrington Bank Quay ▼ d.		1121		1221		1321		1421	
Manchester Piccadilly a.	1154	1158	1258	1358	1358	1458	1556	
Crewe a.	1113	1140	1205	1208	1240	1308	1305	1340	1405	1401	1440	1441	1501	1518
London Euston 550 a.	1319y													

Holyhead d.	…	1330	…	1330	…			1402		1425		1508			1530	1555			1549	
Bangor d.	…	1359	1408	1422		1446	1500	1517	1537	1608	1622	1626	
Penmaenmawr d.		│	│			1529x	│	│	1639x	
Conwy d.		│	│			1535x	│	│	1645x	
Llandudno 557 d.	1353	│	1410	│	1451	1450	│	1552	1610	1625	1650	
Llandudno Junction 557 d.	1402	1418	1418	1426	1441	1500	1458	1504	1541	1555	1602	1618	1626	1641	1645	1650	1700
Colwyn Bay d.	1408	1424	1447	1506	──	1510	1547	1602	1608	──	1632	1647	1656	1706
Abergele and Pensarn d.			1455		1518	1555		1655	1704	│
Rhyl d.	1419	1435	1502	1517	1525	1602	1613	1619	1642	1702	1711	1717
Prestatyn d.	1425	1508	1523	1531	1608	1625	1708	1717	1723
Flint d.	│	1521	│	1544	1621	│	1721	│	1731	│
Chester d.	1457	1510	1517	1521	1539	1521	1608	1617	1618	1628	1639	1647	1652	1657	1717	1721	1739	1742	1752	1806	1755
Warrington Bank Quay ▼ d.	1521	1538	│	1621	│	1721	│	1902	1821
Manchester Piccadilly a.	1558	1621v	1658	1731	1758	1858
Crewe a.	1540	1547	1601	1631	1640	1649	1701	1716	1715	1740	1746	1802	1815	1827
London Euston 550 a.	1811	1921y	2018	

Holyhead d.	…	1610	1655	…	1657				1750	1822		1817	1858				2037	2155	2155
Bangor d.	…	1645	1722	1723	1727	1739x	1803x		1917t	1924	2009	2035	2105	2113	2226	2222
Penmaenmawr d.	1657x	1703x	1745x	1809x		1929x	2118x	2125x
Conwy d.	1703x	1745x	1809x	1935x	2130x	
Llandudno 557 d.	1657	│	│	1753	│	1855	1929	│	2115	│
Llandudno Junction 557 d.	1706	1709	1741	1742	1751	1802	1815	1841	1905	1936	1941	1943	2028	2053	2123	2137	2243	2245
Colwyn Bay d.	1712	1747	1748	1757	1808	1821	1847	1911	1947	1949	2034	2059	2134	2143	2249	2251
Abergele and Pensarn d.			1805	│	1855	│	1955	1957	2107	2142	2151	│
Rhyl d.	1723	1758	1759	1812	1819	1832	1902	1922	2002	2004	2045	2114	2149	2158	2300	2303
Prestatyn d.	1729	1818	1825	1838	1908	1928	2008	2010	2051	2120	2155	2204
Flint d.	1743	│	1831	│	1921	│	2021	2024	2105	2134	2208	2218
Chester d.	1814	1817	1830	1838	1852	1851	1857	1906	1927	1941	1957	2001	2041	2057	2059	2104	2140	2155	2233	2241	2330	2335
Warrington Bank Quay ▼ d.			1921	2022	2122	2221
Manchester Piccadilly a.	1958	2012	2058	2158	2218	2258	2348
Crewe a.	1840	1853	1901	1915	1915	1948	2005	2024	2105	2124	2201	2307	2359
London Euston 550 a.													

B – 🚆 Holyhead - Birmingham International.
r – From 16 Apr.
t – Arrives 1852.
v – Manchester Victoria.
x – Stops on request.
y – Arrive 10 minutes later on ⑥.
▼ – Chester - Warrington Bank Quay on ⑦: see previous page.

Table 556 — ISLE OF MAN RAILWAYS

☎ : (01624) 663366

Manx Electric Railway

	A		B	C		B		C	A	C	B	C	B		C		B		C	E		E
Douglas Derby Castle ▲ d.	0920	…	1000	1030	1100	1200	1300	1310	1330	1400	1430	1500	1600	1700	1745	1800	1930
Laxey (for Snaefell) d.	0950	1030	1100	1130	1230	1330	1340	1400	1430	1500	1530	1630	1730	1815	1830	2000
Ramsey a.	1035	1115	1145	1215	1315	1415	1425	1445	1515	1545	1615	1715	1815	1915	2045

	C		B		C	A	C	B	C	D	B	C	B		C		E		E
Ramsey d.		1000	1130	1140	1200	1230	1330	1430	1500	1530	1600	1630	1730	1830	2115
Laxey (for Snaefell) d.	0945	1045	1215	1225	1245	1315	1415	1515	1545	1615	1645	1715	1815	1915	2200
Douglas Derby Castle a.	1015	1115	1245	1255	1315	1345	1445	1545	1615	1615	1645	1715	1745	1845	1945	2230

Isle of Man Steam Railway

	F	D	F		F		H	D	D				F		F		F		D	D
Douglas Railway Station ▲ d.	1010	1050	1145	1410	1555	1610	1655	Port Erin d.	1015	1205	1415	1515	1615	1615
Ballasalla d.	1045	1130	1220	1445	1630	1645	1730	Castletown d.	1038	1228	1438	1538	1638	1638
Castletown d.	1052	1137	1228	1452	1637	1652	1737	Ballasalla d.	1045	1235	1445	1545	1645	1645
Port Erin a.	1115	1200	1250	1515	1700	1715	1800	Douglas Railway Station a.	1120	1310	1520	1620	1720	1720

A – ①–⑤ Jan. 9 - Apr. 7.
B – Daily Apr. 10 - Oct. 29.
C – Daily May 21 - Sept. 10.
D – ①–④ July 3 - Aug. 31.
E – ①–⑥ July 3 - Aug. 26.
F – Daily Apr. 14 - Oct. 1, Oct. 21–29.
H – Daily Apr. 14 - Jul. 2, Sept. 1 - Oct.1, Oct. 21–29; ⑤–⑦ Jul. 7 - Aug. 27.
▲ – A 🚆 service connects Derby Castle and the Steam Railway Station.

Snaefell Mountain Railway: operates daily Apr. 14 - Oct. 1, subject to weather conditions. First departure from Laxey 1030, last departure 1530. Journey time to summit: 30 minutes.
Groudle Glen Railway (6 km, 10 minutes from Douglas by Manx Electric): operates 1100 - 1630 on ⑦ Apr. 16, Apr. 30 - Oct. 1 (daily Aug. 20–28, also Apr. 17, May 8, 29) and 1900 - 2100 on ③ July 5 - Aug. 23 (special connecting services on Manx Electric every 30 minutes 1845 - 2045 from Douglas, 1900 - 2100 from Groundle).

Table 557 — LLANDUDNO - BLAENAU FFESTINIOG

2 class only

km																		
0	Llandudno 555 d.	…	…	0758		1043	1105	…	1326	…	1552	…	1625	1753	…	…	2050
5	Llandudno Junction 555 d.	0518	…	0807	1052	1125	1335	1600	1610	1645	1800	1817	2110
24	Llanrwst d.	0537	0827	1112	1148	1353	1630	1708	1837	2140
30	Betws y Coed d.	0543	0833	1118	1158	1401	1636	1718	1843	2147
50	Blaenau Ffestiniog a.	0615	0907	1152	1230	1435	1710	1750	1917	2205

Blaenau Ffestiniog d.		0645	0930		1158	1305		1507		1714	1825	1850	1947	1947
Betws y Coed d.	0712	0957	1225	1340	1534	1741	1900	1915	2014	2014
Llanrwst d.	0718	1003	1231	1350	1540	1747	1910	1927	2020	2020
Llandudno Junction 555 d.	0745	1031	1259	1415	1606	1610	1813	1823	1935	1945	2058	2105
Llandudno 555 a.	0753	1038	1307	1430	1624	1833	1950	2000	2103	2110

🚌 – Service 84 operated on ☓ by Crosville Cymru and on ⑦ by Empire on behalf of Gwynedd County Council. Rail tickets are valid on these journeys.

Table 559 DERBY - MATLOCK

2 class only

From Derby:

⚒ : 0617⑥, 0624Ⓐ, 0706, 0820⑥, 0825Ⓐ, 0943⑥, 0952Ⓐ, 1101⑥, 1105Ⓐ, 1228, 1346⑥, 1349Ⓐ, 1503, 1623, 1744, 1858⑥, 1902Ⓐ, 2026, 2156 **E**, 2255 🚌.

⑦ **U** : 1438, 1558, 1723, 1855, 2019, 2134.

From Matlock:

⚒ : 0608, 0659, 0741⑥, 0748Ⓐ, 0855⑥, 0901Ⓐ, 1020⑥, 1027Ⓐ, 1148, 1304Ⓐ, 1307⑥, 1425, 1540, 1700, 1821⑥, 1825Ⓐ, 1940, 2100, 2232 **E**.

⑦ **U** : 1519, 1638, 1815, 1936, 2054, 2215.

E – Ⓐ (also ⑥ Jan. 14 - May 20). **U** – Sept. 25 - Oct. 30, Apr. 16 - May 27 only. 28 km Journey time: 30 minutes.

Table 560 LONDON - LEICESTER - DERBY - SHEFFIELD

for additional services Leicester - Nottingham see Table 574; Nottingham - Sheffield see Table 585

km		Ⓐ🍷	⑥🍷	Ⓐ🍷	Ⓐ🍴	⑥🍷	Ⓐ🍴	Ⓐ🍴	⑥🍷	Ⓐ🍴	⑥🍷	⑦🍷	Ⓐ🍴	Ⓐ🍴	⑥🍷	Ⓐ🍷	⑦🍷	⑥🍷	Ⓐ🍷	Ⓐ🍷	⑥🍷	Ⓐ🍷	⑦🍷	⑥🍷
0	**London St Pancras** d.	...	0630	0700	0730	0730	0800	0830	0830	0900	0915	0915	0930	1000	1000	1030	1030	1045	1100	1130	1130	1200	1200	1215
48	Luton ✈ **533 537** d.	...	0653	0723	0753	0753	|	0853	0853	0923	|	0937	|	1023	1023	|	1052	1108	1123	1153	|	|	1222	1238
80	Bedford d.	0640	0709	|	|	0811	0836	|	|	|	0952	0959	1006	|	|	|	1114	|	1140	|	1206	|	|	|
105	Wellingborough d.	0654	0723	0748	|	0824	0850	0923	0918	|	1005	1014	1020	|	|	|	1129	1134	1155	|	|	|	1254	1303
116	Kettering d.	0704	0731	0757	|	0832	0858	|	0926	0953	1013	1028	|	1053	1053	|	1143	1142	1203	1223	1224	1249	1308	1311
134	Market Harborough d.	0715	0742	0807	|	0843	0909	|	|	1003	1024	1039	|	|	|	1125	1154	1152	1215	|	|	1300	1319	1322
159	**Leicester** d.	0739	0758	0824	0843	0859	0926	0948	0951	1020	1040	1100	1048	1117	1118	1141	1214	1209	1231	1248	1248	1317	1339	1338
180	Loughborough d.	0752	0810	|	0855	0911	0937	|	|	1032	|	1122	|	|	1128	1154	1237	|	|	|	1300	1328	1402	|
204	**Nottingham 561** a.	|	|	0847	|	0927	0953	|	|	1048	1104	|	|	1145	|	|	1312	1232	1255	|	|	1348	|	1402
208	**Derby 561** d.	0812	0829	...	0914	...	...	1014	1017	...	...	1148	1115	...	1148	1213	...	...	...	1314	1319	...	1428	...
246	Chesterfield d.	0835	0852	...	0937	...	...	1037	1040	...	...	1233	1138	...	1210	1235	...	...	...	1337	1342	...	1456	...
265	**Sheffield** a.	0852	0911	...	0953	...	...	1053	1057	...	...	1250	1154	...	1226	1251	...	...	...	1354	1358	...	1513	...
	Leeds **520** a.	...	...	...	...	...	...	...	...	...	...	...	...	...	...	...	...	...	...	...	...	...	...	...

	Ⓐ🍷	Ⓐ🍷	⑥🍷	Ⓐ🍷	⑦🍷	⑥🍷	Ⓐ🍷	Ⓐ🍷	⑥🍷	⑦🍷	Ⓐ🍷	⑥🍷	Ⓐ🍷	⑦🍷	Ⓐ🍷	⑥🍷	⑦🍷	Ⓐ🍷	⑥🍷	Ⓐ🍷	⑦🍷	Ⓐ**P**	Ⓐ🍷	⑥🍷
London St Pancras d.	1230	1300	1300	1330	1330	1345	1400	1430	1430	1430	1500	1515	1530	1530	1600	1600	1615	1630	1645	1700	1700	1715	1720	1730
Luton ✈ **533 537** d.	|	1323	1323	|	1352	|	|	1453	1453	1452	1523	1538	1553	|	|	|	1637	1653	1708	|	1722	|	|	|
Bedford d.	1307	|	|	|	1415	1421	1436	|	|	|	|	|	|	1610	1636	1636	|	|	|	|	1744	|	|	1806
Wellingborough d.	1322	|	|	|	1431	1434	1449	|	|	|	|	1603	1619	1623	1650	|	1709	|	1734	1744	|	|	1808	1820
Kettering d.	|	1353	1353	|	1439	1442	1457	1523	1523	1529	1553	1611	|	1631	1658	1654	1717	1724	1742	1752	1804	|	1818	1828
Market Harborough d.	|	|	|	1425	1456	1453	|	|	|	1539	1604	1622	|	1642	1708	1704	|	1736	1752	|	1814	|	1831	|
Leicester d.	1351	1417	1417	1441	1509	1509	1522	1547	1547	1556	1621	1638	1647	1659	1725	1721	1742	1752	1809	1817	1831	1824	1850	1852
Loughborough d.	|	|	1428	1454	1526	|	|	|	1559	1609	1632	|	|	1711	1737	1732	|	1804	1820	|	1844	|	1903	|
Nottingham 561 a.	|	1448	|	|	1544	1533	1548	|	|	|	1648	1702	|	1726	1753	|	|	|	1837	1841	1859	|	|	|
Derby 561 d.	1418	...	1448	1513	...	...	...	1613	1618	1626	...	...	1714	...	...	1752	1808	1826	...	...	...	1848	1925	1919
Chesterfield d.	1441	...	1511	1535	...	...	...	1637	1641	1648	...	...	1737	...	...	1814	1831	1848	...	...	...	1910	...	1941
Sheffield a.	1456	...	1527	1551	...	...	...	1653	1657	1704	...	...	1753	...	...	1830	1847	1904	...	...	...	1926	...	1956
Leeds **520** a.	...	...	...	...	...	...	...	...	...	...	...	...	...	...	...	...	1931	...	...	...	...	...	...	2046

	Ⓐ🍷	⑦🍷	Ⓐ🍴	⑦🍷	⑥🍷	Ⓐ🍷	⑥🍷	⑦🍷	Ⓐ🍴	⑥🍷	⑦🍷	Ⓐ🍷	Ⓐ🍷	⑥🍷	⑦🍷	⑦🍷	Ⓐ🍷	⑥**B**	⑦🍷	Ⓐ🍷	⑦🍷	⑦	**C**	⑤🍷
London St Pancras d.	1740	1740	1800	1800	1815	1820	1830	1830	1850	1900	1915	1920	2000	2000	2000	2045	2100	2100	2130	2200	2215	2300	2320	2335
Luton ✈ **533 537** d.	|	|	|	|	1838	|	|	1852	|	1923	1937	1946	2023	|	|	2107	|	2123	2152	2223	|	2322	2344	2358
Bedford d.	|	|	|	1840	|	|	1906	|	1926	|	|	|	|	2036	2040	|	2137	2140	|	|	2255	|	0001	0015
Wellingborough d.	1825	|	|	1855	|	1904	1919	1924	1939	1948	|	2011	2048	2049	2055	2139	2150	2153	|	2248	2310	2354	0014	0028
Kettering d.	1833	|	1849	1903	1908	1913	|	1932	1948	1957	2014	2019	2056	2058	2103	2147	2158	2207	2229	2256	2318	0002	0022	0036
Market Harborough d.	|	|	|	1914	1918	1925	|	|	|	2007	2024	2030	|	2108	2114	|	2209	2218	2239	|	2329	0012	0032	0047
Leicester d.	1859	1856	1914	1931	1935	1941	1948	1957	2014	2024	2041	2046	2121	2125	2130	2212	2225	2238	2256	2321	2344	0028	0048	0104
Loughborough d.	1911	|	|	1943	1946	|	1959	|	2027	2035	2054	|	2133	2136	2143	|	2237	2253	2309	2334	2357	0041	0101	0116
Nottingham 561 a.	1929	|	|	|	2005	2005	|	2020	|	|	|	2112	|	2153	2158	|	2253	|	2324	|	|	0058	0124	0132
Derby 561 d.	...	|	1940	2001	|	|	2021	|	2048	2057	2111	...	2152	2221	...	2238	2328	2318	2353	2352v	0022	0131	0158	0200
Chesterfield d.	...	1946	2003	2024	2049	2048	2044	2101	2109	2120	2134	...	2214	...	...	2301	...	2359	...	0014v	...	...	...	...
Sheffield a.	...	2002	2018	2040	2104	2103	2059	2116	2125	2139	2149	...	2232	...	...	2317	...	0015	...	0030v	...	...	...	...
Leeds **520** a.	...	2059	2110	...	...	2205	2154	2210	2216	...	2240	...	...	...	...	...	...	...	...	...	...	...	...	...

	⚒	Ⓐ🍴	⑥🍷	Ⓐ🍴	Ⓐ🍷	Ⓐ🍴	Ⓐ🍴	⑥🍷	⑥🍷	Ⓐ**P**	Ⓐ**P**	Ⓐ🍷	⑦🍷	⑥🍷	Ⓐ🍷	⑥🍷	Ⓐ🍷	⑥🍷	Ⓐ🍷		⑥🍷	⑦🍷	Ⓐ🍷	Ⓐ🍷
Leeds **520** d.	...	...	...	...	...	...	...	...	...	...	...	...	...	0635	0635	...	0725	0754	...	...	...	...	...	...
Sheffield d.	...	...	...	...	...	...	0622	0622	...	0632	0720	...	...	0741	0740	0750	0824	0839	...	...	...	0850	0924	...
Chesterfield d.	...	...	...	...	...	...	0635	0635	...	0645	0733	...	...	0754	0753	0803	0836	0852	...	...	...	0905	0937	...
Derby 561 d.	0505	...	...	0600	0620	...	0700	0659	...	|	0756	...	0824	0817	|	|	0902	0915	...	...	...	0952	1002	...
Nottingham 561 d.	|	0537	0558	|	|	0638	|	|	0729	0738	|	0800	|	|	0838	0846	|	|	0933	...	0947	|	|	1039
Loughborough d.	|	|	0612	0616	|	0656	0717	0716	0746	|	|	0817	0840	|	|	0903	|	|	0947	...	1001	1010	|	|
Leicester d.	0530	0600	0630	0630	0650	0710	0730	0730	0800	0800	|	0830	0900	0845	0900	0915	0930	0945	1000	...	1015	1030	1030	1100
Market Harborough d.	|	0614	0645	0644	|	0724	0745	|	0814	|	|	|	0919	|	0915	0931	|	|	1015	...	1031	1049	|	|
Kettering d.	0552	0625	0656	0654	0715	0735	0756	0752	0824	|	|	0853	0929	0907	0927	0943	|	|	1025	...	1041	1058	|	1125
Wellingborough d.	0600	0632	0704	0702	0725	0744	0804	0759	0832	|	|	0901	0937	0914	0934	|	|	1011	|	...	1049	1107	1056	|
Bedford a.	0614	0647	|	|	|	|	|	|	0846	|	|	|	1006	|	0949	|	|	1025	|	...	|	1136	1110	|
Luton ✈ **533 537** a.	0632	0704	0730	0728	|	|	|	|	0904	|	|	|	1023	|	|	1013	1021	|	|	...	1115	1153	|	1155
London St Pancras a.	0659	0731	0757	0755	0818	0832	0853	0848	0931	0914	0931	0950	1059	1003	1029	1040	1048	1105	1118	...	1142	1229	1150	1222

	⑥🍷	Ⓐ🍷	⑥🍷	Ⓐ🍷		⑦🍷	Ⓐ🍷	⑥🍷	Ⓐ🍷	⑦🍷	⑥🍷	Ⓐ🍷	⑥🍷	Ⓐ🍷	⑦🍷	Ⓐ🍷	⑥🍷	⑦🍷	Ⓐ🍷		Ⓐ🍷	⑥🍷	⑦🍷	⑦🍷
Leeds **520** d.	0836	...	...	...	...	...	...	...	...	1010	...	...	...	...	...	...	...	1154	...	...	...	...	...	...
Sheffield d.	0954	1024	...	...	...	...	1124	1124	...	1121	...	1224	1254	...	...	1324	...	1310	...	...	1424	1424	...	1450
Chesterfield d.	1007	1037	...	...	...	...	1137	1137	...	1135	...	1237	1307	...	...	1337	...	1324	...	...	1437	1437	...	1504
Derby 561 d.	1031	1102	...	...	...	1030	1202	1201	...	1222	...	1302	1331	...	...	1402	...	1411	...	...	1502	1502	...	1527
Nottingham 561 d.	|	|	1124	1137	...	1110	|	|	1233	|	1254	|	|	1339	1323	|	1424	|	1438	...	|	|	1505	|
Loughborough d.	1048	1118	|	|	...	1140	|	1218	1247	1240	|	|	1348	|	1352	1418	|	|	|	...	|	1518	|	1546
Leicester d.	1100	1130	1145	1200	...	1200	1230	1230	1300	1300	1315	1330	1400	1400	1400	1430	1445	1445	1500	...	1530	1530	1530	1600
Market Harborough d.	|	1146	1201	1214	...	1219	|	|	1315	1319	1332	|	|	|	|	1446	1459	1504	|	...	|	|	|	|
Kettering d.	1124	|	1212	1226	...	1229	1253	1254	1325	1328	1343	|	1424	1426	1426	|	1511	1513	1524	...	1553	1555	1554	|
Wellingborough d.	1132	|	1219	1233	...	1237	|	|	|	1337	1352	1356	|	|	1434	|	1519	1522	1532	...	|	|	1601	|
Bedford a.	|	|	1234	1248	...	|	|	1313	|	1406	|	1410	|	|	|	|	1534	1536	1546	...	|	1614	1616	|
Luton ✈ **533 537** a.	1158	|	|	1305	...	1317	1323	|	|	|	1418	|	1454	1457	|	|	|	1556	|	...	1623	|	1635	|
London St Pancras a.	1225	1246	1314	1332	...	1353	1350	1353	1418	1455	1445	1450	1521	1524	1536	1546	1614	1625	1626	...	1650	1654	1705	1716

	Ⓐ🍷	⑥🍷	Ⓐ🍷	⑦🍷	Ⓐ🍷	⑦🍷	⑥🍷	Ⓐ🍷	⑦🍷	⑥🍷	⑦🍷	Ⓐ🍷	Ⓐ🍷	⑥🍷	⑦🍷	⑦🍷	Ⓐ🍷	⑥	⑦🍷	Ⓐ🍷	⑥🍷	⑦🍷	Ⓐ🍷	Ⓐ
Leeds **520** d.	...	...	...	...	...	...	...	...	1524	...	...	...	...	...	...	...	...	...	...	...	...	1840	...	...
Sheffield d.	...	...	1524	...	...	...	1554	1624	1624	...	1652	...	1724	1724	...	1820	...	...	...	1924	1924	1935	2006	...
Chesterfield d.	...	...	1537	...	...	...	1607	1637	1637	...	1708	...	1737	1737	...	1834	...	...	...	1937	1937	1949	2018	...
Derby 561 d.	...	...	1602	1600	...	...	1631	1702	|	...	1733	...	1802	1801	...	1858	...	...	...	2002	2002	2013	2047	2108
Nottingham 561 d.	1533	1552	|	|	1633	1636	|	|	|	1724	|	1733	|	|	1802	|	1903	1903	1932	|	|	|	...	2133
Loughborough d.	1547	|	|	1616	1647	|	1648	1718	|	|	|	1747	1818	1818	1816	1916	1917	1917	1946	|	2018	2031	...	2147
Leicester d.	1600	1615	1630	1630	1700	1700	1700	1730	1730	1745	1800	1800	1830	1830	1830	1930	1930	1930	2000	2030	2030	2045	...	2200
Market Harborough d.	1615	1631	|	1644	1715	1714	|	1746	|	1801	|	1815	|	|	1844	1944	1945	1946	|	2044	2046	2059	...	2215
Kettering d.	1627	1642	|	1655	1726	1724	1723	1757	1752	1812	1822	1826	1854	1855	1854	1954	1955	1956	2022	2056	2057	2109	...	2225
Wellingborough d.	|	1649	1656	1703	1734	|	1732	|	1759	1820	|	1833	|	|	1902	|	2003	2004	2029	2103	2105	2117	...	2233
Bedford a.	|	|	1710	|	|	|	|	|	1814	1835	|	1848	|	|	|	|	2017	2018	2044	|	2119	2131	...	2247
Luton ✈ **533 537** a.	1658	1715	|	1730	|	1757	1758	1828	|	|	1854	|	1924	1927	1930	2027	2035	2036	2103	2129	2141	2151	...	2305
London St Pancras a.	1725	1742	1750	1759	1822	1826	1825	1855	1858	1915	1924	1928	1951	1954	1959	2056	2102	2103	2133	2203	2210	2220	...	2338

– Oct. 1 - Jan. 7. **C** – ①②③④. **P** – Pullman service and 🍴 available in 1 cl. **v** – 14 minutes later on ①②③④.

Table 561 — NOTTINGHAM - DERBY - STOKE - CREWE

2 class only

km		⚒	⚒	⚒	⚒	⚒	⚒	⚒	⑦v	⑦v	⚒	⚒	⚒	⑦	Ⓐ	⑥	⑦	⑦	⚒	⑥	⑦	Ⓐ	⑦	⑦	⚒
0	Nottingham 520 .... d.	0604	0808	0912	1008	1112	1217	1312	1325	1415	1419h	1518	1520	1619	1619	1810	1720	1724	1817	1820	1829	1920	2056	2038
26	Derby 520 .... a.	0632	0836c	0939	1040	1138	1245	1342	1344	1444	1444h	1545	1548	1651	1651	1656	1746	1753c	1846	1846	1856	1946	2051	2106
26	Derby .... d.	0636	0845	0948	1045	1154	1250	1345	1400	1448	1455	1548	1552	1656	1712	1700	1750	1805	1856	1857	1900	1950	2055	2112
57	Uttoxeter .... d.	0657	0906	1009	1110	1215	1311	1406	1421	1509	1516	1609	1613	1717	1733	1721	1811	1826	1917	1918	1921	2011	2116	2133
84	Stoke-on-Trent........ d.	0721	0936	1034	1137	1239	1336	1432	1456	1544	1540	1637	1641	1742	1758	1746	1836	1853	1944	1946	1944	2036	2145	2133
108	Crewe .... a.	0749	1004	1101	1201	1303	1402	1457	1525	1610	1604	1705	1710	1810	1826	1815	1902	1921	2010	2015	2010	2102	2213	2230c

		⑥	Ⓐ	⚒	⚒	⚒	⚒	⚒	⚒	⑦	⚒	⚒	⚒	⚒	⑥	Ⓐ	⑦	⑦	Ⓐ	⑦	⑦	⑥	⑦	⑦	⚒
	Crewe .... d.	0704	0710	0815	0920	1018	1118	1218	1316	1415	1417	1517	1530	1615	1615	1718	1720	1818	1820	1834	1915	1930	2020	2030	2120
	Stoke-on-Trent .... d.	0730	0736	0841	0943	1041	1141	1241	1339	1440	1440	1540	1555	1640	1641	1745	1745	1841	1845	1857	1940	1953	2045	2057	2145
	Uttoxeter .... d.	0753	0759	0904	1005	1103	1203	1304	1401	1503	1502	1603	1618	1703	1704	1808	1810	1904	1908	1920	2003	2015	2108	2120	2208
	Derby .... a.	0816	0822	0928	1030	1128	1230	1325c	1428	1535	1528	1629	1646	1726	1727	1830	1831	1928	1928	1944	2029	2043r	2131	2143	2232
	Derby 520 .... d.	0823	0826	0932	1033c	1131	1236	1340p	1432	1539	1543r	1635	1650	1730	1734	1835	1932	1932	1952	2038	2047	2135	2148	2237
	Nottingham 520 .... a.	0851	0855	1002	1101	1158	1302	1406p	1458	1605	1611r	1704	1716	1802	1805	1903	1959	2018	2104	2118	2201	2216	2307

c – 3 minutes later on ⑥.
h – 3 minutes earlier on ⑥.
p – ⑥ only.

r – 4 minutes earlier on ⑥.
v – Runs Sept. 25 - 5 Mar.

Additional journeys **Derby - Crewe** at 0545⚒ and 0732⚒.
Additional journey **Crewe - Derby** at 0602⚒.

Table 562 — LEEDS - LANCASTER and CARLISLE

2 class only

km		⚒	⚒		⚒	⚒	⑦c	Ⓐ⚕	⚒		⚒	⚒	⑦c	⑦	⚒		⚒	⑦	⚒	⑦c		⚒
0	Leeds .... d.	...	...	...	0845	0901	0900	0949	...	1049	...	1249	1301	1332	1405	1449	...	1631	1705	1725	1732	...	1837
17	Shipley .... d.	...	...	...	0900	0919	0915	1004	...	1104	...	1304	1317	1347	1420	1504	...	1647	1720	1740	1747	...	1852
27	Keighley .... d.	...	...	...	0908	0931	0925	1012	...	1112	...	1312	1331	1355	1433	1512	...	1700	1733	1753	1755	...	1905
42	Skipton .... d.	0535	...	...	0927	0953	0941	1029	...	1128	...	1328	1353	1411	1453	1528	...	1722	1753	1816	1816	...	1925
103	Carnforth .... d.	0637	...	...	1055								1455		1555			1826	1857				
113	Lancaster .... a.	0652	...	...	1105								1506		1606			1836	1908				
66	Settle .... d.	...	...	...	0945	...	0959	1053	...	1147	...	1345	...	1428	...	1545	...	...	1840	1834	...	1949
76	Horton in Ribblesdale d.	...	...	...	0954	...	1008	1102	...	1156	...	1354	...	1437	...	1554	...	...	1849	1843	...	1958
84	Ribblehead .... d.	...	...	...	1002	...	1016	1110	...	1204	...	1402	...	1445	...	1602	...	...	1857	1851	...	2008
94	Dent .... d.	...	...	...	1011	...	1025	1119	...	1213	...	1411	...	1454	...	1611	...	...	1906	1900	...	...
99	Garsdale .... d.	...	...	...	1016	...	1030	1124	...	1219	...	1417	...	1500	...	1617	...	...	1911	1905	...	...
115	Kirkby Stephen ...... d.	...	0727	...	1029	...	1042	1136	...	1231	...	1429	...	1512	...	1629	...	...	1924	1917	...	...
132	Appleby .... d.	...	0740	...	1042	...	1055	1150	...	1245	...	1442	...	1525	...	1642	...	...	1937	1930	...	...
166	Armathwaite .... d.	...	0807	...	1109	...	1123	1218	...	1313	...	1509	...	1552	...	1709	...	...	2004	1958	...	...
182	Carlisle .... a.	...	0824	...	1128	...	1141	1236	...	1331	...	1529	...	1611	...	1720	...	...	2022	2016	...	...

		⚒		⚒		⚒	⑦c	Ⓐ⚕	⚒		⚒	⚒		⚒	⑦c	⚒	Ⓐ⚕	⑦c		⚒	⑥	⚒	⑦
	Carlisle .... d.	...	...	...	0856	...	0948	...	1140	...	1348	1416	...	1520	...	1626	1649	...	1745	1821	...	...
	Armathwaite .... d.	...	...	...	0909	...	1001	...	1153	...	1401	1430	...	1533	...	1640	1702	...	1758	1834	...	...
	Appleby .... d.	...	...	...	0938	...	1030	...	1222	...	1430	1459	...	1602	...	1709	1731	...	1827	1903	...	...
	Kirkby Stephen ...... d.	...	...	...	0953	...	1045	...	1237	...	1445	1514	...	1617	...	1724	1746	...	1842	1918	...	...
	Garsdale .... d.	...	...	...	1006	...	1058	...	1250	...	1458	1528	...	1630	...	1738	1759	...	1855	1931	...	...
	Dent .... d.	...	...	...	1011	...	1103	...	1255	...	1503	1533	...	1635	...	1743	1804	...	1900	1936	...	...
	Ribblehead .... d.	0657	...	...	1021	...	1113	...	1305	...	1513	1542	...	1645	...	1752	1814	...	1910	1946	...	...
	Horton in Ribblesdale d.	0703	...	...	1027	...	1119	...	1311	...	1519	1548	...	1651	...	1758	1820	...	1916	1952	...	...
	Settle .... d.	0711	...	...	1035	...	1127	...	1319	...	1527	1556	...	1659	...	1806	1828	...	1924	2000	...	...
	Lancaster .... d.	...	...	0704					1152				1528								1947	2000	...	...
	Carnforth .... d.	...	...	0727					1203				1537								1956	2008	...	...
	Skipton .... d.	0738	...	0837	1058	...	1152	...	1306	1342	...	1550	1620	1640	...	1728	...	1830	1851	...	1947	2025	2101	2110
	Keighley .... d.	0754	...	0853	1109	...	1203	...	1319	1357	...	1601	1632	1655	...	1739	...	1842	1902	...	1958	2036	2116	2125
	Shipley .... d.	0807	...	0907	1117	...	1211	...	1333	1413	...	1609	1643	1709	...	1749	...	1851	1910	...	2006	2044	2129	2139
	Leeds .... a.	0826	...	0926	1140	...	1230	...	1355	1434	...	1628	1704	1726	...	1808	...	1910	1928	...	2028	2103	2147	2156

A – Runs Apr. 15 and May 27.　　c – Sept. 25 - Oct. 30 and Apr. 16 - May 27.　　For additional local services between **Leeds** and **Skipton**, see Table 563 below.

Table 563 — LEEDS and BRADFORD local services

2 class only

LEEDS - SKIPTON　43 km.　Journey time: 47 minutes.
From Leeds:
⚒ : 0606Ⓐ, 0652, 0724Ⓐ, 0801, 0831 and half-hourly to 1631, then 1703, 1725, 1748, 1801, 1837, 1901, 1931, 2001, 2115.
⑦ : 0900A, 0914B, 1005, 1105 and hourly to 1805, then 1912, 2012, 2112.
For additional (faster) services Leeds - Skipton, see Table 562 above.

From Skipton:
⚒ : 0600, 0628Ⓐ, 0650, 0715Ⓐ, 0738, 0807, 0837, 0901, 1005, 1038, 1058, 1105, 1138, 1205, 1238, 1342, 1405, 1438, 1505, 1538, 1609, 1620, 1640, 1708, 1743, 1808, 1830, 1838, 1906, 1947, 1958, 2101.
⑦ : 0904, 1004 and hourly to 2104.　A – Nov. 6 - Apr. 9　B – Sept. 25 - Oct. 10 and Apr. 16 - May 21.

LEEDS - ILKLEY　26 km.　Journey time: 31 minutes.
From Leeds:
⚒ : 0635Ⓐ, 0703, 0718Ⓐ, 0737⑥, 0741Ⓐ, 0810, 0839, 0907, 0940, and at 07 and 40 mins. past each hour to 1640, then 1709, 1740, 1807⑥, 1816Ⓐ, 1840, 1907, 1940, 2007, 2121.
⑦ : 0908, 0938, 1038 and hourly to 2038.

From Ilkley:
⚒ : 0618, 0646Ⓐ, 0718, 0743Ⓐ, 0812, 0847, 0919, 0943, 1016, 1042 and at 16 and 4 mins. past each hour to 1542, then 1610, 1642, 1710, 1751, 1815Ⓐ, 1826⑥, 1842, 1919, 2016, 2121.
⑦ : 0945, 1045 and hourly to 2045, 2130.

LEEDS - DONCASTER　48 km.　Journey time: 46 minutes.
From Leeds:
Ⓐ : 0625, 0731, 0821, 0921 and hourly to 1721, then 1830, 1921, 2021, 2126, 2239.
⑥ : 0625, 0720, 0821, 0921 and hourly to 2021, 2128.
⑦ : 0946A, 1003B, 1146A, 1203B, 1346A, 1400B, 1600, 1800, 2000, 2100.
A – Sept. 25 - Jan. 8　　B – Jan. 15 - May 21.

For InterCity services, see Table 570.
From Doncaster:
Ⓐ : 0625, 0725, 0750, 0828, 0924, 1014, 1114 and hourly to 1614, then 1713, 1825, 1924, 2033, 2140, 2230.
⑥ : 0625, 0725, 0828, 0924, 1014, 1114, 1214, 1322, 1414, 1514C, 1522D, 1624, 1714C, 1725D, 1814C, 1825D, 1924, 2033, 2120.
⑦ : 0836A, 0900B, 1100B, 1110A, 1258A, 1307B, 1507, 1700, 1916, 2103.
C – Jan. 14 - May 27　　D – Oct. 1 - Jan. 7.

BRADFORD - SKIPTON　30 km.　Journey time: 39 mins. (57 mins. on ⑦)
From Bradford Forster Square:
⚒ : 0709Ⓐ, 0817, 0902, 1001, 1101 and hourly to 1601, then 1625Ⓐ, 1705, 1746Ⓐ, 1814, 1901, 2001, 2104Ⓐ, 2115⑥.
⑦ : (Change at Keighley) 0955, 1155, 1355, 1555, 1755, 1955.

All trains call at Keighley – 21 minutes from Bradford, 14 minutes from Skipton.
From Skipton:
⚒ : 0611Ⓐ, 0707, 0747, 0815, 0915 and hourly to 1415, then 1514, 1625, 1655Ⓐ, 1716⑥, 1816, 1915, 2015.
⑦ : (Change at Keighley) 1004, 1204, 1404, 1604, 1804, 2004.

BRADFORD - ILKLEY　22 km.　Journey time: 33 minutes.
From Bradford Forster Square:
⚒ : 0653Ⓐ, 0751Ⓐ, 0830⑥, 0835Ⓐ, 0857, 0930, 1030 and hourly to 1530, 1632, 1720Ⓐ, 1735⑥, 1802Ⓐ, 1849, 1930, 2030, 2128.
⑦ : 1106, 1306, 1506, 1706, 1906

From Ilkley:
⚒ : 0628Ⓐ, 0729Ⓐ, 0800, 0833Ⓐ, 0910, 0950, 1050 and hourly to 1550, then 1633⑥, 1650⑥, 1723Ⓐ, 1802, 1851, 1950, 2048.
⑦ : 0915, 1115, 1315, 1515, 1715, 1915.

For an explanation of standard symbols see page 4

Table 564 HULL - YORK

2 class

km		Ⓐ🍷	⑥🍷	Ⓐ	⑥	⚒		⚒🍷	⚒	⚒	⚒🍷	⚒	⚒	⚒🍷	⚒	⚒		⚒	⑦🍷	⑦	⚒	⑦🍷	⑦	⚒
0	**Hull** d.	0602	0610	...	...	0653	...	0818	...	0900	1018	...	1102	1218	...	1300	...	1420	1446	...	1602	1646	...	1725
50	Selby d.	0643	0650	0652	0655	0736	...	0849	0900	0938	1049	1058	1142	1249	1258	1342	...	1456	1517	1530	1640	1717	1730	1815
78	**York** a.	...	...	0726	0726	0811	...	...	0931	1010	...	1124	1216	...	1321	1411	...	1527	...	1554	1706	...	1757	1840

		⚒	⑦🍷	⑦	⚒🍷	⚒	⑦	⑦	⚒	⑥
Hull d.	...	1845	1846	...	1959	...	2106	...	2117	...
Selby d.	...	1920	1917	1923	2030	2045	2137	2143	2150	2157
York a.	...	1948	...	1946	...	2109	...	2205	...	2219

	⑥	Ⓐ	⚒	⚒	⑥	Ⓐ	⚒🍷	⚒	⚒
York d.	0625	0650	...	0734	0823	0830	...	0952	1022
Selby d.	0646	0711	0721	0759	0844	0851	0906	1011	1044
Hull a.	...	...	0813	0846	...	...	0942	1059	...

	⚒🍷	⚒	⚒	⚒🍷		⚒	⑦	⑦🍷	⚒	⑦	⑦🍷	⚒	⚒	⚒	⑦	⑦🍷	⚒	⚒	⑦	⑦🍷	⑥	⑥	Ⓐ	⚒🍷
York d.	...	1149	1222	...	...	1349	1400	...	1502	1603	...	1612	1712	1752	1823	...	1930	...	2016	...	2034	2130	2146	...
Selby d.	1100	1208	1244	1301	...	1414	1422	1436	1521	1625	1637	1640	1738	1822	1845	1855	1952	2001	2037	2055	2053	2151	2205	2216
Hull a.	1136	1255	...	1338	...	1500	...	1515	1601	...	1713	1733	1828	1911	...	1932	...	2037	...	2131	2141	...	2253	2255

Table 565 HULL - DONCASTER - SHEFFIELD

2 class

km		⚒	⚒ C	⚒	⚒ A	⚒🍷	⚒🍷	⑦	⚒🍷	⚒🍷	⑦🍷	⚒🍷	⚒🍷	⑦🍷	⚒🍷	⑦🍷	⚒🍷	⑦🍷	⑥🍷	Ⓐ🍷	⑦🍷	⑦ A	⚒🍷	⑦🍷
0	**Hull** d.	0521	0606	0640	0705	0746	0848	0848	0945	1045	1105	1147	1247	1314	1347	1403	1447	1504	1544	1544	1603	1638	1643	1704
38	Goole d.	0547	0641	0715	|	0823	0921	0916	1018	1120	1133	1220	1320	1342	1420	1431	1520	1532	1618	1618	1631	|	1720	1737
66	**Doncaster** a.	0616	0712	0746	0755	0852	0948	0945	1048	1148	1202	1248	1348	1410	1448	1457	1548	1601	1645	1648	1657	1727	1747	1806
66	**Doncaster 520** d.	0625	...	0749	*0809*	0854	0950	0955	1050	1150	1205	1250	1350	1412	1450	*1509*	1550	1602	1650	1651	1659	...	1749	1808
87	Rotherham d.	0650	...	0811	|	0917	1012	1017	1112	1212	1227	1312	1412	1434	1512	*1532*	1616	1625	1707	1714	1722	...	1811	1832
96	**Sheffield 520** a.	0708	...	0830	*0833*	0935e	1030	1038	1130	1230	1248	1330	1430	1452	1530	*1547*	1634	1644	1730	1732	1739	...	1830	1849

	⚒	⑦🍷	⑦🍷	⚒🍷	⑦🍷	⚒🍷	⑦🍷	⚒	①-④	⑤⑥
Hull d.	1739	1757	1854	1900	1954	2011	2112	...	2235	2235
Goole d.	1814	1825	1922	1933	2022	2044	2145	2141	2307	2307
Doncaster a.	1839	1851	1953	1959	2048	2109	2214	2212	2340	2340
Doncaster 520 d.	1841	1856	1955	2001	2050	2111	2216	2212	...	...
Rotherham d.	1909	1922	2017	2024	2112	2133	2238	2238	...	...
Sheffield 520 a.	1926	1940	2035	2042	2130	2151	2256	2256	...	...

	⚒	⚒	⚒🍷	⚒🍷	⑦🍷	⚒🍷	⚒🍷	⑦🍷	⚒🍷
Sheffield 520 d.	0535	*0636*	0744	0848	0900	0942	1041	1055	1143
Rotherham d.	0547	*0647*	0756	0900	0912	0956	1055	1107	1157
Doncaster 520 a.	0612	*0715*	0820	0927	0940	1021	1121	1135	1222
Doncaster d.	0614	0725	0821	0935	0941	1022	1123	1144	1226
Goole d.	0639	0752	0844	0957	1008	1049	1148	1210	1248
Hull a.	0722	0833	0922	1037	1042	1128	1228	1249	1328

	⚒🍷	⑦🍷	⚒🍷	⑦🍷	Ⓐ🍷	⑥🍷	⑦🍷	⚒🍷	⑦🍷	⚒🍷	⑦🍷	Ⓐ🍷	⑥🍷	⑦🍷	⑥ B	Ⓐ B	⚒🍷	⑦🍷	⚒🍷	⑦ B	⚒🍷	⑦	⑦	⚒
Sheffield 520 d.	1241	1302	1343	1420	1441	1441	1515	1541	1613	1643	1710	1746	1746	1814	*1814*	*1829*	1857	1912	1942	*2007*	2059	2123	2214	2226
Rotherham d.	1255	1314	1357	1432	1456	1455	1527	1557	1625	1656	1722	1801	1801	1826	|	*1842*	1909	1924	1955	|	2111	2135	2226	2238
Doncaster 520 a.	1321	1342	1422	1457	1521	1519	1552	1620	1652	1726	1750	1826	1830	1851	*1840*	*1910*	1938	1951	2024	*2034*	2136	2202	2251	2303
Doncaster d.	1323	1343	1426	1507	1522	1520	1555	1624	1653	1728	1800	1831	1832	1902	1907	1930	1942	1958	2029	2107	2141	2203	2302	2305
Goole d.	1348	1412	1448	1529	1548	1548	1621	1646	1716	1753	1826	1858	1858	1925	|	|	2008	2024	2051	|	2204	2229	2326	2332
Hull a.	1429	1446	1528	1603	1627	1628	1700	1725	1749	1838	1900	1937	1937	1958	2001	2025	2052	2057	2126	2202	2241	2303	2359	...

A – [12] and 🍷 (⚒ on Ⓐ) Hull - London Kings Cross.
B – [12] and 🍷 London Kings Cross - Hull.
C – Runs 8 minutes earlier on ⑥.
e – Arrives 5 minutes earlier on ⑥.

Table 566 HULL - BRIDLINGTON - SCARBOROUGH

2 class

km		⚒	⚒	⚒	⚒	⚒	⚒	⚒	⚒	⚒	⚒	⚒	⑦	⚒	⚒	⚒	⑦	⚒	⚒	⑦	⚒	⚒	⑦	⚒	⚒
0	**Hull** d.	0623	0653	0723	0823	0923	0953	1053	1123	1223	1253	1353	1450	1453	1523	1553	1650	1723	1753	1850	1853	1946	2050	2105	2230
13	Beverley d.	0636	0706	0736	0836	0936	1006	1106	1136	1236	1306	1406	1503	1506	1536	1606	1703	1736	1806	1903	1906	1959	2103	2118	2243
31	Driffield d.	0648	0723	0750	0850	0950	1018	1118	1150	1253	1318	1418	1517	1518	1553	1620	1717	1751	1821	1917	1923	2013	2117	2132	2300
50	**Bridlington** d.	0705	0742	0810	0909	1008	1039	1137	1209	1310	1339	1437	1537	1539	1610	1639	1737	1817	1840	1937	1942	2031	2137	2152	2319
72	Filey d.	...	0805	...	0932	...	1102	...	1232	...	1402	...	...	1602	...	1702	...	1840	...	...	2005	...	...	...	...
87	**Scarborough** a.	...	0822	...	0950	...	1119	...	1249	...	1419	...	...	1619	...	1719	...	1902	...	...	2022	...	...	...	...

	⚒	⚒	⚒	⚒	⚒	⚒	⚒	⚒	⚒	⚒	⚒	⑦	⚒	⚒	⑦	⚒	⚒	⚒	⑦	⚒	⚒	⚒	⑦	⚒	⚒
Scarborough d.	...	...	...	0704	...	0831	...	1001	...	1131	...	...	1301	...	...	1501	...	1639	...	...	1740	...	...	1946	...
Filey d.	...	...	...	0718	...	0845	...	1015	...	1145	...	...	1315	...	...	1515	...	1653	...	...	1754	...	...	2000	...
Bridlington d.	0610	0648	0718	0748	0818	0918	1018	1048	1148	1218	1318	1345	1348	1448	1545	1548	1628	1718	1745	1748	1818	1848	1945	2024	2200
Driffield d.	0625	0701	0733	0801	0833	0931	1031	1103	1203	1231	1331	1400	1403	1503	1600	1603	1643	1734	1800	1803	1834	1903	2000	2040	2215
Beverley d.	0640	0718	0748	0818	0848	0948	1045	1116	1216	1245	1348	1415	1416	1516	1615	1616	1700	1748	1815	1818	1848	1918	2015	2054	2230
Hull a.	0658	0735	0805	0835	0905	1005	1102	1132	1232	1305	1404	1431	1432	1532	1631	1632	1717	1805	1831	1834	1905	1936	2031	2111	2246

Additional services **Hull - Bridlington** on ⚒ : 0853, 1023, 1153, 1323, 1423, 1653.
Additional services **Bridlington - Hull** on ⚒: 0948, 1118, 1248, 1418, 1518.

Table 567 LEEDS - HARROGATE - YORK

2 class

km		⚒	⚒	⚒		⚒	⚒	⚒	⚒	⚒	⚒	⑦	⚒	⚒	⚒	⚒	⑦	⚒	⚒	⚒	⚒	⑦	⚒	⚒
0	**Leeds** d.	0609	0638	0715	...	0758	0828	0858	0928	0958	1028	1051	1058	1128	1158	1228	1251	1258	1328	1358	1428	1451	1458	1528
29	**Harrogate** d.	0646	0715	0752	...	0834	0904	0934	1004	1034	1104	1128	1134	1204	1234	1304	1328	1334	1404	1434	1504	1528	1534	1604
36	Knaresborough d.	0655	0724	0801	...	0845	0914	0945	1014	1045	1114	1137	1145	1214	1245	1314	1337	1345	1414	1445	1514	1537	1545	1614
62	**York** a.	0723	0751	0828	...	...	0941	...	1049	...	1149	1204	...	1241	...	1344	1404	...	1444	...	1544	1605	...	1641

	⑦	⚒	⚒	⑦	⚒	⚒	⚒	⑦	⚒	⚒	⑦	⚒	⑦	⚒		⑦	⚒		⑦	⚒		⚒	⑦	
Leeds d.	1551	1558	1628	1651	1658	1713	1728	1751	1758	1834	1851	1928	1951	2017	...	2111	2117	...	2211	2215	...	2315	2325	...
Harrogate d.	1628	1634	1706	1728	1734	1750	1804	1826	1834	1911	1928	2010	2028	2054	...	2148	2154	...	2248	2253	...	2353	0002	...
Knaresborough d.	1637	1645	1720	1737	1745	1800	1814	1840	1845	1920	1937	2019	2043	2103	...	2157	2204	...	...	...	...	...	...	...
York a.	1705	...	1747	1804	...	...	1842	1907	...	1947	2007	2049	2112	2130	...	...	...	...	...	...	...	...	...	...

		Ⓐ	⚒		⚒	A⚒	⚒	⚒	⚒	⑦	⚒	⚒	⚒	⚒	⑦	⚒	⚒	⑦	⚒	⚒	⚒	⚒	⑦	⚒
York d.	...	...	0652	...	...	...	0758	...	0906	...	...	1010	...	1110	...	...	1206	1216	...	1310	...	1410	1412	...
Knaresborough d.	...	0707	0716	...	0804	...	0822	0904	0934	...	1004	1034	1104	1134	1140	1204	1234	1240	1304	1334	1404	1434	1440	1504
Harrogate d.	...	0717	0742	...	0814	0830	0844	0914	0944	0951	1014	1044	1114	1144	1151	1214	1244	1251	1314	1344	1414	1444	1451	1514
Leeds a.	...	0755	0819	...	0852	0857	0922	0952	1022	1029	1052	1122	1152	1222	1229	1252	1322	1329	1352	1422	1452	1522	1529	1552

	⚒	⚒	⚒	⑦	⚒	⚒	⑦	⚒	⚒	⚒	⑦		⑦	⚒		⑥	Ⓐ	⑦		⑦	⚒	⑦		
York d.	1510	...	1608	1611	...	1654	1711	1715	...	1806	1814	...	1911	1916	...	2010	2012	2017	...	2124	2151	...	...	...
Knaresborough d.	1534	1604	1634	1640	1704	1718	1740	1740	1804	1834	1840	...	1940	1940	...	2039	2039	2040	...	2148	2215	...	...	...
Harrogate d.	1544	1614	1644	1651	1714	1728	1751	1750	1814	1844	1851	...	1951	1952	...	2049	2114b	2051	...	2158	2230	2258	...	...
Leeds a.	1622	1652	1722	1729	1752	1805	1829	1828	1852	1922	1929	...	2029	2030	...	2127	2152	2129	...	2236	2308	2336	...	...

A – [12] and 🍷 Harrogate - London Kings Cross.
b – Arrives 1045 on ⑥.
r – Arrives 2048.

For an explanation of standard symbols see page 4

323

Table 568 — SHEFFIELD - HUDDERSFIELD and LEEDS
2 class only

km			⑥		⑥		⑥			⑥			⑥		⑦▲	⑥		⑦	☓	☓	☓	☓	☓
0	Sheffield d.	0550	0607	0612	0639	0647	0657	0702	0727	0737	0804	0834	0837	0845	0905	0934	0954	1007	1034	1054	1107	1154	1207	1234
26	Barnsley d.	0615	0635	0640	0707	0717	0721	0730	0755	0806	0832	0905	0832	0905	0915	0934	1005	1019	1034	1105	1118	1134	1219	1234	1305
60	Huddersfield a.	0705					0810	0814			0845	0856				0955	1005		1054	1108		1208		1308	
44	Wakefield Kirkgate a.		0654	0658	0725			0749			0849	0922				0951			1052	1122		1152		1252	1322
71	Leeds a.		0730	0737	0802			0828			0928	0958				1027			1128	1158		1228		1328	1358

	⑦▲	⑥	⑦	☓	☓	☓	☓	☓	☓	⑦	⑥	⑥	⑥	⑦▲	⑥	⑥	⑥	⑦
Sheffield d.	1254	1307	1334	1354	1407	1437	1454	1507	1537	1554	1607	1635	1637	1655	1706	1707	1731	1737	1752	1805	1826	1836	1837	1907
Barnsley d.	1319	1334	1405	1419	1434	1505	1519	1534	1605	1619	1635	1707	1705	1707	1734	1736	1803	1805	1819	1834	1854	1915	1905	1935
Huddersfield a.	1408		1454	1508		1608		1654	1708			1809	1827					1854	1910		1950	2005		
Wakefield Kirkgate a.		1352			1452	1522		1552			1652	1724	1722		1755	1820		1852			1922	1952
Leeds a.		1428			1529	1559		1627			1731	1801	1758		1831	1902		1928			1957	2029

	⑦▲	⑦	⑥	⑦	☓	⑥	⑥	①-④	①-④	⑦			⑥			⑥	☓			⑥	☓	☓	⑥
Sheffield d.	1937	1937	1937	2008	2037	2050	2109	2110	2206	2237		Leeds d.	0534			0633			0709	0734
Barnsley d.	2005	2005	2016	2036	2105	2118	2137	2138	2234	2305		Wakefield Kirkgate d.	0606			0708			0745	0808	
Huddersfield a.	2054	2055	2105		2208	2227						Huddersfield a.		0558	0605		0708	0704			0740
Wakefield Kirkgate a.				2053	2122			2155	2251	2322		Barnsley d.	0624	0649	0656	0725	0756	0752	0815	0826	0830
Leeds a.				2129	2158			2231	2327	2358		Sheffield a.	0658	0722	0731	0807	0827	0827	0851	0903	0905

	⑦▲	⑥	⑥	⑥			⑥		☓	☓	⑦▲	☓	☓	☓	⑦▲	☓		☓	☓	☓	⑦▲
Leeds d.	0754		0832	0834			0934		1022	1034			1134		1222	1234			1334		1422	1434
Wakefield Kirkgate d.	0825		0903	0907			1005		1053	1105			1205		1253	1305			1405		1453	1505
Huddersfield d.		0817			0918	0927		1028			1115	1128		1227			1315	1328		1428		
Barnsley d.	0843	0905	0920	0925	1008	1015	1025	1116	1110	1125	1203	1216	1225	1316	1310	1325	1403	1416	1425	1516	1510	1525
Sheffield a.	0918	0940	0959	0959	1042	1044	1059	1145	1147	1158	1241	1245	1259	1345	1346	1358	1437	1446	1459	1545	1544	1558

	☓		☓	☓	⑦▲	⑥			⑥		⑥		⑥	⑥	⑥			⑥		⑥	⑥	⑥	①-④
Leeds d.	1534		1622	1634	1710				1737		1822		1834					1934		2022		2034	2134	2222	2305
Wakefield Kirkgate d.	1605		1653	1705	1742				1810		1853		1903					2005		2053		2105	2205	2253	2305
Huddersfield d.		1627				1715	1718	1727		1749		1827		1834	1915	1915		2015		2027		
Barnsley d.	1623	1716	1710	1710	1804	1803	1813	1816	1835	1856	1910	1916	1925	1932	2003	2005	2025	2105	2110	2115	2125	2225	2310	2305
Sheffield a.	1657	1746	1744	1754	1834	1836	1845	1853	1910	1931	1944	1949	1959	2005	2038	2039	2059	2139	2144	2150	2159	2258	2342	2359

▲ – On ⑦ Jan. 22 - Mar. 5 a 🚌 service will replace trains on part of this route. Arrive Huddersfield 57 minutes later than shown. Depart Huddersfield 55 minutes earlier than shown.

Additional services –
Sheffield - Wakefield: 0823⑥, 0937⑥, 1037⑥, 1137⑥, 1237⑥, 1337⑥, 1437⑥, 1537⑥, 1736⑥; Sheffield - Barnsley: 0823⑦, 2007⑥, 2037⑥, 2110⑥, 2137⑦, 2206⑤⑥, 2318①-⑤;
Wakefield - Sheffield: 0934⑥, 1034☓, 1134☓, 1234☓, 1334☓, 1434☓, 1534☓, 1634☓, 1834⑥; Barnsley - Sheffield: 0551☓, 0624⑥, 0740☓, 0910⑦, 2125⑥, 2214⑦, 2237⑤⑥.

Table 569 — PETERBOROUGH - LINCOLN - SHEFFIELD and DONCASTER
2 class only

km		☓	☓	☓	☓	☓	☓	⑥		⑥	☓		⑥	☓			⑥		⑥	⑥		⑥	☓
0	Peterborough d.					0836	0931d		1036		1139	1149		1234		1331	1345		1509	
26	Spalding d.					0902	1006		1102		1204	1211		1302		1402	1410		1536	
57	Sleaford d.			0716	0809	0926	1030		1126		1231	1241		1326		1427	1435		1604	
91	Lincoln Central d.	0645		0749	0910	1002	1102	1111	1202	1302	1302	1311	1311	1350	1400	1459	1506	1510	1550	1635	1713
116	Gainsborough Lea Road d.	0714		0812	0935	1026	1126	1135	1226	1326	1326	1335	1335	1413	1426	1523	1528	1530	1535	1613	1737
	Retford d.	0701	0740	0850		0951	1050		1151		1351		1351	1431		1551		1551	1631	1753
	Worksop d.	0713	0755	0902		1004	1102		1204		1404		1404	1443		1604		1604	1643	1838
	Sheffield a.	0752	0828	0936		1036	1136		1236		1436		1436	1514		1638		1636	1714
150	Doncaster a.			0852				1102	1156		1302	1356	1402		1502		1555	1557

	⑦	⑥	⑥	☓	☓	☓	⑦	☓	⑥	☓			☓	☓	☓	⑥	⑥	⑦	⑦
Peterborough d.		1609	1622							0920
Spalding d.		1636	1648							
Sleaford d.		1700	1712	1738	1749		2015				Doncaster d.			0622		0841	
Lincoln Central d.	1740	1746	1745	1815	1823	1929	1949	2047	2107		Sheffield d.			0651		0908	
Gainsborough Lea Road d.	1803	1810	1810	1838	1847	1953	2012	2111c	2131		Worksop d.			0702		0919	
Retford d.	1821		1855		2009	2030		2147	2239		Retford d.			0941	0942	0950	
Worksop d.	1833		1906		2022	2042		2200	2250		Gainsborough Lea Road d.	0634	0734	0749	0803	0905	1006	1010	1015	1104
Sheffield a.	1904		1940		2055	2113		2232	2326		Lincoln Central d.	0710	0805		0835	0939		1046	1138
Doncaster a.		1838	1837	1924							Sleaford d.			0859	1004		1111	1203
											Spalding d.			0925	1024		1133	1227
											Peterborough a.			0925	1024		1133	1227

	☓		☓	☓	☓		☓		☓		⑦	⑥	☓	⑦	⑦			⑥	⑦	⑥	⑥	⑦	⑦
Doncaster d.	1110		1210		1346	1424		1510			1610				1850		1950	1956				
Sheffield d.		1046		1246			1357		1446			1533		1639	1716	1743	1756		1846			1920	2117
Worksop d.		1113		1313			1422		1513			1558		1706	1745	1822	1831		1913			1945	2142
Retford d.		1123		1323			1432		1523			1631h		1716	1755	1822	1831		1922			2025f	2158
Gainsborough Lea Road d.	1135	1145	1235	1345	1417	1451	1455	1538	1545		1631	1645		1739	1817	1844	1854	1915	1945	2015	2021	2047
Lincoln Central d.	1200	1210	1303	1410	1446	1514	1520	1607	1613	1619	1656	1719	1747	1802	1805	1841	1908	1919	1939	2009	2049	2113
Sleaford d.	1235		1337		1517			1638		1650	1730		1818	1833				2010		2120	2120
Spalding d.	1302		1402		1542			1702													
Peterborough a.	1325		1422e					1727													

c – Not ⑥.   e – Arrive 1429 on ⑥.   h – Arrive 1608.
d – Depart 0939 on Ⓐ.   f – Arrive 1955.

Additional trains Retford - Sheffield: 1250☓, 1450☓, 1651☓, 1921⑥, 2038☓, 2125⑤.
Additional trains Sheffield - Retford: 0542☓, 0741☓, 0803⑥, 0946☓, 1146☓, 1346☓, 1546☓, 1946☓, 2146☓.
Additional trains Peterborough - Spalding: 0634☓, 0728Ⓐ, 0730⑥, 1731Ⓐ, 1738⑥, 1835⑥, 1859Ⓐ, 1959⑥, 2006Ⓐ, 2100☓.
Additional trains Spalding - Peterborough: 0701☓, 0759⑥, 0809Ⓐ, 1808☓, 1924⑥, 1928Ⓐ, 2026⑥, 2031Ⓐ, 2135☓.

Table 569a — BERWICK - CARLISLE rail link bus services (🚌)

km		☓	☓	⑥	Ⓐ	⑥		☓		⑦		⑦		Ⓐ	⑥		Ⓐ	⑦	⑤⑥	⑦	⑦
0	Berwick upon Tweed d.			0657	0817	0827		1047		1252		1252		1507	1517		1707	1712	1747		1907	195☓
68	Galashiels d.	0615	0810	0837	1005	1005	1015	1130	1228	1230	1430	1430	1445	1540	1600	1655	1655	1730	1900	1850	1925	1930	2100	213☓
77	Selkirk d.	0630	0825				1030	1145		1245		1445		1555	1627			1745		1945	
97	Hawick d.	0650	0850				1050	1205		1305		1505		1615	1647			1805		2005	
166	Carlisle a.	0820	1015				1215	1325		1430		1630		1735	1812			1925		2130	

	Ⓐ	⑥	Ⓐ	⑥	☓		☓		☓		☓		⑦	Ⓐ		⑥	⑥	⑦	⑦	⑥⑦
Carlisle d.					0910		1215		1355	1415		1510		1615		1710	1830	2020	2110	210☓
Hawick d.					1030		1335		1515	1537		1630		1733		1838	1950	2140	2230	234☓
Selkirk d.					1052		1355		1535	1557		1652		1755		1900	2010	2200	2250	000☓
Galashiels d.	0740	0815	0825	1050	1110	1235	1250	1412	1435	1450	1550	1612	1630	1632	1710	1725	1810	1830	1915	2025	2215	2305	001☓
Berwick upon Tweed a.	0928	1003	1003	1228		1429	1428		1628	1628		1822	1810		1903		2022

Operator: Lowland Omnibuses Ltd for Borders Regional Council.   Rail tickets are valid on this service.

For an explanation of standard symbols see page 4

Table 570 LONDON - LEEDS, YORK, EDINBURGH and GLASGOW

1, 2 class

km		Ⓐ M	Ⓐ ⓣ	Ⓐ ⓣ	Ⓐ ⓣ	Ⓐ ⓣ	Ⓐ ⓣ	Ⓐ M	Ⓐ G	Ⓐ M	Ⓐ ⓣZ	Ⓐ L	Ⓐ B	Ⓐ M	Ⓐ ✕	Ⓐ ✕	Ⓐ ⓣP	Ⓐ ⓣP	Ⓐ M
0	London Kings Cross .... d.									0600				0700	0730	0750	0800		
44	Stevenage .... d.									0619				0719	0749u	0809u			
123	Peterborough 585 .... d.									0656				0749			0844		
170	Grantham 585 .... d.									0716				0809					
193	Newark Northgate .... d.									0728				0821					
223	Retford .... d.									0743				0836					
251	Doncaster .... d.					0620			0746	0805		0842		0855	0903				
283	Wakefield Westgate .... d.													0912	0934s				
299	Leeds 551 .... d.	0344				0620	0650	0710		0752		0824		0852	0931	0953			0952
303	York 551 .... d.	0433		0550		0645	0705	0718	0734	0819 0823	0830	0852	0911	0921		0928		0952	1021
339	Thirsk .... d.	0456		0613			0724	0738			0845								1040
352	Northallerton .... d.	0505		0621			0733	0747			0853		0916		0949				1049
386	Middlesbrough .... a.	0534		0703n				0822			0925				1024				1122
374	Darlington .... d.			0634			0712	0747		0803	0858	0930	0941		0956			1020	1026
410	Durham .... d.						0729	0806		0820	0915	0949	0958		1013				1048
432	Newcastle .... d.			0630			0747	0827		0838	0933	1010	1020		1030			1052	1110
540	Berwick-upon-Tweed .... d.			0720						0922	1018								
633	Edinburgh .... a.			0809		0920				1016	1109							1215	
633	Edinburgh .... d.		0650	0811		0850	0920			1016	1109							1215	
725	Glasgow Central .... a.		0757	0915		0955	1026			1020								1219	
	Aberdeen 600 .... a.									1250								1319	

	Ⓐ L	Ⓐ	Ⓐ	Ⓐ B	Ⓐ M	Ⓐ ✕	Ⓐ	Ⓐ ✕	Ⓐ E	Ⓐ M	Ⓐ ✕	Ⓐ	Ⓐ L	Ⓐ ✕	Ⓐ M	Ⓐ ✕	Ⓐ N	Ⓐ D	Ⓐ M	Ⓐ ⓣ	Ⓐ	Ⓐ ✕	Ⓐ L
London Kings Cross .... d.		0820	0900			0910	0930	1000		1010	1030		1100		1110	1130	1200			1210	1230	1300	
Stevenage .... d.							0949									1149							
Peterborough 585 .... d.		0904	0944			0954	1019	1044		1054	1115		1144		1154	1219	1245			1254	1314		
Grantham 585 .... d.						1014									1214						1334		
Newark Northgate .... d.			0931			1025									1225								
Retford .... d.						1040									1240								
Doncaster .... d.		0956	1034			1056	1109		1142		1144		1234		1256	1309				1343	1409		
Wakefield Westgate .... d.		1014				1114					1202				1314						1401		
Leeds 551 .... d.	1017	1034		1050	1054	1134			1152	1220		1217		1254	1334			1350	1354	1420			1417
York 551 .... d.	1045		1100	1117	1126		1134	1153	1209	1221		1226	1245	1300		1334	1357	1417	1426		1434	1449	1454
Thirsk .... d.				1147						1242				1348				1447					
Northallerton .... d.	1109			1156					1251			1309		1357				1456					1518
Middlesbrough .... a.				1227					1321					1432				1526					
Darlington .... d.	1123		1128	1147			1202		1239			1323	1328			1402		1447			1502	1516	1532
Durham .... d.	1142			1205			1219		1256			1342				1419		1505			1519		1551
Newcastle .... d.	1211		1159	1226			1238	1247	1313			1321	1410	1400		1437	1457	1526			1538	1547	1612
Berwick-upon-Tweed .... d.			1245											1445									1631
Edinburgh .... a.			1338				1412					1452		1530				1626					1725
Edinburgh .... d.							1415					1457		1533									
Glasgow Central .... a.							1519							1643									
Aberdeen 600 .... a.									1725														

	Ⓐ M	Ⓐ ✕	Ⓐ ⓣ	Ⓐ	Ⓐ J	Ⓐ M	Ⓐ	Ⓐ	Ⓐ ⓣP	Ⓐ	Ⓐ L	Ⓐ C	Ⓐ	Ⓐ	Ⓐ ✕	Ⓐ M	Ⓐ	Ⓐ T	Ⓐ	Ⓐ R	Ⓐ M	Ⓐ	Ⓐ ⓣ	Ⓐ ✕	Ⓐ L
London Kings Cross .... d.		1310	1330	1400			1410	1430	1500			1510	1530				1550	1600				1620	1630	1700	
Stevenage .... d.			1349													1610u							1649u		
Peterborough 585 .... d.		1354	1419				1454	1514				1554	1614				1705	1719				1705	1719		
Grantham 585 .... d.		1414										1615					1725					1725			
Newark Northgate .... d.		1425					1521					1625										1746			
Retford .... d.		1440										1640										1745			
Doncaster .... d.		1456	1509		1530		1546	1604				1656	1704			1723		1742				1802			
Wakefield Westgate .... d.		1514					1603					1714				1741						1819			
Leeds 551 .... d.	1452	1534			1552	1623			1617	1650	1734				1800			1752				1839			1822
York 551 .... d.	1521		1535	1552	1600	1621		1629	1647	1645	1717		1729	1726		1751	1812	1826				1832	1848	1855	
Thirsk .... d.	1540				1640			1708					1749					1847							
Northallerton .... d.	1557				1649			1717					1749	1757				1857				1852		1919	
Middlesbrough .... a.	1626				1723									1832				1926							
Darlington .... d.			1602	1619			1657			1733	1747		1802			1819	1842					1905	1916	1933	
Durham .... d.			1619				1714			1752	1805		1819			1859						1922		1952	
Newcastle .... d.			1637	1650			1732	1742		1814	1823		1838			1851	1918					1939	1947	2013	
Berwick-upon-Tweed .... d.				1735							1908					1935	2002								
Edinburgh .... a.			1809	1824						1905	2005					2024	2055							2114	
Edinburgh .... d.			1812	1835						1909						2035									
Glasgow Central .... a.			1919							2013															
Aberdeen 600 .... a.				2110												2310									

	Ⓐ M	Ⓐ ✕	Ⓐ ⓣP	Ⓐ ⓣP	Ⓐ H	Ⓐ ✕	Ⓐ D	Ⓐ M	Ⓐ ✕	Ⓐ ✕	Ⓐ ⓣ	Ⓐ ①-④	Ⓐ⑤ ✕	Ⓐ L	Ⓐ	Ⓐ ✕	Ⓐ ⓣ	Ⓐ	Ⓐ	Ⓐ ⓣ	Ⓐ	Ⓐ M	Ⓐ
London Kings Cross .... d.		1705	1720	1730	1735	1749	1800		1810	1830	1850	1900	1900		1930	2000		2030		2200		2310	
Stevenage .... d.					1754u																		
Peterborough 585 .... d.		1749	1804	1814		1834	1844u		1855	1915	1934	1944	1944		2014	2044		2116		2244		2357	
Grantham 585 .... d.		1809		1837					1915		1954				2034			2135		2312		0022	
Newark Northgate .... d.			1831			1901				1941					2045			2146		2323		0034	
Retford .... d.			1848							1955					2100			2201					
Doncaster .... d.		1842	1910			1930		1945	1948	2013	2027	2034	2034		2116	2134		2218		2350		0109s	
Wakefield Westgate .... d.		1859		1923s					2006		2044				2134			2235				0127s	
Leeds 551 .... d.	1852	1918		1944				1952	2023		2104		2117		2154			2255				0155	
York 551 .... d.	1921		1939	1925		1955	2013	2021	2039			2059	2059	2145		2159	2330		0019				
Thirsk .... d.	1944							2040						2204			2354						
Northallerton .... d.	1952							2049	2059					2213		2227	0004						
Middlesbrough .... a.	2023							2118															
Darlington .... d.			1952			2022	2044		2115			2127	2127	2227		2240	0021		0053				
Durham .... d.			2009				2101		2132			2144	2144	2246		2257	0043		0112				
Newcastle .... d.			2025			2053	2122		2152			2204	2204	2320		2329	0117		0146				
Berwick-upon-Tweed .... d.			2124			2138						2254											
Edinburgh .... a.			2218			2223						2341											
Edinburgh .... d.						2226																	
Glasgow Central .... a.						2334																	
Aberdeen 600 .... a.																							

— 🚋 and ✕ London - Newcastle.
— 🚋 and ✕ Bristol - Newcastle.
— 🚋 and ⓣ Penzance - Edinburgh.
— 🚋 and ⓣ Paignton - Newcastle.
— 🚋 and ⓣ Plymouth - Newcastle.
— 🚋 and ⓣ Derby - York.

H – 🚋 and ⓣ London - Hull (arrive 2025).
J – 🚋 and ⓣ Bristol - York.
L – 🚋 and ⓣ Liverpool - Newcastle.
M – 🚋 and ⓣ Manchester Airport ✈ - Middlesbrough.
N – 🚋 and ✕ London - Inverness (arrive 2010).
P – Pullman service and ✕ available in 1 cl.

R – 🚋 and ⓣ Bournemouth - Edinburgh.
T – 🚋 and ⓣ London - Bradford Forster Square (arrive 1836).
Z – Also stops at Huntingdon, depart 0640.
n – Via Darlington.
s – Stops to set down only.   u – Stops to pick up only.

Table 570 — LONDON - LEEDS, YORK, EDINBURGH and GLASGOW

1, 2 class

⑥

Station																					
	M ☕	☕	☕	☕	☕	☕	M ☕	☕	M	Z	L	B	M	☕	M	L		B	M
London Kings Cross d.									0600		0700			0800			0810	0900		
Stevenage d.									0619					0819u			0829u	0919u		
Peterborough 585 d.									0656		0744			0849			0859	0949		
Grantham 585 d.									0716		0804						0919			
Newark Northgate d.									0728		0815						0931			
Retford d.						0610			0743											
Doncaster d.									0805		0842	0846		0939			0956	1038		
Wakefield Westgate d.							0620	0650	0710	0752		0824		0852		0952	1017	1034	1014	
Leeds 551 d.	0344			0550	0634	0705	0718	0734	0823	0830	0852	0908	0913	0921	1006	1021	1045		1050	1054
York 551 d.	0433		0550	0613		0724	0738		0845					0940	1040		1104	1117	1126	
Thirsk d.	0456		0613			0733	0747		0853		0916			0949	1049	1109			1147	
Northallerton d.	0505		0621		0652			0822	0925					1022	1121				1156	
Middlesbrough a.	0534		0703n																1227	
Darlington d.			0637		0705	0747		0803		0858	0930	0936	0943	1034		1123		1132	1147	
Durham d.						0722	0806		0820	0915	0949	0954	1001	1051		1142			1205	
Newcastle d.		0630			0740	0827		0838	0933	1008	1014	1020	1109		1211		1203	1226	
Berwick-upon-Tweed d.		0720				0832		0922		1018		1059		1247				1247	
Edinburgh a.		0809			0917			1013	1109		1144			1242			1337		
Edinburgh d.		0650	0810		0850	0920		1020			1153						1340		
Glasgow Central a.		0755	0915		0955	1026					1254						1445		
Aberdeen 600 a.								1250											

⑥

Station																							
	☕	☕	E	M	☕	☕	L	☕	M	☕	N	D	M	☕	☕	M	☕	J	M	L		
London Kings Cross d.	0910	0930	1000		1010	1030		1100	1130	1200			1230	1300	1330		1400			1430	
Stevenage d.		0949u						1119u						1319							
Peterborough 585 d.	0954	1019	1044		1054	1115		1149	1215	1245			1314	1349		1414		1445		1514	
Grantham 585 d.	1014								1234						1442				1549	
Newark Northgate d.	1025								1245						1453					
Retford d.	1040							1238	1300				1438		1508		1524	1527	1543		1614
Doncaster d.	1056	1108	1133	1142		1143			1316		1402	1438		1542		1636	
Wakefield Westgate d.	1114				1202				1337			1420		1452	1602		1552	1617	1659	
Leeds 551 d.	1134		1152	1220		1217	1254	1357		1350	1354	1417	1443		1527		1610	1621	1648	
York 551 d.		1134	1200	1209	1221		1226	1245	1304	1327		1357	1417	1428	1454		1504	1527		1555	1640	1709
Thirsk d.					1242				1349			1447			1546				1649	1719
Northallerton d.					1251		1309		1401			1456	1527		1555				1722	
Middlesbrough a.					1321				1440				1526		1626				
Darlington d.		1202	1228	1239		1323	1332		1447	1541	1532		1638	1733
Durham d.		1219	1256			1336	1349		1505	1600	1550			1752
Newcastle d.		1237	1259	1313		1321	1404	1407		1457	1526	1621	1607		1709	1815
Berwick-upon-Tweed d.		1322			1452			1657			
Edinburgh a.		1409	1428		1452	1538		1626	1748		1838
Edinburgh d.					1457	1541			1751		1855
Glasgow Central a.						1645			1854	
Aberdeen 600 a.					1725				2130	

⑥

Station																							
	⑥	C	M		☕	☕	U	M	L	☕	M	H	☕	D	M	☕	☕	☕	L	☕	☕	T
London Kings Cross d.	1500			1530	1600				1630	1700		1710	1730	1800			1830	1840	1900		2000	2030
Stevenage d.									1649		1749u						1919				
Peterborough 585 d.	1544			1614	1644				1719	1744		1755	1819	1844			1914	1924	1949		2045	2115
Grantham 585 d.				1642					1746		1823				1942				2113	
Newark Northgate d.				1654					1759		1834					1959			2124	
Retford d.				1709							1849				2003				2139	
Doncaster d.	1641			1726	1739	1744			1824	1841	1906	1915	1941	1945		2020	2025	2046		2156	2213	2231
Wakefield Westgate d.				1749					1844		1932			1952		2038			2213	2253
Leeds 551 d.		1650	1654	1811		1752	1820	1905		1852		1952	2058			2117	2232	2310
York 551 d.	1707	1717	1726			1806	1812	1821	1853		1907	1921		2007	2015	2021		2051	2112	2145	2240
Thirsk d.			1745					1840		1940				2043			2207	
Northallerton d.			1754			1849	1917		1949				2052		2139	2216	
Middlesbrough a.			1824			1923		2018			2120			
Darlington d.	1739	1747			1835	1843	1931		1937		2043	2053		2127	2152	2230		2316
Durham d.	1758	1805				1900	1950		1956		2110		2145	2209	2249		2333
Newcastle d.	1817	1826			1906	1919	2011		2015		2114	2131		2204	2228	2310		2352
Berwick-upon-Tweed d.	1901	1911			1951	2003				2209			
Edinburgh a.	1948	2005			2038	2055		2146		2256			
Edinburgh d.	1951							2149			
Glasgow Central a.	2055							2250			
Aberdeen 600 a.											

⑦

Station																							
	M	☕		M	☕	L		☕	☕	M	G	☕	☕	☕	L	☕	B	M			☕	
London Kings Cross d.							0830	0900		1000	1010	1030		1100			1200	1210
Stevenage d.							0855	0925		1025	1035	1055		1125			1225	1235
Peterborough 585 d.							0937	1007		1107	1117	1137	1207			1307	1317
Grantham 585 d.							1011			1151				1351
Newark Northgate d.							1024			1204				1404
Retford d.						1015	1040			1220				1436	1501
Doncaster d.							1121	1136		1150	1226	1301	1307		1336	1346			1517
Wakefield Westgate d.						1116	1137			1317			1351	1537
Leeds 551 d.	0751			0951		1144	1156		1151		1337		1316		1425	1506
York 551 d.	0823	0900		1020	1044		1206	1220	1230	1306		1336	1348	1406	1416	
Thirsk d.	0846			1043		1207		1239		1407		1444	
Northallerton d.	0854	0920		1051		1215		1248		1416		1453	
Middlesbrough a.	0956n			1135n				1335n				1522
Darlington d.	0910	0943		1109	1122	1229		1236	1309		1336	1406	1430	1436	1446		1536
Durham d.		1001			1139	1248		1253		1423	1449	1504		1614
Newcastle d.		1021			1200	1310		1314	1410		1451	1514	1510	1526		1659
Berwick-upon-Tweed d.		1118			1244		1359		1536			1746
Edinburgh a.		1232			1352		1508		1559	1630	1640		1748
Edinburgh d.		1233						1600	1630		1850
Glasgow Central a.		1415					1707		1905	
Aberdeen 600 a.										

B – 🚃 and ☕ Bristol - Newcastle.
C – 🚃 and ☕ Penzance - Newcastle.
D – 🚃 and ☕ Paignton - Newcastle.
E – 🚃 and ☕ Plymouth - Newcastle.
G – 🚃 and ☕ Derby - York.
H – 🚃 and ☕ London - Hull (arrive 2001).

J – 🚃 and ☕ Bristol - York.
L – 🚃 and ☕ Liverpool - Newcastle.
M – 🚃 and ☕ Manchester Airport ✈ - Middlesbrough.
N – 🚃 and ☕ London - Inverness (arrive 2010).
S – 🚃 and ☕ Bournemouth - Edinburgh.
T – 🚃 and ☕ Glasgow - Doncaster - Leeds.

U – 🚃 and ☕ Bournemouth (not Feb. 11 - Mar. 4) - Reading - Edinburgh.
Z – Also stops at Huntingdon depart 0640.

n – Via Darlington.
u – Stops to **pick up** only.

Table 570 LONDON - LEEDS, YORK, EDINBURGH and GLASGOW

1, 2 class except where shown

	⑦ 🍷	⑦ X	⑦ J	⑦ N	⑦ L	⑦ 🍷	⑦ M	⑦ 🍷	⑦ J	⑦ 🍷		⑦ 🍷	⑦ L	⑦ R	⑦ 🍷	⑦ M	⑦ 🍷	⑦ 🍷		⑦ 🍷	⑦ L		⑦ 🍷	⑦ 🍷
London Kings Cross d.	1210	...	...	1300	...	1330	...	1400	...	1410	...	1500	...	...	1530	...	1600	1610	...	1700	...	...	1710	1730
Stevenage d.	1235	...	...	1325	...	1355	...	1425	...	1435	...	1525	...	...	1555	...	1625	1635	...	|	...	...	|	1750
Peterborough 585 d.	1317	...	...	1407	...	1437	...	1507	...	1517	...	1607	...	...	1632	...	1657	1707	...	1747	...	...	1757	1822
Grantham **585** d.	1351	1410	...	|	...	|	...	|	...	1551	...	|	...	...	1706	...	|	|	...	|	...	...	1831	|
Newark Northgate d.	1404	1431	...	|	...	|	...	|	...	1604	...	|	...	...	1719	...	|	|	...	|	...	...	|	1904
Retford d.	1420	...	...	|	...	|	...	|	...	1620	...	|	...	...	|	...	|	1800	...	|	...	...	|	|
Doncaster d.	1501	...	1509	1516	...	1546	...	1616	1633	1641	...	1716	...	1740	1750	...	1806	1821	...	1856	...	...	1910	1935
Wakefield Westgate d.	1517	...	|	|	...	|	...	|	1649	1657	...	|	...	|	|	...	|	1838	...	|	...	...	1929	|
Leeds 551 d.	1537	...	|	|	1516	|	...	|	1710	1717	...	|	1718	|	|	1751	|	1902	...	|	1916	...	1947	|
York 551 d.	...	...	1541	1546	1552	1616	1624	1646	1739	...	...	1746	1752	1810	1820	1826	1836	...	...	1926	1946	...	...	2005
Thirsk d.	...	...	...	|	1611	|	1643	|	...	...	...	|	1811	|	|	1845	|	...	...	|	2005	...	...	|
Northallerton d.	...	...	...	1607	1620	|	1652	|	...	...	...	|	1820	|	1841	1859	|	...	...	|	2014	...	...	2026
Middlesbrough a.	...	...	...	|	|	|	1721	|	...	...	...	|	|	|	|	1928	|	...	...	|	|	...	...	|
Darlington d.	...	...	...	1620	1634	1646	...	1716	...	...	...	1816	1834	1840	1854	...	1906	...	...	1956	2028	...	...	2040
Durham d.	...	...	...	1637	1653	|	...	1734	...	...	...	|	1853	1857	1911	...	|	...	...	2014	2047	...	...	2057
Newcastle d.	...	...	...	1658	1714	1720	...	1754	...	...	...	1850	1914	1918	1932	...	1940	...	...	2034	2108s	...	...	2118
Berwick-upon-Tweed d.	...	...	...	|	...	1805	...	1839	...	...	...	1935	...	2003	...	...	|	...	...	2119	...	...	...	...
Edinburgh a.	...	...	...	1836	...	1901	...	1930	...	...	...	2024	...	2100	...	...	2112	...	...	2206	...	...	...	...
Edinburgh d.	...	...	...	...	...	1910	...	1934	...	...	...	...	...	...	...	...	...	...	...	2208	...	...	...	...
Glasgow Central a.	...	...	...	...	...	|	...	2040	...	...	...	...	...	...	...	...	...	...	...	2315	...	...	...	...
Aberdeen **600** a.	...	...	...	...	...	2145	...	...	...	...	...	...	...	...	...	...	...	...	...	...	...	...	...	...

	⑦ C	⑦ M	⑦ 🍷	⑦ Q		⑦ 🍷	⑦ X	⑦ B	⑦ 🍷	⑦ L	⑦ H	⑦ 🍷		⑦ 🍷		⑦ 🍷		⑦ 🍷	⑦	⑦ 🍷		⑦ 🍷		⑦
London Kings Cross d.	...	...	1800	...	...	1830	...	...	1900	...	1910	1930	...	2000	...	2030	...	2100	...	2110	...	2200	...	2310
Stevenage d.	...	...	|	...	...	|	...	...	|	...	|	1950	...	|	...	|	...	|	...	|	...	|	...	|
Peterborough 585 d.	...	...	1848	...	...	1917	...	...	1948	...	1957	2022	...	2048	...	2117	...	2148	...	2157	...	2248	...	2357
Grantham **585** d.	...	...	1921	...	...	|	1953	...	|	...	2031	|	...	|	...	2151	...	|	...	2231	...	|	...	0031
Newark Northgate d.	...	...	|	...	...	1959	2009	...	|	...	2044	|	...	|	...	2204	...	|	...	2244	...	|	...	0044
Retford d.	...	...	|	...	...	2015	...	...	|	...	|	|	...	|	...	2220	...	|	...	2300	...	|	...	|
Doncaster d.	...	...	2000	2009	...	2037	...	2034	2056	...	2114	2130	...	2156	...	2241	...	2256	...	2321	...	2356	...	0114s
Wakefield Westgate d.	...	...	|	|	...	2054	...	|	|	...	...	2147	...	|	...	2257	...	|	...	2337	...	|	...	|
Leeds 551 d.	1945	1951	|	|	...	2119	...	|	|	2116	...	2209	...	|	...	2320	...	|	...	0004s	...	|	...	0153
York 551 d.	2011	2020	2030	2045	...	...	...	2104	2127	2144	...	...	...	2226	...	...	...	2326	2332	...	...	0026	...	...
Thirsk d.	|	2039	|	...	...	...	...	|	|	2203	...	...	...	|	...	...	...	|	2356	...	...	|	...	...
Northallerton d.	|	2053	|	...	...	...	...	|	|	2212	...	...	...	|	...	...	...	|	0006	...	...	|	...	...
Middlesbrough a.	|	2122s	|	...	...	...	...	|	|	|	...	...	...	|	...	...	...	|	|	...	...	|	...	...
Darlington d.	2046	...	2100	...	...	...	...	2134	2157	2226	...	...	...	2256	...	...	...	0004	0023	...	...	0104	...	...
Durham d.	2103	...	|	...	...	...	...	2152	2214	2245	...	...	...	2314	...	...	...	0022	0045	...	...	0122	...	...
Newcastle d.	2124	...	2134	...	...	...	...	2215	2236	2306	...	...	...	2335s	...	...	...	0044	0108	...	...	0144	...	...
Berwick-upon-Tweed d.	2209	...	2225	...	...	...	...	...	...	...	...	...	...	...	...	...	...	...	...	...	...	...	...	...
Edinburgh a.	2305	...	2318	...	...	...	...	...	...	...	...	...	...	...	...	...	...	...	...	...	...	...	...	...
Edinburgh d.	...	...	...	...	...	...	...	...	...	...	...	...	...	...	...	...	...	...	...	...	...	...	...	...
Glasgow Central a.	...	...	...	...	...	...	...	...	...	...	...	...	...	...	...	...	...	...	...	...	...	...	...	...
Aberdeen **600** a.	...	...	...	...	...	...	...	...	...	...	...	...	...	...	...	...	...	...	...	...	...	...	...	...

Ⓐ

	②-⑤	①	Ⓐ W	②-⑤	①	Ⓐ 🍴	Ⓐ 🍷	Ⓐ 🍷	Ⓐ 🍴	Ⓐ 🍷	Ⓐ 🍷P	Ⓐ 🍷P	Ⓐ 🍷P	Ⓐ M	Ⓐ L	Ⓐ 🍷P	Ⓐ D	Ⓐ F	Ⓐ B	Ⓐ 🍷P	Ⓐ 🍴	Ⓐ 🍷
Aberdeen **600** d.	...	...	...	...	...	...	...	...	...	...	...	...	...	...	...	...	...	...	...	...	...	...
Glasgow Central d.	...	...	...	...	...	...	...	...	...	...	...	...	...	...	...	...	...	...	...	...	...	...
Edinburgh a.	...	...	...	...	...	...	...	...	...	...	...	...	...	...	...	...	...	...	...	...	...	...
Edinburgh d.	...	...	...	...	...	...	...	...	...	...	...	...	...	...	...	...	...	...	...	...	...	...
Berwick-upon-Tweed d.	...	...	...	...	...	...	...	...	...	...	...	...	...	...	...	...	...	...	...	...	...	...
Newcastle d.	0145	0200	...	...	...	...	...	...	...	...	0600	...	...	...	0610	0630	...	...	0640	0700	0710	...
Durham d.	0201	0216	...	...	...	...	...	...	...	...	0612	...	...	...	0627	0642	...	...	0652	0712	|	...
Darlington d.	0224	0239	...	...	...	...	...	...	...	...	0630	...	...	...	0646	0700	...	...	0710	0730	0736	...
Middlesbrough d.	|	|	...	...	...	...	...	...	...	...	|	...	...	0621	|	|	...	...	|	|	|	...
Northallerton d.	|	|	...	...	...	...	...	...	...	...	|	...	...	0647	0659	0712	...	...	|	|	|	...
Thirsk d.	|	|	...	...	...	...	...	...	...	...	|	...	...	0656	0708	|	...	...	|	|	|	...
York 551 d.	0325	0325	0348	0425	0440	...	...	0600	...	0635	0700	...	...	0718	0736h	0735	...	...	0742	|	0805	...
Leeds 551 d.	...	...	0418	|	|	0500	...	|	0615	|	|	0700	0720	0747	0805	|	...	0738	|	|	|	0805
Wakefield Westgate d.	...	...	...	|	|	0513	...	|	0628	|	|	0714	0733	...	...	|	...	0750	|	|	|	0818
Doncaster d.	...	...	...	0515	0515	0535	...	0623	|	0657	|	0730	|	...	...	|	0755	|	0809	|	|	0835
Retford d.	...	...	...	...	...	0551	...	|	0655	|	|	|	|	...	...	|	|	|	...	|	0839	|
Newark Northgate d.	...	...	...	...	...	0605	...	0646	0709	0721	|	|	|	...	...	|	|	0826	...	|	|	0859
Grantham **585** d.	...	...	...	...	...	0618	...	0659	0722	0734	|	|	|	...	...	|	|	0839	...	|	|	0912
Peterborough 585 d.	...	...	...	...	...	0640	0700	0720	0740	0755	0805	|	|	...	...	|	0845	|	...	|	0916	0932
Stevenage d.	...	...	...	...	...	|	|	|	|	|	|	|	|	...	...	0907s	|	|	...	|	|	1006s
London Kings Cross a.	...	...	...	...	...	0734	0751	0812	0835	0849	0857	0904	0918	...	...	0930	0940	0948	...	0950	1011	1031

		Ⓐ L	Ⓐ E	Ⓐ 🍷	Ⓐ 🍷P		Ⓐ T	Ⓐ M	Ⓐ 🍴	Ⓐ S	Ⓐ 🍷	Ⓐ 🍴	Ⓐ M	Ⓐ L	Ⓐ 🍴	Ⓐ 🍴	Ⓐ C	Ⓐ M	Ⓐ 🍴	Ⓐ 🍷	Ⓐ 🍴		Ⓐ M	Ⓐ L
Aberdeen **600** d.	...	...	...	...	...	...	...	...	...	...	...	...	...	...	...	...	...	...	...	...	...	...	...	...
Glasgow Central d.	...	...	...	...	...	...	...	...	...	...	...	...	...	...	0700	...	...	...	0800	...	...	...	...	...
Edinburgh a.	...	...	...	...	...	...	...	...	...	...	...	...	...	...	0759	...	...	...	0859	...	...	...	...	...
Edinburgh d.	...	...	...	0600	0630	...	...	...	0700	0707	...	...	...	...	0800	...	0805	...	0900	0930	...	...	...	...
Berwick-upon-Tweed d.	...	...	...	0644	|	...	...	...	0739	0746	...	...	...	...	|	...	0848	...	0942	1014	...	...	...	...
Newcastle d.	...	0713	...	0742	0755	...	...	...	0830	0837	0900	...	...	0912	0933	...	0940	...	1033	1105	...	...	...	1112
Durham d.	...	0731	...	0754	|	...	...	...	0843	0850	0912	...	...	0929	|	...	0952	...	1046	|	...	...	...	1129
Darlington d.	...	0750	...	0812	|	...	...	...	0901	0908	0930	...	...	0948	1000	...	1010	...	1104	1133	...	...	...	1148
Middlesbrough d.	...	|	0745	|	|	...	...	0814	|	|	|	...	0921	|	|	...	|	1018	|	|	...	...	1121	|
Northallerton d.	...	0803	0811	|	|	...	...	0843	|	|	0942	...	0947	1001	|	...	|	1047	|	|	...	...	1147	1201
Thirsk d.	...	0812	|	|	|	...	...	0852	|	|	|	...	0956	|	|	...	|	1056	|	|	...	...	1156	|
York 551 d.	...	0836	0843k	0843	0848	...	...	0919	0932	0942	1004	...	1019	1037	1031	...	1043	1118	1137	1204	...	...	1219	1237
Leeds 551 d.	...	0905	0913	|	|	...	0905	0946	|	|	|	1005	1046	1105	|	1105	1112	1145	|	|	1205	...	1246	1305
Wakefield Westgate d.	...	...	...	|	|	...	0918	...	|	|	|	1018	...	...	|	1118	...	...	|	|	1218	...	...	...
Doncaster d.	...	...	...	0910	|	...	0935	...	0956	1008	1028	1035	...	...	1057	1136	...	...	1201	|	1236	...	...	...
Retford d.	...	...	...	|	|	...	|	...	|	...	|	1051	...	...	|	|	...	...	|	|	1251	...	...	...
Newark Northgate d.	...	...	...	|	|	...	1000	...	|	...	|	1105	...	...	|	|	...	...	|	|	1305	...	...	...
Grantham **585** d.	...	...	...	|	|	...	1012	...	|	...	|	1118	...	...	|	|	...	...	|	|	1317	...	...	...
Peterborough 585 d.	...	...	...	1000	|	...	1032	...	1044	...	1115	1138	...	...	1144	1224	...	...	|	1309	1338	...	...	...
Stevenage d.	...	...	...	|	|	...	|	...	|	...	1148s	|	...	...	|	|	...	...	|	|	|	...	...	...
London Kings Cross a.	...	...	...	1055	1039	...	1127	...	1139	...	1214	1232	...	...	1240	1316	...	...	1338	1404	1430	...	...	...

– [12] and 🍷 Bristol - Newcastle and v.v.
– [12] and 🍷 Penzance - Edinburgh and v.v.
– [12] and 🍴 Hull (depart 0705) - London.
– [2] and 🍷 Middlesbrough - Blackpool North.
– [12] and 🍴 Bradford Forster Sq. (depart 0704) - London.
– [12] and 🍷 Dundee (depart 0640) - Penzance.
– [12] and 🍷 London - Hull (arrive 2210).

J – [12] and 🍷 Bristol - York.
L – [2] and 🍷 Liverpool - Newcastle and v.v.
M – [2] and 🍷 Manchester Airport ✈ - Middlesbrough and v.v.
N – [12] and 🍷 London - Inverness (arrive 2220).
P – Pullman service and 🍴 available in 1 cl.
Q – [12] and 🍷 Poole - York.

R – [12] and 🍷 Bristol - Edinburgh.
S – [12] and 🍷 Edinburgh - Bournemouth.
T – [12] and 🍷 Harrogate (depart 0830) - London.
W – [2] and 🍷 York - Manchester Airport ✈.
X – [2] Grantham - Lincoln.
h – Arrive 0727.
k – Arrive 0835.
s – Stops to set down only.

Table 570 — GLASGOW, EDINBURGH, YORK and LEEDS - LONDON

1, 2 class

Note: In the tables below ✕ denotes a restaurant/buffet (knife-and-fork) service and ⚲ denotes a refreshment (wine glass) service. Ⓐ = service runs Mondays to Fridays; ⑥ = service runs Saturdays. A vertical line (|) in the original indicates the train passes without calling; "..." indicates no service.

Panel 1 — Ⓐ

Station	⚲	✕	E	✕	M	✕	N	✕	M	L	✕	Q	✕	⚲	⚲	M	✕	E	✕	L	⚲	⚲	M
Aberdeen 600 d.	0755										0955												
Glasgow Central d.					1000											1200	1259						
Edinburgh a.		1020			1059						1220					1259	1300						
Edinburgh d.		1030			1100	1130		1142			1230	1309				1300			1400				1444
Berwick-upon-Tweed d.																							
Newcastle d.	1130	1157	1203				1233	1300		1314	1330	1338	1400			1430	1500			1513	1535	1555	
Durham d.	1143		1215				1246			1331	1343	1350				1443	1512			1530		1608	
Darlington d.	1201	1233					1305			1350	1401	1409				1501	1530			1549	1601	1626	
Middlesbrough d.				1213				1321						1415				1521	1547	1602			1615
Northallerton d.				1239				1347	1403	1413				1441				1556					1644
Thirsk d.				1248				1356						1450									1653
York 551 d.	1232	1251	1305	1315		1337	1354	1418	1431	1437	1443	1454		1519	1532	1602	1619	1637j	1632	1655	1705		1743
Leeds 551 d.			1305	1343				1405	1445	1505		1512		1505		1546		1605	1646	1705			
Wakefield Westgate d.			1318					1418						1518				1618					
Doncaster d.	1256	1330	1339			1401		1436			1501			1535	1549	1558	1630	1635			1719		
Retford d.								1451						1603									
Newark Northgate d.								1505						1616							1751		
Grantham 585 d.								1518						1636	1645						1751		
Peterborough 585 d.	1344	1400	1427			1448	1503	1539			1548		1621s	1645s			1753s			1722	1737	1810s	1839s
Stevenage d.	1414s																						
London Kings Cross a.	1441	1457	1520			1543	1600	1632			1648		1654	1708	1731		1741			1820	1835	1906	

Panel 2 — Ⓐ

Station	⚲ P	⚲	G	⚲	B	M	L	✕	✕	✕	⚲	⚲ Z	M	M	⚲	M	M	⚲
Aberdeen 600 d.										1455								
Glasgow Central d.	1400								1600		1720		1800			2010		2111
Edinburgh a.	1459								1659				1859			2115		
Edinburgh d.	1500					1600			1700	1730			1900			2115		2159
Berwick-upon-Tweed d.						1639				1815			1947			2159		
Newcastle d.	1628		1650	1700		1709	1730		1840	1905			2038	2120		2300		
Durham d.			1702	1712		1726			1853				2051	2138		2313		
Darlington d.			1721	1730		1745	1757		1911	1932			2109	2202	2220	2331		
Middlesbrough d.					1718		1745	1758	1820		1846		1921	2021		2153n		
Northallerton d.					1753	1807			1855				1947	2047		2233		
Thirsk d.													1956	2056		2242		
York 551 d.	1720		1727	1751	1802	1817	1837	1827	1919	1942	2003		2019	2121	2139	2308		0026
Leeds 551 d.		1705			1846	1905					2015	2046		2148		2338		
Wakefield Westgate d.		1718					1815	1828			2028							
Doncaster d.		1740	1754	1815	1830		1852	1858	2008	2029	2045			2205				
Retford d.		1756						1912			2101							
Newark Northgate d.		1810	1839				1926		2032		2115			2229				
Grantham 585 d.							1939				2127			2242				
Peterborough 585 d.		1838	1907				2000		1938	2000	2148		2118	2302				
Stevenage d.		1913s	1939s				2011s	2033s		2128s	2152s	2229s		2339s				
London Kings Cross a.	1910	1937	2007				2038	2058		2155	2226	2259		0010				

Panel 3 — ⑥

Station	⑥ W	⑥ ⚲	⑥ ⚲	⑥ ⚲	⑥ ⚲	⑥ H	⑥ M	⑥ L	⑥ B	⑥ ⚲	⑥ F	⑥ L	⑥ X	⑥ ⚲	⑥ T	⑥ M	⑥ S	⑥ ⚲	⑥ M
Aberdeen 600 d.																			
Glasgow Central d.																			
Edinburgh a.																			
Edinburgh d.															0655	0700			
Berwick-upon-Tweed d.															0734	0743			
Newcastle d.	0145				0600	0610	0640	0700		0705		0800			0828	0840			
Durham d.	0201				0612	0627	0652	0712		0722		0812			0841	0853			
Darlington d.	0224				0630	0646	0710	0730		0741		0830			0859	0911			
Middlesbrough d.						0621	0647	0659	0742		0754	0811			0835				0921
Northallerton d.						0656	0708				0803				0844				0947
Thirsk d.						0718	0736h	0741	0805		0836v	0843	0900		0919r	0933	0942		0956 1019
York 551 d.	0325	0348		0600	0700	0747	0805			0805	0905	0913		0905	0946		1005	1019	1046
Leeds 551 d.		0418	0500	0615		0700			0805		0818			0918		0959	1005	1035	
Wakefield Westgate d.			0513	0628		0713													
Doncaster d.			0535	0622	0645	0723	0730	0755		0809	0835		0924	0935				1050	
Retford d.			0551	0701							0852					1000		1105	
Newark Northgate d.			0605	0715	0754		0829				0905				1012			1118	
Grantham 585 d.			0618	0727		0809	0822	0849			0917		1011	1032			1052	1138	
Peterborough 585 d.			0640	0710	0748	0809	0822	0849		0910	0937	0943s					1121s		
Stevenage d.			0734	0803	0842	0902	0916	0944				1009	1032	1105	1127		1151	1233	
London Kings Cross a.																			

Panel 4 — ⑥

Station	⑥ L	⑥ ⚲	⑥ ⚲	⑥ C	⑥ M	⑥ ⚲	⑥ ⚲	⑥ M	⑥ L	⑥ ⚲	⑥ ⚲	⑥ A	⑥ ⚲	⑥ M	⑥ N	⑥ M	⑥ L	⑥ ⚲	⑥ Q	⑥ ⚲	⑥ M
Aberdeen 600 d.											0755								0955		
Glasgow Central d.		0700			0800					1000				1059				1220			
Edinburgh a.		0759			0859					1020				1059				1230			
Edinburgh d.		0800		0805	0900		0848			1030		1100	1130		1142			1239			
Berwick-upon-Tweed d.				0848	0942				1044												
Newcastle d.	0912	0933		0940	1033		1118	1134	1157	1203		1233	1300		1314	1330	1338	1400			
Durham d.	0929			0952	1046		1135	1148		1215		1246			1331	1343	1350				
Darlington d.	0948	1000		1010	1104		1154	1206		1233		1305			1350	1401	1409				1415
Middlesbrough d.				1018					1118				1213		1321						1441
Northallerton d.	1001			1047			1144	1207		1239				1347	1403	1413					1450
Thirsk d.				1056			1153			1248				1356							1510
York 551 d.	1037	1031		1043	1118	1137	1219	1237	1236	1251	1305		1315	1337	1354	1418	1431	1437	1443	1454	1505
Leeds 551 d.	1105	1105	1112	1145		1205	1246	1305			1305	1343		1405	1445	1505			1512		1518
Wakefield Westgate d.		1118				1218					1318			1418							
Doncaster d.		1057	1135		1201	1235		1302	1330	1339		1401		1436			1501				1535
Retford d.					1251									1451							
Newark Northgate d.					1305									1505							1559
Grantham 585 d.					1318									1518							
Peterborough 585 d.		1146	1222		1248	1338			1349	1400		1426		1448	1503	1539			1548		1627
Stevenage d.			1255s						1422s										1628s		1705s
London Kings Cross a.		1238	1321		1342	1432			1449	1501		1527		1549	1606	1640			1653	1659	1733

A – 🚃 and ⚲ Newcastle - Exeter.
B – 🚃 and ⚲ Newcastle - Bristol.
C – 🚃 and ⚲ Edinburgh - Penzance.
E – 🚃 and ⚲ Newcastle - Plymouth.
F – 🚃 and ⚲ Bradford Forster Square (depart 0733) - London.
G – 🚃 and ⚲ York - Derby.
H – 🚃 and ⚲ Hull (depart 0705) - London.
L – 🚃 and ⚲ Newcastle - Liverpool.
M – 🚃 and ✕ Middlesbrough - Manchester Airport ✈.
N – 🚃 and ✕ (⚲ on ⑥) Inverness - London.
P – Pullman service and ✕ available in 1 cl.
Q – 🚃 and ⚲ Newcastle - Swansea.
S – 🚃 and ⚲ Edinburgh - Bournemouth.
T – 🚃 and ⚲ Harrogate (depart 0830) - London.
W – 🚃 and ⚲ York - Manchester Airport ✈.
X – 🚃 and ⚲ Middlesbrough - Blackpool North.
Z – Also stops at Huntingdon, depart 2202.
h – Arrive 0727.
j – Arrive 1626.
n – Via Darlington.
r – Arrive 0906.
s – Stops to set down only.
v – Arrive 0822.

Table 570 — GLASGOW, EDINBURGH, YORK and LEEDS - LONDON

1, 2 class except where shown

Block 1 — ⑥ (Saturdays)

		E		M	L			M	G		B	M	L					Z	M	M		M
Aberdeen 600 d.	…	…	…	…	…	…	…	…	…	…	…	…	…	…	…	…	…	1455	…	…	…	…
Glasgow Central d.	1200	…	…	…	…	…	…	1400	…	…	1600	…	…	…	…	1800						
Edinburgh a.	1259	…	…	…	…	…	1459	…	…	1659	1720	…	…	…	1859							
Edinburgh d.	1300	…	…	1400	…	…	1500	…	…	1600	1700 1730	…	…	1900								
Berwick-upon-Tweed d.	…	…	…	…	1444	…	…	…	…	1639	1814	…	…	1946								
Newcastle d.	1430	1500	…	1513	1535	…	…	1630	1700	1709	1730	…	1840	1905	…	2045	2120					
Durham d.	1443	1512	…	1530	…	…	…	1643	1712	1726	…	1853	…	2059	2138							
Darlington d.	1501	1530	…	1549	1601	…	…	1701	1730	1745	1757	…	1911	1932	…	2117	2202	2220				
Middlesbrough d.	…	…	1521	…	…	1615	…	…	…	1718	…	1820	…	1920	2019	…	2153n					
Northallerton d.	…	…	1547	1602	…	1644	…	…	1745	1800	…	1846	…	1946	2045	…	2233					
Thirsk d.	…	…	1556	…	…	1653	…	…	1753	1808	…	1855	…	1955	2054	…	2242					
York 551 d.	1532	1602	…	1619 1626 1637	…	1715 1725 1732 1802	1817 1837 1827	…	1919 1942 2003	…	2021 2121 2158	2308										
Leeds 551 d.	…	1605 1646 1705	…	1705 1742	…	1846 1905	…	1815 1946	…	2015 2048 2148 2310t	2338											
Wakefield Westgate d.	…	1618	…	1718	…	1828	…	1946	…	2028	2253t											
Doncaster d.	1558	1630 1635	…	1656 1735	…	1752 1758 1830	…	1852 1854	…	2008 2029 2045	…	2225										
Retford d.	…	1651	…	…	…	…	…	1910	…	2101												
Newark Northgate d.	…	1705	…	…	…	…	…	1924	…	2116												
Grantham 585 d.	…	1717	…	…	…	…	…	1936	…	2129												
Peterborough 585 d.	1645	1738	…	1745 1822	…	1845	…	1938 1957	…	2055 2118 2149												
Stevenage d.	…	1818s	…	1822s 1902s	…	…	…	2018s 2035s	…	2135s 2159s 2235s												
London Kings Cross a.	1746	1843	…	1851 1928	…	1946	…	2044 2102	…	2200 2224 2301												

Block 2 — ⑦ (Sundays)

				L			E		M	X	L			C	M	
Aberdeen 600 d.	…	…	…	…	…	…	…	…	…	…	…	…	…	…	…	…
Glasgow Central d.	…	…	…	…	…	…	…	…	…	…	…	…	…	…	…	…
Edinburgh a.	…	…	…	…	…	…	…	…	…	…	…	…	…	…	…	…
Edinburgh d.	…	…	…	…	…	…	…	0900	…	…	1000	…	1035	…	1100	
Berwick-upon-Tweed d.	…	…	…	…	…	…	…	…	…	…	1040	…	1115	…		
Newcastle d.	0730	…	0830	0910 0930	…	1005	…	1050	1117	1153	…	1228	…	1250		
Durham d.	0742	…	0842	0925	…	1018	…	1104	1132	…	1242	…	1303			
Darlington d.	0800	…	0900	0944 0956	…	1036	…	1106 1122	1151	1221	…	1300	…	1312 1321		
Middlesbrough d.	…	…	…	…	…	1037n	…	…	…	…	…	…	1244n			
Northallerton d.	…	…	…	0957 1009	…	…	1119	…	1204	…	…	…	1325			
Thirsk d.	…	…	…	1006	…	…	1127	…	1213	…	…	…	1333			
York 551 d.	0839	…	0939	1037 1043	…	1115	…	1207 1201	1240	1252	…	1331	…	1407 1352		
Leeds 551 d.	…	0840	…	1104	…	1040	…	1234	…	1307	…	1245	…	1434		
Wakefield Westgate d.	…	0852	…	…	…	1053	…	…	…	1301						
Doncaster d.	0908	0915	1008	1110 1117 1144	…	…	1229	…	1320 1327	…	1400	…	1421			
Retford d.	…	0931	…	…	1132	…	…	…	1343							
Newark Northgate d.	…	0946	…	…	1147	…	…	1328	1358							
Grantham 585 d.	…	0959	…	…	1200	…	…	1359	1411							
Peterborough 585 d.	1028	1045	1128	1228 1246	…	…	1344	…	1435 1457	…	1516					
Stevenage d.	1112s	1131s	1212s	1313s 1332s	…	…	1431s	…	1517s 1543s	…	1602s					
London Kings Cross a.	1157	1212	1257	1357 1412	…	…	1511	…	1602 1623	…	1642					

Block 3 — ⑦ (Sundays)

Q	L		R				D		M		L	N			H	X	M	
Aberdeen 600 d.	…	…	…	…	0935	…	…	…	…	…	…	…	…	…	…	1135	…
Glasgow Central d.	…	…	…	1025	…	…	…	…	…	…	…	1225	…	…	…	…	…
Edinburgh a.	…	…	1156	…	1218	…	…	…	…	…	1356	…	…	1418				
Edinburgh d.	…	…	1145 1200	…	1230	…	1235 1300	…	…	1330	1400	…	…	1430				
Berwick-upon-Tweed d.	…	…	1225 1243	…	…	…	1325 1339	…	…	…	1439	…	…	…				
Newcastle d.	1307	1330	1339 1357	…	1424	…	1438 1453	…	1502 1520	…	1553	…	…	1620				
Durham d.	1322	…	1353	…	…	…	1452 1506	…	1517	…	1606							
Darlington d.	1341	1356	1411 1425	…	1452	…	1510 1524	…	1536 1547	…	1624	…	…	1647				
Middlesbrough d.	…	…	…	…	…	1503	…	…	…	…	…	1603						
Northallerton d.	…	1354	1408	…	…	1529	…	1549	…	…	…	1629						
Thirsk d.	…	1403	…	…	…	1538	…	1558	…	…	…	1638						
York 551 d.	1418	1440f	1432 1447 1456	…	1523	…	1541 1555	1606	1640 1618	…	1655	…	1707 1718					
Leeds 551 d.	…	1507	…	1500	…	1540	…	1633	1707	…	1640	…	1734	…	1730			
Wakefield Westgate d.	…	…	…	1513	…	1553	…	…	…	…	1653	…	…	1743				
Doncaster d.	1449	…	1500 1519 1524	1531 1551	…	1610 1615 1624	…	…	1647	…	1710 1724 1730	…	1747 1800					
Retford d.	…	…	…	1546	…	…	…	…	…	…	1744							
Newark Northgate d.	…	…	…	1601	1636	…	…	…	1735	1759	…	1828						
Grantham 585 d.	…	…	…	1613	1649	…	…	…	1748	1811	…	1843						
Peterborough 585 d.	…	1555	…	1619 1640 1646 1715	…	1721	…	…	1814 1820 1838	…	1844 1855							
Stevenage d.	…	1641s	…	1705s	…	1807s	…	…	1906s	…	1939s							
London Kings Cross a.	…	1711	…	1735 1751 1758 1827	…	1837	…	1848	1926 1936 1949	…	1955 2011							

Block 4 — ⑦ (Sundays)

	E			L		M	J		L			M	G	M	
Aberdeen 600 d.	…	…	…	…	1335	…	…	…	…	…	…	…	…	…	…
Glasgow Central d.	…	…	…	…	1425	…	…	…	1650	…	1850	…	1950		
Edinburgh a.	…	…	…	…	1556	1618	…	…	1756	…	1956	…	2056		
Edinburgh d.	1500	…	…	…	1600	1630	1700	…	1800	…	2000	…	2100		
Berwick-upon-Tweed d.	1539	…	…	…	1639	…	1739	…	1839	…	2045	…	2145		
Newcastle d.	1653	1700	1710	…	1713	1738	1809	…	1833 1917	…	1938	…	2144	2245	
Durham d.	…	1712	1722	…	1730	1751	…	…	1846 1932	…	1952	…	2157		
Darlington d.	1720	1730	1740	…	1749	1809	…	…	1904 1951	…	2010	…	2215		
Middlesbrough d.	…	…	…	…	…	1758	…	…	…	2005	…	2208			
Northallerton d.	…	…	…	1802	1821 1826	…	…	2004	2023 2031	…	2228 2234				
Thirsk d.	…	…	…	1811	1835	…	…	2013	2040	…	2258 2243				
York 551 d.	1751	1801	1811	1838	1845 1907v 1904 1918 1935	…	2037	2047 2107 2120	…	2307					
Leeds 551 d.	…	…	…	1830	1905	1934	…	2104	2134	…	2334				
Wakefield Westgate d.	…	…	…	1843	…	…	…	…	…	…					
Doncaster d.	1820	1830	1840	1902	1913	1932 1943 2004	…	2116	2152						
Retford d.	…	…	…	1918	…	…	…	2131							
Newark Northgate d.	…	…	…	1933	1957	…	…	2146							
Grantham 585 d.	…	1913	…	…	2009	…	…	2158							
Peterborough 585 d.	1915	1940	2008	…	2014	2036	2059	…	2225						
Stevenage d.	2001s	2026s	2054s	…	2100s	2122s	2145s	…	2311s						
London Kings Cross a.	2031	2056	2124	…	2131	2152	2215	…	2341						

B – 🚊 and ♍ Newcastle - Bristol.
C – 🚊 and ♍ Edinburgh - Penzance.
D – 🚊 and ♍ Edinburgh - Oxford.
E – 🚊 and ♍ Newcastle - Plymouth.
G – 🚊 and ♍ York - Derby.
H – 🚊 and ♍ Hull (depart 1638) - London.

J – 🚊 and ♍ York - Bristol.
L – 🚊 and ♍ Newcastle - Liverpool.
M – 🚊 and ♍ Middlesbrough - Manchester Airport ✈.
N – 🚊 and ♍ Inverness (depart 0940) - London.
Q – 🚊 and ♍ York - Poole.
R – 🚊 and ♍ Edinburgh - Bristol.

X – 🚊 Lincoln - Grantham.
Z – Also stops at Huntingdon, depart 2203.
f – Arrive 1424.
n – Via Darlington.
s – Stops to set down only.
v – Arrive 1856.

Table 571 LONDON - PETERBOROUGH stopping trains

1, 2 class

km		Ⓐ	Ⓐ	Ⓐ	Ⓐ	Ⓐ	Ⓐ	Ⓐ	Ⓐ	Ⓐ		Ⓐ	Ⓐ	Ⓐ	Ⓐ	Ⓐ	Ⓐ	Ⓐ	Ⓐ	Ⓐ	Ⓐ	Ⓐ	Ⓐ
0	**London Kings Cross** d.	Ⓐ	0038	0138	0548	0638	0712	0738	0822	0838	and at the	1522	1538	1622	1640	1650	1710	1720	1740	1750	1819	1820	1837
44	Stevenage d.		0114	0214	0628	0714	0737	0814	0848	0914	same mins	1548	1614	1648	|	1718	|	1748	|	1814	|	1847	|
95	Huntingdon d.		0152	0252	0706	0751	0814	0851	0925	0951	past each	1625	1651	1726	1730	1755	1758	1826	1830	1851	1910	1926	1929
123	**Peterborough** a.		0227	0327	0721	0811	0832	0913	...	1006	hour until	...	1711	1753	...	1817	...	1850	...	1908	...	1948	...

	Ⓐ	Ⓐ	Ⓐ	Ⓐ	Ⓐ	Ⓐ	Ⓐ	Ⓐ		⑥	⑥	⑥	⑥	⑥	⑥	⑥		⑥	⑥		⑥	⑥
London Kings Cross d.	1850	1910	1922	2005	2023	2123	2223	2323	⑥	0038	0138	0548	0638	0712	0738	0822	and at the	1322	1338	then at the	1922	1938
Stevenage d.	1914	|	1948	2030	2046	2146	2246	2346		0114	0214	0628	0714	0737	0814	0848	same mins	1348	1414	same mins	1948	2014
Huntingdon d.	1951	1959	2025	2107	2124	2224	2324	0025		0152	0252	0705	0751	0814	0851	0925	past each	1430	1451	past each	2030	2051
Peterborough a.	2008	...	...	2125	2139	2239	2343	0044		0227	0327	0720	0806	0832	0906	...	hour until	...	1511	hour until	...	2111

	⑥	⑥	⑥	⑥	⑥	⑥	⑥			⑦		⑦	⑦		⑦	⑦	⑦	⑦	⑦	⑦	⑦	⑦	⑦	
London Kings Cross d.	2022	2038	2122	2138	2222	2238	2338	...	⑦	0038	...	0710	0823	and	1523	1623	1722	1822	1922	2022	2122	2230	2330	...
Stevenage d.	2048	2114	2148	2214	2248	2314	0017	...		0117	...	0738	0902	hourly	1602	1702	1746	1846	1946	2046	2146	2305	0005	...
Huntingdon d.	2125	2151	2225	2251	2325	2351	0102	...		0202	...	0823	0942	until	1642	1739	1823	1923	2023	2123	2223	2342	0042	...
Peterborough a.	2146	2211	2246	2311	2346	0014	...	...		...	...	...	1007		1706	1805	1845	1945	2045	2145	2245	0007	0107	...

		Ⓐ	Ⓐ	Ⓐ	Ⓐ	Ⓐ	Ⓐ	Ⓐ	Ⓐ	Ⓐ	Ⓐ	Ⓐ	Ⓐ	Ⓐ	Ⓐ	Ⓐ	Ⓐ		Ⓐ	Ⓐ	Ⓐ	Ⓐ	Ⓐ
Peterborough d.	Ⓐ	0415	0510	0557	...	0645	...	0707	...	0732	...	0748	...	0817	0839	0921	...	and at the	1621	...	1716	...	1814
Huntingdon d.		0430	0525	0612	0651	0700	0711	0722	0731	0747	0752	0803	0821	0832	0902	0936	1002	same mins	1636	1702	1736	1757	1836
Stevenage d.		0512	0607	0649	|	0737	|	0759	|	0826	|	0842	|	0911	0939	1013	1039	past each	1713	1739	1813	1834	1913
London Kings Cross a.		0549	0634	0716	0740	0807	0801	0830	0825	0857	0843	0909	0913	0938	1005	1052	1106	hour until	1752	1806	1852	1902	1952

	Ⓐ	Ⓐ	Ⓐ	Ⓐ	Ⓐ		⑥	⑥	⑥	⑥	⑥	⑥	⑥	⑥	⑥	⑥	⑥	⑥	⑥	⑥	⑥	⑥	⑥	⑥
Peterborough d.	1847	1921	2021	2121	2221	⑥	0415	0510	0547	0621	...	0721	...	0816	...	0921	...	1021	...	1121	...	1216	...	1321
Huntingdon d.	1902	1936	2036	2136	2236		0437	0525	0602	0636	0702	0736	0802	0836	0902	0936	1002	1036	1102	1136	1202	1236	1302	1336
Stevenage d.	1939	2013	2113	2213	2313		0512	0607	0639	0713	0739	0813	0839	0913	0943	1013	1043	1113	1139	1213	1243	1313	1343	1413
London Kings Cross a.	2006	2052	2152	2256	2356		0549	0637	0706	0752	0806	0852	0906	0952	1021	1052	1121	1152	1206	1252	1321	1352	1421	1452

	⑥	⑥		⑥	⑥	⑥	⑥		⑦	⑦	⑦	⑦	⑦		⑦	⑦	⑦	⑦	⑦	⑦	⑦	⑦	
Peterborough d.	...	1416	and at the	2016	...	2121	2221	⑦	*0455b*	*0555b*	*0655b*	*0755b*	0924	and	1524	1624	1724	1824	1924	2024	2124	2232	...
Huntingdon d.	1357	1431	same mins	2030	2057	2136	2236		0538	0638	0738	0838	0938	hourly	1538	1638	1738	1838	1938	2038	2138	2246	...
Stevenage d.	1439	1513	past each	2113	2139	2218	2318		0621	0721	0821	0921	1021	until	1621	1716	1816	1916	2016	2116	2216	2324	...
London Kings Cross a.	1506	1552	hour until	2152	2206	2301	0001		0706	0806	0906	1006	1106		1706	1750	1850	1950	2050	2150	2258	0004	...

b – By 🚌.

Table 573 CLEETHORPES - NEWARK and MANCHESTER

2 class only

km		⑥	Ⓐ	⑥	Ⓐ	⚒	⚒ 🍷	⚒	⑥ 🍷	Ⓐ 🍷	⚒	⚒ 🍷	⚒ 🍷	⚒	⚒ 🍷	⑦ 🍷	⑦	⚒ 🍷		⑥	Ⓐ	⚒ 🍷	⑦ 🍷	⑦	⚒
0	**Cleethorpes** d.	0520	0526	0531	0547	0557	0712	0719	0820	0826	0913	0926	1026	...	1126	1135	...	1226	...	...	...	1326	1339	...	...
5	Grimsby Town d.	0527	0533	0538	0554	0604	0719	0726	0827	0833	0920	0933	1033	1122	1133	1142	...	1233	...	1303	1304	1333	1346	...	1428
	Market Rasen d.	|	|	0614	0630	|	|	0800	|	|	0954	|	|	1155	|	|	...	|	...	1336	1347	|	|	...	1503
	Lincoln Central d.	|	|	0635	0652	|	|	0821	|	|	1018	|	|	1216	|	|	1305	|	...	1357	1409	|	|	1510	1524
	Newark Northgate a.	|	|	0702	0711	|	|	0847	|	|	1041	|	|	1239	|	|	1327	|	...	1424	1431	|	|	1532	1547
46	Scunthorpe d.	0600	0606	...	...	0637	0752	...	0900	0906	...	1006	1106	...	1206	1215	...	1306	...	...	...	1406	1419	...	...
83	**Doncaster** a.	0639	0645	...	...	0714	0823	...	0932	0940	...	1040	1140	...	1240	1300	...	1342	...	...	...	1439	1505	...	...
83	**Doncaster** d.	0648	0648	...	...	0716	0828	...	0932	0942	...	1042	1142	...	1242	1306	...	1342	...	...	...	1440	1509	...	...
114	**Sheffield** a.	0730	0730	...	...	0757	0852	...	1000	1007	...	1107	1208	...	1307	1350	...	1408	...	...	...	1506	1547	...	...
114	**Sheffield 585** d.		...	...	...	0803	0909	...	1009	1009	...	1109	1209	...	1309	...	...	1409	...	...	...	1509	1552	...	...
125	Stockport **585** d.		...	...	...	0852	0952	...	1052	1052	...	1152	1252	...	1352	...	...	1452	...	...	...	1552	1639	...	...
183	**Manchester Piccadilly 585** a.		...	...	...	0906	1006	...	1106	1106	...	1206	1306	...	1406	...	...	1506	...	...	...	1606	1650	...	...

	⚒ 🍷	⑦ 🍷	⚒ 🍷	⑥	⑦	⑦ 🍷	⚒ 🍷	Ⓐ		⑦ R🍷	⚒ 🍷	⑦	⑦ 🍷	Ⓐ	⑥ R	Ⓐ R🍷	⑥	⑦ R🍷	⚒ 🍷	⚒	⑦ 🍷	Ⓐ R🍷	⑥ 🍷	⑦ 🍷	Ⓐ
Cleethorpes d.	1426	1439	1526	...	...	1608	1607	1615	...	1710	1714	...	1756	...	1815	1815	...	1910	1915	...	1957	2015	2015	2050	2115
Grimsby Town d.	1433	1446	1533	1603	...	1615	1614	1623	...	1717	1721	...	1803	1807	1822	1822	1828	1917	1922	1936	2004	2022	2022	2057	2122
Market Rasen d.	|	|	|	1636	...	|	|	1656	...	|	|	...	|	1841	|	|	1901	|	|	2009	|	|	|	|	2155
Lincoln Central d.	|	|	|	1657	1700	|	|	1717	...	|	|	1805	|	1900	|	|	1921	|	|	2032	|	|	|	|	2216
Newark Northgate a.	|	|	|	1727	1722	|	|	1747	...	|	|	1827	|	...	|	|	...	|	|	2103	|	|	|	|	...
Scunthorpe d.	1506	1519	1606	...	...	1648	1652	...	...	1750	1754	...	1836	...	1855	1855	...	1950	1955	...	2037	2055	2055	2136	...
Doncaster a.	1537	1608	1638	...	...	1719	1725	...	...	1822	1825	...	1917	...	1925	1926	...	2021	2034	...	2108	2127	2127	2206	...
Doncaster d.	1541	1612	1640	...	...	1720	1726	...	...	1824	1825	...	1920	...	1926	1932	...	2022	2036	...	2109	2128	2128	...	...
Sheffield a.	1607	1644	1706	...	...	1748	1804	...	...	1851	1903	...	2000	...	2003	2007	...	2049	2118	...	2141	2206	2207	...	...
Sheffield 585 d.	1609	1657	1709	...	...	1751	1809	...	...	1854	1906	...	...	...	2009	2009	...	2052	...	...	...	2209	...	...	...
Stockport **585** d.	1652	1739	1752	...	...	1837	1856	...	...	1938	1952	...	...	...	2052	2052	...	2134	...	...	...	2252	...	...	...
Manchester Piccadilly 585 a.	1706	1752	1806	...	...	1849	1908	...	...	1949	2006	...	...	...	2106	2106	...	2147	...	...	...	2306	...	...	...

km		⚒ 🍷	⚒	Ⓐ R🍷	⑥ R🍷	Ⓐ	Ⓐ 🍷	⑥ 🍷	⑥	⚒ 🍷	⚒	⚒ 🍷	⚒ 🍷	⚒	⑦ 🍷	⚒ 🍷	⑦ 🍷	⚒ 🍷	⑦	⚒	⑦	⚒ 🍷	⑦ R🍷	⚒ 🍷	⑦
	Manchester Piccadilly 585 d.	...	...	0716	0716	...	0816	0816	...	0916	...	1016	1116	...	...	1216	...	1316	...	...	...	1416	1508	1516	...
	Stockport **585** d.	...	...	0726	0726	...	0826	0826	...	0926	...	1026	1126	...	...	1226	...	1326	...	...	...	1426	1518	1526	...
	Sheffield 585 a.	...	...	0807	0807	...	0907	0907	...	1008	...	1107	1208	...	...	1307	...	1408	...	...	...	1507	1559	1608	...
	Sheffield d.	0636	...	0810	0810	...	0910	0910	...	1010	...	1110	1210	...	1214	1310	1403	1410	...	...	...	1510	1603	1610	...
	Doncaster a.	0715	...	0838	0846	...	0937	0946	...	1038	...	1135	1238	...	1254	1339	1428	1436	...	...	...	1538	1628	1639	...
	Doncaster d.	0722	...	0841	0848	...	0941	0948	...	1041	...	1136	1241	...	1257	1341	1430	1442	...	...	1540	1541	1630	1641	...
	Scunthorpe d.	0749	...	0907	0914	...	1007	1014	...	1107	...	1207	1307	...	1325	1407	1456	1508	...	...	1606	1607	1656	1707	...
0	**Newark Northgate** d.	|	...	|	|	0854	|	|	0940	|	1045	|	|	1245	|	|	|	|	1433	1436	|	|	|	|	1623
25	**Lincoln Central** d.	|	0752	|	|	0920	|	|	1006	|	1111	|	|	1312	|	|	|	|	1458	1502	|	|	|	|	1648
49	Market Rasen d.	|	0808	|	|	0937	|	|	1023	|	1128	|	|	1328	|	|	|	|	...	1518	|	|	|	|	...
93	Grimsby Town d.	0833	0848	0945	0950	1021	1047	1052	1105	1145	1209	1247	1345	1409	1418	1447	1541	1546	...	1557	1651	1647	1734	1744	...
102	**Cleethorpes** a.	0842	0859	0954	1000	...	1057	1058	...	1154	...	1257	1354	...	1427	1457	1558	1555	...	1606h	1709	1657	1743	1755	...

	Ⓐ	⑥	⑦ 🍷	⑥	Ⓐ 🍷	⑦	⚒	⑦	⑥ 🍷	T 🍷	⑦ 🍷	⚒	⚒ 🍷	Ⓐ	⑥	⑦	Ⓐ	⑦ J🍷	⑦ M🍷	⚒ 🍷	Ⓐ	⚒	⑦	Ⓐ	⑥
Manchester Piccadilly 585 d.	...	...	1608	1616	1616	...	...	1708	1716	1716	1808	...	1816	...	...	...	...	1908	1908	1916	...	...	...	...	...
Stockport **585** d.	...	...	1618	1626	1626	...	...	1718	1725	1725	1818	...	1826	...	...	...	...	1918	1918	1926	...	...	...	...	...
Sheffield 585 a.	...	...	1659	1707	1707	...	...	1800	1812	1812	1859	...	1907	...	...	...	...	1951	1951	2010	...	...	...	...	...
Sheffield d.	...	...	1703	1710	1710	...	...	1803	1814	1814	1903	...	1910	...	...	...	...	2003	2003	2013	2043	...	...	2150	2151
Doncaster a.	...	...	1728	1735	1736	...	...	1831	1840	1849	1928	...	1956	...	...	...	...	2029	2029	2052	2120	...	...	2227	2228
Doncaster d.	...	...	1730	1737	1745	...	...	1833	1845	1851	1938c	...	1958	...	...	...	...	2030	2041	2054	2129	...	2215	2228	2236
Scunthorpe d.	...	...	1756	1808	1812	...	...	1901	1911	1917	2004c	...	2024	...	...	...	...	2056	2107	2122	2206	...	2241	2300	2308
Newark Northgate d.	1635	1652	|	|	|	1728	1754	|	|	|	|	1912	|	1950	1957	2010	2056	|	|	|	...	2206	|	|	|
Lincoln Central d.	1704	1714	|	|	|	1753	1824	|	|	|	|	1945	|	2023	2024	2036	2128	|	|	|	...	2234	|	|	|
Market Rasen d.	1720	1735	|	|	|	...	1840	|	|	|	|	2001h	|	2043	2043	...	...	|	|	|	...	...	|	|	|
Grimsby Town d.	1800	1816	1834	1847	1850	...	1925	1939	1949	1955	2042c	2053h	2108	...	...	...	...	2134	2145	2200	...	...	2319	2337	2344
Cleethorpes a.	...	...	1843	1855	1900	...	...	1948	1956	2004	2051c	2100h	2114	...	...	...	...	2144	2154	2209	...	...	2328	2347	2352

J – Until Jan. 8. M – From Jan. 15. R – To or from Manchester Airport ✈. T – Ⓐ, also ⑥ from Jan. 14. c – 6 minutes later from Jan. 15. h – Not ⑥.

Table 574 LINCOLN - NOTTINGHAM - COVENTRY

km			⚒	⚒	Ⓐ	⑥	N⑥	NⒶ	⚒	⚒	⚒	⑥	Ⓐ	⑦	Ⓐ	⑥	Ⓐ	⑥	⑦	⚒	⑦	⚒	⚒	⑦	⚒
0	**Lincoln Central**	d.	...	...	0555	0607	0635	0652	...	0731	0841	0952	0952	...	1051	1051	1150	1155	...	1243	...	1352	1441	...	1557
26	Newark Castle	d.	...	...	0639	0639	0733	0733	...	0801	0906	1017	1017	...	1116	1116	1228	1228	...	1306	...	1423	1506	...	1616
49	**Nottingham 560**	d.	0601	0617	0726	0726	0806	0806	...	0849	0949	1043	1043	1150	1154	1153	1251	1257	1307	1345	1444	1453	1603	1650	1643
75	Loughborough **560**	d.	0622	0639	...	...	...	...	0735	0907	1008	1101	1101	1206	|	|	1309	1315	1339	|	1501	1510	1622	1708	1704
95	**Leicester 560**	d.	0637	0702	...	...	...	...	0749	0922	1022	1116	1116	1225	1224	1224	1325	1330	1356	1416	1520	1525	1640	1724	1718
118	Hinckley	d.	0657	0723	...	...	...	...	0807	0941	1044	1136	1136	|	1245	1245	1344	1349	1415	1434	1539	1547	1700	1743	1739
125	Nuneaton	d.	0707	0740	...	...	...	...	0820	0952	1054	1151	1151	1247	1255	1255	1357	1401	1428	1444	1552	1559	1710	1756	1749
141	**Coventry**	a.	0729	0758	...	...	...	...	...	1011	1112	1209	1209	...	1313	1313	1415	1419	1448	1502	1614	1617	...	1813	1808

		⑥	Ⓐ	⑦	⚒	⚒	⑦	⚒	C⚒	⑦	Ⓐ
Lincoln Central	d.	1636	1644	...	1810	1912	...	1952	2032	...	2216
Newark Castle	d.	1708	1717	...	1841	1940	...	2019	2123	...	2244
Nottingham 560	d.	1751	1751	1832	1911	2007	2040	2052	2152	2225	2317
Loughborough **560**	d.	1814	1814	1853	1934	2038	2057	...	2210	2242	...
Leicester 560	d.	1836	1836	1915	1955	2059	2113	...	2227	2259	...
Hinckley	d.	1856	1856	1934	2016	2119	2132	...	2248	2318	...
Nuneaton	d.	1906	1906	1946	2026	2129	2144	...	2258	2327	...
Coventry	a.	1924	1924	2003	2044	2147	2201	...	2319	...	...

		⚒	⚒	⚒	⚒	⑥	Ⓐ	Ⓐ	⑥	⚒
Coventry	d.	...	...	0615	0715	0734	0734	0807	0807	...
Nuneaton	d.	...	...	0636	0738	0800	0800	0830	0830	0936
Hinckley	d.	...	...	0643	0745	0808	0808	0836	0836	0943
Leicester 560	d.	...	...	0704	0805	0830	0830	0856	0905	1007
Loughborough **560**	d.	...	...	0725	0818	0850	0850	0909	0918	1020
Nottingham 560	d.	0603	0655	0752	0841	0915	0915	0938	0941	1042
Newark Castle	d.	0637	0726	0830	0903	...	...	1003	1015	1112
Lincoln Central	a.	0709	0758	0856	0936	...	...	1034	1042	1144

		⚒	⑥	Ⓐ	⑦	⚒	⚒	⑦	Ⓐ	⑥	⚒	⑦	⚒	KⒶ	⑦	⑥	Ⓐ	⑥	Ⓐ	⑦	⚒	⑦	Ⓐ	⑦	⚒
Coventry	d.	1021	1116	1116	1145	1216	1325	1358	1420	1420	1512	1515	1619	...	1715	...	...	1820	1820	1845	1941	2012	...	2115	2115
Nuneaton	d.	1042	1136	1136	1210	1239	1347	1421	1439	1439	1533	1537	1640	...	1736	...	1836	1849	1849	1907	2002	2034	...	2136	2136
Hinckley	d.	1049	1143	1143	1216	1246	1353	1427	|	|	|	1543	1650	...	1742	...	1843	1856	1856	1913	2008	2040	...	2142	2142
Leicester 560	d.	1109	1204	1204	1239	1309	1412	1448	1503	1516	1607	1609	1709	...	1807	...	1906	1919	1919	1936	2031	2102	...	2204	2203
Loughborough **560**	d.	1123	1222	1217	1252	1322	1425	1501	1516	1529	1626	1622	1722	...	1820	...	|	1932	1932	1949	2051	2115	...	2217	2223
Nottingham 560	d.	1144	1245	1240	1325	1344	1444	1521	1544	1551	1646	1644	1744	1829	1839	1831	1937	1956	1956	2008	2122	2135	2210	2236	2250
Newark Castle	d.	1208	1315	1316	...	1411	1516	...	1613	1620	1715	...	1818	1858	...	1858	...	2030	2030	...	2154	...	2240	...	...
Lincoln Central	a.	1240	1341	1342	...	1439	1544	...	...	...	1801	...	1850	1943	...	1943	...	2102	2128	...	2234	...	2305	...	...

C – 2 Grimsby - Coventry.
K – 2 Nottingham - Cleethorpes Ⓐ, Lincoln ⑥.
N – 2 Cleethorpes - Nottingham.

Table 575 NEWCASTLE - HEXHAM - CARLISLE

2 class only

km			⚒	⚒	⚒	⚒	⑦	⚒	⚒	⑦	⚒	⚒	⑦	⚒	⑦	⚒	⑦	⚒	⑦	⚒	⚒	⑦	⚒	⑦	⚒
0	**Newcastle ▲**	d.	0635	0825	0910	1025	1055	1125	1237	1255	1325	1425	1430	1518	1530	1625	1630	1710	1730	1748	1825	1840	1915	2042	2110
34	Hexham ▲	d.	0711	0905	0948	1054	1132	1154	1306	1333	1354	1457	1508	1548	1608	1703	1708	1742	1808	1826	1903	1918	1953	2120	2148
60	Haltwhistle	d.	0734	0927	1006	1112	1155	1216	1324	1352	1412	1515	1527	1611	1631	1722	1727	1804	1827	1848	1921	1941	2011	2139	2210
96	**Carlisle**	a.	0807	1002	1037	1148	1300	1253	1401	1438	1443	1546	1613	1645	1721	1753	1813	1840	1858	1919	1955	2018	2043	2210	2244

		⚒	⚒	⚒	⚒	⚒	⚒	⑦	⚒	⚒	⑦	⚒	⑦	⚒	⚒	⑦	⚒	⑦	⚒	⑦	⚒	⑦	⚒	⑦	⚒
Carlisle	d.	0640	0707	0747	0848	0935	1030	1030	1137	1237	1300	1330	1425	1443	1517	1522	1610	1625	1722	1728	1818	1850	1932	2026	2115
Haltwhistle	d.	0708	0738	0820	0919	1003	1058	1102	1205	1305	1329	1401	1454	1512	1545	1554	1641	1654	1753	1757	1846	1922	2000	2055	2146
Hexham ▲	d.	0732	0802	0842	0941	1022	1117	1125	1224	1324	1347	1423	1512	1531	1604	1617	1703	1712	1812	1815	1905	1945	2019	2113	2208
Newcastle ▲	a.	0812	0844	0919	1022	1053	1152	1234	1259	1355	1443	1455	1608	1603	1635	1713	1738	1809	1847	1858	1946	2026	2059	2157	2255

▲ – Additional trains run between Newcastle - Hexham and v.v.

Table 576 MIDDLESBROUGH - SUNDERLAND - NEWCASTLE

2 class only

km			⚒	Ⓐ	⚒	⚒	⚒	⚒	⚒	⚒	⚒	⑦	⚒	⚒	⚒	⑦	⚒	⚒	⑦	⚒	⑦	⚒	⚒	⑦	⚒
0	**Middlesbrough**	d.	...	...	0705	0739	...	0902	1000	1032	1134	1230	1233	...	1334	1418	1434	1534	1538	1703	1733	1803	1903	1933	2027
9	Stockton	d.	...	...	0715	0749	...	0912	1010	1042	1144	1240	1243	...	1344	1428	1444	1544	1548	1713	1743	1813	1913	1943	2037
28	Hartlepool	d.	...	...	0735	0809	...	0932	1028	1100	1202	1259	1302	...	1402	1447	1502	1602	1607	1732	1802	1831	1932	2002	2057
58	Sunderland ▲	d.	0700	0735	0805	0840	0930	1000	1100	1130	1230	1345	1330	1400	1430	1515	1530	1630	1635	1800	1830	1900	2000	2030	2125
79	**Newcastle ▲**	a.	0727	0803	0827	0908	0951	1020	1120	1150	1251	1427	1352	1420	1450	1556	1551	1656	1702	1820	1857	1921	2021	2057	2151

		⑥	Ⓐ	⚒	⚒	⚒	⚒	⑦	⚒	⑦	⚒	⚒	⑦	⚒	⚒	⑦	⚒	⚒	⚒	⑦	⚒	⚒	⚒	⑦	⚒
Newcastle ▲	d.	0645	0653	0815	0900	1000	1100	1045	1200	1300	1300	1400	1430	1500	1600	1630	1710	1745	1820	1830	1920	2000	2100	2100	2220
Sunderland ▲	d.	0707	0715	0840	0920	1021	1121	1126	1220	1341	1321	1420	1511	1520	1622	1656	1733	1811	1841	1856	1946	2026	2126	2126	2247
Hartlepool	d.	0731	0739	0905	0945	1045	1145	1150	1245	1405	1345	1445	1535	1545	1646	1720	1757	1836	1905	1920	...	2050	...	...	...
Stockton	d.	0750	0758	0924	1002	1103	1203	1210	1304	1425	1403	1502	1555	1602	1706	1740	1817	1853	1925	1940	...	2110	...	...	...
Middlesbrough	a.	0804	0812	0938	1016	1125	1218	1240	1318	1455	1418	1522	1610	1616	1720	1758	1836	1907	1939	1955	...	2124	...	...	...

▲ – A frequent local service operates between Newcastle and Sunderland and v.v.

Table 577 MIDDLESBROUGH - DARLINGTON - NEWCASTLE

1, 2 class

km			⚒	⚒	⑦	⑥	Ⓐ	⑦	Ⓐ	⑥	⑦	⑥	Ⓐ	⑦	⑦	⚒	⑦	⚒	⑦	Ⓑ	⑥	⑦	⚒	⑦	⚒
0	**Middlesbrough**	d.	0652	0848	0907	0956	0956	1024	1124	1130	1136	1154	1200	1223	1234	1254	1319	1354	1409	1526	1537	1609	1618	1642	1652
24	**Darlington 570**	d.	0723	0918	0936	1021	1026	1048	1154	1203	1204	1219	1228	1253	1258	1320	1347	1426h	1440	1555	1607	1639	1647	1710	1722
60	Durham **570**	d.	0745	0939	...	1042	1048	...	...	...	...	1247	1250	...	...	...	...	1448	...	...	...	...	1708	...	...
84	**Newcastle 570**	a.	0806	1000	...	1104	1110	...	...	...	...	1311	1310	...	...	...	...	1509	...	...	...	...	1730	...	...

		⑦	⑦	⑦	⚒	⑦	⚒	⑦	⚒	⑦	⑦
Middlesbrough	d.	1728	1811	1851	1926	1951	1957	2111	2120	2156	2237
Darlington 570	d.	1800	1840	1920	1950	2021	2029	2139	2150	2226	2301
Durham **570**	d.	1821	...	...	...	...	...	...	...	...	...
Newcastle 570	a.	1839	...	...	...	...	...	...	...	...	...

		⚒	⑦	⚒	⑦	⑥	Ⓐ	⑦	⑦	⑦
Newcastle 570	d.	0811	...	0842	...	1004	1010	1000	...	...
Durham **570**	d.	0829	...	0900	...	1022	1028	1015	...	...
Darlington 570	d.	0854	0920	0925	0950	1047	1053	1055	1117	1145
Middlesbrough	a.	0919	0946	0951	1016	1109	1116	1119	1143	1211

		⚒	⑦	⚒	⑦	⑦	Ⓐ	⑥	⑦	⚒	⑦	⑦	⑦	⚒	⑦	⑦	⚒	⑦	⑦	⑦	⑥	Ⓐ	⑦	⑥	Ⓐ
Newcastle 570	d.	...	...	1206	...	...	...	...	...	1410	...	...	...	1605	...	...	1740	...	...	...	...	...	...	...	...
Durham **570**	d.	...	...	1221	...	...	...	...	...	1428	...	...	...	1623	...	...	1758	...	...	...	...	...	...	...	...
Darlington 570	d.	1228	1232	1248	1326	1348	1405	1412	1442	1452	1517	1600	1631	1647	1725	1825	1829n	1945	2022	2110	2137	2143	2231	2235	2246
Middlesbrough	a.	1252	1256	1310	1352	1414	1428	1434	1506	1516	1541	1626	1655	1711	1751	1849	1853	2011	2046	2136	2203	2209	2256	2301	2312

Additional trains **Middlesbrough - Darlington** on ⚒: 0555, 0735, 0817, 0828, 1024, 1054, 1224, 1324, 1424, 1454, 1554, 1721, 1754, 1824, 1854, 2153.
Additional trains **Darlington - Middlesbrough** on ⚒: 0627, 0637, 0714, 0753, 0815, 0954, 1020⑥, 1027Ⓐ, 1125**e**,1156, 1330, 1427, 1556, 1629, 1715, 1800, 1927, 2000, 2030**e**.
e – 5 minutes later on ⑥. h – Arrive 1420. n – Arrive 1820

Table 578 MIDDLESBROUGH - WHITBY

No Sunday Service in Winter. 2 class only

km			⚒		⚒		⚒			⚒
0	**Middlesbrough**	d.	0712	...	1036	...	1425	...	...	1740
71	Grosmont	d.	0820	...	1138	...	1531	...	...	1846
81	**Whitby**	a.	0844	...	1205	...	1554	...	...	1909

			⚒			⚒		⚒			⚒
Whitby	d.	...	0902	...	...	1248	...	1605	...	...	1921
Grosmont	d.	...	0918	...	...	1304	...	1622	...	...	1937
Middlesbrough	a.	...	1026	...	...	1416	...	1736	...	...	2049

11 *For explanation of standard symbols, see page 4* 331

Table 579 NORWICH - CROMER - SHERINGHAM

2 class

km			⚒	⚒	⚒	⚒	⚒	⚒	⑦p	⚒	⑦q	⚒	⑦p	⚒	⑦q	⑦p	⚒	⑦q	⚒	⑦p	⚒	⑦q	⚒	⚒
0	**Norwich**	d.	0520	0552	0716	0845	0947	1042	1045	1143	1145	1243	1305	1353	1405	1505	1540	1601	1642	1745	1747	1805	1853	2050
14	Hoveton and Wroxham ▲	d.	0534	0607	0732	0900	1001	1056	1100	1157	1200	1258	1319	1407	1419	1519	1555	1615	1657	1800	1802	1820	1907	2105
26	North Walsham	d.	0544	0624	0749	0913	1016	1112	1113	1212	1213	1316	1329	1421	1429	1529	1611	1625	1715	1813	1819	1833	1925	2121
43	**Cromer**	d.	0610v	0646	0809	0934	1033	1130	1134	1230	1234	1337	1347	1439	1447	1547	1632	1643	1736	1834	1840	1854	1943	2142
49	**Sheringham** △	a.	0616	0654	0817	0942	1040	1137	1143	1238	1243	1346	1355	1447	1455	1555	1641	1651	1745	1843	1849	1903	1950	2151

		⚒	⚒	⚒	⚒	⚒	⚒	⚒	⑦p	⚒	⑦q	⚒	p⑦	⚒	⑦q	⑦p	⚒	⑦q	⚒	⑦p	⚒	⑦q	⚒	⚒
Sheringham △	d.	...	0630	0718	0821	0945	1044	1144	1154	1245	1254	1354	1401	1454	1501	1601	1647	1701	1749	1854	1854	1910	1955	2158
Cromer	d.	0605	0643	0729	0832	0956	1054	1154	1205	1256	1305	1404	1411	1505	1511	1611	1657	1711	1800	1905	1905	1921	2005	2209
North Walsham	d.	0621	0700	0746	0849	1013	1109	1209	1222	1313	1322	1419	1426	1522	1526	1626	1712	1726	1817	1922	1922	1938	2020	2226
Hoveton and Wroxham ▲	d.	0633	0712	0758	0901	1023	1119	1219	1234	1325	1334	1429	1436	1534	1536	1636	1722	1736	1829	1934	1934	1940	2030	2238
Norwich	a.	0649	0728	0814	0917	1037	1133	1236	1250	1345	1350	1446	1450	1550	1550	1650	1736	1750	1845	1950	1955	2006	2045	2254

p – Dec. 18 - Apr. 9.
q – Apr. 16 - May 27.
v – Arrives 0559.
▲ – Station for Bure Valley Railway ☎ (01263) 733858.
△ – Station for North Norfolk Railway ☎ (01263) 822045.

Table 580 LONDON - IPSWICH - NORWICH

Service on ⑦ valid to Apr. 9 — 1, 2 class

km			⚒	⚒		Ⓐ🍷	⑥🍷	Ⓐ✕	⑥🍷	Ⓐ🍷		⚒R	⚒🍷		⚒🍷	⚒R		Ⓐ🍷	⑥🍷	⚒🍷	Ⓐ🍷	Ⓐ🍷
0	**London Liverpool Street**	d.	0625	0630	...	0725	0730	0800	0800	0804	...	0830	0900	and at	1500	1530	...	1555	1600	1630	1645	1700
84	**Colchester**	d.	0713	0735	...	0812	0817	|	0903e	0908e	...	0917	0958e	the same	1558e	1617	...	1645	1658	1717	1749e	|
97	Manningtree 584	d.	0722	0744	...	0823	0827	|	0912	0917	...	|	1009	minutes	1607	|	...	1656	1707	|	1758	|
111	**Ipswich**	d.	0733	0757	...	0835	0838	0900	0924	0929	...	0935	1023	past	1619	1635	...	1711	1719	1735	1810	1801
130	Stowmarket	d.	0744	...	...	0849	0849	|	...	...	...	0946	...	each	...	1646	...	...	...	1746	...	|
153	Diss	d.	0756	...	...	...	0901	0920	...	...	...	0958	...	hour	...	1658	...	...	...	1758	...	|
185	**Norwich**	a.	0820	...	...	...	0925	0944	...	...	...	1022	...	until	...	1722	...	...	...	1824	...	1836

		⑥🍷	Ⓐ	⑥🍷	Ⓐ🍷	⑥🍷	Ⓐ🍷	⑥🍷	Ⓐ	⑥🍷	Ⓐ✕	⑥🍷	Ⓐ✕	Ⓐ🍷	⑥🍷	P🍷	Ⓐ✕	Q🍷	Ⓐ	P	Ⓐ🍷	P🍷	Q🍷		Ⓐ
London Liverpool Street	d.	1700	1710	1730	1730	1755	1800	1800	1802	1830	1830	1930	1930	1948	2000	2030	2030	2050	2102	2102	2200	2200	2200	...	2330
Colchester	d.	1758e	1810	1817	|	1846	|	1858	1903	1917	|	2017	|	2048e	2058e	2117	2117	2213	2204e	2209e	2247	2256	2317	...	0027s
Manningtree 584	d.	1807	1819	|	1830	|	|	1907	1912	|	1927	|	2027	2057	2107	|	2127	|	2213	2218	2257	2307	2327	...	0037s
Ipswich	d.	1819	1834	1835	1840	1904	1905	1919	1926	1935	1937	2035	2038	2109	2119	2135	2138	2231	2225	2230	2308	2317	2338	...	0048s
Stowmarket	d.	...	...	1846	1851	1915	1916	...	...	1946	1949	2046	2049	...	...	2146	2149	2242	...	...	2319	2328	2348	...	0058s
Diss	d.	...	...	1858	1903	1927	1929	...	...	1958	2002	2058	2102	...	...	2158	2201	2254	...	...	2331	2340	0001	...	0120s
Norwich	a.	...	...	1922	1926	1951	1953	...	...	2022	2026	2122	2126	...	...	2222	2225	2318	...	...	2355	0016	0037	...	0141

		⑦	⑦	⑦		⑦	⑦🍷		⑦	⑦🍷		⑦	⑦🍷		⑦🍷	⑦	⑦🍷	⑦	⑦🍷	⑦	⑦
London Liverpool Street	d.	*0732c*	*0802c*	*0832c*	...	*0932c*	*1002c*	and at	*1332c*	*1402c*	...	1502	1530	and at	1930	2002	2030	2102	2200	2202	2330
Colchester	d.	0902	0923	1002	...	1102	1123	the same	1502	1523	...	1602	1622	the same	2022	2102	2122	2202	2252	2302	0022s
Manningtree 584	d.	0911	|	1011	...	1111	|	minutes	1511	|	...	1611	|	minutes	|	2111	2133	2211	2303	2311	0032s
Ipswich	d.	0923	0940	1023	...	1123	1140	past	1523	1540	...	1623	1640	past	2040	2123	2143	2223	2313	2323	0043s
Stowmarket	d.	...	0951	...	...	...	1151	each	...	1551	...	...	1651	each	2051	...	2154	...	2324	...	0053s
Diss	d.	...	1003	...	...	...	1203	hour	...	1603	...	...	1703	hour	2103	...	2206	...	2336	...	0115s
Norwich	a.	...	1029	...	...	...	1229	until	...	1629	...	...	1727	until	2127	...	2230	...	2359	...	0136

		⚒🍷	Ⓐ🍷	Ⓐ✕	⑥🍷	Ⓐ	⑥🍷	Ⓐ🍷	⑥🍷	Ⓐ✕	⑥🍷	Ⓐ🍷	Ⓐ✕	Ⓐ🍷	Ⓐ🍷	⑥🍷	Ⓐ🍷	⑥🍷	⑥🍷	⚒🍷	⚒🍷	
Norwich	d.	0505	0530	0600	0605	...	...	0630	0705	0705	...	...	0755	0805	...	0830	0905	0905	0935	...	1005	and at
Diss	d.	0522	0547	0618	0622	...	...	0648	0722	0723	...	...	|	0822	...	0847	0923	0922	|	...	1022	the same
Stowmarket	d.	0533	0558	0630	0633	...	...	0700	0733	0735	...	...	|	0833	0900	0858	0934	0933	|	...	1033	minutes
Ipswich	d.	0545	0610	0642	0645	0700	0700	0712	0745	0747	0800	0804	0830	0845	0912	0910	0946	0945	1009	1000	1045	past
Manningtree 584	d.	0554	0619	0651	|	0711	0711	|	|	|	0811	0814	|	|	0921	|	|	|	|	1011	|	each
Colchester	d.	0605	0632	0704	0703	0722	0730t	0732	0803	|	0830t	0833t	|	0906	0932	|	|	1003	|	1030t	1103	hour
London Liverpool Street	a.	0653	0722	0757	0753	0819	0828	0826	0853	0900	0925	0931	0933	0955	1020	1022	1051	1053	1122	1123	1153	until

		⚒🍷	⚒🍷		⚒🍷	⚒🍷	Ⓐ🍷	⚒R	⑥🍷	Ⓐ	⚒R	⑥	⑥🍷	⚒🍷	⑥	Ⓐ	P	Q	Ⓐ	⑥	Ⓐ	Ⓐ		Ⓐ2	⑥2
Norwich	d.	1505	...	...	1605	...	...	1705	...	...	1805	...	1905	1905	...	2040	2040	2040	...	...	2140	...	...	2300	2300
Diss	d.	1522	...	...	1622	...	...	1722	...	...	1822	...	1922	1922	...	2057	2057	2057	...	...	2201	...	...	2321	2321
Stowmarket	d.	1533	...	...	1633	...	...	1733	...	...	1833	...	1933	1933	...	2108	2108	2108	...	...	2218	...	...	2338	2338
Ipswich	d.	1545	1600	...	1645	1700	1718	1745	1800	1820	1845	1900	1945	1945	2000	2120	2120	2120	2200	2200	2233	2245	...	2354	2355
Manningtree 584	d.	|	1611	...	|	1711	1727	|	1811	1830	|	1911	|	|	2011	|	|	|	2211	2211	...	2256	...	0005	...
Colchester	d.	1603	1630t	...	1703	1730t	1739	1803	1830t	1842	1903	1930t	2003z	2003	2030t	2140	2138	2141	2230t	2230t	...	2307	...	0017	...
London Liverpool Street	a.	1653	1723	...	1758g	1828g	1830	1854	1923	1949	1953	2043v	2053z	2053	2158v	2228	2234	2255	2349	2346z	...	0018	...	...	...

		⑦🍷	⑦	⑦🍷	⑦	⑦	⑦🍷		⑦🍷	⑦	⑦🍷	⑦		⑦🍷	⑦	⑦	⑦	⑦	⑦	⑦	
Norwich	d.	0705	...	0905	...	...	1105	and at	1305	...	1405	...	and at	1905	...	...	2040	...	...	2300	...
Diss	d.	0722	...	0922	...	...	1122	the same	1322	...	1422	...	the same	1922	...	...	2057	...	...	2321	...
Stowmarket	d.	0733	...	0933	...	...	1133	minutes	1333	...	1433	...	minutes	1933	...	...	2108	...	...	2338	...
Ipswich	d.	0745	0900	0945	1000	1100	1145	past	1345	1400	1445	1500	past	1945	2000	2100	2120	2200	2245	2354	...
Manningtree 584	d.	0754	0910	|	1010	1110	|	each	|	1410	|	1510	each	|	2010	2110	|	2210	2256	0005	...
Colchester	d.	0806	0922	1003	1022	1122	1202	hour	1402	1421	1502	1521	hour	2002	2021	2121	2139	2221	2307	0017	...
London Liverpool Street	a.	*0956c*	*1056c*	*1156c*	*1156c*	*1256c*	*1356c*	until	*1556c*	*1556c*	1557	1626	until	2057	2126	2226	2233	2326	0018	...	...

P – ⑥ Dec. 17 - Apr. 8.
Q – ⑥ Apr. 15 - May 27.
R – ✕ on Ⓐ, 🍷 on ⑥.
c – Special train / 🚌 service during line closure due to engineering works. Passengers join and alight from Ipswich / Norwich trains at Witham.
e – Arrives 6 minutes earlier.
g – Arrives 5 minutes earlier on ⑥.
s – Stops to set down only.
v – Arrives 15 minutes earlier Dec. 17 - Apr. 8.
z – 17 Dec. - Apr. 8 only.

Table 581 LONDON - CAMBRIDGE - KINGS LYNN

1, 2 class

km			⚒	⚒	Ⓐ	⚒	Ⓐ	⑥	⑦	⚒	⚒	⑦	⚒	⚒	⑦	⚒	Ⓐ	⑥	Ⓐ	⑦	⚒	⑦		⚒	⑦
0	**London Kings Cross**	d.	...	0608	0652	0743	0845	0845	...	0945	1045	...	1145	1245	...	1345	1445	1445	1515	...	1543	1545	...	1643	1645
	London Liverpool Street	d.	...	|	|	|	|	|	0913	|	|	1113	|	|	1313	|	|	|	|	1513	|	|	...	|	|
	Bishops Stortford ▲	d.	...	|	|	|	|	|	1000	|	|	1200	|	|	1400	|	|	|	|	1600	|	|	...	|	|
93	**Cambridge 586**	d.	0635	0735	0806	0848	0938	0939	1030	1038	1138	1230	1238	1338	1430	1438	1538	1538	1609	1628	1638	1716p	...	1737	1751
117	**Ely 586**	d.	0650	0750	0822	0904	0952	0954	1045	1054	1152	1246	1254	1352	1445	1454	1551	1554	1626	1644	1654	1736	...	1753	1809
142	Downham Market	d.	0707	0807	0839	0921	1007	1011	1102	1111	1208	1303	1311	1408	1502	1511	...	1611	1643	1700	1711	1753	...	1810	1826
159	**Kings Lynn**	a.	0722	0821	0853	0935	1021	1025	1116	1126	1221	1318	1325	1421	1516	1525	...	1625	1657	1715	1726	1807	...	1824	1840

			Ⓐ	⑥	Ⓐ	⑦	Ⓐ	⑥	Ⓐ	⑦	Ⓐ	⑥	Ⓐ	⑦	⑥	Ⓐ	⑦	⚒	⑦		⑦	②-⑤	①	⑥	
London Kings Cross	d.	...	...	1745	1743	1745	...	1845	1843	1845	1913	1945	1943	1945	2043	2043	2045	2143	2145	...	2245	2300	2300	2305	...
London Liverpool Street	d.	...	1703	|	|	|	1803	|	|	|	|	|	|	|	|	|	|	|	|	...	|	|	|	|	...
Bishops Stortford ▲	d.	...	1740	|	|	|	1840	|	|	|	|	|	|	|	|	|	|	|	|	...	|	|	|	|	...
Cambridge 586	d.	...	1815	1839	1848	1849	1919	1938	1947	1949	2014	2038	2044	2049	2144	2144	2149	2244	2249	...	2349	0001s	0011s	0008	...
Ely 586	d.	...	1831	1858	1904	1905	1935	1959	2003	2005	2030	2058	2100	2105	2159	2159	2205	2259	2304	...	0004	0018	0028	0023	...
Downham Market	d.	...	1848	1914	1921	1922	1952	2015	2020	2022	2047	2114	2116	2122	2216	2216	2222	2316	...	...	...	...	...	...	...
Kings Lynn	a.	...	1902	1929	1935	1938	2006	2030	2034	2037	2101	2129	2131	2136	2230	2234	2236	2331	...	...	...	...	...	...	...

h – Arrives 1653.
p – Arrives 1710.
s – Stops to set down only.
▲ – Passengers from Stansted Airport ✈ change here for Cambridge and beyond.

For additional services London - Cambridge, see next page.

Table 581

KINGS LYNN - CAMBRIDGE - LONDON

1, 2 class

	Ⓐ	Ⓐ	⑥	Ⓐ	⑥	Ⓐ		Ⓐ		⑥	Ⓐ	Ⓐ	⑦	Ⓐ	⑦	Ⓐ			⚒	⑦	Ⓐ	⑦	Ⓐ		⑦
Kings Lynn .... d.	0543	0608	0613	0635	0657	0705	...	0734	...	0801	0805	0835	0910	1001	1005	1005	...	1110	1201	1205	1205	1308	...	1401
Downham Market ... d.	0556	0621	0626	0649	0708	0718	...	0747	...	0814	0818	0848	0921	1014	1018	1018	...	1121	1214	1218	1218	1319	...	1414
Ely 586 .... d.	0614	0639	0644	0707	0724	0736	0744	0805	...	0832	0836	0906	0938	1032	1036	1036	...	1138	1232	1236	1236	1336	...	1432
Cambridge 586 ..... d.	0632	0657	0702	0732	0740	0754	0802	0823	...	0850	0854	0924	0954	1050	1054	1054	...	1154	1250	1254	1254	1354	...	1450
Bishops Stortford ▲ .. d.	0701			0801			0831		...	0915			1115				...	1315					...	1515
London Liverpool Street . a.	0742			0843			0912		...	1003			1203				...	1403					...	1603
London Kings Cross ...... a.		0759	0821		0840	0846		0928	...		0946	1016	1046		1146	1151	...	1246	...	1346	1350	1446	...	

		Ⓐ	⑥		Ⓐ		⑥	Ⓐ	Ⓐ		⑥	⑦	Ⓐ	⑦	Ⓐ	Ⓐ		⚒	⑦	⚒	⑦		⑥	Ⓐ
Kings Lynn .... d.	1405	1505	1510	...	1605	1615	1705	1718	...	1805	1809	1818	1842	1910	1918	...	1942	2018	2042	2118	...	2142	2217
Downham Market ... d.	1418	1518	1521	...	1618	1628	1718	1731	...	1818	1822	1831	1855	1921	1931	...	1955	2031	2055	2131	...	2155	2230
Ely 586 .... d.	1436	1536	1538	...	1610	1636	1649	1736	1749	...	1836	1840	1849	1913	1938	1949	...	2013	2049	2113	2149	...	2213	2248
Cambridge 586 ..... d.	1454	1554	1554	...	1628	1654	1707	1754	1807	...	1854	1858	1907	1931	1954	2007	...	2031	2107	2131	2207	...	2231	2310
Bishops Stortford ▲ .. d.				...					...							...					...		
London Liverpool Street . a.				...					...							...					...		
London Kings Cross ...... a.	1546	1649	1649	...	1736	1748	1810	1847	1910	...	1946	1950	2010	2037	2046	2110	...	2137	2210	2239	2310	...	2345	0030

Additional services London - Cambridge:

From Kings Cross:

Ⓐ : 0008, 0708, 0815, 0915 and hourly to 1415, then 1508, 1613, 1713, 1813, 2013, 2038, 2108, 2208, 2308.

⑥ : 0008, 0652, 0708, 0815, 0915 and hourly to 1915, then 2008, 2108, 2208.

⑦ : 0008, 0645, 0745 and hourly to 1645, then 2004, 2104, 2135, 2235.

From Liverpool Street via Bishops Stortford:

Ⓐ : 0633, 0703, 0733, 0803, 0833, 0908, 0938 and half-hourly to 1538, then 1603, 1633, 1733, 1833, 1903, 1933, 2003, 2033, 2103, 2233, 2333.

⑥ : 0640, 0710 and half-hourly to 2340.

⑦ : 0813, 1013, 1213, 1413, 1613, 1713 and hourly to 2313.

▲ – Passengers from Cambridge and beyond change here for Stansted Airport +.

Additional services Cambridge - London:

To Kings Cross:

Ⓐ : 0551, 0641, 0716, 0845, 1024, 1124 and hourly to 1924, then 2002, 2102, 2202, 2231.

⑥ : 0631, 0831, 0924, 1024 and hourly to 1824, then 1902, 2002, 2102, 2202, 2305.

⑦ : 0717, 0817 and hourly to 1617, then 1642, 1746, 1842, 1946, 2042.

To Liverpool Street via Bishops Stortford:

Ⓐ : 0425, 0602, 0632, 0702, 0732, 0832, 0905, 0958, 1018, 1058 and at 18 and 58 mins past each hour to 1458, then 1508, 1535, 1605, 1635, 1720, 1748, 1818, 1835, 1920, 1935, 2005, 2105, 2205, 2305.

⑥ : 0425, 0648, 0721, 0758 and at 21 and 58 mins past each hour to 1921, then 1948, 2048, 2148, 2248

⑦ : 0750, 0850 and hourly to 2250.

Table 582

IPSWICH - LOWESTOFT

2 class

km		⚒	⚒	⚒	⑦a	⚒	⑦b	⑦a	⚒	⑦b	⑦a	⚒	⑦b	⑦a	⚒	⑦a	⚒	⑦a	⚒	⑦b	⑦a	⚒	⑦b	⚒	⚒
0	Ipswich .... d.	0715	0812	0905	0950	1045	1050	1150	1245	1250	1350	1445	1450	1550	1645	1650	1717	1750	1850	1850	2005	2013	2050	2150	2200
17	Woodbridge ...... d.	0732	0829	0922	1007	1102	1107	1207	1302	1307	1407	1502	1507	1607	1702	1707	1734	1807	1907	1907	2022	2030	2124h	2207	2217
36	Saxmundham ...... d.	0752	0849	0942	1027	1122	1127	1227	1322	1327	1427	1522	1527	1627	1722	1727	1754	1827	1927	1927	2042	2050	2144	2227	2237
65	Beccles .... d.	0822		1012	1057	1152	1157	1257	1352	1357	1457	1552	1557	1657	1752	1757	1824	1857	1957	1957	2112	2120	2214	2257	2307
79	Lowestoft .... a.	0839		1029	1115	1209	1215	1315	1409	1415	1515	1609	1615	1715	1809	1815	1841	1915	2014	2015	2130	2137	2231	2315	2324

		⚒	⚒	⑦a		⑦b	⑦a	⑦a		⚒	⑦a		⚒	⑦a		⚒	⑦a	⚒	⚒	⑦b	⑦a	⚒	⑦b	⑦a	⚒	
Lowestoft .... d.	0541	0712		0810	0906	0910	1010	1056	1110	1210	1256	1310	1410	1450	1510	1610	1705	1710	1810	1845	1910	2005	2020	2025	...
Beccles .... d.	0556	0727		0825	0921	0925	1025	1111	1125	1225	1311	1325	1425	1505	1525	1625	1720	1725	1825	1900	1925	2020	2035	2040	...
Saxmundham .... d.	0625	0756	0853	0854	0950	0954	1054	1140	1154	1254	1340	1354	1454	1534	1554	1654	1705e	1754	1854	1929	1954	2049	2104	2109	...
Woodbridge .... d.	0645	0816	0913	0914	1010	1014	1114	1200	1214	1314	1400	1414	1514	1554	1614	1714	1815	1814	1914	1949	2014	2109	2124	2129	...
Ipswich .... a.	0703	0834	0931	0932	1028	1032	1132	1218	1232	1332	1418	1432	1532	1612	1632	1732	1833	1832	1932	2007	2032	2127	2142	2147	...

a – Dec. 18 - Apr. 9.   b – Apr. 16 - May 21.   e – Arrives 1749.   h – Arrives 2106.

Table 583

IPSWICH - CAMBRIDGE

2 class

km		⚒	⚒		⚒	⚒	⑦	⚒	⑦		⑦		⑦	⚒	⑦	⑦	⑦		⑦		⑦		⚒	⚒	⑦	⚒
0	Ipswich .... d.	0515	0645	...	0806	0816	0850	0943	0950	...	1025	...	1205	1212	1245	1322	...	1415	...	1441	...	1530	1620
19	Stowmarket .... d.	0529	0701	...	0818	0832	0906	0957	1006	...	1039	1120	1221	1228	1259	1336	...	1429	...	1457	1512	1544	1636
42	Bury St Edmunds ... d.	0550	0722	...	0835	0853	0926	1014	1027	...	1056	1137	1242	1249	1316	1353	1430	1447	...	1517	1535	1601	1657
66	Newmarket .... d.	0609	0741	...		0912		1047		...	1154		1302		1335		1448		...	1552			
89	Cambridge .... a.	0633	0805	...		0936		1110		...	1217		1325		1359		1510		...	1615			
	Peterborough 585 ... a.	0743	0921	...	0936	1102	...	1121	...	1212	1332	...	1446	1408	1456	1459	1646	1605	...	1729	1705	1805

		⚒		⚒	⚒	⚒		⚒	⚒	⚒					Ⓐ	⚒	⚒		⑥	⑥	⚒	⑦	
Ipswich .... d.		1705	...	1807	1832	1942	...	2005	2200	2200		Peterborough 585 .... d.	...	0710	...	0858	0918	1015	...	
Stowmarket .... d.		1721	...	1823	1846	1958	...	2021	2216	2216		Cambridge .... d.	0649	0815	...	1015	1015		1118	...
Bury St Edmunds .... d.	1713	1742	...	1844	1903	2019	...	2042	2236	2237		Newmarket .... d.	0710	0836	...	1036	1036		1139	...
Newmarket .... d.	1732	1802	...			2038	...	2102		2257		Bury St Edmunds ...... d.	0557	0730	0856	0942	1056	1056	1123	1200	...
Cambridge .... d.	1756	1825	...			2102	...	2125		2320		Stowmarket .... d.	0618	0752	0918	1003	1112	1112	1140	1221	...
Peterborough 585 .... a.	1941	1956	...	1952	2007		...					Ipswich .... a.	0635	0809	0935	1020			1155	1238	...

		Ⓐ	⑥	⚒	⑦			⚒	⑦		⚒	⚒	⑦	⚒		⑦		⚒		⑦	⑥	Ⓐ
Peterborough 585 .... d.	1052	1132	1211	1248	...	1254	1450	...	1500	1558	1613	1632	...	1805	1811	...	2007	...	2058	...	2205
Cambridge .... d.	1228	1228		1343	...	1410		1518	1621		1802		...	1840		2110	...	2140	...	2338
Newmarket .... d.	1249	1249		1403	...	1431		1539	1642		1823		...	1901		2131	...	2201	...	2359
Bury St Edmunds .... d.	1307	1307	1319	1406	1423	...	1451	1556	1606	1706	1706	1722	1843	...	1915	1920	1922	2117	2151	...	2206	2222	2245	0020
Stowmarket .... d.	1324	1324	1341	1423	...	1507	1613	1621	1723	1723	1744	1905	...	1938	1938	1943	2134	2213	...	2223	2243	2306	0041
Ipswich .... a.	1340	1340	1358	1438	...	1628	1638	1740	1738	1759	1922	...	1949	1952	2000	2149	2230	...	2238	2300	2323	0058

Table 584

HARWICH and FELIXSTOWE

HARWICH - MANNINGTREE and v.v.   18 km.   Journey time: 21 minutes.   Trains call at **Harwich Parkeston Quay**, 5 mins from Harwich Town, 16 mins from Manningtree.   1, 2 class

For boat trains to and from London, see Tables 15, 21, 23; to and from Peterborough, see Table 585.

From Harwich Town:

Ⓐ : 0555, 0647, 0715, 0748, 0845, 0945, 1041 and hourly to 1641, then 1754, 1826A, 1941, 2041, 2141, 2220.

⑥ : 0555, 0647, 0748, 0841 and hourly to 2141, then 2245C, 2309D.

⑦E : 0845 and hourly to 2145.   ⑦F : 0910 and hourly to 2110.

From Manningtree:

Ⓐ : 0622, 0714, 0817, 0921, 1014 and hourly to 1614, then 1719, 1801, 1835, 1932, 2033, 2131, 2216, 2300H, 2352H.

⑥ : 0622, 0714 and hourly to 2114, then 2220C, 2239D, 2310CH, 2336DH.

⑦E : 0815, 0914 and hourly to 2214, 2348H.   ⑦F : 0840, 0939 and hourly to 2139, 2336H.

A – Change at Harwich Parkeston Quay.   C – To Apr. 8.   D – From Apr. 15.   E – To Apr. 9.   F – From Apr. 16.   H – To Harwich Parkeston Quay only.

IPSWICH - FELIXSTOWE and v.v.   25 km.   Journey time: 26 minutes.   2 class   No service on ⑦.

From Ipswich:

⚒ : 0600, 0710, 0845, 0940, 1040, 1240, 1440, 1617, 1745, 1846, 1956, 2055.

From Felixstowe:

⚒ : 0630, 0740, 0914, 1010, 1110, 1310, 1510, 1647, 1815, 1925, 2026, 2127.

Table 585 NORWICH - LIVERPOOL

2 class only

km			⚒ 🍷	⚒ 🍷	⚒ 🍷	⚒ 🍷	⑦r 🍷	⚒ 🍷	⑦r 🍷	⚒ 🍷	⑦ 🍷	⚒ 🍷	⚒ 🍷	⑦r 🍷	⑦t 🍷	⚒	⚒ 🍷	⑦t 🍷	⑦r 🍷	⑦	⚒ 🍷	⑦ 🍷	⚒ 🍷	⚒	⑦ 🍷
0	**Norwich**	d.	...	...	...	0554	...	0700	...	0753	...	...	0900	...	...	...	0958	...	...	...	1100	1145	1140	...	1301
49	Thetford	d.	...	...	...	0627	...	0727	...	0826	...	...	0927	...	...	...	1031	...	...	...	1127	1212	1221	...	1328
	Harwich Parkeston Quay	d.	...	...	...	|	...	|	...	|	...	0740	|	...	...	...	|	...	...	...	|	|	|	...	|
	Ipswich **583**	d.	...	...	...	|	...	|	...	|	...	0806	|	...	...	0943	|	...	...	1025	|	|	|	1212	|
86	**Ely**	a.	...	...	...	0652	...	0749	...	0853	...	0900	0949	...	...	1040	1056	...	...	1124	1149	1237	1252	1318	1352
86	**Ely**	d.	...	...	...	0656	...	0755	...	0857	...	0901	0953	...	...	1041	1102	...	...	1125	1153	1241	1258	1325	1356
112	March	d.	...	...	...	0712	...	0811	...	|	...	|	|	...	...	1059	|	...	...	1142	|	|	1314	1346	|
136	**Peterborough**	d.	...	...	...	0735	...	0828	...	0931	...	0936	1030	...	...	1121	1136	...	...	1212	1229	1327	1334	1408	1430
182	Grantham	d.	...	...	0652	0805	...	0859	...	1000	...	...	1107q	...	...	...	1210	...	...	...	1258	1405	1409	...	1500
224	Loughborough	d.	...	...	|	|	...	|	...	|	...	...	|	...	...	...	|	...	...	...	|	|	|	...	|
219	**Nottingham**	a.	...	...	0731	0842	...	0933	...	1034	...	...	1141	...	...	...	1244	...	...	...	1330	1438	1443	...	1533
219	**Nottingham**	d.	0525	0635	0733	0844	0910	0944	1037	1047	1134	...	1147	1237	1241	...	1245	1335	1339	...	1347	1440	1444	...	1540
	Derby **520 561**	d.	|	|	|	|	|	|	|	|	|	...	|	|	|	...	|	|	|	...	|	|	|	...	|
265	Chesterfield	d.	0559	0715	0822	0924	1005	1024	1118	1124	1215	...	1225	1318	|	...	1324	|	1417	...	1424	1520	1524	...	1617
284	**Sheffield**	a.	0613	0732	0839	0939	1025	1039	1133	1139	1231	...	1239	|	|	...	1339	|	1432	...	1439	1536	1539	...	1632
284	**Sheffield**	d.	0617	0736	0842	0942	1024	1042	1137	1142	1234r	...	1242	|	|	...	1342	|	1438	...	1442	1539	1542	...	1636
343	Stockport	d.	0725	0825	0925	1025	1127	1125	1226	1225	1326r	...	1325	1426	1426	...	1425	1526	1526	...	1525	1626	1625	...	1726
353	**Manchester Piccadilly**	a.	0736	0836	0936	1036	1136	1136	1236	1236	1336r	...	1336	1436	1436	...	1436	1536	1536	...	1536	1636	1636	...	1736
353	**Manchester Piccadilly**	d.	0737	0837	0937	1037	1137	1137	1237	1237	1337r	...	1337	1437	1437	...	1437	1537	1537	...	1537	1637	1637	...	1737
379	Warrington Central	a.	0757	0857	0957	1057	|	1157	|	1257	1357r	...	1357	|	|	...	1457	1557	|	...	1557	|	1657	...	|
409	**Liverpool Lime Street**	a.	0829	0929	1029	1129	1229	1229	1329	1329	1429r	...	1429	1529	1529	...	1529	1629	1629	...	1629	1729	1729	...	1829

		⚒ 🍷	⑦	⑦ 🍷	⚒ 🍷	⚒	⑦ 🍷	⚒ 🍷		⑦	⑦ 🍷	⚒ 🍷		⚒	⑦ 🍷		⑥ 🍷	Ⓐ 🍷	⚒	⚒	⑦	⑦ C🍷	⚒ B🍷	⑦ 🍷	⚒
Norwich	d.	1300	...	1353	1354	...	1455	1508	...	...	1550	1555	...	...	1650	...	1722	1726	...	...	...	1845	1843	1925	1925
Thetford	d.	1327	...	1420	1427	...	1522	1536	...	...	1617	1628	...	...	1722	...	1755	1759	...	...	...	1917	1923	1952	1958
Harwich Parkeston Quay	d.	|	...	|	|	...	|	|	...	...	|	|	...	...	|	...	|	|	...	...	...	|	|	|	|
Ipswich **583**	d.	|	1322	|	|	1415	|	|	...	1530	|	|	...	1620	|	...	|	|	...	1807	1832	|	|	|	|
Ely	a.	1349	1421	1444	1452	1513	1544	1556	...	1629	|	1654	...	1725	1744	...	1820	1824	...	1912	1931	1944	1954	2014	2023
Ely	d.	1353	1422	1451	1456	1525	1553	1600	...	1630	|	1658	...	1726	1753	...	1824	1828	...	1913	1932	1953	1958	2018	2027
March	d.	|	1440	|	|	1544	|	|	...	1647	|	|	...	1744	|	...	|	|	...	1931	1949	|	2014	|	|
Peterborough	d.	1427	1459	1525	1529	1605	1627	1634	...	1705	1717	1731	...	1805	1829	...	1858	1902	...	1952	2007	2027	2033	2052	2100
Grantham	d.	|	...	|	|	...	1657	1707	...	...	|	|	...	...	1859	...	1931	1941	...	...	...	2057	2111	2128	|
Loughborough	d.	1522	...	1618	1620	...	|	|	...	...	1814	1821	...	...	|	...	|	|	...	...	...	|	|	|	2203
Nottingham	a.	1539	...	1636	1640	...	1730	1743	...	...	1831	1837	...	...	1932	...	2005	2015	...	...	...	2132	2143	2201	2219
Nottingham	d.	1547	...	1640	1645	...	1740	1744	...	...	1840	1843	...	...	1940	...	2016	2016	...	...	...	2134	2144	...	...
Derby **520 561**	d.	|	...	|	|	...	|	|	...	...	|	|	...	...	|	...	|	|	...	...	...	2159	2209	...	...
Chesterfield	d.	1624	...	1720	1725	...	1820	1824	...	...	1920	1923	...	...	2017	...	2057	2057	...	...	...	...	...	...	...
Sheffield	a.	1639	...	1738	1739	...	1836	1839	...	...	1936	1939	...	...	2032	...	2112	2112	...	...	...	...	...	...	...
Sheffield	d.	1642	...	1742	1742	...	1839	1842	...	...	1940	1942	...	...	2036	...	2115	2115	...	...	...	...	...	...	...
Stockport	d.	1725	...	1826	1825	...	1926	1925	...	...	2026	2027	...	...	2126	...	2158	2158	...	...	...	...	...	...	...
Manchester Piccadilly	a.	1736	...	1836	1836	...	1936	1936	...	...	2036	2036	...	...	2142	...	2209	2209	...	...	...	...	...	...	...
Manchester Piccadilly	d.	1737	...	1837	1837	...	1937	1937	...	...	...	2037	...	...	...	...	...	...	2318	...	...	...	...	...	...
Warrington Central	a.	1802	...	|	1857	...	|	1957	...	...	...	2057	...	...	...	...	...	...	2356	...	...	...	...	...	...
Liverpool Lime Street	a.	1834	...	1929	1929	...	2029	2029	...	...	...	2129	...	...	...	...	...	...	0027	...	...	...	...	...	...

km			Ⓐ	⑥	⚒	⑥ 🍷	Ⓐ 🍷	⑥ 🍷	Ⓐ 🍷	⚒	⚒ 🍷	⚒ 🍷	⚒	⑦	⚒ 🍷	⑦ 🍷		⚒ 🍷	⚒	⚒ 🍷	⑦ 🍷	⚒ 🍷	⑦	⚒	⑦ 🍷
0	**Liverpool Lime Street**	d.	...	...	...	...	...	...	...	...	0648	0748	...	...	0851	...	...	0951	...	1051	...	1151	...	...	...
30	Warrington Central	d.	...	...	...	...	...	...	...	...	0714	0815	...	...	0917	...	...	1017	...	1117	...	1217	...	...	...
56	**Manchester Piccadilly**	a.	...	...	...	...	...	...	...	...	0741	0841	...	...	0941	...	...	1041	...	1141	...	1241	...	...	...
56	**Manchester Piccadilly**	d.	...	...	0549	...	...	...	...	...	0743	0843	...	...	0943	...	...	1043	...	1143	...	1243	...	...	1243
65	Stockport	d.	...	...	0558	...	...	...	...	...	0756	0853	...	...	0953	...	...	1053	...	1153	...	1253	...	...	|
125	**Sheffield**	a.	...	...	0655	...	...	...	...	...	0848	0935	...	...	1043	...	...	1135	...	1235	...	1335	...	...	1341
125	**Sheffield**	d.	...	...	...	...	...	...	...	...	0851	0938	...	...	1046	...	...	1138	...	1246	...	1338	...	...	1345
144	Chesterfield	d.	...	...	...	...	...	...	...	...	0906	0952	...	...	1100	...	...	1152	...	1301	...	1353	...	...	1359
	Derby **520 561**	d.	...	...	...	0711	0711	0803	0803	...	|	|	...	...	|	...	...	|	...	|	...	|	...	...	|
190	**Nottingham**	a.	...	...	...	0732	0735	0824	0824	...	0943	1025	...	...	1137	...	...	1227	...	1338	...	1428	...	...	1432
190	**Nottingham**	d.	0457	0457	...	0738	0741	0825	0833	...	0945	1029	...	...	1139	1204	...	1236	...	1342	1349	1429	...	...	1442
214	Loughborough	d.	0513	0513	...	0753	0756	|	|	...	|	1044	...	...	|	1230	...	1251	...	1358	|	|	...	...	|
226	Grantham	d.	|	|	...	|	|	0900	0907	...	1017	|	...	...	1218	|	...	|	...	|	1433	1502	...	...	1535
273	**Peterborough**	d.	0622	0622	...	0855	0858	0930	0947n	1015	1052e	1148	1211	1248	1253	1355	...	1348	1450	1500	1508	1536	1558	1613	1616
297	March	d.	0637	0637	...	|	|	|	|	1033	|	|	1229	1305	|	|	...	|	1508	|	|	1553	1606	1631	|
322	**Ely**	a.	0659	0700	...	0928	0931	1003	1021	1054	1124	1222	1248	1336	1327	1428	...	1421	1527	1532	1541	1611	1636	1651	1652
322	**Ely**	d.	0703	0708	...	0935	0935	1007	1025	1055	1127	1225	1249	1337	1333	1432	...	1425	1528	1539	1545	1614	1637	1652	1656
	Ipswich **583**	a.	|	|	...	|	|	|	|	1155	|	|	1358	1438	|	|	...	|	1628	|	|	|	1738	1759	|
	Harwich Parkeston Quay	a.	|	|	...	|	|	|	|	...	|	|	...	...	|	|	...	|	...	|	|	|	...	...	|
360	Thetford	d.	0732	0735	...	0959	0959	1028	1048	...	1156	1247	...	...	1357	1455	...	1446	...	1603	1606	1636	...	...	1719
409	**Norwich**	a.	0813	0813	...	1033	1033	1055	1116	...	1240	1315	...	...	1433	1524	...	1515	...	1637	1635	1705	...	...	1753

		⚒ 🍷	⑦ 🍷	⚒ 🍷	⑦ 🍷	⑦	⚒	Ⓐ 🍷	⑥ 🍷	⑦ 🍷	⑦ 🍷	⚒ 🍷	⚒	⑦ 🍷	⚒ 🍷	⑦	⚒ 🍷	⑦ 🍷	⚒ 🍷	⑦	⑦	⚒ 🍷	⚒	⑦	⚒ 🍷
Liverpool Lime Street	d.	1251	1251	1351	1351	...	...	1451	1451	1451	1551	1551	...	1651	1651	...	1751	1751	1851	1851	1951	1951	2055	2121	...
Warrington Central	d.	1317	|	1417	|	...	...	1517	1517	|	|	1617	...	|	1717	...	1817	|	1917	|	|	2017	2145	|	...
Manchester Piccadilly	a.	1341	1341	1441	1441	...	...	1541	1541	1541	1641	1641	...	1741	1741	...	1841	1841	1941	1941	2041	2041	2211	2211	...
Manchester Piccadilly	d.	1343	1343	1443	1443	...	...	1543	1543	1543	1643	1643	...	1743	1743	...	1843	1843	1943	1943	2043	2043	...	2213	2228
Stockport	d.	1353	1353	1453	1453	...	...	1553	1553	1553	1653	1653	...	1753	1753	...	1853	1853	1953	1953	2053	2053	...	2223	2238
Sheffield	a.	1435	1440	1535	1542	...	...	1635	1635	1636	1734	1743	...	1840	1835	...	1935	1940	2035	2036	2134	2135	...	2321	2337
Sheffield	d.	1438	1443	1538	1545	...	...	1638	1638	1640	1738	1746	...	1843	1846	...	1946	1944	2038	2042	2138	2138	...	2325	2340
Chesterfield	d.	1453	1458	1552	1559	...	...	1654	1654	1654	1752	1801	...	1859	1859	...	2000	1957	2052	2056	2152	2152	...	2339	2354
Derby **520 561**	d.	|	|	|	|	...	...	|	|	|	|	|	...	|	|	...	|	|	|	|	|	|	...	|	|
Nottingham	a.	1530	1533	1628	1633	...	...	1732	1732	1729	1827	1837	...	1932	1934	...	2038	2032	2130	2131	2227	2230	...	0016	0027
Nottingham	d.	1532	1546	1636	1640	...	...	1734	1736	1738	1836	1841	...	...	...	...	2046	2036	...	...	...	...	...	...	...
Loughborough	d.	|	1602	1652	|	...	...	|	|	1754	|	1857	...	...	...	...	|	2051	...	...	...	...	...	...	...
Grantham	d.	1606p	|	|	1722	...	...	1814	1813	|	1917	|	...	...	...	...	2120	|	...	...	...	...	...	...	...
Peterborough	d.	1652	1701	1755	1755	1805	1811	1852	1857	1851	1949	1959	2007	...	...	2058	2155	2151	...	...	...	...	...	...	...
March	d.	|	|	1810	1810	1823	1829	|	|	|	|	|	2028	...	...	2116	|	|	...	...	...	...	...	...	...
Ely	a.	1727	1734	1830	1829	1844	1850	1923	1929	1924	2022	2032	2048	...	...	2136	2228	2224	...	...	...	...	...	...	...
Ely	d.	1733	1746	1838	1833	1845	1851	1927	1932	1928	2026	2036	2049	...	...	2137	2231	2228	...	...	...	...	...	...	...
Ipswich **583**	a.	|	|	|	|	1949	1952	|	|	|	|	|	2149	...	...	2238	|	|	...	...	...	...	...	...	...
Harwich Parkeston Quay	a.	|	|	|	|	2016	2021	|	|	|	|	|	...	...	...	...	|	|	...	...	...	...	...	...	...
Thetford	d.	1755	1808	1902	1856	...	...	1950	1954	1951	2047	2100	...	...	...	...	2253	2251	...	...	...	...	...	...	...
Norwich	a.	1824	1837	1936	1933	...	...	2026	2028	2026	2116	2129	...	...	...	...	2327	2325	...	...	...	...	...	...	...

B – ② Norwich - Derby (- Birmingham New Street on Ⓐ, arrives 2306).
C – ② Norwich - Derby - Birmingham New Street (arrives 2254).

e – Arrives 1045.
n – Arrives 0940.
p – On ⑥ departs 1612.

q – Arrives 1059.
r – Sept. 25 - Jan. 8, Apr. 16 - May 21.
t – Jan. 15 - Apr. 9.

Other trains:
Ely - Peterborough and v.v.: Table **586**.
Peterborough - Grantham and v.v.: Table **570**.
Grantham - Nottingham and v.v.: Table **587**.
Loughborough - Nottingham - Sheffield and v.v.: Table **560**.
Sheffield - Manchester and v.v.: Table **573**.
Manchester - Liverpool and v.v.: Table **551**.

For an explanation of standard symbols see page 4

Table 586 CAMBRIDGE - PETERBOROUGH - BIRMINGHAM

2 class only

km		⚒	⚒	⚒ 🍷	⑥ 🍷	Ⓐ 🍷	⚒ 🍷	⑥ 🍷	Ⓐ 🍷	⑦ 🍷	⚒ 🍷		⚒ 🍷	⑦ 🍷	⚒ 🍷		⑦ 🍷	⚒ 🍷	⑦ 🍷	⚒ 🍷		⑦ 🍷	⚒ 🍷	⑥ 🍷
0	**Cambridge** d.	...	0520	0629	0645	0645	0829	1005	1005	1040	1105	...	1205	1243	1305	...	1355	1405	1455	1505	...	1555	1603	1654
	Norwich **585** d.	...	|	|	|	|	|	|	|	|	|	...	|	|	|	...	|	|	|	|	...	|	|	|
24	**Ely** a.	...	0535	0644	0700	0700	0844	1022	1022	1055	1120	...	1221	1258	1320	...	1410	1420	1510	1520	...	1610	1620	1709
24	**Ely 585** d.	...	0537	0646	0702	0702	0846	1024	1024	1057	1122	...	1223	1300	1322	...	1412	1422	1512	1522	...	1612	1622	1711
49	March **585** d.	...	0554	0702	0722	0722	0902	1040	1040	1113	1138	...	1239	1316	1338	...	1428	1438	1528	1538	...	1628	1638	1727
73	**Peterborough 585** d.	...	0616	0725	0747	0747	0922	1100	1104	1145	1157	...	1301	1348	1357	...	1448	1457	1548	1557	...	1648	1657	1747
93	Stamford d.	...	0629	0737	0800	0800	0934	1112	1116	1157	1210	...	1313	1404	1409	...	1500	1510	1600	1610	...	1700	1710	1759
114	Oakham d.	0617	0644	0751	0814	0814	0948	1126	|	1211	1224	...	1327	1417	1423	...	1514	1524	1614	1624	...	1714	1724	1815
133	Melton Mowbray d.	0627	0656	0801	0824	0824	0958	1137	1138	1222	1234	...	1337	1428	1434	...	1525	1534	1624	1634	...	1725	1734	1827
157	**Leicester 574** d.	0644	0717	0822	0840	0843	1018	1155	1155	1244	1255	...	1357	1450	1455	...	1551	1554	1644	1655	...	1747	1756	1850
187	Nuneaton **574** d.	0722e	0747	0844	0911	0911	1042	1219	1219	1308	1317	...	1417	1512	1517	...	1612	1617	1711	1719	...	1809	1834	1916
221	**Birmingham New Street** a.	0759	0822	0920	0954	0954	1112	1252	1252	1354	1350	...	1450	1540	1550	...	1651	1650	1743	1750	...	1841	1904	1950

	Ⓐ 🍷	⑦ 🍷		⚒ 🍷	⑦ 🍷	⚒ 🍷	⑦ 🍷	⑦ C 🍷	Ⓐ C 🍷	⚒ D 🍷
Cambridge d.	1654	1655	...	1748	1810	1852	1905	...	...	...
Norwich **585** d.	|	|	...	|	|	|	|	1845	1843	1925
Ely a.	1709	1710	...	1805	1825	1907	1920	1944	1954	2023
Ely 585 d.	1711	1712	...	1807	1827	1909	1922	1953	1958	2027
March **585** d.	1727	1728	...	1825	1843	1925	1938	|	2014	|
Peterborough 585 d.	1747	1748	...	1844	1903	1943	1958	2027	2033	2100
Stamford d.	1759	1800	...	1857	1915	1955	2010	|	|	2112
Oakham d.	1815	1816	...	1911	1929	2011	2024	|	|	2126
Melton Mowbray d.	1827	1828	...	1921	1940	2023	2035	|	|	2137
Leicester 574 d.	1850	1851	...	1950	2005	2046	2057	|	|	...
Nuneaton **574** d.	1921	1918	...	2016	2027	2108	2126	|	|	...
Birmingham New Street a.	1950	1952	...	2050	2059	2142	2158	2254	2306	...

	⚒ E 🍷	Ⓐ 🍷	⑥ 🍷		⑥ 🍷	Ⓐ 🍷	⑥ 🍷	Ⓐ 🍷	
Birmingham New Street d.	...	...	...	...	0639	0639	0717	0738	...
Nuneaton **574** d.	...	...	...	...	0706	0706	0747	0805	...
Leicester 574 d.	...	...	...	...	0732	0732	0820	0836	...
Melton Mowbray d.	0537	...	...	...	0749	0749	0838	0853	...
Oakham d.	0549	...	...	...	0801	0801	0850	0905	...
Stamford d.	0602	0656	...	...	0814	0814	0903	0918	...
Peterborough 585 d.	0622	0710	0710	...	0833	0833	0918	0937	...
March **585** d.	0637	0728	0728	...	0848	0848	0933	0953	...
Ely 585 a.	0700	0751	0751	...	0907	0912	0952	1011	...
Ely d.	0703	0752	0752	...	0908	0913	0953	1012	...
Norwich **585** a.	0813	|	|	...	|	|	|	|	...
Cambridge a.	...	0809	0809	...	0925	0932	1009	1029	...

	⑥ 🍷	Ⓐ 🍷	⑥ 🍷	Ⓐ 🍷	⚒ 🍷	⚒ 🍷	⑦ 🍷	⚒ 🍷		⚒ 🍷	⑦ 🍷	⑦ 🍷	⚒ 🍷	⑦ 🍷	⚒ 🍷	⑦ 🍷	⚒ 🍷	⑥ 🍷	⑦ 🍷	⚒ 🍷	⚒ 🍷	⑦ 🍷	⚒ 🍷	⑦ 🍷
Birmingham New Street d.	0838	0838	0938	0942	1037	1136	1217	1238	...	1338	1328	1420	1436	1530	1536	1630	1636	1638	1730	1737	1836	1910	2008	2010
Nuneaton **574** d.	0905	0909	1005	1011	1108	1204	1303	1306	...	1405	1413	1505	1504	1558	1608	1702	1709	1709	1801	1805	1904	1940	2036	2042
Leicester 574 d.	0928	0935	1031	1038	1131	1226	1327	1331	...	1431	1437	1529	1531	1626	1634	1727	1736	1736	1826	1831	1929	2005	2104	2110
Melton Mowbray d.	0948	0952	1048	1054	1148	1245	1345	1348	...	1448	1455	1547	1548	1644	1653	1745	1753	1754	1844	1848	1946	2023	2121	2129
Oakham d.	1000	1004	1100	1106	1200	1257	1357	1400	...	1500	1507	1559	1600	1656	1705	1757	1805	1806	1856	1900	1958	2035	2133	2141
Stamford d.	1013	1017	1113	1118	1213	1310	1410	1413	...	1513	1520	1612	1613	1709	1718	1810	1818	1819	1909	1913	2011	2048	2146	2155
Peterborough 585 d.	1040r	1040r	1132	1136	1232	1330	1430	1435	...	1532	1540	1631	1632	1730	1738	1830	1837	1837	1929	1932	2035	2108	2205	2215
March **585** d.	1055	1055	1148	1152	1248	1346	1445	|	...	|	1555	1646	1653	1745	1757	1845	1852	1852	1944	1952	2050	2123	2224	2230
Ely 585 a.	1111	1111	1206	1210	1306	1404	1504	1508	...	1606	1614	1705	1710	1804	1816	1904	1912	1910	2003	2017	2109	2142	2243	2250
Ely d.	1112	1112	1207	1211	1307	1405	1505	1509	...	1607	1615	1706	1711	1805	1817	1907	1913	1918	2005	2018	2110	2143	2244	2251
Norwich **585** a.	|	|	|	|	|	|	|	|	...	|	|	|	|	|	|	|	|	|	|	|	|	|	|	|
Cambridge a.	1128	1128	1224	1228	1324	1422	1521	1525	...	1623	1631	1722	1728	1821	1833	1923	1930	1934	2021	2034	2126	2159	2300	2307

C – Via Nottingham and Derby. See Table **585**.
D – [2] and 🍷 Norwich - Nottingham (arrives 2203). See Table **585**.
E – [2] and 🍷 Nottingham (departs 0457) - Norwich. See Table **585**.
e – Arrives 0714.
r – Arrives 1035.

Table 587 NOTTINGHAM - SKEGNESS

2 class only

km		⚒	⚒	⚒	⚒	⚒	N⚒	⑥	Ⓐ	⚒	⚒	⑥p	Ⓐ	⑥	⑦	⚒	⚒	⑦	⚒	⑦	⚒	⑦	⑦	⚒
0	**Nottingham** d.	...	0554	...	0625	...	0655	0825	0833	...	0917	0937	1004	1004	...	1100	1139	1145	1200	1200	1304	1349	1425	1429
36	Grantham a.	...	0635	...	0707	...	|	0859	0907	...	|	|	1048	1048	...	1143	1218	1229	1242	1253	1349	1431	1518	1501
36	Grantham d.	...	...	0648	...	0729	|	...	...	0910	|	|	1052	1104	...	1148	...	...	1248	1300	1425	...	1530	...
60	Sleaford d.	...	...	0716	...	0755	0834	...	...	0933	1007	|	1116	1132	...	1217	...	...	1317	1323	1448	...	1557	...
87	Boston d.	0642	...	0740	...	0821	...	...	...	0956	1029	1049	1139	1155	1228	1243	...	...	1341	1352	1520	...	1621	...
126	**Skegness** a.	0717	...	0818	...	...	...	...	...	1031	1104	1123	1214	1230	1303	1319	...	...	1416	1427	1555	...	1656	...

	⑦	⚒	⑦	⚒	⚒	⑥	Ⓐ	⑦	Ⓐ	⑥	⑦	⚒	⑦	⑥	Ⓐ	⑦	Ⓐ	⑥	⑦	⚒	Ⓐ	⑥	Ⓐ	⑥
Nottingham d.	1442	1500	1525	1532	...	1606	1606	1640	1655	1700	1710	1734	1750	1803	1803	1836	1910	1911	1945	2046	2050	2050	2130	2149
Grantham a.	1528	1542	1608	1605	...	1649	1649	1713	1740	1745	1755	1812	1835	1849	1847	1911	1954	1954	2035	2119	2133	2133	2218	2232
Grantham d.	...	1546	1615	...	...	1653	1712	...	1745	1748	...	...	1845	1901	1905	...	2007	1957	2040	...	2142	2146	...	...
Sleaford d.	...	1611	1638	...	1653	1716	1749	...	1813	1814	...	...	1911	1931	1931	...	2033	2023	2102	...	2205	2209	...	...
Boston d.	...	1650	1703	...	1715	1800	1818	...	1843	1843	...	...	1934	1958	2000	...	2057	2108	...	...	2228	2231	...	...
Skegness a.	...	1726	1738	...	...	1838	1855	...	1920	1920	...	...	...	2033	2035	...	2132	2143	...	...	...	...	...	...

	⚒	⚒	⚒	⚒	Ⓐ	Ⓐ	⑥	⑥	⚒	⚒	⚒	⚒	⚒	⑦q	⚒	⑦	⚒	⑦	⚒	⚒	⑦	⑦	⚒	⚒
Skegness d.	...	...	...	...	0725	...	0725	...	...	...	0921	...	1036	...	...	...	1147	...	...	1241	...	1320	1330	1430
Boston d.	0548	...	0624	...	0800	...	0800	...	...	0838	1002	...	1109	...	...	...	1221	...	...	1316	...	1354	1406	1504
Sleaford d.	0614	...	0645	...	0826	...	0826	...	...	0904	1023	...	1131	...	...	...	1247	...	...	1347	...	1424	1428	1526
Grantham a.	0643	...	0714	...	0857	...	0903	...	...	0933	1051	...	1157	...	...	...	1310	...	...	1422	...	1452	1454	1557
Grantham d.	...	0652	...	0733	...	0859	...	0913	0921	0938	1056	1210	1225	1242	1258	1255	1322	1405	1409	1429	1500	1505	1505	1606
Nottingham a.	...	0731	...	0813	...	0933	...	0943	1002	1021	1135	1243	1306	1326	1330	1345	1401	1438	1443	1509	1533	1555	1544	1646

	⑦	Ⓐ	⑥	⑥	⑦	Ⓐ	⚒	⑦	⑦	⚒	⑦	⑥	Ⓐ	⑦	⑦	⑥	Ⓐ	⚒	⑦	⑦	Ⓐ	⑥	⚒	Ⓐ
Skegness d.	...	...	...	1600	1605	1610	...	...	...	1744	1745	...	...	1905	...	1922	1927	...	...	...	2045	2055	2147	...
Boston d.	...	...	...	1632	1639	1646	1722	...	...	1820	1819	...	...	1939	...	1958	2005	...	...	...	2118	2128	2220	...
Sleaford d.	...	...	...	1653	1700	1718	1749	...	...	1845	1840	...	...	2000	...	2027	2027	...	...	2135	2141	2151	...	...
Grantham a.	...	...	...	1724	1727	1744	...	...	...	|	1908	...	...	2032	...	2056	2056	...	...	2204	2207	2217	...	...
Grantham d.	1657	1707	1712	1733	1748	1748	...	1810	1859	|	1920	1931	1941	2047	2057	2102	2102	2111	2128	2208	2210	2220	...	2230
Nottingham a.	1730	1743	1743	1812	1828	1827	...	1850	1932	1934	2000	2005	2015	2127	2132	2140	2140	2143	2201	2248	2252	2300	...	2312

N – [2] Derby - Sleaford - Spalding - Peterborough.
p – Apr. 15 - May 26. q – Sept. 25 - Jan. 8, Apr. 16 - May 21.

Additional trains **Nottingham - Grantham**: 0517Ⓐ, 0803⚒, 0945⚒.
Additional trains **Grantham - Nottingham**: 0602Ⓐ, 0805Ⓐ, 0809⑥, 1000⚒, 1107⚒.

Table 588 NORWICH - GREAT YARMOUTH and LOWESTOFT

2 class only

NORWICH - GREAT YARMOUTH 33 km. Journey time: 29 - 35 minutes.

⚒ : 0543, 0632 **R**, 0703, 0748 **R**, 0818, 0935, 1035 **R**, 1137, 1235, 1340, 1435, 1532, 1635, 1658, 1740, 1844, 1945, 2135, 2300.

⑦ A: 0745, 1040 **R**, 1240 **R**, 1440 **R**, 1640 **R**, 1740 **R**, 1840 **R**, 2140 **R**, 2240 **R**.

⑦ B: 0845, 1040 **R**, 1140 **R**, 1240 **R**, 1340 **R**, 1440 **R**, 1540 **R**, 1640 **R**, 1740 **R**, 1840 **R**, 1940 **R**, 2140 **R**, 2240 **R**.

NORWICH - LOWESTOFT 38 km. Journey time: 33 - 43 minutes.

⚒ : 0525, 0605 **R**, 0708 **R**, 0800 **R**, 0903, 0952 **R**, 1101, 1201 **R**, 1301, 1349 **R**, 1501, 1601 **R**, 1650 **R**, 1735 **R**, 1830 **R**, 1900 **R**, 2000 **R**, 2143 **R**, 2250 **R**.

⑦ A: 0850 **R**, 1050, 1250 **R**, 1450, 1650 **R**, 1850, 2050 **R**.

⑦ B: 0950 **R**, 1150, 1350 **R**, 1550, 1750 **R**, 1950, 2150 **R**.

GREAT YARMOUTH - NORWICH

⚒ : 0624, 0712, 0759, 0829, 0924, 1024, 1119 **R**, 1224, 1311, 1424, 1523, 1609, 1710, 1740 **R**, 1818, 1920, 2025, 2211, 2335 **R**.

⑦ A: 0820 **R**, 1120 **R**, 1320 **R**, 1520 **R**, 1720 **R**, 1820 **R**, 1955 **R**, 2225 **R**, 2325 **R**.

⑦ B: 0920 **R**, 1120 **R**, 1220 **R**, 1320 **R**, 1420 **R**, 1520 **R**, 1620 **R**, 1720 **R**, 1820 **R**, 1955 **R**, 2225 **R**, 2325 **R**.

LOWESTOFT - NORWICH

⚒ : 0602 **R**, 0708 **R**, 0800 **R**, 0847 **R**, 0950, 1040 **R**, 1150, 1248 **R**, 1350, 1440 **R**, 1540 **R**, 1615, 1750 **R**, 1820, 1850, 1950 **R**, 2050, 2150 **R**, 2230, 2340.

⑦ A: 1000 **R**, 1205, 1400 **R**, 1605, 1800 **R**, 1945, 2200 **R**, 2325 **R**.

⑦ B: 1100 **R**, 1305, 1500 **R**, 1705, 1900 **R**, 2050, 2210 **R**, 2325 **R**.

A – Sept. 25, Oct. 2, Dec. 18, Jan. 1 - Apr. 9 B – Oct. 9 - Dec. 11, Apr. 16 - May 21. R – Calls at **Reedham** 19 mins from Norwich, 13 mins from Yarmouth, 22 mins from Lowestoft.

03 *For an explanation of standard symbols see page 4* 335

Table 589 GLASGOW - KILMARNOCK - DUMFRIES - CARLISLE

km		⚒	⚒	⚒ G	⚒ 🍷	⑥	⚒		⚒ 🍷	⑦	⚒ N	⑦	⚒ 🍷		⚒	⑦	⚒	⚒	Ⓐ	⚒	⑦		⚒	⑦
0	**Glasgow Central** d.	...	...	...	0828	...	0958	...	1103	...	...	...	1303	...	...	1535	1548	1730	...	...	...	...	2203	2220
39	**Kilmarnock** d.	...	...	0740	0907	...	1034	...	1140	...	1250	...	1344	...	...	1604	1624	1809	...	...	...	...	2240	2249
85	Kirkconnel d.	...	...	0815	0941	...	1108	...	1214	...	1323	...	1418	...	...	1638	1658	1843	...	...	...	...	2314	2323
132	**Dumfries** d.	0650	0737	0849	1013	1041	1141	...	1247	1305	1355	1450	1458	...	1653	1710	1731	1915	2118	2214	2214	...	2347	2355
157	Annan d.	0705	0752	0905	1029	1056	1157	...	1303	1320	1411	1505	1513	...	1708	1726	1747	1931	2133	2229	2229	...	0003	0011
186	**Carlisle** a.	0727	0814	0926	1050	1118	1218	...	1324	1342	1435	1527	1537	...	1732	1750	1812	1952	2155	2251	2251	...	0024	0032
282	*Newcastle* **575** a.	...	...	1053	...	...	...	...	...	...	1603	...	...	...	...	...	1946	...	...	...	...	...	...	...

	⚒	⚒	⚒		⚒	⑥	⚒ 🍷	⑦	⚒		⑦	⚒ N	⚒ 🍷	⚒		⚒ 🍷	⚒ S	⑦		⚒	⚒	⑦		⚒
Newcastle **575** d.	...	...	...	...	0635	...	...	...	...	...	...	1237	...	...	...	...	1710	...	...	...	...	...	...	2110
Carlisle d.	0555	0612	0645	...	0812	0948	1110	1240	1310	...	1354	1423	1454	1558	...	1748	1855	1920	...	2018	2112	2112	...	2257
Annan d.	0615	0632	0705	...	0831	1008	1129	1259	1329	...	1414	1444	1513	1618	...	1808	1914	1939	...	2038	2132	2132	...	2317
Dumfries d.	0632	0650	0722	...	0848	1025	1146	1316	1346	...	1431	1501	1529	1635	...	1825	1931	1956	...	2055	2149	2149	...	2334
Kirkconnel d.	...	0721	...	...	0919	...	1217	1347	1417	...	...	1532	1600	...	...	1856	2002	2027	...	...	...	...	...	...
Kilmarnock d.	...	0758	...	...	0956	...	1253	1423	1453	...	...	1609	1635	...	...	1950	2039	2103	...	...	...	...	...	...
Glasgow Central a.	...	0837	...	...	1041	...	1330	1452	1530	...	...	...	1712	...	...	2027	...	2132	...	...	...	...	...	...

G – [2] and 🍷 Girvan - Newcastle. N – [2] and 🍷 Stranraer Harbour - Newcastle and v.v. S – [2] and 🍷 Newcastle - Ayr.

Table 590 EDINBURGH - FALKIRK - GLASGOW

1, 2 class (most with 🍷)

km		⚒	⚒	⚒	⚒	Ⓐ	⚒	⚒	⑦		⚒	⑦	⚒	⑦		⚒	⑦	⚒	⚒		⚒	⑦
0	**Edinburgh** d.	0550	0620	0700	0730	0742	0800	0830	0830	and at the	1800	1805	1830	1830	and at the	2200	2230	2230	2300	...	2330	2330
41	Falkirk High d.	0620	0650	0727	0757	0812	0827	0857	|	same mins.	1827	|	1857	|	same mins.	2227	|	2257	2330	...	2359	|
	Falkirk Grahamston d.	|	|	|	|	|	|	|	0900	past each	|	1830	|	1900	past each	|	2300	|	|	...	|	2359
76	**Glasgow Queen Street** a.	0644	0714	0750	0820	0841	0850	0920	0935	hour until	1850	1858	1920	1940	hour until	2250	2328	2325	0005	...	0027	0028

	Ⓐ	⚒	⚒	⚒		⚒	⑦	⚒		⚒	⑦	⚒	⑦		⑦	⚒	⚒	⑦	⚒	⚒	⚒	⑦
Glasgow Queen Street d.	0555	0622	0655	0730	...	0800	0800	0830	and at the	1800	1800	1830	1830	and at the	2130	2130	2200	2230	2230	2300	2330	2330
Falkirk Grahamston d.	|	|	|	|	...	|	0823	|	same mins.	|	1823	|	1853	same mins.	2153	|	|	2253	|	|	|	2353
Falkirk High d.	0615	0645	0717	0750	...	0820	|	0850	past each	1820	|	1850	|	past each	|	2150	2220	|	2250	2320	2350	|
Edinburgh a.	0649	0718	0750	0820	...	0850	0902	0920	hour until	1850	1859	1920	1922	hour until	2222	2220	2250	2329	2320	2353	0025	0029

Table 591 GLASGOW - AYR - STRANRAER HARBOUR

2 class only

km		⚒	⚒	⚒ 🍷	⚒	⚒ 🍷	K	K	K	⚒ 🍷	⑦	K	⚒	⑦ 🍷	K	K	K	⚒ N	⑦ 🍷	K	⚒	K	Ⓐ	⑥
0	**Glasgow Central ▲** d.	0600	0700	0723	0800	0823	0900	1000	1100	1123	...	1200	...	1257	1300	1400	1500	...	1537	1600	...	1700	...	...
11	Paisley Gilmour Street d.	0610	0710	0734	0810	0834	0910	1010	1110	1134	...	1210	...	1308	1310	1410	1510	...	1548	1610	...	1710	...	...
43	Kilwinning d.	0629	0729	0754	0833	0854	0929	1031	1129	1154	...	1229	...	1325	1329	1431	1529	...	1605	1629	...	1731	...	...
48	Irvine d.	0633	0733	|	0837	|	0933	1035	1133	|	...	1233	...	|	1333	1435	1533	...	|	1633	...	1735	...	...
56	Troon d.	0639	0739	|	0844	|	0939	1041	1139	|	...	1242	...	|	1339	1441	1539	1622	|	1639	...	1743	...	...
61	Prestwick Airport ✈ d.	0643	0743	|	0848	|	0943	1045	1143	|	...	1244	...	|	1343	1445	1543	|	|	1643	...	1747	...	...
68	**Ayr** a.	0652	0752	0811	0858	0911	0952	1054	1152	1211	...	1255	...	1342	1352	1454	1552	1633	1628	1652	...	1800	...	...
68	**Ayr** d.	...	...	0818	...	0912	...	...	...	1218	1218	...	1332	1345	...	...	...	1635	1635	...	1700	...	1810	1830
82	Maybole d.	...	...	0830	...	0923	...	...	...	1229	1229	...	1343	1356	...	...	...	1647	1647	...	1711	...	1821	1841
101	Girvan d.	...	...	0844	...	0937	...	...	...	1243	1243	...	1357	1410	...	...	...	1701	1701	...	1727	...	1837	1855
121	Barrhill d.	...	...	0905	...	0958	...	...	...	1304	1304	...	1418	1431	...	...	...	1722	1722	...	...	...	...	1917
163	**Stranraer Harbour** a.	...	...	0940	...	1034	...	...	...	1340	1340	...	1454	1512	...	...	...	1800	1800	...	...	...	...	1952

	K	⚒	Ⓐ	K	K	⚒ S	K	K	⚒	K
Glasgow Central ▲ d.	1800	1830	...	1900	2000	...	2100	2200	2223	2300
Paisley Gilmour Street d.	1810	1840	...	1910	2010	...	2110	2210	2234	2310
Kilwinning d.	1831	1901	...	1929	2029	...	2129	2229	2254	2329
Irvine d.	1835	1905	...	1933	2033	...	2133	2233	|	2333
Troon d.	1842	1912	...	1939	2039	2052	2139	2239	|	2339
Prestwick Airport ✈ d.	1846	1916	...	1943	2043	|	2143	2243	|	2343
Ayr a.	1856	1926	...	1952	2052	2102	2152	2252	2311	2352
Ayr d.	...	...	1932	...	...	...	...	...	2312	...
Maybole d.	...	...	1943	...	...	...	...	...	2323	...
Girvan d.	...	...	1958	...	...	...	...	...	2337	...
Barrhill d.	...	...	2019	...	...	...	...	...	2358	...
Stranraer Harbour a.	...	...	2054	...	...	...	...	...	0034	...

	⚒	⚒	⚒ G	⚒	⚒	⚒	K	K	⚒ 🍷
Stranraer Harbour d.	...	...	...	...	0702	...	...	...	1012
Barrhill d.	...	...	...	...	0736	...	...	...	1050
Girvan d.	...	...	0645	...	0755	...	...	...	1110
Maybole d.	...	...	0701	...	0811	...	...	...	1126
Ayr a.	...	...	0713	...	0827	...	...	...	1138
Ayr ▲ d.	0543	0643	0715	0718	0828	0843	0943	1043	...
Prestwick Airport ✈ d.	0550	0651	|	0726	|	0850	0950	1050	...
Troon d.	0554	0655	0723	0730	|	0854	0954	1054	...
Irvine d.	0602	0703	...	0738	|	0900	1000	1100	...
Kilwinning d.	0606	0708	...	0743	|	0905	1005	1105	...
Paisley Gilmour Street d.	0632	0726	...	0807	0859	0923	1023	1123	...
Glasgow Central a.	0643	0738	...	0818	0911	0934	1034	1134	...

	K	⚒ N	⑦	K	K	K	K	⚒ 🍷	⑦ 🍷	⚒	⚒	K	K	⚒	⚒	K	Ⓐ	⚒	K 🍷	K	⑥	K	Ⓐ	K
Stranraer Harbour d.	...	1100	1100	...	...	...	...	1430	1450	...	1516	...	...	...	...	...	...	...	1840	...	2018	...	2105	...
Barrhill d.	...	1134	1134	...	...	...	...	1509	1524	...	1550	...	...	...	...	...	...	...	1914	...	2052	...	2139	...
Girvan d.	...	1153	1153	...	...	...	...	1528	1544	...	1609	...	...	1734	...	...	1842	...	1934	...	2111	...	2158	...
Maybole d.	...	1209	1210	...	...	...	...	1544	1600	...	1625	...	...	1750	...	...	1858	...	1953	...	2127	...	2214	...
Ayr a.	...	1222	1224	...	...	...	...	1554	1610	...	1638	...	...	1802	...	...	1908	...	2004	...	2139	...	2227	...
Ayr ▲ d.	1143	1225	1225	1243	1343	1443	1543	1555	1610	1613	...	1643	1743	...	1813	1843	...	1943	2005	2043	2140	2143	2227	2300
Prestwick Airport ✈ d.	1150	|	|	1250	1350	1450	1550	|	|	1621	...	1650	1750	...	1821	1850	...	1950	|	2050	|	2150	|	2307
Troon d.	1154	1233	|	1254	1354	1454	1554	|	|	1625	...	1654	1754	...	1825	1854	...	1954	|	2054	|	2154	|	2311
Irvine d.	1200	...	|	1300	1400	1500	1600	|	|	1633	...	1701	1800	...	1833	1900	...	2000	|	2100	|	2200	|	2319
Kilwinning d.	1205	...	1240	1305	1405	1505	1605	1610	1629	1638	...	1706	1805	...	1838	1905	...	2005	2020	2105	2156	2205	2243	2324
Paisley Gilmour Street d.	1223	...	1303	1323	1423	1523	1623	1633	1650	1658	...	1724	1828	...	1858	1923	...	2023	2043	2123	2215	2225	2303	2344
Glasgow Central a.	1234	...	1318	1334	1434	1534	1634	1645	1703	1709	...	1735	1841	...	1909	1934	...	2034	2055	2134	2228	2236	2317	2358

G – [2] and 🍷 Girvan - Newcastle.
K – Runs daily (On ⑦ may run up to 12 minutes later).
N – [2] and 🍷 Stranraer Harbour - Newcastle and v.v.
S – [2] and 🍷 Newcastle - Ayr.
▲ – Additional local trains (⚒ only) run Glasgow - Ayr and v.v.: **From Glasgow**: 0630⚒ and hourly until 2330⚒. **From Ayr**: 0613⚒, 0743⚒, 0813⚒ and hourly until 2213⚒.

Table 592 GLASGOW - ARDROSSAN - LARGS

2 class only

km		⚒	⚒		⚒		Ⓐ	⚒		⚒	⚒			⚒		⑦	⚒		⚒		⚒			⚒
0	**Glasgow Central** d.	0615	0645	...	0715	...	0815	0833	...	0845	0915	0945	...	1015	1045	1115	1115	1145	1215	1245	1315	1345	...	1415
11	Paisley Gilmour Street d.	0625	0655	...	0725	...	0825	0843	...	0855	0925	0955	...	1025	1055	1125	1125	1155	1225	1255	1325	1355	...	1425
43	Kilwinning d.	0652	0720	...	0752	...	0852	0910	...	0918	0952	1020	...	1052	1118	1146	1152	1218	1252	1320	1352	1418	...	1452
50	Ardrossan South Beach d.	0703	0728	...	0802	...	0900	0918	...	0926	1000	1028	...	1100	1126	1154	1200	1226	1300	1328	1400	1426	...	1500
51	Ardrossan Town a.	|	0732	...	|	...	...	0922	...	|	1004	|	...	1104	|	|	1204	|	1304	|	1404	|	...	1504
52	**Ardrossan Harbour** a.	|	...	...	|	...	...	0925	...	|	...	|	...	...	|	1209	1207	|	...	|	...	|	...	1507
64	Fairlie d.	0714	...	...	0814	...	...	...	...	0937	...	1039	...	...	1137	...	...	1237	...	1339	...	1437	...	...
69	**Largs** a.	0721	...	...	0820	...	...	...	...	0944	...	1053	...	...	1153	...	...	1253	...	1353	...	1453	...	...

For an explanation of standard symbols see page 4

Table 592 — GLASGOW - ARDROSSAN - LARGS
2 class only

	✕	✕	✕	⑦	✕	⑦	✕	✕	✕	✕		✕	✕	✕	✕	✕	✕	✕	✕	✕		✕	⑦	✕
Glasgow Central d.	1445	1515	1545	1620	1645	1650	1655	1720	1735	1745	...	1815	1845	1915	1945	2015	2045	2115	2145	2215	...	2245	2245	2315
Paisley Gilmour Street d.	1455	1525	1555	1630	1655	1700	1706	1731	1745	1755	...	1825	1855	1925	1955	2025	2055	2125	2155	2225	...	2255	2255	2325
Kilwinning d.	1518	1552	1618	1657	1720	1725	1727	1754	1812	1820	...	1852	1918	1952	2018	2052	2118	2152	2218	2252	...	2318	2325	2352
Ardrossan South Beach a.	1526	1600	1626	1710	1728	1734	1735	1802	1820	1828	...	1900	1926	2004	2026	2100	2126	2200	2226	2300	...	2326	2333	2359
Ardrossan Town a.		1604				1738			1824				1904		2007		2104		2204			2304		
Ardrossan Harbour a.						1742	1743																	
Fairlie d.	1537		1637	1722	1740			1813		1839			1937		2037		2137		2237			2337	2344	0011
Largs a.	1553		1653	1728	1746			1820		1848			1946		2046		2146		2246			2344	2350	0017

	✕	✕	Ⓐ	⑦	Ⓐ	⑥	Ⓐ	Ⓐ	⑥	✕	R	✕	R	✕	R	✕	⑦	R	✕	R	✕
Largs d.	...	0642	...	0725	0742	...	0828	...	0853	...	0953	...	1053	...	1153	...	...	1253	...	1353	...
Fairlie d.	...	0647	...	0730	0747	...	0833	...	0858	...	0958	...	1058	...	1158	...	...	1258	...	1358	...
Ardrossan Harbour d.										0930			1033	1133				1230	1235		
Ardrossan Town d.	0633				0814	0833			0933			1033	1133		1233			1333			1433
Ardrossan South Beach d.	0636	0658		0741	0758	0817	0836	0844	0909	0909	0936	1009	1036	1109	1136	1209	1236	1240	1309	1336	1409	1436
Kilwinning d.	0645	0711		0750	0808	0826	0844	0853	0918	0918	0945	1018	1045	1118	1145	1218	1245	1249	1318	1345	1418	1445
Paisley Gilmour Street d.	0711	0735		0813	0834	0852	0911	0917	0940	0940	1011	1040	1111	1140	1211	1240	1311	1310	1340	1411	1440	1511
Glasgow Central a.	0722	0748		0824	0846	0904	0922	0930	0953	0953	1022	1052	1122	1152	1222	1252	1322	1328	1352	1422	1452	1522

	R	✕	R	✕	✕	⑦	✕	✕	⑦	⑦	✕	R	✕	R	✕	R	✕	R	✕	✕
Largs d.	1453	...	1553	...	1650	1658	...	1735	...	1758	...	1853	...	1953	...	2053	...	2153	...	2253
Fairlie d.	1458	...	1558	...	1655	1703	...	1740	...	1803	...	1858	...	1958	...	2058	...	2158	...	2258
Ardrossan Harbour d.		1530							1803	1803				2030						
Ardrossan Town d.		1533		1633			1738		1806			1833		1933		2033		2133	2233	
Ardrossan South Beach d.	1509	1536	1609	1636	1706	1714	1740	1751	1809	1809	1814	1836	1909	1936	2009	2036	2109	2136	2209	2236	2309
Kilwinning d.	1518	1545	1618	1645	1715	1723	1747	1800	1818	1818	1823	1845	1918	1945	2018	2045	2118	2145	2218	2245	2318
Paisley Gilmour Street d.	1540	1611	1640	1711	1741	1748	1811	1822	1840	1838	1848	1911	1940	2011	2040	2111	2140	2211	2242	2311	2340
Glasgow Central a.	1552	1622	1652	1722	1754	1759	1822	1834	1852	1850	1859	1922	1952	2022	2052	2122	2152	2222	2254	2322	2352

R – Daily (On ⑦ runs 5 minutes later Largs - Paisley, arrives Glasgow 14 minutes later).

Table 593 — GLASGOW - OBAN, FORT WILLIAM and MALLAIG
2 class only

km		G✕	✕	✕	✕✕	✕J	✕✕	E	E✕
	London Euston 550 d.	1950v							
0	Glasgow Queen Street ▲ d.	...			0812 0812	1242 1242		1812	1812
26	Dumbarton Central ▲ d.				0836 0836	1306 1306		1836	1836
41	Helensburgh Upper ▲ d.	0508s			0853 0853	1323 1323		1853	1853
52	Garelochhead d.	0523s			0904 0904	1334 1334		1905	1905
69	Arrochar and Tarbet d.	0546s			0924 0924	1355 1355		1925	1925
82	Ardlui d.	0602s			0943 0943	1410 1410		1947	1947
96	Crianlarich a.	0623s			0959 0959	1425 1425		2002	2002
96	Crianlarich d.				1005 1011	1431 1437		2008	2014
123	Dalmally d.				1029	1455		2032	
142	Taynuilt d.				1147	1514		2052	
163	Oban a.				1110	1537		2115	
116	Bridge of Orchy d.	0654s			1036	1502			2039
140	Rannoch d.	0721s			1057	1523			2106
178	Roy Bridge d.	0812s			1135	1601			2144
183	Spean Bridge d.	0818s			1141	1607			2150
198	Fort William a.	0835			1154	1620			2203
198	Fort William d.		0845		1200	1625			2210
223	Glenfinnan d.		0917		1232	1700			2242
252	Arisaig d.		0950		1306	1732			2315
260	Morar d.		0958		1314	1740			2323
264	Mallaig a.		1005		1325	1747			2330

	✕✕	✕	✕✕	✕J		E✕	E	✕	K⑦	LⒶ
Mallaig d.	0600		1030			1610		1815		
Morar d.	0607		1037			1617		1822		
Arisaig d.	0616		1046			1626		1831		
Glenfinnan d.	0648		1118			1659		1903		
Fort William a.	0720		1153			1731		1935		
Fort William d.	0730		1203			1738			1900	1950
Spean Bridge d.	0743		1216			1751			1918u	2007u
Roy Bridge d.	0749		1222			1757			1924u	2013u
Rannoch d.	0829		1304			1836			2014u	2107u
Bridge of Orchy d.	0849		1324			1855			2043u	2131u
Oban d.		0805		1235			1808			
Taynuilt d.		0827		1257			1830			
Dalmally d.		0847		1316			1851			
Crianlarich a.	0919	0919	1348	1346		1922	1922			
Crianlarich d.	0925	0925	1353	1353		1928	1928		2121u	2202u
Ardlui d.	0942	0942	1411	1411		1946	1946		2141u	2222u
Arrochar and Tarbet d.	0957	0957	1426	1426		2000	2000		2159u	2238u
Garelochhead d.	1016	1016	1449	1449		2019	2019		2226u	2302u
Helensburgh Upper ▲ d.	1028	1028	1501	1501		2031	2031		2240u	2315u
Dumbarton Central ▲ d.	1045	1045	1515	1515		2045	2045			
Glasgow Queen Street ▲ a.	1114	1114	1544	1544		2114	2114			
London Euston 550 a.	...	...	...	...		...	...		0747	0747

G – Runs ⑧ only (not Jan. 1) from London: [sleeper] 1, 2 cl. London - Fort William.
E – Runs daily.
J – Also runs ⑦ Sept. 25 - Oct. 30.
K – Runs ⑦ only (not Jan. 1): [sleeper] 1, 2 cl. Fort William - London.
L – Runs Ⓐ only: [sleeper] 1, 2 cl. Fort William - London.

s – Stops to set down only.
u – Stops to pick up only.
v – Departs 1950 on ⑦, 2025 on Ⓐ.
▲ – Frequent local services operate: Glasgow - Helensburgh Lower and v.v.
✧ – Timings subject to confirmation.

Table 594 — ⛴ MALLAIG - KYLE OF LOCHALSH
Summer only service

Service operates ⑤ only May 19 - Sept. 15.   Journey time 2 hours.   A ✕ service is available on the ship.   **Operator:** Caledonian MacBrayne ☎ (01475) 650100 Fax : (01475) 637607

From Mallaig: 1230.   From Kyle of Lochalsh: 1530.

Table 595 — ABERDEEN - ELGIN - INVERNESS
1, 2 class

km							Ⓐ G♀				⑦ ♀	♀	⑦ ♀			♀	Ⓐ ♀	⑦ ♀		Ⓐ	♀ H♀			♀	⑦ ♀	♀
0	Aberdeen .... d.	...	...	0628	0727	0824	0847	...	0922	1000	1137	1300	...	1518	1633	1714	1714	1741	1812	...	2000	2048	2140
10	Dyce + ... d.	...	...	0637	0739	0833	0856	...	0931	1009	1146	1309	...	1527	1642	1724	1724	1750	1821	...	2012	2057	2149
27	Inverurie .... d.	...	...	0650	0755			...	0943	1021	1158	1321	...	1542	...	1736	1736	...	1834	...	2024	2109	2201
44	Insch .... d.	...	...	0703	0807			...	0956	1034	1211	1333	...	1555	...	1749	1749	...	1847	...	2037	2122	2214
66	Huntly .... d.	...	...	0723	0824	0910		...	1019	1051	1228	1350	...	1613	...	1806	1806	...	1904	...	2054	2139	2230
85	Keith .... d.	0620	...	0736	0838	0932		...	1033	1106	1242	1404	...	1632	...	1819	1819	...	1918	...	2107	2159	2244
116	Elgin .... d.	0644	...	0759	0901			...	1058	1129	1304	1434	...	1655	...	1843	1848	...	1941	...	2130	2222	2305
135	Forres .... d.	0659	...	0814	0916			...	1117	1144	1318	1449	...	1710	...	1858	1903	...	1956	...	2145	2237	2320
150	Nairn .... d.	0710	...	0827	0927			...	1128	1155	1329	1500	...	1728	...	1909	1914	...	2007	...	2158	2248	2331
174	Inverness .... a.	0730	...	0847	0947			...	1148	1215	1350	1520	...	1748	...	1929	1934	...	2027	...	2218	2308	2350

				Ⓐ G♀		Ⓐ	⑥			⑦ ♀	E♀	♀		Ⓐ K♀	♀		Ⓐ		♀	⑦ ♀	♀	⑦ ♀	♀
Inverness .... d.	0454	...	0600	...	...	0807	0807	...	0955	1045	1222	...	1352	...	1523	...	...	1706	1752	1806	2045	2135	2137
Nairn .... d.	0511	...	0617	...	0831	0831	...	1012	1102	1239	1409	...	1540	...	...	1725	1809	1823	2102	2152	2201
Forres .... d.	0522	...	0628	...	0842	0841	...	1023	1113	1250	1420	...	1551	...	...	1736	1820	1834	2113	2203	2212
Elgin .... d.	0538	...	0644	...	0905	0905	...	1038	1129	1309	1435	...	1606	...	...	1750	1836	1850	2131	2219	2228
Keith .... d.	0601	...	0706	...	0928	0928	0944	1101	1152	1332	1458	...	1629	...	...	1813	...	1913	2154	...	...
Huntly .... d.	0619	...	0722	...		0942	0958	1118	1206	1351	1512	...	1643	...	...	1831	...	1930	2208	...	...
Insch .... d.	0636	...	0740	...		1000	1014	1134	1222	1407	1528	...	1658	...	...	1847	...	1946	2224	...	...
Inverurie .... d.	0651	...	0754	...		1012	1026	1146	1234	1419	1541	...	1710	...	...	1859	...	1958	2236	...	...
Dyce + ... d.	0703	0713	0806	0902	1020	1024	1038	1158	1246	1431	1553	1652	1725	...	1755	1911	...	2011	2248	...	...
Aberdeen .... a.	0714	0756	0818	0913	1032	1036	1050	1210	1258	1443	1605	1702	1738	...	1805	1922	...	2022	2300	...	...

E – 🚇 and ♀ Inverness - Edinburgh.
G – 🚇 and ♀ Glasgow Queen Street - Dyce and v.v.
H – 🚇 and ♀ Glasgow Queen Street - Inverness.
K – 🚇 and ♀ Dyce - Edinburgh.
L – 🚇 and ♀ Glasgow Queen Street - Perth - Inverness - Elgin.

Table 596 — INVERNESS - OBAN

		G ⤬	H ⤬	G ⤬	H ⤬	H ⤬	G ⤬	H ⤬	H ⤬	H ⑦	G ⤬
Inverness (Bus Station)........ d.		...	...	1000	1110	1330	1455	1740	1915	1950	
Fort Augustus..................... d.		...	...	1058	1208	1425	1610	1838	2013	2045	
Fort William (An Aird)........... a.		...	...	1150	1300	1515	1702	1930	2105	2135	
Fort William (An Aird)........... d.		0645	0720	0945		1330	...				
Ballachulish (Square)............ d.		0730	0745f	1015		1353					
Oban (Rail Station)............... a.		0835	0848	1120		1500					

	H ⤬	H ⤬	H ⤬	G ⑦	H ⤬	H ⑦	G ⤬	G ⤬	H
Oban (Rail Station)............. d.	...	...	0915	1300	...	1605	...	1600	
Ballachulish (Square)........ d.	...	...	1018f	1405	...	1710	...	1707	
Fort William (An Aird)....... a.	...	...	1043	1432	...	1737	...	1730	
Fort William (An Aird)....... d.	0728	0850	1050	...	1520	1700	...	1755	
Fort Augustus.................. d.	0820	0942	1142	...	1612p	1752	...	1845	
Inverness (Bus Station)...... a.	0926	1040	1240	...	1710p	1850	...	1940	

G – Operated by Gaelic Bus, Ballachulish (timings subject to conformation): ☎ (018552) 229.
H – Operated by Highland Bus & Coach, Inverness: ☎ (01463) 233371.
f – Ballachulish Ferry (Hotel).
p – 13 mins later on schooldays.

Table 597 — INVERNESS - KYLE OF LOCHALSH, THURSO and WICK
No Sunday service during Winter
2 class only

	⤬ ♀	⤬	⤬	⤬	⤬		⤬	⤬	⤬
Inverness .... d.	0720	...	0800	1040	1100	...	1532	1800	1838
Muir of Ord .... d.	0736	...	0816	1059	1117	...	1548	1816	1854
Dingwall .... d.	0746	...	0826	1109	1126	...	1558	1826	1914
Garve .... d.		...	0850	1132		...			1935
Achnasheen............ d.		...	0917	1203		...			2002
Strathcarron .... d.		...	0945	1233		...			2030
Stromeferry .... d.		...	1003	1251		...			2048
Plockton .... d.		...	1015	1303		...			2059
Kyle of Lochalsh ..... a.		...	1030	1320		...			2115
Invergordon .... d.	0802	...			1142	...	1614	1847	...
Tain .... d.	0818	...			1158	...	1629	1903	...
Ardgay .... d.	0838	...			1213	...		1918	...
Lairg .... d.	0856	...			1230	...		1935	...
Golspie .... d.	0918	...			1252	...		1959	...
Brora .... d.	0928	...			1307	...		2009	...
Helmsdale .... d.	0943x	...			1322x	...		2024x	...
Georgemas Junction .. a.	1042	...			1422	...		2124	...
Georgemas Junction .. d.	1045	1045			1425	1425		2127	2127
Thurso .... a.	1100				1440			2142	
Wick .... a.	...	1104				1444			2146

	⤬	⤬ ♀	⤬	⤬	⤬	⤬ ♀	⤬	⤬	⤬
Wick .... d.	...	0605	...	1124	...	...	1530	...
Thurso .... d.	...		0613		1132	1538		...
Georgemas Junction . a.	...	0621	0626	1140	1145	1551	1546	
Georgemas Junction . d.	...		0631		1150		1600	
Helmsdale .... d.	...		0729		1248x		1659x	
Brora .... d.	...		0745		1306		1714	
Golspie .... d.	...		0754		1315		1724	
Lairg .... d.	...		0818		1338		1750	
Ardgay .... d.	...		0837		1354		1806	
Tain .... d.	...		0852		1409	1642	1821	
Invergordon .... d.	...		0912		1429	1702	1844	
Kyle of Lochalsh . d.	0710		1148				1705	
Plockton .... d.	0723		1201				1718	
Stromeferry.......... d.	0735		1213				1730	
Strathcarron .... d.	0753		1234				1748	
Achnasheen.......... d.	0821		1302				1817	
Garve .... d.	0849	:..	1330				1844	
Dingwall .... d.	0914		0930	1355		1448	1720	1906	1916
Muir of Ord .... d.	0923		0939	1404		1457	1729	1915	1925
Inverness .... a.	0939		0957	1420		1513	1745	1935	1948

x – Stops on request.

Table 599 — ⛴ SCOTTISH ISLAND FERRIES
⛴ CalMac

Caledonian MacBrayne operate numerous services linking the Scottish mainland with the Western Isles as well as inter-island services. Some routes are seasonal. Principal routes are shown on the map (page 276), although others are also operated. For further details contact the operator: Caledonian MacBrayne ☎ (01475) 650100 Fax (01475) 637607.

Table 600

EDINBURGH and GLASGOW - ABERDEEN

For additional services Edinburgh and Glasgow - Perth, see Table 605

1, 2 class

Block 1

km	Station																					
		ⓑ	✕	✕D	✕	⊗	⊗	⊗	⊗	⊗	⑦	⑦2	⊗	⑦	⑦F	⊗	⑦	⑦2	⊗	⊗	
	London Kings Cross 570 d.	2105r																			
0	Edinburgh d.				0648	0705		0810		0840	0855	0910	0915		1020		1055	1110	1115		1210
42	Kirkcaldy d.	0532s			0721	0740		0842		0917	0931	0943	1000		1057		1130	1142	1200		1243
54	Markinch d.				0730	0749		0851		0926		1008					1151	1208			1252
82	Leuchars (for St Andrews) d.	0601s				0811		0911		0951	0955	1009	1030		1121		1154	1211	1230		1314
	Glasgow Queen Street d.			0550			0725		0825			0925	0925		1025				1125	1125	
	Stirling d.			0621			0753		0853			0953	0956		1053				1153	1156	
	Perth d.		0625	0700	0808		0829		0927			1027	1034		1127				1227	1234	
95	Dundee d.	0620s	0648	0723	0833	0827	0852	0926	0950	1006	1010	1024	1050	1050	1057	1135	1150	1208	1226	1250 1257	1326
123	Arbroath d.	0640s	0707	0742		0844	0909	0947	1007		1026	1041		1107	1114	1152	1209	1225	1243	1307	1314 1345
145	Montrose d.	0658s	0722	0759		0859	0924	1002			1042	1056		1122	1129	1207	1224	1240	1258	1322	1329 1402
184	Stonehaven d.	0726s	0745	0822		0922	0947	1025			1104			1145	1152	1229	1247	1303		1345	1352
210	Aberdeen a.	0750	0807	0844		0942	1009	1045	1100		1136	1138		1205	1219	1250	1307	1332	1338	1405	1419 1442

Block 2

	⊗	⑦	⑦2	⊗	⑦	⊗	⑦2	⑦E	⊗	Ⓐ	⑥	⑦	⑥	Ⓐ	⊗	⑦	⑦2	⊗	⊗	
London Kings Cross 570 d.						1030						1030								
Edinburgh d.		1310	1315		1410		1457	1515			1620	1630		1620		1700	1700	1715	1714	
Kirkcaldy d.		1342	1400		1443		1532	1600			1659	1707		1659		1735	1735	1758	1759	
Markinch d.		1351	1408		1452			1608			1708			1708		1745		1806	1808	
Leuchars (for St Andrews) d.		1411	1430		1514		1556	1630			1729	1737		1729		1806	1806	1828	1835	
Glasgow Queen Street d.	1225			1325	1325		1425			1525	1525		1625			1625			1725	1725
Stirling d.	1253			1353	1356		1453			1553	1556		1653			1653			1756	1753
Perth d.	1327			1427	1434		1527			1627	1634		1722			1727			1829	1832
Dundee d.	1350	1426	1450	1450	1457	1526	1550	1610	1650	1650	1657		1744	1743	1751	1750	1750		1820	1820 1846 1849 1852 1855
Arbroath d.	1407	1446		1507	1514	1545		1627		1710	1714		1759	1807	1809	1809			1837	1837 1909 1914
Montrose d.		1501		1522	1529	1600		1642		1725	1729		1815	1823	1824	1824			1852	1852 1924 1929
Stonehaven d.				1545	1552			1704		1748	1752		1837	1837	1845	1847	1847		1915	1915 1947 1952
Aberdeen a.	1500	1541		1605	1619	1641	1659	1725		1808	1812		1858	1900	1905	1907	1907		1935	1937 2007 2014

Block 3

	⊗	Ⓐ	⑥	⊗	⑦	2	⊗	⑦	2	Ⓐ	⑦K	⑥	2	⑦	⑦2	⊗	2	⊗
London Kings Cross 570 d.		1400	1400		1330				1600									
Edinburgh d.	1810	1835	1855		1910	1915			2015	2035	2052	2110	2122		2125		2225	2310
Kirkcaldy d.	1847	1910	1930		1945	1958			2058	2111	2126	2144	2205		2208		2308	2350
Markinch d.	1856					2006			2106		2153	2213			2216		2316	2359
Leuchars (for St Andrews) d.	1918	1934	1955		2015	2028			2128	2135	2150	2215	2235		2238		2338	0021
Glasgow Queen Street d.				1825			1925	1925		2025				2125		2125		2333c
Stirling d.				1853			1953	1956		2053				2153		2156		0013
Perth d.				1932			2027	2034		2130				2227		2234		0052
Dundee d.	1932	1950	2009	1957	2030	2046	2050	2057	2143	2153	2156	2205	2229	2249	2254	2255	2300	2355 0036
Arbroath d.	1949	2006	2025	2014	2046		2107	2114		2212	2221	2246		2313		2319		
Montrose d.	2004	2025	2046	2029	2102		2122	2129		2228	2237	2301		2328		2334		
Stonehaven d.		2047	2108	2052	2124		2145	2152		2250	2259	2324		2351		2357		
Aberdeen a.	2044	2110	2130	2115	2145		2205	2212		2310	2322	2345		0013		0017		

Block 4 (Aberdeen → Edinburgh/Glasgow)

	2	Ⓐ	S	2	⑦	⊗	⑥	⑦	⑦	⊗	⊗	2	⊗	⑦K	⑦	⑦D	⑦	✕	2
Aberdeen d.		0512			0627	0650	0707	0710		0724		0755		0828	0910		0910 0926	0935	0955
Stonehaven d.		0531			0646	0707	0724	0727				0812		0845	0927		0927 0943	0952	1012
Montrose d.		0554			0709	0730				0801		0834		0908	0949		0950 1006	1014	1034
Arbroath d.		0608			0723	0744				0815		0848		0922	1004		1004 1020	1029	1049
Dundee d.	0618	0637	0640		0722	0727	0745	0805	0818	0817 0832	0836	0839	0906	0927	0945		1020 1027	1032 1045	1101 1106 1127
Perth d.		0700				0808		0840	0840	0840 0855		0904		1008			1055 1108		
Stirling d.		0737				0840		0910		0931		0940		1040			1131 1140		
Glasgow Queen Street a.		0814				0913		0943	0940	1014		1010		1110			1211 1210		
Leuchars (for St Andrews) d.	0631		0652		0735	0739		0817		0848		0919	0939		1034	1039		1114 1119	1139
Markinch d.	0655		0717		0801	0803		0841		0912			1003			1103			1203
Kirkcaldy d.	0704		0725		0811	0812		0850		0921		0943	1012		1100	1112		1138 1143	1212
Edinburgh a.	0748		0804		0853	0858		0926		0957		1020	1058		1140	1150		1218 1220	1259
London Kings Cross 570 a.												1501						1758 1659

Block 5

	✕	✕	⑦	⑦	⑦	⑦	⑦K	2	⊗	⊗	⑦J	⑦	⑦	⑦	2	✕	✕	⑦	⑦
Aberdeen d.		1030		1110	1117	1135	1135	1150	1216		1235	1310	1310	1335	1335		1420	1435	1455 1500 1525 1523 1525
Stonehaven d.		1047		1127		1152	1207	1235			1327	1327		1352			1437		1512 1520 1542 1540 1542
Montrose d.		1110		1150	1154		1214	1229	1258			1350	1350		1414		1500		1534 1542 1605 1602 1605
Arbroath d.		1124		1204	1208	1224	1229	1244	1312		1324	1404	1404	1424	1424		1514		1549 1557 1619 1617 1619
Dundee d.	1132	1145		1232	1227	1245	1301	1316	1327	1327	1345	1427	1432	1445	1445	1501	1530	1545	1606 1627 1643 1645 1645
Perth d.		1208		1255		1308			1408		1455	1508			1608				1708 1708
Stirling d.		1240		1331		1340			1440		1531	1540			1640				1740 1744
Glasgow Queen Street a.		1310		1411		1412			1510		1611	1610			1710				1814 1824
Leuchars (for St Andrews) d.	1144			1239	1314	1329	1342	1339		1439		1514	1539	1542		1619	1639		1657
Markinch d.	1208			1303			1403	1403		1503			1603	1603			1723		
Kirkcaldy d.	1217			1312		1338	1356	1412	1412	1512		1538	1612	1612		1643	1704		1732
Edinburgh a.	1253			1348		1418	1439	1448	1458	1548		1618	1658	1648		1720	1741		1809
London Kings Cross 570 a.				1955									2152				2226		

Block 6

	✕	⑦		✕	⊗	✕		✕		✕	✕	✕	⑦	⑦	✕	⑦H	✕	✕	Ⓐ	ⓑ
		2		B			2				2			2		H			H	
Aberdeen d.	1615		1630		1712	1748	1815		1826		1900	1932	1932	2000		2025	2032	2050	2114 2130	2230
Stonehaven d.			1647		1732	1807	1832		1843		1917	1951	1951			2045u	2049	2109	2131 2150u	2249
Montrose d.	1652		1710		1754	1830	1854		1906		1940	2013	2013	2037		2112u	2112	2134	2154 2217u	2312
Arbroath d.	1706		1724		1809	1844	1909		1920		1954	2028	2028	2051		2130u	2126	2148	2208 2235u	2326
Dundee d.	1727	1727	1745		1827	1907	1927	1927	1944	1953	2012	2045	2045	2109	2127	2127	2150u	2145	2205 2227 2255u	2347
Perth d.			1808		1930		2007				2108	2108				2208			0011
Stirling d.			1840		2001		2042				2140	2147				2240			
Glasgow Queen Street a.			1912		2042		2110				2212	2220				2314			
Leuchars (for St Andrews) d.	1739	1739		1839		1940	1939		2006	2025			2122	2139	2140	2205u		2219	2239 2310u	
Markinch d.	1803	1803		1905			2003		2030				2203	2204					
Kirkcaldy d.	1812	1812		1914		2004	2012		2039	2052			2147	2212	2213	2235u		2244	2312 2340u	
Edinburgh a.	1848	1858		1950		2042	2058		2123	2127			2223	2258	2257			2320	2357	
London Kings Cross 570 a.															0710e			0710v	

A – 🛏 1, 2 cl. and 🍴 London Euston - Aberdeen.
B – 🍴 and ♀ Dyce - Edinburgh.
D – 🍴 and ♀ Glasgow - Dyce and v.v.
E – 🍴 and ♀ Glasgow - Inverness.
F – 🍴 and ♀ Leeds - Aberdeen.

H – 🛏 1, 2 cl. and 🍴 Aberdeen - London Euston.
J – 🍴 and ♀ Inverness - Edinburgh.
K – 🍴 and ♀ Plymouth - Birmingham - Aberdeen and v.v.
S – 🍴 and ♀ Dundee - Birmingham - Penzance.

c – Depart 2340 on ⑦.
e – London Euston.
r – London Euston. Depart 2205 on Ⓐ.
s – Stops to set down only.   u – Stops to pick up only.
v – London Euston. Arrive 0715 on ⑥.

For an explanation of standard symbols see page 4

Table 605 — GLASGOW and EDINBURGH - INVERNESS

For additional services Glasgow and Edinburgh - Perth, see Table **600**

1, 2 class

Inverness-bound (morning/midday)

km	Station	⑧ A	times
	London Kings Cross 570 d.	1950f	
0	Glasgow Queen Street d.		0710 · 0925 · 0925 · 1155 · 1355
	Edinburgh d.		0645 · 0648 · 0748 · 0848 · 0935 · 0940 · 0948 · 1048 · 1125 · 1148 · 1248 · 1340
	Kirkcaldy d.		0721 · 1010 · 1013 · 1200 · 1413
	Markinch d.		0730 · 1022 · 1209
	Falkirk Grahamston d.		0715 · 0818 · 0918 · 1018 · 1118 · 1218 · 1318
47	Stirling d.	0508s	0733 · 0738 · 0836 · 0936 · 0953 · 0956 · 1036 · 1136 · 1223 · 1236 · 1336 · 1423
	Perth a.	0551s	0804 · 0815 · 1025 · 1033 · 1048 · 1055 · 1242 · 1259 · 1453 · 1500
100	Perth d.		0815 · 1050 · 1057 · 1300 · 1506
147	Pitlochry d.	0629s	0846 · 1122 · 1127 · 1331 · 1536
157	Blair Atholl d.	0641s	0856 · 1132 · 1137 · 1341 · 1546
211	Newtonmore d.	0725s	0931 · 1208 · 1417 · 1625
216	Kingussie d.	0731s	0936 · 1213 · 1214 · 1422 · 1638
235	Aviemore d.	0749s	0949 · 1226 · 1227 · 1435 · 1638
246	Carrbridge d.		0959 · 1236 · 1444
290	Inverness a.	0840	1032 · 1310 · 1312 · 1515 · 1725

Inverness-bound (afternoon/evening)

Station	⑦ E	times
London Kings Cross 570 d.		1200 · 1300
Glasgow Queen Street d.	1355	1525 · 1625 · 1625 · 1755 · 1925
Edinburgh d.	1340	1348 · 1448 · 1540 · 1548 · 1640 · 1648 · 1714 · 1727 · 1740 · 1748 · 1844 · 1848 · 1940 · 2018 · 2118 · 2218 · 2318
Kirkcaldy d.	1415	1615 · 1759 · 1813 · 2013
Markinch d.		1624 · 1808 · 1836 · 2022
Falkirk Grahamston d.		1426 · 1518 · 1618 · 1705 · 1718 · 1818 · 1915 · 1918 · 2048 · 2148 · 2248 · 2348
Stirling d.	1426	1436 · 1536 · 1553 · 1636 · 1653 · 1721 · 1736 · 1826 · 1836 · 1932 · 1936 · 1953 · 2106 · 2206 · 2306 · 0006
Perth a.	1455	1506 · 1625 · 1659 · 1721 · 1725 · 1758 · 1845 · 1911 · 1853 · 1903 · 2009 · 2025 · 2055 · 2249 · 2349
Perth d.	1515	1700 · 1800 · 1905 · 2010 · 2057
Pitlochry d.	1546	1732 · 1830 · 1935 · 2043 · 2127
Blair Atholl d.	1556	1742 · 1945 · 2137
Newtonmore d.	1633	1817 · 2020 · 2213
Kingussie d.	1638	1822 · 1913 · 2025 · 2131 · 2218
Aviemore d.	1652	1835 · 1932 · 2041 · 2143 · 2231
Carrbridge d.	1701	2050 · 2241
Inverness a.	1733	1915 · 2010 · 2127 · 2220 · 2312

Glasgow/Edinburgh-bound (morning/midday)

Station	times
Inverness d.	0638 · 0750 · 0940 · 1035 · 1213
Carrbridge d.	0710 · 1010 · 1251
Aviemore d.	0719 · 0825 · 1018 · 1113 · 1300
Kingussie d.	0732 · 0838 · 1030 · 1125 · 1312
Newtonmore d.	0736 · 1035 · 1129 · 1316
Blair Atholl d.	0811 · 1109 · 1202 · 1350
Pitlochry d.	0820 · 0919 · 1120 · 1212 · 1359
Perth a.	0855 · 0950 · 1154 · 1245 · 1431
Perth d.	0856 · 0904 · 0920 · 0952 · 1008 · 1155 · 1245 · 1252 · 1435 · 1500
Stirling d.	0632 · 0649 · 0723 · 0705 · 0810 · 0902 · 0940 · 0958 · 1002 · 1027 · 1040 · 1102 · 1202 · 1232 · 1302 · 1327 · 1402 · 1509 · 1532
Falkirk Grahamston d.	0652 · 0742 · 0829 · 0922 · 1016 · 1022 · 1045 · 1122 · 1222 · 1247 · 1300 · 1322 · 1422 · 1552
Markinch d.	0736 · 0928 · 1330
Kirkcaldy a.	0745 · 0937 · 1530 · 1539
Edinburgh a.	0725 · 0816 · 0826 · 0902 · 0955 · 1013 · 1055 · 1118 · 1157 · 1256 · 1318 · 1355 · 1410 · 1455 · 1615 · 1625
Glasgow Queen Street a.	0732 · 1010 · 1110 · 1335 · 1409 · 1541
London Kings Cross 570 a.	1606k · 1848

Glasgow/Edinburgh-bound (afternoon/evening)

Station	⑧ A	times
Inverness d.	2030	1310 · 1435 · 1610 · 1645 · 1830 · 1830 · 2005 · 2010
Carrbridge d.		1343 · 1643 · 1908 · 1908
Aviemore d.	2122u	1351 · 1521 · 1653 · 1725 · 1916 · 1916 · 2044 · 2102u
Kingussie d.	2137u	1403 · 1533 · 1705 · 1737 · 1928 · 1928 · 2056 · 2117u
Newtonmore d.	2143u	1408 · 1709 · 1741 · 1933 · 1933 · 2100 · 2123u
Blair Atholl d.	2225u	1443 · 1609 · 1742 · 1819 · 2006 · 2006 · 2138 · 2205u
Pitlochry d.	2237u	1453 · 1618 · 1751 · 1831 · 2016 · 2016 · 2147 · 2217u
Perth a.		1526 · 1652 · 1823 · 1903 · 2050 · 2049 · 2219
Perth d.	2320u	1530 · 1550 · 1655 · 1708 · 1828 · 1906 · 1910 · 2050 · 2050 · 2108 · 2108 · 2220 · 2255u
Stirling d.	0005u	1602 · 1605 · 1704 · 1740 · 1802 · 1902 · 1905 · 1939 · 2006 · 2032 · 2132 · 2140 · 2147 · 2250 · 2302 · 2340u
Falkirk Grahamston d.		1622 · 1722 · 1822 · 1922 · 2022 · 2052 · 2152 · 2322
Markinch d.		1729 · 1941
Kirkcaldy a.		1626 · 1738 · 1950 · 2128 · 2132
Edinburgh a.		1655 · 1703 · 1755 · 1814 · 1856 · 1955 · 2026 · 2056 · 2125 · 2206 · 2210 · 2227 · 2355
Glasgow Queen Street a.		1640 · 1814 · 1945 · 2012 · 2212 · 2220 · 2320
London Kings Cross 570 a.		0747e · 0747e

Notes

A – 1, 2 cl. London **Euston** (Table 550) - Inverness and v.v.
B – and ⚍ Glasgow - Aberdeen (Table 600) and v.v.
C – Edinburgh - Dundee (Table 600).
E – and ⚍ Glasgow - Inverness - Elgin (Table 595).
N – and ⚍ Glasgow - Aberdeen - Inverness (Table 595).
Q – Dundee (Table 600) - Glasgow.

b – Conveys ✕ on ⑥.
e – London **Euston**.
f – London **Euston**. Depart 2025 on ⑥.
g – Ⓐ only.
h – Ⓑ only.
k – Arrive 1600 on ⑥.
s – Stops to **set down** only.
u – Stops to **pick up** only.

TAILOR YOUR OWN TOUR WITH A LITTLE HELP FROM . . .

NEW *On the Rails around Britain and Ireland*

Day Trips and Holidays by Train

Covers over 200 places of interest

40 rail routes connecting all main sightseeing destinations

Ideal for days out by train or extended rail tours

NEW *On the Rails around France, Belgium, The Netherlands and Luxembourg*

The Practical Guide to Holidays by Train

Inter-Rail passes now cover these countries as a single zone

Over 40 expertly chosen rail routes and descriptions of over 150 popular destinations

- Dozens of recommended routes, accompanied by at-a-glance route diagrams and practical details of rail connections
- Clear maps of cities and regions
- Detailed descriptions of towns and cities with up-to-date advice on public transport, accommodation, entertainment, sightseeing and lots more
- Suggestions for side-trips and stopovers
- Selection of ready-made themed tours
- Essential travel information
- Practical advice on rail passes and other fare bargains and how to get the best out of the rail network

The *On the Rails* series of touring handbooks (price £9.95 each) are obtainable from UK bookshops, Thomas Cook UK retail shops, or by post at £11.45 (UK), £13.45 (Europe), or £15.45 (overseas) from Thomas Cook Publishing (TPO/FE) at PO Box 227, Peterborough PE3 8BQ. ☎ (01733) 505821/268943

Thomas Cook

IRELAND

Operators:	Northern Ireland Railways (NIR); Iarnród Éireann (IE); Bus Éireann (BE).
Timings:	Rail services - valid until further notice. Trains between Belfast and Dublin are subject to delay during major engineering works. Bus services - valid to **May 7, 1995**.
Services:	In Northern Ireland, most trains on the Belfast - Dublin line convey First Class accommodation; all other trains are Standard class only and are shown as "2" in the tables. In the Republic of Ireland, First class is available on all lines except Dublin - Rosslare, and Limerick - Rosslare (Tables **637** and **643**). In business hour trains on the Dublin to Cork line, a premium service (**CityGold**) replaces ordinary ordinary first class accommodation, and a higher fare is charged. Restaurant and buffet cars are operated by both **NIR** and **IE**. CityGold and First class passengers can usually be served meals at their seats.
	Bus services are shown to areas where there is no rail service, or to improve upon the number of daily journeys possible. Bus services may not call at the rail station, but usually stop nearby. On longer routes, a change of bus may be required. Full details of bus services should be obtained from Bus Éireann. Dublin Busaras is 5 minutes walk (down the ramp) from Dublin Connolly station; DART 🚃 **90** connects Connolly and Heuston stations at frequent intervals (10–20 minutes journey).

Table 630 — BELFAST - DUNDALK - DUBLIN

1, 2 class except where shown

km		2⚒	2⚒	2⚒	2⚒		2⚒	⚒		2⚒	⚒	⚒		2⚒	2⑦ KX		⑧	2⚒		2⚒	2⑥	2⑤
0	Belfast Central 633 ...... d.	...	...	...	0800	...	0900	...	1000	1100	...	1430	1500	...	1700	...	1715	1800	...	1800	1805	1900
14	Lisburn 633 ...... d.	...	...	...	0918	...	1018	...	1446		...	1718	...	1739	...	...	1823	1847	1918
40	Portadown ...... d.	...	...	0833u	0941	...	1042	1135	...	1510	1535	...	1742	1810	1808	...	1835	1852	1916	1946
70	Newry ...... d.	...	...		1002	...	1103	1156	...	1532	1556	...	1803	1832	1832	...	1858	1918	1941	2010
94	Dundalk ...... d.	0553	0632	0724	0813		1018	...	1122	1214	...	1551	1611	...	1819	1853	1903	...	1917	1937	2000
130	Drogheda ...... d.	0620	0700	0752	0837	1005	1046	1130	1149	1243	1531	1618	1638	1748	1846	1917	...	1935	1944	...
181	Dublin Connolly ...... a.	0725	0807	0859	0928	1000	1106	1125	1232	1223	1325	1618	1652	1720	1853	1925	1955	...	2005	2037	2018

	2⑥		2⚒	2⚒	⚒	2⚒		⚒	2⚒	⚒	⚒		⑦ KX	⚒		⑦ ⚒	⑦		⑥	⑧	⑧
Dublin Connolly ...... d.	...	0755	0847	1015	1100	...	1300	1350	1500	1500	...	1719	1748	1755	1820	...	1820	...	1833	1915	2015	2200
Drogheda ...... d.	...	0832	0945	1051	1137	...	1337	1452	1536	1537	...	1812	1900	...	1857	...	1925	2018	2051	2056	2258
Dundalk ...... d.	...	...	0859	...	1119	1204	...	1404	...	1604	1604	...	1844	...	1926	...	2010	2045	2119	2123	2325
Newry ...... d.	0730	0807	0919	...	1138	1224	...	1424	...	1623	1624	1840	...	1919	...	1945s	2000	2032	...	2138	2142
Portadown ...... d.	0800	0807	0945	...	1212	1250	1300	1450	...	1649	1650	1906	...	1945	1953s	2005	2011s	2027	2055	...	2204	2207
Lisburn 633 ...... d.	0828	0835	...	1235		1327	1513	...	1712		1934	...	2010	...	2032	2031s	2055	2123	...	2227	2230
Belfast Central 633 ...... a.	0845	0855	1019	...	1250	1324	1353	1528	...	1730	1724	1951	...	2031	2027	2054	2048	2120	2148	...	2244	2247

Major engineering work near Belfast and Dublin may affect trains until further notice especially on ⑦.   Passengers requiring further information: ☎ + 1 703 366222.

K – Not Apr. 16.
X – Timings subject to confirmation **locally**.
u – Stops to **pick up** only.
s – Stops to **set down** only.

Additional local trains run between Drogheda and Dublin Connolly:
From Drogheda: 0716⚒, 0732⚒, 1307⚒, 1345⚒, 1712⚒, 1816⚒;   **From Dublin:**   0600⚒, 0813⚒, 1112⚒, 1215⚒, 1510⚒, 1546⚒, 1632⚒, 1658⚒, 1734⚒.

Table 631 — COLERAINE - PORTRUSH

2 class only

Rail service Coleraine - Portrush and v.v.   9 km.   Journey time: 13 minutes.
From Coleraine: 0705Ⓐ, 0800⑥, 0802Ⓐ, 0900Ⓐ, 0950Ⓐ, 1010⑥, 1037Ⓐ, 1100⑥, 1144Ⓐ, 1200⑥, 1220Ⓐ, 1310Ⓐ, 1313⑥, 1440⚒, 1505⑦, 1530Ⓐ, 1553⑥, 1555Ⓐ, 1602Ⓐ, 1700⑦, 1704Ⓐ, 1715Ⓐ, 1745⑦, 1755Ⓐ, 1757⑥, 1902Ⓐ, 1920Ⓐ, 2000⚒, 2007⑦, 2121⚒, 2140⑦, 2223⑥, 2225Ⓐ, 2235⑦.
From Portrush: 0635Ⓐ, 0645⑥, 0725Ⓐ, 0825Ⓐ, 0830Ⓐ, 0916⚒, 0930Ⓐ, 1015⚒, 1030⑥, 1053Ⓐ, 1140⑥, 1200Ⓐ, 1240Ⓐ, 1250Ⓐ, 1330⑥, 1335Ⓐ, 1500⚒, 1525⑦, 1546Ⓐ, 1610⑥, 1615⑦, 1637Ⓐ, 1720⑦, 1735⚒, 1830⚒, 1835⑦, 1935Ⓐ, 1937⚒, 2020⚒, 2030⑦, 2200⚒, 2210⑦, 2240⑥, 2241Ⓐ, 2251⑦.

Table 632 — BELFAST - LARNE HARBOUR

NIR   2 class only

Rail service Belfast - Larne and v.v.   39 km.   Journey time: 33 - 50 minutes.   The new link across Belfast to Central Station is now open.
From Belfast Central: 0635Ⓐ, 0640⑥, 0655⑥, 0745⑥, 0755⑥, 0847⑥, 0905⑥, 0908⑥, 1000⑥, 1005Ⓐ, 1100⚒, 1115⑦, 1135Ⓐ, 1245Ⓐ, 1317Ⓐ, 1321⑥, 1350⑦, 1410⚒, 1452⑥, 1500⑦, 1535⑥, 1550⑦, 1615⑥, 1635Ⓐ, 1726Ⓐ, 1730⚒, 1752Ⓐ, 1800⑦, 1808Ⓐ, 1810⑥, 1915⑥, 1917⑥, 2057⚒, 2100⑦, 2155⚒.
From Larne Harbour: 0620Ⓐ, 0625⑥, 0640Ⓐ, 0725Ⓐ, 0753⑥, 0800⑥, 0843⑥, 0857⑥, 1005⚒, 1020⑥, 1030⑥, 1105⚒, 1155Ⓐ, 1205⑦, 1220⑦, 1245Ⓐ, 1350Ⓐ, 1415⚒, 1450⑦, 1500⑥, 1515⑥, 1550⑥, 1645⑥, 1648⑥, 1735⚒, 1825⑥, 1855⑦, 1905⚒, 2010⚒, 2152⚒, 2155⑦.

Trains call at **Carrickfergus**, approx. 17 minutes from Belfast, **Whitehead**, approx. 25 minutes from Belfast, and **Larne Town**, approx. 45 minutes from Belfast.   Additional services operate to or from **Larne Town** and do **not** serve the Harbour station.   Connections are available at Larne Harbour to/from **Stranraer/Cairnryan** 🚢. (Tables 1025, 1030).

Table 633 — BELFAST - COLERAINE - PORTRUSH and LONDONDERRY

2 class only

km		Ⓐ	⑥	Ⓐ	FⒶ	⑦	⑥	Ⓐ	⑥	⑦	⑥	⑦	⑥	⑥	⑥	Ⓐ	⑥	⑦	⑥	⑥	⑦
0	Belfast Central 630 ...... d.	0715	0825	0850	1000	1010	1120	1130	1255	1300	1340	1410	1410	1441	1605	1605	1705	1730	1810	1815	1825	2035	2035	2045
14	Lisburn 630 ...... d.	0733	0843	0908	1018	1028	1138	1148	1313	1328	1358	1428	1428	1514	1623	1624	1733	1748	1833	1843	2053	2053	2107
46	Antrim ...... d.	0808	0917	0943	1054	1100	1212	1222	1351	1404	1430	1500	1500	1547	1659	1701	1814	1824	1900	1907	1917	2130	2132	2142
65	Ballymena ...... d.	0822	0931	0957	1109	1114	1226	1236	1404	1417	1444	1514	1514	1600	1713	1715	1828	1840	1917	1921	1931	2144	2146	2156
111	Coleraine ...... a.	0855	1006	1032	1142v	1147	1303	1309		1517	1547	1547	...	1748	1750	1901	1915	1950	1954	2004	2217	2219	2229
111	Coleraine ...... d.	0857	1008	1033	1144v	1149	1306	1311	...	1521	1549	1549	...	1752	1752	1902	1916	1954	1956	2006	2218	2220	2231
120	Portrush 631 ...... a.					1157v										1915	1929		2019			
165	Londonderry ...... a.	0934	1047	1112		1228	1345	1350		1600	1626	1628	...	1831	1831	...	...	2033	2035	...	2257	2259	2308

	Ⓐ	Ⓐ	⑥	Ⓐ	Ⓐ		⑥	①-④	⑦	Ⓐ	Ⓐ	⑥	⑤	⑥	⑥	Ⓐ	⑥	⑦	Ⓐ	Ⓐ	⑥
Londonderry ...... d.	...	0610	0620	0805	0810	...	0945	...	1105	1120	1135	...	1440	1440	...	1700	1705	1705	...	1900	1910	1910
Portrush 631 ...... d.	...					0925						1335							1835		
Coleraine ...... a.	...	0650	0657	0845	0849	0938	1025	...	1144	1157	1215	...	1348	1520	1519	1739	1745	1744	1848	1939	1949	1949
Coleraine ...... d.	0600	0651	0700	0855	0851	0940	1033	...	1150	1200	1218	...	1352	1524	1523	1741	1751	1753	1850	1942	1953	1953
Ballymena ...... d.	0637	0730	0737	0929	0931	1022	1110	1130	1227	1237	1252	1415	1429	1558	1601	1715	1815	1825	1828	1934	2019	2030	2033
Antrim ...... d.	0651	0744	0751	0943	0931	1036	1124	1145	1241	1251	1306	1430	1445	1613	1615	1729	1829	1842	1948	2033	2044	2047
Lisburn 630 ...... d.	0728	0821	0830	1015	1017	1114	1201	1225	1313	1324	1318	1507	1514	1522	1647	1650	1806	1908	1914	1916	2021	2106	2119	2122
Belfast Central 630 ...... a.	0753	0839	0851	1032	1034	1131	1219	1242	1330	1341	1356	1524	1539	1539	1705	1707	1831	1925	1931	1933	2038	2123	2136	2139

F – ①-④ to Ballymena, ⑤ to Portrush.   v – ⑤ only.

Table 634 — DUBLIN - DONEGAL

Bus Éireann

		⚒		⚒	⑤		⚒			⑥		⚒			
Dublin Busaras ...... d.	...	0900	...	1145	...	1430	1715	1800	**Donegal 635** ...... d.	0800	...	0900	...	1100	...	1500	...	173
Navan ...... d.	...	0947	...	1232	...	1517		1847	Ballyshannon **635** ...... d.	0825	...	0925	...	1125	...	1525	...	175
Kells ...... d.	...	1002	...	1247	...	1532		1902	Enniskillen ...... d.	0910	...	1010	...	1210	...	1610	...	184
Cavan ...... a.	...	1040	...	1325	...	1610	1855	1940	Cavan ...... a.	1000	...	1120	...	1320	...	1720	...	195
Cavan ...... d.	...	1055	...	1340	...	1625	1900	1955	Cavan ...... d.	1015	...	1135	...	1335	...	1735	...	200
Enniskillen ...... d.	...	1205	...	1450	...	1735	1950	2105	Kells ...... d.	1055	...			1412	...	1812	...	204
Ballyshannon **635** ...... d.	...	1250	...	1535	...	1820	2035	2150	Navan ...... d.	1110	...			1427	...	1827	...	205
Donegal **635** ...... a.	...	1315	...	1600	...	1845	2105	2215	Dublin Busaras ...... a.	1200	...	1315	...	1515	...	1915	...	214

Table 635 — LONDONDERRY AND BALLINA - GALWAY - CORK
Bus Éireann 111, 119, 259

	Ⓐ	✕✕	⑦	⑦	✕✕	✕✕	✕✕	✕✕	⑦	✕✕	⑦	✕✕	②⑤	③⑥	✕✕	⑭	⑦	✕✕	⑦
Londonderry Ulsterbus Depot . d.						0850					1145	1200					1440		1600
Letterkenny ... d.						0927					1222	1237					1515		1637
Donegal Abbey Hotel 634 .. d.						1020					1315	1330					1608		1730
Ballyshannon 634 ... d.						1045					1340	1355					1633		1755
Sligo Rail Station ... a.						1125					1425	1440					1720		1840
Sligo Rail Station ... d.					0945	1145					1440	1500					1735		1900
Ballina ... d.				0830		1130		1230			1515	1630	1630		1630	1705			
Knock ... d.				0930	1105	1301				1601	1616	1615				1851		2016	
Claremorris ... d.				0950	1120			1350			1635			1835					
Tuam Old Rail Station ... d.				1025	1151	1351	1425			1650	1706	1710			1941		2106		
Galway Rail Station ... a.				1100	1225	1415	1425	1500		1730	1740	1745	1920	1935		1950	1945	2015	2140
Galway Rail Station ... d.		0900	0900	1115	1115	1250		1515	1515	1645		1800	1800		1945		2030		
Ennis ... d.		1012	1012	1227	1227	1447		1627	1627	1757		1912	1920		2100		2142		
Limerick Rail Station ... a.		1055	1115	1310	1310	1450		1710	1710	1840		2000	2005		2140		2225		
Limerick Rail Station ... d.	0900	1110	1130	1330	1330	1505		1730	1730	1900		2015	2015						
Charleville ... d.	0725	0940	1150	1210	1410	1410	1545		1810	1810	1940		2055	2055					
Mallow Town Park ... d.	0750	1010	1220	1240	1440	1440	1615		1840	1840	2010		2125	2125					
Cork Parnell Place ... a.	0845	1050	1300	1320	1520	1520	1655		1920	1920	2050		2205	2205					

	②⑤	③	⑥	⑭	✕✕	✕✕	✕✕	⑦	⑦	✕✕	✕✕	⑤	⑦	✕✕	✕✕	⑦	✕✕	⑦
Cork Parnell Place ... d.						0930	0930			1115	1200		1300		1530	1530	1700	1800	2015
Mallow Town Park ... d.						1010	1010			1155	1240		1340		1610	1610	1740	1840	2055
Charleville ... d.						1040	1040			1225	1310		1410		1640	1640	1810	1910	2125
Limerick Rail Station ... a.						1120	1120			1305	1350		1450		1720	1720	1850	1950	2205
Limerick Rail Station ... d.					0900	1135	1135	1300	1320	1405		1505		1735	1730	1905	2015	2020	
Ennis ... d.					1005	1230	1230	1405	1408	1450		1550		1818	1820	1948	2105	2105	
Galway Rail Station ... a.					1115	1340	1340	1515	1520	1600		1700		1930	1930	2100	2210	2215	
Galway Rail Station ... d.	0805	0805	0805	0805	0900	1200	1400		1400		1600		1615	1630	1715	1715	1830		2000	2100	2115
Tuam Old Rail Station ... d.					0934	1234	1435		1434		1634		1650		1749	1750			2035	2134	2150
Claremorris ... d.						1308	1510						1825	1825			2110	2205	
Knock ... d.					1024	1323			1524		1724		1740		1837	1842		2127	2240	
Ballina ... d.	1050	1100	1110	1120		1630						1930		1945	2120		2230	2320	
Sligo Rail Station ... d.					1140	1440		1640		1840		1855	1955				2355		
Sligo Rail Station ... d.					1200	1500		1700		1900		1910							
Ballyshannon 634 ... d.					1245	1545		1745		1945		1955							
Donegal Abbey Hotel 634 .. d.					1310	1610		1810		2010		2020							
Letterkenny ... d.					1403	1703		1903		2103		2113							
Londonderry Ulsterbus Depot . a.					1440	1740		1940		2140		2150							

Table 636 — DUBLIN - SLIGO and BALLINA
Trains 1, 2 class except where shown Bus Éireann 92, 93

km		✕✕	2 ⑦	🚌	🚌	✕✕	✕✕	2 ⑦	✕✕		⑦		2 ⑤	🚌 ⑦	⑦	🚌	✕✕	✕✕	⑦🍸	2 ✕✕
0	Dublin Connolly ... d.	0840	0900			1325	1340				1500		1705	1715			1745		1815	1830
	Dublin Busaras ... d.			0900			1130		1330						1730					
82	Maynooth ... d.	0905	0925			1204	1350	1405	1404		1534		1733	1800	1804		1819		1840	1855
124	Mullingar ... d.	0947	1007	1030		1300	1438	1447	1500		1630		1825	1851	1900		1915		1922	1938
159	Longford ... d.	1024	1046	1125b	1125	1350	1516	1520	1555b	1555	1720b	1725	1908		1950	1950b	2005b	2005	2001	2015
173	Carrick on Shannon ... d.	1057	1119		1203		1549	1601		1633		1803	1940		2028		2043	2034	2048
218	Boyle ... d.	1109	1131		1218		1601	1613		1648		1818	1953		2043		2058	2046	2100
	Sligo ... a.	1150	1212		1300		1642	1654		1730		1900	2036		2125		2140	2127	2143
	Ballina ... a.			1330		1545			1800		1915			2145		2200		

	2 ①	2 ②-⑥	✕✕	🚌 ⑦	🚌 ⑦	2 ⑦	🚌 ⑦		✕✕	✕✕ ⑦			🚌 ⑦	🍸	⑦	✕✕		2 ⑦🍸	2 ⑦
Ballina ... d.				0745			0915		1110			1600				1715			
Sligo ... d.	0450		0750	0800		0855	0930		1140		1325	1435	1630		1740	1730		1810	
Carrick on Shannon ... d.	0532		0830	0842		0935	1012		1222		1405	1515	1712		1820	1812		1850	
Boyle ... d.	0544		0842	0857		0947	1027		1237		1417	1527	1727		1832	1827		1902	
Longford ... d.	0618		0914	0935	0950	1019	1105	1120	1315	1330	1450	1559	1805	1820	1904	1905	1910	1934	
Mullingar ... d.	0657	0657	0950		1030	1054	1200		1410		1524	1634	1900		1940		2000	2010	2010
Maynooth ... d.	0748	0748	1031			1136			1606	1716			2022			2051	2105	
Dublin Busaras ... a.				1145			1315		1525				2025			2125		
Dublin Connolly ... a.	0832	0832	1100		1205				1635	1745			2050				2120	2153

- Arrives in time to connect with the Sligo 🚌 in next column.

Table 637 — DUBLIN - ROSSLARE HARBOUR
Trains are 2 class only Bus Éireann 59, 81

km		✕✕	✕✕ ✕✕	🍸 ⑦	⑦	⑦		✕✕	🍸 ✕✕	🚌	🚌	Ⓐ N	🚌		⑦	⑦	✕✕	🍸 ⑦	🚌	🚌 ✕✕	🚌 ⑦
0	Dublin Connolly ▲. d.		0935		1025			1335				1726			1830		1830				
	Dublin Busaras ... d.			1000		1030	1300		1400	1500	1600	1615		1745	1800			2000	2010	2100	
11	Dun Laoghaire ▲ ... d.	0932		1017				1334				1745			1827		1832				
23	Bray ... d.	0950	1002	1035	1049		1352	1359	1440		1655	1806		1840	1845	1854	1857	2040	2050	
49	Wicklow ... d.		1031	1110u		1117	1140	1410u		1428	1530	1610u		1710u	1745	1837		1923		1926	2130	2140
82	Arklow ... d.		1107	1135		1153	1205	1435		1504		1635		1735	1910		1930		1959	2003		2225
99	Gorey ... d.		1123	1155		1210	1225	1455		1520		1655		1750		1950		2014	2016		2240
128	Enniscorthy ... d.		1147	1220		1234	1250	1520		1544		1720		1815	1930		2015		2035	2038		2300
154	Wexford ... d.		1210	1240		1257	1310	1540		1607		1740		1835	2010	2057		2057	2059		2320
163	Rosslare Strand ... d.		1228			1315			1625					2113		2117			2340
168	Rosslare Harbour ... a.		1240	1300		1325	1330	1600		1635		1800		1900	2035	2100		2130	2129		2340

	🚌	✕✕	✕✕	✕✕	🍸	✕✕	⑦	⑦	⑦		✕✕	✕✕			🍸	⑦	🚌	🚌	⑦	⑦	🚌
Rosslare Harbour ... d.			0725	0730		0815		0915		0930		1300		1455		1630	1730	1730	1800		1830	1930
Rosslare Strand ... d.				0735			0920						1500				1805	1835		
Wexford ... d.			0800	0753		0835		0938		0950		1320		1518		1650	1750	1750	1823		1853	1950
Enniscorthy ... d.				0816		0900		1002		1010		1340		1545		1710		1820	1846		1916	2010
Arklow ... d.	0657	0800	0855	0854		0930		0950		1040		1410		1610		1735	1845	1909		1939	2035
Gorey ... d.			0840	0839		0930		1025		1035		1410		1610		1755					
Wicklow ... d.	0700	0730	0905	0926		1030	1117		1120	1200	1300	1430		1755		1905	1924		2000		2030	2050
Bray ... d.		0805	0945	1000	1007		1121	1153	1200		1250	1440		1636	1733	1745		2033	2037	2106	2110
Dun Laoghaire ▲ ... d.		0820			1023			1216						1801				2053		2126	
Dublin Busaras ... a.	0830		1030	1020			1115	1200		1230	1330	1520	1600	1715		1930	2010	2030			2215
Dublin Connolly ▲ ... a.		0846e		1030				1216						1805					2057	2130	

- Does **not** connect with 2030 sailing to Fishguard.
- Stops to **pick up** only.

▲ – Suburban trains operate every 10-15 minutes (half-hourly on ⑦) between Connolly and Dun Laoghaire. Allow 20 minutes at Connolly for connection to main line services.

Table 638 — DUBLIN - NENAGH - LIMERICK - TRALEE
Iarnród Éireann   Bus Éireann 86, 87

km				2											2					2	2	
			⑦	✕ ⑦			⑦		⑦		⑦					✕		⑦		⑦	⑦	
0	Dublin Heuston 640 645....d.	...	0900								1740							1830		...
	Dublin Busaras........d.	0745		0930	0930	1200	1230	1400	1515	1600	1615		1745	1745	1815			2000
48	Kildare 640 645........d.	0845	0932	1025	1037	1307		1437			1715	1832	1852		1857		2055
82	Portlaoise 640........d.	0913	0958	1051	1105	1335		1505		1725	1745	1850	1920		1923		2123
102	Ballybrophy 640........d.		1015	1020								1850	1855		1941	1945	
118	Roscrea........d.	1005	1033	1140	1200	1430		1600		1735	1820	1850	1908	1955	2015	1958	2205
149	Nenagh........d.	1035	1103	1210	1232	1505	1632		1805	1850	1922	1935	2025	2050	2026	2310
193	Limerick Rail Station......d.	1110	1150	1245	1310	1540	1540	1710	1710	1840	1930	2000	2020	2100	2055	2125	2125	2055	2106	2310
	Limerick Rail Station......d.	1125		1330	1330		1550		1735	1900	1935		2100	2130
	Listowel Square........d.	1310		1500	1515		1720		1920	2030	2100		2230	2300
	Tralee Rail Station........a.	1340		1530	1545		1750		1950	2100	2130		2300	2330

		2		2										2					2	⑤
		✕		✕				⑦		⑦				✕		⑦			⑦	
Tralee Rail Station............d.					0630		0855	0855		1145		1240			1445		1530		1700	1750c
Listowel Square................d.					0655		0925	0925		1215		1310			1515		1600		1730	1825
Limerick Rail Station........a.					0825		1110	1110		1345		1455			1650		1735		1900	1900
Limerick Rail Station........d.	0700	0730	0750	0820	0835	0845	0930	1120	1120	1120	1320	1400	1440	1510	1510	1545		1715	1715	1745	1745	1800	1900
Nenagh ....d.	0805	0833		0920	1000		1200	1158	1355		1435		1548	1627		1750		1815	1841	1950
Roscrea ....d.	0835	0902		0950	1030		1230	1236	1425		1505		1626	1655		1820		1845	1910	2020
Ballybrophy 640 ....d.	0917	0925										1710	1715				1925	2115
Portlaoise 640 ....d.	0826	0915	0940	1045	1110	1322	1316	1517		1557		1706	1730		1912		2140
Kildare 640 645 ....d.	0848	0943		1138	1348	1343	1545		1623		1733	1755		1912		
Dublin Busaras ....d.		1045		1145	1200	1245	1430	1440	1445	1500	1645	1710	1720	1830	1850		2025	2040	2055	2055	
Dublin Heuston 640 645........a.	0925		1025											1825		2230

Trains are 1, 2 class except where shown.

c – Depart 1800 on ⑦.

Table 640 — DUBLIN - MALLOW - TRALEE and CORK
1, 2 class except where shown.

km		2 ✕	2 ⑦	Ⓐ	⑥	2 ⑦	2 ⑦	✕	2 ✕	2 ⑦		2 ⑦	✕	2 ⑦		2 ⑦		2 ⑦			2 ⑦	2 ⑧	⑦	✕	2
		C	GX	GX						C		GX	C			GX	CD	⑨	⑨			C	GX		
0	Dublin Heuston 645.d.			0730	0815	0850		0900		1020	1015		1045		1320		1330	1320	1340	1455		1645	1730	1735	1740
48	Kildare 645 ....d.					0932			1045	1112				1354	1409			1715				1819
67	Portarlington ....d.					0946		1100	1126	1357		1409	1424	1531		1730		
82	Portlaoise ....d.		0813		0937	0958		1112	1138	1410		1422	1437	1543		1743		1818t	1832	1851
107	Ballybrophy ....d.					1016		1131										1853	1912
139	Thurles ....d.		0844		1012	1040		1157		1215	1446		1457	1517	1615		1839	1853	1934
172	Limerick Junction ....a.		0902	0938	1033	1102		1144	1217		1234	1505		1515	1517	1540	1634		1841	1855	2015
172	Limerick Junction 641 ....d.		0904	0940	1035	1104		1146	1219		1236	1507		1517	1519	1555	1636			1940	2050
207	Limerick 641 ....a.														1621			
208	Charleville ....d.					1059		1127			1245	1300	1532		1545		1905		
232	Mallow ....a.		0938	1015	1117	1143		1220	1301	1317		1548	1603		1711		1922	1930
232	Mallow ....d.	0905	0933	0939	1016	1119	1122	1147	1150	1222	1302	1308	1318	1319	1553	1553	1559	1604		1712	1907v	1923	1931
	Millstreet 643 ....a.				1147	1214			1339	1346	1624	1626		
298	Killarney 643 ....a.				1218	1243			1413	1416	1653	1655		
333	Tralee 643 ....a.				1255	1315			1455	1500	1730	1733		1740	1945	1950	2000
266	Cork 643 ....a.	0935	1000	1005	1045		1150		1220	1250	1330		1345		1620		1630			1740	1945	1950	2000

		2 ⑤	⑦	✕	⑦	⑦	✕	2 ✕	✕				2 ✕	2 ✕		✕		✕	2	2 ⑦	2
			GX						⑨						GX			C			
Dublin Heuston 645....d.	1740	1750	1815	1830	1855	1855	1915		2100	2130		Cork 643 ....d.	0520		0735		0820			0900	0910
Kildare 645 ....d.			1857		1927			2134	2205		Tralee 643 ....d.					0730	0750		
Portarlington ....d.	1819		1910		1940			2149	2219		Killarney 643 ....d.					0802	0824		
Portlaoise ....d.	1832		1923		1953			2202	2232		Millstreet 643 ....d.					0832	0855		
Ballybrophy ....d.	1851		1941		2011						Mallow ....a.	0547		0759		0848	0858	0922	0924	0934
Thurles ....d.	1912		1929	2004	2012	2034	2025		2239	2312		Mallow ....d.	0548		0800		0859		0925	0935
Limerick Junction ....a.					2033	2053	2044		2259	2332		Charleville ....d.	0604				0916		0942	0952
Limerick Junction 641 ....d.					2035	2055	2046		2301	2334		Limerick Junction 641 ....d.		0700		0820				1005
Limerick 641 ....a.				2055								Limerick Junction ....a.	0627		0833				1003	1014
Charleville ....d.	2006		2008			2119	2110		2333	0001		Limerick Junction ....d.	0629		0835				1005	1016
Mallow ....a.	2006	2025	2D	2112	2136	2127		2351	0017		Thurles ....d.	0653	0746		0904		0955	1027	1038	1050
Mallow ....d.	2008	2027	2113	2137	2128	2137		2352	0018		Ballybrophy ....d.	0718			0925			1053	1117
Millstreet 643 ....a.	2036		2056		2156						Portlaoise ....d.	0735	0826		0940			1109	1135
Killarney 643 ....a.	2107		2125		2225						Portarlington ....d.	0748						1120	1147
Tralee 643 ....a.	2145		2200		2300						Kildare 645 ....d.	0802	0848					1134	1202
Cork 643 ....a.		2010	2055	2140	2205		2200	0020	0045		Dublin Heuston 645........a.	0840	0925	1005	1025		1110	1210	1150	1235

		2 ⑦	2 ⑤		2	2 ✕	2 ⑤		⑦	2 ⑦	⑦			⑦	2 ✕	⑦	✕				✕	2 ✕	2
			CD	GX	C	C			G⑦		✕				J		G⑦	GX			CD		
Cork 643 ....d.	1050		1120	1230	1240	1345		1415	1430	1445		1515		1730	1730		1710		1830		1900	1955	2050
Tralee 643 ....d.		0955	0955						1340	1420		1710		1730	1735	1745
Killarney 643 ....d.		1032	1032						1411	1452		1745	1806	1810	1820
Millstreet 643 ....d.		1103	1103						1442	1523		1816	1838	1838	1848
Mallow ....a.	1117	1131	1131	1144	1257	1307	1410		1440	1455	1509	1510	1542	1550		1754		1844	1855	1907	1906	1915	1924	2020	2120
Mallow ....d.		1132		1147		1411		1441	1456	1510	1511		1551		1755		1845	1856		1925
Charleville ....d.			1205					1513	1527	1529				1916		1942
Limerick 641 ....d.														1815		
Limerick Junction 641 ....a.		1209		1228				1514	1535	1549	1551		1626	1829		1938		2006
Limerick Junction ....d.		1211		1230				1516	1537	1551	1552		1628	1831	1902	1940		2008
Thurles ....d.		1235		1252		1502		1600	1613	1618		1649	1853	1902	2003		2028
Ballybrophy ....d.								1645			1715		1929	2030
Portlaoise ....d.			1329					1649	1701	1730		1946	2047		2104
Portarlington ....d.		1321		1341				1714	1741		1958	2100		2116
Kildare 645 ....d.			1355					1727	1755			2114		2133
Dublin Heuston 645........a.	1410		1425		1615	1645	1720	1735	1805	1825	1950	2005	2045	2055	2145		2200

C – 🚌 Cork - Tralee and v.v.   D – ①②③④⑥.   G – City Gold service - see heading.   J – Through service Cork to Tralee on ①②③④⑥.   t – Not ⑤.   v – Depart 1914 on ①②③④⑥

Table 641 — LIMERICK JUNCTION - LIMERICK
Iarnród Éireann; Bus Éireann 113, 21

km			2 Ⓐ	2 ⑥	2 ⑦	2 ✕	2	2			2	2 ⑦	⑦			2 ⑤			2 ✕	2 ⑦		2 ⑦	2	2 ⑦	2 ⑦⑨
	Dublin Heuston 640 .. d.		0730	0815	0850	0900	1015	1045		1320	1320	1340		1455	1645	1730t	1735	1740		1830	1915	1855		2100	213t
	Cork 640 .... d.	0520t	0735	0900	0910		1050c	1120		1415	1430	1445t	1515p	1730	1730		1900	1830		
0	Limerick Junction ... d.	0749	0905	1008	1037	1107	1222	1238	1420	1512	1522	1555	1610	1638	1843	1925		2015	2015	2048	2058	2225	2305	2314
35	Limerick .... d.	0844	0932	1035	1105	1134	1249	1305	1455	1539	1549	1621	1650	1705	1910	2000		1940	2050	2050	2055	2115	2125	2315	2332	000

K – ①②③④⑥.   c – Additional change at Mallow necessary.   p – Connection by train. Additional change at Mallow necessary.   t – Connection by train.

Table 641 — LIMERICK - LIMERICK JUNCTION
Iarnród Éireann; Bus Éireann 113, 213

		2	2	✗		2	2	2⑦	✗	🚌	2	🚌	2	2	2		2	2⑦	2		2
Limerick	d.	...	0700	0805	0820	...	0910	0935	0945	1005		1120	1200	1330		1445	1510	1555		1630	1800	1815	1910	...	1935
Limerick Junction	a.			0832		...	0937	1002	1012			1200	1227	1403		1512	1542	1622		1705	1827		1937	...	2002
Cork 640	a.			1005		...	1045	1220c	1150c			1330n	1345	1620t		1630		1740		2000		2140		...	2205
Dublin Heuston 640	a.	...	0925	1005	1025	...	1210	1210	1150	1235			1425			1645	1735	1825		2005	2045	2145			2200

c – Additional change at Mallow necessary.   n – ⑦ only.   t – Connection by train.

Table 642 — DUBLIN - WATERFORD
1, 2 class except where shown

km		✗	2⑦	✗		2⑦	✗	2⑤	✗	2⑦			②①	✗	2⑦	✗		2⑦	2⑦	✗
0	Dublin Heuston 638 640 d.	0735	0950	1135	...	1450	1500	1715	1810	1815		Waterford d.	0600	0730	0945	1050	...	1445	1515	1800	1825
48	Kildare 638 640 d.	0810	1025	1202	...	1525	1535		1842	1847		Kilkenny d.	0650	0817	1032	1139	...	1526	1602	1850	1913
72	Athy d.	0829	1044	1224	...	1544	1554	1802	1902	1907		Carlow d.	0721	0850	1105	1211	...	1558	1639	1923	1947
90	Carlow d.	0848	1105	1243	...	1600	1609	1817	1916	1925		Athy d.	0735	0904	1119	1226	...	1617	1654	1938	2002
130	Kilkenny d.	0935	1148	1325	...	1640	1653	1903	2005	2009		Kildare 638 640 d.	0756	0922	1138	1247	...	1638	1713	1959	2023
177	Waterford a.	1020	1225	1405	...	1730	1740	1950	2045	2050		Dublin Heuston 638 640 a.	0830	0950	1215	1325	...	1720	1750	2035	2100

Table 643 — LIMERICK and TRALEE - ROSSLARE
Bus Éireann 101/102/104/113; Iarnród Éireann

km		🚌	🚌	🚌		🚌	2		🚌	2		🚌	2			🚌	🚌	🚌	2
			Ⓐ	✗			✗		✗	✗					⑦	✗	✗	⑦	⑤⑦	⑦
0	Limerick d.	...	...	0900	...	1120	...	1330	...	1555	1630	...				1740	1915	2015	...
35	Limerick Junction d.	...	...	0940	...	1200	...	1403		1645	1705v						1813	2010		...
40	Tipperary d.	...	...	0945	...	1205	...	1410		1700	1715						1820	2018	2105	...
62	Cahir d.	...	...	1015	...	1230	...	1435		1722	1745						1855	2045	2130	...
	Tralee Rail Station d.	...				0850			1200			1400			1605				1800
	Killarney d.					0925			1235			1435			1640				1835
	Millstreet d.					1005			1315			1515			1720				1915
	Cork Parnell Place a.					1120			1430			1630			1830				2030
	Cork Parnell Place d.		0900			1135			1445			1645	1730	1800				2045
79	Clonmel Rail Station d.	...	0730		1035		1255		1500		1739	1805				1915	2110	2150	
102	Carrick-on-Suir d.	...	0755		1055		1315		1523		1759	1825				1940	2130	2215	
124	Waterford Bus Station a.	...	0830	1115	1125		1345	1350	1555		1700	1821r	1855	1900		1945	2015	2015h	2200	2240	2250
124	Waterford Bus Station d.	0700					1400	1400		1700r		1823r	1930	1930						
	Wexford Rail Station d.	0800					1500	1500					2030	2030						
187	Rosslare Harbour a.	0820					1520	1520		1817			1930	2050	2050					

		🚌	2	🚌	🚌		🚌	2	🚌	🚌		🚌	🚌	🚌	2	🚌	🚌	🚌	2
			✗	✗	✗		✗	Ⓐ	✗	⑦		✗	✗	⑤⑦		⑦	✗	✗	⑦	⑦	2
Rosslare Harbour d.		...	0715	0720	0720	...						1440					1900	...	1940
Wexford Rail Station d.				0740	0740							1500					1920		
Waterford Bus Station a.			0825r	0840	0840							1600					2020		2046r
Waterford Bus Station d.		0800		0900	0900	1040	1100	1100	1135	1230	1430	1445	1630	1630		1645	1730	1800	1915	...	2045	2045	2048r
Carrick-on-Suir d.				0930		1110		1150		1300		1515		1655			1805		1950		2115	2111
Clonmel Rail Station d.				0955		1135		1215		1325		1540		1720			1830		2015		2135	2133
Cork Parnell Place a.		1015			1115		1315		1350		1645		1845			1900	1945		2015		2250	
Cork Parnell Place d.					1125		1325				1735		1915								
Millstreet d.					1240		1440				1850		2025								
Killarney d.					1320		1520				1930		2105								
Tralee Rail Station d.					1355		1555				2005		2140								
Cahir d.				1020		1200		1240		1350		1605		1740			1855		2050		2155	2152
Tipperary d.				1045		1225		1305		1415		1630		1805			1920		2115		2220	2214
Limerick Junction a.				1050		1230				1420		1635					1925		2123		2225	2225n
Limerick a.				1125		1305		1345		1455		1710		1855			2000		2210		2315	2332

n – Arrive 2005 on ⑦.   n – Depart 2305.   r – Rail station.   v – ⑦ only.

Table 645 — DUBLIN - GALWAY, WESTPORT and BALLINA
1, 2 class except where shown   Bus Éireann 90 91

km		✗✗	✗✗	2	2⑦✗	⑦	✗		2	✗✗	1300		2 ✗✗✗	⑦	2 ✗	2 ✗		⑤⑦	①-④	✗✗	⑦✗	⑦		✗✗	⑦✗	🚌	⑦
0	Dublin Heuston d.	0800	0830	...	0920		...		1105	1300		...	1410	1410		...		1700	1700	1805	1800		...	1845	1845	...	2020
	Dublin Busaras d.						0900					1230				1400	1600									2000	
48	Kildare d.	0829			0950				1135	1332			1440	1445				1730	1740		1832			1912		2049
67	Portarlington d.	0844	0906		1004				1149	1346			1453	1459				1744	1753	1841	1846			1926		2104
93	Tullamore d.	0907	0931		1025				1207	1407			1513	1520				1806	1812	1903	1907		1937	1957		2126
130	Athlone a.	0947	1012		1107		...		1105	1239	1438		1435	1544	1554	1605	1805	1839	1839	1935	1948		2009	2030	2200	2158
130	Athlone d.	0949	1013		1109	1120			1115	1243	1439		1445	1545	1555	1625	1815	1840		1936	1950		2010	2031	2200	2200
152	Ballinasloe d.	1007			1128				1142	1303			1512	1604	1613		1842						2028	2049	2227	2218
187	Athenry d.	1039			1203					1333				1638	1640								2050	2122		2245
208	Galway a.	1055			1220		...		1245	1350			1615	1655	1655		1945						2115	2140	2330	2305
160	Roscommon d.	...	1041			1148				1508						1700		1910	1910		2006	2020		...	
222	Claremorris d.	...	1135			1242				1601						1825		2011	✗	2059	2115		...	
239	Manulla Junction d.	...	1150	1151		1257	1257			1617	1617							2115	2114	2129	2130		...	
246	Castlebar d.	...	1157			1304				1624					1855			2121	2137				...	
264	Westport d.	...	1215			1325				1645					1915			2140	2155				...	
277	Ballina a.	...	1225			1330				1650						2100	2150					2205	

		2 Ⓐ✗	✗✗	2 ✗	2 ✗✗	⑦	2 ⑦✗			✗✗			2 ✗	✗✗	2 ⑦✗	2 ✗✗	⑦		🚌	⑦		2 ⑦	⑦✗	2 ✗	2 ✗✗
Ballina d.		...	0715										1325				1505					1740		1815	
Westport d.				0725	0755						0740			1330				1510	1500				1745		1825
Castlebar d.				0741	0811						0800			1346				1526	1520				1801		1840
Manulla Junction d.			0745	0750								1355	1356			1535	1536			1810	1812	1846	1850
Claremorris d.				0803	0831				0830				1409			1552	1550					1825		1903
Roscommon d.				0857	0925				0950				1507			1648	1710			⑦	1920		2005
Galway d.			0800			0850	0900	1030	1135		1330			1450	1515			1630	1745	1805	1810		
Athenry d.			0814			0904		1150						1505	1530				1820	1826		
Ballinasloe d.			0840			0938	1003	1131	1222		1431			1531	1605			1733	1848	1852	1903		
Athlone a.			0859			0926	0954	0957	1030	1155	1241	1310	1410	1455		1539	1550	1605		1718	1810	1800	1915	1911	1923	1949	2037
Athlone d.		0635	0900			0927		1000	1040	1205	1242	1325	1425		1545	1555	1629		1719	1805	1805	1925	1913	1924	1950	2039
Tullamore d.		0703	0932			1001		1031		1311			1616	1626	1659		1752			1959	1958	2023	2058
Portarlington d.		0725				1022		1053		1332			1637	1648	1722		1815			2020	2021	2044	2110
Kildare d.		0739				1107				1346			1703				1831			2035	2036	2058	2149
Dublin Busaras a.									1245	1400		1520	1620						2035	2035	2130			
Dublin Heuston a.		0825	1030			1100		1140		1420			1715	1745	1806		1905			2110	2110	2135	2220

04

345

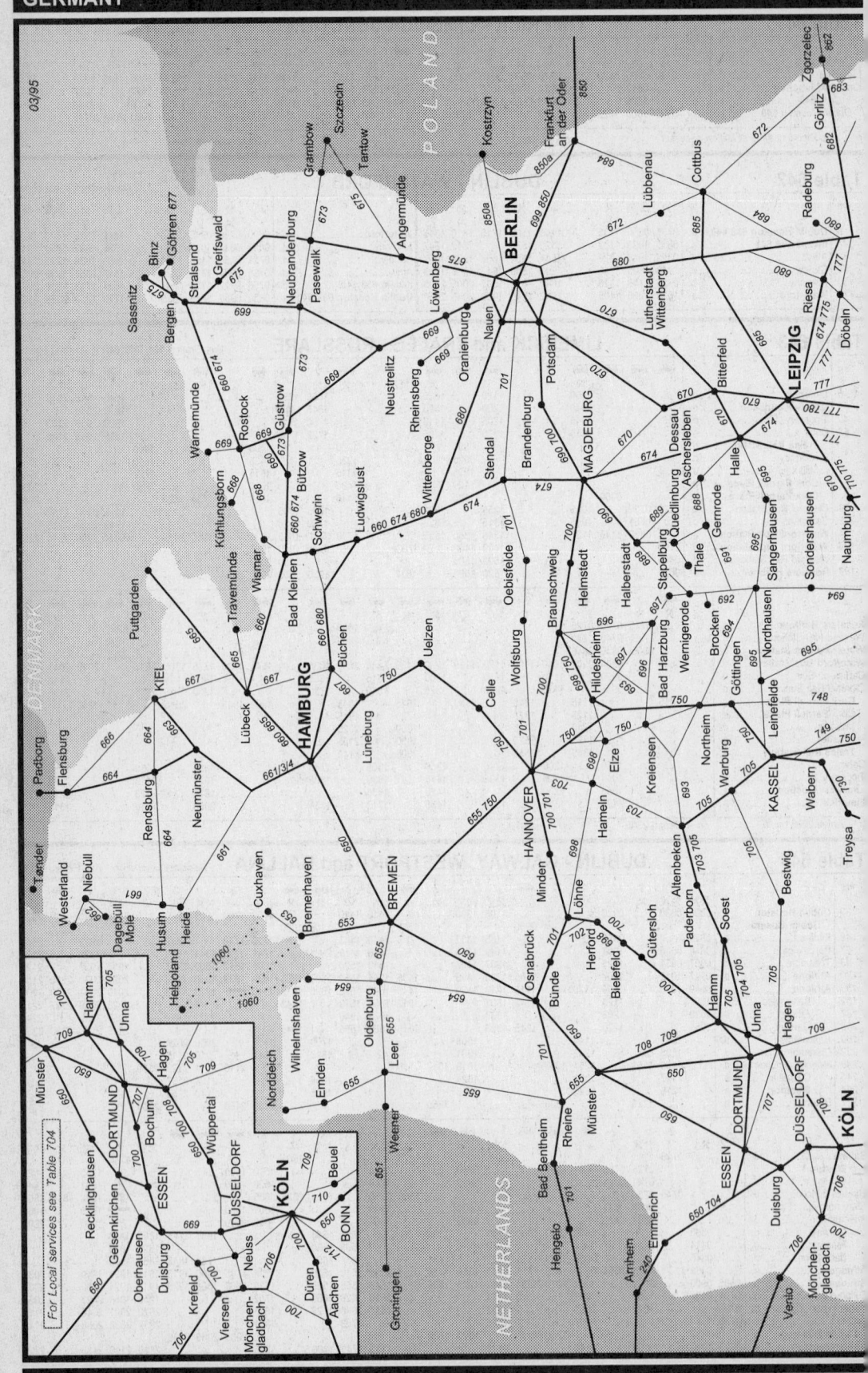

03/95

For Local services see Table 704

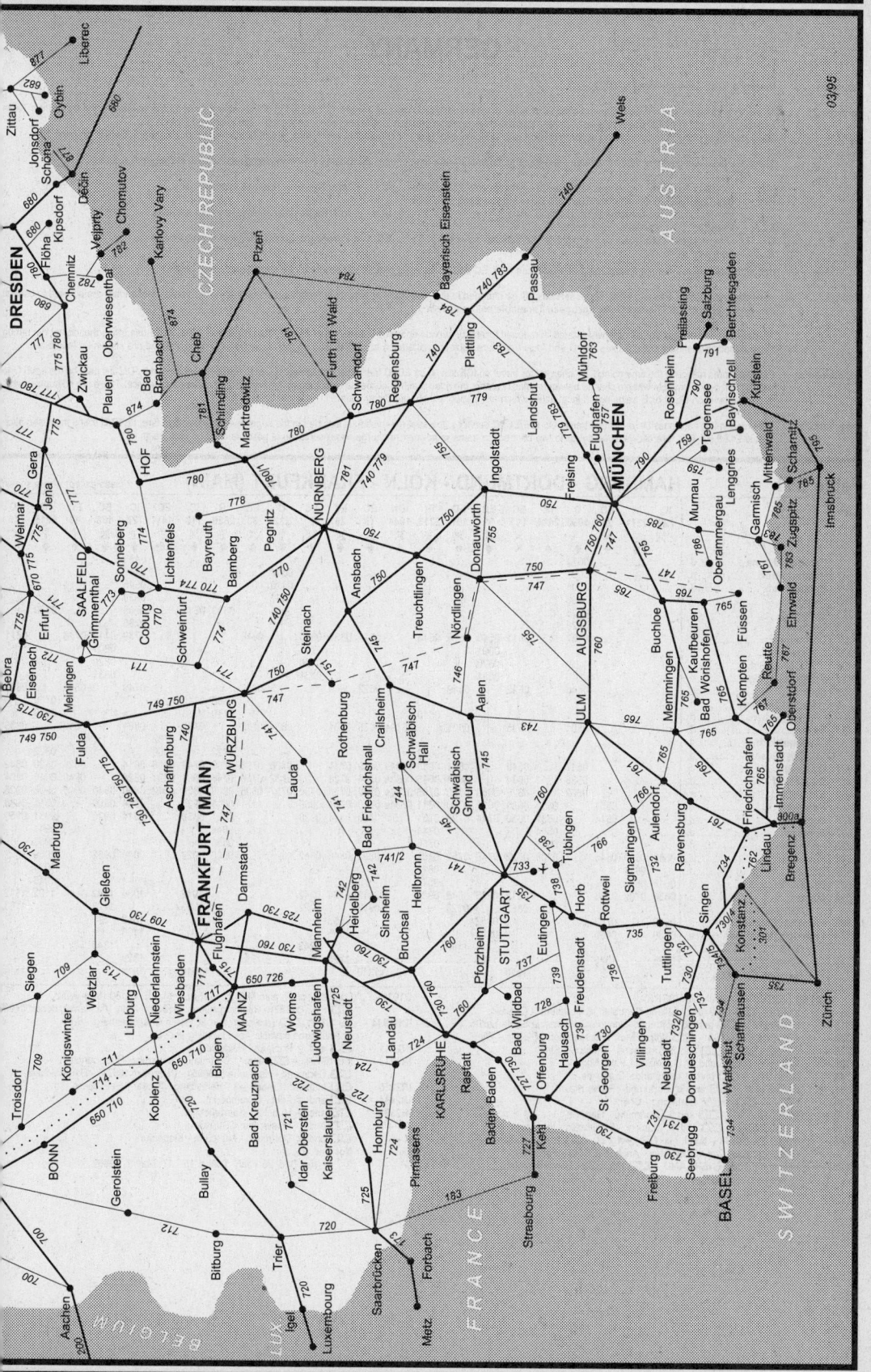

GERMANY

Operators: Deutsche Bahn Aktiengesellschaft (DB).

Services: All daytime trains convey First and Second classes of travel unless otherwise shown by a figure "2" at the top of the column, or in a note situated to the right of the Table heading. Overnight **D** or **EN** trains may only convey Second class seats in addition to sleeping accommodation - see individual footnotes.
Many overnight trains convey sleeping accommodation; eg: sleeping cars (🛏), or couchettes (🛏) which are of normal European standard. Details on page **10**.

There are eight categories of fast and/or semi-fast trains in Germany - the type of train is indicated by the following letter codes above each column:

ICE:	**InterCity Express** high speed services travelling at up to 250 km/hour.		**IC:**	**InterCity** long distance express trains.
ICN:	**InterCityNight** hotel-standard overnight trains e.g. sleeping cars with shower/toilet in the compartments; reclining seats.		**IR:**	**InterRegio** inter-regional express services.
EC:	**EuroCity** international express trains.			
D:	Other express trains (usually overnight or international services).		**EN:**	**EuroNight** quality overnight express trains.
E:	Semi-fast trains.			

ICE and **ICN** services require the payment of a premium fare; **EC** and **IC** services require the payment of a supplement - see below.

Timings: Valid **Sept. 25, 1994 - May 27, 1995**. Some services will be changed in our April issue and minor amendments made from time to time. Passengers are advised to consult the latest edition of the **Thomas Cook European Timetable** before travelling.

All trains run daily unless unless otherwise stated. A reduced **InterCity** service operates between April 14 - 17, 30, and May 1, 1995, and those trains that do not run during these periods are shown in the Tables. **IR, D** and local trains are subject to alteration or cancellation on the above dates. Trains affected are shown by footnote.

Supplements: Premium fares reflecting the time gained are charged for travel on **ICE** trains; on **EC/IC** trains the supplement is DM 6. Rates are increased by DM 2 if paid on the train. One supplement only is payable when a change between trains is made, provided that the journey is continued by the first onward connecting service. There are no supplements to pay for travel on **IR, D** or **E** trains nor in local trains which are shown without qualifying letter.

Reservations: Seat reservations are possible on all fast trains. On **ICE/EC/IC** services, the seat reservation is included in the supplementary/premium fare; on **IR/D** trains the reservation cost is DM 6.00. This fare allows travel by up to two connecting trains without extra charge. No reservation is possible on **E** or local trains.

Table 650 — HAMBURG - DORTMUND - KÖLN - FRANKFURT (MAIN)   1, 2 class except where shown

km		IC 723 ⚡✕ ◆	IR 2211 ⚟ ◆	EC 23 ◆	D 1930 ◆	IR 2434 ⚟ ◆	EC 113 ✕ K	EC 51 ✕ ◆	EC 107 ✕ ◆	IR 2213 ⚟ ◆	ICN 1944 ◆	EC 13 ✕ ◆	EC 25 ⚟ ◆	EC 5 ✕ ◆	D 232 ◆	EC 30 ✕ ◆	IR 2538 ⚟ ◆	IC 119 ✕ ◆	EC 141 ⚟ A❖	IC 725 ⚟ ◆	EC 103 ✕ ◆	EC 48 ⚟ ◆	IC 2215 ⚟ ◆	EC 115 ✕ K
0	Hamburg Altona .... d.	...	...	...	0015	...	...	...	...	...	...	...	...	...	...	...	...	...	...	0433	...	...	...	...
7	Hamburg Hbf .... d.	...	...	...	0037	...	...	...	...	...	...	...	...	0312	...	...	...	...	...	0447	...	...	...	...
122	Bremen Hbf .... d.	...	...	...	0201	...	...	...	...	...	...	...	...	0420	...	...	...	...	...	0545	...	...	...	...
245	Osnabrück .... d.	...	...	...	0306	...	...	...	...	...	...	...	...	0532	...	...	...	...	...	0639	...	...	...	...
295	Münster .... d.	...	...	...	0338	...	...	...	...	...	...	...	...	0604	...	0630	0644	...	...	0705	...	...	0730	...
351	Dortmund .... a.	...	...	...	0428	...	...	...	...	...	...	...	...	...	...	...	...	...	...	0736	...	...	...	...
351	Dortmund .... d.	...	...	...	0432	...	0511	0540	0538	0548	...	0611	0638	0640	...	0648	...	...	...	0738	0740	0748	...	0811
380	Hagen .... d.	...	...	...	...	...	...	0601	...	...	...	...	...	0701	...	...	...	...	...	...	0801	...	...	...
406	Wuppertal Hbf .... d.	...	...	...	...	...	...	0620	...	...	...	...	...	0720	...	...	...	...	...	...	0820	...	...	...
424	Solingen Ohligs .... d.	...	...	...	...	...	...	0631	...	...	...	...	...	0731	...	...	...	...	...	...	0831	...	...	...
369	Bochum .... d.	...	...	...	0446	...	0522	...	0549	...	...	0622	0649	...	...	0700	...	...	...	0749	...	0800	0758	...
	Recklinghausen .... d.	...	...	...	...	...	...	...	...	...	...	...	...	...	...	...	0658	0712	...	...	...	...	...	...
	Gelsenkirchen .... d.	...	...	...	...	...	...	...	0610	...	...	...	...	...	...	...	0710	0723	...	...	...	...	0810	...
385	Essen .... d.	...	...	...	0501	...	0535	...	0601	...	0619s	0635	0701	...	0654	0712	...	0735	...	0801	...	0812	...	0835
	Emmerich 🚉 .... d.	...	...	...	...	...	...	...	...	...	...	...	...	...	...	...	...	...	0732	...	...	...	...	...
	Oberhausen .... d.	...	...	...	...	...	...	...	0622	...	...	...	...	...	...	...	0722	...	0800	...	...	...	0822	...
404	Duisburg .... d.	...	...	...	0517	...	0549	...	0614	0630	0634s	0649	0714	...	0708	0725	0730	0749	0808	0814	...	0825	0830	0849
418	Düsseldorf Hbf .... d.	...	...	...	0536	...	0604	...	0628	0645	0653s	0704	0728	...	0732	0740	0745	0804	0821	0828	...	0840	0845	0904
452	Köln Hbf .... a.	...	...	...	0602	...	0626	0650	0650	0700	0720s	0726	0750	0757	0805	0808	0826	0842	0850	0850	0850	0905	0908	0930
452	Köln Hbf .... d.	...	...	0554	...	0611	0630	0654	0700	0711	0734s	0730	0754	0800	...	0811	0830	...	0854	0900	...	0911	0930	
487	Bonn Hbf .... d.	...	...	0614	...	0631	0650	0714	0720	0731	0755	0750	0814	0820	...	0831	0850	...	0914	0920	...	0931	0950	
507	Remagen .... d.	...	...	...	...	0644	...	...	0744	...	...	...	...	...	0844	...	...	...	...	...	...	0944		
528	Andernach .... d.	...	...	...	...	0656	...	...	0756	...	...	...	...	...	0856	...	...	...	...	...	...	0956		
546	Koblenz .... d.	0543	0609	0646	...	0708	0722	0746	0752	0809	...	0822	0846	0852	...	0908	0922	...	0946	0952	...	1009	1022	
565	Boppard .... d.	...	0621	...	...	...	...	...	0821	...	...	...	...	...	...	...	...	...	...	1021			
607	Bingen Hbf .... d.	0618	0646	...	...	...	...	...	0846	...	...	...	...	...	...	...	...	...	...	1046			
637	Mainz .... d.	0636	0702	0736	...	...	0812	0836	0842	0902	...	0912	0936	0942	...	...	1012	...	1036	1042	...	1102	1112	
	Mannheim .... a.	...	...	...	...	...	0853	...	0923	...	...	0953	...	1023	...	...	1053	...	...	1123	...	...	1153	
665	Frankfurt Flughafen ✈ . a.	0652	...	0752	...	...	0852	...	...	0952	...	...	...	...	...	...	1052	...	...	...				
674	Frankfurt (Main) Hbf .. a.	0706	...	0806	...	...	0906	...	...	1006	...	...	...	...	...	...	1106	...	...	...				
	Basel SBB 730 .... a.	...	...	...	...	1143	...	...	...	...	1243	...	...	...	...	1343								
	Nürnberg 750 .... a.	0925	...	1025	...	...	1125	...	...	1225	...	...	...	...	1328	...	...	...						
	München Hbf 760 ..... a.	...	...	...	1210	...	...	1310	...	...	...	...	1410	...	1518	...	...	1510						

◆ – **NOTES** (LISTED BY TRAIN NUMBERS)

EC5 – VERDI – 🍴 Dortmund - Milano Centrale; ✕ Dortmund - Chiasso.
EC13 – PAGANINI – 🍴 and ✕ Dortmund - Innsbruck - Venezia Santa Lucia.
EC23 – JOHANN STRAUSS – 🍴 Köln - Wien Westbahnhof; ✕ Bonn - Wien.
EC25 – FRANZ LISZT – 🍴 and ⚟ Dortmund - Budapest Keleti.
EC30 – MOLIÈRE – 🍴 and ✕ Dortmund - Paris Nord.
EC48 – MEMLING – 🍴 and ⚟ Dortmund - Oostende.
EC51 – KARLSTEIN – 🍴 and ✕ Dortmund - Praha Hlavni.
EC103 – RÄTIA – 🍴 and ✕ Dortmund - Chur.
EC107 – MONT BLANC – 🍴 and ✕ Dortmund - Genève.
IC119 – KARWENDEL – 🍴 and ✕ Münster - Mittenwald - Innsbruck.
D232 – NORD EXPRESS – 🛏 1,2 cl. (T2), 🛏 2 cl., 🍴 and 🍴 København - Oostende; 🛏 1,2 cl. København - Aachen (EC30) - Paris Nord.
IC725 – BERCHTESGADENER LAND – 🍴 Hamburg - Berchtesgaden; ⚟ Bremen - Freilassing.

D1930 – Daily except ⑥, also May 27, **not** Apr. 14, 15, 16, 30 (from Kiel): 🍴 Kiel (D2883) - Hamburg Altona (D1930) - Köln. Via Hamm, depart 0409.
ICN1944 – 🛏 1,2 cl., 🍴 (reclining) and ✕ Berlin Charlottenburg - Bonn. Special fares payable - see heading above.
IR2211 – 🍴 and ⚟ Koblenz - Heidelberg.
IR2213 – MURGTAL – 🍴 and ⚟ Dortmund - Karlsruhe - Freudenstadt; 🍴 Dortmund - Karlsruhe (E3005) - Pforzheim (6077) - Bad Wildbad.
IR2215 – 🍴 Münster (Emden ✗) - Heidelberg; ⚟ Leer - Heidelberg.
IR2434 – 🍴 and ⚟ Köln - Luxembourg.
IR2538 – 🍴 and ⚟ Münster - Saarbrücken.
A – 🍴 and ⚟ Amsterdam CS - Köln.
K – 🍴 and ✕ Dortmund - München - Klagenfurt.
❖ – **Not** Dec. 25, Jan. 1.
✗ – ① - ⑥ (**not** Dec. 25 - Jan. 1, Apr. 15 - 17, May 1, **1995**).

Table 650 — HAMBURG - DORTMUND - KÖLN - FRANKFURT (MAIN)

1, 2 class except where shown

Upper table

	EC 143 A	EC 27 ✗	EC 9 ✗	IR 2432 ♀	IC 715 ✗	IC 727 ✗♀	IC 548 ✗	EC 105 ✗	IR 2217 ♀	IC 513 ♀	EC 29 ✗	IC 546 ✗♀	EC 3 ✗	IR 2536 ♀	IC 613 ✗	IC 621 ♀	EC 109 ✗	EC 38 ✗	IR 2219 ♀	EC 19 ✗	EC 145 A	IC 729 ✗	IC 501 ✗	IR 2336 B ♀
Hamburg Altona d.		0533			0633						0733					0833						0933		
Hamburg Hbf d.		0547			0647						0747					0847						0947		
Bremen Hbf d.		0645	0702		0745						0845				0902	0945						1045		1102
Osnabrück d.		0739	0802		0839						0939				1002	1039						1139		1202
Münster d.		0805	0830	0844	0905					0930	1005				1030	1044	1105		1130			1205		1230
Dortmund a.		0833			0933						1033						1133					1233		
Dortmund d.		0840	0838		0938	0940		1011		1038	1040				1140		1138	1146		1211		1238	1240	
Hagen d.		0901				1001					1101						1201					1301		
Wuppertal Hbf d.		0920				1020					1120						1220					1320		
Solingen Ohligs d.		0931				1031					1131						1231					1331		
Bochum d.			0849		0949				1022	1049							1149	1158		1222		1249		
Recklinghausen d.				0858	0912				0958					1058	1112			1158						1258
Gelsenkirchen d.				0910	0923				1010					1110	1123			1210						1310
Essen d.	0832		0901		0935	1001			1035	1101				1135			1201	1210		1235		1301		
Emmerich 🚫 d.									0934				1034					1232						
Oberhausen d.	0900			0922				1004	1022				1104	1122				1222		1300				1322
Duisburg d.	0908		0914		0949	1008	1014	1019	1030	1049			1119	1130	1149		1214	1224	1230	1249		1308	1314	1330
Düsseldorf Hbf d.	0921		0928	0945	1004		1028	1034	1045	1104			1128	1134	1145	1204		1228	1239	1245	1304	1328		1345
Köln Hbf a.	0942	0950	1008	1026	1050	1050	1057	1108	1126	1150	1150	1157	1208	1226	1250	1250	1304	1308	1326	1342	1350	1350		1408
Köln Hbf d.		0954	1000	1011	1030	1054		1100	1111	1130	1154		1200	1211	1230	1254	1300	1311	1330	1354	1400	1411		
Bonn Hbf d.		1014	1020	1031	1050	1114		1120	1131	1150	1214		1220	1231	1250	1314	1320	1331	1350	1414	1420	1431		
Remagen d.					1044					1144					1244					1344		1444		
Andernach d.					1056					1156					1256					1356		1456		
Koblenz d.		1046	1052	1108	1122	1146		1152	1209	1222	1246		1252	1308		1346	1352	1409	1422	1446	1452	1508		
Boppard d.									1221										1421					
Bingen Hbf d.									1246										1446					
Mainz d.		1136	1142	1212	1236			1242	1302	1312	1336		1342	1412		1436	1442	1502	1512	1536	1542			
Mannheim a.		1223		1253				1323	1353				1423		1453		1523		1553		1623			
Frankfurt Flughafen ✈ a.		1152			1252				1352						1452				1552					
Frankfurt (Main) Hbf a.		1206			1306				1406						1506				1606					
Basel SBB 730 a.			1443			1543					1643					1743					1843			
Nürnberg 750 a.		1425			1525				1625						1725				1825					
München Hbf 760 a.										1710		1625				1810	1918		1910					

Lower table

	IC 615 ✗	IC 521	EC 46 ✗	IC 603	IR 2311 ♀	IC 617	EC 147 A ♀	IC 823 ✗	EC 605 ✗	IR 2430 ♀	IC 719 ✗	IC 523 ✗	IC 503 ♀	IR 2313 ♀	IC 517 ✗	EC 149 A ♀	IC 625 ♀	IC 505 ✗	IR 2334 ♀	IC 619 ♀✗	IC 527 ♀	IC 507 ✗	IR 2315 ♀
Hamburg Altona d.		1033					1133				1233					1333				1433			
Hamburg Hbf d.		1047					1147				1247					1347				1447			
Bremen Hbf d.		1145					1245	1302			1345					1445	1502			1545			
Osnabrück d.		1239					1339	1402			1439					1539	1602			1639			
Münster d.	1244	1305			1330		1405	1430	1444		1505		1530			1605	1630	1644		1705			1730
Dortmund a.		1333					1433				1533					1633				1733			
Dortmund d.		1340	1338			1411	1438	1440			1540	1538			1611	1640	1638			1738	1740		
Hagen d.		1401						1501			1601					1701				1801			
Wuppertal Hbf d.		1420						1520			1620					1720				1820			
Solingen Ohligs d.		1431						1531			1631					1731				1831			
Bochum d.			1349			1422		1449					1549		1622			1649			1749		
Recklinghausen d.	1312				1358				1458	1512			1558					1658	1712				1758
Gelsenkirchen d.	1323				1410				1510	1523			1610					1710	1723				1810
Essen d.	1335		1401			1435		1501			1535			1549			1635		1701	1735	1801		
Emmerich 🚫 d.							1432								1632								
Oberhausen d.					1422		1500		1522					1622			1700		1722				1822
Duisburg d.	1349		1414	1430	1449		1508	1514	1530	1549			1614	1630	1649		1708	1714	1730	1749			1830
Düsseldorf Hbf d.	1404		1428	1445	1504	1521	1528	1545	1604		1628		1645	1704	1721	1728	1745		1804	1828		1845	
Köln Hbf a.	1426	1450	1450	1500	1511	1526	1542	1550	1600	1611	1626	1650	1650	1708	1726	1742	1750	1750	1800	1811	1830	1850	1850
Köln Hbf d.	1430	1454		1500	1511	1530		1554	1600	1611	1630	1654	1700	1711	1730		1754	1800	1811	1830	1900	1911	
Bonn Hbf d.	1450	1514		1520	1531	1550		1614	1620	1650	1650	1714	1720	1731	1814		1820	1831	1850	1914	1920	1931	
Remagen d.					1544					1644				1744				1844				1944	
Andernach d.					1556					1656				1756				1856				1956	
Koblenz d.	1522	1546		1552	1609	1622		1646	1652	1708	1722	1746	1752	1809	1822		1846	1908	1922	1946	1952	2007	
Boppard d.					1621									1821									
Bingen Hbf d.					1646									1846									
Mainz d.	1612	1636		1642	1702	1712		1736	1742	1812	1836	1842	1902	1912		1936	1942		2010	2036	2042		
Mannheim a.	1653			1723	1753			1822	1853			1923	1953			2023					2123		
Frankfurt Flughafen ✈ a.		1652			1752				1852				1952			2052					2106		
Frankfurt (Main) Hbf a.		1706			1806				1906				2006			2106							
Basel SBB 730 a.			1943						2043				2143					2243					
Nürnberg 750 a.		1925			2025				2127				2227			2243				2327			
München Hbf 760 a.	2010				2110				2127				2311										

◆ — NOTES (LISTED BY TRAIN NUMBERS)

EC3 – REMBRANDT – 🛏 and ✗ Amsterdam Schiphol ✈ - Chur.
EC9 – TIZIANO – 🛏 Hannover (Braunschweig /) - Milano; ✗ Hannover - Chiasso.
IC19 – ANDREAS HOFER – 🛏 and ✗ Dortmund - Innsbruck.
IC27 – JOSEPH HAYDN – 🛏 and ✗ Hamburg - Wien Westbahnhof.
IC29 – PRINZ EUGEN – 🛏 and ✗ Kiel - Wien Westbahnhof.
EC38 – JACQUES BREL – 🛏 and ✗ Dortmund - Paris Nord.
EC46 – ALEXANDER VON HUMBOLDT – 🛏 and ✗ Berlin Zoo - Brussels.
EC105 – BERNER OBERLAND – 🛏 and ✗ Amsterdam Schiphol ✈ - Interlaken Ost.
EC109 – THUNERSEE – 🛏 and ✗ Berlin Zoo - Interlaken Ost.
IC503 – MARK BRANDENBURG – 🛏 and ♀ Berlin Zoo - Basel SBB.
IC505 – KAISERSTUHL – 🛏 and ✗ Berlin Zoo - Basel SBB.
IC507 – STOLZENFELS – 🛏 Berlin Zoo - Karlsruhe; ✗ Berlin - Mainz.
IC517 – FRIEDRICH SCHILLER – daily except ⑥ (**not** Apr. 14 - 16, 30, **1995**): 🛏 and ✗ Dortmund - Stuttgart; extended on ⑦ also Apr. 17, May 1, **not** Apr. 16, 30 to München.
IC523 – WESTFÄLISCHER FRIEDE – 🛏 and ✗ Kiel - Nürnberg.
IC527 – GORCH FOCK – 🛏 and ♀ Kiel - Nürnberg.
IC546 – WESERBERGLAND – 🛏 and ✗ Leipzig - Köln.
IC548 – GÜRZENICH – 🛏 and ✗ Hannover (Braunschweig /) - Köln.
EC605 – HEINRICH DER LÖWE – 🛏 and ✗ Braunschweig - Basel SBB.
IC613 – BACCHUS – 🛏 and ✗ Münster - Stuttgart (München ♣).
IC619 – GUTENBERG – 🛏 and ♀ Münster - Stuttgart.

IC621 – KONSUL – 🛏 and ✗ Kiel - Nürnberg (München ♣).
IC625 – WALHALLA – 🛏 and ♀ Hamburg - Frankfurt/Main (Regensburg ♣).
IC715 – NEBELHORN – 🛏 and ✗ Münster - Oberstdorf.
IC719 – ALLGÄU – 🛏 and ✗ Stuttgart (Kempten ♣) - Dortmund.
IC727 – LORELEY – 🛏 and ♀ Hamburg - Nürnberg; conveys on ⑥: 🛏 Hamburg Altona - Nürnberg (**IC927**) - Zwiesel.
IC729 – PASSAVIA – 🛏 and ♀ Hamburg - Passau.
IC823 – NORDFRIESLAND – 🛏 and ✗ Westerland - Passau; conveys ⑥⑦ Mar. 24 - Apr. 30, daily May 1 - 27: 🛏 Dagebüll - Passau.
IR2217 – HÖLLENTAL – 🛏 and ♀ Emden - Seebrugg.
IR2219 – 🛏 and ♀ Norddeich - Heidelberg.
IR2311 – 🛏 and ♀ Emden - Stuttgart.
IR2313 – 🛏 and ♀ Norddeich - Karlsruhe.
IR2315 – 🛏 and ♀ Emden - Koblenz.
IR2334 – 🛏 Rostock (Binz on ⑥, **not** Apr. 15, May 27) - Saarbrücken; ♀ Rostock - Merzig.
IR2336 – 🛏 and ♀ Rostock (Stralsund /) - Saarbrücken.
IR2430 – 🛏 and ♀ Cuxhaven - Luxembourg.
IR2432 – 🛏 and ♀ Münster (Bremerhaven /) - Luxembourg.
IR2536 – 🛏 and ♀ Cuxhaven - Saarbrücken.
A – 🛏 and ♀ Amsterdam CS - Köln.
/ – ① - ⑥ (**not** Dec. 25 - Jan. 1, Apr. 15 - 17, May 1, **1995**).
♣ – Daily except ⑥ (**not** Dec. 24 - 31, Apr. 14 - 16, Apr. 30, **1995**).

Table 650 — HAMBURG - DORTMUND - KÖLN - FRANKFURT (MAIN)

1, 2 class except where shown

	D 1205	EC 151	IC 827	IC 607	IR 2530	D 223	D 201	IC 738	IC 509	D 201	D 353	IR 2317	D 1125	ICE 638	D 1125	D 1015	EC 153	IC 609	IC 736
	🚻R	A										C		✕			A		
Hamburg Altona ... d			1533					1633						1743					
Hamburg Hbf ... d			1547					1647						1757					
Bremen Hbf ... d			1645		1702			1745											1845
Osnabrück ... d			1739		1802			1839											1939
Münster ... d			1805		1830			1905				1930		1949					2005
Dortmund ... a			1833					1933											2033
Dortmund ... d	1755		1838	1840		1905	1909	1940	1938				1954			2000	2040		2038
Hagen ... d				1901					2001								2101		
Wuppertal Hbf ... d				1920					2020								2120		
Solingen Ohligs ... d				1931					2031								2131		
Bochum ... d	1808u		1849		1918		1923u		1949			1958	2007			2013			2049
Recklinghausen ... d					1858						2010								
Gelsenkirchen ... d					1910														
Essen ... d	1821u		1901			1931	1935u		2001				2020	2034		2025			2101
Emmerich 🚩 ... d		1832										2022					2100		
Oberhausen ... d		1900			1922							←				2042			
Duisburg ... d	1836u		1908	1914	1930		1947	1947f		2014	2019u		2030	2037	2045	2108			2114
Düsseldorf Hbf ... d	1853u		1921	1928	1945	2005	→		2050	2050	2102u	2112	2045	2057	2101	2113	2121		2128
Köln Hbf ... a	1920		1942	1950	1950	2032	2037	2050	2054	2100	2106u	2111		2122		2130	2156	2154	
Köln Hbf ... d	1929u		1954	2000	2011	2037	2054	2100	2106u	2114	2120	2127u	2133	2142	2152	2217b	2214		
Bonn Hbf ... d	1950u		2014	2020	2031	2059		2114	2120	2127u	2133		2142		2152	2217b	2214		
Remagen ... d					2044														
Andernach ... d					2056														
Koblenz ... d	2027u		2046	2052	2108	2135		2146	2152	2203		2209		2232	2257		2246		
Boppard ... d																	2320		
Bingen Hbf ... d																			
Mainz ... d	2123u		2136	2142		2228		2236	2242	2258u		2305		2326					
Mannheim ... a	2207u			2223					2328	2339u									
Frankfurt Flughafen ✈ ... a			2152					2252											
Frankfurt (Main) Hbf ... a			2206			2300		2306			2330			2354					
Basel SBB 730 ... a	0100e																		
Nürnberg 750 ... a						0200						0222							
München Hbf 760 ... a																0404o			

	D 1219	IC 544	IC 734	D 1215	IR 2319	D 1925	D 403	D 1019	D 830	D 203	D 1019	ICE 640	D 1203	IC 730	EN 225	D215 EN225	D 215	IC 925	E 4768	E 4802	E 7500	E 4700
									K			✕		K		L			V			V
Hamburg Altona ... d			1833						1933				2033									
Hamburg Hbf ... d			1847						1947				2047									
Bremen Hbf ... d			1945						2045				2145									
Osnabrück ... d			2039						2139				2239									
Münster ... d			2105		2130		2101		2205				2305							0234		
Dortmund ... a			2133					2141u	2233				2333									
Dortmund ... d	2140		2138			2143u	2205	2222	2240			2248							0302	0301		0354
Hagen ... d	2201								2301											0326		
Wuppertal Hbf ... d	2220								2320													
Solingen Ohligs ... d	2231								2331													
Bochum ... d			2149				2156u	2218	2235										0315	0311		0407
Recklinghausen ... d					2158															0324		
Gelsenkirchen ... d					2210																	
Essen ... d			2201				2209u	2231	2251	2157	2236		2306				2250	2250	0327			0419
Emmerich 🚩 ... d						2134	2209			2236					2328	2328				0338		
Oberhausen ... d			2214	2218		2230	2224u	2243	2307	2304		2317	2325		2338	2338			0340	0345		0432
Duisburg ... d			2228	2234		2245	2259u		2324	2321	←	2330	2342u		2356	2356	0312c	0353c	0355c	0358c		0445c
Düsseldorf Hbf ... d			2250	2250	2300	2308	2326u		2355	2350	2347	2355	2352	0007u		0022	0022	0348				
Köln Hbf ... a	2234	2254		2305			2336u		2359	2359		0011u		0044	0044	0049	0350					
Köln Hbf ... d	2257b	2314		2328			2358u	→	0021	0021b		0033u		0111	0411							
Remagen ... d																						
Andernach ... d																						
Koblenz ... d	2338	2344		0016			0036u		0057	0104				0146	0446							
Boppard ... d																						
Bingen Hbf ... d																						
Mainz ... d									0151x				0240x									
Mannheim ... a													0321									
Frankfurt Flughafen ✈ ... a									0208								0554					
Frankfurt (Main) Hbf ... a																	0606					
Basel SBB 730 ... a									0626		0625e											
Nürnberg 750 ... a				0559o			0714									0514	0514					
München Hbf 760 ... a																		0736				

NOTES (LISTED BY TRAIN NUMBERS)

D201 – Sept. 24 - May 26: 🛏 1,2 cl., ⊣ 2 cl., and ⊟ Dortmund - Milano.

D215 – 🛏 1,2 cl., ⊣ 2 cl. and ⊟ Amsterdam CS - München; 🛏 1,2 cl. ⊣ 2 cl. and ⊟ Oostende (EN225) - München.

D223 – DONAU KURIER – 🛏 1,2 cl., ⊣ 2 cl., and 🍴 Dortmund - Wien; 🛏 1,2 cl. and ⊟ Dortmund - Budapest Keleti; conveys Jan. 9 - Mar. 30: 🛏 1,2 cl., ⊣ 2 cl. and ⊟ Dortmund - Praha.

EN225 – 🛏 1,2 cl., ⊣ 2 cl. and ⊟ Oostende - Wien.

D353 – Mar. 31 - May 27: 🛏 1,2 cl., ⊣ 2 cl., and 🍴 Köln - Praha.

IC509 – RHEINFELS – ⊟ and 🍴 Berlin Zoo - Karlsruhe.

IC544 – ELSE LASKER-SCHÜLER – ⊟ and 🍴 Berlin Zoo - Koblenz.

IC607 – GAMBRINUS – ⊟ and 🍴 Berlin Zoo - Karlsruhe.

IC609 – FRIEDRICH HARKORT – ⊟ and 🍴 Braunschweig - Wiesbaden (arrive 2343).

ICE640 – SPREE-KURIER – ⊟ and ✕ Berlin Zoo - Köln.

IC730 – WESTFALEN – ⊟ and 🍴 Kiel - Dortmund.

IC734 – KAROLINGER – ⊟, not Apr. 14 - 16, 30: ⊟ Kiel - Aachen; 🍴 Kiel - Köln.

IC736 – RÜGEN – ⊟ Stralsund - Köln (Aachen ♦); starts from Binz ⑥⑦ Apr. 29 - May 27; 🍴 to Köln.

IC738 – KIELER FÖRDE – ⊟ and 🍴 Kiel - Frankfurt/Main.

IC827 – THEODOR STORM – ⊟ and 🍴 Westerland - Frankfurt/Main; ⊟ Dagebüll Mole - Frankfurt/Main.

IC830 – DEICHGRAF – ⊟ and 🍴 Westerland - Köln; conveys May 1 - 27: ⊟ Dagebüll Mole - Köln.

D1015 – ⑤ Jan. 6 - Apr. 7: 🛏 2 cl., 🍴 and ⊟ Dortmund - Garmisch - Innsbruck; 🛏 1,2 cl., ⊣ 2 cl. and ⊟ Dortmund - München (D1115) - Kufstein - Innsbruck; ⊣ 2 cl. and ⊟ (also 🛏 1,2 cl. to Mar. 17) München (D1115) - Wörgl (D1615) - Schwarzach St Veit; conveys to Mar. 17: 🛏 1,2 cl. Dortmund - Garmisch.

D1019 – VORARLBERG EXPRESS – ⑤ Jan. 6 - Apr. 7: 🛏 1,2 cl., ⊣ 2 cl. and ⊟ Dortmund - Innsbruck; ⊣ 2 cl. and ⊟ (also 🛏 1,2 cl. to Mar. 3) Dortmund - Oberstdorf; 🍴 Dortmund - Lindau. No stops Koblenz - Ulm (Table 761).

D1125 – DOLOMITEN EXPRESS – ⑤ Jan. 6 - Mar. 24: 🛏 1,2 cl., ⊣ 2 cl., ⊟ and 🍴 Dortmund - Bolzano; 🛏 1,2 cl., ⊣ 2 cl. and ⊟ Dortmund - Villach; 🛏 1,2 cl. Dortmund - Graz.

D1205 – ITALIA EXPRESS – Mar. 31 - May 27: 🛏 2 cl., 🍴 and ⊟ (also 🛏 1,2 cl. exce on Mar. 31, Apr. 1) Dortmund - Brig - Roma. [R]

D1215 – ⑤ Jan. 6 - Apr. 24: ⊣ 2 cl. and 🍴 Amsterdam CS - Villach; conveys from Koblenz: ⊣ 2 cl. and ⊟ Oostende - Villach.

D1219 – ⑤ Jan. 6 - Mar. 24: ⊣ 2 cl. and ⊟ Oostende - Villach for train D1215 at Kobler

D1925 – LUNA – 🛏 1,2 cl., ⊣ 2 cl. and 🍴 Münster (Norddeich Mole on ⑤⑥⑦ Apr. 7 - May 27 also Apr. 17) - München. Via Hamm, depart 2122u.

IR2319 – ⊟ Norddeich Mole - Köln.

IR2530 – ⊟ Cuxhaven - Trier (Saarbrücken ♦); 🍴 Cuxhaven - Koblenz.

A – ⊟ and 🍴 Amsterdam CS - Köln.

C – ⊟ and 🍴 Norddeich Mole - Köln.

K – SCHWEIZ EXPRESS – see Tables 38 and 78.

L – 🛏 1,2 cl., ⊣ 2 cl. and ⊟ Amsterdam CS - Wien.

V – Not Dec. 25.

b – Bonn Beuel.

d – Düsseldorf Flughafen ✈.

e – Basel Bad. Stops to **pick up** only. Depart 2019.

f – Stops to **pick up** only.

o – München Ost.

u – Stops to **pick up** only.

x – ② - ⑥ **only.**

✜ – **Not** Dec. 25, Jan. 1.

❖ – Daily except ⑥ (**not** Dec. 24 - 31, Apr. 14 - 16, Apr. 30, **1995**).

Table 650 — FRANKFURT (MAIN) - KÖLN - DORTMUND - HAMBURG

1, 2 class except where shown

km	IC 831	IR 2316	D 214	EN224 D214	EN 224	IC 731	IR 2533	D 1018	D 1202	D 202	IC 733	ICE 641	D 1014	ICE 639	D 402	D 1214	D 1924	IR 2314	IC 545	IC 735	EC 140	IR 2335
	München Hbf 760 d.			2211									2318				2341o	2317					
	Nürnberg 750 d.				0024	0024							2318										
	Basel SBB 730 d.									2358e	2325												
	Frankfurt (Main) Hbf d.																						
	Frankfurt Flughafen + d.										0335												
	Mannheim d.			0211																			
	Mainz d.			0256x							0355x												
	Bingen Hbf d.																						
	Boppard d.																						
	Koblenz d.			0350						0434	0449			0459			0525	0542s		0612			0646
	Andernach d.																						0659
	Remagen d.																						0712
	Bonn Hbf d.			0425					0511	0515s	0523			0539b		0600	0600	0618s		0645			0725
	Köln Hbf a.			0447	0450	0450			0537	0540s	0545			0559		0621	0600	0622	0639s	0645		0705	0725
0	Köln Hbf d.			0510	0510		0540		0545s	0550	0552	0605		0602	0626		0632	0642s	0645	0710	0709	0717	0748
40	Düsseldorf Hbf d.			0546	0546		0611		0612s	0620		0626		0640	0647		0701	0717s	0714	0733	0739		0813
64	Duisburg d.			0613	0613		0628		0629			0655		0638	0658	0658	0711	0721	0733s	0728	0746	0752	0827
72	Oberhausen d.			0626	0626							0703				0706	0729			0735		0758	0835
	Emmerich a.			0704	0704											0740	0806						0826
	Essen d.						0642					0649			0710	0725		0747s			0759		
80	Gelsenkirchen d.													0721						0746			0846
95	Recklinghausen d.																			0759			0859
	Bochum d.						0653									0737			0758s		0809		
	Solingen Ohligs d.										0610											0728	
	Wuppertal Hbf d.										0624											0742	
	Hagen d.										0641											0759	
	Dortmund a.						0705				0702	0705			0749	0745			0810s		0820	0820	
152	Dortmund d.	0525	0550					0625			0708				0745			0814s		0825			
	Münster d.	0556	0628					0656	0727		0756			0752				0855		0828	0856		0930
	Osnabrück d.	0621						0721	0757		0821									0921			0957
	Bremen Hbf a.	0716						0816	0857		0916									1016			1100
	Hamburg Hbf a.	0811						0911			1011				0946					1111			1206
	Hamburg Altona a.	0824						0924			1024				0959					1124			

	D 352	IC 737	IC 608	D 200	D 1124	IR 2312	IC 508	IC 739	EC 142	D 222	IC 518	IC 222	IR 2531	IC 506	IC 826	D 1204	IC 618	D 1204	IR 2310
München Hbf 760 d.				0157o															
Nürnberg 750 d.	0304								0406		0528								
Basel SBB 730 d.																0457e			
Frankfurt (Main) Hbf d.	0544							0651		0658				0751					
Frankfurt Flughafen + d.									0704					0804					
Mannheim d.				0549s			0636												
Mainz d.	0610			0632s	0638		0654	0718	0724	0728				0748					
Bingen Hbf d.			0638				0710												
Boppard d.							0735												
Koblenz d.	0705		0713	0725s	0732		0748	0807	0813	0823		0837		0845	0907	0913	0926s	0937	0948
Andernach d.							0759					0859							0959
Remagen d.							0812					0912							1012
Bonn Hbf d.	0739		0745	0759s			0825	0839	0845	0859		0909		0925	0939	0945	0959s	1009	1025
Köln Hbf a.	0801	0805		0821s	0833		0845	0859	0905			0921		0939	0945	0959s	1009	1021	1025
Köln Hbf d.		0809	0810	0825s	0836	0848	0910	0909	0917	0926	0933			0948	1009	1010	1035s	1033	1048
Düsseldorf Hbf d.		0833		0854s	0916	0913			0933	0939	1001	0957		1001	1013	1033	1057	1106s	1113
Duisburg d.		0846		0910s	0933	0927			0946	0952			1011	1019	1027	1046	1111	1124s	1127
Oberhausen d.						0935			0958				1035						1135
Emmerich a.									1026										
Essen d.		0859	0925s	0947					0959		1025	1033		1059		1124	1139s		1146
Gelsenkirchen d.								0946						1059			1133		1159
Recklinghausen d.								0959									1145		
Bochum d.				0936s	0958				1009					1036	1044		1150s		
Solingen Ohligs d.			0828					0928						1028					
Wuppertal Hbf d.			0842					0942						1042					
Hagen d.			0859					0959						1059					
Dortmund a.		0920	0920	0948	1010			1020	1020			1048	1056		1120	1120		1203	
Dortmund d.	0925				1010			1025							1120	1120		1125	
Münster d.	0956					1028		1056					1130	1156		1214			1228
Osnabrück d.	1021							1121					1157	1221					
Bremen Hbf a.	1116							1216					1257	1316					
Hamburg Hbf a.	1211							1311						1411					
Hamburg Altona a.								1324						1424					

NOTES (LISTED BY TRAIN NUMBERS)

200 – Sept. 25 - May 27: 1,2 cl. and couchette Milano - Dortmund.

214 – 1,2 cl., 2 cl. and couchette München - Amsterdam CS; 1,2 cl., 2 cl. and couchette München - Köln (EN224) Oostende.

222 – DONAU KURIER – 1,2 cl., 2 cl., couchette and ♀ Wien - Dortmund; 1,2 cl., 2 cl. and couchette Budapest - Dortmund; conveys Jan. 8 - Mar. 29 (from Praha): 1,2 cl., 2 cl. and couchette Praha - Dortmund.

N224 – 1,2 cl., 2 cl. and couchette Wien - Oostende.

352 – Mar. 30 - May 27 (from Praha): 1,2 cl., 2 cl., couchette and ♀ Praha - Köln.

506 – STOLZENFELS – restaurant and ♀ Karlsruhe - Berlin Zoo.

508 – RHEINFELS – restaurant and ♀ Karlsruhe - Berlin Zoo.

518 – OSKAR SCHLEMMER – restaurant and ♀ Stuttgart - Dortmund.

545 – ELSE LASKER-SCHÜLER – restaurant and ♀ Koblenz - Berlin Zoo.

608 – FRIEDRICH HARKORT – restaurant and ♀ Wiesbaden (dep 0616) - Braunschweig. Train does not call at Mainz.

618 – GUTENBERG – restaurant and ♀ Stuttgart - Münster.

E641 – SPREE-KURIER – restaurant and ♀ Köln - Berlin Zoo.

731 – WESTFALEN – restaurant and ♀ Dortmund - Kiel.

735 – KAROLINGER – ① - ⑥, not Apr. 15 - 17, May 1: restaurant and ✗ Aachen - Kiel.

737 – RÜGEN – restaurant Köln (Aachen ✗) - Stralsund. Extended to Binz on ⑤⑥ Apr. 28 - May 27; ♀ from Köln.

739 – KIELER FÖRDE – restaurant and ♀ Frankfurt/Main - Kiel.

826 – THEODOR STORM – restaurant and ✗ Nürnberg - Westerland; conveys May 1 - 27: restaurant Nürnberg - Dagebüll Mole.

831 – DEICHGRAF – restaurant and ♀ Dortmund - Westerland; couchette Dortmund - Dagebüll Mole.

1014 – ⑥ Jan. 7 - Apr. 8: 2 cl., couchette and ♀ (from Innsbruck) Innsbruck - Garmisch - Dortmund; 1,2 cl., 2 cl. and couchette Innsbruck (D1114) - Kufstein - München - Dortmund; 2 cl. and couchette (also 1,2 cl. to Mar. 18) Schwarzach St Veit (1614) - Wörgl (D1114) - München - Dortmund; conveys to Mar. 18: 1,2 cl. Garmisch - Dortmund.

D1018 – VORARLBERG EXPRESS – ⑥ Jan. 7 - Apr. 8 (from Innsbruck): 1,2 cl., 2 cl. and couchette Innsbruck - Dortmund; 1,2 cl., 2 cl. and couchette Oberstdorf - Dortmund; ♀ Lindau - Dortmund.

D1124 – DOLOMITEN EXPRESS – ⑥ Jan. 7 - Mar. 25 (from Bolzano): 1,2 cl., 2 cl., couchette and ♀ Bolzano - Dortmund; 1,2 cl. and couchette Villach - Dortmund; couchette 2 cl. Graz - Dortmund.

D1204 – ITALIA EXPRESS – Mar. 31 - May 27 (from Roma): 2 cl. and ♀ (also 1,2 cl. except on Mar. 31, Apr. 1) Roma - Brig - Dortmund.

D1214 – ⑥ Jan. 7 - May 27 (from Villach): 1,2 cl., 2 cl. and ♀ Villach - Amsterdam; conveys to Köln: 2 cl. and couchette Villach - Oostende for D1118.

D1924 – LUNA – ⑤⑥⑦ Apr. 7 - May 27: 2 cl. and ♀ München - Münster (Norddeich Mole on ⑤⑥⑦ Apr. 7 - May 27, also Apr. 17 from München). Via Hamm, arrive 0833s.

IR2310 – restaurant and ♀ Emden - Emden.

IR2312 – restaurant and ♀ Karlsruhe - Norddeich; ♀ Heidelberg - Norddeich.

IR2314 – restaurant and ♀ Köln - Emden.

IR2316 – restaurant and ♀ Dortmund - Norddeich. Via Hamm, depart 0609.

IR2335 – restaurant and ♀ Koblenz - Rostock.

IR2531 – restaurant and ♀ Trier (Saarbrücken ✗) - Cuxhaven.

IR2533 – restaurant and ♀ Münster - Cuxhaven.

A – restaurant and ♀ Köln - Amsterdam CS.

K – SCHWEIZ EXPRESS – see Tables 38 and 78.

L – 1,2 cl., 2 cl. and ♀ Wien - Amsterdam CS.

b – Bonn Beuel.

e – Basel Bad.

o – München Ost.

s – Stops to set down only.

x – ②③④⑤⑥.

✗ – ① - ⑥ (not Dec. 25 - Jan. 1, Apr. 15 - 17, May 1, 1995).

Table 650 — FRANKFURT (MAIN) - KÖLN - DORTMUND - HAMBURG
1, 2 class except where shown

First part

	IC 504 ✕	IC 526 ◆	EC 144 🍴A	IC 516	IR 2337 🍴	IC 604 ◆	IC 822 ◆	IC 616 ✕	IR 2218 🍴	IC 502 ✕	IC 524 ◆	EC 146 🍴A	IC 718 🍴	IR 2431 🍴	IC 500 ✕	IC 522 ✕	IR 2216 🍴	IC 602 ◆	EC 47 ◆	IC 620 ◆	IC 148 🍴A	EC 18 ◆
München Hbf 760 d.						0650				0638					0850							0950
Nürnberg 750 d.		0628					0728				0832					0932				1032		
Basel SBB 730 d.	0620e			0717				0817					0917					1017			1251	
Frankfurt (Main) Hbf d.		0851			0951	1004				1051	1104					1151		1204				1304
Frankfurt Flughafen ✈ d.		0904																1207	1237			1307
Mannheim d.	0837		0907	0937	1007		1037					1107	1137		1207		1237			1324		1348
Mainz d.	0918	0924	0948	1018	1024	1048	1054	1118	1124			1148	1218	1224	1248	1254	1318		1324			1348
Bingen Hbf d.							1110									1310						
Boppard d.							1135									1335						
Koblenz d.	1007	1013	1037	1045	1107	1113	1137	1148	1207	1213		1237	1245	1307	1313	1337	1348	1407		1413		1437
Andernach d.					1059			1159					1259			1359						
Remagen d.					1112			1212					1312			1412						
Bonn Hbf d.	1039	1045	1109	1125	1139	1145	1209	1229	1239	1245		1309	1325	1339	1345	1409	1425	1439		1445		1509
Köln Hbf a.	1059	1105	1129	1145	1159	1205	1229	1245	1259	1305		1329	1345	1359	1405	1429	1445	1459		1505		1529
Köln Hbf d.	1109	1110	1133	1148	1210	1229	1233	1248	1309	1310	1317	1333	1348	1410	1409	1433	1457	1513	1509	1510	1517	1539
Düsseldorf Hbf d.	1133	1139		1213	1227		1233	1257		1313	1333	1339	1357	1413		1433	1457	1513		1533		1557
Duisburg d.	1146	1152	1211	1227		1246	1311	1327	1346			1352	1411	1427		1446	1511	1527		1546		1611
Oberhausen d.		1158	1226	1235				1335				1358	1435					1535			1558	
Emmerich 🚇 a.												1426									1626	1625
Essen d.	1159		1225			1259	1324		1359				1446			1459	1524			1559		1625
Gelsenkirchen d.				1246			1333	1346								1533	1546					
Recklinghausen d.				1259			1345	1359					1459			1545	1559					
Bochum d.	1209		1236			1309			1409				1436			1509				1609		1636
Solingen Ohligs d.		1128			1228					1328					1428					1528		
Wuppertal Hbf d.		1142			1242					1342					1442					1542		
Hagen d.		1159			1259					1359					1459					1559		
Dortmund a.	1220	1220	1248		1320	1320			1420	1420			1448			1520	1520			1620	1620	1648
Dortmund d.		1225				1325				1425					1530			1556	1614	1628		1656
Münster d.		1256			1330		1356	1414	1428	1456					1557			1621		1721		
Osnabrück d.		1321			1357		1421			1521					1657			1716		1816		
Bremen Hbf d.		1416			1500		1516			1616								1811		1911		
Hamburg Hbf a.		1511			1606		1611			1711								1811		1911		
Hamburg Altona a.		1524			1624					1724								1824		1924		

Second part

	IR 2537 🍴	EC 102 ◆	IC 728 🍴	IC 612 🍴	IR 2214 🍴	EC 108 ◆	IC 520 🍴	IC 150 🍴A	EC 112 ✕	IR 2433 🍴	EC 104 ◆	EC 28 ✕	IC 547 ✕	IR 118 🍴	IR 2212 🍴	EC 2 ◆	IC 724 🍴	IC 549 ✕	IR 714 ✕	IR 2539 🍴	EC 39 ✕	EC 8 ✕	EC 26 ✕	EC 114 ✕
München Hbf 760 d.				1050			1038	1150						1250		1238								1450
Nürnberg 750 d.			1132			1232				1332				1417		1432				1517		1532		
Basel SBB 730 d.		1117			1217			1317				1551			1651						1751		1804	
Frankfurt (Main) Hbf d.			1351			1451		1504				1604			1704									
Frankfurt Flughafen ✈ d.			1404																					
Mannheim d.		1337	1418	1407	1437		1507	1518	1524		1548		1607	1637	1648	1654	1718	1724		1748		1818	1824	1848
Mainz d.			1424	1448	1454	1518	1524		1548		1618	1624			1710					1707	1737			
Bingen Hbf d.				1510											1735									
Boppard d.				1535																				
Koblenz d.	1445	1507	1513	1548	1607	1613		1637	1645	1707	1713		1737	1748	1807	1813			1837	1846	1907	1913	1937
Andernach d.	1459			1559					1659						1759					1859				
Remagen d.	1512			1612					1712						1812					1912				
Bonn Hbf d.	1525	1539	1545	1609	1625	1639	1645		1709	1725	1739	1745		1809	1825	1839	1845		1909	1925	1939	1945	2009
Köln Hbf a.	1545	1559	1605	1629	1645	1705		1729	1745	1759	1805		1829	1845	1859	1905			1929	1945	1959	2005	2029
Köln Hbf d.	1548	1609	1610	1633	1648	1710	1709	1709	1717	1733	1757	1813	1826	1833	1857	1913	1810	1833	1848	1902	1909	1910	1933	1948	1951	2009	2010	2033	2057
Düsseldorf Hbf d.	1613	1633		1657	1713		1733	1739	1757	1813	1826	1833		1857	1911	1927	1948v	1946		2011	2027	2034	2046	2057
Duisburg d.	1627	1646		1711	1727		1746	1752	1811	1827	1848t	1846		1911	1927	1948v	1946		1935	1955		2035		2111
Oberhausen d.	1635			1735			1758		1835	1855										2024				
Emmerich 🚇 a.							1826			1924											2048	2059		2125
Essen d.		1659		1724			1759		1825		1859			1925				1959		2024			2048	2125
Gelsenkirchen d.	1646			1733	1746				1846					1946						2033	2046			
Recklinghausen d.	1659			1745	1759				1859					1959						2045	2059			2136
Bochum d.		1709					1809		1836		1909			1936				2009						
Solingen Ohligs d.			1628			1728				1828					1928				1928				2028	
Wuppertal Hbf d.			1642			1742				1842					1942				1942				2042	
Hagen d.			1659			1759				1859					1959				1959				2059	
Dortmund a.		1720	1720			1820	1820		1848		1920	1920	1948				2020	2020			2111	2120	2120	2148
Dortmund d.			1725				1825				1925					2025					2125			
Münster d.	1730		1756	1814	1828		1856		1928		1956				2028		2056		2114	2128		2156		
Osnabrück d.	1757		1821				1921				2021				2121					2221				
Bremen Hbf d.	1857		1916				2016				2116				2216					2311				
Hamburg Hbf a.			2011				2111				2211				2311					0011				
Hamburg Altona a.			2024				2124								2324									

◆ – NOTES (LISTED BY TRAIN NUMBERS)

EC2 – REMBRANDT – 🚊 and ✕ Chur - Amsterdam CS.
EC8 – TIZIANO – 🚊 Milano - Hannover; ✕ Chiasso - Hannover.
EC18 – ANDREAS HOFER – 🚊 and ✕ Innsbruck - Dortmund.
EC26 – JOSEPH HAYDN – 🚊 and ✕ Wien Westbahnhof - Hamburg.
EC28 – PRINZ EUGEN – 🚊 and ✕ Wien Westbahnhof - Kiel.
EC39 – JACQUES BREL – 🚊 and ✕ Paris Nord - Dortmund.
EC47 – ALEXANDER VON HUMBOLDT – 🚊 and ✕ Berlin Zoo - Brussels.
EC102 – RÄTIA – 🚊 and ✕ Chur - Berlin Zoo.
EC104 – BERNER OBERLAND – 🚊 and ✕ Interlaken Ost - Amsterdam Schiphol ✈.
EC108 – THUNERSEE – 🚊 and ✕ Interlaken Ost - Berlin Zoo.
EC112 – WÖRTHERSEE – 🚊 and ✕ Klagenfurt - Dortmund.
EC114 – BLAUER ENZIAN – 🚊 and ✕ Klagenfurt - Dortmund.
IC118 – KARWENDEL – 🚊 and ✕ Innsbruck - Mittenwald - Dortmund.
IC500 – MARIE LUISE KASCHNITZ – 🚊 and ✕ Basel SBB - Braunschweig.
IC502 – MARK BRANDENBURG – 🚊 and ✕ Basel SBB - Berlin Zoo.
IC504 – KAISERSTUHL – 🚊 and 🍴 Basel Bad - Berlin Zoo.
IC516 – FRIEDRICH SCHILLER – 🚊 and 🍴 Stuttgart - Dortmund.
IC520 – SPESSART – 🚊 and 🍴 Nürnberg (München ① - ⑥, not Dec. 25 - Jan. 1, Apr. 15 - 17, May 1) - Hamburg; conveys on ⑥: Zwiesel - Hamburg. Extended to Kiel on dates in Table 663.
IC522 – WESTFÄLISCHER FRIEDE – 🚊 and ✕ Passau - Hamburg.
IC524 – HANSEAT – 🚊 and 🍴 Nürnberg (München ✗) - Kiel.
IC526 – GORCH FOCK – 🚊 and 🍴 Frankfurt/Main (Nürnberg ✗) - Kiel.
IC547 – WESERBERGLAND – 🚊 and ✕ Köln - Leipzig.
IC549 – GÜRZENICH – 🚊 and ✕ Köln - Hannover.

IC604 – HEINRICH DER LÖWE – 🚊 and 🍴 Basel SBB - Braunschweig.
IC620 – KONSUL – 🚊 and 🍴 Nürnberg - Hamburg.
IC714 – NEBELHORN – 🚊 and ✕ Oberstdorf - Münster.
IC718 – ALLGÄU – 🚊 and ✕ Stuttgart (Kempten ✗) - Dortmund.
IC724 – BERCHTESGADENER LAND – 🚊 Berchtesgaden - Hamburg; 🍴 Freilassing - Bremen.
IC728 – PASSAVIA – 🚊 and ✕ Passau - Hamburg.
IC822 – NORDFRIESLAND – 🚊 and 🍴 Frankfurt/Main (Regensburg ✗) - Westerland; conveys May 1 - 27: 🚊 Nürnberg/Regensburg - Dagebüll Mole.
IR2212 – MURGTAL – 🚊 Freudenstadt - Münster (Emden ◆); 🚊 Bad Wildbad (E3022) - Karlsruhe - Münster (Emden ◆); 🍴 Freudenstadt - Lingen.
IR2214 – 🚊 and 🍴 Heidelberg - Norddeich.
IR2216 – HÖLLENTAL – 🚊 and 🍴 Seebrugg - Norddeich Mole.
IR2218 – 🚊 and 🍴 Heidelberg - Norddeich.
IR2337 – 🚊 and 🍴 Saarbrücken - Stralsund (Rostock on Dec. 24, 31).
IR2431 – 🚊 and 🍴 Luxembourg - Cuxhaven.
IR2433 – 🚊 and 🍴 Luxembourg - Münster.
IR2537 – 🚊 and 🍴 Saarbrücken - Münster (Bremerhaven ◆).
IR2539 – 🚊 and 🍴 Saarbrücken - Münster.
A – 🚊 and 🍴 Köln - Amsterdam CS.
e – Basel Bad.
t – Arrive 10 minutes earlier. Connects out of EC28.
v – Arrive 10 minutes earlier. Connects out of IC724.
◆ – Daily except ⑥ (not Dec. 24 - 31, Apr. 14 - 16, Apr. 30, 1995).
✗ – ① - ⑥ (not Dec. 25 - Jan. 1, Apr. 15 - 17, May 1, 1995).

Table 650

FRANKFURT/MAIN - KÖLN - DORTMUND - HAMBURG

1, 2 class except where shown

	IR 2210 ♀♐♦	EC 49 ♀♦	EC 106 ✕♦	IC 726 ♐♀♦	EC 152 ♀ A	IC 512 ✕✕♦	IR 2439 ♀♦	EC 31 ♦	D 233 ♀	EC 4 ✕♦	EC 24 ✕♦	EC 12 ✕♦	ICN 1945 ♀	IR 2318 ✕♦	EC 50 ✕♦	D 1931 ♦	EC 22 ✕♐	IC 722 ♐♀	IC 924 ♦
München Hbf 760 .... d.	...	...	...	...	...	1550	...	...	...	...	...	1650	...	...	...	...	...	...	...
Nürnberg 750 .... d.	...	...	...	1632	...	...	...	...	...	1732	...	...	...	1832	...	...	1932	2032	...
Basel SBB 730 .... d.	...	...	1617	...	...	...	...	...	1717	...	...	...	...	...	...	...	...	...	...
Frankfurt/Main Hbf .... d.	...	...	...	1851	...	...	...	...	...	...	1951	...	...	...	2051	...	2151	2251	2356
Frankfurt Flughafen ✈ ..... d.	...	...	...	1904	...	...	...	...	...	...	2004	...	...	...	2104	...	2204	2304	0008
Mannheim .... d.	...	...	1837	...	...	1907	...	...	1937	...	2007	...	...	...	...	...	...	...	...
Mainz .... d.	1854	...	1918	1924	...	1948	...	...	2018	2024	2048	...	...	2124	...	...	2224	2324	...
Bingen Hbf .... d.	1910	...	...	...	...	...	...	...	...	...	...	...	...	...	...	...	...	...	...
Boppard .... d.	1935	...	...	...	...	...	...	...	...	...	...	...	...	...	...	...	...	...	...
Koblenz .... d.	1948	...	2007	2013	...	2037	2045	...	2107	2113	2137	...	...	2213	...	...	2315	0014	0118
Andernach .... d.	1959	...	...	...	...	...	2059	...	...	...	...	...	...	...	...	...	...	...	...
Remagen .... d.	2012	...	...	...	...	...	2112	...	...	...	...	...	...	...	...	...	...	...	...
Bonn Hbf .... d.	2025	...	2039	2045	...	2109	2125	...	2139	2145	2209	2215	...	2245	...	...	2347	...	0150
Köln Hbf .... a.	2045	...	2059	2105	...	2129	2145	...	2159	2205	2229	2238u	...	2305	...	...	0007	...	0210
Köln Hbf .... d.	2048	2051	2109	2110	2117	2133	...	2152	2200	2210	2209	2245u	2309	2310	...	...	...	...	0212
Düsseldorf Hbf .... d.	2113	2119	2133	...	2139	2157	...	2218	2226	...	2233	2257	2325u	2338	...	2336	...	0006	0247c
Duisburg .... d.	2127	2134	2146	...	2152	2211	...	2233	2242	...	2246	2311	2341u	2353	...	...	...	0024	...
Oberhausen .... d.	2135	...	...	...	2158	...	...	...	...	...	...	...	...	...	...	...	...	...	...
Emmerich 🚉 .... a.	...	...	...	...	2226	...	...	...	...	...	...	...	...	...	...	...	...	...	...
Essen .... d.	...	2147	2159	...	...	2224	...	2246	2256	...	2259	2325	2355u	0019	...	0040	...	...	...
Gelsenkirchen .... d.	2146	...	...	...	...	2233	...	...	...	...	...	...	...	...	...	...	...	...	...
Recklinghausen .... d.	...	...	...	...	...	2245	...	...	...	...	...	...	...	...	...	...	...	...	...
Bochum .... d.	...	2157	2209	...	...	...	...	2256	...	...	2309	2336	...	0019	...	0053	...	...	...
Solingen Ohligs .... d.	...	...	...	2128	...	...	...	...	2228	...	...	...	...	2328	...	...	...	...	...
Wuppertal Hbf .... d.	...	...	...	2142	...	...	...	...	2242	...	...	...	...	2342	...	...	...	...	...
Hagen .... d.	...	...	...	2159	...	...	...	...	2259	...	...	...	...	2359	...	...	...	...	...
Dortmund .... a.	2209	2209	2220	2220	...	2308	...	...	2320	2320	2348	...	0030	0020	...	0105	...	...	...
Dortmund .... d.	...	...	...	...	...	...	...	...	...	...	...	...	...	...	...	0113	...	...	...
Münster .... d.	...	...	...	2314	...	...	...	2353	...	...	...	...	...	...	...	0206	...	...	...
Osnabrück .... d.	...	...	...	...	...	...	...	0024	...	...	...	...	...	...	...	0245	...	...	...
Bremen Hbf .... d.	...	...	...	...	...	...	...	0130	...	...	...	...	...	...	...	0400	...	...	...
Hamburg Hbf .... a.	...	...	...	...	...	...	...	0235	...	...	...	...	...	...	...	0504	...	...	...
Hamburg Altona .... a.	...	...	...	...	...	...	...	...	...	...	...	...	...	...	...	0524	...	...	...

— NOTES (LISTED BY TRAIN NUMBERS)

C4 — VERDI – 🛏 Milano Centrale - Dortmund; ✕ Chiasso - Dortmund.
C12 — PAGANINI – 🛏 and ✕ Venezia Santa Lucia - Innsbruck - Dortmund.
C22 — JOHANN STRAUSS – 🛏 Wien Westbahnhof - Köln; ✕ Wien - Bonn.
C24 — FRANZ LISZT – 🛏 and ✕ Budapest Keleti - Dortmund.
C31 — MOLIÈRE – 🛏 and ♀ Paris Nord - Dortmund.
C49 — MEMLING – 🛏 and ♀ Oostende - Dortmund.
C50 — KARLSTEIN – 🛏 Praha - Dortmund; ✕ Praha - Köln.
C106 — MONT BLANC – 🛏 and ✕ Genève - Dortmund.
233 — NORD EXPRESS – 🛏 1,2 cl. (T2), 🛏 2 cl., 🛏 and ♀ Oostende - København; 🛏 1,2 cl. Paris Nord (EC31) - Aachen - København.

IC512 — ANNETTE KOLB – 🛏 München - Münster; ✕ München - Essen.
D1931 — Daily except ⑥, also May 27, not Dec. 25, Apr. 14, 15, 16, 30: 🛏 Köln - Hamburg (D2882) - Kiel. Via Hamm, depart 0109.
ICN1945 — 🛏 1,2 cl., 🛏 (reclining) and ✕ Bonn - Berlin Charlottenburg. Special fares payable - see heading on page 348.
IR2210 — 🛏 Heidelberg - Dortmund; ♀ Heidelberg - Düsseldorf.
A — 🛏 and ♀ Köln - Amsterdam CS.
c — Düsseldorf Flughafen ✈.
u — Stops to pick up only.
♦ — Daily except ⑥ (not Dec. 24 - 31, Apr. 14 - 16, Apr. 30, 1995).

Table 651

GRONINGEN - LEER

1, 2 class

Rail service Groningen - Leer.   72 km.   Journey time: 64 - 71 minutes.
From Groningen: 0802, 1034 ✕, (also Nov. 17, Apr. 1, May 12), 1704.

Customs/ticket point is Weener 🚉.
From Leer: 0922, 1321 ✕ (also Nov. 17, Apr. 1, May 12), 2028.

Table 653

CUXHAVEN - BREMEN

1, 2 class

km		E 4503 Ⓐ	IR 2432 ♀	5421	E 4507	ICE 883 ✕	IR 2536 ♀	5427	E 4511	E 4513	E 4513	IR 2430 ♀	E 4521	E 4525	IR 2530 Ⓒ	E 4531	5457	E 4533	5461	E 4535	E 4465	E 4539	E 4567	E 4541 Ⓐ
0	Cuxhaven .... d.	0458	...	...	0625	...	0721	...	0818	...	0946	1121	1237	1346	1521	1624	...	1746	...	S 1857	S ...	S 1941	S ...	Ⓐ 2138
40	Bremerhaven Lehe .. d.	0545	0617	0653	0714	...	0807	0836	0906	0941	1032	1207	1319	1432	1604	1721	1736	1833	1841	1938	1941	2027	2041	2220
43	Bremerhaven Hbf .... a.	0550	0621	0657	0719	...	0811	0840	0911	0945	1036	1211	1323	1436	1611	1726	1741	1838	1845	1942	1945	2031	2045	2225
43	Bremerhaven Hbf .... d.	0559	0623	0659	0742	0734	0823	0842	...	0947	1042	1223	1342	1442	1623	1742	1742	...	1847	...	1947	...	2047	2224
106	Bremen .... a.	0656	0700	0754	0837	0808	0900	0937	...	1037	1137	1300	1437	1537	1700	1837	1837	...	1937	...	2037	...	2137	2329

		E 4502 ✕	E 5410	E 4506	E 5424	E 2533 ♀	E 4514	E 4518	IR 2531 ♀	E 4524	E 5440 ✕	E 4528 Ⓐ	E 4530	IR 2431 ♀	E 4536	E 4538	E 2537 ♀	E 4538	E 5468	E 4542 S	E4546 E5478	ICE 880	E4546 E5478	E 5482
	Bremen .... d.	0522	0622	0722	0822	0900	1022	1122	1300	1322	1422	...	1522	1700	1722	1822	1900	...	1922	...	2022	2122	2151	2222
	Bremerhaven Hbf .... a.	0617	0717	0817	0917	0936	1111	1217	1346	1417	1517	...	1617	1736	1817	1917	1936	...	2011	...	2117	2211	2225	2317
	Bremerhaven Hbf .... d.	0629	0720	0821	0919	0948	1120	1232	1348	1429	1530	1605	1638	1748	1826	...	1938	1942	2020	2031	2117	2222	←	2319
	Bremerhaven Lehe .. d.	0634	0724	0826	0923	0953	1148	1237	1353	1434	1534	1610	1643	1753	1831	...	1942	1947	2024	2036	2123	→	2237	2323
	Cuxhaven .... a.	0719	...	0909	...	1035	1212	1325	1424	1519	...	1653	1726	1840	1923	...	2031	...	2119	...	...	2320h	2237	2323

— NOTES (LISTED BY TRAIN NUMBERS)

E880 — VEIT STOSS – 🛏 and ✕ München - Bremerhaven.
E883 — PAULA MODERSOHN-BECKER – 🛏 and ✕ Bremerhaven - München.
2430/1 — 🛏 and ♀ Cuxhaven - Luxembourg and v.v.
2432 — 🛏 and ♀ Bremerhaven - Luxembourg.
2530 — 🛏 Cuxhaven - Trier (Saarbrücken ♣); ♀ Cuxhaven - Koblenz.
2531 — 🛏 and ♀ Trier (Saarbrücken ✎) - Cuxhaven.

IR2533 — 🛏 and ♀ Münster - Cuxhaven.
IR2536 — 🛏 and ♀ Cuxhaven - Saarbrücken.
IR2537 — 🛏 and ♀ Saarbrücken - Bremerhaven.
S — Not Dec. 24, 31.
h — Not ⑥.
♣ — ① - ⑥ (not Dec. 25 - Jan. 1, Apr. 15 - 17, May 1, 1995).
♦ — Daily except ⑥ (not Dec. 24 - 31, Apr. 14 - 16, Apr. 30, 1995).

Table 654

WILHELMSHAVEN - OSNABRÜCK

1, 2 class

km		E 7312 ✕♐	E 7314	E 7318	E 7320	E 7322	E 2583 B♀	IR 7324 C	E 7326	E 8416	E 7330	E 7332	IR 2585 B♀	E 7336 C	E 7338	E 8424	IR 2587 S	E 7342	E 7348 S	IR 7350 S	E 8432 K♀	E 7352 G	E 8434 ⑦♣	E 8436
0	Wilhelmshaven ... d.	0527	0632	...	0823	...	0939	1032	...	1144	1232	...	1339	1432	...	1543	1632	1739	1832	...	1944	2039	2039	...
52	Oldenburg .... a.	0611	0718	...	0910	...	1027	1118	...	1229	1318	...	1427	1518	...	1629	1718	1827	1918	...	2029	2127	2127	2132
52	Oldenburg .... d.	0614	0735	0816	0935	1016	...	1135	1216	...	1335	1416	...	1535	1616	...	1735	...	1935	2016	...	2135	...	2218
95	Osnabrück .... a.	0758	0932	0958	1132	1158	...	1332	1358	...	1531	1558	...	1731	1758	...	1931	...	2200	2336	...	...	...	...

🛏 and ♀ Wilhelmshaven - Hannover - Hildesheim and v.v.
Daily to Oldenburg, ✕ to Osnabrück.
Not when IR2589 runs.
🛏 and ♀ Wilhelmshaven - Hannover and v.v.

K — ⑧, not Dec. 24 - 31, Apr. 14 - 16, Apr. 30: 🛏 and ♀ Wilhelmshaven - Bremen.
S — Not Dec. 24, 31.
♣ — Not Dec. 25, Jan. 1.

Table 654 OSNABRÜCK - WILHELMSHAVEN

1, 2 class

	E	E	IR	E	E	E	IR	E	E	E	E	IR	E	E	E	E	E	IR	E	E	E	E	E	E	E
	7309	7311	2588	8411	7315	7317	2586	7321	7323	7327	7329	2584	7333	7335	7339	7341	8431	2582	7345	8433	7347	7351	8437	7353	7355
	C	❖	J🍷				B🍷	⚒				B🍷		C		C	G	A🍷	S		S⚒	S	S	⑦❖	⑦❖
Osnabrück d.	0513	0625	...	...	0759	0826	...	0959	1026	1159	1226	...	1359	1427	1559	1626	...	...	1759	...	1856	1959	...	2057	2201
Oldenburg a.	0716	0824	...	...	0939	1024	...	1139	1224	1339	1424	...	1539	1624	1739	1824	...	...	1941	...	...	2139	...	2249	2339
Oldenburg d.	0734	...	0829	0927	...	1042	1129	...	1242	...	1442	1529	...	1642	...	1842	1929	1929	...	2048	...	2143	2242	...	...
Wilhelmshaven a.	0823	...	0919	1015	...	1130	1219	...	1330	...	1530	1619	...	1730	...	1930	2019	2019	...	2136	...	2231	2330	...	...

A – Ⓑ, **not** Dec. 24 - 31, Apr. 14 - 16, Apr. 30: [12] and 🍷 Hildesheim - Wilhelmshaven.
B – [12] and 🍷 Hildesheim - Hannover - Wilhelmshaven.
C – Daily to Oldenburg, ⚒ to Osnabrück.
G – **Not** when **IR2582** runs.
J – [12] and 🍷 Hannover - Wilhelmshaven.
S – **Not** Dec. 24, 31.
❖ – **Not** Dec. 25, Jan. 1.

Table 655 NORDDEICH - MÜNSTER and HANNOVER

1, 2 class

km		IR	E	IC	IR	IR	E	E	E	E	IR	IR	E	E	E	IR	IR	E	E	IR	IR	IR	E	E
		2481	6405	541	2581	2215	6407	3117	3254	6411	2483	2217	3125	3258	6417	2583	2219	3133	3262	2743	2311	2511	3141	3141
		⚡🍷	⚒	⚡🍷 ♦	🍷	⚡🍷	❖				🍷	🍷 ♦				🍷	🍷			🍷 ♦	🍷 ♦	🍷 ♦	A	B
0	**Norddeich Mole** d.	...	...	...	...	...	...	...	...	...	0700	...	0735	...	...	...	0900	0926	...	1100	...	1128	1128	...
1	**Norddeich** d.	...	...	...	...	*0507*f	...	0543**d**	...	0619	0702	...	0736	...	...	...	0902	0927	...	1102	...	1130	1130	...
35	Emden a.	...	...	...	...	*0535*f	...	0611**d**	...	0702	0733	...	0805	...	...	...	0933	0956	...	1133	...	1201	1201	...
35	Emden d.	...	...	...	...	0540	...	0614	0631	0712	0735	0743	0807	0832	0909	...	0943	1003	1038	1135	1143	1203	1203	...
61	Leer a.	...	...	...	...	0556	...	0630	0647	0728	0751	0759	0824	0849	0925	...	0959	1020	1054	1151	1159	1223	1223	...
61	Leer d.	...	...	...	...	0558	0606	0639	0650	0739	0802	0801	0839	0852	0935	...	1001	1039	1103	1202	1201	1226	1236	1236
	Meppen d.	...	...	...	...	0635	|	|	0740	|	|	0835	|	0948	|	...	1035	|	1148	|	1235	1303	|	|
	Lingen d.	...	...	...	...	0647	|	|	0756	|	|	0847	|	1003	|	...	1047	|	1203	|	1247	1316	|	|
	Rheine a.	...	...	...	...	0704	|	|	0820	|	|	0904	|	1026	|	...	1104	|	1226	|	1304	1333	|	|
	Rheine d.	...	...	...	...	0705	|	|	0828	|	|	0905	|	1028	|	...	1105	|	1228	|	1305	1345	|	|
	Münster a.	...	...	...	...	0728	|	|	0855	|	|	0928	|	1055	|	...	1128	|	1255	|	1328	1408	|	|
	Köln Hbf **650** a.	...	...	...	...	0908	|	|	...	|	|	1108	|	...	|	...	1308	|	...	|	1508	...	|	|
	Heidelberg **730** a.	...	...	...	...	1159	|	|	...	|	|	1359	|	...	|	...	1559	|	...	|	1759	...	|	|
	Wilhelmshaven **654** d.	...	0457	...		...	|	|	...	|	|	...		...		0939	...	|	...	|	...	...	|	|
116	Oldenburg d.	...	0549	0606	...	...	0649	0726	...	0822	0837	...	0926	...	1024	1037	...	1126	...	1237	...	...	1326	1326
161	**Bremen** a.	...	0633	0637	...	...	0733	0802	...	...	0907	...	1002	...	...	1107	...	1202	...	1307	...	...	1402	1402
161	**Bremen 750** d.	0510	...	0641	0710	...	...	0821	...	...	0910	...	1021	...	...	1110	...	1221	...	1310	...	...	1421	1421
283	**Hannover Hbf 750** a.	0615	...	0742	0815	...	...	0940	...	...	1015	...	1140	...	...	1215	...	1340	...	1415	...	...	1540	1540
	Hildesheim **697** a.	0647	...	...	0840	...	...	...	...	...	1040	...	...	...	...	1240	...	...	...	...	...	...	...	...
	Bad Harzburg **697** a.	0802	...	...	...	...	...	...	...	...	1202	...	...	...	...	...	...	...	...	...	...	...	...	...

	E	E	IR	IR	E	E	IR	IR	E	E	E	IR	IR	E	E	E	D	IR	IR	E	E	E	IR	E
	3266	6429	2585	2313	3149	3270	2487	2315	3157	3274	6441	2587	2317	3165	3278	6447	1925	2489	2319	6451	6451	3282	2589	3177
	K		🍷	🍷 ♦			🍷 ♦	🍷 ♦		L		🍷	🍷		S		🍷 ♦	🍷	🍷 ♦	Ⓒ	Ⓐ	C	🍷 ♣	S
Norddeich Mole d.	...	...	...	1300	1330	...	1500	...	1528	...	...	...	1700	1729	...	...	1823	...	1900	1928	...	...	...	2033
Norddeich d.	...	...	...	1302	1332	...	1502	...	1530	...	...	...	1702	1731	...	...	1825**u**	...	1902	1930	...	...	...	2035
Emden a.	...	...	...	1333	1406	...	1533	...	1559	...	...	...	1733	1801	...	...	1902**u**	...	1930	1959	...	...	...	2108
Emden d.	1243	1311	...	1343	1409	1446	1535	1543	1603	...	1711	...	1743	1803	1845	1906	1913**u**	1935	1943	2003	2003	2042	...	2110
Leer a.	1259	1327	...	1359	1425	1502	1551	1559	1620	...	1727	...	1759	1820	1901	1922	1928**u**	1951	1959	2019	2019	2058	...	2126
Leer d.	1303	1336	...	1401	1439	1503	1602	1601	1635	1640	1736	...	1801	1839	1903	1939	1930**u**	2002	2001	2035	2035	2100	...	2135
Meppen d.	1348	|	...	1435	|	1548	|	1635	|	1657	|	...	1835	|	1948	|	2004**u**	|	2035	|	|	2145	...	|
Lingen d.	1403	|	...	1447	|	1603	|	1647	|	1748	|	...	1847	|	2003	|	2017**u**	|	2047	|	|	2159	...	|
Rheine a.	1426	|	...	1504	|	1626	|	1704	|	1826	|	...	1904	|	2026	|	2034**u**	|	2104	|	|	2222	...	|
Rheine d.	1428	|	...	1505	|	1628	|	1705	|	1828	|	...	1905	|	2027	|	2036**u**	|	2105	|	|	2223	...	|
Münster a.	1455	|	...	1528	|	1655	|	1728	|	1855	|	...	1928	|	2054	|	2059**u**	|	2128	|	|	2255	...	|
Köln Hbf **650** a.	...	|	...	1708	|	...	|	1908	|	...	|	...	2112	|	...	|	...	|	2308	|	|	...	...	|
Heidelberg **730** a.	...	|	...	1959	|	...	|	...	|	...	|	...	...	|	...	|	...	|	...	|	|	...	...	|
Wilhelmshaven **654** d.	...	|	1339	...	|	...	|	...	|	...	|	1739	...	|	...	|	...	|	...	|	|	...	2039	|
Oldenburg d.	...	1424	1437	...	1526	...	1637	...	1726	...	1824	1837	...	1926	...	2021	...	2037	...	2119	2119	...	2137	2226
Bremen a.	...	...	1507	...	1602	...	1707	...	1802	...	...	1907	...	2002	...	...	...	2107	...	...	...	...	2207	2302
Bremen 750 d.	...	...	1510	...	1621	...	1710	...	1821	...	...	1910	...	2021	...	...	...	2110	...	...	...	...	*2221*	2317
Hannover Hbf 750 a.	...	...	1615	...	1740	...	1815	...	1940	...	...	2015	...	2140	...	...	...	2215	...	...	...	...	*2340*	004[illegible]
Hildesheim **697** a.	...	...	1640	...	...	...	1840	...	...	...	...	...	...	...	...	...	...	...	...	...	...	...	...	...
Bad Harzburg **697** a.	...	...	...	...	...	...	1954	...	...	...	...	...	...	...	...	...	...	...	...	...	...	...	...	...

km		E	E	IR	E	IR	E	E	IR	IR	D	E	E	E	IR	IR	E	E	E	IR	IR	E	E	IR
		6402	6404	2316	3104	2588	6414	3259	2314	2488	1924	3261	3116	3120	2312	2586	6422	3265	3124	2310	2742	3269	3132	251[illegible]
		F		🍷 ♦	❖	🍷			🍷	🍷 ♦	🍷 ♦				🍷 ♦	🍷				🍷 ♦	🍷 ♦	K	B	🍷 ♦
	Bad Harzburg **697** d.	...	...	...	...	...	...	...	...	0607	...	...	...	...	...	...	...	...	...	...	...	...	...	...
	Hildesheim **697** d.	...	...	...	...	...	...	...	...	0716	...	...	...	...	...	0916	...	...	...	...	...	...	...	...
	Hannover Hbf 750 d.	...	...	...	0517	0643	...	...	...	0744	...	...	0817	0917	...	0943	...	...	1017	...	1143	...	1217	...
	Bremen 750 a.	...	...	...	0637	0748	...	...	...	0848	...	...	0937	1037	...	1048	...	...	1137	...	1248	...	1337	...
	Bremen d.	0439	0546	...	0653	0751	...	...	...	0851	...	...	0953	...	...	1051	...	...	1153	...	1251	...	1353	...
	Oldenburg d.	0527	0632	...	0734	0821	0837	...	...	0923	...	...	1033	...	...	1121	1133	...	1237	...	1323	...	1433	...
	Wilhelmshaven **654** a.	|	|	...	|	0919	|	...	...	|	...	...	|	...	...	1219	|	...	|	...	|	...	|	...
	Heidelberg **730** d.	|	|	...	|	...	|	...	...	|	...	...	|	...	0558	...	|	...	|	0758	|	...	|	...
	Köln Hbf **650** d.	|	|	...	|	...	|	...	0648	|	...	...	|	...	0848	...	|	...	|	1048	|	...	|	...
0	**Münster** d.	|	|	0630	|	...	|	0804	0830	|	0857	0904	|	...	1030	...	|	1104	|	1230	|	1304	|	135
39	Rheine a.	|	|	0651	|	...	|	0830	0851	|	0919**s**	0930	|	...	1051	...	|	1130	|	1251	|	1330	|	141
39	Rheine d.	|	|	0653	|	...	|	0832	0853	|	0923**s**	0932	|	...	1053	...	|	1132	|	1253	|	1332	|	142
70	Lingen d.	|	|	0711	|	...	|	0854	0911	|	0941**s**	0946	|	...	1111	...	|	1146	|	1311	|	1356	|	144
91	Meppen d.	|	|	0724	|	...	|	0907	0924	|	0954**s**	1013	|	...	1124	...	|	1213	|	1324	|	1413	|	145
154	**Leer** a.	0604	0709	0757	0815	...	0919	0951	0957	0956	1026**s**	1059	1109	...	1157	...	1214	1259	1316	1357	1356	1459	1509	153
154	**Leer** d.	0613	0718	0800	0824	...	0928	0952	0959	1007	1028**s**	1101	1118	...	1159	...	1223	1301	1325	1359	1407	1501	1518	153
180	Emden a.	0628	0734	0820	0840	...	0944	1010	1015	1026	1044**s**	1119	1134	...	1215	...	1239	1319	1341	1415	1423	1519	1534	155
180	Emden d.	0630	0742	0827	...	...	0958	...	...	1027	1046**s**	...	1137	...	1227	...	...	...	1344	...	1427	...	...	160
214	**Norddeich** a.	0658	0816	0858	...	...	1026	...	...	1058	1120**s**	...	1212	...	1258	...	...	...	1413	...	1458	...	...	163
215	**Norddeich Mole** a.	0706	0820	0905	...	...	1029	...	...	1105	1135	...	1216	...	1305	...	...	...	1417	...	1505	...	...	163

♦ – **NOTES** (LISTED BY TRAIN NUMBERS)

IC541 – ROLAND – [12] and 🍷 Oldenburg - Berlin Zoo.
D1924/5 – LUNA – ⑤⑥⑦ Apr. 7 - May 27, also Apr. 17 (from München and Norddeich): 1,2 cl., 2 cl. and 🍷 München - Norddeich Mole and v.v.
IR2217 – HÖLLENTAL – [12] and 🍷 Emden - Seebrugg.
IR2310/1 – [12] and 🍷 Emden - Stuttgart and v.v.
IR2312 – [12] Karlsruhe - Norddeich Mole; 🍷 Heidelberg - Norddeich Mole.
IR2313 – [12] and 🍷 Norddeich Mole - Karlsruhe.
IR2315 – [12] and 🍷 Emden - Koblenz.
IR2316 – [12] and 🍷 Dortmund - Norddeich Mole.
IR2319 – [12] Norddeich Mole - Köln; 🍷 Norddeich Mole - Rheine.
IR2487 – [12] and 🍷 Norddeich Mole - Hannover (Bad Harzburg ♣).
IR2510/1 – May 1 - 27: [12] and 🍷 Norddeich Mole - Frankfurt and v.v.
IR2742 – [12] and 🍷 Dresden (Leipzig on Dec. 25, Jan. 1) - Norddeich Mole.
IR2743 – [12] and 🍷 Norddeich Mole - Görlitz (Dresden on Dec. 24, 31).

A – Nov. 1 - Apr. 30.
B – May 1 - 27.
C – Ⓑ, **not** Dec. 24, 31 from Emden; daily from Rheine.
F – **Not** Dec. 24, 31 from Bremen; daily from Oldenburg.
K – Ⓑ Emden - Münster and v.v; daily Rheine - Münster and v.v.
L – Ⓑ, also Dec. 25, Jan. 1, **not** Dec. 24, 31 from Emden; daily from Rheine.
S – **Not** Dec. 24, 31.
f – ⚒ only.
u – Stops to **pick up** only.
⚡ – ① - ⑥ (**not** Dec. 25 - Jan. 1, Apr. 15 - 17, May 1, **1995**).
♣ – Daily except ⑥ (**not** Dec. 24 - 31, Apr. 14 - 16, Apr. 30, **1995**).
d – Ⓐ only.
s – Stops to **set down** only.
❖ – **Not** Dec. 25, Jan. 1.

Table 655 HANNOVER and MÜNSTER - NORDDEICH

1, 2 class

	E 3132	IR 2218	IR 2584	E 6434	E 3273	E 3140	IR 2486	IR 2216	IR 2486	E 3277	E 3148	IR 2214	IR 2582	E 6446	E 3281	E 3156	E 3160	IR 2212	E 3283	IR 2482	E 3285	E 3164	IC 540	E 3287
	A	🍷	🍷		K		🍷	🍷 ♦	🍷		F	🍷	🍷 ♦			C		♣🍷 ♦	K	🍷	S		♣🍷 ♦	S
Bad Harzburg **697** .... d.	...	...	...	...	...	...	1405	...	...	...	...	...	...	...	...	...	...	...	...	1805	...	...	...	...
Hildesheim **697** .... d.	...	...	1316	...	...	...	1516	...	...	...	...	...	1716	...	...	...	...	...	...	1916	...	...	...	...
annover Hbf 750 .... d.	1217	...	1343	...	...	1417	1543	...	...	...	1617	...	1743	...	...	1817	1917	...	...	1943	...	2017	2157	...
remen 750 .... a.	1337	...	1448	...	...	1537	1648	...	...	...	1737	...	1848	...	...	1937	2037	...	...	2048	...	2137	2259	...
remen.............................. d.	1353	...	1451	...	...	1553	1651	...	...	...	1753	...	1851	...	...	1953	━━	...	...	2051	...	2153	2301	...
ldenburg .... d.	1433	...	1521	1533	...	1637	1723	...	...	...	1832	...	1921	1933	...	2037	...	...	...	2123	...	2233	2330	...
Wilhelmshaven **654** .... a.	|	...	1619	|	...	|	|	...	...	...	|	...	2019	|	...	|	E	...	...	|	...	|	...	...
Heidelberg **730** .... d.	|	0958	...	|	...	|	|	1158	...	...	|	1358	...	|	...	|	**3283**	1558	...	|	...	|	...	...
Köln Hbf **650** .... d.	|	1248	...	|	...	|	|	1448	...	...	|	1648	...	|	...	|	K	1848	...	|	...	|	...	...
ünster............................. d.	|	1430	...	|	1504	|	|	1630	...	1704	|	1830	...	|	1904	|	2004	2030	...	|	2110	|	...	2210
heine................................. a.	|	1451	...	|	1530	|	|	1651	...	1730	|	1851	...	|	1930	|	2030	2051	...	|	2142	|	...	2242
heine................................. d.	|	1453	...	|	1532	|	|	1653	...	1732	|	1853	...	|	1932	|	2032	2053	...	|	2153	|	...	2300
ingen .... d.	|	1511	...	|	1556	|	|	1711	...	1746	|	1911	...	|	1946	|	2054	2111	...	|	2215	|	...	2323
leppen................................ d.	|	1524	...	|	1613	|	|	1724	←	1813	|	1924	...	|	2013	|	2107	2124	...	|	2227	|	...	2338
eer .... a.	1509	1557	...	1614	1659	1716	1756	1757	1756	1859	1909	1957	...	2014	2059	2116	2151	2157	...	2156	2311	2313t	...	0025
eer .... d.	1518	1559	...	1625	1701	1725	→	1759	1807	1901	1918	1959	...	2023	2101	2125	2152	2159	←	2207	2312	2322t	...	0027
mden .... a.	1534	1615	...	1639	1719	1741	...	1815	1823	1920	1934	2015	...	2039	2120	2141	2210	2215	2210	2223	2330	2338t	...	0045
mden .... d.	1601	1627	...	...	...	1803	...	1828	...	...	1936	2019	...	...	...	2144	→	...	2231	...	...	...	...	...
orddeich .... a.	1633	1658	...	...	...	1837	...	1858	...	...	2010	2052	...	...	...	2213	...	...	2300	...	...	...	...	...
orddeich Mole .... a.	1636	1705	...	...	...	1840	...	1905	...	...	2014	...	...	...	...	...	...	...	...	...	...	...	...	...

– **NOTES** (LISTED BY TRAIN NUMBERS)

540 – ROLAND – [12] and 🍷 Berlin Zoo - Oldenburg.
2212 – MURGTAL – [12] and 🍷 Freudenstadt - Emden; [2] Bad Wildbad - Emden. 🍷 Freudenstadt - Lingen.
2216 – HÖLLENTAL – [12] and 🍷 Seebrugg - Emden.
2582 – [12] and 🍷 Hildesheim - Bremen (Wilhelmshaven ♣).
– Nov. 1 - Apr. 30.

C – Daily to Oldenburg; Ⓑ to Norddeich.
F – Daily to Emden; ⑥⑦ and holidays to Norddeich Mole.
K – Ⓑ Emden - Münster and v.v; daily Rheine - Münster and v.v.
S – **Not** Dec. 24, 31.
t – **Not** Dec. 24, 31.
♣ – Daily except ⑥ (**not** Dec. 24 - 31, Apr. 14 - 16, Apr. 30, **1995**).

Table 660 HAMBURG - ROSTOCK - STRALSUND

1, 2 class except where shown

km		IR 2231	E 3757	IR 2635	IR 2233	E 3761	IR 2235	E 3763	IR 2335	IC 737	E 3767	IR 2237	E 3769	IR 2637	IR 2337	E 3773	E3815 E3817	IR 2239	E 3777	IR 2339	IR 2833	E 3781	D 477	E 3819
		🍷 ❖		🍷 ♦	🍷 ♦	Ⓐ	🍷	2	🍷 ♦	🍷 ♦	Ⓐ	🍷 ♦		🍷 ♦	🍷 ♦	2		🍷 ♦	S	🍷 ♦	🍷 ♦	Ⓑ	🍷 C	Ⓑ
0	**Hamburg Altona** .... d.	0603	...	0718	0803	...	1003	...	...	...	...	1403	...	1518	...	...	...	1738	...	2003	...	...	2153	...
7	**Hamburg Hbf 665** .... d.	0619	0721	0731	0819	0921	1019	1121	1219	1219	1321	1419	1511	1531	1619	1721	...	1759	1921	2019	2119	2121	2221	*2204*
69	Lübeck **665** .... d.	0707	|	|	0907	|	1107	|	1307	|	|	1507	|	|	1707	|	1750t	1907	|	2107	2212	|	|	2307
	Büchen .... d.	|	0811	0826	|	1011	|	1211	|	|	1411	|	1601	1626	|	1811	|	|	2011	|	|	2211	2306	|
	Hagenow Land .... d.	|	0844	0856	|	1042	|	1242	|	|	1442	|	1636	1656	|	1842	|	|	2042	|	|	2242	|	|
	Ludwigslust .... d.	|	|	0920	|	|	|	|	|	|	|	|	|	1720	|	|	|	|	|	|	|	|	2351	|
	Magdeburg **674** .... a.	|	|	1103	|	|	|	|	|	|	|	|	|	1903	|	|	|	|	|	|	|	|	0144	|
	Schwerin 668..................... d.	|	0906	...	|	1104	|	1309	|	1356	1504	|	1706	...	|	1904	|	|	2104	|	|	2304	...	|
131	Bad Kleinen **668** .... d.	0757	...	...	0957	...	1157	...	1357	|	...	1557	...	...	1757	...	1910	1957	...	2157	2301	...	...	2359
172	Bützow .... d.	0822	...	...	1022	...	1222	...	1422	|	...	1622	...	...	1828	...	1938	2022	...	2225	2325	...	...	0026
202	**Rostock**............................ a.	0851	...	...	1051	...	1251	...	1451	1501	...	1651	...	...	1855	...	2005	2051	...	2257	2354	...	...	0053
202	**Rostock**............................ d.	0900	...	...	1100	...	...	...	...	1510	...	1702	...	...	1903	...	2021	2102	...	...	...	...	...	...
231	Ribnitz-Damgarten West ..... d.	0923	...	...	1123	...	...	...	...	1533	...	1725	...	...	1930	...	2050	2125	...	...	...	...	...	...
274	**Stralsund Hbf** .... a.	0953	...	...	1153	...	...	...	...	1603	...	1755	...	...	2002	...	2121	2157	...	...	...	...	...	...
	Binz **675** .... a.	1047	...	...	1246	...	...	...	...	1656	...	...	...	...	...	...	...	...	...	...	...	...	...	...

km		D 476	D 476	IR 2338	E 3756	IR 2336	E 3760	IR 2238	E 3762	IR 2334	IR 2636	E 3008	IR 2236	E 3816	E 3768	IC 736	IR 2234	E 3772	IR 2232	IR 2634	IR 2832	E 3776	IR 2230	E 3780	E 3818
		🍷 A	🍷 B	🍷 ♦		🍷 ♦	2	🍷	Ⓐ	🍷 ♦	🍷 ♦	G	🍷		2	🍷 ♦	🍷		🍷	🍷 ♦	🍷 ♦	S	🍷 ♦	2 Ⓑ	Ⓑ
	Binz **675** .... d.	...	...	...	...	...	...	...	...	0905	...	...	...	...	...	1251	...	...	...	...	...	...	1705	...	...
0	**Stralsund Hbf** .... d.	...	...	...	...	0602	...	0804	...	1004	...	1004	1204	...	...	1347	...	...	...	...	*1620*	...	1804	...	1911
43	Ribnitz-Damgarten West.. d.	...	...	...	...	0634	...	0834	...	1034	...	1036	1234	...	...	1418	...	...	...	...	*1728*	...	1834	...	1949
72	**Rostock**................... a.	...	...	...	...	0658	...	0858	...	1058	...	1058	1258	...	...	1444	...	...	...	...	*1753*	...	1858	...	2013
72	**Rostock**................... d.	...	...	0501	...	0707	...	0907	...	1107	...	━━	1307	1337	...	1452	1507	...	1707	...	1758	...	1907	...	2024
02	Bützow .... d.	...	...	0530	...	0734	...	0934	...	1134	...	**E3766**	1334	1405	...	|	1534	...	1734	...	1825	...	1934	...	2052
43	Bad Kleinen **668** ...... d.	...	...	0600	...	0800	...	1000	...	1200	...	Ⓐ	1400	1433	...	|	1600	...	1800	...	1851	...	2000	...	2119
59	**Schwerin 668**........ d.	...	0450	|	0659	|	0859	|	1059	|	...	1259	|	|	1459	1558	|	1659	|	...	|	1859	|	2059	|
	Magdeburg **674** .. d.	0228	|	|	|	|	|	|	|	|	1020	|	|	|	|	|	|	|	|	1620	|	|	|	|	|
	Ludwigslust .... d.	0423	|	|	|	|	|	|	|	|	1213	|	|	|	|	|	|	|	|	1813	|	|	|	|	|
88	Hagenow Land ...... d.	0439	|	|	0717	|	0917	|	1117	|	1227	1317	|	|	1517	|	|	1717	|	1827	|	1917	|	2117	|
35	Büchen .... d.	0509	|	|	0749	|	0949	|	1149	|	1254	1349	|	|	1549	|	|	1749	|	1854	|	1949	|	2149	|
	Lübeck .... a.	|	0610	0651	|	0851	|	1051	|	1251	|	|	1451	1531	|	|	1651	|	1851	|	1951	|	2051	|	2210
82	**Hamburg Hbf** .... a.	0604	0708	0739	0839	0939	1039	1139	1239	1339	1340	1439	1539	*1650*	1739	1734	1739	1839	1939	1940	2039	2039	2139	2239	*2354*
89	**Hamburg Altona** ...... a.	0630	0730	0754	...	...	...	1154	...	...	1355	...	1554	...	...	...	1754	...	1954	2000	...	...	2154	...	...

– **NOTES** (LISTED BY TRAIN NUMBERS)

36 – RÜGEN – [12] Stralsund - Köln (Aachen ♣); starts from Binz ⑥⑦ Apr. 29 - May 27; 🍷 to Köln.
37 – RÜGEN – [12] Köln (Aachen ⁄) - Stralsund. Extended to Binz on ⑤⑥ Apr. 28 - May 27; 🍷 from Köln.
230/3 – [12] and 🍷 Hamburg - Stralsund (Binz on ⑥⑦ Apr. 29 - May 27) and v.v.
237 – [12] and 🍷 Hamburg - Rostock (Stralsund on ⑤, also Apr. 13, May 24, **not** Apr. 14, May 26.
239 – [12] and 🍷 Hamburg - Rostock (Stralsund daily except ⑥, **not** Apr. 14 - 16, Apr. 30).
334 – [12] Rostock (Binz on ⑥, **not** Apr. 15, May 27) - Saarbrücken; 🍷 Rostock - Merzig.
335 – [12] and 🍷 Koblenz - Köln - Hamburg - Rostock.
336 – [12] and 🍷 Rostock (Stralsund ① - ⑥, **not** Apr. 15 - 17, May 1) - Saarbrücken.
337 – [12] and 🍷 Saarbrücken - Stralsund (Rostock on Dec. 24, 31).
338 – ① - ⑥, **not** Apr. 15 - 17, May 1: [12] Rostock - Hamburg; 🍷 Bad Kleinen - Hamburg.

IR2339 – Daily except ⑥, **not** Apr. 14 - 16, 30: [12] and 🍷 Hamburg - Rostock.
IR2634 – [12] and 🍷 Dresden Hbf - Hamburg.
IR2635 – [12] and 🍷 Hamburg - Dresden Hbf.
IR2636 – [12] and 🍷 Dresden Hbf (Magdeburg on Dec. 25) - Hamburg.
IR2637 – [12] and 🍷 Hamburg - Dresden Hbf (Magdeburg on Dec. 24).
IR2832/3 – ⑦, also Apr. 17, May 1, **not** Apr. 16, 30: [12] and 🍷 Hamburg - Rostock and v.v.
A – Daily except ⑥ (from Praha): 🛏 1,2 cl., ▬ 2 cl., [12] and 🍷 Praha Hlavni - Hamburg.
B – ⑥ (from Praha): 🛏 1,2 cl., ▬ 2 cl., [12] and 🍷 Praha Hlavni - Hamburg.
C – 🛏 1,2 cl., ▬ 2 cl. and [12] Hamburg - Praha Hlavni.
G – Ⓑ, also Apr. 15, May 27, **not** Apr. 14, May 26.
S – **Not** Dec. 24, 31.
t – ⑤⑥. On ①②③④⑦ depart Lübeck 1804.
❖ – **Not** Dec. 25, Jan. 1.

Table 661 — HAMBURG - WESTERLAND

1, 2 class except where shown

km		E 5804	5712	5718	3704	IC 831 ♟	3708	5732	5736	3712	IC 632 ✕	5750	3716	IC 826 ✕	3720	IC 822 ♟	3724	5770	5774	3728	E 5778 S	E 5782 S	E 3732 S	E 5786 S
		✕✕	❖			0814					1104			1414		1614								
0	Hamburg Hbf....d.	...	...	0559	0729	0844	0929	0959	1059	1129	1145	1259	1349	1445	1529	1645	1729	1759	1859	1929	1959	2059	2129	2159
	Hamburg Altona....d.	...	...	0646	0809		1009	1046	1148	1209	1145	1346	1409		1609		1809	1846	1948	2009	2046	2146	2209	2256
64	Itzehoe....d.	...	...	0729	0842	0957	1042	1129	1230	1242	1257	1427	1442	1557	1643	1757	1842	1929	2030	2042	2129	2229	2242	2322
123	Heide....d.	...	0602	0701	0809	0904	1023	1104	1154	1254	1304	1323	1454	1504	1623	1707	1823	1904	1959	2054	2104	2158	2254	0003
157	Husum....d.	...	0602	0701	0809	0904	1023	1104	1154	1254	1304	1323	1454	1504	1623	1707	1823	1904	1959	2054	2104	2158	2254	0003
197	Niebüll....d.	...	0637	0735	0834	0941	1102	1137			1335	1405		1535	1702	1737	1902	1937	2030		2136	2230	...	2335
237	Westerland....a.	...	0711	0816	0910	1018	1126	1211			1412	1432		1607	1728	1813	1928	2006	2104		2203	2301	...	0007

		5709	3709	E 5719	3713	IC 823 ✕	5727	E 3719	5729	3723	IC 633 ✕	827	5747	3727	5751	5753	3733	5759	IC 830 ♟	E 3737	5771	5777	4441 3743 S	E 5783 S	5787
			❖			✕					✕								♟				S	S	
	Westerland....d.	...	0535	0646	0740	0839	...	0937	...	1128	1139	1239		1336			1527		1636	1730	...	1855	1940	...	2040
	Niebüll....d.	...	0617	0729	0816	0912	...	1004	...	1153	1213	1312		1413			1605		1712	1804	...	1929	2017	...	2127
	Husum....d.	0601	0645	0801	0843	0938	1001	1032	1101	1224	1248	1338	1401	1443	1501	1601	1633	1701	1739	1832	1901	1957	2044	2101	2201
	Heide....d.	0626	0707	0826	0907	1000	1026	1056	1126	1246	1301	1400	1426	1501	1526	1626	1656	1726	1802	1856	1926	...	2107	2126	2227
	Itzehoe....d.	0710	0742	0910	0942		1110	1129	1210	1320			1510	1542	1610	1710	1729	1810		1929	2010	...	2142	2210	2307
	Hamburg Altona....a.	0758	0823	0958	1023	1113	1158	1209	1258	1403	1413	1513	1558	1623	1658	1758	1809	1858	1913	2012	2107	...	2225	2300	2359
	Hamburg Hbf....a.				1143							1448	1543							1943					

♦ — NOTES (LISTED BY TRAIN NUMBERS)

IC632/3 — EMIL NOLDE – 🛏 and ✕ Berlin Zoo - Westerland and v.v; conveys May 1 - 27: 🛏 Berlin - Dagebüll Mole and v.v.

IC822 — NORDFRIESLAND – 🛏 and ♟ Frankfurt/Main (Regensburg ✗) - Westerland; conveys May 1 - 27: 🛏 Frankfurt/Regensburg - Dagebüll Mole.

IC823 — NORDFRIESLAND – 🛏 and ✕ Westerland - Passau; conveys ⑥⑦ Mar. 24 - Apr. 30, daily May 1 - 27: 🛏 Dagebüll Mole - Passau.

IC826 — THEODOR STORM – 🛏 and ✕ Nürnberg - Westerland; conveys May 1 - 27: 🛏 Nürnberg - Dagebüll Mole.

IC827 — THEODOR STORM – 🛏 and ♟ Westerland - Frankfurt/Main; 🛏 Dagebüll Mole - Frankfurt/Main.

IC830 — DEICHGRAF – 🛏 and ♟ Westerland - Köln; conveys May 1 - 27: 🛏 Dagebüll Mole - Köln.

IC831 — DEICHGRAF – 🛏 and ♟ Hamburg (Dortmund ✗) - Westerland; 🛏 Hamburg/Dortmund - Dagebüll Mole.

S – Not Dec. 24, 31.

❖ – Not Dec. 25, Jan. 1.

✗ – ① - ⑥ (not Dec. 25 - Jan. 1, Apr. 15 - 17, May 1, 1995).

Table 662 — NIEBÜLL - DAGEBÜLL MOLE

service Nov. 1 - Apr. 30

2 class only

km		1 Ⓐ	🚐 P	103 Ⓐ	3 Ⓐ	109	13	🚐 P	117 S	🚐			🚐 2 Ⓐ	4 Ⓐ	🚐	10 ♦	14 ♦	🚐	🚐 S
	Niebüll....d.	...	...	...	...	1105	1405	...	1655	...	Dagebüll Mole....d.	0605	0655	0825	1110	1225	1453	1650	...	195
0	Niebüll NVAG ▲....d.	0601	0645	0736	0740	1111	1416	1450	1701	1940	Niebüll NVAG ▲....a.	0620	0719	0849	1125	1249	1517	1705	...	201
14	Dagebüll Mole....a.	0625	0700	0758	0804	1135	1440	1505	1722	1955	Niebüll DB....a.	...	...	0855	...	1255	1523	...		

♦ — NOTES (LISTED BY TRAIN NUMBERS)

Details of through cars attached/detached at Niebüll to or from DB InterCity services:

4 — Mar. 24 - Apr. 30: 🛏 Dagebüll - Passau for **IC823**.

10 — 🛏 Dagebüll - Frankfurt/Main for **IC827**.

109 — 🛏 Dortmund/Hamburg –Dagebüll from **IC831**.

P – Ⓐ, not Dec. 23 - Jan. 6, Apr. 10 - 21.

S – Not Dec. 24, 31.

▲ – Niebüll NVAG is adjacent to the DB station. Ordinary DB rail tickets (but not railpasses) are valid on this line.

Table 663 — HAMBURG - KIEL

Engineering work in connection with electrification may affect services

1, 2 class

km		D1931 D1882 C	D 1882	E 3518 ♟	5524 ⑦	E 3522 Ⓐ	3526	E 3530	IC 731 ♟			3534	3538	IC 735 ♟	3540			E 3546	IC 739 ♟	E 3550	3554	IC 526 ♟	3558	3562	IC 524 ♟	E 356
			0406						0914					1114					1314			1514			1714	
0	Hamburg Hbf....d.				0620	0720	0820	0920	0939			1020	1120	1139	1220			1320	1339	1420	1520	1539	1620	1720	1739	182
7	Hamburg Altona....d.	0537	0537	0620	0620	0720	0820	0920	0939			1020	1120	1139	1220			1320	1339	1420	1520	1539	1620	1720	1739	182
73	Neumünster....d.	0632	0632	0711	0724	0811	0911	1011	1022			1111	1211	1222	1312			1411	1422	1511	1611	1622	1711	1812	1822	191
111	Kiel....a.	0656	0656	0735	0752	0835	0935	1035	1048			1135	1235	1248	1335			1435	1448	1535	1635	1648	1735	1835	1848	191

		3572	IC 534 ✕	3574	3578 S	IC 520 ♦		3582	EC 28 ✕	3586			E 3503	E 3507	EC 29 ✕	E 3509	E 3513 ♦	IC 621 ♟	E 3515		E 35
			1904		2114			2214					0513	0541	0608	0619	0642	0708	0721	...	08
	Hamburg Hbf....d.											Kiel....d.	0513	0541	0608	0619	0642	0708	0721	...	08
	Hamburg Altona....d.		1914	1939	2020	2122	2140		2220	2240	2334	Neumünster....d.	0537	0611	0630	0645	0706	0730	0745	...	08
	Neumünster....d.		2011	2022	2111	2211	2223		2311	2323	0023	Hamburg Altona....a.	0628	0708	0718	0743	0809	0818	0838	...	09
	Kiel....a.		2035	2048	2135	2235	2249		2335	2349	0043	Hamburg Hbf....a.			0743				0843		

		IC 535 ✕	3521	3525	IC 523 ✕	3529	3533	IC 527 ♟	3537			3541	IC 738 ♟	3545	3549	IC 734 ♟♟	E3553 E3555	E 3557	IC 730 ♟	3561	3565	3569	3577	D 1883	D1930	35
								♟											♟			S	S	B	B	
	Kiel....d.	0908	0921	1021	1108	1121	1221	1308	1321			1421	1508	1521	1621	1708	1721 1745	1821	1908	1921	2021	2121	2221	2245	2245	23
	Neumünster....d.	0930	0945	1045	1131	1145	1245	1330	1345			1445	1530	1545	1645	1730	1745 1818	1845	1930	1945	2044	2145	2245	2310	2310	23
	Hamburg Altona....a.	1018	1038	1138	1218	1238	1338	1418	1438			1538	1618	1638	1738	1818	1838 1938	2018	2038	2141	2238	2338	0004	0004	00
	Hamburg Hbf....a.	1048			1243			1443					1643					2043						0043		

♦ — NOTES (LISTED BY TRAIN NUMBERS)

EC28/9 — PRINZ EUGEN – 🛏 and ✕ Wien Westbahnhof - Kiel and v.v.

IC520 — SPESSART – ⑥, not Dec. 24 - 31, Apr. 14 - 17, 30, May 1.

IC523 — WESTFÄLISCHE FRIEDE – 🛏 and ✕ Kiel - Nürnberg.

IC524 — HANSEAT – 🛏 and ✕ Nürnberg (München ✗) - Kiel.

IC526 — GORCH FOCK – 🛏 and ♟ Frankfurt/Main (Nürnberg ✗) - Kiel.

IC527 — GORCH FOCK – 🛏 and ♟ Kiel - Nürnberg.

IC534/5 — KÄTHE KOLLWITZ – 🛏 and ✕ Berlin Zoo - Kiel and v.v.

IC621 — KONSUL – 🛏 and ✕ Kiel - Nürnberg (München ♣).

IC730/1 — WESTFALEN – 🛏 and ♟ Kiel - Dortmund and v.v.

IC734 — KAROLINGER – daily except ⑥, not Dec. 25, Apr. 14 - 16, 30: 🛏 Kiel - Aachen; ♟ Kiel - Köln.

IC735 — KAROLINGER – ① - ⑥, not Dec. 26, Apr. 15 - 17, May 1: 🛏 and ✕ Aachen - Kiel.

IC738/9 — KIELER FÖRDE – 🛏 and ♟ Kiel - Frankfurt/Main and v.v.

D1882 — 🛏 and ♟ Hamburg - Kiel; 🚭 1,2 cl., 🛏 2 cl. and 🛏 München (Innsbruck on ⑤ Jan. 7 - Mar. 25) - Hamburg - Kiel.

D1883 — 🛏 and ♟ Kiel - Hamburg; 🚭 1,2 cl., 🛏 2 cl. and 🛏 Kiel - München (Innsbruck on ⑤ Jan. 6 - Mar. 24).

B – Daily except ⑥, also May27, not Dec. 25, Apr. 14, 15, 16, 30: 🛏 Kiel - Köln.

C – Daily except ⑥, also May 27, not Dec. 25, Apr. 14, 15, 16, 30 (from Köln: 🛏 Köln - Kiel.

S – Not Dec. 24, 31.

✗ – ① - ⑥ (not Dec. 25 - Jan. 1, Apr. 15 - 17, May 1, 1995).

♦ – Daily except ⑥ (not Dec. 24 - 31, Apr. 14 - 16, Apr. 30, 1995).

Table 664

NEUMÜNSTER and KIEL - HUSUM and FLENSBURG

Electrification work between Hamburg and Neumünster may affect services

1, 2 class

km		3604 ⑦	3608 ✗	3610 ⑦	4410	3612	4404 4460	IR 2078	4414	3616	4464	D 276 ♦	4418	3620	4468	IR 2076 G	4422	3624	4472	D 274 ♦	4426	3628	4476 S	IR 2074 G
	Hamburg Hbf 663 ....d.	...	...	...	...	...	0819	...	...	...	...	1011	...	...	...	1219	...	...	...	1411	...	...	...	1619
	Hamburg Altona 663 ....d.	...	...	...	...	...	0839	...	...	...	...	1039	...	...	...	1239	...	...	...	1439	...	...	...	1639
0	Neumünster ....d.	0637	0704	0717	...	0817	0924	...	0924	...	1017	1124	...	...	1217	1324	...	1417	...	1524	...	1617	...	1724
	Kiel ....d.				0729		0829	0929		1029			1129	1229			1329		1429		1529		1629	
39	Rendsburg ....d.	0708	0733	0746	0800	0846	0900	0951	1000	1046	1100	1151	1200	1246	1300	1351	1400	1446	1500	1551	1600	1646	1700	1751
63	Schleswig ....d.	0727	0741	0806	0820	0906	0920	1010	1020	1106	1120	1210	1220	1306	1320	1410	1420	1506	1520	1610	1620	1706	1720	1810
75	Jübek ....d.	0735	0752	0815	0829	0915	0929		1029	1115	1129		1229	1315	1329		1429	1515	1528		1629	1715	1729	
	Husum ....a.				0851		0951	1051		1151			1251	1351			1451		1551		1651		1751	
101	Flensburg ....a.	0755	0819	0835		0935	1034		1135		1234		1335		1434		1535		1634		1735		1834	

		4430	3632	4480	D 272	4434	3636	4484	IR 2072	4488	3640		3607	4409	IR 2073 G	4459	3611	4413	D 273 ♦	4033	3615
		S		S	1811	S		S	2019	S	S										
	Hamburg Hbf 663 ....d.				1811				2019												
	Hamburg Altona 663 ....d.				1839				2039												
	Flensburg ....d.												0618	...	0720	0803	0818	...	0920	...	1018
	Husum ....d.												...	0700			...	0902		1003	
	Neumünster ....d.	...	1817	...	1924	...	2017	...	2124	...	2228										
	Jübek ....d.												0637	0724		0822	0837	0924		1026	1037
	Kiel ....d.	1729		1829		1928		2029		2129			0647	0734	0744	0834	0847	0934	0944	1036	1047
	Schleswig ....d.																				
	Rendsburg ....d.	1800	1846	1900	1951	2000	2046	2100	2151	2200	2259		0707	0755	0803	0855	0907	0955	1003	1056	1107
	Schleswig ....d.	1820	1906	1920	2010	2020	2106	2120	2210	2220	2321										
	Kiel ....a.												0707	0755	0803	0855	0907	0927		1027	1127
	Jübek ....d.	1829	1915	1929		2029	2115	2129		2229	2331										
	Neumünster ....a.												0737		0833		0937		1033	1137	
	Husum ....a.	1851		1951		2051		2151		2251											
	Hamburg Altona 663 ....a.													0918					1118		...
	Flensburg ....a.			1935		2034		2135		2234	2351			0938					1141		...

		4417	IR 2075 G	4439	3619	4421	D 275	4473	3623	4425	IR 2077	4477	3627	4479	D 277	4063	3631	4481	IR 2079	4485	4441 ℐ	3635	4487	3647	3639 ℐ	4489	3643
													S		S		S		S		S		S	S		S	S
	Flensburg ....d.		1120		1218		1320		1418		1520		1618		1720		1818		1920			2018		2118		2218
	Husum ....d.	1102		1203		1302		1403		1502		1603		1702		1803		1902		2003		2102		2203		
	Jübek ....d.	1124		1226	1237	1324		1426	1437	1524		1626	1637	1724		1826	1837	1924		2026		2124	2137	2226		2227
	Schleswig ....d.	1134	1144	1236	1247	1334	1344	1436	1447	1534	1544	1636	1647	1734	1744	1836	1847	1934	1944	2036	2047	2134	2147	2236		2247
	Rendsburg ....d.	1155	1203	1256	1307	1355	1403	1456	1507	1555	1603	1656	1707	1755	1803	1856	1907	1955	2003	2056	2107	2155	2207	2259		2307
	Kiel ....a.	1227		1327		1427		1527		1627		1727		1827		1927		2027		2127		2227		2331		2337
	Neumünster ....a.		1233		1337		1433		1537		1633		1737		1833		1937		2033		2137		2236		
	Hamburg Altona 663 ....a.		1318				1518				1718				1918				2118						
	Hamburg Hbf 663 ....a.		1338				1541				1738				1941				2141						

NOTES (LISTED BY TRAIN NUMBERS)

272/3 – 🚃 Hamburg Altona - Fredericia and v.v.
274/7 – 🚃 Hamburg Altona - Århus and v.v.
275/6 – 🚃 Hamburg Altona - Frederikshavn and v.v.
2072 – 🚃 Göttingen - Flensburg; ♀ Göttingen - Neumünster.

IR2077 – 🚃 Flensburg - Göttingen (Erfurt ♣); ♀ Flensburg - Göttingen.
IR2078 – 🚃 Kassel Hbf - Flensburg; ♀ Göttingen - Flensburg.
G – 🚃 and ♀ Göttingen - Flensburg and v.v.
S – **Not Dec. 24, 31.**
♣ – Daily except ⑥ (**not** Dec. 24 - 31, Apr. 14 - 16, Apr. 30, **1995**).

Table 665

HAMBURG - LÜBECK - PUTTGARDEN

1, 2 class except where shown

km		E 3002 ✗	E 3102	E 3004	E 3106	IR 2231 ♀	E 3006	E 3110	EC 180 ✗ K	E 3014	IR 2233 ♀	E 3018	EC 182 ✗ K	E 3024	IR 2235 ♀		E 3028	E 3126	IR 2335 ♀	E 3130	E 3040	EC 188 ✗ K	E 3134	IR 2237 ♀
0	Hamburg Hbf 660 ....d.	0504	...	0602	0602	0619	0704	...	0719	0804	0819	0904	0919	1004	1019		...	1104	...	1219	...	1304	1326	1419
62	Lübeck 660 ....a.	0548	...	0647	0647	0659	0748	...	0756	0847	0859	0948	0955	1047	1059		...	1148	...	1259	...	1348	1400	1459
62	Lübeck ....d.	...	0604	...	0704	...	...	0804	0758	0904	...	1004	0957	1104	...		1204	...	1304	...	1402	1404	...	...
117	Travemünde ▲ ....d.	...	0618	...	0718	...	...	0818	...	0918	...	1018	...	1118	...		1218	...	1318	...	1419	...	...	...
153	Oldenburg Holstein........d.	...	...	...	...	...	...	...	0828	...	...	...	1029	...	...		...	...	...	...	1432	...	...	...
	Puttgarden 🚢 ....a.	...	...	...	...	...	...	...	0852	...	...	...	1055	...	...		...	...	...	...	1455	...	...	...

		E 3138	EC 186 ✗ K	E 3142	E 3052	IR 2337 ♀	E 3146	E 3060		E 3062	IR 2239 ♀ S	E 3070	EC 188 ✗ K	E 3074		IR 2339 ♀	E 3162	E 2833 J	E 3092 ♦	E 3096		D 233 ✗ ♀	D 482 ✗ ♀
	Hamburg Hbf 660 ....d.	...	1519	...	1604	1619	...	1704		1734	1759	1804	1826	1904		...	2019	...	2119	2204	2304		0245	0405
	Lübeck 660 ....a.	...	1555	...	1647	1659	...	1748		1818	1842	1847	1900	1947		...	2059	...	2159	2248	2350		0330	0443
	Lübeck ....d.	1504	1557	1604	...	...	1704	1804		1823	...	1905	1902	2004		...	2105	...	...	...	...		0332	0445
	Travemünde ▲ ....d.	1518	...	1619	...	...	1719	1818		1919	...	1919	...	2019		...	2119	...	...	...	...		...	...
	Oldenburg Holstein........d.	...	1629	...	...	...	...	...		1942	...	1936	...	...		...	...	...	...	...	...		0440	0545
	Puttgarden 🚢 ....a.	...	1655	...	...	...	...	...		2005	...	1959	...	...		...	...	...	...	...	...		...	...

km		E 3007	D 476 ✗ ♀ ♦	E 3011 ④ S	E 3105 ④	IR 2338 ♀	E 3017 ✗	E 3107	E 3021		E 4121 ✗	E 3111	IR 2336 ♀	E 3027	IR 2238 ♀	E 3031		EC 189 ✗ K	E 3123	E 3035	E 3127	IR 2334 ♀		EC 187 ✗ K	E 3131
	Puttgarden 🚢 ....d.	...	...	...	...	0541	...	...	...		0716	...	...	...	...	...		1052	...	...	...	...		1250	...
	Oldenburg Holstein........d.	...	...	...	...	0608	...	...	...		0741	...	...	...	...	...		1115	...	...	...	...		1314	...
0	Travemünde ▲ ....d.	...	...	...	0635	...	0735	...	...		...	0835	...	0935	...	1035		...	1143	...	1235	...		...	1343
18	Lübeck ....d.	...	...	...	0649	...	0716	0749	...		0829	0849	...	0949	...	1049		1148	1157	...	1249	...		1348	1357
18	Lübeck 660 ....d.	0605	0623	0629	...	0700	0736	...	0805		...	...	0900	1007	1100	1109		1150	...	1209	...	1300		1350	...
80	Hamburg Hbf 660 ....a.	0650	0708	0716	...	0739	0816	...	0850		...	...	0939	1054	1139	1154		1225	...	1254	...	1339		1429	...

NOTES (LISTED BY TRAIN NUMBERS)

233 – NORD EXPRESS – 🛏 1,2 cl. (T2), 🛏 2 cl., 🚃 and ♀ Oostende - København; 🛏 1,2 cl. Paris Nord (EC31) - Aachen - København.
476 – ♂ (from Praha Hlavni): 🚃 and ♀ Praha Hlavni - Hamburg.
482 – 🛏 1,2 cl., 🛏 2 cl., 🚃 and ♀ München (Innsbruck on ⑥ Jan. 7 - Mar. 25) - København.
2338 – ① - ⑥, **not** Dec. 26, Apr. 15 - 17, May 1.

IR2339 – Daily except ⑥, **not** Dec. 25, Apr. 14 - 16, 30.
IR2833 – ⑦, also Apr. 17, May 1, **not** Dec. 25, Apr. 16, 30.
J – ⑧, **not** Nov. 1, Jan. 6.
K – 🚃 and ♀ Hamburg - København and v.v.
S – **Not** Dec. 24, 31.
▲ – Skandinavienkai - for sailings to/from Trelleborg and Helsinki. See Tables **1225**, **1250**.

Table 665 — PUTTGARDEN - LÜBECK - HAMBURG

1, 2 class except where shown

	E 3043	E 3135	IR 2236 ♀	E 3139	E 3053	EC 185 ♀ K	E 3143	IR 2234 ♀	E 3067	IR 2232 ♀	E 3075	EC 183 ♀ K	IR 2832 ♦	E 3079	IR 2230 ♀ S	E 3085	EC 181 ♀ K	E 3089	E 3091	D 483 ♦	D 232 ♀ ♦
Puttgarden 🚢 .... d.	...	...	...	...	...	1546	...	...	...	...	...	1850	...	...	...	2046	...	...	...	2300	0105	...
Oldenburg Holstein............ d.	...	...	...	...	...	1608	...	...	...	...	...	1914	...	...	...	2108	...	...	...			...
Travemünde ▲........... d.	...	1435	...	1535	...		1635	...	1735	...	1835		1935	...	2035			...	...	2358	0210	...
Lübeck .... d.	...	1449	...	1549	...	1642	1649	...	1749	...	1849	1946	1949	...	2049	2137		...	...		0212	...
Lübeck 660 .... d.	1409	...	1500	...	1605	1644	...	1700	1809	1900	1909	1948	2000	2009	2100	2109	2139	2205	2305	0000	0212	...
Hamburg Hbf 660 .... a.	1454	...	1539	...	1650	1722	...	1739	1854	1939	1954	2027	2039	2055	2139	2154	2215	2254	2354	0040	0300	...

♦ – NOTES (LISTED BY TRAIN NUMBERS)
D232 – NORD EXPRESS – 🛏 1,2 cl. (T2), ➛ 2 cl., ⛟ and ♀ København - Oostende; 🛏 1,2 cl. København - Aachen (EC30) - Paris Nord.
D483 – 🛏 1,2 cl., ➛ 2 cl., ⛟ and ♀ København - München (Innsbruck on ⑤ Jan. 6 - Mar. 24).
IR2832 – ⑦, also Apr. 17, May 1, not Dec. 25, Apr. 16, 30.
K – ⛟ and ♀ København - Hamburg.
S – Not Dec. 24, 31.

Table 666 — FLENSBURG - KIEL

1, 2 clas

km		3515 ♒	4249 ♒	4253		4257	4261	4263		4265	4269	4271		4275	4279	4281		4285 S	4287 S	4289 S		4291 S	4293 Ⓐ S	4295 S
0	Flensburg .... d.	0603	0702	0801	...	0901	1001	1101	...	1201	1301	1401	...	1501	1601	1701	...	1801	1901	2001	...	2101	2201	2301
50	Eckenförde..................... d.	0649	0746	0846	...	0946	1046	1146	...	1246	1346	1446	...	1546	1646	1746	...	1846	1946	2046	...	2146	2246	2346
81	Kiel.............................. a.	0713	0813	0913	...	1013	1113	1213	...	1313	1413	1513	...	1611	1710	1810	...	1913	2013	2113	...	2213	2313	0023

	4242 Ⓐ	4244 ♒	4250 ♒	4258	4260		4262	4264	4266		4270	4272	4276	4278	4280		4284 S	4286 S	4288 S		4290 S	4292 S		4294 S
Kiel.............................. d.	0435	0541	0642	0743	0843	...	0943	1043	1143	...	1243	1343	1443	1541	1640	...	1740	1843	1943	...	2043	2143	...	2243
Eckenförde..................... d.	0504	0609	0708	0807	0907	...	1007	1107	1207	...	1307	1407	1507	1607	1707	...	1807	1907	2007	...	2107	2207	...	2307
Flensburg .... a.	0546	0653	0752	0851	0951	...	1051	1151	1251	...	1351	1451	1551	1651	1751	...	1851	1951	2051	...	2151	2251	...	2351

S – Not Dec. 24, 31.

Table 667 — KIEL - LÜBECK - LÜNEBURG

1, 2 clas

km		E 4005	E 4013	E 3025	E 4021	E 15221	E 4023	E 4031	E 15229	E 4033	E 4037	E 4041	E 4043	E 15249	E 4045	E 4049	E 4055	E 15257	E 4057	E 15261	E 4063	E 4067	E3091 E4441	E 4075
0	Kiel............................. d.	0537	0640	0740	0840	...	0940	1040	...	1140	1240	1340	...	1440	...	1540	1640	1740	...	1840	...	1940	2040	2140	2240
33	Plön............................ d.	0613	0713	0813	0913	...	1013	1113	...	1213	1313	1413	...	1513	...	1613	1713	1813	...	1913	...	2013	2113	2213	2313
47	Eutin........................... d.	0629	0729	0829	0929	...	1029	1129	...	1229	1329	1429	...	1529	...	1629	1729	1829	...	1929	...	2029	2129	2229	2329
80	Lübeck .... a.	0653	0753	0853	0953	...	1053	1153	...	1253	1353	1453	...	1553	...	1653	1753	1853	...	1953	...	2053	2153	2253	2353

		E 4107	E 15215	E 15219		E 15225			E 15233	E 15237			E 15245			E 15253			E 15265		
80	Lübeck .... d.	0700	0800	0900	...	1000	1100	...	1200	1300	1400	...	1500	1600	1640	...	1800	...	1900	...	2000	2100
102	Ratzeburg .... d.	0716	0816	0916	...	1016	1116	...	1216	1316	1416	...	1516	1616	1656	...	1816	...	1916	...	2016	2116
111	Mölln .... d.	0723	0823	0923	...	1023	1123	...	1223	1323	1423	...	1523	1623	1709	...	1823	...	1923	...	2023	2123
130	Büchen......................... d.	0739	0839	0939	...	1039	1139	...	1239	1339	1439	...	1539	1639	1724	...	1839	...	1939	...	2039	2159d
159	Lüneburg .... a.	0801	0901	1001	...	1101	1201	...	1301	1401	1501	...	1601	1701	1746	...	1901	...	2001	...	2101	2229

	E 3002	E3004 E4404	E 15206	E 15210	E 4022	E 15214	E 15218	E 4030	E 15222	E 15226	E 4038	E 15230	E 15234	E 4046	E 15236	E 15242	E 15246	E 4060	E 15250	E 15254	E 15258	E4076 E4492	E 4194	E3099 E408
Lüneburg .... d.			0619	0712		0812	0912		1012	1112		1219	1312		1412	1512	1620		1710	1812	1912		2012	2156
Büchen........................ d.			0651	0740		0840	0940		1040	1140		1251	1340		1440	1540	1654		1746	1840	1940		2040	2222
Mölln .... d.			0705	0754		0854	0954		1054	1154		1305	1354		1454	1554	1708		1801	1854	1954		2054	2236
Ratzeburg .... d.			0717	0803		0903	1003		1103	1203		1317	1403		1503	1603	1717		1817	1903	2003		2103	2244
Lübeck .... a.			0731	0824		0924	1024		1124	1224		1331	1424		1524	1632	1732		1832	1933	2024		2124	2258

		E 4020			E 4028			E 4032			E 4042			E 4050	E 4056			E 4064	E 4066		E 4496
Lübeck .... d.	0601	0701	0801	...	0901	1001	...	1101	1201	...	1301	1359	...	1501	1601	1701	...	1801	1859	2001	...	2101	2201	230
Eutin........................... d.	0627	0727	0827	...	0927	1027	...	1127	1227	...	1327	1427	...	1527	1627	1727	...	1827	1927	2027	...	2127	2227	232
Plön............................ d.	0642	0742	0842	...	0942	1042	...	1142	1242	...	1342	1442	...	1542	1642	1742	...	1842	1942	2042	...	2142	2242	232
Kiel............................. a.	0713	0813	0913	...	1013	1113	...	1213	1313	...	1413	1513	...	1613	1713	1813	...	1913	2013	2113	...	2213	2313	001

d – Arrive 2137.

Table 668 — ROSTOCK - WISMAR - SCHWERIN

1, 2 class except where show

km		IR 2031 ✎ M	5708 2	4107 2 Y	5712 2	E 3658	4109 2	E 2035 ♀ A	3906 2	IR 2733 ♀ H	5716 2	E 2037 2 B	5718 2	5720 2	4514 2	5724 2 C	IR 2039 ✎	3916 2	5726 2	4127 2	5730 2 S	5732 2 S	4133 2	5736 2	512 2
0	Rostock....................... d.		0450		0647			0903		0958		1154	1256		1358		1507	1600		1656	1800		2009			
16	Bad Doberan ▲ ..... d.		0517		0710			0923		1021		1217	1319		1421		1527	1622		1723	1823		2032			
57	Wismar....................... a.		0618		0812			1018		1131		1327	1421		1530		1623	1722		1847	1929		2132			

		4105 2					4111 2		4115 2		4117 5121 2		4121 2		4123 4125 2			4129 2		
57	Wismar....................... d.	0612	0631	0738	...	0818	0938	1012	1022	...	1138	1212	1332	1446	...	1538	1612	1632	1738	1823	...	1938	2023	...	213
72	Bad Kleinen.................. d.	0623	0645	0752	...	0829	0952	1023	1035	...	1152	1223	1346	1500	...	1552	1623	1646	1752	1836	...	1951	2036	...	215
72	Bad Kleinen 660 674... d.	0625	0646	0803	...	0906	1003	1025	...	1039	1203	1225	1403	...	1507	1603	1625	1649	1803	1848	...	2003	2046	...	
89	Schwerin 660 674...... a.	0637	0701	0817	...	0920	1017	1037	...	1052	1217	1237	1417	...	1521	1617	1637	1704	1817	1903	...	2017	2101	...	

A – ① - ⑤: ⛟ and ♀ Wismar - Berlin Lichtenberg.
B – ⛟ Wismar - Berlin Lichtenberg - Cottbus - Görlitz.
C – ⛟ and ♀ Wismar - Cottbus - Görlitz (Berlin Lichtenberg on Dec. 24).
H – ⛟ and ♀ Rostock - Magdeburg - Dresden Hbf.
M – ⛟ Wismar - Berlin Lichtenberg.

S – Not Dec. 24, 31.
Y – Not Dec. 25, 26, Jan. 1.
✎ – ① - ⑥ (not Dec. 25 - Jan. 1, Apr. 15 - 17, May 1, **1995**).

Additional trains Rostock - Bad Doberan: 0549, 0746, 1112, 1912 **S**.

▲ – Steam hauled narrow gauge service between Bad Doberan and Ostseebad Kühlungsborn West (15 km, 2 class only, journey time 45 minutes):
From Bad Doberan: 0529 Ⓐ, 0654, 0829, 0930, 1033 (see below), , 1127, 1332, 1432, 1530, 1629, 1729, 1835, 1946 (not Dec. 24, 31), 2038 (Apr. 29 - May 27).
From Kühlungsborn: 0433 Ⓐ, 0526, 0657, 0825, 0927, 1021, 1228, 1329 (see below) 1428, 1527, 1625, 1726, 1831 (not Dec. 24, 31), 1943 (Apr. 29 - May 27).
On ⑥⑦ Mar. 11 - May 27 a special train with higher fare and a stop en-route for photographers replaces the 1033 from Bad Doberan and the 1329 from Kühlungsborn.

Table 668 — SCHWERIN - WISMAR - ROSTOCK

1, 2 class except where shown

	4102 2	E 3907 2	4507 2	5715 2	4108 2	4110 2	4112 2	IR 2038 2 C	4116 2	4118 2	5721 2	4120 2	4122 2	IR 2036 2 B	4124 2	E 3915 2	IR 2034 2 A	4128 2	5731 2 S	4130 2	4132 2	5735 2 F	IR 2030 2	4136 2	4138 2 ⑦
Schwerin 660 674 ..... d.	0540	...	0736	...	0850	0936	1036	1057	1136	1236	...	1336	1407	1457	1536	...	1657	1736	...	1849	1936	...	2057	2136	2242
Bad Kleinen 660 674 .. a.	0554	...	0750	...	0904	0950	1050	1110	1150	1250	...	1350	1421	1510	1550	...	1710	1750	...	1903	1950	...	2110	2150	2256
Bad Kleinen............. d.	0604	...	0810	...	0915	0954	1052	1111	1204	1251	...	1404	1421	1511	1604	...	1711	1804	...	1914	2004	...	2111	2205	2304
Wismar.................. a.	0623	...	0829	...	0930	1008	1106	1121	1223	1306	...	1418	1437	1521	1623	...	1721	1818	...	1929	2018	...	2121	2219	2318

	5711 2					5717 2	5719 2					5723 2	5727 2												
Wismar................ d.	0635	0824	...	0911	...	1020	...	1215	...	...	1311	1423	...	1606	...	1725	...	...	1822	...	...	2022	...	...	
Bad Doberan ▲ ..... d.	0741	0924	...	1023	...	1120	...	1321	...	1423	1529	...	1722	...	1825	...	...	1922	...	...	2128	...	...		
Rostock............... a.	0804	0944	...	1046	...	1143	...	1344	...	1446	1552	...	1744	...	1845	...	...	1945	...	...	2150	...	...		

A – Daily except ⑤⑥: [12] and ♀ Berlin Lichtenberg - Wismar.
B – [12] and ♀ Görlitz - Cottbus - Berlin Lichtenberg - Wismar.
C – [12] Görlitz (Berlin Lichtenberg on Dec. 25) - Wismar; ♀ Berlin - Wismar.
F – ⑤ also Apr. 13, May 24, not Apr. 14, May 26: [12] Berlin Lichtenberg - Wismar.

S – Not Dec. 24, 31.
Additional trains Bad Doberan - Rostock: 0827, 1156, 1627, 2033 S.

▲ – Narrow gauge service Bad Doberan - Kühlungsborn see foot of page 358.

Table 669 — BERLIN - ROSTOCK - WARNEMÜNDE

1, 2 class except where shown

km		IR 2378 ♥	4706 2	8608 2	4778 2	E 3282 2	IC 818	IR 2278 ♥	E3150 E3152	E 3284 2	4782	4714 2	IR 2016 2 ♦	IR 2276 ♦	E 3286 2	4786 2	4720 2	D 304 ♥ Ⓐ	3512 2	E 4790 2	4724
0	Berlin Lichtenberg .... d.	0651	...	...	...	0750	0816h	...	0851	...	0905	0920	...	...	...	1051	1251	1315	...	...	1451
38	Oranienberg .... d.	0716	...	...	0755	0816	0848	...	0916	...	0936	0947	...	1035	1048	1116	1316	1341	1353	1448	1516
55	Löwenberg .... d.	...	...	...	0815	0827	...	...	...	...	0953	0958	...	1055	1103	...	...	1354	1413	1504	...
	Rheinsberg .... a.	...	...	...	0923	...	...	...	...	...	1046	...	1202	...	...	...	...	1523	...	...	1747
109	Neustrelitz .... a.	0756	...	...	...	0901	...	0956	...	1031	...	...	1150	1156	1356	1427	...	1550	1556	...	...
109	Neustrelitz .... d.	0758	0801	...	...	0902	...	0958	...	1032	...	1203	1158	1358	1428	...	1551	1558	1606	...	...
	Neubrandenburg .... d.		0829	0841	...	0928	0954		...	1102	...	1231			1457	...	1620		1634	...	1839
	Stralsund Hbf................. a.			1018	...	1034	1055		...	1222	...				1603	...	...	1748	...		
145	Waren .... d.	0821	...	...	...	...	...	1021	...	...	...	...	1221	1421	...	...	1621	...	...	...
190	Güstrow .... d.	0857	...	...	...	...	...	1057	...	...	...	...	1257	1457	...	...	1657	...	...	...
224	Rostock ▲ .... a.	0925	...	...	...	...	...	1125	...	...	...	...	1325	1525	...	...	1725	...	...	...
237	Warnemünde ▲ .... a.	0956	...	...	...	...	...	...	...	...	...	...	1356	1556	...	...	1745	...	...	...

	IR 2274 ♥	3288 2	4792 2	IR 2272 ♥	E 3516 2	8624 2	4796 2 A	4728 2 Ⓐ	IR 2151 ♥ B	D 308 ♥
Berlin Lichtenberg .... d.	1651	1711	...	1851	...	...	...	...	2147	2352
Oranienberg .... d.	1716	1737	1748	1916	...	2028	2048	2212	2017	0017
Löwenberg .... d.	...	1749	1808	...	...	2048	2103	...	...	...
Rheinsberg .... a.	...	...	1922	...	...	2156	...	...	...	...
Neustrelitz .... a.	1756	1823	...	1956	...	...	2150	2255	0058	
Neustrelitz .... d.	1758	1825	...	...	2003	...	2201	2257	0100	
Neubrandenburg .... d.		1900	...	...	2035	2045	...	2229	2321	
Stralsund Hbf................ a.		2012	...	...	2213	...	...			
Waren .... d.	1821									
Güstrow .... d.	1857									0123
Rostock ▲ .... a.	1925									0158
Warnemünde ▲ .... a.	1956									0227

	D 309 §	IR 2652 2	4709	IR 2373 ♦	4779 2	E 3283 2	4713 2	IR 2273 ♥	E 3285 2
Warnemünde ▲ .... d.	0408	...	...	0550	...	...	0750	...	
Rostock ▲ .... d.	0425	...	0632	...	...	0832	...		
Güstrow .... d.	0453	...	0700	...	...	0900	...		
Waren .... d.	0528	...	0734	...	...	0934	...		
Stralsund Hbf................. d.				0720	...	...		0818	
Neubrandenburg .... d.				0830	...	...		1021	
Neustrelitz .... a.	0549	...	0755	...	0855	...	0955	1054	
Neustrelitz .... d.	0551	0655	0720	0757	...	0857	0917	0957	1056
Rheinsberg .... d.					0751		...	...	
Löwenberg .... d.		0809	...	0907	0932	1009		1132	
Oranienberg .... d.	0637	0738	0824	0840	0926	0943	1024	1040	1143
Berlin Lichtenberg .... a.	0704	0803	...	0905	...	1011	...	1107	1211

	IR 2275 ♥	4785	4719 2	E 3509 2 A	D 305 ♥ Ⓐ	4787 2	E 3287 2	3511 2	E 2017 2	4791 2	IR 3155 2 A	4725 2 S	E 3517 2	IR 2279 2	4793 2 B	E 3159 2	E 3289 2 C	4727 2 S	E 3519 2	IR 2379 ♥ S	4795 2	IC 819 ♥	E 2879 2
Warnemünde ▲ .... d.	0950	...	...	1201	...	...	...	1350	...	1550	...	...	...	...	...								1950
Rostock ▲ .... d.	1032	...	...	1232	...	...	...	1432	...	1632	...	...	...	1832	...								2032
Güstrow .... d.	1100	...	...	1300	...	...	...	1500	...	1700	...	...	...	1900	...								2059
Waren .... d.	1134	...	...	1334	...	...	...	1534	...	1734	...	...	...	1934	...								2132
Stralsund Hbf................. d.	...	1057	1201	...	1330	...	...	1427	1616	...	1708	...	1814	...	1901								
Neubrandenburg .... d.	...	1236	1322	...	1437	1525	...	1636	1725	...	1825	1925	...	2003									
Neustrelitz .... a.	1155	1311	1347	1355	1509	1550	1555	1705	1750	1755	1850	1950	1955	2153									
Neustrelitz .... d.	1157	...	1321	1357	1510		1557	1708	1757		1853	1920	1957	2155									
Rheinsberg .... d.		1222		1351			1527	1619		1752	1755		1927										
Löwenberg .... d.		1329	1409		1507	1546		1636	1725	1809	1902	1902	1932	2009	2037								
Oranienberg .... d.	1240	1348	1424	1440	1527	1557	1640	1655	1741	1824	1840	1922	1910	1943	2024	2040	2055	2109	2240				
Berlin Lichtenberg .... a.	1307	...	1507	1625	1707		1816		1907	1940	2011		2107	2140h	2307								

NOTES (LISTED BY TRAIN NUMBERS)

04 – NEPTUN – [12] Dresden Hbf - København; ♀ Dresden - Warnemünde.
05 – NEPTUN – [12] København - Chemnitz; ♀ Warnemünde - Chemnitz.
08 – OSTSEE EXPRESS – ♥ 1,2 cl., ▭ 2 cl. and [12] Berlin - København. Not Dec. 24, 31.
09 – OSTSEE EXPRESS – ♥ 1,2 cl., ▭ 2 cl. and [12] København - Berlin.
318 – CASPAR DAVID FRIEDRICH – ⑥⑦ Apr. 29 - May 27: [12] and ♀ Berlin - Stralsund - Binz.
319 – CASPAR DAVID FRIEDRICH – ⑤⑥ Apr. 28 - May 26: [12] and ♀ Binz - Stralsund - Berlin.
2016/7 – [12] and ♀ Leipzig - Rostock and v.v.
2151 – ⑥, not Dec. 25, Apr. 14 - 16, 30.
2272 – [12] and ♀ Berlin (Chemnitz ♣) - Rostock. Not Dec. 24, 31.
2273/4 – [12] and ♀ Rostock - Chemnitz and v.v.
2275 – [12] and ♀ Rostock - Berlin (Chemnitz daily except ⑥, not Dec. 25, Apr. 14 - 16, 30).

IR2278 – [12] and ♀ Chemnitz (Berlin on Dec. 25, Jan. 1) - Warnemünde.
IR2279 – [12] and ♀ Rostock - Chemnitz (Berlin on Dec. 24, 31).
IR2373 – [12] and ♀ Rostock - Dresden Hbf. Not Dec. 25, Jan. 1.
IR2652 – ① - ⑥, not Dec. 26, Apr. 15 - 17, May 1.
IR2879 – ⑦, also Apr. 17, not Dec. 25, Apr. 16: [12] Rostock - Berlin.
E3283 – ① - ⑥ from Stralsund; daily from Neubrandenburg.
A – Daily Berlin - Neubrandenburg, ⑧ Berlin - Stralsund.
C – [12] and ♀ Chemnitz - Rostock.
G – ① - ⑥ Stralsund - Berlin (daily from Neubrandenburg).
S – Not Dec. 24, 31.
h – Berlin Hbf.
✧ – ...
§ – Train number D1309 Sept. 24 - Dec. 15 (from København)..
♣ – Daily except ⑥ (not Dec. 24 - 31, Apr. 14 - 16, Apr. 30, 1995).
▲ – Frequent S-Bahn services run between these points.

Table 670 — BERLIN - HALLE - ERFURT

1, 2 class except where shown

Part 1

km	Station	IR 2573	IR 2201	IR 2603	E 4403	IR 2150	IC 801	E 3453	IR 2203	E 4405	IC 2652	IC 813	IR 3964	E 2013	IR 4407	IR 2152	IC 705	IR 2205	E 4409	IC 2654	IC 707	IR 3966	IR 2015	E 4411
		◆	🍴 Q	◆	Y	🍴	✕		🍴		🍴	✕ K	◆			🍴		🍴		✕ R	◆		◆	
0	Berlin Hbf d.						0706				0906						1106				1306			
	Berlin Lichtenberg d.			0612	0618				0818				0936		1018			1218					1336	
	Berlin Zoo d.		0538																					
	Berlin Charlottenburg d.									0740									1140					
	Berlin Wannsee d.		0551							0751									1151					
19	Berlin Schönefeld + d.		0631			0637	0725		0837		0925			0955		1037	1125			1237	1325		1355	
79	Jüterbog d.					0725		0754			0925						1125			1237	1325		1349	
111	Lutherstadt Wittenberg d.				0656	0749		0821			0949				1100		1149			1300				1500
	Magdeburg a.										0846	0953	1049	1102	1153			1246	1353		1449	1502	1553	
	Dessau a.	0539	0646		0753			0846	0953			1049	1102	1153			1246	1353		1449	1502	1553		
148	Bitterfeld a.	0555	0701		0809	0813		0846	0901	1009	1013		1106	1119	1209	1213		1301	1409	1413		1506	1513	1609
148	Bitterfeld d.	0557	0703		0819	0814		0847	0903	1019	1014		1107	1121	1219	1214		1303	1419	1414		1507	1521	1619
182	Leipzig a.			0824	0845			0907	0917	1045			1107	1245			1307		1445	1507		1545		1645
178	Halle a.	0627	0732			0844			0932			1044	1138			1244		1332		1444			1539	
178	Halle 770 d.		0735			0848			0935			1048				1248		1335		1448				
221	Naumburg 770 775 a.		0811			0923		0954	1024			1123	1154			1323	1354	1411		1523			1554	
262	Weimar 775 a.		0841			0950						1150				1350		1441		1550				
284	Erfurt 775 a.		0857			1005						1205				1405		1457		1605				
	Frankfurt/Main 775 a.					1338												1757						
	Würzburg 771 a.		1157																					
	Saalfeld 770 a.							1102	1142			1302				1502				1702				
	Nürnberg 770 a.							1318	1415			1518				1718				1918				
	München Hbf 770 a.						1501	1503				1706				1903				2103				

Part 2

Station	IR 2154	IC 709	E 3656	E 3455	E 4413	IR 2156	IC 805	IR 2207	IR 2017	E 4415	IC 2656	IC 807	E 3206	IR 2647	E 3970	D 1209	IR 2658	D 1907	IC 809	D 7419	D 1183	D 358	ICN 1901	D 1954
	🍴	✕	A	T		🍴	✕		🍴		🍴 Q	✕		H			🍴	◆	✕	◆	T	🍴	♣ ✕	◆
Berlin Hbf d.		1506					1706				1906							2018	2022	2106				
Berlin Lichtenberg d.	1418					1618			1736		1818								2022		2058	2119		2349
Berlin Zoo d.			1626				1740						1934									2203		
Berlin Charlottenburg d.				1635			1751									2022				2125	2151	2230		0003
Berlin Schönefeld + d.	1437	1525			1637	1725		1755		1837	1925						2037	2043	2125					
Jüterbog d.	1525				1725					1925							2125							
Lutherstadt Wittenberg d.	1549			1700	1749			1900		1949			2009				2100							
Magdeburg a.			1649	1752	1753			1846	1903	1953			2046	2055	2059	2119			2206	2253	2246			0129
Dessau a.	1613		1706	1757	1809	1813		1901	1920	2009	2013		2111	2116		2213			2231		2302			
Bitterfeld a.	1614		1707	1758	1819	1814		1903	1921	2019	2014		2112	2117		2214			2234		2303			
Leipzig a.		1707		1828	1845		1907		1945	2045		2107		2143			2243	2307	2308					
Halle a.	1644		1739			1844		1932			2044		2139	2158	2244				2310	2334	0006	0214		
Halle 770 d.	1648					1848		1935			2048				2248				2323			0008	0216	
Naumburg 770 775 d.	1723	1754				1923	1954	2024			2123				2323				2350					0311
Weimar 775 d.	1750					1950					2150				2350									0328
Erfurt 775 d.	1805					2005					2205				0005									0703
Frankfurt/Main 775 a.	2138																							
Würzburg 771 a.																								
Saalfeld 770 a.		1902					2102	b			2323								0435				0645	
Nürnberg 770 a.		2118					2323												0619					
München Hbf 770 a.		2303																						

Part 3

Station	D 359	IR 2744	D 1906	IC 808	IR 2659	E 4404	D 1182	IC 3450	IR 2206	E 2016	IC 806	IR 2157	IR 4406	E 3961	IC 804	IR 2155	IR 4408	E 3655	IR 2014	IC 708	IR 2657	E 4410	IR 2204	IC 706
	◆	🍴	🍴	✕	🍴		V	✕	🍴	🍴	🍴 ✕	🍴		Y	✕ K	🍴 V		A	🍴	✕	🍴		🍴	✕
München Hbf 770 d.			2308n								0453									0656				0856
Nürnberg 770 d.			0105								0637									0840				1040
Saalfeld 770 d.									0612		0855									1055				1255
Würzburg 771 d.																						0948		
Frankfurt/Main 775 d.																								
Erfurt 775 d.					0548				0748			0948				1148				1204		1306		
Weimar 775 d.					0604				0804			1004				1204				1231		1306		
Naumburg 770 775 d.					0631			0733	0831			1002	1031			1231				1311		1332	1402	
Halle 770 d.					0711			0813	0911			1111			1002	1311			1014			1311	1410	
Halle d.	0554	0614	0622	0648	0714		0720		0816		0914		1014		1114	1214				1314			1413	
Leipzig d.						0710		0753		0825	0848			0910			1110		1048		1225	1248		1310
Bitterfeld a.	0626	0642		0744	0737		0820	0846	0851			0944	0937	1044		1144	1137	1244	1249		1344	1337	1443	1448
Bitterfeld d.	0635	0644		0746	0748		0847	0852			0946	0948	1045		1146	1148	1245	1250		1346	1344	1444	1501	
Dessau a.	0649	0705			0805	0810	0838	0859	0910			1005	1102			1205	1302	1310			1405	1453		
Magdeburg a.		0750			0809		0853				1009					1209					1409			
Lutherstadt Wittenberg d.					0833					1033						1233					1433			
Jüterbog d.			0818	0830	0914				1018	1030	1114			1230	1314			1418	1430	1514				1630
Berlin Schönefeld + a.	0815		0838	0830	0932		0908	1002	0956			1230	1314			1438	1532				1553			164
Berlin Wannsee a.							0908	1002	0956												1601			
Berlin Charlottenburg a.							1012	1004																
Berlin Zoo a.	0839						1038		1132		1332					1438	1532							
Berlin Lichtenberg a.			0838	0849					1049		1249									1449				
Berlin Hbf a.																								

NOTES (LISTED BY TRAIN NUMBERS)

◆ — NOTES (LISTED BY TRAIN NUMBERS)

D358/9 — 🛏 1,2 cl., ⊒ 2 cl., ⊒ and 🍴 Berlin - Basel SBB and v.v.

IC706 — BERTOLT BRECHT - ①⑤⑥⑦ also Apr. 13: ⊒ and ✕ München - Saalfeld - Berlin.

IC801 — THERESE GIEHSE - ⊒ and ✕ Berlin - München. Extended to Innsbruck and Bischofshofen on ⑥ Jan. 7 - Apr. 8, May 20 - 27, also Dec. 17, 23, 25, 26.

IC807 — CAROLINE NEUBER - ⊒ Berlin - Gera; ✕ Berlin - Leipzig. Not Dec. 24.

IC808 — FRIEDICH LUDWIG JAHN - ⊒ Gera - Berlin; ✕ Leipzig - Berlin. Not Dec. 24.

IC813 — WETTERSTEIN - ⊒ and ✕ Berlin - Garmisch- Mittenwald. Extended to Seefeld in Tirol on ⑥ Jan. 7 - Apr. 8, also Dec. 17, 21, 22, 23, 26.

D1182 — SPREE-ALPEN EXPRESS - ⑥ Jan. 7 - Apr. 22, also Dec. 17, 23, 26, Apr. 17, not Apr. 15: 🛏 2 cl., ⊒ and 🍴 Verona - Berlin; 🛏 1,2 cl. Innsbruck - Berlin.

D1183 — SPREE-ALPEN EXPRESS - ⑤ Jan. 6 - Apr. 21, also Dec. 16, 22, 25, Apr. 13, not Apr. 14: 🛏 2 cl., ⊒ and 🍴 Berlin - Verona; 🛏 1,2 cl. Berlin - Innsbruck.

D1209 — ⑤ Jan. 6 - Apr. 7, also Dec. 16, 22, 25: 🛏 1,2 cl. Berlin-Villach.

ICN1901 — 🛏 1,2 cl., ⟨⟩ (reclining) and ✕ Berlin - München. Special fare payable - see heading on page 348.

D1906/7 — 🛏 1,2 cl., ⊒ 2 cl., ⊒ and 🍴 Berlin - Hof - Nürnberg - Stuttgart and v.v; ⊒ 2 cl. and 🍴 Berlin - München and v.v./to/from trains D1960/1 at Hof.

D1954 — 🛏 1,2 cl., ⊒ 2 cl., ⊒ and 🍴 Berlin - Frankfurt/Main. Not Nov. 19.

IR2013 — ⊒ and 🍴 Berlin - Leipzig (from Stralsund daily except Dec. 25, 26, Jan. 1).

IR2014/5 — ⊒ and 🍴 Binz - Stralsund - Berlin - Leipzig and v.v.

IR2016/7 — ⊒ and 🍴 Rostock - Leipzig and v.v.

IR2154 — Not Dec. 25: ⊒ and 🍴 Berlin - Erfurt (Frankfurt ⑦), not Dec. 25, Apr. 30, May 1

IR2207 — ⊒ and 🍴 Berlin - Saalfeld; ⊒ connection on to Saalfeld.

IR2573 — ⊒ and 🍴 Dessau - Nordhausen - Kassel - Konstanz. Not Dec. 25, Jan. 1.

IR2603 — ⊒ and 🍴 Berlin - Regensburg - München - Oberstdorf; ⊒ Berlin - Reichenbach (D367) - Karlovy Vary.

IR2647 — ⊒ and 🍴 Aachen - Hannover - Leipzig. Not Dec. 24, 31.

IR2658 — ⊒ and 🍴 Berlin - Erfurt; 🍴 Berlin - Halle. Not Dec. 24.

IR2744 — ⊒ and 🍴 Leipzig - Hannover - Aachen. Not Dec. 25, Jan. 1.

E3970 — Not Dec. 24, 25, 31: ⊒ Dessau - Nordhausen.

A — ⊒ Northeim - Nordhausen - Dessau.

H — Not Dec. 25, Apr. 14, 16, 30.

K — ⊒ Dessau - Nordhausen - Kassel and v.v.

Q — Not Dec. 24.

R — Not Dec. 24, 25.

T — Not Dec. 24, 25, 31.

V — Not Dec. 25.

Y — Not Dec. 25, 26, Jan. 1.

∕ — Daily except ⑥ (not Dec. 24 - 31, Apr. 14 - 16, Apr. 30, 1995).

① - ⑥ — (not Dec. 25 - Jan. 1, Apr. 15 - 17, May 1, 1995).

b — Connection by 🚌. See note for IR2207.

n — Train number D1961.

Table 670 — ERFURT - HALLE - BERLIN

1, 2 class except where shown

	IC 706	IR 2153	E 4412	E 3458	E 3657	IR 2012	IC 812	IR 2655	E 4414	E 2200	IC 800	IC 800	E 4416	IR 2151	IR 2576	E 2602	IR 2202	E 5664	IC 704	IR 2653	E 3967	D 1955	D 1208	ICN 1900
	✕	⟡				⟡	✕	⟡		⟡	✕	✕		⟡	⟡	⟡	⟡	2	✕	⟡	⟡	⟡	⟡	✕
	◆				A			Q		Q	◆	B	T						◆					◆
München Hbf 770 .... d.	0856					1056					1256	1256			1257			1456						2306
Nürnberg 770 .... d.	1040					1240					1440	1440			1542			1640						
Saalfeld 770 .... d.					1455						1655				1814			1855						
Würzburg 771 .... d.						1348																		
Frankfurt/Main 775 ..... d.		1018									1418							2323						
Erfurt 775 .... d.	1348					1548		1650			1748						1948		0257					
Weimar 775 .... d.	1404					1604		1706			1804					2004		0314						
Naumburg 770 775 ..... d.	1431			1602	1631		1732	1802			1831			1932		2002	2015							
Halle 770 .... a.	1511				1711	1810				1911			2010		2111	2108								
Halle .... d.	1514		1614		1714	1813				1914	1936		2014		2114	2214	0412	0512	0558					
Leipzig .... d.	1508	1510	1601		1625	1648	1710			1848	1908	1910			1934		2048		0410		0551			
Bitterfeld .... a.		1544	1537	1626	1643	1648		1744	1737	1843		1937	1944	2007		2043			2144	2244				
Bitterfeld .... d.		1546	1543	1627	1645	1650		1746	1743	1844		1943	1948	2008		2044			2146	2246				
Dessau .... d.			1605		1702	1710			1805	1901		2005		2025		2101	2104			2302	0458	0603		
Magdeburg .... d.			1654							1852				2210										
Lutherstadt Wittenberg . d.		1609		1656			1809					2009				2209								
Jüterbog .... d.		1633		1719			1833					2033				2233								
Berlin Schönefeld ✈ ... a.	1700	1714			1818	1830	1914			2030	2100		2114		2130		2230	2314						
Berlin Wannsee .... a.										1953						2153					0628			0738
Berlin Charlottenburg .. a.										2001														0753
Berlin Zoo .... a.																2203					0641	0700		
Berlin Lichtenberg ..... a.		1732				1838							2132		2150					2332				
Berlin Hbf .... a.	1719					1849				2049	2119							2249						

NOTES (LISTED BY TRAIN NUMBERS)

◆ –

IC706 – BERTOLT BRECHT – ②③④, not Apr. 13: ⌷ and ✕ München - Berlin.

IC800 – THERESE GIEHSE – ①⑤⑥⑦ also Apr. 13: ⌷ and ✕ München - Berlin; conveys ⑥⑦ Jan. 7 - Apr. 9, May 20 - 27, also Dec. 18, 24, 26, 27, Jan. 2, 6, Apr. 18, 22: ⌷ and ✕ Bischofshofen - Innsbruck - München - Berlin.

IC812 – WETTERSTEIN – ⌷ and ✕ Mittenwald - Garmisch - Berlin. Starts Seefeld in Tirol ⑥ Jan. 14 - Apr. 8, also Jan. 2 - 8).

D1208 – ⑥ Jan. 7 - Apr. 8, also Dec. 17, 23, 26 (from Villach): ⇌ 1,2 cl., ⇌ 2 cl., ⌷ and ⟡ Villach - Berlin.

ICN1900 – ⇌ 1,2 cl., ⌷ (reclining) and ✕ München - Berlin. Special fare payable - see heading on page 348.

D1955 – ⇌ 1,2 cl., ⇌ 2 cl., ⌷ and ⟡ Frankfurt/Main - Berlin. Not Nov. 19.

IR2012 – ⌷ and ⟡ Leipzig - Stralsund (Berlin on Dec. 24).

IR2151 – ⑧, not Dec. 25, Apr. 14 - 16, 30).

IR2202 – ⌷ Nürnberg - Berlin; ⟡ Nürnberg - Dessau.

IR2576 – ⌷ and ⟡ Konstanz - Kassel - Nordhausen - Dessau. Not Dec. 24, 31.

IR2602 – ⌷ and ⟡ Oberstdorf - München - Regensburg - Berlin; ⌷ Karlovy Vary (D366) - Reichenbach - Berlin.

IR2653 – ⌷ Erfurt - Berlin; ⟡ Erfurt - Halle. Not Dec. 24, 25.

E3967 – ⌷ Kassel - Nordhausen - Dessau. Not Dec. 24, 25, 31.

A – Northeim - Nordhausen - Dessau.

B – THERESE GIEHSE – ②③④, not Apr. 13: ⌷ and ✕ München - Berlin.

C – ⑧, not Dec. 25, Apr. 14, 16, 30.

Q – Not Dec. 24.

T – Not Dec. 24, 25, 31.

Y – Not Dec. 25, 26, Jan. 1.

Table 672 — BERLIN - COTTBUS - GÖRLITZ

1, 2 class except where shown

km		E 5357	IR 3131	IR 2251	E 3133	E 5359		E 3135	E 5361		IR 2133	E 3137	E 5363	E 3139	E 5367	IR 2037	E 3141	E 5369	E 3143	E 5371	IR 2039	E 5373	IR 2139	E 3009
		2				2			2				2		2			2		S		T		
0	Berlin Lichtenberg ... d.		0600	0700	0800			1000			1123	1200		1400		1523	1600		1800		1923		2130	2322
	Berlin Schöneweide .. d.		0612		0812			1012				1212		1412			1612		1812					2334
31	Königs Wusterhausen . d.		0627	0724	0827			1027			1148	1227		1427		1548	1627		1827		1948		2155	2349
78	Lübben .... d.		0658	0754	0858			1058			1218	1258		1458		1618	1658		1858		2018		2225	0024
89	Lübbenau .... d.		0706	0803	0906			1106			1226	1306		1506		1626	1706		1906		2026		2233	0032
119	Cottbus .... a.		0729	0820	0925			1129			1244	1325		1530		1644	1725		1925		2044		2251	0051
119	Cottbus .... d.	0655		0830		1001			1201		1254		1401		1601	1654		1801		2001	2054	2222		
143	Spremberg .... d.	0713		0849		1024			1225		1313		1424		1624	1713		1824		2024	2113	2224		
161	Weißwasser .... d.	0749		0903		1051			1252		1328		1452		1652	1728		1840		2052	2128	2300		
191	Horka .... d.	0814				1117			1319		1359		1519		1727	1749		1923		2119	2149			
212	Görlitz .... a.	0833		0938		1141			1338		1418		1538		1746	1808		1942		2138	2208			

		IR 2138	E 3132	IR 2038	E 5354	E 3134	E 5358	E 3136	IR 2036	E 5360	E 3138	E 5362	E 3140	IR 2132	E 5364	E 3142		E 5366	E 3144	E 5368	IR 2250	E 3946	E 3918	E 5370	E 3948
					2		2			2		2			2					2		2	2	2	
		◆												◆							S	Q			⑧
Görlitz .... d.				0540	0600		0755		0940	1006		1206		1340	1356			1606		1810	1838			2006	
Horka .... d.				0558	0624		0818		0958	1024		1224		1358	1424			1624		1830	1856			2024	
Weißwasser .... d.				0621	0654		0846		1021	1057		1254		1421	1457			1654		1857	1919			2054	
Spremberg .... d.				0635	0714		0914		1035	1114		1314		1435	1514			1714		1914	1933			2114	
Cottbus .... a.				0653	0735		0935		1053	1135		1335		1453	1535			1735		1935	1951			2135	
Cottbus .... d.	0510	0540	0705		0757			1105		1200		1400	1500		1600			1800	2003	2025			2230	
Lübbenau .... d.	0528	0559	0724		0820			1124		1220		1420	1524		1620			1827	2022	2058	2141		2258	
Lübben .... d.		0606	0732		0827		1027	1132		1227		1427	1532		1627			1827	2030	2104	2150		2304	
Königs Wusterhausen . d.		0636	0802		0858		1058	1202		1258		1458	1602		1658			1858	2100		2234			
Berlin Schöneweide ... d.		0649			0911		1111			1311		1511			1711			1911			2247			
Berlin Lichtenberg ... a.	0624	0700	0825		0923		1123	1225		1323		1523	1625		1723			1923	2122		2300			

NOTES (LISTED BY TRAIN NUMBERS)

◆ –

IR2036 – ⌷ Görlitz - Wismar; ⟡ Cottbus - Wismar.

IR2037 – ⌷ Wismar - Görlitz; ⟡ Berlin - Görlitz.

IR2038 – ⌷ Görlitz - Berlin - Wismar. Not Dec. 25.

IR2039 – ⌷ Wismar - Görlitz. Not Dec. 24.

IR2132/3 – ⌷ Lübeck - Berlin - Görlitz and v.v.

IR2138 – ① - ⑥, not Dec. 25: ⌷ and ⟡ Cottbus - Lübeck.

IR2139 – ⑧: ⌷ and ⟡ Lübeck - Cottbus.

IR2251 – ⌷ Berlin - Görlitz; ⟡ Berlin - Cottbus. Not Dec. 25.

Q – Not Dec. 24.

S – Not Dec. 24, 31.

T – Not Dec. 24, 25, 31.

V – Not Dec. 25.

❖ – Not Dec. 25, Jan. 1.

h – Berlin Hbf.

Table 673 — BÜTZOW - GÜSTROW - PASEWALK - SZCZECIN

2 class only

km		8651	E3305 5305	E3307 8669	E3313 8655	8657	E 3315	E 3317	E 3319	7385			E 3304	E 3306	E 3308	5314	8654 7370	E 3314	8656 E3316	8658
		❖			B			S	S	S							C	S	H	J
0	Bützow .... d.		0547	0753	1025	1425	1635	1825	2025			Szczecin Glowny ...... d.				1205		1555		1800
14	Güstrow .... d.		0603	0806	1037	1437	1649	1837	2037			Grambow ▥ .... a.				1239		1632		1838
101	Neubrandenburg ...... d.		0759	0920	1222	1553	1812	2007	2152	2158		Grambow ▥ .... d.				1247		1640		1847
154	Pasewalk .... a.		0900	1004	1240	1630	1850	2045		2248		Pasewalk .... a.				1315		1709		1910
154	Pasewalk .... d.	0804		1009	1242	1636						Pasewalk .... d.	0555	0917	1149	1337	1440	1710		
181	Grambow ▥ .... d.	0828		1033	1306	1700						Neubrandenburg ...... d.	0558	0637	0959	1244	1428	1527	1759	
181	Grambow ▥ .... d.	0838			1314	1708						Güstrow .... a.	0717	0749	1117	1417		1645	1915	
196	Szczecin Glowny ...... a.	0906			1343	1751						Bützow .... a.	0727	0805	1127	1439		1727	1927	

B – Daily to Pasewalk; not Dec. 24, 31, Apr. 15 Pasewalk - Szczecin.

C – Daily from Pasewalk; not Dec. 25, Jan. 1 from Szczecin.

▥ – Daily Szczecin - Pasewalk; not Dec. 24, 32 Szczecin - Bützow.

J – Not Dec. 24, 31, Apr. 15.

S – Not Dec. 24, 31.

❖ – Not Dec. 25, Jan. 1.

Table 674 DRESDEN - MAGDEBURG - ROSTOCK - STRALSUND

1, 2 class except where shown

For other trains between Schwerin and Stralsund see Table 660

km	Station	6054	IR 2638	IC 546	D 452	IR 2738	IR 2742	4415	IR 2636	E 3013
		2	🍷 ✤	⚡🍴 ◆	🍷 ◆	🍷	🍷 ◆	2	🍷 ◆	✤
0	**Dresden Hbf 775** d.	...	...	...	0511	...	0608	...	0711	...
4	**Dresden Neustadt 775** d.	...	...	...	0519	...	0616	...	0719	...
54	Riesa d.	...	...	...	0554	...	0654	...	0754	...
67	Oschatz d.	...	...	...	0604	...	0704	...	0804	...
120	**Leipzig 775** a.	...	...	...	0645	...	0745	...	0845	...
120	**Leipzig** d.	...	...	0555	▬	0653	0813	...	0853	...
158	**Halle** a.	...	...	0620	...	0718	0839	...	0918	...
158	**Halle** d.	0549	...	0623	...	0722	0842	...	0922	...
193	Köthen d.	0625	...	|	...	0745	0905	...	0945	...
244	**Magdeburg** a.	0711	...	0716	...	0816	0938	...	1016	...
244	**Magdeburg** d.	▬	0600	▬	...	0820	...	...	1020	...
301	Stendal d.	...	0643	...	...	0859	...	...	1055	...
356	Wittenberge d.	**E**	0732**c**	...	...	0932	...	...	1132	...
400	Ludwigslust d.	**3005**	0805	...	...	1005	...	...	1203	...
437	**Schwerin** a.	2	0828	...	...	1028	...	...	*1254*	...
437	**Schwerin** d.	0709	0831	...	...	1031	...	...	...	1304
453	Bad Kleinen d.	0722	0846	**4409**	...	1046	...	...	...	1319
494	Bützow d.	0748	0910	2	...	1110	...	...	...	1344
524	**Rostock** a.	0812	0937	...	...	1137	...	...	...	1409
524	**Rostock** d.	0822	...	0949	...	...	...	1301	...	1433
553	Ribnitz-Damgarten West d.	0850	...	1024	...	...	...	1334	...	1509
596	**Stralsund** a.	0921	...	1110	...	...	...	1442	...	1550

Station	IR 2646	E 3017	IR 2736	E 3021	IR 2644	IR 2734	4421	IR 2448	IR 2634	E 3214	4425	IR 2446	IR 2732	IR 2444
	🍷 ◆		🍷	Ⓐ	🍷 A	🍷 ◆	2	🍷 ◆	🍷 ◆		2	🍷 ◆	🍷 ◆	🍷 ◆
Dresden Hbf 775 d.	*0754*	...	0911	...	1011	1111	...	...	1311	...	...	1411	1511	...
Dresden Neustadt 775 d.	0819	...	0919	...	1019	1119	...	...	1319	...	...	1419	1519	...
Riesa d.	0854	...	0954	...	1054	1154	...	...	1354	...	...	1454	1554	...
Oschatz d.	0904	...	1004	...	1104	1204	...	...	1404	...	...	1504	1604	...
Leipzig 775 a.	0945	...	1045	...	1145	1245	...	...	1445	...	...	1545	1645	...
Leipzig d.	1013	...	1053	...	1213	1253	...	1413	1453	...	...	1613	1653	1813
Halle a.	1039	...	1118	...	1239	1318	...	1439	1518	...	...	1639	1718	1839
Halle d.	1042	...	1122	...	1242	1322	...	1442	1522	...	...	1642	1722	1842
Köthen d.	1105	...	1145	...	1305	1345	...	1505	1545	...	...	1705	1745	1905
Magdeburg a.	1137	...	1216	...	1337	1416	...	1537	1616	...	...	1738	1816	1937
Magdeburg d.	...	...	1220	...	...	1420	...	...	1620	...	...	...	1820	...
Stendal d.	...	...	1255	...	...	1455	...	...	1655	...	...	...	1855	...
Wittenberge d.	...	...	1332	...	...	1532	...	...	1732	...	...	...	1932	...
Ludwigslust d.	...	...	1405	...	...	1605	...	...	1803	1809	...	...	2005	...
Schwerin a.	...	...	1428	...	...	1628	...	...	...	1833	...	...	2028	...
Schwerin d.	...	...	1431	1525	...	1631	...	...	...	...	...	...	2031	...
Bad Kleinen d.	...	...	1446	1539	...	1646	...	...	...	...	...	...	2046	...
Bützow d.	...	...	1536**e**	1605	...	1710	...	...	...	...	...	...	2110	...
Rostock a.	...	...	1603	1629	...	1737	...	...	...	...	...	...	2137	...
Rostock d.	...	1526	...	1637	...	...	1819	...	...	...	1936	...	...	...
Ribnitz-Damgarten West d.	...	1551	...	1702	...	...	1859	...	...	...	2015	...	...	...
Stralsund a.	...	1634	...	1740	...	...	1944	...	...	...	2104	...	...	...

Station	IR 2730	IR 2440	IR 2632	6076	D 1948	D 450	D 476	D 476	E 3203	D 351
	🍷 ◆	♣🍴 ◆	🍷		🍷 ◆	🍷 ◆	Ⓑ🍷 G	⑥🍷 G	Ⓑ	🍷 ◆
Dresden Hbf 775 d.	1711	1811	1911	...	2101	...	2311	2311	...	...
Dresden Neustadt 775 d.	1719	1819	1919	...	2109	2243	2319	2319	...	...
Riesa d.	1754	1854	1954	...	2144	2333	2354	2354	...	...
Oschatz d.	1804	1904	2004	...	2154	2343	0004	0004	...	...
Leipzig 775 a.	1845	1945	2045	...	2239	0025	0045	0045	...	...
Leipzig d.	1853	2013	▬	...	2252	...	0055	0055	...	...
Halle a.	1918	2039	...	...	2318	...	0121	0121	...	...
Halle d.	1922	2042	**6658**	2152	2323	...	0128	0128	...	0332
Köthen d.	1945	2105	2	2225	2346	...	|	|	...	|
Magdeburg a.	2016	2137	**T**	2311	0020	...	0222	0222	...	0425
Magdeburg d.	2020	2146	2258	...	...	...	0225	0225	...	0428
Stendal d.	2054	2221	2342	...	...	...	0301	0301	...	|
Wittenberge d.	2132	...	...	...	...	...	0348**c**	0348**c**	...	0539
Ludwigslust d.	2205	...	...	...	...	...	0418	0423	0432	|
Schwerin a.	2228	...	...	...	...	...	...	0448	0456	0629
Schwerin d.	2231	...	...	...	...	...	...	...	0458	0631
Bad Kleinen d.	2246	...	...	...	...	...	...	...	0511	0646
Bützow d.	2310	...	...	...	...	...	...	...	0535	|
Rostock a.	2337	...	...	...	...	...	...	...	0559	0734
Rostock d.	...	...	...	...	...	...	...	...	0609	0743
Ribnitz-Damgarten West d.	...	...	...	...	...	...	...	...	0636	|
Stralsund a.	...	...	...	...	...	...	...	...	0715	0841

Station	IR 2641	D 1949	IR 2441	IR 2633	IR 2443	IR 2731	E 3004	IR 2445	E 3306
	⚡🍷	🍷 ◆	⚡🍷	🍷 V	🍷 ◆	🍷 ◆	✤	🍷 ◆	
Stralsund d.	...	...	...	...	...	...	...	...	...
Ribnitz-Damgarten West d.	...	...	...	...	...	...	...	...	...
Rostock a.	...	...	...	...	...	...	...	...	...
Rostock d.	...	...	...	...	...	0545	0640	...	...
Bützow d.	...	...	...	...	...	0613	0707	...	0806
Bad Kleinen d.	...	...	...	...	...	0639	0732	...	0833
Schwerin a.	...	...	...	...	...	0652	0744	...	0846
Schwerin d.	...	...	...	...	...	0654	...	...	0848
Ludwigslust d.	...	...	...	...	...	0720	...	...	0914
Wittenberge d.	...	...	...	...	...	0752	...	...	...
Stendal d.	...	...	0536	...	...	0828	...	...	...
Magdeburg a.	...	...	0613	...	...	0903	...	...	...
Magdeburg d.	...	0518	0618	0718	0821	0922	...	1021	...
Köthen d.	...	0552	0654	0754	0854	0954	...	1054	...
Halle a.	...	0616	0716	0816	0916	1016	...	1116	...
Halle d.	...	0623	0723	0823	0923	1023	...	1123	...
Leipzig a.	...	0649	0749	0849	0949	1049	...	1149	...
Leipzig 775 d.	0601	...	0801	0907	1001	1107	...	...	...
Oschatz d.	0641	...	0841	0948	1041	1148	...	...	...
Riesa d.	0652	...	0852	0959	1052	1159	...	...	...
Dresden Neustadt 775 a.	0727	...	0927	1034	1127	1234	...	...	...
Dresden Hbf 775 a.	0735	...	0935	1042	1135	1242	...	...	...

Station	IR 2635	E 3006	IR 2447	IR 2733	4410	IR 2449	IR 2735	4412	IR 2743	IR 2737	D 453
	🍷 ◆	Ⓐ	🍷 A	🍷	2	🍷 ◆	🍷	2	🍷 ◆	🍷	🍷 ◆
Stralsund d.	...	0645	...	...	0902	...	...	1059	...	...	...
Ribnitz-Damgarten West d.	...	0717	...	...	0955	...	...	1155	...	...	...
Rostock a.	...	0741	...	...	1025	...	...	1225	...	...	...
Rostock d.	...	0753	...	0950	...	...	1150	...	...	1350	...
Bützow d.	...	0820	...	1016	...	...	1216	...	...	1416	...
Bad Kleinen d.	...	0845	...	1039	...	...	1239	...	...	1439	...
Schwerin a.	...	0857	...	1052	...	...	1252	...	...	1452	...
Schwerin d.	...	...	...	1054	...	...	1254	...	...	1454	...
Ludwigslust d.	0920	...	...	1120	...	...	1320	...	...	1520	...
Wittenberge d.	0952	...	...	1152	...	...	1352	...	...	1552	...
Stendal d.	1028	...	...	1228	...	...	1428	...	...	1628	...
Magdeburg a.	1103	...	...	1303	...	...	1503	...	...	1703	...
Magdeburg d.	1121	...	1221	1321	...	1421	1521	...	1621	1721	...
Köthen d.	1154	...	1254	1354	...	1454	1554	...	1654	1754	...
Halle a.	1216	...	1316	1416	...	1516	1616	...	1716	1816	...
Halle d.	1223	...	1323	1423	...	1523	1623	...	1723	1823	...
Leipzig a.	1249	...	1349	1449	...	1549	1649	...	1749	1849	...
Leipzig 775 d.	1307	...	1401	1507	...	...	1707	...	1801	...	1905
Oschatz d.	1348	...	1441	1548	...	...	1748	...	1841	...	1948
Riesa d.	1359	...	1452	1559	...	...	1759	...	1852	...	1959
Dresden Neustadt 775 a.	1434	...	1527	1634	...	...	1834	...	1930	...	2034
Dresden Hbf 775 a.	1442	...	1535	1642	...	...	1842	...	*1946*	...	...

Station	4414	E 3212	IR 2637	4418	E 3016	IR 2739	IC 547	IR 2639	D 350	4426	E 3218	D 477	D 451
	2		🍷 ◆	2		🍷 ◆	♣🍴 ◆	🍷 ◆	🍷 ◆	2	S	🍷 G	🍷 ◆
Stralsund d.	1229	...	...	1421	1525	*1609*	...	*1822*	2006	2013	...	...	...
Ribnitz-Damgarten West d.	1311	...	...	1507	1609	*1704*	...	*1909*	|	2106	...	...	...
Rostock a.	1349	...	...	1545	1633	*1744*	...	*1945*	2058	2143	...	...	...
Rostock d.	▬	1538	...	...	1641	1750	...	1950	2116	...	2156	...	...
Bützow d.	...	1606	...	...	1708	1816	...	2016	|	...	2223	...	...
Bad Kleinen d.	...	1633	...	...	1734	1839	...	2039	2202	...	2248	...	...
Schwerin a.	...	1645	...	...	1746	1852	...	2052	2215	...	2300	...	...
Schwerin d.	...	1650	...	...	...	1854	...	2054	2217	...	2312	...	...
Ludwigslust d.	**IR**	1715	1720	...	...	1920	...	2120	|	...	2336	2351	...
Wittenberge d.	**2645**	...	1752	...	...	1952	...	2152	2307	...	...	0031**c**	...
Stendal d.	🍷	...	1828	...	...	2028	...	2229	|	...	...	0108	...
Magdeburg a.	◆	...	1903	...	...	2103	...	2303	0016	...	...	0144	...
Magdeburg d.	1821	...	1921	...	...	2121	2245	...	0027	...	...	0149	...
Köthen d.	1854	...	1954	...	...	2154	|	...	|	...	...	|	...
Halle a.	1916	...	2016	...	...	2216	2336	...	0118	...	...	0240	...
Halle d.	1923	...	2023	...	...	2223	2339	...	...	...	...	0247	...
Leipzig a.	1949	...	2049	...	...	2249	0005	...	...	...	...	0314	...
Leipzig 775 d.	2001	...	2107	...	...	...	...	...	...	...	...	0324	0507
Oschatz d.	2041	...	2148	...	...	...	...	...	...	...	...	0406	0548
Riesa d.	2052	...	2159	...	...	...	...	...	...	...	...	0417	0559
Dresden Neustadt 775 a.	2127	...	2234	...	...	...	...	...	...	...	...	0452	0638
Dresden Hbf 775 a.	2135	...	2242	...	...	...	...	...	...	...	...	0505	...

◆ – NOTES (LISTED BY TRAIN NUMBERS)

D350/1 – 🛏 1,2 cl., ▬ 2 cl., [2] and 🍷 Stralsund (Binz **b**) - Basel and v.v; 🛏 1,2 cl., ▬ 2 cl. and [2] Stralsund (Binz **b**) - Bebra (**D482/3**) - München and v.v.
D450/1 – 🛏 1,2 cl., ▬ 2 cl., [12] and 🍷 Warszawa - Frankfurt/Main and v.v; ▬ 2 cl. and [2] Kraków - Frankfurt/Main and v.v; 🛏 1,2 cl. Moskva - Frankfurt/Main and v.v.
D452/3 – 🛏 1,2 cl., ▬ 2 cl., [12] and 🍷 Warszawa - Leipzig and v.v; 🛏 1,2 cl. and [2] Kraków - Leipzig and v.v.
IC546/7 – WESERBERGLAND – [12] and 🍴 Leipzig - Köln and v.v.
D1948/9 – 🛏 1,2 cl., ▬ 2 cl. and [12] Dresden - Köln and v.v; 🛏 1,2 cl., ▬ 2 cl. and [2] Dresden - Halle (**D358/9**) - Basel SBB.
IR2440 – [12] and 🍷 Dresden - Magdeburg (Stendal on dates in note **W**).
IR2443 – [12] and 🍷 Hannover (Leipzig on Dec. 25, Jan. 1) - Dresden.
IR2444 – [12] and 🍷 Leipzig - Hannover. **Not** Dec. 24, 31.
IR2445 – [12] Hannover (Köln ① - ⑥, **not** Dec. 26, Apr. 15 - 17, May 1) - Leipzig; 🍷 Mülheim - Leipzig.
IR2446 – [12] and 🍷 Dresden - Hannover (Köln Ⓑ, **not** Dec. 25, Apr. 14 - 16, 30).
IR2448/9 – [12] and 🍷 Leipzig - Aachen and v.v.
IR2634 – [12] and 🍷 Dresden - Hamburg (Magdeburg on Dec. 24).
IR2635 – [12] and 🍷 Hamburg (Magdeburg on Dec. 25) - Dresden.
IR2636 – [12] and 🍷 Dresden (Magdeburg on Dec. 25) - Hamburg.
IR2637 – [12] and 🍷 Hamburg - Dresden (Magdeburg on Dec. 24).
IR2639 – [12] and 🍷 Rostock - Magdeburg. Runs on dates in note **W**.
IR2645 – [12] and 🍷 Aachen - Dresden (Leipzig on Dec. 24, 31).
IR2646 – [12] and 🍷 Görlitz (Dresden Neustadt on Dec. 25, Jan. 1) - Aachen.
IR2730 – [12] and 🍷 Dresden - Stendal ♣; extended to Rostock on dates in note **W**.
IR2731 – [12] and 🍷 Rostock (Schwerin on Dec. 25) - Dresden.
IR2732 – [12] and 🍷 Dresden - Rostock (Schwerin on Dec. 24).
IR2734 – [12] and 🍷 Leipzig (Dresden ⚡) - Rostock.
IR2739 – **Not** Dec. 24, 31: [12] and 🍷 Rostock - Magdeburg (Leipzig Ⓑ, **not** Dec. 25, Apr. 14 - Apr. 16, 30.
IR2742 – [12] and 🍷 Dresden (Leipzig on Dec. 25, Jan. 1) - Norddeich Mole.
IR2743 – [12] and 🍷 Norddeich Mole - Görlitz (Dresden Neustadt on Dec. 24, 31).
A – [12] and 🍷 Dresden - Aachen and v.v.
G – 🛏 1,2 cl., ▬ 2 cl., [12] and 🍷 Praha Hlavni - Hamburg and v.v.
S – **Not** Dec. 24, 31.
T – **Not** Dec. 24, 25, 31.
W – ⑦, also Dec. 26, Apr. 17, May 1, **not** Dec. 25, Apr. 16, 30.
V – **Not** Dec. 25.
b – Train is extended to/from Binz on ⑥ Apr. 8 - May 27, also Apr. 14, 17, May 25, **not** Apr. 15.
c – Arrive 10 - 15 minutes earlier.
e – Arrive 1508.
✤ – **Not** Dec. 25, Jan. 1.
⚡ – ① - ⑥ (**not** Dec. 25 - Jan. 1, Apr. 15 - 17, May 1, **1995**).
♣ – Daily except ⑥ (**not** Dec. 24 - 31, Apr. 14 - 16, Apr. 30, **1995**).

Table 675 — BERLIN - SZCZECIN, STRALSUND and SASSNITZ

1, 2 class except where shown

Berlin → Szczecin / Stralsund / Sassnitz

km	Station	6409 2	3182	351	328	2118 2	6413 2	6417 2	IC 818	6419 2	2233	2116	7902 2	3186	6423 2	2376	3188	316	IC 737	3018 2	6431 2	2014 2	7908
	Berlin Schönefeld + 670 .. d																1026					1420	
0	Berlin Lichtenberg d			0632	0700				0815h			0900					1100	1300				1420	
29	Bernau d			0653	0721							0921					1121	1321				1521	
51	Eberswalde d			0708	0736							0936					1136	1336				1536	
76	Angermünde d			0731	0754							0954	1030				1154	1354				1554	1600
	Tantow § d			0757									1107										1637
	Szczecin Gumience ⌂ a			0814									1121										1651
	Szczecin Gumience ⌂ d			0833									1140										1708
	Szczecin Glowny a			0838									1145										1713
114	Prenzlau d				0816							1016					1216	1416				1616	
138	Pasewalk d		0725		0833							1033			1125		1233	1433				1633	
215	Greifswald d		0822		0926							1126			1222		1326	1526				1622	1726
247	Stralsund Hbf a		0841		0945			1055				1145			1241		1345	1545				1745	
247	Stralsund Hbf d	0735	0852			0933	1033	1105	1119		1156	1206		1233	1343			1555	1605		1735	1800	1833
251	Stralsund Rügendamm d	0740				0940		1040		1124		1238			1348						1740		1838
277	Bergen d	0806	0918			1006		1106	1130	1151	1221	1232		1303	1413			1619	1631		1813	1827	1903
285	Lietzow ▲ a	0817				1017		1117		1200		1313			1423						1824	1827	1916
	Binz ▲ a		0951						1155									1656			1852		
298	Sassnitz Hbf a	0832				1032		1132		1215		1254	1328		1442			1642			1839		1931
299	Sassnitz Hafen ⌂ a														1659								

Berlin → Stralsund / Sassnitz (continued) — and return

Station	3190 2	2112	326	3192 2	2012	2110	3146 2	320	318	1010		3133 2	2013	6406	2111	7901	6408	7211	6410	2334
Berlin Schönefeld + 670 .. d				1820							Sassnitz Hafen ⌂ d									
Berlin Lichtenberg d		1700		1900	2100	2200	2225	2238h		0354	Sassnitz Hbf d			0641			0742		0842	
Bernau d		1721		1921	2121	2222	2245				Binz ▲ d									0905
Eberswalde d		1736		1936	2136	2238	2301	2359			Lietzow ▲ d			0702			0759		0859	
Angermünde d		1754	1800	1954	2154	2259	2320				Bergen d			0711			0809		0909	0931
Tantow § d			1826					2348			Stralsund Rügendamm d			0736			0834		0934	
Szczecin Gumience ⌂ a			1845					0008			Stralsund Hbf a		0630	0740		0830		0912	0938	0955
Szczecin Gumience ⌂ d			1904					0037			Stralsund Hbf d		0630		0830			0912		
Szczecin Glowny a			1909					0042			Greifswald d		0652		0852			0946		
Prenzlau d		1816			2016	2216	2320				Pasewalk d		0744		0944			1053		
Pasewalk d	1725	1833			1931	2033	2233	2336			Prenzlau d		0759		0959					
Greifswald d	1822	1926	6435	2028	2126	2324			0137	0603	Szczecin Glowny d					0910				
Stralsund Hbf a	1841	1945	2	2047	2145	2343				0622	Szczecin Gumience ⌂ d					0917 E				
Stralsund Hbf d			1935							0633	Szczecin Gumience ⌂ d					0935 3137				
Stralsund Rügendamm d			1940						0156		Tantow § d					0955 2				
Bergen d			2006						0216	0659	Angermünde d	0701	0824		1024	1032	1101			
Lietzow ▲ a			2017								Eberswalde d	0719	0840		1040		1119			
Binz ▲ a											Bernau d	0736	0857		1057		1136			
Sassnitz Hbf a			2032						0239	0721	Berlin Lichtenberg a	0757	0916		1116		1157			
Sassnitz Hafen ⌂ a									0256	0737	Berlin Schönefeld + 670 .. a		0953							

Sassnitz / Stralsund → Berlin

Station	2015	7905	6414	2113	6420	327	IC 736	317	7223	6424		2115	3315	6428	2230	2117	IC 819	329	6434	350	2119	1011	319	321
Sassnitz Hafen ⌂ d						1311																		
Sassnitz Hbf d			1042		1235		1330		1447					1644		1729		1859				2215	0323	
Binz ▲ d	0917						1251								1705		1801		1914			2234	0342	
Lietzow ▲ d			1059		1257			1502						1700		1917								
Bergen d	0951		1109		1305		1317	1511					1709	1731	1753	1827		1926	1940		2257	0406	
Stralsund Rügendamm d			1134		1329			1536						1734		1951							0427	
Stralsund Hbf a	1015		1138		1334		1341	1418	1540				1738	1755	1817	1851		1955	2004		2321			
Stralsund Hbf d	1030			1230				1430	1518		1630	1715			1830	1901				2030	2343			
Greifswald d	1052			1252				1452	1547		1652	1741			1852					2052	0005	0447		
Pasewalk d	1144			1344				1544	1653		1744	1903			1944					2144				
Prenzlau d	1159			1359				1559			1759	1917			1959					2159				
Szczecin Glowny d			1235			1450											2000						0500	
Szczecin Gumience ⌂ a			1242			1457											2007						0507	
Szczecin Gumience ⌂ d			1305			1524											2022						0539	
Tantow § d			1323			1544											2042						0559	
Angermünde d	1224	1400	1424			1610		1624			1824	1941			2024	2108		2224				0630		
Eberswalde d	1240		1440			1640		1640			1840	1958			2040	2124		2240		0622	0649			
Bernau d	1257		1457			1657		1657			1857				2057	2141		2257			0708			
Berlin Lichtenberg a	1316		1516			1716		1716			1916				2116	2140h	2200	2316	0211	0701h	0728			
Berlin Schönefeld + 670 .. a	1353					1742																		

NOTES (LISTED BY TRAIN NUMBERS)

D316 – BERLINAREN – [sleeper]2 and ♀ Berlin - Sassnitz; [couchette] Berlin - Malmö.

D317 – BERLINAREN – [couchette] Malmö - Berlin; [sleeper] Sassnitz - Plauen; ♀ Sassnitz - Reichenbach.

D318/9 – SASSNITZ EXPRESS – [sleeper]1,2 cl., [couchette] 2 cl. and [couchette] Berlin - Malmö and v.v.

D320/1 – GEDANIA – [sleeper]1,2 cl., [couchette] Berlin - Gdynia and v.v.; conveys (except on Apr. 15, 16 from Berlin, and Apr. 16, 17 from Kaliningrad): [sleeper]1,2 cl. Berlin - Kaliningrad and v.v.

D328/9 – MARE BALTICUM – [couchette] and ♀ Berlin - Gdynia and v.v.

D350/1 – ARKONA – ⑥ Apr. 8 - May 27 to Apr. 14, 17, May 25, not Apr. 15: (from Binz and Basel) [sleeper]1,2 cl., [couchette] 2 cl., [couchette] and ♀ Basel - Basel SBB and v.v.; [sleeper]1,2 cl., [couchette] 2 cl. and [couchette] Binz - Bebra (D482/3) - München and v.v.

IC736 – RÜGEN – ⑥⑦ Apr. 29 - May 27: [couchette] Köln (Aachen ♣); ♀ to Köln.

IC737 – RÜGEN – ⑤⑥ Apr. 28 - May 27: [couchette] Köln (Aachen ✈) - Binz. ♀ from Köln.

IC818 – CASPAR DAVID FRIEDRICH – ⑥⑦ Apr. 29 - May 27: [couchette] and ♀ Berlin Hbf - Neubrandenburg - Binz.

IC819 – CASPAR DAVID FRIEDRICH – ⑤⑥ Apr. 28 - May 27: [couchette] and ♀ Binz - Neubrandenburg - Berlin.

D1010 – CSÁRDÁS – Apr. 6 - May 27 (from Budapest): [sleeper]1,2 cl. and [couchette] 2 cl. Budapest Keleti - Malmö; [couchette] Budapest - Sassnitz; [couchette] Trelleborg - Malmö.

D1011 – CSÁRDÁS – Apr. 7 - May 27 (from Malmö): [sleeper]1,2 cl. and [couchette] 2 cl. Malmö - Budapest Keleti; [couchette] Sassnitz - Budapest; [couchette] Malmö - Trelleborg.

IR2012 – [couchette] and ♀ Leipzig - Stralsund.

IR2013 – [couchette] and ♀ Stralsund - Leipzig.

IR2014/5 – [couchette] and ♀ Leipzig - Binz and v.v.

IR2233 – ⑥⑦ May 27: [couchette] and ♀ Hamburg - Binz and v.v.

IR2334 – ⑥, not Apr. 15, May 27: [couchette] Binz - Saarbrücken; ♀ Binz - Merzig.

IR2376 – [couchette] and ♀ Plauen - Stralsund.

G – Not Dec. 25, 31.

K – ⑦, also Apr. 17, May 1, not Apr. 16, 30.

Q – Not Dec. 24.

S – Not Dec. 24, 31.

U – Not Apr. 14, 16, 17, May 1.

h – Berlin Hbf.

§ – Ticket point.

♦ – Daily except ⑥ (not Apr. 14 - 16, Apr. 30, 1995).

▲ – Local service Lietzow to Binz and v.v. – see below.

▲ – Local services Lietzow - Binz and v.v.   12 km.   Journey time: 16 minutes.   2 class only.

From Lietzow: 0516, 0621, 0721, 0947, 1128, 1320, 1520, 1726, 1932, 2120.

From Binz: 0538, 0642, 0837, 1010, 1208, 1437, 1619, 1812, 2042, 2120.

Table 677 — BERGEN - PUTBUS - GÖHREN

2 class only

Rail service Bergen - Putbus. 10 km. Journey time: 15 minutes.
From Bergen: 0550 ✧, 0715, 0919, 1115, 1315, 1515, 1715, 1930 ⑥, 2120 ⑥. **From Putbus:** 0647 ✧, 0847, 1047, 1248, 1448, 1648, 1843, 2047 ⑥, 2146 ⑥.

Steam hauled narrow gauge services operate between Putbus and Göhren. 24 km. Journey time 65 - 85 minutes.
From Putbus: 0940 ✧, 1020 **B**, 1140 **C**, 1340, 1540 **C**, 1735 **E**, 1950 **D**. **From Göhren:** 0720 **F**, 0926 **C**, 1126, 1326 **C**, 1416 **B**, 1526 **E**, 1721 **D**, 1936 **D**.

B – Traditionszug: ③⑥ Mar. 25 - May 27. Special fares apply. **C** – Dec. 26 - Jan. 4, Apr. 14 - 18, Apr. 29 - May 27. **D** – Apr. 29 - May 27. **E** – Not Dec. 24, 31.
F – Sept. 26 - Apr. 28. ✧ – Not Dec. 25, Jan. 1. Deutsche Bahn AG, Bahnhof Putbus, Bahnhofstraße 9, 18581 Putbus. ☎ – 03 83 01 456

Table 680 — HAMBURG - BERLIN - DRESDEN - PRAHA

Hamburg - Dresden/Praha trains will NOT serve Berlin Hbf until further notice

1, 2 class except where shown

km		EC 1773	IR 171 ✕ ✧	E 2271 ✧	EC 3255 F	IR 173 ✕	IR 2031 ♀	IC 2373 ♀	IC 531 X	EC 175 ✕ ✧	IR 2133 ♀	IR 2273 ♀	E 3259 ♀	IC 533 X	EC 177 ✕ ✧	IR 2035 ①-⑤	IR 2135 ♀	IR 2275 ♀	E 3261 F	IC 535 ✕	IC 871 ✕	IR 2037 ♀	D 305 ♀
0	Hamburg Altona .... d.	...	...	...	...	...	...	...	0638	...	...	...	...	0838	...	...	...	...	...	1038	...	...	...
7	Hamburg Hbf .... d.	...	...	...	...	...	...	...	0651	...	0721	...	...	0851	...	...	0914	...	...	1051	...	...	...
	Lübeck 665 .... d.	...	...	...	...	...	...	...		...		...	...		...	1012		...	...		...	1212	...
	Wismar 668 .... d.	...	...	...	...	0612	...	...		...		...	...	0840	...	1040	1040	...	...		...	1240	...
	Schwerin 660 668 .... d.	...	...	...	...	0640	...	...		...		...	...	0904	...	1104	1104	...	...		...	1304	...
122	Ludwigslust 660 .... d.	...	...	...	...	0704	...	...		...	0840	...	...	0932	...	1132	1132	...	...		...	1332	...
166	Wittenberge .... d.	...	...	...	...	0732	...	...		...	0904	...	...		...			...	...	1315	1324	1426	...
257	Nauen .... d.	...	...	...	...	0826	0915	0924	1026	...	0932	...	1115	1124	1226	1226		...	1337				...
	Berlin Spandau .... d.	...	...	...	...		0937			...		...	1137			1150		...	1350				...
297	**Berlin Zoo** .... a.	...	...	...	...	0911	0950		1005	1111		...	1205	1311	1311			...	1405	1511			...
	Berlin Lichtenberg .... a.	...	0621	0724		0821		0924	1021	1124		...	1221			1324		...	1421	1524			...
	Berlin Lichtenberg .... d.	...	0643	0743		0843		0943	1043	1143		...	1243			1343		...	1443	1543			...
325	Berlin Schönefeld ✈ .... d.	...		0826				1026		1226		...				1426		...		1626			...
418	Doberlug-Kirchhain .... d.	...		0842	0855			1039		1239	1255	...				1439	1455	...		1639			...
438	Elsterwerda .... d.	...		0900						1300		...				1500		...		1700			...
	Riesa .... d.	...		0918						1318		...				1518		...		1718			...
	Döbeln .... d.	...								1351		...				1551		...		1751			...
	Chemnitz .... a.	...		0951								...						...					...
491	Dresden Neustadt .... d.	...	0804		0936	1004		1113		1206		1336		1406				1536		1606			...
495	**Dresden Hbf** .... a.	...	0812		*0946*	1012		1119		1212		*1346*		1412				*1556*		1612			...
495	**Dresden Hbf** .... d.	...	0825			1025				1225				1425								1775	...
535	Bad Schandau ▥ § .... d.	...	0857			1057			1257	**1617**				1457								S	...
557	Děčín .... a.	...	0918			1118			1318					1518								1741	...
557	Děčín .... d.	0757	0922			1122			1322	1407				1522								1804	...
580	Usti nad Labem Hlavni .... d.	0820	0943			1143			1343	1431				1543									...
686	Praha Holešovice .... a.		1059			1259			1459					1659								1940	...
686	Praha Masarykovo .... a.	0951								1603													...
689	**Praha Hlavni** .... a.		1113																				...

	E 3263 F	IC 537 ✕ X	EC 179 ✕ ✧	IR 2137 ♀	D 317 ♀	371 M	IC 633 ✕	IC 875 ♀	D 379 ♀	IR 2039 ♀	IR 2279 ♀	E 3267 F	IC 539 ✕ K	ICE 679 ♀ Q	IC 877 ♀ Q	IR 2139 ♀ Q	D 377 ♀	IC 635 ✕	IC 879 ♀	IC 637 ✕ ♣	D 373 ♀	D 1011 ✕	IR 1771 ✕	D 477 ♀
Hamburg Altona .... d.	...	1238	...	...	...	1438	...	...	...	...	...	...	1638	...	...	...	...	1838	...	2038	...	...	...	2153
Hamburg Hbf .... d.	...	1251	...	...	...	1451	...	...	...	...	...	...	1651	...	1721	...	...	1851	...	2051	...	...	...	2221
Lübeck 665 .... d.	...		...	1321	...		...	...	...	1612	...	...		...		...	...		...		...	...	...	
Wismar 668 .... d.	...		...	1440	...		...	...	...	1640	...	...		...	1840	...	...		...		...	...	...	2351
Schwerin 660 668 .... d.	...		...	1504	...		...	...	...	1704	...	...		...	1904	...	...		...		...	...	...	0031
Ludwigslust 660 .... d.	...	1515	1524	1532	...		...	1715	1724	1732	...	...	1915	...	1932	...	2024		...		...	...	...	
Wittenberge .... d.	...	1538		1626	...		...	1738		1826	...	...	1937	...		1924	2026	2115	2134		...	...	...	
Nauen .... d.	...	1550			...	1715	1724	1750			...	...	1950	2020			2139	2139	2337		...	...	...	
Berlin Spandau .... d.	...		1605	1711	...		1805		1911	...	...	...			1945	2111	2152	2152	2347	2205	...	...	...	
Berlin Zoo .... a.	...		1621		...		1821	1848		1924	...	...						2224			2348	0214	...	
Berlin Lichtenberg .... a.	...		1643	1723	...		1843	1907		1943	...	...						2243			0007		...	
Berlin Lichtenberg .... d.	...			1742	...					2026	...	...											...	
Berlin Schönefeld ✈ .... d.	1655			1826	...					2039	2055	...											...	0417
Doberlug-Kirchhain .... d.				1839	...					2100		...											...	
Elsterwerda .... d.					...					2118		...											...	
Riesa .... d.					...					2151		...											...	
Döbeln .... d.					...							...											...	
Chemnitz .... a.	1736	1806		1911	...		2006	2039		2136		...	0010					0137					...	0452
Dresden Neustadt .... d.	*1746*	1812			...		2012	2047		*2146*		...	0018		2218			0143	0412				...	0525
Dresden Hbf .... a.		1825			1955			2109				...	0028					0153	0458				...	0605
Dresden Hbf .... d.		1857	1777		2030			2150				...	0101					0253	0458				...	0626
Bad Schandau ▥ § .... d.		1918	T		2051			2211				...	0122					0314	0519				...	
Děčín .... a.		1922	1947		2119			2226				...	0139					0336	0536	0605	0640		...	
Děčín .... d.		1943	2010		2141			2247				...	0159					0357	0557	0628	0701		...	
Usti nad Labem Hlavni .... d.		2059	2135		2309			0007				...	0314					0514	0714		0802		...	0815
Praha Holešovice .... a.												...											...	0831
Praha Masarykovo .... a.		2113	2149									...											...	
Praha Hlavni .... a.												...											...	

♦ – NOTES (LISTED BY TRAIN NUMBERS)

EC173 – VINDOBONA – 🍴 and ✕ Berlin - Wien Südbahnhof.
EC175 – HUNGARIA – 🍴 and ✕ Nauen - Budapest Keleti.
D305 – NEPTUN – 🍴 København - Chemnitz; ♀ Warnemünde - Chemnitz.
D317 – BERLINAREN – 🍴 Malmö - Plauen (Berlin on Dec. 24, 31); 🍴 and ♀ Sassnitz (Berlin on Dec. 25, Jan. 1) - Plauen. No through cars from Malmö on Dec. 25, Jan. 1.
D373 – BALT ORIENT EXPRESS – 🛏 1, 2 cl., 🛏 2 cl., 🍴 and ♀ Berlin - Bucureşti; 🍴 Berlin - Budapest - Lökösháza.
D377 – SANSSOUCI – 🛏 1,2 cl., 🛏 2 cl., 🍴 and ♀ Berlin - Wien Südbahnhof; 🍴 Berlin - Dresden.
D379 – METROPOL – 🛏 1,2 cl., 🛏 2 cl., 🍴 and ♀ Berlin - Budapest Nyugati.
D477 – 🛏 1,2 cl., 🛏 2 cl., 🍴 and ♀ Hamburg - Magdeburg - Dresden - Praha.
IC535 – KÄTHE KOLLWITZ – 🍴 Kiel - Berlin.
IC633 – EMIL NOLDE – 🍴 and ✕ Westerland - Berlin; conveys May 1 - 27: 🍴 Dagebüll - Berlin.
D1011 – CSARDAS – Nov. 1 - 6, Apr. 7 - May 27: 🛏 1,2 cl. and 🛏 2 cl Malmö - Budapest Keleti; 🍴 Sassnitz - Budapest; ✕ Dresden - Budapest.
IR2031 – 🍴 and ♀ Schwerin (Wismar ✎) - Berlin.
IR2037 – 🍴 Wismar - Görlitz; ♀ Schwerin - Berlin.

IR2039 – 🍴 Wismar - Görlitz (Berlin on Dec. 24); ♀ Berlin - Görlitz.
IR2133 – 🍴 and ♀ Lübeck - Görlitz.
IR2135 – ⑥⑦: 🍴 and ♀ Kiel - Berlin.
IR2273 – 🍴 and ♀ Rostock - Chemnitz.
IR2275 – 🍴 and ♀ Rostock - Berlin (Chemnitz ⑥, not Dec. 25, Apr. 14 - 16, 30).
IR2279 – 🍴 and ♀ Rostock - Chemnitz (Berlin on Dec. 24, 31).
IR2373 – 🍴 and ♀ Rostock (Berlin on Dec. 25, Jan. 1) - Dresden.
F – 🍴 Frankfurt/Oder - Dresden.
K – Passengers for Dresden should change at Berlin Zoo.
M – Not Dec. 24, 31: 🍴 Dresden - Košice; 🛏 1,2 cl., 🛏 2 cl., and ✕ Děčín - Košice.
Q – Not Dec. 24.
S – Not Dec. 24, 31.
T – Not Dec. 24, 25, 31.
X – Passengers from Hamburg for Dresden and the Czech Republic MUST change at Nauen (easy cross-platform interchange) and **not** in Berlin.
✧ – Not Dec. 25, Jan. 1.
① - ⑥ (not Dec. 25 - Jan. 1, Apr. 15 - 17, May 1, **1995**).
♣ – Daily except ⑥ (not Dec. 24 - 31, Apr. 14 - 16, Apr. 30, **1995**).
§ – Ticket point is **Schöna**.

11

Table 680

PRAHA - DRESDEN - BERLIN - HAMBURG

Praha/Dresden - Hamburg trains will NOT serve Berlin Hbf until further notice

1, 2 class except where shown

	IC 636	D 372	IR 2138	IC 878	IC 632	D 376	D 378	IR 2038	IR 2278	IC 876	ICE 678	IC 538	IR 2136	IR 2376	226 370	IC 874	IC 634	1616	E 3258	IR 2276	EC 178	IC 536	IR 2034	IR 2134
	✗🍴	🍴	◆	🍴	🍴	✗	◆	🍴	✗	🍴	◆	◆	🍴	◆	M	X	🍴	❖	F	C	✗	✗	🍴	◆
Praha Hlavni d.																								
Praha Masarykovo d.																		0753						
Praha Holešovice d.		0035				0205	0312									0612					0847			
Usti nad Labem Hlavni a.		0201				0330	0437									0750		0921			1008			
Děčín a.		0223				0351	0459									0811		0941			1029			
Děčín d.		0241				0411	0509									0831					1033			
Bad Schandau § d.		0301				0434	0534									0850					1055			
Dresden Hbf a.		0335				0505	0603									0925					1125			
Dresden Hbf d.		0347				0519	0613				0727				0846	0936		1017			1136			
Dresden Neustadt d.		0355				0527	0621								0854	0944		1026			1144			
Chemnitz d.									0617				1017											
Döbeln d.									0651				1051											
Riesa d.									0710				1110											
Elsterwerda d.								0656			0727		0927					1107		1127				
Doberlug-Kirchhain d.								0707			0739		0939							1139				
Berlin Schönefeld + a.		0524				0654	0754			0824					1024	1106				1224	1306			
Berlin Lichtenberg a.		0544				0714	0814			0847					1044	1129				1247	1329			
Berlin Lichtenberg d.			0627	0745					0827		0945		1027		1145			1227			1345		1427	1427
Berlin Zoo d.	0600			0800							0927	1000				1200					1400			
Berlin Spandau d.	0612			0812								1012				1211					1412			
Nauen d.			0707	0823				0836	0907		1023	1036	1107			1223	1236	1307			1423	1436	1507	1507
Wittenberge d.	0726		0803								1003					1203		1403					1603	1603
Ludwigslust 660 d.			0832								1032					1232		1432					1603	1603
Schwerin 660 668 a.			0854								1054					1254		1454					1632	1632
Wismar 668 a.								1121										1521					1721	
Lübeck 665 a.			1010										1416											
Hamburg Hbf a.	0859			1059							1259							1459			1659			
Hamburg Altona a.	0915			1115							1315							1515			1715			

	D 304	IC 870	IC 534	IR 2132	E 3262	2274	EC 176	IC 532	IR 2030	E 3264	IR 2272	1772	EC 174	IC 530	E 3266	IR 2270	EC 172	EC 170	D 476	D 476	D 1010
	🍴	✗	✗	◆	🍴		F	✗	◆	F		◆	✗	Q🍴		S	◆	S	H🍴	K🍴	◆
Praha Hlavni d.						1233												1833	1946	1946	
Praha Masarykovo d.											1310										
Praha Holešovice d.						1247							1447				1647	1847	1958	1958	2249
Usti nad Labem Hlavni a.						1408					1451		1608				1808	2008	2126	2126	0015
Děčín a.						1429					1511		1633				1829	2029	2147	2147	0036
Děčín d.						1433						1547	1655				1833	2033	2202	2202	0046
Bad Schandau § d.						1455						1607	1725				1855	2055	2226	2226	0110
Dresden Hbf a.						1525						1656	1745				1925	2125	2256	2256	0140
Dresden Hbf d.	1246	1336			1417	1536		1617				1736		1817			1936	2136	2311	2311	0150
Dresden Neustadt d.	1254	1344			1426	1544		1626				1744		1826			1944	2144	2319	2319	
Chemnitz d.					1417						1617					1817					
Döbeln d.					1451						1651					1851					
Riesa d.					1510						1710					1910					
Elsterwerda d.	1327				1507	1527					1707	1727		1907		1927					
Doberlug-Kirchhain d.	1339				1539						1739			1939							
Berlin Schönefeld + a.	1424		1506			1624		1706			1824		1906			2024	2106	2306			
Berlin Lichtenberg a.	1447		1529			1647		1726			1847		1929			2044	2129	2329			
Berlin Lichtenberg d.			1545		1627			1745			1827					1945					0351
Berlin Zoo d.		1600							1800							2000					
Berlin Spandau d.		1612							1812							2012					
Nauen d.		1623	1636						1823	1836	1907					2023	2036				
Wittenberge d.			1803						2003										0348	0348	
Ludwigslust 660 d.			1832						2032										0423	0423	
Schwerin 660 668 a.			1854						2054											0448	
Wismar 668 a.									2121												
Lübeck 665 a.				2010															0610		
Hamburg Hbf a.			1859						2059							2259			0604	0708	
Hamburg Altona a.			1915						2115							2315			0630	0730	

◆ – NOTES (LISTED BY TRAIN NUMBERS)

EC172 – VINDOBONA – 🛏 and ✗ Wien Südbahnhof - Berlin.
EC174 – HUNGARIA – 🛏 and ✗ Budapest Keleti - Nauen. Passengers for Hamburg must change at Nauen. See note X.
D304 – NEPTUN – 🛏 Dresden - København; 🍴 Dresden - Warnemünde.
D372 – BALT ORIENT EXPRESS – 🛏 1, 2 cl., 🛏 2 cl., 🛏 and 🍴 Bucureşti - Berlin; 🛏 Lökösháza - Budapest - Berlin.
D376 – SANSSOUCI – 🛏 1,2 cl., 🛏 2 cl., 🛏 and 🍴 Wien Südbahnhof - Berlin; 🛏 Dresden - Berlin.
D378 – METROPOL – 🛏 1,2 cl., 🛏 2 cl., 🛏 and Budapest Nyugati - Berlin.
IC534 – KÄTHE KOLLWITZ – 🛏 and ✗ Berlin - Kiel.
IC632 – EMIL NOLDE – 🛏 and ✗ Berlin - Westerland; conveys May 1 - 27: 🛏 Berlin - Dagebüll.
D1010 – CSÁRDÁS – Apr. 6 - May 27 (from Budapest); 🛏 1,2 cl. and 🛏 2 cl. Budapest Keleti - Malmö; 🛏 Budapest - Dresden.
IR2030 – 🛏 Berlin - Schwerin (Wismar on ⑤, also Apr. 13, May 24, not Apr. 14, May 26); 🍴 Berlin - Schwerin.
IR2034 – ①②③④⑦: 🛏 and 🍴 Görlitz - Schwerin.
IR2036 – 🛏 and 🍴 Görlitz - Wismar.
IR2038 – 🛏 Görlitz - Wismar; 🍴 Berlin - Wismar.

IR2132 – 🛏 and 🍴 Görlitz - Lübeck.
IR2134 – ⑤⑥: 🛏 and 🍴 Berlin - Kiel.
IR2272 – 🛏 and 🍴 Berlin (Chemnitz ⑥, not Apr. 14 - 16, Apr. 30) - Rostock.
IR2278 – 🛏 and 🍴 Chemnitz - Warnemünde.
IR2376 – 🛏 and 🍴 Plauen - Stralsund.
C – 🛏 and 🍴 Chemnitz - Rostock.
F – 🛏 Dresden - Frankfurt/Oder.
H – ⑥ (from Praha): 🛏 1,2 cl., 🛏 2 cl., 🛏 and 🍴 Praha - Dresden - Magdeburg - Büchen - Hamburg.
K – ⑥ (from Praha): 🛏 1,2 cl., 🛏 2 cl., 🛏 and 🍴 Praha - Dresden - Magdeburg - Lübeck - Hamburg.
M – 🛏 Košice - Dresden; 🛏 1,2 cl., 🛏 2 cl., 🛏 and ✗ Košice - Děčín.
Q – Not Dec. 24.
S – Not Dec. 24, 31.
V – Not Dec. 25.
X – Passengers from the Czech Republic and Dresden bound for Hamburg MUST change trains at Nauen (easy cross-platform interchange) and not in Berlin.
❖ – Not Dec. 25, Jan. 1.
✗/ – ① - ⑥ (not Dec. 25 - Jan. 1, Apr. 15 - 17, May 1, **1995**).
§ – Ticket point is **Schöna**.

▲ – Narrow gauge steam hauled trains run between **Radebeul Ost** and **Radeburg** (17 km, journey 56 minutes, 2 class only) and between **Freital Hainsberg** and **Kurort Kipsdorf** (26 km, journey approx. 1 hour 30 minutes, 2 class only). Radebeul Ost and Freital Hainsberg are in the Dresden suburbs, 10 km from Dresden Hbf and connection is made by regular S-Bahn services.

From Radebeul Ost: 0558, 0732, 1013, 1213, 1413, 1603 ©, 1613 Ⓐ, 1803, 2013.
From Radeburg: 0600 Ⓐ, 0610 ©, 0740, 0909, 1215, 1415, 1605, 1805.
From Freital Hainsberg: 0619 Ⓐ, 0624 ©, 0820 Ⓐ, 0919, 1020 ©, 1155, 1418, 1522 ©, 1625 Ⓐ, 1752 ©, 1925. **From Kurort Kipsdorf:** 0637 ✗, 0832, 1126, 1231, 1334 Ⓐ, 1424 ©, 1607, 1707 ©, 1938.

Both railways run additional short distance trains and/or special **Traditionszüge** for enthusiasts. For more details enquire locally.

Postfach 010256, Radebeul 01436. ☎ – 03 51 4 61 41 00.

Bahnhof Freital Hainsberg ☎ – 03 51 4 61 23 74.

Table 682 — DRESDEN - ZITTAU and GÖRLITZ
1, 2 class

km		E 15416	E 4481	D 451	D 4483	E 5507 2	IR 2053	E 4485	E 1855	E 4487	E 5511 2	IR 2055	E 4489	IR 2057	E 4491	IR 457	IR 2065	E 4493	E 15496	IR 2743	E 15500	E 4495	D 453	D 4497	E 1859
		◆				2	♀				2	♀		♀		♀	♀			♀	S		S	♀	T	◆
0	Dresden Hbf ▲ ..... d.	0626	...	...	...	0850	0940	...	1140	...	1250	1340	...	1532	...	1740	1817.	...	1924	...	2026	...	...	...	2340
4	Dresden Neustadt ▲ .. d.	0632	0648	0654	0848	0858	0948	1048	1148	1248	1348	1448	1540	1648	1748	1825	1839	1930	1948	2032	2039	2048	2248	2348
26	Arnsdorf bei Dresden.. d.	...	0710	...	0910	0925	...	1110	...	1310	1325	...	1510	...	1710	...	1903	...	...	2103	...	2310	...
41	Bischofswerda ...... d.	...	0723	...	0923	0941	...	1123	...	1323	1341	...	1523	...	1722	...	1917	...	...	2116	...	2322	...
93	Oberoderwitz .... d.	...	0824	...	1024	...	...	1223	...	1424	...	...	1624	...	1824	...	2024	...	...	2224	...	0021	...
105	Zittau § .... a.	...	0833	...	1033	...	...	1232	...	1433	...	...	1633	...	1833	...	2033	...	...	2233	...	0030	...
	Bautzen .... d.	...	...	0747	...	1000	1032	...	1231	...	1400	1433	...	1625	...	1832	1911	...	2039	...	...	2140	...	0031
	Löbau .... d.	...	...	0810	...	1024	1053	...	1251	...	1430	1500	...	1646	...	1853	1932	...	2101	...	...	2204	...	0051
	Görlitz .... a.	...	...	0832	...	1050	1115	...	1312	...	1457	1521	...	1708	...	1914	1954	...	2122	...	...	2227	...	0112

km		E 4480	IR 2668	IR 2646	E 15431	E 5506 2	E 4482	E 456	E 4484	E 5510 2	E 4486	IR 2056	E 4488	E 1854	E 5514 2	E 4490	IR 2054	E 4492	IR 2052	E 4494	D 450	E 15507	E 4496	E 5520 2	D 452
		♀		♀		2	♀			2		◆			2		♀		♀		♀			2	♀
0	Görlitz .... d.	...	0546	0630	...	0707	...	0932	...	1102	...	1233	...	1423	1507	...	1633	...	1833	...	2059	...	...	2230	0321
24	Löbau .... d.	...	0607	0652	...	0732	...	0952	...	1132	...	1254	...	1445	1532	...	1654	...	1854	...	2122	...	...	2255	0343
66	Bautzen .... d.	...	0626	0713	...	0755	...	1010	...	1155	...	1314	...	1505	1555	...	1714	...	1914	...	2142	...	...	2318	0404
	Zittau § .... d.	0523	...	...	...	0720	...	0919	...	1119	...	1319	...	1519	...	1719	...	1920	...	2119	...	...	...
	Oberoderwitz .... d.	0534	...	...	...	0730	...	0930	...	1130	...	1330	...	1530	...	1730	...	1931	...	2130	...	...	...
	Bischofswerda ...... d.	0635	...	...	0816	0839	...	1039	1216	1239	...	1439	...	1616	1639	...	1839	...	2033	...	2239	2339	...
	Arnsdorf bei Dresden.. d.	0647	...	...	0831	0851	...	1051	1231	1251	...	1451	...	1631	1651	...	1851	...	2045	...	2251	2354	...
102	Dresden Neustadt ▲ .. d.	0705	0713	0800	0819	0855	0909	1054	1111	1255	1309	1400	1509	1549	1657	1709	1800	1909	2000	2103	2231	2249	2309	0019	0453
106	Dresden Hbf ▲ ...... d.	0714	0722	...	0826	0904	...	1102	...	1304	...	1408	...	1600	...	1800	1808	...	2008	...	...	2256	...	0030	0501

◆ – NOTES (LISTED BY TRAIN NUMBERS)

D450/1 – 🛏 1,2 cl., ➔ 2 cl., ⊡ and Warszawa - Frankfurt/Main and v.v; ➔ 2 cl. and ⊡ Kraków - Frankfurt/Main and v.v; 🛏 1,2 cl. Moskva - Frankfurt and v.v.
D452/3 – 🛏 1,2 cl., ➔ 2 cl. and ♀ Warszawa - Leipzig and v.v; 🛏 1,2 cl. and ⊡ Kraków - Leipzig and v.v.
D456/7 – ⊡ and ♀ Wroclaw - Dresden and v.v.
D1854 – Daily except ⑥, not Dec. 25, Apr. 14 - 16, 30.
D1855 – ① - ⑥, not Dec. 26, Apr. 15 - 17, May 1.

D1859 – ⑤, also Apr. 14, May 24, not Apr. 14, May 26.
IR2065 – ⊡ and ♀ Oberstdorf - München - Hof - Dresden - Görlitz.
IR2646 – ⊡ and ♀ Görlitz - Dresden - Magdeburg - Aachen. Not Dec. 25, Jan. 1.
IR2668 – ⊡ and ♀ Görlitz - Dresden - Hof - Nürnberg - Stuttgart - Karlsruhe.
IR2743 – ⊡ and ♀ Norddeich Mole - Görlitz. Not Dec. 24, 31.
E4481/92 – ⊡ Dresden - Zittau - Liberec and v.v.
S – Not Dec. 24, 31.
Y – Not Dec. 25, 26, Jan. 1.
T – Not Dec. 24, 25, 31.
▲ – Frequent local service between these points.

§ – Narrow gauge steam hauled trains operate from Zittau to the resorts at Oybin and Jonsdorf:

km		Ⓐ														S	S
0	Zittau .... d.	0508	...	0800	0854	0940	...	1055	...	1238	...	1324	...	1408	...	1538	...	1721	...
9	Bertsdorf .... d.	0544	...	0832	0927	1013	1015	...	1128	1130	1310	1311	...	1357	1402	1446	1447	1529	...	1617	1619	1754	1755
12	Kurort Oybin .... a.	...	...	...	0941	1027	...		1142		...	1325	...	1410	...		1500	1543	...	1631		1808		
13	Kurort Jonsdorf ...... a.	0555	...	0844	...		1027	...		1142	1322	...		1414	1458	...		1631	...	1807

		Ⓐ														S	S
	Kurort Jonsdorf ...... d.	0628	...	0950	...	1105	...	...	1208	1338	...	...	1505	...	1554	...	...	1647	...	...	1903
	Kurort Oybin .... d.	...		0954		1109	...	1202		1338	1423	...		1513		1557	...		1647	1826	
	Bertsdorf .... d.	0551	0640	1001	1014	1116	1129	1216	1220	1349	1358	1436	1516	1528	1605	1618	1658	1702	1841	1915
	Zittau .... a.	0621	0710	...	1046	...	1201	...	1256	...	1431	...	1600	...	1650	...	1739	1913	1946

S – Not Dec. 24, 31.

Table 683 — GÖRLITZ – ZITTAU
2 class only

Rail service Görlitz - Zittau.   34 km.   Journey time: 45 minutes.

From Görlitz: 0538 Ⓐ, 0627, 0838, 0950, 1217, 1358, 1509 Ⓐ, 1627, 1820, 2003, 2213 ⑥⑦ (Apr. 1 - May 27).
From Zittau: 0450, 0540, 0630 Ⓐ, 0841, 1101, 1238, 1447, 1535 Ⓐ, 1655, 1732, 2103 Ⓐ (Apr. 1 - May 27), 2115 (⑥⑦ Apr. 1 - May 27).

Table 684 — DRESDEN - COTTBUS - FRANKFURT/ODER
1, 2 class

km		E 3254	E 3256	E 3258	E 3260	E 3262	E 3264	D 2855	E 3266	D 2759	E 3268			E 3253	D 2854	E 3255	E 3257	E 3259	E 3261	E 3263	E 3265	E 3267	E 3269
								S A		C T				Y F									
0	Dresden Neustadt ... d.	0626	0826	1026	1226	1426	1626	...	1826	...	2026	Frankfurt/Oder ..... d.	...	0500	0640	0840	1040	1240	1440	1640	1840	2040
63	Elsterwerda .... d.	0709	0909	1109	1309	1509	1709	...	1909	...	2109	Eisenhüttenstadt..... d.	...	0517	0657	0857	1057	1257	1457	1657	1857	2057
105	Senftenberg........... d.	0742	0942	1142	1342	1542	1742	...	1942	...	2142	Guben .... d.	...	0535	0716	0916	1116	1316	1516	1716	1916	2116
141	Cottbus .... d.	0811	1011	1211	1411	1611	1811	1948	2011	2148	2211	Cottbus .... d.	0549	0602	0752n	0952n	1152n	1352n	1552n	1752n	1952n	2143
179	Guben .... d.	0838	1038	1238	1438	1638	1838	2011	2045	2215	...	Senftenberg........... d.	0619	...	0821	1021	1221	1421	1621	1821	2021	...
204	Eisenhüttenstadt...... d.	0856	1056	1256	1456	1656	1856	2033	2102	2233	...	Elsterwerda .... d.	0653	...	0855	1055	1255	1455	1655	1855	2055	...
228	Frankfurt/Oder ...... a.	0912	1112	1312	1512	1712	1912	2050	2119	2250	...	Dresden Neustadt ... a.	0732	...	0936	1136	1336	1536	1736	1938	2136	...

A – Not Dec. 25, 31: ⊡ Erfurt - Cottbus (Frankfurt/Oder ① - ⑥, not Dec. 26, Apr. 15 - 17, May 1).
C – Not Dec. 24: ⊡ Erfurt - Cottbus (Frankfurt/Oder on ⑦, also Dec. 26, Apr. 17, May 1, not Dec. 25, Apr. 16, 30).
F – Not Dec. 25, 26, Jan. 1, Apr. 16, 17, May 1. ⊡.
S – Not Dec. 24, 31.
T – Not Dec. 24, 25, 31.
Y – Not Dec. 25, 26, Jan. 1.
n – Arrive 9 minutes earlier.

Table 685 — LEIPZIG - COTTBUS
1, 2 class

km		D§ 2851	D§ 2853	D§ 2751	D§ 2753	D§ 2755	D§ 2757	D§ 2855	D§ 2759	D§ 2857			D§ 2856	D§ 2854	D§ 2758	D§ 2756	D§ 2754	D§ 2752	D§ 2750	D§ 2852	D§ 2850
		B		N				G	P	H			B	K				A	M	H	
	Erfurt 775 .... d.	...	...	0820	1018	1220	1420	1620	1820	2020	Cottbus .... d.	0500	0605	0805	1005	1205	1405	1605	1805	2005
0	Leipzig .... d.	0601	0801	1001	1201	1401	1601	1801	2001	2201	Calau .... d.	0516	0621	0821	1021	1221	1421	1621	1821	2021
52	Torgau .... d.	0636	0836	1036	1236	1436	1636	1836	2036	2236	Doberlug-Kirchhain .. d.	0537	0642	0842	1042	1242	1442	1642	1842	2042
70	Falkenberg .... d.	0650	0850	1050	1250	1450	1650	1850	2050	2250	Falkenberg .... d.	0554	0659	0859	1059	1259	1459	1659	1859	2059
93	Doberlug-Kirchhain .. d.	0705	0906	1106	1306	1506	1706	1906	2106	2306	Torgau .... d.	0608	0712	0912	1112	1312	1512	1712	1912	2112
125	Calau .... d.	0728	0928	1128	1328	1528	1728	1928	2128	2328	Leipzig .... a.	0646	0751	0951	1151	1351	1551	1751	1951	2151
149	Cottbus .... a.	0743	0943	1143	1343	1543	1743	1943	2143	2343	Erfurt 775 .... a.	...	0938	1138	1338	1538	1739	1938	2138	...

A – ⊡ Cottbus - Erfurt (Leipzig on Dec. 24, 25).
B – ① - ⑥, not Dec. 26, Apr. 15 - 17, May 1.
C – ⊡ Cottbus - Erfurt (Leipzig on Dec. 24).
G – Not Dec. 24, 31: ⊡ Erfurt - Cottbus (Frankfurt/Oder ① - ⑥, not Dec. 26, Apr. 15 - 17, May 1).
K – Not Dec. 25, Jan. 1: ⊡ Frankfurt/Oder (Cottbus on Dec. 24, Apr. 16, 17, May 1) - Erfurt.

M – ⊡ Cottbus - Leipzig (Erfurt on ⑦, also Dec. 26, Apr. 17, May 1, not Dec. 25, Apr. 16, 30).
N – ⊡ Leipzig (Erfurt except on Dec. 25, Jan. 1) - Cottbus.
P – Not Dec. 24: ⊡ Erfurt - Cottbus (Frankfurt/Oder on ⑦, also Dec. 26, Apr. 17, May 1, not Dec. 25, Apr. 16, 30).
§ – Express trains on this route will become InterRegio (IR) during 1994/5.

11

Table 688 QUEDLINBURG - ASCHERSLEBEN

2 class only

km		8735	8737	8739	8741	8743	8745 C	8747	8749 B	8751	8753
0	**Quedlinburg** d.	0615	0815	1015	1215	1415	1515	1615	1721	1815	2015
9	Gernrode d.	0629	0829	1029	1229	1428	1528	1629	1733	1829	2029
37	**Aschersleben** a.	0733	0933	1133	1333	...	...	1733**b**	...	1933	2133

	8736	8738	8740	8742	8744 C	8746	8748 B	8750	8752	8754 T
Aschersleben d.	0631	0831	1031	1231	1339	1431	1539	1631**h**	1831	2031
Gernrode d.	0735	0935	1135	1335	1443	1535	1643	1740	1935	2135
Quedlinburg a.	0746	0946	1146	1346	1454	1552	1654	1751	1946	2146

B – Ⓑ, **not** Dec. 25, Jan. 6, Apr. 14, 16, 30.
C – Ⓐ, **not** Jan. 6.
T – **Not** Dec. 24, 25, 31.
h – ©, also Jan. 6. On other dates depart at 1636.
b – ⑥ only.

Table 689 HALLE - WERNIGERODE - STAPELBURG

1, 2 class except where shown

km		5862 2	6502 2	5890 2	E 4962 Y	5864 2	E 4964	5866 2	E 4966	5868 2	E 4968	5870 2	5872 2Ⓐ	E 4970	5874 2	E 4972	5876 2	E 4974	5878 2	E 4976 T	5880 2	6518 2	E 4978 B	8794 5882 T
0	**Halle** d.	...	0412	...	0531	...	0731	...	0931	...	1131	...	...	1331	...	1531	...	1731	...	1931	...	2015	2131	...
58	Aschersleben d.	...	0518	...	0624	...	0824	...	1024	...	1224	...	...	1424	...	1624	...	1824	...	2024	...	2124	2219	2226
91	**Halberstadt** a.	...	0558	...	0653	...	0853	...	1053	...	1253	...	...	1453	...	1653	...	1853	...	2053	...	2158	...	2300
91	**Halberstadt** d.	0551	...	0618	0656	0742	0856	0942	1056	1142	1256	1342	1420	1456	1542	1655	1742	1856	1942	2056	2142	...	...	2309
91	Wernigerode a.	0621	...	0653	0725	0812	0925	1012	1125	1212	1325	1412	1455	1525	1612	1727	1812	1925	2012	2125	2212	...	...	2344
113	Wernigerode ▲ d.	0622	...	0702	...	0818	0927	1018	1127	1218	1327	1418	...	1527	1618	1728	1818	...	2018	2127	2218	...	...	...
123	Ilsenburg ▲ d.	0641	...	0720	...	0843	0938	1043	1145	1243	1345	1443	...	1545	1643	1746	1843	...	2043	2145	2236	...	...	...
126	**Stapelburg** ▲ a.	0648	...	...	...	0850	...	1050	...	1250	...	1450	...	...	1650	...	1850	...	2050	...	...	...	...	...

	8793 2H	E 4961 Y	5863 2	E 4963	6507 2	5865 2	E 4965	5867 2	E 4967	6511 2	5869 2	E 4969	5871 2	5873 2Ⓐ	E 4971	5875 2	E 4973	6517 2	5877 2	E 4975 T	6519 2	5879 2	5881 2	5893 2T
Stapelburg ▲ d.	...	...	0634	...	...	0834	...	1034	...	...	1234	...	1434	...	...	1634	...	...	1834	...	...	2034	2144	...
Ilsenburg ▲ d.	...	0548	0642	0752	...	0842	...	1042	1157	...	1242	1352	1442	...	1552	1642	1757	...	1842	1957	...	2042	2152	2242
Wernigerode ▲ a.	...	0606	0700	0810	...	0900	...	1100	1210	...	1300	1410	1500	...	1610	1700	1810	...	1900	2010	...	2100	2210	2300
Wernigerode d.	...	0607	0701	0814	...	0901	1014	1101	1214	...	1301	1414	1501	1546	1614	1701	1814	...	1901	2014	...	2101	2214	2301
Halberstadt a.	...	0638	0729	0838	...	0929	1038	1129	1238	...	1329	1438	1529	1618	1639	1729	1838	...	1929	2038	...	2129	2242	2329
Halberstadt d.	0528	0640	...	0840	0909	...	1040	...	1240	1309	...	1440	...	...	1640	...	1840	1909	...	2040	2109	...	...	...
Aschersleben d.	0609	0711	...	0911	0951	...	1111	...	1311	1351	...	1511	...	...	1711	...	1911	1951	...	2111	2151	...	...	...
Halle a.	0718	0813	...	1013	1109	...	1213	...	1413	1409	...	1614	...	...	1813	...	2013	2109	...	2213	2312	...	...	...

B – Ⓑ, **not** Dec. 25, Jan. 6, Apr. 14, 16, 30.
H – ⚒, also Nov. 16, Apr. 14, May 25, **not** Jan. 7, Apr. 15.
T – **Not** Dec. 24, 25, 31.
Y – **Not** Dec. 25, 26, Jan. 1.
▲ – For 🚌 service to/from Bad Harzburg see Table **697**.

Table 690 BERLIN - MAGDEBURG - HALBERSTADT - THALE

1, 2 class except where shown

km		8704 2	5704 2	D§ 2148 V	8706 2	5706 2	E 3502	8708 2	5708 2	D§ 2146	8710 2	5710 2	E 3504	8712 2	5712 2	D§ 2144	8714 2	5714 2	D§ 2142	8716 2	5716 2	E 3506 B	5718 2	D§ 2140 Q	5720 2
0	**Berlin Wannsee** d.	...	...	0544	...	...	...	...	...	0952	...	...	*1123*z	...	...	1352	...	...	1552	...	...	...	...	1952	...
9	Potsdam Stadt d.	...	...	0606	...	...	...	...	...	1003	...	...	*1145*	...	...	1403	...	...	1603	...	...	...	...	2003	...
45	Brandenburg d.	...	...	0638	...	...	0836	...	...	1038	...	...	1234	...	...	1438	...	...	1638	...	...	1834	...	2038	...
124	**Magdeburg** a.	...	...	0740	...	...	0942	...	...	1140	...	...	1340	...	...	1540	...	...	1742	...	...	1942	...	2140	...
124	**Magdeburg** d.	...	0624	0745	...	0824	0945	...	1024	1145	...	1224	1345	...	1424	1545	...	1624	1745	...	1824	1945	2024	2145	2224
163	Oschersleben d.	...	0712	0811	...	0912	1011	...	1112	1211	...	1312	1411	...	1512	1611	...	1712	1811	...	1912	2011	2112	2211	2312
183	**Halberstadt** a.	...	0737	0826	...	0937	1026	...	1137	1226	...	1337	1426	...	1537	1626	...	1737	1826	...	1937	2026	2137	2226	2337
183	**Halberstadt** d.	0647	0747	...	0847	0947	...	1047	1147	...	1247	1347	...	1447	1547	...	1647	1747	...	1847	1947	*2047*	2147	*2247*t	...
201	Quedlinburg d.	0711	0811	...	0911	1011	...	1111	1211	...	1311	1411	...	1511	1611	...	1711	1811	...	1911	2011	*2111*	2211	*2311*t	...
211	**Thale** a.	0823	0823	...	0923	1023	...	1123	1223	...	1323	1423	...	1523	1623	...	1723	1823	...	1923	2023	*2123*	2223	*2323*t	...

	D§ 2141 V	8701 2	5705 2	8703 2	D§ 2143	5707 2	E 3503	5709 2	8707 2	D§ 2145	5711 2	8709 2	E 3505	5713 2	8711 2	D§ 2147	5715 2	8713 2	D§ 2149 Q	5717 2	8715 2	E 3507 2T	5719 2	8717 2	8719 2T
Thale d.	...	0556	0636	0756	...	0836	*0956*	1036	1156	...	1236	1356	...	1436	1556	...	1636	1756	...	1836	1956	...	2036	2136	2236
Quedlinburg d.	...	0612	0648	0812	...	0848	*1012*	1048	1212	...	1248	1412	...	1448	1612	...	1648	1812	...	1848	2012	...	2048	2148	2248
Halberstadt a.	...	0635	0717	0835	...	0917	*1035*	1117	1235	...	1317	1435	...	1517	1635	...	1717	1835	...	1917	2035	...	2117	2217	2317
Halberstadt d.	0550	...	0740	...	0850	0940	1050	1140	...	1250	1340	...	1450	1540	...	1650	1740	...	1850	1940	...	2047	2140	...	...
Oschersleben d.	0605	...	0805	...	0905	1005	1105	1205	...	1305	1405	...	1505	1605	...	1705	1805	...	1905	2005	...	2102	2205	...	...
Magdeburg a.	0632	...	0857	...	0932	1057	1132	1257	...	1335	1457	...	1532	1657	...	1732	1857	...	1932	2057	...	2129	2257	...	...
Magdeburg d.	0644	...	...	...	0944	...	1144	...	...	1344	...	...	1544	...	...	1744	...	...	1942	...	...	...	...	...	...
Brandenburg d.	0745	...	...	...	1045	...	1248	...	...	1445	...	...	1648	...	...	1845	...	...	2045	...	...	...	...	...	...
Potsdam Stadt a.	0814	...	...	...	1114	...	*1338*	...	...	1514	...	...	*1814*	...	...	1914	...	...	2114	...	...	...	...	...	...
Berlin Wannsee a.	0823	...	...	...	1123	...	...	...	...	1523	...	...	...	...	...	1923	...	...	2123	...	...	...	...	...	...

B – Ⓑ, **not** Dec. 25, Apr. 14, 16, 30.
Q – **Not** Dec. 24.
T – **Not** Dec. 24, 25, 31.
V – **Not** Dec. 25.
t – **Not** Dec. 24, 25, 31.
z – Berlin **Zoo**.
§ – Train will become InterRegio (**IR**) during 1994.

Table 691 GERNRODE - HARZGERODE and HASSELFELDE

Harzer Schmalspurbahnen Gmbh

Oct. 25 - Apr. 30 **Most trains are steam hauled** **2 class only.**

km		8951	8961	8973	8953	8963	8955	8957	8965 Q	8959 Q	8979 Q
0	**Gernrode** § d.	0735	...	...	1025	1111	...	1402	1435	1645	...
10	Mägdesprung d.	0809	...	...	1059	1146	...	1436	1510	1719	...
	Harzgerode d.	|	0845	...	|	|	...	|	|	|	...
15	Alexisbad a.	0824	0855	...	1114	1201	...	1451	1525	1734	...
15	Alexisbad d.	0825	0912	...	1115	1208	1208	1452	1532	1735	...
18	**Harzgerode** a.	0835	|	...	1125	|	1218	1505	|	1745	...
18	Silberhütte d.	...	0927	...	...	1222	...	—	1546	—	...
22	Straßberg *(Harz)* d.	...	0941	...	...	1237	...	...	1601	...	...
28	Güntersberge d.	...	0950	...	...	1246	...	...	1610	**8978**	...
36	Stiege a.	...	1005	...	...	1301	...	...	1625	**Q**	...
	Stiege d.	...	|	...	...	1302	...	**8975**	|	1734	...
41	**Hasselfelde** a.	...	|	...	...	1321	...	**Q**	|	1753	...
	Hasselfelde d.	...	|	1049	...	...	...	1554	|	...	1803
	Stiege a.	...	|	1108	...	...	...	1615	|	...	1822
36	Stiege d.	...	1006	1116	...	...	...	...	1626	...	1823
46	Eisfelder Talmühle a.	...	1030	1138	...	...	...	...	1650	...	1845
46	Eisfelder Talmühle d.	...	*1037*	1145	...	...	...	...	*1653*	...	1852
63	**Nordhausen Nord** § a.	...	*1125*	1229	...	...	...	...	*1737*	...	1935

	8972	8962	8954	8964	8974 H	8976 Q	8977 Q	8966 Q	8958 Q	8968 Q
Nordhausen Nord § d.	0853	*0944*	...	...	1343	...	...	*1610*	...	...
Eisfelder Talmühle a.	0935	*1025*	...	...	1424	...	...	*1651*	...	...
Eisfelder Talmühle d.	0942	1047	...	...	1431	...	...	1707	...	...
Stiege a.	1004	1109	...	...	1453	...	...	1729	...	...
Stiege d.	1010	|	...	...	1454	1630	...	|	...	...
Hasselfelde a.	1029	|	...	...	1513	1649	...	|	...	...
Hasselfelde d.	—	|	...	1322	...	...	1700	|	...	...
Stiege d.	...	|	...	1351	...	...	1719	|	...	...
Stiege d.	...	1110	...	1352	...	...	—	1730	...	...
Güntersberge d.	...	1128	...	1408	...	...	...	1747	...	...
Straßberg *(Harz)* d.	**8952**	1137	...	1417	...	...	**8956**	1757	...	...
Silberhütte d.	...	1151	...	1432	...	...	...	1811	...	...
Harzgerode d.	1141	|	1228	|	...	...	1512	|	1810	1855
Alexisbad a.	1151	1206	1238	1446	...	...	1522	1825	1820	1905
Alexisbad d.	...	1213	1245	1453	...	...	1529	1835	1827	1912
Harzgerode a.	...	|	|	|	...	...	|	1845	|	|
Mägdesprung d.	...	1228	1301	1511	...	...	1545	...	1843	1928
Gernrode § a.	...	1302	1335	1544	...	...	1620	...	1916	2002

H – Daily to Eisfelder Talmühle; daily except Dec. 24 to Hasselfelde.
Q – **Not** Dec. 24.
§ – Adjacent to main line railway stations.

All trains are shown. Both directions of the Table should be read in order to work out all connectional possibilities.

Table 692 WERNIGERODE - NORDHAUSEN

Harzer Schmalspurbahnen Gmbh

Oct. 25 - Apr. 30 — Most trains are steam hauled — 2 class only

km			8901	8931 ↯			8933 ↯		8903	8920 D↯			8905	8922 D↯			8935		8941	8921 D↯			8909
0	**Wernigerode** § d.	...	0816	0827	...	...	0940	...	1051	...	...	...	1225	...	...	...	1400	...	1446	...	...	...	1616
14	Drei Annen Hohne a.	...	0857	0910	...	...	1021	...	1135	...	...	...	1308	...	...	...	1444	...	1527	...	...	...	1657
14	Drei Annen Hohne d.	...	0904	0917	...	...	1028	...	1142	1151	...	...	1315	1310	...	...	1451	...	...	1539	...	...	1704
	Schierke d.	...	|	0936	...	...	1048	...	|	1211	...	...	|	1329	...	...	1521	...	...	|	...	...	|
	Brocken a.	...	|	1006	...	...	1118	...	|	1241	...	...	|	1359	...	...	1551	...	...	|	...	...	|
19	Elend d.	...	0915	...	...	...	...	...	1154	...	...	...	1326	...	...	...	...	...	...	1550	...	...	1716
27	Sorge d.	...	0934	...	...	...	...	...	1213	...	...	...	1345	...	...	...	...	...	...	1608	...	...	1735
31	Benneckenstein d.	...	1001g	...	...	...	...	...	1221	...	...	...	1354	...	...	...	...	...	...	1617	...	...	1743
43	Eisfelder Talmühle a.	...	1030	...	...	...	...	...	1251	...	...	...	1424	...	...	...	...	...	...	1646	...	...	1813
43	Eisfelder Talmühle **691** d.	...	1037	...	...	...	...	...	1258	...	...	...	1431	...	...	...	...	...	...	1653	...	...	1820
61	**Nordhausen Nord 691** § a.	...	1125	...	...	...	...	...	1341	...	...	...	1517	...	...	...	...	...	...	1737	...	...	1903

km			8902			8920 D↯	8932 ↯			8922 D↯	8934		8910 Q	8940 ↯		8921 ↯	8974	8904		8942	8936 ↯		8906
	Nordhausen Nord 691 § d.	...	0830	...	...	0944	...	...	...	1049	...	...	1246	...	...	...	1343	...	...	...	...	...	1610
	Eisfelder Talmühle **691** a.	...	0911	...	...	1025	...	...	...	1143	...	...	1330	...	...	...	1424	...	...	...	...	...	1651
	Eisfelder Talmühle d.	...	0918	...	...	1035	...	...	...	1150	...	...	...	...	...	...	...	1426	...	...	...	...	1658
	Benneckenstein d.	...	0948	...	...	1102	...	...	...	1222	...	...	...	...	...	...	...	1456	...	...	...	...	1744c
	Sorge d.	...	0956	...	...	1110	...	...	...	1230	...	...	...	...	...	...	...	1504	...	...	...	...	1757
	Elend d.	...	1016	...	...	1130	...	...	...	1250	...	...	...	...	...	...	...	1524	...	...	...	...	1812
0	**Brocken** d.	...	|	...	...	|	1017	...	...	|	1140	...	...	1257	...	1440	...	|	...	...	1620	...	|
14	**Schierke** d.	...	|	...	...	|	1121	...	...	|	1240	...	...	1329	...	1520	...	|	...	...	1650	...	|
19	Drei Annen Hohne a.	...	1026	...	...	1140	1133	...	...	1300	1253	...	...	1352	...	1532	...	1535	...	...	1702	...	1822
19	Drei Annen Hohne d.	...	1037	...	...	...	1152	...	...	...	1312	...	...	1359	...	...	...	1542	...	1602	1709	...	1829
34	**Wernigerode** § a.	...	1123	...	...	...	1235	...	...	...	1354	...	...	1444	...	...	...	1626	...	1648	1751	...	1911

D – To or from Brocken. Q – **Not** Dec. 24. c – Arrive 1722. g – Arrive 0942. ↯ – Train subject to alteration or cancellation in bad weather. § – Adjacent to main line stations.

Table 693 PADERBORN - KREIENSEN - BRAUNSCHWEIG

1, 2 class

km		E 6007 ⚒	E 3513 ⚒	E 6011 ⚒	E 3683 A	E 7406 ⚒	E 6013	E 6017	E 6915	E 6021	E 6919	E 3657 B	E 5979	E 6027	E 6031	E 6929	E 6035 Q	E 5983 Q	E 6763 C	E 6041 S	E 5987 S	E 5933 S	E 6943 Ⓑ	E 5939 Ⓑ	E 5943 S
0	**Paderborn 703 705** d.	...	...	...	...	0607	...	0755	...	0955	...	...	*1155*	1155	1355	...	1555	...	...	1755	...	*1848*f	...	1955	*2048*f
17	Altenbeken **703 705** d.	...	...	...	0534	0620	0626**b**	0812	...	1012	...	1133	*1212*	1212	1412	...	1612	...	1733	1812	...	1912	...	2012	2112
48	Ottbergen d.	...	0534	...	0605	...	0654	0843	0845	1041	1045	1200	1245	1259	1441	1445	1641	1645	1800	1841	1845	1941	2000	2041	2141
	Bad Karlshafen d.	...	|	...	0621	...	|	|	0904	|	1104	1216	1304	|	|	1504	|	1704	1816	|	1904	|	2016	|	|
	Northeim a.	...	|	...	0709	...	|	|	0945	|	1145	1304	1345	|	|	1545	|	1745	1904	|	1945	|	2105	|	|
58	Höxter Rathaus d.	...	0543	...	...	...	0704	0854	...	1052	...	...	...	1311	1452	...	1652	...	...	1852	...	1952	...	2052	2152
66	Holzminden d.	...	0555	...	...	...	0720	0905	...	1120	...	...	...	1321	1520	...	1720	...	...	1920	...	2018	...	2107	2207
110	**Kreiensen** a.	...	0631	...	...	...	0758	0942	...	1158	...	...	...	1358	1558	...	1758	...	...	1958	...	2055	...	...	...
110	**Kreiensen 696** d.	0611	...	0719	...	...	0800	1000	...	1200	...	...	...	1400	1600	...	1800	...	...	2000	...	...	...	...	...
116	Bad Gandersheim **696** d.	0617	...	0725	...	...	0806	1006	...	1206	...	...	...	1406	1606	...	1806	...	...	2006	...	...	...	...	...
130	Seesen **696** d.	0628	...	0737	...	...	0817	1017	...	1217	...	...	...	1417	1617	...	1817	...	...	2017	...	...	...	...	...
151	Salzgitter Ringelheim d.	0643	...	0753	...	...	0833	1033	...	1237	...	...	...	1434	1637	...	1833	...	...	2033	...	...	...	...	...
182	**Braunschweig** a.	0707	...	0816	...	...	0857	1057	...	1301	...	...	...	1459	1701	...	1857	...	...	2057	...	...	...	...	...

km		E 5910	E 6910 ⚒	E 5914 ⚒	E 6002 ⚒	E 6914	E 5916	E 3650 G	E 5976	E 6008	E 6924	E 6014	E 5980	E 6018	E 3684 A	E 6934	E 6024	E 3654 G	E 5984 Q	E 6030 Q	E 6940 Ⓑ	E 5986 S	E 6034 S	E 6038 S	E 6042 Ⓑ
	Braunschweig d.	...	...	...	0627	...	...	...	...	0855	...	1058	...	1255	...	...	1455	...	...	1655	...	...	1858	2041	2209
	Salzgitter Ringelheim d.	...	...	...	0655	...	...	...	...	0919	...	1119	...	1319	...	...	1514	...	...	1719	...	...	1919	2103	2235
	Seesen **696** d.	...	...	...	0712	...	...	...	...	0936	...	1136	...	1336	...	...	1536	...	...	1736	...	...	1936	2118	2252
	Bad Gandersheim **696** d.	...	...	...	0724	...	...	...	...	0948	...	1148	...	1348	...	...	1548	...	...	1748	...	...	1948	2129	2303
	Kreiensen 696 a.	...	...	...	0731	...	...	...	...	0955	...	1155	...	1355	...	...	1555	...	...	1755	...	...	1955	2136	2309
	Kreiensen d.	0552**b**	...	...	...	...	0801	...	...	1001	...	1214	...	1401	...	...	1601	...	...	1801	...	...	2012	...	...
	Holzminden d.	0701	...	...	...	...	0845	...	...	1049	...	1301	...	1449	...	...	1649	...	...	1849	...	...	2049	...	...
	Höxter Rathaus d.	0712	...	...	...	...	0901	...	...	1100	...	1317	...	1500	...	...	1700	...	...	1900	...	...	2100	...	...
0	**Northeim** d.	|	0641	...	...	0811	|	0850	1011	|	1211	|	1411	|	1450	1611	|	1650	1811	|	1835	2011	|	...	...
47	Bad Karlshafen d.	|	0738	...	...	0853	|	0938	1053	|	1253	|	1453	|	1538	1653	|	1743	1853	|	1922	2053	|	...	...
64	Ottbergen d.	0727	0753	0812	...	0907	0912	0953	1107	1112	1307	1327	1507	1512	1553	1707	1712	1753	1907	1912	1936	2107	2112	...	...
95	Altenbeken **703 705** d.	0807	...	0841	...	...	0944	1023	...	1147	...	1400	...	1547	1623	...	1747	1823	...	1947	*2041*	...	2143	...	...
112	**Paderborn 703 705** a.	0820	...	*0903*f	...	...	0957	...	...	1201	...	1414	...	1601	...	...	1800	...	...	2000	...	...	2157	...	...

A – [12] Altenbeken - Erfurt and v.v.
B – [12] Altenbeken - Dessau.
C – [12] Altenbeken - Nordhausen.
G – [12] Halle - Altenbeken.
Q – **Not** Dec. 24.
b – ⚒ only.
S – **Not** Dec. 24, 31.
f – IR supplement payable.

Table 694 NORTHEIM - NORDHAUSEN - ERFURT

1, 2 class except where shown

km		E 4281 ⚒	E 6711 ⚒	E 3683	6611 2	E 6719	E 3655	6613 2	E 6727	E 3687	6619 2	E 6735	E 3657 H	6627 2	E 6743	E 3691	6631 2	E 6751	E 3659 Q	6635 2	E 6757 S	E 6763 S	6639 2Ⓑ	E 6767 S
	Altenbeken 693 d.	...	...	0536t	...	...	...	...	...	...	...	...	1133	...	...	...	...	...	...	...	...	1733	...	...
0	**Northeim** d.	...	...	0711	...	0811	0911	...	1011	1111	...	1211	1311	...	1411	1511	...	1611	1712	...	1811	1911	...	2034
27	Herzberg d.	...	0639	0739	...	0839	0939	...	1039	1139	...	1239	1339	...	1439	1539	...	1639	1739	...	1839	1939	...	2110
47	Bad Sachsa d.	...	0658	0758	...	0858	0958	...	1058	1158	...	1258	1358	...	1458	1558	...	1658	1758	...	1858	1958	...	2120
50	Walkenried d.	...	0704	0804	...	0904	1004	...	1109	1204	...	1304	1404	...	1504	1604	...	1704	1804	...	1904	2004	...	2126
70	**Nordhausen** a.	...	0734	0838	...	0938	1038	...	1138	1238	...	1338	1438	...	1534	1638	...	1738	1838	...	1938	2038	...	2155
70	**Nordhausen** d.	0647	...	0847	0910	...	1052	1110	...	1247	1308	...	1452	1510	...	1647	1708	...	1852	1910	...	...	2117	...
90	Sondershausen d.	0707	...	0907	0939	...	|	1139	...	1307	1339	...	|	1539	...	1707	1739	...	|	1938	...	...	2145	...
150	**Erfurt** a.	0806	...	1002	1043	...	|	1251	...	1402	1443	...	|	1645	...	1802	1843	...	|	2045	...	...	2250	...
	Halle 695 a.	...	...	...	...	...	1211	...	...	...	...	...	1611	...	...	...	...	...	2011	...	...	...	...	...

	E 6710	E 3650	6606 2❖	E 6716	E 3680	E 6726	6610 2	E 3652	E 6734	6612 2	E 3684	E 6742	6616 2	E 3654	E 6750	6620 2	E 3688	E 6758 S	6628 2	E 3656 G	E 6766 S	6632 2	E 4288 Ⓑ	6636 2
Halle 695 d.	...	0542	...	...	...	...	...	0942	...	...	...	...	...	1342	...	...	...	...	...	1742	...	...	...	...
Erfurt d.	...	|	0549	...	0753	...	0908	|	...	1108	1153	...	1308	|	...	1508	1553	...	1708	|	...	1908	2031	2148
Sondershausen d.	...	|	0710	...	0848	...	1017	|	...	1217	1248	...	1417	|	...	1617	1648	...	1817	|	...	2017	2126	2257
Nordhausen a.	...	0705	0742	...	0910	...	1042	1100	...	1242	1310	...	1442	1502	...	1642	1710	...	1842	1905	...	2039	2144	2321
Nordhausen d.	0618	0715	...	0818	0918	1020	...	1118	1218	...	1318	1418	...	1515	1618	...	1718	1820	...	1918	2018	...	...	...
Walkenried d.	0649	0749	...	0849	0949	1049	...	1149	1249	...	1349	1449	...	1549	1649	...	1749	1849	...	1949	2050	...	...	...
Bad Sachsa d.	0656	0756	...	0856	0956	1056	...	1156	1256	...	1356	1456	...	1556	1656	...	1756	1856	...	1956	2057	...	...	...
Herzberg d.	0716	0816	...	0916	1016	1116	...	1216	1316	...	1416	1516	...	1616	1716	...	1816	1916	...	2016	2116	...	...	...
Northeim a.	0745	0845	...	0945	1045	1145	...	1245	1345	...	1445	1545	...	1645	1745	...	1845	1945	...	2045	2145	...	...	...
Altenbeken 693 a.	...	1024	...	...	...	...	...	...	...	...	1624	...	...	1824v	...	...	...	...	...	...	...	...	...	...

G – [12] Dessau - Northeim. H – [12] Altenbeken - Dessau. Q – **Not** Dec. 24. S – **Not** Dec. 24, 31. t – ⚒ only. v – Ⓑ only. ❖ – **Not** Dec. 25, Jan. 1.

Table 695 HALLE - NORDHAUSEN - KASSEL

1, 2 class except where shown

km		8907	E 3950	6402	8909	E 3650 A	7608 2	IR 2573 ♦🍷	8911	E 4272	6404	8913	E 3962	IR 2173 K🍷	E 3773	E 3952	6406	8917	E 3652	7514 2	6408	8921	E 3964	IR 2175 K🍷	E 3781
	Dessau **670** d.	...	...	...	...	...	...	0539	...	...	...	...	...	...	...	...	...	...	...	...	...	...	1049	...	...
0	**Halle** d.	...	...	0444	...	0542	...	0635	...	...	0635	...	0742	...	...	...	0844	...	0942	...	1044	...	1142	...	...
38	Lutherstadt Eisleben d.	...	...	0527	...	0615	...	0706	...	...	0727	...	0815	...	...	...	0927	...	1015	...	1127	...	1215	...	...
60	Sangerhausen d.	...	...	0549	...	0633	...	0723	...	...	0750	...	0833	...	...	...	0950	...	1033	...	1150	...	1233	...	...
98	**Nordhausen** d.	...	...	0626	...	0705	...	0749	...	...	0826	...	0902	...	...	...	1026	...	1100	...	1226	...	1302	...	...
	Erfurt d.	...	...	|	...	...	...	|	...	0718	|	...	|	...	...	0927	|	...	▬	1102	|	...	|	...	...
	Gotha Ost d.	...	...	|	...	...	0639	|	...	0740	|	...	|	...	...	0950	|	...	...	|	|	...	|	...	...
	Mühlhausen d.	...	...	|	...	...	0722	|	...	0816	|	...	|	...	...	1018	|	...	**8919**	1215	|	...	|	...	...
140	Leinefelde d.	...	0637	0708	...	...	0755	0818	...	0843	0908	...	0937	...	...	1041	1108	...	...	1243	1308	...	1337	...	...
	Göttingen d.	0627	|	|	0731	...	...	|	0831	...	|	0931	|	1017	1057	|	|	1131	1231	...	|	1331	|	1417	1457
171	Eichenberg d.	0647	0711	0736	0747	...	...	0844	0847	...	0936	0947	1002	1032	1112	1120	1136	1147	1247	...	1336	1347	1402	1432	1512
194	Hann Münden d.	0707	0731	...	0807	...	...	0902	0907	...	...	1007	1020	1049	...	1138	...	1207	1307	...	...	1407	1420	1449	...
218	**Kassel Hbf** a.	0730	0749	...	0830	...	...	0921	0930	...	...	1030	1038	1107	...	1156	...	1230	1330	...	...	1430	1438	1507	...

	E 3954	6410	8925	E 3654	E 4274 S⚒	IR 2673 ♦🍷	8927	6412	8929	E 4276	E 3966	IR 2177 ♦🍷	E 3789	E 3956	6414	8933	E 3656 B	7530 2	6416	8937	E 4278	E 3968 C	IR 2179 ♦	6418	E 3970 T
Dessau **670** d.	...	...	...	...	...	...	...	...	...	...	1449	...	...	...	...	...	1649	...	...	...	...	...	...	...	2059
Halle d.	...	1244	...	1342	...	1423	...	1444	...	...	1542	...	...	...	1644	...	1742	...	1844	...	...	1942	...	2044	2142
Lutherstadt Eisleben d.	...	1327	...	1415	...	1454	...	1527	...	...	1615	...	...	...	1727	...	1815	...	1927	...	...	2015	...	2127	2215
Sangerhausen d.	...	1349	...	1433	...	1512	...	1550	...	...	1633	...	...	...	1750	...	1833	...	1950	...	...	2033	...	2150	2233
Nordhausen d.	...	1426	...	1500	...	1540	...	1626	...	...	1702	...	...	...	1826	...	1905	...	2026	...	...	2103	...	2223	2300
Erfurt d.	1327	|	...	...	1421	|	...	|	...	1555	|	...	...	1727	|	...	▬	1902	|	...	2018	|	...	...	...
Gotha Ost d.	1350	|	...	...	1444	|	...	|	...	1619	|	...	...	1750	|	...	...	|	|	...	2040	|	...	...	...
Mühlhausen d.	1418	|	...	...	1520	|	...	|	...	1650	|	...	...	1818	|	...	**8935**	2015	|	...	2106	|	...	...	...
Leinefelde d.	1441	1508	...	...	1550	1612	...	1708	...	1716	1737	...	...	1841	1908	...	...	2043	2108	...	2133	2137	...	...	...
Göttingen d.	|	|	1531	...	...	|	1631	|	1731	...	|	1817	1857	|	|	1931	2031	...	|	2131	...	|	2217	...	...
Eichenberg d.	1520	1536	1547	...	...	1639	1647	1736	1747	...	1802	1832	1912	1920	1936	1947	2047	...	2136	2147	...	2202	2232	...	...
Hann Münden d.	1538	...	1607	...	...	1656	1707	...	1807	...	1820	1849	...	1938	...	2007	2107	...	...	2207	...	2220	2249	...	...
Kassel Hbf a.	1556	...	1630	...	...	1716	1730	...	1830	...	1838	1907	...	1956	...	2030	2130	...	...	2230	...	2238	2307	...	...

km		6403	E 4271	IR 2078 ♦	E 3653	8902	6405	E 3951	6483	E 3961	8906	6407	7513 2	8908	IR 2478 ♦🍷	E 3655	8910	6409	E 3953	IR 2174 ♦🍷	E 3963	7619 E4273 ⚒	8914	6411	7519 2
0	**Kassel Hbf** d.	...	...	0452	...	0529	...	0603	...	0715	0729	...	...	0829	0841	...	0929	...	1003	1052	1115	...	1129	...	...
24	Hann Münden d.	...	...	0509	...	0549	...	0620	...	0732	0749	...	...	0849	0858	...	0949	...	1020	1109	1132	...	1149	...	...
47	Eichenberg d.	...	...	0527	...	0610	0619	0640	...	0752	0810	0819	...	0910	0917	...	1010	1019	1040	1127	1152	...	1210	1219	...
	Göttingen a.	...	...	0539	...	0624	|	|	...	|	0824	|	...	0924	|	...	1024	|	|	1139	|	...	1224	|	...
78	Leinefelde d.	...	0519	...	...	...	0648	0718	0735	0819	...	0848	0910	...	0944	...	...	1048	1116	...	1219b	1220	...	1248	1311
105	Mühlhausen d.	...	0547	...	...	...	|	0740	|	|	...	|	0941	...	|	...	...	|	1139	...	|	1305	...	|	1339
142	Gotha Ost d.	...	0618	...	...	...	|	0807	|	|	...	|	|	...	|	...	...	|	1207	...	|	1335	...	|	|
172	**Erfurt** a.	...	0640	...	...	...	|	0829	|	|	...	|	1058	...	|	...	...	|	1229	...	|	1357	...	|	1501
	Nordhausen d.	0531	...	...	0653	...	0731	...	0819	0853	...	0931	...	...	1016	1053	...	1131	...	...	1253	...	...	1331	...
	Sangerhausen a.	0604	...	...	0722	...	0804	...	...	0922	...	1004	...	...	1044	1122	...	1204	...	...	1322	...	...	1404	...
	Lutherstadt Eisleben d.	0625	...	...	0740	...	0825	...	...	0940	...	1025	...	...	1103	1140	...	1225	...	...	1339	...	...	1425	...
	Halle a.	0709	...	...	0811	...	0909	...	...	1011	...	1109	...	...	1132	1211	...	1309	...	...	1414	...	...	1509	...
	Dessau **670** a.	...	...	...	...	...	...	...	...	1102	...	...	...	...	...	1303	...	...	...	...	...	...	...	...	...

	8916	E 3657 G	8918	6413	E 3955	IR 2172 K🍷	E 3965	8922	6415	8924	IR 2576 ♦🍷	E 4277	E 3659 H	8926	6417	E 3957	IR 2170 ♦🍷	E 3967 F	8930	6419	7641 2	8932	E 3969 Ⓑ	8934	8936
Kassel Hbf d.	1229	...	1329	...	1403	1452	1515	1529	...	1629	1641	...	...	1729	...	1755	1852	1915	1929	...	...	2029	2117	2129	2239
Hann Münden d.	1249	...	1349	...	1420	1509	1532	1549	...	1649	1658	...	...	1749	...	1817	1909	1932	1949	...	...	2049	2134	2149	2259
Eichenberg d.	1310	...	1410	1419	1450	1527	1552	1610	1619	1711	1717	...	...	1810	1819	1850	1927	1952	2010	2019	...	2110	2154	2210	2320
Göttingen a.	1324	...	1424	|	|	1539	|	1624	|	1725	|	...	...	1824	|	|	1939	|	2024	|	...	2124	|	2224	2334
Leinefelde d.	...	...	...	1448	1516	...	1619	...	1648	...	1744	1748	...	...	1848	1916	...	2019	...	2048	2140	...	2225	...	...
Mühlhausen d.	...	...	...	|	1538	...	|	...	|	...	|	1817	...	...	|	1939	...	|	...	|	2220	...	|	...	...
Gotha Ost d.	...	...	...	|	1607	...	|	...	|	...	|	1846	...	...	|	2007	...	|	...	|	2312	...	|	...	...
Erfurt a.	...	...	...	|	1629	...	|	...	|	...	|	1907	...	...	|	2029	...	|	...	|	...	...	|	...	...
Nordhausen d.	...	1453	...	1531	...	...	1653	...	1731	...	1816	...	1853	...	1931	...	...	2053	...	2131	...	...	2307	...	...
Sangerhausen a.	...	1522	...	1604	...	...	1722	...	1804	...	1844	...	1922	...	2004	...	...	2122	...	2204	...	...	...	...	...
Lutherstadt Eisleben d.	...	1540	...	1625	...	...	1740	...	1825	...	1903	...	1940	...	2025	...	...	2140	...	2225	...	...	...	...	...
Halle a.	...	1611	...	1709	...	...	1811	...	1909	...	1932	...	2011	...	2109	...	...	2211	...	2309	...	...	...	...	...
Dessau **670** a.	...	1702	...	...	...	...	...	...	...	...	2025	...	...	...	...	...	...	2302	...	...	...	...	...	...	...

♦ – **NOTES** (LISTED BY TRAIN NUMBERS)

R2078 – 🚃12 Kassel - Hamburg - Flensburg.
R2170 – 🚃12 Kassel - Hamburg; 🚃12 Konstanz - Hamburg; 🍷 Kassel - Celle.
R2174/7 – 🚃12 and 🍷 Hamburg - Kassel; 🚃12 Hamburg - Karlsruhe.
R2179 – 🚃12 Hamburg - Kassel.
R2478 – 🚃12 and 🍷 Frankfurt/Main (Kassel on Dec. 25, Jan. 1) - Halle.
R2573 – 🚃12 and 🍷 Dessau - Konstanz. **Not** Dec. 25, Jan. 1.
R2576 – 🚃12 and 🍷 Konstanz - Halle. **Not** Dec. 24, 31.
R2673 – 🚃12 Halle - Karlsruhe ⑥, Halle - Konstanz Ⓑ; 🍷 Halle - Karlsruhe.
A – 🚃12 Nordhausen (Dessau except on Dec. 25, 26, Jan. 1) - Altenbeken.

B – 🚃12 Dessau - Nordhausen (Northeim Ⓑ).
C – 🚃12 Nordhausen (Halle except on Dec. 24, 25, 31) - Kassel.
F – Daily Kassel - Nordhausen. Extended to Halle except on Dec. 24, 25, 31.
G – 🚃12 Altenbeken - Dessau.
H – 🚃12 Northeim - Halle. **Not** Dec. 24, 25, 31.
K – 🚃12 and 🍷 Hamburg - Kassel and v.v; 🚃12 Hamburg - Konstanz and v.v.
M – 🚃12 Kassel - Nordhausen (Halle except on Dec. 24, 25, 31).
S – **Not** Dec. 24, 31.
T – **Not** Dec. 24, 25, 31.
b – Arrive 1217.

Table 696 BRAUNSCHWEIG - BAD HARZBURG - GÖTTINGEN

1, 2 class

km		E 3504 Ⓐ	E 3504 ⑥	E 3506 ⚒	E 3506 ⑦	E 3510	E 3512	E 3514	E 3516	E 3518 ⚒	E 3522	E 3524 ⚒	E 3528	E 3530 G	E 3532 Ⓐ	E 3534 H	E 3536 Q	E 3538 Ⓐ	E 3540 S	E 3542 S	E 3544 S	E 3548 S⑥	E 3548 SⒷ	E 3550 Ⓑ
0	**Braunschweig** d.	0517	...	0559	...	0721	0823	0923	1023	1121	1221	1321	1423	1523	1552	1623	1723	1752	1823	1923	2008	2121	2121	2213
12	Wolfenbüttel d.	0527	...	0609	...	0732	0834	0934	1034	1131	1233	1333	1434	1534	1605	1634	1734	1805	1834	1934	2018	2132	2132	2224
49	**Bad Harzburg** a.	0602	...	0645	...	0807	0909	1009	1109	1205	1309	1409	1509	1609	|	1709	1809	|	1909	2009	2051	2207	2207	|
49	**Bad Harzburg 697** d.	0616	...	0656	...	0815	0915	1015	1115	1211	1315	1415	1515	1615	|	1715	1815	|	1915	2015	2057	2213	2213	|
60	Goslar **697** d.	0630	0630	0714	0714	0830	0930	1030	1130	1225	1330	1430	1530	1630	1645	1730	1830	1845	1930	2030	2109	2224	2225	2304
83	Seesen **693** d.	0649	0649	0736	0736	0849	0950	1049	1150	1244	1350	1449	1550	1649	...	1750	1849	...	1949	2049	2128	...	2244	...
97	Bad Gandersheim **693** d.	0700	0700	0748	0748	0859	1003	1059	1202	1255	1402	1459	1602	1659	...	1802	1859	...	1959	2059	2138	...	2254	...
103	**Kreiensen 693** a.	0706	0706	0755	0755	0906	1009	1106	1209	1302	1409	1506	1609	1706	...	1809	1906	...	2006	2106	2145	...	2301	...
103	**Kreiensen 750** d.	...	...	0812	0812	...	1012	...	1212	...	1412	...	1612	...	...	1812	...	...	2014	...	...	...	...	...
122	Northeim **750** d.	...	...	0828	0828	...	1028	...	1228	...	1428	...	1628	...	...	1828	...	...	2030	...	...	...	...	...
142	**Göttingen 750** a.	...	...	0844	0844	...	1044	...	1244	...	1444	...	1644	...	...	1844	...	...	2045	...	...	...	...	...

G – Ⓑ, also Dec. 24, 31.
H – Daily to Goslar; **not** Dec. 24 to Göttingen.
Q – **Not** Dec. 24.
S – **Not** Dec. 24, 31.

Table 696 GÖTTINGEN - BAD HARZBURG - BRAUNSCHWEIG

1, 2 class

	E	E	E	E	E	E	E	E	E	E	E	E	E	E	E	E	E	E	E	E	E	E	E	E
	3501	3503	3505	3507	3507	3509	3513	3513	3515	3517	3519	3521	3525	3529	3531	3535	3537	3539	3543	3545	3547	3549	6045	6047
	Ⓐ	Ⓐ	⚒	Ⓐ	⑥	S⚒	⚒	⑦				⚒		⚒		SⒶ		Q	Q	S	S	S	Ⓐ	⑦
Göttingen 750 d.	...	...	...	...	...	...	...	...	0712	...	0912	...	1112	...	1312	...	1512	...	1712	...	1912	...	2112	2212
Northeim **750** d.	...	...	...	...	...	...	...	...	0727	...	0928	...	1127	...	1327	...	1527	...	1727	...	1927	...	2127	2226
Kreiensen 750 d.	...	0446	...	0547	...	...	0647	...	0747	0847	0947	1047	1147	1247	1347	1447	1547	1647	1747	1847	1947	2047	2200	2247
Bad Gandersheim d.	...	0452	...	0553	...	...	0653	...	0753	0853	0953	1053	1153	1253	1353	1453	1553	1653	1753	1853	1953	2053	2206	2253
Seesen d.	...	0503	...	0605	...	...	0705	...	0806	0906	1006	1105	1206	1306	1406	1506	1606	1706	1806	1906	2006	2106	2217	2305
Goslar **697** d.	0450	0524	0605	0628	0628	0718	0727	0727	0829	0929	1029	1127	1229	1329	1429	1529	1629	1729	1829	1929	2029	2130	|	|
Bad Harzburg 697 a.	|	0537	|	0642	0642	|	0740	0740	0843	0943	1043	1140	1243	1343	1443	1543	1643	1743	1843	1943	2043	2143	|	|
Bad Harzburg d.	|	0543	|	0650	0650	|	0748	0748	0849	0949	1049	1146	1249	1349	1449	1549	1649	1749	1849	1949	2053	2149	|	|
Wolfenbüttel d.	0528	0619	0646	0728	0728	0756	0823	0823	0924	1024	1124	1222	1322	1427	1522	1622	1724	1822	1924	2024	2126	2224	|	|
Braunschweig a.	0538	0630	0657	0739	0739	0807	0834	0834	0935	1035	1135	1233	1333	1439	1533	1633	1735	1833	1935	2035	2137	2235	2257	2342

Q – **Not** Dec. 24. S – **Not** Dec. 24, 31.

Table 697 HANNOVER - BAD HARZBURG - (🚌) WERNIGERODE

1, 2 class Hannover - Bad Harzburg

km		E	IR	E	E	IR	E	E	IR	E	IR	E3621	E	IR	E	IR	E	E	E3633	IR	E	E	E	E
		3603	2481	3605	3611	2581	3613	3615	2483	3619	2583	E3623	3625	2643	3629	2585	3631	3543	E3635	2487	3637	3637	3639	3645
		⚒	🍷	⚒					🍷		🍷			🍷			⚒		Ⓑ	♣	⑥	Ⓑ		
			♦			♦			M		C			♦		C				M	S	S	S	S
0	**Hannover Hbf** d.	0533	0624	0633	0733	0818	0833	0933	1018	1133	1218	1233	1333	1438	1533	1618	1633	...	1733	1818	1833	1833	1933	2133
36	Hildesheim a.	0604	0647	0704	0804	0840	0904	1004	1040	1204	1240	1304	1404	1503	1604	1640	1704	...	1804	1840	1904	1904	2004	2204
36	Hildesheim d.	0607	0658	0707	0807	...	0907	1007	1051	1207	...	1340	1407	1505	1607	...	1707	...	1807	1851	1907	...	2007	2207
70	Salzgitter Ringelheim d.	0640	0728	0740	0840	...	0940	1040	1122	1240	...	1418	1440	1536	1640	...	1740	...	1840	1922	1940	...	2042	2240
89	Goslar **696** d.	0657	0750	0759	0857	...	0959	1057	1150	1257	...	1440	1457	1556	1657	...	1755	1829	1857	1942	1957	...	2104	2255
100	**Bad Harzburg 696** a.	0714	0802	0813	0911	...	1013	1111	1202	1311	...	1454	1511	1608	1711	...	...	1843	1911	1954	2011	...	2118	...
100	**Bad Harzburg** ▲ d.	...	*0820*	*0850*	*0950*	...	...	...	*1250*	*1350*	...	...	...	*1700*	*1815*	...	...	...	...	...	...	...	...	...
111	Stapelburg **689** ▲ d.	...	*0842*	*0912*	*1012*	...	...	...	*1312*	*1412*	...	...	...	*1722*	*1837*	...	...	...	...	...	...	...	...	...
114	Ilsenburg **689** ▲ d.	...	*0848*	*0918*	*1018*	...	...	...	*1318*	*1418*	...	...	...	*1728*	*1843*	...	...	...	...	...	...	...	...	...
124	**Wernigerode 689** ▲ a.	...	*0908*	*0938*	*1038*	...	...	...	*1338*	*1438*	...	...	...	*1748*	*1903*	...	...	...	...	...	...	...	...	...

	E	E	E	IR	E		E	IR	E	IR	E		E	IR	E3626	E	IR	E		E	IR	E		E
	3604	3610	3610	2488	3608	🚌	3612	2586	3614	2642	3622	🚌	3624	2584	E3628	3630	2486	3634	🚌	3638	2482	3642	🚌	3646
	Ⓐ	Ⓐ	⑥	⌿🍷				🍷		🍷				🍷			🍷			Ⓐ	🍷			
	S	S		♦				C		♦				C			N				N	S		S
Wernigerode 689 ▲ d.	...	...	...	...	...	0640	...	...	*0750*	...	*0950*	1045	...	...	...	...	...	*1420*	1545	...	...	...	1945	...
Ilsenburg **689** ▲ d.	...	...	...	...	...	0701	...	...	*0811*	...	*1011*	1106	...	...	...	...	...	*1441*	1606	...	...	...	2006	...
Stapelburg **689** ▲ d.	...	...	...	...	...	0707	...	...	*0817*	...	*1017*	1112	...	...	...	...	...	*1447*	1612	...	...	...	2012	...
Bad Harzburg ▲ a.	...	...	...	...	...	0726	...	...	*0836*	...	*1036*	1131	...	...	...	...	...	*1506*	1631	...	...	...	2031	...
Bad Harzburg d.	...	0542	...	0607	...	...	0742	...	0845	0950	1045	...	1142	...	1245	1345	1405	1545	...	1645	1805	1845	...	2045
Goslar d.	0458	0558	0558	0624	0646	...	0800	...	0900	1014	1100	...	1200	...	1300	1400	1424	1600	...	1700	1824	1900	...	2100
Salzgitter Ringelheim d.	0513	0613	0613	0650	0701	...	0816	...	0916	1028	1116	...	1216	...	1316	1416	1438	1616	...	1716	1838	1916	...	2116
Hildesheim a.	0546	0646	0646	0706	0731	...	0846	...	0946	1055	1146	...	1246	...	1346	1446	1506	1646	...	1746	1906	1946	...	2146
Hildesheim d.	0549	0649	0649	0716	0749	...	0849	0916	0949	1057	1149	...	1249	1316	1349	1449	1516	1649	...	1749	1916	1949	...	2149
Hannover Hbf a.	0623	0723	0723	0740	0822	...	0923	0940	1023	1123	1223	...	1323	1340	1423	1523	1540	1723	...	1823	1940	2023	...	2223

♦ – **NOTES** (LISTED BY TRAIN NUMBERS)
IR2481 – [12] and 🍷 Hannover (Bremen ⌿) - Bad Harzburg.
IR2488 – [12] and 🍷 Bad Harzburg - Norddeich Mole.
IR2581 – [12] and 🍷 Bremen - Hildesheim.
IR2642 – [12] and 🍷 Bad Harzburg - Aachen.
IR2643 – [12] and 🍷 Köln (Aachen ⌿) - Bad Harzburg.
C – [12] and 🍷 Hildesheim - Bremen - Wilhelmshaven and v.v.

M – [12] and 🍷 Norddeich Mole - Bremen - Bad Harzburg.
N – [12] and 🍷 Bad Harzburg - Bremen - Emden.
S – **Not** Dec. 24, 31.
⌿ – ① - ⑥ (**not** Dec. 25 - Jan. 1, Apr. 15 - 17, May 1, **1995**).
♣ – Daily except ⑥ (**not** Dec. 24 - 31, Apr. 14 - 16, Apr. 30, **1995**).
▲ – Connection is by 🚌 service. Stops are adjacent to rail stations.

Table 698 BIELEFELD - HAMELN - HILDESHEIM - BRAUNSCHWEIG

1, 2 class

km		E	E	E	E	E	E	E	E	E	E	E	E	E	E	E	E	E	E	E	E	E	E	E
		5613	5617	3705	3705	5623	5629	3711	5631	5637	3715	5641	5645	3719	5647	5653	3723	3725	3727	7131	3729	5665	5673	7135
		⚒	⚒	⚒	⑦														S		S	S	Ⓑ	
0	**Bielefeld** d.	...	...	...	...	...	...	0944	...	...	1144	...	...	1344	...	...	1544	1646	1745	...	1845	...	...	...
14	Herford d.	...	...	...	...	...	...	0957	...	...	1157	...	...	1357	...	...	1557	1659	1758	...	1857	...	...	...
24	Löhne d.	...	0626	...	...	...	...	1006	...	...	1206	...	...	1406	...	...	1606	1708	1808	...	1906	...	2050	...
77	**Hameln** a.	...	0716	...	...	...	...	1056	...	...	1256	...	...	1456	...	...	1707	1807	1907	...	1956	...	2140	...
77	**Hameln** d.	0626	0727	0826	0826	0926	1026	...	1126	1226	...	1343	1426	...	1526	1626	1726e	1826e	1926	...	...	2026	...	...
106	Elze d.	0655	0756	0855	0855	0955	1055	...	1155	1255	...	1413	1455	...	1555	1655	1755e	1855e	1955	2033	...	2055	...	2315
124	**Hildesheim** a.	0713	0815	0913	0913	1013	1113	...	1213	1313	...	1438	1513	...	1613	1713	1813e	1913e	2013	2053	...	2113	...	2335

	E	E	E	E	E	E	E	E	E	E	E	E	E	E	E	E	E	E	E	E	E	E	E	E
	3706	5608	5614	3710	5618	7108	5622	3714	5624	7112	5630	3718	7116	5638	3722	7120	3724	3726	7124	3728	5658	7128	5664	5666
	⚒	⚒																	Q	S	S	S	S	S
Hildesheim d.	0541	0641	0741	...	0841	0905	0941	...	1041	1105	1141	1241	1305	1341	1441	1505	1541	1641	1705	1741	1841	1905	1941	2041
Elze d.	0601	0701	0801	...	0901	0923	1001	...	1101	1123	1201	1301	1323	1413	1501	1523	1601	1701	1723	1801	1901	1923	2001	2101
Hameln a.	0629	0729	0829	...	0929	...	1029	...	1129	...	1229	1329	...	1441	1529	...	1629	1729	...	1829	1929	...	2029	2129
Hameln d.	0651	...	...	0914	...	...	...	1114	...	...	...	1343	...	...	1543	...	1643	1743e	...	1843	...	...	...	...
Löhne d.	0754	...	...	1005	...	...	...	1205	...	...	...	1438	...	...	1638	...	1738	1838e	...	1938	...	...	...	...
Herford d.	0802	...	...	1013	...	...	...	1213	...	...	...	1446	...	...	1647	...	1747	1847e	...	1947	...	...	...	...
Bielefeld a.	0814	...	...	1025	...	...	...	1225	...	...	...	1459	...	...	1659	...	1800	1859e	...	1959	...	...	...	...

Q – **Not** Dec. 24. S – **Not** Dec. 24, 31. e – **Not** Dec. 24, 31.

Local trains Hildesheim - Braunschweig. 43 km. Journey time: 33 minutes. For **ICE** express services see Table **750**.
From Hildesheim: 0459⚒, 0548⚒, 0652⚒, 0728, 0823⚒, 0918, 1117, 1317, 1502, 1623⚒, 1703**Q**, 1823Ⓑ, 1914**S**, 2112**S**.
From Braunschweig: 0511⚒, 0601⚒, 0639⚒, 0809, 1009, 1209, 1409, 1458⚒, 1610, 1658Ⓑ, 1809, 1927⚒**S**, 2027**S**, 2202**S**.

Table 699 BERLIN LOCAL and S-BAHN SERVICES (subject to change without notice)

Rail service Berlin Hbf - Frankfurt (Oder) and v.v. 80 km. Journey time: 52 minutes (47 by express). **L** – To or from Berlin **Lichtenberg**. ❖ – **Not** Dec. 25, Jan. 1

From Berlin Hbf: 0531, 0638, 0738, 0810 ❖ (**EC41**), 0838 and hourly until 1538, 1632 **S** (**EC43**), 1638 and hourly until 1938, 2024**L**, 2038, 2207**L**, 2224, 0045.
From Frankfurt (Oder): 0538, 0603**L**, 0638, 0709**L**, 0738 and hourly until 1038, 1131 ❖ **EC42**), 1138 and hourly until 1538, 1635, 1738, 1838, 1938, 2048, 2207**S** (**EC40**), 2248.

S-Bahn services **S3**, **S5**, **S7**, **S9** and **S75** combine to form frequent city centre services, linking all major stations. Early morning/late evening and weekend frequencies are a little less an some services may only run for part of the full route shown below. Some delays are possible during the rebuilding of the parallel main line tracks (closed for 2 - 3 years from September 1994
S3 route: Potsdam Stadt - Wannsee - Westkreuz - Charlottenberg - Zoo - Friedrichstraße - Alexanderplatz - Hauptbahnhof - Ostkreuz - Karlshorst - Erkner.
S5 route: Charlottenberg - Zoo - Friedrichstraße - Alexanderplatz - Hauptbahnhof - Ostkreuz - Lichtenberg - Strausberg - Strausberg Nord.
S7 route: Potsdam Stadt - Wannsee - Westkreuz - Charlottenberg - Zoo - Friedrichstraße - Alexanderplatz - Hauptbahnhof - Ostkreuz - Lichtenberg - Ahrensfelde.
S9 route: Westkreuz - Charlottenberg - Zoo - Friedrichstraße - Alexanderplatz - Hauptbahnhof - Ostkreuz - Baumschulenweg - Schöneweide - Schönefeld ✈.
S75 route: Westkreuz - Charlottenberg - Zoo - Friedrichstraße - Alexanderplatz - Hauptbahnhof - Ostkreuz - Lichtenberg - Wartenberg.
The recently re-opened Südring services **S45, S46** form a useful link between Westkreuz and Tempelhof ✈, Baumschulenweg, Schöneweide and Schönefeld ✈.

Table 700 AACHEN - HANNOVER - MAGDEBURG - BERLIN

1, 2 class except where shown

km		D 243	IC 649	IR 2443	IC 541	E 3909	IR 2445	3003	ICE 641	IC 543	ICE 696	D 231	IR 2455	IR 2241	E 3915	3205	3005	3159	IC 735	IC 545	IR 2447	3007	3161	IC 737	IC 608
		🍷 ♦	✕ ♦	🍷 ❖	⫽✕ ♦		🍷 ♦	❖	⫽✕	⫽🍷	✕ ♦	🍷 ♦	🍷 ♦	🍷 ♦		❖	❖	❖ B	✕ ♦	🍷 ♦	🍷	❖	❖ A	🍷 ♦	🍷 ♦
0	**Aachen** d.	...	...	...	...	...	...	0404	...	...	...	0501	...	...	...	...	0512	0604	0558	...	0634	0550	0704	0658	...
	Mönchengladbach d.	...	...	...	...	...	...	|	...	...	...	|	...	...	...	0625	|	0652	|	...	0718	|	0752	|	...
	Viersen d.	...	...	...	...	...	...	|	...	...	...	|	...	...	...	0633	|	|	|	...	0725	|	|	|	...
	Krefeld d.	...	...	...	...	...	...	|	...	...	...	|	...	...	...	0644	|	|	|	...	0738	|	|	|	...
31	Düren d.	...	...	...	...	...	...	0430	...	...	...	|	...	...	...	|	0540	|	0620	...	|	0629	|	0720	...
70	**Köln Hbf** a.	...	...	...	...	...	...	0509	...	...	...	0550	...	...	...	|	0609	|	0642	...	|	0709	|	0742	...
70	**Köln Hbf** d.	...	0332	...	...	...	0513	0516	0605	...	...	0555	...	...	...	|	0611	|	0709	0710	|	0716	|	0809	0810
	Neuss d.	...	|	...	...	...	|	|	|	...	...	|	...	...	...	|	|	0706	|	|	|	|	0806	|	|
117	**Düsseldorf Hbf** d.	...	0356	...	...	...	0542	0550	0626	...	...	0629	...	...	...	|	0650	0718	0733	|	|	0750	0818	0833	|
141	Duisburg d.	...	0409	...	...	...	0557	0605	0638	...	...	0644	...	...	...	0701	0705	|	0746	|	0757	0805	|	0846	|
151	Mülheim (Ruhr) d.	...	|	...	...	...	0603	0611	|	...	...	|	...	...	...	...	0711	|	|	|	0803	0811	|	|	|
160	**Essen** d.	...	0422	...	...	...	0612	0619	0649	...	...	0658	...	...	...	...	0719	|	0759	|	0812	0819	|	0859	|
176	Bochum d.	...	0432	...	...	...	0622	0631	|	...	...	0709	...	...	...	...	0731	|	0809	|	0822	0831	|	0909	|
	Solingen Ohligs d.	...	|	...	...	...	|	|	|	...	...	|	...	...	...	...	|	|	|	0728	|	|	|	|	0828
	Wuppertal Hbf d.	...	|	...	...	...	|	|	|	...	...	|	...	...	...	...	|	0736	|	0742	|	|	0836	|	0842
	Hagen d.	...	|	...	...	...	|	|	|	...	...	|	...	...	...	...	|	0805	|	0759	|	|	0905	|	0859
194	**Dortmund** a.	...	0443	...	...	...	0632	0643	0705	...	...	0722	...	...	...	...	0743	...	0820	0820	0832	0843	...	0920	0920
194	**Dortmund** d.	...	0445	...	...	...	0634	0645	0707	...	...	...	0736	...	...	...	0745	...	...	0827	0834	0845	...	...	0927
225	Hamm d.	...	0504	...	...	...	0653	0727	0724	...	...	...	0755	...	...	...	0819	...	...	0846	0853	0919	...	...	0946
275	Gütersloh d.	...	|	...	...	...	0713	0801	|	...	...	...	...	...	...	...	0852	...	...	|	0913	0952	...	...	|
292	Bielefeld d.	0437	0530	...	...	0626	0723	0815	0749	...	...	...	...	...	0824	...	0906	...	...	0913	0923	1006	...	...	1013
306	Herford d.	|	|	...	...	0637	0732	...	|	...	...	...	...	...	0836	...	...	...	...	|	0932	...	...	...	|
316	Löhne d.	|	|	...	...	0644	|	...	|	...	...	...	...	...	0843	...	...	...	...	|	|	...	...	...	|
337	Bad Oeynhausen d.	|	|	...	...	0649	0741	...	|	...	...	...	...	...	0848	...	...	...	...	|	0941	...	...	...	|
337	Minden d.	|	|	...	...	0703	0750	...	|	...	...	...	...	...	0903	...	...	...	...	|	0950	...	...	...	|
402	**Hannover Hbf** a.	0556	0620	...	...	0752	0819	...	0837	...	...	...	...	...	0952	...	...	...	...	1002	1019	...	...	...	1102
402	**Hannover Hbf** d.	0600	0623	0629	0746	...	0823	...	0839	0904	...	...	...	0930	...	...	...	...	...	1004	1023	...	...	...	1104
463	**Braunschweig** d.	0640	0706	0713	0832	...	0914	...	|	0947	1003	...	...	1020	...	...	...	...	...	1047	1110	...	...	...	1145
499	Helmstedt d.	|	|	0738	|	...	0938	...	|	|	|	...	...	|	...	...	...	...	...	|	1135	...	...	...	...
547	**Magdeburg** a.	0729	0750	0804	0917	...	1004	...	|	1032	1050	...	...	1114	...	...	...	...	...	1132	1202	...	...	...	...
547	**Magdeburg** d.	0732	0753	0821	0921	...	1021	...	|	1044	1052	...	...	1126	...	...	...	...	...	1135	1221	...	...	...	...
	Halle **660** a.	|	|	0916	|	...	1116	...	|	|	|	...	...	|	...	...	...	...	...	|	1316	...	...	...	...
	Leipzig **660** a.	|	|	0949	|	...	1149	...	|	|	|	...	...	|	...	...	...	...	...	|	1349	...	...	...	...
	Dresden Hbf **660** a.	|	|	1135	|	...	...	...	|	|	|	...	...	|	...	...	...	...	...	|	1535	...	...	...	...
627	Brandenburg d.	|	|	...	|	...	...	...	|	1143	|	...	...	1238	...	...	...	...	...	|	...	...	...	...	...
663	Potsdam Stadt ▲ a.	|	|	...	|	...	...	...	|	1216	|	...	...	|	...	...	...	...	...	|	...	...	...	...	...
672	**Berlin Wannsee** ▲ a.	0844	0858	...	1027	...	...	...	|	|	1157	...	...	1308	...	...	...	...	...	1241	...	...	...	...	...
687	**Berlin Zoo** ▲ a.	0858	0912	...	1040	...	...	...	1108	1240	1210	...	...	1326	...	...	...	...	...	1254	...	...	...	...	...

	ICE 694	E 3919	IR 2457	3209	3009	3163	IC 508	IR 2449	3011	D 411	3165	IC 506	ICE 598	IR 2243	E 3923	IR 2459	3213	3013	D 413	3167	IC 504	IR 2643	IR 2743	3015	3169
	✕ ♦		🍷 ♦	❖	❖	B	🍷 G	🍷		🍷 O	A	🍷 G	✕ ♦	🍷 ♦		🍷 ♦			🍷 O	B	✕ ♦	🍷 ♦	🍷 ♦		A
Aachen d.	...	...	...	...	0712	0804	...	0834	0812	0853	0904	...	...	...	...	...	...	0912	0953	1004	...	1034	...	1012	1104
Mönchengladbach d.	...	...	...	0825	|	0852	...	0913	|	|	0952	...	...	...	...	...	1025	|	|	1052	...	1118	...	|	1152
Viersen d.	...	...	...	0833	|	|	...	0925	|	|	|	...	...	...	...	...	1033	|	|	|	...	1125	...	|	|
Krefeld d.	...	...	...	0844	|	|	...	0938	|	|	|	...	...	...	...	...	1044	|	|	|	...	1138	...	|	|
Düren d.	...	...	...	|	0740	|	...	|	0840	0915	|	...	...	...	...	...	|	0940	1015	|	...	|	...	1040	|
Köln Hbf a.	...	...	...	|	0809	|	...	|	0909	0942	|	...	...	...	...	...	|	1009	1042	|	...	|	...	1109	|
Köln Hbf d.	...	...	...	|	0816	|	0910	|	0916	...	|	1009	...	...	...	...	|	1016	...	|	1109	|	...	1116	|
Neuss d.	...	...	...	|	|	0906	|	|	|	...	1006	|	...	...	...	...	|	|	...	1106	|	|	...	|	1206
Düsseldorf Hbf d.	...	...	0840	|	0850	0918	|	|	0950	...	1018	1033	...	...	...	1040	|	1050	...	1118	1133	|	...	1150	1218
Duisburg d.	...	...	0857	0901	0905	|	|	0957	1005	...	|	1046	...	...	...	1057	1101	1105	...	|	1146	1157	...	1205	|
Mülheim (Ruhr) d.	...	...	0904	...	0911	|	|	1003	1011	...	|	|	...	...	...	1104	...	1111	...	|	|	1203	...	1211	|
Essen d.	...	...	0913	...	0919	|	|	1012	1019	...	|	1059	...	...	...	1113	...	1119	...	|	1159	1212	...	1219	|
Bochum d.	...	...	0923	...	0931	|	|	1022	1031	...	|	1109	...	...	...	1123	...	1131	...	|	1209	1222	...	1231	|
Solingen Ohligs d.	...	...	|	...	|	|	0928	|	|	...	|	|	...	...	...	|	...	|	...	|	|	|	...	|	|
Wuppertal Hbf d.	...	...	|	...	|	0936	0942	|	|	...	1036	|	...	...	...	|	...	|	...	1136	|	|	...	|	1236
Hagen d.	...	...	|	...	|	1005	0959	|	|	...	1105	|	...	...	...	|	...	|	...	1205	|	|	...	|	1305
Dortmund a.	...	...	0934	...	0943	...	1020	1032	1043	...	...	1120	...	...	...	1134	...	1143	...	...	1220	1232	...	1243	...
Dortmund d.	...	...	0936	...	0945	...	1027	1034	1045	...	...	1127	...	...	...	1136	...	1145	...	...	1227	1234	...	1245	...
Hamm d.	...	...	0955	...	1019	...	1046	1053	1119	...	...	1146	...	...	...	1155	...	1219	...	...	1246	1253	...	1319	...
Gütersloh d.	...	...	...	...	1052	...	|	1113	1152	...	...	|	...	...	...	...	...	1252	...	...	|	1313	...	1352	...
Bielefeld d.	...	1024	...	...	1106	...	1113	1123	1206	...	...	1213	...	...	1224	...	...	1306	...	...	1313	1323	...	1406	...
Herford d.	...	1036	...	...	...	...	|	1132	...	...	...	|	...	...	1236	...	...	...	...	...	|	1332	...	...	...
Löhne d.	...	1043	...	...	...	...	|	|	...	...	...	|	...	...	1243	...	...	...	...	...	|	|	...	...	...
Bad Oeynhausen d.	...	1048	...	...	...	...	|	1141	...	...	...	|	...	...	1248	...	...	...	...	...	|	1341	...	...	...
Minden d.	...	1103	...	...	...	...	|	1150	...	...	...	|	...	...	1303	...	...	...	...	...	|	1350	...	...	...
Hannover Hbf a.	...	1152	...	...	...	...	1202	1219	...	...	...	1302	...	...	1352	...	...	...	...	...	1402	1419	...	...	...
Hannover Hbf d.	...	...	...	...	...	...	1204	1223	...	...	...	1304	...	1330	...	...	...	...	...	...	1404	...	1429	...	...
Braunschweig d.	1203	...	...	...	...	...	1247	1310	...	...	...	1347	1403	1420	...	...	...	...	...	...	1447	...	1513	...	...
Helmstedt d.	|	...	...	...	...	...	|	1335	...	...	...	|	|	|	...	...	...	...	...	...	|	...	1538	...	...
Magdeburg a.	1250	...	...	...	...	...	1332	1402	...	...	...	1432	1450	1514	...	...	...	...	...	...	1532	...	1604	...	...
Magdeburg d.	1252	...	...	...	...	...	1335	1421	...	...	...	1444	1452	1526	...	...	...	...	...	...	1535	...	1621	...	...
Halle **660** a.	|	...	...	...	...	...	|	1516	...	...	...	|	|	|	...	...	...	...	...	...	|	...	1716	...	...
Leipzig **660** a.	|	...	...	...	...	...	|	1549	...	...	...	|	|	|	...	...	...	...	...	...	|	...	1749	...	...
Dresden Hbf **660** a.	|	...	...	...	...	...	|	...	...	...	...	|	|	|	...	...	...	...	...	...	|	...	1930n	...	...
Brandenburg d.	|	...	...	...	...	...	|	...	...	...	...	1543	|	1638	...	...	...	...	...	...	|	...	...	...	...
Potsdam Stadt ▲ a.	|	...	...	...	...	...	|	...	...	...	...	1616	|	1708	...	...	...	...	...	...	|	...	...	...	...
Berlin Wannsee ▲ a.	1357	...	...	...	...	...	1441	...	...	...	...	|	1557	|	...	...	...	...	...	...	1641	...	...	...	...
Berlin Zoo ▲ a.	1410	...	...	...	...	...	1454	...	...	...	...	1640	1610	1726	...	...	...	...	...	...	1654	...	...	...	...

♦ – **NOTES** (LISTED BY TRAIN NUMBERS)

D231 – 🛏 2 cl., (12) and 🍷 (also 🛌 1,2 cl. **not** Dec. 24, 31) Paris Nord - Dortmund.
D243 – 🛌 1,2 cl., 🛏 2 cl., (2) and 🍷 Paris Nord - Berlin; 🛏 2 cl. Oostende - Berlin.
IC504 – KAISERSTUHL – (12) and ✕ Basel **Bad** - Köln - Berlin.
IC541 – ROLAND – (12) and ✕ Oldenburg - Berlin.
IC545 – ELSE LASKER-SCHÜLER – (12) and 🍷 Koblenz - Berlin.
ICE598 – LEO VON KLENZE – (12) and ✕ München - Kassel - Berlin.
IC608 – FRIEDRICH HARKORT – (12) and 🍷 Wiesbaden - Berlin.
IC649 – ADOLPH VON MENZEL – (12) and ✕ Hannover (Köln on ①, also Dec. 27, Apr. 18, May 2, **not** Dec. 26, Apr. 17, May 1) - Berlin.
ICE694 – RICARDA HUCH – (12) and ✕ Stuttgart (München ⫽) - Kassel - Berlin.
ICE696 – BETTINA VON ARNIM – (12) and ✕ Frankfurt (Stuttgart ⫽) - Kassel - Berlin.
IC735 – KAROLINGER – ① - ⑥, **not** Dec. 26, Apr. 15 - 17, May 1: (12) and ✕ Aachen - Kiel.
IC737 – RÜGEN – (12) Köln (Aachen ⫽) - Stralsund. Extended to Binz on ⑤⑥ Apr. 28 - May 27. 🍷 from Köln.
IR2241 – ⑥⑦, **not** Dec. 24, 25, 31, Jan. 1, Apr. 15, 16: (12) and 🍷 Bad Bentheim - Berlin.
IR2243 – ⑥, **not** Dec. 24, 31, Apr. 15: (12) and 🍷 Amsterdam Schiphol ✈ - Berlin.
IR2445 – (12) Hannover (Köln ① - ⑥, **not** Dec. 26, Apr. 15 - 17, May 1) - Leipzig; 🍷 Mülheim - Leipzig.
IR2455 – (12) Dortmund - Paderborn - Kassel - Bebra; 🍷 on ① - ⑥.
IR2457 – (12) and 🍷 Düsseldorf - Paderborn - Kassel - Bebra - Erfurt - Chemnitz.
IR2459 – (12) and 🍷 Düsseldorf - Paderborn - Kassel - Bebra.
IR2643 – (12) and 🍷 Hannover (Aachen ① - ⑥, **not** Dec. 26, Apr. 15 - 17, May 1) - Bad Harzburg.
IR2743 – (12) and 🍷 Norddeich Mole - Görlitz (Dresden Neustadt on Dec. 24, 31)..
A – (12) Aachen - Hagen (Iserlohn Ⓐ, **not** Nov. 1).
B – (12) Aachen - Iserlohn.
G – (12) and 🍷 Karlsruhe - Berlin.
O – (12) and 🍷 Oostende - Köln.
n – Dresden **Neustadt**.
❖ – **Not** Dec. 25, Jan. 1.
⫽ – ① - ⑥ (**not** Dec. 25 - Jan. 1, Apr. 15 - 17, May 1, **1995**).
▲ – Frequent S-Bahn services run between these points.

Table 700 AACHEN - HANNOVER - MAGDEBURG - BERLIN

1, 2 class except where shown

	IC 604	ICE 596	E 3927	IR 2551	3217	3017	D 417	EC 33	3171	IC 502	IR 2645	3019	D 419	3173	IC 500	ICE 594		E 3931	IR 2553	3221	3021	3175	EC 47	IR 2647	3023
	🍷 H	🍴 M		🍷 ◆			🍷 O	🍴 ◆	B	🍴 ◆	🍷 ◆		🍷 O	A	🍷 H	🍴 M			🍴 ◆			B	🍴 ◆	🍷 ◆	
Aachen d.	...	...	...	...	...	1112	1153	1202	1204	...	1234	1212	1253	1304	...	...	...	...	...	...	1312	1404	1358	1434	1412
Mönchengladbach d.	...	...	...	...	1225	|	|	|	1252	...	1318	|	|	1352	...	...	...	...	...	1425	|	1452	|	1518	|
Viersen d.	...	...	...	...	1233	|	|	|	|	...	1325	|	|	|	...	...	...	...	...	1433	|	|	|	1525	|
Krefeld d.	...	...	...	...	1244	|	|	|	|	...	1338	|	|	|	...	...	...	...	...	1444	|	|	|	1538	|
Düren d.	...	...	...	...	|	1140	1215	|	|	...	|	1240	1315	|	...	...	...	...	...	|	1340	|	|	|	1440
Köln Hbf a.	...	...	...	...	|	1209	1242	1248	|	...	|	1309	1342	|	...	...	...	...	...	|	1409	|	1442	|	1509
Köln Hbf d.	1210	...	...	...	|	1216	...	...	|	1309	|	1316	...	|	1410	...	...	...	...	|	1416	|	1509	|	1516
Neuss d.	|	...	...	...	|	|	...	...	1306	|	|	|	...	1406	|	...	...	...	...	|	|	1506	|	|	|
Düsseldorf Hbf d.	|	...	...	1240	|	1250	...	...	1318	1333	|	1350	...	1418	|	...	...	...	1440	|	1450	1518	1533	|	1550
Duisburg d.	|	...	...	1257	1301	1305	...	...	|	1346	1357	1405	...	|	|	...	...	...	1457	1501	1505	|	1546	1557	1605
Mülheim (Ruhr) d.	|	...	...	1304	...	1311	...	...	|	|	1403	1411	...	|	|	...	...	...	1504	...	1511	|	|	1603	1611
Essen d.	|	...	...	1313	...	1319	...	...	|	1359	1412	1419	...	|	|	...	...	...	1513	...	1519	|	1559	1612	1619
Bochum d.	|	...	...	1323	...	1331	...	...	|	1409	1422	1431	...	|	|	...	...	...	1523	...	1531	|	1609	1622	1631
Solingen-Ohligs d.	1228	...	...	|	...	|	...	...	|	|	|	|	...	|	1428	...	...	...	|	...	|	|	|	|	|
Wuppertal Hbf d.	1242	...	...	|	...	|	...	...	1336	|	|	|	...	1436	1442	...	...	...	|	...	|	1536	|	|	|
Hagen d.	1259	...	...	|	...	|	...	...	1405	|	|	|	...	1505	1459	...	...	...	|	...	|	1605	|	|	|
Dortmund a.	1320	...	...	1334	...	1343	...	...	...	1420	1432	1443	...	...	1520	...	...	...	1534	...	1543	...	1620	1632	1643
Dortmund d.	1327	...	...	1336	...	1345	...	...	...	1427	1434	1445	...	...	1527	...	...	...	1536	...	1545	...	1627	1634	1645
Hamm d.	1346	...	...	1355	...	1419	...	...	...	1446	1453	1519	...	...	1546	...	...	...	1555	...	1619	...	1646	1653	1719
Gütersloh d.	|	...	...	...	...	1452	...	...	...	|	1513	1552	...	...	|	...	...	...	...	...	1652	...	|	1713	1752
Bielefeld d.	1413	...	1424	...	...	1506	...	...	...	1513	1523	1606	...	...	1613	...	...	1624	...	...	1706	...	1713	1723	1806
Herford d.	|	...	1436	...	...	...	...	...	...	|	1532	...	...	...	|	...	...	1636	...	...	...	...	|	1732	...
Löhne d.	|	...	1443	...	...	...	...	...	...	|	|	...	...	...	|	...	...	1643	...	...	...	...	|	|	...
Bad Oeynhausen d.	|	...	1448	...	...	...	...	...	...	|	1541	...	...	...	|	...	...	1648	...	...	...	...	|	1741	...
Minden d.	|	...	1503	...	...	...	...	...	...	|	1550	...	...	...	|	...	...	1703	...	...	...	...	|	1750	...
Hannover Hbf a.	1502	...	1552	...	...	...	...	...	...	1602	1619	...	...	...	1702	...	...	1752	...	...	...	...	1802	1819	...
Hannover Hbf d.	1504	...	...	...	...	...	...	...	...	1604	1623	...	...	...	1704	...	...	...	...	...	...	...	1804	1823	...
Braunschweig d.	1545	1603	...	...	...	...	...	...	...	1647	1710	...	...	...	1745	1803	...	...	...	...	...	...	1847	1910	...
Helmstedt d.	...	|	...	...	...	...	...	...	...	|	1735	...	...	...	...	|	...	...	...	...	...	...	|	1935	...
Magdeburg a.	...	1650	...	...	...	...	...	...	...	1732	1802	...	...	...	...	1850	...	...	...	...	...	...	1932	2002	...
Magdeburg d.	...	1652	...	...	...	...	...	...	...	1735	1821	...	...	...	...	1852	...	...	...	...	...	...	1935	2005	...
Halle **660** a.	...	|	...	...	...	...	...	...	...	|	1916	...	...	...	...	|	...	...	...	...	...	...	|	|	...
Leipzig **660** a.	...	|	...	...	...	...	...	...	...	|	1949	...	...	...	...	|	...	...	...	...	...	...	|	2143	...
Dresden Hbf **660** a.	...	|	...	...	...	...	...	...	...	|	2135	...	...	...	...	|	...	...	...	...	...	...	|	...	...
Brandenburg d.	...	|	...	...	...	...	...	...	...	|	...	...	...	...	...	|	...	...	...	...	...	...	|	...	...
Potsdam Stadt ▲ a.	...	|	...	...	...	...	...	...	...	|	...	...	...	...	...	|	...	...	...	...	...	...	|	...	...
Berlin Wannsee ▲ a.	...	1757	...	...	...	...	...	...	...	1841	...	...	...	...	...	1957	...	...	...	...	...	...	2041	...	...
Berlin Zoo ▲ a.	...	1810	...	...	...	...	...	...	...	1854	...	...	...	...	...	2010	...	...	...	...	...	...	2054	...	...

	3177	EC 102	ICE 592	E 3935	IR 2555	3225 3227	3029	D 425	3179	EC 108	IR 2649	3033	3181	IC 547	ICE 17590	ICE 590	IR 2557	3231	3037	D 429	3183	IC 549	IR 2749	D 241	3039
	A	🍴 ◆	🍴 ◆		🍷 ◆			🍷 O	B	🍴 ◆	🍷 ◆		AS	♣🍴 ◆	🍴 ◆	🍴 ◆	🍷 ◆	S		🍷 O	BS	🍴	🍷 ◆	🍷 ◆	
Aachen d.	1504	...	...	...	...	...	1512	1553	1604	...	1634	1600	1704	...	...	...	...	...	1712	1751	1804	...	1834	1808	1812
Mönchengladbach d.	1552	...	...	...	...	1625	|	|	1652	...	1718	|	1752	...	...	...	...	1825	|	|	1852	...	1918	|	|
Viersen d.	|	...	...	...	...	1633	|	|	|	...	1725	|	|	...	...	...	...	1833	|	|	|	...	1925	|	|
Krefeld d.	|	...	...	...	...	1644	|	|	|	...	1738	|	|	...	...	...	...	1844	|	|	|	...	1938	|	|
Düren d.	|	...	...	...	...	|	1540	1615	|	...	|	1630	|	...	...	...	...	|	1740	1815	|	...	|	|	1840
Köln Hbf a.	|	...	...	...	...	|	1609	1642	|	...	|	1709	|	...	...	...	...	|	1809	1842	|	...	|	1902	1909
Köln Hbf d.	|	1609	...	...	...	|	1616	...	|	1710	|	1716	|	1810	...	...	...	|	1816	...	|	1910	|	1916	1916
Neuss d.	1606	|	...	...	...	|	|	...	1706	|	|	|	1806	|	...	...	...	|	|	...	1906	|	|	|	|
Düsseldorf Hbf d.	1618	1633	...	...	1640	|	1650	...	1718	|	|	1750	1818	|	...	...	1840	|	1850	...	1918	|	|	1945u	1950
Duisburg d.	|	1646	...	...	1657	1701	1705	...	|	|	1757	1805	|	|	...	...	1857	1901	1905	...	|	|	1957	2001u	2005
Mülheim (Ruhr) d.	|	|	...	...	1704	...	1711	...	|	|	1803	1811	|	|	...	...	1904	—	1911	...	|	|	2003	|	2011
Essen d.	|	1659	...	...	1713	...	1719	...	|	|	1812	1819	|	|	...	...	1913	...	1919	...	|	|	2012	2016u	2019
Bochum d.	|	1709	...	...	1723	...	1731	...	|	|	1822	1831	|	|	...	...	1923	...	1931	...	|	|	2022	|	2031
Solingen-Ohligs d.	|	|	...	...	|	...	|	...	|	1728	|	|	|	1828	...	...	|	...	|	...	|	1928	|	|	|
Wuppertal Hbf d.	1636	|	...	...	|	...	|	...	1736	1742	|	|	1836	1842	...	...	|	...	|	...	1936	1942	|	|	|
Hagen d.	1705	|	...	...	|	...	|	...	1805	1759	|	|	1905	1859	...	...	|	...	|	...	2005	1959	|	|	|
Dortmund a.	...	1720	...	...	1734	...	1743	...	...	1820	1832	1843	...	1920	...	...	1934	...	1943	...	...	2020	2032	2037u	2043
Dortmund d.	...	1727	...	...	1736	...	1745	...	...	1827	1834	1845	...	1927	...	...	1936	**E**	1945	...	...	2027	2034	2040u	2045v
Hamm d.	...	1746	...	...	1755	...	1819	...	...	1846	1853	1919v	...	1946	...	...	1955	**3939**	2019	...	...	2046	2053	2107u	2119v
Gütersloh d.	...	|	...	...	...	...	1852	...	...	|	1913	1952v	...	|	...	...	...	...	2052	...	...	|	2113	|	2152v
Bielefeld d.	...	1813	...	1824	...	...	1906	...	...	1913	1923	2006v	...	2013	...	...	...	2024	2106	...	...	2113	2123	2148u	2206v
Herford d.	...	|	...	1836	...	...	...	...	...	|	1932	...	...	|	...	...	...	2036	...	...	...	|	2132	|	...
Löhne d.	...	|	...	1843	...	...	...	...	...	|	|	...	...	|	...	...	...	2043	...	...	...	|	|	|	...
Bad Oeynhausen d.	...	|	...	1848	...	...	...	...	...	|	1941	...	...	|	...	...	...	2048	...	...	...	|	2141	|	...
Minden d.	...	|	...	1903	...	...	...	...	...	|	1950	...	...	|	...	...	...	2103	...	...	...	|	2150	|	...
Hannover Hbf a.	...	1902	...	1952	...	...	...	...	...	2002	2019	...	...	2102	...	...	...	2152	...	...	...	2202	2224	2257u	...
Hannover Hbf d.	...	1904	...	...	...	...	...	...	...	2004	2023	...	...	2104	...	...	...	...	...	...	...	...	...	2309u	...
Braunschweig d.	...	1947	2003	...	...	...	...	...	...	2047	2110	...	...	2147	2159	2203	...	...	...	...	...	...	...	2351u	...
Helmstedt d.	...	|	|	...	...	...	...	...	...	|	2134	...	...	|	|	|	...	...	...	...	...	...	...	|	...
Magdeburg a.	...	2032	2050	...	...	...	...	...	...	2132	2203	...	...	2232	2247	2250	...	...	...	...	...	...	...	0039u	...
Magdeburg d.	...	2044	2052	...	...	...	...	...	...	2135	...	...	...	2245	2249	2252	...	...	...	...	...	...	...	0042u	...
Halle **660** a.	...	|	|	...	...	...	...	...	...	|	...	...	...	2336	|	|	...	...	...	...	...	...	...	...	...
Leipzig **660** a.	...	|	|	...	...	...	...	...	...	|	...	...	...	0005	|	|	...	...	...	...	...	...	...	...	...
Dresden Hbf **660** a.	...	|	|	...	...	...	...	...	...	|	...	...	...	...	|	|	...	...	...	...	...	...	...	...	...
Brandenburg d.	...	2143	|	...	...	...	...	...	...	|	...	...	...	...	|	|	...	...	...	...	...	...	...	...	...
Potsdam Stadt ▲ a.	...	2216	|	...	...	...	...	...	...	|	...	...	...	...	|	|	...	...	...	...	...	...	...	...	...
Berlin Wannsee ▲ a.	...	|	2157	...	...	...	...	...	...	2241	...	...	...	...	2355	2357	...	...	...	...	...	...	...	...	...
Berlin Zoo ▲ a.	...	2240	2210	...	...	...	...	...	...	2254	...	...	...	...	0008	0010	...	...	...	...	...	...	...	...	...

◆ – **NOTES** (LISTED BY TRAIN NUMBERS)

- **EC33** – PARSIFAL – 🚃12 and 🍴 Paris Nord - Köln.
- **EC47** – ALEXANDER VON HUMBOLDT – 🚃12 and 🍴 Brussels - Berlin.
- **EC102** – RÄTIA – 🚃12 and 🍴 Chur - Basel SBB - Berlin.
- **EC108** – THUNERSEE – 🚃12 and 🍴 Interlaken Ost - Basel SBB - Berlin.
- **D241** – OST-WEST EXPRESS – see Table **24**.
- **IC502** – MARK BRANDENBURG – 🚃12 and 🍴 Basel SBB - Berlin.
- **IC547** – WESERBERGLAND – 🚃12 and 🍴 Köln - Leipzig.
- **ICE590** – ANDREAS SCHLÜTER – 🚃12 and 🍴 München - Kassel - Berlin. **Not** Dec. 24, 31.
- **ICE592** – WALTER GROPIUS – 🚃12 and 🍴 München - Kassel - Berlin. **Not** Dec. 24.
- **IR2551** – 🚃12 and 🍷 Düsseldorf - Paderborn - Bebra - Chemnitz (Erfurt on Dec. 24).
- **IR2553** – 🚃12 and 🍷 Düsseldorf - Paderborn - Bebra.
- **IR2555** – 🚃12 and 🍷 Düsseldorf - Paderborn - Erfurt (Bebra on Nov. 19, Dec. 24, 31).
- **IR2557** – 🚃12 Düsseldorf - Kassel Wilhelmshöhe; 🍷 Düsseldorf - Altenbeken.
- **IR2645** – 🚃12 and 🍷 Aachen - Dresden (Leipzig on Dec. 24, 31).
- **IR2647** – 🚃12 and 🍷 Aachen - Dessau - Leipzig (Magdeburg on Dec. 24, 31).
- **IR2649** – 🚃12 Aachen - Magdeburg (Hannover Dec. 24, 31); 🍷 Aachen-Braunschweig
- **IR2749** – 🚃12 Aachen - Hannover; 🍷 Aachen - Hamm.
- **ICE17590** – ⑤⑦, also Dec. 22, 26, Apr. 12, 13, 17, 18, May 1, 24, **not** Dec. 25, Apr. 14, 16 Apr. 30, May 26: 🚃12 and 🍴 Frankfurt/Main - Berlin.
- **A** – 🚃12 Aachen - Hagen (Iserlohn Ⓐ, **not** Nov. 1).
- **B** – 🚃12 Aachen - Iserlohn.
- **H** – 🚃12 and 🍷 Basel SBB - Braunschweig.
- **M** – 🚃12 and 🍴 München - Kassel - Berlin.
- **O** – 🚃12 and 🍷 Oostende - Köln.
- **S** – **Not** Dec. 24, 31.
- **t** – ⚒, **not** Nov. 1.
- **u** – Stops to **pick up** only.
- **v** – **Not** Dec. 24, 31.
- **♣** – Daily except ⑥ (**not** Dec. 24 - 31, Apr. 14 - 16, Apr. 30, **1995**).
- **▲** – Frequent S-Bahn trains run between these points.

Table 700 — AACHEN - HANNOVER - MAGDEBURG - BERLIN

1, 2 class except where shown

	EC 39	3185	EC 8	E 3943	IR 2559	3235	3041	3187	EC 49	3237	3043 / 3045	EC 31	3189	D 233	3239	3047	D 1219	ICN 1945	EC 37	D 1949	3049	D 341	D 439	EN 225
	✗	◆	G	S	◆	S			AS	AS		✗		AS			S	◆	◆			S	O	◆
Aachen d	1856	1904	…	…	…	…	1912	…	2004	1958	…	2004b	2102	2104	2106	…	2112	2135	…	2155	…	2204	2253	2332
Mönchengladbach d		1952	…	…	…	2025	…	2052	…	2125	…		2152	…	2225	2233								
Viersen d						2033				2133					2233	2244								
Krefeld d						2044				2144					2244									
Düren d			…	…			1940		2042		2030b									2230		2315		
Köln Hbf a	1942		…	…			2009	2042	2109		2149	2155		2209	2227		2242			2254		2309	2342	0017
Köln Hbf d	1951	2009	…	…			2016	2051	2116		2152	2200		2216					2245	2254		2316		
Neuss d		2006						2106					2206											
Düsseldorf Hbf d	2018	2018	2033	…		2040		2050	2118	2119	2150	2218	2218	2226		2250	2325u		2332	2350				
Duisburg d	2034	2046	2057	2101		2105		2134	2201	2205	2233	2242	2301	2305		2305	2341u		2350	0005				
Mülheim (Ruhr) d			2104	…		2111				2211				2311					2350	0011				
Essen d	2048	2059	2113			2119		2147	2219	2246		2253		2319			2355u		0004	0019				
Bochum d	2059	2109	2123			2131		2157	2231	2256				2331					0023	0031				
Solingen-Ohligs d																								
Wuppertal Hbf d		2036				2136						2236												
Hagen d		2105				2205						2305												
Dortmund a	2111		2120	2134		2143		2209	2243	2308		2343							0035	0043				
Dortmund d			2127	2136	2151v				2245			2345							0042					
Hamm d			2146	2155	2222v				2319			0015							0113					
Gütersloh d					2255v				2352															
Bielefeld d			2213	2224	2309v				0006										0203					
Löhne d				2236																				
Herford d				2243																				
Bad Oeynhausen d				2248																				
Minden d			2235	2304																				
Hannover Hbf a			2305	2400																				
Hannover Hbf d																				0319			0349	
Braunschweig d																				0326			0438	
Helmstedt d																				0409				
Magdeburg a																				0500			0532	
Magdeburg d																				0518			0536	
Halle 660 a																				0616				
Leipzig 660 a																				0649				
Dresden Hbf 660 a																				0842				
Brandenburg a																								
Potsdam Stadt ▲ a																								
Berlin Wannsee ▲ a																		0642				0647		
Berlin Zoo ▲ a																						0706		

	EN 224	EC 36	D 1948	D 1118	3004	3200	D 412	ICN 1944	3006	3202	3152	D 232	EC 30	D 340	3010	IR 2748	3154	EC 48	3012	3206	IR 2558	D 240	E 3904	EC 9
	◆	✗	♀	◆	❖	L	◆	✗ / O		❖	A	◆	✗	♀	❖	♀	♀ A	♀	◆	❖	♀	♀	✗	◆
Berlin Zoo ▲ d														2340										
Berlin Wannsee ▲ d								2300						2354										
Potsdam Stadt ▲ d																								
Brandenburg d																								
Dresden Hbf 660 d			2101																					
Leipzig 660 d			2252																					
Halle 660 d			2323																					
Magdeburg a			0020											0106										
Magdeburg d			0045											0110								0413s		
Helmstedt d																								
Braunschweig d			0135											0240								0502s		0615
Hannover Hbf a			0233											0342								0547s		0655
Hannover Hbf d			0238											0402		0538						0601s	0605	0657
Minden d														0444		0607						0653		0726
Bad Oeynhausen d																0615							0705	
Löhne d																0625							0711	
Herford d																							0718	
Bielefeld d			0343											0559	0634			0650				0716s	0728	0748
Gütersloh d														0612	0643			0703						
Hamm d			0426											0651	0705			0745				0759	0804s	0815
Dortmund a			0446											0714	0722			0814				0819	0824s	0833
Dortmund d			0450	0516				0616						0716	0724			0748	0816			0821	0826s	0838
Hagen d											0652						0752							
Wuppertal Hbf d											0713						0813							
Solingen-Ohligs d																								
Bochum d			0502		0527			0627					0700		0727	0735		0800		0827		0832		0849
Essen d			0514		0539		0619s	0639	0655			0654	0712		0739	0745		0812	0839			0844	0905s	0901
Mülheim (Ruhr) d					0546			0646							0746	0752		0846				0851		
Duisburg d			0529		0555	0557		0634s	0655	0657		0708	0725		0755	0804		0825	0855	0857		0919s		0914
Düsseldorf Hbf d			0548	0610		0653s	0710				0739	0732	0740		0810	0839	0840	0910			0914	0935s		0928
Neuss d															0749			0849						
Köln Hbf a			0629		0645			0720	0744			0757	0805		0847			0905	0947			1000		0950
Köln Hbf d	0508	0630		0638	0650		0714		0750			0802	0814		0850			0914	0950			1006		
Düren d					0717		0739		0817						0917				1017					
Krefeld d				0617				0717								0821				0915				
Viersen d				0627				0727								0835				0926				
Mönchengladbach d				0633				0733	0800							0843	0900			0932				
Aachen a	0555	0707		0732	0745		0758		0845	0847	0848	0855			0945	0919	0947	0955	1045			1055s		

NOTES (LISTED BY TRAIN NUMBERS)

C8 – TIZIANO – 🛏 Milano - Hannover; ✗ Chiasso - Hannover.
C9 – TIZIANO – 🛏 Hannover (Braunschweig ✗) - Milano; ✗ to Chiasso.
C30/1 – MOLIÈRE – 🛏 and ✗ Dortmund - Paris Nord and v.v.
C36/7 – FELIX TIMMERMANS – 🛏 and ✗ Köln - Brussels Midi and v.v.
C39 – JACQUES BREL – 🛏 and ✗ Paris Nord - Brussels Midi - Dortmund.
C48/9 – MEMLING – 🛏 and ♀ Oostende - Dortmund and v.v.
N224/5 – DONAUWALZER – 🛏 1,2 cl., ➡ 2 cl. and 🛏 Oostende - Wien; 🛏 1,2 cl., ➡ 2 cl. and 🛏 Oostende - Köln (D214) - München.
232/3 – NORD EXPRESS – see Tables 21 and 50.
240 – OST-WEST EXPRESS – see Table 24.
340/1 – 🛏 1,2 cl., ➡ 2 cl., 🛏 and ♀ Berlin - Amsterdam CS and v.v.
1118 – ⑦ Jan. 8 - Mar. 26, also Jan. 2: conveys ➡ 2 cl. and 🛏 Villach - Oostende from train D1214 (Villach depart previous night).
1219 – ⑤ Jan. 6 - Mar. 24, also Dec. 23: conveys ➡ 2 cl. and 🛏 Oostende - Villach for train D1215 at Koblenz.
N1944/5 – 🛏 1,2 cl., 🛏 (reclining) and ✗ Berlin Charlottenburg (depart 2230, arrive 0657) - Bonn and v.v. Special fares payable - see heading on page 352.

D1948/9 – 🛏 1,2 cl., ➡ 2 cl., 🛏 and ♀ Köln - Dresden Hbf and v.v.
IR2558 – 🛏 and ♀ Kassel Hbf - Düsseldorf.
IR2559 – 🛏 and ♀ Düsseldorf - Paderborn.
IR2748 – ① - ⑥, not Dec. 26, Apr. 15 - 17, May 1: 🛏 and ♀ Hannover - Aachen.
A – 🛏 Aachen - Hagen (Iserlohn Ⓐ, not Nov. 1) and v.v.
G – Not Dec. 24, 31: 🛏 Aachen - Hagen (Iserlohn Ⓑ).
L – ✗, not Nov. 1.
O – 🛏 and ♀ Oostende - Köln and v.v.
S – Not Dec. 24, 31.
b – On Ⓐ depart Aachen 2012, Düren 2040.
s – Stops to set down only.
u – Stops to pick up only.
v – Not Dec. 24, 31.
❖ – Not Dec. 25, Jan. 1.
▲ – Frequent S-Bahn services run between these points.

Table 700   BERLIN - MAGDEBURG - HANNOVER - AACHEN

1, 2 class except where show[n]

	3156	3014	IR 2648	3158	IC 548	D 420	3016	3210	IR 2556	E 3908	3160	ICE 591	IC 546	D 422	3018	IR 2744	EC 109	3162	EC 38	3020	3214	IR 2554	E 3912	ICE 593
	A		♦	B	✕	O			♀	♦	A	✕/M	⚡✕	O		♦	✕	B	✕			♀	♦	M
Berlin Zoo ▲ d.	…	…	…	…	…	…	…	…	…	…	0548	…	…	…	…	…	0707	…	…	…	…	…	…	0748
Berlin Wannsee ▲ d.	…	…	…	…	…	…	…	…	…	…	0601	…	…	…	…	…	0720	…	…	…	…	…	…	0801
Potsdam Stadt ▲ d.																								
Brandenburg d.																								
Dresden Hbf 660 d.												0555												
Leipzig 660 d.												0623				0614								
Halle 660 d.																								
Magdeburg a.	…	…	…	…	…	…	…	…	…	…	0707	0716	…	…	…	0750	0827	…	…	…	…	…	…	0907
Magdeburg d.	…	…	0553	…	…	…	…	…	…	…	0709	0730	…	…	…	0755	0830	…	…	…	…	…	…	0909
Helmstedt d.			0623													0823								
Braunschweig d.	…	…	0650	0715	…	…	…	…	…	…	…	0754	…	…	…	0850	0815	…	0915	…	…	…	…	0954
Hannover Hbf a.	…	…	0733	0755	…	…	…	…	…	…	…	…	…	…	…	0855	0933	…	0955	…	…	…	…	…
Hannover Hbf d.	…	…	0738	0757	…	…	…	…	…	0805	…	…	…	…	…	0857	0938	…	0957	…	…	…	1005	…
Minden d.			0807							0853							1007						1053	
Bad Oeynhausen d.			0815							0905							1015						1105	
Löhne d.										0911													1111	
Herford d.			0825							0918							1025						1118	
Bielefeld d.	…	0751	0834	…	0846	…	0850	…	…	0928	…	…	…	0946	…	…	0950	1034	1046	…	…	1050	1128	…
Gütersloh d.	…	0804	0843	…	0903	…	…	…	…	…	…	…	…	1003	…	…	1043	…	1103	…	…	…	…	…
Hamm d.	…	0845	0905	…	0915	…	0945	0959	…	…	…	1015	…	1045	1105	1115	…	…	1145	1159	…	…	…	…
Dortmund a.	…	0914	0922	…	0933	…	1014	1019	…	…	…	1033	…	1114	1122	1133	…	…	1214	1219	…	…	…	…
Dortmund d.	…	0916	0924	…	0940	…	1016	1021	…	…	…	1040	…	1116	1124	1138	…	1146	1216	1221	…	…	…	…
Hagen d.	0852			0952	1001					1052				1101				1152	1213					
Wuppertal Hbf d.	0913			1013	1020					1113				1120				1213						
Solingen-Ohligs d.				1031										1131										
Bochum d.		0927	0935				1027	1032							1127	1135	1149		1158	1227	1232			
Essen d.		0939	0945				1039	1044							1139	1145	1201		1210	1239	1244			
Mülheim (Ruhr) d.		0946	0952				1046	1051							1146	1152				1246	1251			
Duisburg d.		0955	1004				1055	1057	1059						1155	1204	1214		1224	1257	1259			
Düsseldorf Hbf d.	0939	1010		1039			1110		1114	1139				1210		1228	1239	1239	1310		1314			
Neuss d.	0949			1049					1149							1249								
Köln Hbf a.		1045		1050			1145		1150				1150	1245	1250			1304	1347					
Köln Hbf d.		1050				1114	1150						1214	1250				1314	1350					
Düren d.		1117				1139	1217						1239	1317					1417					
Krefeld d.		1021						1115							1221					1315				
Viersen d.		1035						1126							1235					1326				
Mönchengladbach d.	1000	1043	1100					1132			1200				1243		1300			1332				
Aachen a.	1047	1145	1119	1147			1200				1247			1258	1345	1319			1345	1355	1445			

	3164	IC 501	D 426	3022	IR 2742	IR 2642	EC 46	3166	3024	3218	IR 2552	E 3916	ICE 595	3168	IC 605	D 430	3026	3056	IR 2646	IC 503	3170	EC 32	3028	3226	IR 2550	392[?]
	A	✕	O		♀	♀	✕	B			♀	♦	✕/M	A	✕/O				♀	✕	B	✕			♀	
Berlin Zoo ▲ d.	…	0723	…	…	…	0907	…	…	…	…	…	…	0948	A	…	…	…	…	…	1107	…	…	…	…	…	…
Berlin Wannsee ▲ d.						0920							1001							1120						
Potsdam Stadt ▲ d.			0745																							
Brandenburg d.			0820																							
Dresden Hbf 660 d.					0608												0819n									
Leipzig 660 d.					0813												1013									
Halle 660 d.					0842												1042									
Magdeburg a.		0918				0938		1027					1107	A			1137	1227								
Magdeburg d.		0930				0955		1030					1109				1155	1230								
Helmstedt d.						1023											1223									
Braunschweig d.		1015				1050		1115					1154		1215		1250	1315								
Hannover Hbf a.		1055				1133		1155							1255		1333	1355								
Hannover Hbf d.		1057			1138	1157				1205					1257		1338	1357								140
Minden d.					1207					1253						1407										145
Bad Oeynhausen d.					1215					1305						1415										150
Löhne d.										1311																151
Herford d.					1225					1318						1425										151
Bielefeld d.		1146		1150	1234	1246		1250		1328					1346	1434	1443			1446			1450		1503	152
Gütersloh d.				1203		1243		1303							1415	1445	1505	1515					1545			
Hamm d.		1215		1245	1305	1315		1345	1359						1415	1433	1514	1522	1533				1545	1559		
Dortmund a.		1233		1314	1322	1333		1414	1419			1421			1433	1440	1516	1524	1538				1614	1619		
Dortmund d.		1240		1316	1324	1338		1416	1421			1421			1440	1516	1524	1538				1616	1621			
Hagen d.	1252	1301						1352								1452	1501				1552			1613		
Wuppertal Hbf d.	1313	1320						1413								1513	1520				1613					
Solingen-Ohligs d.		1331														1531										
Bochum d.				1327	1335	1349		1427	1432						1527	1535	1549				1627	1632				
Essen d.				1339	1345	1401		1439	1444						1539	1546	1552				1646	1651				
Mülheim (Ruhr) d.				1346	1352			1446	1451						1546	1552					1655	1657	1659			
Duisburg d.				1355	1404	1414		1455	1457	1459					1555	1604	1614				1655	1657	1659			
Düsseldorf Hbf d.	1339			1410		1428	1439	1510		1514					1610		1628	1639			1710			1714		
Neuss d.	1349					1449									1549			1649								
Köln Hbf a.		1350		1445		1450		1547		1550					1645	1650			1708	1750			1747			
Köln Hbf d.				1414	1450			1514		1550					1614	1650				1708	1750			1817		
Düren d.				1439	1517					1617					1639	1717					1817					
Krefeld d.								1421			1515					1621						1715				
Viersen d.								1435			1526					1635						1726				
Mönchengladbach d.	1400							1443		1500	1532					1643	1700					1733				
Aachen a.	1447	1458	1545		1519	1557	1547	1645						1647		1658	1745	1719		1747	1749	1845				

♦ — NOTES (LISTED BY TRAIN NUMBERS)

EC32 – PARSIFAL – [café] and ✕ Köln - Paris Nord.
EC38 – JACQUES BREL – [café] and ✕ Dortmund - Paris Nord.
EC46 – ALEXANDER VON HUMBOLDT – [café] and ✕ Berlin - Brussels Midi.
EC109 – THUNERSEE – [café] and ✕ Berlin - Köln - Basel - Interlaken Ost.
IC501 – MARIE LUISE KASCHNITZ – [café] and ✕ Berlin - Köln - Basel SBB.
IC503 – MARK BRANDENBURG – [café] and ♀ Berlin - Köln - Basel SBB.
IC548 – GÜRZENICH – [café] and ✕ Hannover (Braunschweig ⚡) - Köln.
ICE591 – ANDREAS SCHLÜTER – [café] and ✕ Berlin (Braunschweig on Dec 25) - München.
IC605 – HEINRICH DER LÖWE – [café] and ✕ Braunschweig - Basel SBB.
IR2550 – [café] Erfurt (Chemnitz on Dec 25) - Düsseldorf.
IR2552 – [café] and ♀ Bebra - Paderborn - Düsseldorf.
IR2554 – [café] Erfurt (Chemnitz ①-⑥, not Dec 26, Apr 15-17, May 1; Bebra on Dec 25, Jan 1) Paderborn - Düsseldorf; ♀ Erfurt - Düsseldorf.

IR2556 – [café] and ♀ Kassel - Paderborn - Düsseldorf.
IR2642 – [café] and ♀ Bad Harzburg - Aachen.
IR2646 – [café] and ♀ Görlitz (Dresden Neustadt on Dec 25, Jan 1) - Aachen.
IR2648 – [café] and ♀ Magdeburg (Hannover on Dec 25, Jan 1) - Aachen.
IR2742 – [café] and ♀ Dresden (Leipzig on Dec 25, Jan 1) - Norddeich Mole.
IR2744 – [café] and ♀ Leipzig (Magdeburg on Dec 25, Jan 1) - Aachen.
A – [café] Hagen (Iserlohn ⑥, not Nov 1) - Aachen.
B – [café] Iserlohn - Aachen.
M – [café] and ✕ Berlin - Kassel - München.
O – [café] and ♀ Köln - Oostende.
n – Dresden Neustadt.
⚡ – ①-⑥ (not Dec 25 - Jan 1, Apr 15-17, May 1, **1995**).
▲ – Frequent S-Bahn trains run between these points.

Table 700 BERLIN - MAGDEBURG - HANNOVER - AACHEN

1, 2 class except where shown

	IR 2242	ICE 597	IC 505	3172	D 434	3032	IR 2644	3174	IC 507	3034	3230	IR 2458	E 3924	3176	ICE 17599	ICE 599	IC 646	3038	IR 2448	IC 509	3178	3044	3234	E 3928	IR 2240
	🍷	🍴	🍴		🍷		🍷		🍴			🍷			🍴	🍴	🍷		🍷	🍷					🍷
	◆	M	◆	A	O			BS	◆		S	◆		AS	◆	M				◆	BS		S		◆
Berlin Zoo ▲ d.	1034	1148	1123	...	...	...	...	...	1307	...	...	...	...	...	1345	1348	...	...	...	1507	...	...	...	...	1434
Berlin Wannsee ▲ d.	|	1201	|	...	...	...	...	...	1320	...	...	...	...	...	1356	1401	...	...	...	1520	...	...	...	...	|
Potsdam Stadt ▲ d.	1055	|	1145	...	...	...	...	...	|	...	...	...	...	...	|	|	...	...	...	|	...	...	...	...	1455
Brandenburg d.	1129	|	1220	...	...	...	...	...	|	...	...	...	...	...	|	|	...	...	...	|	...	...	...	...	1535
Dresden Hbf **660** d.	|	|	|	...	...	...	1011	...	|	...	...	...	...	...	|	|	...	...	...	|	...	...	...	...	|
Leipzig **660** d.	|	|	|	...	...	...	1213	...	|	...	...	...	...	...	|	|	...	...	1413	|	...	...	...	...	|
Halle **660** d.	|	|	|	...	...	...	1242	...	|	...	...	...	...	...	|	|	...	...	1442	|	...	...	...	...	|
Magdeburg a.	1238	1307	1318	...	...	...	1337	...	1427	...	...	...	...	...	1501	1507	...	...	1537	1627	...	...	...	...	1638
Magdeburg d.	1256	1309	1330	...	...	...	1355	...	1430	...	...	...	...	...	1503	1509	...	...	1555	1630	...	...	...	...	1656
Helmstedt d.	|	|	|	...	...	...	1423	...	|	...	...	...	...	...	|	|	...	...	1623	|	...	...	...	...	|
Braunschweig d.	1346	1354	1415	...	...	...	1450	...	1515	...	...	...	...	...	1552	1554	1615	...	1650	1715	...	...	...	...	1746
Hannover Hbf a.	1425	...	1455	...	...	...	1533	...	1555	...	...	...	...	...	...	▬	1655	...	1733	1755	...	...	...	...	1825
Hannover Hbf d.	1438	...	1457	...	...	...	1538	...	1557	...	...	...	1605	...	...	...	1657	...	1738	1757	...	...	...	1805	1838
Minden d.	1511	...	|	...	...	...	1607	...	|	...	...	...	1653	...	...	...	|	...	1807	|	...	...	...	1853	1911
Bad Oeynhausen d.	1520	...	|	...	...	...	1615	...	|	...	...	...	1705	...	...	...	|	...	1815	|	...	...	...	1905	1920
Löhne d.	...	...	|	...	...	...	|	...	|	...	...	...	1711	...	...	...	|	...	|	|	...	...	...	1911	...
Herford d.	...	...	|	...	...	...	1625	...	|	...	...	...	1718	...	...	...	|	...	1825	|	...	...	...	1918	...
Bielefeld d.	...	...	1546	...	...	1550	1634	...	1646	1650	...	...	1728	...	...	...	1746	1750	1834	1846	...	1850	...	1928	...
Gütersloh d.	...	...	|	...	...	1603	1643	...	|	1703	...	...	...	...	...	...	|	1803	1843	|	...	1903	...	...	...
Hamm d.	...	...	1615	...	...	1645	1705	...	1715	1745	...	1759	...	...	...	...	1815	1845	1905	1915	...	1945	...	...	...
Dortmund a.	...	...	1633	...	...	1714	1722	...	1733	1814	...	1819	...	...	...	...	1833	1914	1922	1933	...	2014	...	...	...
Dortmund d.	...	...	1638	...	...	1716	1724	...	1740	1816	...	1821	...	...	...	...	...	1916	1924	1938	...	2016	...	...	...
Hagen d.	...	...	|	1652	...	|	|	1752	1801	|	...	|	...	1852	...	...	...	|	|	|	1952	|	...	...	...
Wuppertal Hbf d.	...	...	|	1713	...	|	|	1813	1820	|	...	|	...	1913	...	...	...	|	|	|	2013	|	...	...	...
Solingen-Ohligs d.	...	...	|	|	...	|	|	|	1831	|	...	|	...	|	...	...	...	|	|	|	|	|	...	...	...
Bochum d.	...	...	1649	|	...	1727	1735	|	|	1827	...	1832	...	|	...	...	...	1927	1935	1949	|	2027	...	...	...
Essen d.	...	...	1701	|	...	1739	1745	|	|	1839	...	1844	...	|	...	...	...	1939	1945	2001	|	2039	...	...	...
Mülheim (Ruhr) d.	...	...	|	|	...	1746	1752	|	|	1846	...	1851	...	|	...	...	...	1946	1952	|	|	2046	...	...	...
Duisburg d.	...	...	1714	|	...	1755	1804	|	|	1855	1857	1859	...	|	...	**D**	...	1955	2004	2014	|	2055	2057	...	...
Düsseldorf Hbf d.	...	...	1728	1739	...	1810	|	1839	|	1910	|	1914	...	1939	...	**438**	...	2010	|	2028	2039	2110	|	...	...
Neuss d.	...	...	|	1749	...	|	|	1849	|	|	|	...	...	1949	...	🍷	...	|	|	|	2049	|	|	...	...
Köln Hbf a.	...	...	1750	|	...	1845	|	|	1850	1947	|	...	...	|	...	O	...	2045	|	2050	|	2147	|	...	...
Köln Hbf d.	...	...	...	|	1814	1850	|	|	...	1950	|	...	...	|	...	2014	...	2050v	|	...	|	2150v	|	...	...
Düren d.	...	...	...	|	1839	1917	|	|	...	2017	|	...	...	|	...	2039	...	2117v	|	...	|	2217v	|	...	...
Krefeld d.	...	...	...	|	|	|	1821	|	...	|	1915	...	...	|	...	|	...	|	2021	...	|	|	2115	...	...
Viersen d.	...	...	...	|	|	|	1835	|	...	|	1926	...	...	|	...	|	...	|	2035	...	|	|	2126	...	...
Mönchengladbach d.	...	...	...	1800	|	|	1843	1900	...	|	1932	...	...	2000	...	|	...	|	2043	...	2100	|	2132	...	...
Aachen a.	...	...	...	1847	1858	1945	1919	1947	...	2045	...	...	...	2047	...	2058	...	2145v	2119	...	2147	2245v	...	...	...

	ICE 17695	ICE 695	IC 609	IC 736	3048	3236	IR 2446	3182	IC 544	IC 734	3052	E 3932	ICE 697	IC 542	E 3036	E 3038	ICE 640	D 230	3054	IR 2444	IC 540	E 3936	IC 648	E 3940	D 242
	🍴	🍴	♣🍷	🍷			🍷		🍷	🍷			🍴	♣🍷			♣🍴	🍷		🍷	♣🍷		🍷		🍷
	◆	◆	◆	◆		S	◆	BS	◆	◆	S		◆		⑥	⑧		◆	S	S	◆	S	◆	⑧	◆
Berlin Zoo ▲ d.	1537	1548	...	...	...	...	...	...	1707	...	...	...	1748	1723	...	...	1847	...	...	...	1907	...	1947	...	2049
Berlin Wannsee ▲ d.	|	1601	...	...	...	...	...	...	1720	...	...	...	1801	|	...	...	|	...	...	...	1920	...	2000	...	2103
Potsdam Stadt ▲ d.	|	|	...	...	...	...	...	...	|	...	...	...	|	1745	...	...	|	...	...	...	|	...	|	...	|
Brandenburg d.	|	|	...	...	...	...	...	...	|	...	...	...	|	1820	...	...	|	...	...	...	|	...	|	...	|
Dresden Hbf **660** d.	|	|	...	...	...	...	1411	...	|	...	...	...	|	|	...	...	|	...	...	...	|	...	|	...	|
Leipzig **660** d.	|	|	...	...	...	...	1613	...	|	...	...	...	|	|	...	...	|	...	...	1813	|	...	|	...	|
Halle **660** d.	|	|	...	...	...	...	1642	...	|	...	...	...	|	|	...	...	|	...	...	1842	|	...	|	...	|
Magdeburg a.	1704	1707	...	...	...	...	1738	...	1827	...	...	...	1907	1919	...	...	|	...	...	1937	2027	...	2102	...	2218
Magdeburg d.	1706	1709	...	...	...	...	1755	...	1830	...	...	...	1909	1930	...	...	|	...	...	1954	2030	...	2109	...	2223
Helmstedt d.	|	|	...	...	...	...	1823	...	|	...	...	...	|	|	...	...	|	...	...	2032	|	...	|	...	|
Braunschweig d.	1752	1754	1815	...	...	...	1850	...	1915	...	...	...	1954	2015	...	...	|	...	...	2053	2115	...	2156	...	2312
Hannover Hbf a.	▬	▬	1855	...	...	...	1933	...	1955	...	...	...	...	2055	...	...	2118	...	...	2135	2155	...	2236	...	2354
Hannover Hbf d.	...	...	1857	...	...	...	1938	...	1957	...	...	2005	...	...	2105	2105	2120	...	...	...	▬	2205	...	2305	2359
Minden d.	...	...	|	...	...	...	2007	...	|	...	...	2053	...	...	2152	2203	|	...	...	...	...	2252	...	2352	|
Bad Oeynhausen d.	...	...	|	...	...	...	2015	...	|	...	...	2105	...	...	2204	2215	|	...	...	...	...	2303	...	0004	|
Löhne d.	**IR**	...	|	...	...	...	|	...	|	...	...	2111	...	...	2209	2220	|	...	...	...	**3058**	2308	...	0010	|
Herford d.	**2456**	...	|	...	...	...	2025	...	|	...	...	2118	...	...	...	...	|	...	...	...	**S**	2315	...	0019	|
Bielefeld d.	🍷	...	1946	...	1950	...	2034	...	2046	...	2050	2128	...	...	...	...	2207	...	2150	...	2250	2323	...	0031	0054
Gütersloh d.	◆	...	|	...	2003	...	2043	...	|	...	2103	▬	...	...	...	...	|	...	2203	...	2303	...	...	...	...
Hamm d.	1959	...	2015	...	2045	...	2105	...	2115	...	2145	...	...	...	...	...	2232	...	2245	...	2345	...	...	...	...
Dortmund a.	2019	**3180**	2033	...	2114	...	2122	...	2133	...	2214	...	...	...	...	...	2247	...	2314	...	0006	...	...	...	...
Dortmund d.	2021	**AS**	2040	2038	2116v	...	2124	...	2140	2138	2216	...	...	...	...	...	2248	2237	2316	...	...	...	...	...	...
Hagen d.	|	2052	2101	|	|	...	|	2152	2201	|	|	...	...	...	...	...	|	|	|	...	...	...	...	...	...
Wuppertal Hbf d.	|	2113	2120	|	|	...	|	2213	2220	|	|	...	...	...	...	...	|	|	|	...	...	...	...	...	...
Solingen-Ohligs d.	|	|	2131	|	|	...	|	|	2231	|	|	...	...	...	...	...	|	|	|	...	...	...	...	...	...
Bochum d.	2032	|	|	2049	2127v	...	2135	|	|	2149	2227	...	...	...	...	...	|	2248	2327	...	...	...	...	...	...
Essen d.	2044	|	|	2101	2139v	...	2145	|	|	2201	2239	**3238**	...	...	...	...	2306	2300	2339	...	...	...	...	...	...
Mülheim (Ruhr) d.	2051	|	|	|	2146v	...	2151	|	|	|	2246	**S**	...	...	...	...	|	|	2346	...	...	...	...	...	...
Duisburg d.	2059	|	|	2114	2155v	2157	2159	|	|	2214	2255	2257	...	...	...	...	2317	2321	2353	...	...	...	...	...	...
Düsseldorf Hbf d.	2114	2139	|	2128	2210v	|	2214	2239	|	2228	2310	|	...	...	...	...	2330	2338	...	...	...	...	...	...	...
Neuss d.	...	2149	|	|	|	|	|	2249	|	|	|	|	...	...	...	...	|	|	...	...	...	...	...	...	...
Köln Hbf a.	...	|	2150	2150	2247v	|	2243	|	2250	2250	2341	|	...	...	...	...	2352	0003	...	...	...	...	...	...	...
Köln Hbf d.	...	|	...	2214	2250v	|	...	|	...	2314	2350v	|	...	...	...	...	...	0007	...	...	...	...	...	...	...
Düren d.	...	|	...	2236	2317v	|	...	|	...	2336	0017v	|	...	...	...	...	...	|	...	...	...	...	...	...	...
Krefeld d.	...	|	...	|	|	2215	...	|	...	|	|	2315	...	...	...	...	...	|	...	...	...	...	...	...	...
Viersen d.	...	|	...	|	|	2226	...	|	...	|	|	2326	...	...	...	...	...	|	...	...	...	...	...	...	...
Mönchengladbach d.	...	2200	...	|	|	2232	...	2300	...	|	|	2332	...	...	...	...	...	|	...	...	...	...	...	...	...
Aachen a.	...	2247	...	2256	2345v	...	...	2347	...	2356	0045v	...	...	...	...	...	...	0054	...	...	...	...	...	...	...

– **NOTES** (LISTED BY TRAIN NUMBERS)

230 – 🛏 2 cl., [12] and 🍷 (also 🛏 1,2 cl. except on Dec. 24, 31): Dortmund - Paris Nord.
242 – 🛏 1,2 cl., 🛏 2 cl., [2] and 🍷 Berlin - Paris Nord; 🛏 2 cl. Berlin - Oostende.
505 – KAISERSTUHL – [12] and 🍴 Berlin - Köln - Basel SBB.
507 – STOLZENFELS – [12] Berlin - Köln - Karlsruhe; 🍴 Berlin - Mainz.
509 – RHEINFELS – [12] and 🍷 Berlin - Köln - Karlsruhe.
540 – ROLAND – [12] and 🍴 Berlin - Oldenburg.
544 – ELSE LASKER-SCHÜLER – [12] and 🍷 Berlin - Koblenz.
609 – FRIEDRICH HARKORT – [12] and 🍷 Braunschweig - Wiesbaden.
648 – ADOLPH VON MENZEL – [12] Berlin - Hannover (Köln on ⑦, also Dec. 26, Apr. 17, May 1, **not** Dec. 25, Apr. 16, 30); 🍷 Berlin - Hannover.
E695 – RICARDA HUCH – [12] and 🍴 Berlin - Kassel - Stuttgart.
E697 – BETTINA VON ARNIM – [12] and 🍴 Berlin (Braunschweig on Dec. 24) - Kassel - Frankfurt/Main.
734 – KAROLINGER – ⑧, **not** Dec. 25, Apr. 14 - 16, 30: [12] Kiel - Aachen; 🍷 Kiel - Köln.
736 – RÜGEN – [12] Stralsund - Köln (Aachen ♣); starts from Binz on ⑥⑦ Apr. 29 - May 27; 🍷 to Köln.
2240 – ⑥, **not** Dec. 24, 31, Apr. 15: [12] and 🍷 Berlin - Amsterdam Schiphol ✈.
IR2242 – ⑥⑦, **not** Dec. 24, 25, 31, Jan. 1, Apr. 15, 16: [12] and 🍷 Berlin - Amsterdam Schiphol ✈.
IR2446 – [12] and 🍷 Dresden - Hannover (Köln ⑧, **not** Dec. 25, Apr. 14 - 16, 30).
IR2456 – [12] and 🍷 Chemnitz - Erfurt - Paderborn - Aachen.
IR2458 – [12] and 🍷 Bebra - Paderborn - Düsseldorf.
ICE17599 – ⑤⑦, also Nov. 1, Dec. 22, 26, Jan. 2, Apr. 12, 13, 17, 18, May 1, 24, **not** Dec. 25, Apr. 14, 16, 30, May 26: [12] and 🍴 Berlin - Kassel - Frankfurt/Main.
ICE17695 – ⑤⑦, also Nov. 1, Dec. 22, Jan. 2, Apr. 12, 13, 17, 18, May 24, **not** Dec. 25, Apr. 14, 16, 30, May 26: [12] and 🍴 Berlin - Kassel - Frankfurt/Main.
A – [12] Iserlohn - Aachen.
B – [12] Hagen (Iserlohn Ⓐ, **not** Nov. 6) - Aachen.
M – [12] and 🍴 Berlin - Kassel - München.
O – [12] and 🍷 Köln - Oostende.
S – **Not** Dec. 24, 31.
v – **Not** Dec. 24, 31.
♣ – Daily except ⑥ (**not** Dec. 24 - 31, Apr. 14 - 16, Apr. 30, **1995**).
▲ – Frequent S-Bahn trains run between these points.

Table 701 HENGELO - HANNOVER - STENDAL - BERLIN

1, 2 class except where shown

Timings between Oebisfelde and Berlin subject to alteration

km		E	IR	E	IR	E	E	E	E	E	IR	IR	E	E	E	IR	E	E	E	E	IR	IR	E	E
		3571	2349	3003	2541	3573	3411	3007	7025	3855	2543	2241	3415	3011	3857	2341	3575	3419	3015	3859	2343	2243	3423	3019
			🍷		🍷	2					🍷	🍷				🍷	2				🍷	🍷		
		G	◆	⚒	❖	J			⚒	B	◆	◆			B	◆	J			B	◆	◆		
0	**Hengelo** d.	...	...	...	...	...	...	...	...	...	...	...	...	...	...	0858	...	...	...	...	1058	1058	...	...
26	Bad Bentheim 🏛 d.	...	...	...	...	...	...	...	0617	...	0726	0726	...	...	...	0926t	...	...	...	...	1126t	1126t	...	...
47	Rheine d.	...	...	...	...	...	...	...	0636	0712	0739	0739	...	...	0912	0939	...	...	...	1112	1139	1139	...	1212
95	**Osnabrück** d.	...	...	0510	0603	...	...	0652	0713	0752	0805	0805	...	0852	0952	1005	...	...	1052	1152	1205	1205	...	1252
132	Bunde d.	...	...	0534	0625	...	...	0717	...	0816	0825	0825	...	0917	1016	1025	...	...	1117	1216	1225	1225	...	1317
142	Löhne d.	...	...	0544	|	...	...	0728	...	...	|	|	...	0928	...	|	...	...	1128	...	|	|	...	1328
148	Bad Oeynhausen **700** d.	...	...	0550	0636	...	...	0733	...	...	0836	0836	...	0933	...	1036	...	...	1133	...	1236	1236	...	1333
163	Minden **700** d.	...	...	0603	0646	...	...	0758	...	...	0846	0846	...	1003	...	1046	...	...	1203	...	1246	1246	...	1403
228	**Hannover 700** a.	...	...	0652	0719	...	...	0852	...	...	0919	0919	...	1052	...	1119	...	...	1252	...	1319	1319	...	1452
228	**Hannover 700** d.	...	0525	...	...	0727	0827	...	...	...	0930	0930	1027	...	...	...	1125	1227	...	...	1330	1330	1422	...
	Magdeburg **700** a.	...	|	...	...	|	|	...	...	...	|	1114	|	...	...	...	|	|	...	...	|	1514	|	...
303	Wolfsburg d.	...	0628	...	...	0851	0955	...	...	...	1028	|	1145	...	...	...	1251	1355	...	...	1428	|	1545	...
316	Oebisfelde d.	...	0643	...	...	0905	...	...	...	...	1044	|	...	...	...	...	1305	...	...	...	1444	|	...	...
378	**Stendal** d.	0556	0734	...	...	1006	...	...	...	...	1134	|	...	...	...	...	1403	...	...	...	1534	|	...	...
413	Rathenow d.	0630	0811	...	...	1040	...	...	...	...	1211	|	...	...	...	...	1437	...	...	...	1611	|	...	...
471	Berlin Spandau a.	0721	0900	...	...	1145	...	...	...	...	1300	|	...	...	...	...	1545	...	...	...	1700	|	...	...
482	**Berlin Zoo 700** a.	...	0916	...	...	1159c	...	...	...	...	1315	1326	...	...	...	...	...	...	...	...	1715	1726	...	...

	E	IR	E	E	E	E	IR		E	E	E	E	IR	E	E	E	IR	E	E	E	E			D
	3863	2545	3577	3431	3023	3865	2345		3437	3027	7075	3867	2547	3579	3031	3869	2347	3445	3035	3873	7097	3875		341
		🍷					🍷						🍷				🍷					Ⓑ		🍷
	B		K			B	◆		Q			B		S		B	◆	F	S	BS	Ⓑ	B		◆
Hengelo d.	...	1258	...	...	...	...	1458	...	...	...	...	...	1658	...	...	...	1858	...	...	...	...	...	...	0037
Bad Bentheim 🏛 d.	...	1326t	...	...	...	...	1526t	...	...	...	1603	...	1726t	...	...	...	1926t	...	...	...	2132	...	...	0110e
Rheine d.	1312	1339	...	...	...	1512	1539	...	...	...	1636f	1712	1739	...	...	1912	1939	...	...	2112	2153	...	...	0130
Osnabrück d.	1352	1405	...	...	1452	1552	1605	...	...	1652	1713	1752	1805	...	1852	1952	2005	...	2052	2152	2231	2252	...	0205
Bunde d.	1416	1425	...	...	1517	1616	1625	...	...	1717	...	1816	1825	...	1917	2016	2025	...	2117	2216	...	2321	...	|
Löhne d.	...	|	...	...	1528	...	|	...	...	1728	...	...	|	...	1928	...	|	...	2128	...	...	...	...	|
Bad Oeynhausen **700** d.	...	1436	...	...	1533	...	1636	...	...	1733	...	...	1836	...	1933	...	2036	...	2133	...	...	...	...	|
Minden **700** d.	...	1446	...	...	1603	...	1646	...	...	1803	...	...	1846	...	2003	...	2046	...	2203	...	...	...	...	0241
Hannover 700 a.	...	1519	...	...	1652	...	1719	...	...	1852	...	...	1919	...	2052	...	2119	...	2252	...	...	...	...	0325
Hannover 700 d.	...	...	1527	1627	...	...	1730	...	1827	...	...	...	...	1927	...	...	...	2129	...	...	...	...	...	0349
Magdeburg **700** a.	...	...	|	|	...	...	|	...	|	...	...	...	...	|	...	...	...	|	...	...	...	...	...	0532
Wolfsburg d.	...	...	1651	1755	...	...	1828	...	1945	...	...	...	...	2051	...	...	...	2256	...	...	...	...	...	|
Oebisfelde d.	...	...	1705	...	...	...	1844	...	...	...	...	...	...	2104	...	...	...	...	...	...	...	...	...	|
Stendal d.	...	...	1756	...	...	...	1934	...	...	...	...	...	...	...	...	...	...	...	...	...	...	...	...	|
Rathenow d.	...	...	1830	...	...	...	2011	...	...	...	...	...	...	...	...	...	...	...	...	...	...	...	...	|
Berlin Spandau a.	...	...	1921	...	...	...	2100	...	...	...	...	...	...	...	...	...	...	...	...	...	...	...	...	|
Berlin Zoo 700 a.	...	...	...	...	...	...	2115	...	...	...	...	...	...	...	...	...	...	...	...	...	...	...	...	0706

	E	E	IR	E	E	E	IR	E	E	E	IR		E	E	E	E	IR	E	E	E	IR	IR	E	E
	7006	3004	2346	3852	3008	3570	2546	3854	3012	3414	2344		3856	3016	3418	3572	2544	3858	3020	3422	2342	2242	3862	3024
			🍷				🍷				🍷						🍷				🍷	🍷		
	❖	⚒	◆	B				B			◆		B			J		B			◆	◆	B	
Berlin Zoo 700 d.	...	...	...	...	...	...	...	...	...	...	0638	...	...	...	...	...	...	...	...	...	1038	1034	...	...
Berlin Spandau d.	...	...	...	...	...	...	...	...	...	...	0654	...	...	...	...	0833	...	...	...	...	1054	|	...	...
Rathenow d.	...	...	...	...	...	...	...	...	...	...	0743	...	...	...	...	0922	...	...	...	...	1143	|	...	...
Stendal d.	...	...	...	...	...	...	...	...	...	...	0815	...	...	...	...	0955	...	...	...	...	1215	|	...	...
Oebisfelde d.	...	...	...	...	...	0644	...	...	...	...	0907	...	...	...	...	1044	...	...	...	...	1307	|	...	...
Wolfsburg d.	...	...	...	...	...	0701	...	...	...	0756	0920	...	...	...	0951	1101	...	...	...	1201	1320	|	...	...
Magdeburg **700** d.	...	...	...	...	...	|	...	...	...	|	|	...	...	...	|	|	...	...	...	|	|	1256	...	...
Hannover a.	...	...	...	...	...	0829	...	...	...	0929	1025	...	...	...	1129	1229	...	...	...	1329	1425	1425	...	...
Hannover 700 d.	...	0500	0638	...	0705	...	0838	...	0905	...	1038	...	...	1105	...	...	1238	...	1305	...	1438	1438	...	1505
Minden **700** d.	...	0612	0711	...	0812	...	0911	...	1012	...	1111	...	...	1212	...	...	1311	...	1412	...	1511	1511	...	1612
Bad Oeynhausen **700** d.	...	0624	0720	...	0824	...	0920	...	1024	...	1120	...	...	1224	...	...	1320	...	1424	...	1520	1520	...	1624
Löhne d.	...	0630	|	...	0830	...	|	...	1030	...	|	...	...	1230	...	...	|	...	1430	...	|	|	...	1630
Bunde d.	...	0640	0733	0740	0840	...	0933	0940	1040	...	1133	...	1140	1240	...	...	1333	1340	1440	...	1533	1533	1540	1640
Osnabrück d.	0643	0710	0755	0810	0904	...	0955	1012	1104	...	1155	...	1212	1304	...	...	1355	1412	1504	...	1555	1555	1610	1704
Rheine d.	0723	0749	0819	0848	...	...	1019	1048	...	...	1219	...	1248	...	...	...	1419	1448	...	...	1619	1619	1648	...
Bad Bentheim 🏛 d.	0741	...	0841t	...	...	...	1041t	...	...	...	1241t	...	...	...	...	...	1441t	...	...	...	1641t	1641t	...	...
Hengelo a.	...	...	0858	...	...	...	1058	...	...	...	1300	...	...	...	...	...	1458	...	...	...	1700	1700	...	...

	E	E	IR	E	E	E	IR	IR	E	E	E	E	IR	E	E	E	E		IR	E	E	E		D
	3426	3574	2542	3864	3028	3430	2340	2240	3866	3032	3434	3576	2540	3868	3036	3038	3439		2348	3442	3444	3578		340
			🍷				🍷	🍷					🍷						🍷		⚒			🍷
		J		B			◆	◆	B		Q	K	S	BS	◆	◆	S		F	S	S	F		◆
Berlin Zoo 700 d.	...	...	...	...	...	...	1438	1424	...	...	...	...	...	...	...	...	...	...	1838	...	...	...	...	2340
Berlin Spandau d.	...	1233	...	...	...	...	1454	|	...	...	...	1633	...	...	...	...	...	...	1854	...	...	2025	...	|
Rathenow d.	...	1322	...	...	...	...	1543	|	...	...	...	1722	...	...	...	...	...	...	1943	...	...	2122	...	|
Stendal d.	...	1355	...	...	...	...	1615	|	...	...	...	1755	...	...	...	...	...	...	2015	...	...	2153	...	|
Oebisfelde d.	...	1444	...	...	...	...	1707	|	...	...	...	1844	...	...	...	...	...	...	2107	...	...	...	...	|
Wolfsburg d.	1351	1501	...	...	...	1601	1720	|	...	...	1751	1901	...	...	...	...	2001	...	2120	2146	2213	...	...	|
Magdeburg **700** d.	|	|	...	...	...	|	|	1656	...	...	|	|	...	...	...	...	|	...	|	|	|	...	...	0110
Hannover a.	1529	1629	...	...	...	1729	1825	1825	...	...	1929	2029	...	...	...	...	2130	...	2225	2306	2340	...	...	0332
Hannover 700 d.	...	...	1638	...	1705	...	1838	1838	...	1905	...	...	2038	...	2105	2105	...	...	...	...	...	...	...	0402
Minden **700** d.	...	...	1711	...	1812	...	1911	1911	...	2012	...	...	2111	...	2152	2203	...	...	...	...	...	...	...	0444
Bad Oeynhausen **700** d.	...	...	1720	...	1824	...	1920	1920	...	2024	...	...	2120	...	2204	2215	...	...	...	...	...	...	...	|
Löhne d.	...	...	|	...	1830	...	|	|	...	2030	...	...	|	...	2210	2221	...	...	...	...	...	...	...	|
Bunde d.	...	...	1733	1740	1840	...	1933	1933	1940	2040	...	...	2133	2140	2221	2232	...	...	...	...	...	...	...	|
Osnabrück d.	...	...	1755	1812	1904	...	1955	1955	2010	2104	...	...	2156	2210	2246	2257	...	...	...	...	...	...	...	0538
Rheine d.	...	...	1819	1848	...	...	2019	2019	2048	...	...	...	...	2248	...	...	...	...	...	...	...	...	...	0610
Bad Bentheim 🏛 d.	...	...	1841t	...	...	...	2041t	2041t	...	...	...	...	...	...	...	...	...	...	...	...	...	...	...	0653
Hengelo a.	...	...	1858	...	...	...	2100	2100	...	...	...	...	...	...	...	...	...	...	...	...	...	...	...	0713

◆ – **NOTES** (LISTED BY TRAIN NUMBERS)

D340/1 – 🛏 1,2 cl., couchette 2 cl., [2] and 🍷 Amsterdam CS - Berlin and v.v.
IR2240/3 – ⑥, **not** Dec. 24, 31, Apr. 15: [12] and 🍷 Amsterdam Schiphol ✈ - Berlin and v.v.
IR2241/2 – ⑥⑦, **not** Dec. 24, 25, 31, Jan. 1, Apr. 15, 16.
IR2340 – Ⓑ, also Apr. 15: [12] and 🍷 Berlin - Amsterdam Schiphol ✈; also runs between Berlin and Osnabrück on Dec. 24, 31.
IR2341 – [12] and 🍷 Amsterdam Schiphol ✈ (Osnabrück Dec. 25, Jan. 1) - Hannover.
IR2342 – ① - ⑤, also Dec. 24, 25, 31, Jan. 1, Apr. 15, 16: [12] and 🍷 Berlin - Schiphol ✈.
IR2343 – Ⓑ, also Dec. 24, 31, Apr. 15: [12] and 🍷 Amsterdam Schiphol ✈ - Berlin.
IR2344 – [12] and 🍷 Berlin (① - ⑥, **not** Apr. 17), Hannover ⑦ - Amsterdam Schiphol ✈.
IR2345 – [12] and 🍷 Amsterdam Schiphol ✈ - Berlin Ⓑ, Hannover ⑥. **Not** Apr. 16.
IR2346/7 – [12] and 🍷 Amsterdam Schiphol ✈ - Hannover and v.v.
IR2349 – ① - ⑥, **not** Dec. 26, Apr. 15 - 17, May 1.
IR2543 – ① - ⑤, also Dec. 24, 25, 31, Jan. 1, Apr. 15, 16, **not** Dec. 26, Apr. 17 between Hengelo and Bad Bentheim).

E3036 – ⑥, also Dec. 25 - 30, Apr. 14, 16, 30, **not** Dec. 24, 31.
E3038 – Ⓑ, **not** Dec. 25 - 30, Apr. 14, 16, 30.
B – [12] Rheine - Bielefeld and v.v.
G – ⚒, also Nov. 16, Apr. 14, May 25, **not** Apr. 15.
F – Ⓑ, **not** Dec. 25, Apr. 13, 14, 16, 30.
J – [12] Hannover - Oebisfelde (Berlin Spandau ① - ⑤) and v.v.
K – [12] Hannover - Oebisfelde (Berlin Spandau Ⓑ).
Q – **Not** Dec. 24.
S – **Not** Dec. 24, 31.
c – Berlin **Charlottenburg**.
e – Arrive 0046.
f – Arrive 1621.
h – Arrive 0625.
t – Arrive 10 minutes earlier.
❖ – **Not** Dec. 25, Jan. 1.

GERMAN RAIL MAP - STRECKENKARTE DER DEUTSCHEN BAHNEN

Table 702 — BÜNDE - BIELEFELD
1, 2 class

km		E 7901 Ⓐ	E 7753 J	E 3853	E 7755 L	E 7759 L	E 3855 B	E 7761 L	E 7763 L	E 3857 B	E 7767	E 3859		E 7771 L	E 3863 B	E 7773 J	E 7775 L	E 3865 B	E 7779 J	E 3867 B	E 7783 J	E 3869 B	E 7873 BS	E 3875 Ⓑ
0	Bünde .... d.	0520	0545	0616	0649	0753	0816	0849	0953	1016	1153	1216	...	1353	1416	1431	1553	1616	1753	1816	1953	2016	2216	2321
14	Herford 698 700 .... d.	0538	0600	0630	0704	0808	0829	0904	1008	1029	1208	1229	...	1408	1429	1451	1608	1629	1808	1829	2008	2029	2229	2334
28	Bielefeld 698 700 .... a.	0550	0612	0640	0715	0820	0839	0920	1020	1039	1220	1239	...	1420	1439	1504	1620	1639	1820	1839	2020	2039	2239	2344

		E 7754 J	E 3852 B	E 7758 L	E 3854 B	E 7764 L	E 3856 B	E 7768 L	E 7419	E 7770 L	E 3858 B	E 7772	E 3927	E 7914	E 3862 B	E 7776 L	E 7778 J	E 3864 B	E 7780 J	E 7782 B	E 3866 J	E 7784 BS	E 3868 Ⓑ	E 7924 S	E 3872 S
Bielefeld 698 700 .... d.		0617	0716	0735	0916	0932	1116	1132	1218	...	1316	1332	1424	...	1516	1532	1640	1716	1732	1839	1916	1932	2116	2234	2323
Herford 698 700 .... d.		0635	0728	0749	0928	0946	1128	1146	1228	1235	1328	1346	1434	1446	1528	1546	1654	1728	1746	1855	1928	1946	2128	2246	2335
Bünde .... a.		0648	0738	0843	0938	0958	1153	1158	...	1248	1338	1358	...	1458	1538	1558	1706	1738	1758	1907	1938	2000	2138	2258	2347

B – 🚃 Rheine - Bielefeld and v.v.
J – Ⓐ, not Nov. 1.
L – 🏃 not Nov. 1.
S – Not Dec. 24, 31.

Table 703 — PADERBORN - HAMELN - HANNOVER
1, 2 class

km		5805 🏃	3801	3803 ❖	5811	3805	3807	5815	3811	5819	3815	5823	3817 🏃	3817 ⑦	3819	5827	3823	5831	3827	5835	3835	5839 S	3839 S	3841 S
0	Paderborn 693 705 ..... d.	...	0503e	0535	...	0631	0714	...	0914	...	1114	...	...	1314	...	1514	...	1714	...	1914	...	2114	2300
17	Altenbeken 693 705 .... d.	...	0517e	0550	...	0647	0729	...	0929	...	1129	...	1254	1254	1329	...	1529	...	1729	...	1929	...	2129	2313
56	Bad Pyrmont .... d.	0504	0552e	0625	0704	0721	0804	0904	1004	1104	1204	1304	1329	1329	1404	1504	1604	1704	1804	1900	2004	2104	2204	2346
75	Hameln .... a.	0519	0608e	0640	0719	0737	0819	0919	1019	1119	1219	1319	1344	1344	1419	1519	1619	1719	1819	1915	2019	2119	2219	2400
75	Hameln .... d.	0523	0617	0645	0723	0745	0822	0923	1022	1123	1223	1322	1354	...	1422	1523	1622	1723	1822	1923	2023	2123	2223	...
130	Hannover Hbf .... a.	0609	0709	0740	0809	0840	0909	1009	1109	1209	1309	1409	1440	...	1509	1609	1709	1809	1909	2009	2109	2209	2309	...

		3800 🏃	3802 Ⓐ	3804 🏃	E3741 L	3808	5808	3814	5812	3818	5816	3822	5820	3826 Ⓐ	3824	3832	3836	5828	3830 Ⓐ	5830	3838	5834 S	3840 S	3842 S	5838 S
Hannover Hbf .... d.		...	0448	...	...	0648	0748	0848	0948	1048	1148	1248	1348	1448	1514	1548	1648	1714	1748	1814	1848	1948	2048	2148	2248
Hameln .... a.		...	0533	...	...	0735	0833	0935	1033	1135	1233	1335	1433	1535	1609	1635	1735	1809	1835	1909	1937	2001	2135	2233	2337
Hameln .... d.		0503	0537	0603	...	0737	0837	0937	1037	1137	1237	1337	1437	1538	1616	1638	1738	1816	1837	...	1939	2033	2137	2237	...
Bad Pyrmont .... d.		0529	0553	0622	...	0753	0851	0953	1051	1153	1251	1353	1451	1553	1632	1652	1753	1832	1851	...	1954	2037	2153	2253	...
Altenbeken 693 705 .... d.		0556	0630	0657	0703	0830	...	1030	...	1230	...	1430	...	1630	1709	...	1830	1915	...	...	2030	2051	2230	2330	...
Paderborn 693 705 ..... a.		0608	0642	...	0715	0842	...	1042	...	1242	...	1442	...	1642	1722	...	1842	1928	...	...	2042	...	2242	2342	...

– 🏃, not Nov. 1.   S – Not Dec. 24, 31.   ❖ – Not Dec. 25, Jan. 1.   e – Ⓐ only.

Table 704 — RHEIN - RUHR LOCAL and S-BAHN SERVICES
1, 2 class

Rail service Dortmund - Iserlohn and v.v.   38 km.   Journey time: 47 minutes.   All trains call at Schwerte, 21 minutes from Dortmund, 26 minutes from Iserlohn.
From Dortmund: 0521 Ⓐ, 0551 Ⓐ, 0621 Ⓐ, 0651 🏃, 0721 Ⓐ, 0751 🏃, 0851, 0951, 1051, 1151, 1251, 1351, 1451, 1551, 1621 Ⓐ, 1651 Q, 1721 Ⓐ, 1751 Q, 1851 ⒷQ, 1951 ⒷQ, 2051 ⒷQ.
From Iserlohn: 0522 Ⓐ, 0616 Ⓐ, 0646 Ⓐ, 0716 🏃, 0746 🏃, 0816 🏃, 0916 🏃, 1016, 1116, 1216, 1316, 1416, 1516, 1616, 1646 Ⓐ, 1716, 1744 Ⓐ, 1816 Q, 1916 Q, 2016 ⒷQ, 2116 ⒷQ.

Rail service Hagen - Iserlohn and v.v.   27 km.   Journey time: 25 minutes.   Most trains run through to or from Aachen, Table 700.
From Hagen: 0522 J, 0622 L, 0722 L, 0822, 0922 J, 1022, 1122 J, 1222, 1322 J, 1422, 1522 J, 1622, 1722 J, 1822 Q, 1922 J, 2022 S, 2122 Ⓑ, 2222 🏃 (not Nov. 1, Dec. 24, 31).
From Iserlohn: 0614 J, 0714 L, 0814 L, 0914, 1014 J, 1114, 1214 J, 1314, 1414 J, 1514, 1614 J, 1714, 1814 J, 1914 Q, 2014 J, 2114 S, 2212 Ⓑ, 2314 🏃 (not Nov. 1, Dec. 24, 31).

Rail service Köln - Krefeld and v.v.   65 km.   Journey time: 43 minutes.   All trains call at Neuss, 24 minutes from Köln, 15 minutes from Krefeld.
From Köln: 0527 J, 0627 ❖, 0727 ❖, 0827 and hourly until 1527, 1557 J, 1627, 1727, 1827, 1927 S, 2027 S, 2127 S, 2227 S, 2327 S.
From Krefeld: 0557 L, 0648 ❖, 0748 ❖, 0848 ❖, 0948 and hourly until 1948, 2048 S, 2148 S, 2248 S, 2348 S.

Rail service Düsseldorf - Krefeld and v.v.   27 km.   Journey time: 25 minutes.
From Düsseldorf Hbf: 0620 ❖, 0720 ❖, 0820 ❖, 1020 and hourly until 1620, 1720 S, 1820 S, 1855 J, 1920 S, and hourly until 2320 S.
From Krefeld: 0516 J, 0616 L, 0716 ❖, 0816 ❖, 0916 ❖, 1016 ❖, 1116 and hourly until 1716, 1816 S, and hourly until 2316 S.

Rail service Dortmund - Witten and v.v.   16 km.   Journey time: 16 minutes.
From Dortmund: 0439 L, 0509 L, 0539 ❖, 0609 ❖, 0639 ❖, 0709 and half hourly until 1739, 1809 Q, 1839 Q and half hourly until 2139 Q, 2209 J, 2239 Q, 2309 J, 2339 Q.
From Witten: 0504 L, 0534 L, 0604 ❖, 0634 ❖, 0704 ❖, 0734 and half hourly until 1804, 1834 Q, 1904 Q, and half hourly until 2134 Q, 2204 J, 2234 Q, 2334 Q.

Rail service Dortmund - Soest and v.v.   53 km.   Journey time: 46 minutes.   All trains call at Unna, 23 minutes from Dortmund, 23 minutes from Soest.
From Dortmund: 0510 J, 0540 J, 0610 J, 0640 and every hour (30 minutes on dates in note J) until 1810, 1840 Q, 1910 J, 1940 Q, 2040 Q, 2140 Q, 2240 S, 2342 S.
From Soest: 0532 L, 0602 J, 0632, 0702 J, 0732 and every hour (30 minutes on dates in note J) until 1802 J, 1832 Q, 1902 J, 1932 Q, 2002 J, 2032 Q, 2132 Q, 2232 S, 2332 S.

Rail service Dortmund - Hagen and v.v.   24 km.   Journey time: 36 minutes.   For express services see Table 650.
From Dortmund: 0535 J, 0635 L, 0735 L, 0835, 0935 L, 1035, 1135 L, 1235, 1335, 1435, 1535, 1635, 1735 Q, 1835 Q, 1935 Q, 2035 Q.
From Hagen: 0556 J, 0603 L, 0703 L, 0803, 0903 L, 1003, 1103 L, 1203, 1303 L, 1403, 1503, 1603, 1703 Q, 1803 Q, 1903 Q, 2003 Q.

Rail service Duisburg - Emmerich and v.v. 69 km. Journey time: 65 minutes.   Trains call at Oberhausen, Dinslaken and Wesel, 7, 20 and 32 minutes from Duisburg, 31, 43 and 57 minutes from Emmerich.
From Duisburg: 0555 L, 0623 L, 0644, 0755, 0855 and hourly until 1555, 1623 J, 1655 Q, 1723 J, 1755, 1855, 1955, 2055 S, 2155 S.
From Emmerich: 0429 J, 0456 L, 0532 J, 0552, 0625 J, 0652, 0736 L, 0756, 0856 and hourly until 1856, 1956 S, 2056 S.

Notes for all services above:
Ⓑ – Ⓐ, not Nov. 1.   L – 🏃, not Nov. 1.   Q – Not Dec. 24.   R – Not Dec. 25.   S – Not Dec. 24, 31.   ❖ – Not Dec. 25, Jan. 1.

Table 704 – continued RHEIN – RUHR LOCAL and S-BAHN SERVICES

1,2 class

S-Bahn services run daily, every 20-30 minutes (**S21** is hourly) from approximately 0500 - 2330 throughout the **Rhein-Ruhr** conurbation, linking most major towns and cities. Stops are frequent so these trains more useful for short journeys as a supplement would be payable by faster **InterÇity** services. The most useful routes are shown below - **time taken to travel between** stations is shown alongside the station name.

LINE **S 1** Dortmund - Bochum (21) - Essen (39) - Mülheim Ruhr (50) - Duisburg (59) - Düsseldorf Unterrath (79) (**change** for Düsseldorf Flughafen ✈ - **S 7**) - Düsseldorf Hbf (89).
LINE **S 2** Dortmund - Herne (26) - Wanne Eickel (29) - Gelsenkirchen (34) - Oberhausen (51) - Duisburg (58). **S 2** is hourly but another local service alternates to make a 30 minute service.
LINE **S 3** Oberhausen - Mülheim Ruhr (8) - Essen (18).
LINE **S 6** Köln - Leverkusen Mitte (19) - Düsseldorf Hbf (53) - Essen (95).
LINE **S 8** Mönchengladbach - Neuss (16) - Düsseldorf Hbf (33) - Wuppertal Hbf (65) - Hagen Hbf (100).
LINE **S 11** Köln - Neuss (43) - Düsseldorf Hbf (65).

LINE S 7 – DÜSSELDORF FLUGHAFEN ✈ - DÜSSELDORF HBF - SOLINGEN OHLIGS

km		✣	Ⓐ	⑥✣	Ⓐ	✣	Ⓐ	⑥✣	Ⓐ		Ⓐ	⑥	Ⓐ		Ⓐ					
0	**Düsseldorf Flughafen ✈** ... d.	0505	0525	0535	0545	0605	0625	0635	0645	0705	0725	0735	0745	and at the	1845	1905	1935	and at the	2335	0005
3	Düsseldorf Unterrath .... d.	0508	0528	0538	0548	0608	0628	0638	0648	0708	0728	0738	0748	same	1848	1908	1938	same	2338	0008
10	**Düsseldorf Hbf** .... a.	0516	0536	0546	0556	0616	0636	0646	0656	0716	0736	0746	0756	minutes past	1856	1916	1946	minutes past	2346	0016
10	**Düsseldorf Hbf** .... d.	0518	0538	0548	0558	0618	0638	0648	0658	0718	0738	0748	0758	each hour	1858	1918	1948	each hour	0000	...
29	**Solingen Ohligs** .... a.	0539	0559	0609	0619	0639	0659	0709	0719	0739	0759	0809	0819	until:	1919	1939	2009	until:	0021	...

		Ⓐ	Ⓐ	✣	Ⓐ	⑥✣	Ⓐ		Ⓐ	⑥✣	Ⓐ		Ⓐ	⑥		Ⓐ				
Solingen Ohligs .... d.	0349	0505	0525	0545	0605	0615	0625	0645	0705	0715	0725	0745	0805	0815	and at the	1825	1845	1915	and at the	2345
Düsseldorf Hbf .... a.	0405	0526	0546	0606	0626	0636	0646	0706	0726	0736	0746	0806	0826	0836	same	1846	1906	1936	same	0006
Düsseldorf Hbf .... d.	0406	0528	0548	0608	0628	0640	0648	0708	0728	0740	0748	0808	0828	0840	minutes past	1848	1908	1940	minutes past	0010
Düsseldorf Unterrath .... d.	|	0537	0557	0617	0637	0649	0657	0717	0737	0749	0757	0817	0837	0849	each hour	1857	1917	1949	each hour	0019
Düsseldorf Flughafen ✈ ..... a.	0413	0540	0600	0620	0640	0652	0700	0720	0740	0752	0800	0820	0840	0852	until:	1900	1920	1952	until:	0022

LINE S 21 – DÜSSELDORF FLUGHAFEN - ESSEN - DORTMUND direct services

km		Ⓒ✣	Ⓐ	Ⓒ✣	Ⓐ	Ⓒ	Ⓐ	Ⓒ	Ⓐ		Ⓐ	Ⓒ	Ⓐ	Ⓒ	Ⓐ	Ⓒ	Ⓐ					
0	**Düsseldorf Flughafen ✈** ... d.	0537	0547	0637	0709	0737	0809	0837	0847	and at the	1547	1637	1709	1737	1809	1837	1847	1937	2037	2137	2237	2337
20	Duisburg .... d.	0600	0610	0700	0730	0800	0830	0900	0910	same	1610	1700	1730	1800	1830	1900	1910	2000	2100	2200	2300	0000
29	Mülheim (Ruhr) .... d.	0607	0617	0707	0737	0807	0837	0907	0917	minutes past	1617	1707	1737	1807	1837	1907	1917	2007	2107	2207	2307	0007
39	**Essen Hbf** .... d.	0618	0628	0718	0748	0818	0848	0918	0928	each hour	1628	1718	1748	1818	1848	1918	1927	2018	2118	2218	2318	0018
56	Bochum Hbf .... d.	0636	0646	0736	0806	0836	0906	0936	0946	until:	1646	1736	1806	1836	1906	1936	*2006*	2036	2136	2236	2336	0036
76	**Dortmund** .... a.	0657	0707	0757	0827	0857	0927	0957	1007		1707	1757	1827	1857	1927	1957	*2027*	2057	2157	2257	2357	0057

		Ⓐ	Ⓒ		Ⓐ	Ⓒ	Ⓐ	Ⓒ														
Dortmund .... d.	...	0417	0427	and at	1717	1727	1817	1827	1927	...	2027	...	...	2127	...	...	2227	2257	...	...	2327	2357
Bochum Hbf .... d.	...	0439	0449	the same	1739	1749	1839	1849	1949	...	2049	...	...	2149	...	...	2249	2319	...	...	2349	0019
Essen Hbf .... d.	...	0458	0508	minutes	1758	1808	1858	1908	1958	...	2058	...	...	2158	...	...	2308	2338	...	...	0014	0038
Mülheim (Ruhr) .... d.	...	0507	0517	past each	1807	1817	1907	1917	2008	...	2108	...	...	2208	...	...	2317	2347	...	...	0023	0047
Duisburg .... d.	...	0516	0526	hour	1816	1826	1926	1926	2026	...	2126	...	...	2226	...	...	2326	2355	...	...	0031	0055
Düsseldorf Flughafen ✈ ..... a.	...	0536	0546	until	1836	1846	1946	1946	2046	...	2146	...	...	2246	...	...	...	...	...	...	...	...

Table 705 DORTMUND and HAGEN - KASSEL

1, 2 class

	IR 2451	IR 2453	E 6855	E 3881	E 3457	IR 2455	E 3883	E 3459	IR 2457	E 3885	E 3463	IR 2459	E 3887	E 3467	IR 2551	E 3889	E 3469	IR 2553	E 3891	E 3473	IR 2555	E 3893	E 3479	IR 2557	IR 2559
	🍷	🍷 ♦		L		🍷 ♦		G	🍷 ♦			🍷			🍷 ♦			🍷			🍷 ♦			🍷	🍷
Düsseldorf Hbf **700** .... d.	...	...	...	...	...	...	...	...	0840	...	...	1040	...	...	1240	...	...	1440	...	...	1640	...	...	1840	2040
Essen **707** .... d.	...	...	...	0503	0603n	...	0706	0803	0913	...	1003	1113	...	1203	1313	...	1403	1513	...	1603	1713	...	1803	1913	2113
Dortmund .... d.	...	...	...	|	|	0736	|	|	0936	...	|	1136	...	|	1336	...	|	1536	...	|	1736	...	|	1936	2136
Hagen .... d.	...	...	...	0606	0712	|	0812	0912	|	1012	1112	|	1212	1312	|	1412	1512	|	1612	1712	|	1812	1912	|	|
Schwerte .... d.	...	...	...	0617	0722	|	0822	0922	|	1022	1122	|	1222	1322	|	1422	1522	|	1622	1722	|	1822	1922	|	|
Arnsberg .... d.	...	...	...	0650	0755	|	0855	0955	|	1055	1155	|	1255	1355	|	1455	1555	|	1655	1755	|	1855	1955	|	|
Meschede .... d.	...	...	...	0710	0815	|	0915	1015	|	1115	1215	|	1315	1415	|	1515	1615	|	1715	1815	|	1915	2015	|	|
Bestwig .... d.	...	...	...	0717	0822	|	0922	1022	|	1122	1222	|	1322	1422	|	1522	1622	|	1722	1822	|	1922	2022	|	|
Brilon Wald .... d.	...	...	...	0733	0838p	|	0938	1038	|	1138	1238	|	1338	1438x	|	1538	1638x	|	1738	1838x	|	1938v	2038x	|	|
Hamm .... d.	...	...	0611	|	|	0802	|	|	1002	|	|	1202	|	|	1402	|	|	1602	|	|	1802	|	|	2002	2202
Soest .... d.	...	...	0633	|	|	0816	|	|	1016	|	|	1216	|	|	1416	|	|	1616	|	|	1816	|	|	2016	2216
Lippstadt .... d.	...	...	0649	|	|	0828	|	|	1028	|	|	1228	|	|	1428	|	|	1628	|	|	1828	|	|	2028	2228
Paderborn .... d.	0548	0648	0718	|	|	0848	|	|	1048	|	|	1248	|	|	1448	|	|	1648	|	|	1848	|	|	2048	2246
Altenbeken .... d.	0602	0702	...	|	|	0902	|	|	1102	|	|	1302	|	|	1502	|	|	1702	|	|	1902	|	|	2102	...
Warburg .... d.	0625	0725	...	0816	0919p	0925	1016	1119	1125	1216	1319	1325	1416	1519x	1525	1616	1719x	1725	1816	1919x	1925	2016v	2124x	2125	...
Kassel Hbf .... a.	|	|	...	0856	...	|	1056	...	|	1256	...	|	1456	...	|	1656	...	|	1856	...	|	2056v	...	|	...
Kassel Hbf .... d.	|	|	...	0903	...	|	1103	...	|	1303	...	|	1503	...	|	1703	...	|	1903	...	|	2103v	...	|	...
Kassel Wilhelmshöhe ... a.	0701	0759	...	0907	...	0959	1107	...	1159	1307	...	1359	1507	...	1559	1707	...	1759	1907	...	1959	2107v	...	2201	...
Bebra **750** .... a.	...	0834	...	...	...	1034	...	...	1234	...	...	1434	...	...	1634	...	...	1834	...	...	2034	...	...	...	...

km		IR 2558	3462	E 3880	IR 2556	E 3464	E 3882	IR 2554	E 3466	E 3884	IR 2552	E 3468	E 3886	IR 2550	E 3472	E 3888	IR 2458	E 3476	E 3890	IR 2456	E 3478	E 3892	E 3894	IR 2454	IR 2452
		🍷	G	G	🍷	G		🍷 ♦	G		🍷	G		🍷 ♦			🍷	Q		🍷 ♦	S	J	⑦	🍷	🍷 ♦
	Bebra **750** .... d.	...	...	...	...	...	...	0921	...	...	1121	...	...	1321	...	...	1521	...	...	1721	...	...	...	1921	2121
0	**Kassel Wilhelmshöhe** ... d.	...	...	...	0757	...	0850	0957	...	1050	1157	...	1250	1357	...	1450	1557	...	1650	1757	...	1850	1850	1957	2157
4	**Kassel Hbf** .... a.	...	...	...	|	...	0854	|	...	1054	|	...	1254	|	...	1454	|	...	1654	|	...	1854	1854	|	|
4	**Kassel Hbf** .... d.	0546	...	0701p	|	...	0901	|	...	1101	|	...	1301	|	...	1501	|	...	1701	|	...	1901	1901	|	|
57	Warburg .... d.	0627	0629p	0740p	0827	0836p	0940	1027	1036p	1140	1227	1236p	1340	1427	1436	1540	1627	1636x	1740	1827	1836x	1940	1940	2027	2227
94	Altenbeken .... d.	0650	|	|	0850	|	|	1050	|	|	1250	|	|	1450	|	|	1650	|	|	1850	|	|	|	2050	2250
113	**Paderborn** .... d.	0704	|	|	0904	|	|	1104	|	|	1304	|	|	1504	|	|	1704	|	|	1904	|	|	|	2104	2303
145	Lippstadt .... d.	0720	|	|	0920	|	|	1120	|	|	1320	|	|	1520	|	|	1720	|	|	1920	|	|	|	2120	...
165	Soest .... d.	0736	|	|	0936	|	|	1136	|	|	1336	|	|	1536	|	|	1736	|	|	1936	|	|	|	2136	...
191	**Hamm** .... d.	0752	|	|	0952	|	|	1152	|	|	1352	|	|	1552	|	|	1752	|	|	1952	|	|	|	2152	...
	Brilon Wald .... d.	|	0717p	0822p	|	0922p	1022	|	1122p	1222	|	1322p	1422	|	1522	1622	|	1722x	1822	|	1922x	2022	2022	|	...
	Bestwig .... d.	|	0736	0836	|	0936	1036	|	1136	1236	|	1336	1436	|	1536	1636	|	1736	1836	|	1936	2036	2036	|	...
	Meschede .... d.	|	0744	0844	|	0944	1044	|	1144	1244	|	1344	1444	|	1544	1644	|	1744	1844v	|	1944	2044	2044	|	...
	Arnsberg .... d.	|	0802	0902	|	1002	1102	|	1202	1302	|	1402	1502	|	1602	1702	|	1802	1902v	|	2002	2102	2102	|	...
	Schwerte .... d.	|	0836	0936	|	1036	1136	|	1236	1336	|	1436	1536	|	1636	1736	|	1836	1936v	|	2036	2136	2136	|	...
	Hagen .... a.	|	0846	0946	|	1046	1146	|	1246	1346	|	1446	1546	|	1646	1746	|	1846	1946v	|	2046	2146	2146	|	...
222	**Dortmund** .... a.	0819	|	...	1019	|	...	1219	|	...	1419	|	...	1619	|	...	1819	|	|	2019	|	|	|	2219	...
	Essen **707** .... a.	0842	0953	...	1042	1153	...	1242	1353	...	1442	1553	...	1642	1753	...	1842	1953	2053v	2042	2153	2253	2253	...	...
	Düsseldorf Hbf **700** .. a.	0914	...	...	1114	...	...	1314	...	...	1514	...	...	1714	...	...	1914	...	...	2114	...	...	...	...	...

♦ – **NOTES** (LISTED BY TRAIN NUMBERS)
IR2452/3 – [12] and 🍷 Chemnitz - Paderborn.
IR2456/7 – [12] and 🍷 Chemnitz - Düsseldorf and v.v.
IR2550/1 – [12] and 🍷 Chemnitz - Düsseldorf and v.v.
IR2554 – [12] Erfurt (Chemnitz ① - ⑥, **not** Apr. 15 - 17) - Düsseldorf; 🍷 Erfurt - Düsseldorf.
IR2555 – [12] and 🍷 Düsseldorf - Erfurt.
G – **Not** Nov. 1.

J – **Not** Nov. 1, Jan. 6.
L – ⚒, **not** Nov. 1, Jan. 6.
Q – **Not** Dec. 24.
S – **Not** Dec. 24, 31.
p – **Not** ⑦.
x – **Not** ⑥.

Table 706 KÖLN - MÖNCHENGLADBACH - VENLO

1, 2 class

km		8114 ❖	D1802 G	8124	D1804 G	8130	8134	D1808 G	8140	8144	D1812 G	8150	8154	D1816 G	8160	8164	D1820 G	8170	8174	D1824 G	8180	D1826 L	8184	8190 S	8194 S
0	**Köln Hbf** d.	0624	0717	0824	0917	0924	1024	1117	1124	1224	1317	1324	1424	1517	1524	1624	1717	1724	1824	1917	1924	2017	2024	2124	2224
35	Grevenbroich d.	0653	|	0853	|	0953	1053	|	1153	1253	|	1353	1453	|	1553	1653	|	1754	1853	|	1953	|	2053	2153	2253
54	Rheydt Hbf d.	0711	|	0912	|	1011	1111	|	1211	1311	|	1411	1511	|	1611	1711	|	1811	1911	|	2011	|	2111	2211	2311
57	**Mönchengladbach** a.	0715	0756	0916	0956	1015	1115	1156	1215	1315	1356	1415	1515	1556	1615	1715	1756	1815	1915	1956	2015	2056	2115	2215	2315
57	**Mönchengladbach 700** d.	0734	0758	0934	0958	1034	1134	1158	1234	1334	1358	1434	1534	1558	1634	1734b	1758	1834b	1934b	1958	2034b	2058	2134b	2234	...
66	Viersen **700** d.	0741	0805	0941	1005	1041	1141	1205	1241	1341	1405	1441	1541	1605	1643	1741b	1805	1841b	1941b	2005	2041b	2105	2141b	2241	...
84	Kaldenkirchen d.	0759	|	0959	|	1059	1159	|	1259	1359	|	1459	1559	|	1701	1759b	|	1859b	1959b	|	2059b	|	2159b	2259	...
94	**Venlo** 🏛 a.	...	0821	...	1021	...	...	1221	...	...	1421	...	...	1621	...	...	1821	...	...	2021	...	2121	...	...	...

	8115	8121	D1803 J	8125	8131	D1807 G	8135	8141	D1811 G	8145	8151	D1815 G	8155	8161	D1819 G	8165	8171	D1823 G	8175	8181 S	D1827 G	8185 S	8191 S	D1829 G	8195 S
Venlo 🏛 d.	...	...	0812	...	...	1012	...	...	1212	...	...	1412	...	...	1612	...	...	1812	...	...	2012	...	...	2212	...
Kaldenkirchen d.	...	0723c	|	0823	0923	|	1023	1123	|	1223	1323	|	1423	1523	|	1623	1723b	|	1823b	1923	|	2023	2123	|	2223
Viersen **700** d.	...	0741c	0831	0841	0941	1031	1041	1141	1231	1241	1341	1431	1441	1541	1631	1641	1741b	1831	1841b	1941	2031	2041	2141	2231	2241
Mönchengladbach 700 a.	...	0748c	0837	0848	0948	1037	1048	1148	1237	1248	1348	1437	1448	1548	1637	1648	1748b	1837	1848b	1948	2037	2048	2148	2237	2248
Mönchengladbach d.	0653	0753	0839	0853	0953	1039	1053	1153	1239	1252	1353	1439	1453	1553	1639	1653	1753	1839	1853	1953	2039	2053	2153	2239	2253
Rheydt Hbf d.	0657	0757	|	0857	0957	|	1057	1157	|	1257	1357	|	1457	1557	|	1657	1757	|	1857	1957	|	2057	2157	|	2257
Grevenbroich d.	0715	0815	|	0915	1015	|	1115	1215	|	1315	1415	|	1515	1615	|	1715	1815	|	1915	2015	|	2115	2215	|	2315
Köln Hbf a.	0746	0846	0919	0946	1046	1119	1146	1245	1319	1346	1446	1519	1546	1646	1719	1746	1846	1919	1946	2046	2119	2146	2246	2319	2346

G – [12] Köln - Den Haag and v.v.
J – [12] Venlo (Den Haag ① - ⑥, **not** Dec. 26, Apr. 17) - Köln.
L – [12] Köln - Den Haag (Venlo on Dec. 24, 25, 31, Apr. 16).
S – **Not** Dec. 24, 31.
b – **Not** Dec. 24, 31.
c – **Not** Dec. 25, Jan. 1.
❖ – **Not** Dec. 25, Jan. 1.

Table 707 ESSEN - BOCHUM - HAGEN

1, 2 class

km		❖					S	S
0	**Essen** d.	0603	0706	0803	and at the	1903	2003	2103
16	Bochum d.	0617	0720	0817	same minutes	1917	2017	2117
30	Witten d.	0629	0731	0829	past each	1929	2029	2129
45	**Hagen** a.	0644	0745	0844	hour until:	1944	2044	2144

	❖	❖				Q	S	S
Hagen d.	0514	0614	0714	and at the	1914	2014	2114	2214
Witten d.	0529	0629	0729	same minutes	1929	2029	2129	2229
Bochum d.	0540	0640	0740	past each	1940	2040	2140	2240
Essen a.	0553	0654	0753	hour until:	1953	2053	2153	2253

Q – **Not** Dec. 24.
S – **Not** Dec. 24, 31.
❖ – **Not** Dec. 25, Jan. 1.

Table 708 KÖLN - HAMM - MÜNSTER

For InterCity services see Table 650

1, 2 class

km		E 3101 ❖	E 3103 ❖	E 3105	E 3107	E 3109	E 3111	E 3113	E 3115	E 3117	E 3119	E 3121	E 3125 ⑥⑦	E 3127 Ⓐ	E 3131 ⑥⑦	E 3133 Ⓐ	E 3135 G	E 3135 S	E 3137 Q	E 3139 S	E 3139	E3141 E3147 S	E3141 E3147 S	E3143 E3145 S
0	**Köln Hbf** d.	0513	0613	0713	0813	0913	1013	1113	1213	1313	1413	1513	1613	1619	1713	1720	1813	1813	1913	2013	...	2113	...	2213
18	Opladen d.	0532	0632	0732	0832	0932	1032	1132	1232	1332	1432	1532	1632	1637	1732	1738	1832	1832	1933	2032	...	2132	...	2232
28	Solingen-Ohligs d.	0544	0644	0744	0844	0944	1044	1144	1244	1344	1444	1543	1644	1646	1744	1747	1844	1844	1944	2044	...	2147	...	2244
46	**Wuppertal Hbf** d.	0604	0704	0804	0904	1004	1104	1204	1304	1404	1504	1604	1704	1706	1804	1806	1904	1904	2002	2104	...	2206	...	2304
73	**Hagen 709** d.	0633	0733	0833	0933	1033	1133	1233	1333	1433	1533	1633	1733	1733	1833	1833	1930	1933	2033	2130	2212	2230	2312	2330
86	Schwerte **709** d.	0645	0745	0845	0945	1045	1145	1245	1345	1445	1545	1645	1745	1745	1845	1845	...	1945	2045	...	2222	...	2322	...
102	Unna **709** d.	0658	0758	0858	0958	1058	1158	1258	1358	1458	1558	1658	1758	1758	1858	1858	...	1958	2058	...	2236	...	2336	...
121	**Hamm 709** a.	0712	0812	0912	1012	1112	1212	1312	1412	1512	1612	1712	1812	1812	1912	1912	...	2012	2112	...	2250	...	2356	...
121	**Hamm 709** d.	0713c	0823	...	1023	...	1223	1321h	1423	...	1623	...	1826	1823	...	...	...	2023	...	...	2311	...	...	...
157	**Münster 709** a.	0743c	0848	...	1048	...	1248	1358h	1448	...	1648	...	1851	1848	...	...	...	2048	...	...	2343	...	...	...

	E 3100 ❖	E 3102 ❖	E 6960 Ⓐ	E 3108	E 3110	E 3112	E 3114	E 3116	E 3118	E 3120	E 3122	E 3124	E 3126 ⑥⑦	E 3146 Ⓐ	E 3128	E 3130	E 3132	E 3134 ⑥⑦	E 3134 Ⓐ	E 3136 S	E 3138 S	E 3144 SⒸ	E 3140 Ⓐ	E 3142 S
Münster 709 d.	...	...	...	0505c	...	0710c	...	0910	...	1110	...	1310	...	1414	1510	1614h	1710	...	1814	1910	...	2110	2110	...
Hamm 709 a.	...	...	...	0535c	...	0739c	...	0935	...	1135	...	1335	...	1444	1535	1644h	1735	...	1844	1935	...	2139	2139	...
Hamm 709 d.	...	...	0503	0547c	0647h	0747	0847	0947	1047	1147	1247	1347	1447	1447	1547	1647	1747	1847	1847	1947	2047	2147	2147	2251
Unna **709** d.	...	...	0516	0600c	0700h	0800	0900	1000	1100	1200	1300	1400	1500	1500	1600	1700	1800	1900	1900	2000	2100	2200	2200	2304
Schwerte **709** d.	...	...	0529	0615c	0715h	0815	0915	1015	1115	1215	1315	1415	1515	1515	1615	1715	1815	1915	1915	2015	2115	2215	2215	2317
Hagen 709 d.	0432	0529	0540	0629	0729	0829	0959	1029	1129	1229	1329	1429	1528	1528	1629	1729	1829	1926	1929	2029	2129	2229	2226	2328
Wuppertal Hbf d.	0456	0554	*0620*v	0654	0754	0854	0954	1054	1154	1254	1354	1454	1554	1557	1654	1754	1854	...	1954	2054	2154	2254	2249	...
Solingen-Ohligs d.	0513	0613	*0631*v	0713	0813	0913	1013	1113	1213	1313	1413	1513	1613	1614	1713	1813	1913	...	2013	2113	2213	2313	2317	...
Opladen d.	0522	0622	|	0722	0822	0922	1022	1122	1222	1322	1422	1522	1622	1622	1722	1822	1922	...	2022	2122	2222	2322	2326	...
Köln Hbf a.	0541	0642	*0650*v	0742	0842	0942	1042	1142	1242	1342	1442	1542	1642	1642	1742	1842	1942	...	2042	2142	2242	2344	2344	...

G – Dec. 24, 31.
Q – **Not** Dec. 24.
S – **Not** Dec. 24, 31.
❖ – **Not** Dec. 25, Jan. 1.
c – ⚒ only.
h – Ⓐ only.
v – InterCity supplement payable.

Table 709 MÜNSTER and KÖLN - SIEGEN - FRANKFURT (MAIN)

1, 2 class

km		IR 2411 A🍷	E 3305 L	IR 2413 🍷	E 3307	E 3503	E 3309	IR 2415 🍷	E 3311	E 3505	E 3313	E 3315	IR 2417 🍷	E 3507	E 3317	E 3319	IR 2419 🍷	E 3509	E 3321	E 3323	IR 2511 B🍷	E 3511	E 3325	E 3329
0	**Münster 708** d.	...	...	0610	...	...	...	0810	...	...	...	...	1010	...	...	...	1210	...	...	...	1410	...	...	...
36	Hamm **708** d.	...	...	0631	...	...	...	0831	...	...	...	...	1031	...	...	...	1231	...	...	...	1431	...	...	...
55	Unna **708** d.	...	...	0642	...	...	...	0842	...	...	...	...	1042	...	...	...	1242	...	...	...	1442	...	...	...
71	Schwerte **708** d.	...	...	0653	...	...	...	0853	...	...	...	...	1053	...	...	...	1253	...	...	...	1453	...	...	...
84	**Hagen 708** a.	...	...	0703	...	...	...	0903	...	...	...	...	1103	...	...	...	1303	...	...	...	1503	...	...	...
84	**Hagen** d.	...	...	0710	...	0816	...	0910	...	1016	...	...	1110	1216	...	...	1310	1416	...	...	1510	1616	...	...
123	Werdohl d.	...	...	0738	...	0848	...	0938	...	1048	...	...	1138	1248	...	...	1338	1448	...	...	1538	1648	...	...
168	Siegen Weidenau d.	...	...	0825	...	0943	...	1025	...	1143	...	...	1225	1343	...	...	1425	1544	...	...	1625	1743	...	...
	Köln Hbf 711 d.	...	0614	|	0710	|	0819	|	0919	|	1019	1119	|	|	1219	1319	|	|	1419	1519	|	|	1619	1719
	Troisdorf **711** d.	...	0630	|	0736	|	0836	|	0936	|	1036	1136	|	|	1236	1336	|	|	1436	1536	|	|	1636	1736
	Siegburg d.	...	0634	|	0741	|	0841	|	0941	|	1041	1141	|	|	1241	1341	|	|	1441	1541	|	|	1641	1741
	Betzdorf d.	...	0726	|	0831	|	0931	|	1031	|	1131	1231	|	|	1331	1431	|	|	1531	1631	|	|	1731	1831
	Siegen a.	...	0748	|	0847	0946	0948	|	1048	1146	1148	1248	|	1346	1348	1448	|	1547	1548	1648	|	1743	1748	1848
	Siegen d.	0619	0754	|	*0854*h	...	0954	|	*1054*h	...	1154	...	|	...	1354	...	|	...	1554	...	|	...	1754	...
200	Dillenburg d.	0645	0819	0848	*0919*h	...	1019	1048	*1119*h	...	1219	...	1248	...	1419	...	1448	...	1619	...	1648	...	1819	...
228	Wetzlar **714** d.	0704	0838	0905	*0938*h	...	1038	1105	*1138*h	...	1238	...	1305	...	1438	...	1505	...	1638	...	1705	...	1838	...
241	**Gießen 714** a.	0714	0848	0914	*0947*h	...	1048	1114	*1147*h	...	1248	...	1314	...	1448	...	1514	...	1648	...	1714	...	1848	...
241	**Gießen 730** d.	0721	...	0921	...	...	...	1121	...	...	...	...	1321	...	...	...	1521	...	...	...	1721	...	...	...
297	**Frankfurt (Main) Hbf 730** a.	0804	...	1001	...	...	...	1201	...	...	...	...	1401	...	...	...	1601	...	...	...	1801	...	...	...

A – [12] and 🍷 Gießen (Siegen ⚡) - Frankfurt/Main.
B – [12] and 🍷 Münster (Norddeich Mole May 1 - 27) - Frankfurt/Main.
L – ⚒, **not** Nov. 1.
h – Ⓐ only.
⚡ – ① - ⑥ (**not** Dec. 25 - Jan. 1, Apr. 15 - 17, May 1, **1995**).

Table 709 MÜNSTER and KÖLN - SIEGEN - FRANKFURT (MAIN)

1, 2 class

	IR 2513 🍷	E 3513	E 3333	E 3335	IR 2515 A🍷	E 3515	E 3337 SⒷ	IR 2517 H	E 3339 S	E 3341 Ⓑ
Münster 708 d.	1610	...	...	...	1810	...	...	2010	...	...
Hamm 708 d.	1631	...	...	...	1831	...	...	2031	...	...
Unna 708 d.	1642	...	...	...	1842	...	...	2042	...	...
Schwerte 708 d.	1653	...	...	...	1853	...	...	2053	...	...
Hagen 708 a.	1703	...	...	...	1903	...	...	2103	...	...
Hagen d.	1710	1816	...	...	1910	2016	...	2110	...	...
Werdohl d.	1738	1848	...	...	1938	2048	...	2138	...	...
Siegen Weidenau d.	1825	1943	...	...	2025	2143	...	2225	...	...
Köln Hbf 711 d.	|	|	1819	1919	|	|	2019	|	2113	2219
Troisdorf 711 d.	|	|	1836	1936	|	|	2036	|	2131	2237
Siegburg d.	|	|	1841	1941	|	|	2041	|	2136	2241
Betzdorf d.	|	|	1931	2031	|	|	2131	|	2235	2340
Siegen a.	|	1946	1948	2048	|	2146	2148	2228	2253	2358
Siegen d.	|	...	1954	...	|	...	2154	...	...	...
Dillenburg d.	1848	...	2019	...	2048	...	2219	...	...	...
Wetzlar 714 d.	1905	...	2038	...	2105	...	2238	...	...	...
Gießen 714 a.	1914	...	2048	...	2114	...	2248	...	...	...
Gießen 730 d.	1921	...	...	...	2121	...	...	...	...	...
Frankfurt (Main) Hbf 730 a.	2001	...	...	...	2201	...	...	...	...	...

	IR 2516 K	E 3304 L	E 3308 ❖	IR 2514 🍷	E 3310	E 3504	E 3312	IR 2512 🍷	E 3314
Frankfurt (Main) Hbf 730 d.	...	...	...	0555	...	...	...	0755	...
Gießen 730 a.	...	...	...	0635	...	...	...	0835	...
Gießen 714 d.	...	...	...	0642	0708	...	...	0842	0908
Wetzlar 714 d.	...	...	...	0651	0719	...	...	0851	0919
Dillenburg d.	...	...	...	0707	0741	...	...	0907	0941
Siegen a.	...	...	...	|	0805	...	...	|	1005
Siegen d.	0525	0603	0709	|	0809	0810	0909	|	1009
Betzdorf d.	|	0626	0726	|	0826	|	0926	|	1026
Siegburg d.	|	0716	0815	|	0915	|	1015	|	1115
Troisdorf 711 d.	|	0721	0820	|	0920	|	1020	|	1120
Köln Hbf 711 a.	|	0739	0839	|	0939	|	1039	|	1139
Siegen Weidenau d.	0529	...	...	0729	...	0814	...	0929	...
Werdohl d.	0617	...	...	0817	...	0909	...	1017	...
Hagen a.	0647	...	...	0847	...	0942	...	1047	...
Hagen 708 d.	0654	...	...	0854	...	...	...	1054	...
Schwerte 708 d.	0705	...	...	0905	...	...	...	1105	...
Unna 708 d.	0715	...	...	0915	...	...	...	1115	...
Hamm 708 d.	0729	...	...	0929	...	...	...	1129	...
Münster 708 a.	0748	...	...	0948	...	...	...	1148	...

	E 3506	IR 2510 J	E 3316	E 3318	E 3508	IR 2418 🍷	E 3320	E 3322	E 3512	IR 2416 🍷	E 3324	E 3326	E 3516	E 3328	IR 2414 🍷	E 3330	E 3518	E 3332	IR 2412 B🍷	E 3334	E 3520	E 3334 Ⓑ	IR 2410 M	E3338 E3340 ⑦
Frankfurt (Main) Hbf 730 d.	...	0955	...	...	...	1155	...	...	...	1355	...	...	...	...	1555	...	...	...	1755	...	...	...	1955	...
Gießen 730 a.	...	1035	...	...	...	1235	...	...	...	1435	...	...	...	...	1635	...	...	...	1835	...	...	...	2035	...
Gießen 714 d.	...	1042	...	1108	...	1242	...	1308	...	1442	...	1508	...	*1610*h	1642	1708	...	*1810*h	1842	1908	...	...	2042	2108
Wetzlar 714 d.	...	1051	...	1119	...	1251	...	1319	...	1451	...	1519	...	*1619*h	1651	1719	...	*1819*h	1851	1919	...	...	2051	2119
Dillenburg d.	...	1107	...	1141	...	1307	...	1341	...	1507	...	1541	...	*1641*h	1707	1741	...	*1841*h	1907	1941	...	...	2110	2141
Siegen a.	...	|	...	1205	...	|	...	1405	...	|	...	1605	...	*1705*h	|	1805	...	*1905*h	|	2005	...	...	2135	2205
Siegen d.	1010	|	1109	1209	1210	|	1309	1409	1410	|	1509	1609	1610	1709	|	1809	1810	1909	|	2009	2010	2110	...	2210
Betzdorf d.	|	|	1126	1226	|	|	1326	1426	|	|	1526	1626	|	1726	|	1826	|	1926	|	2026	|	2126	...	2226
Siegburg d.	|	|	1215	1315	|	|	1415	1515	|	|	1615	1714	|	1815	|	1915	|	2015	|	2115	|	2222	...	2318
Troisdorf 711 d.	|	|	1220	1320	|	|	1420	1520	|	|	1620	1720	|	1820	|	1920	|	2021	|	2120	|	2227	...	2323
Köln Hbf 711 a.	|	|	1239	1339	|	|	1439	1539	|	|	1639	1739	|	1839	|	1939	|	2039	|	2139	|	2245	...	2341
Siegen Weidenau d.	1014	1129	...	...	1214	1329	...	...	1414	1529	...	...	1614	...	1729	...	1814	...	1929	...	2014	...	...	...
Werdohl d.	1109	1217	...	...	1309	1417	...	...	1514	1617	...	...	1714	...	1817	...	1909	...	2017	...	2109	...	...	...
Hagen a.	1142	1247	...	...	1342	1447	...	...	1547	1647	...	...	1747	...	1847	...	1942	...	2047	...	2142	...	...	...
Hagen 708 d.	...	1254	...	...	...	1454	...	...	...	1654	...	...	...	...	1854	...	...	...	2054	...	...	...	...	...
Schwerte 708 d.	...	1305	...	...	...	1505	...	...	...	1705	...	...	...	...	1905	...	...	...	2105	...	...	...	...	...
Unna 708 d.	...	1315	...	...	...	1515	...	...	...	1715	...	...	...	...	1915	...	...	...	2115	...	...	...	...	...
Hamm 708 d.	...	1329	...	...	...	1529	...	...	...	1729	...	...	...	...	1929	...	...	...	2129	...	...	...	...	...
Münster 708 a.	...	1348	...	...	...	1548	...	...	...	1748	...	...	...	...	1948	...	...	...	2148	...	...	...	...	...

A – [12] Münster - Frankfurt (Main); 🍷 Münster - Wetzlar.
B – [12] Frankfurt (Main) - Münster; 🍷 Frankfurt (Main) - Schwerte.
H – [12] Münster - Hagen (Siegen ♣); 🍷 Münster - Hagen.
K – [12] and 🍷 Hagen (Siegen ⚡) - Münster; 🍷 Werdohl - Münster.
J – [12] and 🍷 Frankfurt (Main) - Münster (Norddeich May 1 - 27).
L – ⚒, **not** Nov. 1.
M – [12] and 🍷 Frankfurt (Main) - Gießen (Siegen ♣).
h – Ⓐ only.
❖ – **Not** Dec. 25, Jan. 1.
⚡ – ① - ⑥ (**not** Dec. 25 - Jan. 1, Apr. 15 - 17, May 1, **1995**).
♣ – Daily except ⑥ (**not** Dec. 24 - 31, Apr. 14 - 16, Apr. 30, **1995**).
S – **Not** Dec. 24, 31.

Table 710 KÖLN - KOBLENZ - MAINZ

1, 2 class

km		3353	3355 ❖	E 3505	E3509 E3511 ❖		E3513 E3515	E 3517	E 3521	E 3525	E 3529	E 3533	6021	E 3537	E 3541	E 3545	E 3549	E3553 E3555	E 3377 S	E 3557	E 3561 S	E 3383 S	E 3563 ⑥⑦	E 3565 Ⓐ	7367 S
0	**Köln Hbf** d.	...	...	0619	0717	...	0819	0919	1019	1119	1219	1319	...	1419	1519	1619	1717	1819	...	1919	2019	...	2115	2115	2201
35	**Bonn Hbf** d.	...	...	0653	0753	...	0853	0953	1053	1153	1253	1353	...	1453	1553	1653	1753	1853	...	1953	2046	...	2150	2150	2249
55	Remagen d.	...	...	0708	0808		0908	1008	1108	1208	1308	1408	...	1508	1611	1711	1808	1908	...	2008	2103	...	2207	2212	2307
65	Bad Breisig d.	...	...	0717	0817		0917	1017	1117	1217	1317	1417	...	1517	1619	1719	1817	1917	...	2017	2118	...	2215	2220	2315
76	Andernach d.	...	...	0727	0824	...	0924	1024	1124	1224	1324	1424	...	1524	1627	1727	1824	1924	...	2024	2127	...	2222	2228	2324
94	**Koblenz** a.	...	...	0740	0837	...	0937	1037	1137	1237	1337	1437	...	1537	1637	1738	1837	1939	...	2037	2140	...	2234	2240	2340
				E 3357	6011		E 3359	6013	E 3363	6019	E 3365			E 3367	6025	E 3373	6029			6033 S					
94	**Koblenz** d.	0613	0657	0757	0857	...	0957	1057	1157	1256	1357	...	1457	1557	1657	1757	1856	...	2001	2101	...	2220	...	...	...
113	Boppard d.	0630	0713	0810	0913	...	1010	1113	1210	1313	1410	...	1513	1610	1713	1810	1918	...	2017	2117	...	2235	...	...	...
118	Bad Salzig d.	0634	0717	0814	0917	...	1014	1121	1214	1317	1414	...	1517	1614	1717	1814	1922	...	2021	2121	...	2239	...	...	...
128	St Goar d.	0644	0726	0821	0926	...	1021	1126	1221	1326	1421	...	1526	1621	1726	1821	1929	...	2030	2130	...	2246	...	...	...
135	Oberwesel d.	0650	0732	0827	0932	...	1027	1132	1227	1332	1427	...	1532	1627	1732	1827	1935	...	2036	2136	...	2252	...	...	...
141	Bacharach d.	0655	0738	0832	0938	...	1032	1138	1232	1338	1432	...	1538	1632	1738	1832	1940	...	2041	2141	...	2257	...	...	...
155	Bingen Hbf a.	0708	0751	0841	0951	...	1041	1151	1241	1351	1441	...	1551	1641	1751	1841	1952	...	2053	2153	...	...	...	...	...
155	Bingen Hbf d.	0709	0758	0858	0958	...	1058	1158	1300	1358	1458	...	1558	1658	1758	1858	1959	...	2103	...	...	...	...	...	...
156	Bingen Stadt d.	0711	0801	0901	1001	...	1101	1201	1303	1401	1501	...	1601	1701	1801	1901	2002	...	2106	...	...	...	...	...	...
185	**Mainz Hbf** a.	0731	0831	0931	1031	...	1131	1231	1331	1431	1531	...	1631	1731	1831	1931	2031	...	2131	...	...	...	...	...	...

	6002 ❖	E 3352 ❖	E3516 E3518	6008 ⚒	E 3354	E 3354	6010	E3528 E3530	E 3358	6018	E 3360	6024	E3544 E3546	E 3366	6026	E 3372	E3556 E3558	6030	E 3380	E 3564 Ⓑ	7374 S	E 3384	6038 Ⓐ	6040 Ⓐ	6040 SⒸ
Mainz Hbf d.	0528	0642	...	0657	0757	...	0857	...	1027	*1127*	1227	1327	...	1427	1527	1635	...	1727	1827	...	...	1957	2127	2227	2227
Bingen Stadt d.	0558	0704	...	0727	0827	0904	0927	...	1057	*1157*	1304	1357	...	1504	1557	1704	...	1757	1857	...	...	2027	2157	2257	2257
Bingen Hbf a.	0600	0706	...	0729	...	0907	0929	...	1104	*1159*	1307	1359	...	1507	1559	1707	...	1759	1904	...	...	2029	2159	2259	2259
Bingen Hbf d.	0602	0713	...	0806	...	0913	1006	...	1113	1206	1313	1406	...	1513	1606	1713	...	1806	1907	...	...	2043	2200	...	2301
Bacharach d.	0614	0725	...	0819	...	0925	1019	...	1125	1219	1325	1419	...	1525	1619	1723	...	1819	1925	...	...	2055	2212	...	2313
Oberwesel d.	0619	0730	...	0824	...	0930	1024	...	1130	1224	1330	1424	...	1530	1624	1728	...	1824	1930	...	...	2100	2224	...	2318
St Goar d.	0625	0736	...	0830	...	0936	1030	...	1136	1230	1336	1430	...	1536	1630	1735	...	1830	1936	...	...	2106	2230	...	2324
Bad Salzig d.	0634	0743	...	0839	...	0943	1039	...	1143	1239	1343	1439	...	1543	1639	1742	...	1839	1943	...	...	2113	2239	...	2333
Boppard d.	0639	0748	...	0844	...	0948	1044	...	1148	1244	1348	1444	...	1548	1644	1747	...	1844	1948	...	...	2118	2244	...	2338
Koblenz a.	0656	0801	...	0901	...	1001	1101	...	1201	1301	1401	1501	...	1601	1701	1801	...	1901	2001	...	...	2131	2301	...	2354
	E3512 E3514			E3520 E3522		E3524 E3596			E 3532	E 3536	E 3540			E 3548	E3552 E3554			E 3560	E 3562 ⑥			E 3568 S			
Koblenz d.	0717	...	0817	0917	...	1021	...	1121	1221	1317	1421	...	1521	1621	1721	...	1821	1921	2021	2021	2117	2221	...	...	...
Andernach d.	0728	...	0828	0928	...	1032	...	1132	1232	1328	1432	...	1532	1632	1732	...	1832	1932	2032	2032	2134	2232	...	...	...
Bad Breisig d.	0735	...	0835	0935	...	1039	...	1139	1239	1339	1439	...	1539	1639	1739	...	1839	1939	2039	2039	2144	2239	...	...	...
Remagen d.	0749	...	0848	0948	...	1048	...	1148	1248	1348	1448	...	1548	1648	1748	...	1848	1948	2048	2048	2159	2248	...	...	...
Bonn Hbf d.	0809	...	0912	1012	...	1112	...	1212	1312	1412	1512	...	1612	1712	1812	...	1912	2012	2104	2112	2219	2304	...	...	...
Köln a.	0838	...	0938	1038	...	1138	...	1238	1338	1438	1538	...	1638	1738	1838	...	1938	2038	2132	2138	2250	2331	...	...	...

S – **Not** Dec. 24, 31.
❖ – **Not** Dec. 25, Jan. 1.

Table 711 KOLN - KOBLENZ - WIESBADEN

1, 2 class

km		E	E	E	E	E	E	E	E		E	E	E	E	E	E	E	E	E	E	E	E		E	E
		3481	6153	6313	6317	3407	6321	3411	3487	6129	6325	6329	3415	6337	3419	3491	6341	3423	6345	6349	3427	6357	6361	3431	6365
				❖	L		L		Ⓒ	Ⓐ						Ⓒ			L	Ⓑ		Ⓑ	S	Ⓑ	S
0	**Köln Hbf 709** d.	...	...	0636	0713	0813	0913	1013	...	...	1113	1142	1213	1313	1413	...	1513	1613	1636	1713	1813	1913	*2019*	2122	2213
21	Troisdorf **709** d.	...	...	0653	0730	0831	0930	1031	...	...	1130	1159	1231	1330	1431	...	1530	1631	1653	1730	1831	1930	2039	2140	2233
30	Bonn Beuel d.	...	...	0703	0740	0838	0940	1038	...	...	1140	1209	1238	1340	1438	...	1540	1640	1703	1740	1838	1940	2048	2149	2242
38	Königswinter d.	...	...	0712	0749	0844	0949	1044	...	...	1149	1218	1244	1349	1444	...	1549	1646	1712	1749	1845	1949	2057	2159	2251
43	Bad Honnef d.	...	...	0718	0755	0849	0955	1049	...	...	1155	1224	1249	1355	1449	...	1555	1651	1718	1755	1851	1955	2106	2204	2257
53	Linz am Rhein d.	...	...	0728	0805	0858	1005	1058	...	...	1205	1234	1258	1405	1458	...	1605	1700	1728	1805	1903	2005	2120	2214	2307
60	Bad Hönningen d.	...	...	0735	0812	0904	1012	1104	...	...	1212	1241	1304	1412	1504	...	1612	1706	1735	1812	1910	2012	2126	...	...
76	Neuwied d.	...	...	0749	0826	0917	1026	1117	...	...	1226	1255	1317	1426	1517	...	1626	1719	1749	1826	1923	2026	2140	...	...
91	**Koblenz** a.	...	...	0802	0841	0931	1041	1131	...	...	1241	1308	1330	1441	1531	...	1641	1732	1802	1841	1941	2041	2156	...	...
				E		E							E						E		E				
				3483	6155	3485	6157	6127			6159	6109	3489	6161	3499		6163		3493	6165	3495	6167			
				⚒				Ⓐ				Ⓐ			Ⓐ		Ⓒ				Ⓐ				
91	**Koblenz 713** d.	0613	0655	0813	0858	1013	1058	1158	1213	1228	1258	1318	1413	1458	1608	1613	1658	...	1813	1928	2013	2128	...	...	...
96	Niederlahnstein **713** d.	0619	0704	0819	0904	1019	1104	1204	1219	1234	1304	1324	1419	1504	1614	1619	1704	...	1819	1934	2019	2134	...	...	...
102	Braubach d.	0601	0711	0825	0911	1025	1111	1211	1225	1241	1311	1331	1425	1511	1621	1625	1711	...	1825	1941	2025	2141	...	...	...
114	Kamp-Bornhofen d.	0633	0722	0835	0922	1035	1122	1222	1235	1252	1322	1342	1435	1522	1632	1635	1722	...	1835	1952	2035	2151	...	...	...
126	St Goarshausen d.	0643	0733	0843	0933	1043	1133	1233	1243	1303	1333	1353	1443	1533	1643	1643	1733	...	1843	2003	2043	2202	...	...	...
137	Kaub d.	0651	0741	0849	0941	|	1141	1241	1251	1311	1341	...	|	1541	1651	1651	1741	...	1851	2011	2051	2210	...	...	...
143	Lorch d.	0656	0748	0856	0948	1056	1148	1248	1256	1318	1348	...	1456	1548	1656	1656	1748	...	1856	2017	2056	2216	...	...	...
151	Aßmannshausen d.	0701	0754	|	0954	|	1154	1254	|	1333	1354	...	|	1554	|	|	1754	...	|	2024	|	2222	...	...	...
155	Rüdesheim d.	0705	0758	0905	0958	1105	1158	1258	1305	1338	1358	...	1505	1558	1705	1705	1758	...	1905	2028	2105	2226	...	...	...
185	**Wiesbaden Hbf** a.	0729	0829	0928	1028	1128	1229	1330	1328	1409	1428	...	1528	1628	1728	1728	1829	...	1928	2100	2128	2257	...	...	...

		E			E		E		E		E		E	E		E	E		E	E		E			
	6102	6314	6118	6120	3480	6152	3482	6154	3484	6124	3418	6186	3486	6338	6158	3488	3490	6160	3492	6346	6162	3494	6164	6196	6108
	Ⓐ	L	⚒	⚒						Ⓐ		Ⓐ					Ⓐ	Ⓒ		S					
Wiesbaden Hbf d.	...	...	0610	0655	0730	0830	0930	1030	1130	1155	...	1304	1330	...	1430	1530	1630	1630	1730	...	1830	1930	2030	2140	2304
Rüdesheim d.	...	...	0646	0735	0753	0901	0953	1101	1153	1228	...	1335	1353	...	1501	1553	1653	1701	1753	...	1901	1953	2101	2211	2335
Aßmannshausen d.	...	...	0652	0739	|	0906	|	1106	|	1232	...	1339	|	...	1506	|	|	1706	|	...	1906	|	2106	...	...
Lorch d.	...	...	0659	0745	0802	0912	1002	1112	1202	1238	...	1345	1402	...	1512	1602	1702	1712	1802	...	1912	2002	2112	...	...
Kaub d.	...	...	0706	0752	0807	0918	|	1118	1207	1245	...	1352	|	...	1518	1607	1707	1718	1807	...	1918	2007	2118	...	...
St Goarshausen d.	0557	...	0714	0801	0815	0927	1015	1127	1215	1254	...	1401	1415	...	1527	1615	1715	1727	1815	...	1927	2015	2127	...	...
Kamp-Bornhofen d.	0607	...	0724	...	0824	0937	1024	1137	1225	1304	...	...	1424	...	1537	1624	1726	1737	1824	...	1937	2024	2137	...	...
Braubach d.	0618	...	0736	...	0834	0948	1034	1148	1235	1316	...	...	1434	...	1548	1634	1737	1748	1834	...	1948	2034	2148	...	...
Niederlahnstein **713** d.	0625	...	0744	...	0842	0955	1042	1155	1242	1324	...	...	1442	...	1555	1642	1745	1755	1842	...	1955	2042	2155	...	...
Koblenz 713 a.	0634	...	0751	...	0849	1003	1049	1203	1249	1331	...	...	1449	...	1603	1649	1752	1803	1849	...	2003	2049	2204	...	...
	E		E		E	E	E	E	E				E			E	E	E			E	E			
	3402		3406		6322	3410	6326	3414	6330				6334			6342	3426	3426			3428	6350			
	L																					S			
Koblenz d.	0600	0652	0826	...	0917	1026	1117	1226	1317	...	1426	...	1517	1552	...	1717	1826	1826	...	1917	2017	2124	...	...	...
Neuwied d.	0612	0705	0838	...	0930	1038	1130	1238	1330	...	1438	...	1530	1605	...	1730	1838	1838	...	1930	2038	2137	...	...	...
Bad Hönningen d.	0625	0719	0852	...	0944	1052	1144	1251	1344	...	1452	...	1544	1619	...	1744	1852	1852	...	1943	2052	2150	...	...	...
Linz am Rhein d.	0631	0726	0857	...	0951	1057	1151	1257	1351	...	1457	...	1551	1626	...	1751	1857	1857	...	1950	2057	2157	...	...	...
Bad Honnef d.	0641	0736	0902	...	1001	1107	1201	1307	1401	...	1507	...	1601	1636	...	1801	1907	1907	...	2000	2107	2207	...	...	...
Königswinter d.	0645	0742	0911	...	1007	1111	1207	1311	1407	...	1511	...	1607	1642	...	1807	1911	1911	...	2004	2111	2213	...	...	...
Bonn Beuel d.	0651	0751	0918	...	1016	1118	1216	1318	1416	...	1518	...	1616	1651	...	1816	1918	1918	...	2010	2118	2222	...	...	...
Troisdorf **709** d.	0701	0801	0926	...	1026	1126	1226	1326	1426	...	1526	...	1626	1701	...	1826	1926	1926	...	2017	2126	2232	...	...	...
Köln Hbf 709 a.	0723	0823	0945	...	1045	1145	1245	1345	1445	...	1545	...	1645	1720	...	1845	1945	1945	...	2039	2145	2253	...	...	...

L – ⚒, **not** Nov. 1. S – **Not** Dec. 24, 31. ❖ – **Not** Dec. 25, Jan. 1.

Table 712 KÖLN - GEROLSTEIN - TRIER

1, 2 class

km		E3603	E	E	E	E	E3645	E		E
		E3605	3613	3621	3629	3637	E3647	3649	6555	3653
		❖						Ⓐ	Ⓐ	S
0	**Köln Hbf** d.	0721	0923	1123	1323	1523	1720	1823	...	1923
41	Euskirchen d.	0758	0958	1158	1358	1558	1758	1858	...	1958
81	Blankenheim d.	0832	1032	1232	1432	1632	1832	1935	...	2032
113	**Gerolstein** d.	0901	1101	1301	1501	1701	1901	2008	2031	2059
143	Bitburg-Erdorf d.	0928	1128	1328	1528	1728	1928	...	2105	...
182	**Trier** a.	1004	1204	1404	1604	1804	2004	...	2152	...

	E	E	E	E	E	E	E	E	
	3614	3618	3622	3630	3638	3646	3652	3656	6552
	⚒	⚒					S	K	S⚒
Trier d.	0744	...	0949	1151	1341	1546	1743	1951	2050
Bitburg-Erdorf d.	0826	...	1027	1227	1428	1627	1827	2027	2134
Gerolstein d.	0856	0945	1056	1256	1456	1656	1855	2056	2208
Blankenheim d.	0924	1021	1124	1324	1524	1727	1924	2124	...
Euskirchen d.	0959	1059	1159	1359	1559	1801	1959	2159	...
Köln Hbf a.	1034	1134	1234	1434	1634	1834	2034	2235	...

K – ⑦, **not** Dec. 25, Apr. 16, 30. S – **Not** Dec. 24, 31. ❖ – **Not** Dec. 25, Jan. 1.

Table 713 KOBLENZ - LIMBURG - GIESSEN

1, 2 class

km				E		E			E					E			E		E		E		E		
		6983	6911	3905	6919	3907	6923	6925	3909	6917	6929	6991	6933	3913	6937	3915	3917	6943	3921	6949	3925	6957	3929	6961	6965
		Ⓐ	⚒	Ⓐ		⚒			⚒	Ⓒ	Ⓐ	Ⓐ	Ⓐ		Ⓒ	Ⓐ			Ⓑ			Ⓑ	⑦	⚒	Ⓐ
0	**Koblenz 711** d.	...	...	0733	0753	0843	0913	0953	1043	1113	1113	...	1203	1243	1313	1333	1443	1513	1643	1713	1843	1913	2043	2053	2153
5	Niederlahnstein **711** d.	...	...	0739	0759	0849	0919	0959	1049	1119	1119	...	1209	1249	1319	1339	1449	1519	1649	1719	1849	1919	2049	2101	2159
18	Bad Ems d.	...	...	0756	0816	0902	0936	1016	1102	1136	1136	...	1226	1302	1336	1356	1502	1536	1702	1736	1902	1936	2102	2116	2216
26	Nassau d.	...	...	0805	0825	0910	0945	1025	1110	1145	1145	...	1235	1310	1345	1405	1510	1545	1710	1745	1910	1945	2110	2125	2225
49	Diez d.	...	...	0833	0852	0932	1012	1052	1132	1212	1212	...	1302	1332	1412	1433	1532	1612	1732	1812	1932	2012	2132	2152	2252
52	**Limburg** d.	0634	0719	0839	0857	0939	1019	1057	1139	1219	1217	1234	1309	1339	1419	1439	1539	1619	1739	1819	1939	2019	2139	2157	2257
55	Eschofen d.	0638	0723	0843	...	0943	1023	...	1143	1223	...	1239	1313	1343	1457	1443	1543	1623	1743	1823	1943	2023	2143	...	...
81	Weilburg d.	0702	0757	0907	...	1007	1057	...	1207	1257	...	1312	1347	1407	1500	1507	1607	1657	1807	1857	2007	2057	2207	...	...
104	Wetzlar **709** d.	0728	0828	0928	...	1028	1128	...	1228	1328	...	1338	1413	1428	1528	1528	1628	1725	1828	1925	2028	2128	2228	...	...
117	**Gießen 709** a.	0739	0839	0939	...	1039	1139	...	1239	1339	...	1349	1424	1439	1539	1539	1639	1734	1839	1934	2039	2139	2239	...	...

						E			E		E				E		E			E		E		E	
	6910	6916	6918	6920	6920	3902	6926	6926	3904	6932	3906	6988	6940	6942	3910	6948	3914	6982	6954	3918	6958	3920	6992	3924	6994
	⚒	Ⓐ	Ⓐ	⑥	⑦	⚒	⚒	⑦	⚒			Ⓐ	Ⓒ	Ⓐ				Ⓐ					Ⓑ	⑦	Ⓐ
Gießen 709 d.	...	0525	0600	0615	...	0715	0815	...	0915	1015	1115	1155	1215	1235	1315	1415	1515	1545	1615	1715	1815	1915	2015	2115	2115
Wetzlar **709** d.	...	0535	0610	0625	...	0725	0825	...	0925	1025	1125	1205	1225	1245	1325	1425	1525	1555	1625	1725	1825	1925	2025	2125	2125
Weilburg d.	...	0556	0636	0651	...	0744	0851	...	0944	1051	1144	1231	1251	1311	1344	1451	1544	1621	1651	1744	1851	1944	2051	2144	2150
Eschofen d.	...	0628	0713	0723	...	0808	0923	...	1008	1123	1208	1303	1323	1343	1408	1520	1608	1653	1723	1808	1923	2008	2123	2208	...
Limburg d.	0550	0640	0720	0730	0730	0814	0930	0930	1014	1130	1214	1310	1330	1350	1414	1530	1614	1656	1730	1814	1930	2014	2128	2214	...
Diez d.	0554	0644	0724	0734	0734	0818	0934	0934	1018	1134	1218	1314	1334	1354	1418	1534	1618	...	1734	1818	1934	2018	...	2218	...
Nassau d.	0620	0710	0750	0800	0800	0840	1000	1000	1040	1200	1240	1340	1400	1420	1440	1600	1640	...	1800	1840	2000	2040	...	2240	...
Bad Ems d.	0628	0718	0758	0808	0808	0848	1008	1008	1048	1208	1248	1348	1408	1428	1448	1608	1648	...	1811	1848	2008	2048	...	2248	...
Niederlahnstein **711** d.	0648	0738	0818	0828	0828	0900	1028	1028	1101	1228	1300	1408	1428	1448	1500	1628	1700	...	1828	1900	2028	2100	...	2300	...
Koblenz 711 a.	0655	0745	0825	0835	0835	0907	1035	1035	1107	1235	1307	1415	1435	1455	1507	1635	1707	...	1835	1907	2035	2107	...	2307	...

Table 714 — KÖLN - KOBLENZ - MAINZ (Rhein Ship Services)

Operator: Köln - Düsseldorfer Deutsche Rheinschiffahrt AG, Frankenwerft 15, 50667 Köln. ☎ 02 21 20 88 318 or 02 21 20 88 319.   Fax: 02 21 20 88 229

Summer service only (April 1 - October 29, 1995).   (See note ▲ below for exceptions).

Station	37 Z/	33 S	31 S	3 B	J	17 C	11 J	27 D	29 E	13 S	47 H	19 K	21 O	7 V	S	25 J
Köln Rheingarten ...... d.	0900											0930	0930	0930		1030
Bonn .... d.	0940							0815	0815		0945	1210	1210	1210		1310
Königswinter .... d.	0955							0900	0900		1030	1310	1310	1310		1410
Bad Honnef .... d.	│							0920	0920		1050	1330	1330	1330		1430
Remagen .... d.	1010							0955	0955		1125	1405	1405	1405		1505
Linz am Rhein .... d.	1015							1015	1015		1145	1425	1425	1425		1525
Bad Breisig .... d.	1025			0830				1045	1145		1215	1455		1455		1555
Bad Hönningen .... d.	│			0835				1050	1050		1220	1500		1500		1600
Andernach .... d.	1035			0920				1135	1135		1305			1550		1645
Neuwied .... d.	│			0940				1155	1155		1325					1705
Koblenz .... a.	1100			1055				1325	1325							1825
Koblenz .... d.	1105		0900	1100		1230	1230	1330	1330	1400					1800	
Winningen (Mosel) ...... d.									1440							
Niederlahnstein .... d.	│		0930	1130		1255	1255			1430					1825	
Braubach .... d.	│		1000	1200		1325	1325	1430		1500					1855	
Boppard .... d.	1130	0900	1050	1250		1410	1410	1515		1550					1925	
Kamp-Bornhofen .... d.	│	0910	1100	1300		1420	1420			1600						
Bad Salzig .... d.	│	0920	1110	1310		1430	1430			1610						
St Goarshausen .... d.	│	1010	1200	1400	1500	1520	1530			1700						
St Goar .... d.	1150	1015	1205	1405	1505	1525	1535			1705						
Oberwesel .... d.	│	1045	1230	1430	1530	1550	1600			1730						
Kaub .... d.	│	1100	1245	1445	1545	1605	1615			1745						
Bacharach .... d.	1210	1120	1305	1505	1605	1625	1635			1805						
Lorch .... d.	│	x	x	x	x	x	x			x						
Aßmannshausen .... d.	│	1230	1400	1600	1700	1720	1730			1900						
Bingen .... d.	1230	1255	1430	1630	1730	1750	1800			1930						
Rüdesheim .... d.	1235	1310	1440	1640	1740	1800	1810			1940						
Eltville .... d.	│				1750	1850	1910									
Wiesbaden Biebrich ..... d.	1305				1835	1935	1955									
Mainz .... a.	1315				1900	2000	2015									

Summer service only (April 1 - October 29, 1995).   (See note ▲ below for exceptions).

Station	36 Z/	10 J	6 C	20 P	24 O	24 K	2 G	2 A	2 V	16 H	2 J	26 D	26 E	32 S	18 J	30 F	30 R
Mainz .... d.	1425						0900	0900	0900	1000	1000						
Wiesbaden Biebrich ..... d.	1430						0925	0925	0925	1020	1020						
Eltville .... d.	│						0950	0950	0950	1040	1040						
Rüdesheim .... d.	1500	0900	0900	1000			1045	1045	1045	1130	1130			1400		1550	1620
Bingen .... d.	1505	0910	0915	1015			1100	1100	1100	1145	1145			1415		1605	1635
Aßmannshausen .... d.	│	0925	0930	1030			1115	1115	1115	1200	1200			1430		1620	1650
Lorch .... d.	│	x	x	x			x	x	x	x	x			x		x	x
Bacharach .... d.	│	0955	1000	1100			1145	1145	1145	1230	1230			1505		1650	1720
Kaub .... d.	│	1005	1010	1110			1155	1155	1155	1245	1245			1515		1705	1735
Oberwesel .... d.	│	1015	1025	1125			1205	1205	1205	1255	1255			1525		1715	1745
St Goar .... d.	1540	1035	1045	1145			1230	1230	1230	1315	1315			1550		1730	1800
St Goarshausen .... d.	1540	1045	1055	1155			1240	1240	1240	1325	1325			1600		1740	1810
Bad Salzig .... d.	│		1120	1220			1305	1305	1305	1350				1625		1800	1830
Kamp-Bornhofen .... d.	1555	1115	1130	1230			1315	1315	1315	1400		1550		1635		1810	1840
Boppard .... d.	1555	1120	1140	1240			1330	1330	1330	1410		1615		1645		1820	1850
Braubach .... d.	│	1145	1210	1310			1355		1355			1645		1715		1850	1920
Niederlahnstein .... d.	│		1240	1340			1425		1425					1735		1910	1910
Winningen (Mosel) ...... d.													1600				
Koblenz .... a.	1615	1220	1250	1350			1455		1455			1700	1700	1755		1930	2000
Koblenz .... d.	1620						1505		1505			1705	1705	1830			
Neuwied .... d.	│					1425	1550		1550			1750	1750	1915			
Andernach .... d.	1635					1440	1555	1605	1605			1805	1805	1930			
Bad Hönningen .... d.	│				1510	1510	1625	1630	1630			1830	1830	1955			
Bad Breisig .... d.	1650				1515	1515	1630	1635	1635			1840	1840	2000			
Linz am Rhein .... d.	1655			1435	1535	1535	1655	1655	1705			1905	1905				
Remagen .... d.	1700			1450	1550	1550	1710	1710	1715			1915	1915				
Bad Honnef .... d.	│			1515	1615	1615	1735	1735	1740			1940	1940				
Königswinter .... d.	1720			1530	1630	1630	1750	1750	1800			2000	2000				
Bonn .... d.	1730			1600	1700	1700	1820	1820	1830			2030	2015				
Köln Rheingarten .... a.	1805			1730	1830	1830v	1950		2000								

A – Apr. 14 - 30, Oct. 4 - 8.
B – May 1 - Oct. 3.
C – Apr. 14 - July 1, Aug. 29 - Oct. 8.
D – ①⑦ May 1 - Oct. 3.
E – ⑦ July 2 - Aug. 28.
F – Oct. 4 - 29.
G – May 1 - July 1, Aug. 29 - Oct. 3. Extended on ⑦ to Köln.

H – May 1 - July 1, Aug. 29 - Oct. 3.
J – July 2 - Aug. 28.
K – Apr. 13 - 30, July 2 - Aug. 28, Oct. 4 - 22.
O – ⑤⑥ May 1 - July 1, Aug. 29 - Oct. 3.
P – Apr. 1 - 13, July 2 - Aug. 28, Oct. 9 - 29.
R – Apr. 1 - Oct. 3.
S – ①②③④⑦ May 1 - July 1, Aug. 29 - Oct. 3.
V – ①②③④⑦ May 1 - July 1, Aug. 29 - Oct. 3.

Z – ②③④⑤⑥⑦ Apr. 14 - Oct. 22.
v – ⑦ only.
x – Calls at Lorch are by request only.
/ – Express services operated by Hydrofoils Rheinpfeil and Rheinjet. Higher fare applies.
▲ – Restricted service on May 6, July 1, Aug. 12, Sep. 9, 16 (enquire locally).

Table 715 — FRANKFURT FLUGHAFEN ✈

Local S-Bahn services run daily, every 20 - 30 minutes from early morning to late evening, (typically 0500-2330) linking **Frankfurt (Main) Hbf, Frankfurt Flughafen ✈, Mainz** and **Wiesbaden**. These services are recommended for use by airport passengers travelling within this area - ie. not requiring InterCity connections to other parts of Germany. Stops are more freuquent so these trains are more useful for short journeys for which a supplement is payable on faster **InterCity** services. The most important routes are shown below - **time taken to travel between stations** is shown in figures alongside the station name. For longer distance travel, on **InterCity** trains carrying supplements, see the tables indicated at the bottom of this panel.

LINE **S 14**   Frankfurt (Main) Hbf - Frankfurt Flughafen ✈ (9) - Rüsselsheim (22) - Mainz (35) - Wiesbaden (48).

LINE **S 15**   Frankfurt (Main) Hbf - Frankfurt Flughafen ✈.

From **Frankfurt (Main) Hbf** at: 0414, 0434, 0454 and every 20 minutes to 2354. From **Frankfurt Flughafen** ✈ at: 0433, 0453, 0513 and every 20 minutes to 2353, also 0033. Journey time 11 minutes.   Services may be reduced on ⑥⑦, also Dec. 24, 31 and holidays.

Non-stop Airport Expresses:

From **Frankfurt Flughafen** ✈ direct to Stuttgart Hbf: 0916 (**IC901**), 1316 (**IC903**), 1716 (**IC905**), 2129 (**IC907**).
From **Stuttgart Hbf** direct to **Frankfurt Flughafen** ✈ : 0637 (**IC900**), 1105 (**IC902**), 1505 (**IC904**), 1905 (**IC906**).   All trains convey ♀. Journey time: 1 hour 25 minutes.

For **InterCity** services from Frankfurt Flughafen ✈ to Bonn, Köln, Düsseldorf, Essen, Dortmund, Bremen and Hamburg - see Table 650.
For **InterCity** services from Frankfurt Flughafen ✈ to Würzburg, Nürnberg, Regensburg, Passau, Linz and Wien - see Table 740.

There are no **InterCity** services running **directly** from Frankfurt Flughafen ✈ to München, Mannheim, Karlsruhe, Offenburg, Freiburg, Basel SBB or other destinations in Switzerland and Italy. Passengers must change at Frankfurt (Main) Hbf for München and at Frankfurt (Main) Hbf **or** Mainz for other destinations, whichever offers the best connection; it is often quicker via **Mainz**.

Table 717 — FRANKFURT/MAIN and MAINZ - WIESBADEN
1, 2 class

Rail service Frankfurt/Main - Wiesbaden and v.v. *41 km.* Journey time: 30 minutes by InterCity, 42 minutes by S-Bahn. **NOTE** : S - Bahn trains use the underground platforms at Frankfurt.

From Frankfurt/Main Hbf: Inter-City services with supplement - (seat reservations not possible) at 0653, 0853, 1053, 1253, 1453, 1653, 1853.
Other S-Bahn services are available every 20 minutes (less frequently on ⑥⑦) between 0518 and 2118, 2218, 2318, 0018.
From Wiesbaden: Inter-City services with supplement - (seat reservations not possible) at 0735, 0935, 1135, 1335, 1535, 1735, 1935.
Other S-Bahn services are available every 20 minutes (less frequently on ⑥⑦) between 0447 and 1907, 1927 Ⓐ, 2007, 2107, 2207, 2307, 0007.

- -

Rail service Mainz - Wiesbaden and v.v. *10 km.* Journey time: 11 minutes.

From Mainz: Inter-City services with supplement - (seat reservations not possible) at 0821 and hourly until 2021, 2120, 2220 (daily except ⑥ (not Dec. 24 - 31, Apr. 14 - 16, Apr. 30, **1995**),
2320 (daily except ⑥ (not Dec. 24 - 31, Apr. 14 - 16, Apr. 30, **1995**).
From Wiesbaden: Inter-City services with supplement - (seat reservations not possible) at 0629, 0729, 0751, 0856 and hourly until 1956.
Other S-Bahn and local services run between Mainz and Wiesbaden and v.v. at frequent intervals on ① - ⑤, reduced to approximately 30 minutes on ⑥⑦.

- -

Table 720 — KOBLENZ - LUXEMBOURG and SAARBRÜCKEN
1, 2 class except where shown

Block 1

km	Station	E 5807	E 3753	E 3755	E 3757	3032	IR 2265	E 3953	3034 (2)	3036	IR 2434	IR 461	E 3955	3038	IR 2538	3040	E 3959	3044	IR 2432	3185
	(symbols)	L	Ⓐ	Ⓐ	L	L	◆		✗		◆		①–⑥		◆		◆		◆	
	Köln Hbf 650 d.											0611			0811				1011	
0	Koblenz d.						0558					0719	0817		0919			1017	1119	
47	Cochem d.						0632					0752	0851		0952			1051	1152	
59	Bullay d.						0640					0801	0859		1001			1059	1201	
76	Wittlich d.				0553d		0655					0814	0912		1014			1112	1214	
112	Trier a.				0621d		0721					0839	0936		1039			1136	1239	
112	Trier d.	0428	0525	0547	0622	0630	0735	0647	0730	0825	0840	0848	0938	0942	1041	1044	1138	1225	1241	1244
126	Wasserbillig ⛑ ▲ d.					0650			0750	0839	0856			0958		1058		1239	1256	
163	Luxembourg a.					0722			0818	0905	0923			1024		1124		1305	1323	
135	Saarburg d.	0448	0544	0613	0641		0703	0753					0956				1156			1300
161	Merzig d.	0510	0606	0641	0703		0722	0813				0922	1017		1115		1217			1322
177	Saarlouis d.	0528	0621	0656	0716		0732	0827				0932	1029		1126		1229			1335
200	Saarbrücken a.	0554	0642	0718	0734		0748	0845				0948	1045		1142		1245			1354

Block 2

Station	E 3963	IR 3046	2536	E 3048	3967	E 3050	IR 2336	E 3052	3971	3054	IR 2430	3191	E 3973	3058	IR 2334	E 3977	3062	IR 2530	E 3979
(symbols)		♀	♀				♀				♀	S		S		S		◆	®
Köln Hbf 650 d.			1211								1611						1811	2011	
Koblenz d.		1217	1319		1417		1519		1617		1719			1817	1919		2017	2119	2219
Cochem d.		1251	1352		1451		1552		1651		1752			1851	1952		2051	2152	2255
Bullay d.		1259	1401		1459		1601		1659		1801			1859	2001		2100	2201	2303
Wittlich d.		1312	1414		1512		1614		1714		1814			1912	2014		2112	2214	2315
Trier a.		1336	1439		1536		1639		1736		1839			1936	2039		2136	2239	2341
Trier d.	1338	1342	1441	1444	1538	1542	1641	1644	1738	1742	1841	1845	1938	1946	2041	2138	2144	2241	2341
Wasserbillig ⛑ ▲ d.	1358		1458			1556				1800				2000		2158		2355	
Luxembourg d.	1426		1524			1622				1826				2026		2224		0022	
Saarburg d.		1356		1556					1756		1902		1956				2156		2258
Merzig d.		1417		1515			1617		1715		1817		1926		2017		2115	2217	2317
Saarlouis d.		1429		1526			1629		1726		1829		1939		2029		2126	2229	2328
Saarbrücken a.		1445		1542			1645		1742		1846		1958		2045		2142	2245	2344

Block 3

Station	E 3950	E 3952	E 3954	3029	2531	3031 (2)	3033	IR 3956	3035	2337	3037	3960	3174	2431	3041	3964	3043	2537	3045	3968
(symbols)	Ⓐ	L		①–⑥	⑦	◆ L		❖		♀			S	♀		S		♀		®
Saarbrücken d.					0613		0712		0815		0912		1000		1112		1215			1312
Saarlouis d.					0628		0728		0830		0928		1018		1128		1230			1328
Merzig d.					0638		0740		0840		0940		1031		1140		1240			1340
Saarburg d.					0658		0800				1000		1052		1200					1400
Luxembourg d.			0537	0624			0637		0730		0830	0930		1033	1130		1230		1328	
Wasserbillig ⛑ ▲ d.			0604	0651			0704		0800		0857	0957		1100	1157		1257		1355	
Trier a.			0618	0710	0715	0725	0813	0819	0910	0915	1010	1019		1110	1115	1210	1219	1310	1315	1408 1419
Trier d.	0413	0500	0620		0717		0821		0917		1021		1110	1117		1221		1317		1421
Wittlich d.	0436	0524	0643		0741		0844		0941		1044		1141		1244		1317			1444
Bullay d.	0449	0536	0656		0754		0857		0954		1057		1154		1257		1354			1457
Cochem d.	0457	0546			0803		0905		1003		1105		1203		1305		1403			1505
Koblenz a.	0535	0625	0740		0837		0941		1037		1141		1237		1341		1437			1541
Köln Hbf 650 a.			0945						1145				1345				1545			

Block 4

Station	3178	2433	3047	3049	E 3972	7469 (2)	3051	IR 2539	3053	E 3976	3057	IR 2437	3057	E 3978	IR 2264	2435	3982	5862	IR 2266	3846	5868
(symbols)	◆	♀				✗ Ⓐ		♀ S	S			♀		◆	®	◆	S ®	◆	®	®	®
Saarbrücken d.	1400				1512			1615		1712			1815		1912	2010	2113	2130	2210	2215	2330
Saarlouis d.	1418				1528			1630		1728			1830		1928	2025	2130	2152	2225	2234	2352
Merzig d.	1431				1540			1640		1740			1840		1940	2035	2143	2207	2235	2255	0007
Saarburg d.	1452				1600					1800			2000				2204		2254	2316	
Luxembourg d.		1433	1445	1530			1630		1719		1830	1930			2033						
Wasserbillig ⛑ ▲ d.		1500	1512	1557			1657		1748		1857	1957			2100						
Trier a.	1510	1515	1525	1613	1619	1710	1715	1807	1819	1910	2013	2019	2109	2115	2224				2311	2336	
Trier d.	1517				1621	1631		1717	1821		1917			2021	2117						
Wittlich d.	1541				1644	1707		1741	1844		1941			2046	2141						
Bullay d.	1554				1657	1722		1754	1857		1954			2059	2154						
Cochem d.	1603				1705	1734		1803	1905		2003			2107	2203						
Koblenz a.	1637				1741	1825		1837	1941		2037			2141	2237						
Köln Hbf 650 a.	1745					1945															

NOTES (LISTED BY TRAIN NUMBERS)

◆ –
R461 – 🚉 and ⛑ Trier - Landeck.
R2264 – 🚉 and ⛑ Friedrichshafen Stadt - Trier.
R2265 – 🚉 and ⛑ Trier (Saarbrücken on Dec. 25, Jan. 1) - Friedrichshafen Stadt.
R2266 – 🚉 Friedrichshafen Stadt - Trier. Not Dec. 24, 31.
R2334 – 🚉 and ⛑ Rostock (Binz on ⑥ also Apr. 14, May 27, **1995**) - Saarbrücken
⛑ Rostock - Merzig.
R2336 – 🚉 and ⛑ Rostock (Stralsund ⚡) - Saarbrücken.
R2337 – 🚉 and ⛑ Saarbrücken - Stralsund (Rostock on Dec. 24, 31).
R2430/1 – 🚉 and ⛑ Cuxhaven - Luxembourg and v.v.
R2432 – 🚉 and ⛑ Münster (Bremerhaven ⚡) - Luxembourg.
R2433 – 🚉 and ⛑ Luxembourg - Münster.
R2434 – 🚉 and ⛑ Köln (Trier on Dec. 25, Jan. 1) - Luxembourg.
R2435 – 🚉 and ⛑ Luxembourg - Koblenz (Trier on Dec. 24, 31).

IR2530 – 🚉. Cuxhaven - Trier (Saarbrücken ♣).
IR2531 – 🚉 and ⛑ Trier (Saarbrücken ⚡) - Cuxhaven.
IR2536 – 🚉 and ⛑ Cuxhaven - Saarbrücken.
IR2537 – 🚉 and ⛑ Saarbrücken - Münster (Bremerhaven ♣).
IR2538/39 – 🚉 and ⛑ Münster - Saarbrücken and v.v.
E3953 – Ⓐ, not Nov. 1 Koblenz - Trier; daily Trier - Saarbrücken.
L – ✗, not Nov. 1.
S – Not Dec. 24, 31.
d – ⑥ only.
❖ – Not Dec. 25, Jan. 1.
⚡ – ① - ⑤ (not Dec. 25 - Jan. 1, Apr. 15 - 17, May 1, **1995**).
✗ – Daily except ⑥ (not Dec. 24 - 31, Apr. 14 - 16, Apr. 30, **1995**).
▲ – Ticket point is Igel.

11

Table 721 MAINZ - IDAR OBERSTEIN - SAARBRÜCKEN

1, 2 class

km		4308 L	3862 Ⓐ	3742 L	3744 L	3400 ❖	3402 L	3404	3406 L	3408	3412 L	3414	3416	3420	3426	3428 Ⓐ	3430	3432 Ⓐ	3434 S	3436 S	3438 Ⓑ	4396 ⑦	4394 Ⓐ	3746 ⑦
0	**Mainz** d.	...	...	...	...	0734	0835	0935	1035	1135	1235	1335	1435	1535	1628	1706	1735	1806	1835	1935	2035	...	...	...
41	Bad Kreuznach d.	...	...	0535	0643	0810	0911	1010	1111	1210	1310	1410	1511	1610	1710	1741	1810	1840	1911	2010	2110	...	...	2136
92	Idar Oberstein d.	...	...	0631	0736	0852	0951	1052	1151	1252	1352	1452	1551	1652	1752	1835	1852	1934	1951	2052	2152	...	...	2217
116	Türkismühle d.	0452	0602	0658	0802	0912	1012	1112	1212	1312	1414	1512	1612	1712	1814	1901	1912	2000	2013	2112	...	...	...	2240
131	St Wendel d.	0510	0619	0716	0819	0923	1023	1123	1223	1323	1425	1523	1623	1723	1825	1918	1923	2017	2024	2123	...	2236	2240	2251
166	**Saarbrücken** a.	0553	0654	0753	0854	0955	1055	1155	1255	1355	1455	1555	1655	1755	1855	...	1955	...	2055	2155	...	2318	2323	2325

	3401 Ⓐ	3405 ⚒	3409 A	3413 ❖	4325 ❖	3415 L	3417	3419 L	3421	3423 L	3427	3431	3435	3441	4371	3445 Ⓑ	3447 S	3749 Ⓑ	4387 Ⓑ	4389 S	3879 Ⓑ	4393	3881 SⒷ	
Saarbrücken d.	...	0445	0602	0654	0737	0802	0902	1002	1102	1202	1302	1402	1501	1601	1633	1702	1802	1851	1933	2029	2102	2133	2202	...
St Wendel d.	0455	0519	0633	0727	0820	0834	0934	1034	1134	1234	1334	1434	1535	1633	1716	1736	1834	1925	2018	2114	2136	2216	2240	...
Türkismühle d.	0506	0532	0643	0745	0837	0845	0945	1045	1145	1245	1345	1445	1545	1645	1733	1746	1845	1943	2035	2131	...	2233	2257	...
Idar Oberstein d.	0528	0556	0704	0806	...	0904	1006	1104	1206	1305	1406	1504	1606	1705	...	1806	1904	2004	...	...	...	...	...	...
Bad Kreuznach d.	0613	0643	0747	0847	...	0947	1047	1147	1247	1347	1447	1547	1647	1747	...	1847	1947	2044	...	...	...	...	...	...
Mainz a.	0647	0720	0824	0921	...	1022	1121	1222	1321	1422	1522	1621	1721	1822	...	1921	2022	...	...	...	...	...	...	...

A – ⚒, **not** Nov. 1, Dec. 25, Jan. 1. L – ⚒, **not** Nov. 1. S – **Not** Dec. 24, 31. d – Ⓐ only. e – Ⓒ only. ❖ – **Not** Dec. 25, Jan. 1.

Table 722 BINGEN - KAISERSLAUTERN - PIRMASENS

1, 2 class

km		3706 Ⓐ	3706 ⑥	3562 Ⓑ	3708	3710 L	3712 L	3712 ⑦	3714	3716	3566	3718	3568	3720 L	3720 ⑦	3722	3724	3726	3728 Ⓑ	3728 ⑥	3732 S	3736 S	3738 S	3748 Ⓑ
0	**Bingen** d.	0554	0554	...	0651	0714	0806	...	0852	0942	...	1052	...	1146	...	1252	1404	1452	1604	...	1652	1804	1852	2115
16	Bad Kreuznach a.	0613	0613	...	0710	0734	0820	...	0906	1002	...	1106	...	1206	...	1306	1423	1506	1618	...	1706	1823	1906	2135
16	Bad Kreuznach d.	0615	0615	...	0712	0740	0822	...	0917	1016	...	1122	...	1216	...	1321	1425	1518	1620	...	1716	1824	1918	...
79	**Kaiserslautern** a.	0720	0720	...	0816	0843	0919	...	1018	1117	...	1219	...	1317	...	1421	1525	1619	1720	...	1821	1925	2019	...
79	**Kaiserslautern** d.	...	0734	0734	0834	...	0934	0934	1034	...	1134	...	1234	1334	1334	1434	1534	1634	1734	1734	1834	1934	2034	...
108	Pirmasens Nord a.	...	0804	0804	0904	...	1004	1004	1104	...	1204	...	1304	1404	1404	1504	1604	1704	1804	1804	1904	2004	2104	...
108	Pirmasens Nord d.	...	0810	0810	0910	...	1010	1010	1110	...	1210	...	1310	1410	1410	1510	1610	1710	1810	1810	1910	2010	2105	...
115	**Pirmasens Hbf** a.	...	0818	0818	0918	...	1018	1018	1118	...	1218	...	1318	1418	1418	1518	1618	1718	1818	1818	1918	2018	2113	...

	3701 L	3703 L	3705 Ⓐ	3707 L	3709	4206 ❖	3711 L	3561 ⑦❖	3713	3715	3717	3719	3721 B	3723	3725	3727 ⑥	3727 Ⓑ	3731 Ⓒ	3731 Ⓐ	3733 S	3735 S	3737 SⒷ	3567 S	3569 S
Pirmasens Hbf d.	...	...	0539	...	0642	0733	...	0742	0842	0942	1042	1142	...	1242	1342	1442	1442	1542	1542	1642	1742	1842	1942	2042
Pirmasens Nord a.	...	...	0546	...	0649	0740	...	0749	0849	0949	1049	1149	...	1249	1349	1449	1449	1549	1549	1649	1749	1849	1949	2049
Pirmasens Nord d.	...	...	0547	...	0650	...	0750	0750	0850	0950	1050	1150	...	1250	1350	1450	1450	1550	1550	1650	1750	1850	1950	2050
Kaiserslautern a.	...	...	0620	...	0724	...	0824	0824	0924	1024	1124	1224	...	1324	1424	1524	1524	1624	1624	1724	1824	1924	2024	2124
Kaiserslautern d.	0538	0609	0632	0717	0744	...	0843	...	0938	1036	1144	1236	1308	1344	1436	...	1538	...	1638	1739	1839	1944	...	...
Bad Kreuznach a.	0636	0707	0733	0818	0839	...	0941	...	1036	1134	1239	1334	1406	1439	1534	...	1633	...	1737	1835	1940	2040	...	...
Bad Kreuznach d.	0645	0709	0734	0821	0850	...	0942	...	1050	1135	1250	1335	1414	1450	1535	...	1650	...	1750	1850	...	2051	...	...
Bingen a.	0704	0728	0753	0840	0903	...	1002	...	1103	1154	1303	1354	1433	1503	1548	...	1703	...	1810	1903	...	2110	...	...

B – ⚒, **not** Nov. 1, Dec. 24, 31. L – ⚒, **not** Nov. 1. S – **Not** Dec. 24, 31. ❖ – **Not** Dec. 25, Jan. 1.

Table 724 PIRMASENS - SAARBRÜCKEN, NEUSTADT and KARLSRUHE

km		4200 L	4491 Ⓐ	3765 L	4451 ⑥❖	3767	4204 ❖	3769	4206 ❖	4457	3771	4208	4461	3773	4210	4463	3775	4212	4465	3777	4214	4467	3779	4216
0	**Pirmasens Hbf** d.	0529	0547	...	0601	...	0629	...	0733	0801	...	0833	0901	...	0933	1001	...	1033	1101	...	1133	1201	...	1233
7	Pirmasens Nord a.	0536	0554	...	0608	...	0636	...	0740	0808	...	0840	0908	...	0940	1008	...	1040	1108	...	1140	1208	...	1240
7	Pirmasens Nord d.	0537	0558	...	0619	...	0643	...	0744	0819	...	0844	0919	...	0944	1019	...	1044	1119	...	1144	1219	...	1243
	Zweibrücken d.	0603	|	...	|	...	0716	...	0811	|	...	0911	|	...	1011	|	...	1111	|	...	1211	|	...	1311
	Saarbrücken a.	0645	|	...	|	...	0805	...	0849	|	...	0949	|	...	1049	|	...	1149	|	...	1249	|	...	1349
40	Annweiler d.	...	0642	...	0701	...	...	...	...	0901	...	...	1001	...	...	1101	...	...	1201	...	...	1301	...	...
	Neustadt (Weinstrasse) d.	...	|	0652	|	0803	...	0903	...	|	1003	...	|	1103	...	|	1203	...	|	1303	...	|	1403	...
55	Landau (Pfalz) d.	...	0702	0706	0721	0815	...	0915	...	0921	1015	...	1021	1115	...	1121	1215	...	1221	1315	...	1321	1415	...
73	**Neustadt** (Weinstrasse) a.	...	0724	|	0742	|	...	|	...	0942	|	...	1042	|	...	1142	|	...	1242	|	...	1342	|	...
95	**Karlsruhe** a.	...	...	0746	...	0849	...	0949	...	...	1049	...	...	1149	...	...	1249	...	...	1349	...	...	1449	...

	4469	3781	4218	4473	3783	4222	4475	4224	4479	3785	3787	4226	4481	3789	4228	4485 S	3791	4230	4487 S	4498 Ⓐ	4232 S	4489 S	3793	4234 S
Pirmasens Hbf d.	1301	...	1333	1401	...	1433	1501	1533	1601	...	...	1633	1701	...	1733	1801	...	1833	1901	...	1933	2001	...	2033
Pirmasens Nord a.	1308	...	1340	1408	...	1440	1508	1540	1608	...	...	1640	1708	...	1740	1808	...	1840	1908	...	1940	2008	...	2040
Pirmasens Nord d.	1319	...	1344	1419	...	1444	1519	1544	1619	...	...	1644	1719	...	1744	1819	...	1844	1919	1918	1944	2019	...	2044
Zweibrücken d.	|	...	1411	|	...	1511	|	1611	|	...	...	1711	|	...	1811	|	...	1911	|	1946	2011	|	...	2109
Saarbrücken a.	|	...	1449	|	...	1549	|	1649	|	...	...	1749	|	...	1850	|	...	1949	|	2020	2049	|	...	2147
Annweiler d.	1401	...	...	1501	...	...	1601	...	1701	...	...	...	1801	...	...	1901	...	...	2001	...	...	2101	...	...
Neustadt (Weinstrasse) d.	|	1503	...	|	1603	...	|	...	|	1703	1803	...	|	1903	...	|	2003	...	|	...	...	|	2103	...
Landau (Pfalz) d.	1421	1515	...	1521	1615	...	1621	...	1712	1715	1815	...	1821	1915	...	1927	2015	...	2021	...	...	2121	2124	...
Neustadt (Weinstrasse) a.	1442	|	...	1542	|	...	1642	...	*1738*	|	|	...	1842	|	...	1948	|	...	2042	...	...	2142	|	...
Karlsruhe a.	...	1549	...	...	1649	...	...	...	...	1749	1849	...	...	1949	...	...	2049	...	...	...	...	...	2208	...

km		4308 L	4454 Ⓐ	4205 L	4207 ❖	3762 L	4458	3764 L	3766	4209	4462	4211	4464	4213	3768	3770	4466	4215	4468	4217	3772	4219 Ⓐ	3774	4470
	Karlsruhe d.	0526	...	...	...	0607	...	0712	0806	...	...	...	...	...	0907	1007	...	...	...	...	1107	...	1207	...
	Neustadt (Weinstrasse) d.	|	*0601*	...	...	|	0718	|	|	...	0816	...	0916	...	|	|	1016	...	1116	...	|	...	|	1216
	Landau (Pfalz) d.	0614	0624	...	...	0647	0741	0756	0846	...	0847	...	0941	...	0946	1046	1047	...	1141	...	1146	...	1246	1247
	Neustadt (Weinstrasse) a.	0636	|	...	...	0709	|	0813	0858	...	|	...	|	...	0958	1058	|	...	|	...	1158	...	1258	|
	Annweiler d.	...	0642	...	...	...	0800	...	...	...	0900	...	1000	...	...	...	1100	...	1200	...	...	...	...	1300
0	**Saarbrücken** d.	...	|	0613	0709	...	|	...	...	0809	|	0909	|	1009	...	...	|	1109	|	1209	...	1239	...	|
36	Zweibrücken d.	...	|	0715	0748	...	|	...	...	0847	|	0947	|	1047	...	...	|	1147	|	1247	...	1311	...	|
60	Pirmasens Nord a.	...	0718	0740	0826	...	0840	...	...	0916	0940	1016	1040	1116	...	...	1140	1216	1240	1316	...	1337	...	1340
60	Pirmasens Nord d.	...	0723	*0751*n	...	...	0851	...	...	0918	0951	1018	1051	1118	...	...	1151	1218	1251	1318	...	...	...	1351
67	**Pirmasens Hbf** a.	...	0731	*0759*n	...	...	0859	...	...	0926	0959	1026	1059	1126	...	...	1159	1226	1259	1326	...	...	...	1359

	4221	4472	4223	3776	3778	4476	4225	4478	4227	3780	3782	4480	4229	4484 S	4229	3784	3786	4486 S	4233 S	4488 S	4235 S	3788	3790	4490 S
Karlsruhe d.	...	...	...	1307	1407	...	...	...	...	1509	1605	...	...	...	...	1707	1807	...	...	...	...	1907	2007	...
Neustadt (Weinstrasse) d.	...	1316	...	|	|	1416	...	1516	...	|	|	1616	...	1716	...	|	|	1816	...	1916	...	|	|	2016
Landau (Pfalz) d.	...	1341	...	1346	1446	1447	...	1541	...	1546	1646	1647	...	1741	...	1746	1846	1847	...	1941	...	1946	2046	2047
Neustadt (Weinstrasse) a.	...	|	...	1358	1458	|	...	|	...	1558	1658	|	...	|	...	1758	1858	|	...	|	...	1958	2058	|
Annweiler d.	...	1400	...	...	...	1500	...	1600	...	...	...	1700	...	1800	...	...	...	1900	...	2000	...	...	...	2100
Saarbrücken d.	1308	|	1409	...	...	|	1509	|	1608	...	...	|	1709	|	1809	...	...	|	1909	|	2009	...	...	|
Zweibrücken d.	1347	|	1447	...	...	|	1547	|	1647	...	...	|	1747	|	1847	...	...	|	1947	|	2047	...	...	|
Pirmasens Nord a.	1416	1440	1516	...	...	1540	1616	1640	1716	...	...	1740	1816	1840	1916	...	...	1940	2016	2040	2116	...	...	2113
Pirmasens Nord d.	1418	1451	1518	...	...	1551	1618	1651	1718	...	...	1751	1818	1851	1918	...	...	1951	2018	2051	2118	...	...	2120
Pirmasens Hbf a.	1426	1459	1526	...	...	1559	1626	1659	1726	...	...	1759	1826	1859	1926	...	...	1959	2026	2059	2126	...	...	2148

L – ⚒, **not** Nov. 1. S – **Not** Dec. 24, 31. n – **Not** Dec. 25, Jan. 1. ❖ – **Not** Dec. 25, Jan. 1.

Table 725

SAARBRÜCKEN - MANNHEIM
1, 2 class

km		IR 361	EC 15 ✗ ◆	IC 653 ◆	E 3505	IR 2265	E 3179	IC 651 ◆	E 3507	IR 461 ◆	E 3181	IC 559 ◆ A	E 3509	IR 2267	E 3183	EC 57 ✗ ◆	E 3511	IR 2365	E 3185	IC 557 ◆ B	E 3513	IR 2367	E 3187	EC 55 ✗ ◆ C
0	Saarbrücken .... d.	0548	0626	0651	0702	0750	0801	0851	0901	0950	1001	1051	1101	1150	1201	1251	1301	1350	1401	1451	1501	1550	1601	1650
31	Homburg .... d.	0608	0647	0711	0735	0810	0829	0911	0929	1010	1029	1111	1129	1210	1229	1311	1329	1410	1429	1511	1529	1610	1610	1710
51	Landstuhl .... d.	0618			0750		0844		0944		1044		1144		1244		1344		1444		1544		1644	
67	Kaiserslautern .... d.	0628	0706	0730	0802	0828	0902	0930	0930	1028	1100	1130	1200	1228	1300	1300	1400	1428	1500	1528	1602	1628	1703	1730
100	Neustadt (Weinstrasse) ...... d.	0650	0730	0752	0830	0850	0930	0952	1030	1050	1130	1152	1230	1250	1330	1352	1430	1450	1530	1552	1630	1650	1731	1752
128	Ludwigshafen 726 .... d.	0707	0748		0900	0907	0959		1059	1107	1159		1259	1307	1359		1459	1507	1530		1659	1707	1759	
131	Mannheim 726 .... a.	0711	0752	0811	0904	0911	1011	1011	1103	1111	1203	1211	1303	1311	1403	1411	1503	1511	1603	1611	1703	1711	1803	1811
	Frankfurt (Main) Hbf 730 d.				0906	...	...	1106	...	...	1306	...	...	...	1506	...	...	...	1706	...	...	...	...	1906

		E 3515	IR 2269 ◆	IC 3189 ♀	E 553 ♀ ⊞	IR 3517	E 2369	IC 3191 ♀	E 53 ✗ ◆ C	E 3521	
	Saarbrücken .... d.	1701	1750	1801	1851	1901	1950	2002	2058	2301	...
	Homburg .... d.	1729	1810	1829	1911	1929	2010	2029	2118	2329	...
	Landstuhl .... d.	1744		1844		1944		2044		2344	...
	Kaiserslautern .... d.	1800	1828	1900	1930	2000	2028	2100	2138	2355	...
	Neustadt (Weinstrasse) ...... d.	1830	1850	1930	1952	2030	2050	2130	2200	0024	...
	Ludwigshafen 726 .... d.	1859	1907	1956		2059	2107	2159		0049	...
	Mannheim 726 .... a.	1903	1911	2000	2011	2103	2111	2203	2219	0053	...
	Frankfurt (Main) Hbf 730 a.	...	...	2106	...	...	...	2315	...	...	...

		IR 2337 ⓐ	E 7202	EC 52 ✗ ◆	IR 2268 ◆	E 3508	E 3902 ⑦	IR ♪ ♪	E 552 ♀	IC 3176 ◆	IR 2368 ♀ B
	Frankfurt (Main) Hbf 730 .. d.			0727					0851		
	Mannheim 726 .... d.	0646	0659	0822	0848	0856	0946	0946	0957	1048
	Ludwigshafen 726 .... d.	0652	0704		0854	0903		1003	1054
	Neustadt (Weinstrasse) ..... d.	0708	0729	0843	0909	0929	1005	1005	1029	1109
	Kaiserslautern .... d.	0731	0804	0904	0931	1004	1028	1028	1104	1131
	Landstuhl .... d.	0741	0815		1015		1115	
	Ludwigshafen 726 .... d.	0752	0831	0923	0948	1031	1046	1046	1131	1148
	Homburg .... d.	0752	0831	0923	0948	1031	1046	1046	1131	1148
	Saarbrücken .... a.	0813	0856	0944	1008	1056	1107	1107	1156	1208

		E 3510	EC 54 ✗ ◆ C	E 3178	IR 2366 ◆	E 3512	IC 556 ♀	E3178 E3180	IR 460 ◆	E 3514	EC 56 ✗ ◆	E 3182	IR 360 ◆ A	E 3516	IC 558 ◆	E 2264	IR 3518	E 650 ♀ A	IC 3186	IR 2266 ◆ A	EC 14 ✗ ◆	E 3520	IC 652 ♀	IR 2262 H
	Frankfurt (Main) Hbf 730 . d.	...	1051	...	...	...	1251	...	...	...	1451	...	...	...	1651	...	...	...	1851	...	...	...	2051	...
	Mannheim 726 .... d.	1057	1146	1157	1248	1257	1346	1357	1448	1457	1546	1557	1648	1657	1746	1848	1857	1946	1956	2048	2107	...	2146	2248
	Ludwigshafen 726 .... d.	1103		1203	1254	1303		1403	1454	1503		1603	1654	1703		1854	1903		2002	2054	2113	...		2254
	Neustadt (Weinstrasse) ...... d.	1129	1205	1229	1309	1329	1405	1429	1509	1529	1605	1629	1709	1734	1805	1909	1929	2005	2032	2109	2128	...	2205	2309
	Kaiserslautern .... d.	1204	1228	1304	1331	1404	1428	1504	1531	1602	1628	1704	1731	1807	1828	1931	2004	2028	2101	2131	2151	2204	2228	2331
	Landstuhl .... d.	1215		1315		1415		1515		1616		1715		1818			2015		2112		2215		2340
	Saarbrücken .... a.	1231	1247	1331	1348	1431	1446	1531	1548	1631	1646	1731	1748	1833	1846	1948	2031	2046	2130	2148	2209	2231	2246	2350
	Saarbrücken .... a.	1257	1307	1357	1408	1431	1456	1507	1556	1608	1656	1707	1756	1808	1857	1907	2008	2056	2230	2256	2307			0011

NOTES (LISTED BY TRAIN NUMBERS)

- **EC14/5** – PATSCHERKOFEL – 🚃 and ✗ Innsbruck - Saarbrücken and v.v.
- **EC56/7** – 🚃 and ✗ Dresden Hbf - Paris Est and v.v.
- **IR360/1** – 🚃 and ♀ Saarbrücken - Bregenz and v.v.
- **IR460** – 🚃 and ♀ Landeck - Saarbrücken.
- **IR461** – 🚃 and ♀ Trier - Landeck.
- **IC552** – PFALZER WALD – 🚃 and ♀ Erfurt - Saarbrücken.
- **IC556** – GOTTFRIED SEMPER – 🚃 and ✗ Dresden Hbf - Saarbrücken.
- **IC557** – GOTTFRIED SEMPER – 🚃 and ✗ Saarbrücken - Dresden Hbf.
- **IR2264** – 🚃 and ♀ Friedrichshafen Stadt - Trier.
- **IR2265** – 🚃 and ♀ Trier - Friedrichshafen Stadt.
- **IR2266** – 🚃 Friedrichshafen Stadt - Trier; ♀ Friedrichshafen - Neustadt.
- **IR2267** – 🚃 and ♀ Saarbrücken - Friedrichshafen Stadt.
- **IR2268** – 🚃 and ♀ Ulm - Saarbrücken.
- **IR2269** – 🚃 and ♀ Saarbrücken - Ulm.
- **IR2366** – 🚃 and ♀ Lindau - Saarbrücken.
- **A** – 🚃 and ✗ Saarbrücken - Dresden Hbf and v.v.
- **B** – 🚃 and ♀ Saarbrücken - Lindau and v.v.
- **C** – 🚃 and ✗ Frankfurt/Main - Paris Est and v.v.
- **H** – Daily except ⑥: 🚃 and ♀ Heidelberg - Saarbrücken and v.v.
- **◆** – Daily except ⑥ (**not** Dec. 24 - 31, Apr. 14 - 16, Apr. 30, **1995**).
- **♪** – ① - ⑥ (**not** Dec. 25 - Jan. 1, Apr. 15 - 17, May 1, **1995**).

Table 726

MAINZ - WORMS - MANNHEIM
1, 2 class except where shown

km		E 6407 ⓐ	E 3051 L	ICE 995 L	E 3053	EC 101	3055	E 6427 ✗	3057	E 6437	3059	E 6447	3061	E 6455 ⓐ	E 6457	3063	E 6467	3065	E 6475 ⓐ	E 6477	6481	D 1205	IC 509 ◆	6491 S
0	Mainz .... d.	0502	0602	0642	0658	0742	0800	0900	1000	1100	1200	1300	1400	1432	1500	1617	1658	1758	1832	1900	2018	2123	2242	2339
46	Worms .... d.	0546	0641	0708	0739	0809	0853	0953	1053	1153	1253	1353	1453	1522	1553	1657	1753	1853	1922	1953	2114	2150	2308	0025
67	Ludwigshafen 725 .... d.	0606	0700		0758		0914	1014	1114	1214	1314	1412	1514	1545	1614	1714	1814	1914	1941	2014	2135		2324	
70	Mannheim 725 .... a.	0610	0703	0724	0802	0823	0918	1018	1118	1218	1318	1418	1518	1549	1618	1718	1818	1918	1945	2018	2139	2207	2328	

		E 3050 ✗	IC 508 ◆	E 6414 ♣	D 1204 ◆	E 6418	3054	E 6428 ✗	3056	E 6438	6440	3058	E 6446	6448	3060	E 6458	E 6460	3062	E 6468	3066	E 6478	EC 100 ◆◆	IC 600 ◆◆	ICE 994 ⓐ	6490 ⓐ
	Mannheim 725 .... d.	0536	0636	0651	0742	0750	0844	0950	1044	1150	1200	1244	1350	1444	1550	1600	1642	1750	1844	1950	2037	2137	2235	2251
	Ludwigshafen 725 .... d.	0542		0658		0755	0853	0955	1053	1155	1224	1253	1324	1355	1453	1555	1623	1653	1755	1853	1955				2256
	Worms .... d.	0608	0651	0720	0758	0824	0924	1024	1124	1224	1255	1324	1355	1424	1524	1623	1653	1724	1824	1924	2024	2052	2152	2252	2314
	Mainz .... d.	0648	0716	0804	0830	0908	1008	1108	1124	1224	1321	1342	1408	1442	1508	1608	1708	1742	1808	1908	2008	2108	2118	2318	0001

NOTES (LISTED BY TRAIN NUMBERS)

- **IC100/1** – MATTERHORN – 🚃 and ♀ Wiesbaden - Brig and v.v. (Wiesbaden depart 0729, arrive 2131).
- **1204/5** – ITALIA EXPRESS – see Table 650. Not available for local journeys.
- **ICE994/5** – RHEINGAU – 🚃 and ✗ München Hbf - Wiesbaden and v.v. (Wiesbaden depart 0629, arrive 2330).
- **IC508/9** – RHEINFELS – 🚃 and ♀ Karlsruhe - Berlin Zoo and v.v.
- **IC600** – BADENIA – 🚃 and ♀ Basel SBB - Wiesbaden (arrive 2231).
- **L** – ✗, not Nov. 1, Jan. 6.
- **S** – Not Dec. 24, 31.
- **◆◆** – Not Dec. 25, Jan. 1.
- **♣** – Daily except ⑥ (**not** Dec. 24 - 31, Apr. 14 - 16, Apr. 30, **1995**).

Table 727

KARLSRUHE and OFFENBURG - STRASBOURG
1, 2 class except where shown

km		E 3252	EC 68 ✗ ◆	E 1864	E 3262	EC 66 ✗ ◆	E 1866	E 1868	E 1870	E 3274	EC 64 ✗ ◆	E 1872	E 3276	D 1173	E 1874	D 260 ◆	D 262
	München Hbf 760 .... d.	...	...	...	...	0750	...	...	...	...	1350	...	...	...	...	2106	0034n
	Stuttgart 760 .... d.	...	0612	...	...	1015	...	...	...	...	1615	...	...	...	...	2335	0303
0	Karlsruhe .... d.	...	0704	...	...	1107	...	...	...	...	1707	...	1842	...	...	0049	0402
32	Baden Baden .... d.	...	0719	...	...	1125	...	...	...	...	1725	...	1900	...	...	0106	
	Offenburg .... d.	0639		1009	1131	1209	1409	1609	1731	1809	1839	2009		0143	0452
79	Kehl 🚃 .... d.	0654	0745	1026	1146	1155	1226	1426	1626	1746	1757	1826	1854	1937	2026	0143	0452
87	Strasbourg .... a.		0753	1035		1204	1235	1435	1635		1806	1835		1947	2035	0152	0501

NOTES

- **EC64** – MOZART – 🚃 and ♀ Paris Est - Wien and v.v.; 🚃 Paris - Graz and v.v.
- **EC66** – MAURICE RAVEL – 🚃 and ✗ Paris Est - München Hbf.
- **EC68** – MARIE CURIE – 🚃 and ✗ Paris Est - Stuttgart and v.v.
- **260** – See Table 30.
- **D262** – See Table 32.
- **D1173** – Mar. 30 - May 27. See Table 79.
- **n** – München **Ost**.

4   385

Table 727 — STRASBOURG - OFFENBURG and KARLSRUHE

1, 2 class except where shown

		E 1863	D .1172	E 1865		E 1867	EC 65 ✕	E 3263		E 1869		E 1871		E 1873	EC 67 ✕	E 3275	E 1875		EC 69 ✕	E 3283		D 263		D 261
Strasbourg	d.	0721			◆										◆				◆			◆		◆
Strasbourg	d.	0721	0908	0921		1121	1157			1321		1521		1721	1757		1921		2144			0000		0351
Kehl ⌂	d.	0732	0928	0932		1132	1207	1216		1332		1532		1732	1807	1816	1932		2155	2202		0013		0418
Offenburg	a.	0747		0947		1147		1231		1347		1547		1747		1831	1947		2217					0445
Baden Baden	d.		0954				1233								1833			2220						0504
Karlsruhe	a.		1013				1251								1851			2240			0056		0504
Stuttgart 760	a.						1346								1946			2338			0157		0620
München Hbf 760	a.						1610								2210						0423n		0850

EC65 – MOZART – ⊡ and ✕ Paris Est - Wien and v.v.; ⊡ Paris - Graz and v.v.
EC67 – MAURICE RAVEL – ⊡ and ✕ Paris Est - München Hbf.
EC69 – MARIE CURIE – ⊡ and ✕ Paris Est - Stuttgart and v.v.
D261 – See Table 30.
D263 – See Table 32.
D1172 – Mar. 30 - May 27. See Table 79.
n – München Ost.

Table 728 — KARLSRUHE - RASTATT - FREUDENSTADT

1, 2 class except where shown

km		8303	8305 ✕	8309 ✕	8311	8315	8319	8321	8327 2	2213 C ☕	8381	8331	8335	8337	8339 2	8343	8345	8347 2Ⓐ	8353 Ⓒ	8351	8355	8357	8363 Ⓑ	8367 Ⓑ	8371
0	Karlsruhe 730 d.	0459p	0526		0700	0826	0910		1026	1041	1126		1226	1310		1426	1505			1626	1710		1826	1910	2020
24	Rastatt 730 a.	0520p	0549		0723	0840	0933		1040	1055	1148		1240	1333		1440	1528			1640	1733		1840	1933	2043
24	Rastatt d.	0529	0554		0746	0841	0934		1041	1057	1150		1241	1334		1441	1534			1641	1734		1841	1946	2045
40	Gernsbach d.	0559	0616		0812	0859	0958		1059	1143	1217		1259	1358		1459	1558			1659	1758		1859	2010	2108
51	Forbach-Gausbach d.	0617	0654		0839	0916	1017		1116	1141	1235		1316	1417		1516	1617			1716	1817		1916	2031	2127
37	Schönmünzach d.	0629	0706		0850	0927	1031		1127	1153	1248		1327	1431		1527	1637			1727	1831		1927	2042	2138
74	Baiersbronn d.	0647	0725	0730	0913	0944	1050	1100	1144	1210	1302	1310	1344	1451	1458	1544	1651	1658	1708	1744	1851	1858	1944		
79	Freudenstadt Stadt d.	0657		0740	0922	0953		1109	1153	1221		1328	1353		1508	1553		1708	1713	1753		1908	1953		
82	Freudenstadt Hbf a.	0702		0745	0927	0958		1113	1158	1226		1333	1358		1513	1558		1713	1723	1758		1913	1958		

		8300 Ⓐ	8304 Ⓐ	8308 ✕	8310 ✕	3700	8312 ✕	3702	8316 ⑦	8322	8320	8330	8324	3154 2	8340 2	2212 H ☕	8342	3156 2	8348	8350	3160 2	8356 2Ⓐ	8358 Ⓑ	8360 Ⓑ	8370
	Freudenstadt Hbf d.		0555		0710		0756	0855	0857n	1000	1038		1213	1252		1320	1400	1438		1600	1638	1648		1800	1925
	Freudenstadt Stadt d.		0601		0716		0801	0900	0902n	1005	1046		1221	1257		1328	1405	1445		1605	1645	1655		1805	1932
	Baiersbronn d.		0546	0610		0723	0730	0810	0907	0910	1014	1055	1108	1230	1305	1308	1345	1414	1453	1508	1614	1653	1703	1708	1814	1943
	Schönmünzach d.	0529	0604	0627	0630		0744	0826		0929	1030		1129	1248		1329	1401	1430		1529	1630			1729	1830	2003
	Forbach-Gausbach d.	0540	0619		0641		0755	0838		0940	1041		1140	1259		1340	1418	1441		1540	1641			1759	1859	2022
	Gernsbach d.	0558	0638		0656		0810	0859		0959	1059		1159	1314		1359	1432	1459		1559	1659			1820	1914	2043
	Rastatt a.	0619	0700		0712		0825	0914		1021	1114		1220	1332		1421	1454	1514		1621	1714			1823	1916	2047
	Rastatt 730 d.	0620	0704		0715		0827	0916		1024	1116		1224	1333		1424	1456	1516		1624	1716			1847	1929	2055
	Karlsruhe 730 a.	0644	0728		0738		0851	0929		1048	1129		1247	1356		1448	1512	1529		1648	1729			1847	1929	2055

C – ⊡ and ☕ Dortmund - Freudenstadt.
H – ⊡ and ☕ Freudenstadt - Münster (Emden ♣).
n – ✕ only.
p – Ⓐ only.
♣ – Daily except ⑥ (not Oct. 2, Dec. 24 - 31, Apr. 14 - 17, Apr. 30, 1995).

Table 730 — KASSEL - FRANKFURT (MAIN) - KONSTANZ and BASEL

1, 2 class except where shown

km		E3551 E3559 K	D 358 ☕ ◆	E 3449	E 3553	IC 601 ☕☕	D 1999 ☕	IR 2473 ☕	E 3175	ICE 995 ✕✕	E 271 ✕	E 3555	D 350 ☕	IR 2211 ☕	EC 52 ✕	IR 2671 ☕	ICE 997 ✕✕	EC 101 ✕	IR 2671 ✕✕	8655 E3601	E 3177	ICE 999 ✕✕	EC 107 ✕	E 3557	IC 552 ✕
	Hamburg Hbf 750 d.						2302									0529			0604		0500				
0	Kassel Hbf d.															0536	0613		0609		0713				
4	Kassel Wilhelmshöhe d.			0315												0554			0644						
34	Wabern d.															0611			0701						
62	Treysa d.															0635			0733						
104	Marburg d.						0435									0654		←	0752						
134	Gießen d.						0515									0735	0739		0735	0835		0839			
200	Frankfurt (Main) Hbf a.					0540	0523			0640			0628		0727	0757	0743		0747						
200	Frankfurt (Main) Hbf d.															0747 →				0538			0852		
	Dortmund 650 d.																			0628					
	Düsseldorf Hbf 650 d.																			0700					
	Köln Hbf 650 d.							0642							0742					0842					
	Mainz					0544						0649	0724	0747		0806							091		
228	Darmstadt d.												0736			0818									
250	Bensheim d.												0745			0826									
264	Weinheim d.																								
288	Mannheim a.			0508		0623		0724	0723				0820		0824	0823			0924	0923		094			
288	Mannheim 742 d.					0631		0731							0831				0931						
	Heidelberg 742 d.			0535			0624	0642			0724	0759			0842	0821									
	Bruchsal d.			0557			0649	0658			0744				0858	0904									
341	Karlsruhe 728 d.			0546	0612	0656	0710	0715	0730		0756	0802			0856	0912	0928		0956						
365	Rastatt 728 d.				0624		0727	0743							0924		0941								
373	Baden Baden d.			0605	0630	0711	0733	0749			0820			0911	0930	0947									
414	Offenburg d.			0627	0659	0729	0754	0823		0828	0842			0951	1021	1028									
414	Offenburg d.	0535	0629	0700	0704	0731		0756		0830	0837	0844		0953		1030	1037								
	Hausach d.	0603			0723		0816			0905				1013			1105								
	Triberg d.	0627			0744		0838			0932				1036			1132								
	St Georgen d.	0643			0759		0853			0948				1051			1148								
	Villingen d.	0658			0809		0905			1000				1103			1200								
	Donaueschingen d.	0709			0820		0915			1012				1114			1212								
	Immendingen d.	0723			0832		0926			1030				1125			1230								
	Singen 734 d.	0749			0856		0950			1054				1150			1254								
	Radolfzell 734 d.	0800			0905		0959			1106				1159			1306								
	Konstanz ⌂ a.	0817			0919		1012			1122				1212			1322								
476	Freiburg (Breisgau) d.		0710	0736		0801				0901		0921		1001			1101								
538	Basel Bad Bf ⌂ a.		0803	0814		0834				0934		1008		1036			1135								
543	Basel SBB a.		0818			0843				0943		1023		1043			1143								

NOTES (LISTED BY TRAIN NUMBERS)
EC52 – GOETHE – ⊡ and ✕ Frankfurt/Main - Saarbrücken - Paris Est.
EC101 – MATTERHORN – ⊡ and ☕ Wiesbaden - Worms - Mainz - Brig.
EC107 – MONT BLANC – ⊡ and ✕ Dortmund - Genève.
ICE271 – JOHANNA SPYRI – ⊡ and ✕ Frankfurt/Main - Zürich Hbf.
D350 – ☛ and ☕ Stralsund (Binz ⑥ Apr. 8 - May 27 also Apr. 14, 17, May 25 not Apr. 15) - Bebra - Basel.
  ☛ 1,2 cl. and 2 cl. København (D483) - Bebra - Basel; ☕ Bebra - Basel.
D358 – ☛ 1,2 cl., ← 2 cl., ⊡ and ☕ Berlin Zoo - Basel; ☛ 1,2 cl., ← 2 cl. and ⊡ Dresden Hbf (D1948) - Halle - Basel.

IC552 – PFALZER WALD – ⊡ and ☕ Erfurt - Saarbrücken.
ICE995 – RHEINGAU – ⊡ and ✕ Wiesbaden - Worms - Mainz - München.
D1999 – ☛ 1,2 cl., ← 2 cl., ⊡ and ☕ Hamburg Altona - Stuttgart.
IR2211 – ⊡ and ☕ Koblenz - Heidelberg.
IR2473 – ⊡ and ☕ Karlsruhe (Heidelberg ① - ⑤, not Apr. 14 - 17, May 1, 25) - Konstanz.
IR2671 – ⊡ and ☕ Frankfurt/Main (Kassel Hbf ① - ⑥) - Konstanz.
K – ✕ from Offenburg; daily from Villingen.
✕ – ① - ⑥ (not Dec. 25 - Jan. 1, Apr. 15 - 17, May 1, 1995).

Table 730 — KASSEL - FRANKFURT/MAIN - KONSTANZ and BASEL

1, 2 class except where shown

Upper table

Station	IR 2213	IR 2571	ICE 791	EC 5	IR 2571	E 3603	ICE 771	E 3179	ICE 591	EC 103	E 3561	EC 54	IR 2215	IR 2573	ICE 573	ICE 793	EC 9	IR 2573	E 3605	ICE 575	E 3181	ICE 593	EC 105	E 3563	IC 556
Hamburg Hbf 750 ...d.			0600				0636									0737	0802					0837			
Kassel Hbf ...d.		0729			0819									0929						1019					
Kassel Wilhelmshöhe ...d.		0736	0813		0825	0845			0913					0936	0945	1013		1025	1045			1113			
Wabern ...d.		0754												0954				1045							
Treysa ...d.		0811				0923								1011				1102							
Marburg ...d.		0835				0933								1035				1133							
Gießen ...d.		0854				←0952								1054				←1152							
Frankfurt/Main Hbf ...a.		0935	0939		0935	1035	1005		1039					1135				1235	1135			1239			
Frankfurt/Main Hbf ...d.	0548	0947	0943	0640	0947			1009	1043	0740		1051		1147	1109	1143	0838	1147		1209		1243			1251
Dortmund 650 ...d.	0548	→		0640						0740				→		0838									
Düsseldorf Hbf 650 ...d.	0645									0845						0928							1034		
Köln Hbf 650 ...d.	0711			0800						0911						1000							1034		
Mainz ...d.	0904			0942												1142							1242		
Darmstadt ...d.	0924			1006							1111	1124					1142		1206				1242		1311
Bensheim ...d.	0936			1018								1136							1218						1311
Weinheim ...d.	0945			1026								1145							1226						
Mannheim ...a.			1024	1022			1050		1124	1123		1144		1150	1224	1223			1250			1324	1323		1344
Mannheim 742 ...d.			1031				1058			1131				1158		1231			1258				1331		
Heidelberg 742 ...d.	1001			1042				1021				1159				1242					1221		1331		
Bruchsal ...d.	1017			1058				1104								1258					1304				
Karlsruhe 728 ...d.	1041		1056	1112				1123	1130		1156				1221	1256		1312			1321	1328		1356	
Rastatt 728 ...d.	1055			1124					1143		1149							1324			1341	1347			
Baden Baden ...d.			1111	1130					1149							1311		1330			1347				
Offenburg ...a.				1151				1156	1221		1228							1351			1421		1428		
Offenburg ...d.				1153				1158			1230	1237						1353					1430	1437	
Hausach ...d.				1213								1305						1413					1430	1505	
Triberg ...d.				1236								1332						1436						1532	
St Georgen ...d.				1251								1348						1451						1548	
Villingen ...d.				1303								1400						1503						1600	
Donaueschingen ...d.				1314								1412						1514						1612	
Immendingen ...d.				1325								1430						1525						1630	
Singen 734 ...d.				1350								1454						1550						1654	
Radolfzell 734 ...d.				1359								1506						1559						1706	
Konstanz ...a.				1412								1522						1612						1722	
Freiburg (Breisgau) ...d.			1201					1229			1301					1401						1501			
Basel Bad Bf ...a.			1235					1303			1336					1435						1536			
Basel SBB ...a.			1243					1310			1343					1443						1543			

Lower table

Station	IR 2217	IR 2575	ICE 577	ICE 895	EC 3	IR 2575	E 3607	ICE 71	E 3183	ICE 595	EC 109	EC 56	IR 2219	IR 2577	ICE 579	ICE 897	IC 501	IR 2577	E 3609	ICE 77	E 3185	ICE 597	IC 603	E 3569
Hamburg Hbf 750 ...d.		0742	0937					1037						1137						1237				
Kassel Hbf ...d.		1129					1219							1329					1419					
Kassel Wilhelmshöhe ...d.		1136	1145	1213			1225	1245		1313				1336	1345	1413		1425	1445			1513		
Wabern ...d.		1154					1245							1354				1445						
Treysa ...d.		1211					1302							1411				1502						
Marburg ...d.		1235					1333							1435				1533						
Gießen ...d.		1254					←1352							1454				←1552						
Frankfurt/Main Hbf ...a.		1335	1305	1339		1335	1435	1405		1439				1535				1635	1535			1639		
Frankfurt/Main Hbf ...d.		1347	1309	1343		1347		1409		1443		1451		1547	1509	1543	1240	1547		1609		1643		
Dortmund 650 ...d.		→								1138				→		1240								
Düsseldorf Hbf 650 ...d.	1045			1134						1228		1245											1500	
Köln Hbf 650 ...d.	1111			1200						1300		1311				1400							1500	
Mainz ...d.	1304			1342						1442		1504				1542							1642	
Darmstadt ...d.	1324				1406						1511	1524					1606						1642	
Bensheim ...d.	1336				1418							1536					1618							
Weinheim ...d.	1345				1426							1545					1626							
Mannheim ...a.			1350	1424	1423			1450		1524	1523	1544		1550	1624	1623			1650			1724	1723	
Mannheim 742 ...d.			1358		1431			1458			1531			1558		1631			1658				1731	
Heidelberg 742 ...d.	1402				1442				1421			1559				1642					1621			
Bruchsal ...d.	1418				1458				1504							1658					1704			
Karlsruhe 728 ...d.	1433		1421	1456	1512				1523	1528	1556				1621	1656		1712			1723	1728		1756
Rastatt 728 ...d.	1445				1524				1541									1724			1741	1747		
Baden Baden ...a.	1451			1511	1530				1547							1730					1747			
Offenburg ...a.	1512				1551				1556	1621		1628				1728	1751				1756	1821		1828
Offenburg ...d.	1514				1553				1558			1630	1637			1730	1753				1758		1830	1837
Hausach ...d.					1613							1705				1813							1905
Triberg ...d.					1636							1732				1836							1932
St Georgen ...d.					1651							1748				1851							1948
Villingen ...d.					1703							1800				1903							2000
Donaueschingen ...d.					1714							1812				1914							2012
Immendingen ...d.					1725							1830				1925							2030
Singen 734 ...d.					1750							1854				1950							2054
Radolfzell 734 ...d.					1759							1906				1959							2106
Konstanz ...a.					1812							1922				2012							2122
Freiburg (Breisgau) ...d.	1548			1601				1629			1701					1801				1829		1901		
Basel Bad Bf ...a.				1635				1703			1735					1835				1903		1935		
Basel SBB ...a.				1643				1710			1743					1843				1910		1943		

NOTES (LISTED BY TRAIN NUMBERS)

3 – REMBRANDT – [2] and X Amsterdam Schiphol +– Chur.
5 – VERDI – [2] Dortmund - Milano Centrale; X Dortmund - Chiasso.
9 – TIZIANO – [2] and X Hannover (Braunschweig /) - Milano Centrale; X Hannover - Chiasso.
54 – GUSTAVE EIFFEL – [2] and X Frankfurt/Main - Saarbrücken - Paris Est.
56 – HEINRICH HEINE – [2] and X Dresden Hbf - Saarbrücken - Paris Est.
103 – RÄTIA – [2] and X Dortmund - Chur.
105 – BERNER OBERLAND – [2] and X Amsterdam Schiphol +– Interlaken Ost.
109 – THUNERSEE – [2] and X Berlin Zoo - Interlaken Ost.
501 – MARIE LUISE KASCHNITZ – [2] and X Berlin Zoo - Basel.

IC556 – [2] and X Dresden Hbf (Leipzig on Dec. 25) - Saarbrücken.
IR2213 – MURGTAL – [2] and ♀ Dortmund - Freudenstadt; [2] Dortmund - Karlsruhe (E3005) - Pforzheim (6077) - Bad Wildbad.
IR2215 – [2] Münster (Emden /) - Heidelberg; ♀ Leer - Heidelberg.
IR2217 – HÖLLENTAL – [2] and ♀ Emden - Seebrugg.
IR2219 – [2] and ♀ Norddeich Mole - Heidelberg.
IR2573 – [2] and ♀ Dessau (Kassel Hbf on Dec. 25, Jan. 1) - Konstanz.
C – [2] and ♀ Kassel - Konstanz; [2] Hamburg Altona - Konstanz.
M – [2] and X Hamburg Altona - Zürich Hbf.
/ – ① - ⑥ (not Dec. 25 - Jan. 1, Apr. 15 - 17, May 1, 1995).

Table 730 — KASSEL - FRANKFURT (MAIN) - KONSTANZ and BASEL

1, 2 class except where shown

	IC 558 ✕ M	IR 2311 ♦	IR 2579 ✕	ICE 671 2	D 1173 ✕	ICE 899 ✕	IC 605 ♦ ⚑	IR 2579 ♦	E 3611	ICE 775 ✕	E 3187	ICE 599 ⚑	IC 503 ✕	E 3571	IC 650 ♦ M	IR 2313 ♦	IR 2673 ✕	ICE 673 ♦	E 3065	ICE 795 ⚑	IC 505 ⚑	E 3469	IR 2673	E 3613	ICE 777 ♣✕
Hamburg Hbf 750 ... d.			1142	1337					1437								1729	1537		1602			1819		1637
Kassel Hbf .... d.		1529							1619														1825		
Kassel Wilhelmshöhe .. d.			1536	1545	1613		1625		1645	1713							1736	1745		1813			1845		1845
Wabern .... d.			1554						1645								1754						1902		
Treysa .... d.			1611						1702								1811						1933		
Marburg .... d.			1635						1733								1835						1952		
Gießen .... d.			1654						←1752								1854								
Frankfurt (Main) Hbf . a.			1735	1705	1739		1735		1835	1805		1839					1935	1905		1939			2035	2035	2005
Frankfurt (Main) Hbf . d.	1651		1747	1709	1743	1717	1747			1809		1843	1851				1947	1909		1943			1947		2009
Dortmund 650 ..... d.					1440							1538			1628		1645			1638	1728				
Düsseldorf Hbf 650 . d.		1445										1628			1700	1711					1800				
Köln Hbf 650 ..... d.		1511			1600							1700			1904					1942					
Mainz .... d.		1704			1742							1842	1911		1924						2006				2029
Darmstadt .... d.	1711	1724				1806									1911	1924			1950		2006		2018		2029
Bensheim .... d.		1736				1818									1936	1945							2018		2026
Weinheim .... d.		1745				1826									1945								2024	2023	2026
Mannheim .... a.	1744					1823		1850				1924	1923	1931	1944				1950		2024	2023	2031		
Mannheim 742 .... d.		1759		1758	1807	1824	1831				1842												2042		2103
Heidelberg 742 .... d.								1858					1821			2002					2018		2058		
Bruchsal .... d.								1858								2031							2112		2131
Karlsruhe 728 ..... d.				1821	1840		1856	1912		1923	1928		1956			2031			2036		2051		2124		2131
Rastatt 728 .... d.							1924			1941											2057		2130		
Baden Baden ...... d.				1900			1911	1930		1947											2128	2111	2151		
Offenburg .... a.							1951	1956	2021		2028									2136	2153			2204	2206
Offenburg .... d.							1953	1958			2030	2037									2213				
Hausach .... d.								2013				2105									2236				
Triberg .... d.								2036				2132									2251				
St Georgen .... d.								2051				2148									2303				
Villingen .... d.								2103				2200									2314				
Donaueschingen ... d.								2114				2212									2325				
Immendingen ...... d.								2125				2230									2350				
Singen 734 .... d.								2150				2254									2359				
Radolfzell 734 .... d.								2159				2306									0014				
Konstanz .... a.								2214				2322										2201	2220		2235
Freiburg (Breisgau) .. d.					2001				2029				2101									2236	2304		
Basel Bad Bf ...... a.					2036				2103				2136									2243			
Basel SBB .... a.					2043				2110				2143												

	ICE 695 ✕	IC 507 ✕ ♦	IC 762 ✕♦	IC 652 M	ICE 677 ♣✕	D 1005 ♦	D 1205 ⚑	IR 2477 ⚑	ICE 797 ✕	IC 607 ♦⚑	E 3499 Ⓐ	IR 2477 ♦	E 3615	ICE 697 ✕	IC 509 ⚑	IC 201 ♦	IC 401 ♦	IC 939 ♦	IC 949 ♦	IR 2479	ICE 799 S	E 3617	D 203 K	D 1203 K	D 471
Hamburg Hbf 750 ... d.						1542	1802														2002				2132
Kassel Hbf .... d.						1929							2019												
Kassel Wilhelmshöhe .. d.	1913			1945		1936	2013						2025	2113						2129	2136	2216	2225		
Wabern .... d.						1954							2045							2154		2211	2245		
Treysa .... d.						2011							2102							2211		2235	2302		
Marburg .... d.						2035							2133							2235		2254	2333		
Gießen .... d.						2054							←2152							2335		2341	2352		
Frankfurt (Main) Hbf . a.	2039			2105		2135	2139		2135	2235	2248							2255	2256	2259		2335	2341		0035
Frankfurt (Main) Hbf . d.	2043			2051	2109	2115	2147		2143		2147														
Dortmund 650 ..... d.		1740				1755	1853u			1840				1938	1909								2321	2342	
Düsseldorf Hbf 650 . d.						1929u				2000				2028	2036	2100	2106u						2359	0011	
Köln Hbf 650 ..... d.		1900				2123u				2142				2100	2106u			2242	2258u				0150v		
Mainz .... d.		2042				2135u				2206								2314u		2320			0236		
Darmstadt .... d.				2111		2135u				2218				2226											
Bensheim .... d.										2218				2226											
Weinheim .... d.										2226															
Mannheim .... a.	2124	2123		2144	2150	2207u		2224	2223									2328	2339u	2345	2355				
Mannheim 742 .... d.		2131			2153	2211u			2231									2331	2341u	2348	0002				
Heidelberg 742 .... d.					2211u					2243	3461			2259	E			2353e	2349f	0001	0015		0315		
Bruchsal .... d.										2259	⑥⑦									0019	0033		0357		
Karlsruhe 728 ..... d.			2154	2204		2215	2240u	2302u		2254	2306	2315	2323		2357t	0038u	0040								
Rastatt 728 .... d.											2318		2335										0415		
Baden Baden ...... d.			2220				2320u				2323		2341										0437	0459s	0510
Offenburg .... a.			2240				2342u				2350			0009									0442	0501s	0513
Offenburg .... d.			2241				2345u				2351			0010											
Hausach .... d.																									
Freiburg (Breisgau) .. d.			2310				0021u				0029			0048									0520	0535s	055?
Basel Bad Bf ...... a.			2345				0100u				0111			0130									0600	0625	0630
Basel SBB .... a.			2352				0126																0626		065?

♦ — NOTES (LISTED BY TRAIN NUMBERS)

D201 — ⛴ 1,2 cl., ⛴ 2 cl. and ⎚ Dortmund - Milano; ⛴ 1,2 cl., ⛴ 2 cl. and ⎚ Frankfurt/Main (D401) - Heidelberg - Milano.
D401 — Conveys Milano cars for D201 at Heidelberg and Paris cars for D260 at Karlsruhe.
D471 — KOMET – ⛴ 1,2 cl. (T2), ⛴ 1,2 cl., ⎚ 2 cl. and ⛐ Hamburg Altona - Basel.
IC503 — MARK BRANDENBURG - ⎚ and ⛐ Berlin Zoo - Basel.
IC505 — KAISERSTUHL – ⎚ and ✕ Berlin Zoo - Basel.
IC507 — STOLZENFELS – ⎚ Berlin Zoo - Karlsruhe; ✕ Berlin - Mainz.
IC509 — RHEINFELS – ⎚ and ⛐ Berlin Zoo - Karlsruhe.
IC605 — HEINRICH DER LÖWE – ⎚ and ✕ Braunschweig - Basel.
IC762 — BADEN KURIER – ⎚ and ✕ München Hbf - Karlsruhe - Basel.
IC939 — ① - ⑤: ⎚ Frankfurt Flughafen ✈ (depart 2236) - Stuttgart.
IC949 — ⑥⑦: ⎚ Frankfurt Flughafen ✈ (depart 2237) - Stuttgart.
D1005 — ITALIA EXPRESS – Mar. 31 - May 27: conveys Roma cars for D1205.
D1173 — Mar. 31 - May 27. See Table 79.
D1205 — ITALIA EXPRESS – Mar. 31 - May 27: ⛴ 1,2 cl., ⎚ 2 cl. and ⎚ Dortmund - Roma Termini; ⛴ 1,2 cl., ⎚ 2 cl. and ⎚ Frankfurt/Main (D1005) - Karlsruhe - Roma.

IR2311 — ⎚ and ⛐ Emden - Heidelberg - Heilbronn - Stuttgart.
IR2313 — ⎚ and ⛐ Norddeich Mole - Karlsruhe.
IR2477 — ⎚ Kassel - Karlsruhe; ⎚ Hamburg - Karlsruhe; ⛐ Kassel - Gießen.
IR2579 — ⎚ Kassel - Karlsruhe; ⎚ Hamburg - Konstanz; ⛐ Kassel - Villingen.
IR2673 — ⎚ Halle - Karlsruhe ⑥, Konstanz ⑦; ⛐ Halle - Karlsruhe.
C — ⎚ and ✕ Kassel - Konstanz; ⎚ Hamburg Altona - Konstanz.
K — SCHWEIZ EXPRESS – see Table 38.
M — ⎚ and ✕ Dresden Hbf - Saarbrücken.
S — Not Dec. 24, 31.
e — Stops to pick up only. Departs 0006.
f — Stops to pick up only. Departs 0010..
s — Stops to set down only.
t — On ⑥⑦, also Apr. 14, 17, May 1, 25 arrive 0012.
u — Stops to pick up only.
v — ②③④⑤⑥ only.
♣ — Daily except ⑥ (not Dec. 24 - 31, Apr. 14 - 16, Apr. 30, 1995).

Table 730 — BASEL and KONSTANZ - FRANKFURT/MAIN - KASSEL

1, 2 class except where shown

km		E 3600	IC 938	IC 948	IR 2478	D 200	D 400	IR 2312	IC 508	ICE 696 / E3650 E3602	IC 518	ICE 672	IR 2476	IC 763	IC 506	ICE 796	IR 2476	D 1204	IR 2310	D 1004	ICE 776	IC 653	E 3550
	Basel SBB .... d.													0512				0457s					
	Basel Bad Bf ▲ .... d.																						
	Freiburg (Breisgau) .. d.													0546				0538s				0633	
0	Konstanz ▲ .... d.																						
20	Radolfzell 734 ...... d.																						
30	Singen 734 .... d.																						
60	Immendingen .... d.																						
79	Donaueschingen .... d.																						0545
93	Villingen .... d.																						0556
108	St Georgen .... d.																						0605
123	Triberg .... d.																						0620
146	Hausach .... d.																						0642
179	Offenburg .... a.											0614						0610s			0700		0710
179	Offenburg .... d.											0616						0619s			0702		
220	Baden Baden ...... d.											0635						0641s					
228	Rastatt 728 .... d.																						
252	Karlsruhe 728 ..... d.		0429	0429	0500s	0519		0523	0602			0626	0642		0653	0702		0706s		0721s		0737	
273	Bruchsal .... d.							0537							0658								
306	Heidelberg 742 .... d.		0449	0449	0534s	0550s		0558			0651	0655	0716							0758	0804s		
323	Mannheim 742 ..... a.		0501	0501	0546s				0627			0706			0727			0740s		0802			
323	Mannheim .... d.		0503	0508	0549s	0636	0635					0708			0737	0735		0742s		0808		0813	
	Weinheim .... d.							0611							0730					0811			
	Bensheim .... d.			0531											0738					0820			
	Darmstadt .... d.			0544		0626s		0633				0726			0751				0833	0837s		0846	
	Mainz .... a.					0630s		0652	0716		0746		0816					0830s		0852			
	Köln Hbf 650 ...... a.					0821s		0845	0859		0929		0959					1021s		1045			
	Düsseldorf Hbf 650 . a.							0851	0911		0955		1031					1103s		1111			
	Dortmund 650 ..... a.							0948	1020		1048		1120					←		1203			
	Frankfurt/Main Hbf .. a.		0552	0605			0652			0714		0747	0808			0814	0808				0859	0847	0906
	Frankfurt/Main Hbf .. d.	0519		0622						0718		0751	0822			0818	0822					0851	
	Gießen .... d.	0605		0704						0808			0904										
	Marburg .... d.	0622		0722						0825			0922										
	Treysa .... d.	0652		0745						0855			0945										
	Wabern .... d.	0708		0802						0911			1002										
	Kassel Wilhelmshöhe . a.	0727		0824						0842 0930		0911						0944	1024		1011		
	Kassel Hbf .... a.	0735		0831						0938		0911							1031				
	Hamburg Hbf 750 .. a.									1121								1156	1416		1221		

		IC 504	ICE 694	E 3604	ICE 670	IR 2672	IC 604	E 788	ICE 3056	IR 2672	ICE 76	IR 2218	IC 651	E 3556	IC 502	ICE 598	E 3606	D 1172	E 3178	IR 2578	ICE 774	IR 2578	IC 500	ICE 896	IR 2578	IR 2216
	Basel SBB .... d.					0717						0752			0817						0852		0917			
	Basel Bad Bf ▲ .... d.	0620				0724						0759			0824						0859		0924			
	Freiburg (Breisgau) .. d.	0654				0758						0833			0858						0933		0958			1012
	Konstanz ▲ .... d.								0547				0634						0747							
	Radolfzell 734 ...... d.								0603				0655						0803							
	Singen 734 .... d.								0613				0705						0812							
	Immendingen .... d.								0634				0727						0833							
	Donaueschingen .... d.								0646				0741						0844							
	Villingen .... d.								0658				0805						0854							
	St Georgen .... d.								0707				0815						0903							
	Triberg .... d.								0722				0830						0918							
	Hausach .... d.								0744				0852						0939							
	Offenburg .... a.	0723						0826	0804				0900				0926		0958	1000	0958					1045
	Offenburg .... d.	0725					0835	0828	0806				0902				0928			1006	1006	1002				1047
	Baden Baden ...... d.	0744					0906	0831	0825								0954 1006	1012		1025		1044				1105
	Rastatt 728 .... d.						0912		0831									1012								1112
	Karlsruhe 728 ..... d.	0802					0927	0902	0846		0927		0937			1002	1016	1034		1037	1046	1102				1127
	Bruchsal .... d.							0858			0954									1057						1139
	Heidelberg 742 .... d.							0916			1026		0958							1057	1116					1158
	Mannheim 742 ..... a.	0827					0927				1002				1027	1053				1102		1127				
	Mannheim .... d.	0837	0835				0937	0937			1008		1013		1037	1056	1035			1108		1137	1135			
	Weinheim .... d.				0930							1011										1130				1211
	Bensheim .... d.				0938							1020										1138				1220
	Darmstadt .... d.				0951						1046	1033										1151				1233
	Mainz .... a.	0916			1016						1052				1116					1216						1252
	Köln Hbf 650 ...... a.	1059			1159						1245				1259					1359						1445
	Düsseldorf Hbf 650 . a.	1131			1320						1311				1331											1511
	Dortmund 650 ..... a.	1220			1320						1420				1420					1520		←				
	Frankfurt/Main Hbf .. a.		0914		1008				1014	1008	1047		1106				1114		1201		1147	1208		1214	1208	
	Frankfurt/Main Hbf .. d.		0918	0922	0952	1022			1018	1022	1051				1118	1122				1208	1151	1222		1218	1222	
	Gießen .... d.			1008						1104						1208									1304	
	Marburg .... d.			1025						1122						1225									1322	
	Treysa .... d.			1055						1145						1255									1345	
	Wabern .... d.			1111						1202						1311									1402	
	Kassel Wilhelmshöhe . a.	1044	1130	1111					1142	1224	1211								1244		1311			1344	1424	
	Kassel Hbf .... a.		1138							1231						1338									1431	
	Hamburg Hbf 750 .. a.				1321					1356	1421										1521				1816	

♦ – **NOTES** (LISTED BY TRAIN NUMBERS)

ICE76 – PANDA – ⊡ and X Zürich Hbf - Hamburg Altona.
D200 – ⊨ 1,2cl., ⊡ 2cl. and ⊡ Milano Dortmund; ⊨ 1,2cl., ⊡ 2cl. and ⊡ Milano - Heidelberg (D400) - Frankfurt/Main.
D400 – Conveys Paris cars of D261 and Milano cars of D200 from Karlsruhe.
IC500 – MARIE LUISE KASCHNITZ – ⊡ and Y Basel - Braunschweig.
IC502 – MARK BRANDENBURG – ⊡ and X Basel - Berlin Zoo.
IC504 – KAISERSTUHL – ⊡ and X Basel Bad - Berlin Zoo.
IC506 – STOLZENFELS – ⊡ and X Karlsruhe - Berlin Zoo.
IC508 – RHEINFELS – ⊡ and X Karlsruhe - Berlin Zoo.
IC518 – OSKAR SCHLEMMER – ⊡ and X Stuttgart - Dortmund.
IC604 – HEINRICH DER LÖWE – ⊡ and X Basel - Braunschweig.
ICE696 – BETTINA VON ARNIM – ⊡ and X Frankfurt/Main (Stuttgart ✗) - Berlin Zoo.
IC763 – BADEN KURIER – ⊡ and X Basel Bad - München Hbf.
IC938 – ①-⑥: ⊡ Stuttgart - Frankfurt Flughafen ✈ (arrive 0616).
IC948 – ⑦: ⊡ Stuttgart - Frankfurt Flughafen ✈ (arrive 0623).
D1004 – ITALIA EXPRESS – Nov. 1 - 5, Mar. 31 - May 27: conveys Roma cars from D1204.

D1172 – Mar. 31 - May 27. See Table 79.
D1204 – ITALIA EXPRESS – Nov. 1 - 5, Mar. 31 - May 27 (from Roma): ⊨ 2cl. and ⊡ (also ⊨ 1,2cl. except on Nov. 4, 5) Roma Termini - Dortmund; ⊨ 1,2cl., ⊨ 2cl. and ⊡ Roma - Karlsruhe (D1004) - Frankfurt/Main.
IR2216 – HÖLLENTAL – ⊡ and X Seebrugg - Norddeich.
IR2218 – ⊡ and Y Heidelberg - Norddeich Mole.
IR2310 – ⊡ and Y Stuttgart - Heilbronn - Heidelberg - Emden.
IR2312 – ⊡ Karlsruhe - Norddeich Mole; Y Heidelberg - Norddeich.
IR2476 – ⊡ and Y Karlsruhe - Kassel; ⊡ Karlsruhe - Hamburg Altona.
IR2478 – ⊡ and Y Karlsruhe - Kassel; ⊡ Dec. 25, Jan. 1.
IR2672 – ⊡ and Y Karlsruhe (Konstanz ①-⑥) - Kassel.
C – ⊡ Konstanz - Kassel; ⊡ Konstanz - Hamburg.Altona.
L – ⊡ Konstanz - Kassel; ⊡ Konstanz - Dresden Hbf.
M – ⊡ Konstanz - Saarbrücken - Dresden Hbf.
s – Stops to set down only.
✗ – ①-⑥ (not Dec. 25 - Jan. 1, Apr. 15 - 17, May 1, 1995).

Table 730 — BASEL and KONSTANZ - FRANKFURT (MAIN) - KASSEL

1, 2 class except where shown

	ICE 578 ✗	IC 559 ✗ M	E 3560	IC 602 ✗	ICE 596 ✗	E 3608	E 3180	ICE 576 ✗	IR 2576 ♦	EC 102 ✗♦	ICE 794 ✗	IR 2576 ♦	ICE 574 ✗	IR 2214 ♦	EC 57 ✗♦	E 3562	EC 108 ✗	ICE 594 ✗	E 3610	E 3182	ICE 70 ✗♦	IR 2574 ♀C	EC 104 ✗	ICE 894 ✗	IR 2574 ♀C
Basel SBB d				1017					1117								1217				1252		1317		
Basel Bad Bf d				1024					1124								1224				1259		1324		
Freiburg (Breisgau) d				1058					1158								1258				1333		1358		
Konstanz d			0850					0949								1050						1149			
Radolfzell 734 d			0908					1003								1108						1203			
Singen 734 d			0917					1013								1117						1213			
Immendingen d			0939					1034								1139						1234			
Donaueschingen d			0953					1046								1153						1246			
Villingen d			1005					1058								1205						1258			
St Georgen d			1015					1107								1215						1307			
Triberg d			1030					1122								1230						1322			
Hausach d			1052					1144								1252						1344			
Offenburg a			1118	1126				1204								1318	1326				1400	1404			
Offenburg d				1128		1135			1206								1328		1335		1402	1406			
Baden Baden d						1206			1225	1244											1406	1425	1444		
Rastatt 728 d						1212			1231												1412	1431			
Karlsruhe 728 d	1137			1202		1234	1237	1246		1302			1337				1402				1434	1437	1446	1502	
Bruchsal d							1301		1258												1501		1458		
Heidelberg 742 d							1333	1316						1358							1533	1516			
Mannheim 742 a	1202			1227					1302	1327			1402				1427				1502		1527		
Mannheim d	1208	1213		1237	1235			1308	1337	1335			1408		1413		1437	1435			1508		1537	1535	
Weinheim d									1330					1411	1420							1530			
Bensheim d									1338					1420								1538			
Darmstadt a		1246							1351					1433	1446							1551			
Mainz a				1316					1416					1452			1516					1616			
Köln Hbf 650 a				1459					1559					1645			1659					1759			
Düsseldorf Hbf 650 a				1631					1631					1711								1824			
Dortmund 650 a				1720								←		1820								←			
Frankfurt (Main) Hbf a	1247	1306		1314				1347	1408		1414	1408	1447		1506			1514			1547	1608		1614	1608
Frankfurt (Main) Hbf d	1251			1318	1322			1351	1422		1418	1422	1451		1504			1518	1522		1551	1622		1618	1622
Gießen d					1408						→			1522					1608				→		1704
Marburg d					1425									1545					1625						1722
Treysa d					1455									1602					1655						1802
Wabern d					1511														1711						
Kassel Wilhelmshöhe a	1411				1444	1530		1511					1542	1624	1611			1644	1730		1711			1744	1824
Kassel Hbf a						1538								1631					1738						1831
Hamburg Hbf 750 a	1621							1721					1821								1921				2216

	IR 2212 ♀♦	ICE 572 ✗	IC 557 ✗M	E 3566	EC 2 ♦	ICE 592 ✗	E 3184	IR 2572 ♀	ICE 770 ✗	IR 2572 ♀	EC 8 ✗	ICE 792 ✗	IR 2572 ♀	E 3066	ICE 570 ♣✗	IR 2210 ♀	EC 55 ✗	E 3568	EC 106 ✗	ICE 590 ✗	E 3614	IR 2570 ♀	EC 4 ✗	ICE 892 ✗	IR 2570 ♀
Basel SBB d						1417			1452		1517									1617			1717		
Basel Bad Bf d						1424			1459		1524									1624			1724		
Freiburg (Breisgau) d						1458			1533		1558									1658			1758		
Konstanz d			1250					1349												1549					
Radolfzell 734 d			1308					1403												1603					
Singen 734 d			1317					1412												1613					
Immendingen d			1339					1433												1634					
Donaueschingen d			1353					1444												1646					
Villingen d			1405					1454												1658					
St Georgen d			1415					1503												1707					
Triberg d			1430					1518												1722					
Hausach d			1452					1539												1744					
Offenburg a			1518	1526				1558	1600	1558								1718	1726			1804			
Offenburg d				1528			1535	1606	1602	1558						1632			1728			1806			
Baden Baden d							1606		1625	1644						1703						1825	1844		
Rastatt 728 d	1456						1612		1631							1709						1831			
Karlsruhe 728 d	1527	1537				1602	1634		1637	1646	1702				1734	1737			1802			1846	1902		
Bruchsal d	1539								1657						1754							1858			
Heidelberg 742 d	1558								1716		1716				1826					1916					
Mannheim 742 a		1602				1627			1702		1727				1802				1827			1927			
Mannheim d		1608	1613			1637	1635		1708		1737	1735			1808	1813		1837	1835			1930	1937		1935
Weinheim d	1611								1730					1811								1930			
Bensheim d	1620								1738					1820								1938			
Darmstadt a	1633		1646						1751					1833	1847							1951			
Mainz a	1652				1716				1816					1852			1916					2016			
Köln Hbf 650 a	1845				1859				1959					2045			2059					2159			
Düsseldorf Hbf 650 a	1911				1924		E		2031					2111			2131								
Dortmund 650 a							3612		2120					2209			2220					2320			
Frankfurt (Main) Hbf a		1647	1706			1714			1747	1808		1814	1808		1847		1906			1914	1922	2008		2014	2008
Frankfurt (Main) Hbf d		1651				1718	1722		1751	1822		1818	1822		1851			1918			2008	2022		2018	2022
Gießen d						1808				→			1904					1922			2025			2122	
Marburg d						1825							1922					1945			2055			2122	
Treysa d						1855							1945					2011			2111			2202	
Wabern d						1911							2002					2111							
Kassel Wilhelmshöhe a	1811					1842	1930		1911				1944	2024	2011			2042	2130			2144		2224	
Kassel Hbf a						1938							2031					2138						2231	
Hamburg Hbf 750 a		2021							2122		2158														

♦ – NOTES (LISTED BY TRAIN NUMBERS)
EC2 – REMBRANDT – 🚗 and ✗ Chur - Amsterdam CS.
EC4 – VERDI – 🚗 Milano Centrale - Dortmund; ✗ Chiasso - Dortmund.
EC8 – TIZIANO – 🚗 Milano Centrale - Hannover; ✗ Chiasso - Hannover.
EC55 – GUSTAVE EIFFEL – 🚗 and ✗ Paris Est - Saarbrücken - Frankfurt/Main.
EC57 – HEINRICH HEINE – 🚗 and ✗ Paris Est - Saarbrücken - Dresden Hbf.
ICE70 – HELVETIA – 🚗 and ✗ Zürich Hbf - Hamburg Altona.
EC102 – RÄTIA – 🚗 and ✗ Chur - Berlin Zoo.
EC104 – BERNER OBERLAND – 🚗 and ✗ Interlaken Ost - Amsterdam Schiphol +.

EC106 – MONT BLANC – 🚗 and ✗ Genève - Dortmund.
EC108 – THUNERSEE – 🚗 and ✗ Interlaken Ost - Berlin Zoo.
IR2212 – MURGTAL – 🚗 Freudenstadt - Münster (Emden ♣); 🚗 Bad Wildbad (E3022) - Karlsruhe - Münster (Emden ♣); ♀ Freudenstadt - Lingen.
IR2214 – 🚗 and ♀ Heidelberg - Norddeich.
IR2576 – 🚗 and ♀ Konstanz - Dessau (Kassel on Dec. 24, 31).
C – 🚗 and ♀ Konstanz - Kassel; 🚗 Konstanz - Hamburg Altona.
M – 🚗 and ✗ Saarbrücken - Dresden Hbf;
♣ – Daily except ⑥ (not Dec. 24 - 31, Apr. 14 - 16, Apr. 30, 1995).

Table 730 — BASEL and KONSTANZ - FRANKFURT (MAIN) - KASSEL
1, 2 class except where shown

	IC 553	D 351	E 3570	EC 100	ICE 790	E 3616	D 351	E 3188	IR 2670	IC 600	ICE 996	E 3618	E 3574	EC 53	ICE 270	ICE 994	E 3190	D 1998	IR 2472	D 359	E 3576	E3434 E3448	D 470	D 202	D 1202
	◆♀				◆✖					◆	✖			✖	✖	✖	◆	♀	♀			◆		K	K
Basel SBB d.		1749		1817						1917					2020					2117				2318	2325
Basel Bad Bf m d.		1757		1824						1924					2027					2135			2340u	2353	2358
Freiburg (Breisgau) d.		1838		1858						1958					2101					2214			0021u	0033	0040u
Konstanz m d.			1646						1749				1850					1949			2055				
Radolfzell 734 d.			1708						1803				1908					2003			2109				
Singen 734 d.			1719						1813				1917					2013			2117				
Immendingen d.			1740						1834				1939					2034			2139				
Donaueschingen d.			1754						1846				1953					2046			2150				
Villingen d.			1805						1858				2005					2058			2200				
St Georgen d.			1815						1907				2014					2107			2209				
Triberg d.			1830						1922				2028					2122			2224				
Hausach d.			1852						1944				2050					2136			2245				
Offenburg a.		1910	1918	1926					2004				2115		2128			2144		2251	2305			0053u	0105
Offenburg d.		1913		1928					1935	2006					2129		2135	2206		2254	2311		0055u	0112	0117
Baden Baden a.		1936					1936	2006	2025	2044					2206			2225		2316	2337				0134
Rastatt 728 d.		→						2012	2031						2212			2231		2343					
Karlsruhe 728 d.				2002				2009	2034	2046	2102				2203		2227	2232	2246	2338	2358			0202	
Bruchsal d.									2023	2058								2245	2302		0011				
Heidelberg 742 d.									2045	2116					2310		2320		0008		0032			0235	
Mannheim 742 a.				2027						2127					2227					2227					
Mannheim d.	2013			2037	2035					2137	2135			2221	2236	2235									
Weinheim d.										2130															
Bensheim d.										2138															
Darmstadt d.	2046							2130		2151					2255			2344						0309	
Mainz a.				2118						2218					2318									0353	
Köln Hbf 650 a.																								0545	0540s
Düsseldorf Hbf 650 a.																						E 3656		0617	0612
Dortmund 650 a.																									
Frankfurt (Main) Hbf a.	2106			2114		2154			2208		2214			2315	2316			0006							
Frankfurt (Main) Hbf d.				2118	2122				2222		2222				2325	0015									
Gießen d.							2208		2304		2321		0058												
Marburg d.							2225		2322		2325		0045												
Treysa d.							2255		2345		2355														
Wabern d.							2311		0002		0011														
Kassel Wilhelmshöhe a.						2244	2331		0023		0030							0223							
Kassel Hbf a.							2338		0028		0038														
Hamburg Hbf 750 ...																		0651					0831		

◆ – NOTES (LISTED BY TRAIN NUMBERS)

EC53 – GOETHE – [1,2 cl. car] and [restaurant] Paris Est - Saarbrücken - Frankfurt/Main.
EC100 – MATTERHORN – [car] and [restaurant] Brig - Mainz - Worms - Wiesbaden (arrive 2131).
ICE270 – JOHANNA SPYRI – [car] and [restaurant] Zürich Hbf - Frankfurt/Main.
D351 – ARKONA – [sleeper] 1,2 cl., [couchette] 2 cl., [car] and [restaurant] Basel - Stralsund (Binz on ⑥ Apr. 8 - May 27, and Apr. 14, 17, May 25, not Apr. 15); [sleeper] 1,2 cl. and [couchette] 2 cl. Basel - Bebra (D482) - København.
D359 – [sleeper] 1,2 cl., [couchette] 2 cl., [car] and [restaurant] Basel - Berlin Zoo; [sleeper] 1,2 cl., [couchette] 2 cl. and [car] Basel - Halle (D1949) - Dresden Hbf. Train does not stop between Heidelberg and Halle.

D470 – KOMET – [sleeper] 1,2 cl. (T2), [sleeper] 1,2 cl., [couchette] 2 cl. and [restaurant] Basel - Hamburg Altona.
IC553 – PFÄLZER WALD – [car] and [restaurant] Saarbrücken - Frankfurt/Main.
IC600 – BADENIA – [car] and [restaurant] Basel - Wiesbaden (arrive 2231).
ICE994 – RHEINGAU – [car] and [restaurant] Basel - Wiesbaden (arrive 2330).
D1998 – [sleeper] 1,2 cl., [couchette] 2 cl., [car] and [restaurant] Stuttgart - Hamburg Altona.
IR2472 – [car] Konstanz - Karlsruhe [restaurant], Heidelberg ⑦, also Apr. 17, May 1, not Apr. 16, 30; [restaurant] Konstanz - Villingen.
IR2670 – [car] Konstanz - Frankfurt/Main ⑥, Kassel ⑧; [restaurant] Konstanz - Frankfurt/Main.
K – SCHWEIZ EXPRESS – see Table 38.
s – Stops to set down only.
u – Stops to pick up only.

Table 731 — FREIBURG - NEUSTADT and SEEBRUGG
36 km to Neustadt, 50 km to Seebrugg. 1, 2 class

Rail services Freiburg (Breisgau) - Neustadt (Schwarzwald) and Seebrugg. All trains call at Titisee 37 minutes from Freiburg, 28 minutes from Seebrugg and 5 minutes from Neustadt.

From Freiburg - Neustadt: 0558 Ⓐ, 0630 ✕, 0743, 0841, 0941, 1041, 1141, 1211 Ⓐ, 1241, 1341, 1441, 1511 © A, 1541, 1641, 1741, 1841, 1911, 1941 Ⓑ, 2011, 2041 ⑦, 2111 Ⓑ.
From Neustadt - Freiburg: 0540 Ⓐ, 0618 ✕, 0649 ✕, 0731, 0801 Ⓑ, 0831, 0931, 1331, 1431, 1531 © A, 1431, 1531, 1631, 1731, 1831, 1931, 2031, 2131 ⑦.
From Freiburg - Seebrugg: 0708, 0811, 0911, 1011⑦, 1111, 1211©, 1311, 1411, 1611 Ⓑ, 1711, 1811.
From Seebrugg - Freiburg: 0838 C, 0938, 1038, 1138⑦, 1238, 1338©, 1438, 1538, 1638, 1740, 1838, 1940.

A – © also Nov. 1, Jan. 6: [car] Freiburg - München and v.v. See Tables 732, 733, 765. B – IR2217 – [car] and [restaurant] Emden - Seebrugg. C – IR2216 and [car] Seebrugg - Norddeich.

Table 732 — NEUSTADT - DONAUESCHINGEN - ULM
1, 2 class

km		E3349 L	3351	3353	3355	3357	3359	E3211	3361	3365 G©
0	Neustadt (Schwarzwald) 736 d.		0726	0930	1130	1330	1530	1556	1730	1930
40	Donaueschingen 736 a.		0811	1008	1208	1410	1608	1638	1808	2008
40	Donaueschingen d.	0528	0815	1017	1217	1417	1617	1651	1817	2017
59	Immendingen d.	0541	0830	1030	1230	1430	1630	1705	1830	2030
68	Tuttlingen a.	0549	0838	1038	1238	1438	1638	1712	1838	2038
68	Tuttlingen d.	0550	0849	1049	1253	1449	1649	1721	1849	
111	Sigmaringen d.	0627	0930	1130	1330	1530	1730	1802	1932	
139	Riedlingen d.	0650	0952	1152	1352	1552	1752		1954	
170	Ehingen d.	0714	1015	1215	1415	1615	1815		2017	
204	Ulm a.	0755	1044	1244	1444	1644	1844		2045	

	3350 B	3352	3354	E3210 G©	3356	3358	3360	3364	3366 L
Ulm d.	0549	0815	1015		1215	1415	1615	1815	1915
Ehingen d.	0616	0845	1045		1245	1445	1647	1847	1952
Riedlingen d.	0651	0907	1107		1307	1507	1707	1909	2024
Sigmaringen a.	0724	0931	1131	1150	1331	1531	1729	1931	
Tuttlingen a.	0800	1009	1209	1226	1409	1609	1809	2009	
Tuttlingen d.	0811	1011	1211	1248	1411	1611	1811	2011	
Immendingen d.	0822	1022	1222	1256	1422	1622	1822	2022	
Donaueschingen a.	0835	1035	1235	1308	1435	1635	1835	2035	
Donaueschingen 736 d.	0849	1049	1249	1320	1449	1649	1849	2049	
Neustadt (Schwarzwald) 736 a.	0925	1125	1325	1400	1525	1725	1925	2125	

B – ✕ from Ulm; daily from Tuttlingen. G – [car] Freiburg - München and v.v. See Tables 731, 733, 765. L – ✕, not Nov. 1, Jan. 6.

[bus] service Donaueschingen (Bf) - Blumberg (Zollhaus). Journey time: 30 minutes. Operator: SBG Südbadenbus, Villingen.
From Donaueschingen: 0650 ✕, 0840 Ⓐ, 0940, 1100 Ⓐ, 1145 Ⓑ, 1240 Ⓐ, 1300 ⑥⑦, 1615 ✕, 1650 Ⓑ, 1730 Ⓐ, 1800 Ⓐ, 1920 Ⓐ, 1940.
From Blumberg: 0659 ✕, 0730 ✕, 0908 Ⓑ, 1024 ⑦, 1129 Ⓐ, 1215 ⑥, 1349, 1504 Ⓐ, 1636 Ⓐ, 1654 Ⓐ, 1726 ⑥⑦, 1829 Ⓐ, 1954 Ⓐ, 2014 ⑥⑦.

[bus] service Waldshut (Bus Bf) - Blumberg (Zollhaus). Journey time: 80 minutes. Operator: SBG Südbadenbus, Waldshut.
From Waldshut: 0755 ✕, 0903 ⑦, 0924 Ⓐ, 1110 ⑥, 1120 Ⓐ, 1247 ✕, 1420 ✕, 1525 ✕, 1600 ⑦, 1650 Ⓐ, 1720 Ⓐ.
From Blumberg: 0730 ✕, 0831 ✕, 1040 ⑦, 1122 Ⓐ, 1204 Ⓑ, 1300 Ⓑ, 1352 Ⓐ, 1519 Ⓐ, 1650 ✕, 1724 Ⓐ, 1740 ⑦, 1843 Ⓐ, 1946 Ⓐ.

Table 733 — STUTTGART FLUGHAFEN ✈
Rail service Stuttgart Hbf (low level) - Flughafen Stuttgart ✈. 20 km. Journey time: 27 minutes. Services are reduced on Jan. 6.

From Stuttgart: 0518, 0538⑦, 0548⑦, 0608Ⓐ, 0618Ⓐ, 0628Ⓐ, 0638⑦, 0648⑦, 0708Ⓐ, 0718©, 0728Ⓐ, 0738⑦, 0748✕, 0808Ⓐ, 0818, 0838Ⓑ, 0848⑦, 0908Ⓐ, 0918, 0938Ⓐ, 0948✕, 1008Ⓐ, 1018, 1038Ⓑ, 1048✕, 1108Ⓐ, 1118, 1138Ⓑ, 1148✕, 1208Ⓐ, 1218, 1238Ⓑ, 1248✕, 1308Ⓐ, 1318, 1338Ⓑ, 1348, 1408Ⓐ, 1418, 1438Ⓑ, 1448, 1508Ⓐ, 1518, 1538Ⓑ, 1548, 1608Ⓐ, 1618, 1638Ⓑ, 1648, 1708Ⓐ, 1718, 1738Ⓑ, 1748, 1808Ⓐ, 1818, 1838Ⓐ, 1848, 1908Ⓐ, 1918, 1938Ⓐ, 1948, 2008, 2018, 2038, 2048Ⓐ, 2118, 2138, 2218, 2238, 2318, 2338.

From Stuttgart ✈: 0501Ⓐ, 0531⑦, 0551Ⓐ, 0601©, 0611Ⓐ, 0631⑦, 0641⑦, 0651Ⓐ, 0701©, 0711Ⓐ, 0731⑦, 0741Ⓑ, 0801, 0811Ⓐ, 0831⑦, 0841Ⓑ, 0901, 0911Ⓐ, 0931⑦, 0941Ⓑ, 1001, 1011Ⓐ, 1031⑦, 1041Ⓑ, 1101, 1111Ⓐ, 1131⑦, 1141Ⓑ, 1201, 1211Ⓐ, 1231⑦, 1241Ⓑ, 1301, 1311Ⓐ, 1331⑦, 1341Ⓑ, 1401, 1411Ⓐ, 1431⑦, 1441Ⓑ, 1501, 1511Ⓐ, 1531Ⓐ, 1601, 1611Ⓐ, 1631, 1641Ⓐ, 1701, 1711Ⓐ, 1731, 1741Ⓐ, 1801, 1811Ⓐ, 1831, 1841Ⓐ, 1901, 1911Ⓐ, 1931, 1941Ⓐ, 2001, 2011Ⓐ, 2031Ⓑ, 2041✕, 2101, 2131Ⓐ, 2141, 2201, 2241, 2301, 2341.

Table 734 — BASEL - SCHAFFHAUSEN - LINDAU
1, 2 class except where shown

km	Train											
		E3835E3863 / E4471E3778 (®A)	E / 3899 (2✕)	E3837E3865E3839E3867E3841E3869 / E4505E3780E4509E3784E4513E3786	E / 3843	E3871E3847E3873 / E3788E4483E3790 (A)	E / 3849	E3875E3851E3877E3895 / E3796E3743E3745E3747	E / 3879	5657 (2®)	E / 3897 (⑥)	E / 3897 (®)

km	Station										
0	Basel Bad Bf .... d.				0608	0818	1016	1216	1416	1615 1815	2015 2100
15	Rheinfelden (Baden) ... d.				0622	0830	1029	1229	1429	1628 1828	2029 2125
32	Bad Säckingen .... d.				0634	0841	1041	1241	1441	1641 1841	2041 2142
55	Waldshut .... d.				0652	0857	1057	1257	1457	1657 1857	2057 2204
75	Erzingen .... d.				0710	0913	1113	1313	1513	1713 1913	2113
94	Schaffhausen 735 ..... a.				0727	0929	1129	1329	1529	1729 1929	2129
113	Singen 735 .... a.				0745	0946	1146	1346	1546	1746 1946	2146
113	Singen 730 .... d.	0500 0547 0623	0754 0856	0954 1054	1154 1254	1354 1454	1554 1654	1754 1850	1954 2054	2154	2250
113	Radolfzell 730 .... d.	0508 0558 0635 0710	0804 0910	1004 1110	1204 1310	1404 1510	1604 1710	1804 1910	2004 2110	2203	2310 2310
138	Überlingen .... d.	0529 0619 0701 0733	0825 0933	1025 1133	1224 1333	1425 1533	1625 1733	1825 1933	2025 2133	2222	2333 2333
172	Friedrichshafen Stadt 761 .. d.	0606 0656 0734 0806	0857 1007	1100 1207	1257 1407	1500 1606	1659 1807	1900 2006	2103 2208	2328	0005 0005
206	Lindau 761 .... a.	0639 0735 0756e 0840	0931 1039	1131 1236	1332 1439	1528 1639	1732 1836	1931 2038	2132 2237	0002	
	Kempten 765 .... a.	0754 0853	0954 1052	1154 1255	1354 1452			2052 2151	2252 2357		
	Ulm 765 .... a.	0958	1158	1358	1558			2158			
	München Hbf 765 ...... a.	1129	1329	1529							

	Train											
		E / 5606 (2✕)	E / 3862 (✕)	E / 3864	E / 3866	E / 3868	E3732E3734E4502E3775E4506E3777E4474E3781E4510E3785 / E3836E3872E3838E3874E3840E3876E3842E3878E3844E3880 (A)	E4514E3789 / E3846E3882	5390 (2)	E4518E3791E4522E3793 / E3848E3884E3890E3892	E / 3120 (⑧)

	Station										
	München Hbf 765 ...... d.					0620	0820	1220	1415	1614	1820
	Ulm 765 .... d.				0800	1000	1200	1400	1600	1800	2000
	Kempten 765 .... d.			0602 0700 0805	0900 1005	1100 1205	1303 1405	1500 1603	1700 1803	1900 2005	2105
	Lindau 761 .... d.		0525 0614 0721	0828 0928	1028 1128	1222 1328	1428 1528	1628 1730	1818 1842	1928 2018	2130 2226 2302
	Friedrichshafen Stadt 761 .. d.		0555 0607 0657	0807 0858	1007 1058	1207 1258	1407 1458	1607 1658 1730	1807 1858 1925	2007 2058	2207 2258 0002
	Überlingen .... d.		0640 0734	0842 0934	1042 1134	1242 1334	1442 1534	1642 1734	1842 1934	2042 2134	2242 2334
	Radolfzell 730 .... d.		0702 0757	0902 0957	1102 1157	1302 1357	1502 1557	1702 1757	1902 1957	2102 2157	2303 2357
	Singen 730 .... a.		0805 0915	1005 1115	1205 1315	1405 1515	1605 1715	1805 1915	2005 2115	2205 2310	0005
	Singen 735 .... d.	0608	0814	1014	1214	1414	1614	1814 1902	2014		
	Schaffhausen 735 ..... d.	0630	0836	1036	1236	1436	1636	1836 1931	2036		
	Erzingen .... d.	0645	0851	1051	1251	1451	1651	1851 1957	2051		
	Waldshut .... d.	0618 0706	0910	1110	1310	1510	1710	1910 2016	2110		
	Bad Säckingen .... d.	0641 0723	0925	1125	1325	1525	1725	1925	2126		
	Rheinfelden (Baden) ... d.	0657 0734	0936	1136	1336	1536	1736	1936	2139		
	Basel Bad Bf .... a.	0712 0747	0948	1148	1348	1548	1748	1948	2150		

A – 🚃 Radolfzell - Augsburg and v.v.

Table 735 — STUTTGART - SINGEN - SCHAFFHAUSEN - ZÜRICH
1, 2 class except where shown

km	Station	1557	1559	1565	1567	EC 155 ✕	E 383	E 6505	E 1571	D 481 ◆	E 1577	E 6507	E 387 Ⓨ A	E 6509	E 1583	E 381 Ⓨ A	E 6511	IC 587 ⑤	D 6513 Ⓨ	E 389	E 6515	1593
0	Stuttgart .... d.					0656	0742	0827		0942	1025	1142	1225		1342	1425		1510	1542		1625
26	Böblingen .... d.						0803	0849		1004	1047	1204	1247		1404	1447		1532	1604		1647
67	Horb .... d.					0740	0831	0918		1031	1117	1231	1317		1431	1517		1608	1631		1717
110	Rottweil .... d.					0812	0900	0959		1100	1159	1300	1359		1500	1559		1643	1700		1756
138	Tuttlingen .... d.						0917	1019		1117	1219	1317	1419		1517	1618			1717		→
172	Singen .... d.					0848	0940	1044		1140	1244	1340	1444		1540				1740		
172	Singen 734 .... a.					0854	0952			1152		1352			1552				1752		
191	Schaffhausen 734 ... a.					0909	1005			1205		1405			1605				1805		
191	Schaffhausen .... d.	0607	0707	0809	0909	0912	1009		1109	1209	1309	1409		1509	1609		1709		1809		1909
219	Bülach .... d.	0630	0730	0830	0930		1030		1130	1230	1330	1430		1530	1630		1730		1830		1930
239	Zürich Hbf .... a.	0647	0747	0847	0947	0955	1047		1147	1247	1347	1447		1547	1647		1747		1847		1947

	Station	EC 159 ✕♥	E 6515	E 6517 ①-④	D 485 ◆	E 6519 G	7891	D 487	E 6521 ⑧	E 6523		Station	E 6502 Ⓐ	E 6506		E 6508	EC 158 ✕♥	E 6508	D 480	1558	E 6510
	Stuttgart .... d.	1652		1710	1742	1825		1942	2025	2225		Zürich Hbf ..... d.				0630		0713	0813		
	Böblingen .... d.			1732	1804	1847		2004	2047	2247		Bülach .... d.				0730		0830			
	Horb .... d.	1735		1808	1831	1917		2031	2117	2317		Schaffhausen ... a.				0704		0751	0851		
	Rottweil .... d.	1803	1810	1843	1900	2000		2100	2159	2350		Schaffhausen 734 d.				0705		0755			
	Tuttlingen .... d.	1819	1829		1919	2019		2117	2219			Singen 734 ..... a.				0718		0808			
	Singen .... a.	1845			1940	2044		2140	2244			Singen .... d.		0605d		0722		0819			0910d
	Singen 734 .... d.	1854			1952			2152				Tuttlingen ..... d.		0638		0726	0744	0842			0938
	Schaffhausen 734 ... a.	1909			2005			2205				Rottweil .... d.	0540	0659		0745	0800	0902			0959
	Schaffhausen .... d.	1912			2009		2052	2209				Horb .... d.	0613	0733		0823	0828	0835	0932		1035
	Bülach .... d.				2030		2130	2230				Böblingen ...... d.	0652	0803				0904	0959		1104
	Zürich Hbf .... a.	1955			2047		2147	2247				Stuttgart ...... a.	0714	0826		0913	0927	1022			1127

	Station	D 484	E 6512	D 1560	D 1084 ◆	E 486	E 6514	E 1568	D 386 ✚	E 6516	E 1572		D 388	E 6518	E 1576	D 380	E 6520	EC 154 ✕♥	E 6520	E 1582	D 382	1588	1590	7890	7894
	Zürich Hbf .... d.	0913		1013	1028	1113		1213	1313		1413		1513		1613	1713		1811		1813	1913	2013	2113	2213	2313
	Bülach .... d.	0930		1030	1046	1130		1230	1330		1430		1530		1630	1730				1830	1930	2030	2130	2230	2330
	Schaffhausen .... a.	0951		1051	1121s	1151		1251	1351		1451		1551		1653	1751		1849		1853	1951	2051	2151	2302	0002
	Schaffhausen 734 ... d.	0955			1136s	1155		1355			1555		1755		1850	1955									
	Singen 734 .... a.	1008			1150	1208		1408			1608		1808		1903	2008									
	Singen .... d.	1019	1110		1219	1310		1419	1510		1619		1819			1908				2019					
	Tuttlingen .... d.	1042	1138		1242	1338		1442	1538		1642		1725		1842	1920				2042					
	Rottweil .... d.	1102	1159		1302	1359		1502	1559		1702		1746		1902	1939	1947	1959		2102					
	Horb .... d.	1132	1235		1332	1435		1532	1635		1732		1835		1932		2015	2035		2132					
	Böblingen .... d.	1159	1304		1359	1504		1559	1704		1759		1904		1959					2159					
	Stuttgart .... a.	1222	1327		1422	1527		1622	1727		1822		1927		2022		2100	2127		2222					

♦ – NOTES (LISTED BY TRAIN NUMBERS)

D380 –	🚃 Milano Centrale - Stuttgart.
D382/3 –	🚃 Genova Porta Principe - Chiasso - Stuttgart and v.v.
D386 –	🚃 Milano Centrale - Chiasso - Zürich Hbf - Nürnberg; Ⓨ Chiasso - Singen.
D388 –	⊨ 2 cl. and 🚃 Lecce - Stuttgart; 🚃 Chiasso - Stuttgart.
D389 –	⊨ 2 cl. and 🚃 Stuttgart - Lecce; 🚃 Stuttgart - Chiasso; Ⓨ Singen - Chiasso.
D481 –	🚃 Nürnberg - Zürich Hbf - Locarno.
D485 –	🚃 Stuttgart - Chiasso.
D486 –	🚃 Chiasso - Stuttgart; conveys Napoli - Stuttgart cars of D1084 from Singen.

D487 –	🚃 Stuttgart - Zürich Hbf; conveys on Apr. 13: ⊨ 2 cl. and 🚃 Stuttgart - Zürich Hbf (1085) - Napoli.
D1084 –	Runs Apr. 16 only (from Napoli): ⊨ 2 cl. and 🚃 Napoli - Singen (D486) - Stuttgart.
A –	🚃 Stuttgart - Chiasso - Milano Centrale; Ⓨ Singen - Chiasso.
G –	Daily except ⑥ Stuttgart - Rottweil; ⑤⑦ Stuttgart - Singen.
d –	✕ only.
s –	Stops to set down only.
✓ –	① - ⑥ (not Dec. 1, Jan. 1, Apr. 15 - 17, May 1, 1995).
✗ –	① - ⑤ (not Dec. 24 - Jan. 1, Apr. 14 - 17, May 1, 1995).
♣ –	Daily except ⑥ (not Oct. 2, Dec. 24 - 31, Apr. 14 - 16, Apr. 30, 1995).

Table 736 NEUSTADT - VILLINGEN - ROTTWEIL

1, 2 class except where shown

km		3326 L	3328	3330	3332	3334	3336	3338	3340	3342 Ⓑ
0	**Neustadt** (Schwarzwald) **732** .. d.	0648	0830	1030	1230	1432	1630	1830	2030	2130
40	Donaueschingen **732** .... a.	0733	0910	1110	1310	1510	1710	1910	2110	2207
40	Donaueschingen **730** .... d.	0736	0916	1114	1314	1514	1714	1914	2114	2212
54	**Villingen 730** .... a.	0747	0927	1125	1325	1525	1725	1925	2125	2224

km		8402	E 8404	E 3088 2 C	E 8408	E 8410	E 8412	E 8414 S	...	...
54	**Villingen** .... d.	0829	1029	1142	1429	1629	1829	2029	...	...
65	Trossingen Bahnhof ▲........ d.	0844	1044	1157	1444	1644	1844	2044	...	...
77	**Rottweil** .... a.	0856	1056	1209	1456	1656	1856	2056	...	...

	3327 L	3329	3331	3333	3335	3337	3339	8401 S	3571
Rottweil .... d.	0647	0904	1104	1304	1504	1704	1904	2104	...
Trossingen Bahnhof ▲...... d.	0659	0916	1116	1316	1516	1716	1916	2116	...
Villingen .... a.	0718	0931	1131	1331	1531	1731	1931	2131	...
	|	|	|	|	|	|	|		
Villingen 730 .... d.	0730	0935	1135	1335	1535	1735	1935	...	2200
Donaueschingen **730** .... a.	0741	0946	1146	1346	1546	1746	1946	...	2210
Donaueschingen **732** .... d.	0747	0947	1147	1347	1547	1747	1947	...	...
Neustadt (Schwarzwald) **732** a.	0825	1025	1225	1427	1625	1825	2025	...	...

C – ⚒, **not** Nov. 1, Dec. 24, 31, Jan. 6, 7, Apr. 15. L – ⚒, **not** Nov. 1, Jan. 6. S – **Not** Dec. 24, 31.

▲ – Local service (2 class only; 5 km; 8 minutes journey) Trossingen Bahnhof - Trossingen Stadt. Operator: Trossinger Eisenbahn, Bahnhof, 78647 Trossingen Stadt. ☎: 74 25 94 02 22
From Trossingen Bf: 0630 Ⓐ 🚌, 0715 Ⓐ, 0846 Ⓐ, 0918 Ⓐ, 1159 Ⓐ **C**, 1159 ⑥ **C** 🚌, 1333 Ⓐ, 1446 Ⓐ, 1518 Ⓐ, 1646 Ⓐ, 1732 Ⓐ, 1846 Ⓐ 🚌, 1933 Ⓐ 🚌.
From Trossingen Stadt: 0648 Ⓐ, 0833 Ⓐ, 0905 Ⓐ, 1146 Ⓐ **C**, 1147 ⑥ **C**, 1305 Ⓐ, 1505 Ⓐ, 1633 Ⓐ, 1705 Ⓐ, 1812 Ⓐ 🚌, 1905 Ⓐ 🚌.

Table 737 PFORZHEIM - HORB and BAD WILDBAD

1, 2 class

km		E 6153 L	E 6155	E 6159	E 6163	E 6165 L	E 6169 L	E 6171	E 6173 Ⓑ	E 6177 Ⓑ✤	E 6179 Ⓑ✤
0	**Pforzheim**................ d.	0632	0751	0938	1138	1238	1438	1538	1638	1838	1938
19	Bad Liebenzell........... d.	0658	0815	0958	1158	1258	1458	1558	1658	1858	1958
26	Calw........................ d.	0707	0823	1006	1206	1306	1506	1606	1706	1906	2006
46	Nagold...................... d.	0733	0848	1030	1230	1330	1530	1630	1730	1930	2030
56	Hochdorf bei Horb..... d.	0744	0858	1040	1240	1340	1540	1640	1740	1940	2040
71	**Horb** .... a.	0756	0911	1052	1252	1352	1552	1653	1753	1952	2052

	E 6156 J	E 6160	E 6164	E 6168 L	E 6172 L	E 6174 Ⓑ	E 6176 L	E 6178 Ⓑ✤	E 6180 Ⓑ✤	E 6182 Ⓑ✤
Horb .... d.	0627	0803	1003	1203	1403	1503	1603	1703	1803	1903
Hochdorf bei Horb... d.	0640	0816	1016	1216	1416	1516	1616	1716	1816	1916
Nagold..................... d.	0650	0828	1028	1228	1428	1528	1628	1728	1828	1928
Calw........................ d.	0717	0847	1047	1247	1447	1547	1647	1747	1847	1947
Bad Liebenzell......... d.	0726	0859	1059	1259	1459	1559	1659	1759	1859	1959
Pforzheim.............. a.	0745	0919	1119	1319	1519	1619	1719	1819	1919	2019

Additional trains: **From Pforzheim** at: 0838 **J**, 1338 Ⓑ and 1738 Ⓑ✤. **From Horb** at: 0503 **J**, 0539 **L**, 1103 Ⓑ and 1303 Ⓑ.

Rail service Pforzheim - Bad Wildbad. 23 km. Journey time 29 minutes.
From Pforzheim: 0551 **J**, 0642 **L**, 0742 **L**, 0842, 0942, 1042, 1142 **G**, 1242, 1342 **L**, 1442, 1542 **S**, 1632 Ⓑ, 1737 **J**, 1842 Ⓑ✤.
From Bad Wildbad: 0546 **J**, 0637 **L**, 0737 **L**, 0837 **L**, 0937, 1037, 1137, 1237 Ⓑ, 1337 **H**, 1437 **L**, 1537, 1627 **S**, 1732 **J**, 1751 **O**, 1837 **J**.

G – Conveys 2 Dortmund - Bad Wildbad. J – Ⓐ, **not** Nov. 1, Jan. 6. O – ⑦, also Nov. 1, Jan. 6.
H – Conveys 2 Bad Wildbad - Emden. L – ⚒, **not** Nov. 1, Jan. 6. S – **Not** Dec. 24, 31. ✤ – **Not** Dec. 25, Jan. 1.

Table 738 STUTTGART - TÜBINGEN - HORB

1, 2 class

km		E 3603 Ⓑ	E 3605 J	E 3607	E 3609	E 3611	E 3651 L	E 3613	E 3615	E 3653 J	E 3617	E 3619	E 3655 J	E 3621	E 3623 J	E 3625	E 3627 J	E 3629	E 3631 J	E 3633	E 3635 J	E 3637	E 3639	E 3641 Ⓑ	E 3643 S
0	**Stuttgart 760** .... d.	0642	0721	0815	0915	1015	1045	1115	1215	1245	1315	1415	1445	1515	1545	1615	1645	1715	1745	1815	1844	1915	2015	2115	2215
22	Plochingen **760** .... d.	0705	0743	0837	0937	1037	|	1137	1237	|	1337	1437	1507	1537	1607	1637	1707	1737	1807	1837	1907	1937	2037	2137	2237
57	Reutlingen.................. d.	0734	0812	0906	1006	1106	1124	1206	1306	1324	1406	1506	1536	1606	1636	1706	1736	1806	1836	1906	1936	2006	2106	2206	2306
71	**Tübingen**.................. a.	0745	0821	0916	1016	1116	1134	1216	1316	1334	1416	1516	1546	1616	1646	1716	1746	1816	1846	1916	1946	2016	2116	2216	2316

	E 3600 L	E 3602 ✤	E3658 E3604 L	E 3682 J	E 3606 ✤	E 3608 L	E 3610	E 3612	E 3652 L	E 3614	E 3616	E 3654 J	E 3618	E 3620	E 3656 J	E 3622	E 3624	E 3628	E 3632	E 3634	E 3636	E3650 E3638	E 3640 S	E 3642 Ⓑ	E 3644 F
Tübingen..................... d.	0447	0526	0611	0632	0638	0713	0734	0834	0912	0934	1034	1110	1134	1234	1310	1334	1445	1534	1634	1734	1834	1930	2034	2145	2230
Reutlingen.................... d.	0458	0537	0623	0642	0649	0724	0745	0845	0922	0945	1045	1120	1145	1245	1320	1345	1456	1545	1645	1745	1845	1945	2045	2156	2245
Plochingen **760** .... d.	0526	0608	0655	|	0720	0753	0815	0915	|	1015	1115	|	1215	1315	|	1415	1526	1615	1715	1815	1915	2015	2115	2226	2317
Stuttgart 760 .... a.	0546	0630	0718	0726	0739	0813	0835	0935	1001	1035	1135	1201	1235	1335	1401	1435	1546	1635	1735	1835	1935	2035	2135	2246	2338

Rail service Tübingen - Horb. 32 km. Journey time: 34 minutes. F – ⚒, **not** Dec. 24, 31, Jan. 6. J – Ⓐ, **not** Jan. 6 L – ⚒, **not** Jan. 6. S – **Not** Dec. 24, 31. ✤ – **Not** Dec. 25, Jan. 1.
From Tübingen: 0600 **J**, 0658, 0750, 0844, 0954, 1024 **J**, 1154, 1224 ⑥, 1254 **J**, 1354, 1424 **J**, 1554, 1624 Ⓑ, 1653 **J**, 1754, 1826 **J**, 1853 **J**, 1950 **S**, 2022 Ⓑ.
From Horb: 0525 **J**, 0616 **J**, 0653 **L**, 0804 **L**, 0835, 0939, 1039 **J**, 1139, 1239 **L**, 1339, 1439 **J**, 1539, 1639 **J**, 1739, 1839 **J**, 1935, 2036 Ⓑ, 2135 **S**.

Table 739 HAUSACH - FREUDENSTADT - STUTTGART

for connections between Hochdorf bei Horb and Horb see Table 737

2 class only

km		E 3084 ⚒	E 6506	E 3098 ⑦	E 3152 Ⓐ	E 3072 ⑥	5905 5907	E 6508	E 3074	E 8334	E 3076	E 3154	E 3078 ⚒	E 8342 ⑦	E 3156 Ⓐ	E 3080 ⑦	E3158 E8350 ⚒	E 6516	E 3160 Ⓐ	E 8360	E 3082	E 6518	E 8370 Ⓑ	E 6179	E 6520
0	**Hausach** .... d.	0604	...	...	0719	0719	...	...	0906	1106	...	1149	1306	1306	1349	1506	1506	...	1549	1706	...	...	1820	...	...
4	Wolfach...................... d.	0609	...	...	0724	0724	...	...	0911	1111	...	1154	1311	1311	1354	1511	1511	...	1554	1711	...	...	1824	...	...
14	Schiltach .... d.	0621	...	...	0735	0735	...	...	0926	1126	...	1206	1326	1326	1406	1526	1526	...	1606	1726	...	...	1836	...	...
23	Alpirsbach .... d.	0639	...	...	0747	0747	...	...	0938	1138	...	1220	1338	1338	1420	1538	1538	...	1620	1738	...	...	1848	...	...
39	**Freudenstadt Hbf** .... a.	0701	...	...	0804	0804	...	...	0955	1155	...	1237	1355	1355	1437	1555	1555	...	1637	1755	...	...	1904	...	...
39	**Freudenstadt Hbf** .... d.	0706	...	0800	*0807*	0807	...	...	1002	...	1202	...	1402	*1402*	...	1602	*1602*	...	...	...	1802	...	...	2002	...
64	Hochdorf bei Horb ..... d.	0731	...	0826	*0830*	0830	...	...	1027	...	1227	...	1427	*1427*	...	1627	*1627*	...	...	...	1827	...	...	2027	...
69	Eutingen im Gau .... d.	0742v	0742	0831	0835	0835	0842n	0843	1033	...	1233	...	1433	*1433*	...	1632	1632	1643	...	...	1836	1843	...	2032	2043
	Horb .... a.	0750	|	...	...	...	0850n	|	|	...	|	...	|	|	...	...	...	|	...	...	1843	|	...	...	|
84	Herrenberg ▲ .... d.	...	0753	...	...	...	...	0854	1048	...	1248	...	1448	*1448*	...	...	...	1654	...	...	...	1854	...	...	2054
126	**Stuttgart Hbf** ▲ .... a.	...	0826	...	...	...	...	0927	*1127*	...	*1327*	...	*1527*	1527	...	...	...	1727	...	...	...	1927	...	...	2127

	E 3151 ⚒	E 3071 Ⓐ	E 3071 ⑥	5903 Ⓐ	E 3073 ⚒	E 3099 ⑦	E 6505	E 3075	E 8315	E 3077	E 8327	E 3155 Ⓐ	E 3079 Ⓑ	E 8335 Ⓑ	E 3079 ⑥	E 3159 Ⓐ	E 3081	E 8343	E 3163	E 6515	6131	E 6519 Ⓑ	E 3085 Ⓑ	E 6521	6133 Ⓑ
Stuttgart Hbf ▲ .... d.	...	...	...	*0703*	...	...	0827	...	...	*1025*	...	...	*1225*	...	*1225*	...	*1428*	...	...	1625	...	1825	...	2025	...
Herrenberg ▲ .... d.	...	...	...	0748	...	...	0859	...	...	1110	...	...	1310	...	1310	...	1510	...	...	1657	...	1857	...	2057	...
Horb .... d.	...	*0613*	...	|	0809	0809	|	...	...	|	...	...	|	...	|	...	|	...	...	|	*1635h*	|	...	|	...
Eutingen im Gau .... d.	...	0628	...	0804	0821	|	0908	0912	...	1126	...	...	1326	...	1326	...	1526	...	...	1706	1717	1906	1917	2106	2110
Hochdorf bei Horb .... d.	...	0635	...	...	0831	0827	...	0918	...	1132	...	...	1332	...	1332	...	1532	...	...	...	1723	...	1923	...	2116
Freudenstadt Hbf ...... a.	...	0704	...	...	0854	0851	...	0944	...	1156	...	...	1356	...	1356	...	1556	...	...	...	1748	...	1948	...	2141
Freudenstadt Hbf ...... d.	0616	0705	0705	...	0856	0856	...	...	0959	...	1159	1255	...	1359	1402	1455	...	1559	1655	...	...	...	2002	...	...
Alpirsbach .... d.	0634	0722	0722	...	0913	0913	...	...	1020	...	1220	1312	...	1420	1420	1512	...	1620	1712	...	...	...	2019	...	...
Schiltach .... d.	0646	0737	0737	...	0924	0924	...	...	1031	...	1231	1324	...	1431	1431	1524	...	1631	1724	...	...	...	2031	...	...
Wolfach....................... d.	0658	0747	0747	...	0935	0935	...	...	1042	...	1242	1335	...	1442	1442	1535	...	1642	1735	...	...	...	2042	...	...
Hausach.................... a.	0702	0751	0751	...	0940	0940	...	...	1047	...	1247	1340	...	1447	1447	1540	...	1647	1740	...	...	...	2047	...	...

h – Daily. A later departure of 1703 (changing Hochdorf) possible on Ⓑ. See Table **737**.
n – 15 minutes later on Ⓒ.
v – Arrives 0736. Connects with 0742 to Stuttgart.
▲ – Stuttgart S-Bahn services run between these points.

Table 740 — FRANKFURT/MAIN - NÜRNBERG - PASSAU - LINZ

1, 2 class except where shown

km		E 1823	EN 225	3309 (2)	E 3467	IC 821	IC 721	3131	IC 723	3817	EC 23	3133	EC 51	3319 (2)	3821	EC 25	3135	689	IC 725	3825	E 1825	EC 27	3137	IC 727
		✗	◆			✗			◆		N		✗			✗ N				P		◆		◆
	Hamburg Hbf 650 750 d.																	0807f	0447		0547			0647
	Dortmund 650 d.												0540			0638			0738		0840			0938
	Düsseldorf Hbf 650 d.															0728			0828					1028
	Köln Hbf 650 d.		0044								0554		0654			0754			0854		0954			1054
0	Frankfurt Flughafen ✈ d.								0654		0754					0854			0954		1054	1154		1254
11	**Frankfurt/Main Hbf** d.					0542	0614		0714	0745	0814		0845	0914	0945	1014	1045	1114	1145		1214	1245	1314	1345
57	Aschaffenburg d.					0613	0644		0714		0814		0845	0914	0945		1041		1141			1241	1341	
95	Lohr d.								0741		0841		0941				1041						1341	
107	Gemünden/Main d.								0752		0852		0952			1052			1152			1252	1352	
147	**Würzburg** a.					0654	0726		0815	0826	0915		0926	1026		1115	1126	1215	1158f	1226	1315	1326	1415	1426
147	**Würzburg** 750 d.						0728		0828		0928		1028			1128		1219	1228		1328			1428
249	**Nürnberg** 750 a.		0514						0825		0925		1025		1125	1225		1323	1328		1425			1525
249	**Nürnberg** 779 d.		0517		0716				0828				1028			1228			1328		1428			1553z
350	**Regensburg** 779 d.		0621		0822				0931				1131			1331			1515		1531			1656z
415	**Plattling** d.				0904				1006	3315			1204			1404			1604		1604			1736z
467	**Passau** 🚢 a.		0730		0940				1037	2			1239			1439			1548		1639			1809z
467	**Passau** 🚢 d.	0606	0746	0930								1128			1328		1444				1550	1644		
481	**Schärding** d.	0618	0759	0946								1144		1259			1459				1604	1659		
519	**Neumarkt Kallham** d.	0648	0824	1029								1228		1329			1529				1637			
550	**Wels** 800 a.	0714	0843	1100								1259		1352			1552				1700	1756		
575	**Linz** 800 a.	0741	0900	1125								1325		1412			1525	1611			1718	1811		
	Wien Westbahnhof 800 a.		1058	1325								1605						1805			1935	2005		

		E 1927 (2)	EC 3829	29	3139	3333 (2)	IC 621	E3042	3833	IC 729	3337 (2)	3143	IC 521	E3044	3837	IC 823	3145	IC 523	3841	IC 625	3147	IC 527	3843	D 223	D 353	EN 491	D 1125
				✗			✗ J						✗			✗ ♣		J	(B)	J				◆			◆
	Hamburg Hbf 650 750 d.			0747			0847			0947			1047			1147		1247		1347		1447		1905		2037	
	Dortmund 650 d.		1038				1140			1238			1340			1438		1540		1640		1738		2005			
	Düsseldorf Hbf 650 d.		1128							1328			1528			1828								2005	2101		
	Köln Hbf 650 d.		1154				1254			1354			1454			1554		1654		1754		1854		2037	2111		2127
	Frankfurt Flughafen ✈ d.		1354				1454			1554			1654			1754		1854		1954		2054					
	Frankfurt/Main Hbf d.		1414				1514	1534h	1614		1634		1714	1734h	1814		1845	1914		2014		2114					0002
	Aschaffenburg d.		1414	1445	1514		1545	1614	1645		1714	1745	1814	1845		1914	1945	2010	2045	2114	2145		2210	2358		0024	
	Lohr d.	1441		1541			1641		1652		1741		1841		1852		1952		2052		2152		2252	0032			
	Gemünden/Main d.	1452		1552			1652		1752		1752		1852		1952		2052		2152		2252		2315			0120	
	Würzburg a.	1515	1526	1615	1626		1715	1726		1815	1826	1915	1926	2015	2026	2115	2126	2215	2226	2315		0054	0115				
	Würzburg 750 d.		1528		1628			1728		1828		1928		2028		2128		2228				0057	0119				
	Nürnberg 750 d.		1625		1725			1825		1925		2025		2127		2227		2327		0200	0222	0249					
	Nürnberg 779 d.		1628									2028				2230				0205	0253	0357					
	Regensburg 779 d.		1731					1804		1931		2006		2131		2206				0311	0357						
	Plattling d.									2037										0417	0502						
	Passau 🚢 a.		1839							2037										0417	0502						
	Passau 🚢 d.	1815	1844	1928						2116										0433	0520						
	Schärding d.	1829	1859	1946						2132										0445	0532						
	Neumarkt Kallham d.	1859	1929	2028						2212										0508	0554						
	Wels 800 a.	1922	1956	2059						2246										0527	0614						
	Linz 800 a.	1950	2011	2125						2313										0544	0630						
	Wien Westbahnhof 800 a.		2205							0058										0740	0830						

		IC 826	3812	IC 526	3816	IC 822	3132	IC 524	3818	IC 522	3134	IC 620	3822	3302	3306 (2)	E 1822	728	3136	IC 520	688	3826	IC 2310 (2)	EC 28	3138	E 1824
		✗		✗ N		✗ N		J		P		N				✗	✗						◆		
	Wien Westbahnhof 800 d.													0540			0742					0640	0800		0844
	Linz 800 d.													0534	0742							0834	0949		1114
	Wels 800 d.													0609	0703	0802						0900	1005		1132
	Neumarkt Kallham d.													0635	0737	0827						0933			1156
	Schärding d.													0717	0817	0858						1013	1054		1226
	Passau 🚢 a.													0731	0832	0910						1028	1108		1240
	Passau 🚢 d.									0720							0920		0941y	0957			1118		
	Plattling d.									0752							0952		1025y	1043			1154		
	Regensburg 779 d.								0623	0828							1028		1109y	1232	1228		1329		
	Nürnberg 779 d.								0725	0929							1129		1210y	1232			1329		
	Nürnberg 750 d.	0528		0628		0728		0832		0932		1032				1132		1232	1236		1332		1428		
	Würzburg 750 d.	0628		0728		0828		0928		1028		1128				1228		1328	1338		1428				
	Würzburg d.	0630	0622	0730	0743	0830	0843	0930	0943	1030	1043	1130	1143			1230	1243	1330	1357g	1343		1430	1443		
	Gemünden/Main d.		0647		0807		0907		1007		1107		1207			1307		1407				1507			
	Lohr d.		0657		0817		0917		1017		1117		1217			1317		1417				1517			
	Aschaffenburg d.	0713	0724	0813	0843	0913	0943	1013	1043	1113	1143	1213	1243			1313	1343	1413		1443		1513	1543		
	Frankfurt/Main Hbf a.	0743		0843		0943		1043		1143		1243				1343		1443				1513	1543		
	Frankfurt Flughafen ✈ a.	0802		0902		1002		1102		1202		1302				1402		1502				1602			
	Köln Hbf 650 a.	1005		1105		1205		1305		1405		1505				1605		1705				1805			
	Düsseldorf Hbf 650 a.							1231				1431				1731						1831			
	Dortmund 650 a.	1120		1220		1320		1420		1520		1620				1720		1820				1920			
	Hamburg Hbf 650 750 a.	1411		1511		1611		1711		1811		1911				2011		2111	1751g			2211			

◆ – NOTES (LISTED BY TRAIN NUMBERS)

EC25 – FRANZ LISZT – 🚪 and ✗ Dortmund - Budapest Keleti.
EC28/9 – PRINZ EUGEN – 🚪 and ✗ Wien - Kiel and v.v.
EC51 – KARLSTEIN – 🚪 and ✗ Dortmund - Praha Hlavni.
D223 – DONAU KURIER – 🛏 1,2 cl., 🛌 2 cl. and 🚪 Dortmund - Wien; 🛏 1,2 cl., 🛌 2 cl. and 🚪 Dortmund - Budapest Keleti; conveys Nov. 1 - Dec. 15, Jan. 9 - Mar. 30: 🛏 1,2 cl., 🛌 2 cl. and 🚪 Dortmund - Praha.
EN225 – DONAUWALZER – 🛏 1,2 cl., 🛌 2 cl. and 🚪 Oostende - Wien; 🛏 1,2 cl., 🛌 2 cl. and 🚪 Amsterdam CS - Wien.
D353 – Dec. 16 - Jan. 8, Mar. 31 - May 27 (from Köln): 🛏 1,2 cl., 🛌 2 cl., 🚪 and ♈ Köln Hbf - Praha Hlavni.
EN491 – HANS ALBERS – 🛏 1,2 cl., 🛌 2 cl., 🚪 and ✗ Hamburg Altona - Wien.
IC520 – 🚪 and ♈ Nürnberg (München ✗) - Hamburg Altona; conveys on ⑥: 🚪 Zwiesel - Hamburg Altona (train IC926 Passau - Nürnberg).
IC526 – GORCH FOCK – 🚪 and ♈ Nürnberg - Kiel.
IC688/9 – ROTTALER LAND – 🚪 Hamburg Altona - Passau and v.v.; 🚪 Hamburg Altona and v.v. Train no. IC780/1 between Hamburg and Würzburg.
IC723 – MAINFRANKEN – 🚪 and ✗ Koblenz - Nürnberg.
IC725 – BERCHTESGADENER LAND – 🚪 Hamburg Altona - Berchtesgaden; 🚪 Bremen - Freilassing.
IC727 – LORELEY – 🚪 and ♈ Hamburg Altona - Nürnberg; conveys on ⑥: 🚪 Hamburg - Zwiesel (train IC927 from Nürnberg).

IC821 – FRANKEN KURIER – 🚪 and ✗ Frankfurt/Main - Ansbach - München Hbf.
IC822 – NORDFRIESLAND – 🚪 and ♈ Regensburg - Westerland; conveys May 1 - 27: 🚪 Regensburg - Dagebüll Mole.
IC823 – NORDFRIESLAND – 🚪 and ✗ Westerland - Passau; conveys ⑥⑦ Mar. 24 - Apr. 30, daily May 1 - 27: 🚪 Dagebüll Mole - Passau.
IC826 – THEODOR STORM – 🚪 and ✗ Nürnberg - Westerland; conveys May 1 - 27: 🚪 Nürnberg - Dagebüll Mole.
D1125 – DOLOMITEN EXPRESS – ⑤ Jan. 6 - Mar. 24, also Dec, 16, 20, 22, 25, Jan. 4 (from Dortmund): 🛏 1,2 cl., 🛌 2 cl., 🚪 and ♈ Dortmund - Bolzano; 🛏 1,2 cl., 🛌 2 cl. and 🚪 Dortmund - Klagenfurt; 🛌 2 cl. Dortmund - Graz.
J – 🚪 and ♈ Kiel - Nürnberg and v.v.
N – ✗, not Nov. 1, Jan. 6.
P – Ⓐ, not Nov. 1, Jan. 6.
f – Train number IC781.
g – Train number IC780.
h – Ⓐ only.
y – ⑥ only - train number IC926.
z – ⑥ only - train number IC927.
♣ – Daily except ⑥ (not Dec. 24 - 31, Apr. 14 - 16, Apr. 30, **1995**).
✗ – ① - ⑥ (not Dec. 25 - Jan. 1, Apr. 15 - 17, May 1, **1995**).

11

Table 740 LINZ - PASSAU - NÜRNBERG - FRANKFURT (MAIN)

1, 2 class except where shown

	IC 724 🍷 ♦	3830	EC 26 ✕	3140	IC 726 🍷♣	3836	E 1826 2 ⚒	EC 24 ✕ ♦	3142	EC 50 ✕ ♦	3840	EC 22 ✕	3144	E 1924	IC 722 🍷♣ ♦	3842 Ⓑ	IC 720 🍷	3328 2	3844	EN 224 ♦	EN 490 🍷 ♦	D 352 🍷 ♦	D 1124 🍷 ♦	D 222 🍷 ♦
Wien Westbahnhof **800** d.	...	...	1000	...	...	...	*1040*	1200	...	...	...	1400	...	*1440*	...	...	...	*1600*	...	1844	2000	...	...	2218
Linz 800 d.	...	...	1149	...	...	...	1256	1349	...	...	...	1549	...	1648	...	...	...	1815	...	2039	2150	...	...	0010
Wels 800 d.	...	...	1205	...	...	...	1315	1405	...	...	...	1605	...	1715	...	...	...	1851	...	2056	2207	...	...	0026
Neumarkt Kallham d.	...	...	1225	...	...	...	1341	1425	...	...	...	1625	...	1742	...	...	...	1949	...	2120	2229	...	...	|
Schärding d.	...	...	1254	...	...	...	1415	1454	...	...	...	1654	...	1807	...	...	...	2004	...	2145	2252	...	...	|
Passau 🏛 a.	...	...	1308	...	...	...	1429	1508	...	...	...	1708	...	1819	...	...	...	...	...	2158	2305	...	...	0122
Passau 🏛 d.	...	...	1318	...	...	...	...	1518	...	...	...	1718	...	...	...	...	1920	...	...	2211	2317	...	...	0142
Plattling d.	...	...	1354	...	...	...	...	1554	...	...	...	1754	...	...	...	...	1952	...	...	|	|	...	...	|
Regensburg **779** d.	...	...	1428	...	...	...	...	1628	...	...	...	1828	...	...	...	...	2027	...	...	2320	0023	...	...	0252
Nürnberg 779 a.	...	...	1529	...	...	...	...	1729	...	...	...	1929	...	...	...	...	2126	...	...	0022	0123	...	...	0354
Nürnberg 750 d.	1432	...	1532	...	1632	...	...	1732	...	1832	...	1932	...	...	2032	...	2138	...	...	0024	0136	0304	...	0406
Würzburg 750 a.	1528	...	1628	...	1728	...	...	1828	...	1928	...	2028	...	...	2128	...	2234	...	...	|	|	0404	...	0506
Würzburg d.	1530	1543	1630	1643	1730	1743	...	1830	1843	1930	1943	2030	2043	...	2130	2143	2236	...	2243	|	|	0414	0436	0510
Gemünden/Main d.	|	1607	|	1707	|	1807	...	|	1907	|	2007	|	2107	...	|	2207	|	...	2307	|	|	|	|	0531
Lohr d.	|	1617	|	1717	|	1817	...	|	1917	|	2017	|	2117	...	|	2217	|	...	2317	|	|	|	|	|
Aschaffenburg d.	1613	1643	1713	1743	1813	1843	...	1913	1943	2013	2043	2113	2143	...	2213	2243	2319	...	2343	|	|	0508	|	0606
Frankfurt (Main) Hbf a.	1643	...	1743	...	1843	...	...	1943	...	2043	...	2143	...	...	2243	...	2348	...	...	|	|	0536	0601	0643
Frankfurt Flughafen ✈ a.	1702	...	1802	...	1902	...	...	2002	...	2102	...	2202	...	...	2302	...	...	...	...	|	|	|	|	|
Köln Hbf **650** a.	1905	...	2005	...	2105	...	...	2205	...	2305	...	0007	...	...	...	...	...	...	...	0450	|	0801	0833	0859
Düsseldorf Hbf **650** a.	1931	...	|	...	|	...	...	2231	...	|	...	...	...	...	...	...	...	...	...	...	|	...	0916	1001
Dortmund **650** a.	2020	...	2120	...	2220	...	...	2320	...	0020	...	...	...	...	...	...	...	...	...	...	|	...	1010	1056
Hamburg Hbf **650 750** a.	2311	...	0011	...	...	...	...	...	...	...	...	...	...	...	...	...	...	...	...	...	0751	...	...	...

♦ – **NOTES** (LISTED BY TRAIN NUMBERS)

EC24 – FRANZ LISZT – [12] and ✕ Budapest Keleti - Dortmund.
EC50 – KARLSTEIN – [12] Praha Hlavni - Dortmund; ✕ Praha - Köln.
D222 – DONAU KURIER – 🛏 1,2 cl., ▬ 2 cl., [2] and 🍷 Wien - Dortmund; 🛏 1,2 cl., ▬ 2 cl. and [2] Budapest Keleti - Dortmund; conveys Oct. 31 - Dec. 14, Jan. 8 - Mar. 29 (from Praha): 🛏 1,2 cl., ▬ 2 cl. and [2] Praha - Dortmund.
EN224 – DONAUWALZER – 🛏 1,2 cl., ▬ 2 cl. and [2] Wien - Oostende; 🛏 1,2 cl., ▬ 2 cl. and [2] Wien - Amsterdam CS.
D352 – Dec. 15 - Jan. 7, Mar. 30 - May 27 (from Praha): 🛏 1,2 cl., ▬ 2 cl., [12] and 🍷 Praha Hlavni - Köln.
EN490 – HANS ALBERS – 🛏 1,2 cl., ▬ 2 cl., [2] and 🍷 Wien - Hamburg Altona.
IC722 – MAINFRANKEN – [12] and 🍷 Nürnberg - Koblenz.
IC724 – BERCHTESGADENER LAND – [12] Berchtesgaden - Hamburg Altona; 🍷 Freilassing - Bremen.
D1124 – DOLOMITEN EXPRESS – ⑥ Jan. 7 - Mar. 25, also Dec. 17, 21, 23, Jan. 1, 5: (from Bolzano): 🛏 1,2 cl., ▬ 2 cl., [2] and 🍷 Bolzano - Dortmund; 🛏 1,2 cl., ▬ 2 cl. and [2] Villach - Dortmund; ▬ 2 cl. Graz - Dortmund.
♣ – Daily except ⑥ (**not** Dec. 24 - 31, Apr. 14 - 16, Apr. 30, **1995**).

Table 741 STUTTGART - HEILBRONN - WÜRZBURG

1, 2 class

km		IR 2310 A🍷	E 3852	E 4004	E 3732 ❖	E 4008	E 3734	E 4010	E 3854	E 3736	E 3738	E 4014	E 3742	E 4016	E 3746	E 4018	E 3856 S	E 3752	E 4020	E 3754 V	E 4022 ⑥	E 4022 Ⓑ	E 3756	E 3758 S	E 3760 U
0	**Stuttgart** d.	0607	0630	0700	0815	0901	1015	1101	1115	1148	1215	1301	1415	1501	1619	1701	1715	1815	1901	1948	2029	2029	2115	2229	2331
53	**Heilbronn** d.	0646	0714	0745	0902	0945	1101	1145	1201	1234	1301	1345	1501	1545	1709	1745	1801	1901	1945	2034	2111	2117	2201	2316	0017
64	Bad Friedrichshall-Jagstfeld d.	...	0741	0754	...	0954	...	1154	1220	...	...	1354	...	1554	1719	1754	1821	...	1954	...	...	2127	...	...	...
102	Osterburken d.	...	...	0822	...	1022	...	1222	...	...	...	1422	...	1622	1747	1824	...	...	2023	...	...	2155	...	...	...
137	Lauda d.	...	...	0845	...	1045	...	1245	...	...	...	1445	...	1645	1809	1847	...	...	2045	...	...	2218	...	...	...
180	**Würzburg** a.	...	...	0915	...	1115	...	1315	...	...	...	1515	...	1715	...	1917	...	...	2115	...	...	2248	...	...	...

	E 3733	E 3765 O	E 3737 L	E 3739 L	E 4003 ①-⑥	E 3741	E 4005 ⑦	E 3743 ①-⑥	E 3853	E 4007	E 3747	E 3751	E 4011	E 3855	E 3753	E 4013	E 3755	E 3757	E 4017	E 3857 S	IR 2311 A🍷	E 4019	E 3759 U	E 4021	E 3761
Würzburg d.	...	...	...	...	0652	...	0801	...	...	1040	...	...	1240	...	...	1440	...	...	1640	...	...	1840	...	2045	...
Lauda d.	...	...	...	0637	0723	...	0832	...	...	1110	...	...	1310	...	...	1510	...	...	1710	...	...	1910	...	2114	...
Osterburken d.	...	...	0639	0702	0748	...	0857	0914	...	1135	...	...	1335	...	...	1535	...	...	1735	...	...	1935	...	2138	...
Bad Friedrichshall-Jagstfeld d.	...	...	0720	0736	0817	...	0925	0942	1043	1203	...	...	1403	1442	...	1603	...	...	1803	1840	...	2003	...	2205	...
Heilbronn d.	0630	0710	0734	0800	0829	0856	0936	1000	1101	1214	1251	1350	1414	1500	1550	1614	1700	1750	1814	1858	1919	2014	2052	2216	2246
Stuttgart a.	0718	0758	0820	0846	0915	0941	1020	1045	1145	1257	1341	1434	1457	1545	1634	1657	1746	1835	1857	1941	2001	2059	2140	2259	2333

A – [12] and 🍷 Stuttgart - Heidelberg - Emden and v.v.
L – ⚒, **not** Nov. 1, Jan. 6.
O – ⑦, also Nov. 1, Jan. 6.
S – **Not** Dec. 24, 31.
U – **Not** Dec. 24, 25, 31, Jan. 1.
V – **Not** Dec. 25.
❖ – **Not** Dec. 25, Jan. 1.

Table 742 MANNHEIM - HEIDELBERG - HEILBRONN

1, 2 class except where shown

km		7327	7913 ⚒	E 3217	7915	3381	E 3221	7921	3383	E 3223	7925	3385	E 3227 2	7929	3387	E 3231 2	E 3397	7933	E 3233 Ⓑ	3389	IR 2311 A🍷	7935 2	E 3235	E 3391	E 3393
0	**Mannheim** ▲ d.	...	...	0837	0900	0937	1037	1100	1137	1237	1300	1337	1437	1458	1537	1637	...	1702	...	1737	...	1800	1837	1937	...
17	**Heidelberg** ▲ d.	0729	0818	0856	0918	0956	1056	1118	1157	1256	1318	1356	1456	1518	1557	1656	1700	1718	1725	1756	1813	1818	1856	1956	2130
29	Neckargemünd d.	0741	0830	0908	0930	1007	1108	1130	1208	1308	1330	1408	1508	1530	1608	1707	1712	1730	1736	1808	|	1830	1908	2008	2142
	Meckesheim d.	|	0844	|	0944	|	|	1144	|	|	1344	|	|	1544	|	|	|	1744	|	|	|	1844	|	|	|
	Sinsheim d.	|	0857	|	1000	|	|	1200	|	|	1400	|	|	1600	|	|	|	1800	|	|	|	1900	|	|	|
	Steinsfurt d.	|	0904	|	1004	|	|	1204	|	|	1404	|	|	1604	|	|	|	1804	|	|	|	1904	|	|	|
50	Eberbach d.	0801	|	0926	|	1026	1126	|	1226	1326	|	1426	1526	|	1626	1726	|	|	1755	1826	1838	|	1926	2026	2200
69	Neckarelz d.	0822	|	0943	|	1047	1143	|	1247	1343	|	1447	1543	|	1647	1743	|	|	1815	1844	1855	|	1943	2047	2217
87	Bad Friedrichshall-Jagstfeld d.	0839	0931	*1001*	1031	1108	*1207*	1231	1308	*1407*	1431	1508	*1607*	1631	1708	*1807*	1754	1830	*1840*	1903	|	1931	*2007*	2108	2232
98	**Heilbronn** a.	0849	0945	*1014*	1045	1121	*1220*	1245	1321	*1420*	1445	1521	*1620*	1645	1721	*1820*	1805	...	*1850*	1912	1917	1945	*2020*	2121	2242

km		IR 2310 A🍷	7914 ⚒	E 3374	7916	E 3220 2	3376	7920	E 3226	7922 ⚒	3378	7924 2	E 3230	3380	7932	E 3234	7934 Ⓐ	3382 3394	7936 2	E 3238 2	3384	7942 Ⓐ	E 3242 2	3386	E 3392 2Ⓑ
0	**Heilbronn** d.	0647	0701	0719	0824	*0841*	0935	1017	*1041*	1117	1135	1217	*1241*	1335	1417	*1441*	1517	1535	1617	*1641*	1735	1817	*1841*	1935	2121
11	Bad Friedrichshall-Jagstfeld d.	|	0723	0730	0835	*0852*	0949	1032	*1052*	1132	1149	1232	*1252*	1349	1432	*1452*	1532	1549	1632	*1652*	1749	1832	*1852*	1949	2131
	Neckarelz d.	0707	|	0745	|	0914	1011	|	1114	|	1211	|	1314	1411	|	1514	|	1611	|	1714	1811	|	1914	2011	2147
	Eberbach d.	0723	|	0801	|	0930	1030	|	1130	|	1230	|	1330	1430	|	1530	|	1630	|	1730	1831	|	1930	2030	2204
34	Steinsfurt d.	|	0750	|	0902	|	|	1102	|	1155	|	1302	|	|	1502	|	1555	|	1702	|	|	1902	|	|	|
37	Sinsheim d.	|	0802	|	0906	|	|	1106	|	1159	|	1306	|	|	1506	|	1559	|	1706	|	|	1906	|	|	|
47	Meckesheim d.	|	0818	|	0918	|	|	1118	|	1211	|	1318	|	|	1518	|	1611	|	1718	|	|	1918	|	|	|
57	Neckargemünd d.	|	0832	0819	0932	0948	1048	1132	1148	1225	1248	1332	1348	1448	1532	1548	1625	1648	1732	1748	1850	1932	1948	2048	2221
69	**Heidelberg** ♠ d.	0749	0846	0836	0946	1003	1103	1146	1203	1239	1303	1346	1404	1503	1546	1603	1639	1703	1746	1803	1903	1946	2003	2103	2236
86	**Mannheim** ♠ a.	...	0858	0849	0948	1019	1119	1158	1219	1258	1319	1358	1419	1519	1558	1619	1658	1719	1758	1819	1919	1958	2019	2119	...

A – [12] and 🍷 Emden - Köln - Mainz - Darmstadt - Heidelberg - Stuttgart and v.v.

▲ – **IC/EC** services (supplement payable) see Table **760**. Additional local services run as follows: 0511, 0534, 0558, 0612⚒, 0634⚒, 0642⚒, 0645 Ⓑ, 0653Ⓐ, 0711, 0730⚒, 0800, 0844Ⓐ, 0920, 1006, 1120, 1200, 1206, 1310, 1320, 1400, 1406, 1520, 1558Ⓐ, 1606, 1641⚒, 1720, 1806, 1900, 1920, 2002, 2039, 2113Ⓑ, 2140, 2206, 2237, 2323, 2354Ⓑ.

♠ – **IC/EC** services (supplement payable) see Table **760**. Additional local services run as follows: 0457, 0510⚒, 0518Ⓐ, 0553Ⓐ, 0601, 0609Ⓐ, 0618Ⓐ, 0628⚒, 0636, 0647Ⓐ, 0703, 0722Ⓐ, 0746Ⓐ, 0803, 0812, 0903, 0935, 1028, 1039⚒, 1135, 1228, 1335, 1428, 1439⚒, 1535, 1619, 1630, 1735, 1828, 1839⚒, 1930, 2028, 2135, 2155, 2233Ⓑ, 2343.

Table 743 AALEN - ULM

1, 2 class except where shown

km		E 3501 L	5515 L	E 3503	E 3505 L		E 3507 2	E 3509	E 3511 L	5535 O	E 3535 L	E 3527 O	E 3515 L	E 3517 2 J		E 3519	5557 2 J	E 3123 2 L	5549 2 O	E 3523	E3521 E3525 Ⓑ	E 3529 ⑥	E 3529 2 J	E 3125 2
0	**Aalen** d.	0608	0616	0739	0835	...	0935	1035	1135	1226	1235	1307	1333	1435	...	1535	1628	1707	1710	1735	1842	1932	1932	2046
14	Königsbronn d.	0621	0632	0752	0852	...	0949	1049	1149	1239	1249	1321	1349	1449	...	1549	1641	1723	1727	1749	1855	1945	1945	2058
23	Heidenheim d.	0629	0646	0801	0900	...	1000	1100	1200	1249	1300	1328	1400	1502	...	1600	1651	1731	1736	1802	1903	1952	1953	2107
57	Langenau d.	0701	0726	0835	0929	...	1029	1129	1229	1327	1329	1357	1431	1535	...	1629	1726	1800	1814	1833	1934	...	2028	2137
73	**Ulm** a.	0714	0744	0848	0944	...	1044	1143	1242	1347	1344	1409	1444	1548	...	1642	1746	1813	1839	1845	1947	...	2041	2150

	5506 L	5514 L	E 3500 L	5520 2 J	E 3122 2	E 3502 L	E 3504 2	E 3506 L		E 3530	E 3516 O	E 3510 L	E 3512 L	E 3514 L		E 3128 2 L	E 3528 O	5546 O	E 3518 J	E 3520	E 3524 2		E 3522	E 3526 Ⓑ
Ulm d.	0444	0532	0620	0659	0746	0812	0914	1014	...	1112	1214	1214	1312	1414	...	1512	1518	1609	1614	1712	1814	...	1913	2013
Langenau d.	0456	0545	0634	0717	0759	0824	0930	1030	...	1130	1226	1230	1330	1432	...	1524	1530	1631	1630	1727	1832	...	1935	2030
Heidenheim d.	0533	0630	0713	0800	0834	0900	1000	1100	...	1200	1300	1300	1400	1502	...	1604	1604	1707	1704	1804	1904	...	2007	2107
Königsbronn d.	0543	0641	0721	0809	0841	0908	1008	1108	...	1208	1308	1308	1408	1510	...	1611	1611	1716	1712	1812	1912	...	2015	2115
Aalen a.	0558	0654	0732	0824	0853	0920	1020	1120	...	1220	1323	1320	1420	1522	...	1624	1624	1729	1725	1824	1924	...	2027	2127

J – Ⓐ, **not** Nov. 1, Jan. 6. L – ⚒, **not** Nov. 1, Jan. 6. O – ⑦, also Nov. 1, Jan. 6.

Table 744 HEILBRONN - SCHWÄBISCH HALL - CRAILSHEIM

1, 2 class except where shown

km		7703 2 L	E 3573 2 L	E 4053 L	7731 2 J	E 3101	E 3575	7707 2 J	7739 2 ⑥	E 3577	7711 7741 L	7713 J	E 4057	E 3579 2 J	7717 2 J	E 3103	E 3581	7719 2 J	D 386	7721 2 J	E 4063	E 3583 V	E 3585 Ⓑ	E 4067	E 3587 J
0	**Heilbronn** d.	0628	0756	...	0906	...	0956	1107	1125	1156	1243	1315	...	1356	1534	...	1556	1630	...	1712	...	1809	1935	...	2125
27	Öhringen d.	0658	0816	...	0936	...	1016	1143	1157	1216	1317	1350	...	1416	1606	...	1616	1702	...	1747	...	1829	1957	...	2150
54	Schwäbisch Hall d.	0723	0841	...	0958	...	1041	1208	1219	1241	1346	1415	...	1441	1628	...	1641	1725	...	1811	...	1853	2020	...	2214
61	Schwäbisch Hall Hessental d.	0730	0848	0855	1005	1008	1050	1216	1226	1250	1353	1423	1441	1450	1635	1639	1650	1732	1751	1818	1840	1902	2027	2037	2221
88	**Crailsheim** a.	...	...	0915	...	1027	1111	...	...	1311	...	...	1501	1511	...	1659	1711	...	1810	...	1900	1920	...	2057	...

	7702 2 J	8154 2 J	E 3572 J	D 1907	7706 2 ⑥	7706 J	D 481	E 3586 O	E 4058	E 3574 2 L	7710 Z	E 3576 2	E 4060 ⑥	E 4060 O	7712 2 L	E 3578 2 J	E 3100	7716 J	E 3580 2 J	E 4062	7718	E 3582	E 3102	7720	E 3584 ⒷV
Crailsheim d.	0518	0604	...	0635	...	0644	0816	...	0839	...	...	1048	1102	1102	...	1248	1356	...	1448	1517	...	1648	1730	...	1928
Schwäbisch Hall Hessental d.	0538	0624	0631	0655	0704	0704	0833	0838	0857	0902	1028	1109	1121	1121	1155	1309	1416	1420	1509	1536	1550	1709	1749	1754	1948
Schwäbisch Hall d.	0545	...	0638	...	0711	0711	...	0845	...	0909	1035	1116	...	...	1202	1316	...	1427	1516	...	1557	1716	...	1801	1955
Öhringen d.	0608	...	0701	...	0734	0734	...	0907	...	0932	1058	1139	...	...	1230	1339	...	1448	1539	...	1620	1739	...	1822	2017
Heilbronn a.	0643	...	0726	...	0807	0807	...	0929	...	0955	1131	1200	...	...	1301	1400	...	1520	1600	...	1653	1800	...	1854	2039

J – Ⓐ, **not** Nov. 1, Jan. 6.
L – ⚒, **not** Nov. 1, Jan. 6.
O – ⑦, also Nov. 1, Jan. 6.
V – **Not** Dec. 25.
Z – **Not** Nov. 1, Dec. 24, 31, Jan. 6.

Table 745 STUTTGART - AALEN/BACKNANG - NÜRNBERG

1, 2 class

Electrification work may cause some minor delays to services

km		IR 2663 🍷 ♦	E 3193 G	E 4053 L	IR 2465 🍷	E 3101	IR 2467 🍷	E 4055 O	IR 2669 🍷	E 4057	IR 2561 🍷	E 3197 T	E 3103	IR 2563 🍷	E 4061 J	D 386 ♦	E 4063	IR 2565 🍷 ♦	E 4065 Ⓑ V	E 4067	IR 2567 🍷 ♦	E 4069 Ⓐ	E 4069 K	D 357 🍷 ♦	D 1906 🍷 ♦
	Karlsruhe **760** d.	0506	...	...	0707	...	0910	...	1110	...	1310	...	...	1510	...	...	...	1710	...	...	1910	...	...	...	...
0	**Stuttgart** d.	0607	0635	0743	0807	0901	1007	1128	1207	1328	1407	1521	1527	1607	1631	1650	1728	1807	1822	1928	2007	2126	2126	2144	2229
51	Schwäbisch Gmünd d.	0640	0715	|	0840	|	1040	|	1240	|	1440	1603	|	1640	|	|	|	1840	|	|	2040	|	|	2223	|
76	Aalen d.	0658	0735	|	0858	|	1058	|	1258	|	1458	1622	|	1658	|	|	|	1858	|	|	2058	|	|	2242	2330
92	Ellwangen d.	0709	...	|	0909	|	1109	|	1309	|	1509	...	|	1709	|	|	|	1909	|	|	2109	|	|	2253	|
	Backnang d.	|	...	0816	|	0931	|	1200	|	1400	|	...	1557	|	1703	1717	1800	|	1851	1959	|	2156	2157	|	|
113	Schwäbisch Hall Hessental d.	|	...	0855	|	1008	|	1237	|	1441	|	...	1639	|	1742	1751	1840	|	1927	2037	|	...	2234	|	|
113	Crailsheim d.	0725	...	0915	0925	1028	1125	1257	1325	1501	1525	...	1704	1725	1802	1812	1900	1925	1946	2057	2125	...	2252	2310	2356
159	Ansbach d.	0751	...	...	0951	1059	1151	...	1351	...	1551	...	1738	1751	...	1839	...	1951	...	...	2151	...	...	2336	0026
203	**Nürnberg** a.	0816	...	...	1016	1129	1216	...	1416	...	1616	...	1810	1816	...	1913	...	2016	...	...	2216	...	...	0003	0053
	Hof **780** a.	1026	...	...	1226	...	1426	...	1626	...	1826	...	...	2026	...	...	...	...	...	...	...	...	...	...	0300
	Dresden Hbf **780** a.	1406	...	...	...	...	...	...	2006	...	...	...	...	...	...	...	...	...	...	...	...	...	...	...	0713z

	E 4054 J	8154 J	D 1907 🍷 ♦	IR 2566 🍷 ❖	D 1907 🍷 ♦	D 356 🍷 ♦	E 4056 Q	D 481 ♦	IR 2564 🍷 ♦	E 4058	IR 2562 🍷	E 4060 H	IR 2560 🍷	E 3100	IR 2668 🍷 ♦	E 4062	E 3196 G	E 4064 J	IR 2466 🍷	E 3102	IR 2464 🍷	E 4066 S	3190 ⑦ F	IR 2662 🍷 ♦	IR 2660 ♦
Dresden Hbf **780** d.	...	...	2226v	...	...	...	...	...	...	...	...	...	...	...	0752	...	...	...	...	...	...	...	...	1352	1552
Hof **780** d.	...	...	0230	...	...	...	...	...	...	...	0731	...	0931	...	1131	...	...	...	1331	...	1531	...	...	1731	1931
Nürnberg d.	...	...	0508	0540	...	0605	...	0719	0745	...	0945	...	1145	1241	1345	...	...	...	1545	1619	1745	...	...	1945	2140
Ansbach d.	...	...	0549	0604	←	0632	...	0748	0809	...	1009	...	1209	1318	1409	...	...	...	1609	1650	1809	...	...	2009	2205
Crailsheim d.	0534	0604	0624	0631	0635	0702	0714	0816	0836	0839	1036	1102	1236	1356	1436	1517	...	1621	1636	1730	1836	1937	...	2036	2234
Schwäbisch Hall Hessental d.	0555	0625	→	|	0658	|	0734	0834	|	0858	|	1122	|	1417	|	1540	...	1641	|	1752	|	1954	...	|	|
Backnang d.	0635	0712	...	|	0731	|	0815	0902	|	0931	|	1159	|	1457	|	1616	...	1731	|	1831	|	2029	...	|	|
Ellwangen d.	|	|	...	0646	|	0723	|	|	0852	|	1052	|	1252	|	1452	|	...	|	1652	|	1852	|	...	2052	2254
Aalen d.	|	|	...	0701	|	0736	|	|	0904	|	1104	|	1304	|	1504	|	1631	|	1704	|	1904	|	2031	2104	2305
Schwäbisch Gmünd d.	|	|	...	0718	|	0754	|	|	0920	|	1120	|	1320	|	1520	|	1650	|	1720	|	1920	|	2050	2120	2321
Stuttgart a.	0701	0741	...	0753	0806	0831	0846	0925	0953	1004	1153	1225	1353	1526	1553	1645	1735	1802	1753	1901	1953	2058	2135	2153	2355
Karlsruhe **760** a.	...	...	...	0848	...	...	...	...	1048	...	1248	...	1448	...	1648	...	...	...	1848	...	2048	...	...	2251	...

♦ – **NOTES** (LISTED BY TRAIN NUMBERS)

D356/7 – 🛏 1,2 cl., 🛏 2 cl., [12] and 🍷 Praha Hlavni - Stuttgart and v.v.
D386 – [12] Milano Centrale - Nürnberg.
D481 – [12] Nürnberg - Zürich Hbf - Locarno.
D1906 – 🛏 1,2 cl., 🛏 2 cl., [12] and 🍷 Stuttgart - Berlin Lichtenberg; 🛏 2 cl. and [2] Stuttgart - Hof (**D1961**) - Dresden Hbf.
D1907 – 🛏 1,2 cl., 🛏 2 cl., [12] and 🍷 Berlin Lichtenberg - Stuttgart; 🛏 2 cl. and [2] Dresden Hbf (**D1960**) - Hof - Stuttgart.
IR2564 – [12] and 🍷 Coburg (Nürnberg on Dec. 25, Jan. 1) - Karlsruhe.
IR2565 – [12] Karlsruhe - Coburg (Nürnberg on Dec. 24, 31); 🍷 Karlsruhe - Erlangen.
IR2567 – [12] Karlsruhe - Nürnberg; 🍷 Karlsruhe - Aalen. **Not** Dec. 24, 31.
IR2660 – ⑦, also Nov. 1, Apr. 17, May 1, **not** Dec. 25, Apr. 16, 30: [12] Dresden Hbf - Stuttgart.
IR2662 – [12] Dresden Hbf - Stuttgart (Karlsruhe ♣); 🍷 Dresden - Aalen.
IR2663 – [12] Stuttgart (Karlsruhe ⚡) - Dresden Hbf; 🍷 Stuttgart - Dresden.
IR2668 – [12] and 🍷 Görlitz - Karlsruhe.
F – ⑦, also Nov. 1, Jan. 6, **not** Dec. 25: [12] Donauwörth - Stuttgart; also runs on Ⓐ from Aalen as train **3472**.

G – [12] München - Donauwörth - Stuttgart and v.v.
H – ⑥⑦, also Nov. 1, Jan. 6 Crailsheim - Stuttgart; daily Backnang - Stuttgart.
J – Ⓐ, **not** Nov. 1, Jan. 6.
K – Ⓒ, also Nov. 1, Jan. 6, **not** Dec. 24, 31.
L – ⚒, **not** Nov. 1, Jan. 6.
O – ⑦, also Nov. 1, Jan. 6.
Q – **Not** Dec. 24.
S – **Not** Dec. 24, 31.
T – **Not** Dec. 24, 25, 31.
V – **Not** Dec. 25.
v – Train number **D1960** from Dresden to Hof.
z – Train number **D1961** from Hof to Dresden.
❖ – **Not** Dec. 25, Jan. 1.
⚡ – ① - ⑥ (**not** Dec. 25 - Jan. 1, Apr. 15 - 17, May 1, **1995**).
♣ – Daily except ⑥ (**not** Dec. 24 - 31, Apr. 14 - 16, Apr. 30, **1995**).

Table 746 AALEN - DONAUWÖRTH

1, 2 class except where shown

km		3171 Ⓐ	3193 B	3173 ⚒	3175 Ⓐ	3177	3179	3183 Ⓐ	3185 Ⓐ	3197 2	3189 Ⓑ
0	**Aalen** d.	0612	0744	0927	1027	1127	1227	1326	1527	1632	1735
39	Nördlingen d.	0650	0817	1000	1056	1200	1317	1400	1600	1719	1820
68	**Donauwörth** a.	0714	0841	1022	1122	1219v	1340	1423	1626	1745	1856

	3170 ⚒	3192	3172 ⚒	3176 Ⓐ	5060 2	3178 Ⓐ	3196 B	3182	3198 Ⓐ	3190 ⑦
Donauwörth d.	0809	0910	1029	1223	1344	1430	1530	1630	1723	1937
Nördlingen d.	0840	0939	1055	1253	1415	1454	1601	1654	1752	2001
Aalen a.	0916	1019	1126	1326	...	1526	1630	1726	...	2030

B – (12) Stuttgart - Donauwörth - Augsburg - München and v.v.   v – **Not** ⑥.

Table 747 ROMANTISCHE STRASSE (EUROPABUS 🚌)

Dates of operation - see below Table

	189E	190		190A	190
Frankfurt/Main (Hbf) (Bussteig 9) d.	...	0800	...	...	...
Würzburg (Hbf) (Omnibusbahnhof Bussteig 13) d.	...	1000	...	...	...
Bad Mergentheim (Hans - Heinrich Ehrter Platz) d.	...	1100	...	...	...
Heidelberg (Hbf) d.	0800	|	...	...	...
Neckargemünd (Bf) d.	0820	|	...	...	...
Eberbach (Neckaranlagen) d.	0840	|	...	...	...
Heilbronn (Marktplatz) a.	1000	|	...	...	...
Heilbronn (Marktplatz) d.	1015	|	...	...	...
Schwäbisch Hall (Omnibusbahnhof - Salinenstraße) d.	1125	|	...	...	...
Rothenburg ob der Tauber (Bahnhof) a.	1310	1245	...	...	...
Rothenburg ob der Tauber (Bahnhof) d.	...	1445	...	...	...
Feuchtwangen (Omnibusbahnhof) d.	...	1510	...	...	←
Dinkelsbühl (Schweinemarkt) a.	...	1525	...	...	1525
Dinkelsbühl (Schweinemarkt) d.	...	1630	...	1615	1630
Nördlingen (Rathaus) a.	...	→	...	|	1710
Nördlingen (Rathaus) d.	...	...	...	|	1710
Donauwörth (Stadtpfarrkirche) d.	...	...	...	|	1745
Augsburg (Hbf) (Bussteig F) a.	...	...	...	1815	1845
Augsburg (Hbf) (Bussteig F) d.	...	...	...	1825	1855
München (Hbf) a.	...	...	...	|	2000
Schwangau (Verkehrsbüro) a.	...	...	...	2050	...
Hohenschwangau a.	...	...	...	2055	...
Füssen (Kaiser - Maximiliansplatz) a.	...	...	...	2100	...

	190	190A		190	189E
Füssen (Kaiser - Maximiliansplatz) d.	...	0800	...	...	...
Hohenschwangau d.	...	0805	...	...	...
Schwangau (Verkehrsbüro) d.	...	0810	...	...	...
München (Hbf) d.	0900	|	...	...	...
Augsburg (Hbf) (Bussteig F) a.	1000	1045	...	...	...
Augsburg (Hbf) (Bussteig F) d.	1015	1055	...	...	...
Donauwörth (Kaufhaus Nossl) d.	1115	1155	...	...	...
Nördlingen (Rathaus) a.	1150	1220	...	...	...
Nördlingen (Rathaus) d.	1205	1230	...	←	...
Dinkelsbühl (Schweinemarkt) a.	1245	1305	...	1245	...
Dinkelsbühl (Schweinemarkt) d.	1400	...	...	1400	...
Feuchtwangen (Omnibusbahnhof) d.	→	...	...	1415	...
Rothenburg ob der Tauber (Bahnhof) a.	...	...	...	1440	...
Rothenburg ob der Tauber (Bahnhof) d.	...	...	...	1615	1615
Schwäbisch Hall (Omnibusbahnhof - Salinenstraße) d.	...	...	...	|	1735
Heilbronn (Marktplatz) a.	...	...	...	|	1845
Heilbronn (Marktplatz) d.	...	...	...	|	1855
Eberbach (Neckaranlagen) d.	...	...	...	|	2000
Neckargemünd d.	...	...	...	|	2020
Heidelberg (Hbf) a.	...	...	...	|	2045
Bad Mergentheim (Hans - Heinrich Ehrter Platz) a.	...	...	...	1730	...
Würzburg (Hbf) (Omnibusbahnhof Bussteig 13) a.	...	...	...	1830	...
Frankfurt/Main (Hbf) (Bussteig 9) a.	...	...	...	2030	...

Services **190, 190A** operate Apr. 1 - Oct. 31, 1995; service **189E** operates May 13 - Sept. 30, 1995.
Reservation is recommended for travel by these services (at least 3 days in advance), especially in the summer, and is essential if break of journey is required.
🚌 operator: Deutsche Touring Gmbh, Am Römerhof 17, 60486 Frankfurt/Main. ☎: + 49 69 7 90 32 56. Fax: + 49 69 7 90 32 19.
Hotel and general information is available from: Touristik Arbeitsgemeinschaft, Romantische Straße, Marktplatz, 91550 Dinkelsbühl. ☎: + 49 98 51 9 02 71. Fax: + 49 98 51 9 02 79.

Table 748 GÖTTINGEN - BEBRA

Rail service Göttingen - Bebra and v.v. 81 km. Journey time: 59 minutes (IR services take 52 minutes). 1, 2 class. All trains except IR services call at **Eichenberg**, 15 minutes from Göttingen, 41 minutes from Bebra. See also Table **695** for other services Göttingen - Eichenberg and v.v.

From Göttingen: 0457⚒, 0557, 0657, 0757, 0857, 0917 (**IR2683**), 0957, 1057, 1157, 1257, 1357, 1457, 1557, 1657, 1757, 1857, 2017 (**IR2077**), 2057.
From Bebra: 0553⚒, 0644 (**IR2176**), 0800, 0900, 1000, 1100, 1200, 1300, 1400, 1500, 1600, 1626 (**IR2682**), 1700, 1800, 1900, 2000, 2100, 2200.

IR2077 – ⑥, **not** Dec. 24 - 31, Apr. 14 - 16, 30: (12) Flensburg - Erfurt.
IR2176 – ① - ⑥, **not** Dec. 25 - Jan. 1, Apr. 15 - 17, May 1: (12) Erfurt - Hamburg Altona.
IR2682/3 – ALPENLAND – (12) and 🍷 Oberstdorf - Hamburg Altona and v.v.

Table 749 KASSEL - FRANKFURT (MAIN)

(for **ICE** services see Table **750**) 1, 2 class

km		E 3801	E 3803	E 3877 Ⓐ	E 3841 Ⓒ	E 3843 Ⓐ	E3551 E3807	E3553 E3809	E 3281 2⚒	E3555 E3811	E3557 E3813	E 3283	E3559 E3815	IR 2683 F🍷	E3561 E3817	E 3285 2	E3563 E3819	E 3287 Ⓐ	E3565 E3821	E 3279 Ⓒ	E3567 E3823	E3569 E3825	E 3289	E3571 E3827
0	**Kassel Hbf** d.	...	...	...	...	...	0514	0609	...	0714	0809	...	0914	...	1009	...	1114	...	1209	...	1314	1409	...	1514
4	**Kassel Wilhelmshöhe** d.	...	...	...	...	...	0520	0615	...	0720	0815	...	0920	...	1015	...	1120	...	1215	...	1320	1415	...	1520
58	Bebra d.	0320	...	0525	...	...	0601	0656	...	0801	0856	...	1001	...	1056	...	1201	...	1256	...	1401	1456	...	1601
72	Bad Hersfeld d.	0328	...	0534	...	...	0610	0705	...	0810	0905	...	1010	...	1105	...	1210	...	1305	...	1410	1505	...	1610
114	**Fulda** a.	0358	...	0603	...	...	0637	0732	...	0837	0932	...	1037	...	1132	...	1237	...	1333	...	1437	1532	...	1637
114	**Fulda** d.	0400	0518	0606	0609	0624	0709	0809	0754	0859	0959	0954	1059	1101	1159	1154	1259	1331	1359	1354	1459	1559	1554	1659
189	Gemünden (Main) a.	|	|	|	|	|	|	|	0847	|	|	1047	|	1130	|	1247	|	1428	|	1447	|	|	1647	|
	Würzburg **740** a.	|	|	|	|	|	|	|	*0915*	|	|	*1115*b	|	1150	|	*1315*h	|	*1515*	|	*1515*	|	|	*1715*	|
195	Hanau ▲ d.	0510	0622	0658	0709	0731	0809	0909	...	1009	1109	...	1209	...	1309	...	1409	...	1509	...	1609	1709	...	1809
208	Offenbach (Main) ▲ d.	0523	0632	|	0718	0744	0818	0918	...	1018	1118	...	1218	...	1318	...	1418	...	1518	...	1618	1718	...	1818
218	**Frankfurt (Main)** ▲ a.	0540	0645	0720	0731	0758	0813	0931	...	1031	1131	...	1231	...	1331	...	1431	...	1531	...	1631	1731	...	1831

	E3573 E3829	E 3291	E3575 E3831	E3577 E3833	E 3293	E3579 E3835	E3581 E3837	E3583 E3839	8537 Ⓐ	8539
Kassel Hbf d.	1609	...	1714	1809	...	1914	2009	2117	2223	2320
Kassel Wilhelmshöhe d.	1615	...	1720	1815	...	1920	2015	2121	2228	2326
Bebra d.	1656	...	1801	1856	...	2001	2056	2201	2323	0016
Bad Hersfeld d.	1705	...	1810	1905	...	2010	2105	2210	...	...
Fulda a.	1733	...	1837	1932	...	2037	2132	2237	...	...
Fulda d.	1759	1754	1859	1959	1954	2109	2209	2301	...	...
Gemünden (Main) a.	|	1847	|	|	2047	|	|	|	...	...
Würzburg **740** a.	|	*1915*	|	|	*2115*c	|	|	|	...	...
Hanau ▲ d.	1909	...	2009	2109	...	2209	2309	0001	...	...
Offenbach (Main) ▲ d.	1918	...	2018	2118	...	2218	2318	0012	...	...
Frankfurt (Main) ▲ a.	1931	...	2031	2131	...	2231	2331	0023	...	...

	E 3470 ⚒	E 3550	E3800 E3552	E 3280 2⚒	E3802 E3554 K	E3804 E3556	E 3282 2	E3806 E3558	E3808 E3560
Frankfurt (Main) ▲ d.	...	...	0526	...	0626	0726	...	0826	0926
Offenbach (Main) ▲ d.	...	...	0538	...	0638	0738	...	0838	0938
Hanau ▲ d.	...	...	0548	...	0648	0748	...	0848	0948
Würzburg **740** d.	...	...	|	*0622*	|	|	*0843*	|	|
Gemünden (Main) d.	...	...	|	0709	|	|	0909	|	|
Fulda a.	...	...	0648	0803	0748	0855	1003	0955	1055
Fulda d.	0544	0624	0720	...	0825	0920	...	1025	1120
Bad Hersfeld d.	0611	0653	0747	...	0852	0947	...	1052	1147
Bebra d.	0621	0702	0757	...	0902	0957	...	1102	1157
Kassel Wilhelmshöhe d.	0706	0743	0838	...	0943	1038	...	1143	1238
Kassel Hbf a.	0711	0748	0843	...	0948	1043	...	1148	1243

	E 3284	E3810 E3562	E3812 E3564	E 3286	E3814 E3566		E3816 E3568	E 3288	IR 2682 F🍷	E3818 E3570	E 3820 Ⓐ	E3820 E3572 Ⓒ	E3876 E3572 Ⓐ	E3822 E3478 Ⓐ	E 3842 Ⓐ	E3290 E3574	E3824 E3576	E 3292	E3826 E3578	E3828 E3580	E3830 E3582	8540	E 3832	E 3834
Frankfurt (Main) ▲ d.	...	1026	1126	...	1226	...	1326	...	...	1426	1526	1526	1604	1626	1655	...	1726	...	1826	1926	2026	...	2126	2226
Offenbach (Main) ▲ d.	...	1038	1138	...	1238	...	1338	...	...	1438	1538	1538	|	1638	|	...	1738	...	1838	1938	2038	...	2138	2238
Hanau ▲ d.	...	1048	1148	...	1248	...	1348	...	...	1448	1548	1548	|	1648	1714	...	1748	...	1848	1948	2048	...	2148	2246
Würzburg **740** d.	*1043*	|	|	*1243*	|	...	|	*1443*	1500	|	|	|	|	|	|	*1643*	|	*1843*	|	|	|	...	|	...
Gemünden (Main) d.	1109	|	|	1309	|	...	|	1509	1520	|	|	|	|	|	|	1709	|	1909	|	|	|	...	|	...
Fulda a.	1203	1155	1255	1403	1355	...	1455	1603	1548	1555	1655	1655	1710	1755	1811	1803	1855	2003	1955	2048	2148	...	2248	...
Fulda d.	...	1224	1320	...	1425	...	1520	...	...	1624	...	1720	1720	1758	...	1825	1920	...	2025	2120	2220	...	...	...
Bad Hersfeld d.	...	1253	1347	...	1452	...	1547	...	...	1653	...	1747	1747	1831	...	1852	1947	...	2052	2147	2247	...	...	...
Bebra d.	...	1302	1357	...	1502	...	1557	...	...	1702	...	1757	1757	1840	...	1902	1957	...	2102	2202	2255	2325	...	...
Kassel Wilhelmshöhe d.	...	1343	1438	...	1543	...	1638	...	...	1743	...	1838	1838	...	...	1943	2038	...	2143	2243	...	0020	...	...
Kassel Hbf a.	...	1348	1443	...	1548	...	1643	...	...	1748	...	1843	1843	...	...	1948	2043	...	2148	2248	...	0024	...	...

F – ALPENLAND – (12) and 🍷 Hamburg - Oberstdorf and v.v.
K – ⑥⑦ is through train to Kassel; on Ⓐ, passengers change trains at Fulda.
b – ⚒, **not** Jan. 6.   c – **Not** ⑥.
h – Ⓐ, **not** Jan. 6.
▲ – Frequent local services also operate between Frankfurt (Main) and Hanau and v.v. A tram service is also available as far as Offenbach (Main).

Table 750 — HAMBURG - FRANKFURT (MAIN), NÜRNBERG and MÜNCHEN

1, 2 class except where shown

km		IC 981	D 1989	IR 2095	ICE 983	E 3001	E 3281	D 358	E 1999	ICE 3003	D 985	D483 D350 (B)	D 1954	IC 821	ICE 997	E 3193 (G)	ICE 987	E 3327	E 4171	E 3251	E 3201	ICE 999	ICE 783
0	Hamburg Altona ... d.		2203					2248			0033x											0446	
7	Hamburg Hbf ... d.		2222					2302			0100	0100										0500	
56	Lüneburg ... d.																						
92	Uelzen ... d.																				0509		
144	Celle ... d.																				0544		
	Bremen 655 ... d.		2334u					0014u															
185	Hannover 655 ... a.		0046u					0120u			0227	0227									0609	0615	
185	Hannover ... d.		0052u					0124u			0229	0229		0520							0619	0620	
	Berlin Zoo 700 ... d.								2119				2349										
	Magdeburg 700 ... d.																						
	Braunschweig 698 ... d.																						0552
	Hildesheim 698 ... d.																						0617
218	Elze ... d.							via				via									0647	0700	
235	Alfeld ... d.							Halle				Halle									0700	→	
254	Kreiensen 696 ... d.																				→		
273	Northeim 696 ... d.																						
285	Göttingen 696 ... d.								0223					0553	0613		0620t					0653	0700c
330	Kassel Wilhelmshöhe ... d.								0312		0437	0441		0512								0713	0721
384	Bebra ▲ ... d.										0511	0515		0550			0643	0650				0743	0750
420	Fulda ... d.										0620			0703	0739		0824					0839	0924
	Frankfurt (Main) Hbf ... a.								0515				0620										
	Mannheim 730 ... a.							0458							0759								
	Karlsruhe 730 ... a.							0543	0710														
	Basel SBB 730 ... a.							0818							1023								
	Stuttgart 760 ... a.								0837								0906					1006	
	Ulm 760 ... a.														1005		1005					1105	
513	Würzburg ... a.										0619						0721						0821
513	Würzburg ... d.										0621			0656			0723	0744					0823
	Steinach bei Rothenburg ... d.																0827						
	Ansbach ... d.													0748			0855						
615	Nürnberg ... a.										0723						0820						0920
615	Nürnberg ... d.	0524		0555	0624	0600			0655	0724	0730				0824					0845		0933	0924
677	Treuchtlingen ... d.			0629	0648	0703			0743	0835	0804				0842					0940		1018	1031
	Ingolstadt ... d.					0740					0835												
711	Donauwörth ... d.	0614		0648	0719				0814						0842		0931			0954			
755	Augsburg 760 ... d.	0634		0626s	0709	0731			0842		0831			0849	0916		0931			1024			1031
811	München Pasing 760 ... d.	0657		0731	0752	0827			0852		0903				0948		0952			1109			1052
819	München Hbf 760 ... a.	0706		0717	0741	0803	0837		0835		0903			0921	0920		0958			1003			1103

		IR 2085	E 3201	E 3007	E 3287	IR 2171	ICE 791	ICE 881	IC 701	E 3365	IR 2171	ICE 771	IR 2683	ICE 591	ICE 583	E 3253	EC 11	EC 51	E 3009	ICE 573	IR 2173	ICE 793	ICE 883	IR 2683	IR 2173
	Hamburg Altona ... d.						0528	0546				0622	0628		0651						0723	0728		0748	
	Hamburg Hbf ... d.						0542	0600				0636	0642		0705						0737	0742		0802	
	Lüneburg ... d.						0612					0712									0812				
	Uelzen ... d.						0629					0729									0829				
	Celle ... d.						0650					0750									0850				
	Bremen 655 ... d.							0617														0817			
	Hannover 655 ... a.						0709	0715				0749	0809		0821						0849	0909	0915	0915	
	Hannover ... d.						0712	0720	0727			0751	0812		0827						0851	0912	0920	0927	
	Berlin Zoo 700 ... d.										0548d	0709													
	Magdeburg 700 ... d.										0709														
	Braunschweig 698 ... d.										0756														
	Hildesheim 698 ... d.										0822														
	Elze ... d.								0730			←									0930				
	Alfeld ... d.		0700						0740			0740									0940				
	Kreiensen 696 ... d.		0714									0753		0853											
	Northeim 696 ... d.		0729									0805		0905											
	Göttingen 696 ... d.		0743					0753	0800			0815	0824	0917	0853	0900					0924		0953	1000	1017
	Kassel Wilhelmshöhe ... d.							0813	0821				0845		0913	0921				1019	0945		1013	1021	
	Bebra ▲ ... d.							0843	0850				0943	0950									1043	1050	1101
	Fulda ... d.																								
	Frankfurt (Main) Hbf ... a.							0939				1005	1039								1105		1139		
	Mannheim 730 ... a.							1024				1050			1124						1150		1224		
	Karlsruhe 730 ... a.											1121									1221				
	Basel SBB 730 ... a.											1310													
	Stuttgart 760 ... a.							1106							1206						1306				
	Ulm 760 ... a.							1205							1305						1405				
	Würzburg ... a.									0921									1021			1121		1150	
	Würzburg ... d.	0841								0923				0944					1023	1028		1123		1152	
	Steinach bei Rothenburg ... d.	0913								1028														1243	
	Ansbach ... d.	0933								1050									1125			1220			
	Nürnberg ... a.									1020				1024	1028				1045	1124		1145		1224	
	Nürnberg ... d.			0945																1140		1233			1317
	Treuchtlingen ... d.	1002		1033	1035					1131															
	Ingolstadt ... d.	1034			1114					1133									1218			1254			1339
	Donauwörth ... d.			1054														1208	1231			1324			1401
	Augsburg 760 ... d.			1124						1131								1208	1231	1324		1331			1401
	München Pasing 760 ... d.									1152								1252				1352			
	München Hbf 760 ... a.	1116		1209						1203	1217				1238	1309	1303					1403			

◆ – NOTES (LISTED BY TRAIN NUMBERS)

EC11 – MIMARA – 🛋 and ✗ Leipzig - Salzburg - Zagreb.

D358 – 🛏 1,2 cl., 🛋 2 cl., 🛋 and ✗ Berlin - Halle - Basel; 🛏 1,2 cl., 🛋 2 cl. and 🛋 Dresden Hbf (D1948) - Halle - Basel. Train runs non-stop from Halle to Mannheim.

D483 – 🛏 1,2 cl., 🛋 2 cl., 🛋 and 🍴 København - München (Innsbruck on ⑤ Jan. 6 - Mar. 24); 🛏 1,2 cl., 🛋 2 cl. and 🛋 Kiel (D1883) - Hamburg - München/Innsbruck; conveys from Bebra: 🛏 1,2 cl., 🛋 2 cl. and 🛋 Stralsund (Binz on ⑥ Apr. 8 - May 27, also Apr. 14, 17, May 25, not Apr. 15) - Stralsund - Rostock - München.

IC701 – SAALETAL – 🛋 and 🍴 Halle - Saalfeld - München.

IC821 – FRANKEN KURIER – 🛋 and ✗ Frankfurt/Main.

ICE883 – PAULA MODERSOHN-BECKER – 🛋 and ✗ Bremerhaven - München.

D1954 – 🛏 1,2 cl., 🛋 2 cl. and 🛋 Berlin - Halle - Erfurt - Frankfurt/Main.

D1999 – METEOR – 🛏 1,2 cl. (T2), 🛋 2 cl. and 🛋 Hamburg - München.

D1999 – 🛏 1,2 cl., 🛋 2 cl., 🛋 and 🛋 Hamburg - Karlsruhe - Stuttgart.

IR2095 – 🛋 and 🍴 Nürnberg - Salzburg.

IR2683 – ALPENLAND – 🛋 and 🍴 Hamburg - Augsburg - Kempten - Oberstdorf.

B – 🛋 Stuttgart - Aalen - Donauwörth - München.

G – 🛋 Stuttgart - Aalen - Donauwörth - München.

K – 🛋 and 🍴 Hamburg - Kassel Hbf; 🛋 Hamburg - Offenburg - Konstanz. See Tables 695, 730.

c – Arrives 0646, connects with ICE999.

d – Not Dec. 25 from Berlin Zoo.

s – Stops to set down only.

t – From Kassel Hbf depart 0614.

u – Stops to pick up only.

x – Train number D1883 from Hamburg Altona.

❖ – Not Dec. 25, Jan. 1.

↗✗ – ① - ⑥ (not Dec. 25 - Jan. 1, Apr. 15 - 17, May 1, 1995).

▲ – For other services Göttingen - Bebra see Table 748.

Table 750 — HAMBURG - FRANKFURT (MAIN), NÜRNBERG and MÜNCHEN

1, 2 class except where shown

	E 3255	IC 781	ICE 575	ICE 593	E 3211	ICE 585	IC 801	IC 725	E 3329	E 3013	ICE 577	E 3211	IR 2073	ICE 895	ICE 785	IR 2089	IR 2073	ICE 71	E 3257	ICE 595	E 3215	ICE 587	IC 813
		Y	✕	✕		✕♦	✕♦	♦			✗✕		♦F	✕	✕	Y	♦F	Y	♦	✕		✕	♦
Hamburg Altona .... d.		0753	0823			0853					0923		0928		0948			1023				1053	
Hamburg Hbf .... d.		0807	0837		0802	0907					0937		0942		1002			1037			1007	1107	
Lüneburg .... d.			0838		0845								1012								1045		
Uelzen .... d.			0854		0916								1029								1116		
Celle .... d.			0916		0951								1050								1151		
Bremen 655 .... d.																1017							
Hannover 655 .... a.			0934	0949		1016	1021				1049		1109	1115	1115			1149			1216	1221	
Hannover .... d.			0937	0951		1023	1027				1051		1112	1120	1127			1151			1223	1227	
Berlin Zoo 700 .... d.				0748																			
Magdeburg 700 .... d.				0909																0948			
Braunschweig 698 ..... d.				0956																1109			
Hildesheim 698 .... d.				1022																1156			
Elze .... d.													←	1130			1130				1247		
Alfeld .... d.											1100			1100			1140				1300		
Kreiensen 696 .... d.											→			1114			1153				→		
Northeim 696 .... d.														1129			1205						
Göttingen 696 .... d.		1016	1024			1053					1100	1143	1124	1153	1200			1215		1224	1253	1300	
Kassel Wilhelmshöhe .. d.		1049n	1045			1113					1121		1145	1213	1221			1245			1313	1321	
Bebra ▲ .... d.																							
Fulda .... d.				1143		1150							1243	1250							1343	1350	
Frankfurt (Main) Hbf .. a.				1205		1239					1305			1339				1405		1439			
Mannheim 730 .... a.				1250		1324					1350							1450					
Karlsruhe 730 .... a.				1321							1421							1524					
Basel SBB 730 .... a.																		1521					
Stuttgart 760 .... a.																		1710					
Ulm 760 .... a.				1406		1505																	
Würzburg .... a.			1158			1221																1421	1423
Würzburg .... d.			1202			1223		1228	1244														
Steinach bei Rothenburg d.									1327														
Ansbach .... d.									1355														
Nürnberg .... a.								1328															
Nürnberg .... d.	1245									1324	1335	1345											
Treuchtlingen .... d.	1340									1429	1433							1445		1540			1524
Ingolstadt .... d.	1418										1435									1534			1620
Donauwörth .... d.										1454	1524												
Augsburg 760 .... a.						1408				1431	1524									1531			
München Pasing 760 ... a.		1435o								1452										1552		1608	1631
München Hbf 760 ...... a.	1509						1438	1503	1518		1603	1616						1710				1638	1706

	IC 727	E 3333	E 3015	ICE 579	E 3215	IR 2175	ICE 897	E 787	ICE 3259	IR 2175	ICE 77	ICE 597	E 3219	ICE 589	IC 705	IC 621	E 3335	E 3021	E 3289	ICE 671	E 3219	ICE 2075	ICE 899
	✗✕			✕		Y K	✕			Y K	✕♦	✕		✕	♣✕	♣✕				✕		Y F	
Hamburg Altona .... d.			1123		1128			1148			1223			1253					1323			1328	
Hamburg Hbf .... d.			1137		1142			1202			1237			1307					1337			1342	
Lüneburg .... d.					1212						1245			1316								1412	
Uelzen .... d.					1229						1316											1429	
Celle .... d.					1250						1351											1450	
Bremen 655 .... d.							1217																1415
Hannover 655 .... a.			1249		1309		1315	1315			1349			1416	1421				1449		1509	1515	
Hannover .... d.			1251		1312		1320	1327			1351			1423	1427				1451		1512	1520	
Berlin Zoo 700 .... d.									1148														
Magdeburg 700 .... d.									1309														
Braunschweig 698 ..... d.									1356														
Hildesheim 698 .... d.									1422														
Elze .... d.				1330					← 1330											1530			
Alfeld .... d.				1300		1340			1340					1447					1500				
Kreiensen 696 .... d.				1314		1353			1353					1500					1514				
Northeim 696 .... d.				1329		1405			1405										1529				
Göttingen 696 .... d.			1324	1343		1353	1400	1417	1424	1453	1500			1524					1543				1553
Kassel Wilhelmshöhe .. d.			1345			1413	1421	1445	1513	1521				1545									1613
Bebra ▲ .... d.										*													
Fulda .... d.				1443	1450			1543	1550														1643
Frankfurt (Main) Hbf .. a.				1505	1539			1605	1639										1705				1739
Mannheim 730 .... a.				1550	1624			1650	1724										1750				1824
Karlsruhe 730 .... a.				1621				1721											1821				
Basel SBB 730 .... a.								1910															
Stuttgart 760 .... a.					1706			1806											1906				
Ulm 760 .... a.					1805			1905											2005				
Würzburg .... a.						1521			1621														
Würzburg .... d.	1428	1444				1523			1623			1628	1644										
Steinach bei Rothenburg d.		1527											1727										
Ansbach .... d.		1555											1755										
Nürnberg .... a.	1528					1620																	
Nürnberg .... d.						1624	1645					1724	1735					1745					
Treuchtlingen .... d.		1629	1633				1740							1829	1833	1834							
Ingolstadt .... d.							1818									1916							
Donauwörth .... d.		1654					1731																
Augsburg 760 .... a.		1724				1752						1808	1831					1859	1939				
München Pasing 760 ... a.						1852							2022										
München Hbf 760 ...... a.						1803	1909					1838	1903	1918					2030		2010		

♦ – NOTES (LISTED BY TRAIN NUMBERS)

ICE71 – HELVETIA – ⊡ and ✕ Hamburg - Zürich Hbf.
ICE77 – PANDA – ⊡ and ✕ Hamburg - Zürich Hbf.
ICE585 – ERNST BARLACH – ⊡ and ✕ Hamburg - München ⑧, Garmisch Partenkirchen ⑥.
IC621 – KONSUL – ⊡ and ✕ Kiel - Köln - Frankfurt/Main - München.
IC705 – SOPHIE SCHOLL – ⊡ and ✕ Berlin Hbf - Saalfeld - München.
IC725 – BERCHTESGADENERLAND – ⊡ Hamburg - Berchtesgaden; Y Bremen - Freilassing.
IC781 – KÖNIGSEE – ⊡ and Y Hamburg - Freilassing; ⊡ Hamburg - Freilassing (5525) - Berchtesgaden; ⊡ Hamburg - Würzburg (IC689) - Passau; ⊡ Hamburg - Würzburg (IC689) - Zwiesel.

IC801 – THERESE GIEHSE – ⊡ and ✕ Berlin Hbf - Saalfeld - München (extended to Bischofshofen on ⑥ Jan. 7 - Apr. 8 also Dec. 17, 23, 25, 26, May 20, 27).
IC813 – WETTERSTEIN – ⊡ and ✕ Berlin Hbf - Saalfeld - Mittenwald.
F – ⊡ and Y Flensburg - Göttingen.
K – ⊡ and Y Hamburg - Kassel Hbf; ⊡ Hamburg - Offenburg - Konstanz. see Tables 695, 730.
n – Arrive 1038, connects with ICE575.
o – München Ost.
✗/ – ① - ⑥ (not Dec. 25 - Jan. 1, Apr. 15 - 17, May 1, 1995).
♣ – Daily except ⑥ (not Dec. 24 - 31, Apr. 14 - 16, Apr. 30, 1995).
▲ – For other services Göttingen - Bebra see Table 748.

Table 750 — HAMBURG - FRANKFURT (MAIN), NÜRNBERG and MÜNCHEN

1, 2 class except where shown

Station	ICE 789 ✕	IR 2075 ✕ F	ICE 775 ✕	IC 17599 ◆	ICE 599 ✕	E 3223	ICE 681 ✕	E 3261	IC 707 B	IC 521 ✕	E 3337	ICE 673 ✕	E 3223	IR 2177 ✕	ICE 795 ✕	ICE 885 ◆✕	IR 2177 ✕	ICE 777 ◆✕	ICE 17695 ✕	ICE 695 ✕	E 3227	ICE 683 ◆✕	IC 709 B	IC 523 ✕
Hamburg Altona d.	1348		1423				1453					1523			1528	1548			1623			1653		
Hamburg Hbf d.	1402	1437		1402	1507							1537			1542	1602			1637			1707		
Lüneburg d.				1445											1612				1645				1716	
Uelzen d.				1516											1629				1716				1751	
Celle d.				1551											1650				1751					
Bremen 655 d.																1617								
Hannover 655 a.	1515		1549				1616	1621				1649			1709	1715	1715		1749			1816	1821	
Hannover d.	1527	1551					1623	1627				1651			1712	1720	1727		1751			1823	1827	
Berlin Zoo 700 d.			1345	1348															1537	1548				
Magdeburg 700 d.			1503	1509															1706	1709				
Braunschweig 698 d.			1554	1556															1754	1756				
Hildesheim 698 d.			1618	1622															1820	1822				
Elze d.		1530					1647								1730			1730				1847		
Alfeld d.		1540					1700					1700		→	1740			1740				1900		
Kreiensen 696 d.		1553					→					1714			1753			1753				→		
Northeim 696 d.		1605										1729			1805			1805						
Göttingen 696 d.	1600	1615	1624	1650	1653		1700					1724	1743		1753	1800	1817	1824	1851	1853		1900	1921	
Kassel Wilhelmshöhe d.	1621		1645	1712	1713		1721					1745			1813	1821		1845	1912	1913		1921		
Bebra ▲ d.																								
Fulda d.	1650			1742	1743		1750								1843	1850			1942	1943		1950		
Frankfurt (Main) Hbf a.			1805	1838	1839							1905			1939			2005	2037	2039				
Mannheim 730 a.			1850		1924							1950			2024					2124				
Karlsruhe 730 a.			1921																					
Basel SBB 730 a.			2110																					
Stuttgart 760 a.		IR			2006										2106			E 3339			2208			
Ulm 760 a.		2183			2105										2205					2021				
Würzburg a.	1721 𝖸					1821									1921							2023		2028
Würzburg d.	1723	1741				1823			1828	1844					1923	1944						2023		2028
Steinach bei Rothenburg d.		1813								1927	E 3025					2028								
Ansbach d.		1833								1955						2055								
Nürnberg a.	1820					1925									2020									2125
Nürnberg d.	1824						1845	1924				1945			2024							2124		
Treuchtlingen d.		1902					1940			2029	2033					2129								
Ingolstadt d.		1934					2018																	
Donauwörth d.										2054														
Augsburg 760 a.	1931					2008		2031		2124					2131							2208	2231	
München Pasing 760 a.	1952					2030		2052							2152							2230	2252	
München Hbf 760 a.	2003					2038	2109	2103							2203							2303		

Station	IR 2187 𝖸	E 3027	ICE 677 ◆𝖸	E 3227	IR 2077 𝖸	ICE 797 ✕	ICE 887 ◆✕𝖸	IR 2077 𝖸	ICE 697 ✕	E 3231	ICE 989 ✕	E 3231	ICE 893 ◆𝖸	IR 2179 𝖸	ICE 799 ◆✕	E 1125 𝖸	IC 1299 𝖸	E 3235	EN 491 A	D1981 C	E 3235 A	D 1089 S	IR 2779	D 471
Hamburg Altona d.			1723		1728	1748					1848			1928	1948		1938		2023	2023		2053	2128	2112
Hamburg Hbf d.			1737		1742	1802			1802		1902			1942	2002		1952	2002	2037	2037		2107	2142	2132
Lüneburg d.					1812				1845					2012				2034	2039			2141u	2214	
Uelzen d.					1829				1916					2029				2057	2103			2231		
Celle d.					1850				1951				1955	2050				2131	2136			2257		
Bremen 655 d.								1817																2245u
Hannover 655 a.			1849		1909	1915	1915		2016	2021		2056	2109	2115		2157	2210	2220	2220	2210	2247u	2319	2350u	
Hannover d.			1851		1912	1920	1927		2023	2027		2112	2123		2202	2228	2224	2224	2228	2251u		2356u		
Berlin Zoo 700 d.									1748n											→				
Magdeburg 700 d.									1909															
Braunschweig 698 d.									1956															
Hildesheim 698 d.									2022															
Elze d.					1930				1930	1940	2047				2130						2252			
Alfeld d.				1900	→				1940	2100		2100			2140						2304			
Kreiensen 696 d.				1914					1953		→				2153						2317			
Northeim 696 d.				1929					2005					2129	2205						2331			
Göttingen 696 d.			1924	1943	1953	2000	2015	2053		2100	2143			2217	2156		2259		2321	2321	2344	2349u		
Kassel Wilhelmshöhe d.			1945		2013	2021	2113			2121				2216										
Bebra ▲ d.							2109																	
Fulda d.					2043	2050		2154t		2150				2245										
Frankfurt (Main) Hbf a.			2105		2139			2248						2341										
Mannheim 730 a.			2150		2224																			
Karlsruhe 730 a.			2215																					
Basel SBB 730 a.																								0651
Stuttgart 760 a.						2306			E 3381													0554		
Ulm 760 a.								2121	⑧		2221						0127							
Würzburg d.	2041						2123	2144			2223						0122 0129							
Steinach bei Rothenburg d.	2113							2228																
Ansbach d.	2133							2250																
Nürnberg a.							2220				2320						0249 0249							
Nürnberg d.			2145				2224										0411							
Treuchtlingen d.	2202	2233															0446							
Ingolstadt d.	2234																0505							
Donauwörth d.		2254															0529							
Augsburg 760 a.		2324					2331									0404o 0409o	0556							
München Pasing 760 a.							2352										0607							
München Hbf 760 a.	2316						0003																	

◆ — NOTES (LISTED BY TRAIN NUMBERS)

D471 – KOMET – [sleeper] 1,2 cl., [couchette] 1,2 cl. (T2), [restaurant] 2 cl. and 𝖸 Hamburg - Basel.

EN491 – HANS ALBERS – [sleeper] 1,2 cl., [couchette] 2 cl., [restaurant] and 𝖸 Hamburg - Wien Westbahnhof.

ICE777 – SCHAUINSLAND – [restaurant] and ✕ Hamburg Altona - Karlsruhe - Freiburg.

ICE887 – LUDWIG QUIDDE – [restaurant] and ✕ Bremen - Nürnberg; extended to München on ⑦, also Nov. 1, Dec. 26, Apr. 17, May 1.

D1089 – ⑤ Jan. 6 - Apr. 7, also Dec. 16, 22, 25, Jan. 4: [sleeper] 1,2 cl., [couchette] 2 cl. and 𝖸 Hamburg - Oberstdorf; [couchette] 2 cl. (also Apr. 7) Hamburg - Innsbruck.

D1125 – DOLOMITEN EXPRESS – ⑤ Jan. 6 - Mar. 24, also Dec. 16, 20, 22, 25, Jan. 4: [sleeper] 1,2 cl., [couchette] 2 cl., [restaurant] and 𝖸 Dortmund - Bolzano; [sleeper] 1,2 cl., [couchette] 2 cl. and [restaurant] Dortmund - Villach; [couchette] 2 cl. Dortmund - Graz.

D1299 – KÄRNTEN EXPRESS – ⑤ Jan. 6- Mar. 24, also Dec. 16, 20, 22, 25, Jan. 4: [sleeper] 1,2 cl., [couchette] 2 cl., [restaurant] and 𝖸 Hamburg - Villach; [sleeper] 1,2 cl., [couchette] 2 cl. and [restaurant] Hamburg - Graz; conveys except on Mar. 20, 24: [sleeper] 1,2 cl. and [couchette] 2 cl. Hamburg - Rosenheim (D1125) - Bischofshofen - Schwarzach St. Veit.

IR2077 – [restaurant] Flensburg - Göttingen (Erfurt ▲); 𝖸 Flensburg - Göttingen.

IR2177 – [restaurant] and 𝖸 Hamburg - Kassel Hbf; [restaurant] Hamburg - Karlsruhe.
See Tables 695, 730.

IR2179 – [restaurant] Hamburg - Kassel Hbf (arrive 2307, Table 695); 𝖸 Hamburg - Hannover.

ICE17599 – ⑤⑦, also Nov. 1, Dec. 22, 26, Jan. 2, Apr. 12, 13, 17, 18, May 1, 24, not Dec. 25, Apr. 14, 16, 30, May 26.

ICE17695 – ⑤⑦, also Nov. 1, Dec. 22, Jan. 2, Apr. 12, 13, 17, 18, May 24, not Dec. 25, Apr. 14, 16, 30, May 26.

A – [restaurant] Hamburg - Göttingen (Hannover on Dec. 24, 31).

B – [restaurant] and ✕ Berlin Hbf - Saalfeld - München.

C – [restaurant] Hamburg - München; conveys from Nürnberg as train D1981. [sleeper] 1,2 cl., [couchette] 2 cl. and [restaurant] Praha Hlavni (D352) - Nürnberg - München.

F – [restaurant] and 𝖸 Flensburg - Göttingen.

S – Not Dec. 24, 31.

n – Not Dec. 24.

o – München Ost.

t – Arrives 2141, connects with ICE989.

u – Stops to pick up only.

◆ – Daily except ⑥ (not Dec. 24 - 31, Apr. 14 - 16, Apr. 30, 1995).

▲ – For other services Göttingen - Bebra see Table 748.

12

Table 750 MÜNCHEN, NÜRNBERG and FRANKFURT (MAIN) - HAMBURG

1, 2 class except where shown

		IR 2078	D 1088	E 3210	ICE 988	D 1298	D 1124	IR 2176	ICE 886	ICE 798	IR 2176	E 3214	IC 804	ICE 684	ICE 696	IR 2186	ICE 672	IR 2076	ICE 884	E 3000	ICE 796	IR 2076	E 3368	E 3218	IC 524
		🍷 ◆	🍷 ◆	◆	↗🍴	🍷 ◆	🍷 ◆	🍷 ◆	↗🍴	↗🍴	🍷 ◆		↗🍷 ◆	🍴	🍴 ◆	🍷	🍴	🍷 F	↗🍴		🍴	🍷 F			🍴 ◆
München Hbf 760	d.	...	...	...	...	...	...	...	...	...	...	...	0453	...	...	0537	...	...	0556	...	...	...	...	...	0638
München Pasing **760**	d.	...	...	...	...	0152o	0157o	...	...	...	...	...	0501	...	...	|	...	...	0604	...	...	...	...	...	|
Augsburg 760	d.	...	...	...	...	|	|	...	...	...	...	...	0525	...	...	|	...	...	0628	...	...	...	...	...	|
Donauwörth	d.	...	...	...	...	|	|	...	...	...	...	...	|	...	...	|	...	...	|	0627	...	...	...	...	|
Ingolstadt	d.	...	...	...	...	|	|	...	...	...	...	...	|	...	...	0617	...	...	|	|	...	...	...	...	0719
Treuchtlingen	d.	...	...	...	...	|	|	...	...	...	...	...	|	...	...	0650	...	...	|	0705	...	...	...	...	|
Nürnberg	a.	...	...	...	...	|	|	...	...	...	...	...	0631	...	...	|	...	...	0734	0750	...	...	...	...	0824
Nürnberg	d.	...	...	...	...	|	|	...	0538	...	...	...	...	0640	...	|	...	...	0738	...	...	...	...	...	0832
Ansbach	d.	...	...	...	...	|	|	...	|	...	...	...	...	|	...	0720	...	...	|	...	...	...	0801	...	|
Steinach bei Rothenburg	d.	...	...	...	...	|	|	...	|	...	...	...	...	|	...	0739	...	...	|	...	...	...	0822	...	|
Würzburg	a.	...	...	...	...	0428	0433	...	0634	...	...	...	...	0734	...	0812	...	...	0834	...	...	...	0907	...	0928
Würzburg	d.	...	...	...	...	0431	...	...	0636	...	...	...	...	0736	...	...	...	...	0836	...	...	...	...	...	...
Ulm **760**	d.	...	2343	...	...	|	...	...	|	...	...	...	...	|	...	...	...	...	|	...	...	...	...	...	...
Stuttgart **760**	d.	...	|	...	...	|	...	...	|	...	...	...	...	|	0553	...	...	...	|	...	0653	...	...	...	...
Basel SBB **730**	d.	...	|	...	...	|	...	...	|	...	...	...	...	|	|	...	...	...	|	...	|	...	...	...	...
Karlsruhe **730**	d.	...	|	...	...	|	...	...	|	...	...	...	...	|	|	...	0626	...	|	...	|	...	...	...	...
Mannheim **730**	d.	...	|	...	...	|	...	...	|	...	...	...	...	|	0635	...	0708	...	|	...	0735	...	...	...	...
Frankfurt (Main) Hbf	d.	...	|	...	...	|	...	...	|	0618	...	...	...	|	0718	...	0751	...	|	...	0818	...	...	...	...
Fulda	d.	...	|	...	...	|	...	...	0708	0716	...	...	...	0808	0816	...	|	...	0908	...	0916	...	...	...	...
Bebra ▲	d.	...	|	...	...	|	...	0644	|	|	...	...	...	|	|	...	|	...	|	...	|	...	...	...	...
Kassel Wilhelmshöhe	d.	...	|	...	0636t	|	...	|	0738	0746	...	...	...	0838	0846	...	0913	...	0938	...	0946	...	...	...	...
Göttingen **696**	d.	0541	0558s	0612	0658	0659	...	0741	0758	0805	...	0812	...	0858	0906	...	0932	0941	0958	...	1005	...	...	1012	...
Northeim **696**	d.	0552	|	0626	|	|	...	0753	|	|	←	0826	...	|	|	...	|	0953	|	...	|	←	...	1026	...
Kreiensen **696**	d.	0605	|	0642	|	|	...	0805	|	|	0805	0842	...	|	|	...	|	1005	|	...	|	1005	...	1042	...
Alfeld	d.	0617	|	0657	|	|	...	→	|	|	0817	0857	...	|	|	...	|	→	|	...	|	1017	...	1057	...
Elze	d.	0627	|	0710	|	|	...	...	|	|	0827	0910	...	|	|	...	|	...	|	...	|	1027	...	1110	...
Hildesheim **698**	d.	|	|	|	|	|	...	...	|	|	|	|	...	|	0934	...	|	...	|	...	|	|	...	→	...
Braunschweig **698**	a.	|	|	|	|	|	...	...	|	|	|	|	...	|	1001	...	|	...	|	...	|	|	...	...	...
Magdeburg **700**	a.	|	|	|	|	|	...	...	|	|	|	|	...	|	1050	...	|	...	|	...	|	|	...	...	...
Berlin Zoo **700**	a.	|	|	|	|	|	...	...	|	|	|	|	...	|	1210	...	|	...	|	...	|	|	...	...	...
Hannover	a.	0646	0658s	0735	0731	0757	...	...	0831	0838	0846	0935	...	0931	...	...	1005	...	1031	...	1038	1046	...	...	...
Hannover 655	d.	0649	0701s	0742	0737	0803	...	...	0843	0843	0849	0942	...	0937	...	...	1007	...	1043	...	1043	1049	...	...	...
Bremen 655	a.	|	|	|	|	|	...	...	0943	|	|	|	...	|	...	...	|	...	1143	...	|	|	...	...	...
Celle	d.	0709	0725s	0807	|	0826	...	...	...	|	0909	1007	...	|	...	...	|	...	...	...	|	1109	...	...	...
Uelzen	d.	0730	0753s	0846	|	0854	...	...	...	|	0930	1046	...	|	...	...	|	...	...	...	|	1130	...	...	...
Lüneburg	d.	0746	0813s	0909	|	0915	...	...	...	|	0946	1109	...	|	...	...	|	...	...	...	|	1146	...	...	...
Hamburg Hbf	a.	0816	0847	0951	0851	0956	...	...	...	0956	1016	1151	...	1051	...	...	1121	...	...	...	1156	1216	...	...	...
Hamburg Altona	a.	0829	0900	...	0905	1014	...	...	...	1010	1029	...	...	1105	...	...	1134	...	...	...	1210	1229	...	...	...

		IC 708	ICE 776	E 3272	E 3002		ICE 682	ICE 694	E 3218	ICE 670	IR 2174	ICE 788	ICE 898	IR 2174	E 3222	E 3004	E 3324	ICE 76	E 3276	IC 620	IC 706	ICE 680	ICE 598	E 3222	E 3252
		🍴 B	↗🍴 ◆				↗🍴	🍴 ◆		↗🍴	🍷 K	🍴	🍴	🍷 K				🍴 ◆		🍷	🍴 B	🍴	🍴		
München Hbf 760	d.	0656	...	...	...	...	0721	...	...	...	...	0756	...	...	...	...	...	...	0755	...	0856	0921	...	...	0855
München Pasing **760**	d.	0704	...	...	...	...	0727	...	...	...	...	0804	...	...	...	...	...	...	|	...	0904	0927	...	...	|
Augsburg 760	d.	0728	...	...	0702	...	0751	...	...	...	...	0828	...	...	...	0831	...	...	|	...	0928	0951	...	...	|
Donauwörth	d.	|	...	...	0748	...	|	...	...	...	...	|	...	...	...	0900	...	...	|	...	|	|	...	...	|
Ingolstadt	d.	|	...	0727	|	...	|	...	...	...	...	|	...	...	...	|	...	...	0851	...	|	|	...	...	0944
Treuchtlingen	d.	|	...	0812	0821	...	|	...	...	...	...	|	...	...	...	0921	0924	...	0938	...	|	|	...	...	1021
Nürnberg	a.	0834	...	...	0906	...	|	...	...	...	...	0934	...	...	...	1006	|	...	...	...	1034	|	...	...	1106
Nürnberg	d.	...	...	...	...	...	|	...	...	...	...	0938	...	...	...	...	|	...	...	1032	...	|	...	...	...
Ansbach	d.	...	...	...	...	...	|	...	...	...	...	|	...	...	...	...	1003	...	...	|	...	|	...	...	...
Steinach bei Rothenburg	d.	...	...	...	...	...	|	...	...	...	...	|	...	...	...	...	1024	...	...	|	...	|	...	...	...
Würzburg	a.	...	...	...	...	...	0934	...	...	...	...	1034	...	...	...	...	1107	...	...	1128	...	1134	...	...	...
Würzburg	d.	...	...	...	...	...	0936	...	...	...	...	1036	...	...	...	...	...	...	...	...	...	1136	...	...	...
Ulm **760**	d.	...	...	...	...	...	|	0654	...	...	...	|	0754	...	...	...	...	...	...	...	...	|	0854	...	...
Stuttgart **760**	d.	...	...	...	...	...	|	0753	...	...	...	|	0853	...	...	...	...	...	...	...	...	|	0953	...	...
Basel SBB **730**	d.	...	...	...	...	...	|	|	...	...	...	|	|	...	...	...	...	0752	...	...	...	|	|	...	...
Karlsruhe **730**	d.	...	0737	...	...	...	|	|	...	...	...	|	|	...	...	...	...	0937	...	...	...	|	|	...	...
Mannheim **730**	d.	...	0808	...	...	...	|	0835	...	...	...	|	0935	...	...	...	...	1002	...	...	...	|	1035	...	...
Frankfurt (Main) Hbf	d.	...	0851	...	...	...	|	0918	...	0952	...	|	1018	...	...	...	...	1051	...	...	...	|	1118	...	...
Fulda	d.	...	|	...	...	...	1008	1016	...	|	...	1108	1116	...	...	...	...	|	...	...	...	1208	1216	...	...
Bebra ▲	d.	...	|	...	...	...	|	|	...	|	...	|	|	...	...	...	...	|	...	...	...	|	|	...	...
Kassel Wilhelmshöhe	d.	...	1013	...	...	...	1038	1046	...	1113	...	1138	1146	...	...	...	...	1213	...	...	...	1238	1246	...	...
Göttingen **696**	d.	...	1032	...	...	...	1058	1106	...	1132	1141	1158	1205	...	1212	...	...	1232	...	...	...	1258	1306	...	...
Northeim **696**	d.	...	|	...	...	...	|	|	...	|	1153	|	|	←	1226	...	...	|	...	...	...	|	|	...	...
Kreiensen **696**	d.	...	|	...	...	...	|	|	...	|	1205	|	|	1205	1242	...	...	|	...	...	...	|	|	...	...
Alfeld	d.	...	|	...	...	...	|	|	←	|	→	|	|	1217	1257	...	...	|	...	...	...	|	|	←	...
Elze	d.	...	|	...	...	...	|	|	1110	|	...	|	|	1227	1310	...	...	|	...	...	...	|	|	1310	...
Hildesheim **698**	d.	...	|	...	...	...	|	1134	|	|	...	|	|	|	→	...	...	|	...	...	...	|	1334	|	...
Braunschweig **698**	a.	...	|	...	...	...	|	1201	|	|	...	|	|	|	...	...	...	|	...	...	...	|	1401	|	...
Magdeburg **700**	a.	...	|	...	...	...	|	1250	|	|	...	|	|	|	...	...	...	|	...	...	...	|	1450	|	...
Berlin Zoo **700**	a.	...	|	...	...	...	|	1410	|	|	...	|	|	|	...	...	...	|	...	...	...	|	1610	|	...
Hannover	a.	...	1105	...	...	...	1131	...	1135	1205	...	1231	1238	1246	...	...	...	1305	...	...	...	1331	...	1335	...
Hannover 655	d.	...	1107	...	...	...	1137	...	1142	1207	...	1243	1243	1249	...	...	...	1307	...	...	...	1337	...	1342	...
Bremen 655	a.	...	|	...	...	...	|	...	|	|	...	|	1343	|	...	...	...	|	...	...	...	|	...	|	...
Celle	d.	...	|	...	...	...	|	...	1207	|	...	|	...	1309	...	...	...	|	...	...	...	|	...	1407	...
Uelzen	d.	...	|	...	...	...	|	...	1246	|	...	|	...	1330	...	...	...	|	...	...	...	|	...	1446	...
Lüneburg	d.	...	|	...	...	...	|	...	1309	|	...	|	...	1346	...	...	...	|	...	...	...	|	...	1509	...
Hamburg Hbf	a.	...	1221	...	...	...	1251	...	1351	1321	...	1356	...	1416	...	...	...	1421	...	...	...	1451	...	1551	...
Hamburg Altona	a.	...	1234	...	...	...	1305	...	...	1334	...	1410	...	1429	...	...	...	1434	...	...	...	1505	...	...	...

◆ – **NOTES** (LISTED BY TRAIN NUMBERS)

- **ICE76** – PANDA – (12) and 🍴 Zürich Hbf - Hamburg.
- **IC524** – HANSEAT – (12) and 🍴 Nürnberg (München ↗) - Frankfurt/Main - Kiel.
- **ICE694** – RICARDA HUCH – (12) and 🍴 Stuttgart (München ↗) – Berlin Zoo.
- **ICE696** – BETTINA VON ARNIM – (12) and 🍴 Frankfurt (Stuttgart ↗) – Berlin Zoo.
- **ICE776** – SCHAUINSLAND – (12) and 🍴 Freiburg - Karlsruhe - Hamburg.
- **IC804** – HANS SACHS – (12) and 🍷 München - Saalfeld - Berlin Hbf.
- **D1088** – ⑥ Jan. 7 - Apr. 8 (from Oberstdorf): 🛏 1,2 cl., ▬ 2 cl. and 🍷 Oberstdorf - Hamburg; ▬ 2 cl. (also 🛏 1,2 cl. except on Apr. 1, 8) Innsbruck - Hamburg.
- **D1124** – DOLOMITEN EXPRESS – ⑥ Jan. 7 - Mar. 25, also Dec. 17, 21, 23, Jan. 1, 5 (from Bolzano): 🛏 1,2 cl., ▬ 2 cl., (2) and 🍷 Bolzano - Dortmund; 🛏 1,2 cl., ▬ 2 cl. and (2) Villach - Dortmund; ▬ 2 cl. Graz - Dortmund.
- **D1298** – KÄRNTEN EXPRESS – ⑥ Jan. 7 - Mar. 25, also Dec. 17, 21, 23, Jan. 1, 5 (from Villach): 🛏 1,2 cl., ▬ 2 cl., (12) and 🍷 Villach - Hamburg; ▬ 2 cl. and (12) Graz - Hamburg; 🛏 1,2 cl. and ▬ 2 cl. Bolzano - Hamburg; conveys except on Mar. 17, 21, 25: 🛏 1,2 cl. and ▬ 2 cl. Schwarzach St Veit (**1614**) - Wörgl (**1114**) - Kufstein (**1124**) - Rosenheim - Hamburg.
- **IR2078** – (12) Kassel Hbf (depart 0452, Table **695**) - Flensburg; 🍷 Göttingen - Flensburg.
- **IR2176** – (12) Göttingen (Erfurt ↗) - Hamburg; 🍷 Eisenach - Hamburg.
- **E3210** – (12) Göttingen (Hannover on Dec. 25, Jan. 1) - Hamburg.
- **B** – (12) and 🍴 München - Saalfeld - Berlin Hbf.
- **F** – (12) and 🍷 Göttingen - Flensburg.
- **K** – (12) and 🍷 Kassel Hbf - Hamburg; (12) Karlsruhe - Hamburg. See Tables **695**, **730**.
- **o** – München **Ost**.
- **s** – Stops to **set down** only.
- **t** – From Kassel Hbf depart 0620.
- ↗ – ① - ⑥ (**not** Dec. 25 - Jan. 1, Apr. 15 - 17, May 1, **1995**).
- ▲ – For other services Bebra - Göttingen see Table **748**.

Table 750   MÜNCHEN, NÜRNBERG and FRANKFURT (MAIN) - HAMBURG
1, 2 class except where shown

	IR 2182 ♀	ICE 774 ✗	IR 2074 ♀F	ICE 786 ✗	ICE 896 ✗	IR 2074 ♀F	E 3226	E 3008	E 3328	IC 520 ♦	ICE 578 ✗	IC 812 ♦	E 3254	ICE 588 ♦	ICE 596 ✗	E 3226	ICE 576 ♦	IC 780 ♦	IR 2172 K	E 3374 J	ICE 882 ✗	ICE 794 ✗	IR 2172 ♀K	E 3230	E 3010
München Hbf 760 .....d	0938		0956							1038	1056	1053	1121									1156			
München Pasing 760 d			1003								1104								1114o			1228			1231
Augsburg 760 ....d			1028					1031			1128			1151								1228			1231
Donauwörth.............d								1100																	1302
Ingolstadt...............d	1017								1119			1144													1321
Treuchtlingen ....d	1050							1121	1124			1221													1321
Nürnberg ....a			1134				1206		1224	1234	1306										1334				1406
Nürnberg ....d			1138						1232												1338				
Ansbach ....d	1120						1203												1315						
Steinach bei Rothenburg d	1139						1224												1336						
Würzburg ....a	1212		1234				1307		1328			1334					1338		1421		1434				
Würzburg ....d			1236									1336							1357		1436				
Ulm 760 ....d				0954										1054								1154			
Stuttgart 760 ....d				1053										1153								1253			
Basel SBB 730 ....d		0852																							
Karlsruhe 730 ....d		1037							1137								1237								
Mannheim 730 ....d		1108		1135					1208					1235			1308					1335			
Frankfurt (Main) Hbf .d		1151		1218					1251					1318			1351					1418			
Fulda.....................d				1308	1316									1408	1416							1508	1516		
Bebra ▲ ....d																									
Kassel Wilhelmshöhe d		1313		1338	1346						1413			1438	1446				1513	1517		1538	1546		
Göttingen 696 ....d		1332	1341	1358	1405		1412				1432			1458	1506			1532	1539	1541		1558	1605		1612
Northeim 696 ....d			1353				1426													1553				←	1626
Kreiensen 696 ....d			1405				1405	1442												1605				1605	1642
Alfeld...................d			→				1417	1457												1617				1617	1657
Elze.....................d							1427	1510									1510			1627				1627	1710
Hildesheim 698 ....d								→							1534									→	
Braunschweig 698 ..a															1601										
Magdeburg 700 ...a															1650										
Berlin Zoo 700 ...a															1810										
Hannover ....a		1405		1431	1438	1446					1505			1531	1535			1605	1615			1631	1638	1646	
Hannover 655 ....d		1407		1443	1443	1449					1507			1537	1542			1607	1622			1643	1643	1649	
Bremen 655 ....a					1543																	1743			
Celle.....................d					1509										1607			1642						1709	
Uelzen..................d					1530										1646			1704						1730	
Lüneburg................d					1546										1709			1721						1746	
Hamburg Hbf ....a		1521		1556	1616						1621			1651	1751			1721	1751			1756	1816		
Hamburg Altona ...a		1534		1610	1629						1634			1705	1751			1734	1804			1810	1829		

	E 3332	IR 2682 ♀ ♦	IC 724 ♀ ♦	ICE 800 ✗ ♦	IC 3256	E 586	ICE 594 ✗	E 3230	IR 2682 ♀ ♦	ICE 70	IR 2088	IR 2072 ♀	ICE 784 ✗	ICE 894 ✗	IR 2072 ♀	E 3234	E 3014	E 3334	ICE 572 ♣✗ B	ICE 3196 ♣♀✗	IC 726 ✗	IC 704 ✗	ICE 584 ✗	ICE 592 ✗
München Hbf 760 .....d			1238	1256	1255		1321			1338			1356						1410		1456	1521		
München Pasing 760 d				1304								1404				1418				1504				
Augsburg 760 ....d		1303		1328			1351					1428			1431		1500	1503		1528	1551			
Donauwörth.............d		1321									1417										1527			
Ingolstadt...............d			1319			1344					1450					1521	1524							
Treuchtlingen ....d	1324	1341				1421					1450					1521	1524							
Nürnberg ....a			1424		1434	1506						1534				1606				1632		1634		
Nürnberg ....d			1432									1538												
Ansbach ....d	1415n	1407									1520						1603							
Steinach bei Rothenburg d	1436										1539						1624							
Würzburg ....a	1521	1458	1528				1534				1612			1634			1707			1728		1734		
Würzburg ....d		1500					1536				1636													1736
Ulm 760 ....d								1254					1354											1454
Stuttgart 760 ....d								1353					1453											1553
Basel SBB 730 ....d									1252															
Karlsruhe 730 ....d				1337				1437							1535			1537						1635
Mannheim 730 ....d				1408				1435	1508						1535			1608						1635
Frankfurt (Main) Hbf .d				1451				1518	1551						1618			1651					1808	1718
Fulda.....................d		1550						1608	1616						1708	1716							1808	1814
Bebra ▲ ....d		1626								1626														
Kassel Wilhelmshöhe d		→		1613				1638	1646		1713			1738	1746			1813					1838	1840
Göttingen 696 ....d				1632				1658	1706		1721	1732		1741	1758	1805		1812		1832			1858	1906
Northeim 696 ....d														1753			1826							
Kreiensen 696 ....d									←					1805	1805	1842		1817	1857					
Alfeld...................d																	1817	1857		1910				
Elze.....................d							1710										1827	1910						
Hildesheim 698 ....d								1734									→							1934
Braunschweig 698 ..a								1801																2001
Magdeburg 700 ...a								1850																2050
Berlin Zoo 700 ...a								2010																2210e
Hannover ....a				1705			1731		1735	1800	1805			1831	1838	1846				1905		1931		
Hannover 655 ....d				1707			1737		1742	1802	1807			1843	1843	1849				1907		1937		
Bremen 655 ....a															1943									
Celle.....................d							1807	1827						1909										
Uelzen..................d							1852	1849						1930										
Lüneburg................d							1915	1905						1946										
Hamburg Hbf ....a				1821			1951	1936	1921		1956			2016				2021				2051		
Hamburg Altona ...a				1834			1905	1949	1934		2010			2029				2034				2105		

♦ – NOTES (LISTED BY TRAIN NUMBERS)

ICE70 – HELVETIA – [train] and ✗ Zürich Hbf - Hamburg.
IC520 – SPESSART – [train] and ♀ Nürnberg (München ✗) - Hamburg.
ICE574 – GÖTTINGER SIEBEN – [train] Karlsruhe - Hamburg; ✗ Frankfurt/Main - Hamburg.
ICE588 – MAX PLANCK – [train] and ✗ Garmisch Partenkirchen ⑥, München ⑧ - Hamburg.
IC704 – SOPHIE SCHOLL – [train] and ✗ München - Saalfeld - Berlin Hbf.
IC724 – BERCHTESGADENERLAND – [train] Berchtesgaden - Hamburg; ♀ Freilassing - Bremen.
IC780 – KÖNIGSEE – [train] and ♀ Freilassing - Hamburg; [train] Berchtesgaden (5508) - Hamburg; ✗ Zwiesel (IC888/688) - Würzburg - Hamburg; [train] Passau (IC688) - Würzburg - Hamburg.
IC800 – THERESE GIEHSE – [train] and ✗ München (Bischofshofen on ⑥⑦ Jan. 7 - Apr. 9, also Apr. 2, 6, 18, 22, May 20, 27) - Saalfeld - Berlin Hbf.

IC812 – WETTERSTEIN – [train] and ✗ Mittenwald - München - Saalfeld - Berlin Hbf.
IR2072 – [train] Göttingen - Flensburg; ♀ Göttingen - Neumünster.
IR2682 – ALPENLAND – [train] and ♀ Oberstdorf - Kempten - Augsburg - Hamburg.
B – [train] München - Donauwörth - Aalen - Stuttgart.
F – [train] and ♀ Göttingen - Flensburg.
J – Ⓐ, not Nov. 1, Jan. 6.
K – [train] and ♀ Kassel Hbf - Hamburg; [train] Konstanz - Hamburg.
See tables 695, 730.
e – Not Dec. 24.
n – Arrive 1359, connects with IR2682.
o – München Ost.
♣ – Daily except ⑥ (not Dec. 24 - 31, Apr. 14 - 16, Apr. 30, 1995).
▲ – For other services Bebra - Göttingen see Table 748.

Table 750 **MÜNCHEN, NÜRNBERG and FRANKFURT (MAIN) - HAMBURG** 1, 2 class except where shown

	E 3234	E 3258	E 3376	ICE 770	IR 2170	ICE 3280	ICE 880	ICE 792	IR 2170	E 3238	E 3018	E 3338	ICE 570	IR 2084	E 4184	EC 50	EC 10	E 3260	ICE 582	ICE 17590	ICE 590	E 3238	E 3342	IC 700	ICE 782
				P	✗		P	⚍					♦✗	⚍		✗	✗		✗	✗	✗			♣⚍	✗
München Hbf 760 ...d.		1455				1529	1556						1639				1656	1721						1738	1756
München Pasing 760 ...d.						1604											1704								1804
Augsburg 760 ...d.						1628						1631				1700	1728	1751							1828
Donauwörth ...d.												1700			1749										
Ingolstadt ...d.		1544				1625							1719					1744							
Treuchtlingen ...d.		1621	1624			1712				1721	1724		1751	1811				1821					1824		
Nürnberg ...a.		1706									1806							1834	1906					1929	1934
Nürnberg ...d.						1738											1832								1938
Ansbach ...d.			1701									1803	1820											1901	
Steinach bei Rothenburg ...d.			1722									1824	1839											1922	
Würzburg ...a.			1807			1834						1907	1912		1928				1934				2007	2034
Würzburg ...d.						1836													1936						2036
Ulm 760 ...d.								1554											1654						
Stuttgart 760 ...d.								1653											1753						
Basel SBB 730 ...d.			1452																						
Karlsruhe 730 ...d.			1637									1737													
Mannheim 730 ...d.			1708					1735					1808						1835						
Frankfurt (Main) Hbf ...d.			1751					1818					1851						1916	1918					
Fulda ...d.							1908	1916											2008	2011	2016				2108
Bebra ▲ ...d.																									
Kassel Wilhelmshöhe ...d.			1913				1938	1946					2013						2038	2042	2046				2138
Göttingen 696 ...d.			1932	1941			1958	2005			2012		2032						2058	2102	2106				2158
Northeim 696 ...d.				1953							2026														
Kreiensen 696 ...d.				2005							2005	2042													
Alfeld ...d.											2017	2057													
Elze ...d.	1910										2027	2110									2110				
Hildesheim 698 ...d.																			2128	2134					
Braunschweig 698 ...a.																			2157	2201					
Magdeburg 700 ...a.																			2247	2250					
Berlin Zoo 700 ...a.																			0008	0010e					
Hannover ...a.	1935		2005				2031	2038	2046				2105						2131				2135		2231
Hannover 655 ...d.	1942		2007				2043	2043	2049				2107						2137				2148		2243
Bremen 655 ...a.									2143																
Celle ...d.	2007										2109												2214		
Uelzen ...d.	2046										2130												2247		
Lüneburg ...d.	2109										2146												2310		
Hamburg Hbf ...a.	2151		2122					2158	2216				2222						2253				2349		2358
Hamburg Altona ...a.			2135					2212	2229				2235						2307						0012

	ICE 892	IR 2778	E 3242	E 3020	E 3344	ICE 986	ICE 790	E 3242	E 4186	D351 D482	D 482	D 1955	D 984	E 3290	ICE 982	E 3026	D 980	E 2094	ICE 1998	IR 359	D 2178	D1980 EN490	EN 490	D 470
	✗	♣	S		S	✦✗	✦✗			B		⚍	♦		⚍		⚍		⚍	⚍	❖	⚍	C	♦
München Hbf 760 ...d.						1856						1928	1956	1955	2056		2156	2217				2301	2312	
München Pasing 760 ...d.						1904							2004		2104		2204						2320	
Augsburg 760 ...d.			1831			1928			1931				2028		2128	2131		2228				2339u	2356	
Donauwörth ...d.			1900						2013							2200								
Ingolstadt ...d.											2011		2055					2258						
Treuchtlingen ...d.			1921	1924					2032		2046		2141		2221			2330				0036		
Nürnberg ...a.			2006		2034						2123				2234	2306	2334	0003				0113		
Nürnberg ...d.					2038						2133											0136	0136	
Ansbach ...d.				2003																				
Steinach bei Rothenburg ...d.				2024																				
Würzburg ...a.				2107	2134						2230													
Würzburg ...d.					2136						2233													
Ulm 760 ...d.	1754				1854																			
Stuttgart 760 ...d.	1853				1953																			2318
Basel SBB 730 ...d.											1749									2117				
Karlsruhe 730 ...d.											2009									2232	2338			
Mannheim 730 ...d.	1935				2035																			
Frankfurt (Main) Hbf ...d.	2018				2118					2216		2323												
Fulda ...d.	2116				2208	2216				2341	2341	0028												
Bebra ▲ ...d.										0036	0036	0121												
Kassel Wilhelmshöhe ...d.	2146				2236v	2246														0226				
Göttingen 696 ...d.	2205		2212		2305															0314		0505	0505	
Northeim 696 ...d.			2226																					
Kreiensen 696 ...d.			2242									via Halle												
Alfeld ...d.			2257																					
Elze ...d.			2310																					
Hildesheim 698 ...d.																								
Braunschweig 698 ...a.																								
Magdeburg 700 ...a.																								
Berlin Zoo 700 ...a.												0641								0831				
Hannover ...a.	2238		2333			2338	2333			0222	0222								0423		0520s	0602	0602	0608s
Hannover 655 ...d.	2243	2249	2348				2348			0224	0224								0435		0521	0532s	0606	0613s
Bremen 655 ...a.	2343		→																0540		0646			0721
Celle ...d.		2311						0022												0541				
Uelzen ...d.		2336						0055												0606				
Lüneburg ...d.		2352																		0624				
Hamburg Hbf ...a.		0013g						0355		0355									0651	0656	0756	0751	0751	0831
Hamburg Altona ...a.								0416											0709	0709	0809	0804	0804	0850

♦ **NOTES (LISTED BY TRAIN NUMBERS)**

EC10 — MIMARA – [car] and ✗ Zagreb - Salzburg - Leipzig.
E359 — [couchette]1,2 cl., [seat]2 cl. and [diner] Basel SBB - Halle - Berlin;
  [couchette]1,2 cl., [seat]2 cl. and [car] Basel - Halle (D1949) - Dresden Hbf.
D470 — KOMET – [sleeper]1,2 cl., [couchette]1,2 cl. (T2), [seat]2 cl. and [car] Basel - Hamburg.
D482 — [sleeper]1,2 cl., [seat]2 cl. and [car] München (Innsbruck on ⑥ Jan. 7 - Mar. 25) -
  København; [couchette]1,2 cl., [seat]2 cl. and [car] München/Innsbruck - Hamburg (D1882) -
  Kiel; conveys to Bebra: [sleeper]1,2 cl., [seat]2 cl. and [car] München - Stralsund (Binz from
  May 27, also Apr. 13, 16, May 24, not Apr. 14).
N490 — HANS ALBERS – [sleeper]1,2 cl., [seat]2 cl., [car] and [diner] Wien Westbahnhof - Hamburg.
C700 — SAALETAL – [car] and [diner] München - Saalfeld - Halle.
CE880 — VEIT STOSS – [car] and ✗ München - Bremerhaven.
C980 — LUCAS CRANACH – ⑦, also Apr. 17, May 1, not Apr. 16, 30; [car] and [diner] München -
  Nürnberg.
D1955 — [sleeper]1,2 cl., [seat]2 cl., [car] and [diner] Frankfurt/Main - Erfurt - Halle - Berlin.
D1988 — METEOR – [sleeper]1,2 cl., [couchette]1,2 cl. (T2), [seat]2 cl. and [car] München - Hamburg.
D1998 — [sleeper]1,2 cl., [seat]2 cl., [car] and [diner] Stuttgart - Karlsruhe - Hamburg.
E2094 — [car] and [diner] Salzburg - Nürnberg.

IR2170 — [car] Kassel Hbf - Hamburg; [car] Konstanz - Hamburg; [diner] Kassel - Celle.
  See Tables 695, 730.
ICE17590 — ⑥⑦, also Apr. 12, 13, 18, 19, May 1, 24, not Apr. 14, 16, 30, May 26.
B — [couchette]1,2 cl., [seat]2 cl. and [diner] Basel - København.
C — [car] München - Hamburg; conveys to Nürnberg: [sleeper]1,2 cl., [seat]2 cl. and [car]
  München - Nürnberg (D353) - Praha Hlavni.
K — [car] and [diner] Kassel Hbf - Hamburg; [car] Konstanz - Hamburg (Tables 695, 730).
P — Ⓐ, not Nov. 1, Jan. 6.
e — Not Dec. 24, 31.
e — Not nights of Dec. 24/25 and Dec. 31/Jan. 1.
g — Hamburg Harburg. Connection by S-Bahn train departs Hamburg Harburg 0023,
  arrives Hamburg Hbf 0035 and Hamburg Altona 0048.
s — Stops to set down only.
u — Stops to pick up only.
v — Continues to Kassel Hbf arrive 2244.
❖ — Daily except ⑥ (not Dec. 24 - 31, Apr. 14 - 16, Apr. 30, 1995).
▲ — For other services Bebra - Göttingen see Table 748.

Table 751 — STEINACH - ROTHENBURG OB DER TAUBER
2 class only

Rail service Steinach bei Rothenburg - Rothenburg ob der Tauber.   12 km.   Journey time: 15 minutes (22 by 🚌).
From Steinach: 0556 Ⓐ, 0727, 0830, 1033, 1141 ✗, 1230, 1341, 1441 ✗, 1541 Ⓑ, 1624 ⑥ 🚌, 1730 Ⓐ, 1756 Ⓒ, 1841 Ⓐ, 1923 🚌, 2024 Ⓑ 🚌.
From Rothenburg: 0501 Ⓐ, 0620 Ⓐ, 0631 ⑥, 0801, 0852, 1101 ✗, 1203, 1308, 1415 ✗, 1503 Ⓑ, 1511 ⑥ 🚌, 1603 Ⓐ, 1753 Ⓑ, 1849 Ⓒ 🚌, 1903 Ⓐ, 1955 Ⓑ 🚌.

Table 755 — ULM - DONAUWÖRTH - INGOLSTADT - REGENSBURG
1, 2 class except where shown

km		6131 E3159	E 3161	E 3827	6113	3165	6145	6107	6141	3169	6151	3831
		2 N	2	2 P		2	2 P	2	2		2 K	2 K
0	Ulm .... d.	0458	0742	0945	1111	1309	1420n	1508	1620n	1729	1820n	2209
24	Günzburg ...... d.	0526	0759	1003	1154	1328	1440	1544	1650	1748	1850	2228
48	Dillingen ...... d.	0544	0815	1022	1215	1346	1502	1608	1711	1812	1910	2254
74	Donauwörth ... a.	0608	0836	1045	1238	1406	1527	1632	1741	1831	1933	2316
				6985 N								
74	Donauwörth ... d.	0628	0902	...	1258	1408	1536	1705	1748h	1843	1938	...
106	Neuburg (Donau) d.	0700	0924	...	1327	1437	1611	1742	1816h	1906	2008	...
127	Ingolstadt ...... a.	0716	0936	...	1344	1451	1628	1804	1831h	1919	2022	...
127	Ingolstadt ...... d.	0730	0947	...	1353	1457	1708	...	...	1938	...	...
155	Neustadt (Donau) d.	0749	1004	...	1421	1513	1731	...	...	1959	...	...
201	Regensburg ... a.	0825	1037	...	1501	1548	1812	...	...	2035	...	...

		E 3160	E 3162	6102	E 3164	6138	6142	6150	E 3166	E 3168	6988 E3158
		2 N		2 P		2 P	2 P	2 F		2	2
	Regensburg .... d.	0616	0846	...	1237	1324	...	1624v	1723	1723	1903
	Neustadt (Donau).... d.	0659	0920	...	1315	1407	...	1716v	1807	1807	1947
	Ingolstadt .... a.	0717	0936	...	1334	1430	...	1738v	1826	1826	2008
	Ingolstadt .... d.	0728	0948	1153	1348	1453	1552	1746	1840	1840	...
	Neuburg (Donau) .... d.	0742	1001	1209	1403	1511	1610	1803	1853	1853	...
	Donauwörth .... a.	0807	1023	1237	1424	1536	1635	1833	1920	1920	...
	Donauwörth .... d.	0811	1025	1240	1426	1542	1704	1840	1921	1937	...
	Dillingen .... d.	0834	1042	1303	1444	1607	1728	1902	1947	1956	...
	Günzburg .... d.	0853	1059	1327	1504	1625	1745	1920	2002	2012	...
	Ulm .... a.	0916	1119	1346	1523	1734	1834	1938n	2019	2037	...

F – Ⓑ, not Dec. 25, Apr. 16.
K – Ⓑ, not Dec. 15, Apr. 16, 30.
N – ✗, not Nov. 1, Jan. 6.
O – Ⓒ, also Nov. 1, Jan. 6.
P – Ⓐ, not Nov. 1, Jan. 6.
h – Ⓑ only.
n – InterRegio supplement payable on connecting train.
v – On ⑦, connection departs Regensburg 1610, Neustadt 1654, arriving Ingolstadt 1712.

Table 757 — FLUGHAFEN MÜNCHEN ✈
2 class only

km							
0	München Pasing .... d.	0313	and every	2353	...	0013	0033
7	München Hbf Low Level .. d.	0322	20	0002	...	0022	0042
11	München Ostbahnhof .... d.	0332	minutes	0012	...	0032	0052
44	Flughafen München ✈ ...... a.	0401	until	0041	...	0101	0121

	Flughafen München ✈ .. d.	0355	and every	2355	0015	0035	0055	0115
	München Ostbahnhof .... d.	0427	20	0027	0047	0107	0127	0147
	München Hbf Low Level . d.	0436	minutes	0036	0056	0116	0136	0156
	München Pasing .... a.	0445	until	0045	0105	0125	0145	0205

🚌 635 operates daily from **München Flughafen** ✈ - **Freising Bahnhof** and v.v. (Tables 779/783) connecting with trains to/from Nürnberg, Coburg, Regensburg, Passau and Dresden. Journey time: 15 minutes.   **Operator:** M.V.V.

From **München Flughafen** ✈ : 0555, 0635, 0647, 0715, 0747, 0835, 0847, 0915, 0947, 1035, 1047, 1115, 1147, 1235, 1247, 1315, 1347, 1435, 1447, 1515, 1547, 1635, 1647, 1715, 1747, 1835, 1847, 1915, 1947, 2035, 2128, 2235, 2328.   From **Freising Bhf** : 0536, 0616, 0656, 0723, 0756, 0816, 0856, 0916, and at 16 and 56 minutes past each hour until 2056, 2213, 2256.

Table 759 — MÜNCHEN - BAYRISCHZELL, TEGERNSEE and LENGGRIES
1, 2 class

km		E 4063	4031	6281	E 4001	4081	E 4003	6275	🚌	4033	6283	4067	4083	E 4003	4035	6285	4069	4085	E 4007	E4037	6287	E4087	6255	E 4011
		P✗	O	P✗	O	P	O	P		O	O	P✗	O	P✗	O	O	P	O	P	✗	P	①–⑤	⑤	
0	München Hbf .... d.	0628	0630		0650	0730	0746	...		0830		0853	0930	0930	1030		1054	1130	1148	1230		1330		1348
37	Holzkirchen .... d.	0702	0700	0700	0722	0800	0816	0901		0902	0925	1000	0958	1100	1102	1124	1200	1216	1300	1302	1400	1406	1417
61	Schliersee .... d.			0725		0748		0846			0930			1028	1130			1241	1330			1440	1440
78	Bayrischzell .... a.			0756		0830b		0912			0956			1054	1156			1320b	1356			1506	1516
47	Schaftlach .... d.	0713		0712		0816		0829			0912	0936	1011			1112	1136	1211			1312	1411
47	Schaftlach .... d.	0719		0715		0817		0832	0832		0915	0942	1017			1115	1142	1217			1314	1415
59	Tegernsee .... a.	0738				0834			0854			1001	1034				1201	1234				1435
57	Bad Tölz .... d.	0733		0730		0827		0843			0930	0954	1027			1130	1153	1227			1326	1425
67	Lenggries .... a.	0746		0743		0840		0856			0943	1007	1040			1143	1206	1240			1343	1440

		E 4041	6289	E 4013	4073	4089	589	E 4015	4075	4043	6291	4017	E4091	4019	4045	6293	4021	6279	🚌	4093	4079	🚌	4047	4023	6295
		O		O	P✗	O	O	P✗	O	P		P✗		O	O	P	O	C	O✗	P		P	O	P	O
	München Hbf .... d.	1430		1510	1526	1530		1610	1628	1630		1650	1730	1750	1830		1854			1930	1954		2054	2054	
	Holzkirchen .... d.	1500	1502	1539	1558	1600		1639	1700	1700	1702	1718	1800	1819	1900	1902	1921	1927		2000	2022		2121	2121	2134
	Schliersee .... d.	1530		1610				1710		1730		1750		1850	1930		1952				2150	2150
	Bayrischzell .... a.	1556		1636				1736		1756		1816		1916	1956		2018				2215h	2225g
	Schaftlach .... a.		1512		1609	1611			1711		1712		1811			1912		1937		2011	2033		2134
	Schaftlach .... a.		1515		1613	1617	1615		1716		1715		1817			1915		1942	1940	2017	2037	2037	2137
	Tegernsee .... a.				1633		1635			1734			1835					2000	2034		2057
	Bad Tölz .... a.	1530			1624	1627			1727		1730		1827			1930		1953		2027	2048		2148
	Lenggries .... a.	1543			1637	1640			1740		1743		1840			1943		2006		2040	2101		2201

		🚌	E 4060	6280	E 4030	4002	4062	4080	6250	🚌	4064	🚌	E 4004	6282	4032	E 4066	4082	4006	6284	4034	4068	4084	598	6276	4008
		P	O		⑥	P	O✗	P	P		P		P✗	O	P	O✗	P	O		O✗	P	O	P	P	
	Lenggries .... d.		0608	0615		0646	0716			0719		0811		0909	0916		1011		1107	1116		1210	
	Bad Tölz .... d.		0621	0628		0659	0729			0734		0828		0922	0929		1028		1110	1117	1223	
	Tegernsee .... d.	0606				0647	0718		0719				0910	0917				1112		1212
	Schaftlach .... d.	0629	0631	0638		0709	0739		0742	0745		0838		0932	0939		1038		1132	1139	1231	1233
	Schaftlach .... d.	0634	0640		0715	0745			0747		0840		0938	0945		1040		1138	1145	1235
	Bayrischzell .... d.			0604	0601			0651		0735		0804		0953		1004				1146
	Schliersee .... d.			0636	0634			0723		0810	0820	0836		1025		1036				1218
	Holzkirchen .... d.	0646	0650	0700	0700	0727	0758	0752	0759		0849	0850	0900	0949	0958	1049	1050	1100	1149	1158	1245	1249
	München Hbf .... a.	0716		0726	0728	0756	0824		0827		0916		0926	1016	1024	1116		1126	1216	1224	1316

		6286	E 4036	4070	4086	4072	6288	4038	4010	4074	4088	4012	6290	4042	4014	4090	4076	6292	4044	6256	4078	4092	4018	6294	4046
		O	P✗	O	P✗	O	P	O	P✗	O✗	P	O	P✗	O	P	O✗	P✗	O	O	P✗	O✗	P	O	P	O
	Lenggries .... d.	1211		1310	1316	1410	1411			1506	1516		1611			1716	1743	1811			1910	1916		2011	
	Bad Tölz .... d.	1228		1325	1329	1426	1428			1521	1529		1628			1729	1757	1828			1923	1929		2028	
	Tegernsee .... d.			1313	1317					1510	1518					1718	1746				1911	1918	
	Schaftlach .... d.	1238		1335	1339	1436	1438			1531	1543		1638			1739	1807	1838			1933	1939		2038
	Schaftlach .... d.	1240		1341	1345	1438	1440			1537	1545		1640			1745	1813	1840			1939	1945		2040
	Bayrischzell .... d.		1204					1404	1411			1541		1604	1641				1804	1821			1923		2004
	Schliersee .... d.		1236					1436	1445			1613		1636	1718				1836	1853			1956		2036
	Holzkirchen .... d.	1250	1352	1358	1449	1450	1500	1510	1548	1558	1639	1650	1700	1749	1758	1820	1900	1916	1950	1958	2020	2050	2100
	München Hbf .... a.	1326	1420	1424	1516		1527	1536	1616	1624	1706		1727	1816	1824	1856		1927	2017	2024	2046		2116

O – Ⓒ, also Nov. 1, Jan. 6.
P – Ⓐ, not Nov. 1, Jan. 6.
b – Connection is by 🚌.
g – **Not** ⑤ or Nov. 15, Jan. 5, Apr. 13, May 24.
h – ⑦ only.
✗ – Conveys through carriages München - Tegernsee and München - Lenggries and v.v.

Table 760 — MANNHEIM - STUTTGART - MÜNCHEN

1, 2 class except where shown

km		IC 811	D 1925	D 215	IR 2095	IR 2663	EC 63	D 261	E 3405	E 3031	IR 2191	ICE 991	ICE 993	IR 2191	IC 763	E 3405	IR 2465	IR 361	ICE 995	IR 361	ICE 3001	D 1999	EC 15	IR 2193
		◆	⟟	◆	⟟	⟟	✕	◆			J	⟟	⤢✕	◆	⟟	⤢✕		L	H	⟟	✕	⟟	✕	⟟
	Dortmund 650 d.	…	2143	…	…	…	…	…	…	…	…	…	…	…	…	…	…	…	…	…	…	…	…	…
	Duisburg 650 d.	…	2224	2338	…																			
	Düsseldorf Hbf 650 d.	…	2259	2356	…																			
	Köln Hbf 650 d.	…	2336	0049	…																			
	Frankfurt (Main) Hbf 730 d.											0631												
0	Mannheim 742 d.	…		0323				0457				0627	0709			0642		0713		0727			0755	
17	Heidelberg 742 d.	…		0337				0510					0656										0807	
	Karlsruhe 730 d.	…			0506		0519			0607				0655	0707		0707	0723					0810	
	Pforzheim d.						0540			0630				0717			0734	0753					0830	
50	Bruchsal 730 d.				0520		0537		0603	0638				0718	0722									
83	Mühlacker d.								0603	0638				0725			0743	0802					0838	
91	Vaihingen d.				0538				0610	0645						0744		0750					0845	
130	Stuttgart a.			0454	0555		0620		0641		0701	0750		0756	0800	0806		0825	0837	0850			0901	
130	Stuttgart d.		0502				0600	0627	0633		0716	0711	0716	0757		0816	0811	0816			0857		0916	
152	Plochingen d.						0614		0656		0731						0831							
172	Göppingen d.		0527				0652	0711			0744						0844							
191	Geislingen d.							0727			0756						0856							
224	Ulm d.	0554	0605				0658	0728	0751		0805	0820	0856				0905	0918					0956	
308	Augsburg 750 d.	0639	0655	0709			0739	0813			0846	0903	0937				0946						1037	
362	München Pasing 750 a.	0702			0731		0801					0924	0959										1059	
370	München Hbf 750 a.	0712	0714	0736	0741		0812	0850			0915	0941	0935	1010			1015						1110	
523	Salzburg 790 a.				0940			0955					1140										1245	

	ICE 997	IR 2193	E 3037	E 3020	EC 113	IR 2467	IR 2265	EC 999	IR 2265	EC 3003	EC 13	IR 2195	ICE 791	IR 2195	E 3039	IC 119	IR 2669	IR 461	ICE 591	IR 461	E 3005	EC 115	IR 2197
	⤢✕	⟟			✕ H	⟟	✕		✕		✕		⤢✕		◆	◆ N			◆		◆	✕	⟟
Dortmund 650 d.	…	…	…	…	0511	…	…	…	…	0611	…	…	…	…	…	0749	…	…	…	…	…	0811	…
Duisburg 650 d.	…				0549					0649						0804						0849	
Düsseldorf Hbf 650 d.	…				0604					0704						0804						0904	
Köln Hbf 650 d.	…				0630					0730						0830						0930	
Frankfurt (Main) Hbf 730 d.	0743								0843				0943						1043				
Mannheim 742 d.	0827				0855		0913	0927			0955	1027				1055		1113	1127			1155	
Heidelberg 742 d.				0811	0907						1007					1011	1107					1207	
Karlsruhe 730 d.			0834			0910					0908	1010						1110			1108		1210
Pforzheim d.			0858								0932	1030									1133		1230
Bruchsal 730 d.			0833			0921									1033	1121							
Mühlacker d.			0858	0903							0942	1038			1058			1143					1238
Vaihingen d.			←0904	0915				0943			0949	1045			1104			←1149					
Stuttgart a.	0906	0901	0935	0946	0950	0956	1000	1006	1000	1024	1050	1101	1106	1101	1135	1150	1156	1200	1206	1200	1223	1250	1301
Stuttgart d.	0911	0916			0957		1016	1011	1016		1057	1116	1111	1116		1157		1216	1211	1216		1257	1316
Plochingen d.					0931			→			1031			1131				1231					
Göppingen d.					0944						1044			1144				1244					
Geislingen d.					0956						1056			1156				1256					
Ulm d.	1005				1056			1105	1118		1156	1205	1220			1256			1305	1318		1356	
Augsburg 750 d.	1046	1103			1137			1146			1237	1246	1303			1337			1346			1437	
München Pasing 750 a.		1124			1159						1259		1324			1359						1459	
München Hbf 750 a.	1115	1135			1210			1215			1310	1315	1335			1410			1415			1510	
Salzburg 790 a.		1340			1355			1355				1455	1540			1645			1655				

	ICE 793	IR 2197	E 3041	IC 715	EC 65	IR 2561	IC 715	IR 2267	IR 593	IR 2267	E 3007	IC 513	IR 2199	ICE 895	IR 2199	E 3043	IC 613	IR 2563	IR 2365	ICE 595	IR 2365	E 3009	EC 19
	✕	⟟		✕	◆	⟟	✕ H	◆	⟟	◆	✕			✕	⟟		✕ H	◆	◆	✕	◆		✕
Dortmund 650 d.	…	…	…	…	…	…	…	…	…	…	1011	…	…	…	…	…	…	…	…	…	…	…	1211
Duisburg 650 d.				0949							1049						1149						1249
Düsseldorf Hbf 650 d.				1004							1104						1204						1304
Köln Hbf 650 d.				1030							1130						1230						1330
Frankfurt (Main) Hbf 730 d.	1143								1243				1343						1443				
Mannheim 742 d.	1227			1255				1313	1327		1355		1427		1455		1513	1527					1555
Heidelberg 742 d.			1211	1307							1407				1411	1507							1607
Karlsruhe 730 d.					1253	1310						1308	1410						1510				
Pforzheim d.					1314							1332	1430						1532				
Bruchsal 730 d.			1233			1321									1433	1521							
Mühlacker d.			1258									1343	1438		1458				1542				
Vaihingen d.			←1304									1350			←1504				1543		1549		
Stuttgart a.	1306	1301	1335	1350	1346	1350	1401	1406	1401	1426	1450	1501	1506	1501	1535	1550	1601	1606	1601	1623	1650		
Stuttgart d.	1311	1316		1402	1357		1402	1416	1411	1416		1457	1516	1511	1516		1557	1616	1611	1616		1657	
Plochingen d.				1331	→		→			1431			1531				1631						
Göppingen d.				1344						1444			1544				1644						
Geislingen d.				1356						1456			1556				1656						
Ulm d.	1405	1420		1456	1459		1505	1518		1556	1605	1620			1656		1705	1718			1756		
Augsburg 750 d.	1446	1503		1537	1546					1637	1646	1703			1737		1746				1837		
München Pasing 750 a.		1524		1559						1659		1724			1759						1859		
München Hbf 750 a.	1515	1535		1610	1615					1710	1715	1735			1810						1910		
Salzburg 790 a.		1740			1753					1753					1955						1910		

NOTES (LISTED BY TRAIN NUMBERS)

C13 — PAGANINI – 🛏 and ✕ Dortmund - Kufstein - Venezia Santa Lucia.
C15 — PATSCHERKOFEL – 🛏 and ✕ Saarbrücken - Kufstein - Innsbruck.
C19 — ANDREAS HOFER – 🛏 and ✕ Dortmund - Kufstein - Innsbruck.
C63 — BARTÓK BÉLA – 🛏 and ✕ Stuttgart - Budapest Keleti.
C65 — MOZART – 🛏 and ✕ Paris Est - Kehl - Wien West; 🛏 Paris - Graz.
C113 — WÖRTHERSEE – 🛏 and ✕ Dortmund - Klagenfurt.
C115 — BLAUER ENZIAN – 🛏 and ✕ Dortmund - Klagenfurt.
C119 — KARWENDEL – 🛏 and ✕ Münster - Mittenwald - Innsbruck.
215 — 🛏 1,2 cl., ⊷ 2 cl. and ✕ Amsterdam CS - München;
🛏 1,2 cl., ⊷ 2 cl. and 🍴 Oostende - München.
261 — 🛏 and ✕ Paris Est - Kehl - Karlsruhe - München.
361 — 🛏 and 🍴 Saarbrücken - Lindau - Bregenz.
461 — 🛏 and 🍴 Trier - Landeck.
613 — 🛏 and ✕ Münster - Stuttgart (München ♣).
715 — NEBELHORN – 🛏 and ✕ Münster - Kempten - Oberstdorf.
763 — BADEN KURIER – 🛏 and ✕ Basel Bad - München.
811 — ELIAS HOLL – ① - ⑤, **not** Apr. 14 - 17, May 1, 25: 🛏 Ulm - München.

ICE993 — ISAR-SPRINTER – ① - ⑤, **not** Apr. 14 - 17, May 1, 25: 🛏 and ✕ Frankfurt Main - München.
D1925 — LUNA – 🛏 1,2 cl., ⊷ 2 cl. and 🍴 Münster (Norddeich Mole on ⑤⑥⑦) Apr. 7 - May 27, also Apr. 17) - München.
D1999 — 🛏 1,2 cl., ⊷ 2 cl., 🛏 and 🍴 Hamburg Altona - Karlsruhe - Stuttgart.
IR2095 — 🛏 and 🍴 Nürnberg - Salzburg.
IR2265 — 🛏 and 🍴 Trier (Saarbrücken on Dec. 25, Jan. 1) - Friedrichshafen Stadt.
IR2267 — 🛏 and 🍴 Saarbrücken - Friedrichshafen Stadt.
IR2365 — 🛏 and 🍴 Saarbrücken - Lindau.
IR2663 — 🛏 Stuttgart (Karlsruhe ⤢) - Nürnberg - Dresden Hbf; 🍴 Stuttgart - Dresden.
E3005 — 🛏 Karlsruhe - Stuttgart; 🛏 Dortmund (IR2213) - Karlsruhe - Pforzheim (6077) - Bad Wildbad.
H — 🛏 and 🍴 Karlsruhe - Nürnberg - Hof.
J — ⑥, **not** Nov. 1, Jan. 6.
L — ✕, **not** Nov. 1, Jan. 6.
N — 🛏 and 🍴 Karlsruhe - Nürnberg - Hof - Dresden Hbf.
❖ — Not Dec. 25, Jan. 1.
⤢ — ① - ⑥ (**not** Dec. 25 - Jan. 1, Apr. 15 - 17, May 1, **1995**).
♣ — Daily except ⑥ (**not** Dec. 24 - 31, Apr. 14 - 16, Apr. 30, **1995**).

Table 760 — MANNHEIM - STUTTGART - MÜNCHEN

1, 2 class except where shown

	IR 2291	ICE 897	IR 2291	E 3045	IC 615	IR 2565	IR 2367	ICE 597	IR 2367	E 3011	IC 617	IR 2293	ICE 899	IR 2293	E 3047	EC 67	IC 719	IR 2567	EC 67	IR 2269	ICE 599	IR 2269	E 3013
Dortmund 650 d.											1411												
Duisburg 650 d.				1349							1449						1549						
Düsseldorf Hbf 650 d.				1404							1504						1604						
Köln Hbf 650 d.				1430							1530						1630						
Frankfurt (Main) Hbf 730 d.		1543						1643					1743								1843		
Mannheim 742 d.		1627			1655		1713	1727			1755		1827				1855			1913	1927		
Heidelberg 742 d.				1611			1707				1807					1811	1907						
Karlsruhe 730 d.	1610					1708	1710				1810					1853				1910			1908
Pforzheim d.	1630									1732	1830						1914						1935
Bruchsal 730 d.				1633			1721				1742		1838				1858				1833		1945
Mühlacker d.	1638			1658						1704			1845			1904				1943			1952
Vaihingen d.	1645		←				1743				1749		1845			1904							
Stuttgart a.	1701	1706	←	1735	1750	1756	1800	1806	1808	1823	1850	1901	1906	1901	1935	1946	1950	1956	1946	2000	2006	2000	2026
Stuttgart d.	1716	1711	1716		1757		1816	1811	1816		1857	1916	1911	1916		2002	1957		2002	2016	2011	2016	
Plochingen d.	→		1731						→	1831			1931			→					2031		
Göppingen d.			1744							1844			1944								2044		
Geislingen d.			1756							1856			1956								2056		
Ulm d.		1805	1820		1856			1905		1918	1956		2005	2020			2052		2057	2105	2118		
Augsburg 750 d.		1846	1903		1937			1946			2037		2046	2103			2137			2146			
München Pasing 750 a.			1924		1959						2059						2159						
München Hbf 750 a.		1915	1935		2010			2015			2110		2115	2140			2210			2215			
Salzburg 790 a.			2140					2245v			2340										0024		

	E 3437	IC 517	IC 517	IR 2295	E 795	E 3431	E 3049	IR 2569	E 619	ICE 695	IR 2299	E 3015	ICE 797	E 3439	E 3017	EC 69	IC 939	IC 949	D 263	D 1015	D 1215
Dortmund 650 d.		1611	1611						1749											2000	
Duisburg 650 d.		1649	1649						1804											2042	2218
Düsseldorf Hbf 650 d.		1704	1704						1830											2113	2234
Köln Hbf 650 d.		1730	1730					2043				2143								2156	2305
Frankfurt (Main) Hbf 730 d.				1943		2027				2127			2227						2348	0002	
Mannheim 742 d.		1955	1955			2027		2011	2107				2227							0002	
Heidelberg 742 d.		2007	2007																0001	0015	
Karlsruhe 730 d.				2007				2107		2108				2208	2249					0058	
Pforzheim d.				2030						2132				2232	2308						
Bruchsal 730 d.							2033	2121		2142				2242					0020	0034	
Mühlacker d.				2038			2058			2149				2249					0044	0058	
Vaihingen d.				2045			2104	2139		2149											
Stuttgart a.		2050	2050	2101	2106	2116	2135	2156	2203	2208	2228	2306	2324	2349	0118	0132	0157				
Stuttgart d.	2035		2057	2111	2116		2135				2216		2316				0206				
Plochingen d.	2054				2135						2231		2339								
Göppingen d.	2109				2154						2244		0001								
Geislingen d.	2124				2209						2256		0017								
Ulm d.	2149		2156		2205	2234					2320		0042							0358	0429/0516
Augsburg 750 d.			2237		2246						0003										0516
München Pasing 750 a.			2259		2307						0024						0423o			0436	0559o
München Hbf 750 a.			2310		2318						0035										0733
Salzburg 790 a.			0101														0553				

km		ICE 696	IC 518	ICE 672	IR 2568	EC 68	E 3032	E 3404	E 796	IR 2296	E 3410	IC 618	E 3000	IR 2268	IC 694	IR 2268	IR 2566	E 516	E 3034	E 3414	IR 2294	ICE 990	ICE 898	IR 2294
	Salzburg 790 d.																					0435		
	München Hbf 750 d.											0542									0622	0638	0646	
	München Pasing 750 d.											0550									0629	0645		
	Augsburg 750 d.											0614									0653		0714	
	Ulm d.							0516		0554		0640	0654						0708	0744	0754			
	Geislingen d.							0542		0618		0702							0736	0807				
	Göppingen d.							0559		0633		0716							0753	0819				
	Plochingen d.							0614		0646		0727							0807	0830				
	Stuttgart a.							0634		0704		0744	0749	0744					0826	0844				
0	Stuttgart d.	0553	0557		0603	0612	0620		0653	0657		0711	0736	0800	0753	0800	0805	0811	0821		0857		0853	0857
39	Vaihingen d.				0618		0650		0713			0808	→		0816				0851		0849			0913
47	Mühlacker d.					0657			0720			0816							0859					0920
60	Bruchsal 730 d.				0635				0726			0837							0926					0929
91	Pforzheim a.				0648	0641			0729			0826				0848								0948
	Karlsruhe 730 a.				0648	0702			0749			0850								0947				
	Heidelberg 742 d.		0651	0655				0747			0754			0832	0846				0854	0947				
	Mannheim 742 a.	0632	0706					0732			0804			0904								0932		
	Frankfurt (Main) Hbf 730 a.	0714	0747					0814			0914										0948	1014		
	Köln Hbf 650 a.		0929							1029								1129						
	Düsseldorf Hbf 650 a.		0955							1055								1155			1209			
	Duisburg 650 a.		1009															1209						
	Dortmund 650 a.		1048															1248						

◆ – NOTES (LISTED BY TRAIN NUMBERS)

EC67 — MAURICE RAVEL – ✕ Paris Est - Kehl - Karlsruhe - München.
EC68/9 — MARIE CURIE – 🛌 and ✕ Paris Est - Kehl - Karlsruhe - Stuttgart and v.v.
D263 — ORIENT EXPRESS – 🛌 2 cl. and 🛌 Paris Est - Kehl - Karlsruhe - Budapest Keleti; 🛌 1,2 cl. Paris Est - Wien Westbahnhof.
IC615 — DRACHENFELS – 🛌 and ✕ Münster - Mannheim.
IC618/9 — GUTENBERG – 🛌 and ☕ Münster - Stuttgart and v.v.
ICE672 — MARKGRAF – 🛌 and ✕ Karlsruhe - Hamburg Altona.
ICE694 — RICARDA HUCH – 🛌 and ✕ Stuttgart (München ✈) - Berlin Zoo.
IC719 — ALLGÄU – 🛌 and ✕ Münster - Stuttgart (Kempten ♣).
IC939 — ①-⑥: 🛌 Frankfurt Flughafen ✈ (depart 2236) - Stuttgart.
IC949 — ⑥⑦: 🛌 Frankfurt Flughafen ✈ (depart 2237) - Stuttgart.
ICE990 — RHEIN SPRINTER – ①-⑤, not Apr. 14 - 17, May 1, 25: 🛌 and ✕ München - Frankfurt/Main.
D1015 — ⑤ Jan. 6 - Apr. 7: 🛌 2 cl., 🛌 and 🛌 Dortmund - Garmisch - Innsbruck; 🛌 1,2 cl., 🛌 2 cl. and 🛌 Dortmund - München (D1115) - Kufstein - Innsbruck; (also 🛌 to Mar. 17) - München (D1115) - Wörgl (D1615) - Schwarzach St Veit; conveys to Mar. 17: 🛌 1,2 cl. Dortmund - Garmisch.
D1215 — ⑤ Jan. 6 - Mar. 24: 🛌 1,2 cl., 🛌 2 cl., 🛌 and ☕ Amsterdam - Villach; conveys from Koblenz: 🛌 2 cl. and 🛌 Oostende - Villach.

IR2268 — 🛌 and ☕ Ulm - Saarbrücken.
IR2269 — 🛌 and ☕ Saarbrücken - Ulm.
IR2291 — 🛌 Karlsruhe - Salzburg; ☕ Karlsruhe - Traunstein.
IR2293 — 🛌 Karlsruhe - Salzburg; ☕ Karlsruhe - Stuttgart.
IR2294 — 🛌 and ☕ Münster - Karlsruhe.
IR2367 — 🛌 and ☕ Saarbrücken - Lindau.
IR2565 — 🛌 Karlsruhe - Nürnberg - Coburg; ☕ Karlsruhe - Erlangen.
IR2566 — 🛌 and ☕ Nürnberg - Karlsruhe.
IR2567 — 🛌 Karlsruhe - Nürnberg. ☕ Karlsruhe - Aalen.
B — FRIEDRICH SCHILLER – ⑦, also Apr. 17, May 1, not Apr. 16, 30: 🛌 and ✕ Dortmund - München.
S — Not Dec. 24, 31.
U — Not Dec. 24, 25, 31, Jan. 1.
Y — Not Dec. 25, 26, Jan. 1.
o — München Ost.
v — Not Dec. 24, 31.
❖ — Not Dec. 25, Jan. 1.
✗ — ①-⑥ (not Dec. 25 - Jan. 1, Apr. 15 - 17, May 1, 1995).
♣ — Daily except ⑥ (not Dec. 24 - 31, Apr. 14 - 16, Apr. 30, 1995).

Table 760 — MÜNCHEN - STUTTGART - MANNHEIM

1, 2 class except where shown

	IC 616 ✕◆	E 3416 L	E 3002	IR 2368 ⟐M	ICE 598 ✕◆	IR 2368 ⟐M	EC 66 ✕◆	IR 2564 ⟐	IC 718 ✕◆	EC 66 ✕◆	E 3036	IR 2198 ⟐	ICE 896 ✕	IR 2198 ⟐	IC 614 ✕◆	E 3416	E 3004	IR 2366 ⟐M	ICE 596 ✕◆	IR 2366 ⟐M	IR 2562 ⟐H	EC 18 ✕◆	E 3038
Salzburg 790 .... d.	...	...	...	0518d	...	...	...	...	...	...	0618	...	...	...	...	...	...	...	0715	...	...	...	...
München Hbf 750 .... d.	0650			0746		0750					0826	0846		0850					0946			0950	
München Pasing 750 .. d.	0658			0758		0758					0833			0858					0958			0958	
Augsburg 750 .... d.	0722			0814		0822					0857	0914		0922				1014			1022		
Ulm .... d.	0805	0810		0840	0854	0902		0907			0940	0954		1005		1011		1040	1054			1105	
Geislingen .... d.		0835		0902							1002					1035		1102					
Göppingen .... d.		0851		0916							1016					1051		1116					
Plochingen .... d.		0905		0927				←			1027					1105		1127			←		
Stuttgart .... a.	0903	0925		0944	0949	0944	0958		1003	0958	1044	1049		1044	1103	1125		1144	1149	1144		1203	
Stuttgart .... d.	0911	...	0936	1000	0953	1000	1015	1005	1011	1015	1057	1057	1053	1053	1111		1136	1200	1153	1200	1205	1211	1221
Vaihingen .... d.			1008	→	1016	→						1051	→	1113			1208	→		1216			1251
Mühlacker .... d.			1016									1059		1120			1216						1300
Bruchsal 730 .... d.						1037					1126			1129						1237			1326
Pforzheim .... d.			1026						1045								1226						
Karlsruhe 730 .... a.			1050					1048		1105				1148			1250					1248	
Heidelberg 742 .... a.	0954								1054		1147				1154							1254	1347
Mannheim 742 .... a.	1004			1032	1046				1104			1132		1204				1232	1246			1304	
Frankfurt (Main) Hbf 730 .. a.				1114								1214						1314					
Köln Hbf 650 .... a.	1229								1329					1429								1529	
Düsseldorf Hbf 650 .... a.	1255								1355					1455								1555	
Duisburg 650 .... a.	1309								1409					1509								1609	
Dortmund 650 .... a.									1448													1648	

	IR 2196 ⟐	ICE 794 ✕	IR 2196 ⟐	IC 612 ✕◆	E 3006	E 3022 ✕	IR 460 ⟐	ICE 594 ✕◆	IR 460 ⟐	IR 2560 ⟐	EC 112 ✕◆H	E 3040	IR 2194 ⟐	ICE 894 ✕	IR 2194 ⟐	IC 118 ✕◆	E 3426	E 3008	IR 360 ⟐	ICE 592 ✕◆	IR 360 ⟐	IR 2668 ⟐	IC 714 ✕◆
Salzburg 790 .... d.	0818	0905	...	...	...	...	...	1005	...	...	1005	...	1018	...	...	...	...	...	...	1209	...	...	...
München Hbf 750 .... d.	1026	1046		1050				1146			1150		1226	1246		1250				1346			
München Pasing 750 .. d.	1033			1058							1158		1233			1258							
Augsburg 750 .... d.	1057	1114		1122				1214			1222		1257	1314		1322				1414			
Ulm .... d.	1140	1154		1205			1240	1254			1305		1340	1354		1405	1410		1440	1454			1500
Geislingen .... d.	1202						1302						1402				1435		1502				
Göppingen .... d.	1216						1316						1416				1451		1516				
Plochingen .... d.	1227						1327			←			1427				1505		1527				
Stuttgart .... a.	1244	1249	1244	1303			1344	1349	1344		1403		1444	1449	1444	1503	1525		1544	1549	1544		1558
Stuttgart .... d.	1257	1253	1257	1311	1336		1400	1353	1400	1405	1411	1421	1457	1453	1457	1511		1534	1600	1553	1600	1605	1611
Vaihingen .... d.	→		1313		1408		→		1416			1451	→		1513			1608	→		1616		→
Mühlacker .... d.			1320		1416							1500			1520			1616					
Bruchsal 730 .... d.											1437	1526										1637	
Pforzheim .... d.			1329		1426	1430									1529			1626					
Karlsruhe 730 .... a.			1348		1450	1456					1448				1548			1649				1648	
Heidelberg 742 .... a.				1354							1454	1547				1554							
Mannheim 742 .... a.		1332		1404						1432	1446	1504				1532		1604			1632	1646	
Frankfurt (Main) Hbf 730 .. a.		1414								1514						1614					1714		
Köln Hbf 650 .... a.				1629							1729					1829							
Düsseldorf Hbf 650 .... a.				1655							1755					1855							
Duisburg 650 .... a.				1709							1809					1909							
Dortmund 650 .... a.											1848					1948							

	EC 64 ✕◆	IC 714 ✕◆	E 3042	IR 2192 ⟐	ICE 792 ✕◆	IR 2192 ⟐	EC 114 ✕◆	E 3428	E 3010	IR 2264 ⟐	E 590 ✕	IR 2264 ⟐	IR 2466 ⟐H	IC 512 ✕◆	E 3046	IR 2190 ⟐	ICE 892 ✕	IR 2190 ⟐	IC 12 ✕◆	E 3012	IR 2266 ⟐	ICE 790 ✕✕◆	IR 2266 ⟐	IR 2464 ⟐H
Salzburg 790 .... d.	1209	...	...	1218	1305	...	1305	...	...	...	1318	...	...	...	...	1418	1505	...	...	...	...	1518	...	...
München Hbf 750 .... d.	1350			1426	1446		1450				1546				1550	1626	1646		1650			1746		
München Pasing 750 .. d.	1358			1433			1458								1558	1633			1658					
Augsburg 750 .... d.	1422			1457	1514		1522				1614				1622	1657	1714		1722			1814		
Ulm .... d.	1505			1540	1554		1605	1610		1640	1654				1705	1740	1754		1805		1840	1854		
Geislingen .... d.				1602				1636		1702						1802			1902					
Göppingen .... d.				1616				1653		1716						1816			1916					
Plochingen .... d.			←	1627			←	1707		1727					←	1827			1927					
Stuttgart .... a.	1603	1558		1644	1649	1644	1703	1726		1744	1749	1744			1803	1844	1849	1844	1903		1944	1949	1944	
Stuttgart .... d.	1615	1611	1623	1657	1653	1657	1711		1736	1800	1753	1800	1805	1811	1821	1857	1853	1857	1911	1937	2000	1953	2000	2005
Vaihingen .... d.			1653	→		1713			1808	→		1816			1852	→		1913		2008	→		2016	
Mühlacker .... d.			1700			1720			1816						1900			1920		2016				
Bruchsal 730 .... d.			1726										1837		1926									2037
Pforzheim .... d.	1645			1729					1826						1929					2026				
Karlsruhe 730 .... a.	1705			1748					1851				1848		1947					2050				2048
Heidelberg 742 .... a.		1654	1747				1754							1854					1954					
Mannheim 742 .... a.		1704				1732	1804					1832	1846	1904			1932		2004			2032	2046	
Frankfurt (Main) Hbf 730 .. a.						1814						1914					2014					2114		
Köln Hbf 650 .... a.		1929					2029						2129					2229						
Düsseldorf Hbf 650 .... a.		1955					2055						2155					2255						
Duisburg 650 .... a.		2009					2109						2209					2309						
Dortmund 650 .... a.							2148											2348						

— **NOTES** (LISTED BY TRAIN NUMBERS)

C12 – PAGANINI – 🛏 and ✕ Venezia Santa Lucia - Kufstein - Dortmund.
C18 – ANDREAS HOFER – 🛏 and ✕ Innsbruck - Kufstein - Dortmund.
C64 – MOZART – 🛏 and ✕ Wien West - Kehl - Paris Est; 🛏 Graz - Paris Est.
C66 – MAURICE RAVEL – 🛏 and ✕ München - Karlsruhe - Kehl - Paris Est.
C112 – WÖRTHERSEE – 🛏 and ✕ Klagenfurt - Dortmund.
C114 – BLAUER ENZIAN – 🛏 and ✕ Klagenfurt - Dortmund.
C118 – KARWENDEL – 🛏 and ✕ Innsbruck - Mittenwald - Dortmund.
R360 – 🛏 and ⟐ Bregenz - Saarbrücken.
R460 – 🛏 and ⟐ Landeck - Saarbrücken.
R512 – ANNETTE KOLB – 🛏 and ✕ München - Münster.
R612 – BACCHUS – 🛏 and ⟐ München - Münster.
R616 – LUDWIG UHLAND – 🛏 and ✕ München - Münster.
R614 – DRACHENFELS – 🛏 and ✕ München - Münster.
R714 – NEBELHORN – 🛏 and ✕ Oberstdorf - Münster.
R718 – ALLGÄU – 🛏 and ✕ Stuttgart (Kempten ✗) - Dortmund.

IR2198 – 🛏 and ⟐ Salzburg (München on Dec. 25, Jan. 1) - Karlsruhe.
IR2264 – 🛏 and ⟐ Friedrichshafen Stadt - Trier.
IR2266 – 🛏 Friedrichshafen Stadt - Trier (Saarbrücken on Dec. 24, 31);
⟐ Friedrichshafen - Neustadt.
IR2564 – 🛏 and ⟐ Nürnberg (Coburg except on Dec. 25, Jan. 1) - Karlsruhe.
IR2668 – 🛏 and ⟐ Görlitz - Dresden - Hof - Nürnberg - Karlsruhe.
E3022 – 🛏 Bad Wildbad - Karlsruhe (IR2212) - Emden.
– 🛏 and ⟐ Hof - Nürnberg - Karlsruhe.
J – ⑥, not Nov. 1, Jan. 6.
L – ✕, not Nov. 1, Jan. 6.
M – 🛏 and ⟐ Lindau - Saarbrücken.
d – ⑦, also Nov. 1, Jan. 6; on all other dates depart Salzburg 0527.
✗ – ① - ⑥ (not Dec. 25 - Jan. 1, Apr. 15 - 17, May 1, 1995).
♣ – Daily except ⑥ (not Dec. 24 - 31, Apr. 14 - 16, Apr. 30, 1995).

3

Table 760 — MÜNCHEN - STUTTGART - MANNHEIM

1, 2 class except where shown

	EC 14	E 3048	IR 2098	ICE 996	IR 2098	IC 1998	D 3434	E 2662	ICE 994	IR 3014	E 2096	EC 62	E 3016	D 260	IC 810	D 214		D 1924	D 1014	D 1214	IC938 262 IC948
	✕			✕		✕			✕										♦	♦	♦
	♦		T							S			♦		♦			♦	♦	♦	H
Salzburg 790 .... d.			1618					1718							1918	2018				2307	
München Hbf 750 .... d.	1750		1826	1846		1850			1946		2026	2050		2106	2150	2211		2317	2318		
München Pasing 750 .. d.	1758		1833			1858					2033	2058		2158						2341o0034o	
Augsburg 750 .... d.	1822		1857	1914		1922			2014		2057	2122		2142	2222	2246			2356	0027	
Ulm .... d.	1905		1940	1954		2005		2010	2054		2140	2205		2229	2304	2334			0042	0118	
Geislingen .... d.			2002			2035		2035			2202										
Göppingen .... d.			2016			2051		2051			2216			2304							
Plochingen .... d.			2027		←	2105		2105			2227	2254		2346							
Stuttgart .... a.	2003		2044	2049	2044	2103		2125	2149		2244	2311		2328	2400	0032				0255	
Stuttgart .... d.	2011	2021	2057	2053	2057	2111	2115		2153	2215			2318	2335		0041				0303	0331
Vaihingen .... d.			2052		2113					2221	2246		2350								0404
Mühlacker .... d.			2100			2132	2149			2254			2358								0429
Bruchsal 730 .... d.			2126			2132			2238				0010	0020							
Pforzheim .... d.						2141	2159			2304			0033	0040						0400	
Karlsruhe 730 .... d.						2145	2202	2219		2251	2329					0157					0449
Heidelberg 742 .... d.	2054	2147		2132				2232					0209b								
Mannheim 742 .... a.	2104			2214									0447								
Frankfurt (Main) Hbf 730 .. a.				2214									0537				0639	0559	0622		
Köln Hbf 650 .... a.													0559				0707	0637	0658		
Düsseldorf Hbf 650 .... a.																	0731	0700	0715		
Duisburg 650 .... a.																	0810	0745			
Dortmund 650 .... a.																					

NOTES (LISTED BY TRAIN NUMBERS)

EC14 – PATSCHERKOFEL – 🛏 and ✕ Innsbruck - Kufstein - Saarbrücken.
EC62 – BARTÓK BÉLA – 🛏 and ✕ Budapest Keleti - Stuttgart.
D214 – 🛏 1,2 cl., 🛏 2 cl. and 🛏 München - Amsterdam CS; 🛏 1,2 cl., 🛏 2 cl. and 🛏 München - Oostende.
D260 – 🛏 1,2 cl., 🛏 2 cl. and 🛏 München - Karlsruhe - Kehl - Paris Est.
D262 – ORIENT EXPRESS – 🛏 2 cl. and 🛏 Budapest Keleti - Paris Est.
IC762 – BADEN-KURIER – 🛏 1,2 cl., 🛏 2 cl. and 🛏 München - Karlsruhe - Basel Bad.
IC810 – EDUARD MÖRIKE – ⑦, also Nov. 1, Dec. 26, Apr. 17, May 1, not Dec. 25, Apr. 16, 30.
D1014 – ⑥ Jan. 7 - Apr. 8, also Dec. 23, Jan. 1, 5 (from Innsbruck): 🛏 2 cl., 🛏 and ♀ Innsbruck - Garmisch - Dortmund; 🛏 1,2 cl., 🛏 2 cl. and 🛏 Innsbruck (D1114) - Kufstein - München - Dortmund; 🛏 also 🛏 1,2 cl. to Mar. 18) Schwarzach St Veit (1614) - Wörgl (D1114) - München - Dortmund; conveys to Mar. 18: 🛏 1,2 cl. Garmisch - Dortmund.

D1214 – ⑥ Jan. 7 - Mar. 25, also Jan. 1 (from Villach): 🛏 1,2 cl., 🛏 2 cl., 🛏 and ♀ Villach - Amsterdam; conveys to Köln: 🛏 2 cl. and 🛏 Villach - Oostende for D1118.
D1924 – LUNA – 🛏 1,2 cl., 🛏 2 cl. and ♀ München - Münster (Norddeich Mole on ⑤⑥⑦ Apr. 7 - May 27, also Apr. 17).
D1998 – 🛏 1,2 cl., 🛏 2 cl., 🛏 and ♀ Stuttgart - Karlsruhe - Hamburg Altona.
IR2096 – 🛏 Salzburg - Stuttgart; ♀ Salzburg - Augsburg.
IR2098 – 🛏 Salzburg - Karlsruhe; ♀ Salzburg - Stuttgart.
IR2662 – 🛏 Dresden Hbf - Hof - Nürnberg - Karlsruhe; ♀ Dresden - Aalen.
H – 🛏 Stuttgart - Frankfurt Flughafen ✈ (arrive 0616 ① - ⑥, 0623 ⑦).
S – Not Dec. 24, 31.
T – Not Dec. 24, 25, 31.
b – ② - ⑥ only.
o – München Ost.
♦ – Daily except ⑥ (not Dec. 24 - 31, Apr. 14 - 16, Apr. 30, 1995).

Table 761 — ULM - FRIEDRICHSHAFEN - LINDAU

1, 2 class except where shown

km		IR 2261	D 1019	E 3545	E 3107	E 3547	IR 361	E 3109	E 3121	IR 2265	E 3111	E 3551	IR 461	E 3113	E 3105	IR 2267	E 3115	E 3555	IR 2365	E 3117	IR 2367	E 3561	E 3119	E 3565
		✠	♀				♦			♦			♦			♦			F		F			
	Stuttgart 760 .... d.						0816			1016			1216			1416			1616		1816			
0	Ulm .... d.	0616	0626	0719	0811	0911	0927	1011	1111	1127	1211	1311	1327	1411	1511	1527	1611	1711	1727	1811	1927	2011	2111	2211
37	Biberach .... d.	0639	0651	0742	0835	0935	0947	1035	1135	1150	1235	1335	1347	1435	1535	1550	1635	1735	1750	1835	1950	2035	2135	2235
62	Aulendorf .... d.	0756	0709	0800	0852	0952	1001	1052	1152	1206	1252	1352	1401	1452	1552	1606	1652	1752	1806	1852	2006	2052	2152	2252
84	Ravensburg .... d.	0713	0726	0815	0908	1008	1018	1108	1208	1222	1308	1408	1418	1508	1608	1622	1708	1808	1822	1908	2022	2108	2208	2308
103	Friedrichshafen Stadt .... a.	0728	0740	0830	0923	1023	1039	1123	1223	1237	1323	1423	1432	1523	1623	1637	1723	1823	1837	1923	2037	2123	2223	2323
103	Friedrichshafen Stadt ▲ .. d.	0737	0749	0835	0930	1028	1039	1130	1230n	1257	1330	1428	1439	1530	1629p	1659	1731	1830	1850	2048	2208	2230h	2248	
104	Friedrichshafen Hafen ▲ . a.			0837		1030				1430				1830										
127	Lindau .... a.	0756	0809		0956		1058	1156	1309n	1332	1356		1458	1554	1656p	1732	1754		1910	1959	2109	2237	2300h	0002

		E3538 E3544	IR 2368	E 3546	IR 3108	E 2366	E 3548	IR 3110	E 460	E 3550	IR 3112	E 360	IR 3552	E 3114	IR 2264	E 3554	IR 3116	IR 2266	E 3106	IR 3118	E 3558	IR 2260	E 3560	E 3562	D 1018
		♦			♦			♦			♦					♦			♦				S			♦
			F			F																				♀
	Lindau .... d.		0649		0805	0851		1005	1100		1204	1251		1405	1428		1605	1628	1705p	1804		2004	2018	2130	2150	
	Friedrichshafen Hafen ▲ .. d.			0725			0925			1127			1324			1525					1924					
	Friedrichshafen Stadt ▲ .. a.		0710	0727	0827	0910	0927	1027	1119	1129	1226	1310	1326	1427	1458	1527	1657	1727p	1833	1928	1926	2023	2045	2200	2210	
	Friedrichshafen Stadt .... d.	0623	0720	0733	0833	0933	0933	1033	1126	1133	1233	1320	1333	1433	1520	1532	1649	1735	1833	1933	1949	2031	2101	2211	2220	
	Ravensburg .... d.	0639	0735	0749	0849	0935	0949	1049	1141	1155	1249	1335	1349	1452	1535	1549	1704	1752	1804	1904	2004	2059	2131	2243	2253	
	Aulendorf .... d.	0654	0752	0803	0904	0952	1004	1104	1155	1204	1304	1352	1404	1504	1552	1604	1704	1752	1822	1922	2022	2114	2149	2302	2310	
	Biberach .... d.	0712	0808	0822	0922	1008	1022	1122	1209	1221	1322	1408	1422	1522	1608	1722	1722	1808	1822	1922	2022	2114	2149	2302	2310	
	Ulm .... a.	0741	0830	0846	0946	1030	1046	1146	1230	1246	1346	1430	1446	1546	1630	1646	1746	1830	1844	1944	2046	2134	2213	2327	2334	
	Stuttgart 760 .... a.		0944			1144			1344			1544			1744			1944								

NOTES (LISTED BY TRAIN NUMBERS)

IR360 – 🛏 and ♀ Bregenz - Saarbrücken.
IR361 – 🛏 and ♀ Saarbrücken - Bregenz.
IR460 – 🛏 and ♀ Landeck - Saarbrücken.
IR461 – 🛏 and ♀ Saarbrücken - Landeck.
D1018 – VORARLBERG EXPRESS – 🛏 1,2 cl., 🛏 2 cl. and 🛏 Innsbruck - Dortmund; conveys except on Dec. 23, Jan. 1, 5: 🛏 2 cl. Innsbruck - Hamburg Altona; also conveys except on Dec. 23, Jan. 1, 8: 🛏 1,2 cl. Innsbruck - Hamburg Altona; ♀ Lindau - Dortmund.
D1019 – VORARLBERG EXPRESS – 🛏 1,2 cl., 🛏 2 cl. and 🛏 Dortmund - Innsbruck; 🛏 2 cl. (also 🛏 1,2 cl. except on Mar. 31, Apr. 7) Hamburg Altona - Innsbruck; ♀ Dortmund - Lindau.
IR2264 – 🛏 and ♀ Friedrichshafen Stadt - Trier.
IR2265 – 🛏 and ♀ Trier (Saarbrücken on Dec. 25, Jan. 1) - Friedrichshafen Stadt.

IR2266 – 🛏 Friedrichshafen Stadt - Trier (Saarbrücken on Dec. 24, 31); ♀ Friedrichshafen - Neustadt.
IR2267 – 🛏 and ♀ Saarbrücken - Friedrichshafen Stadt.
F – 🛏 and ♀ Saarbrücken - Lindau and v.v.
S – Not Dec. 24, 31.
h – ⑧, not Nov. 15, Dec. 25, Jan. 5, Apr. 13, 16, 30, May 24.
n – ✕, not Nov. 1, Jan. 6.
p – ④, not Nov. 1, Jan. 6.
✠ – Not Dec. 25, Jan. 1.
▲ – Additional trains Friedrichshafen Stadt - Friedrichshafen Hafen: 0735, 0928, 1128, 1228, 1328, 1528, 1628, 1728, 1928.
Friedrichshafen Hafen - Friedrichshafen Stadt: 0826, 1024, 1224, 1426, 1624, 1724, 1824, 1955, 2024 S.

Table 762 — BREGENZ - LINDAU - KONSTANZ (BODENSEE ⛴ SERVICE)

The main ship service operates May 29 - September 25 (with less frequent services in April and October). The schedule is too complex to be shown in detail, and is subject to cancellation or delay during bad weather. Principal points on the lake are: Bregenz, Lindau, Friedrichshafen, Meersburg, Mainau and Konstanz. Details of sailings should be obtained from German National Tourist Offices, or direct from the operator shown below. Distances to rail stations (in metres): Bregenz 800, Lindau 150, Friedrichshafen Hafen 100, Konstanz 300. Passengers bound for Switzerland via Konstanz should take care to enter the rail station via the Customs terminal and not by any other entrance.

Operator: Bodensee Schiffsbetriebe der Deutschen Bahn AG, Hafenstraße 6, 78462 Konstanz.

Table 763 — MÜNCHEN - MÜHLDORF

1, 2 clas

Rail service München - Mühldorf and v.v. 85 km. Journey time: 65 minutes.
From München: 0708, 0811, 0911 and hourly until 1511, 1611 ⑥, 1630 ⑧, 1711 P, 1734, 1811 P, 1835 O, 1925, 2036, 2130, 2230 ⑦, 2334.
From Mühldorf: 0523 N, 0633 O, 0642 P, 0733 and hourly until 1533, 1633 O, 1733, 1833, 2033, 2144 ⑦.

N – ✕, not Nov. 1, Jan. 6.
O – ⑤, also Nov. 1, Jan. 6.
P – ⑧, not Nov. 1, Jan. 6.

Table 765 — MÜNCHEN, AUGSBURG and ULM - SOUTHERN BAVARIA

1, 2 class except where shown

Block 1

km		5801	E3732 E3836 (2)	E 3202	E 4500	E 3771	E 4370	E 4734	E 3701	E 4264	14104	E 4402	14106	E 4402	E 4462	E 4266	D 1089	E 3705	E 3904	E 4304 (2)	E4502 E3838	E 3206	E 4270	IR 2166
		N	C	Ⓐ	Ⓐ	◆	Ⓐ		Ⓒ		Ⓐ		Ⓒ		◆	◆	◆			K		Ⓐ		♀
0	München Hbf ..... d.				0501					0540			0540								0619	0652		0722
7	München Pasing ..... d.				0509					0548			0548								0628	0700		0730
	Augsburg ..... d.					0517				0537		0603		0603					0637				0715	
68	Buchloe ..... a.				0552	0552				0610		0631		0631	0638	0638			0708	0711	0745	0740		0809
68	Buchloe ..... d.				0555	0559				0612	0613	0636	0645	0639	0640			0652	0717	0713	0747	0748		0811
88	Kaufbeuren ..... d.				0608					0626		0652	0655						0726			0801		0824
	Türkheim ..... d.						0605			0620		0643	0652						0700	0732		0754		
	Bad Wörishofen ..... a.									0626		0649								0738				
	Mindelheim ..... d.						0617					0700							0708			0802		
	Marktoberdorf ..... d.									0643					0713							0817		
	Füssen ..... a.									0725					0754							0857		
	Ulm ..... d.				0600										0608	0700								
	Memmingen ..... a.				0627	0644									0727	0731					0824			
	Memmingen ..... d.			0636	0628				0650				0723		0729	0736					0838			
131	Kempten ..... a.			0639	0647			0650		0722			0722		0737	0754				0759			0851	
131	Kempten ..... d.	0541	0602	0646			0700	0724							0739	0756				0802			0853	
152	Immenstadt ..... a.	0556	0618	0702			0718	0740							0758	0811				0818			0908	
152	Immenstadt ..... d.	0616	0619	0712			0719	0744							0813	0822		E 0819				0919		
160	Sonthofen ..... d.	0629		0724				0754							0823	0835		6603 (2)				0928		
173	Oberstdorf ..... a.	0647		0743				0817							0842	0856						0947		
	Kißlegg 766 ..... d.			0716														0816	0837		0916			
	Aulendorf 766 ..... a.																	0847						
	Wangen ..... d.			0727															0847		0927			
	Hergatz ..... d.		0656	0732														0852	0856		0932			
220	Lindau ..... a.		0714	0750				0814										0914	0950					

Block 2

		E3775 E3874 (2)	E 4306	E 4272	E 3707	E 3210	EC 92	E 4376	E 6605 (2)	E3840 14120	E 4544	E 3876	E 3136	IR 2164 (2)	E 4312	E 4472 (2)	E 3709	E 3912	E 4274	E 4410	E4474 E3842	E 4546	E3878 3138	IR 2068
		M				G	H			K		M		♀		Ⓐ					C		M	♀
	München Hbf ..... d.					0753	0810			0819		0850		0920					1019		1050			1120
	München Pasing ..... d.					0800				0828		0858		0928					1028		1058			1128
	Augsburg ..... a.		0737	0803					0837			0903		0937	0937	1003		1037			1107			
	Buchloe ..... a.		0808	0838		0842	0853	0908		0911		0942	0938	1009	1008	1008		1042	1038	1111	1108	1142	1138	1209
	Buchloe ..... d.		0818	0845		0843	0854			0913	0923	0944	0945	1011	1018	1022		1045	1045	1118	1114	1144	1145	1211
	Kaufbeuren ..... d.			0900						0926		0958		1024	1038			1100		1127	1159			1224
	Türkheim ..... d.		0832			0850				0930		0952		1031				1106		1128			1152	
	Bad Wörishofen ..... a.		0838							0936				1037						1134				
	Mindelheim ..... d.			0917		0911						1000						1114	1115			1216	1200	
	Marktoberdorf ..... d.			0917						1016								1115		1216				
	Füssen ..... a.			0957						1057								1257						
	Ulm ..... d.	0800			0900					1000					1100				1200					
	Memmingen ..... a.	0834			0927	0931	0922				1027	1023			1127	1134						1227	1223	
	Memmingen ..... d.	0835			0928	0935	0923				1028	1045			1128	1136						1228	1236	
	Kempten ..... a.	0855			0954					0959	1047		1051		1113	1154		1159		1247			1251	
	Kempten ..... d.	0902	5813		0956					1002	1102		1053		1118	1156		1202		1303			1256	
	Immenstadt ..... a.	0918			1011					1018	1118		1108		1134	1211		1218		1319			1312	
	Immenstadt ..... d.	0919	0948		1021					1019	1119		1119		1142	1221		1219		1320			1326	
	Sonthofen ..... d.		0958		1031						1128		1156		1231	E 3483 (2)							1335	
	Oberstdorf ..... a.		1023		1053						1147		1223		1251								1353	
	Kißlegg 766 ..... d.					1013				1037				1117			1216		1237			1316		
	Aulendorf 766 ..... a.					1047											1247							
	Wangen ..... d.					1047								1128			1247					1327		
	Hergatz ..... d.					1052	1056							1133			1252	1256				1332		
	Lindau ..... a.	1014				1022				1114				1214	1151		1314					1414	1350	

Block 3

		E 4318	3711	3914	4276	6609 (2)	EC 94	E4510 E3844	4322	4548	E3785 E3880	3140	IR 2066	4324	EC 166	3916	4280	IR 2683	3713 E3846	4328	IC 715	4550 E3882	3142	IR 2603
		◆					✗ H	K			M		♀		✗			♀	K		✗		M	♀
	München Hbf ..... d.					1150	1210	1219		1250		1320		1402			1415			1450			1520
	München Pasing ..... d.					1158		1228		1258		1328					1424			1458			1528
	Augsburg ..... a.	1137			1207			1240			1307	1337				1407	1420		1440			1507	
	Buchloe ..... a.	1208		1242	1238		1253	1311	1308	1342	1338	1409	1408		1438	1451	1510	1508	1542	1538	1609	
	Buchloe ..... d.	1218		1243	1245		1254	1313	1323	1344	1345	1411	1418		1445	1448	1453	1513	1518	1544	1545	1611	
	Kaufbeuren ..... d.				1259			1326		1359		1424			1501	1511		1526		1558		1624	
	Türkheim ..... d.	1228	1249					1330		1352	1428		1452			1528			1552			
	Bad Wörishofen ..... a.	1234						1336			1434					1534						
	Mindelheim ..... d.			1311					1416		1400			1500		1516			1615			1600	
	Marktoberdorf ..... d.			1317					1416							1516			1615				
	Füssen ..... a.			1401					1457							1557			1657				
	Ulm ..... d.		1300					1400						1424				1512		1600			
	Memmingen ..... a.		1327	1331		1322			1432	1423			1523			1518			1550	1627	1623	
	Memmingen ..... d.		1328	1336		1323			1433	1436			1536			1528			1552	1628	1638	
	Kempten ..... a.		1349					1359		1457	1451		1518			1545	1554	1559		1621	1647		1651
	Kempten ..... d.		1356					1402	5827	1500	1453		1520			1547	1556	1603		1623	1700		1653
	Immenstadt ..... a.		1411					1418		1516	1508					1604	1613	1621		1638	1716		1708
	Immenstadt ..... d.		1421					1419	1441	1519	1519					E 6611 (2)	1615	1624	1622		1649	1719		1719
	Sonthofen ..... d.		1431						1454	1528	1547						1627	1638		1659			1728
	Oberstdorf ..... a.		1451						1519								1646	1657		1718			1747
	Kißlegg 766 ..... d.			1416	1437						1515			1624	1637			1718				
	Aulendorf 766 ..... a.			1447										1648								
	Wangen ..... d.				1447						1526			1647				1729				
	Hergatz ..... d.			1452	1456						1531			1652				1658				
	Lindau ..... a.				1422	1514				1614	1549			1622						1813	1749	

NOTES (LISTED BY TRAIN NUMBERS)

166 – ALBERT EINSTEIN – 🍴 and ✗ Praha Hlavni - Furth im Wald - München - St. Gallen - Zürich Hbf - Bern.

715 – NEBELHORN – 🍴 and ✗ Münster - Stuttgart - Ulm - Oberstdorf.

089 – ⑤ Jan. 6 - Apr. 7 (from Hamburg): ⇌ 1,2 cl., ⇌ 2 cl. and ♀ Hamburg - Oberstdorf; ⇌ 2 cl. and 🍴 (also ⇌ 1,2 cl. to Mar. 3) Dortmund - Oberstdorf.

2066 – 🍴 and ♀ Dresden Hbf - Hof - Oberstdorf.

2068 – Hof (Chemnitz ✗) - Oberstdorf; ♀ Hof - Oberstdorf.

2164 – 🍴 Regensburg (Hof ✗) - Oberstdorf; ✗ Marktredwitz - Oberstdorf.

2166 – 🍴 and ✗ München (Regensburg ✗) - Oberstdorf.

2603 – 🍴 and ♀ Berlin Lichtenberg - Leipzig - Hof - Oberstdorf.

IR2683 – ALPENLAND – 🍴 and ♀ Hamburg Altona - Oberstdorf.

E3705 – ⑥⑦ from Ulm; daily from Memmingen.

E3734 – 🍴 Kempten - Lindau (Basel Bad on ✗, train E3872 from Lindau).

E3904 – Ⓐ from Buchloe; daily from Memmingen.

E4276 – 🍴 Augsburg - Marktoberdorf ⑥⑦, Füssen Ⓐ.

C – 🍴 Augsburg - Radolfzell.

G – 🍴 München - Aulendorf (- Sigmaringen - Neustadt - Freiburg on Ⓒ).

H – 🍴 and ✗ München - St. Gallen - Zürich Hbf.

K – 🍴 München - Radolfzell.

M – 🍴 Ulm - Singen - Schaffhausen - Basel Bad.

N – 🍴 Kempten - Radolfzell.

✗ – ① - ⑥ (not Dec. 25 - Jan. 1, Apr. 15 - 17, May 1, 1995).

Table 765 MÜNCHEN, AUGSBURG and ULM - SOUTHERN BAVARIA

1, 2 class except where shown

	E 4330	E 3715	E 3920	E 3922 (2)	E 4282	E 4334	E 4518 / E 3848	E 4418	E 4482	E 3791 / E 3884	E 3144	E 4552	IR 2064 ♦	E 4336	E 3924	E 4286	E 4288	E 3717	E 4522 / E 3890	E 4340 (2)	EC 98 ⚡ H	E 4554	E 3793	E 3146	E 4590 (2) G
			父				K	Ⓐ	Ⓐ	B					Ⓐ	Ⓒ			K						
München Hbf d.	...	...	1550	...	...	1615	1636	...	...	...	...	1649	1722	...	1750	...	...	1819	...	1837	1850	...	...	...	1920
München Pasing d.	...	...	1558	...	...	1624	1645	...	...	...	...	1658	1730	...	1758	...	...	1828	...	1858	...	...	1904	...	1928
Augsburg d.	1537	...	...	1607	1640	...	...	1654	...	1707	...	...	1737	...	1803	1807	...	...	1837	...	...	1911	1908	1920	1942
Buchloe a.	1608	1642	...	1638	1708	1710	1730	1727	...	1738	1744	1809	1808	1842	1838	1838	...	...	1911	1908	...	1938	1945
Buchloe d.	1618	1644	...	1645	1709	1712	1731	1733	...	1747	1748	1811	1818	1843	1845	1845	...	...	1913	1915	1922	1944
Kaufbeuren d.	...	...	...	1700	...	1727	...	1747	...	...	1801	1824	...	...	1900	1900	...	...	1926	...	1958	...
Türkheim d.	1628	1701	...	...	1718	...	1737	...	...	1754	...	...	1828	1850	...	...	...	1923	...	...	1952
Bad Wörishofen a.	1634	...	...	...	1724	...	...	...	...	...	...	1834	...	...	...	1929	...	...	...
Mindelheim d.	...	1709	...	...	...	1745	...	1802	...	...	1816	...	1858	...	...	...	...	...	...	2002
Marktoberdorf d.	...	...	...	1717	...	...	1857	...	...	...	1917	1917	...	...	2016	...
Füssen d.	...	...	...	1757	...	...	...	...	...	...	1957	1957	...	...	2057	...
Ulm d.	...	1700	...	...	1808	...	1800	...	...	...	1900	...	1927	...	...	2000	...
Memmingen a.	1727	1729	...	...	1827	1824	...	...	1920	...	1927	...	1948	2027	2025
Memmingen d.	1728	1736	1736	...	1828	1836	...	...	1922	...	1928	...	1949	2028	2041
Kempten a.	1754	...	...	1804	1847	1851	...	1954	1959	2047	2051
Kempten d.	1756	...	...	1804 5835	1902	1853	...	1956	2002	2102
Immenstadt a.	1811	...	1820	1918	1908	...	2011	2018	2118
Immenstadt d.	1821	...	E 6613 2	1821	1843	1919	...	2021	2019	2119
Sonthofen d.	1831	...	...	1856	...	1928	...	2031	...
Oberstdorf d.	1851	...	...	1919	...	1947	...	2051	...
Kißlegg 766 d.	...	1816	1816	1837	...	1916	...	2001	...	2132
Aulendorf 766 a.	...	1847	1847	...	...	2031	...	2143
Wangen d.	...	...	1847	...	1927	...
Hergatz d.	...	...	1852	1858	1932	...	2114	2056	2214 2204
Lindau a.	...	...	1915	2013	1950	...	2114	2056	2214 2204

	IR 2062 (2) ♣♀	E 4342 (2)	E 4422	IC 719 ♣✕	E 3795	E 6616 (2)	E 4290	E 4488	E 4424	E 3746	E 4556	E 4394 (2)	E 3723	E 6618 (2)	IR 2607 ♣	E 4594	E 3748 (2)	E 4348 (2)	E 4428	E 3799	E 4294	E 4596	E 4350 (2)	E 4432	E 4490
				G											G										
München Hbf d.	1920	...	1950	...	...	...	2019	...	2050	...	...	2120	2120	...	2150	...	...	2219	...	2250	...
München Pasing d.	1928	...	1958	...	...	...	2028	...	2058	...	...	2128	2128	...	2158	...	...	2228	...	2258	...
Augsburg d.	...	1937	...	...	2003	2037	...	2103	...	...	2209	2209	...	2137	...	2203	2237	...	2303
Buchloe a.	2009	2008	2012	...	2038	2108	2111	...	2142	2138	...	2211	2211	...	2208	2242	2238	2311	2308	2342	2345
Buchloe d.	2011	2018	2044	...	2045	2114	2118	...	2144	2145	...	2218	2245	...	2245	2313	2318	2345	2345
Kaufbeuren d.	2024	...	...	2100	2127	...	2158	...	2224	2224	...	2300	2326	...	2359
Türkheim d.	...	2028	2101	...	...	2128	...	2152	...	...	2228	2252	...	2328	2352
Bad Wörishofen a.	...	2034	...	...	2134	...	...	...	2234	...	2334
Mindelheim d.	...	...	2109	...	...	...	2200	...	...	2300	...	0000
Marktoberdorf d.	...	...	...	2117	...	2216	...	2317	...
Füssen d.	...	...	...	2157	...	2257	...	2357	...
Ulm d.	...	...	2102	2102	...	...	2200	...	2300	...
Memmingen a.	...	2130	2132	2132	...	...	2223	2227	...	2324	2327	...	0023
Memmingen d.	...	2133	2133	2135	...	...	2228	2236	...	2328	...
Kempten a.	2051	...	2155	2155	...	2159	...	2254	2256	...	2251	2251	...	2354	2359	...	0031
Kempten d.	...	5845	...	...	...	2207 5851	2256	...	2302	...
Immenstadt a.	...	...	...	...	2224	2311	...	2318	...
Immenstadt d.	...	2121	...	E 6615 2	...	2225 2227	2321	...	2319	...
Sonthofen d.	...	2133	...	⑧	...	2237	2331	...
Oberstdorf d.	...	2151	...	...	2256	2351	...
Kißlegg 766 d.	...	...	...	2212	2244	...	2332	...
Aulendorf 766 a.	...	...	...	2237	...
Wangen d.	...	...	...	2254	...	2343	...
Hergatz d.	...	...	...	2259	2302	...	2348	...	2356
Lindau a.	...	...	...	2320	...	0014

km		IR 2606 ♦	E 4405	E 4463	E 4581	E 4375	E 4467	E 3905	E 4267	E 4379	E 4583	E 4583	E 3731 (2)	E 3700	IR 2063 ♦	E 4587	E 14109	E 4381	E 14113	E 3133	E 3733 (2)	E 4543	E 5804	E 3835 / E 4471	E 4409
					Ⓐ		Ⓐ	父	Ⓒ	Ⓐ	Ⓒ										Ⓐ			父	C
0	Lindau d.	...	...	...	...	...	...	0537	...	...	...	...	...	...	...	...	0600	0610	...	...	0645
23	Hergatz d.	...	...	...	...	...	...	0553	...	...	...	...	...	0618	0627	...	0703
29	Wangen d.	...	...	...	...	...	...	0624	...
	Aulendorf 766 d.	...	...	...	...	...
42	Kißlegg 766 d.	...	...	...	...	0530	...	...	...	0636
	Oberstdorf d.	...	...	...	0558	...	...	...	0704
	Sonthofen d.	...	...	...	0618	...	...	...	0725
	Immenstadt a.	...	...	0629	0627	...	...	0701	...	0735	0739
	Immenstadt d.	...	...	0630	0643	...	...	0703	...	0740
	Kempten a.	...	...	0646	0658	...	...	0720	...	0754
	Kempten d.	0502	...	...	0545	...	0612	...	0638	...	0700	0702	0702	...	...	0756
85	Memmingen a.	...	...	...	...	0610	...	...	0726	...	0719	...
85	Memmingen d.	...	...	...	...	0611	...	0634	...	0728	...	0734	...
137	Ulm d.	...	...	...	...	...	...	0758	...	0701	...
	Füssen d.	...	...	...	0600	...	...	0750	...
	Marktoberdorf d.	...	...	...	0645	...
112	Mindelheim d.	...	...	...	0632	...	0700	...	0802	...
	Bad Wörishofen d.	...	...	...	...	...	0720	0758	...
123	Türkheim d.	...	...	...	0641	...	0709	...	0726	0730	0805	0810
	Kaufbeuren d.	0529	...	...	0642	0659	0707	...	0730	0730	...	0806	...	0825
131	Buchloe a.	0540	...	0618	0653	0649	0712	0716	0718	...	0741	0741	0738	...	0817	0817	0836 0839
131	Buchloe d.	0542	0558	0558	0633	0633	0654	0657	0721	...	0722	0722	0743	0743	0748	...	0823	0822	0849 0844
171	Augsburg a.	...	0631	...	0706	0725	0753	...	...	...	0819	0852	...	0905	0919
	München Pasing a.	0621	0640	...	0721	...	0740	...	0807	0807	...	0822	0822	...	...	092...
	München Hbf a.	0630	0649	...	0733	...	0749	...	0815	0815	...	0831	0831	...	0913	093...

Table 765 — SOUTHERN BAVARIA - MÜNCHEN, AUGSBURG and ULM

1, 2 class except where shown

	E3702	IC718	E6602 2	E3911	E3205	E3778	IR2065	E4311	E3137	E6604 2	E3837 E4505	E3704	E4313	E3913	EC99	E4273	E5810 2	E3865 E3780	E4317	IR2602	E4547	IR2682	E3139	E6608 E4509 2
	♦	✗✗	©		Ⓐ		♦				K				✗ H			M		🍴		🍴	♦	K
Lindau d.						0743			0800		0846					0937		0945				1000		1046
Hergatz d.			0658			0800			0818	0858	0903											1018	1058	1103
Wangen d.			0703						0824		0903											1024		1103
Aulendorf 766 d.				0707	0707							0907												
Kißlegg 766 d.			0713	0736	0736					0836	0913	0933											1036	1113
Oberstdorf d.						0805						0908				0948			1012		1034			
Sonthofen d.						0824						0928				1008			1031		1053			
Immenstadt a.								0834	0832		0939	0937				1016		1035	1039		1102			1139
Immenstadt d.								0836	0850		0940	0945				1036		1050			1113			1140
Kempten a.								0852	0904		0954	1000				1052		1104			1129			1154
Kempten d.	0802	0802						0858	0906		0956	1002				1107		1106			1131			1156
Memmingen a.	0822	0822	0819	0819	0922				0917		1026	1019	1043			1126					1122			
Memmingen d.	0823	0823	4271	0840	0840	0928			0934	4545	1028	1026	1044			1128					1135			
Ulm a.	0853	0853			0958						1058					1158								
Füssen d.			0805						0905						1005				1104					
Marktoberdorf d.			0850						0950						1050				1147					
Mindelheim d.				0907	0907				1000				1047		E	1200								
Bad Wörishofen d.								0920			1022			3913	1120									
Türkheim d.				0914	0914			0930	1009		1029	1055			1128				1209					
Kaufbeuren a.			0905				0934		1006	1027		1105	←		1134	1158	1204		1227					
Buchloe a.			0918	0921	0919		0945	0938	1016	1017	1038	1037	1102	1110	1118	1102		1136	1145	1210	1217	1216		1238
Buchloe d.			0919	0922	0927		0947	0949	1023	1022	1040	1049	1122	1112	1123	1122		1149	1147	1222	1219	1228		1240
Augsburg a.			0944		0956				1019	1052		1120			1152			1219			1245	1258		
München Pasing a.				1005					1025			1104	1122		1205			1225			1305			1322
München Hbf a.				1013					1035			1112	1130		1155			1213			1234	1313		1330

	E3706	E4319	EC167	E3207	E5814 E3784	IR2067	E4323	E3141	E6608 2	IC714	E3841 E4513	E4325	E3708	E4279	E3921	IR2069	E3869 E3786	E4329	E3143	E4551	E6610 2	E4517	E4331	E3923
					M	🍴				✗ K						🍴	M						A	
Lindau d.			1137		1146			1200		1246						1343			1400				1446	
Hergatz d.					1204			1218	1258	1303						1400			1418	1458		1503		
Wangen d.								1224	1303										1424	1503				
Aulendorf 766 d.				1108									1307											1508
Kißlegg 766 d.				1136				1236	1313				1333						1436	1513				1536
Oberstdorf d.	1108			1133		1212			1253		1304				1412									
Sonthofen d.	1128			1156		1231			1313		1325				1431									
Immenstadt a.	1137			1205	1239	1239			1322	1339	1337				1439	1434						1539		
Immenstadt d.	1145				1240	1249			1333	1340	1346				1450	1436						1540		
Kempten a.	1200		1240		1256	1303			1348	1354	1401				1504	1452						1554		
Kempten d.	1202		1242		1258	1304			1350	1356	1403				1505	1507						1556		
Memmingen a.	1226			1219	1322			1317	1409		1427	1419			1526	1519						1619		
Memmingen d.	1228			1240	1328			1334	4549	1411		1433	1435		1528	1534						1624		
Ulm a.	1258				1358				1445			1532			1558									
Füssen d.								1308											1505					
Marktoberdorf d.								1353					1451						1550					
Mindelheim d.				1307				1400					1500						1600					
Bad Wörishofen d.		1220				1320			1420				1520						1620				1645	
Türkheim d.		1228	1314			1331	1409		1428			1509			1528	1609			1628				1652	
Kaufbeuren a.					1331		1407				1505	1532			1606			1627						
Buchloe a.	1236		1322		1342	1339	1416	1418		1438	1436	1518	1516	1543		1536	1616	1617		1638	1636	1700		
Buchloe d.	1249		1323		1344	1349	1423	1422		1440	1449	1523	1522	1545		1549	1623	1640		1649	1722			
Augsburg a.	1321		1352			1419	1452			1520		1552			1619	1652						1720		
München Pasing a.			1357		1422			1505	1522			1605	1623				1705	1722			→			
München Hbf a.					1431			1513	1530			1613	1633				1713	1730						

	EC95	E3710	E4775 2	E4281	E3923	E3871 E3788	E4335	IR2165	E3145	E6612 2	E4483	E4421	E3712	E4285	E3925	E5832	E3873 E3790	IR2167	E4341	E3147	E6614 2	E4521	E4343	E3716	E3211
	✗ H		Ⓐ			M		🍴			C						M	🍴							B
Lindau d.	1537					1545		1600		1646						1743		1800		1846					
Hergatz d.								1618	1658	1703						1800		1818	1859	1903					
Wangen d.								1624	1703					1708				1824	1903						
Aulendorf 766 d.														1736											1908
Kißlegg 766 d.								1639	1713									1836	1914						1936
Oberstdorf d.		1508					1608			1705		1748		1812								1908			
Sonthofen d.		1528					1627			1728		1808		1831								1928			
Immenstadt a.		1537			1635		1635			1739	1737	1817	1834	1839								1939	1937		
Immenstadt d.		1545			1636		1647			1740	1745	1836	1850									1940	1945		
Kempten a.		1600			1652		1702			1754	1800	1852	1904									1954	2000		
Kempten d.		1602	1624		1707		1708			1756	1802	1907	1906									1956	2002		
Memmingen a.	1637	1626			1726			1721	E		1826	1819	1926				1918	E					2026	2023	
Memmingen d.	1639	1628			1728			1733	4553		1828	1833	1928				1934	4555					2028x	2026	
Ulm a.	1658				1758						1858		1958										2058x		
Füssen d.			1605					1705				1805						1905							
Marktoberdorf d.			1650					1750				1850						1950							
Mindelheim d.							1802					1858						2002					2045		
Bad Wörishofen d.					1710					1815				1914					2020				2045		
Türkheim d.					1718		1810			1826		1906		1928	2010				2028				2052		
Kaufbeuren a.			1657	1705	←		1734	1817	1806	1825		1905		1934				2006	2027						
Buchloe a.	1705		1710	1718	1700		1726	1745	1820	1817	1836	1834	1918	1913		1945	1936	2017	2017	2038	2036		2100		
Buchloe d.	1707		1723	1722			1749	1747	1855	1822	1837	1840	1920	1921		1947	1948	2020	2022	2040	2048		2122		
Augsburg a.			1752				1820			1903			1955				2019	2055			2118	→			
München Pasing a.				1805				1826		1905		1922		2005			2026			2105	2122				
München Hbf a.	1751			1813				1835		1913		1930		2035			2035			2113	2130				

NOTES (LISTED BY TRAIN NUMBERS)

C167 – ALBERT EINSTEIN – [12] and ✗ Interlaken Ost - Bern - Zürich Hbf - St Gallen - München - Fürth im Wald - Praha Hlavni.
714 – NEBELHORN – [12] and ✗ Oberstdorf - Ulm - Stuttgart - Münster.
718 – ALLGÄU – [12] and ✗ Kempten - Ulm - Stuttgart - Dortmund.
2065 – [12] Oberstdorf - Hof - Dresden Hbf - Görlitz.
2067 – [12] and 🍴 Oberstdorf - Hof - Dresden Hbf; 🍴 Oberstdorf - Chemnitz.
2069 – [12] Oberstdorf - Hof (Chemnitz ♣); 🍴 Oberstdorf - Plauen.
2165 – [12] Oberstdorf - Schwandorf (Hof ♣); 🍴 Oberstdorf - Schwandorf.
2167 – [12] Oberstdorf - München (Regensburg ♣); 🍴 Oberstdorf - Freising.
2602 – [12] and 🍴 Oberstdorf - Hof - Leipzig - Berlin Lichtenberg.

IR2682 – ALPENLAND – [12] and 🍴 Oberstdorf - Hamburg Altona.
E3702 – ⑦, also Apr. 15, 17, May 1.
B – [12] Aulendorf (© Freiburg - Neustadt - Sigmaringen) - München.
C – [12] Radolfzell - Augsburg.
H – [12] and ✗ Zürich Hbf - St. Gallen - München.
K – [12] Radolfzell - München.
M – [12] Basel Bad - Schaffhausen - Singen - Ulm.
x – ⑥⑦ only.
♦ – ① - ⑥ (not Dec. 25 - Jan. 1, Apr. 15 - 17, May 1, 1995).
♣ – Daily except ⑥ (not Dec. 24 - 31, Apr. 14 - 16, Apr. 30, 1995).

Table 765 — SOUTHERN BAVARIA - MÜNCHEN, AUGSBURG and ULM

1, 2 class except where shown

	E 3794	EC 93	E3875 5836	E E3796	E 4525	E 3219	E 3213 2	E 4557	D 1088	E3851 E3743	E 4597	E 4349	E 3718 E6623	E 4293	E3495 4431 2	E 5848	E3877 E3745	E 3798	E 4351	E 4599	14177 2	E 3149	E 4559	E 3747
	Ⓐ	✗ H	M	Ⓐ	♦				♦	G							B							
Lindau .... d.	…	1937	…	1946	…	…	2008	…	2042	…	…	…	…	…	…	…	2143	…	…	…	…	2209	…	2249
Hergatz .... d.	…						2026		2100								2200					2231		2306
Wangen .... d.	…						2036																	
Aulendorf .... d.	…							2013					2103									2243		
Kißlegg .... d.	…					2047	2050						2133											
Oberstdorf .... d.	…		1933	2003					2029			2100			2155									
Sonthofen .... d.	…		1956	2019					2108			2120			2212									
Immenstadt .... a.	…		2005	2035 2032					2117 2136			2133			2222	2234								2340
Immenstadt .... d.	…		2036	2042					2126 2137			2145				2236								2341
Kempten .... a.	…		2052	2057					2143 2151			2200				2252								2357
Kempten .... d.	…		2100	2105					2145	2154		2202				2259					2306	2322		
Memmingen .... a.	…	2038	E 4291	2119			2128					2226	2217				2326					2334		
Memmingen .... d.	2030	2039		2121			2135					2228			2234		2328							
Ulm .... a.	2124			2158		E 4347			2341			2325					2400							
Füssen .... d.	…		2005				2105					2205				2300							2305	
Marktoberdorf .... d.	…		2050		2		2150					2250											2350	
Mindelheim .... d.	…				2200							2300												0000
Bad Wörishofen .... d.	…		3211		2120							2220					2320					2342		
Türkheim .... d.	…		F	2128	2209				2228			2309					2328			2400	0009			
Kaufbeuren .... a.	…		2105	2134			2206		2226			2305					2336			0006				
Buchloe .... a.	…	2105	2117	2100 2145	2136	2216 2217			2239	2236		2318	2316			2336	2346		0016	0017				
Buchloe .... a.	…	2107	2120	2122 2147	2148	2220 2222			2240	2248		2319	2321			2349	2347			0022				
Augsburg .... a.	…	2155			2220	2255				2319		2349				0019								
München Pasing .... a.	…	2204	2226			2305			2322			0005					0026			0110				
München Hbf .... a.	…	2148	2212 2235			2313			2330			0013					0035			0118				

♦ – NOTES (LISTED BY TRAIN NUMBERS)

D1088 – ⑥ Jan. 7 - Apr. 8: ⇐1,2 cl., ⇐2 cl. and ⑨ Oberstdorf - Hamburg; ⇐2 cl. and ▭ (also ⇐1,2 cl. to Mar. 24) Oberstdorf - Dortmund.

E3219 – ▭ Lindau - Kißlegg - Aulendorf.

B – ▭ Basel Bad - Schaffhausen - Singen - Kempten.

F – ▭ Aulendorf (ⓒ Freiburg - Neustadt - Sigmaringen) - München.

G – ▭ Radolfzell - Kempten.

H – ▭ and ✗ Zürich Hbf - St. Gallen - München Hbf.

M – ▭ Basel Bad - Schaffhausen - Singen - Ulm.

Table 766 — TÜBINGEN - SIGMARINGEN - AULENDORF - HERGATZ

1, 2 class except where shown

km		E 6601 2	E 6603 2	E 3481 H	E 6605	E 3937 ✗	E 3483 2	E 3941 ⑦	E 3499 2	E 6609 ✗	E 3485	E 3487	E 6611 2	E 3947	E 3489 Ⓐ	E 6613 K	E 3949	E 3211	E 3491	E 3493 2Ⓑ	E 6333 2Ⓐ	E 3497 ⑦	E 6615 Ⓑ	E 3935
0	Tübingen .... d.	…	0615	…	0749	0926	…	1126	…	…	1326	…	…	…	1526	…	…	…	1726	1826	1928	1932		
25	Hechingen .... d.	…	0656		0815	0951	1151		1156	1352					1552				1752	1902	1957	1957		
42	Balingen .... d.	…	0713		0832	1007	1208		1216	1408					1608				1808	1919	2014	2014		
60	Albstadt-Ebingen .... d.	…	0739		0851	1030	1229		1255	1430		1532	1630		1732				1831	1935	2034	2031		
87	Sigmaringen .... a.	0650	0809	0900	0918	1100	1200	1255	1300	1322	1500	1600	1700	1800	1804	1900	2002	2101	2059		220?			
132	Aulendorf .... a.	0742	0848	0946	1046	1146	1246		1346	1446	1546	1646	1746		1846	1846	1947	2048		2146		2238		
132	Aulendorf 765 .... d.	0607	0807		1007	1208		1407			1608			1808		1908						2204		
162	Kißlegg 765 .... d.	0637t	0837t		1037t	1237t		1437t			1640t			1837t		1934						2244t		
175	Wangen .... d.	0647	0847		1047	1247		1447			1650			1847								2254		
181	Hergatz .... a.	0652	0852		1052	1252		1452			1655			1852								220?		

	E 6306 2✗	E 6312 ✗	E 3932 2	E 3480 H	E 6602 2	E 3482 K	E 6604 2	E 3210	E 3484 2	E 6606 Ⓐ	E 3486	E 6608 2	E 6314 2	E 3488 2	E 6610 ⑥	E 3490 Ⓐ	E 6612 ⑦	E 3494	E 3494 2	E 3946	E 6614	E3948	E 3219 G	E 3936
Hergatz .... d.	…	…	…	0658	0858		1058	1258		1458	1700							1858		2026				
Wangen .... d.	…	…	0503	0703	0903		1103	1303		1503	1704							1903		2036				
Kißlegg 765 .... d.	…	…	0518t	0616	0703b		0918t	1013	1119t	1318t	1518t	1720t						1918t		2051t				
Aulendorf 765 .... d.	…	…	0546	0647	0747		0947	1047	1148	1347	1548	1747						1948		2121				
Aulendorf .... d.	…	0601	0701	0809	1009	1048	1209	1309	1409	1509	1609	1709	1811	1909	1909	2014	2201	2301						
Sigmaringen .... d.	0550	0645	0741	0856	1002	1054	1202	1254	1402	1458	1602	1654	1709	1804	1854	2000	2004	2004	2055	2155	2247	2344		
Albstadt-Ebingen .... d.	0618	0711	0809		1029		1228		1428	1525	1545	1629		1830		2035	2033							
Balingen .... d.	0639	0738	0831		1046		1244		1444		1613	1644		1845		2050	2048							
Hechingen .... d.	0656	0754	0847		1102		1300		1500		1632	1701		1900		2111	2104							
Tübingen .... a.	0724	0826	0907		1122		1322		1522		1659	1722		1926		2132	2125							

G – ▭ Lindau - Aulendorf.

H – ✗ Tübingen - Aulendorf and v.v.; daily Sigmaringen - Aulendorf and v.v.

K – ⓒ only: ▭ Freiburg - Neustadt - Donaueschingen - Kißlegg - München and v.v.

t – Arrives 4 - 5 minutes earlier.

Table 767 — KEMPTEN - REUTTE IN TIROL - GARMISCH PARTENKIRCHEN

2 class only except where shown

km		5901	5903	5457	5905	5907	5461	5909	5911	5465	5915	5917	5469	5919	5921	5473	5923	5925	5477	5929	5481 Ⓐ	5481	5931	593?
0	Kempten .... d.	0550	0656	…	0804	0900	…	1004	1100	…	1204	1301	…	1404	1500	…	1604	1700	…	1804	…	…	1900	2000
18	Oy-Mittelberg .... d.	0621	0729		0829	0929		1029	1129		1229	1325		1429	1529		1629	1729		1829			1941	2020
24	Nesselwang .... d.	0641	0741		0841	0941		1041	1141		1241	1341		1441	1541		1641	1741		1841			1952	2055
31	Pfronten-Ried .... d.	0651	0752		0850	0952		1050	1152		1251	1351		1450	1552		1650	1752		1851			1955	…
33	Pfronten-Steinach ▦ .... a.	0654	0755			0955		1155		1254	1355		1555		1755	1854		1958						
33	Pfronten-Steinach ▦ .... d.	0702b		0758		0958		1158		1358		1558		1758	1858		2006							
38	Vils .... d.	0710b		0806		1003		1206		1406		1606		1806	1906									
48	Reutte in Tirol .... d.	0725b		0823		1023		1224		1424		1623		1823	1925	1925	2021							
68	Lermoos .... d.			0848		1048		1249		1449		1648		1848	1950	1950								
71	Ehrwald Zugspitzbahn .... d.			0856		1056		1256		1456		1656		1856	1956	1956								
93	Garmisch-Partenkirche .... a.			0922		1122		1322		1522		1722		1922	2022	2022								

	5900	5902	5904	5454	5906	5460	5910	5912	5464	5916	5918	5468	5920	5472	5924	5926	5476	5930	5932	5480 Ⓐ	5934	5936	5484	593?
Garmisch-Partenkirche .... d.	…	…	…	0628b	…	0828	…	1028	…	…	1228	1428	…	…	1628	…	…	1828	…	…	2028			
Ehrwald Zugspitzbahn .... d.				0659b		0859		1056			1259	1459			1659			1856			2056			
Lermoos .... d.				0703b		0903		1100			1300	1503			1703			1900			2100			
Reutte in Tirol .... d.				0629b	0729	0929		1129			1329	1529			1729			1929			2124			
Vils .... d.				0645b	0745	0945		1145			1345	1545			1745			1945						
Pfronten-Steinach ▦ .... a.				0653b	0753	0953		1153			1353	1553			1753			1953						
Pfronten-Steinach ▦ .... d.			0700		0800	1000		1200	1300		1401		1600			1800	1900		2000					
Pfronten-Ried .... d.	0558	0625	0705		0805	1005	1105	1205	1304		1405	1605	1705		1805	1905		2005	2105		220?			
Nesselwang .... d.	0608	0635	0715		0815	1015	1115	1215	1313		1415	1615	1715		1815	1915		2015	2115		221?			
Oy-Mittelberg .... d.	0621	0647	0729		0829	1029	1129	1229	1329		1429	1629	1729		1829	1929		2029	2129		221?			
Kempten .... a.	0649	0711	0752		0855	1055	1152	1255	1346		1455	1655	1752		1855	1952		2055	2152		222?			

b – ✗ only.

Table 770 NÜRNBERG - COBURG, HALLE and LEIPZIG

1, 2 class except where shown

Electrification work between Saalfeld and Jena will affect services until further notice. Delays and alterations likely.

km		IR 2206 🍷 ♦	7312 2	D 2751 ❖	6216	E 3710	IC 804 ✕ ♦	6218	E3462 E3714	IC 708 ✕ M	6222	E 3032	IC 706 ✕ M	D 2916 K	E 3034	IC 812 ✕ ♦	6232	E 3036	IC 800 ✕ ♦	D 2910 K	6238	IR 2202 🍷 ♦	E 3038	IC 704 ✕ M
	München Hbf **750** d.	...	...	...	...	...	0453	...	...	0656	...	0748	0856	...	0948	1056	...	1148	1256	...	...	...	1348	1456
	Augsburg **750** d.	...	...	...	...	...	0525	...	...	0728	...	|	0928	...	|	1128	...	|	1328	...	...	...	|	1528
	Regensburg **779** d.	...	...	...	...	...	|	...	0710	|	...	0916	|	...	1116	|	...	1316	|	...	...	...	1516	|
0	**Nürnberg** d.	...	...	...	...	0600	0637	...	0824	0840	...	1024	1040	...	1224	1240	...	1424	1440	...	...	1540	1624	1640
24	Erlangen d.	...	...	...	...	0616	0654	...	0842	0854	...	1042	1054	...	1242	1254	...	1442	1454	...	...	1600	1642	1654
62	Bamberg d.	...	...	...	...	0642	0714	...	0906	0914	...	1106	1114	...	1306	1314	...	1506	1514	...	...	1623	1708	1714
94	Lichtenfels d.	...	...	...	...	0711	0730	...	0925	0930	...	1125	1130	...	1325	1330	...	1525	1530	...	...	1640	1725	1730
115	**Coburg** a.	...	...	...	...	0731	|	...	0940	|	...	1140	|	...	1340	|	...	1540	|	...	...	|	1740	|
157	Probstzella a.	...	...	...	...	...	0816	...	...	1016	...	...	1216	...	▬	1416	...	...	1616	...	...	1729	...	1816
157	Probstzella d.	...	...	...	...	...	0829	...	...	1029	...	...	1229	...	...	1429	...	...	1629	...	...	1743	...	1829
182	**Saalfeld** d.	0612	0655	...	...	...	0855	...	...	1055	...	...	1255	...	**6226**	1455	...	...	1655	...	...	1814	...	1855
232	Jena Saalbahnhof d.	0655	0813	...	...	...	0934	...	...	1134	...	...	1334b	1334	...	1534	...	...	1734b	1734	...	1855	...	1934
260	Naumburg **775** d.	0733	0849	0903	0908	...	1002	1008	...	1202	1208	...	1402b	1402	1408	1602	1608	...	1802b	1802	1808	1933	...	2002
274	Weißenfels **775** d.	0746	...	0915	0921	...	|	1021	...	|	1221	...	|	|	1421	|	1621	...	|	|	1821	1946	...	|
306	**Halle 775** a.	0813	...	|	0952	...	|	1052	...	|	1252	...	|	|	1452	|	1652	...	|	|	1852	2013	...	|
314	**Leipzig** a.	...	...	0945	...	...	1040	...	...	1240	...	...	1440b	1440	...	1640	...	...	1840b	1840	...	...	...	2040

	6242	E 3046	EC 10 ✕ ♦	6246	IC 700 ♣🍷	IC 555 ✕ S	E 3736	IR 2565 🍷 ♦	7348 G	ICN 1900 ✕ ♦
München Hbf **750** d.	...	1548	1656	...	1738	...	...	...	...	2306
Augsburg **750** d.	...	|	1728	...	|	...	...	...	...	2347u
Regensburg **779** d.	...	1716	|	...	|	...	...	...	...	|
ürnberg d.	...	1823	1840	...	1942	...	1946	2042	...	|
rlangen d.	...	1839	1854	...	1956	...	2004	2059	...	|
amberg d.	...	1906	1914	...	2016	...	2031	2123	...	|
ichtenfels d.	...	1925	1930	...	2032	...	2059	2140	...	|
Coburg a.	...	1940	|	...	|	...	2119	2155	...	|
robstzella a.	...	...	2016	...	2118	...	...	...	...	|
robstzella d.	...	...	2029	...	2131	...	...	...	...	|
aalfeld d.	...	...	2055	...	2157	...	...	...	2215	|
ena Saalbahnhof d.	...	...	2134	...	2236	...	...	...	2325	|
laumburg **775** d.	2008	...	2202	2208	2304	2316	...	...	...	|
Veißenfels **775** d.	2021	...	|	2221	|	|	...	...	...	|
Halle 775 a.	2052	...	|	2252	2355	|	...	...	...	0551
eipzig a.	...	...	2240	...	...	2355	...	...	...	...

	IR 2564 🍷 ♦	E3715 E3035	E 3037	IC 554 ✕	IC 701 ⚡🍷	6213	EC 11 ✕ ♦	E 3039	6217
Leipzig d.	...	...	...	0604	...	...	0715	...	...
Halle 775 d.	...	...	...	|	0600	0705	|	...	0905
Weißenfels **775** d.	...	...	...	|	|	0736	|	...	0936
Naumburg **775** d.	...	...	...	0639	0645	0746	0754	...	0946
Jena Saalbahnhof d.	...	...	...	...	0720	...	0822	...	...
Saalfeld d.	...	...	...	...	0801	...	0904	...	...
Probstzella d.	...	...	...	...	0826	...	0929	...	...
Probstzella d.	...	...	...	...	0838	...	0941	...	...
Coburg d.	0602	...	0800	...	|	...	|	1017	...
Lichtenfels d.	0619	...	0816	...	0924	...	1027	1034	...
Bamberg d.	0637	0648	0837	...	0941	...	1044	1055	...
Erlangen d.	0700	0718	0859	...	1000	...	1103	1117	...
Nürnberg a.	0719	0735	0916	...	1016	...	1118	1134	...
Regensburg **779** a.	...	0841	1041	...	|	...	|	1241	...
Augsburg **750** a.	...	|	|	...	|	...	1229	|	...
München Hbf **750** a.	...	1011	1211	...	1217	...	1303	1413	...

	IC 801 ✕ ♦	E 3041	IR 2203 🍷 ♦	6221	IC 813 ✕ ♦	E 3045		6225	IC 705 ✕ M	E 3049	6229	IC 707 ✕ M	E 3053	6237	IC 709 ✕ M	E 3057 N	D 1609 ♦	6241	IC 805 ✕ ♦	IR 2207 🍷 ♦	IC 656 🍷	6243	7345 2	ICN 1901 ✕ ♦
eipzig d.	0915	...	...	...	1115	...	...	...	1315	...	...	1515	...	...	1715	...	...	...	1915	...	2004	...	...	...
Halle 775 d.	|	...	0935	1105	|	...	...	1305	|	...	1505	|	...	1705	|	...	1800	1905	|	1935	|	2005	...	0008
Veißenfels **775** d.	|	...	1000	1136	|	...	...	1336	|	...	1536	|	...	1736	|	...	1824	1936	|	2000	|	2036	...	|
laumburg **775** d.	0954	...	1024	1146	1154	...	...	1346	1354	...	1546	1554	...	1746	1754	...	1835	1946	1954	2024	2039	2046	2059	|
ena Saalbahnhof d.	1022	...	1100	...	1222	...	...	...	1422	...	...	1622	...	...	1822	...	1904	...	2022	2051	...	...	2142	|
aalfeld d.	1104	...	1151	...	1304	...	...	...	1504	...	...	1704	...	...	1904	...	1953	...	2104	...	...	...	2246	|
robstzella d.	1129	...	1215	...	1329	...	...	...	1529	...	...	1729	...	...	1929	...	2017	...	2129	...	...	...	...	|
robstzella d.	1141	...	1228	...	1341	...	...	...	1541	...	...	1741	...	...	1941	...	2029	...	2141	...	...	...	...	|
Coburg d.	|	1217	|	...	|	1417	...	...	|	1617	...	|	1817	...	|	2003	|	...	|	...	...	...	...	|
ichtenfels d.	1227	1234	1318	...	1427	1434	...	...	1627	1634	...	1827	1834	...	2027	2034	2121	...	2227	...	...	...	...	|
amberg d.	1244	1255	1335	...	1444	1455	...	...	1644	1655	...	1844	1855	...	2044	2055	2138	...	2244	...	...	...	...	|
rlangen d.	1303	1317	1357	...	1503	1517	...	...	1703	1717	...	1903	1917	...	2103	2117	2200	...	2303	...	...	...	...	|
ürnberg a.	1318	1334	1415	...	1518	1534	...	...	1718	1734	...	1918	1934	...	2118	2134	2216	...	2323	...	...	...	...	|
Regensburg **779** a.	|	1441	...	...	|	1641	...	...	|	1841	...	|	2041	...	|	2241	...	...	...	...	...	...	...	|
Augsburg **750** a.	1429	|	...	...	1629	|	...	...	1829	|	...	2029	|	...	2229	...	...	...	...	...	...	...	...	0601s
München Hbf **750** a.	1504	1611	...	...	1706	1811	...	...	1903	2011	...	2103	2211	...	2303	...	...	...	...	...	...	...	...	0645

♦ – **NOTES** (LISTED BY TRAIN NUMBERS)

C10/1 – MIMARA – [12] and ✕ Zagreb - Leipzig and v.v.
C800 – THERESE GIEHSE – [12] and ✕ München (Bischofshofen on ⑥⑦ Jan. 7 - Apr. 9, also Dec. 18, 24, 26, 27, Jan. 2, 6, 18, 22, May 20, 27) - Berlin Hbf.
C801 – THERESE GIEHSE – [12] and ✕ Berlin Hbf - München (Bischofshofen on ⑥ Jan. 7 - Apr. 8, also Dec. 17, 23, 25, 26, May 20, 27).
C804 – HANS SACHS – [12] and ✕ Nürnberg (München ⚡) - Berlin Hbf.
C805 – HANS SACHS – [12] and ✕ Berlin Hbf - Nürnberg.
C812/3 – WETTERSTEIN – [12] and ✕ Mittenwald - Berlin Hbf and v.v.
1609 – ⑦, also Nov. 1, Apr. 17, May 1, **not** Dec. 25, Apr. 16, 30: [12] Halle - Nürnberg.
CN1900/1 – 🛏 1,2 cl., [2] (reclining) and ✕ München - Berlin Charlottenburg and v.v. Special fares payable - see heading on page **352**.
R2202 – [12] Nürnberg - Berlin Zoo; 🍷 Nürnberg - Dessau.
R2203 – [12] and 🍷 Berlin Charlottenburg - Nürnberg.

IR2206 – [12] and 🍷 Saalfeld - Berlin Charlottenburg. **Not** Dec. 25.
IR2207 – **Not** Dec. 24: [12] and 🍷 Berlin Charlottenburg - Jena; 🚌 connection to Saalfeld.
IR2564 – [12] and 🍷 Coburg - Nürnberg - Stuttgart - Karlsruhe. **Not** Dec. 25, Jan. 1.
IR2565 – [12] Karlsruhe - Nürnberg - Coburg; 🍷 Karlsruhe - Erlangen. **Not** Dec. 24, 31.
K – ②③④, **not** Apr. 13.
M – [12] and ✕ München - Berlin Hbf and v.v.
N – [12] Coburg - Regensburg - Landshut.
G – ⑧, **not** Dec. 25, Apr. 14, 16, 30.
S – **Not** Dec. 24, 31.
b – Does **not** call Jena or Naumburg ②③④ (runs Apr. 13); Leipzig arrive 20 minutes later.
s – Stops to **set down** only. **u** – Stops to **pick up** only.
❖ – **Not** Dec. 25, Jan. 1.
⚡ – ① - ⑥ (**not** Dec. 25 - Jan. 1, Apr. 15 - 17, May 1, **1995**).
♣ – Daily except ⑥ (**not** Dec. 24 - 31, Apr. 14 - 16, Apr. 30, **1995**).

Table 771 SCHWEINFURT - MEININGEN - ERFURT

1 2 class except where shown

km		6814 2	6816 2	E 3972 Ⓐ	6878 2	E 3974	6820 2	6811 2	E 3976 C	7717	E 3978	6817 2	14915	IR 2204 🍷 M	14914	6826 2	14921 2	E 3982	E 3984	14916	14923	IR 2200 🍷 N	6825 H	6834 2	6838 2 S
	Würzburg **774** d.	...	...	...	...	...	...	...	...	...	...	...	...	0948	...	...	...	...	...	...	...	1348	...	...	...
0	**Schweinfurt 774** d.	...	...	0545	...	0645	...	...	0729	...	0915	...	...	1023	...	...	...	1246	1315	...	...	1423	...	...	...
40	Bad Neustadt (Saale) d.	...	...	0630	...	0724	...	...	0804	...	0945	...	...	1034	...	...	...	1317	1350	...	...	1453	...	...	...
54	Mellrichstadt d.	...	...	0641	...	0734	...	...	0825	...	0955	...	...	1053	...	...	...	1327	1402	...	...	|	...	...	...
87	Grimmenthal a.	...	...	|	...	0754	...	...	|	...	1009	...	...	1116	...	...	...	|	1416	...	...	1516	...	...	...
	Grimmenthal d.	...	...	|	...	|	...	0811	|	...	|	1016	...	|	1136	...	...	|	|	1428	...	|	1520	...	...
80	**Meiningen** a.	...	...	0720	...	|	...	0819	0905		|	1024	...	|	1145	...	...	1358	|	1437	...	|	1528	...	...
80	**Meiningen 773** d.	0545	0636	...	0724	|	0759	...	...	0954	|	...	1102	|	...	1243	1354	...	|	...	1504	|	...	1531	1636
	Grimmenthal **773** a.	0553	0644	...	0733	|	0807	...	...	1003	|	...	1111	|	...	1251	1403	...	|	...	1513	|	...	1540	1644
87	Grimmenthal d.	0554	0655	...	0738	0756	0814	...	...	...	1010	...	...	1118	...	1253	...	...	1418	...	...	1518	...	1541	1649
107	Suhl d.	0615	0722	...	0804	0814	0834	...	...	...	1036	...	...	1135	...	1313	...	...	1436	...	...	1535	...	1611	1713
113	Zella-Mehlis d.	0622	0740	...	0812	0822	0842	...	...	...	1045	...	...	1143	...	1321	...	...	1445	...	...	1543	...	1618	1721
118	Oberhof d.	0629	0746	...	...	0829	0848	...	...	...	1052	...	...	1150	...	1328	...	...	1452	...	...	1550	...	1625	1728
149	Arnstadt d.	0705	0822	...	...	0900	0928	...	...	...	1125	...	...	1228	...	1401	...	...	1525	...	...	1628	...	1702	1802
172	**Erfurt** a.	0722	0839	...	...	0918	0951	...	...	...	1141	...	...	1245	...	*1430*	...	...	1541	...	...	1645	...	1725	*1830*

C – [12] Schweinfurt - Meiningen - Eisenach.
H – ⚒, **not** Dec. 24, 31, Apr. 15.
M – [12] and 🍷 Würzburg - Halle - Berlin Charlottenburg.
N – [12] and 🍷 Würzburg - Halle - Berlin Charlottenburg. **Not** Dec. 24.
S – **Not** Dec. 24, 31.

Table 771 SCHWEINFURT - MEININGEN - ERFURT

1, 2 class except where shown

	E 3990 J	6890 2	E 3992	6833 2	E 3994 C	6840 2	14929	E 3996	6837 2	E 3998
Würzburg 774 d.	...	...	1556	...	...	...	...	...	...	...
Schweinfurt 774 d.	1546	...	1636	...	1731	...	...	1917	...	2118
Bad Neustadt (Saale) d.	1627	...	1713	...	1808	...	...	1957	...	2156
Mellrichstadt d.	1643	...	1729	...	1820	...	...	2007	...	2206
Grimmenthal a.	|	...	1754	...	|	...	...	2021	...	|
Grimmenthal d.	|	...	|	1819	|	...	...	|	2025	|
Meiningen a.	1717	...	|	1828	1850	...	...	|	2033	2237
Meiningen 773 d.	...	1722	|	...	...	1917	2010	|	...	*2245*
Grimmenthal 773 a.	...	1731	|	...	...	1925	2019	|	...	2254
Grimmenthal d.	...	1732	1755	...	...	1931	...	2023	...	*2255*
Suhl d.	...	1801	1810	...	...	1951	...	2040	...	*2317*
Zella-Mehlis d.	...	1809	1817	...	...	1959	...	2048	...	*2326*
Oberhof d.	...	...	1823	...	...	2005	...	2056	...	...
Arnstadt d.	...	...	1857	...	...	2040	...	2125	...	...
Erfurt a.	...	...	1915	...	...	2100	...	2141	...	...

	E 3973	E 3975 J	6878 2	E 3977	14906	6811 2	E 3979 C	6882 2	6817 2	IR 2201 🍷 N
Erfurt d.	...	...	...	0611	...	0633	...	...	0831	0900
Arnstadt d.	...	...	...	0631	...	0658	...	...	0855	0925
Oberhof d.	...	...	...	0708	...	0732	...	...	0932	0955
Zella-Mehlis d.	...	...	...	0714	...	0739	...	...	0938	1002
Suhl d.	...	...	...	0721	...	0746	...	...	0946	1010
Grimmenthal a.	...	...	...	0736	...	0810	...	...	1006	1025
Grimmenthal 773 d.	...	...	...	|	0740	0811	...	...	1017	|
Meiningen 773 a.	...	...	...	|	0749	0819	...	...	1025	|
Meiningen d.	0548	0639	0724	|	...	...	0825	1005	...	|
Grimmenthal a.	|	|	0733	|	...	...	|	1014	...	|
Grimmenthal d.	|	|	...	0737	...	...	|	...	...	1026
Mellrichstadt d.	0618	0709	...	0754	...	...	0854	...	...	|
Bad Neustadt (Saale) d.	0631	0722	...	0803	...	...	0904	...	...	1053
Schweinfurt 774 a.	0710	0753	...	0838	...	...	0939	...	...	1122
Würzburg 774 a.	...	...	...	...	...	...	...	...	...	1157

	7724	6824 2	E 3983	14914	E 3985	6823 2	14923	6825 2 H	E 3987	E 3991 Ⓐ	14918	6827 2	IR 2205 🍷 M	6885 2 Ⓐ	E 3993	6829 2 Ⓐ	E 3995 J	6833 2	6840 2	E 3997	6891 2	E 3999 C	6837 2	6843 2	6845 2
Erfurt d.	...	...	1010	...	...	1231	...	*1321*	1410	...	...	1431	1500	...	...	1527	...	1631	...	1810	...	...	1831	2031	2302
Arnstadt d.	...	...	1028	...	...	1255	...	1355	1428	...	...	1455	1525	...	...	1548	...	1655	...	1829	...	...	1855	2052	2326
Oberhof d.	...	...	1058	...	...	1331	...	1430	1458	...	...	1530	1555	...	...	1628	...	1731	...	1900	...	...	1931	2131	0001
Zella-Mehlis d.	...	...	1101	...	...	1338	...	1445	1504	...	...	1544	1602	1619	...	1635	...	1738	...	1906	...	...	1938	2138	0008
Suhl d.	...	...	1111	...	...	1346	...	1452	1511	...	...	1551	1610	1626	...	1645	...	1743	...	1913	...	...	1955	2145	0015
Grimmenthal a.	...	...	1132	...	...	1406	...	1511	1532	...	...	1610	1625	1646	...	1704	...	1808	...	1929	...	...	2014	2204	0034
Grimmenthal 773 d.	1031	...	|	1136	...	1407	...	1520	|	...	1542	1612	|	1647	...	1706	...	1809	...	|	1933	...	2025	2205	0035
Meiningen 773 a.	1040	...	|	1145	...	1415	...	1528	|	...	1551	1620	|	1656	...	1714	...	1818	...	|	1942	...	2033	2213	0043
Meiningen d.	...	1120	|	...	1235	...	1504	...	|	1546	...	...	|	...	1659	...	1808	...	1917	|	...	2017	...	...	...
Grimmenthal a.	...	1128	|	...	|	...	1513	...	|	|	...	...	|	...	|	...	|	...	1925	|	...	|	...	...	...
Grimmenthal d.	...	...	1133	...	|	...	...	...	1533	|	...	...	1626	...	|	...	|	...	...	1930	...	|	...	...	...
Mellrichstadt d.	...	...	1150	...	1305	...	...	...	1552	1616	...	...	|	...	1730	...	1842	...	...	1946	...	2047	...	...	...
Bad Neustadt (Saale) d.	...	...	1201	...	1319	...	...	...	1602	1626	...	...	1653	...	1741	...	1852	...	...	1957	...	2057	...	...	...
Schweinfurt 774 a.	...	...	1236	...	1401	...	...	...	1634	1659	...	...	1722	...	1819	...	1930	...	...	2032	...	2131	...	...	...
Würzburg 774 a.	...	...	...	...	...	...	...	...	...	...	...	...	1757	...	...	...	...	...	...	...	...	...	...	...	...

C – [12] Schweinfurt - Meiningen - Eisenach and v.v.
H – ⚒, **not** Dec. 24, 31, Apr. 15.
J – Ⓐ, **not** Jan. 6.
M – [12] and 🍷 Berlin Charlottenburg - Halle - Erfurt - Würzburg.
N – [12] and 🍷 Berlin Zoo - Halle - Erfurt - Würzburg. **Not** Dec. 25.

Table 772 EISENACH - MEININGEN

1, 2 class except where shown

km		E 3979	7717	7719 2	7723 2	7729	7737 2	6144 7743 2	E 3999 2	7753	7757 2Ⓑ
0	**Eisenach** d.	0724	0838	0953	1112	1343	1553	1728	1908	2038	2215
27	Bad Salzungen a.	0744	0905	1019	1138	1409	1619	1754	1934	2104	2245
27	Bad Salzungen d.	0745	0905	1024	1144	1421	1620	1759	1935	2105	2246
41	Wernshausen d.	0758	0920	1038	1158	1435	1657	1813	1948	2120	2301
61	**Meiningen** a.	0815	0944	1058	1228	1455	1716	1832	2005	2139	2320
	Schweinfurt 771 a.	0939	...	...	...	...	...	...	2131	...	...

	7718 2	E 3976	7724 2	7728 2	7732 2	7738 2	7746 2	E 3994	7756 2	7758 Ⓑ
Schweinfurt 771 d.	...	0729	...	...	...	...	...	1731	...	...
Meiningen d.	0826	0931	1108	1214	1345	1506	1632	1900	2014	2142
Wernshausen d.	0846	0948	1128	1234	1405	1526	1653	1917	2034	2202
Bad Salzungen a.	0859	1000	1141	1247	1418	1540	1707	1929	2047	2215
Bad Salzungen d.	0907	1002	1142	1248	1420	1541	1708	1937	2048	2217
Eisenach a.	0934	1030	1209	1320	1446	1607	1735	1958	2120	2243

Additional journeys from Eisenach at 0436 ⚒, 0507 Ⓐ, 0625, 1238, 1439 ⚒, 1636 Ⓐ.

Additional journeys from Meiningen at 0418 ⚒, 0546, 0633 ⚒, 1542 Ⓐ, 1723 Ⓐ, 1750 Ⓒ.

Table 773 MEININGEN - SONNEBERG - COBURG

2 class only Meiningen - Sonneberg

km		14903 Ⓐ	7013 2N	14911	14915	14917 ⚒	14921	14923	14925 Ⓐ	14927	14931 Ⓑ
0	**Meiningen 771** d.	0435	...	0822	1102	1256	1354	1504	1622	1840	2153
7	Grimmenthal 771 a.	0444	...	0831	1111	1305	1403	1513	1631	1849	2202
7	Grimmenthal d.	0445	...	0832	1122	1311	1421	1536	1632	1850	2210
21	Themar d.	0505	...	0852	1136	1324	1435	1550	1646	1904	2223
48	Eisfeld d.	0545	...	0928	1224	1402	1530	1644	1756	1950	2259
64	Rauenstein d.	0622	...	1005	1301	1438	1608	1720	1832	2025	...
80	**Sonneberg** a.	0656	...	1033	1329	1507	1636	1748	1902	2054	...
		7053 P		7017 2	7029	7037	7041 2		7047 2Ⓑ		
80	**Sonneberg** d.	0659	0836	1036	1336	1547	1641	...	1936	...	...
100	**Coburg** a.	0725	0858	1058	1358	1608	1702	...	1958	...	...

	14904 Ⓐ	7052 N	15203 ⚒	14910	7012 2N	7024 N	14918	7030 2	7034 2P	7042 Ⓑ
Coburg d.	...	0502	...	...	0802	1102	...	1402	1610	1710
Sonneberg a.	...	0524	...	...	0823	1123	...	1423	1630	1730
		14906			14914	14916		14922	14924 Ⓐ	14926
Sonneberg d.	0436	0527	0627	...	0914	1212	...	1536	1648	1800
Rauenstein d.	0517	0613	0710	...	0956	1252	...	1616	1728	1839
Eisfeld d.	0556	0640	0736	0813	1023	1319	1427	1648	1754	1906
Themar d.	0632	0716	...	0849	1059	1359	1513	1736	...	1942
Grimmenthal a.	0647	0731	...	0904	1114	1414	1528	1751	...	1957
Grimmenthal 771 d.	0648	0740	...	0905	1136	1428	1542	1752	...	1958
Meiningen 771 a.	0657	0749	...	0914	1145	1437	1551	1801	...	2007

Additional trains Sonneberg - Coburg: 0536 **L** ♠, 0613 **J**, 0736 **L**, 0936 **L**, 1136 **L**, 1236 ♠, 1252 **J** ♠, 1436 **J** ♠, 1736 Ⓑ.
Additional trains Coburg - Sonneberg: 0617 **J**, 0709 **L**, 0902 **L**, 1002 ♠, 1202 ♠, 1302, 1332 **J** ♠, 1513 **J**, 1548 **O**, 1822 **J** ♠, 1902 **O** ♠.

J – Ⓐ, **not** Jan. 6. L – ⚒, **not** Jan. 6. O – ⑦, also Jan. 6. ♠ – 2 class only.

Table 774 WÜRZBURG - BAMBERG - HOF

1, 2 class

km		E 3783	E 3785	E 3787	E 3789	E 3791	E 3793	E 3795	E 3797	E 3645	E 3649
0	**Würzburg 771** d.	0637	0842	1042	1242	1442	1642	1842	1942	2042	2254
43	Schweinfurt 771 a.	0711	0911	1111	1311	1517	1711	1911	2014	2111	2322
43	Schweinfurt d.	0720	0913	1113	1313	1519	1713	1913	2015	2113	2324
100	**Bamberg** a.	0800	0955	1155	1355	1602	1755	1955	2055	2155	0002
100	**Bamberg 770** d.	0809	1009	1212	1409	1627	1806	2021	2109	...	...
132	Lichtenfels 770 a.	0828	1028	1231	1428	1649	1825	2041	2128	...	...
132	Lichtenfels d.	0837	1037	1237	1437	1650	1837	2043	2143	...	...
162	Kulmbach d.	0858	1058	1258	1458	1711	1858	2104	2204	...	...
174	Neuenmarkt Wirsberg d.	0908	1108	1308	1508	1721	1914	2114	2214	...	...
182	Marktschorgast d.	0918	1118	1318	1518	1731	1924	2124	2224	...	...
203	Münchberg d.	0938	1138	1338	1538	1751	1944	2144	2244	...	...
227	**Hof** a.	1001	1201	1401	1601	1814	2007	2207	2307	...	...

	E 3610 L	E 3780	E 3782	E 3784	E 3786	E 3788	E 3790	E 3792	E 3794	E 3796
Hof d.	...	0559	0757	1001	1201	1401	1601	1801	2004	...
Münchberg d.	...	0625	0819	1023	1223	1423	1623	1823	2026	...
Marktschorgast d.	...	0645	0839	1043	1243	1443	1643	1843	2046	...
Neuenmarkt Wirsberg d.	...	0653	0847	1051	1252	1451	1651	1851	2054	...
Kulmbach d.	...	0702	0856	1100	1301	1500	1700	1900	2103	...
Lichtenfels a.	...	0723	0917	1121	1322	1521	1721	1921	2124	...
Lichtenfels 770 d.	...	0727	0930	1127	1327	1527	1727	1927	2125	...
Bamberg 770 a.	...	0747	0950	1147	1347	1546	1747	1947	2145	...
Bamberg d.	0645	0803	1003	1203	1403	1555	1803	2003	2157	2313
Schweinfurt a.	0724	0842	1042	1242	1442	1634	1842	2042	2236	2352
Schweinfurt 771 d.	0725	0844	1044	1244	1444	1640	1844	2044	2238	2355
Würzburg 771 a.	0757	0915	1115	1315	1515	1715	1915	2115	2312	0026

L – ⚒, **not** Jan. 6.

Table 775 FRANKFURT/MAIN - ERFURT - LEIPZIG - DRESDEN

1, 2 class except where shown

km		IR 2351 🍷 M	IC 659 🍷 Q	8707	D§ 2751 F❖	IC 657 🍷 ♦	IR 2453 🍷 ♦	D§ 2753 F	IC 655 🍴	D§ 2755 F	IC 653 🍴	IR 2153 🍷 H	IR 2457 🍷 C	D§ 2757 F	IC 651 🍴	D 1659 K	D§ 2855 ♦	IC 559 🍴	IR 2151 🍷 ♦	IR 2551 🍷 ♦	D§ 2759 ♦	EC 57 🍴 ♦	D 1657 KL	D§ 2857 ♦
	Saarbrücken **725** d.	...	...	...	...	...	...	...	...	...	0651	...	...	...	0851	...	...	1051	...	...	...	1251	...	...
0	**Frankfurt/Main Hbf** d.	...	...	...	...	0522	...	...	0722	...	0922	1018	...	...	1122	1301	...	1322	1418	...	...	1522	1622	...
104	Fulda d.	...	...	...	...	0620	...	...	0820	...	1020	1131	...	...	1220	1404	...	1420	1531	...	...	1620	|	...
170	Bebra a.	...	...	...	...	0651	...	...	0851	...	1051	1209	...	...	1251	1438	...	1451	1605	...	...	1651	1749	...
170	Bebra d.	...	...	0608	...	0701	0846	...	0901	...	1101	1215	1246	...	1301	1447	...	1501	1615	1646	...	1701	1800	...
215	Eisenach d.	...	...	0702	...	0740	0926	...	0940	...	1140	1253	1326	...	1340	1525	...	1540	1653	1726	...	1740	1835	...
244	Gotha d.	...	...	0734	...	|	0949	...	|	...	|	1317	1349	...	|	1548	...	|	1717	1749	...	|	1859	...
271	**Erfurt** a.	...	...	0759	...	0824	1010	...	1024	...	1224	1336	1410	...	1424	1607	...	1624	1736	1810	...	1824	1920	...
271	**Erfurt 670 777** d.	0613	0637	...	0820	0837	1013	1018	1037	1220	1237	1348	1413	1420	1437	1611	1620	1637	1748	1813	1820	1837	1927	2020
302	Weimar **670 777** d.	0630	0652	...	0836	|	1030	1034	1052	1236	|	1404	1430	1436	|	1628	1636	|	1804	1830	1836	|	1944	2036
	Jena West **777** d.	0651	|	...	|	|	1051	|	|	|	|	|	1451	|	|	1702	|	|	|	1851	|	|	2004	|
	Gera 777 d.	0732	|	...	|	|	1132	|	|	|	|	|	1532	|	|	1749	|	|	|	1932	|	|	2047	|
	Glauchau d.	0824	|	...	|	|	1224	|	|	|	|	|	1624	|	|	...	|	|	|	2024	|	|	...	|
	Chemnitz a.	0850	|	...	|	|	1250	|	|	|	|	|	1650	|	|	...	|	|	|	2050	|	|	...	|
344	Naumburg d.	...	0717	...	0903	|	...	1103	|	1303	|	1431	...	1503	|	...	1703	|	1831	...	1903	1916	...	2103
358	Weißenfels d.	...	|	...	0915	|	...	1115	|	1315	|	1444	...	1515	|	...	1715	|	1844	...	1915	|	...	2115
	Halle **670** a.	...	|	...	|	|	...	|	|	|	|	1511	...	|	|	...	|	|	1911	...	|	|	...	|
397	**Leipzig** a.	...	0755	...	0945	0955	...	1145	1155	1345	1355	...	...	1545	1555	...	1745	1755	...	...	1945	1955	...	2145
397	**Leipzig 674** d.	...	0807	...	...	1007	...	...	1207	...	1407	...	...	...	1607	...	...	1807	...	...	...	2007	...	...
513	Dresden Neustadt **674** a.	...	0932	...	...	1132	...	...	1332	...	1532	...	...	...	1732	...	...	1934	...	...	...	2132	...	...
517	**Dresden Hbf 674** a.	...	0940	...	...	1140	...	...	1340	...	1540	...	...	...	1740	...	...	1942	...	...	...	2140	...	...

	IC 557 🍴 ♦	6246	IR 2651 🍷 ♦	D§ 2859 Z	IR 2555 🍷 S	IC 555 🍴 S	IR 2077 ♣ ♦	D 351 🍷 ♦	D 1955 🍷 ♦	D 451 🍷 ♦
Saarbrücken **725** d.	1451	...	...	...	...	...	...	...	...	...
Frankfurt/Main Hbf d.	1722	...	...	...	...	1922	...	2216	2323	2359
Fulda d.	1820	...	...	...	...	2020	...	2331	0028	0113
Bebra a.	1851	...	...	...	...	2051	...	0007	0107	0146
Bebra d.	1901	...	...	...	2046	2101	2121	0042	0121	0156
Eisenach d.	1940	...	...	...	2126	2140	2202	|	0201	0238
Gotha d.	|	...	...	...	2149	|	2226	|	|	0306
Erfurt a.	2024	...	...	...	2210	2224	2247	0159	0245	0327
Erfurt 670 777 d.	2037	2109	2148	2155	...	2237	...	0217	0257	0340
Weimar **670 777** d.	2052	2133	2204	2211	...	|	...	|	0314	0357
Jena West **777** d.	|	|	|	|	...	|	...	|	|	|
Gera 777 d.	|	|	|	|	...	|	...	|	|	|
Glauchau d.	|	|	|	|	...	|	...	|	|	|
Chemnitz a.	|	|	|	|	...	|	...	|	|	|
Naumburg d.	|	2208	2231	2238	...	2316	...	|	|	|
Weißenfels d.	|	2221	2244	2250	...	|	...	|	|	|
Halle **670** a.	|	2252	2311	|	...	|	...	0327	0410	|
Leipzig a.	2155	...	...	2320	...	2355	...	...	...	0501
Leipzig 674 d.	2207	...	...	...	...	...	...	...	...	0507
Dresden Neustadt **674** a.	2332	...	...	...	...	...	...	...	...	0638
Dresden Hbf 674 a.	2340	...	...	...	...	...	...	...	...	...

	IC 552 ⚡🍷	6114	IC 554 🍴 ❖	D§ 2858 ❖	IR 2554 🍷 ♦	IR 2650 🍷 ♦	IC 556 🍴 ♦	D§ 2854 ♦	IR 2150 🍷 H
Dresden Hbf 674 d.	...	...	...	...	...	...	0622	...	...
Dresden Neustadt **674** d.	...	...	...	...	...	...	0630	...	...
Leipzig 674 a.	...	...	...	...	...	...	0751	...	...
Leipzig d.	...	...	0604	0612	...	...	0804	0812	...
Halle **670** d.	...	...	|	|	...	0700	|	|	0848
Weißenfels d.	...	...	|	0643	...	0728	|	0843	0913
Naumburg d.	...	...	0641	0653	...	0738	|	0853	0923
Chemnitz d.	...	...	|	|	0508	|	|	|	|
Glauchau d.	...	...	|	|	0533	|	|	|	|
Gera 777 d.	...	...	|	|	0625	|	|	|	|
Jena West **777** d.	...	...	|	|	0705	|	|	|	|
Weimar **670 777** d.	...	...	0708	0721	0730	0808	|	0921	0949
Erfurt 670 777 a.	...	...	0724	0738	0746	0824	0922	0938	1005
Erfurt d.	0552	0708	0734	...	0749	...	0934	...	1015
Gotha d.	|	0736	|	...	0810	...	|	...	1037
Eisenach d.	0617	0808	0817	...	0833	...	1017	...	1100
Bebra a.	0655	...	0855	...	0910	...	1055	...	1138
Bebra d.	0705	...	0905	...	...	...	1105	...	1148
Fulda d.	0739	...	0939	...	...	...	1139	...	1228
Frankfurt/Main Hbf a.	0835	...	1035	...	...	...	1235	...	1338
Saarbrücken **725** a.	1107	...	...	...	...	...	1507	...	...

	EC 56 🍴 ♦	D§ 2758 F	IR 2550 🍷 ♦	IC 558 🍴	D§ 2756 F	IR 2152 🍷 H	IC 650 🍴	D§ 2754 F	IR 2456 🍷 C	D 1656 Z	IC 652 🍴	D§ 2752 Fh	IR 2154 🍷 ♦	IC 654 🍴	IR 2452 🍷 ♦	D§ 2750 🍷 FR	IC 656 🍷	D§ 2852 FZ	6245		IC 658 🍷 ♣	D 450 🍷 ♦	D 350 🍷 ♦	D 1954 🍷 ♦
Dresden Hbf 674 d.	0822	...	...	1022	...	...	1222	...	...	...	1422	...	...	1622	...	...	1822	...	...	...	2022	...	...	...
Dresden Neustadt **674** d.	0830	...	...	1030	...	...	1230	...	...	...	1430	...	...	1630	...	...	1830	...	...	...	2030	...	...	...
Leipzig 674 a.	0951	...	...	1151	...	...	1351	...	...	...	1551	...	...	1751	...	...	1951	...	...	...	2151	...	...	...
Leipzig d.	1004	1012	...	1204	1212	...	1404	1412	...	...	1604	1612	...	1804	...	1812	2004	2012	...	...	2204	0035	...	...
Halle **670** d.	|	|	...	|	|	1248	|	|	...	...	|	|	1648	|	...	|	|	|	2105	...	|	|	0125	0216
Naumburg d.	|	1043	...	|	1243	1313	|	1443	...	...	|	1643	1713	|	...	1843	|	2043	2136	...	|	|	|	|
Weißenfels d.	1041	1053	...	|	1253	1323	|	1453	...	...	|	1653	1723	|	...	1853	2041	2053	2147	...	2241	|	|	|
Chemnitz d.	|	|	0908	|	|	|	|	|	1308	...	|	|	|	|	1708	|	|	|	|	...	|	|	|	|
Glauchau d.	|	|	0933	|	|	|	|	|	1333	...	|	|	|	|	1733	|	|	|	|	...	|	|	|	|
Gera 777 d.	|	|	1025	|	|	|	|	|	1425	...	|	|	|	|	1825	|	|	|	|	...	|	|	|	|
Jena West **777** d.	|	|	1105	|	|	|	|	|	1505	...	|	|	|	|	1905	|	|	|	|	...	|	|	|	|
Weimar **670 777** d.	|	1121	1130	|	1321	1349	|	1521	1530	1643	1706	1722	1749	|	1930	1921	2108	2121	2229	...	2308	0138	|	0311
Erfurt 670 777 a.	1122	1138	1146	1322	1338	1405	1522	1538	1546	1659	1722	1739	1805	1922	1946	1938	2124	2138	2246	...	2324	0155	0234	0328
Erfurt d.	1134	...	1149	1334	...	1415	1534	...	1549	1702	1734	...	1815	1934	1949	...	...	...	...	...	...	0207	0246	0339
Gotha d.	|	...	1210	|	...	1437	|	...	1610	1723	|	...	1837	|	2010	...	...	...	...	...	...	0232	|	|
Eisenach d.	1217	...	1233	1417	...	1500	1617	...	1633	1747	1817	...	1900	2017	2033	...	...	...	...	...	...	0256	|	0424
Bebra a.	1255	...	1310	1455	...	1538	1655	...	1710	1822	1855	...	1938	2055	2110	...	...	...	...	...	...	0338	0408	0501
Bebra d.	1305	...	...	1505	...	1548	1705	...	...	1832	1905	...	1948	2105	...	...	...	...	...	...	...	0350	0441	0512
Fulda d.	1339	...	...	1539	...	1628	1739	...	...	1914	1939	...	2028	2139	...	...	...	...	...	...	...	0430	0515	0550
Frankfurt/Main Hbf a.	1435	...	...	1635	...	1738	1835	...	...	2026	2035	...	2138	2235	...	...	...	...	...	...	...	0600	0620	0703
Saarbrücken **725** a.	1707	...	...	1907	...	...	2107	...	...	...	2107	...	...	...	...	...	...	...	...	...	...	...	...	...

♦ – **NOTES** (LISTED BY TRAIN NUMBERS)

- **EC56/7** – HEINRICH HEINE – [12] and 🍴 Paris Est - Dresden and v.v.
- **D350/1** – ARKONA – daily from Stralsund and Basel (extended to/from Binz on ⑥ Apr. 8 - May 27 also Apr. 14, 17, May 25, **not** Apr. 15: 🛏 1,2 cl., ▬ 2 cl. and [2] Stralsund/Binz - Halle - Basel SBB and v.v; 🛏 1,2 cl., ▬ 2 cl. and [2] Stralsund/Binz - Bebra (**D482/3**) - München and v.v.
- **D450/1** – 🛏 1,2 cl., ▬ 2 cl., [12] and 🍷 Warszawa Wschodnia - Wroclaw - Görlitz - Dresden - Frankfurt/Main and v.v; ▬ 2 cl. and [2] Kraków - Frankfurt and v.v; 🛏 1,2 cl. Moskva - Frankfurt and v.v.
- **IC556** – [12] and 🍴 Dresden (Leipzig on Dec. 25) - Saarbrücken.
- **IC557** – [12] and 🍴 Saarbrücken - Dresden (Leipzig on Dec. 24).
- **IC657** – ANDREAS SCHUBERT – [12] and 🍷 Frankfurt/Main - Dresden.
- **D1954/5** – 🛏 1,2 cl., ▬ 2 cl., [12] and 🍷 Frankfurt/Main - Berlin and v.v.
- **IR2077** – [12] Flensburg - Erfurt.
- **IR2151** – [12] and 🍷 Frankfurt/Main - Berlin Lichtenberg.
- **IR2154** – **Not** Dec. 25: [12] and 🍷 Berlin Lichtenberg - Erfurt. Extended to Frankfurt on ⑦, **not** Dec. 25, Apr. 30, May 1.
- **IR2452** – [12] and 🍷 Chemnitz - Paderborn. **Not** Dec. 24, 31.
- **IR2453** – [12] and 🍷 Paderborn - Chemnitz. **Not** Dec. 25, Jan. 1.
- **IR2550** – [12] and 🍷 Chemnitz (Erfurt on Dec. 25) - Düsseldorf.
- **IR2551** – [12] and 🍷 Düsseldorf - Chemitz (Erfurt on Dec. 24).
- **IR2554** – **Not** Dec. 25, Jan. 1: [12] Erfurt (Chemnitz ① - ⑥, **not** Dec. 26, Apr. 15 - 17, May 1) - Düsseldorf; 🍷 Erfurt - Düsseldorf.
- **IR2650** – ① - ⑥, **not** Dec. 26, Apr. 17, May 1: [12] and 🍷 Halle - Erfurt.
- **IR2651** – ① - ⑤, **not** Dec. 26, Apr. 17: [12] and 🍷 Erfurt - Halle.
- **D2759** – **Not** Dec. 24: [12] Erfurt - Cottbus; [12] Erfurt - Frankfurt/Oder (**Z**).
- **D2854** – [12] Frankfurt/Oder - Erfurt. Starts at Cottbus on Dec. 26, Apr. 16, 17, May 1, and at Leipzig on Dec. 25, Jan. 1.
- **D2855** – **Not** Dec. 24, 31: [12] Erfurt - Cottbus (Frankfurt/Oder ① - ⑥, **not** Dec. 26, Apr. 15 - 17, May 1). On Dec. 24, 31 runs Erfurt - Leipzig only.
- **D2857** – [12] Erfurt - Leipzig daily except Dec. 24, 25; [12] Erfurt - Cottbus (**Z**).
- **C** – [12] and 🍷 Düsseldorf - Chemnitz and v.v.
- **F** – [12] Erfurt - Cottbus and v.v.
- **H** – [12] and 🍷 Frankfurt/Main - Berlin Lichtenberg and v.v.
- **K** – ⑤, also Apr. 13, May 24, **not** Dec. 30, Apr. 14, May 26.
- **L** – [12] Frankfurt/Main - Gera.
- **Q** – **Not** Dec. 24.
- **R** – **Not** Dec. 24, 25.
- **S** – **Not** Dec. 24, 31.
- **Z** – ⑦, also Dec. 26, Apr. 17, May 1, **not** Dec. 25, Apr. 16, 30.
- **h** – **Not** Dec. 24.
- ❖ – **Not** Dec. 25, Jan. 1.
- ⚡ – ① - ⑥ (**not** Dec. 25 - Jan. 1, Apr. 15 - 17, May 1, **1995**).
- ♣ – Daily except ⑥ (**not** Dec. 24 - 31, Apr. 14 - 16, Apr. 30, **1995**).
- § – These express trains will become InterRegio (**IR**) during 1994.

Table 777　OTHER SERVICES IN THE LEIPZIG, CHEMNITZ AND DRESDEN AREAS

Rail service Leipzig - Gera and v.v.　72 km.　Journey time: 70 minutes (semi-fast), 1 hour 40 (slow - 2 class only).
From Leipzig:　(semi-fast) – 0756, 0956, 1156, 1356, 1556, 1756, 1956, 2115 (not Dec. 24 - **IC807**);　(slow) – 0432, 0525 **Y**, 0632, 0832, 1032, 1232, 1432, 1632, 1832, 2032, 2313 **T**.
From Gera:　(semi-fast) – 0539 (not Dec. 25 - **IC808**) 0723, 0923, 1123, 1323, 1523, 1723, 1923 **S**, 2123 **T**;　(slow) – 0521 **Y**, 0628, 0828, 1028, 1228, 1428, 1628, 1828, 2227.

Rail service Saalfeld - Gera and v.v.　67 km.　Journey time: 67 minutes (semi-fast), 1 hour 47 (slow - 2 class only).
From Saalfeld:　(semi-fast) – 0613, 0907, 1107, 1307, 1507, 1707, 1907, 2107, 2200 ⊀;　(slow) – 0658, 0933, 1133, 1333, 1524, 1815, 1931 **S**.
From Gera:　(semi-fast) – 0649 ⁄, 0743, 0938, 1138, 1338, 1538, 1738, 1938, 2112 **S**;　(slow) – 0849, 1020, 1221, 1441, 1604, 1835, 2019 Ⓐ, 2228.

Local trains Erfurt - Gera and v.v.　89 km.　Journey time: 90 minutes.　Trains call at Weimar and Jena West 16 and 36 minutes from Erfurt, 41 and 61 minutes from Gera. See also Table **775**.
From Erfurt:　0715, 0842, 1242, 1516 Ⓑ (not Dec. 25, Apr. 14, 16, 30), 1642, 1741, 1842⊀ (2 class only), 2042 **S**, 2231.
From Gera:　0441 (2 class only), 0514 ❖, 0750, 0911, 1150, 1311 (2 class only), 1709 (2 class only), 1932, 2111.

Rail service Leipzig - Chemnitz and v.v.　87 km.　Journey time; 1 hour 24 - 1 hour 40.　1, 2 class.
From Leipzig:　0454, 0628, 0654, 0828, 0854, 1028, 1054, 1228, 1428, 1628, 1654, 1828, 1854, 2028, 2228 Ⓐ.
From Chemnitz:　0641, 0739, 0841, 0939, 1041, 1139, 1241, 1339, 1441, 1539, 1641, 1739, 1841, 1939, 2041, 2139.

Rail service Leipzig - Zwickau and v.v.　90 km.　Journey time: 74 minutes.　1, 2 class.　**From Zwickau:**　0420 ❖, 0620, 0820, 1020, 1220, 1420, 1620, 1820, 2020.
From Leipzig:　0613, 0813, 1013, 1213, 1413, 1613, 1813, 2013, 2213 **S**.

Rail service Leipzig - Dresden.　134 km.　1, 2 class.　A frequent S-Bahn service also operates between Dresden and Meißen and v.v. for most of the day.
All trains call at Döbeln (66 km, journey time 1 hour 7 minutes from both Leipzig and Dresden), and Meißen (107 km, journey time 1 hour 54 minutes from Leipzig, 24 minutes from Dresden).
From Leipzig:　0618, 0818, 1018, 1218, 1418, 1618, 1818, 2018.　**From Dresden Hbf:**　0458, 0704, 0901, 1101, 1301, 1501, 1701, 1901.

Additional notes for Table 777:
IC807/8 –　🚃 Berlin Hbf - Gera and v.v; ✗ Berlin - Leipzig and v.v.
S –　Not Dec. 24, 31.
T –　Not Dec. 24, 25, 31.

Y –　Not Dec. 25, 26, Jan. 1.　　❖ –　Not Dec. 25, Jan. 1.
⁄ –　① - ⑥ (not Dec. 25 - Jan. 1, Apr. 15 - 17, May 1, **1995**).
⊀ –　Daily except ⑥ (not Dec. 24 - 31, Apr. 14 - 16, Apr. 30, **1995**).

Table 778　　NÜRNBERG - BAYREUTH　　　1, 2 class

km		0549	0649	0749	and at the	2149	2249	2349		0510	0610	0710	and at the	2010	2110	2210
0	Nürnberg ...... d.	0549	0649	0749	and at the	2149	2249	2349	Bayreuth ...... d.	0510	0610	0710	and at the	2010	2110	2210
28	Hersbruck (rechts Pegnitz) ...... d.	0606	0706	0806	same minutes	2206	2306	0006	Pegnitz ...... a.	0528	0628	0728	same minutes	2028	2128	2228
67	Pegnitz ...... d.	0630	0730	0830	past each	2230	2330	0030	Hersbruck (rechts Pegnitz) ...... d.	0552	0652	0752	past each	2052	2152	2252
94	Bayreuth ...... a.	0646	0746	0846	hour until:	2246	2346	0046	Nürnberg ...... a.	0609	0709	0809	hour until:	2109	2209	2309

Table 779　　MÜNCHEN - REGENSBURG - NÜRNBERG　　　1, 2 class

km		IC 822 ⁄✗🍽	IR 2606 🍽	E 3032	IR 2063 🍽	E 3034	IC 688 🍽	IR 2065 🍽	E 3036	IR 2602 🍽	E 3038	EC 167 ✗		IR 2067 🍽	E 3046	IR 2069 🍽	E 3050	IR 2165 🍽	E 3054	E 3486 ⊀🍽	IR 2167 🍽	E 3056	D 1961 🍽	IR 2169 🍽
				C		C		C		C				C				C						
0	München Hbf 783 ... d.	...	...	0657	0748	0857	0948	...	1057	1148	1257	1348	1408	...	1457	1548	1657	1748	1857	1948	...	2057	2148	2308	2328
42	Freising 783 ...... d.	...	...	0721	0811	0921	1011	...	1121	1211	1321	1411	...	...	1521	1611	1721	1811	1921	2011	...	2121	2211	2331	2351
76	Landshut 783 ...... d.	...	...	0741	0831	0941	1031	...	1141	1231	1341	1431	1450	...	1541	1631	1741	1831	1941	2031	...	2141	2231	2354	0011
138	Regensburg ...... a.	...	...	0820	0913	1020	1113	...	1220	1313	1420	1513	1529	...	1620	1713	1820	1913	2020	2113	...	2220	2313	0034	0050
138	Regensburg 740 ...... d.	0623	...	0916	...	1116	1127	...	1316	...	1516	...	...	...	1716	...	1916	...	2120	2200	...	...	...	...
202	Neumarkt (Oberpfalz)... d.	0702	...	0959	...	1159	1207	...	1359	...	1559	...	...	...	1759	...	1959	...	2218	2242	...	...	...	...
239	Nürnberg 740 ...... a.	0725	...	1021	...	1221	1232	...	1421	...	1621	...	...	...	1821	...	2021	...	2254	2306	...	...	...	...

		IR 2166 ⁄🍽	E 3031	E 3033	E 3461	IR 2164 🍽	E 3035	IR 2068 🍽	E 3037	IR 2066 🍽	EC 166 ✗	E 3039	IR 2603 🍽	E 3041	IC 689 🍽	E 3043	IR 2064 🍽	E 3045	IR 2062 🍽	E 3049	IR 2607 🍽	E 3053	IR 2160 ⊀🍽	IR 2162 ⊀🍽	E 3057	IC 625 ⊀🍽	D 1960 🍽
			L		L		C		C		C		C		C		C		C		C		F	C		F	
	Nürnberg 740 ...... d.	...	...	0623	...	0737	...	0937	...	...	...	1137	...	...	1328	1337	...	1537	...	1737	...	1937	...	...	2137	2230	...
	Neumarkt (Oberpfalz).. d.	...	...	0649	...	0759	...	0959	...	...	1159	...	...	1351	1359	...	1559	...	1759	...	1959	...	...	2159	2254	...
	Regensburg 740 ...... a.	...	...	0733	...	0841	...	1041	...	...	1241	...	...	1431	1441	...	1641	...	1841	...	2041	...	...	2241	2334	...
	Regensburg ...... d.	0546	0604	0700	...	0737	0844	0937	1044	1137	1233	1244	1337	...	1444	1537	1644	1737	1844	1937	2044	2137	2150	2244	...	0445
	Landshut 783 ...... d.	0627	0651	0745	...	0817	0928	1017	1128	1217	1311	1328	1417	...	1528	1617	1728	1817	1928	2017	2128	2217	2228	2326	...	0532
	Freising 783 ...... d.	0647	0714	0807	...	0836	0947	1036	1147	1236		1347	1436	...	1547	1636	1747	1846	1947	2036	2147	2236	2248	...	...	0554
	München Hbf 783 ...... a.	0712	0740	0831	...	0901	1011	1101	1211	1301	1351	1413	1501	...	1611	1701	1811	1901	2011	2101	2211	2301	2312	...	...	0619

C –　To or from Coburg, Table 770.
F –　⑥, also Dec. 24 - 31, Apr. 14 - 16, 30.
L –　✗, not Nov. 1, Jan. 6.

S –　Not Dec. 24, 31.
⁄ –　① - ⑥ (not Dec. 25 - Jan. 1, Apr. 15 - 17, May 1, **1995**).
⊀ –　Daily except ⑥ (not Dec. 24 - 31, Apr. 14 - 16, Apr. 30, **1995**).

Table 780　　REGENSBURG and NÜRNBERG - DRESDEN　　1, 2 class except where shown
Engineering work taking place between Plauen and Hof in November and May will affect services.

km		IR 2376 🍽	E 4405	IR 2061 ⁄🍽	E 4407	IR 2661 ⁄🍽	E 2161 🍽	IR 2663 ⁄🍽	IR 2606 🍽	IR 2663 ⁄🍽	E 5910	IR 2465 🍽	IR 2063 🍽	IR 2467 🍽	E 2065 🍽	E 4415	D 1669	366	IR 2669 🍽	IR 2602 🍽	E 6366	D 4417	IR 1667 🍽	IR 2561
		♦		⁄		⁄	✗	♦		♦		H		H			A	2	♦		M	A		
	München Hbf 779 ... d.	...	...	...	...	...	0657	...	...	...	0857	...	1057	...	...	...	1257	...	1428	...				
0	Regensburg ...... d.	...	...	...	...	0631	...	0831	...	0918	0952	1031	1231	...	...	...	1431	...	1601	...				
42	Schwandorf ...... d.	...	...	...	...	0659	...	0859	...	0952	1059	1259	...	...	...	1459	...	1629	...					
86	Weiden ...... d.	...	...	...	...	0729	...	0929	...	1033	1129	1329	...	...	...	1529	...	1658	...					
	Nürnberg 781 ...... d.	...	...	...	0634	0834		1034	1234		...	...	1354	...	1434	...	...	...	...	1634				
137	Marktredwitz 781 ... d.	...	...	...	0756	0807	0956	1007	1118	1156	1207	1356	1407	...	1556	1607	...	1740	1756					
179	Hof ...... a.	...	...	...	0826	0836	1026	1037	1156	1226	1237	1426	1437	...	1626	1637	...	1808	1826					
179	Hof ...... d.	...	...	0639	...	0840		1029	1039		...	1239	...	1439	...	1556	1629	1639	...	1811				
228	Plauen ...... d.	...	0543	0719	...	0919		1109	1119	⁄	...	1319	...	1519	...	1635	1700	1709	1719	1753	...	1851		
252	Reichenbach ...... d.	...	0605	0742	...	0942	E	1132	1142	1132	E	1342	E	1542	...	1658	1724	1732	1742t	1815	...	1914		
252	Reichenbach ...... d.	...	0616	0751	...	0951	4409	1156	1145	1156	4411	1351	4413	1551	...	1709	1745	1755	1824	...	1923			
	Leipzig ▲ ...... a.	...	...	...	...	...	2	→	1305				2	...	...	...	1915	⁄						
275	Zwickau ...... d.	...	0644	0714	0818	0914	1018	1114		1218	1314		1418	1514	1618	1714	1733	...	1818	...	1843	1914	1943	
291	Glauchau ...... d.	...	0657	0726	0831	0926	1031	1126		1231	1326		1431	1526	1631	1726	1745	...	1831	...	...	1926	1957	
324	Chemnitz ...... d.	...	0726	0753	0858	0953	1058	1153		1258	1353		1458	1553	1659	1753	1812	...	1858	...	...	1953	2026	
363	Freiberg (Sachs) ...... d.	...	0757	0829	0929	1029	1129	1229		1329	1429		1529	1629	1732	1829	1844	...	1929	...	...	2029	2057	
403	Dresden Hbf ...... a.	...	0833	0907	1001	1107	1206	1307		1406	1507		1606	1707	1807	1907	1924	...	2006	...	...	2107	2134	

♦ –　NOTES (LISTED BY TRAIN NUMBERS)
D366 –　🚃 Karlovy Vary - Berlin for train **IR2602** at Reichenbach.
IR2063 –　🚃 and 🍽 München (Kempten ⁄) - Dresden.
IR2065 –　🚃 and 🍽 Oberstdorf - Görlitz.
IR2376 –　🚃 Plauen - Stralsund. Not Dec. 25, Jan. 1.
IR2602 –　🚃 and 🍽 Oberstdorf - Berlin Lichtenberg; conveys 🚃 Karlovy Vary -
Berlin from Reichenbach.
IR2606 –　🚃 München (Kempten ⁄) - Leipzig; 🍽 Buchloe - Leipzig.

IR2663 –　🚃 Stuttgart (Karlsruhe ⁄) - Dresden; 🍽 Stuttgart - Dresden.
IR2669 –　🚃 and 🍽 Karlsruhe - Dresden.
A –　⑤, also Apr. 13, May 24, May 26. Not Dec. 30, Apr. 14, May 26.
H –　🚃 and 🍽 Karlsruhe - Hof.
t –　Connects with 1745 to Dresden (**IR2669**).
⁄ –　① - ⑥ (not Dec. 25 - Jan. 1, Apr. 15 - 17, May 1, **1995**).
▲ –　Additional services are available to Leipzig via Zwickau (Table **777**).

Table 780 — REGENSBURG and NÜRNBERG - DRESDEN

1, 2 class except where shown

Engineering work taking place between Plauen and Hof in November and May will affect services.

	IR 2067 🍴	IR 2563 🍴 H	IR 2069 🍴	3589	E 5942	2165	3593	E 5944	D 1906 ♦	D 1961 ♦
München Hbf 779 d.	1457	—	1657	—	1857	—	—	—	—	2308
Regensburg d.	1631	1831	—	1917	2031	—	2118	—	—	0052
Schwandorf d.	1659	1859	—	1948	2059	—	2149	—	—	0123
Weiden d.	1729	—	1929	—	2032	2129	—	2228	—	0154
Nürnberg 781 d.	|	1834	—	1949	—	—	2149	—	0105	|
Marktredwitz 781 d.	1807	1956	2011	2107	2116	2211	2307	2314	0230	0239
Hof a.	1837	2026	2039	2130	2146	2239	2330	2344	0300	0311
Hof d.	1839	—	2041	—	—	—	—	—	0333	0344
Plauen d.	1919	—	2121	—	—	—	—	—	0412	0426
Reichenbach d.	1942	E	2144	—	—	—	—	—	0435	0450
Reichenbach d.	1951	4419	2156	—	—	—	—	—	0444	0500
Leipzig ▲ a.	—	—	—	—	—	—	—	—	—	0605
Zwickau d.	2018	2114	2218	—	—	—	—	—	—	—
Glauchau d.	2031	2126	2231	—	—	—	—	—	—	0522
Chemnitz d.	2058	2153	2255	—	—	—	—	—	—	0535
Freiberg (Sachs) d.	2129	2229	—	—	—	—	—	—	—	0604
Dresden Hbf a.	2206	2307	—	—	—	—	—	—	0637	0713

	IR 2164 ✗	3564	IR 2068 🍴	IR 2562 M	E 6363 2	IR 2066 🍴	IR 2560	E 4400	IR 2603 ♦
Dresden Hbf d.	↗	—	—	—	—	0544	—	0640	—
Freiberg (Sachs) d.	—	—	—	—	—	0623	—	0720	—
Chemnitz d.	—	—	0503	—	—	0701	—	0757	—
Glauchau d.	—	—	0527	—	—	0727	—	0822	—
Zwickau d.	—	—	0542	—	0640	0743	—	0833	—
Leipzig ▲ d.	—	—	—	—	—	—	—	—	0833
Reichenbach a.	—	—	0559	—	0656	0800	—	—	1001
Reichenbach d.	—	—	0609	—	0706	0812	—	—	1012
Plauen d.	—	—	0632	—	0727	0835	—	—	1035
Hof a.	—	—	0714	—	—	0917	—	—	1117
Hof d.	0516	0628	0716	0731	—	0919	0931	—	1119
Marktredwitz 781 d.	0553	0651	0746	0801	—	0948	1001	—	1148
Nürnberg 781 a.	—	0809	—	0924	—	—	1124	—	|
Weiden d.	0632	—	0828	—	—	1028	—	—	1228
Schwandorf d.	0700	—	0855	—	—	1055	—	—	1255
Regensburg a.	0729	—	0925	—	—	1125	—	—	1325
München Hbf 779 a.	0901	—	1101	—	—	1301	—	—	1501

	IR 2668 🍴	D 367 ♦	E 4402 F	IR 2064	IR 2466 H	E 4404	IR 2062	IR 2464 ✗	E 4406 H	IR 2662 🍴
Dresden Hbf d.	0752	—	0840	0952	—	1040	1152	—	1240	1352
Freiberg (Sachs) d.	0830	—	0920	1030	—	1120	1230	—	1320	1430
Chemnitz d.	0903	—	0957	1103	—	1157	1303	—	1357	1503
Glauchau d.	0927	—	1022	1127	—	1222	1327	—	1422	1527
Zwickau d.	0952	—	1033	1143	—	1233	1343	—	1433	1543
Leipzig ▲ d.	—	—	—	—	—	—	—	1453	←	—
Reichenbach a.	1009	—	—	1200	—	—	1400	1611	—	1600
Reichenbach d.	1022	1030	—	1212	—	—	1412	1622	—	1613
Plauen a.	1045	1118	—	1235	—	—	1435	→	—	1635
Hof a.	1128	—	—	1317	—	—	1517	—	—	1717
Hof d.	1131	—	—	1319	1331	—	1519	1531	—	1719
Marktredwitz 781 d.	1201	—	—	1348	1401	—	1548	1601	—	1748
Nürnberg 781 a.	1324	—	—	1524	—	—	1724	—	—	1924
Weiden d.	—	—	1428	—	—	1628	—	—	1828	—
Schwandorf d.	—	—	1455	—	—	1655	—	—	1855	—
Regensburg a.	—	—	1525	—	—	1725	—	—	1925	—
München Hbf 779 a.	—	—	1701	—	—	1901	—	—	2101	—

	IR 2607	IR 2662	IR 4408	IR 2160	IR 2660	D 1666 W	E 4410 F	E 4412	IR 2060	E 4414	D 317	E 4416	E 4418	D 1907	D 1960
Dresden Hbf d.	—	—	—	—	1440	1552	1640	1640	1752	1840	1936	2040	2145	—	2226
Freiberg (Sachs) d.	—	—	—	—	1520	1630	1718	1720	1830	1920	2014	2120	2225	—	2305
Chemnitz d.	—	—	—	—	1557	1703	1752	1757	1903	1957	2046	2157	2302	—	2339
Glauchau d.	—	—	—	—	1622	1727	1815	1822	1927	2022	2109	2227	2327	—	0003
Zwickau d.	—	—	—	—	1633	1743	1829	1833	1943	2033	2122	2233	2339	—	0019
Leipzig ▲ d.	—	—	—	—	—	—	—	—	—	—	2256	—	—	—	—
Reichenbach a.	—	—	—	—	1800	1846	—	—	2000	—	—	—	2138	0013	0036
Reichenbach d.	—	—	—	—	1811	1856	—	—	2012	—	—	—	2148	0023	0046
Plauen a.	1635	1645	—	—	1834	1920	3592	—	2035	—	—	—	2117	0048	0117
Hof a.	1717	1728	—	—	1916	2003	—	—	2117	—	—	—	—	0134	0157
Hof d.	1719	1731	—	1920	2008	2028	—	—	—	—	—	—	—	0218	0308
Marktredwitz 781 d.	1748	1801	—	1949	2001	2051	—	—	—	—	—	—	—	0251	0308
Nürnberg 781 a.	1924	—	—	2124	2153	2209	—	—	—	—	—	—	—	—	0435
Weiden d.	1828	—	—	2028	—	—	—	—	—	—	—	—	—	0331	—
Schwandorf d.	1855	—	—	2055	—	—	—	—	—	—	—	—	—	0401	—
Regensburg a.	1925	—	—	2125	—	—	—	—	—	—	—	—	—	0435	—
München Hbf 779 a.	2101	—	—	2301	—	—	—	—	—	—	—	—	—	0619	—

NOTES (LISTED BY TRAIN NUMBERS)

317 – 🛏 Malmö - Plauen; 🍴 Berlin - Plauen.
367 – 🛏 Berlin - Karlovy Vary from train IR2603 at Reichenbach.
1906/7 – 🛌 1,2 cl., ➡ 2 cl. and 🛏 Stuttgart - Hof (D1960/1) - Dresden Hbf and v.v.;
 ➡ 2 cl. and 🛏 Stuttgart - Hof (D1960/1) - Dresden Hbf and v.v.
1960/1 – 🛌 1,2 cl., ➡ 2 cl. and 🛏 München - Dresden Hbf and v.v.;
 ➡ 2 cl. and 🛏 München - Hof (D1906/7) - Berlin Lichtenberg and v.v.
2062 – 🛏 and 🍴 Dresden - München (Kempten ♣).
2067 – 🛏 Oberstdorf - Dresden; 🍴 Oberstdorf - Chemnitz.
2068 – 🛏 Hof (Chemnitz ✗) - Oberstdorf; 🍴 Hof - Oberstdorf.
2069 – 🛏 Oberstdorf - Hof (Chemnitz ✗); 🍴 Oberstdorf - Plauen.
2160 – 🛏 Hof - München; 🍴 Hof - Schwandorf.
2164 – 🛏 Regensburg (Hof ♣) - Oberstdorf; 🍴 Hof - Karlsruhe.
2165 – 🛏 Oberstdorf - Schwandorf (Hof ♣); 🍴 Oberstdorf - Schwandorf.

IR2603 – 🛏 and 🍴 Berlin Lichtenberg - Oberstdorf; conveys 🛏 Berlin - Karlovy Vary to Reichenbach.
IR2607 – 🛏 Leipzig - München (Kempten ♣); 🍴 Leipzig - München.
IR2660 – 🛏 Dresden - Nürnberg (Stuttgart see note W); 🍴 Dresden - Nürnberg.
IR2662 – 🛏 Dresden - Stuttgart (Karlsruhe ✗); 🍴 Dresden - Aalen.
IR2668 – 🛏 and 🍴 Görlitz - Karlsruhe.
F – 🛏 and 🍴 Dresden - Oberstdorf.
G – 4 - 10 minutes later when train D1666 runs.
H – 🛏 and 🍴 Hof - Karlsruhe.
M – 🛏 Zwickau - Plauen - Bad Brambach - Mariánské Lázne and v.v.
W – ⑦, also Apr. 17, May 1, not Apr. 16, 30.
① - ⑥ (not Dec. 25 - Jan. 1, Apr. 15 - 17, May 1, 1995).
♣ – Daily except ⑥ (not Dec. 24 - 31, Apr. 14 - 16, Apr. 30, 1995).
▲ – Additional services are available to/from Leipzig via Zwickau (Table 777).

Full service Bad Brambach ▥ - Plauen (2 class only): 0617, 0817, 1017, 1217, 1417, 1558 (D366), 1617, 1650 (M), 1817, 2017.
Plauen - Bad Brambach (2 class only): 0638, 0727 (M), 0838, 1038, 1118 (D367), 1238, 1438, 1638, 1838, 2038.

Table 781 — NÜRNBERG - CHEB

1, 2 class except where shown

km		D357 ♀	D353 ♦	E7381 2	7409	3507	IC169 ✗	7411	D259 1713 K		3511	6511	EC51 ♦✗	3515	E7383 2	3519	E6515		3521 ♦✗	EC167	3523	E7385 2	3529	3533
0	Nürnberg d.	0025	0240	—	—	0744	0755	—	K		0944	—	1135	1144	—	1344	—		1444	—	1544	—	1844	2044
	Regensburg 780 d.																			1538				
	Schwandorf a.	|	|	0841	0902	—	—	1041	—		1241	1441	—	—	—	1541	1607	1641	—	—	1941	1943
	Schwandorf d.			0850	0904	—	—	1045	1253		—	1446	—	—	—	1615	1703	—	—	1950	2153
	Cham a.			0919	—	—	1133	1326	—		1526	—	—	1732	—	—	2023	2222
	Furth im Wald ▥ a.			0640	1002b	1105	—	1715b
	Ceská Kubice a.			0657	1030b	1119	—	1743b
	Domažlice a.			0732	1043	1133	—	1756
125	Marktredwitz d.	0200	0426	0811	—	1011	—	1254	1411	—	1811
139	Schirnding d.	0214	0440	0826	—	1024	—	1426	—	1826
152	Cheb a.	0229	0455	0839	—	1037	—	1321	1439	—	1839
	Plzeň 870 a.	0425	0650	0857	1136	1249	1503	1848
	Praha Hlavni 870 a.	0611	0839	1326	1503v	1613n	1645

km		7400 Q✗	3508	E7380 2	7406	7452 2	3516	D258 K	EC166 ♦	3518	E7382	3524	3528	EC50 P	7414	7456 2	6518 P	3530	E7384 2	3532	IC168 ✗	D352	7424	D356
	Praha Hlavni 870 d.			—	0420	—	—	0623	0723	—	—	1308	1122	—	—	1623	2050	2352
0	Pizeň 870 d.	0354		0636	—	0913	—	1446	1436	—	1811	2241	2244	0148
	Cheb d.	0712	1113	1512	1632	—	1912	—	0053	0347
	Schirnding d.	0727	1128	1527	—	1927	—	0110	0404
	Marktredwitz d.	0740	1140	1540	1701	—	1940	—	0126	0422
59	Domažlice d.	0519	0542	0801	0820	1008	—	1624	1629	—	1915	0010
70	Ceská Kubice d.	0557	0836	1035b	—	1644	—	1943b
82	Furth im Wald ▥ d.	0613	0846	1024	1100b	1424	—	1654	1710	—	1824	2008b
101	Cham d.	0625	3512	1036	—	3520	1436	—	1733	—	1836
	Schwandorf a.	0653	1104	1143	1504	—	1808	—	1904	2050
149	Schwandorf d.	0711	0911	1111	1151	1211	1311	1511	1711	—	1811	—	1911	2052
	Regensburg 780 a.	1221
243	Nürnberg a.	0814	1014	—	1214	—	1314	1414	1614	1814	1819	—	1914	—	2014	2203	0250	0547

EC50 – KARLSTEIN – 🛏 Praha - Dortmund; ✗ Praha - Köln.
EC51 – KARLSTEIN – 🛏 and ✗ Dortmund - Praha.
EC167 – ALBERT EINSTEIN – 🛏 and ✗ Interlaken Ost - Praha.
EC168 – ALBERT EINSTEIN – 🛏 and ✗ Praha - Bern.
852/3 – 🛌 1,2 cl. ➡ 2 cl., 🛏 and 🍴 Köln - Praha and v.v.
856/7 – 🛌 1,2 cl. ➡ 2 cl., 🛏 and 🍴 Stuttgart - Praha and v.v.

K – 🛏 Praha - Karlovy Vary - Marktredwitz and v.v.
P – Ⓐ, not Nov. 1, Jan. 6.
b – Arrive 15 minutes earlier.
n – Praha Holešovice.
v – Praha Smichov.

Table 782 CHEMNITZ - FLÖHA - VEJPRTY - CHOMUTOV

2 class only

No service Cranzahl - Vejprty - Chomutov on Dec. 24, 25, 26, 31, Jan. 1.

km		E3911	5867 Ⓐ	5869	5871 Ⓐ	5873	5875	5879	5881 Ⓒ	5883	5885
	Chemnitz d.	0641	0734	0817	...	1017	1217	1417	1617	1717	1823
0	**Flöha** d.	0656	0750	0839	...	1039	1236	1435	1634	1734	1838
51	Cranzahl ▲ d.	0811	0934	1006	1022	1208	1408	1607	1802	1909	2008
61	Bärenstein d.	0828	...	...	1041	▬	1427	1626	...	1928	...
63	**Vejprty** a.	0831	...	...	1044	...	1430	1629	...	1931	...
		16805			**16807**	**16809**		**16811**		**16813**	
63	**Vejprty** 🛃 d.	0849	...	...	1129	1333	...	1702	...	1944	...
121	**Chomutov** a.	1027	...	...	1310	1512	...	1850	...	2126	...

	16800	16802	5872 Ⓐ	5874	16804	16806	5880	5882	16808	16810
Chomutov d.	0548	0740	...	...	1140	1344	...	...	1715	1955
Vejprty 🛃 a.	0733	0924	...	...	1323	1528	...	...	1859	2138
	5868	**5870**			▬	**E3912**			**5886**	
Vejprty d.	0743	0947	1105	...	**5876**	1545	1639	...	1951	...
Bärenstein d.	0749	0953	1111	...	...	1551	1645	...	1957	...
Cranzahl ▲ d.	0812	1011	1127	1220	1409	1606	1702	1813	2014	...
Flöha a.	0936	1136	...	1347	1533	1732	1833	1947	2138	...
Chemnitz a.	0955	1155	...	1406	1555	1745	1851	2002	2155	...

▲ – Narrow gauge steam hauled services operate between Cranzahl and Kurort Oberwiesenthal.
From Cranzahl: 0531 Ⓐ, 0656, 0812, 1023, 1223, 1420, 1609, 1819, 2037. **From Oberwiesenthal**: 0401 Ⓐ, 0502, 0651, 0907, 1018 Ⓐ, 1053 Ⓒ, 1300, 1457, 1707, 1917.

Table 783 MÜNCHEN - PASSAU

1, 2 class

km		E 3066	E 3068	E 3072	E 3076	E 3080 Ⓑ	E 3082 L	E 3084	E 3086 L	E 3088	E 3092
0	**München Hbf 779** d.	0728	0928	1128	1328	1528	1607	1728	1808	1928	2128
42	Freising **779** d.	0752	0952	1152	1352	1552	1633	1752	1832	1952	2152
76	Landshut **779** d.	0815	1015	1215	1415	1615	1702	1815	1902	2015	2215
121	Landau (Isar) d.	0842	1042	1242	1442	1642	1737	1842	1937	2042	2244
139	Plattling **740** d.	0856	1056	1256	1456	1656	1756	1856	1956	2056	2259
191	**Passau 740** 🛃 a.	0932	1132	1332	1532	1732	1832	1932	2032	2132	2335

	E 3061 L	E 3063	E 3065	E 3067	E 3071	E 3075	E 3079 Ⓑ	E 3083	E 3087
Passau 740 🛃 d.	0445	0610	0823	1023	1223	1423	1623	1823	2023
Plattling **740** d.	0523	0649	0901	1101	1301	1501	1701	1901	2101
Landau (Isar) d.	0538	0704	0913	1113	1313	1513	1713	1913	2113
Landshut **779** d.	0611	0743	0944	1144	1344	1544	1744	1944	2144
Freising **779** d.	0634	0807	1007	1207	1407	1607	1807	2007	2207
München Hbf 779 a.	0700	0831	1031	1231	1431	1631	1831	2031	2231

L – ⚒, **not** Nov. 1, Jan. 6.

Table 784 PLATTLING - BAYERISCH EISENSTEIN - PLZEŇ

2 class only

km		7468	7472	7476	7480	7482	7484	IC889 N	7488	IC929 M	7492
0	**Plattling** d.	0700	0908	1108	1308	1408	1508	1525	1708	1750	1808
58	Zwiesel d.	0811	1011	1211	1411	1511	1611	1629	1811	1844	1914
72	**Bayerisch Eisenstein** 🛃 d.	0825	1025	1225	1425	1525	1625	▬	1825	...	1928
		7501	**7503**	**7557** Ⓐ	**7505**	**7507** A	**7555** Ⓐ		**7511**		**7573**
72	**Bayerisch Eisenstein** 🛃 d.	0844	1102	1232	1502	1602	1656	**7533**	1835	...	1935
76	Železná Ruda Město ▲ d.	0857	1113	1243	1514	1617	1708	...	1846	...	1945
131	Klatovy d.	1009	1223	1447h	1634	1738	1817	1830	1951	...	2011
170	**Plzeň** a.	1117	1340	1557	1750	1842	...	1946	2102	...	...

	7502 Ⓐ	IC928 M	IC888 N	7504 Ⓒ	7506	7510	7524 Ⓐ	7512	7514	7530
Plzeň d.	0531	...	...	0618	0812	1050	1225	1510	1640	1904
Klatovy d.	0713	...	...	0713	0920	1214	1450v	1641	1739	2022
Železná Ruda Město ▲ d.	0820	...	...	0821	1038	1327	1559	1750	1859	2142z
Bayerisch Eisenstein 🛃 a.	0829	...	...	0830	1047	1336	1608	1759	1908	...
	7471			**7473**	**7477**	**7483**	**7487**	**7493**	**7495**	
Bayerisch Eisenstein 🛃 d.	0834	...	...	0934	1134	1434	1634	1837	1937	...
Zwiesel d.	0848	0910	0923	0948	1148	1448	1648	1851	1951	...
Plattling a.	0948	1006	1030	1048	1248	1548	1748	1948	2051	...

A – ⑥⑦ (**not** Dec. 24, 31).
M – ⑥ only: (2) Hamburg Altona - Zwiesel and v.v.
N – (2) Hamburg Altona - Zwiesel and v.v.
h – Arrive 1344.
v – Arrive 1335.
z – **Not** Dec. 24, 25, 31.
▲ – Eisenstein Stadt.

Table 785 MÜNCHEN - MITTENWALD - INNSBRUCK

1, 2 class

km	*German Train Number*		D1015	E3603	E3605	E3607	E3609	E3611	E3613	E3615	E3617	E3619	⁄585	IC119	E3621	E3623	E3627	IC813	E3629	E3631	E3633	E3635	E3637	E3639
	Austrian Train Number	E5401		E5403	5405	E5407		E5411	5413	E5415	5417	E5419		E119	5421	E5423			E5429					
		⚒	N🍷										F✕	A✕	G			H✕	M			S	S	S
0	**München Hbf** d.	...	0457	0554	0659	0800	0900	1000	1100	1200	1300	1400	1443	1421	1500	1600	1700	1718	1800	1900	2000	2100	2200	2300
7	München Pasing d.	...	|	0601	0706	0807	0907	1007	1107	1207	1307	1407	|	|	1507	1607	1707	|	1807	1907	2007	2107	2207	2307
54	Weilheim d.	...	0536	0635	0739	0839	0939	1038	1139	1239	1339	1439	|	1456	1539	1639	1739	1757	1839	1939	2039	2139	2239	2339
75	Murnau d.	...	0553	0658	0758	0854	0958	1054	1158	1254	1358	1454	|	1522	1558	1654	1758	1821	1858	1958	2054	2158	2254	2358
101	**Garmisch-Partenkirchen** a.	...	0620	0723	0823	0916	1023	1116	1223	1316	1423	1516	1601	1551	1623	1716	1823	1848	1923	2023	2116	2223	2316	0023
101	**Garmisch-Partenkirchen** d.	0626	0637	0726	0826	0926	1026	1126	1226	1326	1426	1526	...	1606	1626	1726	1826	1904	1926	2026	2126	2226	2326	...
118	**Mittenwald** d.	0650	0703	0748	0848	0948	1046	1148	1248	1348	1448	1548	...	1639	1704n	1748	1846	1931	1959c	2046	2146	2246	2346	...
125	Scharnitz 🛃 d.	0658	0712	0756	0857	0955	...	1155	1257	1355	1457	1555	...	1652	1712	1755	...	...	2007	...	...	...	...	...
135	Seefeld in Tirol d.	0712	0727	0809	0910	1008	...	1208	1311	1408	1511	1608	...	1706	1726	1808	...	...	2017	...	...	...	...	...
160	**Innsbruck Hbf** a.	0747	0801	0846	0948	1039	...	1241	1348	1441	1548	1643	...	1746	1804	1842	...	...	2054	...	...	...	...	...

Austrian Train Number					E5410		5412		E5414	E118		E5418	5420	E5422	5424	E5426	5428	E5430		E5442	E5434			5438
German Train Number	E3600	E3602	E3606	E3608	E3610	IC812	E3612	⁄588	E3614	IC118	E3616	E3618	E3620	E3622	E3624	E3626	E3628	E3630	E3632		E3634	D1014	E3636	E3638
	J	L				H✕		F✕		A✕										Ⓐ		P🍷	S	
Innsbruck Hbf d.	...	...	...	...	0707	...	0759	...	0907	0943	...	1107	1200	1307	1400	1507	1600	1705	...	1835	1907	1949	...	2105
Seefeld in Tirol d.	...	...	...	...	0742	...	0840	...	0941	1021	...	1141	1239	1342	1439	1541	1639	1740	...	1912	1940	2023	...	2142
Scharnitz 🛃 d.	...	...	...	...	0755	...	0855	...	0955	1033	...	1155	1255	1355	1455	1555	1655	1755	...	1925	1952	2035	...	2155
Mittenwald d.	...	...	0556	0703	0803	0848	0903	...	1003	1048	1103	1203	1303	1403	1503	1603	1703	1803	1903	1932	2003	2048	2103	2203
Garmisch-Partenkirchen a.	...	...	0617	0724	0824	0909	0924	...	1024	1109	1124	1224	1324	1424	1524	1624	1724	1824	1924	...	2024	2108	2124	2224
Garmisch-Partenkirchen d.	0450	0534	0627	0734	0827	0919	0934	0953	1027	1119	1134	1227	1334	1427	1534	1627	1734	1831	1934	...	2027	2118	2134	2227
Murnau d.	0517	0558	0654	0758	0854	0942	0958	|	1054	1142	1158	1254	1358	1454	1558	1654	1800	1858	1958	...	2054	2142	2158	2254
Weilheim d.	0536	0613	0713	0813	0913	1002	1013	|	1113	1202	1213	1313	1413	1513	1613	1714	1815	1916	2013	...	2113	2203	2213	2313
München Pasing a.	0606	0645	0745	0844	0944	|	1044	|	1144	|	1244	1344	1444	1544	1644	1745	1845	1946	2044	...	2144	|	2244	2344
München Hbf a.	0614	0653	0753	0852	0952	1038	1052	1117	1152	1239	1252	1352	1452	1552	1652	1753	1853	1954	2052	...	2152	2243.	2252	2352

A – (12) and ✕ Dortmund - Innsbruck and v.v.
F – ⑥: (12) and ✕ Hamburg Altona - Garmisch-Partenkirchen and v.v.
G – (12) München - Mittenwald (Innsbruck on Ⓐ, **not** Nov. 1, Jan. 6).
H – (12) and ✕ Berlin Hbf - Saalfeld - München - Mittenwald and v.v.
J – Ⓐ, **not** Nov. 1, Jan. 6.
L – ⚒, **not** Nov. 1, Jan. 6.
M – Through train to Innsbruck on Ⓒ also Nov. 1, 16, Jan. 6, Apr. 14, **not** Dec. 8; on other days **change trains** at Mittenwald.
N – ⑤ Jan. 6 - Apr. 7, also Dec. 16, 22, 25, Jan. 4 (from Dortmund): 🛏 2 cl., (2) and 🍷 Dortmund - Innsbruck; conveys to Mar. 17: 🛏 1,2 cl. Dortmund - Garmisch.
P – ⑥ Jan. 7 - Apr. 8, also Dec. 23, Jan. 1, 5: 🛏 2 cl., (2) and 🍷 Innsbruck - Dortmund; conveys to Mar. 18: 🛏 1,2 cl. Garmisch - Dortmund.
S – **Not** Dec. 24, 31.
c – Arrive 10 minutes earlier.
n – Arrive 1646.
⁄ – InterCity Express service (**ICE**). Premium fare payable.

Table 786 MURNAU - OBERAMMERGAU

1, 2 class

Rail service Murnau - Oberammergau and v.v. *24 km.* Journey time: 41 minutes.
From Murnau: 0607 **P** 🚌, 0701, 0807, 0857, 1007, 1057, 1207, 1309, 1407, 1507, 1607, 1607, 1707, 1807, 1907, 2007, 2107 **S**, 2207 **A**, 2307 **S**.
From Oberammergau: 0506 **P** 🚌, 0607, 0700, 0807, 0857, 1007, 1057, 1207, 1309, 1407, 1507, 1610, 1709, 1807, 1907, 2007 **S**, 2107 **S**, 2207 **S**, 2307 ⑦.
A – ⑤⑥⑦ and holidays, also Nov. 1, **not** Dec. 24, 31. P – Ⓐ, **not** Nov. 1, Jan. 6. S – **Not** Dec. 24, 31.

Table 788 ZUGSPITZE

A local rack rail service runs between Garmisch-Partenkirchen and the nearby Zugspitz mountain. Journey time to Eibsee 40 minutes, Zugspitzplatt 80 minutes. For details contact the operator: **Bayerische Zugspitzbahn AG**, Postfach 1246, 82452 Garmisch-Partenkirchen. ☎ 88 21 797 0. A cable car operates between **Zugspitzplatt** and **Zugspitzgipfel** (summit). Other cable cars run between **Eibsee** and **Zugspitzgipfel** and (from Austria, operator Tiroler Zugspitzbahn, A-6632, Ehrwald-Obermoos; ☎ 56 73 23 09) between **Ehrwald** and **Zugspitzwestgipfel** and v.v.

Table 790 — MÜNCHEN - SALZBURG

1, 2 class except where shown

km		IR 2093	E 3501	IR 2095	EC 63	E 3507	IR 2191	E 3513	IR 2193	EC 113	E 3519	EC 11	IR 2195	IC 781	E 3525	EC 115	IC 725	IR 2197	EC 65	E3533/E3535	IR 2199	EC 17	E 3539	IR 2291
0	München Hbf 795 d.	0600	0650	0751	0825	0850	0951	1050	1151	1225	1250	1325	1351	1450o	1450	1525	1551	1551	1625	1650	1751	1850	1951	
65	Rosenheim 795 d.	0641	0732	0832		0932	1032	1132	1232		1332		1432	1521	1532		1614	1632		1732	1832		1932	2032
90	Prien-am-Chiemsee d.	0700		0851	0853	0951	1053	1151	1253		1351		1453	1542	1551		1635	1653		1752	1853		1951	2051
118	Traunstein d.	0719	0816	0912		1016	1112	1216	1312		1416		1512	1605	1616		1659	1712		1817	1912		2016	2112
147	Freilassing d.	0739	0837	0932		1037	1132	1237	1332		1437		1532	1624	1637		1719	1732		1838	1932		2037	2132
153	Salzburg a.	0746	0845	0940	0955	1045	1140	1245	1340	1355	1445	1455	1540		1645	1655		1740	1753	1845	1940	1955	2045b	2140

	E 3543	IR 2293	D 297	D 269	D 3549	D 1299	D 263	D 1209
München Hbf 795 d.	2050	2151	2246	2319	2350	0411o	0426o	...
Rosenheim 795 d.	2132	2233	2327	0005	0032	0509		0529
Prien-am-Chiemsee d.	2151	2254			0051			0550
Traunstein d.	2216	2313			0114			0612
Freilassing d.	2237	2333			0133	0600		0634
Salzburg a.	2245b	2340	0024	0101		0607	0553	0642

	E 3502	E 3504	IR 2198	E 3510	IR 2196	EC 16	E 3516	IC 780	EC 112
Salzburg d.	0518	0527	0618	0715	0818	0905	0918	...	1005
Freilassing d.	0526	0535	0626	0726	0826		0926	0934	
Traunstein d.	0545	0556	0645	0745	0845		0945	0953	
Prien-am-Chiemsee d.	0607	0619	0703	0807	0903		1007	1013	
Rosenheim 795 d.	0629	0640	0704	0829	0924		1029	1035	
München Hbf 795 a.	0710	0723	0807	0910	1007	1035	1110	1114o	1138

	IR 2194	IC 724	D 3522	EC 64	E 2192	EC 114	D 3528	IR 2190	EC 10	E 3534	E 2098	E 3540	IR 2096	EC 62	D 3544	IR 2094	D 1208		IR 2092	D 262	D 1298	D 268	D 296
Salzburg d.	1018		1118	1209	1218	1305	1318	1418	1505	1518	1618	1718	1818	1905	1918	2018	2039		2215	2307	2358	0408	0435
Freilassing d.	1026	1034	1126		1226		1326	1426		1526	1626	1726	1826		1926	2025	2048		2222		0006		
Traunstein d.	1045	1054	1145		1245		1345	1445		1545	1645	1745	1845		1945	2043	2109		2240				
Prien-am-Chiemsee d.	1103	1122	1207		1303		1407	1503		1607	1703	1807	1903		2007	2100	2130		2300				
Rosenheim 795 d.	1124	1144	1229		1324		1429	1524		1629	1724	1829	1924		2029	2122	2148		2320		0118	0505	
München Hbf 795 a.	1207	1223	1310	1338	1407	1435	1510	1607	1635	1710	1807	1910	2007	2036	2110	2200			2400	0031o	0149o	0603	0613

NOTES (LISTED BY TRAIN NUMBERS)

C10/1 – MIMARA – [train] Leipzig - Zagreb and v.v.
C16/7 – MAX REINHARDT – [train] and X München - Wien West and v.v.
C62/3 – BARTÓK BÉLA – [train] X Stuttgart - Budapest Keleti and v.v.
C64/5 – MOZART – [train] and X Paris Est - Wien West and v.v.; [train] Paris - Graz and v.v.
262/3 – [train] 2 cl. and [train] Paris Est - Budapest Keleti and v.v.; [train] 2 cl. Paris - Wien and v.v.
268/9 – [train] 1,2 cl., [train] 2 cl. and [train] München - Budapest Keleti and v.v.; [train] München - Wien West and v.v. and [train] München - Bucuresti and v.v.
296/7 – [train] 1,2 cl., [train] 2 cl. and [train] München - Zagreb and v.v.; [train] 2 cl. [train] München - Rijeka and v.v.
724/5 – BERCHTESGADENER LAND – [train] Hamburg Altona - Berchtesgaden and v.v; [train] Bremen - Freilassing and v.v.
780/1 – KÖNIGSEE – [train] Hamburg - Berchtesgaden and v.v; [train] to or from Freilassing.
1208/9 – ⑤ Jan. 6 - Apr. 7, also Dec. 16, 22, 25 (from Berlin); ⑥ Jan. 7 - Apr. 8 (from Villach): [train] 1,2 cl., [train] 2 cl. [train] and [train] Berlin Wannsee - Villach and v.v.

D1298/9 – KÄRNTEN EXPRESS – ⑤ Jan. 6 - Mar. 24, also Dec. 16, 20, 22, 25, Jan. 4 (from Hamburg), ⑥ Jan. 7 - Mar. 25, also Dec. 17, 21, 23, Jan. 1, 5 (from Villach): [train] 1,2 cl., [train] 2 cl. and [train] Hamburg - Villach and v.v; [train] 2 cl. and [train] Hamburg - Graz and v.v. For other cars see Table 795.
IR2094 – [train] Salzburg - Nürnberg; [train] Salzburg - Prien-am-Chiemsee.
IR2095 – [train] and [train] Nürnberg - Salzburg.
IR2096 – [train] Salzburg - Stuttgart; [train] Salzburg - Augsburg.
IR2098 – [train] Salzburg - Karlsruhe; [train] Salzburg - Stuttgart.
IR2291 – [train] Karlsruhe - Salzburg; [train] Karlsruhe - Traunstein.
IR2293 – [train] Karlsruhe - Salzburg. Not Dec. 24, 31.
K – [train] and [train] Karlsruhe - Salzburg and v.v.
L – [train] and [train] Dortmund - Klagenfurt and v.v.
P – ⑦, also Nov. 1, Jan. 6.
b – Not Dec. 24, 31.

S – Not Dec. 24, 31. o – München Ost. ❖ – Not Dec. 25, Jan. 1.

Table 791 — FREILASSING - BERCHTESGADEN

33 km. Journey 49 minutes (64 by bus). 1, 2 class

from Freilassing: 0635 P, 0654 O, 0725 P, 0742 O, 0842, 0942, 1042, 1142, 1242, 1342, 1442, 1542, 1642 A, 1734 A, 1842, 1940 [bus], 2042 S, 2245 S [bus]
from Berchtesgaden: 0450 P [bus], 0607 ⑦, 0625 N, 0715 P, 0733 O, 0822 A, 0914, 0934 A, 1033, 1133, 1233, 1333, 1433, 1533, 1633, 1721, 1833, 1933, 2115 O [bus]

[train] Hamburg - Berchtesgaden and v.v. N – X, not Nov. 1, Jan. 6. O – ⑦, also Nov. 1, Jan. 6. P – ⑧, not Nov. 1, Jan. 6. S – Not Dec. 24, 31.

Table 795 — MÜNCHEN - INNSBRUCK

1, 2 class except where shown

km		EC 81	D 1183	D 489	EC 85	D 483	EC 160	D 15	EC 13	D 283	EC 87	D 801	IC 3557	D 516	EC 285	D 19	EC 287	D 1289	EC 289	D1125/D1299	D1299/D1125	D 1115	D 1117
0	München Hbf 790 d.	0700		0830	0930	0935	0951t	1130	1330	1430	1530	1537	1612		1730	1930	2030	2143	2330	0405o 0405o	0411o	0512	
65	Rosenheim 790 d.		0712	0908	1008	1015	1036	1208	1408	1508	1608	1635	1656		1808	2008	2108	2222	0009	0509 0538	0538	0605	
99	Kufstein d.	0759	0734	0934	1034	1046	1152	1234	1434	1534	1634	1709	1727		1834	2034	2134	2255	0040	0618	0618	0642	0713
113	Wörgl d.	0808	0945	1045	1057	1203	1245	1445	1545	1645	1718	1806	1845		2045	2145	2306	0053		0633	0633	0654	0727
148	Jenbach d.	0827	1000		1115		1300	1500	1600	1753h		1820	1900							0649	0649	0710	0743
183	Innsbruck Hbf a.	0836	0849	1020	1136	1236	1320	1520	1620	1718	1823h		1840	1920	2118	2218	2339	0126		0709	0709	0730	0803

	D 288	IC 967	D 3552	D 1288	EC 286	EC 18	D 282	IC 284	EC 86	EC 163	EC 12	EC 14	D 84	D 482	D 488	IC 969	D 1114	EC 80	D 1182		D1116/D1124	D1124/D1298	D1298/D1124
Innsbruck Hbf d.	0437	0504		0621	0641	0739	0839		1039	1241	1324	1441	1539	1641	1705	1837	1956	2008	2103	2040	2134	2248	2248
Jenbach d.		0522				0800	0900		1100				1600		1726	1859	2015	2029		2104	2156	2309	2309
Wörgl d.	0514	0536		0659	0716	0816	0916	1040	1116	1316	1359	1516	1616	1716	1744	1916	2034	2053		2122	2220	2325	2325
Kufstein d.	0530	0544	0600	0720	0728	0828		1052	1128	1328	1408	1528	1628	1728	1802	1928	2114	2143	2208		2229	2356	2356
Rosenheim 790 d.	0555		0634	0743	0750	0850	0950	1124	1350	1431	1550	1650	1750	1824	1950	2115	2139		2237		0125	0118	0125
München Hbf 790 a.	0635		0714	0825	0830	0930	1030	1218	1430	1507t	1630	1730	1830	1903	2030	2200t	2224	2240			0155o	0149o	0155o

NOTES (LISTED BY TRAIN NUMBERS)

C12/3 – PAGANINI – [train] and X Dortmund - Venezia Santa Lucia and v.v.
C14/5 – PATSCHERKOFEL – [train] and X Saarbrücken - Innsbruck and v.v.
C18/9 – ANDREAS HOFER – [train] and X Dortmund - Innsbruck and v.v.
C84/5 – MICHELANGELO – [train] and X München - Roma Termini and v.v.
282 – [train] Innsbruck (Bolzano ① - ⑤, not Dec. 17 - Jan. 8, Apr. 14 - 17) - München.
284 – [train] Innsbruck (Bolzano daily Dec. 17 - Jan. 8, Apr. 14 - 17) - München.
285 – [train] München - Bolzano.
286/7 – [train] 2 cl. and [train] München - Roma - Napoli Centrale and v.v.
288/9 – [train] 1,2 cl., [train] 2 cl. and [train] München - Firenze and v.v.; [train] 2 cl. and [train] München - Genova and v.v; [train] 2 cl. and [train] München - Venezia S. L. and v.v.
482/3 – ⑤ Jan. 6 - Mar. 24 (from København), ⑥ Jan. 7 - Mar. 25 (from Innsbruck): [train] 1,2 cl., [train] 2 cl. and [train] København - Innsbruck and v.v.; [train] 2 cl. [train] Kiel - Innsbruck and v.v.
488/9 – [train] München - Verona and v.v.
800/1 – THERESE GIEHSE – ⑤ Jan. 7 - Apr. 8, also Dec. 17, 23, 25, 26, May 20, 27 (from Berlin), ⑥⑦ Jan. 7 - Apr. 9 also Dec. 18, 24, 26, 27, Jan. 2, 6, Apr. 18, 22, May 20, 27 (from Bischofshofen): [train] and [train] Berlin Hbf - Bischofshofen and v.v.
1114 – ⑥ Jan. 7 - Apr. 8, also Dec. 23, Jan. 1, 7: [train] 1,2 cl., [train] 2 cl. and [train] Innsbruck - Dortmund; [train] 2 cl. and [train] (also 1,2 cl. to Mar. 18) Schwarzach St Veit (1614) - Wörgl - Dortmund; [train] Innsbruck - München.
1115 – ⑤ Jan. 7 - Apr. 8, also Dec. 17, 23, 26, Jan. 5: [train] 1,2 cl., [train] 2 cl. and [train] Dortmund - Innsbruck; [train] 2 cl. (also 1,2 cl. to Mar 17) Dortmund - Wörgl (1615) - Schwarzach St Veit; [train] München - Innsbruck.

D1116/7 – SKI-EXPRESS – ⑤ Dec. 23 - Apr. 7 (from Brussels), ⑥ Dec. 31 - Apr. 15 (from Lienz): [train] 1,2 cl. (T2), [train] 2 cl. Brussels - Lienz and v.v; [train] 1,2 cl. (T2), [train] and [train] Brussels - Wörgl - Schwarzach St Veit and v.v.
D1124/5 – DOLOMITEN EXPRESS – ⑤ Jan. 6 - Mar. 24, also Dec. 16, 20, 22, 25, Jan. 4 (from Dortmund), ⑥ Jan. 7 - Mar. 25, also Dec. 17, 21, 23, Jan. 1, 5 (from Bolzano): [train] 1,2 cl., [train] 2 cl. and [train] Dortmund - Bolzano and v.v.
D1182/3 – SPREE-ALPEN EXPRESS – ⑤ Jan. 6 - Apr. 21, also Dec. 16, 22, 25, Apr. 13, not Apr. 14, (from Berlin), ⑥ Mar. 24 - Apr. 22, also Dec. 17, 23, 26, Apr. 18, not Apr. 14 (from Verona), ⑤ Jan. 7: [train] and [train] Berlin - Verona and v.v; [train] 2 cl. Berlin - Innsbruck and v.v.
D1288/9 – May 19 - 27 (from München), May 20 - 27 (from Pescara): [train] 2 cl., [train] and [train] München - Pescara and v.v.
B – ⑥ Jan. 7 - Mar. 25, also Dec. 17, 21, 23, Jan. 1, 5: [train] 1,2 cl. and [train] 2 cl. Bolzano - Hamburg; [train] and X München - Milano and v.v.
C – ⑥ Jan. 7 - Mar. 25, also Dec. 17, 21, 23, Jan. 1, 5: [train] 1,2 cl. and [train] 2 cl. Bolzano - Hamburg; also conveys except on Dec. 17, 21, 23, Jan. 1, 5: [train] 2 cl. Schwarzach St Veit - Hamburg.
G – ⑥ Jan. 7 - Mar. 25, also Dec. 17, 21, 23, Jan. 1, 5: [train] 1,2 cl., [train] 2 cl. and [train] Villach - Dortmund; [train] 2 cl. Graz - Dortmund.
H – ⑤ Jan. 6 - Mar. 24, also Dec. 16, 20, 22, 25, Jan. 4 (from Dortmund): [train] 1,2 cl., [train] 2 cl. and [train] Dortmund - Villach; [train] 2 cl. and [train] Dortmund - Graz.
J – ⑤ Jan. 6 - Mar. 24, also Dec. 16, 20, 22, 25, Jan. 4 (from Hamburg): [train] 1,2 cl. and [train] 2 cl. Hamburg - Bolzano; conveys to Mar. 7: [train] 2 cl. and [train] Hamburg - Wörgl - Schwarzach St Veit. P – ⑧, not Nov. 1, Jan. 6. h – ⑥ only. Train E1727.
o – München Ost. t – Change at Kufstein and Rosenheim.

BOOKS AND MAPS BY MAIL ORDER FROM THOMAS COOK PUBLISHING

BOOKS FOR THE RAIL TRAVELLER

AUSTRALIA BY RAIL
A handy illustrated guide on how to make the most of your Austrailpass – with routes, services, itineraries and maps.

INDIA BY RAIL
A fascinating and practical guide to the mysteries of rail travel in India. Essential pre-reading for the adventurous or for the armchair traveller. Lavishly illustrated.

SRI LANKA BY RAIL
A complete guide to the country and its people.

MEXICO BY RAIL
A unique handbook which explains how to use Mexico's remarkable and inexpensive rail network, joining and leaving at any point.

SILK ROUTE BY RAIL
This guide shows you how to arrange a trip between Moscow and Beijing using the recently-opened line between Alma Ata and Urumqi, stopping off in Samarkand, Bukhara and many of the other cities on the Silk Route.

SPAIN AND PORTUGAL BY RAIL
Ideal for rail pass users.

THAILAND, MALAYSIA AND SINGAPORE BY RAIL
How to make the most of a rail pass to explore these popular Asian tourist destinations.

EASTERN EUROPE BY RAIL
Czech Republic, Slovakia, Romania, Bulgaria and eastern Germany.

TRANS-SIBERIAN HANDBOOK
The third edition of this new 300+ page guide to the most famous rail route of them all.

USA BY RAIL
A guide to Amtrak's extensive network of long-distance train journeys, and much more. Includes Canada.

RAIL MAPS

GERMANY
Scale 1:750 000. Covers DB (including former DR) and most museum lines. Includes ICE and new lines under construction. Laminated and folded.

SWITZERLAND
Scale 1:300 000. A full-colour map of the railways and post-bus routes, with city plans.

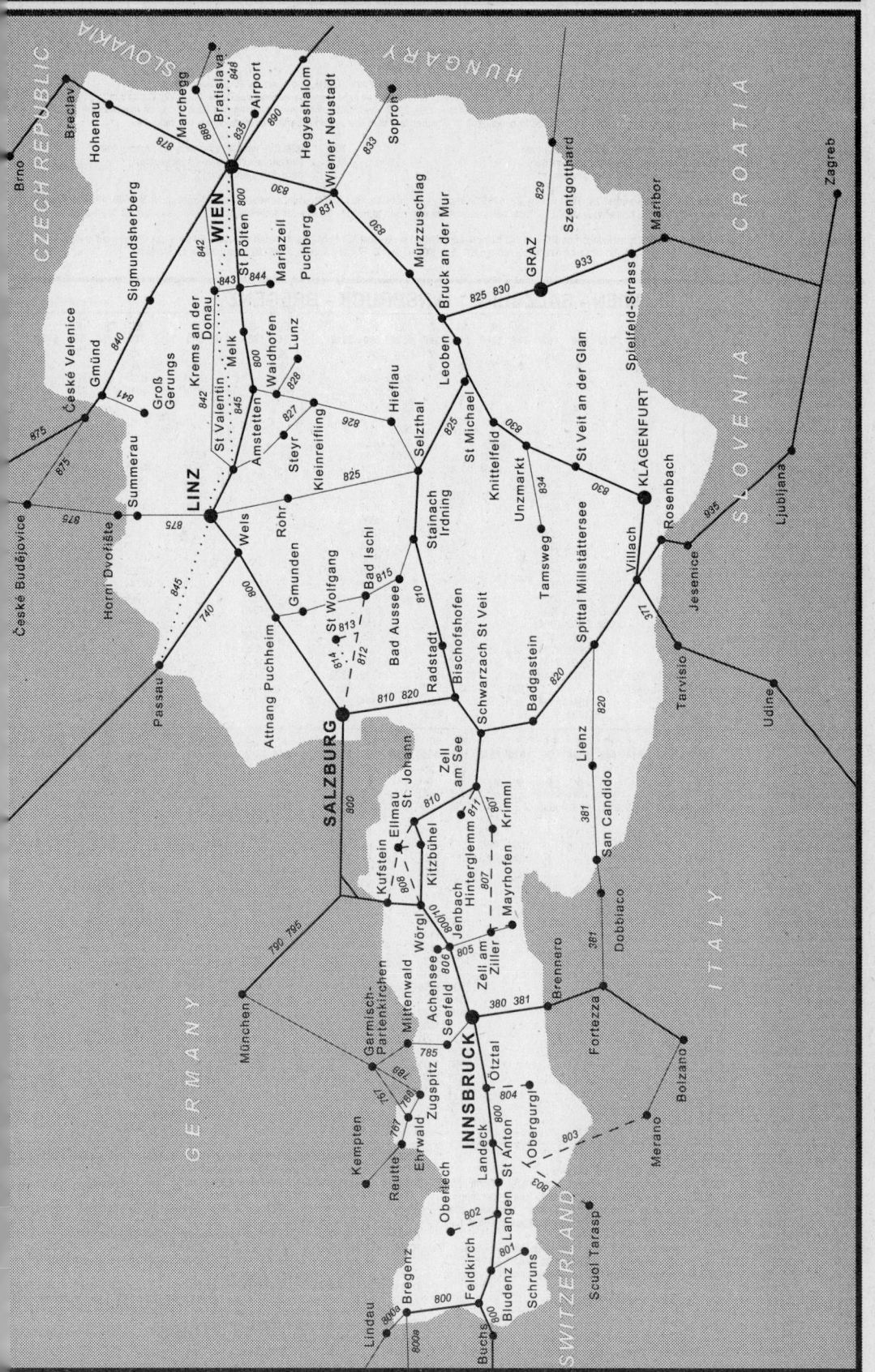

AUSTRIA

Operator: Except where stated otherwise railways are operated by Österreichisches Bundesbahnen (ÖBB), and buses by PAST Bundesbus.

Services: All **EC**, **SC** and **IC** trains convey First and Second class accommodation. Most **E** and all local trains are second class only. Overnight **D** trains may only convey Second class seats in addition to sleeping accommodation – see individual footnotes. Many overnight trains convey sleeping cars (🛏) and/or couchettes (🛏) which are of the normal European types. Some trains offer four berth couchettes at a higher fare than the usual six berth. For more details see page **10**.

Types of train:

EC:	**EuroCity** quality international express train	**IC:**	**InterCity** national long distance express train
EN:	**EuroNight** quality overnight express train	**D:**	Ordinary express train (Schnellzüge)
SC:	**SuperCity** fast limited stop business train	**E:**	Semi-fast train (Eilzüge)

Timings: Railway services valid **September 24, 1994** to **May 27, 1995** unless stated otherwise. Bus and shipping services are valid throughout **May 29, 1994** to **May 27, 1995**. All services run daily unless stated otherwise but local services may be amended at holiday times – for details of public holidays in Austria see page 2.

Supplements: For travel in First Class accommodation on **EC** and **SC** trains a supplement is payable: 50 schillings if paid in advance, 60 schillings if paid on the train.

Reservations: Seat reservations are possible on all fast trains in categories **EC**, **EN**, **SC**, **IC** and **D**. Reservations are not available on **E** or local trains.

Table 800 — WIEN - SALZBURG - INNSBRUCK - BREGENZ

Local trains 2 class only

km		IC 860 ✕ ♦	D 348 ♦	D 5310	D 460 ⍾ ♦	IC 862 ✕ ♦	D 448 ♦	E 1800 ✕	IC 844 ♦	D 360 ⍾ ♦	E 1520	IC 560 ✕	5718	EC 16 ✕ ♦	E 1780	IC 2010	IC 540 ✕ ♦	E 2012	EC 160 ✕ ♦	E 1780	IC 562 ✕	5720
0	Wien Westbahnhof........d.	...	...	...	...	...	...	...	...	...	0440	0540	...	0600	...	...	0640	...	0735	...	0740	...
60	St Pölten Hbf..............d.	...	...	...	...	...	...	...	...	...	0555	0621	...	0641	...	0645	0721	0725	0816	...	0821	...
85	Melk...........................d.	...	...	...	...	...	...	...	...	...	0611		...		...	0708		0748		...		...
94	Pöchlarn....................d.	...	...	...	...	...	...	...	...	...	0618		...		...	0715		0755		...		...
108	Ybbs an der Donau......d.	...	...	...	...	...	...	...	...	...	0625		...		...	0727		0813		...		...
126	Amstetten..................d.	...	...	...	...	...	0504	...	...	...	0640	0654	...		...	0743	0754	0829		...	0854	...
166	St Valentin.................d.	...	...	...	...	...	0534	...	...	...	0709	0716	...		...	0816				...	0916	...
190	Linz Hbf 740...............d.	...	...	...	0534	...	0554	0634	...	...	0727	0734	...	0748	...	0834		0923	0934	...	0934	...
215	Wels 740....................d.	...	...	...	0549	...		0649	...	...		0749	...		...	0849		0937	0949	...	0949	...
246	Attnang Puchheim.......a.	...	...	...	0610	...		0710	...	...		0810	...		...	0910			1010	...	1010	...
317	Salzburg Hbf...............a.	...	...	...	0655	...		0755	...	...		0855	...	0900	...	0955		1035	1055	...	1055	...
317	Salzburg Hbf...............d.	0500	...	...	0700	...			...	...		0900	...		...			1038	1100	...	1100	...
440	Kufstein 790...............d.	0614	...	...	0814	...			...	...		1014	...		...			1152	1214	...	1214	...
453	Wörgl 790 810.............d.	0624	...	...	0824	...			...	...		1024	...		...		1203		1224	...	1224	...
478	Jenbach 790 810..........d.	0638	...	...	0838	...			...	...		1038	...		...				1238	...	1238	...
513	Innsbruck Hbf 790 810 ....a.	0658	...	...	0858	...			...	...		1058	...		...		1236		1258	...	1258	...
513	Innsbruck Hbf..............d.	0702	...	0717	0902	...			...	...		1102	...	1153	...		1244		1302	...		...
560	Ötztal........................d.	0729	...	0806	0930	...			...	...		1130	...	1232	...		1309		1330	...		...
570	Imst Pitztal................d.	0741	...	0822	0939	...			...	...		1139	...	1243	...				1339	...		...
588	Landeck.....................d.	0755	...	0839	0863 0954	...			...	...		1154	...	1307	...		1331		1354	...		...
615	St Anton am Arlberg.......d.	0825	...		0917 1025	...			...	...		1225	...	1338	...		1359		1425	...		...
626	Langen am Arlberg........d.	0835	...		0927 1035	...			...	...		1235	...	1350	...		1408		1435	...		...
651	Bludenz.....................d.	0901	...		0958 1101	...			...	...		1301	...	1422	...		1434		← 1501	...		...
672	Feldkirch....................d.	0919	0931		1013 1119	1134			...	...		1319	1324	1455t	...		1452	1455	1519	1531		...
	Buchs 🚉...................a.		0947				1150		...	...			1351	→	...		1508			1554		...
711	Bregenz 🚉..................a.	0944	...		1040 1144				...	...		1344	...		...			1531	1544			...
	Lindau 800a...............a.		...		1050			1227 1238	...	...			...		...							...

		E 1604 ⍾	EC 28 ✕	E 2014	IC 542 ✕	E 1824 ⍾	EC 64 ✕	E 1824 ⍾	IC 2016	EC 162 ✕	IC 564 ✕	5722	EC 26 ✕	IC 2018	IC 544 ✕	IC 2020	EC 168 ✕	IC 1868	IC 566 ✕	EC 24 ✕	IC 2022	D 1018 ♦	D 364 ♦
	Wien Westbahnhof........d.	0745	0800	...	0840	0844	0900	...	...	0935	0940	...	1000	...	1040	...	1140	1200	...	...	...	...	...
	St Pölten Hbf..............d.	0826	0841	0845	0921	0932	0940	...	0945	1016	1021	...	1041	1045	1121	...	1221	1241	1245	...	...	...	...
	Melk...........................d.	0839		0908		0947		...	1008			...		1108		1208			1308	...	...	...	...
	Pöchlarn....................d.			0915		1000	←	...	1015			...		1115		1215			1315	...	...	...	...
	Ybbs an der Donau......d.			0927		1008	1008	1027			...		1127		1227			1327	...	...	...	...
	Amstetten..................d.	0900		0943	0954	→		1021	1043		1054	...		1143		1243			1343	...	...	...	...
	St Valentin.................d.	...		1016			1051	1116			...		1216		1316				...	...	...	...
	Linz Hbf 740...............d.	...	0949	1034		1046	1114	1123	1134		1149		1234		1334	1349		...	...	...	...
	Wels 740....................d.	...	1002	1049			1129		1149	1202		1249		1349	1402		...	...	...	...
	Attnang Puchheim.......d.	...		1108				1210			1310		1410			...	...	...	...
	Salzburg Hbf..............a.	...		1152		1158		1235 1255			1355		1455			...	...	...	...
	Salzburg Hbf..............d.	...						1238 1300					1500			...	...	...	...
	Kufstein 790...............d.	...						1352 1414					1614			...	...	...	...
	Wörgl 790 810.............d.	...						1403 1424				1611	1624			...	...	...	...
	Jenbach 790 810..........d.	...						1438				1625	1638			...	...	...	...
	Innsbruck Hbf 790 810 ....a.	...						1436 1458				1645	1658			...	...	...	...
	Innsbruck Hbf..............d.	...						1444 1502				1653	1702			...	1805 1844
	Ötztal........................d.	...						1509 1530				1717	1730			...	1833 1909
	Imst Pitztal................d.	...						1539				1739			...	1846
	Landeck.....................d.	...						1531 1554				1740	1754			...	1904 1932
	St Anton am Arlberg.......d.	...						1559 1625				1807	1825			...	1935 1959
	Langen am Arlberg........d.	...						1608 1635				1817	1835			...	1947 2008
	Bludenz.....................d.	...						1634 1701				1843	1901			...	2020 2034
	Feldkirch....................d.	...						1652 1719	1746			1901	1903 1919			...	2054 2042
	Buchs 🚉...................a.							1708	1811			1917			...	2108
	Bregenz 🚉..................a.											1934	1946		...	2126 ...
	Lindau 800a...............a.							1744				1956			...	2136 ...

♦ – NOTES (LISTED BY TRAIN NUMBERS)

EC16 –	MAX REINHARDT – 🍽 and ✕ Wien - München.
EC24 –	FRANZ LISZT – 🍽 and ✕ Budapest - Frankfurt (Main) - Köln - Dortmund.
EC26 –	JOSEPH HAYDN – 🍽 and ✕ Wien - Frankfurt (Main) - Köln - Hamburg.
EC28 –	PRINZ EUGEN – 🍽 and ✕ Wien - Frankfurt (Main) - Köln - Hamburg - Kiel.
EC64 –	MOZART – 🍽 and ✕ Wien - München - Stuttgart - Strasbourg - Paris Est.
EC160 –	MARIA THERESIA – 🍽 and ✕ Wien - Zürich.
EC162 –	TRANSALPIN – 🍽 (observation car), 🍽 and ✕ Wien - Zürich - Basel.
EC168 –	ROBERT STOLZ – 🍽 (observation car), 🍽 and ✕ Graz - Zürich; 🍽 Graz - Feldkirch; 🍽 Klagenfurt (train EC198) - Schwarzach St Veit - Zürich.
D348 –	🍽 Feldkirch - Zürich.
D360 –	🍽 and ⍾ Bregenz - Lindau - Stuttgart - Saarbrücken.
D364 –	🍽 Innsbruck - Zürich.
D448 –	🍽 Feldkirch - Zürich.
D460 –	🍽 and ⍾ Landeck - Lindau - Stuttgart - Saarbrücken.
IC540 –	KITZSTEINHORN – 🍽 and ✕ Wien - Salzburg - Zell am See - Wörgl.
IC542 –	HAHNENKAMM – 🍽 and ✕ Wien - Salzburg - Zell am See - Wörgl; 🍽 Wien - Schwarzach St Veit - Villach.
IC544 –	JAKOB PRANDTAUER – 🍽 and ✕ Wien - Salzburg - Zell am See - Innsbruck; 🍽 Wien - Schwarzach St Veit - Villach.
IC564 –	ALEMANNIA – 🍽 and ✕ Wien - Bregenz; 🍽 Wien - Attnang Puchheim - Stainach Irdning.
IC844 –	🍽 and ✕ Linz - Salzburg - Zell am See - Wörgl.
IC860 –	MARKUS SITTIKUS – 🍽 and ✕ Salzburg - Bregenz. Conveys on Dec. 23 - Jan. 6, and ⑤ Jan. 13 - Mar. 31, also Dec. 16 (from Wien): 🛏 2 cl. Wien (train D248) - Innsbruck - Bregenz.
D1018 –	VORARLBERG EXPRESS – Runs ⑥ Oct. 1 - 8 (**not** 🛏 1, 2 cl.), ⑥ Jan. 7 - Apr. 8, also Dec. 23, Jan. 1, 5: 🛏 1, 2 cl., 🛏 2 cl. and 🍽 Innsbruck - Dortmund; conveys on above dates except Apr. 1, 8: 🛏 1, 2 cl. and 🛏 2 cl. Innsbruck - Heidelberg (train D1088) - Hamburg.
E1604 –	Runs ⑥: 🍽 and ⍾ Wien - Bischofshofen.
E1824 –	🍽 and ⍾ Wien - Passau.
t –	Arrive 1439.

Table 800 — WIEN - SALZBURG - INNSBRUCK - BREGENZ

Local trains 2 class only

	IC 546 ✕	E 1524	IC 15568	IC 568 ✕	EC 22 ✕	2026	IC 548 ✕	E 1526	5672	IC 660 ✕	D 1168 ♦	E 1528 Ⓐ	EC 62 ✕	2030	5113	IC 640 ✕	E 1620	SC 968 ⟟✕	IC 610	IC 762 ✕	E 1622 Ⓐ	5542
Wien Westbahnhof....d.	1240	1226	1335	1340	...	1400	...	1440	1426	...	1540	...	1526	1600	...	1640	1626	1700	...	1740	1726	...
St Pölten Hbf....d.	1321	1325	1416	1421	...	1441	1445	1521	1525	...	1621	...	1625	1641	1645	1721	1725	1742	...	1821	1825	...
Melk....d.		1341			...	1508		1541		...		...	1645		1708		1741		...		1841	...
Pöchlarn....d.		1349			...	1515		1549		...		...	1649		1715		1749		...		1849	...
Ybbs an der Donau....d.		1357			...	1527		1557		...		...	1657		1727		1757		...		1857	...
Amstetten....d.	1354	1407		1454	...	1543	1554	1607		1654		...	1707		1743	1754	1807		...	1854	1907	...
St Valentin....d.	1416			1516	...		1616			1716		...				1816		...		1916		...
Linz Hbf 740....d.	1434		1523	1534	1549		1634			1734		1748				1834		1848		1934		...
Wels 740....d.	1449		1538	1549	1602		1649			1749						1849				1949		...
Attnang Puchheim....d.	1510		1559	1610			1710			1810						1910				2010		...
Salzburg Hbf....a.	1555		1644	1655			1755			1855		1900				1955		2000		2055		...
Salzburg Hbf....d.	...	...	...	1700	...		...			1900								2002				...
Kufstein 790....d.	...	...	...	1814	...		...			2014												...
Wörgl 790 810....d.	...	...	...	1824	...		...			2024	2010									2206		...
Jenbach 790 810....d.	...	...	...	1838	...		...			2038	2024		2041							2220		...
Innsbruck Hbf 790 810....a.	...	...	...	1858	...		...			2058	2044		2115					2150	2240			...
Innsbruck Hbf....d.	...	...	...	1902	...		...			2102	2110		2137					2152	2240			2319
Ötztal....d.	...	...	...	1930	...		...			2130	2141		2232						2310			0014
Imst Pitztal....d.	...	...	...	1939	...		...			2139	2153		2247						2320			0025
Landeck....d.	...	...	...	1954	...		...			2154	2214		2304					2246	2334			0044
St Anton am Arlberg....d.	...	...	...	2025	...		...			2225	2247							2312				
Langen am Arlberg....d.	...	...	...	2035	...		...			2235	2301											
Bludenz....d.	...	...	...	2101	...		...		2206	2301	2333							2345				
Feldkirch....d.	...	...	...	2119	...		...		2228	2319	2349							0001				
Buchs 🚲....a.	...	...	...		...		...			0004												
Bregenz 🚲....a.	...	...	...	2144	...		...		2312	2344								0023				
Lindau 800a....a.	...	...	...		...		...															

	2034	SC 966 ✕	IC 740 ✕	EN 224	2036	D 262 ♦	E 1624	EN 490	IC 742 ✕	2056	EN 466 ✕	5602	E 1626	D 464 ♦	EN 246	D 222 ♦	5712	D 1275 ♦	D 248	D 268	5614	5616
Wien Westbahnhof....d.	...	...	1833	1840	1844	...	1940	1926	2000	2040	...	2125	...	2140	...	2210	2218	...	2330	0047h		
St Pölten Hbf....d.	...	1848		1921	1927	1933	2021	2025	2042	2121	2125	2207	...	2227	...	2252	2300	...	0012			
Melk....d.	...	1911				1956		2041			2146		...	2242				...	0027			
Pöchlarn....d.	...	1918				2004		2049			2152		...	2249				...				
Ybbs an der Donau....d.	...	1932				2016		2057			2203		...	2258				...	0048			
Amstetten....d.	...	1948		1954		2032	2055	2107		2154	2215		...	2309	2326	2334		...	0110			
St Valentin....d.	...			2016						2216			...	2330		2348		...				
Linz Hbf 740....d.	...		2009	2034	2039		2134		2150	2234	2315		2345	0015b	0010		0121	0127	0230			
Wels 740....d.	...		2024	2049	2054		2149		2205	2249	2330			0030	0024		0136	0142				
Attnang Puchheim....d.	...			2110			2210			2313				0051			0155	0203				
Salzburg Hbf....a.	...	2118	2155				2255				0012						0242	0248	0353			
Salzburg Hbf....d.	...	2120									0033			0043			0302					
Kufstein 790....d.	...	2231																0549				
Wörgl 790 810....d.	...	2240																0603				
Jenbach 790 810....d.	...	2254																0626				
Innsbruck Hbf 790 810....a.	...	2312									0235			0447								
Innsbruck Hbf....d.	...										0240			0430	0502							
Ötztal....d.	...														0528							
Imst Pitztal....d.	...														0537							
Landeck....d.	...													0516	0554							
St Anton am Arlberg....d.	...													0550	0625							
Langen am Arlberg....d.	...													0559	0635							
Bludenz....d.	...													0625	0701						0736	0806
Feldkirch....d.	...										0501a	0458		0652	0723e		0721		0744		0758	0828
Buchs 🚲....a.	...										0518			0708			0708					
Bregenz 🚲....a.	...											0542			0751		0744				0842	0912
Lindau 800a....a.	...																					

♦ — NOTES (LISTED BY TRAIN NUMBERS)

EC22 — JOHANN STRAUSS – 🍴 Wien - Frankfurt (Main) - Köln; ✕ Wien - Bonn.
EC62 — BÉLA BARTÓK – 🍴 and ✕ Budapest - München - Stuttgart.
D222 — DONAU KURIER – 🛏 1, 2 cl., ━ 2 cl. and ✕ Dortmund; 🛏 1, 2 cl., ━ 2 cl. and 🚃 Budapest (train 466) - Wien - Dortmund.
EN224 — DONAUWALZER – 🛏 1, 2 cl., ━ Wien - Oostende; 🛏 1, 2 cl., ━ 2 cl. and 🚃 Wien - Köln (train D214) - Amsterdam; 🚃 Wien - Passau.
EN246 — WEST KURIER – 🛏 1, 2 cl., ━ 1, 2 cl. (T2), ━ 2 cl. and 🚃 Wien - Bregenz. Train does not stop at Salzburg Hbf.
D248 — 🛏 2 cl. and 🚃 Wien - Salzburg (train D268) - München; ━ 2 cl. (Dec. 16, 23 - Jan. 6, ⑤ Jan. 13 - Mar. 31 from Wien extended to Bregenz) and 🚃 Wien - Innsbruck; conveys Dec. 16, 23 - Jan. 6, ⑤ Jan. 13 - Mar. 31 (from Wien): ━ 2 cl. Wien - Innsbruck (train IC860) - Bregenz.
D262 — ORIENT EXPRESS – 🛏 1, 2 cl. and ━ 2 cl. Wien - Paris Est; ━ 2 cl. and 🚃 Budapest - Paris Est; 🚃, and 🚃 Budapest - Salzburg.
D268 — KÁLMÁN IMRE – 🛏 1, 2 cl., ━ 2 cl. and 🚃 Budapest - München; 🚃 Bucureşti (train 21) - Curtici (train 374) - Budapest - München.
D464 — 🛏 1, 2 cl., ━ 2 cl. and 🚃 Graz - Zürich - Basel; ━ 2 cl. and 🚃 Villach (train D894) - Schwarzach St Veit - Basel.

EN466 — WIENER WALZER – 🛏 1, 2 cl. Wien - Zürich - Basel; ━ 2 cl. and 🚃 (sleeperette with supplement) Budapest (train D466) - Wien - Basel.
EN490 — HANS ALBERS – 🛏 1, 2 cl., ━ 2 cl. and 🚃 Wien - Hamburg.
IC546 — WILDER KAISER – 🚃 and ✕ Wien - Salzburg - Zell am See - Innsbruck.
IC548 — PONGAU – 🚃 and ✕ Salzburg - Zell am See - Wörgl.
IC610 — SCHÖCKL – 🚃 and ⟟ Graz - Landeck.
IC640 — KARL HEINRICH WAGGERL – 🚃 and ✕ Wien - Salzburg - Saalfelden.
IC740 — SCHMITTENHÖHE – 🚃 and ✕ Wien - Salzburg - Saalfelden.
D1168 — ARLBERG EXPRESS – Runs ⑥ Feb. 4 - Mar. 25, also Dec. 17, 24, 31: 🛏 1, 2 cl. and ━ 2 cl. Zell am Zee - Paris Est; ━ 2 cl. Innsbruck - Basel (train 298) - Brussels.
D1275 — Runs ⑤ Dec. 16 - Jan. 6 and Apr. 7 - May 26 (from Praha): 🛏 1, 2 cl., ━ 2 cl. and 🚃 Praha - Linz - Salzburg - Villach - Venezia Santa Lucia.
IC15568 — Runs ⑤, also Dec. 26, Apr. 17, 18, May 1, not Dec. 25, Apr. 16, 30.
a — Arrive 0448.
b — Arrive 0003.
e — Arrive 0717.
h — Wien Hütteldorf.
u — Stops to pick up only.

Table 800a — ST MARGRETHEN - BREGENZ - LINDAU

Supplements on EC trains are not payable for local journeys

2 class only except where shown

km		5560 ✕	5562 ✕	5851 ✕	5564	5568	5855	EC99 C	5572	5857 ✕	5859 A	EC167	5578	5865	5584	5867	5871	EC95 C	5586	5588	5873	5590	5877 5592	5879	EC93 C
	Zürich Hbf 308....d.	...	...	...	...	...	...	0740	...	...	0940	...	...	...	...	...	...	1340	...	...	...	...	...	...	1740
0	St Margrethen 🚲....d.	...	...	0700	...	...	0843	0906	...	1005	1043	1106	...	1243	...	1333	1443	1506	...	...	1643	...	1737	1843	1906
14	Bregenz 🚲 ▲....a.	...	...	0718	...	...	0902	0919	...	1026	1104	1119	...	1302	...	1351	1504	1519	...	...	1704	...	1756	1902	1919
14	Bregenz 🚲 ▲ 800....d.	0617	0652	...	0721	0820	...	0921	0947	...	1121	1147	...	1347	...	...	1521	1547	1645	...	1748	1815	...	1921
24	Lindau 800....a.	0628	0704	...	0733	0831	...	0930	0958	...	1130	1158	...	1358	...	...	1530	1558	1656	...	1759	1826	...	1930
	München Hbf 765....a.	...	...	...	...	...	...	1151	...	...	1356	...	...	...	...	...	...	1748	...	...	...	...	...	...	2145

A – ALBERT EINSTEIN – 🚃 and ✕ Interlaken Ost - Zürich - Praha.
C – 🚃 and ✕ Zürich - St Gallen - Lindau - München.

▲ – Passengers joining or alighting EC trains at Bregenz should use the carriage marked 'Für Reisenden von und nach Bregenz'.

🛏 – Sleeping car   ━ – Couchette car   🚃 – Through carriage (1 and 2 class)

Table 800 BREGENZ - INNSBRUCK - SALZBURG - WIEN

Local trains 2 class only

km		IC 765 ✕	EN 491 ◆	E 1565	D 263 ✕ ◆		SC 967 ✕	2013	IC 741 ✕ ◆	2015	EN 225 ◆	IC 743 ✕ ◆	2017	IC 561 ✕	IC 513 🍷 ◆	2019	EC 63 ✕ ◆	IC 541 ✕ ◆	2021	5711	IC 563 ✕	D 1169 ◆		2023
	Lindau **800a** d.	...	...	...	...	...	...	...	...	...	...	...	...	...	...	...	...	...	...	...	...	...	...	...
	Bregenz 🏨 d.	...	...	...	...	...	...	...	...	...	...	...	...	0410	...	...	...	...	...	...	0614	...	...	...
0	**Buchs** 🏨 d.	...	...	...	...	...	...	...	...	...	...	...	...	|	...	...	...	...	...	0615	|	0628s	...	...
19	Feldkirch d.	...	...	...	...	...	...	...	...	...	...	...	...	0444	...	...	...	...	...	0637	0643	0651s	...	...
40	Bludenz d.	...	...	...	...	...	...	...	...	...	...	...	...	0500	...	...	...	...	...	...	0700	0711s	...	...
65	Langen am Arlberg d.	...	...	...	...	...	...	...	...	...	...	...	...	0526	...	...	...	...	...	...	0726	0741s	...	...
76	**St Anton am Arlberg** d.	...	...	...	...	...	...	...	...	...	...	...	...	0537	...	...	...	...	...	...	0737	0807s	...	...
103	Landeck d.	...	...	...	...	...	...	...	...	...	...	...	...	0609	0618	...	...	...	...	...	0809	0840s	...	...
121	Imst Pitztal d.	...	...	...	...	...	...	...	...	...	...	...	...	0623	0634	...	...	...	...	...	0823	0901s	...	...
131	Ötztal d.	...	...	...	...	...	...	...	...	...	...	...	...	0632	0646	...	...	...	...	...	0832	0912s	...	...
178	**Innsbruck Hbf** a.	...	...	...	...	...	...	...	...	...	...	...	...	0658	0717	...	...	...	...	...	0858	0940	...	...
178	**Innsbruck Hbf 790 810** d.	...	...	...	...	...	0504	...	...	...	...	...	...	0702	0720	...	...	...	...	...	0902	...	...	...
213	Jenbach **790 810** d.	...	...	...	...	...	0522	...	...	...	...	...	...	0722	0740	...	...	...	...	...	0922	...	...	...
238	Wörgl **790 810** d.	...	...	...	...	...	0536	...	...	...	...	...	...	0737	0754	...	...	...	...	...	0937	...	...	...
252	Kufstein **790** d.	...	...	...	...	...	0545	...	...	...	...	...	...	0747	...	...	...	...	...	...	0947	...	...	...
374	**Salzburg Hbf** a.	...	...	...	...	...	0657	...	...	...	...	...	...	0900	...	...	...	...	...	...	1100	...	...	...
374	**Salzburg Hbf** d.	0505	...	0511	0605	...	0700	...	0705	...	...	0805	...	0905	...	...	1000	1005	...	...	1105	...	...	...
445	Attnang Puchheim d.	0552	...	0610	0652	...	|	...	0752	...	...	0852	...	0952	...	...	|	1052	...	...	1152	...	...	...
476	**Wels 740** d.	0611	0616	0635	0711	...	|	...	0811	...	0845	0911	...	1011	...	...	|	1111	...	...	1211	...	...	...
501	**Linz Hbf 740** d.	0627	0632	0652	0727	...	0809	...	0827	...	0902	0927	...	1027	...	...	1114	1127	...	...	1227	...	...	...
525	St Valentin d.	0642	|	0711	0742	...	|	...	0842	...	|	0942	...	1042	...	...	|	1142	...	...	1242	...	...	...
565	Amstetten d.	0704	|	0736	0804	...	|	0825	0904	0915	|	1004	1015	1104	...	1115	|	1204	1215	...	1304	...	...	1315
583	Ybbs an der Donau d.	|	|	0746	|	...	|	0850	|	0930	|	|	1030	|	...	1130	|	|	1230	...	|	...	...	1330
597	Pöchlarn d.	|	|	0756	|	...	|	0903	|	0943	|	|	1043	|	...	1143	|	|	1243	...	|	...	...	1343
606	Melk d.	|	|	0804	|	...	|	0910	|	0950	|	|	1050	|	...	1150	|	|	1250	...	|	...	...	1350
631	**St Pölten Hbf** d.	0739	0744	0819	0839	...	|	0933	0939	1013	1010	1039	1113	1139	...	1213	1219	1239	1313	...	1339	...	...	1413
691	**Wien Westbahnhof** a.	0825	0830	0905	0925	...	0945	...	1025	...	1058	1125	...	1225	...	...	1305	1325	...	...	1425	...	...	...

	IC 543 ✕ ◆	2025	E 1787	E 1861 ⚒	EC 23 ✕ ◆	5713	IC 565 ✕	2027	D 365 ◆	E 1623 ◆	D 1019 ◆	IC 545 ✕ ◆	2029	EC 25 ✕ ◆		IC 567 ✕		EC 163 ✕ ◆	2031		IC 547 ✕ ◆	E 1825	2033	D 361 🍷 ◆
Lindau **800a** d.	...	...	...	0652	...	...	0802	...	...	...	0823	...	...	...	...	...	...	...	...	...	...	...	...	1108
Bregenz 🏨 d.	...	...	0648	0707	...	...	0817	...	...	...	0834	...	...	...	...	1017	...	...	...	...	...	...	...	1118
Buchs 🏨 d.	...	...	|	|	...	0803	|	...	0852	...	|	...	...	...	...	|	...	1052	...	...	...	...	...	...
Feldkirch d.	...	...	0720	0741	...	0825	0844	...	0911	...	0916	...	...	...	...	1044	...	1111	...	...	...	...	...	...
Bludenz d.	...	...	0737	...	...	...	0900	...	0927	...	0941	...	...	...	...	1100	...	1127	...	...	...	...	...	...
Langen am Arlberg d.	...	...	0806	...	...	...	0926	...	0953	...	1016	...	...	...	...	1126	...	1153	...	...	...	...	...	...
St Anton am Arlberg d.	...	...	0821	...	...	...	0937	...	1003	...	1029	...	...	...	...	1137	...	1203	...	...	...	...	...	...
Landeck d.	...	...	0856	...	...	...	1009	...	1030	...	1100	...	...	...	...	1209	...	1230	...	...	...	...	...	...
Imst Pitztal d.	...	...	0912	...	...	...	1023	...	|	...	1117	...	...	...	...	1223	...	|	...	...	...	...	...	...
Ötztal d.	...	...	0922	...	...	...	1032	...	1051	...	1128	...	...	...	...	1232	...	1251	...	...	...	...	...	...
Innsbruck Hbf a.	...	...	0958	...	...	...	1058	...	1116	...	1153	...	...	...	...	1258	...	1316	...	...	...	...	...	...
Innsbruck Hbf 790 810 d.	...	...	...	...	...	...	1107	...	...	...	...	...	...	...	...	1302	...	1324	...	...	...	...	...	...
Jenbach **790 810** d.	...	...	...	...	...	...	|	...	...	...	...	...	...	...	...	1322	...	|	...	...	...	...	...	...
Wörgl **790 810** d.	...	...	...	...	...	...	|	...	...	...	...	...	...	...	...	1337	...	1359	...	...	...	...	...	...
Kufstein **790** d.	...	...	...	...	...	...	1147	...	...	...	...	...	...	...	...	1347	...	1409	...	...	...	...	...	...
Salzburg Hbf a.	...	...	...	...	...	...	1300	...	...	...	...	...	...	...	...	1500	...	1522	...	...	...	...	...	...
Salzburg Hbf d.	1205	...	...	...	...	...	1305	...	...	...	...	1405	...	...	...	1505	...	1525	...	...	1605	...	...	...
Attnang Puchheim d.	1252	...	...	...	...	...	1352	...	...	1355	...	1452	...	...	...	1552	...	|	...	...	1652	...	...	...
Wels 740 d.	1311	...	...	...	1356	...	1411	...	...	1418	...	1511	...	1556	...	1611	...	|	...	...	1711	1703	...	...
Linz Hbf 740 d.	1327	...	...	...	1414	...	1427	...	...	1445	...	1527	...	1614	...	1627	...	1639	...	...	1727	1721	...	...
St Valentin d.	1342	...	...	...	|	...	1442	...	...	1506	...	1542	...	|	...	1642	...	|	...	...	1742	1739	...	...
Amstetten d.	1404	1415	...	...	|	...	1504	1515	...	1534	...	1604	1615	|	...	1704	...	|	1715	...	1804	1811	1815	...
Ybbs an der Donau d.	|	1430	...	...	|	...	|	1530	...	1545	...	|	1630	|	...	|	...	|	1730	...	|	1821	1830	...
Pöchlarn d.	|	1443	...	...	|	...	|	1543	...	1554	...	|	1643	|	...	|	...	|	1743	...	|	1831	1843	...
Melk d.	|	1450	...	...	|	...	|	1550	...	1602	...	|	1650	|	...	|	...	|	1750	...	|	1838	1850	...
St Pölten Hbf d.	1439	1513	...	...	1519	...	1539	1613	...	1621	...	1639	1713	1719	...	1739	...	1744	1813	...	1839	1853	1913	...
Wien Westbahnhof a.	1525	...	...	...	1605	...	1625	...	...	1711	...	1725	...	1805	...	1825	...	1830	...	...	1925	1940	...	...

◆ – **NOTES** (LISTED BY TRAIN NUMBERS)

EC23 – JOHANN STRAUSS – [12] Köln - Frankfurt (Main) - Wien; ✕ Bonn - Wien.
EC25 – FRANZ LISZT – [12] and ✕ Dortmund - Köln - Frankfurt (Main) - Budapest.
EC63 – BÉLA BARTÓK – [12] and ✕ Stuttgart - München - Budapest.
EC163 – TRANSALPIN – [1] (observation car), [12] and ✕ Basel - Wien.
EN225 – DONAUWALZER – 🛏 1, 2 cl., ▬ 2 cl. and [2] Oostende - Wien; 🛏 1, 2 cl., ▬ 2 cl. and [2] Amsterdam (train **215**) - Köln - Wien; [12] Passau - Wien.
D263 – ORIENT EXPRESS – 🛏 1, 2 cl. and ▬ 2 cl. Paris Est - Wien; ▬ 2 cl. and [2] Paris Est - Budapest; [12] and ✕ Salzburg - Budapest.
D361 – [12] and 🍷 Saarbrücken - Stuttgart - Bregenz.
D365 – [12] Zürich - Innsbruck.
EN491 – HANS ALBERS – 🛏 1, 2 cl., ▬ 2 cl. and [2] Hamburg - Wien; [12] and 🍷 Passau - Wien.
IC513 – [12] and 🍷 Landeck - Graz.
IC541 – KITZSTEINHORN – [12] and ✕ Innsbruck - Zell am See - Salzburg - Wien.
IC543 – HAHNENKAMM – [12] and ✕ Innsbruck - Zell am See - Schwarzach St Veit - Salzburg - Wien; [12] Villach - Schwarzach St Veit - Wien.
IC545 – JAKOB PRANDTAUER – [12] and ✕ Wörgl - Zell am Zee - Salzburg - Wien.
IC547 – WILDER KAISER – [12] and ✕ Wörgl - Zell am See - Schwarzach St Veit - Salzburg - Wien; [12] Villach - Schwarzach St Veit - Wien.
IC741 – SCHMITTENHÖHE – [12] and ✕ Saalfelden - Zell am See - Salzburg - Wien.
IC743 – HOCHKÖNIG – [12] and ✕ Saalfelden - Zell am See - Salzburg - Wien.
D1019 – VORARLBERG EXPRESS – Runs ⑤ Sept. 30 - Oct. 7 (**not** 🛏 1, 2 cl.), ⑤ Jan. 6 - Apr. 7, also Dec. 16, 22, 25, Jan. 4 (from Germany): 🛏 1, 2 cl., ▬ 2 cl. and [2] Dortmund - Innsbruck; conveys on above dates **except** Mar. 31, Apr. 7: 🛏 1, 2 cl. and ▬ 2 cl. Hamburg (train **D1089**) - Heidelberg - Innsbruck.
D1169 – ARLBERG EXPRESS – Runs ⑤ Feb. 3 - Mar. 24, also Dec. 16, 23, 30 (from Paris/Brussels): 🛏 1, 2 cl. and ▬ 2 cl. Paris Est - Zell am See; ▬ 2 cl. Brussels (train **299**) - Basel - Innsbruck.
E1623 – [12] Stainach Irdning - Attnang Puchheim - Wien.
s – Stops to **set down** only.

Table 800a LINDAU - BREGENZ - ST MARGRETHEN

Supplements on **EC** trains are **not** payable for local journeys

2 class only except where shown

	5850 ⚒	E1861 ⚒	5565 ⚒	5854	5571 5856	5858	5573	EC92 C	5862	5579	5864	5866	5585	EC94 C	5868	5589	EC166 B		5591 5872	5593 5874	5595	5597	5599		EC98 C
München Hbf **765** d.	...	...	...	...	...	...	...	0811	...	...	...	...	...	1211	...	...	1402	...	...	...	...	...	...	...	1839
Lindau 🏨 **800** d.	...	0652	0721	...	0921	...	1003	1029	...	1203	...	...	1403	1419	...	1603	1629	...	1701	1803	1903	2003	2020	...	2104
Bregenz 🏨 ▲ **800** a.	...	0703	0732	...	0932	...	1014	1038	...	1214	...	...	1414	1438	...	1614	1638	...	1713	1814	1914	2014	2031	...	2113
Bregenz 🏨 ▲ d.	0609	...	...	0800	0933	1000	...	1040	1200	...	1310	1400	...	1440	1600	...	1640	...	1714	1815	...	...	...	...	2115
St Margrethen 🏨 a.	0627	...	...	0818	0951	1018	...	1054	1218	...	1328	1418	...	1454	1618	...	1654	...	1733	1834	...	...	...	...	2128
Zürich Hbf **308** a.	...	...	...	...	...	...	...	1221	...	...	...	...	...	1621	...	...	1823	...	...	...	...	...	...	...	2256

B – ALBERT EINSTEIN – [12] and ✕ Praha - Zürich - Bern.
C – [12] and ✕ München - Lindau - St Gallen - Zürich.

▲ – Passengers joining or alighting **EC** trains at Bregenz should use the carriage marked 'Für Reisenden von und nach Bregenz'.

424 Ⓑ – Daily except Saturdays ◆ – See footnote Ⓒ – Saturdays, Sundays and holidays 04

Table 800

BREGENZ - INNSBRUCK - SALZBURG - WIEN

Local trains 2 class only

	EC 27 ✕ ◆	E 1605 ▯ ◆	IC 569 ✕ ◆	IC 769 ◆	EC 169 ✕ ◆	EC 65 ✕ ◆	E 1629 ◆	IC 549 ✕ ◆	2037	EC 29 ✕ ◆	5719	IC 661 ✕ ◆	E 1863 ▯ ◆	EC 161 ✕ ◆	D 461 ▯ ◆	EC 17 ✕ ◆	IC 641 ✕ ◆	2041	5721	IC 663 ✕ ◆	
Lindau 800a .... d.	...	...	...	...	...	...	...	...	...	...	...	...	...	...	1508	...	...	...	...	...	...
Bregenz 🏬 .... d.	...	...	1217	...	...	...	...	...	...	...	...	1417	1443	...	1522	...	...	...	...	1617	...
Buchs 🏬 .... d.	...	...	...	...	1244	...	...	...	...	1403	...	...	...	1452	...	...	...	1603	...	...	...
Feldkirch .... d.	...	...	1244	...	1309	...	...	...	...	1425	1444	1508	1511	1550	...	...	...	1625	1644	...	
Bludenz .... d.	...	...	1300	...	1325	...	...	...	...	1500	1527	1607	...	...	...	1700	...				
Langen am Arlberg ... d.	...	...	1326	...	1350	...	...	...	...	1526	1553	1649	...	...	...	1726	...				
St Antoṅ am Arlberg ... d.	...	...	1337	...	1400	...	...	...	...	1537	1603	1700	...	...	...	1737	...				
Landeck .... d.	...	...	1409	...	1427	...	...	...	...	1609	1630	1725	...	...	...	1809	...				
Imst Pitztal .... d.	...	...	1423	...	...	...	...	...	...	1623	...	...	...	...	...	1823	...				
Ötztal .... d.	...	...	1432	...	1448	...	...	...	...	1632	1651	...	...	...	...	1832	...				
Innsbruck Hbf .... a.	...	...	1458	...	1513	...	...	...	...	1658	1716	...	...	...	...	1858	...				
Innsbruck Hbf 790 810 .. d.	...	...	1502	...	1523	...	...	...	...	1702	1724	...	...	...	...	1902	...				
Jenbach 790 810 .... d.	...	...	1522	...	1542	...	...	...	...	1722	...	...	...	...	...	1922	...				
Wörgl 790 810 .... d.	...	...	1537	...	1556	...	...	...	...	1737	1759	...	...	...	...	1937	...				
Kufstein 790 .... d.	...	...	1547	...	...	...	...	...	...	1747	1809	...	...	...	...	1947	...				
Salzburg Hbf .... a.	...	...	1700	...	...	...	...	...	...	1900	1922	...	...	...	...	2100	...				
Salzburg Hbf .... d.	...	...	1705	...	...	1800	...	1805	...	1905	1925	...	2000	2005	...	2105	...				
Attnang Puchheim ..... d.	...	...	1752	1752	...	...	...	1852	...	1952	...	...	...	2052	...	2152	...				
Wels 740 .... d.	1756	...	1811b	1811	...	...	...	1911	...	2011	2023	...	...	2111	...	2211	...				
Linz Hbf 740 .... d.	1814	...	1827b	1827	...	1914	...	1927	...	2027	2039	...	2114	2127	...	2227	...				
St Valentin .... d.			1842b	1842	...	...	1942	...	...	2042	...	...	...	2142	...	2242	...				
Amstetten .... d.		1859	1904b	1904	...	...	1949	2004	2015	2104	...	...	2204	2219	...	2304	...				
Ybbs an der Donau ..... d.					...	...	1959	...	2030	...	...	...	...	2234	...						
Pöchlarn .... d.					...	...	2008	...	2043	...	...	...	...	2247	...						
Melk .... d.					...	...	2016	...	2050	...	...	...	...	2254	...						
St Pölten Hbf .... d.	1919	1934	1939b	1939	...	2019	2034	2039	2113	2119	...	2139	2144	...	2219	2239	2317	...	2339		
Wien Westbahnhof .... a.	2005	2020	2025b	2025	...	2105	2120	2125	...	2205	...	2225	2230	...	2305	2325	...	...	0025		

	SC 5723	D 969 ▯	D 449 ◆	5725	IC 863 ✕ ◆	D 269 ◆	D 1274	D 349 ◆	E 865 ◆	D 249 ◆	E 1529 ✕	EN 247 ✕	D 465 ◆	D 223 ◆	2007 ✕	E 1621 ✕	EN 467 ✕ ◆
Lindau 800a .... d.	...	...	...	...	...	...	...	...	...	...	...	...	...	...	...	...	...
Bregenz 🏬 .... d.	...	1718	...	...	1817	...	...	2017	...	...	2138	...	...	...	...	...	...
Buchs 🏬 .... d.	1718	...	1750	1819		...	2018	...	...	...		2253	...	...	...	...	0007
Feldkirch .... d.	1740	1744	1812	...	1841	1844	...	2034	2044	...	2211	2323	...	...	...	...	0028
Bludenz .... d.	...	1759	...	...	...	1900	...	...	2100	...	2228	2345	...	...	...	...	
Langen am Arlberg ..... d.	...	...	...	...	...	1926	...	...	2126	...	2301	0014	...	...	...	...	
St Anton am Arlberg ... d.	...	1839	...	...	...	1937	...	...	2137	...	2313	0025	...	...	...	...	
Landeck .... d.	...	1904	...	...	...	2009	...	...	2209	...	2342	0052	...	...	...	...	
Imst Pitztal .... d.	...	...	...	...	...	2023	...	...	2223	...	2357		...	...	...	...	
Ötztal .... d.	...	...	...	...	...	2032	...	...	2232	...	0007		...	...	...	...	
Innsbruck Hbf .... a.	...	1951	...	...	...	2058	...	...	2258	...	0034	0137	...	...	...	...	0246
Innsbruck Hbf 790 810 .. d.	...	1956	...	...	2114	...	...	...	...	2310	...	0048	...	...	...	...	0252
Jenbach 790 810 .... d.	...	2015	...	...	2134	...	...	...	...	2332	...	...	...	...	...	...	
Wörgl 790 810 .... d.	...	2030	...	...	2149	...	...	...	...	2350	...	...	...	...	...	...	
Kufstein 790 .... d.	...	2041	...	...	2159	...	...	...	...		...	...	...	...	...	...	
Salzburg Hbf .... a.	...	2154	...	...	2312	...	...	...	...	0240	...	...	...	...	...	...	0445
Salzburg Hbf .... d.	...	2157	...	...	...	0116	0155	...	...	0305	...	...	...	...	...	...	0453
Attnang Puchheim ..... d.	...	2241	...	...	...	...	0241	...	...	0352	...	0450	...	...	...	...	
Wels 740 .... d.	...	2259	...	...	...	...	0300	...	...	0411	...	0510	...	0529	...	...	0556
Linz Hbf 740 .... d.	...	2315	...	...	...	0233	0314	...	...	0430	0510	0530	...	0546	...	...	0612
St Valentin .... d.	...	...	...	...	...	...	...	...	...	0445	0526	0545	...		...	...	
Amstetten .... d.	...	...	...	...	...	...	...	...	...	0508	0550	0608	...		0622	...	
Ybbs an der Donau ..... d.	...	...	...	...	...	...	...	...	...		0602	...	...		0637	...	
Pöchlarn .... d.	...	...	...	...	...	...	...	...	...		0611	...	...	0635	0645	...	
Melk .... d.	...	...	...	...	...	...	...	...	...		0619	...	...	0642	0653	...	
St Pölten Hbf .... d.	...	0017	...	...	...	...	...	...	...	0544	0639	0644	...	0652	0707	0710	0720
Wien Westbahnhof .... a.	...	0058	...	...	...	0416h	...	...	...	0632	0725	0735	...	0740	0818	...	0805

◆ – NOTES (LISTED BY TRAIN NUMBERS)

EC17 – MAX REINHARDT – 🛏 and ✕ München - Wien.
EC27 – JOSEPH HAYDN – 🛏 and ✕ Hamburg - Köln - Frankfurt (Main) - Wien.
EC29 – PRINZ EUGEN – 🛏 and ✕ Kiel - Hamburg - Köln - Frankfurt (Main) - Wien.
EC65 – MOZART – 🛏 and ✕ Paris Est - Strasbourg - Stuttgart - München - Wien.
EC161 – MARIA THERESIA – 🛏 and ✕ Zürich - Wien.
EC169 – ROBERT STOLZ – 🛏 (observation car), 🛏 and ✕ Zürich - Graz; 🛏 Feldkirch - Graz; 🛏 Zürich - Schwarzach St. Veit (train **EC199**) - Klagenfurt.
D223 – DONAU KURIER – 🛌 1, 2 cl., ▭ 2 cl. and 🛏 Dortmund - Wien; 🛌 1, 2 cl., ▭ 2 cl. and 🛏 Dortmund - Wien (train **D467**) - Budapest.
EN247 – WEST KURIER – 🛌 1, 2 cl., 🛌 1, 2 cl. (T2), ▭ 2 cl. and 🛏 Bregenz - Wien. Train does **not** stop at Salzburg Hbf.
D249 – ▭ 2 cl. and 🛏 München (train **D269**) - Salzburg - Wien; ▭ 2 cl. and 🛏 Innsbruck - Wien; conveys daily Dec. 23 - Jan. 7, ⑥ Jan. 14 - Apr. 1, also Dec. 17 (from Bregenz): ▭ 2 cl. Bregenz (train **E865**) - Innsbruck - Wien.
D269 – KÁLMÁN IMRE – 🛌 1, 2 cl., ▭ 2 cl. and 🛏 München - Wien Hütteldorf - Budapest; 🛏 München - Budapest (train 375) - Curtici (train 22) - Bucureşti.
D349 – 🛏 Zürich - Feldkirch.
D361 – 🛏 and ▯ Saarbrücken - Mannheim - Stuttgart - Bregenz.
D449 – 🛏 Sargans - Feldkirch.
D461 – 🛏 and ▯ Trier - Saarbrücken - Mannheim - Stuttgart - Landeck.

D465 – 🛌 1, 2 cl., ▭ 2 cl. and 🛏 Basel - Zürich - Graz; 🛌 2 cl. and 🛏 Basel - Zürich - Schwarzach St. Veit (train **D895**) - Villach.
EN467 – WIENER WALZER – 🛌 1, 2 cl. Basel - Zürich - Wien; ▭ 2 cl. and 🛏 (sleeperette with supplement) Basel - Wien (train **D467**) - Budapest; 🛏 Salzburg - Wien.
IC549 – PONGAU – 🛏 and ✕ Wörgl - Zell am See - Salzburg - Wien.
IC569 – BODENSEE – 🛏 and ✕ Bregenz - Wien. Train **D15569** from Attnang Puchheim on ⑦ also Dec. 26, Apr. 17, 18, May 1, **not** Dec. 25, Apr. 16, 30.
IC641 – KARL HEINRICH WAGGERL – 🛏 and ✕ Wörgl - Zell am See - Salzburg - Wien.
IC769 – Runs ⑦, also Dec. 26, Apr. 17, 18, May 1, **not** Dec. 25, Apr. 16, 30: 🛏 Stainach Irdning (train 3429) - Attnang Puchheim - Wien.
E865 – 🛏 Bregenz - Innsbruck; conveys daily Dec. 23 - Jan. 7, ⑥ Jan. 14 - Apr. 1, also Dec. 17: ▭ 2 cl. Bregenz - Innsbruck (train **D249**) - Wien.
D1274 – Runs ⑥ Dec. 17 - Jan. 7 and Apr. 8 - May 27 (from Venezia SL): 🛌 1, 2 cl., ▭ 2 cl. and 🛏 Venezia Santa Lucia - Villach Westbf - Salzburg - Linz - Praha.
E1605 – Runs ⑥: 🛏 and ▯ Bischofshofen - Selzthal - Amstetten - Wien.
E1629 – Runs ⑦, **not** Dec. 25, Apr. 16, 30.
b – On ⑦ also Dec. 26, Apr. 17, 18, May 1, **not** Dec. 25, Apr. 16, 30, runs 5 minutes later as **IC15569**.
h – Wien **Hütteldorf**.

Table 801 BLUDENZ - SCHRUNS

2 class only. Montafonerbahn

km		8917 ⚒	8919	8921	8923	8925	8927	8929	8931	8933	8935	8937	8939	8941	8943	8945	8947	8949	8951	8953	8955	8957	8959	8961	8963
0	**Bludenz** d.	0620	0704	0734	0804	0834	0904	1004	1104	1208	1234	1330	1404	1504	1609	1634	1704	1734	1804	1834	1904	2004	2104	2204	2304
7	St Anton im Montafon d.	0632	0716	0745	0815	0845	0914	1014	1114	1219	1245	1341	1414	1514	1620	1645	1715	1745	1815	1845	1914x	2014x	2114x	2214x	2314x
13	**Schruns** a.	0641	0728	0755	0825	0855	0924	1024	1124	1229	1256	1351	1424	1524	1630	1655	1725	1755	1825	1855	1924	2024	2124	2224	2324

	8916 ⚒	8918	8920	8922	8924	8926	8928	8930	8932	8934	8936	8938	8940	8942	8944	8946	8948	8950	8952	8954	8956	8958	8960	8962
Schruns d.	0532	0620	0704	0734	0804	0834	0930	1034	1134	1208	1234	1330	1434	1534	1609	1634	1704	1734	1804	1834	1934	2034	2134	2234
St Anton im Montafon d.	0541x	0632	0716	0745	0815	0845	0939	1043	1143	1219	1245	1341	1443	1543	1620	1645	1715	1745	1815	1845	1943x	2043x	2143x	2243x
Bludenz a.	0552	0642	0728	0755	0825	0855	0950	1054	1154	1229	1255	1351	1454	1554	1630	1655	1725	1755	1825	1855	1954	2054	2154	2254

x – Stops on request.

Operator: Montafonerbahn AG, ☎ Schruns (0 55 56) 723 82.

Table 802 🚌 LANGEN and ST ANTON - OBERLECH

🚌 services (**4248/4274**)

km		A	E	K	G	A	E	A	E	A	K	G	E	K	G	G	E	H	K	E		H	K⑦	K⑥
0	**Langen am Arlberg** d.	0840	0840	1000	...	1045	1050	1200	1200	1330	1330	...	1415	1455	1530	...	1625	1730	1730	1825	1840	1930	1930	1950
	St Anton im Arlberg d.	|	|	|	1000	|	|	|	|	|	|	1315	|	|	|	1610b	|	|	|	|	|	|	|	|
3	Stuben Post d.	0845	0850	1010	|	1050	1055	1205	1205	1334	1334	|	1420	1500	1534	|	1630	1735	1735	1830	1845	1935	1935	1955
5	Rauzalpe d.	0850	0857	1012	1023	1055	1100	1211	1210	1339	1339	1339	1427	1511	1540	1630b	1641	1740	1740	1835	1850	1940	1940	2000
10	Zurs Post d.	0855	0905	1020	1032	1102	1110	1220	1220	1350	1350	1350	1435	1515	1547	1636b	1645	1745	1745	1840	1855	1945	1945	2007
15	**Lech** d.	0900	0917	1033	1037	1107	1119	1225	1228	1357	1400	1357	1448	1526	1554	1642b	1658	1748	1748	1845	1900	1950	1952	2012
18	**Oberlech** ‡ a.	0905	0920	1035	1040	1109	1120	1230	1230	1400	1405	1400	1450	1530	1600	1645b	1700	1750	1750	1850	1905	1955	1955	2015

		K		A	E	E	K	H⚒	G	E	A	H	E		K	K		E	G	A	E		H	K
Oberlech ‡ d.	0725	0750	...	0915	0915	0945	1040	1050	1050	1240	1245	1315	1350	...	1500	1530	...	1630	1645	1645	1710	...	1750	1810
Lech d.	0727	0755	...	0917	0920	0950	1045	1051	1055	1245	1250	1320	1355	...	1505	1535	...	1635	1647	1646	1715	...	1751	1815
Zurs Post d.	0735	0805	...	0925	0928	1000	1055	1059	1103	1255	1255	1330	1405	...	1515	1545	...	1645	1655	1654	1725	...	1759	1825
Rauzalpe d.	0744	0815	...	0935	0934	1013	1102	1104	1110	1304	1304	1340	1415	...	1525	1552	...	1652	1702	1701	1737	...	1806	1835
Stuben Post d.	0750	0822	...	0940	0940	1017	1108	1109	|	1310	1310	|	1422	...	1532	1558	...	1658	|	1705	1742	...	1810	1842
St Anton am Arlberg a.	|	|	...	|	|	|	|	|	1130	|	|	1355	|	...	|	|	...	|	1720	|	|	...	|	|
Langen am Arlberg a.	0755	0830	...	0945	0945	1025	1114	1114	...	1315	1315	...	1430	...	1540	1605	...	1705	...	1710	1750	...	1815	1847

A – Runs May 29 - Nov. 11 and Apr. 24 - May 27.
E – Runs Nov. 12 - Apr. 23.
G – Runs July 9 - Oct 9.
H – Runs July 9 - Sept. 11.
K – Runs Dec. 10 - Apr. 23.
b – Sept. 12 - Oct. 9: Runs 20 minutes later.
‡ – Lech PG. (Oberlech Seilbahnstation).

Table 803 🚌 LANDECK - SCUOL TARASP and MERANO

🚌 services (**4218/4220/4224**), SAD (**101**)

km					N		⚒			N	⑥	Ⓐ	N			N				N		N	Ⓐ	
0	**Landeck** Bf d.	...	0735	...	...	...	...	...	1045	...	1205	1240	...	...	1340	...	...	1610	...	...	1730	...	1815	...
2	Landeck Stadt d.	...	0740	...	...	...	...	...	1050	...	1210	1245	...	...	1345	...	...	1615	...	...	1735	...	1820	...
18	Ried im Oberinntal Post d.	...	0800	...	...	...	...	...	1110	...	1230	1305	...	...	1406	...	...	1635	...	...	1755	...	1838	...
32	Pfunds Post d.	...	0815	...	...	...	...	...	1125	...	1250	1328	...	1340	1425	...	...	1700	...	...	1818	...	1858	1905
45	**Nauders** Post a.	...	0835	...	...	...	...	...	1143	...	1320	1350	...	|	1445	...	...	1719	...	...	1835	...	1920	|
45	**Nauders** Post d.	...	▬	0840	0845	...	...	...	1145	1225	▬	...	1425	|	1445	1535	...	1720	...	1725	...	1840	...	|
53	Martina 🏛 d.	...	...	0900	|	...	...	...	1205	|	...	...	|	1410	1510	|	...	1739	1810	|	...	|	...	1925
73	**Scuol Tarasp** Post d.	...	...	0925	|	...	...	...	1229	|	...	...	|	1435	1535	|	...	...	1841	|	...	|	...	1955
73	**Scuol Tarasp** Bf a.	...	...	0927	|	...	...	...	1232	|	...	...	|	1437	1537	|	...	...	1843	|	...	|	...	1958
50	Resia ‡ d.	0625	*0720*e	...	0857	...	*1005*	...	...	1232	...	...	1437	...	...	1547	...	...	...	1737	...	1852	...	...
74	Malles d.	0655	0755	...	0927	1005	1105	1210	...	1307	1350	...	1507	...	...	1617	1705	...	...	1807	...	1922	...	...
79	Sluderno d.	0705	0805	...	0937	1015	1115	1220	...	1317	1400	...	1517	...	...	1625	1715	...	...	1817	...	1930	...	...
83	Spondigna d.	0713	0813	...	0945	1023	1123	1228	...	1325	1408	...	1525	...	...	1632	1723	...	...	1825	...	1936	...	...
97	Silandro d.	0740	0840	...	1010	1050	1150	1300	...	1355	1435	...	1550	...	...	1657	1750	...	...	1850	...	1958	...	...
132	**Merano** Bus Bf a.	0840	0940	...	1110	1150	1250	1400	...	1455	1535	...	1650	...	...	1751	1850	...	...	1950	...	2055	...	...

	N		⚒	⚒	N				N			N	⚒		N					⚒	N			
Merano Bus Bf d.	0605	...	0645	0745	0845	...	0940	...	1030	1150	...	1245	...	1340	1430	...	...	...	...	1510	1540	1700	1755	2010
Silandro d.	0700	...	0745	0845	0950	...	1045	...	1135	1300	...	1345	...	1440	1535	...	...	...	...	1615	1645	1800	1900	2110
Spondigna d.	0725	...	0812	0910	1015	...	1110	...	1159	1325	...	1410	...	1505	1600	...	...	...	...	1640	1710	1825	1925	2130
Sluderno d.	0733	...	0818	0918	1023	...	1118	...	1206	1333	...	1418	...	1513	1608	...	...	...	...	1648	1718	1833	1933	2137
Malles d.	0743	...	0828	0928	1033	...	1128	...	1215	1343	...	1428	...	1523	1622	...	...	...	...	1658	1728	1843	1943	2145
Resia ‡ d.	0813	...	*0910*	...	1103	...	...	...	1243	▬	...	1458	...	...	1648	...	...	...	...	...	1758	1913	2010e	...
Scuol Tarasp Bf d.	|	0740	▬	...	|	...	...	1135	|	...	1235	|	...	...	|	1615	...	1710	1815	...	|	▬	...	...
Scuol Tarasp Post d.	|	0743	...	...	|	...	...	1138	|	...	1237	|	...	...	|	1617	...	1712	1817	...	|	...	...	...
Martina 🏛 d.	|	0808	...	...	|	...	...	1204	|	...	1303	|	...	...	|	1644	...	1738	1843	...	|	...	...	...
Nauders Post a.	0825	0828	...	...	1115	...	...	1224	1255	...	|	1510	...	...	1700	1704	...	*1800*	|	...	1810	...	...	...
Nauders Post d.	...	...	0840	...	...	1130	...	...	...	1305	|	...	1540	...	...	...	1705	...	|	...	...	1845	...	...
Pfunds Post d.	...	...	0900	...	...	1145	...	...	...	1322	1323	...	1600	...	...	...	1725	...	1903	...	...	1905	...	...
Ried im Oberinntal Post d.	...	...	0923	...	...	1215	...	...	...	...	1339	...	1623	...	...	...	1745	...	...	...	...	1920	...	...
Landeck Stadt a.	...	...	0948	...	...	1235	...	...	...	...	1402	...	1648	...	...	...	1807	...	...	...	...	1945	...	...
Landeck Bf a.	...	...	0950	...	...	1240	...	...	...	...	1405	...	1650	...	...	...	1810	...	...	...	...	1950	...	...

N – Daily **except** Dec. 25, Jan. 1, Apr. 3, May 1.
e – ⚒ only.
‡ – 🏛 is Reschenpass/Passo Resia.

Operators: Dienstleitung, Postautostelle A-6500 Landeck, Austria and SAD – Servizi Autobus Dolomiti, Via Conciapelli 60, 39100 Bolzano, Italy. ☎ Bolzano (0471) 971259, Fax: 970042.

Table 804 🚌 IMST - ÖTZTAL - OBERGURGL

🚌 service (**4194**)

km			v			t⑧	⚒					⚒												
0	**Imst** Post d.	...	...	...	1020	1120	1215	...	1515r	1635	...	1740	1825	...	...	...	...	...	...	...	...	...	...	...
13	**Ötztal** Bahnhof d.	0732	0810	0942	1052	1150	1240	1415	1540	1655	1745	1810	1843	...	...	...	...	...	...	...	...	...	...	...
20	Oetz Post d.	0745	0822	0956	1104	1205	1255	1428	1555	1710	1758	1825	1859	...	...	...	...	...	...	...	...	...	...	...
53	Sölden Post d.	0837	0908	1048	1154	1251	1345	1512	1640	1754	1840	1909	...	...	...	...	...	...	...	...	...	...	...	...
57	Zwieselstein d.	0846	0918	1100	1202	1257	1354	1521	1649	1802	1849	1915	...	...	...	...	...	...	...	...	...	...	...	...
67	**Obergurgl** Post a.	0906	0932	1118	1220v	1314	1414z	1534	1700	1825v	1902	1935	...	...	...	...	...	...	...	...	...	...	...	...

	Ⓐ		⚒					t	⚒		p											
Obergurgl Post d.	...	...	...	0745t	0945	1135	1320	1400	1455z	1550	1630	1755	...	...	...	...	...	...	...	...	...	...
Zwieselstein d.	0532	0605	0714	0800	1000	1154	1335	1415	1511	1604	1646	1811	...	...	...	...	...	...	...	...	...	...
Sölden Post d.	0542	0615	0725	0815	1013	1205	1345	1425	1522	1618	1700	1825	...	...	...	...	...	...	...	...	...	...
Oetz Post d.	0625	0702	0811	0905	1100	1247	1429	1508	1605	1700	1748	1913	...	...	...	...	...	...	...	...	...	...
Ötztal Bahnhof a.	0638	0715	0826	0912	1113	1302	1444	1522	1619	1712	1800	1925	...	...	...	...	...	...	...	...	...	...
Imst Post a.	...	0735	0845	...	...	1340	1500	...	1635	...	1819	1945n	...	...	...	...	...	...	...	...	...	...

n – ⑦ only.
p – Runs ⚒, also daily July 10 - Oct. 2 and Apr. 10 - May 27.
r – ⚒ only.
t – July 10 - Sept. 9 **only**.
v – July 10 - Oct. 2 and Dec. 17 - Apr. 23 **only**.
z – ⚒ July 11 - Oct. 1 and Dec. 19 - Apr. 22 **only**.

For explanation of standard symbols see page 4

Table 805

JENBACH - MAYRHOFEN

A bus service also serves **Mayrhofen - Jenbach** and intermediate points

2 class only. Narrow gauge. ZV
🚌 service (**8330**)

km		8821	8823		8825		8827		8811 S 🚂	8829	8831		8833		8835	8837	8813 T 🚂	8839		8841		8843	8845	🚌	🚌
0	**Jenbach Zillertal Bf.** d.	0650	0750	...	0850	...	0950	...	1030	1050	1150	...	1250	...	1350	1450	1455	1550	...	1650	...	1750	1850	1925	2050
7	Schlitters d.	0702	0802	...	0902	...	1002	...	1048	1102	1202	...	1302	...	1402	1502	1517	1602	...	1702	...	1802	1902	1938d	2103d
11	Fügen d.	0709	0809	...	0909	...	1009	...	1059	1109	1209	...	1309	...	1409	1509	1525	1609	...	1709	...	1809	1909	1943d	2108d
13	Uderns d.	0714	0814	...	0914	...	1014	...	1106	1114	1214	...	1314	...	1414	1514	1531	1614	...	1714	...	1814	1914	1948	2113
17	Kaltenbach d.	0721	0821	...	0921	...	1021	...	1125	1121	1221	...	1321	...	1421	1521	1545	1621	...	1721	...	1821	1921	1956	2121
21	Aschau im Zillertal d.	0727	0827	...	0927	...	1027	...	1139	1127	1227	...	1327	...	1427	1527	1554	1627	...	1727	...	1827	1927	2005	2130
25	**Zell am Ziller** d.	0734	0834	...	0934	...	1034	...	1151	1134	1234	...	1334	...	1434	1534	1603	1634	...	1734	...	1834	1934	2012	2137
32	**Mayrhofen** a.	0747	0847	...	0947	...	1047	...	1210	1147	1247	...	1347	...	1447	1547	1620	1647	...	1747	...	1847	1947	2024	2149

		8818		8820		8822	8824		8826	8828		8830	8812 S 🚂	8832		8834		8836	8838		8814 T 🚂	8840		8842	🚌
Mayrhofen d.	...	0620	...	0720	...	0820	0920	...	1020	1120	...	1220	1247	1320	...	1420	...	1520	1620	...	1700	1720	...	1820	1850
Zell am Ziller d.	...	0633	...	0733	...	0833	0933	...	1033	1133	...	1233	1304	1333	...	1433	...	1533	1633	...	1718	1733	...	1833	1905
Aschau im Zillertal d.	...	0640	...	0740	...	0840	0940	...	1040	1140	...	1240	1313	1340	...	1440	...	1540	1640	...	1727	1740	...	1840	1912
Kaltenbach d.	...	0646	...	0746	...	0846	0946	...	1046	1146	...	1246	1322	1346	...	1446	...	1546	1646	...	1737	1746	...	1846	1920
Uderns d.	...	0651	...	0751	...	0851	0951	...	1051	1151	...	1251	1331	1351	...	1451	...	1551	1651	...	1746	1751	...	1851	1926
Fügen d.	...	0656	...	0756	...	0856	0956	...	1056	1156	...	1256	1338	1356	...	1456	...	1556	1656	...	1808	1756	...	1856	1932d
Schlitters d.	...	0702	...	0802	...	0902	1002	...	1102	1202	...	1302	1348	1402	...	1502	...	1602	1702	...	1818	1802	...	1902	1937d
Jenbach Zillertal Bf a.	...	0713	...	0813	...	0913	1013	...	1113	1213	...	1313	1406	1413	...	1513	...	1613	1713	...	1834	1813	...	1913	1950

S – Daily Sept. 25 - Oct. 29, Dec. 25 - Jan. 8, Apr. 14 - 17 and Apr. 29 - May 27.
T – ⑥ Oct. 1 - 29 and Apr. 29 - May 27.
d – Buses stop at Schlitters **Dorf** and Fügen **Dorf**.
🚂 – Steam train. Special fares apply.
Operator: ZV – Zillertaler Vehrkehrsbetriebe AG, Jenbach.

Table 806

JENBACH - ACHENSEE

Rack railway operated by steam locomotives. Special fares apply.

Narrow gauge. Achenseebahn
2 class only

km			C				C		C	
0	**Jenbach ÖBB Bahnhof** d.	...	1035	...	...	...	1320	...	1520	...
1	Burgeck d.	...	1042	...	...	...	1327	...	1527	...
4	Eben d.	...	1103	...	...	...	1348	...	1548	...
5	Maurach d.	...	1108	...	...	...	1353	...	1553	...
7	**Achensee Schiffstation** a.	...	1120	...	...	...	1405	...	1605	...

			C		C		C		
Achensee Schiffstation d.	...	...	1205	...	1410	...	1610	...	...
Maurach d.	...	...	1212	...	1417	...	1616	...	...
Eben d.	...	...	1215	...	1421	...	1619	...	...
Burgeck d.	...	...	1237	...	1442	...	1639	...	...
Jenbach ÖBB Bahnhof a.	...	...	1245	...	1450	...	1645	...	...

C – Runs Sept. 26 - Oct. 23 and May 1 - 28.
Operator: Achenseebahn AG, 6200 Jenbach, ☎ Jenbach (0 52 44) 22 43.

Table 807

MAYRHOFEN - KRIMML - ZELL AM SEE

🚌 **Mayrhofen - Krimml**

2 class only. Narrow gauge. ÖBB
🚌 services (**4090/4**)

km		5901 ⚒	5903	5905	5907	🚌 E	🚌 A	🚌 D	5909	🚌 A		5911	🚂 H	🚌 AE	🚌 A	5913	5915	🚌 DE	🚌 B	5917	🚌 C		🚌 DE⚒	🚌 A
0	**Mayrhofen Bf** d.	...	...	...	...	...	0922	...	...	1107	...	...	...	...	...	...	...	...	1527	...	1627	...	...	1822
8	Zell am Ziller Bf d.	...	...	...	...	0935	0935	1035	...	1120	...	...	...	1240	...	...	...	1535	1540	...	1640	...	1835	1835
9	Zell am Ziller Dorf d.	...	...	...	...	0937	0938	1037	...	1123	...	...	...	1242	...	...	...	1537	1542	...	1642	...	1837	1837
26	**Gerlos Ort** d.	...	...	...	...	1009	1014	1109	...	1159	...	...	...	1314	...	...	...	1614	1614	...	1714	...	1909	1909
35	Königsleiten (Sesselift) d.	...	...	...	...	1025	1030	...	...	1215	...	...	...	1330	1450	...	...	...	1630	...	1730	...	...	...
51	Mautstelle Ost ‡ d.	...	...	...	...	...	1054	...	...	1239	...	...	...	...	1514	...	...	...	1654	...	1754	...	...	...
54	**Krimml Bf** a.	...	...	...	...	...	1059	...	...	1244	...	...	...	...	1519	...	...	...	1659	...	1759	...	...	...
54	**Krimml Bf** d.	0437	0537	0737	0937	...	...	...	1154	...	...	1337	1548	...	...	1537	1637	...	...	1737	...	...	...	...
79	Mittersill d.	0516	0616	0816	1016	...	...	...	1245	...	...	1416	|	...	...	1616	1716	...	...	1816	...	...	...	...
108	**Zell am See Bf** a.	0610	0710	0910	1110	...	...	...	1336	...	...	1510	1811	...	...	1710	1810	...	...	1910	...	...	...	...

	🚌 A⚒	🚌 A⑦		5900	🚌 A	🚌 E	🚌 D⚒	5902	🚌 A	🚂 H	5904	🚌 E	🚌 D	🚌 A		5908	🚌 D⚒	🚌 E	5910	🚌 A	5912	5914	5916	5918 ⑧n
Zell am See Bf d.	...	...	...	0649	...	...	...	0849	...	0930	1049	...	...	...	...	1349	...	...	1449	...	1549	1649	1749	1849
Mittersill d.	...	...	...	0742	...	...	...	0942	...	|	1142	...	...	...	...	1442	...	...	1542	...	1642	1742	1842	1942
Krimml Bf a.	...	...	...	0823	...	...	...	1023	...	1153	1223	...	...	...	...	1523	...	...	1623	...	1723	1823	1923	2023
Krimml Bf d.	...	...	...	...	0826	...	...	...	1106	...	...	...	...	1331	...	...	...	...	...	1631	...	...	...	...
Mautstelle Ost ‡ d.	...	...	...	...	0830	...	...	...	1113	...	...	...	...	1338	...	...	...	...	...	1638	...	...	...	...
Königsleiten (Sesselift) d.	...	...	...	...	0900	...	...	...	1140	...	...	1330	...	1405	...	...	...	...	...	1705	...	...	...	...
Gerlos Ort d.	0651	0756	...	...	0916	1151	1156	...	1156	...	...	1346	1351	1421	...	...	1651	1651	...	1721	...	...	...	...
Zell am Ziller Dorf a.	0722	0827	...	...	0947	1222	1227	...	1227	...	...	1417	1422	1457	...	...	1722	1722	...	1752	...	...	...	...
Zell am Ziller Bf a.	0724	0829	...	...	0950	1225	1230	...	1230	...	...	1420	1425	1500	...	...	1725	1725	...	1755	...	...	...	...
Mayrhofen Bf a.	...	...	...	...	1003	...	...	...	...	...	...	...	...	1513	...	...	...	...	...	1808	...	...	...	...

A – May 29 - Sept. 24.
B – May 29 - July 8 and Sept. 12 - 24.
C – July 9 - Sept. 11.
D – Sept. 25 - Dec. 17.
E – Dec. 18 - May 27.
H – Runs ②④ July 5 - Aug. 30 also ⑥ Sept. 3 - 24 **only**.
n – Will **not** run Aug. 14, Dec. 25, Apr. 16, 30.
🚂 – Steam train, special fares apply. **Information**: Krimml Dampfzug, Marktplatz 4, A–5730 Mittersill. ☎ Mittersill (0 65 62) 53 91 40; Fax: (0 65 62) 53 91 80.
‡ – Bus stop for Krimml Waterfalls – the highest in Europe. A shuttle bus connects with most trains to/from **Krimml Bf**.

Table 808

🚌 KUFSTEIN and WÖRGL - ELLMAU - KITZBÜHEL

🚌 services (**4006/8/24/60**)

km		⚒	⚒	⚒	⚒						⚒		L	⚒			⑦	⚒	R		K	Ⓐ		
*	München Flughafen* ✈ d.	...	...	...	...	...	...	...	...	...	...	...	1200	...	...	...	...	...	1500	...	...	...	...	...
0	**Kufstein Bf** d.	...	0555	...	...	...	0850	...	1120	...	1240	...	|	...	1355	...	1530	1600	|	...	...	1720	...	1835
	Wörgl Bf d.	...	|	...	0815	...	|	1002	|	1205	|	...	|	1340	|	1510	|	|	|	...	1710	|	1825	|
12	Söll (Crossroads) d.	...	0612	0801	|	...	0910	|	1140	|	1300	...	|	|	1415	|	1550	1620	|	...	|	1740	|	1855
15	Söll (Post) d.	...	0618	|	0845	...	0915	1029	1145	1236	1305	...	|	1415	1420	1540	1555	1625	|	...	1740	1745	1855	1900
17	Scheffau Ort d.	...	0633	0805z	...	...	0928	...	1200	1248	...	...	|	...	1433	1553d	1604z	1638	|	...	...	1800	...	1912
20	Ellmau Dorf/Post d.	0625	0646	0812	...	0905	0941	...	1210	1259	...	1315	1415	...	1446	...	1614	1651	1715	1715	...	1810	...	1922
30	**St Johann in Tirol Bf** a.	|	0713	0830	...	|	1005	...	1230	...	...	|	1425t	...	1510	...	1637	1715	1725t	|	...	1830	...	1940
47	**Kitzbühel Bf** a.	0700	...	...	...	0940	...	...	...	...	...	1350	1435	...	...	...	...	...	1735	1750	...	...	...	...

	⚒	⚒	L	⚒	⚒	⚒	⚒			R				⚒			⚒	K	Ⓐ		⚒			
Kitzbühel Bf d.	...	...	0630	...	...	0750	...	...	...	1000	...	...	1215	...	...	...	...	...	...	...	1620	...	1820	...
St Johann in Tirol Bf d.	0550	...	0645t	...	0730	|	...	0810	...	1010t	...	1045	|	...	...	1320	...	...	1600	1640	|	...	|	1855
Ellmau Dorf/Post d.	0614	...	0655	...	0748	0830	...	0834	...	1020	...	1109	1255	...	1300	1344	...	...	1624	1704	1700	...	1900	1918
Scheffau Ort d.	0628	...	|	...	0755z	...	...	0848	...	|	...	1123	...	...	1313	1358	...	1600d	1638	1718	...	...	...	1926z
Söll (Post) d.	0640	0650	|	0715	|	...	0755	0900	0920	|	1035	1135	...	1315	1325	1410	1420	1615	1650	1730	...	1745	...	1935
Söll (Crossroads) d.	0645	|	|	0720	0800	...	0800	0905	|	|	|	1140	...	1320	|	1415	|	|	1655	1735	...	|	...	1940
Wörgl Bf a.	|	0721	|	|	*0845*	...	|	|	0950	|	1105	|	...	|	1355	|	1450	1655	|	|	...	1815	...	|
Kufstein Bf a.	0705	...	|	0740	...	...	0820	0925	...	|	...	1200	...	1340	...	1435	...	...	1715	1755	...	...	...	2000
München Flughafen* ✈ d.	...	...	0905	...	...	...	...	...	...	1235	...	...	...	...	...	...	...	...	...	...	...	...	...	...

K – ⚒ May 29 - Dec. 21 and Apr. 3 - May 27, also daily Dec. 22 - Apr. 2.
L – ⑥⑦ Dec. 17 - Mar. 19.
R – ⑥ Dec. 17 - Mar. 18.
d – Dec. 22 - Apr. 2.
t – St Johann in Tirol **Steinlechnerplatz**.
z – Scheffau **Gasthof zum Wilder Kaiser**.
* – *177km* from **Kitzbühel**, pick-up/set-down at Terminal 2.

11

🚌 – Bus or coach service

427

Table 810 INNSBRUCK - KITZBÜHEL - BISCHOFSHOFEN - SELZTHAL

1, 2 class except where shown

km		IC 711	3509	IC 741	IC 713	IC 743	D 819	5001	IC 511	IC 891	3515	5003	IC 541	E 1615	5005	E 1617	IC 513	IC 791	3517	5007		IC 543	5009	IC 515
		🍷	2	🍴	🍷	🍴	🍷	2	🍷	🍷	2	2	🍴		2		🍷	🍷	2	2		🍴	2	🍷
			A		♦		♦				A	⚒		♦		♦	♦		A	⚒				
0	**Innsbruck Hbf 790 800** ..... d.	...	...	...	...	...	...	...	0520	...	...	...	0617	...	...	...	0720	...	...	...	...	0817	...	0920
35	Jenbach **790 800** ..... d.	...	...	...	...	...	...	...	0540	...	...	...	0639	...	...	...	0740	...	...	...	...	0839	...	0940
60	Wörgl **790 800** ..... d.	...	...	...	...	...	...	0510	0556	...	...	0601	0657	0706	0710	0733	0756	...	...	0810	...	0857	0910	0956
64	Bruckhäusl ‡ ..... d.	...	...	...	...	...	...	0514	|	...	...	0605	|	|	0714	|	|	...	...	0814	...	|	0914	|
79	Westendorf ..... d.	...	...	...	...	...	...	0530	|	...	...	0623	|	|	0730	|	|	...	...	0832	...	|	0930	|
86	Kirchberg in Tirol ..... d.	...	...	...	...	...	...	0537	0618	...	...	0631	0720	0729	0737	0755	0818	...	...	0840	...	0920	0937	|
96	**Kitzbühel** ..... d.	...	...	...	...	...	...	0548	0628	...	...	0642	0729	0742	0748	0806	0828	...	...	0851	...	0929	0948	1025
105	St Johann in Tirol ..... d.	...	...	...	...	...	...	0558	0636	...	...	0653	0737	0753	0758	0815	0836	...	...	0902	...	0937	0958	1033
141	Saalfelden ..... d.	...	...	0503	...	0609	...	0636	0704	...	...	0732	0808	0827	0836	0847	0904	...	...	0942	...	1008	1036	1104
154	**Zell am See** ..... d.	...	...	0513	...	0620	...	0648	0715	...	...	0756	0820	0842	0848	0900	0915	...	...	0956	...	1020	1048	1115
187	**Schwarzach St Veit** ..... a.	...	...	0544	...	0650	...	0724	0745	...	...	0832	0850	0912	0924	0930	0945	...	...	1032	...	1050	1124	1145
187	**Schwarzach St Veit** ..... d.	...	...	0545	...	0653	...	0727	0747	0757	...	0834	0853	...	0927	...	0947	0957	...	1034	...	1056	1130	1147
192	St Johann im Pongau ..... d.	...	...	0551	...	0659	...	0732	|	|	...	0839	0859	...	0932	...	|	|	...	1039	...	1101	1136	|
201	**Bischofshofen** ..... a.	...	...	0558	...	0706	...	0741	0759	0809	...	0848	0906	...	0941	...	0959	1009	...	1048	...	1109	1145	1159
201	**Bischofshofen 820** ..... d.	0428	0508	0600	0601	0709	0717	0751	0801	0811	0814	0850	0910	...	0951	...	1001	1011	1014	1050	...	1111	1151	1201
255	**Salzburg 820** ..... a.	|	|	0646	|	0753	|	0849	|	0853	|	0949	0953	...	1049	...	|	1053	|	1149	...	1152	1249	|
	Wien Westbahnhof **800** a.	|	|	1025	|	1125	|	...	|	...	|	...	1325	...	...	...	|	...	|	...	...	1525	...	|
225	Radstadt ..... d.	0450	0538	...	0624	...	0740	...	0824	...	0842	...	...	...	...	...	1024	...	1042	...	...	...	...	1224
244	Schladming ..... d.	0506	0557	...	0640	...	0757	...	0840	...	0902	...	...	...	...	...	1040	...	1102	...	...	...	...	1240
284	**Stainach Irdning** ..... d.	0545	0642	...	0710	...	0828	...	0910	...	0947	...	...	...	...	...	1110	...	1148	...	...	...	...	1310
297	Liezen ..... d.	0558	0654	...	0721	...	0838	...	0921	...	1000	...	...	...	...	...	1121	...	1200	...	...	...	...	1321
303	**Selzthal** ..... a.	0605	0700	...	0728	...	0845	...	0928	...	1007	...	...	...	...	...	1128	...	1207	...	...	...	...	1328
	Graz **825** ..... a.	0810	...	...	0920	...	1050	...	1120	...	...	...	...	...	...	...	1320	...	...	...	...	...	...	1520

	EC 114	3519	5011	D 1169	IC 545	5013	IC 517	EC 10		3521	E 1605		5015	IC 547	5017	IC 519	IC 593	3523	5019	IC 549	5021	EC 169	IC 595	3569
	🍴	2	2		🍴	2	🍷	🍴		2			2	🍴	2	🍷	🍷	2	2	🍴	2	🍴	🍷	2
		A	⚒	♦						A	♦©		⚒					A	⚒			♦		
Innsbruck Hbf 790 800 ..... d.	...	...	...	0948	*0951*	...	1120	...	...	...	...	...	...	*1151*	...	1320	...	...	...	*1351*	...	1523	...	...
Jenbach **790 800** ..... d.	...	...	...	1007	*1025*	...	1140	...	...	...	...	...	...	*1225*	...	1340	...	...	...	*1425*	...	1542	...	...
Wörgl **790 800** ..... d.	...	...	1010	1024	1057	1110	1156	...	...	...	...	...	1210	1257	1310	1356	...	...	1410	1457	1510	1558	...	...
Bruckhäusl ‡ ..... d.	...	...	1014	|	|	1114	|	...	...	...	...	...	1214	|	1314	|	...	...	1414	|	1514	|	...	...
Westendorf ..... d.	...	...	1032	|	|	1130	|	...	...	...	...	...	1232	|	1330	|	...	...	1432	|	1530	|	...	...
Kirchberg in Tirol ..... d.	...	...	1040	1046	1120	1137	1218	...	...	...	...	...	1240	1320	1337	1418	...	...	1440	1520	1537	1619	...	...
Kitzbühel ..... d.	...	...	1051	1055	1129	1148	1228	...	...	...	...	...	1251	1329	1348	1428	...	...	1451	1529	1548	1628	...	...
St Johann in Tirol ..... d.	...	...	1102	1103	1137	1158	1236	...	...	...	...	...	1302	1337	1358	1436	...	...	1502	1537	1558	1636	...	...
Saalfelden ..... d.	...	...	1142	1132	1208	1236	1304	...	...	...	...	...	1342	1408	1436	1504	...	...	1542	1608	1636	1704	...	...
Zell am See ..... d.	...	...	1156	1142	1220	1248	1315	...	...	...	...	...	1356	1420	1448	1515	...	...	1556	1620	1648	1715	...	...
Schwarzach St Veit ..... a.	...	...	1232	...	1250	1324	1345	...	...	...	...	...	1432	1450	1524	1545	...	...	1632	1650	1724	1744	...	...
Schwarzach St Veit ..... d.	1157	...	1234	...	1253	1327	1347	1357	...	...	...	...	1434	1456	1527	1547	1557	...	1634	1653	1727	1747	1757	...
St Johann im Pongau ..... d.	|	...	1239	...	1259	1332	|	|	...	...	...	...	1439	1501	1532	|	|	...	1639	1659	1732	|	|	...
Bischofshofen ..... a.	1209	...	1248	...	1306	1341	1359	1409	...	...	...	...	1448	1509	1541	1559	1609	...	1648	1706	1741	1759	1809	...
Bischofshofen 820 ..... d.	1211	1214	1250	...	1309	1351	1401	1411	...	1414	1508	...	1450	1511	1551	1601	1611	1614	1650	1709	1751	1801	1811	1814
Salzburg 820 ..... a.	1253	|	1349	...	1353	1449	|	1453	...	|	|	...	1549	1553	1649	|	1653	|	1749	1753	1849	|	1853	|
Wien Westbahnhof **800** . a.	...	|	...	...	1725	...	|	...	...	|	|	...	...	1925	...	|	...	|	...	2125	...	|	...	|
Radstadt ..... d.	...	1242	...	...	...	...	1424	...	...	1442	1537	...	...	...	...	1624	...	1642	...	...	...	1824	...	1842
Schladming ..... d.	...	1302	...	...	...	...	1440	...	...	1502	1553	...	...	...	...	1640	...	1702	...	...	...	1840	...	1902
Stainach Irdning ..... d.	...	1349	...	...	...	...	1510	...	...	1554	1629	...	...	...	...	1710	...	1749	...	...	...	1910	...	1948
Liezen ..... d.	...	1401	...	...	...	...	1521	...	...	1608	1639	...	...	...	...	1721	...	1801	...	...	...	1921	...	2000
Selzthal ..... a.	...	1407	...	...	...	...	1528	...	...	1614	1646	...	...	...	...	1728	...	1808	...	...	...	1928	...	2007
Graz **825** ..... a.	...	...	...	...	...	...	1720	...	...	...	...	...	...	...	...	1920	...	...	...	...	...	2120	...	...

	5023	EC 117	IC 641	5025	D 801	IC 613	IC 597	3571		5081	5027	5029	IC 715		IC 691	3573		5031		D 249	EN 247	D 465		
	2	🍷	🍴	2	🍴	🍷	🍷	2		2	2	2	🍷		🍷	2		2						
	⚒	♦			♦															♦	♦	♦		
Innsbruck Hbf 790 800 ..... d.	...	...	*1539*	...	...	1720	...	...	...	...	...	...	1920	...	...	...	...	...	...	2320	0048	0140	...	...
Jenbach **790 800** ..... d.	...	...	*1600*	...	...	1740	...	...	...	...	...	...	1940	...	...	...	...	...	...	2332	|	|	...	...
Wörgl **790 800** ..... d.	1610	...	1657	1710	1728	1756	...	...	...	1810	...	1901	1956	...	...	...	...	2056	...	2350	|	|	...	...
Bruckhäusl ‡ ..... d.	1614	...	|	1714	|	|	...	...	...	1814	...	1904	|	...	...	...	...	|	...	|	|	|	...	...
Westendorf ..... d.	1632	...	|	1730	1748	|	...	...	...	1832	...	1921	|	...	...	...	...	2114	...	|	|	|	...	...
Kirchberg in Tirol ..... d.	1640	...	1720	1737	1756	1818	...	...	...	1840	...	1928	2018	...	...	...	...	2121	...	0013	|	|	...	...
Kitzbühel ..... d.	1651	...	1729	1748	1806	1828	...	...	...	1851	...	1939	2028	...	...	...	...	2131	...	0022	|	|	...	...
St Johann in Tirol ..... d.	1702	...	1739	1758	1814	1836	...	...	...	1902	...	1947	2036	...	...	...	...	2138	...	0030	|	|	...	...
Saalfelden ..... d.	1742	...	1808	1836	1851	1904	...	...	...	1941	...	...	2104	...	...	...	...	...	...	0058	|	|	...	...
Zell am See ..... d.	1756	...	1820	1848	1907	1915	...	...	...	...	...	...	2115	...	...	...	...	...	...	0110	|	|	...	...
Schwarzach St Veit ..... a.	1832	...	1850	1924	1955	1945	...	...	...	...	...	...	2145	...	...	...	...	...	...	0140	|	0348	...	...
Schwarzach St Veit ..... d.	1834	...	1853	1927	...	1947	1957	...	...	...	2034	...	2147	...	2157	...	...	...	...	0144	|	0353	...	...
St Johann im Pongau ..... d.	1839	...	1859	1932	...	|	|	...	...	...	2039	...	2153	...	|	...	...	...	...	|	|	|	...	...
Bischofshofen ..... a.	1848	...	1906	1941	...	1959	2009	...	...	...	2048	...	2200	...	2209	...	...	...	...	0156	|	0405	...	...
Bischofshofen 820 ..... d.	1850	1856	1909	1951	...	2001	2011	2014	...	...	2050	...	...	...	2211	2221	...	...	...	0157	|	0410	...	...
Salzburg 820 ..... a.	1949	|	1953	2049	...	|	2053	|	...	...	2149	...	...	...	2253	|	...	...	...	0240	|	|	...	...
Wien Westbahnhof **800** . a.	...	|	2325	...	...	|	...	|	...	...	...	...	...	...	...	|	...	...	...	0632	0735	|	...	...
Radstadt ..... d.	...	1920	...	...	...	2024	...	2042	...	...	...	...	...	...	...	2249	...	...	...	...	...	|	...	...
Schladming ..... d.	...	1938	...	...	...	2040	...	2102	...	...	...	...	...	...	...	2306	...	...	...	...	...	|	...	...
Stainach Irdning ..... d.	...	2007	...	...	...	2110	...	2148	...	...	...	...	...	...	...	...	...	...	...	...	...	|	...	...
Liezen ..... d.	...	2017	...	...	...	2121	...	2200	...	...	...	...	...	...	...	...	...	...	...	...	...	|	...	...
Selzthal ..... a.	...	2024	...	...	...	2128	...	2207	...	...	...	...	...	...	...	...	...	...	...	...	...	0527	...	...
Graz **825** ..... a.	...	2205	...	...	...	2320	...	...	...	...	...	...	...	...	...	...	...	...	...	...	...	0732	...	...

♦ – **NOTES** (LISTED BY TRAIN NUMBERS)

EC117 – MOZART – [2] and 🍷 Salzburg - Graz; [12] Paris Est (train **EC65**) - München - Salzburg - Graz.

EC169 – ROBERT STOLZ – [1] (observation car), [2] and 🍴 Zürich - Graz; [12] Zürich - Schwarzach St Veit (train **EC199**) - Klagenfurt.

EN247 – WEST KURIER – See Table **800**. Train does **not** stop at Salzburg Hbf.

D249 – 🛏 2 cl. and [12] Innsbruck - Wien; conveys Dec. 23 - Jan. 7, ⑥ Jan. 14 - Apr. 1, also Dec. 17 (from Bregenz): 🛏 2 cl. Bregenz (train **E865**) - Innsbruck - Wien.

D465– 🛌 1, 2 cl., 🛏 2 cl. and [2] Basel - Zürich - Graz; 🛏 2 cl. and [12] Basel - Schwarzach St Veit (train **D895**) - Villach.

IC513 – DACHSTEIN – [12] and 🍷 Landeck - Graz.

IC713 – KARL BÖHM – [12] and 🍷 Salzburg - Graz.

D801 – THERESE GIEHSE – Runs ⑥ Oct. 1 - 29, Jan. 7 - Apr. 8, May 20, 27, also Dec. 17, 23, 25, 26: [12] and 🍴 Berlin Hbf (train **IC801**) - München - Bischofshofen.

D819 – Runs daily Sept. 24 - Oct. 28, Mar. 31 - May 27, and ⑤ Jan. 6 - Mar. 24, also Dec. 16, 20, 22, 25, Jan. 4 (from Germany): 🛏 2 cl. and [12] Hamburg (train **D1299**) - Bischofshofen - Graz; 🛏 2 cl. Dortmund (train **D1123**; **D1125** on ⑤ Jan. 6 - Mar. 24, also Dec. 16, 20, 22, 25, Jan. 4) - Rosenheim (train **D1299**) - Bischofshofen - Graz.

D1169 – ARLBERG EXPRESS – Runs ⑤ Feb. 3 - Mar. 24, also Dec. 16, 23, 30 (from Paris/Brussels): 🛌 1, 2 cl. and 🛏 2 cl. Paris Est - Zell am See; 🛏 2 cl. Brussels (train **299**) - Basel - Innsbruck.

E1605 – Runs © only; [12] and 🍷 Bischofshofen - Amstetten - Wien.

E1615 – Runs ⑤ Jan. 6 - Apr. 7 also Dec. 16, 22, 25, Jan. 4 (from Germany): 🛌 1, 2 cl. (**not** Mar. 24, 30, Apr. 7), 🛏 2 cl. and [2] Dortmund (train **D1015**) - München (train **D1115**) - Wörgl - Schwarzach St Veit; Conveys on ⑤ Jan. 6 - Mar. 17 also Dec. 16, 22, 25, Jan. 4 (from Germany): 🛌 1, 2 cl. and 🛏 2 cl. Hamburg (train **D1299**) - Rosenheim (train **D1125**) - Wörgl - Schwarzach St Veit.

E1617 – SKI EXPRESS – Runs ⑤ Dec. 23 - Apr. 7 (from Brussels): 🛌 1, 2 cl. (T2), 🛏 2 cl. and [2] Brussels (**D1117**) - Wörgl - Schwarzach St Veit.

A – [2] Bischofshofen - Selzthal - Amstetten.

‡ – Formerly **Söll Leukental**.

♦ – See footnote

Table 810 — SELZTHAL - BISCHOFSHOFEN - KITZBÜHEL - INNSBRUCK

1, 2 class except where shown

Section 1

	IC 5074 2	IC 713 ♥	IC 712 ♥	5076 2	5000 2 ✕	3550 2	IC 590 2 ♥	IC 714 2 ♥	D 800 ◆	5002 2	IC 844 2 ✕	3586 2	IC 5004 2 ✕ A	3504 2 A	IC 592 2 ♥	IC 510 2 ♥	5006 2	IC 540 ✕	EC 116 2 ♥	5008 2	3510 2 A	IC 594 2 ♥
Graz 825 d																0640			0757			
Selzthal d						0528	0632							0753		0831			0938			0953
Liezen d						0535	0639							0800		0838			0945			1000
Stainach Irdning d						0549	0649							0812		0849			0955			1013
Schladming d						0640	0722					0901		0821		0921			1023			1101
Radstadt d						0658	0738					0920		0842		0937			1043			1120
Wien Westbahnhof 800 d																		0640				
Salzburg 820 d		0508			0611			0708	0713	0808	0811		0908		0911		1008	1011		1108		
Bischofshofen 820 a		0551			0715	0726	0750	0759	0811	0851	0908		0912	0950		0959	1008	1051	1105	1112	1148	1150
Bischofshofen d			0553		0717		0752	0801	0813	0853	0914		0952	1001		1012		1053	1114			1152
St Johann im Pongau d			0601		0727		0812	0822	0901	0924			1001	1022		1101		1124				
Schwarzach St Veit a			0606		0732		0804	0813	0818	0827	0906		0929	1004	1013	1027		1106		1129		1204
Schwarzach St Veit d			0607		0733		0815	0821	0832	0909	0932		1015	1032		1109		1132				
Zell am See d			0637		0809		0846	0855	0909	0941			1009	1046		1109		1141	1209			
Saalfelden d	0609		0647		0823		0856	0909	0922	0951			1023	1056		1122		1151	1223			
St Johann in Tirol d	0647		0716	0757	0902		0924	0942	1000	1021			1102	1124		1302						
Kitzbühel d	0656		0725	0806	0912		0933	0952	1009	1031			1112	1133	1209	1231		1312				
Kirchberg in Tirol d	0705		0734	0818	0923		0942	1001	1019	1040			1123	1142	1219	1240		1323				
Westendorf d	0712			0825	0931			1008	1026				1131	1226		1331						
Bruchhäusl ‡ d	0729			0843	0948			1043					1148	1243		1348						
Wörgl 790 800 d	0740		0758	0848	0953		1006	1028	1048	1103			1153	1206	1248	1303		1353				
Jenbach 790 800 d	0800		0812				1020	1134						1220	1334							
Innsbruck Hbf 790 800 a	0828		0832				1040	1212						1240	1409							

Section 2

	IC 512 ♥	5010 2	542 ✕	E 1604 ◆©	5012 2 ✕	3512 2	IC 596 ♥	EC 168 ✕	5014 2	IC 544 ✕	5016 2 A	3514 2	EC 11 ✕	IC 516 ♥	5018 2	IC 546 ✕	5020 2 A	3518 2 A	EC 115 ✕	IC 518 ♥	D 1168
Graz 825 d	0840						1040				1240										1440
Selzthal d	1031			1113		1153	1231				1353	1431					1547	1631			1631
Liezen d	1038			1121		1200	1238				1400	1438					1553	1638			1638
Stainach Irdning d	1049			1132		1213	1249				1413	1449					1614	1649			1649
Schladming d	1121			1207		1301	1321				1501	1521					1701	1721			1721
Radstadt d	1137			1223		1320	1337				1520	1537					1701	1737			1737
Wien Westbahnhof 800 d			0840							1040							1240				
Salzburg 820 d		1111		1208			1308			1408	1411			1511	1608		1611		1708		
Bischofshofen 820 a	1159	1210	1251	1253	1312	1348	1350	1359	1410	1451	1512	1548	1550	1559	1611	1651	1712	1748	1752	1759	
Bischofshofen d	1201	1212	1253		1314		1352	1401	1412	1453	1514	1552	1601	1615	1653	1714			1752	1801	
St Johann im Pongau d		1222	1301		1324			1422		1501	1524		1625	1701	1724						
Schwarzach St Veit a	1213	1227	1306		1329		1404	1413	1427	1506	1529	1604	1613	1630	1706	1729			1804	1813	
Schwarzach St Veit d	1215	1232	1309		1332			1423	1432	1509	1535	1615	1635	1709	1732					1815	
Zell am See d	1246	1309	1341		1409		1453	1509	1541	1609	1646	1713	1741	1809		1846				1852	
Saalfelden d	1256	1322	1351		1423		1503	1522	1551	1623	1656	1726	1751	1823		1856				1902	
St Johann in Tirol d	1325	1400	1421		1502		1530	1600	1621	1702	1719	1804	1821	1902		1924				1930	
Kitzbühel d	1334	1412	1431		1512		1539	1609	1631	1712	1726	1814	1831	1912		1933				1939	
Kirchberg in Tirol d	1343	1419	1440		1523		1547	1619	1640	1723	1735	1825	1840	1921		1942				1948	
Westendorf d		1426			1531			1626		1731			1832	1931							
Bruchhäusl ‡ d		1443			1548			1643		1748			1849	1948							
Wörgl 790 800 d	1406	1448	1503		1553		1611	1648	1706	1753	1806		1854	1906		1953			2006	2010	
Jenbach 790 800 d	1420		1534		1609		1625		1720		1820			1920					2020	2024	
Innsbruck Hbf 790 800 a	1440		1609		1645		1743		1840		1943			2040					2044		

Section 3

	E 1614 ◆	5022 2	5082 2	IC 548 ✕	E 1616 ◆	3520 2	IC 890 ♥	IC 610 ♥	IC 640 ✕	5034 2	3522 2	IC 892 ♥	IC 612 ♥	IC 818 ✕	IC 740 ✕	IC 710 ♥	5066 2	D 464 ◆	EN 246 ◆	D 248 ◆
Graz 825 d				1640					1840	1900		2040						2200		
Selzthal d				1753	1831				1953	2031	2113	2231						0013		
Liezen d				1800	1838				2001	2038	2121	2238								
Stainach Irdning d				1813	1849				2014	2049	2132	2250								
Schladming d				1901	1921				2101	2121	2203	2324								
Radstadt d				1920	1937				2120	2137	2219	2341								
Wien Westbahnhof 800 d				1440					1640			1840							2210	2330
Salzburg 820 d	1711			1814			1908		2008	2011		2108	2208		2323					0302
Bischofshofen 820 a		1812		1856		1948	1950	1959	2053	2112	2148	2150	2159	2242	2251	0007	0022	0136		0343
Bischofshofen d		1814		1858	1906	1952	2001		2054	2114	2152		2253			0024		0141		0345
St Johann im Pongau d		1824		1906					2103	2124			2301			0033				
Schwarzach St Veit a		1829		1911		2004	2013		2108	2129		2204	2306			0038		0153		0357
Schwarzach St Veit d	1828	1835		1913		2015			2109				2309					0212		0359
Zell am See d	1905	1912		1943		2035		2046	2145				2341							0431
Saalfelden d	1918	1925		1953		2046		2056	2154				2350							0441
St Johann in Tirol d	1950		2002	2023		2116		2124												0509
Kitzbühel d	2005		2011	2032		2127		2133												0517
Kirchberg in Tirol d	2016		2021	2041		2137		2142												0526
Westendorf d			2028																	
Bruchhäusl ‡ d			2045																	
Wörgl 790 800 d	2038		2050	2103		2158		2206												0549
Jenbach 790 800 d				2128		2220														0604
Innsbruck Hbf 790 800 a				2209		2240												0421	0447	0624

♦ – NOTES (LISTED BY TRAIN NUMBERS)

EC116 – MOZART – 🍴 and ♥ Graz - Bischofshofen; ⬜ Graz - Salzburg (train EC64) - Paris Est.

EC168 – ROBERT STOLZ – ⬜ (observation car), ⬜ and ✕ Graz - Zürich; ⬜ Klagenfurt (train EC198) - Schwarzach St Veit - Zürich.

EN246 – WEST KURIER – See Table 800. Train does **not** stop at Salzburg Hbf.

D248 – ⬜ 2 cl. and ⬜ Wien - Innsbruck; Conveys Dec. 23 - Jan. 6, ⑤ Jan. 13 - Mar. 31, also Dec. 16 (from Wien): ⬜ 2 cl. Wien - Innsbruck (train IC860) - Bregenz.

D464 – ⬜ 1, 2 cl., ⬜ 2 cl. and ⬜ Graz - Zürich - Basel; ⬜ and ⬜ Villach (train D894) - Schwarzach St Veit - Basel.

IC610 – SCHÖCKL – ⬜ and ♥ Graz - Landeck.

IC612 – KARL BÖHM – ⬜ and ♥ Graz - Salzburg.

D800 – THERESE GIEHSE – Runs ⑥⑦ Sept. 25 - Oct. 30, Jan. 7 - Apr. 9, and May 20, also Dec. 18, 24, 26, 27, Jan. 2, 6, Apr. 18, 22: ⬜ and ✕ Bischofshofen - München (train IC800) - Berlin Hbf.

D818 – Runs daily Sept. 25 - Oct. 29, Apr. 1 - May 27, and ⑥ Jan. 7 - Mar. 25, also Dec. 17, 21, 23, Jan. 1, 5: ⬜ Graz - Bischofshofen; ⬜ 2 cl. and ⬜ Graz - Bischofshofen (train D1298) - Hamburg; ⬜ Graz - Bischofshofen (train D1298) - Rosenheim (train D1122; D1124 on ⑥ Jan. 7 - Mar. 25, also Dec. 17, 21, 23, Jan. 1, 5) - Dortmund.

IC844 – PINZGAU – ⬜ and ✕ Linz - Salzburg - Wörgl.

D1168 – ARLBERG EXPRESS – Runs ⑥ Feb. 4 - Mar. 25, also Dec. 17, 24, 31: ⬜ 1, 2 cl. and ⬜ 2 cl. Zell am Zee - Paris Est; ⬜ 2 cl. Innsbruck - Basel (train 298) - Brussels.

E1604 – Runs © only; ⬜, and ♥ Wien - Amstetten - Selzthal - Bischofshofen.

E1614 – Runs ⑥ Jan. 7 - Apr. 8, also Dec. 23, and Jan. 1, 5: ⬜ 1, 2 cl. (not Mar. 25, Apr. 1, 8), ⬜ 2 cl. and ⬜ Schwarzach St Veit - Wörgl (train D1114) - München (train D1014) - Dortmund; Conveys on ⑥ Jan. 7 - Mar. 18, also Dec. 23, and Jan. 1, 5: ⬜ 1, 2 cl. and ⬜ 2 cl. Schwarzach St Veit - Wörgl (train D1114) - Kufstein (train D1124) - Rosenheim (train D1298) - Hamburg.

E1616 – SKI EXPRESS – Runs ⑥ Dec. 31 - Apr. 15: ⬜ 1, 2 cl. (T2), ⬜ 2 cl. and ⬜ Schwarzach St Veit - Wörgl (train D1116) - Brussels.

A – ⬜ Amstetten - Selzthal - Bischofshofen.
‡ – Formerly Söll Leukental.

Table 811 ZELL AM SEE - HINTERGLEMM

service (3406)

km		⚒						C					C					C							⚒
0	**Zell am See** Bf ... d.	0623	0658	...	0820	...	0920	1020	...	1120	1220	...	1320	...	1420	...	1520	1620	...	...	1720	...	1820	1920
20	Saalbach Ort ... d.	0651	0730	...	0855	...	0955	1055	...	1155	1255	...	1355	...	1455	...	1555	1655	...	...	1755	...	1855	1955
23	**Hinterglemm** Ost ... a.	0659	0738	...	0902	...	1002	1102	...	1202	1302	...	1402	...	1502	...	1602	1702	...	...	1802	...	1902	2002

	⚒		⚒							C						C			C					⑥
Hinterglemm Ost ... d.	0632	...	0702	...	0755	0925	...	1025	...	1125	...	1225	...	1325	...	1425	1525	...	1625	...	1725	...	1825	1920
Saalbach Ort ... d.	0640	...	0710	...	0805	0935	...	1035	...	1135	...	1235	...	1335	...	1435	1535	...	1635	...	1735	...	1835	1928
Zell am See Bf ... a.	0707	...	0737	...	0837	1007	...	1107	...	1207	...	1307	...	1407	...	1507	1607	...	1707	...	1807	...	1907	1957

C – Runs ⚒, also daily Dec. 24 - Apr. 17.

Table 812 SALZBURG - STROBL - BAD ISCHL

services (**2560, 3000**)

km		⚒	⚒			A			⚒	⑦		B	C	D	E				F	BC	⚒		B	C
0	**Salzburg Hbf** ... d.	...	0645	0815	0915	1015	1125	1215	1315	1315	1415	1515	1515	1615	1615	1625x	1715	1725x	1815	1815	1915	2030	2205	2300
1	Salzburg Mirabellplatz ... d.	...	0649	0819	0919	1019	1129	1219	1319	1319	1419	1519	1519	1619	1619	1629x	1719	1729x	1819	1819	1919	2034	2209	2304
32	St Gilgen ... d.	0605	0736	0905	1010	1105	1220	1310	1410	1410	1510	1605	1605	1705	1710	1710	1805	1810	1904	1905	2005	2120	2245	2340
45	Strobl ... d.	0620	0756	0921	1031	...	1241	1331	1431	1429	1531	1619	1621	...	1729	1731	...	1831	...	1921	2021	...	...	...
57	**Bad Ischl Bahnhof** ... a.	0643	0820	0945	1055	...	1305	1355	1455	...	1555	...	1645	...	...	1755	...	1855	...	1945	2045	...	...	...

	⚒	Ⓐ	Ⓐ	Ⓒ	Ⓒ	⚒	⚒		M	C					C	K	N						G	C
Bad Ischl Bahnhof ... d.	0505	...	0605	0605	...	0645	...	0750	...	...	0915	*1015*x	1125	1215	1315	...	*1330*	1415	1515	1615	1715	1815	2010	2010
Strobl ... d.	0523	...	0628	0628	...	0710	...	0815	...	0941	0941	1041x	1153	1241	1341	...	*1355*	1441	1541	1641	1741	1841	2032	2033
St Gilgen ... d.	0540	0600	0645	0643	0647	...	0750	0835	0935	1005	1005	1105	1220	1310	1405	1415	1415	1505	1605	1705	1805	1905	...	2051
Salzburg Mirabellplatz ... d.	0621	0646	0726	...	0736	...	0836	0921	1021	1041	1051	1151	1306	1356	1451	1501	1501	1551	1651	1751	1851	1951	...	2136
Salzburg Hbf ... a.	0625	0650	0730	...	0740	...	0840	0925	1025	1045	1055	1155	1310	1400	1455	1505	1505	1555	1655	1755	1855	1955	...	2140

A – ⚒ May 29 - July 8 and Sept. 12 - May 27, also daily July 10 - Sept. 11.
B – Ⓐ May 29 - July 8 and Sept. 12 - May 26.
C – Daily July 9 - Sept. 11.
D – Daily May 29 - July 10 and Sept. 10 - May 27, also Ⓒ July 11 - Sept. 9.
E – Ⓐ July 11 - Sept. 9.
F – Ⓒ May 29 - July 3 and Sept. 17 - May 27.
G – Daily May 29 - July 8 and Sept. 12 - May 27.
K – ⑥ June 4 - July 9 and Sept. 10 - May 27.
M – Ⓐ May 30 - Sept. 23.
N – Ⓐ May 29 - July 8 and Sept. 12 - May 27.
t – Runs on schooldays.
x – Ⓐ only.

Table 813 ST WOLFGANG - STROBL - BAD ISCHL

service (**2560, 3000**)

km		Ⓐ	⚒	A	⚒							⑦	C	B			F	BC		BC		C	C
0	**St Wolfgang Schafbergbahnhof** ‡ d.	0520	...	0615	0650	...	0740	...	0905	...	...	1005	1005	1005	1210	1315	1505	1505	1615	1715	1815	1905	2000
1	St Wolfgang Marktplatz ... d.	0522	...	0617	0655	...	0745	...	0910	...	...	1010	1010	1010	1215	1320	1510	1510	1620	1720	1818	1910	2005
7	Strobl ... d.	0532	0620	0628	0706	...	0754	0756	0920	0921	...	1020	1020	1020	1225	1330	1520	1520	1630	1730	1831	1920	2015
19	**Bad Ischl Bahnhof** ... a.	0555	0643	0655	0730	...	...	0820	...	0945	...	1045	*1045*	*1055*	1250t	1355	...	1545	1655	1755	1855	*1942*	*2045*

	⚒	⚒	⑦	⚒	⚒		C	⑦			C	B				A				BC		C	
Bad Ischl Bahnhof ... d.	0645	...	0825	0910	1015	...	*1125*	1125	1215	...	*1315*	1330	1415	...	1515	1615	...	1715	...	1815	...	...	2010
Strobl ... d.	0710	0815	|	0940	1040	...	1150	1150	1240	...	1340	1355	1440	...	1540	1640	...	1740	...	|	1840	1925	2035
St Wolfgang Marktplatz ... d.	0721	0826	0856	0951	1051	...	1201	1201	1251	...	1351	1406	1451	...	1551	1651	...	1751	...	1846	1851	1936	2046
St Wolfgang Schafbergbahnhof ‡ a.	0725	0830	0900	0955	1055	...	1205	1205	1255	...	1355	1410	1455	...	1555	1655	...	1755	...	1851	1855	1940	2050

For explanation of letter codes see under Table **812**.

‡ – Narrow gauge steam rack railway (Schafbergbahn) operates May 7 - October 9 to Schafbergspitze. Special fares are payable. Trains leave from a terminal station adjacent to ferry/buses. Services run subject to demand (minimum 20 passengers). Return journeys must be booked **immediately on arrival** at the summit.

Table 814 ST. GILGEN - STROBL (WOLFGANGSEE)

services

	L	L	E	L	E	L	E	L	L	E	L	E	L	E		L	E	W	E			E	E
St Gilgen ... d.	...	0908	0920	1005	1035	1105	1150	1220	1325	1340	1440	1455	1545	1612	...	1650	1730	1810	1810	...	...	1920	2040
St Wolfgang Schafbergbahnhof ‡.. d.	0807	0941	0945	1038	1100	1138	1215	1254	1359	1404	1514	1520	1619	1637	...	1724	1755	1844	1844	...	...	1954	2112
St Wolfgang Markt ... d.	0815	0948	0952	1045	1107	1145	1222	1301	1406	1410	1521	1527	1626	1644	...	1731	1802	1850	1851	...	...	2001	2118
Strobl ... a.	0830	1003	...	1100	...	1200	...	1316	1421	...	1536	...	1641	...	...	1754	...	...	1914	...	...	2024	...

	L	E	L	E	L	E	L	L	E	L	E	L		E	L	E	L			E	W	E	E
Strobl ... d.	...	...	0835	...	1005	...	1110	1218	...	1325	...	1440	...	...	1550	...	1700	...	...	1800	1800	1930	2030
St Wolfgang Markt ... d.	0800	0840	0858	0955	1020	1110	1125	1233	1305	1340	1415	1455	...	1535	1605	1650	1715	...	...	1815	1822	1955	2045
St Wolfgang Schafbergbahnhof ‡.. d.	0807	0847	0905	1002	1027	1117	1132	1240	1311	1347	1422	1502	...	1542	1612	1657	1722	...	...	1822	1828	2002	2051
St Gilgen ... a.	0841	0912	0939	1027	1100	1142	1206	1314	1335	1421	1447	1536	...	1607	1646	1722	1756	...	...	1856	...	2034	...

E – June 18 - Sept. 18.
L – May 29 - Oct. 9.
W – May 29 - June 17 and Sept. 19 - Oct. 9.
‡ – See note under Table **813**.

Table 815 ATTNANG PUCHHEIM - STAINACH IRDNING

1, 2 class except where shown

km		3440	3400	75700	3404	E3406	3408		E3410	3412	E3414	3416	E3418	3420	E3422		3424	3426	E3428	3430	E3432	3434	3436	
		2⚒	2⚒	2⚒	2	2			2	2	2	X	2	2	2		2	2Ⓐ	2	2	2	2	2	
0	**Attnang Puchheim** ... d.	...	...	0527	0627	0725	0825	...	0925	1025	1125	1225	1325	1425	1525	...	1625	1700	1725	1825	1925	2025	2125	...
12	**Gmunden** ... d.	...	...	0555	0644	0744	0844	...	0944	1044	1144	1243	1344	1444	1544	...	1644	1714	1744	1844	1944	2044	2143	...
17	Altmünster am Traunsee ... d.	...	...	0604	0649	0749	0849	...	0949	1049	1149	1248	1349	1449	1549	...	1649	1721	1749	1849	1949	2049	2148	...
22	Traunkirchen ... d.	...	...	0609	0654	0754	0854	...	0954	1054	1154	1254	1354	1454	1554	...	1654	1726	1754	1854	1954	2054	2154	...
28	Ebensee Landungsplatz ... d.	...	...	0617	0702	0802	0902	...	1002	1102	1202	1302	1402	1502	1602	...	1702	1734	1802	1902	2002	2102	2202	...
46	**Bad Ischl** ... d.	...	0539	0645	0725	0822	0925	...	1022	1125	1222	1325	1422	1525	1622	...	1725	1759	1822	1925	2022	2124	2223	...
65	Hallstatt ... d.	...	0604	0719	0750	0846	0950	...	1046	1150	1246	1350	1446	1550	1646	...	1750	...	1846	1950	|	|	...	...
67	Obertraun Dachsteinhöhlen . d.	...	0614	0723	0753	0850	0953	...	1050	1153	1250	1353	1450	1553	1650	...	1753	...	1850	1953	2048	2151	...	...
78	Bad Aussee ... d.	0534	0628**d**	0736	0811	0906	1011	...	1106	1211	1306	1411	1506	1611	1706	...	1811	...	1906	2005	2100	2203	...	...
108	**Stainach Irdning** ... a.	0609	0705**d**	...	0846	0942	1046	...	1142	1246	1342	1446	1542	1646	1747	...	1846	...	1954	...	...	...	...	...

	3401	3403	3405	3407	3409	E3411		3413	E3415	3417	E3419	3421	E3423		3425	E3427	3429	E3431	3433	3435	E3437	3439		
	2	2⚒	2	2	2⚒	2⑦		2	2	2	2	Y	2		2	2	Z	2	2Ⓐ	2Ⓒ	2	2		
Stainach Irdning ... d.	...	...	...	...	0610	0627	...	0718	0819	0918	1019	1118	1219	...	1318	1419	1518	1619	1654	1718	1819	1918	...	...
Bad Aussee ... d.	...	...	0524	0602	0646	0709	...	0806	0906	1006	1106	1206	1306	...	1406	1506	1606	1706	1739	1806	1906	2006	...	...
Obertraun Dachsteinhöhlen ... d.	...	...	0536	0614	0658	0722	...	0818	0920	1018	1120	1218	1320	...	1418	1520	1618	1720	1753	1818	1920	2018	...	...
Hallstatt ... d.	...	...	|	0618	0701	0725	...	0821	0923	1021	1123	1221	1323	...	1421	1523	1621	1723	1756	1821	1923	2021	...	...
Bad Ischl ... d.	0449	0530	0604	0647	0747	0750	...	0847	0950	1047	1150	1247	1350	...	1447	1550	1647	1750	1835	1847	1950	2047	...	...
Ebensee Landungsplatz ... d.	0510	0551	0625	0708	0808	0808	...	0908	1008	1108	1208	1308	1408	...	1508	1608	1708	1808	1907	1908	2008	2108	...	...
Traunkirchen ... d.	0518	0559	0633	0716	0816	0816	...	0916	1016	1116	1216	1316	1416	...	1516	1616	1716	1816	1914	1916	2016	2116	...	...
Altmünster am Traunsee ... d.	0523	0604	0638	0721	0821	0821	...	0921	1021	1121	1221	1321	1421	...	1521	1621	1721	1821	1919	1921	2021	2121	...	...
Gmunden ... d.	0529	0610	0644	0727	0827	0827	...	0927	1027	1127	1227	1327	1427	...	1527	1627	1727	1827	1927	1927	2027	2127	...	...
Attnang Puchheim ... a.	0545	0626	0700	0743	0843	0843	...	0943	1043	1143	1243	1343	1443	...	1543	1643	1743	1843	1943	1943	2043	2143	...	...

X – (12) Wien - Attnang Puchheim - Stainach Irdning.
Y – (12) Stainach Irdning - Attnang Puchheim - Wien.
Z – (12) Stainach Irdning - Attnang Puchheim; conveys on ⑦ also Dec. 26, Apr. 17, 18, May 1, **not** Dec. 25, Apr. 16, 30: (12) Stainach Irdning - Attnang Puchheim - Wien.
d – Runs daily.

Table 820   SALZBURG and LIENZ - VILLACH - KLAGENFURT

1, 2 class except where shown

km		IC 4627 2 ☆	IC 532 ⚑	IC 713 ◆	E 1734	4905 2	D 1299 A	D 1299 B	D 1209 ◆	590 ⚑	D 1209 E	D 1209 F	D 1215 ◆ C	4613 2	IC 844 ✕	4907 2	IC 592 ⚑	4635 2	E 1738	4615 2 C	IC 540 ✕	4909 2	4639 2	IC 594 ⚑
0	Salzburg Hbf d.			0508		0541	0623	0623	0657	0708			0757		0808		0908				1008			1108
54	Bischofshofen a.			0551		0642	0705	0705	0741	0750			0840		0851		0950				1051			1150
54	Bischofshofen d.			0551		0643	0709	0709	0742	0752			0844		0853	0859	0952				1053			1152
63	St Johann im Pongau d.					0653	0718	0718	0751				0853		0901	0908					1101			
68	Schwarzach St Veit a.					0658	0724	0724	0757	0804			0859		0906	0913	1004				1106			1204
68	Schwarzach St Veit d.					0715	0728	0728	0759	0807			0903		0916		1007					1114		1207
88	Bad Hofgastein d.					0734	0750	0750	0818	0824			0923		0935		1024					1133		1224
99	Badgastein d.			4633		0750	0804	0804	0843	0837	0843	0843	0942		0950		1037					1147		1237
103	Böckstein d.			2		0755				→					0954							1152		
115	Mallnitz Obervellach ‡ d.					0805	0820	0820	0851	0858	0858		0959		1004		1051				1202			1251
151	Lienz d.	0508	0631	0746										0930					1043	1126	1210			
151	Spittal Millstättersee d.	0616	0724	0840		0854	0850	0850	0920	0931	0931		1031		1041		1120	1143		1231	1239		1310	1320
188	Villach Hbf a.	0654	0746			0926	0914	0914	0943	0954	0954		1054		1115		1143	1217			1314			1343
188	Villach Hbf 830 d.	0710	0750		0836				0917				1000				1150	1236						1350
204	Velden am Wörthersee 830 d.		0801		0848				0929				1014				1201	1248						
212	Pörtschach am Wörthersee 830 d.				0854				0936				1022					1254						1405
226	Klagenfurt Hbf 830 a.	0733	0814		0905				0948				1014		1034		1214	1305						1414
	Wien Südbahnhof 830 a.		1240														1440				1640			1840

		E 1830 C	4617 2 ✕ W	IC 542 X	4913 2	4641 ✕	IC 596 ⚑	4643 2	EC 113 ✕	IC 544 ✕	4917 N	EC 11 ⚑	IC 430 2 C	4619 2	IC 546 Ⓐ	4919 2	E 1710 ◆	EC 199 ◆	EC 115 ✕	IC 634 ⚑	EC 117 ✕	4623 2 ✕	IC 548 ⚑	4923 2	IC 890 ⚑
	Salzburg Hbf d.			1208		1308	1400		1408	1508			1608		1628		1708		1808		1814			1908	
	Bischofshofen a.			1251		1350	1442		1451	1550			1651		1718		1750		1848		1856			1950	
	Bischofshofen d.			1253		1352	1444		1453	1552			1653		1720		1752		1858					1952	
	St Johann im Pongau d.			1301						1501			1701		1728				1906						
	Schwarzach St Veit a.			1306		1404	1457		1506	1604			1706		1734		1804		1911					2004	
	Schwarzach St Veit d.				1320	1407	1502			1515		1607			1716		1753	1807					1915	2007
	Bad Hofgastein d.				1340	1424			1523		1535	1623			E 1735		1809	1823					1935	2026
	Badgastein d.				1354	1437			1540		1550	1638		1814	1750		1822	1838					1950	2044
	Böckstein d.				1358						1556				1756								1955	2044
	Mallnitz Obervellach ‡ d.				1408		1451		1555		1607	1652			1806		1836	1852					2005	2054
	Lienz d.		1335			1410			1521					1631	1717			1817		1914					
	Spittal Millstättersee d.	1434		1445	1510	1520	1621	1626		1645	1721	1725b	1826		1850		1912	1921	1925		2023		2047	2126
	Villach Hbf a.		1519		1543	1649			1719	1744	1748				1925		1935	1944	1950		2122		2151
	Villach Hbf 830 d.	1436			1550	1652		1750			1831				1937	1946	1952					
	Velden am Wörthersee 830 d.	1448			1601	1704				1846				1948	2003				
	Pörtschach am Wörthersee 830 d.	1454			1711			1805	1854				1954				
	Klagenfurt Hbf 830 a.	1505			1614	1723		1814	1907				2006	2010	2016		
	Wien Südbahnhof 830 a.			2040						2240							0040

		E 1819	4276 2	IC 640 ✕	4925 2	IC 892 ⚑	D 297	D 1275	D 248	D 895
	Salzburg Hbf d.			2008		2108	0045	0256	.0302	
	Bischofshofen a.			2053		2150	0126	0336	0343	
	Bischofshofen d.			2054		2152	0128	0337	0345	
	St Johann im Pongau d.			2103						
	Schwarzach St Veit a.			2108		2204	0141	0349	0357	
	Schwarzach St Veit d.				2127	2207	0145	0354		0410
	Bad Hofgastein d.				2146	2224		0411		0428
	Badgastein d.				2201	2237	0211	0424		0441
	Böckstein d.				2206					
	Mallnitz Obervellach ‡ d.				2217	2251		0438		0454
	Lienz d.	2030								
	Spittal Millstättersee d.	2131		2300	2320		0257	0508		0523
	Villach Hbf a.	2205		2337	2343		0324v	0532v		0545
	Villach Hbf 830 d.		2213		2345					
	Velden am Wörthersee 830 d.		2228		2355					
	Pörtschach am Wörthersee 830 d.		2235		0001					
	Klagenfurt Hbf 830 a.		2249		0012					

		IC 741 ✕	4900 2	4902 2	4904 2 ✕	4630 2	IC 891 ⚑	EC 112 ◆	4614 2 C	IC 791 ⚑
	Wien Südbahnhof 830 d.									
	Klagenfurt Hbf 830 d.						0546	0645		0746
	Pörtschach am Wörthersee 830 d.						0557	0658		
	Velden am Wörthersee 830 d.						0603	0705		0800
	Villach Hbf 830 a.						0615	0717		0810
	Villach Hbf d.		0500	0531			0619	0723		0819
	Spittal Millstättersee d.	0541	0614	0624			0645	0749	0754	0844
	Lienz d.					0735			0901	
	Mallnitz Obervellach ‡ d.	0510	0616		0652		0715	0820		0914
	Böckstein d.	0520	0627		0703					
	Badgastein d.	0525	0633		0708		0728	0835		0928
	Bad Hofgastein d.	0539	0647		0721		0740	0847		0940
	Schwarzach St Veit a.	0559	0705		0742		0755	0905		0955
	Schwarzach St Veit d.	0601	0714		0750	0545	0757	0907		0957
	St Johann im Pongau d.	0606	0719		0755	0551				
	Bischofshofen a.	0614	0728		0803	0558	0809	0919		1009
	Bischofshofen d.	0615	0729			0600	0811	0921		1011
	Salzburg Hbf a.	0707	0825			0646	0853	1000		1053

◆ – NOTES (LISTED BY TRAIN NUMBERS)

EC11 – MIMARA – [couchette] and ✕ Leipzig - Nürnberg - München - Ljubljana - Zagreb.

EC112/3 – WÖRTHERSEE – [couchette] and ✕ Klagenfurt - München - Köln - Dortmund and v.v.

EC115 – BLAUER ENZIAN – [couchette] and ✕ Dortmund - Köln - München - Klagenfurt.

EC117 – MOZART – [couchette] and ✕ Paris Est (train EC65) - Salzburg - Graz.

EC199 – ROBERT STOLZ – [couchette] and ⚑ Schwarzach St Veit - Klagenfurt; [couchette] Zürich (train EC169) - Schwarzach St Veit - Klagenfurt.

D297 – ⇌ 1, 2 cl., ⬩ 2 cl. and [couchette] München - Zagreb; ⬩ 2 cl. and [couchette] München - Ljubljana (train 481) - Rijeka.

IC430 – VAL PUSTERIA/PUSTERTAL – [couchette] and ⚑ Lienz - Wien; [couchette] Innsbruck (train IC433) - San Candido - Lienz - Wien.

IC592 – GASTEINERTAL – [couchette] and ⚑ Salzburg - Wien; [couchette] Salzburg - Villach (train EC31) - Roma; [couchette] Venezia Santa Lucia (train D232) - Villach - Wien.

IC713 – KARL BÖHM – [couchette].

D895 – ⬩ 2 cl. and [couchette] Basel (train D465) - Schwarzach St Veit - Villach.

D1209 – Runs ⑤ Sept. 30 - Oct. 7 and Jan. 6 - Apr. 7, also Dec. 16, 22, 25 (from Berlin); ⇌ 1, 2 cl., ⬩ 2 cl. and [couchette] Berlin Wannsee - Villach (- Klagenfurt on Oct. 1, 8 only).

D1215 – Runs ⑤ Jan. 6 - Mar. 24, also Dec. 23 (from Amsterdam); ⇌ 1, 2 cl., ⬩ 2 cl. and [couchette] Amsterdam - Klagenfurt; ⬩ 2 cl. and [couchette] Oostende (train D1219) - Koblenz - Klagenfurt.

D1275 – Runs ⑤ Dec. 16 - Jan. 6 and Apr. 7 - May 26 (from Praha); ⇌ 1, 2 cl., ⬩ 2 cl. and [couchette] Praha - České Budějovice - Linz - Venezia Santa Lucia.

A – KÄRNTEN EXPRESS – Runs ⑤ Jan. 6 - Mar. 24, also Dec. 16, 20, 22, 25, Jan. 4 (from Germany); ⇌ 1, 2 cl., ⬩ 2 cl. and [couchette] Hamburg - Villach; ⇌ 1, 2 cl., ⬩ 2 cl. and [couchette] Dortmund (train D1125) - Rosenheim - Villach; For Hamburg and Dortmund - Graz cars see Table 810.

B – KÄRNTEN EXPRESS – Runs daily Sept. 24 - Oct. 28 and Mar. 26 - May 27 (from Germany); ⇌ 1, 2 cl. (Sept. 24 - Oct. 28 only), ⬩ 2 cl. and [couchette] Hamburg - Klagenfurt; ⇌ 1, 2 cl., ⬩ 2 cl. and [couchette] Dortmund (train D1123) - Rosenheim - Klagenfurt; For Hamburg and Dortmund - Graz cars see Table 810.

C – [couchette] San Candido - Spittal Millstättersee and v.v.

E – Runs Oct. 1, 8 only.

F – Runs ⑥ Jan. 7 - Apr. 8, also Dec. 17, 23, 26.

N – [couchette] and ✕ Wien - Innsbruck; [couchette] Wien - Schwarzach St Veit - Villach.

W – [couchette] and ✕ Wien - Wörgl; [couchette] Wien - Schwarzach St Veit - Villach.

X – [couchette] Wien - Schwarzach St Veit - Villach.

b – Arrive 1715 to connect with train EC11 to Ljubljana and Zagreb.

t – Arrive 0830.

v – Villach Westbahnhof.

‡ – For car trains through the Tauern Tunnel – see panel below.

‡ – TAUERN TUNNEL CAR CARRYING TRAINS

km																						
0	Böckstein d.		0630	0730	0830	0930		1030	1130	1230	1330		1430	1530	1630		1730	1830	1930	2030	2130	2230
12	Mallnitz Obervellach a.		0642	0742	0842	0942		1042	1142	1242	1342		1442	1542	1642		1742	1842	1942	2042	2142	2242

	Mallnitz Obervellach d.	0600	0700		0800	0900	1000	1100		1200	1300	1400	1500	1600		1700	1800	1900		2000	2100	2200
	Böckstein a.	0612	0712		0812	0912	1012	1112		1212	1312	1412	1512	1612		1712	1812	1912		2012	2112	2212

Ⓑ – Daily except Saturdays   Ⓒ – Saturdays, Sundays and holidays   ⑦ – Sundays

Table 820 — KLAGENFURT - VILLACH - LIENZ and SALZBURG

1, 2 class except where shown

	4908	IC 543	E 1731	EC 4632	114	4634	4910	IC 545	E 1813	IC 431	EC 10	4616	EC 198	4261	IC 547	4916	4636	E 1735	IC 593	4638	4918	IC 549	E 1737	4640
	X	✕ N		2 C	✕	2 ◆	2	✕		⬚	✕	2	⬚ C	2	✕ W	2	2 ✕		⬚	2		✕	✕ F	2
Wien Südbahnhof 830 .... d.										0722									0922					
Klagenfurt Hbf 830 ...... d.			0855		0952		1007		1053	1146		1203				1253	1346					1453		
Pörtschach am Wörthersee 830 . d.			0907				1021		1105			1215				1307	1355					1505		
Velden am Wörthersee 830 . d.			0913				1028		1111	1200		1222				1315						1511		
Villach Hbf 830 .... a.			0925		1016		1043		1123	1210		1233				1328	1410					1523		
Villach Hbf .... d.	0843				1019		1045			1214	1218	1235	1222		1259		1419		1443					
Spittal Millstättersee .... d.	0918		EC 116	0937	1044	1057	1128			1239	1244	1302	1300	1326	1339		1444	1450	1518					1536
Lienz .... a.			1036		1156					1325		1405			1438		1552							1639
Mallnitz Obervellach ‡ ...... d.	0954		◆		1115		1202				1315		1330	1402		1450		1514		1555				
Böckstein .... d.	1004						1212						1341	1412		1501				1606				
Badgastein .... d.	1011				1219		1218				1329		1343	1417		1508		1528		1612				
Bad Hofgastein .... d.	1024			1140	1231						1340		1354	1431		1522		1540		1625				
Schwarzach St Veit .... a.	1042			1155	1249						1355		1410	1448		1541		1555		1643				
Schwarzach St Veit .... d.		1056		1157			1253				1357			1456			1557			1653				
St Johann im Pongau ...... d.		1101					1259							1501					1659					
Bischofshofen .... a.		1109		1209			1306				1409			1509			1609			1706				
Bischofshofen .... d.		1111	1116	1211			1309				1411			1511			1611			1709				
Salzburg Hbf .... a.		1152	1155	1253			1353				1453			1553			1653			1753				

	IC 595	4642	4920	4604	D 1208	D 1208	1739	IC 597	4644	D 1214	4924	4646	E 1831	IC 691	D 1298	D 1298	4648	E 1613	4926	IC 533	D 1274	D 249	D 894	D 296
	⬚	2	2	2 ◆	G	H		⬚	2		2	2	⬚		J	K	2		2	⬚	◆	◆	◆	◆
Wien Südbahnhof 830 .... d.	1122						1322						1522					1722						
Klagenfurt Hbf 830 ...... d.	1546				1634	1653	1746			1854	1946	1950			2053		2146							
Pörtschach am Wörthersee 830 . d.					1647	1705				1906		2004			2105		2155							
Velden am Wörthersee 830 . d.	1600				1654	1711				1912	2000	2011			2111									
Villach Hbf 830 .... a.	1610				1706	1723	1810			1924	2010	2023			2123		2210							
Villach Hbf .... d.	1619		1650		1720	1720		1819		1849	1834		2019	2026	2026			2141	2310v		0008	0137u		
Spittal Millstättersee .... d.	1644	1645	1725	1728	1749	1749		1844	1846	1914	1929n	1924	IC 612	2046	2056	2056	2128	2216	2244	2335		0033	0206	
Lienz .... a.		1750		1825						1945		2029					2225		2336					
Mallnitz Obervellach ‡ ...... d.	1714		1803		1824	1824		1914		1948	2007		⬚	2116	2132	2132		2250		0007		0105		
Böckstein .... d.			1814	IC							2017		◆			2259								
Badgastein .... d.	1728		1820	641	1842	1842		1928		2002	2025		2129	2148	2148			2305		0020		0120		
Bad Hofgastein .... d.	1740		1833	✕	1853	1853		1940		2014	2042		2140	2159	2159			2319		0031		0131		
Schwarzach St Veit .... a.	1755		1850		1911	1911		1955		2029	2101		2155	2221	2221			2337		0047		0147	0318	
Schwarzach St Veit .... d.	1757			1853	1913	1913		1957		2030	2113		2157	2223	2223					0049	0144			0320
St Johann im Pongau ...... d.				1859	1919	1919				2036	2118			2229	2229									
Bischofshofen .... a.	1809			1906	1927	1927		2009		2044	2127		2209	2238	2238					0101	0156			0332
Bischofshofen .... d.	1811			1909	1935	1935		2011		2047	2150		2205	2211	2257	2257				0102	0159			0334
Salzburg Hbf .... a.	1853			1953	2017	2017		2053		2128	2245		2248	2253	2341	2341				0142	0240			0415

◆ – NOTES (LISTED BY TRAIN NUMBERS)

EC10 – MIMARA – 🚌 and ✕ Zagreb - Ljubljana - München - Nürnberg - Leipzig.
EC114 – BLAUER ENZIAN – 🚌 and ✕ Klagenfurt - München - Köln - Dortmund.
EC116 – MOZART – 🚌 Graz - Salzburg (train EC64) - Paris Est.
EC198 – ROBERT STOLZ – 🚌 and ♈ Klagenfurt - Schwarzach St Veit; 🚌 Klagenfurt - Schwarzach St Veit (train EC168) - Zürich.
D296 – 🛏 1, 2 cl., ➡ and 🚌 Zagreb - München; ➡ 2 cl. and 🚌 Rijeka (train 480) - Ljubljana - München.
IC431 – VAL PUSTERIA/PUSTERTAL – 🚌 and ♈ Wien - Lienz; 🚌 Wien - Lienz - San Candido (train IC432) - Innsbruck.
IC612 – KARL BÖHM – 🚌 and ♈ Graz - Salzburg.
D894 – ➡ 2 cl. and 🚌 Villach - Schwarzach St Veit (train D464) - Basel.
D1214 – Runs ⑥ Jan. 7 - Mar. 25, also Jan. 1: 🛏 1, 2 cl., ➡ 2 cl. and 🚌 Villach - Amsterdam; ➡ 2 cl. and 🚌 Villach - Köln (train D1118) - Oostende.
D1274 – Runs ⑥ Dec. 17 - Jan. 7 and Apr. 8 - May 27 (from Venezia): 🛏 1, 2 cl., ➡ 2 cl. and 🚌 Venezia Santa Lucia - Linz - České Budějovice - Praha.
4604 – 🚌 Spittal Millstättersee - San Candido - Innsbruck.

C – 🚌 Spittal Millstättersee - San Candido.
N – 🚌 and ♈ Innsbruck - Wien; 🚌 Villach - Schwarzach St Veit - Wien.
F – 🚌 Spittal Millstättersee - Lienz - Sillian.
G – Runs Oct.1, 8: 🛏 1, 2 cl., ➡ 2 cl. and 🚌 Klagenfurt - Berlin Wannsee.
H – Runs ⑥ Jan. 7 - Apr. 8, also Dec. 17, 23, 26: 🛏 1, 2 cl., ➡ 2 cl. and 🚌 Villach - Berlin Wannsee.
J – KÄRNTEN EXPRESS – Runs Sept. 25 - Oct. 29 and Apr. 1 - May 27: 🛏 1, 2 cl. (Sept. 25 - Oct. 29 only), ➡ 2 cl. and 🚌 Klagenfurt - Hamburg; 🛏 1, 2 cl., ➡ 2 cl. and 🚌 Klagenfurt - Rosenheim (train D1122) - Dortmund; For Graz - Hamburg and Dortmund cars see Table 810.
K – KÄRNTEN EXPRESS – Runs ⑥ Jan. 7 - Mar. 25, also Dec. 17, 21, 23, Jan. 1, 5: 🛏 1, 2 cl., ➡ 2 cl. and 🚌 Villach - Hamburg; 🛏 1, 2 cl., ➡ 2 cl. and 🚌 Villach - Rosenheim (train D1124) - Dortmund; For Graz - Hamburg and Dortmund cars see Table 810.
W – 🚌 and ♈ Wörgl - Wien; 🚌 Villach - Schwarzach St Veit - Wien.
X – 🚌 Villach - Schwarzach St Veit - Wien.
n – Arrives 1910, connects with 1924 to Lienz.
v – Villach Westbahnhof.
‡ – For car trains through the Tauern Tunnel, see panel on page 431.

Table 825 — LINZ - SELZTHAL - GRAZ

1, 2 class except where shown

km		D 465	IC 711	IC 713	IC 501	IC 819	IC 511	3911	IC 503	IC 513	3913	IC 505		IC 515	3915	IC 507	IC 517	3917	IC 509	IC 519	3919		IC 601	EC 169
		◆	♈	♈	♈		♈ N		♈	♈		♈ N		♈ N		♈	♈		♈	♈			♈	✕
0	Linz Hbf .... d.				0640		0737	0840		0937	1040				1137	1240		1337	1440		1537			1640	
28	Rohr .... d.				0700		0810	0900		1010	1100				1210	1300		1411	1500		1609			1700	
32	Kremsmünster Markt ... d.				0705		0815	0905		1015	1105				1214	1305		1415	1505		1613			1705	
49	Kirchdorf an der Krems .. d.				0723		0837	0923		1036	1123				1236	1323		1436	1523		1636			1723	
67	Hinterstoder .... d.						0859			1059					1259			1459			1659				
81	Windischgarsten .... d.				0753		0915	0953		1115	1153				1315	1353		1515	1553		1715			1753	
87	Spital am Pyhrn .... d.				0800		0920	1000		1120	1200				1320	1400		1520	1600		1720			1800	
104	Selzthal .... a.				0816		0937	1016		1137	1216				1337	1416		1539	1616		1737			1816	
104	Selzthal .... d.		0533	0615	0732	0818	0852	0932		1018	1132		1218		1332		1418	1532		1618	1732			1818	1933
121	Trieben .... d.			0631	0747		0910	0947			1147				1347			1547			1747				1947
167	St Michael .... d.		0622	0704		0903	0943			1103			1303			1503			1703					1903	
179	Leoben Hbf .... d.		0636	0717	0829	0917	0957	1029		1117	1229		1317		1440	1517	1629		1717	1829			1917	2029	
195	Bruck an der Mur ..... a.		0648	0728	0840	0928	1008	1040		1128	1240		1328		1440	1528	1640		1728	1840			1928	2040	
195	Bruck an der Mur 830 ... d.		0658	0736	0845	0936	1015	1045		1136	1245		1340		1445	1536	1645		1736	1845			1936	2045	
249	Graz Hbf 830 .... a.		0732	0810	0920	1010	1050	1120		1210	1320		1414		1520	1610	1720		1810	1920			2010	2120	

◆ – NOTES (LISTED BY TRAIN NUMBERS)

EC169 – ROBERT STOLZ – 🚌 (observation car), 🚌 and ✕ Zürich - Graz.
D465 – 🛏 1, 2 cl., ➡ 2 cl. and 🚌 Basel - Innsbruck - Bischofshofen - Graz.
IC513 – DACHSTEIN – 🚌 and ♈ Landeck - Innsbruck - Bischofshofen - Graz.
IC711 – 🚌 and ♈ Bischofshofen - Graz.
IC713 – KARL BÖHM – 🚌 and ♈ Salzburg - Graz.

D819 – Runs daily Sept. 25 - Oct. 29, Apr. 1 - May 27, and ⑥ Jan. 7 - Mar. 25, also Dec. 17, 21, 23, 26, Jan. 5 (Departs Germany previous day): 🚌 Bischofshofen - Graz; ➡ 2 cl. and 🚌 Hamburg (train D1299) - Bischofshofen - Graz; ➡ 2 cl. Dortmund (train D1123, D1125 on ⑤ Jan. 6 - Mar. 24, also Dec. 16, 20, 22, 25, Jan. 4) - Rosenheim (train D1299) - Bischofshofen - Graz.
N – 🚌 and ♈ Innsbruck - Bischofshofen - Graz.

🛏 – Sleeping car   🚌 – Through carriage (1 and 2 class)   ➡ – Couchette car   11

Table 825 LINZ - SELZTHAL - GRAZ

1, 2 class except where shown

		3923	E 1707	IC 603	EC 117	IC 613	3925	2137	3939	
		2	2 Ⓐ	🍷	🍷 ♦	🍷 N	2	2 Ⓐ	2	
Linz Hbf d.	...	1737	1806	1840	...	...	1937	2137	2217	...
Rohr d.	...	1811	1834	1900	...	...	2011	2211	2249	...
Kremsmünster Markt d.	...	1815	1839	1905	...	...	2015	2215	2254	...
Kirchdorf an der Krems d.	...	1836	1859	1923	...	...	2036	2235	2314	...
Hinterstoder d.	...	1859	1920	|	...	...	2059	...	...	...
Windischgarsten d.	...	1915	1933	1953	...	...	2115	...	...	...
Spital am Pyhrn d.	...	1920	1939	2000	...	...	2120	...	...	...
Selzthal a.	...	1937	1958	2016	...	...	2137	...	...	...
Selzthal d.	...	...	...	2018	2029	2132	...	...	...	...
Trieben d.	...	...	...	|	|	2147	...	...	...	...
St Michael d.	...	...	...	2103	|	|	...	...	...	...
Leoben Hbf d.	...	...	...	2117	2123	2229	...	...	...	...
Bruck an der Mur a.	...	...	...	2128	|	2240	...	...	...	...
Bruck an der Mur 830 d.	...	...	...	2140	|	2245	...	...	...	...
Graz Hbf 830 a.	...	...	...	2215	2205	2320	...	...	...	...

	E 1708	3900	IC 500	3902	IC 510	EC 116	IC 502	3904	IC 512
	2 ⚒	2	🍷	2	🍷 N	🍷 ♦	🍷	2	🍷 N
Graz Hbf 830 d.	...	...	0550	...	0640	0757	0750	...	0840
Bruck an der Mur 830 a.	...	...	0624	...	0715	|	0824	...	0915
Bruck an der Mur d.	...	...	0632	...	0720	|	0832	...	0920
Leoben Hbf d.	...	...	0644	...	0731	0840	0844	...	0931
St Michael d.	...	...	0657	...	|	|	0857	...	|
Trieben d.	...	...	|	...	0812	|	|	...	1012
Selzthal a.	...	...	0742	...	0827	0931	0942	...	1027
Selzthal d.	0532	0614	0744	0820	...	...	0944	1020	...
Spital am Pyhrn d.	0549	0638	0800	0838	...	...	1000	1038	...
Windischgarsten d.	0555	0644	0807	0843	...	...	1007	1044	...
Hinterstoder d.	0608	0700	|	0858	...	...	|	1100	...
Kirchdorf an der Krems d.	0628	0722	0837	0922	...	...	1037	1122	...
Kremsmünster Markt d.	0649	0747	0855	0943	...	...	1055	1143	...
Rohr d.	0700	0751	0900	0948	...	...	1100	1148	...
Linz Hbf a.	0722	0824	0920	1024	...	...	1120	1224	...

	IC 504	3906		EC 168	IC 506	3908	IC 516		E 1704	IC 508	3910	IC 518	3928	IC 600	3912	IC 610		IC 602	3914	IC 612	D 818		IC 710	D 464
	🍷	2		✕ ♦	🍷	2	🍷 N		2	🍷	2	🍷 N	2	🍷	2	🍷 ♦		🍷	2	🍷 ♦	🍷 ♦		🍷 ♦	♦
Graz Hbf 830 d.	0950	...	...	1040	1150	...	1240	...	...	1350	...	1440	...	1550	...	1640	...	1750	...	1840	1900	...	2040	2200
Bruck an der Mur 830 a.	1024	...	...	1115	1224	...	1315	...	...	1424	...	1515	...	1624	...	1715	...	1824	...	1915	1935	...	2115	2235
Bruck an der Mur d.	1032	...	...	1120	1232	...	1320	...	...	1432	...	1520	...	1632	...	1720	...	1832	...	1920	1945	...	2120	2245
Leoben Hbf d.	1044	...	...	1131	1244	...	1331	...	...	1444	...	1531	...	1644	...	1731	...	1844	...	1931	1958	...	2131	2300
St Michael d.	1057	...	...	|	1257	...	|	...	...	1457	...	|	...	1657	...	|	...	1857	...	|	2013	...	|	2314
Trieben d.	|	...	...	1212	|	...	1412	...	...	|	...	1612	...	|	...	1812	...	|	...	2012	2048	...	2212	|
Selzthal a.	1142	...	...	1226	1342	...	1427	...	...	1542	...	1627	...	1742	...	1827	...	1942	...	2027	2104	...	2227	0001
Selzthal d.	1144	1220	...	...	1344	1420	...	...	1526	1544	1620	...	1651	1744	1820	...	...	1944	2020	...	...	...	...	...
Spital am Pyhrn d.	1200	1238	...	...	1400	1438	...	...	1542	1600	1638	...	1709	1800	1838	...	...	2000	2038	...	...	...	...	...
Windischgarsten d.	1207	1244	...	...	1407	1444	...	...	1552	1607	1644	...	1721	1807	1844	...	...	2007	2044	...	...	...	...	...
Hinterstoder d.	|	1300	...	...	|	1500	...	...	1605	|	1659	...	1740	|	1900	...	...	|	2100	...	...	...	...	...
Kirchdorf an der Krems d.	1237	1322	...	...	1437	1522	...	...	1625	1637	1722	...	1811	1837	1923	...	...	2037	2122	...	...	...	...	...
Kremsmünster Markt d.	1255	1343	...	...	1455	1543	...	...	1642	1655	1744	...	1835	1855	1943	...	...	2055	2143	...	...	...	...	...
Rohr d.	1300	1348	...	...	1500	1548	...	...	1645	1700	1748	...	1842	1900	1948	...	...	2100	2148	...	...	...	...	...
Linz Hbf a.	1320	1424	...	...	1520	1624	...	...	1711	1720	1824	...	...	1920	2024	...	...	2120	2224	...	...	...	...	...

♦ – **NOTES** (LISTED BY TRAIN NUMBERS)

EC116/7 – MOZART – [12] Graz - Salzburg (trains **EC64/5**) - München - Paris Est and v.v.; [2] and 🍷 Graz - Bischofshofen and Salzburg - Graz.

EC168 – ROBERT STOLZ – [1] (observation car), [2] and ✕ Graz - Zürich.

D464 – 🛏 1, 2 cl., ▬ 2 cl. and [2] Graz - Bischofshofen - Innsbruck - Basel.

IC610 – SCHÖCKL – [12] and 🍷 Graz - Bischofshofen - Innsbruck - Landeck.

IC612 – KARL BÖHM – [12] and 🍷 Graz - Salzburg.

IC710 – [12] and 🍷 Graz - Selzthal - Bischofshofen.

D818 – Runs daily Sept. 25 - Oct. 29, Apr. 1 - May 27, and ⑥ Jan. 7 - Mar. 25, also Dec. 17, 21, 23, Jan. 1, 5: [2] Graz - Bischofshofen; ▬ 2 cl. and [12] Graz - Bischofshofen (train **D1298**) - Hamburg; ▬ 2 cl. Graz - Bischofshofen (train **D1298**) - Rosenheim (train **D1122**; **D1124** on ⑥ Jan. 7 - Mar. 25, also Dec. 17, 21, 23, Jan. 1, 5) - Dortmund.

N – [12] and 🍷 Graz - Bischofshofen - Innsbruck and v.v.

Table 826 AMSTETTEN - KLEINREIFLING - SELZTHAL

2 class only, except where shown

km		3504	E1803	3510	3516	3530	3532	E1604	3512	3534	3514	3536	3518	3538	3538	3520	3540	3522	E1620	4167	3524	3659	3548	3526
			S	⚒	⑦	⚒		B						©	Ⓐ				L	⚒				
0	**Amstetten** d.	0510	...	0632	0702	0717	0810	0902	0910	1010	1110	1210	1310	1410	1410	1510	1610	1710	1810	...	1910	...	2010	2110
23	Waidhofen an der Ybbs d.	0540	...	0710	0732	0800t	0839	0922	0940	1039	1140	1240	1340	1439	1440	1540	1640	1740	1840	...	1940	...	2039	2140
45	**Kleinreifling** a.	0608	...	0738	0805	0827	...	0943	1008	...	1208	1308	1408	...	1508	1608	1708	1808	1908	...	2008	...	...	2208
45	**Kleinreifling** d.	0614	0656	0758	0806	...	...	0944	1016	...	1219	...	1419	...	...	1619	...	1819	1910	...	...	2014	...	...
81	Hieflau d.	0655	0733	0840	0844	...	...	1020	1100	...	1300	...	1500	...	...	1700	...	1900	1949	1951	...	2053	...	...
106	Admont d.	0722	0757	0908	0909	...	...	1047	1127	...	1327	...	1527	...	...	1728	...	1927	2013b	2013	...	...	...	...
120	**Selzthal** a.	0736	0809	0921	0923	...	...	1059	1141	...	1341	...	1541	...	...	1741	...	1941	2026b	2026	...	...	...	...
	Bischofshofen **810** a.	0948	...	1148	1148	...	...	1253	1348	...	1548	...	1748	...	...	1948	...	2148	...	...	...	...	...	...

	3541	3543	3600	3545	3501	3511		3509	3509	3513	3533	3602	3515	3535	3517	3537	3519	3539	3521	E1605	3531	3523	3525	E1802
	⚒				⚒			⚒	⑦			S⚒				Ⓐ				B				S
Bischofshofen **810** d.	...	...	...	...	...	...	...	0508	...	...	...	...	0814	...	1014	...	1214	...	1414	1508	...	1614	...	...
Selzthal d.	...	...	...	...	0542	...	...	0721	*0737*	...	...	0940	1019	...	1219	...	1419	...	1619	1700	...	1819	...	1947
Admont d.	...	...	...	...	0558	...	...	0741	*0756*	...	...	0953	1033	...	1233	...	1433	...	1633	1714	...	1833	...	2001
Hieflau d.	...	...	0532	...	0625	...	...	0814	*0822*	...	...	1020	1101	...	1301	...	1501	...	1701	1737	...	1901	...	2026
Kleinreifling a.	...	...	0613	...	0713	...	...	0859	*0900*	...	...	1112	1141	...	1351	...	1541	...	1741	1813	...	1941	...	2109
Kleinreifling d.	0428	0550	...	0635	...	0750	...	0901	0901	0950	...	...	1150	1250	1352	1453	1550	1650	1750	1818	1850	1950	2050	...
Waidhofen an der Ybbs d.	0457	0621	...	0708	...	0821	...	0922	0922	1021	1121	...	1221	1321	1421	1521	1621	1721	1821	1840	1921	2021	2121	...
Amstetten a.	0526	0650	...	0734	...	0850	...	0950	0950	1050	1150	...	1250	1350	1450	1550	1650	1750	1850	1858	1950	2050	2150	...

B – Runs © **only**: [12] and 🍷 Wien - Amstetten - Selzthal - Bischofshofen and v.v.

L – [2] Wien - Hieflau Ⓐ, Selzthal ©.

S – [2] Linz - Selzthal and v.v.

b – ⑦ only.

t – Arrive 0747.

Table 827 ST VALENTIN - STEYR - KLEINREIFLING

2 class only

km		E1803	3611	E1805	3641	3613	E1807	3643	3615	E1809	3645	3617	E1901	3647	3631	3649	3621	E1905	E1905	3659	3623	E1907	3653	3625	3627
		S													Ⓐ			Ⓑ	⑥						
0	*Linz* **800** d.	0515	0656	0800	...	0848	1000	...	1054	1200	...	1254	1400	...	1531	1618d	1654	1800	1800	1818d	1854	2000	...	2054	...
24	**St. Valentin** d.	0536	0721	0821	0851	0921	1021	1051	1121	1221	1251	1321	1421	1451	1558	1651	1721	1821	1821	1851	1921	2021	2051	2121	2259
44	Steyr d.	0554	0748	0838	0915	0948	1038	1115	1147	1238	1315	1348	1438	1515	1623	1715	1748	1838	1838	1915	1948	2038	2115	2146	2322
46	Garsten d.	0557	0751	0841	0919	0951	1041	1119	1154	1241	1319	1352	1441	1519	1626	1719	1751	1842	1842	1919	1951	2041	2118	2153	2325
94	**Kleinreifling** a.	0644	0843	...	1014	...	...	1214	1247b	...	1414f	1447d	...	1614	1720	1814	...	1936	...	2014	...	...	...	2249	...

	E1804	3630	E1806	3612	3640	E1808	3614	3642	E1900	3602	3644	E1902	3618	3646	E1904	3620	3648	E1906	3622	3650	E1908	3624	3652	3626	E1802
	Ⓐ									S															S
Kleinreifling d.	0452	...	*0614*	...	0743	...	...	0945	...	1113b	1145	...	...	1345	...	...	1545	...	...	1725	1815	...	1945	...	2110
Garsten d.	0548	0639	0718	0807	0841	0918	1007	1041	1118	1207	1241	1318	1407	1441	1511	1607	1641	1710	1807	1830	1918	2002	2041	2110	2154
Steyr d.	0552	0642	0721	0810	0845	0921	1010	1045	1121	1210	1245	1321	1410	1445	1515	1610	1645	1719	1810	1839	1921	2010	2045	2114	2157
St. Valentin a.	0610	0705	0739	0835	0908	0937	1035	1108	1137	1235	1308	1337	1435	1508	1537	1635	1708	1737	1835	1908	1937	2035	2108	2138	2212
Linz **800** a.	...	...	0759	0907	...	0957	1107	...	1157	1307	...	1357	1507	1542d	1557	1707	1742d	1757	1907	...	1957	2107	...	2207	2240

S – [2] Linz - Selzthal and v.v.

b – ⚒ only.

d – Ⓐ only.

f – © only.

Table 828 WAIDHOFEN AN DER YBBS - LUNZ AM SEE

2 class only. Narrow gauge. ÖBB

Rail service Waidhofen an der Ybbs - Lunz am See. *54 km.* Journey time: 85 - 105 minutes.

From Waidhofen an der Ybbs: 0552⚒, 0710⚒, 0750⑦, 0945, 1118⑥, 1213Ⓐ, 1245©, 1314Ⓐ, 1350, 1542, 1645, 1845.

From Lunz am See: 0452⚒, 0532, 0752, 0942, 1135Ⓐ, 1213⑥, 1350, 1540, 1635Ⓐ, 1742.

Table 829 — GRAZ - SZENTGOTTHARD - SZOMBATHELY

1, 2 class except where shown. ÖBB, MÁV

km			H	2	2	2	2		2	
0	Graz Hbf	d.	0618	...	0925	1142	1232	1325	...	1625	...
62	Fehring	d.	0752	...	1022	1244	1343	1438	...	1739	...
82	Szentgotthard ⓜ	a.	0817	...	1045	1306	1405b	1500	...	1800	...
						2Ⓐ	⤬				
82	Szentgotthard ⓜ	d.	0842	...	1130	1345	1447	1610	...	1830	2235
146	Szombathely	a.	0955	...	1240	1455	1603	1723	...	1938	2340

			2	2	Ⓐ	2	2	H	2	
Szombathely		d.	0505	...	0728	1011	1311	1431	1637	1853
Szentgotthard ⓜ		a.	0619	...	0832	1121	1421	1538	1748	2000
			2⤬		2	2	2Ⓐ	2		
Szentgotthard ⓜ		d.	0655d	...	0850	1140	1435	1600	1820	...
Fehring		d.	0718d	...	0751	0914	1202	1502	1622	1844	...
Graz Hbf		a.	...	0900	1028	1315	1618	1731	1944	...

H – ⟥ Graz - Budapest and v.v.   b – ⤬ only.   d – Runs 30 minutes later on ⑦.

Table 830 — WIEN - BRUCK AN DER MUR - GRAZ and VILLACH

1, 2 class except where shown

km			E 1839	IC 791 🍴	E 4283 2 ⤬	E 1731	IC 4257 2	IC 531 🍴	E 711 🍴	IC 4259 2	E 1553 🍴	IC 551	E 1813	E 1555 🍴	EC 31 ⤬ ◆	IC 4261 2	IC 431 2 ◆	E 501 🍴	E 1557	IC 4287 2	E 151 ⤬ ◆	IC 1735 🍴	E 1559 2	E 4263 2
0	Wien Südbahnhof	d.	...	...	...	...	...	0522	...	0552	0622	...	0652	0718	...	0722	...	0752	...	0822	...	0852	...
4	Wien Meidling	d.	...	...	...	...	...	0528	...	0557	0628	...	0657	...	...	0728	...	0757	...	0828	...	0857	...
50	Wiener Neustadt	d.	...	...	...	...	...	0556	...	0632	0656	...	0732	0749	...	0756	...	0832	...	0856	...	0932	...
106	Semmering	d.	...	...	...	...	...	...	...	0731	...	...	0827	...	...	...	...	0928	...	...	...	1031	...
119	Mürzzuschlag	d.	...	...	...	...	...	0652	...	0748	0752	...	0841	...	...	0852	...	0942	...	0952	...	1048	...
160	Bruck an der Mur	a.	...	...	...	...	...	0717	...	...	0817	...	...	0912	...	0917	...	...	...	1017	...	...	...
160	Bruck an der Mur 825	d.	...	0524	...	0627	...	0724	0736	...	0820	0822	...	0914	...	0924	0936	...	1020	1027	...	...
214	Graz 825	a.	...	...	...	...	0810	...	...	0855	...	...	...	1010	...	1055	...	...	...
	Leoben Hbf	d.	...	0535	...	0640	...	0736	...	...	0836	...	0936	...	1040	...	...
	Knittelfeld	d.	...	0559	...	0704	...	0800	...	...	0900	...	1000	...	1104	...	...
	Zeltweg	d.	...	0605	...	0711	...	0807	...	...	0907	...	1007	...	1111	...	...
	Judenburg	d.	...	0613	...	0718	...	0815	...	...	0915	...	1015	...	1118	...	...
	Unzmarkt	d.	...	0627	...	0732	...	0830	...	...	0930	...	1030	...	1132	...	...
	St Veit an der Glan	d.	0633	0730	...	0836	0903	0930	...	...	1036	...	1130	...	1236	...	1303
	Klagenfurt Hbf	a.	0650	0744	...	0852	0923	0944	...	1051	...	1144	...	1251	...	1324
	Klagenfurt Hbf 820	d.	0653	0746	0750	0855	0925	0946	1007	1053	1121	1130	1146	1215	1253	1326
	Pörtschach am Wörthersee 820	d.	0705	...	0804	0907	0941	0955	1021	1105	1144	1230	1307	1340
	Velden am Wörthersee 820	d.	0712	0800	0811	0913	0949	...	1028	1111	1151	1200	1238	1315	1347
	Villach Hbf 820	a.	0727	0810	0825	0925	1006	1010	1043	1123	1145	1206	1210	1254	1328	1402

			IC 593 🍴 S	IC 503 🍴	E 1651	IC 4289 2	E 555 🍴	E 1737	IC 1653 🍴	E 4267 2	IC 595 🍴 S	IC 505 🍴	E 4269 2	IC 1655 🍴	E 557	E 1739	IC 1657	IC 597 🍴 ◆	E 507 🍴	E 1659	IC 4295 2	E 559 🍴	E 1831	E 1751 🍴	E 4273 2
Wien Südbahnhof	d.		0922	...	0952	...	1022	...	1052	...	1122	...	...	1152	1222	...	1252	1322	...	1352	...	1422	...	1452	...
Wien Meidling	d.		0928	...	0957	...	1028	...	1057	...	1128	...	...	1157	1228	...	1257	1328	...	1357	...	1428	...	1457	...
Wiener Neustadt	d.		0956	...	1032	...	1056	...	1132	...	1156	...	...	1232	1256	...	1332	1356	...	1430	...	1456	...	1532	...
Semmering	d.			...	1131	...		...	1231	...		...	...	1331		1431			...		...	1631		
Mürzzuschlag	d.		1052	...	1148	...	1152	...	1248	...	1252	...	...	1348	1352	...	1448	1452	...	1552	...	1648	
Bruck an der Mur	a.		1117	...		...	1217	...		...	1317	...	...	1417		...	1517	1617	...		...
Bruck an der Mur 825	d.		1124	1136	...	1220	1227	...	1324	1340	...	1420	1427	...	1524	1536	1620	1627	...
Graz 825	a.			1210	...	1255	...	...	1414	...	1455	...	1610	...	1655	...
Leoben Hbf	d.		1136	...	1240	...	1336	...	...	1440	...	1536	...	1640	...
Knittelfeld	d.		1200	...	1304	...	1400	...	...	1504	...	1600	...	1704	...
Zeltweg	d.		1207	...	1311	...	1407	...	...	1511	...	1607	...	1711	...
Judenburg	d.		1215	...	1318	...	1415	...	...	1518	...	1615	...	1718	...
Unzmarkt	d.		1230	...	1332	...	1430	...	...	1532	...	1630	...	1732	...
St Veit an der Glan	d.		1330	...	1436	...	1504	1530	1611	1636	...	1730	...	1836	1904
Klagenfurt Hbf	a.		1344	...	1451	...	1524	1544	1630	1652	...	1744	...	1852	1923
Klagenfurt Hbf 820	d.		1346	...	1354	1453	1530	1546	1639	1653	...	1746	1810	1854	1930
Pörtschach am Wörthersee 820	d.		1355	...	1409	1505	1544	...	1653	1705	...	1825	1906	1944
Velden am Wörthersee 820	d.			...	1418	1511	1551	1600	1700	1711	...	1834	1912	1951
Villach Hbf 820	a.		1410	...	1434	1523	1606	1610	1714	1723	...	1810	1850	1924	2006

			IC 691 🍴 S	IC 509 🍴	E 1855 2 Ⓑ	E 4297 2	E 159 ⤬ ◆	IC 1613	E 1755 🍴	IC 533 🍴	E 601 🍴	IC 1757 ◆	IC 653 ◆	E 1835	IC 1759 ◆	IC 631 🍴	E 235 ◆	IC 603 🍴	E 1635	IC 1235 2 ◆	E 655 🍴	IC 4243 2	IC 633 🍴	EN 237 ◆	E 1639 2
Wien Südbahnhof	d.		1522	...	1552	...	1622	...	1652	1722	...	1752	1822	...	1852	1922	1945	...	1952	2015	2022	...	2122	2222	2315
Wien Meidling	d.		1528	...	1557	...	1628	...	1657	1728	...	1757	1828	...	1857	1928		...	1957		2028	...	2128	2228	2320
Wiener Neustadt	d.		1556	...	1630	...	1656	...	1732	1756	...	1832	1856	...	1932	1956	2012u	...	2032	2043	2056	...	2156	2300	2351
Semmering	d.			...	1734	...		...	1831		...	1931		...	2031			...				...	2240		
Mürzzuschlag	d.		1652	...	1748	...	1752	...	1848	1852	...	1948	1952	...	2048	2052		...		2152		...	2254	0010	0055
Bruck an der Mur	a.		1717	...		...	1817	...		1917	...		2017	...		2117	2134u	...	2204	2217		...	2325	0036	
Bruck an der Mur 825	d.		1724	1736	...	1820	1827	...	1924	1936	2020	2027	...	2124	2136u	2140	...	2206	2220	2222	...		0041	
Graz 825	a.			1810	...	1855	...	...	2010	...	2055	...	2215	...	2255	...			
Leoben Hbf	d.		1736	...	1840	...	1936	...	...	2040	...	2136	2150u	...	2219	...	2238	...	0056	
Knittelfeld	d.		1800	...	1906	...	2000	...	...	2104	...	2200	...		2315	...	0123	
Zeltweg	d.		1807	...	1908	...	2007	...	...	2111	...	2206	...		2322	...	
Judenburg	d.		1815	...	1912	...	2015	...	...	2118	...	2214	...		2329	...	
Unzmarkt	d.		1830	...	1935	...	2030	...	...	2133	...	2228	...		2345	...	
St Veit an der Glan	d.		1930	...	2036	...	2130	...	...	2236	...	2325	...			...	
Klagenfurt Hbf	a.		1944	...	2051	...	2144	...	...	2251	...	2338	2345u	...	0010	...	0254	
Klagenfurt Hbf 820	d.		1946	...	2012	2053	2146	...	...	2253	...	2340	2347u	...	0012	...	0257	
Pörtschach am Wörthersee 820	d.			...	2027	2105	2155	...	...	2308	...			...		...	
Velden am Wörthersee 820	d.		2000	...	2036	2111	...	...	...	2316	...	2354		...		...	0322	
Villach Hbf 820	a.		2010	...	2052	2123	2210	...	...	2332	...	0005	0010u	...	0035	...		

◆ – NOTES (LISTED BY TRAIN NUMBERS)

EC31 – ROMULUS – ⟥ and ⤬ Wien - Roma.
IC151 – EMONA – ⟥ and ⤬ Wien - Ljubljana; ⟥ Wien - Ljubljana (train 483) - Rijeka.
IC159 – CROATIA – ⟥ and ⤬ Wien - Zagreb; ⟥ Wien - Maribor (train 513) - Ljubljana.
D235 – REMUS – 🛏 1, 2 cl., ⇥ 2 cl. and ⟥ Wien - Roma; conveys daily Sept. 26 - Dec. 25, Jan. 9 - Apr. 6, and Apr. 24 - May 18: 🛏 1, 2 cl., ⇥ 2 cl. and ⟥ Wien - Venezia (train IC642) - Milano.
EN237 – SAN MARCO – 🛏 1, 2 cl. (T2), ⇥ 2 cl. and ⟥ Wien - Venezia Santa Lucia; ⟥ Wien - Villach.
IC431 – VAL PUSTERIA/PUSTERTAL – ⟥ and 🍴 Wien - Villach - Lienz; ⟥ Wien - Lienz - San Candido (train IC432) - Innsbruck.
IC533 – EGGER LIENZ – ⟥ and 🍴 Wien - Villach - Lienz.
IC597 – CARINTHIA – ⟥ and 🍴 Wien - Villach - Salzburg; ⟥ Wien - Villach (train D233) - Venezia Santa Lucia.
IC653 – ALEXANDER GIRARDI – ⟥ and 🍴 Wien - Graz; conveys on ⑤, also Dec. 7, Jan. 5, May 24, not Jan. 6: ⟥ and 🍴 Wien - Bruck an der Mur (train E1835) - Villach.

D1235 – Runs daily Dec. 26 - Jan. 8, Apr. 7 - 23, and May 19 - 27: ⇥ 2 cl. and ⟥ Wien - Firenze; 🛏 1, 2 cl., ⇥ 2 cl. and ⟥ Wien - Venezia (train IC642) - Milano.
E1835 – ⟥ Bruck an der Mur - Villach; conveys on ⑤, also Dec. 7, Jan. 5, May 24, not Jan. 6: ⟥ and 🍴 Wien (train IC653) - Bruck an der Mur - Villach.
S – ⟥ and 🍴 Wien - Villach - Salzburg. For Wien - Salzburg direct service see Table 800.
u – Stops to pick up only.

Table 830 VILLACH and GRAZ - BRUCK AN DER MUR - WIEN

1, 2 class except where shown

km		SC 950 🍷 ⚒		IC 500 🍷	IC 630 🍷	D 1234 ◆	D 234 ◆	E 1630	IC 510 🍷	E 1610	SC 932 🍷 ⚒	IC 550 🍷	E 1650 2	IC 502 🍷	IC 530 🍷	E 1652 2	4850 2 ⚒	E 1732	IC 552 🍷	4282 2 ⚒	E 1654 2	4284 2	IC 504 🍷	IC 532 🍷 B
0	**Villach Hbf 820** d.	...	...	...	0349	0411	0424s	...	...	0434	0521	...	...	...	0550	...	0554	0631	...	0650	...	0730	...	0750
16	Velden am Wörthersee **820** d.	...	...	...	0401	|	|	...	...	0446	|	...	...	...	|	...	0609	0645	...	0706	...	0747	...	0801
24	Pörtschach am Wörthersee **820** d.	...	...	...	|	|	|	...	...	0452	|	...	...	...	0605	...	0616	0651	...	0714	...	0755	...	|
38	**Klagenfurt Hbf 820** a.	...	...	...	0415	0435	0447s	...	...	0503	0542	...	...	...	0614	...	0630	0702	...	0729	...	0810	...	0814
38	**Klagenfurt Hbf** d.	...	...	...	0417	0437	0449s	...	...	0505	0543	...	...	...	0616	...	0632	0707	...	...	...	...	...	0816
58	St Veit an der Glan d.	...	...	...	0430	|	|	...	...	0521	0557	...	...	...	0630	...	0653	0723	...	...	...	...	...	0830
128	Unzmarkt d.	...	...	...	0531	|	|	...	...	0627	|	...	...	...	0730	...	0759	0828	...	...	...	...	...	0930
147	Judenburg d.	...	...	...	0545	|	|	...	...	0643	|	...	...	...	0745	...	...	0842	...	...	...	...	...	0945
154	Zeltweg d.	...	...	...	0553	|	|	...	...	0650	|	...	...	...	0753	...	...	0850	...	...	...	...	...	0953
162	Knittelfeld d.	...	...	...	0559	|	|	...	...	0657	|	...	...	...	0800	...	...	0856	...	...	...	...	...	1000
196	Leoben Hbf d.	...	...	...	0625	0631	0643s	...	...	0723	0728	...	...	...	0825	...	...	0920	...	...	...	...	...	1025
	Graz 825 d.	0530	...	0550	|	|	|	0622	0640	|	|	0705	...	0750	|	...	...	|	0905	...	...	...	0950	|
212	Bruck an der Mur **825** a.	0601	...	0624	0638	0644	0655s	0659	0715	0736	0739	0740	...	0824	0836	...	...	0933	0940		...	...	1024	1036
212	Bruck an der Mur d.	0602	...	...	0640	0647	0658s	0701	...	...	0740	0743	...	...	0843	...	...	...	0943	...	...	...	...	1043
253	Mürzzuschlag d.	0627	...	...	0709	|	|	0735	...	...	|	0809	0813	...	0909	0913	...	...	1009	...	1013	...	...	1109
266	Semmering d.	|	...	...	|	|	|	0747	...	...	|	|	0828	...	|	0928	...	...	|	...	1028	...	...	|
312	Wiener Neustadt d.	0722	...	...	0805	0810	0822s	0830	...	...	|	0905	0930	...	1005	1030	...	...	1105	...	1130	...	...	1205
358	**Wien Meidling** a.	0748	...	...	0833	0844	0850s	0903	...	...	0919	0933	1003	...	1033	1103	...	...	1133	...	1203	...	...	1233
362	**Wien Südbahnhof** a.	0753	...	...	0840	0850	0857	0908	...	...	0925	0940	1008	...	1040	1108	...	...	1140	...	1208	...	...	1240

	E 1656 2	4258 2 ⚒	E 1734	IC 158 ✕ ◆	E 1658	IC 506 🍷	IC 590 🍷 S	E 1750 2	4260 2	E 1736	IC 556 🍷		E 1634 2	4286 2	IC 508 🍷	IC 592 🍷 ◆	E 1752	4262 2	E 1738	IC 558 🍷	E 1754 2	4288 2	IC 600 🍷	IC 594 🍷 S
Villach Hbf 820 d.	...	0754	0836	...	...	...	0950	...	0954	1036	...	...	...	1130	...	1150	...	1154	1236	...	...	1310	...	1350
Velden am Wörthersee **820** d.	...	0809	0848	...	...	...	|	...	1009	1048	...	...	...	1147	...	1201	...	1209	1248	...	...	1327	...	|
Pörtschach am Wörthersee **820** d.	...	0816	0854	...	...	...	|	...	1016	1054	...	...	...	1155	...	|	...	1216	1254	...	...	1335	...	1405
Klagenfurt Hbf 820 a.	...	0830	0905	...	...	...	1014	...	1030	1105	...	...	...	1210	...	1214	...	1230	1305	...	...	1350	...	1414
Klagenfurt Hbf d.	...	0836	0906	...	...	...	1016	...	1033	1106	...	...	...	...	...	1216	...	1236	1307	...	...	...	...	1416
St Veit an der Glan d.	...	0854	0923	...	...	...	1030	...	1053	1123	...	...	...	...	...	1230	...	1254	1323	...	...	...	...	1430
Unzmarkt d.	...	...	1028	...	...	...	1130	...	...	1228	...	...	...	...	...	1330	...	...	1428	...	...	...	...	1530
Judenburg d.	...	...	1042	...	...	...	1145	...	...	1243	...	...	...	...	...	1345	...	...	1442	...	...	...	...	1545
Zeltweg d.	...	...	1050	...	...	...	1153	...	...	1251	...	...	...	...	...	1353	...	...	1450	...	...	...	...	1553
Knittelfeld d.	...	...	1056	...	...	...	1200	...	...	1258	...	...	...	...	...	1400	...	...	1456	...	...	...	...	1600
Leoben Hbf d.	...	...	1120	...	...	...	1225	...	...	1322	...	...	...	...	...	1425	...	...	1520	...	...	...	...	1625
Graz 825 d.	...	...	|	1105	...	1150	|	...	...	|	1305	...	...	...	1350	|	...	...	|	1505	...	...	1550	|
Bruck an der Mur **825** a.	...	...	1133	1140	...	1224	1236	...	...	1335	1340	...	...	...	1424	1436	...	...	1533	1540	...	...	1624	1636
Bruck an der Mur d.	...	...	...	1143	...	...	1243	...	...	...	1343	...	...	...	...	1443	...	...	...	1543	...	...	...	1643
Mürzzuschlag d.	1113	...	...	1209	1213	...	1309	1313	...	...	1409	...	*1413*	...	...	1509	1513	...	...	1609	1613	...	...	1709
Semmering d.	1128	...	...	|	1228	...	|	1328	...	...	|	...	*1428*	...	...	|	1528	...	...	|	1628	...	...	|
Wiener Neustadt d.	1230	...	...	1305	1330	...	1405	1430	...	...	1505	...	1530	...	...	1605	1630	...	...	1705	1730	...	...	1805
Wien Meidling a.	1303	...	...	1333	1403	...	1433	1503	...	...	1533	...	1603	...	...	1633	1703	...	...	1733	1803	...	...	1833
Wien Südbahnhof a.	1308	...	...	1340	1408	...	1440	1508	...	...	1540	...	1608	...	...	1640	1708	...	...	1740	1808	...	...	1840

	E 1756 2	4266 2	E 1830	IC 650 🍷	IC 602 🍷	IC 596 🍷 S	4270 2	EC 30 ✕ ◆	E 1758 2	E 1832	IC 150 ✕ ◆	4292 2		IC 430 🍷 ◆	E 1814	IC 654 🍷	SC 938 🍷 ⑦	D 464 ◆	IC 634 🍷 B	4274 2	4298 2 ⑧	4276 2	EN 236 ◆	
Villach Hbf 820 d.	...	1354	1436	...	...	1550	1554	1613	...	1631	...	1724	...	1750	1831	...	1930	...	1952	1956	2108	2213	0127	...
Velden am Wörthersee **820** d.	...	1409	1448	...	...	1601	1609	|	...	1645	...	1741	...	|	1846	...	|	...	2003	2011	2125	2228	|	...
Pörtschach am Wörthersee **820** d.	...	1416	1454	...	...	|	1616	|	...	1651	...	1749	...	1805	1854	...	|	...	|	2018	2133	2235	|	...
Klagenfurt Hbf 820 a.	...	1430	1505	...	...	1614	1630	1637	...	1702	...	1804	...	1814	1907	...	1953	...	2016	2032	2148	2249	0150	...
Klagenfurt Hbf d.	...	1434	1507	...	...	1616	1631	1639	...	1706	...	...	...	1816	1908	...	1954	...	2018	2034	2200	2253	0153	...
St Veit an der Glan d.	...	1453	1523	...	...	1630	1654	|	...	1723	...	...	...	1830	1923	...	2008	...	2032	2054	2221	2310	|	...
Unzmarkt d.	...	...	1628	...	...	1730	...	|	...	1828	...	...	...	1930	2030	...	|	...	2130	...	...	...	|	...
Judenburg d.	...	...	1642	...	...	1745	...	|	...	1842	...	...	...	1945	2045	...	|	...	2145	...	...	...	|	...
Zeltweg d.	...	...	1649	...	...	1753	...	|	...	1850	...	...	...	1953	2053	...	|	...	2153	...	...	...	|	...
Knittelfeld d.	...	...	1656	...	...	1800	...	|	...	1856	...	...	...	2000	2100	...	|	...	2200	...	...	...	0323	...
Leoben Hbf d.	...	...	1720	...	...	1825	...	1835	...	1920	...	...	...	2025	2125	...	2146	...	2225	...	...	...	0349	...
Graz 825 d.	...	...	|	1705	1750	|	...	|	...	|	1905	...	...	|	|	2105	|	2200	|	...	...	...	|	...
Bruck an der Mur **825** a.	...	...	1733	1740	1824	1836	...	1847	...	1933	1940	...	...	2036	2137	2140	2157	2235	2236	...	...	...	0401	...
Bruck an der Mur d.	...	...	...	1743	...	1843	...	1849	...	...	1943	...	...	2043	...	2143	2158	...	2243	...	...	...	0405	...
Mürzzuschlag d.	1713	...	...	1809	...	1909	...	|	1919	...	2009	...	...	2109	...	2209	|	...	2309	...	...	...	0437	...
Semmering d.	1728	...	...	|	...	|	...	|	1933	...	|	...	...	|	...	|	|	...	|	...	...	...	|	...
Wiener Neustadt d.	1830	...	...	1905	...	2005	...	2012	2030	...	2105	...	...	2205	...	2305	|	...	0005	...	...	...	0542	...
Wien Meidling a.	1903	...	...	1933	...	2033	...	2040	2103	...	2133	...	...	2233	...	2333	2340	...	0033	...	...	...	0616	...
Wien Südbahnhof a.	1908	...	...	1940	...	2040	...	2046	2108	...	2140	...	...	2240	...	2340	2346	...	0040	...	...	...	0623	...

◆ – **NOTES** (LISTED BY TRAIN NUMBERS)

EC30 – ROMULUS – [12] and ✕ Roma - Wien.

IC150 – EMONA – [12] and ✕ Ljubljana - Wien; [12] Rijeka (train **482**) - Ljubljana - Wien.

IC158 – CROATIA – [12] and ✕ Zagreb - Wien; [12] Ljubljana (train **512**) - Maribor - Wien.

D234 – REMUS – 🛏 1, 2 cl., ▬ 2 cl. and [12] Roma - Wien; conveys daily Sept. 25 - Dec. 24, and Jan. 8 - Apr. 5, Apr. 23 - May 17 (from Milano): 🛏 1, 2 cl., ▬ 2 cl. and [12] Milano (train **2113**) - Venezia - Wien.

EN236 – SAN MARCO – 🛏 1, 2 cl. (T2), ▬ 2 cl. and [12] Venezia Santa Lucia - Wien; [12] Villach - Wien.

IC430 – VAL PUSTERIA/PUSTERTAL – [12] Innsbruck (train **IC433**) - San Candido - Lienz - Villach - Wien; [12] and 🍷 Lienz - Villach - Wien.

D464 – 🛏 1, 2 cl., ▬ 2 cl. and [2] Graz - Bischofshofen - Innsbruck - Basel.

IC592 – GASTEINERTAL – [12] and 🍷 Salzburg - Villach - Wien; [12] Venezia Santa Lucia (train **D232**) - Villach - Wien.

D1234 – Runs daily Dec. 25 - Jan. 7, Apr. 6 - 22, and May 18 - May 27 (from Italy): ▬ 2 cl. and [2] Firenze - Wien; 🛏 1, 2 cl., ▬ 2 cl. and [12] Milano (train **2113**) - Venezia - Wien.

B – [12] and 🍷 Lienz - Villach - Wien.

S – [12] and 🍷 Salzburg - Villach - Wien. For Salzburg - Wien **direct** service see Table **800**.

s – Stops to **set down** only.

Table 831 WIENER NEUSTADT - PUCHBERG AM SCHNEEBERG

2 class only

km		6401 Ⓐ	6403 ⚒	6405	6407		6409	6441 Ⓒ	6411		6413	6415		6417	6419	6421		6423	6425	6427		6429	6431
0	**Wiener Neustadt** d.	0440	0514	0636	0736	...	0836	0936	1036	...	1136	1236	...	1336	1436	1536	...	1636	1736	1836	...	1936	2036
21	Grünbach am Schneeberg d.	0516	0552	0712	0812	...	0912	1012	1112	...	1212	1312	...	1412	1512	1612	...	1712	1812	1912	...	2012	2112
28	**Puchberg am Schneeberg** ‡ a.	0530	0605	0726	0826	...	0926	1026	1126	...	1226	1326	...	1426	1526	1626	...	1726	1826	1926	...	2026	2126

	6400 Ⓐ	6402 ⚒		6404 ⚒	6406	6408	6410		6442 Ⓒ	6412	6414		6416	6418	6420	6422	6424		6426	6428		6430	6432
Puchberg am Schneeberg ‡ d.	0502	0537	...	0607	0637	0737	0837	...	0937	1037	1137	...	1237	1337	1437	1537	1637	...	1737	1837	...	1937	2037
Grünbach am Schneeberg d.	0516	0552	...	0621	0652	0752	0852	...	0952	1052	1152	...	1252	1352	1452	1552	1652	...	1752	1852	...	1952	2052
Wiener Neustadt a.	0548	0623	...	0652	0723	0823	0923	...	1023	1123	1223	...	1323	1423	1523	1623	1723	...	1823	1923	...	2023	2123

‡ – Narrow gauge steam rack railway (Puchbergbahn) operates May - October to Hochschneeberg. Special fares are payable. Trains leave from a station adjacent to the main ÖBB station, taking 90 minutes for the ascent of the mountain. Services run subject to demand with extra trains at busy times. Return journeys must be booked **immediately on arrival** at the summit.

Table 833 — WIENER NEUSTADT - SOPRON

2 class only

Rail service Wiener Neustadt - Sopron 🚆, connecting with GySEV/MÁV services to/from Budapest (Table **890**). *34 km*. Journey time: 45 minutes.

From Wiener Neustadt: 0432⚒, 0836, 1136, 1405⚒, 1436⑦, 1736.

From Sopron: 1039, 1339, 1655Ⓐ, 1939.

Table 834 — UNZMARKT - TAMSWEG

2 class only. Murtalbahn narrow gauge/🚌 service (**8620**)

km		8701 ⚒		8703 ⚒	🚌		8705 ⚒		🚌 ⑦	8707 ⚒	8741 D🚂	8743 B🚂	🚌 ⚒	8709 ⚒	🚌 E	8745 C🚂	🚌 ⑦	8711 Ⓐ	8711 ⑥	🚌	8713 Ⓐ	🚌 ⑦		🚌 ⑤⑦
0	**Unzmarkt Bhf** d.	...	...	0635	0835	...	0935	...	1235	1235	...	...	1405	1535	1605	...	1635	1735	1735	1835	1935	1940	...	2035
27	**Murau Stolzalpe** a.	...	...	0726	0919	...	1015	...	1319	1315	...	...	1450	1615	1650	...	1717	1815	1815	1920	2015	2020	...	2115
27	**Murau Stolzalpe** d.	0625	...	0745	0920	...	1017	...	1320	1317	1335	1335	...	1617	...	1700	1718	1817	...	...	...	...	...	...
35	St Lorenzen ob Murau d.	0637	...	0757	0932	...	1030	...	1332	1330	1352	1352	...	1630	...	|	|	1830	...	...	...	...	...	...
44	Stadl an der Mur d.	0655	...	0817	0947	...	1046	...	1347	1346	1418	1418	...	1646	...	1740	1743	1846	...	...	...	...	...	...
57	Ramingstein Thomatal d.	0716	...	0838	1004k	...	1109	...	1404k	1409	|	...	...	1709	...	1813	1759k	1909	...	...	...	...	...	...
65	**Tamsweg** a.	0730	...	0852	1020	...	1122	...	1420	1422	1505	...	...	1722	...	1830	1812	1922	...	...	...	...	...	...

	8700 ⚒	🚌 Ⓐ	🚌 ⑥	8702 ⚒	🚌 ⑦	8704 ⚒	8706 ⚒	🚌 Ⓒ	🚌 Ⓐ	8708 ⑥	🚌 Ⓐ	8740 C🚂	8710 Ⓐ	8742 B🚂	🚌 ⑦	8712 ⚒	🚌 Ⓐ	🚌 ⑥	🚌 ⑦		8744 D🚂	🚌 ⑦	8714 Ⓐ	🚌 ⑦
Tamsweg d.	...	...	...	0620	...	0740	0940	1040	...	1140	1205	1300	1340	...	...	1540	...	...	1635	...	1650	...	1740	1840
Ramingstein Thomatal d.	...	...	...	0633	...	0753	0953	1053k	...	1153	1218k	1315	1353	...	...	1553	...	...	1648k	...	|	...	1753	1852k
Stadl an der Mur d.	...	0607	...	0656	...	0816	1016	1109	...	1216	1236	1350	1416	1500	...	1616	...	...	1704	...	1740	...	1816	1907
St Lorenzen ob Murau d.	...	0620	...	0712	...	0831	1031	1123	...	1231	1252	|	1431	1520	1518	1631	...	...	1718	...	1801	...	1831	1922
Murau Stolzalpe a.	...	0630	...	0724	...	0843	1043	1135	...	1243	1304	1425	1443	1535	1531	1643	...	...	1730	...	1815	...	1843	1934
Murau Stolzalpe d.	0545	0630	0630	...	0730	0845	1045	1135	1135	1245	1310	...	1445	...	1535	1645	1705	1730	1730	...	...	1830	1845	1935
Unzmarkt a.	0615	0720	0720	...	0820	0925	1125	1222	1222	1325	1355	...	1525	...	1620	1725	1755	1820	1820	...	...	1920	1925	2020

B – Runs July 9, 23, Aug. 6, 20.
C – Runs ③ June 29 - Sept. 14.
D – Runs ② June 28 - Sept. 13.
E – Schooldays, except ⑥.
k – Ramingstein **Karneralm**.
🚂 – Steam train. Special fares apply.

Table 835 — WIEN - FLUGHAFEN WIEN SCHWECHAT ✈

2 class only

S-Bahn rail service (line S7) **Wien Nord** - **Flughafen Wien Schwechat** ✈ (most S7 line services show final destination **Wolfsthal**). *21 km*. Journey time: 31-40 minutes.
All services call at **Wien Mitte** (adjacent to Central 🚌 station at Landstraße/Hauptstraße) 3-4 minutes from **Wien Nord**.

From **Wien Nord**: 0509, 0547, 0623, 0647, 0729, 0753, 0829, 0853, 0929, 0953, 1029, 1053, 1129, 1153, 1229, 1253, 1329, 1353, 1429, 1453, 1529, 1553Ⓒ, 1607Ⓐ, 1629, 1653Ⓒ, 1707Ⓐ, 1729, 1753, 1829, 1853, 1929, 1953, 2029, 2053, 2145.

From **Flughafen Wien Schwechat**: 0511Ⓐ, 0529⚒, 0611, 0634, 0705⚒, 0712⚒, 0727, 0739, 0803, 0839, 0903, 1003, 1039, 1103, 1139, 1203, 1239, 1303, 1339, 1403, 1439, 1503, 1539, 1603, 1639, 1703, 1739, 1803, 1839, 1903, 1939, 2003, 2039, 2103, 2139, 2216.

🚌 service operates **Wien Westbf** - **Wien Südbf** - **Flughafen Wien Schwechat** ✈. Journey time: 35 - 40 minutes from Wien Westbf, 20 - 25 minutes from Wien Südbf.

From **Wien Westbf** (**Wien Südbf** 15 minutes later): 0540, 0640, 0740, 0840, 0910**b**, 0940, 1010**b**, 1040, 1110**b**, 1140, 1210**b**, 1240, 1310**b**, 1340, 1410**b**, 1440, 1510**b**, 1540, 1610**b**, 1640, 1710**b**, 1740, 1840, 1940, 2040, 2140, 2240, 2340.

From **Flughafen Wien Schwechat**: 0330**c**, 0430**c**, 0530**c**, 0640, 0740, 0840, 0940, 1010**b**, 1040, 1110**b**, 1140, 1210**b**, 1240, 1310**b**, 1340, 1410**b**, 1440, 1510**b**, 1540, 1610**b**, 1640, 1710**b**, 1740, 1840, 1940, 2040, 2140, 2240.

b – ⑤⑥⑦ Apr. 1 - Oct. 2 **only**. c – Apr. 1 - Oct. 31 **only**.

Table 840 — WIEN - GMÜND

1, 2 class except where shown

Service valid: **Mar. 6 - May 27, 1995**. Minor alterations to the service below apply **Mar. 1 - 6, 1995**

km		2100 2⚒	E 1570 2	2116 2⚒	2104 2	E 1572	2106 2	E 1574	2108 2	2154 2	E 1576 2	2110 2	E 15271 T	D 270 S	E 1578 2	2112 2	E 1676 2Ⓐ	E 1670 2	E 1778 2Ⓐ	D 272 Ⓑ	E 1678 2Ⓐ	E 1672	E 1674	6196 2
0	**Wien Franz Josefs Bhf 842** d.	0430	0640	0651	0710f	0840	0910	1040	1110	...	1240	1310	1407	1407	1440	1510	1555	1640	1700	1724	1735	1840	2000	2040
3	Heiligenstadt **842** d.	0434	0644	0655	0714f	0844	0914	1044	1114	...	1244	1314	1411	1411	1444	1514	1600	1644	1704	1728	1739	1844	2004	2044
36	Tulln **842** d.	0501	0704	0735	0739	0904	0940	1104	1140	...	1304	1340	1433	1433	1504	1542	1622	1704	|	1749	1800	1904	2024	2108
47	Absdorf Hippersdorf **842** d.	0517	0712	...	0748	0913	0959	1113	1206	...	1313	1359	|	|	1512	1559	1633	1712	|	|	1809	1912	2033	2117
82	Eggenburg d.	0609	0740	...	0827	0940	1035	1140	1244	...	1340	1436	1502	1502	1540	1637	1702	1740	|	1821	1838	1943	2059	*2154h*
92	**Sigmundsherberg** a.	0619	0748	...	0837	0948	1045	1148	1253	...	1348	1445	1509	1509	1548	1646	1710	1748	|	1829	1846	1951	2107	*2202h*
92	**Sigmundsherberg** d.	*0621*	0756	...	*0904*	1003	...	1156	...	...	1356	...	1514	1522	1556	...	1719	1800f	|	1837	1859	2004	2115	...
126	Göpfritz d.	*0656*	0825	...	*0930*	1033	...	1225	...	1346	1425	...	1546	1549	1625	...	1749	1829f	1825	1905	1936	2032	2143	...
143	Schwarzenau d.	*0710*	0840	...	*0947*	1047	...	1239	...	1404	1440	...	1558	1603	1640	...	1804	1844f	1838	1920	1953	2046	2158	...
167	**Gmünd NÖ** 🚆 a.	*0732*	0901	...	*1018*b	1115b	...	1308b	...	1434b	1507b	...	1620	1621	1701	...	1826	1912f	1859	1938	2017	2109	2219	...
354	*Praha Hlavni* **875** a.	...	...	...	...	...	...	...	...	...	...	...	*1935*	1935	...	...	...	...	...	2304	...	...	...	...

	D 273 ⚒	E 1571 2⚒	E 1573 ⚒	E 1575 2⚒	E 1779 2Ⓐ	E 1577 2	E 15279	2103 2	E 1579 2	E 15271 T	D 271 S	2105 2	2107 2	E 1671	2109 2	E 1673	2111 2	E 1675 2	2113 2	E 1775 2⑦e	E 1773 2	2135 2	E 1677 2⑦	
Praha Hlavni **875** d.	0011	...	...	...	...	...	...	...	...	*0623*	0623	...	...	...	...	...	...	...	...	...	...	...	...	...
Gmünd NÖ 🚆 d.	0355	...	0419	0507k	0536	...	0619	*0747*	0833	0955	0959	...	...	1231b	...	1432b	...	1648	...	1803	1859	1925	1953	...
Schwarzenau d.	0414	...	0442	0531k	0557	...	0641	*0810*	0855	1016	1018	...	...	1257	...	1456	...	1711	...	1826	1920	1952	2015	...
Göpfritz d.	0429	...	0458	0547k	0611	...	0656	*0825*	0911	1029	1033	...	...	1313	...	1512	...	1729	...	1844	1936	2008	2032	...
Sigmundsherberg a.	0451	...	0524	0612k	|	...	0722	*0851*	0938	1100	1055	...	...	1341	...	1539	...	1756	...	1912	2003	2039	2058	...
Sigmundsherberg d.	0459	0518	0534	0620	|	0648	0730	0912	0949	1104	1104	1111	1311	1354	1510	1554	1653	1812	1847	1920	2010	2051	2108	...
Eggenburg d.	0507	0526	0542	0628	|	0656	0739	0922	0957	1112	1112	1121	1321	1402	1520	1602	1702	1821	1857	1928	2018	2100	2116	...
Absdorf Hippersdorf **842** d.	|	|	0616	0657	|	0726	0807	1005	1029	|	|	1205	1405	1430	1605	1631	1805	1849	1944	1951	2047	2127	2145	...
Tulln **842** d.	0541	|	0626	0705	|	0738	0815	|	1037	1142	1142	|	|	1439	|	1640	|	1857	2002	1959	2055	2136	2153	...
Heiligenstadt **842** a.	0601	0620	0647	0725	0732	0759	0835	|	1057	1202	1202	|	|	1459	|	1700	|	1918	2028	2020	2116	2156	2213	...
Wien Franz Josefs Bhf 842 a.	0606	0625	0651	0730	0736	0804	0840	1037n	1102	1207	1207	1237n	1437n	1503	1637n	1705	1837n	1922	2033	2025	2120	2201	2217	...

S – SMETANA – Runs Ⓒ only: (12) and ✕ Wien - Praha and v.v.
T – Runs Ⓐ only: By rail **Wien - Sigmundsherberg** and v.v., then by 🚌 **Sigmundsherberg - Gmünd** and v.v.
b – On Ⓐ service liable to replacement 🚌 from **Pürbach-Schrems** (*160 km* from Wien) and not shown in the above table, to **Gmünd NÖ** and v.v. (7 kilometres).
e – Will **not** run Apr. 16, 30.
f – Ⓒ only.
h – Ⓐ only.
k – ⑥ only.
n – Wien **Nord**.

Table 841 — GMÜND - GROß GERUNGS

2 class on
Narrow gauge. ÖB

Service valid: Dec. 5, **1994** - May 27, **1995**

km		7573 a	7553 a	7555	7577 Ⓐ	7557 a	7559		7581	7565 Ⓐ	7567 Ⓒ
0	**Gmünd NÖ** d.	0830	0904	1135	1240	1332	1515	...	1640	1905	1917
14	Weitra d.	0854	0934	1200	1308	1357	1549	...	1709	1930	1942
24	Steinbach Groß Pertholz d.	...	0955	1219	1329	1416	1608	...	1730c	1949	2001
36	Langschlag d.	...	1018	1241b	...	1438	1630	...	...	2011	2023
43	**Groß Gerungs** a.	...	1032	1254b	...	1451	1644	...	...	2024	2036

	7570 ⚒	7550	7574 a	7554 a	7580 Ⓐ		7558		756
Groß Gerungs d.	...	0705	...	1100	...	...	1455	...	173
Langschlag d.	...	0718	...	1115	...	...	1508	...	174
Steinbach Groß Pertholz d.	0630	0740	...	1138	1336	...	1530	...	180
Weitra d.	0650	0759	0931	1200	1356	...	1550	...	182
Gmünd NÖ a.	0720	0825	0953	1229	1426	...	1619	...	185

a – Daily Dec. 5 - Apr. 7 and Ⓐ Apr. 10 - May 27.
b – Ⓒ Apr. 8 - May 27.
c – Ⓐ only.

🚂 Steam trains operate on Ⓒ Apr. 8 - Oct. 26: **Gmünd NÖ** depart 0906, 1332. **Groß Gerungs** arrive 1059, 1524; **Groß Gerungs** depart 1127, 1610, **Gmünd NÖ** arrive 1315, 1758.

For Airport – City Centre services see Table 5

Table 842 WIEN - KREMS AN DER DONAU - ST VALENTIN

1, 2 class except where shown

km		6100	6102	1870	6122	6160	1872	6104	1874	6106	1876	6108	1878	6110	6170	1970	6114	1774	1972	6116	1974	1976	6196	1978
				E			E		E		E		E			E		E	E		E	E		E
		2⚒	2	2	2⚒	2⚒		2		2	2	2		2©	2Ⓐ	2	2	2Ⓐ		2	2Ⓐ		2	2
0	**Wien Franz Josefs Bf 840** d.	...	...	0609	...	...	0740	...	0940	...	1140	...	1340	...	...	1540	...	1630	1740	...	1810	1940	2040	2140
3	Heiligenstadt **840** d.	...	...	0613	...	...	0744	...	0944	...	1144	...	1344	...	...	1544	...	1635	1744	...	1814	1944	2044	2144
47	Tulln **840** d.	...	...	0634	...	...	0805	...	1005	...	1205	...	1405	...	...	1605	...	1657	1805	...	1836	2005	2108	2205
47	Absdorf Hippersdorf **840** d.	...	...	0643	...	...	0813	...	1013	...	1213	...	1413	...	...	1614	...	|	1814	...	1844	2014	2118	2213
79	**Krems an der Donau** a.	...	...	0715	...	...	0839	...	1039	...	1239	...	1439	...	...	1639	...	1730	1840	...	1910	2039	2156	2237
79	**Krems an der Donau** d.	0450	0652	...	0731	...	...	0847	...	1045	...	1247	...	1450	*1450*	...	1651	*1738*	▬	1850	...	...	...	...
86	Dürnstein Oberloiben d.	0500	0700	...	0745	...	...	0858	...	1056	...	1258	...	1501	*1501*	...	1702	*1748*	**6174**	1901	...	...	...	...
92	Weißenkirchen in der Wachau d.	0507	0710	...	0754	...	...	0906	...	1104	...	1306	...	1509	*1509*	...	1711	*1755*	2	1909	...	...	...	...
98	Spitz an der Donau d.	0517	0719	...	0806	...	...	0917	...	1113	...	1315	...	1518	*1518*	...	1721	*1804*	...	1918	...	...	...	...
107	Aggsbach Markt d.	0531	0731	...	0819	...	...	0929	...	1125	...	1328	...	1529	*1529*	...	1733	*1815*	...	1929	...	...	...	...
125	Klein Pöchlarn d.	0557	0756	...	0850	...	...	0955	...	1151	...	1354	...	1555	*1555*	...	1759	*1840*	...	1955	...	...	...	...
130	Marbach Maria Taferl d.	0616	0802	...	0859	...	...	1004	...	1203	...	1405	...	1601	*1601*	...	1805	*1845*	...	2009	...	...	...	...
160	Grein Bad Kreuzen d.	0657	0843	...	0945	0956	...	1043	...	1243	...	1444	...	1642	1707	...	1845	...	1944	2047	...	...	...	...
191	Mauthausen d.	0750	0927	...	...	1039	...	1126	...	1326	...	1527	...	1726	1758	...	1929	...	2026	...	...	...	...	...
199	**St Valentin** a.	0758	0935	...	...	1047	...	1134	...	1335	...	1535	...	1734	1807	...	1938	...	2034	...	...	...	...	...

	1873	1875	6183	6103	1877	6185	6105	1879	6187	6107	1971	6189	6109	1973	6191	6111	1975	6193	6113	1977	6117	1979	6119	6171
	E	E			E			E			E			E			E			E		E		
	2Ⓐ	2	2	2	2	2	2		2	2		2	2	2	2	2		2	2	2	2		2	2
t Valentin d.	...	...	...	...	...	...	0614	...	...	0822	...	...	1031	...	...	1225	...	...	*1347*	...	1606	...	1838	1948
authausen d.	...	...	...	...	...	...	0624	...	...	0831	...	...	1040	...	...	1234	...	...	*1356*	...	1615	...	1846	1957
rein Bad Kreuzen d.	...	...	...	0521	...	...	0724	...	...	0926	...	...	1125	...	...	1326	...	...	1520	...	1706	...	1930	2042
arbach Maria Taferl d.	...	...	...	0602	...	...	0812	...	...	1013	...	...	1216	...	...	1405	...	...	1606	...	1805	...	2009	▬
lein Pöchlarn d.	...	...	...	0608	...	...	0817	...	...	1018	...	...	1221	...	...	1411	...	...	1611	...	1810	...	2015	E
ggsbach Markt d.	...	...	...	0634	...	...	0843	...	...	1043	...	...	1246	...	...	1448	...	...	1639	...	1836	...	2041	**1777**
pitz an der Donau d.	...	...	...	0646	...	...	0855	...	...	1055	...	...	1258	...	...	1500	...	...	1655	...	1857	...	2053	2
Veißenkirchen in der Wachau d.	...	...	...	0655	...	...	0905	...	...	1104	...	...	1307	...	...	1509	...	...	1709	...	1907	...	2101	...
ürnstein Oberloiben d.	...	...	...	0702	...	...	0912	...	...	1111	...	...	1314	...	...	1516	...	...	1717	...	1915	...	2108	...
rems an der Donau a.	...	...	...	0713	...	...	0923	...	...	1122	...	...	1325	...	...	1527	...	...	1728	...	1926	...	2119	...
rems an der Donau d.	0602	0618	0646	...	0732	0820	...	0938	1020	...	1138	1220	...	1332	1420	...	1538	1618	...	1732	...	1938	...	2138
bsdorf Hippersdorf **840** d.	0636	0643	0721	...	0757	0856	...	1003	1056	...	1203	1256	...	1403	1456	...	1603	1658	...	1805	...	2004	...	|
ulln **840** d.	0644	0652	0730	...	0806	0908	...	1011	1108	...	1211	1308	...	1411	1508	...	1611	1712	...	1813	...	2012	...	2207
eiligenstadt **840** a.	0705	0713	0755	...	0826	0932	...	1031	1132	...	1231	1332	...	1431	1532	...	1631	1737	...	1833	...	2032	...	2227
Vien Franz Josefs Bf 840 a.	0710	0719	0801	...	0831	0938	...	1037	1138	...	1237	1338	...	1437	1538	...	1637	1742	...	1838	...	2037	...	2231

Table 843 ST PÖLTEN - KREMS AN DER DONAU

2 class only

ail service St Pölten Hbf - Krems an der Donau and v.v. *31 km*. Journey time: 32 - 45 minutes.

om **St Pölten Hbf**: 0502⚒, 0626, 0653, 0728, 0852, 0926, 1053, 1126, 1212⑥, 1253, 1326, 1453, 1526, 1617Ⓐ, 1649, 1726, 1852, 1926⚒, 1935⑦, 2050.

From **Krems an der Donau**: 0440⚒, 0503Ⓐ, 0547, 0604⚒, 0626, 0649, 0804, 0849, 1002, 1049, 1202, 1249, 1402, 1449, 1601, 1648, 1802, 1849, 2049.

Table 844 ST PÖLTEN - MARIAZELL

2 class only. Narrow gauge. ÖBB

km		6801	E1961	6883	6805	6807	6809	6811	6831 Ⓐ	6835
0	**St Pölten Hbf** ▲ d.	0600	0730	0930	1130	1328	1528	1730	1830	2030
31	Kirchberg an der Pielach ▲ d.	0711	0830	1030	1230	1430	1630	1829	1931	2129
39	Schwarzenbach an der Pielach ▲ d.	0726	0843	1044	1244	1444	1644	1842	1944	2142x
49	Laubenbachmühle ▲ d.	0745	0859	1059	1259	1459	1659	1904	2000	2157
58	Winterbach d.	0802	0914	1113	1313	1513	1713	1919**b**	...	...
68	Gösing d.	0824	0934	1133	1333	1533	1735	1936**b**	...	...
81	Mitterbach d.	0850	0959	1157	1357	1557	1805	2000**b**	...	...
85	**Mariazell** a.	0856	1006	1203	1403	1603	1811	2006**b**	...	...

	6800	6802	6828 ⚒	6880	6882	6884	6804	6806 ©	E1968
Mariazell d.	0535e	0752	...	1100	1300	1500d	1549e	1700	1756
Mitterbach d.	0541e	0758	...	1106	1306	1506d	1559e	1706	1803
Gösing d.	0606e	0823	...	1131	1331	1531d	1625e	1731	1829
Winterbach d.	0622e	0840	...	1147	1347	1547d	1642e	1747	1846
Laubenbachmühle ▲ d.	0638	0900	...	1202	1402	1602	1702	1802	1902
Schwarzenbach an der Pielach ▲ d.	0654	0915	...	1216	1416	1616	1716	1817	1916
Kirchberg an der Pielach ▲ d.	0709	0929	1029	1229	1429	1629	1729	1832	1930
St Pölten Hbf ▲ a.	0813	1027	1127	1327	1527	1727	1827	1929	2028

– Runs ⑧, **not** Dec. 25, Apr. 16, 30.
– ⑦ only.

e – ⚒ only.
x – Request stop.

▲ – Additional trains operate **St Pölten Hbf - Laubenbachmühle** and v.v.:
From St Pölten Hbf: 1030, 1230, 1430, 1630.
From Laubenbachmühle: 0528, 0800, 1226⚒, 1300⑦, 1426Ⓐ, 1500©, 1725Ⓐ.

Table 845 WIEN - KREMS - MELK - LINZ - PASSAU

1995 Service. All services convey ✕

DDSG

	Q	K			N	J		M		M
ien Reichsbrücke ▲ d.	...	...	...	...	0800	0800	...	...	...	...
ılln d.	...	...	...	...	1045	1045	...	...	...	...
ems an der Donau d.	...	1030	...	...	1310	1310	...	1430	...	1600
ırnstein d.	...	1105	...	...	1345	1345	...	1505	...	1635
eißenkirchen in der Wachau d.	...	1130	...	...	...	1410	...	1530	...	1700
ɔitz an der Donau d.	...	1200	...	...	...	1440	...	1600	...	1730
ggsbach Dorf d.	...	1245	...	...	...	1525	...	1645	...	...
elk d.	...	1330	...	...	...	1610	...	1730	...	...
öchlarn d.	...	...	...	...	...	1700n	...	1820n	...	...
arbach Maria Taferl d.	...	...	...	...	...	1720n	...	1840n	...	...
bbs an der Donau d.	...	...	...	...	...	1755n	...	1915n	...	...
rein d.	...	...	...	...	...	1920n	...	...	...	...
nz a.	0800	...	...	...	...	2255n	...	...	...	...
assau a.	1430	...	...	...	...	...	...	...	...	...

	M		K		N	J		M	Q
Passau d.	...	...	...	...	...	...	...	...	1515
Linz d.	...	...	...	...	...	0900	...	...	2040
Grein d.	...	...	...	...	...	1155	...	...	...
Ybbs an der Donau d.	0930	...	...	...	...	1300	...	...	...
Marbach Maria Taferl d.	0955	...	...	...	...	1325	...	...	...
Pöchlarn d.	1010	...	...	...	...	1340	...	...	...
Melk d.	1120	...	1400	...	...	1440	...	...	...
Aggsbach Dorf d.	1145	...	1425	...	...	|	...	...	...
Spitz an der Donau d.	1215	...	1455	...	...	1525	...	1735	...
Weißenkirchen in der Wachau d.	1230	...	1510	...	...	1540	...	1750	...
Dürnstein d.	1245	...	1525	...	1555	1555	...	1805	...
Krems an der Donau d.	1305	...	1545	...	1615	1615	...	1825	...
Tulln d.	...	...	...	...	1805	1805n	...	...	...
Wien Reichsbrücke ▲ a.	...	...	...	...	2015	2015n	...	...	...

– Daily May 18 - Sept. 24.
– Daily Apr. 8 - Oct. 29.
– Daily Apr. 29 - Sept. 24.

N – ④⑤⑥⑦ Apr. 27 - May 14, also May 1.
Q – ④⑤⑥⑦ Apr. 27 - May 14, daily May 18 - Sept. 24, also May 1.
n – Will **not** run June 24.

▲ – DDSG Schiffahrtszentrum (main landing stage) - close to Vorgartenstraße U-Bahn station (Line U1).

able 848 WIEN - BRATISLAVA and BUDAPEST

1995 Service. All services convey 🍸

Hydrofoil or hovercraft services
DDSG, SPD

km		X	Y	A	B	C	X	B	A	C
0	**Wien Reichsbrücke** ▲ d.	0800z	0900z	0900	0900	0930	1450z	1545	1815	1845
62	**Bratislava** a.	❖	❖	1000	1030	1100	❖	1715	2015	2015
62	**Bratislava** d.	❖	❖	...	...	...	❖	...	...	...
282	**Budapest** § a.	1300	1400	...	...	...	1950	...	...	...

	A	D	X		Y	B	A	C	X
Budapest § d.	...	...	0740z	...	0900z	...	...	...	1400z
Bratislava a.	...	...	❖	...	❖	...	...	...	❖
Bratislava d.	0715	0715	❖	...	❖	1530	1630	1630	❖
Wien Reichsbrücke ▲ a.	0830	0900	1340	...	1500	1715	1745	1815	2000

– May 1 - 31, also ④⑤⑥⑦ Apr. 13 - 30.
– Sept. 4 - 24, also ④⑤⑥⑦ Sept. 25 - Oct. 15.
– June 1 - Sept. 3.
– June 1 - Sept. 24, also ④⑤⑥⑦ Sept. 25 - Oct. 15.

X – May 20 - Sept. 3.
Y – Apr. 8 - May 19 and Sept. 4 - Oct. 29.
z – Check-in closes **15 minutes before departure**.
❖ – Information not available.

▲ – DDSG Schiffartszentrum (main landing stage) - close to Vorgartenstraße U-Bahn station (Line U1).
§ – Nemzetkozi hajoallomas (International shipping quay).

erators: DDSG – DDSG Donaureisen. ☎ Wien (0222) 72 75 00; SPD – Slovenská Plavba Dunajská (Slovak Danube Navigation), Bratislava.

Thomas Cook
NEW RAIL MAP OF EUROPE

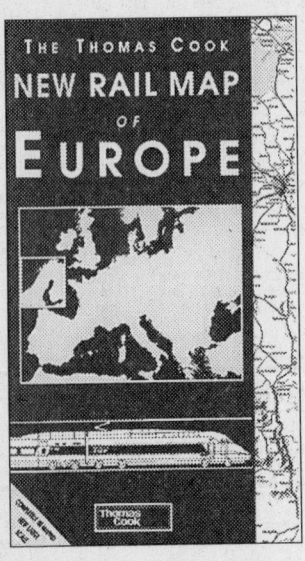

The Thomas Cook Rail Map of Europe has been an essential requirement for rail travellers in Europe for many years. Over 100,000 copies have been sold to date.

Business and leisure rail travellers – especially holders of the Inter-Rail and Eurail passes – find it an indispensable aid to planning and enjoying a European rail trip.

This brand-new edition has been entirely re-compiled. New mapping techniques enhance the clear and colourful design, giving a highly visible, attractive product.

Researched by the editorial team of the world-famous *Thomas Cook European Timetable.*

★ Passenger railways of Europe from the Atlantic to Moscow.

★ New 1:3.75 million scale (Scandinavia 1:7.5 million). Central Europe enlarged to 1:1.5 million on reverse for extra detail.

★ High-speed lines and scenic routes colour-coded.

★ Channel Tunnel and other major tunnels, passenger and rail ferries marked.

★ Shows over 5000 cities and towns, plus major airports.

★ Ski and beach resort areas, main tourist regions, major mountain ranges and rivers.

 Légende en français!

 Legende auf deutsch!

 ¡Leyenda en español!

Obtainable through Thomas Cook UK retail shops at £4.95, or by post at £5.65 (UK), £6.25 (Europe), £6.85 (overseas air mail) from:

Thomas Cook Publishing (TPO/FE), PO Box 227, PETERBOROUGH PE3 8BQ, UK.

☎ (01733) 505821/268943.

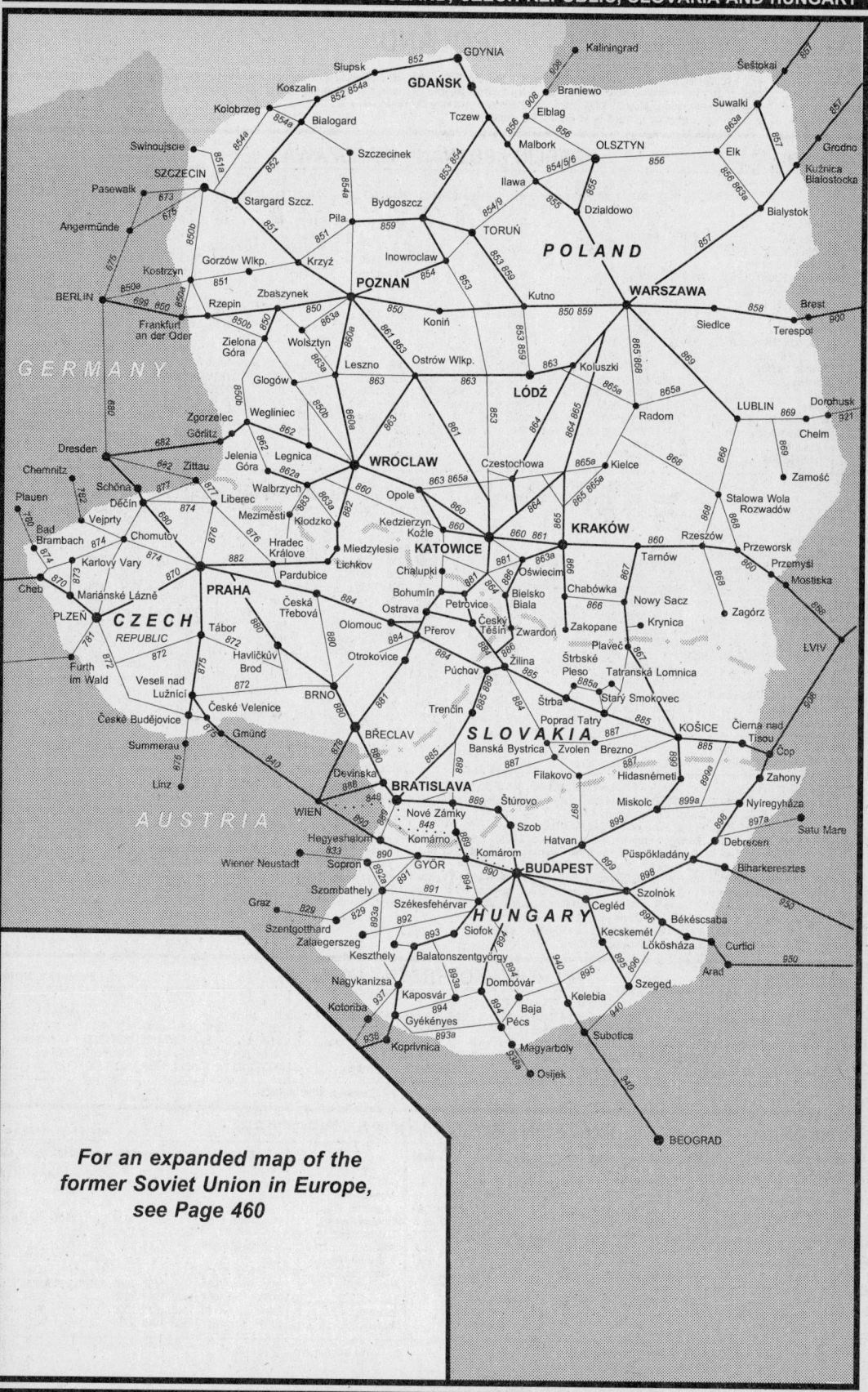

For an expanded map of the former Soviet Union in Europe, see Page 460

POLAND

Operator: Polskie Koleje Państwowe (PKP).
Services: Trains convey first and second class seats, shown as '1' and '2' or [12] in the tables. Sleeping cars (🛏) and couchette cars (▬) are of the normal European types, see page 10 for more details. Russian sleeping car services cannot be used for journeys in or between Poland and Germany, unless seating cars are shown.
Timings: **September 25, 1994** to **May 27, 1995**. International services valid **May 29, 1994** to **May 27, 1995**.
Tickets: A higher fare is payable for travel by all **EC**, **IC**, **Ex**, and **IR** trains.

Table 850 BERLIN - POZNAŃ - WARSZAWA

1, 2 class except where shown. DB, PKP

km		IC 7102 [R]✕ ⚒k	241 2🍷 O	Ex 7200 [R]✕ Z	IR 77110	Ex 8110 [R]✕ S	EC 41 [R]✕ Vn	2	83102 ✕ W	Ex 7202 [R]✕ U	247 🛏 M	247 🛏 K		Ex 7100 [R]✕ r	Ex 8112 [R]✕ S	IR 77116	EC 43 [R]✕ Bp	1249 🛏 ①⑥A	336	449 🍷 Q	77100	81000 ✕ G	345 R	299 🛏 L
	Köln **700** d.	...	1916	...	...	...	...	...	...	...	...	...	...	...	...	...	...	...	...	...	...	...	...	...
0	**Berlin** Hbf d.	...	|	...	...	...	0810	...	...	...	...	...	...	...	...	...	1632	...	...	...	...	...	...	...
	Berlin Lichtenberg d.	...	|	...	...	...	|	...	...	...	1140	1140	...	...	...	...	|	1513	...	2024	...	...	2207	2300
82	Frankfurt (Oder) a.	...	0310	...	...	...	0857	...	...	...	1245	1245	...	...	...	...	1719	1624	...	2119	...	...	2259	0004
82	Frankfurt (Oder) ▦ d.	...	0341	...	...	...	0900	...	...	...	1320	1320	...	...	...	...	1722	1645	...	2145	...	...	2319	0024
93	Kunowice ▦ d.	...	|	...	...	...	|	...	...	...	1340	1340	...	...	...	...	|	1701	...	2208	...	...	2337	0045
105	Rzepin a.	...	0409	...	...	...	0918	...	...	...	1352	1352	...	...	...	...	1740	1713	...	2225	...	...	2349	0057
105	Rzepin d.	...	0424	...	...	...	0928	...	...	...	1407	1407	...	...	...	...	1750	1727	...	...	...	...	0005	0115
	Zielona Góra d.	...	|	0506	0745	...	|	*1035*	...	...	|	|	...	...	...	1708	|	|	1840	...	2235	...	|	|
	Zbaszynek d.	...	|	0610	0845	...	|	1153	...	...	1506	1506	...	...	...	1810	|	1848	1955	...	2337	...	0105	0211
261	**Poznań** Glówny a.	...	0625	0703	0950	...	1109	1320	...	...	1605	1605	...	...	...	1915	1928	1955s	2120	...	0045	...	0200	0315
261	**Poznań** Glówny d.	0622	0630	0708	...	1007	1112	...	1440	1503	1625	1625	...	1718	1820	...	1931	1956s	...	...	...	0205	0220	0330
361	Konin d.	|	0742	0805	...	1108	1213	...	1540	1609	1735	1735	...	1813	1915	...	2025	2152	...	...	...	0316	0330	0437
440	Kutno d.	|	0842	0854	...	1203	1305	...	1639	1702	1829	1829	...	1905	2007	...	2115	2251	...	...	...	0411	0421	0534
569	**Warszawa** Centralna a.	0930	1015	1030	...	1330	1430	...	...	1830	2010	2010	...	2030	2130	...	2240	|	...	...	...	0550	0615	|
572	**Warszawa** Wschodnia a.	0944	1029	1054	...	1344	1449	...	...	1854	2024	2024	...	2044	2144	...	2254	0032g	...	...	...	0604	0629	0720g
	Brest **858** a.	...	1616	...	...	...	...	...	...	...	0151	0256	...	...	...	...	...	0540	...	...	...	1204	...	...
	Moskva **900** a.	...	1206	...	...	...	...	...	...	...	2210	...	...	...	...	...	...	...	...	...	...	...	...	...

	331	1248 🛏 ①⑥A	EC 42 [R]✕ Bn	Ex 1811 [R]✕ S	IR 77113	Ex 2701 [R]✕ U	38103 ✕ W	IR 77115		246 🛏 K	246 🛏 M	Ex 1701 [R]✕ r	335	Ex 1813 ✕ S	77103	IC 1703 [R]✕ Ⓑr	339 2	EC 40 [R]✕ Vp	Ex 2703 [R]✕ Z	240 2[R]🍷 O	298 🛏 L	448 [R]🍷 Q	18001 ✕ G	344 [R] R
Moskva **900** d.	...	...	...	...	...	...	...	...	...	...	1309	...	...	...	...	...	...	...	...	2015	...	...	...	...
Brest **858** d.	...	2353	...	...	...	...	...	...	...	0305	0800	...	...	...	...	...	...	...	...	1436	...	...	1945	...
Warszawa Wschodnia d.	...	0307g	0600	0615	...	0910	...	...	...	1038	1038	1115	...	1325	...	1515	...	1635	1715	1910	2206g	...	2315	2340
Warszawa Centralna d.	...	|	0615	0630	...	0930	...	...	...	1050	1050	1130	...	1340	...	1530	...	1650	1730	1925	|	...	2330	2355
Kutno d.	...	0455	0737	0753	...	1056	1113	...	...	1225	1225	1258	...	1506	...	|	...	1812	1853	2055	2348	...	0103	0133
Konin d.	...	0552	0821	0837	...	1144	1201	...	...	1319	1319	1345	...	1555	...	|	...	1856	1937	2144	0044	...	0154	0229
Poznań Glówny a.	...	0727s	0915	0937	...	1250	1307	...	...	1425	1425	1450	...	1700	...	1836	...	1950	2037	2245	0155	...	0315	0350
Poznań Glówny d.	0440	0729s	0918	...	1115	...	...	1420	...	1445	1445	...	1505	...	1750	...	1900	1953	2042	2250	0215	...	...	0405
Zbaszynek d.	0611	0846	|	...	1217	...	...	1522	...	1546	1546	...	1635	...	1855	...	2030	|	2135	|	0316	...	...	0501
Zielona Góra a.	0720	|	|	...	1320	...	...	1622	...	|	|	...	1740	...	2000	...	2134	|	2237	|	|	...	...	|
Rzepin a.	...	0946	1057	...	...	...	...	...	...	1638	1638	...	...	...	...	...	...	2133	...	0040	0412	...	...	0558
Rzepin d.	...	1008	1108	...	...	...	...	...	...	1653	1653	...	...	...	...	...	...	2144	...	0100	0430	0503	...	0615
Kunowice ▦ d.	...	1031	|	...	...	...	...	...	...	1711	1711	...	...	...	...	...	...	|	...	|	0450	0531	...	0637
Frankfurt (Oder) ▦ a.	...	1043	1128	...	...	...	...	...	...	1723	1723	...	...	...	...	...	...	2204	...	0127	0502	0543	...	0649
Frankfurt (Oder) d.	...	1103	1131	...	...	...	...	...	...	1743	1743	...	...	...	...	...	...	2207	...	0147	0522	0603	...	0709
Berlin Lichtenberg a.	...	1207	|	...	...	...	...	...	...	1847	1847	...	...	...	...	...	...	|	...	|	0627	0702	...	0802
Berlin Hbf a.	...	...	1218	...	...	...	...	...	...	...	...	...	...	...	...	...	...	2254	...	|	...	...	...	...
Köln **700** a.	...	...	...	...	...	...	...	...	...	...	...	...	...	...	...	...	...	...	...	1000	...	...	...	...

A – Runs ①⑥ from Berlin, ④⑥ from Saratov (⑤⑦ from Brest): 🛏 2 cl. Berlin - Ryazan - Saratov and v.v.; conveys also 🛏 2 cl. Berlin - Saratov - Vpronezh, Rostov-na-Donu, and Tselinograd (Kazakhstan) and v.v. See Table **900**.
B – BEROLINA – [12] and ✕ Berlin - Warszawa and v.v.
G – 🛏 1, 2 cl., ▬ 2 cl., [12] and ✕ Szczecin - Warszawa - Brest and v.v.
K – KIEW EXPRESS – 🛏 2 cl. Berlin - Warszawa Wschodnia (trains **249/8**) - Brest (trains **68/67**) - Kyïv and v.v.
L – ST. PETERSBURG EXPRESS – 🛏 1, 2 cl. Berlin - Sankt Peterburg and v.v.; 🛏 2 cl. Berlin - Vilnius - Riga and v.v.
M – MOSKWA EXPRESS – 🛏 1, 2 cl. Berlin - Brest (trains **14/13**) - Moskva and v.v.
O – OST-WEST EXPRESS – : ▬ 2 cl. and [2] and 🍷 Brussels - Warszawa and v.v.; 🛏 1, 2 cl. Brussels - Brest (trains **16/15**) - Moskva and v.v.; conveys on ⑦ from Brussels, ⑤ from Kyïv: 🛏 1, 2 cl. Brussels - Brest (trains **684/3**) - Kyïv and v.v.; conveys on ①⑤ (also ③ June 1 - Sept. 21) from Brussels, ③⑥ (also ① May 30 - Sept. 19) from Sankt Peterburg: 🛏 1, 2 cl. Brussels - Brest - Orsha - Sankt Peterburg and v.v.
Q – 🛏 1, 2 cl., ▬ 2 cl., [12] and 🍷 Berlin - Wroclaw - Kraków and v.v.
R – 🛏 1, 2 cl., ▬ 2 cl. and [12] Berlin - Warszawa and v.v.
S – [12] and ✕ Warszawa - Szczecin and v.v.
U – [12] and ✕ Poznań - Warszawa - Lublin and v.v.
V – VARSOVIA – [12] and ✕ Berlin - Warszawa and v.v.
W – WAWEL – [12] and ✕ Świnoujście - Kraków and v.v.
Z – [12] Zielona Góra - Warszawa - Lublin and v.v.
g – Warszawa **Gdańska**.
k – Will **not** run Dec. 26, Apr. 17, May 1.
n – Will **not** run Dec. 25, Jan. 1.
p – Will **not** run Dec. 24, 31.
r – Will **not** run Dec. 25, Apr. 16, 30.
s – Poznań **Staroleka**.

Table 850a BERLIN - KOSTRZYN - GORZÓW

2 class only. DB, PKP

km										
0	**Berlin Lichtenberg** d.	0700	...	0900	1100	1300	1500	1700	...	1900
30	Strausberg d.	0720	...	0920	1120	1320	1520	1720	...	1920
	Frankfurt an der Oder d.	*0717*k	0917	|	*1117*k	*1317*k	*1517*k	*1717*k	1917	|
92	Kostrzyn ▦ **851** a.	0830	*1015*k	1015	1230	1413	1630	1830	*2013*k	2013
132	**Gorzów Wlkp. 851** a.	...	...	1120b	...	...	...	...	...	2112b

Gorzów Wlkp. 851 d.	...	0805b	...	...	...	...	...	1807b	...	...
Kostrzyn ▦ **851** d.	0650	0910	0910	1050	1310	1450	1650	1912	1912	2050
Frankfurt an der Oder a.	*0818*k	|	*1018*k	*1218*k	*1418*k	*1618*k	*1818*k	|	*2018*k	|
Strausberg a.	0803	1004	...	1203	1404	1603	1803	2006	...	2203
Berlin Lichtenberg a.	0823	1023	...	1223	1423	1623	1823	2025	...	2223

b – Runs ⑤⑥⑦, **not** Dec. 24, 25, 31, Jan. 1, Apr. 16.
k – Change at **Küstrin-Kietz**.

Table 850b SZCZECIN - ZIELONA GÓRA - WROCLAW

1, 2 class except where shown

km		73102 🍷	8620 🍷		8732	7642	2	86102 🍷 n	449 🍷 K	2	86202 J
0	**Szczecin** Glówny d.	...	0955	...	1335	...	1655	1750	...	2005	2315
104	Kostrzyn d.	...	1134	...	1534	...	1857	1918	...	2156	0050
136	Rzepin d.	...	1203	...	1630	...	1954	1945	2245	2230	0124
207	**Zielona Góra** d.	0600	1313	1424	1750	1800	2109	2040	2340	...	0235
	Wegliniec d.	|	|	1712	...	|	...	|	|	...	0428
	Jelenia Góra a.	|	|	1843	...	|	...	|	|	...	0543
260	Glogów d.	0647	1408	...	...	1857	...	2123	0026	...	...
	Legnica **862** a.	|	1527	...	...	|	...	|	|	...	...
360	**Wroclaw** Glówny a.	0815	1644	...	...	2049	...	2248	0158	...	...
540	*Katowice* **860** a.	1115	...	...	...	...	...	...	0507	...	...
618	*Kraków* **860** a.	1242	...	...	...	...	...	...	0636	...	...

	2	6741	68103 🍷 n	2	7831	6821 🍷		37103 🍷	68203 J	448 [R]🍷 K
Kraków **860** d.	...	...	...	...	...	...	...	1612	...	2102
Katowice **860** d.	...	...	...	...	...	...	...	1742	...	2232
Wroclaw Glówny d.	...	0652	0730	...	...	1438	...	2051	...	013
Legnica **862** d.	...	|	|	...	...	1545	...	|	...	|
Glogów d.	...	0848	0910	...	...	1701	...	2222	...	0309
Jelenia Góra d.	...	|	|	...	...	|	1525	|	2223	|
Wegliniec d.	...	|	|	...	...	|	1710	|	0004	|
Zielona Góra d.	0635	0945	1001	...	1437	1801	1936	2305	0200	035
Rzepin d.	0750	...	1052	1404	1552	1915	...	...	0254	044
Kostrzyn d.	0831	...	1120	1440	1635	2000	...	...	0325	*053*
Szczecin Glówny a.	1050	...	1317	1647	1848	2218	...	...	0531	*074*

K – 🛏 1, 2 cl., ▬ 2 cl., [12] and 🍷 Berlin - Kraków and v.v.
J – 🛏 1, 2 cl., ▬ 2 cl. and [12] Szczecin - Jelenia Góra and v.v.
n – Will **not** run Dec. 25, Apr. 16.

 [R] – Reservation obligatory ✕ – Restaurant car 🍷 – Buffet car

Table 851 — SZCZECIN and KOSTRZYN - POZNAŃ

1, 2 class except where shown

km		IC 8102	88204 87104	87104	85102	Ex 8110		86100	83102	81106		Ex 8112	83206		83204	82200	254	84202	82202	81202	88700	81700	81000	85200	83200
		[R]✕ ⚒n		✕	✕ T	[R]✕	2	✕	✕ V	✕ L	2	[R]✕	✕ Z	2	✕ P	✕ N	[R] B	✕ p	✕ C	E	🛌 W	🛌 W	✕ Y	✕ O	✕ K
	Świnoujście **851a** .. d.	...	...	...	...	...	...	...	0941	...	...	...	...	...	...	...	1830**b**	...	...	...	2027	...	...	...	2054
0	**Szczecin** Główny ...... d.	0510	...	0545	0635	0720	...	0945	1140	1350	...	1530	1545	...	1740	1955	2010	2040	2100	...	|	2155	2225	2300	2325
15	Szczecin Dabie .... d.	0523	...	0600	0650	0733	...	0959	1154	1408	...	1545	1604	...	1759	2010	2031	2059	2115	...	|	2210	2243	2316	2340
40	Stargard Szczeciński . d.	0546	...	0628	0715	0756	...	1024	1219	1434	...	1609	1632	...	1828	2039	2058	2129	2142	...	2247	2247	2311	2343	0008
	Kostrzyn .... d.	|	*0542*	|	|	|	0835	|	|	|	1417	|	|	1632	|	|	|	|	|	2240	|	|	|	|	|
	Gorzów Wlkp .... d.	|	0640	|	|	|	0936	|	|	|	1524	|	|	1734	|	|	|	|	|	2325	|	|	|	|	|
130	Krzyż .... d.	0652	0752	0752	0844	0902	1052	1142	1330	1551	1643	1716	1750	1849	1945	2158	2213	2246	2300	0022	|	|	0033	0110	0127
	Pila .... a.	|	|	|	0937	|	...	|	|	|	*1834*	*1834*	|	*2159*	*2159*	|	|	|	|	0113	|	|	|	0209	|
214	**Poznań** Główny .... a.	|	0855	0855	...	0958	...	1245	1430	1650	...	1811	1855	...	2055	2305	2315	2355	0005	|	|	|	0140	...	0235
	Wrocław **860a** .... a.	|	...	...	...	|	...	1505	...	...	...	|	2115	...	...	...	0145	...	...	|	|	|	|	...	0500
	Warszawa **850** ...... a.	1055	...	...	...	1330	...	...	...	...	...	2130	...	...	...	...	...	...	...	0720	0742	0742	0550	...	...

	38205	255		38207	Ex 1811	18107		38103		78105	78105 88205	58101	Ex 1813	IC 1803		68101	58201	28203	38201		18701	18701	18001	28201	18203
	✕ P	B	2	Z	[R]✕	✕ L	2	✕ V	2	✕		✕ T	[R]✕	[R]✕ Ⓑt	2	✕	✕ O	✕ C	✕ K	2	🛌 W	🛌 W	✕ Y	✕ N	E
Warszawa **850** .... d.	...	...	...	...	0630	...	...	...	...	...	...	...	1340	1655	...	...	...	...	...	...	2228	2228	2330	...	2301
Wrocław **860a** .... d.	...	0310	...	0550	|	...	...	...	...	...	...	...	|	|	...	1750	...	...	2350	...	|	|	|	...	|
Poznań Główny .... d.	0500	0610	...	0820	0947	1020	...	1317	...	1520	1520	...	1715	|	...	2020	...	0200	0220	...	|	|	0335	0420	|
Pila .... d.	|	|	*0635*	|	*0925*	|	*0925*	|	1311	|	|	1654	|	|	1925	|	2104	|	|	...	|	|	|	|	0446
Krzyż .... d.	0614	0712	0907	0928	1044	1128	1225	1420	1423	1633	1703	1756	1812	2034	2043	2129	2216	0308	0331	0412	|	|	0443	0529	0555
Gorzów Wlkp .... a.	|	|	1013	|	|	|	1334	|	1533	|	1758	|	|	|	2152	|	|	|	|	0521	|	|	|	|	0646
Kostrzyn .... a.	|	|	1114	|	|	|	*1528*	|	1630	|	*1913*	|	|	|	*2327*	|	|	|	|	0620	|	|	|	|	0730
Stargard Szczeciński ... d.	0730	0819	...	1039	1142	1237	...	1526	...	1741	...	1901	1910	2132	...	2237	2324	0417	0443	...	0658	0716	0553	0640	...
Szczecin Dabie .... a.	0747	0835	...	1058	1159	1253	...	1542	...	1758	...	1917	1926	2149	...	2253	2340	0435	0502	...	0722	|	0611	0658	...
Szczecin Główny .... a.	0806	0848	...	1114	1212	1311	...	1601	...	1816	...	1932	1939	2202	...	2309	2357	0452	0517	...	0740	|	0625	0715	...
Świnoujście **851a** .... a.	...	1039**b**	...	...	...	...	...	1756	...	...	...	...	...	...	...	...	...	...	0737	...	...	0900	...	...	...

B – BALTIC – May 29 - Sept. 24: 🛌 2 cl. and [12] Świnoujście - Praha and v.v.; Sept. 25 - May 27: 🛏 1, 2 cl. and [12] Szczecin - Praha and v.v.
C – 🛏 1, 2 cl., [12] and 🍷 Szczecin - Ostrów - Kielce and v.v.
E – 🛏 1, 2 cl. and [12] Kostrzyn - Toruń - Warszawa and v.v.
K – 🛏 1, 2 cl., 🛌 2 cl. and [12] Świnoujście - Kraków and v.v.; 🍷 Szczecin - Kraków and v.v.
L – [12] Szczecin - Ostrów - Lódź and v.v.
N – 🛏 1, 2 cl., 🛌 2 cl., [12] and 🍷 Szczecin - Lódź - Lublin and v.v.
O – [12] Szczecin - Olsztyn and v.v.
P – 🛏 1, 2 cl., 🛌 2 cl., [12] and ✕ Szczecin - Kraków - Przemyśl and v.v.
T – [12] Szczecin - Toruń and v.v.
V – WAWEL – [12] and ✕ Świnoujście - Kutno - Kraków and v.v.
W – 🛏 1, 2 cl. and 🛌 2 cl. Świnoujście and Szczecin - Warszawa and v.v.
Y – 🛏 1, 2 cl., 🛌 2 cl., [12] and ✕ Szczecin - Brest and v.v.
Z – 🛏 1, 2 cl., 🛌 2 cl. and [12] Szczecin - Katowice - Zakopane and v.v.
b – May 29 - Sept. 24 **only**.
n – Will **not** run Dec. 28, Apr. 17, May 1.
p – Will **not** run Dec. 24, 25, 31, Apr. 16.
t – Will **not** run Dec. 25, Apr. 16, 30.

Table 851a — SZCZECIN - ŚWINOUJŚCIE

1, 2 class except where shown

km		38100		255			38103	58106			
		K✕	2n	B	2	2n	W✕	G✕	2	2	2
0	**Szczecin** Główny ...... d.	0535	0810	0850	1245	1420	1610	1625	1750	1945	2140
15	Szczecin Dabie .... d.	0552	0828	0908	1303	1438	1628	1643	1806	2002	2158
116	**Świnoujście** .... a.	0737	1028	1039	1451	1636	1756	1810	1957	2147	2323

		83102	85106					254	83100	
	2	W✕	G✕	2	2n	2	2	B	K✕	2
Świnoujście .... d.	0740	0941	1000	1200	1334	1518	1643	1830	2054	2216
Szczecin Dabie .... a.	0942	1122	1147	1400	1537	1722	1824	2010	2237	2400
Szczecin Główny .... a.	0958	1135	1201	1417	1552	1739	1841	2028	2252	0016

B – Runs May 28 - Sept. 24 **only**: See Table **851**.
G – [12] and ✕ Świnoujście - Gdynia and v.v.
K – 🛏 1, 2 cl., 🛌 2 cl., [12] Świnoujście - Kraków and v.v.
W – WAWEL – [12] and ✕ Świnoujście - Kutno - Kraków and v.v.
n – Will **not** run Dec. 25, Apr. 16.

Table 852 — SZCZECIN - KOSZALIN - GDYNIA - GDAŃSK

All trains 1, 2 class

km		Ex 8108	Ex 8502	328	85106		Ex 8504	81204	81200	320
		[R]✕	[R]✕ ⚒	✕ M	✕ S		[R]✕	✕ B	W	G
	Berlin Lichtenberg **675** .... d.	...	...	0632	...	...	...	...	...	2225
0	**Szczecin** Główny .... d.	...	0620	0850	1220	...	1610	1835	...	0055
15	Szczecin Dabie .... d.	...	0633	0907	1235	...	1623	1850	...	0114
40	Stargard Szczeciński .... d.	...	0656	0931	1303	...	1646	1918	...	0142
151	Bialogard .... d.	...	0809	1046	1447	...	1803	2057	...	0308
	Kolobrzeg .... d.	...	|	*0909*	*1359*	...	*1631*	|	2032	|
175	**Koszalin** .... d.	0435	0829	1104	1510	...	1825	2121	2146	0332
242	Slupsk .... d.	0525	0916	1152	1614	...	1916	2229	2254	0430
294	Lebork .... d.	0607	0955	1233	1707	...	1955	2314	2337	0511
353	**Gdynia** .... a.	0646	1033	1315	1752	...	2037	0001	0032	0604
353	**Gdynia** ▲ .... d.	0648	1035	...	...	...	2040	0020	0055	...
362	Sopot ▲ .... a.	0657	1043	...	...	...	2048	0029	0107	...
374	**Gdańsk** ▲ .... a.	0708	1059	...	...	...	2104	0046	0124	...
406	**Tczew 855** .... a.	0732	1125	...	...	...	2130	0115	0153	...
	Warszawa Centralna **855** a.	1042	...	...	...	...	...	...	0547	...

	18205	Ex 5801	58105		329	Ex 5803	Ex 1807	321	18201
	✕ B	[R]✕ ⚒	✕ S		[R]✕ M	[R]✕	[R]✕	[R] G	W
Warszawa Centralna **855** d.	...	...	...	...	...	...	1602	...	2152
Tczew 855 .... d.	0258	0525	...	...	...	1625	1913	...	0143
Gdańsk ▲ .... d.	0325	0550	...	...	...	1650	1936	...	0210
Sopot ▲ .... d.	0342	0605	...	...	...	1705	1948	...	0228
Gdynia ▲ .... a.	0355	0615	...	...	...	1714	1957	...	0241
Gdynia .... d.	0415	0618	1120	...	1530	1716	2000	2330	0300
Lebork .... d.	0511	0700	1210	...	1615	1756	2042	0021	0348
Slupsk .... d.	0606	0738	1303	...	1656	1833	2120	0106	0435
Koszalin .... d.	0717	0828	1355	...	1743	1921	2210	0206	0620
Kolobrzeg .... a.	|	*0958*	|	...	*1850*	*2120*	*2327*	|	0743
Bialogard .... d.	0747	0845	1416	...	1802	1938	...	0230	...
Stargard Szczeciński .... d.	0936	0959	1548	...	1916	2052	...	0406	...
Szczecin Dabie .... a.	0953	1015	1604	...	1932	2108	...	0424	...
Szczecin Główny .... a.	1008	1028	1620	...	1945	2121	...	0438	...
Berlin Lichtenberg **675** .. a.	...	...	...	...	2200	...	...	0728	...

– 🛏 1, 2 cl., 🛌 2 cl. and [12] Szczecin - Bialystok and v.v.
– GEDANIA – 🛏 1, 2 cl., 🛌 2 cl. and [12] Berlin - Gdynia and v.v.; 🛏 1, 2 cl. Berlin - Gdynia (trains **55000/2**) - Kaliningrad and v.v.
M – MARE BALTICUM – [12] and ✕ Berlin - Szczecin - Gdynia and v.v.
S – [12] and ✕ Świnoujście - Gdynia and v.v.
W – 🛏 1, 2 cl., 🛌 2 cl. and [12] Kolobrzeg - Warszawa and v.v.
▲ – Frequent local trains run between **Gdynia** and **Gdańsk**.

Table 853 — GDYNIA - LÓDŹ, KATOWICE and KRAKÓW

1, 2 class except where shown

km		Ex5108	54100	54102	51104	53700	54202	53206	54204	51200
		[R]🍷	🍷 k	🍷	🍷	🛌 Zp	🍷 A	K	An	🍷 L
0	**Gdynia 854** .... d.	0500	0657	1200	1650	1933	2048	...	2207	2245
9	Sopot **854** .... d.	0510	0706	1210	1659	1944	2059	...	2217	2255
21	**Gdańsk 854** .... d.	0530	0726	1230	1720	2007	2120	...	2238	2315
53	Tczew **854** .... d.	0553	0750	1256	1745	2032	2146	...	2305	2345
181	Bydgoszcz **854** .... d.	0717	0919	1428	1926	2205	2318	2323	0034	|
	Toruń Główny **859** .... d.	0802	|	|	2013	2251	|	0018	|	|
	Wloclawek **859** .... d.	0839	|	|	2051	|	|	0057	|	|
	Kutno **859** .... d.	0921	|	|	2135	|	|	0141	|	0539
	Lódź Kaliska **859** .... a.	1026	|	|	2240	|	|	0259	|	0712
227	Inowroclaw **854** .... d.	...	0952	1511	...	|	2356	|	0111	...
	Czestochowa Osobowa ▲ .. d.	...	1305	1845	...	|	|	0608	0452	...
552	**Katowice** .... a.	...	1430	2008	...	|	0452	|	0618	...
	Kraków Główny ▲ .... a.	...	...	...	...	0556	...	0813	...	...

	15105	45101	Ex1509	45103	45201	45203	15201	35209	35701
	🍷	🍷	[R]🍷	🍷 k	An	🍷 A	🍷 L	K	🛌 Zr
Kraków Główny ▲ .... d.	...	...	...	...	...	...	...	2121	2242
Katowice .... d.	...	0800	...	1430	2030	2202	...	|	|
Czestochowa Osobowa ▲ d.	...	0925	...	1655	2202	|	...	2320	|
Inowroclaw **854** .... d.	...	1252	...	1924	0138	0309	...	|	|
Lódź Kaliska **859** .... d.	0611	|	1549	|	|	|	2325	0216	|
Kutno **859** .... d.	0718	|	1653	|	|	|	0052	0323	|
Wloclawek **859** .... d.	0802	|	1737	|	|	|	|	0407	|
Toruń Główny **859** .... d.	0840	|	1814	|	|	|	|	0512	0603
Bydgoszcz **854** .... d.	0945	1335	1917	2003	0217	0352	|	0557	0658
Tczew **854** .... d.	1119	1507	2036	2136	0350	0528	0559	...	0824
Gdańsk 854 .... a.	1140	1533	2058	2157	0413	0553	0621	...	0846
Sopot **854** .... a.	1159	1551	2117	2218	0436	0624	0641	...	0908
Gdynia 854 .... a.	1209	1602	2130	2229	0450	0635	0655	...	0920

– 🛏 1, 2 cl., 🛌 2 cl. and [12] Gdynia - Katowice and v.v.
– 🛌 2 cl. and [12] Bydgoszcz and Olsztyn - Kraków and v.v.
– [12] Gdynia - Lódź and v.v.
– 🛏 1, 2 cl., 🛌 2 cl. and [12] Gdynia - Kraków - Krynica and v.v.
Z – 🛏 1, 2 cl. and 🛌 2 cl. Gdynia - Kraków - Zakopane and v.v.
n – **Not** Dec. 24, 25, 31, Apr. 16.
▲ – Additional journeys **Czestochowa - Kraków** and v.v. Journey: approx. 2 hours. From **Czestochowa** 0708**k**; from **Kraków** 1740**k**.
k – **Not** Dec. 25, Apr. 16.
p – **Not** Dec. 24, 30, Apr. 15.
r – **Not** Dec. 25, 31, Apr. 16.

[12] – Through carriage (1 and 2 class)

A higher fare is payable for travel by **EC**, **IC**, **Ex** *and* **IR** *trains in Poland*

Table 854 GDYNIA and OLSZTYN - POZNAŃ

1, 2 class except where shown

km		Ex 5600 R🍷	56104 n	56100 🍷	16110 🍷	57100 🍷	Ex 5602 R🍷 n	254 🍴 B	53206 K	56200 W
0	**Gdynia 853** d.	0500	...	1000	...	1300	1600	1800	...	2100
9	Sopot **853** d.	0510	...	1009	...	1310	1610	1809	...	2110
21	**Gdańsk 853** d.	0530	...	1030	...	1330	1630	1830	...	2130
53	Tczew **853** d.	0553	...	1054	...	1355	1652	1853	...	2155
181	Bydgoszcz **853** d.	0715	...	1225	...	1529	1810	2016	...	2328
	Olsztyn 859 d.	|	0607	|	1219	|	|	|	2130	|
	Ilawa d.	|	0702	|	1320	|	|	|	2224	|
	Toruń Glówny **859** d.	|	0841	|	1453	|	|	|	0003	|
227	Inowroclaw **853** d.	0746	0909	1300	1522	1602	1841	2052	...	0009
283	Gniezno d.	0824	0951	1350	1606	1646	1924	2136	...	0100
334	**Poznań** Glówny a.	0905	1035	1435	1650	1730	2005	2220	...	0145
	Wroclaw **860a** a.	1108	1312	1705	1915	...	2158	0145	...	0415

	35209 K	65203 W	255 🍴 B	Ex 6503 R🍷 n	61111 🍷	65101 🍷	65105 n	Ex 6501 R🍷	75101 🍷
Wroclaw **860a** d.	...	2250	0310	0720	0855	1050	1350	1520	...
Poznań Glówny d.	...	0115	0615	0920	1120	1315	1615	1710	2010
Gniezno d.	...	0204	0703	1004	1205	1400	1701	1754	2057
Inowroclaw **853** d.	...	0250	0747	1044	1249	1446	1744	1834	2140
Toruń Glówny **859** d.	0510	|	|	|	1318	|	1824	|	|
Ilawa d.	0634	|	|	|	1434	|	1945	|	|
Olsztyn 859 a.	0729	|	|	|	1526	|	2040	|	|
Bydgoszcz **853** d.	...	0330	0828	1115	...	1525	...	1917	2217
Tczew **853** d.	...	0500	0953	1233	...	1657	...	2036	2344
Gdańsk 853 a.	...	0522	1014	1254	...	1725	...	2101	0006
Sopot **853** a.	...	0544	1034	1307	...	1740	...	2117	0026
Gdynia 853 a.	...	0556	1044	1317	...	1751	...	2130	0038

B – BALTIC – 🛏 1, 2 cl., ▬ 2 cl., (12) and 🍴 Gdynia - Poznań - Praha and v.v.
K – ▬ 2 cl. and (12) Olsztyn - Kraków (- Zakopane in summer) and v.v.
W – 🛏 1, 2 cl., ▬ 2 cl. and (12) Gdynia - Wroclaw and v.v.
n – Will **not** run Dec. 25, Apr. 16.

Table 854a KOLOBRZEG - POZNAŃ

1, 2 class except where shown

km		2	87100 🍴	87500 2e	2	87440 🍴	704 2n	84200 Kp🍴	88202 W	83202 R	86200 S
0	**Kolobrzeg** d.	0305	...	...	1045	1405	1610	1920	2232	2258	...
	Slupsk 852 d.	|	0526	...	|	|	|	|	|	|	2330
	Koszalin **852** d.	|	0616	0852	|	|	|	|	|	|	0029
36	Bialogard **852** d.	|	0645	0917	|	1451	1641	2006	2318	2335	0053
	Szczecin Glówny a.	0626	|	|	*1417*d	|	1852	|	|	|	|
100	Szczecinek d.	...	0740	1009	...	1615	...	2106	0029	0040	0151
171	Pila d.	...	0835	1112	...	1730	...	2204	0120	0136	0252
267	**Poznań** Glówny a.	...	0950	1235	...	1906	...	2325	...	0315	0420
	Wroclaw **860a** a.	...	...	...	...	...	...	...	...	...	0709

	703 2n	78441 🍴	2	78503 2e	78103 🍴	2	48201 Kt🍴	68201 S	38203 R	88203 W
Wroclaw **860a** d.	...	...	...	...	...	...	...	2335	...	...
Poznań Glówny d.	...	1220	...	1350	1835	...	0110	0210	0250	...
Pila d.	...	1422	...	1519	1957	...	0245	0359	0420	0432
Szczecinek d.	...	1534	...	1616	2103	...	0341	0501	0519	0535
Szczecin Glówny d.	0740	|	1420	|	|	2030	|	|	|	|
Bialogard **852** d.	1003	1645	|	1719	2156	|	0438	0610	0616	0647
Koszalin **852** a.	|	|	|	1737	2213	|	|	0638	|	|
Slupsk 852 a.	|	|	|	...	2305	|	|	0756	|	|
Kolobrzeg a.	1040	1731	*1758*d	...	...	0002	0522	...	0653	0738

K – 🛏 1, 2 cl., ▬ 2 cl. and (12) Kolobrzeg - Katowice and v.v.
R – 🛏 1, 2 cl., ▬ 2 cl. and (12) Kolobrzeg - Kraków and v.v.
S – 🛏 1, 2 cl. and (12) Slupsk - Wroclaw and v.v.
W – Conveys 🛏 1, 2 cl. Kolobrzeg - Pila - Warszawa and v.v.
e – Runs June 24 - Aug. 31, Oct. 29 - Nov. 1 **only**.
p – Will **not** run Dec. 24, 25, 31, Apr. 16.
d – Change at **Goleniów**.
n – Will **not** run Dec. 25, Jan. 1, Apr. 16.
t – Will **not** run Dec. 25, 26, Jan. 1, Apr. 16.

Table 855 GDYNIA - GDAŃSK - WARSZAWA

1, 2 class except where shown

km		66208	81200 K	2	Ex 5300 R🍷	IC 5100 R🍷 ⚒n	2 T	Ex 5112 R🍷	Ex 8108 R🍷 S	51112 T	2	Ex 5102 R🍷	Ex 5302 R🍷 P	2	Ex 5200 R🍷 E	IC 5304 R🍷	66106	70110 🍷 T	IC 5104 R🍷 Ⓑn	Ex 51400 R🍷	2	52200 🍷 L	53508 🍷 M	51200 🍷 D
0	**Gdynia 856** d.	...	0055	...	0444	0540	0550	...	0648	0745	...	0842	1042	...	1245	1445	...	1610	1645	1843	...	2140	2217	2245
9	Sopot **856** d.	...	0108	...	0453	0550	0559	...	0658	0754	...	0852	1051	...	1255	1455	...	1619	1655	1853	...	2150	2227	2255
21	**Gdańsk 856** d.	...	0130	...	0510	0610	0615	...	0710	0815	...	0910	1110	...	1310	1510	...	1640	1710	1910	...	2210	2248	2315
53	Tczew **856** d.	...	0158	...	0532	|	0641	...	0733	0838	...	0932	1132	...	1332	1532	...	1705	|	1932	...	2245	2322	2345
	Elblag d.	...	|	...	*0448*	|	|	...	*0708*	|	...	*0859*	*1051*	...	*1308*	*1450*	...	|	|	*1901*	...	*2204*	|	*2316*
72	Malbork **856** d.	...	0219	...	0546	|	0656	...	0749	0900	...	0947	1147	...	1347	1547	...	1724	|	1947	...	2308	2344	0004
	Olsztyn d.	0220	|	0513	|	|	|	0700	|	|	0849	|	|	1215	|	*1503*	1720	|	|	|	2230	|	|	|
141	Ilawa d.	|	0309	0616	0630	|	0744	|	0831	0950	|	1029	1229	|	1430	1628	|	1810	|	2029	2333	0001	0035	0049
201	Dzialdowo d.	0336	0349	...	0707	|	...	0804	|	...	1017	1105	1305	1332	1507	1705	1829	...	|	2105	...	0045	0117	...
251	Ciechanów d.	0409	0426	...	|	|	...	0837	|	...	...	1134	1334	1414	|	|	1904	...	|	2137	...	0123	0153	...
345	**Warszawa** Wschodnia a.	0517	0537	...	0837	0922	...	0938	1033	...	...	1237	1437	1550	1637	1837	2012	...	2022	2239	...	0232	0303	...
350	**Warszawa** Centralna a.	0527	0547	...	0852	0932	...	0948	1042	...	...	1247	1452	1555	1657	1852	2022	...	2032	2249	...	...	0317	...
	Kraków Glówny **865** a.	...	...	...	1140	...	...	...	...	...	...	...	1737	...	...	2137	...	...	...	...	...	...	0828	...

	25201 🍷 L	15201 🍷 D	35509 🍷 M	2	70103 🍷 T	Ex 15401 R🍷	IC 1501 R🍷 ⚒n	15101	IC 3501 R🍷		Ex 2501 R🍷 E	Ex 3503 R🍷 P	2	2 T	Ex 1505 R🍷	2	15113 T	Ex 1807 R🍷 S	IC 1507 R🍷 Ⓑn	Ex 1511 R🍷	Ex 3505 🍷		18201 K	66201
Kraków Glówny **865** d.	...	...	2115	...	...	...	...	...	0615	...	...	1015	...	...	...	...	...	...	...	...	1615	...	...	...
Warszawa Centralna d.	...	...	0222	...	...	0602	0702	0707	0857	...	1057	1257	...	...	1502	...	...	1602	1702	1757	1857	1952	2152	2302
Warszawa Wschodnia d.	0129	...	0237	...	...	0612	0712	0718	0912	...	1112	1312	...	...	1512	...	...	1612	1712	1807	1912	2002	2202	2312
Ciechanów d.	0238	...	0344	...	...	0712	|	0824	|	...	|	1412	...	...	1612	...	...	|	|	1907	|	2122	2308	0020
Dzialdowo d.	0317	...	0421	...	...	0745	|	0900	1040	...	1239	1442	...	...	1642	...	...	|	|	1942	2039	2203	2347	0056
Ilawa d.	0358	0450	0501	0510	0748	0821	|	|	1115	1130	1315	1518	1523	1601	1718	1725	1758	1812	|	|	2114	|	0028	|
Olsztyn a.	|	|	|	0613	|	|	|	1010	|	1234	|	|	1626	|	|	1828	|	|	|	2045	|	2313	|	0201
Malbork **856** d.	0450	0539	0549	...	0834	0905	|	...	1157	...	1356	1601	...	1648	1801	...	1844	1856	|	...	2157	...	0122	...
Elblag a.	|	|	*0629*	...	|	*0946*	|	...	*1236*	...	*1458*	*1704*	...	|	*1837*	...	|	*1934*	|	...	*2304*	...	|	...
Tczew **856** d.	0510	0559	0610	...	0853	0921	|	...	1212	...	1414	1618	...	1703	1818	...	1901	1913	|	...	2213	...	0143	...
Gdańsk 856 a.	0536	0621	0633	...	0916	0942	1023	...	1234	...	1435	1639	...	1727	1839	...	1922	1934	2023	...	2235	...	0205	...
Sopot **856** a.	0557	0641	0654	...	0934	1001	1039	...	1248	...	1449	1657	...	1746	1858	...	1940	1947	2042	...	2254	...	0227	...
Gdynia 856 a.	0608	0655	0705	...	0945	1012	1051	...	1300	...	1500	1708	...	1756	1909	...	1950	1957	2054	...	2304	...	0241	...

D – (12) and 🍷 Gdynia - Lódź and v.v.
E – (12) and 🍷 Gdynia - Warszawa - Kielce and v.v.
K – 🛏 1, 2 cl., ▬ 2 cl. and (12) Kolobrzeg - Warszawa and v.v.
L – 🛏 1, 2 cl. and (12) Gdynia - Lublin and v.v.
M – 🛏 1, 2 cl., ▬ 2 cl. and (12) Gdynia - Kraków and v.v.
P – (12) and 🍷 Gdynia - Warszawa - Kraków - Przemyśl and v.v.
S – From/to Koszalin (Table **852**).
T – To/from Olsztyn (Table **856**).
n – **Not** Dec. 25, 26, Apr. 16, 17.

Table 856 GDYNIA - GDAŃSK - OLSZTYN - BIALYSTOK

1, 2 class except where shown

km		81204 C	2	55000 BR🍷	51112		2	2	70110 🍷		51000 G🍷
0	**Gdynia 855** d.	0020	0550	0631	0745	...	...	1450	1610	...	1925
9	Sopot **855** d.	0030	0559	0641	0754	...	...	1458	1619	...	1935
21	**Gdańsk 855** d.	0052	0615	0700	0815	...	1020	1514	1640	...	1955
53	Tczew **855** d.	0120	0641	0723	0838	...	1045	1540	1705	...	2021
72	Malbork **855** d.	0141	0656	0741	0900	...	1101	1556	1724	...	2044
101	Elblag d.	0218	|	0815	|	...	1120	1616	|	...	2115
	Kaliningrad **908** a.	|	|	1330	|	...	|	▬	|	...	|
	Ilawa d.	|	0750	...	1006	...	|	...	1825	...	|
200	**Olsztyn** a.	0403	0838	...	1058	...	*1409*	🍷	1920	...	2257
200	**Olsztyn** d.	0428	*0854*	...	1124	1241	...	1543	...	2050	2307
320	Giżycko d.	0646	*1128*	...	|	1514	...	1817	...	2325	0104
367	Elk **863a** a.	0735	*1215*	...	1612	1608	...	1903	...	0012	0149
471	**Bialystok 863a** a.	0929	...	...	...	...	...	...	...	...	0339

	70102 🍷	2	2	🍷	2	15112	15001 G🍷	55002 B🍷		1820 C
Bialystok 863a d.	...	...	...	...	...	...	1303	...	...	1940
Elk **863a** d.	...	...	...	0843	...	1201	1430	...	1804	2126
Giżycko d.	...	...	...	0931	...	|	1511	...	1900	2212
Olsztyn a.	...	...	...	1207	...	1630	1709	...	2125	0014
Olsztyn d.	0646	...	*0836*	...	1503	1647	1722	...	...	0026
Ilawa d.	0748	...	|	...	1601	1758	|	...	...	|
Kaliningrad **908** d.	|	...	|	...	|	|	|	1712	...	|
Elblag d.	|	0830	1144	...	|	|	1855	2050	...	0215
Malbork **855** d.	0834	0851	1207	...	1648	1844	1919	2123	...	0240
Tczew **855** d.	0853	0907	1223	...	1703	1901	1937	2143	...	0258
Gdańsk 855 a.	0916	0928	1246	...	1727	1922	2012	2206	...	0320
Sopot **855** a.	0934	0943	...	...	1746	1940	2033	2227	...	0341
Gdynia 855 a.	0945	0952	...	...	1756	1950	2045	2238	...	0355

B – Will **not** run Dec. 24, 25, 26, 31, Jan. 1, Apr. 16, 17 (one day **earlier** from Berlin): 🛏 1, 2 cl. Berlin (trains **320/1**) - Szczecin - Gdynia - Kaliningrad and v.v.; (12) Gdynia - Kaliningrad and v.v.
C – 🛏 1, 2 cl., ▬ 2 cl. and (12) Szczecin - Bialystok and v.v.
G – (12) Gdynia - Grodno and v.v.; 🛏 1, 2 cl. Gdynia - Bialystok (trains **58/7**) - St Peterbu and v.v.; 🛏 1, 2 cl. Gdynia - Bialystok - Grodno.

For explanation of standard symbols see page 4

Table 857

WARSZAWA - BIALYSTOK - VILNIUS

1, 2 class except where shown. PKP, BČ, LG

km		99011 2	77201	99013	094	51000	11113 58		77101	99015	096		299 26	299 26		11101	77103	77105	79011	14 1 R	36	11109	77107	77109	99043	77111	11105 28
		G	n			W	S		k	n			L	R					B	B	M		k		n	®	V
0	Warszawa Centralna ...... d.	...	0012	...	...	...	0712	...	...	...	...	...	...	...	0912	1112	1312	1437	...	...	1712	1912	...	2112	2117
5	Warszawa Wschodnia ...... d.	...	0040	...	...	0043g	0722	...	...	0758g	0758g	0922	1122	1322	1447	...	...	1722	1922	...	2122	2144
184	Bialystok .... a.	...	0252	...	...	0315	0930	...	...	1030	1030	1130	1330	1530	1641	...	...	1930	2130	...	2330	2355
184	Bialystok .... d.	...	0317	...	0410	0445	0553	0945	...	...	1100	1100	1135	1348	...	1645	...	1813	1937	...	2147	...	0003
225	Sokółka .... d.	...	0410	...	0454	0607	0656	1040	...	...	1150	1150	1209	1448	...	1730	...	1904	2030	...	2229	...
324	Suwalki .... a.	0400	0613	0710		...	0854	1212	1600	...	...	...	...	1644	...	1856	...	2221	...	...
350	Trakiszki ⊞ .... a.	...	0450	0805				1655	...	...	...	...	...	1950r	...	...
377	Šeštokai .... § d.	0700		1015	1120			1905	2000	...	...	...	...	2200r	2225	...
471	Kaunas .... § a.			1310					2150	...	...	...	...	0002	...
241	Kuźnica Bialostocka ...... a.				0505	0623				...	1205	1205	1221	...	...	1926	...	2243	...	0046
241	Kuźnica Bialostocka ⊞ .... a.				0620	0915				...	1500	1500	1343	...	...	2158	...	2340	...	0330
268	Grodno ⊞ .... ‡ a.				0812	1106				...	1649	1649	1535	...	...	2346	...	0135	...	0526
268	Grodno ⊞ .... d.					1146				...	1729	1729	...	...	...	...	...	0601
425	Vilnius .... § a.			1455						...	2334	2038	2038	...	...	...	...	0950
	Riga 919 .... a.					d				...	...	0810	...	0606	...	...
	Tallinn 914 .... a.									...	...	...	...	1310	...	...
	Sankt Peterburg 905 ...... a.				0910					...	...	1250	...	...	...

		99044 2	77100	77122	35 11110	77104	99012 2	57 11114	2 13 R	79014	15001	77106	77108	093 2	99014	77110	25 298	25 298		11102	095	27 11106	99016	77222
		p	k	M		S	B	B	W		®			n	k	L	R		V	n	G
Sankt Peterburg 905 .... d.	...	...	1210	...	...	...	...	...	...	2025	...	...	...
Tallinn 914 .... d.	...	...	1710	...	...	...	...	...	...	...	...	...
Riga 919 .... d.	...	...	d	0025	...	...	...	...	2205	...	...	...
Vilnius .... § d.	...	...	...	0815	...	...	0656	...	1022	1022	...	1545	1715	...
Grodno ⊞ .... ‡ d.	...	...	0412	0855	...	1040	...	1354	1354	...	2056	...
Kuźnica Bialostocka ⊞ ... a.	0324	...	0411	0847	...	1045	...	1434	1434	1651	2136	...
Kuźnica Bialostocka ...... a.	0418	...	0706	1057	...	1127	...	1429	1429	1705	2130	...
Kaunas .... § d.				0625	...	0833	...	1710	1710	1812	0018	...
Šeštokai .... § d.				0740	0805	0900r	...	1030	1100	...	1723	...
Trakiszki ⊞ .... d.				0850	0930r	...	1210	...	1920	2045	...
Suwalki .... d.			0457	0920	...	1025	1041	1245	1509	1525	2155	...
Sokółka .... a.	0434	0700		1153	1212	1247	...	1642	1727	1826	0049	0105	...
Bialystok .... a.	0515	0734	0749	1152	1232	1247	1333	...	1723	1808	1808	1830	1859	0121	0140	...
Bialystok .... d.		0540	0740	0940	1158	1240	1340	1540	...	1740	1818	1818	1914	0136	0153	...
Warszawa Wschodnia ...... a.		0825	1025	1225	1501g	1525	...	1625	1825	2025	2132g	2132g	2158	0411	0440	...
Warszawa Centralna ...... a.		0837	1037	1237		1537	...	1637	1837	2037		2212	0447	0507	...

- BALTI – ⬛, ⬛ Warszawa - Šeštokai and v.v.; BALTI EKSPRESS – ⬛ 1, 2 cl., ⬛ and ✕ Šeštokai - Tallinn and v.v.
- ⬛ Łódź - Warszawa - Suwalki and v.v.
- ST. PETERSBURG EXPRESS – ⬛ 1, 2 cl. Berlin - Sankt Peterburg and v.v.
- ⬛ 2 cl. and ♀ Moskva - Minsk - Grodno - Bialystok and v.v.
- ⬛ 2 cl. Berlin - Vilnius (trains 221/2) - Riga and v.v.; ⬛ 2 cl. Warszawa - Riga and v.v.
- ⬛ 1, 2 cl. and ♀ Warszawa - Sankt Peterburg and v.v.; ⬛ 1, 2 cl. Gdynia (trains 51000/15001) - Bialystok - Sankt Peterburg and v.v.

- V – ⬛ 2 cl. Warszawa - Vilnius and v.v.
- W – ⬛ 1, 2 cl. Gdynia - Grodno; ⬛ Gdynia - Grodno and v.v.
- d – Via Novosokolniki and Lida – See map. (Transit visas for Lithuania/Latvia not required.)
- g – Warszawa Gdańska.
- k – Will not run Dec. 25, 26, Apr. 16.
- n – Will not run Dec. 24, 25, 26, 31, Jan. 1, Apr. 15, 16, 17.
- p – Will not run Dec. 25, 26, 27, Jan. 1, 2, Apr. 16, 17, 18.
- r – Note R applies.
- ‡ – Belarus time (one hour ahead of Polish time).
- § – Lithuanian time (one hour ahead of Polish time).

Table 858

WARSZAWA - BREST

1, 2 class except where shown

km		1249 ⬛ ⑦J	40 ⬛ L	2	81001 ✕ S	22 ⬛ JL	241 ⬛	10003 2	10 ⬛ J	126 ⬛ Jh	110 ⬛ L	11011 n	11209 ⬛ J	104 ⬛	247 ⬛ J	249 ⬛ K	11015 n
0	Warszawa Centralna .... d.	...	...	...	0557	0902	1022	...	1237	1454	...	1732	1907	1942	2017	2017	...
5	Warszawa Wschodnia .... d.	0050g	0050g	...	0627	0937	1111	1043	1248	1509	1430g	1523	1630g	1944	2010	2023	2043	2158	2310
93	Siedlce .... d.	0209	0235	...	0608	0746	1048	1220	1204	1358	1429	1620	1632	1648	1807	1856	2030	2122	2211	2311	0035
173	Biala Podlaska .... d.	...	...	0732	...	0845	...	1337	1501	1602	...	1820	...	2000	2128	...	0140
210	Terespol .... a.	0333	0426	...	0812	...	0915	1215	1338	1418	1535	1643	1730	1755	1902	1940	2031	2200	2246	2335	0036	0213
217	Brest ⊞ .... ‡ a.	0540	0652	...	1204	1434	1616	1746	...	1906	2008	2209	2351	...	0102	...	0151	0256	0456
	Moskva 900 .... a.	...	...	...	1025	1206	...	1217	1602	...	...	...	2210	...

		109 ⬛ Jh	125 ⬛ K	248 ⬛ J	103 ⬛ J	11008 n	9 ⬛	11206	246 2	11012 2 n		2	21 ⬛ J	240 ⬛ JL		10000	18000 ⬛ S	11018 n		39 ⬛ L	1248 ⬛ ⑤⑦J
		L	Jh	K	J		n							J	JL						L
Moskva 900 .... d.	...	0901	...	...	1517	...	1309	...	1901	2015	...		...
Brest ⊞ .... ‡ d.	0105	0210	0305	0415	0505	0635	...	0800	...	1000	...	1325	1436	...	1620	...	1945	2100	...	2353	2353
Terespol .... d.	0208	0228	0300	0405	0503	0558	0655	0743	...	1006	...	1330	1500	...	1648	...	1955	2047	...	2345	2345
Biala Podlaska .... d.	...	...	0439	0537	...	0726	...	1038	...	1720	...	2026	2118	...	...
Siedlce .... d.	0332	0353	0424	0553	0640	0720	0824	0904	...	1143	...	1434	1618	1634	1825	...	2126	2245	...	0109	0109
Warszawa Wschodnia .... a.	0454g	0532g	0536	0727	0752	0834	0935	1018	...	1254	...	1610	1615	1725	1810	1952g	...	2235	...	0238g	0238g
Warszawa Centralna .... a.	...	...	1045	0742	0807	0847	0952	1045	...	1307	...	1632	1917	...	2322	...	...

- For composition see Table 900.
- KIEW EXPRESS – ⬛ 2 cl. and ♀ Berlin (trains 247/6) - Warszawa - Kyїv and v.v.
- For days of running and composition see Table 920.

- S – ⬛ 1, 2 cl., ⬛ 2 cl., ⬛ and ✕ Szczecin - Warszawa - Brest and v.v.
- g – Warszawa Gdańska.
- h – May 29 - Sept. 24 only.
- n – Will not run Dec. 23 - 27, 31, Jan. 1, 2, Apr. 15 - 18.
- ‡ – See Table 857.

Table 859

PILA - BYDGOSZCZ - TORUŃ - WARSZAWA

1, 2 class except where shown

km		Ex 8104 R♀	Ex 5108 R♀ G	85102 2	51102 ♀	51108 ♀	51104 ♀ G	81202 ♀ E	85200			15105 ♀ G	15109 ♀	15103 ♀	58101 ♀ G	Ex 1509 R♀	58201 ♀	Ex 1805 R♀	2	18203 E
	Szczecin Główny 851 ..... d.	...	...	0635	...	...	...	2300		Warszawa Wschodnia ...... d.	...	0625	...	...	1640	...	2245
0	Pila .... d.	0454c	...	0952	...	0138	0224		Warszawa Centralna ...... d.	...	0640	...	...	1655	...	2301
87	Bydgoszcz Główny 853 .. a.	0611	0717	0954	1056	1428	1735	1926	0259	0334		Łódź Kaliska 853 ▲ ..... d.	0611	...	0941	...	1549	...	1819	...
138	Toruń Główny 853 ...... d.	0656	0802	1051	1141	1511	1824	2013	0355	0429		Kutno 853 .... d.	0718	0815	1107	...	1653	...	1827	2010	0050
	Olsztyn 854 .... d.	...	...	...	0647		Włocławek 853 .... d.	0802	0859	1150	...	1737	...	1912	2108	0134
193	Włocławek 853 .... d.	0733	0839	1148	1549	1900	2051	0434		Olsztyn 854 .... d.	...	...	1635	...
248	Kutno 853 .... d.	0815	0921	1311	1656	1943	2135	0528		Toruń Główny 853 .... a.	0840	0936	1228	1455	1814	1901	1949	2204	0214
	Łódź Kaliska 853 ▲ .... a.		1026	1432	1800	2240		Bydgoszcz Główny 853 ... a.	0925	1020	1312	1541	1855	1949	2040	2257	0320
375	Warszawa Centralna ..... a.	0945		2116	0710		Pila .... a.	...	1639	...	2046	2143b	...	0422
380	Warszawa Wschodnia .... a.	0959		2134	0729		Szczecin Główny 851 ..... a.	...	1932	...	2357	...

- ⬛ 1, 2 cl., ⬛ 2 cl. and ⬛ Kostrzyn - Gorzów - Warszawa and v.v.;
- ⬛ 1. Kolobrzeg - Pila - Warszawa and v.v.
- From/to Gdynia (Table 853).
- b – ⑧ (not Apr. 30) only.
- c – ✕ (not May 1) only.

- ▲ – Additional trains (2 class only) Kutno - Łódź and v.v. (journey 70-90 minutes):
  From Kutno: 0357, 0457, 0613, 0839, 1141, 1415, 1554, 1800, 2028, 2152.
  From Łódź Kaliska: 0355, 0455, 0624, 0832, 1246, 1503, 1611, 2010, 2151.

Don't forget you may require a Belarus transit visa for Warszawa - Vilnius services via Grodno

Table 860 WROCLAW - KATOWICE - KRAKÓW - PRZEMYŚL

1, 2 class except where shown

km		33107	43111	83200	6302 6303	6420	73102	44 43	6304	451 63000	Ex 5303		6306	6320	391	63102	62206	62202	83206	6310	83204	6300	453 63006	63200	449
		✕	✕ n	🍷 S	🍷 V		🍷 Y	🛏 N🍷	🍷	🍷 F	[R]✕ G		🍷		[R] B	🍷		R	🍷 Z	🍷 W	✕ Q	🍷	🍷 L	J	🍷 H
	Szczecin **851** .... d.	...	...	2325	...	...	...	...	...	...	...	...	...	...	1130d	...	...	...	1545	...	1740	...	...	...	...
	Poznań **860a** .... d.	...	...	0255	...	...	...	...	...	...	...	...	...	...	|	...	...	...	1910	...	2115	...	...	...	...
0	**Wroclaw** Glówny ...... d.	...	...	0525	0625	0700	0835	0918	1025	1325	...	...	1525	...	1710	1725	1925	...	2137	2225	|	0025	0155	...	0225
82	Opole Glówny .... d.	...	...	0626	0724	0826	0935	1013	1124	1425	...	...	1624	...	1804	1824	2025	...	2242	2324	|	0124	0256	...	0324
	Jelenia Góra .... d.	...	...	|	|	|	|	|	|	|	...	...	|	1145	|	|	|	...	|	|	|	|	|	2247	|
	Walbrzych .... d.	...	...	|	|	|	|	|	|	|	...	...	|	1250	|	|	|	...	|	|	|	|	|	2340	|
	Klodzko .... d.	...	...	|	|	|	|	|	|	|	...	1327	|	|	|	|	|	1944	|	|	|	|	|	|	|
125	Kedzierzyn Koźle ...... d.	...	...	|	0757	0929	|	|	1157	1459	...	1617	1657	1752	1838	1857	2059	2226	2314	2357	|	0157	0329	0341	0357
	Racibórz .... a.	...	...	|	|	|	|	|	|	|	...	...	|	|	1908	|	|	|	|	|	|	|	|	|	|
	Rybnik .... d.	...	...	|	|	1017	|	|	|	|	...	...	|	1840	...	|	|	|	|	|	|	|	|	|	|
	Oświecim .... d.	...	...	|	|	...	|	|	|	|	...	...	|	2009	...	|	|	|	|	|	|	|	|	|	|
152	Gliwice .... d.	...	0632	0733	0833	...	1041	1119	1233	1533	...	...	1735	|	...	1933	2133	2301	2350	0033	|	0233	0404	0413	0432
180	**Katowice** .... a.	...	0707	0807	0907	...	1115	1207	1307	1607	...	...	1807	|	...	2007	2207	2335	0023	0107	|	0307	0437	0447	0507
180	**Katowice** ▲............ d.	...	0715	0815	0915	...	1120	1215	1315	1615	...	...	1815	|	...	2015	2215	...	...	0115	|	0315	0447	0455	0515
258	**Kraków** Glówny ▲ ... a.	...	0837	0937	1037	...	1242	1337	1437	1732	...	...	1937	2131	...	2137	2335	...	...	0237	0339	0437	0614	0626	0636
258	**Kraków** Glówny .... d.	0645	0845	...	1045	...	...	1345	1445	...	1745	...	2000	...	...	*2300*	2345	...	...	0245	0351	0445	...	...	...
263	Kraków Plaszów........ d.	0652	0854	...	1054	...	...	1353	1454	...	1753	...	2008	...	...	*2310*	2353	...	...	0254	0403	0454	...	...	...
336	Tarnów .... d.	0753	1001	...	1201	...	...	1500	1601	...	1850	...	2114	...	...	*0019*	0057	...	...	0401	0514	0601	...	...	...
416	Rzeszów .... d.	0853	1109	...	1309	...	...	1608	1709	...	1948	...	2222	...	...	*0124*	...	...	...	0509	0620	0709	...	...	...
663	Przeworsk .... d.	0919	1137	...	1337	...	...	1634	1737	...	2011	...	2251	...	...	*0150*	...	...	...	0538	0648	0737	...	...	...
678	Jaroslaw.................. d.	0932	1151	...	1351	...	...	1649	1751	...	2023	...	2304	...	...	...	...	...	...	0551	0702	0751	...	...	...
503	**Przemyśl** .... a.	1000	1221	...	1421	...	...	1720	1821	...	2050	...	2334	...	...	...	...	...	...	0621	0732	0821	...	...	...

	390	26203	26206		36101	3600	3621	3602	Ex 3502	36001 450	3604	44 43	4620	37103	3606	33106	38201	36007 452	448	34112	36201	38204	38207	3610
	B	R		2	🍷	🍷		🍷	[R]✕ G	🍷 F		🛏 N🍷		🍷 Y	🍷	V	🍷 S	[R]🍷 L	[R]🍷 H	✕ p	J	✕ Q	🍷 Z	🍷 W
Przemyśl .... d.	...	...	...	...	...	0331	...	0531	0705	...	1031	1130	...	...	1331	1453	...	...	...	1725	...	1825	...	2231
Jaroslaw......................... d.	...	...	...	...	...	0401	...	0601	0732	...	1101	1201	...	...	1401	1521	...	...	...	1754	...	1855	...	2300
Przeworsk .... d.	...	...	...	...	...	0415	...	0615	0744	...	1115	1216	...	...	1415	1533	...	...	...	1809	...	1909	...	2315
Rzeszów .... d.	...	...	...	...	...	0446	...	0646	0809	...	1146	1246	...	...	1446	1600	...	...	...	1840	...	1940	...	2346
Tarnów............................. d.	...	...	0259	...	...	0554	...	0754	0908	...	1254	1352	...	...	1554	1700	...	...	...	1948	...	2049	...	0054
Kraków Plaszów.................. d.	...	...	0401	...	...	0657	...	0857	1002	...	1357	1456	...	...	1657	1757	...	...	...	2049	...	2154	...	0157
Kraków Glówny .... a.	...	...	0406	...	...	0702	...	0902	1007	...	1402	1502	...	...	1702	1802	...	...	...	2054	...	2159	...	0202
Kraków Glówny ▲ .... d.	...	...	0412	...	0612	0712	0754	0912	*1017*	1200	1412	1512	...	1612	1712	...	1912	1942	2102	2112	2130	2217	...	0212
Katowice ▲..................... a.	...	...	0537	...	0737	0837	|	1037	*1137*	1317	1537	1637	...	1737	1837	...	2037	2102	2222	2237	2257	|	...	0337
Katowice .... d.	...	0427	0542	...	0742	0842	|	1042	...	1327	1542	1642	...	1742	1842	...	2050	2107	2232	2247	2302	|	0242	0342
Gliwice .... d.	...	0509	0621	...	0821	0921	|	1121	...	1406	1621	1744	...	1821	1921	...	2127	2147	2310	2321	2341	|	0321	0421
Oświecim........................... d.	...	|	|	...	|	|	0929	|	...	|	|	|	...	|	|	...	|	|	|	...	|	|	|	|
Rybnik .... d.	...	|	|	0657	|	|	1100	|	...	|	|	|	1717	|	|	...	|	|	|	...	|	|	|	|
Racibórz .... d.	0459	|	|	|	|	|	|	|	...	|	|	|	|	|	|	...	|	|	|	...	|	|	|	|
Kedzierzyn Koźle .... d.	0533	0600	0655	0744	0855	0955	1200	1155	...	1438	1655	|	1810	|	1955	...	|	2219	2344	...	0032	|	0355	0455
Klodzko .... a.	|	0818	|	|	|	|	|	|	...	|	|	|	|	|	|	...	|	|	|	...	|	|	|	|
Walbrzych.......................... a.	|	...	|	|	|	|	1621	|	...	|	|	|	|	|	|	...	|	|	|	...	0421	|	|	|
Jelenia Góra..................... a.	|	...	|	|	|	|	1725	|	...	|	|	|	|	|	|	...	|	|	|	...	0515	|	|	|
Opole Glówny .... d.	0606	...	0729	0846	0939	1029	...	1229	...	1512	1729	1847	1854	1931	2029	...	2229	2256	0017	...	...	|	0428	052
Wroclaw Glówny .... a.	0700	...	0825	1001	1037	1125	...	1325	...	1605	1825	1940	2017	2025	2125	...	2325	2350	0110	...	...	|	0525	062
Poznań **860a** .... a.	|	...	...	...	...	...	...	...	...	...	...	...	...	...	...	...	0155	...	...	...	...	0440	0755	...
Szczecin **851** .... a.	1255d	...	...	...	...	...	...	...	...	...	...	...	...	...	...	...	0517	...	...	...	...	0806	1114	...

B – BEM – 🛏 1, 2 cl. and [12] (Szczecin -) Wroclaw - Budapest and v.v. Extended from/to Szczecin: May 29 - Sept. 24 from Szczecin, May 30 - Sept. 25 from Budapest.
F – [12] Wroclaw - Kraków and v.v.; ▬ 2 cl. and [2] Frankfurt (Main) - Kraków and v.v.
G – [12] and ✕ Gdynia - Warszawa - Kraków - Przemyśl and v.v.
H – 🛏 1, 2 cl., ▬ 2 cl., [12] and 🍷 Berlin - Rzepin - Wroclaw - Kraków and v.v.
J – 🛏 1, 2 cl. and [12] Jelenia Góra - Kraków and v.v.
L – 🛏 1, 2 cl. and [2] Leipzig - Wroclaw - Kraków and v.v.; [12] Wroclaw - Kraków and v.v.
N – 🛏 1, 2 cl. and 🍷 Wroclaw - Lvov - Kyïv and v.v.
Q – 🛏 1, 2 cl., ▬ 2 cl., [12] and ✕ Szczecin - Ostrów - Kraków - Przemyśl and v.v.
R – ▬ 2 cl. and [12] Klodzko - Katowice - Lublin and v.v.
S – 🛏 1, 2 cl., ▬ 2 cl. and [12] Świnoujście - Kraków and v.v.; 🍷 Szczecin - Kraków and v.v.
V – [12] Wroclaw - Przemyśl and Przemyśl - Kraków; 🛏 2 cl. Kraków - Przemy (trains **107/8**) - Odesa and v.v.
W – ▬ 2 cl. and [12] Wroclaw - Kraków - Przemyśl and v.v.
Y – [12] and 🍷 Zielona Góra - Wroclaw - Kraków and v.v.
Z – 🛏 1, 2 cl. and [12] Szczecin - Katowice - Zakopane and v.v.
d – May 29 - Sept. 24 **only**.
n – Will **not** run Dec. 25, 26, Apr. 16.
p – Will **not** run Dec. 24, 25, Apr. 15.
▲ – Additional trains **Katowice - Kraków** and v.v. Journey time: 90 minutes.
From Katowice: 0620**s**, 1055, 1515**n**, 1715, 1920**s**, 2315**p**.
From Kraków Glówny: 1112**n**, 1532, 1720**s**, 1819Ⓑ, 1847**n**, 2020**s**, 2300n
s – Slow train. Journey time: 110 minutes.

Table 860a POZNAŃ - WROCLAW

Summary Table. All trains 1, 2 cla

km		56200	83200	86200	16500	Ex 5600	56104	86100	56100	16110	83206	Ex 5602	254
			🍷	🍷	🍷	[R]✕	n	✕	✕		✕	[R]✕ n	[R]✕ B
0	**Poznań** . d.	0205	0255	0445	0705	0920	1100	1300	1500	1710	1910	2010	2340
69	Leszno .. d.	0255	0345	0540	0757	1003	1155	1350	1553	1800	2000	2053	0030
165	**Wroclaw** a.	0415	0500	0709	0908	1108	1312	1505	1705	1915	2115	2158	0145

	255	38207	Ex 6503	61111	65101	65105	Ex 6501	68101	61501	65203	68201	382
	✕ B	✕	[R]✕ n	✕	✕	n	[R]✕	✕	🍷		🍷	🍷
Wroclaw d.	0310	0550	0720	0855	1050	1350	1520	1750	1950	2250	2335	235
Leszno d.	0440	0705	0821	1010	1204	1505	1621	1905	2105	0005	0050	010
Poznań a.	0540	0755	0905	1100	1255	1555	1705	1955	2155	0055	0140	015

B – BALTIC – Gdynia and Świnoujście/Szczecin - Praha and v.v. – See Table **882**.
n – Will **not** run Dec. 25, Apr. 16.

Table 861 POZNAŃ - OSTRÓW - KATOWICE - KRAKÓW

All trains 1, 2 cla

km		82202	83200	83202	73100	83102	74100	83206	83204	73200	84200
		🍷 K	🍷 S	C	✕	✕ W	🍷 p	🍷 Z	✕ Q	En	✕ Dt
	Szczecin **851** .... d.	2100	2325	...	...	...	...	1545	1740	...	...
0	**Poznań** Glówny .... d.	0030	0255	0340	0555	1440	1535	1910	2115	2150	2345
	Wroclaw **860** .... d.	|	0525	|	|	|	|	2137	|	|	|
114	Ostrów Wielkopolski .. d.	0210	|	0520	0723	|	1704	|	2255	2322	0120
201	Kluczbork .... d.	0323	|	0635	0837	|	1819	|	0011	0031	0230
	Czestochowa Stradom d.	0450	|	0755	|	|	|	|	0133	|	|
	Kielce..................... a.	0632	|	|	|	|	|	|	|	|	|
302	Bytom....................... d.	...	|	|	1018	|	1955	|	|	0212	0412
320	**Katowice** .... a.	...	0807	|	1047	|	2025	0023	|	0242	0442
398	**Kraków** Glówny .... a.	...	0937	0956	1218	2010	...	...	0339	0408	...

	38207	47101	38102	37101	48201	28203	38201	38203	38205	372
	🍷 Z	🍷 v	✕ W	🍷	✕ Dt	🍷 K	🍷 S	✕ C	✕ Q	E
Kraków Glówny ...... d.	...	...	0745	1532	...	...	1912	2002	2217	23
Katowice .... d.	0242	0622	|	1702	1952	...	2050	|	|	00
Bytom...................... d.	|	0651	|	1731	2021	...	|	|	|	01
Kielce.................... d.	|	|	|	|	|	1940	|	|	|	|
Czestochowa Stradom d.	|	|	|	|	|	2135	|	2217	0024	|
Kluczbork .... d.	|	0829	|	1913	2203	2252	|	2331	0143	02
Ostrów Wielkopolski d.	|	0938	|	2025	2324	0012	|	0050	0304	04
Wroclaw **860** .... a.	0525	|	|	|	|	|	2325	|	|	|
Poznań Glówny ...... a.	0755	1105	1307	2155	0055	0145	0155	0225	0440	05
Szczecin **851** ...... a.	1114	...	...	...	...	0452	0517	...	0806	.

C – 🛏 1, 2 cl., ▬ 2 cl. and [12] Kolobrzeg - Kraków and v.v.
D – 🛏 1, 2 cl., ▬ 2 cl., [12] Kolobrzeg - Katowice and v.v.
E – ▬ 2 cl. and [12] Poznań - Kraków - Zakopane and v.v.
K – 🛏 1, 2 cl., [12] and 🍷 Szczecin - Kielce and v.v.
Q – 🛏 1, 2 cl., ▬ 2 cl., [12] and ✕ Szczecin - Kraków - Przemyśl and v.v.
S – 🛏 1, 2 cl., ▬ 2 cl. and [12] Świnoujście - Kraków and v.v.; 🍷 Szczecin - Kraków and v.v.
W – WAWEL – [12] and ✕ Świnoujście - Poznań - Kutno - Kraków and v.v.
Z – 🛏 1, 2 cl. and [12] Szczecin - Katowice - Zakopane and v.v.
n – Will **not** run Dec. 24, Apr. 15.
p – Will **not** run Dec. 24, Apr. 16.
r – Will **not** run Dec. 25, Apr. 16.
t – Will **not** run Dec. 24, 25, 31, Apr. 16.
v – Will **not** run Dec. 25, Apr. 17.

[R] – Reservation obligatory 🛏 – Sleeping car ▬ – Couchette car

Table 862 GÖRLITZ - WROCLAW

1, 2 class except where shown

km		514	451	451	518	520	522	66224	457		453
		2		2		2	2		🍷	2	🍷
			F	K							L
0	*Leipzig* **674** .... d.	...	0507	0507	...	...	...	...	...	...	1905
116	*Dresden N* **682** ..... d.	...	0654	0654	...	...	...	...	1748	...	2048
218	**Görlitz** .... d.	...	0900	0900	...	...	...	...	1935	...	2255
220	Zgorzelec 🏛.............. d.	...	0906	0906	1230	1430	...	1757	1941	...	2301
248	Wegliniec .... d.	0622	0950	0955	1320	1521	1701	1847	2016	2046	2340
322	Jelenia Góra **862a** . a.	|	|	1100	|	|	|	|	|	2209	|
273	Boleslawiec .... d.	0645	1009	|	1344	1545	1725	1913	2033	...	2359
317	Legnica .... d.	0735	1044	|	1432	1632	1809	2009	2106	...	0032
383	**Wroclaw** Glówny ...... a.	0845	1137	1309	1543	1742	1921	2122	2156	...	0122
573	*Katowice* **860** .... a.	...	|	1607	...	...	...	...	...	...	0437
651	*Kraków* **860** .... a.	...	|	1732	...	...	...	...	...	...	0614
768	*Warszawa* **863** ...... a.	...	1725	...	...	...	...	...	...	...	0735

		456	513	515	517	519	36001	450	523	452
	2	🍷		2			2[R]	[R]	2	[R]🍷
							K	F		L
Warszawa **863** ..... d.	...	...	...	...	...	...	...	1220	...	1825
Kraków **860** ..... d.	...	...	...	...	...	...	1200	|	...	1942
Katowice **860** .. d.	...	...	...	...	...	...	1327	|	...	2107
Wroclaw Glówny .... d.	...	0642	0847	1045	1415	1634	1615	1750	2135	0012
Legnica .... d.	...	0734	1002	1200	1534	1753	|	1845	2246	0108
Boleslawiec .... d.	...	0803	1046	1245	1620	1837	|	1919	2331	0139
Jelenia Góra **862a** d.	0630	|	|	|	|	|	1823	|	|	|
Wegliniec .... d.	0800	0835	1123	1322	1657	1914	1959	1959	2354	0214
Zgorzelec 🏛........... d.	...	0902	1202	1401	1736	1953	2033	2033	...	0247
Görlitz .... a.	...	0908	...	...	...	...	2038	2038	...	0252
Dresden N **682** ... a.	...	1054	...	...	...	...	2231	2231	...	0453
Leipzig **674** .... a.	...	...	...	...	...	...	0025	0025	...	0645

F – 🛏 1, 2 cl., ▬ 2 cl. and [12] Frankfurt (Main) - Wroclaw - Warszawa and v.v.;
🛏 1, 2 cl. Frankfurt (Main) - Warszawa (trains **247/6**) - Moskva and v.v.

K – ▬ 2 cl. and [2] Frankfurt (Main) - Wegliniec (trains **63000/36001**) - Kraków and v.v.

L – 🛏 1, 2 cl., ▬ 2 cl. and [12] Leipzig - Warszawa and v.v.;
🛏 1, 2 cl., [2] and 🍷 Leipzig - Wroclaw (trains **63006/36007**) - Kraków and v.v.

Table 862a JELENIA GÓRA - WALBRZYCH - WROCLAW

1, 2 class except where shown

km				63000		61100		61500	61204	62200	61200
				K🍷	2	W🍷	2		W	L	W🍷
0	**Jelenia Góra** .... d.	0632	0732	1103	1254	1500	1629	1705	2045	2114	2200
47	Walbrzych Glówny .... d.	0734	0846	1151	1356	1551	1733	1756	2141	2206	2253
77	Jaworzyna Ślaska ..... d.	0818	0928	1230	1442	1630	1817	1838	2223	2247	2333
126	**Wroclaw** Glówny ...... a.	0908	1015	1309	1535	1705	1906	1913	2305	2325	0010

	16201	16205	26201	16501		16101		36001		
	W🍷	W	L			W🍷		K🍷		
Wroclaw Glówny .... d.	0350	0500	0617	0935	1050	1215	1515	1615	1755	2056
Jaworzyna Ślaska ... d.	0427	0551	0656	1012	1140	1252	1608	1652	1845	2149
Walbrzych Glówny .. d.	0512	0635	0743	1054	1222	1334	1653	1732	1928	2234
Jelenia Góra .... a.	0603	0740	0838	1148	1326	1425	1759	1820	2030	2341

K – See Table **862**.

L – 🛏 1, 2 cl. and [12] Jelenia Góra - Wroclaw - Czestochowa - Lublin and v.v.

W – To/from Warszawa – for composition see Table **863**.

Table 863 WROCLAW - LÓDŹ - WARSZAWA

All trains 1, 2 class

km		253	453	33100	3300	Ex 6102	Ex 6100	71100	33102	33104	33106	451	33108	33110	Ex 6104	61100	81106	77200		82200	61204	61200	71202	
						[R]🍴	[R]🍴	🍷				🍴			[R]🍴	🍷	🍷			🍷				
		B	L	⚒		n			p	p		F	p	p				W		N	J	R	S	
	Jelenia Góra **862a** .... d.	...	...	...	...	...	...	...	...	...	...	...	...	...	...	1500	...	...	...	...	2045	2200	...	...
0	**Wroclaw** Glówny .... d.	0130	0151	...	...	0505	0543	...	...	...	...	1200	...	...	1625	1730	...	...	1815	...	2330	0035	...	...
	Szczecin **851** .... d.	|	|	...	...	|	|	...	...	...	...	|	...	...	|	|	1350	...	|	1955	|	|	...	...
	Poznań Glówny.............. d.	|	|	...	...	|	|	0730	...	...	...	|	...	...	|	|	1715	...	|	2330	|	|	...	...
	Zielona Góra .... d.	|	|	...	...	|	|	|	...	...	...	|	...	...	|	|	|	...	|	|	|	|	2217	...
	Glogów.......................... d.	|	|	...	...	|	|	|	...	...	...	|	...	...	|	|	|	...	|	|	|	|	2320	...
106	Ostrów Wielkopolski.......... d.	0254	0314	...	...	|	0702	0908	...	...	...	1330	...	...	|	1846	1900	...	2050	0115	|	0202	0212	...
130	Kalisz .... d.	0322	0342	...	...	|	0728	0935	...	...	...	1358	...	...	|	1913	1928	...	2123	0144	|	0232	0245	...
243	**Lódź** Kaliska.................... d.	0449	0520	...	...	|	0847	1101	...	...	...	1529	...	...	|	2040	2053	...	2319	0308	|	0404	0427	...
	Lódź Fabryczna................ d.	|	|	0640	0750	|	|	...	1040	1240	1440	|	1640	1840	|	|	...	2210	...	...	|	|	|	...
	Opole............................. d.	|	|	|	|	0601	|	...	|	|	|	|	|	|	1720	|	...	|	...	...	0034	|	|	...
	Czestochowa Osobowa ... d.	|	|	|	|	0720**s**	|	...	|	|	|	|	|	|	1838**s**	|	...	|	...	...	0215	|	|	...
279	Koluszki............................ d.	|	0602	0705	|	|	|	...	1105	1305	1505	|	1705	1905	|	|	...	2235	...	...	0418	|	0521	...
319	Skierniewice .... d.	|	0628	0730	|	|	|	...	1130	1330	1530	|	1730	1930	|	|	...	2300	...	...	0446	|	0549	...
405	**Warszawa** Centralna .... a.	0643	0735	0830	0925	0940	1035	...	1230	1435	1630	1725	1835	2035	2100	2230	...	2400	...	...	0600	0620	0653	...
410	**Warszawa** Wschodnia .... a.	0657	0748	0844	0939	0954	1049	...	1249	1457	1644	1744	1849	2049	2114	2244	...	0019	...	...	0614	0634	0706	...

	77203	18107	Ex 1605	16101	22101		22103	22105	450	22107	17101	22109	Ex 1601	3303	Ex 1603		252	452	22111	17201	16201	16205	28201	
		🍷	[R]🍴	🍴					🍴		🍷		[R]🍴		[R]🍴		[R]	[R]			🍴		🍷	
	W				⚒			p	F	p		p			n		B	L	p	S	R	J	N	
Warszawa Wschodnia .... d.	0500	...	0535	0640	0705	...	0905	1105	1205	1305	...	1505	1540	1710	1705	...	1805	1810	1905	2050	2130	2200	...	...
Warszawa Centralna .... d.	0515	...	0550	0655	0720	...	0915	1120	1220	1320	...	1520	1555	1725	1720	...	1820	1825	1920	2110	2145	2215	...	...
Skierniewice........................ d.	0619	...	|	|	0824	...	1014	1224	|	1424	...	1624	|	1824	|	...	|	1922	2024	2210	|	2313	...	...
Koluszki.............................. d.	0653	...	|	|	0850	...	1040	1250	|	1450	...	1650	|	1849	|	...	|	1950	2050	2236	|	2340	...	...
Czestochowa Osobowa ..... d.	|	...	0812**s**	|	|	...	|	|	|	|	...	|	|	|	1942**s**	...	|	|	|	|	|	0207	...	...
Opole.................................. d.	|	...	0933	|	|	...	|	|	|	|	...	|	|	|	2103	...	|	|	|	|	|	0341	...	...
Lódź Fabryczna.................. a.	0725	...	|	|	0915	...	1105	1315	|	1515	...	1715	|	1910	|	...	|	|	2115	|	|	|	...	...
Lódź Kaliska....................... d.	...	0620	|	0847	...	1040	...	...	1413	...	1555	...	1742	...	|	...	2021	2040	...	2334	2346	|	2359	...
Kalisz .... d.	...	0747	|	1015	...	1240	...	...	1538	...	1721	...	1906	...	|	...	2153	2206	...	0105	0114	|	0135	...
Ostrów Wielkopolski............... d.	...	0822	|	1040	...	1311	...	...	1604	...	1751	...	1929	...	|	...	2220	2232	...	0138	0142	|	0217	...
Glogów............................ a.	...	|	|	|	...	|	...	...	|	...	|	...	|	...	|	...	|	|	...	0422	|	|	|	...
Zielona Góra .... a.	...	|	|	|	...	|	...	...	|	...	|	...	|	...	|	...	|	|	...	0532	|	|	|	...
Poznań Glówny................... a.	...	0955	|	|	...	|	...	...	|	...	1920	...	|	...	|	...	|	|	...	...	|	|	0400	...
Szczecin **851** .... a.	...	1311	|	|	...	|	...	...	|	...	...	...	|	...	|	...	|	|	...	...	|	|	0715	...
Wroclaw Glówny .... a.	...	...	1027	1159	...	1553	...	...	1728	...	...	...	2046	...	2157	...	2345	2355	...	...	0330	0440	...	...
Jelenia Góra **862a** .... a.	...	...	...	1425	...	...	...	...	...	...	...	...	...	...	...	...	...	...	...	...	0603	0740	...	...

B – BOHEMIA – 🛏 1, 2 cl. (also ▬ 2 cl. May 29 - Sept. 24) and [12] Warszawa - Praha and v.v.; 🛏 1, 2 cl. Moskva - Praha and v.v.

F – 🛏 1, 2 cl., ▬ 2 cl. and [12] Frankfurt (Main) - Warszawa and v.v.;
🛏 1, 2 cl. Frankfurt (Main) - Warszawa (trains **247/6**) - Moskva and v.v.

J – 🛏 1, 2 cl., ▬ 2 cl. and [12] Jelenia Góra - Warszawa and v.v.

L – 🛏 1, 2 cl., ▬ 2 cl. and [12] Leipzig - Warszawa and v.v.

N – 🛏 1, 2 cl., ▬ 2 cl. and [12] Szczecin - Poznań - Lódź - Lublin and v.v.

R – KARKONOSZE – 🛏 1, 2 cl. and [12] Jelenia Góra - Warszawa and v.v.; 🛏 1, 2 cl., ▬ 2 cl. and [12] Klodzko - Warszawa and v.v.

S – 🛏 1, 2 cl. and [12] Zielona Góra - Warszawa and v.v.

W – [12] Lódź - Warszawa - Suwalki and v.v.

n – Will **not** run Dec. 25, Apr. 16, May 1.

p – Will **not** run Dec. 25, Apr. 16.

s – Czestochowa **Stradom**.

Table 863a LOCAL RAILWAYS

Mostly 2 class only

km								Ⓐ		
0	**Zbaszynek**...................... d.	...	0500	0600	...	1147	1500	1640	1815	2246
28	Wolsztyn .... d.	0424	0610	0705	...	1234	1539	1733	1854	2324
75	**Leszno** .... a.	0532	0720	0830	...	1340	1654	1836	1956	...

						Ⓐ			
Leszno .... d.	...	0543	0740	...	1250	1432	1606	2045	2230
Wolsztyn .... d.	0433	0649	0838	1045	1412	1541	1711	2149	2336
Zbaszynek...................... a.	0517	0730	...	1125	1450	1620	1750	2227	...

BIALYSTOK - ELK *104* km Journey 140 minutes (see also Table **856**). From **Bialystok** 0319, 0536, 0943, 1343, 1543, 1731, 2140. From **Elk** 0348, 0552, 1140, 1528, 1723, 1935, 2355.

ELK - SUWALKI *66* km Jny 110 minutes (🚌 2½ hours). From **Elk** 0440, 0700🚌, 0830🚌, 1250🚌, 1530, 2110🚌. From **Suwalki** 0440, 0520🚌, 0910🚌, 1240🚌, 1525, 1800🚌.

KATOWICE - OŚWIECIM *33* km Journey 65 minutes. From **Katowice**: 0440, 0520Ⓐ, 0600, 0708, 0920, 1125, 1250Ⓐ, 1405, 1505, 1545, 1645, 1830, 2020, 2105, 2230.
From **Oświecim**: 0418, 0518Ⓐ, 0554, 0655Ⓐ, 0821, 0956, 1238, 1330, 1414Ⓐ, 1506, 1548, 1653, 1814, 2050, 2221.

KRAKÓW - OŚWIECIM *70* km Journey 105 minutes. From **Kraków** Glówny: 0519**p**, 0603**p**, 0650, 0742**p**, 1200**p**, 1310Ⓐ**p**, 1444**p**, 1445, 1548**p**, 1640**p**, 1725**p**, 1825, 1942**p**, 2226**p**.
From **Oświecim**: 0353**p**, 0509**p**, 0558, 0634**p**, 0811**p**, 1050**p**, 1245**p**, 1400, 1410**p**, 1516Ⓐ**p**, 1621**p**, 1754**p**, 1908, 1920**p**, 2009, 2038**p**, 2148, 2343**p**. **p** – From/to Kraków **Plaszów**.

POZNAŃ - WOLSZTYN *81* km Journey 2 - 2¼ hours. Service partly operated by Steam Locomotives. Please note that the steam service detailed below is liable to change.
From **Poznań** Glówny: 0555, 0750 (🚂 on Ⓐ), 1340🚂, 1540, 1940Ⓐ🚂, 2040🚂. From **Wolsztyn**: 0427Ⓐ🚂, 0517🚂, 0815, 1115 (🚂 on Ⓐ), 1544🚂, 1937.

WALBRZYCH - KLODZKO *51* km Journey 95 minutes. From **Walbrzych** 0515Ⓐ, 0810, 1400Ⓐ, 1530, 1958. From **Klodzko** 0540, 0701Ⓐ, 1325Ⓐ, 1555, 1935.

12 *For explanation of standard symbols see page 4* 445

Table 864 WARSZAWA - KATOWICE - BIELSKO BIALA

1, 2 class except where shown

km		IC	Ex				EC	IC			Ex		Ex			IC	IC	Ex						
		106	1401	14101	14121		105	131	22103	14103	1405		1407	22107	14105	1409	1411	1413	14107	337	200	203	16205	14201
		[R] ✕	[R] ✕				[R] ✕	[R] ✕			[R] ✕		[R] ✕			[R] ✕	[R] ✕	[R] ✕		[R] ✕	[R]	[R]		
		D	p	Zp			E	P		p	p		Ⓑp	p		Ⓑp		Ⓐt	p	B	S	C	J	Gn
0	**Warszawa** Wschodnia d.	0555	0655	...	0605	...	0855	1055	0905	...	1255	...	1455	1305	...	1620	1655	1755	*1600*d	1855	1950	2020	2200	2256
5	**Warszawa** Centralna d.	0610	0710	...	0618	...	0910	1110	0915	...	1310	...	1510	1320	...	1635	1710	1810	*1615*d	1910	2005	2045	2215	2310
	Koluszki d.	|	|	...	0748	...	|	|	1040	1044	|	...	|	1450	1454	|	|	|	*1749*d	|	|	|	2340	0037
	Lódź Fabryczna d.	|	|	0620	|	...	|	|	1105	b	|	...	|	1515	c	|	|	|	1820	|	|	|	|	|
	Piotrków Trybunalski d.	|	|	0732	0840	...	|	|	...	1135	|	...	|	...	1545	|	|	|	1933	|	|	|	0035	0133
	Czestochowa Osobowa d.	|	|	0855	1000	1005	|	|	...	1255	|	...	|	...	1705	|	|	|	2055	|	|	|	0157	0257
255	Zawiercie d.	|	0905	0930	...	1040	|	|	...	1320	1505	...	1705	...	1742	|	1905	2005	2130	2138	2231	2253	...	0332
390	Sosnowiec d.	0834	0934	1004	...	1114	|	1334	...	1404	1534	...	1734	...	1816	1859	1934	2034	2204	2212	2301	2323	...	0406
298	**Katowice** a.	0848	0948	1018	...	1128	1148	1348	...	1418	1548	...	1748	...	1830	1913	1948	2048	2218	2228	2315	2337	...	0420
298	**Katowice 866** d.	...	0953	1025	...	...	...	...	...	1427	1557	...	1753	...	1835	1917	1953	2057	*2247*	...	...	...	...	0428
	Gliwice a.	...	|	|	...	...	...	...	...	1500	1630	...	|	...	1908	1950	|	2130	*2321*	...	...	...	...	|
353	**Bielsko Biala 866** a.	...	1053	1122	...	...	...	...	...	...	...	...	1853	...	...	...	2053	...	...	...	...	...	...	0530

km						IC			IC	Ex		Ex	Ex			EC		IC	Ex			IC		
		336		201	202	4100	41122	41100	4102	4106	41102	4108	4110	33106		104	41104	130	4112	41124	41106	107	41200	61204
		[R] ✕	2	[R]	[R]	[R] ✕			[R] ✕	[R] ✕		[R] ✕	[R] ✕			[R] ✕		[R] ✕	[R] ✕			[R] ✕		
		B		S	C	⚒r				⚒r	p	Ⓐt	p			E	p	P	p		Zp	D	Gn	J
	Bielsko Biala d.	...	...	...	...	...	...	...	0625	0825	...	...	1225	...	...	...	...	...	...	...	1730	...	2245	...
0	Gliwice d.	...	...	...	...	0519	...	0549	|	|	...	1049	|	...	...	...	1447	...	1749	...	|	...	|	...
28	**Katowice** a.	...	...	...	...	0552	...	0622	0725	0925	...	1122	1325	...	...	...	1520	...	1822	...	1830	...	2350	...
28	**Katowice** d.	0335	...	0400	0445	0600	...	0630	0730	0930	1120	1130	1330	...	1400	1500	1530	1700	1830	...	1835	2000	2355	...
36	Sosnowiec d.	0351	...	0416	0501	0614	...	0646	0744	0944	1136	1144	1344	...	1416	|	1546	1714	1844	...	1851	2014	0011	...
71	Zawiercie d.	0421	0429	0446	0533	|	...	0716	|	1014	1206	1214	1414	...	1446	|	1616	|	1914	...	1921	|	0041	...
114	**Czestochowa** Osobowa d.	|	0521	|	|	|	0607	0755	|	|	1251	|	|	...	1520	|	1655	|	|	1747	2000	|	0120	0215
199	Piotrków Trybunalski d.	|	...	|	|	|	0714	0853	|	|	1357	|	|	...	...	|	1753	|	|	1854	2059	|	0220	0315
*265	**Lódź** Fabryczna a.	|	...	|	|	|	|	1015	|	|	e	|	|	1440	...	|	1930	|	|	|	2220	|	|	|
238	Koluszki d.	|	...	|	|	|	0817	...	|	|	1458	|	|	1505	...	|	...	|	|	1958	...	|	0322	0418
344	**Warszawa** Centralna a.	0647	...	0715	0750	0840	0955	...	1010	1210	...	1410	1610	1630	...	1740	...	1940	2110	2140	...	2245	0455	0600
349	**Warszawa** Wschodnia a.	0701	...	0734	0804	0859	1009	...	1024	1224	...	1424	1629	1644	...	1754	...	1954	2129	2154	...	2259	0509	0614

B – BÁTHORY – 🛏 1, 2 cl., ▬ 2 cl., [12] and ✕ Warszawa - Žilina - Budapest and v.v.; 🛏 1, 2 cl., ▬ 2 cl. and [2] Warszawa - Žilina - Bratislava and v.v.
C – CHOPIN – 🛏 1, 2 cl., ▬ 2 cl. and [12] Warszawa - Wien and v.v.; 🛏 1, 2 cl. Moskva - Warszawa - Wien and v.v.
D – PRAHA – [12] and ✕ Warszawa - Praha and v.v.
E – SOBIESKI – [12] and ✕ Warszawa - Wien and v.v.
G – 🛏 1, 2 cl., ▬ 2 cl. and [12] Warszawa - Bielsko Biala and v.v.
J – 🛏 1, 2 cl., ▬ 2 cl. and [12] Warszawa - Jelenia Góra and v.v.
P – POLONIA – [12] and ✕ Warszawa - Žilina - Budapest and v.v.
S – SILESIA – 🛏 1, 2 cl., ▬ 2 cl. and [12] Warszawa - Praha and v.v.
Z – [12] Lódź - Żywiec and v.v.
b – From **Lódź Fabryczna** (depart 1005).
c – From **Lódź Fabryczna** (depart 1415).
d – Change at Piotrków Trybunalski (arrive 1840).
e – To **Lódź Fabryczna** (arrive 1536).
* – *km* via Koluszki.
n – Will **not** run Dec. 24, 25, 31, Apr. 16.
p – Will **not** run Dec. 25, Apr. 16.
r – Will **not** run Dec. 26, Apr. 17.
t – Will **not** run May 1, 2.

Table 865 WARSZAWA - KRAKÓW

All trains 1, 2 class

km					Ex		IC	Ex		IC		IC		Ex		IC		Ex	Ex		IC	IC			
		53509	381	13101	1301	13109	1303	5301	12113	1305	12115	1307	23113	5303	13107	1313	13103	1315	5201	12135	1317	5305	12117	13209	13201
		🍷	✕	🍷	[R] ✕		[R] ✕	[R] ✕	🍷	[R] ✕	🍷	[R] ✕		[R] ✕		[R] ✕		[R] ✕	[R] ✕		[R] ✕	[R] ✕	🍷		
		G	K				⚒		x	n	x	n	n		p	Ⓑn	n				Ⓑn		Ⓑ	Y	Z
	Gdynia **855** d.	2217	...	...	...	...	...	0444	...	...	...	...	...	1042	...	...	...	...	1245	...	...	1445	...	...	...
0	**Warszawa** Wschodnia d.	0310	0545	...	0645	0651	0745	0845	0850	1046	1041	1245	...	1445	1440	1545	1550	1645	1650	...	1745	1845	1840	2125	2248
5	**Warszawa** Centralna d.	0325	0600	...	0700	0705	0800	0900	0905	1100	1105	1300	...	1500	1505	1600	1605	1700	1705	...	1800	1900	1905	2140	2305
	Lódź Fabryczna d.	|	|	0610	|	|	|	|	|	|	|	|	...	|	|	|	|	|	|	1540	|	|	|	|	|
	Radom d.	0513	|	|	|	0838	|	|	1033	|	1230	|	...	|	1645	|	1750	|	1828	1855	|	|	2041	2317	0057
	Skarżysko Kamienna d.	0548	|	|	|	0907	|	|	1102	|	1258	|	1455	|	1720	|	1820	|	1856	...	|	|	2110	2350	0133
	Kielce d.	0642	|	|	|	*0951*	|	|	1140	|	1335	|	1533	|	1805	|	...	|	1934	...	|	|	2148	0032	0218
292	**Kraków** Glówny a.	0828	0837	0926	0937	...	1040	1140	...	1340	...	1540	1713	1737	1950	1837	...	1937	...	...	2037	2137	...	0223	0404
297	Kraków Plaszów a.	...	0911	...	0951	...	...	...	...	...	...	...	1744	1751	...	...	...	1951	...	...	...	...	...	0234	0431
	Zakopane **866** a.	...	|	...	1239v	...	...	...	...	...	...	...	...	|	...	...	...	|	...	...	...	...	...	|	0838
	Nowy Sacz **867** a.	...	1226	...	...	...	...	...	...	...	...	...	...	|	...	...	...	2220	...	...	...	...	...	0558	...
	Przemyśl **860 868** a.	...	...	...	...	...	...	...	...	...	...	...	...	2050	...	...	...	...	...	...	...	...	...	...	...

km						Ex	IC	Ex	Ex			IC	Ex		IC		IC		Ex		IC		Ex		
		31200	21136	31202	21112	3500	3100	2500	3102	31102	31106	3104	3502	32112	3108	21114	3110	21116	3504	31100	3114	22108	3116	380	35508
					🍷	[R] ✕	[R] ✕	[R] ✕	[R] ✕			[R] ✕	[R] ✕		[R] ✕	🍷	[R] ✕	🍷	[R] ✕	🍷	[R] ✕		[R] ✕	✕	🍷
		Z		Y	⚒		⚒t			n	p	⚒t		n	⚒		n				n			K	G
	Przemyśl **860 868** d.	...	...	...	...	...	...	...	...	...	...	...	0705	...	...	...	...	...	...	...	...	...	...	...	...
	Nowy Sacz **867** d.	...	...	2241	...	...	...	...	0535	...	...	...	|	...	...	...	...	...	...	...	...	...	...	1653	...
	Zakopane **866** d.	2118	...	|	...	...	...	...	|	...	...	...	|	...	...	...	...	...	...	...	...	...	1617v	|	...
	Kraków Plaszów d.	0054	...	0201	...	...	...	...	0802	...	0813	...	1002	0956	...	...	...	...	...	...	...	...	1902	1948	2055
0	**Kraków** Glówny d.	0110	...	0215	...	0615	0715	...	0815	...	0833	0915	1015	1025	1215	...	1415	...	1615	1732	1815	...	1915	2015	2115
132	Kielce d.	0251	...	0410	0605	|	|	0815	|	...	1022	|	|	1212	|	1405	|	1600	|	|	|	1817	|	|	2315
176	Skarżysko Kamienna d.	0332	...	0455	0645	|	|	0852	|	0959	1105	|	|	1250	|	1444	|	1640	|	|	|	1920	|	|	2359
217	Radom d.	0410	0435	0535	0717	|	|	0921	|	1034	1140	|	|	...	|	1517	|	1717	|	|	|	1955	|	|	0040
	Lódź Fabryczna a.	|	0740	|	|	|	|	|	|	|	|	|	|	...	|	|	|	|	|	2040	|	|	|	|	|
320	**Warszawa** Centralna a.	0540	...	0730	0845	0850	0950	1045	1050	1205	1325	1150	1250	...	1450	1645	1650	1845	1850	...	2050	2145	2150	2253	0215
325	**Warszawa** Wschodnia a.	0554	...	0744	0900	0904	1004	1104	1109	1219	1339	1204	1304	...	1506	1659	1704	1909	1904	...	2104	2209	2204	2314	0229
	Gdynia **855** a.	...	...	...	...	1300	...	1500	...	...	...	...	1708	...	...	...	...	...	2304	...	...	...	...	...	0705

G – 🛏 1, 2 cl., ▬ 2 cl. and [12] Gdynia - Kraków and v.v.
K – KARPATY – [12] Warszawa - Košice - Bucureşti and v.v.; ✕ Warszawa - Plaveč and v.v.
Y – 🛏 1, 2 cl., ▬ 2 cl. and [12] Warszawa - Krynica and v.v.
Z – 🛏 1, 2 cl., ▬ 2 cl. and [12] Warszawa - Zakopane and v.v.
n – Will **not** run Dec. 25, Apr. 16.
t – Will **not** run Dec. 26, Apr. 17.
v – Runs on dates in Table **866**.
x – Train liable to cancellation without notice.
p – Will **not** run Dec. 25, Apr. 16, 30.

Table 865a LUBLIN - WROCLAW, KATOWICE and KRAKÓW

All trains 1, 2 class

km		24100	24100	23100	24102	23102	28200		26200	26202
					n	🍷	P 🍷		J	L
0	**Lublin** d.	0555	0555	0640	1410	1735	1940	...	2205	2225
128	Radom **865** d.	0735	0735	0813	1545	1908	2118	...	2340	0027
169	Skarżysko Kamienna d.	0807	0807	0843	1618	1940	|	...	0014	0100
	Lódź Kaliska a.	|	|	|	|	|	2342	...	|	|
213	Kielce **865** d.	0900	0915	0920	1700	2017	...	...	0112	0142
326	Czestochowa Stradom d.	|	1058	|	|	|	...	...	0300	|
421	Opole d.	|	|	|	|	|	...	...	|	|
503	**Wroclaw** Glówny a.	|	1330	|	|	|	...	...	0546	|
386	**Katowice** a.	1118	...	|	1956	|	...	...	...	0422
350	**Kraków** Glówny **865** a.	...	...	1102	...	2159	...	...	...	...

	82201	32100	42100		32102	42102	62103	62202	6220
	P 🍷	🍷	n					L	J
Kraków Glówny **865** d.	...	0600	...	...	1653	...	...	...	...
Katowice d.	...	|	0750	...	|	1630	...	2345	...
Wroclaw Glówny d.	...	|	|	...	|	|	1410	|	2345
Opole d.	...	|	|	...	|	|	|	|	|
Czestochowa Stradom d.	...	|	|	...	|	|	1648	|	0231
Kielce **865** d.	...	0740	1034	...	1834	1900	1900	0232	0435
Lódź Kaliska d.	0326	|	|	...	|	|	|	|	|
Skarżysko Kamienna d.	|	0820	1120	...	1913	1943	1943	0318	0518
Radom **865** d.	0606	0850	1155	...	1946	2016	2016	0420	0553
Lublin a.	0740	1019	1324	...	2116	2145	2145	0610	0727

J – 🛏 1, 2 cl., ▬ 2 cl. and [12] Lublin - Wroclaw - Jelenia Góra and v.v.
L – ▬ 2 cl. and [12] Lublin - Katowice - Klodzko and v.v.
P – 🛏 1, 2 cl., ▬ 2 cl. and [12] Lublin - Lódź - Poznań - Szczecin and v.v.
n – Will **not** run Dec. 25, Apr. 16.

446 *A higher fare is payable for travel by* **EC**, **IC**, **Ex** *and* **IR** *trains in Poland* 1

Table 866   KRAKÓW - ZAKOPANE

1, 2 class except where shown

km		83207	73201	2		13201	53701	33101		2		Ex1301	2	2	2	2	2	2	43107	2	2	2	2
		S	Pk ✕	✕		A	Gn					ℝ v							C				
	Warszawa Centralna 865 ... d.	...	...	2305	...	...	...	...	...	...	0700												
0	Kraków Główny .... d.	...	0415	...	0425	0604	0636	...	0810	0945		...	...	...	...	...	1536	1827		...	...	...	
5	Kraków Płaszów .... d.	...	0439	...	0459	0622	0644	...	0823	1003		...	...	...	1431	...	1533	1600	1835	...	...	...	2014
	Katowice .... d.	0032							1108			1100	1410					1813					
	Bielsko Biała .... d.	0148			0417					1706													
	Nowy Sącz .... d.							0635			1023					1535				1721	1931		
103	Chabówka .... d.	0440	0719	0658	0743	0840	0823	0922		1154	1303	1340	1415	1656	1714	1837	1842		2018	2011	2204	2307	
126	Nowy Targ .... d.	0508	0747		0815	0913	0849			1221		1414		1800		1921			2044		2353	
147	Zakopane .... a.	0530	0807		0838	0930	0905			1239		1442		1828		2000			2100		0019	

		2	34106	2	2		2		2		2		Ex3116	33102		35700		37200	38206		31200
			C										ℝ v			Gn		✕ Pk	S		A
	Zakopane .... d.	...	0502	0630	...	0841	...	1221	...	1520	...	1617	1730		1902	1926	2102	2118			
	Nowy Targ .... d.	...	0529	0647	...	0912	...	1251	...	1542	...	1635	1747		1920	1948	2122	2144			
	Chabówka .... d.	0553	0615	0714	...	0826	1008	1205	1322	1525	1618	1710	1734	1814		1957	2028	2210	2230		
	Nowy Sącz .... d.	0847				1100		1450			1757		2039					0123			
	Bielsko Biała .... d.			0653														0227			
	Katowice .... d.																		0040	
	Kraków Płaszów .... a.		0837	0849	0916		1235		1601		1825	1852		1950		2157	2218			
	Kraków Główny .... a.		0857	0934							1907	1957		2223	2238			0100
	Warszawa Centralna 865 ... a.										2150							0540

A – 🛏 1, 2 cl., ◼ 2 cl. and ⊡ Warszawa - Zakopane and v.v.
C – ⊡ Częstochowa - Zakopane and v.v.
P – ◼ 2 cl. and ⊡ Poznań - Zakopane and v.v.
S – 🛏 1, 2 cl., ⊡ Szczecin - Zakopane and v.v.; ◼ 2 cl. Wrocław - Zakopane and v.v.
k – Will not run Dec. 24, Apr. 15 from Poznań, Dec. 25, Apr. 16 from Zakopane.
n – Will not run Dec. 24, 30, Apr. 15 from Gdynia, Dec. 25, 31, Apr. 16 from Zakopane.
v – Daily Dec. 16 - Mar. 5, Apr. 8 - Apr. 19, also ⓒ Sept. 25 - Oct. 23, Mar. 11 - Apr. 2, Apr. 22 - May 27, and May 3.

Table 867   KRAKÓW - KRYNICA and KOŠICE

All trains 1, 2 class

km		43201	13209		381	33105	1315	Ex 311			310	Ex 3102	33104	44100	380		31202
		n	F ✕		ℝ ✕ KⓉ		ℝ✕	ℝ✕ CⓉ			ℝ✕ CⓉ	ℝ✕			p	KⓉ	F ✕
	Warszawa Centralna 865 d.	...	2140	...	0600	...	...	1700		Budapest 897 .... d.	1905						
	Katowice 860 .... d.	2315								Košice .... d.	0005				1244		
0	Kraków Główny 860 ..... d.	0046	0227	...	0905	1009	1645	1945	2105	Prešov .... d.	0051				1332		
78	Tarnów 860 .... d.	0207	0405	...	1045	1204	1757	2051	2220	Plaveč 🚉 .... a.	0206				1447		
167	Nowy Sącz 860 .... d.	0400	0601	...	1233	1409	1926	2220	2357	Plaveč 🚉 .... d.	0244				1540		
217	Muszyna .... d.	0510	0712	...	1329	1541			0054	Krynica .... d.		0304	0415	1350		1802	2115	2220
228	Krynica .... a.	0525	0728		1558					Muszyna .... d.	0304	0439	1416	1601		1832	2143	2248
231	Plaveč 🚉 .... a.			1347				0112		Nowy Sącz 860 .... d.	0359	0535	0636	1519	1653	1954	2241	2358
231	Plaveč 🚉 .... d.			1450				0210		Tarnów 860 .... d.	0533	0708	0806	1722	1845	2208	0025	0208
285	Prešov .... a.			1605				0325		Kraków Główny 860 .... a.	0647	0807	0906	1837	1953	0104	0207	0342
318	Košice .... a.			1638				0356		Katowice 860 .... a.				2010			0730	
	Budapest 899 .... a.							0842		Warszawa Centralna 865 a.	1050			2253			

C – CRACOVIA – 🛏 1, 2 cl., ◼ 2 cl., ⊡ and ✕ Kraków - Budapest and v.v.
F – 🛏 1, 2 cl., ◼ 2 cl. and ⊡ Warszawa - Krynica and v.v.
K – KARPATY – ⊡ Warszawa - Košice - Miskolc - Bucureşti and v.v.; ✕ Warszawa - Plaveč and v.v.
n – Will not run Dec. 24, Apr. 15 from Katowice.
p – Will not run Dec. 25, Apr. 16.
✕ – Supplement payable in Slovakia.

Table 868   WARSZAWA - PRZEMYŚL - LVIV

1, 2 class except where shown

km		23105	13109	107	6303 107	75 2	43	Ex 5303	13103	13205		31102	Ex 3502	43 44	107 108	33106	31108	32104	75 76 2	31206
				LⓈ	L● S			KⓉ	d	Z		ℝ✕ n	d	KⓉ L●	🛏 S					Z
0	Warszawa Wschodnia ...... d.	...	0651	0810g	...	...	1445	1550	2045		Odesa 925 .... d.	...	...	1925	1925					
5	Warszawa Centralna .... d.	...	0705	...	...	1500	1505	2105		Kyïv (Kiev) 925 .... d.	...	1906						0736	
108	Radom .... d.	...	0838			1750	2240		Chernivtsi 922 .... d.									
	Lublin .... d.	0645	1105				0154		Lviv .... d.		0702	0927	0927	1106b			1344	
276	Stalowa Wola Rozwadów .. d.	0848	1131	1305		2046		Mostiska II .... d.		0923	1143	1143	1325b			1603	
	Kraków 860 .... a.			1045	1345	1745		Medyka 🚉 .... d.		0907	1127	1127	1309b			1547	
	Rzeszów 860 .... a.			1309	1608	1948	0335		Przemyśl .... d.		0929	1149	1149	1331b			1609	
	Krosno .... a.						0622		Przemyśl 860 .... d.	0523	0705	1130	1448	1453	1446	1554		
	Sanok .... a.						0738		Jarosław 860 .... d.	0553	0732	1201	1459	1521	1515	1624		
	Zagórz .... a.						0750		Zagórz .... d.									2000
360	Jarosław 860 .... d.	1014	1304	1430	1351	1649	2023	2247		Sanok .... d.									2012
395	Przemyśl 860 .... a.	1043	1334	1506	1421	1720	2050	2243		Krosno .... d.									2133
395	Przemyśl .... d.	1456b	1803	1811	1931		Rzeszów 860 .... d.	0809	1246	1600					2359
408	Medyka 🚉 .... d.	1545b	1739	1739	1840	2010		Kraków 860 .... d.	1015	1502	1802					
415	Mostiska II .... d.	1812b	2006	2006	2110	2237		Stalowa Wola Rozwadów.. d.	0733		1640	1649	1807			0150
513	Lviv .... a.	1953b	2147	2147	2251	0018		Lublin .... a.		1831	1945					
	Chernivtsi 922 .... a.					0440		Radom .... d.	1034		1955					0455
	Kyïv (Kiev) 925 .... a.	...	...	1116	1116		1226		Warszawa Centralna .. a.	1205	1250	2145					0657
	Odesa 925 .... a.							Warszawa Wschodnia a.	1219	1304	2158g	2209				0724

– 🛏 2 cl. and Ⓨ Wrocław - Kraków - Przemyśl - Kyïv and v.v.
– 🛏 2 cl. and ✕ Kraków - Przemyśl - Odesa and v.v.; conveys on alternate days only: 🛏 2 cl. and Ⓨ Warszawa - Odesa and v.v.
– 🛏 2 cl. Kraków - Przemyśl - Odesa and v.v.
Z – 🛏 1, 2 cl., ◼ 2 cl. and ⊡ Warszawa - Zagórz and v.v.
b – Train 63 from Przemyśl, 64 from Lviv.
d – To/from Gdynia (Table 855).
g – Warszawa Gdańska.
n – Will not run Dec. 25, Apr. 16.
● – Warszawa - Przemyśl and v.v. alternate days only.

Table 869   WARSZAWA - LUBLIN - CHELM and ZAMOŚĆ

All trains 1, 2 class

km		52201	12101	Ex 12103	7201	12105	12107	12109	Ex 7203	12111	12201		Ex 2700	21100	21102	21104	Ex 2702	21106	21108	21110	25200	21200
		G	C	✕p	Z	C		P	ℝ✕		Cn		ℝ P	C			ℝ✕ Z		C	ℝ●np	G	Cn
0	Warszawa Centralna d.	...	0647	0847	1047	1247	1447	1647	1847	2047	2317		Zamość .... d.	...	0535	0726	...	...	...	1517	...	...	2321
5	Warszawa Wschodnia d.	0245	0657	0857	1102	1257	1457	1657	1857	2057	2327		Chelm .... d.	0530	0700	0906	1054	1247	1418	1644	1904	2037	0058
175	Lublin .... d.	0508	0911	1111	1307	1511	1711	1911	2102	2311	0147		Lublin .... a.	0635	0805	1023	1225	1402	1536	1827	2019	2150	0220
175	Lublin .... d.		0915	1125	1335	1527	1715	1930	2121	2320	0152		Lublin .... d.	0700	0830	1030	1230	1500	1630	1830	2030	2250	0230
249	Chelm .... a.		1052	1244	1454	1643	1830	2049	2240	0053	0310		Warszawa Wschodnia a.	0905	1047	1247	1447	1705	1847	2047	2247	0111	0450
293	Zamość .... a.	1225			2010					0442			Warszawa Centralna a.	0917	1057	1257	1457	1722	1857	2102	2300	0127	0502

⊡ Warszawa - Chelm and v.v.; ⊡ Warszawa - Zamość and v.v.
◼ 2 cl. and ⊡ Gdynia - Warszawa - Lublin and v.v.
P – ⊡ Poznań - Warszawa - Lublin and v.v.
Z – ⊡ Zielona Góra - Poznań - Warszawa - Lublin and v.v.
n – Will not run Dec. 24, Apr. 16.
p – Will not run Dec. 26, Apr. 17.

ℝ Reservation obligatory   🚉 – Frontier station   ⊡ – Through carriage (1 and 2 class)

CZECH REPUBLIC

SEE MAP PAGE 439

Operator: České Dráhy (ČD).

Services: Trains convey first and second classes of accommodation, shown as '1' and '2' or 🚋 in the tables. Sleeping cars (🛏) and couchette cars (⊨) are of the normal European types, see page 10 for more details.

Timings: Valid **May 29, 1994** to **May 27, 1995.** A Sunday service operates on public holidays – for dates of public holidays see page 2. Certain services, including some long-distance expresses, are liable to withdrawal over the Christmas and New Year period. Intending passengers should check locally before travelling during this period.

Reservations: It is possible to reserve seats on most Express trains.
Supplements: All **EC/IC** and certain International/Express trains carry supplements.

Table 870 — PRAHA - PLZEŇ - CHEB and NÜRNBERG

1, 2 class except where shown. ČD, DB

km		420	1860 2	640	258	EC166	1862 2	650		652	7044 2	EC50	654	1864	IC168			242	674		7046 2	352	356
0	Praha Hlavni .... d.	0406	0540	0559	0623	0723	0750	0855	...	1122	...	1308	1432	1528	1623	...	...	1712	1916	...	...	2050	2352
4	Praha Smichov .... d.	0420	0550	0610		0801	0905		...	1133	...		1443	1539		...	...	1723	1927	...	...		
43	Beroun .... d.	0503	0624	0644		0836	0938		...	1207	...		1518	1613		...	...	1755	2001	...	...	2132	0033
114	Plzeň .... a.	0611	0733	0743	0857	0944	1041		...	1304	...	1443	1625	1719	1757	...	...	1851	2059	...	...	2231	0133
114	Plzeň .... d.	0620			0913		1051		...	1314	...	1446	1637		1811	...	...	1900	2114	...	...	2241	0148
190	Mariánské Lázně 874 .... d.	0735			1008		1203		...	1426	1423	1549	1748			...	...	2014	2225	...	2220	2353	0300
	Karlovy Vary 874 .... d.				1008				...		1423					...	...			...	2220		
220	Cheb △ .... a.	0801			1058		1235		...	1500	1536	1617	1817		w	...	...	2043	2254	...	2329	0020	0331
263	Schwandorf .... d.				1151				...							...	...			...			
371	Nürnberg 780 .... d.				1324p				...			1819			2203	...	...			...		0250	0547
443	München 780 .... a.				1351				...							...	...			...		0607	

		1861 2	357	1863 2	651	353	7003 2	441	643	IC169		243		EC51	653	1691		655	EC167		421	7315	7051
	München 780 .... d.	...	...	...	2312	...	...	...	...	...		...		...	...	...		1408	...		...	...	...
	Nürnberg 780 .... d.	...	0025	...	0240	...	...	0755	...	...		1135		...	...	...			...		...	...	...
	Schwandorf △ .... d.	...	...	...	...	...	...	0904	...	...		...		...	...	...		1615	...		...	...	...
	Cheb .... d.	...	0250	...	0432	0517	0611	0607	w	...		1210		1336	1454	1505		1649	w		1933	2148	2301
	Karlovy Vary 874 .... a.	...	...	...	...	...	0709	...	...	...		...		...	...	1553		...	...		...	...	2400
	Mariánské Lázně .... d.	...	0322	...	0503	0547		0638		...		1240		1402	1524			1721	...		1958	...	...
	Plzeň .... a.	...	0425	...	0609	0643		0755		1136		1355		1503	1633			1831	1848		2109	0006	...
	Plzeň .... d.	0315	0431	0545	0627	0659		0810	0958	1149		1410		1506	1640			1841	1903		2118		...
	Beroun .... d.	0427	0526	0646	0731	0755		0921	1102			1521			1742			1941			2219		...
	Praha Smichov .... a.	0501	0600	0720	0805	0828		0955	1136	1315		1555		1633	1816			2015	2029		2253		...
	Praha Hlavni .... a.	0511	0611	0731	0816	0839		1006	1147	1326		1606		1645	1827			2026	2039		2304		...

◆ – **NOTES** (LISTED BY TRAIN NUMBERS)
EC50/1 – KARLSTEIN – 🚋 Praha - Dortmund and v.v.; ✗ Praha - Köln and Dortmund - Praha.
EC166/7 – ALBERT EINSTEIN – 🚋 and ✗ Praha - Bern and Interlaken Ost - Praha.
242/3 – BEČVA – 🚋 Žilina - Praha - Cheb and v.v.; ✗ Praha - Cheb and v.v.
258 – 🚋 Praha - Karlovy Vary - Cheb - Marktredwitz.
352/3 – 🛏 1, 2 cl., ⊨ 2 cl. and 🚋 Praha - Nürnberg (D1981/0) - München and v.v.; For Praha - Köln and Dortmund cars see Table 33.
356/7 – 🛏 1, 2 cl., ⊨ 2 cl. and 🚋 Praha - Nürnberg - Stuttgart and v.v.
420/1 – EXCELSIOR – 🛏 1, 2 cl., ⊨ 2 cl. and 🚋 Košice - Praha - Cheb and v.v.

441 – 🚋 and ✗ Cheb - Praha - Bohumín - Žilina.
640 – 🚋 Bohumín - Praha - Plzeň.
643 – 🚋 Plzeň - Praha - Český Těšín.
674 – 🚋 and ✗ Břeclav - Praha - Cheb.
p – Change at Marktredwitz (Note ✗ applies: Marktredwitz - Nürnberg).
w – Via Furth im Wald (Table 781).
✗ – Supplement payable.
△ – 🏛 is at Cheb/Schirnding.

Table 872 — PLZEŇ - ČESKÉ BUDĚJOVICE - BRNO

1, 2 class except where shown. ČD

km		1661 2	663 2		665 2	1761 2		761 2			667 2			763 2	661 2		765 K	1796 2		767 2	⑥p
0	Plzeň .... d.	...	...	0330	0621	0621		0810		...	1110		1403			...	1545		...	1902	
76	Strakonice .... d.	...	...	0530	0722	0722		0912		...	1302		1510			...	1647		...	2010	
	Tábor .... d.	...	...	0911						...						...			...		
136	České Budějovice .... a.	...	...	0700		0817		1000		...	1437		1600			...	1733		...	2100	
136	České Budějovice .... d.	...	0517	0545	0740	0841	0933		1134	...	1403		1459	1648	1653		1812	1916	...	2103	2250
	České Velenice 875 ...... d.	...	0659	0846		0921	1044		1245	...			1606		1758		1901	2024	...	2156	2343
175	Veseli nad Lužnici 875 .... d.	...	0549						1436	...			1730						...		
268	Jihlava .... d.	0535	0738			1112			1504	1635						...		1922	...		
309	Třebič .... d.	0618	0820			1154			1609	1722						H			...		
372	Brno .... a.	0734	0929			1300			1748	1833						2122			...		

		760 2		666 2	762 2		1760 2		660 2		1762 2	764 2		1560 2			662 2	766 2	664 2	
	Brno .... d.	...	...	0221	K		...	...	0650		...	0928		1109	⑤⑦n		1401		1535	...
	Třebič .... d.	...	...		J		...	...	0802		...	1101		1248			1511		1648	1947
	Jihlava .... d.	...	...	0435			...	...	0903		...	1208		1350			1603		1740	2046
	Veseli nad Lužnici 875 ... d.	...	...	0621			...	...	1046		...	1416		1610			1751			
	České Velenice 875 ...... d.	0406	0541				0751	0936		1129	1256		1450		1646			1958	2133	
	České Budějovice .... a.	0509	0641	0651			0858	1021		1117	1230	1339	1525	1556	1720	1747	1820	2049	2225	
	České Budějovice .... d.	0536				0715			1030				1345		1647		1852		2117	
	Tábor .... d.	...	...														1934			
	Strakonice .... d.	0627		0805			1145					1433		1734			1941	2116	2227	
	Plzeň .... a.	0733		0906			1327					1536		1834			2044	2222		

H – Via Havlíčkův Brod (depart 1956).
J – Via Havlíčkův Brod (depart 0405).
K – 🚋 České Budějovice - Brno and v.v.; 2 cl. and 🚋 České Budějovice - Brno - Bohumín - Žilina - Košice and v.v.

n – Will not run July 3, 4, 5.
p – Will not run July 6.
q – Will not run July 4.

Table 873 — KARLOVY VARY - MARIÁNSKÉ LÁZNĚ

2 class only. ČD

km		⑥n																
0	Karlovy Vary .... d.	0404	0531	0838	1000	1256	1412	1535	1741	1928		Mariánské Lázně 870 ..... d.	...	0440	0612	0932	1241	1344	1508	1722	2237
53	Mariánské Lázně 870 ...... a.	0543	0720	1016	1133	1432	1554	1707	1927	2056		Karlovy Vary .... a.	...	0631	0741	1116	1407	1530	1645	1900	0015

n – Will not run July 5, Oct. 28, Dec. 24, 25, Apr. 16, 30, May 7.

Table 874 PRAHA - CHOMUTOV - KARLOVY VARY - CHEB

1, 2 class except where shown. ČD

km		7050 ✕ ◆	2	1793 n	770 2✕ ◆	258 M	1710 2	1690		672 ◆	2	366 2 ◆	2	240 ◆	1894 2	2	1712 2	1774 2	2	1791 ◆	1694 p	1896 2 p	1714 2 p	1898 2 np
	Praha Hlavni **680** d.	...	...	...	0400	0623	...	...	...	...	...	...	...	...	...	...	...	...	...	...	...	1932	...	2345
0	**Praha** Holešovice **680** d.	...	...	...	0430	|	...	...	...	0943	...	...	...	1204	...	...	...	...	...	...	...	|	...	|
0	**Praha** Masarykovo d.	...	...	...	|	|	0629	...	...	|	...	...	*0938*	|	1420	...	1546	1535	...	...	...	|	1918	|
	Liberec d.	...	...	...	|	|	|	0534	...	|	...	...	|	|	|	...	|	|	...	1514	1729	|	|	|
	Děčín **680** d.	...	...	0500	|	|	|	0752	...	|	...	...	|	|	|	...	|	|	...	1748	1953	|	|	|
106	Ústí nad Labem Hlavni **680** d.	...	0429	0522	0610**z**	|	|	0816	...	1121**z**	...	...	|	1346**z**	|	...	|	1717**z**	...	1817	2021	|	|	|
123	Teplice d.	...	0459	0545	0631	|	|	0837	...	1141	...	...	|	1405	|	...	|	1736	...	1841	2047	|	|	|
	Louny d.	...	|	|	|	|	0816	|	...	|	...	...	|	|	|	...	1733	|	...	|	|	|	2114	|
152	**Most** d.	...	0537	0613	0702	|	0846	0909	...	1206	...	...	|	1434	|	...	1802	1807	...	1917	2116	|	2143	|
	Kladno d.	...	|	|	|	0712	|	|	...	|	...	...	*1037*	|	1501	...	...	|	...	|	|	2020	|	0031
177	**Chomutov** a.	...	0604	0642	0725	|	0916	0935	...	1231	...	...	*1314*	1459	1651	...	...	1835	...	1944	2142	2214	2212	0217
177	**Chomutov** d.	...	0618	0653	0737	*0817*	...	0948	...	1243	...	...	1348	1516	1702	...	...	*1841*	1959	1956**v**	...	...	2218	...
	Plzeň a.	...	|	0905	|	|	...	|	...	|	...	...	|	|	|	...	...	|	|	2215**v**	...	...	|	...
236	**Karlovy Vary** a.	...	0733	▬	0836	0958	...	1050	...	1340	...	...	1504	1620	1807	...	...	*1954*	2112	...	...	...	2320	...
236	**Karlovy Vary** d.	0447	0745	2	0846	1008	...	1100	...	...	1423	1430	1514	1631	...	1813	...	*2011*	2122	...	...	...	2322	...
259	Sokolov d.	0516	0817	...	0912	1032	...	1124	...	...	1502	1451	1543	1659	...	1841	...	*2041*	2152	...	...	...	2347	...
	Bad Brambach 🏛 d.	|	|	0824	|	|	...	|	...	...	|	1555	|	|	...	|	...	|	|	...	...	...	...	...
	Plauen **780** a.	|	|	|	|	|	...	|	...	...	|	1659	|	|	...	|	...	|	|	...	...	...	...	...
288	**Cheb** a.	0557	0856	0908	0939	1058	...	1151	...	...	1536	...	1623	1729	...	1917	...	*2119*	2230	...	...	...	...	...

	1711 2 n	1695 n	1891 2	2	1790 ◆	241 ◆		1713 2 M	2	367 2 ◆	673 ◆	1893 2	2	1691	2	2	1895	1792 2 p	771 2✕ ◆	2 p	2	2 np	2	7051 ◆
Cheb d.	...	...	0400	0604	...	0847	...	1100	1240	...	...	...	1350	1505	1550	1633	...	...	1735	...	1834	...	2055	2301
Plauen **780** d.	...	...	|	|	...	|	...	|	|	1118	...	...	|	|	|	|	...	...	|	...	|	...	|	|
Bad Brambach 🏛 d.	...	...	|	|	...	|	...	|	|	1215	...	...	|	|	1647	|	...	...	|	...	|	...	|	|
Sokolov d.	...	...	0429	0644	...	0918	...	1136	1317	1323	...	...	1432	1532	▬	1713	...	...	1805	...	1918	...	2135	2335
Karlovy Vary a.	...	...	0451	0709	...	0941	...	1203	1351	1343	...	...	1459	1553	...	1740	...	...	1827	...	1945	...	2202	2400
Karlovy Vary d.	...	...	0501	0720	...	0952	...	1215	...	▬	1410	...	1509	1603	...	...	1744	...	1837	...	2005	...	2213	*0005*
Plzeň d.	...	...	|	|	0619**r**	|	...	|	...	...	|	...	|	|	...	...	|	1646	|	...	|	...	|	|
Chomutov a.	...	...	0600	0834	0908**r**	1055	...	1324	...	...	1509	...	1621	1704	**1717**	...	1847	1906	1933	...	2120	...	2323	*0115*
Chomutov d.	0531	0540	0612	...	0921	1105	...	1330	...	...	1519	1530	...	1717	2	...	1855	1917	1942	2014	...	2222	...	...
Kladno d.	|	|	0810	...	|	|	...	|	...	...	|	1734	...	|	...	...	2050	|	|	2237	...	|	...	...
Most d.	0600	0609	|	...	0951	1134	...	1354	...	**1697**	1546	|	...	1745	1841	...	|	1946	2013	|	...	2257	...	...
Louny d.	0632	|	|	...	|	|	...	1426	...	**2p**	|	|	...	|	1914	...	|	|	|	|	...	|	...	...
Teplice d.	|	0638	|	...	1023	1210	...	|	...	...	1612	|	...	1817	|	...	|	2019	2043	|	...	2336	...	...
Ústí nad Labem Hlavni **680** d.	|	0702	|	...	1050	1230**z**	...	|	...	1530	1631**z**	|	...	1843	|	...	|	2041	2102**z**	|	...	2400	...	...
Děčín **680** d.	|	0734	|	...	1121	|	...	|	...	1603	|	|	...	1910	|	...	|	2118	|	|	...	...	...	...
Liberec a.	|	0953	|	...	1345	|	...	|	...	1813	|	|	...	2124	|	...	|	...	|	|	...	...	...	...
Praha Masarykovo a.	0826	...	0845	...	...	|	...	1613	...	...	|	1810	...	...	2058	...	|	...	|	2319	...	...	...	...
Praha Holešovice **680** a.	...	...	...	...	...	1400	...	...	...	...	1800	...	...	...	...	...	|	...	2232	...	...	...	...	...
Praha Hlavni **680** a.	...	...	...	...	...	...	...	...	...	...	...	...	...	...	...	...	2135	...	2254	...	...	...	...	...

◆ – **NOTES** (LISTED BY TRAIN NUMBERS)

240/1 – VSACAN – [12] Žilina - Praha - Cheb and v.v.
366/7 – KARLEX – [2] Karlovy Vary - Reichenbach (trains **2602/3**) - Berlin.
672 – BRNĚNSKÝ DRAK – [12] and ✕ Břeclav - Brno - Praha - Karlovy Vary.
673 – BRNĚNSKÝ DRAK – [12] and ✕ Karlovy Vary - Praha - Brno.
770/1 – 🛏 1, 2 cl. and [2] Bratislava (trains **378/9**) - Praha Holešovice - Cheb and v.v.;
🛏 1, 2 cl., ▬ 2 cl., [2] and ✕ Košice (trains **420/1**) - Praha - Cheb and v.v.
1790/1 – [12] Plzeň - Děčín - Zittau - Liberec and v.v.
7050 – [12] and ✕ Karlovy Vary - Cheb (train **441**) - Plzeň - Praha - Žilina.
7051 – [12] Břeclav - Praha - Plzeň (train **674**) - Cheb - Karlovy Vary.
M – [12] Praha - Marktredwitz and Marktredwitz (train **D259**) - Cheb - Karlovy Vary.
n – Will **not** run Dec. 25, Jan. 1.
p – Will **not** run Dec. 24, 31.
r – Not ⑦ Nov. 6 - Apr. 9, Dec. 24.
v – Not ⑥ Nov. 5 - Apr. 8, Dec. 25.
z – Ústí nad Labem **Západ**.

Table 875 PRAHA - ČESKÉ BUDĚJOVICE - LINZ and GMÜND

1, 2 class except where shown. ČD

km		273 ⚒	273 931 ⚒	18003 2t	28201 2	1761 2	271 ◆	271 1277	8205 2	18207 2	1531 ⑥n	18005 2	28205 2	8233 2	8207 2	631	1273	2	1273 1975	1796 2	633	633 1973	635	1275 ◆
0	**Praha** Hlavni d.	0011	0011	...	...	...	0623	0623	0749	...	0838	...	...	*0900*	1100	1352	1503	...	1503	...	1752	1752	1929	2011
49	Benešov d.	0101	0101	...	...	...	0716	0716	0852	...	0932	...	...	1033	1220	1445	1556	...	1556	...	1845	1845	2022	|
103	Tábor d.	0146	0146	...	...	...	0803	0803	0956	...	1017	...	...	1150	1353	1536	1640	...	1640	...	1932	1932	2109	2147
130	Veseli nad Lužnicí a.	0210	0210	...	...	...	0827	0827	1026	...	1040	...	...	1220	1428	1600	1704	...	1704	...	1956	1956	2138	2209
130	Veseli nad Lužnicí d.	0227	0218	...	...	...	0842	0834	1028	1056	1043	...	...	*1239*	1437	1601	1712	...	1733	...	2003	2010	2140	2211
169	**České Budějovice** a.	|	0247	...	...	...	|	0905	1111	|	1115	...	...	*1328*	1525	1635	1742	...	|	...	2033	|	2210	2241
169	**České Budějovice** d.	|	...	0545	0523	0841	|	0920	▬	|	...	1134	1140	...	...	...	1759	...	|	1812	...	|	...	2255
225	Horní Dvořiště 🏛 d.	|	...	|	0707	|	|	1035	2	|	...	|	1332	...	...	...	1904	...	|	|	...	|	...	0002
232	Summerau 🏛 a.	|	...	|	0716	|	|	1044	...	|	...	|	1341	...	...	...	1913	...	|	|	...	|	...	0011
232	Summerau d.	|	...	|	*0720*	|	|	1057**b**	1131	|	...	|	*1351*	...	...	...	1927**b**	1948	|	|	...	|	...	0026
294	**Linz** Hbf. a.	|	...	|	*0835*	|	|	1151**b**	1250	|	...	|	*1508*	...	...	...	2022**b**	2103	|	|	...	|	...	0119
151	Třeboň d.	0244	...	|	...	|	0900	...	...	1122	...	|	...	...	...	...	...	...	1750	|	...	2030	...	...
185	České Velenice a.	0311	...	0659	...	0921	0928	...	...	1207	...	1245	...	...	...	...	...	...	1818	1901	...	2058	...	...
185	České Velenice d.	0341	...	*0728*	...	...	0942	...	...	...	...	*1308*	...	...	...	...	...	...	1833	...	...	2103	...	...
187	**Gmünd N.Ö.** 🏛 a.	0345	...	*0733*	...	...	0946	...	...	...	...	*1313*	...	...	...	...	...	...	1837	...	...	2107	...	...
354	*Wien Franz-Josefs Bf* **840** a.	0606	...	...	...	...	*1207*	...	...	...	...	...	...	...	...	...	...	...	...	...	...	...	...	...

	630	1274 ◆	632	1972 632	18004 2	1760 2	2	1272	1762 2	634	1974 634	18208 2	18008 2	2	1276	661	270 ◆	1530 ⑦p	18010 2	636	272 Ⓑ	930 272 Ⓑ	18012 2	28214 2	8212
Wien FJ Bf **840** d.	...	...	...	...	...	...	...	...	...	...	...	...	...	...	...	...	*1407*	...	...	...	1724	...	...	...	...
Gmünd N.Ö. 🏛 d.	...	...	...	0700	*0740*	...	...	...	...	...	1245	*1410*	...	...	...	...	1632	...	...	...	1951	...	...	...	...
České Velenice a.	...	...	...	0704	*0745*	...	...	...	...	...	1249	*1415*	...	...	...	...	1636	...	...	...	1955	...	...	...	...
České Velenice d.	...	...	...	0709	0751	0936	...	...	1256	...	1254	1448	1450	...	...	...	1643	...	1646	...	2003	...	1958	...	...
Třeboň d.	...	...	...	0737	|	|	...	...	|	...	1323	|	|	...	...	...	1711	...	|	...	2030	...	|	...	...
Linz Hbf. d.	...	0316	...	|	|	|	0701**d**	0738**c**	|	...	|	|	|	1157	1336**b**	...	|	...	|	...	|	...	|	*1757*	...
Summerau a.	...	0408	...	|	|	|	0824	0833**c**	|	...	|	|	|	1313	1430**b**	...	|	...	|	...	|	...	|	*1919*	...
Summerau 🏛 d.	...	0435	...	|	|	|	*0856*	0845**c**	|	...	|	|	|	*1408*	1444**b**	...	|	...	|	...	|	...	|	1925	...
Horní Dvořiště 🏛 d.	...	0500	...	|	|	|	*0905*	0908	|	...	|	|	|	*1417*	1502	...	|	...	|	...	|	...	|	1942	...
České Budějovice a.	...	0601	...	|	0858	1021	...	1013	1339	...	|	|	1556	...	1601	...	|	...	1747	...	|	...	2049	2104	...
České Budějovice d.	0528	0616	0733	|	...	...	...	...	...	1318	|	|	...	...	1617	1648	|	1802	...	1855	|	2014	...	...	2125
Veseli nad Lužnicí a.	0558	0646	0801	0753	...	...	...	...	...	1346	1339	1558	...	...	1645	1722	1727	1835	...	1925	2046	2049	...	...	2208
Veseli nad Lužnicí d.	0600	0647	0811	0811	...	...	...	...	...	1359	1359	...	...	...	1647	...	1739	1841	...	1930	2102	2102	...	...	2226
Tábor d.	0626	0711	0839	0839	...	...	...	...	...	1426	1426	...	...	...	1717	...	1801	1905	...	2002	2128	2128	...	...	2300
Benešov d.	0710	|	0923	0923	...	...	...	...	...	1514	1514	...	...	...	|	...	1844	1954	...	2053	2212	2212	...	...	...
Praha Hlavni a.	0802	0850	1014	1014	...	...	...	...	...	1606	1606	...	...	...	1850	...	1935	2048	...	2145	2304	2304	...	...	...

◆ – **NOTES** (LISTED BY TRAIN NUMBERS)

270/1 – SMETANA – [12] and ✕ (Wien -) Gmünd N.Ö. - Praha and v.v.
1274 – Runs ⑥ Dec. 17 - Jan. 7 and Apr. 8 - May 27 from Venezia:
🛏 1, 2 cl., ▬ 2 cl. and [12] Venezia Santa Lucia - Praha.
1275 – Runs ⑤ Dec. 16 - Jan. 6 and Apr. 7 - May 26 from Praha:
🛏 1, 2 cl., ▬ 2 cl. and [12] Praha - Venezia Santa Lucia.

b – June 24 - Sept. 11 **only**.
c – June 25 - Sept. 12 **only**.
d – On ⑦ depart 0711.
n – Runs also July 1, 5, Oct. 28, Dec. 23; will **not** run Oct. 29, Dec. 24.
p – Runs also July 1; will **not** run July 5, Oct. 28, Dec. 24, 25, Apr. 16, 30, May 7.
t – Will **not** run Dec. 25, Jan. 1.

450 ◆ – See footnote

Table 876 — LIBEREC - PRAHA and PARDUBICE

1, 2 class except where shown. ČD

km		1941 2※	1601 2※	1943	681	1603 2⑧	1945	683 2⑤	1605 2	1947 2	1689 2
0	Liberec .... d.			0539	0553	1304	1304	1508	1723	1723	2130
38	Turnov .... d.	0415	0404	0636	0635	1350	1353	1557	1812	1814	2218
68	Mladá Boleslav.. d.	0502		0712			1434		1854		
140	Praha Hlavní .... a.	0621		0824		1548			2010		
	Jičín.................. d.		0524		1442			1903			
139	Hradec Králové. a.		0626		0842	1543		1804	2002		0006
139	Hradec Králové. d.		0640		0847	1605		1809	2014		0014
161	Pardubice 880 a.		0715		0904	1630		1826	2039		0031
312	Brno 880 ...... a.				1141b			2110			

		1688 2Z	1940 2	1600 2	1942 2	682 2⑧	1602 2⑤	1944 2⑧	1604 2	1682 2	1946 2	680
	Brno 880 .... d.				0520				1406		1609	
	Pardubice 880 ...... d.	0501		0635		0806	1211		1532	1700		1855
	Hradec Králové ... a.	0519		0653		0823	1234		1600	1717		1913
	Hradec Králové ... d.	0529		0656		0829	1300		1615	1722		1920
	Jičín.................. d.			0805			1408		1720			
	Praha Hlavní ...... d.		0002		0651			1315			1740	
	Mladá Boleslav ... d.		0125		0810			1434			1855	
	Turnov................ a.	0732	0241	0857	0905	1054	1502	1516	1807	1930	1944	2129
	Liberec.............. a.	0812		0940	1003	1143	1550	1604	1906	2012	2030	2211

b – Subject to alteration on Ⓐ. (Engineering work: Brno - 8 kms North thereof). Z – 🚻 Pardubice - Liberec - Zittau.

Table 877 — LIBEREC - ZITTAU - DĚČÍN

2 class only, except where shown. ČD

km				Z								
0	Liberec .... d.	0400	0530	0816	1014	1215	1514	1609	1720	1819	2234
15	Zittau 🚻 .... a.	0428	0627	0843	1053	1251	1551	1648	1802	1856	2314
45	Varnsdorf 🚻 ..... a.		0647		1113		1611	1709	1823		2334
106	Děčín 874 .... a.						1734		2110		

					J							
	Děčín 874 .... d.				1121						1849
	Varnsdorf .... d.		0547		0906	1250		1440	1719		2116
	Zittau 🚻 .... d.	0434	0609	0900	0928	1312	1422	1502	1741	1906	2138
	Liberec.............. a.	0520	0700	0929	1009	1345	1501	1544	1817	1947	2227

J – 🚻 Liberec - Zittau - Děčín - Chomutov - Plzeň and v.v. Z – 🚻 Pardubice - Liberec - Zittau.

Table 878 — BŘECLAV - WIEN

1, 2 class except where shown. ČD, ÖBB

km		D203 C	D377 N	2317 2		EC105 ※ S	EC173 ※ V	2325 2	EC9 ※
	Brno 880 .... d.		0639				1620		2020
0	Břeclav 🚻 .... d.	0502	0730	1208		1605	1707	1908	2105
19	Hohenau 🚻 .... d.	0608	0808	1226		1620	1721	1926	2120
84	Wien Nord .... a.			1328				2028	
91	Wien Südbahnhof .. a.	0652	0852			1704	1804		2203

		EC8 ※ A	2304 2	EC104 ※ S		EC172 ※ V	2314 2	2318 2	D376 N	D202 C
	Wien Südbahnhof .. d.	0739		0939		1139			2025	2150
	Wien Nord .... d.		0839				1439	1639		
	Hohenau 🚻 .... a.	0824	0944	1026		1226	1540	1740	2125	2304
	Břeclav 🚻 .... a.	0837	1000	1039		1239	1557	1757	2139	2319
	Brno 880 .... a.	0922				1325			2232	

A – ANTONÍN DVOŘÁK – 🚻 and ※ Wien - Praha and v.v.
C – CHOPIN – 🛏 1, 2 cl., ⊷ 2 cl. and 🚻 Wien - Warszawa and v.v.; ⊷ 2 cl. and 🚻 Wien - Warszawa - Berlin and v.v.
       ⊷ Wien - Kraków and v.v.; 🛏 1, 2 cl. Wien - Warszawa - Brest - Moskva and v.v.
N – SANSSOUCI – 🛏 1, 2 cl., ⊷ 2 cl. and 🚻 Wien - Praha - Berlin and v.v.
S – SOBIESKI – 🚻 and ※ Wien - Warszawa and v.v.
V – VINDOBONA – 🚻 and ※ Wien - Praha - Děčín - Dresden - Berlin and v.v.

Table 880 — PRAHA - BRNO - BRATISLAVA

1, 2 class except where shown. ČD, ŽSR

km		377 ◆ B	231 ☐	373 ◆	1011 ※☐	681 L	277 ◆		2 EC173 ※	233 ☐ B	1571 e	671 ◆	EC175 ※	471 ☐	EC9 ※ S	275 ◆		683 L	661 K	673 ◆	375 ☐		379 ☐
	Praha Holešovice.... d.	0324		0558	0739			1311			1353	1511		1441	1711			1810			0028	
0	Praha Hlavní .... d.					0912					1353	1433		1441	1736				2222		0028	
62	Kolín.................. d.	0408		0642	0824	1001	1355			1523	1555	1531		1824				1855	2313			
136	Havlíčkův Brod ..... d.	0514		0749	0930	1121	1458			1559	1634	1658		1859	1931			1956	2003	0028	0218	
	Pardubice 884 ...... d.					0911					1555							1837				
	Česká Třebová 884 . d.					1011					1650							1934				
	Svitavy .... d.					1030					1713							1954				
257	Brno .... a.	0634		0917	1050	1141b	1253		1617	1727	1806	1817	1823	2017	2051			2110	2122	2136	0156		0340
257	Brno .... d.	0639		0934	1055		1308	1425	1620		1810	1820	1840	2020	2055				2255	0211		0348
316	Břeclav .... a.	0717		1014	1135		1347	1535	1657		1847	1857	1919	2057	2131				2400	0250		0427
316	Břeclav △ .... a.	0726	0726	1019	1137		1349	1552	1707	1726		1900	1921	2055	2133					0316		0431
	Wien Südbf 878 .... a.	0852							1804						2203							
398	Bratislava Hlavní ... a.		0842	1130	1248		1459	1727		1839				2000	2034	2233				0427		0539
	Budapest Nyugati 889 .... a.				1628											2242					0858	
	Budapest Keleti 889 ...... a.			1442																0747		

		670	682 L	672 ◆	274 ◆ S	EC8 ※	232 ☐ B	EC174 ※		EC172 ※	470 ☐	674 ◆	680 L	276 ◆ B	230 ☐	1010 ※☐	372 ◆		2	376 ☐		378 ☐		666 K	374 ☐
	Budapest Keleti 889 ..... d.					0655									1320	1500									2120
	Budapest Nyugati 889 ... d.																			1825					
	Bratislava Hlavní .... d.			0355	0548		0805	0943		1153			1451	1649	1718	1818	1800			2145					0043
	Wien Südbf 878 .... d.					0739				1139						2025									
	Břeclav △ .... a.			0530	0640	0805	1015	1047		1239	1309		1600	1600	1827	1929	1944	2139		2256					0153
	Břeclav .... a.			0537	0649	0845		1047		1247	1312	1440		1604	1831	1931	1950	2154		2258					0206
	Brno .... a.	0500		0615	0726	0922		1125		1325	1352	1517		1643	1907	2010	2100	2232		2337				0221	0245
	Brno .... d.	0500		0620	0730	0925		1128		1328	1406	1521	1609	1654	1914	2017		2237		2341					0252
	Svitavy .... d.		0644								1536		1726												
	Česká Třebová 884 .... d.		0712								1602		1756												
	Pardubice 884 .... d.		0800								1653		1845												
	Havlíčkův Brod .... d.	0634		0743	0853	1045		1249		1449		1649		1834	2038	2144				0001		0105		0351	0427
	Kolín.................... d.	0740			0956			1350		1550	1715	1750		1945	2140	2249								0533	
	Praha Hlavní .... a.	0832			1050			1437		1637		1812	1851	2040											0629
	Praha Holešovice...... a.			0933		1232									2228	2337		0148		0253					

◆ – NOTES (LISTED BY TRAIN NUMBERS)

EC8/9 – ANTONÍN DVOŘÁK – 🚻 and ※ Wien - Praha and v.v.
EC172/3 – VINDOBONA – 🚻 and ※ Wien - Praha - Děčín - Dresden - Berlin and v.v.
EC174/5 – HUNGARIA – 🚻 and ※ Budapest - Berlin - Nauen (- Hamburg) and v.v.
*76/7 – DEVÍN – 🚻 Štúrovo - Nové Zámky - Bratislava - Praha and v.v.
72/3 – BALT ORIENT EXPRESS – 🛏 1, 2 cl., ⊷ 2 cl. and 🚻 București - Budapest - Praha - Dresden - Berlin and v.v.; ⊷ Lökösháza - Budapest - Berlin and v.v.; 🚻 Štúrovo - Praha and v.v.
74/5 – PANNONIA – 🛏 1, 2 cl., ⊷ 2 cl. and 🚻 București - Budapest - Praha and v.v.; 🛏 1, 2 cl., ⊷ 2 cl. and 🚻 Budapest - Praha and v.v.
76/7 – SANSSOUCI – 🛏 1, 2 cl., ⊷ 2 cl. and 🚻 Wien - Praha - Berlin and v.v.
*78/9 – METROPOL – 🚻 Budapest - Berlin and v.v.; 🛏 1, 2 cl. Bratislava - Berlin and v.v.; 🛏 1, 2 cl. and 🚻 Bratislava - Praha (trains 770/1) - Karlovy Vary - Cheb and v.v.
*70/1 – PODLUŽAN – 🚻 Štúrovo - Bratislava - Praha and v.v.
72/3 – BRNĚNSKÝ DRAK – 🚻 Břeclav - Brno - Praha - Karlovy Vary and Karlovy Vary - Praha - Brno.
*74 – 🚻 and ※ Břeclav - Praha - Plzeň - Cheb; 🚻 Břeclav - Cheb (train 7051) - Karlovy Vary.

1010/1 – CSÁRDÁS – Runs May 29 - Nov. 5, also Apr. 6 - May 27, 1995 (from Budapest), May 29 - Nov. 6, also Apr. 7 - May 27, 1995 (from Malmö, next day from Praha): 🛏 1, 2 cl. and ⊷ 2 cl. Budapest - Praha - Berlin - Malmö and v.v.; 🚻 Budapest - Berlin - Sassnitz and v.v.; ⊷ 2 cl. Bratislava - Malmö and v.v.; ※ Budapest - Dresden and v.v.
B – 🚻 Štúrovo - Bratislava - Břeclav - Přerov - Bohumin and v.v.
K – 🚻 České Budějovice - Brno and v.v.; ⊷ 2 cl. and 🚻 České Budějovice - Brno - Bohumín - Žilina - Košice and v.v.
L – 🚻 Liberec - Brno and v.v.
S – SLOVENSKÁ STRELA – 🚻 Bratislava - Praha and v.v.
b – Subject to alteration on Ⓐ. (Engineering work: Brno - 8 kms North thereof).
e – Will not run July 8.
v – Brno Královo Pole.
△ – 🚻 is at Lanžhot/Kúty.
🖊 – Supplement payable.
☐ – Supplement payable in Slovakia.

Table 881 KATOWICE - OSTRAVA - BŘECLAV
1, 2 class except where shown. PKP, ČD

km		231	1630	4208 2	3363 2	4210 2	3365 2	705	106 IC RX	105 EC RX	233	3367	131 IC RX	1808	701 X	3369 2	490	1538	4222 R	391 R	337 RX	200 R	203 2R K	34005 203 R
									◆	◆	S		◆		X		J	⑦n	◆	◆	RX	R	K	K
0	Warszawa Centralna 864 ... d.	...	...	...	...	...	...	0610	0910	...	...	1110	...	...	...	...	1640	...	...	1910	2005	...	2045
321	Katowice ... d.	...	...	...	...	...	...	0853	1153	...	...	1353	...	...	...	...	...	...	...	2233	2320	...	2347
	Kraków Glówny 863a ... d.																				2235		
	Oświecim 863a ... d.																				2339		
395	Zebrzydowice ▥ ... d.	...	...	...	...	...	...	0955	1250	...	...	1455	...	...	...	1747	...	...	2340	0028	0105	0105
401	Petrovice ▥ ... a.	...	...	...	...	...	...	1005	1258	...	...	1504	...	...	...	1757	...	...	2350	0038	0115	0115
401	Petrovice ▥ ... d.	...	...	...	...	...	...	1018	1311	...	...	1518	...	...	...	1815	...	...	0005	0109	0135	0135
	Wroclaw 860 ... d.										1420		1708					1710				
	Racibórz ▥ ... d.			0648		0826					1443		1743					1910				
	Chalupki ▥ ... d.			0756		0850											1933				
415	Bohumin 884 ... d.	0426	0540	0804	0847	0858	1035	1327	1434	1451	1545	1518	1730	1833	1856	2018	0128	0154	0154
	Český Těšín ... a.														2052	0035		
423	Ostrava Hlavní 884 ... d.	0442	0556		0904		1049	1342	1451		1543	1746	1847	1911			0144	0216	0216
478	Hranice na Morave 884 ... d.	0531	0649		1001		1425	1534		1634	1839	2001			
	Praha Hlavní 884 ... d.						0835d	1459			1512d	1712d		0612		
507	Přerov ... d.	0556	0714	0920		1105		1220	1447	1600	1702	1910	2022	2108		0316	0316
535	Otrokovice ... d.	0621	0738	0955		1145		1244	1506	1626	1726	1934		2135		0336	0336
587	Hodonín ... d.	0705	0823	1105		1244		1326		1707	1808	2025		2232	
607	Břeclav ... a.	0722	0840	1129		1307		1343	1557	1724	1824	2042		2253	
689	Bratislava Hlavní 880 ... a.	0842						1459			1839				0426	0426
753	Wien Südbf 878 ... a.								1704						0652	0652

		390 R	3362 2	491	700	1807	4205 2	232	4207	104 EC RX	4209 2	130 IC RX	3366 2	1809	3368 2	3313 2	107 IC RX	1633 2	3317 2	230	4225 2	336 RX	201 R	202 2R K	202 43004 R
		◆		J	X			S		RX		RX					X	⑦n		S		◆	R	K	K
	Wien Südbf 878 ... d.								0939																2150	2150
	Bratislava Hlavní 880 ... d.						0805						1153							1649				2344	2344
	Břeclav ... d.			0333	0610	0755	0922	0908	1053	1058		1328				1453	1605	1816	2040		2344	2344
	Hodonín ... d.			0359	0638	0822	0941	0932		1346				1518	1630	1834	2104		0036	0036
	Otrokovice ... d.			0453	0727	0930	1024	1044	1144	1223		1430			1605	1726	1917	2158		0100	0100
	Přerov ... d.			0532	0751	1003	1052	1125	1207	1255		1452	1615	1631	1806	1944	2236		2116
	Praha Hlavní 884 ... d.			0914a				1518a			1340					
	Hranice na Morave 884 ... d.			0629	0821	3364	1115	1229		1524	1646	1712	1658	1836	2007	2319
	Ostrava Hlavní 884 ... d.			0701	0732	0911	2	1205	1310		1615	1743	1756	1749	1943	2056	0027	0142	0206	0206
	Český Těšín 889 ... d.	0324								1458							0124	
	Bohumin 884 ... d.	0428	0659	0717	0746	0928	0943	1219	1323	1539	1632	1725	1757	1811	1803	1956	2110	0042	0158	0222	0222
	Chalupki ▥ ... d.	0440	0707			0953				1549	1733				
	Racibórz ▥ ... a.	0456	0741			1014				1610	1814				
	Wroclaw 860 ... a.	0700													
	Petrovice ▥ ... d.				0733			1339	1524		1827			0152	0215	0239	0239
	Petrovice ▥ ... d.				0753			1352	1540		1840			0210	0230	0300	0300
	Zebrzydowice ▥ ... d.				0806			1400	1540		1850			0223	0245	0330	0340
	Oświecim 863a ... d.															0436
	Kraków Glówny 863a ... a.															0535
	Katowice ... a.			0912				1456	1655		1955			0326	0348	0438
	Warszawa Centralna 864 ... a.							1740	1940		2245			0647	0715	0804

◆ – NOTES (LISTED BY TRAIN NUMBERS)

EC104/5 – SOBIESKI – ⊑ and X Wien - Warszawa and v.v. Supplement payable.
IC106/7 – PRAHA – ⊑ and X Warszawa - Praha and v.v. Supplement payable.
IC130/1 – POLONIA – ⊑ and X Budapest - Warszawa and v.v. Supplement payable.
200/1 – SILESIA – 〓 1, 2 cl., 〓 2 cl. and ⊑ Warszawa - Praha and v.v.
202/3 – CHOPIN – 〓 1, 2 cl., 〓 2 cl. and ⊑ Wien - Warszawa and v.v.; 〓 1, 2 cl. Wien - Warszawa (245/4) - Brest (74/3) - Minsk - Moskva and v.v.
336/7 – BATHORY – 〓 1, 2 cl., 〓 2 cl., ⊑ and X Budapest - Warszawa and v.v.; 〓 1, 2 cl., 〓 2 cl. and ⊑ Bratislava - Žilina - Warszawa and v.v.
390/1 – BEM – 〓 1, 2 cl. and ⊑ Budapest - Wroclaw (- Szczecin in Summer) and v.v.
700/1 – ⊑ and X Břeclav - Přerov - Praha and v.v.

4207 – ⊑ Břeclav - Přerov (train 702) - Praha.
4222 – ⊑ Praha (train 707) - Přerov - Břeclav.
J – Runs ⑤⑥⑦ only. Also runs Apr. 17, May 1, 8, not Dec. 24, 25, Jan. 1.
K – CHOPIN – 〓 2 cl. and ⊑ Kraków - Wien and v.v.
R – ⓡ (reservation obligatory) in Poland.
S – ⊑ Štúrovo - Břeclav - Bohumin and v.v.
a – Arrival time.
d – Departure time.
n – Will not run July 3, 5, 6, Oct. 28, Dec. 24, 25, 26, Apr. 16, 30, May 7.
t – Will not run Oct. 29.

Table 882 PRAHA - HRADEC KRALOVÉ - WROCLAW
1, 2 class except where shown. ČD, PKP

km		1751	15253 2	330	1755	1753	1757	253	255
		E		⑤⑦x		E	B	K	X K
0	Praha Hlavni ... d.	0717	...	...	1212	1506	1618	1813	2012
	Pardubice 884 ... d.	...						
50	Nymburk ... d.	0813	...	1308	1601	1716	1901	2101
116	Hradec Králové ... d.	0921	...	1416	1706	1825	2005	2205
137	Týniště nad Orlici 883 ... d.	0951	...	1437	1740	1845	2035	2235
178	Letohrad ... d.	1040			1839	2014	2129	2323
199	Lichkov ... d.	1102	1813	1934	2204	0001
209	Miedzylesie ... a.		1825	2217	0014
209	Miedzylesie ... d.		1943	2257	0039
245	Klodzko ... d.		2030	2345	0118
339	Wroclaw ... a.		2215	0104	0240
740	Warszawa Centralna 863 ... a.			0643

		252	1756	254	1752	1754	1750	1758	317 2
		B	E	X K		E	⑤⑦x	④E	©
	Warszawa Centralna 863 ... d.	1820						1357
	Wroclaw ... d.	0020	0208					1357
	Klodzko ... d.	0140	0325					1538
	Miedzylesie ... a.	0230	0400					1622
	Miedzylesie ... d.	0309	0446					1844
	Lichkov ... d.	0325	0502	1006	1521	1713	1858
	Letohrad ... d.	0347	0406	0527	1044	1407	1547	1748	1930
	Týniště nad Orlici 883 ... d.	0444	0521	0629	1148	1539	1642	1856	2032
	Hradec Králové ... d.	0506	0545	0656	1211	1606	1704	1921	2113
	Nymburk ... d.	0610	0647	0753	1314	1714	1811	2029
	Pardubice 884 ... d.						
	Praha Hlavni ... a.	0703	0740	0843	1402	1805	1902	2120

B – BOHEMIA – 〓 1, 2 cl., 〓 2 cl. and ⊑ Warszawa - Wroclaw - Praha and v.v.; 〓 1, 2 cl. Moskva - Minsk - Brest (trains 21/2) - Warszawa - Praha and v.v.; Conveys on ③⑦ from Minsk, ⑭ from Praha: 〓 1, 2 cl. Praha - Minsk and v.v.
E – Conveys ⊑ Praha - Týniště nad Orlici - Meziměsti and v.v.

K – BALTIC – 〓 1, 2 cl., 〓 2 cl., and ⊑ and X Praha - Poznań - Gdynia and v.v.; 〓 1, 2 cl., 〓 2 cl. and ⊑ Praha - Szczecin (- Świnoujście in Summer) and v.v.
c – Subject to confirmation.
x – Will not run July 5, Oct. 28, Dec. 25, Apr. 16, 30, May 7.

Table 883 PRAHA - WALBRZYCH
1, 2 class except where shown. ČD, PKP

km		2	1850	77734 2	2	2	77736 2	1757
			E					E
0	Praha Hlavni 882 ... d.		0717				1506	1618
137	Týniště nad Orlici ... d.	0741	1001	1149	1526	1737	1859
174	Náchod ▥ ... d.	0841	1044	1252	1634	1742	1843	1934
205	Meziměsti ▥ ... d.	0933	1129	1255	1352	1729	1905	1943	2015
211	Mieroszów ▥ ... d.		1307	1917
232	Walbrzych Glówny ... a.		1326	1936

		1756	77731		1851	77735	
		E	2	2	2	④E	2 2⑦n 2
	Walbrzych Glówny ... d.		0830			1521
	Mieroszów ▥ ... d.		0856			1545
	Meziměsti ▥ ... d.	0347	0423	0906	0949	1324	1511	1612	1631	1841
	Náchod ▥ ... d.	0427	0520	1044	1416	1550	1654	1718	1937
	Týniště nad Orlici ... d.	0505	0622	1138	1514	1624	1812	2031
	Praha Hlavni 882 ... a.	0740	0843	1402	1902	2120

E – ⊑ Praha - Týniště nad Orlici - Meziměsti and v.v.

n – Runs ⑦ only. Will not run July 3, 5, 6, Oct. 28, Dec. 24, 25, Apr. 16, 30, May 7.

---

①-⑦ – Monday - Sunday   X – Daily except Sunday and holidays   2 – 2 class only

Table 884 PRAHA - OSTRAVA - ŽILINA - ZVOLEN

1, 2 class except where shown. ČD, ŽSR

km		433	Ex505	245	232	681	EC104	705	321	IC131	441	733	643	IC107	241	737	471	701	IC503	230	243	667	707	683	IC501
		⊡	✕	⊡			✕↯	✕	✕⊡	✕↯	✕⊡			✕↯	⊡			✕	✕↯		✕⊡				✕↯
					S	L	♦	B		♦	♦		♦	♦	♦		♦	B		S	♦	♦	B	L	
0	**Praha** Hlavni ..... d.	...	0606	0652	...	...	...	0835	0906	...	1040	...	1212	1340	1425h	...	1441	1512	1540	...	1625	...	1712	...	1745h
62	Kolín ..... d.	...	0653	0746	...	...	...	0922	0953	...	1130	...	1300	1426	1516	...	1528	1559	|	...	1716	...	1800	...	1828
104	Pardubice ..... d.	...	0721	0814	...	0911	...	0953	1021	...	1203	...	1330	1453	1545	...	1555	1628	1654	...	1743	...	1832	1837	1855
164	Česká Třebová ..... d.	...	0807	0900	...	1011	...	1041	1105	...	1258	...	1420	1535	1631	...	1650	1720	1740	...	1829	...	1921	1934	1934
252	Olomouc ..... d.	...	0912	1005	...	|	...	1155	1213	...	1415	...	1530	1638	1740	...	|	1833	1844	...	1935	...	2039	|	2033
	Brno ..... d.	0620	|	|	...	1141g	...	|	|	...	|	1220	|	|	|	1650	1823	|	|	...	|	1850	|	2110	|
274	Přerov ..... d.	0759	|	1041	1052	...	1207	1215	|	...	1453	1458	1602	|	1828	1834	...	1852	|	1944	|	2037	2057	...	|
303	Hranice na Morave ..... d.	0823	0949	1104	1115	...	|	...	1249	...	1517	1527	1625	1712	1851	1859	...	▬	1922	2007	2013	2059	...	...	2107
	Valašské Meziříčí ..... d.	|	|	1132	|	...	|	...	|	...	|	|	|	|	1917	|	...	...	|	|	2046	|	...	...	|
	Vsetín 🏛 ..... d.	|	|	1154	|	...	|	...	|	...	|	|	|	|	1935	|	...	**391**	|	|	2104	|	...	...	|
	Púchov ..... d.	|	|	1250	|	...	|	...	|	...	|	|	|	|	2035	|	...	🍷⊡	|	|	2201	|	...	...	|
358	**Ostrava** Hlavni ..... d.	0914	1035	|	1205	...	1310	...	1327v	...	1613	1618	1702v	1756	|	1948	...	♦	2013	2056	|	2149	...	...	2155
366	Bohumín ..... a.	0928	1049	|	1219	...	1322	...	|	...	1627	1632	|	1810	|	2002	...	...	2027	2110	|	2203	...	...	2209
366	Bohumín ..... d.	0930	...	|	...	...	...	...	|	...	1644	▬	|	...	|	...	...	2018	...	...	|	...	...	...	...
397	Český Těšín 🏛 ..... d.	1007	...	|	...	...	...	...	1402	1547	1720	...	1738	...	|	...	...	2054	...	...	|	...	...	...	...
435	Čadca ..... d.	1105	...	|	...	...	...	...	1450	1623	1810	**841**	...	...	|	...	...	2140	...	...	|	...	...	...	...
466	**Žilina 885** ..... a.	1130	...	1333	...	...	...	...	1515	1648	1835	...	...	...	2118	...	...	2205	...	...	2244	...	...	...	...
466	**Žilina 885** ..... d.	...	...	1350	...	...	...	...	1521	...	...	1915	...	...	...	...	...	2217	...	...	...	...	...	...	...
	Poprad Tatry **885** .. a.	...	...	|	...	...	...	...	1719	...	...	|	...	...	...	...	...	|	...	...	...	...	...	...	...
494	Martin ..... d.	...	...	1426	...	...	...	...	|	...	...	1951	...	...	...	...	...	2252	...	...	...	...	...	...	...
563	Banská Bystrica ..... a.	...	...	1550	...	...	...	...	|	...	...	2106	...	...	...	...	...	0011	...	...	...	...	...	...	...
584	**Zvolen** ..... a.	...	...	1613	...	...	...	...	|	...	...	2130	...	...	...	...	...	0032	...	...	...	...	...	...	...
708	*Košice* **885** ..... a.	...	...	...	...	...	...	...	1837	...	...	...	...	...	...	...	...	...	...	...	...	...	...	...	...

	221	709	225	431	201	202	341	227	421	641
	🛏		⊡	✕⊡			⊡	✕⊡	✕⊡	
	♦		♦	♦	♦	♦	♦	♦	♦	
Praha Hlavni ..... d.	1835	1902	2059	...	2116	...	2159	2327h	2336	0035
Kolín ..... d.	|	1952	2146	...	2202	...	2248	0012	0025	0124
Pardubice ..... d.	1948	2019	2214	...	2231	...	2318	0042	0054	0155
Česká Třebová ..... d.	2032	2104	2257	...	2320	...	0005	0126	0138	0245
Olomouc ..... d.	2139	2208	0002	...	0026	...	0117	0232	0247	0359
Brno ..... d.	|	|	|	2240	|	...	|	|	|	|
Přerov ..... d.	|	2228	|	0019	|	0100	0151	|	0321	0440
Hranice na Morave ..... d.	|	*2319*	0038	0042	|	|	0214	0310	|	0503
Valašské Meziříčí ..... d.	2246	|	0108	|	|	|	|	0339	|	|
Vsetín 🏛 ..... d.	2308	|	0129	|	|	|	|	0359	|	|
Púchov ..... d.	0008	|	0231	|	|	|	|	0457	|	|
Ostrava Hlavni ..... d.	|	*0027*	|	0127	0142	0206	0251v	|	0439	0601
Bohumín ..... a.	|	*0042*	|	0141	0156	0220	|	|	0453	0615
Bohumín ..... d.	|	...	|	0143	...	...	|	|	0458	0617
Český Těšín 🏛 ..... d.	|	...	|	0220	...	...	0329	|	0532	0650
Čadca ..... d.	|	...	|	0310	...	...	0420	|	0620	...
Žilina 885 ..... a.	0048	...	0314	0335	...	...	0445	0536	0645	...
Žilina 885 ..... d.	0106	...	0320	0340	...	...	0456	0540	0653	...
Poprad Tatry **885** ..... a.	0303	...	0518	0543	...	...	|	0738	0849	...
Martin ..... d.	|	...	|	|	...	...	0536	|	|	...
Banská Bystrica ..... a.	|	...	|	|	...	...	0713	|	|	...
Zvolen ..... a.	|	...	|	|	...	...	0737	|	|	...
Košice **885** ..... a.	0431	...	0637	0705	...	...	...	0905	1006	...

	IC500	430	700	231	390	IC502	220	240	730	3708
	✕↯		✕		🍷⊡	✕↯	🛏			2
		♦	B	S	♦		♦	♦		
Košice **885** ..... d.	...	2215	...	...	...	...	0040	...	...	...
Zvolen ..... d.	...	|	...	...	2344	...	|	...	...	...
Banská Bystrica ..... d.	...	|	...	...	0009	...	|	...	...	...
Martin ..... d.	...	|	...	...	0137	...	|	...	...	...
Poprad Tatry **885** ..... d.	...	2345	...	...	|	...	0157	...	...	...
Žilina ..... a.	...	0144	...	...	0204	...	0349	...	...	...
Žilina ..... d.	...	0148	...	...	0209	...	0405	0508	...	...
Čadca 🏛 ..... d.	...	0225	...	...	0249	...	|	|	...	0638
Český Těšín ..... d.	...	0304	...	...	0324	...	|	|	...	0738
Bohumín ..... a.	...	0337	...	...	0359	...	|	|	...	0815
Bohumín ..... d.	0343	0349	...	0426	▬	0508	|	|	0616	0847
Ostrava Hlavni ..... d.	0400	0405	...	0442	...	0524	|	|	0633	0904
Púchov 🏛 ..... d.	|	|	...	|	...	|	0451	0553	|	|
Vsetín ..... d.	|	|	...	|	...	|	0549	0647	|	|
Valašské Meziříčí ..... d.	|	|	...	|	**682**	|	0609	0707	|	|
Hranice na Morave ..... d.	0451	0459	...	0531	L	0611	|	0730	0723	1001
Přerov ..... d.	|	0535c	0530	0553	...	|	|	0805d	0758	1035
Brno ..... a.	|	0710	|	...	0520	|	|	|	0920	|
Olomouc ..... d.	0528	...	0551	...	|	0648	0714	0830	...	1100
Česká Třebová ..... d.	0630	...	0704	...	0712	0751	0818	0937	...	...
Pardubice ..... d.	0712	...	0756	...	0800	0831	0906	1023	...	...
Kolín ..... d.	|	...	0823	...	...	0856	|	1051	...	...
Praha Hlavni ..... a.	0824h	...	0914	...	...	0947	1026	1139h	...	...

	840	IC106	242	440	732	EC105	470	320	233	680	734	Ex504	IC130	244	736	432	2938	420	666	640	226	200	203	224	340
		✕↯	✕⊡	✕⊡		✕↯		✕⊡				✕	✕↯	⊡	2	⊡	2	✕⊡			✕⊡			⊡	
		♦	♦			♦	♦		S	L			♦	♦				♦	♦	♦	♦	♦	♦	♦	♦
Košice **885** ..... d.	...	...	...	...	...	...	...	0920	...	...	...	...	...	...	...	...	...	1615	...	...	2007	...	...	2135	...
Zvolen ..... d.	0530	...	...	...	...	...	...	|	...	...	...	...	...	1355	...	...	...	|	...	...	|	...	...	|	2145
Banská Bystrica ..... d.	0552	...	...	...	...	...	...	|	...	...	...	...	...	1422	...	...	...	|	...	...	|	...	...	|	2214
Martin ..... d.	0700	...	...	...	...	...	...	|	...	...	...	...	...	1551	...	...	...	|	...	...	|	...	...	|	2354
Poprad Tatry **885** ..... d.	|	...	...	...	...	...	...	1040	...	...	...	...	...	|	...	...	...	1745	...	...	2136	...	...	2259	|
Žilina ..... a.	0736	...	...	...	...	...	...	1234	...	...	...	...	...	1618	...	...	...	1944	...	...	2334	...	...	0053	0021
Žilina ..... d.	▬	...	1025	1005	...	...	...	1240	...	...	...	...	1355	1627	...	1640	1727	1950	...	...	2340	...	...	0059	0030
Čadca 🏛 ..... d.	...	...	|	1045	...	...	...	1320	...	...	...	...	1425	|	...	1720	1820	2030	...	...	|	...	...	|	0110
Český Těšín ..... d.	...	...	|	1123	...	...	...	1352	...	...	...	...	1456	|	1654	1801	1924	2109	...	...	|	...	...	|	0211
Bohumín ..... a.	...	...	|	1157	...	...	...	|	...	...	...	...	▬	|	1728	1911	1958	2145	...	...	|	...	...	|	|
Bohumín ..... d.	...	1035	|	1212	1205	1327	...	|	1434	...	1518	1540	...	|	1730	|	...	2200	2250	0006	|	0128	0154	|	|
Ostrava Hlavni ..... d.	...	1049	|	1229	1221	1342	...	1425v	1451	...	1543	1557	...	|	1746	w	...	2224	2319	0022	|	0144	0216	|	0249v
Púchov 🏛 ..... d.	...	|	1112	|	|	|	...	|	|	...	|	|	...	1711	|	...	...	|	|	|	0025	|	|	0158	|
Vsetín ..... d.	**702**	|	1210	|	|	|	...	|	|	...	|	|	...	1808	|	...	...	|	|	|	0122	|	|	0255	|
Valašské Meziříčí ..... d.	**B**	|	1229	|	|	|	...	|	|	...	|	|	**704**	1827	|	...	...	|	|	|	0142	|	|	0314	|
Hranice na Morave ..... d.	...	|	1258	1322	1311	1425	...	1503	1534	...	1634	1643	...	1853	1839	...	...	2312	0010	0114	0209	|	|	|	0328
Přerov ..... d.	1125	|	|	1355b	1350	1444	...	|	1555	...	1710	|	1735	1930f	1922e	...	...	2345	0044	0148	|	|	0313	|	0405
Brno ..... a.	|	|	|	|	1527	...	1406	|	...	1609	1836	|	|	|	2050	...	...	|	0206	|	|	|	...	|	|
Olomouc ..... d.	1151	1205	1339	1418	...	...	|	1539	...	|	...	1721	1801	1955	...	...	...	0011	...	0212	0249	0303	...	0419	0430
Česká Třebová ..... d.	1300	1305	1450	1525	...	...	1602	1640	...	1756	...	1824	1913	2105	...	...	...	0122	...	0319	0357	0406	...	0528	0543
Pardubice ..... d.	1353	1347	1539	1609	...	...	1653	1722	...	1845	...	1908	2005	2155	...	...	...	0211	...	0410	0440	0453	...	0612	0637
Kolín ..... d.	1421	|	1608	1636	...	...	1720	1748	...	...	...	1935	2036	2223	...	...	...	0240	...	0438	0508	0521	...	0642	0707
Praha Hlavni ..... a.	1518	1459	1659	1729	...	...	1812	1845	...	...	...	2026	2127	2314	...	...	...	0328	...	0529	0556h	0612	...	0733	0759

♦ – **NOTES** (LISTED BY TRAIN NUMBERS)

C104/5 – SOBIESKI – [12] and ✕ Wien - Břeclav - Katowice - Warszawa and v.v.
C106/7 – PRAHA – [12] and ✕ Warszawa - Katowice - Praha and v.v.
C130/1 – POLONIA – [12] and ✕ Budapest - Warszawa and v.v.
00/1 – SILESIA – 🛏 1, 2 cl., ▬ 2 cl. and [12] Praha - Katowice - Warszawa and v.v.
02/3 – CHOPIN – See Table **881**.
20/1 – DUKLA – 🛏 1, 2 cl. Moskva (trains **7/8**) - Kyïv - Lviv - Chop (trains **220/1**) - Praha and v.v.; 🛏 2 cl. St Peterburg (trains **183/4**) - Vilnius - Lviv (trains **7/8**) - Chop - Praha and v.v.; 🛏 2 cl. Kyïv and Chop - Praha and v.v.
24/5 – VIHORLAT – 🛏 1, 2 cl., ▬ 2 cl. and [12] Košice - Praha and v.v.; 🛏 1, 2 cl. and ▬ 2 cl. Bratislava (trains **614/5**) - Púchov - Praha and v.v.
26/7 – LABOREC – 🛏 1, 2 cl., ▬ 2 cl., [12] and ✕ Košice - Praha - Děčín and v.v.; [12] Košice - Děčín (trains **370/1**) - Dresden and v.v. **Not** Dec. 24, 31.
0/1 – VSACAN – [12] Žilina - Praha Holešovice - Karlovy Vary - Cheb and v.v.
42/3 – BEČVA – [12] and ✕ Žilina - Praha - Plzeň - Cheb and v.v.
44 – DETVAN – Conveys on ⑦: [2] Bohumín (train **736**) - Přerov - Praha.
40/1 – HRON – ▬ 2 cl. and [12] Zvolen - Praha and v.v.
0/1 – BEM – 🛏 1, 2 cl., [12] and 🍷 Budapest - Wroclaw (- Szczecin in Summer) and v.v.
20 – EXCELSIOR – 🛏 1, 2 cl., ▬ 2 cl. and [12] Košice - Praha - Plzeň - Cheb; ▬ 2 cl. and [2] Košice - Bohumín (train **666**) - Brno - České Budějovice; 🛏 1, 2 cl., ▬ 2 cl., [2] and ✕ Košice - Praha (train **676**) - Karlovy Vary (- Cheb).

421 – EXCELSIOR – 🛏 1, 2 cl., ▬ 2 cl. and [12] Cheb - Plzeň - Praha - Košice; 🛏 1, 2 cl., ▬ 2 cl., [2] and ✕ (Cheb -) Karlovy Vary (train **771**) - Praha - Košice.
430/1 – PETROV – 🛏 1, 2 cl., ▬ 2 cl. and [12] Košice - Brno and v.v.; train **431** conveys also: ▬ 2 cl. and [2] České Budějovice (train **661**) - Brno - Košice.
441 – [12] Cheb - Plzeň - Praha - Bohumín - Žilina; [12] and ✕ Karlovy Vary (train **7050**) - Cheb - Žilina.
470/1 – PODLUŽAN – [12] Štúrovo - Bratislava - Česká Třebová - Praha and v.v.; For Athínai/Sofija/Beograd/Budapest - Praha cars see Tables **889** and **96b**.
640 – LEOŠ JANÁČEK – [12] Bohumín - Praha - Plzeň.
643 – [12] Plzeň - Praha - Český Těšín.
666/7 – ODRA – [12] Bohumín - Brno - České Budějovice and v.v.; train **666** conveys also ▬ 2 cl. and [2] Košice (train **420**) - Bohumín - Brno - České Budějovice.
B – [12] Praha - Přerov - Břeclav and v.v.
L – [12] Liberec - Brno and v.v.
S – [12] Štúrovo - Bratislava - Břeclav - Přerov - Bohumín and v.v.
b – Arrive 1343.
c – Arrive 0520.
d – Arrive 0750.
e – Arrive 1900.
f – Arrive 1914.
g – Subject to alteration on Ⓐ.
h – Praha **Holešovice**.
v – Ostrava **Vitkovice**.
w – Via Ostrava Vitkovice (depart 1834) and Ostrava Hlavni (depart 1857).
↯ – Supplement payable.
⊡ – Supplement payable in Slovakia.

[12] – Through carriage (1 and 2 class) ♦ – See footnote ✕ – Restaurant car

SLOVAKIA

SEE MAP ON PAGE 439

Operator: Železnic Slovenskej Republiky (ŽSR).
Services: Trains convey first and second classes of accommodation, shown as '1' and '2' or 🚃12 in the tables. Sleeping cars (🛏) and couchette cars (▬) are of the normal European types, see page 10 for more details.
Timings: Valid **May 29, 1994** to **May 27, 1995**. A Sunday service operates on public holidays – for dates of public holidays see page 2. Certain services, including some long-distance expresses, are liable to withdrawal over the Christmas and New Year period. Intending passengers should check locally before travelling during this period.
Reservations: It is possible to reserve seats on most Express trains.
Supplements: All **EC/IC**, and most International and Express trains carry supplements, as stated in the relevant table footnotes.

Table 885 BRATISLAVA - ŽILINA - KOŠICE - CHOP

1, 2 class except where shown. ŽSR, ČD

km		601	225	431	227	901	421	IC511	333	603	313	605	607	321	609	335	611	IC513	223	903	905	725	221	613	615
		⚡	⚡ ◆	⚡ ◆	✕⚡ ◆		✕⚡ ◆	✕⚡ Ⓡ◆	✕⚡ ◆	✕⚡	✕⚡ ◆	✕⚡	✕⚡	✕⚡	✕⚡	⚡ ◆	✕⚡	✕⚡ Ⓡ◆	🛏 ◆	⚡	◆	⚡ ◆	🛏 ◆	⚡ ◆	⚡ ◆
0	**Bratislava** Hlavni ...... d.	0015	...	...	...	0350	...	0545	0550	0750	...	0950	1150	...	1350	1450	1550	1715	1735	1750	1950	2050	...	2250	2300
46	Trnava .... d.	0046	...	...	...	0423	...	0615	0623	0823	...	1023	1223	...	1423	1523	1623	|	|	1823	2023	2123	...	2323	2331
81	Piešťany .... d.	0116	...	...	...	0451	...	|	0651	0851	...	1051	1251	...	1451	1551	1651	|	1830	1851	2051	2222	...	2351	0000
99	Nové Mesto .... d.	0129	...	...	...	0504	...	|	0704	0904	...	1104	1304	...	1504	1604	1704	|	|	1904	2104	|	...	0004	0013
123	Trenčin .... d.	0149	...	...	...	0524	...	0702	0724	0924	...	1124	1324	...	1524	1624	1724	|	1900	1924	2124	2251	...	0024	0032
	Praha Hlavni **884** .. d.	|	2059	...	2327h	|	2336	|	|	|	...	|	|	0906	|	|	|	|	|	|	|	|	1835	|	|
158	Púchov **884** .... d.	0217	0231	...	0457	0551	|	|	0751	0951	...	1151	1351	|	1551	1651	1751	|	|	1951	2151	2320	0008	0051	0147
203	**Žilina 884** .... a.	0300	0314	...	0536	0634	0645	0755	0834	1034	...	1234	1434	1515	1634	1734	1834	1918	2005	2034	2234	2400	0048	0134	0226
203	**Žilina 884** .... d.	0327	0320	0340	0540	...	0653	0759	*0840*	1040	...	1240	1440	1521	1640	...	1840	1922	2017	...	...	...	0106	0140	0240
325	Štrba .... d.	0518	0505	0530	0725	...	0836	|	*1025*	1225	...	1425	1625	1706	1825	...	2025	|	|	...	...	...	|	0325	0432
344	Poprad-Tatry **885a** ... d.	0537	0521	0546	0746	...	0851	0942	*1044*	1244	1354	1444	1644	1722	1844	...	2044	2105	2203	...	...	...	0309	0344	0451
370	Spišská Nová Ves ..... d.	0600	0543	0608	0808	...	0912	|	*1108*	1308	1416	1508	1708	1743	1908	...	2108	|	|	...	...	...	|	0408	0516
445	**Košice** .... a.	0657	0637	0705	0905	...	1006	1050	*1205*	1405	1513	1605	1805	1837	2005	...	2205	2213	2313	...	...	...	0431	0505	0612
445	**Košice** .... d.	...	...	...	...	...	...	...	...	...	...	1617	...	...	...	...	...	...	2328	...	...	...	0453	...	0642
507	Slovenské Nové Mesto d.	...	...	...	...	...	...	...	...	...	...	1711	...	...	...	...	...	...	|	...	...	...	|	...	0746
541	Čierna nad Tisou ⊞ .. a.	...	...	...	...	...	...	...	...	...	...	1743	...	...	...	...	...	...	0050	...	...	...	0616	...	0820
551	**Chop** ⊞ .... a.	...	...	...	...	...	...	...	...	...	...	...	...	...	...	...	...	...	0240	...	...	...	0813	...	...
827	*Lviv* **925** .... a.	...	...	...	...	...	...	...	...	...	...	...	...	...	...	...	...	...	1017	...	...	...	1613	...	...
1458	*Kyïv (Kiev)* **925** ...... a.	...	...	...	...	...	...	...	...	...	...	...	...	...	...	...	...	...	2131	...	...	...	0319	...	...
2325	*Moskva* **924** .... a.	...	...	...	...	...	...	...	...	...	...	...	...	...	...	...	...	...	1503	...	...	...	2028	...	...

	606	612	220	904	902	900	IC512	608	604	320	334	610	312	600	602	IC510	420	332	710	226	224	430	337	222	614
	⚡	⚡ ◆	🛏 ◆	⚡	⚡ ◆		✕⚡ Ⓡ◆	✕⚡	✕⚡	✕⚡	⚡ ◆	✕⚡	✕⚡ ◆	✕⚡	✕⚡	✕⚡ Ⓡ◆	✕⚡ ◆	✕⚡ ◆	✕	✕⚡ ◆	⚡ ◆	⚡ ◆	⚡ ◆	🛏 ◆	⚡ ◆
Moskva **924** .... d.	...	...	1300	...	...	...	...	...	...	...	...	...	...	...	...	...	...	...	...	...	...	...	...	1147	...
Kyïv (Kiev) **925** .... d.	...	...	0352	...	...	...	...	...	...	...	...	...	...	...	...	...	...	...	...	...	...	...	...	0229	...
Lviv **925** .... d.	...	...	1533	...	...	...	...	...	...	...	...	...	...	...	...	...	...	...	...	...	...	...	...	1407	...
Chop ⊞ .... d.	...	...	2300	...	...	...	...	...	...	...	...	...	...	...	...	...	...	...	...	...	...	...	...	2115	...
Čierna nad Tisou ⊞ .... d.	...	...	2301	...	...	...	...	...	0626	...	...	...	...	...	...	...	...	...	...	...	...	...	...	2128	2104
Slovenské Nové Mesto d.	...	...	|	...	...	...	...	...	0655	...	...	...	...	...	...	...	...	...	...	...	...	...	...	|	2134
Košice .... a.	...	...	0020	...	...	...	...	...	0746	...	...	...	...	...	...	...	...	...	...	...	...	...	...	2245	2235
Košice .... d.	2315	0015	0040	...	...	...	0555	0615	0815	0920	...	1015	1036	1215	1415	1600	1615	...	1815	2007	2135	2215	...	2255	2300
Spišska Nová Ves .... d.	0019	0119	|	...	...	...	|	0719	0919	1018	...	1119	1138	1319	1519	|	1719	...	1919	2113	2235	2319	...	|	0001
Poprad-Tatry **885a** ..... d.	0045	0145	0157	...	...	...	0707	0745	0945	1040	...	1145	1158	1345	1545	1712	1745	...	1945	2136	2259	2345	...	0015	0024
Štrba .... d.	0102	0200	|	...	...	...	|	0802	1002	1057	...	1202	...	1402	1602	|	1802	...	2002	2153	|	0002	...	|	0040
Žilina 884 .... a.	0244	0344	0349	...	...	...	0850	0944	1144	1234	...	1344	...	1544	1744	1853	1944	...	2144	2334	0053	0144	...	0209	0216
Žilina 884 .... d.	0250	0350	0405	0450	0550	0750	0854	0950	1150	1240	1250	1350	...	1550	1750	1857	1950	1950	...	2340	0059	...	0202	0221	0243
Púchov .... d.	0334	0434	0451	0534	0634	0834	|	1034	1234	|	1334	1434	...	1634	1834	|	|	2034	...	0025	0158	...	0243	|	0342
Praha Hlavni **884** .... a.	|	|	1026	|	|	|	|	|	|	1845	|	|	...	|	|	|	0328	|	...	0556h	0733	...	|	|	|
Trenčin .... d.	0401	0501	...	0601	0701	0901	0948	1101	1301	...	1401	1501	...	1701	1901	1951	...	2101	...	...	...	...	0308	0321	0510
Nové Mesto .... d.	0419	0519	...	0619	0719	0919	|	1119	1319	...	1419	1519	...	1719	1919	|	...	2119	...	...	...	...	|	|	0532
Piešťany .... d.	0432	0532	...	0632	0732	0932	1014	1132	1332	...	1432	1532	...	1732	1932	|	...	2132	...	...		...	0336	0351	0546
Trnava .... d.	0459	0559	...	0659	0759	0959	|	1159	1359	...	1459	1559	...	1759	1959	2037	...	2159	...	...	...	...	0511	|	0632
Bratislava Hlavni .... a.	0530	0630	...	0730	0830	1030	1102	1230	1430	...	1530	1630	...	1830	2030	2105	...	2230	...	...	...	...	0540	0446	0701

◆ – **NOTES** (LISTED BY TRAIN NUMBERS)

220/1 – DUKLA – 🛏 1, 2 cl. Moskva (trains **7/8**) - Chop (trains **220/1**) - Praha and v.v.; 🛏 2 cl. Kyïv - Praha and v.v.; 🛏 2 cl. Sankt Peterburg (trains **183/4**) - Vilnius - Lviv (trains **7/8**) - Chop - Praha and v.v.; 🛏 2 cl. Sankt Peterburg - Žilina (trains **902/5**) - Bratislava and v.v.; 🛏 2 cl. Praha - Chop and v.v.

222/3 – SLOVAKIA – 🛏 1, 2 cl. Moskva (trains **51/2**) - Chop (trains **222/3**) - Bratislava and v.v.; 🛏 1, 2 cl. Moskva - Bratislava (trains **401/4**) - Wien and v.v.; 🛏 1, 2 cl. Chop - Bratislava and v.v.; conveys on ③⑤⑦ from Kyïv (also ② from Lviv), ①④⑥ (also ③ to Lviv) from Wien: 🛏 1, 2 cl. Kyïv - Lviv - Wien and v.v.

224/5 – VIHORLAT – 🛏 1, 2 cl., ▬ 2 cl., 🚃12 and ✕ Košice - Praha and v.v.; 🛏 1, 2 cl., ▬ 2 cl. and 🚃12 Bratislava (trains **615/4**) - Púchov - Praha and v.v.

226/7 – LABOREC – 🛏 1, 2 cl., ▬ 2 cl., 🚃12 and ✕ Košice - Praha - Děčín and v.v.; 🚃12 Košice - Děčín (trains **370/1**) - Dresden and v.v. **Not** Dec. 24, 31.

312/3 – RÁKOCZI – Runs Dec. 11 - Jan. 22, also ⑤⑥⑦ Jan. 27 - Feb. 19: 🚃12 and ✕ Budapest - Košice - Poprad Tatry and v.v.

332/3/4/5 – 🚃12 Kraków - Žilina - Bratislava and v.v.

337 – 🛏 1, 2 cl., ▬ 2 cl. and 🚃2 Warszawa - Leopoldov (train **724**) - Bratislava.

420/1 – EXCELSIOR – 🛏 1, 2 cl., ▬ 2 cl. and 🚃12 Košice - Praha - Plzeň - Cheb and v.v.; 🛏 1, 2 cl., ▬ 2 cl., 🚃2 and ✕ Košice - Praha (trains **770/1**) - Cheb (via Karlovy Vary) and v.v.; train **420** conveys also: ▬ 2 cl. and 🚃2 Košice - Bohumín (train **666**) - Brno - České Budějovice.

430/1 – PETROV – 🛏 1, 2 cl., ▬ 2 cl. and 🚃12 Košice - Brno and v.v.; train **431** conveys also: ▬ 2 cl. and 🚃2 České Budějovice (train **661**) - Brno - Košice

IC510/1 – TATRAN – 🚃12 and ✕ Košice - Žilina - Bratislava.

IC512/3 – KRIVAŇ – 🚃12 and ✕ Košice - Žilina - Bratislava.

612/3 – ZEMPLÍN – 🛏 1, 2 cl., ▬ 2 cl. and 🚃12 Košice - Bratislava and v.v.

614/5 – HORNÁD – 🛏 1, 2 cl. and ▬ 2 cl. Čierna nad Tisou - Bratislava and v.v. 🛏 1, 2 cl., ▬ 2 cl. and 🚃12 Praha - Púchov (trains **225/4**) - Bratislava and v.v

725 – 🛏 1, 2 cl., ▬ 2 cl. and 🚃2 Bratislava - Leopoldov (train **336**) - Warszawa.

902/5 – Conveys 🛏 2 cl. Sankt Peterburg (trains **183/4**) - Lviv (trains **7/8**) - Chop (trains **220/1**) - Žilina - Bratislava and v.v.

h – Praha **Holešovice**.

⚡ – Supplement payable.

Table 885a TATRA LOCAL RAILWAYS

2 class only. ŽSR

POPRAD TATRY - TATRANSKÁ LOMNICA *17 km*. Journey 25-35 minutes.

From Poprad Tatry: 0406, 0524**c**, 0558**c**, 0749, 0956**c**, 1111, 1150**c**, 1400**c**, 1447**c**, 1543, 1743, 1824**c**, 2009, 2120**c**.
c – Change at Studený Potok.

From Tatranská Lomnica: 0558**c**, 0633, 0841**c**, 0952, 1103**c**, 1240**c**, 1318**c**, 1358**c**, 1507, 1616, 1811**c**, 1901, 2037**c**, 2152**c**, 2309.
c – Change at Studený Potok.

POPRAD TATRY - STARÝ SMOKOVEC - ŠTRBSKÉ PLESO *29 km*. Journey 40-50 minutes to Starý Smokovec, 70-90 minutes to Štrbské Pleso. Approximately 25 journeys in each direction.

STARÝ SMOKOVEC - TATRANSKÁ LOMNICA *6 km*. Journey 15 minutes. Approximately 20 journeys in each direction.

ŠTRBA - ŠTRBSKÉ PLESO Rack railway, *5 km*. Journey 14-18 minutes. Approximately 24 journeys in each direction.

Table 886 BRATISLAVA - ŽILINA - KRAKÓW

1, 2 class except where shown. ŽSR, PKP

km					333			41106	335	
			2	2	✕⚡	2	2	Z	⚡	2
0	*Bratislava Hlavni* **885** .... d.	...	...	...	0550	...	...	...	1450	...
203	**Žilina 885** .... d.	...	...	...	0844	...	...	...	1750	...
234	Čadca .... d.	...	0635	0740	0923	1055	1445	...	1828	1941
248	Skalité Serafínov ⊞ .... d.	...	0735	0844	|	1153	1541	...	|	2033
255	Zwardoń ⊞ .... d.	...	0738	0847	1015n	1156	1544	...	1920n	2036
292	Żywiec .... d.	...	...	...	1119n	...	...	1659	2020n	...
313	**Bielsko Biala 864** .... d.	...	...	...	1145n	...	...	1725	2048n	...
345	Oświecim **863a** .... d.	...	...	...	1250n	...	...	...	2148n	...
410	**Kraków** Glówny **863a** .... a.	...	...	...	1347n	...	...	...	2245n	...

			334	14101			332		
	2	2	⚡	Z	2	2	✕⚡	2	
Kraków Glówny **863a** .... d.	...	...	0728n	...	...	...	1445n	...	...
Oświecim **863a** .... d.	...	...	0854n	...	...	...	1547n	...	...
Bielsko Biala 864 .... d.	...	...	0948n	1127	...	...	1643n	...	...
Żywiec .... d.	...	...	1013n	1153	...	...	1717n	...	...
Zwardoń ⊞ .... d.	0800	0918	1120n	...	1342	1645	1827n	2050	...
Skalité Serafínov ⊞ .... d.	0803	0921	|	...	1345	1648	|	2053	...
Čadca .... d.	0840	1009	1207	...	1422	1731	1915	2132	...
Žilina 885 .... a.	...	...	1232	...	...	...	1940	...	...
Bratislava Hlavni **885** ..... a.	...	...	1530	...	...	...	2230	...	...

Z – 🚃12 Żywiec - Lódź and v.v.

n – Sept. 25 - Dec. 2, also Mar. 26, **1995**: will **not** run Čadca - Kraków and v.v.

⚡ – Supplement payable in Slovakia.

⊞ – Frontier station Ⓐ – Mondays to Fridays only, except holidays ⑦ – Sundays only

Table 887 — BRATISLAVA - ZVOLEN - KOŠICE

1, 2 class except where shown. ŽSR

km		801	395	811	823	803		805	831	
		↗	↗	↗	↗	↗	2	↗	R	2
		P	U				✕	R		
0	Bratislava Hlavni .... d.	0001	...	0635	...	1135	...	1355	1642	...
89	Šurany .... d.	0105	...	0745	...	1240	...	1502	1756	...
131	Levice .... d.	0149	...	0827	...	1324	...	1547	1843	...
	Banská Bystrica 884 .... d.	...	0630							
209	Zvolen .... a.	0307	0656	0952	...	1447	...	1712	2005	...
209	Zvolen 884 .... d.	0326	0710	1012	1004	1452	1508	1735	2033	2040
230	Banská Bystrica 884 .... d.	...	...	1036	...		1547			2115
272	Brezno .... d.	...	...	1128	...		1720			2204
263	Lučenec .... d.	0423	0802	...	1055	1545	...	1831	2145	...
279	Filakovo .... d.	0440	0815	...	1113	1600	...	1904	2205	...
370	Rožňava .... d.	0626	...	...	1244	1720	...	2039	...	...
442	Košice .... a.	0732	...	1447	1344	1817	...	2145	...	...

		830	820		804	832	822	810	394	800
		↗	↗	2	↗	↗	↗	↗	↗	↗
		R		n					U	P
	Košice .... d.	...	0528	...	0955	...	1536	1502	...	2247
	Rožňava .... d.	...	0641	...	1103	...	1642	...	...	0000
	Filakovo .... d.	...	0817	...	1235	1534	1815	...	1854	0127
	Lučenec .... d.	...	0830	...	1249	1605	1833	...	1907	0144
	Brezno .... d.	0400	...	1202				1829		
	Banská Bystrica 884 .... d.	0507	...	1306				1919		
	Zvolen 884 .... a.	0529	0927	1347	1350	1729	1932	1941	1956	0250
	Zvolen .... d.	0539	...	...	1415	1742	...	2001	2010	0310
	Banská Bystrica 884 .... d.	...	...	...				2030		
	Levice .... d.	0658	...	...	1548	1911	...	2123	...	0435
	Šurany .... d.	0746	...	...	1631	1955	...	2204	...	0521
	Bratislava Hlavni .... a.	0901	...	...	1745	2106	...	2315	...	0631

P – POLANA – ⛆ 1, 2 cl., ➡ 2 cl. and ⊡ Bratislava - Zvolen - Košice and v.v.
R – ⊡ Bratislava - Košice and Košice - Zvolen; ⊡ and ✕ Budapest - Filakovo - Košice and v.v.
U – URPÍN – ⊡ Budapest - Banská Bystrica and v.v.; ⊡ and ✕ Budapest - Filakovo - Košice and v.v.

n – Will **not** run ①②③④⑥⑦ July 1 - Aug. 25.
↗ – Supplement payable.

Table 888 — BRATISLAVA - WIEN

2 class except where shown. ŽSR, ÖBB

km		401	403	405	407
0	Bratislava Hlavni .... d.	0606	1006	1406	1806
17	Marchegg ▣ .... a.	0632	1032	1432	1832
17	Marchegg ▣ .... d.	0634	1034	1434	1834
64	Wien Südbahnhof .... a.	0713	1113	1513	1913

		E400	E402	E404	E408
				◆	
	Wien Südbahnhof .... d.	0800	1200	1600	2110
	Marchegg .... a.	0839	1239	1639	2152
	Marchegg ▣ .... d.	0841	1241	1641	2201
	Bratislava Hlavni .... a.	0907	1307	1707	2227

◆ – NOTES (LISTED BY TRAIN NUMBER)
401 – ⊡ Bratislava - Wien; ⛆ 1, 2 cl. Moskva (train 51) - Kyїv - Lviv - Chop (train 222) - Košice - Žilina - Bratislava - Wien; conveys on ③⑤⑦ from Kyїv (also ② from Lviv); ⛆ 1, 2 cl. Kyїv - Lviv - Wien.

E404 – ⊡ Wien - Bratislava; ⛆ 1, 2 cl. Wien - Bratislava (train 223) - Žilina - Košice - Chop (train 52) - Lviv - Kyїv - Moskva; conveys on ①④⑥ (also ③ to Lviv only) ⛆ 1, 2 cl. Wien - Lviv - Kyїv.

Table 889 — BRATISLAVA - BUDAPEST

1, 2 class except where shown. ŽSR, MÁV

km			379	475	411	231	1015	373	1011	413	277	251		473	IC131	233	EC175	471		337	375
		2	↗	↗	↗	↗	↗	↗	↗	↗	↗	2	↗	✕	↗	✕	↗		✕	↗
							B		◆						◆	B				◆	◆
	Praha Holešovice 880 .... d.	...	0028				0558	0739								1511					...
0	Praha Hlavni 880 .... d.	...																		2222
257	Brno 880 .... d.	...	0348				0934	1055		1308					1820	1840				0211
398	Bratislava Hlavni .... d.	...	0606	0748		0847	1127	1145	1306		1508	1521		1740		1845	2005	2054		0442
	Bratislava Nové Mesto . d.	0615					1150				1532		1740							
	Rajka .... a.	0650					1225	1345			1605		1815							
	Rajka .... d.	0705					1240	1400			1620		1837							
	Győr 890 .... a.	0805					1330	1442			1720		1935							
	Český Těšín 881 .... d.														1547				0038	
	Žilina 884 885 .... d.														1658				0202	
	Púchov 884 885 .... d.																		0243	
	Trenčín 885 .... d.														1758				0308	
489	Nové Zámky .... d.		0710	0858	0903	0956	1243		1528c	1614			1848	1926	1951	2101	2158		0454	0547
533	Štúrovo .... d.		0755	0940		1023	1325			1642			1930	1958	2018	2132	2240		0536	0630
549	Szob ▣ .... d.		0806	0951			1337						1941						0546	0641
	Komárno .... d.				0945					1645										
	Komárom 890 .... d.				1010					1716	1757									
617	Budapest Nyugati .... a.		0858	1050	1256					1956			2035							
633	Budapest Keleti .... a.						1442	1628							2112		2242		0647	0747

			232	EC174	250	410		470	IC130	472	276	474	230	1010	1014	412	372		378	336		374
		2	↗	✕	↗	2		↗	✕	↗	↗	↗	↗	✕	↗	2	↗	2	↗	✕		↗
				B	◆				ℝ				B		◆				◆	ℝ		◆
	Budapest Keleti .... d.	...		0655				0920					1320		1500			1850			2120
	Budapest Nyugati .... d.	...				0620			0950		1250			1255		1825					
	Komárom 890 .... d.	...			0914	0915								1550							
	Komárno .... d.	...				0925								1600							
	Szob ▣ .... d.	...							1044		1344				1604						
	Štúrovo .... d.	...	0620	0811				1005	1040	1110	1305	1410	1501		1630	1914	1954			2224
	Nové Zámky .... d.	...	0652	0840		1015		1037	1110	1141	1338	1441	1533		1640 1701	2016	2056			2255	2327
	Trenčín 885 .... a.							1242								2251				
	Púchov 884 885 .... a.															2320				
	Žilina 884 885 .... a.							1345								2400				
	Český Těšín 881 .... a.							1456								0121				
	Győr 890 .... d.	0545			0941								1503	1530		1720		•		
	Rajka .... a.	0648			1040								1550	1615		1820				
	Rajka .... d.	0710			1056								1620	1635		1840				
	Bratislava Nové Mesto . a.	0747			1130								1712			1917				
	Bratislava Hlavni .... a.		0800	0938	1144			1144		1253	1444	1553	1644	1703	1723		1800	2120		0030
	Brno 880 .... a.			1125				1352			1643		1907		2010		2337		0245
	Praha Hlavni 880 .... a.							1812			2040								0629
	Praha Holešovice 880 .... a.			1437									2228		2337	0253			

◆ – NOTES (LISTED BY TRAIN NUMBERS)
C130/1 – POLONIA – ⊡ and ✕ Budapest - Warszawa and v.v.
EC174/5 – HUNGARIA – ⊡ and ✕ Budapest - Berlin - Nauen (- Hamburg) and v.v.
436/7 – BATHORY – ⛆ 1, 2 cl., ➡ 2 cl., ⊡ and ✕ Budapest - Warszawa and v.v.
472/3 – BALT ORIENT EXPRESS – ⛆ 1, 2 cl., ➡ 2 cl. and ⊡ Bucureşti - Praha - Děčín - Dresden - Berlin and v.v.; ⊡ Lőkösháza - Budapest - Berlin and v.v.; ⛆ Štúrovo - Praha and v.v.
474/5 – PANNONIA – ⛆ 1, 2 cl., ➡ 2 cl. and ⊡ Bucureşti - Budapest - Praha and v.v.; ⛆ 1, 2 cl. and ⊡ Budapest - Praha and v.v.
478/9 – METROPOL – ⛆ 1, 2 cl., ➡ 2 cl. and ⊡ Budapest - Praha - Berlin and v.v.; ⛆ 1, 2 cl. Bratislava - Berlin and v.v.

1010/1 – CSÁRDÁS – Runs May 29 - Nov. 5, also Apr. 6 - May 27, **1995** (from Budapest), May 29 - Nov. 6, also Apr. 7 - May 27, **1995** (from Malmö, next day from Praha): ⛆ 1, 2 cl. and ➡ 2 cl. Budapest - Praha - Berlin - Malmö and v.v.; ⊡ Budapest - Berlin - Sassnitz and v.v.; ✕ Budapest - Dresden and v.v.
1014/5 – Runs Nov. 8 - Apr. 7 from Bratislava, Nov. 6 - Apr. 5 from Győr: ⊡ Bratislava - Győr and v.v.

B – ⊡ Štúrovo - Bratislava - Břeclav - Přerov - Bohumín and v.v. (Table 881).
c – ✕ only.
↗ – Supplement payable.

HUNGARY

SEE MAP ON PAGE 439

Operator: Magyar Államvasutak (MÁV), except the Györ - Sopron line (Table 890) which is operated by Györ - Sopron - Ebenfurthi Vasút (GySEV).
Services: Trains convey first and second classes of accommodation, shown as '1' and '2' or 🚃 in the tables. Sleeping cars (🛏) and couchette cars (🛏) are of the normal European types, see page 10 for more details.
Timings: September 25, 1994 to May 27, 1995. Certain trains are liable to be withdrawn over the Christmas and New Year holiday period.
Tickets: A supplement is payable for travel by EuroCity (EC) and InterCity (IC) trains. Reservation is not normally possible on internal trains, except those marked Ⓡ where reservation is compulsory.

Table 890 — WIEN - HEGYESHALOM - GYÖR - BUDAPEST

1, 2 class except where shown

km		D269 K	947 n	937 Ⓡ	2	EC41 L	D345 A	D467 W	935	263 O	945	596	2	EC63 B	D343 R	933	251 S	2	941 Ⓡ p	931 Ⓡ p	EC25 F	2 Ⓐ	D347 D	D341 E
0	Wien Westbf d.								0830		1005				1320	1505					1820		1905	2300
	Wien Südbf d.	0420h				0711	0803				1043			1402	1542					1902		1947	2343
41	Bruck an der Leitha d.	0458				0735	0828	0908		1043				1423	1603					1923		2008	0005
79	Hegyeshalom a.	0519				0755	0848	0928		1103				1426	1613	1635				1926		2023	0025
79	Hegyeshalom 🚃 d.	0553	0605			0758	0858	0938		1113	1253				1621	1648		1900					
89	Mosonmagyaróvár d.		0614				0906			1304			1528				1828					
	Sopron a.			0628					0928		1228											
126	Györ a.	0621	0640	0732		0825	0927	1006	1030	1141	1330	1330		1453	1643	1632	1720	1925	1930	1953		2051	0056
126	Györ d.	0623	0642	0742	0810	0827	0928	1008	1042	1143	1342	1342	1445	1455	1644	1647	1722	1725	1940	1940	1955	2017	2053	0057
163	Komárom d.		0710	0810	0852				1110		1410	1410	1527		1708	1714	1748	1801	2005	2005	2051		
194	Tatabánya d.		0740	0840	0927				1140		1440	1440	1602		1736	1743		1842	2035	2035	2130		
254	Budapest Kelenföld a.		0824	0924	1024				1224		1524	1524	1659			1825		1939	2115	2115	2214		0229
264	Budapest Déli a.					1003										1948						
273	Budapest Keleti a.	0808	0843	0943	1043		1108	1153	1243	1328	1543	1543	1718	1638	1833	1843		2133	2133	2138	2233	2238	

		340 E	346 D	932 Ⓡ	932 Ⓡ	250 S	EC24 F	242 R	934		EC62 B	595	595 O	262	936	936	466 W	938 p	344 A	EC40 L	4918 p	3918 K	268	3818
	Budapest Keleti d.		0555	0700	0700		0825	0955	1000	1135	1230	1330	1330	1530	1600	1600	1725	1800	1830		1845	2035	2120	2235
	Budapest Déli d.																			1905				
	Budapest Kelenföld d.	0213		0718	0718			1018	1154		1348	1348		1618	1618	1818				1854	2050		2254
	Tatabánya d.			0801	0801		1049	1101	1251		1431	1431		1701	1701	1901				2001	2156		2351
	Komárom d.			0831	0831	0914		1118	1131	1341		1501	1501		1731	1731	1931				2037	2237		0025
	Györ a.	0341	0733	0857	0857	0939	1004	1143	1157	1432	1409	1527	1527	1712	1757	1757	1903	1957	2012	2037	2112	2312	2258	
	Györ d.	0342	0734	0901	0910	0941	1006	1145	1201		1411	1542	1530t	1714	1801	1810	1904	2001	2014	2038			2259	
	Sopron a.			1004				1304			1644		1644		1904			2104					
	Mosonmagyaróvár d.			0936	1014		1210				1553t			1835			2036					
	Hegyeshalom 🚃 a.	0413	0805	0945	1025	1037	1219		1442		1602t	1745		1935			2045	2109		2330		
	Hegyeshalom d.	0425	0815			1040	1229		1445			1755		1945			2055	2112		2347		
	Bruck an der Leitha d.	0448	0838			1103	1252		1508			1818		2008			2116	2132		0009		
	Wien Südbf a.																	2145	2156		0044h	
	Wien Westbf a.	0530	0920			1146	1334		1550			1900		2050								

A – AVALA – 🚃 and ✕ Wien - Beograd and v.v.
B – BÉLA BARTÓK – 🚃 and ✕ Stuttgart - München - Budapest and v.v.
D – DACIA EXPRESS – 🚃 and ✕ Wien - Budapest and v.v.; 🛏 1, 2 cl., 🛏 2 cl. and 🚃 Wien - Bucureşti and v.v.; 🚃 Wien - Budapest (trains 335/4) - Beograd - Athínai and v.v.
E – BEOGRAD EXPRESS – 🛏 1, 2 cl., 🛏 2 cl. and ✕ Wien - Beograd and v.v.; 🛏 2 cl. Wien - Beograd (trains 493/2) - Niš (trains 213/2) - Skopje and v.v.; 🚃 Wien - Szeged and v.v.
F – FRANZ LISZT – 🚃 and ✕ Dortmund - Frankfurt - Budapest and v.v.
K – KÁLMÁN IMRE – 🛏 1, 2 cl., 🛏 2 cl. and 🚃 München - Budapest and v.v.; München - Budapest - Arad - Bucureşti and v.v.
L – LEHÁR – 🚃 and ✕ Wien - Budapest and v.v.

O – ORIENT EXPRESS – 🚃 and ✕ Salzburg - Budapest and v.v.; 🛏 2 cl. and 🚃 Paris - Salzburg - Budapest and v.v.
R – ARRABONA – 🚃 and 🍽 Wien - Budapest and v.v.
S – SOPIANAE – 🚃 Bratislava - Pécs and v.v.
W – WIENER WALZER – 🚃 and ✕ Wien - Budapest and v.v.; 🛏 2 cl. and 🚃 Basel Budapest and v.v.; 🛏 1, 2 cl., 🛏 2 cl. and 🚃 Dortmund - Budapest and v.v.
h – Wien Hütteldorf.
n – Will not run Dec. 25, Jan. 1.
p – Will not run Dec. 24, 31.
t – Nov. 6 - Apr. 5 only.

Table 891 — BUDAPEST - SZOMBATHELY

1, 2 class

km		9210 Ⓡ	900	9212	934	904 G	595	906	908	938 p			927 Ⓡ	907	9217	925	905 G	903	923	901 Ⓡ	9211
	Budapest Keleti d.				1000		1330			1800p	Szombathely d.			0600	0615	0835	1010	1255	1435	1815	1840
0	Budapest Déli 892/3 d.		0600		1220		1500	1715			Celldömölk d.	0618	0639	0710	0917	1052	1339	1521	1855	1937
4	Budapest Kelenföld d.		0608	1018	1229	1348	1509	1722	1818p	Pápa d.	0646		0754	0945		1552		2009
67	Székesfehérvár 892/3 d.		0703		1329		1606	1819			Györ 890 a.	0730		0854	1030		1637		2113
90	Várpalota d.		0725		1349		1627	1840			Ajka d.		0711		1129	1413		1927	
112	Veszprém d.		0747		1415		1648	1902			Veszprém d.		0748		1202	1446		1959	
148	Ajka d.		0821		1455		1721	1941			Várpalota d.		0807		1224	1509		2020	
	Györ 890 d.		0524	1037	1207		1537		2010	Székesfehérvár 892/3 d.		0839		1255	1541		2052	
	Pápa d.		0626	1134	1250		1623		2053	Budapest Kelenföld 892/3 a.	0924	0925		1224	1344	1626	1825	2140
191	Celldömölk d.		0718	0855	1216	1317	1538	1650	1755	2019	2120	Budapest Déli 892/3 a.		0933			1353	1633		2148
236	Szombathely a.		0808	0935	1309	1357	1615	1730	1835	2100	Budapest Keleti a.	0943		1243		1843

G – 🚃 Budapest - Graz and v.v.
p – Will not run Dec. 24, 31.

Table 892 — BUDAPEST - ZALAEGERSZEG

1, 2 class

km		9752	950	9712	9734	954	9714	9716	956 Ⓡ	9718			9717	957 Ⓡ	9725	9715	955	9713	9711	951 Ⓡ	9751
0	Budapest Déli 891/3 d.		0630	0720	1040	1155	1320	1515	1720	1810	Zalaegerszeg d.		0532			1155		1714	
4	Budapest Kelenföld 891/3 d.		0637	0729	1047	1204	1329	1524	1727	1818	Zalaszentiván d.				1205		1724	
67	Székesfehérvár 891/3 d.	0520	0736	0826	1204	1303	1429	1622	1824	1921	Ukk d.		0619		1244		1802	
117	Balatonalmádi d.	0625	0830	0928	1309	1350	1536	1728	1911	2027	Tapolca d.	0440	0648	0825	1025	1315	1410	1636	1833	2030
132	Balatonfüred d.	0650	0845	0957	1332	1407	1605	1756	1927	2055	Révfülöp d.	0519	0714	0908	1109	1345	1455	1716	1903	2110
157	Révfülöp d.	0731	0907	1038		1429	1645	1835	1949	2135	Balatonfüred d.	0601	0756	0956	1152	1408	1538	1759	1926	2154
184	Tapolca d.	0809	0942	1115		1504	1723	1917	2021	2213	Balatonalmádi d.	0625	0749	1010	1216	1423	1602	1823	1940	2212
212	Ukk d.		1022			1544			2058		Székesfehérvár 891/3 d.	0734	0844	1126	1322	1518	1709	1930	2034	2311
243	Zalaszentiván d.		1051			1614					Budapest Kelenföld 891/3 a.	0830	0931	1218	1414	1608	1804	2021	2121	
252	Zalaegerszeg a.		1100			1623		2135			Budapest Déli 891/3 a.	0838	0938	1228	1423	1618	1813	2028	2128	

Table 892a — LOCAL RAILWAYS

2 class or

BUDAPEST - ESZTERGOM:	From Budapest Nyugati 9-12 times daily (53 km, journey time 90-110 minutes).
BUDAPEST - GÖDÖLLO:	From Budapest Keleti 25 times daily (36 km, journey time 30-40 minutes), also frequent suburban trains from Budapest Örs vezér tere (26 km, 50 minutes).
BUDAPEST - SZENTENDRE:	Frequent HÉV suburban trains from Budapest Batthyány tér (21 km, journey time 40 minutes). Operated by HÉV.
BUDAPEST - VÁC:	Frequent service from Budapest Nyugati (34 km, journey time 45 minutes).
SZOMBATHELY - KÖSZEG:	Approximately 13 trains daily (18 km, journey time 30 minutes).
SZOMBATHELY - SOPRON:	From Szombathely: 0355k, 0522, 0725, 1008, 1143, 1457, 1647✕, 1812, 2005Ⓐ, 2135Ⓒ, 2241Ⓐ. (62 km, journey time 95 minutes).
	From Sopron: 0328, 0430, 0538k, 0705, 1111, 1426, 1558, 1735, 1932, 2224Ⓐ. **k** – Will not run Dec. 25, 26, Jan. 1.

Table 893 BUDAPEST - SIOFOK - NAGYKANIZSA

1, 2 class except where shown

km		8510	9562	242	9542	862	8512	9544		202 864	202	8614	8614	204 866	204	8616	8526	1866	240 868	240	8518	9568	208	8718
			2	D✕	2	🍷		2		B🍷	B			🍷	M	2		⑤		V		2	R	
0	**Budapest** Déli **891/2** ... d.	0400	...	...	...	0700	0715	...	...	...	...	1315	1315	1425	1425	1545	...	1645	...	...	1805	...	1935	2030
	Budapest Keleti ... d.	|	...	0600	...	|	|	...	...	1015	1015	|	|	|	|	|	...	|	1730	1730	|	...	|	|
4	Budapest Kelenföld **891/2** .. d.	0408	...	0617	...	0709	0724	...	...	1032	1032	1324	1324	1434	1434	1554	...	1654	1747	1747	1813	...	1944	2039
	Komárom ... d.	|	...	|	...	|	|	...	...	|	|	|	|	|	|	|	...	|	|	|	|	...	|	|
67	**Székesfehérvár 891/2** ... d.	0518	...	0703	...	0800	0816	...	...	1127	1127	1418	1418	1528	1528	1708	...	1744	1835	1835	1910	...	2039	2147
115	Siófok ... d.	0618	...	0743	...	0841	0915	...	...	1209	1209	1506	1506	1609	1609	1803	...	1831	1917	1917	2010	...	2122	2242
130	Balatonföldvár ... d.	0639	...	0757	...	0857	0935	...	...	1229	1229	1527	1527	1624	1624	1824	...	1847	1934	1934	2032	...	2138	2300
149	Balatonboglár ... d.	0706	...	|	...	0918	1000	...	...	1251	1251	1553	1553	1648	1648	1847	...	1911	2021	2021	2101	...	2200	2322
157	Fonyód ... d.	0716	...	0821	...	0927	1011	...	...	1303	1303	1604	1604	1656	1656	1858	...	1921	2009	2009	2111	...	2209	2329
181	Balatonszentgyörgy ... a.	0747	...	0840	...	0948	1040	...	...	1324	1324	1635	1635	1720	1720	1927	...	1943	2035	2035	2140	...	2230	...
181	Balatonszentgyörgy ... d.	0757	0815	0852	0910	0951	1052	1120	...	1327	1336	1639	1650	1723	1732	1930	1942	1944	2038	2047	2150	2145	2242	...
191	Keszthely ... a.	|	0829	|	0921	1002	|	1133	...	1338	|	1650	|	1734	|	1942	|	1955	2049	|	|	2156	|	...
221	**Nagykanizsa** ... a.	0842	...	0930	...	...	1135	...	...	...	1412	...	1732	...	1809	...	2028	...	...	2124	2226	...	2321	...
352	*Zagreb* **937 938** ... a.	...	...	...	...	...	...	...	...	...	1619	...	...	...	2125	...	...	...	...	2332	...	...	0145	...

	209	869	859 869	8527	8617	867 241	241	8705	9517	8515	865 205	205	863	853 863	8513	861 203	203	8533	1861		8521	8601	243	14851
	R	🍷	🍷				V	2			🍷	M	🍷	🍷		B🍷	B		⑦				D✕	2
Zagreb **937 938** ... d.	0115	...	...	...	...	...	0554	...	...	...	...	0835	...	...	...	...	1350	...	...	...	...	...	...	...
Nagykanizsa ... d.	0349	...	0535	0605	...	...	0815	...	...	0950	...	1151	...	1413	1440	...	1600	1625	...	...	1740	...	1929	...
Keszthely ... d.	|	0600	|	|	0635	0840	|	...	1022	|	1215	|	1435	|	|	1625	|	|	1737	...	|	1820	|	...
Balatonszentgyörgy ... a.	0427	0611	0613	0647	0646	0851	0851	...	1035	1030	1226	1228	1446	1450	1521	1636	1637	1713	1748	...	1824	1831	2006	...
Balatonszentgyörgy ... d.	0439	0623	0623	...	0702	0904	0904	...	...	1041	1240	1240	1458	1458	1532	1649	1649	...	1749	...	...	1843	2018	2036
Fonyód ... d.	0503	0643	0643	...	0739	0929	0929	...	...	1113	1306	1306	1521	1521	1605	1715	1715	...	1820	...	...	1918	2040	2054
Balatonboglár ... d.	0510	0650	0650	...	0748	0936	0936	...	...	1122	1313	1313	1528	1528	1614	1724	1724	...	1827	...	...	1927	|	|
Balatonföldvár ... d.	0531	0709	0709	...	0815	0958	0958	...	...	1145	1334	1334	1550	1550	1637	1744	1744	...	1853	...	...	1949	2103	|
Siófok ... d.	0549	0726	0726	...	0839	1016	1016	1120	...	1208	1352	1352	1608	1608	1706	1804	1804	...	1915	...	...	2012	2120	2143
Székesfehérvár 891/2 ... d.	0630	0813	0813	...	0931	1057	1057	1214	...	1304	1434	1434	1650	1650	1803	1845	1845	...	1959	...	...	2055	2158	2220
Komárom ... a.	|	|	|	...	|	|	|	|	...	|	|	|	|	|	|	|	|	...	|	...	...	|	|	...
Budapest Kelenföld **891/2** ... a.	0720	0859	0859	...	1019	1141	1141	1313	...	1353	1521	1521	1738	1738	1854	1933	1933	...	2044	...	...	2144	2241	...
Budapest Keleti ... a.	|	|	|	...	|	1158	1158	|	...	|	|	|	|	|	|	1953	1953	...	|	...	...	|	2258	...
Budapest Déli **891/2** ... a.	0728	0908	0908	...	1028	...	...	1323	...	1403	1528	1528	1748	1748	1903	...	...	...	2053	...	...	2153	...	...

B – AVAS – [12] Nyiregyháza - Miskolc - Budapest - Zagreb and v.v.; [12] and 🍷 Nyiregyháza - Milkolc - Budapest - Keszthely and v.v.

D – DRAVA – [12] and ✕ Budapest - Ljubljana - Trieste and v.v.; [2] Budapest - Ljubljana - Trieste - Venezia and v.v.

M – MAESTRAL – [12] Budapest - Zagreb and v.v.

R – ADRIATICA – 🛏 1, 2 cl. and [12] Budapest - Rijeka and v.v.

V – VENEZIA EXPRESS – 🛏 1, 2 cl., ▬ 2 cl. and [12] Budapest - Zagreb - Venezia and v.v.; [12] Budapest - Nagykanizsa - Gyékényes and v.v.; 🛏 1, 2 cl. Moskva - Zagreb and v.v. Conveys on ③⑦ from Moskva, ③⑥ from Venezia: 🛏 1, 2 cl. Moskva - Zagreb - Venezia and v.v.

Table 893a SZOMBATHELY - PÉCS

1, 2 class

km		980	8817	9812	8914	9814	8916	8801	9513	896	9818
											2
0	**Szombathely** ... d.	0530	0635	0735	...	1141	...	...	1440	1737	1842
	Zalaegerszeg ... d.	|	|	*0835*	...	*1155*	...	...	|	*1805*	*1930*
49	Zalaszentiván ... d.	0619	|	0900	...	1259	...	...	|	1822	1955
102	**Nagykanizsa** ... d.	0708	|	0957	1040	1357	1510	...	|	1910	2100
131	Gyékényes ... d.	0738	|	▬	1123	▬	1606	...	|	|	...
	Celldömölk ... d.	|	0718	...	|	...	|	...	1558	|	...
	Tapolca ... d.	|	0820	...	|	...	|	1625	1714	|	...
	Keszthely ... d.	|	0853	...	|	...	|	1704	...	|	...
	Fonyód ... d.	|	0954	...	|	...	|	1807	...	|	...
	Kaposvár ... d.	0843	1058	...	|	...	|	1918	...	|	...
	Dombóvár alsó ... d.	0910	...	...	|	...	|	1948	...	|	...
186	Barcs ... d.	|	...	0900	1235	1545	1716	|	...	2049	...
216	Szigetvár ... d.	|	...	0940	1315	1625	1802	|	...	2120	...
250	**Pécs** ... a.	0957	...	1022	1355	1715	1848	2040	...	2150	...

	897	8917	8800	8915	8913	9811	8911	8816	981	8941
Pécs ... d.	0540	0705	0700	1030	1305	...	1540	...	1640	1905
Szigetvár ... d.	0612	0745	|	1116	1354	...	1625	...	|	2000
Barcs ... d.	0646	0823	|	1200	1436	...	1708	...	|	2040
Dombóvár alsó ... d.	|	|	0755	|	|	...	|	...	1738	...
Kaposvár ... d.	|	|	0832	|	|	...	|	1650	1805	...
Fonyód ... d.	|	|	0930	|	|	...	|	1810	|	...
Keszthely ... d.	|	|	1025	|	|	...	|	1900	|	...
Tapolca ... d.	|	|	1100	|	|	...	|	1932	|	...
Celldömölk ... d.	|	|	▬	|	|	...	|	2028	|	...
Gyékényes ... d.	0739	0927	...	1301	1543	...	1810	|	1920	...
Nagykanizsa ... d.	0811	1008	1452	1335	1620	1828	1845	|	1952	...
Zalaszentiván ... a.	0858	...	1600	...	...	1934	...	|	2040	...
Zalaegerszeg ... a.	*0913*	...	*1623*	...	...	|	...	|	*2052*	...
Szombathely ... a.	0943	...	1730	...	...	2050	...	2118	2125	...

Table 894 BUDAPEST - BAJA and PÉCS

1, 2 class except where shown

km			IC 200	200 810	8302	IC 800		812		IC 804	4114	8054	8204	8204	8086	IC 806		816	828	8008	8008	IC 808	251	
		2	A		🍷	🍷[R]	2	🍷		🍷[R]	2		🍷	🍷		🍷[R]	2		🍷[R]			E[R]	S	
0	**Budapest** Déli ... d.	...	0635	0635	0645	0730	...	1005	...	1130	1225	...	1330	1330	1430	1530	...	1630	1735	1755	1755	1930	...	...
4	Budapest Kelenföld ... d.	...	0645	0645	0654	|	...	1014	...	|	1234	...	1339	1339	1439	|	...	1639	1744	1804	1804	|	...	...
	Györ 890 ... d.	...	|	|	|	|	...	|	...	|	|	...	|	|	|	|	...	|	|	|	|	|	1728	...
	Komárom **890** ... d.	...	|	|	|	|	...	|	...	|	|	...	|	|	|	|	...	|	|	|	|	|	1758	...
	Székesfehérvár ... d.	0640	|	|	|	|	1015	|	...	|	|	...	|	|	|	|	1645	|	|	|	|	|	1932	...
84	Sárbogárd ... d.	0744	0755	0755	0823	|	1110	1122	...	|	1351	1400	1451	1502	1617	|	1740	1749	1848	1912	1941	|	2038	...
149	Szekszárd ... a.	▬	|	|	0944	|	...	|	...	|	...	|	|	1623	|	|	...	|	|	|	2108	|	|	...
188	**Baja** ... a.	...	|	|	1035	|	...	|	...	|	...	|	|	1712	|	|	...	|	|	|	2158	|	|	...
164	Dombóvar ... a.	2	0846	0846	...	|	...	1229	...	|	...	1544	1559	...	1750	|	...	1849	1955	2022	...	|	2144	...
164	Dombóvar ... d.	0638	0849	0857	...	|	...	1231	1233	|	...	1609	1601	...	...	|	...	1853	1957	2028	...	|	2146	2145
195	Kaposvár ... a.	0722	0919	|	...	|	...	|	1315	|	...	|	1629	...	...	|	...	|	2024	|	...	|	|	2230
265	Gyékényes ... a.	0900	1025	|	...	|	...	|	1535	|	...	|	1735	...	...	|	...	|	2135	|	...	|	|	0015
228	**Pécs** ... a.	...	...	0945	...	1005	...	1320	...	1405	...	1735	...	...	...	1805	...	1945	...	2120	...	2205	2237	...

	8219	250	IC 809	827	8007	8307	8017	IC 805		815	8203	8303		IC 803	813		8011	8051	IC 801	8301	811 201	IC 201		14801
	2	S	🍷[R]	🍷[R]	🍷	🍷		🍷[R]	2	🍷	🍷	🍷	2	🍷[R]		2			E[R]	🍷		A	2	Ⓐ
Pécs ... d.	...	0500	0610	...	0615	...	...	1010	...	1055	...	...	...	1410	1425	...	1435	1625	1810	...	1835	...	...	1855
Gyékényes ... d.	0325	|	|	0525	|	...	...	|	...	|	1130	...	...	|	|	...	|	|	|	...	|	1750	...	|
Kaposvár ... d.	0504	|	|	0636	|	...	...	|	1102	|	1320	...	...	|	|	1445	|	|	|	...	|	1901	...	|
Dombóvar ... a.	0546	0550	|	0702	0708	...	...	|	1142	1143	1348	...	...	|	1513	1530	1546	1748	|	...	1923	1926	...	1949
Dombóvar ... d.	...	0552	|	0706	0709	...	0720	|	▬	1145	1350	...	...	|	1515	▬	1610	1815	|	...	1937	1937	...	2030
Baja ... d.	...	|	|	|	|	0535	|	|	...	|	|	1230	...	|	|	...	|	|	|	1730	|	|	...	|
Szekszárd ... d.	...	|	|	|	|	0625	|	|	2	|	|	1318	...	|	|	2	|	|	|	1816	|	|	...	|
Sárbogárd ... d.	...	0701	|	|	0818	0818	0911	|	0910	1301	1457	1457	1503	|	1617	1652	1750	2000	|	1948	2036	2036	2040	2214
Székesfehérvár ... a.	...	0745	|	|	|	|	|	|	1005	|	|	|	1558	|	|	1755	|	...	|	|	|	|	2135	|
Komárom **890** ... a.	...	0905	|	|	|	|	|	|	...	|	|	|	...	|	|	...	|	...	|	|	|	|	...	|
Györ 890 ... a.	...	0939	|	|	|	|	|	|	...	|	|	|	...	|	|	...	|	...	|	|	|	|	...	|
Budapest Kelenföld ... a.	...	...	|	0853	0923	0923	1039	|	...	1404	1604	1604	...	|	1724	...	1919	...	|	2050	2134	2134	...	2317
Budapest Déli ... a.	...	...	0843	0903	0933	0933	1048	1243	...	1413	1613	1613	...	1643	1733	...	1928	...	2043	2058	2143	2143	...	2333k

A – AGRAM – [12] Budapest - Zagreb - Rijeka and v.v.

E – ⑤⑦ (daily May 29 - Aug. 28).

S – SOPIANAE – [12] Bratislava - Györ - Pécs and v.v.

k – Budapest **Keleti**.

Table 895 — BUDAPEST - SZEGED

1, 2 class except where shown

km		14700	7020	IC 700	710	572	17802	IC 702 ©	712			IC 704	714	716	IC 706	718	1578 ⑦	7808	578 ※	7008	489 P
		2	2						2	2	2					2					
0	Budapest Nyugati d.	0120	0350	0700	0705	...	1030	...	1100			1400	1425	1625	1730	1825	...	...	...	1925	
	Miskolc 899 d.				0535												1605	1700			
	Szolnok d.				0830												1903	1955		2315	
73	Cegléd d.	0215	0509	0802	0910	...		1200	1340			1518	1718			1919	1930	2030	2030		
106	Kecskemét d.	0252	0541	0813	0831	0941	1143	1227	1145	1513	1545	1749	1843			1948	1959	2110	2110	2359	
	Pécs d.					0555										1640					
	Baja d.					0843	0917									1923					
	Kiskunhalas d.					0957	1040	1125		1420						2035					
131	Kiskunfélegyháza d.	0325	0610		0850	1001	1040	1215	1247	1511	1514	1605	1810		1812	1905	2007	2016	2116	2136	2136	0019
191	Szeged a.	0418	0731	0910	0935	1054	1136	1240	1335		1634	1610	1705	1859	1940	2018	2050	2103	2226	2226	0100

		488 P	719	7807	IC 709	717	577	IC 707	7005	7025	IC 705	715	713	571	17801	IC 703	7001	1470	17001
								2	2								2②	2©
	Szeged d.	0340	0520		0620	0635	0635	0745	0950	1025	1150	1320	1340	1530	1530	1618	1650	1810	1935	2021
	Kiskunfélegyháza d.	0425	0606	0610		0724	0724	0910	1010	1111	1307	1315	1422	1622	1622	1625	1730	1901	2036	2132
	Kiskunhalas d.			0700					1105		1405					1717	1815	1820	
	Baja d.			0814					1226							1925	1942	
	Pécs d.			1050												2200	
	Kecskemét d.	0445	0625		0718	0744	0744	1048	1129	1333		1418	1446	1642	1642		1748	1921	2109	2153
	Cegléd d.		0655			0831	0831	1200	1406			1522	1712	1720			1951	2147	2221
	Szolnok a.	0528				0855							1741	
	Miskolc 899 a.					1142							2033	
	Budapest Nyugati a.		0748		0830	0926		1200	1256			1530	1618	1805			1900	2046	2245	2316

P – PUSKIN – 🛏 1, 2 cl. Beograd - Moskva and v.v.; ▭ Beograd - Záhony and v.v.
Conveys 🛏 1, 2 cl. Athínai/Thessaloníki - Moskva and v.v. on dates in Table 94c.

Table 896 — BUDAPEST and SZEGED - BÉKÉSCSABA - GYULA

1, 2 class except where shown

km		7702	7320	742	7712	7212	375	7714	7324	744	7716	1734	373	7706	738	7718	7206	353	381	347
				2	2	2	R	2		2		⑤	R	2				R[R]	K	K
0	Budapest Keleti d.	...	...	0620	...	...	0855	...	...	1200	...	1400	1515	...	1715	...	...	1925	...	2315
0	Budapest Nyugati 898 d.															1705				
73	Cegléd d.															1806				
100	Szolnok 898 d.			0632	0740	0745	1005	1020	1132	1325	1350	1525	1638	1643	1842	1845	2050	2150	0040
174	Szentes a.			0930		1145				1540			1832	1958				
141	Mezőtúr d.			0724	0815		1049		1212	1354		1554	1707	1912		2119	2221	
159	Gyoma d.			0745	0829		1102		1232	1408		1608	1720	1926		2132	2236	
	Szeged d.		0625			0820		1105			1440			1625	1905			
	Hódmezővásárhely d.		0701			0918	1236	1146			1517			1703	1959	2039		
	Orosháza d.		0739			1005		1222			1605			1737	2035			
196	Békéscsaba a.		0815	0827		0904	1045	1135	1311	1443		1644	1644	1754	1815	2000	2120	2206	2309	0148
196	Békéscsaba d.		0835			0924	1050		1345	1448	1555	1705	1705		1835	2010		2240	
212	Gyula a.		0852			0940	1110		1405	1512	1615	1725	1725		1854	2028		2259	

		346	737	380	352	7207	7707	7327	7727	7717	7715	372	743	7723	7303	7713	7323	374	7701	1473
		R		K	R				2			R						R		2②
	Gyula d.		0520		0621				0725		0941		1235		1453		1619	1730	1815	
	Békéscsaba a.		0540		0641				1000				1250		1510		1638	1749	1830	
	Békéscsaba d.	0156	0550	0607	0647		0655	0720	0750	0920	1100	1108	1313	1415	1450	1515	1650	1755	1820	1850	1930
	Orosháza d.						0736		0833	1006	1148		1507		1612			1859	
	Hódmezővásárhely d.					0555	0807		0918	1041	1230		1541		1705			1930	
	Szeged a.					0845			1005	1128	1310		1617		1750			2008	
	Gyoma d.		0625	0641	0720				0803			1151		1349		1531	1736	1828	1931	2023
	Mezőtúr d.		0640	0655	0737				0823			1205		1407		1548	1752	1840	1946	2042
	Szentes d.					0650				0815			1230		1430		1628		
	Szolnok 898 d.	0314	0713	0723	0810	0820		0900	0952			1237	1418	1438	1610	1629	1800	1838	1913	2018	2115
	Cegléd d.					0842											1937		
	Budapest Nyugati 898 a.					0937													
	Budapest Keleti a.	0502	0837		0932							1407		1602		1757			2037	2142

K – KARPATY – ▭ Warszawa - București and v.v.; 🛏 1, 2 cl. and ◼ 2 cl. Košice - București and v.v.
R – International train to/from Romania – for composition see Table 950.

Table 897 — BUDAPEST - SALGÓTARJÁN - LUČENEC

1, 2 class except where shown

km		5810	5822	392	5814	5824	394	394	5826	390	5838
		2	2		2	2	U	2	2	B	2
0	Budapest Keleti d.			0730			1520	1520		1920	
67	Hatvan 899 d.	0400	0712	0848	1150	1340	1627	1627	1829	2022	2200
126	Salgótarján d.	0541	0851	1006	1331	1517	1753	1753	2008	2129	2333
132	Somoskőújfalu 🏠 d.	0556		1022	1345		1810	1810	2140		
132	Somoskőújfalu 🏠 d.	0653		1045	1400		1830	1830	2156		
145	Filakovo 887 d.	0713		1104	1420		1846	1846	2212		
161	Lučenec 887 a.	0736		1133			1905		2226		
	Košice 887 a.						2145				

		391	5807	5817	395	395	5837	5825	393	5831	5811
		B	2	2	U	U	2	2	2	2	2
	Košice 887 d.				0528						
	Lučenec 887 d.	0142			0802				1430		1911
	Filakovo 887 d.	0158	0610	0837	0837				1459		1946
	Somoskőújfalu 🏠 d.	0216	0630	0855	0855				1521		2007
	Somoskőújfalu 🏠 d.	0250	0645	0910	0910				1606		2030
	Salgótarján d.	0303	0625	0658	0924	0924	1010	1235	1618	1818	2046
	Hatvan 899 d.	0426	0809	0844	1045	1045	1149	1426	1752	1954	2226
	Budapest Keleti a.	0522	0907		1137	1137			1847		

B – BEM – 🛏 1, 2 cl. and ▭ Budapest - Wroclaw and v.v. (Budapest - Szczecin and v.v. May 29 - Sept. 24).
U – URPÍN – ▭ and ※ Budapest - Košice and v.v.; ▭ Budapest - Banská Bystrica and v.v.

Table 897a — DEBRECEN - MÁTÉSZALKA/BAIA MARE

1, 2 class except where shown

km		6322	632	6824	6324	1634	6326	427	636	6328
				2		⑤				
	Budapest Nyugati 898 d.	...	...	...	...	1230	...	1405	1500	...
0	Debrecen d.	0720	1120	1444	1435	1547	1640	1710	1805	1938
30	Nyírábrány d.			1539				1808		
39	Valea lui Mihai 🏠 § d.			1651				2027		
70	Carei § d.			1749				2053		
106	Satu Mare 950 § a.			1842				2127		
165	Baia Mare 950 § a.							2235		
58	Nyírbátor a.	0831	1228		1546	1642	1751		1854	2047
78	Mátészalka a.	0854	1256		1612	1704	1819		1914	2110

		426	637	6337	6325	6825	6323	1631	6821	6321	6331
						2		⑦	2		
	Mátészalka d.	...	0445	0730	1110		1415	1653		1727	1933
	Nyírbátor d.	...	0505	0754	1138		1436	1714		1757	1955
	Baia Mare 950 § d.	0043							1427		
	Satu Mare 950 § d.	0148				0751			1555		
	Carei § d.	0220				0845			1645		
	Valea lui Mihai 🏠 § d.	0445				1220			1800		
	Nyírábrány d.	0427				1215			1800		
	Debrecen d.	0500	0600	0910	1245	1543	1543	1811	1840	1908	2103
	Budapest Nyugati 898 a.	0851	0914				2131				

§ – Romanian time.

①②....⑦ – Monday, Tuesday.... Sunday   Ⓐ – Mondays to Fridays, except holidays

Table 898   BUDAPEST - DEBRECEN - NYÍREGYHÁZA - CHOP

1, 2 class

km		488 P	360 620 ♀	360 R	IC 600 ♀℞	6102	IC 602 ♀✕	6104	302 R℞	IC 604 R℞	6106	427 B	366 636	IC 366 R	606 ♀℞	616	16 T	668 ℞	406 R℞ A	6008	343	618	IC 1608 ⑦℞	6000
0	Budapest Nyugati............d.		0605	0605	0720	0800	1020	1105	1200	1320	1300	1405	1500	1500	1620	1600	1610k	1700	1700	1800	1845k	1900	1920	2100
73	Cegléd.......................d.		0702	0702		0902		1206	1257		1359	1502	1557	1557		1657		1754	1754	1905		1957		2204
100	Szolnok......................d.	0533	0720	0720		0926		1231	1318		1429	1523	1618	1618		1729	1745	1815	1815	1931	2017	2018		2229
162	Karcag.......................d.		0808	0808		1017		1322	1407		1520	1609	1703	1703		1822	1828	1856	1856	2023	2057	2104		2321
177	Püspökladány.................d.		0824	0834		1030		1335	1425		1533	1622	1720	1731		1835	1840	1911	1930	2042	2108	2117		2333
228	Biharkeresztes 950 ....a.			0925				1517					1818					2015						
201	Hajdúszoboszló...............a.		0842		0928	1049	1228	1354		1528	1552	1640	1739		1828	1854	1857	1928		2101	2124	2136	2128	2352
221	Debrecen.....................a.	0653	0856		0941	1105	1241	1410		1541	1608	1655	1754		1841	1911	1911	1942		2117	2137	2159	2141	0009
221	Debrecen.....................d.	0656	0859		0944	1109	1244	1414		1544	1610			1844		1915	1944			2140		2144		
270	Nyíregyháza..................d.	0728	0933		1015	1155	1315	1500		1615	1648			1915		1949	2019			2211		2215		
313	Kisvárda.....................a.		1005													2021				2239				
335	Záhony ▣....................a.	0818	1033													2042				2300				
341	Chop ▣.......................a.	1010	1300													2240								
607	Lviv 925 ....a.	1734														0620								
1243	Kyïv (Kiev) 925 ....a.	0433														1755								
2106	Moskva 924 ....a.	2141														1121								

		405 R	426 B	637	342 A	IC 609 ♀℞	617	367 R	367	6237 15 T	655 ♀	IC 607 ♀℞	6105	IC 605 ♀℞	615 ♀	613 ♀	IC 603 ♀℞	361 R	IC 361 ♀	1601 ⑦℞	301 R	661 IC 301 ✕	1611 2⑦	9 489 P
	Moskva 924 ....d.									2032														0956
	Kyïv (Kiev) 925 ....d.									1205														0023
	Lviv 925 ....d.									0002														1202
	Chop ▣.......................d.									0725								1455						1920
	Záhony ▣....................d.				0525					0550 0725								1525						1935
	Kisvárda....................d.				0547					0621 0750								1545						
	Nyíregyháza..................d.		0430		0614	0625	0617			0710 0823	0845	0925	1035	1225	1235	1435	1525		1617	1825		1825	1905	2045
	Debrecen.....................a.		0516		0700	0711	0700			0755 0900	0929	0955	1117	1255	1317	1518	1555		1649	1855		1907	1943	2124
	Debrecen.....................d.		0556	0617	0646	0658	0703			0803 0903	0934	0958	1120	1258	1321	1521	1558		1652	1858		1911	1947	2130
	Hajdúszoboszló...............d.		0611	0633	0700	0713	0717			0820 0918	0949	1013	1136	1313	1336	1535	1613		1707	1913		1926	2004	
	Biharkeresztes 950 ....d.	0325							0743									1557			1830			
	Püspökladány.................d.	0447	0628	0652	0715		0734	0855	0936	1007		1154		1353	1552		1733	1733		1958	1958	2023	
	Karcag......................d.		0640	0703	0726		0746	0907	0907	0948	1019		1205		1405	1604		1745	1745		2010	2010	2035	
	Szolnok......................d.	0552	0728	0752	0805		0836	1005	1005	1035	1115		1254		1452	1654		1832	1832		2059	2059	2123	2257
	Cegléd.......................d.	0623	0751	0814			0859	1030	1030		1138		1318		1515	1717		1855	1855		2122	2122	2147	
	Budapest Nyugati............a.	0730	0851	0914	0927k	0920	0952	1132	1132	1204p	1237	1220	1419	1520	1613	1810	1820	1953	1953	2120	2220	2220	2244

A – ARRABONA – ▣, and ✕ Wien - Budapest - Záhony and v.v.
B – To/from Baia Mare (Table 897a).
P – PUSKIN – ◢ 1, 2 cl. Beograd - Moskva and v.v.; ▣ Beograd - Záhony and v.v.;
     conveys ◢ 1, 2 cl. Athínai/Thessaloníki - Moskva and v.v. on dates in Table 94c.
R – International train to/from Romania – for composition see Table 950.

T – TISZA EXPRESS – ◢ 1, 2 cl. Budapest - Moskva and v.v.; ◢ 2 cl. Budapest -
     Sankt Peterburg and v.v.; ◢ 2 cl. Moskva - Zagreb and v.v.; ▣ Budapest -
     Chop and v.v.; conveys ◢ 1, 2 cl. Moskva - Venezia and v.v. on dates in Table 94c.
k – Budapest Keleti.

Table 899   BUDAPEST - MISKOLC - KOŠICE

1, 2 class

km		5310 2	312 R	IC 500 ♀℞	552	380 K	577	IC 502 ♀℞	5202	514	514 554	IC 504 ✕℞	5314 2	1514 ♀	5004	516	IC 506 ♀℞	596	318	571 S	5506 ⑦℞	IC 1508 C℞	310 K	203 V
0	Budapest Keleti..............d.		0605	0700	0730			1000	1020	1215	1215	1300		1330	1405	1505	1600	1605	1705		1805	1900	1905	2005
	Szolnok......................d.					0727	0904												1751					
	Jászberény...................d.					0811	0949												1837					
67	Hatvan.......................d.		0659		0834	0850	1016	1113	1309	1309				1430	1508	1554		1700	1755	1907	1910		1959	2059
126	Füzesabony...................d.		0741		0917	0933	1100	1158	1356	1406				1519	1606	1635		1740	1837	1948	2015		2043	2139
143	Eger.........................d.					0935			1223		1423			1538				1804	1903		2033			2214
139	Mezőkövesd...................d.		0750			0943	1109	1210	1406					1529	1618	1645		1750	1847	1958			2053	2149
183	Miskolc......................a.		0822	0852		1015	1142	1152	1255	1437		1452		1604	1700	1719	1752	1821	1918	2033		2052	2125	2220
183	Miskolc......................d.	0639	0835		1033							1458											2140	
244	Hidasnémeti ▣................a.	0801	0935		1125							1615											2238	
244	Hidasnémeti ▣ ‡.............d.	0835	0950		1155							1655											2306	
270	Košice.......................a.	0915	1032		1237							1740											2347	

		519	572 S	311 C	IC 509 ♀℞	557	319	202 V	5317 2	IC 507 ♀		595 ♀	IC 505 ♀℞	555 513 ♀	513	5003 2	5313 ℞	IC 503 ♀℞	551	1578 ⑦S	313 ℞	IC 1501 ⑦℞	381 K	317 ♀	14501 2④
	Košice.......................d.			0423					0723					1328						1523		1653			
	Hidasnémeti ▣ ‡.............a.			0500					0805					1410						1600		1730			
	Hidasnémeti ▣................d.			0520					0820					1425						1616		1750			
	Miskolc......................a.			0618					0945					1545						1715		1845			
	Miskolc......................d.	0410	0535	0630	0700		0705	0730	1000			1055	1300		1320	1430		1600		1605	1730	1900	1905	1930	2030
	Mezőkövesd...................d.	0442	0610	0702			0739	0802				1127			1352	1511				1637	1802		1935	2002	
	Eger.........................d.				0658					1011			1337			1450			1640		1920				
	Füzesabony...................d.	0452	0620	0712		0715	0748	0812		1030		1137		1412	1412	1523			1658	1655	1812		1945	2012	2124
	Hatvan.......................d.	0535	0703	0749		0809	0830	0855		1220			1455	1455	1618				1752	1738	1855		2032	2055	2220
	Jászberény...................d.		0731																	1805			2101		
	Szolnok......................d.		0820																	1850			2146		
	Budapest Keleti..............a.	0632		0842	0852	0907	0922	0952		1152		1312	1452	1547	1547	1717		1752	1802	1847	1952	2052		2152	2312

C – CRACOVIA – ◢ 1, 2 cl., ◢ 2 cl., ▣ and ✕ Budapest - Kraków and v.v.
K – KARPATY – ▣ Bucureşti - Warszawa and v.v.; ◢ 1, 2 cl. and ◢ 2 cl. Košice -
     Bucureşti and v.v.
R – RÁKOCZI – ▣ and ♀ Budapest - Košice (- Poprad Tatry on dates in Table 885) and v.v.

S – ▣ Miskolc - Szeged and v.v.
V – AVAS – ▣ Zagreb/Keszthely - Budapest - Miskolc - Nyíregyháza and v.v.
‡ – Ticket point is Čaňa.

Table 899a   MISKOLC - SLOVENSKÉ NOVÉ MESTO and NYÍREGYHÁZA

1, 2 class

km		655	316	5122 2	5224 2	5134 2	5624 2	5136 2	318	203			319 ♀	202 V	5607 2	5215 2	5213 2	5125 2	5121 2	317 ♀	5621 2
0	Budapest Keleti 899 ....d.		0605						1705	2005		Nyíregyháza 898 ....d.		0600	0800			1130	1700		1920
183	Miskolc......................d.	0720	0826	0900	1200	1400	1503	1730	1922	2230		Tokaj.........................d.		0628	0832			1207	1733		1959
221	Szerencs.....................d.	0747	0900	0938	1247	1440	1543	1808	2000	2255		Slovenské Nové Mesto ...a.	0521							1725	
257	Sárospatak...................a.		0940		1335							Sátoraljaújhely ....a.	0531			0758	1055			1752	
267	Sátoraljaújhely ▣...........a.		0951		1346				2052			Sárospatak ....a.	0543			0810	1108			1806	
269	Slovenské Nové Mesto ...a.		1009						2119			Szerencs......................a.	0632	0647	0848	0910	1201	1228	1758	1859	2025
239	Tokaj........................d.	0802		0958		1500	1603	1827		2312		Miskolc......................a.	0701	0716	0923	0950	1244	1309	1840	1926	2107
272	Nyíregyháza 898 ....a.	0829		1033		1536	1640	1900		2340		Budapest Keleti 899 ......a.	0922	0952						2152	

V – AVAS – ▣ Zagreb/Keszthely - Budapest - Miskolc - Nyíregyháza and v.v.

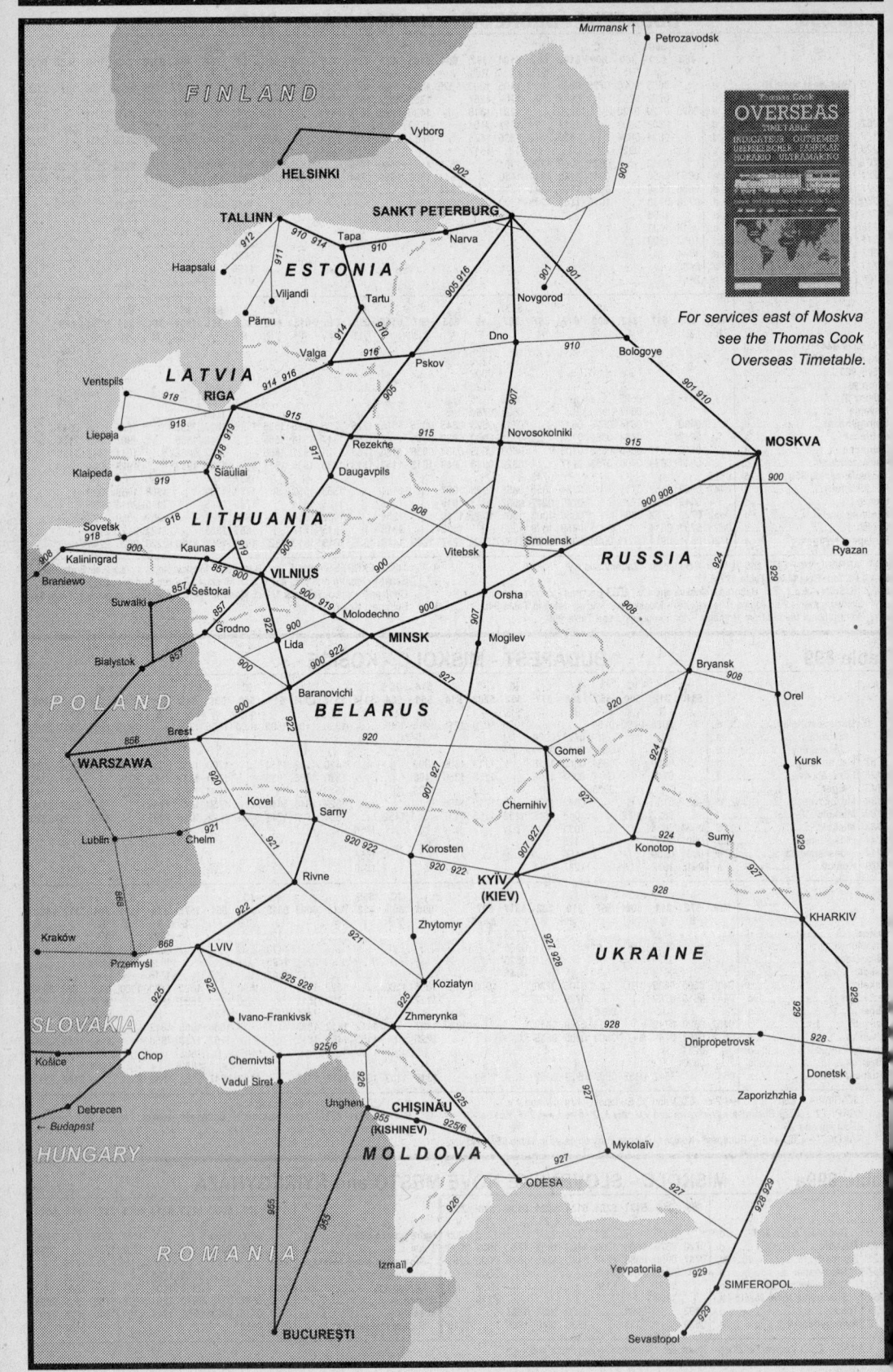

For services east of Moskva
see the Thomas Cook
Overseas Timetable.

RUSSIA, BELARUS and LITHUANIA

Operator: Русский Железный Дороги – Russki Zhelezny Dorogi (РЖД – RŽD), Беларуская Чыгунка – Belaruskaya Chygunka (БЧ – BČ), Lietuvos Geležinkeliai (LG).

Services: **International Services** (to points outside the former Soviet Union): The through sleeping cars to points in Western and Central Europe, Scandinavia and Greece are of Western European ("RIC") type, with single and double compartments in first class, and 3- or 4-berth compartments in second class, all with full bedding. Composition of international services is shown in the tables. Most railways of the former Soviet Union are of broad gauge (1520mm), and on through services to other European countries, the bogies are changed at the frontier. For services east of Moskva, see the **Thomas Cook Overseas Timetable**.
Internal Services (within the former Soviet Union): Two classes of accommodation are provided: **Soft class**, (shown as 🛏 2 cl.) with fully upholstered seats in large 4-berth couchette type compartments with bedding supplied; **Hard class** (shown as 'H' or ⊟) consists of bunks with plastic or leather seats in open non-compartment type coaches, bedding is available at an extra charge. Trains convey Soft (🛏 2 cl.) and Hard (⊟) Classes of accommodation **unless stated otherwise** in table footnotes, or by 🛏 in the train column heading which denotes the train conveys Soft class sleeping cars only. Some services also convey hard class cars with seated accommodation for daytime journeys. The most prestigious express trains also convey International style sleeping cars with 2-berth compartments (shown as 🛏 1 cl. in the tables). Trains running only **by day** are one class (hard) only. The * symbol denotes details of train composition are not available.

Timings: Valid **May 29, 1994 to May 27, 1995**. All timings are shown in local time (Moskva time is one hour ahead of Belarus, the Baltic States and the Ukraine). Due to the economic situation trains are liable to cancellation.

Tickets: Prior reservation is necessary, except for purely local trains.

Table 900 — MOSKVA - MINSK - BREST and VILNIUS - KALININGRAD

Note Ⓡ applies to all services — RŽD, BČ, LG — 🛏 2 cl. and ⊟ except where shown

km		69	125	35	211	103	193	25	13	29	27	57	77	9	79	103	5	73	49	21
		1248	125	11110		103			246			11114		9					240	21
		④⑥A		✕	✕	✕	✕		✕	✕	H✕		✕	✕	✕			✕	✕	✕
				h	B	d	W		M			S		R					L*	P
	Ryazan II .... d.	2336																		
0	**Moskva Smolenskaya ‡ 907/8** d.		0901	0908			0936	1047	1309	1323	1421	1438	1517				1800	1717	1745	1901
419	Smolensk Moskovski ⊙ 907/8 d.	1236	1550	1601			1829	1819	2027	2048	2145	2225	2124				2316	0035	0111	0218
	Sankt Peterburg Vit. 907 . d.													1210v	1520v	1510				
538	Orsha Centralnaya 907 ...... d.	1409	1703	1724			1956	1939	2143	2209	2300	2350	2218				0153	0229	0316	0331
750	Minsk .... a.	1655	1943	2006			2310	2250	0029	0104	0136	0235	0044 b				0431	0513	0603	0611
750	**Minsk 919** .... d.	1705	1953	2021	2036	2145	2339		0044	0119	0146	0250	0054				0446	0523	0618	0624
828	Molodechno 919 .... d.			2200	2210		0100			0241		0352	0412				0608			
944	**Vilnius ▣ 919** .... a.			0113			0410			0530			0617				0924			
944	**Vilnius** .... d.			0133			0425			0548			0632							
956	Lida .... d.			0040								0611	0633							
1101	Grodno .... d.			0310								0815	0859							
1048	Kaunas .... d.			0318				0607		0731			0820							
1289	**Kaliningrad ⊙** .... d.			0852				1220		1257			1423							
898	Baranovichi Centralni ... d.	1913		2150					0304	2344	0342							0722	0822	0839
1100	**Brest** .... d.	2129		0005					0530	0201	0620			0440				1002	1118	1050
1321	Warszawa Centralna 858 . a.	0238g		0532g					1045	0727		1501g		0847						1632

		1	87	15	23	3	149	51				104	247	11109	1249		11113
				240								104	14	36	70	614	58	52
			♀			H✕	✕					W	M	B	②⑦A	*	✕	S
				O													
Ryazan II .... d.									Warszawa Centralna 858 ... d.	1942	2017		0050g		0043g	
Moskva Smolenskaya ‡ 907/8 d.	1915	1936	2015	2038	2132		2207		Brest .... a.	0255	0405		0720			
Smolensk Moskovski ⊙ 907/8 d.	0230	0300	0326	0412	0500		0535		Baranovichi Centralni .... a.	0516	0632		0942			
Sankt Peterburg Vit. 907 .... d.						1842			**Kaliningrad ⊙** .... d.							
Orsha Centralnaya 907 ...... d.	0353	0413	0447	0536	0624	0656	0808		Kaunas .... d.							
Minsk .... a.	0642	0702	0726	0835	0940	1007	1101		Grodno .... d.					0051		1146
Minsk 919 .... d.		0718	0739	0850		1026			Lida .... d.					0319		1356
Molodechno 919 .... d.			0855	1020		1204			Vilnius .... a.							
Vilnius ▣ 919 .... a.			1213	1341		1452			**Vilnius ▣ 919** .... d.					0701		
Vilnius .... d.				1408		1512			Molodechno 919 .... d.					0601		1626
Lida .... d.				1548		1651			**Minsk 919** .... a.	0723	0830	0734	1141	1236		1502
Grodno .... d.						2255			Minsk .... d.		0842	0754	1151			1837
Kaunas .... d.									Orsha Centralnaya 907 .... a.		1157	1147	1519			
Kaliningrad ⊙ .... d.									Sankt Peterburg Vitebski 907 .. a.					0915v		0955
Baranovichi Centralni ... d.		0938							Smolensk Moskovski ⊙ 907/8 .. a.		1500	1450	1822			
Brest .... d.		1153							**Moskva Smolenskaya ‡ 907/8** a.		2210		2200			
Warszawa Centralna 858 . a.		1917							Ryazan II .... a.				0657			

		664	194	104	26	50	2	6	22	4	28	78	74	241	241	88	80	10	212	126	24	150
									22					16/62				10		126		
			✕				✕	✕	✕	H✕	H✕	✕	✕	✕	②⑥	♀	✕		✕	✕	♀	✕
									P					O		K		R	d	h		
Warszawa Centralna 858 ... d.									0902					1022	1022			1454		1430g		
Brest .... a.					1250		1630		1600			1715	1810	1810				2053		2150		
Baranovichi Centralni ..... a.					1542		1853		1917			2005	2033	2033						0013		
Kaliningrad ⊙ .... d.			0050				0830									1135	1240				1520	
Kaunas .... d.		0651	0710				1341									1726	1847			1950	2101	
Grodno .... d.											1348											
Lida .... d.											1646											
Vilnius .... a.		0844	0855				1526									1904	2025		2137	2241		
Vilnius ▣ 919 .... d.		0922					1424	1541				1932				1924	2045		2149	2301		
Molodechno 919 .... d.		1251					1737	1815									2346		0104			
Minsk 919 .... a.		1421				1745	1913	1952	2047	2105	2046	2212	2227	2227	2308		0041	0117	0212	0223	0300	
Minsk .... d.		1436	1555			1801	1920	2007	2100	2128	2115	2122	2257	2253	2324		0051	0222	0237	0315		
Orsha Centralnaya 907 ... d.		1844	1950			2117	2231	2241	2339	0009	0027	0028	0043	0137	0145	0208	0236	0328	0535	0550	0710	
Sankt Peterburg Vit. 907 .. a.							1145									1233v						
Smolensk Moskovski ⊙ 907/8 a.		2217	2247	2258		0152	0202	0243	0313	0330	0353	0346	0440	0448		0540		0554	0838	0853	1030	
Moskva Smolenskaya ‡ 907/8 a.		0547	0627	0605		0906	0925	0956	1025	1052	1120	1103	1154	1206		1303		1217	1602	1607	1826	
Ryazan II .... a.																						

A— The most outlandish train in Europe – Runs ①⑥ from Berlin, ④⑥ from Saratov (and Ryazan): 🛏 2 cl. Berlin - Ryazan - Saratov and v.v.; conveys 🛏 2 cl. Berlin - Voronezh, Rostov-na-Donu, and Tselinograd (Kazakhstan) and v.v. *For timings beyond Ryazan see the Thomas Cook Overseas Timetable.*
B— 🛏 2 cl. and ♀ Moskva - Bialystok and v.v.; 🛏 2 cl., ⊟ and ✕ Moskva - Grodno and v.v.
H— Conveys ⊟, no first/soft class.
K— Runs ①⑤ (also ③ June 1 - Sept. 21) from Brussels: 🛏 1, 2 cl. Brussels - Orsha - Sankt Peterburg.
L— Runs daily; conveys on ③⑥ (also ① May 30 - Sept. 19) from Sankt Peterburg: 🛏 1, 2 cl. Sankt Peterburg - Brest - Warszawa - Brussels.
M— MOSKWA EXPRESS – 🛏 1, 2 cl. Moskva - Berlin and v.v.; 🛏 1, 2 cl. Moskva - Warszawa Wschodnia (trains 450/1) - Frankfurt (Main) and v.v.
O— OST-WEST EXPRESS – 🛏 1, 2 cl. Moskva - Warszawa - Brussels and v.v.; 🛏 1, 2 cl. Moskva - Warszawa (trains 204/3) - Wien and v.v.; 🛏 ✕ Moskva - Brest and v.v.
P— 🛏 1, 2 cl. Moskva - Praha and v.v.
R— POLONEZ – 🛏 1, 2 cl. Moskva - Warszawa and v.v.
S— 🛏 2 cl. Sankt Peterburg - Warszawa and v.v.; 🛏 1, 2 cl. Sankt Peterburg - Bialystok - Gdynia and v.v.; 🛏 2 cl. and ✕ Sankt Peterburg - Grodno and v.v.
L— LIETUVA – 🛏 1, 2 cl. and ✕ Moskva - Vilnius and v.v.

W— 🛏 2 cl. Minsk - Warszawa and v.v.
b— To/from Sankt Peterburg, via Pskov (Table 905).
d— To/from Kharkhiv (Table 927).
g— Warszawa Gdanska.
h— Runs May 29 - Sept. 24 (Sept. 23 from Moskva) only: 🛏 2 cl. Moskva - Warszawa and v.v.
v— Sankt Peterburg Varshavski.
‡— Formerly Moskva Byelorusski station.
◐— 🚋 is at Kybartai/Nesterov.
◑— 🚋 is at Gudogay/Kena.
◒— 🚋 is at Krasnoye/Osinovka.
*— Details of train composition not available.

🛏 – Sleeping car   ⊟ – Hard class car (former USSR only)   ①-⑦ – Monday - Sunday

Table 901

MOSKVA - SANKT PETERBURG
The Oktober Railway

RŽD

km		16 ✕	20	10	112	30	666 •		158 ER200 ⑤	48 H✕	162 •	24 H Y	8 L	160 H✕ A	32 ✕	18 H	14 H A	28 H	42	26	6 T	2 K	4
0	Moskva Oktyabrskaya ¶ .... d.	0035	0105	0113	0120	0156	...		1221	1226	...	1328	...	1718	1817	1822	2035	2200	2210	2300	2310	2355	2359
167	Tver........................... d.	0235		0328			...		1421	...	1537	1812	1850	2037	2044	2245	2355	0009	0103			0202
331	Bologoye...................... d.	0430	0505	0515	0520	0611	...		1620	...	1745	2000	2013	2242	2254	0051	0148	0210	0302	0310	0344	0352
331	Bologoye...................... d.	0440	0515	0525	0530	0621	...		1630	...	1800	2010	2023	2252	2304	0101	0158	0220	0312	0320	0354	0402
	Novgorod...................... d.						0705			1750									0734			...
650	Sankt Peterburg Glavny ‡ .... a.		0916	0920		1030	1105		1720	2015	2035	2236	2348	2319		0902	0515	0548	...	0710	0735	0825	0829
	Helsinki 495 .... a.															0902							...
	Petrozavodsk 903 .... a.	1637		1707											1058							...
	Murmansk 903 .... a.	1442		1540																		...

		15 ✕	31 ✕	17 H A	13	111		161 •	47 H✕	157 ER200 ④	23 H Y	159 H✕ A	7 L	665 •	29	42 H	27	19	9	25	5 T	1 K	3
	Murmansk 903 .... d.	1925				2020																...
	Petrozavodsk 903 .... d.	1746		1912		1859																...
	Helsinki 495 .... d.		1708																			...
	Sankt Peterburg Glavny ‡ .... d.				0035				0655	0830	1215	1305	1550	1720	1755	2020		2155	2230	2245	2310	2333	2355	2359
	Novgorod...................... d.							0935							2205		2040							...
	Bologoye...................... a.	0405	0507	0549	0451	0644			1234		1651	1845	2124			0053	0143	0153	0212	0244	0250	0325	0345	0350
	Bologoye...................... a.	0415	0517	0559	0501	0657			1244		1701	1855	2134			0113	0153	0203	0222	0257	0302	0335	0355	0400
	Tver........................... a.	0622	0702	0817	0801	0907			1440		1918	2021	2317			0301	0357	0402	0414		0500		0602
	Moskva Oktyabrskaya ¶ ...... a.	0850	0910	1025	1057	1117			1658	1714	2209	2150				0456	0556	0622	0635	0710	0719	0743	0825	0830

A – AVRORA.
H – Conveys ⛌ , no first/soft class.
K – KRASNAYA STRELA (The Red Arrow).
L – NEVA – 🛏 1, 2 cl., ⛌ and ✕ Sankt Peterburg - Sevastopol and v.v.

T – INTURIST.
Y – YUNOST.

ER200 – High Speed ER200 train. Higher fare payable.
¶ – Formerly Moskva **Leningradski** station.
‡ – Formerly Sankt Peterburg **Moskovski** station.
∗ – Details of train composition not available.

Table 902

SANKT PETERBURG - HELSINKI

RŽD, VR

km		32 🛏 T✕	33 R R✕	35 R S✕					35 R S✕	33 R R✕	31 🛏 T✕
	Moskva Oktyabrskaya 901 d.	1817			...	Helsinki 495 .... d.		0630	1532	1708
0	Sankt Peterburg Finlandski d.		0805	1555	...	Kouvola..................... d.		0824	1742	1912
129	Vyborg....................... a.	0414	0941	1740	...	Vainikkala................... d.		0913	1848	2007
129	Vyborg 🏬.................... a.	0455	1016	1815	...	Vainikkala 🏬............... d.		0941	1920	2052
147	Luzhaika..................... d.	0516	1035	1834	...	Luzhaika.................... a.		1106	2046	2221
160	Vainikkala 🏬............... d.	0445	1000	1800	...	Vyborg 🏬.................. a.		1125	2105	2240
160	Vainikkala................... a.	0530	1050	1842	...	Vyborg....................... a.		1200	2135	2320
251	Kouvola...................... a.	0626	1146	1932	...	Sankt Peterburg Finlandski. a.		1355	2320	
443	Helsinki 495 .... a.	0902	1403	2134	...	Moskva Oktyabrskaya 901 a.				0910

R – REPIN – 🛏 and ✕. **S –** SIBELIUS – 🛏 and ✕. **T –** TOLSTOI – 🛏 1, 2 cl. and ✕.

Table 903

SANKT PETERBURG - MURMANSK
Details of train composition not available

RŽD

km		106 🍴	186 🍴	18 🍴	16 ✕	112 ✕	56 ✕	22 ✕	658 🍴			105 🍴	657 🍴	55 🍴	185 ✕	21 🍴	15 ✕	111 ✕	17 🍴
	Moskva Oktyabrskaya 901 d.			1822	0030	0114					Murmansk .... d.		0055	2354	0835	1930	2015		...
0	Sankt Peterburg Glavny ‡.. d.	0045	0058				1430	1730	2150		Kandalaksha .... d.		0633	0742	1418	0058	0201		...
121	Volkhovstroy I .... d.	0302	0322	0456	1024	1116b	1700	2003	0023		Belomorsk .... d.		1438	1749	2219	0903	1012		...
401	Petrozavodsk................. d.	0813	1003	1020	1543	1620	2248	0116	0708		Petrozavodsk .... d.	0040	2230	2310	0414	0610	1720	1823	1925
780	Belomorsk.................... d.		2041		2326	0027	0650	0850			Volkhovstroy I .... d.	0645	0615	0420	1205	1101	2209	0003b	0028
1168	Kandalaksha.................. d.		0626		0704	0822	1448	1650			Sankt Peterburg Glavny ‡.a.	0924	0841	0625	1414	1302			...
1445	Murmansk.................... a.		1440		1226	1418	2024	2243			Moskva Oktyabrskaya 901 a.						0857	1126	1025

b – Volkhovstroy II. **‡ –** Formerly Sankt Peterburg **Moskovski** station.

Table 905

SANKT PETERBURG - VILNIUS

RŽD, LVD, LG

km		189 ✕ R	57 ✕ W	79 ✕ K	53 ✕ V		25 🍴 B	191 ✕	183 🍴 P			54 ✕ VR		184 ✕ P		190 ✕ W	58 ✕	192 ✕ K	80 ✕	26 🍴 B
0	Sankt Peterburg Varshavski d.	1205	1221	1520	1610		2025	2050	2240		Berlin Lichtenberg 850 ... d.						0043			2300
274	Pskov.......................... d.	1725		2050	2132		0105	0203	0406		Warszawa Gdańska 857 d.					0043				0758
368	Pytalovo ❶................... a.	1851		2236	2337		0219	0342	0539		Lviv 922 .... d.	0641		1722		1616				
368	Pytalovo ❶................... d.	1955		2341	0113		0323	0514	0700		Vilnius .... § d.	2218		1042		1435		1708	1924	2120
445	Rezekne I.................. § d.	2059		0046	0224		0420	0612	0818		Daugavpils .... § a.	0232		1522		1905	d	2145	2325	0126
533	Daugavpils .... § a.	2222	d	0200	0345		0531	0745	0957		Daugavpils .... § d.	0252		1542		1934		2208	2350	0144
533	Daugavpils .... § d.	2242		0220	0405		0551	0805	1024		Rezekne I................... § d.	0440		1735		2137		2344	0131	0307
707	Vilnius .... § a.	0318		0617	0821		1004	1257	1510		Pytalovo ❶.................. d.	0753		2048		0059		0246	0435	0607
	Lviv 922 .... a.	2251			0125				1013		Pytalovo ❶.................. d.	0902		2134		0221		0412	0547	0655
	Warszawa Gdańska 857 . a.		1501				2132				Pskov......................... d.	1050		2315		0351		0552	0733	0819
	Berlin Lichtenberg 850 .. a.						0627				Sankt Peterburg Varshavski a.	1535		0545		0852	0915	1115	1233	1057

B – ST. PETERBURG EXPRESS – 🛏 1, 2 cl. and 🍴 Sankt Peterburg - Berlin and v.v.; 🛏 2 cl., ⛌ , no first/soft class.
   🛏 2 cl. Riga - Berlin and v.v.; 🛏 2 cl., ⛌ and ✕ St Peterburg - Grodno and v.v.
K – 🛏 2 cl., ⛌ and ✕ Sankt Peterburg - Kaliningrad and v.v. (Table 900).
P – 🛏 2 cl. Sankt Peterburg - Lviv (trains 7/8) - Chop (trains 220/1) - Praha and v.v.;
   🛏 2 cl. Sankt Peterburg - Žilina (trains 902/7) - Bratislava and v.v.; 🛏 2 cl., ⛌ and
   ✕ Sankt Peterburg - Lviv and v.v.
R – Conveys 🛏 2 cl. Sankt Peterburg - Lviv (trains 15/6) - Budapest and v.v.

V – 🛏 2 cl. Sankt Peterburg - Bucureşti and Sofija and v.v.; 🛏 2 cl. and ✕ Sankt Peterburg - Chernivtsi and v.v.
W – 🛏 1, 2 cl. and 🍴 Sankt Peterburg - Warszawa and v.v.; 🛏 1, 2 cl. Sankt Peterburg - Białystok - Gdynia and v.v.; 🛏 2 cl. and ✕ Sankt Peterburg - Grodno and v.v.
d – Via Lida and Grodno (Tables 907/900). Transit visas for Lithuania/Latvia **not** required.
❶ – 🏬 is at Skangali/Karsava.
§ – Lithuanian time.

🛏 – Sleeping car   🏬 – Frontier station   R – Reservation obligatory

Table 907 SANKT PETERBURG - ORSHA - GOMEL - KYÏV

RŽD, BČ, UZ

km		31 🍷*	57 ✕ W	187 ✕	49 🍷 BK*	55 🍷*	19 ✕	51 🍷*	53 ✕	61 ✕
0	**Sankt Peterburg** Vitebski ... d.	...	1221v	1252	1510	...	1730	1842	2153	2314
245	Dno ... d.	...	1730	1834	1935	...	2215	2334	0231	0412
421	Novosokolniki ◐ ... d.	...	2032	2327	2248	...	0140	0308	0613	0729
568	Vitebsk ... d.	...	...	0252	0132	...	0436	0614	0916	1010
	Moskva Smolenskaya **900** d.	0958	...	|	|	1949	|	|	|	|
	Smolensk Mosk. ● **900** ... d.	1733	...	|	|	0336	|	|	|	|
651	Orsha Centralna **900** ... a.	2015	...	0430	0300	0440	0605	0753	1046	1146
651	Orsha Centralna ... d.	1944	...	0445	0316	0508	0620	0808	1100	1202
	Minsk **900** ... a.	|	...	|	0603	|	|	1101	|	|
724	Mogilev **I** ... d.	2112	...	0618	...	0658	0754	...	1235	1339
937	**Gomel** ... a.	...	...	1110	...	1130	|	...	1634	|
937	**Gomel** ⊙ ... d.	...	...	1140	...	...	|	...	1659	|
	Chernihiv ... d.	...	...	1505	...	...	|	...	1954	|
1101	Korosten ⊖ ... d.	...	...	|	...	...	1638	...	|	2250p
1257	**Kyïv** (Kiev) ... a.	...	...	1947	...	...	|	...	2332	|
1183	Zhytomyr ... d.	...	...	...	...	...	1832	...	...	0030
1259	**Koziatyn I** ... a.	...	...	...	...	...	2010	...	...	0224
	Chişinău (Kishinev) **925** ... a.	...	...	...	...	...	|	...	...	1444
	Odesa **925** ... a.	...	...	...	...	...	0521	...	...	...

	20 ✕	188 ✕	58 ✕ W	52 🍷*	32 🍷*	50 🍷 B*	54 ✕	56 🍷*	62 ✕ K
Odesa **925** ... d.	1232	...	...	...	...	...	...	...	...
Chişinău (Kishinev) **925** . d.	|	...	...	...	...	...	...	...	2334
Koziatyn I ... d.	2101	...	...	...	...	...	...	...	1155
Zhytomyr ... d.	2242	...	...	...	...	...	...	...	1341
Kyïv (Kiev) ... d.	|	2237	...	...	...	...	0908	...	|
Korosten ⊖ ... d.	0030	|	...	...	...	...	|	...	1524p
Chernihiv ... d.	|	0305	...	...	...	...	1305	...	|
Gomel ⊙ ... a.	|	0612	...	...	...	...	1556	...	|
Gomel ... d.	|	0642	...	...	...	...	1625	1925	|
Mogilev **I** ... d.	0942	1237	...	...	1849	...	2100	2351	0015
Minsk **900** ... d.	|	|	...	1502	|	1801	|	|	|
Orsha Centralna ... a.	1050	1430	...	1819	2013	2102	2243	0135	0146
Orsha Centralna **900** ... d.	1113	1503	...	1837	2043	2117	0002	0205	0208
Smolensk Mosk. ● **900** . a.	|	|	...	|	2307	|	|	0439	|
Moskva Smolenskaya **900** a.	|	|	...	|	0655	|	|	1240	|
Vitebsk ... d.	1414	1707	...	2043	...	2306	0210	...	0416
Novosokolniki ◐ ... d.	1906	2240	0125	0148	...	0400	0719	...	0954
Dno ... d.	2253	0348	✤	0520	...	0738	1041	...	1304
Sankt Peterburg Vitebski . a.	0517	0929	0915	0955	...	1145	1533	...	1742

B – Sankt Peterburg - Brest and v.v. (Table **900**).
K – Conveys 🛏 1, 2 cl. St Peterburg - Orsha - Brussels and v.v. on dates in Table **900**.
W – Sankt Peterburg - Warszawa and Gdynia and v.v.; for composition see Table **905**.
p – Korosten **Podilskyi**.
v – Sankt Peterburg **Varshavski**.
✤ – Information not available.
* – Details of train composition not available.
◐ – 🏛 is at Zaverezhye/Yezerishche.
● – 🏛 is at Krasnoye/Osinovka.
⊙ – 🏛 is at Lisichki/Gornostaïvka.
⊖ – 🏛 is at Ovruch.

Table 908 KALININGRAD - KLAIPEDA - MOSKVA

RŽD, LG, LVD, BČ

km		901 ⚒Ⓡ	91126 2	270 V✕	903 Ⓡ	91128 2	102 ⊗🍷*	55002 GⓇ	278 🍷*	
0	**Kaliningrad** ... d.	0740	...	...	1315	...	...	1712	...	...
	Braniewo 🏛 ... § d.	1010	1319	...	1550	1700	...	2000	...	...
	Elblag **855** ... § a.	...	1430	...	...	1801	...	2045	...	...
124	Sovetsk 🏛 ... d.	...	...	...	...	...	...	...	...	...
216	**Klaipeda** ... d.	...	...	...	...	...	1525	...	...	...
	Šiauliai ... d.	...	...	...	...	...	1839	...	...	...
	Panevezys ... d.	...	...	...	...	...	2010	...	...	...
	Riga **917** ... d.	...	...	1435	...	...	|	...	...	...
399	**Daugavpils** 🏛 ... d.	...	...	1800	...	...	2358	...	...	...
560	Polotsk ... d.	...	...	2305	...	...	0428	...	1540	...
661	Vitebsk ... d.	...	...	0127	...	...	0645	...	1800	...
799	**Smolensk** Mosk. ● **900/7** .. d.	...	...	0628	...	...	1055	...	2231	...
	Bryansk Orlovski ... d.	...	...	1407	...	...	|	...	|	...
	Orel II ... a.	...	...	1850	...	...	|	...	|	...
1218	**Moskva** Smolenskaya ‡ ... a.	...	...	...	...	...	1831	...	0523	...

	55000 GⓇ	269 V✕		902 ⚒Ⓡ	91125 2	904 Ⓡ	277 🍷*	101 ⊗🍷*	
Moskva Smolenskaya ‡ ... d.	...	...	...	...	...	...	1700	2236	...
Orel II ... d.	...	0927	...	...	...	...	|	|	...
Bryansk Orlovski ... d.	...	1308	...	...	...	...	|	|	...
Smolensk Mosk. ● **900/7** d.	...	2114	...	...	...	...	0102	0553	...
Vitebsk ... d.	...	0102	...	...	...	...	0515	0843	...
Polotsk ... d.	...	0248	...	...	...	...	0726	1035	...
Daugavpils 🏛 ... d.	...	0735	...	...	...	...	...	1500	...
Riga **917** ... a.	...	1045	...	...	...	...	...	|	...
Panevezys ... d.	...	...	...	...	...	...	...	1916	...
Šiauliai ... d.	...	...	...	...	...	...	...	2102	...
Klaipeda ... d.	...	...	...	...	...	...	...	0005	...
Sovetsk 🏛 ... d.	...	...	...	...	...	...	...	...	...
Elblag **855** ... § d.	0815	...	...	...	1545	...	...	...	...
Braniewo 🏛 ... § d.	0930	...	...	1200	1647	1830	...	...	...
Kaliningrad ... a.	1330	...	...	1520	...	2130	...	...	...

V – Runs alternate days only, even dates from Riga, uneven dates from Orel: 🛏 2 cl., (H) and ✕ Riga - Orel (- Voronezh) and v.v.
G – (2) Kaliningrad - Gdańsk - Gdynia and v.v.; conveys daily **except** Dec. 23, 24, 25, 30, 31, Apr. 15, 16 from Berlin, one day later from Kaliningrad: 🛏 1, 2 cl. Kaliningrad - Gdynia (trains **321/0**) - Szczecin - Berlin and v.v.
⊗ – Service currently suspended.
● – 🏛 is at Zaolsha.
‡ – Formerly Moskva **Byelorusski** station.
§ – Polish time.
* – Details of train composition not available.

Trans-Siberian Railway

RŽD, CR

For full details of this and other services east of Moskva, see the Thomas Cook Overseas Timetable in the blue cover

km	*Moskva time*	2 R		4 ②		20 ⑤⑥	
0	**Moskva** Yaroslavski ... d.	1400	*1st day*	1945	*1st day*	2025	*1st day*
1818	Yekaterinburg ... d.	1959	*2nd day*	0009	*3rd day*	0039	*3rd day*
2716	Omsk ... d.	0750	*3rd day*	1202	*3rd day*	1231	*3rd day*
5184	**Irkutsk** ... d.	0057	*5th day*	0346	*5th day*	0427	*5th day*
6304	Ulan Bator ... d.	|		0930	*6th day*	|	
9001	**Beijing** (Pekin) ... a.	|		1533	*7th day*	0632	*8th day*
8531	Khabarovsk ... a.	1335	*7th day*	...		...	
9297	**Vladivostok** ... a.	0245	*8th day*	...		...	

	19 ⑤⑥		3 ③		1 R	
Vladivostok ... d.	...		...		1755	*1st day*
Khabarovsk ... d.	...		...		0748	*2nd day*
Beijing (Pekin) ... d.	2032	*1st day*	0740	*1st day*	|	
Ulan Bator ... d.	|	|	1350	*2nd day*	|	
Irkutsk ... d.	1230	*4th day*	0920	*3rd day*	2004	*4th day*
Omsk ... d.	0434	*6th day*	0109	*5th day*	1309	*6th day*
Yekaterinburg ... d.	1631	*6th day*	1304	*5th day*	0143	*7th day*
Moskva Yaroslavski ... a.	2030	*7th day*	1725	*6th day*	0645	*8th day*

R – ROSSIYA – Runs on uneven dates from Moskva and Vladivostok: 🛏 1, 2 cl. and ✕ Vladivostok - Moskva and v.v.

Operator: CR – Chinese Railways.

ESTONIA AND LATVIA

SEE MAP PAGE 460

Operator: Eesti Vabariigi Raudtee (EVR), Latvijas Dzelzceļš (LVD).
Services: For details see the heading for Russia above Table **900**.
Timings: Valid **May 29, 1994** to **May 27, 1995**. However, timings cannot be guaranteed. All timings are shown in local time (Moskva time is one hour ahead of Belarus, the Baltic States and the Ukraine).
Tickets: Prior reservation is obligatory for most long-distance services, but is not possible on local trains.

Table 910 TALLINN - SANKT PETERBURG and MOSKVA

EVR, RŽD

km		220	222 ⑤⑦	24	176 Ⓡ✕ T	34 ✕ E	650 Ⓡ T	18 🍷 A	70 Ⓡ P	
0	**Tallinn** ... d.	0738	1030	1522	1610	1825	2010	2300	...	...
77	Tapa ... d.	0911	1138	1627	1720	1936	2122	0010	...	...
104	Rakvere ... d.	0940	1208	1656	|	2004	2155	0040	...	...
210	Narva 🏛 ... a.	1150	1420	1855	|	2145	0021	0235	...	...
210	Narva 🏛 ... d.	...	...	...	|	2230	0112	0320	...	...
368	**Sankt Peterburg** Varshavski a.	...	...	...	|	|	0715	0945	...	...
	Tartu ... d.	...	...	...	1902	|	...	...	...	...
	Pechory 🏛 ... d.	...	...	...	2330	|	...	...	...	...
	Pskov ... d.	...	...	...	0040	|	...	...	1810	...
	Dno ... d.	...	...	...	0227	|	...	...	2009	...
677	Bologoye **901** ... d.	...	...	...	0842	0716	...	...	0252	...
841	Tver **901** ... d.	...	...	...	1056	0916	...	...	0448	...
1008	**Moskva** Oktyabrskaya ‡ ... a.	...	...	...	1317	1131	...	...	0655	...

	175 Ⓡ✕ T	33 ✕ E	69 Ⓡ P	221	223 ⑤⑦	25	17 🍷 A	649 Ⓡ T	
Moskva Oktyabrskaya ‡ ... d.	1600	1725	1945	...	...	...	...	...	...
Tver **901** ... d.	1816	2008	2214	...	...	...	...	...	...
Bologoye **901** ... d.	2055	2258	0030	...	...	...	...	...	...
Dno ... d.	0314	|	0705	...	...	...	...	...	...
Pskov ... d.	0458	|	0900	...	...	...	...	...	...
Pechory 🏛 ... d.	0650	|	...	...	...	...	...	...	...
Tartu ... a.	0817	|	...	...	...	...	...	...	...
Sankt Peterburg Varshavski d.	|	|	...	...	...	...	2128	2325	...
Narva 🏛 ... a.	|	0545	...	...	...	...	0124	0400	...
Narva 🏛 ... d.	|	0635	...	0815	1235	1700	0207	0445	...
Rakvere ... d.	|	0820	...	1019	1439	1903	0323	0708	...
Tapa ... d.	1000	0852	...	1049	1513	1934	0431	0743	...
Tallinn ... a.	1105	0955	...	1220	1630	2035	0535	0845	...

– ADMIRALTEYETS – 🛏 1, 2 cl. and 🍷 Tallinn - Sankt Peterburg and v.v.
– TALLINNA EKSPRESS – 🛏 1, 2 cl. and ✕ Tallinn - Moskva and v.v.
P – 🛏 2 cl. and (H) Pskov - Moskva and v.v.
T – 🛏 2 cl. and (2) .
‡ – Formerly Moskva **Leningradski** station.

Table 911 TALLINN - VILJANDI and PÄRNU — EVR

km										®	
0	Tallinn .... d.	0610	0800	1015	1350	1500	1718	1815	2117	...	
72	Lelle .... d.	0752	0947	1153	1531	1613	1919	1958	2257	...	
98	Türi .... d.		1016			1652		2027	2325	...	
151	Viljandi .... a.		1112			1737		2124		...	
141	Pärnu .... a.	0921		1320	1658		2143			...	

			✕						
Pärnu .... d.		0541		1020		1427	1740		
Viljandi .... d.	...		0634		1302			1825	
Türi .... d.	0520		0731		1359			1915	
Lelle .... d.	0555	0710	0800	1153	1428	1613	1917	1959	
Tallinn .... a.	0734	0850	0920	1327	1600	1754	2054	2137	

Table 912 TALLINN - HAAPSALU — EVR

km		r					r	r	
0	Tallinn .... d.	0605	1000	1852	Haapsalu............. d.	0547	0956	1737
104	Haapsalu .... a.	0907	1306	2152	Tallinn .... a.	0846	1257	2042

r – Change at Riisipere.

Table 914 TALLINN - RIGA — EVR, LVD

km		603	607	110 Ⓡ	210	609	176 M✕	2 B✕	14	214	188 V✕
0	Tallinn .... d.			0718	1340		1610	1710	1740	1900	2330
77	Tapa............... d.			0837	1514		1720		1844	2007	0042
190	Tartu.............. d.			1043	1730		1900	1950	2010	2213	0222
273	Valga .... d.			1230				2115			0345
273	Valga ⓜ.......... d.	1120g	1500g			1919g		2135			0433
321	Valmiera .... d.	1207	1545			2004				0005	0601
441	Riga .... a.	1440	1825			2242				0005	0820

		211	175 M✕	1 B✕	604 Ⓡ	15	608	610	215	6854	187 V✕
Riga .... d.				0625	0723		1117	1531		2120	2338
Valmiera .... d.					1003		1341	1810		2355	0138
Valga ⓜ.......... d.				0855	1050g		1428g	1857g			0305
Valga .... d.				0915		1320					0350
Tartu.............. d.			0707	0817	1045		1456			1858	0528
Tapa............... d.			0903	1000			1625			2118	0705
Tallinn .... a.			1026	1105	1310		1729			2250	0810

B – Ⓡ: BALTI EKSPRESS – ⇌ 1, 2 cl., ⊑⊒ and ✕ Tallinn - Šeštokai (- Warszawa) and v.v.
M – Ⓡ: ⇌ 2 cl., ⊑⊒ and ✕ Tallinn - Moskva and v.v. (Table 910).
V – Ⓡ: ⇌ 2 cl., ⊑⊒ and ✕ Minsk - Vilnius - Riga and v.v.
g – Lugaži station (Latvian ⓜ), 277 km from Tallinn, 164 km from Riga.

Table 915 RIGA - MOSKVA — LVD, RŽD

km		696	688	664 Ⓡ*	662 Ⓡ*		606	2 A✕	4 B✕
0	Riga .... d.	0706	1103			1547	1740	1830
129	Krustpils (Jekabpils) .. d.	0917	1310			1752	1919	2014
224	Rezekne II............. d.	1054	1445			1935	2035	2137
	Sebez ⓜ.............. d.					0020	0118	
445	Velikiye Luki .... d.			1750	2010		0255	0403
686	Rzhev.................. d.			0033	0150		0647	0808
922	Moskva Rizhski ‡ ..... a.			0550	0649		1046	1206

		605	1 A✕	3 B✕	661 Ⓡ*	663 Ⓡ*	695	687
Moskva Rizhski ‡ ...... d.			1930	2050	2154	2327	...	
Rzhev................... d.			2332	0055	0230	0451	...	
Velikiye Luki .... d.			0320	0445	0650	1116	...	
Sebez ⓜ............... d.			0653	0824			...	
Rezekne II.............. d.		0459	0759	0928			1325	1725
Krustpils (Jekabpils) .... d.		0635	1040	1044			1502	1925
Riga .... a.		0846		1055	1225		1705	2140

A – LATVIJAS EKSPRESIS – ⇌ 1, 2 cl. and ✕ Moskva - Riga and v.v.
B – JURMALA – Ⓡ: ⇌ 2 cl., ⊑⊒ and ✕ Moskva - Riga and v.v.
* – Details of train composition not available.
‡ – Formerly Moskva Riga Station.

Table 916 RIGA - ST PETERBURG — LVD, EVR, RŽD

km		190	294	390	38 A♀
0	Riga 914................. d.	...	...	...	1900
121	Valmiera 914............ d.	...	...	...	2050
168	Valga ⓜ 914.......... d.	0620	1240	1800	2222
	Võru .... d.	0745	1357	1917	2313
264	Pechory ⓜ............ d.	...	...	...	0045
310	Pskov 905 .... d.	...	...	...	0305
584	Sankt Peterburg Vars. 905 a.	...	...	...	0805

		291	293	191	37 A♀
Sankt Peterburg Vars. 905 . d.	...	...	...	2155
Pskov 905 .... d.	...	...	...	0245
Pechory ⓜ................ d.	...	...	...	0515
Võru .... d.	0624	1522	1758	0453
Valga ⓜ 914.............. d.	0740	1638	1922	0600
Valmiera 914.............. d.	...	...	...	0729
Riga 914.................. a.	...	...	...	0917

A – BALTIYA – Ⓡ: ⇌ 1, 2 cl., ⊑⊒ and ♀ Riga - Sankt Peterburg and v.v.

Table 917 RIGA - DAUGAVPILS — LVD

km		6302	690 Ⓡ		692 Ⓡ	270 Ⓡ	20 Ⓡ✕		698 Ⓡ	684
0	Riga .... d.	...	0800		1326	1435	1540	...	1645	2000
129	Krustpils (Jekabpils) .. d.	0520	1030		1535	1629	1718	...	1840	2215
217	Daugavpils........... a.	0705	1202		1710	1800	1822	...	2010	2313

		19 Ⓡ✕	697 ♀	269 V✕	689 Ⓡ		6301		691 Ⓡ
Daugavpils............... d.	...	0640	0650	0735	1335		1720		1850
Krustpils (Jekabpils) .... d.	...	0752	0816	0852	1512		1934		2036
Riga .... a.	...	0930	1020	1045	1748				2300

V – Riga - Orel (- Voronezh) and v.v. Ⓡ. For days of running and composition see Table 908.

Table 918 RIGA - BALTIC COAST — LVD, LG, RŽD

		611 Ⓡ	951 Ⓡ	667 Ⓡ♀	657 Ⓡ✕	21 Ⓡ	663 Ⓡ♀	17 Ⓡ	669 Ⓡ	273 K♀
0	Riga .... d.	0640		0648	1700	1730	1805	1845	1934	2245
43	Jelgava .... d.	0733		0743	1755	1813	1852		2042	2313
207	Ventspils .... d.	1057	0730		2115		2320	2130		
223	Liepaja .... d.		1102	1140		2115	2320			0236
135	Šiauliai ⓜ............. d.									0236
294	Sovetsk ⓜ............. d.									0706
418	Kaliningrad .... a.									1041

		670 Ⓡ♀	18 Ⓡ✕	22 Ⓡ♀	274 Ⓡ♀	658 Ⓡ♀	664 Ⓡ♀	612 Ⓡ	952 Ⓡ	668 Ⓡ
Kaliningrad .... d.			2240							
Sovetsk .... d.			0245							
Šiauliai .... d.			0648							
Liepaja .... d.				0626			0655		1620	1700
Ventspils .... d.		0632			0650		1710	1952		
Jelgava .... a.		0725		0939	0945	1014	1131	2036		2108
Riga .... a.		0817	0915	1015	1030	1055	1209	2115		2152

K – Ⓡ: Runs ②④ from Riga, ①③ from Kaliningrad: ⇌ 2 cl., ⊑⊒ , ⊑⊒ and ♀ Riga - Kaliningrad and v.v.

On the Rails Around EUROPE

Gives you all the facts and practical advice you need to plan and enjoy the trip of a lifetime . . .

See the back of this book for details and order form.

Table 919 RIGA - VILNIUS - MINSK — LVD, LG, BČ

km		188 Ⓡ✕ W	75 Z✕ ③⑥	257 Z✕ ②⑤	032 Ⓡ♀	259 ✕	664 Ⓡ	221 Ⓡ♀ A	1 14 B✕
0	Tallinn 914 .... d.	2330	...	...	...	...	...	...	1710
0	Riga .... d.	0820	1315	1352	...	...	2205	0025	...
	Jelgava .... d.	0909	1408	1443	...	...	2251	0109	...
	Klaipeda .... d.				1710	2220			
135	Šiauliai ⓜ............. d.	1217	1708	1742	1941		0206	0326	0335
155	Radviliškis .... d.	1243	1727	1808	2005		0244	0352	0401
	Kaunas .... a.						0548	0610	0612
348	Vilnius .... a.	1600	2037	2115	2257		0745	0700	...
348	Vilnius ⓜ 900.......... d.	1620	2054	2135		0424			...
	Lviv 922 .... d.			1443					...
	Molodechno 900....... d.	2002	0007						...
542	Minsk 900 .... a.	2201	0129						...
	Kyïv (Kiev) 922 927 ... d.		1413			2352			...
	Simferopol 927 928 .... d.					2205			...

		031 Ⓡ✕	258 Z✕ ④⑦	260 ✕	187 Ⓡ✕ W	13 2 B✕	663 Ⓡ	222 Ⓡ♀ A	76 Z✕ ②⑤
Simferopol 927 928 ... d.		2252						0842
Kyïv (Kiev) 922 927 .... d.		1919						2126
Minsk 900 .... d.			1047					2305
Molodechno 900....... d.			1213					
Lviv 922 .... d.	1913							
Vilnius ⓜ 900.......... d.		1230	1318	1545				
Vilnius .... d.	0650	1250		1607		2218	2303	0242
Kaunas .... a.					0015	0032	0120	...
Radviliškis .... d.	0929	1543	1926	0232	0333	0355	0543	
Šiauliai ⓜ............. d.	0956	1616	1956	0259	0407	0422	0613	
Klaipeda .... d.	1224				0738			
Jelgava .... a.		1916	2239	0521		0712	0908	
Riga .... a.		2000	2338	0606		0810	0950	
Tallinn 914 .... a.				0810	1319			

A – ⇌ 2 cl., ⊑⊒ and ♀ Riga - Vilnius and v.v.; ⇌ 2 cl. Riga - Vilnius (25/6) -
Warszawa - Berlin and v.v.; ⇌ 2 cl. Riga - Warszawa and v.v.; conveys on ③⑦
from Riga, ③⑥ from Sofija; ⇌ 2 cl. Riga - Vilnius - Chernivtsi - Sofija and v.v.

B – Ⓡ: BALTI EKSPRESS – ⇌ 1, 2 cl., ⊑⊒ and ✕ Tallinn - Šeštokai (- Warszawa) and v.v.
W – ⇌ 2 cl., ⊑⊒ and ✕ Tallinn - Riga - Vilnius - Minsk and v.v.
Z – ⇌ 2 cl. and ⊑⊒, ● applies.   ● – Runs on alternate days (See Table 927)

UKRAINE AND MOLDOVA

SEE MAP PAGE 460

Operator: Українські Залізниці – Ukraïnski Zaliznitsi (УЗ – UZ), Căile Ferate Moldova (CFM).
Services: For details see the heading for Russia above Table 900.
Timings: **May 29, 1994 to May 27, 1995.** All services are subject to alteration without notice, and timings cannot be guaranteed.
All timings are shown in local time (Moskva time is one hour ahead of Belarus, the Baltic States and the Ukraine).
Tickets: Prior reservation is necessary, except for purely local trains.

Table 920 — BREST - GOMEL and KYÏV

BČ, RŽD, UZ

km		110 R K	68 ✗	40 Wn	230 *	684 ⑦	274		39 Wp	109 R	67 ✗ K	273		229 *	683 ⑤ B
	Berlin Lichtenberg 850 .... d.		1140				...	Kyïv (Kiev) .... d.	0608	0850	1110	1358	...		1805
	Warszawa Centralna 858 .. d.	1630g	2017	0050g		...	1022y	Korosten .... d.	0940	1155	1410	1705	...		2120
0	Brest .... d.	0010	0500	0830	...	1505	1700 1910	Sarny .... d.	1348	1519	1736		...		0121
	Kalinkovichi .... d.				0047		0318	Kovel ▯ .... d.	1655	1838	2035				0520
	Gomel .... a.				0255			Bryansk Orlovski .... d.						1607	
	Zlynka ▩ .... d.				0531			Zlynka ▩ .... d.						2116	
	Bryansk Orlovski .... d.				1030			Gomel .... d.						2156	
124	Kovel ▯ .... d.	0415	0900	1220	...		2130	Kalinkovichi .... d.				2138		0035	
266	Sarny .... d.	0739	1200	1515	...	0122		Brest .... a.	2110	2248	0037	0605		0955	1112
421	Korosten .... d.	1106	1530	1900	...	0520	0820	Warszawa Centralna 858 .. a.	0238g	0454g	1045				1917z
577	Kyïv (Kiev) .... a.	1346	1805	2152	...	0801	1120	Berlin Lichtenberg 850 ..... a.			1847				

B – Conveys on ⑦ from Brussels, ⑤ from Kyïv: ⬛ 1, 2 cl. Brussels - Brest - Kyïv and v.v.
K – KIEW EXPRESS – ⬛ 2 cl. and ♀ Kyïv - Warszawa Wschodnia (trains 246/7) - Berlin and v.v.; ✗ Kyïv - Brest and v.v.
R – Runs ③⑥ (**not** Dec. 24, Apr. 4, 7, 15, 19) from Russia and (**not** Dec. 23, 27, 30, Jan. 3, 6, Apr. 14, 18) from Kyïv: ⬛ 2 cl. Kyïv - Warszawa and v.v.
W – Runs ①③④ from Warszawa, ①②⑥ from Kyïv: ⬛ 2 cl. Warszawa - Kyïv and v.v.

g – Warszawa **Gdańska**.
n – Will **not** run Dec. 26, 28, 29, Jan. 2, 4, 5, 9, 11, 12, Apr. 13, 17, 19, 20.
p – Will **not** run Dec. 24, 26, 27, 31, Jan. 2, 3, 7, 9, 10, Apr. 11, 15, 17, 18.
y – ① only.
z – ⑥ only.
* – Details of train composition not available.
▯ – ▩ is at Khotislav/Zabolottia.

Table 921 — LUBLIN - CHELM - KOVEL - KYÏV

PKP, UZ, RŽD

km		12121	1111	72	670	78 ✗	12105 ♀	58 ✗	96		71	1146	95		57 ✗	21104	669	77 ✗
	Warszawa Centralna 869 d.	0040	...	...	...	1447		...	...	Moskva Kievskaya 924 ...d.	...	1509		...	...		0700
0	Lublin 869 .... d.	0402	0605	...	...	1719		...	...	Kyïv (Kiev) .... d.	...	0716		1925	...	2054	2248
74	Chelm 869 .... d.	0544	0720	0850	...	1834	1955	...	Koziatyn I .... d.			2223		2359	0147
95	Dorohusk ▩ .... d.		0753	1000	...		2224	...	Zhytomyr .... d.	...	1148		...			
102	Yagodyn ▩ .... d.			1237	...		2344	...	Rivne .... d.	...	0253		0555	0718
161	Kovel 920 .... d.		1410	1700	2123		0120	...	Lutsk .... d.	...	0449		0752	0920
232	Lutsk .... d.			1925	2348		0340	...	Kovel 920 .... d.	1616		0720		1010	1124
297	Rivne .... d.			2124	0137		0525	...	Yagodyn ▩ .... d.	1905		1025			
	Zhytomyr .... d.							1310	Dorohusk ▩ .... d.	1925		1100			
529	Koziatyn I .... d.		0309	0645		1007	Chelm 869 .... d.	1948	2052		1134	1216	
706	Kyïv (Kiev) .... d.		0615	0940		1250	1752	Lublin 869 .... d.	...	2210		1321		
	Moskva Kievskaya 924 ... a.		0353		1147	Warszawa Centralna 869 a.			1557		

Table 922 — VILNIUS - KYÏV, LVIV and CHERNIVTSI

LG, BČ, UZ

km		172 M	667 ③⑦ C	189 ✗ B	76 P	259 ●	195 R	53 ✗ S	183 ✗ D	76 ③⑥	257 ✗ ②⑤		171 ✗ M	75 P	184 ✗ D	258 ③⑥	260 ●	190 ✗	54 ✗ SB	630 RV	75 ②⑤
	Sankt Peterburg 905 . d.	...	...	1205	...	...	...	1612	2240	...	...	Sofija 960 .... d.	...	...	...	...	2140	...			
	Riga 919 .... d.	...	...	...	...	...	...	1315	1352	Bucureşti 955 .... d.	...	...	...	...	0906			
0	Vilnius .... d.	...	...	0338	...	0424	...	0856	1530	2054	2135	Chernivtsi .... d.	0324	0736	...	...	2342			
95	Lida ▯ .... d.	...	...	0633	...	0800	...	1208	1854	...	0059	Ivano-Frankivsk .... d.	0620	1040	...	...	0229			
	Minsk 900 .... d.	2342	...	...	...	0930	...	...	0144	...	Lviv .... a.	...	1314	...	...	0506			
	Baranovichi Polesski . d.	0203	0831	...	1031	1145	1410	2108	...	0304	Lviv .... d.	...	1722	1913	...	1616	0641		
422	Sarny .... d.	...	1352	...	1650	1859	0318	...	0829	Rivne .... d.	...	2123	2320	...	2359	1005		
	Korosten .... d.	...	...	...	2102	...	...	1118	Simferopol 927/8 .... d.	...	2252			
	Kyïv (Kiev) .... a.	...	...	...	2352	...	...	1413	Kyïv (Kiev) .... d.	...	1919		0842	
	Simferopol 927/8 .... a.	...	...	...	1936	...	Korosten .... d.	...	2220		1137	
509	Rivne .... a.	...	1604	...	...	2055	0540	...	1043	Sarny .... a.	...	2319	0124	0217	0230	1153		
716	Lviv .... a.	...	2251	...	...	0100	0955	...	1443	Baranovichi Polesski .... a.	...	0505	0712	0800	0835	1703	1959	
716	Lviv .... d.	...	...	2309	...	0125	...	Minsk 900 .... a.	...	...	...	...	2238	2106		
929	Ivano-Frankivsk .... d.	2112	...	0205	...	0440	...	Lida ▯ .... d.	...	0720	0920	1020	1057	1900		
1055	Chernivtsi .... a.	0045	...	0440	...	0755	...	Vilnius .... d.	...	1022	1230	1318	1415	2158		0227
	Bucureşti 955 .... a.	...	...	...	2102	...	Riga 919 .... d.	...	2000		0950	
	Sofija 960 .... a.	...	...	...	0920	...	Sankt Peterburg 905 ..... a.	...	0545	...	0852	1535		

B – ⬛ 2 cl., ▭ and ✗ Sankt Peterburg - Lviv and v.v.; ⬛ 2 cl. Sankt Peterburg - Lviv (trains 15/6) - Budapest and v.v.; for ⬛ 2 cl. Minsk - Budapest and v.v. see notes **C** and **V**.
C – Runs ③⑦ from Minsk: ⬛ 2 cl. Minsk - Baranovichi (train 189) - Lviv (train 15) - Budapest.
D – ⬛ 2 cl., ▭ and ✗ Sankt Peterburg - Lviv and v.v.; ⬛ 2 cl. Sankt Peterburg - Lviv (trains 7/8) - Chop (trains 220/1) - Praha and Bratislava and v.v.
M – ⬛ 1, 2 cl., ▭ and ✗ Moskva - Kyïv - Chernivtsi - Ivano-Frankivsk and v.v.
P – ▭ Przemyśl - Lviv - Chernivtsi and v.v.
R – ⬛ 2 cl. Minsk - Baranovichi (trains 53/4) - Chernivtsi - Sofija and v.v.

S – ⬛ 2 cl. and ✗ Sankt Peterburg - Chernivtsi and v.v.; ⬛ 2 cl. Sankt Peterburg - Bucureşti and Sofija and v.v.; conveys on ③⑦ from Riga, ③⑥ from Sofija: ⬛ 2 cl. Riga (trains 221/2) - Vilnius - Sofija and v.v.; For ⬛ 2 cl. Minsk - Sofija and v.v. see note **R**.
V – Conveys on ②⑤ from Budapest: ⬛ 2 cl. Budapest (train 16) - Lviv (train 54) - Baranovichi - Minsk.
● – Runs on alternate days (See Table 927).
▯ – ▩ is at Šalčininkai/Benyakone.

Table 924 — MOSKVA - BRYANSK - KYÏV
RŽD, UZ

km		119 ✕ M	77 ✕	73 ✕	9 🛏 P✕		51 ✕ S🛏	35 ✕	7 ✕ D✕	89 ✕	57 ✕	3 🍴	59 🛏 F✕	95 🛏 Z	33 ✕	171 🛏 A	5 🛏 R	13 ✕ N	185		1	23 ✕	15 🛏 T	41 🍴	47 ✕
0	Moskva Kievskaya .... d.	0046	0700	0917	0956	....	1147	1154	1300	1307	1350	1420	1444	1509	1600	1607	1645	1645	1652		1903	1944	2032	2100	2250
387	Bryansk Orlovski .... d.	0905	1508	1703	1729	...	1935	1958	2057	2105	2216	2246	2315	2323	2345	0035	0100	0100	0118		0305	0340	0436	0501	0653
	Suzemka 🏛 .... d.		1714	1908		...		2156		2300						0145	0230			0320			0541		0658	
	Zernove 🏛 .... d.			1855		...							0014			0215				0305			0525			
651	Konotop .... d.	1337	1905	2113	2055	...	2250	0003	0015	0038	0250	0240	0230	0331	0352	0506	0420	0420	0600		0627	0757	0808	0859	1052
780	Sumy .... a.					...							0625						0940						
	Chernihiv .... a.																									
872	Kyïv (Kiev) .... a.	1725	2228	0045	0001	...	0157	0316	0324	0330		0600	0553	0657	0730	0843	0745	0745			0930	1118	1127	1245	1412
	Odesa 925 .... a.				1505																	2241			
	Chişinău 925 .... a.																2104	2104							0545
	Lviv 925 .... a.	0534		1259	1139		1344		1510					1851								2337			

		60 🛏 F✕	48 ✕	120 🛏 R	6 🛏 R	14 🛏 N	8 ✕ D✕	10 🛏 P✕		78 ✕ M	36 ✕	74 🛏	58 ✕	2	90 🍴	4 🛏 T	16 🛏 T	186	96 🛏 Z	34 ✕	172 🛏 A		52 🛏 S✕	42 🛏	24 ✕
	Lviv 925 .... d.		...	1455		1631	1749		...		0008			...		0626		...	0715			1032			
	Chişinău 925 .... d.	...	1208		1315	1315																			
	Odesa 925 .... d.	...								2330															1126
	Kyïv (Kiev) .... d.	0130	0212	0219	0322	0322	0336	0450		1000	1122	1228		1645	1707	1710	1755		1807	1830	1836		2200	2150	2231
	Chernihiv .... d.											1225													
	Sumy .... d.																1650								
	Konotop .... d.	0524	0544	0555	0711	0711	0719	0841		1338	1500	1603	1700	2021	2112	2042	2155		2115	2205	2213	2234		0157	0134	0217
	Zernove 🏛 .... d.		0831	0846									1959					0003		0100				0500
	Suzemka 🏛 .... d.			1035						1812	1928	2040	2143	0017		0108			0147		0254				0644
	Bryansk Orlovski ...... d.	1152	1205	1225	1338	1338	1242	1402		2010	2137	2255	2357	0146g	0243	0250g	0312	0345	0422	0450	0458		0725	0824	0904
	Moskva Kievskaya ..... a.	1933	1946	1951	2114	2114	2028	2141		0353	0509	0616	0655	0909	1007	1030	1121	1140	1147	1237	1244		1503	1550	1625

For notes, composition and days of operation see Table **925**.

Table 925 — KYÏV - ODESA, CHERNIVTSI, CHIŞINĂU and LVIV
UZ, CFM

km		61 ✕ L	9 🛏 P✕	73 ✕	51 ✕	35 ✕	89 ✕	7 ✕	59 🛏 F✕	33 ✕	5 🛏 R	13 🛏 N	171 🛏 A	23 ✕		15 ✕ T	47 ✕	19 ✕	119 🛏 L	85 🛏 B🍴	43 🛏 K🍴	91	55	225	107 🛏 W✕
0	Moskva Kievskaya 924 ... d.		0956	0917	1147	1154	1307	1300	1444	1600	1645	1645	1607	1944		2033	2250		0046						
872	Kyïv (Kiev) .... d.		0023	0100	0229	0335	0345	0352	0614	0753	0800	0800	0900	1133		1155	1436		1740	1853	1906	1951	2041		
1031	Koziatyn I .... d.		0224	0308	0357	0511	0607	0618	0628	0856	1037	1032	1032	1159		1428	1542	1737	2026	2036	2140	2150	2240	2336	
1093	Vinnytsia .... d.		0325	0410	0507	0613	0710	0726	0734	0958		1134	1134	1325		1532	1558	1840	2133	2154	2245	2250	2348	0044	
	Odesa Hlavna .... d.																							1838	1925
1140	Zhmerynka .... d.		0429	0513	0620	0716	0819	0814	0837	1012		1236	1236	1435		1635	1702	1944	2240	2257	2335	0005	0052	0143	0150	0227
1526	Odesa Hlavna .... a.					1505								2241			0521			0809					
1466	Chernivtsi .... a.								1940					0302					0852						
1497	Tiraspol .... a.	1255										1919	1919				0300								
1572	Chişinău (Kishinev) ..... a.	1444										2104	2104				0545								
	Bucureşti 955 .... a.									0737		1049	1049							2102					
	Sofija 960 .... a.									1902			2235							0856					
1239	Khmelnytskyi .... d.		0556	0805	0900				1025					1900				0040		0150	0244		0348	0420	
1362	Ternopil .... d.		0908	1025	1113				1239					2108				0304		0405	0502		0648	0635	
1503	Lviv .... a.		1139	1259	1344				1510		1851			2337				0534		0643	0734		0920	0912	
1503	Lviv .... d.		1202		1407				1533					0002				0557							
1728	Mukacheve .... d.		1631		1834				2007					0428				1043							
1769	Chop .... d.		1729		1930				2105					0525				1150							
	Košice 885 .... a.				2245				0020																
	Budapest 898 .... a.													1202											

		90 ✕	16 ✕ T	172 ✕ A	34 ✕	52 🛏 S✕	24 ✕	20 ✕ L	60 🛏 F✕	48 ✕	120 🛏 R	6 🛏 R	14 🛏 N	8 ✕ D✕	10 🛏 P✕	92	226	56	108 🛏 W✕		36	86 🛏 B🍴	74 🛏 K🍴	44 🛏 L	62 ✕
	Budapest 898 .... d.	...	1610																						
	Košice 885 .... d.	...				2328					0453														
	Chop .... d.	...	0035		0440				0849			1030	1200												
	Mukacheve .... d.	...	0136		0541				0952			1131	1301												
	Lviv .... a.	...	0608		1017				1440			1613	1734												
	Lviv .... d.	...	0626	0715	1032				1455			1631	1749	1937	2018		2202				0008	0037		
	Ternopil .... d.	...	0851		1304				1728			1902	2020	2209	2254		2034				0257	0311		
	Khmelnytskyi .... d.	...	1114		1510				1942			2112	2227	0026	0128		0252				0517	0530		
	Sofija 960 .... d.								1245			1115						2140							
	Bucureşti 955 .... d.								2355			2316	2316					0906							
	Chişinău (Kishinev) ..... d.								1300			1315	1315											2334	
	Tiraspol .... d.								1357			1543	1543											0126	
	Chernivtsi .... d.			0105						1154											2131				
	Odesa Hlavna .... d.						1126	1232										2140		2330					
	Zhmerynka .... d.	1218	1302	1311		1657	1732	1857	2051	2115	2132	2246	2246	2259	0013	0221	0326	0413	0443		0607	0653	0720	0741	0934
	Odesa Hlavna .... a.																	1024		1116					
	Vinnytsia .... d.	1313	1348	1406		1745	1834	1944	2136	2205	2218	2332	2332	2344	0056	0318		0508			0701	0739	0805	0826	1027
	Koziatyn I .... d.	1420	1450	1513	1525	1849	1940	2101	2238	2316	2324	0034	0034	0050	0158	0434		0613			0810	0845	0909	0930	1155
	Kyïv (Kiev) .... a.	1707	1738	1819	1812	2134	2215		0113	0156	0203	0306	0306	0319	0433	0717		0900			1107	1126	1205	1226	
	Moskva Kievskaya 924 ... a.	1007	1121	1244	1237	1503	1625		1933	1946	1951	2114	2114	2028	2141				0509		0616				

NOTES FOR TABLES 924 AND 925

A – 🛏 1, 2 cl., 🚃 and ✕ Moskva - Chernivtsi - Ivano-Frankivsk and v.v.

B – BULGARIA EXPRESS – 🛏 2 cl. and 🍴 Kyïv - Sofija and v.v.; 🛏 2 cl. Sankt Peterburg (trains 53/4) - Chernivtsi - Bucureşti and Sofija and v.v.; 🛏 2 cl. Minsk - Baranovichi - Sofija and v.v.; Conveys 🛏 2 cl. Riga - Sofija and v.v. on dates in Table 922.

D – DUKLA – 🛏 1, 2 cl. and 🍴 Moskva - Chop (trains 220/1) - Praha and v.v.; 🛏 2 cl. Kyïv - Praha and v.v.; 🛏 2 cl. Sankt Peterburg (trains 183/4) - Vilnius - Lviv (trains 8/9) - Chop - Praha and Bratislava and v.v.; 🛏 2 cl. and ✕ Moskva - Chop and v.v.

F – SOFIJA EXPRESS – 🛏 1, 2 cl. and 🍴 Moskva - Sofija and v.v.; 🛏 2 cl. and ✕ Moskva - Chernivtsi and v.v.

K – 🛏 2 cl. and 🍴 Kyïv - Lviv - Przemyśl - Kraków - Wrocław and v.v.

L – To/from Sankt Peterburg (Table 907).

M – 🛏 1, 2 cl., 🚃 and ✕ Moskva - Koziatyn - Rivne - Kovel and v.v.

N – DANUBIUS EXPRESS – Runs ①⑤ from Moskva, ①④ from Sofija: 🛏 1, 2 cl. and 🍴 Moskva - Sofija and v.v.; 🛏 2 cl. Chişinău - Sofija and v.v.; 🛏 2 cl., 🚃 and ✕ Moskva - Ungheni and v.v.

P – PUSKIN – 🛏 1, 2 cl. and 🍴 Moskva - Chop (trains 489/8) - Beograd and v.v.; 🛏 2 cl. and ✕ Moskva - Chop and v.v.; For Moskva - Athinai and Thessaloniki cars see Table 94c.

R – ROMANIA EXPRESS – Runs daily except ①⑤ from Moskva, ②⑤ from Ungheni/Chişinău (when train N runs): 🛏 2 cl., 🚃 and ✕ Moskva - Ungheni and v.v.; Conveys on ③④⑦ from Moskva, ②⑤⑥ from Bucureşti: 🛏 1, 2 cl. and 🍴 Moskva - Bucureşti and v.v.

S – SLOVAKIA – 🛏 1, 2 cl. and 🍴 Moskva - Chop (trains 222/3) - Bratislava and v.v.; 🛏 1, 2 cl. Moskva - Bratislava (trains 401/6) - Wien and v.v.; 🛏 2 cl. and ✕ Moskva - Chop and v.v.; conveys on ③⑤⑦ from Kyïv, ①④⑥ from Wien: 🛏 2 cl. Kyïv - Wien and v.v.

T – TISZA EXPRESS – 🛏 1, 2 cl. and 🍴 Moskva and Lviv - Budapest and v.v.; 🛏 1, 2 cl. Moskva - Budapest (trains 202/3) - Zagreb and v.v.; 🛏 2 cl. Sankt Peterburg (trains 53/4) - Lviv - Budapest and v.v.; conveys on ③⑦ from Minsk, ②⑤ from Budapest: 🛏 2 cl. Minsk (trains 659/60) - Baranovichi (trains 183/4) - Lviv - Budapest and v.v.; 🛏 2 cl. and v.v.; conveys 🛏 2 cl. Moskva - Zagreb - Venezia and v.v. on dates in Table 94c.

W – 🛏 2 cl. and ✕ Odesa - Przemyśl and v.v. (extended to/from Warszawa on alternate days).

Z – 🛏 1, 2 cl. and 🚃 Moskva - Zhytomyr and v.v.

g – Bryansk Lgovski.

Table 926 — ODESA - CHERNIVTSI and IZMAÏL
UZ, CFM

km		660	804	642	236		252	644	686	
		*	*	*	⚑		⚑	*	*	
0	Odesa Hlavna .... d.	0611	0630	1204	1319	...	1700	1752	2049	...
288	Izmaïl .... a.		1331						0520	...
72	Rozdilna I 🚂 .... d.	❖		❖	1516	...		❖		
117	Tiraspol .... d.	0951		1527	1621	...		2121		
190	Chişinău (Kishinev) .... a.	1200		1725	1805	...		2314		
190	Chişinău (Kishinev) .... d.	...		...	1834	...				
382	Bălţi .... d.	...			2240					
473	Okniţa 🚂 .... d.				0112					
645	Chernivtsi .... d.				0555	1022				
771	Ivano-Frankivsk .... a.				0910					

		686	235	251	641	804		643	659
		*	⚑	⚑	*	*		*	*
	Ivano-Frankivsk .... d.		1107		...	...		...	...
	Chernivtsi .... d.		1420	1530	...	...		...	...
	Okniţa 🚂 .... d.		1857						
	Bălţi .... d.		2128						
	Chişinău (Kishinev) .... a.		0210						
	Chişinău (Kishinev) .... d.		0235	0656				1237	1622
	Tiraspol .... d.		0429	0844				1427	1848
	Rozdilna I 🚂 .... d.		0533		❖	❖		❖	❖
	Izmaïl .... d.	2116			0655				
	Odesa Hlavna .... a.	0540	0800	0949	1134	1337		1732	2228

* – Details of train composition not available.   ❖ – Information not available.

Table 927 — MINSK - KYÏV and SEVASTOPOL
BČ, UZ, RŽD

km		110 A✗	106 M⚑	100 ✗	650 *	76 W✗	212 K✗	28 ⚑	181 V✗	259 R✗
	Riga 919 .... d.	...	...	...	1315	...	...	...	...	...
	Vilnius 919 922 .... d.	...	...	...	2054	2045	...	...	...	0424
0	Minsk .... d.	1740	2210	2238	0144	0153	...	0310	...	...
300	Gomel .... d.	2355	0415	0425		0835	...	0931	...	...
522	Konotop 🔲 .... d.	0536		0935		1506			y	
651	Sumy .... d.	0910	1348			1845				
846	Kharkhiv .... a.	1358	1808			2349				
	Chernihiv ❶ .... d.		0730						1255	
	Korosten ❶ 922 .... d.					1116				2058
	Kyïv (Kiev) .... d.		1141			1413		1912		0010
	Odesa Hlavna .... d.				1819				x	
	Mykolaïv .... d.				2340			0540		1140
	Kherson .... d.				0105			0649		1320
	Simferopol 929 .... a.				0703	0732		1212	1409	1936
	Sevastopol 929 .... a.							1415		

		109 A✗	211 K✗	75 Z✗	99 ✗	182 V✗	649 *	27 ⚑	105 M⚑	260 R✗
	Sevastopol 929 .... d.	...	...	...	...	...	1715	...	...	...
	Simferopol 929 .... d.	...	...	1150	1427	1740	1918	...	...	2252
	Kherson .... d.	...	...	...	0004	0054		...	...	0522
	Mykolaïv .... d.	...	...	0125	0203			...	...	0649
	Odesa Hlavna .... a.	...	...	x	0647			...	...	...
	Kyïv (Kiev) .... d.	...	...	0842		...		1225	1738	1919
	Korosten ❶ 922 .... d.	...	1137			...				2220
	Chernihiv ❶ .... d.	...	...	...	1500			2250		
	Kharkhiv .... d.	2150	0040		0100					
	Sumy .... d.	0210	0518		0553					y
	Konotop 🔲 .... d.	0601	0910		1031					
	Gomel .... d.	1159	1515		1550	1910		0235		
	Minsk .... a.	1739	2036	2106	2122	0028		0808		
	Vilnius 919 922 .... d.	...	0113	0227						1318
	Riga 919 .... d.	...	0950							

A – 🛏 2 cl. and ✗ Minsk - Kharkhiv (- Adler) and v.v.
K – From/to Kaliningrad (Table 900).
M – 🛏 1, 2 cl., 🛏 and ⚑ Minsk - Kyïv and v.v.
R – Runs alternate days only, uneven dates from Vilnius, even dates from Simferopol.
V – Runs alternate days only, even dates from Minsk and Simferopol.
W – Runs ③⑥ from Riga only.
Z – Runs ②⑤ from Kyïv only.
x – Via Table 928.
y – Via Table 922.
🔲 – 🚂 is at Terekhovka/Khorobychi.
❶ – 🚂 is at Lisichki/Gornostaïvka.
❷ – 🚂 is at Ovruch.
* – Details of train composition not available.

Table 928 — LVIV and KYÏV - DONETSK and SIMFEROPOL
UZ, RŽD

km		11 ⚑	181 ✗ R❶	224 ✗	176 ✗ M	37 ✗	64 ✗	17 ✗ A	80 ✗	106 ✗	206 ✗
	Lviv 925 .... d.	...	...	...	...	...	...	...	...	2248	2357
	Ternopil 925 .... d.	...	...	...	...	...	...	...	...	0130	0218
	Khmelnytskyi 925 .... d.	...	...	...	...	...	...	...	...	0352	0538
	Zhmerynka 925 .... d.	...	...	...	...	...	...	...	...	0553	0738
0	Kyïv (Kiev) .... d.	1520		...	1700	1733	2003	2010	2034	2143	...
351	Poltava (Kyïvskaya) .... d.		0155				0418				
491	Kharkhiv .... d.						0815				
592	Dnipropetrovsk .... d.	0127	0324		0400	0637		0745	0755	1943	2221
871	Dnipropetrovsk .... d.	0215y	0423		0507	0714		0828	0835	2022	2314y
1083	Donetsk .... a.			1343	0950	1230					0427
723	Zaporizhzhia I .... d.	0450	0650				2055			2308	
835	Melitopol .... d.	0648	0858							0111	
1079	Simferopol .... a.	1140	1409							0519	

		106 ✗	18 ✗ A	206 ✗	79 ✗	38 ✗	63 ✗	12 ⚑	223 ✗	182 ✗ R❶	175 ✗ M
	Simferopol .... d.	0804		...	...	...	...	1433		1427	...
	Melitopol .... d.	1223		...	...	...	...	1802		1927	...
	Zaporizhzhia I .... d.	1425		...	...	...	...	2010		2118	...
	Rostov-na-Donu 🔲 d.		0830								
	Donetsk .... d.			1255		1530			1914		2202
	Dnipropetrovsk .... d.	1703	1833	1920	2038	2027		2241		2258	0323
	Dnipropetrovsk .... d.	1748	1910	2002	2114	2104		2316		0036	0401
	Kharkhiv .... d.						2000				
	Poltava (Kyïvskaya) .... d.						2350		0620		
	Kyïv (Kiev) .... a.		0629		0803	0741	0752	0909	1426		1500
	Zhmerynka 925 .... d.	0818		1216							
	Khmelnytskyi 925 .... d.	1033		1428							
	Ternopil 925 .... d.	1256		1701							
	Lviv 925 .... a.	1535		1937							

A – 🛏 1, 2 cl. and ✗ Kiev - Rostov-na-Donu (- Adler) and v.v.
M – 🛏 1, 2 cl., 🛏 and ⚑ Kiev - Donetsk (- Mariupol) and v.v.
R – 🛏 2 cl., 🛏 and ✗ Minsk - Simferopol and v.v.
y – Dnepropetrovsk Yuzhny (South).
❶ – Runs on alternate days (See Table 927).
🔲 – 🚂 is at Ilovaysk/Taganrog II.

Table 929 — MOSKVA - KHARKHIV - SEVASTOPOL
RŽD, UZ

For services Moskva - Kharkhiv - Rostov-na-Donu and beyond, see the Thomas Cook Overseas Timetable in the blue cover

km		17 ✗ S	25 ✗	31 ✗	9 ✗	67 ✗		15 ✗	19 ✗	195 H✗	7 ✗ L
0	Moskva Kurski .... d.	0805	0925	1025	1320	1455	...	1926	2040	2056	...
194	Tula I .... d.	1138	1258	1404	1707	1828	...	2303	0010	0031	0531
383	Orel .... d.	1509	1616	1745	2012	2134	...	0212	0318	0351	0844
537	Kursk .... d.	1740	1902	2025	2238	2358	...	0433	0546	0622	1110
697	Belgorod .... d.	2029	2136	2336	0114	0247	...	0722	0826	0832	1422
781	Kharkhiv .... a.	2139	2341	0050	0307	0322	...	0838	0911	1106	1557
781	Kharkhiv .... d.	2159	0001	0110	0228	0355	...	0900	...	1120	1627
	Donetsk .... a.				0914						
	Dnipropetrovsk .... a.							1410			
1108	Zaporizhzhia I .... d.	0332	0541	0627		0937	...		1703	2200	
1220	Melitopol .... d.	0543	0750	0835		1149	...		1930	0013	
	Yevpatoriia .... d.		1034								
1464	Simferopol 927 .... a.			1145	1221	1522	...		0022	0520	
1542	Sevastopol 927 .... a.			1351			...			0721	

		10 ✗	20 ✗	68 ✗ L	8 ✗	16 ✗	196 H✗		18 ✗ S	32 ✗	26 ✗
	Sevastopol 927 .... d.	...	...	0847	...	...	...		...	...	0002
	Simferopol 927 .... d.	...	...	0852	1053	...	1030		...	2358	0156
	Yevpatoriia .... d.	...	...	...	...	...	1700				
	Melitopol .... d.	...	...	1256	1511	...	1601		2155	0423	0547
	Zaporizhzhia I .... d.	...	...	1448	1716	...	1817		0003	0646	0737
	Dnipropetrovsk .... d.	...	...	...	1728	...	...				
	Donetsk .... d.	1134									
	Kharkhiv .... a.	1815		2002	2240	2246	2329		0525	1230	1333
	Kharkhiv .... d.	1855	1805	2042	2320	2308	2349		0602	1310	1413
	Belgorod .... d.	2228	2240	2351	0241	0345	0330		0918	1642	1755
	Kursk .... d.	0107	0115	0236	0449	0518	0610		1157	1930	2034
	Orel .... d.	0320	0328	0445	0724	0740	0826		1418	2204	2254
	Tula I .... d.	0630	0639	0759	1038	1057	1207		1735	0120	0215
	Moskva Kurski .... a.	0955	1013	1131	1436	1540			2125	0444	0540

H – Conveys 🛏, no first/soft class.
L – NEVA – 🛏 1, 2 cl., 🛏 and ✗ Sankt Peterburg - Sevastopol and v.v.
S – Runs May 28 - Sept. 24 only.
* – Details of train composition not available.
❶ – 🚂 is at Tolokonnoye/Kozacha Lopan.

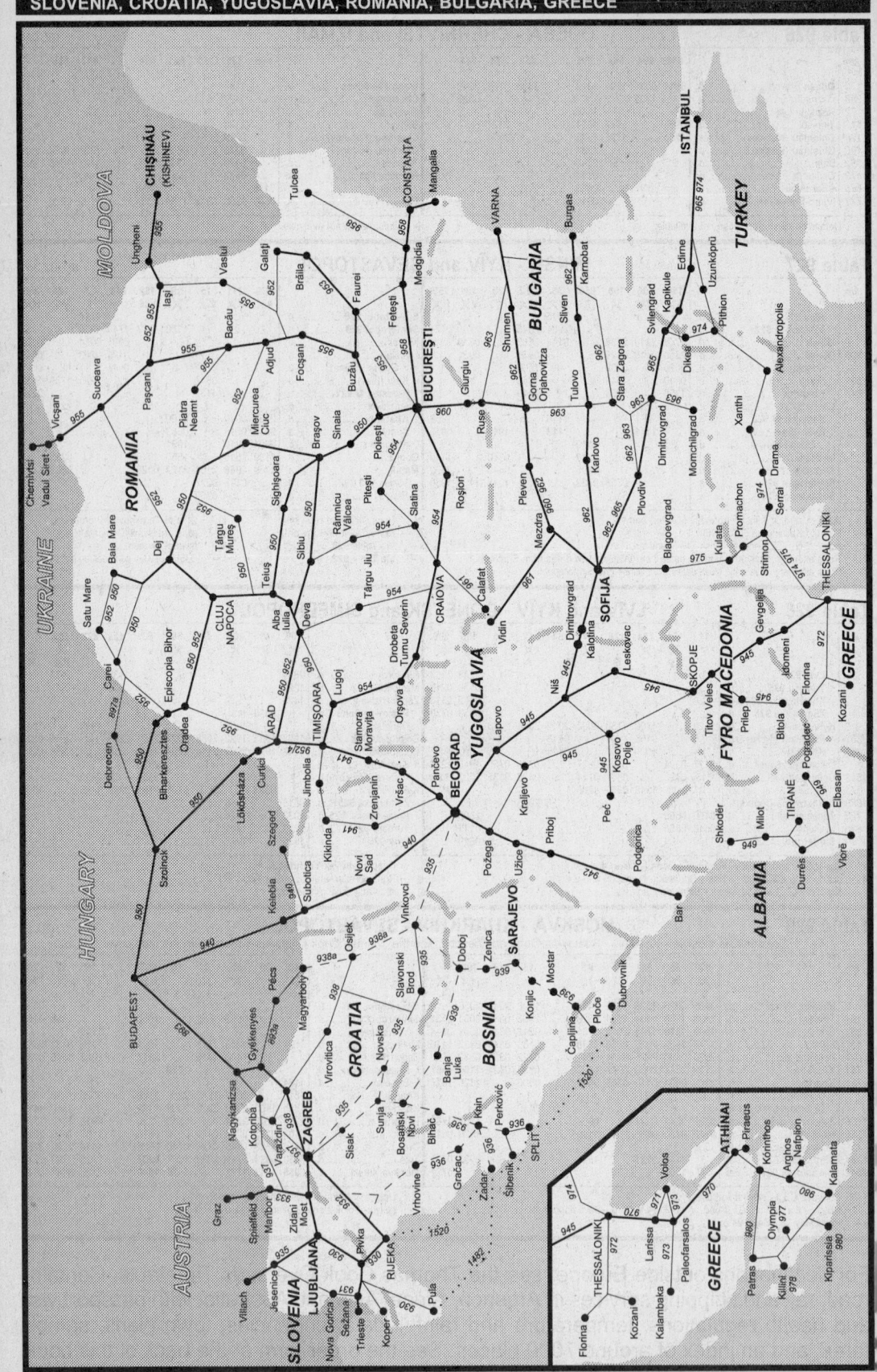

SLOVENIA and CROATIA
INCLUDING BOSNIA - HERZEGOVINA

Operators: Slovenske Železnice (SŽ); Hrvatske Željeznice (HŽ); Zeljeznice Bosne I Hercegovine (ZBH).

Services: Trains convey first and second classes of accommodation, shown as '1' and '2' or 🛳 in the tables. Sleeping cars (🛏) and couchette cars (🛋) are of the normal European types, see page **10** for more details. Rail distances are shown in tariff - kilometres.

Timings: **May 29, 1994 to May 27, 1995.** The information shown is thought to represent the actual services running at the time of publication. However, changes may occur at short notice due to the political situation. All services in Bosnia - Herzegovina are believed to be suspended at present and there are no services running between Croatia and Yugoslavia.

Tickets: A supplement is payable for travel by internal (IC) express trains. Reservation of seats is possible on most express trains.

Table 930 — LJUBLJANA - RIJEKA, PULA, KOPER and TRIESTE

1, 2 class except where shown. SŽ HŽ

km		IC 240 ◆	460 ◆	IC 481 2	IC 2750 2	2632 2	IC264 264	473 2	IC 503 ✕	2600 2	2602 2🎌	2648 2🎌	IC 242 ✕◆	IC 2752 2 E	483 2	IC 2604 2	472 ◆	IC 220 ◆	2614 2	509 ◆	IC302 ®♀ ◆	IC 2606 2	485 2	2608 2	2610 2
	Zagreb 935 ....d.	0020					0540	0540										1410			1535				
	Maribor 933 ....d.								0700					1207					1500						
0	Ljubljana ....d.	0320	0450	0550	0600	0725	0805	0805	0930	1025	1200	1315	1355	1430	1505	1540		1645	1700	1725	1745	1900	2040		2235
76	Postojna ....a.	0415	0551	0648	0702	0829	0858	0858	1022	1128	1303	1416	1446	1533	1604	1642		1741	1803	1820	1837	2003	2143		2338
91	Pivka ....a.	0427	0603	0701	0714	0841	0911	0911	1034	1141	1316	1428	1458	1546	1616	1654		1753	1816	1831	1848	2016	2156		2351
91	Pivka ....d.			0702									1617						1836				2157	2200	
144	Opatija-Matulji △ ...a.			0800									1715						1950e				2255		
155	Rijeka ....a.			0810									1725						2000e				2305		
91	Pivka ....d.	0428	0604		0715	0842	0912	0912	1035	1142	1317	1429	1459		1655			1754	1816	1832	1849	2017			
118	Divača ....d.	0449	0628		0738	0905	0933	0933	1055	1204	1340	1451	1519		1718			1814	1841	1853	1910	2040		2222	
118	Divača ....d.		0640		0741				0950	1058		1440	1611					1854	1915						
258	Pula ▲ ....a.		0925t					1220				1835g				1640			2135						
175	Koper ....a.				0832				1145					1700					1940						
118	Divača ....d.	0451	0629		0906	0940			1205	1341	1452	1520			1719			1815	1842			2041		2223	
129	Sežana ....d.	0501	0639		0917	0950			1216	1352	1502	1530			1730	1840		1825	1853			2052		2233	
129	Sežana 🏛 ....a.	0531	0649			1005					1546							1845							
136	Villa Opicina 🏛 ....a.	0540	0657			1014					1555							1854							
165	Trieste Centrale.....a.	0628				1057					1650							1949							
	Venezia S.L. 376 ...a.	0918									1918							2219v							

		2601 2	2603 2🎌	IC303 ®♀ ◆	2605 2	4201 ◆	508 ◆	IC 484 2	2615 2	IC 221 ◆	2751 2	2714 2	2609 2	IC 243 ◆ E	482 2	2611 2🎌	2649 2🎌	IC 502 ✕	2710 2	2613 2	472 ◆	472 ◆	IC 265 2	2753 2	IC 480 ◆	IC 241 2
	Venezia S.L. 376 ...d.									0708v			0940													2122
	Trieste Centrale......d.									0916			1204										1758			2343
	Villa Opicina 🏛 ....d.					0707				1005			1300								z		1840			0031
	Sežana 🏛 ....a.					0715				1014			1308										1840	1848		0040
	Sežana ....a.			0500		0622	0725		0810	0935	1035			1300	1323			1420	1510		1740		1902	1902	1955	0100
	Divača ....a.			0510		0632			0820	0945	1045			1310	1333			1430	1520		1750		1912	1912	2006	0110
	Koper ....d.						0650				1010						1450					1920				
	Pula ▲ ....d.			0400					0650t										1430g	1610	z					
	Divača ....d.			0617		0735	0739		0821	0930	1057						1539		1717	1912			2012			
	Pivka ....d.			0511	0618	0633	0742		0821	0946	1059		1311	1334		1431	1521	1541		1751	1913	1913	2013			0111
	Pivka ....a.			0533	0638	0656	0803		0845	1009	1107	1121		1334	1454	1454	1602		1813	1934	1934	1934	2036			0132
	Rijeka ....d.							0730					1255					1530b					1838e	2035		
	Opatija-Matulji △ ...d.							0742					1305					1542b					1849e	2046		
	Pivka ....a.							0851					1410					1650					1952	2150		
	Pivka ....d.	0435	0534	0639	0657		0804	0852	1010	1108	1122	1225	1335	1355	1411	1455	1545	1603	1651	1814	1935	1935	2038	2151	0133	
	Postojna ....a.	0448	0547	0651	0710		0816	0906	1023	1121	1135	1238	1348	1407	1424	1508	1558	1617	1704	1827	1948	1948	1948	2204	0146	
	Ljubljana ....a.	0550	0650	0741	0812		0912	1010	1125	1215	1236	1340	1450	1500	1520	1610	1700	1712	1806	1928	2042	2042	2042	2150	2258	0240
	Maribor 933 ....a.							1145						1751				1947								
	Zagreb 935 ....a.			0945					1450												2255	2255	2255			0505

◆ — NOTES (LISTED BY TRAIN NUMBERS)

C150/1 – EMONA – 🛳 and ✕ Ljubljana - Wien and v.v.; 🛳 Rijeka (trains IC482/3) - Ljubljana - Wien and v.v.
C220/1 – SIMPLON EXPRESS – 🛏 1, 2 cl., 🛋 2 cl. and 🛳 Zagreb - Trieste - Venezia - Genève and v.v.
C240/1 – VENEZIA EXPRESS – 🛏 1, 2 cl., 🛋 2 cl. and 🛳 Budapest - Venezia and v.v.; conveys on ③⑥ from Venezia, ③⑦ from Moskva: 🛏 1, 2 cl. Venezia - Zagreb - Budapest (trains 16/5) - Moskva and v.v.
C242/3 – DRAVA – 🛳 and ✕ Budapest - Ljubljana - Venezia and v.v.
C264/5 – KRAS – 🛳 Zagreb - Trieste and v.v.
C302/3 – ARENA – 🛳 and ♀ Zagreb - Pula and v.v.; 1 class fares apply for internal journeys in Slovenia.
472 – 🛳 Pula - Sežana - Divača - Ljubljana - Zagreb.
C480/1 – 🛋 2 cl. (also 🛏 1, 2 cl. May 29 - Sept. 24) and 🛳 Rijeka - Ljubljana - München and v.v.

E – Conveys 🛳 Wien (IC151/0) - Ljubljana - Rijeka and v.v.
b – Change at Illirska Bistrica.
e – Change at Šapjane.
g – Change at Lupoglav.
t – Change at Buzet.
v – Venezia Mestre.
z – From Pula (depart 1610).
▲ – 🏛 Ticket point is Rakitovec/Buzet.
△ – 🏛 Ticket point is Ilirska Bistrica/Sapjane.

Table 931 — JESENICE - NOVA GORICA - SEŽANA

2 class only. SŽ

km						600 L									601 L				
0	Jesenice 935 ....d.	0420	0620	1127 Ⓐ		1416		1648	...	1812	Sežana 930 ....d.	...	...	0525	...	0800	...	1426	...	1856
12	Bled Jezero ....d.	0435	0636	1142		1431		1706	...	1827	Nova Gorica ....a.	...	...	0600	...	0850	...	1515	...	1951
32	Bohinjska Bistrica ...d.	0501	0702	1202		1451		1726	...	1846	Nova Gorica ....d.	0345	0545	...	0700	...	1133	1532	...	2006
67	Most na Soči ....d.	0536	0742	1237		1527		1801	...	1921	Most na Soči ....d.	0421	0622	...	0740	...	1210	1609	...	2044
108	Nova Gorica ....d.	0623	0820	1315		1612		1840	...	1958	Bohinjska Bistrica ...d.	0450	0701	...	0819	...	1255	1645	...	2122
108	Nova Gorica ....d.	0625		1318	1520				...	1845	Bled Jezero ....d.	0519	0721	...	0839	...	1314	1705	...	2142
149	Sežana 930 ....a.	0720		1415	1617				...	1940	Jesenice 935 ....a.	0535	0735	...	0854	...	1330	1720	...	2158

▪ – 🛳 Ljubljana - Jesenice - Nova Gorica and v.v.

Table 932 — ZAGREB - RIJEKA

1, 2 class. HŽ

km		208 R	IC500 ®♀	IC200 ✕ A	4000	502 ®♀	IC504 R			IC503 ®♀	IC505 R	IC201 ✕ A	4001	IC501 ®♀	209 R
0	Zagreb ....d.	0210	0600	1220	1320	1640	1945	Rijeka ....d.	0545	0825	1210	1335	1650	2050
56	Karlovac ....d.	0251		1256	1429		2025	Delnice ....d.		0934	1314	1459	...	2159
115	Ogulin ....d.	0345	0722	1345	1540	1802	2115	Srpske Moravice .....d.	0729	1013	1353	1550	1831	2245
147	Srpske Moravice .....d.	0430	0801	1427	1630	1841	2153	Ogulin ....d.	0803	1041	1427	1631	1859	2315
178	Delnice ....d.	0508		1458	1707		2228	Karlovac ....d.		1129	1515	1750	...	0010
243	Rijeka ....a.	0635	0930	1600	1835	2010	2330	Zagreb ....a.	0925	1200	1550	1850	2020	0050

A – AGRAM – 🛳 and ✕ Budapest - Zagreb - Rijeka and v.v.
R – ADRIATICA – 🛏 1, 2 cl. and 🛳 Budapest - Rijeka and v.v.

Ⓡ – Reservation obligatory   ✕ – Restaurant car   🏛 – Frontier station   **469**

Table 933 — GRAZ - MARIBOR - ZAGREB and LJUBLJANA

1, 2 class except where shown. ÖBB, SŽ, HŽ

km		507	2001	IC 501	2003	IC 503	2901	IC 505	2005	2007	IC 151	221	483	2009	2011	509	2013	IC 511	2015	1515	2017	159	IC159 513	2907	3403
		2	2	1℞℗ 2	2	✕	2	Ⓐ	2	2	✕			Ⓐ	2		1℞℗ 2	1℞℗ 2	2	2	2	✕		Ⓐ	2
				Ⓐ		K		Ⓐ			◆		◆			K	Ⓐ	Ⓐ							
	Wien Südbf 830 .... d.	...	...	...	...	...	...	...	...	...	0822	...	...	...	...	...	...	...	...	1622	1622	...	...	...
0	Graz .... d.	...	...	...	...	...	...	...	...	...	1058	...	...	...	...	...	...	...	...	1858	1858	...	...	...
47	Spielfeld-Strass 🚻 .... a.	...	...	...	...	...	...	...	...	...	1129	...	...	...	...	...	...	...	...	1929	1929	...	...	...
47	Spielfeld-Strass 🚻 .... d.	...	...	...	...	...	...	...	...	...	1141	...	...	...	...	...	...	...	...	1939	1939	...	...	...
68	Maribor .... a.	...	...	...	...	...	...	...	...	...	1159	...	...	...	...	...	...	...	...	1956	1956	...	...	...
68	Maribor .... d.	0410	0515	0600	0615	0700	0715	0900	0915	1015	1207	...	1315	1415	1500	1712	1800	1915	2001	2010	2015	2213
144	Celje .... d.	0520	0625	0657	0725	0757	0825	0957	1025	1125	1258	...	1425	1525	1557	1635	1657	1824	1857	2025	2107	2126	2326
173	Zidani Most 935 .... d.	0547	0652	0722	0752	0822	0852	1022	1052	1152	1322	1326	1452	1552	1622	1702	1722	1852	1922	2052	2132	2155	...
229	Dobova 935 🚻 .... a.											1425						2210				
258	Zagreb 935 .... a.											1450						2235				
246	Ljubljana .... a.	0647	0755	0820	0855	0920	0955	1120	1155	1255	1418	...	1505	1555	1655	1720	1805	1820	1955	2020	2155	...	2230	2300
401	Rijeka 930 .... a.										1725											

		2900	2800	2000	IC 510	512 IC158	IC 158	2002	508	2004	2006	IC 504	2010	IC 500	2012	IC 518	482	220	IC 150	2014	IC 502	2016	3400	506	2018
		2	2	2	1℞℗ 2		2	2	2	2	2	Ⓐ	2	1℞℗ 2	2	1℞℗ 2			✕	2	2	2	2	2	2
					Ⓐ		◆		K	Ⓐ		Ⓐ		Ⓐ		℞			✕		K				
	Rijeka 930 .... d.																1255								
	Ljubljana .... d.	...	0440	0545	0615	0715	...	0755	0925	0945	1045	1125	1245	1325	1345	1425	1520	...	1540	1545	1722	1745	1845	1950	2050
	Zagreb 935 .... d.						0715										1410							
	Dobova 935 🚻 .... d.						0755										1455							
	Zidani Most 935 .... d.	0455	0550	0650	0714	0814	...	0900	1024	1050	1150	1224	1350	1424	1450	1524	...	1535	1635	1650	1821	1850	2000	2049	2155
	Celje .... d.	0520	0616	0716	0740	0840	0854	0926	1050	1116	1216	1250	1416	1450	1516	1547	...	1658	1716	1846	1916	2026	2115	2220
	Maribor .... a.	0630	0728	0825	0835	0935	0945	1035	1145	1225	1325	1345	1526	1545	1625	1655p	...	1751	1825	1947	2025	2135	2212	2329
	Maribor .... d.			0955	0955														1758				
	Spielfeld-Strass 🚻 ...... a.			1013	1013														1815				
	Spielfeld-Strass 🚻 ...... a.			1025	1025														1825				
	Graz .... a.			1055	1055														1855				
	Wien Südbf 830 .... a.			1340	1340														2140				

◆ – NOTES (LISTED BY TRAIN NUMBERS)
IC150/1 – EMONA - 🚋 and ✕ Ljubljana - Wien and v.v.; 🚋 Rijeka (trains IC482/3) - Ljubljana - Wien and v.v.
IC158/9 – CROATIA - 🚋 and ✕ Zagreb - Wien and v.v.; 🚋 Ljubljana (trains 512/3) - Maribor - Wien and v.v.
IC482/3 – 🚋 Rijeka - Ljubljana (trains IC150/1) - Wien and v.v.

K – 🚋 Maribor - Koper and v.v.
p – Change at Pragersko.

Table 935 — VILLACH - LJUBLJANA - ZAGREB - VINKOVCI

1, 2 class except where shown. SŽ, HŽ , ÖBB

km		241	741	2251	IC 297	2401	2403	2405	IC 303	601	IC 311	IC 221	431	2409	4973	2411	2415	2417	EC 11	IC 265	EC 115	315	2211	4989
			🍴	2	2	2	2	2℞🍴	◆	◆	2	2		2	✕	2	2	2	✕		✕		2	2
		V			Ⓐ	Ⓐ			◆	◆	◆	◆			✕	Ⓐ							Ⓐ	
	München 790 .... d.				2246														1325		1525			
	Salzburg 820 .... d.				0045														1508		1708			
0	Villach Hbf. .... d.	...	...	...	...	...	...	...	...	1040	...	...	...	1352	...	...	...	...	1753	...	1949	1956	...	2222
1	Villach Westbf. .... d.				0327									1355										2226
25	Rosenbach 🚻 .... d.				0352					1102				1430					1818		2021			2259
38	Jesenice 🚻 .... a.				0405					1114				1442					1830		983 2033			2311
38	Jesenice .... d.				0430	0452	0538	0622		0740	1120			1414	1505	1700	1800	1844		941 2045			
52	Lesce - Bled .... d.				0443	0508	0553	0636		0755	1134			1430	1519	1715	1818	1858		S 2058			
79	Kranj .... d.				0554	0531	0617	0700		0818	1155			1455	1545	1738	1843			2118			
112	Ljubljana .... a.				0525	0600	0645	0726		0849	1220			1521	1612	1805	1913	1937		2140			
112	Ljubljana .... d.	0253		0440	0540					0745	...	1230	1510					1940	2045		2145	2240
185	Zidani Most 933 .... d.	0348		0550	0637					0839		1326	1610						2140		2242	2344
241	Dobova 🚻 933 .... d.	0440		0636	0735					0920		743	1425	1710				2125	2231		2339	
272	Zagreb 933 .... a.	0505		0724	0800					0945		1450	1735					2150	2255		0004	
272	Zagreb ▲ △ .... d.		0547							1342										2343		
	Sisak ▲ .... d.																					
384	Novska △ .... Σ d.																			0550		
476	Slavonski Brod .... d.		1142							1929										0733		
545	Vinkovci 🚻 .... d.		1233							2023												
705	Beograd .... Σ a.																					

		2400	2402	432	940 980	IC 264	IC 310	EC 10	2404	2406	4974	2408	600	740	2412	IC 220	314	IC 302	2414	2416	430	742	IC 296	240
		2	2				2	✕	2			2			2			2℞🍴	2	2		🍴		
		Ⓐ			S		◆	◆		Ⓐ	✕		◆			◆		Ⓐ					◆	V
	Beograd 🚻 .... Σ d.													0530								1318		
	Vinkovci .... d.				2218									0639								1419		
	Slavonski Brod .... Σ d.				2308																			
	Novska △ .... d.													1216								2009		
	Sisak ▲ .... d.																							
	Zagreb ▲ △ .... a.				0523																			
	Zagreb 933 .... d.			0435		0540		0810						1410		1535			1805		2100	0020
	Dobova 🚻 933 .... d.			0518		0620		0847						1455		1610			1845		2144	0116
	Zidani Most 933 .... d.			0602		0704								1536		1646			1927		2223	0154
	Ljubljana .... a.			0703		0800		1017						1635		1740			2030		2320	0250
	Ljubljana .... d.	0415	0630				0825	1020	1240	1338		1428	1532		1623		1725		1845	2005		2335
	Kranj .... d.	0443	0659				0848	1308	1406		1454	1600		1651		1752		1917	2032		2358
	Lesce - Bled .... d.	0508	0724				0910	1100	1331	1430		1518	1623		1715		1817		1941	2057		0020
	Jesenice .... a.	0523	0739				0925	1114	1347	1445		1533	1636		1730		1830		1956	2113		0035
	Jesenice 🚻 .... d.						0930	1129			1452					1840						0057
	Rosenbach 🚻 .... d.						0943	1144			1506					1855						0114
	Villach Westbf. .... d.										1535											0134
	Villach Hbf. .... a.						1005	1206			1539					1918						0415
	Salzburg 820 .... a.						1453															0415
	München 790 .... a.						1634															0613

◆ – NOTES (LISTED BY TRAIN NUMBERS)
EC10/1 – MIMARA - 🚋 and ✕ Zagreb - Leipzig and v.v.
IC220/1 – SIMPLON EXPRESS - 🛏 1, 2 cl., 🛏 2 cl. and 🚋 Zagreb - Trieste - Venezia - Genève and v.v.
IC264/5 – KRAS - 🚋 Trieste - Zagreb and v.v.
IC296/7 – 🛏 1, 2 cl., 🛏 2 cl. and 🚋 München - Zagreb and v.v.; 🛏 2 cl. (also 🛏 1, 2 cl. May 29 - Sept. 24) and 🚋 München - Ljubljana (trains 480/1) - Rijeka and v.v.
IC302/3 – ARENA - 🚋 and 🍴 Zagreb - Pula and v.v.; 1 class fares apply for internal journeys in Slovenia.
IC310/1 – TRIGLAV - 🚋 Ljubljana - Villach and v.v.; 🚋 Ljubljana - Jesenice and v.v.
600/1 – 🚋 Ljubljana - Jesenice - Nova Gorica and v.v.
S – 🛏 1, 2 cl, 🛏 2 cl. and 🚋 Zagreb - Slavonski Brod and Vinkovci - Zagreb.

V – VENEZIA EXPRESS – See Table 930.
Σ – Novska - Slavonski Brod and Vinkovci - Beograd service suspended.
▲ – For Zagreb - Sisak service see Table 939.
△ – Local service Zagreb - Novska (Journey 90-100 minutes)
From Zagreb: 0501, 0634, 0755, 1007Ⓐ, 1152, 1333, 1450Ⓐ, 1545, 1645, 1800, 1918, 2234.
From Novska: 0359, 0520, 0728, 0843, 1114Ⓐ, 1218, 1403, 1520Ⓐ, 1657, 1752, 1900, 2016, 2200.

🚋 – Through carriage (1 and 2 class)   Ⓐ – Mondays - Fridays, except holidays   ✕ – Daily except Sundays and holidays   02

Table 936 — ZAGREB - ZADAR and SPLIT

2 class only. HŽ, ZBH

km			921	5800	5503	923	5806	5808	5507
0	Zagreb	d.	...	...	...	...	...	...	...
56	Karlovac	d.	...	...	...	...	...	...	...
109	Oštarije	d.	...	...	...	...	...	...	...
177	Vrhovine	d.	...	...	...	...	...	...	...
227	Gospić	d.	...	...	...	...	...	...	...
273	Gračac	d.	...	...	...	...	...	...	...
	Sisak	d.	...	...	...	...	...	...	...
	Novska	d.	...	...	...	...	...	...	...
	Sunja	d.	...	...	...	...	...	...	...
	Bosanski Novi	d.	...	...	...	...	...	...	...
	Bihać	d.	...	...	...	...	...	...	...
341	Zadar	a.	...	...	...	...	...	...	...
341	Knin	d.	...	...	...	...	...	...	...
442	Zadar	d.	...	...	...	...	...	...	...
	Šibenik	d.	0600	...	0710	...	1405	1533	1930
398	Perković	a.	0626	...	0746	0948	1430	1604	2001	2129
449	Split	a.	0735	...	...	1056	1547	...	2238

Service suspended

			5502	5803	920	922	5506
Split		d.	0710	...	1140	1400	1910	...
Perković		d.	0825	0836	1246	1505	2014	...
Šibenik		a.	...	0905	1312	1531	...	...
Zadar		a.	...	...	...	...	...	...
Knin		a.	...	...	...	...	...	...
Knin		d.	...	...	...	...	...	...
Bihać		d.	...	...	...	...	...	...
Bosanski Novi		d.	...	...	...	...	...	...
Sunja		d.	...	...	...	...	...	...
Novska		d.	...	...	...	...	...	...
Sisak		d.	...	...	...	...	...	...
Gračac		d.	...	...	...	...	...	...
Gospić		d.	...	...	...	...	...	...
Vrhovine		d.	...	...	...	...	...	...
Oštarije		d.	...	...	...	...	...	...
Karlovac		d.	...	...	...	...	...	...
Zagreb		a.	...	...	...	...	...	...

Service suspended

Table 937 — ZAGREB - VARAŽDIN - NAGYKANIZSA

1, 2 class except where shown. HŽ

km			7600 2	3000 2	205 ✕ M	7602 2	3006 2	3008 2	IC590 ⚍	243 ✕ D	3020 2
0	Zagreb	d.	...	0455	0835	...	1115	1325	1605	...	2105
41	Zabok	d.	...	0551	0910	...	1217	1428	1640	...	2158
110	Varaždin	d.	0530	0743	1019	1332	1356	1613	1800	...	2328
	Ljubljana 933	d.	...	...	...	...	...	...	...	1503	...
	Pragersko	d.	...	...	...	...	...	...	...	1710	...
122	Čakovec	d.	0548	0752	1037	1342	1405	1626	1809	1819	...
154	Kotoriba	d.	0619	0830	1101	1423	...	1657	...	1852	...
160	Murakeresztúr	d.	0637	...	1136	1445	...	...	...	1915	...
174	Nagykanizsa	a.	0705	...	1148	1500	...	...	...	1927	...
	Budapest Déli 893	a.	...	...	1528	...	...	...	...	2258k	...

			991	IC591 ⚍	7601 2	242 ✕ D	3011 2	7603 2	3015 2	3017 2	993	204 M
Budapest Déli 893		d.	...	...	...	0600k	...	...	...	...	...	1425
Nagykanizsa		d.	...	...	0715	0933	...	1115	...	...	...	1811
Murakeresztúr		d.	...	...	0745	1000	...	1150	...	...	...	1836
Kotoriba		d.	0510	...	0805	1010	...	1202	...	1450	1713	1853
Čakovec		d.	0546	0730	0837	1044f	1036	1236	...	1534	1746	1921
Pragersko		a.	...	...	...	1143	...	...	...	...	...	...
Ljubljana 933		a.	...	...	...	1350	...	...	...	...	...	...
Varaždin		d.	0557	0744	0846	...	1047	1246	1425	1605	1757	1937
Zabok		d.	0715	0855	...	...	1216	...	1612	1744	1916	2049
Zagreb		a.	0754	0934	...	...	1305	...	1710	1828	1956	2125

D – DRAVA – 🛌 and ✕ Venezia - Trieste - Budapest and v.v.   **M –** MAESTRAL – 🛌 Zagreb - Budapest and v.v.   **f –** Arrive 1034.   **k –** Budapest **Keleti**.

Table 938 — ZAGREB - KOPRIVNICA - NAGYKANIZSA and OSIJEK

1, 2 class except where shown. HŽ

km			241 2V	IC583 ⚍	IC585 ⚍ S	203	981 A✕	IC201 1🚻⚍	IC581 ⚍	207	983 Z	209 R
	Rijeka 932	d.	...	...	...	...	1210	...	...	1735	...	2050
0	Zagreb	d.	0555	0618	0953	1350	1411	1605	1640	...	2343	0115
60	Križevci	d.	0638	0713	1037	1434	1459	1647	1721	1819	0034	0159
	Varaždin	d.	...	0657	...	...	...	...	...	...	...	...
92	Koprivnica	d.	0717	0744	1107	1505	1537	1720	1750	1850	0120	0235
	Gyékényes 🚉	d.	0750	...	1533	...	1750	...	1903	...	0320	...
	Nagykanizsa	a.	0814	...	1558	...	...	...	...	...	0345	...
	Budapest Déli 893/4	a.	1158k	...	1953k	2143	...	...	...	...	0728	...
161	Virovitica	d.	...	0849	1203	...	1655	...	1843	...	0223	...
236	Našice	a.	...	0949	1309	...	1801	...	1940	...	0344	...
288	Osijek	a.	...	1025	1345	...	1843	...	2014	...	0502	...

			208 R	980 Z	770	206	IC580 1🚻⚍	IC200 A✕	IC582 ⚍ S	202	IC584 ⚍	240 2V
Osijek		d.	...	0035	...	0600	...	1140	...	1630	...	...
Našice		d.	...	0126	...	0634	...	1218	...	1709	...	...
Virovitica		d.	...	0241	...	0733	...	1318	...	1818	...	...
Budapest Déli 893/4		d.	1935	...	...	...	0635	...	1015k	...	1730k	...
Nagykanizsa		d.	2320	...	...	...	...	...	1413	...	2126	...
Gyékényes 🚉		d.	0012	...	0805	...	1040	...	1450	...	2205	...
Koprivnica		d.	0040	0354	0609	0828	0833	1103	1428	1516	1938	2230
Varaždin		a.	...	...	...	...	...	...	...	...	2009	...
Križevci		d.	0102	0427	0643	0850	0857	1125	1459	1537	2001	2252
Zagreb		a.	0145	0523	0729	0931	0936	1206	1545	1619	2042	2332
Rijeka 932		a.	0635	...	...	...	1600	...	...	...	...	...

A – AGRAM – 🛌 and ✕ Rijeka - Budapest and v.v.   **Z –** 🛏 1, 2 cl., 🛏 2 cl. and 🛌 Zagreb - Osijek and v.v.
R – ADRIATICA – 🛏 1, 2 cl. and 🛌 Budapest - Rijeka and v.v.   **k –** Budapest **Keleti**.
S – AVAS – 🛌 Zagreb - Budapest - Nyíregyháza and v.v.
V – VENEZIA EXPRESS – 🛏 1, 2 cl., 🛏 2 cl. and 🛌 (also 🛌 May 29 - Sept. 25) Venezia - Trieste - Zagreb - Budapest and v.v.;
🛏 1, 2 cl. Zagreb - Budapest (trains **16/5**) - Moskva and v.v.; conveys on ③⑥ from Venezia, ③⑦ from Moskva: 🛏 1, 2 cl. Venezia - Zagreb - Moskva and v.v.

Table 938a — VINKOVCI - OSIJEK - PÉCS

1, 2 class except where shown. HŽ , MÁV

km			8139	8127	8137	8117	8125 2	8123	8111 2	8151
0	Vinkovci	d.	...	...	...	...	...	...	...	...
36	Osijek	a.	...	...	...	...	...	...	...	...
36	Osijek	d.	...	...	...	...	...	...	...	...
64	Beli Manastir 🚉	d.	...	...	...	...	...	...	...	...
76	Magyarbóly	d.	0432v	0535v	0734v	0920	1137v	1502v	1640	1942
118	Pécs	a.	0535	0650	0845	1000	1250	1620	1745	2055

Service suspended

			8120 2	8110	8122 2	8124	8154	8134	8126 2	8118	8138 ⑥
Pécs		d.	0500	0550	0700	1105	1330	1440	1645	1905	2240
Magyarbóly		d.	0630v	0645	0810v	1225v	1442	1550v	1805v	2001	2343
Beli Manastir 🚉		d.	...	...	...	...	...	...	...	...	...
Osijek		a.	...	...	...	...	...	...	...	...	...
Osijek		d.	...	...	...	...	...	...	...	...	...
Vinkovci		a.	...	...	...	...	...	...	...	...	...

Service suspended

v – Change at Villány.

Table 939 — ZAGREB - SARAJEVO - PLOČE

2 class only. HŽ, ZBH

km			5901	5903	5905	5907	5909	5911
0	Zagreb ▲	d.	...	...	...	...	...	...
53	Sisak ▲	d.	...	...	...	...	...	...
77	Sunja	d.	...	...	...	...	...	...
	Bihać	d.	...	...	...	...	...	...
119	Bosanski Novi	d.	...	...	...	...	...	...
221	Banja Luka 🚉	d.	...	...	...	...	...	...
	Vinkovci	d.	...	...	...	...	...	...
331	Doboj 🚉	d.	...	...	...	...	...	...
443	Zenica	d.	...	...	...	...	...	...
536	Sarajevo	a.	...	...	...	...	...	...
536	Sarajevo	d.	...	...	...	...	...	...
615	Konjic	d.	...	...	...	...	...	...
688	Mostar	d.	...	...	...	...	...	...
729	Čapljina 🚉	d.	0455	0639	0818	1251	1656	2030
764	Ploče	a.	0550	0730	0912	1347	1750	2125

Service suspended

			5900	5902	5904	5906	5908
Ploče		d.	0610	1055	1415	1845	2145
Čapljina 🚉		d.	0721	1148	1511	1941	2241
Mostar		d.	...	...	...	...	...
Konjic		d.	...	...	...	...	...
Sarajevo		a.	...	...	...	...	...
Sarajevo		d.	...	...	...	...	...
Zenica		d.	...	...	...	...	...
Doboj 🚉		d.	...	...	...	...	...
Vinkovci		a.	...	...	...	...	...
Banja Luka 🚉		d.	...	...	...	...	...
Bosanski Novi		d.	...	...	...	...	...
Bihać		d.	...	...	...	...	...
Sunja		d.	...	...	...	...	...
Sisak ▲		d.	...	...	...	...	...
Zagreb ▲		a.	...	...	...	...	...

Service suspended

▲ – Local trains are operating **Zagreb - Sisak Caprag** (Journey 55-60 minutes):
From Zagreb: 0420, 0523, 0546, 0650, 0920, 1055, 1350, 1500, 1628, 1741, 1955, 2055.
From Sisak Caprag: 0416, 0530, 0628, 0718, 0816, 1030, 1215, 1508, 1617, 1750, 1915, 2120.

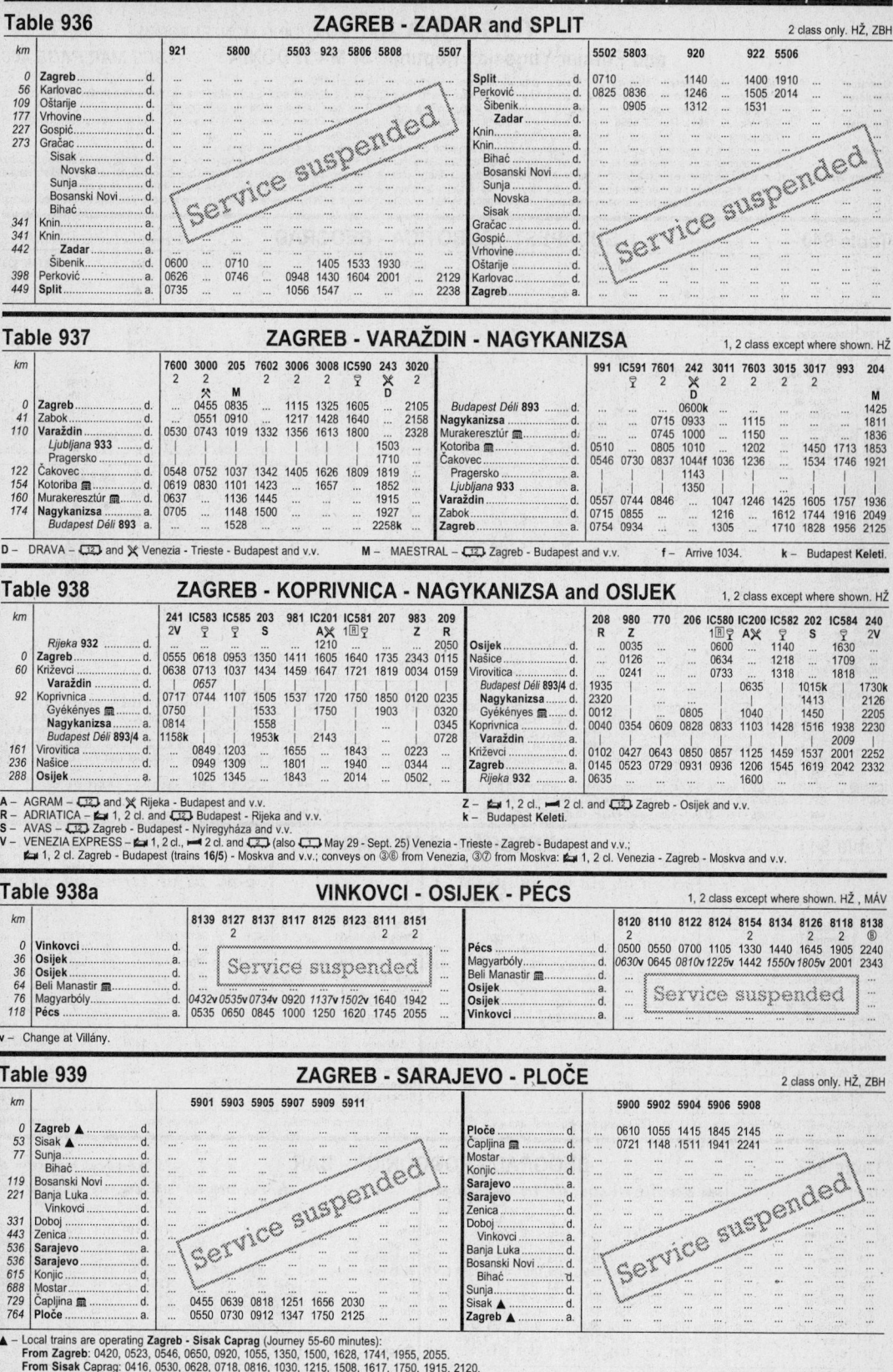

All long-distance rail services in Bosnia, and some services in Croatia, are suspended.

YUGOSLAVIA (INCLUDING MONTENEGRO)
and Former Yugoslav Republic of MACEDONIA

SEE MAP PAGE 468

Operator: Zajednica Jugoslovenskih Železnica (JŽ); Македонски Железници - Makedonski Železnici (МЖ - MŽ).

Services: Trains convey first and second classes of accommodation, shown as '1' and '2' or (12) in the tables. Sleeping cars (🛏) and couchette cars (▬) are of the normal European types – see page **10** for more details. Rail distances in Yugoslavia and F.Y.R.O. Macedonia are shown in tariff-kilometres.

Timings: Valid **May 29, 1994** to **May 27, 1995**. There are currently no through services to Croatia or Bosnia. Expect delays at all frontiers with consequent late running. Services in Yugoslavia (including Montenegro) are subject to alteration or cancellation due to fuel shortages.

Tickets: A supplement is payable for travel by internal express trains. Reservation of seats is possible on most express trains.

Visas: Most nationals require a visa (double-entry visa if going beyond Yugoslavia and returning). These must be obtained **in advance** or entry into Yugoslavia may be refused.

Security Warning: Due to the desperate economic situation travel on international trains is **dangerous**, as they now attract gangs of thieves and bandits especially at night. Tickets issued outside Yugoslavia may not be honoured, so you may wish to consider an alternative route via Romania/Bulgaria (Table **961**). If necessary to travel to or through Yugoslavia couchette/sleeping car accommodation is recommended for better security (though is still far from safe) and you are advised to take appropriate precautions.

Table 940 BUDAPEST - SUBOTICA - BEOGRAD

1, 2 class except where shown. MÁV, JŽ

km			489		335	501	341					IC339					345		503		491			881	IC333
			2			2Ⓡ🍷	2			2	2	Ⓡ✕	2	2	2	2	Ⓡ✕	2	Ⓡ🍷	2		2	2	🍷	Ⓡ✕
			◆		◆		◆					◆					◆				◆			◆	◆
0	**Budapest Keleti**	d.	...	...	0030	...	...	...	...	...	...	0625	...	...	...	...	1125	...	...	...	1510	...	...	...	1715
7	Budapest Ferencváros	d.	...	...	|	...	0230k	...	...	...	...	|	...	...	...	...	|	...	...	...	|	...	...	...	|
124	Kiskunhalas	d.	...	...	0249	...	|	...	...	...	...	0834	...	...	...	...	1329	...	...	...	1724	...	...	...	1926
163	Kelebia	a.	...	...	0310	...	0520	...	...	...	...	0855	...	...	...	...	1350	...	...	...	1745	...	...	...	1947
163	Kelebia 🏛	d.	...	...	0350	...	0550	...	...	...	...	0910	...	...	...	...	1400	...	...	...	1800	...	...	...	2000
	Szeged 895	d.	0130	...	|	...	|	...	...	...	0700	|	...	0930	...	1200	|	...	...	...	|	...	1800	...	|
	Röszke 🏛	d.	0255	...	|	...	|	...	...	...	0734	|	...	1008	...	1225	|	...	...	...	|	...	1834	...	|
	Horgoš 🏛	d.	0320	...	|	...	|	...	...	...	0800	|	...	1045	...	1249	|	...	...	...	|	...	1903	...	|
175	**Subotica** 🏛	a.	0351	...	0400	...	0600	...	...	...	0831	0920	...	1116	...	1320	1410	...	...	...	1810	...	1934	...	2010
175	**Subotica**	d.	0405	...	0430	0602	0636	...	...	0644	...	0945	1119	...	*1224*	...	1437	1447	1648	...	1845	...	...	1950	2048
274	Novi Sad	d.	0520	...	0557	0726	0751	...	...	0856	...	1101	1324	...	1436	...	1559	1643	1816	1906	2006	2014	...	2150	2209
354	**Beograd**	a.	0634	...	0709	0847	0907	...	...	1035	...	1218	1501	...	1620	...	1712	1814	1938	2041	2128	2223	...	2328c	2338

			IC332		880		490					344		500		IC338				340	502	334	488		
		2	Ⓡ✕	2	🍷			2	2	2	2	Ⓡ✕	2	2Ⓡ🍷		Ⓡ✕	2		2	2	Ⓡ🍷		2	2	
			◆		◆		◆					◆				◆				◆		◆	◆		
Beograd	d.	...	0610	...	0523c	...	0650	0725	0910	...	1130	1155	...	1325	...	1430	1550	...	1810	1920	2010	2145	2205	2300	...
Novi Sad	d.	...	0742	...	0755	...	0843	0916	1110	...	1309	1323	...	1456	...	1600	1739	...	1955	2054	2140	2320	2334	0036	...
Subotica	a.	...	0854	...	0930	...	1009	1054	1255	...	...	1432	...	1616	...	1715	...	...	...	2205	2300	0036	0045	...	...
Subotica 🏛	d.	0725	0925	0900	...	...	1110	...	...	1340	...	1525	1603	...	...	1745	...	...	...	2220	...	0130	0100	...	...
Horgoš 🏛	d.	0817	|	0952	...	...	|	...	...	1431	...	|	1653	...	...	|	...	...	...	|	...	|	0206	...	...
Röszke 🏛	d.	0846	|	1021	...	...	|	...	...	1500	...	|	1722	...	...	|	...	...	...	|	...	|	0300	...	...
Szeged 895	a.	0900	|	1035	...	...	|	...	...	1514	...	|	1736	...	...	|	...	...	...	|	...	|	0315	...	...
Kelebia 🏛	a.	...	0935	...	...	...	1120	...	...	...	...	1535	...	...	...	1755	...	...	...	2245	...	0140	...	...	...
Kelebia	d.	...	0950	...	...	...	1140	...	...	...	...	1545	...	...	...	1810	...	...	...	2305	...	0205	...	...	...
Kiskunhalas	d.	...	1012	...	...	...	1201	...	...	...	...	1607	...	...	...	1832	...	...	...	|	...	0257	...	...	...
Budapest Ferencváros	a.	...	|	...	...	...	|	...	...	...	...	|	...	...	...	|	...	...	...	0211k	...	|	...	...	...
Budapest Keleti	a.	...	1218	...	...	...	1413	...	...	...	...	1818	...	...	...	2043	...	...	...	...	...	0513	...	...	...

◆ – **NOTES** (LISTED BY TRAIN NUMBERS)

IC332/3 – IVO ANDRIĆ – (12) and ✕ Beograd - Budapest and v.v. Supplement payable.

334/5 – HELLAS EXPRESS – 🛏 1, 2 cl., ▬ 2 cl. and (2) Athínai - Budapest and v.v.; (2) Athínai - Budapest (trains **346/7**) - Wien and v.v.; conveys May 28 - Sept. 24: 🛏 1, 2 cl. Beograd - Budapest (trains **1074/5**) - Štúrovo (trains **470/1**) - Praha and v.v.; for ▬ 2 cl. Athínai - Budapest - Bratislava/Praha and v.v. see Table **96b**.

IC338/9 – HUNYADI – (12) and ✕ Beograd - Budapest and v.v. Supplement payable.

340/1 – BEOGRAD EXPRESS – 🛏 1, 2 cl., ▬ 2 cl. and (2) Beograd - Wien and v.v.; ▬ 2 cl. Skopje (trains **212/3**) - Niš (trains **492/3**) - Beograd - Wien and v.v.

344/5 – AVALA – (12) and ✕ Beograd - Wien and v.v.

488/9 – PUSKIN – 🛏 1, 2 cl. Beograd - Chop (train **10**) - Moskva and Moskva (train **9**) - Chop - Beograd; (2) Beograd - Szeged - Záhony and v.v.; conveys 🛏 2 cl. Athínai/Thessaloniki (trains **334/5**) - Beograd - Moskva on dates in Table **94c**.

490/1 – BALKAN EXPRESS – ▬ 1, 2 cl. and (2) Istanbul - Budapest and v.v.; 🛏 1, 2 cl., ▬ 2 cl. and (12) Sofija - Budapest and v.v.; (12) Beograd - Budapest and v.v.

880/1 – 🛏 1, 2 cl., ▬ 2 cl., (12) and 🍷 Bar - Beograd - Subotica and v.v.

c – Beograd **Centar**.

k – Budapest **Kelenföld**.

Table 941 BEOGRAD - TIMIŞOARA

1, 2 class except where shown. JŽ, CFR

km			1243 1202	6717	1182	2303	1586	2305	2355	1245 1204	241 12
			2	2		2		2	2	2	Ⓡ B
0	**Beograd** Dunav	d.	...	...	...	...	...	...	...	...	1915
	Beograd Centar	d.	...	...	...	*0732*	...	*1207*	*1427*	...	|
18	Pančevo Glavna	a.	...	...	...	*0802*	...	*1241*	*1501*	...	1933
18	Pančevo Glavna	d.	...	...	...	0915	...	1250	1510	...	1935
100	Zrenjanin	d.	...	...	...	1120	...	1446	|	...	|
179	Kikinda ‡	d.	...	0630	...	1314	*1425*	1642	|	...	|
198	Jimbolia 🏛 §	a.	...	0748	...	...	*1543*	...	|	...	|
198	Jimbolia	d.	...	...	0826	...	1725	...	|	...	|
84	Vršac	a.	...	...	|	...	|	...	1622	...	2045
84	Vršac 🏛 ‡	d.	0615c	...	|	...	|	...	...	1920c	2145
103	Stamora Moraviţa 🏛 §	a.	0735c	...	|	...	|	...	...	2040c	2306
103	Stamora Moraviţa	d.	0820	...	|	...	|	...	...	2145	2351
159	**Timişoara** Nord	a.	0935	...	0927	...	1821	...	...	2300	0039
	Bucureşti **954**	a.	...	...	...	...	...	...	...	...	0840

		1201 1242	2352	11 240	1581	2302	1583	1203 1244	2358	2306
		2	2	Ⓡ B		2		2	2	2
Bucureşti **954**	d.	...	...	2200	...	...	...	...	...	...
Timişoara Nord	d.	0405	...	0614	0631	...	1605	1650	...	...
Stamora Moraviţa	a.	0518	...	0710	|	...	|	1750	...	...
Stamora Moraviţa 🏛 §	d.	0555c	...	0800	|	...	|	1850c	...	...
Vršac 🏛 ‡	a.	0515c	...	0720	|	...	|	1816c	...	...
Vršac	d.	...	0755	0815	|	...	|	...	1915	...
Jimbolia	a.	...	|	|	0725	...	1704	...	|	...
Jimbolia 🏛 §	d.	...	|	|	*0912*	...	*1710*	...	|	...
Kikinda ‡	d.	...	|	|	*0830*	1100	*1628*	...	|	1743
Zrenjanin	d.	...	|	|	...	1300	...	...	|	1925
Pančevo Glavna	a.	...	0908	0935	...	1505	...	...	2045	2118
Pančevo Glavna	d.	...	*0930*	0938	...	*1520*	...	...	*2110*	2120
Beograd Centar	a.	...	*0955*	|	...	*1545*	...	...	*2135*	|
Beograd Dunav	a.	...	...	0955	...	...	...	...	...	2150

B – BUCUREŞTI EXPRESS – 🛏 1, 2 cl. and (12) Beograd - Bucureşti and v.v.

c – Subject to confirmation. ‡ – Yugoslav time. § – Romanian time.

Table 942 BEOGRAD - PODGORICA - BAR

1, 2 class except where shown. JŽ

km			6861	6863	2711	871	575	577	873	9661	1877	881
			2	2			1Ⓡ 🍷	2	H	▬ E	J	🍷 S
0	**Beograd**	d.	...	...	0730	1030	1400	1730	2140	2240	...	2340c
93	Valjevo	d.	...	...	0926	1206	1530	1905	2317	|	...	0103
159	Požega	d.	...	...	1037	1307	1629	2013	0027	|	0158	0223
186	Užice	d.	...	...	1109	1338	1653	2039	0101	0130	0218	0247
255	Priboj	d.	...	...	1215	1430	1747	2133	0159	|	0316	0340
288	Prijepolje	d.	...	...	1242	1500	1812	2155	0222	|	0339	0404
338	Bijelo Polje	d.	0703	1246	...	1547	1854	...	0308	0350	0425	0450
468	**Podgorica**	d.	0859	1435	...	1735	2034	...	0455	0533	0607	0629
514	Sutomore	a.	0939	1521	...	1812	2108	...	0529	|	0648	0710
524	**Bar**	a.	0948	1531	...	1821	2116	...	0537	0618	0656	0718

		576	2700	2740	870	574	6864	1876	880	9660	872
		2	2			1Ⓡ 🍷	2	J	🍷 S	▬ E	H
Bar	d.	...	...	...	1010	1410	1600	2030	2120	2200	2230
Sutomore	d.	...	...	...	1022	1421	1611	2043	2133	|	2241
Podgorica	d.	...	...	...	1100	1500	1650	2126	2210	2300	2325
Bijelo Polje	d.	...	0600	1015	1243	1640	1851	2310	2355	0045	0113
Prijepolje	d.	0421	0642	1059	1324	1719	...	2346	0034	|	0157
Priboj	d.	0445	0708	1125	1350	1747	...	0009	0058	|	0226
Užice	d.	0542	0827	1237	1453	1845	...	0118	0156	0316t	0340
Požega	d.	0606	0901	1259	1521	1906	...	0137	0240	|	0412
Valjevo	d.	0702	1007	...	1619	2003	...	...	0336	|	0508
Beograd	a.	0836	1152c	...	1749	2132	...	...	0523c	0549	0639

E – Runs May 30 - Sept. 26: 🛏 1, 2 cl. and ▬ 2 cl. Beograd - Bar and v.v.

H – 🛏 1, 2 cl., ▬ 2 cl. and (12) Beograd - Bar and v.v.

J – Runs June 11 - Sept. 18: 🛏 1, 2 cl., ▬ 2 cl. and (12) Požega - Bar and v.v.

S – 🛏 1, 2 cl., ▬ 2 cl. and (12) and 🍷 Subotica - Beograd Centar - Bar and v.v.

c – Beograd Centar.

t – Užice **Teretna**.

Table 945 — BEOGRAD - NIŠ - SKOPJE - GEVGELIJA

1, 2 class except where shown. JŽ, MŽ, BDŽ

km			771	761			335	593		493	213			591	763		291	521		495	775	491
		2	2	2	2	2	⛾	ℝ		♦	♦	2	2	ℝ	2		2			2 ⓑ	⛾	⛾
0	Beograd ....d.	...	...	0550	0620	...	...	0740	...	...	1045	1045	...	...	1410	1420	...	1800	1835	...	2055	2200
110	Lapovo ....d.	...	...	0516	0812	0845	...	0948	...	...	1300	1300	...	...	1619	1659	...	2005	2048	...	2314	0011
139	Kragujevac ....d.	...	...	0555	...	0922	...	...	...	...			...	...	1735	...	...			...	...	...
195	Kraljevo ....d.	0222	...	0735	...	1035	...	...	...	1455			...	...	1905	...	...			...	...	...
325	Kosovska Mitrovica ....d.	0526	...	1028	...	1312	...	...	...	1731			...	...	2134	...	...			...	...	...
359	Kosovó Polje ....d.	0635	0830	1112	...	1345	1400	...	...	1820	1900		...	...	2208	2352	...			...	...	...
441	Peć ....d.		1016		...		1545	...	...	2045			...	...		0137	...			...	...	...
136	Jagodina ....d.	...	...	...	0831	...	...	1007	...	...	1319	1319	...	...	1639	...	...	2023	2107	...	2336	0031
244	Niš ....a.	...	...	...	1015	...	...	1140	...	...	1452	1452	...	...	1808	...	...	2150	2235	...	0110	0205
244	Niš ....d.	...	...	...	1022	...	...	1150	...	...	1510	1505	...	...	1824	...	...	2200	...	2350	0130	0226
	Dimitrovgrad ....d.	...	...	...	...	...	...	...	1730	...			...	...		...	...			0300	...	0450
	Kalotina ▥ ....d.	...	...	...	...	...	...	...	1915	...			...	...		...	...			0438	...	0628
	Dragoman ★ ....d.	...	...	...	...	...	...	...	1943	...			...	...		...	...			0512	...	0702
417	Sofija ....d.	...	...	...	...	...	...	...	2032	...			...	...		...	...			0619	...	0738
288	Leskovac ⓞ ....d.	...	...	...	1100	...	...	1227	...	...	1541		...	...	1900	...	...	2236	...	...	0210	...
472	Skopje ....a.	0930	...	...	...	...	...	...	...	...	1945	2115	...	...	2259	...	...	0224	...	...	0624	...
472	Skopje ....d.	...	1119	...	...	...	1445	1650	1705	2007			...	...		...	0233	0244	...	0610	...	...
535	Titov Veles ....d.	...	1211	...	...	...	1535	1729	1744	2100			...	...		...	0318	0322	...	0659	...	...
643	Prilep ....d.	...	1404	...	...	...	1731		1914	2249			...	...		...	0516		...	0903	...	...
701	Bitola ....a.	...	1449	...	...	...	1816		1945	2322			...	...		...	0602		...	0948	...	...
678	Gevgelija ▥ ....a.	...	...	...	...	...	...	1847	...	...			...	...		...	0445	...	...	...	...	...
757	Thessaloniki 970 ....a.	...	...	...	...	...	...	2218	...	...			...	...		...	0725	...	...	...	...	...
1267	Athínai 970 ....a.	...	...	...	...	...	...	0703	...	...			...	...		...		...	...	...	...	...

	520		492	212	592	770		334	762	590		2		494		2548	490	774		2		760	290
	2		♦	♦	ℝ			⛾ ⛾	2	⛾		2		✕		2	♦	⛾		2			ℝ ♦
Athínai 970 ....d.	...	...	...	...	...	...	...	2330	...	...	...	...	...	...	...	...	...	...	...	...	...	...	...
Thessaloniki 970 ....d.	...	...	...	...	...	...	...	0826	...	...	...	...	...	...	...	...	...	...	...	...	...	...	2100
Gevgelija ▥ ....d.	...	...	...	...	...	...	...	1000	...	...	...	...	...	...	...	...	...	...	...	...	...	...	2215
Bitola ....d.	...	...	0300	...	0620	0707	...		...	...	...	...	...	1214	...	...	1540	...	...	...	1954	...	...
Prilep ....d.	...	...	0337	...	0656	0754	...		...	...	...	...	...	1300	...	...	1627	...	...	...	2040	...	...
Titov Veles ....d.	...	...	0520	...	0817	0941	...	1123	...	...	...	...	...	1441	...	...	1822	...	...	...	2220	2346	...
Skopje ....a.	...	...	0607	...	0857	1028	...	1200	...	...	...	...	...	1533	...	...	1913	...	...	...	2307	0023	...
Skopje ....d.	...	...	...	0815	...	...	1100	1220	1400	...	...	...	...		...	...	2150	...	2115	...	...	0045	...
Leskovac ⓞ ....d.	...	...	...	1205	...	1512	...	1624	1756	...	...	...	...		...	...	0209	...	...	...	...	0440	...
Sofija ....d.	...	2	0935	...	2	...	...		...	...	...	...	...	1650	...	...	2255	...	2	...	...	...	...
Dragoman ★ ....d.	...	...	1020	...	...	...	...		...	...	...	...	...	1748	...	...	2342	...	...	...	...	...	...
Kalotina ▥ ....d.	...	...	1107	...	...	...	...		...	...	...	...	...	1840	...	...	0032	...	...	...	...	...	...
Dimitrovgrad ....d.	...	...	1045	...	...	...	...		...	...	...	...	...	1900	...	...	0012	...	...	...	...	...	...
Niš ....a.	...	...	1234	1247	1553	...	...	1700	1838	...	...	...	...	2120	...	...	0201	0245	...	...	...	...	0516
Niš ....d.	...	0620	1315	1315	1603	...	...	1715	1845	...	...	...	...		...	2330	0220	0300	...	...	...	...	0535
Jagodina ....d.	...	0758	1453	1453	1745	...	...	1853	2016	...	...	...	...		...	0208	0354	0437	...	...	...	...	0706
Peć ....d.	...		0435	...	1105	...	...		1605	...	...	...	...		...		2115	...	...	...	...	...	...
Kosovo Polje ....d.	0225	...	0630	...	1255	...	1413		1500	1755	1828	...	...		...		2305	0020	0026	...	...	...	...
Kosovska Mitrovica ....d.	0316	...	0712	...		...	...		1532		1908	...	...		...				0101	...	...	...	...
Kraljevo ....d.	0610	...	0951	...		...	...		1807		2212	...	...		...				0338	...	...	...	...
Kragujevac ....d.	0725	...		...		...	...		1910		2325	...	...		...				0442	...	...	...	...
Lapovo ....d.	0802	0817	1513	1513	1806	...	...	1912	1955	2036	0003	...	...		...	0240	0414	0457	...	...	...	0531	0726
Beograd ....a.	...	1025	1716	1716	2034	...	...	2115	2159	2239		...	...		...		0619	0714	...	...	...	0738	0927

♦ – NOTES (LISTED BY TRAIN NUMBERS)

42/3 – ◢ 2 cl. and 🛏 Skopje - Niš (trains 492/3) - Beograd and v.v.; ◢ 2 cl. Skopje - Beograd (trains 340/1) - Budapest - Wien and v.v.

90/1 – AKROPOLIS EXPRESS – ◢ 1, 2 cl. and ◢ 2 cl. and 🛏 Thessaloniki - Beograd and v.v.

34/5 – HELLAS EXPRESS – ⚄ 1, 2 cl., ◢ 2 cl. and 🛏 Athínai - Budapest (trains 346/7) - Wien and v.v.; conveys May 28 - Sept. 24: ⚄ 1, 2 cl. Beograd - Budapest (trains 1074/5) - Štúrovo (trains 470/1) - Praha and v.v.; conveys ◢ 2 cl. Athínai - Budapest - Bratislava/Praha and v.v. on dates in Table 96b.; conveys ⚄ 2 cl. Moskva (trains 9/10) - Chop (trains 489/8) - Beograd - Thessaloniki and Athínai and v.v. on dates in Table 94c

490/1 – BALKAN EXPRESS – ◢ 1, 2 cl. and 🛏 Istanbul - Budapest and v.v.; ⚄ 1, 2 cl., ◢ 2 cl. and 🛏 Sofija - Budapest and v.v.; ◢ 2 cl. and 🛏 Istanbul - Beograd and v.v.

492/3 – BEOGRAD SOFIJA EXPRESS – 🛏 Sofija - Beograd and v.v.; ⛾ Dimitrovgrad - Beograd and v.v.

774/5 – ◢ 1, 2 cl., ◢ 2 cl. and 🛏 and ⛾ Skopje - Beograd and v.v.

c – Beogard Centar.

ⓞ – ▥ is at Preševo/Tabanovci.

★ – Change here for the Bolshevik branch.

ALBANIA

SEE MAP PAGE 468

Operator: Hekurudhë ë Shqipërisë (HSH).

Services: Trains conveys one class of accommodation only. Reservation is compulsory, and seats are often sold out one or two days in advance.

Timings: Timings are believed to be correct as at **May 1994**, but are subject to alteration at short notice.

Table 949 — ALBANIAN RAILWAYS

One class only. HSH

km																						
0	Tiranë ....d.	...	0540	0740	0925	1220	1355	1525	1700	1745	1930	Vlorë ....d.	...	...	0520	...	...	1330	...	...	...
51	Milot ....d.	...			1100			1825				Ballsh ....d.	...	0440		0710	...		1550	...	...
98	Shkodër ....a.	...			1250			2005				Fier ....d.	...	0530	0620	0810	...	1413	1640	...	...
36	Durrës ....a.	...	0646	0850	1330	1505	1630		1846	2040		Lushnjë ....d.	...	0717		1505	...		...	...	...
36	Durrës ....d.	...	0700	0905		1525	1645		1900			Pogradec ....d.	...	0530	...		...	...	1340	...	...
	Elbasan ....d.	...	0937			1753			2120			Elbasan ....d.	...	0520	0800		...	...	1625	...	...
189	Pogradec ....a.	...	1245			2055						Durrës ....d.	...	0741	0855	1030	...	1640	1850	...	...
	Lushnjë ....a.	...		1040			1820					Durrës ....d.	0600	0800	0920	1050	1410	1700	1915	...	...
121	Fier ....a.	0545		1134	1352			1913	1930			Shkodër ....d.		0515			1315		...	...	...
146	Ballsh ....a.	0640			1515			2030				Milot ....d.		0650			1450		...	...	...
155	Vlorë ....a.	...		1240			2025					Tiranë ....a.	0710	0840	0905	1030	1206	1520	1640	1815	...	2025

ROMANIA

SEE MAP PAGE 46

Operator: Societatea Naţională a Căilor Ferate Române (CFR).
Services: Trains convey first and second classes of accommodation, shown as '1' and '2' or ⬛ in the tables. Sleeping cars (🛏) and couchette cars (🛏) are of the norm European types, see page **10** for more details.
Timings: Valid **May 29, 1994 - May 27, 1995**.
Tickets: Supplements are payable for travel by certain express trains, except by passengers holding tickets bought outside Romania. Reservation is obligatory for travel by mos services (except local trains), and passengers without reservations have to pay a surcharge.

Table 950 (BUDAPEST) - ARAD/CLUJ NAPOCA - BRAŞOV - BUCUREŞTI

1, 2 class except where shown. CF

km		468 352 ℝ✕ G	468 462 462 ℝ✕	38 463 ℝ	360 87 3202 ℝ✕	316 ℝ✕	471 316 ℝ	362 ℝ	375 22 P	432 F	226 847 F	302 S	366 3204 ℝ	439 322 E	322 E	373 34 2ℝ	426 ℝ	422 E	224 ℝ	406 ℝ	353 206 C	381 26 K	347 24 D
0	Budapest Keleti 896 ..... d.	...	...	...	...	...	...	...	0855	...	...	...	...	...	...	1515	...	...	...	...	1925	...	2315
	Budapest Nyugati 898 .... d.	...	...	...	0605	...	...	...			1200	1500			...		...	...	1700			...	
100	Szolnok 896 898 .... d.	...	...	...	0723	...	1020	...			1318	1618			...	1638	...	...	1815	2050	2150	0040
	Biharkeresztes 🚩 § 898 .. d.	...	...	...	0948	...	...	...			1540	1845			...		...	...	2045			
	Episcopia Bihor 🚩 ‡ ..... d.	...	...	...	1140	...	...	...			1742	2038			...		...	...	2242			
	Satu Mare .... d.	...	0508	...	...	...	...	...							...		1850	...				
	Carei .... d.	...	0600	...	...	...	...	...							...		1922	...				
	Baia Mare .... d.	...		0650	...	...	...	...							...	1946	...					
	Dej Călători .... d.	...		0924	0924	...	...	...							...	2216	...					
	Oradea 952 .... d.	0622			1148	1200	...	...			1754	2046			...	2111	...	2252			
	Cluj Napoca 952 .... a.	0902	1014	1014	▬	1419	...	...			2019			...	2346	...	0111			
	Cluj Napoca .... d.	0914	1025	1025	...	1433	1530	...			2031		2204	...	0001	...	0123			
	Târgu Mureş .... d.	...			...	1416	...	...			2243	2148	...		...				
	Teiuş .... d.	1048	1155	1155	...	1621	1621	1704				2358	2358	...	0135	...			
	Gheorghieni .... d.	...			...				2339					0151	...	0518			
	Miercurea Ciuc .... d.	...			...				0039					0301	...	0620			
196	Békéscsaba 896 .... d.	...	259		...		1136	...			1816			...		2208	2320	0151
225	Lököshaza 🚩 § .... d.	...	222		...		1225	...			1915			...		2252	0010	0240
236	Curtici 🚩 ‡ .... d.	...	ℝ		...		1410	...			2106			...		0042	0209	0437
253	Arad .... a.	...	✕		...		1425	...			2121			...		0056	0215	0452
253	Arad .... d.	...			...		1427	1845			2123			...		0058	0217	0458
	Timişoara Nord 954 ..... d.	...			0830									...	0149			
401	Deva .... d.	...			1140		1615	2044			2311			...		0404	0643
411	Simeria .... d.	...			1204			2112						...		0431	
465	Alba Iulia .... d.	...			...	1722	1706				0003			...		0738
500	Blaj .... d.	1108	1214	1214	...	1640	1640	1738		0017	0017	0035	0157	...		0810
540	Mediaş .... d.	1148	1249	1249	...	1714	1714	1807		0057	0057	0110	0233	...		0840
579	Sighişoara .... d.	1219	1331	1331	...	1745	1745	1836		0130	0130	0140	0304	...		0911
	Sibiu .... d.	...			1439		1916		2345				0350	...	0646	
	Făgăraş .... d.	...			1627				0119				0520	...	0800	
706	Braşov .... a.	1414	1514	1514	1738	1929	1929	2016	0207	0223	0328	0328	0320	0431	0452	0620	0745	0856	1056
706	Braşov .... d.	1427	1527	1527	1718	1756	1941	1941	2028	0219	0235	0338	0338	0330	0443	0504	0635		0912	1107
733	Predeal .... d.	1505	1604	1604	1753	1836	2020	2020	2105	0258	0314	0417	0417	0406	0522	0543	0712		0947	1148
752	Sinaia .... d.	1535	1629	1629	1817	1908	2049	2049	2130	0323	0339	0442	0442	0431	0548	0611	0742		1017	1208
814	Ploieşti Vest .... d.	1633	1724	1724	1906	2011	2141	2141	2218	0414	0430	0538	0538	0526	0646	0707	0843		1117	1256
873	Bucureşti Nord .... a.	...	1803	1803	1945	2050	2220	2220	2257	0453	0509	0617	0617	0559	0725	0746	0927		0936	1158	1339
	Constanţa 958 .... a.	...			2238					0818r					1235		

		33 372 2ℝ B	361 364 ℝ	3201 361 ℝ	461 ℝ	21 466 ℝ✕	354 374 ℝ✕	88 301 P	315 351 ✕	37 221 ℝ✕	315 ℝ✕	223 ℝ	405 ℝ	23 346 C	431 ℝ D	421 ℝ F	380 ℝ E	25 352 ℝ K	205 367 ℝ O	3203 425 ℝ	848 225 ℝ E	321 440 ℝ E	321 ℝ E
	Constanţa 958 .... d.	...	...	...	...	...	...	...	0620	...	...	...	...	...	...	...	1825	...	1910r	...	...	...	
	Bucureşti Nord .... d.	0110	...	...	0638	0638	0821	...	0900	0920	0920	1310	1310	1500		1625	1850	1945	2008	2120		2125	2210	2326	2320
	Ploieşti Vest .... d.	0152	...	...	0720	0720	0904	...	0911	0944	1003	1352	1352	1541		1707	1932	2027	2050		2207	2251	0008	0008
	Sinaia .... d.	0243	...	...	0815	0815	0955	...	1016	1035	1104	1448	1448	1640		1758	2028	2133	2140		2305	2347	0104	0104
	Predeal .... d.	0310	...	...	0842	0842	1022	...	1045	1102	1138	1518	1518	1711		1823	2101	2201	2207		2341	0014	0131	0131
	Braşov .... a.	0339	...	...	0911	0911	1053	...	1121	1142	1207	1547	1547	1740		1852	2131	2230	2236		0011	0044	0201	0201
	Braşov .... d.	0354	...	...	0922	0922	1105	...	1136		1222	1559	1559	1755	1809	1904	2145	2244	2251		0025	0059	0213	0213
	Făgăraş .... d.	...	...	...	...	...	...	1325				1857				...	2345				0212		
	Sibiu .... d.	...	0640	...	...	...	...	1509				2017				...	0110				0354		
	Sighişoara .... d.	0529			1113	1113	1239	1334			1740	1740		2038			0024				0359	0359
	Mediaş .... d.	0603			1150	1150	1314	1410			1814	1814		2112			0059				0433	0433
	Blaj .... d.	0639			1236	1236	1346	1446			1847	1847		2143			0134				0508	0508
	Alba Iulia .... d.	0710	0831				1415							2213								
	Simeria .... d.						...			1738						0318				0620		
	Deva .... d.	0801					1505			1750				2303		0327				0631		
	Timişoara Nord 954 .... d.						...			2053						0513						
	Arad .... d.	0950					1653							0051		0515	0601			0830		
	Arad .... d.	0953					1655							0053		0517	0603					
	Curtici 🚩 ‡ .... d.	1100					1750							0150		0610	0650					
	Lököshaza 🚩 § .... d.	1040					1725							0125		0540	0620					
	Békéscsaba 896 .... a.	1104					1755							0149		0604	0644					
	Miercurea Ciuc .... d.						...						1934	2312					0207			
	Gheorghieni .... d.						...						2033	0014					0318			
	Teiuş .... d.		0850		1256	1256	1507			1907	1907				0155				0528	0528
	Târgu Mureş .... d.						1300			2047									0726	
	Cluj Napoca .... a.		1021		1428	1428	1511	1640		2042		0027			0325					0707
	Cluj Napoca 952 .... a.				1443	1443	1523	1652		2054		0039			0340					
	Oradea 952 .... d.		1527				1749	1929		2311		0251			0619		0713			
	Dej Călători .... d.				1545	1545	...											0653		
	Baia Mare .... d.				1750		...											0900		
	Carei .... d.				1923		...									0739				
	Satu Mare .... a.				1954		...									0810				
	Episcopia Bihor 🚩 ‡ .... d.		1620				1850					0342			0810		0722			
	Biharkeresztes 🚩 § 898 .. d.		1532				1802					0254			0722					
	Szolnok 896 898 .... a.	1235	1829		1910	2057						0549	0312			0723	0807	0957		
	Budapest Nyugati 898 ... a.		1953			2220						0730					1132			
	Budapest Keleti 896 .... a.	1407			2037							0502			0932				

B – BALT ORIENT EXPRESS – 🛏 1, 2 cl., 🛏 2 cl. and 🛏 Berlin - Praha - Budapest - Bucureşti and v.v.; ⬛ Berlin - Lököshaza and v.v.
C – CORONA – 🛏 2 cl. and ⬛ Budapest - Braşov and v.v.
D – DACIA EXPRESS – 🛏 1, 2 cl., 🛏 2 cl. and ⬛ Wien - Bucureşti and v.v.; ⬛ Wien - Bucureşti - Athínai and v.v.; ⬛ Curtici - Bucureşti and v.v.
E – Conveys 🛏 1, 2 cl., 🛏 2 cl. and ⬛.
F – Conveys 🛏 1, 2 cl. and ⬛.
G – ⬛ Oradea - Galaţi and v.v.

K – KARPATY – ⬛ Warszawa - Košice and v.v.; 🛏 1, 2 cl. and 🛏 2 cl. Košice - Bucureşti and v.v.
O – OVIDIUS – 🛏 1, 2 cl., 🛏 2 cl. and ⬛ Budapest - Constanţa and v.v.
P – PANNONIA EXPRESS – 🛏 1, 2 cl., 🛏 2 cl. and ⬛ Praha - Budapest - Bucureşti and v.v.; ⬛ München - Wien - Bucureşti and v.v.
S – CLAUDIOPOLIS – ⬛ Budapest - Tirgu Mureş and v.v.
r – July 2 - Sept. 19 **only**.
§ – Hungarian time.
‡ – Romanian time.

For explanation of standard symbols see page 4 1

Table 952

TIMIŞOARA - ARAD - CLUJ NAPOCA - IAŞI

All trains 1, 2 class. CFR

km		456 Ⓡ	343 ⓇⓍ	3113	657 Ⓡ	423 Ⓡ	347 Ⓡ F	746 Ⓡ F	746 648 Ⓡ F	3115	437 Ⓡ			341 ⓇⓍ	458 Ⓡ	438 Ⓡ	655 Ⓡ	424 Ⓡ	748 Ⓡ F	647 Ⓡ F	3112	345 Ⓡ F	3114
0	Timişoara Nord 954 .....d.	...	0640	1304	1445	1555	1720	1850	1850	1957	2315	Galaţi.............d.	...	0820	...	...	1605	...	...	...	...	...
57	Arad 954 ....d.	...	0751	1435	1526n	1659		1931n	1931n	2138		Iaşi.................d.	0530	1233	...	1436		...	1526	...	2030	
178	Oradea ....d.	...	0957	1725		1905				0010		Paşcani ....d.	0645	1341	...	1546		...	1632t	...	2140	
311	Satu Mare...........d.	...				2132						Suceava ....d.	0745	1426	...	1657		...		...	2240	
369	Baia Mare...........d.	...				2235						Dej Călători ....d.	1338	...	2155	2236		...		...	0447	
205	Deva 950 ....d.	...		1738			2023	2144	2144		0217	Cluj Napoca ......a.	1432	...	2250	2327		...		...	0539	
269	Alba Iulia 950 ......d.	...		1853			2139	2303	2303		0334	Cluj Napoca ......d.	1445	...	2302	2343		...		...	0552	
	Târgu Mureş ....d.	...						0114	0114			Târgu Mureş ....d.		...				0112	0112	...		
331	Cluj Napoca ....a.	...	1233		2048		2336				0529	Alba Iulia 950 .....d.		0055	0142		0316	0316		...	0746	
331	Cluj Napoca ....d.	...	1245		2106		2348				0544	Deva 950 ....d.		0215	0256		0433	0433		...	0903	
390	Dej Călători ....d.	...	1340		2209		0043				0635	Baia Mare 950 ....d.				0043				...		
656	Suceava ....d.	1306	1944		0424		0625					Satu Mare 950 ....d.				0148				...		
717	Paşcani ....d.	1401	2040		0527		0741		0947t			Oradea 950 ....d.	1728			0413				0510		1441
793	Iaşi ....a.	1504	2143		0630		0844		1050			Arad 954 ....d.	1942			0510n	0614	0648n	0648n	0807		1738
1048	Galaţi ....a.	1920					1020					Timişoara Nord 954 a.	2030	0520	0557	0710	0745	0745	0918	1208	1848	

F – Conveys 🛏 1, 2 cl. and 🛋 . n – Arad Nou. t – Paşcani Triaj.

Table 953

BUCUREŞTI - GALAŢI

All trains 1, 2 class. CFR

km		731 Ⓡ		75 Ⓡ	352 Ⓡ G	862		733 Ⓡ			354 Ⓡ	732 ⓇⓍ	752 Ⓡ G		734 Ⓡ		76 Ⓡ	
0	Bucureşti Nord 955 ....d.	0600	...	1510	...	...	1615	1925	Galaţi.............d.	0525	0615	0634	0800	1305	1520	1700	1935	1945
59	Ploieşti Sud 955 ....d.	0643	...	1552	1643			2007	Brăila............d.	0612	0651	0710	0836	1353	1556	1750	2008	2032
128	Buzău 955 ....d.	0742	...	1513	1645	1739		2103	Făurei............d.	0721	0735	0754	0938	1518	1640	1926		2141
	Constanţa 958 ....d.	...	0510	...		1615			Constanţa 958 ...a.	...			1206		2323			
168	Făurei ....d.	0819	0915	1215	1612	1811	1909	1938	2135	Buzău 955 ....d.	0818	0809	0828			1714		2119	2233
228	Brăila ....d.	0906	1030	1330	1720	1756	1857	1954	2048	2220	Ploieşti Sud 955 ..d.	...	0901	0924			1806		2209	
259	Galaţi ....a.	0940	1115	1420	1805	1826	1930	2027	2133	2253	Bucureşti Nord 955 d.	...	1005			1835	1845		2248	

G – 🛋 and Ⓧ Oradea - Cluj Napoca - Galaţi and v.v.

Table 954

ARAD - TIMIŞOARA - CRAIOVA - BUCUREŞTI

All trains 1, 2 class. CFR

km		140 Ⓡ	12 Ⓡ B	28 83 Ⓡ	206 801 Ⓡ O	232 Ⓡ		14 Ⓡ	122 Ⓡ		138 Ⓡ	254 138 ⓇⓍ	227 242 ⓇⓍ	124 Ⓡ	336 ⓇⓍ		255 258 Ⓡ C	294 258	288 188 Ⓡ V	188 843 Ⓡ V	244 Ⓡ D	132 Ⓡ	16 Ⓡ E
	Budapest Keleti 896......d.	...	...	...	1925	...	...	...	...	...	...	...	...	...	...	...	...	...	...	...	...	2035	...
0	Arad 952 ....d.	...	...	...	0058	...	...	...	...	...	...	...	...	...	...	...	...	...	...	...	...	2125	...
	Beograd Dunav 941 ....d.	...	1915	...		...	...	...	...	...	...	...	...	...	...	...	...	...	...	...	...		...
57	Timişoara Nord 952 .....a.	...	...	0044	0146		...	...	...	...	...	...	...	...	...	...	...	...	...	...	...	2125	...
57	Timişoara Nord ....d.	...	0100	...	0149		0640	0650		...	...	...	...	1345		...	...	1845	2225	2310			
116	Lugoj ....d.	...	0143	...	0232			0747		...	...	...	...	1428		...	...	1939	2318	2350			
155	Caransebeş ....d.	...	0218	...	0307			0824		...	...	...	...	1505		...	...	2022	2356	0031			
226	Băile Herculane ....d.	...	0341	...	0427		0903	0938		...	...	...	...	1618		...	...	2157	0111	0146			
244	Orşova ....d.	...	0402	...	0448			0957		...	...	...	...	1639		...	...	2220	0138	0207			
268	Drobeta Turnu Severin ....d.	...	0436	...	0522		0950	1028	1505	...	...	...	...	1710		...	...	2255	0219	0248			
	Cluj Napoca ....d.	...		...						0931	...	...	1121			...	...						
	Deva ....d.	...		...						1325	...	...		1926	2135								
	Târgu Jiu ....d.	...		0510					1451	1636		2246		0101									
	Braşov ....d.	...		...								1323											
	Sibiu ....d.	...		...						1504		1513											
	Râmnicu Vâlcea ....d.	...		...	0546					1712	1732	1732											
382	Craiova ....a.	...	0614	0637	0700		1121	1214	1703	1703	1809	1856	1949	1949	0023	0043	0236	0411	0439				
382	Craiova ....d.	0525	0626	0644	0712		1133	1226	1713	1713	1821	1908			0054	0054	0248	0423	0451				
	Slatina ....d.	...							1917									0528					
	Piteşti ....d.	...							2100									0707					
435	Caracal ....d.	0602		0748	0807		1303		1749	1749	1857	1945			0130	0130	0325						
491	Roşiori Nord ....d.	0645		0828	0848		1348		1830	1830	1940	2025			0210	0210	0404						
591	Bucureşti Nord ....a.	0755	0840	0858	0936	0958	1345	1456	1940	1940	2050	2135	2240		0325b	0325b	0514	0848	0705				
	Constanţa 958 ....a.	...			1140	1235									0611	0611							

		241 Ⓡ D	256 257 C	256 293	137 Ⓡ	137 253 ⓇⓍ		121 ⓇⓍ	231 Ⓡ	131 Ⓡ	13 Ⓡ		243 228 ⓇⓍ	139 ⓇⓍ		335 ⓇⓍ	84 27 Ⓡ		844 187 W	187 287 W	802 205 O	11 Ⓡ B	15 Ⓡ E	123 Ⓡ
	Constanţa 958 ....d.	...	...	...	...	...	...	...	...	...	...	...	...	...	...	1605	1758	1758	1825	...	...	...	...
	Bucureşti Nord..............d.	0025	...	0620	0620		1120	1350	1355	1430		1610	1735		1905	1905	2037b	2037b	2120	2230	2300	2340	
	Roşiori Nord ....d.	0138	...	0730	0730		1241	1501				1723	1848				2154	2154	2228			0052	
	Caracal ....d.	0220	...	0813	0813		1321	1600				1807	1932				2235	2235				0132	
	Piteşti ....d.	...	...						1542						2053								
	Slatina ....d.	...	...						1702						2217								
	Craiova ....a.	0300	...	0853	0853		1401		1808	1649		1847	2012		2124		2315	2315	2344	0050	0120	0212	
	Craiova ....d.	0313	0815	0815	0905	0905	1412		1820	1702		1859			2136		2326	2340	2354	0100	0132	0222	
	Râmnicu Vâlcea ....a.	...	1040	1040				1803						0031									
	Sibiu ....a.	...		1301										0235									
	Braşov ....a.	...	1457																				
	Târgu Jiu ....a.	0502			1110							2039			2305		0123						
	Deva ....a.	0815										0010			0440								
	Cluj Napoca ....a.	...										0308		0619									
	Drobeta Turnu Severin ....d.	...			1105		1607		2008	1844						0111		0135	0242	0314	0410		
	Orşova ....d.	...					1640		2036							0139		0208	0310	0343	0450		
	Băile Herculane ....d.	...					1701		2056	1930						0205		0229	0331	0413	0511		
	Caransebeş ....d.	...					1816		2208							0345		0357	0446	0543	0629		
	Lugoj ....d.	...					1850		2240							0420		0431	0520	0618	0704		
	Timişoara Nord ....d.	...					1930		2325	2150						0500		0510	0600	0707	0752		
	Timişoara Nord 952 ....d.	...																0513	0616	0755			
	Beograd Dunav 941 ....a.	...																	0955				
	Arad 952 ....a.	...																0601	0300	0911			
	Budapest Keleti 896........a.	...																0932					

◄ – BUCUREŞTI EXPRESS – 🛏 1, 2 cl. and 🛋 Beograd - Bucureşti and v.v.
 – 🛋 Iaşi - Braşov - Craiova and v.v.
◄ – 🛏 1, 2 cl. and 🛋 Deva - Bucureşti and v.v.
◄ – 🛏 1, 2 cl., 🛋 2 cl. and 🛋 Timişoara - Bucureşti and v.v.
◄ – OVIDIUS – 🛏 1, 2 cl., 🛋 2 cl. and 🛋 Budapest - Timişoara - Constanţa and v.v.

V – Runs July 1 - Sept. 18 only.
W – Runs July 2 - Sept. 19 only.
b – Bucureşti Băneasa.

---

1 | 🛏 – Sleeping car | Ⓡ – Reservation obligatory | 🛋 – Couchette car |

Table 955 — CHERNIVTSI and CHIŞINĂU - BUCUREŞTI

1, 2 class except where shown. UZ, CFM, CFR

km		255 258 ℝ C	66 ℝ✗	522 ℝ✗	546 522 ℝ	663 662 ℝ V	628 ℝ	532 ℝ✗	524 ℝ	624	503 502 ℝ B♉	52 ℝ✗	61 52 ℝ	526 ℝ	105 610 ⇶ K	63 54 ℝ F	54 ℝ F	626 ℝ	542	507 512 ⇶ S♉	554 ℝ E	603 602 2ℝ R♉	603 602 2ℝ D♉
	Moskva 924 .... d.	...	...	...	...	...	...	...	...	...	...	...	...	...	...	...	...	...	...	1444	...	1645	1645
	Kyïv (Kiev) 925 ... d.	...	...	...	...	...	...	...	...	...	1850	...	...	...	...	...	...	...	...	0615	...	0807	0807
0	Chernivtsi .... d.	...	...	...	...	...	...	...	...	...	0938	...	...	...	...	...	...	...	...	1955	...		
42	Vadul Siret ▥ ... d.	...	...	...	...	...	...	...	...	...	1240	...	...	...	...	...	...	...	...	2300	...		
52	Vicşani ▥ .... d.	...	...	...	...	...	...	...	...	...	1352	...	...	...	...	...	...	...	...	0100	...		
89	Suceava Nord ..... d.	...	...	0629	...	...	...	...	1403	...	1449	...	2300	...	...	...	...	...	...	0153	...		
	Suceava .... d.	...	...	0635	...	...	...	...	1409	...	...	1620	2306	...	0030	...	...	...	...		0217		
	Chişinău (Kishinev).. d.	...	...	...	...	...	...	...	...	...	...	...	1710	...	...	...	...	...	...			2135	2135
	Ungheni ▥ ...... d.	...	...	...	...	...	...	...	...	...	...	...	2130	...	...	...	...	...	...			0214	0214
	Iaşi .... d.	0500	0610	...	...	0911	1156	...	1445	...	...	1555	2313	...	2330	2359	...	...	...			0416	0416
	Vaslui .... d.		0712	...	...		1259	...	1548	...	...			...		0118	...	...	...				
	Bârlad .... d.		0751	...	...		1338	...	1636	...	...			...		0214	...	...	...				
152	Paşcani .... d.	0606t		0723	...	1039	1249	1457		1534	1718	1718	0007	0016t	0158	0158	...	...	...	0238	0301	0519t	0519t
192	Roman .... d.	0635		0753	...	1110	1320	1527		1748	1748	0037	0047		...		...	...	...	0330	0550	0550	
	Piatra-Neamţ ..... d.				0713											0209							
236	Bacău .... d.	0704		0832	0832	1142	1359	1556		1642	1825	1825	0112	0124	0254	0254	...	...	...	0322	0346	0405	0629	0629
294	Adjud .... a.	0755		0915	0915	1233	1443	1647		1732	1905	1905	0158	0210		...	...	...	...	0413	0432	0449	0715	0715
	Braşov .... a.	1303			1736																		
340	Focşani .... d.		0924	0957	0957		1512	1527	1730	1819	...	1949	1949	0241	0254	0410	0410	0348	0456		0533	0757	0757
410	Buzău .... d.		1015	1048	1048		1605	1618	1822	1912	1902	2042	2042	0330	0346	0458	0458	0439	0549	0602	0626	0907	0907
479	Ploieşti Sud ..... d.		1107	1143	1143		1657	1709	1914	2002	2019	2133	2133	0422	0438	0546	0546	0528	0638	0654	0715	1004	1004
538	Bucureşti Nord .... a.		1148	1230	1230		1736	1748	1953	2041	2102	2212	2212	0501	0521	0625	0625	0607	0717	0737	0754	1049	1049

km		51 ℝ✗	106 62 ℝ	501 B♉	627 ℝ V	521 ℝ✗	541 ℝ	621 ℝ	523 ℝ	523 545 ℝ C	257 256 ⇶ K	65 ℝ✗	609 620 ⇶ E	553 ℝ	661 ℝ	664 ⇶ R♉	531 ℝ	525 ℝ	102 601 2ℝ D♉	102 601 2ℝ F	53 ℝ F	64 625 ℝ	104 511 ⇶ S♉
0	Bucureşti Nord..... d.	0608	0608	0906	1120	1200	1300	1320	1555	1555	...	1720	1932	2050	...	2220	2310	2316	2316	2335	2335	2345	2385
59	Ploieşti Sud ..... d.	0651	0651	1005	1204	1244	1342	1402	1637	1637	...	1802	2017	2132	...	2302	2351	0001	0001	0016	0016	0027	0040
128	Buzău .... d.	0748	0748		1300	1342	1436	1456	1734	1734	...	1909	2114	2226	...	2358	0044	0058	0058	0109	0109	0120	
199	Focşani .... d.	0840	0840		1353	1435	1527	1547	1825	1825	...	2000	2206	2318	...	0049	0132	0150	0150	0157	0157	0211	
	Braşov .... d.										1509				1959								
244	Adjud .... d.	0921	0921	1239		1524	1612		1906	1906	2014	...	2243	2359	...	0051	0130	0213	0233	0233	...	...	0258
303	Bacău .... d.	1010	1010	1331		1603	1704		1955	2024	2054	...	2334	0046	...	0131	0217	0300	0324	0324	0310	0310	0349
	Piatra-Neamţ ..... a.				1759				2119														
346	Roman .... d.	1038	1038		1632		...		2023	...	2123	...	0005	0115	...	0200	0246	0329	0355	0355	...	...	
384	Paşcani .... d.	1117	1130	1435	1705		...		2056	...	2154t	...	0039t	0148	...	0249	0317	0402	0429t	0429t	0416	0451	0452
	Bârlad .... d.				1529		1721		2132												0345		
	Vaslui .... d.				1625		1759		2210												0423		
460	Iaşi .... d.		1231		1735		1905		2257	2316	0154	...		0349	...	0544	0544	...	0552	0532			
483	Ungheni ▥ ...... a.										0605	...				1014	1014						
591	Chişinău (Kishinev).. a.										0810	...				1303	1303						
	Suceava .... a.	1201			1757		2142			0232	...			0444			0501						
	Suceava Nord ..... a.			1534	1803		2148						0450									0612	
	Vicşani ▥ ...... a.			1700																		0747	
	Vadul Siret ▥ ... a.			1937																		1012	
	Chernivtsi .... a.			2050																		1125	
	Kyïv (Kiev) 925 ... a.			1125											0306	0306						0113	
	Moskva 924 .... a.														2011	2114						1823	

B – BULGARIA EXPRESS – ⇶ 2 cl. and ♉ Kyïv - Chernivtsi - Bucureşti - Sofija and v.v.; ⇶ 2 cl. Sankt Peterburg (trains 53/4) - Chernivtsi - Bucureşti and Sofija and v.v.; ⇶ 2 cl. Minsk (trains 195/630) - Baranovichi (trains 53/4) - Sofija and v.v.; conveys ⇶ 2 cl. Riga - Vilnius - Bucureşti - Sofija and v.v. on dates in Table 922.
C – ⌑ Iaşi - Craiova and v.v.
D – DANUBIUS EXPRESS – Runs ①⑤ from Moskva, ①④ from Sofija (and Bucureşti): ⇶ 1, 2 cl. and ♉ Moskva - Chişinău - Sofija and v.v.; ⇶ 2 cl. Chişinău - Sofija and v.v.; ⌑ Ungheni - Bucureşti and v.v.
E – Also conveys ⇶ 1, 2 cl. and ⇥ 2 cl.
F – Also conveys ⇶ 1, 2 cl.
K – PRIETENIA – ⇶ 2 cl. Chişinău - Bucureşti and v.v.
R – ROMANIA EXPRESS – Runs ③④⑦ from Moskva, ②⑤⑥ from Bucureşti: ⇶ 1, 2 cl and ♉ Moskva - Bucureşti and v.v.; ♉ Ungheni - Bucureşti and v.v.
S – SOFIJA EXPRESS – ⇶ 1, 2 cl. and ♉ Moskva - Chernivtsi - Sofija and v.v.
V – Runs ①⑤⑥⑦ only.
t – Paşcani Triaj.

Table 958 — BUCUREŞTI - CONSTANŢA - MANGALIA

1, 2 class except where shown. CFR

km		821 ℝ	666 865 ℝ g	188 843 ℝ	226 847 ℝ	823 ℝ✗	831 ℝ✗ h	881 ℝ✗	85 83 ℝ✗ T	28 861 ℝ O	752 801 ℝ	206 825 ℝ	827	829 ℝ✗	87 ℝ✗ B	38 8051 F
0	Bucureşti Nord...... d.	0100	...	0338b	0540	0605	0710	0710	0810	0915	...	0957	1325	1620	...	1900	...	2015	2314o
	Iaşi 955 .... d.		2259														
	Galaţi 953 ...... d.							0800									
146	Feteşti .... d.	0253	0420	0512		0741	0842	0842		1050	1126	1457	1752	...	2032	...	0201
190	Medgidia .... d.	0339	0503	0617	0700	0824	0908	0945	0943		1135	1209	1540	1544	1836	1905	2115	...	0312
334	Tulcea .... a.				1008		1200	1215					1852		2211	...	0611
225	Constanţa .... a.	0412	0530	0611	0710	0818	0851		1011	1036	1140	1206	1235	1607	...	1903	...	2142	2238	...
225	Constanţa .... d.	...	0545	0639	0739	0830	0910		1055		1226h	1634	...	1924	...	2155f	...
239	Eforie Nord ...... d.	...	0615	0657	0803	0848	0928		1113		1245h	1703	...	1950	...	2213f	...
268	Mangalia .... a.	...	0711	0750	0905	0930	1015		1155		1340h	1805	...	2042	...	2255f	...

		88 37 ℝ✗ B	822 ℝ✗	824	826 ℝ	866 665 ℝ	84 27 ℝ✗ T	862 751 ℝ✗ h	86 ℝ✗	832 ℝ	882 832 ℝ C	844 187 ℝ O	802 205 ℝ A	848 225 ℝ	828	830 ℝ e	8052 F
	Mangalia .... d.		0525	0735	...	1240		1440h	1539		1620		1817	1936	...	2050	2335	...
	Eforie Nord ...... d.		0613	0820	...	1331		1533h	1634		1720		1752	1900	2035	...	2135	0018	...
	Constanţa .... a.		0640	0843	...	1400		1551h	1652		1738		1810	1922	2059	...	2158	0040	...
	Constanţa .... d.	0620	0700	0850	1320	1419	1605	1615	1710	...	1718	1758	1825	1910	1935	...	2110	...	0052	...
	Tulcea .... d.				0722					1510				1902	...	...	2340
	Medgidia .... d.		0733	0921	1029	1450	1646		1800	1800		1856		2006	2154	2205	...	0128	0259
	Feteşti .... d.		0822	1006	1436	1535	1731		1846	1846		1942		2051	2302	...	0216	0318
	Galaţi 953 ...... a.						2027										
	Iaşi 955 .... a.				2122											
	Bucureşti Nord .... a.	0841	0950	1135	1600	1826	1932	2010	2010	2024b	2105	2140	2218	...	0410	0640o

A – Runs July 2 - Sept. 19: ⇶ 1, 2 cl. and ⌑ Arad - Sibiu - Bucureşti - Mangalia and v.v.
B – BRAŞOVIA EXPRESS – ⌑ and ✗ Braşov - Bucureşti - Constanţa and v.v.
C – Runs July 2 - Sept. 19 (one day earlier from Timişoara): ⇶ 1, 2 cl. and ⌑ Timişoara Nord - Craiova - Mangalia and v.v.
F – Also conveys ⇶ 1, 2 cl.
O – OVIDIUS – ⇶ 1, 2 cl., ⇥ 2 cl. and ⌑ Budapest - Timişoara - Constanţa and v.v.
T – OLTENIA EXPRESS – ⌑ and ✗ Tirgu Jiu - Craiova - Constanţa and v.v.

b – Bucureşti Băneasa.
e – May 29 - Sept. 23 only.
f – May 29 - Sept. 24 only.
g – May 30 - Sept. 24 only.
h – July 1 - Sept. 18 only.
k – Runs July 2 - Sept. 19 only.
o – Bucureşti Obor.

⌑ – Through carriage (1 and 2 class)　　♉ – Buffet car　　✗ – Restaurant car

BULGARIA

SEE MAP PAGE 468

Operator: Български Държавни Железници – Bulgarski Durzhavni Zheleznitzi (БДЖ - BDŽ).
Services: Trains convey first and second class of accommodation, shown as '1' and '2' or 🚋 in the tables. Sleeping cars (🛏) and couchette cars (🛌) are of the normal European types, see page 10 for more details. Reservation of seats is possible on most express trains.
Timings: Valid May 29, 1994 - May 27, 1995.

Table 960

BUCUREŞTI - RUSE - SOFIJA

1, 2 class except where shown. CFR, BDŽ

km		740 Ⓡ✕	742 Ⓡ✕	103 484 S 🍴	822 ✕	111 841 2Ⓡ✕	101 402 T	109 744 D🍴	105 482 F	B🍴
0	Bucureşti Nord........ d.	...	...	0826	...	1027	1128	1925	...	2140
91	Giurgiu Nord............ a.	...	...	0956	...	1206	1258	2047	...	2313
91	Giurgiu Nord 🚢.......... d.	...	...	1046	...	1333	1421	2141	...	0006
108	Ruse 🚢.................. a.	...	...	1110	...	1357	1445	2205	...	0030
108	Ruse.................... d.	0610	1010	1210	1325	1505	1535	2310	...	0130
219	Gorna-Orjahovitza .... d.	0830	1222	1443	1552	1716	1823	0136	...	0415
319	Pleven 962 .... d.	0951	1351	1603	1716	...	1943	0301	...	0541
425	Mezdra 962 .... d.	1111	1513	1732	1838	...	2103	0421	...	0717
513	Sofija 962 .... a.	1243	1645	1902	2015	...	2235	0600	...	0856

		840 112 2Ⓡ✕ T	821 Ⓡ✕	401 102 D🍴	741 Ⓡ✕	483 104 S 🍴	743 ✕	485 106 B🍴	823 110 F
	Sofija 962............. d.	...	0830	1115	1230	1300	1515	...	2140	2300
	Mezdra 962........... d.	...	1002	1246	1404	1431	1645	...	2311	0035
	Pleven 962............ d.	...	1121	1410	1524	1542	1801	...	0025	0201
	Gorna-Orjahovitza .. d.	0855	1245	1554	1648	1718	1926	...	0210	0332
	Ruse.................. a.	1105	1450	1835	1900	1940	2140	...	0445	0550
	Ruse.................. d.	1245	...	1930	...	2020	...	...	0530	0635
	Giurgiu Nord 🚢....... a.	1309	...	1954	...	2044	...	...	0554	0659
	Giurgiu Nord.......... d.	1354	...	2050	...	2200	...	...	0653	0748
	Bucureşti Nord....... a.	1518	...	2217	...	2327	...	...	0823	0912

B – BULGARIA EXPRESS – 🛏 2 cl. and 🍴 Kyïv - Chernivtsi - Bucureşti - Sofija and v.v.; 🛏 2 cl. Sankt Peterburg (trains 53/4) - Chernivtsi - Bucureşti - Sofija and v.v.; 🛏 2 cl. Minsk (trains 195/630) - Baranovichi (trains 53/4) - Sofija and v.v.; conveys 🛏 2 cl. Riga - Vilnius - Sofija and v.v. on dates in Table 922.
D – DANUBIUS EXPRESS – Runs ①⑤ from Moskva, ①④ from Sofija: 🛏 1, 2 cl. and 🍴 Moskva - Kyïv - Chişinău - Sofija and v.v.; 🛏 2 cl. Chişinău - Sofija and v.v.

F – 🛏 1, 2 cl., 🛌 2 cl., 🚋 and 🍴 Bucureşti - Sofija and v.v.
S – SOFIJA EXPRESS – 🛏 1, 2 cl. and 🍴 Moskva - Kyïv - Chernivtsi - Sofija and v.v.
T – BUCUREŞTI ISTANBUL EXPRESS – Runs daily May 29 - Sept. 24, **only** when required Sept. 25 - May 27: 🚋 Bucureşti - Istanbul and v.v.
✕ – Conveys Sleeping car passengers from/to the Ukraine and Russia **only**; service **not** available for journeys Bucureşti - Sofija and v.v.

Table 961

CRAIOVA - CALAFAT - VIDIN - SOFIJA

1, 2 class except where shown. CFR, BDŽ

km			2						
0	Craiova 954............ d.	...	0514	0805	...	1425	1606	...	2035
107	Calafat................ a.	...	0736	1031	...	1646	1826	...	2253
	🚢		670		672	2	674		
0	Vidin.................. d.	0730	...	1255	1420	1655	...	2300
88	Mezdra................ a.	...	...	...	1831	...	...	0306
269	Sofija................. a.	1217	...	1736	...	2152	...	0530

			2		671		673	675
	Sofija................. d.	...	2340	...	0715	...	1245	1700
	Mezdra................ d.	...	0201	...	...	...	...	...
	Vidin.................. a.	...	0620	...	1154	...	1726	2130
	🚢							
	Calafat................ d.	0400	0600	...	1200	1312	...	1540
	Craiova 954........... a.	0632	0827	...	1420	1537	...	1817

🚢 operates from **Calafat** to **Vidin** (journey time: 15 minutes) across the Danube river.   **Operator:** CFR – Societatea Naţională a Căilor Ferate Române.

Table 962

SOFIJA - PLOVDIV - BURGAS and VARNA

1, 2 class except where shown. BDŽ

km		627	781 Ⓡ🍴	521 Ⓡ✕	581 Ⓡ🍴	631 🍴	881 ✕	711 Ⓡ🍴	681 🍴	621 ✕	783 🍴	633 ✕	523 Ⓡ✕	683 🍴	531 Ⓡ🍴	811 Ⓡ🍴	883 Ⓡ🍴	525 Ⓡ🍴	713 🍴	785 J	721 🍴	625 V	685 H	637 K
0	Sofija .... d.	...	0630	0630	0700	0815	0915	1015	1030	1215	1335	1415	1415	...	1600	1615	1715	1715	1815	...	2015	2200	2245	2300
120	Pazardzhik ... d.	...	...	0813	...	1001	1110	1202	...	1402	...	...	1602	...	...	1811	1902	2011	...	...	...	0045	...	
156	Plovdiv .... a.	...	...	0837	...	1027	1135	1229	...	1429	...	...	1629	...	...	1836	1929	2036	...	...	...	0113	...	
156	Plovdiv .... d.	...	0637	0842	...	1033	...	1237	...	1438	...	...	1637	...	...	...	1934	...	...	2245	...	0125	...	
149	Karlovo .... d.	...	...	...	0913	...	...	...	1553	...	...	...	...	1807	...	...	...	...	...	...	...	0115	
223	Tulovo .... d.	...	...	...	1041	...	...	...	1658	...	...	...	...	...	...	...	...	...	...	...	...	0224	
299	Sliven .... d.	...	...	...	1201	...	...	...	1816	...	...	...	...	2023	...	...	...	...	...	...	...	0346	
262	Stara Zagora . d.	...	0831	1020	...	1213	...	1433	...	1620	...	1821	...	...	...	...	2117	...	...	0050	...	0323	...	
340	Jambol .... d.	...	0940	1124	...	...	...	1540	...	1728	...	1929	...	...	...	...	2225	...	...	0200	...	0431	...	
389	Karnobat ..... d.	...	1023	1201	1244	...	...	1621	...	1809	1902	2013	...	2103	...	...	...	...	...	0247	...	0517	0437	
450	Burgas .... a.	...	...	1240	1335	...	...	1705	...	...	1950	2100	...	2145	...	...	...	...	...	...	...	0610	...	
88	Mezdra 960 ... a.	...	...	0800	...	...	...	...	1201	...	...	1545	...	...	...	1846	...	...	...	2152	2337	...	...	
194	Pleven 960 ... a.	0540	0917	...	...	...	...	...	1319	...	...	1702	...	...	...	2001	...	...	...	2318	0058	...	...	
294	Gorna-Orjahovitza .. a.	0710	1039	...	...	...	...	...	1448	...	...	1824	...	...	...	2117	...	...	...	0052	0234	...	...	
435	Shumen .... a.	0910	1227	...	...	...	...	...	1644	...	...	2012	...	...	...	...	...	...	...	0254	0437	...	...	
543	Varna .... a.	1053	1240	1356	...	...	...	...	1822	2030	...	2140	...	...	...	...	...	...	0515	...	0622	...	0705	

		720	710	520 Ⓡ🍴	810 Ⓡ🍴	880 Ⓡ🍴		532 Ⓡ🍴	682 🍴	522 Ⓡ✕		782 🍴	632 🍴	684 ✕	622 Ⓡ✕	712 🍴	526 Ⓡ✕	634 🍴	582 Ⓡ🍴	784 🍴	626 H	686 K	638 V	628 🍴 J	786
	Varna .... d.	...	0124	...	...	...	...	0710	...	0810	...	...	...	1030	...	1400	...	...	1625	1735	...	2215	2242	2310	
	Shumen ...... d.	...	0335	0535	...	...	...	0835	...	1036	...	...	1206	1526	...	1914	...	...	2120	...	0018	...	...	...	
	Gorna-Orjahovitza ... d.	...	0500	0657	...	...	...	1156	...	1412	...	...	1722	1840	...	2120	...	...	2235	...	0233	...	...	...	
	Pleven 960 ... d.	...	0624	0815	...	...	...	1314	...	1535	...	...	1840	1958	...	...	...	...	0400	...	...	...	...	...	
	Mezdra 960 .. d.	...	...	...	...	...	...	...	...	1656	...	...	...	...	...	0520	...	...	...	...	...	...	...	...	
	Burgas .... d.	...	...	...	...	...	0600	0630	...	...	1030	1100	...	...	1510	1600	...	2310	...	...	...	...	0133	...	
	Karnobat ..... d.	...	...	...	...	0645	0717	...	1028	1117	1158	...	1557	1644	1851	...	2358	0035	...	...	...	0215	...		
	Jambol .... d.	...	...	0505	...	0756	...	1106	1236	...	1720	1933	...	0039	...	...	...	0345	...	...	...			
	Stara Zagora . d.	...	...	0716	...	0913	...	1218	1354	...	1825	2049	...	0208	...	...	...							
	Sliven .... d.	...	...	...	...	0726	...	1202	...	1642	...	0119	...	...	...									
	Tulovo .... d.	...	...	...	...	...	1315	...	1804	...	0242	...	...	...										
	Karlovo .... d.	...	...	...	0934	...	1417	...	1913	...	0344	...	...	...										
	Plovdiv .... a.	...	...	0854	...	1054	...	1356	1550	...	1955	2231	0350	...	0525									
	Plovdiv .... d.	...	0600	0800	0900	...	1100	...	1400	1600	1700	2000	...	0400	...									
	Pazardzhik ... d.	...	0629	0829	0929	...	1129	...	1429	1629	1730	2026	...	0433	...									
	Sofija .... a.	0759	0819	0945	1020	1110	...	1144	1310	1445	...	1610	1648	1813	1919	2130	2136	2205	...	0627	0607	0701	...		

🍴 – 🛏 1, 2 cl., 🛌 2 cl. and 🚋 and 🍴 Sofija - Plovdiv - Burgas and v.v.
🍴 – 🛏 1, 2 cl., 🚋 and 🍴 Plovdiv - Varna and v.v.

K – 🛏 1, 2 cl., 🛌 2 cl. and 🚋 Sofija - Varna and v.v.
V – 🛏 1, 2 cl., 🚋 and 🍴 Sofija - Varna and v.v.

Table 963 — RUSE - VARNA and PLOVDIV

1, 2 class except where shown. BDŽ

km		823	2403 2	641	643	645	841 2℞T	821	647 V♈	647 V
0	Ruse 960 .... d.	0605	...	...	...	1455	1505	1500	2145	2145
	Varna .... a.	1010	...	...	...			1853		
111	Gorna Orjahovitza .... d.	...	0525	0730	0840	1728	1738	...	0005	0005
125	Veliko-Turnovo .... d.	...	0550	0758	0902	1750	1801	...	0026	0026
226	Tulovo .... d.	...	0822	1029	1121	2003		...	0241	0241
253	Stara Zagora .... d.	...	0905	1113	1156	2035	2112	...	0330	0330
310	Dimitrovgrad .... d.	...	...	1209			2225	...	0440	
411	Momchilgrad .... a.	...	...	...				...	0722	
359	Plovdiv 962 .... a.	...	...	...	1340			...		0525

km		840 2℞T	640	822	2404 2	642	824	644	646 V♈	646 V
	Plovdiv 962 .... d.	...	...	...	1415	...	...	...		2245
	Momchilgrad .... d.	...	...	...	...	...	...	...	2135	
	Dimitrovgrad .... d.	0450	...	...	...	...	...	1627	2348	
	Stara Zagora .... d.	0600	0630	...	0828	1600	...	1740	0100	0100
	Tulovo .... d.		0710	...	0903	1633	...	1823	0134	0134
	Veliko-Turnovo ...... d.	0830	0928	...	1132	1853	...	2048	0405	0405
	Gorna Orjahovitza ... d.	0855	0955	...	1200	1912	...	2221	0415	0415
0	Varna .... d.	...	...	0930	...	...	1816	...		
226	Ruse 960 .... a.	1105	1205	1315	...	...	2214	...	0640	0640

T – BUCUREŞTI ISTANBUL EXPRESS – Runs daily May 29 - Sept. 24, **only when** required Sept. 25 - May 27: ☐☐ Bucureşti - Istanbul and v.v.

V – ☒ 1, 2 cl., ☐☐ and ♈ Ruse - Momchilgrad and v.v.; ☒ 1, 2 cl. and ☐☐ Ruse - Plovdiv and v.v.

TURKEY IN EUROPE

SEE MAP PAGE 468

Operator: Türkiye Cumhuryeti Devlet Demiryollan (TCDD).

Services: Trains convey first and second class of accommodation, shown as '1' and '2' or ☐☐ in the tables. Sleeping cars (☒) and couchette cars (►) are of the normal European types, see page 10 for more details. Reservation of seats is possible on most express trains. Services covering Turkey in Asia and beyond are given in the **Thomas Cook Overseas Timetable**.

Timings: Valid **May 29, 1994 - May 27, 1995**.

Table 965 — SOFIJA - ISTANBUL

1, 2 class except where shown. BDŽ, TCDD

km		82861 2	81721	1143	491 ℞ B	81711		751 2 S	499 1191 2℞T
	Bucureşti 960 .... d.	...	...	...	...	...	...	...	1027
	Beograd 945 .... d.	...	...	...	2200	...	...	...	...
0	Sofija 962 .... d.	...	...	...	0805	...	...	...	...
120	Pazardzhik 962 .... d.	...	...	...	0946	...	...	...	...
156	Plovdiv 962 .... d.	...	...	0850	1024	...	...	...	...
234	Dimitrovgrad .... d.	...	...	1031	1142	...	...	...	2315
299	Svilengrad .... d.	...	...	1150	1250	...	...	...	0030
299	Svilengrad ☒ .... a.	...	...		1325	...	...	...	0110
318	Kapikule ☒ .... d.	...	...		1345	...	...	...	0130
318	Kapikule .... d.	...	0730		1445	...	...	...	0220
339	Edirne .... d.	...	0800		1506	...	...	...	0242
*20	Uzunköprü .... d.	0805				1555	...	0205		
385	Pehlivanköy .... d.	0830	0855		1547	1622	...	0229	0323
407	Alpullu .... d.		0922		1609	1648	...	0252	0346
506	Çerkezköy .... d.	...	...		✧	✧	...	✧	✧
636	Istanbul Sirkeci .... d.	...	1420		1955	2145	...	0720	0755

		81712	2144	490 12℞ B	81722	82862 2	498 2℞T T	750 2 S
Istanbul Sirkeci .... d.		0815	...	1000	1510	...	1935	2340
Çerkezköy .... d.		✧	...	✧	✧	...	✧	✧
Alpullu .... d.		1332	...	1351	2026	...	2353	0359
Pehlivanköy .... d.		1358	...	1416	2052	2114	0019	0423
Uzunköprü .... a.		1420	...	/		2140	/	0445
Edirne .... d.		...	...	1500	2150	...	0101	...
Kapikule .... a.		...	...	1520	2210	...	0121	...
Kapikule ☒ .... d.		...	...	1620		...	0220	...
Svilengrad ☒ .... a.		...	...	1640		...	0240	...
Svilengrad .... d.		...	1600	1715	...	...	0330	...
Dimitrovgrad .... d.		...	1732	1828	...	...	0450	...
Plovdiv 962 .... d.		...	1911	2005	...	...		...
Pazardzhik 962 .... d.		...	...	2032	...	...		...
Sofija 962 .... a.		...	...	2211	...	...		...
Beograd 945 .... a.		...	...	0619	...	...		...
Bucureşti 960 .... a.		...	...		...	...	1518	...

B – BALKAN EXPRESS – ► 1, 2 cl. and ☐☐ Budapest - Istanbul and v.v.

S – ☐☐ Thessaloniki (trains 614/3) - Pithion - Istanbul and v.v.

T – BUCUREŞTI ISTANBUL EXPRESS – Runs daily May 29 - Sept. 24, **only when** required Sept. 25 - May 27: ☐☐ Bucureşti - Istanbul and v.v.

✧ – Information not available.

* – km ex Pehlivanköy.

Operator: BDŽ – Bulgarski Durzhavni Zheleznitzi (Bulgarian State Railways).

Table 966 — BOSPHORUS FERRIES

🚢 service **Istanbul Karaköy - Haydarpaşa** (for Asian rail services) and v.v. *2 km*. Journey: 20-25 minutes. **Operator:** TDI – Türkiye Denizcilik İşletmeleri.

From Istanbul Karaköy: 0000, 0615Ⓒ, 0630, 0650Ⓐ, 0700Ⓒ, 0705Ⓐ, 0720Ⓐ, 0730Ⓒ, 0745Ⓒ, 0750Ⓒ, 0755Ⓐ, 0810, 0830, 0850, 0910, 0930, 0945Ⓐ, 0950Ⓒ, 1010, 1030, 1050, and at xx10, xx30, xx50 minutes past each hour until 1610, 1630Ⓒ, 1640Ⓐ, 1650Ⓒ, 1705Ⓐ, 1710Ⓒ, 1720Ⓐ, 1730Ⓒ, 1735Ⓐ, 1750Ⓒ, 1755Ⓐ, 1810Ⓒ, 1815Ⓐ, 1830, 1845Ⓐ, 1850Ⓒ, 1905Ⓐ, 1910Ⓒ, 1930, 1940Ⓐ, 1950Ⓒ, 2000Ⓐ, 2010Ⓒ, 2020Ⓐ, 2030Ⓒ, 2040Ⓐ, 2100, 2130, 2200, 2230, 2300, 2330.

From Haydarpaşa: 0010, 0620Ⓐ, 0635, 0705, 0720Ⓐ, 0725Ⓒ, 0735Ⓐ, 0745Ⓒ, 0750Ⓒ, 0805Ⓒ, 0810Ⓐ, 0825, 0840Ⓐ, 0845Ⓒ, 0855Ⓐ, 0905Ⓒ, 0915Ⓐ, 0925Ⓒ, 0935Ⓐ, 0945Ⓒ, 0955Ⓐ, 1010Ⓒk, 1025Ⓐ, 1030Ⓒk, 1045Ⓐ, 1050Ⓒk, 1105Ⓐ, 1110Ⓒk, 1130k, 1150k, and at xx10k, xx30k, xx50k minutes past each hour until 1605Ⓒk, 1610Ⓒk, 1630h, 1650h, 1705Ⓐ, 1710Ⓒk, 1730h, 1750h, 1805Ⓐ, 1810Ⓒk, 1820Ⓒk, 1830Ⓒk, 1840Ⓐ, 1850Ⓒk, 1905Ⓐ, 1910Ⓒk, 1920Ⓐ, 1930h, 1945Ⓐ, 1950Ⓒk, 2005Ⓐ, 2010Ⓒk, 2025Ⓐ, 2030Ⓒk, 2045, 2105, 2135, 2205, 2240, 2305, 2340.

h – Runs daily; on Ⓒ journey time 35-40 minutes (calls at **Kadiköy**).

k – Journey time 35-40 minutes (calls at **Kadiköy**).

Frequent (TDI) ferry services also operate: **Eminönü (Sirkeci) - Üsküdar** and v.v. (0630-2245); **Eminönü (Sirkeci) - Kadiköy** and v.v. (0740-1950); **Karaköy - Kadiköy** and v.v. (0630-2400).

For explanation of standard symbols see page 4

GREECE

SEE MAP PAGE 468

perator: Οργανισμος Σιδηροδρομων Ελλαδος - Organismos Sidirodromon Ellados/Chemins de Fer Helleniques (ΟΣΕ - OSE/CH).
ervices: Trains convey first and second classes of accommodation, shown as '1' and '2' or [12] in the tables. Sleeping cars (🛏) and couchette cars (▬) are of the normal European types, see page **10** for more details.
imings: Valid **May 29, 1994** to **May 27, 1995**.
ickets: Reservation of seats is possible (and recommended) on most express trains. **IC** trains carry a supplement of Drachma 3,500,–.

Table 970 ATHÍNAI - LARISSA - THESSALONIKI - GEVGELIJA

1, 2 class except where shown. CH

km		1590		IC70 🍷⚡ A	1510		500 ✕	IC50 🍷⚡	1592	IC40 🍷⚡ V	1520	IC52 🍷⚡	290 K	1594	1512	602 🍷 S	IC42 🍷⚡	IC54 🍷⚡	1522	502 ✕		504 ▬ N🍷		604 🍷 D	334 H
0	**Athínai** d.	...	...	0700	0615	...	0810	1000	...	1100	1200	1300	...	...	1400	1500	1600	1700	1715	1800	...	2200	...	2300	2330
61	Inoi d.	...	...	0749	0716	...	0908	|	...	|	1256	|	...	...	1454	1554	|	|	1812	1857	...	2302	...	0001	0043
90	Thivæ d.	...	...	|	0738	...	0929	|	...	|	1314	|	...	...	1514	1615	|	|	1830	1916	...	|	...	0025	0106
132	Levadia d.	...	...	0825	0808	...	0952	|	...	1224	1340	|	...	...	1538	1637	|	|	1856	1941	...	|	...	0054	0134
171	Amfiklia d.	...	...	|	0857	...	1020x	|	...	|	1413	|	...	...	1607	1702x	|	|	1940	2017	...	|	...	0126x	|
213	Lianokladi d.	...	...	0928	1003	...	1120	1220	...	1326	1454	1526	...	...	1709	1747	1825	1925	2025	2108	...	0100	...	0224	0302
293	Paleofarsalos **973** d.	...	...	|	1152	...	1245	|	...	1433	...	|	...	...	1831	1906	1935	|	...	2225	...	0227	...	0349	0432
339	**Larissa 971** a.	...	...	1058	1228	...	1313	1353	...	1459	...	1659	...	...	1901	1936	2000	2102	...	2254	...	0256	...	0418	0500
339	**Larissa** d.	0715	...	1100	...	...	1318	1355	1409	...	...	1701	...	1810	...	1940	...	2104	...	2300	...	0300	...	0422	0505
412	Litohoro △ d.	0840	...	|	...	...	1418	|	1514	...	...	|	...	1918	...	2035x	...	|	...	2357	...	|	...	0519x	0602x
425	Katerini d.	0907	...	1155	...	...	1427	1451	1525	...	...	1756	...	1931	...	2045	...	2159	...	0006	...	0407	...	0532	0616
473	Plati **972** d.	0959	...	1226	...	...	1501	1522	1619	...	...	1827	...	2022	...	2126	...	2230	...	0041	...	0448	...	0614	0659
510	**Thessaloniki** a.	1034	...	1255	...	...	1532	1551	1654	...	...	1857	...	2057	...	2158	...	2259	...	0111	...	0517	...	0643	0728
510	**Thessaloniki** d.	...	...	...	...	...	...	...	...	...	...	...	2100	...	...	...	...	...	...	...	...	...	...	...	0826
586	Idomeni 🏛 a.	...	...	...	...	...	...	...	...	...	...	...	2200	...	...	...	...	...	...	...	...	...	...	...	0939
586	Idomeni 🏛 d.	...	...	...	...	...	...	...	...	...	...	...	2235	...	...	...	...	...	...	...	...	...	...	...	1020
589	**Gevgelija** ‡ a.	...	...	...	...	...	...	...	...	...	...	...	2140	...	...	...	...	...	...	...	...	...	...	...	0925
	Beograd **945** a.	...	...	...	...	...	...	...	...	...	...	...	0927	...	...	...	...	...	...	...	...	...	...	...	2115

	1521 2	1511	IC41 🍷⚡ V		603 🍷 S	1591	IC51 🍷⚡	291 K	501 ✕		1593	IC71 🍷⚡ A	1523	1515	IC53 🍷⚡	IC43 🍷⚡ V		IC55 🍷⚡	503 ✕	1595		605 🍷 D	335 H		505 ▬ N🍷
Beograd **945** d.	...	...	...	...	...	...	...	1800	...	...	...	...	...	...	...	...	...	...	...	...	...	...	0740	...	...
evgelija ‡ d.	...	...	...	...	...	...	...	0505	...	...	...	...	...	...	...	...	...	...	...	...	...	...	1922	...	...
omeni 🏛 a.	...	...	...	...	...	...	...	0555	...	...	...	...	...	...	...	...	...	...	...	...	...	...	2027	...	...
omeni 🏛 d.	...	...	...	...	...	...	...	0615	...	...	...	...	...	...	...	...	...	...	...	...	...	...	2110	...	...
essaloniki a.	...	...	...	...	...	...	...	0725	...	...	...	...	...	...	...	...	...	...	...	...	...	...	2218	...	...
essaloniki d.	...	...	...	...	0607	0620	0707	...	0800	...	1112	1307	...	...	1507	...	...	1707	1800	1825	...	2204	2240	...	2330
ati **972** d.	...	...	...	...	0637	0659	0737	...	0830	...	1148	1337	...	...	1538	...	...	1738	1830	1901	...	2235	2311	...	0001
aterini d.	...	...	...	...	0715	0748	0809	...	0908	...	1240	1410	...	...	1610	...	...	1814	1908	1956	...	2314	2346	...	0046
ohoro △ d.	...	...	...	...	0723x	0801	|	...	0915x	...	1253	|	...	...	|	...	...	|	1917x	2010	...	|	2357	...	|
arissa a.	...	...	...	...	0816	0918	0903	...	1008	...	1356	1503	...	...	1704	...	...	1906	2008	2119	...	0020	0047	...	0148
arissa 971 d.	...	0700	0733	...	0821	...	0905	...	1015	...	...	1505	...	1530	1706	1804	...	1908	2013	...	...	0025	0050	...	0200
aleofarsalos **973** d.	...	0732	0758	...	0852	...	|	...	1046	...	...	|	...	1606	|	1830	...	|	2041	...	...	0100	0125	...	0235
anokladi d.	0630	0928	0906	...	1026	...	1038	...	1222	...	...	1636	1701	1800	1839	1939	...	2042	2206	...	...	0228	0302	...	0418
nfiklia d.	0712	1021	|	...	1122x	...	|	...	1308x	...	...	|	1753x	1855	|	|	...	|	2247x	...	...	0322x	|	...	|
vadia d.	0745	1052	1008	...	1148	...	|	...	1335	...	...	|	1824	1945	|	2039	...	2142	2316	...	...	0350	0426	...	0534
ivæ d.	0811	1120	|	...	1215	...	|	...	1400	...	...	|	1851	2020	|	|	...	|	2338	...	...	0416	0500	...	0604
oi d.	0831	1141	1238	...	1238	...	|	...	1421	...	...	1811	1911	2046	|	|	...	|	2358	...	...	0437	0523	...	0626
hínai a.	0926	1236	1130	...	1338	...	1302	...	1519	...	...	1858	2003	2151	2104	2204	...	2305	0058	...	...	0544	0628	...	0726

– [12] and 🍷 Athínai - Alexandropolis Port and v.v.
– 🛏 1, 2 cl., ▬ 2 cl., [12] and 🍷 Athínai - Ormenion and Dikea - Athínai. Reservation recommended.
– HELLAS EXPRESS – 🛏 1, 2 cl., ▬ 2 cl. and [2] Budapest - Athínai and v.v.; [2] Wien (trains **D347/6**) - Budapest - Athínai and v.v.; conveys ▬ 2 cl. Praha and Bratislava (trains **471/0**) - Budapest - Athínai and v.v. on dates in Table **96b**; conveys 🛏 2 cl. Moskva (trains **9/10**) - Chop (trains **489/8**) - Beograd - Thessaloniki and Athínai and v.v. on dates in Table **94c**.
– AKROPOLIS EXPRESS – 🛏 1, 2 cl., ▬ 2 cl. and [12] Thessaloniki - Beograd and v.v.
– 🛏 1, 2 cl., ▬ 2 cl. and 🍷 Athínai - Thessaloniki and v.v.

S – ▬ 2 cl., [12] and 🍷 Athínai - Ormenion and v.v.
V – [12] and 🍷 Athínai - Volos and v.v.
x – Stops on request.
⚡ – Supplement payable. Reservation obligatory.
‡ – Yugoslav time.
△ – **Litohoro** is the alighting point for **Mount Olympus**.

able 971 LARISSA - VOLOS

All trains 1, 2 class. CH

km													IC40							IC42			
0	**Larissa 970** d.	0400	0510	...	0644	0830	...	1020	1148	...	1300	1420	...	1502	1550	...	1714	...	1854	...	2003	2030	...	2204
61	**Volos** a.	0456	0608	...	0752	0931	...	1117	1246	...	1359	1521	...	1545	1652	...	1815	...	1954	...	2046	2129	...	2305

			IC41													IC43								
los d.	...	0525	0648	...	0710	0850	...	1035	1140	...	1255	1417	...	1549	...	1719	...	1735	1850	...	2048	2150	...	2310
rissa 970 a.	...	0624	0730	...	0809	0948	...	1137	1241	...	1353	1518	...	1645	...	1801	...	1833	1947	...	2145	2247	...	0006

trains operate from/to Athínai (Table **970**) and are Ⓡ with supplement payable.

able 972 THESSALONIKI - KOZANI and FLORINA

All trains 1, 2 class. CH

km		🍷	🍷	🍷		🍷		🍷	🍷	🍷		🍷
0	**Thessaloniki** d.	0558	0730	0915	...	1203	...	1447	1612	1806	...	2130
38	Plati **970** d.	0631	0809	0950	...	1239	...	1526	1648	1842	...	2208
69	Veria d.	0700	0843	1024	...	1310	...	1601	1722	1919	...	2245
12	Edessa d.	0746	0933	1119	...	1359	...	1654	1808	2011	...	2334
62	Aminteon a.	0836	1025	1209	...	1450	...	...	1858	2102	...	...
62	Aminteon d.	0837	1031	1213	1220	1502	1500	...	1901	2104	2115	...
89	Ptolemais a.	|	1053	1237	|	1523	|	...	|	2125	|	...
22	Kozani a.	|	1120	1309	|	1553	|	...	|	2155	|	...
96	**Florina** a.	0917	...	...	1258	...	1540	...	1940	...	2154	...

		🍷	🍷	🍷	🍷		🍷	🍷		🍷
Florina d.	0605	...	0755	0944	...	1405	...	...	1720	...
Kozani d.	|	0555	|	|	1203	|	1353	...	|	1715
Ptolemais d.	|	0626	|	|	1238	|	1423	...	|	1746
Aminteon a.	0645	0649	0835	1024	1300	1445	1446	...	1800	1808
Aminteon d.	▬	0651	0839	1026	1303	...	1451	...	...	1810
Edessa d.	0430	0748	0934	1120	1357	...	1547	1725	...	1910
Veria d.	0523	0844	1025	1208	1443	...	1638	1822	...	2000
Plati **970** d.	0601	0916	1055	1240	1514	...	1708	1904	...	2033
Thessaloniki a.	0639	0952	1129	1314	1548	...	1744	1944	...	2108

ew daily **IC** service Athínai - Kozani and v.v. will commence from May 28, **1995**.

able 973 VOLOS - PALEOFARSALOS - KALAMBAKA

2 class only. Narrow gauge. CH

km											
0	**Volos** d.	...	0540	...	...	1050	...	1409	...	1715	2025
82	Paleofarsalos a.	...	0727	...	...	1237	...	1557	...	1905	2215
82	Paleofarsalos **970** d.	0400	0735	0903	1048	1248	1454	1615	1843	1940	2231
11	Karditsa d.	0436	0811	0939	1124	1323	1532	1651	1919	2018	2309
40	Trikala d.	0507	0842	1010	1159	1357	1603	1722	1950	2049	2340
62	**Kalambaka** a.	0527	0902	1030	1219	1417	1623	1742	2010	2109	2400

Kalambaka d.	0600	0719	0910	1115	1255	1440	1700	1755	2027	2318
Trikala d.	0621	0740	0931	1136	1316	1501	1723	1816	2050	2341
Karditsa d.	0651	0812	1005	1206	1349	1531	1752	1845	2122	0011
Paleofarsalos **970** a.	0726	0847	1040	1241	1424	1604	1825	1923	2158	0046
Paleofarsalos d.	0737	...	...	1250	...	1620	...	1930	2232	...
Volos a.	0920	...	...	1437	...	1803	...	2113	0013	...

🏛 – Frontier station 🛏 – Sleeping Car ▬ – Couchette Car

Table 974 — THESSALONIKI - ALEXANDROPOLIS - ISTANBUL

1, 2 class except where shown. CH, TCDD

km		1690	1680	1630	604 D♈	610 ♈	IC 70 ♈	1694	614 ST♈	1634	602 M♈
	Athínai 970 .... d.	...	...	...	2300	...	0700	...	...	...	1500
0	Thessaloniki .... d.	...	...	0602	0750	0931	1330	...	1504	1735	2230
130	Strimon .... d.	...	...	0814	0951	1132		...	1704	1955	0021
162	Serrai .... d.	...	...	0844	1017	1159	1518	...	1733	2030	0049
232	Drama .... d.	...	0601		1132	1300	1611	...	1841	2132	0158
327	Xanthi .... d.	...	0734	1692	1312	1429	1732	...	2015		0332
374	Komotini .... d.	...	0813		1349	1508	1801	...	2055		0410
442	Alexandropolis .... a.	0758	0907	1138				1857		751	0513
443	Alexandropolis Port .. d.	0805	0924	1145	1504	1627	1901	1904	2225	2S	0545
444	Alexandropolis .... a.	0812	0930	1152				1910			0555
557	Pithion .... d.	1014	...	1344	1707	...	2043	0015	0100	0739
574	Nea Orestias .... a.	1036	...	1406	1724	...	2059	0034		0756
610	Dikea .... a.	1114	...	1443	1757	...	2126	0104		0829
618	Ormenion .... a.	1145	...	1456	1815	...	...	...		0844
626	Svilengrad ⌑ 965 ... d.	1156	...							
573	Uzunköprü ⌑ 965 .... d.	...	...					0205		
844	Istanbul Sirkeci 965. a.	...	...					0720		

km		1691	IC 71 ♈✗	750 2S	613 ST♈	605 D♈	615 ♈	1695	1681	1697	603 M♈
	Istanbul Sirkeci 965 d.	...	2340								
	Uzunköprü ⌑ 965 ... d.	...	0538								
	Svilengrad ⌑ 965 ... d.	...						1230			
	Ormenion .... d.	...						1246		1500	1825
	Dikea .... d.	0500			0605	1024		1330		1542	1959
	Nea Orestias .... d.	0527			0639	1059		1405		1617	1959
	Pithion .... d.	0541	0558		0710	1115		1433		1636	2016
	Alexandropolis .... a.	0713	0701		0853	1256	1518	1626	1611	1827	2158
	Alexandropolis Port .. d.	0728	0708		0925	1323	1525	1643	1618	1832	2208
	Alexandropolis .... a.	0732	0720		0932	1330	1532	1647	1635		2230
	Komotini .... d.		0812		1040	1435	1632		1733		2334
	Xanthi .... d.	1631	0842	1633	1118	1516	1710		1813		0013
	Drama .... d.	0600	1003		1301	1708	1842		1950		0156
	Serrai .... d.	0658	1054		1330	1358	1810	1942			0253
	Strimon .... d.	0730		1303	1440	1840	2009				0318
	Thessaloniki .... a.	0946	1243	1519	1642	2042	2259				1338
	Athínai 970 .... a.	...	1858			0544					1338

D – ⌑ 1, 2 cl., ⌑ 2 cl., ⌑, ⌑ and ♈ Athínai - Ormenion and Dikea - Athínai. Reservation recommended.
M – ⌑ 2 cl., ⌑ and ♈ Athínai - Ormenion and v.v.; ⌑ 1, 2 cl. Thessaloniki - Alexandropolis and v.v. Reservation recommended.

S – ⌑ Thessaloniki (trains 614/3) - Pithion (trains 751/0) - Istanbul and v.v.
T – ⌑ and ♈ Thessaloniki - Dikea and v.v.
✗ – Supplement payable. Reservation obligatory.
Operator: TCDD – Türkiye Cumhuryeti Devlet Demiryollan (Turkish State Railways).

Table 975 — SOFIJA - ATHÍNAI

1, 2 class except where shown. BDŽ, CH

km			1661 613 J♈		653 2		655 2	657 2	
0	Sofija .... d.	...	0740	...	1300	...	1600	1800	...
33	Pernik .... d.	...	0832	...	1346	...	1651	1845	...
91	Dupnitza .... d.	...							...
123	Blagoevgrad .... d.	...	1027	...	1527	...	1841	2046	...
210	Kulata .... a.	...	1222	...	1714	...	2022	2242	...
210	Kulata ⌑ .... d.	...	1300						
213	Promachon ⌑ .... d.	...	1305						
213	Promachon .... d.	...	1355						
227	Strimon .... d.	...	1440						
357	Thessaloniki .... a.	...	1642						
867	Athínai 970 .... a.	...	0058						

km				652 2	654 2	604 1660 K♈		656 ♈	658 2	
	Athínai 970 .... d.	...	...	...	2300	...	...	...
	Thessaloniki .... d.	...	...	...	0750	...	...	...
	Strimon .... d.	...	...	...	1015	...	...	...
	Promachon .... a.	...	...	...	1030	...	...	...
	Promachon ⌑ .... a.	...	...	...	1135	...	...	...
	Kulata ⌑ .... a.	...	...	...	1140	...	...	...
	Kulata .... d.	...	0350	0620	1335	...	1505	1600	...
	Blagoevgrad .... d.	...	0548	0808	1526	...	1655	1808	...
	Dupnitza .... d.	...							...
	Pernik .... d.	...	0740	1000	1800	...	1840	2020	...
	Sofija .... a.	...	0830	1047	1849	...	1927	2107	...

J – TRANSBALKAN – ⌑ Sofija - Thessaloniki; Conveys once weekly May 29 - Sept. 24 from Bucureşti; ⌑ 1, 2 cl. Bucureşti (train 371) - Sofija - Thessaloniki.
K – TRANSBALKAN – ⌑ Thessaloniki - Sofija; Conveys ⑤ June 3 - Sept. 23: ⌑ 1, 2 cl. Thessaloniki - Sofija (train 526) - Bucureşti.

Table 977 — PIRGHOS - OLYMPIA

2 class only. CH

km							
0	Pirghos .... d.	0630	0915	1130	1400	1850
21	Olympia .... a.	0706	0951	1206	1436	1926

Olympia............... d.	0725	1015	1220	1540	1935
Pirghos .... a.	0801	1051	1259	1616	2011

Table 978 — KAVASSILA - KILLINI

2 class only. C

km							
0	Kavassila 980 .... d.	0823	0950	1205	1410	1605
16	Killini .... a.	0859	1024	1239	1444	1639

Killini .... d.	0902	1100	1245	1510	1710
Kavassila 980 .... a.	0936	1134	1319	1544	1744

Table 980 — PIRAEUS - ATHÍNAI - PATRAS and KALAMATA

1, 2 class except where shown. C

km		1342	302	422	IC 10 ♈	1420	IC 20 ♈✗	424	304 ♈	IC 12 ♈✗	IC 22 ♈✗	306	426	1422	IC 24 ♈✗	IC 14 ♈✗
0	Piraeus ▲ .... d.	...	...	0600	0600	0732	...	0802	0830	...	0850	0920	1137	1310	...	1432	1432	1540	1640	1851
8	Athínai Pelop. ▲ ...... d.	...	...	0630	0630	0756	...	0830	0854	...	0928	0950	1202	1343	...	1459	1459	1609	1709	1911
99	Korinthos .... d.	...	...	0818	0820	0927	...	1014	1024	...	1119	1152	1331	1513	...	1647	1650	1803	1839	2041
	Arghos .... a.	...	...		0918		...	1110		...	1218	1220		1355		1650		1750	1903	
	Nafplion .... a.	...	...				...	1128		...		1238		1413		1708		1921	
	Tripolis .... d.	...	...		1037		...			...	1334					1907		
133	Xylocastron .... d.	...	...	0858		0957	...		1054	...		1231	1402	1546		1719		1909	2118
177	Diakoptó .... d.	...	0900	0942		1030	1052		1130	1150	...	1328	1352	1435	1620	1625	1803		1942	2156
190	Kalávrita .... a.	...	1009				1203			1300	...		1503		1734				2027	2124
230	Patras .... a.	...		1039		1115			1215		...	1438		1520	1705		1905		2030	
230	Patras .... d.	0608		1045					1218		...	1440			1708		1914		2133	
295	Kavassila 978 .... d.	0728		1203					1321		...	1601			1809		2032		2200	
329	Pirghos 977 .... d.	0805		1240					1350		...	1655			1838		2108		
391	Kiparissia .... a.	0922		1351					1449		...	1814			1937		2219		
391	Kiparissia .... d.	0925									...	1819						
458	Kalamata .... a.	1112			1300			1555			...	2003					2130		

km		1421	IC 11 ♈✗	IC 21 ♈✗	421	301	IC 23 ♈✗	13 ♈✗	423	303	1343	IC 15 ♈✗	1423	IC 25 ♈✗	425	305	1341
0	Kalamata .... d.	...	...		0630	...	...	...	1000	...	0800	...		1540	...	...	1501
	Kiparissia .... a.	...	...			...	...	...		...	0944	...			...	...	1643
	Kiparissia .... d.	...	...		0624	0810	...	...		...	0949	...		1528	...	1605	1654
	Pirghos 977 .... d.	...	...	0605	0737	0910	...	...	1108	1325	...		1629	...	1718	1811
	Kavassila 978 .... d.	...	...	0632	0813	0937	...	...	1151	1405	...		1656	...	1754	1853
	Patras .... a.	...	...	0736	0930	1040	...	...	1319	1524	...		1800	...	1913	2012
	Patras .... d.	...	0600	0738	0935	1042	1241	...	1325	...	...	1557		1803	...	1916	
	Kalávrita .... d.	0555	0710			1010	1215		1310	...	1505		1735			2011	
	Diakoptó .... d.	0646	0819	0824	1031	1121	1131	1325	1327	1421	1436	1614	1644	1849	1844	1849	
	Xylocastron .... d.	0719		0857	1117	1204		1401		1524		1718		1925		2055	
115	Tripolis .... d.	...	...	0855					1228	...	...		1808		...	
	Nafplion .... d.	0555			1147			1322		...	1610	1730		1927		
183	Arghos .... d.	0615		1018	1205			1340	1353	...	1628	1751		1925	1945	
236	Korinthos .... d.	0710	0750	0928	1120	1156	1236	1431	1453	1557	1746	1847	1955	2031	2131	
327	Athínai Pelop. ▲ ...... a.	0853	0917	1057	1302	1342	1402	1558	1638	1753	1912	2046	2122	2213	2322	
335	Piraeus ▲ .... a.	0916	0945	1123	1337	1407	1430	1623	1708	1823	1938	2110	2148	2236	2349	

✗ – Supplement payable.   ▲ – Frequent local trains run between Athínai Omonia and Piraeus on the Athínai Electric Railway, journey approximately 20 minut...

✗ – Restaurant Car   ♈ – Buffet Car   ⌑ – Through carriage (1 and 2 class)

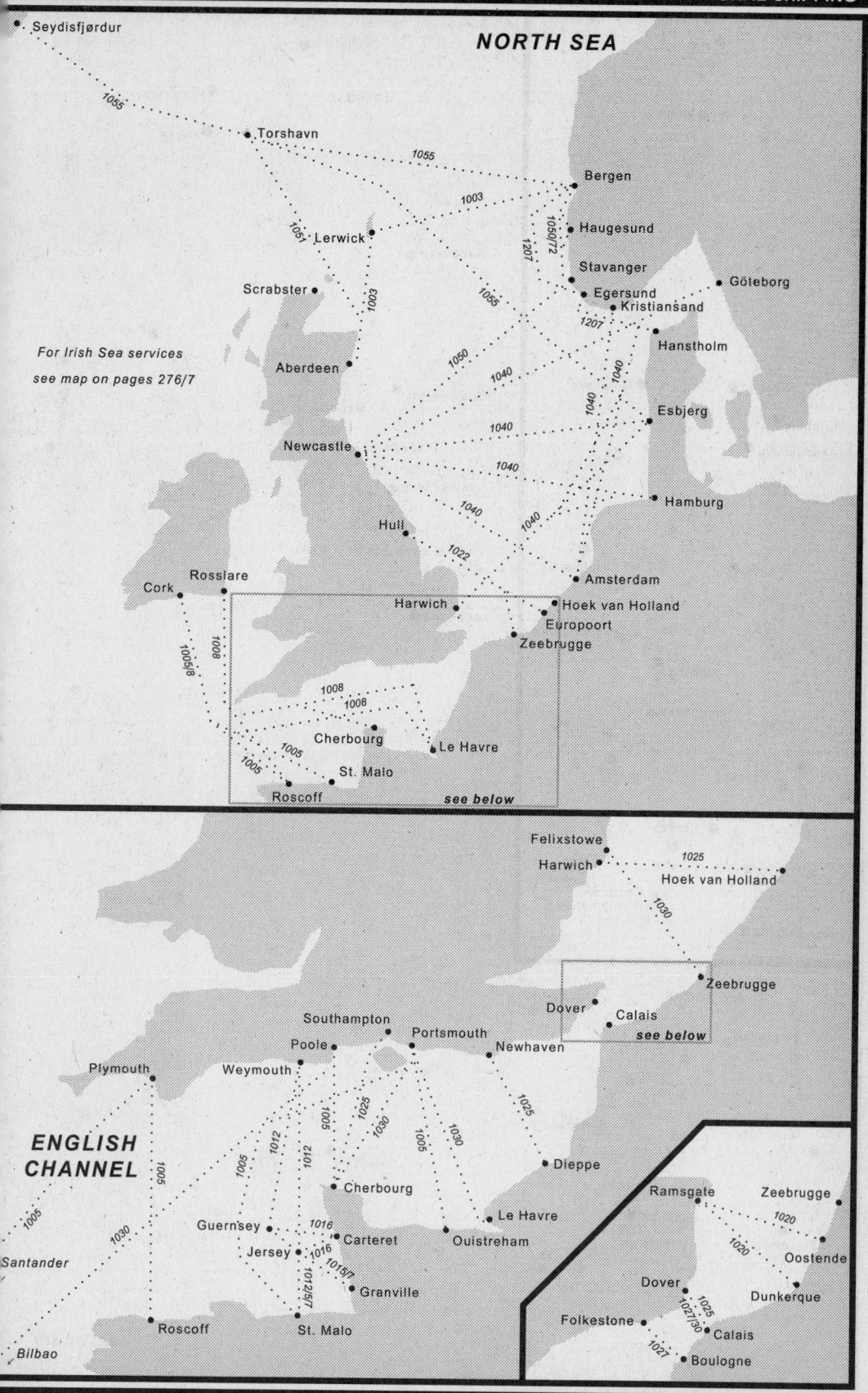

NORTH SEA

Seydisfjørdur

1055

Torshavn

1055

Bergen

1003

Haugesund

1051 Lerwick

1050/72

1207

Stavanger

Scrabster

1003

1055

Egersund
Kristiansand

Göteborg

1207

Hanstholm

For Irish Sea services
see map on pages 276/7

Aberdeen

1050

1040

1040

Esbjerg

1040

1040

Newcastle

1040

1040

Hamburg

1040

1040

Hull

1022

Rosslare

1005/8

1008

Cork

Harwich

Amsterdam

Hoek van Holland
Europoort
Zeebrugge

1008

1008

Cherbourg

Le Havre

1005

1005

St. Malo

Roscoff

see below

Felixstowe
Harwich

1025

Hoek van Holland

1030

Zeebrugge

see below

Dover Calais

Southampton
Poole

Portsmouth

Newhaven

Plymouth Weymouth

1025

**ENGLISH
CHANNEL**

1012

1005

1030

1005

1030

Dieppe

1005

Cherbourg

Le Havre

1005

1030

Guern'sey

1016

Carteret

Ouistreham

Jersey

1016

1012/5/7

1012/5/7 Granville

Ramsgate

Zeebrugge

1020

1020

Oostende

Dover

Dunkerque

1025

Santander

Folkestone

1027/30

Calais

Roscoff

St. Malo

1027

Boulogne

Bilbao

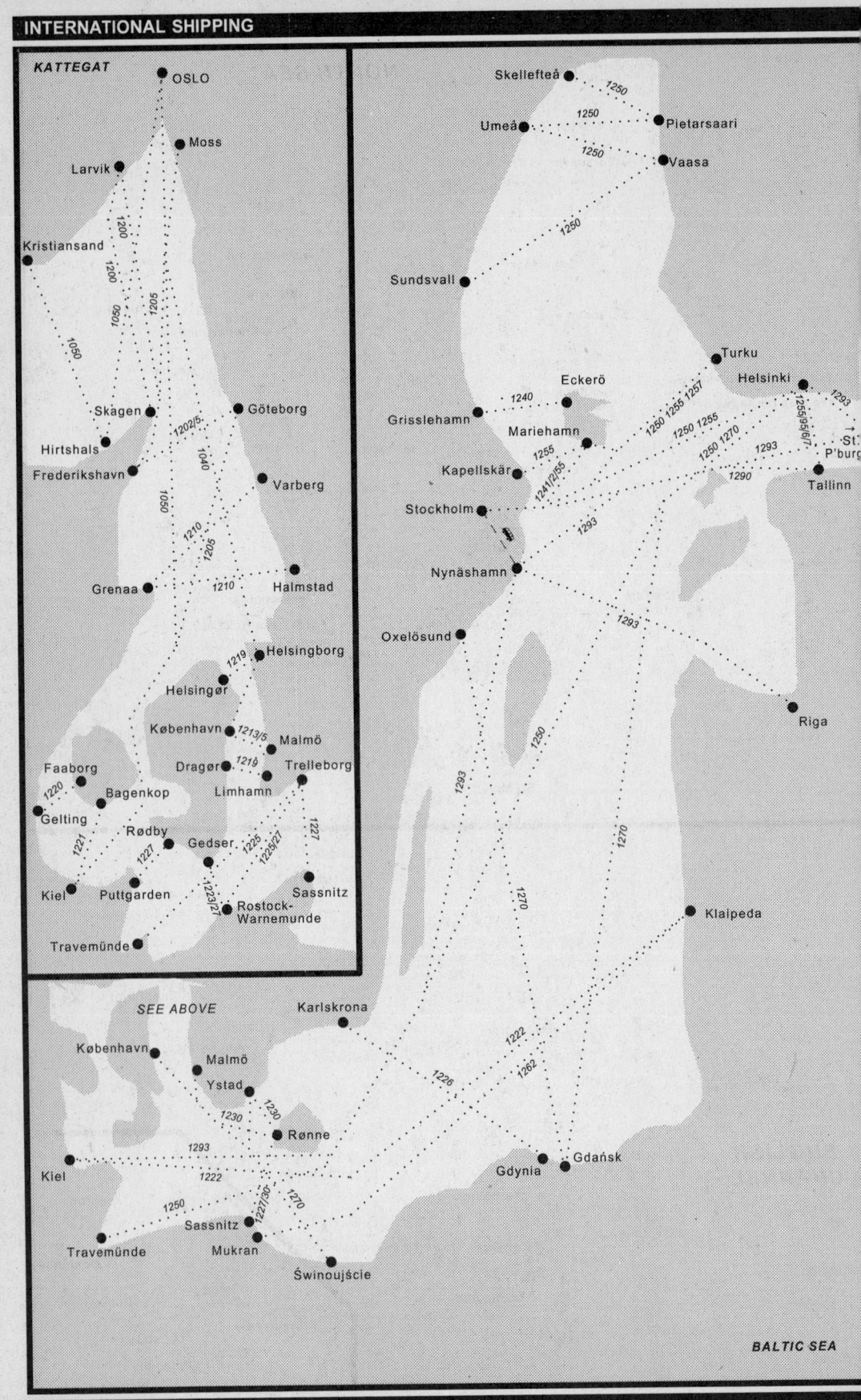

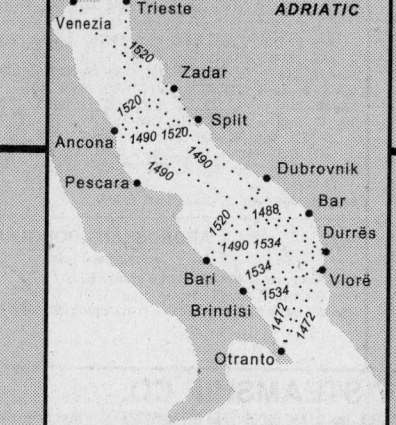

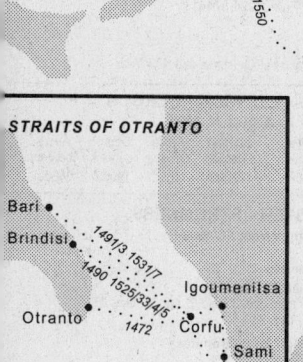
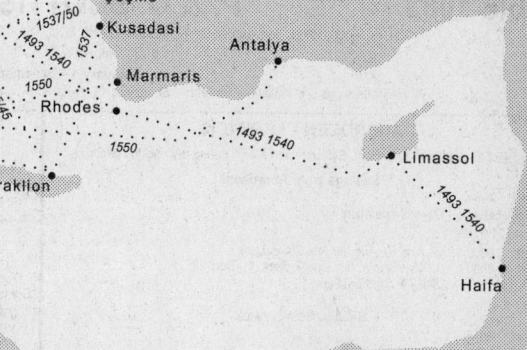

STRAITS OF GIBRALTAR

Algeciras · Gibraltar
Tanger
Sebta
1400/10 · 1400

Sète · Marseille · Toulon
Genova · La Spezia · Livorno
Bastia · Porto Vecchio
Valencia · Palma · Ibiza · Porto Torres · Napoli
Malaga · Almeria · Cagliari · Palermo
Tanger · Melilla · Oran · Alger · Bejaia · Skikda · Annaba · Tunis · Trapani · Licata · Catania · Siracusa · Pozzallo
Gozo · Malta

WESTERN MEDITERRANEAN

ADRIATIC

Venezia · Trieste · Zadar · Split · Ancona · Pescara · Dubrovnik · Bar · Durrës · Vlorë · Bari · Brindisi · Otranto

EASTERN MEDITERRANEAN

Venezia · Trieste · Ancona · Dubrovnik · Durrës · Bari · Corfu · Igoumenitsa · Piraeus · Patras
Istanbul · Izmir · Çeşme · Kusadasi · Marmaris · Rhodes · Antalya
Heraklion · Limassol · Haifa · Alexandria

For Turkey - Cyprus services
see the Thomas Cook
Overseas Timetable

STRAITS OF OTRANTO

Bari · Brindisi · Otranto · Igoumenitsa · Corfu · Sami · Patras

Table 1001 — ISLE OF MAN STEAM PACKET CO.

P. O. Box 5, Douglas, Isle of Man. ☎ 01624 661661   Fax 01624 661065
m.v. *King Orry*,   m.v. *Lady of Mann*,   Catamaran *SeaCat Isle of Man*
January 5 - September 30, 1995

HEYSHAM - DOUGLAS

Sailings from Heysham Sea Terminal

Depart Heysham	Arrive Douglas	Days of operation
0100	0600	① Jan. 9 - Sept. 25, also Apr. 13, May 12,26-31, June 1-9, Aug. 20,25-28, Sept. 3,12..
1330	1715	Apr. 9, 23 only.
1415	1800	①②③④⑤ Jan. 5 - May 19 (also May 7,14); daily May 21 - Sept. 29.

Sailings from Douglas

Depart Douglas	Arrive Heysham	Days of operation
0830	1215	①②③④⑤ Jan. 5 - May 31 (also Apr. 9,23, May 7,14,21,28); daily June 1 - Sept. 29 (depart 0800 May 26 - June 4).
1830	2215	⑦ Jan. 8 - Apr. 16, also Apr. 30.
1930	2315	⑦ May 7 - Sept. 24 (also Apr. 7,20, May 29, June 2-12, Aug. 19, 25-28,31, Sept. 1,2,16 (depart 2000 June 5,6, Sept. 1-3; depart 2030 June 7-12, depart 1900 Aug. 28).

FLEETWOOD - DOUGLAS

By *SeaCat*, journey 2 hours (* - By ship, 3 hours, 20 minutes)

Sailings from Fleetwood

May 28: 1030*, 2300*. June 14: 1030, 2300. June 20: 0900, 2100. June 27: 1000, 2200. July 5: 0800, 1400, 2000. July 11: 1000, 2200. July 18: 1400, 2000. July 25: 1000, 2200. Aug. 1: 1300. Aug. 2: 0100. Aug. 8: 1000, 2200. Aug. 15: 1300. Aug. 16: 0100. Aug. 22: 1000, 2200. Aug. 29: 1200, 2359. Sept. 5: 1000, 2200. Sept. 12: 1200, 2359. Sept. 19: 1000, 2200.

Sailings from Douglas

May 28: 0600*, 1900*. June 14: 0730, 2000. June 20: 0600, 1800. June 27: 0700, 1900. July 5: 0500, 1100, 1700. July 11: 0700, 1900. July 18: 1100, 1700. July 25: 0700, 1900. Aug. 1: 1000, 2200. Aug. 8: 0700, 1900. Aug. 15: 1000, 2200. Aug. 22: 0700, 1900. Aug. 29: 0900, 2100. Sept. 5: 0700, 1900. Sept. 12: 0900, 2100. Sept. 19: 0700, 1900.

DOUGLAS - DUBLIN and BELFAST

Departure times vary.

DOUGLAS - DUBLIN By *SeaCat*, journey 2 hours 45 minutes (* - By ship, 5 hours). From Douglas and Dublin: Apr. 14*,18*, May 24,30, June 4,6; ④⑦ June 11 - Sept. 24.

DOUGLAS - BELFAST By *SeaCat*, journey 2 hours 45 minutes (* - By ship, 4½ hours). From Douglas and Belfast: Apr. 15*§,19*§, May 26,29, June 4,5,11*; ①⑤ June 16 - Sept. 22 (also July 8,9,16; also Sept. 14 from Belfast, Sept. 16 from Douglas). § - Next day from Belfast.

LIVERPOOL - DOUGLAS

By *SeaCat*, journey 2½ hours (* - By ship, 4½ hours)

Sailings from Liverpool

Jan. 7 - May 24: ⑥: 0815* (also 0130* on Apr. 14,18).
May 25 - June 13: May 25: 1030, 2100. May 26: 1500*,2100. May 27: 1030, 1815*, 2100. May 28: 1300, 2100. May 29: 1500*,2100. May 30: 1500*. May 31: 0115, 0915, 1400*,1715. June 1-2: 0115, 0915, 1400*,1715. June 3: 0115, 0530*, 0915, 1715, 2100*. June 4: 0115, 1500*. June 5: 0115. June 7: 0115, 1300. June 8: 1300. June 9-10: 0900, 1800. June 11: 0900. June 12: 1345, 2115. June 13: 1030, 2100.
June 16 - July 3: ①: 2100. ③: 1030, 2100. ⑤: 2100. ⑥: 1030, 1730. ⑦: 2100.
July 4 - 9: July 4: 1030, 2100. July 7: 2100. July 8: 1800.
July 10 - Aug. 18: ①: 2100. ③: 1030, 2100. ⑥:0130*, 0930, 1630, 2330.
Aug. 19 - Sept. 3: Aug. 19: 0130*, 0930, 1730. Aug. 20: 0030. Aug. 21: 2100. Aug. 23: 1030, 2100. Aug. 26: 0230, 1015, 1800. Aug. 27: 0230, 2100. Aug. 28: 1700, 2359. Aug. 30: 1030, 2100. Sept. 1: 2115. Sept. 2: 0630, 1430, 2215. Sept. 3: 0630, 2100.
Sept. 4 - 24: ①: 2100. ③: 1030, 2100. ⑤: 2100. ⑥: 1300, 2100 (0930, 1630 on Sept. 16). ⑦: 2100.
Sept. 25 - 30: ⑥: 1815.

Sailings from Douglas

Jan. 7 - May 24: ⑥: 0815* (also 1900* on Apr. 13,17).
May 25 - June 13: May 25: 0700, 1730. May 26: 1730. May 27: 0600, 0815*, 1730. May 28: 0930, 1730. May 29: 0900*, 1730. May 30: 1730. May 31: 1315, 2115. June 1: 1315. June 2: 1315, 2115. June 3: 0515, 1315, 2115. June 4: 0900*. June 5: 1730. June 6: 1500*, 2130. June 7-8: 0930, 1730, 1900*. June 9: 0530, 1330, 1500*, 2200. June 10: 0300*, 0530, 1330, 1500*, 2200. June 11: 0530, 2200. June 12: 1015, 1200*, 1745. June 13: 0600, 1730.
June 16 - July 3: ①: 1730. ③: 0700, 1730. ⑤: 1730. ⑥: 0700, 1400. ⑦: 1730.
July 4 - 9: July 4: 0700, 1730. July 7: 1730. July 8: 1430.
July 10 - Aug. 18: ①: 1730. ③: 0700, 1730. ⑥: 1900*. ⑦: 0600, 1300, 2000.
Aug. 19 - Sept. 3: Aug. 19: 0600, 1300, 2100. Aug. 21: 1730. Aug. 23: 0700, 1730. Aug. 25: 2200. Aug. 26: 0600, 1345, 2130. Aug. 27: 1730. Aug. 28: 1330, 2030. Aug. 30: 0700, 1730. Sept. 1: 1745. Sept. 2: 0200, 1100, 1845. Sept. 3: 0300, 1745.
Sept. 4 - 24: ①: 1730. ③: 0700, 1730. ⑤: 1730. ⑥: 0930, 1730 (0600, 1300 on Sept. 16). ⑦: 1730.
Sept. 25 - 30: Sept. 25: 0930. Sept. 30: 0815.

ARDROSSAN - DOUGLAS

Sailing time 8 hours.
From Ardrossan: ⑥ May 27 - Sept. 2 (depart 0830).
From Douglas: ⑦ May 28 - Sept. 3 (depart 1130).
Operated by Caledonian MacBrayne in association with Isle of Man Steam Packet.

Table 1002 — ISLES OF SCILLY STEAMSHIP CO.

The Weighbridge, Quay Street, Penzance, Cornwall, TR18 4BD. ☎ 01736 62009 Fax 01736 51223   m.v. *Scillonian III*
April 8 - October 28, 1995 (*sailings are available at other times by cargo vessel*)

PENZANCE - ST. MARY'S

Sailings from Penzance, Lighthouse Pier

Depart Penzance	Arrive St. Mary's	Days of operation
0630	0910	⑥ May 27, June 3, ⑥ July 22 - Aug. 26.
0915	1155	①②③④⑤ Apr. 10 - Oct. 6, also Aug 6; ②③⑤⑥ Oct. 10 - 28.
1100	1340	⑥ Apr. 8 - May 20, ⑥ June 10 - July 15, ⑥ Sept. 2 - Oct. 7.
1345	1625	⑥ May 27, June 3, ⑥ July 22 - Aug. 26.

Sailings from St. Mary's

Depart St. Mary's	Arrive Penzance	Days of operation
0945	1225	⑥ May 27, June 3, ⑥ July 22 - Aug. 26.
1500	1740	⑥ Apr. 8 - May 20, ⑥ June 10 - July 15, ⑥ Sept. 2 - Oct. 7.
1630	1910	①②③④⑤ Apr. 10 - Oct. 6, also Aug 6; ②③⑤⑥ Oct. 10 - 28.
1700	1940	⑥ May 27, June 3, ⑥ July 22 - Aug. 26.

Table 1003 — P. & O. SCOTTISH FERRIES

P.O. Box 5, Jamieson's Quay, Aberdeen AB9 8DL. ☎ 01224 572615, Telex 73344, Fax 01224 574411
m.v. *St. Ola*, m.v. *St. Clair*, m.v. *St. Sunniva*
January 1 - December 31, 1995
Additional sailings are available Aberdeen - Stromness - Lerwick and v.v. All services are subject to alteration at Christmas and New Year

ABERDEEN - LERWICK

Subject to alteration in January, February and March during dry docking period.

Sailings from Aberdeen

Depart Aberdeen	Arrive Lerwick next day	Days of operation
1200	0800	② June 6 - Aug. 29 (via Stromness).
1800	0800	①②③④⑤ Jan. 3 - June 2; Sept. 4 - Dec. 29; ①③④⑤ June 5 - Sept. 1.

Sailings from Lerwick

Depart Lerwick	Arrive Aberdeen next day	Days of operation
1200	0800	⑤ Apr. 1 - Sept. 30, also ③ June 8 - Aug. 31 (via Stromness).
1800	0800	①②③④⑦ Jan. 3 - June 1; Sept. 3 - Dec. 31. ①②④ June 5 - Aug. 31.
1900	0900	⑦ June 4 - Aug. 27.

ABERDEEN - LERWICK - BERGEN

June 2 - August 27, 1995

Depart Aberdeen	Arrive Lerwick	Depart Lerwick	Arrive Bergen	Depart Bergen	Arrive Lerwick	Depart Lerwick	Arrive Aberdeen
1800⑤	0700⑥	1000⑥	2330⑥		1400⑦	1900⑦	0800①

SCRABSTER - STROMNESS

Sailings from Scrabster

Depart Scrabster	Arrive Stromness	Days of operation
0600	0745	①②③④⑤ Apr. 3 - Oct. 31.
1200	1345	①②③④⑤⑥ from Jan. 3 (also ⑦ Apr. 2 - Oct. 29).
1745	1930	⑤⑥ Apr. 1 - Oct. 28.

Sailings from Stromness

Depart Stromness	Arrive Scrabster	Days of operation
0800	0945	⑦ Jan. 8 - Mar. 26, Nov. 5 - Dec. 31.
0845	1030	①②③④⑤⑥ from Jan. 3 (also ⑦ Apr. 2 - Oct. 29).
1500	1645	Daily Apr. 1 - Oct. 31.
2000	2145	① Apr. 17 - Oct. 23.

Table 1005   BRITTANY FERRIES

Millbay, Plymouth, PL1 3EW ☎ 01752 221321 Telex 45380 Fax 01752 661308.
Wharf Road, Portsmouth, PO2 8RU ☎ 01705 827701 Telex 86878
42 Grand Parade, Cork ☎ 021 277801
Gare Maritime Roscoff, Port du Bloscon, F-29211 ☎ 98 61 22 11 Telex 940360.
Modesto Pineiro & Co., 27 Paseo de Pereda, Santander ☎ 942 214500 Telex 35913.

m.v. Bretagne, m.v. Duc de Normandie, m.v. Quiberon, m.v. Normandie, m.v. Barfleur, m.v. Val de Loire, m.v. Duchesse Anne.

March 1 - December 31, 1995

PLYMOUTH - ROSCOFF

Sailings from Plymouth Millbay

Depart Plymouth	Arrive Roscoff	Days of operation
0800	1500	①②④ Mar. 13 - Apr. 4; ②③⑤⑦ Apr. 7 - Sept. 10 (not May 2,3); ①②④ Sept. 12 - Oct. 5; daily Oct. 9-14,18-21,24-28,31, Nov. 1-4,7-11,14.
1200	1900	①⑦ Jan. 8 - Mar. 12; ⑦ Nov. 19 - Dec. 31 (also Nov. 15,16,20, 27, Dec. 4,11,18).
1500h	2200	③⑤⑥⑦ Mar. 15 - Apr. 5; ①④⑤⑥ Apr. 6 - July 1 (also May 28, June 4,11); ①④⑤⑥⑦ July 3 - Sept. 9, also Sept. 11; ③⑤⑥⑦ Sept. 13 - Oct. 8; ① Oct. 23 - Nov. 13.
2330	0630	⑤ Jan. 6 - Mar. 10; ②④⑤ Mar. 14 - Apr. 4; ③⑤⑦ Apr. 7 - Sept. 10; daily Sept. 14,15,19,21,22,26,28,29, Oct. 3,5,6; ⑤⑥⑦ Oct. 13 - Nov. 12; ⑤ Nov. 17 - Dec. 29.

Sailings from Roscoff

Depart Roscoff	Arrive Plymouth	Days of operation
0830	1330	③⑤⑥⑦ Mar. 15 - Apr. 5; ①④⑥ Apr. 8 - July 1 (also May 28, June 4,11); ①④⑥⑦ July 3 - Sept. 9; daily Sept. 11,15-17,20, 22-24,27,29,30, Oct. 1,4,6-8; ① Oct. 23 - Nov. 13.
1630c	2130c	②④ Mar. 14 - Apr. 4; ③⑤⑦ Apr. 7 - Sept. 10; also Sept. 14,19,21,26,28, Oct. 3,5; ⑥⑦ Oct. 14 - Nov. 12.
2330	0600	④⑥⑦ Jan. 5 - Mar. 12; ①③⑤⑦ Mar. 13 - Apr. 5; ①②④⑥⑦ Apr. 6 - Sept. 12; daily Sept. 13,16-18,20,23-25,27,30, Oct. 1,2,4,7-14,17-21,23-28,30,31, Nov. 1-4,6-11,13-16,18,19, 23,25,26,30, Dec. 2,3,7,9,10,14,16,17,21,23,28,30.

c - 30 minutes earlier Sept. 24 - Oct. 21.
h - Depart 1600 Sept. 24-30; depart 1530 Oct. 1-8.

PLYMOUTH - SANTANDER

Sailings from Plymouth Millbay
(Sailings Jan. 8 - Mar. 12 and Nov. 19 - Dec. 30 are from Portsmouth)

Depart Plymouth	Arrive Santander next day	Days of operation
0830	0930	① Apr. 10 - Sept. 11.
1200	1300	③ Mar. 15 - Nov. 8; ⑦ Mar. 19 - Apr. 2 and Sept. 17 - Nov. 12.
1200▲	2100§	From Portsmouth: ⑦ Feb. 5 - Mar. 12; ⑦ Nov. 19 - Dec. 17, also Dec. 30.

Sailings from Santander
(Sailings from Santander Jan. 1 - March 14 and Nov. 21 - Dec. 19 arrive Portsmouth)

Depart Santander	Arrive Plymouth next day	Days of operation
1100	1000	② Apr. 11 - Sept. 12.
1200	1900♥	② Jan. 10 - Mar. 14; ② Nov. 21 - Dec. 19 (to Portsmouth).
1430	1330	④ Apr. 6 - Sept. 7.
1900	1800	①④ Mar. 16 - Apr. 3; ①④ Sept. 14 - Nov. 13.

▲ - Sailings Feb. 5 - Mar. 12 and Nov. 19 - Dec. 30 are from **Portsmouth**.
♥ - Sailings from Santander Jan. 1 - Mar. 14 and Nov. 21 - Dec. 19 arrive at **Portsmouth**.
§ - Passengers may normally spend the second night on board the ship at Santander (disembarking at 0800).

CORK - ROSCOFF / ST MALO

Sailings from Cork, Ringaskiddy

Depart Cork	Arrive Roscoff	Arrive St Malo	Days of operation
1430	0530	...	② May 16 - Sept. 26.
1530	0630	...	⑥ Mar. 18 - Oct. 7.
2000	1100	...	② Apr. 11, 18, 25.
2359	→	1900	③ May 17 - Sept. 27.

Sailings from Roscoff or St Malo

Depart St Malo	Depart Roscoff	Arrive Cork	Days of operation
...	0800	2100	③ May 17 - Sept. 27.
...	2000	0900	③ Apr. 12, 19, 26.
1900	→	1200	① May 15 - Sept. 25.
...	2359	1300	⑤ Mar. 17 - Oct. 6.
2100	→	1400	① Apr. 10, 17, 24.

CONNECTIONS

🚌 services are available between
Portsmouth Continental Ferry Port and Portsmouth Harbour station
and between Ouistreham and Caen station (journey 45 minutes)
to connect with most sailings.

PORTSMOUTH - ST MALO

Sailings from Portsmouth Continental Ferry Port

Depart Portsmouth	Arrive St. Malo	Days of operation
2030	0800	③⑤ Mar. 1-10; daily Mar. 15 - Nov. 17; ③⑤ Nov. 22 - Dec. 29.

Sailings from St. Malo

Depart St. Malo	Arrive Portsmouth	Days of operation
1000	1745	Daily Oct. 1-21.
1045	1830	Daily Mar. 16 - Sept. 30, Oct. 22 - Nov. 17, also Dec. 28.
2100	0645	④⑥ Mar. 2-11 and Nov. 18 - Dec. 23.

PORTSMOUTH - OUISTREHAM (CAEN)

Sailings from Portsmouth Continental Ferry Port

Depart Portsmouth	Arrive Ouistreham	Days of operation
0745	1445b	Daily except Mar. 4,11, Nov. 18,25, Dec. 2,9,16,24-27,30,31.
1430a	2130	①②④⑤⑥⑦ to Nov. 7 (also Mar. 1,8); daily Nov. 9 - Dec. 24, Dec. 27-29, 31.
2245	0630	Daily Mar. 1 - Dec. 23, Dec. 27-30.

Sailings from Ouistreham

Depart Ouistreham	Arrive Portsmouth	Days of operation
0800	1300a	Daily Mar. 1-3, 5-10; ①②④⑤⑥⑦ Mar. 12 - Nov. 12; ①②③④⑤⑦ Nov. 13 - Dec. 17; daily Dec. 19-24, 28,29,31.
1545	2145	Daily Sept. 24 - Oct. 21.
1615	2115	Daily Mar. 1 - Sept. 23, Oct. 22 - Dec. 23, Dec. 27-30.
2300	0615	Daily Mar. 1 - Dec. 23, Dec. 27-29.

a - One hour later Sept. 24 - Oct. 21.
b - One hour earlier Sept. 24 - Oct. 21.

POOLE - CHERBOURG   *Truckline*

Sailings from Poole

Depart Poole	Arrive Cherbourg	Days of operation
0830	1345	③⑤⑦ Jan. 4 - May 17 (not Apr. 14,16,21,23); ③ May 24 - July 5; ③ Sept. 13 - 27; ③⑤⑦ Oct. 1 - Dec. 31 (not Dec. 27).
1230	1745	Apr. 13-16, 20-23; ④⑤⑥⑦ May 18 - July 2; ②③④⑤⑥⑦ July 6 - Sept. 10; also Sept. 14-17, 21-23.
1600	2115	②④⑥ Jan. 3 - May 16 (not Apr. 13,15,20,22); ② May 23 - July 4; ② Sept. 12 - 26; ②④⑥ Sept. 30 - Dec. 30 (not Dec. 26).
2345	0630	①③⑤⑦ Jan. 4 - May 14 (also Apr. 13,15,20,22); ①③④⑤⑥⑦ May 15 - July 3; daily July 5 - Sept. 11; daily Sept. 13-18,20-25,27-29; ①③⑤⑦ Oct. 1 - Dec. 22, Dec. 27,29.

Sailings from Cherbourg

Depart Cherbourg	Arrive Poole	Days of operation
0800	1115	②④⑤⑥⑦ Apr. 13-23 and May 18 - July 9; ②③④⑤⑥⑦ July 11 - Sept. 10; ②④⑤⑥⑦ Sept. 12 - 30.
0930	1245	②④⑥ Jan. 3 - Apr. 11 and Apr. 25 - May 16; ②④⑥ Oct. 3 - Dec. 23, also Dec. 28,30.
1830	2145	①③⑤⑦ Jan. 4 - Mar. 31; ①③⑤⑦ Oct. 1 - Dec. 22, also Dec. 27,29.
1900	2215	①③⑤⑦ Apr. 2 - May 14 (also Apr. 13,15,20,22); ①③④⑤⑥⑦ May 15 - July 3; daily July 5 - Sept. 10; ①③④⑤⑥⑦ Sept. 11 - 30.
2345	0630	②④⑥ Jan. 3 - May 13 (not Apr. 13,15,20,22); ② May 16 - July 4; ② Sept. 12 - 26; ②④⑥ Oct. 3 - Dec. 23, also Dec. 28,30.

POOLE - ST. MALO

Sailings from Poole

Depart Poole	Arrive St. Malo	Days of operation
0800	1700	①⑥⑦ Apr. 8-30; ①⑤⑥⑦ May 12 - Sept. 30.

Sailings from St. Malo

Depart St. Malo	Arrive Poole	Days of operation
2130	0600	⑤⑥⑦ Apr. 7 - 29; ④⑤⑥⑦ May 11 - Sept. 30.

Table 1008 IRISH FERRIES

P.O. Box 19, Alexandra Rd, Dublin 1. See also Table **1009**.
☎ (01) 855 2222   Telex 30303
m.v. *St. Patrick II* 7,984 tons,   m.v. *St. Killian II* 10,256 tons.
January 1 - December 31, 1995. No service Dec. 22-26.

ROSSLARE - CHERBOURG

Depart Rosslare	Arrive Cherbourg next day	Days of operation
1500	0900	⑥ May 27 - July 15.
1530	0930	① July 17 - Sept. 11.
1600	1000	Daily Apr. 7,13,21,27, May 5,11,19,25.
1700	1100	⑥ July 22 - Sept. 16.
2230	1730	⑤ Jan. 6 - Mar. 31; ⑤ Sept. 22 - Dec. 15, also Dec. 29.

Depart Cherbourg	Arrive Rosslare next day	Days of operation
1930	1200	Daily Apr. 8,14,22,28, May 6,12,20,26; ② July 18 - Sept. 12.
2000	1230	⑦ July 23 - Sept. 17.
2030	1300	⑦ May 28 - July 16.
2030	1400	⑥ Jan. 7 - Apr. 1; ⑥ Sept. 23 - Dec. 16, also Dec. 30.

ROSSLARE - LE HAVRE

Depart Rosslare	Arrive Le Havre next day	Days of operation
1500	1300	③ July 19 - Sept. 13.
1600	1400	Daily Apr. 5,9,11,15,17,19,23,25,29, May 1,3,7,9,13,15,17,21,2 3, Sept. 18.
1700	1500	①③ May 29 - July 12; ②④ July 18 - Sept. 14.
1800	1600	③⑦ Jan. 1 - Apr. 2; ③⑦ Sept. 20 - Dec. 31 (also Oct. 30, not Oct. 29).

Depart Le Havre	Arrive Rosslare next day	Days of operation	
1700	1300	Daily Apr. 4,6,10,12,16,18,20,24,26,30, May 2,4,8,10,14,16,18,22,24.	
1800	1400	①② May 29 - July 11; ①③⑤ July 17 - Sept. 15.	
1900	1500*	② Jan. 3 - Mar. 28; ② Sept. 19 - Dec. 19.	* – 1 hour later Sept. 27 - Oct. 20.
2000	1600*	④ Jan. 5 - Mar. 30; ④ Sept. 21 - Dec. 28.	

ROSSLARE - ROSCOFF

Depart Rosslare next day	Arrive Roscoff	Period of operation	Depart Roscoff next day	Arrive Roscoff	Days of operation
1700②	1000③	May 27 - July 16.	1930③	1030④	May 27 - July 16.
1700④	0830⑤	May 27 - July 16.	1930⑤	1030⑥	May 27 - July 16.
			1930⑥	1030⑦	Sept. 16 only.

CORK - ROSCOFF and LE HAVRE
May 28 - September 15 only

Depart Cork	Arrive Roscoff	Arrive Le Havre	Depart Le Havre	Depart Roscoff	Arrive Cork
1700⑤	1000⑥	...	1800④	→	1430⑤
1530⑦	→	1400①	...	1930⑥	1030⑦

Table 1009 IRISH FERRIES
FORMERLY B & I LINE

Reliance House, Water Street, Liverpool, Merseyside. L2 8TP
☎ 0151 227 3131   Fax: 0151 236 0562
m.v. *Isle of Innisfree, Isle of Inishmore*
January 1 - December 31, 1995

HOLYHEAD - DUBLIN
Sailings from Holyhead and Dublin Ferryport

Ships may sail up to 75 minutes earlier on Jan. 1,2,29-31, Feb. 27,28 due to tidal variations.
Last sailing before Christmas: 1545 on Dec. 24, recommencing 0930 on Dec. 27.

Depart Holyhead	Arrive Dublin	Notes	Depart Dublin	Arrive Holyhead	Notes
0330	0730	Jan. 1 - May 22.	0930	1330	Jan. 1 - May 22.
0345	0715	From May 23.	0945	1315	From May 23.
1530	1930	Jan. 1 - May 22.	2130	0130	Jan. 1 - May 22.
1545	1915	From May 23.	2145	0115	From May 23.

PEMBROKE - ROSSLARE
Sailings from Pembroke and Rosslare

Depart Pembroke	Arrive Rosslare	Notes	Depart Rosslare	Arrive Pembroke	Notes
0245	0700	Not Dec. 25-27.	0830	1245	Not Dec. 24-27.
1415	1830	Not Dec. 24-27.	2030	0045	Not Dec. 24-26.

Table 1010 SWANSEA CORK FERRIES

52 South Mall, Cork, Ireland ☎ 021 271166 fax 021 275061
Swansea: ☎ 01792 456116 fax 01792 644356
m.v. *Superferry*
March 10, 1995 - January 11, 1996 (no service Feb. 1995)

SWANSEA - CORK
Sailings from Swansea (on July 8, Aug. 6, sailings are from Pembroke)

Depart Swansea	Arrive Cork	Days of operation
2100b	0700	②④⑤⑦ Mar. 10 - June 20 (also Apr. 12, June 3); ①③④⑤⑥⑦ June 22 - Sept. 17; ②④⑤⑦ Sept. 19 - Dec. 22 (not Nov. 3); daily Dec. 23,28,29,31, Jan. 2,4,7,9,11.

Sailings from Cork (Ringaskiddy)

Depart Cork	Arrive Swansea	Days of operation
0900b	1900	⑤ Mar. 10 - June 16 (also Apr. 12,13,16, June 3,4); ①③④⑤⑥⑦ June 23 - Sept. 17; ⑤ Sept. 22 - Dec. 29 (also Dec. 23; not Nov. 3).
2100b	0700	①③⑥ Mar. 11 - June 21 (not Apr. 12,15, June 3); ①③⑥ Sept. 18 - Dec. 20, also Dec. 27,30, Jan. 1,3,5,8,10.

b - Due to tidal variations, departure times may vary by up to two hours.

Table 1012 CONDOR FERRIES

P.O. Box 10, Bulwer Avenue, St. Sampson, Guernsey GY1 3AF.   ☎ (Weymouth) 01305 761551, (Jersey) 01534 607080.
Catamaran *Condor 8*, fast ferry *Condor 11*, m.v. *Havelet* (sailings by m.v. *Havelet* are shown as 🚢 in the tables).
Services to/from Weymouth also carry cars, other services are passenger only.
1995 services

WEYMOUTH - ST. PETER PORT - ST. HELIER - ST. MALO

Dates of operation:	March 17 - September 23										September 24 - November 12										
	D	J	D	A	B	D	E	F	J🚢	J	U	R	J	T	W	P	R	S	L	N	J🚢	J
Weymouth .... d.	...	0650	...	...	...	...	...	...	1535	2245	...	0650	...	...	...	...	...	...	...	...	1535	2245
Alderney .... d.	...		...	...	...	1605	...	...			...		...	...	...	...	...	...	...	...		
St. Peter Port (Guernsey) ..... a.	...	0905	...	...	...	...	1650	1750	0730	...	...	0905	...	...	...	...	...	...	1750	0730	
St. Peter Port (Guernsey) ..... d.	...	0925	...	...	1610	...	1640	1710	1815	0830	...	0925	...	1510	...	...	1640	1710	1815	0830	
Sark .... d.	...		...	...	...	1715	...				...		...	...	...	...	1715				
St. Helier (Jersey) .... a.	...	1025	...	...	1700	...	1800	1800	1915	1030	...	1025	...	...	1600	...	1800	1800	1915	1030	
St. Helier (Jersey) .... d.	0845	...	1450	1720	1720	1750	1820	1820	...	...	0930	1000	...	1030	1620	1620	1750	1820	1820	...	
St. Malo .... a.	1055	...	1700	1930	1930	2000	2030	2030	...	...	1140	1110	...	1140	1830	1830	1900	1930	1930	...	

Dates of operation:	March 17 - September 23										September 24 - November 12										
	D	A	B	F	E	J	J🚢	D	D	J	R	W	P	J🚢	K	N	L	J	U	R	T	J
St. Malo .... d.	0815	0900	0900	0900	0900	...	...	1115	1720	...	0830	0900	0900	...	0900	0900	0900	...	1550	1620	1650	...
St. Helier (Jersey) .... a.	0825	0910	0910	0910	0910	...	...	1125	1730	...	0940	0910	0910	...	1010	1010	1010	...	1600	1730	1800	...
St. Helier (Jersey) .... d.	...	...	0930	0930	0930	0830	1055	...	...	1945	...	...	0930	0830	...	1030	1030	1055	...	...	...	1945
Sark .... a.	...	...	...	1015	...						...	...	...			1115			...	...	...	
St. Peter Port (Guernsey) ..... a.	...	...	1020	1020	1050	1030	1155	...	...	2045	...	...	1020	1030	...	1120	1150	1155	...	...	...	2045
St. Peter Port (Guernsey) ..... d.	...	...	...	1040	...	1115	1220	...	...	2105	...	...	1115	...	...		1220		...	...	...	2105
Alderney .... a.	...	...	...	1125	...						...	...	...						...	...	...	
Weymouth .... a.	...	...	...	...	1615	1435	...	...	...	2310	...	...	...	1615	...	...	1435	...	...	...	...	2310

A - Daily Mar. 17 - Apr. 4.	K - Daily Sept. 24 - Oct. 21.	T - ②④⑥⑦ Oct. 16-21.
B - ①③⑥ Mar. 17 - Apr. 4.	L - ①-⑥ Sept. 24 - Oct. 15; ①③⑤ Oct. 16-21.	U - ②④⑥⑦ Oct. 22 - Nov. 12.
D - Daily Apr. 5 - Sept. 23.	N - ⑦ Sept. 24 - Oct. 15.	W - Daily Oct. 22 - Nov. 12.
E - ①-⑥ Apr. 5 - Sept. 23.	P - ①③⑤ Oct. 22 - Nov. 12.	
F - ⑦ Apr. 9 - Sept. 17.	R - Daily Sept. 24 - Oct. 15.	🚢 - Service operated by m.v. *Havelet*.
J - Daily Apr. 1 - Oct. 31.	S - Daily Oct. 16-21.	

Table 1015
EMERAUDE LINES

Elizabeth Harbour, St Helier, Jersey
☎ 0534 66566 Telex 4192311 Fax 0534 68741
m.v. *Solidor II*, *Trident* catamarans.

1995 services (catamaran services not yet received)

ST. MALO - ST. HELIER (by car ferry)

**Sailings from St. Malo (Gare Maritime du Naye)
and St. Helier Elizabeth Harbour**

April 1 - October 1 ❖

Depart St. Malo	Arrive St. Helier	Notes	Depart St. Helier	Arrive St. Malo	Notes
0800	0945	Daily ▲	1045	1430	Note E ❶
1500	1645	Note E ⊠	1700	2115	Daily ♣

E - ①③⑥ Apr. 8 - Sept. 25; also ⑤ May 26 - Sept. 8. Also May 9, July 25, Aug. 8; not May 15, July 24, Aug. 11.
▲ - Sails up to 30 minutes earlier on Apr. 17, June 14, July 13,14, Aug. 12, 26-28.
⊠ - Departure time varies on Apr. 15, June 14,17, July 12, Aug. 12.
♣ - Departure time varies between 1700 and 1800. Depart 1845 on Apr. 15, Sept. 25; depart 1900 on July 13, Sept. 9.
❶ - Depart 0945 Aug. 12, depart 1000 Apr. 17, June 14, Aug. 26,28, depart 1130 July 12, Sept. 25, depart 1145 Apr. 15, depart 1200 Sept. 9.
❖ - Outside this period, sailings operate 4 - 6 times weekly. Contact operator for details.

ST. MALO - ST. HELIER (by catamaran)

May 21 - September 24, 1994

A reduced service also operates Apr. 1 - May 20 and Sept. 25 - Oct. 22.

Depart St. Malo	Arrive St. Helier	Notes	Depart St. Helier	Arrive St. Malo	Notes
0815	0830	Daily.	0900	1115	Daily.
1015	1030	①-⑥.	1730	1945	①-⑥.
1745	1800	①-⑥.	1830	2045	Daily.

Additional 'Trident' catamaran services operate
during the summer between the following points:

St. Malo and St Peter Port (journey 2 hours)
St. Helier and St. Peter Port (journey 1 hour)
Granville and Jersey (journey 1 hour 10 minutes),
Carteret and Gorey (journey 30 minutes),
Portbail and Gorey (journey 40 minutes),
St. Quay Portrieux (near St. Brieuc) and St. Helier (journey 1½ hours),
and between St. Helier and Sark (journey 1 hour).

Table 1016
SERVICE MARITIME CARTERET

B.P. 15, 50270 Barneville-Carteret.
☎ 33.53.87.21. Telex 170477F Carsey Fax 33 04 54 61
m.v. *Pegasus*.
Irregular sailings, subject to confirmation

Carteret - Gorey and v.v. journey 30 minutes.	Mar. 30-Sept. 15.
Portbail - Gorey and v.v. journey 30 minutes.	Mar. 30-Sept. 15.
Carteret - St. Peter Port and v.v. journey 1 hour.	Mar. 28-Nov. 13.
Portbail - St. Peter Port and v.v. journey 1 hour 15 minutes.	Mar. 28-Nov. 13.

Table 1017
CHANNILAND

3 ter, Rue Georges Clémenceau, 50403 Granville
☎ 33 51 77 45   fax 33 51 12 10
U.K. agent: Southern Ferries (see Table **1400** for address etc.)

Saint Malo - St. Helier and v.v. (by Catamaran)	April to November
Granville - St. Helier and v.v. (by Catamaran)	April to October
St. Helier - St. Peter Port and v.v. (by Catamaran)	April to November

Table 1020
SALLY FERRIES

INCLUDING OOSTENDE LINES

Argyle Centre, York Street, Ramsgate, CT11 9DS.
☎ 01843 595522   Fax 01843 589329 Telex 96389

Ramsgate - Dunkerque: m.v. *Sally Star*, m.v. *Sally Sky*.

Ramsgate - Oostende: operated by Oostende Lines (RTM)
in association with Sally Lines. For Jetfoil see Table **12**.
m.v. *Reine Astrid*, m.v. *Prins Albert*, m.v. *Prins Filip*

January 1 - December 31, 1995

RAMSGATE - DUNKERQUE

Sailings from Ramsgate and Dunkerque Ouest

Depart Ramsgate	Arrive Dunkerque	Days of operation	Depart Dunkerque	Arrive Ramsgate	Days of operation
0845	1215	Not Dec. 25,26.	0830b	1000	Not Dec. 25,26.
1130	1500	Not Dec. 25,26.	1330b	1500	Not Dec. 25,26.
1600	1930	Not Dec. 25,26.	1700b	1830	Not Dec. 24,25.
1930	2300	Not Dec. 24,25.	2030b	2200	Not Dec. 24,25.
2300	0230	Not Dec. 24,25.	2359b	0130	Not Dec. 24,25.

b – Depart one hour earlier Sept. 24 - Oct. 21.

RAMSGATE - OOSTENDE

For rail connections and the Jetfoil service see Table 12.
Sailings from Ramsgate and Oostende

Depart Ramsgate	Arrive Oostende	Days of operation	Depart Oostende	Arrive Ramsgate	Days of operation
0045	0530c	Not Dec. 25,26.	0030	0330b	Not Dec. 25,26..
0430b	0915	Not Dec. 25,26.	0545b	0930	Not Dec. 25.
1030	1600c	Not Dec. 25.	0945c	1245	Not Dec. 25.
1345	1830c	Not Dec. 25.	1350k	1650k	Not Dec. 25.
1800h	2215	Not Dec. 25.	1715c	2100	Not Dec. 24-31.
2200	0330c	Not Dec. 24,25.	2045c	2345	Not Dec. 24,25,31.

b - One hour later Sept. 24 - Oct. 21.
c - One hour earlier Sept. 24 - Oct. 21.
h - Sept. 24 - Oct. 21 depart 1830, arrive 2230.
k - Sept. 24 - Oct. 21 depart 1330, arrive Ramsgate 1730.

Table 1022
NORTH SEA FERRIES

Beneluxhavn, Europoort, P.O. Box 1123, 3180 AC Rozenburg Z.H.
☎ 01819 55500 Telex 29571 Fax 01819 55215
King George Dock, Hedon Road, Hull HU9 5QA.
☎ 01482 377177 Telex 592349 Fax 01482 706438

Hull - Rotterdam: m.v. *Norsea*, m.v. *Norsun*.
Hull - Zeebrugge: m.v. *Norland*, m.v. *Norstar*.

January 1 - December 31, 1995

HULL - ROTTERDAM

Sailings from Hull King George Dock and Rotterdam Europoort

Depart Hull	Arrive Rotterdam		Depart Rotterdam	Arrive Hull	
1830	0800	Daily.	1830	0800	Daily.

HULL - ZEEBRUGGE

Sailings from Hull King George Dock and Zeebrugge Leopold II Dam

Depart Hull	Arrive Zeebrugge		Depart Zeebrugge	Arrive Hull	
1815	0830	Daily.	1815	0800	Daily.

🚆 connections (reservation recommended):

Hull railway station (depart 1700) - King George Dock and v.v.
Rotterdam Centraal Station (depart 1605) - Europoort and v.v.
Amsterdam Centraal Station (depart 1515) - Europoort and v.v.
Bruges Station (depart 1700) - Zeebrugge and v.v.

Table 1025

STENA SEALINK LINE

Charter House, Park Street, Ashford, Kent, TN24 8EX. ☎ 01233 647047

Dover - Calais: m.v. *Stena Fantasia, Fiesta, Cote d'Azur, Stena Invicta, Stena Challenger,* **Newhaven - Dieppe:** m.v. *Stena Londoner, Stena Parisien*
Southampton - Cherbourg: m.v. *Stena Normandy,* **Harwich - Hoek van Holland:** m.v. *Stena Europe, Koningin Beatrix*
Irish Services: m.v. *Stena Cambria, Stena Hibernia, Stena Felicity, Stena Caledonia, Stena Galloway, Stena Antrim,* **Catamarans** *Stena Sea Lynx, Stena Sea Lynx II*

February 1 - September 23, 1995

DOVER - CALAIS

Sailings from Dover Eastern Docks and Calais Journey 90 minutes

January 9 - February 9

Depart Dover : 0045, 0245, 0430, 0600, 0800, 0930, 1115, 1245, 1430, 1545, 1715, 1900, 2015, 2145, 2330.

Depart Calais : 0100, 0245, 0430, 0630, 0800, 0945, 1130, 1315, 1430, 1600, 1745, 1900, 2030, 2215, 2330.

February 10 - September 23

Depart Dover : 0015, 0100, 0245, 0345, 0530, 0615, 0700, 0800, 0900, 1000, 1045, 1130, 1230, 1330, 1430, 1515, 1600, 1700, 1800, 1900, 1945, 2030, 2130, 2230, 2330.

Depart Calais : 0045, 0145, 0315, 0400, 0500, 0645, 0745, 0845, 0930, 1015, 1115, 1215, 1315, 1400, 1445, 1545, 1645, 1745, 1830, 1915, 2015, 2115, 2300, 2345.

HARWICH - HOEK VAN HOLLAND

Sailings from Harwich Parkeston Quay and Hoek van Holland

Depart Harwich	Arrive Hoek	Notes	Depart Hoek	Arrive Harwich	Notes
1130	1900	Not Dec. 25,26,31.	1200	1800b	Not Dec. 25,26,31.
2130	0700	Not Dec. 25,26,31.	2200	0700	Not Dec. 25,26,31.

b – Arrive 1900 Sept. 24 - Oct. 21.

NEWHAVEN - DIEPPE

Sailings from Newhaven

Depart Newhaven	Arrive Dieppe	Days of operation
0545♦	0900♦	Daily June 16 - Sept. 23.
0715	1215	Daily Feb. 12 - Sept. 23 (not Mar. 7, May 10)
1015	1515	Daily.
1115♦	1430♦	Daily June 16 - Sept. 23.
1645♦	2000♦	Daily June 16 - Sept. 23.
1930	0030	Daily Feb. 12 - Sept. 23 (not Mar. 25).
2230	0330	Daily except Mar. 11, May 6.
2300♦	0215♦	Daily July 14 - Sept. 3.

Sailings from Dieppe

Depart Dieppe	Arrive Newhaven	Days of operation
0200	0500	Daily Feb. 12 - Sept. 23 (not Mar. 26, May 10).
0245♦	0400♦	Daily July 15 - Sept. 4.
0530	0830	Daily except Mar. 12, May 7.
0930♦	1045♦	Daily June 16 - Sept. 23.
1400	1700	Daily Feb. 12 - Sept. 23.
1500♦	1615♦	Daily June 16 - Sept. 23.
1730	2030	Daily. Depart 1600 on Feb. 11.
2030♦	2115♦	Daily June 16 - Sept. 23.

♦ - Service by *Sea Lynx* catamaran.

SOUTHAMPTON - CHERBOURG

Sailings from Southampton

Depart S'thampton	Arrive Cherbourg	Days of operation
1100	1700	Apr. 13-15, 22,23; ①③④⑤⑥⑦ May 23 - Sept. 18.
2200	0800	Daily Jan. 9 - May 22 (not Apr. 13-15, 22,23); daily Sept. 19 - Dec. 23.
2300	0500	Apr. 13-15, 22,23 and daily May 23 - Sept. 18 (arrive 0800 on Apr. 16,24).

Sailings from Cherbourg

Depart Cherbourg	Arrive S'thampton	Days of operation
0600	1000	Apr. 13-15, 22,23; ①③④⑤⑥⑦ May 23 - Sept. 18.
0900	1400	② May 23 - Sept. 18.
1500	2000b	Daily Jan. 9 - May 22 (not Apr. 13-15, 22,23); daily Sept. 19 - Dec. 23.
1800	2200	Apr. 13-15, 22,23; ①③④⑤⑥⑦ May 23 - Sept. 18.

b – Arrive one hour later Sept. 24 - Oct. 21.

CONNECTIONS

🚌 services are available between
Dover Eastern Docks and Dover Priory Station and
Southampton Docks and Southampton Central Station
to connect with most sailings.

HOLYHEAD - DUN LAOGHAIRE

Sailings from Holyhead and Dun Laoghaire (no service Dec. 25,26)

Depart Holyhead	Arrive Dun Laoghaire	Notes	Depart Dun Laoghaire	Arrive Holyhead	Notes
		January 9 - May 27			
0130	0530		0915	1245	
0330	0700		0930♦	1120♦	Mar. 25 - May 27.
0700♦	0850♦	Mar. 25 - May 27.	1130	1500	
1200	1350♦		1515♦	1705♦	
1430	1800		2030	2400	
1645	2045	Depart 1700 to Apr. 30.	2100♦	2250♦	
1745♦	1935♦		2230	0200	
		May 28 - September 30			
0130	0530		0620♦	0810♦	
0330	0700		0915	1245	
0400♦	0550♦		1105♦	1255♦	
0845	1035♦		1130	1500	
1345♦	1535♦		1615♦	1805♦	
1430	1800		2030	2400	
1700	2045		2100♦	2250♦	
1840♦	2030♦		2230	0200	

♦ - Service by *Sea Lynx* catamaran.

FISHGUARD - ROSSLARE

Sailings from Fishguard and Rosslare (no service Dec. 25,26)

Depart Fishguard	Arrive Rosslare	Notes	Depart Rosslare	Arrive Fishguard	Notes
0100♦	0240♦	⑥ July 14 - Sept. 3.	0315♦	0455♦	⑥ July 14 - Sept. 3.
0315	0645	See note E.	0900	1230	See note E.
0700♦	0840♦	Mar. 25 - Oct. 12.	0915♦	1055♦	Mar. 25 - Oct. 12.
1130♦	1310♦	Mar. 13 - Dec. 29.	1345♦	1525♦	Mar. 13 - Dec. 29.
1500	1830		1815♦	1955♦	Mar. 13 - Dec. 29.
1600♦	1740♦	Mar. 13 - Dec. 29.	2150	0120	Depart 1950 Dec. 24.
2030♦	2210♦	July 14 - Sept. 3.	2245♦	0025♦	July 14 - Sept. 3.

♦ - Service by *Sea Lynx* catamaran.
E - Not Feb. 27, Mar. 27, Apr. 24, May 22, Oct. 9, Nov. 13, Dec. 11, 25-27.

STRANRAER - LARNE

Sailings from Stranraer and Larne (no service Dec. 25,26)

Depart Stranraer	Arrive Larne	Days of operation	Depart Larne	Arrive Stranraer	Days of operation
0300	0520	②③④⑤⑥.	0130	0350	①-⑥.
0300	0520	⑦ June 30 - Aug. 28.	0130	0350	⑦ June 30 - Aug. 28.
0530	0650	See note H.	0345	0605	See note K.
0715	0935		0800	1020	
1130	1350		0930	1150	See note J.
1330	1550	See note J.	1130	1350	
1600	1820		1530	1750	
1900	2120		1700	1920	⑥⑦ (n).
2045	2305	⑥⑦ (n).	1800	2020	①-⑤.
2145	0005	①-⑤.	2000	2220	
2359	0220	①-⑤.	2300	0120	①-⑤.
2359	0220	⑥ June 30 - Aug. 28.	2300	0120	⑥ June 30 - Aug. 28.

H - ①-⑥ (daily June 30 - Aug. 28). Not May 20, June 3,10, Oct. 21, Nov. 4,11.
J - ⑤, also daily Mar. 31, Apr. 1-17, 28-30, May 1,26-29, June 26 - Sept. 3, Sept. 9,10, 16,17,23,24,30, Oct. 1,27,30, Dec. 16-24.
K - ②-⑥ (also ⑦ June 30 - Aug. 28).
n - Not May 20, June 3,10, Oct. 21, Nov. 4,11.

Table 1026   HOVERSPEED

IRISH SEA SERVICE

☎ 0345 523523
For other details see Table **1027**.

February 16 - December 31, 1995
Suspended Jan. 9 - Feb. 15, 1995. No service Dec. 25,26, Jan. 1.

STRANRAER - BELFAST

by 'Seacat' catamaran
Sailings from Stranraer West Pier and Belfast Donegall Quay

Depart Stranraer	Arrive Belfast	Notes	Depart Belfast	Arrive Stranraer	Notes
0600	0730	Daily.	0100	0230	①④⑤⑥⑦ June 24 - Sept. 11.
1015	1145	Daily.			
1430	1600	Daily.	0800	0930	Daily.
1845	2015	Daily.	1215	1345	Daily.
2300	0030	③④⑤⑥⑦ June 23 - Sept. 10.	1630	1800	Daily.
			2045	2215	Daily.

Table 1027 HOVERSPEED

International Hoverport, Marine Parade, Dover, Kent, CT17 9TG ☎ 01304 240241 Fax 01304 240088
International Hoverport, Calais ☎ 21 46 14 14 Fax 21 46 14 56. For **Stranraer - Belfast** service see Table **1026**.
February 1 - September 24, 1995

DOVER - CALAIS

Departures from Dover Hoverport and Calais Hoverport

By HOVERCRAFT (journey 35 minutes)

February 1 - March 30 (by SEACAT):

Depart Dover : 0800, 1100, 1430, 1730.
Depart Calais : 1030, 1400, 1700, 2000.

March 31 - June 29 and September 5 - 24:

Depart Dover : 0600J, 0700, 0800, 0900, 1000E, 1100, 1300, 1400, 1500E, 1600, 1800, 2000.
Depart Calais : 0800J, 0900, 1000, 1100, 1200E, 1300, 1500, 1600, 1700E, 1800, 2000, 2200.

June 30 - September 4:

Depart Dover : 0600 and hourly to 1300; 1500 and hourly to 1900, also 2100.
Depart Calais : 0800 and hourly to 1500; 1700 and hourly to 2100, also 2300.

E - ①⑤⑥⑦ (also May 25,30).
J - ①⑤⑥⑦ May 26 - June 26 (also May 25,30).
N - ①⑤⑥⑦ only.

FOLKESTONE - BOULOGNE

Departures from Folkestone Harbour and Boulogne Maritime

By SEACAT (journey 55 minutes)

January 4 - March 30:

NO SERVICE

March 31 - June 29 and September 5 - 24:

Depart Folkestone : 0500K, 0800, 1115, 1430, 1800, 2145M.
Depart Boulogne : 0015N, 0430 (Sept. 5 only), 0730K, 1030, 1400, 1715, 2115.

June 30 - September 4:

Depart Folkestone : 0500, 0800, 1115, 1430, 1800, 2230.
Depart Boulogne : 0430, 0730, 1030, 1400, 1715, 2115.

K - ⑤⑥ May 19 - June 24 and Sept. 5 - 24.
M - ④⑤ Mar. 31 - May 18; ④-⑦ May 19 - June 29 and Sept. 5 - 24.
N - ⑤⑥ Apr. 1 - May 18; ①⑤⑥⑦ May 19 - June 29.

CONNECTIONS

🚌 services are available between
Calais Hoverport and Calais Ville station.

Table 1030 P. & O. EUROPEAN FERRIES

Channel House, Channel View Road, Dover, Kent CT17 9TJ. ☎ 01304 212121.
Portsmouth: ☎ 01705 827677. Calais: ☎ 21 46 04 40. Le Havre: ☎ 35 19 78 50. Zeebrugge: ☎ 050 / 54 22 22. Bilbao: (94) 423 44 77.
19 Rue des Mathurins, F-75009 Paris. ☎ (1) 44 51 0051

Dover - Calais: m.v. *Pride of Dover, Pride of Calais, Pride of Kent, Pride of Bruges, Pride of Burgundy*
Portsmouth - Le Havre: m.v. *Pride of Le Havre, Pride of Portsmouth,* **Portsmouth - Cherbourg:** m.v. *Pride of Hampshire, Pride of Cherbourg*
Felixstowe - Zeebrugge: m.v. *Pride of Suffolk, Pride of Flanders,* **Portsmouth - Bilbao:** m.v. *Pride of Bilbao,* **Cairnryan - Larne:** m.v. *Pride of Ailsa, Pride of Rathlin*
February 1 - September 23, 1995

DOVER - CALAIS

Sailings from Dover Eastern Docks and Calais Journey 75 minutes

February 1 - September 23

Depart Dover : 0100, 0300, 0400, 0500, 0545A, 0630, 0800, 0845, 0930, 1015B, 1100, 1230, 1315, 1400, 1445B, 1530, 1700, 1745, 1830, 1915B, 2000, 2130, 2215, 2300, 2359C.

Depart Calais : 0100, 0200, 0300, 0400E, 0500, 0630, 0730, 0815, 0900F, 0945, 1115, 1200, 1245, 1330G, 1415, 1545, 1630, 1715, 1800G, 1845, 2015, 2100, 2145, 2230G, 2315.

A - Feb. 17 - 27, Apr. 11 - Sept. 24.   E - Feb. 18 - 27, Apr. 11 - Sept. 23.
B - Feb. 17 - 27, Apr. 10 - Sept. 24.   F - Feb. 17 - 27, Apr. 11 - Sept. 23.
C - Feb. 17 - 26, Apr. 10 - Sept. 23.   G - Feb. 17 - 27, Apr. 10 - Sept. 23.

CAIRNRYAN - LARNE

Sailings from Cairnryan

Depart Cairnryan	Arrive Larne	Days of operation
0400	0615	②③④⑤⑥ (not Dec. 26,27).
0730	0945	Daily Jan. 2 - Feb. 13, Mar. 24 - Dec. 24, Dec. 27-31.
1130	1345	Daily except Dec. 25,26, Jan. 1.
1530	1745	Daily Jan. 2 - Feb. 13, Mar. 24 - Dec. 24, Dec. 27-31.
1930	2145	Daily except Dec. 24-26, Jan. 1.
2359	0215	①②③④⑤ Jan. 2 - Feb. 13, Mar. 24 - Dec. 22, Dec. 27-29.

Sailings from Larne

Depart Larne	Arrive Cairnryan	Days of operation
0400	0615	②③④⑤⑥ Jan. 3 - Feb. 11, Mar. 24 - Dec. 23, Dec. 28-30.
0800	1015	Daily except Dec. 25,26, Jan. 1.
1130	1345	Daily Jan. 2 - Feb. 13, Mar. 24 - Dec. 24, Dec. 27 - 31.
1530	1745	Daily except Dec. 25,26, Jan. 1.
2000	2215	Daily Jan. 2 - Feb. 13, Mar. 24 - Dec. 23, Dec. 27 - 31.
2330	0145	①②③④⑤ (not Dec. 25,26).

PORTSMOUTH - BILBAO

Sailings from Portsmouth Continental Ferry Port and Bilbao (Santurtzi)

Santurtzi is located approximately 13 km to the north west of the city centre.

Depart Portsmouth	Arrive Bilbao 3rd day	Days of operation	Depart Bilbao	Arrive Portsmouth 3rd day	Days of operation
2030	0830	②⑥ (not Dec. 23).	1300	1800	①④ (not Dec. 25).

FELIXSTOWE - ZEEBRUGGE

Sailings from Felixstowe and Zeebrugge

Depart Felixstowe	Arrive Zeebrugge	Days of operation	Depart Zeebrugge	Arrive Felixstowe	Days of operation
1100	1745a	Feb. 16 - Dec. 24.	1200a	1645	Not Dec. 25,26, Jan. 1.
2300	0800a	Not Dec. 24-26,31.	2359a	0700	Feb. 16 - Dec. 23.

a - One hour **earlier** Sept. 24 - Oct. 21.

PORTSMOUTH - LE HAVRE

**Sailings from Portsmouth Continental Ferry Port and
Le Havre Quai de Southampton**

Depart Portsmouth	Arrive Le Havre	Days of operation	Depart Le Havre	Arrive Portsmouth	Days of operation
0800	1430a	See note G.	0830	1300b	See note G.
1445b	2115	Daily.	1630a	2100	Daily.
2230	0700	Daily.	2300	0600	Daily.

G - ②-⑦ (daily Jan. 1 - Mar. 31 and June 13 - Sept. 10, also Apr. 17, May 8,29).
a – One hour **earlier** Sept. 24 - Oct. 21.
b – One hour **later** Sept. 24 - Oct. 21.

PORTSMOUTH - CHERBOURG

Sailings from Portsmouth Continental Ferry Port and Cherbourg

Depart Portsmouth	Arrive Cherbourg	Days of operation	Depart Cherbourg	Arrive Portsmouth	Days of operation
0815	1415	See note N.	0800	1200	See note P.
1330	1930	Mar. 18 - Sept. 23.	1300	1700	⑥ Apr. 8 - Sept. 23.
2030	0815	⑤ Apr. 7 - Sept. 22.	1715	2115	Jan. 3 - Sept. 23.
2300	0700	Jan. 2 - Dec. 23.	2300	0615	Mar. 1 - Dec. 23.

N - ①③④⑤⑥⑦ Mar. 17 - Dec. 23 (daily June 14 - Sept. 11).
P - ①③④⑤⑥⑦ Mar. 18 - Dec. 24 (daily June 14 - Sept. 11).

🚌 CONNECTIONS (connecting with most sailings):

Dover Eastern Docks - Dover Priory Station: from Eastern Docks every 45 minutes
0530 - 0100 (also 0420⚡); from Dover Priory every 45 minutes 0545 - 0115.

Calais Port - Calais (Place d'Armes) via Calais Ville station:
from Calais Port on arrival of ship; from Place d'Armes 0540
and every 45 minutes 0655 - 2125.

Portsmouth Continental Ferry Port - Portsmouth Harbour Station.

Zeebrugge - Bruges (operated by *De Lijn*).

Table 1040   SCANDINAVIAN SEAWAYS

Axelborg Vesterbrogade 4A, DK-1620 København V. ☎ 33 156341 Telex 22983 Fax 33 936330
Scandinavia House, Parkeston Quay, Harwich CO12 4QG. ☎ 01255 240240 Telex 987542 Fax 01255 244382
Skandiahamnen, P.O. Box 8895, S-402 72 Göteborg. ☎ 031 65 06 00 Telex 21724 Fax 031 54 3925
Van-den-Smissen Strasse 4, D-2000 Hamburg 50. ☎ 040 389 0371 Telex 02161759 Fax 040 389 03120
P.O. Box 1418, NL-1000 BK, Amsterdam. ☎ 20 116615 Telex 14561 Fax 20 119585

København - Oslo: m.v. *Queen of Scandinavia*, m.v. *Crown of Scandinavia*,
British routes: m.v. *Dana Anglia*, m.v. *Prince of Scandinavia*, m.v. *Princess of Scandinavia*, m.v. *King of Scandinavia*, m.v. *Winston Churchill*, m.v. *Hamburg*.

January 16 - December 31, 1995 (rail connections valid to May 27, 1995)

HARWICH - ESBJERG

Sailings from Harwich Parkeston Quay

Depart London by train ◆	Depart Harwich ◆	Arrive Esbjerg next day	Arrive København	Days of operation
1425	1700	1345	1848 🗓	②④⑥ Jan. 17 - June 24; even numbered dates June 26-30, July 2-30, Sept. 2-14; uneven numbered dates Aug. 1-31; ②④⑥ Sept. 16 - Dec. 23, also Dec. 27,29,31.

Sailings from Esbjerg Englandskajen

Depart København by train	Depart Esbjerg	Arrive Harwich next day ◆	Arrive London by train ◆	Days of operation
1255 🗓	1800	1230	1430	①③⑤ Jan. 16 - June 23; uneven numbered dates June 25-29, July 1-31, Sept. 1-13; even numbered dates Aug. 2-30; ①③⑤ Sept. 15 - Dec. 22, also Dec. 26,28,30.

◆ - All UK times are one hour later Sept. 24 - Oct. 21.

NEWCASTLE - ESBJERG

Sailings from Newcastle Tyne Commission Quay and Esbjerg Englandskajen

Depart Newcastle	Arrive Esbjerg next day	Arrive København by train		Depart København by train	Depart Esbjerg	Arrive Newcastle next day ◆
1730E	1330E	1843		1055	1630G	1030G

E - Depart Newcastle Apr. 11,15,19,23,27, May 1,5,9,13,17,21,25,29, June 2,6,10,14,18, 22,26,30, July 4,8,12,16,20,24,28, Aug. 1,5,9,13,17,21,25,29, Sept. 2,6,10,14,18,22,26, 30, Oct. 4,8,12,16,21,26,30.
G - Depart Esbjerg Apr. 8,12,16,20,24,28, May 2,6,10,14,18,22,26,30, June 3,7,11,15,19, 23,27, July 1,5,9,13,17,21,25,29, Aug. 2,6,10,14,18,22,26,30, Sept. 3,7,11,15,19,23,27, Oct. 1,5,9,13,18,23,27.
◆ - All UK times are one hour later Sept. 24 - Oct. 21.

HARWICH - GÖTEBORG

Sailings from Harwich Parkeston Quay and Göteborg Skandiahamnen

Depart London by train ◆	Depart Harwich ◆	Arrive Göteborg	Notes	Depart Göteborg	Arrive Harwich	Arrive London by train ◆	Notes
January 5 - May 22 and September 16 - December 31							
1025⑤	1300⑤	1400⑥		1100④	1900⑤	1230⑥	
1645⑦	1900②	2000①	B	1700⑥	1600⑦	1830⑦	B
May 27 - September 13							
1620②	2030②	2100③		1900①	1730②	2000②	
1325⑦	1600⑦	1600①		1400⑥	1300⑦	1530⑦	

B - Also Dec. 25 (not Dec. 23) from Göteborg and Dec. 26 (not Dec. 24) from Harwich.
◆ - All UK times are one hour later Sept. 24 - Oct. 21.

NEWCASTLE - GÖTEBORG

Sailings from Newcastle Tyne Commission Quay and Göteborg Skandiahamnen

Depart Newcastle	Arrive Göteborg next day	Days of operation		Depart Göteborg	Arrive Newcastle next day	Days of operation
1200	1100	⑤ May 26 - Sept. 15.		1000	0900	④ May 25 - Sept. 14.

NEWCASTLE - AMSTERDAM

Sailings from Newcastle Tyne Commission Quay and Amsterdam (IJmuiden)

Depart Newcastle	Arrive IJmuiden next day	Days of operation
1730n	0930n	May 21,23,26,28,30; uneven numbered dates June 1-29, July 1-31, Sept. 1-13; even numbered dates Aug. 2-30.
2100	1500	May 19 only.

Depart IJmuiden	Arrive Newcastle next day	Days of operation
1500	0900	May 22 only.
1830	0900	May 18,20,25,27,29,31; even numbered dates June 2-30, July 2-30, Sept. 2-12; uneven numbered dates Aug. 1-31.

n - On ② depart Newcastle 1630, arrive IJmuiden 0830.

HARWICH - HAMBURG

Sailings from Harwich Parkeston Quay

Depart London by train ◆	Depart Harwich ◆	Arrive Hamburg next day	Days of operation
1325	1530	1300	③⑤ Jan. 25 - Mar. 31; even numbered dates Apr. 2-30, May 2-30, Aug. 2-30; uneven numbered dates June 1-29, July 1-31, Sept. 1-29 (not Sept. 11), Oct. 1-15; ③⑤ Oct. 18 - Dec. 22, also Dec. 26,28,30.
1525	1730	1500	⑦ Jan. 8 - Mar. 26; ⑦ Oct. 22 - Dec. 17.

Sailings from Hamburg Fischereihafen

Depart Hamburg	Arrive Harwich next day ◆	Arrive London by train ◆	Days of operation
1630	1200	1430	②④⑥ Jan. 3 - Mar. 30; uneven numbered dates Apr. 1-29, May 1-31, Aug. 1-31; even numbered dates June 2-30, July 2-30, Sept. 2-30 (not Sept. 10), Oct. 2-14; ②④⑥ Oct. 17 - Dec. 21, also Dec. 25,27,29,31.

◆ - All UK times are one hour later Sept. 24 - Oct. 21.

NEWCASTLE - HAMBURG

Sailings from Newcastle Tyne Commission Quay and Hamburg Fischereihafen

Depart Newcastle	Arrive Hamburg next day ◆	Days of operation		Depart Hamburg	Arrive Newcastle next day ◆	Days of operation
1300	1330	See note J.		1630	1500	See note K.

J - Apr. 9,13,17,21,25,29, May 3,7,11,15,19,23,27,31, June 4,8,12,16,20,24,28, July 2,6,10,14,18,22,26,30, Aug. 3,7,11,15,19,23,27,31, Sept. 4,8,12,16,20,24,28, Oct. 2,6,10,14,19,24,28.
K - Apr. 10,14,18,22,26,30, May 4,8,12,16,20,24,28, June 1,5,9,13,17,21,25,29, July 3,7,11,15,19,23,27,31, Aug. 4,8,12,16,20,24,28, Sept. 1,5,9,13,17,21,25,29, Oct. 3,7,11,15,20,25,29.
◆ - All UK times are one hour later Sept. 24 - Oct. 21.

KØBENHAVN - HELSINGBORG - OSLO

Sailings from København Kvaesthusbroen

Depart København	Depart Helsing.	Arrive Oslo next day	Days of operation
1700	1900	0900	Daily except Apr. 18,21, Dec. 23,24.

Sailings from Oslo Utstikker

Depart Oslo	Arrive Helsing.	Arrive København	Days of operation
1700	0645	0915	Daily except Apr. 19,21,23, Dec. 24,25.

AMSTERDAM - GÖTEBORG

Sailings from Amsterdam (IJmuiden) and Göteborg Skandiahamnen

Depart IJmuiden	Arrive Göteborg	Notes		Depart Göteborg	Arrive IJmuiden	Notes
April 9 - May 24 and September 14 - October 28						
1700②	1700③			1800④	1600⑤	
1400⑥	1200⑦			1800⑦	1600①	
May 26 - September 13						
1300③	1030④			1530⑤	1230⑥	
1700⑥	1400⑦			1700⑦	1400①	

AMSTERDAM - KRISTIANSAND

Sailings from Amsterdam (Ijmuiden) and Kristiansand

May 29 - September 13

Depart IJmuiden	Arrive Krist'sand	Notes		Depart Krist'sand	Arrive IJmuiden	Notes
1700①	1030②			1600②	1000③	

CONNECTIONS

Rail services are available between Harwich Parkeston Quay and London Liverpool Street (substitute bus will operate on certain Saturdays and Sundays) and between Esbjerg Havn and København to connect with most sailings.

🚌 services are available between
Hamburg Fischereihafen and Hamburg Altona station (depart Altona 1515),
Göteborg Skandiahamnen and Göteborg station (depart station 1½ hours before sailing)
Ijmuiden and Amsterdam Centraal station (depart station 1½ hours before sailing)
and between Newcastle Tyne Commission Quay and Newcastle station (depart Newcastle station 2½ and 1¼ hours before sailings).

Table 1050 COLOR LINE

Postboks 1422 Vika, 0115 Oslo. ☎ 22 94 44 00 Telex 71 697 Fax 22 83 07 76
Royal Quays, North Shields, Tyne & Wear, NE29 6EE. ☎ 0191 296 1313 Telex 537275 Fax 0191 296 1540

m.v. *Skagen*, m.v. *Christian IV*, m.v. *Prinsesse Ragnhild*, m.v. *Kronprins Harald*, m.v. *Color Festival*, m.v. *Color Viking*.

January 1 - December 31, 1995

BERGEN - STAVANGER - NEWCASTLE

Sailings from Bergen Skoltegrunnskaien and Stavanger Strandkaien

Depart Bergen	Depart Haugesund	Depart Stavanger	Arrive Newcastle	Days of operation (from Bergen)
1100⑤	→	1730⑤	0930⑥	⑤ June 9 - Sep. 1.
1100①	1515①	1800①	1200②	① Jan. 2 (▲) - May 29, Sept. 4 - Dec. 18.
1400⑥	1815⑥	2100⑥	1600⑦	⑥ Dec. 30 only.
1600⑦	→	2200⑦	1430①	⑦ June 4 - Aug. 27.
1600②	2015②	2300②	1800③	② Dec. 26 only.
1700②	2115②	2345②	1600③	② June 6 - Aug. 29.
1700④	2115④	0000⑤	1900⑤	④ Jan. 5 (▲) - May 25, Sept. 7 - Dec. 14.

Sailings from Newcastle Tyne Commission Quay

Depart Newcastle	Arrive Stavanger	Arrive Haugesund	Arrive Bergen	Days of operation (from Newcastle)
1330⑥	0800⑦	→	1400⑦	⑥ June 3 - Aug. 26.
1700③④	1300④⑤	1530④⑤	1945④⑤	③ Dec. 20, ④ Dec. 28 only.
1800①	2315②**B**	2045②**B**	1515②	① June 5 - Aug. 28.
1830②⑥	1430③⑦	1700③⑦	2115③⑦	②⑥ Jan. 3 (▲) - May 30, Sept. 2 - Dec. 16.
1900③	1500④	1730④	2100④.	③ June 7 - Aug. 30.

B – Via Bergen. ▲ – No sailings Jan. 9 - 18.

OSLO - HIRTSHALS

Sailings from Oslo Color Line Terminalen, Hjortnes

Depart Oslo	Arrive Hirtshals next day	Days of operation
1930	0800	①②③④⑤⑥ (not Dec. 23, 30).
1930	0800	⑦ Apr. 16, June 4, June 18 - Aug. 13.

Sailings from Hirtshals

Depart Hirtshals	Arrive Oslo	Days of operation
1000	1830	②③④⑤⑥ (also Apr. 16, 17; not Dec. 24, 31).
1900	0800	⑦ (not Dec. 25).

🚌 CONNECTIONS

Services to connect with most sailings are available between:

- Newcastle Tyne Commission Quay and Newcastle rail station
- Oslo Color Line Terminal and Oslo Sentral rail station (Hotel Royal Christiania)
- Kiel Oslo-Kai and Hamburg ZOB (Central Bus Station).

KRISTIANSAND - HIRTSHALS

Sailings from Kristiansand

Depart Kristiansand	Arrive Hirtshals	Days of operation
0030	0630	Daily June 17 - Aug. 20.
0800	1215	Daily June 16 - Aug. 20.
0815	1245	②③④⑤⑥⑦ (also ① Jan. 2, 9, Apr. 17, May 1, June 5, Aug. 21; not Dec. 24).
1330	1745	Daily June 16 - Aug. 8.
1330	1800	⑤⑥ Jan. 20 - Mar. 25.
1915	2345	Daily Jan. 2 - 19, Mar. 26 - June 15, Aug. 21 - Dec. 23, Dec. 26-30; ①②③④⑦ Jan. 22 - Mar. 23.
2030	0700	Jan. 1; daily Jan. 16 - June 15, Aug. 21 - Dec. 22, Dec. 25-31.

Sailings from Hirtshals

Depart Hirtshals	Arrive Kristiansand	Days of operation
0030	0630	Daily June 16 - Aug. 20.
0045	0700	Daily Jan. 3 - 20, Mar. 27 - June 15, Aug. 21 - Dec. 24, Dec. 27–31; ①②③④⑤ Jan. 23 - Mar. 24.
0800	1230	⑤⑥ Jan. 20 - Mar. 25; daily June 16 - Aug. 20.
1330	1745	Daily June 16 - Aug. 20.
1345	1815	Daily Jan. 2–19, Dec. 26–30; ①②③④⑦ Jan. 22 - Mar. 26; ②③④⑤⑥⑦ Mar. 28 - Jun. 15, Aug. 22 - Dec. 23 (also ① Apr. 17, May 1, June 5).
1500	1930	Jan. 1; daily Jan. 16 - June 15, Aug. 21 - Dec. 23, Dec. 26 - Dec. 30.
1900	2315	Daily June 16 - Aug. 20.
2030	0700	⑤⑥ Jan. 20 - Mar. 25.

OSLO - KIEL

Sailings from Oslo Color Line Terminalen, Hjortnes

Depart Oslo	Arrive Kiel next day	Arrive Hamburg by bus	Days of operation
1330	0900	*1120*	①③⑤ (not Jan. 16, 18, 20, 30, Feb. 1, 6, 8, Sept. 15, Dec. 23, 31).
1630	1200	*1420*	②④⑥⑦ (not Jan. 10, 12, 14, 22, 24, 26, 28, Feb. 4).

Sailings from Kiel Oslo-Kai

Depart Hamburg by bus	Depart Kiel	Arrive Oslo next day	Days of operation
1030	1330	0900	②④ (not Jan. 17, 19, 31, Feb. 2, 7).
1130	1430	1000	⑦ (not Jan. 15, 29, Feb. 5, Dec. 24, 31).
1400	1630	1200	①③⑤⑥ (not Jan. 9, 11, 13, 21, 23, 25, 27, Feb. 3, Sept. 14).

Table 1051
STRANDFARASKIP LANDSINS

Yviri vid Strond 4, Postboks 88, FR-110 Tórshavn.
☎ +298 14550 Telex 81295 Fax +298 16000.

UK agent: P&O Scottish Ferries, PO Box 5, Aberdeen AB9 8DL
☎ 01224 572615 Telex 73344 Fax 01224 574411

m.v. *Smyril*.

January 1 - August 28, 1995

TÓRSHAVN - ABERDEEN

Sailings from Tórshavn

Depart Tórshavn	Arrive Aberdeen	Days of operation
1030⑤	0930⑥	
1600②	1500③	May 2 - Aug. 22.
1730②	1730③	Jan. 3 - Apr. 25.

Sailings from Aberdeen

Depart Aberdeen	Arrive Tórshavn	Days of operation
0800④	0820⑤	Jan. 5 - Apr. 28.
1000④	0845⑤	May 4 - Aug. 24.
1700⑦	1500①	May 7 - Aug. 27.
1900⑥	1925⑦	Jan. 7 - Apr. 29.

Table 1055
SMYRIL LINE

Jonas Broncksgota 25, Postboks 370, FR-110 Tórshavn.
☎ +298 15900 Telex 81296 Fax +298 15707.

UK agent: P&O Scottish Ferries, PO Box 5, Aberdeen AB9 8DL
☎ 01224 572615 Fax 01224 574411

m.v. *Norröna*.

June 3 - September 2, 1995 (no winter service)

TÓRSHAVN - ESBJERG

Depart Tórshavn	Arrive Esbjerg		Depart Esbjerg	Arrive Tórshavn
0830⑤	1900⑥		2200⑥	1000①

TÓRSHAVN - BERGEN

Depart Tórshavn	Arrive Bergen		Depart Bergen	Arrive Tórshavn
1400①	1200②		1500②	1100③

TÓRSHAVN - SEYDISFJÖRDUR (ICELAND)

Depart Tórshavn	Arrive Seydisfjördur		Depart Seydisfjördur	Arrive Tórshavn
1500③	0700④		1100④	0500⑤

Table 1057   EIMSKIP

Iceland Steamship Company Ltd, P.O. Box 220, 121 Reykjavík
☎ 354 1 697100 fax 354 1 28216
1995 service

Weekly cargo service with limited passenger accommodation:
Reykjavík ③ - Immingham ⑦ - Hamburg ① -
Rotterdam ③ - Immingham ④ - Reykjavík ⑦
Other services: Icelandic coastal service, also Reykjavík - Scandinavia.

Table 1060   HELGOLAND

SUMMER SERVICES

Route .... Operator

Cuxhaven - Helgoland and v.v. .... K. G. Seetouristik
Cuxhaven - Helgoland and v.v. .... Cassen Eils
Busum - Helgoland and v.v............ Cassen Eils
Bremerhaven - Helgoland and v.v....... Bremer Seebaderdienst
Wilhelmshaven - Helgoland and v.v. ..... Harle Express Seetouristik

Table 1070   HURTIGRUTEN

(NORWEGIAN COASTAL VOYAGE)

TFDS, Postboks 548, 9001 Tromsø,
☎ 77 68 60 88 Telex 64457 Fax 77 68 87 10
m.v. *Nordlys, Kong Harald, Midnatsol, Harald Jarl, Ragnvald Jarl*

OVDS, Postboks 43, 8501 Narvik,
☎ 76 92 37 00 Telex 64040 Fax 76 92 37 25
m.v. *Richard With, Narvik, Vesterålen, Nordnorge,. Kong Olav*

FFR, Postboks 308, 9601 Hammerfest,
☎ 78 41 10 00 Telex 64 257 Fax 78 41 46 55
m.v. *Lofoten*

October 1, 1994 - September 30, 1995. Only principal points are shown.

BERGEN - TRONDHEIM - TROMSØ - KIRKENES

Sailings from Bergen (daily)			day		Sailings from Kirkenes (daily)			day
Bergen	d.	2200▲	A		Kirkenes	d.	1130d	A
Florø	d.	0445	B		Vardø	d.	1800e	A
Måløy	d.	0730	B		Honningsvåg	d.	0645	B
Ålesund	a.	1200	B		Hammerfest	a.	1115▲	B
Ålesund	d.	1500	B		Hammerfest	d.	1300§	B
Molde	d.	1800▲	B		Tromsø	a.	2345	B
Kristiansund	a.	2300	B		Tromsø	d.	0130	C
Trondheim	a.	0600	C		Finnsnes	d.	0445	C
Trondheim	d.	1200	C		Harstad	d.	0845	C
Rørvik	a.	2115	C		Stokmarknes	d.	1515§	C
Brønnøysund	d.	0100	D		Svolvaer	d.	1915§	C
Sandnessjøen	d.	0415	D		Bodø	a.	0100	D
Bodø	a.	1230	D		Bodø	d.	0400	D
Bodø	d.	1500	D		Sandnessjøen	d.	1330	D
Svolvaer	d.	2200	D		Brønnøysund	d.	1700	D
Stokmarknes	d.	0100	E		Rørvik	d.	2130	D
Harstad	d.	0815	E		Trondheim	a.	0630	E
Finnsnes	d.	1230	E		Trondheim	d.	1000	E
Tromsø	a.	1515	E		Kristiansund	a.	1700	E
Tromsø	d.	1830	E		Molde	d.	2115	E
Hammerfest	a.	0530	F		Ålesund	a.	2345	E
Hammerfest	d.	0800	F		Ålesund	d.	0045	F
Honningsvåg	d.	1730a	F		Måløy	d.	0515§	F
Vardø	d.	0615b	G		Florø	d.	0730▲	F
Kirkenes	a.	1145c	G		Bergen	d.	1400▲	F

a - 1445 Oct. 1 - Mar. 31.
b - 0500 Oct. 1 - Mar. 31.
c - 1015 Oct. 1 - Mar. 31. Arrive 2 hours earlier on ①③⑤⑥ (via Vadsø ②④⑦).
d - 0945 Oct. 1 - Mar. 31. Depart 2 hours later on ②④⑦ (via Vadsø ①③⑤⑥).
e - 1630 Oct. 1 - Mar. 31.
▲ - 30 minutes later from Apr. 1, 1995.
§ - 15 minutes later from Apr. 1, 1995.

Table 1071
NORDLANDSEKSPRESSEN

OVDS, Bodø ☎ 75 52 10 20 Fax 75 52 08 35
m.v. *Skogøy,* m.v. *Børtind*

1994/95 service

SVOLVAER - NARVIK

Depart Svolvaer	Arrive Narvik	Days of operation	Depart Narvik	Arrive Svolvaer	Days of operation
0815	1130	②③④⑤	1200	1600	⑦
1800	2120	⑦	1515	1845	①②③④⑤
2100	0050	⑤			

Table 1072   FLAGGRUTEN

Partrederiet Flagruten ANS, Postboks 2005 Nordnes, 5024 Bergen
☎ 55 23 87 00 Fax 55 23 87 01
Catamarans: *Sleipner, Draupner, Tjelden, Tedno*
May 1, 1994 - April 30, 1995

BERGEN - HAUGESUND - KOPERVIK - STAVANGER

Sailings from Bergen

Depart Bergen	Depart Haugesund	Depart Kopervik	Arrive Stavanger	Days of operation
...	0700	0720	0825	Ⓐ
...	0830	0850	0955	Ⓑ
0800	1035	1055	1155	Daily execpt ⑦
0930	1255	1315	1420	Ⓐ
...	1255	1315	1420	Ⓑ⑦
1230	1515	1535	1635	Daily
...	1830	1850	1955	Ⓐ
...	1900	1920	2025	⑦
1730	2005	2025	2125	Daily except ⑥

Sailings from Stavanger

Depart Stavanger	Depart Kopervik	Depart Haugesund	Arrive Bergen	Days of operation
0720	0815	0840	1115	Daily except ⑦
0910	1005	1030	1325	Ⓐ
1030	1130	1155	...	Ⓑ
1230	1325	1350	1625	Daily
1630	1730	1755	...	Daily
1730	1825	1850	2125	Daily except ⑥
2030	2130	2155	...	Daily except ⑥

Table 1200   LARVIK LINE

Hoffsveien15, Postboks 265, Skøyen, 0212 Oslo
☎ 22 52 55 00 Fax 22 52 15 40
Postboks 30, 9900 Fredrikshavn ☎ 99 20 40 60 Fax 98 20 40 50.
m.v. *Peter Wessel,* catamaran *Juan. L.*
January 3 - December 23, 1995 (special service operates Dec. 24 - Jan. 2).

LARVIK - FREDERIKSHAVN   *by ship*
Jan. 3 - Mar. 19
From Larvik : 0800⑤⑦ (arrive 1400); 1530⑥ (arrive 2130); 2030①②③ (arrive 0800);
2200⑦ (arrive 0800); 2230⑤ (arrive 0700).
From Frederikshavn : 0830⑥ (arrive 1430); 1330①②③ (arrive 1930); 1500⑦ (arrive 2100);
1530⑤ (arrive 2130); 2030④ (arrive 0700); 2230⑥ (arrive 0700).

Mar. 20 - May 30 and Aug. 28 - Dec. 22 (no service Apr. 18 - 27)
From Larvik : 2030 daily (arrive 0800). On Apr. 17, depart 1500.
From Frederikshavn : 1330 daily (arrive 1945). On Apr. 17, depart 0800, 2200.

May 31 - June 21 and Aug. 14 - 27
From Larvik : 0800⑤ (arrive 1415); 2030①②③⑥⑦ (arrive 0800); 2230⑤ (arrive 0800).
From Frederikshavn : 1330①②③⑥⑦ (arrive 1945); 1530⑤ (arr. 2145); 2030④ (arr. 0700).

June 22 - Aug. 13
From Larvik : 0800③⑤⑦ (arrive 1415); 1530①②④⑥ (arrive 2145); 2230③⑤⑦ (arr. 0700).
From Frederikshavn : 0800①④⑥ (arr. 1415); 1530③⑤⑦ (arr. 2145); 2230①②④⑥ (arr. 0700).

LARVIK - SKAGEN   *by catamaran, journey 2 hours 45 minutes*
May 5 - 30 and Aug. 28 - Sept. 29
From Larvik : 0830⑤⑥⑦, 1530 daily.   From Skagen : 1200⑤⑥⑦, 1900 daily.

May 31 - June 21 and Aug. 14 - 27
From Larvik : 0830⑤⑦, 1200④, 1430⑤, 1530①②③⑥⑦, 1900④.
From Skagen : 1100⑤, 1200⑥⑦, 1530④, 1800⑤, 1900①②③⑥⑦.

June 22 - Aug. 13
From Larvik : 0700①④⑥, 1030②③⑤⑦, 1400①④⑥, 1730③⑤⑦, 2100①②④⑥.
From Skagen : 0700②③⑤⑦, 1030①④⑥, 1400③⑤⑦, 1730①②④⑥, 2100③⑤⑦.

Table 1202   SEACAT

Sea Containers Sweden AB, Box 4040, S-40040 Göteborg
☎ 031 775 4200   Fax 031 420015
SeaCat Terminal Göteborg ☎ 031 775 0800, Fredrikshavn ☎ 98 42 8300
UK agents: Hoverspeed Dover ☎ 01304 240241 Fax 01304 240088

SeaCatamaran Danmark
January 1, 1995 - March 31, 1996 No sailings Dec. 25 or Jan. 9 - Mar. 9, 1996

GÖTEBORG - FREDERIKSHAVN
Sailings from Göteborg and Frederikshavn

Depart Göteborg	Arrive Frederikshavn	Notes	Depart Frederikshavn	Arrive Göteborg	Notes
0245	0430	A	0500	0645	A
0730	0915	B	1000	1145	B
1215	1400		1500e	1645e	
1730	1915	C	2000g	2145g	C
2215	2400	D	0030	0215	D

A – ⑥⑦ July 1 - Aug. 6.
B – ①②③④⑤⑥ to Apr. 1;
daily from Apr. 2 (not Jan. 1).
C – ①②③④⑤⑦ to Mar. 31;
daily from Apr. 1 (not Dec. 24, 31).
D – Daily Jun. 16 - Aug. 13; also
Jun. 2, 5, 9, 11, Aug. 18, 20, 25, 27.
e – 15 minutes later Jan. 1 - Mar. 19, 1995.
g – 15 minutes earlier Jan. 1 - Mar. 19, 1995.

Table 1205 STENA LINE

Masthuggskajen, S-405 19 Göteborg. ☎ 031 858000   Fax 031 858025.
Trafikhavn, DK-9900 Frederikshavn. ☎ 98 424366   Fax 98 422750.
UK bookings: Stena Line ☎ 01233 615777

m.v. *Stena Germanica*, m.v. *Stena Scandinavia*, m.v. *Stena Danica*,
m.v. *Stena Jutlandica*, m.v. *Stena Nordica*, m.v. *Stena Saga*.
February 1 - December 31, 1995

FREDERIKSHAVN - GÖTEBORG

Sailings from Frederikshavn Trafikhavn and Göteborg

Depart Frederikshavn	Arrive Göteborg	Notes	Depart Göteborg	Arrive Frederikshavn	Notes
February 2 - June 22 and August 7 - December 23					
0345	0700	②③④⑤⑥ (b).	0745	1100	See note H.
0900	1215	See note G.	0930	1245	
1230	1545	See note H.	1300r	1615r	See note G.
1430	1745		1630	1945	
2015	2330		1830	2145	(Depart 1900 on ⑥).
2215	0130		2355	0310	①②③④⑤ h
June 23 - August 6					
0330	0645		0330	0645	
0730	1045		0730	1045	
0900	1215		0930	1245	
1130	1445		1130	1445	
1330	1645		1300	1615	
1530	1845		1530	1845	
1930	2245		1930	2245	
2330	0245		2330	0245	

G - Not ② June 19. or ② Aug. 29 - Dec. 19.
H - Not ① Feb. 6 - Apr. 24 or Sept. 25 - Dec. 19.
b - Not Apr. 15,18, May 26,27, June 6.
h - Not Apr. 14,17, May 25,26, June 5.
r - One hour later on ⑤ Feb. 3 - Mar. 10, ④ Mar. 16 - June 22, ④ Aug. 17 - Dec. 21.

FREDERIKSHAVN - OSLO

Sailings from Frederikshavn Trafikhavn and Oslo Utstikker 2

Depart Frederikshavn	Arrive Oslo	Notes	Depart Oslo	Arrive Frederikshavn	Notes
February 1 - March 12					
0945	1830	③④⑦ (not Feb. 4-19).			
1830	0800	①⑤.	1930	0800	②③④⑥⑦.
2100	0930	⑥ Feb. 4 - 19.			
March 13 - June 22 and August 13 - December 17					
0945	1830	①②③⑥⑦	1930	0800	Daily except ④.
1830	0800	④			
June 23 - August 12					
0945	1830	Daily	1930	0745	Daily

FREDERIKSHAVN - MOSS

Sailings from Frederikshavn Trafikhavn and Moss Faerge Terminal

Depart Frederikshavn	Arrive Moss	Notes	Depart Moss	Arrive Frederikshavn	Notes
1700	2355	Not Dec. 23-31.	0045	0815	Not Dec. 23-31.

KIEL - GÖTEBORG

Sailings from Kiel Schwedenkai and Göteborg

Depart Kiel	Arrive Göteborg	Notes	Depart Göteborg	Arrive Kiel	Notes
1900	0900	Not Dec. 24,25.	1900	0900	Not Dec. 24,25.

Table 1207 FJORD LINE

Slottsgatan 1, postboks 4088, 5023 Bergen
☎ +47 55 323770   fax +47 55 323815
m.v. *Bergen*
January 2 - December 31, 1995

BERGEN - EGERSUND - HANSTHOLM

January 2 - June 18 and August 21 - December 31

Depart Bergen	Depart Egersund	Arrive Hanstholm	Depart Hanstholm	Depart Egersund	Arrive Bergen
1630①③⑤	0045②④⑥	0900②④⑥	1630②④	2330②④	0900③⑤
...	2100⑥	0900⑦	1300⑥	2015⑥	...
			1400⑦	2115⑦	0700①
June 19 - August 20					
1630①③⑤	0045②④⑥	0800②④⑥	0845②④⑥	1515②④⑥	...
...	1600②④⑥	2245②④⑥	2345②④	0645③⑤	1445③⑤
...	0800⑦	1445⑦	2345⑤	0715⑦	...
...	...	...	1545⑤	2215⑦	0700①

A connecting bus service operates between Egersund and Stavanger.

Table 1210
LION FERRY

Box 94 S-432 22, Varberg.   ☎ 340 19010   Telex 3462   Fax 340 85125.
Box 60 S-301 03, Halmstad.   ☎ 35 135170   Telex 38338   Fax 35 140875
Box 150 DK-8500, Grenaa.   ☎ 86 320300   Telex 63490   Fax 86 327525.

m.v. *Lion Queen*,   m.v. *Lion Prince*.
January 3 - October 1, 1995

GRENAA - HALMSTAD

Sailings from Grenå and Halmstad Kattegatt Hamnen

Depart Grenaa	Arrive Halmstad	Days of running	Depart Halmstad	Arrive Grenaa	Days of running
January 2 - April 2					
0800	1215	②③④⑤⑥	0800	1215	⑦
1400	1815	⑦	1330	1745	①②③④⑤
1900	2315	①②③④⑤	1800	2215	⑥
2359	0530	⑥⑦	1900	2315	⑦
			2359	0530	①②③④⑤
April 3 - June 21 and August 14 - October 1					
0800	1230	Daily	1330	1800	Daily
1900	2315	Daily	2359	0530	Daily
June 22 - August 13					
0815	1230	Daily	1330	1800	Daily
1900	2315	Daily	2359	0715	Daily

GRENAA - VARBERG

Sailings from Grenå and Varberg

Depart Grenaa	Arrive Varberg	Days of running	Depart Varberg	Arrive Grenaa	Days of running
January 2 - April 2					
1300	1715	⑤	0800	1200	⑤
1400	1815	①②③④	0900	1300	①②③④⑥
2230	0225	⑤	1400	1815	⑦
2359	0530	①②③④	1800	2200	⑥
			1900	2315	①②③④
			2359	0630	⑥
April 3 - June 21 and August 14 - October 1					
1400	1800	Daily	0900	1300	Daily
2359	0530	Daily (not June 21).	1900	2315	Daily
June 22 - August 13					
0200	0555	①④⑥	0200	0555	③⑤⑦
0700	1100	③⑤⑦	0700	1100	①②④⑥
1200	1545	①②④⑥	1200	1545	③⑤⑦
1630	2015	③⑤⑦	1630	2015	①②④⑥
2100	0045	①②④⑥	2100	0045	③⑤⑦

Table 1215
FLYVEBÅDENE

Havnegade 49, DK-1020 København K.
☎ 33 12 80 88   Fax 33 93 33 10
Catamarans
January 9 - April 12, 1995
Subject to minor alterations from April 13

KØBENHAVN - MALMÖ   Journey 45 minutes.

Sailings from København Nyhavn : 0030Ⓐ, 0100Ⓑ⑦, 0600Ⓐ, 0700, 0800⚒, 0900, 1000, 1100, 1200, 1300, 1400, 1500, 1600, 1700, 1800⚒, 1900, 2000⚒, 2100, 2300.

Sailings from Malmö Skeppsbron : 0600, 0700Ⓐ, 0800, 0900⚒, 1000, 1100, 1200, 1300, 1400, 1500, 1600, 1700, 1800, 1900⚒, 2000, 2100⚒, 2200, 2345①②③④⑦, 2359⑤⑥.

Table 1216
MOLS-LINIEN

Faergehavnen, 8400 Ebeltoft.   ☎ 89 52 52 52   Fax 89 52 52 92
m.v. *Mette Mols*   m.v. *Maren Mols*   m.v. *Mie Mols*

From March 1, 1995
Subject to alteration on holidays

EBELTOFT - SJAELLANDS ODDE   Journey 1 hour 40 minutes.

Sailings from Ebeltoft : 0200Ⓐ, 0600Ⓐ, 0800, 1000⚒, 1200, 1400, 1500Ⓑ, 1600, 1800, 1900Ⓑ, 2000, 2200Ⓑ, 2359Ⓑ.

Sailings from Sjaellands Odde : 0200Ⓐ, 0600Ⓐ, 0800, 1000⚒, 1200, 1300Ⓑ, 1400, 1600, 1700Ⓑ, 1800, 2000, 2100Ⓑ, 2200Ⓑ, 2359Ⓑ.

Table 1217 S A S

Hammerichsgade 1, DK-1611 København V.
☎ 32 326868 Fax 32 326448.

Catamarans

KØBENHAVN LUFTHAVN (AIRPORT) - MALMÖ Journey 30 minutes.
10 - 12 flights daily

Table 1218
DSB (DANISH RAILWAYS)

DSB Rederidivisionen, Sølvgade 40, DK-1349 København K.
☎ 33 148880 Telex 27105

Rødby - Puttgarden and v.v.	Journey 60 minutes.	30 - 40 sailings daily.
Gedser - Warnemünde and v.v.	Journey 2 hours.	See Table 1227.
Halsskov - Knudshoved and v.v.	Journey 60 minutes.	20 - 35 sailings daily.
Kalundborg - Århus and v.v.	Journey 3 hours.	See Table 451.
Kalundborg - Samsø and v.v.	Journey 2 hours.	2 - 3 sailings daily.
Esbjerg - Fanø and v.v.	Journey 20 minutes.	17 - 30 sailings daily.
Bøjden - Fynshav and v.v.	Journey 50 minutes.	7 - 8 sailings daily.

Table 1219 SCANDLINES

Terminalgatan 1, Box 44, S 252 78 Helsingborg
☎ 042 186100   Fax 042 187410   (Helsingør: ☎ 49 26 26 81)

January 9 - May 27, 1995

HELSINGØR - HELSINGBORG AND V.V.   Journey approx 25 minutes

Sailings from Helsingør : 0010, 0110, 0210, 0410, 0450, 0530, 0610, 0630Ⓐ, 0650, 0710Ⓐ, 0730, 0750※, 0810, 0830※, 0850, 0910※, 0930, 0950※, 1010, 1030※, 1050, 1110※, 1130, 1150※, 1210, 1230※, 1250, 1310 then every 20 minutes until 1650, 1710Ⓑ, 1730, 1750, 1810, 1830Ⓑ, 1850, 1910, 1930, 1950Ⓑ, 2010, 2030, 2050, 2130, 2150※, 2210, 2250, 2330.

Sailings from Helsingborg : 0010, 0110, 0210, 0410, 0450, 0530, 0610, 0630Ⓐ, 0650, 0710Ⓐ, 0730, 0750※, 0810, 0830※, 0850, 0910※, 0930, 0950※, 1010, 1030※, 1050, 1110※, 1130, 1150※, 1210, 1230※, 1250, 1310 then every 20 minutes until 1650, 1710, 1730, 1750Ⓑ, 1810, 1830, 1850, 1910Ⓑ, 1930, 1950, 2010, 2030Ⓑ, 2050, 2110※, 2130, 2210, 2250, 2330.

DRAGØR - LIMHAMN AND V.V.   Journey 55 minutes
14 - 18 sailings daily.

Table 1220
FAABORG - GELTING LINIEN

Odensevej 95, DK-5600, Faaborg.   ☎ 62 611533   Fax 62 619376.
m.v. *Gelting Syd.*

February 10 - December 30, 1995

Sailings from Faaborg and Gelting

Depart Faaborg	Arrive Gelting	Days of operation	Depart Gelting	Arrive Faaborg	Days of operation
0830	1030	①b ②③④⑤⑥⑦.	1115	1315	①b ②③④⑤⑥⑦.
1400	1600	①b ②③④⑤⑥⑦.	1645	1845	①b ②③④⑤⑥⑦.
1930	2145	Daily July 7 - Aug. 6 g.	2215	0015	Daily July 7 - Aug. 6 g.

b – For dates of sailings on ① Feb. 13 - May 29, please contact the shipping company.
g – Also ⑤ June 23, 30, Aug. 11, 18, 25, and ⑥ Apr. 8 - July 1, Aug. 12 - Dec. 16.

Table 1221
LANGELAND - KIEL LINIEN

Fahrhafen, DK-5935 Bagenkop.
☎ 62 561400   Fax 62 561959.
m.v. *Langeland III*

January 1 - December 31, 1995. No service Jan. 4 - Feb. 16, Dec. 24,25,31.

BAGENKOP - KIEL   Journey 2 hours 30 minutes.
Sailings from Bagenkop : 0800, 1400, 1930g.
Sailings from Kiel Oslo Kai : 1100, 1645, 2215g.

g – ⑤ Mar. 3 - Dec. 15; ⑥ Apr. 29 - Dec. 16, also Apr. 13,15,16,May 24, June 4.

Table 1222 LISCO

Lithuanian Shipping Company, 24 Jenonio, Klaipeda 5813, Lithuania
☎ and fax: (370 61) 55943
Krantas Maritime Agency, Klaipeda, ☎ (370 61) 56116, fax (370 61) 18479
m.v. *Vilnius*, m.v. *Kaunas*, m.v. *Mercuri I*

KIEL - KLAIPEDA   *Subject to confirmation*

Depart Kiel	Arrive Klaipeda	Depart Klaipeda	Arrive Kiel
2200①	2359②	2200①	0800③
1200②	1800③	1200③	1500④
1500③	1800④	2359③	0700⑤
2200④	2359⑤	2359④	0800⑥
1500⑥	2100⑦	1200⑦	1500①

Table 1223 EUROPA-LINIEN

Moltzaugade 5, DK-4874 Gedser.
☎ 53 879233 Fax 53 870075

m.v. *Rostock Link*, m.v. *Falster Link*, m.v. *Baltavia*
Joint service with DSB (m.v. *Knudshoved*)

October 14, 1994 - May 27, 1995

GEDSER - ROSTOCK AND V.V.   Journey 2 hours

Sailings from Gedser : 0300③④⑥ (not Apr. 17), 0600 (not Dec. 25, Jan. 1), 0900, 1200, 1500, 1800 (not Dec. 24,31), 2100.
Sailings from Rostock Überseehafen : 0600① - ⑥ (not Apr. 17), 0900 (not Dec. 25, Jan. 1), 1200, 1500, 1800, 2100 (not Dec. 24,31), 2359②③⑤⑥⑦.

Table 1225 TT-LINE / TR-LINE

Mattentwiete 8, 20457 Hamburg.
☎ 040/3601 442 - 446   Fax 040/3601 407   Telex 215185

m.v *Peter Pan*, m.v. *Nils Holgersson*, m.v. *Nils Dacke*, m.v. *TT-Traveller*,
m.v. *Saga Star*, m.v. *Nord Neptunus*, m.v. *Kahleberg*.

January 1 - December 31, 1995
Services liable to alteration over the Christmas period.

TRAVEMÜNDE - TRELLEBORG

Sailings from Travemünde Skandinavienkai and Trelleborg

Depart Travemünde	Arrive Trelleborg	Days of operation	Depart Trelleborg	Arrive Travemünde	Days of operation
January 1 - June 15 and August 21 - December 31					
0230	1000	②③④⑤⑥.	1000	1715	Daily.
0400	1130	①.	1230	2000	②③④⑦.
1000	1715	Daily.	1300	2030	⑥.
1300	2030	⑥.	1715	0030	①②③④⑤.
2200	0600	①②③④.	1715	0200	⑦.
2230	0730	Daily.	2030	0430	⑤.
2300	0630	⑥.	2200	0700	Daily.
June 16 - August 20					
0230	1000	②③④⑤⑥.	0730	1430	②③⑥⑦.
0400	1130	①.	1000	1715	①④⑤.
0730	1430	②③⑥⑦.	1230	2000	②③④⑦.
1000	1715	①④⑤.	1300	2030	⑥.
1300	2030	⑥.	1530	2230	②③⑥⑦.
1530	2230	②③⑥⑦.	1715	0030	①②③④⑤⑦.
2200	0600	①②③④⑥.	2030	0430	⑤.
2230	0630	①⑤.	2200	0630	①⑤.
2230	0730	④.	2200	0700	④.
2330	0730	②③⑥⑦.	2330	0700	②③⑥⑦.

ROSTOCK - TRELLEBORG

Sailings from Rostock Überseehafen and Trelleborg

Depart Rostock	Arrive Trelleborg	Days of operation	Depart Trelleborg	Arrive Rostock	Days of operation
January 9 - December 21					
0730	1330	②③④⑤⑥⑦.	0730	1330	②③④⑤⑥⑦.
1500	2100	Daily.	1500	2100	Daily.
2300	0530	①②③④⑤⑥.	2300	0530	①②③④⑤⑥.
2300	0630	⑦.	2300	0630	⑦.
January 1 - 8 and December 22 - 31					
1300	1900	Daily.	1300	1830	Daily.
2300	0630	Daily.	2300	0530	Daily.

Table 1226 CORONA LINE

ul. Kwiatkowskiego 60, 81-127 Gdynia, Poland
☎ (48 58) 213241 fax (48 58) 216667

February 20 - December 20, 1994

KARLSKRONA - GDYNIA

Depart Karlskrona	Arrive Gdynia	Days of operation	Depart Gdynia	Arrive Karlskrona	Days of operation
February 11 - July 1 and August 15 - December 20					
1100	2100	⑦.	1800	0900	②④⑥ (arr. next day)
1800	0900	①③⑤ (arr. next day).	2200	1100	① (arrive next day)
July 2 - August 14					
2100	0700	Daily (arr. next day).	0900	1900	Daily (arr. next day).

THOMAS COOK TRAVELLERS
AMSTERDAM

See the order form at the back of this book for details.

Table 1227   DFO (HANSAFERRY)

Deutsche Fährgesellschaft Ostsee, Industriestrasse 8, 18069 Rostock
Sassnitz :   ☎ 03 83 92 22267   Fax 03 83 92 22266
Warnemünde :   ☎ 0381 51406   Fax 0381 51409
m.v. *Knudshoved*, m.v. *Warnemünde*, m.v. *Rostock*, m.v. *Sassnitz*,
m.v. *Trelleborg*, m.v. *Götaland*, m.v. *Rügen*

1995 sailings (subject to confirmation)

WARNEMÜNDE - GEDSER
Sailings from Warnemünde and Gedser

Depart Warnemünde	Arrive Gedser	Notes	Depart Gedser	Arrive Warnmünde	Notes
0100	0310	Daily except ② (b).	0100	0320	Not Dec. 25,31.
0330	0605	Not Dec. 25.	0400	0610	Daily except ② (b).
0700	0900	Daily except ② (b).	0700	0855	Daily except ② (b).
1000	1205		0925	1120	
1200	1400		1300	1500	
1600	1805		1525	1720	
1800	2000		1900	2100	
2200	2400	Not Dec. 24,31.	2125	2220	Not Dec. 24,31.

b – Not Dec. 25.

ROSTOCK - TRELLEBORG
Sailings from Rostock and Trelleborg

Depart Rostock	Arrive Trelleborg	Notes	Depart Trelleborg	Arrive Rostock	Notes
0800	1345	Daily except ①.	0800	1345	Daily except ①.
1445	2030		1445	2030	
2200	0500		2200	0600	

SASSNITZ - TRELLEBORG
Sailings from Sassnitz and Trelleborg

Depart Sassnitz	Arrive Trelleborg	Notes	Depart Trelleborg	Arrive Sassnitz	Notes
0330	0730		0330	0730	
0830	1215		0830	1215	
1300	1700		1300	1700	
1800	2130		1800	2130	
2230	0215		2230	0215	

SASSNITZ - RØNNE   *1994 sailings*
Sailings from Sassnitz

Depart Sassnitz	Arrive Rønne	Days of running
0400	0715	Daily June 1 - Sept. 14.
1030	1400	③⑥⑦ Jan. 1-Mar. 30; ①④⑤⑥⑦ Mar. 31-May 1; ③⑥⑦ Oct. 26 - Dec. 21 (also Dec. 22,23,26-31).
1400	1730	①③④⑤⑥⑦ May 4 - Oct. 24 (daily June 1 - Sept. 14). ·

Sailings from Rønne

Depart Rønne	Arrive Sassnitz	Days of running
0815	1130	①④⑤⑥⑦ May 4 - Oct. 24 (daily June 1 - Sept. 14).
1700	2030	③⑥⑦ Jan. 1-Mar. 30; ①④⑤⑥⑦ Mar. 31-May 1; ③⑥⑦ Oct. 26 - Dec. 21 (also Dec. 22,23,26-31).
1900	2245	① May 4 - Oct. 24 (daily June 1 - Sept. 14).

PUTTGARDEN - RØDBY

Frequent sailings (30-40 daily). Sailing time 55 minutes.

Table 1240   ECKERÖ LINJEN

Storagatan 8, Box 158, SF-22100 Mariehamn.
☎ +358 28 28000   Fax +358 28 12011.
Grisslehamn ☎ 0175 309 20 Fax 0175 308 20
m.v. *Roslagen*, m.v. *Ålandia*.

February 17, 1995 - January 7, 1996

Grisslehamn - Eckerö and v.v.	Journey 2 hours.

February 17 - June 8 and August 21 - January 7

Sailings from Grisslehamn : 1000, 1500, 2000④⑤⑥⑦.
Sailings from Eckerö : 0830①⑤⑥⑦, 1330, 1830 (1845 on ⑦).

No sailings December 24, 25

June 9 - August 20

Sailings from Grisslehamn : 1000, 1130, 1500, 1700, 2000.
Sailings from Eckerö : 0930, 1330, 1530, 1830, 2015.

🚌 connections:
Stockholm (Tekniska Högskolan T-banan station) - Grisslehamn and v.v., departing 2 hours before ship departure.
Eckerö - Mariehamn and v.v.

Table 1230 BORNHOLMSTRAFIKKEN

Havnen, 3700 Rønne. ☎ 56 95 18 66   Fax 56 91 07 66
m.v. *Peder Olsen*, m.v. *Jens Kofoed*, m.v. *Povl Anker*.

January 1 - December 30, 1995   Not Dec. 25.

YSTAD - RØNNE	Journey 2½ hours.

Sailings from Ystad :

Jan. 9 - June 23: 1115, 1300⑥ (not June 3-17), 1915, 2100N.
June 24 - Aug. 13: 1000①⑤⑥⑦, 1115, 1300③, 1700①⑤⑥⑦, 1915, 2100②④.
Aug. 14 - 31: 1000⑥, 1115, 1300⑤⑦ (not Aug. 18), 1700①⑥ (not Aug. 21), 1915.
Sept. 1 - Dec. 31: 1115 (not Nov. 2,5,9), 1300⑥ (not Sept. 2-23), 1915 (not Dec. 24,31).

Sailings from Rønne :

Jan. 9 - June 23: 0800, 0930⑥ (not June 3-17), 1600, 1730N.
June 24 - Aug. 13: 0630①⑤⑥⑦, 0800, 0930③, 1330①⑤⑥⑦, 1600, 1730②④.
Aug. 14 - 31: 0630⑥, 0800, 0930⑤⑦ (not Aug. 18), 1300① (not Aug. 21), 1330⑥, 1600.
Sept. 1 - Dec. 31: 0800 (not Nov. 2,5,9), 0930⑥ (not Sept. 2-23), 1600 (not Dec. 24,31).

KØBENHAVN - RØNNE	Subject to confirmation	Journey 7 hours.

Sailings from København Kvaesthusbroen : 0830E, 2330.
Sailings from Rønne : 1515E, 2330.

NEU MUKRAN (SASSNITZ) - RØNNE	Subject to confirmation	Journey 3½ hours

Sailings from Neu Mukran : 1130G. Sailings from Rønne : 0700G.

E - ①②④⑤⑥⑦ June 18 - Aug. 7.
G - ④⑥ Jan. 1 - May 28 (also Apr. 1,4, May 1,15,16,22,23); ①④⑥⑦ May 29 - Sept. 24.
N - Apr. 17, May 14,24,25,27,28, June 2,5 only.

Table 1235 GOTLANDSLINJEN

Box 27304, 102 54 Stockholm ☎ 08 - 666 60 70   Fax 08 - 666 60 25
m.v. *Graip*, m.v. *Nord Gotlandia*.

January 1 - December 30, 1995 (no service Dec. 24, 25, 31).

Nynäshamn - Visby and v.v.	Journey 5½ hours.

January 1 - June 8 and August 21 - December 30

Sailings from Nynäshamn : 1215E, 1230⑥b, 1530G, 2330⑥.
Sailings from Visby : 0700⑥, 0700E, 0800G, 1600⑤⑦h, 1700N.

June 9 - August 20

Sailings from Nynäshamn : 1215, 1315J, 1530K, 2345 (not June 23).
Sailings from Visby : 0630, 0715J, 0800K, 1800 (not June 23), 1900J.

Oskarshamn - Visby and v.v.	Journey 4½ hours.

January 1 - June 8 and August 21 - December 30

Sailings from Oskarshamn : 1200①n, 1200⑥ (also Apr. 14), 2330②③④⑤⑦ (not Apr. 14).
Sailings from Visby : 0700①①n, 0700R, 1530W, 1630S, 1715②③④ (not Apr. 13), 1745V.

June 9 - August 20

Sailings from Oskarshamn : 1215, 1315P, 2330 (not June 23, Aug. 19).
Sailings from Visby : 0700, 0800P, 1730 (not June 23, Aug. 19).

E - ①③⑤⑦ May 1 - June 8 (also Apr. 12,13,17,18, June 5, Nov. 3,5; not May 3,26).
G - ⑤⑦ Aug. 25 - Sept. 10.   **J** - ⑤⑥⑦ June 30 - Aug. 20.   **K** - ⑤⑥⑦ June 9 - 29.
N - ①②③④ (depart 1745 on Apr. 12,13,17,18, May 1, June 5 and ③ May 10 - June 8).
P - ①②③④ June 30 - Aug. 20.   **R** - ⑥ Apr. 22 - June 8 and Aug. 26 - Sept. 9 (not Apr. 14).
S - ⑤ Jan. 1 - May 4 and Aug. 21 - Dec. 30 (also Apr. 13; not Apr. 14).
V - ⑤⑦ May 5 - June 8.   **W** - ⑦ (not May 7 / June 8).
b - On Mar. 4 depart 1800   **h** - Depart 1745 on Nov. 3,11.
n - On Apr. 17, May 1,25, June 5 depart Visby 1530, depart Oskarshamn 2330.

🚌 service Stockholm City Terminal - Nynäshamn connects with most sailings.

Table 1241   ÅNEDIN LINJEN

Vasagatan 4, S-11181 Stockholm.
☎ 08 247985   Telex 12824 Fax 08 100741
m.v. *Baltic Star*.

January 1 - April 29 and September 9 - December 31, 1994

Stockholm - Mariehamn and v.v.	24 hour cruises	Journey 7 hours.

Sailings from Stockholm Skeppsbron : 1600①④, 1800②⑤, 1900⑥.
Sailings from Mariehamn : 0930②⑤, 1100③⑥, 1200⑦.

From May to September there will be three 24-hour cruises per week from Stockholm to Mariehamn and two 36-hour cruises per week from Stockholm to the island of Saaremaa (Ösel) in Estonia.

Table 1242   BIRKA CRUISES

Box 15131, Södermalmstorg 2, S-104 65 Stockholm.
☎ 08 714 5510 Telex 11947 Fax 08 714 9830
m.v. *Birka Princess*.

January 19 - December 30, 1995

Stockholm - Mariehamn and v.v.	24 hour cruises	Journey 6 - 8 hours.

Sailings from Stockholm Stadsgården : 1400①, 1500②, 1600③, 1700④, 1800⑤b, 1900⑥b.
Sailings from Mariehamn (Swedish time): 0800②, 0900③, 1000④, 1100⑤, 1200⑥b, 1300⑦b.

b - No sailings ⑤⑥ June 23 - Aug. 11 (next day from Mariehamn) - replaced by weekend cruises to Gotland and Bornholm.

Table 1250   SILJA LINE

Mannerheimintie 2, SF-00100 Helsinki.
☎ 90 18041   Fax 90 1804 279
Stockholm - Helsinki: m.v. *Silja Serenade*, m.v. *Silja Symphony*.
Stockholm - Turku: m.v. *Silja Europa*, m.v. *Silja Scandinavia*.
Travemünde - Helsinki: g.t.v. *Finnjet*.
Vaasa/Skellefteå routes: m.v. *Fennia*, m.v. *Wasa Queen*, m.v. *Silja Festival*
January 1 - October 27, 1995

STOCKHOLM - HELSINKI

Sailings from Stockholm Värtahamnen and Helsinki Eteläsatama.

Depart Stockholm	Arrive Helsinki	Notes		Depart Helsinki	Arrive Stockholm	Notes
1800	0830	Daily.		1800	0830	Daily.

STOCKHOLM - TURKU

Sailings from Stockholm Värtahamnen.

Depart Stockholm	Depart Mariehamn	Arrive Turku	Days of operation
0800	→	1900	Daily except May 29,30, Sept. 4,5.
2000	0215	0800	Daily except May 21,22, Sept. 10,11.

Sailings from Turku

Depart Turku	Depart Mariehamn	Arrive Stockholm	Days of operation
1000	→	1900	Daily except May 22,23, Sept. 11,12.
2000	0200	0700	Daily except May 28,29, Sept. 3,4.

TRAVEMÜNDE - HELSINKI   SILJA FINNJET LINE

Sailings from Travemünde Skandinavienkai and Helsinki Katajanokka

Depart Travemünde	Arrive Helsinki	Notes		Depart Helsinki	Arrive Travemünde	Notes
January 3 - June 12, August 27 - October 27						
1800④	0830⑥	Not Apr. 6.		1300⑥	1700⑦	Not Mar. 4, Apr. 8.
2000⑦	1000②	Not Apr. 9.		1900②	0930④	Not Apr. 11.
June 13 - August 26						
1630③	1630④			1700②	1900③	
1800⑤	1800⑥			1800④	1600⑤	
1900⑦	1000②			1930⑥	1730⑦	

VAASA - SUNDSVALL

Journey 8½ hours (11-15 hours overnight)

April 13 - June 18 and August 14 - December 22
Sailings from Vaasa : 1800①, 1900③, 1000④, 1100⑤, 1200⑥, 1300⑦.
Sailings from Sundsvall : 1700②, 1800③, 1900④, 2000⑤, 2000⑥, 2100⑦.

June 19 - August 13
Sailings from Vaasa : 1200.
Sailings from Sundsvall : 2000.

VAASA - UMEÅ (HOLMSUND)

Journey 4 hours.

January 2 - February 15 and March 6 - April 9
Sailings from Vaasa : 1300①, 1730②, 1000④, 1600⑤, 1700⑥, 1100⑦.
Sailings from Umeå : 0900②, 1200③, 1800④, 2030⑤, 2100⑥, 1600⑦.

February 16 - March 5
Sailings from Vaasa : 1300①, 1730②, 1000⑤ (also Feb. 23, Mar. 2), 2100⑤, 1530⑥, 1100⑦. Also sails Feb. 16 at 1800.
Sailings from Umeå : 0900②, 1200③, 1430⑤, 0900⑥, 2100⑥, 1600⑦. Also sails Feb. 16 at 2200 and Feb. 23, Mar. 2 at 1800.

April 10 - June 30 and August 8 - December 22
Sailings from Vaasa : 1700① G, 0900② G, 2200②, 1700③, 1000④⑤, 2330⑤, 1700⑥, 0900⑦, 1900⑦.
Sailings from Umeå : 0900① G, 2100① G, 1700②, 0900③, 2100③, 1800④, 1800⑤, 1100⑥, 2100⑥, 1300⑦.

July 1 - August 6
Sailings from Vaasa : 0900, 1330①②③④, 1800.
Sailings from Umeå : 0800①②③④, 1230, 2130.

G - Not May 22 - June 6, Aug. 28 - Sept. 12 (also 0900 from Umeå cancelled Apr. 10).

PIETARSAARI - SKELLEFTEÅ   Journey 5 hours

June 19 - 30 and August 7 - 13 (no winter service)
Sailings from Pietarsaari : 1800①, 1100③, 1800④, 2030⑤, 1600⑥, 1000⑦.
Sailings from Skellefteå : 1500②, 1800③, 1400⑤, 0900⑥, 2015⑥, 1500⑦.

July 1 - August 6
Sailings from Pietarsaari : 0900⑤, 2200⑤, 1600⑥, 0930⑦.
Sailings from Skellefteå : 1530⑤, 0900⑥, 2100⑥, 1415⑦.

PIETARSAARI - UMEÅ   Journey 5 hours

From Pietarsaari : **May 22 - June 5, Aug. 28 - Sept. 12:** 1700①, 0900②;
July 2 - Aug. 3: 2030⑦, 2245①②③. Also sails Aug. 13 at 2130. No winter service.
From Umeå : **May 22 - June 5, Aug. 28 - Sept. 12:** 0900①, 2100①;
July 2 - Aug. 3: 1630①②③④. No winter service.

Table 1255   VIKING LINE

P.O. Box 35, SF-22101 Mariehamn.
☎ +358 28 26011 Telex 63122 Fax +358 28 15811
UK agent: Finnman Travel, Leigh, WN7 1AZ ☎ 01942 262662
m.v. *Isabella*, m.v. *Mariella*, m.v. *Amorella*, m.v. *Rosella*, m.v. *Ålandsfärjan*
January 1 - April 30, 1995

STOCKHOLM - HELSINKI

Sailings from Stockholm Stadsgården and Helsinki Katajanokka.

Depart Stockholm	Arrive Helsinki	Notes		Depart Helsinki	Arrive Stockholm	Notes
1800	0900			1800	0900	

STOCKHOLM - MARIEHAMN - TURKU

Sailings from Stockholm Stadsgården and Turku Linnansatama.

Depart Stockholm	Depart Mariehamn	Arrive Turku	Notes		Depart Turku	Depart Mariehamn	Arrive Stockholm	Notes
0800	1440	2010			1000	1535	2010	
2115	→	0805			2130	→	0700	

(STOCKHOLM) - KAPELLSKÄR - MARIEHAMN

Sailings from Kapellskär and Mariehamn

Depart Stockholm	Depart Kapellskär	Arrive Mariehamn		Depart Mariehamn	Arrive Kapellskär	Arrive Stockholm
January 1 - April 12						
0815♦	1000	1330		0700	0830	1015♦
1615♦	1800	2130		1500	1615	1800♦
April 13 - 30						
0715♦	0900	1230		0700	0815	1000♦
1315♦	1500	1830		1300	1415	1600♦
1845♦	2030	2400		1900	2015	2200♦

♦ - Connecting bus service to/from Stockholm Central station (Cityterminalen).

HELSINKI - TALLINN   *Catamarans 'Viking Express I and II'*

Sailings from Helsinki Makasiiniterminaali and Tallinn

April 15 - December 15 (weather permitting in winter)

Depart Helsinki	Arrive Tallinn			Depart Tallinn	Arrive Helsinki	
0830 §	1010			0700	0845	☼ June 1 - Aug. 31.
0930	1115	☼ June 1 - Sept. 30.		1115 §	1255	
1455	1645			1230	1415	June 1 - Sept. 30
1715 §	1905	June 1 - Sept. 30.		1800	1945	
2030	2215	June 1 - Aug. 31.		2000 §	2140	June 1 - Sept. 30.

§ - Also conveys cars from June 1 *(Viking Express I)*. Other sailings are passenger only.

Connecting 🚌 services:
Stockholm Central station - Slussen metro station - Viking Line terminal and v.v.
Stockholm Arlanda Airport - Viking Line terminal and v.v. (depart Arlanda 1420④, 1550④,
1550⑦, 1600⑥, 1620④; depart Viking Line Terminal 0930 daily).
Helsinki railway station – Viking Line terminal and v.v. (bus no. 13).

Table 1257   SEAWIND

SeaWind Line Ab, Linnankatu 84, 20100 Turku
☎ 921 301900 Fax 921 303334 Stockholm : ☎ 020-795 331
m.v. *Sea Wind*
January 28 - December 31, 1995 No sailings Dec. 23-26
For passengers with vehicles (limited passenger facilities).

STOCKHOLM - TURKU

Sailings from Stockholm Värtan and Turku

Depart Stockholm	Arrive Turku	Days of operation		Depart Turku	Arrive Stockholm	Days of operation
January 28 - June 2 and August 16 - December 31						
0845	2015	②		0920	1900	④
2045	0815	③④⑥⑦		0945	1915	⑦
				2145	0715	①②⑤
June 3 - August 15						
0845	2015	Daily		2145	0715	Daily

Table 1262   DEUTSCHE SEEREEDEREI TOURISTIK

Postfach 401405, D-18125 Rostock ☎ (0381) 458 4672 fax (0381) 458 4678
m.v. *Greifswald*
January 1 - December 31, 1995

MUKRAN - KLAIPEDA

Depart Mukran	Arrive Klaipeda	Days of operation		Depart Klaipeda	Arrive Mukran	Days of operation
1500	0900	See note A.		1500	0900	See note B.

A - Alternate days (even dates in Jan., June, July, Sept. and Oct.; uneven dates in Feb., Mar., May, Aug., Nov. and Dec.). No service in April (subject to confirmation).
B - Alternate days (uneven dates in Jan., June, July, Sept. and Oct.; even dates in Feb., Mar., May, Aug., Nov. and Dec.). No service in April (subject to confirmation).

Table 1270 POLFERRIES

Polish Baltic Shipping Co., ul. Portowa 41, PL 78 100 Kolobrzeg
Gdańsk: ☎ +48 58 431877 Telex 512386 Fax +48 58 430975
m.v. *Nieborów*, m.v. *Silesia*, m.v. *Wilanów*, m.v. *Pomerania*, m.v. *Rogalin*.
January 16 - December 31, 1995

YSTAD - ŚWINOUJŚCIE *to April 30*

Depart Ystad	Arrive Świnoujście	Notes	Depart Świnoujście	Arrive Ystad	Notes
1300	2000	Not Apr. 9.	1300	2000	
2300	0800		2300	0800	

MALMÖ - ŚWINOUJŚCIE *from May 1*

Depart Malmö	Arrive Świnoujście	Notes	Depart Świnoujście	Arrive Malmö	Notes
1130 H	2030 H	Not Dec. 23,25.	1130 H	2030 H	Not Dec. 23,24.
2300	0830	Not Dec. 24.	2300	0830	Not Dec. 24,31.

H - No sailing on ① Sept. 4 - Dec. 31.

KØBENHAVN - ŚWINOUJŚCIE

Depart København	Arrive Świnoujście	Days of operation	Depart Świnoujście	Arrive København	Days of operation
1100	2030	⑦	1030	1945	④⑤
2130	0730	①③④⑤	2230b	0830	②⑥⑦ (arr. 0930 ⑦)

No sailings from Świnoujscie Apr. 15, Dec. 23,24,30,31 (next day from København).
b - Depart 2330 June 24 - Aug. 26.

HELSINKI - GDAŃSK

Depart Helsinki	Arrive Gdańsk	Notes	Depart Gdańsk	Arrive Helsinki	Notes
June 4 - August 27					
2100②	0800④		1200④	1730⑤	
2100⑤	0900⑦		2000⑦	1030②	
January 1 - June 3 and August 28 - December 31					
2000②	0900④	E	2000④	1100⑥	E
1500⑥	1830②		2200⑦	1030②	

E – Gdańsk arrive 1100/depart 1900 on ④ Feb. 15 - Apr. 7, May 3-18, Oct. 4-19.

GDAŃSK - OXELÖSUND

Depart Gdańsk	Arrive Oxelösund		Depart Oxelösund	Arrive Gdańsk	
1800	1230	See note A.	1600	1030	See note B.

A - Sails on Feb. 2,5,7,9,16,23, Mar. 2,9,16,23,30, Apr. 6,10,12,17,19,21,24,26, May 4,11, 18,20, 22,24,26,28,30; uneven dates June 1-29, July 1-31; even dates Aug. 2-30; daily Sept. 1,3,5,7,10,12,14,17,19,21,24,26,28, Oct. 5,12,19,22,24,26,29,31, Nov. 2,5,7,9, 12,14,16,19,21,23,26,28,30, Dec. 3,5,7,10,12,14,16,18,20,22,26,28, Jan. 2,4,7,9,11.
B - Sails on Feb. 1,3,6,8,10,15,22, Mar. 1,8,15,22,29, Apr. 5,11,13,18,20,22,25,27, May 3, 10,17,21,23,25,27,29,31; even dates June 2-30, July 2-30; uneven dates Aug. 1-31; daily Sept. 2,4,6,8,11,13,15,18,20,22,25,27,29, Oct. 4,11,18,23,25,27,30, Nov. 1,3,6,8, 10,13,15,17,20,22,24,27,29, Dec. 1,4,6,8,11,13,15,17,19,20,21,23,27,29, Jan. 3,5,8,10,12.

ŚWINOUJŚCIE - RØNNE

Depart Świnoujście	Arrive Rønne	Notes	Depart Rønne	Arrive Świnoujście	Notes
1000	1600	⑥ June 24 - Aug. 26.	1730	2245	⑥ June 24 - Aug. 26.

Table 1290 ESTLINE

Frihamnen Magasin 2, Box 27304, 102 54, Stockholm.
☎ +46 8 667 0001 Fax +46 8 666 6052
m.v. *Mare Balticum*, m.v. *Nord Neptunus*

STOCKHOLM - TALLINN

Depart Stockholm Frihamnen	Arrive Tallinn	Days of operation	Depart Tallinn	Arrive Stockholm Frihamnen	Days of operation
1730	0900	Every other day ▲	1900	1000	Every other day ▲

▲ – Ship sails from Stockholm on uneven dates (even dates from Tallinn) in Jan., Apr., May., Aug., Nov. and Dec. 1995, and on even dates (uneven dates from Tallinn) in Dec. 1994, Feb., Mar., June, July, Sept. and Oct. 1995. On other dates, sailings are by cargo ship m.v. *Nord Neptunus* with limited facilities.
🚌 service available Tallinn Harbour - Central Station - Olümpia Hotel and v.v.

Table 1296 ESTONIAN NEW LINE

Kalevankatu 1 C 51, SF-00100 Helsinki.
☎ (90) 680 2499, Fax (90) 680 2475
'City Jet' service. Catamaran *San Pietro*
Subject to confirmation

HELSINKI - TALLINN

Catamaran sailings from Helsinki Makasiiniterminaali and Tallinn C-terminal

Depart Helsinki	Arrive Tallinn	Days of operation	Depart Tallinn	Arrive Helsinki	Days of operation
0800	0930	②③④⑤.	0700	0830	⑥.
0930	1100	①⑥⑦.	1030	1200	②③④⑤.
1330	1500	⑤.	1200	1330	⑥.
1600	1730	②③④⑥⑦.	1330	1500	⑦.
1900	2030	⑤.	1600	1730	⑤
			1830	2000	Daily except ⑤.

Table 1293 BALTIC LINE

Positionen 118, S-115 74 Stockholm. ☎ (0)8 202795, fax (0)8 100741.
Nynäshamn: ☎ (0)20 290029. Gdynia: ☎ 58 213524
m.s. *Ilich*, m.s. *Anna Karenina*, m.s. *Konstantin Simonov*, m.s. *Balanga Sister*
January 1 - December 31, 1995 Subject to alteration
Revised schedules operate at Christmas/New Year

HELSINKI - ST. PETERBURG

Depart Helsinki	Arrive St. P'burg	Days of operation	Depart St. P'burg	Arrive Helsinki	Days of operation
1700①④	0930②⑤	Apr. 13 - Dec. 18.	0005④⑦	1100④⑦	Apr. 16 - Dec. 21.

STOCKHOLM - ST. PETERBURG

Depart Stockholm	Arrive St. P'burg	Days of operation	Depart St. P'burg	Arrive Stockholm	Days of operation
1600⑤	1830⑥	Mar. 3 - Dec. 15.	1600①	1300②	Mar. 6 - Dec. 18.

(STOCKHOLM 🚌) - NYNÄSHAMN - ST. PETERBURG

Depart Nynäshamn	Arrive St. P'burg	Days of operation	Depart St. P'burg	Arrive Nynäshamn	Days of operation
1930⑦	0900②	Feb. 12 - Apr. 16.	1400③	1700④	Feb. 15 - Apr. 19.
1730⑦	1800①	Apr. 23 - Dec. 17.	1800③	1700④	Apr. 26 - Dec. 20.

(STOCKHOLM 🚌) - NYNÄSHAMN - RIGA

Depart Nynäshamn	Arrive Riga	Days of operation	Depart Riga	Arrive Nynäshamn	Days of operation
1800①	0945②	Mar. 27 - Dec. 22.	1800②	0945③	Mar. 27 - Dec. 22.
1800③	0945④	Mar. 27 - Dec. 22.	1800④	0945⑤	Mar. 27 - Dec. 22.

(STOCKHOLM 🚌) - NYNÄSHAMN - KIEL

Depart Nynäshamn	Arrive Kiel	Days of operation	Depart Kiel	Arrive Nynäshamn	Days of operation
1830④	1930⑤	Feb. 9 - Dec. 14.	1500⑤	1730⑦	Feb. 11 - Apr. 15.
			1500⑥	1600⑦	Apr. 22 - Dec. 16.

BUS CONNECTIONS
🚌 - A special bus service operates between Stockholm Central (Cityterminal) and Nynäshamn to connect with sailings, journey 1½ hours

Table 1295 TALLINK

Eteläranta 14, SF-00130 Helsinki. ☎ (9)0 2282 1277, Fax (9)0 635311
m.v. *Georg Ots*, m.v. *Tallink*, m.v. *Vana Tallinn*
hydrofoils: *Liisa, Laura*
April 1 - September 30, 1995. Subject to alteration.

HELSINKI - TALLINN *by ship*

Depart Helsinki ↗	Arrive Tallinn	Days of operation	Depart Tallinn	Arrive Helsinki ↗	Days of operation
April 1 - 30					
0800	1130	Daily.	0930	1300	①②⑤.
1000	1330	Daily.	1100	1500	③⑥.
1700	2030	②③⑤⑥.	1300	1700	④⑦.
1900	2230	①④⑦.	1730	2100	Daily.
			1830	2200	Daily.
May 1 - September 30 ↗					
0800	1130	Daily.	1230	1600	Daily.
1000	1330	Daily.	1730	2100	Daily.
1800	2130	Daily.	1830	2200	Daily.

↗ - From May 1, Helsinki terminal is Länsisatama (western harbour).

HELSINKI - TALLINN *by hydrofoil. Tallink Express*

Sailings from Helsinki Makasiiniterminaali and Tallinn Linnahall

Depart Helsinki	Arrive Tallinn	Dates of operation	Depart Tallinn	Arrive Helsinki	Dates of operation
0730	0900	Apr. 1 - Sept. 30.	0730	0900	Apr. 1 - Sept. 30.
1030	1200	May 1 - Sept. 30.	1000	1130	May 1 - Sept. 30.
1430	1600	May 1 - Sept. 30.	1500	1630	May 1 - Sept. 30.
1800	1930	Apr. 1 - Sept. 30.	1800	1930	Apr. 1 - Sept. 30.

Table 1297 EESTIN LINJAT

Fabianinkatu 9, 00130 Helsinki. ☎ (90) 66 99 44 fax (90) 66 99 90
m.v. *Alandia*
January 1 - December 31, 1995 No sailings Dec. 24-26.

HELSINKI - TALLINN

Depart Helsinki §	Arrive Tallinn	Depart Tallinn	Arrive Helsinki §
0800	1130	1630	2000

§ - Olympia Terminaali

Table 1400

TRASMEDITERRANEA

Pedro Munez Seca, 2 bajo, 28001 Madrid. ☎ 91 431 07 00 Telex 23189 Fax 91 431 08 04.

U.K. Agent: Southern Ferries, 179 Piccadilly, London W1V 9DB. ☎ 0171 491 4968 Fax 0171 491 3502.

m. v. *Ciudad de Badajoz*, m. v. *Ciudad de Sevilla*, m. v. *Juan March*, m. v. *Ciudad de Compestela*, m.v. *Antonio Lazaro*, m.v. *Vicente Puchol*, m. v. *Las Palmas de Gran Canaria*, m. v. *Ciudad de Salamanca*, m. v. *Santa Cruz de Tenerife*, m. v. *Ciudad de Palma*, m. v. *Ciudad de Santa Cruz de la Palma*, m.v. *Villa de Agaete*, m.v. *Juan Jose Sister*, m.v. *Manuel Soto*.

Balearic Services are valid January 16 - December 31, 1995. All other services are subject to confirmation (1994 details).

CÁDIZ - SANTA CRUZ TENERIFE - LAS PALMAS

Depart Cádiz	Arrive Tenerife	Arrive Las Palmas	Depart Tenerife	Depart Las Palmas	Arrive Cádiz
1800⑥	0900①	1800①	2345②	1700③	0900⑤

LAS PALMAS - SANTA CRUZ TENERIFE

Depart Las Palmas	Arrive Tenerife	Days of operation	Depart Tenerife	Arrive Las Palmas	Days of operation
1000	1400	⑤	1400	1800	①
1400	1800	①②③⑤	1700	2100	①③⑤
1800	2200	⑦	1800	2200	⑦
			2345	0800	②④

Additional service by hydrofoil : 2-4 departures daily, journey 80 minutes.

LAS PALMAS - PUERTO ROSARIO - ARRECIFE

Depart Las Palmas	Arrive P. Rosario	Arrive Arrecife	Depart Arrecife	Depart P. Rosario	Arrive Las Palmas
2345①③⑤	0800②④⑥	1300②④⑥	1800②④⑥	2345②④⑥	0800③⑤⑦

SANTA CRUZ TENERIFE - SANTA CRUZ PALMA

Depart Tenerife	Arrive S.C.Palma	Depart S.C.Palma	Arrive Tenerife
2345①③⑤	0800②④⑥	1300④	2000⑤
		2345②⑥	0800③⑦

ALGECIRAS - SEBTA (CEUTA)

Journey 1 hour 30 minutes

Jan. 3 - Mar. 24, Apr. 4 - June 19 and Sept. 12 - Dec. 18

Sailings from Algeciras : 0800☒, 1000⑦, 1030☒, 1300, 1530☒, 1630⑦, 1800☒, 1900⑦, 2030☒, 2100⑦.

Sailings from Sebta : 0800☒, 1000⑦, 1030☒, 1300, 1530☒, 1630⑦, 1800☒, 1900⑦, 2030☒, 2100⑦.

Mar. 25 - Apr. 3 and Dec. 19 - Jan. 4

Sailings from Algeciras : 0730☒, 0800⑦, 0830☒, 0900⑦, 1030, 1200☒, 1300, 1530, 1700☒, 1800, 2030.

Sailings from Sebta : 0800⑦, 0830☒, 0930☒, 1030, 1300, 1430☒, 1530, 1630⑦, 1800, 1930☒, 2030.

June 20 - Sept. 11

Sailings from Algeciras and Sebta : an increased service will operate (no details available).

Additional service all year by hydrofoil : 4-6 departures daily, journey 30 minutes.

ALGECIRAS - TANGER

Journey 2 hours 30 minutes

Sailings from Algeciras : 0930 (also 1330 June 20 - Sept. 11).
Sailings from Tanger : 1530 (also 0900 June 20 - Sept. 11).

MÁLAGA - MELILLA

Depart Málaga	Arrive Melilla	Days of operation	Depart Melilla	Arrive Málaga	Days of operation
January 1 - June 19 and September 12 - December 31					
1300	2030	①②③④⑤⑥	2300	0630	①②③④⑤⑥
June 20 - September 11					
1300	2030	Daily.	1300	2030	①③⑤.
2330	0700	①③⑤.	2300	0630	Daily.

ALMERÍA - MELILLA

Depart Almería	Arrive Melilla	Days of operation	Depart Melilla	Arrive Almería	Days of operation
January 1 - June 19 and September 12 - December 31					
1300	1930	②③④⑤⑥.	2330	0600	①②③④⑤⑥.
2330	0600	⑦.			
June 20 - 28, July 4 - 10 and July 19 - 25					
0200	0830	①③⑤⑦.	0200	0830	②④⑥.
1000	1630	②④⑥.	1000	1630	①③⑤⑦.
1800	0030	①③⑤⑦.	1800	0030	②④⑥.
June 27 - July 3, July 11 - 18 and July 26 - September 11					
0200	0830	②④⑥.	0200	0830	①③⑤⑦.
1000	1630	①③⑤⑦.	1000	1630	②④⑥.
1800	0030	②④⑥.	1800	0030	①③⑤⑦.

OTHER SERVICES

Las Palmas - Morro Jable and v.v.	2 sailings per week by hydrofoil.
Santa Cruz Tenerife - Morro Jable and v.v.	2 sailings per week by hydrofoil.
S.S. Gomera - Los Cristianos and v.v.	3-4 sailings daily by hydrofoil, 2 sailings daily by ferry.
Valverde - Los Cristianos and v.v.	3 sailings per week by ferry.

BARCELONA - PALMA

Journey 8 hours

Depart Barcelona : Jan. 16 - Apr. 2 2330;
Apr. 3 - Apr. 23 1300②⑥, 2330; **Apr. 24 - May 31** 1300②, 2330;
June 1 - 18 2330; **June 19 - Sept. 10** 1300⑤, 2330;
Sept. 11 - Dec. 31 2330.

Depart Palma : **Jan. 16 - Apr. 2** 1300①②③④, 2330⑥⑦;
Apr. 3 - Apr. 23 1300②④⑥⑦, 2330①②③⑤⑥⑦;
Apr. 24 - May 31 1300②④, 2330①②③⑤⑥⑦; **June 1 - 18** 2330;
June 19 - Sept. 10 1300①②⑥⑦, 2330③④⑤⑦;
Sept. 11 - Oct. 1 1300⑥, 2330①②③④⑤⑦;
Oct. 2 - Nov. 26 1300①②③④, 2330⑤⑥⑦; **Nov. 27 - Dec. 31** 2330.

BARCELONA - IBIZA

Journey 9½ hours

Depart Barcelona : **Jan. 16 - Apr. 2** 2330①③ (also ⑤⑥ via Palma);
Apr. 3 - Apr. 23 2330①③⑤⑥ (also ②④ via Palma);
Apr. 24 - May 31 2330①③⑤ (also ②⑥ via Palma);
June 1 - June 18 2330①③⑤ (also ⑥ via Palma);
June 19 - July 23 and Aug. 28 - Sept. 10 2330①②③⑦ (also ④ via Palma);
July 24 - Aug. 27 0930⑥⑦, 2330①②③ (also ④ via Palma);
Sept. 11 - Oct. 1 and Nov. 27 - Dec. 31 2330①③⑤ (also ⑥ via Palma);
Oct. 2 - Nov. 26 2330①③ (also ⑥ via Palma).

Depart Ibiza : **Jan. 16 - Apr. 2** 1200②④ (also 1730② via Palma);
Apr. 3 - Apr. 23 1200②⑤⑥, 1730③⑤⑦;
Apr. 24 - May 31 1200②⑤, 2330⑦ (also 1730③ via Palma);
June 1 - June 18 1200②④, 2330⑦;
June 19 - July 23 & Aug. 28 - Sept. 10 1200②③④, 1400⑤ (also 1730⑦ via Palma);
July 24 - Aug. 27 1200②③④, 1400⑤, 2200⑥ (also 2015⑦ via Palma);
Sept. 11 - Dec. 31 1200②④ (also 2330⑦ via Palma).

BARCELONA - MAHON

Journey 9 hours

Depart Barcelona : **Jan. 16 - Apr. 2** 2330②④; **Apr. 3 - Apr. 23** 2330②④⑦;
Apr. 24 - June 18 2330②④; **June 19 - Sept. 10** 2330①②④⑥⑦, 2359⑤;
Sept. 11 - Oct. 1 2330②④⑥; **Oct. 2 - Dec. 31** 2330②④.

Depart Mahon : **Jan. 16 - Apr. 2** 1200③⑤; **Apr. 3 - Apr. 23** 1200①③⑤;
Apr. 24 - June 18 1200③⑤; **June 19 - Sept. 10** 1200①②③⑤⑥⑦;
Sept. 11 - Oct. 1 1200③⑤⑦; **Oct. 2 - Dec. 31** 1200③⑤.

VALENCIA - PALMA

Journey 9 hours

Depart Valencia : **Jan. 16 - Apr. 2** 2330①-⑥ (also ⑤ via Ibiza);
Apr. 3 - Apr. 23 1200①, 2330①-⑥; **Apr. 24 - Dec. 31** 2330①-⑥.

Depart Palma : **Jan. 16 - Apr. 2** 1200②③④⑤, 2330⑦ (also 1000⑥ via Ibiza);
Apr. 3 - Apr. 23 1200①-⑥, 2330⑦; **Apr. 24 - Dec. 31** 1200②③④⑤⑥, 2330⑦.m

VALENCIA - IBIZA

Journey 9 hours

Depart Valencia : **Jan. 16 - Apr. 2** 2330⑤; **Apr. 3 - May 31** 2330④;
June 1 - June 18 no service; **June 19 - July 23 and Aug. 28 - Sept. 10** 2130;
July 24 - Aug. 27 and Sept 11 - Dec. 31 2130①-⑥.

Depart Ibiza : **Jan. 16 - Apr. 2** 1500⑥; **Apr. 3 - Apr. 23** 1530④;
Apr. 24 - May 31 1200④; **June 1 - June 18** no service;
June 19 - Dec. 31 1200②-⑥, 2330⑦.

PALMA - IBIZA

Journey 4½ hours

Depart Palma : **Jan. 16 - Apr. 2** 1000⑥⑦; **Apr. 3 - Apr. 23** 1000③⑤;
Apr. 24 - May 31 1000③⑦; **June 1 - June 18** 1000⑦;
June 19 - Sept. 10 0830⑤; **Sept. 11 - Dec. 31** 1000⑦.

Depart Ibiza : **Jan. 16 - Apr. 2** 0800⑥, 1730⑦; **Apr. 3 - Apr. 23** 1730③⑤⑦;
Apr. 24 - May 31 1730③, 2330⑥; **June 1 - June 18** 2330⑥;
June 19 - July 23 and Aug. 28 - Sept. 10 1730⑦; **July 24 - Aug. 27** 2015⑦;
Sept. 11 - Oct. 1 and Nov. 27 - Dec. 31 2330⑥; **Oct. 2 - Nov. 26** 1730⑦.

PALMA - MAHON

Journey 6½ hours

Depart Palma : 0900⑦. Depart Mahon : 1630⑦.

Table 1410 LIMADET FERRY

3 Rue Ibn Rochd, Tanger. ☎ 933621, Telex 33652, Fax 932913.

m.v. *Ibn Batouta*, m.v. *Ibn Batouta 2*, m.v. *C. de Algeciras*.

ALGECIRAS - TANGER

Sailings from Algeciras : 0930, 1130, 1330, 1530, 1800, 2100.
Sailings from Tanger : 0730, 0930, 1230, 1530, 1700, 1900.

Journey 2 hours 30 minutes. Timings subject to confirmation.

Table 1430

S N C M

Société Nationale Maritime Corse Mediterranée, 61, Boulevard des Dames, 13002 Marseille. ☎ 91 56 30 10 Fax 91 56 31 00
UK agent: Southern Ferries, 179 Piccadilly, London W1V 9DB. ☎ 0171 491 4968 Fax 0171 491 3502.
m.v. *Corse*, m.v. *Esterel*, m.v. *Ile de Beaute*, m.v. *Napoleon*, m.v. *Danielle Casanova*, m.v. *Paglia Orba*, ♦ NGV (high speed car ferry)

March 1 - October 31, 1995   Departure times vary. For journey times see foot of page. Journeys marked * and ♦ are daytime sailings.

MARSEILLE - AJACCIO

Departures from Marseille : Mar. 4,8,11,15,17,22,24,29,31,
Apr. 5,7,10,12,14,15,18,21,22,24,26,28, May 5,6,8,10,12,15,17,19,29,31,
June 3,9,12,14,16,19,27,30, July 1,3,5,7,8,10,12,15,17,19,21,22,24,25,26,28,29,31,
Aug. 2,4,5,7,9,11,12,14,17*,18*,19*,21*,22*,23*,24*,25*,26*,28*,29*,31*,
Sept. 1*,2*,4*,5*,6,7,8,11,13,15,18,20,22,25,27,29,
Oct. 2,4,6,9,11,13,16,18,20,23,25,27,30.

Departures from Ajaccio : Mar. 1,5,9,11,12,16,19,23,26,30,
Apr. 2,6,9,11,12,17,19,23,25,27,29, May 4,9,11,14,16,18,21,26,30,
June 1,5,8,11,13,15,18,20,26,28,30*,30,
July 1*,3*,4*,6*,7*,8*,10*,11*,13*,15*,17*,18*,20*,22*,24*,25*,26*,27*,28*,29*,31*,
Aug. 1*,3*,4*,5*,7*,8*,10*,12*,14*,15,17,20,22,24,27,29,31,
Sept. 3,5,7,8,10,12,14,16,17,19,21,24,26,28,
Oct. 1,3,5,8,10,12,15,17,19,22,24,26,29,31.

TOULON - AJACCIO

Departures from Toulon : Apr. 29, May 3,22,24,25,28, June 5*,7,21,23,25,29,
July 2,4,6,9,11,13,14,16,18,20,23,27,30,
Aug. 1,3,6,8,10,13,16*,20*,27*,30*, Sept. 3*,28.

Departures from Ajaccio : Mar. 3, Apr. 15,22,30, May 6,7,23,25,28, June 22,24,
July 2*,5*,9*,12*,14*,16*,19*,21*,23*,30*,
Aug. 6*,9*,11*,13*,16,18,19,21,23,25,26,28,30, Sept. 1,2,4,29.

NICE - AJACCIO   ♦ - NGV (high speed ferry)

Departures from Nice : Mar. 2,5,10,14*, 20,27, Apr. 3,11,19,23,26, May 2,9,16,21,30,
June 6,13,18,21,26*,30*, July 2,5*,8*,9,11,16,19*,21*,23*,24,26*,28*,30*,31,
Aug. 4*,6*,7,9*,11*,13*,14,16*,18*,20*,21,23*,25*,27*,28,30*,
Sept. 1*,3*,4,6*,8*,10*,12*,16*,19♦,21♦,26♦,28♦,
Oct. 4♦,7♦,11♦,14♦,18♦,21♦,25♦,28♦.

Departures from Ajaccio : Mar. 6,14,21,28, Apr. 4,13,20,24,27, May 3,10,17,22,31,
June 7,14,19,22,26, July 3*,5,8,10*,12*,17*,19*,21,23,25*,26*,28,30,
Aug. 1*,4,6,8*,9*,11,13,15*,16*,18,20,22*,23*,25,27,29*,30*,
Sept. 13,5*,6*,8,11*,13*,19♦,21♦,26♦,28♦,
Oct. 4♦,7♦,11♦,14♦,18♦,21♦,25♦,28♦.

MARSEILLE - BASTIA

Departures from Marseille :
Mar. 2,6,10,11,13,18,20,25,27, Apr. 1,3,8,12,20,26,28, May 2,9,13,20,22,24,27,
June 2,6,10,17,21,23,29, July 1,3,4,6,8,10,11,13,15,17,18,20,22,24,27,29,31,
Aug. 1,3,5,7,8,10,12,14,16*,18*,21*,23*,25*,28*,30*,
Sept. 1*,4*,9,12,14,16,19,21,23,26,28,30, Oct. 5,7,12,14,19,21,26,28.

Departures from Bastia :
Mar. 3,7,11,14,17,21,24,28,31, Apr. 4,7,13,18,21,25,27, May 7,10,17,23,28,
June 7,14,22,26,30*, July 1*,3*,5*,7*,8*,8,10*,12*,15*,17*,19*,21*,22*,24*,28*,29*,31*,
Aug. 2*,4*,5*,9*,11*,12*,13,16,18,20,21,22,23,25,27,28,30,
Sept. 1,3,4,5,10,13,15,17,20,22,24,27,29, Oct. 4,6,11,13,18,20,25,27.

TOULON - BASTIA

Departures from Toulon : Mar. 4*, Apr. 15,17,22,24, May 1*,5,7*,16,30,
June 4,13,27,30, July 2,5,7,9,12,14,16,19,21,23,25,26,28,30,
Aug. 2,4,6,9,11,15*,17*,19*,20*,22*,24*,26*,27*,29*,31*,
Sept. 2*,3*,5*,7, Oct. 3,10,17,24,31.

Departures from Bastia: Apr. 16,23,29*, May 1,3,4,14,21,25*,31,
June 3,5,11,18,24,28, July 2*,4*,6*,9*,11*,13*,14*,16*,18*,20*,23*,25*,26*,27*,30*,
Aug. 1*,3*,6*,8*,10*,14,15,17,19,24,26,29,31,
Sept. 2,8, Oct. 1,8,15,22,29.

NICE - BASTIA   ♦ - NGV (high speed ferry)

Departures from Nice : Mar. 7,12,16,23,30, Apr. 6,14,16,21,28,30,
May 4*,7,12,14,19,23,26,28, June 2,4,9,11,14,16,21,28,29*,29*,30*,30,
July 4*,6,7,11*,13*,14*,17♦,18*,20*,20♦,21♦,22♦,22,23♦,24*,24♦,25♦,27*,27♦,
July 28♦,29♦,30*,30♦,31*,31♦, Aug. 1♦,2*,3♦,4♦,5♦,6♦,7*,7♦,8♦,10*,10♦,
Aug 11♦,12♦,12,13♦,14*,14♦,15♦,17*,17♦,18♦,19♦,19,20*,20♦,21*,21♦,22♦,
Aug. 24*,24♦,25♦,26♦,26,27♦,28*,28♦,29♦,31*,31♦, Sept. 1♦,2♦,2,3,4*,4♦,
Sept. 5*,7*,7♦,8♦,9♦,9,10♦,11,13♦,14*,15♦,16♦,17♦,18♦,20,23♦,
Sept. 25♦,27♦,30♦, Oct. 2♦,6♦,9♦,13♦,16♦,20♦,23♦,27♦,30♦.

Departures from Bastia : Mar. 1,4,8,12*,13,19,26, Apr. 2,9,15,17,22,29,
May 1,6,8,13,15,20,24,27,29, June 3,5,10,17,20,24,28*,29,30*,
July 1,4*,7*,11*,13*,14,17♦,18*,20*,20♦,21♦,22,22♦,23*,23♦,24*,24♦,25♦,27♦,27♦,
July 28♦,29♦,30*,30♦,31*,31♦, Aug. 1♦,2*,3♦,4♦,5♦,6♦,7*,7♦,8♦,10*,10♦,
Aug. 11♦,12♦,13♦,14*,14♦,15*,17*,17♦,18,19*,19♦,20*,20♦,21*,21♦,22♦,
Aug. 24*,24♦,25,26♦,27*,27♦,28*,28♦,29*,31*,31♦, Sept. 1♦,2♦,3,4*,4♦,5*,7*,7♦,
Sept. 4*,4♦,5♦,7,7♦,8♦,9♦,10*,10♦,11♦,13*,15*,15♦,16♦,17,18♦,20♦,
Sept. 23♦,25♦,27♦,30♦, Oct. 2♦,6♦,9♦,13♦,16♦,20♦,23♦,27♦,30♦.

NICE - CALVI   ♦ - NGV (high speed ferry)

Departures from Nice :
July 7* (from Marseille), 10*, then ①②③④⑤⑦ July 18 - Sept. 10♦
(depart 0745, arrive 1030; additional sailing on ③: depart 1500, arrive 1745);
Sept. 12♦,14♦,16♦,17♦,22♦,24♦,29♦, Oct. 1♦,8♦,15♦,22♦,29♦.

Departures from Calvi :
June 30*,July 3,7*,10,18♦, then ①②③④⑤⑦ July 19 - Sept. 10♦
(depart 1115, arrive 1400; additional sailing on ③: depart 1830, arrive 2115);
Sept. 12♦,14♦,16♦,17♦,22♦,24♦,29♦, Oct. 1♦, 8♦,15♦,22♦,29♦.

NICE/MARSEILLE/TOULON - ILE ROUSSE

Departures from Nice to Ile Rousse (M - from Marseille; T - from Toulon) :
Mar. 2*,9*,15,22*,29*, Apr. 5*,10*,18*,25*,30*,
May 7*,14*,18*,21*,25*,28*, June 1,8,11*,15*,18*,24M*,25*,27*,29M*,
July 2*,4,5T,6*,7,9*,10T,12*,12T,13,15*,16*,17*,17T,19T,20,22*,25*,26T,27,29*,31T,
Aug. 1*,2T,3,5*,6T,7T,8*,9T,10,12*,15M*,15*,17M*,17,19*,22*,24*,24,26*,29*,31M*,31,
Sept. 2*,5*,7,9*,12T,18T,26T.

Departures from Ile Rousse to Nice (M - to Marseille; T - to Toulon).:
Mar. 2*,9,16*,22,29, Apr. 5,10,18,25,30*,
May 7*,14*,18,21*,25,28*, June 1,9*,11,15,18*,24,25*,27,29*,
July 2*,5,6T*,6,8*,9*,11T*,12,13T*,14*,15*,16*,17,18M*,20T*,21*,22*,25,27T*,28*,29*,
July 29,31M, Sept. 1*,2*,5,8*,9*,13T,19T,27T.

TOULON/MARSEILLE - PROPRIANO

Departures from Toulon to Propriano (M - from Marseille; N - from Nice) :
Apr. 13M,19M,30M, May 4,8,11M,18M,26, June 2,8M,15M,19,25,27M,29,30M,
July 2,3,4,6,7M,9,11,13,14,16,18M,20,21M,23,24,25,27,28M,30,
Aug. 1,2N,3,4M,8,10,11M,12,14*,16*,18*,20*,21*,22M*,23*,25*,27*,28*,29*,30*,
Sept. 1*,3*,4*,5,9,14,16,20,23,30.

Departures from Propriano to Toulon (M - to Marseille; N - to Nice) :
Apr. 14M,20M, May 1M,5M,8M,12M,19M,27, June 2M,4,9M,16M,20,26,28,30*,
July 1*,3*,4*,5*,7*,8*,10*,12*,14*,15*,17*,19*,21M*,22*,24*,25*,26*,28*,29*,31*,
Aug. 2*,3N*,4*,5*,9*,11M*,12*,13,14M,16M,18,20,21M,22,23M,25,27,28,29,30M,
Sept. 1,3,4,6,10,15,17,21,24, Oct. 1M.

LIVORNO/GENOVA - BASTIA   ♦ - NGV (high speed ferry)

Departures from Livorno to Bastia (G - from Genova) :
Apr. 15*,17*,22*,29*, May 6*,20*,27*, June 3*,5*,10*,17*,24*,
July 1*,1G,8*,8G,15G,22♦,22G,29♦,29G,
Aug. 5♦,5G,12♦,12G,19♦,20*,26♦,27G*, Sept. 2♦,3G*,9♦.

Departures from Bastia to Livorno (G - to Genova) :
Apr. 15*,17*,22*,29*, May 6*,20*,27*, June 3*,5*,10*,17*,24*,
July 1*,1G*,8*,8G*,15G*,22♦,22G*,29♦,29G*,
Aug. 5♦,5G*,12♦,12G*,19♦,19G,26♦,26G, Sept. 2♦,2G,9♦.

LIVORNO - PORTO VECCHIO

Departures from Livorno : July 3,8,15,22,29, Aug. 5,12,20*,27*, Sept. 3*,10*.
Departures from Porto Vecchio : July 3*,8*,15*,22*,29*, Aug. 5*,12*,19,26, Sept. 2,9.

TOULON/MARSEILLE - PORTO TORRES

Departures from Toulon (M - from Marseille) :
Apr. 13M,15M,28M,30M, May 4,6M,11M,18M,24,26, June 1,3M,8M,15M,23,
July 1,8,15,22,29, Aug. 5,12,14M,19,26, Sept. 2,9,16,23,30.

Departures from Porto Torres to Toulon (M - to Marseille) :
Apr. 14M,17M,29M, May 1M,5M,7,12M,19M,25,27, June 2M,4,9M,16M,24,
July 2,9,16,23,30, Aug. 6,13,15M,19,26, Sept. 2,10,17,24, Oct. 1M.

MARSEILLE - ALGER

Departures from Marseille :
| Mar. 3,7,10,14,16,18,21,25,28, | Apr. 1,4,8,11,13,15,18,22,25,27,29, |
| May 2,5,9,11,16,18,20,23,27,30, | June 3,6,9,13. |

Departures from Alger :
| Mar. 1,6,8,12,15,19,22,26,29, | Apr. 2,5,9,12,16,19,23,26,29, |
| May 1,3,7,10,14,17,21,24,28,31, | June 4,7,11,14. |

MARSEILLE - ORAN/ANNABA/BEJAIA/SKIKDA

Departures from Marseille to Oran (A - to Annaba; B - to Bejaia; S - to Skikda) :
Mar. 8,21S,28, Apr. 4A,11B,18,25S, May 2,16A,20B,23,30S, June 6B,13.

Departures from Oran (A - from Annaba; B - from Bejaia; S - from Skikda) :
Mar. 8B,16,23S,30, Apr. 6A,13B,20,27S, May 16,18A,23B, June 1S,15B.

MARSEILLE - TUNIS

Departures from Marseille :
| Mar. 1,3,8,10,15,17,22,24,29,31, | Apr. 5,8,12,14,19,21,26,28, |
| May 3,5,10,12,17,19,24,26,31. | |

Departures from Tunis :
①⑦ Jan. 1 - May 29.

JOURNEY TIMES

From Marseille: Ajaccio 9 hours, Bastia 10 hours , Calvi 8 hours, Ile Rousse 8-10 hours,
Porto Vecchio 12 hours, Propriano 12 hours, Porto Torres 16 hours, Alger 20 hours,
Oran 25 hours, Tunis 24 hours.
From Nice: Ajaccio 7 hours (♦ 4 hours), Bastia 7 hours (♦ 3½ hours),
Calvi 5 hours (♦ 2 hours 45 minutes) , Ile Rousse 5-6 hours.
From Toulon: Ajaccio 9 hours, Bastia 9-11 hours, Ile Rousse 11 hours,
Porto Torres 11-16 hours, Propriano 7-9 hours.
From Livorno: Bastia 3 hours (♦ 1 hour 50 minutes), Porto Vecchio 8-11 hours.

All sailings (except those marked * or ♦) are overnight sailings.

Table 1450 CORSICA FERRIES

INCLUDING SARDINIA FERRIES AND ELBA FERRIES
5 bis, Rue Chanoine Leschi, 20296 Bastia.
☎ 95 32 95 95 Fax 95 32 14 71
m.v. *Corsica Regina*, m.v. *Corsica Victoria*, m.v. *Corsica Serena II*,
m.v. *Corsica Marina II*, m.v. *Sardinia Nova*, m.v. *Sardinia Vera*
March 1 - December 31, 1995

MONACO - BASTIA and CALVI

June 1 - Oct. 8 (fast ferry *Corsica Express*)

Depart Monaco	Arrive Calvi	Arrive Bastia		Depart Bastia	Depart Calvi	Arrive Monaco
0815	→	1145		1230	→	1600
1630	1915	...		...	1945	2230

LIVORNO - BASTIA

Depart Livorno	Arrive Bastia	Days of operation
0830	1230	④ Mar. 13 - May 4; daily June 2 - Sept. 10; ②⑤⑥⑦ Sept. 12-24.
1000	1400	④ Mar. 2 - Apr. 6; ④ Oct. 5 - Dec. 28.
1400	1800	① Apr. 10 - Nov. 6; ③ May 24 - Sept. 20; ④ May 11 - Sept. 28; ⑥ Mar. 11 - Dec. 20; also Aug. 4,6,13,18,20,25.
1845	2230	June 23, July 2,9,16,23,24,28,29, Aug. 1,5,7,15,17,19-21,24,27.
2000	2345	⑤⑥ June 24 - Aug. 26; also July 30,31, Aug. 2,3,6,13,20; not Aug.11.

Depart Bastia	Arrive Livorno	Days of operation
0130	0700	⑥⑦ June 25 - July 23, also July 31, Aug. 1,3-5,7,13,14,19,26,27.
0845	1230	① Apr. 10 - Sept. 25; ③ May 24 - Sept. 20; ④ May 11 - Sept. 28; ⑥ Mar. 11 - Sept. 30, also July 28,30, Aug. 4,6,13,18,20,25.
0900	1245	① Oct. 2 - Nov. 6; ⑥ Oct. 7 - Dec. 30.
1200	1600	③ Mar. 1 - Apr. 5; ③ Oct. 4 - Dec. 27.
1330	1730	June 2-23,25-29, July 2-6,9-13,16-20,23-29, Aug. 1,5-7-11,14-17, 19-24,27-31, Sept. 1-10,12,15-17,19,22-24.
1430	1830	③ Apr. 12 - May 3; daily June 24,30, July 1,7,8,14,15,21,22,28-31, Aug. 2-6,12,13,18-20,25,26.
2345	0700	June 23, July 2,9,16,23,24,28,29, Aug. 1,5,7,15,17,19-21,24,27.

LA SPEZIA - BASTIA

Depart La Spezia	Arrive Bastia	Days of operation
0815	1315	②③⑤ Apr. 11 - May 3; daily May 5 - Oct. 1.
1930	0030	⑤⑥ June 24 - July 22, also July 30,31, Aug. 4,6,12,13,18,25,26.

Depart Bastia	Arrive La Spezia	Days of operation
0100	0700	⑥⑦ June 25 - July 23; also July 29-31, Aug. 1,5-7,13,14,19-21,26,27.
1330	1830	⑤⑥ June 24 - July 22; also July 30,31, Aug. 2-4,6,12,13,18,25,26.
1400	1900	②④ Apr. 11 - May 2; daily May 5 - 31.
1430	1930	Daily June 1 - 23; ①②③④⑦ June 25 - July 27; also Aug. 1,7-11, 14-17,21-24,27-31; daily Sept. 1 - Oct. 1.
2200	0700	① Apr. 10 - May 1.

GENOVA - BASTIA

Depart Genova	Arrive Bastia	Days of operation
0815	1415	①②③④⑥ July 1 - Aug. 30.
0830	1430	①⑦ May 20 - June 19; also June 20,24,26-29, Sept. 2,4,8,9,11,15, 16,22,29, Oct. 6,13.
1200	1800	Dec. 31 only.
2300	0800	①⑤ Mar. 6 - Apr. 7; ⑤⑦ Apr. 9 - May 21 (also May 9,16); ②③⑤⑦ May 23 - July 23 and Sept. 1-17; ②-⑦ July 25 - Aug. 30 (not Aug. 10,26); ②⑤⑦ Sept. 19 - Nov. 7 and Dec. 8-19; ①⑤ Nov. 10 - Dec. 4, also Dec. 22,25,26,29.

Depart Bastia	Arrive Genova	Days of operation
1200	1800	⑦ Mar. 5 - Apr. 30; ⑦ Oct. 8 - Dec. 24 (also Dec. 26).
1430	2030	⑤ Apr. 14 - 28.
1530	2130	①⑦ May 20 - June 19, also June 20; ①②③④⑥ July 24 - Aug. 30; ⑤ Sept. 8 - Oct. 13, also Sept. 2,4,9,11,16.
2000	0800	④ Mar. 9 - Apr. 6.
2200	0700	①④⑥ May 4 - 20; ①③④⑥ May 22 - July 22 and Sept. 2-18; ①③④⑤⑥⑦ July 26 - Aug. 31 (not Aug. 11,27); ①④ Sept. 21 - Nov. 9 (also Sept. 23,30); ④ Nov. 16 - Dec. 28 (also Dec. 11,18,30).

LIVORNO - GOLFO ARANCI

Sardinia Ferries, April 7 - October 1 only

Depart Livorno	Arrive Golfo Aranci	Days of operation
0930	1845	Daily Apr. 18, May 2, June 10 - Sept. 4 (not June 14, July 5, Aug. 9), Sept. 7-10,13-17,20-30, Oct. 1.
2130	0715	Daily Apr. 7,8,10,12-15,19,21,22,24,26,28-30, May 3,5-8,10,12 15,17, 19-22,24,26-29,31, June 1-Sept. 18 (not June 6,13, July 4, Sept. 12).

Depart Golfo Aranci	Arrive Livorno	Days of operation
0930	1845	Daily Apr. 8,13-15,22,29,30, May 6-8,13-15,20-22,27-29, June 1 - Sept. 18 (not June 6,7,13, July 4, Aug. 9, Sept. 6,12,13).
2130	0715	Daily Apr. 9,11,17,18,20,23,2527, May 1,2,4,9,11,16,18,23,25,30, June 6, June 10 - Oct. 1 (not June 14, July 5, Sept. 5,11,18).

OTHER SERVICES operate in summer as follows:
Genova - Ile Rousse (2 sailings per week, May 28 - Sept. 10)
Genova - Ajaccio (1-3 sailings per week, May 20 - Sept. 16)
Piombino - Portoferraio (Elba Ferries, 3-4 sailings daily, Apr. 7 - Oct. 1).

Table 1451
CIE. MAROCAINE DE NAVIGATION

7, Boulevard de la Résistance, Casablanca 05.
☎ 30 30 12 Telex 25 952 Fax 30 84 55.
m.v. *Marrakech*.
January 1 - December 31, 1995

SÈTE - TANGER

Depart Sète	Arrive Tanger		Depart Tanger	Arrive Sète
1900	0900 2 days later		1800	1000 2 days later

Sailings from Sète :
Jan. 4, 8, 13, 17, 21, 26 July 3, 7, 11, 15, 19, 23, 27, 3
Feb. 21, 25 Aug. 4, 8, 12, 16, 20, 24, 28
Mar. 1, 5, 9, 14, 18, 22, 28 Sept. 1, 5, 9, 13, 17, 21, 25, 29
Apr. 1, 6, 10, 14, 18, 22, 26, 30 Oct. 4, 8, 12, 16, 20, 25, 29
May 4, 8, 12, 16, 20, 26, 31 Nov. 2, 6, 10, 15, 19, 23, 27
June 4, 8, 12, 16, 20, 24, 29 Dec. 1, 6, 10, 14, 18, 23, 29

Sailings from Tanger :
Jan. 1, 6, 10, 15, 19, 23, 28 July 1, 5, 9, 13, 17, 21, 25, 29
Feb. 23, 27 Aug. 2, 6, 10, 14, 18, 22, 26, 3
Mar. 3, 7, 11, 16, 20, 24, 30 Sept. 3, 7, 11, 15, 19, 23, 27
Apr. 3, 8, 12, 16, 20, 24, 28 Oct. 1, 6, 10, 14, 18, 22, 27, 3
May 2, 6, 10, 14, 18, 22, 29 Nov. 4, 8, 12, 17, 21, 25, 29
June 2, 6, 10, 14, 18, 22, 26 Dec. 3, 8, 12, 16, 20, 25, 31

Table 1455 MOBY LINES

Viale Elba 4, 57037 Portoferraio.
☎ 0565 918101 Telex 590590 Fax 0565 916758
UK agent: Serena Holidays, London ☎ 0171 244 8422 fax 0171 244 9829
m.v. *Moby Fantasy*, m.v. *Moby Blu*, m.v. *Moby King*
m.v. *Moby Vincent*, m.v. *Moby Baby*, m.v. *Sardegna Bella*
1995 services

LIVORNO - BASTIA

Depart Livorno	Arrive Bastia	Days of operation
0830	1230	Daily Mar. 30,31, Apr. 5-7,12-14,18-21,25-28,May 2-5,8-12,16-31, June 1 - Aug. 31, Sept. 1-18,20-25,27-30, Oct. 1,2,4-8.
1000	1400	①④ Oct. 9 - 26.
1400	1800	①⑥ Apr. 1 - May 20, also May 27, June 3,10.
2000	2355	⑤⑥ June 30 - Aug. 26, also July 30,31, Aug. 1,3,6,20,21,23,27,28,30.

Depart Bastia	Arrive Livorno	Days of operation
0100	0600	⑥⑦ July 1 - Aug. 27, also July 31, Aug. 1,2,4,7,21,22,24,28,29,31.
0900	1300	①⑥ Apr. 1 - May 20, also May 27, June 3,10,14.
1200	1600	②⑤ Oct. 10 - 27.
1400	1800	Daily Mar. 30, Apr. 5,6,12,13,18-20,25-27, May 2-4,9-11,16-18,20-31, June 1 - Aug. 31, Sept. 1-18,20-25,27-30, Oct. 1,2,4-8.
2200	0600	① Apr. 3 - May 15.

GENOVA - BASTIA

Depart Genova	Arrive Bastia	Days of operation
1000	1645	Daily June 15 - Aug. 14.
2300	0700	⑤⑦ Mar. 31 - May 21; daily May 22,24-26,28-31, June 1,2,4,5,7-9, 11-13, Aug. 15 - Sept. 17.

Depart Bastia	Arrive Genova	Days of operation
1145	1830	Daily Aug. 15 - Sept. 17.
1200	1800	⑦ Apr. 2 - June 11; also May 22,24-26,19-31, June 1,2,5,7-9,12,13.
1400	2000	⑤ Mar. 31 - May 19.
2200	0700	Daily June 15 - Aug. 13.

PIOMBINO - BASTIA

Depart Piombino	Arrive Bastia	Days of operation		Depart Bastia	Arrive Piombino	
1240	1610	Daily July 8 - Sept. 3.		0150	0520	Aug. 3,4,18,25.
2140	0110	Aug. 2,3,17,24.		1710	2040	Daily July 8 - Sept. 3.

LIVORNO - OLBIA *SARDEGNA LINE*

Depart Livorno	Arrive Olbia	Days of operation
1000	2000	Daily Apr. 17-19,24-26, May 1; daily June 15 - Oct. 8 (not July 5, Aug. Sept. 4,11).
2200	0800	Daily Mar. 30,31, Apr. 1,3,4,6-8,10,11,13-15,20-22,27-29; ①②③⑤⑥⑦ May 2-31; daily June 1-7,9-12,14-30, July 1-3,5-31, Aug. 1-31, Sept. 1-4; ②⑤ Oct. 10 - 27.

Depart Olbia	Arrive Livorno	Days of operation
1000	2000	Daily Mar. 31, Apr. 1,4,7,8,11,14,15,21,22,28,29; ①②③⑤⑥⑦ May 3-3 daily June 1-7,9-13,15-30, July 1-3,5-31, Aug. 1-14,16-31, Sept. 1-4, 7-11,14-17.
2200	0800	Daily Apr. 2,5,9,12,16-19,23-26,30, May 1, June 15 - 30, July 1-4,6-31 Aug. 1-31, Sept. 1-3,5-10,12-30, Oct. 1,2,4-8; ③⑦ Oct. 11 - 29.

OTHER SERVICES

Piombino - Portoferraio (Elba) : 1-6 sailings daily in winter, 13-15 sailings in summer.
Bonifacio (Corsica) - Santa Teresa di Gallura (Sardinia) : 4-10 sailings daily (April 7 to Oct. 8 only).

Table 1460   TOREMAR

Via Calafati 6, Casella Postale 482, 57123 Livorno.
☎ 0586 825511   fax 0586 825624
1995 services

PIOMBINO - PORTOFERRAIO : by ship: 8-15 sailings daily, journey 1 hour.
By hydrofoil: 3-4 journeys daily (also serving Cavo), journey 30-40 minutes.

PIOMBINO - RIO MARINA - PORTO AZZURRO : 2-3 sailings daily, journey 60-85 minutes.
Extended twice weekly to Isola Pianosa.

LIVORNO - GORGONA - CAPRAIA : 1-2 sailings daily, journey 2½ - 3½ hours.

PORTO SANTO STEFANO - ISOLA DEL GIGLIO : 3-6 sailings per day, journey 55 mins.

Table 1463   SICILFERRY

Grandi Traghetti SPA, Via Fieschi 17, 16121 Genova.
☎ (010) 589331 Telex 271132 Fax (010) 5509225
UK agent: Viamare Travel, London ☎ 0171 431 4560 Fax 0171 431 5456
January 1 - December 31, 1995

LIVORNO - PALERMO

Depart Livorno	Arrive Palermo	Days of operation	Depart Palermo	Arrive Livorno	Days of operation
2100	1600	⑤ Jan. 1 - July 11.	2000	1500	④ Jan. 1 - July 11.
2200	1700	⑦ Jan. 1 - July 11.	2200	1700	⑥ Jan. 1 - July 11.
2300	1800	②④⑥.	2300	1800	①③⑤.

LIVORNO - PALERMO - MALTA - TUNIS
January 1 - July 11

Livorno depart 2200⑦ → Palermo arrive 1700①, depart 2300① →
Valletta arrive 1200②, depart 2100② → Tunis arrive 1000③, depart 2100③ →
Palermo arrive 0800④, depart 2000④ → Livorno arrive 1500⑤.

Table 1464   GRANDI NAVI VELOCI

Via Fieschi 17, 16121 Genova ☎ 010 55091 Telex 270164 Fax 010 5509333
UK agent: Viamare Travel, London ☎ 0171 431 4560 Fax 0171 431 5456
m.v. *Majestic*, m.v. *Splendid*
January 1 - December 30, 1995

GENOVA - PALERMO

Depart Genova	Arrive Palermo	Notes	Depart Palermo	Arrive Genova	Notes
2100①	1800②		2000①	1700②	Not July 17 - Sept. 11.
2100②	1800③	Not July 11 - Sept. 12.	2100②	1800③	
2200③	1900④		2100③	1800④	Not July 12 - Sept. 13.
2300④	2000⑤	Not July 13 - Sept. 7.	2200④	1900⑤	
2300⑤	2000⑥		2300⑥	2000⑦	

GENOVA - PORTO TORRES

Depart Genova	Arrive Porto Torres	Days of operation	Depart Porto Torres	Arrive Genova	Days of operation
1000	2000	Aug. 16 - Sept. 12.	1000	1900	July 13 - Aug. 15 (E).
2200	0800	July 12 - Aug. 14 (F).	2200	0800	Aug. 16 - Sept. 12.

E - Not Aug. 10.   F - Not Aug. 9.

GENOVA - PALERMO - TUNIS - MALTA
January 5 - July 7

Genova 2300④ → Palermo depart 2300⑤ → Tunis arrive 0800⑥, depart 2000⑥ →
Valletta arrive 0800⑦, depart 0100① → Palermo arrive 1200① → Genova 1700②

Table 1465   TIRRENIA

Rione Sirignano 2, Casella Postale 438, 80121 Napoli.
☎ (Napoli) 081 720111 Telex 710028.
UK agent: Serena Holidays, London ☎ 0171 244 8422 Fax 0171 244 9829
January 1 - May 31, 1995
▲ - Details of additional summer services not yet received.

GENOVA - PORTO TORRES

Depart Genova	Arrive P. Torres	Days of operation	Depart P. Torres	Arrive Genova	Days of operation
▲1000	2200	Aug. 16 - Sept. 10.	▲1000	2200	June 23 - Aug. 14.
1930	0800	Jan. 1 - Dec. 31.	1930	0800	Jan. 1 - Dec. 31.
▲2400	1230	June 22 - Aug. 14	▲2400	1230	Aug. 15 - Sept. 10.

GENOVA - OLBIA

Depart Genova	Arrive Olbia	Days of operation
▲1000	2215	④ July 23 - Aug. 15; ②⑥ Aug. 17 - Sept. 3.
1800	0630	①③⑤ (daily June 1 - Sept. 30).
▲2345	1230	① June 24 - July 22; ②⑥ July 23 - Aug. 15; ④ Aug. 16 - Sept. 3.

Depart Olbia	Arrive Genova	Days of operation
▲1000	2215	②⑥ July 24 - Aug. 15; ④ Aug. 16 - Sept. 3.
▲1730	0645	③⑦ July 23 - Aug. 15; ①⑤ Aug. 16 - Sept. 3.
2030	0900	②④⑥ (daily June 1 - Sept. 30).
▲2230	1130	Aug. 16 - Sept. 3.

Table 1465   TIRRENIA continued

GENOVA - ARBATAX   *via Olbia*

Depart Genova	Arrive Arbatax	Days of operation
1800	1230	③⑤.

Depart Arbatax	Arrive Genova	Days of operation
1400	0900	④⑥.

GENOVA - CAGLIARI

Depart Genova	Arrive Cagliari	Days of operation	Depart Cagliari	Arrive Genova	Days of operation
▲1645	1330	②④ June 23-Sept.15.	▲1500	1145	③⑦ June 23-Sept. 15.

LA SPEZIA - OLBIA

Depart La Spezia	Arrive Olbia	Days of operation	Depart Olbia	Arrive La Spezia	Days of operation
▲0830	2000	Aug. 17 - Sept. 5.	▲0930	2100	July 23 - Aug. 15.
▲2400	1130	July 23 - Aug. 15.	▲1900	0630	Aug. 16 - Sept. 5.

Hydrofoils:

▲1000	1530	June 1 - July 22.	▲1430	2000	June 23-July 22, Sept.6-30.
▲1000	1530	Sept. 6-30.	▲1630	2200	June 1 - 22.

CIVITAVECCHIA - OLBIA

Depart C.Vecchia	Arrive Olbia	Days of operation	Depart Olbia	Arrive C.Vecchia	Days of operation
▲1100	1830	June 9 - Sept. 15.	▲1100	1830	June 9 - Sept. 15.
2300	0600	Jan. 1 - Dec. 31.	2300	0600	Jan. 1 - Dec. 31.

Hydrofoils:

▲0845	1230	July 23 - Aug. 15.	▲0845	1230	Aug. 16 - Sept. 5.
▲1000	1330	June 1 - July 22.	▲1315	1700	July 23 - Aug. 15.
▲1000	1330	Sept. 6-30.	▲1630	2000	June 1 - July 22.
▲1315	1700	Aug. 16 - Sept. 5.	▲1630	2000	Sept. 6-30.
▲1815	2200	July 23 - Aug. 15.	▲1815	2200	Aug. 16 - Sept. 5.
▲2345	0530	Aug. 16 - Sept. 5.	▲2345	0530	July 23 - Aug. 15.

CIVITAVECCHIA - ARBATAX - CAGLIARI

Depart C.Vecchia	Depart Arbatax	Arrive Cagliari	Days of operation
1830	0600G	0830	Jan. 1 - Dec. 31.

Depart Cagliari	Depart Arbatax	Arrive C.Vecchia	Days of operation
1800	2400H	0830	Jan. 1 - Dec. 31.

G - Calls at Arbatax on ④⑥.
H - Calls at Arbatax on ③⑦.

NAPOLI - CAGLIARI

Depart Napoli	Arrive Cagliari	Days of operation	Depart Cagliari	Arrive Napoli	Days of operation
1915	1015	④⑥.	1830	0930	③⑤.

PALERMO - CAGLIARI

Depart Palermo	Arrive Cagliari	Depart Cagliari	Arrive Palermo
1900⑥	0730⑦	1900⑤	0730⑥

CAGLIARI - TRAPANI - TUNIS

Depart Cagliari	Arrive Trapani	Depart Trapani	Arrive Tunis	Depart Tunis	Arrive Trapani	Depart Trapani	Arrive Cagliari
1900⑦	0600①	0900①	1600①	2000①	0800②	2100②	0830③

GENOVA - PALERMO

Depart Genova	Arrive Palermo	Days of operation	Depart Palermo	Arrive Genova	Days of operation
1200	1100	②④⑥.	1600	1500	①③⑤.

NAPOLI - PALERMO

Depart Napoli	Arrive Palermo	Depart Palermo	Arrive Napoli
2000	0700 Daily.	2000	0700 Daily.

▲ – Details of additional summer services not yet received.

Thomas Cook Travellers - Mallorca

See the back of this book for details

Table 1467 CAREMAR

Campania Regionale Marittima S.p.A., Molo Beverello, 80133 Napoli.
☎ (Napoli) 081 5515384 Telex 720054 Fax (Napoli) 081 5514551
Subject to alteration

CAPRI
Napoli - Capri : 7 - 8 sailings daily by catamaran, 4 - 5 sailings by ship.
Sorrento - Capri : 4 - 5 sailings daily by ship.

ISCHIA and PROCIDA
Napoli - Ischia : 6 - 7 sailings daily by catamaran, 8 - 9 sailings by ship.
Napoli - Procida : 5 - 6 sailings daily by catamaran, 4 - 5 sailings by ship.
Pozzuoli - Procida - Ischia : 3 - 4 sailings daily by ship.

ADDITIONAL SERVICES operate infrequently between Procida and Ischia, Ventotene and Ponza, Formia and Ventotene, Formia and Ponza.

Table 1468 ALILAURO

Via Caracciolo 11, 80122 Napoli.
☎ (Napoli) 081 7614909 Fax (Napoli) 081 7614250
Hydrofoils & Catamarans
1995 services

CAPRI
Sorrento - Capri : 6 - 13 sailings daily by catamaran, also 1 - 6 sailings by ship.
Napoli Mergellina or Beverello - Capri : 5 - 11 sailings daily.
Additional infrequent services to Capri (summer only) operate from Ischia, Castellammare, Torre Annunziata, Positano, Amalfi and Salerno.

ISCHIA
Napoli Mergellina - Ischia : 4 - 15 sailings daily.
Napoli Beverello - Ischia : 2 - 8 sailings daily by ship, 4 - 10 sailings daily by catamaran.
Napoli Mergellina - Forio : 4 sailings daily (summer only).
Pozzuoli - Ischia : frequent service by ship (also Pozzuoli - Procida 4 times daily).
Additional infrequent services to Ischia (summer only) operate from Capri, Sorrento, Castellammare, Torre Annunziata, Positano and Amalfi.

OTHER SERVICES
Napoli (Mergellina or Beverello) - Sorrento : 5 - 9 sailings daily.
Pozzuoli - Procida : 5 - 6 sailings daily.
Fiumicino and S. Felice Circeo - Ponza : summer only, infrequent sailings.
Salerno - Amalfi - Positano - Capri : summer only, infrequent sailinbgs by catamaran.
Napoli - Sorrento - Positano - Amalfi and v.v. : summer only, infrequent sailings.
Napoli - Capri - Agropoli - Palinuro - Marina di Camerota (coastal service) - Summer only.

Table 1470 ALISCAFI SNAV

Via Giordano Bruno 84, 80122 Napoli.
☎ (Napoli) 081 7612348 fax (Napoli) 081 7612141
1995 services *Hydrofoils*

NAPOLI - CAPRI
Journey 35 minutes.
From Napoli Mergellina : 0710A, 0810B, 0910, 1010, 1110, 1210, 1310, 1410D, 1510, 1610D, 1710, 1810D, 1910E.
From Capri : 0810A, 0910B, 1010, 1110C, 1210, 1310, 1410, 1510D, 1610, 1710D, 1810, 1910D, 2010E.
A - ✗ (daily May 1 - Sept. 26). B - ⑦ (daily Jan. 1 - Feb. 28, May 1 - Sept. 26, Nov. 4 - Dec. 31)
C - ⑦ (daily Mar. 1 - Nov. 4). D - Mar. 16 - Oct. 14. E - May 1 - Sept. 26.

NAPOLI - PROCIDA - CASAMICCIOLA (ISCHIA)
Journey 45 minutes.
From Napoli : 0820, 1020, 1220, 1420, 1620, 1820, (also 2020 Apr. 1 - Sept. 30).
From Casamicciola : 0730, 0920, 1120, 1320, 1520, 1720, (also 1920 Apr. 1 - Sept. 30).
Departs Procida 30 minutes after Napoli and 20 minutes after Casamicciola.

NAPOLI - EOLIAN ISLANDS
Daily June 1 - Sept. 30 :
Napoli Mergellina (1430) - Stromboli (1830) - Panarea (1900) - Lipari (1930) - Vulcano (1950) - Rinella (2025) - S.M. Salina (2040).
S.M. Salina (0700) - Lipari (0750) - Vulcano (0810) - Panarea (0845) - Stromboli (0920) - Napoli Mergellina (1320).

EOLIAN ISLANDS Other services
Messina - Lipari, Vulcano and Rinella : 2 journeys per day (5-6 journeys June 1 - Sept. 30).
Messina - S.M. Salina : 1 journey per day (also to Filicudi and Alicudi June 1 - Sept. 30).
Messina - Panarea : 1 - 3 journeys per day.
Milazzo - Lipari : 3 journeys per day (5 journeys June 1 - Sept. 30).
Milazzo - Vulcano and Rinella : 2 - 4 journeys per day.
Milazzo - S.M. Salina : 1 journey per day (also to Filicudi and Alicudi June 1 - Sept. 30).
Milazzo - Panarea : 1 - 2 journeys per day.
Palermo - Filicudi, Rinella, S.M. Salina, Vulcano and Lipari : 2 per day June 1 - Sept. 30.
Palermo - Alicudi, Panarea, Stromboli : 1 journey per day June 1 - Sept. 30.
Reggio di Calabria - Lipari, Vulcano, S.M. Salina and Rinella : 1 journey per day (5-6 journeys per day June 1 - Sept. 30).
Reggio di Calabria - Stromboli, Panarea, Filicudi, Alicudi : 1 - 3 per day June 1 - Sept. 30.

REGGIO DI CALABRIA - MESSINA
Journey 15 minutes.
Sailings from Reggio di Calabria and Messina : 15 - 20 sailings on ✗ , 3 sailings on ⑦ (June 1 - Sept. 30 : 20 - 24 sailings ✗, 10 sailings ⑦).

Table 1471 NAV. LIBERA del GOLFO

Molo Beverello, 80133 Napoli. ☎ (Napoli) 081 5520763 Telex 722661
LINEA JET Subject to alteration

NAPOLI - CAPRI 4 - 9 sailings daily. Journey 40 minutes.
Other services operate in the summer season between Térmoli and Trémiti and between Castellammare di Stábia and Capri.

Table 1472 LINEE LAURO

Piazza Municipio 88, 80133 Napoli ☎ (081) 5513352 fax (081) 5524329.
UK agent: Viamare Travel, London ☎ 0171 431 4560 fax 0171 431 5456.
1995 services

OTRANTO - VLORË and DURRËS
Durrës service is subject to alteration

Depart Otranto	Arrive Vlorë	Arrive Durrës	Depart Durrës	Depart Vlorë	Arrive Otranto
0900①③⑥	1200①③⑥	...		1630①③⑥	1900①③⑥
2300①	→	0800②	1300②	→	2000②
1000④	→	1700④	1300⑤	→	2000⑤

OTRANTO - CORFU - IGOUMENITSA

Depart Otranto	Arrive Corfu	Depart Corfu	Arrive Ig'menitsa	Depart Ig'menitsa	Arrive Corfu	Depart Corfu	Arrive Otranto
July 1 - August 13							
2300③⑥	→	→	0700④⑦	0830④⑦	1000④⑦	1100④⑦	1450④⑦
August 16 - September 3							
2300③⑥	0600④⑦	→	0800④⑦	2100④⑦	→	2300④⑦	0600⑤①

NAPOLI - PALAU (SARDINIA)

Depart Napoli	Arrive Palau	Days of operation	Depart Palau	Arrive Napoli	Days of operation
1800	0800	③⑤ June 16 - Sept. 22.	1800	0800	④⑥ June 17 - Sept. 23.

NAPOLI - PORTO VECCHIO (CORSICA) via Palau

Depart Napoli	Arrive P.Vecchio	Days of operation	Depart P.Vecchio	Arrive Napoli	Days of operation
1800	1130	⑤ June 16 - Sept. 15; ③ July 26 - Aug. 30.	1400	0800	⑥ June 17 - Sept. 16; ④ July 27 - Aug. 31.

NAPOLI - TUNIS

Depart Napoli	Arrive Tunis	Days of operation	Depart Tunis	Arrive Napoli	Days of operation
1400	0800	⑦ June 18 - Sept. 24.	1300	0900	② July 4 - Sept. 5, also June 19,26, Sept.11,18,25

MAZARA DEL VALLO (SICILY) - TUNIS

Depart Mazara V.	Arrive Tunis	Days of operation	Depart Tunis	Arrive Mazara V.	Days of operation
2300	0800	① July 3 - Aug. 28; also Sept. 5.	1100	2000	① July 3 - Aug. 28; also Sept. 4.

CATANIA and SIRACUSA - MALTA
See Table **1477**.

Table 1473 USTICA LINES

☎ (Napoli) 081 5800340 fax 081 5800341. Hydrofoil.
1995 services

NAPOLI - TRAPANI
①④⑥ June 15 - Sept. 16: Napoli 1430 → Ustica 1900 → Favignana 2110 → Trapani 2130.
①④⑥ June 15 - Sept. 16: Trapani 0630 → Favignana 0700 → Ustica 0910 → Napoli 1320.

TRAPANI - KELIBIA (TUNISIA)
③⑤⑦ June 15 - Sept. 16: Trapani 0845 → Pantelleria 1130 → Kelibia 1150 (local time).
③⑤⑦ June 15 - Sept. 16: Kelibia 1350 (local time) → Pantelleria 1630 → Trapani 1910.

Thomas Cook Travellers - Malta

See the back of this book for details

Table 1474 ITALIAN RAILWAYS

Piazza della Croce Rossa, I-00161 Roma.
☎ 39 6 884 0724 Telex 610089 Fax 39 6 883 1108
September 25, 1994 - May 27, 1995

CIVITAVECCHIA - GOLFO ARANCI   Journey 8 hours.

Sailings from Civitavecchia : 1000, 1100E, 2130, 2230G.
Sailings from Golfo Aranci : 1000, 1100J, 2130, 2230E.

E - Daily Jan. 1-15, Apr. 17 - May 1.
G - Daily Dec. 15-30, Apr. 7-15.
J - Daily Dec. 16-31, Apr. 8-16.

VILLA S. GIOVANNI - MESSINA   Journey 35 minutes.

Sailings from Villa S. Giovanni : 0015, 0045, 0140, 0205, 0255, 0450, 0540, 0605, 0730, 0845, 0940, 1005, 1100, 1120, 1215, 1250, 1335, 1405, 1500, 1530, 1610, 1640, 1740, 1810, 1855, 1920, 2015, 2050, 2140, 2205, 2300, 2325.

Sailings from Messina : 0020, 0040, 0135, 0205, 0300, 0325, 0420, 0445, 0540, 0610, 0700, 0725, 0820, 0850, 0940, 1005, 1100, 1125, 1220, 1245, 1340, 1415, 1450, 1520, 1620, 1650, 1730, 1805, 1855, 1935, 2020, 2045, 2140, 2210, 2330, 2355.

REGGIO DI CALABRIA - MESSINA   Journey 45 minutes.

Sailings from Reggio Di Calabria : 0655, 0800, 0910, 1020, 1300, 1420, 1515, 1720, 1930.
Sailings from Messina : 0510, 0655, 0810, 0910, 1200, 1310, 1410, 1620, 1830.

Table 1475 SIREMAR

Sicilia Regionale Marittima, Via Principe di Belmonte 1/c, 90139 Palermo.
☎ 091 582688 Telex 910135 Fax 091 582267.
April 1, 1994 - March 31, 1995 Subject to alteration

NAPOLI - MILAZZO AND V.V. via Stromboli, Ginostra, Panarea, Lipari and Vulcano.
Also serves Rinella and S.M. Salina on certain days.   Journey 16-20 hours.

January 1 - March 31 and September 26 - December 31
Sailings from Napoli : 2100②⑤.   Sailings from Milazzo : 1100①④.
April 1 - May 31
Sailings from Napoli : 2100②⑤.   Sailings from Milazzo : 1300①④.
June 1 - 15
Sailings from Napoli : 2100①④⑥.   Sailings from Milazzo : 1430③⑤⑦.
June 16 - July 7 and September 11 - 25
Sailings from Napoli : 2100②④⑤⑥⑦.   Sailings from Milazzo : 1430①③④⑤⑦.
July 8 - September 10
Sailings from Napoli : 2100①②④⑤⑥⑦.   Sailings from Milazzo : 1430 : ①③④⑤⑥⑦.

MILAZZO - VULCANO - LIPARI AND V.V.   Journey 2 hours.

January 1 - May 31 and September 26 - December 31
Sailings from Milazzo : 0900ex⑦, 1830.
Sailings from Lipari : 0630, 1400③, 1545①②④⑤⑥.
June 1 - September 25
Sailings from Milazzo : 0900, 1830 (also 0700, 1515 July 1 - Sept. 15).
Sailings from Lipari : 0630, 1400③, 1545ex③ (also 1145, 1750 July 1 - Sept. 15).

MILAZZO - VULCANO - LIPARI - PANAREA - GINOSTRA - STROMBOLI AND V.V.
Sailings from Milazzo and Stromboli : 1-3 sailings per week.   Journey 5 hours.

MILAZZO - VULCANO - LIPARI - S. M. SALINA - RINELLA - FILICUDI - ALICUDI.
Sailings from Milazzo and Alicudi : 4-5 sailings per week.   Journey 6 hours.

TRAPANI - FAVIGNANA - LEVANZO - MARETTIMO AND V.V. Journey 3 hours.
Sailings from Trapani and Marettimo : 6-7 sailings per week.

PALERMO - USTICA AND V.V.   5-7 sailings per week.   Journey 2½ hours.

TRAPANI - PANTELLERIA AND V.V.   6-7 sailings per week.   Journey 4½ hours.

PORTO EMPEDOCLE - LINOSA - LAMPEDUSA AND V.V.   Journey 8 hours.
Sailings from Porto Empedocle (Agrigento) and Lampedusa : 6-11 sailings per week.

HYDROFOILS 2-6 sailings per day:
MILAZZO - VULCANO - LIPARI - S. M. SALINA
LIPARI - RINELLA - S. M. SALINA
MILAZZO - VULCANO - LIPARI
MILAZZO - VULCANO - LIPARI - PANAREA - GINOSTRA - STROMBOLI
MILAZZO - VULCANO - LIPARI - RINELLA - FILICUDI - ALICUDI
PALERMO - USTICA
TRAPANI - LEVANZO - FAVIGNANA - MARETTIMO

Table 1477 EUROMALTA EXPRESS

Flagstone Wharf, Marsa HMR 12, Malta ☎ 259 94213 fax 239179
1995 service. Operated in partnership with Linee Lauro.

MALTA (VALLETTA) - CATANIA   ◆ – Catamaran

Depart Valletta	Arrive Catania	Days of operation	Depart Catania	Arrive Valletta	Days of operation
0430◆	0730◆	⑥ June 16 - Sept. 3.	1630	2330	③ June 25 - Sept. 10.
0630◆	0930◆	②④⑤ June 16 - Sept. 3.	1900◆	2200◆	⑥⑦ June 16 - Sept. 3.
0700◆	1400	③ June 25 - Sept. 10.	2030◆	2330◆	②④⑤ June 16 - Sept. 3.
1500◆	1800◆	⑦ June 16 - Sept. 3.			

MALTA (VALLETTA) - SIRACUSA   ◆ – Catamaran

Depart Valletta	Arrive Siracusa	Days of operation	Depart Siracusa	Arrive Valletta	Days of operation
0630◆	0900◆	③ June 16 - Sept. 3.	1700	2200	②④⑤⑥⑦ June 25 - Sept. 10.
0830◆	1330	②④⑤⑥⑦ June 25 - Sept. 10.	1930◆	2200◆	③ June 16 - Sept. 3.

Table 1476 VIRTU RAPID FERRIES

3 Princess Elizabeth Street, Ta' Xbiex MSD 11, Malta.
☎ 317088 Telex 1214 Fax 314533
April 1 - October 10, 1995   Catamarans

MALTA (VALLETTA) - CATANIA

Depart Valletta	Arrive Catania	Days of operation
0530	0830	②⑥.
0700	1100	⑤ July 18 - Sept. 3 (via Pozzallo).
1500	1800	②⑥ July 18 - Sept. 3.
1930	2230	⑦ Aug. 5 - 23.

Depart Catania	Arrive Valletta	Days of operation
1100	1400	②⑥ July 18 - Sept. 3.
1300	1700	⑤ July 18 - Sept. 3 (via Pozzallo).
1930	2230	②⑥ Apr. 1 - July 17; ②⑥ Sept. 4 - Oct. 10.
2000	2300	②⑥ July 18 - Sept. 3.

MALTA (VALLETTA) - POZZALLO

Depart Valletta	Arrive Pozzallo	Days of operation
0700	0830	①④ Apr. 1 - May 31; ①③④⑤ June 1 - Oct. 10.
1500	1630	⑦ Aug. 5 - 23.
1600	1730	⑦ June 1 - Aug. 4; ⑦ Aug. 24 - Oct. 10.
1830	2000	⑤ June 1 - Oct. 10.
1930	2100	④ June 1 - Oct. 10; ① July 18 - Sept. 3; ③ Aug. 5 - 23.

Depart Pozzallo	Arrive Valletta	Days of operation
0900	1030	④ June 1 - Oct. 10; ① July 18 - Sept. 3; ③ Aug. 5 - 23.
1530	1700	⑤ June 1 - Oct. 10.
1700	1830	⑦ Aug. 5 - 23.
1830	2000	⑦ June 1 - Aug. 4; ⑦ Aug. 24 - Oct. 10.
2130	2300	①④ Apr. 1 - May 31; ①③④⑤ June 1 - Oct. 10.

Certain sailings have 🚌 connection to/from Catania.

MALTA (VALLETTA) - LICATA

Depart Valletta	Arrive Licata	Days of operation	Depart Licata	Arrive Valletta	Days of operation
0800	1015	⑦ July 18 - Sept. 3.	1145	1400	⑦ July 18 - Sept. 3.
1200	1415	④ July 18 - Sept. 3.	1600	1815	④ July 18 - Sept. 3.

Table 1478 GOZO CHANNEL

Hay Wharf, Sa Maison, Malta.
☎ 243964 Telex 1580 MW Fax (356) 248007
Mgarr - Cirkewwa: m.v. *Mgarr*, m.v. *Xlendi*.
Malta - Pozzallo: m.v. *Ghawdex*.

CIRKEWWA (MALTA) - MGARR (GOZO) AND V.V.   Journey 25 minutes.

January 1 - May 28, 1995

Sailings from Cirkewwa : 0030 (from Apr. 10), 0645, 0730, 0815, 0915, 0945, 1015, 1100 (from Apr. 3), 1200, 1300, 1415, 1500, 1600, 1645, 1715, 1745, 1845, 2030, 2145, 2300.
Sailings from Mgarr : 0600, 0645, 0730, 0830, 0900, 0930, 1000 (from Apr. 3), 1100, 1200, 1315, 1400, 1500, 1600, 1630, 1700, 1800, 1930, 2115, 2230, 2359 (from Apr. 10).

VALLETTA (MALTA) - POZZALLO (SICILY) AND V.V.

April 6 - October 1, 1995 (no winter service)

Depart Valletta	Arrive Pozzallo	Depart Pozzallo	Arrive Valletta	Days of operation
0900	1230	1500	1830	Apr. 14,28 only.
1000	1330	1630	2000	② July 18 - Aug. 30; ④ Apr. 6,20, May 4 - Sept. 28; ⑥ Aug. 5-26; ⑦ June 4 - Oct. 1.
1800	2130	2300	0230	Apr. 17, May 1 only.

Table 1482
COMPAGNIE TUNISIENNE DE NAVIGATION

Dag Hammarskjoeld Avenue 5, Tunis ☎ (1) 341777 fax (1) 335714
UK Agent: Southern Ferries, London; SNCM, Marseille (see Table **1430**).
February 1 - April 30, 1995

MARSEILLE - TUNIS
From Marseille : ③ Feb. 1 - Apr. 26 (depart Marseille 1100, arrive Tunis 1100 next day).
From Tunis : ① Feb. 6 - Apr. 24 (depart Tunis 1100, arrive Marseille 1100 next day).

GENOVA - TUNIS
From Genova : ⑥ Feb. 4 - Apr. 29 (depart Genova 1530 or 1630, arrive 1630 next day).
From Tunis : ⑤ Feb. 3 - Apr. 28 (depart Tunis 1100, arrive Genova 1100 next day).

NAPOLI - TUNIS
Summer only.

Table 1490 ADRIATICA

Adriatica di Navigazione S.p.a, Zattere 1411, 30123 Venezia.
☎ (Venezia) 041 781611 fax (Venezia) 041 781894 telex 410045
UK agent: Serena Holidays, London ☎ 0171 244 8422 Fax 0171 244 9829

m.v. *Palladio*, m.v. *Sansovino*, m.v. *Laurana*, m.v. *Egitto Express*,
m.v. *Espresso Grecia*, m.v. *Espresso Venezia*.

January 1 - December 31, 1995

BRINDISI - CORFU - PATRAS

Depart Brindisi day 1	Depart Corfu day 2	Depart Igoumenitsa day 2	Arrive Patras day 2	Arrive Athinai by bus ♦	Notes
2000	→	→	1100	*1800*	M
2230	0700	0900	1800	*2200*	N

Depart Athinai by bus ♦	Depart Patras day 1	Depart Igoumenitsa day 2	Depart Corfu day 2	Arrive Brindisi day 2	Notes
0930	1900	→	→	0900	P
1300	2200	0700	0900	1700	Q

M - Alternate days June 21 - 29, July 1 - 31, Aug. 2 - 30, Sept. 1 - 19.
N - ②④⑥ Jan. 3 - Mar. 30; alternate days Apr. 1 - 29, May 1 - 31, June 2 - 30, July 2 - 30, Aug. 1 - 31, Sept. 2 - 30, Oct. 2 - 30; ②④⑥ Nov. 2 - Dec. 30.
P - Alternate days June 22 - 30, July 2 - 30, Aug. 1 - 31, Sept. 2 - 20.
Q - ③⑤⑦ Jan. 1 - Mar. 31; alternate days Apr. 2 - 30, May 2 - 30, June 1 - 29, July 1 - 31, Aug. 2 - 30; Sept. 1 - 29, Oct. 1 - 31; ③⑤⑦ Nov. 3 - Dec. 31.
♦ - 🚌 service, subject to confirmation. July 15 - Sept. 15 only. Athinai departure point is Voyages Liossis, 50 Chalkokondyli Str. (check in time 30 minutes).

Additional daily sailings :

June 21 - Aug. 12 : Brindisi (2200) → Igoumenitsa (0700) → Corfu (1000) → Brindisi (1800).
Aug. 14 - Sept. 20 : Brindisi (1200) → Corfu (2100) → Igoumenitsa (2330) → Brindisi (0800).

ANCONA - SPLIT / ANCONA - DURRËS

Dpart Ancona	Arrive Split	Depart Split	Arrive Ancona	Depart Ancona	Arrive Durrës	Depart Durrës	Arrive Ancona
2200③	0600④	1000④	1800①	1900①	1300②	1900②	1300③
2200⑥	0600⑦	2200⑦	0700⑤	2200④	1700⑤	2200⑤	1600⑥

TRIESTE and BARI - DURRËS

Depart Trieste	Depart Bari	Arrive Durrës	Depart Durrës	Arrive Bari	Arrive Trieste
1300②⑤	→	1400③⑥	1900③⑥	→	2000④⑦
	2200①③⑥	0700②④⑦	1200②④⑦	2100②④⑦	...

TRIESTE - ROVINJ - MALI LOŠINJ *1994 dates*

②-⑦ May 24 - September 30 (calls at Piran ③⑤⑦ only):

Trieste (0800) - Grado or Lignano - Piran - Umag (1020) - Rovinj (1120▲) - Brioni (1200).
Brioni (1630) - Rovinj (1710▲) - Umag (1810) - Piran - Lignano or Grado - Trieste (2030).

▲ - Extended to/from Mali Lošinj on ⑥⑦ July 12 - Sept. 11, not calling at Rovinj.

ISOLE TREMITE

Hydrofoil sailings operate throughout the year to Isole Tremite from Termoli (also less frequently from Ortona, Vasto, Rodi Garganico, Vieste and Manfredonia).

Table 1491 VENTOURIS FERRIES

91 Pireos Avenue, GR 185 41 Piraeus.
☎ (01) 4825.815 fax (01) 4832.919

m.v. *Athens Express*, m.v. *Grecia Express*, m.v. *Saturnus*, m.v. *Polaris*
m.v. *Vega*, m.v. *Venus*.

January 1 - December 31, 1995

BARI - PATRAS

Depart Bari	Arrive Patras	Notes	Depart Patras	Arrive Bari	Notes
2030	1600	See note A.	2130	1600	See note B.

A - Daily except Jan. 1,2, Apr. 23,24, Dec. 25,26. On certain dates, depart Bari 1800, arrive Patras 1200 - contact operator for details.
B - Daily except Jan. 1, Apr. 22,23, Dec. 24,25,31. On certain dates, depart Patras 1800, arrive Bari 1000 - contact operator for details.

Certain sailings (daily July 1 - Sept. 30) also call at **Igoumenitsa**.
From June to September certain sailings (daily July 1 - Sept. 20) also call at **Corfu**.

Certain sailings also call at Kefalonia (Sami): from Bari alternate days July 2 - Aug. 27, (arrive Sami 1300); from Sami (depart 0100) alternate days July 14 - Sept. 10.

🚌 service available Patras - Piraeus - Athinai (26 Amalias Ave) and v.v. (depart Patras one hour after ship's arrival, depart Athinai 1300, Piraeus 1330). Subject to confirmation.

Table 1488 TRANSEUROPA LINE

☎ (Bari) 080 5210022 fax 080 5211204
In association with Prekookeanska Plovidba, Bar: ☎ 85 12809 fax 85 11652
January 1 - December 31, 1995   Subject to alteration

BARI - BAR

Depart Bari	Arrive Bar		Depart Bar	Arrive Bari	
2200	0800	①②④⑤⑥.	1200	1900	②.
			2200	0800	①④⑤⑦.

Table 1493 POSEIDON LINES

32 Alkyonidon Str., 16673 Voula, Athinai
☎ 01 9658300 Telex 215926 Fax 01 9658310
UK agent: Viamare Travel, London ☎ 0171 431 4560 Fax 0171 431 5456

m.v. *Sea Harmony*, m.v. *Sea Wave*, m.v. *Sea Serenade*

1995 services

BARI - PATRAS

Depart Bari	Arrive Igoumenitsa	Arrive Patras	Depart Patras	Depart Igoumenitsa	Arrive Bari
February 13 - August 4 and September 9 - December 31					
2100③	0800③	1600③	2200③	0600 ❖	1400④
2100④	0800⑤	1600⑤	2200⑤	→	1400⑥
1900⑥	0600⑦	...	2200①	1000⑦	1900⑦
2300⑦	1000① ❖	1800①	2200①	0600②	1530②
August 5 - September 8					
1900①	0600②	1400②	1700②	2359④	0900③
1900③	0600④	...	...	2200④	0700⑤
1000⑤	2100⑤	...	...	2359⑤	0900⑥
1900⑥	0600⑦	1400⑦	1700⑦	2359⑦	0900①

❖ - Calls June 12 - Aug. 4 only.

PIRAEUS - LIMASSOL - HAIFA

Depart Piraeus	Depart Heraklion	Arrive Rhodes	Depart Rhodes	Arrive Limassol	Depart Limassol	Arrive Haifa	Notes
1900①	1100②	2000②	2100②	1200③	2000③	0630④	June 26 - Sept. 7.
1900①	→	1200②	1500②	0900③	2000③	0700④	See note E.
1700④	→	1300⑤	1400⑤	1100⑤	1900⑥	0700⑦	Mar. 16 - Oct. 29.

Depart Haifa	Arrive Limassol	Depart Limassol	Arrive Rhodes	Depart Rhodes	Depart Heraklion	Arrive Piraeus	Notes
2000④	0630⑤	1300⑤	0600⑥	1100⑥	2200⑥	0900⑦	June 29 - Sept. 10
2000④	0700⑤	1400⑤	0800⑥	1300⑥	→	0700⑦	See note G.
2000⑤	0700⑥	1400⑥	0800⑦	1300⑦	→	0700①	See note H.
1900⑦	0700①	1200①	0900②	1200②	→	0800③	Mar. 19 - Nov. 1

E - Jan. 2 - June 25 and Sept. 11 - Dec. 31.
G - From Haifa on ④ Jan. 5 - Mar. 30, Apr. 13, May 18, Oct. 26 - Dec. 28.
H - From Haifa on ⑤ Apr. 7, Apr 21 - May 12, May 26 - June 23, Sept. 15 - Oct. 20.

Table 1520 JADROLINIJA

SEE ALSO NEXT PAGE

January 1 - September 30, 1995

DUBROVNIK - BARI

Depart Dubrovnik	Arrive Bari	Depart Bari	Arrive Dubrovnik	Period of operation
2300①	0800②	2200②	0600③	July 24 - Sept. 12.
2300③	0800④	2200④	0600⑤	May 31 - Sept. 28.
2300⑤	0800⑥	2200⑥	0600⑦	Jan. 1 - May 30.

SPLIT - VENEZIA

July 28 - September 16

Depart Split	Depart Zadar	Depart Mali Lošinj	Arrive Venezia	Depart Venezia	Depart Mali Lošinj	Arrive Zadar	Arrive Split
1400⑤	1930⑤	2359⑤	0800⑥	2100⑥	0700⑦	1030⑦	1600⑦

ANCONA - VELA LUKA

June 3 - October 1

Depart Ancona	Arrive Vis	Arrive Stari Grad	Arrive Vela Luka	Depart Vela Luka	Depart Stari Grad	Depart Vis	Arrive Ancona
2100⑥	0600⑦	0845⑦	1200⑦	1600⑦	1915⑦	2200⑦	0800①

PULA - ZADAR

Depart Pula	Depart Mali Lošinj	Arrive Zadar	Depart Zadar	Depart Mali Lošinj	Arrive Pula
April 12 - May 31					
0600⑤	0940⑤	1350⑤	1200③	1630③	1950③
Daily June 1 - 23 and September 6 - 30					
0600	0945	1415	1200	1645	2015

CONTINUED ON NEXT PAGE

Table 1520 — JADROLINIJA

Riva 16, 51000 Rijeka, Croatia. ☎ +385 (51) 330-899 Telex 24225 fax +385 (51) 213-116.
U.K. agent : Dalmatian & Istrian Travel, 28 Denmark Street, London WC2 8NJ ☎ 0171 379 6249 fax 0171 379 6383

January 1 - September 30, 1995

RIJEKA - ZADAR - SPLIT - DUBROVNIK

Depart Rijeka	Depart Rab	Depart Zadar	Arrive Split	Depart Split	Depart Hvar	Depart Korčula	Arrive Dubrovnik	Depart Dubrovnik	Depart Korčula	Depart Hvar	Arrive Split	Depart Split	Depart Zadar	Depart Rab	Arrive Rijeka
January 1 - May 30
0900①	→	1700①	...	...	...	...	...	...	...	...	...	1900①	0035②	→	0730②
1800②	→	0020③	0625③	0800③	1000③	1220③	...	...	...	...	...	0900③	→	1500③
1800③	→	0020④	0625④	...	...	...	...	...	1335③	1615③	1755③	1900③	0035④	0420④	0730④
1800④	2125④	0110⑤	0625⑤	0800⑤	1000⑤	1240⑤	1630⑤	...	...	...	...	1900④	0035⑤	→	0730⑤
1800⑤	2125⑤	0110⑥	0625⑥	0800⑥	1000⑥	1220⑥	...	...	1335⑥	1615⑥	1755⑥	1900⑥	0100⑦	→	0730⑦
1800⑦	→	0020①	0625①	...	...	...	...	0900⑦	1335⑦	1615⑦	1755⑦	1900⑦	0035①	0420①	0730①
June 1 - September 30 (▲ - July 15 - Sept. 9)
2000①	→	→	0700①	...	...	...	...	0800①	1215①	1655①	1835①	1930①	0055②	0420②	0720②
1800②	2125②	0110③	0625③	0800③	1000③	1240③	1630③	...	1335②	1615②	1755②	1900②	0100③	→	0700③
1800③	→	0020④	0625④	0800④	1000④	1220④	...	0900③	1335③	1615③	1755③	1900③	0035④	0420④	0720④
1800④	2125④	0110⑤	0625⑤	0800⑤	1000⑤	1240⑤	1630⑤	...	...	...	...	2000④	→	→	0700⑤
2000⑤	→	→	0700⑥	...	...	...	...	0900⑤	1335⑤	1615⑤	1755⑤	1900⑤	0035⑥	0420⑥	0720⑥
1800⑥	→	→	0625⑦	0730⑦	0920⑦	1405⑦	1750⑦	...	...	...	...	0800⑥▲	1330⑥▲	→	1930⑥▲
2100⑥▲	→	0315⑦▲	0845⑦▲	...	...	...	...	0900⑥	1335⑥	1615⑥	1755⑥	1900⑥	→	→	0700⑦
1800⑦	2125⑦	0110①	0625①	0800①	1000①	1240①	1630①	...	...	...	...	2000⑦	→	→	0700①

ANCONA - ZADAR and SPLIT

Depart Ancona	Arrive Zadar	Arrive Šibenik	Arrive Split	Days of operation
2100	→	→	0700	①③⑤.
2200	→	→	0700	⑥ June 3 - Sept. 30.
2300	0600	1000	...	① June 5 - Sept. 25.
2300	0600	...	...	③ July 19 - Sept. 13.
2300	0700	...	...	⑤ June 2 - Sept. 29.

Depart Split	Depart Šibenik	Depart Zadar	Arrive Ancona	Days of operation
...	1800A	2300	0600	④ June 8 - Sept. 28.
...	1800	2300	0600	② July 18 - Sept. 12.
2100	→	→	0700	②④⑦.
...	...	1000	1730	⑥ June 3 - Sept. 30.
1100	→	→	1900	⑥ June 3 - Sept. 30.

A – ④ June 8 - July 13, also Sept. 21, 28.

FOR OTHER SERVICES SEE PREVIOUS PAGE
Many additional local services operate to the Islands along the Croatian coast.

Table 1525 — HELLENIC MEDITERRANEAN LINES

Electric Railway Station Building, 185 10 Piraeus. ☎ 1 4225341 fax 1 4225317
UK agent: Amathus Travel, 51 Tottenham Court Road, London W1P 0HS ☎ 0171 636 6158 fax 0171 636 3307
m.v. *Apollonia II*, m.v. *Egnatia II*, m.v. *Lydia*, m.v. *Media II*, m.v. *Poseidonia*

1994 services (1995 services not available by press date)

BRINDISI - PATRAS

Depart Brindisi	Arrive Patras	Arrive Athinai ♦	Days of operation
2000	1330	*1745*	Alternate days June 17-29, daily July 1 - Sept. 5, also Sept. 7,9,11.
2200	1500	*1915*	Alternate days Apr. 1-29, May 1-31, June 2-30, July 2-30, Aug. 1-31, Sept. 2-10.
2200	1700	*2115*	③⑤⑦ Mar. 9-30, also Mar. 24,26; daily Sept. 12 - Oct. 10; alternate days Oct. 12-30.

Depart Athinai ♦	Depart Patras	Arrive Brindisi	Days of operation
1100	1700	0930	Alternate days June 16-30; daily July 1 - Sept. 4, also Sept. 6,8,10.
1530	2100	1300	Mar. 29,31; alternate days Apr. 2-30, May 2-30, June 1-29, July 1-31, Aug. 2-30, Sept. 1-9.
1530	2100	1600	②④⑥ Mar. 8-26, also Mar. 23,25,27; daily Sept. 13 - Oct. 9; alternate days Oct. 11 - 29.

♦ – ☷ service operates June 1 - Sept. 30 to/from Athinai (28 Amalias Avenue). Also departs from Piraeus Harbour (Electric Railway Station) 30 minutes later.

For details of services from Piraeus to the Greek Islands, see the Thomas Cook Guide to Greek Island Hopping.

BRINDISI - CORFU - IGOUMENITSA

Depart Brindisi	Arrive* Corfu	Arrive* Igoumenitsa	Days of operation
0900	1830	2000	Daily July 1 - Sept. 12 (not Aug. 16).
2200	0630	0800	③⑤⑦ Mar. 9-20; daily Mar. 23 - Oct. 10; alternate days Oct. 12 - 30.

Depart* Igoumenitsa	Depart* Corfu	Arrive Brindisi	Days of operation
0630	0800	1600	③⑤⑦ Mar. 9-20; daily Mar. 23-28 and Sept. 12 - Oct. 10; alternate days Oct. 12-30.
0900	1030	1730	Daily Mar. 29 - Aug. 15.
0930	1100	1830	Daily Aug. 17 - Sept. 11.
2200	2330	0700	Daily June 30 - Sept. 11.

* - Timings at Corfu and Igoumenitsa are approximate.

OTHER SERVICES

Brindisi - Paxi : From Brindisi alternate days July 2-30, Aug. 1-31. From Paxi alternate days July 1-31, Aug. 2-30, Sept. 1,3.
Brindisi - Kefalonia (Sami) : From Brindisi alternate days June 17 - 29; daily July 1 - Sept. 4. From Kefalonia alternate days June 18-30; daily July 1 - Sept. 4, also Sept. 6,8,10.
Direct sailings also operate from Brindisi to Ithaca and Zante in high summer.

Table 1530 SUPERFAST FERRIES

157 Alkyonidon Avenue, 166 73 Voula, Athinai
☎ (01) 965 7777   fax (01) 899 2060   Telex 215031
UK agent: Viamare Travel, London ☎ 0171 431 4560 fax 0171 431 5456
April 16 - December 31, 1995

ANCONA - PATRAS

Depart Ancona	Arrive Patras	Notes	Depart Patras	Arrive Ancona	Notes
2200①	1900②	From mid-June▲.	2200①	1700②	From Apr. 16.
2200②	1900③	From Apr. 16.	1600③	1100④	From mid-June▲.
1600④	1300⑤	From mid-June▲.	1600④	1100⑤	From Apr. 16.
1600⑤	1300⑥	From Apr. 16.	1900⑤	1400⑥	From mid-June▲.
1900⑥	1600⑦	From mid-June▲.	1900⑥	1400⑦	From Apr. 16.
1900⑦	1600①	From Apr. 16.	2200⑦	1700①	From mid-June▲.

▲ - Start date will depend on delivery of vessel.

Table 1533 FRAGLINE

5a Rethymnou Street, Athinai 10682.
☎ 01 8214171 Telex 218403 FRLN GR Fax 01 8213095.
UK agent: Viamare Travel, London ☎ 0171 431 4560 fax 0171 431 5456

m.v. *Eolos*, m.v. *Ouranos*.

1995 service (subject to confirmation)

BRINDISI - CORFU - IGOUMENITSA - PATRAS

Depart Brindisi	Arrive Corfu	Arrive Igoumenitsa	Arrive Corfu	Arrive Patras	Days of operation
2045	0600	0700	→	1630	See note A.
2045	→	0615	0800	...	See note B.

Depart Patras	Depart Corfu	Depart Igoumenitsa	Depart Corfu	Arrive Brindisi	Days of operation
2130	→	0700	0830	1600	See note C.
...	0830	0700	→	1600	See note D.

A - From Brindisi Mar. 25,27,29, Apr. 1,3,5,8,10,12,15,18,25,29, May 1,9,15,23,29, June 6,12,19,26, July 3,10,17,24,31, Aug. 7,14,21,28, Sept. 4,11,18,25.
B - From Brindisi Mar. 31, Apr. 7,14,17,20-24,27,28, May 3-8,11-14,17-22,25-28,31, June 1-5,8-11,14-18,21-25,28-30, July 1,2,5-9,12-16,19-23,26-30, Aug. 1-6,9-13,16-20, 23-27,30,31, Sept. 1-3,6-10,13-17,20-24,27-30, Oct. 1-3,5-9,11-16.
C - From Patras Mar. 25,27,29,31, Apr. 1,3,5,7,10,12,14,17,20,27, May 1,3,11,17,25,31, June 8,14,21,28, July 5,12,19,26, Aug. 2,9,16,23,30, Sept. 6,13,20,27.
D - Apr. 8,15,18,21-25,28,29, May 4-9,12-15,18-23,26-29, June 1-6,9-12,15-19,22-26,29,30, July 1-3,6-10,13-17,20-24,27-31, Aug. 3-7,10-14,17-21,24-28,31, Sept. 1-4, 7-11,14-18,21-25,28-30, Oct. 1-3,5-9,11-16.

Table 1534 MISANO ALTA VELOCITÀ

Corso Garibaldi 96/98, 72100 Brindisi
☎ 0831 529771   Telex 813384   Fax 0831 527968
Catamaran *Santa Eleonora*

Albanian services are operated in conjunction with Albadria S.A. (vessel not advised).

January 1 - December 31, 1995

BRINDISI - CORFU - PAXI

April 1 - September 24, 1995 (no winter service)

Depart Brindisi	Arrive Corfu	Arrive Paxi	Days of operation
1400	1815	...	④⑤⑥⑦ (daily June 19 - Sept. 3).
1400	1815	2000	Daily July 1 - Sept. 3.

Depart Paxi	Depart Corfu	Arrive Brindisi	Days of operation
...	0900	1115	④⑤⑥⑦ (daily June 19 - Sept. 3).
0700	0900	1115	Daily July 1. - Sept. 3.

BRINDISI - DURRËS/VLORË

Subject to confirmation

Depart Brindisi	Arrive Durrës	Arrive Vlorë	Days	Depart Vlorë	Depart Durrës	Arrive Brindisi	Days
0900	1130	...	⑦.	1500	→	1700	④⑥.
1000	→	1200	④⑥.		1630	1900	②③⑦.
1130	1400		②③.				

BARI - DURRËS

Subject to confirmation

Depart Bari	Arrive Durrës	Days	Depart Durrës	Arrive Bari	Days
0900	1230	①.	0900	1230	②④⑤⑥⑦.
1630	2000	②④⑤⑥.			

Table 1531 ARKADIA LINES

Kifissias Ave 215, 15124 Maroussi, Greece
☎ (01) 6123.402 fax (01) 6126.206 telex 217469
UK agent: Viamare Travel, London ☎ 0171 431 4560 fax 0171 431 5456
1995 services

BARI - IGOUMENITSA

Depart Bari	Arrive Igoumenitsa		Depart Igoumenitsa	Arrive Bari	
2030	0900	Daily June 2 - Oct. 2.	2100	0900	Daily June 1 - Oct. 1.

Table 1535
STRINTZIS LINES - MINOAN LINES
JOINT SERVICE

Strintzis Lines: 26, Akti Possidonos, 185 31 Piraeus.
☎ (01) 422.5000 Telex 212068 Fax (01) 422.5265
UK agent: Magnum Travel, 729 Green Lanes, London N21 3RZ
☎ 0181 360 5353 fax 0181 360 1056
Minoan Lines: 2 Vassileos Konstantinou Ave. (Stadion), 116 35 Athinai.
☎ 01 7512356 Telex 226888 Fax 01 7520540
January 1 - October 17, 1995

ANCONA - IGOUMENITSA - CORFU - PATRAS

Depart Ancona	Arrive Ig'nitsa	Arrive Corfu	Arrive Patras	Depart Patras	Depart Corfu	Depart Ig'nitsa	Arrive Ancona
Daily January 1 - April 7 (January 1 - April 5 from Patras)							
2100	2030	2230	0700	2200	0800	1100	0800
1st day	*2nd day*	*2nd day*	*3rd day*	*1st day*	*2nd day*	*2nd day*	*3rd day*
April 8 - October 17 (April 6 - October 17 from Patras)							
2100①	1930②	2130②	0700③	2230①	0800②	1100②	0800③
1400③	1400④	1200④	2100④	2230②	0800③	1100③	1100④
2100④	2300⑤	2100⑤	0700⑥	2230④	0800④	1100④	0800⑤
2100⑤	1930⑥	2130⑥	0700⑦	2230⑤	0800⑤	1100⑤	0800⑥
1400⑥	1400⑦	1200⑦	2100⑦	1200⑥	→	2000⑥	1900⑦
2100⑦	2300①	2100①	0700②	1200⑦	1930⑦	2200⑦	1800①

🚐 connection Patras - Athinai and v.v. is available (depart Athinai 1700).

ANCONA - PATRAS (direct)

Depart Ancona	Arrive Ig'nitsa	Arrive Corfu	Arrive Patras	Depart Patras	Depart Corfu	Depart Ig'nitsa	Arrive Ancona
January 7 - April 4 (January 5 - April 2 from Patras)							
2000②	→	→	2100③	2000④	→	→	2000⑤
1400⑥	→	→	1500⑦	2100⑦	→	→	2000①
April 7 - July 8 (April 5 - July 6 from Patras)							
1400②	1200③	→	2000③	2350③	→	→	0800⑤
2000②	→	→	2100③	2100④	→	→	2000⑤
1300⑤	→	→	1700⑥	2100⑥	→	→	2300⑦
1600⑥	→	→	1700⑦	2100⑦	→	→	2100①
July 9 - October 17 (July 8 - October 15 from Patras)							
1300①	→	→	1400②	1800②	→	→	1700③
1300②	→	→	1700③	2000③	→	→	2350④
2000②	→	→	2100③	1800④	→	→	1700⑤
2000③	→	→	2100④	1800⑤	→	→	1750⑥
1300⑤	→	→	1700⑥	2200⑥	→	→	2350⑦
2000⑤⑥	→	→	2100⑥⑦	2350⑥⑦	→	→	2300⑦①

VENEZIA - CORFU - PATRAS

Daily April 4 - October 17 (April 6 - October 15 from Patras)

Depart Venezia	Arrive Corfu	Arrive Igoumenitsa	Arrive Patras	Depart Patras	Depart Corfu	Depart Igoumenitsa	Arrive Ancona
1800	2130	2330	0700	2200	0615	0830	1000

BRINDISI - CORFU - IGOUMENITSA

Depart Brindisi	Arrive Corfu	Arrive Ig'nitsa	Dates	Depart Ig'nitsa	Depart Corfu	Arrive Brindisi	Dates
1000	1700	1815	A	2330	0100	0700	E
2230	0530	0700	G				

A - ① Apr. 8 - Sept. 30 (daily June 19 - Sept. 11).
E - ①③⑤⑦ Apr. 7 - June 16 and Sept. 10 - 29; daily June 18 - Sept. 9.
G - ②④⑥ Apr. 8 - June 17 and Sept. 12 - 30..

OTHER SERVICES - MINOAN LINES (subject to confirmation)

PIRAEUS - HERAKLION Journey 12 hours :
From Piraeus and Heraklion : depart 1915 daily (1845 from Nov. 1).

PIRAEUS - CHANEA Journey 12 hours : 3-5 sailings per week.

OTHER SERVICES - STRINTZIS LINES

PATRAS - SAMI - ITHACA daily
Patras 1300 → Sami 1600 → Ithaca 1715
Ithaca 0700 → Sami 0800 → Patras 1145.

KILLINI - POROS daily (journey 1 hour 15 minutes)
From Killini 1200, 1730; from Poros 0900, 1530.

Table 1536 ANEK LINES

32 Akti Possidonos, 185 31 Piraeus.
☎ 01 4118611 Telex 213269 Fax 01 4114188
UK agent: Viamare Travel, London ☎ 0171 431 4560 fax 0171 431 5456
m.v. *Venizelos, Lato, Lissos, Candia, Aptera, Kydon, Rethimnon, Kriti*
1995 services

ANCONA - CORFU - PATRAS

Depart Ancona	Arrive Corfu	Arrive Igoumenitsa	Arrive Patras	Depart Patras	Depart Corfu	Depart Igoumenitsa	Arrive Ancona
March 11 - April 10							
1500③	→	1230④	2030④	2300④	0800⑤	1030⑤	0800⑥
1600⑥	→	1330⑦	2100⑦	2300①	0800②	1030②	0800③
April 12 - June 24							
2100①	2200②	2000②	0700③	2300③	0800④	1030④	0800⑤
1400⑤	1130⑥	1230⑥	2100⑥	2359⑥	0800⑦	1030⑦	0800①
2330⑥	2330⑦	2130⑦	0700①	...	...	...	...
June 26 - October 31							
2100①	→	2200②	0700③	2300③	→	1030④	0800⑤
2100②	2200③	2000③	0700④	2300④	0800⑤	1030⑤	0800⑥
1700⑤	→	1400⑥	2130⑥	2359⑥	→	1030⑦	0800①
1500⑥	1200⑦	1400⑦	2130⑦	2359⑦	0800①	1030①	0800②

TRIESTE - CORFU - PATRAS

Depart Trieste	Arrive Corfu	Arrive Igoumenitsa	Arrive Patras	Depart Patras	Depart Corfu	Depart Igoumenitsa	Arrive Trieste
April 12 - June 24							
1230③	→	1400④	2130④	2359④	0700⑤	1000⑤	1000⑥
1330⑥ A	2330⑦	2130⑦	0700①	2300①	→	0700②	0800③
June 26 - October 31							
1230③	→	1400④	2130④	2359④	0800⑤	1030⑤	1030⑥
1900⑥	2300⑦	2100⑦	0700①	2300①	→	0700②	0800③

A - Via Ancona (see above).

Table 1537 MARLINES

38 Akti Possidonos, 185 31 Piraeus.
☎ (01) 4110777 Telex 241691 Fax (01) 4133727
UK agent: Viamare Travel, London ☎ 0171 431 4560 fax 0171 431 5456
m.v. *Countess M, Crown M, Duchess M, Grace M, Dame M, Charm M, Baroness M*
1995 services

ANCONA - IGOUMENITSA - PATRAS

Depart Ancona	Arrive Corfu	Arrive Ig'itsa	Arrive Patras	Depart Patras	Depart Ig'itsa	Depart Corfu	Arrive Ancona
January 14 - June 30							
2000①	→	2200②	0800③	2200③	1000④	→	0800⑤
1700②	→	1500③	2200③	2400④	1000⑤	→	0800⑥
1300⑤	→	1500⑥	2300⑥	2400⑥	1000⑦	→	1000①
1700⑥	→	1500⑦	2200⑦	2400⑦	1000①	→	0800②
July 1 - Dec. 20 (Dec. 18 from Patras)							
1800①	→	1600②	2300②	2400①	1000②	→	0800⑤
1800③	→	1600④	2300④	2400③	1000④	→	0800⑤
1800⑤	1500⑥	1700⑥	2300⑥	2400④	1000⑤	1200⑤	0800⑥
1800⑥	1500⑦	1700⑦	2300⑦	2400⑥	1000⑦	1200⑦	0800①

ANCONA - HERAKLION - KUSADASI

Depart Ancona	Depart Patras	Arrive Heraklion	Arrive Kusadasi	Depart Kusadasi	Depart Heraklion	Depart Patras	Arrive Ancona
June 24 - September 15							
1800⑥	→	2100①	1200②	1900③	1000④	0800⑤	1400⑥

BARI - CORFU - IGOUMENITSA

Depart Bari	Arrive Corfu	Arrive Igoumenitsa	Depart Igoumenitsa	Depart Corfu	Arrive Bari
January 1 - March 31					
2100②	→	0900③	2100①	→	0800②
2100④	→	1000⑤	2100③	→	0800④
1700⑥	→	0600⑦	2100⑤	→	0800⑥
2200⑦	→	1100①	0900⑦	→	1900⑦
Daily April - December 21					
2100	0800 B	0930	2100	2300 B	1000

B - Calls July 1 - Sept. 10.

BARI - PATRAS - ÇEŞME

Depart Bari	Depart Igoumenitsa	Arrive Patras	Arrive Çeşme	Depart Çeşme	Depart Patras	Depart Igoumenitsa	Arrive Bari
June 24 - August 5							
2000⑥	→	1500⑦	1000①	1700①	1400②	→	0800③
2100③	→	1600④	...	...	2100④	0700⑤	1900⑤
August 6 - September 16							
2100②	→	1500③	1100④	2000④	1700⑤	→	1000⑥
2100⑥	→	1600⑦	...	...	2100⑦	0700①	1900①

Table 1540 VERGINA CRUISES LINES

11 Sachtouri Street, GR-185 36 Piraeus.
☎ 4132392 Telex 211830 Fax 4510500
m.v. *Vergina*
April 21 - October 30, 1994 (no winter service)

PIRAEUS - LIMASSOL - HAIFA

Depart Piraeus	Arrive Rhodes	Arrive Limassol	Arrive Haifa	Depart Haifa	Depart Limassol	Depart Rhodes	Arrive Piraeus
1900④	1230⑤	1100⑥	0700⑦	2000⑦	1200①	1400②	0900③

The April 28 departure from Piraeus will run one day earlier

Table 1545 GREEK ISLANDS

Summary table of regular 🚢 services to the Greek Islands.

Each route is operated by various shipping companies to differing schedules. Further details are given in the **Thomas Cook Guide to Greek Island Hopping**. Additional inter-island routes are operated at less regular intervals.

Piraeus to Aegina, Poros, Hydra, Spetsae, Kythira, Antikythira.
Piraeus to Serifos, Sifnos, Milos, Folegandros.
Piraeus to Paros, Ios, Santorini, Heraklion.
Piraeus to Naxos, Amorgos, Astipalea.
Piraeus to Patmos, Leros, Kalimnos, Kos, Nissiros, Tilos, Symi, Rhodes, Kaupathos, Kassos.
Piraeus to Ikaria, Samos, Chios, Lesbos.
Piraeus and Rafina to Syros, Delos, Mykonos, Tinos, Andros.
Patras to Zante, Kefalonia, Ithaca, Corfu, Igoumenitsa.
Volos Ag. Konstantinos and Kimi to Skiathos, Skopelos, Alonissos, Skyros.
Kavalla to Thassos, Samothrace, Lemnos.

Table 1550 TURKISH MARITIME LINES

Denizyollari Ac. Rihtim Cad. Karaköy, Istanbul.
☎ 249 92 22 Telex 24810 Fax 251 90 25.
m.v. *Ankara*, m.v. *Samsun*, m.v. *Iskenderun*, m.v. *Truva*, m.v. *Ayvalik*
January 1 - December 31, 1995

ANTALYA and MARMARIS - VENEZIA

Depart Antalya	Depart Marmaris	Arrive Venezia	Notes	Depart Venezia	Arrive Marmaris	Arrive Antalya	Notes
1200③	→	1000⑥	Note A.	1600⑥	→	1400②	Note C.
...	1200③	1000⑥	Note B.	1600⑥	1400②	...	Note D.

A - June 14,28, July 12,26, Aug. 9,23, Sept. 6,20, Oct. 4.
B - June 7,21, July 5,19, Aug. 2,16,30, Sept. 13,27.
C - June 10,24, July 8,22, Aug. 5,19, Sept. 2,16,30.
D - June 17, July 1,15,29, Aug. 12,26, Sept. 9,23. Also Oct. 7 to Istanbul.

IZMIR - VENEZIA

Depart Izmir	Arrive Venezia	Dates of running	Depart Venezia	Arrive Izmir	Dates of running
1600③	1100⑥	Mar. 29 - Nov. 15, also Nov. 29, Dec. 13,27.	2100⑥	1200②	Apr. 1 - Nov. 18, also Dec. 2,16,30.

ÇEŞME - VENEZIA

Depart Çeşme	Arrive Venezia	Dates of running	Depart Venezia	Arrive Çeşme	Dates of running
1800③	1000⑥	June 21 - Sept. 27.	2000⑥	1200②	June 24 - Sept. 30.

ISTANBUL - IZMIR

Depart Istanbul	Arrive Izmir	Depart Izmir	Arrive Istanbul
1730⑤	1145⑥	1400②	0900①

For Cyprus - Turkey services and Turkish coastal services see the Thomas Cook Overseas Timetable

---

Other Mediterranean services

Several other operators sail from Italy to Greece and Turkey and from Greece to Cyprus and Israel.
Further details will be found in the
Thomas Cook Guide to Greek Island Hopping
(see the back of this book for details).

U.K. agent for many of these services is
Viamare Travel, 2 Sumatra Road, London NW6 1PU
☎ 0171 431 4560 fax 0171 431 5456.

INTERNATIONAL SERVICES ADVANCE SUMMER TIMINGS

Compiled from the latest available information and updated each month, all timings are subject to confirmation.

Services   All trains convey First and Second classes of seating accommodation unless otherwise noted. Sleeping cars (🛏) and couchettes (🛌) are usually of the normal European types, but some countries (former U.S.S.R. etc.) use their own stock for international trains, see page 10 for more details. Restaurant (✗) and buffet (♀) cars vary considerably from country to country in standard of service offered. The catering car may not be carried or open for the whole journey.

Timings   Valid May 28, 1995 – September 23, 1995.
Services can change at short notice and passengers are advised to consult the latest Thomas Cook European Timetable before travelling.
International trains are not normally affected by public holidays, but can be affected at Christmas and Easter.

Tickets   **Seat reservations** are available for most international trains and are advisable as some trains can get very crowded. **Supplements** are payable on EuroCity (EC) trains in most countries and on most InterCity trains, consult the introduction at the start of each country to see which supplements apply.

Table 10 (Summer)   LONDON - PARIS by Eurostar

train number	9004	9010		9014	9014		9018	9018		9024	9028		9034	9038		9042	9042	9044		9048	9048	9052	
notes	Ⓡ✗	Ⓡ✗		Ⓡ✗	✗		Ⓡ✗	Ⓡ✗		Ⓡ✗	Ⓡ✗		Ⓡ✗	Ⓡ✗		Ⓡ✗	Ⓡ✗	Ⓡ✗		Ⓡ✗	Ⓡ✗	Ⓡ✗	
days of running	①-⑥	①-⑥		①-⑥	⑦	A	①-⑥	①-⑤		⑥⑦	①-⑦	A	⑦			①-⑥	B	⑦		①-⑤	⑥⑦	C	
London Waterloo........ d.	...	0657	0823	...	0910	0923	...	1010	1023	...	1157	1253	...	1423	1510	...	1623	1623	1657	...	1748	1753	1853	...
Calais Fréthun............ a.	...	|	|	...	|	|	...	|	|	...	|	|	...	|	|	...	|	|	|	...	2026	2026	|	...
Paris Nord.................. a.	...	1059	1223	...	1323	1323	...	1417	1417	...	1550	1647	...	1826	1923	...	2023	2023	2056	...	2156	2156	2250	...

train number	9007		9011	9011	9011		9015		9019	9019	9019		9027	9027		9039	9039		9043	9047		9051	9051	9059
notes	Ⓡ✗		Ⓡ✗	Ⓡ✗	✗		Ⓡ✗		Ⓡ✗	Ⓡ✗	✗		Ⓡ✗	Ⓡ✗		Ⓡ✗	Ⓡ✗		Ⓡ✗	Ⓡ✗		Ⓡ✗	Ⓡ✗	Ⓡ✗
days of running	①-⑤		①-⑥	①-⑤	⑦		①-⑥	D	①-⑥	①-⑤	⑦		①-⑥	①-⑤		⑥	E		⑤⑦	①-⑦		①-⑤	F	①-⑦
Paris Nord.................. d.	0713	...	0813	0813	0813	...	0910	...	1019	1019	1019	...	1213	1213	...	1519	1519	...	1613	1710	...	1818	1818	2013
Calais Fréthun............ d.	0839	...	|	0939	0939	...	|	...	|	|	1230	...	|	|	...	|	|	...	1809	1909	...	|	|	|
London Waterloo........ a.	0920	...	1009	1013	1030	...	1109	...	1213	1213	1230	...	1413	1430	...	1713	1713	...	|	|	...	2013	2013	2213

LONDON - PARIS by rail and sea

Rail/sea services for the summer have not been announced
Other services are available by taking normal service trains between London and Dover (Tables 500,506),
Stena Sealink sailings between Dover and Calais (Tables 1025) and normal service trains between Calais and Paris (Table 102),
passengers making their own way between stations and docks at Dover and Calais, allowing at least 1 hour for connections.

Additional services are available via Newhaven and Dieppe: see Tables 505, London - Brighton;
507, Brighton - Lewes - Newhaven; 1025, Newhaven - Dieppe and 115, Dieppe - Rouen - Paris.

French train number							French train number						
classes on trains							classes on trains						
notes (see below)							notes (see below)						
sea crossing							sea crossing						
London Charing Cross ...... d.	...	...	...	...	...	...	Paris Nord.................. d.	...	...	...	...	...	...
Folkestone Harbour...... a.	...	...	...	...	...	...	Amiens....................... d.	...	...	...	...	...	...
Folkestone Harbour 🚢.... d.	...	...	...	...	...	...	Calais Ville .... a.	...	...	...	...	...	...
Dover Priory................ a.	...	...	...	...	...	...	Calais Maritime .... d.	...	...	...	...	...	...
Dover Hoverport ♣ 🚢.... d.	...	...	...	...	...	...	Calais Hoverport ♣ 🚢.... d.	...	...	...	...	...	...
Dover Eastern Docks ♣ 🚢.. d.	...	...	...	...	...	...	Boulogne Ville .... a.	...	...	...	...	...	...
							Boulogne Maritime ♣ 🚢.d.	...	...	...	...	...	...
Boulogne Maritime ♣ 🚢.. a.	...	...	...	...	...	...	Dover Eastern Docks ♣ 🚢.a.	...	...	...	...	...	...
Boulogne Ville .... d.	...	...	...	...	...	...	Dover Hoverport ♣ 🚢.... a.	...	...	...	...	...	...
Calais Hoverport ♣ 🚢.... a.	...	...	...	...	...	...	Dover Priory .... d.	...	...	...	...	...	...
Calais Maritime ♣ 🚢 ..... a.	...	...	...	...	...	...	Folkestone Harbour ...... a.	...	...	...	...	...	...
Calais Ville .... d.	...	...	...	...	...	...	Folkestone Harbour ...... d.	...	...	...	...	...	...
Amiens....................... a.	...	...	...	...	...	...	London Charing Cross ... a.	...	...	...	...	...	...
Paris Nord.................. a.	...	...	...	...	...	...							

CONNECTIONS: Connections are available in Paris from the services shown in this table to all parts of France. Allow at least one hour to cross Paris.

NOTES

A – ①②③④⑤⑥ from July 3.
B – ⑦ from July 2.
C – ①②③④⑤⑦.
D – ①②③④⑤ from July 3.
E – ①②③④⑤⑦ from July 2.
F – ⑥⑦ from July 2.

SC – Seacat service (Hoverspeed). Ⓡ, supplement payable, one class only on catamaran ♀. When bad weather interrupts sailings. passengers are transferred to the next available car-ferry service, see Table 1025, and arrival at destination will be correspondingly later.
🚢 – Ship service (Sealink), one class only on ship, ✗, for additional car-ferry services see Table 1025.
♣ – A free 🚌 connection is provided between the railway station and the port.

EDINBURGH – LONDON
Services for Eurostar passengers only
Runs from July 3
Subject to alteration

	♀Ⓡ ①-⑥			♀Ⓡ ①-⑥
Edinburgh............ d.	0915	Paris Nord............ d.	1019b	
Newcastle .... d.	1044	London Waterloo. a.	1213b	
Darlington............ d.	1111			
York .... d.	1145	Brussels Midi........ d.	1028	
Doncaster............ d.	1208	London Waterloo. a.	1239	
Newark................ d.	1233			
Peterborough ...... d.	1301	London Waterloo. d.	1346	
London Waterloo. a.	1446	Peterborough ...... a.	1520	
		Newark................ a.	1548	
London Waterloo. d.'	1623	Doncaster............ a.	1616	
Paris Nord............ a.	2023	York .... a.	1651	
		Darlington............ a.	1727	
		Newcastle .... a.	1757	
London Waterloo. d.	1627	Edinburgh............ a.	1927	
Brussels Midi........ a.	2046			

b – For days of running see above.

MANCHESTER – LONDON
Services for Eurostar passengers only
Runs from May 28
Subject to alteration

	♀Ⓡ ①-⑥			♀Ⓡ ①-⑥
Manchester Pic ... d.	0737	Paris Nord............ d.	1213	1213
Stockport............. d.	0745	London Waterloo. a.	1413	1413
Crewe .... d.	0813			
Stafford .... d.	0834	Brussels Midi....... d.	1233	1233
Wolverhampton .... d.	0859	London Waterloo. a.	1439	1439
Birmingham N St. d.	0927			
Birmingham Int.... d.	0950	London Waterloo. d.	1542	1546
Coventry.............. d.	1004	Milton Keynes ...... a.	1628	1650
Rugby .:............... d.	1021	Rugby .... a.	1656	1725
Milton Keynes ...... d.	1045	Coventry.............. a.	1719	1737
London Waterloo. a.	1146	Birmingham Int .... a.	1731	1755
		Birmingham N St. a.	1744	1810
London Waterloo. d.	1253	Wolverhampton .... a.	1813	1835
Paris Nord............ a.	1647	Stafford .... a.	1832	1851
		Crewe .... a.	1900	1925
London Waterloo. d.	1227	Stockport............. a.	1930	2000
Brussels Midi....... a.	1644	Manchester Picc.. a.	1940	2013

'LE SHUTTLE'

The shuttle service through the **Channel Tunnel** runs between the British terminal at Folkestone and the French terminal at Calais. Branded **'Le Shuttle'** the journey takes 35 minutes and carries cars and motorcycles with their passengers. Coaches will also be carried from Spring 1995.

The service is operating hourly during the day (0700 - 2300) and two-hourly at night (2300 - 0700). The frequency will increase to four per hour later in 1995.

A 'turn up and go' service operates. Passengers buy tickets at the toll booths when they arrive at the terminal and board the next available shuttle. No reservations will be necessary although vouchers can be purchased from travel agents to exchange for tickets at the Shuttle terminal.

Table 11 (Summer) — LONDON - SOUTHERN FRANCE

	TGV 9004 ①-⑥	532 (R)✗	9112 ①-⑥	TGV 634	TGV 634	TGV 540	9132 ⑦	9132 ①-⑥	542	542	TGV 546	9140 ⑦	9034 B	TGV 648
London Waterloo ... d.	...	0657	...	0723	...	...	1214	1227	...	...	1414	1423	...	...
Lille Europe ... a.		0955		1022			1527	1527				1725	1722	
Lille Europe ... d.	...	1029	...	1217	1217	1310	...	...	1610	1610	1750	...	...	1916
Marne la Vallée EuroDisney ... a.		1140				1419			1710	1710	1800			2102
Lyon Part-Dieu ... a.		1332				1612			1912	1912	2053			2258
Lyon Perrache ... a.														2307
Valence ... a.		1410		1543	1543	1657			1957	1957				
Avignon ... a.		1512		1639	1639	1754			2050	2050				
Nîmes ... a.					1715					2125				
Montpellier ... a.					1742					2151				
Marseille St Charles ... a.		1606			1736	1850				2153				
Toulon ... a.		1651												
St Raphael ... a.		1740												
Cannes ... a.		1808												
Antibes ... a.		1817												
Nice ... a.		1835												

	TGV 561 A	9015 ①-⑥	9121 ⑦	TGV 563	TGV 565	566	9027 ①-⑥	9027 ⑦	TGV 573	9153	TGV 575	576	TGV 579	9059
Nice ... d.	...								0940					
Antibes ... d.	...								0954					
Cannes ... d.	...								1005					
St Raphael ... d.	...								1029					
Toulon ... d.	...								1117					
Marseille St Charles ... d.	...				0636				1202		1325		1408	
Montpellier ... d.						0634						1323		
Nîmes ... d.						0700						1348		
Avignon ... d.					0733	0733			1257		1422	1422	1502	
Valence ... d.					0830	0830			1352		1519	1519	1600	
Lyon Perrache ... d.	0613													
Lyon Part-Dieu ... d.	0624								1439				1645	
Marne la Vallée EuroDisney ... d.	0817			0755	0915	0915			1630				1836	
Lille Europe ... a.	0933			0950	1106	1106			1748		1848	1848	2012	
Lille Europe ... d.		1010	1041	1125	1216	1218	1314	1314		1839				2115
London Waterloo ... a.		1109	1143				1413	1430		1939				2213

NOTES

A – ①②③④⑤⑥.

B – ①-⑥ from July 3.

✗ – Supplement payable.

INTERNATIONAL SERVICES FROM BUDAPEST

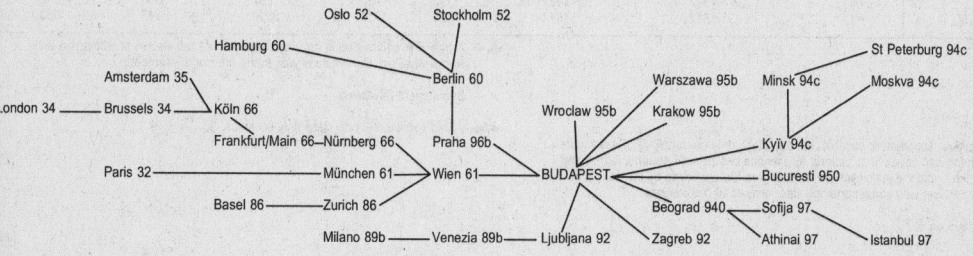

INTERNATIONAL SERVICES FROM PARIS

Table 12 (Summer)   LONDON - BRUSSELS by *Eurostar*

train number	9004	9112		9118	9124		9132	9132			9140	9034		9148		9152	9152
notes (see page 4)	ℝ✕	ℝ✕		ℝ✕	.		✕	ℝ			✕	ℝ✕		ℝ✕		ℝ✕	ℝ✕
notes (see below)												A					
days of running	①–⑥	①–⑥		⑦	①–⑥		⑦	①–⑥			⑦			①–⑦		①–⑤	⑥⑦
London Waterloo........d.	...	0657	0723	...	0857	...	1027	...	1214	1227	...	...	...	1414	1423	...	1627	...	1715	1727
Lille Europe ....a.	...	0955	1022	...		...		...	1527	1527	...	...	...	1725	1722	...		...	2026	2026
Brussels Midi/Zuid ......a.	...	...	1138	...	1317	...	1438	...	1644	1644	...	...	...	...	1838	...	2046	...	2139	2139
Leuven 200 ....a.	...	...	...	...	...	...	...	...	...	...	...	...	...	...	...	...	...	...	...	...
Liège Guillemins 200 ......a.	...	...	...	...	...	...	...	...	...	...	...	...	...	...	...	...	...	...	...	...
Namur 210 ....a.	...	...	...	...	...	...	...	...	...	...	...	...	...	...	...	...	...	...	...	...
Luxembourg 210 ....a.	...	...	...	...	...	...	...	...	...	...	...	...	...	...	...	...	...	...	...	...

train number	9113		9015		9121		9125		9129	9027	9027	9133	9141		9153		9159		9059
notes (see page 4)	ℝ✕		ℝ✕		ℝ✕		ℝ✕		ℝ✕	ℝ✕	ℝ✕	ℝ✕	ℝ✕		ℝ✕		ℝ✕		ℝ✕
days of running	①–⑥		①–⑥		⑦		①–⑥		⑦	①–⑥	⑦	①–⑥	⑦		①–⑦		①–⑦		①–⑦
Luxembourg 210 ....d.	...	...	...	...	...	...	...	...	...	...	...	...	...	...	...	...	...	...	...
Namur 210 ....d.	...	...	...	...	...	...	...	...	...	...	...	...	...	...	...	...	...	...	...
Liège Guillemins 200 ......d.	...	...	...	...	...	...	...	...	...	...	...	...	...	...	...	...	...	...	...
Leuven 200 ....d.	...	...	...	...	...	...	...	...	...	...	...	...	...	...	...	...	...	...	...
Brussels Midi/Zuid ......d.	0731	...	...	...	0928	...	1028	...	1128	...	...	1233	1428	...	1722	...	1856	...	...
Lille Europe ....d.	0844	...	1010	...	1041	...	1141	...	1244	1314	1314			...	1839	...		...	2115
London Waterloo........a.	0943	...	1109	...	1143	...	1239	...	1347	1413	1430	1443	1643	...	1939	...	2109	...	2213

For connections to and from Manchester and Edinburgh, see below Table 10.

LONDON - BRUSSELS by *rail and sea*

train number		512			515			517			439			520			413	
notes (see page 4)		ℝ		ℝ	ℝ			ℝ			ℝ			ℝ			ℝ	
notes (see below)					✕			✕						✕			D ✕		
sea crossing		J		⛴	J			J			⛴			J			J		⛴
London Victoria........d.	...	0805	...	0805	1105	...	1305	...	...	1105	...	...	1605	...	...	1813e	2205	...
Ramsgate ♣ ....a.	...	0947	...	0947	1247	...	1447	...	...	1247	...	...	1751	...	...	2013	2358	...
Ramsgate Port ♣ 🚌 ......d.	...	1025	...	1030	1330	...	1530	...	...	1345	...	...	1830	...	...	2055	0045	...
Oostende 🚢 ....a.	...	1305	...	1600	1605	...	1805	...	...	1830	...	...	2105	...	...	2330	0530	...
Oostende ....d.	...	...	1334	...	...	1634	...	1834	...	...	1934	...	2134	...	...	...	...	0634
Brugge ....a.	...	...	1348	...	...	1648	...	1848	...	...	1948	...	2148	...	...	...	...	0648
Gent Sint Pieters........a.	...	...	1412	...	...	1712	...	1912	...	...	2012	...	2212	...	...	...	...	0712
Brussels Midi..........a.	...	...	1443	...	...	1743	...	1943	...	...	2043	...	2243	...	...	...	...	0743
Brussels Nord..........a.	...	...	1455	...	...	1755	...	1955	...	...	2055	...	2257	...	...	...	...	0755

train number	529		530			412		534				422		540			438	
notes (see page 4)	ℝ		ℝ			ℝ		ℝ		ℝ		ℝ		ℝ			ℝ	
notes (see below)						✕		✕				✕		D ✕				
sea crossing	J		⛴			J		J		⛴		J		J			⛴	
Brussels Nord ....d.	0647	...	0747	...	...	0947	...	1147	...	...	...	1447	...	1747	...	...	2247	...
Brussels Midi ....d.	0659	...	0759	...	...	0959	...	1159	...	...	...	1459	...	1759	...	...	2259	...
Gent Sint Pieters........d.	0730	...	0830	...	...	1030	...	1230	...	...	...	1530	...	1830	...	...	2330	...
Brugge ....d.	0754	...	0854	...	...	1054	...	1254	...	...	...	1554	...	1854	...	...	2354	...
Oostende ....a.	0809	...	0909	...	...	1109	...	1309	...	...	...	1609	...	1909	...	...	0009	...
Oostende ....d.	...	0825	...	0945	...	...	1150	...	1345	1350	...	...	1655	...	1930	...	...	0030
Ramsgate Port ♣ 🚌 ......d.	...	0900	...	1245	...	...	1225	...	1420	1645	...	...	1730	...	2005	...	...	0330
Ramsgate ♣ ....d.	...	0932	...	1332	...	...	1332	...	1532	1732	...	...	1832	...	2055	...	...	0437
London Victoria........a.	...	1117	...	1517	...	...	1517	...	1723	1917	...	...	2019	...	2247	...	...	0630

NOTES

A – ①-⑥ from July 3.

D – June 30 – Sept. 3.

J – Jetfoil service, supplement payable, ℝ, one class only on Jetfoil, ☾. Passengers from London can check-in at Victoria 60 minutes before train departs. When bad weather interrupts the Jetfoil service, passengers are conveyed by the next available car-ferry service, with correspondingly later arrivals at destinations.

e – Depart 1805 on ⑥⑦.

♣ – A free 🚌 connection is provided between the rail station at Ramsgate and Ramsgate Port. Connections with trains are not guaranteed.

✕ – Supplement payable.

🚢 – Ship service, ℝ, one class only on ships, ✕.

Table 15 (Summer) — LONDON - AMSTERDAM by *Eurostar*

Station	9112	2484		9132	9132	285	2490		9140	287	2492		9148	2493	
train type															
notes (see page 4)	Ⓡ✕			Ⓡ✕	Ⓡ✕	Y			Ⓡ✕				Ⓡ✕	✕	
notes	①-⑥			⑦	①-⑥					⑦					
London Waterloo d.	0723			1214	1227				1414				1627		
Lille Europe d.	1022			1527	1527				1725						
Brussels Midi/Zuid a.	1138			1644	1644				1838				2046		
Brussels Midi/Zuid d.		1210				1754	1810			1956	2010			2110	
Brussels Nord/Noord d.		1219				1801	1819			2004	2019			2119	
Antwerpen Berchem a.		1246				1832	1846			2035	2046			2148	
Antwerpen Centraal a.		1254					1854			2057				2200	
Roosendaal a.		1323	1325			1911	1923	1925		2102	2126	2125		2226	2228
Breda a.			1343					1943				2143			2245
Tilburg a.			1409					2009				2209			2309
's-Hertogenbosch a.			1425					2025				2225			2325
Nijmegen a.			1457					2057				2257			2357
Arnhem a.			1512					2112				2312			0013
Dordrecht a.		1345					1945				2148			2249	
Rotterdam CS a.		1401	1437			1950	2001	2037		2138	2203	2237		2305	
Utrecht a.			1513					2113				2313			
Amersfoort a.			1537					2137				2337			
Zwolle a.			1614					2214				0033			
Groningen a.															
Den Haag HS a.		1420				2009	2021			2156	2220			2323	
Leiden a.		1433					2033				2233			2334	
Amsterdam Centraal a.		1508				2102	2108			2248	2308			0010	

Station			2455	9121			2458	EC 82	9133			2464	9159
train type													
notes (see page 4)				Ⓡ✕				✕✓	Ⓡ✕				Ⓡ✕
notes			①-⑤	⑦					①-⑥				
Amsterdam Centraal d.							0825	0853				1425	
Leiden d.							0900					1500	
Den Haag HS d.							0912	0933				1512	
Groningen d.	0613									1218			
Zwolle d.	0713									1319			
Amersfoort d.	0757									1357			
Utrecht d.	0817									1417			
Rotterdam CS d.			0624		0855		0932	0953		1532		1455	
Dordrecht d.			0639				0948			1548			
Arnhem d.						0821					1421		
Nijmegen d.		0530				0838					1438		
's-Hertogenbosch d.		0608				0909					1509		
Tilburg d.		0624				0925					1525		
Breda d.		0647				0949					1549		
Roosendaal d.		0705	0714			1007					1614	1607	
Antwerpen Centraal d.			0749				1014	1032				1649	
Antwerpen Berchem d.			0753					1049				1653	
Brussels Nord/Noord d.			0823				1053	1059				1723	
Brussels Midi/Zuid a.			0835				1123	1132				1730	
Brussels Midi/Zuid d.				0928					1233				1856
Lille Europe a.				1041									
London Waterloo a.				1143					1443				2109

LONDON - AMSTERDAM by *Rail and Sea*

Station	🚢 366			🚢 362 Ⓡ		
London Liverpool Street d.	0925			1900		
Harwich Parkeston Quay d.	1045	1130		2020	2130	
Hoek van Holland a.	1900	1945		0700	0750	
Schiedam-Rotterdam West a.		2005				
Rotterdam CS a.				0815		
Den Haag HS a.		2025		0839		
Leiden a.						
Amsterdam Centraal a.		2117		0925		

Station	🚢 367			🚢 363 Ⓡ		
Amsterdam Centraal d.	0955			1955		
Leiden d.						
Den Haag HS d.	1036			2036		
Rotterdam CS d.						
Schiedam-Rotterdam West d.	1055			2055		
Hoek van Holland d.	1113	1200		2113	2200	
Harwich Parkeston Quay a.		1800	1915		0700	0750
London Liverpool Street a.		2035			0905	

NOTES
✓ – Supplement payable.

INTERNATIONAL SERVICES FROM AMSTERDAM

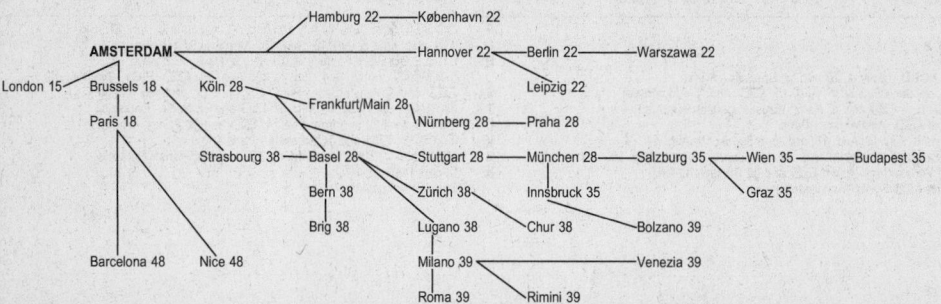

Table 18 (Summer) AMSTERDAM - BRUSSELS - PARIS

train type		TGV												EC								TGV			EC
train number		80	2454	482	482	2455	2455	2456	1182	282	2457		2458	82		2459	2460		284		2461	88		2462	38
notes (see page 4)		Ⓡ	①-⑥			⑥⑦	①-⑤							Ⓡ								Ⓡ			
notes (see below)		V ⚡		H	J				B	S				C ⚡								V ⚡			E ⚡
Amsterdam Centraal . d.	...	...	...	...	...	...	...	0623	...	0657	0725	...	0825	0853	...	0925	1025	...	1052	...	1125	...	...	1225	...
A'dam Schiphol ✈ .... d.	...	...	...	...	...	...	...	0643	...	|	0743	...	0843	|	...	0943	1043	...	|	...	1143	...	...	1243	...
Leiden .... d.	...	...	...	...	...	...	...	0700	...	|	0800	...	0900	|	...	1000	1100	...	|	...	1200	...	...	1300	...
Den Haag HS............. d.	...	...	...	...	...	...	...	0712	...	0741	0812	...	0912	0933	...	1012	1112	...	1136	...	1212	...	...	1312	...
Rotterdam CS .... d.	...	...	0527	...	...	0624	0624	0732	...	0804	0832	...	0932	0953	...	1032	1132	...	1204	...	1232	...	...	1332	...
Dordrecht .... d.	...	...	0543	...	...	0639	0639	0748	...	|	0848	...	0948	|	...	1048	1148	...	|	...	1248	...	...	1348	...
Roosendaal 🏛 .... d.	...	...	0614	...	...	0714	0714	0814	...	0848	0914	...	1014	1032	...	1114	1214	...	1247	...	1314	...	...	1414	...
Antwerpen Centraal . d.	...	...	0649	...	...	0749	0749	0849	...	|	0949	...	1049	|	...	1149	1249	...	|	...	1349	...	...	1449	...
Antwerpen Berchem.... d.	...	...	0653	...	...	0753	0753	0853	...	0914	0953	...	1053	1059	...	1153	1253	...	1315	...	1353	...	...	1453	...
Brussels Nord/Noord d.	...	...	0723	0744	0744	0823	0828	0923	...	0945	1023	...	1123	1132	...	1223	1323	...	1346	...	1423	...	...	1523	1550
Brussels Midi/Zuid .... a.	...	...	0730	0750	0750	0830	0835	0930	...	0951	1030	...	1130	1137	...	1230	1330	...	1352	...	1430	...	...	1530	1556
Brussels Midi/Zuid .... d.	...	0704	...	0800	0800	...	...	...	0954	1006	...	...	...	1154	...	...	...	...	1413	...	...	1504	...	...	1600
Mons (🏛 = Quevy) .... d.	...	|	...	0841	0841	...	...	...	|	1044	...	...	...	|	...	...	...	...	1450	...	...	|	...	...	1639
Lille Europe............. a.	...	0826	...	|	|	...	...	...	|	|	...	...	...	|	...	...	...	...	|	...	...	|	...	...	|
St. Quentin.................. a.	...	|	...	|	0952	...	...	...	|	1141	...	...	...	|	...	...	...	...	1553	...	...	|	...	...	1748
Paris Nord.................. a.	...	0938	...	1055	1115	...	...	...	1247	1258	...	...	...	1425	...	...	...	...	1708	...	...	1740	...	...	1859

train type			TGV				TGV																		
train number		2463	84		2464		86	2465	286		2466	280		2467		2468	2469		2470		2471		288		
notes (see page 4)			Ⓡ				Ⓡ 🍴					🍸													
notes (see below)			V ⚡				⚡		M														G		
Amsterdam Centraal . d.	...	1325	...	...	1425	...	...	1525	1552	...	1625	...	...	1724	...	1825	1925	...	2025	...	2125	...	2215	...	...
A'dam Schiphol ✈ .... d.	...	1343	...	...	1443	...	...	1543	|	...	1643	...	...	1743	...	1843	1943	...	2043	...	2143	...	|	...	...
Leiden .... d.	...	1400	...	...	1500	...	...	1600	|	...	1700	...	...	1800	...	1900	2000	...	2100	...	2200	...	|	...	...
Den Haag HS............. d.	...	1412	...	...	1512	...	...	1612	1636	...	1712	...	...	1812	...	1912	2012	...	2112	...	2212	...	2307	...	...
Rotterdam CS .... d.	...	1432	...	...	1532	...	...	1632	1658	...	1732	...	...	1832	...	1932	2032	...	2132	...	2232	...	2334	...	...
Dordrecht .... d.	...	1448	...	...	1548	...	...	1648	|	...	1748	...	...	1848	...	1948	2048	...	2148	...	2248	...	|	...	...
Roosendaal 🏛 .... d.	...	1514	...	...	1614	...	...	1714	1743	...	1814	...	...	1914	...	2014	2114	...	2214	...	2314	...	0025	...	...
Antwerpen Centraal . d.	...	1549	...	...	1649	...	...	1749	|	...	1849	...	...	1949	...	2049	2149	...	2249	...	2343	...	|	...	...
Antwerpen Berchem.... d.	...	1553	...	...	1653	...	...	1753	1812	...	1853	...	...	1953	...	2053	2153	...	2253	...	...	...	0054	...	...
Brussels Nord/Noord d.	...	1623	...	...	1723	...	...	1823	1845	...	1923	...	...	2026	...	2123	2223	...	2326	...	...	...	0127	...	...
Brussels Midi/Zuid .... a.	...	1630	...	...	1730	...	...	1830	1851	...	1930	...	...	2030	...	2130	2230	...	2330	...	...	...	0134	...	...
Brussels Midi/Zuid .... d.	...	...	1704	...	...	...	1834	...	1907	...	...	2004	...	...	...	...	...	...	...	...	...	...	0153	...	...
Mons (🏛 = Quevy) .... d.	...	...	|	...	...	...	|	...	1946	...	...	2042	...	...	...	...	...	...	...	...	...	...	0232	...	...
Lille Europe............. a.	...	...	1818	...	...	...	1946	...	|	...	...	|	...	...	...	...	...	...	...	...	...	...	|	...	...
St. Quentin.................. a.	...	...	|	...	...	...	|	...	2048	...	...	|	...	...	...	...	...	...	...	...	...	...	|	...	...
Paris Nord.................. a.	...	...	1929	...	...	...	2105	...	2205	...	...	2259	...	...	...	...	...	...	...	...	...	...	0656	...	...

train type					TGV													TGV			TGV				
train number	2478	2479	2480	2481	81		2482		281	2483		2484		2485	483		283	83		2486	89	2487			2488
notes (see page 4)	①-⑥				Ⓡ				🍸									Ⓡ			Ⓡ				
notes (see below)					V ⚡										A		X	U ⚡			T ⚡				
Paris Nord.................. d.	...	...	...	...	0707	...	...	...	0752	...	...	...	...	...	1008	...	1023	1052	...	...	1152	...	...	...	...
St. Quentin.................. d.	...	...	...	...	|	...	...	...	0908	...	...	...	...	...	1122	...	1136	|	...	...	|	...	...	...	...
Lille Europe............. d.	...	...	...	...	0817	...	...	...	|	...	...	...	...	...	|	...	|	1201	...	...	1301	...	...	...	...
Mons (🏛 = Quevy) .... d.	...	...	...	...	|	...	...	...	1010	...	...	...	...	...	1234	...	1239	|	...	...	|	...	...	...	...
Brussels Midi/Zuid .... a.	...	...	...	...	0934	...	...	...	1049	...	...	...	...	...	1315	...	1318	1312	...	...	1415	...	...	...	...
Brussels Midi/Zuid .... d.	0610	0710	0810	0910	...	...	1010	...	1104	1110	...	1210	...	1310	...	...	1329	...	...	1410	...	1510	...	...	1610
Brussels Nord/Noord d.	0619	0719	0819	0919	...	...	1019	...	1112	1119	...	1219	...	1319	...	...	1337	...	...	1419	...	1519	...	...	1619
Antwerpen Berchem.... d.	0646	0746	0846	0946	...	...	1046	...	1147	1146	...	1246	...	1346	...	...	1409	...	...	1446	...	1546	...	...	1646
Antwerpen Centraal . d.	0654	0754	0854	0954	...	...	1054	...	|	1154	...	1254	...	1354	...	...	|	...	...	1454	...	1554	...	...	1654
Roosendaal 🏛 .... d.	0723	0824	0923	1023	...	...	1123	...	1215	1224	...	1323	...	1423	...	...	1442	...	...	1523	...	1623	...	...	1723
Dordrecht .... a.	0745	0845	0945	1045	...	...	1145	...	|	1246	...	1345	...	1445	...	...	|	...	...	1545	...	1645	...	...	1745
Rotterdam CS .... a.	0804	0901	1001	1101	...	...	1201	...	1256	1302	...	1401	...	1501	...	...	1526	...	...	1601	...	1701	...	...	1801
Den Haag HS............. a.	0823	0920	1020	1120	...	...	1220	...	1317	1321	...	1420	...	1520	...	...	1550	...	...	1620	...	1720	...	...	1820
Leiden .... a.	0833	0933	1033	1133	...	...	1233	...	|	1334	...	1433	...	1533	...	...	|	...	...	1633	...	1733	...	...	1833
A'dam Schiphol ✈ .... a.	0849	0949	1049	1149	...	...	1249	...	|	1350	...	1449	...	1549	...	...	|	...	...	1649	...	1749	...	...	1849
Amsterdam Centraal . a.	0908	1008	1108	1208	...	...	1308	...	1402	1408	...	1508	...	1608	...	...	1634	...	...	1708	...	1808	...	...	1908

train number		EC										TGV					EC								1289
train number		39	2489		285	2490		2491		287		85	2492		2493		87		2494		487	487	2495		289
notes (see page 4)					🍸							Ⓡ					Ⓡ				🍴	🍴			
notes (see below)		E ⚡										V ⚡					R ⚡				P	Q			N
Paris Nord.................. d.	...	1346	...	...	1433b	...	...	...	...	1636	...	1725	...	...	...	...	1839	...	...	...	1926	1941	...	...	2322
St. Quentin.................. d.	...	1458	...	...	1604	...	...	...	...	1751	...	|	...	...	...	...	|	...	...	...	2048	|	...	...	0125
Lille Europe............. d.	...	|	...	...	|	...	...	...	...	|	...	|	...	...	...	...	|	...	...	...	|	|	...	...	|
Mons (🏛 = Quevy) .... d.	...	1606	...	...	1702	...	...	...	...	1903	...	|	...	...	...	...	|	...	...	...	2151	2151	...	...	0353
Brussels Midi/Zuid .... a.	...	1645	...	...	1742	...	...	...	...	1942	...	2001	...	...	...	...	2110	...	...	...	2230	2230	...	...	0432
Brussels Midi/Zuid .... d.	...	1655	1710	...	1754	1810	...	1910	...	1956	...	...	2010	...	2110	...	2120	...	2210	...	2239	2239	2310	...	0449
Brussels Nord/Noord d.	...	1701	1719	...	1801	1819	...	1919	...	2004	...	...	2019	...	2119	...	2127	...	2219	...	2246	2246	2319	...	0457
Antwerpen Berchem.... d.	...	...	1746	...	1832	1846	...	1946	...	2035	...	...	2046	...	2146	...	2157	...	2246	...	...	...	2346	...	0531
Antwerpen Centraal . d.	...	...	1754	...	|	1854	...	1954	...	|	...	...	2057	...	2200	...	|	...	2254	...	...	...	2354	...	|
Roosendaal 🏛 .... d.	...	...	1823	...	1911	1923	...	2023	...	2102	...	...	2126	...	2228	...	2225	...	2323	...	...	...	0023	...	0602
Dordrecht .... a.	...	...	1845	...	|	1945	...	2045	...	|	...	...	2148	...	2249	...	|	...	2345	...	...	...	0045	...	|
Rotterdam CS .... a.	...	...	1901	...	1950	2001	...	2101	...	2138	...	...	2203	...	2305	...	2301	...	0001	...	...	...	0107	...	0647
Den Haag HS............. a.	...	...	1920	...	2009	2021	...	2120	...	2156	...	...	2220	...	2323	...	2319	...	...	...	...	...	...	...	0707
Leiden .... a.	...	...	1933	...	|	2033	...	2133	...	|	...	...	2233	...	2334	...	|	...	...	...	...	...	...	...	|
A'dam Schiphol ✈ .... a.	...	...	1949	...	|	2049	...	2149	...	|	...	...	2249	...	2350	...	|	...	...	...	...	...	...	...	|
Amsterdam Centraal . a.	...	...	2008	...	2102	2108	...	2208	...	2248	...	...	2308	...	0010	...	2359	...	...	...	...	...	...	...	0802

NOTES:

- **A** – July 1 - Sept. 3.
- **B** – July 1 - Sept. 4.
- **C** – ETOILE DU NORD – daily: [12] and 🍴 Brussels - Paris; ①②③④⑤⑥, not June 5, July 15, Aug. 15: [12] and 🍸 Amsterdam - Paris.
- **E** – JACQUES BREL – [12] and 🍴 Paris - Brussels - (Dortmund) and v.v.
- **G** – 🛏 1,2 cl. and [12] Amsterdam - Paris.
- **H** – ①⑥, also June 6, July 14, Aug. 16; not June 5, July 15, Aug. 14.
- **J** – ②③④⑤⑦, also June 5, July 15, Aug. 14; not June 6, July 14, Aug. 16.
- **M** – [12] and 🍸 Amsterdam - Paris; [12] and 🍴 Brussels - Paris.
- **N** – 🛏 1,2 cl. and [12] Paris - Amsterdam.
- **P** – ①②③④⑥, also June 4, July 14, Aug. 13; not June 5, July 13, Aug. 15.
- **Q** – ⑤⑦, also June 5, July 13, Aug. 15; June 4, July 14, Aug. 13.
- **R** – ETOILE DU NORD – daily: [12] and 🍴 Paris - Brussels; ①②③④⑤⑦, not June 4, July 14 and Aug. 14: [12] Paris - Amsterdam.
- **S** – [12] and 🍸 Amsterdam - Paris; [12] and 🍴 Brussels - Paris.
- **T** – ①②③④⑤, daily July 1 - Sept. 3: [12] and 🍴 Paris - Brussels.
- **U** – Daily to June 30 and from Sept. 4: [12] and 🍴 Paris - Brussels.
- **V** – ①②③④⑤: [12] and 🍴 Brussels - Paris and v.v.
- **X** – [12] and 🍸 Paris - Amsterdam; [12] and 🍴 Paris - Brussels.
- **b** – Depart 1445 on ⑥⑦.
- ⚡ - Supplement payable.

For explanation of standard symbols see page 4.

Table 20 (Summer) LONDON AND BRUSSELS - KÖLN

EC = EuroCity. Train numbers in the 9000 series are Eurostar services.

	411	413	417	419	9112	47 (EC)	425	9124	429	39 (EC)	9132	9132	35 (EC)	233	9140	517	37 (EC)	50 (EC)	439	9148	225
notes (see page 4)					①-⑥	✕R A✗		①-⑥		✕✗ B	⑦	✕R ①-⑥	✕✗ C		✕R ⑦		✕✗ D	✕✗		R	F
London Waterloo 12 d.					0723			1027			1214	1227			1414					1627	
Lille Europe d.					1022						1527	1527			1725						
Oostende d.	0532	0634	0834	0934			1234		1434				1657	1734		1834			1934		2013
Brugge d.	0548	0650	0850	0950			1250		1450				1712	1750		1850			1950		2028
Gent Sint Pieters d.	0617	0715	0915	1015			1315		1515				1736	1815		1915			2015		2054
Brussels Midi/Zuid a.	0645	0745	0945	1045	1138		1345	1438	1545	1644	1644		1804	1843	1838	1945			2045	2046	2122
Brussels Midi/Zuid d.	0647	0748	0948	1048		1207	1348		1548	1655			1808	1847		1947	2003		2048		2126
Brussels Nord/Noord d.	0657	0757	0957	1057		1216	1357		1557	1703			1817	1857		1957	2012		2057		2134
Leuven d.	0717	0817	1017	1117			1417		1617					1917		2017			2117		
Liège Guillemins a.	0800	0900	1100	1200		1317	1500		1700	1803			1913	2000		2056	2113		2200		2235
Aachen a.	0843	0943	1143	1243		1355	1543		1743	1845			1955	2043			2151		2243		2318
Düren a.	0913	1013	1213	1313			1613		1813										2313		
Köln a.	0942	1042	1242	1342		1442	1642		1842	1942			2042	2116			2242	2155	2342		0017
Düsseldorf 700 a.						1531				2016			2116	2224			2331				
Duisburg a.						1544				2031			2132	2240			2344				
Essen 700 a.						1557				2046			2145	2253			2357				
Dortmund 700 a.						1619				2110			2209				0019				

	224	113 (EC)	36 (EC)	9121	412	9125	232	34 (EC)	9133	420	422	38 (EC)	426	9153	46 (EC)	9159	430	434	438
notes (see page 4)	F	✕✗	✕R D✗	✕R ⑦		R ①-⑥		✕ C✗	✕R ①-⑥			✕✗ B		R	✕R	✕R A			
Dortmund 700 d.			0511									1148			1339				
Essen 700 d.			0535				0654		0812			1212			1401				
Duisburg d.			0549				0708		0825			1225			1414				
Düsseldorf 700 d.			0604				0732		0840			1240			1428				
Köln Hbf d.	0508	0626	0630		0714	0739	0802		0914	1114	1214	1314	1414		1514		1614	1814	2014
Düren d.					0739					1139	1239		1439				1639		
Aachen a.	0606		0710		0805		0905		1001	1205	1305	1410	1505		1607		1705	1905	2105
Liège Guillemins a.	0647		0749		0843		0943		1036	1243	1343	1449	1543		1647		1743	1943	2143
Leuven a.					0924		1024			1324	1424		1624				1824	2024	2224
Brussels Nord/Noord a.	0755		0850		0944		1044		1132	1344	1444	1548	1644		1749		1844	2044	2244
Brussels Midi/Zuid a.	0804	0901			0955		1055		1142	1355	1455	1556	1655		1801		1855	2055	2255
Brussels Midi/Zuid d.	0809			0928	0959	1028	1059	1145	1233	1359	1459		1722	1659		1856	1859	2059	2259
Gent Sint Pieters a.	0838				1027		1127	1212		1427	1527		1727				1927	2127	2327
Brugge a.	0903				1052		1152	1234		1452	1552		1752				1952	2152	2352
Oostende a.	0918				1109		1209	1248		1509	1609		1809				2009	2209	0009
Lille Europe a.				1041		1141								1839		2109			
London Waterloo 12 a.				1143		1239		1443						1939		2109			

NOTES

A – ALEXANDER VON HUMBOLDT – 🚃 and ✕ Brussels - Berlin and v.v., supplement payable in Germany.

B – JACQUES BREL – 🚃 and ✕ (Paris) - Brussels - Dortmund and v.v., supplement payable in Germany.

C – MEMLING – 🚃 and ⑨ Oostende - Dortmund and v.v., supplement payable in Germany.

D – FELIX TIMMERMANS – 🚃 and ✕ Brussels - Köln and v.v., supplement payable in Germany.

F – Second class seats only.

✗ – Supplement payable.

INTERNATIONAL SERVICES FROM LONDON AND BRUSSELS

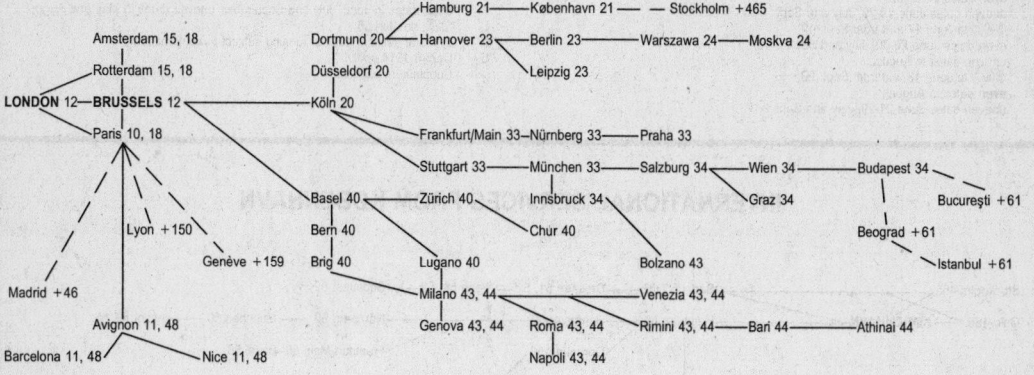

Table 21 (Summer) — LONDON AND BRUSSELS - HAMBURG AND KØBENHAVN

train type / number	IC 411	826	413	IC 526	EC 186	417	IC 524	419	IC 522	EC 188	9112	EC 47	IC 620	425	IC 520	9124	429	IC 724	EC 39	EC 26	9132	233	IN 384	IN 288
notes											①-⑥					①-⑥						D		
London Waterloo 12 d.											0723					1027					1227b			
Lille Europe 12 d.											1022										1527			
Oostende 12 d.	0532		0634			0834		0934						1234			1434					1734		
Brugge d.	0548		0650			0850		0950						1250			1450					1750		
Gent St. Pieters d.	0617		0715			0915		1015						1315			1515					1815		
Brussels Midi/Zuid d.	0647		0748			0947		1047			1138	1207		1347		1438	1547		1655		1644	1847		
Brussels Nord/Noord d.	0657		0757			0957		1057				1216		1357	1500		1557		1703			1857		
Liège Guillemins d.	0800		0900			1100		1200				1317		1500			1700		1803			2000		
Aachen d.	0843		0943			1143		1243				1355			1543		1743		1845			2106		
Köln d.	0942	1010	1042	1110		1242	1310	1342	1409			1442	1510	1642	1709		1842	1909	1942	2010		2200		
Münster a.		1154		1254			1454		1554				1654		1854			2054		2154		2350		
Osnabrück a.		1219		1319			1519		1619				1719		1919			2119		2219		0020		
Bremen Hbf a.		1312		1412			1612		1712				1812		2012			2212		2312		0127		
Hamburg Hbf 50 a.		1407		1507	1512		1707		1807	1827			1907		2107			2307		0007		0235		
Hamburg Altona a.		1421		1521			1721		1821				1921		2121			2321		0021				
Lübeck a.					1550					1902												0330		
Rødby ⛴ a.					1800					2100												0600		
Nykøbing a.					1837					2131														
København 50 a.					2020					2259												0830	0948	0948
Stockholm C a.																								1741
Göteborg C a.																							1435	
Oslo S a.																							1952	

train type / number	IC 727	EC 420	EC 29	422	IC 621	EC 38	EC 729	426	9153	IC 521	EC 46	9159	IC 823	430	EC 189	IC 625	434	EC 187	IC 827	438	IN 385	IN 33	232	9133
notes	L																				D	D		①-⑥
Oslo S d.																					1015			
Göteborg C d.																					1525			
Stockholm C d.																						1212		
København 50 d.															0730	0920					2018	2058	2105	
Nykøbing d.															0902	1057							2246	
Rødby ⛴ d.															0925	1130							2330	
Lübeck d.															1143	1346							0212	
Hamburg Altona d.	0638		0738		0838		0938			1038			1138				1338			1538				
Hamburg Hbf 50 d.	0653		0753		0853		0953			1053			1153		1223	1353	1428	1553					0312	
Bremen d.	0747		0847		0947		1047			1147			1247		1341	1447		1647					0420	
Osnabrück d.	0841		0941		1041		1141			1241			1341		1441	1541		1741					0532	
Münster d.	0906		1006		1106		1206			1306			1406			1606		1806					0603	
Köln Hbf a.	1050	1114	1150	1214	1250	1314	1350	1414		1514	1550		1614		1750	1814		1950	2014				0757	
Aachen a.		1205		1305		1410		1505			1600			1705			1905		2105				0848	
Liège Guillemins a.		1243		1343		1449		1543			1648			1743			1943		2143				0943	
Brussels Nord/Noord a.		1344		1444		1548		1644			1749			1844			2044		2244				1044	
Brussels Midi/Zuid a.		1355		1455		1556		1655	1722		1801	1856		1855			2055		2255				1055	1233
Gent St. Pieters a.		1427		1527				1728						1927			2127		2327				1127	
Brugge a.		1452		1552				1752						1952			2209						1152	
Oostende a.		1509		1609				1809						2009			0009						1209	
Lille Europe a.									1839															
London Waterloo 12 a.									1939			2109												1443

LONDON - HAMBURG AND KØBENHAVN by Sea

446

	B	B ℝ	C ℝ	E	E ℝ
London Liverpool Street d.	1425			1325	
Harwich Parkston Quay d.	1545			1445	
Harwich Parkston Quay d.		1700			1530
Hamburg Fischereihafen a.					1300
Esbjerg Havn a.		1345			
Esbjerg Havn d.			1420		
Odense a.			1610		
København a.			1848		

445

	A ℝ	A ℝ	B	F ℝ	E
København d.	1252				
Odense d.	1535				
Esbjerg Havn a.	1725				
Esbjerg Havn d.			1800		
Hamburg Fischereihfn d.				1630	
Harwich Parkston Quay a.		1230		1200	
Harwich Parkston Quay a.			1305		1305
London Liverpool Street a.			1430		1430

NOTES

A – ①③⑤ to June 16 and from Sept. 18,
　　even dates in August,
　　uneven dates June 19-29, July and Sept. 1-15.
B – ②④⑥ to June 17 and from Sept. 19,
　　even dates June 20-30, July and Sept. 2-16;
　　uneven dates in August.
C – ③⑤⑦ to June 18 and from Sept. 20,
　　even dates in August;
　　uneven dates June 21-29, July and Sept 1-17.

D – NORD EXPRESS –
　　1,2 cl. (T2), 2 cl. and Oostende - København and v.v.
E – Even dates in May and August; uneven dates in June, July and September.
F – Even dates in June, July and September; uneven dates in May and August.
L – ①-⑥, not June 5.
P – Eurostar service, days of running subject to confirmation.
b – Depart 1214 on ⑦.
✗ – Supplement payable.

INTERNATIONAL SERVICES FROM KØBENHAVN

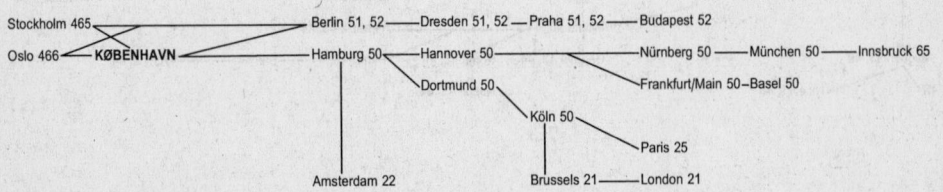

Table 22 (Summer)   AMSTERDAM - HAMBURG AND BERLIN

train type			IC	EC	IR				IC	IC	IR				IC	EC	IR			EC
train number	521	2341	737	43	2449	529	2343	2243	826	504	2741	545	2345	2245	522	47	2647	561	2347	28
notes (see page 4)	Ⓐ	✗		✗Ⓡ	✗		Ⓑ	✗	✗	✗	✗		Ⓑ	✗	✗	✗	✗		✗	✗
Amsterdam Schiphol d.			0648				0848	0848					1248	1248					1648	
Amsterdam Centraal d.		0714					0914	0914					1314	1314					1714	
Rotterdam CS d.	0637					0837						1237						1637		
Utrecht CS d.	0722					0922						1322						1719		
Amersfoort d.	0737	0750				0937	0950	0950				1337	1350	1350				1737	1750	
Duisburg d.																				
Hengelo d.		0858					1058	1058					1458	1458					1858	
Bad Bentheim a.		0914					1114	1114					1514	1514					1914	
Rheine a.		0936					1136	1136					1536	1536					1936	
Osnabrück a.		1002	1021				1202	1202	1221				1602	1602	1621				2002	2021
Bremen Hbf a.			1112						1312						1712				2112	
Hamburg Hbf a.			1207						1407						1807				2207	
Hamburg Altona a.									1421						1821				2221	
Rødby a.																				
København 50 a.																				
Hannover Hbf a.			1113				1313	1313		1403			1713	1713		1803			2113	
Braunschweig a.			1153					1353		1441				1753		1841				
Magdeburg a.			1255		1334			1455		1527	1534			1855		1927	1934			
Halle a.					1426					1626						2026				
Leipzig a.					1454					1654						2054				
Potsdam Stadt a.		1418						1641						2018						
Berlin Zoo a.		1440c					1655c	1702					2058	2042						
Berlin Hbf a.				1621																
Warszawa Centralna 56 a.				2232																

train type		EC					EC
train number	569	153	233	1237	1783	341	41
notes (see page 4)		✗	M	N		B	✗Ⓡ
Amsterdam Schiphol d.							
Amsterdam Centraal d.		1906		2014			2240
Rotterdam CS d.	1837				2207		
Utrecht CS d.	1913	1935			2252		
Amersfoort d.				2052	2307	2320	
Duisburg d.		2106	2242				
Hengelo d.				2214		0037	
Bad Bentheim d.				2234		0056	
Rheine d.				2315		0125	
Osnabrück a.			0020			0157	
Bremen Hbf a.			0127	0046			
Hamburg Hbf a.			0235	0150			
Hamburg Altona a.							
Rødby a.			0600	0500			
København 50 a.			0825	0730			
Hannover Hbf a.						0325	
Braunschweig a.						0434	
Magdeburg a.						0525	
Halle a.							
Leipzig a.							
Potsdam Stadt a.							
Berlin Zoo a.						0724	
Berlin Hbf a.							0817
Warszawa Centralna 56 a.							1440

train type	EC	IR		IR	EC	IC	IR	IR
train number	27	2346	1730	2744	109	729	2244	1746
notes (see page 4)	✗	✗		✗	✗	✗	①-⑥ ⑦	✗
Warszawa Centralna 56 d.								
Berlin Hbf d.								
Berlin Zoo d.							0701	0727
Potsdam Stadt d.								0747
Leipzig d.				0702				
Halle d.				0730				
Magdeburg d.				0823	0830		0916	
Braunschweig d.					0918		1003	
Hannover Hbf d.		0647			0957	1047	1047	
København 50 d.								
Rødby d.								
Hamburg Altona d.	0538				0938			
Hamburg Hbf d.	0553				0953			
Bremen Hbf d.	0647				1047			
Osnabrück d.	0739	0757			1141	1157	1157	
Rheine d.		0822				1222	1222	
Bad Bentheim d.		0843				1243	1243	
Hengelo a.		0901				1301	1301	
Duisburg d.								
Amersfoort a.		1011	1027			1411	1411	1427
Utrecht a.			1043					1443
Rotterdam CS a.			1125					1525
Amsterdam Centraal a.		1048				1448	1448	
Amsterdam Schiphol a.		1114				1514	1514	

train type	IR	IC	IC	IR	IR		EC	IR	IC	IR		EC				EC		
train number	2646	503	625	2342	2242	1762	42	2448	736	2340	1778	40	340	1718	232	140	1726	1236
notes (see page 4)	✗	✗	✗	①-⑤	⑥⑦		✗Ⓡ	✗	✗	✗		✗Ⓡ		B	M	✗		N
Warszawa Centralna 56 d.							0618					1640						
Berlin Hbf d.							1224					2242						
Berlin Zoo d.				1101	1127					1527				2351				
Potsdam Stadt d.					1147					1547								
Leipzig d.	1102								1502									
Halle d.	1130								1530									
Magdeburg d.	1223	1230			1316				1624				0110					
Braunschweig d.		1318			1403					1803			0205					
Hannover Hbf d.		1357		1447	1447					1847			0255					
København 50 d.															2105			2205
Rødby d.															2330			0030
Hamburg Altona d.			1338															
Hamburg Hbf d.			1353						1753						0312			0420
Bremen Hbf d.			1447						1847						0420			0525
Osnabrück d.			1539						1939	1957			0425		0532			
Rheine d.			1622	1622						2022			0455					0657
Bad Bentheim d.			1643	1643						2043			0527					0731
Hengelo a.			1701	1701						2102			0546					0751
Duisburg d.													0706	0752				
Amersfoort a.				1811	1811	1827			2214	2227		0659	0727					0907
Utrecht a.						1843				2243			0743			0923	0947	
Rotterdam CS a.						1925				2325			0825				1025	
Amsterdam Centraal a.				1848	1848				2248			0740				0954		0948
Amsterdam Schiphol a.				1914	1914				2314									

NOTES

Ⓑ – 🛏 1,2 cl., 🚃 2 cl. and 🚗 Amsterdam - Berlin and v.v.

M – NORD EXPRESS – 🛏 1,2 cl. (T2), 🛏 1,2 cl., 🚃 2 cl. and 🚗 (Oostende/Paris) - Duisburg - København and v.v.

N – NORD WEST EXPRESS – June 15 - Aug 27: 🚃 2 cl. and 🚗 Amsterdam - København and v.v.

c – Berlin Charlottenburg

⚡ – Supplement payable.

Table 23 (Summer)   LONDON and BRUSSELS - HANNOVER and BERLIN

train type		IC	IR	IC	IR		IC	IR	IC	IR	IC	IR	9112	EC		EC	IC		IC		9148	IC	IR	IC
train number	411	506	2735	413	504	2485	417	502	2645	419	500	2647	9112	47	425	108	547	429	549	9148	520	2443	657
notes (see page 4)		⚉	⚉	✕	⚉		✕	⚉		✕	⚉	⚉	✕ Ⓡ	N		✕	K		✕	✕ Ⓡ		⚉	✕
notes (see below)													①-⑥	✔			✔		✔		M		
London Waterloo 12 .... d.	...	...	...	...	...	...	...	...	...	...	...	...	0723	...	...	...	...	...	...	...	1627	...	...
Lille Europe 12 .... d.	...	...	...	...	...	...	...	...	...	...	...	...	1022	...	...	...	...	...	...			...	...
Oostende 12 .... d.	0532	...	...	0634	...	...	0834	...	...	0934	...	...		...	1234	...	...	1434	...	...	2134	...	...
Brugge .... d.	0548	...	...	0650	...	...	0850	...	...	0950	...	...		...	1250	...	...	1450	...	...	2150	...	...
Gent St. Pieters .... d.	0617	...	...	0715	...	...	0915	...	...	1015	...	...		...	1315	...	...	1515	...	...	2215	...	...
Brussels Midi/Zuid .... d.	0647	...	...	0748	...	...	0947	...	...	1047	...	...	1138	1207	1347	...	...	1548	...	2046	2250	...	...
Brussels Nord/Noord ...... d.	0657	...	...	0757	...	...	0957	...	...	1057	...	...		1216	1357	...	...	1557	...	...	2259	...	...
Liège Guillemins .... d.	0800	...	...	0900	...	...	1100	...	...	1200	...	...		1317	1500	...	...	1700	...	...	0048	...	...
Aachen 🏛 .... d.	0849	...	...	0949	...	...	1149	...	...	1249	...	...		1355	1549	...	...	1743	...	...	0142	...	...
Köln .... d.	0942	1009	...	1042	1109	...	1242	1309	...	1342	1410	...		1509	1642	1710	1810	1842	1910	...	0428	...	...
Bielefeld .... a.	...	1210	...	...	1310	...	...	1510	...	...	1610	...		1710	...	1910	2010	...	2110	...	0428	...	...
Hannover Hbf .... a.	...	1300	...	...	1400	...	...	1600	...	...	1700	1746		1800	...	2000	2100	...	2203	...	0544	...	...
Braunschweig .... a.	...	1341	...	...	1441	...	...	1641	...	...	1741	1825		1841	...	2041	2141	...	...	...	0637	...	...
Magdeburg .... a.	...	1427	1434	...	1527	1556	...	1727	1734	...	1827e	1920		1927	...	2127	2227	...	...	...	0729	0735	...
Halle .... a.	...		1526	...			...		1826	...		2026			...		2326	...	...	...		0826	...
Leipzig .... a.	...		1556	...		1726	...		1854	...		2054			...		2355	...	...	...		0854	0905
Dresden Hbf .... a.	...		1738	...		1908	...			...					...			...	...	...			1031
Potsdam Stadt .... a.	...			...			...			...					...			...	...	...			
Berlin Zoo .... a.	...			...	1652		...	1852		...					...	2052	2252	...	...	...	0858		
Berlin Lichtenberg .... a.	...	1611		...			...			...		2011e			...			...	...	...			

train type	ICE	IC		IR	EC	EC	IC		IR	EC		IR	IC		IR	IC		IR	IC		IR		IR	IC	9113
train number	591	546	422	2744	109	38	501	426	2740	46	9159	2636	605	430	2734	505	434	2644	507	438	2632	242	9113
notes (see page 4)	✕	⚉		⚉	✕	⚉	✕		⚉	✕ Ⓡ		⚉	⚉		⚉	✕		⚉	✕		⚉		✕ Ⓡ
notes (see below)	✔	L	✔		✔		✔		✔	N	✔				✔			✔			M		①-⑥
Berlin Lichtenberg .... d.	...	...	...	...	...	...	0748f	...	...	...	...	...	0948	...	...	...	...	...	...	...	...	...	...
Berlin Zoo .... d.	0546	...	...	0707	...	...		...	0907	...	...	...		...	1148	...	...	1307	...	2059	...	...	...
Potsdam Stadt .... d.		...	...		...	...		...		...	...	...		...		...	...		...		...	...	...
Dresden Hbf .... d.		...	...		...	...		...		...	0754	...	0954	...		...	...	1754	...		...	...	...
Leipzig .... d.		0602	...	0702	...	...		0902		1002	...	...	1202	...	1302	...	...	2002	...		...	...	...
Halle .... d.		0630	...	0730	...	...		0930		1030	...	...	1230	...	1330	...	...	2030	...		...	...	...
Magdeburg .... d.	0710	0730	...	0823	0830	...	0930f	...	1022	1030	1122	1130	1322	1330	...	1423	1430	...	2124	2225	...
Braunschweig .... d.	0818	...	...	0918	...	1018	...	1118	...	1218	...	1418	...	1518	...	...	2314	...
Hannover Hbf .... d.	0900	...	...	1000	...	1100	...	1200	...	1300	...	1500	...	1600	...	...	0001	...
Bielefeld .... d.	0947	...	...	1047	...	1147	...	1247	...	1347	...	1547	...	1647	...	...	0054	...
Köln .... d.	...	1150	1214	...	1250	1314	1350	1414	...	1514	...	1550	1614	...	1750	1814	...	1850	2014	...	0400	...
Aachen 🏛 .... d.	...		1305	...		1410	...	1505	...	1607	...	...	1705	...		1905	...	...	2105	...	0510	...
Liège Guillemins .... a.	...		1343	...		1449	...	1543	...	1647	...	...	1743	...		1943	...	...	2143	...	0644	...
Brussels Nord/Noord ..... a.	...		1444	...		1548	...	1644	...	1749	...	...	1844	...		2044	...	...	2244	...	0644	...
Brussels Midi/Zuid .... a.	...		1455	...		1556	...	1655	...	1801	1856	...	1855	...		2055	...	...	2255	...	0655	0731
Gent St. Pieters .... a.	...		1527	...			...	1728	...			...	1927	...		2127	...	...	2327	...	0727	
Brugge .... a.	...		1552	...			...	1752	...			...	1952	...		2152	...	...	2352	...	0752	
Oostende 12 .... a.	...		1609	...			...	1809	...			...	2009	...		2209	...	...	0009	...	0809	
Lille Europe 12 .... a.	...			...			...		...			...		...			...	...		...		0844
London Waterloo 12 ..... a.	...			...			...		...	2109		...		...			...	...		...		0943

LONDON - BERLIN by Sea

		🚢		IC633	IC875				IC678	IC538				
	P	P Ⓡ		✕	✕				✔	✕	F Ⓡ	P	
London Liverpool Street ..... d.	1325		...	...	...	Dresden Hbf .... d.	...	0717	...	...	...	...
Harwich Parkeston Quay .... a.	1445		...	...	...	**Berlin Zoo** .... d.	...	0919	1000	...	...	...
Harwich Parkeston Quay .... d.		1530	...	...	...	Nauen .... d.	...		1030	...	...	...
Hamburg Fischereihafen ♣ a.		1300	...	...	...	**Hamburg Altona** ♣ .... a.	...		1316	...	...	...
Hamburg Altona ♠ .... d.			...	1442	...	**Hamburg Fishereihafen** ♣ .. d.	...			1630	...	...
Nauen .... a.			...	1729	1736	Harwich Parkeston Quay ... a.	...			1200	...	...
Berlin Zoo .... a.			...	1800	...	Harwich Parkeston Quay ... d.	...				1305	...
Dresden Hbf .... a.			...	...	2023	**London Liverpool Street** . a.	...				1430	...

NOTES

F – Even dates in June, July and August; uneven dates in May and August.

K – ①②③④⑤⑦, not June 4.

L – ①-⑥, not June 5.

M – 🛏 1,2 cl., 🛏 2 cl. and 🚋 Oostende - Berlin and v.v.

N – ALEXANDER VON HUMBOLDT – 🚋 and ✕ Brussels - Berlin and v.v.

P – Even dates in May and August, uneven dates in June, July and September.

e – Not ⑥, not June 4.

f – Not ⑦, not June 5.

✔ – Supplement payable.

♣ – 🚌 service Hamburg Fischereihafen - Hamburg Altona and v.v.

Table 24 (Summer) LONDON, BRUSSELS AND PARIS - WARSZAWA AND MOSKVA

	TGV					
train number	83	9118	9124	241	241	241
notes (see page 4)	✕ Ⓡ	✕ Ⓡ	✕ Ⓡ			
notes (see below)	ϟ	⑦	①-⑥	A	B	C
London Waterloo 12 .... d.	...	0857	1027	...	...	...
Lille Europe 12 .... d.	...	|	|	...	...	...
Paris Nord .... d.	1052	|	|	...	...	...
Brussels Midi .... d.	1312	1317	1438	1555	1555	1555
Brussels Nord .... d.	...	...	...	1603	1603	1603
Liège Guillemins .... d.	...	...	...	1703	1703	1703
Aachen 🏛 .... d.	...	...	...	1808	1808	1808
Frankfurt/Oder 🏛 .... a.	...	...	...	0309	0309	0309
Kunowice .... a.	...	...	...	0354	0354	0354
Rzepin .... a.	...	...	...	0409	0409	0409
Poznań Glówny .... a.	...	...	...	0625	0625	0625
Warszawa Centralna .... a.	...	...	...	1015	1015	1015
Warszawa Wschodnia .... a.	...	...	...	1029	1029	1029
Terespol .... a.	...	...	...	1338	1338	1338
Brest 🏛 .... a.	...	...	...	1615	1615	1615
Kyïv (Kiev) .... a.	...	...	...	|	1240	|
Minsk .... a.	...	...	...	2227	...	|
Sankt Peterburg Vitebski ... a.	...	...	...	|	...	1742
Smolensk .... a.	...	...	...	0418	...	...
Moskva Smolenskaya .... a.	...	...	...	1206	...	...

Moskva/Kyïv/St. P. train no.	15	273	49		
Warszawa train number	240	240	240	284	9153
notes (see page 4)					✕ Ⓡ
notes (see below)	A	D	E		
Moskva Smolenskaya ..... d.	2015	...	...	...	...
Smolensk .... d.	0326	...	...	...	...
Sankt Peterburg Vitebski d.	|	...	1510	...	...
Minsk .... d.	0736	...	|	...	...
Kyïv (Kiev) .... d.	|	1805	|	...	...
Brest 🏛 .... d.	1436	1436	1436	...	...
Terespol .... d.	1500	1500	1500	...	...
Warszawa Wschodnia ..... d.	1910	1910	1910	...	...
Warszawa Centralna .... d.	1925	1925	1925	...	...
Poznań Glówny .... d.	2250	2250	2250	...	...
Rzepin .... d.	0100	0100	0100	...	...
Kunowice .... d.	0115	0115	0115	...	...
Frankfurt/Oder 🏛 .... d.	0150	0150	0150	...	...
Aachen 🏛 .... a.	1055	1055	1055	...	...
Liège Guillemins .... a.	1159	1159	1159	...	...
Brussels Nord .... a.	1314	1314	1314	...	...
Brussels Midi .... a.	1322	1322	1322	1413	1722
Paris Nord .... a.	...	...	...	1708	|
Lille Europe 12 .... a.	...	...	...	...	1839
London Waterloo 12 .... a.	...	...	...	...	1939

NOTES

A – OST WEST EXPRESS – 🛏 1,2 cl. Brussels - Moskva and v.v. (journey 2 nights); 🛏 1,2 cl., ▬ 2 cl. and [2] Brussels - Warszawa and v.v. (journey 1 night).

B – ②, also ⑦ June 4 - Sept. 10: 🛏 1,2 cl. Brussels - Kyïv (journey 2 nights).

C – ①⑤, also ③ May 31 - Sept. 20: 🛏 1,2 cl. Brussels - Sankt Peterburg (2 nights).

D – ⑦, also ⑤ June 2 - Sept. 8: 🛏 1,2 cl. Kyïv - Brussels (journey 2 nights).

E – ③⑥, also ① May 29 - Sept. 18: 🛏 1,2 cl. Sankt Peterburg - Brussels (2 nights).

ϟ – Supplement payable.

Table 25 (Summer) PARIS - LIÈGE, KÖLN, HAMBURG and BERLIN

train number	EC	IC	IC	EC	EC	EC	EC	EC		487				EC		ICE	ICE
train number	33	502	524	39	8	26	31	31	1233	331	331	243	235	180	239	641	639
notes (see page 4)		✕	✕		✕	✕								🍷		✕	✕
notes (see below)	F ϟ	ϟ	ϟ	D ϟ	ϟ	ϟ	E ϟ	K	V	B	C	N	J	ϟ	G	ϟ	P ϟ
aris Nord .... d.	0737	...	...	1346	...	...	1632	1632	1902	1926	1945	2101	2130	...	2316	...	...
t. Quentin .... d.	0847	...	...	1458	...	...	|	|	|	2053	2104	2215	|	...	0103	...	...
eumont 🏛 .... d.	|	...	...	|	...	...	|	|	2108	2205	2205	|	2342	...	0225	...	...
harleroi Sud .... d.	0954	...	...	|	...	...	1853	1853	2132	2232	2232	2326	0007	...	0248	...	...
amur .... d.	1023	...	...	|	...	...	1922	1922	2202	2300	2300	2355	0037	...	0317	...	...
iège Guillemins .... a.	1059	...	...	1759	...	...	1959	1959	2253	2343	2343	0033	0114	...	0405	...	...
achen 🏛 .... a.	1150	...	...	1845	...	...	2050	2050	2336	...	...	|	|	...	0448	...	...
öln Hbf .... a.	1248	1309	1310	1942	2009	2010	2149	2155	0034	...	...	|	|	...	0550	0600	0625
üsseldorf .... a.	...	1331	|	2016	2031	|	2216	2224	0102	...	...	|	|	...	0628	|	|
uisburg .... a.	...	1344	|	2031	2044	|	2232	2240	|	...	...	|	|	...	0644	|	|
ssen .... a.	...	1357	|	2045	2057	|	2245	2253	|	...	...	|	|	...	0658	|	|
ortmund .... a.	...	1419	1419	2110	2119	2119	2309	|	|	...	...	|	|	...	0723	|	|
Münster .... a.	...	|	1456	...	|	2156	...	2350	|	...	...	|	|	...	...	|	0752
Osnabrück .... a.	...	|	1519	...	|	2219	...	0020	|	...	...	|	|	...	...	|	|
Bremen Hbf .... a.	...	|	1612	...	|	2312	...	0127	|	...	...	|	0600	...	...	|	|
Hamburg Hbf .... a.	...	|	1707	...	|	0007	...	0235	0442	...	...	|	0708	0730	...	|	0942
Hamburg Altona .... a.	...	|	1721	...	|	0021	...	|	|	...	...	|	0731	|	...	|	0956
Rødby F 🏛 .... a.	...	|	...	...	|	...	...	0600	0800	...	...	|	...	1000	...	|	...
København 50 .... a.	...	|	...	...	|	...	...	0830	1030	...	...	|	...	1159	...	|	...
ielefeld .... a.	...	1510	...	...	2210	...	...	...	...	...	...	0437	...	...	...	0750	...
annover Hbf .... a.	...	1600	...	...	2303	...	...	...	...	...	...	0544	...	...	...	0837	...
raunschweig .... a.	...	1641	...	...	...	...	...	...	...	...	...	0637	...	...	...	|	...
agdeburg .... a.	...	1727	...	...	...	...	...	...	...	...	...	0729	...	...	...	|	...
erlin Zoo .... a.	...	1852	...	...	...	...	...	...	...	...	...	0858	...	...	...	1110	...
erlin Hbf .... a.	...	...	...	...	...	...	...	...	...	...	...	...	...	...	...	...	...

train number			EC		EC	IC	EC	IC	IC	EC	IC	ICE		EC		
train number	330	1232	30	232	109	621	38	503	523	32	830	640	238	181	234	242
notes (see page 4)					✕	✕		🍷	✕		✕	✕		🍷		
notes (see below)		W	E ϟ	K	ϟ	ϟ	D ϟ	ϟ	ϟ	F ϟ	ϟ	ϟ	G	ϟ	J	N
erlin Hbf .... d.	...	...	...	...	...	...	...	...	...	...	...	...	...	...	...	...
erlin Zoo .... d.	...	...	...	...	0707	...	...	1107	...	...	...	1848	...	...	...	2059
agdeburg .... d.	...	...	...	...	0830	...	...	1230	...	...	...	|	...	...	...	2225
raunschweig .... d.	...	...	...	...	0918	...	...	1318	...	...	...	|	...	...	...	2314
annover Hbf .... d.	...	...	...	...	1000	...	...	1400	...	...	...	2120	...	...	...	0001
ielefeld .... d.	...	...	...	...	1047	...	...	1447	...	...	...	2206	...	...	...	0054
København 50 .... d.	...	2005	...	2105	|	...	...	|	...	...	...	|	...	1730	...	|
Rødby F 🏛 .... d.	...	2230	...	2330	|	...	...	|	...	...	...	|	...	1925	...	|
Hamburg Altona .... d.	...	|	...	|	|	0838	...	|	1238	...	1938	|	...	|	2223	|
Hamburg Hbf .... d.	...	0145	...	0312	|	0853	...	|	1253	...	1953	|	...	2215	2242	|
Bremen Hbf .... d.	...	|	...	0420	|	0947	...	|	1347	...	2047	|	...	...	2353	|
Osnabrück .... d.	...	|	...	0532	|	1041	...	|	1441	...	2141	|	...	...	|	|
Münster .... d.	...	|	...	0603	|	1104	...	|	1504	...	2204	|	...	...	|	|
ortmund .... d.	...	|	0648	|	1138	1141	1148	1539	1541	...	2234	|	2237	...	|	|
ssen .... d.	...	|	0712	0654	1201	|	1212	1601	|	...	|	|	2300	...	|	|
uisburg .... d.	...	|	0725	0708	1214	|	1225	1614	|	...	|	2321	2326	...	|	|
üsseldorf .... d.	...	0517	0740	0732	1228	|	1240	1628	|	...	|	2333	2342	...	|	|
öln Hbf .... d.	...	0546	0814	0802	1250	1250	1314	1650	1650	1708	2359	2354	0011	...	|	|
achen 🏛 .... d.	...	0643	0909	0909	...	...	1410	...	...	1800	...	...	0104	...	|	|
ège Guillemins .... d.	0700	0735	0959	0959	...	...	1452	...	...	1847	...	...	0155	...	0437	0526
amur .... d.	0740	0822	1039	1039	...	...	|	...	...	1925	...	...	0234	...	0516	0608
harleroi Sud .... d.	0810	0852	1108	1106	...	...	|	...	...	1954	...	...	0304	...	0547	0640
eumont 🏛 .... d.	0837	0927	|	|	...	...	|	...	...	|	...	...	0328	...	0633	|
. Quentin .... d.	0952	|	1215	1215	...	...	1750	...	...	2057	...	...	0444	...	|	|
aris Nord .... a.	1110	1121	1329	1329	...	...	1859	...	...	2208	...	...	0623	...	0840	0908

OTES

– ①②③④⑥ not June 5, July 13, Aug. 15.

– ⑤⑦ also June 5, July 13, Aug. 15.

– JACQUES BREL – [12] and ✕ Paris - Dortmund and v.v.

– MOLIERE – [12] and ✕ Paris - Dortmund and v.v.

– PARSIFAL – [12] and ✕ Paris - Köln and v.v.

– 🛏 1,2 cl., ▬ 2 cl., [12] and 🍷 Paris - Dortmund and v.v.

– 🛏 1,2 cl., ▬ 2 cl. and [2] Paris - Hamburg and v.v; [12] Paris - Liège and v.v.

K – 🛏 1,2 cl. Paris - København and v.v.; [12] Paris - Aachen and v.v.; 🛏 1,2 cl., ▬ 2 cl. and [2] (Oostende) - Aachen - København and v.v.

N – 🛏 1,2 cl., ▬ 2 cl., [2] and 🍷 Paris - Berlin and v.v.

P – ①-⑥, not June 5.

V – VIKING EXPRESS – ①④⑥ June 22-Aug. 28: ▬ 2 cl. and [2] Paris - København.

W – VIKING EXPRESS – ②⑤⑦ June 23-Aug. 29: ▬ 2 cl. and [2] København - Paris.

ϟ – Supplement payable.

Table 28 (Summer) — AMSTERDAM - KÖLN AND FRANKFURT/MAIN

	141	725	103	591	143	27	9	793	105	727	593	3	29	795	145	729	501	797
train type	EC	IC	EC	ICE	EC	EC	EC	ICE	EC	IC	ICE	EC	EC	ICE	EC	IC	IC	ICE
notes (see page 4)	A ∕	✗	✗	✗	B ∕	✗	✗	✗	C ∕	Z ∕	∕	D ∕	✗	✗	E ∕	♀	✗	✗
Amsterdam Centraal d.	0602				0706				0800			0900			1106			
Rotterdam C.S. d.	│				│				│			│			│			
Utrecht C.S. d.	0633				0735				0830			0930			1135			
Arnhem d.	0705				0806				0905			1005			1206			
Emmerich d.	0731				0831				0934			1034			1231			
Oberhausen a.	0759				0859				1002			1102			1259			
Duisburg a.	0806	0814			0906		0914		1010	1014		1110	1114		1306	1314		
Düsseldorf a.	0819	0828			0919		0928		1032	1028		1132	1128		1319	1328		
Köln Hbf a.	0842	0854	0900		0942	0954	1000		1057	1054		1157	1154		1342	1354	1400	
Bonn a.		0912	0919			1012	1018		1118	1112		1218	1212				1412	1418
Koblenz a.		0944	0951			1044	1051		1150	1145		1250	1245				1444	1451
Mainz a.		1034	1042			1134	1142		1240	1236		1340	1336				1534	1542
Frankfurt/Main a.		1107			1207					1307			1407			1607		
Würzburg a.		1225			1325					1425			1525			1725		
Nürnberg a.		1322			1422					1522			1622			1822		
Praha Hlavni 57 a.																		
Regensburg 740 a.					1524								1724			1924		
Mannheim a.			1123	1127			1223	1227	1323		1327	1423		1427			1623	1627
Stuttgart a.				1206				1306			1406			1506				1708
Ulm a.				1304				1404			1504			1604				1804
Augsburg a.				1343				1443			1543			1643				1843
München Hbf a.				1415				1515			1615			1715				1915
Karlsrühe a.			1157				1257		1357			1457					1657	
Baden Baden a.							1313					1513						
Offenburg a.			1231						1431								1731	
Freiberg im Breisgau a.			1302				1402		1502			1602					1802	
Basel SBB a.			1345				1445		1545			1645					1845	

	147	823	605	799	149	625	505	895	151	827	607	353	153	203	215	215
train type	EC	IC	IC	ICE	EC	IC	IC	ICE	EC	IC	IC		EC		EN	EN
notes (see page 4)	F ∕	✗	✗	✗	G ∕	✗	✗	✗	H ∕	♀	♀	N	J ∕	K	L	M
Amsterdam Centraal d.	1306				1506				1700				1906	2005	2056	2056
Rotterdam C.S. d.	│				│				│				│	│	│	│
Utrecht C.S. d.	1335				1535				1729				1935	2047	2130	2130
Arnhem d.	1406				1606				1805				2006	2127	2214	2214
Emmerich d.	1431				1631				1831				2031	2157	2235	2235
Oberhausen a.	1459				1659				1859				2059	2234	2326	2326
Duisburg a.	1506	1514			1706	1714			1906			1946	2106	2244	2335	2335
Düsseldorf a.	1519	1528			1719	1728			1919			2004	2119	2318	2352	2352
Köln Hbf a.	1542	1554	1600		1742	1754	1800		1942	1954	2000	2035	2142	2350	0022	0022
Bonn a.		1612	1618			1812	1818			2012	2018	2055		0022		0109
Koblenz a.		1644	1651			1844	1851			2044	2051	2132		0058		0144
Mainz a.		1734	1742			1934	1942			2134	2142	2226				0238
Frankfurt/Main a.		1807				2007				2207		2300				
Würzburg a.		1925				2125b						0107			0514	
Nürnberg a.		2022				2223b						0211			0618	
Praha Hlavni 57 a.												0812				
Regensburg 740 a.		2124				2328b										
Mannheim a.			1823	1827			2023	2027			2224					0321
Stuttgart a.				1908				2108								0454
Ulm a.				2004				2204								0603
Augsburg a.				2043				2243								0652
München Hbf a.				2115				2316								0736
Karlsrühe a.			1857				2057				2257			0349		
Baden Baden a.			1913				2125							0414		
Offenburg a.							2146							0437		
Freiberg im Breisgau a.			2002				2216							0520		
Basel SBB a.			2045				2245							0640		

NOTES

A – BONIFACIUS – ⊡ and ♀ Amsterdam - Köln.

B – ERASMUS – ⊡ and ♀ Amsterdam - Köln.

C – BERNER OBERLAND – ⊡ and ✗ Amsterdam - Basel - (Interlaken).

D – REMBRANDT – ⊡ and ✗ Amsterdam - Basel - (Chur).

E – FRANZ HALS – ⊡ and ♀ Amsterdam - Köln.

F – PIET MONDRIAAN – ⊡ and ♀ Amsterdam - Köln.

G – JOHANNES VERMEER – ⊡ and ♀ Amsterdam - Köln.

H – JAN PIETERSZ. SWEELINCK – ⊡ and ♀ Amsterdam - Köln.

J – HIERONYMUS BOSCH – ⊡ and ♀ Amsterdam - Köln.

K – SCHWEIZ EXPRESS – 2 cl. and ⊡ Amsterdam - Basel; also ⊟ 1,2 cl. on ⑤⑥.

L – ⊟ 1,2 cl., ⊨ 2 cl. and ⊡ Amsterdam - Regensburg - (Wien).

M – ⊟ 1,2 cl., ⊨ 2 cl. and ⊡ Amsterdam - München.

N – ⊟ 1,2 cl., ⊨ 2 cl. and ⊡ (Dortmund) - Duisburg - Praha.

Z – ①②③④⑤⑥, not June 5.

b – Not ⑥; not June 4.

∕ – Supplement payable.

Table 28 (Summer) — KÖLN AND FRANKFURT/MAIN - AMSTERDAM

	EC	IC	EC		ICE	IC	IC	EC	ICE	IC	IC	EC	ICE	IC	IC	EC
train number	140	739	142	352	694	504	526	144	598	502	524	146	596	602	620	148
notes (see below)	A		B	T				C				D				E
Basel SBB d.										0814			1014			
Freiberg im Breisgau d.						0652				0855			1055			
Offenburg d.						0722				0925			1125			
Baden Baden d.						0741									1251	
Karlsruhe d.						0800				1000			1200			
München Hbf d.							0540f		0745					0945		
Augsburg d.							0611f		0811					1011		
Ulm d.							0651f		0851					1051		
Stuttgart d.							0750		0950					1150		
Mannheim d.						0836	0831		1031	1036			1231	1236		
Regensburg 740 d.																
Praha Hlavni 57 d.				2135												
Nürnberg d.					0357			0633f			0835				1035	
Würzburg d.					0509			0731f			0931				1131	
Frankfurt/Main Hbf d.		0651			0658			0851			1051					
Mainz d.		0724			0728	0916		0924	1116	1124			1316	1324		
Koblenz d.		0813			0823	1005		1013	1205	1213			1405	1413		
Bonn d.		0845			0859	1037		1045	1237	1245			1437	1445		
Köln Hbf d.	0717	0905	0917		0926	1059	1105	1117	1259	1305		1317	1459	1505		1517
Düsseldorf d.	0739		0939		1001		1133	1139	1333			1339				1539
Duisburg d.	0752		0952		1015		1144	1152	1344			1352				1552
Oberhausen a.	0758		0958					1158				1358				1558
Emmerich a.	0826		1026					1226				1426				1626
Arnhem a.	0852		1052					1252				1452				1652
Utrecht C.S. a.	0923		1123					1323				1523				1723
Rotterdam C.S. a.	|		|									|				
Amsterdam Centraal a.	0954		1151					1351				1551				1751

	ICE	EC	IC	EC		ICE	EC	EC		ICE	IC	EC		ICE	EC	IC	EC		EN		EN		
train number	594	108	520	150		794	28	104		592	724	2		590	106	726	152		214		224		202
notes (see below)				F				M				N				Y	G		H		J		K
Basel SBB d.		1214				1314						1414			1614								2325
Freiberg im Breisgau d.		1255				1355						1455			1655								0033
Offenburg d.		1325										1525			1725								0112
Baden Baden d.						1441																	0134
Karlsruhe d.		1400				1500						1600			1800								0158
München Hbf d.	1145							1245		1345				1545					2211				
Augsburg d.	1211							1311		1411				1611					2246				
Ulm d.	1251							1351		1451				1651					2334				
Stuttgart d.	1350							1450		1550				1750					0041				
Mannheim d.	1431	1436				1531		1536		1631		1636		1831	1836								
Regensburg 740 d.																					2320		
Praha Hlavni 57 d.							1232																
Nürnberg d.			1235				1335				1435					1632					0024		
Würzburg d.			1331				1431				1531					1730							
Frankfurt/Main Hbf d.			1451				1551				1651					1851							
Mainz d.	1516	1524				1616		1624		1724		1716		1916	1924								
Koblenz d.	1605	1613				1705		1713		1813		1805		2005	2013				0350				0449
Bonn d.	1637	1645				1737		1745		1845		1837		2037	2045				0425				0523
Köln Hbf d.	1659	1709		1717		1802		1805		1909		1902		2109	2105		2117		0510		0510		0550
Düsseldorf d.	1733			1739		1826		1833		1933		1926		2133			2139		0545		0545		0620
Duisburg d.	1744			1752		1848		1844		1944		1948		2144			2152		0613		0613		0655
Oberhausen a.				1758				1855				1955					2158		0626		0626		0703
Emmerich a.				1826				1924				2024					2226		0704		0704		0740
Arnhem a.				1852				1952				2052					2252		0741		0741		0825
Utrecht C.S. a.				1923				2023				2123					2323		0823		0823		0906
Rotterdam C.S. a.				|								|							|				
Amsterdam Centraal a.				1951				2051				2151					2351		0857		0857		0940

NOTES

A – HIERONYMUS BOSCH – 🛏 and ♥ Köln - Amsterdam.

B – JAN PIETERSZ. SWEELINCK – 🛏 and ♥ Köln - Amsterdam.

C – JOHANNES VERMEER – 🛏 and ♥ Köln - Amsterdam.

D – PIET MONDRIAAN – 🛏 and ♥ Köln - Amsterdam.

E – FRANS HALS – 🛏 and ♥ Köln - Amsterdam.

F – ERASMUS – 🛏 and ♥ Köln - Amsterdam.

G – BONIFACIUS – 🛏 and ♥ Köln - Amsterdam.

H – 1,2 cl., 2 cl. and 🛏 München - Amsterdam.

J – 1,2 cl., 2 cl. and 🛏 (Wien) - Regensburg - Amsterdam.

K – SCHWEIZ EXPRESS – 2 cl. and 🛏 Basel - Amsterdam, also 1,2 cl. on ⑥⑦.

M – BERNER OBERLAND – 🛏 and ✗ (Interlaken) - Basel - Amsterdam.

N – REMBRANDT – 🛏 and ✗ (Chur) - Basel - Amsterdam.

T – 1,2 cl., 2 cl. and 🛏 Praha - Duisburg - (Dortmund).

Y – ①②③④⑤⑦, not June 4.

f – Not ⑦, not June 5.

✗ – Supplement payable.

Table 30 (Summer) PARIS - FRANKFURT/MAIN, LEIPZIG AND PRAHA

train type		EC	IC	ICE			EC	IC	ICE	IC			EC	D	D							IC	IC	ICE
train number		57	621	594			55	523	590	555			53	1955	353			1251		261	1253	723	655	696
notes (see page 4)			✕	✕				🍷	✕	✕												🍷	✕	✕
notes (see below)		C ⚡	⚡	⚡			B ⚡	⚡	⚡	⚡			G ⚡	W	S			F		L	V	H ⚡	⚡	⚡
Paris Est d.	...	0854	...	...	...	...	1256	...	...	...	...	...	1716	...	...	...	...	1955	...	2230	2300	...	...	...
Metz d.	...	1151	...	...	...	...	1551	...	...	...	...	...	2006	...	...	...	...	2307	...	0205	|	...	...	...
Forbach 🏛 d.	...	1239	...	...	...	...	1639	...	...	...	...	...	2051	...	...	...	...	2355	...	|	0308	...	...	...
Saarbrücken a.	...	1249	...	...	...	...	1648	...	...	...	...	...	2058	...	...	...	...	0005	...	|	0316	...	...	...
Kaiserlautern a.	...	1328	...	...	...	...	1728	...	...	...	...	...	2138	...	...	...	...	|	...	|	0357	...	...	...
Mannheim **742** a.	...	1410	...	1434	...	...	1810	...	1834	...	...	...	2221	...	...	...	...	|	...	|	0444	...	...	...
Heidelberg **742** a.	...	|	...	|	...	...	|	...	|	...	...	...	|	...	...	...	...	|	...	0548	0458	...	...	...
Darmstadt a.	...	|	...	|	...	...	|	...	|	...	...	...	|	...	...	...	...	|	...	0624	0624	...	...	...
Frankfurt/Main a.	...	1500	1515	1519	...	...	1900	1915	1919	1923	...	...	2310	2338	2327	...	...	|	...	0652	0652	0715	0723	0719
Würzburg a.	...	|	1625	|	...	...	...	2025	|	|	...	...	...	|	0107	...	...	|	...	...	...	0825	|	|
Nürnberg a.	...	|	1722	|	...	...	...	2123	|	|	...	...	...	|	0211	...	...	|	...	...	...	0922	|	|
Fulda a.	...	1617	...	1616	...	...	...	...	2016	2019	...	...	...	0111	|	...	...	|	...	...	...	...	0819	0816
Bebra a.	...	|	...	|	...	...	...	...	|	|	...	...	...	|	|	...	...	|	...	...	...	...	|	|
Erfurt a.	...	1741	...	|	...	...	...	...	|	2241	...	...	...	|	|	...	...	|	...	...	...	...	0941	|
Leipzig a.	...	1857	...	|	...	...	...	...	|	2300	...	...	...	|	|	...	...	0556	...	...	...	...	1057	|
Dresden Hbf a.	...	2031	...	|	...	...	...	...	|	...	...	...	...	|	|	...	...	0735	...	...	...	...	1231	|
Děčin 🏛 a.	...	2125	...	|	...	...	...	...	|	...	...	...	...	|	|	...	...	0831	...	...	...	...	...	|
Cheb 🏛 a.	...	|	...	|	...	...	...	...	|	...	...	...	...	|	0438	...	...	|	...	...	...	...	...	|
Plzeň Hlavni a.	...	|	...	|	...	...	...	...	|	...	...	...	...	|	0634	...	...	|	...	...	...	...	...	|
Praha Holešovice a.	...	2302	...	|	...	...	...	...	|	...	...	...	...	|	|	...	...	1020	...	...	...	...	...	|
Praha Hlavni a.	...	2316	...	|	...	...	...	...	|	...	...	...	...	|	0812	...	...	1036	...	...	...	...	...	|
Kassel Wilhelmshöhe a.	...	...	...	1644	...	...	...	...	2044	...	...	...	...	|	...	...	...	...	...	...	...	...	...	0844
Magdeburg a.	...	...	...	1849	...	...	...	...	2249	...	...	...	...	|	...	...	...	...	...	...	...	...	...	1049
Berlin Zoo a.	...	...	...	2011	...	...	...	...	0011	...	...	...	...	0639	...	...	...	...	...	...	...	...	...	1211
Berlin Hbf a.	...	...	...	...	...	...	...	...	...	...	...	...	...	...	...	...	...	...	...	...	...	...	...	...

train type			D		EC			IC	ICE	IC	EC			ICE	IC	EC			IC	IC				
train number			352	1954	52			554	591	524	54			595	520	56			654	722	401	1252		1250
notes (see page 4)								✕	✕	✕				✕	🍷				✕	✕				
notes (see below)			S	W	G ⚡			⚡	⚡	⚡	B ⚡			⚡	⚡	C ⚡			⚡	Q ⚡	R	Z		D
Berlin Hbf d.	...	...	...	...	...	...	...	...	...	...	...	...	...	...	...	...	...	...	...	...	...	...	...	...
Berlin Zoo d.	...	...	...	2321	...	...	...	...	0546	...	...	...	...	0946	...	...	...	...	...	...	...	...	...	...
Magdeburg d.	...	...	...	|	...	...	...	...	0710	...	...	...	...	1110	...	...	...	...	...	...	...	...	...	...
Kassel Wilhelmshöhe d.	...	...	...	|	...	...	...	...	0913	...	...	...	...	1313	...	...	...	...	...	...	...	...	...	...
Praha Hlavni d.	...	...	2135	|	...	...	...	...	|	...	...	...	...	|	...	...	...	...	...	...	...	...	...	1846
Praha Holešovice d.	...	...	|	|	...	...	...	...	|	...	...	...	...	|	...	0633	...	...	...	...	...	...	...	1859
Plzeň Hlavni d.	...	...	2313	|	...	...	...	...	|	...	...	...	...	|	...	|	...	...	...	...	...	...	...	|
Cheb 🏛 d.	...	...	0120	|	...	...	...	...	|	...	...	...	...	|	...	|	...	...	...	...	...	...	...	|
Děčin 🏛 d.	...	...	|	|	...	...	...	...	|	...	...	...	...	|	...	0816	...	...	...	...	...	...	...	2045
Dresden Hbf d.	...	...	|	|	...	...	...	...	|	...	...	...	...	|	...	0921	...	...	1721	...	...	...	...	2139
Leipzig d.	...	...	|	|	...	...	...	0659	|	...	...	...	...	|	...	1059	...	...	1900	...	...	...	...	2316
Erfurt d.	...	...	|	|	...	...	...	0814	|	...	...	...	...	|	...	1214	...	...	2014	...	...	...	...	|
Bebra d.	...	...	|	|	...	...	...	|	|	...	...	...	...	|	...	|	...	...	|	...	...	...	...	|
Fulda d.	...	...	|	0545	...	...	...	0938	0941	...	...	...	...	1341	...	1340	...	...	2138	...	...	...	...	|
Nürnberg d.	...	...	0357	|	...	...	...	|	|	0835	...	...	...	|	1235	|	...	...	|	2035	...	...	...	|
Würzburg d.	...	...	0509	|	...	...	...	|	|	0931	...	...	...	|	1331	|	...	...	|	2131	...	...	...	|
Frankfurt/Main d.	...	...	0643	0646	0727	...	...	1035	1039	1043	1058	...	...	1439	1443	1458	...	...	2235	2243	2255	2255	...	|
Darmstadt d.	...	...	...	...	0747	...	...	...	|	...	|	...	...	|	...	|	...	...	...	...	2314	2314	...	|
Heidelberg **742** d.	...	...	...	...	|	...	...	...	|	...	|	...	...	|	...	|	...	...	...	...	0010	0003	...	|
Mannheim d.	...	...	...	...	0822	...	...	...	1124	...	1150	...	...	1524	...	1550	...	...	...	...	|	0017	...	|
Kaiserlautern d.	...	...	...	...	0904	...	...	...	...	...	1231	...	...	...	...	1631	...	...	...	...	|	0103	...	|
Saarbrücken d.	...	...	...	...	0946	...	...	...	...	...	1312	...	...	...	...	1712	...	...	...	...	|	0153	...	0544
Forbach 🏛 a.	...	...	...	...	0953	...	...	...	...	...	1320	...	...	...	...	1721	...	...	...	...	|	0201	...	0552
Metz a.	...	...	...	...	1040	...	...	...	...	...	1407	...	...	...	...	1808	...	...	...	...	0337	|	...	0638
Paris Est a.	...	...	...	...	1338	...	...	...	...	...	1711	...	...	...	...	2108	...	...	...	...	0705	0645	...	0938

NOTES

- B – GUSTAVE EIFFEL – [12] and ✕ Paris - Frankfurt/Main and v.v.
- C – HEINRICH HEINE – [12] and ✕ Paris - Praha and v.v.
- D – June 24 - Sept. 2: 🛏 1,2 cl., ▬ 2 cl. and [2] Praha - Paris.
- F – June 23 - Sept. 1: 🛏 1,2 cl., ▬ 2 cl. and [2] Paris - Praha.
- G – GOETHE – [12] and ✕ Paris - Frankfurt/Main and v.v.
- H – ①②③④⑤⑦, not June 4.
- L – May 28 - June 28 and Sept. 3 - 23: ▬ 2 cl. and [2] Paris - Frankfurt/Main; also 🛏 1,2 cl. (T2) daily except ⑥, not June 4.
- Q – ①②③④⑤⑦, not June 4.
- R – May 28 - June 29 and Sept. 4 - 23: ▬ 2 cl. and [2] Frankfurt/Main - Paris; also 🛏 1,2 cl. (T2) daily except ⑥, not June 4.
- S – 🛏 1,2 cl., ▬ 2 cl. and [2] (Dortmund) - Frankfurt/Main - Praha and v.v.
- V – June 29 - Sept. 2: ▬ 2 cl. and [2] Paris - Frankfurt/Main; also 🛏 1,2 cl. daily except ⑥, not July 14, Aug. 13,14.
- W – 🛏 1,2 cl., ▬ 2 cl., [12] and 🍷 Berlin - Frankfurt/Main and v.v.
- Z – June 30 - Sept. 3: ▬ 2 cl. and [2] Frankfurt/Main - Paris; also 🛏 1,2 cl. daily except ⑥, not July 14, Aug. 13,14.
- ⚡ – Supplement payable.

Table 31 (Summer) PARIS - INNSBRUCK

train type										
train number						469	443	669		
notes (see page 4)										
notes (see below)						B				
Paris Est d.	...	...	...	...	...	2240	...	...	...	...
Mulhouse d.	...	...	...	...	...	0504	...	...	...	...
Basel SBB 🏛 d.	...	...	...	...	...	0600	0625	...	...	...
Zürich Hbf d.	...	...	...	...	...	0657	0733	...	...	...
Buchs 🏛 a.	...	...	...	...	...	...	0845	...	...	...
Feldkirch a.	...	...	...	...	...	...	0907	0911	...	...
Bludenz a.	...	...	...	...	...	...	...	0925	...	...
Langen am Arlberg a.	...	...	...	...	...	...	...	0953	...	...
St. Anton am Arlberg a.	...	...	...	...	...	...	...	1002	...	...
Landeck a.	...	...	...	...	...	...	...	1028	...	...
Ötztal a.	...	...	...	...	...	...	...	1051	...	...
Innsbruck a.	...	...	...	...	...	...	...	1116	...	...
Kirchberg in Tirol a.	...	...	...	...	...	...	...	...	...	...
Kitzbühel a.	...	...	...	...	...	...	...	...	...	...
St. Johann in Tirol a.	...	...	...	...	...	...	...	...	...	...
Saalfelden a.	...	...	...	...	...	...	...	...	...	...
Zell am See a.	...	...	...	...	...	...	...	...	...	...

train type									
train number			566	448	468				
notes (see page 4)									
notes (see below)					B				
Zell am See d.	...	...	...	...	...	...	...	...	...
Saalfelden d.	...	...	...	...	...	...	...	...	...
St. Johann in Tirol d.	...	...	...	...	...	...	...	...	...
Kitzbühel d.	...	...	...	...	...	...	...	...	...
Kirchberg in Tirol d.	...	...	...	...	...	...	...	...	...
Innsbruck d.	...	...	1702	...	...	...	...	...	...
Ötztal d.	...	...	|	...	...	...	...	...	...
Landeck d.	...	...	1754	...	...	...	...	...	...
St. Anton am Arlberg d.	...	...	1825	...	...	...	...	...	...
Langen am Arlberg d.	...	...	|	...	...	...	...	...	...
Bludenz d.	...	...	|	...	...	...	...	...	...
Feldkirch d.	...	...	1917	1931	...	...	...	...	...
Buchs 🏛 d.	...	...	...	2005	...	...	...	...	...
Zürich Hbf d.	...	...	...	2126	2300	...	...	...	...
Basel SBB 🏛 a.	...	...	...	2235	0005	...	...	...	...
Mulhouse a.	...	...	...	...	0054	...	...	...	...
Paris Est a.	...	...	...	...	0648	...	...	...	...

NOTES

- B – 🛏 1,2 cl., ▬ 2 cl. and [2] Paris - Zürich - (Chur) and v.v.

Table 32 (Summer) PARIS - MÜNCHEN AND WIEN

train type			EC	EC	IC				EC				EC				IC	IC	IC				IR	
train number			65	65	890				67	269	269		69			263	590	511	503			261	2191	
notes (see page 4)					🍷												🍷	🍷	🍷				🍷	
notes (see below)			B /	C /					D /	E	H		F /			A						G		
Paris Est d.	...	...	0751	0751	...	...	...	...	1345	...	...	...	1719	...	...	1943	...	...	...	...	...	2230	...	...
Nancy d.	...	...	1029	1029	...	...	...	...	1632	...	...	...	2005	...	...	2226	...	...	...	...	...	|	...	...
Strasbourg d.	...	...	1157	1157	...	...	...	...	1758	...	...	...	2145	...	...	0003	...	...	...	...	...	0351	...	...
Kehl 🛃 a.	...	...	1205	1205	...	...	...	...	1806	...	...	...	2154	...	...	0013	...	...	...	...	...	0402	...	...
Baden Baden a.	...	...	1229	1229	...	...	...	...	1830	...	...	...	2220	...	...	|	...	...	...	...	...	0444	...	...
Karlsruhe a.	...	...	1248	1248	...	...	...	...	1850	...	...	...	2239	...	...	0056	...	...	...	...	...	0504	...	...
Stuttgart a.	...	...	1344	1344	...	...	...	...	1944	...	...	...	2341	...	...	0157	...	...	...	...	...	0620	...	...
Ulm a.	...	...	1453	1453	...	...	...	...	2053	...	...	...	...	...	...	|	...	...	...	...	...	0726	...	...
Augsburg a.	...	...	1534	1534	...	...	...	...	2134	...	...	...	...	...	...	|	...	...	...	...	...	0811	...	...
München Pasing a.	...	...	1559	1559	...	...	...	...	2159	...	...	...	...	...	...	|	...	...	...	...	...	|	...	...
München Hbf a.	...	...	1610	1610	...	...	...	...	2210	2319	2319	...	...	...	...	|	...	...	...	...	...	0850	0951	...
Salzburg 🛃 a.	...	...	1753	1753	1908	...	...	...	...	0101	0101	...	...	...	...	0553	0708	...	...	...	...	...	1140	...
Bischofshofen a.	...	...	|	1848	1950	...	...	...	...	|	|	...	...	...	...	|	0750	0801	...	...	...	...	...	...
Schwarzach St. Veit a.	...	...	|	|	2004	...	...	...	...	|	|	...	...	...	...	|	0804	|	...	...	...	...	...	...
Badgastein a.	...	...	|	|	2037	...	...	...	...	|	|	...	...	...	...	|	0835	|	...	...	...	...	...	...
Villach Hbf a.	...	...	|	|	2151	2213	...	...	...	|	|	...	...	...	...	|	0943	|	...	...	...	...	...	...
Klagenfurt a.	...	...	|	|	...	2249	...	...	...	|	|	...	...	...	...	|	1014	|	...	...	...	...	...	...
Linz a.	...	...	1912	|	...	...	...	...	...	0231	0425	...	...	...	...	0725	...	|	0840	...	...	...	...	...
Radstadt a.	...	...	|	1918	...	...	...	...	...	|	|	...	...	...	...	|	...	0822	|	...	...	...	...	...
Stainach Irdning a.	...	...	|	2006	...	...	...	...	...	|	|	...	...	...	...	|	...	0909	|	...	...	...	...	...
Selzthal a.	...	...	|	2024	...	...	...	...	...	|	|	...	...	...	...	|	...	0928	1016	...	...	...	...	...
Graz a.	...	...	|	2205	...	...	...	...	...	|	|	...	...	...	...	|	...	1120	1210	...	...	...	...	...
Wien Westbahnhof a.	...	...	2105	...	...	...	...	...	...	|	0632	...	...	...	...	0925	...	...	...	...	...	...	...	...
Hegyeshalom 🛃 a.	...	...	...	...	...	...	...	...	...	0519	...	...	...	...	...	1056	...	...	...	...	...	...	...	...
Györ a.	...	...	...	...	...	...	...	...	...	0621	...	...	...	...	...	1132	...	...	...	...	...	...	...	...
Budapest Keleti a.	...	...	...	...	...	...	...	...	...	0808	...	...	...	...	...	1308	...	...	...	...	...	...	...	...

train type		EC					EC			IC	EC	EC			EC				IC	IC	IC			
train number		68			268	248	66			791	64	116			62	260			602	612	691	262		
notes (see page 4)										🍷					✕				🍷	🍷	🍷			
notes (see below)		F /			E	H	D /				B /	C /			/	G						A		
Budapest Keleti d.	...	...	...	...	2120	...	...	...	...	...	...	...	...	...	1225	...	...	...	...	...	...	1540	...	...
Györ d.	...	...	...	...	2259	...	...	...	...	...	...	...	...	...	1404	...	...	...	...	...	...	1719	...	...
Hegyeshalom 🛃 d.	...	...	...	...	2347	...	...	...	...	...	...	...	...	...	1445	...	...	...	...	...	...	1755	...	...
Wien Westbahnhof d.	...	...	...	...	|	2330	...	...	...	...	0900	...	...	...	1600	...	...	...	...	...	...	1940	...	...
Graz d.	...	...	...	...	|	|	...	...	...	...	|	0757	...	...	|	...	...	...	1750	1840	...	|	...	...
Selzthal d.	...	...	...	...	|	|	...	...	...	...	|	0937	...	...	|	...	...	...	1944	2031	...	|	...	...
Stainach Irdning d.	...	...	...	...	|	|	...	...	...	...	|	0954	...	...	|	...	...	...	|	2049	...	|	...	...
Radstadt d.	...	...	...	...	|	|	...	...	...	...	|	1042	...	...	|	...	...	...	|	2137	...	|	...	...
Linz d.	...	...	...	...	0213	0127	...	...	...	...	1046	|	...	...	1748	...	...	...	2120	|	...	2134	...	...
Klagenfurt d.	...	...	...	...	|	|	...	...	...	0746	|	|	...	...	|	...	...	...	...	|	1946	|	...	...
Villach Hbf d.	...	...	...	...	|	|	...	...	...	0819	|	|	...	...	|	...	...	...	...	|	2019	|	...	...
Badgastein d.	...	...	...	...	|	|	...	...	...	0928	|	|	...	...	|	...	...	...	...	|	2129	|	...	...
Schwarzach St. Veit d.	...	...	...	...	|	|	...	...	...	0957	|	|	...	...	|	...	...	...	...	|	2157	|	...	...
Bischofshofen d.	...	...	...	...	|	|	...	...	...	1011	|	1116	...	...	|	...	...	...	...	2159	2211	|	...	...
Salzburg 🛃 d.	...	...	...	...	0408	0408	...	...	...	1053	1209	1209	...	...	1905	...	...	...	...	2248	2253	2307	...	...
München Hbf d.	...	...	...	...	0603	0603	0749	...	...	...	1349	1349	...	...	2036	2100	...	...	...	...	...	|	...	...
München Pasing d.	...	...	...	...	...	...	0757	...	...	...	1357	1357	...	...	...	|	...	...	...	...	...	|	...	...
Augsburg d.	...	...	...	...	...	...	0823	...	...	...	1423	1423	...	...	...	2136	...	...	...	...	...	|	...	...
Ulm d.	...	...	...	...	...	...	0905	...	...	...	1505	1505	...	...	...	2226	...	...	...	...	...	|	...	...
Stuttgart d.	...	0612	...	...	...	...	1015	...	...	...	1615	1615	...	...	...	2335	...	...	...	...	...	0303	...	...
Karlsruhe d.	...	0704	...	...	...	...	1111	...	...	...	1711	1711	...	...	...	0049	...	...	...	...	...	0405	...	...
Baden Baden d.	...	0719	...	...	...	...	1129	...	...	...	1729	1729	...	...	...	0106	...	...	...	...	...	|	...	...
Kehl 🛃 d.	...	0744	...	...	...	...	1157	...	...	...	1758	1758	...	...	...	0143	...	...	...	...	...	0452	...	...
Strasbourg a.	...	0753	...	...	...	...	1206	...	...	...	1807	1807	...	...	...	0152	...	...	...	...	...	0501	...	...
Nancy a.	...	0927	...	...	...	...	1335	...	...	...	1934	1934	...	...	...	|	...	...	...	...	...	0643	...	...
Paris Est a.	...	1213	...	...	...	...	1622	...	...	...	2222	2222	...	...	...	0705	...	...	...	...	...	0934	...	...

NOTES

A – ORIENT EXPRESS – 🛏 1,2 cl., 🛌 2 cl. and [2] Paris - Wien and v.v.; 🛌 2 cl. and [2] Paris - Budapest and v.v.; [12] and ✕ Salzburg - Budapest and v.v.; [12] and 🍷 Paris - Strasbourg and v.v.

B – MOZART – [12] and ✕ Paris - Wien and v.v.

C – [12] Paris - Graz and v.v.; ✕ Paris - Salzburg and v.v.; 🍷 Bischofshofen - Graz and v.v.

D – MAURICE RAVEL – [12] and ✕ Paris - München and v.v.

E – KÁLMÁN IMRE – 🛏 1,2 cl., 🛌 2 cl. and [12] München - Budapest and v.v.

F – MARIE CURIE – [12] and ✕ Paris - Stuttgart and v.v.

G – 🛏 1,2 cl., 🛌 2 cl., [2] and 🍷 Paris - München and v.v.

H – 🛌 2 cl. and [12] München - Wien and v.v.

/ – Supplement payable.

Table 33 (Summer) LONDON AND BRUSSELS - FRANKFURT/MAIN AND MÜNCHEN

train type		EC	EC	ICE		IC	IC	ICE			IC	EC	ICE			IC	IC	ICE			EC	IC	IC	ICE
train number	411	27	9	793	413	727	105	593		417	621	109	595		419	729	501	797		9112	47	521	603	597
notes (see page 4)		✕	✕	✕		✕	✕	✕			✕	✕	✕			🍷	✕	✕		✕ R	✕	✕	✕	✕
notes (see below)		/	/	/		M /	/	/			/	/	/			/	/	/		①-⑥	/	/	/	/
London Waterloo 12 d.	...	...	...	...	...	...	...	...	...	...	...	...	...	...	...	...	...	...	...	0723	...	...	...	...
Lille Europe **12** d.	...	...	...	...	...	...	...	...	...	...	...	...	...	...	...	...	...	...	...	1022	...	...	...	...
Oostende d.	0532	...	...	...	0634	...	...	...	...	0834	...	...	...	...	0934	...	...	...	...	|	...	...	...	...
Brussels Midi/Zuid d.	0647	...	...	...	0748	...	...	...	...	0947	...	...	...	...	1047	...	...	...	...	1138	1203	...	...	...
Brussels Nord/Noord d.	0657	...	...	...	0757	...	...	...	...	0957	...	...	...	...	1057	...	...	...	...	...	1212	...	...	...
Liège Guillemins d.	0800	...	...	...	0900	...	...	...	...	1100	...	...	...	...	1200	...	...	...	...	...	1313	...	...	...
Aachen 🛃 a.	0843	...	...	...	0943	...	...	...	...	1143	...	...	...	...	1243	...	...	...	...	...	1351	...	...	...
Köln a.	0942	0954	1000	...	1042	1054	1100	...	...	1242	1254	1300	...	...	1342	1354	1400	...	...	...	1442	1454	1500	...
Bonn a.	...	1012	1018	...	...	1112	1118	...	...	...	1312	1318	...	...	...	1412	1418	...	...	...	...	1512	1518	...
Koblenz a.	...	1045	1151	...	...	1145	1151	...	...	...	1345	1351	...	...	...	1445	1451	...	...	...	...	1545	1551	...
Mainz a.	...	1136	1142	...	...	1236	1242	...	...	...	1436	1442	...	...	...	1536	1542	...	...	...	...	1636	1642	...
Frankfurt/Main a.	...	1207	|	...	...	1307	|	...	...	...	1507	|	...	...	...	1607	|	...	...	...	...	1707	|	...
Würzburg a.	...	1325	|	...	...	1425	|	...	...	...	1625	|	...	...	...	1725	|	...	...	...	...	1825	|	...
Nürnberg a.	...	1422	|	...	...	1522	|	...	...	...	1722	|	...	...	...	1822	|	...	...	...	...	1922	|	...
Praha Hlavni **57** a.	...	|	|	...	...	...	|	...	...	...	...	|	...	...	...	|	|	...	...	...	...	...	|	...
Regensburg **740** a.	...	1524	|	...	...	...	|	...	...	...	...	|	...	...	...	1924	|	...	...	...	...	...	|	...
Mannheim a.	...	...	1223	1227	...	...	1323	1327	...	...	...	1523	1527	...	...	...	1623	1627	...	...	...	...	1723	1727
Stuttgart a.	...	...	...	1306	...	...	...	1408	...	...	...	...	1608	...	...	...	...	1708	...	...	...	...	...	1808
Ulm a.	...	...	...	1404	...	...	...	1503	...	...	...	...	1703	...	...	...	...	1803	...	...	...	...	...	1903
Augsburg a.	...	...	...	1443	...	...	...	1545	...	...	...	...	1745	...	...	...	...	1845	...	...	...	...	...	1944
München Hbf a.	...	...	...	1515	...	...	...	1615	...	...	...	...	1815	...	...	...	...	1915	...	...	...	...	...	2015

NOTES

M – ①-⑥, not June 5.

/ – Supplement payable.

04 For explanation of standard symbols see page 4. 521

Table 33 (Summer) — LONDON AND BRUSSELS - FRANKFURT/MAIN AND MÜNCHEN

Table 1

	425	523	503	599	9124	429	527	507	695	39	827	353	9132	9132	35	738	9148	225	225
train type		IC	IC	ICE			IC	IC	ICE	EC	IC				EC	IC		EN	
notes (see page 4)		🍷	🍷	✗	✗Ⓡ		🍷	✗	✗	✗	🍷		✗Ⓡ	✗Ⓡ	✗	🍷	✗Ⓡ		
notes (see below)				✗	①-⑥			C	✗	✗		N	⑦	①-⑥	✗	✗		A	B
London Waterloo 12 d.	…	…	…	…	1027	…	…	…	…	…	…	…	1214	1227	…	…	1627	…	…
Lille Europe 12 d.	…	…	…	…	…	…	…	…	…	…	…	…	1527	1527	1657	…	…	2013b	2013b
Oostende d.	…	1234	…	…	…	1434	…	…	…	…	…	…			…	…	…	…	…
Brussels Midi/Zuid d.	1348	…	…	…	1438	…	1548	…	…	1655	…	…	1644	1644	…	1808	2046	2125	2125
Brussels Nord/Noord d.	1357	…	…	…	…	1557	…	…	…	1703	…	…	…	…	1817	…	…	2134	2134
Liège Guillemins d.	1500	…	…	…	…	1700	…	…	…	1803	…	…	…	…	1913	…	…	2235	2235
Aachen m a.	1543	…	…	…	…	1743	…	…	…	1845	…	…	…	…	1955	…	…	2318	2318
Köln a.	1642	1654	1700	…	…	1842	1854	1900	…	1942	1954	2035	…	…	2042	2054	…	0017	0017
Bonn a.	…	1712	1718	…	…	…	1912	1918	…	…	2012	2057	…	…	2112	…	…	0109	
Koblenz a.	…	1745	1751	…	…	…	1945	1951	…	…	2045	2134	…	…	2145	…	…	0144	
Mainz a.	…	1836	1842	…	…	…	2036	2042	…	…	2136	2228	…	…	2236	2307	…		
Frankfurt/Main a.	…	1907	…	…	…	…	2107	…	…	…	2207	2300	…	…	…	…	…	0107	
Würzburg a.	…	2025		…	…	…	2225		…	…		0107	…	…	…	…	…		
Nürnberg a.	…	2123		…	…	…	2325		…	…		0211	…	…	…	…	…	0514	
Praha Hlavni 57 a.	…	…	…	…	…	…	…	…	…	…	…	0812	…	…	…	…	…	0618	
Regensburg 740 a.	…	…	…	…	…	…	…	…	…	…	…	…	…	…	…	…	…		
Mannheim a.	…	…	1923	1927	…	…	…	2123	2127	…	…	…	…	…	…	…	…		0321
Stuttgart a.	…	…	…	2006	…	…	…	…	2207	…	…	…	…	…	…	…	…		0454
Ulm a.	…	…	…	2104	…	…	…	…	…	…	…	…	…	…	…	…	…		0603
Augsburg a.	…	…	…	2143	…	…	…	…	…	…	…	…	…	…	…	…	…		0652
München Hbf a.	…	…	…	2215	…	…	…	…	…	…	…	…	…	…	…	…	…		0736

Table 2

	739	34	9133	352	694	504	526	420	898	604	822	422	598	502	524	38	796	500	522	426	9153
train type	IC	EC	✗Ⓡ		ICE	IC	IC		ICE	IC	IC		ICE	IC	IC	EC	ICE	IC	IC		Ⓡ✗
notes (see page 4)	🍷	✗	✗Ⓡ		✗	✗	🍷	✗	✗	🍷	✗	✗	✗	✗	🍷	✗	✗	🍷	✗		Ⓡ
notes (see below)			①-⑥	N					✗		✗										
München Hbf d.	…	…	…	…	…	…	…	…	0645	…	…	…	0745	…	…	…	0845	…	…	…	…
Augsburg d.	…	…	…	…	…	…	…	…	0711	…	…	…	0811	…	…	…	0911	…	…	…	…
Ulm d.	…	…	…	…	…	…	…	…	0751	…	…	…	0851	…	…	…	0951	…	…	…	…
Stuttgart d.	…	…	…	…	0750	…	…	…	0850	…	…	…	0950	…	…	…	1050	…	…	…	…
Mannheim d.	…	…	…	…	0831	0836	…	…	0931	0936	…	…	1031	1036	…	…	1131	1136	…	…	…
Regensburg 740 d.	…	…	…	…	…	…	…	…	…	…	0628c	…	…	…	…	…	…	…	0832	…	…
Praha Hlavni 57 d.	…	…	…	2135	…	…	…	…	…	…	…	…	…	…	…	…	…	…	…	…	…
Nürnberg d.	…	…	…	0357	…	…	…	…	…	…	0733c	…	…	…	0835	…	…	…	0935	…	…
Würzburg d.	…	…	…	0509	…	…	…	…	…	…	0831c	…	…	…	0931	…	…	…	1031	…	…
Frankfurt/Main d.	0651	…	…	0658	…	…	…	0851	…	…	0951	…	…	…	1051	…	…	…	1151	…	…
Mainz d.	0724	…	…	0728	…	…	0918	0924	…	1018	1024	…	…	1118	1124	…	…	1218	1224	…	…
Koblenz d.	0813	…	…	0823	…	1007	1013	…	…	1107	1113	…	…	1207	1213	…	…	1307	1313	…	…
Bonn d.	0845	…	…	0859	…	1039	1045	…	…	1139	1145	…	…	1239	1245	…	…	1339	1345	…	…
Köln d.	0905	0914	…	0921	…	1059	1105	1114	1159	1205	1214	…	1259	1305	1314	…	1359	1405	1414	…	…
Aachen m a.	…	1001	…	…	…	…	…	1205	…	…	…	1305	…	…	…	1410	…	1505	…	…	…
Liège Guillemins a.	…	1036	…	…	…	…	…	1243	…	…	…	1343	…	…	…	1449	…	1543	…	…	…
Brussels Nord/Noord a.	1132	…	…	…	…	…	…	1344	…	…	…	1444	…	…	…	1548	…	1644	…	…	…
Brussels Midi/Zuid a.	1142	1233	…	…	…	…	…	1355	…	…	…	1455	…	…	…	1556	…	1655	…	1722	…
Oostende a.	…	1248	…	…	…	…	…	1509	…	…	…	1609	…	…	…	…	…	1809	…	…	…
Lille Europe 12 a.	…	…	…	…	…	…	…	…	…	…	…	…	…	…	…	…	…	…	…	…	1839
London Waterloo 12 a.	…	…	1443	…	…	…	…	…	…	…	…	…	…	…	…	…	…	…	…	…	1939

Table 3

	596	602	620	46	9159	796	102	728	430	794	104	28	434	792	8	26	438	224	214	9121	9125
train type	ICE	IC	IC	EC	Ⓡ✗	ICE	EC	IC		ICE	EC	EC	✗	ICE	EC	EC	✗	EN		Ⓡ✗	Ⓡ✗
notes (see page 4)	✗	✗	🍷	✗	Ⓡ	✗	✗	✗	✗	✗	✗	✗	✗	✗	✗	✗	✗			Ⓡ	Ⓡ
notes (see below)																		A	B	⑦	①-⑥
München Hbf d.	…	0945	…	…	…	1045	…	…	…	1245	…	…	…	1445	…	…	…	…	2211	…	…
Augsburg d.	…	1011	…	…	…	1111	…	…	…	1311	…	…	…	1511	…	…	…	…	2246	…	…
Ulm d.	…	1051	…	…	…	1151	…	…	…	1351	…	…	…	1551	…	…	…	…	2334	…	…
Stuttgart d.	1150	…	…	…	…	1250	…	…	…	1450	…	…	…	1650	…	…	…	…	0041	…	…
Mannheim d.	1231	1236	…	…	…	1331	1336	…	…	1531	1536	…	…	1731	1736	…	…	…	0211	…	…
Regensburg 740 d.	…	…	…	…	…	…	…	1032	…	…	…	…	1232	…	…	1432	…	2325	…	…	…
Praha Hlavni 57 d.	…	…	…	…	…	…	…	…	…	…	…	…	…	…	…	…	…	…	…	…	…
Nürnberg d.	…	…	1035	…	…	…	…	1135	…	…	…	…	1335	…	…	1535	…	0028	…	…	…
Würzburg d.	…	…	1131	…	…	…	…	1231	…	…	…	…	1431	…	…	1631	…	…	…	…	…
Frankfurt/Main d.	…	…	1251	…	…	…	…	1351	…	…	…	…	1551	…	…	1751	…	…	…	…	…
Mainz d.	…	1318	1324	…	…	…	1418	1424	…	…	1618	1624	…	…	1818	1824	…	0256	…	…	…
Koblenz d.	…	1407	1413	…	…	…	1507	1513	…	…	1707	1713	…	…	1907	1913	…	0350	…	…	…
Bonn d.	…	1439	1445	…	…	…	1539	1545	…	…	1739	1745	…	…	1939	1945	…	0424	…	…	…
Köln d.	…	1459	1505	1514	…	…	1559	1605	1614	…	1759	1805	1814	…	1959	2005	2014	0508	0508	0606	0606
Aachen m a.	…	…	…	1607	…	…	…	…	1705	…	…	…	1905	…	…	…	2105	…	0606	…	…
Liège Guillemins a.	…	…	…	1648	…	…	…	…	1743	…	…	…	1943	…	…	…	2143	…	0647	…	…
Brussels Nord/Noord a.	…	…	…	1749	…	…	…	…	1844	…	…	…	2044	…	…	…	2244	…	0755	…	…
Brussels Midi/Zuid a.	…	…	…	1801	1856	…	…	…	1855	…	…	…	2055	…	…	…	2255	0804	0804	0928	1028
Oostende a.	…	…	…	…	…	…	…	…	2009	…	…	…	2209	…	…	…	0009	0918b	0918b	…	…
Lille Europe 12 a.	…	…	…	…	…	…	…	…	…	…	…	…	…	…	…	…	…	…	…	1041	1141
London Waterloo 12 a.	…	…	…	…	2109	…	…	…	…	…	…	…	…	…	…	…	…	…	…	1143	1239

NOTES

A – 🛏 1,2 cl., 🛏 2 cl. and 🚗 Oostende - Regensburg - (Wien) and v.v.

B – 🛏 1,2 cl., 🛏 2 cl. and 🚗 Oostende - München and v.v.

C – ①②③④⑤⑦, not June 4.

N – 🛏 1,2 cl., 🛏 2 cl. and 🚗 (Dortmund) - Köln - Praha and v.v.

Z – Eurostar service, days of running subject to confirmation.

b – Daily to Sept. 3.

c – ①-⑥, not June 5.

✗ – Supplement payable.

Table 34 (Summer)   LONDON AND BRUSSELS - WIEN AND INNSBRUCK

train number	9132	1219	1219	1219	9148	EN 225	EC 63	IC 505
notes (see page 4)	R ✕				R ✕	✕		♟
notes (see below)		B	C	D		A ⁄		
London Waterloo 12 d.	1227n	...	...	...	1627	...	...	...
Lille Europe .... d.	1527	...	...	...	...	...	...	...
Oostende .... d.		1807	1807	1807		2013b	...	...
Brussels Midi/Zuid ... d.	1644	1923	1923	1923	2046	2125	...	...
Brussels Nord/Noord d.		1932	1932	1932		2134	...	...
Liège Guillemins .... d.		2034	2034	2034		2235	...	...
Aachen .... a.		2118	2118	2118		2318	...	...
Köln Hbf .... a.		2227	2227	2227		0017	...	...
Namur .... d.								
Luxembourg .... d.								
Metz .... d.								
Strasbourg .... d.								
Basel .... d.								
Zürich .... d.								
Buchs .... a.								
Feldkirch .... a.								
Bludenz .... a.								
Langen am A. ...... a.								
St. Anton am A. ... a.								
Landeck .... a.								
Ötztal .... a.								
Kufstein .... a.		0640	0640					
Wörgl .... a.		0655	0655					
Innsbruck .... a.		0738						
Kirchberg in Tirol .... a.		...	0727					
Kitzbühel .... a.			0735					
St. Johann in Tirol ... a.			0744					
Saalfelden .... a.			0815					
Zell am See .... a.			0825					
Passau .... a.						0729		
Linz .... a.						0900		1040
Graz .... a.							1414	
Wien Westbahnhof ... a.						1058		1320
Budapest Keleti ... a.							1643	
Salzburg .... a.				0733				
Bischofshofen ...... a.				0840				
Schwarzach St. Veit a.				0859				
Badgastein .... a.				0938				
Villach Hbf .... a.				1054				
Klagenfurt .... a.				1128				

train number	IC 600	EC 62	EN 224	9121	1216	1618	1218	9125
notes (see page 4)	♟	✕	A	R ⑦		R ✕		R ✕ ①–⑥
notes (see below)			⁄		E	F	G	
sea crossing								
Klagenfurt .... d.	...	...	...	...	1805	...	...	...
Villach Hbf .... d.	...	...	...	...	1849	...	...	...
Badgastein .... d.	...	...	...	...	2002	...	...	...
Schwarzach St. Veit .. d.	...	...	...	...	2030	...	...	...
Bischofshofen .... d.	...	...	...	...	2047	...	...	...
Salzburg .... d.	...	...	...	...	2143	...	...	...
Budapest Keleti ... d.	...	1225	...	...	...	...	...	...
Wien Westbahnhof ... d.	...	1550	1844	...	...	...	...	...
Graz .... d.	1550	...	...	...	...	...	...	...
Linz .... d.	1920	...	2039	...	...	...	...	...
Passau .... d.	...	...	2216	...	...	...	...	...
Zell am See .... d.	...	...	...	...	...	2030	...	...
Saalfelden .... d.	...	...	...	...	...	2041	...	...
St. Johann in Tirol .. d.	...	...	...	...	...	2111	...	...
Kitzbühel .... d.	...	...	...	...	...	2120	...	...
Kirchberg in Tirol .... d.	...	...	...	...	...	2128	...	...
Innsbruck .... d.	...	...	...	...	...	...	2115	...
Wörgl .... d.	...	...	...	...	...	2205	2205	...
Kufstein .... d.	...	...	...	...	...	2219	2219	...
Ötztal .... d.								
Landeck .... d.								
St. Anton am A. .... d.								
Langen am Arlberg ... d.								
Bludenz .... d.								
Feldkirch .... d.								
Buchs .... a.								
Zürich .... a.								
Basel .... a.								
Strasbourg .... a.								
Metz .... a.								
Luxembourg .... a.								
Namur .... a.								
Köln Hbf .... a.	...	...	0450	...	0641	0641	0641	...
Aachen .... a.	...	...	0555	...	0732	0732	0732	...
Liège Guillemins ..... a.	...	...	0647	...	0823	0823	0823	...
Brussels Nord/Noord . a.	...	...	0755	...	0923	0923	0923	...
Brussels Midi/Zuid ... a.	...	...	0804	0928	0933	0933	0933	1028
Oostende .... a.	...	...	0918b	...	1045	1045	1045	...
Lille Europe .... a.	...	...	...	1041	...	...	...	1141
London Waterloo 12 ... a.	...	...	...	1143	...	...	...	1239

NOTES

A – DONAUWALZER – [couchette] 1,2 cl., [seat] 2 cl. and [couchette] Oostende - Wien and v.v.
B – ⑤ June 2 - Sept. 22: [seat] 2 cl. Oostende - Innsbruck - (Verona).
C – ⑤ June 2 - Sept. 22: [seat] 2 cl. and [couchette] Oostende - Zell am See.
D – ⑤ June 2 - Sept. 22: [seat] 2 cl. and [couchette] Oostende - Klagenfurt.
E – ⑥ June 3 - Sept. 23: [seat] 2 cl. and [couchette] Klagenfurt - Oostende.

F – ⑥ June 3 - Sept. 23: [seat] 2 cl. and [couchette] Zell am See - Oostende.
G – ⑥ June 3 - Sept. 23: [seat] 2 cl. (Verona) - Innsbruck - Oostende.
H – Eurostar service, days of running subject to confirmation.
b – Daily to Sept. 3 only.
n – Depart 1214 on ⑦.
⁄ – Supplement payable.

Table 35 (Summer)   AMSTERDAM - WIEN AND INNSBRUCK

train number	1217	1217	1217	EN 215	EC 63	IC 505
notes (see page 4)				1,2	1,2 ✕	♟
notes (see below)	P	M	N	R		
Amsterdam Centraal ... d.	1939	1939	1939	2056	...	...
Utrecht .... d.	2025	2025	2025	2130	...	...
Arnhem .... d.	2105	2105	2105	2214	...	...
Emmerich .... d.	2133	2133	2133	2248	...	...
Friedrichshafen Stadt . a.						
Lindau .... a.						
Bregenz .... a.						
Feldkirch .... a.						
Bludenz .... a.						
Langen .... a.						
St. Anton .... a.						
Landeck .... a.						
Ötztal .... a.						
München Hbf .... a.						
Kufstein .... a.		0640	0640			
Wörgl .... a.		0655	0655			
Innsbruck .... a.		0738				
Kirchberg in Tirol ... a.		...	0727			
Kitzbühel .... a.			0735			
St. Johann in Tirol .. a.			0744			
Saalfelden .... a.			0815			
Zell am See .... a.			0825			
Salzburg .... a.	0733					
Bischofshofen ..... a.	0840					
Schwarzach St. Veit a.	0859					
Badgastein .... a.	0938					
Villach Hbf .... a.	1054					
Klagenfurt .... a.	1128					
Passau .... a.				0729		
Linz .... a.				0900		1040
Graz .... a.					1414	
Wien Westbahnhof .. a.				1058		1320
Budapest Keleti ... a.					1643	

train number	IC 600	EC 62	EN 224	1618	1218	1216
notes (see page 4)	1,2 ♟	1,2 ✕	R			
notes (see below)				S	T	V
Budapest Keleti ... d.	...	1225	...	...	...	...
Wien Westbahnhof ... d.	...	1550	1844	...	...	...
Graz .... d.	1550	...	...	...	...	...
Linz .... d.	1920	...	2039	...	...	...
Passau .... d.	...	...	2216	...	...	...
Klagenfurt .... d.	...	...	...	...	...	1805
Villach Hbf .... d.	...	...	...	...	...	1849
Badgastein .... d.	...	...	...	...	...	2002
Schwarzach St. Veit . d.	...	...	...	...	...	2030
Bischofshofen ...... d.	...	...	...	...	...	2047
Salzburg .... d.	...	...	...	...	...	2143
Zell am See .... d.	...	...	...	2030	...	...
Saalfelden .... d.	...	...	...	2041	...	...
St. Johann .... d.	...	...	...	2111	...	...
Kitzbühel .... d.	...	...	...	2120	...	...
Kirchberg .... d.	...	...	...	2128	...	...
Innsbruck .... d.	...	...	...	...	2115	...
Wörgl .... d.	...	...	...	2205	2205	...
Kufstein .... d.	...	...	...	2219	2219	...
München Hbf ...... d.						
Ötztal .... d.						
Landeck .... d.						
St. Anton .... d.						
Langen .... d.						
Bludenz .... d.						
Feldkirch .... d.						
Bregenz .... d.						
Lindau .... d.						
Friedrichshafen Stadt . a.						
Emmerich .... a.	...	...	0702	0815	0815	0815
Arnhem .... a.	...	...	0741	0845	0845	0845
Utrecht .... a.	...	...	0823	0935	0935	0935
Amsterdam Centraal .. a.	...	...	0857	1011	1011	1011

NOTES

M – ⑤ June 2 - Sept. 22: [seat] 2 cl. and [couchette] Amsterdam - Innsbruck - (Verona).
N – ⑤ June 2 - Sept. 22: [seat] 2 cl. and [couchette] Amsterdam - Zell am See.
P – ⑤ June 2 - Sept. 22: [seat] 2 cl. and [couchette] Amsterdam - Klagenfurt.

R – DONAUWALZER – [couchette] 1,2 cl., [seat] 2 cl. and [couchette] Amsterdam - Wien and v.v.
S – ⑥ June 3 - Sept. 23: [seat] 2 cl. and [couchette] Zell am See - Amsterdam.
T – ⑥ June 3 - Sept. 23: [seat] 2 cl. and [couchette] (Verona) - Innsbruck - Amsterdam.
V – ⑥ June 3 - Sept. 23: [seat] 2 cl. and [couchette] Klagenfurt - Amsterdam.

Table 38 (Summer)   AMSTERDAM - ZÜRICH AND INTERLAKEN

train number		EC	IC			EC		IC	IC						
train number		105	1685	337	983		3		839	257	1736		203	203	1706	203	203
notes (see page 4)		B ⚟	⚲	⚲	⚲		A ⚟		✕	⚲			M	E		K	F
Amsterdam Centraal .... d.	...	0800	...	...	...		0900	...	...	...		2005	2005	...	2005	2005	...
Utrecht .... d.	...	0830	...	...	...		0930	...	...	...		2047	2047	...	2047	2047	...
Arnhem .... d.	...	0905	...	...	...		1005	...	...	...		2127	2127	...	2127	2127	...
Emmerich ▥ .... d.	...	0934	...	...	...		1034	...	...	...		2157	2157	...	2157	2157	...
Basel SBB ▥ .... a.	...	1543	1551		1625		1645		1701	1720		0640	0640	...	0640		...
Zürich Hbf .... a.				1723			1803							0815		
Sargans .... a.							1919							0939		
Landquart .... a.							1932	...	1935					0955	1040	
Davos Platz .... a.									2050						1146	
Chur .... a.							1944	1952						1008		1052
St. Moritz .... a.								2158								1258
Olten .... a.	...	1628	1621						1727	1747			0728		0734	
Luzern .... a.			1704							1827			0813			
Arth Goldau .... a.			1740							1858			0844			
Bellinzona .... a.			1951							2047			1029			
Lugano .... a.			2021							2117			1058			
Chiasso .... a.			2056							2142			1123			
Bern .... a.	...	1710		1722					1812		1828		0810	0828		
Thun .... a.	...	1746		1741					1841		1848		0840	0848		
Spiez .... a.	...	1757		1752					1852		1859		0851	0859		
Interlaken West .... a.	...	1814									1916			0916		
Interlaken Ost .... a.	...	1819									1921			0921		
Brig .... a.	...			1859					1959					0958		

train number		EC		EC			IC		EC				IC	336	
train number		96	250	1821	104		1723	820	1670		2			472	1690	890	2544	202
notes (see page 4)		✕	⚲	⚲			⚲	✕			A ⚟			H	K	✕	G	M
Brig .... d.					1001		...		1101							2001		
Interlaken Ost .... d.					1039		1139								1939		
Interlaken West .... d.					1044		1144								1944		
Spiez .... d.				1107	1101		1201	1207							2001	2108	
Thun .... d.				1118	1112		1212	1218							2012	2119	
Bern .... d.				1138	1148		1232	1248							2032	2153	
Chiasso .... d.			0827						0906						1704		
Lugano .... d.			0854						0941						1738		
Bellinzona .... d.			0923						1009						1806		
Arth Goldau .... d.			1120						1256						2018		
Luzern .... d.			1156												2055		
Olten .... d.			1239		1232			1332	1339						2138		2241
St. Moritz .... d.		0805											1800				
Chur .... d.		1007	1023						1107	1115			2007	2032			
Davos Platz .... d.	0905							1005				1905					
Landquart .... d.	1017		1034					1117		1126			2017	2044			
Sargans .... d.			1045							1139				2059			
Zürich Hbf .... d.			1200							1257				2215			
Basel SBB ▥ .... d.			1306	1309		1317		1359	1409		1417				2325		2325	2325
Emmerich ▥ .... a.						1924					2024				0741	0741	0741	0741
Arnhem .... a.						1952					2052				0825	0825	0825	0825
Utrecht .... a.						2023					2123				0906	0906	0906	0906
Amsterdam Centraal .... a.						2051					2151				0940	0940	0940	0940

Table 39 (Summer)   AMSTERDAM - MILANO AND ROMA

train number		IC					
train number		201	533	2093	2183		1217
notes (see page 4)		C	⚟	✕	⚲		D
Amsterdam Centraal .... d.	...	1755	...	...	...		1939	...
Utrecht .... d.	...	1830	...	...	...		2025	...
Arnhem .... d.	...	1905	...	...	...		2105	...
Emmerich ▥ .... d.	...	1933	...	...	...		2133	...
Basel SBB ▥ .... d.								
Chiasso ▥ .... a.		0637						
Como .... a.		0700						
Milano Centrale .... a.		0745	0800	0810	0815			
Brennero ▥ .... a.							0818	
Fortezza .... a.							0914	
Bolzano .... a.							1004	
Verona .... a.					0951		1158	
Venezia Santa Lucia ...... a.					1125			
Genova P. Principe ...... a.				1005				
Ventimiglia .... a.				1250				
Bologna .... a.		1036	0944					
Firenze SMN .... a.			1053					
Roma Termini .... a.			1255					
Napoli Centrale .... a.			1500					
Ravenna .... a.		1143						
Rimini .... a.		1232						

train number				IC	IC	IC		
train number		1218		688	658	544	200
notes (see page 4)		L		⚟	⚟	⚟	C
Rimini .... d.	...	...		...	...	...	1610
Ravenna .... d.	...	...		...	...	...	1718
Napoli Centrale .... d.	...	...		...	...	...	...
Roma Termini .... d.	...	...		...	...	1605	...
Firenze SMN .... d.	...	...		...	...	1807	...
Bologna .... d.	...	...		...	...	1916	1848
Ventimiglia .... d.	...	...		...	...	...	...
Genova P. Principe .... d.	...	...		...	1913	...	...
Venezia Mestre .... d.	...	...		...	1817	...	...
Verona .... d.	...	1632		...	1934	...	...
Bolzano .... d.	...	1814		...	...	...	...
Fortezza .... d.	...	1901		...	...	...	...
Brennero ▥ .... d.	...	2026		...	...	...	...
Milano Centrale .... d.	...	...		2050	2055	2100	2125
Como .... d.	...	...		...	...	...	2205
Chiasso ▥ .... d.	...	...		...	...	...	2230
Basel SBB ▥ .... d.							
Emmerich ▥ .... a.		0815		...	...	...	0956
Arnhem .... a.		0845		...	...	...	1023
Utrecht .... a.		0935		...	...	...	1100
Amsterdam Centraal .... a.		1011		...	...	...	1133

NOTES for Tables 38 and 39.

A – REMBRANDT – ⬛ and ✕ Amsterdam - Chur and v.v.

B – BERNER OBERLAND – ⬛ and ✕ Amsterdam - Interlaken and v.v.

C – ⬛ 1,2 cl., ⬛ 2 cl., ⬛ and ⚲ Amsterdam - Rimini and v.v.

D – ⑤ June 2 - Sept. 22: ⬛ 2 cl. and ⬛ Amsterdam - Verona.

E – SCHWEIZ EXPRESS – ⑤⑥: ⬛ 1,2 cl. and ⬛ 2 cl. Amsterdam - Brig.

F – SCHWEIZ EXPRESS – ⬛ 1,2 cl. and ⬛ 2 cl. Amsterdam - Zürich;
⬛ 2 cl. (also ⬛ 1,2 cl. on ⑤) Amsterdam - Chur.

G – SCHWEIZ EXPRESS – ⑥⑦: ⬛ 1,2 cl. and ⬛ 2 cl. Brig - Amsterdam.

H – SCHWEIZ EXPRESS – ⬛ 1,2 cl. and ⬛ 2 cl. Zürich - Amsterdam;
⬛ 2 cl. (also ⬛ 1,2 cl. on ⑥) Chur - Amsterdam.

K – ⬛ 2 cl. Amsterdam - Chiasso and v.v.

L – ⑥ June 3 - Sept. 23: ⬛ 2 cl. and ⬛ Verona - Amsterdam.

M – ⬛ 1,2 cl., ⬛ 2 cl. and ⬛ Amsterdam - Basel and v.v.

⚟ – Supplement payable.

Table 40 (Summer)   LONDON AND BRUSSELS - BASEL, ZÜRICH AND INTERLAKEN

train type	EC			EC		EC						EC									
train number	91	1728	1679	103		9112	97	1789		2691	893	2443	295	115	9132	299	9152	499	1661	2405	499		499
notes (see page 4)		☼	☼	✕		✕ ®	☼							✕	✕ ®		✕ ®		☼				
notes (see below)	G ⁄					①-⑥	H ⁄							K		D		A			B		C
London Waterloo 12 d.						0723								1227n		1715r							
Brussels Midi/Zuid ....d.	0715					1138	1219						1513	1644	1913	2139	2217		2217		2217		2217
Brussels Nord/Noord d.	0723						1227						1521		1921		2226		2226		2226		2226
Brussels QL ....d.	0733						1238						1531		1931		2238		2238		2238		2238
Namur ....d.	0808						1312						1608		2008		2316		2316		2316		2316
Luxembourg 🚇 ....d.	1001						1459						1802		2201		0118		0118		0118		0118
Metz ....d.	1046						1544						1847		2252		0215		0215		0215		0215
Strasbourg ....d.	1211						1708						2008		0018		0353		0353		0353		0353
Mulhouse ....d.	1315						1803						2106		0117		0453		0453		0453		0453
Basel SBB 🚇 ....a.	1339		1351	1354			1825			1851	1901		2130	2148	0140		0516	0600	0516		0516		0516
Zürich Hbf ....a.				1500			1945	2010						2247				0657					
Sargans ....a.				1613				2119										0819					
Landquart ......a.				1625		1640		2135	2145									0833	0852				
Davos Platz ....a.						1746			2259										1002				
Chur ....a.			1637	1652				2149										0828		0900		
St. Moritz ......a.					1858															1118		
Olten ....a.	1428		1421							1921	1927					0620	0630						
Luzern ....a.			1504								2004						0712						
Arth Goldau ....a.			1540														0744						
Bellinzona ......a.			1751												0505		0951						
Lugano ....a.			1821												0535		1021						
Chiasso ....a.			1856												0602		1056						
Bern ....a.	1510	1528									2012	2028				0710		0728					
Thun ....a.	1540	1548										2048				0741		0748					
Spiez ....a.	1551	1559										2059				0752		0759					
Interlaken West.......a.		1616										2119						0816					
Interlaken Ost ....a.		1621										2123						0821					
Biel ....a.																						0730
Neuchâtel ....a.																						0759
Lausanne ....a.																						0848
Vevey ....a.																						0914
Montreux ....a.																						0919
Aigle ....a.																						0931
Bex ....a.																						0937
Martigny ....a.																						0952
Sion ....a.																						1008
Sierre ....a.																						1019
Visp ....a.																						1046
Brig ....a.	1658															0858						1053

train type	IC			IC	EC			EC				EC	IC							
train number	952	296	9153	1821	104	250		96	1676			1780	1727	90	254	498		1794	1647	9113	298	9125
notes (see page 4)	☼		✕ ®	☼	✕	☼			☼			✕	☼	☼						✕ ®	✕ ®
notes (see below)		K						L ⁄				G ⁄		A				B	E	①-⑥	D	①-⑥
Brig ....d.			1001									1301				2001			1907			
Visp ....d.																			1913			
Sierre ....d.																			1940			
Sion ....d.																			1952			
Martigny ....d.																			2008			
Bex ....d.																			2023			
Aigle ....d.																			2030			
Montreux ....d.																			2043			
Vevey ....d.																			2049			
Lausanne ....d.																			2112			
Neuchâtel ....d.																			2209			
Biel ....d.																			2230			
Interlaken Ost ....d.				1039								1339		2040								
Interlaken West.......d.				1044								1344		2044								
Spiez ....d.			1107	1101								1401	1408	2102	2107							
Thun ....d.			1118	1112								1412	1419	2118								
Bern ....d.			1138	1148								1432	1450	2153								
Chiasso ....d.					0827			1106				1830								2240		
Lugano ....d.					0854			1141				1857								2307		
Bellinzona ......d.					0923			1209				1927								2335		
Arth Goldau ....d.					1120			1420				2114										
Luzern ....d.					1156			1456				2146										
Olten ....d.					1230	1239		1539				1532	2225	2241							
St. Moritz ....d.							0805		1100				1800								
Chur ....d.						1007		1015	1307	1315			2007		2014						
Davos Platz ....d.							0905		1205						1905						
Landquart ......d.						1017		1025	1317	1326					2017	2024					
Sargans ....d.							1039			1339						2039					
Zürich Hbf ......d.	0635					1200				1500						2200					
Basel SBB 🚇 ....d.	0735	0814		1259	1309		1330	1609			1611	1626	2253	2359		2359	2359	0300			
Mulhouse ....d.		0840					1353					1650		0026		0026	0026	0324			
Strasbourg ......d.		0943					1444					1748		0125		0125	0125	0423			
Metz ....d.		1117					1605					1913		0302		0302	0302	0553			
Luxembourg 🚇 ....a.		1200					1649					1956		0357		0357	0357	0647			
Namur ....a.		1347					1837					2143		0552		0552	0552	0836			
Brussels QL ....a.		1422					1910					2218		0630		0630	0630	0911			
Brussels Nord ....a.		1432					1920					2228		0640		0640	0640	0921			
Brussels Midi ....a.		1440	1722				1928					2237		0649		0649	0649	0731	0930	1028
London Waterloo 12 a.			1939															0649	0649	0943	1239

NOTES

A – 🚋 1,2 cl. and ⊣ 2 cl. Brussels - Brig and v.v.

B – ⊣ 2 cl. and 🚋 Brussels - Chur and v.v.

C – ⑤, daily June 23 - Sept. 1: ⊣ 2 cl. Brussels - Sierre - Brig.

D – 🚋 1,2 cl., 🚋 1,2 cl. (T2), ⊣ 2 cl. and 🚋 Brussels - Chiasso - (Milano) and v.v.

E – ⑥, daily June 24 - Sept. 2: ⊣ 2 cl. Brig - Sierre - Brussels.

G – VAUBAN – 🚋 and ✕ Brussels - Chiasso - (Milano) and v.v.

H – IRIS – 🚋 and ✕ Brussels - Zürich.

K – EDELWEISS – 🚋 and ✕ Brussels - Basel and v.v.

L – IRIS – 🚋 and ✕ Chur - Brussels.

Z – Eurostar service, days of operation subject to confirmation.

n – Depart 1414 on ⑦.

r – Depart 1727 on ⑥⑦.

⁄ – Supplement payable.

Table 41 (Summer)   PARIS - ZÜRICH AND LUZERN

train type	EC 113	2677	EC 57	IC 769			1743	IC 977	EC 9	1745	1783	2687	1847	1747	1789	2691		EC 115	2697	469		469
train number			✕	✕				⚑	✕	⚑	⚑				⚑							
notes (see below)	A ✗										G		©	Ⓐ				B ✗		C		D
Paris Est .... d.	0730	...	...	...			0842b	...	1152	...	...	1330	1341	...	...	...		1700	...	2240		2240
Belfort .... d.	1114	...	...	...			1309	...	1544	...	...	1733	1734	...	...	...		2044	...	0413		0413
Mulhouse .... d.	1145	...	...	...			1342	...	1612	...	...	1811	1811	...	...	...		2117	...	0504		0504
Basel SBB/SNCF ⬛ ...... a.	1211	1251	...	...			1408	1425	1507	1637	1649	1651	1836	1836	1849	1851		2140	2202	0530		0530
Zürich Hbf .... a.	1323		1333	1410				1523		1800				2000				2245		0657		
Sargans 310 .... a.	...			1513																0833	0852	
Landquart 310 .... a.	...			1525	1540																1002	
Davos Platz .... a.	...				1646																...	
Chur 310 .... a.	...			1537		1550														0828		0900
St. Moritz .... a.	...					1758																1118
Olten .... a.	...	1321							1533			1721			1921					2228		0630
Luzern .... a.	...	1404							1612			1804			2004					2310		0712
Arth Goldau 290 .... a.	...								1644													0744
Bellinzona 290 .... a.	...		1559						1832													0954
Lugano 290 .... a.	...		1629						1903													1022
Chiasso 290 .... a.	...								1930													1056

train type		5204	EC		IC	IC					EC		1680	1784	1748		256		468
train number		2656	114		302	966	1744		1676		1780	116							
notes (see page 4)			⚑		⚑	✕			⚑		✕		⚑	⚑					
notes (see below)			B ✗									F ✗					E		C
Chiasso .... d.	...	...	...		0730	...	...	1106	...	...	...	...	...	...	...		1930		...
Lugano 290 .... d.	...	...	...		0757	...	...	1141	...	...	...	...	...	...	...		1956		...
Bellinzona .... d.	...	...	...		0827	...	...	1209	...	...	...	...	1409	...	...		2025		...
Arth Goldau .... d.	...	...	0600		1020	...	...	1420	...	...	...	...	1620	...	...		2214		...
Luzern .... d.	...	...	0635		1056	...	...	1456	...	...	...	...	1656	...	...		2245		...
Olten .... d.	...	...	0717		1139	...	...	1539	...	...	...	...	1739	...	...		2331		...
St. Moritz .... d.	...	...	...				...		1100	...	...	...		...	1900		...		2114
Chur 310 .... d.	...	...	...				...		1307	1315	...	...		...	2107		...		2114
Davos Platz .... d.	...	...	...				...		1205		...	...		...			2000		
Landquart 310 .... d.	...	...	...				...		1317	1326	...	...		...			2115		2124
Sargans .... d.	...	...	...				...		1339		...	...		...			2140		2140
Zürich Hbf .... d.	...	...	...		0715		1137			1450	1537	...	1700	...			2300		2300
Basel SBB/SNCF ⬛ ..... d.	...	...	0749	0823	1209	1235	1248		1609		1648	1809	1811	1830		0028		0028
Mulhouse .... a.	...	...	...	0846			1313		...		1710	...	...	1854		0054		0054
Belfort .... a.	...	...	...	0919			1355		...		1736	...	...	1935		0141		0141
Paris Est .... a.	...	...	...	1314			1806		...		2132	...	...	2343		0648		0648

NOTES
A – LE CORBUSIER – ①②③④⑤⑥, not June 5, July 15, Aug. 14,15:
   🛏 Paris - Zürich; ⚑ Paris - Basel.
B – L'ARBALETE – 🛏 and ✕ Paris - Zürich and v.v.
C – 🛏 1,2 cl., ⚼ 2 cl. and 🛏 Paris - Chur and v.v.; 🛏 Paris - Basel and v.v.
D – ⚼ 2 cl. (also 🛏) June 23 - Sept. 1) Paris - Chiasso.

E – ⚼ 2 cl. (also 🛏) June 24 - Sept. 2) Chiasso - Paris.
F – LE CORBUSIER – ①②③④⑤⑦, not June 4, July 14, Aug. 13,14:
   🛏 Zürich - Paris; ⚑ Basel - Paris.
G – ⑤⑥.
b – Depart 0839 on ⑦.
✗ – Supplement payable.

Table 42 (Summer)   PARIS - LAUSANNE AND BERN

train type	TGV EC21	IC 323	1923		TGV EC23	IC 335	1937	423			TGV EC29	IC 329	1536	TGV EC429		TGV EC27	2147	427
train number			✕			⚑	⚑					⚑						
notes (see below)	A ✗				B ✗						C ✗			C ✗		D ✗		
Paris Lyon .... d.	...	0714	...	...	1225	...	...	...		...	1552	...	1731	...		1807	...	...
Dijon .... d.	...	0853	...	...	1403	...	...	...		...	1731	...	1731	...		1946	...	...
Frasne .... d.	...	1015	...	...	1518	...	1521	...		...	1851	...	1855	...		2106	...	2110
Pontarlier ⬛ .... d.	...		...	...		...	1534	...		...		...	1908	...			...	2123
Neuchâtel .... a.	...		...	...		...	1614	...		...		...	1949	...			...	2204
Bern .... a.	...		...	...		...	1647	...		...	1909	...	2022	...			...	2239
Vallorbe ⬛ .... d.	1034		...	...	1535	...		...		...	1945	1953	1956	...		2125	...	...
Lausanne .... a.	1106	1113	1132		1607	1613	1632			...			2047	2104		2157	2202	...
Vevey .... a.			1146				1646			...				2010			2216	...
Montreux .... a.			1151				1651			...				2015			2221	...
Aigle .... a.			1203				1703			...				2028			2223	...
Bex .... a.			1209				1709			...				2034			2239	...
St. Maurice .... a.			1214				1714			...				2044			2244	...
Martigny .... a.			1225				1725			...				2049			2255	...
Sion .... a.		1207	1241			1707	1741			...			2047	2104			2310	...
Sierre .... a.			1255				1755			...				2116			2322	...
Leuk .... a.			1304				1804			...				2126			2331	...
Visp .... a.			1316	1336			1816	1836		...				2145			2348	...
Zermatt .... a.				1445				1945		...								...
Brig .... a.			1236	1323			1736	1823		...			2116	2152			2355	...

train type	TGV EC422	1904	TGV EC22		420	1521	TGV EC20		1918	IC 330	TGV EC24		426	1930	IC 322	TGV EC26		2136	TGV EC28
train number		⚑				⚑				⚑					⚑	⚑			
notes (see below)	C ✗		C ✗				D ✗		A ✗							B ✗		E ✗	
Brig .... d.	...	0525	...		...	0807	...		1036	1116	...		...	1536	1615	...		1807	...
Zermatt .... d.	...		...		0600		0910				...	1410				1610			...
Visp .... d.	...	0532	...		0709	0813	1021		1042	...	...	1521		1542		1721		1813	...
Leuk .... d.	...	0551	...			0830			1054	...	...			1554				1830	...
Sierre .... d.	...	0601	...			0840			1104	...	...			1604				1840	...
Sion .... d.	...	0613	...			0852			1117	1147	...			1617	1645			1852	...
Martigny .... d.	...	0629	...			0908			1134	...	...			1634				1908	...
St. Maurice .... d.	...	0640	...			0918			1145	...	...			1645				1923	...
Bex .... d.	...	0645	...			0923			1150	...	...			1650				1930	...
Aigle .... d.	...	0652	...			0930			1156	...	...			1656				1943	...
Montreux .... d.	...	0703	...			0943			1207	...	...			1707				1949	...
Vevey .... d.	...	0710	...			0949			1213	...	...			1713				...	...
Lausanne .... d.	...	0725	0731			1003	1015		1227	1240	1246			1727	1740	1753		2003	2015
Vallorbe ⬛ .... a.	...		0804				1047				1318					1825			2047
Bern .... d.	0700				0922								1705						
Neuchâtel .... d.	0733				1004								1740						
Pontarlier ⬛ .... a.	0814				1047								1823						
Frasne .... a.	0828		0823		1059		1106				1444		1835			1845		210	
Dijon .... a.	0943		0939				1216									1957		221	
Paris Lyon .... a.	1124		1124				1357				1630					2139		235	

NOTES see next page.

Table 43 (Summer)   LONDON AND BRUSSELS - MILANO AND ROMA

train type	EC	P	IC							P			
train number	91	515	687	2113	9112	295	9136	1291	299	505	2093	2183	1219
notes (see page 4)		℞	✕	♀	℞	✕	℞			℞	✕	♀	
notes (see below)	E	∕	∕	∕		L	T		L	D			G	∕	∕	♀			B
London Waterloo 12 .... d.	...	...	...	...	...	0727	...	...	1327	...	...	...	...
Oostende .... d.	...	...	...	...	...	...	...	...	...	...	...	...	...
Brussels Midi/Zuid .... d.	...	0715	...	...	1134	1513	...	1738	1756	...	1913	...	1807
Brussels Nord/Noord .... d.	...	0723	...	...	...	1521	...	...	1807	...	1921	...	1923
Liège Guillemins .... d.	...	...	...	...	...	...	...	...	...	...	...	...	1932
Aachen ⋒.............................. d.	...	...	...	...	...	...	...	...	...	...	...	...	2034
Namur.................................... d.	...	0808	...	...	...	1608	...	...	1818	...	2008	...	2135
Luxembourg ⋒...................... d.	...	1001	...	...	...	1802	...	...	2043	...	2201	...	...
Metz .... d.	...	1046	...	...	...	1847	...	...	2140	...	2252	...	...
Strasbourg .... d.	...	1211	...	...	...	2008	...	...	2318	...	0018	...	...
Mulhouse .... d.	...	1315	...	...	...	2106	...	...	...	...	0117	...	...
Basel SBB ⋒......................... d.	...	1402	...	...	...	2210	...	0055	...	...	0200	...	...
Domodossola ⋒................... a.	...	1732	...	...	...	...	...	...	...	...	...	...	...
Stresa .... a.	...	1811	...	...	...	...	...	...	...	...	...	...	...
Arona .... a.	...	1825	...	...	...	...	...	...	...	...	...	...	...
Chiasso ⋒............................ a.	...	...	...	...	...	...	...	...	...	...	...	...	...
Como .... a.	...	...	...	...	...	...	...	...	...	0602	...	...	...
Milano Centrale .... a.	...	1915	1940	2010	2010	...	...	...	...	0625	...	...	...
										0710	0750	0810	0815	
Brennero ⋒........................... a.	...	...	...	...	...	...	...	...	...	...	...	...	0818
Fortezza .... a.	...	...	...	...	...	...	...	...	...	...	...	...	0914
Dobbiaco.............................. a.	...	...	...	...	...	...	...	...	...	...	...	...	...
San Candido .... a.	...	...	...	...	...	...	...	...	...	...	...	...	...
Bolzano 380 .... a.	...	...	...	...	...	...	...	...	...	...	...	...	...
Verona .... a.	...	...	...	2151	...	...	...	...	...	...	...	...	1004
Venezia Santa Lucia.......... a.	...	...	...	2325	...	...	...	...	...	0903f	...	0951	1158
Genova P. Principe .... a.	...	...	2147	...	...	...	...	...	...	1050f	...	1125	...
Ventimiglia 355.................... a.	...	...	...	...	...	...	...	...	...	...	1005	1250	...
Bologna................................. a.	...	2115	...	...	...	0528	...	0800	...	0928	...	...	...
Firenze SMN .... a.	...	2212r	...	...	...	0646	...	...	...	1025r	...	...	...
Roma Termini .... a.	...	2353	...	...	...	0945	...	...	...	1205	...	...	...
Napoli Centrale 405 .... a.	...	...	...	...	...	...	...	...	...	...	...	...	...
Ravenna 388 .... a.	...	...	...	...	...	...	...	...	...	...	...	...	...
Rimini 390 .... a.	...	...	...	...	...	...	...	0930	...	...	...	...	...
Ancona 390 .... a.	...	...	...	...	...	...	...	1048	...	...	...	...	...

train number	IC	IC		EC				IC	IC						
train number	674	532	2094	90	1290	9121		544	688	2110	298		1218		1294	9133
notes (see page 4)			♀			℞	✕		✕	♀	♀					℞	✕
notes (see below)	∕	∕		E	∕	A	L		∕	∕		R		C		V	L
Ancona 390 .... d.	...	...	...	...	1508	...	...	...	...	...	...	...	...	...
Rimini 390 .... d.	...	...	...	...	1627	...	...	...	...	...	...	...	...	...
Ravenna 388 .... d.	...	...	...	...	...	...	...	...	...	...	...	...	...	...
Napoli Centrale 405 .... d.	...	...	...	...	...	...	...	...	...	...	...	...	...	...
Roma Termini .... d.	...	...	...	...	...	...	...	1605	...	...	...	...	1630	...
Firenze SMN .... d.	...	0700	...	...	...	...	...	1807	...	...	...	...	1920	...
Bologna................................. d.	...	0816	...	...	1748	...	...	1916	...	...	...	...	2050	...
Ventimiglia 388.................... d.	...	...	...	...	...	...	...	...	...	...	...	...	...	...
Genova P. Principe .... d.	0813	...	...	...	...	...	...	1913	...	...	...	...	...	...
Venezia Santa Lucia........... d.	...	...	0625	...	...	...	...	...	1725	1751f	...	...	...	...
Verona .... d.	...	...	0801	...	...	...	...	...	1901	1934f	...	...	...	...
Bolzano 390 .... d.	...	...	...	...	...	...	...	...	...	...	1632	...	...	...
San Candido .... d.	...	...	...	...	...	...	...	...	...	...	1814	...	...	...
Dobbiaco.............................. d.	...	...	...	...	...	...	...	...	...	...	...	...	...	...
Fortezza .... d.	...	...	...	...	...	...	...	...	...	...	1901	...	...	...
Brennero ⋒........................... d.	...	...	...	...	...	...	...	...	...	...	2026	...	...	...
Milano Centrale .... d.	0950	1000	0945	1025	...	...	...	2100	2050	2045	2135	...	...	...
Como .... d.	...	...	...	...	...	...	...	...	...	...	2216	...	...	...
Chiasso ⋒............................ d.	...	...	...	...	...	...	...	...	...	...	2240	...	...	...
Arona .... d.	...	...	...	1116	...	...	...	...	...	...	...	...	...	...
Stresa .... d.	...	...	...	1129	...	...	...	...	...	...	...	...	...	...
Domodossola ⋒................... d.	...	...	...	1213	...	...	...	...	...	...	...	...	...	...
Basel SBB ⋒......................... a.	...	...	...	1558	...	0207	...	...	...	...	0240	...	0353	...
Mulhouse .... a.	...	...	...	1648	...	...	...	...	...	...	0322	...	0443	...
Strasbourg .... a.	...	...	...	1745	...	0343	...	...	...	...	0420	...	0539	...
Metz .... a.	...	...	...	1911	...	0508	...	...	...	...	0550	...	0709	...
Luxembourg ⋒...................... a.	...	...	...	1956	...	0602	...	...	...	...	0647	...	0804	...
Namur.................................... a.	...	...	...	2143	...	0750	...	...	...	...	0836	...	0953	...
Aachen ⋒.............................. a.	...	...	...	...	...	...	...	...	...	...	...	0932	...	...
Liège Guillemins .... a.	...	...	...	...	...	...	...	...	...	...	...	0823	...	...
Brussels Nord/Noord .... a.	...	...	...	2228	...	0845	...	...	...	...	0921	0923	1040	...
Brussels Midi/Zuid .... a.	...	...	...	2237	...	0853	0928	...	...	...	0930	0933	1048	1233
Oostende .... a.	...	...	...	...	...	...	...	...	...	...	...	1045	...	...
London Waterloo 12 .... a.	...	...	...	...	...	1139	...	...	...	...	...	...	1439	...

NOTES

A – ⑥ June 3 - Sept. 23: 🛏1,2 cl., 🛏 1,2 cl. (T2), ⭲ 2 cl. and 🚃 Ancona - Brussels.
B – ⑤ June 2 - Sept. 22: ⭲ 2 cl Oostende - Verona.
C – ⑥ June 3 - Sept. 23: ⭲ 2 cl. Verona - Oostende.
D – ⑤ June 2 - Sept. 22: 🛏1,2 cl., 🛏 1,2 cl. (T2), ⭲ 2 cl. and 🚃 Brussels - Ancona.
E – VAUBAN – 🚃 and ✕ Brussels - Milano and v.v.
G – 🛏1,2 cl., 🛏 1,2 cl. (T2), ⭲ 2 cl. and 🚃 Brussels - Milano;
⑤⑥: 🛏1,2 cl., 🛏 1,2 cl. (T2), ⭲ 2 cl. and 🚃 Brussels - Venezia.
⋆ – Eurostar service, days of running subject to confirmation.

R – 🛏1,2 cl., 🛏 1,2 cl. (T2), ⭲ 2 cl. and 🚃 Milano - Brussels;
⑥⑦: 🛏1,2 cl., 🛏 1,2 cl. (T2), ⭲ 2 cl. and 🚃 Venezia - Brussels.
T – ⑤, daily June 30 - Sept. 3: 🛏1,2 cl. (T2), ⭲ 2 cl. and 🚃 Brussels - Roma.
V – ⑥, daily June 29 - Sept. 2: 🛏1,2 cl. (T2), ⭲ 2 cl. and 🚃 Roma - Brussels.
e – Roma Tuscolana.
f – ⑥⑦ only.
r – Firenze Rifredi.
t – Roma Tiburtina.
∕ – Supplement payable.

NOTES for Table 42.

A – LUTETIA – 🚃 and ✕ Paris - Lausanne and v.v.
B – CISALPIN – 🚃 and ✕ Paris - Lausanne and v.v.
C – CHAMPS ELYSEES – 🚃 and ✕ Paris - Lausanne and Bern and v.v.

D – VALAIS – 🚃 and ✕ Paris - Lausanne and v.v.
E – LEMANO – ⑤⑦: 🚃 and ✕ Lausanne - Paris.
∕ – Supplement payable.

Table 44 (Summer) PARIS - MILANO AND ROMA

train type / number / notes	TGV EC21 A	IC 323	IC 543	IC 655	IC 679	TGV EC23 C	IC 335	2113	IC 687	TGV EC29 E	IC 329	EN 213 N	EN 223 K	EN 227 L	1127 G	211 P	EN 217 M
Paris Lyon .... d.	0714					1225				1552		1847	2006	2009	2012	2056	2222
Dijon .... d.	0853					1403				1731		2118	2236		2248	2348	0118
Vallorbe .... d.	1034					1535				1909				0049	0103		
Lausanne .... a.	1106	1113				1607	1613			1945	1953			0140	0335		
Domodossola (= Iselle) ... a.		1307					1807				2147						
Stresa .... a.		1343									2232						
Arona .... a.							1854				2246	2352		0248			
Chambéry .... d.																0435	0540
Modane .... d.																0610	0706p
Torino Porta Nuova .. a.																	0845
Milano Centrale ..... a.		1445	1500	1505	1510		1945	2010	2010		2345	0439					
Genova P. Principe .. a.					1647				2147							0827	
Rapallo 360 .... a.																0910	
La Spezia 360 .... a.																0955	
Viareggio 360 .... a.												0630				1035	
Pisa Centrale .... a.																1051	
Livorno 360 .... a.																1110	
Verona .... a.				1624				2151					0640				
Padova .... a.				1719				2250					0805				
Venezia Mestre ...... a.				1740				2313					0833				
Venezia Santa Lucia . a.				1752				2325					0845				
Bologna .... a.			1648											0710	0722		
Rimini 390 .... a.															0844		
Ancona 390 .... a.															1008		
Pescara 390 .... a.															1146		
Bari 390 .... a.															1457		
Brindisi Marittima 390 a.															1640	2000	
Patras .... a.																1300	
Athinai by 1525 ..... a.															0826	1745	
Firenze SMN .... a.			1802											0945			
Roma Termini .... a.			1855													1429r	
Napoli Centrale 405 . a.																1700	

train type / number / notes	IC 672	IC 330	TGV EC24 A	EC 52	2098	2162	IC 322	TGV EC26 C	EN 216 M	EN 226 L	EN 222 K	210 P	1126 H G	EN 212 N
Napoli Centrale 405 . d.												1355		
Roma Termini .... d.				0805								1622r		1922
Firenze SMN .... d.				1007						1945				
Athinai by 1525 ..... d.													1100	
Patras .... d.													1800	
Brindisi Marittima 390 d.													1000	1236
Bari 390 .... d.														1418
Pescara 390 .... d.														1727
Ancona 390 .... d.														1904
Rimini 390 .... d.														2051
Bologna .... d.					1116				2100		2010			2229
Venezia Santa Lucia . d.						1025					2010			
Venezia Mestre ...... d.						1037					2022			
Padova .... d.						1100					2047			
Verona .... d.						1201					2142			
Livorno 360 .... d.												1926		
Pisa Centrale .... d.												1943		2227
Viareggio 360 .... d.												1959		
La Spezia 360 .... d.												2035		
Rapallo 360 .... d.												2121		
Genova P. Principe .. d.	0713											2204		0018
Milano Centrale ..... d.	0850	0905		1300	1345	1345	1400		2100			0015		0213
Torino Porta Nuova .. d.												2240p		0143
Modane .... a.												0018		0312
Chambéry .... d.												0145		
Arona .... d.		0953	1006				1442							
Stresa .... d.		1006					1458							
Domodossola (= Iselle) . d.		1046					1544	1754						
Lausanne .... a.	1240	1246					1740							
Vallorbe .... a.			1318				1827		0325	0342	0601		0733	0737
Dijon .... a.			1444				1957		0432	0530	0537	0906	1003	1006
Paris Lyon .... a.			1630				2137		0722	0825	0834		1003	

NOTES

A – LUTETIA – [couchette] and ✗ Paris - Lausanne and v.v.

C – CISALPIN – [couchette] and ✗ Paris - Lausanne and v.v.

E – CHAMPS ELYSEES – [couchette] and ✗ Paris - Lausanne.

G – PARTHENON – June 30 - Sept. 3: 2 cl. and [couchette] Paris - Brindisi and v.v.;
[sleeper] 1,2 cl. (T2), 2 cl. and [couchette] Paris - Rimini and v.v.

H – Hellenic Mediterranean Lines and Adriatica Lines, for days of running see Tables
1490 and **1525**.

K – RIALTO – [sleeper] 1,2 cl., [sleeper] 1,2 cl. (T2), 2 cl. and ♟ Paris - Venezia and v.v.

L – GALILEI – [sleeper] 1,2 cl., [sleeper] 1,2 cl. (T2), 2 cl. and ♟ Paris - Firenze and v.v.

M – STENDHAL – [sleeper] 1,2 cl., [sleeper] 1,2 cl. (T2), 2 cl. and [couchette] Paris - Milano and v.v.

N – PALATINO – [sleeper] 1,2 cl., [sleeper] 1,2 cl. (T2), 2 cl. and ♟ Paris - Roma and v.v.

P – NAPOLI EXPRESS– [sleeper] 1,2 cl., 2 cl. and [couchette] Paris - Napoli and v.v.

b – Brindisi Centrale.

g – Milano Porta Garibaldi.

p – Torino Porta Susa.

r – Roma Ostiense.

t – Roma Tiburtina.

✗ – Supplement payable.

Table 45 (Summer) — LYON - TORINO

train type / train number / notes (see page 4) / notes (see below)	412 ⚑	TGV 925 ✕ Ⓡ	416 ⚑	TGV 943 ⚑ Ⓡ	218 Ⓡ B
Paris Lyon .... d.	...	1024	...	1432	...
Lyon Perrache .... d.	0704	|	1226	...	1703
Lyon Part Dieu .... d.	0715	|	1238	...	1714
Aix les Bains .... d.	0830	|	1349	...	1826
Chambéry .... d.	0844	1318	1404	1726	1838
Modane 🏔 .... d.	1004	|	1532	...	2001
Torino Porta Nuova .... a.	1130	...	1657	...	2122
Milano Centrale .... a.	...	...	...	...	2305

train type / train number / notes (see page 4) / notes (see below)	214 B	TGV 932 ✕	414 ⚑	TGV 922 ⚑ Ⓡ	418 ⚑	TGV 936 Ⓡ Ⓡ
Milano Centrale .... d.	0710	...	...	...	...	...
Torino Porta Nuova .... d.	0855	...	1225	...	1645	...
Modane 🏔 .... a.	1022	...	1348	...	1807	...
Chambéry .... a.	1143	...	1511	1542	1925	...
Aix les Bains .... a.	1156	1315	1524	|	1939	1957
Lyon Part Dieu .... a.	1308	|	1638	|	2104	|
Lyon Perrache .... a.	1318	|	1648	|	2115	|
Paris Lyon .... a.	...	1616	...	1839	...	2254

NOTES

B – MONT CENIS – 🍴 and ⚑ Lyon - Milano and v.v.   ✗ – Supplement payable.

Table 46 (Summer) — PARIS - MADRID AND LISBOA

train number / notes (see page 4) / notes (see below)	TGV 8515 Ⓡ ✗	200 ⑧⚑	1202 ⚑ ⑥ ✗		313 Ⓡ ✗	TGV 8543 ⚑ ✗	312 A	312 B	204 M		303 E		409 D
Paris Montparnasse ..... d.	1000	...	...	...	...	1555	...	...	...	...	...	...	...
Paris Austerlitz .... d.	...	...	...	...	1354	...	...	...	...	...	1805	...	2000
Bordeaux St. Jean .... d.	1308	...	...	...	1818	1901	...	...	...	...	2241	...	0030
Hendaye .... d.	1523	...	...	...	2048	2123	...	...	...	...	0157	...	0237
Irún .... d.	1528	1545	1545	...	2051	2128	2200	2200	2215	...	0204	...	0253
San Sebastián/Donostia .... a.	...	1601	1601	...	...	...	2218	2218	2245	...	0219	...	|
Burgos .... a.	...	1903	1903	...	...	...	0158	0158	0242	...	0610	...	0541
Valladolid .... a.	...	|	2003	...	...	...	0327	0327	0410	...	0645	...	|
Medina del Campo .... a.	...	|	2025	...	...	...	0359	0359	0451	...	|	...	|
Salamanca .... a.	...	|	|	...	...	...	0453	0453	|	...	|	...	|
Pampilhosa .... a.	...	|	|	...	...	...	1015	1015	|	...	|	...	|
Lisboa Santa Apolónia .... a.	...	|	|	...	...	...	1305	|	|	...	|	...	|
Porto Campanhã .... a.	...	|	|	...	...	...	...	1145	|	...	|	...	|
Madrid Chamartín .... a.	...	2224	2240	...	...	...	...	...	0740	...	0950	...	0835

train number / notes (see page 4) / notes (see below)	203 ⚑	TGV 8596 ✗ Ⓡ	TGV 8598 † ⚑		301 E		407 D		205 M	311 A	316 B	TGV 8530 ✗ ⚑	310 ✗
Madrid Chamartín .... d.	1000	...	...	...	1815	...	1930	...	2300	...	...	...	...
Porto Campanhã .... d.	...	...	...	...	|	...	|	...	|	1805	...	...	...
Lisboa Santa Apolónia .... d.	...	...	...	...	|	...	|	...	|	1703	...	...	...
Pampilhosa .... d.	...	...	...	...	|	...	|	...	|	2000	2000	...	...
Salamanca .... d.	...	...	...	...	|	...	|	...	|	0205	0205	...	...
Medina del Campo .... d.	1210	...	...	...	|	...	|	...	0127	0254	0254	...	...
Valladolid .... d.	1232	...	...	...	2049	...	|	...	0215	0323	0323	...	...
Burgos .... d.	1333	...	...	...	2148	...	2205	...	0343	0445	0445	...	...
San Sebastián/Donostia .... d.	1623	...	...	...	0135	...	|	...	0755	0832	0832	...	...
Irún .... d.	1645	...	...	...	0203	...	0123	...	0825	0856	0856	...	...
Hendaye 🏔 .... a.	1650	1723	1826	...	0208	...	0139	...	0830	0904	0904	0936	0949
Bordeaux St. Jean .... a.	...	1933	2035	...	0550	...	0355	...	|	|	|	1157	1210
Paris Austerlitz .... a.	...	|	|	...	1034	...	0830	...	|	|	|	|	1715
Paris Montparnasse ...... a.	...	2300	2345	...	...	...	...	...	...	...	...	1500	...

NOTES

– SUD EXPRESS – 🛏 1,2 cl., 🛏 2 cl., 🍴 and ✕ Irún - Lisboa and Lisboa - Hendaye.
🛏 2 cl. and 🍴 Irún - Porto and Porto - Hendaye.

D – FRANCISCO DE GOYA – 🛏 1,2 cl. and ✕ Paris - Madrid and v.v.
E – PUERTA DEL SOL – 🛏 2 cl. and ⚑ Paris - Madrid and v.v.
M – 🛏 1,2 cl., 🛏 2 cl. and 🍴 Irún - Madrid and Madrid - Hendaye.
✗ – Supplement payable.

Table 47 (Summer) — PARIS - BARCELONA

train number / notes (see page 4) / notes (see below)	147 471 ⚑				TGV 524 Ⓡ ✗	TGV 853 Ⓡ ✗	71 J ✗			477 H		473 W	463 ⚑	
Paris Austerlitz .... d.	1006	...	...	...	...	...	...	...	...	2115	...	2145	...	...
Paris Lyon .... d.	...	...	...	...	...	1049	...	...	...	|	...	|	...	...
Lille Europe .... d.	...	...	...	...	0834	|	...	...	...	|	...	|	...	...
Montpellier .... d.	...	...	...	...	1452	1459	1510	...	...	|	...	|	...	...
Limoges .... d.	1309	...	...	...	|	|	|	...	...	0021	...	0122	...	...
Cerbère .... d.	2041	...	...	...	|	|	1701	...	...	|	...	0846	...	...
Port Bou 🏔 .... a.	2045	...	2110	...	|	|	1718	...	...	|	...	0850	1030	1035
Figueres .... a.	...	...	2132	...	|	|	1740	...	...	0649	...	|	1050	1057
Girona .... a.	...	...	2201	...	|	|	1806	...	...	0714	...	1116	1126	
Barcelona França .... a.	...	...	|	...	|	|	1920	...	...	0820	...	|	|	
Barcelona Sants .... a.	...	...	2327	...	|	|	|	...	...	|	...	1225	1247	
València Térmi̇no .... a.	...	...	...	...	|	|	|	...	...	|	...	1615	...	...
Alacant Término .... a.	...	...	...	...	|	|	|	...	...	|	...	1829	...	...

train number / notes (see page 4) / notes (see below)	370 ⑤⑥⑦	470		73 J ✗	TGV 862 Ⓡ ✗ ②③④	TGV 862 Ⓡ ⚑ ①⑤	TGV 582 Ⓡ ⚑ ⑥⑦		460 ⚑	472 V				475 H
Alacant Término .... d.	...	...	...	...	...	...	...	...	1100	...	...	...	...	...
València Término .... d.	...	...	...	...	...	...	...	...	1357	...	...	...	...	...
Barcelona Sants .... d.	...	0710	...	...	...	...	...	...	1707	...	...	...	...	...
Barcelona França .... d.	...	|	...	0855	...	...	...	...	|	1720	...	...	...	2100
Girona .... d.	...	0835	...	1001	...	...	...	...	1816	1849	...	...	...	2210
Figueres .... d.	...	0907	...	1027	...	...	...	...	1842	1930	...	...	...	2237
Port Bou 🏔 .... d.	...	0940	...	1103	...	...	...	...	1910	1958	...	...	...	|
Cerbère .... a.	...	0945	1027	1123	...	...	...	...	1915	2003	2035	...	...	0459
Limoges .... a.	...	|	1654	|	...	...	...	...	|	|	0342	...	...	|
Montpellier .... a.	...	|	|	1315	1354	1404	1556	...	|	|	|	...	...	|
Lille Europe .... a.	...	|	|	|	|	|	2212	...	|	|	|	...	...	|
Paris Lyon .... a.	...	|	|	|	1814	1818	|	...	|	|	|	...	...	|
Paris Austerlitz .... a.	...	|	2032	|	...	...	...	...	|	|	0745	...	...	0815

NOTES

JOAN MIRÓ – 🛏 and ✕ Paris - Barcelona and v.v.
CATALAN TALGO – 🍴 and ✕ Montpellier - Barcelona and v.v.

V – 🛏 2 cl. and 🍴 Cerbère - Paris (also 🛏 1,2 cl. (T2) on ①②③④⑥).
W – 🛏 2 cl. and 🍴 Paris - Port Bou (also 🛏 1,2 cl. (T2) on ①②③④⑥).
✗ – Supplement payable.

For explanation of standard signs see page 4

Table 48 (Summer)   AMSTERDAM AND BRUSSELS - SOUTHERN FRANCE AND BARCELONA

train number	TGV 532	1286	1284	286	1186	1236
notes (see below)	🍴🅁	A	B	G	H	E
Amsterdam Centraal ....d.		1452			1647	
Den Haag HS ....d.		1536			1736	
Rotterdam CS ....d.		1557			1807	
Roosendaal ....d.		1646			1848	
Antwerpen Berchem ....d.		1714			1917	
Brussels Midi ....d.	0905	1804	1842	1907	2013	2021
Mons ....d.		1843	1926	1946	2052	
Tournai ....d.						2118
Lille Flandres ....d.	1029e					2150
Marne la Vallée ....a.	1140					
Brive ....a.						0528
Montauban ....a.						0726
Toulouse ....a.						0755
Tarbes ....a.						0941
Lourdes ....a.						1000
Lyon Perrache ....a.	1332p			0406	0427	
Valence ....a.	1418			0513	0535	
Avignon ....a.	1512			0622	0640	
Nîmes ....a.						
Montpellier ....a.						
Sète ....a.						
Agde ....a.						
Béziers ....a.						
Narbonne ....a.		0546	0725			
Perpignan ....a.		0636	0821			
Argelès sur Mer ....a.						
Port Vendres ....a.						
Port Bou ....a.		0727	0908			
Port Bou ....d.		0850	1030			
Girona ....a.						
Barcelona Sants ....a.		1055	1225			
València Término ....a.		1450	1615			
Arles ....a.				0653	0701	
Marseille ....a.	1608			0748	0753	
Toulon ....a.	1651			0846	0846	
St. Raphaël ....a.	1740			0938	0938	
Cannes ....a.	1808			1006	1006	
Juan les Pins ....a.				1017	1017	
Antibes ....a.	1817			1022	1022	
Nice ....a.	1835			1039	1039	
Beaulieu ....a.				1051	1051	
Monaco-Monte Carlo ....a.				1101	1102	
Menton ....a.				1112	1112	
Ventimiglia ....a.				1129	1129	

train number	TGV 573	1280	1280	6708 6709	1180 1181	1230
notes (see below)	🍴🅁	C	D	J	K	F
Ventimiglia ....d.				1742	1742	
Menton ....d.				1755	1755	
Monaco-Monte Carlo ....d.				1806	1805	
Beaulieu ....d.				1816	1815	
Nice ....d.	0930			1840	1835	
Antibes ....d.	0954			1857	1902	
Juan les Pins ....d.				1902	1907	
Cannes ....d.	1005			1912	1920	
St. Raphaël ....d.	1029			1941	1949	
Toulon ....d.	1117			2035	2042	
Marseille ....d.	1202			2125	2125	
Arles ....d.				2213	2226	
València Término ....d.						
Barcelona Sants ....d.		1420				
Girona ....d.						
Cerbère ....a.			1646			
Cerbère ....d.		1803	1803			
Port Vendres ....d.						
Argelès sur Mer ....d.						
Perpignan ....d.		1834	1834			
Narbonne ....d.		1926	1926			
Béziers ....d.						
Agde ....d.						
Sète ....d.						
Montpellier ....d.						
Nîmes ....d.						
Avignon ....d.	1257			2239	2251	
Valence ....d.	1352			2348	2356	
Lyon Perrache ....d.	1439p			0106	0106	
Lourdes ....d.						1823
Tarbes ....d.						1846
Toulouse ....d.						2047
Montauban ....d.						2124
Brive ....d.						2329
Marne la Vallée ....d.	1630					
Lille Flandres ....a.	1758e					0806
Tournai ....a.						0846
Mons ....a.				0824	0824	
Brussels Midi ....a.	1915	0703	0703	0903	0903	1002
Antwerpen Berchem ....a.		0754			0957	
Roosendaal ....a.		0828			1025	
Rotterdam CS ....a.		0925			1107	
Den Haag HS ....a.		0954			1131	
Amsterdam Centraal ....a.		1047			1225	

NOTES

A – CAMINO AZUL – ⑤ June 2 - 30 and Sept. 1 - 22, ③⑤⑦ July 2 - Aug. 25:
🛏 2 cl., 🛏 and 🍴 Amsterdam - Port Bou.

B – CAMINO AZUL – ①②④⑥ July 1 - Aug. 24:
🛏 2 cl. and 🛏 (also 🛏 1,2 cl. (T2) on ①②④) Brussels - Port Bou.

C – CAMINO AZUL – ⑥ June 3 - 24 and Sept. 2 - 23, ①④⑥ July 1 - Aug. 26:
🛏 2 cl., 🛏 and 🍴 Cerbère - Amsterdam.

D – CAMINO AZUL - ②③⑤⑦ July 2 - Aug. 25:
🛏 2 cl. and 🛏 (also 🛏 1,2 cl. (T2) on ②③⑤) Cerbère - Brussels.

E – ⑤, also ⑦ June 30 - Aug. 25: 🛏 1,2 cl., 🛏 2 cl. and 🛏 Brussels - Lourdes.

F – ⑥, also ① July 1 - Aug. 26: 🛏 1,2 cl., 🛏 2 cl. and 🛏 Lourdes - Brussels.

G – FLANDRES RIVIERA – ①②③④⑦ to June 27 and from Sept. 4:
🛏 1,2 cl. (T2) and 🛏 2 cl. Brussels - Ventimiglia.

H – FLANDRES RIVIERA – ⑤⑥ June 2 - 24 and Sept. 8 - 23, daily June 28 - Sept. 3
🛏 2 cl. Amsterdam - Ventimiglia;
🛏 1,2 cl., 🛏 1,2 cl. (T2) and 🛏 2 cl. Brussels - Ventimiglia.

J – FLANDRES RIVIERA – ①②③④⑤ to June 26 and from Sept. 6:
🛏 1,2 cl. (T2) and 🛏 2 cl. Ventimiglia - Brussels.

K – FLANDRES RIVIERA – ⑥⑦ June 3 - 25 and Sept. 9 - 24, daily June 27 - Sept. 5:
🛏 2 cl. Ventimiglia - Amsterdam;
🛏 1,2 cl., 🛏 1,2 cl. (T2) and 🛏 2 cl. Ventimiglia - Brussels.

e – Lille Europe.

p – Lyon Part Dieu.

🍴 – Supplement payable.

INTERNATIONAL SERVICES FROM MADRID AND BARCELONA

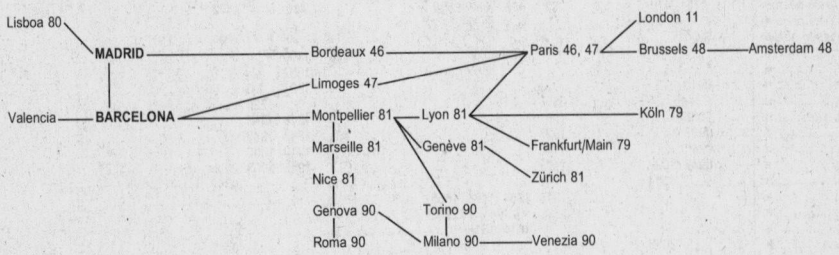

Table 50 (Summer)   KØBENHAVN - HAMBURG AND KÖLN

train type	IN	IN	EC	ICE	IC	ICE	IC	EC	ICE	IC	ICE	IC	EC	ICE	IC	ICE
train number	381	293	189	77	523	589	621	187	775	527	681	521	185	673	736	885
notes (see page 4)	Ⓡ	Ⓡ		✗/	/	/	/		✗/	/	/	/		✗/	/	✗/
notes (see below)	C	J	H					G					F	V		V
Oslo S .... d.	2137	...	...													
Göteborg C .... d.	0220	...	...													
Stockholm C .... d.		2224	...													
København H .... d.	0700	0700	0730					0920					1230			
Nykøbing F .... d.			0902					1057					1402			
Rødby F .... d.			0925					1130					1425			
Puttgarden .... a.			1035					1235					1535			
Lübeck Hbf .... a.			1143					1346					1640			
Hamburg Hbf .... a.			1223					1428					1722			
Hamburg Hbf .... d.			1238	1253	1308			1438	1453	1508			1738	1753	1813	
Bremen .... a.			1347					1547					1847			
Osnabrück .... a.			1441					1641					1941			
Münster .... a.			1504					1704					2004			
Dortmund .... a.			1534					1734					2034			
Essen .... a.								1759					2059			
Duisburg .... a.								1812					2112			
Düsseldorf .... a.								1826					2126			
Köln Hbf .... a.			1650					1850					2150			
Hannover Hbf .... a.				1350		1425			1550		1625			1850	1925	
Frankfurt/Main .... a.				1558					1758					2058		
Mannheim .... a.				1641					1841							
Heidelberg .... a.														2151		
Karlsruhe .... a.				1705					1905							
Offenburg .... a.				1741					1941							
Freiburg im Breisgau .... a.				1811					2011							
Basel SBB .... a.				1854					2054							
Würzburg .... a.					1620	1627				1820	1827				2120	
Nürnberg .... a.						1722				1922					2218	
München Hbf .... a.					1838					2041						
Innsbruck .... a.																

train type	EC	IC	IC25	ICE	IN	EC		IC33	IN	
train number	183	730	IN285	91	393	181	483 / 483	IN289	385	232
notes (see page 4)	D /	/	Ⓡ ✗		Ⓡ ✗	B /	R S	Ⓡ✗ Ⓡ✗		A
Oslo S .... d.				0810					1015e	
Göteborg C .... d.				1215	1227				1525	
Stockholm C .... d.			0812					1212		
København H .... d.	1520		1658		1658	1730	1905 1905	2058	2018	2105
Nykøbing F .... d.	1657					1902	2046 2046			2246
Rødby F .... d.	1730					1925	2130 2130			2330
Puttgarden .... a.	1835					2035	2235 2235			0035
Lübeck Hbf .... a.	1946					2136	0001 0001			0210
Hamburg Hbf .... a.	2028					2215	0040 0040			0300
Hamburg Hbf .... d.		2053					0050 0050			0312
Bremen .... a.		2147								0418
Osnabrück .... a.		2241								0530
Münster .... a.		2304								0559
Dortmund .... a.		2334								...
Essen .... a.										0651
Duisburg .... a.										0706
Düsseldorf .... a.										0722
Köln Hbf .... a.										0757
Hannover Hbf .... a.							0221 0221			
Frankfurt/Main .... a.							0620			
Mannheim .... a.										
Heidelberg .... a.							0722			
Karlsruhe .... a.							0759			
Offenburg .... a.							0842			
Freiburg im Breisgau .... a.							0917			
Basel SBB .... a.							1023			
Würzburg .... a.							0619			
Nürnberg .... a.							0723			
München Hbf .... a.							0921			
Innsbruck .... a.							1136			

NOTES

A – NORD EXPRESS – ⇌ 1,2 cl., ⇌ 1,2 cl. (T2), ⇌ 2 cl. and ⟐ København - Köln - (Oostende/Paris).
B – CHRISTIAN MORGENSTERN – ⟐ and ♀ København - Hamburg.
C – ⇌ 1,2 cl. and ⇌ 2 cl. Oslo - København.
D – THOMAS MANN – ⟐ and ♀ København - Hamburg.
F – BERTEL THORVALDSEN – ⟐ and ♀ København - Hamburg.
G – KAREN BLIXEN – ⟐ and ♀ København - Hamburg.

H – HAMLET – ⟐ and ♀ København - Hamburg.
J – ⇌ 1,2 cl., ⇌ 2 cl. and ⟐ Stockholm - København.
R – ⇌ 1,2 cl. and ⇌ 2 cl. København - Basel.
S – ⇌ 1,2 cl., ⇌ 2 cl. and ⟐ København - München;
   ⑤ June 16 - Aug. 11: ⇌ 1,2 cl., ⇌ 2 cl. and ⟐ København - Innsbruck.
V – Daily except ⑥, not June 4.
e – ⑤⑥⑦ only.
/ – Supplement payable.

INTERNATIONAL SERVICES FROM KÖLN

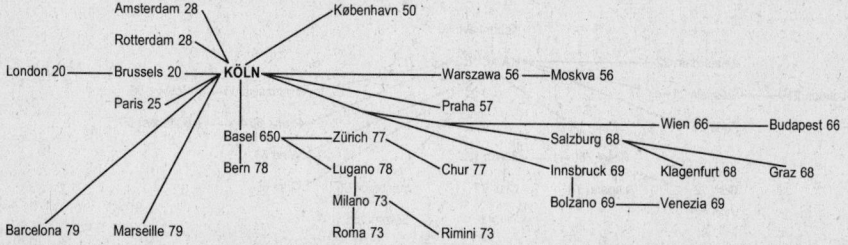

Table 50 (Summer) KÖLN AND HAMBURG - KØBENHAVN

	EC 180	IN 392	ICE 94	IN 284	EC 182	IC 524	ICE 682	IC 739	ICE 774	EC 184	ICE 670	IC 620	ICE 680	IC 526	EC 186
notes (see page 4)		Ⓡ ✗	Ⓡ	Ⓡ		✗	✗	✗	✗	✗	✗	♈	✗	♈	
notes (see below)	B /				D /			V /	/	F /	/	/	/	/	G /
Innsbruck .... d.	...	...	...	...	...	...	...	...	...	...	...	...	0920	...	...
München Hbf .... d.	...	...	...	...	...	...	0720	...	...	...	...	1035	...	...	...
Nürnberg .... d.	...	...	...	...	...	0835	...	...	...	...	...	1129	1137	...	...
Wurzburg .... d.	...	...	...	...	...	0929	0937	...	...	...	...	...	...	...	...
Basel SBB .... d.	...	...	...	...	...	...	...	...	0707	...	...	...	...	...	...
Freiburg im Breisgau ... d.	...	...	...	...	...	...	...	...	0748	...	...	...	...	...	...
Offenburg .... d.	...	...	...	...	...	...	...	...	0818	...	...	...	...	...	...
Karlsruhe .... d.	...	...	...	...	...	...	...	...	0853	...	1007	...	...	...	...
Heidelberg .... d.	...	...	...	...	...	...	...	...	...	...	...	...	...	...	...
Mannheim .... d.	...	...	...	...	...	...	...	...	0917	...	...	...	...	...	...
Frankfurt/Main .... d.	...	...	...	...	...	...	...	...	1000	...	1100	...	...	...	...
Hannover Hbf .... d.	...	...	...	...	...	1135	1208	...	...	...	1308	1335	...	...	...
Köln Hbf .... d.	...	...	...	...	...	...	...	0909	...	...	...	...	...	1110	...
Düsseldorf .... d.	...	...	...	...	...	...	...	0933	...	...	...	...	...		...
Duisburg .... d.	...	...	...	...	...	...	...	0946	...	...	...	...	...		...
Essen .... d.	...	...	...	...	...	...	...	0959	...	...	...	...	...	1225	...
Dortmund .... d.	...	...	...	...	...	...	...	1025	...	...	...	...	...	1256	...
Münster .... d.	...	...	...	...	...	...	...	1056	...	...	...	...	...	1319	...
Osnabrück .... d.	...	...	...	...	...	...	...	1119	...	...	...	...	...		...
Bremen .... d.	...	...	...	...	...	...	...	1212	...	...	...	...	...	1412	...
Hamburg Hbf .... a.	...	...	...	...	...	1252	...	1307	1322	...	1422	1452	...	1507	...
Hamburg Hbf .... d.	0730	...	...	...	0912	...	...	...	...	1330	...	...	...	...	1512
Lübeck Hbf .... d.	0806	...	...	...	0950	...	...	...	...	1406	...	...	...	...	1550
Puttgarden 🚢 .... d.	0905	...	...	...	1105	...	...	...	...	1505	...	...	...	...	1705
Rødby F 🚢 .... a.	1000	...	...	...	1200	...	...	...	...	1600	...	...	...	...	1800
Nykøbing F .... a.	1031	...	...	...	1237	...	...	...	...	1631	...	...	...	...	1837
København H .... a.	1159	1228	...	1315	1420	...	...	...	...	1759	...	...	...	...	2020
Stockholm C .... a.	...	...	...	2141	...										
Göteborg C .... a.	...	1734	1800	...	...										
Oslo S .... a.	...	...	2219	...	...										

	ICE 786	IC 522	ICE 576	EC 188	IN 380	IN 292		233		482	351	IN 384	IN 288
notes (see page 4)	✗	✗	✗		Ⓡ							Ⓡ ✗	Ⓡ ✗
notes (see below)	/	/	/	H /	N	C		A		S	R		
Innsbruck .... d.	...	...	...	...	...	...		...		1705	...	...	...
München Hbf .... d.	...	1155	...	...	...	...		...		1928	...	...	...
Nürnberg .... d.	...	1339	...	...	...	...		...		2131	...	...	...
Wurzburg .... d.	...	1437	...	...	...	...		...		2233	...	...	...
Basel SBB .... d.	...	...	...	...	...	...		...		...	1746	...	...
Freiburg im Breisgau ... d.	...	...	...	...	...	...		...		...	1838	...	...
Offenburg .... d.	...	...	...	...	...	...		...		...	1913	...	...
Karlsruhe .... d.	...	...	...	...	...	...		...		...	2009	...	...
Heidelberg .... d.	1407	...	...	...	...	...		...		...	2045	...	...
Mannheim .... d.	1500	...	...	...	...	...		...		...	2216	...	...
Frankfurt/Main .... d.	...	...	...	...	...	...		...		0224	0224	...	...
Hannover Hbf .... d.	1708	1635	...	...	...	...		...		...	...	...	...
Köln Hbf .... d.	...	...	1409	...	...	...		2200		...	...	...	...
Düsseldorf .... d.	...	...	1433	...	...	...		2226		...	...	...	...
Duisburg .... d.	...	...	1446	...	...	...		2242		...	...	...	...
Essen .... d.	...	...	1459	...	...	...		2256		...	...	...	...
Dortmund .... d.	...	...	1525	...	...	...		2353		...	...	...	...
Münster .... d.	...	...	1556	...	...	...		0024		...	...	...	...
Osnabrück .... d.	...	...	1619	...	...	...		0130		...	...	...	...
Bremen .... d.	...	...	1712	...	...	...		0235		...	...	...	...
Hamburg Hbf .... a.	1822	1801	1807	...	...	...		0245		0352	0352	...	...
Hamburg Hbf .... d.	...	...	...	1827	...	...		0332		0401	0401	...	...
Lübeck Hbf .... d.	...	...	...	1902	...	...		0505		0440	0440	...	...
Puttgarden 🚢 .... d.	...	...	...	2005	...	...		0600		0605	0605	...	...
Rødby F 🚢 .... a.	...	...	...	2100	...	...		0652		0700	0700	...	...
Nykøbing F .... a.	...	...	...	2131	...	...		...		0752	0752	...	...
København H .... a.	...	...	...	2259	2315	2315		0830		0930	0930	0948	0948
Stockholm C .... a.	...	...	...	...	...	0747		...		...	...	...	1747
Göteborg C .... a.	...	...	...	...	0340	...		...		...	...	1435	...
Oslo S .... a.	...	...	...	...	0837	...		...		...	...	1937b	...

NOTES

A – NORD EXPRESS – ▭ 1,2 cl., ▭ 1,2 cl. (T2), ▭ 2 cl. and ▭ (Oostende/Paris) – Köln – København.
B – CHRISTIAN MORGENSTERN – ▭ and ♈ Hamburg – København.
C – ▭ 1,2 cl., ▭ 2 cl. and ▭ København – Stockholm.
D – THOMAS MANN – ▭ and ♈ Hamburg – København.
F – BERTEL THORVALDSEN – ▭ and ♈ Hamburg – København.
G – KAREN BLIXEN – ▭ and ♈ Hamburg – København.

H – HAMLET – ▭ and ♈ Hamburg – København.
N – ▭ 1,2 cl. and ▭ 2 cl. København – Oslo.
R – ▭ 1,2 cl. and ▭ 2 cl. Basel – København.
S – ▭ 1,2 cl., ▭ 2 cl. and ▭ München – København; ⑥ June 17 – Aug. 12: ▭ 1,2 cl., ▭ 2 cl. and ▭ Innsbruck – København.
V – ①-⑥, not June 5.
b – ⑤⑥⑦ only.
/ – Supplement payable.

INTERNATIONAL SERVICES FROM HAMBURG

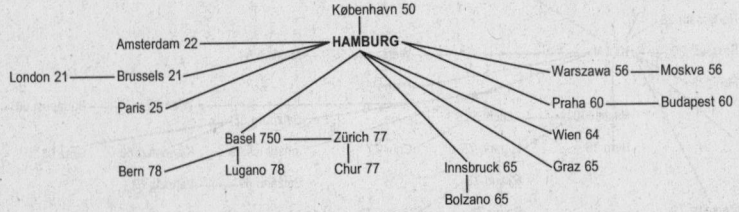

Table 51 (Summer)　　　KØBENHAVN - BERLIN AND PRAHA

train type		EC			IR		EC	EC
train number	305	179	2245		2379	309	41	173
notes (see page 4)		✕		⛴	⚑		✕	✕
notes (see below)	A	✕			⛴	B	✕	✕
København .... d.	0720	...	1241	...	...	2230	...	...
Nykøbing .... d.	0852	...	1434	...	...	0018	...	...
Gedser ▥ .... d.	0925	...	1455	1525	...	0100	...	...
Warnemünde ▥ ..... a.	1120	...	...	1720	1804	0300	...	...
Rostock .... a.	1221	...	...	...	1821	0419	...	...
Berlin Lichtenberg ... a.	1506	1631	...	...	2057	0656	0817b	0831
Poznań Główny ▥ ... a.							1440	
Warszawa Centralna ... a.	...	...	...	...	...	...	1440	...
Dresden Hbf .... a.	...	1823	...	...	...	...	...	1012
Děčín ▥ .... a.	...	1918	...	...	...	...	...	1118
Praha Holešovice .... a.	...	2102	...	...	...	...	...	1302
Praha Hlavní .... a.	...	2116	...	...	...	...	...	...

train type	IR			EC	IR	EC	EC	
train number	2278		2242	178	304	40	170	308
notes (see page 4)	⛴			✕		✕	✕	
notes (see below)				✕	C	✕	✕	B
Praha Hlavní .... d.	...	...	...	...	...	...	...	...
Praha Holešovice .... d.	...	...	...	0833	...	...	1833	...
Děčín ▥ .... d.	...	...	...	1033	...	...	2033	...
Dresden Hbf .... d.	...	...	...	1117	1239	...	2117	...
Warszawa Centralna ... d.	...	...	...	...	...	1640	...	...
Poznań Główny ▥ ... d.	...	...	...	...	...	...	...	...
Berlin Lichtenberg ... d.	0856	...	...	1311	1456	2248b	2311	2352
Rostock .... d.	1128	...	...	...	1728	...	...	0224
Warnemünde ▥ ..... d.	1142	1200	...	...	1800	...	...	0330
Gedser ▥ .... a.	...	1400	1440	...	2000	...	...	0530
Nykøbing .... a.	...	...	1500	...	2100	...	...	0633
København .... a.	...	...	1655	...	2305	...	...	0826

NOTES

A – NEPTUN – ⟦⟧ København - Berlin - (Chemnitz).

B – OSTSEE EXPRESS – ⛏ 1,2 cl., ⟼ 2 cl. and ⟦⟧ København - Berlin and v.v.

C – NEPTUN – ⟦⟧ Dresden - København.

b – Berlin Hbf.

✕ – Supplement payable.

Table 52 (Summer)　　　STOCKHOLM - BERLIN AND PRAHA

train type		IN			ICE	IN	IC		IN	IC	
train number	205	383	317	1013	91	391	29	1011	385	37	319
notes (see page 4)		ℝ			ℝ	✕ℝ✕	ℝ	ℝ	✕ℝ✕	ℝ	
notes (see below)	R	L	K	P					E		M
Oslo Sentral .... d.	...	2137	...	...	0737	...	...	...	...	...	1015f
Göteborg C .... d.	...	0220	...	...	1155	1210	...	1525	...	...	...
Stockholm .... d.	2312						1012			1412	
Malmö .... d.	0645	0632	0747	1200	...	1550	1640	1712	1913	2045	2120
Trelleborg ▥ .... d.	...	...	0830	1300	...	...	...	1800	...	...	2230
Sassnitz Hafen ▥ ... a.	...	...	1200	1700	...	...	...	2130	...	...	0230
Berlin Hbf .... a.	...	...	1618	2116	...	...	...	0200	...	...	
Berlin Lichtenberg ... a.	...	...	...	...	...	...	...	...	...	...	0647
Dresden Hbf .... a.	...	...	...	...	...	...	0406	...	...	...	...
Děčín .... a.	...	...	...	...	...	...	0513	...	...	...	...
Praha Holešovice .... a.	...	...	...	...	...	...	0711	...	...	...	...
Bratislava Hlavní ..... a.	...	...	...	...	...	...	1248	...	...	...	...
Budapest Keleti ..... a.	...	...	...	...	...	...	1638	...	...	...	...

train type	IR	IR	IN		IN	IC	IC		IC	IN	
train number	1012	316	682	206	318	34	606	1010	42	692	
notes (see page 4)			ℝ			ℝ✕	ℝ✕		✕ℝ✕		
notes (see below)	T	K	L	R	M			E			
Budapest Keleti ..... d.	...	...	...	...	...	1330	...	...	...	...	
Bratislava Hlavní ..... d.	...	...	...	...	...	1719	...	...	...	...	
Praha Holešovice ... d.	...	...	...	...	...	2257	...	...	...	...	
Děčín .... d.	...	...	...	...	...	0046	...	...	...	...	
Dresden Hbf .... d.	...	...	...	...	...	0148	...	...	...	...	
Berlin Hbf .... d.	...	...	...	2306	...	...	...	...	...	...	
Berlin Lichtenberg .. d.	0848	1325	...	...	...	...	0354	...	...	...	
Sassnitz Hafen ▥ ... d.	1300	1800	...	0330	...	...	0830	...	...	...	
Trelleborg ▥ .... a.	1700	2130	...	0715	...	...	1200	...	...	...	
Malmö .... a.	1810	2230	2247	2300	0812	0917	0845	1256	1320	1317	
Stockholm .... a.	...	...	0641	...	1541	...	1941	...	...	...	
Göteborg C .... a.	...	...	0340	...	...	1245	...	...	1734		
Oslo Sentral .... a.	...	...	0837	...	...	...	...	...	...	...	

NOTES

E – CSÁRDÁS – ⛏ 1,2 cl. and ⟼ 2 cl. Malmö - Budapest and v.v.;
⟦⟧ Sassnitz - Budapest and v.v.; ✕ Dresden - Budapest and v.v.

K – KURT TUCHOLSKY – ⟦⟧ Berlin - Malmö and v.v.

L – ⟼ 2 cl. and ⟦⟧ Oslo - Malmö and v.v.

M – SASSNITZ EXPRESS – ⛏ 1,2 cl., ⟼ 2 cl. and ⟦⟧ Malmö - Berlin and v.v.

P – June 22 - Aug. 27: ⟦⟧ Malmö - Berlin.

R – ①②③④⑤⑦: ⛏ 1,2 cl., ⟼ 2 cl. and ⟦⟧ Stockholm - Malmö and v.v.

T – June 21 - Aug. 28: ⟦⟧ Berlin - Malmö.

f – ⑤⑥⑦ only.

Table 55 (Summer)　　　FRANKFURT AND DRESDEN - WARSZAWA AND MOSKVA

train number	451	451	IC559	457	EC57	453	453
notes (see page 4)			✕	⛴	✕		
notes (see below)	T	V	✕	✕	✕	W	Y
Frankfurt/Main .... d.	...	2323	2323	...	1323	...	1523	...
Fulda .... d.	...	0113	0113	...	1419	...	1619	...
Bebra .... d.	...	0156	0156	...		...		...
Erfurt .... d.	...	0237	0237	...	1543	...	1743	...
Leipzig .... d.	...	0425	0425	...	1705	...	1857	2005	2005
Dresden Hbf .... d.	...	...	...	1823	...	...	...
Dresden Neustadt ..... d.	...	0611	0611	1823	1831	...	2130	2130
Görlitz .... d.	...	0802	0802	...	2015	...	0005	0005
Zgorzelec ▥ .... d.	...	0807	0807	...	2020	...	0010	0010
Jelenia Góra .... a.	...	...	1201	...		...		...
Legnica .... a.	...	0943		...	2143	...	0139	0139
Wrocław Główny ...... a.	...	1037	1210	...	2230	...	0232	0232
Opole .... a.	...	...	1313	...	...	...	0412	
Katowice .... a.	...	...	1505	...	...	...	0557	
Kraków Główny .... a.	...	...	1630	...	...	...	0734	
Łódź Kaliska .... a.	1415	...	...	...	0616	...	
Warszawa Centralna ... a.	1615	...	...	...	0847	...	
Warszawa Wschodnia ... a.	1629	...	...	...	0901	...	
Brest .... a.	2200	...	...	...		...	
Terespol .... a.	0151	...	...	...		...	
Minsk .... a.	0830	...	...	...		...	
Moskva Smolenskaya ... a.	2000	...	...	...		...	

Moskva train number					456	IC558		9 450	36000		452	36006	IC554
Polish train number													
notes (see page 4)					⛴	✕							
notes (see below)					✕	✕		T	V		W	Y	✕
Moskva Smolenskaya ..... d.	...	...	...	...	1517	...	...	...	...
Minsk .... d.	...	...	...	...	0044	...	...	...	...
Brest ▥ .... d.	...	...	...	...	0800	...	...	...	...
Terespol .... d.	...	...	...	...	0655	...	...	...	...
Warszawa Wschodnia .... d.	...	...	...	...	1249	...	1825	...	...
Warszawa Centralna .... d.	...	...	...	...	1303	...	1840	...	...
Łódź Kaliska .... a.	...	...	...	...	1457	...	2100	...	...
Kraków Główny .... d.	...	...	...	...	1240	...	2002	...
Katowice .... d.	...	...	...	...	1407	...	2132	...
Opole .... d.	...	...	...	...	1552	...	2317	...
Wrocław Główny .... d.	0710	...	1823	1615	...	0022	0022	...
Legnica .... d.	0802	...	1918	...	0118	0118	...
Jelenia Góra .... d.	...	...	1903	...	...	...
Zgorzelec ▥ .... d.	0930	...	2106	2106	...	0257	0257	...
Görlitz .... a.	0935	...	2111	2111	...	0302	0302	...
Dresden Neustadt ...... a.	1120	1129	...	2259	2259	...	0450	0450	...
Dresden Hbf .... d.	1128		...			...			...
Leipzig .... a.	...	1248	...	0044	0044	...	0628	0628	0659
Erfurt .... a.	...	1412	...	0238	0238	...	...		0812
Bebra .... a.	...	...	0338	0338	...	...		
Fulda .... a.	...	1538	...	0428	0428	...	...		0938
Frankfurt/Main .... a.	...	1635	...	0600	0600	...	...		1035

NOTES

– ⛏ 1,2 cl., ⟼ 2 cl., ⟦⟧ and ⛴ Frankfurt/Main-Warszawa and v.v. (journey 1 night);
⛏ 1,2 cl. Frankfurt/Main - Moskva and v.v. (journey 2 nights).

– ⟼ 2 cl. and ⟦⟧ Frankfurt/Main - Kraków and v.v. (journey 1 night)

W – ⛏ 1,2 cl., ⟼ 2 cl., ⟦⟧ and ⛴ Leipzig - Warszawa and v.v.

Y – ⛏ 1,2 cl., ⟦⟧ and ⛴ Leipzig - Kraków and v.v.

✕ – Supplement payable.

Table 56 (Summer) BERLIN - WARSZAWA AND MOSKVA

train type / train number	328	EC 41	IC 49	IC 508	IC 537	EC 43	449	247	247	345	320	299	299	241	241	241
notes (see below)	S	V ✗	A ✗	✗	✗	B ✗	N	K	L	P	E	Q	T	D	W	G
Köln Hbf ... d.				0910										1916	1916	1916
Düsseldorf ... d.														1944	1944	1944
Duisburg ... d.														2000	2000	2000
Essen ... d.														2015	2015	2015
Dortmund ... d.				1023										2040	2040	2040
Bielefeld ... d.				1110										2148	2148	2148
Hannover ... d.				1203										2310	2310	2310
Hamburg Hbf ... d.					1301											
Berlin Zoo ... d.				1452	1600											
Berlin Hbf ... d.		0817	0914			1621										
Berlin Lichtenberg ... d.	0632						2021	2123	2123	2149	2235	2300	2300			
Frankfurt/Oder ... a.		0910	1001			1714	2145	2245	2245	2319		0024	0024	0341	0341	0341
Szczecin Główny ... a.	0844										0047					
Gdynia Główna ... a.	1315										0604					
Gdańsk Główny ... a.											0655					
Kaliningrad ... a.											1330					
Kunowice ... a.							2158	2258	2256	2332		0037	0037			
Rzepin ... a.		0928	1022			1732	2225	2315	2315	2349		0057	0057	0409	0409	0409
Wroclaw Główny ... a.			1322				0156									
Katowice ... a.			1550				0507									
Kraków Główny ... a.			1702				0636									
Poznań Główny ... a.		1119				1920		0130	0130	0200		0315	0315	0625	0625	0625
Warszawa Centralna ... a.		1440				2232		0716	0716	0615		0716	0716	1015	1015	1015
Warszawa Wschodnia ... a.		1459				2248		0730	0730	0629		0730	0730	1029	1029	1029
Grodno ... a.												1649	1649			
Vilnius ... a.												2100	2100			
Riga ... a.													0810			
Terespol ... a.								1112	1112					1338	1338	1338
Brest ... a.								1321	1321					1615	1616	1616
Kyïv (Kiev) ... a.									0920							1240
Minsk ... a.								1944				1210		2227		
St Peterburg Varshavski ... a.															1742p	
Smolensk ... a.								0152						0418		
Moskva Smolenskaya ... a.								0935						1206		

train number / train number	EC 42	IC 507	IC 536	48	329	EC 40	49 / 240	15 / 240	273 / 240	221 / 298	25 / 298	448	7 / 321	141 / 246	13 / 246	344
notes (see below)	B ✗	✗	✗	A ✗	S	V ✗	Y	D	H	T	Q	N	E	L	K	P
Moskva Smolenskaya ... d.								2015								
Smolensk ... d.								0326							0610	
St Peterburg Varshavski ... d.							1510p				2105					
Minsk ... d.								0736							1025	
Kyïv (Kiev) ... d.									1805							
Brest ... d.							1436	1436	1436					1849	1849	
Riga ... d.										2205						
Vilnius ... d.										1022	1022					
Grodno ... d.										1434	1434					
Terespol ... d.																
Warszawa Wschodnia ... d.	0603					1625	1910	1910	1910	2206	2206			2200	2200	2327
Warszawa Centralna ... d.	0618					1640	1925	1925	1925	2220	2220			2214	2214	2342
Kraków Główny ... d.				0930								2102				
Katowice ... d.				1049								2232				
Wroclaw Główny ... d.				1313								0132				
Poznań Główny ... d.	0921					1943	2250	2250	2250	0215	0215			0319	0319	0352
Rzepin ... d.	1110			1614		2134	0100	0100	0100	0430	0430	0501	1712	0534	0534	0602
Kaliningrad ... d.													1712			
Gdańsk Główny ... d.													2211			
Gdynia Główna ... d.					1530								2330			
Szczecin Główny ... d.					1955								0450			
Kunowice ... d.							0115	0115	0115	0447	0447	0521		0552	0552	0624
Frankfurt/Oder ... a.	1131			1635		2154	0127	0127	0127	0459	0459	0533		0605	0605	0636
Berlin Lichtenberg ... a.						2202				0625	0625	0653	0716	0732	0732	0753
Berlin Hbf ... a.	1224			1726		2248										
Berlin Zoo ... a.		1307	1400													
Hamburg Hbf ... a.			1659													
Hannover ... a.		1557					0547	0547	0547							
Bielefeld ... a.		1647					0704	0704	0704							
Dortmund ... a.		1735					0823	0823	0823							
Essen ... a.							0900	0900	0900							
Duisburg ... a.							0917	0917	0917							
Düsseldorf ... a.							0933	0933	0933							
Köln Hbf ... a.		1850					1000	1000	1000							

NOTES

A – WAWEL – [IC] and [sleeper] Berlin - Krakow and v.v.
B – BEROLINA – [IC] and [sleeper] Berlin - Warszawa and v.v.
D – 1,2 cl., 2 cl. and [couchette] (Brussels) - Köln - Warszawa and v.v. (journey 1 night); [sleeper] 1,2 cl. (Brussels) - Köln - Moskva and v.v. (journey 2 nights).
E – GEDANIA – [sleeper] 1,2 cl., 2 cl. and [couchette] Berlin - Gdynia and v.v. (1 night); [sleeper] 1,2 cl. Berlin - Kaliningrad and v.v. (1 night).
G – ②, also ⑦ June 4 - Sept. 10: [sleeper] 1,2 cl. (Brussels) - Köln - Kyïv (2 nights).
H – ⑦, also ⑤ June 2 - Sept. 8: [sleeper] 1,2 cl. Kyïv - Köln (Brussels) (2 nights).
K – MOSKWA EXPRESS – [sleeper] 1,2 cl. and ⛲ Berlin - Moskva and v.v. (2 night).
L – [sleeper] 2 cl. Berlin - Kyïv and v.v. (2 night).
N – [sleeper] 1,2 cl., 2 cl., [couchette] and ⛲ Berlin - Krakow and v.v. (1 night).
P – 1,2 cl., 2 cl. and [couchette] Berlin - Warszawa and v.v. (1 night).
Q – ST. PETERSBURG EXPRESS – [sleeper] 1,2 cl. Berlin - St Peterburg and v.v. (2 nights).
S – MARE BALTICUM – [IC] and ⛲ Berlin - Gdynia and v.v.
T – [sleeper] 2 cl. Berlin - Riga and v.v. (2 nights).
V – VARSOVIA – [IC] and [sleeper] Berlin - Warszawa and v.v.
W – ①⑤, also ③ May 31 - Sept. 20: [sleeper] 2 cl. (Brussels) - Köln - Sankt Peterburg (journey 2 nights).
Y – ③⑥, also ① May 29 - Sept. 18: [sleeper] 2 cl. Sankt Peterburg - Köln - (Brussels) (journey 2 nights).
p – Sankt Peterburg Vitebski.
✗ – Supplement payable.

INTERNATIONAL SERVICES FROM BERLIN

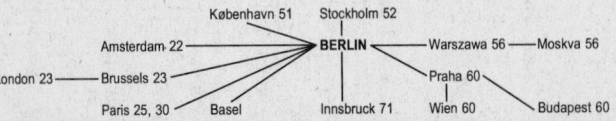

København 51 — Stockholm 52 — Amsterdam 22 — London 23 — Brussels 23 — Paris 25, 30 — Basel — **BERLIN** — Warszawa 56 — Moskva 56 — Innsbruck 71 — Wien 60 — Praha 60 — Budapest 60

Table 57 (Summer) KÖLN, FRANKFURT/MAIN AND MÜNCHEN - PRAHA

(train type / train number)	3507	IR 265	IC 107	IR 2063	IR 2663	259	IR 2161	2465	EC 51	7009	EC 27	3521	IR 2195	EC 167	201	382	1961	353	1980
notes (see page 4)									A					F	H		D	K	C
Dortmund Hbf .... d.									0541		0841						1905		
Hagen Hbf .... d.									0602		0901								
Wuppertal Hbf .... d.									0620		0920								
Düsseldorf Hbf .... d.																			2004
Köln Hbf .... d.									0654		0954								2035
Bonn .... d.									0714		1014								2057
Koblenz .... d.									0746		1046								2134
Mainz .... d.									0838		1136								2228
Frankfurt/Main Hbf .... d.									0915		1215								2327
Würzburg .... d.									1027		1328								0112
Bern .... d.														0816					
Zürich Hb .... d.														0941		1913			
St. Gallen .... d.														1041					
Bregenz .... d.														1121					
Lindau .... d.														1137					
Stuttgart .... d.				0608				0807					1116			2222	2251		
München Hbf .... d.		0657		0657			0857							1335	1408			2312	
Regensburg .... d.		0830		0830			1035					1524			1537				
Nürnberg .... d.	0744				0839			1016		1139			1444				0235	0235	0235
Schwandorf .... d.	0841	0907		0902			1049						1541		1615				
Fürth im Wald .... d.		1006													1715				
Marktredwitz .... d.				1008	0956	1011	1205		1258								0409	0409	0409
Schirnding .... a.						1024											0423	0423	0423
Cheb .... a.						1037			1325	1350							0438	0438	0438
Karlovy Vary .... a.						1203				1459									
Plzeň .... a.		1132							1506						1841		0634	0634	0634
Praha Hlavni .... a.		1316	1343						1640					2023	2123		0812	0812	0812
Warszawa Centralna .. a.			2245												0715				

(train type / train number)	200	EC 166	3518	IR 2192	EC 28	258	2603	IR 2668	7044	EC 50	2062	2662	IC 106	264	3536	352	352	352	383
notes (see page 4)	H	G								A						C	K	D	
Warszawa Centralna ... d.	1955												0555						
Praha Hlavni .... d.	0612	0735								1315			1459	1626		2135	2135	2135	
Plzeň .... d.		0916								1448				1811		2313	2313	2313	
Karlovy Vary .... d.						1008			1423										
Cheb .... d.						1113			1536		1632					0120	0120	0120	
Schirnding .... a.						1126										0135	0135	0135	
Marktredwitz .... a.						1140	1147	1200			1659	1747							
Fürth im Wald .... a.		1045												1947					
Schwandorf .... a.		1143	1211					1306			1906			2049	2111				
Nürnberg .... a.			1314				1319			1819		1945			2214	0320	0320	0320	
Regensburg .... a.		1222		1232				1321			1921			2125					
München Hbf .... a.		1351	1426					1501				2101		2301		0604			
Stuttgart .... a.			1644				1553				2153					0652			0742
Lindau .... a.		1622																	
Bregenz .... a.		1638																	
St. Gallen .... a.		1718																	
Zürich Hb .... a.		1823																	1047
Bern .... a.		1943																	
Würzburg .... a.				1428						1929								0454	
Frankfurt/Main Hbf .... a.				1543						2043								0643	
Mainz .... a.				1624						2122								0726	
Koblenz .... a.				1713						2211								0820	
Bonn .... a.				1745						2243								0857	
Köln Hbf .... a.				1805						2305								0921	
Düsseldorf Hbf .... a.				1831						2331								0951	
Wuppertal Hbf .... a.																			
Hagen Hbf .... a.																			
Dortmund Hbf .... a.				1919						0019								1054	

NOTES
- KARLSTEIN – [1,2 cl.] and ✕ Dortmund - Praha and v.v.
- [1,2 cl.], [2 cl.] and [couchette] München - Praha and v.v.
- [1,2 cl.], [2 cl.] and [couchette] Stuttgart - Praha and v.v.
- ALBERT EINSTEIN – [1,2 cl.] and ✕ (Interlaken) - Bern - Praha.

G – ALBERT EINSTEIN – [1,2 cl.] and ✕ Praha - Bern.
H – SILESIA – [1,2 cl.], [2 cl.] and [couchette] Praha - Warszawa and v.v.
K – [1,2 cl.], [2 cl.] and [couchette] Praha - Warszawa.
/ – Supplement payable.

INTERNATIONAL SERVICES FROM FRANKFURT/MAIN

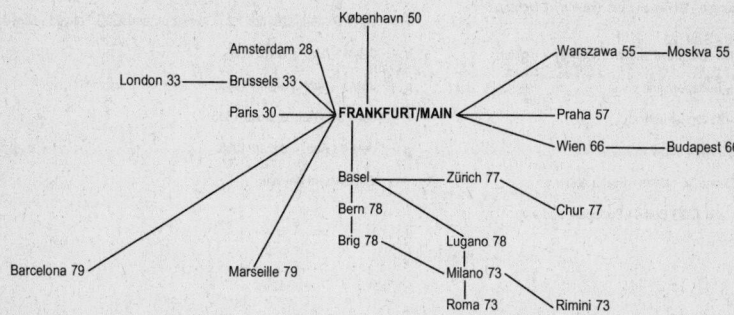

Table 60 (Summer) HAMBURG AND BERLIN - PRAHA AND WIEN

train type		EC	IC	EC	IC	IC	EC	IR	IC	EC	EC	D	IC	IC	EC	IC	EC	D	D	D	D	D
train number	1251	171	657	173	655	531	175	2447	533	177	9	371	559	537	179	875	57	379	453	1279	377	1073
notes (see page 4)	L	G		H			F		X	C		N		X	X	J	M	K	S	A		E
Hamburg Altona ...... d.						0643			0843					1243								
Hamburg Hbf .... d.						0701			0901					1301								
Nauen .... d.						0929	0936			1129	1136			1529	1536							
Berlin Hbf .... d.																						
Berlin Lichtenberg .. d.		0631		0831			1031			1231				1631		1831		1909			2231	2349
Leipzig .... d.	0605		0905		1105		1305						1705				1905		2025			
Bad Brambach .... a.																						
Karlovy Vary .... a.																						
Dresden Hbf .... d.	0737	0837	1031	1037	1231		1237	1432		1437		1822	1831	1837		2023	2037	2120	2153	2220	0035	0155
Bad Schandau .... d.	0810	0905		1105			1305			1505		1856		1905			2106	2152		2253	0108	0253
Děčín .... a.	0831	0925		1125			1325			1525		1916		1925			2125	2212		2315	0128	0314
Praha Holešovice .... a.	1020	1102		1302			1502			1702	1712		2149	2102			2302	0004		0104	0315	0509
Praha Hlavni .... a.	1033													2116			2316					
Pardubice .... a.													2329									
Olomouc .... a.													0123									
Poprad Tatry .... a.													0644									
Košice .... a.													0805									
Brno hlavni .... a.		1417		1617			1817		2017									0342			0634	0855
Břeclav .... a.		1456		1656			1856		2057									0429	0544		0716	0946
Wien Süd .... a.				1803f					2203											0658	0852b	
Bratislava hlavni ... a.		1556					1956											0539				1058
Stúrovo .... a.		1722					2122											0730				
Budapest Nyugati .... a.																		0857				1438
Budapest Keleti ..... a.		1837					2237															
Komárom .... a.																			0850			
Siofok .... a.																			1115			
Fonyód .... a.																			1210			
Lőkőshaza .... a.																						1840
Curtici .... a.																						2025
Bucureşti Nord ...... a.																						0600
Beograd .... a.																						
Sofija .... a.																						

train number	EC 56	IC 874	324	EC 178	IC 536	IC 558	EC 8	EC 176	IC 532	IC 652	EC 174	IC 530	IC 654	EC 172	IC 656	EC 170	1948	1250	33 1072	376	378	IR 2484	1278
notes	M		N	J	X	X	X	C	X	X	F		X	H		G		L	D	A	K		T
Sofija .... d.																							
Beograd .... d.																							
Bucureşti Nord ...... d.																			0115				
Curtici .... d.																			1100				
Lőkőshaza .... d.																			0945				
Fonyód .... d.																							1738
Siofok .... d.																							1835
Komárom .... d.																							2100
Budapest Keleti ..... d.									0650									1050	1400		1825		
Budapest Nyugati .... d.											0808			1208				1333			1950		
Stúrovo .... d.											0933								1744		2145		2257
Bratislava hlavni ... d.											1113	1125g							1947		2254	2025e	0011
Wien Süd .... d.					0725	0845	0925		1033	1113		1233	1313	1433	1513					2154		2254	
Břeclav .... d.																							
Brno hlavni .... d.																			1947	2237	2337		
Košice .... d.			2135																				
Poprad Tatry .... d.			2256																				
Olomouc .... d.			0424																				
Pardubice .... d.			0616																				
Praha Hlavni .... d.							1220											1846					
Praha Holešovice .... d.	0633		0751	0833			1221	1233			1433			1633		1833		1859	0044	0214	0313		0449
Děčín .... d.	0816		1000	1016			1416				1616			1836		2016		2045	0241	0407	0502		0637
Bad Schandau .... d.	0836		1020	1036			1436				1636			1836		2036	2105		0301	0427	0522		0657
Dresden Hbf .... a.	0905	0917	1059	1105	1121			1505	1521		1705	1721	1905	1954	2105	2121	2135		0333	0459	0559	0640	0744
Karlovy Vary .... d.																							
Bad Brambach .... a.																							
Leipzig .... a.	1048		1311		1248		1711	1648			1911			2111	2132	2311	2252	2307	0541	0711	0818		0449
Berlin Lichtenberg .. a.		1111		1311																			0819
Berlin Hbf .... a.																							
Nauen .... a.				1410	1430			1810	1830		2010	2030		2305	2316								
Hamburg Hbf .... a.					1659				2059														
Hamburg Altona ...... a.					1716				2116														

NOTES

A – SANSSOUCI – 1,2 cl. sleeper, 2 cl. couchette and restaurant Berlin - Wien and v.v.

C – PORTA BOHEMICA – restaurant and ✗ Nauen - Praha and v.v.

D – BALT ORIENT EXPRESS – May 28 - Sept. 22: 1,2 cl. sleeper, 2 cl. couchette and restaurant Bucureşti - Berlin and v.v. (journey 2 nights).

E – BALT ORIENT EXPRESS – May 28 - Sept. 23: 1,2 cl. sleeper, 2 cl. couchette and restaurant Berlin - Bucureşti and v.v. (journey 2 nights).

F – HUNGARIA – restaurant and ✗ Nauen - Budapest and v.v.

G – COMENIUS – restaurant and ✗ Berlin - Budapest and v.v.

H – VINDOBONA – restaurant and ✗ Berlin - Wien and v.v.

J – CARL MARIA VON WEBER – restaurant and ✗ Nauen - Praha and v.v.

K – METROPOL – 1,2 cl. sleeper, 2 cl. couchette and restaurant Berlin - Budapest and v.v.

L – restaurant (Paris) - Leipzig - Praha and v.v.

M – HEINRICH HEINE – restaurant and ✗ (Paris) - Leipzig - Praha and v.v.

N – 2 cl. couchette and restaurant Dresden - Košice and v.v.

S – June 16 - Aug. 25: 1,2 cl. sleeper, 2 cl. couchette and restaurant Dresden - Fonyód.

T – June 17 - Aug. 26: 1,2 cl. sleeper, 2 cl. couchette and restaurant Fonyód - Dresden.

b – July 1 - Aug. 3 arrive 0928.

e – July 1 - Aug. 3 depart 1955.

f – June 30 - Aug. 3 arrive 1833.

g – July 1 - Aug. 4 depart 1055.

✗ – Supplement payable.

Table 61 (Summer)   MÜNCHEN AND WIEN - BUDAPEST AND BUCUREŞTI

Services to Beograd are subject to disruption and are not recommended for international travellers.

train type	EC						EC			EC							
train number	41	345			263	491	63	343	25	347	347	341	341			269	
notes (see page 4)																	
notes (see below)	H ⟋		M		A	J	C ⟋	P	E ⟋	L	K	R	Z			B	
Stuttgart Hbf .... d.	...	...	...	...	...	...	0600	...	...	...	...	...	...				
München Hbf .... d.	...	...	...	...	...	...	0825	...	...	...	...	...	...			2319	
Salzburg ⓜ .... d.	...	...	...	...	0605	...	1000	...	...	...	...	...	...			0116	
Linz .... d.	...	...	...	...	0727	...	1114	...	1614	...	...	...	...			0233	
Wien West .... d.	...	...	0905	...	0958	...	1320	1505	1820	1905	1905	2325	2325				
Wien Süd .... d.	0716	...	...	...	...	...	...	...	...	...	...	...	...				
Hegyeshalom ⓜ .... a.	0800	1003	...	...	1056	...	1418	1603	1923	2008	2008	0026	0026			0519	
Győr .... a.	0830	1040	...	...	1132	...	1447	1643	2001	2100	2100	0120	0120			0608	
Budapest Keleti .... a.		...	...	...	1308	1455	1623	1828	2138	2238	2238					0753	
Budapest Déli .... a.	0958	...	...	...	...	...	...	...	...	...	...	...	...				
Záhony 898 .... a.	...	...	...	...	...	...	...	2300	...	...	...	...	...				
Szeged 895 .... a.	...	...	...	...	...	...	...	...	...	...	...	...	0602				
Curtici ⓜ .... a.	...	...	...	...	...	...	...	...	...	...	0350	...	...			1310	
Arad .... a.	...	...	...	...	...	...	...	...	...	...	0445	...	...			1410	
Braşov .... a.	...	...	...	...	...	...	...	...	...	...	1056	...	...			2017	
Bucureşti Nord .... a.	...	...	...	...	...	...	...	...	...	...	1340	...	...			2300	
Kelebia ⓜ .... a.	...	...	1447	...	...	1745	...	...	...	0320	...	0540	...				
Beograd .... a.	...	...	1845	...	...	2128	...	...	...	0714	...	0907	...				
Niš .... a.	...	...	...	...	...	0205	...	...	...	1145	...	1430	...				
Skopje .... a.	...	...	...	...	...	...	...	...	...	1624	...	1944	...				
Thessaloniki .... a.	...	...	...	...	...	...	...	...	...	2218	...	...	...				
Athínai .... a.	...	...	...	...	...	...	...	...	...	0703	...	...	...				
Dimitrovgrad .... a.	...	...	...	...	...	0416	...	...	...	...	...	...	...				
Sofija .... a.	...	...	...	...	...	0738	...	...	...	...	...	...	...				
Svilengrad .... a.	...	...	...	...	...	1250	...	...	...	...	...	...	...				
Kapikule ⓜ .... a.	...	...	...	...	...	1345	...	...	...	...	...	...	...				
Istanbul .... a.	...	...	...	...	...	1959	...	...	...	...	...	...	...				

train number	23			EC		EC						EC		21		7051	212
train number	346	334		24	342	62	490	262			344	40		268		340	340
notes (see page 4)																	
notes (see below)	K	L		E ⟋	P	C ⟋	J	A			M	H ⟋		B		Z	R
Istanbul .... d.	...	...	...	...	...	...	1000	...	...	...	...	...	...	...		...	...
Kapikule .... d.	...	...	...	...	...	...	1620	...	...	...	...	...	...	...		...	...
Svilengrad .... d.	...	...	...	...	...	...	1715	...	...	...	...	...	...	...		...	...
Sofija .... d.	...	...	...	...	...	...	2255	...	...	...	...	...	...	...		...	...
Dimitrovgrad .... d.	...	...	...	...	...	...	0010	...	...	...	...	...	...	...		...	...
Athínai .... d.	...	2330	...	...	...	...		...	...	...	...	...	...	...		...	...
Thessaloniki .... d.	...	0826	...	...	...	...		...	...	...	...	...	...	...		...	...
Skopje .... d.	...	1220	...	...	...	...		...	...	...	...	...	...	...		...	0905
Niš .... d.	...	1715	...	...	...	...	0201	...	...	...	...	...	...	...		...	1400
Beograd .... d.	...	2145	...	...	...	...	0650	...	...	1050	...	...	...	...		...	1930
Kelebia ⓜ .... d.	...	0210	...	...	...	...	1140	...	...	1430	...	...	...	...		...	2305
Bucureşti Nord .... d.	1625		...	...	...	...	...	...	...	...	...	0800	...	...		...	...
Braşov .... d.	1904		...	...	...	...	...	...	...	...	...	1057	...	...		...	...
Arad .... d.	0053		...	...	...	...	...	...	...	...	...	1655	...	...		...	...
Curtici ⓜ .... d.	0150		...	...	...	...	...	...	...	...	...	1750	...	...		...	...
Szeged 895 .... d.			...	...	...	...	...	...	...	...	...	...	...	...		2240	...
Záhony 898 .... d.			...	...	0525	...	...	...	...	...	...	...	...	...		...	...
Budapest Déli .... d.			...	...	...	...	...	...	...	...	...	1840	...	...		...	...
Budapest Keleti .... d.	0600	0600	...	0850	1000	1240	1428	1540	...	...	...	...	2125	...		...	...
Győr .... d.	0738	0738	...	1025	1149	1415	...	1719	...	1909	...	2008	2303	...		0342	0342
Hegyeshalom ⓜ .... d.	0815	0815	...	1055	1229	1445	...	1755	...	1945	...	2038	2347	...		0425	0425
Wien Süd .... a.			...	...	...	...	...	...	...	...	...	2122	...	...		...	...
Wien West .... a.	0920	0920	...	1200	1334	1550	...	1900	...	2050	...	...	0530	...		0530	0530
Linz .... a.	...	...	...	1402	...	1746	...	2131	...	...	...	0228	...	...		...	...
Salzburg ⓜ .... a.	...	...	...	...	...	1900	...	2255	...	...	...	0353	...	...		...	...
München Hbf .... a.	...	...	...	...	...	2036	...	...	...	...	...	0603	...	...		...	...
Stuttgart Hbf .... a.	...	...	...	...	...	2250	...	...	...	...	...	...	...	...		...	...

NOTES

A – ORIENT EXPRESS – 🛏 and ✕ Salzburg - Budapest and v.v.
B – KÁLMÁN IMRE – 🛏 1,2 cl., ⊨ 2 cl. and 🚃 München - Budapest and v.v.;
   🚃 München - Bucureşti and v.v.; 🚃 Budapest - Bucureşti and v.v.
C – BARTÓK BÉLA – 🛏 and ✕ Stuttgart - Budapest and v.v.
E – FRANZ LISZT – 🛏 and ✕ (Dortmund) - Linz - Budapest and v.v.
H – LEHÁR – 🛏 and ✕ Wien - Budapest and v.v.
J – BALKAN EXPRESS – 🛏 1,2 cl., ⊨ 2 cl. and 🚃 Budapest - Sofija and v.v.;
   ⊨ 1,2 cl. and 🚃 Budapest - Istanbul and v.v.; 🚃 Sofija - Istanbul and v.v.

K – DACIA EXPRESS – 🛏 1,2 cl., ⊨ 2 cl. and 🚃 Wien - Bucureşti and v.v.;
   🚃 and ✕ Wien - Budapest and v.v.
L – 🛏 Wien - Athínai and v.v. (journey 2 nights);
   🛏 and ✕ Wien - Budapest and v.v.
   ⊨ 1,2 cl., ⊨ 2 cl. and 🚃 Budapest - Athínai and v.v.
M – AVALA – 🚃 and ✕ Wien - Beograd and v.v.
P – ARRABONA – 🚃 and ✕ Wien - Záhony and v.v.
R – BEOGRAD EXPRESS – 🛏 1,2 cl., ⊨ 2 cl. and 🚃 Wien - Beograd and v.v.;
   ⊨ 2 cl. Wien - Skopje and v.v.
Z – 🚃 Wien - Szeged and v.v.
⟋ – Supplement payable.

Table 62 (Summer)   MÜNCHEN AND VILLACH - LJUBLJANA AND ZAGREB

train number	IC		EC	EC						train number		EC	EC		IC		
train number	590	311	11	115	315		297	297		train number	310	114	10	314	691	296	480
notes (see page 4)	🍴			✕						notes (see page 4)		✕					
notes (see below)			C ⟋	⟋			A	B		notes (see below)		⟋	C ⟋			A	B
Leipzig .... d.	...	...	0740	...	...		...	...		Zagreb .... d.	...	...	0810	...	...	2100	...
Nürnberg .... d.	...	...	1126	...	...		...	...		Zidani Most ⓜ .... d.	...	...		...	...	2223	...
München Hbf .... d.	...	...	1325	1525	...		2248	2248		Rijeka .... d.	...	...		...	...		2030
Salzburg .... d.	0708	...	1508	1708	...		0045	0045		Ljubljana .... d.	0825	...	1022	1725	...	2335	2335
Bischofshofen ... d.	0752	...	1552	1752	...		0128	0128		Jesenice ⓜ .... d.	0930	...	1130	1840	...	0057	0057
Schwarzach St Veit .. d.	0807	...	1607	1807	...		0145	0145		Villach Hbf .... a.	1005	1019	1206	1918	2019	0134e	0134e
Villach Hbf .... d.	0943	1040	1753	1944	1956		0327e	0327e		Schwarzach St Veit .. a.	...	1155	1355	...	2155	0318	0318
Jesenice ⓜ ...... a.	...	1114	1830	...	2033		0405	0405		Bischofshofen ...... a.	...	1209	1409	...	2209	0332	0332
Ljubljana .... a.	...	1220	1937	...	2140		0525	0525		Salzburg .... a.	...	1253	1453	...	2253	0415	0415
Rijeka .... a.	...			...	...		...	0823		München Hbf .... a.	...	1435	1635	...	...	0613	0613
Zidani Most ⓜ .. a.	...			...	2241		0635	...		Nürnberg .... a.	...	...	1831	...	...	...	...
Zagreb .... a.	...		2152	...	0006		0800	...		Leipzig .... a.	...	...	2218	...	...	...	...

NOTES

A – 🛏 1,2 cl., ⊨ 2 cl. and 🚃 München - Zagreb and v.v.
B – 🛏 1,2 cl., ⊨ 2 cl. and 🚃 München - Rijeka and v.v.

C – MIMARA – 🚃 and ✕ Leipzig - Zagreb and v.v.
e – Villach West.
⟋ – Supplement payable.

Table 64 (Summer) — HAMBURG - WIEN

train type	ICE	ICE	EC	ICE	ICE	EC	ICE	ICE	EC	ICE	ICE	EC	IR	EN
train number	791	783	23	793	785	25	795	785	27	797	789	29	2489	491
notes (see page 4)	✗	✗	✗	✗	✗	✗	✗	✗	✗	✗	✗	✗	🥤	
notes (see below)	D	D							B			C		A
Hamburg Altona .... d.	0553				0758			0958	0538		1158	0738		2023
Hamburg Hbf .... d.	0608				0813			1013	0553		1213	0753		2038
Bremen Hbf .... d.		0619		0819			1019		0647	1219		0847	2113	
Hannover Hbf .... d.	0718	0727		0918	0927		1118	1127		1318	1327		2218	2226
Nürnberg .... d.		1018	1025		1218	1225		1418	1425		1618	1625		0255
Passau 🚉 .... d.			1233			1433			1633			1833		0510
Linz .... a.			1354			1554			1754			1954		0630
Wien Westbahnhof .... a.			1547			1747			1947			2147		0830

train type	EC	ICE	ICE	EC	ICE	ICE	EC	ICE	ICE	EC	ICE	ICE	EN	IR
train number	28	786	796	26	784	794	24	782	792	22	880	790	490	2588
notes (see page 4)	✗	✗	✗	✗	✗	✗	✗	✗	✗	✗	✗	✗		🥤
notes (see below)	C			B									A	
Wien Westbahnhof .... d.	0815			1015			1215			1415			2000	
Linz .... d.	1004			1204			1404			1604			2150	
Passau 🚉 .... a.	1125			1325			1525			1725			2312	
Nürnberg .... a.	1332	1339		1532	1539		1732	1739		1932	1939		0132	
Hannover .... a.		1633	1642		1833	1842		2033	2042		2233	2242	0602	0642
Bremen Hbf .... a.	2112	1741		2312	1941			2141						0748
Hamburg Hbf .... a.	2207	1747		0007	1947			2147			2356		0752	
Hamburg Altona .... a.	2221	1801		0021	2001			2201			0010		0806	

NOTES

A – HANS ALBERS – 🛏 1,2 cl., 🛋 2 cl. and 🪑 Hamburg - Wien and v.v.

B – JOSEPH HAYDN – 🛋 and 🍴 Hamburg - (Köln) - Wien and v.v.

C – PRINZ EUGEN – 🛋 and 🍴 (Kiel) - Hamburg - (Köln) - Wien and v.v.

D – ①②③④⑤⑥, not June 5.

↗ – Supplement payable.

Table 65 (Summer) — HAMBURG - INNSBRUCK AND KLAGENFURT

train number	1299	1299	1299	541
notes (see below)	K	J	G	
Hamburg Altona .... d.	2023	2023	2023	
Hamburg Hbf .... d.	2038	2038	2038	
Hannover .... d.	2226	2226	2226	
Lindau 🚉 .... a.				
Bregenz .... a.				
Feldkirch .... a.				
Bludenz .... a.				
Langen am Arlberg .... a.				
St. Anton am Arlberg ..... a.				
Landeck .... a.				
Ötztal .... a.				
Kufstein 🚉 .... a.			0605	
Wörgl .... a.			0627	0657
Kitzbühel .... a.				0729
St. Johann .... a.				0737
Saalfelden .... a.				0807
Zell am See .... a.				0818
Innsbruck .... a.			0709	
Brennero 🚉 .... a.			0802	
Bolzano .... a.			0939	
Salzburg 🚉 .... a.	0703	0703		
Bischofshofen .... a.	0815	0815		
Radstadt .... a.	0854			
Selzthal .... a.	1023			
Graz .... a.	1230			
Schwarzach St Veit .... a.		0834		
Badgastein .... a.		0914		
Villach .... a.		1027		
Klagenfurt .... a.		1100		

train number	5084	1122	1298	818
notes (see below)		G	J	K
Klagenfurt .... d.			1925	
Villach .... d.			2007	
Badgastein .... d.			2125	
Schwarzach St Veit .... d.			2205	
Graz .... d.				1845
Selzthal .... d.				2052
Radstadt .... d.				2158
Bischofshofen .... d.			2239	2239
Salzburg 🚉 .... d.			2338	2338
Bolzano .... d.		2016		
Brennero 🚉 .... d.		2200		
Innsbruck .... d.		2248		
Zell am See .... d.				
Saalfelden .... d.				
St. Johann .... d.	2157			
Kitzbühel .... d.	2205			
Wörgl .... d.	2240	2325		
Kufstein 🚉 .... d.		2356		
Ötztal .... d.				
Landeck .... d.				
St. Anton am Arlberg ..... d.				
Langen am Arlberg .... d.				
Bludenz .... d.				
Feldkirch .... d.				
Bregenz .... d.				
Lindau 🚉 .... d.				
Hannover .... a.		0801	0801	0801
Hamburg Hbf .... a.		1002	1002	1002
Hamburg Altona .... a.		1016	1016	1016

NOTES

G – 🛏 1,2 cl. and 🛋 2 cl. Hamburg - Bolzano and v.v.

J – KÄRNTEN EXPRESS – 🛏 1,2 cl. and 🛋 2 cl. Hamburg - Klagenfurt and v.v.

K – 🛋 2 cl. and 🍴 Hamburg - Graz and v.v.

Table 66 (Summer) KÖLN AND FRANKFURT/MAIN – WIEN AND BUDAPEST

train type train number notes (see page 4) notes (see below)	EC 23	EC 25	EC 27	EC 29	EN 223
	J ⚹	F ⚹	G ⚹	H ⚹	B
Dortmund .... d.	...	...	0638	0841	...	1039	...
Essen .... d.	...	...	0701	...	1101	...
Duisburg .... d.	...	...	0714	...	1114	...
Düsseldorf .... d.	...	...	0728	...	1128	...
Köln Hbf .... d.	0554	0754	0954	1154	2110
Bonn .... d.	0614	0814	1014	1214	2134
Koblenz .... d.	0646	0846	1046	1246	2211
Mainz .... d.	0736	0936	1136	1336	2304
Frankfurt/Main ...... d.	0815	1015	1215	1415	2338
Würzburg .... d.	0927	1127	1327	1527	...
Nürnberg .... d.	1025	1225	1425	1625	...
Regensburg .... d.	1126	1326	1526	1726	...
Passau 🚻 .... d.	1233	1433	1633	1833	...
Linz .... a.	1354	1554	1754	1954	0541
Wien West .... a.	1547	1747	1947	2147	0740
Hegyeshalom .... a.	...	1903	...	...	...
Györ .... a.	...	1932	...	...	...
Budapest Keleti ..... a.	...	2108	...	...	...

train number train number notes (see page 4) notes (see below)	EC 28	EC 26	EC 24	EC 22	EN 222
	H ⚹	G ⚹	F ⚹	J ⚹	B
Budapest Keleti ..... d.	...	...	...	0850	...
Györ .... d.	...	...	...	1025	...
Hegyeshalom .... d.	...	...	...	1055	...
Wien West .... d.	0815	1015	1215	1415	2130
Linz .... d.	1004	1204	1404	1604	2320
Passau 🚻 .... a.	1125	1325	1533	1725		
Regensburg .... a.	1230	1430	1630	1830		
Nürnberg .... a.	1332	1532	1732	1932		
Würzburg .... a.	1429	1629	1829	2029		
Frankfurt/Main ...... a.	1543	1743	1943	2143	0601
Mainz .... a.	1622	1822	2022	2222	0644
Koblenz .... a.	1711	1911	2111	2311	0739
Bonn .... a.	1743	1943	2143	2344	0816
Köln Hbf .... a.	1805	2005	2205	0007	0842
Düsseldorf .... a.	1831	...	2231	...	...
Duisburg .... a.	1844	...	2244	...	...
Essen .... a.	1857	...	2257	...	...
Dortmund .... a.	1919	2119	2319	...	...

NOTES

B – DONAU KURIER – 🛏 1,2 cl. and 🛋 Köln - Wien and v.v.
F – FRANZ LISZT – 🛋 and ✕ Dortmund - Budapest and v.v.

G – JOSEPH HAYDN – 🛋 and ✕ (Hamburg) - Dortmund - Wien and v.v.
H – PRINZ EUGEN – 🛋 and ✕ (Kiel) - Dortmund - Wien and v.v.
J – JOHANN STRAUSS – 🛋 and ✕ Köln - Wien and v.v.
⚹ – Supplement payable.

Table 67 (Summer) MÜNCHEN – WIEN

train type train number notes (see page 4) notes (see below)	IR 2093	E 743	IC 3501	EC 561	IR 63	IC 2191	E 543	EC 3513	IR 565	EC 113	IC 545	EC 11	IC 567	IR 2195	IC 547	EC 115	IC 569	EC 65	3533 3535	IC 661	EC 17	269
	⚇	✕		E ⚹	⚇	✕			✕	✕	✕	✕	✕	⚇	✕	✕		A	✕	D ⚹	C	
Stuttgart .... d.	...	...	...	0600	...	...	...	...	...	...	...	...	...	...	...	...	...	1355	...	...	...	...
Ulm .... d.	...	...	...	0658	...	...	...	...	...	...	...	...	...	...	...	...	...	1455	...	...	...	...
Augsburg .... d.	...	...	...	0739	...	...	...	...	...	...	...	...	...	...	...	...	...	1537	...	...	...	...
München Hbf .... d.	0600	...	0650	...	0825	0951	...	1050	...	1225	...	1325	...	...	...	1525	...	1625	1650	...	1825	2319
Salzburg 🚻 .... a.	0746	0805	0844	0905	0955	1140	1205	1244	1305	1355	1405	1455	1505	1540	1605	1655	1705	1753	1845	1905	1955	0103
Linz .... a.	...	0925	...	1025	1112	...	1325	...	1425	...	1525	...	1625	...	1725	...	1825	1912	...	2025	2112	0425
Wien West .... a.	...	1125	...	1225	1305	...	1525	...	1525	...	1725	...	1825	...	1925	...	2030	2105	...	2225	2305	0632

train type train number notes (see page 4) notes (see below)	EC 16	IC 540	EC 112	IC 562	EC 3522	IC 64	EC 564	IC 114	EC 544	IR 2190	IC 566	EC 10	IC 546	IR 2098	IC 568	E 3540	EC 62	SC 968	EC 2094	IC 740	IR 2092	248
	D ⚹	✕	✕	✕		A ⚹	✕	✕	⚇	✕	✕	✕	✕		E ⚹	⚇	✕	⚇	C			
Wien West .... d.	0600	0640	...	0740	...	0900	0940	...	1040	...	1140	...	1240	...	1340	...	1600	1700	...	1840	...	2330
Linz .... d.	0748	0834	...	0934	...	1046	1134	...	1234	...	1334	...	1434	...	1534	...	1748	1848	...	2034	...	0127
Salzburg 🚻 .... d.	0905	0955	1005	1055	1118	1209	1255	1305	1355	1418	1455	1505	1555	1618	1655	1718	1905	2000	2018	2155	2215	0408
München Hbf .... a.	1035	...	1138	...	1309	1338	...	1435	...	1607	...	1635	...	1807	...	1910	2036	...	2200	...	2400	0603
Augsburg .... a.	...	...	...	...	...	1420	...	...	...	...	...	...	...	...	...	...	2110	...	...	...	...	...
Ulm .... a.	...	...	...	...	...	1503	...	...	...	...	...	...	...	...	...	...	2149	...	...	...	...	...
Stuttgart .... a.	...	...	...	...	...	1603	...	...	...	...	...	...	...	...	...	...	2250	...	...	...	...	...

NOTES

A – MOZART – 🛋 and ✕ (Paris) - Stuttgart - Wien and v.v.
C – 🛏 2 cl. and 🛋 München - Wien and v.v.

D – MAX REINHARDT – 🛋 and ✕ München - Wien and v.v.
E – BARTÓK BÉLA – 🛋 and ✕ Stuttgart - Wien - (Budapest) and v.v.
⚹ – Supplement payable.

Table 68 (Summer) KÖLN AND MÜNCHEN – VILLACH AND GRAZ

train type train number notes (see page 4) notes (see below)	EC 113	EC 113	EC 11	EC 115	EC 65	1123	1123
	R ⚹	X ⚹	T ⚹	S ⚹	W ⚹	M	N
Dortmund .... d.	0511	0511	...	0811	...	1905	1905
Essen .... d.	0535	0535	...	0835	...	1931	1931
Duisburg .... d.	0549	0549	...	0849	...	1946	1946
Düsseldorf .... d.	0604	0604	...	0904	...	2004	2004
Köln Hbf .... d.	0630	0630	...	0930	...	2035	2035
Bonn .... d.	0650	0650	...	0950	...	2057	2057
Koblenz .... d.	0722	0722	...	1022	...	2134	2134
Mainz .... d.	0812	0812	...	1112	...	2228	2228
Frankfurt/Main ...... d.			...	...	...	2327	2327
Mannheim .... d.	0854	0854	...	1154	...		
Heidelberg .... d.	0906	0906	...	1206	...		
Stuttgart .... d.	0955	0955	...	1255	1355		
Ulm .... d.	1055	1055	...	1355	1455		
Augsburg .... d.	1137	1137	...	1437	1537		
München Hbf .... a.	1225	1225	1325	1525	1625		
Salzburg 🚻 .... a.	1355	1355	1455	1655	1753	0703	0703
Bischofshofen .... a.	1441	1441	1550	1750	1848	0815	0815
Selzthal .... a.		1624			2024		1023
Graz .... a.		1805			2205		1230
Schwarzach St Veit . a.	1458		1604	1804		0834	...
Villach Hbf .... a.	1649		1744	1944		1027	...
Klagenfurt .... a.	1723			2010		1100	...

train type train number notes (see page 4) notes (see below)	EC 112	EC 112	EC 116	EC 114	EC 10	1298	818
	R ⚹	X ⚹	W ⚹	Z ⚹	T ⚹	M	N
Klagenfurt .... d.	0636	...	0952	...	1925	...	...
Villach Hbf .... d.	0712	...	1019	1218	2007	...	...
Schwarzach St Veit. d.	0858	...	1157	1357	2205	...	...
Graz .... d.		0557	0757			...	1845
Selzthal .... d.		0737	0937			...	2052
Bischofshofen .... d.	0921	0921	1116	1211	1411	2239	2239
Salzburg 🚻 .... d.	1005	1005	1209	1305	1505	2338	2338
München Hbf .... a.	1138	1138	1338	1435	1635	...	...
Augsburg .... a.	1220	1220	1420	1520			
Ulm .... a.	1303	1303	1503	1603			
Stuttgart .... a.	1403	1403	1603	1703			
Heidelberg .... a.	1452	1452		1752			
Mannheim .... a.	1505	1505		1805			
Frankfurt/Main ...... a.						0643	0643
Mainz .... a.	1546	1546		1846		0726	0726
Koblenz .... a.	1635	1635		1935		0820	0820
Bonn .... a.	1707	1707		2007		0857	0857
Köln Hbf .... a.	1729	1729		2029		0921	0921
Düsseldorf .... a.	1755	1755		2055		0951	0951
Duisburg .... a.	1809	1809		2109		1015	1015
Essen .... a.	1822	1822		2122		1029	1029
Dortmund .... a.	1848	1848				1054	1054

NOTES

M – 🛏 1,2 cl. and 🛏 2 cl. Dortmund - Klagenfurt and v.v.
N – 🛏 2 cl. Dortmund - Graz and v.v.
R – WÖRTHERSEE – 🛋 and ✕ Dortmund - Klagenfurt and v.v.
S – BLAUER ENZIAN – 🛋 and ✕ Dortmund - Klagenfurt.
T – MIMARA – 🛋 and ✕ (Leipzig) - München - Villach - (Zagreb) and v.v.

W – MOZART – 🛋 (Paris) - Stuttgart - Graz and v.v.;
     ✕ Stuttgart - Salzburg and v.v.; ⚇ Salzburg - Graz and v.v.
X – 🛋 Dortmund - Graz and v.v.
Z – BLAUER ENZIAN – 🛋 and ✕ Klagenfurt - Essen - (Münster).
⚹ – Supplement payable.

Table 69 (Summer)   KÖLN AND STUTTGART - INNSBRUCK AND VERONA

	IR	EC		IC	IR	EC			
train type	IR	EC		IC	IR	EC			
train number	361	13		119	461	19		1123	
notes (see page 4)	⚲				⚲				
notes (see below)		D ✗		F ✗		E ✗		H	
Dortmund ....d.		0611				1211		1905	
Essen ....d.		0635		0735		1235		1931	
Duisburg ....d.		0649		0749		1249		1946	
Düsseldorf ....d.		0704		0804		1304		2004	
Köln Hbf ....d.		0730		0830		1330		2035	
Bonn ....d.		0750		0850		1350		2057	
Koblenz ....d.		0822		0922		1422		2134	
Mainz ....d.		0912		1012		1512		2228	
Frankfurt/Main ....d.								2327	
Saarbrücken ....d.	0546				0948				
Mannheim ....d.	0710	0954		1054	1110	1554			
Heidelberg ....d.		1006		1106		1606			
Stuttgart ....d.	0759	1055		1155	1159	1655			
Ulm ....d.	0911	1155		1255	1311	1755			
Lindau 🚉 ....d.	1059				1502				
Bregenz ....a.	1109				1513				
Bludenz ....a.					1605				
Langen am Arlberg ....a.					1648				
St. Anton am Arlberg ......a.					1658				
Landeck ....a.					1725				
Augsburg ....d.		1237		1337		1837			
München Hbf ....d.		1330		1421		1930			
Seefeld in Tirol 🚉 ....a.				1703					
Kufstein 🚉 ....a.		1431				2031		0605	
Wörgl ....a.		1442	1457			2042	2056	0627	0657
Kitzbühel ....a.			1529				2131		0729
St Johann in Tirol ....a.			1537				2138		0737
Saalfelden ....a.			1607				2145		0807
Zell am See ....a.			1618						0818
Schwarzach St Veit ....a.									
Innsbruck 🚉 ....a.		1519		1746		2119		0709	
Brennero 🚉 ....a.		1559						0802	
Bolzano ....a.		1728						0939	
Trento ....a.		1800							
Verona ....a.		1904							
Padova ....a.									
Venezia S. Lucia ....a.									

	EC		IR	IC	IR	EC			
train type	EC		IR	IC	IR	EC			
train number	18		460	118	360	12		1122	
notes (see page 4)			⚲		⚲				
notes (see below)	G ✗			F ✗		D ✗		H	
Venezia S. Lucia ....d.									
Venezia Mestre ....d.									
Padova ....d.									
Verona ....d.						1100			
Trento ....d.						1158			
Bolzano ....d.						1233		2016	
Brennero 🚉 ....d.						1404		2200	
Innsbruck ....d.		0840		0935		1440		2248	
Schwarzach St Veit ....d.									
Zell am See ....d.	0637					1341		2046	
Saalfelden ....d.	0647					1351		2056	
St Johann in Tirol ....d.	0716					1421		2124	
Kitzbühel ....d.	0725					1431		2133	
Wörgl ....d.	0756	0917				1503	1517	2204	2325
Kufstein 🚉 ....d.		0928					1528		2356
Seefeld in Tirol 🚉 ....d.				1010					
München Hbf ....a.	1030			1239		1630			
Augsburg ....a.	1120			1320		1720			
Landeck ....d.			0850						
St. Anton am Arlberg ......d.			0917						
Langen am Arlberg ....d.			0927						
Bludenz ....d.			0958						
Bregenz ....d.			1044		1249				
Lindau 🚉 ....a.			1054		1308				
Ulm ....a.	1203		1243	1403	1443	1803			
Stuttgart ....a.	1303		1357	1503	1557	1903			
Heidelberg ....a.	1352			1552		1952			
Mannheim ....a.	1405		1448	1605	1648	2005			
Saarbrücken ....a.			1610		1810				
Frankfurt/Main ....a.								0643	
Mainz ....a.	1446			1646		2046		0726	
Koblenz ....a.	1535			1735		2135		0820	
Bonn ....a.	1607			1807		2207		0857	
Köln Hbf ....a.	1629			1829		2229		0921	
Düsseldorf ....a.	1655			1855		2255		0951	
Duisburg ....a.	1709			1909		2309		1015	
Essen ....a.	1722			1922		2322		1029	
Dortmund ....a.						2348		1054	

NOTES

D – LEONARDO DA VINCI – 🚃 and ✗ Dortmund - Verona - (Milano) and v.v.

E – ANDREAS HOFER – 🚃 and ✗ Dortmund - Innsbruck.

F – KARWENDEL – 🚃 and ✗ (Munster) - Essen - Innsbruck and v.v.

G – ANDREAS HOFER – 🚃 and ✗ Innsbruck – Münster.

H – DOLOMITEN EXPRESS – 🛏 1,2 cl., ⊟ 2 cl. and 🚃 Dortmund - Bolzano and v.v.

✗ – Supplement payable.

Table 70 (Summer) MÜNCHEN - INNSBRUCK AND ZELL AM SEE

train type			EC	543				EC	IC		EC	IC		EC	IC				EC	IC	D
train number			81	543				85	545		87	547		13	549				89	641	1281
notes (see page 4)									✕			✕			✕					✕	
notes (see below)			C ✗					D ✗			A ✗			B ✗					E ✗		⑥
München Hbf .... d.	...	...	0730	...	...	...	...	0930	...	...	1130	...	...	1330	...	...	...	...	1530	...	1537
Kufstein ▣ .... a.	...	...	0831	...	...	...	...	1031	...	...	1231	...	...	1431	...	...	...	...	1631	...	1706
Wörgl .... a.	...	...	0842	0857	...	...	...	1042	1057	...	1242	1257	...	1442	1457	...	...	...	1642	1657	1718
Kirchberg in Tirol ...... a.	...	...		0920	...	...	...		1120	...		1320	...		1520	...	...	...		1720	1755
Kitzbühel .... a.	...	...		0929	...	...	...		1129	...		1329	...		1529	...	...	...		1729	1804
St. Johann in Tirol ..... a.	...	...		0937	...	...	...		1137	...		1337	...		1537	...	...	...		1739	1813
Saalfelden .... a.	...	...		1007	...	...	...		1207	...		1407	...		1607	...	...	...		1807	1849
Zell am See .... a.	...	...		1018	...	...	...		1218	...		1418	...		1618	...	...	...		1818	1903
Jenbach .... a.	...	...	0857		...	...	...		...	...		...	...	1457	...	...	...	...	1657	...	...
Innsbruck Hbf .... a.	...	...	0919		...	...	...	1118	...	...	1318	...	...	1519	...	...	...	...	1719	...	...

train type		D	IC		EC		D			train type		D	IC	EC
train number		285	715		19	5031	287			train number		286	712	18
notes (see page 4)			⚇							notes (see page 4)			⚇	
notes (see below)					G ✗					notes (see below)				G ✗
München Hbf .... d.	...	1730	...	...	1930	...	2030	...		Innsbruck Hbf .... d.	...	0641	...	0840
Kufstein ▣ .... a.	...	1831	...	...	2031	...	2131	...		Jenbach .... d.	...		...	0901
Wörgl .... a.	...	1842	1956	...	2042	2056	2142	...		Zell am See .... d.	...		0637	
Kirchberg in Tirol .... a.	...		2018	...		2121		...		Saalfelden .... d.	...		0647	
Kitzbühel .... a.	...		2028	...		2131		...		St. Johann in Tirol .... d.	...		0716	
St. Johann in Tirol ... a.	...		2036	...		2138		...		Kitzbühel .... d.	...		0725	
Saalfelden .... a.	...		2103	...		2145		...		Kirchberg in Tirol .... d.	...		0734	
Zell am See .... a.	...		2113	...				...		Wörgl .... d.	...	0717	0756	0917
Jenbach .... a.	...	1857	...	...	2057	...		...		Kufstein ▣ .... d.	...	0728	...	0928
Innsbruck Hbf .... a.	...	1919	...	...	2119	...	2218	...		München Hbf .... a.	...	0830	...	1030

train type		D	IC	D		IC	EC		IC	EC				IC	EC		IC	EC			EC
train number	1280		844	284		540	88		542	12				544	84		546	86			80
notes (see page 4)	⑥		✕			✕			✕								✕				
notes (see below)	⑥						E ✗		B ✗					D ✗			A ✗				C ✗
Innsbruck Hbf .... d.	...	...	...	1040	...	...	1240	...	...	1440	...	...	...	1641	...	...	1841	...	...	...	2040
Jenbach .... d.	...	...	...	1101	...	...	1301	...	...	1501	...	...	...		...	...		...	...	...	2101
Zell am See .... d.	0855	...	0941		...	1141		...	1341		...	...	...	1541		...	1741		...	1943	
Saalfelden .... d.	0909	...	0951		...	1151		...	1351		...	...	...	1551		...	1751		...	1953	
St. Johann in Tirol ... d.	0942	...	1021		...	1221		...	1421		...	...	...	1621		...	1821		...	2023	
Kitzbühel .... d.	0952	...	1031		...	1231		...	1431		...	...	...	1631		...	1831		...	2032	
Kirchberg in Tirol ..... d.	1001	...	1040		...	1240		...	1440		...	...	...	1640		...	1840		...	2041	
Wörgl .... d.	1040	...	1103	1117	...	1303	1317	...	1503	1517	...	...	...	1703	1717	...	1903	1917	...	2103	2117
Kufstein ▣ .... d.	1052	...	...	1128	...	...	1328	...	...	1528	...	...	...	...	1728	...	...	1928	...	...	2128
München Hbf .... a.	1216	...	...	1230	...	...	1430	...	...	1630	...	...	...	...	1830	...	...	2030	...	...	2230

NOTES

A – TIEPOLO – 🚇 and ✕ München - Venezia and v.v.

B – LEONARDO DA VINCI – 🚇 and ✕ (Dortmund) - München - Innsbruck - (Milano) and v.v.

C – GARDA – 🚇 and ✕ München - Innsbruck - (Milano) and v.v.

D – MICHELANGELO – 🚇 and ✕ München - Innsbruck - (Roma) and v.v.

E – PAGANINI – 🚇 and ✕ München - Innsbruck - (Verona) and v.v.

F – GROSSGLOCKNER – ⑥: 🚇 München - Zell am See and v.v.

G – ANDREAS HOFER – 🚇 and ✕ (Dortmund) - München - Innsbruck and v.v.

✗ – Supplement payable.

Table 71 (Summer) BERLIN - INNSBRUCK AND VILLACH

train type	EC					train type	EC		
train number	11		1209	1283		train number	10	1208	1282
notes (see page 4)						notes (see page 4)			
notes (see below)	G ✗		E	A		notes (see below)	G ✗	F	B
Berlin Hbf .... d.	...	...	...	...		Verona .... d.	...	...	1540
Berlin Zoo .... d.	...	...	...	...		Trento .... d.	...	...	1642
Berlin Wannsee .... d.	...	...	1926	2138		Bolzano .... d.	...	...	1756
Halle .... d.	...	...	2140	0008		Brennero .... d.	...	...	1948
Leipzig .... d.	0740	...				Innsbruck .... d.	...	...	2036
Nürnberg Hbf .... d.	1126	...				Seefeld in Tirol .... d.	...	...	
München Hbf .... d.	1325	...				Zell am See .... d.	...	...	
Salzburg .... a.	1455	...	0542			Saalfelden .... d.	...	...	
Bischofshofen .... a.	1550	...	0647			St. Johann .... d.	...	...	
Schwarzach St Veit .. a.	1604	...	0704			Kitzbühel .... d.	...	...	
Villach Hbf .... a.	1744	...	0855			Wörgl .... d.	...	...	2124
Klagenfurt .... a.	...	...	0931			Kufstein ▣ .... d.	...	...	2152
Kufstein ▣ .... a.	...	...		0741		Klagenfurt .... d.	...	1920	
Wörgl .... a.	...	...		0803		Villach Hbf .... d.	1218	2025	
Kitzbühel .... a.	...	...				Schwarzach St Veit .. d.	1357	2209	
St. Johann .... a.	...	...				Bischofshofen .... d.	1411	2227	
Saalfelden .... a.	...	...				Salzburg .... d.	1505	2323	
Zell am See .... a.	...	...				München Hbf .... a.	1635		
Seefeld in Tirol .... a.	...	...				Nürnberg Hbf .... a.	1831		
Innsbruck .... a.	...	...		0848		Leipzig .... a.	2218		
Brennero .... a.	...	...		0938		Halle .... a.	...	0649	0538
Bolzano .... a.	...	...		1120		Berlin Wannsee .... a.	...	0824	0721
Trento .... a.	...	...		1219		Berlin Zoo .... a.	...	...	
Verona .... a.	...	...		1330		Berlin Hbf .... a.	...	...	

NOTES

A – SPREE ALPEN EXPRESS – ⑤: 🛏 2 cl. and 🚇 Berlin - Verona;
🛏 1,2 cl. Berlin - Bolzano.

B – SPREE ALPEN EXPRESS – ⑥: 🛏 2 cl. and 🚇 Verona - Berlin;
🛏 1,2 cl. Bolzano - Berlin.

E – ⑤: 🛏 1,2 cl., 🛏 2 cl., 🚇 and ⚇ Berlin - Klagenfurt.

F – ⑥: 🛏 1,2 cl., 🛏 2 cl., 🚇 and ⚇ Klagenfurt - Berlin.

G – MIMARA – 🚇 and ✕ Leipzig - Villach - (Zagreb) and v.v.

✗ – Supplement payable.

Table 73 (Summer)   KÖLN AND FRANKFURT/MAIN - MILANO AND ROMA

	EC 5	IC 685	P 515	EC 9	IC 689	1205	1005	201	401	IC 533	2183
notes	R ✓	✓	® ✗	S ✓	✓	D	E	A	B	✓	
Dortmund d.	0641			0839		1755					
Essen d.						1821					
Duisburg d.				0914		1836		2019			
Düsseldorf d.				0928		1853		2036			
Köln Hbf d.	0800			1000		1933		2105			
Bonn d.	0820			1020		1954		2127			
Koblenz d.	0852			1052		2028		2203			
Mainz d.	0942			1142		2122		2258			
Frankfurt/Main d.											2115
Mannheim d.	1032			1232		2210		2341			
Heidelberg d.							2211	0006	0006		
Karlsruhe d.	1059			1259		2304	2304	0038	0038		
Offenburg d.						2346	2346				
Freiburg im Breisgau d.	1204			1404		0022	0022				
Basel SBB a.	1311			1511		v	v	v	v		
Domodossola a.						0420	0420				
Arona a.											
Chiasso a.	1730			1930				0637	0637		
Como a.	1754			1954				0700	0700		
Milano Centrale a.	1835	1910	1940	2035	2110			0745	0745	0800	0815
Alessandria a.											
Genova P. Principe a.		2047			2247						1005
San Remo a.		2302									1228
Ventimiglia a.		2320									1250
Bologna a.			2115			0806	0806	1036	1036	0944	
Firenze SMN a.			2212r			0921	0921			1053	
Roma Termini a.			2353			1138	1138			1255	
Napoli Centrale a.										1500	
Ravenna a.								1143	1143		
Rimini a.								1232	1232		

	IC 672	EC 8	IC 675 IC 676	P 500	EC 4	IC 688	IC 544	200	200	1204	1204
notes	✓	S ✓	✓	✓	R ✓	✓	✗	A	B	F	G
Rimini d.						1610	1610				
Ravenna d.						1718	1718				
Napoli Centrale d.											
Roma Termini d.				0655			1605			1805	1805
Firenze SMN d.				0832r			1807			2037	2037
Bologna d.				0930		1916	1848	1848		2150	2150
Ventimiglia d.			0650								
San Remo d.			0709								
Genova P. Principe d.	0713		0913			1913					
Alessandria d.											
Milano Centrale d.	0850	0925	1050	1105	1125	2050	2100	2125	2125		
Como d.		1004			1205			2205	2205		
Chiasso d.		1030			1230			2230	2230		
Arona d.											
Domodossola d.										0144	0144
Basel SBB a.		1449			1649			v	v	0536	0536
Freiburg im Breisgau a.		1553			1753					0610	0610
Offenburg a.										0659	0659
Karlsruhe a.		1657			1857			0456	0456		
Heidelberg a.								0529	0529		0757
Mannheim a.		1726			1927			0546	0652	0740	
Frankfurt/Main a.											0921
Mainz a.		1816			2016			0630		0830	
Koblenz a.		1905			2105			0722		0921	
Bonn a.		1937			2137			0757		0957	
Köln Hbf a.		1959			2159			0821		1021	
Düsseldorf a.		2031						0851		1103	
Duisburg a.		2044						0908		1120	
Essen a.		2057								1137	
Dortmund a.		2119			2319					1204	

NOTES

A – [1,2 cl.], [2 cl.], [couchette] and [restaurant] (Amsterdam) - Duisburg - Rimini and v.v.
B – [1,2 cl.], [2 cl.] and [couchette] Frankfurt/Main - Rimini and v.v.
D – ITALIA EXPRESS – May 28 - Sept. 22: [1,2 cl.], [2 cl.] and [couchette] Dortmund - Roma.
E – ITALIA EXPRESS – May 28 - Sept. 22: [1,2 cl.], [2 cl.] and [couchette] Frankfurt/Main - Roma.
F – ITALIA EXPRESS – May 28 - Sept. 23: [1,2 cl.], [2 cl.] and [couchette] Roma - Dortmund.

G – ITALIA EXPRESS – May 28 - Sept. 23: [1,2 cl.], [2 cl.] and [couchette] Roma - Frankfurt/Main.
R – VERDI – [couchette] and [restaurant] Dortmund - Milano and v.v.; [X] Dortmund - Chiasso and v.v.
S – TIZIANO – [couchette] and [restaurant] (Hannover) - Dortmund - Milano and v.v.; [X] (Hannover) - Dortmund - Chiasso and v.v.
r – Firenze Rifredi
v – Via Basel Bad.
✗ – Supplement payable.

INTERNATIONAL SERVICES FROM MILANO

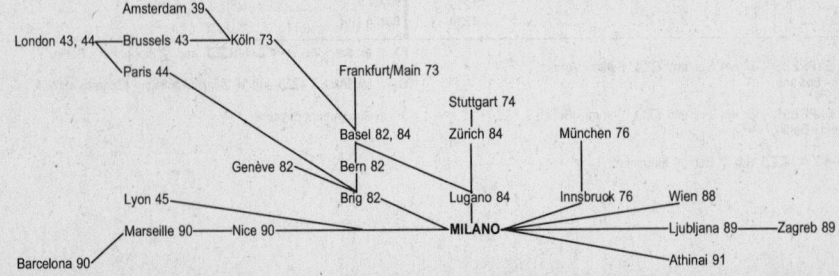

Amsterdam 39 — Brussels 43 — Köln 73
London 43, 44 — Paris 44 — Frankfurt/Main 73
Stuttgart 74 — Zürich 84 — München 76
Basel 82, 84
Genève 82 — Bern 82
Lyon 45 — Brig 82 — Lugano 84 — Innsbruck 76 — Wien 88
Marseille 90 — Nice 90 — MILANO — Ljubljana 89 — Zagreb 89
Barcelona 90 — Athinai 91

Table 74 (Summer) STUTTGART – ZÜRICH AND MILANO

train type train number notes (see page 4) notes (see below)	383	IC 545 ⚇ ✗		385	P 515 D ✗	IC 683 ⚇ ✗		387	IC 687 ⚇ ✗		381 A	2201	823 K		389 C	389 E		485		487 L	
Nürnberg............... d.	...	...	...	...	...	...	...	0919	...	...	...	...	...	...	...	...	...	...	...	...
Stuttgart.............. d.	...	0742	...	0942	...	...	...	1142	...	...	1342	...	...	1542	1542	...	1642	...	1842	...
Singen 🚐.............. d.	...	0953	...	1153	...	...	...	1353	...	...	1553	...	...	1753	1746	...	1853	...	2053	...
Schaffhausen........ a.	...	1006	...	1206	...	...	...	1406	...	...	1606	...	...	1809	1759	...	1906	...	2106	...
Zürich Hb............. a.	...	1047	...	1247	...	...	...	1447	...	...	1647	...	...	1847	1922	...	1947	...	2147	...
Zug....................... a.	...	1133	...	1331	...	...	...	1533	...	...	1731	...	...	1929		...	...	...		...
Arth Goldau.......... a.	...	1148	...	1345	...	...	...	1548	...	...	1745	...	...	1945		...	...	...		...
Bellinzona............ a.	...	1335	...	1535	...	...	...	1735	...	...	1935	...	...	2135		...	...	...		...
Lugano................. a.	...	1404	...	1604	...	...	...	1804	...	...	2004	...	...	2203		...	...	...		...
Chiasso 🚐........... a.	...	1430	...	1630	...	...	...	1830	...	...	2030	...	...	2230	2300	...	...	...	0158	...
Como.................... a.	...	1454	...	1654	...	...	...	1854	...	...	2054	...	...	2254		...	...	...		...
Milano Centrale..... a.	...	1535	1600	1735	1940	1805	...	1935	2010	...	2135	2215	2215	2335		...	...	...		...
Genova P. Principe.. a.	...	1740		...	...	1947	...	...	2147	...	...	0005		...		...	...	...		...
Sestri Levante......... a.	...	1836		...	...		...	...		...	...			...		...	...	...		...
Bologna.................. a.	...		1744	...	2015		...	...		...	...		0048	...		...	...	...		...
Ancona................ a.	...			...	...		...	...		...	...			...	0428	...	...	...		...
Pescara................ a.	...			...	...		...	...		...	...			...	0608	...	...	...		...
Bari..................... a.	...			...	...		...	...		...	...			...	0949	...	...	...		...
Brindisi C............. a.	...			...	...		...	...		...	...			...	1141	...	...	...		...
Lecce................... a.	...			...	...		...	...		...	...			...	1218	...	...	...		...
Firenze SMN......... a.	...	1853		...	2212r		...	...		...	...			...		...	...	...		...
Roma Termini........ a.	...	2055		...	2353		...	...		...	...	0524t		...		...	...	...	0900t	...
Napoli Centrale...... a.	...	2300		...			...	...		...	...	0816		...		...	...	...	1125	...

train type train number notes (see page 4) notes (see below)	480		484 F	1084 M	302 486		1082 B	820 K	2156	386		IC 674 ⚇ ✗	388 C		P 500 Ⓡ Ⓐ ✗ ✗	IC 676 ⚇ ✗	380		P 504 Ⓡ ✗	382
Napoli Centrale...... d.	...	...	...	1857	...	...	1947	...	...	...	...	...	...	...	...	...	...	...	...	...
Roma Termini........ d.	...	...	...	2143t	...	...	2244t	...	...	...	...	...	...	...	0655	...	...	...	0955	...
Firenze SMN......... d.	...	...	...		...	...		...	...	...	...	...	...	...	0832r	...	...	...	1132r	...
Lecce................... d.	...	...	...		2106	...		...	...	...	...	...	...	...		...	...	...		...
Brindisi C............. d.	...	...	...		2152	...		...	...	...	...	...	...	...		...	...	...		...
Bari..................... d.	...	...	...		2352	...		...	...	...	...	...	...	...		...	...	...		...
Pescara................ d.	...	...	...		0326	...		...	...	...	...	...	...	...		...	...	...		...
Ancona................ d.	...	...	...		0501	...		...	...	...	...	...	...	...		...	...	...		...
Bologna.................. d.	...	...	...			...	0345	...	...	...	...	...	...	...	0930	...	...	...	1230	...
Sestri Levante......... d.	...	...	...			...		0548	...	...	...	...	...	...		...	...	...	1122	...
Genova P. Principe.. d.	...	...	...			...		0740	0825	...	0813	...	...	...	0913	...	...	...	1222	...
Milano Centrale..... d.	...	...	...			...	0620	0740	0825	0950	1025	...	1105	1050	1225	...	1405	1425		...
Como.................... d.	...	...	...			...			0905	...	1105	...	...	1305		...	1505			...
Chiasso 🚐........... d.	...	...	...	0640	0730	...	0840		0930	...	1130	...	...	1330		...	1530			...
Lugano................. d.	...	...	...		0755	...			0955	...	1157	...	...	1355		...	1555			...
Bellinzona............ d.	...	...	...		0827	...			1024	...	1224	...	...	1424		...	1624			...
Arth Goldau.......... d.	...	...	...		1012	...			1212	...	1415	...	...	1615		...	1812			...
Zug....................... d.	...	...	...		1031	...			1228	...	1431	...	...	1631		...	1828			...
Zürich Hb............. d.	0630	...	0913	1028	1113	...	1237		1313	...	1513	...	...	1713		...	1913			...
Schaffhausen........ d.	0705	...	0954	1136	1154	...	1336		1354	...	1554	...	...	1754		...	1954			...
Singen 🚐............. a.	0718	...	1007	1150	1207	...	1350		1407	...	1607	...	...	1807		...	2007			...
Stuttgart.............. a.	0922	...	1222	1422	1422	...	1622		1622	...	1822	...	...	2022		...	2222			...
Nürnberg............... a.	...	...	...			...			1913	...		...	...			...				...

NOTES

A – 🚋 Stuttgart - Milano; ⚇ Singen - Chiasso.

B – ⑥ July 8 - Sept. 9: ⊨ 2 cl. and 🚋 Lecce - Stuttgart.

C – 🚋 Stuttgart - Milano and v.v.; ✗ Singen - Chiasso and v.v.

D – 🚋 Stuttgart - Milano; ✗ Singen - Milano.

E – ⑤ July 7 - Sept. 8: ⊨ 2 cl. and 🚋 Stuttgart - Lecce.

F – 🚋 Zürich - Stuttgart; ⚇ Zürich - Singen.

K – 1,2 cl. and 🚋 Napoli - Milano and v.v.

L – 🚋 Stuttgart - Zürich; ⑤ July 7 - Sept. 8: ⊨ 2 cl. and 🚋 Stuttgart - Napoli.

M – ⑥ July 8 - Sept. 9: ⊨ 2 cl. and 🚋 Napoli - Stuttgart.

r – Firenze Rifredi.

t – Roma Tiburtina.

✗ – Supplement payable.

Table 75 (Summer) MÜNCHEN - ZÜRICH

train type train number notes (see page 4) notes (see below)	EC 92 C ✗	IC 924 ⚇	IC 726 ✗	EC 94 D ✗	IC 934	1736	IC 736 ✗	EC 166 B ✗	IC 740	2443	EC 98 E ✗
München Hbf.......... d.	0814	...	...	1214	...	...	1402	...	...	...	1814
Kempten................ d.	...	...	...		...	...	1520	...	...	...	
Lindau 🚐.............. d.	1029	...	...	1429	...	...	1629	...	...	...	2029
Bregenz 🚐............ d.	1038	...	...	1440	...	...	1640	...	...	...	2040
St. Margrethen 🚐... a.	1054	...	...	1454	...	...	1654	...	...	...	2054
St. Gallen............. a.	1118	...	...	1518	...	...	1718	...	...	...	2118
Winterthur............ a.	1158	...	...	1558	...	...	1758	...	...	...	2158
Zürich Hbf.......... a.	1223	1233	1303	1622	1633	...	1703	1823	1903	...	2223
Olten.................... a.	...	...			...	...		...		...	
Bern.................... a.	...	1345	1415	...	1745	1828	1815	1943	2015	2028	
Interlaken West....... a.	...	1444		...		1916		...		2119	
Interlaken Ost........ a.	...	1449		...		1921		...		2123	
Lausanne.............. a.	...	...	1526	...	...		1926	...	2126		
Genève................. a.	...	...	1602	...	...		2002	...	2202		

train type train number notes (see page 4) notes (see below)	EC 99 E ✗	IC 711 ✗	EC 167 A ✗	EC 104 ✗	IC 721 D ✗	EC 95	IC 729 ✗	1729 ⚇	EC 93 C ✗
Genève................ d.	...	0558	...	0958	...	1358	...	...	...
Lausanne.............. d.	...	0634	...	1034	...	1434	...	...	...
Interlaken Ost........ d.	...	...	0711	1039	...		1439	...	...
Interlaken West....... d.	...	...	0716	1044	...		1444	...	...
Bern.................... d.	...	0745	0816	1132	1145	...	1545	1551	...
Olten.................... d.	...					...		1642	...
Zürich Hbf.......... d.	0741	0857	0941		1257	1337	1657	1730	1741
Winterthur............ d.	0803	...	1003		...	1403	...		1803
St. Gallen............. d.	0841	...	1041		...	1441	...		1841
St. Margrethen 🚐... d.	0906	...	1106		...	1506	...		1906
Bregenz 🚐............ d.	0921	...	1121		...	1521	...		1921
Lindau 🚐.............. d.	0930	...	1130		...	1530	...		1930
Kempten................ a.	...	...	1240		...		...		
München Hbf.......... a.	1151	...	1357		...	1748	...		2149

NOTES

A – ALBERT EINSTEIN – 🚋 and ✗ Interlaken - München - (Praha).

B – ALBERT EINSTEIN – 🚋 and ✗ (Praha) - München - Bern.

C – ANGELIKA KAUFFMANN – 🚋 and ✗ Zürich - München and v.v.

D – GOTTFRIED KELLER – 🚋 and ✗ Zürich - München and v.v.

E – BAVARIA – 🚋 and ✗ Zürich - München and v.v.

✗ – Supplement payable.

Table 76 (Summer) MÜNCHEN AND INNSBRUCK - MILANO AND VENEZIA

train type	EC				EC				EC	IC		EC			EC									
train number	81	355	345		85	656	2107		87	660		13			89	2119	285		287	1289		289	289	289
notes (see page 4)																								
notes (see below)	J ⁄				K ⁄				B ⁄	⁄		H ⁄			L ⁄				N	M		S	D	C
München Hbf d.	0730	...	...	...	0930	...	...	...	1130	...	...	1330	...	...	1530	...	1730	...	2030	2125	...	2340	2340	2340
Kufstein 🏛 d.	0833	...	...	...	1033	...	...	...	1233	...	...	1433	...	...	1633	...	1833	...	2133	2255	...	0044	0044	0044
Wörgl d.	0844	...	...	...	1044	...	...	...	1244	...	...	1444	...	...	1644	...	1844	...	2144	2306	...	0056	0056	0056
Innsbruck d.	0922	...	...	...	1122	...	...	...	1322	...	...	1522	...	...	1722	...	1924	...	2222	2345	...	0142	0142	0142
Brennero 🏛 d.	1014	...	...	...	1214	...	...	...	1414	...	...	1614	...	...	1814	...	2026	...	2319	0042	...	0239	0239	0239
Bolzano a.	1128	...	...	...	1328	...	...	...	1528	...	...	1728	...	...	1928	...	2155	...	0034	0155	...	0354	0354	0354
Trento a.	1200	...	...	...	1400	...	...	...	1600	...	...	1800	...	...	2000	...	...	...	0106	0228	...	0432	0432	0432
Verona a.	1304	1328	...	...	1504	1532	1558	...	1704	1732	...	1904	...	...	2104	2158	...	...	0208	0335	...	0540	0540	0540
Padova a.	│	│	...	...	│	│	1650	...	1801	│	...	│	...	...	...	2250	...	...	│	│	...	│	0805	│
Venezia Mestre a.	│	│	...	...	│	│	1713	...	1823	│	...	│	...	...	...	2313	...	...	│	│	...	│	0833	│
Venezia Santa Lucia a.	│	1450	...	...	│	│	1730	...	1835	│	...	│	...	...	...	2330	...	...	│	│	...	│	0845	│
Milano Centrale a.	1450	...	1510	...	│	1655	...	...	...	1855	...	2050	...	...	...	...	...	...	│	│	...	0830	...	│
Genova Porta Principe a.	...	...	1640	...	│	...	...	...	...	...	...	...	...	...	...	...	...	...	│	│	...	...	...	│
Ventimiglia a.	...	...	1908	...	│	...	...	...	...	...	...	...	...	...	...	...	...	...	│	│	...	...	...	│
Bologna a.	...	...	...	...	1635	...	...	...	...	...	...	...	...	...	...	...	...	...	0408	0532	...	...	...	0756
Firenze SMN a.	...	...	...	...	1742	...	...	...	...	...	...	...	...	...	...	...	...	...	│	│	...	...	...	0910
Roma Termini a.	...	...	...	...	1945	...	...	...	...	...	...	...	...	...	...	...	...	...	0815	│	...	...	...	...
Napoli Centrale a.	...	...	...	...	...	...	...	...	...	...	...	...	...	...	...	...	...	...	1038	│	...	...	...	...
Rimini a.	...	...	...	...	...	...	...	...	...	...	...	...	...	...	...	...	...	...	...	0655	...	...	...	...
Ancona a.	...	...	...	...	...	...	...	...	...	...	...	...	...	...	...	...	...	...	...	0826	...	...	...	...
Pescara a.	...	...	...	...	...	...	...	...	...	...	...	...	...	...	...	...	...	...	...	1004	...	...	...	...

train number		EC						EC11	IC	IC	EC		IC	EC	343		EC83			220				
train number	282	18	284		2094	EC88		EC12	649	650	84		863	86	344	2106	EC80		288	288	2121		1288	286
notes (see page 4)		✕							🍷	🍷						🍷								
notes (see below)	F	⁄	W			L ⁄		H ⁄	⁄	⁄	K ⁄		⁄	B ⁄			J ⁄		C	D	S		E	N
Pescara d.	...	...	...	...	...	...	...	...	...	...	...	...	...	...	...	...	...	...	...	...	...	...	1935	...
Ancona d.	...	...	...	...	...	...	...	...	...	...	...	...	...	...	...	...	...	...	...	...	...	...	2113	...
Rimini d.	...	...	...	...	...	...	...	...	...	...	...	...	...	...	...	...	...	...	...	...	...	...	2245	...
Napoli Centrale d.	...	...	...	...	...	...	...	...	...	...	...	...	...	...	...	...	...	...	...	...	...	...	│	1815
Roma Termini d.	...	...	...	...	...	...	...	...	...	...	0815	...	...	...	...	...	...	...	...	...	...	...	│	2035
Firenze SMN d.	...	...	...	...	...	...	...	...	...	...	1019	...	...	...	...	...	...	...	2130	...	...	...	│	│
Bologna d.	...	...	...	...	...	...	...	...	...	...	1126	...	...	...	...	...	...	...	2240	...	...	...	0008	0050
Ventimiglia d.	...	...	...	...	...	...	...	...	...	...	│	...	...	...	1050	...	...	...	│	...	...	...	│	│
Genova P. Principe d.	...	...	...	...	...	...	...	...	...	...	│	...	...	...	1322	...	...	...	│	...	...	...	│	│
Milano Centrale d.	...	...	...	...	...	...	...	0910	1105	...	│	...	1310	...	1450	...	1510	...	│	...	2215	...	│	│
Venezia Santa Lucia d.	...	...	...	...	0620	...	...	│	│	1105	│	...	│	1312	...	1520	│	...	│	2202	│	...	│	│
Venezia Mestre d.	...	...	...	...	0637	...	...	│	│	│	│	...	│	1324	...	1537	│	...	│	2242	│	...	│	│
Padova d.	...	...	...	...	0700	...	...	│	│	│	│	...	│	1349	...	1600	│	...	│	2307	│	...	│	│
Verona d.	...	...	...	...	0755	0900	...	1100	1228	1229	1300	...	1447	1500	...	1658	1700	...	0030	0030	0030	...	0208	0232
Trento d.	...	...	...	...	...	0958	...	1158	...	...	1358	...	...	1558	...	...	1758	...	0130	0130	0130	...	0309	0350
Bolzano d.	0600	...	0800	...	...	1033	...	1233	...	...	1433	...	...	1633	...	...	1833	...	0212	0212	0212	...	0355	0423
Brennero 🏛 d.	0756	...	0956	...	...	1204	...	1404	...	...	1604	...	...	1804	...	...	1900	...	0351	0351	0351	...	0540	0548
Innsbruck a.	0834	0840	1034	...	...	1237	...	1437	...	...	1637	...	...	1837	...	...	2037	...	0424	0424	0424	...	0613	0637
Wörgl a.	...	│	1115	...	...	1315	...	1515	...	...	1715	...	...	1915	...	...	2115	...	0510	0510	0510	...	0657	0715
Kufstein 🏛 a.	...	│	1126	...	...	1326	...	1526	...	...	1726	...	...	1926	...	...	2126	...	0523	0523	0523	...	0708	0726
München Hbf a.	...	1030	1230	...	...	1430	...	1630	...	...	1830	...	...	2030	...	...	2230	...	0635	0635	0635	...	0835	0830

NOTES

B – TIEPOLO – (12) and ✕ München - Venezia and v.v.
C – BRENNER EXPRESS – 🛏 1,2 cl., ▬ 2 cl. and (2) München - Firenze and v.v.
D – ▬ 2 cl. and (2) München - Venezia and v.v.
E – ▬ 2 cl. and (2) Pescara - München, also 🛏 1,2 cl. ⑥ June 3 - Sept. 16.
F – ①②③④⑤ to July 7 and from Sept. 11.
H – LEONARDO DA VINCI – (12) and ✕ (Dortmund) - München - Milano and v.v.
J – GARDA – (12) and ✕ München - Milano and v.v.
K – MICHELANGELO – (12) and ✕ München - Roma and v.v.
L – PAGANINI – (12) and ✕ München - Verona and v.v.
M – ▬ 2 cl. and (2) München - Pescara, also 🛏 1,2 cl. ⑤ to Sept. 15.
N – 🛏 1,2 cl., ▬ 2 cl. and (2) München - Napoli and v.v.
S – 🛏 1,2 cl., ▬ 2 cl. and (2) München - Milano and v.v.
W – ⑥⑦, daily July 8 - Sept. 10.
⁄ – Supplement payable.

Table 77 (Summer) KÖLN AND FRANKFURT/MAIN - ZÜRICH AND CHUR

train type	ICE		ICE	EC	IC	ICE	EC			EC	ICE	IC	ICE	EC		EC	ICE	IC	ICE	EC		ICE	EC	
train number	271	1765	997	101	769	999	107	1769		5	79	773	591	103		9	73	777	593	105	1781	71	3	
notes (see page 4)		✕	①-⑥	✕	🍷	①-⑥	✕	🍷		✕	①-⑥	✕	✕			✕	✕	✕	✕	✕	🍷	✕		
notes (see below)	B ⁄		✕ ⁄	⁄		✕ ⁄	⁄			⁄	✕ ⁄		⁄	C ⁄		⁄	⁄		⁄	⁄		⁄	A ⁄	
Dortmund d.	...	...	b	...	...	b	0539	...	...	0641	...	...	...	0741	...	0839	...	...	...	...	...	...	...	...
Essen d.	...	...	...	...	...	...	0601	...	...	│	...	...	...	│	...	0901	...	...	...	...	...	...	...	...
Duisburg d.	...	...	...	...	...	...	0614	...	...	│	...	...	...	│	...	0914	...	...	...	1019	...	...	1119	...
Düsseldorf d.	...	...	...	...	...	...	0628	...	...	│	...	...	...	│	...	0928	...	...	...	1034	...	...	1134	...
Köln Hbf d.	...	...	...	...	...	...	0700	...	...	0800	...	...	...	0900	...	1000	...	...	...	1100	...	...	1200	...
Bonn d.	...	...	...	...	...	...	0720	...	...	0820	...	...	...	0920	...	1020	...	...	...	1120	...	...	1220	...
Koblenz d.	...	...	...	...	...	...	0752	...	...	0852	...	...	...	0952	...	1052	...	...	...	1152	...	...	1252	...
Mainz d.	...	...	...	0742	...	...	0842	...	...	0942	...	...	...	1042	...	1142	...	...	...	1242	...	...	1342	...
Hamburg Altona d.	...	...	...	│	...	...	│	...	...	│	0620	...	...	│	...	│	...	...	...	│	...	1023	│	...
Hamburg Hbf d.	...	...	...	│	...	...	│	...	...	│	0636	...	...	│	...	│	...	...	...	│	...	1038	│	...
Hannover Hbf d.	...	...	0520	│	...	...	│	...	...	│	0750	...	...	│	...	│	...	...	...	│	...	1150	│	...
Kassel Wilhelmshöhe d.	...	...	0613	│	...	0713	│	...	...	│	0840	...	0913	│	...	│	1029	...	1113	│	...	1240	│	...
Frankfurt/Main Hbf d.	0643	...	0743	│	...	0843	│	...	...	│	1002	...	1043	│	...	│	1203	...	1243	│	...	1402	│	...
Mannheim d.	0731	...	0824	0832	...	0924	0932	...	...	1032	1043	...	1124	1132	...	1232	1243	...	1324	1332	...	1443	1432	...
Karlsruhe d.	0758	...	...	0857	...	...	0957	...	...	1057	1105	...	...	1159	...	1257	1305	...	...	1357	...	1505	1459	...
Freiburg im Breisgau d.	0902	...	...	1002	...	...	1102	...	...	1202	1211	...	...	1304	...	1402	1411	...	...	1502	...	1611	1604	...
Basel SBB 🏛 a.	0942	0951	...	1045	1108	...	1145	1151	...	1245	1254	1308	...	1345	...	1445	1454	1508	...	1545	1551	1654	1645c	...
Zurich Hbf a.	1045	1100	...	...	1203	...	...	1300	...	...	...	1403	...	1500	...	...	...	1603	...	...	1700	→	1803	...
Sargans a.	...	1219	...	...	1319	...	...	1419	...	...	...	1519	...	1619	...	...	...	1719	...	...	1819	...	1919	...
Landquart a.	...	1232	...	...	1332	...	...	1432	...	...	...	1532	...	1632	...	...	...	1732	...	...	1832	...	1932	...
Landquart d.	...	*1240*	...	...	*1340*	...	...	*1440*	...	...	...	*1540*	...	*1640*	...	...	...	*1740*	...	...	*1840*	...	*1935*	...
Davos Platz a.	...	*1346*	...	...	*1446*	...	...	*1546*	...	...	...	*1646*	...	*1746*	...	...	...	*1846*	...	...	*1946*	...	*2050*	...
Chur a.	...	1244	...	...	1344	...	...	1444	...	...	...	1544	...	1644	...	...	...	1744	...	...	1844	...	1944	...
Chur d.	...	*1252*	...	...	*1352*	...	...	*1452*	...	...	...	*1550*	...	*1652*	...	...	...	*1752*	...	...	*1852*	...	*1952*	...
St. Moritz a.	...	*1458*	...	...	*1558*	...	...	*1658*	...	...	...	*1758*	...	*1858*	...	...	...	*1958*	...	...	*2058*	...	*2158*	...

NOTES

A – REMBRANDT – (12) and ✕ (Amsterdam) - Duisburg - Chur.
B – JOHANNA SPYRI – (12) and ✕ Frankfurt/Main - Zürich.
C – RÄTIA – (12) and ✕ (Hannover) - Dortmund - Chur.
b – Not June 5.
c – Depart 1708.
⁄ – Supplement payable.

Table 77 (Summer) KÖLN AND FRANKFURT/MAIN - ZÜRICH AND CHUR

train number	ICE 595	EC 109	1787	IC 501	1789	ICE 77	ICE 597	IC 603	1791	IC 605	1793	ICE 775	ICE 599	IC 503	1795	203	471
notes (see below)	✗	✗	✗	✗	♉	✗ S		✗	♉	✗		✗		♉		N	P
Dortmund d.		1139		1241						1441			1539				
Essen d.		1201											1601				
Duisburg d.		1214											1614			2304	
Düsseldorf d.		1228											1628			2322	
Köln Hbf d.		1300		1400				1500		1600			1700			0001	
Bonn d.		1320		1420				1520		1620			1720			0023	
Koblenz d.		1352		1452				1552		1652			1752			0059	
Mainz d.		1442		1542				1642		1742			1842			0152	
Hamburg Altona d.						1223						1423					2114
Hamburg Hbf d.						1238						1438					2133
Hannover Hbf d.						1350						1550					2356
Kassel Wilhelmshöhe d.	1313					1440	1513					1640	1713				
Frankfurt/Main Hbf d.	1443					1602	1643					1802	1843				
Mannheim d.	1524	1532		1632		1643	1724	1732		1832		1843	1924	1932			
Karlsruhe d.		1557		1657		1705		1757		1857		1905		1957	0349		
Freiburg im Breisgau d.		1702		1802		1811		1902		2002		2011		2102	0520	0600	
Basel SBB ▣ a.		1745	1751	1845	1851	1854	1945	1951		2045	2051	2054	2108	2145	2151	0640	0651
Zürich Hbf a.		1900		2000		2003		2100		2200		2300				0815	0815
Sargans a.		2018		2118				2218								0937b	0937b
Landquart a.		2034		2134				2234								0951b	0951b
Landquart d.		2045		2145													1040
Davos Platz a.		2159		2259													1146
Chur a.		2045		2145				2245								1004b	1004b
Chur d.																	1052
St. Moritz a.																	1258

train type		ICE	IC		IC	ICE	ICE		ICE	IC	ICE	ICE	EC	ICE		EC	ICE	EC	EC	EC	EC	ICE
train number	1750	774	614	1754	502	598	76	1756	500	1760	602	596	102	72	1764	108	594	70	96	104	2	592
notes (see below)	♉	✗	♉		✗	✗	✗ S		✗		✗	✗		✗ T	♉	✗		✗ R		✗ M		✗
St. Moritz d.															0705			0805			0900	
Chur a.															0907			1007			1107	
Chur d.							0614		0714		0815		0915			1015					1115	
Davos Platz d.										0600		0700		0805			0905			1005		
Landquart d.							0624		0724		0817		0917			1017					1117	
Sargans d.							0640		0740		0839		0939			1039					1139	
Zürich Hbf d.	0557		0700		0757	0750		0900			0957→			1100			1157	1200			1257	
Basel SBB ▣ a.	0702	0707		0809	0814		0907	0909	0914	1009	1014	1114c	1107		1209	1214	1307	1306	1314		1414	
Freiburg im Breisgau a.	0748	0755		0855		0948	0955		1055		1155	1148			1255		1348	1355			1455	
Karlsruhe a.	0853	0900		1000		1053	1100		1200			1254	1300		1400		1453	1500			1600	
Mannheim a.	0915	0926		1026	1034	1115	1126		1226	1234	1326	1315		1426	1434	1515			1526		1626	1634
Frankfurt/Main Hbf a.	0956				1155	1156					1315	1355			1515	1556				1626		1715
Kassel Wilhelmshöhe a.	1118				1244	1318				1444		1528			1644	1718						1844
Hannover Hbf a.	1208					1408									1808							
Hamburg Hbf a.	1322					1522									1922							
Hamburg Altona a.	1336					1536									1936							
Mainz a.		1016		1116			1216		1316		1416				1516				1616		1716	
Koblenz a.		1105		1205			1305		1405		1505				1605				1705		1805	
Bonn a.		1137		1237			1337		1437		1537				1637				1737		1837	
Köln Hbf a.		1159		1259			1359		1459		1559				1659				1759		1859	
Düsseldorf a.				1331							1631								1824		1924	
Essen a.				1344							1644								1838		1938	
Dortmund a.		1319		1419			1519				1719				1819							

train type	IC	ICE	EC		EC	ICE		IC	EC	ICE		EC	ICE		ICE	ICE		IC			472 470	472 202
train number	778	78	8	1780	106	590	782	4	790	1784	100	790	1786	270	996	1788	600				W	X
notes (see below)	♉	⑧	✗		✗	✗	♉	✗	♉		✗	①-⑤	✗	♉	⑧	♉	✗				W	X
St. Moritz d.				1100			1200			1300			1400			1500	1800					
Chur a.	1207			1307			1407			1507			1607			1707	2007					
Chur d.	1215			1315			1415			1515			1615			1715					2032b	2032b
Davos Platz d.	1105			1205					1405	1405	1438		1605				1905					
Landquart d.	1217			1317			1417			1517	1607		1717				2017					
Sargans d.	1239			1339			1439			1539			1639			1739					2044b	2044b
Zürich Hbf d.	1357			1500			1557			1700			1800			1900					2059b	2059b
Basel SBB ▣ d.	1451	1507	1514		1609	1614	1651	1714		1809	1814	1909	1914	2009	2014						2215	2215
Freiburg im Breisgau a.		1548	1555			1655			1755			1855		1955		2055					2318	2325
Karlsruhe a.		1653	1700			1800			1900			2000		2102		2201					0021	0033
Mannheim a.		1715	1726		1826	1834		1926	1934		2026	2034	2126	2135	2226							0158
Frankfurt/Main Hbf a.		1756				1915			2015			2115		2215								
Kassel Wilhelmshöhe a.		1918				2044			2144			2244										
Hannover Hbf a.		2008							2240			2353									0609	
Hamburg Hbf a.		2122							2356												0829	
Hamburg Altona a.		2136							0010												0851	
Mainz a.			1816		1916			2016			2116		2218									0355
Koblenz a.			1905		2005			2105														0445
Bonn a.			1937		2037			2137														0520
Köln Hbf a.			1959		2059			2159														0546
Düsseldorf a.			2031		2131																	0619
Essen a.			2044		2144																	0636
Dortmund a.			2057		2157			2319														

NOTES

- REMBRANDT – [12] and ✗ Chur - Duisburg - (Amsterdam).
- 1,2 cl. and ➟ 2 cl. (Amsterdam) - Duisburg - Zürich (Chur on ⑤); [12] and ♉ (Amsterdam) - Duisburg - Basel.
- 1,2 cl. and ➟ 2 cl. Hamburg-Zürich (Chur on ⑤); [12] and ♉ (T2) and ♉ Hamburg - Basel.
- HELVETIA – [12] and ✗ Zürich - Hamburg.

S – PANDA – [12] and ✗ Hamburg - Zürich and v.v.
T – RÄTIA – [12] and ✗ Chur - Dortmund - (Berlin).
W – 1,2 cl. and ➟ 2 cl. Zürich (Chur on ⑥)-Hamburg; [12] 1,2 cl. (T2) and ♉ Basel - Hamburg.
X – 1,2 cl. and ➟ 2 cl. Zürich (Chur on ⑥) - Duisburg - (Amsterdam); [12] and ♉ Basel - Duisburg - (Amsterdam).
b – ⑥ only.
c – Arrive 1051.
➚ – Supplement payable.

Table 78 (Summer) KÖLN AND FRANKFURT/MAIN - BERN AND LUZERN

train number	EC 101	EC 107	EC 5	ICE 79	EC 9	ICE 73	EC 105	EC 109	201	401	203	203	1706
notes (see below)	K ✗	N ✗	F ✗	S ✗	G ✗	R ✗	A ✗	M ✗	C	B	Q	D	♀
Dortmund d.		0539	0641		0839			1139					
Essen d.		0601			0901			1201					
Duisburg d.		0614			0914		1019	1214	2019		2304	2304	
Düsseldorf d.		0628			0928		1034	1228	2036		2322	2322	
Köln Hbf d.	0600e	0700	0800		1000		1100	1300	2105		0002	0002	
Bonn d.	0620e	0720	0820		1020		1120	1320	2127		0024	0024	
Koblenz d.	0652e	0752	0852		1052		1152	1352	2203		0100	0100	
Mainz d.	0742	0842	0942		1142		1242	1442	2258		0152	0152	
Hamburg Altona d.				0621									
Hamburg Hbf d.				0636									
Bremen Hbf d.													
Hannover Hbf d.				0750									
Berlin Zoo d.						0651							
Kassel Wilhelmshöhe d.				0840		1029							
Frankfurt/Main Hbf d.				1002		1203				2255			
Mannheim d.	0832	0932	1032	1043	1232	1243	1332	1532	2341				
Karlsruhe d.	0859	0959	1059	1107	1259	1307	1359	1559	0038	0038	0357	0357	
Freiburg im Breisgau d.	1001	1104	1204	1213	1404	1413	1504	1704			0527	0527	
Basel SBB a.	1045	1145	1245	1254	1445	1454	1545	1745	v	v	0640	0640	
Biel a.		1304											
Neuchâtel a.		1325											
Lausanne a.		1412											
Genève a.		1455											
Olten a.	1128		1337	1332	1537		1628	1828			0734	0728	
Bern a.	1210					1610	1710	1910				0810	0828
Spiez a.	1251					1657	1757	1951				0851	0859
Spiez d.						1659	1759	1953				0853	0901
Interlaken West a.						1714	1814						0916
Interlaken Ost a.						1719	1819						0921
Brig a.	1358							2058				0958	
Luzern a.			1416	1410	1616						0813		
Bellinzona a.			1635		1835				0543	0543	1029		
Lugano a.			1704		1904				0612	0612	1058		
Chiasso a.			1730		1930				0637	0637	1123		

train number	ICE 72	EC 108	EC 104	ICE 78	EC 8	EC 106	EC 4	EC 100	IC 890	336 / 202	1690 / 202	200	200
notes (see below)	R ✗	M ✗	A ✗	T ✗	G ✗	N ✗	F ✗	L ✗	✕	P	Q	C	B
Chiasso d.					1030		1230				1704	2230	2230
Lugano d.					1055		1255				1738	2257	2257
Bellinzona d.					1124		1324				1806	2327	2327
Luzern d.				1351	1342		1542				2055		
Brig d.			0901					1501		2001			
Interlaken Ost d.	0840		1040						1939				
Interlaken West d.	0845		1045						1944				
Spiez a.	0900	1005	1100					1605	1959	2105			
Spiez d.	0902	1008	1102					1608	2001	2108			
Bern d.	0950	1050	1150					1650	2032	2153			
Olten d.	1032	1132	1232	1429	1422		1622	1732		2241	2138		
Genève d.						1308							
Lausanne d.						1348							
Neuchâtel d.						1436							
Biel d.						1457							
Basel SBB d.	1107	1214	1314	1507	1521	1614	1721	1814		2325	2325	v	v
Freiburg im Breisgau a.	1145	1253	1353	1546	1553	1653	1753	1853		0024	0024	0456	0456
Karlsruhe a.	1252	1357	1457	1651	1657	1757	1857	1957		0153	0153	0546	0546
Mannheim a.	1315	1426	1526	1715	1726	1826	1927	2026					0546
Frankfurt/Main Hbf a.	1355			1756									0652
Kassel Wilhelmshöhe a.	1528			1918									
Berlin Zoo a.	1911												
Hannover Hbf a.				2008									
Bremen Hbf a.													
Hamburg Hbf a.				2122									
Hamburg Altona a.				2136									
Mainz a.		1516	1616		1816	1916	2016	2116		0353	0353	0630	
Koblenz a.		1605	1705		1905	2005	2105	2207f		0445	0445	0722	
Bonn a.		1637	1737		1937	2037	2137	2238f		0520	0520	0757	
Köln Hbf a.		1659	1759		1959	2059	2159	2259f		0544	0544	0821	
Düsseldorf a.			1824		2031	2131				0613	0613	0851	
Duisburg a.			1838		2044	2144				0630	0630	0908	
Essen a.					2057	2157							
Dortmund a.		1819			2119	2219	2319						

NOTES

A – BERNER OBERLAND – 🚋 and ✕ (Amsterdam) - Duisburg - Interlaken and v.v.

B – 🛌 1,2 cl., ▬ 2 cl. and 🚋 Frankfurt/Main - Chiasso - (Rimini) and v.v.

C – 🛌 1,2 cl., ▬ 2 cl., 🚋 and ♀ (Amsterdam) - Duisburg - Chiasso - (Rimini) and v.v.

D – 🛌 1,2 cl., ▬ 2 cl. and 🚋 (Amsterdam) - Duisburg - Basel;
⑤⑥: 🛌 1,2 cl. and ▬ 2 cl. (Amsterdam) - Duisburg - Brig.

F – VERDI – 🚋 and ✕ Dortmund - Chiasso - (Milano) and v.v.

G – TIZIANO – 🚋 and ✕ (Hannover) - Dortmund - Chiasso - (Milano) and v.v.

K – MATTERHORN – 🚋 and ✕ (Wiesbaden, Köln on ①) - Mainz - Brig.

L – MATTERHORN – 🚋 and ✕ Brig - Mainz - (Wiesbaden, Köln on ⑦).

M – LÖTSCHBERG – 🚋 and ✕ (Berlin) - Dortmund - Brig and v.v.

N – MONT BLANC – 🚋 and ✕ Dortmund - Genève and v.v.

P – 🛌 1,2 cl., ▬ 2 cl. and 🚋 Basel - Duisburg - (Amsterdam);
⑥⑦: 🛌 1,2 cl. and ▬ 2 cl. Brig - Duisburg - (Amsterdam)

Q – ▬ 2 cl. (Amsterdam) - Duisburg - Chiasso and v.v.

R – THUNERSEE – 🚋 and ✕ Berlin - Interlaken and v.v.

S – ⑥: 🚋 and ✕ Hamburg - Luzern.

T – ⑦: 🚋 and ✕ Luzern - Hamburg.

e – ① only.

f – ⑦ only.

v – Via Basel Bad.

✗ – Supplement payable.

Table 79 (Summer) KÖLN AND FRANKFURT/MAIN - MARSEILLE AND BARCELONA

	1173	1173	1173		1273	1273
train number	J	H	K		C	D
Köln Hbf .... d.	...	...	...	...	1551	1551
Koblenz .... d.	...	...	...	...	1656	1656
Trier .... d.	...	...	...	...	1812	1812
Luxembourg ⑃ ..... d.	...	...	...	...	1925	1925
Metz .... d.	...	...	...	...	2110	2114
Nancy .... d.	...	...	...	...	2200	2211
Frankfurt/Main .... d.	1717	1717	1717	...	...	...
Mannheim .... d.	1805	1805	1805			
Karlsruhe .... d.	1839	1839	1839			
Kehl ⑃ .... d.	1937	1937	1937			
Strasbourg .... d.	2024	2030	2013			
Mulhouse .... d.	2140	2158	2131			
Dijon .... d.	0047	0101	0043			0105
Avignon .... a.	0500	0530	0443			0522
Nîmes .... a.			0513	...	...	0600
Montpellier .... a.			0544	...	...	0643
Béziers .... a.			0632	...	...	0739
Narbonne .... a.			0649	...	...	0757
Perpignan .... a.			0733	...	...	0839
Cerbère .... a.			0820	...	...	0923
Port Bou .... a.			0829	1030	...	0935 1030
Figueres .... a.				...	...	
Girona .... a.				...	...	
Barcelona Sants .... a.				1225	...	1225
Marseille St. Charles .... a.	0613	0645	...	...	0518	...
Toulon .... a.	0715	0745	...	...	0621	
Les Arcs .... a.	0756	0824	...	...	0702	
St. Raphaël .... a.	0815	0841	...	...	0719	
Cannes .... a.	0840	0906	...	...	0747	
Antibes .... a.	0855	0921	...	...	0803	
Nice .... a.	0916	0943	...	...	0822	
Beaulieu .... a.	0934	...				
Monaco .... a.	0944	...				
Menton .... a.	0954	...				
Ventimiglia .... a.	1007	...				

	1172	6694	6690		6646	6630
train number	1171	6695	6691		6647	6631
train number	L	E	F		D	C
Ventimiglia .... d.	...	1847	...	...	...	...
Menton .... d.	...	1859				
Monaco .... d.	...	1909				
Beaulieu .... d.	...	1919				
Nice .... d.	...	1941	2003	...	...	2017
Antibes .... d.	...	2005	2023	...	...	2052
Cannes .... d.	...	2019	2038	...	...	2054
St. Raphaël .... d.	...	2043	2102	...	...	2119
Les Arcs .... d.	...	2102	2120	...	...	2139
Toulon .... d.	...	2154	2202	...	...	2221
Marseille St. Charles .... d.	...	2259	2259	...	...	2314
Barcelona Sants .... d.	1707	...	...	...	1707	...
Girona .... d.	...	...	...	...		...
Figueres .... d.	...	...	...	...		...
Port Bou .... d.	1910	...	...	...	1910	...
Cerbère .... d.	1915	1937	...	...	1915	2030
Perpignan .... d.	...	2028		...	...	2117
Narbonne .... d.	...	2127		...	...	2208
Béziers .... d.	...	2144		...	...	2224
Montpellier .... d.	...	2231		...	...	2313
Nîmes .... d.	...	2259		...	...	2343
Avignon .... d.	...	2328	0010	0007	...	0019
Dijon .... d.	...	0422	0435	0428	...	0439
Mulhouse .... d.	...	0746	0739	0712	...	
Strasbourg .... d.	...	0908	0908	0908	...	
Kehl ⑃ .... a.	...	0918	0918	0918	...	
Karlsruhe .... a.	...	1016	1016	1016	...	
Mannheim .... a.	...	1055	1055	1055	...	
Frankfurt/Main .... a.	...	1148	1148	1148	...	
Nancy .... d.	...	...	...	...	0730	0629
Metz .... d.	...	...	...	...	0820	0719
Luxembourg ⑃ ..... a.	...	...	...	...	0922	0840
Trier .... a.	...	...	...	...	1028	1028
Koblenz .... a.	...	...	...	...	1147	1147
Köln .... a.	...	...	...	...	1301	1301

NOTES

C – June 30 - Sept. 2: 2 cl. and ⬛ Köln - Nice and v.v.

D – June 30 - Sept. 2: 2 cl. and ⬛ Köln - Port Bou and v.v.

E – Daily to June 23 and from Aug. 28, also ①②③④⑤ June 26 - Aug. 25: 2 cl. Ventimiglia - Frankfurt/Main.

F – ⑥⑦ June 24 - Aug. 27: 2 cl. Nice - Frankfurt/Main.

H – ⑤⑥ June 23 - Aug. 26: 2 cl. Frankfurt/Main - Nice.

J – Daily to June 22 and from Aug. 27, also ①②③④⑦ June 25 - Aug. 24: 2 cl. Frankfurt/Main - Ventimiglia.

K – 2 cl. and ⬛ Frankfurt/Main - Port Bou (also 1,2 cl. on ④⑤⑥).

L – 2 cl. and ⬛ Cerbère - Frankfurt/Main (also 1,2 cl. on ⑤⑥⑦).

Table 80 (Summer) MADRID - LISBOA

	30	332
notes	B ⁄	A ⁄
Madrid Chamartín .... d.	... ...	... 2230 ...
Madrid Puerta de Atocha .. d.	... 1405	... ...
Valencia de Alcántara ⑃ ... d.	... 1850	... 0500 ...
Marvão Beirã ⑃ .... a.	... 1904	... 0517
Entroncamento .... d.	... 2044	... 0703
Lisboa Santa Apolónia ..... a.	... 2145	... 0833

	31	335
notes	B ⁄	A ⁄
Lisboa Santa Apolónia ... d.	... 1155	... 2205 ...
Entroncamento .... d.	... 1259	... 2325
Marvão Beirã ⑃ .... a.	... 1445	... 0120
Valencia de Alcántara ⑃ ... a.	... 1500	... 0150
Madrid Puerta de Atocha .. a.	... 1953	... ...
Madrid Chamartín .... a.	... ...	... 0837

NOTES

A – LUSITANIA – 1,2 cl., 2 cl., ⬛ and ✕ Madrid - Lisboa and v.v.

B – LUIS DE CAMOENS – ①②③④⑤⑦: ⬛ and ♀ Madrid - Lisboa and v.v.

⁄ – Supplement payable.

Table 81 (Summer) BARCELONA – LYON, GENÈVE AND MARSEILLE

Train number		TGV	6464	EN		376	364
Train number	73	860/1	6465	272		471	375 365
notes	N ⁄	⁄		L		P	R
Barcelona França ... d.	0855	...	...	2015	...	...	...
Barcelona Sants ...... d.	...	...	...	...	2000	...	
Girona .... d.	...	1001	...	2126	2134	...	
Figueres .... d.	...	1027	...	2153	2201	...	
Port Bou ⑃ .... d.	...	1055			2227	...	
Cerbère ⑃ .... a.	...	1126			2232	2305	2355
Perpignan .... a.	...	1151			2353	0030	
Narbonne .... a.	...	1225			0036	0118	
Montpellier .... a.	...	1315	1330	1349		0157	0253
Nîmes .... a.	...	1357	1415			0228	0325
Avignon .... a.	...	1423				0300	
Marseille .... a.	...		1533				0450
Nice .... a.	...		1835				0742
Ventimiglia ...... a.	...						0853
Valence .... a.	...	1520					0428
Lyon Part Dieu ... a.	...	1603					0600
Genève ⑃ .... a.	...	1744		0552			0820
Lausanne .... a.	...			0640			
Bern .... a.	...			0751			
Zürich .... a.	...			0915			

Train number	164	TGV		71	6950	5511		377	362		EN
Train number	165	868/9						378	363	471	274
notes	⁄	⁄	N	⁄				P	R		⁄
Zürich .... d.	...	...	...	...	...	...	...	...	...		1933
Bern .... d.	...	...	...	...	...	...	...	...	...		2048
Lausanne .... d.	...	...	...	...	...	...	...	...	...		2158
Genève ⑃ .... d.	...	1044	...	...	...	...	2154	...			2250
Lyon Part Dieu ... d.	...	1226		1403			2357				
Valence .... d.	...	1315		1507			0108				
Ventimiglia ...... d.	...	...	...	...	...	2120	...				
Nice .... d.	1030	...	1148			2220	...				
Marseille .... d.	1302	...	1442			0120	...				
Avignon .... d.	...	1411		1607		0207					
Nîmes .... d.	...	1437		1552	1638	0236	0242				
Montpellier .... d.	1426	1502	1510	1636	1714	0306	0315				
Narbonne .... d.	...		1600	1735	1817	0410	0436				
Perpignan .... d.	...		1633		1858	0450	0514				
Cerbère ⑃ .... a.	...		1701		1951	2110	0538	0548	...		
Port Bou ⑃ .... a.	...		1718		1955	2110	0542	0552	0645		
Figueres .... a.	...		1740	...	2132	...	...	0708	0729		
Girona .... a.	...		1806	...	2202	...	...	0735	0756		
Barcelona Sants ...... a.	...		...	...	2327	...	...	0902			
Barcelona França ... a.	...	1920	...	...	...	...	...	...	0910		

NOTES

L – PABLO CASALS – 1,2 cl., ⬛ and ✕ Barcelona - Zürich and v.v.

N – CATALAN TALGO – ⬛ and ✕ Barcelona - Montpellier and v.v.

P – HISPANIA – 1,2 cl. and ⬛ Genève - Port Bou/Cerbère and v.v.

R – 2 cl. and ⬛ Cerbère/Port Bou - Ventimiglia and v.v.

⁄ – Supplement payable.

Table 82 (Summer) GENÈVE AND BERN - MILANO

train type	IC		IC	IC			EC	IC	IC		IC	IC		IC		IC	IC		EC	IC	IC		IC		IC
train number	331		321	321	1808		39	813	677		323	679		333		327	683		91	335	687		337		329
notes (see page 4)	🍷		🍷						🍷		🍴	🍷		🍴		🍷	🍷				🍷		🍷		🍷
notes (see below)				C	D		Q ⚡	⚡	⚡			⚡					⚡		S ⚡		⚡				
Genève d.	...	...	0731	0731	...	...	0820	...	...	...	1034	...	...	...	...	1248	...	...	...	1535	...	...	...	...	1916
Lausanne d.	...	...	0809	0809	...	...	0857	...	...	...	1113	...	...	...	...	1332	...	...	...	1613	...	...	...	...	1953
Montreux d.	...	...	|	|	...	...	|	...	...	...	|	...	...	...	...	1353	...	...	...	|	...	...	...	...	|
Martigny d.	...	...	|	|	...	...	|	...	...	...	|	...	...	...	...	1421	...	...	...	|	...	...	...	...	|
Sion d.	...	...	0904	0904	...	...	0951	...	...	...	1208	...	...	...	...	1438	...	...	...	1708	...	...	...	...	2048
Basel d.	...	...	|	|	...	...	|	0730	...	...	|	...	...	...	...	|	...	...	1401	|	...	...	...	...	|
Bern d.	0650	...	|	|	0756	...	|	0850	...	...	|	...	...	1256	...	|	...	...	1522	|	...	...	1722	...	|
Spiez d.	0722	...	|	|	0828	...	|	0923	...	...	|	...	...	1328	...	|	...	...	1554	|	...	...	1754	...	|
Brig d.	0822	...	0934	0945	0945	...	1031	1031	...	...	1238	...	...	1431	...	1517	...	...	1702	1738	...	...	1902	...	2118
Domodossola 🏛 a.	0850	...	1002	1017	1017	...	1100	1100	...	...	1307	...	...	1500	...	1547	...	...	1732	1807	...	...	1932	...	2147
Stresa a.	0938	...	1045	1107	1107	...	1139	1139	...	...	1344	...	...	1542	...	1632	...	...	1813	|	...	...	2013	...	2233
Arona a.	0950	...	1057	1123	1123	...	1152	1152	...	...	|	...	...	1554	...	1645	...	...	1825	1854	...	...	2025	...	2246
Milano Centrale a.	1045	...	1145	|	|	...	1240	1240	1315	...	1445	1510	...	1645	...	1745	1805	...	1915	1945	2010	...	2115	...	2345
Genova P.P. a.	...	...	...	1332	1332	...	...	...	1451	...	...	1647	...	...	...	...	1947	...	...	...	2147	...	...	...	...
Ventimiglia a.	...	...	...	1640	1640	...	...	...	...	...	...	...	...	...	...	...	...	...	...	...	...	...	...	...	...

train number			IC		IC	IC	EC		IC		IC		IC	EC	EC				1021	1021		IC			IC
train number	320		332		330	674	90		334		322		680	40	40	344	326		1022	1022		682	336		328
notes (see page 4)			🍴			🍷			🍷				🍷			🍷	🍴					🍷			
notes (see below)						⚡	S ⚡						⚡	Q ⚡	⚡				E	F		⚡			
Ventimiglia d.	...	...	...	...	...	...	...	...	...	...	...	...	...	...	...	...	...	...	1225	1225	...	...	...	...	...
Genova P.P d.	...	...	...	...	...	0805	...	...	...	...	...	...	1313	...	...	1354	...	...	1520	1520	...	1513	...	...	...
Milano Centrale d.	0725	...	0825	...	0905	0950	1025	...	1225	...	1400	...	1450	1525	1525	1545	1625	...	|	|	...	1650	1725	...	1905
Arona d.	0816	...	0915	...	0953	...	1116	...	1316	...	1442	...	...	1617	1617	...	1716	...	1741	1741	...	...	1815	...	1952
Stresa d.	0830	...	0929	...	1006	...	1129	...	1329	...	1458	...	...	1630	1630	...	1729	...	1758	1758	...	...	1828	...	2000
Domodossola 🏛 d.	0915	...	1011	...	1046	...	1213	...	1411	...	1544	...	...	1713	1713	...	1813	...	1850	1850	...	...	1913	...	2100
Brig a.	0945	...	1040	...	1114	...	1243	...	1440	...	1613	...	...	1744	1744	...	1843	...	1922	1922	...	...	1944	...	2130
Spiez a.	|	...	1140	...	|	...	1405	...	1540	...	|	...	...	|	1905	...	|	...	|	2053	...	...	2105	...	|
Bern a.	|	...	1212	...	|	...	1438	...	1612	...	|	...	...	|	1940	...	|	...	|	2127	...	...	2140	...	|
Basel a.	|	...	...	...	|	...	1559	...	...	...	|	...	...	|	2058	...	|	...	|	...	...	...	...	...	|
Sion a.	1023	...	...	...	1146	...	...	...	...	...	1644	...	...	1818	...	...	1921	...	2010	...	...	...	...	...	2202
Martigny a.	1040	...	...	...	|	...	...	...	...	...	|	...	...	|	...	...	1938	...	2037	...	...	...	...	...	|
Montreux a.	1105	...	...	...	|	...	...	...	...	...	|	...	...	|	...	...	2005	...	2106	...	...	...	...	...	|
Lausanne a.	1127	...	...	...	1240	...	...	...	...	...	1740	...	...	1914	...	...	2027	...	2127	...	...	...	...	...	2255
Genève a.	1212	...	...	...	1316	...	...	...	...	...	1817	...	...	1951	...	...	2112	...	2212	...	...	...	...	...	2332

Table 83 (Summer) GENÈVE - ROMA AND VENEZIA

train number	EC	IC	EC		EC			IC	IC	IC	IC			IC	IC	EC			EN	EN				
train number	39	813	55		39	813		819	323	543	655		1925	333	657	53		311	311	313		1227	313	221
notes (see page 4)			🍴					🍷	🍴	🍷	🍷		🍷	🍴	🍷	🍴								
notes (see below)	Q ⚡		⚡		R	T				⚡	⚡				⚡	⚡			V	W		L	M	A
Genève d.	0820	...	...	...	0820	...	...	...	1034	...	...	...	1148	...	...	...	...	2025	2025	...	...	2048	...	2302
Lausanne d.	0857	...	...	...	0857	...	...	...	1113	...	...	...	1232	...	...	...	...	2110	2110	...	...	2132	...	2345
Sion d.	0951	...	...	...	|	...	...	...	1208	...	...	...	1343	...	...	...	...	2216	2216	...	...	|	...	0052
Basel d.	|	0730	...	...	|	...	...	0901	|	...	...	...	|	...	...	...	...	|	|	2002	...	|	...	|
Bern d.	|	0850	...	...	|	0850	...	1022	|	...	...	...	|	1256	...	...	...	|	|	2120	...	|	2120	|
Brig d.	1031	1031	...	...	1045	1045	...	1159	1238	...	...	...	1423	1431	...	...	...	230	2332	2332	...	2323	2323	0129
Domodossola 🏛 a.	1100	1100	...	...	1115	1115	...	...	1307	...	...	...	...	1500	...	...	...	2334	|	|	...	2353	2353	0200
Milano Centrale a.	1240	1240	1300	...	|	|	...	...	1445	1500	1505	...	...	1645	1705	1700	...	|	|	|	...	|	|	|
Verona a.	1425	1425	|	...	|	|	...	...	...	|	1624	...	...	...	1824	|	...	|	|	|	...	|	|	0512
Padova a.	1515	1515	|	...	|	|	...	...	...	|	1719	...	...	...	1919	|	...	|	|	|	...	|	|	0613
Venezia Mestre a.	1538	1538	|	...	|	|	...	...	...	|	1740	...	...	...	1940	|	...	|	|	|	...	|	|	0640
Venezia Santa Lucia a.	1550	1550	|	...	|	|	...	...	...	|	1752	...	...	...	...	|	...	|	|	|	...	|	|	0700
Bologna a.	...	...	1444	...	1523	1523	...	...	...	1644	...	...	...	...	...	1844	...	0350	|	|	...	0358	0358	...
Rimini a.	...	...	|	...	1654	1654	...	...	...	|	...	...	...	...	...	|	...	|	|	|	...	0520	0520	...
Ancona a.	...	...	|	...	1820	1820	...	...	...	|	...	...	...	...	...	|	...	|	|	|	...	0640	0640	...
Pescara a.	...	...	|	...	2008	2006	...	...	...	|	...	...	...	...	...	|	...	|	|	|	...	0830	0830	...
Firenze SMN a.	...	...	1551	...	...	...	...	...	...	1753	...	...	...	...	...	1953	...	0514	0631	0631	...	...	...	...
Roma Termini a.	...	...	1755	...	...	...	...	...	...	1955t	...	...	...	...	...	2155	...	0800t	0923	0923	...	...	...	...
Napoli Centrale a.	...	...	...	...	...	...	...	...	...	...	...	...	...	...	...	...	...	1031	...	...	...	...	...	...

train type	EC		IC			P	EC	EC						IC						9720		EN	EN	
train number	52	2098	322	1839		502	40	40		1228	1228		354	536	326	1843		1226	1226	220		314	314	312
notes (see page 4)	🍴	🍷		🍷		[R] 🍴							🍴	🍴	🍴	🍷								
notes (see below)	⚡					⚡	Q ⚡	⚡		G	H			⚡				N	P	A		V	W	
Napoli Centrale d.	...	...	...	...	...	...	...	...	...	...	...	...	...	0857	...	...	...	...	...	...	...	...	...	1915
Roma Termini d.	0805	...	...	...	...	1055	...	...	...	...	...	...	...	1105	...	...	...	...	...	...	...	2100	2100	2155
Firenze SMN d.	1007	...	...	...	...	1236r	...	...	...	...	...	...	...	1307	...	...	...	...	...	...	...	2341	2341	0117
Pescara d.	|	...	...	...	...	|	...	...	...	0755	0755	...	...	|	...	...	...	1925	1925	...	...	|	|	|
Ancona d.	|	...	...	...	...	|	...	...	...	0959	0959	...	...	|	...	...	...	2107	2107	...	...	|	|	|
Rimini d.	|	...	...	...	...	|	...	...	...	1129	1129	...	...	|	...	...	...	2228	2228	...	...	|	|	|
Bologna d.	1116	...	...	...	...	1331	...	...	...	1300	1300	...	...	1416	...	...	...	2342	2342	...	...	|	|	0301
Venezia Santa Lucia d.	|	1025	...	...	...	|	1205	1205	...	|	|	...	1225	|	...	...	...	|	|	2202	...	|	|	|
Venezia Mestre d.	|	1037	...	...	...	|	1217	1217	...	|	|	...	1237	|	...	...	...	|	|	2242	...	|	|	|
Padova d.	|	1100	...	...	...	|	1240	1240	...	|	|	...	1300	|	...	...	...	|	|	2309	...	|	|	|
Verona d.	|	1201	...	...	...	|	1332	1332	...	|	|	...	1401	|	...	...	...	|	|	0010	...	|	|	|
Milano Centrale d.	1300	1345	1400	...	...	1505	1525	1525	...	|	|	...	1545	1600	1625	...	...	|	|	|	...	|	|	0625
Domodossola 🏛 d.	...	...	1544	...	...	...	1713	1713	...	1645	1645	...	...	...	1813	...	...	0335	0335	0325	...	|	|	0813
Brig a.	...	...	1613	1622	...	...	1744	1744	...	1717	1717	...	...	...	1843	1901	...	0405	0405	0357	...	0639	0639	0843
Bern a.	...	...	|	1804	...	...	|	1940	...	|	1905	...	...	...	|	2038	...	|	0602	|	...	|	0840	|
Basel a.	...	...	|	...	...	...	|	2058	...	|	...	...	...	...	|	...	...	|	...	|	...	|	0958	|
Sion a.	...	...	1644	...	...	...	1818	...	...	|	...	...	...	...	1921	...	...	|	...	0448	...	0721	...	0921
Lausanne a.	...	...	1740	...	...	...	1914	...	...	1927	...	...	...	...	2027	...	...	0533	...	0555	...	0827	...	1027
Genève a.	...	...	1817	...	...	...	1951	...	...	2012	...	...	...	...	2112	...	...	0614	...	0639	...	0912	...	1112

NOTES for Tables 82 and 83

- **A –** SIMPLON EXPRESS – ▬ 2 cl. and [2] Genève - Venezia Santa Lucia and v.v.; 🛏 1,2 cl., ▬ 2 cl. and [12] Genève - Venezia Mestre - (Zagreb) and v.v.
- **C –** ⑤⑥, June 3 - Oct. 14: [12] Genève - Ventimiglia.
- **D –** ⑤⑥, June 3 - Oct. 14: [12] Bern - Ventimiglia.
- **E –** ⑥⑦ June 4 - Oct. 15: [12] Ventimiglia - Genève.
- **F –** ⑥⑦ June 4 - Oct. 15: [12] Ventimiglia - Bern.
- **G –** ⑥⑦ July 2 - Aug. 27: [12] Pescara - Genèva.
- **H –** ⑥⑦ July 2 - Aug. 27: [12] Pescara - Bern.
- **L –** ⑤⑥ June 30 - Aug. 12: [12] Genèva - Ancona (Pescara on ⑤).
- **M –** ⑤⑥ June 30 - Aug. 12: [12] Bern - Ancona (Pescara on ⑤).
- **N –** ⑥ July 1 - Aug. 12: [12] Pescara - Genèva.
- **P –** ⑥ July 1 - Aug. 12: [12] Pescara - Bern.
- **Q –** MONTEVERDI – [12] and 🍴 Genève - Venezia and v.v.
- **R –** ⑤⑥ July 1 - Aug. 26: [12] Genèva - Pescara.
- **S –** VAUBAN – [12] and 🍴 (Brussels) - Basel - Milano and v.v.
- **T –** ⑤⑥ July 1 - Aug. 26: [12] Bern - Pescara.
- **V –** ROMA – 🛏 1,2 cl., 🛏 1,2 cl. (T2) and ▬ 2 cl. Genève - Roma and v.v.
- **W –** ROMA – 🛏 1,2 cl. and ▬ 2 cl. Basel - Roma and v.v.
- **r –** Firenze Rifredi.
- **t –** Roma Tiburtina.
- **⚡ –** Supplement payable.

For explanation of standard symbols see page 4

Table 84 (Summer) — ZÜRICH - MILANO

train type	IC 351	2187	IC 251	EC 55	IC 677	IC 357	2189	IC 345	IC 383	EC 53	IC 681	IC 385	IC 683	EC 5	IC 685	IC 387	IC 687	EC 9	IC 689	IC 381	IC 257	IC 389	1087
notes (see page 4)				☕						☕								☕			☕		
notes (see below)	S			P✎		X✎		✎	G	R✎	✎	T	✎	A✎	✎	D	✎	B✎	✎	C		J	V
Zürich Hb .... d.	0707	...	0830	...	0907	...	...	...	1107	...	1111	1307	...	...	1507	...	...	...	1707	...	1907	0006
Basel .... d.	...	0707	...	...	...	...	0911	...	...	1111	...	...	1311	...	...	1511	...	...	1720	...		
Luzern .... d.	...	0819	...	...	...	...	1023	...	...	1223	...	...	1423	...	...	1623	...	...	1834	...		
Arth Goldau .... d.	0752	...	...	...	0952	...	...	1052	1152	1252	...	1452	...	1552	...	1652	...	1749	1900	1949	
Bellinzona .... d.	0938	1028	1057	1137	...	1238	1338	1438	...	1538	...	1638	...	1738	...	1838	...	1938	2049	2138	
Lugano .... d.	1007	1059	1124	1207	...	1307	1407	1507	...	1607	...	1707	...	1807	...	1907	...	2007	2119	2206	
Chiasso ▥ .... d.	1048	1141	1158	1248	...	1348	1448	1548	...	1648	...	1748	...	1848	...	1948	...	2048	2200	2248	0355
Como .... a.	1054	1146	1206	1254	...	1356	1454	1554	...	1654	...	1754	...	1854	...	1954	...	2054	2205	2254	0400
Milano Centrale ... a.	1135	1215	1230	1245	1315	1335	1405	1435	1535	1635	1710	1735	1805	1835	1910	1935	2010	2035	2110	2135	2240	2335	0440
Genova P P .... a.	...	1405	...	...	1451	...	1559	1640	...	1740	...	1847	...	1947	...	2047	...	2147	...	2247	...	...	0652
Sestri Levante .. a.	...	...	...	...	...	...	...	...	1836	...	...	...	...	...	...	...	...	...	...	...	...	...	
Ventimiglia ...... a.	...	...	...	...	...	1901	...	...	...	...	...	...	...	...	...	...	...	...	...	...	...	...	
Nice .... a.	...	...	...	...	...	2000	...	...	...	...	...	...	...	...	...	...	...	...	...	...	...	...	1000

train number	250	386	IC 672	EC 8	IC 674	388	IC 676	EC 4	380	IC 678	EC 52	382	IC 356 / IC343 IC344	IC 354	EC 682	EC 54	254	1089 1086	2164	IC 256	IC 684	384
notes (see page 4)	☕				☕		☕								☕			☕	☕	☕		
notes (see below)			H	B✎		K		A✎	D		R✎	G	X✎		S	P✎		V			T✎	
Nice .... d.	...	...	...	...	...	...	...	...	...	1000	...	...	...	...	...	...	...	...	...	...	
Ventimiglia ...... d.	...	...	...	...	...	...	...	...	...	1059	...	...	...	...	...	...	1255	...	...	...	
Sestri Levante .. d.	...	...	...	...	...	...	...	...	...	...	1122	...	...	...	...	...	...	...	...	...	
Genova P P .... d.	...	...	0713	...	0813	...	0913	...	1113	...	1222	...	1322	...	1513	...	...	1602 1554	...	1713	
Milano Centrale ... d.	0725	0825	0850	0925	0950	1025	1050	1125	1225	1305	1325	1425	1500	1525	1625	1650	1725	1725	...	1745	1825	1850	1925
Como .... a.	0804	0905	...	1004	...	1105	...	1205	1305	...	1405	1505	1538	1605	1705	...	1805	1806	1839	...	1905	...	1959
Chiasso ▥ .... a.	0812	0912	...	1012	...	1112	...	1212	1312	...	1412	1512	1545	1612	1712	...	1812	1812	1845	...	1912	...	2005
Lugano .... a.	0851	0952	...	1052	...	1154	...	1252	1352	...	1452	1552	1630	1652	1752	...	1852	1854	1925	...	1954	...	2038
Bellinzona .... a.	0920	1021	...	1121	...	1221	...	1321	1421	...	1521	1621	1659	1721	1821	...	1921	1924	1954	...	2024	...	2108
Arth Goldau .... a.	1111	1208	...	1308	...	1411	...	1508	1611	...	1708	1808	1845	1908	2008	...	2108	2111	2140	...	2211	...	2256
Luzern .... a.	1146		1335					1535			1735		1935				2139			2239		
Basel .... a.	1309		1449					1649			1849		2049				2253			2359		
Zürich Hb .... a.	...	1253	...	1453	...	1653	...	1853	...	1928	...	2053	...	2153	...	2226	...	2337

Table 85 (Summer) — ZÜRICH - ROMA AND VENEZIA

train type / number	IC 351	EC 55	EC 39	IC 357	IC 541	2101	IC 383	IC 545	2105	1571	EC 53	IC 657	IC 385	IC 559	2109	IC 387	2113	IC 389	301	1593	EN 303
classes			✕		✕	☕		☕	☕			☕		☕	☕						
notes (see below)	S	P✎	✎	X✎	✎		G	✎	✎		R✎	✎	T✎	✎		D		J	N	M	L
Zürich Hb .... d.	0707	0830	...	0907	...	...	1107	...	...	1203	...	...	1307	...	...	1507	...	1907	...	2007	2207
Basel .... d.			...		...	...		...	...	1111	...	...		...	...		...		1911		
Luzern .... d.			...		...	...		...	...	1223	...	...		...	...		...		2023		
Arth Goldau .... d.	0752	...	...	0952	...	...	1152	...	...	1245	1252	...	1552	...	1949	2100	2100	2250
Bellinzona .... d.	0938	1057	...	1137	...	...	1338	...	...	1438	...	1538	1738	...	2138	2252	2252	0035
Lugano .... d.	1007	1124	...	1207	...	...	1407	...	...	1507	...	1607	1807	...	2206	2321	2321	0102
Chiasso ▥ ...... d.	1048	1158	...	1248	...	...	1448	...	...	1548	...	1648	1848	...	2248	0005	0005	
Milano Centrale ... a.	1135	1245	1305	1335	1400	1410	1535	1600	1610	...	1635	1705	1735	1755	1810	1935	2010	2335		
Verona .... a.	...	...	1325	...	1424	...	...	1751	...	1824	...	1951	...	2151		
Padova .... a.	...	...	1415	...	1519	...	...	1850	...	1919	...	2050	...	2250		
Venezia Mestre .. a.	...	...	1438	...	1540	...	...	1913	...	1940	...	2113	...	2313		
Venezia Santa Lucia .. a.	...	...	1450	...	1552	...	...	1925	...	...	2125	...	2325		
Bologna .... a.	...	1444	...	1544	...	...	1744	...	1844	...	1958	...	0220	0350	0350
Ancona .... a.	...	...	...	...	...	...	...	0428		
Pescara .... a.	...	...	...	...	...	...	...	0608		
Bari .... a.	...	...	...	...	...	...	...	0949		
Brindisi Centrale ... a.	...	...	...	...	...	...	...	1141		
Lecce .... a.	...	...	...	...	...	...	...	1218		
Firenze SMN ... a.	...	1551	...	1653	...	1853	...	1951	...	2110	...	0514	0514	0631
Roma Termini ... a.	...	1755	...	1855	...	2055	...	2155	...	...	0800t	0800t	0923
Napoli Centrale .. a.	...	...	2100	...	2307	...	...	1031	1031	

train type / number	EC 52	1582	P 504	2100	EC 56	IC 536	354	EC 40	EC 54	2104	P 506	IC 256	IC 540	IC 656	EN 384	314	312	312	388
classes			✕ Ⓡ			✕		✕			Ⓡ ✕		✕	☕					
notes (see below)	R✎		✎		X✎		S	P✎	✎		✎		T✎		L		N	M	K
Napoli Centrale .. d.	...	...	...	...	0857	...	...	...	...	...	...	...	...	1915	1915	...
Roma Termini ... d.	...	0805	...	0955	...	1105	...	1205	...	1355	1405	...	2100	2155t	2155t	...
Firenze SMN ... d.	...	1008	...	1132r	...	1307	...	1407	...	1532r	1607	...	2341	0117	0117	...
Lecce .... d.	...	...	...	...	...	...	...	...	...	...	...	...	...	2106
Brindisi Centrale ... d.	...	...	...	...	...	...	...	...	...	...	...	...	...	2152
Bari .... d.	...	...	...	...	...	...	...	...	...	...	...	...	...	2352
Pescara .... d.	...	...	...	...	...	...	...	...	...	...	...	...	...	0326
Ancona .... d.	...	...	...	...	...	...	...	...	...	...	...	...	...	0501
Bologna .... d.	...	1115	...	1230	...	1416	...	1516	...	1630	...	1716	...	0301	0301	0746
Venezia Santa Lucia .. d.	...	...	...	1125	...	1305	1405	...	1425	...	1605		
Venezia Mestre .. d.	...	...	...	1137	...	1317	1417	...	1437	...	1617		
Padova .... d.	...	...	...	1200	...	1340	1439	...	1500	...	1639		
Verona .... d.	...	...	...	1301	...	1432	1534	...	1601	...	1734		
Milano Centrale ... d.	1325	...	1405	1445	1500	1600	1625	1655	1725	1745	1805	1825	1900	1855	1925				1025
Chiasso ▥ .... a.	1412	...	1545	...	1712	1812	...	1912	...	2005	...	0715	0715	1112
Lugano .... a.	1452	...	1630	...	1752	1852	...	1954	...	2038	0552	0752	0752	1154
Bellinzona .... a.	1521	...	1659	...	1821	1921	...	2024	...	2108	0621	0821	0821	1224
Arth Goldau .... a.	1708	1715	...	1845	...	2008	2108	...	2211	...	2256	0808	1008	1008	1411
Luzern .... a.	1735								2239				1044		
Basel .... a.	1849								2359			1207		
Zürich Hb .... a.	...	1757	...	1928	...	2053	2153	...	2337	0853	...	1053	1457

NOTES for Tables 84 and 85

- V — VERDI – 🚃 (Dortmund) - Basel - Milano and v.v.; ✕ Basel - Chiasso and v.v.
- TIZIANO – 🚃 (Hannover) - Basel - Milano and v.v.; ✕ Basel - Chiasso and v.v.
- 🚃 (Stuttgart) - Zürich - Milano; ✕ Zürich - Chiasso.
- 🚃 Milano - Zürich - (Stuttgart) and v.v.
- 🚃 (Stuttgart) - Zürich - Sestri Levante and v.v.
- 🚃 Milano - Zürich - (Nürnberg); ✕ Chiasso - Zürich.
- ⊢ 2 cl. and 🚃 (Stuttgart) - Zürich - Lecce; 🚃 and ✕ Zürich - Chiasso.
- ⊢ 2 cl. and 🚃 Lecce - Zürich - (Stuttgart).
- ROMA – ⊢ 1,2 cl. and ⊢ 2 cl. Zürich - Roma and v.v.

- M — 🚃 Zürich - Napoli and v.v.
- N — 🚃 Basel - Napoli and v.v.
- P — RAFFAELLO – 🚃 and ✕ Zürich - Roma and v.v.
- R — COLOSSEUM – 🚃 and ✕ Basel - Roma and v.v.
- S — CANALETTO – 🚃 and ✕ Zürich - Venezia and v.v.
- T — GOTTARDO – 🚃 and ☕ Zürich - Milano and v.v.
- V — ⑥ June 10 - Oct. 7: 🚃 Zürich - Ventimiglia and v.v.
- X — TICINO – 🚃 and ✕ Zürich - Milano and v.v.
- r — Firenze Rifredi.
- t — Roma Tiburtina.
- ✎ — Supplement payable.

Table 86 (Summer) — ZÜRICH - INNSBRUCK AND WIEN

train type	443	IC 669	IC 596		EC 163	IC 519			EC 161	IC 613		IC 449	863		EN 465	EN 465	EN 467
notes (see page 4)		✕	⛉			⛉				⛉			✕				
notes (see below)					B ↗	↗			F ↗						H	J	A
Basel SBB .... d.	...	0625	...	...	0825	...	...	...	...	...	...	...	...	...	...	...	...
Zürich Flughafen ✈ ...... d.	0713		...	...	0905	...	...	1316		...	...	...	...	2105	...	...	...
Zürich Hbf .... a.	0723	0723	...	...	0918	0923	...	1326		...	...	...	...	2118	...	...	...
Zürich Hbf .... d.	...	0733	...	...	0933		...	...	1333	...	...	1709	...	...	2133	2133	2144
St Gallen .... d.	...		...	...			...	...		...	...		...	...			2250
Sargans .... d.	...	0833	...	...	1033		...	...	1433	...	1808		...	...			
Buchs ▥ .... d.	...	0852	...	...	1052		...	...	1452	...	1825		...	...	2253	2253	0005
Feldkirch .... a.	...	0907	0912	...	1108		...	...	1509	...	1840	1844	...	...	2308	2308	
Bludenz .... a.	...	0927		...	1125		...	...	1525	...		1858	...	...			
Langen am Arlberg ...... a.	...	0953		...	1152		...	...	1552	...		1926	...	...			
St. Anton am Arlberg ... a.	...	1003		...	1201		...	...	1601	...		1935	...	...			
Landeck .... a.	...	1030		...	1228		...	...	1628	...		2007	...	...			
Ötztal .... a.	...	1051		...	1250		...	...	1650	...		2032	...	...			
Innsbruck Hbf .... a.	...	1116		...	1316	1320	...	...	1716	1720		2058	...	...			
Kitzbühel .... a.	...	1228		...		1427	...	...		1827			...	...			
Zell am See .... a.	...	1313		...		1513	...	...		1913			...	...			
Schwarzach St. Veit ...... a.	...	1345	1407	...		1545	...	...		1945			...	...			
Bischofshofen .... a.	...	1359		...		1559	...	...		1959			...	...			
Selzthal .... a.	...	1528		...		1728	...	...		2128			...	...	0527	0527	
Graz .... a.	...	1720		...		1920	...	...		2320			...	...	0732		
Villach Hbf ▥ .... a.	...			...			...	...					...	...			
Klagenfurt .... a.	...			1614			...	...					...	...			
Salzburg .... a.	...			...	1522		...	...	1922				2300	...			
Linz .... a.	...			...	1637		...	...	2037					...			0600
St. Pölten .... a.	...			...	1743		...	...	2143					...			0718
Wien West .... a.	...			...	1830		...	...	2230					...			0805
Hegyeshalom ▥ .... a.	...			...			...	...						...			
Sopron .... a.	...			...			...	...						...	0920		
Györ .... a.	...			...			...	...						...	1027		
Budapest Keleti .... a.	...			...			...	...						...	1208		

train type	IC 860	442			IC 510	EC 160			IC 512	EC 162		EC 10	IC 668	IC 566	448		EN 466		434	EN 464
notes (see page 4)	✕					⛉				⛉			✕	✕						
notes (see below)						F ↗				B ↗							A		J	H
Budapest Keleti .... d.	...	...	...	...	...	...	...	...	...	...	...	...	...	...	...	...	...	...	1725	...
Györ .... d.	...	...	...	...	...	...	...	...	...	...	...	...	...	...	...	...	...	...	1904	...
Sopron .... d.	...	...	...	...	...	...	...	...	...	...	...	...	...	...	...	...	...	...	2013	...
Hegyeshalom ▥ .... d.	...	...	...	...	...	...	...	...	...	...	...	...	...	...	...	...	...	...		...
Wien West .... d.	...	...	...	...	0735		...	...	0935		...	...	1140		...	...	2125	...		...
St. Pölten .... d.	...	...	...	...	0816		...	...	1016		...	...	1221		...	...	2207	...		...
Linz .... d.	...	...	...	...	0923		...	...	1123		...	...	1334		...	...	2315	...		...
Salzburg .... d.	...	...	...	...	1038		...	...	1238		...	...	1500		...	...		...		...
Klagenfurt .... d.	...	...	...	...			...	...			...	1218			...	...		...		...
Villach Hbf .... d.	...	...	...	...			...	...			...				...	...		...		2200
Graz .... d.	...	...	...	...	0640		...	...	0840		...		1040		...	...		...		2200
Selzthal .... d.	...	...	...	...	0831		...	...	1031		...		1231		...	...		0013	0013	
Bischofshofen .... d.	...	...	...	...	1001		...	...	1201		...		1401		...	...		...		
Schwarzach St. Veit ...... d.	...	...	...	...	1015		...	...	1215		...	1355	1415		...	...		...		
Zell am See .... d.	...	...	...	...	1046		...	...	1246		...		1446		...	...		...		
Kitzbühel .... d.	...	...	...	...	1133		...	...	1333		...		1533		...	...		...		
Innsbruck Hbf .... d.	0702	...	...	...	1240	1244	...	...	1440	1444	...	1644	1702		...	...		...		
Ötztal .... d.	0729	...	...	...		1309	...	...		1509	...	1711	1730		...	...		...		
Landeck .... d.	0755	...	...	...		1331	...	...		1531	...	1740	1754		...	...		...		
St Anton am Arlberg ...... d.	0825	...	...	...		1359	...	...		1559	...	1807	1825		...	...		...		
Langen am Arlberg ...... d.	0835	...	...	...		1408	...	...		1608	...	1817	1835		...	...		...		
Bludenz .... d.	0901	...	...	...		1434	...	...		1634	...	1844	1901		...	...		...		
Feldkirch .... d.	0917	0931	...	...		1452	...	...		1652	...	1858	1917	1931	...	...		0640	0640	
Buchs ▥ .... a.	...	0947	...	...		1508	...	...		1708	...		1947		...	0540		0708	0708	
Sargans .... a.	...	1017	...	...		1527	...	...		1727	...		2017		...			...		
St Gallen .... a.	...		...	...			...	...			...				...	0709		...		
Zürich Hbf .... a.	...	1126	...	...		1626	...	...		1826	...		2126		...	0825		0826	0826	
Zürich Hbf .... d.	...		1139	...		1639	...	...		1837	1845	...		2137	2145	...		...		0839
Zürich Flughafen ✈ ...... d.	...		1151	...		1651	...	...		1856	...	...			2156	...		...		0850
Basel SBB .... a.	...			...			...	...		1935	...	...			2235	...		...		

NOTES

A – WIENER WALZER – ⛏ 1,2 cl., ⛉ and ⛉ Zürich - Wien and v.v.
B – TRANSALPIN – ⛉ and ✕ Basel - Wien and v.v.
F – MARIA THERESIA – ⛉ and ✕ Zürich - Wien and v.v.

H – ZURICHSEE – ⛏ 1,2 cl. and ⛏ 2 cl. Zürich - Graz and v.v.; ✕ Selzthal - Graz and v.v.
J – ⛏ 2 cl. and ⛉ Zürich - Budapest and v.v.
↗ – Supplement payable.

Table 87 (Summer) — ROMA - ATHÍNAI

train type		IC 565	E 969					train type		E AD	HM	1950 B	E 950	E 956 C
notes (see page 4)		✕	⛉					notes (see page 4)						
notes (see below)		↗		HM	AD			notes (see below)		AD	HM	B		C
Milano Centrale .... d.	...	0705	...	...	...	...		Athínai (by 🚌) .... d.	...	1300	1530	...	...	...
Bologna .... d.	...	0859	...	...	...	...		Patras .... d.	...	2200	2100	...	...	...
Rimini .... d.	...	1005	...	...	...	...		Brindisi Marittima ...... d.	...	1700	1600	...	...	...
Ancona .... d.	...	1100	...	...	...	...		Brindisi Centrale ...... d.	...			2002	2059	2241
Pescara .... d.	...	1220	...	...	...	...		Bari Centrale .... a.	...			2137	2231	0022
Roma Termini .... d.	...		1310	...	...	...		Foggia .... a.	...			2318	0052	0214
Napoli Centrale .... d.	...		1430	...	...	...		Caserta .... a.	...				0420	0537
Caserta .... d.	...		1503	1531	...	...		Napoli Centrale ...... a.	...				0500	
Foggia .... d.	...	1413	1802	...	...	...		Roma Termini .... a.	...					0750
Bari Centrale .... d.	...	1540	1927	...	...	...		Pescara .... a.	...			0126		
Brindisi Centrale ...... a.	...	1654	2054	...	...	...		Ancona .... a.	...			0259		
Brindisi Marittima ...... d.	...			2200	2230	...		Rimini .... a.	...					
Patras .... a.	...			1700	1800	...		Bologna .... a.	...			0523		
Athínai (by 🚌) .... a.	...			2115	2200	...		Milano Centrale ...... a.	...			0900		

NOTES

B – ⛏ 1,2 cl., ⛏ 1,2 cl. (T2) and ⛏ 2 cl. Brindisi - Milano.
C – ⛏ 1,2 cl., ⛏ 2 cl. and ⛉ Brindisi - Roma.

↗ – Supplement payable.
AD – ADRIATICA DI NAVIGAZIONE SPA, for days of running see **Table 1490**.
HM – HELLENIC MEDITERRANEAN LINES, for days of running see **Table 1525**.

Table 88 (Summer) WIEN - VENEZIA AND MILANO

train number / notes (see page 4) / notes (see below)	EC 31	IC 592	2847 ①-⑥	2106 ☲		IC597 233	2855		IC 892 ☲	235	235		1235	1235		1135		EN 237	2841 ①-⑥	EC 12 ✗
	D ✗	E ✗								H	J		L	N		B		A		
Wien Süd .... d.	0718	...	...	...		1322	...		...	1945	1945		2015	2015		2102		2222	...	...
Bruck an der Mur .... d.	0914	...	...	...		1524	...		...	2136	2136		2206	2206		2308		0041	...	...
Klagenfurt............... d.	1121	...	...	...		1746	...		...	2347	2347		0012	0012		0120		0257	...	...
Salzburg Hbf .... d.		0908	...	...		...	...		2108	...	...		...	...		...		...	...	...
Villach Hbf............. d.	1200	1200	...	...		1827	...		2343	0014	0014		0054	0054		0146		0332	...	...
Tarvisio 🚉 .... a.	1225	1225	...	...		1852	...		...	0042	0042		0118	0118		0212		0420	...	...
Udine .... a.	1357	1357	1430	...		2038	2047		...	0218	0218		0254	0254		0405		0606	0646	...
Trieste .... a.			1539	...		...	2156		...	...	...		...	...		...		...	0754	...
Venezia Mestre .... a.	1516	1516	...	1537		2210	...		...	0343	0343		0420	0420		0526		0831	...	0906
Venezia Santa Lucia ...... a.	1527	1527	...	...		2222	...		...	...	0403		...	0440		...		0842	...	...
Padova .... a.	1617	1617	...	...		...	...		...	0420	0556		0459	0556		0607		...	...	0927
Verona .... a.			...	1658		...	...		...	...	0656		...	0656		...		...	...	1050
Milano Centrale .... a.			...	1845		...	...		...	...	0850		...	0850		...		...	...	...
Bologna .... a.	1735	1735	...	...		...	...		...	0540	...		0627	...		...		...	...	...
Firenze SMN .... a.	1842	1842	...	...		...	...		...	0656	...		0753	...		...		...	...	...
Roma Termini .... a.	2045	2045	...	...		...	...		...	0930	...		...	...		...		...	...	...
Ravenna .... a.			...	...		...	...		...	...	...		...	...		...		0809	...	...
Rimini .... a.			...	...		...	...		...	...	...		...	...		...		0910	...	...
Ancona .... a.			...	...		...	...		...	...	...		...	...		...		1044	...	...

train type / train number / notes (see page 4) / notes (see below)	2842 ①-⑥	232		2846	IC 647 ☲ ✗	EC 30 D ✗	EC 30 E ✗		2107	872	EN 239		1134		1234	2119		234	2119
											A		C		M	P		H	K
Ancona .... d.	...	...		...	...	...	...		...	...	...		1720		...	...		...	...
Rimini .... d.	...	...		...	...	...	...		...	...	...		1856		...	...		...	...
Ravenna .... d.	...	...		...	...	...	...		...	...	...		2012		...	...		...	...
Roma Termini .... d.	...	...		...	0715	0715	...		...	...	...				...	1920		...	...
Firenze SMN .... d.	...	...		...	0919	0919	...		...	...	...				1943	2152		...	...
Bologna .... d.	...	...		...	1026	1026	...		...	...	...				2115	2300		...	...
Milano Centrale .... d.	...	...		0905	...	...	...		1710	...	...				...	2015		...	2015
Verona .... d.	...	...		1027	...	...	...		1854	...	...				...	2158		...	2158
Padova .... d.	...	...		1122	1207	1207	...		...	...	2220				2304	2256		0022	2256
Venezia Santa Lucia ...... d.	...	0730		...	1236	1236	...		...	2035	...				2355	2355		...	2355
Venezia Mestre .... d.	...	0742		1140	1247	1247	...		2013	2046	2306				0006	0006		0105	0105
Trieste .... d.	0735	...		1224	...	...	...		...	2118	...				...	...		...	...
Udine .... d.	0848	0924		1336	1404	1404	...		...	2230	2256		0043		0132	0132		0224	0224
Tarvisio 🚉 .... a.	...	1109		...	1535	1535	...		...	...	0043		0250		0328	0328		0358	0358
Villach Hbf............. a.	...	1133		...	1600	1600	...		...	...	0111		0317		0351	0351		0422	0422
Salzburg Hbf .... a.	...	...		...	...	1853	...		...	...	...				...	...		...	...
Klagenfurt............... a.	...	1214		...	1637	...	...		...	0150	...		0347		0435	0435		0447	0447
Bruck an der Mur .... a.	...	1436		...	1847	...	...		...	0401	...		0607		0644	0644		0654	0654
Wien Süd .... a.	...	1640		...	2046	...	...		...	0623	...		0850		0850	0850		0857	0857

NOTES

A – SAN MARCO – 🛏 1,2 cl. (T2), 🍽 2 cl. and 🛌 Wien - Venezia and v.v.
B – ⑤ June 9 - Sept. 1: 🛏 1,2 cl., 🍽 2 cl. and 🛌 Wien - Ancona.
   ⑥ June 10 - Sept. 9: 🛏 1,2 cl., 🍽 2 cl. and 🛌 Ancona - Wien.
C – ROMULUS – 🛌 and 🍽 Wien - Roma and v.v.
   🛌 Salzburg - Roma and v.v.; 🍽 Villach - Roma and v.v.
D – REMUS – 🛏 1,2 cl., 🍽 2 cl. and 🛌 Wien - Roma and v.v.
   ①②③④ June 19 - Sept. 21: 🛏 1,2 cl., 🍽 2 cl. and 🛌 Wien - Milano.

K – ①②③⑦ June 18 - Sept. 20: 🛏 1,2 cl., 🍽 2 cl. and 🛌 Milano - Wien.
L – Daily to June 18, also ⑤⑥⑦ June 23 - Sept. 24: 🍽 2 cl. and 🛌 Wien - Firenze.
M – Daily to June 18, also ⑤⑥⑦ June 23 - Sept. 23: 🍽 2 cl. and 🛌 Firenze - Wien.
N – Daily to June 18, also ⑤⑥⑦ June 23 - Sept. 24:
   🛏 1,2 cl., 🍽 2 cl. and 🛌 Wien - Milano.
P – Daily to June 17, also ④⑤⑥ June 22 June 23:
   🛏 1,2 cl., 🍽 2 cl. and 🛌 Milano - Wien.
✗ – Supplement payable.

Table 89a (Summer) WIEN - LJUBLJANA AND ZAGREB

train number / notes (see page 4) / notes (see below)	4093	505 ①-⑥	IC 151	IC 151		515	511 ①-⑥		IC 159	IC 159
		E	A				E		C	
Wien Süd .... d.	...	...	0822	0822		...	...		1622	1622
Graz .... d.	0825	...	1058	1058		1528	...		1858	1858
Spielfeld-Strass .... a.	0908	0915	1141	1141		1559	1605		1939	1939
Maribor 🚉 .... a.	...	0932	1207	1159		...	1623		1956	1956
Zidani Most .... a.	...	1101	1322			...	1746		...	2131
Zagreb .... a.	...	...		1450		...	...		2237	...
Ljubljana .... a.	...	1200	1420	...		...	1845		...	2230
Rijeka .... a.	...	...	1725	...		...	...		...	...

train number / notes (see page 4) / notes (see below)	510 ①-⑥	4058	IC 158	IC 512	504 ①-⑥	558		436	IC482 IC150
	E		C	E					A
Rijeka .... d.	...	...	...	...	...	...		...	1250
Ljubljana .... d.	0605	...	...	0715	1130	...		...	1535
Zagreb .... d.	...	...	0710		...	1450		...	...
Zidani Most .... d.	0704	...	...	0814	1229	...		...	1631
Maribor 🚉 .... d.	0829	...	0955	0955	1357	...		1758	1758
Spielfeld-Strass .... a.	0847	0855	1013	1013	1415	1425		1815	1815
Graz .... a.	...	0938	1055	1055	1455	1455		1855	1855
Wien Süd .... a.	...	...	1340	1340	...	1740		2140	2140

NOTES

C – CROATIA – 🛌 and 🍽 Wien - Zagreb and v.v.
E – 1st class only.

A – EMONA – 🛌 and 🍽 Wien - Ljubljana and v.v.; 🛌 Wien - Rijeka and v.v.

Table 89b (Summer) VENEZIA – LJUBLJANA, ZAGREB AND BUDAPEST

train type / train number / notes (see page 4) / notes (see below)	221	IC 641 ☲	IC 243		2215	265		2109 ☲	241
	A	✗	C			D			B
Genève .... d.	2302	...	...		...	...		...	...
Lausanne .... d.	2345	...	...		...	...		...	...
Brig ⊚ .... d.	0129	...	...		...	...		...	...
Milano Centrale .... d.		...	0705		...	...		1810	...
Verona .... d.	0516	...	0827		...	...		1954	...
Roma Termini .... d.		...	...		...	...		...	...
Firenze S.M.N. .... d.		...	...		...	...		...	...
Padova .... d.	0615	...	0922		...	...		2053	...
Venezia Santa Lucia .... d.		...	0940		1540	...		...	2140
Venezia Mestre .... d.	0708	0940	0951		1551	...		2113	2151
Trieste .... d.	0917	...	1202		1747	1757		...	0002
Villa Opicina 🚉 .... d.	1005	...	1249		1840	...		...	0050
Ljubljana .... a.	1215	...	1450		2042	...		...	0300
Zagreb .... a.	1452	...			2258	...		...	0532
Budapest Keleti .... a.	...	...	2242		...	...		...	1158

train type / train number / notes (see page 4) / notes (see below)	240	IC 648 ☲		264	2212		IC 242	2114		220
	B	✗		D			C			A
Budapest Keleti .... d.	1730	...		...	...		0620	...		...
Zagreb .... d.	0020	...		0540	...		...	...		1410
Ljubljana .... d.	0320	...		0805	...		1410	...		1645
Villa Opicina 🚉 .... d.	0540	...		1014	...		1610	...		1854
Trieste .... d.	0628	...		1057	1212		1657	...		1948
Venezia Mestre .... a.	0907	1017		...	1407		1907	1937		2214
Venezia Santa Lucia .... a.	0918	...		...	1418		1918	...		...
Padova .... a.		1036		...	...		...	1957		2304
Firenze S.M.N. .... a.		...		...	...		...	...		...
Roma Termini .... a.		...		...	...		...	...		...
Verona .... a.		1131		...	...		...	2058		0002
Milano Centrale .... a.		1300		...	...		...	2245		...
Brig ⊚ .... a.		...		...	...		...	...		0357
Lausanne .... a.		...		...	...		...	...		0555
Genève .... a.		...		...	...		...	...		0639

NOTES

A – SIMPLON EXPRESS – 🛏 1,2 cl., 🍽 2 cl. and 🛌 Genève - Zagreb and v.v.
B – VENEZIA EXPRESS – 🛏 1,2 cl., 🍽 2 cl. and 🛌 Venezia - Budapest and v.v.

C – DRAVA – 🛌 and 🍽 Venezia - Budapest and v.v.
D – KRAS – 🛌 and 🍽 Trieste - Zagreb and v.v.
⊚ – 🚉 is at Domodossola/Iselle.
✗ – Supplement payable.

Table 90 (Summer)   BARCELONA AND MARSEILLE - MILANO

train number				6173				6172									

train number				6173					273		1142	366	6478	6476	6476		IC
train number			347	6172	369		361				1143	367	367	367	367		343
notes (see page 4)																	
notes (see below)				J		H		F		E		C	G	N	P	S		L
Hendaye ...... d.	...	...	...	...	...	...	...	...	...	...	...	...	1810	1850	1850	...	...
Bordeaux ...... d.																	
Toulouse ...... d.	...	...	...	...	...	...	...	...	...	...	...	...	2259	2259	2259	...	...
Barcelona França ...... d.								2015									
Barcelona Sants ...... d.								2126		1923	2052						
Girona ...... d.										2204	2315	2355					
Cerbère 🚇 ...... d.												0151	0151	0151	0200	...	...
Narbonne ...... d.												0257	0257	0257	0303	...	...
Montpellier ...... d.												0502	0502	0502	0513	...	...
Marseille ...... d.				1743								0553	0548	0548	0557	...	...
Toulon ...... d.				1832													
Cannes ...... d.				1952								0632	0709	0709	0718	...	...
Nice ...... d.			1825	2019	2030		2100					0715	0811	0811	0811	0815	...	1000
Monaco Monte Carlo ...... d.			1840		2048							0734	0830	0830	0830	0835	...	
Ventimiglia 🚇 ...... a.			1902		2110		2145					0800	0853	0853	0853	0900	...	1044
San Remo ...... a.					2207							0923	1008	1008	1008	1008	...	
Genova P. Principe ...... a.			2119		0034		0040					1140	1213	1213	1213	1213	...	1310
La Spezia ...... a.					0210								1333	1333	1333	1333	...	
Pisa ...... a.					0305								1430	1430	1430	1430	...	
Roma Termini ...... a.					0655								1805	1805	1805	1805	...	
Torino Porta Susa ...... a.									0706									
Milano Centrale ...... a.				2300					0845			1345					...	1450
Verona ...... a.																	
Venezia Santa Lucia ...... a.								0710									

train number	IC347	6950			IC345				364			1143		EN		358			164		
train number	IC346	6951			IC346	364	364	364	365	472	1142		276		360		368	165	71	
notes (see page 4)																				
notes (see below)	J				L	T	Q	K	G		D		E		F		H		M	
Venezia Santa Lucia ...... d.															2328					
Verona ...... d.																				
Milano Centrale ...... d.		0710			1510						1815		2000							
Torino Porta Susa ...... d.													2132							
Roma Termini ...... d.						1225	1225	1225	1225							2315				
Pisa ...... d.						1559	1559	1559	1559							0311				
La Spezia ...... d.						1658	1658	1658	1658							0410				
Genova P. Principe ...... d.	0852				1652	1816	1816	1816	1816		2020				0530		0545			
San Remo ...... d.						2009	2009	2009	2009		2228						0817			
Ventimiglia 🚇 ...... d.	1110				1916	2120	2120	2130	2120		2312				0825		0900			
Monaco Monte Carlo ...... a.	1131					2143	2143	2151	2143		2332									
Nice ...... a.	1146	1148			2000	2200	2200	2207	2200		2351		0019		0910		0940	1030		
Cannes ...... a.		1219				2245	2245	2257	2245		0019							1059		
Toulon ...... a.		1342				0007	0007	0019	0007									1209		
Marseille ...... a.		1425				0056	0056	0105	0056									1250		
Montpellier ...... a.		1618				0310	0310	0323	0311								1426	1510		
Narbonne ...... a.		1735	1817			0411	0411	0440	0416									1558		
Port Bou 🚇 ...... a.			1955						0552	0645	0636							1718		
Girona ...... a.										0735			0756					1806		
Barcelona Sants ...... a.										0902								1920		
Barcelona França ...... a.													0910							
Toulouse ...... a.		1904				0549	0549	0648									1619			
Bordeaux ...... a.		2153															1823			
Irún ...... a.						1050	1124	1124												

NOTES

C – July 14 - Aug. 30: 🛏 1,2 cl. and 🍴 Cerbère - Milano.
D – July 12 - Aug. 28: 🛏 1,2 cl. and 🍴 Milano - Port Bou.

E – SALVADOR DALI – 🛏 1,2 cl., 🍽 and ✕ Barcelona - Milano and v.v. Special fares apply.

F – 🛏 1,2 cl., 🛏 2 cl. and 🍴 Nice - Venezia and v.v.
G – 🛏 2 cl. and 🍴 Cerbère/Port Bou - Roma and v.v.

H – 🛏 1,2 cl., 1,2 cl. (T2), 🛏 2 cl. and 🍴 Nice - Roma and v.v.
J – LIGURE – 🍴 and ✕ Nice - Milano and v.v.

K – ⑤ to June 23 and from Sept. 8; daily June 29 - Sept. 3: 🍴 Roma - Irún.
L – 🍴 and ✕ Nice - Milano - (Basel) and v.v.

M – CATALAN TALGO – 🍴 and ✕ Montpellier - Barcelona and v.v.
N – ①②③④⑥ to June 27 and from Sept. 2: 🍴 Hendaye - Roma.

P – ⑤ to June 23 and from Sept. 8: 🍴 Hendaye - Roma.
Q – ⑦ to June 25 and from Sept. 10: 🍴 Roma - Irún.

S – ⑦ to June 25 and from Sept. 3, daily June 28 - Sept. 1: 🍴 Hendaye - Roma.
T – ①②③④⑥ to June 28 and from Sept. 4: 🍴 Roma - Irún.

✗ – Supplement payable.

Table 92 (Summer)   BUDAPEST - ZAGREB AND LJUBLJANA

| train number | 8907 | 242 | 200 | 202 | 253 | 204 | 240 | | 208 | 251 |
notes (see below)		R	T	V	L	P	S		M	N
Nyiregyháza França ...... d.				0555						
Miskolc ...... d.				0725						
Budapest Keleti ...... d.				0955			1730			
Budapest Déli ...... d.		0620	0630			1510			1910	
Bratislava ...... d.				0710						1520
Székesfehérvár ...... d.		0703		1127	1127	1602	1835		2002	2002
Nagykanizsa ...... d.		0933		1413	1413	1812	2126		2240	2240
Pécs ...... d.	0545									
Gyékényes ...... d.	0805		1045	1450	1450		2205		2320	2320
Kotoriba 🚇 ...... a.		1027				1855				
Koprivnica 🚇 ...... a.	0818		1058	1503	1503		2218		2333	2333
Zagreb ...... a.	0931		1211	1619	1619	2125	2332		0055	0055
Rijeka ...... a.			1605						0540	0540
Ljubljana ...... a.		1405				0250				
Trieste ...... a.		1657				0628				
Venezia Mestre ...... a.		1907				0907				
Venezia Santa Lucia ...... a.		1918				0918				

| train number | 205 | 203 | 203 | 201 | 207 | 243 | 209 | 209 | 241 |
notes (see below)	P	V	L	T		R	M	Q	
Venezia Santa Lucia ...... d.						0940			214
Venezia Mestre ...... d.						0951			215
Trieste ...... d.						1202			000
Ljubljana ...... d.						1455			031
Rijeka ...... d.				1210			2050	2050	
Zagreb ...... d.	0835	1350	1350	1605	1755		0115	0115	060
Koprivnica 🚇 ...... d.		1508	1508	1720	1912		0235	0235	072
Kotoriba 🚇 ...... d.	1105				1839				
Gyékényes ...... a.		1521	1521	1733	1925		0248	0248	073
Pécs ...... a.					2130				
Nagykanizsa ...... a.	1145	1600	1600				0927	0345	081
Székesfehérvár ...... a.	1442	1842	1842				2156	0625	0625
Bratislava ...... a.			2237						1144
Budapest Déli ...... a.	1538			2143			2242	0728	
Budapest Keleti ...... a.		1958							115
Miskolc ...... a.		2220							
Nyiregyháza França ...... a.		2340							

NOTES

L – 🍴 Bratislava - Zagreb and v.v.
M – ADRIATICA – 🛏 1,2 cl. and 🍴 Budapest - Rijeka and v.v.
N – ⑤ June 16 - Sept. 15: 🛏 2 cl. Bratislava - Rijeka.
P – MAESTRAL – 🍴 Budapest - Zagreb and v.v.

Q – ⑥ June 17 - Sept. 16: 🛏 2 cl. Rijeka - Bratislava.
R – DRAVA – 🍴 and ✕ Budapest - Venezia and v.v.
S – VENEZIA EXPRESS – 🛏 1,2 cl., 🛏 2 cl. and 🍴 Budapest - Venezia and v.v.
T – AGRAM – 🍴 and ✕ Budapest - Rijeka and v.v.
V – AVAS – 🍴 Budapest - Zagreb and v.v.

Table 93 (Summer) — SANKT PETERBURG, RIGA AND VILNIUS - WARSZAWA

train number	2/14	79014	57	57	25	221	27
notes (see page 4)	R	R					
notes (see below)	Y	T	B	A	Z	S	W
St Peterburg Vars...... d.	...	...	1210	1210	...	2105	...
Tallinn...................... d.	1710	...					
Riga........................ d.	0025	...				2205	
Kaunas.................... d.	0625	...					
Šeštokai.................. d.	0805	0900					
Trakiszki 🚂........... d.	...	0930					
Vilnius..................... d.	...				1022	1022	1715
Grodno 🚂............... d.	...		0855	0855	1434	1434	2136
Warszawa Gdańska a.	...		1501				
Warszawa Wschodnia a.	...	1525			2123	2123	0411
Warszawa Centralna . a.	...	1537			2213	2213	0447
Gdynia Główna .... a.	...			2045	...	...	...

train number	299	299	79011	14	11105	11113	15001
notes (see page 4)				R			
notes (see below)	Z	S	T	Y	W	B	A
Gdynia Główna .... d.	...	...	...	...	...	...	1925
Warszawa Centrala ... d.	0723	0723	1437	...	2117	...	
Warszawa Wschodnia... d.	0807	0807	1447	...	2144	...	
Warszawa Gdańska... d.	...					0043	
Grodno 🚂................. a.	1649	1649			0526	1106	1106
Vilnius..................... a.	2100	2100			0950		
Trakiszki 🚂............. a.			1950		...	...	...
Šeštokai.................. a.			2200	2225			
Kaunas.................... a.			...	0002			
Riga........................ a.		0810		0606			
Tallinn..................... a.				1310			
St Peterburg Varshavski.. a.	1210					0910	0910

NOTES

A – 🚋 2 cl. Gdynia - Sankt Peterburg and v.v.
B – 🚋 1,2 cl. Warszawa - Sankt Peterburg and v.v.
S – 🚋 2 cl. Riga - Warszawa - (Berlin) and v.v.

T – BALTI – 🚆 Warszawa - Šeštokai and v.v.
W – 🚋 2 cl. Vilnius - Warszawa and v.v.
Y – BALTI EKSPRESS – 🚋 1,2 cl., 🚆 and ✕ Šeštokai - Tallinn and v.v.
Z – 🚋 1,2 cl. Sankt Peterburg - Warszawa - (Berlin) and v.v.

Table 94a (Summer) — MOSKVA - WARSZAWA, PRAHA AND WIEN

train number	103	9	21	15	15	49	273	141	13	39	109
notes (see below)	P	L	G	N	S	V	X	C	A	D	B
Moskva Smolenskaya .... d.	...	1517	1901	2015	2015	...	...	2250	...	...	...
Smolensk .... d.	...	2124	0208	0326	0326	...	...	0610	...	...	...
Sankt Peterburg Vitebski ... d.	...	...	...	...	...	1510	...	...	...	...	...
Minsk .... d.	2125	0054	0632	0736	0736	...	...	1025	...	...	...
Kyїv (Kiev) .... d.	...	...	...	...	...	1805	2335	...	0608	0850	
Brest .... a.	0415	0635	1325	1436	1436	1436	1436	1849	1849	2353	0105
Terespol .... a.	0333	0553	1243	1354	1354	1354	1354	1800	1800	2311	0023
Warszawa Wschodnia ..... a.	0727	0834	1615	1725	1725	1725	1725	2115	2115	0238g	0454g
Warszawa Centralna .... a.	0742	0847	1812	2027c	1917	1917	1917	2207	2207		
Wrocław Główny .... a.			2345								
Lichkov 🚂..................... a.			0318								
Hradec Králové .... a.			0459								
Praha Hlavní .... a.			0651								
Poznań Główny .... a.				2245	2245	2245		0259	0259		
Katowice .... a.				2337c							
Petrovice 🚂.................. a.				0115c							
Břeclav .... a.				0427c							
Wien Süd .... a.				0652c							

| train number | | | 253 | | | 202 | | | | | |
train number	247	249	11005	241	241	11005	241	10	110	104	40
notes (see below)	A	C	G	O	Q	F	S	L	E	P	M
Wien Süd .... d.	...	...	...	...	...	2150b	...	...	...	...	...
Břeclav .... d.	...	...	...	...	...	2344	...	...	...	...	...
Petrovice 🚂.................. d.	...	...	...	...	...	0300	...	...	...	...	...
Katowice .... d.	...	...	...	...	...	0445	...	...	...	...	...
Poznań Główny .... d.	0150	0150	...	0630	0630		0630	...	...	...	...
Praha Hlavní .... d.			1824								
Hradec Králové .... d.			2014								
Lichkov 🚂..................... d.			2203								
Wrocław Główny .... d.			0130								
Warszawa Centralna .... d.	0723	0723	0650	1022	1022	1022	1022	1454	...	1942	...
Warszawa Wschodnia ...... d.	0840	0840	0937	1111	1111	1111	1111	1509	1630g	2010	0050g
Terespol .... d.	1135	1135	1248	1430	1430	1430	1430	1735	2023	2316	0513
Brest .... a.	1321	1321	1434	1616	1616	1616	1616	1906	2209	0102	0652
Kyїv (Kiev) .... a.		0920			1240				1346		2152
Minsk .... a.	1944		2047			2227	2227	0041		0723	
Sankt Peterburg Vitebski .. a.				1742							
Smolensk .... a.	0152		0242			0418	0418	0550			
Moskva Smolenskaya .... a.	0935		1025			1206	1206	1217			

NOTES

A – MOSKWA EXPRESS – 🚋 1,2 cl. Moskva - Poznań - (Berlin) and v.v.
B – ②⑤ 🚋 2 cl. Kyїv - Warszawa.
C – KIEW EXPRESS – 🚋 1,2 cl. Kyїv - Poznań - (Berlin) and v.v.
D – ①②⑥ 🚋 2 cl. Kyїv - Warszawa.
E – ③⑥ 🚋 2 cl. Warszawa - Kyїv.
F – ②④⑤⑦ 🚋 1,2 cl. Wien - Moskva (journey 2 nights).
G – 🚋 1,2 cl. Moskva - Praha and v.v. (journey 2 nights).
L – POLONEZ – 🚋 1,2 cl. Warszawa - Moskva and v.v.
M – ①③④ 🚋 2 cl. Warszawa - Kyїv.
N – ②③⑤⑦ 🚋 1,2 cl. Moskva - Wien (journey 2 nights).

O – ①③⑤ 🚋 1,2 cl. Brussels - Warszawa ②④⑥ - Sankt Peterburg.
P – 🚋 2 cl. Minsk - Warszawa and v.v.
Q – ②⑦ 🚋 1,2 cl. Brussels - Poznań (①③) - Kyїv.
S – 🚋 2 cl. Moskva - Poznań - (Brussels) and v.v.
V – ①③⑥ 🚋 1,2 cl. St Peterburg - Warszawa - (Brussels).
X – ⑤⑦ 🚋 1,2 cl. Kyїv - Poznań - (Brussels).
b – Depart 2124, July 1 - Aug. 4.
c – June 30 - Aug. 2: Warszawa Centralna arrive 1942, Katowice arrive 2245, Petrovice arrive 0030, Breclav arrive 0345, Wien Süd arrive 0645.
g – Warszawa Gdańska.

Table 94b (Summer)   MOSKVA AND KYÏV - PRAHA AND WIEN

train number	44	51	183	7	183
notes (see below)	Z	H	U	J	K
Moskva Kievskaya............ d.	...	...	1147	...	1300	...
Kyïv (Kiev) .... d.	...	1906	0229	...	0352	...
Sankt Peterburg Varshavski d.	...			2240		2240
Vilnius............................ d.	...			1530		1530
Lviv .... d.	...	0704	1407	1407	1533	1533
Chop ⋔ .... d.	...		2120	2120	2300	2300
Kraków Główny.............. a.	...	1502				
Katowice .... a.	...	1637				
Wrocław Główny............ a.	...	1940				
Košice .... a.	...		2247	2247	0015	0015
Žilina .... a.	...		0151	0151	0321	0321
Bratislava .... a.	...		0431	0431		
Wien Süd .... a.	...		0713b			
Olomouc......................... a.	...				0655	0655
Pardubice....................... a.	...				0846	0846
Praha Hlavní .... a.	...				1002	1002

train number train number	221	221	705	404 223	63002
notes (see below)	J	K	V	L	Z
Praha Hlavní .... d.	1908	1908	...	...	...
Pardubice......................... d.	2020	2020	...	...	...
Olomouc........................... d.	2215	2215	...	...	...
Wien Süd .... d.	...	...	...	1600c	...
Bratislava .... d.	...	...	2010	1740	...
Žilina .... d.	0137	0137	0137	2019	...
Košice .... d.	0505	0505	0505	2329	...
Wrocław Główny................ d.	...	...	...		0918
Katowice .... d.	...	...	...		1215
Kraków Główny.................. d.	...	...	...		1345
Chop ⋔ .... a.	0813	0813	0813	0240	
Lviv .... a.	1613	1613	1613	1017	0018
Vilnius.............................. a.	...	1022	1022		
Sankt Peterburg Vars. ... a.	...	0545	0545		
Kyïv (Kiev) .... a.	0319	...	...	2134	1226
Moskva Kievskaya.............. a.	2028	...	...	1503	

NOTES

H –   SLOVAKIA – 🛏 2 cl. Moskva - Bratislava (journey 2 nights);
   ①④⑥: 🛏 1,2 cl. Moskva - Wien (2 nights); ①③⑥: 🛏 1,2 cl. Kyïv - Wien (1 night).
J –   DUKLA – 🛏 1,2 cl. Moskva - Praha and v.v. (journey 2 nights).
K –   🛏 2 cl. Sankt Peterburg - Praha and v.v. (journey 3 nights).

L –   SLOVAKIA – 🛏 2 cl. Bratislava - Moskva (journey 2 nights);
   ①③⑥: 🛏 1,2 cl. Moskva - Wien (2 nights); ②④⑦: 🛏 1,2 cl. Kyïv - Wien (1 night).
U –   ④: 🛏 2 cl. Sankt Peterburg - Bratislava (journey 3 nights).
V –   ①: 🛏 2 cl. Bratislava - Sankt Peterburg (journey 3 nights).
Z –   🛏 2 cl. Kyïv - Przemyśl - Wrocław and v.v.
b –   July1 - Aug. 3: arrive Wien Nord 0724.
c –   July1 - Aug. 3: depart Wien Nord 1544.

Table 94c (Summer)   MOSKVA AND KYÏV - BUDAPEST, VENEZIA, BEOGRAD AND ATHÍNAI

train number	9	15	15	189	920
notes (see below)	N		K	Y	V	Z
Moskva Kievskaya........... d.	...	0956	...	2033	2033	...	...
Sankt Peterburg Varshavski. d.	...					1125	...
Riga............................... d.	...						1350
Vilnius............................ d.	...						2236
Kyïv (Kiev) .... d.	...	0023		1155	1155	...	...
Minsk.............................. d.	...					0558	0558
Lviv .... d.	...	1202		0002	0002	0002	0002
Chop ⋔ .... d.	...	1925		0730	0730	0730	0730
Szolnok .... a.	...	2257		1038	1038	1038	1038
Budapest Keleti .... a.	...			1207	1207	1207	1207
Siofok .... a.	...				1913		
Zagreb .... a.	...				2332		
Ljubljana .... a.	...				0250		
Trieste .... a.	...				0628		
Venezia Santa Lucia....... a.	...				0918		
Subotica .... a.	...	0329					
Beograd .... a.	...	0629					
Niš .... a.	...	1140					
Skopje............................ a.	...	1624					
Thessaloniki .... a.	...	2218					
Athínai............................ a.	...	0703					

train number train number	334 488	16	241	16	16	16
notes (see below)	A		K	M	R	V	L
Athínai............................. d.	2330	...	...	...	...	...	...
Thessaloniki .... d.	0826	...	...	...	...	...	...
Skopje............................. d.	1220	...	...	...	...	...	...
Niš .... d.	1715	...	...	...	...	...	...
Beograd .... d.	2230	...	...	...	...	...	...
Subotica .... d.	0125	...	...	...	...	...	...
Venezia Santa Lucia...... d.	...			2140			
Trieste .... d.	...			0002			
Ljubljana .... d.	...			0315			
Zagreb .... d.	...			0600			
Siofok .... d.	...			1016			
Budapest Keleti .... d.	...		1615	1615	1615	1615	1615
Szolnok .... d.	0540		1745	1745	1745	1745	1745
Chop ⋔ .... d.	1010		2240	2240	2240	2240	2240
Lviv .... d.	1734		0608	0608	0608	0608	0608
Minsk............................... d.	...				2238		
Kyïv (Kiev) .... a.	0433		1738	1738			
Vilnius.............................. a.	...					2158	2158
Riga................................. a.	...						0810
Sankt Peterburg Var. .... a.	...				1535		
Moskva Kievskaya............. a.	2141		1121	1121			

NOTES

A –   PUŠKIN – 🛏 1,2 cl. Beograd - Moskva (journey 2 nights);
   ③⑦: 🛏 1,2 cl. Athínai - Beograd - Moskva (journey 3 nights).
K –   TISZA EXPRESS – 🛏 2 cl. Moskva - Budapest and v.v. (journey 2 nights).
L –   ⑦: 🛏 2 cl. Budapest - Riga (journey 2 nights).
M –   🛏 1,2 cl. Zagreb - Moskva (journey 2 nights);
   ③⑥: 🛏 1,2 cl. Venezia - Moskva (journey 3 nights).

N –   PUŠKIN – 🛏 1,2 cl. Moskva - Beograd (journey 2 nights);
   ④⑦: 🛏 2 cl. Moskva - Beograd - Athínai (journey 3 nights).
R –   ②⑤: 🛏 2 cl. Budapest - Minsk (journey 2 nights).
V –   🛏 2 cl. Sankt Peterburg - Budapest and v.v. (journey 2 nights).
Y –   ②: 🛏 2 cl. Moskva - Zagreb (journey 2 nights);
   ③⑦: 🛏 2 cl. Moskva - Venezia (journey 3 nights).
Z –   ②④⑤⑥: 🛏 2 cl. Vilnius - Budapest (journey 2 nights);
   ⑤: 🛏 2 cl. Riga - Budapest (journey 2 nights).

Table 94d (Summer)   MOSKVA AND KYÏV - BUCUREŞTI AND SOFIJA

train number	59		85	53	221	195
notes (see below)	F		B	C	D	G
Moskva Kievskaya.............. d.	1444	...	...	...	...	...
Sankt Peterburg Varshavski. d.				1700		
Riga................................. d.					2205	
Vilnius.............................. d.				0856	0856	
Minsk............................... d.						0930
Kyïv (Kiev) .... d.	0614		1853			
Chişinău (Kishinev) .... d.						
Ungheni ⋔ .... d.						
Vadul Siret ⋔ .... d.	2300		1240	1240	1240	1240
Bucureşti Nord .... a.	0737		2102	2102	2102	2102
Ruse ⋔ .... a.	1105		0030	0030	0030	0030
Sofija ⋔ .... a.	1902		0845	0845	0845	0845
Kapikule ⋔ .... a.	0255					
Istanbul .... a.	0955					

train number train number train number	485 501	485 501	485 501	485 501	492 483 104
notes (see below)	B	C	E	G	F
Istanbul .... d.	...	...	...	...	2140
Kapikule ⋔ .... d.	...	...	...	...	0355
Sofija ⋔ .... d.	2140	2140	2140	2140	1300
Ruse ⋔ .... d.	0530	0530	0530	0530	2020
Bucureşti Nord .... d.	0906	0906	0906	0906	2355
Vadul Siret ⋔ .... a.	1728	1728	1728	1728	0815
Chişinău (Kishinev) .... a.	...	...	...	...	
Kyïv (Kiev) .... a.	1125			2248	0113
Minsk.............................. a.	...	...	...	...	
Vilnius............................ a.	...	2158	2158		
Riga................................ a.	...	0810			
Sankt Peterburg Vars. ... a.	1300				
Moskva Kievskaya........... a.	...	...	...	...	1933

NOTES

B –   BULGARIA EXPRESS – 🛏 2 cl. and 🍴 Kyïv - Sofija and v.v. (journey 2 nights).
C –   🛏 2 cl. Sankt Peterburg - Sofija and v.v. (journey 3 nights).
D –   ①③⑤⑦: 🛏 2 cl. Riga - Sofija (3 nights); ③⑤⑦: 🛏 2 cl. Vilnius - Sofija (2 nights).

E –   ①③④⑥: 🛏 2 cl. Sofija - Riga (3 nights); ②⑤⑦: 🛏 2 cl. Sofija - Vilnius (2 nights).
F –   SOFIJA EXPRESS – 🛏 1,2 cl. and 🍴 Moskva - Sofija and v.v. (journey 2 nights);
   conveys twice weekly, 🛏 1,2 cl. Moskva - Istanbul and v.v. (journey 3 nights).
G –   🛏 2 cl. Minsk - Sofija and v.v.

Table 95a (Summer)   WARSZAWA - PRAHA AND WIEN

train number	IC 106 Ⓡ	34102	EC 105 Ⓡ	1750 ①-⑤	1758 ⑥⑦		252	200	34004	34004 203	203	30203	34004	254	57000 254
notes (see below)	G		H				C	F	N	J	K	L	M	D	E
Warszawa Wschodnia ...... d.	0555	...	0855	...	...	...	1805	1950	...	2020	...	1935	...	...	...
Warszawa Centralna .... d.	0610	...	0910	...	...	...	1820	2005	...	2045	...	1950	...	...	...
Gdynia Główna .... d.		...		...	...	...			...		...		...	...	1800
Gdańsk Główny .... d.		...		...	...	...			...		...		...	...	1830
Swinoujscie .... d.		...		...	...	...			...		...		...	1830	
Szczecin Główny .... d.		...		...	...	...			...		...		...	2035	
Poznań Główny .... d.		...		...	...	...			...		...		...	2340	2340
Wrocław Główny .... d.		...		...	1425	...	0020		...		...		...	0208	0208
Wałbrzych .... d.		...		...		...			...		...		...		
Mezimĕsti .... d.		...		1510	1701	...			...		...		...		
Lichkov .... a.		...		...	...	...	0318		...		...		...	0510	0501
Kraków Główny .... d.		...	1017	...	...	...			...	2210	...	2210	...	2210	
Katowice .... d.	0854	1137	1153	...	...	...		2320	...	2347	...	2251	...		
Petrovice ▥ .... a.	1005		1258	...	...	...		0038	0038	0115	0115	0030	0030		
Bohumin .... a.	1034		1326	...	...	...			0126	0152	0152	0110	0110		
Ostrava Hlavni .... a.	1047		1337	...	...	...		0140	0141	0205	0205	0123	0123		
Pardubice .... a.	1345			...	...	...		0448	0450						
Praha Hlavni .... a.	1500			2121	2121	...	0651	0612	0612					0848	0843
Břeclav .... a.	...		1552	...	...	...				0427	0427	0345	0345		
Wien Süd .... a.	...		1701	...	...	...				0652	0652	0645	0645		

train number		1751	EC 104 Ⓡ	42104		IC 107 Ⓡ		253	255	255	201	201	202	202
notes (see below)			H	G				C	D	E	N	F	A	B
Wien Süd .... d.	...	...	0939c	...	...	...	...	...	...	...	...	...	2150b	2150b
Břeclav .... d.	...	...	1053	...	...	...	...	...	...	...	...	...	2344	2344
Praha Hlavni .... d.	...	0719	...	...	...	1343	...	1824	2032	2032	2123	2123	...	...
Pardubice .... d.	...		...	...	...	1454	...				2238	2238	...	...
Ostrava Hlavni .... d.	...		1312	...	...	1758	...		0144	0144			0209	0209
Bohumin .... d.	...			...	...	1811	...						0222	0222
Petrovice ▥ .... d.	...		1352	...	...	1840	...		0230	0230			0300	0300
Katowice .... a.	...		1456	1515	...	1955	...				0348		0438	
Kraków Główny .... a.	...			1637	...	...	...				0535			0535
Lichkov .... d.	...		...	...	...	...	...	2203	0000	0000				
Mezimĕsti .... a.	...	1125	...	...	...	...	...							
Wałbrzych .... a.	...		...	...	...	...	...							
Wrocław Główny .... a.	...	1326	...	...	...	...	...	0130	0250	0250				
Poznań Główny .... a.	...		...	...	...	...	...		0540	0540				
Szczecin Główny .... a.	...		...	...	...	...	...		0843					
Swinoujscie .... a.	...		...	...	...	...	...		1039					
Gdańsk Główny .... a.	...		...	...	...	...	...			1014				
Gdynia Główna .... a.	...		...	...	...	...	...			1044				
Warszawa Centralna .... a.	...		1740	...	...	2245	...	0643			0715		0750	...
Warszawa Wschodnia ...... a.	...		1754	...	...	2259	...	0657			0734		0804	...

NOTES

A – CHOPIN – ⛌ 1,2 cl., ⛌ 2 cl. and ⛌ Wien - Warszawa.
B – ⛌ 2 cl. and ⛌ Wien - Kraków.
C – BOHEMIA – ⛌ 1,2 cl., ⛌ 2 cl. and ⛌ Warszawa - Praha and v.v.
D – BALTIC – ⛌ 2 cl. and ⛌ Swinoujscie - Praha and v.v.
E – BALTIC – ⛌ 1,2 cl., ⛌ 2 cl., ⛌ and ✕ Gdynia - Praha and v.v.
F – SILESIA – ⛌ 1,2 cl., ⛌ 2 cl. and ⛌ Warszawa - Praha and v.v.
G – PRAHA – ⛌ and ✕ Warszawa - Praha and v.v.
H – SOBIESKI – ⛌ and ✕ Warszawa - Wien and v.v.

J – CHOPIN – Daily to June 30 and from Aug. 5:
    ⛌ 1,2 cl., ⛌ 2 cl. and ⛌ Warszawa - Wien.
K – Daily to June 30 and from Aug. 5: ⛌ 2 cl. and ⛌ Kraków - Wien.
L – CHOPIN – July 1 - Aug. 4: ⛌ 2 cl., ⛌ 2 cl. and ⛌ Warszawa - Wien.
M – July 1 - Aug. 4: ⛌ 2 cl. and ⛌ Kraków - Wien.
N – ⛌ 2 cl. Kraków - Praha and v.v.
b – Depart 2124, June 30 - Aug. 2.
c – Depart 0915, July 1 - Aug. 4.
e – Arrive 1726, June 30 - Aug. 3.

Table 95b (Summer)   WARSZAWA - BRATISLAVA, BUDAPEST AND BUCUREŞTI

train number	334	381	IC131	332	391		337	337		311
notes (see below)	✓	P	Q	✓	N		M	T		R
Warszawa Wschodnia ...... d.	...	0600	1055	...	...	...	1855	1855	...	...
Warszawa Centralna .... d.	...	0615	1110	...	...	...	1910	1910	...	...
Katowice .... d.	...		1353	...	...	...	2233	2233	...	...
Szczecin Główny .... d.	...				1130	...			...	...
Poznań Główny .... d.	...					...			...	...
Wrocław Główny .... d.	...				1710	...			...	...
Chalupki ▥ .... d.	...				1933	...			...	...
Bohumin .... a.	...				1941	...			...	...
Kraków Główny .... a.	0748	0905		1445		...			...	2105
Košice ▥ .... a.	...	1536				...			...	0400
Petrovice ▥ .... d.	...		1504			...	2350	2350	...	...
Zwardoń ▥ .... d.	1124		1827			...			...	...
Żilina .... d.	1233	1645	1940	2204		...	0151	0151	...	...
Bratislava hlavni .... a.	1520		2230			...		0540	...	...
Zvolen osob .... a.	...		0032			...			...	...
Filakovo ▥ .... a.	...		0149			...			...	...
Štúrovo ▥ .... a.	...	1945				...	0521		...	...
Komárom ▥ .... a.	...					...			...	...
Budapest Keleti .... a.	...	2102		0522		...	0647		...	0842
Szolnok .... a.	2055					...			...	...
Curtici .... a.	0050					...			...	...
Bucureşti Nord .... a.	1120					...			...	...
Beograd .... a.	...					...			...	...
Niš .... a.	...					...			...	...
Sofija .... a.	...					...			...	...
Istanbul .... a.	...					...			...	...

train number		333	IC130	205 380	335	336	7125		310	390
notes (see below)		✓	Q	P	✓	M	T		R	N
Istanbul .... d.	...	...	...	...	...	...	...	...	...	...
Sofija.............................. d.	...	...	...	...	...	...	...	...	...	...
Niš .... d.	...	...	...	...	...	...	...	...	...	...
Beograd .... d.	...	...	...	...	...	...	...	...	...	...
Bucureşti Nord .... d.	...	...	...	2005	...	...	...	...	...	...
Curtici .... d.	...	...	...	0600	...	...	...	...	...	...
Szolnok .... d.	...	...	...	0725	...	...	...	...	...	...
Budapest Keleti .... d.	...	0940			1850			...	1905	1920
Komárom ▥ .... d.	...		1055		2025			...		
Štúrovo ▥ .... d.	...							...		
Filakovo ▥ .... d.	...							...		2218
Zvolen osob .... d.	...							...		2345
Bratislava hlavni .... d.	...	0610		1510		2050		...		
Żilina .... d.	...	0854	1359	1754	0011	0011		...		0206
Zwardoń ▥ .... a.	...	1002		1902				...		
Petrovice ▥ .... d.	...	1540						...		
Košice ▥ .... d.	...		1213					...	0003	
Kraków Główny .... a.	...	1347	1913	2245				...	0647	
Bohumin .... a.	...							...		0428
Chalupki ▥ .... a.	...							...		0436
Wrocław Główny .... a.	...							...		0700
Poznań Główny .... a.	...							...		
Szczecin Główny .... a.	...							...		1255
Katowice .... a.	...	1655			0326	0326		...		
Warszawa Centralna .... a.	...	1940	2200		0647	0647		...		
Warszawa Wschodnia ...... a.	...	1954	2214		0701	0701		...		

NOTES

M – BATHORY – ⛌ 1,2 cl., ⛌ 2 cl., ⛌ and ✕ Warszawa - Budapest and v.v.
N – BEM – ⛌ 1,2 cl. and ⛌ Szczecin - Budapest and v.v.
P – KARPATY – ⛌ Warszawa - Bucureşti and v.v.;
    ⛌ 2 cl. Košice - Bucureşti and v.v.

Q – POLONIA – ⛌ and ✕ Warszawa - Budapest and v.v.
R – CRACOVIA – ⛌ 1,2 cl., ⛌ 2 cl., ⛌ and ✕ Kraków - Budapest and v.v.
T – ⛌ 1,2 cl. and ⛌ Warszawa - Bratislava and v.v.
✓ – Supplement payable.

Table 96a (Summer) — PRAHA - WIEN AND LINZ

train number	271	271	EC 173	1273	EC 9	1275	273
notes (see page 4)	A		B		C		D / ①-⑥
Praha Holešovice ..... d.			1312		1712		
Praha Hlavni .... d.	0635	0635		1512		2021	0024
Tábor .... d.	0805			1643		2151	0150
České Budějovice .... d.		0919		1757		2255	
Summerau 🛏 .... a.		1044		1913		0011	
Linz 🛏 .... a.		1151		2022		0119	
Villach Westbf ...... a.						0532	
Udine 🛏 .... a.						0741	
Venezia Mestre ...... a.						0928	
Venezia Santa Lucia a.						0939	
Brno .... d.			1620		2020		
Břeclav 🛏 .... d.			1705		2105		
Gmünd 🛏 .... d.	0946						0345
Wien Franz Josefs ... a.	1207						0606
Wien Südbf .... a.			1803e		2203b		

train type / train number	1272	EC 8	EC 172	1276	270	272 ⑧	1274
notes (see page 4)	C	B			A		E
Wien Südbf .... d.		0725c	1125f				
Wien F. Josefs ...... d.					1345	1735	
Gmünd 🛏 .... d.					1610	2010	
Břeclav 🛏 .... a.		0823	1223				
Brno .... a.		0910	1310				
Venezia S. Lucia .... d.							1908
Venezia Mestre ...... d.							1920
Udine 🛏 .... d.							2102
Villach Westbf ...... d.							2310
Linz .... d.	0738		1336				0316
Summerau 🛏 .... a.	0845		1444				0435
České Budějovice .... a.	1013		1604				0602
Tábor 🛏 .... a.			1713	1735	2141		0706
Praha Hlavni .... a.			1838	1908	2308		0840
Praha Holešovice .... a.		1221	1621				

NOTES
A – SMETANA – 🛌 and 🍴 Praha - Wien and v.v.
B – VINDOBONA – 🛌 and 🍴 (Berlin) - Praha - Wien and v.v.
C – ANTONÍN DVOŘÁK – 🛌 and 🍴 Praha - Wien and v.v.
D – ②⑤⑦: 🛏 1,2 cl., 🛏 2 cl. and 🛌 Praha - Venezia.
E – ①③⑥: 🛏 1,2 cl., 🛏 2 cl. and 🛌 Venezia - Praha.
b – June 30 - Aug. 3: Arrive 2233.
c – July 1 - Aug. 4: Depart 0655.
e – June 30 - Aug. 3: Arrive 1833.
f – July 1 - Aug. 4: Depart 1055.

Table 96b (Summer) — PRAHA - BUDAPEST, BUCUREŞTI AND BEOGRAD

train number	IC 1073	77	1011	279	279	EC 175	375	379
notes (see page 4)	R	X	V	N	W	S	M	T
Praha Holešovice ... d.	0536		0741			1512		0032
Praha Hlavni .... d.		0606		1208	1208		2238	
Brno .... d.	0905	0925	1054	1527	1527	1820	0223	0351
Břeclav .... d.	0950	1007	1137	1609	1609	1859	0316	0432
Bratislava Hlavni . d.	1117	1109	1306	1733	1733	2001	0442	0558
Rajka .... d.	1215		1420					
Šturovo 🛏 .... d.		1236		1920	1920	2127	0630	0745
Győr .... a.	1300		1500					
Budapest Nyugati .. a.								0857
Budapest Keleti ... a.	1438	1347	1638	2032	2032	2237	0747	
Subotica 🛏 .... a.					0400			
Beograd .... a.					0714			
Niš .... a.					1145			
Skopje .... a.					1624			
Idomeni 🛏 .... a.					2027			
Thessaloniki ...... a.					2218			
Athínai .... a.					0703			
Curtici 🛏 .... a.	2025							1310
Arad .... a.	2121							1425
Brașov .... a.	0320							2016
Bucureşti Nord .... a.	0600							2300

train number	EC 174	278	278	1010	IC 76	33 1072	378	21 374
notes (see page 4)	S	N	Y	V	X	R	T	M
Bucureşti Nord ..... d.						0115		0800
Brașov .... d.						0354		1105
Arad .... d.						0953		1655
Curtici 🛏 .... d.						1000		1750
Athínai .... d.				2330				
Thessaloniki .... d.				0826				
Idomeni 🛏 .... d.				1020				
Skopje .... d.				1220				
Niš .... d.				1715				
Beograd .... d.				2145				
Subotica 🛏 .... a.				0130				
Budapest Keleti .... d.	0650	0835	0835	1330	1425	1400		2120
Budapest Nyugati ... d.							1825	
Győr .... d.				1508		1538		
Šturovo 🛏 .... a.	0803	0950	0950		1544		1935	2235
Rajka 🛏 .... a.				1550		1617		
Bratislava Hlavni .. a.	0928	1143	1143	1700	1704	1733	2120	0026
Břeclav .... a.	1031	1304	1304	1829	1808	1854	2251	0154
Brno .... a.	1110	1345	1345	1909	1846	1935	2332	0247
Praha Hlavni .... a.		1711	1711		2200			0627
Praha Holešovice ... a.	1421			2227		2313	0249	

NOTES
M – PANNONIA EXPRESS – 🛏 1,2 cl., 🛏 2 cl. and 🛌 Praha - Bucureşti and v.v.
N – SLOVAN – 🛌 and 🍴 Praha - Budapest and v.v.
R – BALT ORIENT EXPRESS –
 🛏 1,2 cl., 🛏 2 cl. and 🛌 (Berlin) - Praha - Bucureşti and v.v.
S – HUNGARIA – 🛌 and 🍴 (Berlin) - Praha - Budapest and v.v.
T – METROPOL – 🛏 1,2 cl., 🛏 2 cl., 🛌 and 🍴 (Berlin) - Praha - Budapest and v.v.
V – CSÁRDÁS – 🛌 (Malmö)- Praha - Budapest and v.v.; 🍴 Praha - Budapest and v.v.
W – 🛏 1,2 cl. Praha - Athínai;
 ③⑤: 🛏 2 cl. Praha - Athínai; ④: 🛏 2 cl. Bratislava - Athínai.
X – MATHIAS CORVINUS – 🛌 and 🍴 Praha - Budapest and v.v.
Y – 🛏 1,2 cl. Athínai - Praha;
 ⑤⑦: 🛏 2 cl. Athínai - Praha; ⑥: 🛏 2 cl. Athínai - Bratislava.

Table 97 (Summer) — BUDAPEST AND BEOGRAD - ATHÍNAI AND ISTANBUL

Due to the political situation, passengers without visas may be prevented from making international journeys via this route.

train number	335 Ⓡ	IC393	493	291	491
notes (see page 4)	F	E	D	C	B
Budapest Keleti ... d.	0035				1455
Kelebia 🛏 .... d.	0350				1800
Beograd .... d.	0750	0940	1020	2000	2200
Niš .... d.	1155	1340	1510	0000	0226
Preševo 🛏 .... d.	1500	1635		0310	
Skopje 🛏 .... d.	1650	1800		0500	
Idomeni 🛏 .... a.	2027	2130		0847	
Thessaloniki ...... a.	2218	2305		1035	
Athínai .... a.	0703				
Dimitrovgrad ...... a.			1710		0415
Kalotina 🛏 .... a.			1838		
Sofija .... a.			2032		0738
Plovdiv .... a.			2325		1010
Kapikule 🛏 .... a.			0255		1355
Istanbul .... a.			0955		1955

train number	490	290	492	IC392	334
notes (see page 4)	B	C	D	E	F
Istanbul .... d.	1000		2140		
Kapikule 🛏 .... d.	1620		0355		
Plovdiv .... d.	2005		0740		
Sofija .... d.	2255		1010		
Kalotina 🛏 .... d.			1142		
Dimitrovgrad ...... d.	0010		1125		
Athínai .... d.					2330
Thessaloniki ...... d.		2100		0600	0826
Idomeni 🛏 .... d.		2240		0805	1020
Skopje 🛏 .... d.		0023		0945	1200
Preševo 🛏 .... d.		0200		1130	1345
Niš .... a.	0200	0514	1316	1433	1658
Beograd .... a.	0619	0927	1807	1832	2115
Kelebia 🛏 .... a.	1120				0140
Budapest Keleti ... a.	1428				0513

NOTES
B – BALKAN EXPRESS – 🛏 1,2 cl. and 🛌 Budapest - Istanbul and v.v.;
 🛏 1,2 cl., 🛏 2 cl. and 🛌 Budapest - Sofija and v.v.;
 🛌 Sofija - Istanbul and v.v.
C – 🛏 1,2 cl., 🛏 2 cl. and 🛌 Beograd - Thessaloniki and v.v.
D – 🛏 1,2 cl., 🛏 2 cl. and 🛌 Beograd - Istanbul and v.v.; 🛌 Beograd - Sofija and v.v.
E – 🛌 and 🍴 Beograd - Thessaloniki and v.v.
F – HELLAS EXPRESS – 🛏 1,2 cl., 🛏 2 cl. and 🛌 Budapest - Athínai and v.v.

Subscription and Sales Agents for Thomas Cook Timetables

Australia	●	Thomas Cook travel shops at Adelaide (45 Grenfell Street), Brisbane (168 Edward Street), Melbourne (159–161 Collins Street), Perth (16 Wesley Centre, William Street) and Sydney (175 Pitt Street).
Austria	●	Österreichisches Verkehrsbüro GmbH, Opernring 5, A-1010 Wien.
Belgium	● ▲	Schuyt & Co. N.V. Suikerrui 5, B–2000 Antwerpen
	●	Thomas Cook Bureau de Change, 4 Grand Place, B–1000 Brussels.
	●	Thomas Cook Bureau de Change, 33 Koningin Astridplein, B–2918 Antwerpen.
Denmark	● ▲	Boghallen, 27 Rådhuspladsen, DK–1585 København V, Denmark
Finland	● ▲	Akateeminen Kirjakauppa, Keskkuskatu 1, SF–00101 Helsinki.
France	● ▲	Thomas Cook Bankers France S.A., Abonnements d'Horaires, 8 Rue Bellini, BP 102-16, 75763 Paris Cédex 16. Fax: 1 47 27 37 22.
		Thomas Cook Bureaux de Change: Bordeaux (Gare St. Jean), Lyon (Gare de Lyon–Part Dieu), Nice (Gare SNCF–Ave. Thiers), and Paris (Eiffel Tower and main-line stations).
Germany	●	Thomas Cook Deutschland Ltd., 2A Domkloster, Köln 1; 11 Kaiserstrasse, 60311 Frankfurt/Main; 39 Ballindamm, 20095 Hamburg; Koblenzer Reisebüro Junges GmbH., 3 Bahnhofplatz, 56068 Koblenz; EurAide office, along track 11, room 7, Hauptbahnhof München.
Ireland (Republic)	●	Thomas Cook Ltd, 118 Grafton Street, Dublin 2.
Italy	● ▲	Anglo American Book Co., Via della Vite 57, 00187 Roma, Italy.
	● ▲	LED, Via Cassini 41, I-10129 Torino. ☎ (011) 568 3837. Fax: (011) 568 3794.
Japan	●	Diamond Student Travel Association, Diamond Building, 1–4–2 Kasumigaseki, Chiyoda-ku, Tokyo (Publishers of the Japanese edition of the European Timetable). UK edition also available in Japan from ● ▲ Japan Travel Bureau, 2–2–3 Hamamatsu-cho, Minato–ku, Tokyo 105 and branches; ● Maruzen & Co. Ltd., 3–10 Nihonbashi 2-chome, Chuo-ku, PO Box 5050, Tokyo 103; ● Map House Co. Ltd., 5th floor, Taiyodo Bldg., 1–10 Jinbo-cho, Kanda, Chiyoda-ku, PO Box 55, Chitose, Tokyo 156. ● Kinokuniya Books, Import Dept, PO Box 55, Chitose, Tokyo 156.
Netherlands	● ▲	Schuyt & Co International BV, Gedempte Oude Grach 35, Postbox 563, 2003 RN Haarlem.
	●	Thomas Cook Nederland BV, 23-25 Dam; 31A Leidseplein; Victoria Hotel, 1-5 Damrak; Munttoren, 12A Muntplein, Amsterdam.
New Zealand	●	Thomas Cook Travel Shop, 10 Commerce Street, Auckland.
Norway	▲	Narvesen A/S, Box 6125, Etterstad, N–Oslo 6.
	▲	Arning Publikasjoner, P.O. Box 3151 Elisenberg, N–0208 Oslo 2.
South Africa	▲	Houston Travel Marketing Services, Ground Floor, M.NET Building, Boeing Road East, Elma Park, Edenvale 1610. (P.O. Box 75262, Gardenview 2047).
South America	● ▲	MFV Representações, Importação Exportação Ltda, Av. Rio Branco 177/21° and., Centro, Rio de Janeiro, RJ 20040-007, Brazil. Fax: 021 262 3182.
Spain	● ▲	Ian Dornan International, Gran Vía 57, Pl. 8 Of. I, 28013 Madrid. ☎ (91) 542 8152. Fax: (91) 542 1396.
Sweden	●	Kartcentrum, Vasagatan 16, Box 322, 10126 Stockholm.
	▲	Wennergren-Williams AB, Box 30004, S–104 25 Stockholm.
Switzerland	● ▲	Verkaufsstelle für ausländische Kursbücher, Hauptbahnhof, 9001 St. Gallen.
U.S.A.	● ▲	Forsyth Travel Library, PO Box 2975, 9154 West 57th Street, Shawnee Mission, Kansas 66201, USA. ☎ (913) 384-3440 or Toll Free within the USA (800) 367-7984. Fax: (913) 384-3553.

● Single copies available.　　　　▲ Subscription Agent.

LIST OF ADVERTISERS

PRICE LIST AND ORDER FORM 1995

X5395C

Thomas Cook Publishing (TPO/FE/5C), P.O. Box 227, Peterborough PE3 8BQ, U.K. ☎ (01733) 505821/268943.

All prices (retail only) are shown in pounds sterling, are applicable for the period 1.1.95–31.12.95, and include postage and packing in:—

▼ UK	▼ Europe	▼ Overseas air mail

THOMAS COOK TIMETABLES ▼
(see also special offers overleaf)

European Timetable Subscription (12 issues)
☐ £101.30 ☐ £126.50 ☐ £143.30

European Timetable – Single copy
☐ £9.10 ☐ £11.20 ☐ £12.60

Overseas Timetable Subscription (6 issues)
☐ £54.60 ☐ £67.20 ☐ £75.60

Overseas Timetable – Single copy
☐ £9.10 ☐ £11.20 ☐ £12.60

Part subscriptions (minimum 6 issues European Timetable or 3 issues Overseas Timetable):-
priced as multiple of single copy rate.

THOMAS COOK TOURING HANDBOOKS ▼

On the Rails Around Europe
☐ £11.45 ☐ £13.45 ☐ £15.45

On the Rails Around Britain and Ireland
☐ £11.45. ☐ £13.45 ☐ £15.45

On the Rails Around France, Belgium, the Netherlands and Luxembourg
☐ £11.45 ☐ £13.45 ☐ £15.45

On the Road Around California
☐ £12.45 ☐ £14.45 ☐ £16.45

THOMAS COOK PHRASEBOOKS ▼

European Traveller's Phrasebook
☐ £5.65 ☐ £6.25 ☐ £6.85

European Rail Traveller's Phrasebook
☐ £4.65 ☐ £5.25 ☐ £5.85

THOMAS COOK RAIL MAPS ▼

New Rail Map of Europe
☐ £5.65 ☐ £6.25 ☐ £6.85

Visitor's Rail Map of Britain and Ireland
☐ £5.65 ☐ £6.25 ☐ £6.85

THOMAS COOK GUIDES ▼

Guide to Greek Island Hopping 1995
☐ £12.45 ☐ £14.45 ☐ £16.45

North American Rail and Bus Guide 1995
☐ £7.95 ☐ £8.95 ☐ £10.75

▼ UK	▼ Europe	▼ Overseas air mail

THOMAS COOK TRAVELLERS ▼

Travellers – 1993/1994 titles @ :-
☐ £7.99 ☐ £8.99 ☐ £10.79

Please indicate title(s) required:-
☐ The Algarve
☐ Amsterdam
☐ Belgium
☐ Boston & New England
☐ California
☐ Cyprus
☐ Eastern Caribbean
☐ Egypt
☐ Florence & Tuscany
☐ Florida
☐ Ireland
☐ Kenya
☐ London
☐ Malta
☐ Munich & Bavaria
☐ New York
☐ Paris
☐ Prague
☐ Singapore & Malaysia
☐ Sydney & New South Wales
☐ Thailand
☐ Turkey
☐ Vancouver & British Columbia
☐ Vienna

Total no. 1993/4 titles required _____ @ £ . =

Travellers – new 1995 titles @ :-
☐ £8.99 ☐ £9.99 ☐ £11.79

Please indicate title(s) required:-
☐ Berlin
☐ Budapest
☐ Greece (Mainland)
☐ Java & Bali
☐ Madeira
☐ Mallorca
☐ Mexico
☐ Morocco
☐ Normandy
☐ Provence
☐ Rome
☐ Venice

Total no. 1995 titles required _____ @ £ . =

SUB-TOTAL CARRIED FORWARD £

CONTINUED OVERLEAF

X5395C

PRICE LIST AND ORDER FORM 1995
(CONTINUED FROM PREVIOUS PAGE)

Thomas Cook Publishing (TPO/FE/5C), P.O. Box 227, Peterborough PE3 8BQ, U.K. ☎ **(01733) 505821/268943**

All prices (retail only) are shown in pounds sterling, are applicable for the period 1.1.95–31.12.95, and include postage and packing in:—

▼ UK ▼ Europe ▼ Overseas air mail   ▼ UK ▼ Europe ▼ Overseas air mail

OTHER BOOKS BY MAIL ORDER ▼

Australia by Rail
☐ £9.95 ☐ £10.95 ☐ £12.75

India by Rail
☐ £12.45 ☐ £14.45 ☐ £16.45

Sri Lanka by Rail
☐ £12.45 ☐ £14.45 ☐ £16.45

Mexico by Rail
☐ £12.45 ☐ £14.45 ☐ £16.45

Silk Route by Rail
☐ £11.45 ☐ £13.45 ☐ £15.45

Thailand, Malaysia & Singapore by Rail
☐ £10.95 ☐ £11.95 ☐ £13.75

Trans-Siberian Handbook
☐ £11.45 ☐ £13.45 ☐ £15.45

USA by Rail
☐ £12.45 ☐ £14.45 ☐ £16.45

Eastern Europe by Rail
☐ £10.95 ☐ £11.95 ☐ £13.75

Spain and Portugal by Rail
☐ £12.45 ☐ £14.45 ☐ £16.45

OTHER MAPS BY MAIL ORDER ▼

Rail Map of Germany
☐ £7.95 ☐ £8.55 ☐ £9.15

Rail Map of Switzerland
☐ £7.95 ☐ £8.55 ☐ £9.15

SPECIAL OFFERS ▼

EUROPEAN RAIL COLLECTION 'A'
Buy European Timetable and New Rail Map of Europe together and save £1.00
☐ £13.75 ☐ £16.45 ☐ £18.45

EUROPEAN RAIL COLLECTION 'B'
Buy On the Rails around Europe and European Rail Traveller's Phrasebook together and save £1.50
☐ £17.80 ☐ £21.60 ☐ £23.90

SUB-TOTAL £

SUB-TOTAL FROM PREVIOUS PAGE £

TOTAL ENCLOSED £

WAYS TO PAY:

● £ Sterling cheque drawn on UK bank.
● Bank transfer to Midland Bank plc, Cathedral Square, PETERBOROUGH, UK. Account no. 21029452, sort code 40-36-15. In this case, please send separate advice of payment to the address at the top of this form.
● Credit card: Mastercard, Visa or American Express. (Any bank or similar charges incurred to be paid by remitter).
● Eurocheque in Sterling.

FOR VAT/TVA/IVA REGISTRATIONS:

If you are registered for one of the above (or similar) taxes, please enter your registration number here:

Please help us to give you a better service by completing the following:

TIMETABLE ISSUE REQUIRED:
(For single copy)

REASONS FOR PURCHASE:
☐ Business Travel   ☐ Independent Travel
☐ Student Inter-Rail   ☐ Rail enthusiast
☐ Other (please specify)

AGE GROUP:
☐ Under 26   ☐ 26-39   ☐ 40-59   ☐ Over 60

FOR CREDIT CARD PAYMENTS – please complete:

☐ Mastercard   ☐ Visa   ☐ American Express

Cardholder's details:

Name _____

Signature _____

Card number:

|_|_|_|_|_| |_|_|_|_|_| |_|_|_|_|_| |_|_|_|_|_|

Card expiry date _____

Address _____

_____

_____

Postcode _____

Delivery details (if different from above):

Name _____

Address _____

_____

_____

Postcode _____

VAT Registration No. GB 239 384 1 42